M·A·N·U·FA·C·T·U·R·I·N·G
& D·I·S·T·R·I·B·U·T·I·O·N
USA

Fourth Edition

Industry Analyses,
Statistics and Leading Companies

ISSN 1529-7659

M·A·N·U·F·A·C·T·U·R·I·N·G
&·D·I·S·T·R·I·B·U·T·I·O·N
USA

Fourth Edition

Industry Analyses,
Statistics and Leading Companies

Volume 3

Arsen J. Darnay, Managing Editor

Joyce P. Simkin, Editor

THOMSON

GALE

Detroit • New York • San Francisco • New Haven, Conn. • Waterville, Maine • London • Munich

THOMSON
GALE

Manufacturing & Distribution USA, Fourth Edition
Joyce P. Simkin, Editor

Project Editors
Julie Gough
Virgil L. Burton III

Editorial
Arsen J. Darnay

Editorial Support Services
Scott Flaugher

Manufacturing
Rita Wimberley

ISBN 0-7876-7440-0 (set)
ISBN 0-7876-7441-9 (v.1)
ISBN 0-7876-7442-7 (v.2)
ISBN 0-7876-7443-5 (v.3)
ISSN 1529-7659

Printed in the United States of America
10 9 8 7 6 5 4 3 2 1

TABLE OF CONTENTS

Volume I

Preface vii
Introduction xxxi
Overview of Content and Sources. xxxvii
Part I - Manufacturing by Annual Survey of Manufactures' NAICS Code, NAICS 311111-33211P. 1

Volume II

Preface vii
Introduction xxxi
Overview of Content and Sources xxxvii
Part I - Manufacturing by Annual Survey of Manufactures' NAICS Code, NAICS 33221N-339999 . . . 885

Volume III

Preface vii
Introduction xxxi
Overview of Content and Sources xxxvii
Part II - Manufacturing by NAICS Code, NAICS 423110-454390 1757

Indexes 2233
NAICS Index 2235
Product/Activity Index 2245
Company Index 2289

Appendices 2443
ASM NAICS to 2002 NAICS Conversion Guide 2445
2002 NAICS to ASM NAICS Conversion Guide 2453

Preface

Manufacturing: The Big Picture

This section will provide an overview of the U.S. manufacturing sector. This will serve as the "big picture" of which the individual NAICS chapters are distinct views. In this section, the focus will be on changes between 1982 and 2004.

In recent years an important subject of political debate has been the loss of U.S. manufacturing jobs. Manufacturing jobs have long been considered one of the highest paying sources of income, especially for those who do not have an advanced college degree. According to the U.S. Census Bureau, 72.3 percent of the population 25 years old and over had less than a bachelor's degree in 2004. Manufacturing jobs have been and continue to be outsourced to countries such as Mexico and China. Some consider this a signal of an economy in transition. Just as in the 19th century our economy switched from agrarian to industrial, the 20th century ushered in a transition from an economy based on manufacturing to one based on services and increasingly one based on high tech services. However, in the 21st century, information technology jobs, such as those held by computer programmers and analysts, were also being outsourced to foreign countries.

Those in favor of outsourcing argue that despite the loss of manufacturing jobs, the manufacturing sector and the economy as a whole are prospering. Productivity has been on the rise. A workforce with high skills using more advanced production processes allows industries to produce more product with fewer workers. Other sectors of the economy have been expanding. The overall unemployment rate declined in the past 23 years. Foreign investment in U.S. manufacturing now surpasses U.S. investment in manufacturing abroad.

Those opposed to outsourcing argue that the jobs created in the last 23 years do not pay as well as the manufacturing jobs that have been lost. The trade deficit continues to rise. Despite numerous free trade agreements, exports have not kept pace with imports. Many see the importing of goods, especially goods needed for national defense, as a dangerous trend.

In this section we will state the facts as they are reported in national statistics. The policy implications, of course, must be drawn by those charged with setting the nation's economic course.

Data in the section entitled *Issues in Manufacturing* are drawn from government as well as non-governmental sources. All other data are drawn from five economic censuses. These are surveys of nearly all manufacturing establishments. Also included are data from the most recent *Annual Survey of Manufactures* (ASM), which is a partial sampling of industrial activity and not at the same level of precision as the other years. Gross Domestic Product (GDP) data have been taken from the Bureau of Economic Analysis website (http://www.bea.gov/).

Prior to 1997, data were classified using Standard Industrial Classification (SIC) coding. In 1997, data were reclassified using the North American Industrial Classification System (NAICS). As a result of this reclassification, 259 new industries were created by merging two or more parts of SIC coded industries; 214 industries remained unchanged after this transition. However, this was not the first reclassification of industries. In 1987, the SIC coding system underwent a change from the 1972 SIC coding. As a result, data prior to 1987 for 35 of the 214 industries taken over without changes to the NAICS system only provide comparable data back to 1987.

In 2003 the U.S. Census Bureau made another important change in how it collects and reports data in the Annual Survey of Manufacturers. Starting in 2003, the ASM no longer reports on all 6 digit NAICS manufacturing industries. Instead a subset of the total has been created by the Census Bureau and it is this subset on which it reports in the ASM. This change reflects the shrinking of U.S. manufacturing.

In preparing *MDUSA* the editors have done a great deal of work to restructure this title so that it adheres to the new, shorter ASM industry list. The ASM industry list contains 6 digit NAICS industries as well as industries made up of two or more 6 digit NAICS industries. For any ASM industry that is a combination of 6 digit NAICS industries, a new code is used. The new ASM code is a 5 digit number and a letter. Whenever such a new industry code is presented in this work, a list is provided for the user of the component NAICS industries that are covered by the new single ASM NAICS code. In addition, two new appendices are proivded, one that offers a conversion from ASM NAICS codes to 2002 NAICS codes and the other providing a look-up guide in the other direction—2002 NAICS codes to ASM NAICS codes.

Of the 322 manufacturing industries presented in this work, 234 are "straight" 6 digit NAICS industries and 88 are new ASM industries (industries made up of more than one 6 digit NAICS industry).

When discussing the manufacturing sector as a whole, all 322 ASM industries are included in the statistics. Only the 137 ASM industries for which historical data are available are included when details about the manufacturing sector are discussed.

Sources for the graphics in this section are listed under *Graphics Sources*. An annotated source list follows.

The General State of Manufacturing

Figure 1. The Importance of Manufacturing to the U.S. Economy, 1947-2004

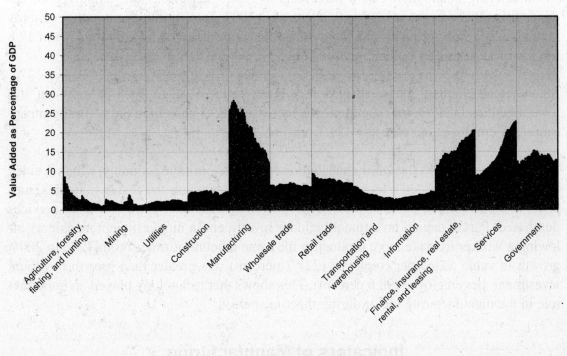

Manufacturing continues to slip in overall importance in the economy. As a percentage of Gross Domestic Product (GDP), Manufacturing, in terms of value added by labor, went from 25.6 percent in 1947 to 12.1 percent of GDP in 2004, a decline of more than 13.5 percent. Nearly half of that decline occurred in the years 1982 to 2004. In 1982, manufacturing was nearly 19 percent of GDP; in 2004, 12.1 percent. The slippage in share of GDP suggests that other sectors of the economy have been expanding more rapidly.

As Figure 1 shows, in the post-World War II era, the Service sector expanded the most rapidly (a 14.0 percent gain), followed by Finance, Insurance, Real Estate, Rental, and Leasing (+10.1 percent) and Information (+2.1 percent). From 1982 to 2004, the gains in these industries were 7.2 percent, 4.0 percent, and 0.8 percent, respectively. The year 1986 was pivitol, it was the first year that the Service sector surpassed the Manufacturing sector as the largest sector in the economy. By 2004, in terms of value added, Services and Finance, Insurance, Real Estate, Rental, and Leasing each outperformed Manufacturing by a ratio of nearly 2 to 1. Gross domestic product value of Services was $2.7 trillion. Finance, Insurance, Real Estate, Rental, and Leasing GDP was $2.4 trillion. Manufacturing GDP was $1.4 trillion.

Note, however, that Manufacturing—along with agriculture, forestry, mining, transportation, and construction—are basic economic activities. All other sectors depend upon these.

Therefore, the expansion of the services sector is in a real sense *enabled* by the productivity of these basic sectors.

Manufacturing employment, as a percentage of total nonagricultural employment, declined from 18.5 percent in 1982 to 9.8 percent in 2004. Total employment in the economy increased. Manufacturing employment shrank by more than 4.4 million jobs, from 17.8 million in 1982 to 13.4 million in 2004.

Manufacturing output, measured in dollars, grew in the 1982 to 2004 period—but at a lower rate than GDP. Output per employee increased 189.3 percent in the period, compensation per employee increased by 121.7 percent.

Value added represents the *labor* contribution to this sector of the economy, which is aided by machines. Value added represents the value of shipments less the cost of materials, supplies, containers, fuel, purchased electrical power, and contract work and other services purchased. Part of capital investment includes investment in more efficient machinery allowing a worker to make more product in the same amount of time. From 1982 to 2004, growth in value added per employee (227.7 percent) was greater than growth in capital investment per employee (98.6 percent). This shows that technology played an important role in the manufacturing sector during this time period.

Indicators of Manufacturing

Establishments. Despite the decline in employment, the total number of manufacturing establishments increased from 348,000 in 1982 to 350,000 in 2002. Establishment counts in 2003 (last available year) were down from the 2002 level, but establishment data for non-census years come from the County Business Patterns, a statistical data collection system based on sampling rather than, as in census years, 100 percent reporting by manufacturers.

Employment. Manufacturing employment showed a decline in 2004 from 1982 (see Figure 2). Manufacturing employed more than 17.8 million people in 1982 and more than 13.4 million people in 2004. Manufacturing employment as a percentage of the total labor force dropped from 18.5 percent in 1982 to 9.8 percent in 2004 (nonagricultural payrolls). In the period 1982 to 2004, the total labor force rose 42.5 percent and manufacturing employment dropped by 24.8 percent.

Hourly production employment, representing most manufacturing jobs, decreased at a lower rate (24.5 percent) than employment of administrative, sales, and technical forces (a decline of 25.3 percent), in the 1982 to 2004 period. The latter segment is relatively small and is also most subject to "outsourcing"—as, for instance, by purchasing contract services such as payroll support, computer support, and engineering services. The numbers suggest that corporate "downsizing" is continuing to show up in manufacturing statistics. This is the more probable because production labor actually *increased* from 1992 to 1997 while the administrative, sales, and technical segment continued to lose ground.

Figure 2. Employment in the Manufacturing Sector, 1982-2004

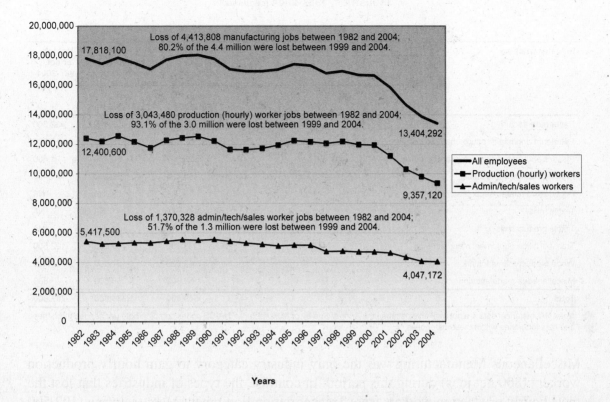

The picture was not so bleak for all industries in the manufacturing sector. Despite the decline in hourly production worker employment throughout the manufacturing sector, some industries gained hourly production worker jobs. Table 1 lists the employment gains and losses for the 137 unchanged ASM NAICS industries by major industrial category.

Table 1. Hourly Production Worker Employment Gains and Losses in Unchanged ASM NAICS Industries, 1987-2004

Industry category	Number of hourly production worker jobs gained 1987-2004	Number of hourly production worker jobs lost 1987-2004	Net job effect, 1987-2004
Apparel manufacturing	NA	NA	NA
Beverage and tobacco product manufacturing	10,900	15,700	-4,800
Chemical manufacturing	24,800	51,400	-26,600
Computer and electronic product manufacturing	63,400	253,800	-190,400
Electrical equipment, appliance, and component manufacturing	65,500	132,100	-66,600
Fabricated metal product manufacturing	38,700	70,900	-32,200
Food manufacturing	19,100	28,200	-9,100
Furniture and related product manufacturing	38,100	80,800	-42,700
Leather and allied product manufacturing	0	57,200	-57,200
Machinery manufacturing	27,400	63,700	-36,300
Nonmetallic mineral product manufacturing	34,800	79,300	-44,500

Table 1. Hourly Production Worker Employment Gains and Losses in Unchanged ASM NAICS Industries, 1987-2004 [continued]

Industry category	Number of hourly production worker jobs gained 1987-2004	Number of hourly production worker jobs lost 1987-2004	Net job effect, 1987-2004
Paper manufacturing	22,800	55,100	-32,300
Petroleum and coal products manufacturing	2,400	18,200	-15,800
Plastics and rubber products manufacturing	29,000	30,400	-1,400
Primary metal manufacturing	34,000	55,900	-21,400
Printing and related support activities	NA	NA	NA
Textile mills	NA	NA	NA
Textile product mills	NA	NA	NA
Transportation equipment manufacturing	38,100	230,600	-192,500
Wood product manufacturing	42,900	57,500	-14,600
Miscellaneous manufacturing	56,600	55,800	+800
Total	**549,000**	**1,336,600**	**-787,600**

Note: NA: historical data are not available because the *Annual Survey of Manufactures'* NAICS codes combine both unchanged industries and new industries within these categories.

Miscellaneous Manufacturing was the only industry category to gain hourly production workers (800 net jobs) during this period. In contrast, the types of industries that lost the most hourly production workers were Transportation Equipment Manufacturing (192,500 net jobs), Computer and Electronic Product Manufacturing (190,400 net jobs), and Electrical Equipment, Appliance, and Component Manufacturing (66,600 net jobs). Table 2 shows the top 5 industries that gained production workers and the top 5 industries that lost production workers.

Table 2. Top 5 Unchanged ASM NAICS Industries With Hourly Production Worker Gains in Employment and Top 5 Unchanged ASM NAICS Industries With Hourly Production Worker Losses in Employment, 1987-2004

NAICS	Industry description	Number of employees	NAICS	Industry description	Number of employees
332721	Precision turned product manufacturing	21,500	336411	Aircraft manufacturing	-58,600
327991	Cut stone and stone product manufacturing	6,900	31621M	Footwear manufacturing	-57,200
336213	Motor home manufacturing	6,900	336414	Guided missile and space vehicle manufacturing	-47,500
327320	Ready-mix concrete manufacturing	6,500	334111	Electronic computer manufacturing	-42,600
321991	Manufactured home (mobile home) manufacturing	5,700	336412	Aircraft engine and engine parts manufacturing	-42,300
339950	Sign manufacturing	5,700			
326160	Plastics bottle manufacturing	4,900			

Compensation. Aggregate compensation levels rose 66.8 percent from 1982 to 2004. Salaries rose faster than hourly wages overall. Compensation in industries with available historical data grew 28.3 percent.

As shown in Figure 3, average yearly income in the manufacturing sector outpaced the average yearly income of the civilian workforce in general. This gap widened between 1982 and 2004. In 1982, the average manufacturing worker made $4,900 more a year than the average civilian worker. In 2004, the average manufacturing worker made $15,000 more a year.

During the 1987 to 2004 period, the yearly wages of hourly production workers in the unchanged ASM NAICS industries were higher than the average hourly production worker overall. The same holds true for the yearly salaries of administrative/technical/sales workers (see Table 3).

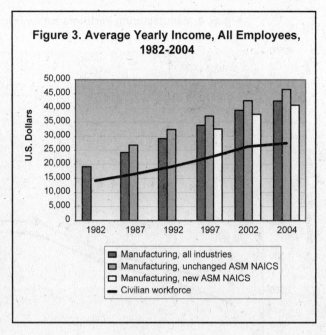

Figure 3. Average Yearly Income, All Employees, 1982-2004

From 1982 to 2004, aggregate hourly wages increased at a lower rate than value of shipments. However, aggregate administrative/technical/sales salaries increased at a higher rate than value of shipments. Aggregate hourly wages increased by 114.8 percent. Administrative/technical/sales salaries increased by 132.7 percent and value of shipments increased by 117.6 percent.

Table 3. Employee Compensation, 1982-2004

[Data in dollars per year. Numbers in **bold** show the highest values per category.]

	1982	1987	1992	1997	2002	2004	Growth (%) 1982-2004	Growth (%) 1987-2004
All employees								
All industries	$19,161	$24,183	$29,153	$33,907	$39,217	42,480	121.7	**75.6**
Unchanged ASM NAICS industries	-	**26,792**	**32,389**	**37,154**	**42,599**	**46,568**	-	73.8
New ASM NAICS industries	-			32,605	37,800	41,029	-	-
Hourly production worker wages								
All industries	16,514	20,476	24,185	28,036	32,598	35,468	114.8	**73.2**
Unchanged ASM NAICS industries	-	**22,551**	**26,567**	**30,569**	**35,349**	**38,655**		71.4
New ASM NAICS industries	-			27,120	31,437	34,375		
Administrative, technical, and sales employee salaries								
All industries	25,218	32,557	40,047	48,850	54,937	58,691	132.7	**80.3**
Unchanged ASM NAICS industries	-	**35,376**	**43,757**	**51,874**	**58,202**	**63,305**		70.9
New ASM NAICS industries	-			47,278	53,405	56,926		

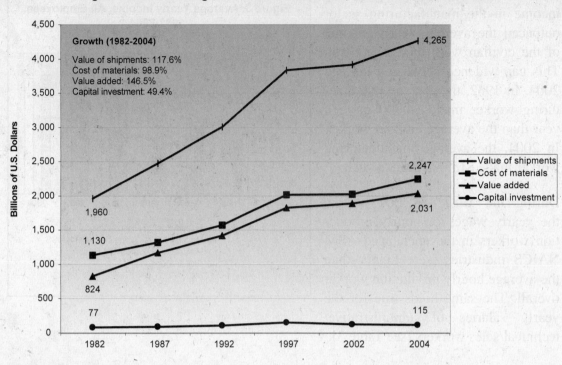

Figure 4. Manufacturing Performance and Growth, Current Dollars, 1982-2004

Performance. In the 1982 to 2004 period, manufacturing shipments declined relative to GDP. Measured as a percent of GDP, manufacturing shipments (roughly equivalent to sales) represented 60.2 percent in 1982 and 36.4 percent in 2004.

In current dollars, costs have grown at nearly twice the rate as capital investment. (See Figure 4). Cost of materials grew 98.9 percent, from $1.1 trillion to $2.2 trillion. Capital investment grew 49.4 percent, from $77 billion to $115 billion. Value added grew the most in this period, 28.9 percentage points higher than the growth in value of shipments. Value added grew 146.5 percent, from $824 billion to $2.0 trillion. Value in shipments rose 117.6 percent, from nearly $2.0 trillion to nearly $4.3 trillion.

In industries for which historical data are available, value of shipments rose at a slower rate than capital investment, but at a faster rate than cost of materials. Value of shipments rose 76.9 percent from $790.7 billion in 1987 to $1.4 trillion in 2004. Capital investment rose 57.0 percent from $26.0 billion to $40.8 billion. Cost of materials rose 73.4 percent from $451.7 billion to $783.1 billion. Growth in value added surpassed growth in value of shipments,s cost of materials, and capital investment. Value added rose 80.2 percent from $343.2 billion in 1987 to $618.4 billion in 2004.

Adjusting for inflation, in the manufacturing sector as a whole, cost of materials and capital investment showed a decline. However, value of shipments and value added grew by 4.2 percent and 18.0 percent, respectively, from 1982 to 2004.

From 1987 to 2004, only capital investment did not outpace inflation in the industries for which historical data are available. It declined by 6.2 percent. Cost of materials grew 3.6 percent, value added grew 7.7 percent and value of shipments grew 5.7 percent.

Figure 5. Manufacturing Productivity, 1987-2004

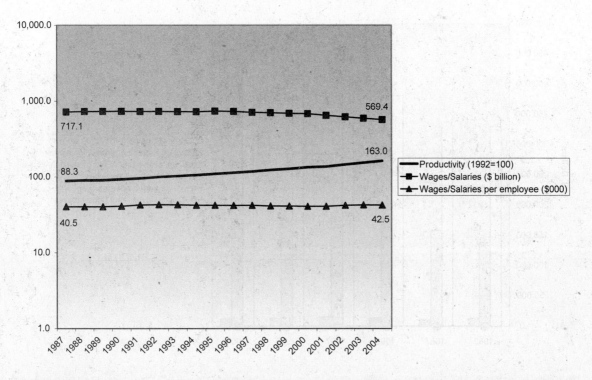

Productivity. Productivity (output per hour) is expressed as an index, with 1992 pegged at 100 (see Figure 5).[1] Wages and salary data are shown in constant 2004 dollars. From 1987 to 2004, productivity rose faster than aggregate wages and salaries and also faster than wages and salaries per employee. In fact, aggregate wages and salaries fell an average of 1.3 percent yearly during this time period—from $717.1 billion to $569.4 billion. The average annual percentage increase in productivity was 3.7 percent. Average annual increase in wages and salaries per employee was 0.3 percent. Conventional wisdom links productivity increases to increases in pay, but the two, in practice, do not always go hand in hand.

Productivity arises from human skills, technology and management. Aggregate wages and salaries declined during this time period while productivity increased. This may mean that technology played a bigger role in manufacturing during this time period than human skill. Other measures indicative of productivity are shown in Figure 6. These measurements confirm the effect of technology on manufacturing productivity. Capital investment, shipments, and value added per employee and per production worker increased from 1982 to 2004. During this period manufacturing jobs overall declined by more than 4.4 million and production worker jobs declined by more than 3.0 million. The manufacturing sector produced more with fewer workers.

Issues in Manufacturing

Free Trade. In 1993, in a debate with Al Gore over the North American Free Trade Agreement (NAFTA), Ross Perot coined the phrase "giant sucking sound" to describe the loss of U.S. jobs to Mexico if NAFTA was ratified. During the debate, he and Pat Choate,

Figure 6. Other Factors in Manufacturing Productivity, 1982-2004

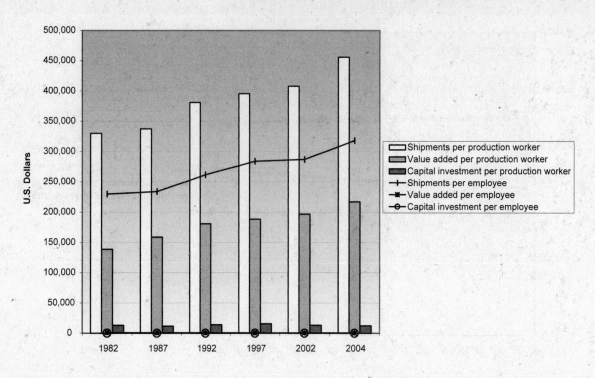

political economist and former vice presidential candidate, claimed that 5 million U.S. jobs would be lost. On January 1, 1994, NAFTA took effect and its consequences are still being debated twelve years later.

On January 1, 1995 the World Trade Organization (WTO) was founded. It is a successor to the General Agreement on Tariffs and Trade (GATT), which was first signed in 1947. The WTO's purpose is to "help trade flow smoothly, freely, fairly, and predictably" by negotiating trade agreements, resolving trade disputes, and providing technical assistance and training to developing countries.[2] Member nations must adhere to a set of rules: agreements that were the result of negotiations between members. These agreements outline the rights and obligations of member nations in order to ensure a "non-discriminatory trading system".[2]

As of August 31, 2005, the WTO had 149 member countries, including the United States. In 2004, trade among WTO members represented 93.7 percent of exports in the world and 95.8 percent of imports in the world. This equated to more than $8.9 trillion in exports and more than $9.2 trillion in imports.

From 1992 (first year of available comparable data) to 2005, export of goods from the United States and import of goods to the United States, on average, trended upward. However, once a country becomes a member of the WTO, the average yearly increase in exports to that country from the U.S. slows. From 1992 to the year a country becomes a member of the WTO, exports from the United States increased an average of 13.1 percent a year. After a country becomes a member of the WTO, exports from the United States slowed to an average increase of 12.9 percent yearly. In contrast, imports of goods from individual countries to the United States increased from an average of 35.0 percent[3] a year before a country joins the WTO to an average of 40.5 percent per year after that country joins the WTO. Table 4 shows the top five WTO member countries the United States exports to and imports from.

The United States did not increase its exports and imports to all member countries during this time period, however. The United States shipped fewer goods to twenty three member countries after their entry into the WTO, most notably Japan ($8.9 billion less) and Venezuela ($2.7 billion less). The United States imported fewer goods from twenty nine member countries after their entry into the WTO. The amount of imports from Singapore and Hong Kong decreased the most: $3.4 billion and $1.3 billion, respectively.

Table 4. Top 5 WTO Member Countries the United States Exports To and Imports From, 1992 to 2005

	EXPORTS			IMPORTS		
Country (Year of WTO Entry)	Total, ($ mil)	Average Total Per Year ($ mil)	Average, Total Per Year, ($ mil)	Country (Year of WTO Entry)	Total, ($ mil)	Average Total Per Year, ($ mil)	Average Total Per Year, ($ mil)
	Year of Entry to 2005		1992 to Year of Entry		Year of Entry to 2005		1992 to Year of Entry
Canada (1995)	84,123.0	7,647.5	9,157.9	Canada (1995)	143,800.3	13,045.5	11,435.0
Mexico (1995)	73,756.0	6,705.1	1,424.9	China (2001)	141,183.9	35,296.0	7,655.1
China (2001)	22,654.2	5,663.5	1,176.3	Mexico (1995)	108,097.5	9,827.0	6,722.3
Germany (1995)	11,754.9	1,068.6	286.5	Germany (1995)	47,968.6	4,360.8	2,005.9
Netherlands (1995)	9,938.0	903.5	701.5	Ireland (1995)	24,542.3	2,231.1	454.2

Employment. Between 1982 and 1992, nearly 760,000 hourly production worker jobs were lost in the United States. In the next 5 years, from 1992 to 1997, more than 424,000 jobs were created. After one more year of upturn, production worker jobs declined again. From 1997 to 2004, more than 2.7 million production worker jobs were lost. Despite the slight upturn from 1992 to 1998, overall, the United States lost more than 3.0 million production worker jobs between 1982 and 2004. From 1982 to 2004, more than 1.3 million administrative, technical, and sales jobs were lost also, with the greatest loss during the 1992 to 1997 period. Overall, from 1982 to 2004, the manufacturing sector lost more than 4.4 million jobs.

Not all of these job losses can be attributed to companies exporting jobs to foreign countries. As discussed earlier, from 1982 to 2004, technology played an important role in manufacturing. Value added per employee increased while the number of workers decreased. However, job losses due to NAFTA were anticipated. The NAFTA-Transitional Adjustment Assistance Program (NAFTA-TAA) was established as part of the NAFTA Implementation Act of 1993. This program was set up to help workers whose companies were directly or indirectly affected by trade with or by production shifting to Mexico or Canada. This program provided up to 52 weeks of unemployment benefits and worker retraining. According to the U.S. Department of Labor, from 1994 to 2003, more than 525,000 workers were certified as eligible for this program and its successor, the Trade Adjustment Assistance Reform Act of 2002 (TAA).

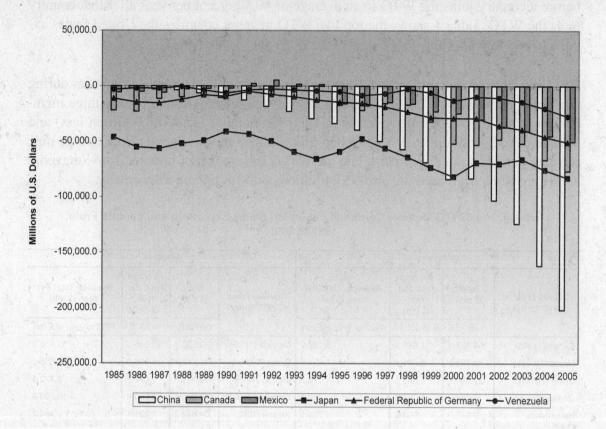

Figure 7. Countries with the Largest Trade Deficits with the United States, 1985-2005

In 2002, the NAFTA-TAA program was replaced by the TAA. This program added to the benefits of NAFTA-TAA by providing health care assistance to displaced workers. Under Section 113 of this act, "workers may be eligible to apply ... if they were laid off as a result of increased imports or if their companies shifted production out of the United States to certain foreign countries."[4] The TAA also increased the number of foreign countries covered and included not only Canada and Mexico, but Israel, Jordan, most of the countries in Africa, and many countries in Central and South America and the Caribbean. However, China and Japan were not on this list. Yet, these two countries had the highest and second highest merchandise trade deficit with the United States since 1991 (see Figure 7).

Merchandise trade deficit. Much debate in recent years has centered around the trade deficit. From 1982 to 2005 the trade deficit has grown more than 2,042 percent from $36.4 billion in 1982 to $781.6 billion in 2005.

World Trade. From 1982 to 2001, United States merchandise exports as a percentage of total world exports remained constant at around 11 percent. However, from 2001 to 2004, United States merchandise exports as a percentage of total world exports trended downward, from 11.6 percent to 8.8 percent. In contrast, merchandise imports into the United States as a percentage of total world imports trended upward from 12.8 percent in 1982 to 15.4 percent in 2004.

Figure 8. U.S. Investment in Manufacturing Abroad vs. Foreign Investment in Manufacturing in the U.S., 1982-2004

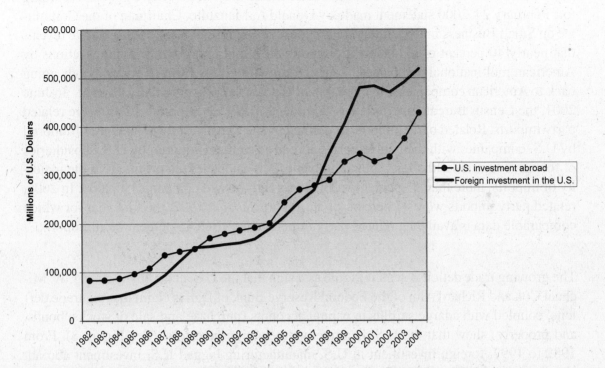

Globalization. Companies closing their factories in the U.S. and moving their manufacturing plants overseas or across the border are growing in number. In the 1990s, some industrialized nations were offering multi-million dollar grants, tax holidays, and other financial incentives to entice American manufacturers to build plants in their countries. Because of this, some high-tech companies moved their manufacturing operations to countries like Northern Ireland, Japan, and Italy.

But for many companies that have closed U.S. plants, and others that have not yet done so, outsourcing to foreign manufacturing companies offers a more economical alternative. Low labor costs and savings from eliminating factory overhead costs entice U.S. firms to outsource to countries such as Mexico, Singapore, Pakistan, Malaysia, Taiwan, Korea, and China.

According to Martha Ojeda, director of the Coalition for Justice in the Maquiladoras, in 2004, the government-mandated minimum wage for workers in assembly plants in Mexico was $4.20 a day, the same as in 1994 when NAFTA took effect. A gallon of milk in Tijuana, Mexico cost $3.[5] In comparison, the Federal minimum wage in the United States was $5.15 per hour and, according to the Bureau of Labor Statistics, the median hourly wage for production workers was $12.74 in 2004. But, despite the comparatively low wages, by 2003, foreign companies who have done business in Mexico were now looking to outsource to countries such as China and Sri Lanka. By 2006, U.S. corporations were contemplating relocation of their factories to "lower-cost countries such as Vietnam and Indonesia"[6] due to labor shortages, an average 14 percent employee turnover rate, and rising wages in China. At one factory in Dongguan, wages in 2005 rose 40 percent to an average of $160 a month.

Globalization and the trade deficit. As companies outsource or move manufacturing plants across the border or overseas, the United States must import more goods. According to a February 24, 2000 statement made by Donald A. Manzullo, Chairman of the Committee on Small Business in the United States House of Representatives, "one estimate reveals that nearly 40 percent of all American imports are simply intra-company transactions by American multinational companies."[7] Therefore, with profits from imported goods going back to American companies, the trade deficit is not as large as originally thought. In June 2001, the Census Bureau reported that 47 percent of all U.S. imports in 2000 were related party imports. Related party imports, as defined by the Census Bureau, "includes [imports] by U.S. companies with their subsidiaries abroad as well as [imports] by U.S. subsidiaries of foreign countries with their parent companies."[8] That leaves the profits from the majority of imports, more than 53 percent, going to foreign-owned companies in 2000. In 2005, related party imports were 47 percent of all imports also. In 1992, the first year for which comparable data is available, related party imports comprised 45 percent of all imports.

The growing trade deficit is seen by some as a sign that the U.S. economy is strong. W. Michael Cox and Richard Alm of the Federal Reserve Bank of Dallas claim that big trade deficits, coupled with a large surplus in capital accounts (purchase and sale of stocks, bonds, and property) show that the U.S. is attractive to foreign investors. (See Figure 8). From 1982 to 1997, foreign investment in U.S. manufacturing lagged U.S. investment abroad. However, from 1998 to 2004, foreign investment in U.S. manufacturing far exceeded U.S. investment in manufacturing abroad. In 2004, foreign companies invested $91 billion more in the U.S. manufacturing sector than the U.S. invested in the manufacturing sector abroad. However, as a percentage of total U.S. investment by foreign companies, manufacturing investment by foreign companies declined slightly from 35.3 percent in 1982 to 34.0 percent in 2004.

In comparison, U.S. investment in manufacturing abroad increased from more than $83 billion in 1982 to more than $428 billion in 2004. And, like foreign investment in U.S. manufacturing, U.S. manufacturing investment abroad as a percentage of total investment abroad declined. But this decline was more substantial, from 40.2 percent in 1982 to 20.7 percent in 2004. This decline signals an increase in investment into other sectors of foreign economies, most notably the Management of Companies and Enterprises sector. By 2004, 34.4 percent of the U.S. investment dollars abroad went to this sector of foreign economies. More than 99 percent of it was invested in the management of non-bank holding companies. The Finance, Insurance, Real Estate, Rental, and Leasing sector garnered 22.9 percent of the U.S. investment dollars abroad.

Those opposed to large trade deficits point to the loss of manufacturing jobs in the U.S. as a sign that the trade deficit and globalization are detrimental to the economy. However, total employment increased from 1982 to 2004 and the unemployment rate went from 9.7 in 1982 to 5.5 in 2004. Productivity also rose during this time period. Total corporate profits rose from $191.0 billion in 1982 to slightly more than $1 trillion in 2004. Corporate profits in manufacturing rose from $67.1 billion in 1982 to $118.9 billion in 2004.

Opponents to globalization argue that the jobs that were created do not pay as well as the jobs that were lost. Most often cited are jobs in the retail and service sector, such as the pay of retail sales personnel, of cashiers, and of waiters and waitresses. According to the U.S. Bureau of Labor Statistics (BLS), in 2005, the median hourly wage for these workers ranged from $6.83 for waiters and waitresses up to $9.20 for retail sales persons. The median hourly wage for production workers was $13.33.

But, as Table 5 shows, not all jobs created were waiters, waitresses, cashiers, or retail sales persons. Many jobs created paid, on average, close to if not above the average hourly manufacturing wage. According to the BLS, from 1982 to 2005, the number of workers being paid at or below the Federal minimum wage dropped by 4.6 million. In 1982, almost 6.5 million workers, or 12.8 percent of the hourly paid worker population, were paid at or below the Federal minimum wage. In 2005, 1.9 million workers, or 2.5 percent of the hourly paid worker population, were being paid wages at or below the Federal minimum wage.

Table 5. Change in Employment and Average Hourly Wages, by Economic Sector, 1982-2005

[Average hourly wages for manufacturing production workers was $16.56 in 2005]

Sector	Change in Employment, 1982-2005 (000)	Average Hourly Wage ($)		Hourly Wage Difference Between Current Sector and Manufacturing Sector, 2005
		1982	2005	
Education and health services	9,827.0	7.00	16.72	+0.16
Professional and business services	9,034.0	8.30	18.07	+1.51
Leisure and hospitality	5,928.0	4.52	9.14	-7.42
Retail trade	4,883.2	6.34	12.36	-4.20
Construction	3,253.0	11.04	19.46	+2.90
Financial activities	2,932.0	6.82	17.94	+1.38
Other services	2,462.0	6.11	14.33	-2.23
Transportation and warehousing	1,530.1	10.67	16.71	+0.15
Wholesale trade	1,175.0	8.81	18.16	+1.60
Information	749.0	10.76	22.07	+5.51

Buy American. In 1933, President Herbert Hoover signed the Buy American Act (BAA). The Act imposed restrictions on Federal government contracts. The Federal government was now obligated to buy products that were at least 50 percent manufactured in the United States. However, the Act exempted the Federal government if the government agency concerned determined American-made products "to be inconsistent with the public interest, or the cost to be unreasonable."[9] No clarification was given in the law as to what "inconsistent with the public interest" or "cost to be unreasonable" meant. Also, this law exempted government agencies from buying American products if the products would be used outside of the United States or if those American-made manufactured items would be unavailable "in sufficient and reasonably available commercial quantities and of a satisfactory quality."

Because of these exemptions, complying with the Buy American Act did not always result in the selection of American companies that employ a majority of American workers.

Many American companies vying for government contracts, including Department of Defense contracts, have moved some or all of their manufacturing operations overseas. In response to this trend, U.S. Senator Russ Feingold of Wisconsin introduced the Buy American Improvement Act (BAIA) in 2003. A similar bill was introduced in the House of Representatives in 2004 by Ohio Representatives Sherrod Brown and Tim Ryan.

In an attempt to limit the Buy American Act waivers, the bill would require the U.S. Commerce Secretary to appoint a panel composed of industry, labor, and academic representatives in order to define "consistent with the public interest" and "cost to be unreasonable" as stated in the original 1933 bill. It would also increase the percentage of American made parts per product from 50 percent to 75 percent. U.S. companies would be granted preference for a government contract if their bids were comparable to foreign companies' bids or if they were the only U.S. company producing that particular product.

The BAIA would apply to Congress, the Legislative Branch, and U.S. agencies operating outside the U.S. (military bases, embassies, other government facilities), all of which were exempted from the BAA. Also under the BAIA, each agency must file an annual report with Congress providing an itemized list of BAA waivers and the dollar amount for each. These reports will be made public giving "the American people a clear picture of each agency's commitment to U.S. companies." [10]

In a response to the findings in the Government Accountability Office (GAO) report *Federal Procurement: International Agreements Result in Waivers of Some U.S. Domestic Source Restrictions*, released January 2005, U.S. Senator Russ Feingold reintroduced the BAIA, renamed the Buy American Improvement Act of 2005. The GAO report found that "current trade agreements result in the waiver of the Buy American Act...for certain products from 45 countries.... [These] waivers...allow products from the countries involved to compete in a comparable manner [with U.S.-made products]." [11] On February 16, 2005, the Act was referred to the Committee on Homeland Security and Governmental Affairs.

In May 2005, United States Representative Donald A. Manzullo introduced a controversial amendment to the Homeland Security Authorization Act of 2006. The amendment, similar to the BAIA, would require "that more than 50 percent of the components in end products purchased by the Department of Homeland Security...be mined, produced or manufactured inside the U. S." [12] The amendment would also prevent waivers of the Buy American Act without approval of Congress. In a U.S. House of Representatives Press Release, Representative Manzullo declared: "when U.S. taxpayers' dollars are spent, we must make sure the federal government is buying as much of their goods and services as possible from U.S. manufacturers." [13]

The president of the Information Technology Association of America, Harris Miller, countered Representative Manzullo's statements by saying "... I guess (the department) will have to learn to do without computers and cell phones.... I cannot think of a single U.S. manufacturer that could meet this 50 percent threshold for these devices..." According to Miller, the amendment also would increase the government's cost and adversely affect global trade by opening up the possibility of other countries imposing trade restrictions on the United States.[14] United States Representative Tom Davis, in a statement opposing the amendment, expressed a similar viewpoint when he said "this restriction would have a devastating effect on the Department of Homeland Security's ability to buy the most high-tech and sophisticated products at a reasonable price to support our critical anti-terror efforts.... [T]his provision will require the Department to pay an artificially high price for products it needs to protect us against terror.... We should not be wasting our Homeland Security dollars...."[12]

In May 2005, the amendment passed in the United States House of Representatives. It was then attached to the Defense Department Reauthorization Act, in addition to becoming a part of the Department of Homeland Security Authorization Act. However, when these bills were passed by Congress they no longer contained the full amendment.

[1] 1987-2004 data are based on the North American Industrial Classification System. Prior data are based on the Standard Industrial Classification; therefore, 1982-1986 data are not comparable to later data and are not included with the aggregate productivity statistics.

[2] *Source:* "The World Trade Organization In Brief," World Trade Organization, Geneva, Switzerland [Online] http://www.wto.org/english/thewto_e/whatis_e/whatis_e.htm [accessed May 24, 2006]

[3] The import averages for 1992 to the year of entry into the WTO do not include Chad. In 1992, goods imported from Chad into the United States totalled $100,000. In 2004, when Chad entered the WTO, imports from Chad totalled nearly $1.4 billion, a total increase of 1,497,300 percent or an average increase of 115,176.9 percent per year.

[4] *Source:* "NAFTA-Transitional Adjustment Assistance (1994-2002)," Public Citizen, Washington, DC [Online] http://www.citizen.org/trade/formas/taa_search.cfm?dataset=1 [accessed February 4, 2004]

[5] *Source:* Bacon, David, "More Poverty as NAFTA Turns 10," Organic Consumers Association, Little Marais, MN, January 19, 2004, reprint of article in the *San Francisco Monitor*, January 14, 2004 [Online] http://www.organicconsumers.org/corp/nafta011904.cfm [accessed February 5, 2004]

[6] *Source:* Dexter Roberts, "How Rising Wages Are Changing The Game in China," *BusinessWeek Online,* March 27, 2006 [Online] http://www.businessweek.com/magazine/content/06_13/b3977049.htm [accessed May 25, 2006]

[7] *Source:* Manzullo, Donald A. and Carolyn McCarthy, "Remarks of the Honorable Donald A. Manzullo Before the Trade Deficit Review Commission," U.S. House of Representatives, Washington, DC, February 24, 2000 [Online] http://www.ustdrc.gov/hearings/24feb00/smanzullo.pdf [accessed February 4, 2004]

[8] *Source:* "U.S. Goods Trade: Imports & Exports by Related Parties: 2000," *United States Department of Commerce News,* Economics and Statistics Administration, U.S. Census Bureau, Washington, DC, June 26, 2001 [Online] http://www.census.gov/foreign-trade/Press-Release/2000pr/aip/related-party.html [accessed May 26, 2006]

[9] *Source*: "Section 10a. American materials required for public use," *FindLaw for Legal Professionals,* Mountain View, CA, January 2, 2001 [Online] http://caselaw.lp.findlaw.com/casecode/uscodes/41/chapters/1/sections/section10a.html [accessed February 10, 2004]

[10] *Source*: "Brown, Ryan Introduce Bill to Strengthen 'Buy American' Laws," *Press Release,* United States House of Representatives, Washington, DC, January 30, 2004 [Online] http://www.house.gov/sherrodbrown/buyamerican13004.html [accessed February 10, 2004]

11 *Source: Federal Procurement: International Agreements Result in Waivers of Some U.S. Domestic Source Restrictions,* GAO-05-188, United States Government Accountability Office, Washington, DC, January 2005 [Online] http://www.gao.gov/ [accessed May 30, 2006]

12 *Source:* "Department of Homeland Security Authorization Act For Fiscal Year 2006 – (House of Representatives - May 18, 2005)," *Congressional Record for the 109th Congress – House,* U.S. Government Printing Office, Washington, DC, May 18, 2005 [Online] http://thomas.loc.gov/cgi-bin/query/F?r109:29:./temp/~r109o5TVf6:e458159: [accessed May 30, 2006]

13 *Source:* "U.S. House Approves Manzullo Amendment to Require Department of Homeland Security to Buy American," *Press Release,* U.S. House of Representatives, Washington, DC, May 18, 2005 [Online] http://manzullo.house.gov/HoR/IL16/news/Press+Releases/Press+Releases+2005/House+Passes+Manzullo+Provision+to+Require+Department+of+Homeland+Security+to+Buy+American.htm [accessed May 30, 2006]

14 *Source:* Frauenheim, Ed, "'Buy American' Legislation Draws Fire," *CNET News.com,* May 20, 2005 [Online] http://news.com.com/Buy+American+legislation+draws+fire/2100-1022_3-5715486.html [accessed May 30, 2006]

Graphics Sources

Figure 1: Adapted from "Value Added by Industry in Current Dollars, Quantity Indexes by Industry, and Price Indexes by Industry, 1947-1997; Value Added by Industry, Gross Output by Industry, Intermediate Inputs by Industry, and the Components of Value Added by Industry, 1987-1997" and "Value Added by Industry, Gross Output by Industry, Intermediate Inputs by Industry, The Components of Value Added by Industry, and Employment by Industry," *Gross Domestic Product (GDP) by Industry Data*, U.S. Department of Commerce, Bureau of Economic Analysis, Washington, DC, April 27, 2006 [Online] http://www.bea.gov/bea/dn2/gdpbyind_data.htm [accessed May 16, 2006]

Figure 2, Table 1, Table 2, Figure 4, Figure 6: Adapted from "Table 1. Statistics for All Manufacturing Establishments: 2004 and Earlier Years," *Annual Survey of Manufactures*, U.S. Census Bureau, Washington, DC, December 20, 2005

Figure 3, Table 3: Adapted from *1982, 1987, 1992, 1997,* and *2002 Economic Census* and *Annual Survey of Manufactures*, U.S. Census Bureau, Washington, DC, various publication dates; "Average Weekly Earnings of Production Workers, Total Private: Not Seasonally Adjusted," *Employment, Hours, and Earnings from the Current Employment Statistics Survey (National),* U.S. Department of Labor, Bureau of Labor Statistics, Washington, DC [Online] http://www.bls.gov/ces/home.htm [accessed May 19, 2006]

Figure 5: Adapted from "Table 1. Statistics for All Manufacturing Establishments: 2004 and Earlier Years," *Annual Survey of Manufactures*, U.S. Census Bureau, Washington, DC, December 20, 2005 and "Flat Files (FTP)," *Major Sector Productivity and Costs,* U.S. Department of Labor, Bureau of Labor Statistics, Washington, DC [Online] http://ftp.bls.gov/pub/time.series/pr/pr.data.1.AllData [accessed January 30, 2004 and May 22, 2006]

Table 4: Adapted from "U.S. Trade in Goods (Imports, Exports and Balance) by Country," *Foreign Trade Statistics*, U.S. Census Bureau, Washington, DC, May 11, 2006

[Online] http://www.census.gov/foreign-trade/balance/index.html [accessed June 2, 2006]; "Members and Observers," *Understanding the WTO: The Organization*, World Trade Organization, Geneva, Switzerland [Online] http://www.wto.org/english/thewto_e/whatis_e/tif_e/org6_e.htm [accessed June 2, 2006] and "NAFTA and GATT Intellectual Property Issues," *Ladas & Perry Bulletin*, December 2004, revised April 23, 1996 [Online] http://www.ladas.com/BULLETINS/1994/NAFTAGATT.html [accessed June 2, 2006]

Figure 7: Adapted from "Trade in Goods (Imports, Exports and Trade Balance) with China," "Trade in Goods (Imports, Exports and Trade Balance) with Canada," "Trade in Goods (Imports, Exports and Trade Balance) with Japan," "Trade in Goods (Imports, Exports and Trade Balance) with Federal Republic of Germany," "Trade in Goods (Imports, Exports and Trade Balance) with Mexico," and "Trade in Goods (Imports, Exports and Trade Balance) with Venezuela," *Foreign Trade Statistics,* U.S. Census Bureau, Washington, DC [Online] http://www.census.gov/foreign-trade/balance/ [accessed May 24, 2006]

Figure 8: Adapted from "U.S. Direct Investment Abroad: Balance of Payments and Direct Investment Position Data: Historical Data," U.S. Department of Commerce, Bureau of Economic Analysis, Washington, DC, March 27, 2006 [Online] http://www.bea.doc.gov/bea/di/di1usdbal.htm [accessed May 25, 2006], "Foreign Direct Investment in the US: Balance of Payments and Direct Investment Position Data: Historical Data," U.S. Department of Commerce, Bureau of Economic Analysis, Washington, DC, March 27, 2006 [Online] http://www.bea.doc.gov/bea/di/di1fdibal.htm [accessed May 25, 2006], "Foreign Direct Investment Position in the United States on a Historical-Cost Basis, 2003," *International Economic Accounts,* U.S. Department of Commerce, Bureau of Economic Analysis, Washington, DC [Online] http://www.bea.gov/bea/di/fdipos/fdipos-03.htm [accessed May 25, 2006], and "Foreign Direct Investment Position in the United States on a Historical-Cost Basis, 2004," *International Economic Accounts,* U.S. Department of Commerce, Bureau of Economic Analysis, Washington, DC [Online] http://www.bea.gov/bea/di/fdipos/fdipos-04.htm [accessed May 25, 2006]

Table 5: *Employment, Hours, and Earnings from the Current Employment Statistics Survey (National)*, U.S. Department of Labor, Bureau of Labor Statistics, Washington, DC [Online] http://data.bls.gov/PDQ/servlet/SurveyOutputServlet [accessed May 26, 2006]

Annotated Source List

"1. Employment status of the civilian noninstitutional population, 1940 to date," *Current Population Survey,* U.S. Department of Labor, Bureau of Labor Statistics, Washington, DC [Online] http://www.bls.gov/cps/cpsaat1.pdf [accessed May 17, 2006]

1982, 1987, 1992, 1997, and *2002 Economic Census*, U.S. Census Bureau, Washington, DC, various publication dates

Annual Survey of Manufactures, U.S. Census Bureau, Washington, DC, various publication dates

Bacon, David, "More Poverty as NAFTA Turns 10," Organic Consumers Association, Little Marais, MN, January 19, 2004, reprint of article in the *San Francisco Monitor*, January 14, 2004 [Online] http://www.organicconsumers.org/corp/nafta011904.cfm [accessed February 5, 2004]

"Brown, Ryan Introduce Bill to Strengthen 'Buy American' Laws," *Press Release*, United States House of Representatives, Washington, DC, January 30, 2004 [Online] http://www.house.gov/sherrodbrown/buyamerican13004.html [accessed February 10, 2004]

"College Degree Nearly Doubles Annual Earnings, Census Bureau Reports," *U.S. Census Bureau News*, U.S. Department of Commerce, U.S. Census Bureau, March 28, 2005 [Online] http://www.census.gov/Press-Release/www/releases/archives/education/004214.html [accessed May 16, 2006]

"Congressional Record Statement of Russ Feingold on the Buy American Improvement Act," February 16, 2005 [Online] http://feingold.senate.gov/statements/05/02/2005414B05.html [accessed May 30, 2006]

County Business Patterns, U.S. Census Bureau, Washington, DC, various publication dates

"Department of Homeland Security Authorization Act For Fiscal Year 2006 – (House of Representatives - May 18, 2005)," *Congressional Record for the 109th Congress – House,* Government Printing Office, Washington, DC, May 18, 2005 [Online] http://thomas.loc.gov/cgi-bin/query/F?r109:29:./temp/~r109o5TVf6:e458159: [accessed May 30, 2006]

Employment, Hours, and Earnings from the Current Employment Statistics Survey (National), U.S. Department of Labor, Bureau of Labor Statistics, Washington, DC [Online] http://data.bls.gov/servlet/SurveyOutputServlet [accessed May 26, 2006]

"Employment Level: Not Seasonally Adjusted," *Labor Force Statistics from the Current Population Survey,* U.S. Department of Labor, Bureau of Labor Statistics, Washington, DC [Online] http://data.bls.gov/PDQ/servlet/SurveyOutputServlet [accessed May 26, 2006]

"Exhibit 5. U.S. Trade in Goods," *FT900: U.S. International Trade in Goods and Services March 2006,* U.S. Census Bureau, U.S. Bureau of Economic Analysis, Washington, DC, May 12, 2006 [Online] http://www.census.gov/foreign-trade/Press-Release/current_press_release/exh5.pdf [accessed May 24, 2006]

Federal Procurement: International Agreements Result in Waivers of Some U.S. Domestic Source Restrictions, GAO-05-188, United States Government Accountability Office, Washington, DC, January 2005 [Online] http://www.gao.gov/ [accessed May 30, 2006]

"Flat Files (FTP)," *Major Sector Productivity and Costs,* U.S. Department of Labor, Bureau of Labor Statistics, Washington, DC [Online] ftp://ftp.bls.gov/pub/time.series/pr/pr.data.1.AllData [accessed January 30, 2004 and May 22, 2006]

"Foreign Direct Investment in the U.S.: Balance of Payments and Direct Investment Position Data: Historical Data," U.S. Department of Commerce, Bureau of Economic Analysis, Washington, DC [Online] http://www.bea.gov/bea/di/di1fdibal.htm [accessed May 25, 2006]

"Foreign Direct Investment Position in the United States on a Historical-Cost Basis, 2003," *International Economic Accounts,* U.S. Department of Commerce, Bureau of Economic Analysis, Washington, DC [Online] http://www.bea.gov/di/fdipos/fdipos-03.htm [accessed May 25, 2006]

"Foreign Direct Investment Position in the United States on a Historical-Cost Basis, 2004," *International Economic Accounts,* U.S. Department of Commerce, Bureau of Economic Analysis, Washington, DC [Online] http://www.bea.gov/di/fdipos/fdipos-04.htm [accessed May 25, 2006]

Frauenheim, Ed, "'Buy American' legislation draws fire," *CNET News.com,* May 20, 2005 [Online] http://news.com.com/Buy+American+legislation+draws+fire/2100-1022_3-5715486.html [accessed May 30, 2006]

"Free Trade Agreement and Trade Beneficiary Countries," U.S. Department of Labor, Employment & Training Administration, Washington, DC [Online] http://www.doleta.gov/tradeact/2002act_freetradeagreements.cfm [accessed May 24, 2006]

"Industry: Sectors 31, 32, and 33 - Manufacturing (NAICS code 31-34)," *Occupational Employment Statistics,* U.S. Department of Labor, Bureau of Labor Statistics, Washington, DC [Online] http://data.bls.gov/oes/datatype.do [accessed May 26, 2006]

International Trade Statistics 2005, World Trade Organization, Geneva, Switzerland, 2005 [Online] http://www.wto.org/english/res_e/statis_e/its2005_e/its05_toc_e.htm [accessed May 24, 2005]

LaFranchi, Howard, "A decade later, a tempered vision of NAFTA," *The Christian Science Monitor,* December 30, 3003 [Online] http://www.csmonitor.com/2003/1230/p02s01-usec.html [accessed January 13, 2004]

Manzullo, Donald A. and Carolyn McCarthy, "Remarks of the Honorable Donald A. Manzullo Before the Trade Deficit Review Commission," U.S. House of Representatives, Washington, DC, February 24, 2000 [Online] http://www.ustdrc.gov/hearings/24feb00/smanzullo.pdf [accessed February 4, 2004]

May 2005 National Occupational Employment and Wage Estimates: United States, U.S. Department of Labor, Bureau of Labor Statistics, Washington, DC [Online] http://www.bls.gov/oes/current/oes_nat.htm [accessed May 26, 2006]

"Members and Observers," *Understanding the WTO: The Organization*, World Trade Organization, Geneva, Switzerland [Online] http://www.wto.org/english/thewto_e/whatis_e/tif_e/org6_e.htm [accessed June 2, 2006]

"NAFTA and GATT Intellectual Property Issues," *Ladas & Perry Bulletin*, December 2004, revised April 23, 1996 [Online] http://www.ladas.com/BULLETINS/1994/NAFTAGATT.html [accessed June 2, 2006]

"NAFTA-Transitional Adjustment Assistance," U.S. Department of Labor, Employment & Training Administration, Washington, DC [Online] http://www.dolets.gov/programs/factsht/nafta.cfm [accessed February 4, 2004]

"NAFTA-Transitional Adjustment Assistance (1994-2002)," Public Citizen, Washington, DC [Online] http://www.citizen.org/trade/formas/taa_search.cfm?dataset=1 [accessed February 4, 2004]

"North American Free Trade Agreement - Transitional Adjustment Adjustment Assistance Estimated Number of Workers Covered by Certifications," U.S. Department of Labor, Employment & Training Administration, Washington, DC [Online] http://www.doleta.gov/tradeact/nafta_certs.htm [accessed May 23, 2006]

Porteus, Liza, "'Buy American' Provisions Return for More Congressional Debate," *FoxNews.com*, June 5, 2005 [Online] http://www.foxnews.com/story/0,2933,158462,00,html [accessed May 30, 2005]

Roberts, Dexter, "How Rising Wages Are Changing The Game in China," *BusinessWeek Online*, March 27, 2006 [Online] http://www.businessweek.com/magazine/content/06_13/b3977049.htm [accessed May 25, 2006]

"Section 10a. American materials required for public use," *FindLaw for Legal Professionals*, Mountain View, CA, January 2, 2001 [Online] http://caselaw.lp.findlaw.com/casecode/uscodes/41/chapters/1/sections/section10a.html [accessed February 10, 2004]

"Table 10. Employed wage and salary workers paid hourly rates with earnings at or below the prevailing Federal minimum wage by sex, 1979-2005 annual averages," *Characteristics of Minimum Wage Workers: 2005*, U.S. Department of Labor, Bureau of Labor Statistics, Washington, DC [Online] http://www.bls.gov/cps/minwage2005tbls.htm#10 [accessed May 26, 2005]

"Table B-6. Chain-type quantity indexes for gross domestic product, 1959-2004," *Economic Report of the President: 2005*, U.S. Government Printing Office, Washington, DC, February 2005 [Online] http://www.gpoaccess.gov/eop/2005/2005_ero.pdf [accessed January 17, 2006]

"Table B-91. Corporate profits by industry, 1959-2005," *Economic Report of the President: 2006*, U.S. Government Printing Office, Washington, DC, February 2006 [Online] http://www.gpoaccess.gov/eop/tables06.html [accessed May 26, 2006]

"Table B-103. U.S. international transactions, 1946-2005," *Economic Report of the President: 2006*, U.S. Government Printing Office, Washington, DC, February 2006 [Online] http://www.gpoaccess.gov/eop/tables06.htm#erp9 [accessed May 25, 2006]

"Top Ten Countries With Which the U.S. Has A Trade Deficit for the Month of December 2005," U.S. Census Bureau, Washington, DC [Online] http://www.census.gov/foreign-trade/top/dst/2005/12/deficit.html [accessed May 24, 2006]

"Trade Adjustment Assistance Reform Act of 2002," U.S. Department of Labor, Employment & Training Administration, Washington, DC [Online] http://www.doleta.gov/tradeact/2002act_index.cfm [accessed February 4, 2004]

"Trade Adjustment Assistance (TAA) and Alternative Trade Adjustment Assistance (ATAA) Services and Benefits," U.S. Department of Labor, Employment & Training Administration, Washington, DC [Online] http://www.doleta.gov/tradeact/benefits.cfm#3 [accessed May 23, 2006]

"Trade Deficit Explained," National Center for Policy Analysis, Dallas, TX, 2001 [Online] http://www.ncpa.org/pd/trade/tradea4.html [accessed February 6, 2004]

"Trade in Goods (Imports, Exports and Trade Balance)," *Foreign Trade Statistics,* U.S. Census Bureau, Washington, DC [Online] http://www.census.gov/foreign-trade/balance/index.html [accessed May-June, 2006]

"Total Merchandise Trade," *World Trade Organization Statistics Database,* World Trade Organization, Geneva, Switzerland [Online] http://stat.wto.org/StatisticalProgram/WSDB ViewData.aspx?Language=E [accessed May 25, 2006]

United States, Cong. House of Representatives, 109th Congress, 1st Session, *H.R. 2360 An Act Making Appropriations for the Department of Homeland Security for the Fiscal Year Ending September 30, 2006, and for Other Purposes,* Congressional Bills, GPO Access [Online] http://www.gpoaccess.gov/bills/index.html [accessed June 13, 2006]

United States, Cong. House of Representatives, 109th Congress, 1st Session, *H.R. 2863 An Act Making Appropriations for the Department of Defense for the Fiscal Year Ending September 30, 2006, and for Other Purposes,* Congressional Bills, GPO Access [Online] http://www.gpoaccess.gov/bills/index.html [accessed June 13, 2006]

United States, Cong. Senate, 109th Congress, 1st Session, *S. 395 A Bill to Amend the Buy American Act to Increase the Requirement for American-made Content, to Tighten the Waiver Provisions, and for Other Purposes* [introduced in the Senate February 16, 2005], Congressional Bills, GPO Access [Online] http://www.gpoaccess.gov/bills/index.html [accessed May 30, 2006]

"U.S. Direct Investment Abroad: Detailed Annual Balances of Payments and Position Estimates: Historical Data," U.S. Department of Commerce, Bureau of Economic Analysis, Washington, DC, March 27, 2006 [Online] http://www.bea.gov/bea/di/di1usdbal.htm [accessed May 25, 2006]

"U.S. Goods Trade: Imports & Exports by Related Parties: 2000," *United States Department of Commerce News,* June 26, 2001 [Online] http://www.census.gov/foreign-trade/Press-Release/2000pr/aip/related-party.html [accessed May 26, 2006]

"U.S. Goods Trade: Imports & Exports by Related Parties: 2005," *U.S. Census Bureau News,* May 12, 2006 [Online] http://www.census.gov/foreign-trade/Press-Release/2005pr/aip/related-party.html [accessed May 26, 2006]

"U.S. House Approves Manzullo Amendment to Require Department of Homeland Security to Buy American," *Press Release,* U.S. House of Representatives, Washington, DC, May 18, 2005 [Online] http://manzullo.house.gov/HoR/IL16/news/Press+Release/Press+Releases+2005/House+Passes+Manzullo+Provision+to+Require+Department+of+Homeland+Security+to+Buy+American.htm [accessed May 30, 2006]

"U.S. Senator Russ Feingold on the Buy American Act," *Russ Feingold Speech*, July 29, 2003 [Online] http://feingold.senate.gov/speeches/03/07/2003820902.html [accessed February 10, 2004]

"U.S. Trade in Goods and Services - Balance of Payments (BOP) Basis," U.S. Census Bureau, Foreign Trade Division, March 9, 2006 [Online] http://www.census.gov/foreign-trade/statistics/historical/index.html [accessed May 24, 2006]

"Value Added by Industry, Gross Output by Industry, Intermediate Inputs by Industry, the Components of Value Added by Industry, and Employment by Industry," *Gross-Domestic Product (GDP) by Industry Data,* U.S. Department of Commerce, Bureau of Economic Analysis, Washington, DC, April 27, 2006 [Online] http://www.bea.gov/bea/dn2/gdpbyind_data.htm [accessed May 16, 2006]

"Value Added by Industry in Current Dollars, Quantity Indexes by Industry, and Price Indexes by Industry, 1947-1997; Value Added by Industry, Gross Output by Industry, Intermediate Inputs by Industry, and the Components of Value Added by Industry, 1987-1997," *Gross-Domestic Product (GDP) by Industry Data,* U.S. Department of Commerce, Bureau of Economic Analysis, Washington, DC, April 27, 2006 [Online] http://www.bea.gov/bea/dn2/gdpbyind_data.htm [accessed May 16, 2006]

"The World Trade Organization In Brief," World Trade Organization, Geneva, Switzerland [Online] http://www.wto.org/english/thewto_e/whatis_e/whatis_e.htm [accessed May 24, 2006]

Introduction

Manufacturing and Distribution USA (MDUSA) presents information on manufacturing, the wholesale trade, and the retail sector in a comprehensive 3-volume presentation. Data are drawn from a variety of federal statistical sources and are combined with information on leading public and private corporations obtained from the *Ward's Business Directory of U.S. Private and Public Companies*.

History

Thomson Gale's "USA" series grew out of a need to present federal statistical data, from different agencies, in a more "user friendly" format and, at the same time, combined with data on corporate participation in various industries. The series features preanalyzed data, ratios, and projections — in a standard format — so that all the data are handily available to the analyst or student in one place. This approach continues with *MDUSA*.

MDUSA is a successor of the award-winning *Manufacturing USA* and also holds the contents heretofore published as *Wholesale and Retail Industries USA*. The first edition came at a time when the government's statistical systems were still, as it were, straddling between the old Standard Industrial Classification (SIC) coding and the new 1997 North American Industry Classification System (NAICS). The first edition of *MDUSA* contained data in both formats — and therefore, of necessity, did not have all of the information that users of this series are accustomed to getting. The second edition was entirely coded using the 1997 NAICS coding. Input-output data and occupational data were once more back in their usual places. The third edition follows the familiar layout of the second edition.

The fourth edition of *MDUSA* comes at another time of transition. In 2002, the Federal Government restructured its 1997 NAICS coding. In 2003, the *Annual Survey of Manufactures (ASM)* restructured its data using codes based on the 2002 Federal Government NAICS codes. Many of these codes correspond directly with the 2002 Federal Government NAICS codes. Others, however, encompass two or more Federal Government NAICS codes. For example, ASM NAICS industry 31121M Flour Milling and Malt Manufacturing includes three 2002 NAICS industries: 311211 Flour Milling, 311212 Rice Milling, and 311213 Malt Manufacturing. As a result of the restructured *Annual Survey of Manufactures* data, this edition of *MDUSA* is coded using two different, though related, NAICS coding formats. The Manufacturing section is coded using ASM NAICS codes. The Wholesale and Retail section is coded using the 2002 Federal Government NAICS coding.

'The Most Current Data Available'

MDUSA reports the most current data available at the time of the book's preparation. The objective is to present hard information — data based on actual survey by authoritative bodies — for all manufacturing and distribution industries on a comparable basis. A few industries may collect more recent information through their industry associations or other bodies. Similarly, estimates are published on this or that industry based on the analyses and guesses of knowledgeable individuals. These data are rarely in the same format as the federal data and are not available for a large cross section of industry. Therefore, the data in *MDUSA* are, indeed, the most current at this level of detail and spanning the entirety of manufacturing and distribution activity. It is meant to serve as the foundation on which others can base their own projections.

In addition to presenting current survey data, the editors also provide projected data for most categories from 2005 to the year 2008.

Scope and Coverage

MDUSA presents statistical data on 460 distinct industries — 322 in the manufacturing sector, 138 in the wholesale and retail sectors. Within the manufacturing presentation, 234 industries correspond directly with NAICS-coded industries. Eighty-eight industries are combinations of NAICS-coded industries. These industries are marked with an asterisk and their corresponding NAICS codes are shown at the bottom of the page. One hundred eighteen industries are either identical to a single old SIC industry or are combinations of old SIC industries; consequently, a full time-series is available for these industries going back some period of time. The industries can also be found by ASM NAICS code by looking in the NAICS Index. Conversion guides have been included in this edition to assist the user in transitioning from NAICS to ASM NAICS and vice versa.

Data on 68 NAICS-coded wholesale industries are shown. Within this group, 40 are, again, equivalent to old SIC industries. These industries are marked with an asterisk and their old SIC code is shown at the bottom of the page. The retail sector is covered by 70 NAICS-coded industries; 27 of these have direct SIC equivalents.

Presentation. Data are typically for 1997 to 2004, with some elements taken from surveys for 1998 to 2001 and 2003 to 2004. The NAICS series began in 1997. Those industries that have remained essentially unchanged feature a full time series, from 1987 or 1988 forward, with projections to 2007 or 2008.

ASM NAICS manufacturing tables additionally feature ratios (for 2002), company data, materials consumed (2002), product share details (2002) and state level data (2002). State data, for manufacturing, are still incomplete. This is noted in each table.

The NAICS wholesale and retail presentation (Part II) provides national and state-level data. State coverage is more complete.

SIC and NAICS

The transition between SIC and NAICS was implemented for the 1997 Economic Census. An updating of the industrial classification system was long overdue. Relatively minor modifications had last taken place in 1987. The new NAICS coding — which was used by the U.S., Canada, and Mexico — represented a major revamping. Additional sectors were created (e.g., Information) and the "services" categories greatly increased.

An updating of the 1997 NAICS codes was implemented for the 2002 Economic Census. Fourteen of the twenty sectors remained unchanged, including the Manufacturing sector. However, the 2002 NAICS changes were substantial for the Construction, Wholesale, Retail, and Information sectors. Minor adjustments were made to the Mining and Administrative and Support Services sectors.

In 2003, the *Annual Survey of Manufactures (ASM)* restructured its data into a combination of NAICS and NAICS-based industries. These industries are based on the 2002 Federal Government NAICS structure. Many ASM-coded industries correspond directly to 2002 NAICS-coded industries. Others correspond to two or more 2002 NAICS-coded industries. The ASM-coded industries that correspond to more than a single NAICS-coded industry include a letter in their code and the first page of the presentation on these industries includes a list of the individual NAICS industries that were combined in its creation.

In *MDUSA*, the organization of data is based on the "new order." Industries no longer classified as manufacturing under NAICS are excluded. Data on *Newspapers, Periodicals, Book Publishing, and Miscellaneous Publishing* do not appear in *MDUSA*. These industries, once in manufacturing, have been reclassified as NAICS Sector 51 - Information.

Major changes in the industrial classification system typically mean some loss of information. Restatement of past years in NAICS terms will require some time — provided budgets for it are available. In some cases, no data for years before 1997 will ever be available.

Under the NAICS coding, 6-digit industry codes replace the old 4-digit SIC codes. The first two digits indicate the sector, the last four specify the industry. The code 311110 - Animal Food Manufacturing, can be parsed as follows: 31 is the first sector code used for manufacturing; 311 is Food Manufacturing, the industry group; 1110 is the actual industry designation. In normal practice, all six digits are used to designate the industry. In the NAICS manual, a trailing zero in some codes is suppressed. The trailing zero appears in published data series, however, and is also used in *MDUSA*.

Organization and Content

MDUSA is now divided into three volumes, as follows:

- **Volume I** — includes *Part I - Manufacturing by ASM NAICS Code*. Included in this volume is the range from 311111 - Dog and Cat Food Manufacturing through 33211P – Crown, Closure, and Metal Stamping Manufacturing.

- **Volume II** — concludes Part I, ranging from 33221N – Cutlery, Kitchen Utensil, Pot and Pan Manufacturing through 339999 – Miscellaneous Manufacturing Not Elsewhere Classified.

- **Volume III** — presents Part II, Wholesale and Retail Industries by NAICS Code. The wholesale trade range extends from 423110 – Automobile and Other Motor Vehicle Merchant Wholesalers through 424990 – Other Miscellaneous Nondurable Goods Merchant Wholesalers. Retail begins with 441110 – New Car Dealers and concludes with 454390 – Other Direct Selling Establishments. Volume III concludes with the indexes and the appendices.

Presentation within each part is the same. Tables included are shown for each part below.

Part I - ASM NAICS Manufacturing

1	Trend Graphics	Provided when multiple years of data are available.
2	General Statistics	National statistics.
3	Indices of Change	National data in index format.
4	Selected Ratios	Twenty ratios for the industry.
5	Leading Companies	Up to 75 companies in this industry.
6	Materials Consumed	Purchases of materials and products by quantity and cost.
7	Product Share Details	Product categories within the industry in dollars.
8	Input-Output Table(s)	Industries this NAICS buys from, sells to.
9	Occupations Employed	Occupations employed by the industry group.
10	Maps	States and regions where the industry is active.
11	Industry Data by State	Data on those states available at publication time.

Part II - NAICS Wholesale and Retail

1	Trend Graphics	Provided when multiple years of data are available.
2	General Statistics	National Statistics.
3	Indices of Change	National data in index format.
4	Selected Ratios	Six ratios for the industry.
5	Leading Companies	Up to 75 companies in this industry.
6	Occupations Employed	Occupations employed by the industry group.
7	Maps	States and regions where the industry is active.
8	Industry Data by State	State level statistics.

Each industry begins on a new page. The order of graphics and tables is invariable. In some instances, data may not be available in a category, e.g., company data or geographical data. The absence of data is indicated in each section.

Three indexes (found in Volume III) are:

- **NAICS Index**. Data are presented by number and then alphabetcally. Page references are provided for each entry. Volume numbers are shown in Roman numerals.

- **Product/Activity Index**. This index shows products and commercial activities (printing, stores, etc.). Presentation is alphabetical. References are provided to pages, with volume indication in Roman numerals.

- **Company Index**. All companies appearing in *MDUSA* are shown in alphabetical order. More than 18,300 companies are indexed. Entries show volume and page numbers. NAICS codes are also provided within brackets.

Two appendices (found in Volume III) are:

- **ASM NAICS To 2002 NAICS Conversion Guide.** All 322 ASM NAICS industries appearing in *MDUSA* are shown in ASM NAICS order. Entries show ASM NAICS codes and descriptions in bold, with corresponding 2002 NAICS codes and descriptions indented.

- **2002 NAICS To ASM NAICS Conversion Guide.** All 473 NAICS industries corresponding to the ASM NAICS industries appearing in *MDUSA* are shown in 2002 NAICS order. Entries show 2002 NAICS codes and descriptions in bold, with corresponding ASM NAICS codes and descriptions indented.

For more detailed information on *MDUSA*'s industry profiles, please consult the *Overview of Content and Sources*, which follows.

Comments and Suggestions are Welcome

Comments on or suggestions for improvement of the usefulness, format, and coverage of *MDUSA* are always welcome. Although every effort is made to maintain accuracy, errors may occasionally occur; the editors will be grateful if these are called to their attention. Please contact the editor below with comments and suggestions or, to have technical questions answered, call the editor directly at ECDI at (248) 926-5187.

> Editor
> Manufacturing and Distribution USA
> Thomson Gale
> 27500 Drake Road
> Farmington Hills, MI 48331-3535
> 248-699-GALE

Overview of Content and Sources

Industry Coding Structure

Manufacturing data in *MDUSA* are ordered in conformity with the *Annual Survey of Manufactures'* North American Industry Classification System (ASM NAICS). The codes are based on the 2002 North American Industry Classification System (NAICS). The Wholesale and Retail data in *MDUSA* are ordered in conformity with the 2002 NAICS.

The NAICS coding system was first used in the 1997 Economic Census and revised for the 2002 Economic Census. Many industries were reclassified so that they no longer resembled the former Standard Industrial Classification (SIC) codes. However, a fairly large number of NAICS codes correspond directly — without change — to the older SIC codes. Of the 460 industries presented in *MDUSA*, 118 either have direct SIC equivalents or are combinations of SIC industries. When the industries coincide, longer time series of data are provided. In the manufacturing section, the data are presented under ASM NAICS codes. When an industry is the equivalent of two or more 2002 NAICS industries, an asterisk is used to mark the industry, and the corresponding 2002 NAICS codes are supplied at the bottom of the page. In the wholesale and retail section, the data are presented under NAICS codes, but an asterisk is used to mark the industry, and the equivalent SIC code is supplied at the bottom of the page. New industries that have no SIC equivalent show data and projections from 1997 forward.

Industry Profiles

Each industry profile contains the tables and graphics listed in the *Introduction*. A detailed discussion of each graphic display and table follows; the meaning of each data element is explained, and the sources from which the data were obtained are cited.

Trends Graphics

At the beginning of each industry profile, two graphs are presented showing (1) industry shipments (manufacturing) or sales (wholesale/retail) and (2) employment plotted for the years 1988 to 2008 (or an earlier date) on logarithmic scale. The curves are provided primarily to give the user an at-a-glance assessment of important trends in the industry. The logarithmic scale ensures that the shipment trends and employment trends can be compared visually despite different magnitudes and denominations of the data (millions of dollars for shipments or sales and thousands of employees for employment); in this mode of presentation, if two curves have the same slope, the values are growing or declining at the same rate. If the values fit within a single cycle (1 to 9, 10 to 90, etc.), a single cycle is shown; if the values bridge two cycles, both are shown.

The data graphed are derived from the first table, *General Statistics*. All available years of data are plotted. If data gaps appear in the series, missing points are calculated using a least-squares curve fitting algorithm.

Those portions of curves based on projections by the editors are shown in a dotted-line format.

General Statistics

Manufacturing. This table shows national statistics for the industry for the years 1988-2008 under five groupings: Companies, Establishments, Employment, Compensation, and Production. The last four groupings are further subdivided, as described below.

Data for 1992, 1997, and 2002 are from the Economic Census held in each of those years. Data for other years, through and including 2004, are from the *Annual Survey of Manufactures (ASM)*. Establishment counts in the *ASM* years are from the *County Business Patterns* for those years. New industries created in the 1997 NAICS reclassification will not show data earlier than 1997. New industries created in the 2002 NAICS reclassification will not show data earlier than 2002.

Data for the period 2005-2008 are projected by the editors. A discussion of the methods of projection is presented below. Projected data are followed by the letter "p".

Company counts are available only from the full *Census of Manufactures* conducted every five years.

Establishment data are provided for 1988 through 2004; projections are shown thereafter. Establishment counts in the Census years (1992, 1997, 2002) are from the Economic Census. In other years, values are from the *County Business Patterns*. Establishment counts are typically higher than company counts because many companies operate from more than one facility. Total establishments are shown together with establishments that employ 20 or more people. Comparing the number of large establishments with total establishments will tell the user whether the industry is populated by relatively small operations or is dominated by large facilities. Values shown are absolute numbers of establishments.

The **Employment** grouping is subdivided into total employment, shown in 1,000 employees (thus a value of 134.9 means that the industry employs 134,900 people), production workers (in thousands), and production hours worked (in millions of hours). Dividing hours worked by production workers produces hours worked by a production worker in the year. This value is precalculated for the user in the table of Selected Ratios. A value of around 1,940 hours indicates full-time employment — on average; obviously such aggregate data hide the finer details of day-to-day industrial operation: the presence of part-time workers, overtime clocked, etc.

The **Compensation** grouping shows the industry's total payroll (in millions of dollars) and wages (in dollars per hour). The payroll value includes all forms of compensation subject to federal taxes, including wages, salaries, commissions, bonuses, etc. The *Survey of Manufactures* provides payroll and wage data as aggregates. The wages per hour were calculated by dividing the Survey wage aggregate by the total hours worked in production.

The interested user can reverse this calculation ($/hour times hours will produce wages-in-the-aggregate). Additional calculations can be used to determine the salaries of those employees who are not production workers. The procedure is to calculate aggregate wages and to deduct the result from payroll to obtain salaries paid; next, salaried employees can be calculated by deducting production workers from total employment; finally, salaries paid divided by salaried employment will produce the average annual salary of the administrative/technical workforce in the industry.

The **Production** grouping shows cost of materials, value added in manufacturing, value of shipments, and capital investments, all in millions of dollars; thus a value of 0.9 means that the actual value is $900,000.

Cost of materials includes cost of raw materials, fuels, freight, and contract work associated with production and excludes costs of services (e.g., advertising, insurance), overhead, depreciation, rents, royalties, and capital expenditures.

Value Added by Manufacture represents Value of Shipments less cost of materials, supplies, containers, fuel, purchased electrical power, and contract work plus income for services rendered. The result is adjusted by adding the difference between the cost and sales price of the merchandise by merchandising operations plus net change in finished goods and work-in-process inventories between the beginning and the end of the year. Value Added is a good measure of net value of production because it avoids the duplications inherent in the Value of Shipments measure (below).

Value of Shipments is the net selling value of products leaving production plants in an industry. In industries where two or more production stages for a product are included under the same SIC, the Value of Shipments measure will tend to overstate the economic importance of the industry: the value of product shipments is usually lower than total Value of Shipments. Nonetheless, Value of Shipments corresponds to the sales volume of the industry.

The Capital Investments column shows capital expenditures for equipment and structures made by the industry provided that these expenditures are depreciated rather than expensed in the year of acquisition.

Wholesale and Retail. The General Statistics for the wholesale and retail sectors show four elements of data and three ratios. The data are Establishments and Employment (actual number) and Payroll and Sales (in millions of dollars). Ratios for Employees per Establishment (number), Sales per Establishment (dollars), and Payroll per Employee ($) are provided. Missing data elements are extrapolated, where possible, and marked with the letter "e". Projections, to the year 2007, are marked with the letter "p".

Indices of Change

The data presented in the *General Statistics* table are partially restated as indices for all industries where multiple years of data are available. The purpose of the table is to show the user rapidly how different categories of the industry have changed since 2002. Indices are shown for the census years (1987, 1992, 1997, and 2002) and for years beyond.

The year 2002 is used as the base and is therefore shown as 100 in every category. Other values are expressed in relation to the 2002 value.

Values of 100 indicate no change in relation to the base year; values above 100 mean better and values below 100 indicate worse performance — all relative to the 2002 base. Note, however, that these are indices rather than compounded annual rates of growth or decline.

Indexes based on projections by the editors are followed by a "p".

Selected Ratios

To understand an industry, analysts calculate ratios of various kinds so that the absolute numbers can be placed in a more global perspective. Twenty important industrial ratios are precalculated for the user in the Selected Ratios table. Additionally, the same ratios are also provided for the average of all manufacturing, wholesale, or retail industries; an index, comparing the two categories, is also provided.

The ratios are calculated for the most recent complete year available; that year is usually the year of the most recent Economic Census. In this case, 2002.

The first column of values represents the **Average of All** . . . — be it manufacturing, wholesale, or retail. These ratios are calculated by (1) adding all categories for manufacturing and (2) calculating the ratios based on the totals.

The second column of values shows the ratios for the **Analyzed Industry**, i.e., the industry currently under consideration.

The third column is an **Index** comparing the Analyzed Industry to the Average of All . . . Industries. The index is useful for determining quickly and consistently how the Analyzed Industry stands in relation to all manufacturing, all wholesale, or all retail. Index values of 100 mean that the Analyzed Industry, within a given ratio, is identical to the average of all industries. An index value of 500 means that the Analyzed Industry is five times the average — for instance, that it has five times as many employees per establishment or pays five times as much. An index value of 50 would indicate that the Analyzed Industry is half of the average of all industries (50 percent). Similarly, an index of 105 means 5 percent above average and 95 indicates 5 percent below.

Manufacturing presentations show 20 ratios. For the wholesale and retail sectors, on which less information is available, six ratios are provided.

Leading Companies

The table of *Leading Companies* shows up to 75 companies that participate in the industry. The listings are sorted in descending order of sales and show the company name, address, name of the Chief Executive Officer, telephone, company type, sales (in millions of dollars) and employment (in thousands of employees). The number of companies shown, their total sales, and total employment are summed at the top of the table for the user's convenience.

The data are from the *Ward's Business Directory of U.S. Private and Public Companies* for 2005, Volumes 1 and 2. Public and private corporations, divisions, subsidiaries, joint ventures, and corporate groups are shown. Thus a listing for an industry may show the parent company as well as important divisions and subsidiaries of the same company (usually in a different location).

While this method of presentation has the disadvantage of duplication (the sales of a parent corporation include the sales of any divisions listed separately), it has the advantage of providing the user with information on major components of an enterprise at different locations. In any event, the user should not assume that the sum of the sales (or employment) shown in the *Leading Companies* table represents the total sales (or employment) of an industry. The Shipments or Sales column of the *General Statistics* table is a better guide to industry sales.

The company's type (private, public, division, etc.) is shown on the table under the column headed "Co Type," thus providing the user with a means of roughly determining the total "net" sales (or employment) represented in the table; this can be accomplished by adding the values and then deducting values corresponding to divisions and subsidiaries of parent organizations also shown in the table. The code used is as follows:

P	Public corporation
R	Private corporation
S	Subsidiary
D	Division
J	Joint venture
G	Corporate group

An asterisk (*) placed behind the sales volume indicates an estimate; the absence of an asterisk indicates that the sales value has been obtained from annual reports, other formal submissions to regulatory bodies, or from the corporation. The symbol "<" appears in front of some employment values to indicate that the actual value is "less than" the value shown. Thus the value of "<0.1" means that the company employs fewer than 100 people.

Materials Consumed

The *Materials Consumed* table is drawn from the 2002 Economic Census. This table reports the quantities of materials and products (e.g., containers, packaging) used by the industry. The delivered cost of the materials, in millions of dollars, is also shown. Data are not available for all industries. Where data are missing, the table header is reproduced with the notation that data are not available.

A number of symbols are used to indicate why data are omitted or their basis. (D) means that data are withheld to avoid disclosure of competitive information; "na" is used when data are "not available." (S) means that data are withheld because statistical norms were not met; (X) stands for "not applicable;" (Z) means that less than half of the unit quantity is consumed; "nec" means "not elsewhere classified," and "nsk" abbreviates "not specified by kind." A single asterisk (*) shows instances where 10-19 percent of the data were estimated; two asterisks (**) show a 20-29 percent estimate.

Product Share Details

The table of *Product Share Details* shows the products of the industry broken down by product classes and categories. Data are shown in millions of dollars of product shipments. The source of product data is the 2002 Economic Census.

This table highlights the difference between *industry shipments* and *product shipments*. In practice this means that total product shipments may be higher or lower than data for shipments shown in the General Statistics table. Product shipments will be higher when significant quantities of the product classified under this code are manufactured in other industries. Product shipments will be lower than industry shipments because industry shipments include miscellaneous receipts (e.g., sales of scrap, contract work) as well as product shipments. Duplication is also reflected in industry shipments but excluded from the product shipment data.

Multiple levels of product groups, products, and subcategories are combined to make a table. Product groups are shown in bold. Lower levels are indented.

In some instances, the symbol (D) will appear instead of a value; the symbol appears when data are withheld to prevent disclosure of competitive information. The abbreviation "nec" stands for "not elsewhere classified," and the abbreviation "nsk" stands for "not specified by kind."

Occupations Employed by Industry Group

MDUSA presents data on 132 occupation categories employed by manufacturing industries; since most of these categories combine two or three occupations, more than 260 occupations are covered. The information presented is an extract from the *Industry-Occupation Matrix* produced by the Bureau of Labor Statistics (BLS), Department of Labor.

The table on *Occupations Employed* presents an extract; showing the entire matrix would have required too much space. Thus only those occupations are included that represent 1% or more of total employment in an industry. The advantage of this method is that the data are kept manageable while most of an industry's employment is defined by occupation. The disadvantage is that certain occupations, although employed by an industry, do not make the "cutoff" of 1 percent of total employment.

The data are shown for 2004 (updated from 2002) in percent of Total Employment for an industry group (4-digit NAICS industry level or groupings of 4-digit NAICS industries). Also shown is the Bureau of Labor Statistics' projection of the anticipated growth or decline of the occupation to the year 2014. This value is reported as a percent change to 2014; a value of 5.5, for instance, means that overall employment, in the industry group, will increase 5.5 percent between 2004 and 2014; a negative value indicates a corresponding decline. Note that these are not rates of annual change.

BLS produces most of the data in 4-digit NAICS format. Occupation data for the industries 332710 Machine Shops, 33991M Jewelry and Silverware Manufacturing, 446110 Pharmacies and Drug Stores, and 451110 Sporting Goods Stores are in 5-digit NAICS format. Data have been matched as closely as possible to the 6-digit NAICS codes. But the same table of *Occupations Employed* is reproduced for each industry which matches the BLS's 4-digit or 5-digit NAICS grouping. This approach has been adopted so that the user will find the occupations associated with an industry with other data on that industry.

The user should note the following:

- As already stated, the occupations shown are a subset of total occupations employed: those that account for 1 percent or more of employment in the industry group.

- Since the data are for groups, some occupations listed may appear out of place in a particular NAICS industry; that is because those occupations are employed by a related NAICS industry in the same group.

- Growth or decline indicated for an occupation within an industry group does not mean that the occupation is growing or declining overall. Also, changes introduced by BLS between editions of this series can be quite drastic. An occupation that grew by several percentage points in an industry two years ago is shown suddenly declining to the year 2014 now.

Map Graphics

The geographical presentation of data begins with two maps titled *Location by State* and *Regional Concentration*.

Manufacturing. In the first map, all states in which the industry is present are shaded. In the second, the industry's concentration is shown by Census region. The two maps, together, tell the user at a glance where the industry is active and which regions rank first, second, and third in value of shipments or in number of establishments; establishment counts are used for ranking in those industries where shipment data are withheld (the (D) symbol) for the majority of states. In the case of some industries, only one or two regions are shaded because the industry is concentrated in a few states. The data for ranking are taken from the table on *Industry Data by State* which immediately follows the maps.

Wholesale and Retail. The information above relates to these sectors as well, with one exception. Since wholesale and retail activity occurs most everywhere, only those states are highlighted on the state map where the activity is greater in the state than would be indicated by the state's share of total U.S. population. Shaded states mean intense wholesale or retail activity.

The regional boundaries are those of the Census Regions and are named, from left to right and top to bottom as follows:

Pacific (includes Alaska and Hawaii)	East South Central
Mountain	New England
West North Central	Middle Atlantic
West South Central	South Atlantic
East North Central	

In the case of the Pacific region, all parts of the region are shaded (including Alaska and Hawaii), even if the basis for the ranking is the industry's predominance in California (the usual case).

Although regional data are only graphed and not reported in a separate table, the table of *Industry Data by State* provides all the necessary information for constructing a regional table.

Industry Data by State

Manufacturing. The table on *Industry Data by State* provides ten data elements for each state in which the industry is active. The data are updated in this edition. They come from the 2002 Economic Census, the most recently available data set on states. Even in this series, certain data elements are suppressed by the Bureau of the Census to prevent disclosure of competitive information. This may come about in instances where only a few operations are present in the state or they are operated by a small number of companies. The states are shown in descending order of shipments. The categories of Establishments, Shipments, Total Employment, and Wages are identical to those in the table of *General Statistics*. In addition, six elements of information are provided so that the user can more easily compare the size, performance, and characteristics of the industry from one state to the next:

Shipments are expressed in millions of dollars and as a percent of the total U.S. shipments for the industry. This is useful for determining the relative importance of the state in the industry as a whole. Shipments per Establishment are also provided; this measure gives an insight into the relative size of the factories in the state.

Total employment is shown together with percent of total employment in the U.S. industry and employment per establishment. For some states, employment is shown as the midpoint of a range; these items are marked with an asterisk (*).

Cost data are expressed as percent of Shipments to facilitate the user's analysis of the relative cost advantages of one state over another. The lower the percentile, the lower the cost experience of the industry in the state. This information, however, must be viewed in light of the hourly wage experience in the state.

Investment data are shown as Investments per employee, again to facilitate state-to-state comparisons.

The symbol (D) is used when data are withheld to prevent disclosure of proprietary information. Dashes are used to indicate that the corresponding data element cannot be calculated because some part of the ratio is missing or withheld.

Wholesale and Retail. State data, for these sectors, is organized slightly differently. Categories are Establishments, Employment, Payroll, and Sales. Total establishments are shown together with the percent of U.S. establishments that they represent. Employment is treated in the same way, but Employment per Establishment is also shown. Payroll is shown in millions of dollars and also per employee, in dollars. Sales are expressed in total (millions of dollars), as a percent of the U.S. total, and as Sales per Establishment (in dollars). Where employment is not provided by the Economic Census, a range of employment is provided.

Projected Data Series

As a service to the busy user of this book, *MDUSA* features trend projections of data — when a sufficient number of years of data is available.

How Projections Were Made

Projections are based on a curve-fitting algorithm using the least-squares method. In essence, the algorithm calculates a trend line for the data using existing data points. Extensions of the trend line are used to predict future years of data.

What Values Were Projected

Every category (column) reported under General Statistics has been subject to projection. In those cases where a coherent series exists from 1988 to the present in Part I and 1987 to the present in Part II, the entire series was used. In those cases where the industry definition underwent a change in 1997, trends are calculated from 1997 forward.

Cost of Materials and Value Added by Manufacturer (in the manufacturing industries) were calculated using the 2002 ratio of costs or value added to shipments in 2002 and then applying that ratio to other years using the projected shipment values for those years. Costs and value added were treated in this manner because averaging these data for a long period (1988-1998, for example) would not properly reflect cost savings and productivity changes achieved most recently. Therefore the use of a ratio, based on the most recent survey year, seemed more appropriate.

Limitations of Projections

Projections are simply means of detecting trends — that may or may not hold in the future. The projections in *MDUSA*, therefore, are not as reliable as actual survey data. Most analysts trying to project the future routinely turn to trend projection. In *MDUSA*, the work of doing the projections has been done for the user in advance.

Part II

WHOLESALE AND RETAIL INDUSTRIES BY NORTH AMERICAN CLASSIFICATION SYSTEM (NAICS) CODE

NAICS 423110 - AUTOMOBILE AND OTHER MOTOR VEHICLE MERCHANT WHOLESALERS*

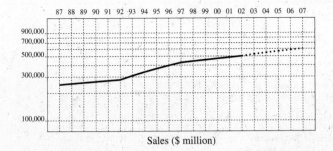

Sales ($ million)

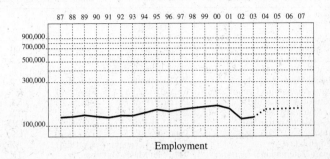

Employment

GENERAL STATISTICS

Year	Establishments (number)	Employment (number)	Payroll ($ million)	Sales ($ million)	Employees per Establishment (number)	Sales per Establishment ($)	Payroll per Employee ($)
1987	7,125	124,448	2,910.5	246,933.2	17.5	34,657,291.2	23,387.3
1988	6,750	126,535	3,174.5	253,329.1 e	18.7	37,530,237.0	25,087.9
1989	6,549	131,501	3,250.7	259,725.0 e	20.1	39,658,726.5	24,720.0
1990	6,433	127,118	3,175.7	266,121.0 e	19.8	41,368,102.0	24,982.3
1991	6,427	123,654	3,140.7	272,516.9 e	19.2	42,401,882.7	25,399.1
1992	7,899	130,098	3,519.9	278,912.9	16.5	35,309,900.0	27,055.8
1993	7,771	129,436	3,657.9	308,801.6 e	16.7	39,737,691.4	28,260.3
1994	7,956	138,918	4,185.4	338,690.3 e	17.5	42,570,424.8	30,128.6
1995	8,123	150,554	4,605.5	368,579.0 e	18.5	45,374,738.4	30,590.4
1996	7,879 e	143,753 e	4,323.9 e	398,467.7 e	18.2 e	50,573,384.9 e	30,078.7 e
1997	7,664	150,947	4,638.9	428,356.4	19.7	55,892,014.6	30,732.0
1998	7,696	156,068	5,189.7	443,089.0 e	20.3	57,573,939.7	33,252.8
1999	7,708	161,232	5,641.4	457,821.7 e	20.9	59,395,651.3	34,989.3
2000	7,805	166,023	5,870.1	472,554.3 e	21.3	60,545,076.2	35,357.3
2001	7,617	153,814	5,826.6	487,287.0 e	20.2	63,973,606.4	37,880.9
2002	7,027	119,019	4,923.7	502,019.6	16.9	71,441,525.5	41,369.0
2003	6,883	123,560	5,181.4	526,128.9 p	18.0	67,774,655.5 p	41,934.0
2004	7,757 p	150,645 p	5,993.3 p	545,502.8 p	19.4 p	70,027,525.3 p	40,931.8 p
2005	7,800 p	151,980 p	6,180.7 p	564,876.8 p	19.4 p	72,280,395.1 p	42,047.1 p
2006	7,843 p	153,315 p	6,368.0 p	584,250.7 p	19.5 p	74,533,264.9 p	43,162.3 p
2007	7,886 p	154,651 p	6,555.4 p	603,624.7 p	19.5 p	76,786,134.7 p	44,277.6 p

Sources: *Economic Census of the United States*, 1987, 1992, 1997, and 2002. Establishment counts, employment, and payroll are from *County Business Patterns* for non-Census years. Values followed by a 'p' are projections by the editors. Sales data for non-Census years are extrapolations, marked by 'e'. Data are the most recent available at this level of detail.

INDICES OF CHANGE

Year	Establishments (number)	Employment (number)	Payroll ($ million)	Sales ($ million)	Employees per Establishment (number)	Sales per Establishment ($)	Payroll per Employee ($)
1987	101.4	104.6	59.1	49.2	103.6	48.5	56.5
1992	112.4	109.3	71.5	55.6	97.6	49.4	65.4
1993	110.6	108.8	74.3	61.5 e	98.8	55.6	68.3
1994	113.2	116.7	85.0	67.5 e	103.6	59.6	72.8
1995	115.6	126.5	93.5	73.4 e	109.5	63.5	73.9
1996	112.1 e	120.8 e	87.8 e	79.4 e	107.7 e	70.8 e	72.7 e
1997	109.1	126.8	94.2	85.3	116.6	78.2	74.3
1998	109.5	131.1	105.4	88.3 e	120.1	80.6	80.4
1999	109.7	135.5	114.6	91.2 e	123.7	83.1	84.6
2000	111.1	139.5	119.2	94.1 e	126.0	84.7	85.5
2001	108.4	129.2	118.3	97.1 e	119.5	89.5	91.6
2002	100.0	100.0	100.0	100.0	100.0	100.0	100.0
2003	98.0	103.8	105.2	104.8 p	106.2	94.9 p	101.4
2004	110.4 p	126.6 p	121.7 p	108.7 p	114.5 p	98.0 p	98.9 p
2005	111.0 p	127.7 p	125.5 p	112.5 p	114.8 p	101.2 p	101.6 p
2006	111.6 p	128.8 p	129.3 p	116.4 p	115.2 p	104.3 p	104.3 p
2007	112.2 p	129.9 p	133.1 p	120.2 p	115.5 p	107.5 p	107.0 p

Sources: Same as General Statistics. The values shown reflect change from the base year, 2002. Values above 100 mean greater than 2002, values below 100 mean less than 2002, and a value of 100 in the 1987-2001 or 2003-2007 period means same as 2002. Values followed by a 'p' are projections by the editors; 'e' stands for extrapolation. Data are the most recent available at this level of detail.

SELECTED RATIOS

For 2002	Avg. of All Wholesale	Analyzed Industry	Index	For 2002	Avg. of All Wholesale	Analyzed Industry	Index
Employees per Establishment	15	17	113	Sales per Employee	791,325	4,217,979	533
Payroll per Establishment	626,122	700,683	112	Sales per Establishment	12,012,387	71,441,526	595
Payroll per Employee	41,161	41,369	101	Expenses per Establishment	na	na	na

Sources: Same as General Statistics. The 'Average of All' column, Wholesale or Retail, represents the average of the sector reported for the most recent complete year available. The Index shows the relationship between the Average and the Analyzed Industry. For example, 100 means that they are equal; 500 that the Analyzed Industry is five times the average; 50 means that the Analyzed Industry is half the national average. The abbreviation 'na' is used to show that data are 'not available'.

*Equivalent to SIC 5012.

LEADING COMPANIES   Number shown: **75**   Total sales ($ mil): **259,372**   Total employment (000): **377.2**

Company Name	Address				CEO Name	Phone	Co. Type	Sales ($ mil)	Empl. (000)
Ford Motor Co.	1 American Rd	Dearborn	MI	48126		313-322-3000	P	171,652	324.9
Toyota Motor Sales U.S.A. Inc.	19001 Southwestern	Torrance	CA	90509	Yoshio Iniaba	310-468-4000	S	36,500*	8.9
Southeast Toyota Distributors Inc.	100 Jim Moran Blvd	Deerfield Beach	FL	33442	Jim Moran	954-429-2000	S	14,027*	2.5
Hyundai Motor America	PO Box 20850	Fountain Valley	CA	92728	Mong-Koo Chung	714-965-3000	S	5,539	1.0
Asbury Automotive Group Inc.	3 Landmark Sq	Stamford	CT	06901	Kenneth B Gilman	203-356-4400	P	5,301	8.0
Subaru of America Inc.	PO Box 6000	Cherry Hill	NJ	08034	Kunio Ishigami	856-488-8500	S	4,100	0.6
Gulf States Toyota Inc.	PO Box 40306	Houston	TX	77040		713-744-3300	S	4,095*	3.2
Akron Auto Auction Inc.	2471 Ley Dr	Akron	OH	44319	Jeff Bailey	330-773-8245	R	2,497*	0.2
Lexus	Park 80	Torrance	CA	90509		310-328-2075	D	2,380*	1.5
Right Honda	7875 E F L Wright	Scottsdale	AZ	85260	Jay Francis	480-778-2510	R	1,586*	0.1
Amparts International Inc.	9117 San Mateo Dr	Laredo	TX	78045	Jerry Gonzales	956-727-3933	S	1,182*	0.1
ADESA Inc.	13085 Hamilton	Carmel	IN	46032	David G Gartzke	317-815-1100	P	912	11.2
W.D. Larson Companies Limited	10700 Lyndale S	Bloomington	MN	55420	William D Larson	952-888-4934	R	646*	0.5
Sanderson Ford Trucks	6400 N 51st Ave	Glendale	AZ	85301	David Kimoly	623-842-8787	R	628*	0.5
Crain M-M Sales Inc.	PO Box 6055	Marietta	GA	30065	Carl Myers	770-428-4421	R	435*	<0.1
Copart Inc.	4665 Business Ctr	Fairfield	CA	94534	A Jayson Adair	707-639-5000	P	401	2.2
Kia Motors America Inc.	PO Box 52410	Irvine	CA	92619	Peter Butterfield	949-470-7000	S	360*	0.3
Barden Companies Inc.	163 Madison Ave	Detroit	MI	48226	Don H Barden	313-496-2900	R	354	4.1
Arrow Truck Sales Inc.	3200 Manchester	Kansas City	MO	64129	Ed Justis	816-923-5000	R	300*	0.3
Subaru of America Inc. West	7801 Lyndale Ave S	Bloomington	MN	55420	Terry Spitzer	952-881-6200	D	280*	<0.1
Insurance Auto Auctions Inc.	850 E Algonquin	Schaumburg	IL	60173	Peter H Kamin	708-492-7000	P	240	1.0
Around The Clock Freightliner	PO Box 272428	Oklahoma City	OK	73137	Charles Bowen	405-917-2047	R	204*	<0.1
Richmond Ford L.L.C.	PO Box 11145	Richmond	VA	23230	Tom Kody	804-358-5521	R	201*	0.2
Big Sky Auto Auction Inc.	PO Box 30717	Billings	MT	59101	Ted Becker	406-259-5999	R	190*	0.2
ABC Minneapolis L.L.C.	18270 Territorial Rd	Dayton	MN	55327		763-428-8777	R	188*	0.2
Greater Kalamazoo Auto Auction	PO Box 697	Schoolcraft	MI	49087	Donald Devries	269-679-5021	R	188*	0.2
Peach State Truck Center	PO Box 808	Norcross	GA	30091	Tom Reynolds	770-449-5300	R	188*	0.2
B/T Western Corp.	4 Upper Newport	Newport Beach	CA	92660	Ronald W Barley	949-476-8426	R	186*	<0.1
Fyda Freightliner Columbus Inc.	1250 Walcutt Rd	Columbus	OH	43228	Timothy Fyda	614-851-0002	R	183*	0.1
Manning Equipment Inc.	PO Box 23229	Louisville	KY	40223	Michael Stich	502-426-5210	R	153*	0.1
Brasher's Cascade Auto Auction	PO Box 55850	Portland	OR	97238	Larry Brasher	503-492-9200	R	151*	0.1
Mid-America Auto Auction Inc.	4716 S Santa Fe St	Wichita	KS	67216	Brad Phillips	316-522-8195	R	151*	0.1
Freightliner of Charlotte	4633 Equipment Dr	Charlotte	NC	28269	Dave Stauffer	704-597-1110	R	125*	0.1
Hartford Springfield Auction	153 Rainbow Rd	East Granby	CT	06026	John Barbarino	860-653-5625	R	125*	0.1
Heritage Pontiac Buick GMC	965 Veterans Mem	Rome	GA	30161		706-291-8820	R	125*	0.1
Imperial Auto Auction	PO Box 2156	Lakeland	FL	33806		863-688-8458	R	125*	0.1
Mayo Global Tranportation	PO Box 337	Chesnee	SC	29323	Curtis Gilbert	864-461-7015	R	125*	0.1
Minuteman Trucks Inc.	2181 Providence	Walpole	MA	02081	Richard Witcher	508-668-3112	R	125*	0.1
Matheny Motor Truck Co.	PO Box 1304	Parkersburg	WV	26101	Mike Matheny	304-485-4418	R	124*	<0.1
Intern. Truck Sales of Richmond	PO Box 6449	Richmond	VA	23230	Thomas Thayer	804-353-5555	R	102*	<0.1
Crossroads Ford Truck Sales Inc.	PO Box 6548	Springfield	IL	62708	John Hogan	217-528-0770	R	100*	<0.1
Harbor Truck Sales & Service Inc.	2723 Annapolis Rd	Baltimore	MD	21230	Edward Dentz	410-685-4474	R	99*	<0.1
Kenworth Sales Company Inc.	PO Box 65829	Salt Lake City	UT	84165	R Kyle Treadway	801-487-4161	R	98*	0.2
University Automotive Group	4260 Atlanta Hwy	Bogart	GA	30622	Ronald L Hill	706-546-7200	R	96	0.2
Hale Trailer Brake and Wheel	PO Box 1400	Voorhees	NJ	08043	Barry Hale	856-768-1330	R	94*	<0.1
Housby Mack Inc.	4747 NE 14th St	Des Moines	IA	50313	Kelly Housby	515-266-2666	R	94*	<0.1
Regional International Corp.	1007 Lehigh Station	Henrietta	NY	14467	James Carello	585-359-2011	R	94*	<0.1
Toyota On The Heights	2950 Mayfield Rd	Cleveland	OH	44118	Lee Seidman	216-321-9100	R	94*	<0.1
Peck Road Ford Truck Sales Inc.	2450 Kella Ave	Whittier	CA	90601	AW Fraser	562-692-7267	R	94*	0.1
Landmark International Trucks Inc.	PO Box 6539	Knoxville	TN	37914	Jim Jablonski	865-637-4881	R	93*	<0.1
Beltway International L.L.C.	1800 Sulphur Spring	Baltimore	MD	21227		410-247-5700	R	88*	<0.1
Duval Auto Auction Inc.	11982 New Kings	Jacksonville	FL	32219	Ronald Seaman	904-764-7653	R	88*	<0.1
Fyda Freightliner Youngstown Inc.	5260 76 Dr	Youngstown	OH	44515		330-797-0224	R	88*	<0.1
Glover Truck Parts	1200 Baucum Ind Dr	N. Little Rock	AR	72117	James Glover	501-945-2000	R	88*	<0.1
Greater Rockford Auto Auction	5937 Sandy Hollow	Rockford	IL	61109	Dwight Clark	815-874-7800	R	88*	<0.1
Ljl Truck Center Inc.	2855 Broadway	Macon	GA	31206	Tim Leskosky	478-784-3100	R	88*	<0.1
Metro Salvage	825 Rankin Rd	Houston	TX	77073	John Nichols	281-821-2300	R	88*	<0.1
Riva World	3671 N Dixie Hwy	Pompano Beach	FL	33064	Steve Bamdas	305-451-3320	R	88*	<0.1
Utility Trailers of Indianapolis Inc.	4255 S Harding St	Indianapolis	IN	46217	Harold Riddle	317-788-0299	R	88*	<0.1
Truck Parts and Equipment Co.	1550 S McCarran	Sparks	NV	89431	Stuart R Engs, Jr	775-359-8840	R	85*	0.3
Kenworth of Tennessee Inc.	550 Spence Ln	Nashville	TN	37210	Lester Turner Jr	615-366-5454	R	83*	0.3
ADESA St Louis	7858 US Hwy 61/67	Barnhart	MO	63012		636-475-9311	R	83*	<0.1
Hidy Motors Inc.	2300 Heller Dr	Dayton	OH	45434	David Hidy	937-426-9564	R	83*	<0.1
Freightliner of Hartford Inc.	222 Roberts St	East Hartford	CT	06108	Lindy Bigliazzi	860-289-0201	R	82*	<0.1
Reganis Auto Center Inc.	PO Box 1245	Scottsbluff	NE	69363	Bruce Dalton	308-632-8200	R	82*	<0.1
Freightliner of San Antonio	PO Box 200410	San Antonio	TX	78220		210-666-6665	R	80*	<0.1
Northern Wholesale Supply Inc.	6800 Otter Lake Rd	Hugo	MN	55038	Nick Gargaro	651-429-1515	R	79*	<0.1
Florida Auto Auction	PO Box 220	Ocoee	FL	34761		407-656-6200	R	77*	1.0
Fresno Truck Center A California	PO Box 80057	Bakersfield	CA	93380		661-393-6950	R	75*	<0.1
Peterbilt of Utah Inc.	PO Box 65616	Salt Lake City	UT	84165	Eric Jackson	801-486-8781	R	75*	<0.1
Rochester-Syracuse Auto Auction	PO Box 129	Waterloo	NY	13165		315-539-5006	R	75*	<0.1
Gage, H L Sales Inc.	PO Box 5170	Albany	NY	12205	Gary Hans	518-456-8871	R	74*	<0.1
Motor Power Equipment Co.	PO Box 80030	Billings	MT	59108	Bruce Sunwall	406-252-5651	R	73*	<0.1
Holcomb Freightliner Inc.	PO Box 1747	Sioux Falls	SD	57101	Dave Larsen	605-336-2995	R	72*	<0.1
Orlando Auto Auction Inc.	571 Mercy Dr	Orlando	FL	32805	Daniel Berry	407-299-3904	R	72*	<0.1

Source: Ward's Business Directory of U.S. Private and Public Companies, Volumes 1 and 2, 2005. The company type code used is as follows: P - Public, R - Private, S - Subsidiary, D - Division, J - Joint Venture, A - Affiliate, G - Group. Sales are in millions of dollars, employees are in thousands. An asterisk (*) indicates an estimated sales volume. The symbol < stands for 'less than'. Company names and addresses are truncated, in some cases, to fit into the available space.

OCCUPATIONS EMPLOYED BY MOTOR VEHICLE & MOTOR VEHICLE PARTS & SUPPLIES

Occupation	% of Total 2004	Change to 2014	Occupation	% of Total 2004	Change to 2014
Sales reps, wholesale & manufacturing, exc tech	8.4	17.9	Motor vehicle operators, nec	1.8	17.9
Truck drivers, light or delivery services	8.1	17.8	Retail salespersons	1.8	17.9
Parts salespersons	7.1	-5.7	Team assemblers	1.7	17.9
Laborers & freight, stock, & material movers, hand	6.7	6.1	Customer service representatives	1.6	20.7
Bus & truck mechanics & diesel engine specialists	5.3	17.9	First-line supervisors/managers of non-retail sales work	1.5	9.0
Stock clerks & order fillers	4.0	-9.7	Truck drivers, heavy & tractor-trailer	1.4	17.9
Office clerks, general	3.3	4.9	First-line supervisors/managers of office workers	1.3	6.8
Automotive service technicians & mechanics	3.0	17.9	Industrial truck & tractor operators	1.2	17.9
Shipping, receiving, & traffic clerks	3.0	6.7	First-line supervisors of mechanics	1.2	17.9
Driver/sales workers	2.8	17.8	Cleaners of vehicles & equipment	1.1	4.1
Bookkeeping, accounting, & auditing clerks	2.4	6.1	First-line supervisors/managers of retail sales workers	1.1	8.4
General & operations managers	2.3	16.6	Order clerks	1.0	-23.4

Source: *Industry-Occupation Matrix*, Bureau of Labor Statistics. These data are reported based on 4-digit NAICS categories but have been matched to corresponding 6-digit NAICS industry codes. The change reported for each occupation to the year 2014 is a percent of growth or decline as estimated by the Bureau of Labor Statistics. The abbreviation nec stands for 'not elsewhere classified.'

LOCATION BY STATE AND REGIONAL CONCENTRATION

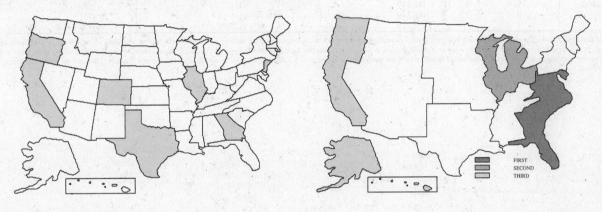

INDUSTRY DATA BY STATE

State	Establishments Total (number)	% of U.S.	Employment Total (number)	% of U.S.	Per Estab.	Payroll Total ($ mil.)	Per Empl. ($)	Sales Total ($ mil.)	% of U.S.	Per Estab. ($)
California	712	10.1	14,152	12.1	20	774.0	54,695	124,565.7	25.8	174,951,798
Georgia	227	3.2	4,572	3.9	20	206.8	45,234	44,938.0	9.3	197,964,731
New Jersey	236	3.4	4,815	4.1	20	269.4	55,957	39,521.8	8.2	167,465,356
Texas	528	7.5	7,600	6.5	14	329.2	43,311	38,812.0	8.0	73,507,572
Illinois	232	3.3	5,221	4.5	23	217.9	41,735	35,873.9	7.4	154,628,741
Colorado	103	1.5	1,905	1.6	18	90.8	47,665	18,545.5	3.8	180,053,650
New York	358	5.1	3,961	3.4	11	158.9	40,123	17,741.6	3.7	49,557,517
Ohio	257	3.7	4,821	4.1	19	175.2	36,349	17,188.2	3.6	66,880,350
Pennsylvania	283	4.0	6,575	5.6	23	256.0	38,936	11,965.1	2.5	42,279,410
Massachusetts	114	1.6	1,464	1.3	13	65.1	44,499	10,380.4	2.1	91,055,842
Missouri	195	2.8	3,187	2.7	16	112.0	35,142	9,579.0	2.0	49,123,200
Oregon	115	1.6	2,189	1.9	19	89.9	41,075	7,291.9	1.5	63,407,617
Tennessee	151	2.2	3,326	2.8	22	124.7	37,504	7,184.2	1.5	47,577,649
Minnesota	144	2.1	3,024	2.6	21	133.5	44,146	7,090.2	1.5	49,237,826
Virginia	152	2.2	2,889	2.5	19	98.6	34,142	6,001.5	1.2	39,483,454
Wisconsin	134	1.9	3,861	3.3	29	136.5	35,350	4,017.7	0.8	29,982,903
Washington	144	2.1	1,652	1.4	11	58.1	35,165	3,987.5	0.8	27,690,868
Kansas	76	1.1	990	0.8	13	36.0	36,398	3,197.9	0.7	42,077,250
North Carolina	224	3.2	3,295	2.8	15	120.3	36,520	3,084.9	0.6	13,771,737
Indiana	184	2.6	3,692	3.2	20	124.0	33,582	1,617.2	0.3	8,788,875
Louisiana	71	1.0	973	0.8	14	32.4	33,269	1,495.2	0.3	21,058,465
Alabama	170	2.4	2,244	1.9	13	75.2	33,533	1,242.1	0.3	7,306,176
Iowa	91	1.3	2,486	2.1	27	83.5	33,585	973.3	0.2	10,695,297
South Carolina	120	1.7	1,377	1.2	11	49.0	35,613	858.0	0.2	7,150,242
Arkansas	98	1.4	1,388	1.2	14	44.9	32,380	635.9	0.1	6,488,316
Utah	51	0.7	1,102	0.9	22	46.3	42,049	587.4	0.1	11,318,373
Oklahoma	88	1.3	1,364	1.2	15	54.8	40,210	583.4	0.1	6,629,398
Connecticut	54	0.8	896	0.8	17	35.4	39,521	563.0	0.1	10,426,111
Mississippi	72	1.0	1,189	1.0	17	40.5	34,084	560.5	0.1	7,784,819
Hawaii	17	0.2	138	0.1	8	8.2	59,457	507.6	0.1	29,857,353
Kentucky	96	1.4	1,292	1.1	13	42.0	32,523	496.7	0.1	5,174,281

Continued on next page.

INDUSTRY DATA BY STATE - Continued

State	Establishments Total (number)	% of U.S.	Employment Total (number)	% of U.S.	Per Estab.	Payroll Total ($ mil.)	Per Empl. ($)	Sales Total ($ mil.)	% of U.S.	Per Estab. ($)
Nebraska	50	0.7	874	0.7	17	35.2	40,247	357.0	0.1	7,139,120
West Virginia	44	0.6	1,034	0.9	23	27.0	26,119	280.3	0.1	6,369,591
North Dakota	29	0.4	370	0.3	13	11.7	31,541	234.1	-	8,074,103
Maine	48	0.7	721	0.6	15	21.6	29,981	232.4	-	4,840,854
New Hampshire	28	0.4	435	0.4	16	19.3	44,425	184.9	-	6,604,071
Idaho	40	0.6	457	0.4	11	16.3	35,663	170.2	-	4,255,700
South Dakota	32	0.5	405	0.3	13	12.9	31,733	167.1	-	5,222,812
Montana	30	0.4	327	0.3	11	11.8	36,076	132.7	-	4,423,867
New Mexico	30	0.4	267	0.2	9	8.7	32,753	102.9	-	3,431,167
Vermont	17	0.2	199	0.2	12	6.5	32,774	67.8	-	3,989,941
Wyoming	12	0.2	132	0.1	11	3.1	23,144	33.3	-	2,778,833
Florida	574	8.2	5K-9999	-	-	(D)	-	(D)	-	-
Michigan	232	3.3	2500-4999	-	-	(D)	-	(D)	-	-
Arizona	139	2.0	1000-2499	-	-	(D)	-	(D)	-	-
Maryland	107	1.5	1000-2499	-	-	(D)	-	(D)	-	-
Nevada	45	0.6	500-999	-	-	(D)	-	(D)	-	-
Delaware	28	0.4	100-249	-	-	(D)	-	(D)	-	-
Rhode Island	19	0.3	100-249	-	-	(D)	-	(D)	-	-
Alaska	16	0.2	100-249	-	-	(D)	-	(D)	-	-
D.C.	1	-	0-19	-	-	(D)	-	(D)	-	-

Source: 2002 *Economic Census*. The states are in descending order of sales or establishments (if sales data are missing for the majority). The symbol (D) appears when data are withheld to prevent disclosure of competitive information. States marked with (D) are sorted by number of establishments. A dash (-) indicates that the data element cannot be calculated. Shaded *states* on the state map indicate those states which have proportionately greater representation in the industry than would be indicated by the states population; the ratio is based on total sales or number of establishments. Shaded *regions* indicate where the industry is regionally most concentrated.

NAICS 423120 - MOTOR VEHICLE SUPPLIES AND NEW PARTS MERCHANT WHOLESALERS

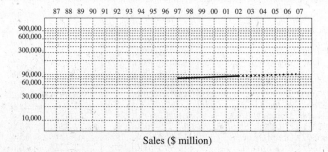

Sales ($ million)

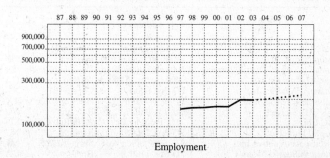

Employment

GENERAL STATISTICS

Year	Establishments (number)	Employment (number)	Payroll ($ million)	Sales ($ million)	Employees per Establishment (number)	Sales per Establishment ($)	Payroll per Employee ($)
1987	-	-	-	-	-	-	-
1988	-	-	-	-	-	-	-
1989	-	-	-	-	-	-	-
1990	-	-	-	-	-	-	-
1991	-	-	-	-	-	-	-
1992	-	-	-	-	-	-	-
1993	-	-	-	-	-	-	-
1994	-	-	-	-	-	-	-
1995	-	-	-	-	-	-	-
1996	-	-	-	-	-	-	-
1997	12,620	156,038	5,065.1	83,214.7	12.4	6,593,874.8	32,460.7
1998	12,158	161,154	5,662.1	85,178.6 e	13.3	7,005,971.4	35,134.7
1999	12,101	162,304	6,010.1	87,142.5 e	13.4	7,201,264.4	37,029.9
2000	12,285	166,430	6,231.9	89,106.4 e	13.5	7,253,268.2	37,444.3
2001	12,083	165,975	6,269.7	91,070.3 e	13.7	7,537,060.3	37,775.1
2002	14,584	197,519	7,154.4	93,034.2	13.5	6,379,196.4	36,221.3
2003	14,495	196,321	7,402.4	94,998.1 p	13.5	7,052,293.8 p	37,705.7
2004	14,398 p	200,427 p	7,721.7 p	96,962.0 p	13.9 p	7,068,633.2 p	38,917.9 p
2005	14,771 p	207,472 p	8,088.0 p	98,925.9 p	14.1 p	7,084,972.6 p	39,584.1 p
2006	15,145 p	214,517 p	8,454.3 p	100,889.8 p	14.2 p	7,101,311.9 p	40,250.3 p
2007	15,518 p	221,561 p	8,820.6 p	102,853.7 p	14.4 p	7,117,651.3 p	40,916.5 p

Source: *Economic Census of the United States*, 1997 and 2002. Establishment counts, employment, and payroll are from *County Business Patterns* for non-Census years. This is a newly defined industry. Data for prior years are unavailable at the time of publication but may become available over time. Values followed by 'p' are projections by the editors. Sales data for non-Census years are extrapolations, marked by 'e'.

INDICES OF CHANGE

Year	Establishments (number)	Employment (number)	Payroll ($ million)	Sales ($ million)	Employees per Establishment (number)	Sales per Establishment ($)	Payroll per Employee ($)
1987	-	-	-	-	-	-	-
1992	-	-	-	-	-	-	-
1993	-	-	-	-	-	-	-
1994	-	-	-	-	-	-	-
1995	-	-	-	-	-	-	-
1996	-	-	-	-	-	-	-
1997	86.5	79.0	70.8	89.4	91.9	103.4	89.6
1998	83.4	81.6	79.1	91.6 e	98.5	109.8	97.0
1999	83.0	82.2	84.0	93.7 e	99.3	112.9	102.2
2000	84.2	84.3	87.1	95.8 e	100.0	113.7	103.4
2001	82.9	84.0	87.6	97.9 e	101.5	118.2	104.3
2002	100.0	100.0	100.0	100.0	100.0	100.0	100.0
2003	99.4	99.4	103.5	102.1 p	100.3	110.6 p	104.1
2004	98.7 p	101.5 p	107.9 p	104.2 p	103.1 p	110.8 p	107.4 p
2005	101.3 p	105.0 p	113.0 p	106.3 p	104.2 p	111.1 p	109.3 p
2006	103.8 p	108.6 p	118.2 p	108.4 p	105.3 p	111.3 p	111.1 p
2007	106.4 p	112.2 p	123.3 p	110.6 p	106.4 p	111.6 p	113.0 p

Sources: Same as General Statistics. The values shown reflect change from the base year, 2002. Values above 100 mean greater than 2002, values below 100 mean less than 2002, and a value of 100 in the 1987-2001 or 2003-2007 period means same as 2002. Values followed by a 'p' are projections by the editors; 'e' stands for extrapolation. Data are the most recent available at this level of detail.

SELECTED RATIOS

For 2002	Avg. of All Wholesale	Analyzed Industry	Index	For 2002	Avg. of All Wholesale	Analyzed Industry	Index
Employees per Establishment	15	14	91	Sales per Employee	791,325	471,014	60
Payroll per Establishment	626,122	490,565	78	Sales per Establishment	12,012,387	6,379,196	53
Payroll per Employee	41,161	36,221	88	Expenses per Establishment	na	na	na

Sources: Same as General Statistics. The 'Average of All' column, Wholesale or Retail, represents the average of the sector reported for the most recent complete year available. The Index shows the relationship between the Average and the Analyzed Industry. For example, 100 means that they are equal; 500 that the Analyzed Industry is five times the average; 50 means that the Analyzed Industry is half the national average. The abbreviation 'na' is used to show that data are 'not available'.

LEADING COMPANIES   Number shown: **75**   Total sales ($ mil): **246,698**   Total employment (000): **543.9**

Company Name	Address				CEO Name	Phone	Co. Type	Sales ($ mil)	Empl. (000)
Ford Motor Co.	1 American Rd	Dearborn	MI	48126		313-322-3000	P	171,652	324.9
Visteon Corp.	17000 Rotunda Dr	Dearborn	MI	48120		313-755-2800	P	18,691	70.0
Southeast Toyota Distributors Inc.	100 Jim Moran Blvd	Deerfield Beach	FL	33442	Jim Moran	954-429-2000	S	14,027*	2.5
Genuine Parts Co.	2999 Circle 75 Pkwy	Atlanta	GA	30339	Thomas C Gallagher	770-953-1700	P	9,097	30.8
Subaru of America Inc.	PO Box 6000	Cherry Hill	NJ	08034	Kunio Ishigami	856-488-8500	S	4,100	0.6
Gulf States Toyota Inc.	PO Box 40306	Houston	TX	77040		713-744-3300	S	4,095*	3.2
CARQUEST Corp.	PO Box 26929	Raleigh	NC	27611	Al Stecklein		R	2,500	25.0
TBC Corp.	7111 Fairway Dr	Palm Bch Grdns	FL	33418	Marvin E Bruce	561-227-0955	P	1,855	9.4
General Parts Inc.	PO Box 26006	Raleigh	NC	27611	O Temple Sloan III	919-573-3000	R	1,754	17.0
O'Reilly Automotive Inc.	233 S Patterson Ave	Springfield	MO	65802	Greg Henslee	417-862-6708	P	1,721	15.6
American Suzuki Motor Corp.	PO Box 1100	Brea	CA	92822	Rick Suzuki	714-996-7040	S	1,222*	0.6
American Tire Distributors Inc.	PO Box 3145	Huntersville	NC	28070	William E Berry	704-992-2000	R	1,112	1.9
Rush Enterprises Inc.	555 IH 35 S, Ste 500	New Braunfels	TX	78130		830-626-5200	P	1,095	1.9
R.B. Matheson Trucking Inc.	PO Box 970	Elk Grove	CA	95759	Robert B Matheson	916-685-2330	R	1,084*	1.0
M and M Knopf Auto Parts Inc.	239 O N Brunswick	Piscataway	NJ	08854	Marshall Knopf	732-981-8040	R	1,050*	<0.1
US Oil Company Inc.	PO Box 25	Combined Locks	WI	54113		920-739-6101	R	980*	0.4
Lacy Diversified Industries	54 Monument Cir	Indianapolis	IN	46204	Andre Lacy	317-237-5400	R	855*	<0.1
GenTek Inc.	90 E Halsey Rd	Parsippany	NJ	07054	John G Johnson Jr	973-515-3221	P	844	6.1
Myers Industries Inc.	1293 S Main St	Akron	OH	44301		330-253-5592	P	803	5.3
Keystone Automotive Industries	700 E Bonita Ave	Pomona	CA	91767	Ronald G Foster	909-624-8041	P	501	3.4
SunSource Inc.	2301 Windsor Ct	Addison	IL	60101	Justin Jacobi	630-317-2700	S	460*	2.1
Barden Companies Inc.	163 Madison Ave	Detroit	MI	48226	Don H Barden	313-496-2900	R	354	4.1
Bing Group L.L.C.	11500 Oakland St	Detroit	MI	48211	David Bing	313-852-3700	R	347	1.1
Mighty Distributing System	650 Engineering Dr	Norcross	GA	30092	Ken Voelker	770-448-3900	R	328*	0.2
Safety Components Intern. Inc.	41 Stevens St	Greenville	SC	29605	John C Corey	864-270-2600	P	248	2.8
Parts Warehouse Inc.	1901 E Roosevelt Rd	Little Rock	AR	72206	E Fletcher Lord Jr	501-375-1215	R	247*	0.3
Insurance Auto Auctions Inc.	850 E Algonquin	Schaumburg	IL	60173	Peter H Kamin	708-492-7000	P	240	1.0
PACCAR Inc. Parts Div.	750 Houser Way N	Renton	WA	98055		425-254-4400	D	233*	0.4
Monroe Truck Equipment Inc.	1051 W 7th St	Monroe	WI	53566	David Quade	608-328-8127	R	199*	0.5
Interstate Battery System of Dallas	12770 Merit Dr	Dallas	TX	75251	Norm Miller	972-991-1444	R	192*	0.9
Peach State Truck Center	PO Box 808	Norcross	GA	30091	Tom Reynolds	770-449-5300	R	188*	0.2
Flowers Auto Parts Co.	PO Box 1118	Hickory	NC	28601	Bobby Flowers	828-322-5414	R	182*	0.1
MCI Service Parts Inc.	1700 E Golf Rd	Schaumburg	IL	60173	Tom Sorrells	847-285-2000	S	177*	0.2
Universal Cooperative Inc.	1300 Corp Ctr	Eagan	MN	55121	Terry Bohman	651-239-1000	R	167*	0.3
Barron Motor Inc.	PO Box 1327	Cedar Rapids	IA	52402	William J Barron	319-393-6220	R	164*	0.1
Medart Inc. (Fenton, Missouri)	124 Manufacturers	Arnold	MO	63010	J Michael Medart	636-282-2300	R	161*	0.1
Coast Distribution System Inc.	350 Woodview Ave	Morgan Hill	CA	95037	Thomas R McGuire	408-782-6686	P	157	0.4
Factory Motor Parts Co.	2855 Eagandale	Eagan	MN	55121	E Badzin	651-405-3500	R	156*	0.1
Sterling Construction Company	2751 Centerville Rd	Wilmington	DE	19803		281-821-9091	P	154	0.7
Manning Equipment Inc.	PO Box 23229	Louisville	KY	40223	Michael Stich	502-426-5210	R	153*	0.1
Motorcycle Stuff Inc.	PO Box 1179	Cape Girardeau	MO	63701	Frank Espanito	573-339-1111	R	148*	<0.1
Bauer Built Inc.	PO Box 248	Durand	WI	54736	Jerry M Bauer	715-672-4295	R	137*	0.5
Bruckner Truck Sales Inc.	8351 E Amarillo	Amarillo	TX	79107	Ben Bruckner Jr	806-376-6273	R	137*	0.2
Nissho Iwai American Corp.	1211 Av Americas	New York	NY	10036	Teruo Matsumura	212-704-6500	S	130*	0.1
Big O Tires Inc.	12650 E Briarwood	Englewood	CO	80112	John Adams	303-728-5500	S	125*	0.5
LeMans Corp.	PO Box 5222	Janesville	WI	53547	Fred Fox	608-758-1111	R	122*	0.5
Automotive Supply Co.	PO Box 145	Appleton	WI	54912	Casey Wewerka	920-734-2651	R	121*	0.1
Hahn Automotive Warehouse Inc.	415 W Main St	Rochester	NY	14608	Daniel Chessin	585-235-1595	R	121	1.1
Integrated Supply Network Inc.	PO Box 90009	Lakeland	FL	33804	Bruce Weber	863-603-0777	R	120*	0.1
Johnson Industries	5944 Peachtree	Norcross	GA	30071	Buddy Johnson	770-441-1133	S	120*	0.2
Pam Oil Inc.	PO Box 5200	Sioux Falls	SD	57117	William G Pederson	605-336-1788	R	112*	0.3
Fred Jones Enterprises L.L.C.	PO Box 25068	Oklahoma City	OK	73125	Scott Weaver	405-272-9261	R	110*	<0.1
Crossroads Ford Truck Sales Inc.	PO Box 6548	Springfield	IL	62708	John Hogan	217-528-0770	R	100*	<0.1
Kenworth Sales Company Inc.	PO Box 65829	Salt Lake City	UT	84165	R Kyle Treadway	801-487-4161	R	98*	0.2
Midwest Auto Parts	2565 Kasota Ave	St. Paul	MN	55108	Herb Lohse	651-644-6448	R	95*	0.8
Hale Trailer Brake and Wheel	PO Box 1400	Voorhees	NJ	08043	Barry Hale	856-768-1330	R	94*	<0.1
Arnold Motor Supply Co.	PO Box 320	Spencer	IA	51301		712-262-1141	R	85*	0.4
Coast Counties Truck & Equip.	PO Box 757	San Jose	CA	95106	Robert Archer	408-453-5510	R	82*	0.1
Capitol Chevrolet Inc.	PO Box 36	Montgomery	AL	36101	Phil Marshall	334-272-8700	R	80*	0.2
Bale Chevrolet Geo Co.	PO Box 22070	Little Rock	AR	72221	John H Bale Jr		R	79*	0.2
Southern Pump and Tank Co.	PO Box 31516	Charlotte	NC	28231		704-596-4373	R	73*	0.2
DBM Technologies L.L.C.	140 S Saginaw St	Pontiac	MI	48342	Lawrence D Crawford	248-836-4823	R	72	0.5
Mattos Inc.	4501 Beech Rd	Temple Hills	MD	20748	John A Mattos	301-423-1142	R	67*	0.1
Nichirin Coupler TEC USA	9600 Plz Cir	El Paso	TX	79927	Toshiaki Fujiwara	915-859-1199	R	67*	0.4
Hedman/TD Performance	16410 Manning Way	Cerritos	CA	90703		562-926-3254	R	65*	<0.1
Frank Edwards Co.	3626 Parkway Blvd	Salt Lake City	UT	84120	Robert Edwards Jr	801-736-8000	R	63*	0.2
Caravan Trailer L.L.C.	PO Box 12595	Kansas City	MO	64116		816-781-1701	R	63*	<0.1
Minn-Dak Inc.	PO Box 11057	Fargo	ND	58106	Ron Ristvedt	701-293-9133	R	63*	<0.1
Western States Equipment	PO Box 38	Boise	ID	83707	Tommy Harris	208-888-2287	R	62*	0.6
Stag/Parkway Inc.	PO Box 43463	Atlanta	GA	30336	Stanley I Sunshine	404-349-1918	R	61*	0.3
Universal Automotive Industries	11859 S Central Ave	Alsip	IL	60803	Arvin Scott	708-293-4050	P	59	0.2
Sosmetal Products Inc.	2945 E Tioga St	Philadelphia	PA	19134	Milton Soskin	215-739-6200	R	58*	0.2
Daewoo International Corp.	85 Challenger Rd	Ridgefield Park	NJ	07660	Young Nam	201-229-4500	R	56*	<0.1
Automotive Parts Headquarters	PO Box 1338	Saint Cloud	MN	56302	John Bartlett	320-252-5411	R	53*	<0.1
Camco Manufacturing Inc.	PO Box 18865	Greensboro	NC	27419	Donald Caine	336-668-7661	R	53*	0.2

Source: Ward's Business Directory of U.S. Private and Public Companies, Volumes 1 and 2, 2005. The company type code used is as follows: P - Public, R - Private, S - Subsidiary, D - Division, J - Joint Venture, A - Affiliate, G - Group. Sales are in millions of dollars, employees are in thousands. An asterisk (*) indicates an estimated sales volume. The symbol < stands for 'less than'. Company names and addresses are truncated, in some cases, to fit into the available space.

OCCUPATIONS EMPLOYED BY MOTOR VEHICLE & MOTOR VEHICLE PARTS & SUPPLIES

Occupation	% of Total 2004	Change to 2014	Occupation	% of Total 2004	Change to 2014
Sales reps, wholesale & manufacturing, exc tech	8.4	17.9	Motor vehicle operators, nec	1.8	17.9
Truck drivers, light or delivery services	8.1	17.8	Retail salespersons	1.8	17.9
Parts salespersons	7.1	-5.7	Team assemblers	1.7	17.9
Laborers & freight, stock, & material movers, hand	6.7	6.1	Customer service representatives	1.6	20.7
Bus & truck mechanics & diesel engine specialists	5.3	17.9	First-line supervisors/managers of non-retail sales work	1.5	9.0
Stock clerks & order fillers	4.0	-9.7	Truck drivers, heavy & tractor-trailer	1.4	17.9
Office clerks, general	3.3	4.9	First-line supervisors/managers of office workers	1.3	6.8
Automotive service technicians & mechanics	3.0	17.9	Industrial truck & tractor operators	1.2	17.9
Shipping, receiving, & traffic clerks	3.0	6.7	First-line supervisors of mechanics	1.2	17.9
Driver/sales workers	2.8	17.8	Cleaners of vehicles & equipment	1.1	4.1
Bookkeeping, accounting, & auditing clerks	2.4	6.1	First-line supervisors/managers of retail sales workers	1.1	8.4
General & operations managers	2.3	16.6	Order clerks	1.0	-23.4

Source: Industry-Occupation Matrix, Bureau of Labor Statistics. These data are reported based on 4-digit NAICS categories but have been matched to corresponding 6-digit NAICS industry codes. The change reported for each occupation to the year 2014 is a percent of growth or decline as estimated by the Bureau of Labor Statistics. The abbreviation nec stands for 'not elsewhere classified.'

LOCATION BY STATE AND REGIONAL CONCENTRATION

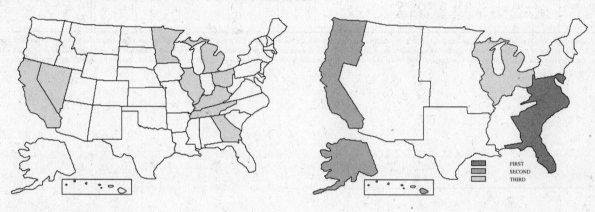

FIRST
SECOND
THIRD

INDUSTRY DATA BY STATE

State	Establishments Total (number)	% of U.S.	Employment Total (number)	% of U.S.	Per Estab.	Payroll Total ($ mil.)	Per Empl. ($)	Sales Total ($ mil.)	% of U.S.	Per Estab. ($)
Michigan	708	4.8	20,010	10.0	28	1,060.5	52,998	18,458.3	19.2	26,071,016
California	1,999	13.7	26,146	13.1	13	970.5	37,118	12,859.9	13.4	6,433,170
Illinois	579	4.0	10,243	5.1	18	391.4	38,211	6,304.2	6.6	10,888,059
Ohio	626	4.3	10,029	5.0	16	353.4	35,236	5,463.0	5.7	8,726,887
Texas	1,048	7.2	14,283	7.2	14	484.1	33,896	5,422.9	5.6	5,174,529
Georgia	463	3.2	6,135	3.1	13	243.5	39,685	4,096.0	4.3	8,846,568
Florida	1,111	7.6	8,838	4.4	8	297.4	33,653	3,351.3	3.5	3,016,429
Tennessee	324	2.2	5,528	2.8	17	190.3	34,423	2,822.3	2.9	8,710,667
New York	844	5.8	8,586	4.3	10	259.9	30,265	2,246.5	2.3	2,661,680
Kentucky	196	1.3	3,007	1.5	15	102.3	34,025	2,075.9	2.2	10,591,102
Indiana	308	2.1	4,594	2.3	15	159.1	34,638	1,930.7	2.0	6,268,354
Pennsylvania	552	3.8	7,698	3.9	14	235.4	30,577	1,892.4	2.0	3,428,279
Minnesota	278	1.9	5,091	2.6	18	185.0	36,346	1,860.8	1.9	6,693,424
Missouri	299	2.0	4,157	2.1	14	141.2	33,975	1,550.0	1.6	5,183,863
Massachusetts	314	2.1	4,333	2.2	14	148.3	34,225	1,382.6	1.4	4,403,264
North Carolina	378	2.6	3,702	1.9	10	109.1	29,458	1,332.2	1.4	3,524,217
Wisconsin	200	1.4	3,202	1.6	16	132.0	41,223	1,182.1	1.2	5,910,405
Washington	273	1.9	3,557	1.8	13	110.6	31,083	1,114.9	1.2	4,083,806
Connecticut	133	0.9	1,676	0.8	13	70.4	42,002	1,042.4	1.1	7,837,444
Maryland	250	1.7	2,723	1.4	11	94.7	34,771	975.4	1.0	3,901,652
Nevada	98	0.7	1,577	0.8	16	63.6	40,320	933.5	1.0	9,525,051
Iowa	171	1.2	2,161	1.1	13	62.5	28,935	900.7	0.9	5,267,497
Arkansas	110	0.8	1,473	0.7	13	45.6	30,955	796.4	0.8	7,240,418
Kansas	139	1.0	1,803	0.9	13	54.7	30,365	705.6	0.7	5,076,460
Oklahoma	143	1.0	2,115	1.1	15	55.6	26,282	628.8	0.7	4,396,874
Alabama	201	1.4	2,439	1.2	12	66.2	27,157	586.9	0.6	2,920,124
Utah	113	0.8	1,589	0.8	14	48.9	30,805	515.7	0.5	4,563,752
South Carolina	177	1.2	1,840	0.9	10	52.2	28,390	495.6	0.5	2,800,017
Mississippi	113	0.8	1,354	0.7	12	39.4	29,095	482.2	0.5	4,267,389
West Virginia	95	0.6	1,361	0.7	14	60.7	44,565	269.8	0.3	2,840,421
Nebraska	94	0.6	1,007	0.5	11	28.3	28,148	211.9	0.2	2,254,255

Continued on next page.

INDUSTRY DATA BY STATE - Continued

State	Establishments Total (number)	% of U.S.	Employment Total (number)	% of U.S.	Per Estab.	Payroll Total ($ mil.)	Per Empl. ($)	Sales Total ($ mil.)	% of U.S.	Per Estab. ($)
Hawaii	48	0.3	759	0.4	16	22.7	29,874	163.3	0.2	3,401,813
Montana	50	0.3	528	0.3	11	15.7	29,731	159.2	0.2	3,184,700
New Mexico	68	0.5	696	0.3	10	18.9	27,101	152.2	0.2	2,237,632
Maine	43	0.3	479	0.2	11	13.6	28,405	127.3	0.1	2,960,837
South Dakota	47	0.3	477	0.2	10	13.8	28,878	107.7	0.1	2,291,979
Vermont	46	0.3	423	0.2	9	12.8	30,305	76.7	0.1	1,667,826
Alaska	18	0.1	220	0.1	12	7.7	35,209	73.1	0.1	4,059,278
Wyoming	18	0.1	177	0.1	10	7.7	43,316	43.1	-	2,393,389
New Jersey	489	3.3	5K-9999	-	-	(D)	-	(D)	-	-
Virginia	359	2.5	2500-4999	-	-	(D)	-	(D)	-	-
Arizona	251	1.7	2500-4999	-	-	(D)	-	(D)	-	-
Colorado	220	1.5	2500-4999	-	-	(D)	-	(D)	-	-
Oregon	193	1.3	1000-2499	-	-	(D)	-	(D)	-	-
Louisiana	169	1.2	1000-2499	-	-	(D)	-	(D)	-	-
Idaho	68	0.5	500-999	-	-	(D)	-	(D)	-	-
Rhode Island	60	0.4	500-999	-	-	(D)	-	(D)	-	-
North Dakota	53	0.4	500-999	-	-	(D)	-	(D)	-	-
New Hampshire	43	0.3	500-999	-	-	(D)	-	(D)	-	-
Delaware	40	0.3	500-999	-	-	(D)	-	(D)	-	-
D.C.	8	0.1	100-249	-	-	(D)	-	(D)	-	-

Source: 2002 *Economic Census*. The states are in descending order of sales or establishments (if sales data are missing for the majority). The symbol (D) appears when data are withheld to prevent disclosure of competitive information. States marked with (D) are sorted by number of establishments. A dash (-) indicates that the data element cannot be calculated. Shaded *states* on the state map indicate those states which have proportionally greater representation in the industry than would be indicated by the states population; the ratio is based on total sales or number of establishments. Shaded *regions* indicate where the industry is regionally most concentrated.

NAICS 423130 - TIRE AND TUBE MERCHANT WHOLESALERS

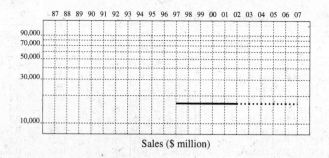

Sales ($ million)

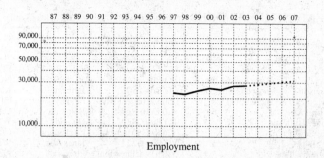

Employment

GENERAL STATISTICS

Year	Establishments (number)	Employment (number)	Payroll ($ million)	Sales ($ million)	Employees per Establishment (number)	Sales per Establishment ($)	Payroll per Employee ($)
1987	-	-	-	-	-	-	-
1988	-	-	-	-	-	-	-
1989	-	-	-	-	-	-	-
1990	-	-	-	-	-	-	-
1991	-	-	-	-	-	-	-
1992	-	-	-	-	-	-	-
1993	-	-	-	-	-	-	-
1994	-	-	-	-	-	-	-
1995	-	-	-	-	-	-	-
1996	-	-	-	-	-	-	-
1997	1,939	22,939	782.9	16,508.9	11.8	8,514,131.0	34,129.6
1998	1,871	22,195	806.0	16,505.0 e	11.9	8,821,507.2	36,314.5
1999	1,925	24,090	883.4	16,501.2 e	12.5	8,572,041.6	36,670.8
2000	2,036	25,752	957.0	16,497.3 e	12.6	8,102,809.4	37,163.6
2001	2,005	24,907	971.2	16,493.5 e	12.4	8,226,164.6	38,991.1
2002	2,264	27,343	987.5	16,489.6	12.1	7,283,392.2	36,115.3
2003	2,239	27,669	1,056.4	16,485.7 p	12.4	7,412,445.6 p	38,180.7
2004	2,292 p	28,600 p	1,102.3 p	16,481.9 p	12.5 p	7,172,189.8 p	38,805.8 p
2005	2,355 p	29,503 p	1,147.7 p	16,478.0 p	12.6 p	6,931,934.0 p	39,308.5 p
2006	2,418 p	30,407 p	1,193.1 p	16,474.2 p	12.7 p	6,691,678.1 p	39,811.2 p
2007	2,481 p	31,311 p	1,238.5 p	16,470.3 p	12.7 p	6,451,422.3 p	40,313.8 p

Source: *Economic Census of the United States*, 1997 and 2002. Establishment counts, employment, and payroll are from *County Business Patterns* for non-Census years. This is a newly defined industry. Data for prior years are unavailable at the time of publication but may become available over time. Values followed by 'p' are projections by the editors. Sales data for non-Census years are extrapolations, marked by 'e'.

INDICES OF CHANGE

Year	Establishments (number)	Employment (number)	Payroll ($ million)	Sales ($ million)	Employees per Establishment (number)	Sales per Establishment ($)	Payroll per Employee ($)
1987	-	-	-	-	-	-	-
1992	-	-	-	-	-	-	-
1993	-	-	-	-	-	-	-
1994	-	-	-	-	-	-	-
1995	-	-	-	-	-	-	-
1996	-	-	-	-	-	-	-
1997	85.6	83.9	79.3	100.1	97.5	116.9	94.5
1998	82.6	81.2	81.6	100.1 e	98.3	121.1	100.6
1999	85.0	88.1	89.5	100.1 e	103.3	117.7	101.5
2000	89.9	94.2	96.9	100.0 e	104.1	111.3	102.9
2001	88.6	91.1	98.3	100.0 e	102.5	112.9	108.0
2002	100.0	100.0	100.0	100.0	100.0	100.0	100.0
2003	98.9	101.2	107.0	100.0 p	102.1	101.8 p	105.7
2004	101.2 p	104.6 p	111.6 p	100.0 p	103.5 p	98.5 p	107.4 p
2005	104.0 p	107.9 p	116.2 p	99.9 p	104.0 p	95.2 p	108.8 p
2006	106.8 p	111.2 p	120.8 p	99.9 p	104.6 p	91.9 p	110.2 p
2007	109.6 p	114.5 p	125.4 p	99.9 p	105.2 p	88.6 p	111.6 p

Sources: Same as General Statistics. The values shown reflect change from the base year, 2002. Values above 100 mean greater than 2002, values below 100 mean less than 2002, and a value of 100 in the 1987-2001 or 2003-2007 period means same as 2002. Values followed by a 'p' are projections by the editors; 'e' stands for extrapolation. Data are the most recent available at this level of detail.

SELECTED RATIOS

For 2002	Avg. of All Wholesale	Analyzed Industry	Index	For 2002	Avg. of All Wholesale	Analyzed Industry	Index
Employees per Establishment	15	12	81	Sales per Employee	791,325	603,065	76
Payroll per Establishment	626,122	436,175	70	Sales per Establishment	12,012,387	7,283,392	61
Payroll per Employee	41,161	36,115	88	Expenses per Establishment	na	na	na

Sources: Same as General Statistics. The 'Average of All' column, Wholesale or Retail, represents the average of the sector reported for the most recent complete year available. The Index shows the relationship between the Average and the Analyzed Industry. For example, 100 means that they are equal; 500 that the Analyzed Industry is five times the average; 50 means that the Analyzed Industry is half the national average. The abbreviation 'na' is used to show that data are 'not available'.

LEADING COMPANIES   Number shown: **71**   Total sales ($ mil): **5,604**   Total employment (000): **16.8**

Company Name	Address				CEO Name	Phone	Co. Type	Sales ($ mil)	Empl. (000)
TBC Corp.	7111 Fairway Dr	Palm Bch Grdns	FL	33418	Marvin E. Bruce	561-227-0955	P	1,855	9.4
American Tire Distributors Inc.	PO Box 3145	Huntersville	NC	28070	William E Berry	704-992-2000	R	1,112	1.9
Johnson Cooperative Grain Co.	PO Box 280	Johnson	KS	67855	Steve Arnold	620-492-6210	R	336*	<0.1
Hercules Tire and Rubber Co.	1300 Morrical Blvd	Findlay	OH	45840	Craig E Anderson	419-425-6400	R	300*	0.4
WheelWorks	120 Cam Real	Belmont	CA	94002		650-592-3200	R	249*	0.4
Bauer Built Inc.	PO Box 248	Durand	WI	54736	Jerry M Bauer	715-672-4295	R	137*	0.5
Big O Tires Inc.	12650 E Briarwood	Englewood	CO	80112	John Adams	303-728-5500	S	125*	0.5
LeMans Corp.	PO Box 5222	Janesville	WI	53547	Fred Fox	608-758-1111	R	122*	0.5
Redburn Tire	3801 W Clarendon	Phoenix	AZ	85019	JD Chastain	602-272-7601	R	109*	0.2
Kumho Tires U.S.A. Inc.	14605 Miller Ave	Fontana	CA	92336	Kyu S Cho	909-428-3999	S	92*	<0.1
Capital Tire Inc.	1001 Cherry St	Toledo	OH	43608	Thomas B Geiger Jr	419-241-5111	R	84*	0.1
Friend Tire Co.	11 Industrial Dr	Monett	MO	65708	Donald L Isbell	417-235-7836	S	82*	0.2
Reliable Tire Distributors Inc.	PO Box 39	Blackwood	NJ	08012	Richard Betz	856-232-0700	R	69*	0.1
Allied Oil and Supply Inc.	PO Box 3687	Omaha	NE	68103	RC Heinson	402-344-4343	R	60*	0.2
Burggraf Tire Supply Inc.	322 Main St	Quapaw	OK	74363	Joe Karnes	918-674-2281	R	50*	<0.1
American Tire Distributors	PO Box 85746	Lincoln	NE	68501		402-473-7500	R	38*	0.1
Solideal Tire Inc.	PO Box 790070	Charlotte	NC	28206	Baldwin Hickey	704-374-9700	R	38*	<0.1
Jack Williams Tire Company Inc.	PO Box 3655	Scranton	PA	18505	William C Williams	570-457-5000	R	35*	0.4
Player Wire Wheels Ltd.	116 S Meridian Rd	Youngstown	OH	44509	Ray Starr	330-799-0128	R	31*	<0.1
Harold's Tire and Auto	709 Liberty Dr	Easley	SC	29640	Robbie Medlin	864-859-3741	R	30*	<0.1
H.C. Gabler Inc.	PO Box 220	Chambersburg	PA	17201	Thomas Gabler	717-264-4184	R	28*	<0.1
Gay Johnson's Inc.	26 Covington Dr	Englewood	CO	80113	Burt Johnson	303-783-2064	R	25*	<0.1
Barron's Wholesale Tire Inc.	1302 Eastport Rd	Jacksonville	FL	32218	David Barron	904-751-2449	R	23*	<0.1
H.C. Lewis Oil Co.	PO Box 649	Welch	WV	24801	HC Lewis Jr	304-436-2148	R	23*	<0.1
Vista Oil Co.	PO Box 5127	McAllen	TX	78502	Mike Broughton	956-381-0976	R	23*	<0.1
Terry Dees Enterprises Inc.	3955 Government	Mobile	AL	36693	Terry Dees	251-666-0840	R	21*	<0.1
TM Tire Company Inc.	4201 Midlothian	Midlothian	IL	60445	Thomas Accomando	708-597-3078	R	21*	<0.1
Mc Court Industries	1314 Centerview Cir	Akron	OH	44321	Charles Mc Court	330-666-0149	R	21*	<0.1
Dealer Tire L.L.C.	3711 Chester Ave	Cleveland	OH	44114		216-432-0088	R	19*	<0.1
Schiebout Tire Co.	PO Box 407	Pella	IA	50219	Dewey Veenstra	641-628-3153	R	19*	<0.1
Gay Johnson's Inc.	PO Box 1829	Grand Junction	CO	81502	Bert Johnson	970-242-3021	R	19*	<0.1
Rott-Keller Supply Co.	PO Box 390	Fargo	ND	58107	Herb F Rott Jr	701-235-0563	R	19*	<0.1
Magnum Tire Corp.	724 N 1st St	Minneapolis	MN	55401	Jerry Ray	612-338-8861	R	18*	<0.1
L & W Service Center Inc.	PO Box 190	Kearney	NE	68848	Marc Loescher	308-237-2185	R	15*	<0.1
Robison Tire Company Inc.	PO Box 545	Laurel	MS	39441	Joe Robison	601-649-8104	R	15*	<0.1
Alpine Tire Service of Spokane	3534 E Trent Ave	Spokane	WA	99202	Kermit Yochum	509-535-0261	R	13*	<0.1
Ball and Prier Tire Inc.	PO Box 136	Golden	MO	65658	Michael Ball	417-271-3299	R	13*	<0.1
Commercial Tire of Louisiana Inc.	PO Box 74010	Baton Rouge	LA	70874	Michael Bueche	225-775-1034	R	13*	<0.1
Toby Sexton Tire Company Inc.	PO Box 1768	Loganville	GA	30052	Tolbert Sexton	770-466-1060	R	12*	<0.1
Tech Supply Inc.	PO Box 14310	Schuylkl Hvn	KS	66285	Jack Clifford	913-492-6440	R	12*	<0.1
Advantage Performance	930 Columbia Ave	Riverside	CA	92507	Marty Miller	951-653-5485	R	12*	<0.1
Bergson Tire Company Inc.	PO Box 1258	Up Saddl Rvr	CT	06066	James Wood	860-872-7729	R	11*	<0.1
Chicago Tire Inc.	16001 Van Drunen	South Holland	IL	60473	John Wagner	708-331-8980	R	11*	<0.1
Tyldin Corp.	171 York St	Rochester	NY	14611	Richard Henry	585-328-4720	R	11*	<0.1
Walter's Tire Service Inc.	PO Box 348	Somerset	PA	15501	James Walters	814-445-4124	R	11*	<0.1
Western Tire Centers Inc.	3545 S Richey Blvd	Tucson	AZ	85713	John Furrier	520-748-1700	R	11*	<0.1
Samaritan Wholesale Tire Inc.	3138 Snelling Ave	Minneapolis	MN	55406	Jay Halvorson	612-729-8000	R	11*	<0.1
Dillon Cross Tire Inc.	10201 Sapp Brothers	Omaha	NE	68138		402-829-1000	R	10*	<0.1
Inland Industrial Tire North Inc.	30900 San Antonio	Hayward	CA	94544	Linda Griffin	510-429-2999	R	10*	<0.1
Speck Sales Inc.	17746 N Dixie Hwy	Bowling Green	OH	43402	Esther Speck	419-353-8312	R	10*	<0.1
Commercial Tire Company Inc.	5790 Washington	Elkridge	MD	21075	Jesse Albright	410-796-4330	R	10*	<0.1
General Tire Service	3375 Richmond St	Philadelphia	PA	19134	John Morrone	215-425-9980	R	10*	<0.1
Toce Brothers Inc.	143 E Main St	Torrington	CT	06790	Dominic Toce	860-496-2080	R	10*	<0.1
King Tire Service Inc.	PO Box 3511	Bluefield	WV	24701	Matthew King	304-589-3756	R	9*	<0.1
Wheel City	4327 E Belknap St	Fort Worth	TX	76117	Johnny Weaver	817-831-4231	R	9*	<0.1
Kent's Tire Service Inc.	1026 E Fort Worth	Wichita Falls	TX	76301	Kent Teague	940-761-1349	R	9*	<0.1
Bruneel Tire Factory Inc.	1519 Main St	Lewiston	ID	83501	Craig Bruneel	208-746-9873	R	8*	<0.1
Heafner Tires and Products 113	243 Ln Ave N	Jacksonville	FL	32254		904-693-9249	R	8*	<0.1
Dan Lewis Enterprises	408 W 8th St	Jacksonville	FL	32206	Daniel Lewis	904-353-8221	R	8*	<0.1
ITD California Inc.	6737 E Washington	Los Angeles	CA	90040	John Farkas	323-722-8542	R	8*	<0.1
LD Willcox and Son Inc.	1113 State Rte 13	Cortland	NY	13045	Newell Willcox	607-753-3344	R	8*	<0.1
Northwest Tire Factory L.L.C.	6102 N Marine Dr	Portland	OR	97203		503-283-6494	R	8*	<0.1
Quality Truck Tires Inc.	PO Box 60366	Midland	TX	79711	Stanley Dickerson	432-563-5301	R	8*	<0.1
Rhino Linings of Wausau	1509 Post Ave	Schofield	WI	54476	Rick Bender	715-355-7963	R	8*	<0.1
Salta's Tire Company Inc.	125 Water St	Laconia	NH	03246	William Salta	603-524-9030	R	8*	<0.1
Statham Commercial Tire	15 Linkwood NW	Atlanta	GA	30311		404-696-8500	R	8*	<0.1
Van Kleeck's Tire Inc.	PO Box 617	Lake Katrine	NY	12449	Clayton Van Kleeck	845-382-1292	R	8*	<0.1
Hanson Tire Service Inc.	510 Hwy 56 W	Le Roy	MN	55951		507-324-5638	R	7*	<0.1
G.A. Sadowsky and Son Inc.	PO Drawer D	Dickinson	ND	58601	AG Sadowsky	701-225-2713	R	6*	<0.1
Millersburg Tire Service Inc.	7375 State Rte 39 E	Millersburg	OH	44654	Brad Schmucker	330-674-1085	R	6*	<0.1
Varga Enterprises Inc.	2350 S Arpt Blvd	Chandler	AZ	85249	George Varga	480-963-6936	R	5*	<0.1

Source: *Ward's Business Directory of U.S. Private and Public Companies,* Volumes 1 and 2, 2005. The company type code used is as follows: P - Public, R - Private, S - Subsidiary, D - Division, J - Joint Venture, A - Affiliate, G - Group. Sales are in millions of dollars, employees are in thousands. An asterisk (*) indicates an estimated sales volume. The symbol < stands for 'less than'. Company names and addresses are truncated, in some cases, to fit into the available space.

OCCUPATIONS EMPLOYED BY MOTOR VEHICLE & MOTOR VEHICLE PARTS & SUPPLIES

Occupation	% of Total 2004	Change to 2014	Occupation	% of Total 2004	Change to 2014
Sales reps, wholesale & manufacturing, exc tech	8.4	17.9	Motor vehicle operators, nec	1.8	17.9
Truck drivers, light or delivery services	8.1	17.8	Retail salespersons	1.8	17.9
Parts salespersons	7.1	-5.7	Team assemblers	1.7	17.9
Laborers & freight, stock, & material movers, hand	6.7	6.1	Customer service representatives	1.6	20.7
Bus & truck mechanics & diesel engine specialists	5.3	17.9	First-line supervisors/managers of non-retail sales work	1.5	9.0
Stock clerks & order fillers	4.0	-9.7	Truck drivers, heavy & tractor-trailer	1.4	17.9
Office clerks, general	3.3	4.9	First-line supervisors/managers of office workers	1.3	6.8
Automotive service technicians & mechanics	3.0	17.9	Industrial truck & tractor operators	1.2	17.9
Shipping, receiving, & traffic clerks	3.0	6.7	First-line supervisors of mechanics	1.2	17.9
Driver/sales workers	2.8	17.8	Cleaners of vehicles & equipment	1.1	4.1
Bookkeeping, accounting, & auditing clerks	2.4	6.1	First-line supervisors/managers of retail sales workers	1.1	8.4
General & operations managers	2.3	16.6	Order clerks	1.0	-23.4

Source: *Industry-Occupation Matrix*, Bureau of Labor Statistics. These data are reported based on 4-digit NAICS categories but have been matched to corresponding 6-digit NAICS industry codes. The change reported for each occupation to the year 2014 is a percent of growth or decline as estimated by the Bureau of Labor Statistics. The abbreviation nec stands for 'not elsewhere classified.'

LOCATION BY STATE AND REGIONAL CONCENTRATION

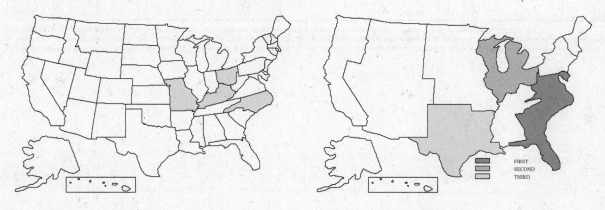

FIRST
SECOND
THIRD

INDUSTRY DATA BY STATE

State	Establishments Total (number)	% of U.S.	Employment Total (number)	% of U.S.	Per Estab.	Payroll Total ($ mil.)	Per Empl. ($)	Sales Total ($ mil.)	% of U.S.	Per Estab. ($)
North Carolina	84	3.7	1,413	5.2	17	63.2	44,698	1,055.3	6.4	12,563,202
Ohio	84	3.7	1,352	4.9	16	54.5	40,305	859.0	5.2	10,226,071
Florida	178	7.8	1,414	5.2	8	49.3	34,885	676.0	4.1	3,797,770
Texas	178	7.8	1,560	5.7	9	49.6	31,776	656.6	4.0	3,688,871
Pennsylvania	97	4.3	1,375	5.0	14	43.8	31,819	580.6	3.5	5,985,165
Kentucky	35	1.5	624	2.3	18	20.8	33,413	387.2	2.3	11,062,143
Missouri	58	2.6	787	2.9	14	25.2	32,057	378.3	2.3	6,523,086
Indiana	62	2.7	913	3.3	15	29.0	31,766	282.4	1.7	4,554,371
Alabama	53	2.3	642	2.3	12	18.0	28,020	202.1	1.2	3,812,585
South Carolina	46	2.0	544	2.0	12	18.1	33,274	196.4	1.2	4,269,500
Mississippi	23	1.0	380	1.4	17	14.1	37,187	138.8	0.8	6,034,957
Arkansas	28	1.2	296	1.1	11	10.4	35,064	94.4	0.6	3,373,000
Iowa	20	0.9	285	1.0	14	8.4	29,421	86.1	0.5	4,302,650
Kansas	25	1.1	243	0.9	10	8.0	32,757	58.4	0.4	2,335,880
Hawaii	10	0.4	86	0.3	9	2.9	34,012	43.0	0.3	4,299,700
New Mexico	16	0.7	136	0.5	9	3.6	26,294	35.8	0.2	2,238,750
Vermont	4	0.2	56	0.2	14	2.5	44,625	28.9	0.2	7,212,500
California	231	10.2	2500-4999	-	-	(D)	-	(D)	-	-
New York	126	5.5	1000-2499	-	-	(D)	-	(D)	-	-
Georgia	105	4.6	1000-2499	-	-	(D)	-	(D)	-	-
New Jersey	70	3.1	500-999	-	-	(D)	-	(D)	-	-
Tennessee	68	3.0	1000-2499	-	-	(D)	-	(D)	-	-
Illinois	62	2.7	500-999	-	-	(D)	-	(D)	-	-
Michigan	62	2.7	500-999	-	-	(D)	-	(D)	-	-
Colorado	47	2.1	250-499	-	-	(D)	-	(D)	-	-
Arizona	44	1.9	250-499	-	-	(D)	-	(D)	-	-
Virginia	39	1.7	250-499	-	-	(D)	-	(D)	-	-
Oklahoma	37	1.6	250-499	-	-	(D)	-	(D)	-	-
Washington	37	1.6	250-499	-	-	(D)	-	(D)	-	-
Minnesota	36	1.6	250-499	-	-	(D)	-	(D)	-	-
Massachusetts	35	1.5	250-499	-	-	(D)	-	(D)	-	-

Continued on next page.

INDUSTRY DATA BY STATE - Continued

State	Establishments Total (number)	Establishments % of U.S.	Employment Total (number)	Employment % of U.S.	Employment Per Estab.	Payroll Total ($ mil.)	Payroll Per Empl. ($)	Sales Total ($ mil.)	Sales % of U.S.	Sales Per Estab. ($)
Louisiana	33	1.5	250-499	-	-	(D)	-	(D)	-	-
Maryland	30	1.3	250-499	-	-	(D)	-	(D)	-	-
Nevada	28	1.2	100-249	-	-	(D)	-	(D)	-	-
Utah	25	1.1	250-499	-	-	(D)	-	(D)	-	-
Wisconsin	20	0.9	100-249	-	-	(D)	-	(D)	-	-
Oregon	19	0.8	100-249	-	-	(D)	-	(D)	-	-
Connecticut	18	0.8	100-249	-	-	(D)	-	(D)	-	-
West Virginia	16	0.7	100-249	-	-	(D)	-	(D)	-	-
New Hampshire	13	0.6	20-99	-	-	(D)	-	(D)	-	-
Nebraska	12	0.5	100-249	-	-	(D)	--	(D)	-	-
Idaho	11	0.5	20-99	-	-	(D)	-	(D)	-	-
Maine	9	0.4	20-99	-	-	(D)	-	(D)	-	-
South Dakota	9	0.4	100-249	-	-	(D)	-	(D)	-	-
Montana	8	0.4	20-99	-	-	(D)	-	(D)	-	-
North Dakota	7	0.3	20-99	-	-	(D)	-	(D)	-	-
Delaware	6	0.3	20-99	-	-	(D)	-	(D)	-	-
Alaska	3	0.1	20-99	-	-	(D)	-	(D)	-	-
Rhode Island	3	0.1	20-99	-	-	(D)	-	(D)	-	-
Wyoming	3	0.1	20-99	-	-	(D)	-	(D)	-	-

Source: 2002 *Economic Census*. The states are in descending order of sales or establishments (if sales data are missing for the majority). The symbol (D) appears when data are withheld to prevent disclosure of competitive information. States marked with (D) are sorted by number of establishments. A dash (-) indicates that the data element cannot be calculated. Shaded *states* on the state map indicate those states which have proportionately greater representation in the industry than would be indicated by the states population; the ratio is based on total sales or number of establishments. Shaded *regions* indicate where the industry is regionally most concentrated.

NAICS 423140 - MOTOR VEHICLE PARTS (USED) MERCHANT WHOLESALERS

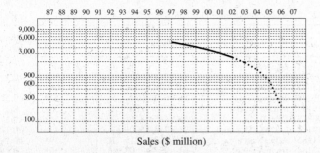

Sales ($ million)

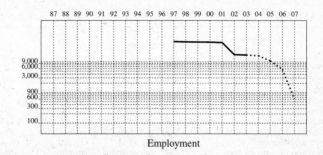

Employment

GENERAL STATISTICS

Year	Establishments (number)	Employment (number)	Payroll ($ million)	Sales ($ million)	Employees per Establishment (number)	Sales per Establishment ($)	Payroll per Employee ($)
1987	-	-	-	-	-	-	-
1988	-	-	-	-	-	-	-
1989	-	-	-	-	-	-	-
1990	-	-	-	-	-	-	-
1991	-	-	-	-	-	-	-
1992	-	-	-	-	-	-	-
1993	-	-	-	-	-	-	-
1994	-	-	-	-	-	-	-
1995	-	-	-	-	-	-	-
1996	-	-	-	-	-	-	-
1997	7,105	45,807	971.8	5,272.1	6.4	742,026.7	21,215.1
1998	6,976	44,770	999.4	4,709.9 e	6.4	675,160.6	22,323.0
1999	6,594	44,223	1,033.4	4,147.7 e	6.7	629,017.3	23,367.9
2000	6,259	43,846	1,070.4	3,585.6 e	7.0	572,864.7	24,413.5
2001	5,867	42,600	1,075.9	3,023.4 e	7.3	515,319.6	25,256.7
2002	2,589	17,342	439.0	2,461.2	6.7	950,637.3	25,314.3
2003	2,357	16,799	462.5	1,899.0 p	7.1	731,575.4 p	27,533.7
2004	2,000 p	15,983 p	492.3 p	1,336.8 p	7.3 p	746,071.9 p	28,035.9 p
2005	1,152 p	10,858 p	399.3 p	774.7 p	7.4 p	760,568.4 p	28,994.0 p
2006	304 p	5,733 p	306.2 p	212.5 p	7.5 p	775,064.9 p	29,952.1 p
2007		608 p	213.1 p		7.6 p	789,561.4 p	30,910.3 p

Source: Economic Census of the United States, 1997 and 2002. Establishment counts, employment, and payroll are from County Business Patterns for non-Census years. This is a newly defined industry. Data for prior years are unavailable at the time of publication but may become available over time. Values followed by 'p' are projections by the editors. Sales data for non-Census years are extrapolations, marked by 'e'.

INDICES OF CHANGE

Year	Establishments (number)	Employment (number)	Payroll ($ million)	Sales ($ million)	Employees per Establishment (number)	Sales per Establishment ($)	Payroll per Employee ($)
1987	-	-	-	-	-	-	-
1992	-	-	-	-	-	-	-
1993	-	-	-	-	-	-	-
1994	-	-	-	-	-	-	-
1995	-	-	-	-	-	-	-
1996	-	-	-	-	-	-	-
1997	274.4	264.1	221.4	214.2	95.5	78.1	83.8
1998	269.4	258.2	227.7	191.4 e	95.5	71.0	88.2
1999	254.7	255.0	235.4	168.5 e	100.0	66.2	92.3
2000	241.8	252.8	243.8	145.7 e	104.5	60.3	96.4
2001	226.6	245.6	245.1	122.8 e	109.0	54.2	99.8
2002	100.0	100.0	100.0	100.0	100.0	100.0	100.0
2003	91.0	96.9	105.4	77.2 p	106.4	77.0 p	108.8
2004	77.3 p	92.2 p	112.1 p	54.3 p	108.8 p	78.5 p	110.8 p
2005	44.5 p	62.6 p	90.9 p	31.5 p	110.6 p	80.0 p	114.5 p
2006	11.8 p	33.1 p	69.7 p	8.6 p	112.4 p	81.5 p	118.3 p
2007		3.5 p	48.5 p		114.2 p	83.1 p	122.1 p

Sources: Same as General Statistics. The values shown reflect change from the base year, 2002. Values above 100 mean greater than 2002, values below 100 mean less than 2002, and a value of 100 in the 1987-2001 or 2003-2007 period means same as 2002. Values followed by a 'p' are projections by the editors; 'e' stands for extrapolation. Data are the most recent available at this level of detail.

SELECTED RATIOS

For 2002	Avg. of All Wholesale	Analyzed Industry	Index	For 2002	Avg. of All Wholesale	Analyzed Industry	Index
Employees per Establishment	15	7	45	Sales per Employee	791,325	141,921	18
Payroll per Establishment	626,122	169,564	27	Sales per Establishment	12,012,387	950,637	8
Payroll per Employee	41,161	25,314	62	Expenses per Establishment	na	na	na

Sources: Same as General Statistics. The 'Average of All' column, Wholesale or Retail, represents the average of the sector reported for the most recent complete year available. The Index shows the relationship between the Average and the Analyzed Industry. For example, 100 means that they are equal; 500 that the Analyzed Industry is five times the average; 50 means that the Analyzed Industry is half the national average. The abbreviation 'na' is used to show that data are 'not available'.

LEADING COMPANIES   Number shown: **75**   Total sales ($ mil): **5,472**   Total employment (000): **28.7**

Company Name	Address				CEO Name	Phone	Co. Type	Sales ($ mil)	Empl. (000)
CARQUEST Corp.	PO Box 26929	Raleigh	NC	27611	Al Stecklein		R	2,500	25.0
M and M Knopf Auto Parts Inc.	239 O N Brunswick	Piscataway	NJ	08854	Marshall Knopf	732-981-8040	R	1,050*	<0.1
Tube City L.L.C.	PO Box 2000	Glassport	PA	15045	Michael Coslov	412-678-6141	R	1,006*	0.9
Tracy Industries Inc.	PO Box 1260	La Puente	CA	91749	Thomas Tracy	562-692-9034	S	142*	0.2
Sosmetal Products Inc.	2945 E Tioga St	Philadelphia	PA	19134	Milton Soskin	215-739-6200	R	58*	0.2
Tell Steel Inc.	2345 W 17th St	Long Beach	CA	90813	Don Tuffli	562-435-4826	R	51*	<0.1
O'Connor Truck Sales Inc.	H St & Hunting Pk	Philadelphia	PA	19124	Larry O'Connor	215-744-8500	R	43*	<0.1
Scheu Steel Supply Co.	PO Box 250	Upland	CA	91785	Allyn Scheu	909-982-1321	R	39*	<0.1
Jack Young Company Inc.	354 Cambridge St	Boston	MA	02134	Irwin Young	617-782-1250	R	36*	0.1
Midwest Wrecking Co.	PO Box 3757	Edmond	OK	73083	Benjamin Kates	405-478-8833	R	26*	<0.1
Boch Olmsmoblie	859 Providence Hwy	Norwood	MA	02062	Ernest Boch	781-255-6243	R	25*	<0.1
B and B Auto Parts Inc.	1255 E 180th St	Bronx	NY	10460	William Bastardi	718-597-4000	R	25*	<0.1
D and W Diesel Inc.	1503 Clark St Rd	Auburn	NY	13021	Douglas Wayne	315-253-5300	R	24*	<0.1
H.C. Lewis Oil Co.	PO Box 649	Welch	WV	24801	HC Lewis Jr	304-436-2148	R	23*	<0.1
Viking Industrial Corp.	620 Clark Ave	Pittsburg	CA	94565	Spencer Brog	925-427-2518	R	21*	<0.1
Pierce-Spafford Metals Inc.	7550 Chapman Ave	Garden Grove	CA	92841	John Spafford	714-895-7756	S	21*	<0.1
Crest Steel Corp.	1250 E 223rd St	Carson	CA	90745	Randall Putnam	310-830-2651	R	19*	<0.1
American Metal Marketing Inc.	5222 Alhambra Ave	Los Angeles	CA	90032	William Dilts	323-225-1288	R	18*	<0.1
Newman Auto Recyclers Inc.	2700 Newman Rd	Mobile	AL	36695	Lon Lindquist	251-639-7447	R	18*	<0.1
Autocenter Chevrolet Inc.	285 E Main Rd 295	Middletown	RI	02842	Richard Gudoian	401-847-0510	R	15*	<0.1
State Pipe & Supply Inc	PO Box 3286	Santa Fe Springs	CA	90670	Honggie Kim	562-695-5555	D	14*	<0.1
Bay Diesel Corp.	PO Box 7009	Portsmouth	VA	23707	J Wheeler	757-485-0075	R	11*	<0.1
Van's Electrical Systems	2541 Kentucky Ave	Indianapolis	IN	46221	Richard Van Vlymen	317-240-5900	R	11*	<0.1
Barker-Jennings Corp.	PO Box 11289	Lynchburg	VA	24506	Tommy S Dinkard	434-846-8471	R	11*	<0.1
Bumper To Bumper Autowares	PO Box 7666	Madison	WI	53707		608-241-1291	R	11*	<0.1
DG Nicholas Co.	PO Box 270	Scranton	PA	18501	James Nicholas	570-342-7683	R	11*	<0.1
Tunnessen's Automotive	PO Box 38	Hazleton	PA	18201	Robert Tunnessen	570-455-7761	R	10*	<0.1
Target Marketing Systems Inc.	146 Alexandra Way	Carol Stream	IL	60188	Richard Koh	630-784-1188	R	10*	<0.1
Border Distributing Company Inc.	PO Box 467	Malone	NY	12953	Robert Lyng	518-483-4801	R	9*	<0.1
CRS Auto Parts Inc.	1985 Ticonderoga	Chester Springs	PA	19425	Nelson Rogers	610-644-9657	R	9*	<0.1
Bokan Brothers Engine Rebuilders	4101 Franklin Blvd	Sacramento	CA	95820	William Bokan	916-451-6541	R	9*	<0.1
Hunts Point Auto Wreckers Inc.	1480 Sheridan Expy	Bronx	NY	10459		718-589-4444	R	8*	<0.1
LD Willcox and Son Inc.	1113 State Rte 13	Cortland	NY	13045	Newell Willcox	607-753-3344	R	8*	<0.1
Superior Wheels	PO Box 631	Eaton	OH	45320		937-456-8746	R	8*	<0.1
Wolf Manufacturing Inc.	1450 E Scotts Ave	Stockton	CA	95205	Carl Blain	209-469-2940	R	8*	<0.1
J and I Automotive Distributors	PO Box 27	Marshfield	MO	65706	Robert Carter	417-468-2439	R	7*	<0.1
River City Truck Parts Inc.	PO Box 18035	Louisville	KY	40261		502-968-5111	R	7*	<0.1
Rose, Morris Auto Parts Inc.	2129 E Michigan	Kalamazoo	MI	49048	Lawrence Rose	269-345-0123	R	7*	<0.1
Nordstrom Auto Recycling	25513 480th Ave	Garretson	SD	57030	Art Nordstrom	605-594-3910	R	7*	<0.1
TTP Diesel Power and Machine	7 Matchet Dr	Pierceton	IN	46562	Don Dickerhoff	574-594-5888	R	7*	<0.1
Bellis Steel Company Inc.	8740 Vanalden Ave	Northridge	CA	91324	Theron Ghrist	818-886-5601	R	6*	<0.1
A and R Auto Salvage Inc.	511 Gap Creek Rd	Duncan	SC	29334	Ronnie Strange	864-242-3561	S	6*	<0.1
Beheydt's Auto Wrecking	15475 Serfass Rd	Doylestown	OH	44230	Maxwell Beheydt	330-658-6109	R	6*	<0.1
Moore, Tony Automotive Parts	PO Box 1167	Decatur	AL	35602	Tony Moore	256-353-3124	R	6*	<0.1
Jantz's Yard 4 Automotive Inc.	2500 Washington Rd	Kenosha	WI	53140	Alfred Jantz	262-658-1392	R	6*	<0.1
EH Burrell Company Inc.	PO Box 629	Salem	OR	97308	Curtis Schott	503-581-2555	R	5*	<0.1
Import Auto Clinic	3820 NW 39th St	Oklahoma City	OK	73112	Sammy Potter	405-789-6828	R	5*	<0.1
Liberty Auto Salvage	PO Box 4240	Evansville	IN	47724	Mark Maurer	812-422-9373	R	5*	<0.1
Midway Auto Parts Inc.	4210 Gardner Ave	Kansas City	MO	64120	Mary Enochs	816-241-0500	R	5*	<0.1
Schram Auto and Truck Parts Inc.	2549 Dixie Hwy	Waterford	MI	48328		248-673-5700	R	5*	<0.1
Jordan Auto Parts Inc.	217 Moffit Rd	Dilliner	PA	15327	David Jordan	724-943-3522	R	4*	<0.1
Garcia & Sons Auto & Used Part	PO Box 3826	Edinburg	TX	78540	Obie Garcia	956-380-6653	R	4*	<0.1
Van Bebber Brothers Inc.	PO Box 760	Petaluma	CA	94953	Rick Van Bebber	707-762-4528	R	4*	<0.1
Chet's Wrecking & Auto Parts Inc.	1735 Page Blvd	Springfield	MA	01104	Kenneth Bousquet	413-543-3247	R	4*	<0.1
Crosstown Used Auto Parts	218 Pascal St N	Saint Paul	MN	55104	Clyde Payne	612-861-3020	R	4*	<0.1
Jean's Used Auto Parts	7144 S 45 Rd	Cadillac	MI	49601	Donald Whaley	231-775-2645	R	4*	<0.1
Palmer Auto Salvage	682 Hwy 78 NW	Monroe	GA	30655		770-267-5965	R	4*	<0.1
Richard J Cassidy Inc.	PO Box 245	Tioga Center	NY	13845	David French	607-687-4100	R	4*	<0.1
Kennedy Diversified Inc.	3844 William Flynn	Slippery Rock	PA	16057	John Kennedy	724-794-6913	R	3*	<0.1
AB and B Auto Parts Inc.	540111 US Hwy 1	Callahan	FL	32011	Barnett Thompson	904-879-3045	R	3*	<0.1
Auto Recyclers Inc.	8209 Old Stage Rd	Moss Point	MS	39562	Todd Peacock	228-475-9100	R	3*	<0.1
Butler A-1 Motors	121 Currie Rd	Uvalda	GA	30473		912-594-8041	R	3*	<0.1
Ingram Auto Parts	2440 E Indian River	Norfolk	VA	23523	Robert Ingram	757-543-3531	R	3*	<0.1
Discovery Auto Parts Inc.	3904 Blue Star Hwy	Holland	MI	49423	Stall Hiegan	616-393-7998	R	3*	<0.1
HI Way Auto Inc.	PO Box 1946	Brownwood	TX	76804	James Cooley	325-646-8254	R	3*	<0.1
U-Pull-It	4172 US 117 S Alt	Dudley	NC	28333		919-734-3446	R	3*	<0.1
Checkered Flag Corp.	19300 San Marcos	Martindale	TX	78655	Michael Ladd	512-357-6200	R	3*	<0.1
Greensboro Auto Parts Inc.	3720 Burlington Rd	Greensboro	NC	27405	Thomas Bigham	336-375-5809	R	3*	<0.1
Doeco Inc.	PO Box 5403	Tucson	AZ	85703	Elizabeth Santilli	520-622-0601	R	3*	<0.1
Motor Warehouse	PO Box 15152	Sacramento	CA	95851	David Kenmonth	916-920-2221	R	3*	<0.1
AGM Automotive Inc.	1000 E Whitcomb	Madison Heights	MI	48071	Robert Blinstrub	248-776-0600	R	2*	<0.1
Arizona Auto and Truck Parts Inc.	2021 W Buckeye Rd	Phoenix	AZ	85009	Michael Pierson	602-253-5111	R	2*	<0.1
Aveyard Enterprises Inc.	2200 Valley Pke	Dayton	OH	45404	John Aveyard	937-233-5481	R	2*	<0.1
B Map Core	PO Box 473	Harrison	NJ	07029	Greg Gartland	973-484-8989	R	2*	<0.1
Bill's Used Auto Parts Inc.	1415 Radford Rd	Christiansburg	VA	24073	Ken Harvey	540-382-3972	R	2*	<0.1

Source: Ward's Business Directory of U.S. Private and Public Companies, Volumes 1 and 2, 2005. The company type code used is as follows: P - Public, R - Private, S - Subsidiary, D - Division, J - Joint Venture, A - Affiliate, G - Group. Sales are in millions of dollars, employees are in thousands. An asterisk (*) indicates an estimated sales volume. The symbol < stands for 'less than'. Company names and addresses are truncated, in some cases, to fit into the available space.

OCCUPATIONS EMPLOYED BY MOTOR VEHICLE & MOTOR VEHICLE PARTS & SUPPLIES

Occupation	% of Total 2004	Change to 2014	Occupation	% of Total 2004	Change to 2014
Sales reps, wholesale & manufacturing, exc tech	8.4	17.9	Motor vehicle operators, nec	1.8	17.9
Truck drivers, light or delivery services	8.1	17.8	Retail salespersons	1.8	17.9
Parts salespersons	7.1	-5.7	Team assemblers	1.7	17.9
Laborers & freight, stock, & material movers, hand	6.7	6.1	Customer service representatives	1.6	20.7
Bus & truck mechanics & diesel engine specialists	5.3	17.9	First-line supervisors/managers of non-retail sales work	1.5	9.0
Stock clerks & order fillers	4.0	-9.7	Truck drivers, heavy & tractor-trailer	1.4	17.9
Office clerks, general	3.3	4.9	First-line supervisors/managers of office workers	1.3	6.8
Automotive service technicians & mechanics	3.0	17.9	Industrial truck & tractor operators	1.2	17.9
Shipping, receiving, & traffic clerks	3.0	6.7	First-line supervisors of mechanics	1.2	17.9
Driver/sales workers	2.8	17.8	Cleaners of vehicles & equipment	1.1	4.1
Bookkeeping, accounting, & auditing clerks	2.4	6.1	First-line supervisors/managers of retail sales workers	1.1	8.4
General & operations managers	2.3	16.6	Order clerks	1.0	-23.4

Source: Industry-Occupation Matrix, Bureau of Labor Statistics. These data are reported based on 4-digit NAICS categories but have been matched to corresponding 6-digit NAICS industry codes. The change reported for each occupation to the year 2014 is a percent of growth or decline as estimated by the Bureau of Labor Statistics. The abbreviation nec stands for 'not elsewhere classified.'

LOCATION BY STATE AND REGIONAL CONCENTRATION

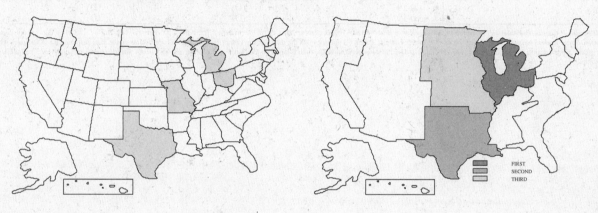

INDUSTRY DATA BY STATE

State	Establishments Total (number)	% of U.S.	Employment Total (number)	% of U.S.	Per Estab.	Payroll Total ($ mil.)	Per Empl. ($)	Sales Total ($ mil.)	% of U.S.	Per Estab. ($)
Texas	218	8.4	1,579	9.3	7	39.2	24,822	211.3	8.6	969,179
Ohio	122	4.7	880	5.2	7	22.6	25,627	144.5	5.9	1,184,180
Michigan	82	3.2	798	4.7	10	27.2	34,079	125.8	5.1	1,534,293
Pennsylvania	128	4.9	841	4.9	7	17.6	20,912	89.9	3.7	701,992
Missouri	63	2.4	394	2.3	6	11.6	29,500	63.3	2.6	1,004,413
North Carolina	62	2.4	362	2.1	6	8.2	22,657	43.9	1.8	707,468
Indiana	36	1.4	269	1.6	7	8.2	30,658	40.5	1.7	1,125,417
Alabama	50	1.9	220	1.3	4	5.0	22,682	32.2	1.3	643,620
Kentucky	39	1.5	263	1.5	7	5.0	18,894	27.8	1.1	712,179
South Carolina	37	1.4	195	1.1	5	4.5	23,282	21.1	0.9	570,568
Iowa	20	0.8	149	0.9	7	3.8	25,826	21.1	0.9	1,054,750
Arkansas	25	1.0	161	0.9	6	3.5	21,658	20.1	0.8	804,000
Mississippi	25	1.0	160	0.9	6	2.9	18,294	15.5	0.6	618,960
Kansas	29	1.1	133	0.8	5	2.9	22,030	14.2	0.6	489,000
New Mexico	17	0.7	81	0.5	5	1.8	22,000	7.3	0.3	428,588
Hawaii	6	0.2	22	0.1	4	0.4	18,455	3.1	0.1	509,833
Vermont	3	0.1	15	0.1	5	0.3	18,133	1.3	0.1	440,333
California	323	12.4	1000-2499	-	-	(D)	-	(D)	-	-
New York	187	7.2	1000-2499	-	-	(D)	-	(D)	-	-
Florida	169	6.5	1000-2499	-	-	(D)	-	(D)	-	-
Illinois	77	3.0	500-999	-	-	(D)	-	(D)	-	-
Georgia	74	2.9	500-999	-	-	(D)	-	(D)	-	-
New Jersey	69	2.7	250-499	-	-	(D)	-	(D)	-	-
Tennessee	66	2.5	250-499	-	-	(D)	-	(D)	-	-
Massachusetts	65	2.5	250-499	-	-	(D)	-	(D)	-	-
Virginia	56	2.2	250-499	-	-	(D)	-	(D)	-	-
Oklahoma	52	2.0	250-499	-	-	(D)	-	(D)	-	-
Washington	50	1.9	250-499	-	-	(D)	-	(D)	-	-
Minnesota	47	1.8	250-499	-	-	(D)	-	(D)	-	-
Wisconsin	44	1.7	250-499	-	-	(D)	-	(D)	-	-
Maryland	38	1.5	250-499	-	-	(D)	-	(D)	-	-

Continued on next page.

INDUSTRY DATA BY STATE - Continued

State	Establishments		Employment			Payroll		Sales		
	Total (number)	% of U.S.	Total (number)	% of U.S.	Per Estab.	Total ($ mil.)	Per Empl. ($)	Total ($ mil.)	% of U.S.	Per Estab. ($)
Arizona	36	1.4	250-499	-	-	(D)	-	(D)	-	-
Louisiana	35	1.3	100-249	-	-	(D)	-	(D)	-	-
Colorado	34	1.3	100-249	-	-	(D)	-	(D)	-	-
Oregon	28	1.1	100-249	-	-	(D)	-	(D)	-	-
Connecticut	23	0.9	100-249	-	-	(D)	-	(D)	-	-
Nebraska	20	0.8	100-249	-	-	(D)	-	(D)	-	-
Rhode Island	19	0.7	100-249	-	-	(D)	-	(D)	-	-
Utah	18	0.7	20-99	-	-	(D)	-	(D)	-	-
New Hampshire	16	0.6	100-249	-	-	(D)	-	(D)	-	-
Maine	15	0.6	20-99	-	-	(D)	-	(D)	-	-
Nevada	13	0.5	20-99	-	-	(D)	-	(D)	-	-
West Virginia	13	0.5	20-99	-	-	(D)	-	(D)	-	-
Delaware	10	0.4	20-99	-	-	(D)	-	(D)	-	-
South Dakota	10	0.4	20-99	-	-	(D)	-	(D)	-	-
Idaho	9	0.3	0-19	-	-	(D)	-	(D)	-	-
Montana	7	0.3	0-19	-	-	(D)	-	(D)	-	-
North Dakota	6	0.2	0-19	-	-	(D)	-	(D)	-	-
Wyoming	3	0.1	0-19	-	-	(D)	-	(D)	-	-
D.C.	1	-	0-19	-	-	(D)	-	(D)	-	-

Source: 2002 *Economic Census*. The states are in descending order of sales or establishments (if sales data are missing for the majority). The symbol (D) appears when data are withheld to prevent disclosure of competitive information. States marked with (D) are sorted by number of establishments. A dash (-) indicates that the data element cannot be calculated. Shaded *states* on the state map indicate those states which have proportionately greater representation in the industry than would be indicated by the states population; the ratio is based on total sales or number of establishments. Shaded *regions* indicate where the industry is regionally most concentrated.

NAICS 423210 - FURNITURE MERCHANT WHOLESALERS

87 88 89 90 91 92 93 94 95 96 97 98 99 00 01 02 03 04 05 06 07

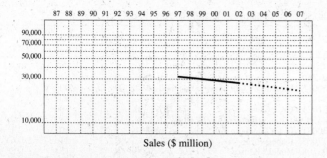

Sales ($ million)

87 88 89 90 91 92 93 94 95 96 97 98 99 00 01 02 03 04 05 06 07

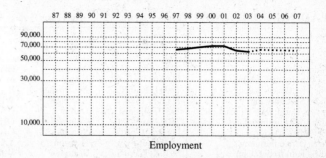

Employment

GENERAL STATISTICS

Year	Establishments (number)	Employment (number)	Payroll ($ million)	Sales ($ million)	Employees per Establishment (number)	Sales per Establishment ($)	Payroll per Employee ($)
1987	-	-	-	-	-	-	-
1988	-	-	-	-	-	-	-
1989	-	-	-	-	-	-	-
1990	-	-	-	-	-	-	-
1991	-	-	-	-	-	-	-
1992	-	-	-	-	-	-	-
1993	-	-	-	-	-	-	-
1994	-	-	-	-	-	-	-
1995	-	-	-	-	-	-	-
1996	-	-	-	-	-	-	-
1997	6,697	65,930	2,415.3	31,898.6	9.8	4,763,117.8	36,634.3
1998	6,728	67,803	2,684.8	30,971.0 e	10.1	4,603,296.7	39,597.1
1999	6,704	70,291	2,845.9	30,043.4 e	10.5	4,481,408.1	40,487.4
2000	6,673	72,457	3,095.2	29,115.7 e	10.9	4,363,215.9	42,717.8
2001	6,521	72,519	3,026.7	28,188.1 e	11.1	4,322,668.3	41,737.3
2002	6,093	64,690	2,627.3	27,260.5	10.6	4,474,068.6	40,613.7
2003	5,941	63,042	2,567.9	26,332.9 p	10.6	4,260,763.6 p	40,733.3
2004	5,948 p	66,296 p	2,826.7 p	25,405.3 p	11.1 p	4,192,040.1 p	42,585.8 p
2005	5,815 p	65,844 p	2,845.4 p	24,477.6 p	11.2 p	4,123,316.5 p	43,142.3 p
2006	5,682 p	65,391 p	2,864.1 p	23,550.0 p	11.4 p	4,054,593.0 p	43,698.7 p
2007	5,549 p	64,939 p	2,882.8 p	22,622.4 p	11.5 p	3,985,869.5 p	44,255.1 p

Source: Economic Census of the United States, 1997 and 2002. Establishment counts, employment, and payroll are from *County Business Patterns* for non-Census years. This is a newly defined industry. Data for prior years are unavailable at the time of publication but may become available over time. Values followed by 'p' are projections by the editors. Sales data for non-Census years are extrapolations, marked by 'e'.

INDICES OF CHANGE

Year	Establishments (number)	Employment (number)	Payroll ($ million)	Sales ($ million)	Employees per Establishment (number)	Sales per Establishment ($)	Payroll per Employee ($)
1987	-	-	-	-	-	-	-
1992	-	-	-	-	-	-	-
1993	-	-	-	-	-	-	-
1994	-	-	-	-	-	-	-
1995	-	-	-	-	-	-	-
1996	-	-	-	-	-	-	-
1997	109.9	101.9	91.9	117.0	92.5	106.5	90.2
1998	110.4	104.8	102.2	113.6 e	95.3	102.9	97.5
1999	110.0	108.7	108.3	110.2 e	99.1	100.2	99.7
2000	109.5	112.0	117.8	106.8 e	102.8	97.5	105.2
2001	107.0	112.1	115.2	103.4 e	104.7	96.6	102.8
2002	100.0	100.0	100.0	100.0	100.0	100.0	100.0
2003	97.5	97.5	97.7	96.6 p	100.1	95.2 p	100.3
2004	97.6 p	102.5 p	107.6 p	93.2 p	104.6 p	93.7 p	104.9 p
2005	95.4 p	101.8 p	108.3 p	89.8 p	106.0 p	92.2 p	106.2 p
2006	93.3 p	101.1 p	109.0 p	86.4 p	107.4 p	90.6 p	107.6 p
2007	91.1 p	100.4 p	109.7 p	83.0 p	108.7 p	89.1 p	109.0 p

Sources: Same as General Statistics. The values shown reflect change from the base year, 2002. Values above 100 mean greater than 2002, values below 100 mean less than 2002, and a value of 100 in the 1987-2001 or 2003-2007 period means same as 2002. Values followed by a 'p' are projections by the editors; 'e' stands for extrapolation. Data are the most recent available at this level of detail.

SELECTED RATIOS

For 2002	Avg. of All Wholesale	Analyzed Industry	Index	For 2002	Avg. of All Wholesale	Analyzed Industry	Index
Employees per Establishment	15	11	71	Sales per Employee	791,325	421,402	53
Payroll per Establishment	626,122	431,200	69	Sales per Establishment	12,012,387	4,474,069	37
Payroll per Employee	41,161	40,614	99	Expenses per Establishment	na	na	na

Sources: Same as General Statistics. The 'Average of All' column, Wholesale or Retail, represents the average of the sector reported for the most recent complete year available. The Index shows the relationship between the Average and the Analyzed Industry. For example, 100 means that they are equal; 500 that the Analyzed Industry is five times the average; 50 means that the Analyzed Industry is half the national average. The abbreviation 'na' is used to show that data are 'not available'.

LEADING COMPANIES   Number shown: **75**   Total sales ($ mil): **27,241**   Total employment (000): **77.5**

Company Name	Address				CEO Name	Phone	Co. Type	Sales ($ mil)	Empl. (000)
Genuine Parts Co.	2999 Circle 75 Pkwy	Atlanta	GA	30339	Thomas C. Gallagher	770-953-1700	P	9,097	30.8
BJ's Wholesale Club Inc.	PO Box 9601	Natick	MA	01760		508-651-7400	P	7,220	18.5
United Stationers Inc.	2200 E Golf Rd	Des Plaines	IL	60016	Richard W Gochnauer	847-699-5000	P	4,000	5.7
School Specialty Inc.	PO Box 1579	Appleton	WI	54912		920-734-5712	P	907	2.8
Farmers Furniture Company Inc.	1851 Telfair St	Dublin	GA	31021	Greg Glass	478-275-3150	S	780*	1.3
Value City Furniture Div.	1800 Moler Rd	Columbus	OH	43207	Jay L Schottenstein	614-221-9200	D	680*	4.9
S.P. Richards Co.	PO Box 1266	Smyrna	GA	30081	Dean Beacham	770-436-6881	S	601*	2.1
Finger Office Furniture	4001 Gulf Fwy	Houston	TX	77003	Robert S Finger	713-221-4441	R	216*	0.6
Pacific Rim Import Corp.	5930 4th Ave S	Seattle	WA	98108	Ronald Benson	206-767-5000	R	154*	0.2
Business Furniture Corp.	6102 victory way	Indianapolis	IN	46278	Deborah Oakes	317-216-1600	R	150*	<0.1
Office Depot Inc. Bus Serv	3366 E Willow St	Signal Hill	CA	90755		562-490-1000	D	149*	0.9
Continental Office Furniture Corp.	2601 Silver Dr	Columbus	OH	43211	Ron Geese	614-262-8088	R	135*	0.4
Haskell Office L.L.C.	231 Haskell Ln	Verona	PA	15147	Rick Symanski	412-828-6000	R	130*	0.4
Coaster Company of America	12928 Sandoval St	Santa Fe Springs	CA	90670		562-944-7899	R	123*	0.7
Champion Industries Inc.	PO Box 2968	Huntington	WV	25728	Toney K Adkins	304-528-2700	P	122	0.8
Wasserstrom Co.	477 S Front St	Columbus	OH	43215	Rodney Wasserstrom	614-228-6525	R	122*	0.5
New WPI L.L.C.	30800 Telegraph Rd	Bingham Farms	MI	48025	Joseph E Eatman	248-430-2345	R	108*	0.3
TAB Products Co.	935 Lakeview Pky	Vernon Hills	IL	60061	John Boustead	847-968-5400	R	104	0.7
Pivot Interiors	2740 Zanker Rd	San Jose	CA	95134	Ken Baugh	408-432-5600	R	101*	0.2
National Business Furniture Inc.	PO Box 514052	Milwaukee	WI	53203	George Mosher	414-276-8511	R	95*	0.2
LaSalle Bristol L.P.	PO Box 98	Elkhart	IN	46515	Larry Campbell	574-295-4400	R	90*	0.2
Cooper Classics	115 Cooper Classics	Rocky Mount	VA	24151	Ashley Cooper	540-483-5774	R	89*	0.3
Hotel Superstore	PO Box 757	Mascotte	FL	34753	Arthur Reiss	561-371-2661	R	85*	0.3
Corporate Express Office Products	9301 Largo Dr W	Upper Marlboro	MD	20774		301-808-7136	R	81*	0.3
A.D. Wynne Company Inc.	710 Baronne St	New Orleans	LA	70113	Arthur Wynne	504-522-9558	R	77*	<0.1
ATD-American Co.	111-149 Greenwood	Wyncote	PA	19095	Jerome Zaslow	215-576-1380	R	65*	0.1
Thomas Interior Systems Inc.	476 Brighton Dr	Bloomingdale	IL	60108	Thomas Klobucher	630-980-4200	R	64*	<0.1
Intern. Contract Furnishings Inc.	704 Executive Blvd	Valley Cottage	NY	10989	Janes Kasschaw	201-784-0200	R	63*	<0.1
Wilson Group Ltd.	1540 Champion Dr	Carrollton	TX	75006	B Don Hill	972-488-4100	R	61	0.1
Legends Furniture Inc.	5555 N 51st Ave	Glendale	AZ	85301	Richard Schmidgall	623-931-6500	R	59*	0.2
Artlite Office Supply & Furniture	1851 Piedmont Rd	Atlanta	GA	30324	Steve Light	404-875-7271	R	57*	<0.1
Fraenkel Wholesale Furniture Inc.	PO Box 15385	Baton Rouge	LA	70895	Ray Crocker	225-275-8111	R	56*	0.3
Miles Treaster and Associates	3480 Industrial Blvd	W. Sacramento	CA	95691	Miles Treaster	916-373-1800	R	56*	<0.1
American Office Equipment Inc.	309 N Calvert St	Baltimore	MD	21202	David Kuntz	410-539-7529	R	55*	0.2
Jofran Sales Inc.	1 Jofran Way	Norfolk	MA	02056	Robert Roy	508-384-6019	R	54*	<0.1
Business Interiors Northwest Inc.	10848 E Marginal S	Tukwila	WA	98168	Rich Lacher	206-762-8818	R	52*	0.1
Dancker, Sellew and Douglas Inc.	100 Broadway	New York	NY	10005	J Scott Douglas	212-267-2200	R	51*	0.1
Business Office Systems Inc.	740 Hilltop Dr	Itasca	IL	60143	Glenn Basgall	630-773-7777	R	50*	0.1
Desks Inc.	600 West Fulton	Chicago	IL	60661	Jim Ford	773-523-3375	R	50*	<0.1
Lucky Coin	1525 Airline Dr	Metairie	LA	70001	John Georges	504-835-3232	R	50*	0.1
Corporate Environments of GA	PO Box 29725	Atlanta	GA	30359	Karen Hughes	404-679-8999	R	46*	0.1
Barclay Dean	1917 120th Ave NE	Bellevue	WA	98005	Scott Harrison	425-451-8940	R	41*	0.1
Advanced Innovations West L.L.C.	8595 Milliken Ave	R. Cucamonga	CA	91730		909-980-3033	R	41*	0.3
Business Interiors	1111 Valley View	Irving	TX	75061	Kathy White	817-858-2000	R	40*	0.1
Workspace Development L.L.C.	5601 6th Ave S	Seattle	WA	98108	Timothy Jones	206-768-8000	R	40*	0.1
Loth Mbi Inc.	3574 E Kemper Rd	Cincinnati	OH	45241	J B Buse	513-554-4900	R	40*	0.1
Ivan Allen Workspace L.L.C.	730 Peachtree St	Atlanta	GA	30308		404-760-8700	R	38*	<0.1
Acme Trading Corp.	19895 Arenth Ave	City of Industry	CA	91748	CHI-Chu Chen	323-589-6589	R	37*	<0.1
Amarillo Hardware Co.	PO Box 1891	Amarillo	TX	79172	Joe Wildman	806-376-4722	R	36*	0.1
Southern Office Furniture	PO Box 49009	Greensboro	NC	27419	Frank Biggerstaff	336-668-4195	R	36*	0.2
Business Furniture Inc.	133 Rahway Ave	Elizabeth	NJ	07202	Dan Morley	908-355-3400	R	35*	<0.1
Morton Mfg and Trade Inc.	1440 E Cedar St	Ontario	CA	91761	WEI Ding	909-923-5818	R	32*	0.1
Thomas W. Ruff of Florida Inc.	3201 Commerce	Miami	FL	33055	Jack Gorman	954-435-7300	S	31*	0.1
Castleberry Office Furnishings	3600 American Dr	Atlanta	GA	30341		770-452-6600	R	29*	<0.1
A. Pomerantz and Co.	701 Market St	Philadelphia	PA	19106	Garry Maddox	215-408-2100	R	28*	<0.1
Maco Furniture Inc.	PO Box 396	Clackamas	OR	97015	Jerry MacDuffee	503-557-3114	R	26*	0.3
Desks Inc.	1385 S Santa Fe Dr	Denver	CO	80223	Jay Stark	303-777-8880	R	25*	<0.1
United Corporate Furnishings Inc.	1780 N Market Blvd	Sacramento	CA	95834	Mark Hoag	916-553-5900	R	25*	<0.1
Kindy Wood Manufacturing Inc.	1945 Wheeler Ave	Fort Smith	AR	72901		479-783-4127	R	24*	<0.1
Interior Investments L.L.C.	625 Heathrow Dr	Lincolnshire	IL	60069		847-325-1000	R	24*	<0.1
Dot Line Corp.	9420 Eton Ave	Chatsworth	CA	91311	Stanley Offman	818-700-9997	R	23*	<0.1
Douron Inc.	30 New Plant Ct	Owings Mills	MD	21117	Eugene L Hux	410-363-2600	R	23*	0.1
Imports by Four Hands L.P.	2090 Woodward St	Austin	TX	78744	Brett Hatton	512-371-7575	R	23	<0.1
US Business Interiors Inc.	8800 Lottsford Rd	Largo	MD	20774	Bernard Walsh	301-350-8700	R	22*	<0.1
Vanguard Legato A California	2121 Williams St	San Leandro	CA	94577		510-351-3333	R	22*	<0.1
Warehouse One Inc.	7800 E 12th St	Kansas City	MO	64126	Mary Jacoby	816-483-6999	R	22*	<0.1
Ameriwest Industries Inc.	1455 E Francis St	Ontario	CA	91761	Lilly Huang	909-930-5658	R	21*	<0.1
Town House Home Furnishings	PO Box 360	Smithville	MS	38870	Kevin Trautman	662-651-5441	R	21*	<0.1
W.B. Wood Co.	890 Mountain Ave	New Providence	NJ	07974	Michael Kopelman	908-771-9000	R	20*	<0.1
Zocalo Imports Inc.	1551 Bancroft Ave	San Francisco	CA	94124	Jeremy Sommer	415-293-1600	R	20*	<0.1
Metro Systems	6775 Shady Oaks Rd	Eden Prairie	MN	55344	James Harmon	952-933-5050	R	19*	<0.1
Office Pavilion	3815 Ingersoll Ave	Des Moines	IA	50312	John Stenberg	515-279-8879	R	19*	<0.1
Carroll's Discount Office Furniture	5615 S Rice Ave	Houston	TX	77081	Frank Carroll	713-667-6668	R	18*	<0.1
ABE Corp.	PO Box 5808	El Monte	CA	91734	Rick Follis	626-336-6665	R	18*	0.1
Parron-Hall Corp.	820 W Ash St	San Diego	CA	92101	James Herr	619-239-0345	R	17*	<0.1

Source: *Ward's Business Directory of U.S. Private and Public Companies*, Volumes 1 and 2, 2005. The company type code used is as follows: P - Public, R - Private, S - Subsidiary, D - Division, J - Joint Venture, A - Affiliate, G - Group. Sales are in millions of dollars, employees are in thousands. An asterisk (*) indicates an estimated sales volume. The symbol < stands for 'less than'. Company names and addresses are truncated, in some cases, to fit into the available space.

OCCUPATIONS EMPLOYED BY FURNITURE & HOME FURNISHINGS WHOLESALE

Occupation	% of Total 2004	Change to 2014	Occupation	% of Total 2004	Change to 2014
Sales reps, wholesale & manufacturing, exc tech	15.5	11.9	Order clerks	2.4	-27.3
Laborers & freight, stock, & material movers, hand	7.4	0.7	Truck drivers, heavy & tractor-trailer	2.3	11.8
Team assemblers	5.3	11.9	First-line supervisors/managers of office workers	1.9	1.4
Shipping, receiving, & traffic clerks	4.7	1.3	Retail salespersons	1.8	11.9
Customer service representatives	4.0	14.5	First-line supervisors/managers of non-retail sales work	1.6	3.5
Industrial truck & tractor operators	3.5	11.9	Interior designers	1.3	7.3
Office clerks, general	3.4	-0.4	Accountants & auditors	1.2	11.9
Packers & packagers, hand	2.9	11.9	Sewing machine operators	1.2	11.9
Stock clerks & order fillers	2.9	-14.3	Secretaries, except legal, medical, & executive	1.2	-5.8
General & operations managers	2.7	10.7	Executive secretaries & administrative assistants	1.1	6.0
Truck drivers, light or delivery services	2.7	11.8	Assemblers & fabricators, nec	1.0	3.8
Bookkeeping, accounting, & auditing clerks	2.6	0.7			

Source: *Industry-Occupation Matrix*, Bureau of Labor Statistics. These data are reported based on 4-digit NAICS categories but have been matched to corresponding 6-digit NAICS industry codes. The change reported for each occupation to the year 2014 is a percent of growth or decline as estimated by the Bureau of Labor Statistics. The abbreviation nec stands for 'not elsewhere classified.'

LOCATION BY STATE AND REGIONAL CONCENTRATION

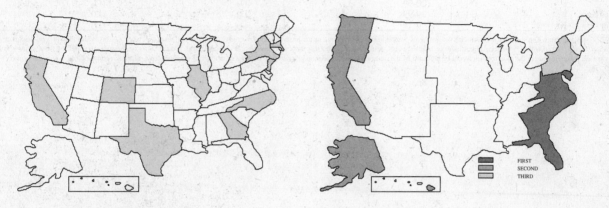

FIRST
SECOND
THIRD

INDUSTRY DATA BY STATE

State	Establishments Total (number)	% of U.S.	Employment Total (number)	% of U.S.	Per Estab.	Payroll Total ($ mil.)	Per Empl. ($)	Sales Total ($ mil.)	% of U.S.	Per Estab. ($)
California	958	15.6	11,569	17.6	12	455.5	39,370	4,819.0	17.3	5,030,228
New York	502	8.2	4,564	6.9	9	242.3	53,087	2,420.1	8.7	4,820,906
North Carolina	294	4.8	3,102	4.7	11	128.3	41,348	2,310.1	8.3	7,857,344
Texas	463	7.6	5,530	8.4	12	206.6	37,356	2,067.4	7.4	4,465,289
Illinois	300	4.9	3,527	5.4	12	168.3	47,727	1,739.2	6.3	5,797,467
New Jersey	242	4.0	2,981	4.5	12	140.6	47,163	1,401.1	5.0	5,789,843
Florida	480	7.8	3,149	4.8	7	110.8	35,187	1,182.4	4.3	2,463,329
Georgia	261	4.3	2,367	3.6	9	86.9	36,722	1,125.8	4.0	4,313,264
Michigan	156	2.5	1,810	2.8	12	84.1	46,472	953.4	3.4	6,111,244
Pennsylvania	209	3.4	2,830	4.3	14	101.5	35,858	884.1	3.2	4,230,206
Ohio	184	3.0	2,120	3.2	12	79.9	37,701	788.5	2.8	4,285,196
Massachusetts	136	2.2	1,483	2.3	11	74.5	50,249	742.5	2.7	5,459,831
Colorado	131	2.1	1,011	1.5	8	38.0	37,551	458.8	1.7	3,502,489
Missouri	95	1.6	973	1.5	10	35.3	36,321	452.0	1.6	4,758,042
Tennessee	91	1.5	871	1.3	10	37.4	42,923	340.1	1.2	3,737,165
Connecticut	66	1.1	1,115	1.7	17	56.3	50,450	305.3	1.1	4,625,106
Alabama	77	1.3	687	1.0	9	25.2	36,678	265.9	1.0	3,453,143
Mississippi	49	0.8	644	1.0	13	18.4	28,618	225.1	0.8	4,594,490
Kentucky	40	0.7	466	0.7	12	16.9	36,296	133.9	0.5	3,348,550
Louisiana	50	0.8	537	0.8	11	16.2	30,173	121.3	0.4	2,425,300
Utah	31	0.5	279	0.4	9	9.2	33,079	115.9	0.4	3,737,677
Iowa	35	0.6	403	0.6	12	15.1	37,412	106.0	0.4	3,029,229
New Hampshire	29	0.5	205	0.3	7	7.9	38,473	81.7	0.3	2,817,897
Maine	16	0.3	295	0.4	18	9.6	32,515	58.5	0.2	3,659,312
New Mexico	28	0.5	240	0.4	9	9.2	38,292	56.6	0.2	2,022,286
Nebraska	22	0.4	217	0.3	10	7.6	34,806	42.8	0.2	1,946,227
West Virginia	18	0.3	143	0.2	8	5.2	36,455	36.8	0.1	2,044,444
North Dakota	11	0.2	112	0.2	10	3.4	30,687	20.1	0.1	1,830,909
Vermont	6	0.1	53	0.1	9	1.9	35,981	18.3	0.1	3,049,833
Montana	9	0.1	55	0.1	6	1.9	34,564	10.1	-	1,121,333
Virginia	148	2.4	1000-2499	-	-	(D)	-	(D)	-	-

Continued on next page.

INDUSTRY DATA BY STATE - Continued

State	Establishments		Employment			Payroll		Sales		
	Total (number)	% of U.S.	Total (number)	% of U.S.	Per Estab.	Total ($ mil.)	Per Empl. ($)	Total ($ mil.)	% of U.S.	Per Estab. ($)
Washington	134	2.2	1000-2499	-	-	(D)	-	(D)	-	-
Minnesota	120	2.0	1000-2499	-	-	(D)	-	(D)	-	-
Maryland	111	1.8	1000-2499	-	-	(D)	-	(D)	-	-
Indiana	96	1.6	1000-2499	-	-	(D)	-	(D)	-	-
Arizona	90	1.5	500-999	-	-	(D)	-	(D)	-	-
Wisconsin	76	1.2	1000-2499	-	-	(D)	-	(D)	-	-
South Carolina	66	1.1	500-999	-	-	(D)	-	(D)	-	-
Oregon	51	0.8	250-499	-	-	(D)	-	(D)	-	-
Kansas	42	0.7	250-499	-	-	(D)	-	(D)	-	-
Oklahoma	39	0.6	250-499	-	-	(D)	-	(D)	-	-
Nevada	35	0.6	250-499	-	-	(D)	-	(D)	-	-
Arkansas	32	0.5	250-499	-	-	(D)	-	(D)	-	-
D.C.	24	0.4	250-499	-	-	(D)	-	(D)	-	-
Hawaii	21	0.3	100-249	-	-	(D)	-	(D)	-	-
Rhode Island	17	0.3	100-249	-	-	(D)	-	(D)	-	-
Delaware	10	0.2	100-249	-	-	(D)	-	(D)	-	-
Idaho	10	0.2	100-249	-	-	(D)	-	(D)	-	-
Alaska	7	0.1	20-99	-	-	(D)	-	(D)	-	-
South Dakota	4	0.1	20-99	-	-	(D)	-	(D)	-	-
Wyoming	2	-	0-19	-	-	(D)	-	(D)	-	-

Source: 2002 *Economic Census*. The states are in descending order of sales or establishments (if sales data are missing for the majority). The symbol (D) appears when data are withheld to prevent disclosure of competitive information. States marked with (D) are sorted by number of establishments. A dash (-) indicates that the data element cannot be calculated. Shaded *states* on the state map indicate those states which have proportionately greater representation in the industry than would be indicated by the states population; the ratio is based on total sales or number of establishments. Shaded *regions* indicate where the industry is regionally most concentrated.

NAICS 423220 - HOME FURNISHING MERCHANT WHOLESALERS

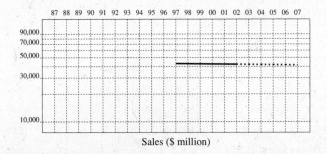

Sales ($ million)

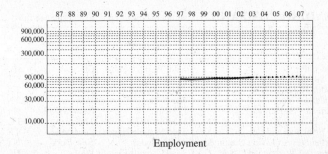

Employment

GENERAL STATISTICS

Year	Establishments (number)	Employment (number)	Payroll ($ million)	Sales ($ million)	Employees per Establishment (number)	Sales per Establishment ($)	Payroll per Employee ($)
1987	-	-	-	-	-	-	-
1988	-	-	-	-	-	-	-
1989	-	-	-	-	-	-	-
1990	-	-	-	-	-	-	-
1991	-	-	-	-	-	-	-
1992	-	-	-	-	-	-	-
1993	-	-	-	-	-	-	-
1994	-	-	-	-	-	-	-
1995	-	-	-	-	-	-	-
1996	-	-	-	-	-	-	-
1997	8,549	91,535	2,901.7	43,107.9	10.7	5,042,449.4	31,700.4
1998	8,287	89,409	3,039.5	42,954.7 e	10.8	5,183,383.6	33,995.5
1999	8,304	91,396	3,277.9	42,801.5 e	11.0	5,154,323.2	35,864.8
2000	8,232	94,946	3,504.5	42,648.3 e	11.5	5,180,794.5	36,910.1
2001	8,024	93,616	3,596.0	42,495.1 e	11.7	5,295,999.5	38,412.7
2002	7,986	96,315	3,713.5	42,341.9	12.1	5,302,016.0	38,555.8
2003	7,827	99,396	4,008.2	42,188.7 p	12.7	5,359,376.2 p	40,325.2
2004	7,737 p	99,461 p	4,146.7 p	42,035.5 p	12.8 p	5,406,866.3 p	41,901.1 p
2005	7,628 p	100,876 p	4,324.7 p	41,882.3 p	13.2 p	5,454,356.4 p	43,241.9 p
2006	7,520 p	102,291 p	4,502.8 p	41,729.1 p	13.5 p	5,501,846.4 p	44,582.7 p
2007	7,411 p	103,706 p	4,680.8 p	41,575.9 p	13.8 p	5,549,336.5 p	45,923.5 p

Source: *Economic Census of the United States*, 1997 and 2002. Establishment counts, employment, and payroll are from *County Business Patterns* for non-Census years. This is a newly defined industry. Data for prior years are unavailable at the time of publication but may become available over time. Values followed by 'p' are projections by the editors. Sales data for non-Census years are extrapolations, marked by 'e'.

INDICES OF CHANGE

Year	Establishments (number)	Employment (number)	Payroll ($ million)	Sales ($ million)	Employees per Establishment (number)	Sales per Establishment ($)	Payroll per Employee ($)
1987	-	-	-	-	-	-	-
1992	-	-	-	-	-	-	-
1993	-	-	-	-	-	-	-
1994	-	-	-	-	-	-	-
1995	-	-	-	-	-	-	-
1996	-	-	-	-	-	-	-
1997	107.0	95.0	78.1	101.8	88.4	95.1	82.2
1998	103.8	92.8	81.9	101.4 e	89.3	97.8	88.2
1999	104.0	94.9	88.3	101.1 e	90.9	97.2	93.0
2000	103.1	98.6	94.4	100.7 e	95.0	97.7	95.7
2001	100.5	97.2	96.8	100.4 e	96.7	99.9	99.6
2002	100.0	100.0	100.0	100.0	100.0	100.0	100.0
2003	98.0	103.2	107.9	99.6 p	105.0	101.1 p	104.6
2004	96.9 p	103.3 p	111.7 p	99.3 p	106.0 p	102.0 p	108.7 p
2005	95.5 p	104.7 p	116.5 p	98.9 p	108.8 p	102.9 p	112.2 p
2006	94.2 p	106.2 p	121.3 p	98.6 p	111.5 p	103.8 p	115.6 p
2007	92.8 p	107.7 p	126.0 p	98.2 p	114.2 p	104.7 p	119.1 p

Sources: Same as General Statistics. The values shown reflect change from the base year, 2002. Values above 100 mean greater than 2002, values below 100 mean less than 2002, and a value of 100 in the 1987-2001 or 2003-2007 period means same as 2002. Values followed by a 'p' are projections by the editors; 'e' stands for extrapolation. Data are the most recent available at this level of detail.

SELECTED RATIOS

For 2002	Avg. of All Wholesale	Analyzed Industry	Index	For 2002	Avg. of All Wholesale	Analyzed Industry	Index
Employees per Establishment	15	12	81	Sales per Employee	791,325	439,619	56
Payroll per Establishment	626,122	465,001	74	Sales per Establishment	12,012,387	5,302,016	44
Payroll per Employee	41,161	38,556	94	Expenses per Establishment	na	na	na

Sources: Same as General Statistics. The 'Average of All' column, Wholesale or Retail, represents the average of the sector reported for the most recent complete year available. The Index shows the relationship between the Average and the Analyzed Industry. For example, 100 means that they are equal; 500 that the Analyzed Industry is five times the average; 50 means that the Analyzed Industry is half the national average. The abbreviation 'na' is used to show that data are 'not available'.

LEADING COMPANIES   Number shown: **75**   Total sales ($ mil): **8,361**   Total employment (000): **24.9**

Company Name	Address				CEO Name	Phone	Co. Type	Sales ($ mil)	Empl. (000)
True Value Co.	8600 W Bryn Mawr	Chicago	IL	60631	Bryan R. Ableidinger	773-695-5000	R	2,024	2.8
GE Supply	PO Box 861	Shelton	CT	06484	WL Meddaugh	203-944-3000	D	1,100*	2.2
Garden Ridge Corp.	19411 Atrium Pl	Houston	TX	77084	John Rice	281-579-7901	R	521*	5.0
Kirkland's Inc.	805 N Pky	Jackson	TN	38305	Robert E Alderson	731-668-2444	P	369	3.7
Andrea by Sadek	PO Box 717	New Rochelle	NY	10802	Jim Sadek	914-633-8090	D	312*	0.2
W.S. Badcock Corp.	PO Box 497	Mulberry	FL	33860	Don Marks	863-425-4921	R	286*	1.2
LD Brinkman and Co.	1655 Waters Ridge	Lewisville	TX	75057	Levon Ezell	972-353-3500	R	270*	1.0
Martha Stewart Living Omnimedia	11 W 42nd St	New York	NY	10036		212-827-8000	P	246	0.5
Waterford-Wedgwood U.S.A.	1330 Campus Pkwy	Wall	NJ	07719	Chris McGillary	732-938-5800	R	232*	0.6
Lillian Vernon Corp.	445 Hamilton Ave	White Plains	NY	10601	Rick Bennett	914-872-2000	R	228*	1.1
Tarkett Inc.	PO Box 354	Florence	AL	35631	Jack Lee	610-266-5500	R	196*	<0.1
Hoboken Wood Flooring Corp.	70 Demarest Dr	Wayne	NJ	07470	Joe Leskowitz	973-694-2888	R	134*	0.2
Koval Marketing Inc.	11208 47th Ave W	Mukilteo	WA	98275	Roy Koval	425-347-4249	R	100*	<0.1
Stark Carpet Corp.	979 Third Ave	New York	NY	10022	John S Stark	212-752-9000	R	94*	0.3
LaSalle Bristol L.P.	PO Box 98	Elkhart	IN	46515	Larry Campbell	574-295-4400	R	90*	0.2
Bradshaw International Inc.	9409 Buffalo Ave	R. Cucamonga	CA	91730	Mike Rodriguez		S	84*	<0.1
Twin City Bottle Inc.	1227 E Hennepin	Minneapolis	MN	55414	Ken Slater	612-331-8880	R	76*	0.3
Back to Basics Products Inc.	675 W 14600 S	Bluffdale	UT	84065	Thomas E Daniels Jr	801-571-7349	R	68	<0.1
Barth and Dreyfuss of California	2255 N Ontario St	Burbank	CA	91504	Warren Munday	818-260-4800	R	68*	<0.1
Charles Sadek Import Inc.	125 Beachwood Ave	New Rochelle	NY	10802	Sanford J Sadek	914-633-8090	R	65*	<0.1
Figi Acquisition Company L.L.C.	3636 Gateway	San Diego	CA	92102	Woody LaForge	619-262-8811	R	61*	0.2
Princess House Inc.	470 Myles Standish	Taunton	MA	02780	James Northrop	508-823-0713	R	61*	0.2
Phoenix Textile Corp.	13652 Lakefront Dr	St. Louis	MO	63145	Palmer A Reynolds	314-291-2151	R	56*	0.1
Carpet Cushions and Supplies Inc.	PO Box 653	Elk Grove Vill.	IL	60009	Aaron Karsen	847-364-6760	R	56*	<0.1
Re:Source New Jersey	220 Evans Way	Branchburg	NJ	08876		908-704-9777	R	53*	0.2
Derr Flooring Co.	PO Box 912	Willow Grove	PA	19090	CH Derr Jr	215-657-6300	R	53*	0.1
Ostrow Co.	PO Box 10550	Rock Hill	SC	29731	Joel J Ostrow	803-324-4284	R	53*	0.6
Heritage Lace Inc.	PO Box 328	Pella	IA	50219	Mark De Cook	641-628-4949	R	52*	0.1
Bennett Brothers Inc.	30 E Adams St	Chicago	IL	60603	GK Bennett	312-263-4800	R	50*	0.1
Cain and Bultman Inc.	PO Box 2815	Jacksonville	FL	32204	Thomas Sandifer	904-356-4812	R	50*	<0.1
Gulf Coast American Blind Corp.	3705 Westview Dr	Naples	FL	34104	Carlos Diaz	239-643-2460	R	49*	0.2
Orrefors Kosta Boda	140 Bradford Dr	West Berlin	NJ	08091	Oyvind Saetre	856-768-5400	R	48*	<0.1
Edward Fields Inc.	232 E 59th St Fl 2	New York	NY	10022	John Fields	212-310-0400	R	46*	<0.1
Dealers Supply Co.	PO Box 2628	Durham	NC	27715	Russell Barringer Jr	919-383-7451	R	44*	0.1
ARC Intern. North America Inc.	PO Box 5001	Millville	NJ	08332	Hubert Idled	856-825-5620	R	43*	0.1
Allure Home Creation Inc.	85 Fulton St	Boonton	NJ	07005	Stanley Ho	973-402-8888	R	42*	<0.1
Fargo Glass and Paint Co.	1801 7th Ave N	Fargo	ND	58102	Gerald Lovell	701-235-4441	R	42*	0.1
Adleta Corp.	1645 Diplomat Dr	Carrollton	TX	75006	Jack Adleta	972-620-5600	R	40*	0.1
Forbo Industries Inc.	PO Box 667	Hazleton	PA	18201	Denis Darrah	570-459-0771	R	40*	0.1
Yves Delorme Inc.	1725 Broadway St	Charlottesville	VA	22902	Dominique Fremaux	434-979-3911	R	38*	<0.1
Acme Trading Corp.	19895 Arenth Ave	City of Industry	CA	91748	CHI-Chu Chen	323-589-6589	R	37*	<0.1
B and F System Inc.	3920 S W Walker	Dallas	TX	75236	John Meyer	214-333-2111	R	37*	0.1
Setzers and Company Inc.	PO Box 24270	Jacksonville	FL	32241	Allen Setzer	904-731-4100	R	34*	<0.1
Global Accents Inc.	801 W Victoria St	Compton	CA	90220	Parham Partielli	310-639-2600	R	33*	0.1
Reader's Wholesale Distributors	PO Box 2407	Houston	TX	77252	Lloyd Burke	713-224-8300	R	33*	<0.1
Door County Cooperative Inc.	92 E Maple St	Sturgeon Bay	WI	54235	Randall Seiler	920-743-6555	R	32*	<0.1
Harbor Linen	2 Foster Ave	Gibbsboro	NJ	08026	Earl Waxman	856-435-2000	R	30*	0.1
Welcome Industrial Corporation	71 E Industry Ct	Deer Park	NY	11729	Tony Lin	631-242-5556	R	30*	0.1
Woodmart Window Coverings	15920 Arminta St	Van Nuys	CA	91406	Richard Decker	818-785-1528	R	30*	0.1
Eastside Wholesale Supply Co.	6450 E 8 Mile Rd	Detroit	MI	48234	Bob Paquette	313-891-2900	R	25	<0.1
Larson Distributing Company Inc.	PO Box 16189	Denver	CO	80216	John L Larson Jr	303-296-7253	R	25*	<0.1
Allison-Erwin Co.	2920 N Tryon St	Charlotte	NC	28206	Bob Allison	704-334-8621	R	24*	<0.1
Harold Import Company Inc.	747 Vassar Ave	Lakewood	NJ	08701	Robert Laub	732-367-2800	R	23*	<0.1
Vanguard Legato A California	2121 Williams St	San Leandro	CA	94577		510-351-3333	R	22*	<0.1
All Tile Inc.	1201 Chase Ave	Elk Grove Vill.	IL	60007	Robert Weiss	847-364-9191	R	21*	<0.1
American Window Concepts	908 W Rd Ste B	Houston	TX	77038	Minh Nguyen	281-999-9002	R	21*	<0.1
Donald E McNabb Carpet Co.	PO Box 448	Milford	MI	48381	Tony Ware	248-437-8146	R	21*	<0.1
Pictures and More Inc.	PO Box 242	Clinton	KY	42031	Joan Rothermel	270-653-2645	R	21*	<0.1
Vector Marketing Corp.	815 S Tacoma Way	Tacoma	WA	98499		253-983-0204	R	21*	<0.1
Eastern Decor Inc.	PO Box 985	Sanford	NC	27331	Eugene Blanton	919-776-7628	R	21*	<0.1
Independent Distribution Services	3000 Waterview	Baltimore	MD	21230	John Mulkey	410-539-3000	R	20*	<0.1
Zocalo Imports Inc.	1551 Bancroft Ave	San Francisco	CA	94124	Jeremy Sommer	415-293-1600	R	20*	<0.1
Stewart Distributors Inc.	464 Brighton Dr	Bloomingdale	IL	60108	George Stewart	630-351-9900	R	20*	<0.1
Gold Lumber Company Inc.	PO Box 683	Farmingdale	NJ	07727	Arie Halpern	732-938-3090	R	19*	<0.1
Blackton Inc.	1714 Alden Rd	Orlando	FL	32803	Michael Blackton	407-898-2661	R	19*	<0.1
Brownstone Gallery Ltd.	295 5th Ave	New York	NY	10016	Mark S Breslos	212-696-4663	R	19*	<0.1
Kreative Kamaaina Enterprises	1804 Hart St	Honolulu	HI	96819		808-841-8731	R	19*	<0.1
Robinson Knife Manufacturing Inc.	PO Box 550	Cheektowaga	NY	14225	James Walsh	716-685-6300	R	19*	<0.1
Midwest Floor Coverings	PO Box 65768	Salt Lake City	UT	84165	John Parrish	801-972-1125	R	18*	<0.1
American Drapery Blind & Carpet	PO Box 896	Renton	WA	98057	Greg Perry	425-255-3893	R	18*	0.1
Interstate Supply Co.	4445 Gustine Ave	St. Louis	MO	63116	Gary K Morrow	314-481-2222	R	18*	<0.1
BP Industries Inc.	5300 Concours	Ontario	CA	91764	Dong Kim	909-481-0227	R	17*	<0.1
Johnson Wholesale Floors Inc.	PO Box 250479	Atlanta	GA	30325	Donald Johnson	404-352-2700	R	17*	<0.1
Valley Wholesale Supply Corp.	10708 Vanowen St	N. Hollywood	CA	91605	David Labowitz	818-769-5656	R	17*	<0.1
United Supply Co.	PO Box 410149	Charlotte	NC	28241	John Hawkins	704-588-3310	R	17*	0.1

Source: Ward's Business Directory of U.S. Private and Public Companies, Volumes 1 and 2, 2005. The company type code used is as follows: P - Public, R - Private, S - Subsidiary, D - Division, J - Joint Venture, A - Affiliate, G - Group. Sales are in millions of dollars, employees are in thousands. An asterisk (*) indicates an estimated sales volume. The symbol < stands for 'less than'. Company names and addresses are truncated, in some cases, to fit into the available space.

OCCUPATIONS EMPLOYED BY FURNITURE & HOME FURNISHINGS WHOLESALE

Occupation	% of Total 2004	Change to 2014	Occupation	% of Total 2004	Change to 2014
Sales reps, wholesale & manufacturing, exc tech	15.5	11.9	Order clerks	2.4	-27.3
Laborers & freight, stock, & material movers, hand	7.4	0.7	Truck drivers, heavy & tractor-trailer	2.3	11.8
Team assemblers	5.3	11.9	First-line supervisors/managers of office workers	1.9	1.4
Shipping, receiving, & traffic clerks	4.7	1.3	Retail salespersons	1.8	11.9
Customer service representatives	4.0	14.5	First-line supervisors/managers of non-retail sales work	1.6	3.5
Industrial truck & tractor operators	3.5	11.9	Interior designers	1.3	7.3
Office clerks, general	3.4	-0.4	Accountants & auditors	1.2	11.9
Packers & packagers, hand	2.9	11.9	Sewing machine operators	1.2	11.9
Stock clerks & order fillers	2.9	-14.3	Secretaries, except legal, medical, & executive	1.2	-5.8
General & operations managers	2.7	10.7	Executive secretaries & administrative assistants	1.1	6.0
Truck drivers, light or delivery services	2.7	11.8	Assemblers & fabricators, nec	1.0	3.8
Bookkeeping, accounting, & auditing clerks	2.6	0.7			

Source: Industry-Occupation Matrix, Bureau of Labor Statistics. These data are reported based on 4-digit NAICS categories but have been matched to corresponding 6-digit NAICS industry codes. The change reported for each occupation to the year 2014 is a percent of growth or decline as estimated by the Bureau of Labor Statistics. The abbreviation nec stands for 'not elsewhere classified.'

LOCATION BY STATE AND REGIONAL CONCENTRATION

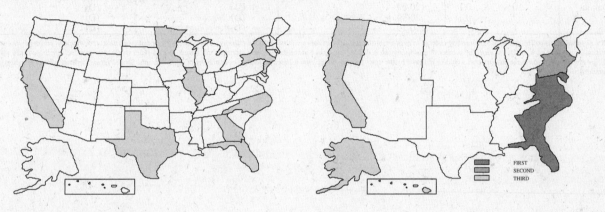

FIRST
SECOND
THIRD

INDUSTRY DATA BY STATE

State	Establishments Total (number)	% of U.S.	Employment Total (number)	% of U.S.	Per Estab.	Payroll Total ($ mil.)	Per Empl. ($)	Sales Total ($ mil.)	% of U.S.	Per Estab. ($)
New York	990	12.4	11,881	12.1	12	511.3	43,035	6,178.0	14.2	6,240,442
California	1,296	16.2	16,757	17.1	13	606.4	36,190	5,797.8	13.3	4,473,615
New Jersey	439	5.5	7,640	7.8	17	386.3	50,567	4,278.8	9.8	9,746,690
Georgia	435	5.4	5,996	6.1	14	240.3	40,071	4,210.7	9.7	9,679,738
Texas	526	6.6	6,690	6.8	13	255.1	38,138	3,818.6	8.8	7,259,772
Illinois	300	3.7	6,009	6.1	20	249.6	41,533	2,823.5	6.5	9,411,563
Florida	655	8.2	5,024	5.1	8	159.9	31,834	2,440.2	5.6	3,725,495
North Carolina	227	2.8	2,527	2.6	11	98.9	39,119	1,500.2	3.4	6,609,031
Ohio	193	2.4	3,014	3.1	16	123.7	41,033	1,402.8	3.2	7,268,244
Pennsylvania	236	2.9	3,299	3.4	14	120.8	36,612	1,370.4	3.1	5,806,932
Minnesota	105	1.3	1,485	1.5	14	63.1	42,522	843.8	1.9	8,035,752
Massachusetts	187	2.3	2,103	2.1	11	91.3	43,428	790.7	1.8	4,228,262
Tennessee	120	1.5	1,896	1.9	16	65.6	34,578	609.8	1.4	5,081,625
Missouri	119	1.5	1,514	1.5	13	52.0	34,318	505.5	1.2	4,248,143
Colorado	153	1.9	1,492	1.5	10	61.6	41,304	450.5	1.0	2,944,471
Oregon	86	1.1	720	0.7	8	26.6	36,918	210.8	0.5	2,450,895
Kentucky	53	0.7	551	0.6	10	15.4	27,875	158.9	0.4	2,997,528
Louisiana	63	0.8	585	0.6	9	19.6	33,586	147.6	0.3	2,342,540
Maine	31	0.4	522	0.5	17	21.1	40,400	130.5	0.3	4,208,548
Utah	59	0.7	683	0.7	12	18.0	26,406	129.2	0.3	2,190,085
Alabama	68	0.8	550	0.6	8	14.3	25,985	117.4	0.3	1,726,132
Iowa	36	0.4	250	0.3	7	9.3	37,036	117.4	0.3	3,260,417
Mississippi	33	0.4	226	0.2	7	7.0	31,049	66.2	0.2	2,007,000
New Mexico	36	0.4	267	0.3	7	8.5	31,850	65.2	0.1	1,812,083
Nebraska	25	0.3	179	0.2	7	5.5	30,603	51.3	0.1	2,052,920
New Hampshire	26	0.3	121	0.1	5	5.0	41,719	29.3	0.1	1,126,192
Montana	22	0.3	90	0.1	4	2.3	25,033	23.5	0.1	1,067,273
Vermont	22	0.3	130	0.1	6	3.9	30,323	21.5	-	979,545
North Dakota	8	0.1	36	-	5	0.9	24,611	8.4	-	1,055,000
Washington	198	2.5	2500-4999	-	-	(D)	-	(D)	-	-
Michigan	148	1.8	1000-2499	-	-	(D)	-	(D)	-	-

Continued on next page.

INDUSTRY DATA BY STATE - Continued

State	Establishments Total (number)	% of U.S.	Employment Total (number)	% of U.S.	Per Estab.	Payroll Total ($ mil.)	Per Empl. ($)	Sales Total ($ mil.)	% of U.S.	Per Estab. ($)
Arizona	138	1.7	1000-2499	-	-	(D)	-	(D)	-	-
Maryland	138	1.7	1000-2499	-	-	(D)	-	(D)	-	-
Virginia	135	1.7	1000-2499	-	-	(D)	-	(D)	-	-
Indiana	93	1.2	500-999	-	-	(D)	-	(D)	-	-
South Carolina	93	1.2	1000-2499	-	-	(D)	-	(D)	-	-
Wisconsin	89	1.1	500-999	-	-	(D)	-	(D)	-	-
Connecticut	81	1.0	500-999	-	-	(D)	-	(D)	-	-
Oklahoma	59	0.7	500-999	-	-	(D)	-	(D)	-	-
Arkansas	49	0.6	250-499	-	-	(D)	-	(D)	-	-
Kansas	46	0.6	250-499	-	-	(D)	-	(D)	-	-
Nevada	46	0.6	250-499	-	-	(D)	-	(D)	-	-
Hawaii	31	0.4	100-249	-	-	(D)	-	(D)	-	-
Rhode Island	31	0.4	250-499	-	-	(D)	-	(D)	-	-
Delaware	19	0.2	100-249	-	-	(D)	-	(D)	-	-
D.C.	17	0.2	20-99	-	-	(D)	-	(D)	-	-
Idaho	16	0.2	100-249	-	-	(D)	-	(D)	-	-
West Virginia	15	0.2	100-249	-	-	(D)	-	(D)	-	-
South Dakota	10	0.1	20-99	-	-	(D)	-	(D)	-	-
Alaska	7	0.1	20-99	-	-	(D)	-	(D)	-	-
Wyoming	1	-	0-19	-	-	(D)	-	(D)	-	-

Source: 2002 *Economic Census*. The states are in descending order of sales or establishments (if sales data are missing for the majority). The symbol (D) appears when data are withheld to prevent disclosure of competitive information. States marked with (D) are sorted by number of establishments. A dash (-) indicates that the data element cannot be calculated. Shaded *states* on the state map indicate those states which have proportionately greater representation in the industry than would be indicated by the states population; the ratio is based on total sales or number of establishments. Shaded *regions* indicate where the industry is regionally most concentrated.

NAICS 423310 - LUMBER, PLYWOOD, MILLWORK, AND WOOD PANEL MERCHANT WHOLESALERS*

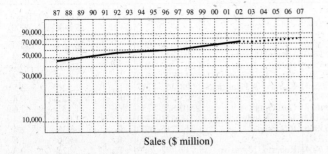

Sales ($ million)

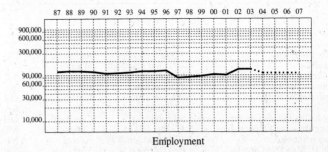

Employment

GENERAL STATISTICS

Year	Establishments (number)	Employment (number)	Payroll ($ million)	Sales ($ million)	Employees per Establishment (number)	Sales per Establishment ($)	Payroll per Employee ($)
1987	8,098	119,796	2,812.4	45,877.5	14.8	5,665,287.7	23,476.6
1988	7,808	123,333	3,091.0	47,902.8 e	15.8	6,135,092.2	25,062.2
1989	7,633	122,607	3,159.2	49,928.2 e	16.1	6,541,097.9	25,766.9
1990	7,677	118,902	3,134.7	51,953.6 e	15.5	6,767,435.2	26,363.7
1991	7,594	109,438	2,982.5	53,979.0 e	14.4	7,108,111.7	27,252.9
1992	8,364	111,626	3,242.3	56,004.4	13.3	6,695,887.1	29,046.1
1993	8,377	115,391	3,591.8	56,894.7 e	13.8	6,791,775.1	31,127.2
1994	8,604	122,835	3,876.1	57,785.0 e	14.3	6,716,062.3	31,555.3
1995	8,584	122,769	3,794.6	58,675.3 e	14.3	6,835,426.4	30,908.5
1996	8,667 e	126,616 e	4,055.4 e	59,565.6 e	14.6 e	6,872,689.5 e	32,029.1 e
1997	6,767	88,905	3,126.4	60,455.9	13.1	8,933,929.4	35,165.6
1998	6,893	91,458	3,406.4	63,068.0 e	13.3	9,149,572.0	37,245.5
1999	7,019	96,929	3,783.2	65,680.1 e	13.8	9,357,472.6	39,030.6
2000	7,105	104,798	4,119.9	68,292.2 e	14.7	9,611,850.8	39,312.7
2001	7,220	101,631	4,097.0	70,904.3 e	14.1	9,820,540.2	40,312.8
2002	8,729	134,915	5,401.9	73,516.4	15.5	8,422,087.3	40,039.3
2003	8,709	135,266	5,751.4	72,954.3 p	15.5	9,741,444.5 p	42,519.4
2004	7,788 p	111,205 p	4,904.2 p	74,621.8 p	14.2 p	9,994,671.0 p	43,515.4 p
2005	7,778 p	110,834 p	5,034.5 p	76,289.4 p	14.1 p	10,247,897.4 p	44,715.1 p
2006	7,769 p	110,464 p	5,164.9 p	77,956.9 p	14.1 p	10,501,123.9 p	45,914.8 p
2007	7,760 p	110,093 p	5,295.2 p	79,624.5 p	14.1 p	10,754,350.3 p	47,114.4 p

Sources: Economic Census of the United States, 1987, 1992, 1997, and 2002. Establishment counts, employment, and payroll are from County Business Patterns for non-Census years. Values followed by a 'p' are projections by the editors. Sales data for non-Census years are extrapolations, marked by 'e'. Data are the most recent available at this level of detail.

INDICES OF CHANGE

Year	Establishments (number)	Employment (number)	Payroll ($ million)	Sales ($ million)	Employees per Establishment (number)	Sales per Establishment ($)	Payroll per Employee ($)
1987	92.8	88.8	52.1	62.4	95.5	67.3	58.6
1992	95.8	82.7	60.0	76.2	85.8	79.5	72.5
1993	96.0	85.5	66.5	77.4 e	89.0	80.6	77.7
1994	98.6	91.0	71.8	78.6 e	92.3	79.7	78.8
1995	98.3	91.0	70.2	79.8 e	92.3	81.2	77.2
1996	99.3 e	93.8 e	75.1 e	81.0 e	94.2 e	81.6 e	80.0 e
1997	77.5	65.9	57.9	82.2	84.5	106.1	87.8
1998	79.0	67.8	63.1	85.8 e	85.8	108.6	93.0
1999	80.4	71.8	70.0	89.3 e	89.0	111.1	97.5
2000	81.4	77.7	76.3	92.9 e	94.8	114.1	98.2
2001	82.7	75.3	75.8	96.4 e	91.0	116.6	100.7
2002	100.0	100.0	100.0	100.0	100.0	100.0	100.0
2003	99.8	100.3	106.5	99.2 p	100.2	115.7 p	106.2
2004	89.2 p	82.4 p	90.8 p	101.5 p	91.5 p	118.7 p	108.7 p
2005	89.1 p	82.2 p	93.2 p	103.8 p	91.2 p	121.7 p	111.7 p
2006	89.0 p	81.9 p	95.6 p	106.0 p	91.0 p	124.7 p	114.7 p
2007	88.9 p	81.6 p	98.0 p	108.3 p	90.7 p	127.7 p	117.7 p

Sources: Same as General Statistics. The values shown reflect change from the base year, 2002. Values above 100 mean greater than 2002, values below 100 mean less than 2002, and a value of 100 in the 1987-2001 or 2003-2007 period means same as 2002. Values followed by a 'p' are projections by the editors; 'e' stands for extrapolation. Data are the most recent available at this level of detail.

SELECTED RATIOS

For 2002	Avg. of All Wholesale	Analyzed Industry	Index	For 2002	Avg. of All Wholesale	Analyzed Industry	Index
Employees per Establishment	15	15	103	Sales per Employee	791,325	544,909	69
Payroll per Establishment	626,122	618,845	99	Sales per Establishment	12,012,387	8,422,087	70
Payroll per Employee	41,161	40,039	97	Expenses per Establishment	na	na	na

Sources: Same as General Statistics. The 'Average of All' column, Wholesale or Retail, represents the average of the sector reported for the most recent complete year available. The Index shows the relationship between the Average and the Analyzed Industry. For example, 100 means that they are equal; 500 that the Analyzed Industry is five times the average; 50 means that the Analyzed Industry is half the national average. The abbreviation 'na' is used to show that data are 'not available'.

*Equivalent to SIC 5031.

LEADING COMPANIES   Number shown: 75   Total sales ($ mil): 57,150   Total employment (000): 198.7

Company Name	Address				CEO Name	Phone	Co. Type	Sales ($ mil)	Empl. (000)
Lowe's Companies Inc.	PO Box 1111	N. Wilkesboro	NC	28656		336-658-4000	P	36,464	123.0
Universal Corp.	PO Box 25099	Richmond	VA	23260	Henry H Harrell	804-359-9311	P	2,271	30.0
Crane Co.	100 First Stamford	Stamford	CT	06902	Robert S Evans	203-363-7300	P	1,890	10.1
Builders FirstSource Inc.	2001 Bryan St	Dallas	TX	75201	Alan Davenport	214-880-3500	S	1,675	6.2
American Builders & Contractors	PO Box 838	Beloit	WI	53511	Kenneth A Hendricks	608-362-7777	R	1,520*	3.5
North Pacific Group Inc.	PO Box 3915	Portland	OR	97208		503-231-1166	R	1,227	0.8
Pacific Supply	1735 24th St	Oakland	CA	94623	Curt Gones	510-832-5734	D	1,131*	2.6
Forest City Enterprises Inc.	50 Public Sq	Cleveland	OH	44113	John W Judy	216-621-6060	P	1,022	4.4
Huttig Building Products Inc.	PO Box 1041	Chesterfield	MO	63006	R S Evans	314-216-2600	P	938	2.4
Bradco Supply Corp.	13 Production Way	Avenel	NJ	07001		732-382-3400	R	850	1.8
John H. Myers and Son Inc.	2200 Monroe St	York	PA	17404	Robert L Myers Jr	717-792-2500	R	625*	0.3
Timber Products Co.	PO Box 269	Springfield	OR	97477	Joseph H Gonyea	541-747-4577	R	600*	1.5
Buckeye Pacific Corp.	PO Box 168	Portland	OR	97207	Jeff Dill	503-228-3330	S	400*	<0.1
Radford Co.	PO Box 2688	Oshkosh	WI	54903	Michael Walsh	920-426-6200	R	356*	0.2
VerHalen Inc.	PO Box 11968	Green Bay	WI	54307	John Calawerts	920-435-3791	R	302*	0.5
Patrick Industries Inc.	1800 S 14th St	Elkhart	IN	46516	Keith V Kankel	219-294-7511	P	302	1.1
Seven D Wholesale	PO Box 67	Gallitzin	PA	16641	Donald A DeGol Sr	814-886-8151	D	300*	0.4
AC Houston Lumber Co.	PO Box 337410	North Las Vegas	NV	89033		702-633-5000	R	253*	0.3
Brockway-Smith Co.	146 Dascomb Rd	Andover	MA	01810	Charles Smith	978-475-7100	R	200	0.7
PDC Glass and Metal Services Inc.	100 Business Ctr Dr	Cheswick	PA	15024	Steve Perilstein	724-274-9050	R	185*	0.1
K and A Lumber Company Inc.	1001 W Mowry Dr	Homestead	FL	33030	Richard Jackson II	305-245-5312	R	179*	0.1
North Amercian Forest Products	PO Box AC	Edwardsburg	MI	49112		269-663-8500	R	139*	0.2
Mid-AM Building Supply Inc.	PO Box 645	Moberly	MO	65270	Joseph I Knaebel	816-263-2140	R	135*	0.2
Central Valley Builders Supply	1100 Vintage Ave	St. Helena	CA	94574	Kathleen Patterson	707-963-3622	R	134*	0.2
Hoboken Wood Flooring Corp.	70 Demarest Dr	Wayne	NJ	07470	Joe Leskowitz	973-694-2888	R	134*	0.2
Pacific Mutual Door Co.	1525 W 31st St	Kansas City	MO	64108	Jon Lambert	816-531-0161	R	131*	0.2
R and K Building Supplies Inc.	PO Box 4740	Mesa	AZ	85211	Chad Coons	480-892-0025	R	130*	0.2
J.E. Higgins Lumber Co.	PO Box 4124	Concord	CA	94524	Jonathan R Long	925-245-4300	R	122*	0.5
Futter Lumber Corp.	PO Box 347	Rockville Centre	NY	11571	Bernard Futter	516-764-4445	R	119*	<0.1
Amerhart Ltd.	PO Box 10097	Green Bay	WI	54307	Mark Kasper	920-494-4744	R	109*	0.2
Lake States Lumber Inc.	PO Box 310	Aitkin	MN	56431	Roger D Wilson	218-927-2125	R	108*	0.1
National Wood Products Inc.	PO Box 65599	Salt Lake City	UT	84165	Donald Meyer	801-977-1171	R	104*	<0.1
Dealers Supply and Lumber Inc.	PO Box 5025, Sta B	Greenville	SC	29606	Knox Wherry	864-242-6571	R	101*	<0.1
Lumberman's Inc.	4418 Stafford SW	Wyoming	MI	49548	Roger A Vanderheide	616-261-3200	R	101*	0.2
Williams Kitchen and Bath	658 Richmond	Grand Rapids	MI	49504	James Williams	616-456-1613	R	97*	0.2
J and M Service Inc.	11532 Anabel Ave	Garden Grove	CA	92843	Mark Sieve	714-530-3325	R	94*	0.1
Mill Creek Lumber and Supply Co.	6201 S 129th E Ave	Tulsa	OK	74012	JD Dunn	918-747-2000	R	92*	0.4
Snavely Forest Products Inc.	PO Box 9808	Pittsburgh	PA	15227	CM Snavely	412-885-4005	R	92*	0.1
Dyke Industries Inc.	309 Ctr St	Little Rock	AR	72201	Fred Edick	501-376-2921	R	91*	<0.1
Howard A. Davidson Lumber Co.	PO Box 27066	Detroit	MI	48227	Howard A Davidson	313-834-6770	R	91*	<0.1
Vidalia Naval Stores Co.	PO Box 1659	Vidalia	GA	30475	Hugh Peterson Jr	912-537-8964	R	85*	0.3
Economy Lumber Yard Inc.	4200 N Ih 35	Laredo	TX	78041	Isaac Epstein	956-721-7300	R	84*	0.1
Hampton Affiliates	9600 SW Barnes Rd	Portland	OR	97225	Michael Phillips	503-297-7691	S	84*	0.1
Griffin Wood Company Inc.	PO Box 669	Marion	AL	36756	Corin Harrison Jr	334-683-9073	R	84*	<0.1
RK Miles Inc.	PO Box 1125	Manchester Ctr	VT	05255	Josiah Miles	802-362-1952	R	81*	0.1
Miller and Company Inc.	PO Box 770	Selma	AL	36702	Bill DeRamus	334-874-8271	R	81*	0.3
Stanford Home Centre	2001 Rte 286	Plum Boro	PA	15239	Carl Piekarski	724-327-6800	R	81*	0.1
Vaughan and Sons Inc.	PO Box 17258	San Antonio	TX	78217	Curtis T Vaughan III	210-590-9300	R	79*	0.3
Cleary Millwork Company Inc.	PO Box 628	Rocky Hill	CT	06067	Kenneth Bussmann	860-721-0520	R	78*	0.1
Building Products Inc.	PO Box 1390	Watertown	SD	57201	Lee Schull	605-886-3495	R	74*	0.1
B. Frank Joy Company Inc.	5355 Kilmer Pl	Hyattsville	MD	20781	T Kenneth Joy	301-779-9400	R	73*	0.5
Star Lumbers New Home	902 E Indianapolis	Wichita	KS	67211		316-269-0481	R	71*	0.1
Wille Brothers Co.	2154 Vermont St	Blue Island	IL	60406	Curt Wille	708-388-0045	R	71*	<0.1
Redwood Empire Inc.	PO Box 1300	Morgan Hill	CA	95038	Rodger Burch	408-779-7354	R	71*	<0.1
East Coast Millwork Distributors	PO Box 349	Elkin	NC	28621		336-835-1182	R	70*	0.1
Pozzi Window Co.	PO Box 5249	Bend	OR	97708		541-382-4411	R	69*	0.5
Adams Building Materials Inc.	1801 7th St SW	Winter Haven	FL	33880	Greg Adams	863-294-0611	R	65*	0.1
Delmarva Millwork Corp.	PO Box 4068	Lancaster	PA	17604	James Bounds	717-299-2364	R	65*	0.1
Hampton Distribution Co's	PO Box 13457	Sacramento	CA	95813		916-929-3191	R	65*	0.1
Hamshaw Lumber Inc.	PO Box 725	Keene	NH	03431	Douglas Hamshaw	603-352-6506	R	65*	0.1
Samuel Feldman Lumber Inc.	330 N Henry St	Brooklyn	NY	11222	Robert Feldman	718-786-7777	R	65*	0.1
Cleveland Wrecking Co.	628 E Edna Pl	Covina	CA	91723	Jim Sheridan	626-967-9799	R	64*	0.6
Western Products Inc.	117 23rd St N	Fargo	ND	58102	Michael J Bullinger	701-293-5310	R	64*	0.1
Builders General Supply Co.	PO Box 95	Little Silver	NJ	07739	Timothy J Shaheen	732-747-0808	R	60*	0.2
Winco Distributors Inc.	PO Box 2401	Houston	TX	77252	Fenton Hord	713-224-5361	D	60*	0.2
T.H. Rogers Lumber Co.	PO Box 5770	Edmond	OK	73083	John M Kennedy	405-330-2181	R	57*	0.2
KC Company Inc.	12100 Baltimore	Beltsville	MD	20705	Kevin Cassidy	301-419-2200	R	52*	<0.1
Maner Builders Supply Co.	PO Box 204598	Augusta	GA	30917	James Broome	706-863-6191	R	52*	<0.1
Millwork Distributors Inc.	PO Box 2465	Oshkosh	WI	54903	Kenneth Huszar	920-235-8110	R	52*	<0.1
Prestige Lumber and Supplies Inc.	1985 State Rd 419	Longwood	FL	32750	Stephen Rominger	407-323-5662	R	52*	<0.1
R-Y Timber Inc.	PO Box 220	Townsend	MT	59644		406-266-3111	R	52*	0.1
Seal Rite Door	PO Box 1414	Pataskala	OH	43062	Scott Miller	740-927-3558	R	52*	<0.1
Tampa Bay Hardwoods & Lumber	8408 Temple Ter	Tampa	FL	33637	Richard Lee	813-987-9663	R	52*	<0.1
Wilson Plywood and Door Inc.	PO Box 461546	Garland	TX	75046	James Preddy	972-494-3545	R	52*	<0.1
Woodland Products Company Inc.	1480 E Grand Ave	Pomona	CA	91766	Rob Robertson	909-623-3434	R	52*	<0.1

Source: Ward's *Business Directory of U.S. Private and Public Companies*, Volumes 1 and 2, 2005. The company type code used is as follows: P - Public, R - Private, S - Subsidiary, D - Division, J - Joint Venture, A - Affiliate, G - Group. Sales are in millions of dollars, employees are in thousands. An asterisk (*) indicates an estimated sales volume. The symbol < stands for 'less than'. Company names and addresses are truncated, in some cases, to fit into the available space.

OCCUPATIONS EMPLOYED BY LUMBER & OTHER CONSTRUCTION MATERIALS WHOLESALE

Occupation	% of Total 2004	Change to 2014	Occupation	% of Total 2004	Change to 2014
Sales reps, wholesale & manufacturing, exc tech	15.9	18.2	Shipping, receiving, & traffic clerks	1.9	7.0
Laborers & freight, stock, & material movers, hand	11.7	6.4	First-line supervisors/managers of non-retail sales work	1.7	9.3
Truck drivers, heavy & tractor-trailer	9.3	18.0	Order clerks	1.4	-23.3
Industrial truck & tractor operators	5.0	6.4	Carpenters	1.1	18.2
Truck drivers, light or delivery services	4.5	18.0	Secretaries, except legal, medical, & executive	1.1	-0.5
Team assemblers	4.3	18.2	First-line supervisors/managers of office workers	1.1	7.1
General & operations managers	2.8	17.0	First-line supervisors/managers of transporation workers	1.0	18.2
Bookkeeping, accounting, & auditing clerks	2.7	6.4	First-line supervisors/managers of production workers	1.0	18.2
Office clerks, general	2.5	5.2	Retail salespersons	1.0	18.2
Stock clerks & order fillers	2.3	-9.5			

Source: *Industry-Occupation Matrix*, Bureau of Labor Statistics. These data are reported based on 4-digit NAICS categories but have been matched to corresponding 6-digit NAICS industry codes. The change reported for each occupation to the year 2014 is a percent of growth or decline as estimated by the Bureau of Labor Statistics. The abbreviation nec stands for 'not elsewhere classified.'

LOCATION BY STATE AND REGIONAL CONCENTRATION

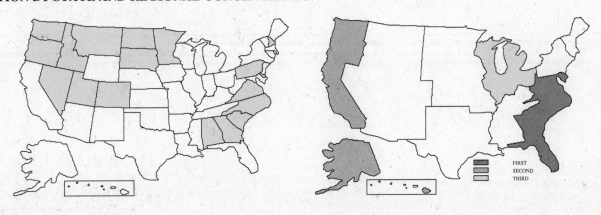

INDUSTRY DATA BY STATE

State	Establishments Total (number)	% of U.S.	Employment Total (number)	% of U.S.	Per Estab.	Payroll Total ($ mil.)	Per Empl. ($)	Sales Total ($ mil.)	% of U.S.	Per Estab. ($)
California	775	8.9	12,498	9.3	16	525.6	42,053	6,362.8	8.5	8,210,025
Pennsylvania	346	4.0	6,444	4.8	19	260.9	40,490	5,755.9	7.7	16,635,474
Oregon	353	4.0	4,392	3.3	12	222.0	50,553	5,637.5	7.5	15,970,266
Texas	501	5.7	10,828	8.0	22	428.4	39,561	4,586.7	6.1	9,155,018
Minnesota	201	2.3	4,075	3.0	20	204.8	50,257	3,355.9	4.5	16,696,055
Florida	525	6.0	6,479	4.8	12	261.5	40,356	3,334.9	4.4	6,352,270
New York	394	4.5	5,675	4.2	14	244.3	43,041	3,327.9	4.4	8,446,497
Washington	367	4.2	4,373	3.2	12	182.1	41,647	3,201.4	4.3	8,723,264
Georgia	362	4.2	5,965	4.4	16	233.3	39,115	3,067.6	4.1	8,473,903
North Carolina	369	4.2	5,144	3.8	14	190.7	37,069	2,419.4	3.2	6,556,515
Virginia	209	2.4	3,370	2.5	16	128.1	38,013	1,992.4	2.6	9,533,115
Colorado	186	2.1	3,937	2.9	21	172.0	43,695	1,973.6	2.6	10,610,909
Ohio	329	3.8	4,590	3.4	14	171.7	37,408	1,945.7	2.6	5,914,049
Illinois	279	3.2	3,595	2.7	13	154.5	42,977	1,757.6	2.3	6,299,559
Massachusetts	165	1.9	2,667	2.0	16	129.3	48,477	1,646.0	2.2	9,976,000
New Jersey	202	2.3	3,564	2.6	18	161.6	45,345	1,629.6	2.2	8,067,158
South Carolina	104	1.2	1,498	1.1	14	57.0	38,083	1,551.4	2.1	14,917,385
Wisconsin	186	2.1	3,496	2.6	19	128.2	36,685	1,396.9	1.9	7,510,419
Alabama	203	2.3	2,383	1.8	12	84.7	35,551	1,311.8	1.7	6,462,222
Maryland	147	1.7	2,987	2.2	20	122.9	41,156	1,302.4	1.7	8,860,014
Tennessee	194	2.2	2,921	2.2	15	104.9	35,925	1,293.3	1.7	6,666,644
Missouri	198	2.3	2,850	2.1	14	108.1	37,947	1,233.5	1.6	6,229,985
Indiana	188	2.2	2,738	2.0	15	106.6	38,929	1,231.3	1.6	6,549,702
Louisiana	128	1.5	1,677	1.2	13	56.5	33,671	994.4	1.3	7,768,492
Idaho	70	0.8	907	0.7	13	36.3	40,019	889.4	1.2	12,705,586
Connecticut	93	1.1	1,744	1.3	19	79.4	45,541	812.4	1.1	8,735,645
New Hampshire	51	0.6	671	0.5	13	41.5	61,915	740.8	1.0	14,525,882
Utah	77	0.9	1,429	1.1	19	52.6	36,826	672.8	0.9	8,737,714
Nevada	75	0.9	1,339	1.0	18	56.2	42,001	625.1	0.8	8,335,280
Arkansas	89	1.0	1,158	0.9	13	35.6	30,737	615.2	0.8	6,912,775
Mississippi	88	1.0	969	0.7	11	35.3	36,443	581.4	0.8	6,606,409
Kentucky	112	1.3	1,304	1.0	12	43.6	33,461	569.9	0.8	5,088,679
Kansas	80	0.9	1,322	1.0	17	52.9	40,018	531.0	0.7	6,638,100

Continued on next page.

INDUSTRY DATA BY STATE - Continued

State	Establishments Total (number)	% of U.S.	Employment Total (number)	% of U.S.	Per Estab.	Payroll Total ($ mil.)	Per Empl. ($)	Sales Total ($ mil.)	% of U.S.	Per Estab. ($)
Oklahoma	74	0.8	886	0.7	12	31.5	35,525	482.1	0.6	6,515,541
Iowa	90	1.0	1,393	1.0	15	45.8	32,887	476.4	0.6	5,292,844
New Mexico	54	0.6	956	0.7	18	33.9	35,486	369.7	0.5	6,846,796
Montana	59	0.7	627	0.5	11	21.6	34,429	356.8	0.5	6,047,610
Maine	47	0.5	568	0.4	12	20.8	36,600	282.7	0.4	6,014,787
Delaware	29	0.3	368	0.3	13	13.2	35,859	231.4	0.3	7,979,000
North Dakota	29	0.3	640	0.5	22	23.1	36,033	225.7	0.3	7,781,310
South Dakota	38	0.4	500	0.4	13	17.8	35,590	219.7	0.3	5,782,211
West Virginia	51	0.6	717	0.5	14	18.6	25,887	182.6	0.2	3,580,235
Nebraska	41	0.5	514	0.4	13	18.3	35,673	164.7	0.2	4,018,293
Hawaii	38	0.4	380	0.3	10	13.3	35,003	161.1	0.2	4,239,816
Vermont	29	0.3	274	0.2	9	10.1	36,730	144.9	0.2	4,995,448
Rhode Island	24	0.3	347	0.3	14	14.1	40,553	106.0	0.1	4,418,250
Wyoming	12	0.1	115	0.1	10	4.4	38,009	75.2	0.1	6,264,500
Michigan	277	3.2	2500-4999	-	-	(D)	-	(D)	-	-
Arizona	161	1.8	2500-4999	-	-	(D)	-	(D)	-	-
Alaska	19	0.2	500-999	-	-	(D)	-	(D)	-	-
D.C.	4	-	20-99	-	-	(D)	-	(D)	-	-

Source: 2002 *Economic Census*. The states are in descending order of sales or establishments (if sales data are missing for the majority). The symbol (D) appears when data are withheld to prevent disclosure of competitive information. States marked with (D) are sorted by number of establishments. A dash (-) indicates that the data element cannot be calculated. Shaded *states* on the state map indicate those states which have proportionally greater representation in the industry than would be indicated by the states population; the ratio is based on total sales or number of establishments. Shaded *regions* indicate where the industry is regionally most concentrated.

NAICS 423320 - BRICK, STONE, AND RELATED CONSTRUCTION MATERIAL MERCHANT WHOLESALERS*

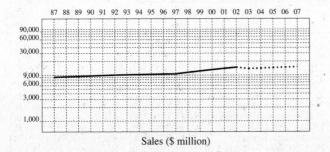

Sales ($ million)

Employment

GENERAL STATISTICS

Year	Establishments (number)	Employment (number)	Payroll ($ million)	Sales ($ million)	Employees per Establishment (number)	Sales per Establishment ($)	Payroll per Employee ($)
1987	3,880	33,252	800.2	9,094.1	8.6	2,343,840.2	24,064.7
1988	3,754	33,941	878.7	9,298.8 e	9.0	2,477,037.8	25,889.0
1989	3,622	33,352	969.8	9,503.5 e	9.2	2,623,826.6	29,077.7
1990	3,746	33,415	929.4	9,708.2 e	8.9	2,591,617.7	27,813.9
1991	3,892	32,419	889.8	9,912.9 e	8.3	2,546,993.8	27,446.9
1992	4,285	32,062	924.8	10,117.7	7.5	2,361,190.2	28,844.1
1993	4,434	33,468	981.5	10,236.5 e	7.5	2,308,637.8	29,326.5
1994	4,618	35,532	1,116.7	10,355.3 e	7.7	2,242,377.7	31,428.0
1995	4,375	35,141	1,103.8	10,474.1 e	8.0	2,394,080.0	31,410.6
1996	4,629 e	34,554 e	1,117.2 e	10,592.9 e	7.5 e	2,288,377.6 e	32,332.0 e
1997	3,026	23,753	761.7	10,711.7	7.8	3,539,887.6	32,067.5
1998	3,103	23,428	858.3	11,530.6 e	7.6	3,715,958.7	36,635.6
1999	3,236	25,998	996.5	12,349.5 e	8.0	3,816,297.9	38,329.9
2000	3,351	29,196	1,141.4	13,168.5 e	8.7	3,929,710.5	39,093.1
2001	3,502	31,621	1,280.7	13,987.4 e	9.0	3,994,111.9	40,500.2
2002	3,568	30,472	1,224.6	14,806.3	8.5	4,149,747.8	40,187.7
2003	3,757	32,347	1,402.9	13,818.0 p	8.6	4,037,288.2 p	43,369.2
2004	3,503 p	28,431 p	1,241.9 p	14,150.7 p	8.1 p	4,164,294.9 p	42,799.9 p
2005	3,468 p	28,100 p	1,266.3 p	14,483.3 p	8.1 p	4,291,301.7 p	43,909.6 p
2006	3,434 p	27,769 p	1,290.7 p	14,816.0 p	8.1 p	4,418,308.4 p	45,019.3 p
2007	3,400 p	27,438 p	1,315.1 p	15,148.6 p	8.1 p	4,545,315.2 p	46,128.9 p

Sources: Economic Census of the United States, 1987, 1992, 1997, and 2002. Establishment counts, employment, and payroll are from County Business Patterns for non-Census years. Values followed by a 'p' are projections by the editors. Sales data for non-Census years are extrapolations, marked by 'e'. Data are the most recent available at this level of detail.

INDICES OF CHANGE

Year	Establishments (number)	Employment (number)	Payroll ($ million)	Sales ($ million)	Employees per Establishment (number)	Sales per Establishment ($)	Payroll per Employee ($)
1987	108.7	109.1	65.3	61.4	101.2	56.5	59.9
1992	120.1	105.2	75.5	68.3	88.2	56.9	71.8
1993	124.3	109.8	80.1	69.1 e	88.2	55.6	73.0
1994	129.4	116.6	91.2	69.9 e	90.6	54.0	78.2
1995	122.6	115.3	90.1	70.7 e	94.1	57.7	78.2
1996	129.7 e	113.4 e	91.2 e	71.5 e	88.2 e	55.1 e	80.5 e
1997	84.8	78.0	62.2	72.3	91.8	85.3	79.8
1998	87.0	76.9	70.1	77.9 e	89.4	89.5	91.2
1999	90.7	85.3	81.4	83.4 e	94.1	92.0	95.4
2000	93.9	95.8	93.2	88.9 e	102.4	94.7	97.3
2001	98.2	103.8	104.6	94.5 e	105.9	96.2	100.8
2002	100.0	100.0	100.0	100.0	100.0	100.0	100.0
2003	105.3	106.2	114.6	93.3 p	101.3	97.3 p	107.9
2004	98.2 p	93.3 p	101.4 p	95.6 p	95.6 p	100.4 p	106.5 p
2005	97.2 p	92.2 p	103.4 p	97.8 p	95.4 p	103.4 p	109.3 p
2006	96.3 p	91.1 p	105.4 p	100.1 p	95.2 p	106.5 p	112.0 p
2007	95.3 p	90.0 p	107.4 p	102.3 p	95.1 p	109.5 p	114.8 p

Sources: Same as General Statistics. The values shown reflect change from the base year, 2002. Values above 100 mean greater than 2002, values below 100 mean less than 2002, and a value of 100 in the 1987-2001 or 2003-2007 period means same as 2002. Values followed by a 'p' are projections by the editors; 'e' stands for extrapolation. Data are the most recent available at this level of detail.

SELECTED RATIOS

For 2002	Avg. of All Wholesale	Analyzed Industry	Index	For 2002	Avg. of All Wholesale	Analyzed Industry	Index
Employees per Establishment	15	9	57	Sales per Employee	791,325	485,899	61
Payroll per Establishment	626,122	343,217	55	Sales per Establishment	12,012,387	4,149,748	35
Payroll per Employee	41,161	40,188	98	Expenses per Establishment	na	na	na

Sources: Same as General Statistics. The 'Average of All' column, Wholesale or Retail, represents the average of the sector reported for the most recent complete year available. The Index shows the relationship between the Average and the Analyzed Industry. For example, 100 means that they are equal; 500 that the Analyzed Industry is five times the average; 50 means that the Analyzed Industry is half the national average. The abbreviation 'na' is used to show that data are 'not available'.

*Equivalent to SIC 5032.

1787

LEADING COMPANIES   Number shown: 75   Total sales ($ mil): 21,418   Total employment (000): 29.9

Company Name	Address				CEO Name	Phone	Co. Type	Sales ($ mil)	Empl. (000)
Oldcastle APG National Inc.	7920 Notes Dr	Manassas	VA	20109	Patrcik O Sullivan	703-361-2777	R	13,120*	<0.1
Lafarge North America Inc.	12950 Worldgate Dr	Herndon	VA	20170	Bertrand Collomb	703-480-3600	P	3,763	15.3
Pacific Supply	1735 24th St	Oakland	CA	94623	Curt Gones	510-832-5734	D	1,131*	2.6
Kiewit Materials Co.	1000 Kiewit Plz	Omaha	NE	68131	Bruce Grewcock	402-271-2947	S	855*	4.5
H and E Equipment Services	11100 Mead Rd	Baton Rouge	LA	70816	John Engquist	225-298-5200	R	414	1.3
Granite Rock Co.	PO Box 50001	Watsonville	CA	95077	Bruce W Woolpert	831-768-2000	R	180*	0.7
American Tile Supply Inc.	PO Box 425	Fort Worth	TX	76107	Harrold Merchant	972-243-2377	R	134*	0.2
Wildish Land Co.	PO Box 7428	Eugene	OR	97401	James A Wildish	541-485-1700	R	92*	0.1
Interceramic Inc.	2333 S Jupiter Rd	Garland	TX	75041	Victor Almeida	214-503-5500	S	85*	0.2
Alpha Tile Distributors Inc.	2443 East Meadow	Tampa	FL	33619	Scott Bennett	813-620-9000	S	81*	<0.1
Vaughan and Sons Inc.	PO Box 17258	San Antonio	TX	78217	Curtis T Vaughan III	210-590-9300	R	79*	0.3
Twin City Bottle Inc.	1227 E Hennepin	Minneapolis	MN	55414	Ken Slater	612-331-8880	R	76*	0.3
Builders General Supply Co.	PO Box 95	Little Silver	NJ	07739	Timothy J Shaheen	732-747-0808	R	60*	0.2
Nu-Way Concrete Forms Inc.	4190 Hofmeister	St. Louis	MO	63125	Gerald Rhomberg	314-544-1214	R	52*	0.2
Cooperative Reserve Supply Inc.	1100 Iron Horse Pk	Billerica	MA	01862		617-864-1444	R	50*	<0.1
Robinson Brick Co.	1845 W Dartmouth	Englewood	CO	80110	Robert Jaster	303-783-3000	R	49*	0.2
Badger Corrugating Co.	PO Box 1837	La Crosse	WI	54601	Michael J Sexauer	608-788-0100	R	49*	0.1
All American Asphalt	PO Box 2229	Corona	CA	92878	Dan Sizemore	949-786-1290	R	47*	0.1
Gary Merlino Construction Inc.	1915 SE Maple	Renton	WA	98055		425-226-1000	S	46*	0.3
Colonial Building Supply L.L.C.	PO Box 459	Centerville	UT	84014	Fred Hale	801-295-9471	R	45*	<0.1
Keystone Aggregate Products Co.	Rte 329	Bath	PA	18014		610-837-2211	R	42*	0.3
Saginaw Asphalt Paving Co.	2981 Carrollton Rd	Saginaw	MI	48604	Albert Birnbaum	989-755-8147	R	42*	0.1
Shelley's Septic Tank	PO Box 249	Zellwood	FL	32798	Barbara Shelley	407-889-8042	R	38*	<0.1
Clark Pacific Inc.	1980 S River Rd	W. Sacramento	CA	95691		916-371-0305	R	37*	0.3
Huntington Tile Group L.P.	PO Box 7292	Fort Worth	TX	76111	David Hyland	817-838-2323	R	37*	0.1
Sylvester Materials Co.	3810 Herr Rd	Sylvania	OH	43560	Charles Stansley	419-885-4658	R	36*	0.1
Barton Leasing Inc.	14800 E Moncrieff	Aurora	CO	80011	Donnie Barton	303-576-2200	R	31*	0.1
Form Services Inc.	PO Box 60	Linthicum H.	MD	21090	Joseph Papparotto	410-247-9500	R	30*	0.1
Harrington and Co.	PO Box 25723	Salt Lake City	UT	84125	Stephen Booth	801-972-3131	R	29*	<0.1
Damons Management Inc.	9500 Diamond Ctr	Mentor	OH	44060	Shannon Foust	440-358-1847	R	24*	<0.1
Carter-Waters Corp.	PO Box 412676	Kansas City	MO	64141	Jeff Hanes	816-471-2570	R	23*	<0.1
Kent Gypsum Supply Inc.	11409 58th Ave E	Puyallup	WA	98373		253-848-8665	R	23*	<0.1
Rose and Walker Supply Inc.	3974 N Indianapolis	Columbus	IN	47201	Ronald Rose	812-372-8181	R	23*	<0.1
Yardville Supply Co.	PO Box 8427	Trenton	NJ	08650	George Smith	609-585-5000	R	22*	<0.1
Associated Asphalt & Materials	3810 Oliver Dr	Santa Fe	NM	87507		505-438-0337	R	21*	<0.1
California Wholesale Material	31625 Hayman St	Hayward	CA	94544		510-429-8877	R	21*	<0.1
L and W Stone Corp.	PO Box 1224	Orland	CA	95963	Scott Laine	530-865-5085	R	21*	<0.1
V-Line Corporation L.L.C.	PO Box 68109	Indianapolis	IN	46268		317-546-1588	R	19*	<0.1
Valley Caliche Products Inc.	PO Box 1086	Mission	TX	78573	R Thompson	956-581-2751	R	19*	<0.1
Desert Equipment Company Inc.	1495 W Melody Dr	Gilbert	AZ	85233	Craig Hills	480-898-7414	R	18*	<0.1
Happy Floors	180 NW 183rd St	Miami	FL	33169	Sol Bonan	305-932-5582	R	18*	<0.1
Fairway Building Products L.P.	53 Eby Chiques Rd	Mount Joy	PA	17552		717-653-6777	R	18*	<0.1
Service Construction Supply Inc.	PO Box 13405	Birmingham	AL	35202	Todd Wallace	205-252-3158	R	18*	<0.1
Marble Granite Tiles Inc.	1022 N Sabina St	Anaheim	CA	92801	N Von Mittenwald	714-502-5700	R	17*	<0.1
Suburban Marble and Granite Inc.	1010 Pulinski Rd	Warminster	PA	18974	John Menarde	215-956-9711	R	16*	<0.1
Dura Sales Inc.	2481 Bull Creek Rd	Tarentum	PA	15084	Roger Costello	724-224-7700	R	16*	<0.1
Witex USA Inc.	1925 Shiloh	Kennesaw	GA	30144	Steve Newman	770-419-9558	R	15*	<0.1
Southwest Stone Supply Inc.	6386 Hwy 54	Osage Beach	MO	65065	Larry Woll	573-302-8855	R	15*	<0.1
Kesseli Morse Company Inc.	242 Canterbury St	Worcester	MA	01603	George P Kustigian Jr	508-752-1901	R	15*	<0.1
Image Asphalt Maintenance Inc.	8174A Solley Rd	Pasadena	MD	21122	Kevin Miller	410-439-9200	R	15*	<0.1
Sun Marble At Fresno Inc.	447 W Fallbrook	Fresno	CA	93711	Wen Shu	559-448-8988	R	15*	<0.1
Worcester Sand and Gravel Inc.	182 Holden St	Shrewsbury	MA	01545	Michael Trotto	508-852-1683	R	15*	<0.1*
Cranesville Aggregate Co's Inc.	427 Sacandaga Rd	Schenectady	NY	12302	Joseph Tesiero	518-346-5749	R	13*	<0.1
Masonry Center Inc.	PO Box 7825	Boise	ID	83707	Ken Chandler	208-375-1362	R	13*	<0.1
Carder Inc.	PO Box 732	Lamar	CO	81052	Ron Peterson	719-336-3479	R	13*	<0.1
Delta Gypsum Inc.	2010 Raleigh Blvd	Raleigh	NC	27604		919-839-0111	R	13*	<0.1
Gebert Floor Covering Inc.	5650 Lincoln Dr	Minneapolis	MN	55436	Richard Schilling	952-945-9295	R	13*	<0.1
Robert F Henry Tile Company Inc.	PO Box 2230	Montgomery	AL	36102	Robert Henry	334-269-2518	R	13*	<0.1
Granite City Ready Mix Inc.	PO Box 1305	St. Cloud	MN	56302	Bob Bogard	320-252-4324	S	12*	0.1
C.A. International Inc.	13524 W 107th St	Schuylkl Hvn	KS	66215	Daniel Shen	913-338-4488	R	12*	<0.1
CJ Langenfelder and Son Inc.	400 Pier Ave	Stevensville	MD	21666	C Langenfelder	410-643-5575	R	12*	<0.1
Corriher Sand and Stone Inc.	225 Corriher Gravel	China Grove	NC	28023	Glenn Corriher	704-857-0166	R	12*	<0.1
Hastings Tile and Bath Inc.	30 Commercial St	Freeport	NY	11520	Michael Homola	516-379-3500	R	12*	<0.1
Paramount Stone Company Inc.	338 Courtland Ave	Stamford	CT	06906	Steve Riviere	203-353-9119	R	12*	<0.1
Landmark Stone Supply Inc.	301 Swiss Dr	Crowley	TX	76036	Travis Nech	817-919-7839	R	11*	<0.1
Pacific Coast Supply L.L.C.	PO Box 3717	Modesto	CA	95352		209-521-2466	R	11*	<0.1
Lincoln Brick and Supply Inc.	PO Box 7559	Grand Rapids	MI	49510	Edward Frey	616-452-6055	R	11*	<0.1
Akdo Intertrade Inc.	PO Box 2065	Bridgeport	CT	06608	Hakki Akbulak	203-336-5199	R	10*	<0.1
Jointa Galusha L.L.C.	PO Box 302	Glens Falls	NY	12801		518-792-5029	R	10*	<0.1
Kobrin Builders Supply of Sarasota	1688 Global Ct	Sarasota	FL	34240	Harvey Kobrin	941-926-4494	R	10*	<0.1
CONCO Co's	PO Box 50685	Springfield	MO	65805	Thomas Baird	417-863-2000	R	10*	<0.1
Marvin L Walker & Associates Inc.	PO Box 5600	Norcross	GA	30091	Marvin Walker	770-446-0030	R	10*	<0.1
Colter's Restaurants Ltd.	921 W Main St	Lewisville	TX	75067		972-434-1616	R	9*	<0.1
Patuxent Materials Inc.	2124 Priest Bridge	Crofton	MD	21114	Francis Gardiner	301-261-3683	R	9*	<0.1
Lippert Corp.	PO Box 1030	Menomonee Fls	WI	53052	Daniel Lippert	262-255-2350	R	9*	<0.1

Source: Ward's Business Directory of U.S. Private and Public Companies, Volumes 1 and 2, 2005. The company type code used is as follows: P - Public, R - Private, S - Subsidiary, D - Division, J - Joint Venture, A - Affiliate, G - Group. Sales are in millions of dollars, employees are in thousands. An asterisk (*) indicates an estimated sales volume. The symbol < stands for 'less than'. Company names and addresses are truncated, in some cases, to fit into the available space.

OCCUPATIONS EMPLOYED BY LUMBER & OTHER CONSTRUCTION MATERIALS WHOLESALE

Occupation	% of Total 2004	Change to 2014	Occupation	% of Total 2004	Change to 2014
Sales reps, wholesale & manufacturing, exc tech	15.9	18.2	Shipping, receiving, & traffic clerks	1.9	7.0
Laborers & freight, stock, & material movers, hand	11.7	6.4	First-line supervisors/managers of non-retail sales work	1.7	9.3
Truck drivers, heavy & tractor-trailer	9.3	18.0	Order clerks	1.4	-23.3
Industrial truck & tractor operators	5.0	6.4	Carpenters	1.1	18.2
Truck drivers, light or delivery services	4.5	18.0	Secretaries, except legal, medical, & executive	1.1	-0.5
Team assemblers	4.3	18.2	First-line supervisors/managers of office workers	1.1	7.1
General & operations managers	2.8	17.0	First-line supervisors/managers of transporation workers	1.0	18.2
Bookkeeping, accounting, & auditing clerks	2.7	6.4	First-line supervisors/managers of production workers	1.0	18.2
Office clerks, general	2.5	5.2	Retail salespersons	1.0	18.2
Stock clerks & order fillers	2.3	-9.5			

Source: Industry-Occupation Matrix, Bureau of Labor Statistics. These data are reported based on 4-digit NAICS categories but have been matched to corresponding 6-digit NAICS industry codes. The change reported for each occupation to the year 2014 is a percent of growth or decline as estimated by the Bureau of Labor Statistics. The abbreviation nec stands for 'not elsewhere classified.'

LOCATION BY STATE AND REGIONAL CONCENTRATION

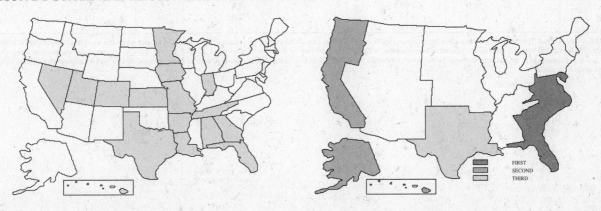

FIRST
SECOND
THIRD

INDUSTRY DATA BY STATE

State	Establishments Total (number)	% of U.S.	Employment Total (number)	% of U.S.	Per Estab.	Payroll Total ($ mil.)	Per Empl. ($)	Sales Total ($ mil.)	% of U.S.	Per Estab. ($)
Texas	340	9.5	3,312	10.7	10	115.8	34,950	1,877.0	12.5	5,520,603
California	398	11.1	4,305	13.9	11	178.7	41,505	1,650.5	11.0	4,147,015
Florida	325	9.0	2,210	7.1	7	82.6	37,390	947.6	6.3	2,915,794
New York	241	6.7	1,692	5.5	7	72.7	42,954	930.0	6.2	3,858,851
Illinois	121	3.4	1,030	3.3	9	46.0	44,619	604.3	4.0	4,994,182
Alabama	57	1.6	630	2.0	11	25.0	39,654	466.5	3.1	8,184,035
Pennsylvania	134	3.7	1,179	3.8	9	43.1	36,557	448.0	3.0	3,343,119
Tennessee	65	1.8	583	1.9	9	24.7	42,331	443.3	3.0	6,820,508
Indiana	68	1.9	774	2.5	11	36.4	47,079	433.8	2.9	6,379,029
Georgia	122	3.4	1,138	3.7	9	44.7	39,243	430.3	2.9	3,527,025
Ohio	114	3.2	857	2.8	8	33.4	39,000	418.2	2.8	3,668,132
Michigan	109	3.0	969	3.1	9	40.8	42,140	403.2	2.7	3,699,229
Minnesota	50	1.4	354	1.1	7	18.7	52,831	367.6	2.5	7,351,360
Missouri	65	1.8	436	1.4	7	17.4	39,940	366.2	2.4	5,633,708
Arkansas	34	0.9	205	0.7	6	5.8	28,356	320.9	2.1	9,438,294
Colorado	88	2.4	763	2.5	9	31.2	40,837	307.9	2.1	3,498,477
Louisiana	64	1.8	694	2.2	11	25.6	36,895	305.0	2.0	4,765,922
North Carolina	94	2.6	667	2.2	7	30.7	45,975	299.5	2.0	3,186,319
Utah	46	1.3	776	2.5	17	30.2	38,867	271.7	1.8	5,906,196
Washington	98	2.7	878	2.8	9	34.6	39,445	267.3	1.8	2,727,327
Maryland	52	1.4	584	1.9	11	24.6	42,110	251.0	1.7	4,826,654
Massachusetts	68	1.9	685	2.2	10	31.3	45,680	244.2	1.6	3,591,324
Kansas	32	0.9	202	0.7	6	8.6	42,550	218.2	1.5	6,817,219
Virginia	71	2.0	523	1.7	7	19.8	37,910	202.0	1.3	2,844,451
Iowa	32	0.9	266	0.9	8	11.7	44,158	195.5	1.3	6,108,344
Wisconsin	52	1.4	332	1.1	6	14.5	43,548	153.6	1.0	2,952,962
Oregon	50	1.4	499	1.6	10	18.7	37,549	152.1	1.0	3,042,760
Oklahoma	44	1.2	232	0.7	5	8.1	34,789	151.0	1.0	3,430,795
South Carolina	39	1.1	266	0.9	7	9.2	34,692	150.1	1.0	3,848,821
Nevada	38	1.1	301	1.0	8	11.2	37,050	128.4	0.9	3,378,974
Hawaii	16	0.4	101	0.3	6	4.3	42,327	110.8	0.7	6,927,625
Rhode Island	9	0.3	89	0.3	10	3.4	38,112	88.1	0.6	9,787,889
Kentucky	23	0.6	205	0.7	9	6.1	29,556	67.1	0.4	2,918,739

Continued on next page.

INDUSTRY DATA BY STATE - Continued

State	Establishments Total (number)	Establishments % of U.S.	Employment Total (number)	Employment % of U.S.	Employment Per Estab.	Payroll Total ($ mil.)	Payroll Per Empl. ($)	Sales Total ($ mil.)	Sales % of U.S.	Sales Per Estab. ($)
New Mexico	26	0.7	158	0.5	6	5.4	34,272	64.9	0.4	2,494,654
Mississippi	28	0.8	111	0.4	4	3.4	30,613	46.5	0.3	1,659,214
South Dakota	5	0.1	119	0.4	24	4.1	34,639	33.3	0.2	6,668,000
West Virginia	18	0.5	49	0.2	3	2.7	55,408	31.9	0.2	1,773,167
Vermont	14	0.4	68	0.2	5	3.1	45,632	29.8	0.2	2,131,429
Montana	23	0.6	76	0.2	3	2.2	29,421	15.5	0.1	676,043
Maine	13	0.4	40	0.1	3	1.3	32,950	12.2	0.1	937,846
New Jersey	100	2.8	500-999	-	-	(D)	-	(D)	-	-
Arizona	79	2.2	500-999	-	-	(D)	-	(D)	-	-
Connecticut	39	1.1	250-499	-	-	(D)	-	(D)	-	-
New Hampshire	24	0.7	100-249	-	-	(D)	-	(D)	-	-
Nebraska	18	0.5	100-249	-	-	(D)	-	(D)	-	-
Idaho	16	0.4	20-99	-	-	(D)	-	(D)	-	-
North Dakota	11	0.3	20-99	-	-	(D)	-	(D)	-	-
Delaware	8	0.2	20-99	-	-	(D)	-	(D)	-	-
Alaska	5	0.1	20-99	-	-	(D)	-	(D)	-	-
Wyoming	5	0.1	0-19	-	-	(D)	-	(D)	-	-
D.C.	1	-	0-19	-	-	(D)	-	(D)	-	-

Source: 2002 *Economic Census.* The states are in descending order of sales or establishments (if sales data are missing for the majority). The symbol (D) appears when data are withheld to prevent disclosure of competitive information. States marked with (D) are sorted by number of establishments. A dash (-) indicates that the data element cannot be calculated. Shaded *states* on the state map indicate those states which have proportionately greater representation in the industry than would be indicated by the states population; the ratio is based on total sales or number of establishments. Shaded *regions* indicate where the industry is regionally most concentrated.

NAICS 423330 - ROOFING, SIDING, AND INSULATION MATERIAL MERCHANT WHOLESALERS

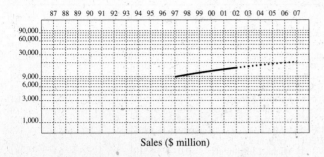

Sales ($ million)

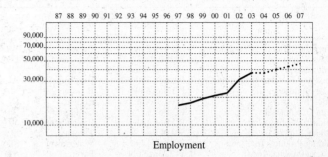

Employment

GENERAL STATISTICS

Year	Establishments (number)	Employment (number)	Payroll ($ million)	Sales ($ million)	Employees per Establishment (number)	Sales per Establishment ($)	Payroll per Employee ($)
1987	-	-	-	-	-	-	-
1988	-	-	-	-	-	-	-
1989	-	-	-	-	-	-	-
1990	-	-	-	-	-	-	-
1991	-	-	-	-	-	-	-
1992	-	-	-	-	-	-	-
1993	-	-	-	-	-	-	-
1994	-	-	-	-	-	-	-
1995	-	-	-	-	-	-	-
1996	-	-	-	-	-	-	-
1997	1,584	16,402	601.8	9,811.5	10.4	6,194,128.8	36,690.6
1998	1,658	17,413	679.6	10,933.6 e	10.5	6,594,439.1	39,028.3
1999	1,777	19,343	773.7	12,055.7 e	10.9	6,784,276.9	39,999.0
2000	1,766	20,899	874.5	13,177.7 e	11.8	7,461,913.9	41,846.2
2001	1,835	22,287	1,003.7	14,299.8 e	12.1	7,792,817.4	45,035.6
2002	2,487	31,293	1,349.6	15,421.9	12.6	6,201,005.2	43,127.9
2003	2,482	36,869	1,594.4	16,544.0 p	14.9	7,268,812.3 p	43,245.6
2004	2,571 p	36,659 p	1,632.2 p	17,666.1 p	14.6 p	7,391,873.9 p	45,982.0 p
2005	2,729 p	39,948 p	1,794.6 p	18,788.1 p	15.2 p	7,514,935.4 p	47,157.0 p
2006	2,886 p	43,238 p	1,957.0 p	19,910.2 p	15.9 p	7,637,997.0 p	48,332.0 p
2007	3,044 p	46,527 p	2,119.4 p	21,032.3 p	16.6 p	7,761,058.5 p	49,507.0 p

Source: *Economic Census of the United States*, 1997 and 2002. Establishment counts, employment, and payroll are from *County Business Patterns* for non-Census years. This is a newly defined industry. Data for prior years are unavailable at the time of publication but may become available over time. Values followed by 'p' are projections by the editors. Sales data for non-Census years are extrapolations, marked by 'e'.

INDICES OF CHANGE

Year	Establishments (number)	Employment (number)	Payroll ($ million)	Sales ($ million)	Employees per Establishment (number)	Sales per Establishment ($)	Payroll per Employee ($)
1987	-	-	-	-	-	-	-
1992	-	-	-	-	-	-	-
1993	-	-	-	-	-	-	-
1994	-	-	-	-	-	-	-
1995	-	-	-	-	-	-	-
1996	-	-	-	-	-	-	-
1997	63.7	52.4	44.6	63.6	82.5	99.9	85.1
1998	66.7	55.6	50.4	70.9 e	83.3	106.3	90.5
1999	71.5	61.8	57.3	78.2 e	86.5	109.4	92.7
2000	71.0	66.8	64.8	85.4 e	93.7	120.3	97.0
2001	73.8	71.2	74.4	92.7 e	96.0	125.7	104.4
2002	100.0	100.0	100.0	100.0	100.0	100.0	100.0
2003	99.8	117.8	118.1	107.3 p	117.9	117.2 p	100.3
2004	103.4 p	117.1 p	120.9 p	114.6 p	115.6 p	119.2 p	106.6 p
2005	109.7 p	127.7 p	133.0 p	121.8 p	120.9 p	121.2 p	109.3 p
2006	116.1 p	138.2 p	145.0 p	129.1 p	126.2 p	123.2 p	112.1 p
2007	122.4 p	148.7 p	157.0 p	136.4 p	131.5 p	125.2 p	114.8 p

Sources: Same as General Statistics. The values shown reflect change from the base year, 2002. Values above 100 mean greater than 2002, values below 100 mean less than 2002, and a value of 100 in the 1987-2001 or 2003-2007 period means same as 2002. Values followed by a 'p' are projections by the editors; 'e' stands for extrapolation. Data are the most recent available at this level of detail.

SELECTED RATIOS

For 2002	Avg. of All Wholesale	Analyzed Industry	Index	For 2002	Avg. of All Wholesale	Analyzed Industry	Index
Employees per Establishment	15	13	84	Sales per Employee	791,325	492,823	62
Payroll per Establishment	626,122	542,662	87	Sales per Establishment	12,012,387	6,201,005	52
Payroll per Employee	41,161	43,128	105	Expenses per Establishment	na	na	na

Sources: Same as General Statistics. The 'Average of All' column, Wholesale or Retail, represents the average of the sector reported for the most recent complete year available. The Index shows the relationship between the Average and the Analyzed Industry. For example, 100 means that they are equal; 500 that the Analyzed Industry is five times the average; 50 means that the Analyzed Industry is half the national average. The abbreviation 'na' is used to show that data are 'not available'.

LEADING COMPANIES   Number shown: **75**   Total sales ($ mil): **6,465**   Total employment (000): **13.2**

Company Name	Address				CEO Name	Phone	Co. Type	Sales ($ mil)	Empl. (000)
American Builders & Contractors	PO Box 838	Beloit	WI	53511	Kenneth A. Hendricks	608-362-7777	R	1,520*	3.5
Pacific Supply	1735 24th St	Oakland	CA	94623	Curt Gones	510-832-5734	D	1,131*	2.6
Bradco Supply Corp.	13 Production Way	Avenel	NJ	07001		732-382-3400	R	850	1.8
Shook and Fletcher Insulation Co.	PO Box 380501	Birmingham	AL	35238	Wayne W Killion	205-991-7606	R	481*	0.3
Harvey Industries Inc.	PO Box 3894	Boston	MA	02241	Alan Marlow	781-899-3500	R	390*	0.1
Patrick Industries Inc.	1800 S 14th St	Elkhart	IN	46516	Keith V Kankel	219-294-7511	P	302	1.1
Seven D Wholesale	PO Box 67	Gallitzin	PA	16641	Donald A DeGol Sr	814-886-8151	D	300*	0.4
Standard Roofings Inc.	PO Box 1410	Eatontown	NJ	07724	John Askin	732-542-3300	R	99*	0.2
Gulfside Supply Inc.	501 N Reo St	Tampa	FL	33609	James Resch	813-636-9808	R	83*	0.3
Building Products Inc.	PO Box 1390	Watertown	SD	57201	Lee Schull	605-886-3495	R	74*	0.1
Western Products Inc.	117 23rd St N	Fargo	ND	58102	Michael J Bullinger	701-293-5310	R	64*	0.1
Sunniland Corp.	PO Box 8001	Sanford	FL	32772	Lee Moore	407-322-2424	R	60*	0.2
Builders General Supply Co.	PO Box 95	Little Silver	NJ	07739	Timothy J Shaheen	732-747-0808	R	60*	0.2
Cooperative Reserve Supply Inc.	1100 Iron Horse Pk	Billerica	MA	01862		617-864-1444	R	50*	<0.1
Badger Corrugating Co.	PO Box 1837	La Crosse	WI	54601	Michael J Sexauer	608-788-0100	R	49*	0.1
J and H Aluminum	187 Enterprise Dr	Somerset	KY	42501	Michael Hill	606-679-8660	R	39*	<0.1
Advanced Building Products Inc.	5501 Jefferson Hwy	New Orleans	LA	70123	Chris Anderson	504-733-8200	R	35*	<0.1
Rhodes Supply Company Inc.	9793 State Rte 303	Mayfield	KY	42066	Gene Rhodes	270-382-2185	R	34*	<0.1
Distribution International	PO Box 23847	Houston	TX	77228		713-428-3900	R	33*	<0.1
Mid-South Building Supply	5640 Sunnyside	Beltsville	MD	20705		301-513-9000	R	30*	<0.1
Heines Insulators Incorporated	PO Box 99	Rockaway	NJ	07866	Steven Raia	973-586-2911	R	29*	<0.1
Roofing Supply Ltd.	PO Box 671627	Houston	TX	77267		281-447-7759	R	28*	<0.1
Insulation Supply Company Inc.	PO Box 1633	Augusta	GA	30903	John Morris	706-724-6222	R	25*	<0.1
Carter-Waters Corp.	PO Box 412676	Kansas City	MO	64141	Jeff Hanes	816-471-2570	R	23*	<0.1
Rose and Walker Supply Inc.	3974 N Indianapolis	Columbus	IN	47201	Ronald Rose	812-372-8181	R	23*	<0.1
Contractors Roofing & Supply Inc.	1760 W Terra Ln	O Fallon	MO	63366	Jerry Schulte	636-946-2710	R	22*	<0.1
Dallas-Fort Worth Roofing Supply	PO Box 540817	Dallas	TX	75354	Vin Perella	214-358-2600	R	22*	<0.1
G and F Roof Supply Inc.	PO Box 3169	Santa Fe Springs	CA	90670	Ron Farrell	562-929-7100	R	22*	<0.1
Pacific Insulation Co.	2741 Yates Ave	Los Angeles	CA	90040	Robert Fults	323-278-8350	R	22*	<0.1
Thomas Mc Lean Inc.	266 Broadway St	Buffalo	NY	14204	James Mc Lean	716-852-2531	R	22*	<0.1
T.J.T. Inc.	PO Box 278	Emmett	ID	83617		208-365-5321	P	20	0.1
Stelwagon Manufacturing Co.	1516 Fayette St	Conshohocken	PA	19428	Charles Ringwalt	610-941-2828	R	20*	<0.1
United Subcontractors Inc.	49 Venture Way	Sykesville	MD	21784	Larry Helminiak	410-795-0600	R	20*	<0.1
Albeni Falls Building Supply Inc.	520 E Hwy 2	Oldtown	ID	83822	David Melbourn	208-437-3153	R	19*	<0.1
V-Line Corporation L.L.C.	PO Box 68109	Indianapolis	IN	46268		317-546-1588	R	19*	<0.1
ABC Supply	4833 Singleton Blvd	Dallas	TX	75212		214-630-3940	R	19*	<0.1
Statewide Wholesale Inc.	PO Box 36216	Denver	CO	80236	Randy Rehbein	303-744-7111	R	19*	<0.1
Denver Fabrication Inc.	PO Box 149	Mooresville	NC	28115		704-663-1261	R	17*	<0.1
Jesus People U S A Full Gospel	2950 N Western Ave	Chicago	IL	60618		773-509-0400	R	17*	<0.1
Central Builder Supplies	6800 NW 22nd St	Gainesville	FL	32653	C Veley	352-372-1111	R	16*	<0.1
Roofline Inc.	PO Box 24038	Eugene	OR	97402	Ron Hagen	541-345-1253	R	15*	<0.1
Wilson Wholesale Supply Co.	405 Barrington Rd	Wauconda	IL	60084	William Wilson	847-487-5055	R	15*	<0.1
Sea Coast Supply	PO Box 957	Englewood	FL	34295		941-474-8185	R	15*	<0.1
Merit Building Supply Inc.	2952 Falling Waters	Lake Villa	IL	60046	Dean Sjong	847-265-5200	R	14*	<0.1
Cordova Floors and Installation	PO Box 1387	Cordova	TN	38088	Scott Gallagher	901-756-0009	R	14*	<0.1
Quality Roofing Supplies Inc.	95 Van Guysling	Schenectady	NY	12305	Frederick Bogdon	518-393-1448	R	13*	<0.1
Urethane Contractors Supply	PO Box 6460	Phoenix	AZ	85005	Jerry Whitaker	602-269-9711	R	13*	<0.1
NB Handy Company Inc.	PO Box 11258	Lynchburg	VA	24506		434-847-2473	R	13*	<0.1
Dixie Building Supplies Inc.	PO Box 31601	Tampa	FL	33631	Larry Comegys	813-871-4811	S	12*	<0.1
Ruffin and Payne Inc.	PO Box 27286	Richmond	VA	23261	George Haw	804-329-2691	R	12*	0.1
Bay Insulation of Kansas City Inc.	2929 Walker Dr	Green Bay	WI	54311	Arnold Schmidt	920-437-5484	R	11*	<0.1
Bigham Insulation and Supply Inc.	PO Box 22146	Fort Lauderdale	FL	33335	Robert Bryant	954-522-2887	R	11*	<0.1
Cameron Ashley Building Prods	6475 E 56th Ave	Commerce City	CO	80022		303-289-4586	R	11*	<0.1
Installed Products USA L.L.C.	3000 Hadley Rd	South Plainfield	NJ	07080		908-756-5455	R	11*	<0.1
Neuse Install	690 Old Johnson Rd	Wendell	NC	27591	Danny Langston	919-796-2491	R	11*	<0.1
Pacific Coast Supply L.L.C.	PO Box 3717	Modesto	CA	95352		209-521-2466	D	11*	<0.1
Roofing Supply of Atlanta Inc.	PO Box 9309	Marietta	GA	30065	Rodney Burns	770-565-1955	R	11*	<0.1
Spartan Supply Co.	PO Box 735	Culver City	CA	90232	Richard Betts	310-837-5351	R	11*	<0.1
Wholesale Roofing Supply Inc.	104 E Trinity Blvd	Grand Prairie	TX	75050	Rick McClaughlin	972-263-8190	R	11*	<0.1
Thomas Roofing Supply Co.	PO Box 374	Seaford	DE	19973	Daniel Thomas	302-629-4521	R	10*	<0.1
Central Coating Company Inc.	670 S Pine St	Madera	CA	93637	John Nolan	559-673-0074	R	10*	<0.1
Climate Guard Construction	4235 170th St	Clinton	IA	52732	Glen Little	563-241-1489	R	10*	<0.1
RS Roofing and Sheet Metal Inc.	39 W Prospect St	Nanuet	NY	10954	Richard Shand	845-623-8404	R	10*	<0.1
Ar-Jay Building Products Inc.	PO Box 10017	Cedar Rapids	IA	52410	Ralph Palmer	319-393-5885	R	9*	0.1
Queens Commercial Service	349 Young Bend Rd	Weatherford	TX	76087	Gary Crawford	817-613-8818	R	9*	<0.1
CWCI Supply Inc.	749 9th Ave	City of Industry	CA	91745	Richard Davis	626-369-4424	R	9*	<0.1
Larry O Crother Inc.	11386 Amalgam	Rancho Cordova	CA	95670	Larry Crother	916-635-7171	R	9*	<0.1
McDonald Metal/Roofing Supply	1 Ave M	Brooklyn	NY	11230	Richard Rosenthal	718-339-0555	R	9*	<0.1
Pace Supply Corp.	PO Box 333	Lansdale	PA	19446	Alger Edwards	215-368-5063	R	9*	<0.1
Seamless Siding Management	111 Canfield Bldg B	Randolph	NJ	07869	Jerry Damora	973-895-4050	R	9*	<0.1
Senez Roofing and Builder, Ernest	1060 E Ind Dr C	Orange City	FL	32763	Ernest Senez	386-774-4950	R	9*	<0.1
Parsons Sales Company Inc.	310 George Ave	Wilkes Barre	PA	18705	Anthony Bartoletti	570-655-3587	R	8*	<0.1
Building & Industrial Wholesale	PO Box 3365	Parkersburg	WV	26103	Revis Stevenson	304-485-6500	S	3*	<0.1
Wesco Cedar Inc.	PO Box 40847	Eugene	OR	97404	LF Plummer	541-688-5020	R	3*	<0.1
Holmquist Lumber Inc.	200 N Logan Ave	Oakland	NE	68045	Calvin Anderson	402-685-5641	R	2*	<0.1

Source: *Ward's Business Directory of U.S. Private and Public Companies*, Volumes 1 and 2, 2005. The company type code used is as follows: P - Public, R - Private, S - Subsidiary, D - Division, J - Joint Venture, A - Affiliate, G - Group. Sales are in millions of dollars, employees are in thousands. An asterisk (*) indicates an estimated sales volume. The symbol < stands for 'less than'. Company names and addresses are truncated, in some cases, to fit into the available space.

OCCUPATIONS EMPLOYED BY LUMBER & OTHER CONSTRUCTION MATERIALS WHOLESALE

Occupation	% of Total 2004	Change to 2014	Occupation	% of Total 2004	Change to 2014
Sales reps, wholesale & manufacturing, exc tech	15.9	18.2	Shipping, receiving, & traffic clerks	1.9	7.0
Laborers & freight, stock, & material movers, hand	11.7	6.4	First-line supervisors/managers of non-retail sales work	1.7	9.3
Truck drivers, heavy & tractor-trailer	9.3	18.0	Order clerks	1.4	-23.3
Industrial truck & tractor operators	5.0	6.4	Carpenters	1.1	18.2
Truck drivers, light or delivery services	4.5	18.0	Secretaries, except legal, medical, & executive	1.1	-0.5
Team assemblers	4.3	18.2	First-line supervisors/managers of office workers	1.1	7.1
General & operations managers	2.8	17.0	First-line supervisors/managers of transporation workers	1.0	18.2
Bookkeeping, accounting, & auditing clerks	2.7	6.4	First-line supervisors/managers of production workers	1.0	18.2
Office clerks, general	2.5	5.2	Retail salespersons	1.0	18.2
Stock clerks & order fillers	2.3	-9.5			

Source: *Industry-Occupation Matrix*, Bureau of Labor Statistics. These data are reported based on 4-digit NAICS categories but have been matched to corresponding 6-digit NAICS industry codes. The change reported for each occupation to the year 2014 is a percent of growth or decline as estimated by the Bureau of Labor Statistics. The abbreviation nec stands for 'not elsewhere classified.'

LOCATION BY STATE AND REGIONAL CONCENTRATION

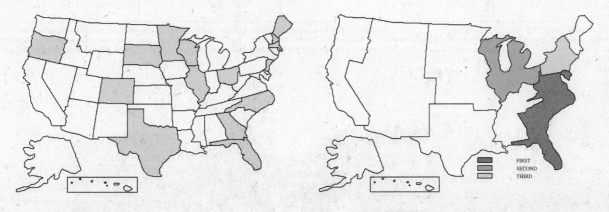

FIRST
SECOND
THIRD

INDUSTRY DATA BY STATE

State	Establishments Total (number)	% of U.S.	Employment Total (number)	% of U.S.	Per Estab.	Payroll Total ($ mil.)	Per Empl. ($)	Sales Total ($ mil.)	% of U.S.	Per Estab. ($)
Texas	183	7.4	2,970	9.4	16	123.5	41,576	1,665.4	10.8	9,100,727
Ohio	132	5.3	2,108	6.7	16	101.1	47,954	1,050.5	6.8	7,958,576
Florida	165	6.6	1,674	5.3	10	67.3	40,218	877.4	5.7	5,317,412
California	160	6.4	1,738	5.5	11	78.3	45,032	816.7	5.3	5,104,344
Illinois	117	4.7	1,391	4.4	12	68.2	49,049	725.2	4.7	6,198,444
Pennsylvania	115	4.6	1,443	4.6	13	62.6	43,396	710.8	4.6	6,181,296
New York	111	4.5	1,400	4.5	13	68.0	48,566	632.0	4.1	5,693,441
New Jersey	78	3.1	1,257	4.0	16	56.7	45,073	580.9	3.8	7,447,795
Wisconsin	52	2.1	944	3.0	18	42.4	44,922	502.1	3.2	9,655,442
Minnesota	42	1.7	868	2.8	21	40.6	46,797	499.8	3.2	11,899,143
Massachusetts	51	2.1	770	2.4	15	40.5	52,553	465.3	3.0	9,122,647
Georgia	105	4.2	897	2.9	9	40.7	45,370	462.4	3.0	4,403,714
North Carolina	90	3.6	1,160	3.7	13	47.8	41,176	445.3	2.9	4,947,611
Colorado	54	2.2	745	2.4	14	30.3	40,728	422.7	2.7	7,827,444
Virginia	69	2.8	837	2.7	12	35.3	42,165	365.3	2.4	5,294,696
Missouri	69	2.8	770	2.4	11	30.5	39,566	304.6	2.0	4,413,971
Washington	65	2.6	764	2.4	12	31.1	40,762	298.2	1.9	4,587,354
Tennessee	66	2.7	484	1.5	7	19.5	40,190	224.7	1.5	3,403,924
Oregon	36	1.4	448	1.4	12	18.5	41,219	217.1	1.4	6,031,222
South Carolina	50	2.0	422	1.3	8	16.6	39,275	210.3	1.4	4,205,440
Alabama	54	2.2	382	1.2	7	14.2	37,291	197.6	1.3	3,658,722
Connecticut	28	1.1	488	1.6	17	23.1	47,381	192.1	1.2	6,862,143
Iowa	34	1.4	440	1.4	13	15.2	34,568	156.2	1.0	4,594,912
Kentucky	23	0.9	389	1.2	17	17.3	44,437	145.9	0.9	6,345,130
Louisiana	42	1.7	382	1.2	9	11.9	31,236	138.1	0.9	3,288,143
New Hampshire	12	0.5	217	0.7	18	10.4	47,880	118.1	0.8	9,840,583
Oklahoma	29	1.2	240	0.8	8	9.0	37,687	99.2	0.6	3,419,241
Maine	12	0.5	215	0.7	18	8.7	40,298	90.3	0.6	7,521,250
Utah	22	0.9	203	0.6	9	7.2	35,433	89.9	0.6	4,085,500
South Dakota	11	0.4	153	0.5	14	6.0	39,242	78.3	0.5	7,122,545
Nebraska	19	0.8	169	0.5	9	7.0	41,254	72.4	0.5	3,812,947
Mississippi	17	0.7	120	0.4	7	4.4	36,783	68.4	0.4	4,022,353
Hawaii	13	0.5	123	0.4	9	5.2	42,276	68.1	0.4	5,242,077

Continued on next page.

INDUSTRY DATA BY STATE - Continued

	Establishments		Employment			Payroll		Sales		
State	Total (number)	% of U.S.	Total (number)	% of U.S.	Per Estab.	Total ($ mil.)	Per Empl. ($)	Total ($ mil.)	% of U.S.	Per Estab. ($)
West Virginia	12	0.5	117	0.4	10	4.4	37,325	54.0	0.3	4,496,667
Nevada	12	0.5	114	0.4	10	4.2	36,860	47.5	0.3	3,962,250
North Dakota	8	0.3	67	0.2	8	2.7	40,254	38.1	0.2	4,758,625
Montana	12	0.5	80	0.3	7	2.6	32,300	36.3	0.2	3,026,500
New Mexico	9	0.4	62	0.2	7	2.4	38,129	31.0	0.2	3,443,444
Idaho	14	0.6	97	0.3	7	3.3	33,784	30.8	0.2	2,199,071
Alaska	5	0.2	35	0.1	7	1.7	47,400	14.1	0.1	2,826,400
Wyoming	7	0.3	10	-	1	0.6	63,900	5.8	-	822,000
Michigan	73	2.9	500-999	-	-	(D)	-	(D)	-	-
Maryland	54	2.2	500-999	-	-	(D)	-	(D)	-	-
Indiana	51	2.1	1000-2499	-	-	(D)	-	(D)	-	-
Arizona	33	1.3	250-499	-	-	(D)	-	(D)	-	-
Arkansas	26	1.0	100-249	-	-	(D)	-	(D)	-	-
Kansas	21	0.8	100-249	-	-	(D)	-	(D)	-	-
Delaware	8	0.3	20-99	-	-	(D)	-	(D)	-	-
Rhode Island	7	0.3	20-99	-	-	(D)	-	(D)	-	-
Vermont	6	0.2	20-99	-	-	(D)	-	(D)	-	-

Source: 2002 *Economic Census*. The states are in descending order of sales or establishments (if sales data are missing for the majority). The symbol (D) appears when data are withheld to prevent disclosure of competitive information. States marked with (D) are sorted by number of establishments. A dash (-) indicates that the data element cannot be calculated. Shaded *states* on the state map indicate those states which have proportionately greater representation in the industry than would be indicated by the states population; the ratio is based on total sales or number of establishments. Shaded *regions* indicate where the industry is regionally most concentrated.

NAICS 423390 - OTHER CONSTRUCTION MATERIAL MERCHANT WHOLESALERS

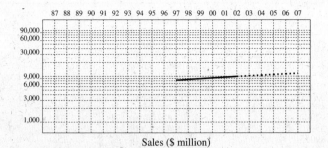

Sales ($ million)

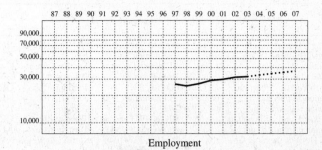

Employment

GENERAL STATISTICS

Year	Establishments (number)	Employment (number)	Payroll ($ million)	Sales ($ million)	Employees per Establishment (number)	Sales per Establishment ($)	Payroll per Employee ($)
1987	-	-	-	-	-	-	-
1988	-	-	-	-	-	-	-
1989	-	-	-	-	-	-	-
1990	-	-	-	-	-	-	-
1991	-	-	-	-	-	-	-
1992	-	-	-	-	-	-	-
1993	-	-	-	-	-	-	-
1994	-	-	-	-	-	-	-
1995	-	-	-	-	-	-	-
1996	-	-	-	-	-	-	-
1997	2,890	26,475	806.2	8,196.7	9.2	2,836,228.4	30,451.4
1998	2,904	25,278	844.0	8,539.0 e	8.7	2,940,413.2	33,388.7
1999	2,869	26,743	949.7	8,881.2 e	9.3	3,095,580.3	35,512.1
2000	2,887	29,044	1,043.9	9,223.5 e	10.1	3,194,832.0	35,943.6
2001	2,922	29,852	1,128.7	9,565.7 e	10.2	3,273,696.1	37,809.0
2002	3,050	31,469	1,180.1	9,908.0	10.3	3,248,524.6	37,500.4
2003	3,028	31,913	1,285.5	10,250.3 p	10.5	3,414,270.6 p	40,281.6
2004	3,044 p	33,226 p	1,361.0 p	10,592.5 p	10.9 p	3,504,572.9 p	41,556.8 p
2005	3,071 p	34,361 p	1,442.8 p	10,934.8 p	11.2 p	3,594,875.2 p	42,985.8 p
2006	3,098 p	35,497 p	1,524.5 p	11,277.0 p	11.5 p	3,685,177.5 p	44,414.8 p
2007	3,125 p	36,633 p	1,606.3 p	11,619.3 p	11.8 p	3,775,479.9 p	45,843.7 p

Source: *Economic Census of the United States*, 1997 and 2002. Establishment counts, employment, and payroll are from *County Business Patterns* for non-Census years. This is a newly defined industry. Data for prior years are unavailable at the time of publication but may become available over time. Values followed by 'p' are projections by the editors. Sales data for non-Census years are extrapolations, marked by 'e'.

INDICES OF CHANGE

Year	Establishments (number)	Employment (number)	Payroll ($ million)	Sales ($ million)	Employees per Establishment (number)	Sales per Establishment ($)	Payroll per Employee ($)
1987	-	-	-	-	-	-	-
1992	-	-	-	-	-	-	-
1993	-	-	-	-	-	-	-
1994	-	-	-	-	-	-	-
1995	-	-	-	-	-	-	-
1996	-	-	-	-	-	-	-
1997	94.8	84.1	68.3	82.7	89.3	87.3	81.2
1998	95.2	80.3	71.5	86.2 e	84.5	90.5	89.0
1999	94.1	85.0	80.5	89.6 e	90.3	95.3	94.7
2000	94.7	92.3	88.5	93.1 e	98.1	98.3	95.8
2001	95.8	94.9	95.6	96.5 e	99.0	100.8	100.8
2002	100.0	100.0	100.0	100.0	100.0	100.0	100.0
2003	99.3	101.4	108.9	103.5 p	102.3	105.1 p	107.4
2004	99.8 p	105.6 p	115.3 p	106.9 p	106.0 p	107.9 p	110.8 p
2005	100.7 p	109.2 p	122.3 p	110.4 p	108.9 p	110.7 p	114.6 p
2006	101.6 p	112.8 p	129.2 p	113.8 p	111.7 p	113.4 p	118.4 p
2007	102.5 p	116.4 p	136.1 p	117.3 p	114.5 p	114.9 p	122.2 p

Sources: Same as General Statistics. The values shown reflect change from the base year, 2002. Values above 100 mean greater than 2002, values below 100 mean less than 2002, and a value of 100 in the 1987-2001 or 2003-2007 period means same as 2002. Values followed by a 'p' are projections by the editors; 'e' stands for extrapolation. Data are the most recent available at this level of detail.

SELECTED RATIOS

For 2002	Avg. of All Wholesale	Analyzed Industry	Index	For 2002	Avg. of All Wholesale	Analyzed Industry	Index
Employees per Establishment	15	10	69	Sales per Employee	791,325	314,850	40
Payroll per Establishment	626,122	386,918	62	Sales per Establishment	12,012,387	3,248,525	27
Payroll per Employee	41,161	37,500	91	Expenses per Establishment	na	na	na

Sources: Same as General Statistics. The 'Average of All' column, Wholesale or Retail, represents the average of the sector reported for the most recent complete year available. The Index shows the relationship between the Average and the Analyzed Industry. For example, 100 means that they are equal; 500 that the Analyzed Industry is five times the average; 50 means that the Analyzed Industry is half the national average. The abbreviation 'na' is used to show that data are 'not available'.

LEADING COMPANIES   Number shown: **75**   Total sales ($ mil): **48,641**   Total employment (000): **149.6**

Company Name	Address				CEO Name	Phone	Co. Type	Sales ($ mil)	Empl. (000)
Lowe's Companies Inc.	PO Box 1111	N. Wilkesboro	NC	28656		336-658-4000	P	36,464	123.0
Allied Building Products Corp.	15 E Union Ave	East Rutherford	NJ	07073	Bob Feury	201-507-8400	S	2,257*	2.0
Building Materials Holding Corp.	4 Embarcadero Ctr	San Francisco	CA	94111	Robert E Mellor	415-627-9100	P	2,092	12.0
AFGD Inc.	1600 Parkwood	Atlanta	GA	30339	John Stilwell	770-951-2343	S	1,825*	1.5
North Pacific Group Inc.	PO Box 3915	Portland	OR	97208		503-231-1166	R	1,227	0.8
Bradco Supply Corp.	13 Production Way	Avenel	NJ	07001		732-382-3400	R	850	1.8
Patrick Industries Inc.	1800 S 14th St	Elkhart	IN	46516	Keith V Kankel	219-294-7511	P	302	1.1
OrePac Building Products	30170 SW Ore Pac	Wilsonville	OR	97070		503-682-5050	R	300*	<0.1
Fontaine International Inc.	5000 Grantswood	Birmingham	AL	35210	Brian Ballard	205-421-4300	S	255*	1.0
AC Houston Lumber Co.	PO Box 337410	North Las Vegas	NV	89033		702-633-5000	R	253*	0.3
Plastival Inc.	1685 Holmes Rd	Elgin	IL	60123	Jim Quinn	847-931-4771	R	231*	0.2
K and A Lumber Company Inc.	1001 W Mowry Dr	Homestead	FL	33030	Richard Jackson II	305-245-5312	R	179*	0.1
United Hardware Distributing Co.	5005 Nathan Ln N	Plymouth	MN	55442	David A Heider	763-559-1800	R	144*	0.4
Mid-AM Building Supply Inc.	PO Box 645	Moberly	MO	65270	Joseph I Knaebel	816-263-2140	R	135*	0.2
H.W. Jenkins Lumber Co.	PO Box 18347	Memphis	TN	38181	HW Jenkins Jr	901-363-7641	R	114*	0.1
Ted Lansing Corp.	PO Box 9489	Richmond	VA	23228	J Lansing	804-266-8893	R	101*	<0.1
Riggs Supply Corp.	320 Cedar St	Kennett	MO	63857	Aldolfis Riggs III	573-888-9501	R	91*	0.4
Butler-Johnson Corp.	PO Box 612110	San Jose	CA	95161	Rolston Johnson	408-259-1800	R	90*	0.1
Everglades Lumber	6991 SW 8th St	Miami	FL	33144	Ovi Vento	305-261-1155	R	85*	0.3
Kobrin Builders Supply Inc.	1924 W Princeton St	Orlando	FL	32806	Harvey Kobrin	407-843-1000	R	72*	0.2
Wille Brothers Inc.	2154 Vermont St	Blue Island	IL	60406	Curt Wille	708-388-0045	R	71*	<0.1
Builders General Supply Co.	PO Box 95	Little Silver	NJ	07739	Timothy J Shaheen	732-747-0808	R	60*	0.2
Drivekore Inc.	PO Box 2004	Mechanicsburg	PA	17055	Dan Emanuel	717-766-7636	R	59*	0.1
T.H. Rogers Lumber Co.	PO Box 5770	Edmond	OK	73083	John M Kennedy	405-330-2181	R	57*	0.2
Hallmark Building Supplies Inc.	6060 N 77th St	Milwaukee	WI	53218	O Joe Balthazar	414-464-5000	R	55*	<0.1
Jamieson Manufacturing Co.	PO Box 763760	Dallas	TX	75376		214-339-8384	R	52*	<0.1
Nu-Way Concrete Forms Inc.	4190 Hofmeister	St. Louis	MO	63125	Gerald Rhomberg	314-544-1214	R	52*	0.2
Prestige Lumber and Supplies Inc.	1985 State Rd 419	Longwood	FL	32750	Stephen Rominger	407-323-5662	R	52*	<0.1
Mentor Lumber and Supply Inc.	7180 N Center St	Mentor	OH	44060	Robert Sanderson	440-255-8814	R	45*	0.2
Fargo Glass and Paint Co.	1801 7th Ave N	Fargo	ND	58102	Gerald Lovell	701-235-4441	R	42*	0.1
Pioneer Industries L.L.C.	PO Box 537	Owensville	MO	65066		573-437-4104	R	41*	0.1
Ellsworth Builders Supply Inc.	261 State St	Ellsworth	ME	04605	Austin Goodyear	207-667-4974	R	37*	0.2
Indiana Supply Corp.	3835 E 21st St	Indianapolis	IN	46218	Dave Draga	317-359-5451	R	37*	<0.1
Rhodes Supply Company Inc.	9793 State Rte 303	Mayfield	KY	42066	Gene Rhodes	270-382-2185	R	34*	<0.1
Dairyman's Supply Co.	PO Box 528	Mayfield	KY	42066	George Cook	270-247-5641	R	31*	<0.1
Lumberyard Suppliers Inc.	3405 N Main St	East Peoria	IL	61611	Troy Reed	309-694-4356	R	30*	<0.1
Mid-South Building Supply	5640 Sunnyside	Beltsville	MD	20705		301-513-9000	R	30*	<0.1
Custom Bilt Metals	9845 Joe Vargas	El Monte	CA	91733	Anthony Chiovare	626-579-5868	R	30*	<0.1
California Panel and Veneer Co.	PO Box 3250	Cerritos	CA	90703	John Fahs	562-926-5834	R	29*	<0.1
W.A. Wilson INC.	PO Box 6712	Wheeling	WV	26003	Robert H Hartong	304-232-2200	R	28*	<0.1
Westshore Glass Corp.	PO Box 15216	Tampa	FL	33684	Ron Brock	813-884-2561	R	28*	0.1
RP Johnson and Son Inc.	10 Mill Rd	Andover	NH	03216	Stephen Johnson	603-735-5544	R	28*	<0.1
Sweetman Construction Co.	1404 N Louise	Sioux Falls	SD	57107	G Sweetman	605-357-6000	R	27*	0.2
Oregon Pacific Building Products	5500 S Federal Way	Boise	ID	83716		208-345-0562	R	26*	<0.1
Dana Kepner Co.	700 Alcott St	Denver	CO	80204	Wayne E Johnson	303-623-6161	R	25*	<0.1
Glazed Products Inc.	PO Box 2404	Martinsville	VA	24113	Kevin Farrell	276-632-7211	R	25*	<0.1
Western Pacific Building Materials	2805 NW 31st Ave	Portland	OR	97210	Ed Meredith	503-224-9142	R	25*	<0.1
Carter-Waters Corp.	PO Box 412676	Kansas City	MO	64141	Jeff Hanes	816-471-2570	R	23*	<0.1
Brin Glass Co.	2300 N 2nd St	Minneapolis	MN	55411	Pat Rome	612-529-9671	R	23*	0.2
Pinkerton Building Supplies Inc.	3215 Lafayette St	Evansdale	IA	50707	Doug Justis	319-233-3361	R	23*	<0.1
Bruce Kreofsky and Sons Inc.	865 Enterprise SW	Plainview	MN	55964	Dennis Kreofsky	507-534-3855	R	21*	<0.1
Winroc Corporation Midwest	5262 Glenbrook N	Saint Paul	MN	55128	Paul Vanderberg	651-777-8222	R	21*	<0.1
Genesee Reserve Supply Inc.	PO Box 20619	Rochester	NY	14602	Richard Buck	585-292-7040	R	21*	<0.1
East Coast Mill Sales Co.	490 Rutherford R	Charlestown	MA	02129		617-241-0440	R	20*	<0.1
Custom Glass Distributors Inc.	1095 E 2nd St	Reno	NV	89502	Kevin Depaoli	775-329-4265	R	20*	<0.1
Stelwagon Manufacturing Co.	1516 Fayette St	Conshohocken	PA	19428	Charles Ringwalt	610-941-2828	R	20*	<0.1
Holmes Drywall Supply Inc.	1821 Broadway St	Kansas City	MO	64108		816-471-7595	R	19*	<0.1
Calrepco Inc.	PO Box 3145	La Habra	CA	90632	Dave Rohrich	562-694-3618	R	19*	<0.1
Cargotec Inc.	12233 Williams St	Perrysburg	OH	43551	Lennart Brelin	419-482-6000	R	18*	<0.1
Cofer Brothers Inc.	PO Box 286	Tucker	GA	30084	Chip Cofer	770-938-3200	R	18*	<0.1
County Home Improvement Center	PO Box 490	Saint Peters	MO	63376	David Hendrix	636-278-5080	R	18*	<0.1
Edward George Co.	4251 W 129th St	Alsip	IL	60803		708-371-0696	R	18*	<0.1
Milwaukee Stove & Furnace	5070 W State St	Milwaukee	WI	53208	Tom Engler	414-258-0300	R	18*	<0.1
Mid-Carolina Steel Recycling Inc.	PO Box 3764	Columbia	SC	29230	Fred Seidenberg	803-786-9888	R	17*	<0.1
Syar Industries Inc.	PO Box 2540	Napa	CA	94558		707-643-3261	R	17*	<0.1
Dillman and Upton Inc.	607 Woodward Ave	Rochester	MI	48307	Todd Upton	248-651-9411	R	17*	<0.1
Fort Worth Lumber Co.	PO Box 969	Fort Worth	TX	76101	Emily Fiesler	817-293-5211	R	17*	<0.1
Caylor Industrial Sales Inc.	PO Box 4659	Dalton	GA	30719	Raymond Caylor	706-226-3198	R	17*	<0.1
American Flat Glass Distributors	2522 Westcott Blvd	Knoxville	TN	37931		865-691-2040	R	16*	<0.1
Gregory Supply Company Inc.	PO Box 448	Burlington	VT	05402	Raymond Heatherton	802-863-3428	R	16*	<0.1
Richard A Johnson Cedar Products	459 E 15th St	Tacoma	WA	98421	Fred Nix	253-383-4603	R	16*	<0.1
Shoreline Glass Company Inc.	1 Mth Plz	Hillside	IL	60162	Lyle Hill	312-829-9500	R	16*	<0.1
Superior Scaffold Services Inc.	520 E Luzerne St	Philadelphia	PA	19124	Gary Bianchini	215-423-0100	R	16*	<0.1
Wholesale Glass Distributors Inc.	1800 Transport Ave	Memphis	TN	38116	Chet Day	901-332-2200	R	16*	<0.1
JRD Trading Inc.	2505 Tweedy Blvd	South Gate	CA	90280	Jose Ramirez	323-563-3333	R	15*	<0.1

Source: *Ward's Business Directory of U.S. Private and Public Companies*, Volumes 1 and 2, 2005. The company type code used is as follows: P - Public, R - Private, S - Subsidiary, D - Division, J - Joint Venture, A - Affiliate, G - Group. Sales are in millions of dollars, employees are in thousands. An asterisk (*) indicates an estimated sales volume. The symbol < stands for 'less than'. Company names and addresses are truncated, in some cases, to fit into the available space.

OCCUPATIONS EMPLOYED BY LUMBER & OTHER CONSTRUCTION MATERIALS WHOLESALE

Occupation	% of Total 2004	Change to 2014	Occupation	% of Total 2004	Change to 2014
Sales reps, wholesale & manufacturing, exc tech	15.9	18.2	Shipping, receiving, & traffic clerks	1.9	7.0
Laborers & freight, stock, & material movers, hand	11.7	6.4	First-line supervisors/managers of non-retail sales work	1.7	9.3
Truck drivers, heavy & tractor-trailer	9.3	18.0	Order clerks	1.4	-23.3
Industrial truck & tractor operators	5.0	6.4	Carpenters	1.1	18.2
Truck drivers, light or delivery services	4.5	18.0	Secretaries, except legal, medical, & executive	1.1	-0.5
Team assemblers	4.3	18.2	First-line supervisors/managers of office workers	1.1	7.1
General & operations managers	2.8	17.0	First-line supervisors/managers of transporation workers	1.0	18.2
Bookkeeping, accounting, & auditing clerks	2.7	6.4	First-line supervisors/managers of production workers	1.0	18.2
Office clerks, general	2.5	5.2	Retail salespersons	1.0	18.2
Stock clerks & order fillers	2.3	-9.5			

Source: Industry-Occupation Matrix, Bureau of Labor Statistics. These data are reported based on 4-digit NAICS categories but have been matched to corresponding 6-digit NAICS industry codes. The change reported for each occupation to the year 2014 is a percent of growth or decline as estimated by the Bureau of Labor Statistics. The abbreviation nec stands for 'not elsewhere classified.'

LOCATION BY STATE AND REGIONAL CONCENTRATION

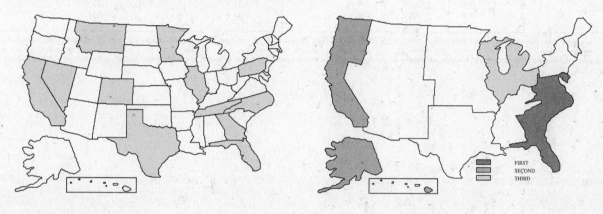

INDUSTRY DATA BY STATE

State	Establishments Total (number)	% of U.S.	Employment Total (number)	% of U.S.	Per Estab.	Payroll Total ($ mil.)	Per Empl. ($)	Sales Total ($ mil.)	% of U.S.	Per Estab. ($)
California	340	11.2	4,027	12.8	12	162.1	40,248	1,242.7	12.7	3,654,853
Illinois	140	4.6	1,888	6.0	13	80.2	42,499	828.1	8.4	5,915,029
Texas	220	7.2	2,742	8.7	12	96.7	35,265	794.4	8.1	3,610,745
Florida	231	7.6	1,641	5.2	7	57.5	35,063	524.4	5.3	2,269,939
Pennsylvania	115	3.8	1,455	4.6	13	62.9	43,210	515.4	5.3	4,481,400
Minnesota	36	1.2	1,002	3.2	28	46.0	45,887	474.2	4.8	13,173,083
Georgia	117	3.8	1,022	3.3	9	40.5	39,649	416.9	4.2	3,563,598
New York	156	5.1	1,347	4.3	9	49.9	37,039	390.0	4.0	2,499,731
Ohio	125	4.1	1,513	4.8	12	53.8	35,547	335.9	3.4	2,687,416
North Carolina	97	3.2	1,143	3.6	12	41.1	35,953	330.1	3.4	3,403,309
Tennessee	74	2.4	982	3.1	13	35.8	36,490	328.7	3.3	4,442,176
Washington	86	2.8	699	2.2	8	23.3	33,343	195.4	2.0	2,272,174
Virginia	72	2.4	684	2.2	10	24.5	35,830	194.1	2.0	2,696,444
Massachusetts	61	2.0	631	2.0	10	26.2	41,544	190.7	1.9	3,126,000
Wisconsin	62	2.0	620	2.0	10	21.1	34,023	161.7	1.6	2,608,790
Missouri	62	2.0	599	1.9	10	20.8	34,693	151.1	1.5	2,437,823
Colorado	67	2.2	529	1.7	8	18.6	35,070	145.0	1.5	2,163,507
Louisiana	54	1.8	465	1.5	9	15.5	33,359	133.1	1.4	2,464,907
Nevada	33	1.1	275	0.9	8	11.2	40,698	116.3	1.2	3,522,818
Alabama	50	1.6	424	1.4	8	14.2	33,559	115.5	1.2	2,309,240
Oregon	46	1.5	409	1.3	9	14.2	34,829	111.8	1.1	2,429,870
Iowa	34	1.1	446	1.4	13	15.7	35,278	106.6	1.1	3,136,147
Kentucky	36	1.2	288	0.9	8	10.4	36,056	87.3	0.9	2,425,694
Oklahoma	37	1.2	261	0.8	7	8.9	34,096	77.5	0.8	2,094,676
South Carolina	29	1.0	270	0.9	9	9.0	33,196	69.8	0.7	2,406,586
Utah	36	1.2	275	0.9	8	9.5	34,556	57.0	0.6	1,583,278
Mississippi	29	1.0	156	0.5	5	4.9	31,564	43.0	0.4	1,481,069
Montana	11	0.4	136	0.4	12	4.4	32,257	42.6	0.4	3,875,545
New Mexico	21	0.7	209	0.7	10	5.9	28,282	40.7	0.4	1,939,810
Hawaii	16	0.5	149	0.5	9	4.9	32,893	40.4	0.4	2,522,063
Maine	8	0.3	61	0.2	8	2.5	40,836	22.1	0.2	2,765,250
West Virginia	15	0.5	106	0.3	7	2.9	27,783	17.3	0.2	1,154,800
South Dakota	5	0.2	12	-	2	0.5	39,167	3.8	-	766,600

Continued on next page.

INDUSTRY DATA BY STATE - Continued

State	Establishments		Employment			Payroll		Sales		
	Total (number)	% of U.S.	Total (number)	% of U.S.	Per Estab.	Total ($ mil.)	Per Empl. ($)	Total ($ mil.)	% of U.S.	Per Estab. ($)
New Jersey	103	3.4	1000-2499	-	-	(D)	-	(D)	-	-
Michigan	83	2.7	500-999	-	-	(D)	-	(D)	-	-
Arizona	65	2.1	500-999	-	-	(D)	-	(D)	-	-
Indiana	64	2.1	500-999	-	-	(D)	-	(D)	-	-
Maryland	42	1.4	250-499	-	-	(D)	-	(D)	-	-
Kansas	31	1.0	250-499	-	-	(D)	-	(D)	-	-
Connecticut	26	0.9	250-499	-	-	(D)	-	(D)	-	-
Arkansas	23	0.8	100-249	-	-	(D)	-	(D)	-	-
Idaho	18	0.6	100-249	-	-	(D)	-	(D)	-	-
New Hampshire	16	0.5	100-249	-	-	(D)	-	(D)	-	-
Nebraska	14	0.5	100-249	-	-	(D)	-	(D)	-	-
Rhode Island	10	0.3	20-99	-	-	(D)	-	(D)	-	-
Alaska	7	0.2	100-249	-	-	(D)	-	(D)	-	-
Delaware	7	0.2	20-99	-	-	(D)	-	(D)	-	-
North Dakota	7	0.2	20-99	-	-	(D)	-	(D)	-	-
Wyoming	6	0.2	20-99	-	-	(D)	-	(D)	-	-
D.C.	2	0.1	0-19	-	-	(D)	-	(D)	-	-
Vermont	2	0.1	0-19	-	-	(D)	-	(D)	-	-

Source: 2002 *Economic Census*. The states are in descending order of sales or establishments (if sales data are missing for the majority). The symbol (D) appears when data are withheld to prevent disclosure of competitive information. States marked with (D) are sorted by number of establishments. A dash (-) indicates that the data element cannot be calculated. Shaded *states* on the state map indicate those states which have proportionately greater representation in the industry than would be indicated by the states population; the ratio is based on total sales or number of establishments. Shaded *regions* indicate where the industry is regionally most concentrated.

NAICS 423410 - PHOTOGRAPHIC EQUIPMENT AND SUPPLIES MERCHANT WHOLESALERS*

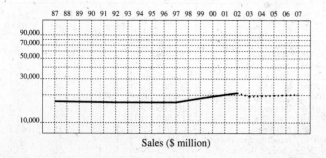

Sales ($ million)

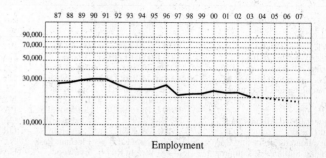

Employment

GENERAL STATISTICS

Year	Establishments (number)	Employment (number)	Payroll ($ million)	Sales ($ million)	Employees per Establishment (number)	Sales per Establishment ($)	Payroll per Employee ($)
1987	1,556	28,123	846.3	17,065.7	18.1	10,967,673.5	30,092.8
1988	1,483	28,840	967.0	16,986.9 e	19.4	11,454,416.7	33,529.8
1989	1,427	30,599	963.2	16,908.2 e	21.4	11,848,773.7	31,478.2
1990	1,372	31,529	1,069.8	16,829.4 e	23.0	12,266,326.5	33,930.7
1991	1,374	31,375	1,119.0	16,750.7 e	22.8	12,191,193.6	35,665.3
1992	1,461	27,372	999.6	16,671.9	18.7	11,411,293.6	36,519.1
1993	1,402	24,645	953.6	16,673.3 e	17.6	11,892,510.7	38,693.4
1994	1,387	24,494	959.9	16,674.8 e	17.7	12,022,206.2	39,189.2
1995	1,386	24,541	1,032.4	16,676.2 e	17.7	12,031,890.3	42,068.4
1996	1,401 e	27,165 e	1,142.5 e	16,677.7 e	19.4 e	11,904,139.9 e	42,057.8 e
1997	1,379	21,195	929.9	16,679.1	15.4	12,095,068.9	43,873.6
1998	1,374	21,787	1,067.0	17,549.0 e	15.9	12,772,168.8	48,974.2
1999	1,358	22,003	1,095.8	18,418.8 e	16.2	13,563,195.9	49,802.3
2000	1,350	23,606	1,246.3	19,288.7 e	17.5	14,287,911.1	52,797.1
2001	1,293	22,533	1,220.0	20,158.5 e	17.4	15,590,518.2	54,141.5
2002	1,143	22,693	1,259.1	21,028.4	19.9	18,397,550.3	55,484.1
2003	1,077	20,563	1,235.7	19,399.8 p	19.1	15,434,178.4 p	60,092.7
2004	1,201 p	19,960 p	1,237.8 p	19,615.7 p	16.9 p	15,744,840.3 p	58,974.4 p
2005	1,183 p	19,347 p	1,257.0 p	19,831.6 p	16.8 p	16,055,502.2 p	60,766.4 p
2006	1,164 p	18,734 p	1,276.2 p	20,047.5 p	16.6 p	16,366,164.1 p	62,558.4 p
2007	1,146 p	18,122 p	1,295.3 p	20,263.4 p	16.4 p	16,676,825.9 p	64,350.4 p

Sources: Economic Census of the United States, 1987, 1992, 1997, and 2002. Establishment counts, employment, and payroll are from *County Business Patterns* for non-Census years. Values followed by a 'p' are projections by the editors. Sales data for non-Census years are extrapolations, marked by 'e'. Data are the most recent available at this level of detail.

INDICES OF CHANGE

Year	Establishments (number)	Employment (number)	Payroll ($ million)	Sales ($ million)	Employees per Establishment (number)	Sales per Establishment ($)	Payroll per Employee ($)
1987	136.1	123.9	67.2	81.2	91.0	59.6	54.2
1992	127.8	120.6	79.4	79.3	94.0	62.0	65.8
1993	122.7	108.6	75.7	79.3 e	88.4	64.6	69.7
1994	121.3	107.9	76.2	79.3 e	88.9	65.3	70.6
1995	121.3	108.1	82.0	79.3 e	88.9	65.4	75.8
1996	122.6 e	119.7 e	90.7 e	79.3 e	97.5 e	64.7 e	75.8 e
1997	120.6	93.4	73.9	79.3	77.4	65.7	79.1
1998	120.2	96.0	84.7	83.5 e	79.9	69.4	88.3
1999	118.8	97.0	87.0	87.6 e	81.4	73.7	89.8
2000	118.1	104.0	99.0	91.7 e	87.9	77.7	95.2
2001	113.1	99.3	96.9	95.9 e	87.4	84.7	97.6
2002	100.0	100.0	100.0	100.0	100.0	100.0	100.0
2003	94.2	90.6	98.1	92.3 p	95.9	83.9 p	108.3
2004	105.1 p	88.0 p	98.3 p	93.3 p	85.2 p	85.6 p	106.3 p
2005	103.5 p	85.3 p	99.8 p	94.3 p	84.2 p	87.3 p	109.5 p
2006	101.9 p	82.6 p	101.4 p	95.3 p	83.3 p	89.0 p	112.8 p
2007	100.3 p	79.9 p	102.9 p	96.4 p	82.3 p	90.6 p	116.0 p

Sources: Same as General Statistics. The values shown reflect change from the base year, 2002. Values above 100 mean greater than 2002, values below 100 mean less than 2002, and a value of 100 in the 1987-2001 or 2003-2007 period means same as 2002. Values followed by a 'p' are projections by the editors; 'e' stands for extrapolation. Data are the most recent available at this level of detail.

SELECTED RATIOS

For 2002	Avg. of All Wholesale	Analyzed Industry	Index	For 2002	Avg. of All Wholesale	Analyzed Industry	Index
Employees per Establishment	15	20	133	Sales per Employee	791,325	926,647	117
Payroll per Establishment	626,122	1,101,575	176	Sales per Establishment	12,012,387	18,397,550	153
Payroll per Employee	41,161	55,484	135	Expenses per Establishment	na	na	na

Sources: Same as General Statistics. The 'Average of All' column, Wholesale or Retail, represents the average of the sector reported for the most recent supplies year available. The Index shows the relationship between the Average and the Analyzed Industry. For example, 100 means that they are equal; 500 that the Analyzed Industry is five times the average; 50 means that the Analyzed Industry is half the national average. The abbreviation 'na' is used to show that data are 'not available'.

*Equivalent to SIC 5043.

LEADING COMPANIES   Number shown: 50   Total sales ($ mil): 5,681   Total employment (000): 8.7

Company Name	Address				CEO Name	Phone	Co. Type	Sales ($ mil)	Empl. (000)
VWR Scientific Products Corp.	1310 Goshen Pkwy	West Chester	PA	19380	Walter Zywotten	610-431-1700	S	2,488*	2.5
Lanier Worldwide Inc.	2300 Parklake NE	Atlanta	GA	30345	Nori Goto	770-496-9500	S	1,087	4.0
Noritsu America Corp.	PO Box 5039	Buena Park	CA	90622	Osame Miki	714-521-9040	R	421*	0.1
Recognition Systems Inc.	30 Harbor Park Dr	Port Washington	NY	11050	John E McCusker	516-625-5000	R	174*	<0.1
Samsung Opto-Electronics Am.	40 Seaview Dr	Secaucus	NJ	07094	JW Ahn	201-902-0347	R	145*	<0.1
Arri Inc.	617 Route 303	Blauvelt	NY	10913	Volker Bahnemann	845-353-1400	S	139*	0.1
BEF Corp.	1670 E Race St	Allentown	PA	18109	Edward Brewer	610-266-8080	R	125*	0.2
Pioneer Photo Albums Inc.	PO Box 2497	Chatsworth	CA	91313	Shell Plutsky	818-882-2161	R	125*	0.2
Witt Co.	15100 SW Koll	Beaverton	OR	97006	Bill Witt	503-681-8557	R	119*	<0.1
Consolidated Purchasing Corp.	11 Vreeland Rd	Florham Park	NJ	07932	Jonathan Sweetwood	973-377-5555	R	58*	<0.1
Imaging Supplies & Equipment	11490 Wright Rd	Lynwood	CA	90262	Charles Bertoni	310-223-0500	R	50*	<0.1
Comp View Inc.	10035 SW Arctic Dr	Beaverton	OR	97005	Scott Birdsall	503-641-8439	R	44*	<0.1
SBC Group Inc.	PO Box 2568	Norcross	GA	30091	Scott Lloyd	770-449-4088	R	42*	<0.1
RE Snader and Associates Inc.	PO Box 8444	San Rafael	CA	94912	John Beritzhoff	415-257-8480	R	38*	<0.1
Supercircuits Inc.	1 Supercircuits Plz	Liberty Hill	TX	78642	Steve Klindworth	512-260-0333	R	35*	<0.1
TechWorks Inc.	4030 W Braker Ln	Austin	TX	78759			R	34*	<0.1
Camcor Inc.	PO Box 1899	Burlington	NC	27216	Raymond Bailey	336-228-0251	R	33*	<0.1
UMI Tech Inc.	16026 Carmenita Rd	Cerritos	CA	90703	Jae Yu	562-802-8461	R	33*	<0.1
The MAC Group	8 Westchester Plz	Elmsford	NY	10523	Jan Lederman	914-347-3300	R	32*	<0.1
Comprehensive Video Group	55 Ruta Ct	S. Hackensack	NJ	07606	Shelly Goldstein	201-229-0025	R	31*	<0.1
North American Video & Sound	PO Box 7266	Huntsville	AL	35807	Danny Bramlett	256-536-8417	R	27*	<0.1
Sinar-Bron Inc.	17 Progress St	Edison	NJ	08820	Jim Bellina	908-754-5800	R	26*	<0.1
National Cinema Supply Corp.	14499 N Dale Mabry	Tampa	FL	33618	Barney Bailey	813-962-2772	R	26*	<0.1
Band Pro Film-Video Inc.	3403 W Pacific Ave	Burbank	CA	91505	Amnon Band	818-841-9655	R	25*	<0.1
Industrial Video Corp.	14885 W Sprague	Cleveland	OH	44136		440-891-9440	R	24*	<0.1
Dot Line Corp.	9420 Eton Ave	Chatsworth	CA	91311	Stanley Offman	818-700-9997	R	23*	<0.1
Industrial Television Services Inc.	3515 Martens St	Franklin Park	IL	60131	Brian Reynolds	847-671-4793	R	23*	<0.1
C.A. M Audio Inc.	2210 Executive Dr	Garland	TX	75041	Dean Harrison	972-271-2800	R	23*	<0.1
Richards & Ellis Graphics Group	311 E Park St	Moonachie	NJ	07074	Harvey Ellis	201-229-9595	R	21*	<0.1
Prinz Ltd.	512 Lindberg Ln	Northbrook	IL	60062	Richard Feldstein	847-291-1560	R	20*	<0.1
Instant Photo Inc.	8120 Jetstar Dr	Irving	TX	75063	Lee Armstrong	972-621-1010	R	19*	<0.1
Royce Photo Graphics Inc.	2140 S 1260 W	Salt Lake City	UT	84119	Roger Bland	801-975-1234	R	19*	<0.1
Southern Colorchrome Inc.	893 Wells Rd	Haughton	LA	71037	Rachel Abshire	318-949-1350	R	19*	<0.1
Buffalo Printers Supply Inc.	3 Peuquet Pkwy	Tonawanda	NY	14150	Thomas Nelson	716-693-7000	R	18*	<0.1
CPQ Colorchrome Inc.	PO Box 8014	Cleveland	TN	37320	Ronald Coppinger	423-479-6186	R	17*	0.2
Mike Crivello's Camera Centers	18110 Bluemnd	Brookfield	WI	53045	Sebastian Crivello	262-782-4303	R	17*	<0.1
Performance Films Distributing	6365 Shier Rings Rd	Dublin	OH	43016	George Lewis	614-766-4602	R	17*	<0.1
USI Inc.	98 Fort Path Rd	Madison	CT	06443	Martin Fagan	203-245-8586	R	15*	<0.1
Murphy Co.	455 W Broad St	Columbus	OH	43215	John L Murphy	614-221-7731	R	10*	<0.1
Photo Systems Inc.	7200 Huron River	Dexter	MI	48130	Alan Fischer	734-426-4646	R	8*	<0.1
Eye Communication Systems Inc.	PO Box 620	Hartland	WI	53029	John Bessent	262-367-1360	R	7*	<0.1
Filmdex Inc.	PO Box 490	Centreville	VA	20122	Ida Slattery	703-631-0600	R	7*	<0.1
Merlin Engineering Works Inc.	1888 Embarcadero	Palo Alto	CA	94303	David Husted	650-856-0900	R	4*	<0.1
Hoag Enterprises Inc.	PO Box 4406	Springfield	MO	65808	Charles Hoag	417-883-8300	R	3*	<0.1
Kinetronics Corp.	4363 Independence	Sarasota	FL	34234	Bill Stelcher	941-951-2432	R	3*	<0.1
UV Process Supply Inc.	1229 W Cortland St	Chicago	IL	60614	Stephen Siegel	773-248-0099	R	3*	<0.1
D/A Mid South Inc.	9000 Jameel Rd	Houston	TX	77040	Richard J Gunn	713-895-0090	R	2*	<0.1
Elden Enterprises	PO Box 3201	Charleston	WV	25332	Ted Elden	304-344-2335	R	2*	<0.1
Central Audio Visual Equipment	375 Roma Jean	Streamwood	IL	60107	Michael Bashir	630-372-8100	R	1*	<0.1
Rainbow Sales Distributing	1637 S 83rd St	West Allis	WI	53214	Daviid Gray	414-774-4949	R	1	<0.1

Source: *Ward's Business Directory of U.S. Private and Public Companies*, Volumes 1 and 2, 2005. The company type code used is as follows: P - Public, R - Private, S - Subsidiary, D - Division, J - Joint Venture, A - Affiliate, G - Group. Sales are in millions of dollars, employees are in thousands. An asterisk (*) indicates an estimated sales volume. The symbol < stands for 'less than'. Company names and addresses are truncated, in some cases, to fit into the available space.

OCCUPATIONS EMPLOYED BY PROFESSIONAL & COMMERCIAL EQUIPMENT & SUPPLIES

Occupation	% of Total 2004	Change to 2014	Occupation	% of Total 2004	Change to 2014
Sales reps, wholesale & manufacturing, exc tech	8.8	20.2	Computer software engineers, systems software	1.7	42.6
Sales reps, wholesale & manufacturing, tech	8.4	20.2	Computer specialists, nec	1.6	20.2
Computer, automated teller, & office machine repairers	8.0	8.2	First-line supervisors/managers of office workers	1.6	9.0
Customer service representatives	3.9	23.6	Truck drivers, light or delivery services	1.5	20.2
Computer systems analysts	2.7	32.3	Team assemblers	1.5	20.2
Computer support specialists	2.6	20.2	Computer software engineers, applications	1.4	44.3
Shipping, receiving, & traffic clerks	2.5	8.8	Business operation specialists, nec	1.3	32.3
Computer programmers	2.5	-1.9	Order clerks	1.2	-21.5
Office clerks, general	2.4	7.0	Sales managers	1.2	28.6
Laborers & freight, stock, & material movers, hand	2.1	8.2	Office machine operators, except computer	1.1	-21.8
Bookkeeping, accounting, & auditing clerks	2.0	8.2	Billing & posting clerks & machine operators	1.1	-3.4
General & operations managers	2.0	19.0	Maintenance & repair workers, general	1.0	20.2
Stock clerks & order fillers	1.9	-7.9	Executive secretaries & administrative assistants	1.0	14.0
First-line supervisors/managers of non-retail sales work	1.8	11.2	Computer & information systems managers	1.0	25.9

Source: *Industry-Occupation Matrix*, Bureau of Labor Statistics. These data are reported based on 4-digit NAICS categories but have been matched to corresponding 6-digit NAICS industry codes. The change reported for each occupation to the year 2014 is a percent of growth or decline as estimated by the Bureau of Labor Statistics. The abbreviation nec stands for 'not elsewhere classified.'

LOCATION BY STATE AND REGIONAL CONCENTRATION

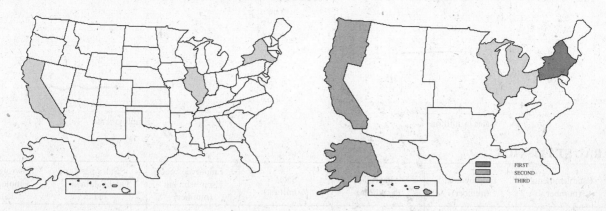

FIRST
SECOND
THIRD

INDUSTRY DATA BY STATE

State	Establishments		Employment			Payroll		Sales		
	Total (number)	% of U.S.	Total (number)	% of U.S.	Per Estab.	Total ($ mil.)	Per Empl. ($)	Total ($ mil.)	% of U.S.	Per Estab. ($)
New York	148	13.1	4,370	19.8	30	244.9	56,031	6,293.4	30.1	42,522,865
California	238	21.0	3,740	17.0	16	192.9	51,572	3,644.7	17.4	15,313,912
Illinois	55	4.9	1,578	7.2	29	85.6	54,265	1,479.4	7.1	26,897,564
Florida	76	6.7	765	3.5	10	43.9	57,441	905.5	4.3	11,915,118
Texas	58	5.1	1,001	4.5	17	52.3	52,224	717.9	3.4	12,377,310
North Carolina	24	2.1	415	1.9	17	22.0	53,039	340.3	1.6	14,180,750
Ohio	33	2.9	553	2.5	17	26.9	48,705	339.6	1.6	10,289,818
Virginia	17	1.5	205	0.9	12	11.5	56,220	241.2	1.2	14,187,941
Tennessee	22	1.9	261	1.2	12	14.8	56,881	184.2	0.9	8,370,727
Indiana	14	1.2	171	0.8	12	6.4	37,620	114.1	0.5	8,149,714
Louisiana	12	1.1	102	0.5	9	4.5	43,873	65.0	0.3	5,416,167
Oklahoma	8	0.7	144	0.7	18	5.3	36,625	62.4	0.3	7,797,125
Wisconsin	14	1.2	252	1.1	18	6.6	26,163	33.6	0.2	2,399,714
Nevada	16	1.4	69	0.3	4	2.9	42,449	22.5	0.1	1,403,688
Iowa	7	0.6	55	0.2	8	1.3	24,218	14.9	0.1	2,125,714
Alabama	5	0.4	16	0.1	3	0.3	20,938	1.7	-	337,800
New Jersey	62	5.5	1000-2499	-	-	(D)	-	(D)	-	-
Georgia	37	3.3	500-999	-	-	(D)	-	(D)	-	-
Massachusetts	31	2.7	1000-2499	-	-	(D)	-	(D)	-	-
Pennsylvania	31	2.7	500-999	-	-	(D)	-	(D)	-	-
Michigan	23	2.0	250-499	-	-	(D)	-	(D)	-	-
Connecticut	22	1.9	250-499	-	-	(D)	-	(D)	-	-
Minnesota	19	1.7	500-999	-	-	(D)	-	(D)	-	-
Missouri	19	1.7	250-499	-	-	(D)	-	(D)	-	-
Washington	19	1.7	100-249	-	-	(D)	-	(D)	-	-
Colorado	18	1.6	250-499	-	-	(D)	-	(D)	-	-
Maryland	17	1.5	100-249	-	-	(D)	-	(D)	-	-
Arizona	12	1.1	100-249	-	-	(D)	-	(D)	-	-
Oregon	8	0.7	20-99	-	-	(D)	-	(D)	-	-
Hawaii	7	0.6	100-249	-	-	(D)	-	(D)	-	-
Kansas	7	0.6	20-99	-	-	(D)	-	(D)	-	-
Kentucky	7	0.6	20-99	-	-	(D)	-	(D)	-	-
Rhode Island	7	0.6	0-19	-	-	(D)	-	(D)	-	-
South Carolina	7	0.6	250-499	-	-	(D)	-	(D)	-	-
Utah	6	0.5	20-99	-	-	(D)	-	(D)	-	-
Nebraska	4	0.4	0-19	-	-	(D)	-	(D)	-	-
New Hampshire	4	0.4	20-99	-	-	(D)	-	(D)	-	-
D.C.	3	0.3	0-19	-	-	(D)	-	(D)	-	-
Montana	3	0.3	0-19	-	-	(D)	-	(D)	-	-
New Mexico	3	0.3	20-99	-	-	(D)	-	(D)	-	-
Arkansas	2	0.2	0-19	-	-	(D)	-	(D)	-	-
Delaware	2	0.2	0-19	-	-	(D)	-	(D)	-	-
Maine	2	0.2	0-19	-	-	(D)	-	(D)	-	-
Vermont	2	0.2	0-19	-	-	(D)	-	(D)	-	-
Alaska	1	0.1	0-19	-	-	(D)	-	(D)	-	-
South Dakota	1	0.1	0-19	-	-	(D)	-	(D)	-	-
West Virginia	1	0.1	0-19	-	-	(D)	-	(D)	-	-

Source: 2002 *Economic Census*. The states are in descending order of sales or establishments (if sales data are missing for the majority). The symbol (D) appears when data are withheld to prevent disclosure of competitive information. States marked with (D) are sorted by number of establishments. A dash (-) indicates that the data element cannot be calculated. Shaded *states* on the state map indicate those states which have proportionately greater representation in the industry than would be indicated by the states population; the ratio is based on total sales or number of establishments. Shaded *regions* indicate where the industry is regionally most concentrated.

NAICS 423420 - OFFICE EQUIPMENT MERCHANT WHOLESALERS

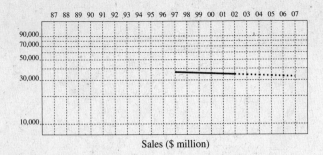

Sales ($ million)

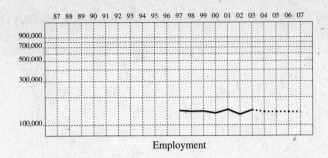

Employment

GENERAL STATISTICS

Year	Establishments (number)	Employment (number)	Payroll ($ million)	Sales ($ million)	Employees per Establishment (number)	Sales per Establishment ($)	Payroll per Employee ($)
1987	-	-	-	-	-	-	-
1988	-	-	-	-	-	-	-
1989	-	-	-	-	-	-	-
1990	-	-	-	-	-	-	-
1991	-	-	-	-	-	-	-
1992	-	-	-	-	-	-	-
1993	-	-	-	-	-	-	-
1994	-	-	-	-	-	-	-
1995	-	-	-	-	-	-	-
1996	-	-	-	-	-	-	-
1997	7,319	143,381	5,421.1	36,646.6	19.6	5,007,050.1	37,809.1
1998	7,235	140,372	5,943.7	36,262.1 e	19.4	5,012,035.9	42,342.5
1999	7,120	141,388	6,058.2	35,877.6 e	19.9	5,038,983.1	42,848.0
2000	7,023	134,340	6,172.8	35,493.0 e	19.1	5,053,828.8	45,949.3
2001	6,779	147,160	6,456.5	35,108.5 e	21.7	5,179,011.7	43,874.2
2002	5,777	130,144	5,501.1	34,724.0	22.5	6,010,732.2	42,269.3
2003	5,857	145,155	6,812.2	34,339.5 p	24.8	5,770,358.7 p	46,930.8
2004	5,638 p	138,940 p	6,578.9 p	33,955.0 p	24.4 p	5,928,478.2 p	47,181.2 p
2005	5,365 p	138,605 p	6,710.5 p	33,570.4 p	25.2 p	6,086,597.7 p	48,189.9 p
2006	5,092 p	138,271 p	6,842.2 p	33,185.9 p	26.0 p	6,244,717.2 p	49,198.7 p
2007	4,819 p	137,937 p	6,973.9 p	32,801.4 p	26.9 p	6,402,836.8 p	50,207.4 p

Source: *Economic Census of the United States*, 1997 and 2002. Establishment counts, employment, and payroll are from *County Business Patterns* for non-Census years. This is a newly defined industry. Data for prior years are unavailable at the time of publication but may become available over time. Values followed by 'p' are projections by the editors. Sales data for non-Census years are extrapolations, marked by 'e'.

INDICES OF CHANGE

Year	Establishments (number)	Employment (number)	Payroll ($ million)	Sales ($ million)	Employees per Establishment (number)	Sales per Establishment ($)	Payroll per Employee ($)
1987	-	-	-	-	-	-	-
1992	-	-	-	-	-	-	-
1993	-	-	-	-	-	-	-
1994	-	-	-	-	-	-	-
1995	-	-	-	-	-	-	-
1996	-	-	-	-	-	-	-
1997	126.7	110.2	98.5	105.5	87.1	83.3	89.4
1998	125.2	107.9	108.0	104.4 e	86.2	83.4	100.2
1999	123.2	108.6	110.1	103.3 e	88.4	83.8	101.4
2000	121.6	103.2	112.2	102.2 e	84.9	84.1	108.7
2001	117.3	113.1	117.4	101.1 e	96.4	86.2	103.8
2002	100.0	100.0	100.0	100.0	100.0	100.0	100.0
2003	101.4	111.5	123.8	98.9 p	110.1	96.0 p	111.0
2004	97.6 p	106.8 p	119.6 p	97.8 p	108.3 p	98.6 p	111.6 p
2005	92.9 p	106.5 p	122.0 p	96.7 p	112.0 p	101.3 p	114.0 p
2006	88.1 p	106.2 p	124.4 p	95.6 p	115.8 p	103.9 p	116.4 p
2007	83.4 p	106.0 p	126.8 p	94.5 p	119.5 p	106.5 p	118.8 p

Sources: Same as General Statistics. The values shown reflect change from the base year, 2002. Values above 100 mean greater than 2002, values below 100 mean less than 2002, and a value of 100 in the 1987-2001 or 2003-2007 period means same as 2002. Values followed by a 'p' are projections by the editors; 'e' stands for extrapolation. Data are the most recent available at this level of detail.

SELECTED RATIOS

For 2002	Avg. of All Wholesale	Analyzed Industry	Index	For 2002	Avg. of All Wholesale	Analyzed Industry	Index
Employees per Establishment	15	23	151	Sales per Employee	791,325	266,812	34
Payroll per Establishment	626,122	952,242	152	Sales per Establishment	12,012,387	6,010,732	50
Payroll per Employee	41,161	42,269	103	Expenses per Establishment	na	na	na

Sources: Same as General Statistics. The 'Average of All' column, Wholesale or Retail, represents the average of the sector reported for the most recent complete year available. The Index shows the relationship between the Average and the Analyzed Industry. For example, 100 means that they are equal; 500 that the Analyzed Industry is five times the average; 50 means that the Analyzed Industry is half the national average. The abbreviation 'na' is used to show that data are 'not available'.

LEADING COMPANIES   Number shown: **75**   Total sales ($ mil): **16,983**   Total employment (000): **31.2**

Company Name	Address				CEO Name	Phone	Co. Type	Sales ($ mil)	Empl. (000)
United Stationers Inc.	2200 E Golf Rd	Des Plaines	IL	60016	Richard W. Gochnauer	847-699-5000	P	4,000	5.7
Canon Business Solutions West	110 W Walnut St	Gardena	CA	90248	Bill Joseph	310-217-3000	S	3,537*	0.7
Lanier Worldwide Inc.	2300 Parklake NE	Atlanta	GA	30345	Nori Goto	770-496-9500	S	1,087	4.0
Savin Corp.	PO Box 10270	Stamford	CT	06904	Thomas Salierno Jr	203-967-5000	S	1,058*	1.9
Brother International Corp. (USA)	100 Somerset Corp.	Bridgewater	NJ	08807	Hideo Kageyama	908-704-1700	S	1,000*	1.1
School Specialty Inc.	PO Box 1579	Appleton	WI	54912		920-734-5712	P	907	2.8
Global Imaging Systems Inc.	PO Box 273478	Tampa	FL	33688	Thomas S Johnson	813-960-5508	P	751	3.2
Imagistics International Inc.	100 Oakview Dr	Trumbull	CT	06611	Marc C Breslawsky	203-365-7000	P	609	3.6
WJS Enterprises Inc.	PO Box 6620	Metairie	LA	70009	Cy Hosch	504-837-5666	R	549*	<0.1
Coast to Coast Business Equipment	8 Vanderbilt	Irvine	CA	92614	Paul Faus	949-261-7105	R	363*	<0.1
Servco Pacific Inc.	PO Box 2788	Honolulu	HI	96803	Mark H Fukunaga	808-521-6511	S	307*	0.9
Funai Corp.	100 North St	Teterboro	NJ	07608	Masao Suwa	201-288-2063	R	269*	<0.1
Embassy Food Beverage	PO Box 1929	Falls Church	VA	22041	Steve Sami	703-845-0800	R	227*	0.8
ITE Distributing	1229 W Washington	Chicago	IL	60607	William Nelson	312-733-1200	R	213*	<0.1
SunCoast Merchandise Corp.	6315 Bandini Blvd	Los Angeles	CA	90040	Kumar Bhavnani	323-720-9700	R	199*	0.2
Ohio Calculating Inc.	20160 Center Ridge	Rocky River	OH	44116	Carl Eichler	440-333-7310	R	142*	<0.1
Witt Co.	15100 SW Koll	Beaverton	OR	97006	Bill Witt	503-681-8557	R	119*	<0.1
Lewan and Associates Inc.	1400 S Colorado	Denver	CO	80222	Jim Arnold	303-759-5440	R	100*	0.5
TRM Corp.	5208 NE 122nd Ave	Portland	OR	97230	Daniel G Cohen	503-257-8766	P	79	0.3
McRae Industries Inc.	PO Box 1239	Mount Gilead	NC	27306		910-439-6147	P	71	0.6
Econ-O-Copy Inc.	4437 Trenton St	Metairie	LA	70006	Johnny Buiton	504-457-0032	R	58*	<0.1
Stargel Office Systems Inc.	1220 Blalock Rd	Houston	TX	77055	Jack Stargel	713-461-5382	R	58*	0.1
Glory Inc.	10 York Ave	Caldwell	NJ	07006	Noraki Sakamoto	973-228-4500	R	57*	<0.1
Lake Business Products Inc.	38322 Apollo Pkwy	Willoughby	OH	44094	Jack Slattery	440-953-1199	R	55*	0.2
Cannon Safe Inc.	216 S 2nd Bldg 932	San Bernardino	CA	92408	Steven Baker	909-382-0303	R	54*	0.2
Offtech Inc.	30 Upton Dr	Wilmington	MA	01887	Stephen Albano	978-988-0700	R	54*	0.2
Capitol Office Solutions Inc.	12301 Kiln Crt	Beltsville	MD	20705	Steve Rolla	301-937-5030	S	50*	<0.1
Tecniflex Inc.	931 N Walnut Ave	Republic	MO	65738	Thomas Black	417-732-7238	R	43*	0.2
TEC America Inc.	4401-A Bankers Cir	Atlanta	GA	30360	Bill Hosken	770-449-3040	S	40*	0.1
A.B. Dick Co.	7400 Caldwell Ave	Niles	IL	60714	Stephen Gray	847-779-1900	S	38*	0.2
Northcoast Business Systems Inc.	7850 Hub Park	Cleveland	OH	44125	Sonny Kumar	216-642-7555	R	38*	0.1
Royal Consumer Information	379 Campus Dr	Somerset	NJ	08875	Solomon Suwalsky	732-627-9977	S	38*	0.3
Nextime Inc.	475 Metroplex Dr	Nashville	TN	37211	Nelson Shields	615-345-8463	R	35*	<0.1
Select Copy Systems	6229 Santos Diaz St	Irwindale	CA	91706	Frank Mendicina	626-334-0383	R	32*	0.2
Advance Business Systems	PO Box 627	Cockeysville	MD	21030	Alan I Elkin	410-252-4800	R	31*	0.2
Innovus Inc.	400 Poydras St	New Orleans	LA	70130	J Brown	504-836-2331	R	28*	<0.1
Arctic Office Machine Inc.	PO Box 100083	Anchorage	AK	99510	William Borchardt	907-276-2322	R	27*	0.1
Copiers Northwest Inc.	601 Dexter Ave N	Seattle	WA	98109	Gregg Petrie	206-282-1200	R	27*	0.1
Triversity Corp.	311 Sinclair Rd	Bristol	PA	19007	David Thomas	215-785-4321	R	27*	0.1
Uinta Business Systems Inc.	332 Bugatti Dr	Salt Lake City	UT	84115	Joseph Weis	801-461-7600	R	27*	0.1
IVCi L.L.C.	108 Adams Ave	Hauppauge	NY	11788		631-273-5800	R	24	<0.1
Cash Register Sales Inc.	2909 Anthony	Minneapolis	MN	55418	David Sanders	612-781-3474	R	22*	<0.1
DocuSource Inc.	1751 Langley Ave	Irvine	CA	92614	Lester Walker	949-862-5270	R	22*	<0.1
Fraser Business Systems	PO Box 7	Reading	PA	19603	William Fraser	610-378-0101	R	21*	<0.1
RK Black Inc.	4111 Perimeter Ctr	Oklahoma City	OK	73112	Chris Black	580-772-3366	R	21*	<0.1
Image IV Systems Inc.	512 S Varney St	Burbank	CA	91502	Ronald Warren	818-841-0756	R	21*	<0.1
Copy Systems Inc.	PO Box 164717	Little Rock	AR	72216	Mike Rebick	501-376-2679	S	20*	<0.1
Dumac Business Systems Inc.	19 Corporate Cir	East Syracuse	NY	13057	Howard Mc Carthy	315-463-1010	R	20*	<0.1
Burtronics Business Systems Inc.	PO Box 1170	San Bernardino	CA	92402	Tom Thompson	909-885-7576	R	19*	<0.1
Imaging Supplies Depot Inc.	1631 S Sinclair St	Anaheim	CA	92806	Paul Doan	714-978-7291	R	19*	<0.1
Gold Type Business Machines Inc.	351 Paterson Ave	East Rutherford	NJ	07073	Richard Picolli	201-935-5090	R	18*	<0.1
Electronic Office Systems	107 Fairfield Rd	Fairfield	NJ	07004	Andrew W Ritshel	973-808-0100	R	18*	<0.1
Standard Duplicating Machine	10 Connector Rd	Andover	MA	01810	L Guy Reny	978-470-1920	R	18*	<0.1
Lucasbilt	1601 Webb St	Asbury Park	NJ	07712	Neil Lucas	732-500-3289	R	17*	<0.1
Diversified Business Solutions Inc.	9765 Clairemont	San Diego	CA	92124	William Bradbury	858-565-2737	R	17*	<0.1
Financial Equipment Company Inc.	PO Box 245	Germantown	WI	53022	Dennis Wick	262-255-6350	R	16*	<0.1
Deluxe Office System Inc.	225 Broadway	New York	NY	10007	Abraham Holtzberg	212-267-0500	R	16*	<0.1
All Copy Products L.L.C.	4141 Colorado Blvd	Denver	CO	80216		303-377-6837	R	15*	<0.1
Imaging Concepts of New Mexico	8600 Pan Am Fwy	Albuquerque	NM	87113	Curt Richter	505-828-2679	R	15*	<0.1
Marimon Business Systems Inc.	7300 Gessner Dr	Houston	TX	77040	Yolanda Marimon	713-856-2000	R	15*	0.1
SIS-USA Inc.	55 Wentworth Ave	Londonderry	NH	03053	Alan Morse	603-432-4495	S	15*	<0.1
USI Inc.	98 Fort Path Rd	Madison	CT	06443	Martin Fagan	203-245-8586	R	15*	<0.1
Copyfax Inc.	6631 Exec Prk Ct	Jacksonville	FL	32216	Larry De Foor	904-296-1600	R	15*	<0.1
Bay Microfilm Inc.	1115 E Arques Ave	Sunnyvale	CA	94085	William D Whitney	408-736-7444	R	14*	0.2
CVI Business Systems	6666 E Stapleton S	Denver	CO	80216	John Kouri	303-393-0027	R	13*	<0.1
Illinois Wholesale Cash Register	PO Box 95405	Hoffman Estates	IL	60195	Al Moorhouse	847-310-4200	R	13*	<0.1
Intern. Trade American Consultant	PO Box 502	Parlin	NJ	08859	Sam Ashor	732-525-3600	R	13*	<0.1
Laser Technologies Inc.	9603 Girard Ave S	Bloomington	MN	55431	Sean Carey	952-888-7375	R	13*	<0.1
Office World Inc.	PO Box 89	Lima	OH	45802	Mark Kitson	419-991-4694	R	13*	<0.1
Rbs Business Solutions L.L.C.	5711 Hillcroft St	Houston	TX	77036	Yandell Rogers	713-787-1200	R	13*	<0.1
Imaging Alliance Group L.L.C.	2818 Washington N	Minneapolis	MN	55411	Corey Tansom	612-588-9944	R	13*	<0.1
Aztec Business Machines Inc.	8670 Argent St	Santee	CA	92071	Rod Jones	619-258-1400	R	13*	<0.1
Whitaker Brothers Business	12410 Washington	Rockville	MD	20852	Joseph Mitchell	301-230-2800	R	13*	<0.1
Gold Circuit Inc.	210 S Beck Ave	Chandler	AZ	85226	James Greenberg	480-829-0404	R	12*	<0.1
Best Image Systems Inc.	PO Box 702985	Dallas	TX	75370	David Rivera	972-386-1860	R	12*	<0.1

Source: Ward's Business Directory of U.S. Private and Public Companies, Volumes 1 and 2, 2005. The company type code used is as follows: P - Public, R - Private, S - Subsidiary, D - Division, J - Joint Venture, A - Affiliate, G - Group. Sales are in millions of dollars, employees are in thousands. An asterisk (*) indicates an estimated sales volume. The symbol < stands for 'less than'. Company names and addresses are truncated, in some cases, to fit into the available space.

OCCUPATIONS EMPLOYED BY PROFESSIONAL & COMMERCIAL EQUIPMENT & SUPPLIES

Occupation	% of Total 2004	Change to 2014	Occupation	% of Total 2004	Change to 2014
Sales reps, wholesale & manufacturing, exc tech	8.8	20.2	Computer software engineers, systems software	1.7	42.6
Sales reps, wholesale & manufacturing, tech	8.4	20.2	Computer specialists, nec	1.6	20.2
Computer, automated teller, & office machine repairers	8.0	8.2	First-line supervisors/managers of office workers	1.6	9.0
Customer service representatives	3.9	23.6	Truck drivers, light or delivery services	1.5	20.2
Computer systems analysts	2.7	32.3	Team assemblers	1.5	20.2
Computer support specialists	2.6	20.2	Computer software engineers, applications	1.4	44.3
Shipping, receiving, & traffic clerks	2.5	8.8	Business operation specialists, nec	1.3	32.3
Computer programmers	2.5	-1.9	Order clerks	1.2	-21.5
Office clerks, general	2.4	7.0	Sales managers	1.2	28.6
Laborers & freight, stock, & material movers, hand	2.1	8.2	Office machine operators, except computer	1.1	-21.8
Bookkeeping, accounting, & auditing clerks	2.0	8.2	Billing & posting clerks & machine operators	1.1	-3.4
General & operations managers	2.0	19.0	Maintenance & repair workers, general	1.0	20.2
Stock clerks & order fillers	1.9	-7.9	Executive secretaries & administrative assistants	1.0	14.0
First-line supervisors/managers of non-retail sales work	1.8	11.2	Computer & information systems managers	1.0	25.9

Source: Industry-Occupation Matrix, Bureau of Labor Statistics. These data are reported based on 4-digit NAICS categories but have been matched to corresponding 6-digit NAICS industry codes. The change reported for each occupation to the year 2014 is a percent of growth or decline as estimated by the Bureau of Labor Statistics. The abbreviation nec stands for 'not elsewhere classified.'

LOCATION BY STATE AND REGIONAL CONCENTRATION

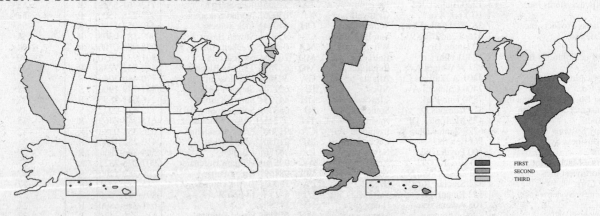

INDUSTRY DATA BY STATE

State	Establishments Total (number)	% of U.S.	Employment Total (number)	% of U.S.	Per Estab.	Payroll Total ($ mil.)	Per Empl. ($)	Sales Total ($ mil.)	% of U.S.	Per Estab. ($)
California	691	11.8	17,121	12.7	25	794.2	46,386	4,826.4	13.4	6,984,661
New Jersey	196	3.4	6,952	5.2	35	363.4	52,275	4,089.0	11.3	20,862,102
Illinois	254	4.3	7,235	5.4	28	315.9	43,668	2,549.1	7.1	10,035,992
Texas	425	7.3	9,594	7.1	23	389.8	40,630	2,501.1	6.9	5,884,995
New York	343	5.9	9,273	6.9	27	415.6	44,819	2,251.7	6.2	6,564,758
Connecticut	85	1.5	6,318	4.7	74	354.2	56,063	1,972.0	5.5	23,200,259
Georgia	186	3.2	4,840	3.6	26	214.9	44,407	1,908.9	5.3	10,262,860
Florida	430	7.4	7,502	5.6	17	305.2	40,682	1,885.9	5.2	4,385,874
Pennsylvania	246	4.2	5,646	4.2	23	234.2	41,476	1,197.4	3.3	4,867,419
Ohio	212	3.6	5,055	3.8	24	194.6	38,498	987.7	2.7	4,658,877
Massachusetts	124	2.1	3,301	2.5	27	151.6	45,918	896.7	2.5	7,231,073
Virginia	129	2.2	3,466	2.6	27	142.6	41,142	758.5	2.1	5,880,000
Minnesota	123	2.1	2,800	2.1	23	115.4	41,232	649.8	1.8	5,282,602
North Carolina	161	2.8	3,178	2.4	20	116.0	36,511	622.5	1.7	3,866,273
Tennessee	149	2.6	2,917	2.2	20	121.0	41,479	579.2	1.6	3,887,268
Washington	115	2.0	2,470	1.8	21	103.0	41,718	520.7	1.4	4,527,939
Indiana	114	2.0	2,512	1.9	22	86.3	34,345	498.7	1.4	4,374,281
Missouri	111	1.9	1,942	1.4	17	77.6	39,947	419.3	1.2	3,777,360
Wisconsin	105	1.8	2,167	1.6	21	81.6	37,675	401.3	1.1	3,822,048
Maryland	95	1.6	1,784	1.3	19	75.7	42,420	387.5	1.1	4,079,295
Iowa	80	1.4	1,528	1.1	19	54.0	35,325	372.7	1.0	4,658,713
Oregon	90	1.5	1,597	1.2	18	66.8	41,831	351.4	1.0	3,904,133
Kansas	50	0.9	1,498	1.1	30	54.1	36,140	310.3	0.9	6,206,560
Alabama	88	1.5	1,382	1.0	16	53.4	38,604	306.1	0.8	3,478,466
Louisiana	88	1.5	1,185	0.9	13	44.6	37,604	249.8	0.7	2,838,284
Kentucky	55	0.9	1,225	0.9	22	48.9	39,944	242.3	0.7	4,405,473
South Carolina	82	1.4	1,184	0.9	14	41.8	35,295	235.7	0.7	2,873,829
Oklahoma	74	1.3	1,114	0.8	15	43.6	39,110	210.5	0.6	2,844,946
Utah	47	0.8	957	0.7	20	38.7	40,489	205.6	0.6	4,375,255

Continued on next page.

INDUSTRY DATA BY STATE - Continued

State	Establishments Total (number)	% of U.S.	Employment Total (number)	% of U.S.	Per Estab.	Payroll Total ($ mil.)	Per Empl. ($)	Sales Total ($ mil.)	% of U.S.	Per Estab. ($)
Nevada	50	0.9	893	0.7	18	34.7	38,822	179.3	0.5	3,585,020
Mississippi	52	0.9	665	0.5	13	21.9	32,911	115.6	0.3	2,223,115
Arkansas	59	1.0	663	0.5	11	23.5	35,373	113.9	0.3	1,930,407
Hawaii	22	0.4	457	0.3	21	19.5	42,593	108.3	0.3	4,920,500
New Mexico	35	0.6	479	0.4	14	16.7	34,889	99.2	0.3	2,833,629
Nebraska	36	0.6	504	0.4	14	17.8	35,224	96.1	0.3	2,668,750
Alaska	20	0.3	329	0.2	16	16.2	49,231	81.7	0.2	4,086,950
West Virginia	26	0.4	441	0.3	17	15.7	35,576	79.0	0.2	3,039,308
Idaho	24	0.4	302	0.2	13	11.2	37,199	46.0	0.1	1,916,000
Maine	26	0.4	277	0.2	11	9.7	34,888	44.3	0.1	1,705,692
South Dakota	27	0.5	264	0.2	10	9.3	35,076	36.8	0.1	1,361,444
Montana	29	0.5	212	0.2	7	6.8	32,151	36.4	0.1	1,253,724
North Dakota	17	0.3	210	0.2	12	8.4	39,886	33.6	0.1	1,977,412
Vermont	15	0.3	168	0.1	11	7.5	44,369	29.7	0.1	1,981,133
Wyoming	10	0.2	82	0.1	8	3.1	38,000	14.6	-	1,463,000
Michigan	154	2.6	2500-4999	-	-	(D)	-	(D)	-	-
Colorado	109	1.9	2500-4999	-	-	(D)	-	(D)	-	-
Arizona	107	1.8	1000-2499	-	-	(D)	-	(D)	-	-
New Hampshire	33	0.6	250-499	-	-	(D)	-	(D)	-	-
Rhode Island	23	0.4	250-499	-	-	(D)	-	(D)	-	-
Delaware	15	0.3	250-499	-	-	(D)	-	(D)	-	-
D.C.	6	0.1	500-999	-	-	(D)	-	(D)	-	-

Source: 2002 *Economic Census*. The states are in descending order of sales or establishments (if sales data are missing for the majority). The symbol (D) appears when data are withheld to prevent disclosure of competitive information. States marked with (D) are sorted by number of establishments. A dash (-) indicates that the data element cannot be calculated. Shaded *states* on the state map indicate those states which have proportionately greater representation in the industry than would be indicated by the states population; the ratio is based on total sales or number of establishments. Shaded *regions* indicate where the industry is regionally most concentrated.

NAICS 423430 - COMPUTER AND COMPUTER PERIPHERAL EQUIPMENT AND SOFTWARE MERCHANT WHOLESALERS

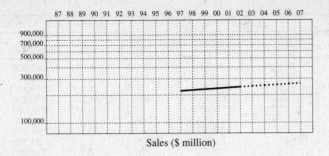

Sales ($ million)

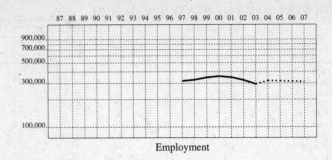

Employment

GENERAL STATISTICS

Year	Establishments (number)	Employment (number)	Payroll ($ million)	Sales ($ million)	Employees per Establishment (number)	Sales per Establishment ($)	Payroll per Employee ($)
1987	-	-	-	-	-	-	-
1988	-	-	-	-	-	-	-
1989	-	-	-	-	-	-	-
1990	-	-	-	-	-	-	-
1991	-	-	-	-	-	-	-
1992	-	-	-	-	-	-	-
1993	-	-	-	-	-	-	-
1994	-	-	-	-	-	-	-
1995	-	-	-	-	-	-	-
1996	-	-	-	-	-	-	-
1997	16,929	317,662	17,305.5	221,447.4	18.8	13,080,949.8	54,477.7
1998	17,309	326,091	20,454.1	225,971.8 e	18.8	13,055,160.9	62,725.1
1999	17,511	346,049	23,187.3	230,496.2 e	19.8	13,162,935.3	67,005.8
2000	17,235	356,853	24,989.9	235,020.5 e	20.7	13,636,236.7	70,028.6
2001	16,524	347,834	24,339.7	239,544.9 e	21.1	14,496,787.7	69,975.0
2002	13,732	324,508	22,130.6	244,069.3	23.6	17,773,762.0	68,197.4
2003	13,048	293,086	21,148.9	248,593.7 p	22.5	17,027,196.4 p	72,159.5
2004	13,215 p	319,568 p	24,227.4 p	253,118.1 p	23.9 p	17,834,689.0 p	75,932.6 p
2005	12,508 p	316,885 p	24,800.1 p	257,642.4 p	24.7 p	18,642,181.7 p	78,324.0 p
2006	11,802 p	314,203 p	25,372.8 p	262,166.8 p	25.4 p	19,449,674.3 p	80,715.4 p
2007	11,095 p	311,520 p	25,945.5 p	266,691.2 p	26.2 p	20,257,167.0 p	83,106.8 p

Source: *Economic Census of the United States*, 1997 and 2002. Establishment counts, employment, and payroll are from *County Business Patterns* for non-Census years. This is a newly defined industry. Data for prior years are unavailable at the time of publication but may become available over time. Values followed by 'p' are projections by the editors. Sales data for non-Census years are extrapolations, marked by 'e'.

INDICES OF CHANGE

Year	Establishments (number)	Employment (number)	Payroll ($ million)	Sales ($ million)	Employees per Establishment (number)	Sales per Establishment ($)	Payroll per Employee ($)
1987	-	-	-	-	-	-	-
1992	-	-	-	-	-	-	-
1993	-	-	-	-	-	-	-
1994	-	-	-	-	-	-	-
1995	-	-	-	-	-	-	-
1996	-	-	-	-	-	-	-
1997	123.3	97.9	78.2	90.7	79.7	73.6	79.9
1998	126.0	100.5	92.4	92.6 e	79.7	73.5	92.0
1999	127.5	106.6	104.8	94.4 e	83.9	74.1	98.3
2000	125.5	110.0	112.9	96.3 e	87.7	76.7	102.7
2001	120.3	107.2	110.0	98.1 e	89.4	81.6	102.6
2002	100.0	100.0	100.0	100.0	100.0	100.0	100.0
2003	95.0	90.3	95.6	101.9 p	95.2	95.8 p	105.8
2004	96.2 p	98.5 p	109.5 p	103.7 p	101.2 p	100.3 p	111.3 p
2005	91.1 p	97.7 p	112.1 p	105.6 p	104.5 p	104.9 p	114.8 p
2006	85.9 p	96.8 p	114.7 p	107.4 p	107.8 p	109.4 p	118.4 p
2007	80.8 p	96.0 p	117.2 p	109.3 p	111.1 p	114.0 p	121.9 p

Sources: Same as General Statistics. The values shown reflect change from the base year, 2002. Values above 100 mean greater than 2002, values below 100 mean less than 2002, and a value of 100 in the 1987-2001 or 2003-2007 period means same as 2002. Values followed by a 'p' are projections by the editors; 'e' stands for extrapolation. Data are the most recent available at this level of detail.

SELECTED RATIOS

For 2002	Avg. of All Wholesale	Analyzed Industry	Index	For 2002	Avg. of All Wholesale	Analyzed Industry	Index
Employees per Establishment	15	24	158	Sales per Employee	791,325	752,121	95
Payroll per Establishment	626,122	1,611,608	257	Sales per Establishment	12,012,387	17,773,762	148
Payroll per Employee	41,161	68,197	166	Expenses per Establishment	na	na	na

Sources: Same as General Statistics. The 'Average of All' column, Wholesale or Retail, represents the average of the sector reported for the most recent complete year available. The Index shows the relationship between the Average and the Analyzed Industry. For example, 100 means that they are equal; 500 that the Analyzed Industry is five times the average; 50 means that the Analyzed Industry is half the national average. The abbreviation 'na' is used to show that data are 'not available'.

LEADING COMPANIES   Number shown: **75**   Total sales ($ mil): **116,732**   Total employment (000): **192.5**

Company Name	Address				CEO Name	Phone	Co. Type	Sales ($ mil)	Empl. (000)
Intel Corp.	2200 Msn College	Santa Clara	CA	95052	Craig R. Barrett	408-765-8080	P	34,209	85.0
Ingram Micro Inc.	PO Box 25125	Santa Ana	CA	92705		714-566-1000	P	25,462	11.3
Tech Data Corp.	5350 Tech Data Dr	Clearwater	FL	33760		727-539-7429	P	17,406	8.4
IKON Office Solutions Inc.	PO Box 834	Valley Forge	PA	19482	Matthew J Espe	610-296-8000	P	4,650	29.4
Avnet Marketing Services Inc	8700 S Price Rd	Tempe	AZ	85284	Steve Tepedino	480-794-6900	S	2,400*	0.6
Storage Technology Corp.	1 StorageTek Dr	Louisville	CO	80028		303-673-5151	P	2,224	7.1
Software House International Inc.	2 Riverview Dr	Somerset	NJ	08873	Leo Koguan	732-764-8888	R	1,739	<0.1
KB Holdings L.L.C.	100 West St	Pittsfield	MA	01201	Michael L Glazer	413-496-3000	S	1,500*	15.0
CompuCom Systems Inc.	7171 Forest Ln	Dallas	TX	75230	James W Dixon	972-856-3600	S	1,455	3.5
Agilysys Inc.	6065 Parkland Blvd	Cleveland	OH	44124		440-720-8500	P	1,403	1.4
Wyle Electronics	15370 Barranca	Irvine	CA	92618	Thomas Beaver	714-753-9953	S	1,378*	1.8
Software Spectrum Inc.	PO Box 848264	Dallas	TX	75284	Keith Coogan	972-840-6600	S	1,213*	2.0
ScanSource Inc.	6 Logue Ct, Ste G	Greenville	SC	29615	Michael L Baur	864-288-2432	P	1,192	0.7
Lanier Worldwide Inc.	2300 Parklake NE	Atlanta	GA	30345	Nori Goto	770-496-9500	S	1,087	4.0
GTSI Corp.	3901 Stonecroft	Chantilly	VA	20151		703-502-2000	P	1,076	0.7
Companion Technologies	633 Davis Dr	Morrisville	NC	27560	Malcolm Sellers	919-286-5509	R	1,070*	<0.1
ASI Corp.	48289 Fremont Blvd	Fremont	CA	94538	Christine Liang	510-226-8000	R	1,000*	0.5
Daisytek Inc.	1025 Central Expwy	Allen	TX	75013	Dale Booth	972-881-4700	S	1,000*	0.3
SED International Inc.	4916 N Ryl Atl	Tucker	GA	30085	Gerald Diamond	770-491-8962	S	944*	0.4
MA Laboratories Inc.	2075 N Capitol Ave	San Jose	CA	95132	Abraham Ma	408-941-0808	R	939*	0.4
Autotote Lottery Corp.	750 Lexington Ave	New York	NY	10022	A Lorne Weil	212-754-2372	S	926*	1.0
Tektronix Inc.	PO Box 500	Beaverton	OR	97077		503-627-7111	P	921	3.8
Pomeroy IT Solutions Inc.	1020 Petersburg Rd	Hebron	KY	41048		859-586-0600	P	742	1.3
World Wide Technology Inc.	60 Weldon Pky	St. Louis	MO	63043	James P Kavanaugh	314-569-7000	S	716	0.4
Military Sales and Service Co.	5301 Westmorelnd	Dallas	TX	75237		214-330-4621	R	554*	0.8
Computer Sales International Inc.	PO Box 16264	St. Louis	MO	63105	Kenneth B Steinback	314-997-7010	R	521*	0.2
Intcomex	9835 NW 14 St	Miami	FL	33172	Michael Shalom	305-477-6230	R	482*	0.5
Navarre Corp.	7400 49th Ave N	New Hope	MN	55428		763-535-8333	P	475	0.4
SHI	2 Riverview Dr	Somerset	NJ	08873	Leo Koguan	732-764-8888	R	443*	0.6
D and H Distributing Co.	PO Box 5961	Harrisburg	PA	17110	Gary Brothers	717-236-8001	R	429*	0.4
McDATA Corp.	380 Interlocken Cres	Broomfield	CO	80021		720-558-8000	P	400	1.0
Itron Inc.	PO Box 15288	Spokane	WA	99215		509-924-9900	P	399	1.5
Brix Group Inc.	541 Division St	Campbell	CA	95008		408-374-7900	R	377*	0.2
SED International Holdings Inc.	4916 N Ryl Atl	Tucker	GA	30085	Jean Diamond	770-491-8962	P	372	0.3
Emulex Corp.	3333 Susan St	Costa Mesa	CA	92626	Paul F Folino	714-662-5600	P	364	0.5
Solarcom	Box 926020	Norcross	GA	30092	Eric Prockow	770-449-6116	P	350*	0.4
En Pointe Technologies Inc.	100 N Sepulveda	El Segundo	CA	90245	Attiazaz Din	310-725-5200	P	279	0.4
Funai Corp.	100 North St	Teterboro	NJ	07608	Masao Suwa	201-288-2063	R	269*	<0.1
Lansa USA Inc.	3010 Highland	Downers Grove	IL	60515	John Siniscal	630-874-7000	R	254*	0.3
Jaco Electronics Inc.	145 Oser Ave	Hauppauge	NY	11788	Joel H Girsky	631-273-5500	P	249	0.4
MultiLing Corp.	PO Box 1998	Provo	UT	84601		801-377-2000	R	233*	0.4
Classic Components Corp.	23605 Telo Ave	Torrance	CA	90505	Arnold Klein	310-539-5500	R	187*	0.3
Parts Now! L.L.C.	3517 W Beltline	Madison	WI	53713		608-276-8688	R	185*	0.3
Manchester Technologies Inc.	160 Oser Ave	Hauppauge	NY	11788	Seth Collins	631-435-1199	P	173	<0.1
Vector Technology Corp.	3445 Executive Ctr	Austin	TX	78731	Tom Flink	512-338-1551	R	172*	0.2
Formosa U.S.A. Inc.	21540 Prairie St	Chatsworth	CA	91311	David Toung	818-407-4965	S	164*	0.2
Sayers Group L.L.C.	1150 Feehanville Dr	Mount Prospect	IL	60056	James V Martin	847-391-4040	R	150	0.2
Canvas Systems L.L.C.	3025 Northwoods	Norcross	GA	30071	Mark Metz	770-662-1881	R	134*	0.2
Agency for Instructional Tech.	1800 N Stonelake Dr	Bloomington	IN	47404		812-339-2203	R	120*	<0.1
Tomba Communications	718 Barataria Blvd	Marrero	LA	70072	Tom Tomba	504-340-2448	R	111*	0.2
Boces Albany	1031 Watervliet	Albany	NY	12205		518-456-7824	R	111*	0.2
AQS Inc.	1325 Walnut Ridge	Hartland	WI	53029	Kevin M Flanagan	262-369-7500	R	108*	0.1
Programmer's Paradise Inc.	1157 Shrewsbury	Shrewsbury	NJ	07702		732-389-8950	P	104	0.1
PCG Trading L.L.C.	4 Technology Dr	Peabody	MA	01960		978-538-8000	R	103*	0.1
Advanced Technologies Intern.	361 Sinclair	Milpitas	CA	95035	John Knight	408-942-1780	R	101*	0.1
Lewan and Associates Inc.	1400 S Colorado	Denver	CO	80222	Jim Arnold	303-759-5440	R	100*	0.5
Rhinotek	PO Box 6205	Carson	CA	90749	Gerald Chamales	310-638-2500	R	99*	0.3
Ensim Corp.	1366 Borregas Ave	Sunnyvale	CA	94089		408-745-3300	R	97*	0.1
Merisel Inc.	1500 Hughes Way	Long Beach	CA	90810	Don Uzzi	310-765-4654	P	96	<0.1
Applied Digital Solutions Inc.	1690 S Congress	Delray Beach	FL	33445	Kevin H McLaughlin	561-805-8000	P	95	0.4
Array Distribution L.L.C.	406 E Anthony Dr	Urbana	IL	61802		217-384-2175	R	95*	0.2
I-Sector Corp.	6401 Southwest Fwy	Houston	TX	77074	Mark T Hilz	713-795-2000	P	93	0.2
Alliance Systems Ltd.	3501 E Plano Pkwy	Plano	TX	75074	Charles Cone	972-633-3400	R	90*	0.1
Greenpages Inc.	PO Box 9001	Kittery	ME	03904	Charles R Hefford	207-439-7310	R	90*	0.1
Digital Storage Inc.	7611 Grn Mdws	Lewis Center	OH	43035	George Babyak	740-548-7179	R	87*	<0.1
Testa Interactive	25 Willowdale Ave	Port Washington	NY	11050		516-767-2500	R	84*	<0.1
Mpower Software Services Inc.	100 Thanet Cir	Princeton	NJ	08540	Naru Narayanan	609-921-0225	R	81*	0.1
Dynamix Group Inc.	604 Macy Dr	Roswell	GA	30076	Chuck Hawkins	912-353-8606	R	80	<0.1
Pacific Magtron International Inc.	1600 California Cir	Milpitas	CA	95035	Theodore S Li	408-956-8888	P	74	<0.1
Alta Computer Services Ltd.	PO Box 510	Salt Lake City	UT	84110		801-972-0679	R	74*	0.1
Ces Computers Inc.	120 Bryant St	Dubuque	IA	52003	Gerald Holt	563-588-9020	R	74*	0.1
IBM Rational Software Corp.	8000 Westpark Dr	Mc Lean	VA	22102		703-761-4400	R	74*	0.1
Kelly Products Inc.	PO Box 44308	Panorama City	CA	91412	Judy Kelly	818-891-4057	R	74*	0.1
Networks Plus Technology Group	13700 Stowe Dr	Poway	CA	92064	James Kernan	858-386-5100	R	74*	0.1
Radware	575 Corporate Dr	Mahwah	NJ	07430	Roy Zisapel	201-512-9771	R	74*	0.1

Source: *Ward's Business Directory of U.S. Private and Public Companies*, Volumes 1 and 2, 2005. The company type code used is as follows: P - Public, R - Private, S - Subsidiary, D - Division, J - Joint Venture, A - Affiliate, G - Group. Sales are in millions of dollars, employees are in thousands. An asterisk (*) indicates an estimated sales volume. The symbol < stands for 'less than'. Company names and addresses are truncated, in some cases, to fit into the available space.

OCCUPATIONS EMPLOYED BY PROFESSIONAL & COMMERCIAL EQUIPMENT & SUPPLIES

Occupation	% of Total 2004	Change to 2014	Occupation	% of Total 2004	Change to 2014
Sales reps, wholesale & manufacturing, exc tech	8.8	20.2	Computer software engineers, systems software	1.7	42.6
Sales reps, wholesale & manufacturing, tech	8.4	20.2	Computer specialists, nec	1.6	20.2
Computer, automated teller, & office machine repairers	8.0	8.2	First-line supervisors/managers of office workers	1.6	9.0
Customer service representatives	3.9	23.6	Truck drivers, light or delivery services	1.5	20.2
Computer systems analysts	2.7	32.3	Team assemblers	1.5	20.2
Computer support specialists	2.6	20.2	Computer software engineers, applications	1.4	44.3
Shipping, receiving, & traffic clerks	2.5	8.8	Business operation specialists, nec	1.3	32.3
Computer programmers	2.5	-1.9	Order clerks	1.2	-21.5
Office clerks, general	2.4	7.0	Sales managers	1.2	28.6
Laborers & freight, stock, & material movers, hand	2.1	8.2	Office machine operators, except computer	1.1	-21.8
Bookkeeping, accounting, & auditing clerks	2.0	8.2	Billing & posting clerks & machine operators	1.1	-3.4
General & operations managers	2.0	19.0	Maintenance & repair workers, general	1.0	20.2
Stock clerks & order fillers	1.9	-7.9	Executive secretaries & administrative assistants	1.0	14.0
First-line supervisors/managers of non-retail sales work	1.8	11.2	Computer & information systems managers	1.0	25.9

Source: Industry-Occupation Matrix, Bureau of Labor Statistics. These data are reported based on 4-digit NAICS categories but have been matched to corresponding 6-digit NAICS industry codes. The change reported for each occupation to the year 2014 is a percent of growth or decline as estimated by the Bureau of Labor Statistics. The abbreviation nec stands for 'not elsewhere classified.'

LOCATION BY STATE AND REGIONAL CONCENTRATION

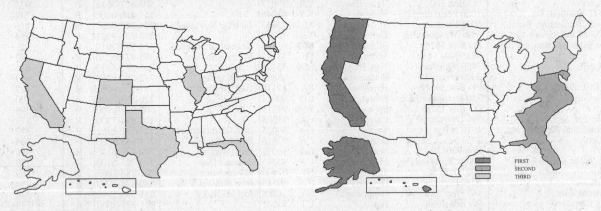

FIRST
SECOND
THIRD

INDUSTRY DATA BY STATE

State	Establishments Total (number)	% of U.S.	Employment Total (number)	% of U.S.	Per Estab.	Payroll Total ($ mil.)	Per Empl. ($)	Sales Total ($ mil.)	% of U.S.	Per Estab. ($)
California	2,837	20.6	64,083	20.2	23	4,436.8	69,236	56,414.1	24.3	19,885,124
Texas	1,059	7.7	25,986	8.2	25	1,544.4	59,434	29,840.7	12.8	28,178,153
Florida	1,087	7.9	14,501	4.6	13	881.7	60,805	18,877.8	8.1	17,366,879
Colorado	308	2.2	14,245	4.5	46	1,138.2	79,902	16,797.4	7.2	54,536,890
Illinois	515	3.7	13,343	4.2	26	998.2	74,811	13,370.2	5.8	25,961,550
Massachusetts	468	3.4	17,869	5.6	38	1,532.9	85,787	9,440.1	4.1	20,171,103
New York	794	5.8	17,394	5.5	22	1,192.4	68,552	9,319.5	4.0	11,737,369
Pennsylvania	403	2.9	9,659	3.1	24	659.2	68,252	7,091.4	3.0	17,596,638
Virginia	360	2.6	8,861	2.8	25	633.3	71,467	4,849.7	2.1	13,471,422
Tennessee	180	1.3	3,392	1.1	19	181.0	53,356	4,041.2	1.7	22,451,078
Washington	338	2.5	6,460	2.0	19	467.9	72,438	3,955.6	1.7	11,703,047
Minnesota	339	2.5	8,110	2.6	24	537.1	66,227	3,855.1	1.7	11,371,941
Maryland	262	1.9	8,776	2.8	33	707.4	80,612	3,648.8	1.6	13,926,641
North Carolina	315	2.3	8,478	2.7	27	989.6	116,721	3,533.5	1.5	11,217,603
Ohio	410	3.0	7,763	2.5	19	519.8	66,955	3,502.9	1.5	8,543,634
Kentucky	86	0.6	3,570	1.1	42	161.7	45,304	3,334.6	1.4	38,773,872
South Carolina	123	0.9	5,186	1.6	42	391.6	75,515	2,811.3	1.2	22,855,829
Indiana	165	1.2	3,650	1.2	22	219.3	60,079	2,242.7	1.0	13,592,333
Connecticut	188	1.4	3,413	1.1	18	256.6	75,180	2,147.9	0.9	11,424,899
Missouri	193	1.4	3,432	1.1	18	242.4	70,633	1,625.9	0.7	8,424,145
Wisconsin	193	1.4	3,687	1.2	19	214.6	58,212	1,451.6	0.6	7,521,166
Utah	125	0.9	2,254	0.7	18	145.5	64,551	1,245.2	0.5	9,961,784
Oregon	168	1.2	2,290	0.7	14	163.3	71,306	1,005.4	0.4	5,984,411
Nebraska	54	0.4	1,468	0.5	27	102.3	69,706	957.4	0.4	17,729,278
Kansas	111	0.8	1,626	0.5	15	82.7	50,832	737.8	0.3	6,646,523
Alabama	107	0.8	1,703	0.5	16	103.7	60,901	648.6	0.3	6,061,636
Oklahoma	114	0.8	1,962	0.6	17	79.1	40,329	636.3	0.3	5,581,982
Iowa	81	0.6	1,054	0.3	13	79.3	75,266	552.8	0.2	6,825,123
New Mexico	61	0.4	772	0.2	13	43.7	56,635	420.4	0.2	6,891,639

Continued on next page.

INDUSTRY DATA BY STATE - Continued

State	Establishments Total (number)	% of U.S.	Employment Total (number)	% of U.S.	Per Estab.	Payroll Total ($ mil.)	Per Empl. ($)	Sales Total ($ mil.)	% of U.S.	Per Estab. ($)
Idaho	41	0.3	514	0.2	13	37.6	73,243	391.3	0.2	9,544,902
Arkansas	59	0.4	782	0.2	13	47.7	61,026	360.1	0.2	6,103,492
Louisiana	98	0.7	1,162	0.4	12	62.4	53,712	346.3	0.1	3,533,908
Nevada	79	0.6	1,077	0.3	14	56.4	52,373	313.4	0.1	3,967,620
Mississippi	50	0.4	544	0.2	11	25.5	46,822	305.0	0.1	6,099,340
Rhode Island	37	0.3	748	0.2	20	52.7	70,468	218.2	0.1	5,897,000
Hawaii	28	0.2	578	0.2	21	48.4	83,763	178.5	0.1	6,373,750
Maine	33	0.2	295	0.1	9	16.9	57,305	111.5	-	3,379,939
West Virginia	27	0.2	199	0.1	7	10.1	50,824	101.3	-	3,752,963
Alaska	10	0.1	154	-	15	8.6	56,084	63.4	-	6,342,700
South Dakota	18	0.1	145	-	8	7.0	48,407	51.2	-	2,844,500
Vermont	20	0.1	81	-	4	3.2	39,062	51.0	-	2,548,200
North Dakota	23	0.2	214	0.1	9	7.6	35,421	35.3	-	1,536,913
Montana	23	0.2	132	-	6	5.7	43,409	32.6	-	1,416,304
New Jersey	567	4.1	10K-24999	-	-	(D)	-	(D)	-	-
Georgia	457	3.3	10K-24999	-	-	(D)	-	(D)	-	-
Michigan	317	2.3	5K-9999	-	-	(D)	-	(D)	-	-
Arizona	232	1.7	2500-4999	-	-	(D)	-	(D)	-	-
New Hampshire	138	1.0	1000-2499	-	-	(D)	-	(D)	-	-
Delaware	32	0.2	250-499	-	-	(D)	-	(D)	-	-
D.C.	16	0.1	500-999	-	-	(D)	-	(D)	-	-
Wyoming	11	0.1	20-99	-	-	(D)	-	(D)	-	-

Source: 2002 *Economic Census*. The states are in descending order of sales or establishments (if sales data are missing for the majority). The symbol (D) appears when data are withheld to prevent disclosure of competitive information. States marked with (D) are sorted by number of establishments. A dash (-) indicates that the data element cannot be calculated. Shaded *states* on the state map indicate those states which have proportionately greater representation in the industry than would be indicated by the states population; the ratio is based on total sales or number of establishments. Shaded *regions* indicate where the industry is regionally most concentrated.

NAICS 423440 - OTHER COMMERCIAL EQUIPMENT MERCHANT WHOLESALERS*

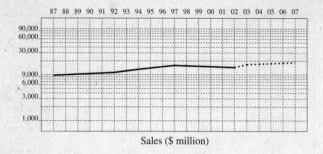

Sales ($ million)

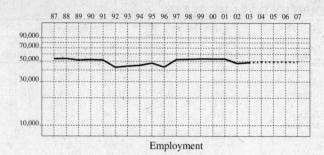

Employment

GENERAL STATISTICS

Year	Establishments (number)	Employment (number)	Payroll ($ million)	Sales ($ million)	Employees per Establishment (number)	Sales per Establishment ($)	Payroll per Employee ($)
1987	5,587	53,157	1,214.5	9,654.8	9.5	1,728,083.0	22,847.4
1988	5,331	53,412	1,337.4	9,964.4 e	10.0	1,869,142.7	25,039.3
1989	4,813	51,486	1,338.2	10,274.1 e	10.7	2,134,656.1	25,991.5
1990	4,801	52,073	1,388.7	10,583.8 e	10.8	2,204,499.1	26,668.3
1991	4,880	51,581	1,418.1	10,893.4 e	10.6	2,232,254.1	27,492.7
1992	4,998	42,924	1,207.9	11,203.1	8.6	2,241,516.6	28,140.4
1993	5,011	44,271	1,274.5	12,145.4 e	8.8	2,423,747.8	28,788.6
1994	5,039	45,117	1,353.7	13,087.7 e	9.0	2,597,281.2	30,004.2
1995	5,141	47,772	1,491.0	14,030.1 e	9.3	2,729,060.5	31,210.8
1996	4,895 e	43,254 e	1,406.6 e	14,972.4 e	8.8 e	3,058,713.0 e	32,519.5 e
1997	5,380	52,186	1,754.7	15,914.7	9.7	2,958,122.7	33,624.0
1998	5,402	52,516	1,899.8	15,609.2 e	9.7	2,889,522.4	36,175.6
1999	5,239	53,097	2,013.7	15,303.7 e	10.1	2,921,110.9	37,924.9
2000	5,152	52,991	2,037.7	14,998.2 e	10.3	2,911,141.3	38,453.5
2001	5,071	53,002	2,060.0	14,692.7 e	10.5	2,897,397.0	38,867.1
2002	4,779	47,547	1,833.8	14,387.2	9.9	3,010,504.3	38,568.2
2003	4,603	48,456	1,940.0	16,643.3 p	10.5	3,273,110.2 p	40,036.0
2004	4,951 p	49,340 p	2,079.0 p	17,074.0 p	10.0 p	3,358,132.3 p	41,750.4 p
2005	4,939 p	49,300 p	2,133.7 p	17,504.7 p	10.0 p	3,443,154.5 p	42,844.5 p
2006	4,926 p	49,261 p	2,188.4 p	17,935.5 p	10.0 p	3,528,176.6 p	43,938.6 p
2007	4,913 p	49,221 p	2,243.1 p	18,366.2 p	10.0 p	3,613,198.7 p	45,032.8 p

Sources: *Economic Census of the United States*, 1987, 1992, 1997, and 2002. Establishment counts, employment, and payroll are from *County Business Patterns* for non-Census years. Values followed by a 'p' are projections by the editors. Sales data for non-Census years are extrapolations, marked by 'e'. Data are the most recent available at this level of detail.

INDICES OF CHANGE

Year	Establishments (number)	Employment (number)	Payroll ($ million)	Sales ($ million)	Employees per Establishment (number)	Sales per Establishment ($)	Payroll per Employee ($)
1987	116.9	111.8	66.2	67.1	96.0	57.4	59.2
1992	104.6	90.3	65.9	77.9	86.9	74.5	73.0
1993	104.9	93.1	69.5	84.4 e	88.9	80.5	74.6
1994	105.4	94.9	73.8	91.0 e	90.9	86.3	77.8
1995	107.6	100.5	81.3	97.5 e	93.9	90.7	80.9
1996	102.4 e	91.0 e	76.7 e	104.1 e	88.9 e	101.6 e	84.3 e
1997	112.6	109.8	95.7	110.6	98.0	98.3	87.2
1998	113.0	110.5	103.6	108.5 e	98.0	96.0	93.8
1999	109.6	111.7	109.8	106.4 e	102.0	97.0	98.3
2000	107.8	111.4	111.1	104.2 e	104.0	96.7	99.7
2001	106.1	111.5	112.3	102.1 e	106.1	96.2	100.8
2002	100.0	100.0	100.0	100.0	100.0	100.0	100.0
2003	96.3	101.9	105.8	115.7 p	106.3	108.7 p	103.8
2004	103.6 p	103.8 p	113.4 p	118.7 p	100.6 p	111.5 p	108.3 p
2005	103.3 p	103.7 p	116.4 p	121.7 p	100.8 p	114.4 p	111.1 p
2006	103.1 p	103.6 p	119.3 p	124.7 p	101.0 p	117.2 p	113.9 p
2007	102.8 p	103.5 p	122.3 p	127.7 p	101.1 p	120.0 p	116.8 p

Sources: Same as General Statistics. The values shown reflect change from the base year, 2002. Values above 100 mean greater than 2002, values below 100 mean less than 2002, and a value of 100 in the 1987-2001 or 2003-2007 period means same as 2002. Values followed by a 'p' are projections by the editors; 'e' stands for extrapolation. Data are the most recent available at this level of detail.

SELECTED RATIOS

For 2002	Avg. of All Wholesale	Analyzed Industry	Index	For 2002	Avg. of All Wholesale	Analyzed Industry	Index
Employees per Establishment	15	10	67	Sales per Employee	791,325	302,589	38
Payroll per Establishment	626,122	383,720	61	Sales per Establishment	12,012,387	3,010,504	25
Payroll per Employee	41,161	38,568	94	Expenses per Establishment	na	na	na

Sources: Same as General Statistics. The 'Average of All' column, Wholesale or Retail, represents the average of the sector reported for the most recent complete year available. The Index shows the relationship between the Average and the Analyzed Industry. For example, 100 means that they are equal; 500 that the Analyzed Industry is five times the average; 50 means that the Analyzed Industry is half the national average. The abbreviation 'na' is used to show that data are 'not available'.

*Equivalent to SIC 5046.

LEADING COMPANIES   Number shown: 75   Total sales ($ mil): 127,128   Total employment (000): 274.4

Company Name	Address				CEO Name	Phone	Co. Type	Sales ($ mil)	Empl. (000)
Philips Consumer Electronics	64 Perimeter Ctr E	Atlanta	GA	31146		770-821-3945	R	107,046*	225.0
EchoStar Communications Corp.	5701 S Santa Fe Dr	Littleton	CO	80120	Charles W Ergen	303-723-1000	P	7,150	26.0
Performance Food Group Co.	12500 W Creek	Richmond	VA	23238	Robert C Sledd	804-484-7700	P	6,149	11.0
Belden Wire and Cable Co.	2200 US Hwy 27 S	Richmond	IN	47374		765-983-5200	R	3,260*	4.0
Enprotech Corp.	335 Madison Ave	New York	NY	10017	M Rabbat	212-818-8204	S	410*	<0.1
Nobel/Sysco Food Services Co.	PO Box 5566	Denver	CO	80217	Chris DeWitt	303-458-4000	S	378*	0.9
Pegler-Sysco Food Services Co.	1700 Center Park Rd	Lincoln	NE	68501	Gary L Rezac	402-423-1031	S	188*	0.5
Wasserstrom Co.	477 S Front St	Columbus	OH	43215	Rodney Wasserstrom	614-228-6525	R	122*	0.5
Agency for Instructional Tech.	1800 N Stonelake Dr	Bloomington	IN	47404		812-339-2203	R	120*	<0.1
Focus Products Group L.L.C.	120 Lakeview Pkwy	Vernon Hills	IL	60061	Keith Jaffee	847-816-6246	R	115*	<0.1
Array Distribution L.L.C.	406 E Anthony Dr	Urbana	IL	61802		217-384-2175	R	95*	0.2
Boelter Companies Inc.	11100 Silver Sprgs	Milwaukee	WI	53225	FW Boelter	414-461-3400	R	87*	0.3
Hotel Superstore	PO Box 757	Mascotte	FL	34753	Arthur Reiss	561-371-2661	R	85*	0.3
Rogers Machinery Company Inc.	PO Box 23279	Portland	OR	97281	Walt Novak	503-639-6151	R	82*	0.2
Next Day Gormet & Superior	510 W County Rd D	St. Paul	MN	55112	Robert M Kurek	651-636-1110	R	80*	0.3
Glacier Water Services Inc.	1385 Park Center Dr	Vista	CA	92081	Brian H McInerney	760-560-1111	P	72	0.3
H.D. Sheldon and Company Inc.	143 W 29th St	New York	NY	10001	Robert Metros	212-924-6920	R	71*	<0.1
Houston's Inc.	9799 SW Freeman	Wilsonville	OR	97070	John Houston	503-582-1121	R	66*	0.2
P.F.G. Lester Company Inc.	PO Box 340	Lebanon	TN	37088		615-444-2963	S	64*	0.2
Burrows Co.	PO Box 747	Wheeling	IL	60090	George J Burrows	847-537-7300	R	61*	0.3
Hubert Co.	PO Box 631642	Cincinnati	OH	45263	Bart Kohler	513-367-8600	R	56*	0.4
Singer Equipment Company Inc.	PO Box 13668	Reading	PA	19612	Fred Singer	610-929-8000	R	56*	0.2
PBI Market Equipment Inc.	PO Box 6097	Signal Hill	CA	90755	Tom L Everson	562-595-4785	R	50*	<0.1
Lucky Coin	1525 Airline Dr	Metairie	LA	70001	John Georges	504-835-3232	R	50*	0.1
Greco and Sons Inc.	280 S Westgate Dr	Carol Stream	IL	60188	Edwardo Greco	630-668-1000	R	46*	0.1
Sunflower Restaurant Supply Inc.	PO Box 1277	Salina	KS	67402	Leroy A Baumberger	785-823-6394	R	45*	<0.1
Brady Distributing Co.	PO Box 19269	Charlotte	NC	28219	Jon P Brady	704-357-6284	R	43*	0.1
Pacific Digital Corp.	2052 Alton Pkwy	Irvine	CA	92606	John Parsa	949-252-1111	R	43*	0.1
TEC America Inc.	4401-A Bankers Cir	Atlanta	GA	30360	Bill Hosken	770-449-3040	S	40*	0.1
Ice-O-Matic	11100 E 45th Ave	Denver	CO	80239		303-371-3737	S	36*	0.2
Mack Boring and Parts Co.	PO Box 3116	Union	NJ	07083	Edward McGovern	908-964-0700	R	35*	<0.1
Advanced Network Inc.	8940 Activity Rd	San Diego	CA	92126	Robert Plunkett	858-578-1533	R	34*	0.1
MG Concept	355 S Technology	Central Islip	NY	11722	Jay Austrien	631-348-1761	R	34*	0.1
Specialty Store Services Inc.	454 Jarvis Ave	Des Plaines	IL	60018	Malcolm Finke	847-470-7000	R	34*	0.1
Struve Distributing Company Inc.	276 West 100 South	Salt Lake City	UT	84101	Preston Struve	801-328-1636	R	34*	<0.1
Asi Holding Inc.	1701B Clint Moore	Boca Raton	FL	33487	Bill Gray	561-241-9599	R	34*	<0.1
Biora Inc.	415 N La Salle St	Chicago	IL	60610	Chris Pallotto	312-832-1414	S	32*	<0.1
Allen Foods Inc.	8543 Page Ave	Overland	MO	63114	Stanley Allen	314-426-4100	S	31*	0.1
Bornquist Inc.	7050 N Lehigh Ave	Chicago	IL	60093	Harry Hultgren	773-774-2800	R	29*	<0.1
Allied Vision	997 Rochester Rd	Troy	MI	48083		248-585-0445	R	28*	<0.1
Wahltek Inc.	2711 Grand Ave	Des Moines	IA	50312	Bruce Fagerstrom	515-309-3935	R	28*	0.1
Resnick Supermarket Equipment	PO Box Q	Mountain Dale	NY	12763	William Resnick	845-434-8200	R	25*	<0.1
Golden West Equipment Inc.	1000 S Euclid St	La Habra	CA	90631	Michael Kennedy	714-879-3850	R	25*	<0.1
Mg's Original Products Co.	13618 SE 272nd Ct	Kent	WA	98042	Richard Gradwohl	253-631-1911	R	24*	<0.1
Store Supply Warehouse Inc.	9801 Page Ave	Saint Louis	MO	63132	Robert Balk	314-427-8887	R	23*	<0.1
Douron Inc.	30 New Plant Ct	Owings Mills	MD	21117	Eugene L Hux	410-363-2600	R	23*	0.1
Premier Technology Inc.	170 E Siphon Rd	Pocatello	ID	83202	Mark Brown	208-238-3036	R	23*	0.1
Partitions and Accessories Co.	1220 S Pasadena	Mesa	AZ	85210	Sandra Borelli	480-969-6606	R	21*	<0.1
Valuecomm Corp.	4410 Roosevelt Rd	Hillside	IL	60162	Phil Hollenberg	708-531-0700	R	20*	<0.1
Henderson Auctions Inc.	PO Box 336	Livingston	LA	70754	Jeffrey Henderson	225-686-2252	R	20*	<0.1
Vic Trenco Inc.	673 Ethel St NW	Atlanta	GA	30318	William Vick	404-876-5002	R	19*	<0.1
Coosa Steel Corp.	PO Box 5624	Rome	GA	30162		706-235-7011	R	19*	<0.1
SS Kemp and Co.	4567 Willow Pkwy	Cleveland	OH	44125	Howard Fishman	216-271-7700	R	18*	<0.1
Le Creuset of America Inc.	PO Box 67	Early Branch	SC	29916	Paul Van Zuydam	803-943-4308	S	18*	<0.1
Rave Computer Association Inc.	36960 Metro Ct	Sterling Heights	MI	48312	Rick Darter	586-939-8230	R	18*	<0.1
A and D Engineering Inc.	1555 McCandless Dr	Milpitas	CA	95035	Paul Huber	408-263-5333	R	18*	<0.1
Midwest Equipment Company Inc.	2511 Cassens Dr	Fenton	MO	63026	James Sramek	636-343-0664	R	18*	<0.1
ABC Industries Inc.	100 Cleveland Ave	Freeport	NY	11520	Howard Schulman	516-867-8400	R	17*	<0.1
Bintz Restaurant Supply Co.	PO Box 1350	Salt Lake City	UT	84110	Roger Brown	801-463-1515	R	17*	<0.1
Digiorgio Costantini Partnership	24 NE 24th Ave	Pompano Beach	FL	33062		954-785-0034	R	17*	<0.1
Noble Gift Packaging	170 Gregg St	Lodi	NJ	07644	Moses Gancfried	201-909-8100	R	17*	<0.1
Partitions Specialties Inc.	20996 Cabot Blvd	Hayward	CA	94545	Randy Squires	650-369-7278	R	16*	<0.1
Idacta	245 El Cajon Way	Los Gatos	CA	95032	Glenn Collyer	408-356-9983	R	16*	<0.1
Southwest Ag Inc.	39927 US Hwy 160	Bayfield	CO	81122	Dennis Hillyer	970-884-4101	R	16*	<0.1
Total Fire and Safety Inc.	6026 Scyene Rd	Dallas	TX	75227	Robert Damesworth	214-381-6116	R	16*	<0.1
Coffee Bean International Inc.	2181 NW Nicolai St	Portland	OR	97210	Margaret Sharp	503-227-4490	R	15*	<0.1
Pars International Computer Inc.	22445 Maple Ct	Hayward	CA	94541		510-733-0103	R	15*	<0.1
American Surplus Inc.	1 Noyes Ave	Rumford	RI	02916	William Di Maio	401-434-4355	R	15*	<0.1
Robert H Ham Associates Ltd.	PO Box 77398	Greensboro	NC	27417	H Elkins	336-299-3422	R	15*	<0.1
Bel Terr Decorating Inc.	367 Taggert Rd	Darlington	PA	16115	Linda Massey	724-843-5674	R	15*	<0.1
Atlantic Scale Company Inc.	136 Washington Ave	Nutley	NJ	07110	Fred Algieri	973-661-7090	R	14*	<0.1
RD Fixtures	889 Erie Ave	N. Tonawanda	NY	14120	William Wicks	716-694-3825	R	14*	<0.1
Taylor Utlimate Services Co.	1780 N Commerce	Fort Lauderdale	FL	33326	Raul Piedra	954-217-9100	R	14*	<0.1
Cliff Weil Inc.	PO Box 427	Mechanicsville	VA	23116	Alvin B Hutzler II	804-746-1321	R	14*	<0.1
Haldeman-Homme Inc.	430 Industrial Blvd	Minneapolis	MN	55413	Ernest R Stalock	612-331-4880	R	14*	<0.1

Source: Ward's Business Directory of U.S. Private and Public Companies, Volumes 1 and 2, 2005. The company type code used is as follows: P - Public, R - Private, S - Subsidiary, D - Division, J - Joint Venture, A - Affiliate, G - Group. Sales are in millions of dollars, employees are in thousands. An asterisk (*) indicates an estimated sales volume. The symbol < stands for 'less than'. Company names and addresses are truncated, in some cases, to fit into the available space.

OCCUPATIONS EMPLOYED BY PROFESSIONAL & COMMERCIAL EQUIPMENT & SUPPLIES

Occupation	% of Total 2004	Change to 2014	Occupation	% of Total 2004	Change to 2014
Sales reps, wholesale & manufacturing, exc tech	8.8	20.2	Computer software engineers, systems software	1.7	42.6
Sales reps, wholesale & manufacturing, tech	8.4	20.2	Computer specialists, nec	1.6	20.2
Computer, automated teller, & office machine repairers	8.0	8.2	First-line supervisors/managers of office workers	1.6	9.0
Customer service representatives	3.9	23.6	Truck drivers, light or delivery services	1.5	20.2
Computer systems analysts	2.7	32.3	Team assemblers	1.5	20.2
Computer support specialists	2.6	20.2	Computer software engineers, applications	1.4	44.3
Shipping, receiving, & traffic clerks	2.5	8.8	Business operation specialists, nec	1.3	32.3
Computer programmers	2.5	-1.9	Order clerks	1.2	-21.5
Office clerks, general	2.4	7.0	Sales managers	1.2	28.6
Laborers & freight, stock, & material movers, hand	2.1	8.2	Office machine operators, except computer	1.1	-21.8
Bookkeeping, accounting, & auditing clerks	2.0	8.2	Billing & posting clerks & machine operators	1.1	-3.4
General & operations managers	2.0	19.0	Maintenance & repair workers, general	1.0	20.2
Stock clerks & order fillers	1.9	-7.9	Executive secretaries & administrative assistants	1.0	14.0
First-line supervisors/managers of non-retail sales work	1.8	11.2	Computer & information systems managers	1.0	25.9

Source: Industry-Occupation Matrix, Bureau of Labor Statistics. These data are reported based on 4-digit NAICS categories but have been matched to corresponding 6-digit NAICS industry codes. The change reported for each occupation to the year 2014 is a percent of growth or decline as estimated by the Bureau of Labor Statistics. The abbreviation nec stands for 'not elsewhere classified.'

LOCATION BY STATE AND REGIONAL CONCENTRATION

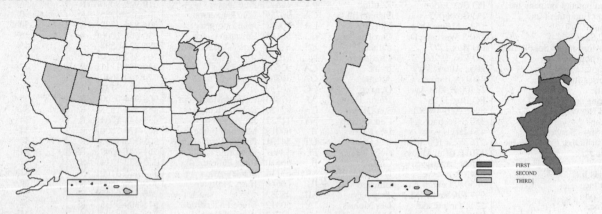

INDUSTRY DATA BY STATE

State	Establishments Total (number)	% of U.S.	Employment Total (number)	% of U.S.	Per Estab.	Payroll Total ($ mil.)	Per Empl. ($)	Sales Total ($ mil.)	% of U.S.	Per Estab. ($)
California	557	11.6	6,026	12.6	11	229.0	38,008	1,706.7	11.8	3,064,117
Ohio	178	3.7	3,213	6.7	18	115.2	35,856	1,194.7	8.3	6,711,562
Illinois	233	4.8	3,484	7.3	15	152.7	43,834	1,044.1	7.2	4,481,159
New York	388	8.1	2,803	5.9	7	108.5	38,694	943.9	6.5	2,432,814
Texas	297	6.2	3,404	7.1	11	118.4	34,775	896.0	6.2	3,016,801
Florida	374	7.8	2,523	5.3	7	91.4	36,221	777.4	5.4	2,078,548
Pennsylvania	197	4.1	1,852	3.9	9	69.7	37,613	474.8	3.3	2,410,371
Georgia	167	3.5	1,540	3.2	9	61.6	40,010	465.1	3.2	2,784,784
Wisconsin	79	1.6	1,347	2.8	17	53.7	39,903	365.2	2.5	4,622,228
Louisiana	78	1.6	691	1.4	9	21.0	30,386	364.0	2.5	4,667,064
North Carolina	132	2.7	1,205	2.5	9	45.7	37,933	355.9	2.5	2,696,174
Washington	127	2.6	1,032	2.2	8	38.7	37,522	314.0	2.2	2,472,394
Massachusetts	104	2.2	965	2.0	9	43.6	45,216	254.8	1.8	2,449,644
Missouri	110	2.3	1,101	2.3	10	39.9	36,204	247.0	1.7	2,245,736
Alabama	52	1.1	493	1.0	9	16.1	32,734	193.7	1.3	3,725,692
Nevada	43	0.9	428	0.9	10	15.9	37,259	173.8	1.2	4,042,442
Rhode Island	19	0.4	417	0.9	22	19.0	45,547	158.8	1.1	8,358,105
Utah	44	0.9	532	1.1	12	16.3	30,583	120.0	0.8	2,727,409
Virginia	88	1.8	497	1.0	6	16.3	32,819	104.1	0.7	1,183,182
Hawaii	29	0.6	290	0.6	10	10.2	35,093	96.0	0.7	3,309,172
Kansas	55	1.1	420	0.9	8	15.7	37,450	90.8	0.6	1,650,127
South Carolina	42	0.9	315	0.7	8	11.1	35,251	77.9	0.5	1,855,738
Oklahoma	45	0.9	374	0.8	8	12.3	32,783	76.6	0.5	1,702,200
Mississippi	28	0.6	234	0.5	8	9.4	40,201	63.4	0.4	2,264,250
New Mexico	27	0.6	203	0.4	8	6.8	33,478	45.6	0.3	1,688,593
Maine	19	0.4	112	0.2	6	3.7	33,375	31.8	0.2	1,673,579
Montana	20	0.4	115	0.2	6	2.9	25,548	21.0	0.1	1,049,400
New Jersey	208	4.3	1000-2499	-	-	(D)		(D)		-
Michigan	137	2.9	1000-2499	-	-	(D)		(D)		-

Continued on next page.

INDUSTRY DATA BY STATE - Continued

State	Establishments		Employment			Payroll		Sales		
	Total (number)	% of U.S.	Total (number)	% of U.S.	Per Estab.	Total ($ mil.)	Per Empl. ($)	Total ($ mil.)	% of U.S.	Per Estab. ($)
Tennessee	106	2.2	500-999	-	-	(D)	-	(D)	-	-
Minnesota	98	2.0	1000-2499	-	-	(D)	-	(D)	-	-
Indiana	93	1.9	1000-2499	-	-	(D)	-	(D)	-	-
Colorado	89	1.9	500-999	-	-	(D)	-	(D)	-	-
Arizona	83	1.7	500-999	-	-	(D)	-	(D)	-	-
Maryland	80	1.7	500-999	-	-	(D)	-	(D)	-	-
Oregon	64	1.3	500-999	-	-	(D)	-	(D)	-	-
Connecticut	56	1.2	500-999	-	-	(D)	-	(D)	-	-
Kentucky	51	1.1	500-999	-	-	(D)	-	(D)	-	-
Iowa	43	0.9	250-499	-	-	(D)	-	(D)	-	-
Arkansas	39	0.8	250-499	-	-	(D)	-	(D)	-	-
New Hampshire	23	0.5	250-499	-	-	(D)	-	(D)	-	-
Nebraska	20	0.4	100-249	-	-	(D)	-	(D)	-	-
West Virginia	18	0.4	100-249	-	-	(D)	-	(D)	-	-
Idaho	16	0.3	100-249	-	-	(D)	-	(D)	-	-
North Dakota	15	0.3	100-249	-	-	(D)	-	(D)	-	-
South Dakota	11	0.2	100-249	-	-	(D)	-	(D)	-	-
Alaska	8	0.2	20-99	-	-	(D)	-	(D)	-	-
Delaware	7	0.1	20-99	-	-	(D)	-	(D)	-	-
Vermont	4	0.1	0-19	-	-	(D)	-	(D)	-	-
D.C.	3	0.1	0-19	-	-	(D)	-	(D)	-	-
Wyoming	3	0.1	20-99	-	-	(D)	-	(D)	-	-

Source: 2002 *Economic Census*. The states are in descending order of sales or establishments (if sales data are missing for the majority). The symbol (D) appears when data are withheld to prevent disclosure of competitive information. States marked with (D) are sorted by number of establishments. A dash (-) indicates that the data element cannot be calculated. Shaded *states* on the state map indicate those states which have proportionately greater representation in the industry than would be indicated by the states population; the ratio is based on total sales or number of establishments. Shaded *regions* indicate where the industry is regionally most concentrated.

NAICS 423450 - MEDICAL, DENTAL, AND HOSPITAL EQUIPMENT AND SUPPLIES MERCHANT WHOLESALERS

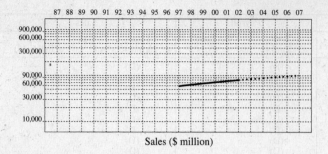

Sales ($ million)

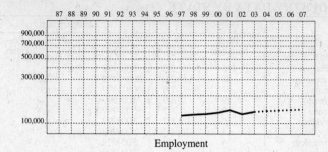

Employment

GENERAL STATISTICS

Year	Establishments (number)	Employment (number)	Payroll ($ million)	Sales ($ million)	Employees per Establishment (number)	Sales per Establishment ($)	Payroll per Employee ($)
1987	-	-	-	-	-	-	-
1988	-	-	-	-	-	-	-
1989	-	-	-	-	-	-	-
1990	-	-	-	-	-	-	-
1991	-	-	-	-	-	-	-
1992	-	-	-	-	-	-	-
1993	-	-	-	-	-	-	-
1994	-	-	-	-	-	-	-
1995	-	-	-	-	-	-	-
1996	-	-	-	-	-	-	-
1997	9,782	121,572	5,746.2	58,791.7	12.4	6,010,192.2	47,265.8
1998	9,826	124,549	6,358.0	62,984.2 e	12.7	6,409,953.2	51,048.2
1999	9,489	126,334	6,980.1	67,176.7 e	13.3	7,079,428.8	55,251.2
2000	9,287	130,855	7,494.3	71,369.2 e	14.1	7,684,849.8	57,271.7
2001	9,212	139,657	8,228.5	75,561.7 e	15.2	8,202,529.3	58,919.4
2002	7,800	126,288	7,560.9	79,754.2	16.2	10,224,897.4	59,870.3
2003	7,906	134,015	8,830.3	83,946.7 p	17.0	10,307,642.7 p	65,890.2
2004	7,621 p	136,771 p	9,157.8 p	88,139.2 p	17.6 p	11,080,690.5 p	67,528.9 p
2005	7,265 p	138,705 p	9,618.8 p	92,331.7 p	18.4 p	11,853,738.4 p	70,285.5 p
2006	6,910 p	140,638 p	10,079.7 p	96,524.2 p	19.2 p	12,626,786.3 p	73,042.1 p
2007	6,554 p	142,571 p	10,540.6 p	100,716.7 p	20.0 p	13,399,834.2 p	75,798.8 p

Source: Economic Census of the United States, 1997 and 2002. Establishment counts, employment, and payroll are from *County Business Patterns* for non-Census years. This is a newly defined industry. Data for prior years are unavailable at the time of publication but may become available over time. Values followed by 'p' are projections by the editors. Sales data for non-Census years are extrapolations, marked by 'e'.

INDICES OF CHANGE

Year	Establishments (number)	Employment (number)	Payroll ($ million)	Sales ($ million)	Employees per Establishment (number)	Sales per Establishment ($)	Payroll per Employee ($)
1987	-	-	-	-	-	-	-
1992	-	-	-	-	-	-	-
1993	-	-	-	-	-	-	-
1994	-	-	-	-	-	-	-
1995	-	-	-	-	-	-	-
1996	-	-	-	-	-	-	-
1997	125.4	96.3	76.0	73.7	76.5	58.8	78.9
1998	126.0	98.6	84.1	79.0 e	78.4	62.7	85.3
1999	121.7	100.0	92.3	84.2 e	82.1	69.2	92.3
2000	119.1	103.6	99.1	89.5 e	87.0	75.2	95.7
2001	118.1	110.6	108.8	94.7 e	93.8	80.2	98.4
2002	100.0	100.0	100.0	100.0	100.0	100.0	100.0
2003	101.4	106.1	116.8	105.3 p	104.6	100.8 p	110.1
2004	97.7 p	108.3 p	121.1 p	110.5 p	108.8 p	108.4 p	112.8 p
2005	93.1 p	109.8 p	127.2 p	115.8 p	113.8 p	115.9 p	117.4 p
2006	88.6 p	111.4 p	133.3 p	121.0 p	118.8 p	123.5 p	122.0 p
2007	84.0 p	112.9 p	139.4 p	126.3 p	123.7 p	131.1 p	126.6 p

Sources: Same as General Statistics. The values shown reflect change from the base year, 2002. Values above 100 mean greater than 2002, values below 100 mean less than 2002, and a value of 100 in the 1987-2001 or 2003-2007 period means same as 2002. Values followed by a 'p' are projections by the editors; 'e' stands for extrapolation. Data are the most recent available at this level of detail.

SELECTED RATIOS

For 2002	Avg. of All Wholesale	Analyzed Industry	Index	For 2002	Avg. of All Wholesale	Analyzed Industry	Index
Employees per Establishment	15	16	108	Sales per Employee	791,325	631,526	80
Payroll per Establishment	626,122	969,346	155	Sales per Establishment	12,012,387	10,224,897	85
Payroll per Employee	41,161	59,870	145	Expenses per Establishment	na	na	na

Sources: Same as General Statistics. The 'Average of All' column, Wholesale or Retail, represents the average of the sector reported for the most recent complete year available. The Index shows the relationship between the Average and the Analyzed Industry. For example, 100 means that they are equal; 500 that the Analyzed Industry is five times the average; 50 means that the Analyzed Industry is half the national average. The abbreviation 'na' is used to show that data are 'not available'.

LEADING COMPANIES Number shown: **75** Total sales ($ mil): **56,936** Total employment (000): **98.8**

Company Name	Address				CEO Name	Phone	Co. Type	Sales ($ mil)	Empl. (000)
Cardinal Distribution L.P.	7000 Cardinal Pl	Dublin	OH	43017	Robert Walter	614-757-5000	S	27,600*	40.0
Fisher Scientific International Inc.	1 Liberty Ln	Hampton	NH	03842	David T Della Penta	603-926-5911	P	4,663	17.5
Owens and Minor Inc.	PO Box 27626	Glen Allen	VA	23060		804-747-9794	P	4,525	3.4
Henry Schein Inc.	135 Duryea Rd	Melville	NY	11747	Stanley M Bergman	516-843-5325	P	4,100	7.9
Toshiba America Medical Systems	PO Box 2068	Tustin	CA	92781	Hiromitsu Igarashi	714-730-5000	S	3,189*	0.1
GMP Companies Inc.	1 E Broward Blvd	Fort Lauderdale	FL	33301	Bart Chernow	954-745-3511	R	2,614*	0.1
Patterson Companies Inc.	1031 Mendota Hts	St. Paul	MN	55120	Peter L Frechette	651-686-1600	P	1,969	5.8
PSS World Medical Inc.	4345 Southpoint	Jacksonville	FL	32216	Clark A Johnson	904-332-3000	P	1,350	3.0
Darby Group Companies Inc.	865 Merrick Ave	Westbury	NY	11590	Carl Ashkin	516-683-1800	R	670*	1.4
West Pharmaceutical Services Inc.	PO Box 645	Lionville	PA	19353		610-594-2900	P	542	4.3
Sicor Inc.	19 Hughes	Irvine	CA	92618	Michael Cannon	949-455-4700	R	456	1.9
Auto Suture Company U.S.A.	150 Glover Ave	Norwalk	CT	06856	Allen Panzer	203-845-1000	S	401*	1.4
VIASYS Healthcare Inc.	227 Washington St	Conshohocken	PA	19428	Thomas I Kuhn	610-862-0800	P	393	1.8
Gaspro	PO Box 30707	Honolulu	HI	96820		808-842-2222	S	320*	0.1
Merriam-Graves Corp.	806 River Rd	Charlestown	NH	03603	Donald Wakeman	603-542-8768	R	237*	0.3
American Medical Systems	10700 Bren Rd W	Minnetonka	MN	55343	Martin J Emerson	952-930-6000	P	209	0.6
Kendall LTP	Two Ludlow	Chicopee	MA	01022			D	192*	0.6
Pegler-Sysco Food Services Co.	1700 Center Park Rd	Lincoln	NE	68501	Gary L Rezac	402-423-1031	S	188*	0.5
Terramarr Inc.	7304 W 130th St	Schuylkl Hvn	KS	66213	Robert Duncan	913-851-0500	R	179*	0.4
Hitachi Medical Systems America	1959 Summit	Twinsburg	OH	44087	Richard L Ernst	330-425-1313	S	142*	0.2
Moore Medical Corp.	PO Box 1500	New Britain	CT	06050	Linda M Autore	860-826-3600	S	142	0.3
Omnicell Inc.	1201 Charleston Rd	Mountain View	CA	94043		650-251-6100	P	124	0.4
Archbold Health Services Inc.	PO Box 1018	Thomasville	GA	31799	Ken E Beverly	912-227-6809	R	122*	0.3
Midwest Veterinary Supply Inc.	11965 Larc Ind Blvd	Burnsville	MN	55337	Guy Flickinger	952-894-4350	R	115*	0.2
Masune First Aid and Safety Co.	PO Box 1050	Tonawanda	NY	14151	Mark Ladouceur	716-695-4999	R	102*	0.2
Chindex International Inc.	7201 Wisconsin	Bethesda	MD	20814	Roberta Lipson	301-215-7777	P	88	0.8
Hotel Superstore	PO Box 757	Mascotte	FL	34753	Arthur Reiss	561-371-2661	R	85*	0.3
Seamens Medical Solutions	209 Gregson Dr	Cary	NC	27511		919-468-7777	R	77*	0.2
ATD-American Co.	111-149 Greenwood	Wyncote	PA	19095	Jerome Zaslow	215-576-1380	R	65*	0.1
MMS, A Medical Supply Co.	13400 Lakefront Dr	Earth City	MO	63045	Gary Reeve	314-291-2900	R	62*	0.1
Burrows Co.	PO Box 747	Wheeling	IL	60090	George J Burrows	847-537-7300	R	61*	0.3
Micro Bio-Medics Inc.	846 Pelham Pkwy	Pelham Manor	NY	10803	Mike Raccioppi	914-738-8400	D	61*	0.2
Crescent City Security Inc.	PO Box 144	Evansville	IN	47701	Stanley Fishburn	812-426-2603	R	59*	0.1
ivpcare Inc.	7164 Technology Dr	Frisco	TX	75034	Von L Best	214-387-3500	R	54*	0.1
Phamatech Inc.	1051 Barnes Cyn	San Diego	CA	92121	Tuan Pham	858-635-5840	R	54*	0.1
Mabis Healthcare Inc.	1931 Norman Dr	Waukegan	IL	60085	Mike Mazza	847-680-6811	R	53*	<0.1
Anderson Bremer Paper Co.	PO Box 151	Canoga Park	CA	91305	Abner Levy	818-999-1888	R	51*	0.1
Atlantic Medco Inc.	520 Kane St	Scranton	PA	18505	Len Mancuso	570-969-4066	R	51*	0.1
Beacon Medical Products L.L.C.	14702 W 105th St	Schuylkl Hvn	KS	66215		913-894-6058	R	51*	0.1
Darrow Medical Corp.	PO Box 1235	Sioux Falls	SD	57101	Sedge Dienst	605-332-6689	R	51*	0.1
Diagnostic Medical Systems	2101 N University	Fargo	ND	58102		701-237-9073	R	51*	0.1
Government Supply Intern. Ltd.	301 Clematis St	W. Palm Beach	FL			561-833-1066	R	51*	0.1
KaVo America Corp.	340 E Main St	Lake Zurich	IL	60047	John Franz	847-550-6800	R	51*	0.1
Mercury Medical	PO Box 20000	Saint Petersburg	FL	33742	Stanley Pangalakis	727-573-0088	R	51*	0.1
Omron Healthcare Inc.	300 Lakeview Pkwy	Vernon Hills	IL	60061	Kazuo Saito	847-680-6200	S	51*	0.1
Pacific Medical Inc.	1264 Stealth St	Livermore	CA	94551	John Petlansky	925-460-0760	R	51*	0.1
Physician Sales and Service Inc.	4105 Royal Dr NW	Kennesaw	GA	30144		678-813-4000	R	51*	0.1
Picker International Inc.	4155 Shackleford Rd	Norcross	GA	30093		770-447-5727	R	51*	0.1
Proseed Inc.	13103 Harland NE	Covington	GA	30014	Bob Mellen	770-786-9051	R	51*	0.1
Saint Elizabeth Home Medical	PO Box 30550	Lincoln	NE	68503	Robert Lanik	402-464-8755	R	51*	0.1
HoMedics-USA Inc.	3000 N Pontiac Trl	Commerce	MI	48390	Ron Ferber	248-863-3000	R	51*	0.2
Zila Inc.	5227 N 7th St	Phoenix	AZ	85014	Douglas D Burkett	602-266-6700	P	49	0.1
MEDICMASTER	3705 St John Pkwy	Sanford	FL	32771	Angel Rivera	407-330-5911	R	47*	0.3
Express-Med Inc.	6530 Campus	New Albany	OH	43054	Charle Poynter		R	44*	0.3
Briggs Corp.	PO Box 1698	Des Moines	IA	50306	Merwyn Dan	515-327-6400	R	42*	0.3
Rigaku MSC Inc.	9009 New Trails Dr	The Woodlands	TX	77381	Yasuhiro Sugiyama	281-363-1033	R	42*	<0.1
Laboratory Supply Company Inc.	PO Box 9289	Louisville	KY	40209		502-363-1891	R	41*	0.2
Ascentra Holdings Inc.	2251 S Jones Blvd	Las Vegas	NV	89146	Jermone Snyder	702-365-1668	R	38*	<0.1
Peterson Medical	468 N Main St	Heber City	UT	84032	Tom Bradley	435-657-0164	R	38*	<0.1
Midland Medical Supply Co.	4850 Old Cheney Rd	Lincoln	NE	68516	Al Borchhardt	402-423-8877	R	38*	<0.1
Clinical Specialties Inc.	6955 Treeline Dr	Brecksville	OH	44141	Edward Rivalsky	440-717-1700	R	38*	<0.1
Holloway Medical Sales Inc.	1736 W Barberry Cir	Louisville	CO	80401	Thomas Holloway	303-661-9805	R	37*	<0.1
A Leventhal and Sons Inc.	PO Box 5150	Scranton	PA	18505	Jeffrey Leventhal	570-342-9106	R	36*	<0.1
Klingensmith's Healthcare	PO Box 151	Ford City	PA	16226	David Knepshield	724-763-8889	R	36*	<0.1
Medco Respiratory Instruments	PO Box 924189	Houston	TX	77292	David Hayden	713-956-5288	R	36*	<0.1
Regional Medical Rental and Sales	10374 S Choctaw Dr	Baton Rouge	LA	70815	Harvey Mitchell	225-272-5919	R	36*	<0.1
Sklar Corp.	889 S Matlack St	West Chester	PA	19382	Don Taylor	610-430-3200	R	36*	<0.1
Sysmex Corporation of America	1 Nelson C White	Mundelein	IL	60060	Tak Kanamari	847-996-4300	R	36*	<0.1
United Health Care Services Inc.	9 Creek Pkwy	Boothwyn	PA	19061	Michael Bronfien	610-364-2700	R	36*	<0.1
Care Rehab & Orthopaedic	PO Box 580	Mc Lean	VA	22101	Christian Hunt	703-448-9644	R	35*	<0.1
Spectranetics Corp.	96 Talamine Ct	Co Springs	CO	80907	Emile J Geisenheimer	719-633-8333	P	35	0.1
Tri-State Surgical Supply	409 Hoyt St	Brooklyn	NY	11231	George Hoffman	718-624-1000	R	34*	<0.1
Boll Medical Inc.	PO Box 11810	Charleston	WV	25339	C Boll	304-345-2944	R	33*	<0.1
Kight's Medical Corp.	PO Box 98237	Raleigh	NC	27624	John Kight	919-878-6666	R	32*	<0.1
Audio Video Supply Inc.	4575 Ruffner St	San Diego	CA	92111	Richard Moore	858-565-1101	R	31*	<0.1

Source: Ward's Business Directory of U.S. Private and Public Companies, Volumes 1 and 2, 2005. The company type code used is as follows: P - Public, R - Private, S - Subsidiary, D - Division, J - Joint Venture, A - Affiliate, G - Group. Sales are in millions of dollars, employees are in thousands. An asterisk (*) indicates an estimated sales volume. The symbol < stands for 'less than'. Company names and addresses are truncated, in some cases, to fit into the available space.

OCCUPATIONS EMPLOYED BY PROFESSIONAL & COMMERCIAL EQUIPMENT & SUPPLIES

Occupation	% of Total 2004	Change to 2014	Occupation	% of Total 2004	Change to 2014
Sales reps, wholesale & manufacturing, exc tech	8.8	20.2	Computer software engineers, systems software	1.7	42.6
Sales reps, wholesale & manufacturing, tech	8.4	20.2	Computer specialists, nec	1.6	20.2
Computer, automated teller, & office machine repairers	8.0	8.2	First-line supervisors/managers of office workers	1.6	9.0
Customer service representatives	3.9	23.6	Truck drivers, light or delivery services	1.5	20.2
Computer systems analysts	2.7	32.3	Team assemblers	1.5	20.2
Computer support specialists	2.6	20.2	Computer software engineers, applications	1.4	44.3
Shipping, receiving, & traffic clerks	2.5	8.8	Business operation specialists, nec	1.3	32.3
Computer programmers	2.5	-1.9	Order clerks	1.2	-21.5
Office clerks, general	2.4	7.0	Sales managers	1.2	28.6
Laborers & freight, stock, & material movers, hand	2.1	8.2	Office machine operators, except computer	1.1	-21.8
Bookkeeping, accounting, & auditing clerks	2.0	8.2	Billing & posting clerks & machine operators	1.1	-3.4
General & operations managers	2.0	19.0	Maintenance & repair workers, general	1.0	20.2
Stock clerks & order fillers	1.9	-7.9	Executive secretaries & administrative assistants	1.0	14.0
First-line supervisors/managers of non-retail sales work	1.8	11.2	Computer & information systems managers	1.0	25.9

Source: Industry-Occupation Matrix, Bureau of Labor Statistics. These data are reported based on 4-digit NAICS categories but have been matched to corresponding 6-digit NAICS industry codes. The change reported for each occupation to the year 2014 is a percent of growth or decline as estimated by the Bureau of Labor Statistics. The abbreviation nec stands for 'not elsewhere classified.'

LOCATION BY STATE AND REGIONAL CONCENTRATION

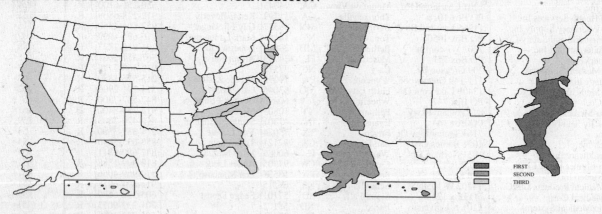

FIRST
SECOND
THIRD

INDUSTRY DATA BY STATE

State	Establishments Total (number)	% of U.S.	Employment Total (number)	% of U.S.	Per Estab.	Payroll Total ($ mil.)	Per Empl. ($)	Sales Total ($ mil.)	% of U.S.	Per Estab. ($)
California	1,060	13.5	20,131	15.7	19	1,284.9	63,828	10,534.3	13.1	9,938,008
Illinois	370	4.7	9,719	7.6	26	590.9	60,797	8,269.2	10.3	22,349,297
Minnesota	168	2.1	6,810	5.3	41	847.0	124,379	7,399.1	9.2	44,042,089
New York	572	7.3	10,717	8.4	19	617.7	57,638	5,690.2	7.1	9,947,983
New Jersey	316	4.0	6,575	5.1	21	436.4	66,372	4,877.9	6.1	15,436,481
Florida	870	11.1	8,494	6.6	10	405.2	47,698	4,681.1	5.8	5,380,571
Massachusetts	203	2.6	5,595	4.4	28	350.3	62,602	3,744.9	4.7	18,447,906
Texas	552	7.0	5,743	4.5	10	278.0	48,410	3,636.6	4.5	6,588,076
Georgia	235	3.0	4,241	3.3	18	239.9	56,573	3,375.5	4.2	14,363,787
Pennsylvania	300	3.8	4,611	3.6	15	271.9	58,978	3,255.1	4.0	10,850,487
Tennessee	163	2.1	3,614	2.8	22	250.9	69,412	2,622.4	3.3	16,088,196
Ohio	304	3.9	4,967	3.9	16	251.9	50,707	2,527.9	3.1	8,315,349
North Carolina	191	2.4	3,362	2.6	18	184.4	54,858	2,307.4	2.9	12,080,372
Michigan	210	2.7	3,701	2.9	18	227.9	61,577	1,959.6	2.4	9,331,310
Indiana	130	1.7	2,162	1.7	17	142.1	65,728	1,654.8	2.1	12,729,392
Connecticut	93	1.2	1,600	1.3	17	98.4	61,479	1,495.7	1.9	16,082,624
Maryland	144	1.8	2,427	1.9	17	133.4	54,965	1,477.8	1.8	10,262,326
Missouri	164	2.1	2,141	1.7	13	115.1	53,771	1,106.9	1.4	6,749,274
Washington	146	1.9	1,992	1.6	14	110.2	55,336	1,034.1	1.3	7,082,644
Louisiana	110	1.4	1,260	1.0	11	57.3	45,485	705.8	0.9	6,415,973
Wisconsin	100	1.3	1,910	1.5	19	96.2	50,340	692.0	0.9	6,920,240
South Carolina	73	0.9	1,195	0.9	16	64.1	53,616	672.0	0.8	9,205,699
Virginia	124	1.6	1,365	1.1	11	70.9	51,976	629.0	0.8	5,072,847
Oklahoma	101	1.3	873	0.7	9	45.8	52,514	473.1	0.6	4,683,782
Nevada	55	0.7	621	0.5	11	30.1	48,496	439.3	0.5	7,987,473
Oregon	69	0.9	644	0.5	9	42.1	65,307	400.3	0.5	5,802,159
Alabama	82	1.0	801	0.6	10	36.4	45,478	393.5	0.5	4,799,390
Kentucky	72	0.9	806	0.6	11	33.0	40,897	365.0	0.5	5,070,097
Nebraska	47	0.6	703	0.5	15	30.5	43,356	290.4	0.4	6,177,681

Continued on next page.

INDUSTRY DATA BY STATE - Continued

State	Establishments		Employment			Payroll		Sales		
	Total (number)	% of U.S.	Total (number)	% of U.S.	Per Estab.	Total ($ mil.)	Per Empl. ($)	Total ($ mil.)	% of U.S.	Per Estab. ($)
Kansas	73	0.9	660	0.5	9	30.3	45,942	279.4	0.3	3,826,808
Utah	71	0.9	1,146	0.9	16	32.0	27,884	260.2	0.3	3,665,282
Mississippi	34	0.4	393	0.3	12	15.3	38,850	153.0	0.2	4,501,324
Iowa	32	0.4	335	0.3	10	12.4	37,158	142.8	0.2	4,463,250
Arkansas	52	0.7	451	0.4	9	15.2	33,752	129.3	0.2	2,486,288
West Virginia	24	0.3	332	0.3	14	11.5	34,642	127.8	0.2	5,324,625
New Hampshire	32	0.4	282	0.2	9	11.5	40,670	109.2	0.1	3,411,781
Hawaii	30	0.4	239	0.2	8	10.7	44,657	103.5	0.1	3,450,300
Maine	19	0.2	282	0.2	15	13.3	47,323	93.7	0.1	4,932,421
New Mexico	40	0.5	234	0.2	6	10.4	44,513	71.9	0.1	1,798,100
Idaho	24	0.3	209	0.2	9	8.8	42,306	67.1	0.1	2,794,417
North Dakota	12	0.2	185	0.1	15	10.7	57,870	64.0	0.1	5,335,333
Montana	12	0.2	94	0.1	8	3.2	34,170	20.0	-	1,665,083
Vermont	9	0.1	52	-	6	2.4	45,269	15.3	-	1,696,556
South Dakota	13	0.2	38	-	3	2.3	61,500	9.9	-	757,846
Alaska	5	0.1	23	-	5	1.0	44,174	8.7	-	1,743,600
Wyoming	4	0.1	23	-	6	0.9	39,696	3.4	-	841,250
Arizona	156	2.0	1000-2499	-	-	(D)	-	(D)	-	-
Colorado	141	1.8	1000-2499	-	-	(D)	-	(D)	-	-
Rhode Island	23	0.3	100-249	-	-	(D)	-	(D)	-	-
Delaware	16	0.2	20-99	-	-	(D)	-	(D)	-	-
D.C.	5	0.1	20-99	-	-	(D)	-	(D)	-	-

Source: 2002 *Economic Census*. The states are in descending order of sales or establishments (if sales data are missing for the majority). The symbol (D) appears when data are withheld to prevent disclosure of competitive information. States marked with (D) are sorted by number of establishments. A dash (-) indicates that the data element cannot be calculated. Shaded *states* on the state map indicate those states which have proportionately greater representation in the industry than would be indicated by the states population; the ratio is based on total sales or number of establishments. Shaded *regions* indicate where the industry is regionally most concentrated.

NAICS 423460 - OPHTHALMIC GOODS MERCHANT WHOLESALERS*

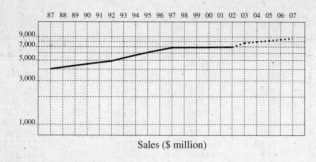

Sales ($ million)

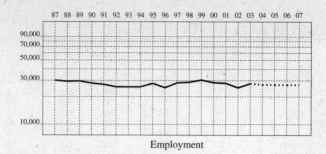

Employment

GENERAL STATISTICS

Year	Establishments (number)	Employment (number)	Payroll ($ million)	Sales ($ million)	Employees per Establishment (number)	Sales per Establishment ($)	Payroll per Employee ($)
1987	1,899	30,134	591.9	4,026.3	15.9	2,120,221.2	19,642.3
1988	1,782	29,289	613.7	4,203.0 e	16.4	2,358,585.9	20,953.3
1989	1,613	29,573	654.9	4,379.6 e	18.3	2,715,189.1	22,145.2
1990	1,603	27,998	652.2	4,556.3 e	17.5	2,842,358.1	23,294.5
1991	1,568	27,149	675.5	4,732.9 e	17.3	3,018,431.1	24,881.2
1992	1,783	25,561	654.4	4,909.6	14.3	2,753,561.4	25,601.5
1993	1,752	25,552	678.9	5,300.7 e	14.6	3,025,513.7	26,569.3
1994	1,740	25,571	716.6	5,691.9 e	14.7	3,271,206.9	28,023.9
1995	1,739	27,880	828.9	6,083.0	16.0	3,497,987.3	29,731.0
1996	1,694 e	25,080 e	783.0 e	6,474.2 e	14.8 e	3,821,841.8 e	31,220.1 e
1997	1,781	28,260	867.8	6,865.3	15.9	3,854,744.5	30,707.7
1998	1,754	28,755	947.1	6,882.2 e	16.4	3,923,740.0	32,936.9
1999	1,712	30,353	1,019.7	6,899.2 e	17.7	4,029,894.9	33,594.7
2000	1,632	28,452	1,011.1	6,916.1 e	17.4	4,237,818.6	35,537.7
2001	1,582	27,990	1,012.5	6,933.1 e	17.7	4,382,465.2	36,172.5
2002	1,396	25,059	868.8	6,950.0	18.0	4,978,510.0	34,670.2
2003	1,368	27,692	964.1	7,701.1 p	20.2	4,815,508.9 p	34,813.9
2004	1,527 p	27,027 p	1,048.1 p	7,932.1 p	17.8 p	4,978,862.4 p	38,362.3 p
2005	1,511 p	26,955 p	1,076.0 p	8,163.0 p	17.9 p	5,142,215.8 p	39,419.0 p
2006	1,495 p	26,884 p	1,103.9 p	8,394.0 p	18.1 p	5,305,569.3 p	40,475.6 p
2007	1,480 p	26,813 p	1,131.9 p	8,625.0 p	18.2 p	5,468,922.8 p	41,532.2 p

Sources: *Economic Census of the United States*, 1987, 1992, 1997, and 2002. Establishment counts, employment, and payroll are from *County Business Patterns* for non-Census years. Values followed by a 'p' are projections by the editors. Sales data for non-Census years are extrapolations, marked by 'e'. Data are the most recent available at this level of detail.

INDICES OF CHANGE

Year	Establishments (number)	Employment (number)	Payroll ($ million)	Sales ($ million)	Employees per Establishment (number)	Sales per Establishment ($)	Payroll per Employee ($)
1987	136.0	120.3	68.1	57.9	88.3	42.6	56.7
1992	127.7	102.0	75.3	70.6	79.4	55.3	73.8
1993	125.5	102.0	78.1	76.3 e	81.1	60.8	76.6
1994	124.6	102.0	82.5	81.9 e	81.7	65.7	80.8
1995	124.6	111.3	95.4	87.5 e	88.9	70.3	85.8
1996	121.3 e	100.1 e	90.1 e	93.2 e	82.2 e	76.8 e	90.0 e
1997	127.6	112.8	99.9	98.8	88.3	77.4	88.6
1998	125.6	114.7	109.0	99.0 e	91.1	78.8	95.0
1999	122.6	121.1	117.4	99.3 e	98.3	80.9	96.9
2000	116.9	113.5	116.4	99.5 e	96.7	85.1	102.5
2001	113.3	111.7	116.5	99.8 e	98.3	88.0	104.3
2002	100.0	100.0	100.0	100.0	100.0	100.0	100.0
2003	98.0	110.5	111.0	110.8 p	112.5	96.7 p	100.4
2004	109.4 p	107.9 p	120.6 p	114.1 p	99.0 p	100.0 p	110.6 p
2005	108.3 p	107.6 p	123.8 p	117.5 p	99.7 p	103.3 p	113.7 p
2006	107.1 p	107.3 p	127.1 p	120.8 p	100.4 p	106.6 p	116.7 p
2007	106.0 p	107.0 p	130.3 p	124.1 p	101.1 p	109.9 p	119.8 p

Sources: Same as General Statistics. The values shown reflect change from the base year, 2002. Values above 100 mean greater than 2002, values below 100 mean less than 2002, and a value of 100 in the 1987-2001 or 2003-2007 period means same as 2002. Values followed by a 'p' are projections by the editors; 'e' stands for extrapolation. Data are the most recent available at this level of detail.

SELECTED RATIOS

For 2002	Avg. of All Wholesale	Analyzed Industry	Index	For 2002	Avg. of All Wholesale	Analyzed Industry	Index
Employees per Establishment	15	18	120	Sales per Employee	791,325	277,345	35
Payroll per Establishment	626,122	622,350	99	Sales per Establishment	12,012,387	4,978,510	41
Payroll per Employee	41,161	34,670	84	Expenses per Establishment	na	na	na

Sources: Same as General Statistics. The 'Average of All' column, Wholesale or Retail, represents the average of the sector reported for the most recent complete year available. The Index shows the relationship between the Average and the Analyzed Industry. For example, 100 means that they are equal; 500 that the Analyzed Industry is five times the average; 50 means that the Analyzed Industry is half the national average. The abbreviation 'na' is used to show that data are 'not available'.

*Equivalent to SIC 5048.

LEADING COMPANIES   Number shown: **38**   Total sales ($ mil): **1,683**   Total employment (000): **11.8**

Company Name	Address				CEO Name	Phone	Co. Type	Sales ($ mil)	Empl. (000)
Sola International Inc.	10590 W Ocean Air	San Diego	CA	92130	Jeremy C. Bishop	858-509-9899	R	650	6.6
Blount International Inc.	PO Box 949	Portland	OR	97222	Eliot M Fried	503-653-8881	P	559	3.3
ABB Optical North America	5360 NW 35th Ave	Fort Lauderdale	FL	33309	Angel Alvarez	954-733-2300	R	111*	0.4
Soderberg Inc.	230 Eva St	Saint Paul	MN	55107	Craig Giles	651-291-1400	R	50*	0.2
New Era Optical Company Inc.	5575 N Lynch Ave	Chicago	IL	60630	Herbert Natkin	773-725-9600	R	39*	0.2
Barbara Creations	8121 Central	Skokie	IL	60076	Al Gluck	847-679-1012	R	23*	<0.1
Limited Editions	PO Box 3519	Chatsworth	CA	91313	Sheldon Lehrer	818-407-1890	R	20*	<0.1
Hoya Optical Inc.	PO Box 580870	Modesto	CA	95358		209-579-7739	R	17*	<0.1
DAC Vision Inc.	3930 Miller Park Dr	Garland	TX	75042	Richard Bulwinkle	972-543-2500	R	15*	0.1
Irwin International Inc.	PO Box 4000	Corona	CA	92880	James Irwin	909-372-9555	R	15*	<0.1
Southwest Lens Corp.	PO Box 567789	Dallas	TX	75356	Robert Dahl	214-634-8109	R	14*	<0.1
Eye Med	401 Meridian St N	Huntsville	AL	35801		256-533-7300	R	13*	<0.1
Logo of The Americas	1840 N Commerce	Fort Lauderdale	FL	33326		954-349-4838	R	13*	<0.1
Celestron International	PO Box 31001-1693	Pasadena	CA	91110	Joe Lupica	310-328-9560	R	11*	<0.1
Wiley X	7491 Longard Rd	Livermore	CA	94551	Myles Freeman	925-243-9810	R	10*	<0.1
Satis Vacuum of America	PO Box 180	Groveport	OH	43125	Larry Clarke	614-409-9401	R	9*	<0.1
Duffins-Langley Optical Inc.	PO Box 419238	Kansas City	MO	64141		913-492-5379	R	8*	<0.1
Moria Inc.	1050 Crosskeys Dr	Doylestown	PA	18901		215-230-7662	R	8*	<0.1
Canyon Eyewear	2 Neil Ct	Oceanside	NY	11572	Edward Chernoff	516-255-0179	R	8*	<0.1
Sun Optics	1785 S 4490 W	Salt Lake City	UT	84104	Bruce Raile	801-924-0440	R	8*	<0.1
Robertson Optical Labratories Inc.	PO Box 1797	Loganville	GA	30052	Calvin Robertson	770-554-3000	R	7*	<0.1
Specto-Optical Co.	4661 Arrow Hwy	Montclair	CA	91763	Brian Morris	909-622-1248	R	7*	<0.1
Visionweb L.P.	8601 Ranch 2222 3	Austin	TX	78730		512-241-8500	R	7*	<0.1
SMI	300 Commerce Blvd	Bogart	GA		Mike Blaesing	706-543-5031	R	6*	<0.1
Co-Optical Ltd.	1010 Executive Dr	Westmont	IL	60559	William Jarrett	630-920-4500	R	6*	<0.1
Pelican Optical Labs Inc.	6850 Whitfield Ind	Sarasota	FL	34243	Dennis Camp	941-751-4437	R	6*	<0.1
Firestone Optics Inc.	PO Box 419142	Kansas City	MO	64141	David Rusch	816-455-0500	R	6*	<0.1
Clips Ltd.	PO Box 8550	Emeryville	CA	94662	David Salk	510-923-0568	R	6*	<0.1
Sans Pareil Inc.	4151 NW 124th Ave	Coral Springs	FL	33065	Steven Lipawsky	954-656-1822	R	6*	<0.1
ACO Optical Lab	2101 S Atlantic Blvd	Los Angeles	CA	90040	Maurice Choi	323-266-3030	R	5*	<0.1
Central Optical Laboratories Inc.	412 Diagonal St	Clarkston	WA	99403	William Scheuerman	509-758-1791	R	5*	<0.1
Optics Inc.	2792 Nationwide	Brunswick	OH	44212	William Wagenlander	330-273-5111	R	5*	<0.1
ILLMO Rx Service Inc.	52 Progress Pkwy	Maryland H.	MO	63043	John Gerber	314-434-6858	R	5*	<0.1
Richmond Optical Company Inc.	29425 Ruus Rd	Hayward	CA	94544	Paul Furr	510-783-1420	R	3*	<0.1
Lifestyle Company Inc.	1800 Rte 34 Ste 401	Belmar	NJ	07719	Thomas Seidner	732-972-8585	R	1*	<0.1
Coyote Vision USA	PO Box 277	Pittsford	NY	14534	Steven Carhart	585-385-7580	R	1*	<0.1
Vision Sciences Research Corp.	130 Ryan Ind Ct	San Ramon	CA	94583	Arthur Ginsburg	925-837-2083	R	1*	<0.1
Rainbow Sales Distributing	1637 S 83rd St	West Allis	WI	53214	Daviid Gray	414-774-4949	R	1	<0.1

Source: *Ward's Business Directory of U.S. Private and Public Companies*, Volumes 1 and 2, 2005. The company type code used is as follows: P - Public, R - Private, S - Subsidiary, D - Division, J - Joint Venture, A - Affiliate, G - Group. Sales are in millions of dollars, employees are in thousands. An asterisk (*) indicates an estimated sales volume. The symbol < stands for 'less than'. Company names and addresses are truncated, in some cases, to fit into the available space.

OCCUPATIONS EMPLOYED BY PROFESSIONAL & COMMERCIAL EQUIPMENT & SUPPLIES

Occupation	% of Total 2004	Change to 2014	Occupation	% of Total 2004	Change to 2014
Sales reps, wholesale & manufacturing, exc tech	8.8	20.2	Computer software engineers, systems software	1.7	42.6
Sales reps, wholesale & manufacturing, tech	8.4	20.2	Computer specialists, nec	1.6	20.2
Computer, automated teller, & office machine repairers	8.0	8.2	First-line supervisors/managers of office workers	1.6	9.0
Customer service representatives	3.9	23.6	Truck drivers, light or delivery services	1.5	20.2
Computer systems analysts	2.7	32.3	Team assemblers	1.5	20.2
Computer support specialists	2.6	20.2	Computer software engineers, applications	1.4	44.3
Shipping, receiving, & traffic clerks	2.5	8.8	Business operation specialists, nec	1.3	32.3
Computer programmers	2.5	-1.9	Order clerks	1.2	-21.5
Office clerks, general	2.4	7.0	Sales managers	1.2	28.6
Laborers & freight, stock, & material movers, hand	2.1	8.2	Office machine operators, except computer	1.1	-21.8
Bookkeeping, accounting, & auditing clerks	2.0	8.2	Billing & posting clerks & machine operators	1.1	-3.4
General & operations managers	2.0	19.0	Maintenance & repair workers, general	1.0	20.2
Stock clerks & order fillers	1.9	-7.9	Executive secretaries & administrative assistants	1.0	14.0
First-line supervisors/managers of non-retail sales work	1.8	11.2	Computer & information systems managers	1.0	25.9

Source: *Industry-Occupation Matrix*, Bureau of Labor Statistics. These data are reported based on 4-digit NAICS categories but have been matched to corresponding 6-digit NAICS industry codes. The change reported for each occupation to the year 2014 is a percent of growth or decline as estimated by the Bureau of Labor Statistics. The abbreviation nec stands for 'not elsewhere classified.'

LOCATION BY STATE AND REGIONAL CONCENTRATION

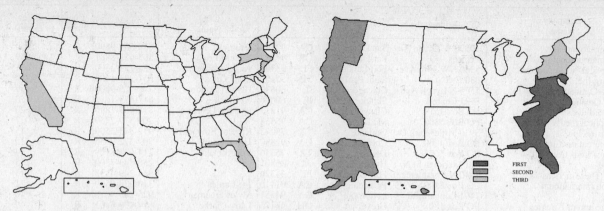

INDUSTRY DATA BY STATE

State	Establishments Total (number)	Establishments % of U.S.	Employment Total (number)	Employment % of U.S.	Employment Per Estab.	Payroll Total ($ mil.)	Payroll Per Empl. ($)	Sales Total ($ mil.)	Sales % of U.S.	Sales Per Estab. ($)
California	239	17.1	3,874	14.9	16	155.2	40,065	1,115.3	16.1	4,666,561
New York	153	11.0	2,789	10.7	18	128.4	46,033	937.5	13.5	6,127,765
New Jersey	53	3.8	3,172	12.2	60	116.3	36,659	887.2	12.8	16,738,868
Florida	180	12.9	1,771	6.8	10	65.3	36,890	542.5	7.8	3,014,133
Texas	76	5.4	1,788	6.9	24	44.3	24,798	346.6	5.0	4,560,158
Ohio	35	2.5	1,078	4.1	31	31.9	29,613	184.5	2.7	5,271,657
Pennsylvania	46	3.3	797	3.1	17	27.5	34,557	166.7	2.4	3,623,391
Virginia	18	1.3	425	1.6	24	18.5	43,419	124.1	1.8	6,893,167
Wisconsin	17	1.2	353	1.4	21	9.7	27,422	107.2	1.5	6,307,235
Colorado	23	1.6	394	1.5	17	13.9	35,282	89.9	1.3	3,909,304
Massachusetts	28	2.0	295	1.1	11	12.7	42,888	80.7	1.2	2,882,750
Oregon	17	1.2	290	1.1	17	7.5	25,914	76.9	1.1	4,526,471
Oklahoma	14	1.0	348	1.3	25	9.9	28,402	66.4	1.0	4,740,857
Kentucky	12	0.9	373	1.4	31	14.3	38,432	64.4	0.9	5,367,500
Iowa	13	0.9	373	1.4	29	10.5	28,016	63.1	0.9	4,854,846
Missouri	32	2.3	387	1.5	12	13.1	33,961	62.4	0.9	1,949,406
Washington	22	1.6	186	0.7	8	5.9	31,677	53.2	0.8	2,416,136
North Carolina	19	1.4	251	1.0	13	6.0	24,008	36.8	0.5	1,936,053
Arizona	26	1.9	190	0.7	7	6.8	35,774	35.2	0.5	1,354,346
Indiana	24	1.7	273	1.0	11	7.0	25,689	30.8	0.4	1,282,833
Utah	17	1.2	97	0.4	6	3.3	33,897	27.0	0.4	1,589,353
Nevada	11	0.8	119	0.5	11	4.2	35,244	18.5	0.3	1,682,091
South Carolina	15	1.1	179	0.7	12	3.8	21,413	17.9	0.3	1,192,733
Montana	6	0.4	88	0.3	15	2.0	22,375	12.4	0.2	2,069,833
Louisiana	11	0.8	88	0.3	8	1.9	21,591	9.8	0.1	894,273
North Dakota	5	0.4	47	0.2	9	1.2	25,106	6.6	0.1	1,324,400
Mississippi	6	0.4	56	0.2	9	1.7	29,589	6.1	0.1	1,021,833
South Dakota	4	0.3	36	0.1	9	0.8	22,694	5.2	0.1	1,291,500
Vermont	3	0.2	39	0.1	13	1.3	32,487	5.0	0.1	1,667,333
New Mexico	4	0.3	20	0.1	5	0.6	27,750	3.1	-	772,000
Maine	6	0.4	32	0.1	5	0.8	24,281	3.0	-	499,167
Wyoming	3	0.2	24	0.1	8	0.4	15,708	2.1	-	710,667
Illinois	53	3.8	500-999	-	-	(D)	-	(D)	-	-
Minnesota	34	2.4	1000-2499	-	-	(D)	-	(D)	-	-
Georgia	32	2.3	500-999	-	-	(D)	-	(D)	-	-
Michigan	31	2.2	250-499	-	-	(D)	-	(D)	-	-
Tennessee	21	1.5	250-499	-	-	(D)	-	(D)	-	-
Maryland	16	1.1	250-499	-	-	(D)	-	(D)	-	-
Connecticut	12	0.9	100-249	-	-	(D)	-	(D)	-	-
Nebraska	11	0.8	100-249	-	-	(D)	-	(D)	-	-
Alabama	10	0.7	20-99	-	-	(D)	-	(D)	-	-
Idaho	7	0.5	20-99	-	-	(D)	-	(D)	-	-
Kansas	7	0.5	250-499	-	-	(D)	-	(D)	-	-
Rhode Island	6	0.4	1000-2499	-	-	(D)	-	(D)	-	-
West Virginia	6	0.4	20-99	-	-	(D)	-	(D)	-	-
Arkansas	5	0.4	20-99	-	-	(D)	-	(D)	-	-
Hawaii	3	0.2	0-19	-	-	(D)	-	(D)	-	-
New Hampshire	3	0.2	20-99	-	-	(D)	-	(D)	-	-
Alaska	1	0.1	0-19	-	-	(D)	-	(D)	-	-
D.C.	1	0.1	0-19	-	-	(D)	-	(D)	-	-

Source: 2002 *Economic Census*. The states are in descending order of sales or establishments (if sales data are missing for the majority). The symbol (D) appears when data are withheld to prevent disclosure of competitive information. States marked with (D) are sorted by number of establishments. A dash (-) indicates that the data element cannot be calculated. Shaded *states* on the state map indicate those states which have proportionately greater representation in the industry than would be indicated by the states population; the ratio is based on total sales or number of establishments. Shaded *regions* indicate where the industry is regionally most concentrated.

NAICS 423490 - OTHER PROFESSIONAL EQUIPMENT AND SUPPLIES MERCHANT WHOLESALERS

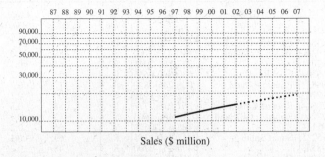

Sales ($ million)

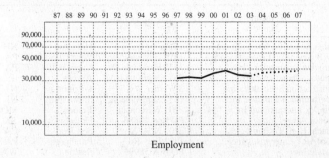

Employment

GENERAL STATISTICS

Year	Establishments (number)	Employment (number)	Payroll ($ million)	Sales ($ million)	Employees per Establishment (number)	Sales per Establishment ($)	Payroll per Employee ($)
1987	-	-	-	-	-	-	-
1988	-	-	-	-	-	-	-
1989	-	-	-	-	-	-	-
1990	-	-	-	-	-	-	-
1991	-	-	-	-	-	-	-
1992	-	-	-	-	-	-	-
1993	-	-	-	-	-	-	-
1994	-	-	-	-	-	-	-
1995	-	-	-	-	-	-	-
1996	-	-	-	-	-	-	-
1997	2,781	31,857	1,267.3	11,038.8	11.5	3,969,363.5	39,780.9
1998	2,769	32,699	1,439.8	11,869.5 e	11.8	4,286,558.3	44,031.9
1999	2,728	31,976	1,452.7	12,700.2 e	11.7	4,655,483.9	45,430.9
2000	2,699	36,045	1,908.6	13,530.8 e	13.4	5,013,279.0	52,950.3
2001	2,615	38,536	1,824.6	14,361.5 e	14.7	5,491,977.1	47,346.7
2002	2,611	34,655	1,559.9	15,192.2	13.3	5,818,537.0	45,012.3
2003	2,529	33,637	1,621.0	16,022.9 p	13.3	6,194,525.0 p	48,191.6
2004	2,507 p	36,460 p	1,821.0 p	16,853.6 p	14.4 p	6,572,236.9 p	50,264.8 p
2005	2,464 p	37,024 p	1,880.8 p	17,684.2 p	14.9 p	6,949,948.9 p	51,304.4 p
2006	2,422 p	37,589 p	1,940.5 p	18,514.9 p	15.3 p	7,327,660.9 p	52,344.0 p
2007	2,380 p	38,154 p	2,000.3 p	19,345.6 p	15.7 p	7,705,372.8 p	53,383.6 p

Source: Economic Census of the United States, 1997 and 2002. Establishment counts, employment, and payroll are from *County Business Patterns* for non-Census years. This is a newly defined industry. Data for prior years are unavailable at the time of publication but may become available over time. Values followed by 'p' are projections by the editors. Sales data for non-Census years are extrapolations, marked by 'e'.

INDICES OF CHANGE

Year	Establishments (number)	Employment (number)	Payroll ($ million)	Sales ($ million)	Employees per Establishment (number)	Sales per Establishment ($)	Payroll per Employee ($)
1987	-	-	-	-	-	-	-
1992	-	-	-	-	-	-	-
1993	-	-	-	-	-	-	-
1994	-	-	-	-	-	-	-
1995	-	-	-	-	-	-	-
1996	-	-	-	-	-	-	-
1997	106.5	91.9	81.2	72.7	86.5	68.2	88.4
1998	106.1	94.4	92.3	78.1 e	88.7	73.7	97.8
1999	104.5	92.3	93.1	83.6 e	88.0	80.0	100.9
2000	103.4	104.0	122.4	89.1 e	100.8	86.2	117.6
2001	100.2	111.2	117.0	94.5 e	110.5	94.4	105.2
2002	100.0	100.0	100.0	100.0	100.0	100.0	100.0
2003	96.9	97.1	103.9	105.5 p	100.0	106.5 p	107.1
2004	96.0 p	105.2 p	116.7 p	110.9 p	108.6 p	113.0 p	111.7 p
2005	94.4 p	106.8 p	120.6 p	116.4 p	111.7 p	119.4 p	114.0 p
2006	92.8 p	108.5 p	124.4 p	121.9 p	114.7 p	125.9 p	116.3 p
2007	91.1 p	110.1 p	128.2 p	127.3 p	117.8 p	132.4 p	118.6 p

Sources: Same as General Statistics. The values shown reflect change from the base year, 2002. Values above 100 mean greater than 2002, values below 100 mean less than 2002, and a value of 100 in the 1987-2001 or 2003-2007 period means same as 2002. Values followed by a 'p' are projections by the editors; 'e' stands for extrapolation. Data are the most recent available at this level of detail.

SELECTED RATIOS

For 2002	Avg. of All Wholesale	Analyzed Industry	Index	For 2002	Avg. of All Wholesale	Analyzed Industry	Index
Employees per Establishment	15	13	89	Sales per Employee	791,325	438,384	55
Payroll per Establishment	626,122	597,434	95	Sales per Establishment	12,012,387	5,818,537	48
Payroll per Employee	41,161	45,012	109	Expenses per Establishment	na	na	na

Sources: Same as General Statistics. The 'Average of All' column, Wholesale or Retail, represents the average of the sector reported for the most recent complete year available. The Index shows the relationship between the Average and the Analyzed Industry. For example, 100 means that they are equal; 500 that the Analyzed Industry is five times the average; 50 means that the Analyzed Industry is half the national average. The abbreviation 'na' is used to show that data are 'not available'.

LEADING COMPANIES   Number shown: **75**   Total sales ($ mil): **8,933**   Total employment (000): **25.1**

Company Name	Address				CEO Name	Phone	Co. Type	Sales ($ mil)	Empl. (000)
Fisher Scientific International Inc.	1 Liberty Ln	Hampton	NH	03842	David T. Della Penta	603-926-5911	P	4,663	17.5
VWR Scientific Products Corp.	1310 Goshen Pkwy	West Chester	PA	19380	Walter Zywotten	610-431-1700	S	2,488*	2.5
Christian Publications Inc.	3825 Hartzdale Dr	Camp Hill	PA	17011		717-761-7044	R	161*	<0.1
Mitutoyo America Corp.	965 Corporate Blvd	Aurora	IL	60504	Noel Ryan	630-820-9666	R	151*	0.2
Construction Specialties Inc.	3 Werner Wy	Lebanon	NJ	08833	Ronald F Dadd	908-236-0800	R	112*	0.7
Programmer's Paradise Inc.	1157 Shrewsbury	Shrewsbury	NJ	07702		732-389-8950	P	104	0.1
Chindex International Inc.	7201 Wisconsin	Bethesda	MD	20814	Roberta Lipson	301-215-7777	P	88	0.8
Radnor Alloys Inc.	PO Box 40880	Houston	TX	77240	Robert L Gilleland	713-466-1600	S	82*	<0.1
Hitachi High Technologies	3100 N 1st St	San Jose	CA	95134		408-432-0520	S	66*	0.2
ALMART Enterprises Inc.	1392 Frey Rd	Pittsburgh	PA	15235	Stuart Smith	412-380-1335	R	63*	<0.1
Carlyle Inc.	PO Box 58999	Seattle	WA	98138		425-251-0700	R	48*	0.2
Shimadzu Scientific Instruments	7102 Riverwood Dr	Columbia	MD	21046	Osamu Ando	410-381-1227	R	41*	0.3
Vet Pharm Inc.	PO Box 167	Sioux Center	IA	51250	Chuck Ploeg	712-722-3836	R	38*	0.1
Alvin and Company Inc.	PO Box 188	Windsor	CT	06095	Scott Shoham	860-243-8991	R	38*	0.2
North Coast Medical Inc.	18305 Sutter Blvd	Morgan Hill	CA	95037	Mark Biehl	408-776-5000	R	38*	0.1
Fiber Optic Center Inc.	23 Center St	New Bedford	MA	02740	Neal H Weiss	508-992-6464	R	31*	<0.1
Gesswein	PO Box 3998	Bridgeport	CT	06605	Dwight Gesswein	203-366-5400	R	30*	0.1
Western Stockmen's	223 Rodeo Ave	Caldwell	ID	83605		208-459-0777	S	29*	<0.1
Cushing and Company Inc.	420 W Huron St	Chicago	IL	60610	C Cushing-Duff	312-266-8228	R	28*	0.1
Thomas Scientific	PO Box 99	Swedesboro	NJ	08085	G Wesner	856-467-2000	R	26*	0.1
A. Daigger and Company Inc.	620 Lakeview Pkwy	Vernon Hills	IL	60061	Jim Woldenberg	847-816-5060	R	25*	<0.1
Heidenhain Corp.	333 E State Pkwy	Schaumburg	IL	60173	Rick Korte	847-490-1191	R	25*	<0.1
Star Guide Corp.	5000 Independence	Arvada	CO	80002		303-424-7300	R	23*	0.1
Robert J Matthews Company Inc.	PO Box 9101	Canton	OH	44711	J Matthews	330-834-3000	R	22*	<0.1
Clearvision Optical Co.	500 Bayview Dr	Miami	FL	33160	David Friedfeld	305-945-5499	R	18*	<0.1
Kurtz Brothers	400 Reed St	Clearfield	PA	16830	Ron Turner	814-765-6561	R	18*	0.2
Broadcasters General Store Inc.	2480 SE 52nd St	Ocala	FL	34480	David Kerstin	352-622-7700	R	18*	<0.1
Jack Rubin and Sons Inc.	PO Box 3005	Compton	CA	90223	Bruce Rubin	310-635-5407	R	15*	<0.1
Intermountain Scientific Corp.	420 N Kays Dr	Kaysville	UT	84037	Gene Platter	801-547-5047	R	14*	<0.1
Ace Educational Supplies Inc.	5595 S University	Fort Lauderdale	FL	33328	Richard Ludwig	954-434-2773	R	13*	<0.1
Learning Labs Inc.	PO Box 1419	Calhoun	GA	30703	David Richardson	706-629-4624	R	13*	<0.1
Sargent-Welch Scientific Co.	PO Box 5229	Buffalo Grove	IL	60089			D	13*	<0.1
BC Industrial Supply Inc.	2720 E Regal	Anaheim	CA	92806	Robert Heavican	714-666-8000	R	13*	<0.1
Foss North America Inc.	7682 Executive Dr	Eden Prairie	MN	55344	Robert Wang	952-974-9892	R	13*	<0.1
Suzanne L Kilmer	3835 J St	Sacramento	CA	95816	Suzanne Kilmer	916-456-0400	R	13*	<0.1
Data Financial Business Services	1100 W Glen Oaks	Mequon	WI	53092	James Holtz	262-243-5511	R	12*	<0.1
Chiral Technologies Inc.	PO Box 564	Exton	PA	19341	Thomas B Lewis	610-594-2100	R	12*	<0.1
Tonini Church Supply Co.	966 Breckenridge Ln	Louisville	KY	40207	Elmore Tonini	502-897-7100	R	12*	<0.1
Eastern Tools and Equipment Inc.	4951 Commerce Dr	Baldwin Park	CA	91706	David Fan	626-960-6299	R	11*	<0.1
Impact Lighting Inc.	50 W Ohio Ave	Richmond	CA	94804	Matthew Guelfi	510-232-5723	R	11*	<0.1
Numax Inc.	117 Rte 303, Ste C	Tappan	NY	10983	Stephen Leber	845-365-2400	S	11*	<0.1
Pyrosequencing Inc.	2200 W Park Dr	Westborough	MA	01581	Jerry Williamson	508-389-9911	R	11*	<0.1
St Jude Shop Inc.	21 Brookline Blvd	Havertown	PA	19083	Louis Di Cocco	610-789-1300	R	11*	<0.1
Ultra Palm Optical	PO Box 600189	Miami	FL	33160	Leonard Cohen	305-651-1373	R	11*	<0.1
Xerographic Solutions Inc.	806 Linden Ave	Rochester	NY	14625	Mark Perlo	585-248-5554	R	11*	<0.1
Atlas Electric Devices Co.	45601 N 47th Ave	Phoenix	AZ	85087		623-465-7356	R	10*	<0.1
Midwest Scientific Inc.	280 Vance Rd	Valley Park	MO	63088	Larry Degenhart	636-225-9997	R	10*	<0.1
Andrzejewski's Marian Church	3535 Bay Rd	Saginaw	MI	48603	Tom Klopp	989-249-9174	R	10*	<0.1
Bancare Equipment Sales Inc.	8 W College Dr	Arlington H.	IL	60004	Joseph Cozzi	847-394-1122	R	9*	<0.1
HL Technologies Inc.	4755 Alpine Rd	Stafford	TX	77477	Colin Zak	281-240-5452	R	9*	<0.1
Krackeler Scientific Inc.	PO Box 1849	Albany	NY	12201	Robert Krackeler	518-462-4281	R	9*	<0.1
Acme Scale	PO Box 1922	San Leandro	CA	94577	Louis Buran	510-638-5040	R	9*	<0.1
Carol School Supply Inc.	17928 Union Tpke	Flushing	NY	11366	Carol Pick	718-380-4203	R	9*	<0.1
Sikora's Religious Art	147 Market St	Passaic	NJ	07055	Arthur Brown	973-473-5246	R	9*	<0.1
Law Enforcement Equipment Co.	2520 Summit St	Kansas City	MO	64108	Kevin Hatfield	816-221-2232	R	8*	<0.1
Scientific Microscopes Inc.	1128 W Evelyn Ave	Sunnyvale	CA	94086	Costa Tsobanakis	408-739-2631	R	8*	<0.1
Cameca Instruments Inc.	204 Spring Hill Rd	Trumbull	CT	06611	George Antier	203-459-0623	R	8*	<0.1
Crown Group Distributing	PO Box 669	Post Falls	ID	83877	Jim Corbett	208-773-9811	R	8*	<0.1
F-D-C Corp.	PO Box 1047	Elk Grove Vill.	IL	60009	RI Hawley	847-437-3990	R	8*	<0.1
Graphaids Inc.	3030 La Cienega	Culver City	CA	90232	Frank Festa	310-204-1212	R	8*	<0.1
Mainpro Inc.	PO Box 154425	Irving	TX	75015	Vernon Freeman	972-438-2096	R	8*	<0.1
Research Products Intern. Corp.	410 N Business Ctr	Mount Prospect	IL	60056	Robert Chudy	847-635-7330	R	8*	<0.1
Scientific Supplies & Technology	7245 NW 43rd St	Miami	FL	33166	Peter Lue	305-593-2137	R	8*	<0.1
Unitech USA	5575 NW 74th Ave	Miami	FL	33166	Carmen De Pierola	305-885-1177	R	8*	<0.1
Hamilton Safe Products Inc.	527 E Hudson St	Columbus	OH	43202	Chester De Bellis	614-268-5530	R	7*	<0.1
Medax International Inc.	224 Plymouth Ave	Salt Lake City	UT	84115	Lori Tokarz	801-265-3413	R	7*	<0.1
Phoenix Equipment Inc.	212 Sheppard St	Penn Yan	NY	14527	Robert Krouse	315-536-0862	R	7*	<0.1
Spectacular Products Inc.	2 Shaker Rd	Shirley	MA	01464	David Marchand	978-929-9911	R	7*	<0.1
Tifton Ophthalmology Inc.	1803 Old Ocilla Rd	Tifton	GA	31794	Larry Moorman	229-386-2181	R	7*	<0.1
WM Management Inc.	299 13th St	Oakland	CA	94612	William Lee	510-839-0369	R	7*	<0.1
Wilkens-Anderson Co.	4525 W Division St	Chicago	IL	60651	Bruce Wilkens	773-384-4433	R	7*	<0.1
IKA-Works Inc.	2635 Northchase SE	Wilmington	NC	28405		910-452-7059	R	7*	<0.1
Corr Tech Inc.	4545 Homestead Rd	Houston	TX	77028	Doris Gottesman	713-674-7887	R	6*	<0.1
MacAlaster Bicknell Company Inc.	PO Box 3257	New Haven	CT	06515		203-624-4191	R	6*	<0.1
Merchandising Incentives Corp.	PO Box 7046	Troy	MI	48007	Richard Williamson	248-362-5060	R	6*	<0.1

Source: Ward's Business Directory of U.S. Private and Public Companies, Volumes 1 and 2, 2005. The company type code used is as follows: P - Public, R - Private, S - Subsidiary, D - Division, J - Joint Venture, A - Affiliate, G - Group. Sales are in millions of dollars, employees are in thousands. An asterisk (*) indicates an estimated sales volume. The symbol < stands for 'less than'. Company names and addresses are truncated, in some cases, to fit into the available space.

OCCUPATIONS EMPLOYED BY PROFESSIONAL & COMMERCIAL EQUIPMENT & SUPPLIES

Occupation	% of Total 2004	Change to 2014	Occupation	% of Total 2004	Change to 2014
Sales reps, wholesale & manufacturing, exc tech	8.8	20.2	Computer software engineers, systems software	1.7	42.6
Sales reps, wholesale & manufacturing, tech	8.4	20.2	Computer specialists, nec	1.6	20.2
Computer, automated teller, & office machine repairers	8.0	8.2	First-line supervisors/managers of office workers	1.6	9.0
Customer service representatives	3.9	23.6	Truck drivers, light or delivery services	1.5	20.2
Computer systems analysts	2.7	32.3	Team assemblers	1.5	20.2
Computer support specialists	2.6	20.2	Computer software engineers, applications	1.4	44.3
Shipping, receiving, & traffic clerks	2.5	8.8	Business operation specialists, nec	1.3	32.3
Computer programmers	2.5	-1.9	Order clerks	1.2	-21.5
Office clerks, general	2.4	7.0	Sales managers	1.2	28.6
Laborers & freight, stock, & material movers, hand	2.1	8.2	Office machine operators, except computer	1.1	-21.8
Bookkeeping, accounting, & auditing clerks	2.0	8.2	Billing & posting clerks & machine operators	1.1	-3.4
General & operations managers	2.0	19.0	Maintenance & repair workers, general	1.0	20.2
Stock clerks & order fillers	1.9	-7.9	Executive secretaries & administrative assistants	1.0	14.0
First-line supervisors/managers of non-retail sales work	1.8	11.2	Computer & information systems managers	1.0	25.9

Source: Industry-Occupation Matrix, Bureau of Labor Statistics. These data are reported based on 4-digit NAICS categories but have been matched to corresponding 6-digit NAICS industry codes. The change reported for each occupation to the year 2014 is a percent of growth or decline as estimated by the Bureau of Labor Statistics. The abbreviation nec stands for 'not elsewhere classified.'

LOCATION BY STATE AND REGIONAL CONCENTRATION

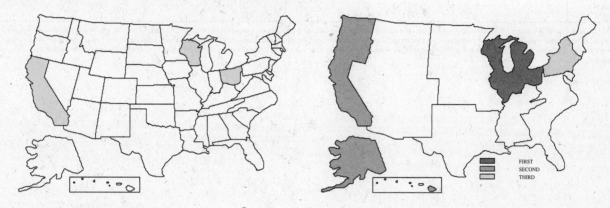

INDUSTRY DATA BY STATE

State	Establishments Total (number)	% of U.S.	Employment Total (number)	% of U.S.	Per Estab.	Payroll Total ($ mil.)	Per Empl. ($)	Sales Total ($ mil.)	% of U.S.	Per Estab. ($)
Ohio	98	3.7	2,367	6.7	24	79.9	33,742	2,149.1	14.2	21,929,316
California	339	12.9	5,053	14.4	15	271.3	53,683	2,011.7	13.3	5,934,118
New York	177	6.7	2,332	6.6	13	118.4	50,756	834.6	5.5	4,715,520
Texas	162	6.2	1,515	4.3	9	67.3	44,448	516.5	3.4	3,188,191
Wisconsin	40	1.5	2,078	5.9	52	66.5	32,024	440.1	2.9	11,002,675
North Carolina	82	3.1	794	2.3	10	37.7	47,438	249.1	1.6	3,038,293
Florida	162	6.2	781	2.2	5	33.8	43,341	228.6	1.5	1,411,056
Michigan	70	2.7	799	2.3	11	38.3	47,909	186.7	1.2	2,667,129
Virginia	59	2.2	512	1.5	9	19.8	38,662	158.5	1.0	2,686,441
Mississippi	17	0.6	546	1.6	32	14.1	25,879	72.8	0.5	4,279,412
Louisiana	37	1.4	246	0.7	7	7.4	29,894	62.0	0.4	1,676,324
Oklahoma	21	0.8	127	0.4	6	4.2	32,906	27.5	0.2	1,309,571
Nevada	20	0.8	79	0.2	4	2.5	31,987	21.9	0.1	1,096,400
Alaska	8	0.3	54	0.2	7	1.8	32,500	12.0	0.1	1,506,000
New Jersey	142	5.4	1000-2499	-	-	(D)	-	(D)	-	-
Illinois	120	4.6	1000-2499	-	-	(D)	-	(D)	-	-
Pennsylvania	114	4.3	1000-2499	-	-	(D)	-	(D)	-	-
Massachusetts	105	4.0	1000-2499	-	-	(D)	-	(D)	-	-
Georgia	84	3.2	1000-2499	-	-	(D)	-	(D)	-	-
Missouri	60	2.3	500-999	-	-	(D)	-	(D)	-	-
Maryland	58	2.2	500-999	-	-	(D)	-	(D)	-	-
Minnesota	54	2.1	250-499	-	-	(D)	-	(D)	-	-
Colorado	52	2.0	250-499	-	-	(D)	-	(D)	-	-
Washington	52	2.0	500-999	-	-	(D)	-	(D)	-	-
Indiana	41	1.6	250-499	-	-	(D)	-	(D)	-	-
Tennessee	41	1.6	250-499	-	-	(D)	-	(D)	-	-
Arizona	40	1.5	250-499	-	-	(D)	-	(D)	-	-
Connecticut	38	1.4	1000-2499	-	-	(D)	-	(D)	-	-
Oregon	38	1.4	250-499	-	-	(D)	-	(D)	-	-

Continued on next page.

INDUSTRY DATA BY STATE - Continued

State	Establishments Total (number)	% of U.S.	Employment Total (number)	% of U.S.	Per Estab.	Payroll Total ($ mil.)	Per Empl. ($)	Sales Total ($ mil.)	% of U.S.	Per Estab. ($)
Alabama	28	1.1	250-499	-	-	(D)	-	(D)	-	-
Kentucky	25	1.0	500-999	-	-	(D)	-	(D)	-	-
Iowa	24	0.9	250-499	-	-	(D)	-	(D)	-	-
South Carolina	21	0.8	100-249	-	-	(D)	-	(D)	-	-
New Hampshire	19	0.7	250-499	-	-	(D)	-	(D)	-	-
Idaho	18	0.7	20-99	-	-	(D)	-	(D)	-	-
Kansas	18	0.7	250-499	-	-	(D)	-	(D)	-	-
Nebraska	17	0.6	20-99	-	-	(D)	-	(D)	-	-
Utah	15	0.6	100-249	-	-	(D)	-	(D)	-	-
Arkansas	14	0.5	20-99	-	-	(D)	-	(D)	-	-
West Virginia	14	0.5	20-99	-	-	(D)	-	(D)	-	-
New Mexico	12	0.5	20-99	-	-	(D)	-	(D)	-	-
Delaware	11	0.4	20-99	-	-	(D)	-	(D)	-	-
Maine	10	0.4	20-99	-	-	(D)	-	(D)	-	-
Rhode Island	9	0.3	20-99	-	-	(D)	-	(D)	-	-
Hawaii	8	0.3	20-99	-	-	(D)	-	(D)	-	-
South Dakota	7	0.3	100-249	-	-	(D)	-	(D)	-	-
Vermont	7	0.3	20-99	-	-	(D)	-	(D)	-	-
Montana	6	0.2	20-99	-	-	(D)	-	(D)	-	-
North Dakota	5	0.2	20-99	-	-	(D)	-	(D)	-	-
Wyoming	5	0.2	20-99	-	-	(D)	-	(D)	-	-

Source: 2002 *Economic Census*. The states are in descending order of sales or establishments (if sales data are missing for the majority). The symbol (D) appears when data are withheld to prevent disclosure of competitive information. States marked with (D) are sorted by number of establishments. A dash (-) indicates that the data element cannot be calculated. Shaded *states* on the state map indicate those states which have proportionately greater representation in the industry than would be indicated by the states population; the ratio is based on total sales or number of establishments. Shaded *regions* indicate where the industry is regionally most concentrated.

NAICS 423510 - METAL SERVICE CENTERS AND OTHER METAL MERCHANT WHOLESALERS*

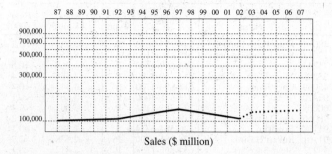

Sales ($ million)

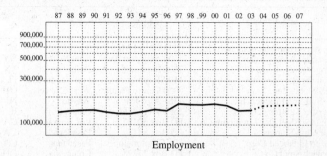

Employment

GENERAL STATISTICS

Year	Establishments (number)	Employment (number)	Payroll ($ million)	Sales ($ million)	Employees per Establishment (number)	Sales per Establishment ($)	Payroll per Employee ($)
1987	10,281	137,009	3,854.4	101,143.3	13.3	9,837,885.4	28,132.5
1988	9,814	141,598	4,354.9	102,081.5 e	14.4	10,401,620.1	30,755.4
1989	9,629	143,818	4,555.4	103,019.6 e	14.9	10,698,888.8	31,674.8
1990	9,673	144,931	4,646.5	103,957.7 e	15.0	10,747,203.6	32,060.1
1991	9,537	137,645	4,431.9	104,895.9 e	14.4	10,998,836.1	32,198.0
1992	10,426	132,741	4,458.1	105,834.0	12.7	10,150,968.7	33,585.0
1993	10,250	132,320	4,667.7	111,806.3 e	12.9	10,907,931.7	35,275.8
1994	10,246	138,724	5,104.7	117,778.6 e	13.5	11,495,081.0	36,797.5
1995	10,331	146,921	5,623.2	123,751.0 e	14.2	11,978,608.1	38,273.6
1996	10,385 e	142,255 e	5,486.0 e	129,723.3 e	13.7 e	12,491,410.7 e	38,564.5 e
1997	11,827	168,950	6,637.6	135,695.6	14.3	11,473,374.5	39,287.4
1998	11,740	166,134	6,762.5	129,977.2 e	14.2	11,071,310.1	40,705.1
1999	11,631	165,112	6,886.9	124,258.8 e	14.2	10,683,411.6	41,710.5
2000	11,465	168,576	7,275.0	118,540.3 e	14.7	10,339,323.2	43,155.7
2001	11,250	162,222	6,967.0	112,821.9 e	14.4	10,028,615.1	42,947.6
2002	10,442	142,825	6,306.3	107,103.5	13.7	10,256,991.0	44,154.0
2003	10,236	144,112	6,471.7	126,612.6 p	14.1	10,963,359.7 p	44,907.6
2004	11,385 p	160,808 p	7,394.9 p	128,034.8 p	14.1 p	10,976,979.5 p	46,576.5 p
2005	11,479 p	162,231 p	7,599.0 p	129,456.9 p	14.1 p	10,990,599.4 p	47,606.6 p
2006	11,572 p	163,655 p	7,803.1 p	130,879.1 p	14.1 p	11,004,219.2 p	48,636.8 p
2007	11,666 p	165,079 p	8,007.2 p	132,301.2 p	14.1 p	11,017,839.0 p	49,667.0 p

Sources: Economic Census of the United States, 1987, 1992, 1997, and 2002. Establishment counts, employment, and payroll are from *County Business Patterns* for non-Census years. Values followed by a 'p' are projections by the editors. Sales data for non-Census years are extrapolations, marked by 'e'. Data are the most recent available at this level of detail.

INDICES OF CHANGE

Year	Establishments (number)	Employment (number)	Payroll ($ million)	Sales ($ million)	Employees per Establishment (number)	Sales per Establishment ($)	Payroll per Employee ($)
1987	98.5	95.9	61.1	94.4	97.1	95.9	63.7
1992	99.8	92.9	70.7	98.8	92.7	99.0	76.1
1993	98.2	92.6	74.0	104.4 e	94.2	106.3	79.9
1994	98.1	97.1	80.9	110.0 e	98.5	112.1	83.3
1995	98.9	102.9	89.2	115.5 e	103.6	116.8	86.7
1996	99.5 e	99.6 e	87.0 e	121.1 e	100.0 e	121.8 e	87.3 e
1997	113.3	118.3	105.3	126.7	104.4	111.9	89.0
1998	112.4	116.3	107.2	121.4 e	103.6	107.9	92.2
1999	111.4	115.6	109.2	116.0 e	103.6	104.2	94.5
2000	109.8	118.0	115.4	110.7 e	107.3	100.8	97.7
2001	107.7	113.6	110.5	105.3 e	105.1	97.8	97.3
2002	100.0	100.0	100.0	100.0	100.0	100.0	100.0
2003	98.0	100.9	102.6	118.2 p	102.8	106.9 p	101.7
2004	109.0 p	112.6 p	117.3 p	119.5 p	103.0 p	107.0 p	105.5 p
2005	109.9 p	113.6 p	120.5 p	120.9 p	103.1 p	107.2 p	107.8 p
2006	110.8 p	114.6 p	123.7 p	122.2 p	103.1 p	107.3 p	110.2 p
2007	111.7 p	115.6 p	127.0 p	123.5 p	103.2 p	107.4 p	112.5 p

Sources: Same as General Statistics. The values shown reflect change from the base year, 2002. Values above 100 mean greater than 2002, values below 100 mean less than 2002, and a value of 100 in the 1987-2001 or 2003-2007 period means same as 2002. Values followed by a 'p' are projections by the editors; 'e' stands for extrapolation. Data are the most recent available at this level of detail.

SELECTED RATIOS

For 2002	Avg. of All Wholesale	Analyzed Industry	Index	For 2002	Avg. of All Wholesale	Analyzed Industry	Index
Employees per Establishment	15	14	92	Sales per Employee	791,325	749,893	95
Payroll per Establishment	626,122	603,936	96	Sales per Establishment	12,012,387	10,256,991	85
Payroll per Employee	41,161	44,154	107	Expenses per Establishment	na	na	na

Sources: Same as General Statistics. The 'Average of All' column, Wholesale or Retail, represents the average of the sector reported for the most recent complete year available. The Index shows the relationship between the Average and the Analyzed Industry. For example, 100 means that they are equal; 500 that the Analyzed Industry is five times the average; 50 means that the Analyzed Industry is half the national average. The abbreviation 'na' is used to show that data are 'not available'.

*Equivalent to SIC 5051.

LEADING COMPANIES   Number shown: **75**   Total sales ($ mil): **110,178**   Total employment (000): **64.7**

Company Name	Address				CEO Name	Phone	Co. Type	Sales ($ mil)	Empl. (000)
ThyssenKrupp Materials N.A. Inc.	22355 W 11 Mile Rd	Southfield	MI	48034	Hans-Erich Forster	248-233-5600	S	45,632*	0.2
Marubeni America Corp.	450 Lexington Ave	New York	NY	10017	Kazuhiko Sakamoto	212-450-0100	S	8,050*	0.2
Commercial Metals Co.	7800 Stemmons	Dallas	TX	75247		214-689-4300	P	4,768	10.6
Republic Services Inc.	110 SE 6th St	Fort Lauderdale	FL	33301	Michael J Cordesman	954-769-2400	P	4,465	13.4
SOS Metals Inc.	9050 Centre Pointe	West Chester	OH	45069	Gary Johns	513-896-2700	S	4,342*	<0.1
LL Building Products Inc.	1361 Alps Rd	Wayne	NJ	07470		973-628-3000	R	3,661*	<0.1
Ryerson Tull Inc.	2621 W 15th Pl	Chicago	IL	60608		773-762-2121	P	3,302	3.4
Reliance Steel and Aluminum Co.	PO Box 60482	Los Angeles	CA	90060	Joe D Crider	213-687-7700	P	2,943	5.2
Blue Chip Stamps	PO Box 831	Pasadena	CA	91102	Bob Bird	626-585-6714	S	2,588*	<0.1
Wesco Financial Corp.	301 E Colorado	Pasadena	CA	91101	Robert H Bird	626-585-6700	P	2,538	2.7
Berwick Steel Co.	PO Box 27278	Columbus	OH	43227	Steve Sakoda	614-866-1338	R	2,412*	<0.1
Worthington Industries Inc.	200 Old Wilson Brg	Columbus	OH	43085	John S Christie	614-438-3210	P	2,379	6.7
Baron Drawn Steel Corp.	PO Box 3275	Toledo	OH	43607	Peter Gasiorski	419-531-5525	S	1,890*	0.2
Metals USA Inc.	1 Riverway	Houston	TX	77056	Daniel W Dienst	713-965-0990	P	1,510	2.4
Fulmer Company Inc.	3004 Venture Ct	Export	PA	15632	Leo Eger	724-325-7140	R	1,500*	<0.1
North Pacific Group Inc.	PO Box 3915	Portland	OR	97208		503-231-1166	R	1,227	0.8
Gibraltar Industries Inc.	PO Box 2028	Buffalo	NY	14219	H N Kornbrekke	716-826-6500	P	1,015	3.8
Olympic Steel Inc.	5096 Richmond Rd	Bedford Heights	OH	44146	Michael D Siegal	216-292-3800	P	894	0.8
Astrocosmos Metallurgical Inc	PO Box 1229	Wooster	OH	44691	Gerhard Doerr	330-264-8639	D	804*	<0.1
Feralloy Corp.	8755 W Higgins Rd	Chicago	IL	60631		773-380-1500	S	743*	<0.1
O'Neal Steel Inc.	PO Box 2623	Birmingham	AL	35202	William Jones	205-599-8000	R	669*	2.1
TW Metals Inc.	PO Box 644	Exton	PA	19341	Peter Gould	610-458-1300	R	650*	<0.1
A.M. Castle and Co.	3400 N Wolf Rd	Franklin Park	IL	60131		847-455-7111	P	543	1.4
J.M. Tull Metals Company Inc.	PO Box 4725	Norcross	GA	30091	S E Makarewicz	770-368-4200	S	540*	0.7
Central Steel and Wire Co.	PO Box 5100	Chicago	IL	60632	John M Tiernan	312-471-3800	R	534*	1.5
Heidtman Steel Products Inc.	2401 Front St	Toledo	OH	43605		419-691-4646	R	490*	<0.1
Phoenix Metals Co.	4685 Buford Hwy	Norcross	GA	30091	Steve Almond	770-447-4211	S	483*	0.2
Feroleto Steel Company Inc.	PO Box 3344	Bridgeport	CT	06605	Harold Wood	203-366-3263	R	480*	<0.1
Lapham-Hickey Steel Corp.	5500 W 73rd St	Chicago	IL	60638	William Hickey	708-496-6111	R	383*	0.4
Trident Co.	PO Box 853900	Richardson	TX	75085	Thomas Bentley	972-231-5176	R	383*	0.2
New Process Steel L.P.	PO Box 55205	Houston	TX	77255		713-686-9631	R	360*	0.3
Tempel Steel Co.	5500 N Wolcott Ave	Chicago	IL	60640		773-250-8000	R	350*	<0.1
Norfolk Iron and Metal Co.	PO Box 1129	Norfolk	NE	68702	Richard Robinson	402-371-1810	R	340*	0.2
Everett J. Prescott Inc.	PO Box 600	Gardiner	ME	04345	PE Prescott	207-582-2006	R	326*	0.2
Alamo Iron Works Inc.	PO Box 231	San Antonio	TX	78291	Anthony Koch	210-223-6161	R	319*	0.4
Lyon Conklin and Company Inc.	2101 Race St	Baltimore	MD	21230	Jenny Allen	301-808-3500	R	296*	0.2
Rafferty-Brown Steel Inc.	PO Box 18927	Greensboro	NC	27419		336-855-6300	R	276*	0.1
Albany Steel Inc.	PO Box 4006	Albany	NY	12204	Peter Hess	518-436-4851	R	264*	0.3
RSDC of Michigan L.L.C.	1775 Holloway Dr	Holt	MI	48842		517-699-7732	R	255*	0.3
Future Metals Inc.	10401 State St	Tamarac	FL	33321	Luis Benitez	954-724-1400	R	243*	0.1
Kenwal Steel Corp.	PO Box 4359	Dearborn	MI	48126	David Bazzy	313-739-1000	R	238*	0.1
Primary Steel Inc.	PO Box 1716	Middletown	CT	06457	Charles E Pompea	860-343-5111	R	238*	0.3
Bohler Uddeholm America Inc.	4902 Tollview Dr	Rch Trgl Pk	IL	60008	Erik Svendsen	847-577-2220	R	234*	0.2
Voss Steel	7925 Beech Daly Rd	Taylor	MI	48180	Jim Piwok	313-291-7500	R	230*	<0.1
Pacesetter Steel Service Inc.	PO Box 100007	Kennesaw	GA	30156	Steven Leebow	770-919-8000	R	215*	<0.1
Sioux City Foundry Co.	PO Box 3067	Sioux City	IA	51102	Andrew Galinsky	712-252-4181	R	196*	<0.1
Commercial Alloys Corp.	1831 E Highland Rd	Twinsburg	OH	44087	Larry Musarra	330-405-5440	R	195*	<0.1
Kataman Metals Inc.	7700 Bonhomme St	St. Louis	MO	63105	Warren J Gelman	314-863-6699	R	193*	<0.1
Empire Resources Inc.	1 Parker Plz	Fort Lee	NJ	07024		201-944-2200	P	184	<0.1
Farwest Steel Corp.	PO Box 889	Eugene	OR	97440	Richard Jones	541-686-2000	R	169*	0.3
Alliance Metals Inc.	905 Fern Hill Rd	West Chester	PA	19380	Bradley B Evans	610-436-8600	R	167*	0.1
Yarde Metals Inc.	45 Newell St	Southington	CT	06489	Craig Yarde	860-406-6061	R	165*	0.5
Grammer Dempsey & Hudson Inc.	PO Box 1059	Newark	NJ	07101	James Hudson	973-589-8000	R	158*	<0.1
Dayton Steel Service Inc.	3911 Dayton	Dayton	OH	45414		937-236-6940	R	150*	<0.1
Mill Steel Co.	PO Box 8827	Grand Rapids	MI	49518	Andrew Samrick	616-949-6700	R	150*	0.2
Magnolia Steel Company Inc.	PO Box 5007	Meridian	MS	39302	Cecil Crowe	601-693-4301	R	149*	0.2
Chatham Steel Corp.	PO Box 2567	Savannah	GA	31402	Burt Tenenbaum	912-233-4182	D	148*	0.3
Alro Metals Service Center	PO Box 3031	Boca Raton	FL	33431	Alvin Glick	561-997-6766	D	145*	0.1
Tubular Steel Inc.	1031 Exec Pkwy	St. Louis	MO	63141	John Hauck	314-851-9200	R	141*	0.3
PDM Steel Service Centers Inc.	PO Box 310	Stockton	CA	95201	Derek Halecky	209-943-0555	S	132*	0.4
Steel and Pipe Supply Inc.	PO Box 1688	Manhattan	KS	66505	Dennis A Mullin	785-587-5100	R	130*	0.3
Chicago Steel L.P.	700 Chase St	Gary	IN	46404		219-949-1111	R	129*	0.1
Ferrous Metal Processing	11103 Memphis Ave	Brooklyn	OH	44144	Eduardo Gonzalez	216-671-6161	R	128*	0.1
AFCO Metals Inc.	PO Box 34287	Little Rock	AR	72203	Steve Makarewicz	501-490-2255	S	126*	0.1
Benedict-Miller L.L.C.	123 N 8th St	Kenilworth	NJ	07033	John Benedict	908-497-1477	R	120*	0.1
Wausau Steel Corp.	PO Box 329	Wausau	WI	54402	Peter Wallach	715-845-4286	R	119*	0.1
Duferco Steel Inc.	100 Matawan Rd Ste	Matawan	NJ	07747	Mike Vignale	732-566-1741	S	117*	<0.1
Friedman Industries Inc.	PO Box 21147	Houston	TX	77226	William E Crow	713-672-9433	P	116	0.1
Columbia Pipe and Supply	1120 W Pershing Rd	Chicago	IL	60609	William D Arenberg	773-927-6600	R	112*	0.3
West Coast Wire Rope & Rigging	PO Box 5999	Portland	OR	97228	Karen Newton	503-228-9353	R	110*	0.1
Metals USA, Plates & Shapes	50 Cabot Blvd E	Langhorne	PA	19047		267-580-2100	D	109*	<0.1
Century Steel L.L.C.	300 E Joe Orr Rd	Chicago Heights	IL	60411		708-758-0900	S	106*	0.1
Lamination Specialties Corp.	235 N Artesian Ave	Chicago	IL	60612	Albert Delighter	312-243-2181	R	106*	<0.1
Clinton Machine Company Inc.	6270 Van Buren Rd	Clinton	OH	44216	Joe Podnar	330-882-6743	R	102*	0.1
Contractors Steel Company Inc.	PO Box 3364	Livonia	MI	48151	Donald Simon	734-464-4000	R	102*	0.2

Source: Ward's Business Directory of U.S. Private and Public Companies, Volumes 1 and 2, 2005. The company type code used is as follows: P - Public, R - Private, S - Subsidiary, D - Division, J - Joint Venture, A - Affiliate, G - Group. Sales are in millions of dollars, employees are in thousands. An asterisk (*) indicates an estimated sales volume. The symbol < stands for 'less than'. Company names and addresses are truncated, in some cases, to fit into the available space.

OCCUPATIONS EMPLOYED BY METAL & MINERAL (EXCEPT PETROLEUM) WHOLESALE

Occupation	% of Total 2004	Change to 2014	Occupation	% of Total 2004	Change to 2014
Sales reps, wholesale & manufacturing, exc tech	13.8	12.5	Team assemblers	2.2	12.5
Laborers & freight, stock, & material movers, hand	10.9	1.3	Stock clerks & order fillers	1.8	-13.8
Truck drivers, heavy & tractor-trailer	4.7	12.5	Truck drivers, light or delivery services	1.7	12.5
Machinists	3.9	12.5	First-line supervisors/managers of non-retail sales work	1.6	4.0
Industrial truck & tractor operators	3.7	12.5	Packaging & filling machine operators & tenders	1.5	6.5
Welders, cutters, solderers, & brazers	3.4	12.5	Sales reps, wholesale & manufacturing, tech	1.4	12.5
General & operations managers	3.0	11.4	Production workers, nec	1.3	-1.4
Shipping, receiving, & traffic clerks	3.0	1.8	Maintenance & repair workers, general	1.2	12.5
Office clerks, general	2.8	0.1	First-line supervisors/managers of office workers	1.2	2.0
Cutting, punching, & press machine setters & operators	2.8	-10.0	Secretaries, except legal, medical, & executive	1.1	-5.3
First-line supervisors/managers of production workers	2.5	12.5	Order clerks	1.0	-26.9
Bookkeeping, accounting, & auditing clerks	2.4	1.2			

Source: Industry-Occupation Matrix, Bureau of Labor Statistics. These data are reported based on 4-digit NAICS categories but have been matched to corresponding 6-digit NAICS industry codes. The change reported for each occupation to the year 2014 is a percent of growth or decline as estimated by the Bureau of Labor Statistics. The abbreviation nec stands for 'not elsewhere classified.'

LOCATION BY STATE AND REGIONAL CONCENTRATION

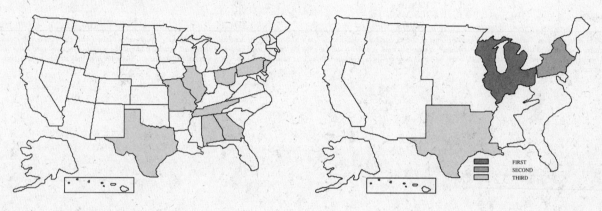

FIRST
SECOND
THIRD

INDUSTRY DATA BY STATE

State	Establishments Total (number)	Establishments % of U.S.	Employment Total (number)	Employment % of U.S.	Employment Per Estab.	Payroll Total ($ mil.)	Payroll Per Empl. ($)	Sales Total ($ mil.)	Sales % of U.S.	Sales Per Estab. ($)
Illinois	715	6.9	13,870	9.6	19	676.5	48,777	11,939.0	11.0	16,697,832
Texas	996	9.5	13,134	9.1	13	591.4	45,026	9,653.7	8.9	9,692,509
Ohio	626	6.0	10,029	7.0	16	449.3	44,799	8,118.7	7.5	12,969,158
Pennsylvania	535	5.1	7,362	5.1	14	341.0	46,322	6,987.7	6.5	13,061,052
New Jersey	377	3.6	4,437	3.1	12	225.3	50,786	4,199.0	3.9	11,137,918
Tennessee	195	1.9	3,487	2.4	18	162.6	46,619	3,906.5	3.6	20,033,364
Georgia	276	2.6	3,875	2.7	14	191.3	49,378	3,453.1	3.2	12,511,134
Florida	560	5.4	4,886	3.4	9	189.4	38,755	2,706.2	2.5	4,832,489
Missouri	254	2.4	3,083	2.1	12	130.8	42,441	2,324.8	2.2	9,152,646
Alabama	187	1.8	3,270	2.3	17	134.0	40,994	1,836.2	1.7	9,819,112
North Carolina	247	2.4	3,067	2.1	12	121.7	39,691	1,507.7	1.4	6,104,227
Maryland	133	1.3	2,104	1.5	16	122.8	58,366	1,266.5	1.2	9,522,662
Louisiana	155	1.5	2,141	1.5	14	78.9	36,872	970.1	0.9	6,258,877
Iowa	91	0.9	1,584	1.1	17	58.7	37,049	844.8	0.8	9,283,473
Kansas	91	0.9	1,324	0.9	15	47.8	36,105	823.3	0.8	9,047,000
Oregon	126	1.2	1,940	1.3	15	78.5	40,448	764.2	0.7	6,065,444
South Carolina	101	1.0	1,186	0.8	12	44.2	37,267	511.2	0.5	5,061,059
Utah	90	0.9	1,076	0.7	12	43.5	40,463	479.7	0.4	5,329,967
Nevada	38	0.4	396	0.3	10	17.6	44,477	125.7	0.1	3,307,053
New Mexico	45	0.4	391	0.3	9	12.8	32,721	124.7	0.1	2,771,689
Montana	32	0.3	230	0.2	7	7.0	30,396	64.4	0.1	2,013,094
Wyoming	21	0.2	131	0.1	6	4.1	31,084	36.2	-	1,724,762
North Dakota	7	0.1	81	0.1	12	2.3	27,864	18.6	-	2,652,286
California	1,184	11.3	10K-24999	-	-	(D)	-	(D)	-	-
New York	562	5.4	5K-9999	-	-	(D)	-	(D)	-	-
Michigan	486	4.7	5K-9999	-	-	(D)	-	(D)	-	-
Indiana	264	2.5	2500-4999	-	-	(D)	-	(D)	-	-
Washington	223	2.1	2500-4999	-	-	(D)	-	(D)	-	-
Massachusetts	197	1.9	1000-2499	-	-	(D)	-	(D)	-	-
Wisconsin	166	1.6	1000-2499	-	-	(D)	-	(D)	-	-
Colorado	163	1.6	1000-2499	-	-	(D)	-	(D)	-	-

Continued on next page.

INDUSTRY DATA BY STATE - Continued

State	Establishments Total (number)	% of U.S.	Employment Total (number)	% of U.S.	Per Estab.	Payroll Total ($ mil.)	Per Empl. ($)	Sales Total ($ mil.)	% of U.S.	Per Estab. ($)
Oklahoma	150	1.4	1000-2499	-	-	(D)	-	(D)	-	-
Minnesota	149	1.4	2500-4999	-	-	(D)	-	(D)	-	-
Connecticut	144	1.4	1000-2499	-	-	(D)	-	(D)	-	-
Arizona	142	1.4	1000-2499	-	-	(D)	-	(D)	-	-
Virginia	134	1.3	1000-2499	-	-	(D)	-	(D)	-	-
Kentucky	125	1.2	1000-2499	-	-	(D)	-	(D)	-	-
Arkansas	83	0.8	1000-2499	-	-	(D)	-	(D)	-	-
Mississippi	56	0.5	500-999	-	-	(D)	-	(D)	-	-
Nebraska	41	0.4	500-999	-	-	(D)	-	(D)	-	-
New Hampshire	41	0.4	500-999	-	-	(D)	-	(D)	-	-
West Virginia	40	0.4	250-499	-	-	(D)	-	(D)	-	-
Rhode Island	38	0.4	250-499	-	-	(D)	-	(D)	-	-
Idaho	36	0.3	250-499	-	-	(D)	-	(D)	-	-
Maine	28	0.3	250-499	-	-	(D)	-	(D)	-	-
Delaware	27	0.3	100-249	-	-	(D)	-	(D)	-	-
Hawaii	18	0.2	100-249	-	-	(D)	-	(D)	-	-
Vermont	15	0.1	100-249	-	-	(D)	-	(D)	-	-
Alaska	12	0.1	100-249	-	-	(D)	-	(D)	-	-
South Dakota	10	0.1	100-249	-	-	(D)	-	(D)	-	-
D.C.	2	-	20-99	-	-	(D)	-	(D)	-	-

Source: 2002 *Economic Census*. The states are in descending order of sales or establishments (if sales data are missing for the majority). The symbol (D) appears when data are withheld to prevent disclosure of competitive information. States marked with (D) are sorted by number of establishments. A dash (-) indicates that the data element cannot be calculated. Shaded *states* on the state map indicate those states which have proportionately greater representation in the industry than would be indicated by the states population; the ratio is based on total sales or number of establishments. Shaded *regions* indicate where the industry is regionally most concentrated.

NAICS 423520 - COAL AND OTHER MINERAL AND ORE MERCHANT WHOLESALERS

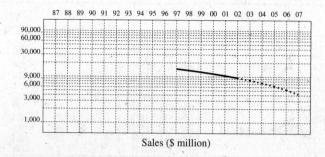

Sales ($ million)

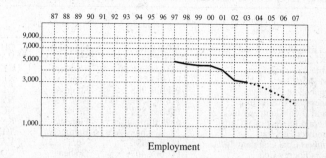

Employment

GENERAL STATISTICS

Year	Establishments (number)	Employment (number)	Payroll ($ million)	Sales ($ million)	Employees per Establishment (number)	Sales per Establishment ($)	Payroll per Employee ($)
1987	-	-	-	-	-	-	-
1988	-	-	-	-	-	-	-
1989	-	-	-	-	-	-	-
1990	-	-	-	-	-	-	-
1991	-	-	-	-	-	-	-
1992	-	-	-	-	-	-	-
1993	-	-	-	-	-	-	-
1994	-	-	-	-	-	-	-
1995	-	-	-	-	-	-	-
1996	-	-	-	-	-	-	-
1997	756	5,079	260.4	14,798.0	6.7	19,574,074.1	51,269.9
1998	729	4,791	270.8	13,743.6 e	6.6	18,852,647.5	56,522.6
1999	695	4,616	265.9	12,689.2 e	6.6	18,257,784.2	57,604.0
2000	661	4,602	289.9	11,634.7 e	7.0	17,601,724.7	62,988.7
2001	649	4,143	256.3	10,580.3 e	6.4	16,302,496.2	61,874.5
2002	529	3,205	187.0	9,525.9	6.1	18,007,372.4	58,346.3
2003	494	3,062	213.8	8,471.5 p	6.2	16,485,347.6 p	69,829.8
2004	469 p	2,829 p	203.9 p	7,417.1 p	6.1 p	16,024,204.1 p	68,862.0 p
2005	425 p	2,483 p	192.6 p	6,362.6 p	6.0 p	15,563,060.7 p	71,133.3 p
2006	381 p	2,136 p	181.2 p	5,308.2 p	5.9 p	15,101,917.2 p	73,404.7 p
2007	337 p	1,790 p	169.9 p	4,253.8 p	5.8 p	14,640,773.7 p	75,676.0 p

Source: Economic Census of the United States, 1997 and 2002. Establishment counts, employment, and payroll are from *County Business Patterns* for non-Census years. This is a newly defined industry. Data for prior years are unavailable at the time of publication but may become available over time. Values followed by 'p' are projections by the editors. Sales data for non-Census years are extrapolations, marked by 'e'.

INDICES OF CHANGE

Year	Establishments (number)	Employment (number)	Payroll ($ million)	Sales ($ million)	Employees per Establishment (number)	Sales per Establishment ($)	Payroll per Employee ($)
1987	-	-	-	-	-	-	-
1992	-	-	-	-	-	-	-
1993	-	-	-	-	-	-	-
1994	-	-	-	-	-	-	-
1995	-	-	-	-	-	-	-
1996	-	-	-	-	-	-	-
1997	142.9	158.5	139.3	155.3	109.8	108.7	87.9
1998	137.8	149.5	144.8	144.3 e	108.2	104.7	96.9
1999	131.4	144.0	142.2	133.2 e	108.2	101.4	98.7
2000	125.0	143.6	155.0	122.1 e	114.8	97.7	108.0
2001	122.7	129.3	137.1	111.1 e	104.9	90.5	106.0
2002	100.0	100.0	100.0	100.0	100.0	100.0	100.0
2003	93.4	95.5	114.3	88.9 p	101.6	91.5 p	119.7
2004	88.6 p	88.3 p	109.0 p	77.9 p	100.5 p	89.0 p	118.0 p
2005	80.3 p	77.5 p	103.0 p	66.8 p	98.9 p	86.4 p	121.9 p
2006	72.0 p	66.7 p	96.9 p	55.7 p	97.3 p	83.9 p	125.8 p
2007	63.7 p	55.9 p	90.9 p	44.7 p	95.7 p	81.3 p	129.7 p

Sources: Same as General Statistics. The values shown reflect change from the base year, 2002. Values above 100 mean greater than 2002, values below 100 mean less than 2002, and a value of 100 in the 1987-2001 or 2003-2007 period means same as 2002. Values followed by a 'p' are projections by the editors; 'e' stands for extrapolation. Data are the most recent available at this level of detail.

SELECTED RATIOS

For 2002	Avg. of All Wholesale	Analyzed Industry	Index	For 2002	Avg. of All Wholesale	Analyzed Industry	Index
Employees per Establishment	15	6	41	Sales per Employee	791,325	2,972,200	376
Payroll per Establishment	626,122	353,497	56	Sales per Establishment	12,012,387	18,007,372	150
Payroll per Employee	41,161	58,346	142	Expenses per Establishment	na	na	na

Sources: Same as General Statistics. The 'Average of All' column, Wholesale or Retail, represents the average of the sector reported for the most recent complete year available. The Index shows the relationship between the Average and the Analyzed Industry. For example, 100 means that they are equal; 500 that the Analyzed Industry is five times the average; 50 means that the Analyzed Industry is half the national average. The abbreviation 'na' is used to show that data are 'not available'.

LEADING COMPANIES   Number shown: 11   Total sales ($ mil): 1,384   Total employment (000): 0.6

Company Name	Address				CEO Name	Phone	Co. Type	Sales ($ mil)	Empl. (000)
Hickman, Williams and Co.	250 E Fifth St	Cincinnati	OH	45202	Paul C. Kjelstrom	513-621-1946	R	793*	0.2
ABC Inc.	5700 Cleveland	Virginia Beach	VA	23462	James Sparts	757-490-2242	R	160*	<0.1
Noble Americas Corp.	333 Ludlow St	Stamford	CT	06902	Vicente Del Castillo	203-324-8555	R	129*	<0.1
HM Royal Inc.	PO Box 28	Trenton	NJ	08601	H Royal	609-396-9176	R	88*	<0.1
Connecticut Coal Inc.	PO Box 368	Stratford	CT	06615	James Osborne	203-377-3871	R	58*	<0.1
Kanematsu U.S.A. Inc.	114 W 47th St	New York	NY	10036	M Shimojima	212-704-9400	S	52*	<0.1
G and B Oil Company Inc.	PO Box 811	Elkin	NC	28621	Jeffery C Eidson	336-835-3607	R	30*	0.1
Emerald International Corp.	6895 Burlington	Florence	KY	41042		859-525-2522	R	26*	<0.1
Summers Fuel Inc.	28 Allegheny Ave	Baltimore	MD	21204	W N Clements III	410-825-8555	R	26*	<0.1
Lambert Coal Company Inc.	PO Box 490	Nora	VA	24272		276-835-8666	R	21*	<0.1
Coors Energy Co.	PO Box 467	Golden	CO	80402		303-277-6042	R	1*	<0.1

Source: Ward's Business Directory of U.S. Private and Public Companies, Volumes 1 and 2, 2005. The company type code used is as follows: P - Public, R - Private, S - Subsidiary, D - Division, J - Joint Venture, A - Affiliate, G - Group. Sales are in millions of dollars, employees are in thousands. An asterisk (*) indicates an estimated sales volume. The symbol < stands for 'less than'. Company names and addresses are truncated, in some cases, to fit into the available space.

OCCUPATIONS EMPLOYED BY METAL & MINERAL (EXCEPT PETROLEUM) WHOLESALE

Occupation	% of Total 2004	Change to 2014	Occupation	% of Total 2004	Change to 2014
Sales reps, wholesale & manufacturing, exc tech	13.8	12.5	Team assemblers	2.2	12.5
Laborers & freight, stock, & material movers, hand	10.9	1.3	Stock clerks & order fillers	1.8	-13.8
Truck drivers, heavy & tractor-trailer	4.7	12.5	Truck drivers, light or delivery services	1.7	12.5
Machinists	3.9	12.5	First-line supervisors/managers of non-retail sales work	1.6	4.0
Industrial truck & tractor operators	3.7	12.5	Packaging & filling machine operators & tenders	1.5	6.5
Welders, cutters, solderers, & brazers	3.4	12.5	Sales reps, wholesale & manufacturing, tech	1.4	12.5
General & operations managers	3.0	11.4	Production workers, nec	1.3	-1.4
Shipping, receiving, & traffic clerks	3.0	1.8	Maintenance & repair workers, general	1.2	12.5
Office clerks, general	2.8	0.1	First-line supervisors/managers of office workers	1.2	2.0
Cutting, punching, & press machine setters & operators	2.8	-10.0	Secretaries, except legal, medical, & executive	1.1	-5.3
First-line supervisors/managers of production workers	2.5	12.5	Order clerks	1.0	-26.9
Bookkeeping, accounting, & auditing clerks	2.4	1.2			

Source: Industry-Occupation Matrix, Bureau of Labor Statistics. These data are reported based on 4-digit NAICS categories but have been matched to corresponding 6-digit NAICS industry codes. The change reported for each occupation to the year 2014 is a percent of growth or decline as estimated by the Bureau of Labor Statistics. The abbreviation nec stands for 'not elsewhere classified.'

LOCATION BY STATE AND REGIONAL CONCENTRATION

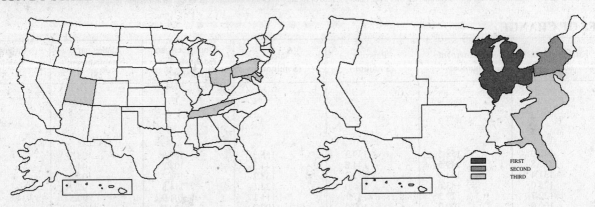

INDUSTRY DATA BY STATE

State	Establishments Total (number)	Establishments % of U.S.	Employment Total (number)	Employment % of U.S.	Employment Per Estab.	Payroll Total ($ mil.)	Payroll Per Empl. ($)	Sales Total ($ mil.)	Sales % of U.S.	Sales Per Estab. ($)
Pennsylvania	67	12.7	366	9.8	5	20.3	55,415	959.7	10.3	14,323,284
Maryland	15	2.8	241	6.5	16	21.8	90,407	648.4	6.9	43,223,600
Ohio	33	6.3	212	5.7	6	13.6	64,387	585.4	6.3	17,738,545
Illinois	24	4.5	160	4.3	7	10.0	62,675	379.4	4.1	15,807,333
Tennessee	13	2.5	502	13.5	39	17.8	35,558	308.0	3.3	23,688,538
Georgia	11	2.1	98	2.6	9	3.8	38,276	140.5	1.5	12,775,545

Continued on next page.

INDUSTRY DATA BY STATE - Continued

State	Establishments		Employment			Payroll		Sales		
	Total (number)	% of U.S.	Total (number)	% of U.S.	Per Estab.	Total ($ mil.)	Per Empl. ($)	Total ($ mil.)	% of U.S.	Per Estab. ($)
Alabama	17	3.2	94	2.5	6	4.9	51,819	130.0	1.4	7,644,294
Utah	7	1.3	54	1.5	8	2.6	48,296	117.1	1.3	16,721,714
South Carolina	8	1.5	90	2.4	11	4.8	53,300	38.4	0.4	4,801,250
Nevada	4	0.8	21	0.6	5	0.9	43,476	18.1	0.2	4,524,750
Oregon	3	0.6	41	1.1	14	1.3	31,829	7.5	0.1	2,501,667
Arizona	7	1.3	14	0.4	2	0.3	22,143	5.1	0.1	734,571
New Mexico	3	0.6	8	0.2	3	0.3	36,750	1.6	-	522,000
New York	40	7.6	100-249	-	-	(D)	-	(D)	-	-
Kentucky	37	7.0	100-249	-	-	(D)	-	(D)	-	-
California	31	5.9	100-249	-	-	(D)	-	(D)	-	-
West Virginia	29	5.5	100-249	-	-	(D)	-	(D)	-	-
Texas	22	4.2	100-249	-	-	(D)	-	(D)	-	-
New Jersey	21	4.0	100-249	-	-	(D)	-	(D)	-	-
Virginia	20	3.8	100-249	-	-	(D)	-	(D)	-	-
Florida	17	3.2	100-249	-	-	(D)	-	(D)	-	-
Indiana	13	2.5	20-99	-	-	(D)	-	(D)	-	-
Colorado	10	1.9	20-99	-	-	(D)	-	(D)	-	-
Louisiana	8	1.5	20-99	-	-	(D)	-	(D)	-	-
Minnesota	7	1.3	20-99	-	-	(D)	-	(D)	-	-
Wisconsin	7	1.3	20-99	-	-	(D)	-	(D)	-	-
Connecticut	6	1.1	20-99	-	-	(D)	-	(D)	-	-
North Carolina	6	1.1	20-99	-	-	(D)	-	(D)	-	-
Washington	6	1.1	0-19	-	-	(D)	-	(D)	-	-
Michigan	5	0.9	0-19	-	-	(D)	-	(D)	-	-
Missouri	5	0.9	20-99	-	-	(D)	-	(D)	-	-
Massachusetts	4	0.8	0-19	-	-	(D)	-	(D)	-	-
Arkansas	3	0.6	0-19	-	-	(D)	-	(D)	-	-
Oklahoma	3	0.6	0-19	-	-	(D)	-	(D)	-	-
Alaska	2	0.4	0-19	-	-	(D)	-	(D)	-	-
Kansas	2	0.4	0-19	-	-	(D)	-	(D)	-	-
North Dakota	2	0.4	0-19	-	-	(D)	-	(D)	-	-
Wyoming	2	0.4	0-19	-	-	(D)	-	(D)	-	-
Idaho	1	0.2	0-19	-	-	(D)	-	(D)	-	-
Maine	1	0.2	0-19	-	-	(D)	-	(D)	-	-
Mississippi	1	0.2	0-19	-	-	(D)	-	(D)	-	-
Nebraska	1	0.2	0-19	-	-	(D)	-	(D)	-	-
New Hampshire	1	0.2	0-19	-	-	(D)	-	(D)	-	-
Rhode Island	1	0.2	0-19	-	-	(D)	-	(D)	-	-
South Dakota	1	0.2	0-19	-	-	(D)	-	(D)	-	-
Vermont	1	0.2	0-19	-	-	(D)	-	(D)	-	-

Source: 2002 *Economic Census*. The states are in descending order of sales or establishments (if sales data are missing for the majority). The symbol (D) appears when data are withheld to prevent disclosure of competitive information. States marked with (D) are sorted by number of establishments. A dash (-) indicates that the data element cannot be calculated. Shaded *states* on the state map indicate those states which have proportionately greater representation in the industry than would be indicated by the states population; the ratio is based on total sales or number of establishments. Shaded *regions* indicate where the industry is regionally most concentrated.

NAICS 423610 - ELECTRICAL APPARATUS AND EQUIPMENT, WIRING SUPPLIES, AND RELATED EQUIPMENT MERCHANT WHOLESALERS

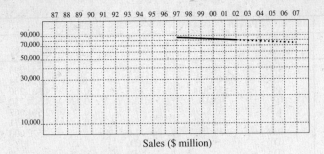

Sales ($ million)

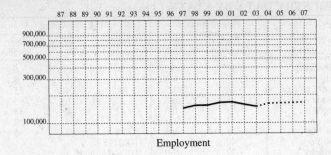

Employment

GENERAL STATISTICS

Year	Establishments (number)	Employment (number)	Payroll ($ million)	Sales ($ million)	Employees per Establishment (number)	Sales per Establishment ($)	Payroll per Employee ($)
1987	-	-	-	-	-	-	-
1988	-	-	-	-	-	-	-
1989	-	-	-	-	-	-	-
1990	-	-	-	-	-	-	-
1991	-	-	-	-	-	-	-
1992	-	-	-	-	-	-	-
1993	-	-	-	-	-	-	-
1994	-	-	-	-	-	-	-
1995	-	-	-	-	-	-	-
1996	-	-	-	-	-	-	-
1997	13,431	144,585	6,028.4	85,861.0	10.8	6,392,748.1	41,694.5
1998	13,768	154,971	6,601.6	84,703.4 e	11.3	6,152,190.6	42,598.9
1999	13,873	155,489	7,105.7	83,545.7 e	11.2	6,022,181.2	45,699.1
2000	13,904	165,955	8,250.9	82,388.1 e	11.9	5,925,494.8	49,717.7
2001	13,878	168,091	8,099.0	81,230.4 e	12.1	5,853,180.6	48,182.1
2002	13,214	158,274	7,261.6	80,072.8	12.0	6,059,694.3	45,879.9
2003	12,462	149,980	7,169.6	78,915.2 p	12.0	5,801,683.0 p	47,803.6
2004	12,931 p	161,820 p	8,036.2 p	77,757.5 p	12.5 p	5,725,712.0 p	49,849.7 p
2005	12,788 p	163,084 p	8,241.1 p	76,599.9 p	12.7 p	5,649,741.0 p	50,827.3 p
2006	12,645 p	164,348 p	8,446.0 p	75,442.2 p	12.9 p	5,573,770.0 p	51,804.9 p
2007	12,502 p	165,612 p	8,650.9 p	74,284.6 p	13.1 p	5,497,799.0 p	52,782.5 p

Source: *Economic Census of the United States*, 1997 and 2002. Establishment counts, employment, and payroll are from *County Business Patterns* for non-Census years. This is a newly defined industry. Data for prior years are unavailable at the time of publication but may become available over time. Values followed by 'p' are projections by the editors. Sales data for non-Census years are extrapolations, marked by 'e'.

INDICES OF CHANGE

Year	Establishments (number)	Employment (number)	Payroll ($ million)	Sales ($ million)	Employees per Establishment (number)	Sales per Establishment ($)	Payroll per Employee ($)
1987	-	-	-	-	-	-	-
1992	-	-	-	-	-	-	-
1993	-	-	-	-	-	-	-
1994	-	-	-	-	-	-	-
1995	-	-	-	-	-	-	-
1996	-	-	-	-	-	-	-
1997	101.6	91.4	83.0	107.2	90.0	105.5	90.9
1998	104.2	97.9	90.9	105.8 e	94.2	101.5	92.8
1999	105.0	98.2	97.9	104.3 e	93.3	99.4	99.6
2000	105.2	104.9	113.6	102.9 e	99.2	97.8	108.4
2001	105.0	106.2	111.5	101.4 e	100.8	96.6	105.0
2002	100.0	100.0	100.0	100.0	100.0	100.0	100.0
2003	94.3	94.8	98.7	98.6 p	100.3	95.7 p	104.2
2004	97.9 p	102.2 p	110.7 p	97.1 p	104.0 p	94.5 p	108.7 p
2005	96.8 p	103.0 p	113.5 p	95.7 p	105.8 p	93.2 p	110.8 p
2006	95.7 p	103.8 p	116.3 p	94.2 p	107.6 p	92.0 p	112.9 p
2007	94.6 p	104.6 p	119.1 p	92.8 p	109.3 p	90.7 p	115.0 p

Sources: Same as General Statistics. The values shown reflect change from the base year, 2002. Values above 100 mean greater than 2002, values below 100 mean less than 2002, and a value of 100 in the 1987-2001 or 2003-2007 period means same as 2002. Values followed by a 'p' are projections by the editors; 'e' stands for extrapolation. Data are the most recent available at this level of detail.

SELECTED RATIOS

For 2002	Avg. of All Wholesale	Analyzed Industry	Index	For 2002	Avg. of All Wholesale	Analyzed Industry	Index
Employees per Establishment	15	12	80	Sales per Employee	791,325	505,913	64
Payroll per Establishment	626,122	549,538	88	Sales per Establishment	12,012,387	6,059,694	50
Payroll per Employee	41,161	45,880	111	Expenses per Establishment	na	na	na

Sources: Same as General Statistics. The 'Average of All' column, Wholesale or Retail, represents the average of the sector reported for the most recent complete year available. The Index shows the relationship between the Average and the Analyzed Industry. For example, 100 means that they are equal; 500 that the Analyzed Industry is five times the average; 50 means that the Analyzed Industry is half the national average. The abbreviation 'na' is used to show that data are 'not available'.

LEADING COMPANIES   Number shown: **75**   Total sales ($ mil): **44,417**   Total employment (000): **72.5**

Company Name	Address				CEO Name	Phone	Co. Type	Sales ($ mil)	Empl. (000)
Arrow Electronics Inc.	50 Marcus Dr	Melville	NY	11747	Daniel W. Duval	631-847-2000	P	10,646	11.2
W.W. Grainger Inc.	100 Grainger Pkwy	Lake Forest	IL	60045	David W Grainger	847-535-1000	P	5,050	14.7
WESCO International Inc.	Commerce Court	Pittsburgh	PA	15219	Ron Haley	412-454-2200	P	3,741	5.3
Anixter International Inc.	2301 Patriot Blvd	Glenview	IL	60025	Robert W Grubbs Jr	224-521-8000	P	3,275	5.0
Hughes Supply Inc.	PO Box 2273	Orlando	FL	32801	Thomas I Morgan	407-841-4755	P	3,253	8.4
Consolidated Electrical Distrib.	31356 Via Colinas	Westlake Village	CA	91362	H Dean Bursch	818-991-9000	R	2,364*	5.0
Hawthorne Machinery Inc.	PO Box 120708	San Diego	CA	92112	Tom J Hawthorne	858-674-7000	R	1,371*	0.6
Audiovox Corp.	150 Marcus Blvd	Hauppauge	NY	11788	John J Shalam	631-231-7750	P	1,324	1.0
State Electric Supply Co.	PO Box 5397	Huntington	WV	25703	Clarence Martin	304-523-7491	R	1,181*	0.5
GE Supply	PO Box 861	Shelton	CT	06484	WL Meddaugh	203-944-3000	D	1,100*	2.2
Cameron and Barkley Co.	PO Box 118007	Charleston	SC	29423	James R Warren	843-745-2400	R	1,078*	2.6
McJunkin Corp.	PO Box 513	Charleston	WV	25322	H Barnard Wehrle III	304-348-5211	R	847*	1.6
Washington Energy Services Co.	2800 Thorndyke W	Seattle	WA	98199	Craig Olsen	206-282-4700	R	719*	0.3
Stanion Wholesale Electric Inc.	PO Drawer F	Pratt	KS	67124	Bill Keller	620-672-5678	R	701*	0.3
AFA Protective Systems Inc.	155 Michael Dr	Syosset	NY	11791	Richard Kleinman	516-496-2322	R	670*	0.3
Western Extralite Co.	1470 Liberty St	Kansas City	MO	64102	Thomas E Isenberg	816-421-8404	R	493*	0.2
Sager Electronics Inc.	97 Libbey Ind Pwy	Weymouth	MA	02189	Frank Flynn	781-682-4844	R	300*	0.6
Power-Lite Electric Supplies	1333 Magnolia St	Bowling Green	KY	42101		270-842-1697	D	295*	0.1
Radiall America	3611 NE 112th Ave	Vancouver	WA	98682	Michael Renard	360-944-7551	R	264*	<0.1
McNaughton-McKay Electric Inc.	1357 E Lincoln Ave	Madison Heights	MI	48071	Don Slominski	248-399-7500	R	259*	0.9
Stuart C. Irby Co.	PO Box 1819	Jackson	MS	39215	Charles Irby	601-969-1811	R	258*	0.6
Interstate Co's Inc.	2601 E 80th St	Bloomington	MN	55425	Jeffrey Caswell	952-854-2044	R	240*	<0.1
Braid Electric Company Inc.	PO Box 23710	Nashville	TN	37202	Ben Gambell	615-242-6511	R	236*	0.1
Steiner Electric Co.	1250 Touhy Ave	Elk Grove Vill.	IL	60007	Harold M Kerman	847-228-0400	R	200*	0.6
Platt Electric Supply Inc.	10605 SW Allen	Beaverton	OR	97005	Harvey Platt	503-641-6121	R	197*	0.8
Seattle Lighting Fixture	1919 NW 19th Ave	Portland	OR	97209		503-225-9009	R	176*	<0.1
Harris Electric Inc.	4020 23rd Ave W	Seattle	WA	98199	Richard A Sundholm	206-282-8080	R	168*	<0.1
Miller Bearings Inc.	17 S Westmoreland	Orlando	FL	32805	Craig Faber	407-425-9078	R	164*	0.1
Summit Electric Supply Inc.	PO Box 6409	Albuquerque	NM	87197	Victor Jury Jr	505-346-9000	R	152*	0.5
Dixon Midland Lighting Co.	PO Box 7992	Chicago	IL	60680		312-364-0150	R	143*	0.2
Eck Supply Co.	PO Box 85618	Richmond	VA	23285	Edgar Eck Jr	804-359-5781	R	136*	0.2
Wille Electric Supply Co.	PO Box 3246	Modesto	CA	95353	LR Robinson III	209-527-6800	R	131*	<0.1
Full Compass Systems Ltd.	8001 Ter Ave	Middleton	WI	53562	Susan Lipp	608-831-7330	R	131*	0.1
Cooper Electric Supply Co.	70 Apple St	Tinton Falls	NJ	07724	Greg Griswold	732-747-2233	R	125*	0.4
Hannan Supply Co.	PO Box 270	Paducah	KY	42002	B Brockenborough	270-442-5456	R	119*	<0.1
Nunn Electric Supply Corp.	PO Box 791	Amarillo	TX	79189	Carl Hare, Jr	806-376-4581	R	119*	0.3
PCG Trading L.L.C.	4 Technology Dr	Peabody	MA	01960		978-538-8000	R	103*	0.1
Thermocoax Inc.	6825 Shiloh Rd E	Alpharetta	GA	30005	Claude Capron	678-947-5510	R	102*	0.2
A and K Railroad Materials Inc.	PO Box 30076	Salt Lake City	UT	84130	Morris Kulmer	801-974-5484	R	100*	0.5
Maurice Electrical Supply Inc.	500 Penn St NE	Washington	DC	20002	Mark Kogod	202-675-9400	R	94*	0.2
Saudi Electric Supply Inc.	1825 Deamerlyn Dr	York	PA	17402	Ali Tamimi	717-757-6016	R	94*	0.2
Emcore Corp.	145 Belmont Dr	Somerset	NJ	08873		732-271-9090	P	93	0.6
Capitol Light and Supply Co.	270 Locust St	Hartford	CT	06141	Mickey Cartin	860-549-1230	R	93*	0.3
RS Electronics Inc.	555 Sparkman Dr	Huntsville	AL	35816	Winston Stalcup	256-721-9999	R	88*	0.2
United Sales	425 Shrewsbury St	Worcester	MA	01604	Tom Andrews	508-752-7073	R	85*	0.1
Fox Valley Fire and Safety Co.	1730 Berkley St	Elgin	IL	60123	Kenneth Volkening	847-695-5990	R	82*	0.1
Billows Electric Supply Co.	9100 State Rd	Philadelphia	PA	19136	Jeff Billows	215-332-9700	R	78*	0.3
Sound Inc.	1550 Shore Rd	Naperville	IL	60563	Todd Channell	630-369-2900	R	75*	0.1
Arizona Wholesale Supply Co.	PO Box 2979	Phoenix	AZ	85062	TW Thomas	602-258-7901	R	73*	0.1
F.D. Lawrence Electric Co.	3450 Beekman St	Cincinnati	OH	45223	Dennis P O'Leary	513-542-1100	R	73*	0.1
A.E. Petsche Company Inc.	2112 W Division St	Arlington	TX	76012	Glenn K Davidson	817-461-9473	R	72*	0.1
Benfield Electric Supply Inc.	25 Lafayette Ave	White Plains	NY	10603	Roy C Kohli	914-948-6660	R	71*	0.2
Walker and Associates Inc.	PO Box 1029	Welcome	NC	27374	Mark Walker	336-731-6391	R	71*	0.1
DBK Concepts Inc.	12905 SW 129th	Miami	FL	33186	Luis Barroso	305-596-7226	R	69*	0.1
Cain Electrical Supply Corp.	PO Box 2158	Big Spring	TX	79721	Tom R Ross	432-263-8421	P	67*	0.3
Georgia Lighting	530 14th St	Atlanta	GA	30318	Robert Nardelli	404-875-4754	S	66*	0.2
Wolff Brothers Supply Inc.	6078 Wolff Rd	Medina	OH	44256	Howard Wolff	330-725-3451	R	65*	0.3
Technical Building Services Inc.	12 Commerce Dr	Ballston Spa	NY	12020	Gerald Jannicelli	518-885-4444	R	65*	0.1
Granite City Electric Supply Co.	19 Quincy Ave	Quincy	MA	02169	Phyllis Godwin	617-472-6500	R	64*	0.2
J.H. Larson Co.	700 Colorado Ave S	Golden Valley	MN	55416	C E Pahl	763-545-1717	R	64*	0.2
Lappin Electric Co.	W165 Continentl N	Waukesha	WI	53188		920-261-6090	R	63*	0.2
American Encoder Repair Service	7115 W Lynwood	Michigan City	IN	46360	Karen Lagrou	219-872-2822	R	63*	0.1
Cmb Components Inc.	630 Broadway Ave	Holbrook	NY	11741		631-244-9800	R	63*	0.1
Litex Industries Inc.	PO Box 535639	Grand Prairie	TX	75053	Mike Miller	972-871-4350	R	63*	0.1
Stoneway Electric Supply Co.	402 N Perry	Spokane	WA	99202	Ed Ralph	509-535-2933	R	62*	0.2
Western States Equipment	PO Box 38	Boise	ID	83707	Tommy Harris	208-888-2287	R	62*	0.6
Zunicom Inc.	1720 Hayden Dr	Carrollton	TX	75006	William K W Tan	972-851-5600	P	61	<0.1
Wichita Falls Nunn Electrical	PO Box 2159	Wichita Falls	TX	76307	Coyal Francis Jr	940-766-4203	R	59*	<0.1
Gross Electric Inc.	PO Box 352377	Toledo	OH	43635	Laurie Gross	419-537-1818	R	58*	<0.1
Amidon Associates Inc.	240 Briggs Ave	Costa Mesa	CA	92626	Robert Yuan	714-850-4660	R	58*	<0.1
Hite Co.	PO Box 1754	Altoona	PA	16603	R Lee Hite	814-944-6121	R	56*	0.2
Ace Mart Restaurant Supply Co.	PO Box 18100	San Antonio	TX	78218	Bud Gustafson	210-323-4400	R	55*	0.3
Martco Inc.	PO Box 7429	Louisville	KY	40257	Spencer Martin	502-635-1600	R	55*	<0.1
Sola Communications Inc.	113 N Pat St	Scott	LA	70583	Gordon Rice	337-235-1515	R	53*	0.3
RGA	PO Box 190007	Little Rock	AR	72219	Jim McGee	501-565-9656	R	52*	0.1

Source: Ward's Business Directory of U.S. Private and Public Companies, Volumes 1 and 2, 2005. The company type code used is as follows: P - Public, R - Private, S - Subsidiary, D - Division, J - Joint Venture, A - Affiliate, G - Group. Sales are in millions of dollars, employees are in thousands. An asterisk (*) indicates an estimated sales volume. The symbol < stands for 'less than'. Company names and addresses are truncated, in some cases, to fit into the available space.

OCCUPATIONS EMPLOYED BY METAL & MINERAL (EXCEPT PETROLEUM) WHOLESALE

Occupation	% of Total 2004	Change to 2014	Occupation	% of Total 2004	Change to 2014
Sales reps, wholesale & manufacturing, exc tech	12.5	21.2	Order clerks	1.7	-20.7
Sales reps, wholesale & manufacturing, tech	6.4	21.2	Sales managers	1.6	29.6
Customer service representatives	4.1	24.1	First-line supervisors/managers of office workers	1.5	9.8
Shipping, receiving, & traffic clerks	4.0	9.7	Secretaries, except legal, medical, & executive	1.5	2.0
Stock clerks & order fillers	3.2	-7.2	Sales engineers	1.5	17.1
Laborers & freight, stock, & material movers, hand	3.1	9.0	Wholesale & retail buyers, except farm products	1.3	14.6
General & operations managers	2.9	19.9	Electronics engineers, except computer	1.2	22.0
Bookkeeping, accounting, & auditing clerks	2.7	9.0	Executive secretaries & administrative assistants	1.2	14.8
Office clerks, general	2.5	7.8	Accountants & auditors	1.1	21.2
First-line supervisors/managers of non-retail sales work	2.4	12.0	Packers & packagers, hand	1.1	21.2
Team assemblers	2.0	21.2	Electrical & electronics repairers	1.1	23.7
Telecommunications equip installers & repairers	2.0	21.2	Retail salespersons	1.1	21.2
Truck drivers, light or delivery services	1.9	21.2	Parts salespersons	1.0	-3.1
Electrical & electronic engineering technicians	1.7	17.1			

Source: Industry-Occupation Matrix, Bureau of Labor Statistics. These data are reported based on 4-digit NAICS categories but have been matched to corresponding 6-digit NAICS industry codes. The change reported for each occupation to the year 2014 is a percent of growth or decline as estimated by the Bureau of Labor Statistics. The abbreviation nec stands for 'not elsewhere classified.'

LOCATION BY STATE AND REGIONAL CONCENTRATION

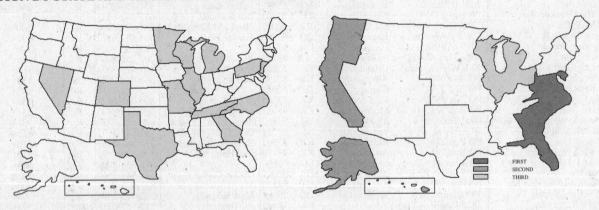

FIRST
SECOND
THIRD

INDUSTRY DATA BY STATE

State	Establishments Total (number)	% of U.S.	Employment Total (number)	% of U.S.	Per Estab.	Payroll Total ($ mil.)	Per Empl. ($)	Sales Total ($ mil.)	% of U.S.	Per Estab. ($)
California	1,750	13.2	20,814	12.7	12	969.5	46,580	9,640.1	11.7	5,508,609
Texas	1,057	8.0	15,054	9.2	14	712.6	47,336	7,457.8	9.1	7,055,640
Illinois	633	4.8	13,037	8.0	21	538.0	41,269	5,668.3	6.9	8,954,638
Pennsylvania	487	3.7	7,392	4.5	15	356.7	48,249	5,620.3	6.8	11,540,593
New York	811	6.1	9,652	5.9	12	447.2	46,328	4,034.6	4.9	4,974,899
Florida	936	7.0	8,532	5.2	9	370.7	43,448	3,785.4	4.6	4,044,192
Ohio	521	3.9	6,769	4.1	13	304.7	45,007	3,477.3	4.2	6,674,200
Michigan	373	2.8	4,788	2.9	13	249.2	52,048	3,321.8	4.0	8,905,729
North Carolina	397	3.0	4,687	2.9	12	222.0	47,360	3,269.3	4.0	8,234,899
Missouri	256	1.9	4,338	2.6	17	194.9	44,939	3,211.4	3.9	12,544,410
Georgia	476	3.6	5,218	3.2	11	252.7	48,436	2,733.7	3.3	5,742,985
New Jersey	454	3.4	5,401	3.3	12	285.2	52,796	2,612.5	3.2	5,754,317
Wisconsin	282	2.1	3,950	2.4	14	180.9	45,809	2,305.6	2.8	8,175,762
Tennessee	282	2.1	3,336	2.0	12	145.6	43,641	1,797.7	2.2	6,374,791
Minnesota	243	1.8	3,652	2.2	15	170.2	46,617	1,716.8	2.1	7,065,078
Indiana	275	2.1	3,106	1.9	11	124.2	39,977	1,630.6	2.0	5,929,564
Massachusetts	307	2.3	3,574	2.2	12	175.4	49,069	1,574.4	1.9	5,128,205
Washington	310	2.3	3,516	2.1	11	154.9	44,052	1,447.3	1.8	4,668,574
Virginia	280	2.1	2,872	1.8	10	133.5	46,485	1,221.4	1.5	4,362,111
Colorado	248	1.9	2,430	1.5	10	113.0	46,505	1,211.5	1.5	4,884,956
Maryland	193	1.5	2,249	1.4	12	107.7	47,888	986.8	1.2	5,113,145
Connecticut	145	1.1	2,256	1.4	16	136.5	60,502	953.8	1.2	6,577,883
Alabama	205	1.5	2,028	1.2	10	88.2	43,495	952.0	1.2	4,643,702
South Carolina	149	1.1	2,115	1.3	14	87.2	41,235	897.0	1.1	6,019,832
Louisiana	197	1.5	2,114	1.3	11	81.6	38,605	866.9	1.1	4,400,736
Oregon	186	1.4	1,843	1.1	10	71.9	39,015	794.3	1.0	4,270,355
Kentucky	133	1.0	1,710	1.0	13	64.0	37,401	779.8	0.9	5,862,902
Arkansas	99	0.7	1,640	1.0	17	43.6	26,613	692.5	0.8	6,994,990
Kansas	146	1.1	1,462	0.9	10	57.8	39,557	601.7	0.7	4,121,397

Continued on next page.

INDUSTRY DATA BY STATE - Continued

State	Establishments Total (number)	% of U.S.	Employment Total (number)	% of U.S.	Per Estab.	Payroll Total ($ mil.)	Per Empl. ($)	Sales Total ($ mil.)	% of U.S.	Per Estab. ($)
Iowa	123	0.9	1,454	0.9	12	58.0	39,863	600.3	0.7	4,880,341
Nevada	95	0.7	963	0.6	10	42.2	43,778	559.5	0.7	5,889,263
Oklahoma	163	1.2	1,383	0.8	8	52.2	37,748	546.2	0.7	3,351,221
Utah	111	0.8	1,012	0.6	9	42.4	41,943	430.9	0.5	3,882,099
Mississippi	75	0.6	712	0.4	9	23.9	33,604	287.7	0.3	3,835,680
New Mexico	66	0.5	493	0.3	7	18.8	38,136	272.5	0.3	4,129,424
Nebraska	67	0.5	536	0.3	8	21.4	39,948	257.8	0.3	3,847,299
Maine	47	0.4	481	0.3	10	19.6	40,713	209.7	0.3	4,460,702
Idaho	72	0.5	497	0.3	7	19.4	39,082	194.7	0.2	2,704,181
South Dakota	27	0.2	401	0.2	15	18.7	46,628	153.9	0.2	5,699,296
North Dakota	25	0.2	297	0.2	12	10.8	36,236	142.9	0.2	5,714,920
Hawaii	38	0.3	316	0.2	8	13.1	41,551	126.2	0.2	3,321,974
Montana	35	0.3	312	0.2	9	10.8	34,561	123.4	0.2	3,524,914
Vermont	25	0.2	249	0.2	10	10.9	43,771	103.8	0.1	4,151,800
Alaska	19	0.1	220	0.1	12	9.4	42,841	98.5	0.1	5,186,211
Wyoming	26	0.2	184	0.1	7	6.3	34,027	68.4	0.1	2,629,846
Arizona	230	1.7	2500-4999	-	-	(D)	-	(D)	-	-
New Hampshire	88	0.7	500-999	-	-	(D)	-	(D)	-	-
West Virginia	48	0.4	250-499	-	-	(D)	-	(D)	-	-
Delaware	32	0.2	250-499	-	-	(D)	-	(D)	-	-
Rhode Island	31	0.2	250-499	-	-	(D)	-	(D)	-	-
D.C.	10	0.1	100-249	-	-	(D)	-	(D)	-	-

Source: 2002 *Economic Census.* The states are in descending order of sales or establishments (if sales data are missing for the majority). The symbol (D) appears when data are withheld to prevent disclosure of competitive information. States marked with (D) are sorted by number of establishments. A dash (-) indicates that the data element cannot be calculated. Shaded *states* on the state map indicate those states which have proportionately greater representation in the industry than would be indicated by the states population; the ratio is based on total sales or number of establishments. Shaded *regions* indicate where the industry is regionally most concentrated.

NAICS 423620 - ELECTRICAL AND ELECTRONIC APPLIANCE, TELEVISION AND RADIO SET MERCHANT WHOLESALERS*

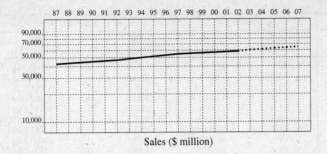

Sales ($ million)

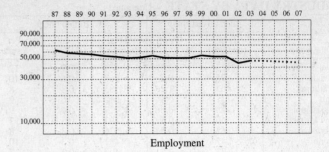

Employment

GENERAL STATISTICS

Year	Establishments (number)	Employment (number)	Payroll ($ million)	Sales ($ million)	Employees per Establishment (number)	Sales per Establishment ($)	Payroll per Employee ($)
1987	3,740	62,722	1,663.1	42,706.7	16.8	11,418,903.7	26,515.4
1988	3,515	58,362	1,702.3	43,541.5 e	16.6	12,387,340.0	29,168.0
1989	3,389	57,280	1,731.4	44,376.2 e	16.9	13,094,187.1	30,227.0
1990	3,385	56,325	1,744.8	45,210.9 e	16.6	13,356,248.2	30,977.4
1991	3,354	54,018	1,731.4	46,045.6 e	16.1	13,728,562.9	32,052.3
1992	3,785	52,910	1,849.4	46,880.3	14.0	12,385,812.4	34,953.7
1993	3,701	51,160	1,837.4	48,441.0 e	13.8	13,088,624.7	35,914.8
1994	3,666	51,754	1,954.9	50,001.7 e	14.1	13,639,307.1	37,772.9
1995	3,674	54,080	2,090.9	51,562.5 e	14.7	14,034,431.1	38,663.1
1996	3,598 e	51,267 e	2,101.6 e	53,123.2 e	14.2 e	14,764,647.0 e	40,993.2 e
1997	3,895	50,922	2,079.7	54,683.9	13.1	14,039,512.2	40,840.9
1998	3,783	51,016	2,193.0	55,422.0 e	13.5	14,650,272.3	42,986.5
1999	3,711	54,202	2,516.2	56,160.1 e	14.6	15,133,403.4	46,422.6
2000	3,595	52,676	2,509.1	56,898.1 e	14.7	15,827,020.9	47,632.7
2001	3,541	52,655	2,647.5	57,636.2 e	14.9	16,276,820.1	50,280.0
2002	3,067	44,668	2,171.4	58,374.3	14.6	19,033,029.0	48,612.0
2003	2,975	47,323	2,442.5	60,376.4 p	15.9	17,065,811.9 p	51,613.9
2004	3,429 p	47,161 p	2,578.3 p	61,515.8 p	13.9 p	17,405,480.1 p	53,165.0 p
2005	3,415 p	46,497 p	2,636.2 p	62,655.2 p	13.7 p	17,745,148.2 p	54,721.7 p
2006	3,402 p	45,833 p	2,694.2 p	63,794.6 p	13.6 p	18,084,816.4 p	56,278.4 p
2007	3,388 p	45,168 p	2,752.1 p	64,934.0 p	13.5 p	18,424,484.6 p	57,835.2 p

Sources: Economic Census of the United States, 1987, 1992, 1997, and 2002. Establishment counts, employment, and payroll are from *County Business Patterns* for non-Census years. Values followed by a 'p' are projections by the editors. Sales data for non-Census years are extrapolations, marked by 'e'. Data are the most recent available at this level of detail.

INDICES OF CHANGE

Year	Establishments (number)	Employment (number)	Payroll ($ million)	Sales ($ million)	Employees per Establishment (number)	Sales per Establishment ($)	Payroll per Employee ($)
1987	121.9	140.4	76.6	73.2	115.1	60.0	54.5
1992	123.4	118.5	85.2	80.3	95.9	65.1	71.9
1993	120.7	114.5	84.6	83.0 e	94.5	68.8	73.9
1994	119.5	115.9	90.0	85.7 e	96.6	71.7	77.7
1995	119.8	121.1	96.3	88.3 e	100.7	73.7	79.5
1996	117.3 e	114.8 e	96.8 e	91.0 e	97.3 e	77.6 e	84.3 e
1997	127.0	114.0	95.8	93.7	89.7	73.8	84.0
1998	123.3	114.2	101.0	94.9 e	92.5	77.0	88.4
1999	121.0	121.3	115.9	96.2 e	100.0	79.5	95.5
2000	117.2	117.9	115.6	97.5 e	100.7	83.2	98.0
2001	115.5	117.9	121.9	98.7 e	102.1	85.5	103.4
2002	100.0	100.0	100.0	100.0	100.0	100.0	100.0
2003	97.0	105.9	112.5	103.4 p	109.0	89.7 p	106.2
2004	111.8 p	105.6 p	118.7 p	105.4 p	95.0 p	91.4 p	109.4 p
2005	111.4 p	104.1 p	121.4 p	107.3 p	94.1 p	93.2 p	112.6 p
2006	110.9 p	102.6 p	124.1 p	109.3 p	93.3 p	95.0 p	115.8 p
2007	110.5 p	101.1 p	126.7 p	111.2 p	92.4 p	96.8 p	119.0 p

Sources: Same as General Statistics. The values shown reflect change from the base year, 2002. Values above 100 mean greater than 2002, values below 100 mean less than 2002, and a value of 100 in the 1987-2001 or 2003-2007 period means same as 2002. Values followed by a 'p' are projections by the editors; 'e' stands for extrapolation. Data are the most recent available at this level of detail.

SELECTED RATIOS

For 2002	Avg. of All Wholesale	Analyzed Industry	Index	For 2002	Avg. of All Wholesale	Analyzed Industry	Index
Employees per Establishment	15	15	97	Sales per Employee	791,325	1,306,848	165
Payroll per Establishment	626,122	707,988	113	Sales per Establishment	12,012,387	19,033,029	158
Payroll per Employee	41,161	48,612	118	Expenses per Establishment	na	na	na

Sources: Same as General Statistics. The 'Average of All' column, Wholesale or Retail, represents the average of the sector reported for the most recent complete year available. The Index shows the relationship between the Average and the Analyzed Industry. For example, 100 means that they are equal; 500 that the Analyzed Industry is five times the average; 50 means that the Analyzed Industry is half the national average. The abbreviation 'na' is used to show that data are 'not available'.

*Equivalent to SIC 5064.

LEADING COMPANIES   Number shown: **75**   Total sales ($ mil): **15,957**   Total employment (000): **27.8**

Company Name	Address				CEO Name	Phone	Co. Type	Sales ($ mil)	Empl. (000)
BJ's Wholesale Club Inc.	PO Box 9601	Natick	MA	01760		508-651-7400	P	7,220	18.5
Audiovox Corp.	150 Marcus Blvd	Hauppauge	NY	11788	John J Shalam	631-231-7750	P	1,324	1.0
Brother International Corp. (USA)	100 Somerset Corp.	Bridgewater	NJ	08807	Hideo Kageyama	908-704-1700	S	1,000*	1.1
Helen of Troy Ltd.	1 Helen of Troy Plz	El Paso	TX	79912		915-225-8000	P	475	0.7
D and H Distributing Co.	PO Box 5961	Harrisburg	PA	17110	Gary Brothers	717-236-8001	R	429*	0.4
Funai Corp.	100 North St	Teterboro	NJ	07608	Masao Suwa	201-288-2063	R	269*	<0.1
Hadco Inc.	325 Horizon Dr	Suwanee	GA	30024	John Drillot	770-932-7282	R	268*	0.1
Directed Electronics Inc.	1 Viper Way	Vista	CA	92081	Jim Minarik	760-598-6200	R	233*	0.2
ABC International Traders Inc.	16730 Schoenborn	North Hills	CA	91343	Isaac Larian	818-894-2525	R	225*	<0.1
Columbia Audio-Video Inc.	1741 2nd St	Highland Park	IL	60035	Gary Rozak	847-433-6010	R	212*	0.1
SunCoast Merchandise Corp.	6315 Bandini Blvd	Los Angeles	CA	90040	Kumar Bhavnani	323-720-9700	R	199*	0.2
City Animation Co.	57 Park Dr	Troy	MI	48083	Eric D Schultz	248-589-0600	R	168*	<0.1
Helen of Troy Texas Corp.	1 Helen of Troy Plz	El Paso	TX	79912	Gerald J Rubin	915-225-8000	S	167*	0.3
Climatic Corp.	PO Box 25189	Columbia	SC	29224	John H Bailey	803-765-2595	R	145*	0.2
Falcon Fine Wire & Wire Products	2401 Discovery	Rockwall	TX	75032	William D LeCount	972-772-8240	R	138*	<0.1
Full Compass Systems Ltd.	8001 Ter Ave	Middleton	WI	53562	Susan Lipp	608-831-7330	R	131*	0.1
Craftmade International Inc.	PO Box 1037	Coppell	TX	75019	James R Ridings	972-393-3800	P	121	0.1
Nunn Electric Supply Corp.	PO Box 791	Amarillo	TX	79189	Carl Hare, Jr	806-376-4581	R	119*	0.3
Samsung Electronics America Inc.	105 Challenger Rd	Ridgefield Park	NJ	07660	Bo-Soon Song	201-229-4000	R	117*	0.3
Apollo Distribution	8309 Sherwick Ct	Jessup	MD	20794	Henry Frederick	410-792-8066	R	114*	0.1
Factory Direct Appliance Inc.	14105 Marshall Dr	Schuylkl Hvn	KS	66215	Dennis Birkestrand	913-888-8028	R	114*	0.1
Electrolux International	3 Parkway Ctr	Pittsburgh	PA	15220	Hans Straberg	412-928-0252	S	107*	<0.1
Appliance Factory Outlet	6005 E Evans Ave	Denver	CO	80222	Chuck Ewings	303-755-8755	R	91*	<0.1
Madison Electric Co.	31855 Van Dyke	Warren	MI	48093	Joseph Schneider	586-825-0200	R	90*	0.2
I Lehrhoff and Company Inc.	351 Mill Rd	Edison	NJ	08837	Daniel Lehrhoff	732-248-3900	R	86*	<0.1
Purcell Murray Company Inc.	185 Park Ln	Brisbane	CA	94005	Timothy Murray	415-468-6620	R	76*	<0.1
Arizona Wholesale Supply Co.	PO Box 2979	Phoenix	AZ	85062	TW Thomas	602-258-7901	R	73*	0.2
Elna USA	1760 Gilsinn Ln	Fenton	MO	63026	Ken Tacony	636-349-3000	D	73*	0.2
Riccar America Co.	1800 E Walnut Ave	Fullerton	CA	92831	Craig Neal	714-525-4400	D	73*	0.2
Securcam Inc.	PO Box 55002	Phoenix	AZ	85078		602-493-2552	R	68*	<0.1
Auto Chlor System Inc.	746 Poplar Ave	Memphis	TN	38105	George Griesbeck	901-579-2300	R	68*	<0.1
Rowenta Inc.	196 Boston Ave	Medford	MA	02155	Paul Pofcher	781-396-0600	S	68*	<0.1
Visual Sound Inc.	485 Park Way	Broomall	PA	19008	John Bogosian	610-544-8700	R	66*	<0.1
Vtech Innovation L.P.	9590 SW Gemini Dr	Beaverton	OR	97008		503-643-8981	R	66*	<0.1
DeLonghi America Inc.	1 Park 80 Plaza W	Saddle Brook	NJ	07663	James McCusker	201-909-4000	R	63*	0.1
CVS Systems L.P.	PO Box 1990	Marion	IN	46952	Tom Collins	765-662-0037	R	63*	<0.1
Impact Merchandising Corp.	PO Box 5042	Livermore	CA	94551	James Hillman	925-373-7900	R	63*	<0.1
Appliance Depot and More	425 E Macewen Dr	Osprey	FL	34229		941-966-0725	R	57*	<0.1
Hite Co.	PO Box 1754	Altoona	PA	16603	R Lee Hite	814-944-6121	R	56*	0.2
Professional Housewares	29309 Clayton Ave	Wickliffe	OH	44092	Dennis Docherty	440-944-3500	R	56*	<0.1
Buckeye Vacuum Cleaner Supply	2780 P Atkinson SE	Smyrna	GA	30080	Kenard Strauss	404-351-7300	R	55*	<0.1
Mercury BE L.L.C.	3255 Saco St	Los Angeles	CA	90058	Nassir Ebrahimi	323-588-4700	R	55*	<0.1
R & B Wholesale Distributors Inc.	2350 S Milliken Ave	Ontario	CA	91761	Robert Burggraf	909-947-0091	R	53*	<0.1
Reliable Parts	PO Box 58544	Tukwila	WA	98138	Doug Loughran	206-575-6774	R	51*	<0.1
C and L Supply Co.	335 S Wilson	Vinita	OK	74301	Fred Kidd		R	50*	0.1
Cain and Bultman Inc.	PO Box 2815	Jacksonville	FL	32204	Thomas Sandifer	904-356-4812	R	50*	<0.1
TEAC America Inc	PO Box 750	Montebello	CA	90640		323-726-0303	D	50*	0.2
Capresso Inc.	PO Box 775	Closter	NJ	07624	Michael Kramm	201-767-3999	R	48*	<0.1
Westar Contract Kitchen & Bath	7255 S Kyrene Rd	Tempe	AZ	85283	Elyse Sioles	602-271-0100	R	48*	<0.1
Ince Distributing Inc.	2233 NW Loop 410	San Antonio	TX	78230	Raymond Ince	210-341-7161	R	48*	0.1
Persinger Supply Co.	PO Box 188	Prichard	WV	25555	Bernice Deskins	304-486-5401	R	46*	<0.1
Dyro Productions	3505 S D Ashford	Houston	TX	77082	Daniel Blalock	281-558-3426	R	46*	<0.1
Excalibur Electronics Inc.	13755 SW 119th	Miami	FL	33186	Shane Samole	305-477-8080	R	46*	<0.1
Jett Racing and Sales Inc.	1301 Lincoln St	Laredo	TX	78040	Wolf Hofman	956-722-3102	R	46*	<0.1
Crystal Promotions Inc.	1820 S Grand Ave	Los Angeles	CA	90015	Arsalan Dokhanian	213-744-0700	R	44*	<0.1
Corner Distributors Inc.	3940 Merritt Ave	Bronx	NY	10466	Francis Vegliante	718-798-1500	R	40*	<0.1
Spina Electric Co.	26801 Groesbeck	Warren	MI	48089	Paul Spina	586-771-8080	R	40*	<0.1
Watson and Associates	5710 High Point	Greensboro	NC	27407	Phil Watson	336-931-0222	R	40*	<0.1
Rieman & Arszman Custom	9652 Inter Ocean Dr	Cincinnati	OH	45246	Ken Rieman	513-874-5444	R	39*	<0.1
Amarillo Hardware Co.	PO Box 1891	Amarillo	TX	79172	Joe Wildman	806-376-4722	R	36*	0.1
Northern Video Systems Inc.	4465 Granite Dr	Rocklin	CA	95677	Mark Haney	916-630-4700	R	35*	<0.1
A and V of The Triad Inc.	4238 Piedmont	Greensboro	NC	27410	Tony Tajalli	336-292-9700	R	34*	<0.1
Eton Corp.	PO Box 2307	Menlo Park	CA	94026	E Hozour	650-903-3866	R	34*	<0.1
GP Systems Inc.	2350 S Bascom Ave	Campbell	CA	95008	Russell Maynard	408-371-9177	R	34*	<0.1
Setzers and Company Inc.	PO Box 24270	Jacksonville	FL	32241	Allen Setzer	904-731-4100	R	34*	<0.1
Star Lucky Industries Inc.	888 Vintage Ave	Ontario	CA	91764	Lee Tim	909-980-1028	R	34*	<0.1
Just In Time Distributors Inc.	6728 Edgewater	Orlando	FL	32810	Mary Gertner	407-302-1535	R	33*	<0.1
Middle Tennessee Natural Gas	P O Box 670	Smithville	TN	37166	Leslie B Enoch II	615-597-4300	R	33*	0.1
Westye Group-Southeast Inc.	9777 Satellite Blvd	Orlando	FL	32837	Jim Donlin	407-857-3777	R	31*	<0.1
Welcome Industrial Corporation	71 E Industry Ct	Deer Park	NY	11729	Tony Lin	631-242-5556	R	30*	0.1
Target Distributing Co.	19560 Amaranth Dr	Germantown	MD	20874	Richard Warsaw	301-296-9400	R	30*	<0.1
Laguna Corp.	96 Hobart St	Hackensack	NJ	07601	Joel Blank	201-489-3370	R	30*	<0.1
Siano Appliance Distributors Inc.	5372 Pleasantview	Memphis	TN	38134	Ralph Siano	901-382-5833	R	29*	<0.1
First Coast Supply Inc.	6860 Phillips Ind	Jacksonville	FL	32256	Timothy Deck	904-388-1217	R	28*	<0.1
JS International Inc.	11733 MO Bottom	Hazelwood	MO	63042		314-731-5677	R	28*	<0.1

Source: Ward's Business Directory of U.S. Private and Public Companies, Volumes 1 and 2, 2005. The company type code used is as follows: P - Public, R - Private, S - Subsidiary, D - Division, J - Joint Venture, A - Affiliate, G - Group. Sales are in millions of dollars, employees in thousands. An asterisk (*) indicates an estimated sales volume. The symbol < stands for 'less than'. Company names and addresses are truncated, in some cases, to fit into the available space.

OCCUPATIONS EMPLOYED BY METAL & MINERAL (EXCEPT PETROLEUM) WHOLESALE

Occupation	% of Total 2004	Change to 2014	Occupation	% of Total 2004	Change to 2014
Sales reps, wholesale & manufacturing, exc tech	12.5	21.2	Order clerks	1.7	-20.7
Sales reps, wholesale & manufacturing, tech	6.4	21.2	Sales managers	1.6	29.6
Customer service representatives	4.1	24.1	First-line supervisors/managers of office workers	1.5	9.8
Shipping, receiving, & traffic clerks	4.0	9.7	Secretaries, except legal, medical, & executive	1.5	2.0
Stock clerks & order fillers	3.2	-7.2	Sales engineers	1.5	17.1
Laborers & freight, stock, & material movers, hand	3.1	9.0	Wholesale & retail buyers, except farm products	1.3	14.6
General & operations managers	2.9	19.9	Electronics engineers, except computer	1.2	22.0
Bookkeeping, accounting, & auditing clerks	2.7	9.0	Executive secretaries & administrative assistants	1.2	14.8
Office clerks, general	2.5	7.8	Accountants & auditors	1.1	21.2
First-line supervisors/managers of non-retail sales work	2.4	12.0	Packers & packagers, hand	1.1	21.2
Team assemblers	2.0	21.2	Electrical & electronics repairers	1.1	23.7
Telecommunications equip installers & repairers	2.0	21.2	Retail salespersons	1.1	21.2
Truck drivers, light or delivery services	1.9	21.2	Parts salespersons	1.0	-3.1
Electrical & electronic engineering technicians	1.7	17.1			

Source: *Industry-Occupation Matrix*, Bureau of Labor Statistics. These data are reported based on 4-digit NAICS categories but have been matched to corresponding 6-digit NAICS industry codes. The change reported for each occupation to the year 2014 is a percent of growth or decline as estimated by the Bureau of Labor Statistics. The abbreviation nec stands for 'not elsewhere classified.'

LOCATION BY STATE AND REGIONAL CONCENTRATION

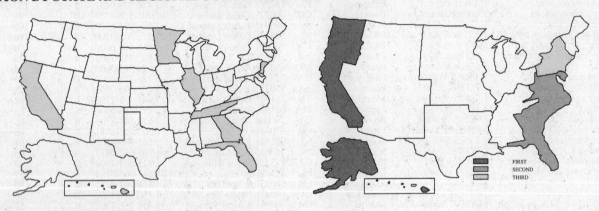

FIRST
SECOND
THIRD

INDUSTRY DATA BY STATE

State	Establishments Total (number)	% of U.S.	Employment Total (number)	% of U.S.	Per Estab.	Payroll Total ($ mil.)	Per Empl. ($)	Sales Total ($ mil.)	% of U.S.	Per Estab. ($)
California	600	19.6	8,968	19.7	15	451.2	50,315	12,250.1	20.5	20,416,913
New Jersey	144	4.7	5,797	12.7	40	385.6	66,510	12,138.6	20.3	84,295,687
Illinois	129	4.2	3,027	6.6	23	178.5	58,981	5,129.0	8.6	39,759,930
Georgia	87	2.8	1,851	4.1	21	94.1	50,820	5,024.8	8.4	57,756,724
Florida	355	11.6	3,169	6.9	9	138.5	43,707	3,529.5	5.9	9,942,299
Texas	204	6.7	2,453	5.4	12	93.9	38,285	2,426.2	4.1	11,892,907
New York	258	8.4	2,555	5.6	10	101.5	39,733	2,164.5	3.6	8,389,609
Tennessee	45	1.5	1,486	3.3	33	66.1	44,511	2,099.2	3.5	46,648,467
Pennsylvania	93	3.0	1,178	2.6	13	49.2	41,729	1,268.0	2.1	13,634,366
Minnesota	30	1.0	309	0.7	10	16.4	52,951	1,175.7	2.0	39,189,667
Ohio	99	3.2	2,047	4.5	21	65.1	31,787	1,067.0	1.8	10,777,848
Massachusetts	92	3.0	1,011	2.2	11	48.2	47,723	884.5	1.5	9,614,337
Virginia	40	1.3	703	1.5	18	45.7	65,006	736.2	1.2	18,405,950
Washington	68	2.2	906	2.0	13	39.4	43,529	580.0	1.0	8,529,971
Missouri	57	1.9	904	2.0	16	39.8	43,996	504.2	0.8	8,844,842
Oregon	33	1.1	564	1.2	17	24.1	42,686	473.3	0.8	14,341,939
Indiana	54	1.8	691	1.5	13	30.5	44,090	387.6	0.6	7,177,481
Wisconsin	40	1.3	491	1.1	12	21.0	42,762	356.3	0.6	8,906,900
Hawaii	22	0.7	239	0.5	11	9.1	38,075	308.8	0.5	14,037,909
Connecticut	21	0.7	445	1.0	21	22.8	51,178	253.8	0.4	12,085,524
North Carolina	56	1.8	406	0.9	7	16.2	40,012	200.6	0.3	3,582,607
Oklahoma	21	0.7	435	1.0	21	14.5	33,384	154.0	0.3	7,332,429
Louisiana	26	0.9	195	0.4	8	6.5	33,349	100.7	0.2	3,872,154
Alabama	33	1.1	234	0.5	7	7.7	33,056	85.8	0.1	2,600,515
Iowa	14	0.5	200	0.4	14	5.9	29,285	65.0	0.1	4,642,786
Nevada	14	0.5	65	0.1	5	2.9	43,908	38.5	0.1	2,750,714
South Carolina	18	0.6	128	0.3	7	4.9	37,953	37.4	0.1	2,076,722
Mississippi	12	0.4	59	0.1	5	1.7	28,068	23.1	-	1,927,833
New Mexico	8	0.3	59	0.1	7	1.5	25,220	16.2	-	2,019,000

Continued on next page.

INDUSTRY DATA BY STATE - Continued

State	Establishments		Employment			Payroll		Sales		
	Total (number)	% of U.S.	Total (number)	% of U.S.	Per Estab.	Total ($ mil.)	Per Empl. ($)	Total ($ mil.)	% of U.S.	Per Estab. ($)
West Virginia	7	0.2	18	-	3	0.4	22,278	1.5	-	208,857
Montana	4	0.1	7	-	2	0.1	10,857	1.2	-	294,000
Michigan	60	2.0	1000-2499	-	-	(D)	-	(D)	-	-
Arizona	54	1.8	1000-2499	-	-	(D)	-	(D)	-	-
Maryland	52	1.7	500-999	-	-	(D)	-	(D)	-	-
Colorado	45	1.5	250-499	-	-	(D)	-	(D)	-	-
Kansas	28	0.9	250-499	-	-	(D)	-	(D)	-	-
Kentucky	25	0.8	250-499	-	-	(D)	-	(D)	-	-
Utah	20	0.7	100-249	-	-	(D)	-	(D)	-	-
Rhode Island	14	0.5	100-249	-	-	(D)	-	(D)	-	-
Arkansas	13	0.4	20-99	-	-	(D)	-	(D)	-	-
Maine	11	0.4	20-99	-	-	(D)	-	(D)	-	-
New Hampshire	11	0.4	20-99	-	-	(D)	-	(D)	-	-
Nebraska	10	0.3	20-99	-	-	(D)	-	(D)	-	-
Idaho	8	0.3	100-249	-	-	(D)	-	(D)	-	-
Alaska	4	0.1	0-19	-	-	(D)	-	(D)	-	-
D.C.	4	0.1	20-99	-	-	(D)	-	(D)	-	-
North Dakota	4	0.1	20-99	-	-	(D)	-	(D)	-	-
Vermont	3	0.1	20-99	-	-	(D)	-	(D)	-	-
Delaware	2	0.1	20-99	-	-	(D)	-	(D)	-	-
South Dakota	2	0.1	0-19	-	-	(D)	-	(D)	-	-
Wyoming	1	-	0-19	-	-	(D)	-	(D)	-	-

Source: 2002 Economic Census. The states are in descending order of sales or establishments (if sales data are missing for the majority). The symbol (D) appears when data are withheld to prevent disclosure of competitive information. States marked with (D) are sorted by number of establishments. A dash (-) indicates that the data element cannot be calculated. Shaded *states* on the state map indicate those states which have proportionately greater representation in the industry than would be indicated by the states population; the ratio is based on total sales or number of establishments. Shaded *regions* indicate where the industry is regionally most concentrated.

NAICS 423690 - OTHER ELECTRONIC PARTS AND EQUIPMENT MERCHANT WHOLESALERS*

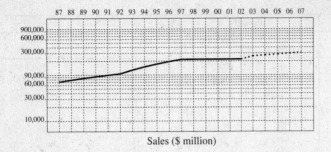

Sales ($ million)

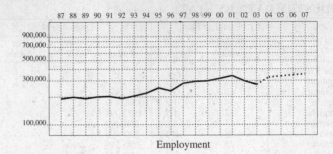

Employment

GENERAL STATISTICS

Year	Establishments (number)	Employment (number)	Payroll ($ million)	Sales ($ million)	Employees per Establishment (number)	Sales per Establishment ($)	Payroll per Employee ($)
1987	14,724	190,845	5,563.9	71,078.1	13.0	4,827,363.5	29,154.0
1988	13,995	199,167	6,494.1	78,095.3 e	14.2	5,580,228.7	32,606.3
1989	13,448	192,042	6,193.1	85,112.5 e	14.3	6,329,008.0	32,248.7
1990	14,320	200,580	6,808.7	92,129.7 e	14.0	6,433,638.3	33,945.1
1991	15,072	202,642	7,260.0	99,146.9 e	13.4	6,578,217.9	35,826.7
1992	17,007	192,552	7,126.5	106,164.0	11.3	6,242,370.8	37,010.8
1993	17,720	204,502	8,216.8	128,360.6 e	11.5	7,243,826.2	40,179.6
1994	18,453	219,455	9,292.9	150,557.2 e	11.9	8,158,955.2	42,345.4
1995	19,488	249,965	11,481.7	172,753.7 e	12.8	8,864,619.3	45,933.2
1996	19,664 e	231,936 e	10,640.3 e	194,950.3 e	11.8	9,914,071.4 e	45,876.0 e
1997	20,908	280,259	14,416.6	217,146.9	13.4	10,385,828.4	51,440.3
1998	21,081	293,828	16,540.2	217,691.9 e	13.9	10,326,448.5	56,292.1
1999	20,928	297,606	19,601.5	218,236.8 e	14.2	10,427,982.6	65,863.9
2000	20,787	316,173	23,149.1	218,781.8 e	15.2	10,524,932.9	73,216.6
2001	20,397	338,488	24,032.2	219,326.7 e	16.6	10,752,892.1	70,998.6
2002	16,923	297,387	19,662.1	219,871.7	17.6	12,992,477.7	66,116.2
2003	15,957	271,624	19,532.0	259,086.9 p	17.0	12,567,640.2 p	71,908.1
2004	20,955 p	326,079 p	23,383.3 p	271,263.3 p	15.9 p	13,049,253.3 p	75,560.3 p
2005	21,317 p	334,995 p	24,569.6 p	283,439.7 p	16.1 p	13,530,866.4 p	78,524.8 p
2006	21,678 p	343,912 p	25,755.9 p	295,616.0 p	16.3 p	14,012,479.5 p	81,489.3 p
2007	22,040 p	352,829 p	26,942.2 p	307,792.4 p	16.6 p	14,494,092.6 p	84,453.7 p

Sources: *Economic Census of the United States*, 1987, 1992, 1997, and 2002. Establishment counts, employment, and payroll are from *County Business Patterns* for non-Census years. Values followed by a 'p' are projections by the editors. Sales data for non-Census years are extrapolations, marked by 'e'. Data are the most recent available at this level of detail.

INDICES OF CHANGE

Year	Establishments (number)	Employment (number)	Payroll ($ million)	Sales ($ million)	Employees per Establishment (number)	Sales per Establishment ($)	Payroll per Employee ($)
1987	87.0	64.2	28.3	32.3	73.9	37.2	44.1
1992	100.5	64.7	36.2	48.3	64.2	48.0	56.0
1993	104.7	68.8	41.8	58.4 e	65.3	55.8	60.8
1994	109.0	73.8	47.3	68.5 e	67.6	62.8	64.0
1995	115.2	84.1	58.4	78.6 e	72.7	68.2	69.5
1996	116.2 e	78.0 e	54.1 e	88.7 e	67.0 e	76.3 e	69.4 e
1997	123.5	94.2	73.3	98.8	76.1	79.9	77.8
1998	124.6	98.8	84.1	99.0 e	79.0	79.5	85.1
1999	123.7	100.1	99.7	99.3 e	80.7	80.3	99.6
2000	122.8	106.3	117.7	99.5 e	86.4	81.0	110.7
2001	120.5	113.8	122.2	99.8 e	94.3	82.8	107.4
2002	100.0	100.0	100.0	100.0	100.0	100.0	100.0
2003	94.3	91.3	99.3	117.8 p	96.7	96.7 p	108.8
2004	123.8 p	109.6 p	118.9 p	123.4 p	90.3 p	100.4 p	114.3 p
2005	126.0 p	112.6 p	125.0 p	128.9 p	91.5 p	104.1 p	118.8 p
2006	128.1 p	115.6 p	131.0 p	134.4 p	92.8 p	107.9 p	123.3 p
2007	130.2 p	118.6 p	137.0 p	140.0 p	94.0 p	111.6 p	127.7 p

Sources: Same as General Statistics. The values shown reflect change from the base year, 2002. Values above 100 mean greater than 2002, values below 100 mean less than 2002, and a value of 100 in the 1987-2001 or 2003-2007 period means same as 2002. Values followed by a 'p' are projections by the editors; 'e' stands for extrapolation. Data are the most recent available at this level of detail.

SELECTED RATIOS

For 2002	Avg. of All Wholesale	Analyzed Industry	Index	For 2002	Avg. of All Wholesale	Analyzed Industry	Index
Employees per Establishment	15	18	118	Sales per Employee	791,325	739,345	93
Payroll per Establishment	626,122	1,161,857	186	Sales per Establishment	12,012,387	12,992,478	108
Payroll per Employee	41,161	66,116	161	Expenses per Establishment	na	na	na

Sources: Same as General Statistics. The 'Average of All' column, Wholesale or Retail, represents the average of the sector reported for the most recent complete year available. The Index shows the relationship between the Average and the Analyzed Industry. For example, 100 means that they are equal; 500 that the Analyzed Industry is five times the average; 50 means that the Analyzed Industry is half the national average. The abbreviation 'na' is used to show that data are 'not available'.

*Equivalent to SIC 5065.

LEADING COMPANIES Number shown: **75** Total sales ($ mil): **170,467** Total employment (000): **148.7**

Company Name	Address				CEO Name	Phone	Co. Type	Sales ($ mil)	Empl. (000)
Morgan Crucible Company PLC	3102 Old Savannah	Augusta	GA	30906		706-796-4200	R	34,492*	14.5
ADT Security Services Inc.	One Town Ctr Rd	Boca Raton	FL	33431	Mike Snyder	561-988-3600	S	31,617*	15.0
Arrow Electronics Inc.	50 Marcus Dr	Melville	NY	11747	Daniel W Duval	631-847-2000	P	10,646	11.2
Avnet Inc.	2211 S 47th St	Phoenix	AZ	85034		480-643-2000	P	10,245	9.9
NTE Electronics Inc.	44 Farrand St	Bloomfield	NJ	07003		973-748-5089	R	9,243*	<0.1
Gerber Radio Supply Co.	PO Box 5690	Norwood	MA	02062	Ben Speigel	781-769-6000	R	8,405*	<0.1
ALLTEL Corp.	1 Allied Dr	Little Rock	AR	72202	Scott T Ford	501-905-8000	P	8,246	20.0
EchoStar Communications Corp.	5701 S Santa Fe Dr	Littleton	CO	80120	Charles W Ergen	303-723-1000	P	7,150	26.0
NEC Business Communication	6535 N State 161	Irving	TX	75039			R	5,586*	<0.1
Toshiba America Electronic	9775 Toledo Way	Irvine	CA	92618	Masaaki Nomi	949-455-2000	R	5,110*	0.3
Graybar Electric Company Inc.	PO Box 7231	St. Louis	MO	63177	Robert A Reynolds Jr	314-512-9200	R	3,803	7.9
Bell Microproducts Inc.	1941 Ringwood Ave	San Jose	CA	95131	W Donald Bell	408-451-9400	P	2,828	1.3
Avnet Marketing Services Inc	8700 S Price Rd	Tempe	AZ	85284	Steve Tepedino	480-794-6900	S	2,400*	0.6
Rexel Inc.	PO Box 9085	Addison	TX	75001	Mark Daniel	972-387-3600	S	2,000	4.8
Brightpoint Inc.	501 Airtech Pky	Plainfield	IN	46168	J Mark Howell	317-707-2355	P	1,866	1.3
CellStar Corp.	1730 Briercroft Ct	Carrollton	TX	75006	Robert A Kaiser	972-466-5000	P	1,793	1.0
Agilysys Inc.	6065 Parkland Blvd	Cleveland	OH	44124		440-720-8500	P	1,403	1.4
Astrokam	9800 Rockside Rd	Cleveland	OH	44125		216-447-0404	R	1,400*	<0.1
Compass Technology of Burlington	Third Fl	Cambridge	MA	02140		617-497-1700	R	1,399*	<0.1
Wyle Electronics	15370 Barranca	Irvine	CA	92618	Thomas Beaver	714-753-9953	S	1,378*	1.8
Audiovox Corp.	150 Marcus Blvd	Hauppauge	NY	11788	John J Shalam	631-231-7750	P	1,324	1.0
Cameron and Barkley Co.	PO Box 118007	Charleston	SC	29423	James R Warren	843-745-2400	R	1,078*	2.6
SED International Inc.	4916 N Ryl Atl	Tucker	GA	30085	Gerald Diamond	770-491-8962	S	944*	0.4
Catalyst Telecom	6 Logue Ct	Greenville	SC	29615	John Black	864-627-1950	D	937*	0.4
GPrime Ltd.	1790 Broadway	New York	NY	10019	John Grou	212-765-3415	R	926*	<0.1
Panasonic Consumer Electronics	1 Panasonic Way	Secaucus	NJ	07094	Don Iwanani	201-348-7000	D	857*	2.0
APW Ltd.	N22 Ridgeview W	Waukesha	WI	53188	David J Gallitano	262-523-7600	P	854	5.6
Hawk Electronics	5718 Arpt Fwy	Fort Worth	TX	76117		817-831-6789	D	746*	0.3
Smith & Associates Intern. Inc.	5306 Hollister Rd	Houston	TX	77040	Robert G Ackerley	713-430-3000	R	711*	0.3
Intermetra Corp.	10100 NW 116	Medley	FL	33178		305-889-1194	R	618*	<0.1
Richardson Electronics Ltd.	PO Box 393	Lafox	IL	60147		630-208-2200	P	520	1.1
CellStar Ltd.	2080 McDaniel Dr	Carrollton	TX	75006	James L Johnson		S	518*	1.0
Siliconix Inc.	PO Box 54951	Santa Clara	CA	95056	King Owyang	408-988-8000	P	466	2.0
D and H Distributing Co.	PO Box 5961	Harrisburg	PA	17110	Gary Brothers	717-236-8001	R	429*	0.4
All American Semiconductor Inc.	16115 NW 52nd	Miami	FL	33014	Bruce M Goldberg	305-621-8282	P	409	0.5
Brix Group Inc.	541 Division St	Campbell	CA	95008		408-374-7900	R	377*	0.2
SED International Holdings Inc.	4916 N Ryl Atl	Tucker	GA	30085	Jean Diamond	770-491-8962	P	372	0.3
Tessco Technologies Inc.	11126 McCormick	Hunt Valley	MD	21031	Robert B Barnhill Jr	410-229-1000	P	353	0.5
Penn Telecom Inc.	2710 Rochester Rd	Cranberry	PA	16066	H Brown		S	350*	0.2
Picolight Inc.	4665 Nautilus Ct S	Boulder	CO	80301	Stan Swirhun	303-530-3189	R	346*	0.1
Nu Horizons Electronics Corp.	70 Maxess Rd	Melville	NY	11747	Arthur Nadata	631-396-5000	P	346	0.5
RMS Communications Group Inc.	4551 NW 44 Ave	Ocala	FL	34482			R	288*	0.1
Power and Telephone Supply Inc.	2673 Yale Ave	Memphis	TN	38112			R	280*	0.4
Integrated Circuit Systems Inc.	2435 Blvd/Generals	Norristown	PA	19403		610-630-5300	P	272	0.5
Funai Corp.	100 North St	Teterboro	NJ	07608	Masao Suwa	201-288-2063	R	269*	<0.1
Golden Companies Inc.	PO Box 2120	Greensboro	NC	27402		336-274-6700	R	267*	<0.1
Heilind Electronics Inc.	58 Jonspin Rd	Wilmington	MA	01887	Robert Clapp	978-657-4870	R	250*	0.1
Jaco Electronics Inc.	145 Oser Ave	Hauppauge	NY	11788	Joel H Girsky	631-273-5500	P	249	0.4
DDI Corp.	1220 Simon Cir	Anaheim	CA	92806	Jay B Hunt	714-688-7200	P	243	1.8
Braid Electric Company Inc.	PO Box 23710	Nashville	TN	37202	Ben Gambell	615-242-6511	R	236*	0.1
JVC Professional Products Co.	1700 Valley Rd	Wayne	NJ	07470	Mike Yoshida	973-317-5000	S	228*	<0.1
Thomas Nelson Inc.	PO Box 141000	Nashville	TN	37214	Michael S Hyatt	615-889-9000	P	223	0.6
DATAVOX Inc.	2000 W S Houston S	Houston	TX	77042	Ross Ferguson	713-881-5300	R	202*	<0.1
Steiner Electric Co.	1250 Touhy Ave	Elk Grove Vill.	IL	60007	Harold M Kerman	847-228-0400	R	200*	0.6
SunCoast Merchandise Corp.	6315 Bandini Blvd	Los Angeles	CA	90040	Kumar Bhavnani	323-720-9700	R	199*	0.2
Telecom Engineering Consultants	8880 NW 15th St	Miami	FL	33172		305-592-4328	R	193*	<0.1
Diodes Inc.	3050 E Hillcrest Dr	Westlake Village	CA	91362	CH Chen	805-446-4800	P	186	1.1
City Animation Co.	57 Park Dr	Troy	MI	48083	Eric D Schultz	248-589-0600	R	168*	<0.1
Reptron Electronics Inc.	13700 Reptron Blvd	Tampa	FL	33626	Mark Holliday	813-854-2000	P	150	1.0
Carlton-Bates Co.	10605 Stebbins Cir	Houston	TX	77043	Bill Carlton	713-461-5554	R	149*	0.5
AdvanTel Inc.	2237 Paragon Dr	San Jose	CA	95131		408-954-5100	R	144*	<0.1
Bell Industries Inc.	1960 E Grand Ave	El Segundo	CA	90245	Russell A Doll	310-563-2355	P	144	0.8
Progressive Concepts Inc.	5718 Arpt Fwy	Fort Worth	TX	76117			R	136*	0.3
Fujitsu Microelectronics America	1280 E Arques Ave	Sunnyvale	CA	94085	Kazuo Iida	408-737-5600	R	134*	0.2
IFM Efector Inc.	805 Springdale Rd	Exton	PA	19341	Joseph Kelly	610-524-2000	R	124*	0.2
Telquest International Corp.	26 Commerce Rd	Fairfield	NJ	07004	Alfred Adel	973-808-4588	R	123*	0.2
Ixia	26601 W Agoura Rd	Calabasas	CA	91302	Jean-Claude Asscher	818-871-1800	P	117	0.3
RedBack Networks Inc.	300 Holger Way	San Jose	CA	95134		408-750-5000	P	116	0.5
Spring Arbor Distribution Inc.	1 Ingram Blvd	La Vergne	TN	37086	Janet McDonald		R	107*	0.5
Force Electronics Inc.	1440 S Priest Dr	Tempe	AZ	85281		480-968-3900	R	100*	0.5
Somera Communications Inc.	301 S Northpoint Dr	Coppell	TX	75019	David W Heard	972-304-5660	P	100	0.2
Bearcom Wireless Worldwide Inc.	PO Box 559001	Dallas	TX	75355	Jerry Denham	214-340-8876	R	99*	0.2
Audio Technica U S Inc.	1221 Commerce Dr	Stow	OH	44224	Phil Cajka	330-686-2600	R	94*	0.1
National Communication Services	PO Box 5525	Bellevue	WA	98006	Ben Hayes	425-378-8080	R	94*	0.1
I-Sector Corp.	6401 Southwest Fwy	Houston	TX	77074	Mark T Hilz	713-795-2000	P	93	0.2

Source: Ward's Business Directory of U.S. Private and Public Companies, Volumes 1 and 2, 2005. The company type code used is as follows: P - Public, R - Private, S - Subsidiary, D - Division, J - Joint Venture, A - Affiliate, G - Group. Sales are in millions of dollars, employees are in thousands. An asterisk (*) indicates an estimated sales volume. The symbol < stands for 'less than'. Company names and addresses are truncated, in some cases, to fit into the available space.

OCCUPATIONS EMPLOYED BY METAL & MINERAL (EXCEPT PETROLEUM) WHOLESALE

Occupation	% of Total 2004	Change to 2014	Occupation	% of Total 2004	Change to 2014
Sales reps, wholesale & manufacturing, exc tech	12.5	21.2	Order clerks	1.7	-20.7
Sales reps, wholesale & manufacturing, tech	6.4	21.2	Sales managers	1.6	29.6
Customer service representatives	4.1	24.1	First-line supervisors/managers of office workers	1.5	9.8
Shipping, receiving, & traffic clerks	4.0	9.7	Secretaries, except legal, medical, & executive	1.5	2.0
Stock clerks & order fillers	3.2	-7.2	Sales engineers	1.5	17.1
Laborers & freight, stock, & material movers, hand	3.1	9.0	Wholesale & retail buyers, except farm products	1.3	14.6
General & operations managers	2.9	19.9	Electronics engineers, except computer	1.2	22.0
Bookkeeping, accounting, & auditing clerks	2.7	9.0	Executive secretaries & administrative assistants	1.2	14.8
Office clerks, general	2.5	7.8	Accountants & auditors	1.1	21.2
First-line supervisors/managers of non-retail sales work	2.4	12.0	Packers & packagers, hand	1.1	21.2
Team assemblers	2.0	21.2	Electrical & electronics repairers	1.1	23.7
Telecommunications equip installers & repairers	2.0	21.2	Retail salespersons	1.1	21.2
Truck drivers, light or delivery services	1.9	21.2	Parts salespersons	1.0	-3.1
Electrical & electronic engineering technicians	1.7	17.1			

Source: Industry-Occupation Matrix, Bureau of Labor Statistics. These data are reported based on 4-digit NAICS categories but have been matched to corresponding 6-digit NAICS industry codes. The change reported for each occupation to the year 2014 is a percent of growth or decline as estimated by the Bureau of Labor Statistics. The abbreviation nec stands for 'not elsewhere classified.'

LOCATION BY STATE AND REGIONAL CONCENTRATION

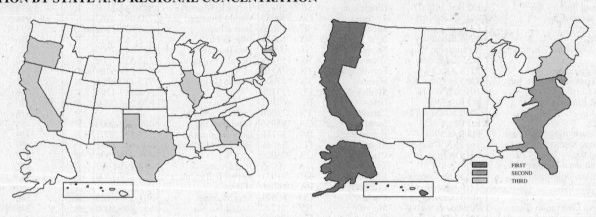

INDUSTRY DATA BY STATE

State	Establishments Total (number)	% of U.S.	Employment Total (number)	% of U.S.	Per Estab.	Payroll Total ($ mil.)	Per Empl. ($)	Sales Total ($ mil.)	% of U.S.	Per Estab. ($)
California	3,555	21.0	79,255	26.4	22	6,272.6	79,145	51,634.4	28.6	14,524,432
Texas	1,290	7.6	27,887	9.3	22	1,839.2	65,953	19,447.0	10.8	15,075,195
Illinois	690	4.1	16,655	5.6	24	1,101.7	66,147	15,672.5	8.7	22,713,748
New Jersey	748	4.4	13,113	4.4	18	911.7	69,527	10,123.3	5.6	13,533,861
New York	1,196	7.0	17,315	5.8	14	1,089.1	62,902	7,927.5	4.4	6,628,356
Florida	1,471	8.7	15,033	5.0	10	844.9	56,206	7,243.3	4.0	4,924,032
Massachusetts	538	3.2	12,846	4.3	24	910.2	70,856	6,611.7	3.7	12,289,474
Georgia	495	2.9	11,143	3.7	23	719.6	64,577	4,914.5	2.7	9,928,283
North Carolina	391	2.3	8,855	3.0	23	538.6	60,828	4,691.6	2.6	11,999,069
Pennsylvania	478	2.8	8,028	2.7	17	482.2	60,066	4,131.7	2.3	8,643,749
Virginia	312	1.8	5,323	1.8	17	359.9	67,613	3,768.1	2.1	12,077,330
Washington	324	1.9	5,138	1.7	16	341.9	66,535	3,439.6	1.9	10,616,179
Oregon	291	1.7	4,986	1.7	17	339.8	68,152	3,095.9	1.7	10,638,742
Minnesota	331	2.0	5,662	1.9	17	318.5	56,244	2,287.6	1.3	6,911,230
Ohio	453	2.7	5,685	1.9	13	258.3	45,438	2,213.2	1.2	4,885,702
Tennessee	225	1.3	4,879	1.6	22	244.6	50,143	1,808.6	1.0	8,038,222
Indiana	233	1.4	3,260	1.1	14	153.1	46,948	1,775.2	1.0	7,619,034
Connecticut	208	1.2	3,238	1.1	16	196.2	60,588	1,629.0	0.9	7,831,779
Missouri	212	1.2	3,122	1.0	15	158.9	50,884	1,169.0	0.6	5,514,165
Alabama	213	1.3	1,806	0.6	8	90.4	50,051	1,017.0	0.6	4,774,714
Wisconsin	204	1.2	2,485	0.8	12	127.8	51,427	982.1	0.5	4,814,348
South Carolina	106	0.6	1,500	0.5	14	74.0	49,353	478.8	0.3	4,516,689
Oklahoma	105	0.6	1,655	0.6	16	96.1	58,091	413.8	0.2	3,940,648
Louisiana	169	1.0	1,751	0.6	10	84.9	48,486	399.1	0.2	2,361,781
Nevada	108	0.6	894	0.3	8	40.0	44,758	290.7	0.2	2,691,667
New Mexico	70	0.4	486	0.2	7	25.8	53,160	254.3	0.1	3,633,100
Iowa	99	0.6	967	0.3	10	52.4	54,176	236.4	0.1	2,387,455
Hawaii	43	0.3	323	0.1	8	15.0	46,542	110.2	0.1	2,562,279
Mississippi	62	0.4	467	0.2	8	20.5	43,829	103.8	0.1	1,673,435

Continued on next page.

INDUSTRY DATA BY STATE - Continued

State	Establishments		Employment			Payroll		Sales		
	Total (number)	% of U.S.	Total (number)	% of U.S.	Per Estab.	Total ($ mil.)	Per Empl. ($)	Total ($ mil.)	% of U.S.	Per Estab. ($)
Montana	36	0.2	221	0.1	6	18.9	85,294	47.7	-	1,325,361
Colorado	381	2.2	5K-9999	-	-	(D)	-	(D)	-	-
Arizona	380	2.2	5K-9999	-	-	(D)	-	(D)	-	-
Michigan	378	2.2	5K-9999	-	-	(D)	-	(D)	-	-
Maryland	255	1.5	2500-4999	-	-	(D)	-	(D)	-	-
New Hampshire	137	0.8	1000-2499	-	-	(D)	-	(D)	-	-
Kansas	128	0.8	1000-2499	-	-	(D)	-	(D)	-	-
Kentucky	110	0.6	1000-2499	-	-	(D)	-	(D)	-	-
Utah	107	0.6	1000-2499	-	-	(D)	-	(D)	-	-
Arkansas	72	0.4	500-999	-	-	(D)	-	(D)	-	-
Idaho	63	0.4	500-999	-	-	(D)	-	(D)	-	-
Nebraska	56	0.3	500-999	-	-	(D)	-	(D)	-	-
Rhode Island	39	0.2	250-499	-	-	(D)	-	(D)	-	-
Maine	32	0.2	250-499	-	-	(D)	-	(D)	-	-
West Virginia	31	0.2	100-249	-	-	(D)	-	(D)	-	-
Delaware	27	0.2	100-249	-	-	(D)	-	(D)	-	-
Alaska	24	0.1	100-249	-	-	(D)	-	(D)	-	-
Vermont	23	0.1	100-249	-	-	(D)	-	(D)	-	-
South Dakota	20	0.1	100-249	-	-	(D)	-	(D)	-	-
North Dakota	18	0.1	100-249	-	-	(D)	-	(D)	-	-
D.C.	17	0.1	250-499	-	-	(D)	-	(D)	-	-
Wyoming	13	0.1	20-99	-	-	(D)	-	(D)	-	-

Source: 2002 *Economic Census*. The states are in descending order of sales or establishments (if sales data are missing for the majority). The symbol (D) appears when data are withheld to prevent disclosure of competitive information. States marked with (D) are sorted by number of establishments. A dash (-) indicates that the data element cannot be calculated. Shaded *states* on the state map indicate those states which have proportionately greater representation in the industry than would be indicated by the states population; the ratio is based on total sales or number of establishments. Shaded *regions* indicate where the industry is regionally most concentrated.

NAICS 423710 - HARDWARE MERCHANT WHOLESALERS

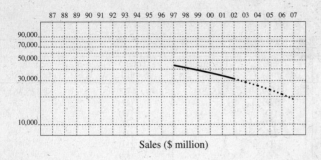

Sales ($ million)

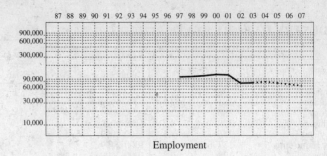

Employment

GENERAL STATISTICS

Year	Establishments (number)	Employment (number)	Payroll ($ million)	Sales ($ million)	Employees per Establishment (number)	Sales per Establishment ($)	Payroll per Employee ($)
1987	-	-	-	-	-	-	-
1988	-	-	-	-	-	-	-
1989	-	-	-	-	-	-	-
1990	-	-	-	-	-	-	-
1991	-	-	-	-	-	-	-
1992	-	-	-	-	-	-	-
1993	-	-	-	-	-	-	-
1994	-	-	-	-	-	-	-
1995	-	-	-	-	-	-	-
1996	-	-	-	-	-	-	-
1997	9,473	110,963	3,865.0	44,063.7	11.7	4,651,504.3	34,831.4
1998	9,524	112,852	4,194.3	41,524.2 e	11.8	4,359,951.7	37,166.4
1999	9,436	117,224	4,536.2	38,984.7 e	12.4	4,131,481.6	38,696.9
2000	9,457	124,860	5,014.7	36,445.1 e	13.2	3,853,773.9	40,162.6
2001	9,387	122,386	5,073.2	33,905.6 e	13.0	3,611,976.1	41,452.6
2002	6,833	80,872	3,168.8	31,366.1	11.8	4,590,384.9	39,182.9
2003	6,684	82,111	3,394.4	28,826.6 p	12.3	3,917,122.3 p	41,338.9
2004	6,714 p	86,559 p	3,760.1 p	26,287.1 p	12.6 p	3,836,344.2 p	42,734.7 p
2005	6,221 p	81,368 p	3,655.6 p	23,747.5 p	12.7 p	3,755,566.2 p	43,674.4 p
2006	5,728 p	76,177 p	3,551.1 p	21,208.0 p	12.8 p	3,674,788.2 p	44,614.1 p
2007	5,235 p	70,986 p	3,446.6 p	18,668.5 p	12.9 p	3,594,010.1 p	45,553.8 p

Source: Economic Census of the United States, 1997 and 2002. Establishment counts, employment, and payroll are from County Business Patterns for non-Census years. This is a newly defined industry. Data for prior years are unavailable at the time of publication but may become available over time. Values followed by 'p' are projections by the editors. Sales data for non-Census years are extrapolations, marked by 'e'.

INDICES OF CHANGE

Year	Establishments (number)	Employment (number)	Payroll ($ million)	Sales ($ million)	Employees per Establishment (number)	Sales per Establishment ($)	Payroll per Employee ($)
1987	-	-	-	-	-	-	-
1992	-	-	-	-	-	-	-
1993	-	-	-	-	-	-	-
1994	-	-	-	-	-	-	-
1995	-	-	-	-	-	-	-
1996	-	-	-	-	-	-	-
1997	138.6	137.2	122.0	140.5	99.2	101.3	88.9
1998	139.4	139.5	132.4	132.4 e	100.0	95.0	94.9
1999	138.1	145.0	143.2	124.3 e	105.1	90.0	98.8
2000	138.4	154.4	158.3	116.2 e	111.9	84.0	102.5
2001	137.4	151.3	160.1	108.1 e	110.2	78.7	105.8
2002	100.0	100.0	100.0	100.0	100.0	100.0	100.0
2003	97.8	101.5	107.1	91.9 p	104.1	85.3 p	105.5
2004	98.3 p	107.0 p	118.7 p	83.8 p	107.2 p	83.6 p	109.1 p
2005	91.0 p	100.6 p	115.4 p	75.7 p	107.9 p	81.8 p	111.5 p
2006	83.8 p	94.2 p	112.1 p	67.6 p	108.6 p	80.1 p	113.9 p
2007	76.6 p	87.8 p	108.8 p	59.5 p	109.3 p	78.3 p	116.3 p

Sources: Same as General Statistics. The values shown reflect change from the base year, 2002. Values above 100 mean greater than 2002, values below 100 mean less than 2002, and a value of 100 in the 1987-2001 or 2003-2007 period means same as 2002. Values followed by a 'p' are projections by the editors; 'e' stands for extrapolation. Data are the most recent available at this level of detail.

SELECTED RATIOS

For 2002	Avg. of All Wholesale	Analyzed Industry	Index	For 2002	Avg. of All Wholesale	Analyzed Industry	Index
Employees per Establishment	15	12	79	Sales per Employee	791,325	387,849	49
Payroll per Establishment	626,122	463,749	74	Sales per Establishment	12,012,387	4,590,385	38
Payroll per Employee	41,161	39,183	95	Expenses per Establishment	na	na	na

Sources: Same as General Statistics. The 'Average of All' column, Wholesale or Retail, represents the average of the sector reported for the most recent complete year available. The Index shows the relationship between the Average and the Analyzed Industry. For example, 100 means that they are equal; 500 that the Analyzed Industry is five times the average; 50 means that the Analyzed Industry is half the national average. The abbreviation 'na' is used to show that data are 'not available'.

LEADING COMPANIES   Number shown: **75**   Total sales ($ mil): **93,801**   Total employment (000): **435.7**

Company Name	Address				CEO Name	Phone	Co. Type	Sales ($ mil)	Empl. (000)
Lowe's Companies Inc.	PO Box 1111	N. Wilkesboro	NC	28656		336-658-4000	P	36,464	123.0
Sears, Roebuck and Co.	3333 Beverly Rd	Hoffman Estates	IL	60179		847-286-2500	D	36,099	250.0
Menard Inc.	4777 Menard Dr	Eau Claire	WI	54703	John R Menard, Jr	715-876-5911	R	6,065*	27.0
Ace Hardware Corp.	2200 Kensington Ct	Oak Brook	IL	60523	David F Hodnik	630-990-6600	R	3,029	5.3
True Value Co.	8600 W Bryn Mawr	Chicago	IL	60631	Bryan R Ableidinger	773-695-5000	R	2,024	2.8
Builders FirstSource Inc.	2001 Bryan St	Dallas	TX	75201	Alan Davenport	214-880-3500	S	1,675	6.2
American Builders & Contractors	PO Box 838	Beloit	WI	53511	Kenneth A Hendricks	608-362-7777	R	1,520*	3.5
Makita U.S.A. Inc.	14930 Northam St	La Mirada	CA	90638	Gary Morikawa	714-522-8088	R	1,048*	0.7
Rock Island Corp.	PO Box 3177	Memphis	TN	38173	Micheal McDonnell	901-529-5700	R	420*	1.5
Lawson Products Inc.	1666 E Touhy Ave	Des Plaines	IL	60018	Jeffrey B Belford	847-827-9666	P	420	0.0
Makino Inc.	7680 Innovation	Mason	OH	45040	Donald Lane	513-573-7200	R	415*	0.2
White Cap Industries Inc.	PO Box 1770	Costa Mesa	CA	92626	Ted Nark	714-850-0900	R	410*	1.4
Maintenance Warehouse/America	PO Box 509055	San Diego	CA	92150	Lew Klessell	858-831-2000	S	283*	1.1
Kar Products	461 N 3rd Ave	Des Plaines	IL	60016	Max Beshears	847-296-6111	S	208*	1.6
Q.E.P. Company Inc.	1081 Holland Dr	Boca Raton	FL	33487	Lewis Gould	561-994-5550	P	170	0.5
Universal Cooperative Inc.	1300 Corp Ctr	Eagan	MN	55121	Terry Bohman	651-239-1000	R	167*	0.3
Moore-Handley Inc.	PO Box 2607	Birmingham	AL	35202	Michael J Gaines	205-663-8011	P	163	0.4
United Hardware Distributing Co.	5005 Nathan Ln N	Plymouth	MN	55442	David A Heider	763-559-1800	R	144*	0.4
Ram Tool and Supply Co.	PO Box 320979	Birmingham	AL	35232	Mariam Head	205-591-2643	R	120*	<0.1
Harvey Gerstman & Associates	2 Irwin Ct	Lynbrook	NY	11563	Dan Gerstman	516-594-4400	R	116*	0.3
Orgil-Frederick Trading Co.	7901 Trading Ln	Frederick	MD	21701	Bill Fondren	301-662-2161	R	107*	0.4
Pleasants Hardware Co.	1010 W Northwest	Winston Salem	NC	27101	Bob Clobes	336-725-3067	R	106*	0.5
Atomicbox Inc.	125 Lena Dr	Aurora	OH	44202	Thomas Bianco	330-995-6110	R	103*	0.1
White Outdoor Products Co.	5903 Grafton Rd	Valley City	OH	44280		330-273-7786	D	94*	0.4
Emery Waterhouse Co.	PO Box 659	Portland	ME	04104	Charles Hildrein Jr	207-775-2371	R	90*	0.3
Blish-Mize Co.	PO Box 249	Atchison	KS	66002	JH Mize Jr	913-367-1250	R	89*	0.3
Ammar's Inc.	710 S College Ave	Bluefield	VA	24605	Keleel A Ammar Jr	276-322-4686	R	85*	0.9
Airgas Rutland Tool & Supply Inc.	PO Box 997	Whittier	CA	90608	Glen Irving	562-566-5000	S	84*	0.4
McLendon Hardware Inc.	440 Rainer Ave S	Renton	WA	98055	Gail McLendon	425-235-3555	R	84*	0.5
Ace Tool Co.	7337 Bryan Dairy	Largo	FL	33777		727-544-6114	S	78*	0.3
Bisco Industries Inc.	1500 N Lakeview	Anaheim	CA	92807	Glen Seiley	714-693-2901	R	74*	0.2
Storis Inc.	300 Littleton Rd	Parsippany	NJ	07054	Donald Surdoval	973-541-9700	R	74*	0.1
Star Sales Company Inc.	PO Box 1503	Knoxville	TN	37901	Neil Foster	865-524-0771	R	69*	0.1
E.B. Bradley Co.	5080 S Alameda St	Los Angeles	CA	90058	Robert E Bradley Jr		R	67*	0.2
U.S. Lock Corp.	77 Rodeo Dr	Brentwood	NY	11717			S	67*	<0.1
Cosmo Store Services L.L.C.	741 N Main St	Orange	CA	92868		714-538-6170	R	65*	0.2
Medal Distributing Co.	330 Vine Ave	Sharon	PA	16146	Dominic Preggi	724-342-6839	D	65*	<0.1
Howard Berger Company Inc.	808 Georgia Ave	Brooklyn	NY	11207	Howard Berger		R	63*	0.2
Ace Mart Restaurant Supply Co.	PO Box 18100	San Antonio	TX	78218	Bud Gustafson	210-323-4400	R	55*	0.3
Jamieson Manufacturing Co.	PO Box 763760	Dallas	TX	75376		214-339-8384	R	52*	<0.1
Rockford International Inc.	612 Harrison Ave	Rockford	IL	61104	Richard Goff	815-397-6000	R	51*	0.1
Brighton-Best Socket Screw Mfg	3105 Medlock	Norcross	GA	30071		770-368-2300	R	50*	0.2
General Tool and Supply Co.	2705 NW Nicolai St	Portland	OR	97210		503-226-3411	R	50*	0.1
Industrial US L.L.C.	PO Box 491085	Minneapolis	MN	55449	Fredrik Molzer	763-792-3125	R	46*	0.1
Fastec Industrial	23348 County Rd 6	Elkhart	IN	46514	J Braddock	574-262-2505	R	45*	0.1
Colonial Commercial Corp.	120 New South Rd	Hicksville	NY	11801	Bernard Korn	516-681-4647	P	45	0.1
House-Hasson Hardware Inc.	3125 Water Plant Rd	Knoxville	TN	37914	Don Hasson	865-525-0471	R	44*	0.2
Eldredge Lumber & Hardware Inc.	PO Box 69	Cape Neddick	ME	03902	Scott Eldredge	207-363-2004	R	42*	0.1
Ziegler Bolt and Parts Co.	PO Box 80369	Canton	OH	44708	William Ziegler	330-478-2542	R	42*	0.1
Bell Fasteners	PO Box 879	Pawtucket	RI	02862		401-725-3880	R	41*	<0.1
Denco Division Belcam	27 Montgomery St	Rouses Point	NY	12979	M Beltram	518-297-3366	R	40*	0.2
Pine Tree Lumber L.P.	707 N Andreasen Dr	Escondido	CA	92029	Michael Wexler	760-745-0411	R	40*	0.1
Thruway Fasteners Inc.	PO Box 776	Syracuse	NY	13205	Peter Jenkins	716-694-1434	R	40*	0.1
M-D Building Material Inc.	953 Seton Ct	Wheeling	IL	60090	Ralph Menn	847-541-0002	R	39*	<0.1
Ellsworth Builders Supply Inc.	261 State St	Ellsworth	ME	04605	Austin Goodyear	207-667-4974	R	37*	0.2
Amarillo Hardware Co.	PO Box 1891	Amarillo	TX	79172	Joe Wildman	806-376-4722	R	36*	0.1
Roadside Lumber & Hardware Inc.	PO Box 339	Agoura Hills	CA	91301	Michael Tuchman	818-991-1880	R	36*	<0.1
H. and E. Brothers Inc.	14021 Amargosa Rd	Victorville	CA	92392	Phillip S Stein	760-241-7540	R	34*	0.3
Contractors Specialties Inc.	408 N Mullan Rd	Spokane	WA	99206	Harry Beckous	509-924-3427	R	34*	<0.1
TriMark Corp.	PO Box 350	New Hampton	IA	50659		641-394-3188	R	33*	0.3
ARC Fasteners Supply Inc.	8715 Boston Pl	R. Cucamonga	CA	91730	Joseph Myers	909-481-8171	R	33*	<0.1
Wright and Wilhelmy Inc.	11005 E St	Omaha	NE	68137	Darcy Michalek	402-593-0600	R	33*	<0.1
Metric & Multistandard	120 Old Saw Mill	Hawthorne	NY	10532	Joseph Voves	914-769-5020	R	32*	<0.1
Buhrman-Pharr Gifts	212 Laurel St 22	Texarkana	AR	71854	Stanley Jones	870-773-3122	R	32*	<0.1
GE Supply Logistics	9500 N Royal Ln	Irving	TX	75063	Jason Jones	817-490-5700	R	31*	0.1
Kentec Inc.	3250 Centerville SW	Lithonia	GA	30038	George W Morgan	770-985-1907	R	30*	0.1
Arena Distributors Inc.	PO Box 1410	Buffalo	NY	14240	Michael Ervolina	716-825-7377	R	29*	<0.1
Colony Hardware Supply Inc.	15 Stiles St	New Haven	CT	06512	Michael Weiner	203-466-5252	R	29*	<0.1
Harrington and Co.	PO Box 25723	Salt Lake City	UT	84125	Stephen Booth	801-972-3131	R	29*	<0.1
Total Door Supply Inc.	4435 S 134th Pl	Seattle	WA	98168	Lael Peterson	206-241-8242	R	29*	<0.1
American Fasteners Inc.	9129 E US Hwy 36	Avon	IN	46123	Jim Delp	317-271-6100	R	28*	<0.1
DoAll Industrial Supply	254 N Laurel Ave	Des Plaines	IL	60016	Michael Wilkie	847-824-1122	R	28*	0.1
Tulnoy Lumber Inc.	1620 Webster Ave	Bronx	NY	10457	H Tulchin	718-901-1700	R	28*	<0.1
RP Johnson and Son Inc.	10 Mill Rd	Andover	NH	03216	Stephen Johnson	603-735-5544	R	28*	<0.1
Totten Tubes Inc.	500 Danlee	Azusa	CA	91702	David Totten	626-812-0220	R	26*	<0.1

Source: Ward's Business Directory of U.S. Private and Public Companies, Volumes 1 and 2, 2005. The company type code used is as follows: P - Public, R - Private, S - Subsidiary, D - Division, J - Joint Venture, A - Affiliate, G - Group. Sales are in millions of dollars, employees are in thousands. An asterisk (*) indicates an estimated sales volume. The symbol < stands for 'less than'. Company names and addresses are truncated, in some cases, to fit into the available space.

OCCUPATIONS EMPLOYED BY HARDWARE, & PLUMBING & HEATING EQUIPMENT & SUPPLIES

Occupation	% of Total 2004	Change to 2014	Occupation	% of Total 2004	Change to 2014
Sales reps, wholesale & manufacturing, exc tech	18.0	16.8	Parts salespersons	2.1	-6.6
Laborers & freight, stock, & material movers, hand	7.0	5.1	Order clerks	1.9	-24.1
Stock clerks & order fillers	5.1	-10.6	Retail salespersons	1.7	16.7
Truck drivers, light or delivery services	4.5	16.8	Truck drivers, heavy & tractor-trailer	1.6	16.7
Shipping, receiving, & traffic clerks	4.4	5.7	First-line supervisors/managers of office workers	1.5	5.8
Heating, air conditioning, & refrigeration mechanics	3.5	16.8	Industrial truck & tractor operators	1.4	16.7
Office clerks, general	3.2	3.9	Wholesale & retail buyers, except farm products	1.4	10.4
Sales reps, wholesale & manufacturing, tech	2.9	16.7	Counter & rental clerks	1.3	22.6
Customer service representatives	2.9	19.5	Secretaries, except legal, medical, & executive	1.3	-1.7
General & operations managers	2.9	15.5	Packers & packagers, hand	1.1	16.8
Bookkeeping, accounting, & auditing clerks	2.8	5.1	Team assemblers	1.0	16.8
First-line supervisors/managers of non-retail sales work	2.7	7.9	Sales managers	1.0	17.5

Source: Industry-Occupation Matrix, Bureau of Labor Statistics. These data are reported based on 4-digit NAICS categories but have been matched to corresponding 6-digit NAICS industry codes. The change reported for each occupation to the year 2014 is a percent of growth or decline as estimated by the Bureau of Labor Statistics. The abbreviation nec stands for 'not elsewhere classified.'

LOCATION BY STATE AND REGIONAL CONCENTRATION

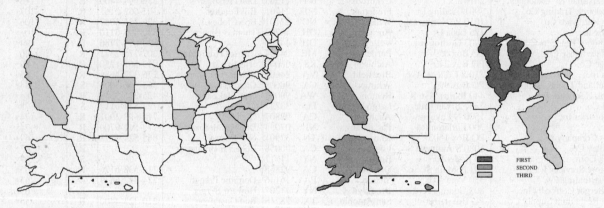

FIRST
SECOND
THIRD

INDUSTRY DATA BY STATE

State	Establishments Total (number)	% of U.S.	Employment Total (number)	% of U.S.	Per Estab.	Payroll Total ($ mil.)	Per Empl. ($)	Sales Total ($ mil.)	% of U.S.	Per Estab. ($)
California	982	14.4	12,417	15.2	13	491.2	39,555	4,933.3	15.0	5,023,703
Illinois	442	6.5	5,857	7.2	13	257.1	43,904	2,897.9	8.8	6,556,412
Indiana	153	2.2	2,077	2.5	14	80.5	38,742	2,136.6	6.5	13,964,889
Texas	543	7.9	5,355	6.6	10	193.8	36,195	1,626.5	5.0	2,995,431
Ohio	308	4.5	4,747	5.8	15	202.9	42,733	1,491.3	4.5	4,841,750
New York	428	6.3	4,159	5.1	10	164.1	39,446	1,355.3	4.1	3,166,689
Wisconsin	143	2.1	2,355	2.9	16	91.5	38,837	1,226.2	3.7	8,575,105
Florida	464	6.8	3,773	4.6	8	130.0	34,452	1,113.0	3.4	2,398,797
Pennsylvania	263	3.8	3,260	4.0	12	137.0	42,034	1,062.7	3.2	4,040,521
North Carolina	211	3.1	3,041	3.7	14	112.5	36,986	1,059.4	3.2	5,020,810
Georgia	204	3.0	2,613	3.2	13	100.5	38,452	1,046.8	3.2	5,131,368
Michigan	255	3.7	3,178	3.9	12	124.8	39,256	1,027.1	3.1	4,027,729
New Jersey	257	3.8	3,021	3.7	12	147.4	48,803	976.0	3.0	3,797,482
South Carolina	70	1.0	865	1.1	12	35.9	41,486	703.5	2.1	10,049,586
Minnesota	138	2.0	1,786	2.2	13	68.8	38,531	686.3	2.1	4,973,051
Connecticut	87	1.3	1,431	1.8	16	82.1	57,393	649.4	2.0	7,463,816
Arkansas	44	0.6	573	0.7	13	18.0	31,462	583.7	1.8	13,266,500
Virginia	141	2.1	1,489	1.8	11	54.1	36,339	557.5	1.7	3,953,603
Washington	161	2.4	1,610	2.0	10	57.6	35,763	541.0	1.6	3,360,292
Tennessee	109	1.6	1,171	1.4	11	41.7	35,623	512.4	1.6	4,700,945
Massachusetts	146	2.1	1,783	2.2	12	80.6	45,183	510.0	1.6	3,493,034
Alabama	83	1.2	1,319	1.6	16	43.5	32,989	491.1	1.5	5,916,325
Colorado	101	1.5	1,226	1.5	12	45.0	36,687	452.8	1.4	4,482,980
Missouri	118	1.7	1,272	1.6	11	49.2	38,706	416.5	1.3	3,529,805
Oregon	88	1.3	900	1.1	10	33.1	36,781	307.5	0.9	3,493,750
Kansas	49	0.7	484	0.6	10	19.7	40,762	188.3	0.6	3,843,020
Utah	49	0.7	526	0.6	11	18.8	35,662	186.2	0.6	3,800,327
Iowa	50	0.7	618	0.8	12	19.9	32,173	172.5	0.5	3,449,880
Kentucky	55	0.8	468	0.6	9	14.4	30,671	143.9	0.4	2,615,855
Maine	15	0.2	418	0.5	28	15.2	36,254	133.6	0.4	8,906,000
North Dakota	16	0.2	161	0.2	10	4.3	26,522	121.5	0.4	7,595,188

Continued on next page.

INDUSTRY DATA BY STATE - Continued

State	Establishments		Employment			Payroll		Sales		
	Total (number)	% of U.S.	Total (number)	% of U.S.	Per Estab.	Total ($ mil.)	Per Empl. ($)	Total ($ mil.)	% of U.S.	Per Estab. ($)
Nevada	47	0.7	417	0.5	9	12.0	28,724	79.3	0.2	1,687,936
Mississippi	33	0.5	248	0.3	8	9.0	36,270	57.9	0.2	1,754,606
New Mexico	30	0.4	219	0.3	7	7.5	34,237	50.9	0.2	1,696,167
Hawaii	24	0.4	188	0.2	8	7.2	38,378	45.5	0.1	1,893,875
Idaho	25	0.4	151	0.2	6	4.2	28,079	31.7	0.1	1,268,760
South Dakota	11	0.2	171	0.2	16	4.4	25,784	25.1	0.1	2,282,182
Vermont	7	0.1	50	0.1	7	1.5	30,720	10.6	-	1,514,000
Wyoming	6	0.1	36	-	6	0.9	25,944	8.7	-	1,451,833
Arizona	128	1.9	1000-2499	-	-	(D)	-	(D)	-	-
Maryland	96	1.4	1000-2499	-	-	(D)	-	(D)	-	-
Oklahoma	61	0.9	1000-2499	-	-	(D)	-	(D)	-	-
Louisiana	60	0.9	500-999	-	-	(D)	-	(D)	-	-
Nebraska	40	0.6	500-999	-	-	(D)	-	(D)	-	-
New Hampshire	27	0.4	100-249	-	-	(D)	-	(D)	-	-
Rhode Island	22	0.3	250-499	-	-	(D)	-	(D)	-	-
Delaware	16	0.2	100-249	-	-	(D)	-	(D)	-	-
West Virginia	16	0.2	100-249	-	-	(D)	-	(D)	-	-
Montana	11	0.2	20-99	-	-	(D)	-	(D)	-	-
Alaska	4	0.1	100-249	-	-	(D)	-	(D)	-	-
D.C.	4	0.1	20-99	-	-	(D)	-	(D)	-	-

Source: 2002 *Economic Census*. The states are in descending order of sales or establishments (if sales data are missing for the majority). The symbol (D) appears when data are withheld to prevent disclosure of competitive information. States marked with (D) are sorted by number of establishments. A dash (-) indicates that the data element cannot be calculated. Shaded *states* on the state map indicate those states which have proportionately greater representation in the industry than would be indicated by the states population; the ratio is based on total sales or number of establishments. Shaded *regions* indicate where the industry is regionally most concentrated.

NAICS 423720 - PLUMBING AND HEATING EQUIPMENT AND SUPPLIES (HYDRONICS) MERCHANT WHOLESALERS

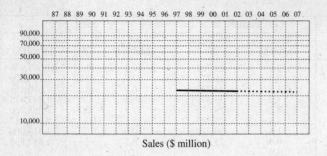

Sales ($ million)

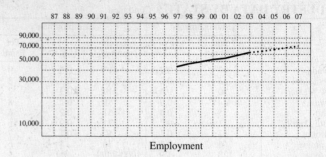

Employment

GENERAL STATISTICS

Year	Establishments (number)	Employment (number)	Payroll ($ million)	Sales ($ million)	Employees per Establishment (number)	Sales per Establishment ($)	Payroll per Employee ($)
1987	-	-	-	-	-	-	-
1988	-	-	-	-	-	-	-
1989	-	-	-	-	-	-	-
1990	-	-	-	-	-	-	-
1991	-	-	-	-	-	-	-
1992	-	-	-	-	-	-	-
1993	-	-	-	-	-	-	-
1994	-	-	-	-	-	-	-
1995	-	-	-	-	-	-	-
1996	-	-	-	-	-	-	-
1997	4,625	43,887	1,582.2	22,928.1	9.5	4,957,427.0	36,051.7
1998	4,800	47,331	1,801.6	22,835.1 e	9.9	4,757,316.7	38,063.8
1999	4,839	49,740	1,971.4	22,742.1 e	10.3	4,699,760.3	39,634.1
2000	4,756	52,669	2,131.8	22,649.2 e	11.1	4,762,228.8	40,475.6
2001	4,912	54,353	2,270.5	22,556.2 e	11.1	4,592,056.2	41,772.8
2002	5,283	58,484	2,451.9	22,463.2	11.1	4,251,978.0	41,924.3
2003	5,470	62,743	2,731.8	22,370.2 p	11.5	4,274,072.1 p	43,539.1
2004	5,466 p	64,671 p	2,855.7 p	22,277.2 p	11.9 p	4,160,913.3 p	44,826.2 p
2005	5,593 p	67,652 p	3,036.0 p	22,184.3 p	12.3 p	4,047,754.5 p	45,980.5 p
2006	5,721 p	70,634 p	3,216.3 p	22,091.3 p	12.6 p	3,934,595.7 p	47,134.9 p
2007	5,849 p	73,616 p	3,396.6 p	21,998.3 p	12.9 p	3,821,436.9 p	48,289.2 p

Source: *Economic Census of the United States*, 1997 and 2002. Establishment counts, employment, and payroll are from *County Business Patterns* for non-Census years. This is a newly defined industry. Data for prior years are unavailable at the time of publication but may become available over time. Values followed by 'p' are projections by the editors. Sales data for non-Census years are extrapolations, marked by 'e'.

INDICES OF CHANGE

Year	Establishments (number)	Employment (number)	Payroll ($ million)	Sales ($ million)	Employees per Establishment (number)	Sales per Establishment ($)	Payroll per Employee ($)
1987	-	-	-	-	-	-	-
1992	-	-	-	-	-	-	-
1993	-	-	-	-	-	-	-
1994	-	-	-	-	-	-	-
1995	-	-	-	-	-	-	-
1996	-	-	-	-	-	-	-
1997	87.5	75.0	64.5	102.1	85.6	116.6	86.0
1998	90.9	80.9	73.5	101.7 e	89.2	111.9	90.8
1999	91.6	85.0	80.4	101.2 e	92.8	110.5	94.5
2000	90.0	90.1	86.9	100.8 e	100.0	112.0	96.5
2001	93.0	92.9	92.6	100.4 e	100.0	108.0	99.6
2002	100.0	100.0	100.0	100.0	100.0	100.0	100.0
2003	103.5	107.3	111.4	99.6 p	103.3	100.5 p	103.9
2004	103.5 p	110.6 p	116.5 p	99.2 p	107.6 p	97.9 p	106.9 p
2005	105.9 p	115.7 p	123.8 p	98.8 p	110.5 p	95.2 p	109.7 p
2006	108.3 p	120.8 p	131.2 p	98.3 p	113.4 p	92.5 p	112.4 p
2007	110.7 p	125.9 p	138.5 p	97.9 p	116.4 p	89.9 p	115.2 p

Sources: Same as General Statistics. The values shown reflect change from the base year, 2002. Values above 100 mean greater than 2002, values below 100 mean less than 2002, and a value of 100 in the 1987-2001 or 2003-2007 period means same as 2002. Values followed by a 'p' are projections by the editors; 'e' stands for extrapolation. Data are the most recent available at this level of detail.

SELECTED RATIOS

For 2002	Avg. of All Wholesale	Analyzed Industry	Index	For 2002	Avg. of All Wholesale	Analyzed Industry	Index
Employees per Establishment	15	11	74	Sales per Employee	791,325	384,091	49
Payroll per Establishment	626,122	464,111	74	Sales per Establishment	12,012,387	4,251,978	35
Payroll per Employee	41,161	41,924	102	Expenses per Establishment	na	na	na

Sources: Same as General Statistics. The 'Average of All' column, Wholesale or Retail, represents the average of the sector reported for the most recent complete year available. The Index shows the relationship between the Average and the Analyzed Industry. For example, 100 means that they are equal; 500 that the Analyzed Industry is five times the average; 50 means that the Analyzed Industry is half the national average. The abbreviation 'na' is used to show that data are 'not available'.

LEADING COMPANIES Number shown: **75**   Total sales ($ mil): **15,097**   Total employment (000): **37.8**

Company Name	Address				CEO Name	Phone	Co. Type	Sales ($ mil)	Empl. (000)
Ferguson Enterprises Inc.	12500 Jefferson Ave	Newport News	VA	23602	Charles A. Banks	757-826-4127	S	5,941	14.8
Hughes Supply Inc.	PO Box 2273	Orlando	FL	32801	Thomas I Morgan	407-841-4755	P	3,253	8.4
McJunkin Corp.	PO Box 513	Charleston	WV	25322	H Barnard Wehrle III	304-348-5211	R	847*	1.6
Noland Co.	80 29th St	Newport News	VA	23607	Lloyd U Noland III	757-928-9000	P	548	1.3
Hajoca Corp.	127 Coulter Ave	Ardmore	PA	19003	Rick Klau	610-649-1430	R	459*	1.3
Lyon Conklin and Company Inc.	2101 Race St	Baltimore	MD	21230	Jenny Allen	301-808-3500	R	296*	0.2
FW Webb Co.	160 Middlesex Tpke	Bedford	MA	01730	John Pope	781-272-6600	R	239*	<0.1
Consolidated Pipe and Supply Inc.	PO Box 2472	Birmingham	AL	35201	Howard Kerr	205-323-7261	R	236*	0.5
R.E. Michel Company Inc.	1 R E Michel Dr	Glen Burnie	MD	21060	JWH Michel	410-760-4000	R	186*	1.0
Cosmopolitan Chemical Div.	50-23 23rd St	Long Island City	NY	11101	R H Seidman	718-729-7200	D	173*	0.1
Bell Industries Inc.	1960 E Grand Ave	El Segundo	CA	90245	Russell A Doll	310-563-2355	P	144	0.8
Keller Supply Co.	PO Box 79014	Seattle	WA	98119	Nick Keller	206-285-3300	R	142*	0.6
Orgil-Frederick Trading Co.	7901 Trading Ln	Frederick	MD	21701	Bill Fondren	301-662-2161	R	107*	0.4
Thos. Somerville Co.	4912 6th St NE	Washington	DC	20017	Pat McGowan	202-635-4100	R	94*	0.3
Temperature Equipment Corp.	17725 Volbrecht Rd	Lansing	IL	60438	FA Mungo	708-418-0900	R	88*	0.2
Trumbull Industries Inc.	PO Box 30	Warren	OH	44482	Murray Miller	330-393-6624	R	87*	0.3
Economy Lumber Yard Inc.	4200 N Ih 35	Laredo	TX	78041	Isaac Epstein	956-721-7300	R	84*	0.1
Goodin Co.	2700 N 2nd St	Minneapolis	MN	55411	Gerard Melgaard	612-588-7811	R	81*	0.3
Waxman Industries Inc.	24460 Aurora Rd	Bedford Heights	OH	44146	Armond Waxman	440-439-1830	R	67	0.4
Medal Distributing Co.	330 Vine Ave	Sharon	PA	16146	Dominic Preggi	724-342-6839	D	65*	<0.1
Wolff Brothers Supply Inc.	6078 Wolff Rd	Medina	OH	44256	Howard Wolff	330-725-3451	R	65*	0.3
J.H. Larson Co.	700 Colorado Ave S	Golden Valley	MN	55416	C E Pahl	763-545-1717	R	64*	0.2
Lee Supply Corp.	PO Box 681430	Indianapolis	IN	46268		317-290-2500	R	61*	0.2
ATR Supply Co.	749 Guilford St	Lebanon	PA	17046	Scott Weaver	717-274-5999	R	55*	0.1
Superior Soft Water Inc.	3536 S 1950 W	Salt Lake City	UT	84119	Gerald Lamborne	801-952-5900	R	55*	0.1
Frank Lill and Son Inc.	656 Basket Rd	Webster	NY	14580	Charles G Lill	585-265-0490	R	53*	0.1
Wholesale Supply Group Inc.	PO Box 4080	Cleveland	TN	37320	Lloyd D Rogers	423-478-1191	R	50*	0.3
Branch Brook Co.	370 Hwy 36	Hazlet	NJ	07730	Kevin Ventrice	732-787-2700	R	50*	<0.1
Parnell-Martin Co.	PO Box 30067	Charlotte	NC	28230	John George	704-375-8651	R	48*	0.2
HPM Building Supply	380 Kanoelehua Ave	Hilo	HI	96720	Robert Fujimoto	808-934-4266	R	47*	0.2
Equipment Sales Corp.	703 Western Dr	Mobile	AL	36607	LH Hughes Sr	251-476-2220	R	45*	<0.1
Best Plumbing Tile and Stone	3333 Crompond Rd	Yorktown H.	NY	10598	Melvin Weiner	914-736-2468	R	44*	<0.1
Bruce Supply Corp.	8805 18th Ave	Brooklyn	NY	11214	Jack Wecksler	718-259-4900	R	44*	<0.1
Elmco Supply	PO Box 920	Canon City	CO	81215	Elmer Smaller	719-275-1544	R	44*	<0.1
Ez-Flo International Inc.	2750 E Mission Blvd	Ontario	CA	91761	Saleem Lahlouh	909-947-5256	R	44*	<0.1
Sunbelt Marketing Inc.	3255 S Sweetwater	Lithia Springs	GA	30122	Ton Menefee	770-739-3740	R	44*	<0.1
Cal-Steam Supply Inc.	1595 Crocker Ave	Hayward	CA	94544		510-512-7700	R	42*	<0.1
Palermo Supply Company Inc.	71 N Washington	Bergenfield	NJ	07621	Thomas Palermo	201-387-1141	R	40*	0.2
J.W. Pierson Co.	89 Dodd St	East Orange	NJ	07019	James Pierson	973-673-5000	R	39*	0.1
W.A. Roosevelt Co.	PO Box 1208	La Crosse	WI	54602	Stephen W Reiman	608-781-2000	R	39*	0.1
US Filter Corp.	2600 S 17th Ave	Broadview	IL	60155		708-345-7290	R	39*	<0.1
Amarillo Hardware Co.	PO Box 1891	Amarillo	TX	79172	Joe Wildman	806-376-4722	R	36*	0.1
Kelly's Pipe and Supply Co.	PO Box 14750	Las Vegas	NV	89114	Brad Shoen	702-382-4957	R	36*	<0.1
United Pipe and Steel Corp.	83 Tpke Rd	Ipswich	MA	01938	David Cohen	978-356-9300	R	36*	<0.1
Buffington and Associates Inc.	5775 Las Positas Rd	Livermore	CA	94551	Darwin Buffington	925-583-1600	R	33*	<0.1
Middle Tennessee Natural Gas	P O Box 670	Smithville	TN	37166	Leslie B Enoch II	615-597-4300	R	33*	0.1
Wright and Wilhelmy Inc.	11005 E St	Omaha	NE	68137	Darcy Michalek	402-593-0600	R	33*	<0.1
Schmidt's Wholesale Inc.	PO Box 5100	Monticello	NY	12701	Gary Schmidt	845-794-5900	R	31*	<0.1
Davidson Pipe Supply Inc.	5002 2nd Ave	Brooklyn	NY	11232	Stewart Krueger	718-439-6300	R	30*	<0.1
Security Supply Corp.	196 Maple Ave	Selkirk	NY	12158	Keith W Bennett	518-767-2226	R	30*	0.1
Legend Valve and Fitting Inc.	51245 Filomena Dr	Shelby	MI	48315	David Hickman	586-566-7400	R	30*	<0.1
HN Hinckley and Sons Inc.	PO Box 578	Vineyard Haven	MA	02568	Nelson Guyther	508-693-0075	R	29*	<0.1
Bornquist Inc.	7050 N Lehigh Ave	Chicago	IL	60646	Harry Hultgren	773-774-2800	R	29*	<0.1
Fresno Distributing Co.	PO Box 6078	Fresno	CA	93703	Steve Cloud	559-442-8800	R	28*	0.1
Torrington Supply Company Inc.	PO Box 2838	Waterbury	CT	06723	Joel S Becker	203-756-3641	R	28*	0.1
California Hydronics Corp.	PO Box 5049	Hayward	CA	94540	David Attard	510-293-1993	R	28*	<0.1
David Gooding Inc.	711 John Mahar	Braintree	MA	02184	David Gooding	781-794-1500	R	28*	<0.1
SG Supply Co.	12900 S Throop St	Calumet Park	IL	60827	Norman E Weiss	708-371-8800	R	27*	0.1
Briggs Incorporated of Omaha	1011 Mason	Omaha	NE	68102		402-342-0778	R	26*	<0.1
Deacon Industrial Supply Inc.	PO Box 62485	King of Prussia	PA	19406	Joseph Pendrak	610-265-5322	R	26*	0.1
Montour Industrial Supply Inc.	1400 2nd Ave	Coraopolis	PA	15108	William Ondrasik	412-262-7460	R	26*	<0.1
US Reclamation Bureau	835 E 2nd Ave	Durango	CO	81301		970-385-6500	R	25*	<0.1
Leonard's Hardware Inc.	PO Box 637	Russellville	AR	72811	Shirley Leonard	479-968-2142	R	25*	0.1
APR Supply Co.	749 Guilford St	Lebanon	PA	17046	Randy Tice	717-274-5999	R	25*	0.1
Dana Kepner Co.	700 Alcott St	Denver	CO	80204	Wayne E Johnson	303-623-6161	R	25*	<0.1
Mountainland Supply Co.	1505 W 130 S	Orem	UT	84058	RJ Rasmussen	801-224-6050	R	25*	<0.1
Carr Supply Inc.	1415 Old Leonard	Columbus	OH	43219	Roger Essig	614-252-7883	R	25*	<0.1
CB and K Supply Inc.	PO Box 1037	Janesville	WI	53547	Rodney Katz	608-755-5100	R	25*	<0.1
Quentzel Henry Plumbing Supply	379 Throop Ave	Brooklyn	NY	11221	Ann Quentzel	718-455-6600	R	25*	<0.1
Benoist Brothers Supply Inc.	PO Box 587	Mount Vernon	IL	62864	Albert Benoist	618-242-0344	R	25*	<0.1
Cabinet and Bath Supply Inc.	882 W Tracker Rd	Nixa	MO	65714	David Pairs	417-725-2525	R	25*	<0.1
Mountain States Pipe & Supply	PO Box 698	Co Springs	CO	80903	Paul Carroll	719-634-5555	R	24*	0.1
Penco Corp.	PO Box 690	Seaford	DE	19973	Kent Peterson	302-629-7911	R	24*	<0.1
WP Law Inc.	303 Riverchase Way	Lexington	SC	29072	Tom Plumblee	803-461-0599	R	24*	<0.1
Gateway Supply Company Inc.	PO Box 56	Columbia	SC	29202	Chris Williams	803-771-7160	R	23*	0.1

Source: Ward's Business Directory of U.S. Private and Public Companies, Volumes 1 and 2, 2005. The company type code used is as follows: P - Public, R - Private, S - Subsidiary, D - Division, J - Joint Venture, A - Affiliate, G - Group. Sales are in millions of dollars, employees are in thousands. An asterisk (*) indicates an estimated sales volume. The symbol < stands for 'less than'. Company names and addresses are truncated, in some cases, to fit into the available space.

OCCUPATIONS EMPLOYED BY HARDWARE, & PLUMBING & HEATING EQUIPMENT & SUPPLIES

Occupation	% of Total 2004	Change to 2014	Occupation	% of Total 2004	Change to 2014
Sales reps, wholesale & manufacturing, exc tech	18.0	16.8	Parts salespersons	2.1	-6.6
Laborers & freight, stock, & material movers, hand	7.0	5.1	Order clerks	1.9	-24.1
Stock clerks & order fillers	5.1	-10.6	Retail salespersons	1.7	16.7
Truck drivers, light or delivery services	4.5	16.8	Truck drivers, heavy & tractor-trailer	1.6	16.7
Shipping, receiving, & traffic clerks	4.4	5.7	First-line supervisors/managers of office workers	1.5	5.8
Heating, air conditioning, & refrigeration mechanics	3.5	16.8	Industrial truck & tractor operators	1.4	16.7
Office clerks, general	3.2	3.9	Wholesale & retail buyers, except farm products	1.4	10.4
Sales reps, wholesale & manufacturing, tech	2.9	16.7	Counter & rental clerks	1.3	22.6
Customer service representatives	2.9	19.5	Secretaries, except legal, medical, & executive	1.3	-1.7
General & operations managers	2.9	15.5	Packers & packagers, hand	1.1	16.8
Bookkeeping, accounting, & auditing clerks	2.8	5.1	Team assemblers	1.0	16.8
First-line supervisors/managers of non-retail sales work	2.7	7.9	Sales managers	1.0	17.5

Source: Industry-Occupation Matrix, Bureau of Labor Statistics. These data are reported based on 4-digit NAICS categories but have been matched to corresponding 6-digit NAICS industry codes. The change reported for each occupation to the year 2014 is a percent of growth or decline as estimated by the Bureau of Labor Statistics. The abbreviation nec stands for 'not elsewhere classified.'

LOCATION BY STATE AND REGIONAL CONCENTRATION

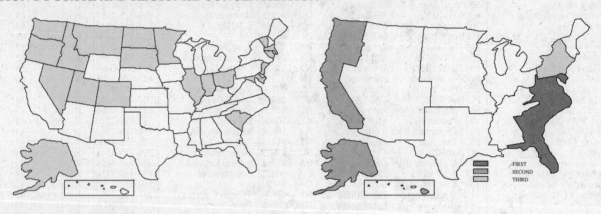

INDUSTRY DATA BY STATE

State	Establishments Total (number)	% of U.S.	Employment Total (number)	% of U.S.	Per Estab.	Payroll Total ($ mil.)	Per Empl. ($)	Sales Total ($ mil.)	% of U.S.	Per Estab. ($)
California	532	9.9	6,279	10.5	12	270.6	43,092	2,414.5	10.6	4,538,617
Illinois	214	4.0	2,808	4.7	13	137.6	49,020	1,552.2	6.8	7,253,388
Texas	321	6.0	3,612	6.0	11	145.9	40,401	1,420.9	6.2	4,426,536
Florida	305	5.7	2,766	4.6	9	114.5	41,382	1,128.4	4.9	3,699,777
Ohio	212	3.9	2,470	4.1	12	97.8	39,588	1,088.6	4.8	5,135,108
Pennsylvania	277	5.2	3,263	5.4	12	128.2	39,289	1,026.9	4.5	3,707,394
New Jersey	158	2.9	2,224	3.7	14	100.5	45,211	887.2	3.9	5,615,386
Washington	160	3.0	1,657	2.8	10	67.0	40,456	663.9	2.9	4,149,619
Massachusetts	145	2.7	1,547	2.6	11	76.4	49,388	648.7	2.8	4,473,572
Colorado	120	2.2	1,399	2.3	12	64.6	46,189	615.4	2.7	5,128,033
Michigan	150	2.8	1,807	3.0	12	77.4	42,821	594.6	2.6	3,964,073
North Carolina	173	3.2	1,649	2.8	10	70.7	42,873	577.5	2.5	3,338,318
Minnesota	115	2.1	1,475	2.5	13	65.8	44,643	569.0	2.5	4,948,087
Virginia	122	2.3	1,630	2.7	13	58.8	36,085	546.7	2.4	4,481,295
Indiana	114	2.1	1,380	2.3	12	53.5	38,791	523.6	2.3	4,592,772
Maryland	100	1.9	1,590	2.7	16	70.8	44,533	460.1	2.0	4,600,760
Wisconsin	90	1.7	961	1.6	11	41.5	43,145	428.3	1.9	4,758,556
South Carolina	70	1.3	712	1.2	10	32.6	45,846	390.9	1.7	5,584,243
Alabama	93	1.7	1,078	1.8	12	40.0	37,121	348.1	1.5	3,742,774
Oregon	79	1.5	960	1.6	12	35.6	37,045	343.0	1.5	4,342,152
Missouri	93	1.7	998	1.7	11	38.5	38,557	314.6	1.4	3,383,011
Connecticut	76	1.4	819	1.4	11	40.8	49,825	314.1	1.4	4,132,342
Nevada	43	0.8	657	1.1	15	31.0	47,207	312.1	1.4	7,259,279
Utah	61	1.1	749	1.3	12	29.7	39,656	267.9	1.2	4,391,295
Oklahoma	100	1.9	600	1.0	6	22.3	37,188	209.4	0.9	2,093,800
Iowa	65	1.2	663	1.1	10	25.0	37,677	205.5	0.9	3,162,015
Louisiana	57	1.1	641	1.1	11	22.3	34,764	167.1	0.7	2,931,211
Nebraska	40	0.7	444	0.7	11	17.6	39,588	129.1	0.6	3,228,200
Alaska	16	0.3	255	0.4	16	11.3	44,165	128.5	0.6	8,031,250
Mississippi	46	0.9	336	0.6	7	12.9	38,509	122.4	0.5	2,659,913
Montana	25	0.5	357	0.6	14	12.3	34,364	118.9	0.5	4,755,000

Continued on next page.

INDUSTRY DATA BY STATE - Continued

State	Establishments Total (number)	% of U.S.	Employment Total (number)	% of U.S.	Per Estab.	Payroll Total ($ mil.)	Per Empl. ($)	Sales Total ($ mil.)	% of U.S.	Per Estab. ($)
Arkansas	43	0.8	398	0.7	9	16.5	41,490	117.9	0.5	2,741,884
Idaho	40	0.7	335	0.6	8	11.1	33,182	114.9	0.5	2,873,625
Vermont	23	0.4	276	0.5	12	12.1	43,739	109.2	0.5	4,749,696
New Mexico	37	0.7	312	0.5	8	10.3	33,077	102.4	0.4	2,767,541
Hawaii	25	0.5	246	0.4	10	9.6	39,224	101.9	0.4	4,075,080
Maine	34	0.6	309	0.5	9	12.7	41,152	100.2	0.4	2,948,147
North Dakota	20	0.4	236	0.4	12	11.4	48,144	97.6	0.4	4,878,300
South Dakota	32	0.6	272	0.5	9	9.9	36,397	93.7	0.4	2,928,875
West Virginia	25	0.5	253	0.4	10	10.9	43,079	83.3	0.4	3,333,320
Wyoming	13	0.2	68	0.1	5	1.9	28,397	21.3	0.1	1,641,154
New York	368	6.9	2500-4999	-	-	(D)	-	(D)	-	-
Georgia	170	3.2	1000-2499	-	-	(D)	-	(D)	-	-
Arizona	100	1.9	1000-2499	-	-	(D)	-	(D)	-	-
Tennessee	88	1.6	1000-2499	-	-	(D)	-	(D)	-	-
Kansas	65	1.2	250-499	-	-	(D)	-	(D)	-	-
Kentucky	50	0.9	500-999	-	-	(D)	-	(D)	-	-
New Hampshire	30	0.6	100-249	-	-	(D)	-	(D)	-	-
Rhode Island	20	0.4	100-249	-	-	(D)	-	(D)	-	-
Delaware	15	0.3	20-99	-	-	(D)	-	(D)	-	-
D.C.	1	-	20-99	-	-	(D)	-	(D)	-	-

Source: 2002 *Economic Census*. The states are in descending order of sales or establishments (if sales data are missing for the majority). The symbol (D) appears when data are withheld to prevent disclosure of competitive information. States marked with (D) are sorted by number of establishments. A dash (-) indicates that the data element cannot be calculated. Shaded *states* on the state map indicate those states which have proportionately greater representation in the industry than would be indicated by the states population; the ratio is based on total sales or number of establishments. Shaded *regions* indicate where the industry is regionally most concentrated.

NAICS 423730 - WARM AIR HEATING AND AIR-CONDITIONING EQUIPMENT AND SUPPLIES MERCHANT WHOLESALERS*

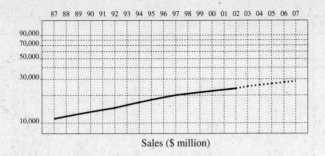

Sales ($ million)

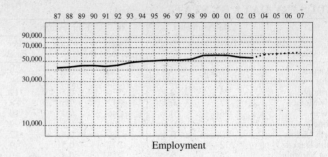

Employment

GENERAL STATISTICS

Year	Establishments (number)	Employment (number)	Payroll ($ million)	Sales ($ million)	Employees per Establishment (number)	Sales per Establishment ($)	Payroll per Employee ($)
1987	5,101	42,414	1,109.8	11,142.6	8.3	2,184,395.2	26,165.9
1988	4,931	43,164	1,217.8	11,838.2 e	8.8	2,400,770.6	28,213.3
1989	4,822	44,753	1,345.0	12,533.8 e	9.3	2,599,294.9	30,053.9
1990	4,837	44,832	1,380.6	13,229.5 e	9.3	2,735,063.1	30,795.0
1991	4,868	43,900	1,377.2	13,925.1 e	9.0	2,860,538.2	31,371.3
1992	5,486	45,129	1,461.4	14,620.8	8.2	2,665,111.2	32,382.7
1993	5,470	48,196	1,623.1	15,709.2 e	8.8	2,871,883.0	33,677.1
1994	5,506	49,661	1,772.0	16,797.6 e	9.0	3,050,781.0	35,681.9
1995	5,571	50,314	1,852.7	17,885.9 e	9.0	3,210,536.7	36,822.8
1996	5,704 e	51,281 e	1,875.5 e	18,974.3 e	9.0 e	3,326,490.2 e	36,573.0 e
1997	5,524	51,252	2,013.5	20,062.7	9.3	3,631,915.3	39,286.3
1998	5,589	52,121	2,210.8	20,791.6 e	9.3	3,720,093.0	42,416.7
1999	5,651	57,424	2,481.8	21,520.5 e	10.2	3,808,264.0	43,218.9
2000	5,710	57,696	2,674.1	22,249.4 e	10.1	3,896,567.4	46,348.2
2001	5,579	57,478	2,705.7	22,978.3 e	10.3	4,118,713.0	47,074.5
2002	5,468	54,791	2,433.6	23,707.2	10.0	4,335,625.5	44,416.1
2003	5,487	53,890	2,569.6	24,884.7 p	9.8	4,349,815.1 p	47,682.4
2004	5,801 p	58,650 p	2,823.2 p	25,768.4 p	10.2 p	4,483,498.9 p	49,430.6 p
2005	5,849 p	59,622 p	2,927.0 p	26,652.1 p	10.3 p	4,617,182.7 p	50,791.0 p
2006	5,897 p	60,594 p	3,030.9 p	27,535.9 p	10.3 p	4,750,866.5 p	52,151.4 p
2007	5,944 p	61,567 p	3,134.7 p	28,419.6 p	10.4 p	4,884,550.3 p	53,511.8 p

Sources: Economic Census of the United States, 1987, 1992, 1997, and 2002. Establishment counts, employment, and payroll are from County Business Patterns for non-Census years. Values followed by a 'p' are projections by the editors. Sales data for non-Census years are extrapolations, marked by 'e'. Data are the most recent available at this level of detail.

INDICES OF CHANGE

Year	Establishments (number)	Employment (number)	Payroll ($ million)	Sales ($ million)	Employees per Establishment (number)	Sales per Establishment ($)	Payroll per Employee ($)
1987	93.3	77.4	45.6	47.0	83.0	50.4	58.9
1992	100.3	82.4	60.1	61.7	82.0	61.5	72.9
1993	100.0	88.0	66.7	66.3 e	88.0	66.2	75.8
1994	100.7	90.6	72.8	70.9 e	90.0	70.4	80.3
1995	101.9	91.8	76.1	75.4 e	90.0	74.1	82.9
1996	104.3 e	93.6 e	77.1 e	80.0 e	90.0 e	76.7 e	82.3 e
1997	101.0	93.5	82.7	84.6	93.0	83.8	88.5
1998	102.2	95.1	90.8	87.7 e	93.0	85.8	95.5
1999	103.3	104.8	102.0	90.8 e	102.0	87.8	97.3
2000	104.4	105.3	109.9	93.9 e	101.0	89.9	104.4
2001	102.0	104.9	111.2	96.9 e	103.0	95.0	106.0
2002	100.0	100.0	100.0	100.0	100.0	100.0	100.0
2003	100.3	98.4	105.6	105.0 p	98.2	100.3 p	107.4
2004	106.1 p	107.0 p	116.0 p	108.7 p	101.5 p	103.4 p	111.3 p
2005	107.0 p	108.8 p	120.3 p	112.4 p	102.5 p	106.5 p	114.4 p
2006	107.8 p	110.6 p	124.5 p	116.1 p	103.5 p	109.6 p	117.4 p
2007	108.7 p	112.4 p	128.8 p	119.9 p	104.4 p	112.7 p	120.5 p

Sources: Same as General Statistics. The values shown reflect change from the base year, 2002. Values above 100 mean greater than 2002, values below 100 mean less than 2002, and a value of 100 in the 1987-2001 or 2003-2007 period means same as 2002. Values followed by a 'p' are projections by the editors; 'e' stands for extrapolation. Data are the most recent available at this level of detail.

SELECTED RATIOS

For 2002	Avg. of All Wholesale	Analyzed Industry	Index	For 2002	Avg. of All Wholesale	Analyzed Industry	Index
Employees per Establishment	15	10	67	Sales per Employee	791,325	432,684	55
Payroll per Establishment	626,122	445,062	71	Sales per Establishment	12,012,387	4,335,625	36
Payroll per Employee	41,161	44,416	108	Expenses per Establishment	na	na	na

Sources: Same as General Statistics. The 'Average of All' column, Wholesale or Retail, represents the average of the sector reported for the most recent complete year available. The Index shows the relationship between the Average and the Analyzed Industry. For example, 100 means that they are equal; 500 that the Analyzed Industry is five times the average; 50 means that the Analyzed Industry is half the national average. The abbreviation 'na' is used to show that data are 'not available'.

*Equivalent to SIC 5075.

LEADING COMPANIES   Number shown: **75**   Total sales ($ mil): **15,603**   Total employment (000): **39.0**

Company Name	Address				CEO Name	Phone	Co. Type	Sales ($ mil)	Empl. (000)
W.W. Grainger Inc.	100 Grainger Pkwy	Lake Forest	IL	60045	David W. Grainger	847-535-1000	P	5,050	14.7
Hughes Supply Inc.	PO Box 2273	Orlando	FL	32801	Thomas I Morgan	407-841-4755	P	3,253	8.4
Watsco Inc.	2665 S Bayshore Dr	Coconut Grove	FL	33133	Albert H Nahmad	305-714-4100	P	1,315	2.6
US Oil Company Inc.	PO Box 25	Combined Locks	WI	54113		920-739-6101	R	980*	0.4
Noland Co.	80 29th St	Newport News	VA	23607	Lloyd U Noland III	757-928-9000	P	548	1.3
Hajoca Corp.	127 Coulter Ave	Ardmore	PA	19003	Rick Klau	610-649-1430	R	459*	1.3
Lyon Conklin and Company Inc.	2101 Race St	Baltimore	MD	21230	Jenny Allen	301-808-3500	R	296*	0.2
FW Webb Co.	160 Middlesex Tpke	Bedford	MA	01730	John Pope	781-272-6600	R	239*	<0.1
Famous Manufacturing Co.	PO Box 1889	Akron	OH	44309	Jay Blaufeild	330-434-5194	R	234*	0.7
R.E. Michel Company Inc.	1 R E Michel Dr	Glen Burnie	MD	21060	JWH Michel	410-760-4000	R	186*	1.0
ACR Group Inc.	3200 Wilcrest Dr	Houston	TX	77042		713-780-8532	P	174	0.4
Climatic Corp.	PO Box 25189	Columbia	SC	29224	John H Bailey	803-765-2595	R	145*	0.2
Bell Industries Inc.	1960 E Grand Ave	El Segundo	CA	90245	Russell A Doll	310-563-2355	P	144	0.8
Mingledorffs Inc.	6675 Jones Mill Ct	Norcross	GA	30092	LB Mingledorff	770-239-2100	R	114*	0.2
Century Air Conditioning Supply	10510 W S Houston	Houston	TX	77099	Dennis Beardan	281-530-2859	R	99*	0.3
Thos. Somerville Co.	4912 6th St NE	Washington	DC	20017	Pat McGowan	202-635-4100	R	94*	0.3
ACR Supply Inc.	8798 Westpark Dr	Houston	TX	77063	Danny Fisher	713-787-6666	S	88*	0.2
Robertshaw Uni-Line	PO Box 2000	Corona	CA	92878		909-734-2600	D	88*	0.2
Temperature Equipment Corp.	17725 Volbrecht Rd	Lansing	IL	60438	FA Mungo	708-418-0900	R	88*	0.2
Goodin Co.	2700 N 2nd St	Minneapolis	MN	55411	Gerard Melgaard	612-588-7811	R	81*	0.3
Three States Supply Co.	PO Box 646	Memphis	TN	38101	Ronald Wigginton	901-948-8651	S	79*	0.3
Bryant-Habegger Co.	4995 Winton Rd	Cincinnati	OH	45232	John Dorr	513-681-6313	R	77*	0.2
Tampa Bay Systems Sales Inc.	PO Box 18547	Tampa	FL	33679	Douglas Cohn	813-877-8251	R	73*	0.2
Gem Products Inc.	7463 Bonnyshire Dr	Chattanooga	TN	37416		423-654-3300	R	68*	0.3
ABCO Refrigeration Supply Corp.	49-70 31st St	Long Island City	NY	11101	JA Gottlieb	718-937-9000	R	67*	0.2
Tom Barrow Company Inc.	2800 P Atkinson SE	Smyrna	GA	30080	Thomas Barrow	404-351-1010	R	66*	<0.1
Wolff Brothers Supply Inc.	6078 Wolff Rd	Medina	OH	44256	Howard Wolff	330-725-3451	R	65*	0.3
J.H. Larson Co.	700 Colorado Ave S	Golden Valley	MN	55416	C E Pahl	763-545-1717	R	64*	0.2
Refrigeration Sales Corp.	9450 Allen Dr	Valley View	OH	44125	Warren W Farr Jr	216-525-8100	R	64*	0.1
CalsonicKansei North America	27000 Hills Tech Ct	Farmington Hills	MI	48331	Shizuo Kato	248-848-4800	S	62*	0.2
ATR Supply Co.	749 Guilford St	Lebanon	PA	17046	Scott Weaver	717-274-5999	R	55*	0.1
Ince Distributing Inc.	2233 NW Loop 410	San Antonio	TX	78230	Raymond Ince	210-341-7161	R	48*	0.1
Climatic Control Company Inc.	5061 W State St	Milwaukee	WI	53208	Larry L Rector	414-259-9070	R	45*	<0.1
Equipment Sales Corp.	703 Western Dr	Mobile	AL	36607	LH Hughes Sr	251-476-2220	R	45*	<0.1
Colonial Commercial Corp.	120 New South Rd	Hicksville	NY	11801	Bernard Korn	516-681-4647	P	45	<0.1
Able Energy Inc.	198 Green Pond Rd	Rockaway	NJ	07866	Timothy Harrington	973-625-1012	P	43	<0.1
NC Filtration Corp.	209 W Ruby Ave	Gastonia	NC	28054		704-868-2940	R	41*	<0.1
Andrews Distributing Inc.	PO Box 17557	Nashville	TN	37217	Peggy Andrews	615-399-1776	R	41*	<0.1
Dakota Electric Supply Co.	PO Box 2886	Fargo	ND	58108	Ben Herr	701-237-9440	R	40*	0.2
Minnesota Electrical Supply Co.	PO Box 997	Willmar	MN	56201	Steve Peterson	320-235-2255	R	39*	0.1
W.A. Roosevelt Co.	PO Box 1208	La Crosse	WI	54602	Stephen W Reiman	608-781-2000	R	39*	0.1
Temperature Systems Inc.	PO Box 8030	Madison	WI	53708	Terry Riker	608-271-7500	R	37*	0.1
Thermal Supply Inc.	717 S Lander St	Seattle	WA	98134	Bob Monroe	206-624-4590	R	37*	<0.1
Charles D Jones and Company Inc.	114 W Linwood	Kansas City	MO	64111	Daniel Ferber	816-561-3761	R	37*	<0.1
Thermo Industries Inc.	PO Box 668109	Charlotte	NC	28266	E Hunt	704-394-7311	R	30*	<0.1
Porter Pipe and Supply Co.	303 S Rohlwing Rd	Addison	IL	60101	James Porter	630-543-8145	R	29*	<0.1
Acme Refrigeration of Baton	11844 S Choctaw Dr	Baton Rouge	LA	70815	AE Kaiser lll	225-273-1740	R	27*	<0.1
Briggs Incorporated of Omaha	1011 Mason	Omaha	NE	68102		402-342-0778	R	26*	<0.1
Koch Filter Corp.	625 W Hill St	Louisville	KY	40201	Joe Cook	502-634-4796	R	26*	0.2
Standard Air and Lite Corp.	PO Box 44445	Pittsburgh	PA	15201	Robert W Wilson	412-920-6505	R	26*	<0.1
Minnesota Air Inc.	6901 Shakopee	Minneapolis	MN	55438	Mike Metzger	952-918-8000	R	26*	<0.1
Golden West Equipment Inc.	1000 S Euclid St	La Habra	CA	90631	Michael Kennedy	714-879-3850	R	25*	<0.1
Benoist Brothers Supply Inc.	PO Box 587	Mount Vernon	IL	62864	Albert Benoist	618-242-0344	R	25*	<0.1
Penco Corp.	PO Box 690	Seaford	DE	19973	Kent Peterson	302-629-7911	R	24*	<0.1
Gateway Supply Company Inc.	PO Box 56	Columbia	SC	29202	Chris Williams	803-771-7160	R	23*	0.1
Marco Sales Inc.	1100 Macklind Ave	St. Louis	MO	63110		314-768-4200	R	23*	<0.1
American Copper and Brass Inc.	PO Box 652	Hillsdale	MI	49242	William Smith	517-439-9368	R	23*	<0.1
AC Installations By Rusher Inc.	19626 Normandie	Torrance	CA	90502	George Rusher	310-323-7201	R	21*	<0.1
Southern Refrigeration Corp.	2026 Salem Ave	Roanoke	VA	24016	John S Lang Jr	540-342-3493	R	20*	<0.1
Star Supply Co.	PO Box 9494	New Haven	CT	06534	Lawrence Cohen	203-772-2240	R	20*	<0.1
Brauer Supply Co.	4260 Forest	St. Louis	MO	63108	James L Truesdell	314-534-7150	R	19*	<0.1
Hvac Distributors Inc.	PO Box 160	Mount Joy	PA	17552	David Mc Ilwaine	717-653-6674	R	19*	<0.1
SWH Supply Co.	242 E Main St	Louisville	KY	40202	Robert Anderson	502-589-9287	R	19*	<0.1
A and A Mechanical Inc.	1101 Ulrich Ave	Louisville	KY	40219	William T Allen	502-968-0121	R	18*	<0.1
Electric Fixture and Supply Co.	PO Box 898	Omaha	NE	68101		402-342-3050	R	18*	<0.1
Air Cleaning Technologies Inc.	10615 Judicial Dr	Fairfax	VA	22030	Peter Laiti	703-383-1344	R	17*	<0.1
Sun-Rys Distributing Corp.	RR 1 Box 337	Moline	IL	61265	Gregory Mosley	309-799-7091	R	17*	<0.1
Bangor Pipe and Supply Inc.	PO Box 1569	Bangor	ME	04402	Thomas Smith	207-942-1200	R	17*	<0.1
Aaron and Company Inc.	PO Box 8310	Piscataway	NJ	08855	Barry Portnoy	732-752-8200	R	16*	<0.1
CK Supply Inc.	1840 Midwest Blvd	Indianapolis	IN	46214	Ken Maddox	317-585-8515	R	16*	<0.1
GAP Supply Corp.	PO Box 1668	Tualatin	OR	97062	Gregory Popma	503-598-7800	R	16*	<0.1
Mid-Way Supply Inc.	2502 Deborah Ave	Zion	IL	60099	Kenneth Sisson	847-872-5481	R	16*	<0.1
Summit Air Industries Inc.	1158 S Creasy Ln	Lafayette	IN	47905	Derek Hookom	765-447-2435	R	16*	<0.1
West Coast Copper and Supply Inc.	12155 Magnolia Ave	Riverside	CA	92503	Brian Mesa	951-637-0720	R	16*	<0.1
Contractors Heating & Supply Co.	70 Santa Fe Dr	Denver	CO	80223	Rick Millard	303-893-6915	S	16*	<0.1

Source: *Ward's Business Directory of U.S. Private and Public Companies*, Volumes 1 and 2, 2005. The company type code used is as follows: P - Public, R - Private, S - Subsidiary, D - Division, J - Joint Venture, A - Affiliate, G - Group. Sales are in millions of dollars, employees are in thousands. An asterisk (*) indicates an estimated sales volume. The symbol < stands for 'less than'. Company names and addresses are truncated, in some cases, to fit into the available space.

OCCUPATIONS EMPLOYED BY HARDWARE, & PLUMBING & HEATING EQUIPMENT & SUPPLIES

Occupation	% of Total 2004	Change to 2014	Occupation	% of Total 2004	Change to 2014
Sales reps, wholesale & manufacturing, exc tech	18.0	16.8	Parts salespersons	2.1	-6.6
Laborers & freight, stock, & material movers, hand	7.0	5.1	Order clerks	1.9	-24.1
Stock clerks & order fillers	5.1	-10.6	Retail salespersons	1.7	16.7
Truck drivers, light or delivery services	4.5	16.8	Truck drivers, heavy & tractor-trailer	1.6	16.7
Shipping, receiving, & traffic clerks	4.4	5.7	First-line supervisors/managers of office workers	1.5	5.8
Heating, air conditioning, & refrigeration mechanics	3.5	16.8	Industrial truck & tractor operators	1.4	16.7
Office clerks, general	3.2	3.9	Wholesale & retail buyers, except farm products	1.4	10.4
Sales reps, wholesale & manufacturing, tech	2.9	16.7	Counter & rental clerks	1.3	22.6
Customer service representatives	2.9	19.5	Secretaries, except legal, medical, & executive	1.3	-1.7
General & operations managers	2.9	15.5	Packers & packagers, hand	1.1	16.8
Bookkeeping, accounting, & auditing clerks	2.8	5.1	Team assemblers	1.0	16.8
First-line supervisors/managers of non-retail sales work	2.7	7.9	Sales managers	1.0	17.5

Source: Industry-Occupation Matrix, Bureau of Labor Statistics. These data are reported based on 4-digit NAICS categories but have been matched to corresponding 6-digit NAICS industry codes. The change reported for each occupation to the year 2014 is a percent of growth or decline as estimated by the Bureau of Labor Statistics. The abbreviation nec stands for 'not elsewhere classified.'

LOCATION BY STATE AND REGIONAL CONCENTRATION

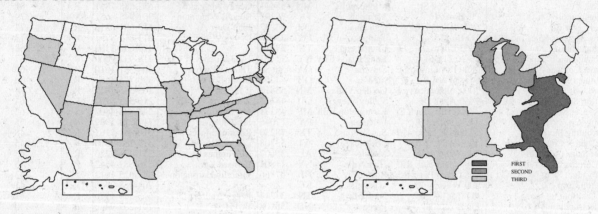

INDUSTRY DATA BY STATE

State	Establishments Total (number)	% of U.S.	Employment Total (number)	% of U.S.	Per Estab.	Payroll Total ($ mil.)	Per Empl. ($)	Sales Total ($ mil.)	% of U.S.	Per Estab. ($)
Texas	472	8.6	5,144	9.4	11	234.2	45,537	3,503.7	14.7	7,423,089
California	391	7.1	3,777	6.9	10	191.7	50,757	1,707.4	7.2	4,366,872
Florida	403	7.3	3,372	6.1	8	146.1	43,334	1,432.0	6.0	3,553,385
Tennessee	152	2.8	4,042	7.4	27	169.0	41,809	1,422.3	6.0	9,357,086
New York	281	5.1	2,670	4.9	10	131.3	49,182	1,002.2	4.2	3,566,520
Illinois	241	4.4	2,311	4.2	10	123.4	53,402	923.9	3.9	3,833,436
Ohio	240	4.4	2,440	4.4	10	97.6	40,009	822.5	3.5	3,427,192
Arkansas	61	1.1	610	1.1	10	24.2	39,603	821.7	3.5	13,470,869
Michigan	189	3.4	1,953	3.6	10	96.3	49,291	787.5	3.3	4,166,481
North Carolina	231	4.2	1,966	3.6	9	78.9	40,153	780.7	3.3	3,379,831
Pennsylvania	223	4.1	1,957	3.6	9	87.5	44,700	731.0	3.1	3,277,960
Missouri	122	2.2	1,407	2.6	12	74.9	53,245	709.5	3.0	5,815,918
Maryland	120	2.2	1,157	2.1	10	53.7	46,395	544.5	2.3	4,537,700
Indiana	126	2.3	1,557	2.8	12	64.0	41,087	538.8	2.3	4,276,222
Virginia	156	2.8	1,331	2.4	9	51.5	38,711	515.7	2.2	3,305,750
Arizona	94	1.7	1,168	2.1	12	51.5	44,097	475.3	2.0	5,055,894
Colorado	75	1.4	804	1.5	11	38.6	47,953	466.0	2.0	6,213,880
Wisconsin	99	1.8	1,121	2.0	11	52.9	47,210	426.9	1.8	4,312,485
Kentucky	87	1.6	1,045	1.9	12	37.9	36,223	364.0	1.5	4,184,092
Oregon	50	0.9	562	1.0	11	23.9	42,521	354.7	1.5	7,094,080
Washington	92	1.7	980	1.8	11	43.2	44,061	336.1	1.4	3,652,935
South Carolina	117	2.1	874	1.6	7	31.6	36,168	321.0	1.3	2,743,709
Louisiana	106	1.9	895	1.6	8	30.2	33,696	309.8	1.3	2,922,226
Connecticut	67	1.2	568	1.0	8	32.3	56,907	251.4	1.1	3,752,015
Nevada	46	0.8	430	0.8	9	18.8	43,723	172.0	0.7	3,739,891
Utah	48	0.9	492	0.9	10	21.5	43,687	170.7	0.7	3,557,167
Kansas	47	0.9	541	1.0	12	25.2	46,614	163.3	0.7	3,474,085
Nebraska	43	0.8	407	0.7	9	16.1	39,587	132.3	0.6	3,075,837
Delaware	23	0.4	270	0.5	12	9.3	34,444	95.5	0.4	4,151,391
Mississippi	50	0.9	278	0.5	6	8.5	30,529	93.2	0.4	1,864,180
West Virginia	43	0.8	253	0.5	6	7.9	31,364	92.3	0.4	2,147,140

Continued on next page.

INDUSTRY DATA BY STATE - Continued

State	Establishments Total (number)	% of U.S.	Employment Total (number)	% of U.S.	Per Estab.	Payroll Total ($ mil.)	Per Empl. ($)	Sales Total ($ mil.)	% of U.S.	Per Estab. ($)
Idaho	30	0.5	180	0.3	6	6.7	37,433	63.9	0.3	2,130,667
New Mexico	25	0.5	127	0.2	5	6.3	49,654	60.7	0.3	2,429,800
Montana	20	0.4	156	0.3	8	6.3	40,513	50.7	0.2	2,532,600
Hawaii	16	0.3	103	0.2	6	5.0	48,155	43.4	0.2	2,712,125
South Dakota	15	0.3	121	0.2	8	5.1	42,041	41.5	0.2	2,763,733
Maine	24	0.4	117	0.2	5	5.4	45,983	40.2	0.2	1,676,000
Vermont	8	0.1	49	0.1	6	1.8	36,061	20.6	0.1	2,579,500
Alaska	7	0.1	40	0.1	6	1.9	47,150	19.3	0.1	2,761,000
Wyoming	4	0.1	15	-	4	0.5	32,667	4.6	-	1,142,750
Georgia	218	4.0	1000-2499	-	-	(D)	-	(D)	-	-
New Jersey	157	2.9	1000-2499	-	-	(D)	-	(D)	-	-
Alabama	108	2.0	500-999	-	-	(D)	-	(D)	-	-
Massachusetts	101	1.8	1000-2499	-	-	(D)	-	(D)	-	-
Minnesota	79	1.4	500-999	-	-	(D)	-	(D)	-	-
Oklahoma	79	1.4	250-499	-	-	(D)	-	(D)	-	-
Iowa	54	1.0	250-499	-	-	(D)	-	(D)	-	-
New Hampshire	25	0.5	100-249	-	-	(D)	-	(D)	-	-
Rhode Island	16	0.3	20-99	-	-	(D)	-	(D)	-	-
North Dakota	10	0.2	20-99	-	-	(D)	-	(D)	-	-
D.C.	1	-	0-19	-	-	(D)	-	(D)	-	-

Source: 2002 Economic Census. The states are in descending order of sales or establishments (if sales data are missing for the majority). The symbol (D) appears when data are withheld to prevent disclosure of competitive information. States marked with (D) are sorted by number of establishments. A dash (-) indicates that the data element cannot be calculated. Shaded states on the state map indicate those states which have proportionately greater representation in the industry than would be indicated by the states population; the ratio is based on total sales or number of establishments. Shaded regions indicate where the industry is regionally most concentrated.

NAICS 423740 - REFRIGERATION EQUIPMENT AND SUPPLIES MERCHANT WHOLESALERS*

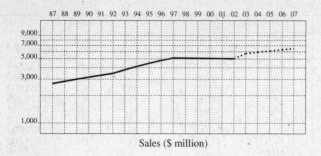

Sales ($ million)

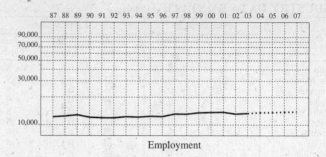

Employment

GENERAL STATISTICS

Year	Establishments (number)	Employment (number)	Payroll ($ million)	Sales ($ million)	Employees per Establishment (number)	Sales per Establishment ($)	Payroll per Employee ($)
1987	1,513	12,218	303.3	2,683.6	8.1	1,773,694.6	24,824.0
1988	1,444	12,446	340.9	2,840.8 e	8.6	1,967,313.0	27,390.3
1989	1,365	12,852	348.3	2,998.0 e	9.4	2,196,337.0	27,100.8
1990	1,340	12,097	353.2	3,155.3 e	9.0	2,354,701.5	29,197.3
1991	1,372	11,948	355.0	3,312.5 e	8.7	2,414,358.6	29,712.1
1992	1,455	11,928	366.9	3,469.7	8.2	2,384,673.5	30,759.6
1993	1,430	12,273	385.2	3,802.8 e	8.6	2,659,300.7	31,386.0
1994	1,421	12,152	417.7	4,135.9 e	8.6	2,910,555.9	34,372.9
1995	1,404	12,407	439.4	4,469.1 e	8.8	3,183,119.7	35,415.5
1996	1,421 e	12,320 e	438.9 e	4,802.2 e	8.7 e	3,379,451.1 e	35,625.0 e
1997	1,572	13,131	517.2	5,135.3	8.4	3,266,730.3	39,387.7
1998	1,540	13,091	526.3	5,116.6 e	8.5	3,322,467.5	40,203.2
1999	1,546	13,566	561.0	5,097.9 e	8.8	3,297,477.4	41,353.4
2000	1,501	13,670	583.4	5,079.2 e	9.1	3,383,877.4	42,674.3
2001	1,445	13,742	612.4	5,060.5 e	9.5	3,502,076.1	44,563.3
2002	1,386	13,159	553.0	5,041.8	9.5	3,637,662.3	42,024.5
2003	1,380	13,330	577.5	5,748.7 p	9.7	3,885,355.1 p	43,321.7
2004	1,466 p	13,584 p	628.2 p	5,938.3 p	9.3 p	4,006,913.1 p	46,608.0 p
2005	1,469 p	13,680 p	647.8 p	6,127.8 p	9.3 p	4,128,471.1 p	47,869.6 p
2006	1,472 p	13,775 p	667.5 p	6,317.4 p	9.4 p	4,250,029.0 p	49,131.2 p
2007	1,474 p	13,871 p	687.1 p	6,506.9 p	9.4 p	4,371,587.0 p	50,392.8 p

Sources: Economic Census of the United States, 1987, 1992, 1997, and 2002. Establishment counts, employment, and payroll are from *County Business Patterns* for non-Census years. Values followed by a 'p' are projections by the editors. Sales data for non-Census years are extrapolations, marked by 'e'. Data are the most recent available at this level of detail.

INDICES OF CHANGE

Year	Establishments (number)	Employment (number)	Payroll ($ million)	Sales ($ million)	Employees per Establishment (number)	Sales per Establishment ($)	Payroll per Employee ($)
1987	109.2	92.8	54.8	53.2	85.3	48.8	59.1
1992	105.0	90.6	66.3	68.8	86.3	65.6	73.2
1993	103.2	93.3	69.7	75.4 e	90.5	73.1	74.7
1994	102.5	92.3	75.5	82.0 e	90.5	80.0	81.8
1995	101.3	94.3	79.5	88.6 e	92.6	87.5	84.3
1996	102.5 e	93.6 e	79.4 e	95.2 e	91.6 e	92.9 e	84.8 e
1997	113.4	99.8	93.5	101.9	88.4	89.8	93.7
1998	111.1	99.5	95.2	101.5 e	89.5	91.3	95.7
1999	111.5	103.1	101.4	101.1 e	92.6	90.6	98.4
2000	108.3	103.9	105.5	100.7 e	95.8	93.0	101.5
2001	104.3	104.4	110.7	100.4 e	100.0	96.3	106.0
2002	100.0	100.0	100.0	100.0	100.0	100.0	100.0
2003	99.6	101.3	104.4	114.0 p	101.7	106.8 p	103.1
2004	105.8 p	103.2 p	113.6 p	117.8 p	97.8 p	110.2 p	110.9 p
2005	106.0 p	104.0 p	117.2 p	121.5 p	98.4 p	113.5 p	113.9 p
2006	106.2 p	104.7 p	120.7 p	125.3 p	98.9 p	116.8 p	116.9 p
2007	106.4 p	105.4 p	124.2 p	129.1 p	99.4 p	120.2 p	119.9 p

Sources: Same as General Statistics. The values shown reflect change from the base year, 2002. Values above 100 mean greater than 2002, values below 100 mean less than 2002, and a value of 100 in the 1987-2001 or 2003-2007 period means same as 2002. Values followed by a 'p' are projections by the editors; 'e' stands for extrapolation. Data are the most recent available at this level of detail.

SELECTED RATIOS

For 2002	Avg. of All Wholesale	Analyzed Industry	Index	For 2002	Avg. of All Wholesale	Analyzed Industry	Index
Employees per Establishment	15	9	64	Sales per Employee	791,325	383,145	48
Payroll per Establishment	626,122	398,990	64	Sales per Establishment	12,012,387	3,637,662	30
Payroll per Employee	41,161	42,024	102	Expenses per Establishment	na	na	na

Sources: Same as General Statistics. The 'Average of All' column, Wholesale or Retail, represents the everage of the sector reported for the most recent supplrte year available. The Index shows the relationship between the Average and the Analyzed Industry. For example, 100 means that they are equal; 500 that the Analyzed Industry is five times the average; 50 means that the Analyzed Industry is half the national average. The abbreviation 'na' is used to show that data are 'not available'.

*Equivalent to SIC 5078.

LEADING COMPANIES   Number shown: **55**   Total sales ($ mil): **2,094**   Total employment (000): **6.1**

Company Name	Address				CEO Name	Phone	Co. Type	Sales ($ mil)	Empl. (000)
Noland Co.	80 29th St	Newport News	VA	23607	Lloyd U. Noland III	757-928-9000	P	548	1.3
R.E. Michel Company Inc.	1 R E Michel Dr	Glen Burnie	MD	21060	JWH Michel	410-760-4000	R	186*	1.0
ACR Group Inc.	3200 Wilcrest Dr	Houston	TX	77042		713-780-8532	P	174	0.4
Refrigeration Supplies Distributor	26021 Atlantic	Lake Forest	CA	92630	Brian Martin	949-380-7878	R	111*	0.4
ACR Supply Inc.	8798 Westpark Dr	Houston	TX	77063	Danny Fisher	713-787-6666	S	88*	0.2
Temperature Equipment Corp.	17725 Volbrecht Rd	Lansing	IL	60438	FA Mungo	708-418-0900	R	88*	0.2
Next Day Gormet & Superior	510 W County Rd D	St. Paul	MN	55112	Robert M Kurek	651-636-1110	R	80*	0.3
ABCO Refrigeration Supply Corp.	49-70 31st St	Long Island City	NY	11101	JA Gottlieb	718-937-9000	R	67*	0.2
Refrigeration Sales Corp.	9450 Allen Dr	Valley View	OH	44125	Warren W Farr Jr	216-525-8100	R	64*	0.1
Young Supply Co.	888 W Baltimore	Detroit	MI	48202	Ronald Vallan	313-875-3280	R	49*	0.1
W.A. Roosevelt Co.	PO Box 1208	La Crosse	WI	54602	Stephen W Reiman	608-781-2000	R	39*	0.1
Thermal Supply Inc.	717 S Lander St	Seattle	WA	98134	Bob Monroe	206-624-4590	R	37*	0.1
Bornquist Inc.	7050 N Lehigh Ave	Chicago	IL	60646	Harry Hultgren	773-774-2800	R	29*	<0.1
Acme Refrigeration of Baton	11844 S Choctaw Dr	Baton Rouge	LA	70815	AE Kaiser Ill	225-273-1740	R	27*	0.1
Resnick Supermarket Equipment	PO Box Q	Mountain Dale	NY	12763	William Resnick	845-434-8200	R	25*	<0.1
Transport Refrigeration Sales	500 Daniel Payne Dr	Birmingham	AL	35214	K Macdonald	205-328-7278	R	21*	<0.1
Southern Refrigeration Corp.	2026 Salem Ave	Roanoke	VA	24016	John S Lang Jr	540-342-3493	R	20*	<0.1
Aquaport USA	414 Plz Dr Ste 302	Westmont	IL	60559	James Trainor	630-734-0633	R	19*	<0.1
Cannon Company Inc.	PO Box 969	Grove City	OH	43123	William Walker	614-875-6390	R	19*	<0.1
SWH Supply Co.	242 E Main St	Louisville	KY	40202	Robert Anderson	502-589-9287	R	19*	<0.1
Refrigeration & Electric Supply	1222 Spring St	Little Rock	AR	72202	Carl H Miller Jr	501-374-6373	R	17*	<0.1
Mid-Way Supply Inc.	2502 Deborah Ave	Zion	IL	60099	Kenneth Sisson	847-872-5481	R	16*	<0.1
Shelby-Skipwith Inc.	PO Box 181112	Memphis	TN	38181	Jon Wallace	901-948-4481	R	16*	<0.1
Frank's Quality Services Inc.	1784 Two Notch Rd	Lexington	SC	29073	Frank Troglauer	803-957-4946	R	16*	<0.1
Hudson Technologies Inc.	275 N Middletown	Pearl River	NY	10965	Brian F Coleman	845-735-6000	P	15	<0.1
Carrier Transcold of Maine	432 Warren Ave	Portland	ME	04103	Jeffery Manning	207-797-9225	R	15*	<0.1
Ice Cold Products	100 Frontier Way	Bensenville	IL	60106	Robert Wartan	630-860-0375	R	15*	<0.1
Richard S Hatfield Inc.	1175 N Knollwood	Anaheim	CA	92801	Richard Hatfield	714-236-3600	R	15*	<0.1
Wittichen Supply Co.	1600 3rd Ave S	Birmingham	AL	35233	David Henderson	205-251-8500	R	15*	<0.1
Luce Schwab and Kase Inc.	9 Gloria Ln	Fairfield	NJ	07004	George Luce	973-227-4840	R	13*	<0.1
Alamo Service Company Inc.	1450 N Flores St	San Antonio	TX	78212	John Stafford	210-227-7571	R	12*	<0.1
Benedict Refrigeration Service Inc.	PO Box 3008	Eau Claire	WI	54702	Timothy Benedict	715-834-3191	R	12*	<0.1
Beverage Control Inc.	5060 N Ryl Atlanta	Tucker	GA	30084	James Young	770-939-9637	R	12*	<0.1
Key Mechanical of Washington	7888 Marathon	Livermore	CA	94550		925-294-8111	R	12*	<0.1
Case Parts Co.	877 Monterey Pass	Monterey Park	CA	91754		323-729-6000	R	12*	<0.1
Totaline of Florida Inc.	9093 Phillips Hwy	Jacksonville	FL	32256		904-783-2441	S	11*	<0.1
Rite Temperature Associates Inc.	101 S Lackawanna	Dalton	PA	18414	David Botscheller	570-563-2923	R	11*	<0.1
Fenco Supply Company Inc.	PO Box 3906	Knoxville	TN	37927	William Fennell	865-637-1821	R	10*	<0.1
Northeast Distributors Inc.	210 Essex St, Ste 3	Whitman	MA	02382	Kenneth Peterson	781-447-0073	R	10*	<0.1
Thermo King of Houston L.L.P.	772 McCarty St	Houston	TX	77029	Kirk Robison	713-671-2700	R	10*	<0.1
Ventana Distributing Company	2825 E Chambers St	Phoenix	AZ	85040	Donald Metzger	602-268-3386	R	10*	<0.1
Brock-McVey Co.	PO Box 55487	Lexington	KY	40555	John M McDonald IV	859-255-1412	S	10*	0.1
Allegheny Refrigeration Service	1228 Brighton Rd	Pittsburgh	PA	15233		412-321-6626	R	10*	<0.1
Carrier Transicold of Utah	PO Box 25415	Salt Lake City	UT	84125	Greg Jenson	801-736-5209	R	10*	<0.1
Chernoff Sales Inc.	3308 Park Central N	Pompano Beach	FL	33064	Joe Andisman	954-972-1414	R	10*	<0.1
Meier Supply Company Inc.	123 Brown St	Johnson City	NY	13790	Frank Meier	607-797-7700	R	10*	<0.1
Benham Enterprises Inc.	PO Box 44188	Tucson	AZ	85733	Earl Benham	520-622-4560	R	9*	<0.1
Dervey Distributing Company Inc.	2580 S Tejon St	Englewood	CO	80110	Don Davis	303-825-0171	R	9*	<0.1
Automatic Ice Machine Inc.	501 E 2nd St	Odessa	TX	79761	A Lewallen	432-337-1681	R	8*	<0.1
HMC Shipping	13138 S Bethel Ave	Kingsburg	CA	93631	Harold McClarty	559-897-4149	R	8*	<0.1
Gardner and Benoit Inc.	PO Box 7246	Charlotte	NC	28241	Karlo Waataja	704-504-1151	R	7*	<0.1
Hockenberg Equipment Co.	2821 Beaver Ave	Des Moines	IA	50310	Don Routh	515-288-0407	R	7*	<0.1
Fetzer Company-Restaurateurs	209 E Main St	Louisville	KY	40202		502-583-2744	R	6*	<0.1
United States Electric Co.	301 N 1st St	Springfield	IL	62702	Paul Branham	217-522-3347	R	6*	<0.1
City Ice Co.	13600 Permilla	Chester	VA	23836	Mark Resnick	804-796-9423	R	1*	<0.1

Source: Ward's Business Directory of U.S. Private and Public Companies, Volumes 1 and 2, 2005. The company type code used is as follows: P - Public, R - Private, S - Subsidiary, D - Division, J - Joint Venture, A - Affiliate, G - Group. Sales are in millions of dollars, employees are in thousands. An asterisk (*) indicates an estimated sales volume. The symbol < stands for 'less than'. Company names and addresses are truncated, in some cases, to fit into the available space.

OCCUPATIONS EMPLOYED BY HARDWARE, & PLUMBING & HEATING EQUIPMENT & SUPPLIES

Occupation	% of Total 2004	Change to 2014	Occupation	% of Total 2004	Change to 2014
Sales reps, wholesale & manufacturing, exc tech	18.0	16.8	Parts salespersons	2.1	-6.6
Laborers & freight, stock, & material movers, hand	7.0	5.1	Order clerks	1.9	-24.1
Stock clerks & order fillers	5.1	-10.6	Retail salespersons	1.7	16.7
Truck drivers, light or delivery services	4.5	16.8	Truck drivers, heavy & tractor-trailer	1.6	16.7
Shipping, receiving, & traffic clerks	4.4	5.7	First-line supervisors/managers of office workers	1.5	5.8
Heating, air conditioning, & refrigeration mechanics	3.5	16.8	Industrial truck & tractor operators	1.4	16.7
Office clerks, general	3.2	3.9	Wholesale & retail buyers, except farm products	1.4	10.4
Sales reps, wholesale & manufacturing, tech	2.9	16.7	Counter & rental clerks	1.3	22.6
Customer service representatives	2.9	19.5	Secretaries, except legal, medical, & executive	1.3	-1.7
General & operations managers	2.9	15.5	Packers & packagers, hand	1.1	16.8
Bookkeeping, accounting, & auditing clerks	2.8	5.1	Team assemblers	1.0	16.8
First-line supervisors/managers of non-retail sales work	2.7	7.9	Sales managers	1.0	17.5

Source: Industry-Occupation Matrix, Bureau of Labor Statistics. These data are reported based on 4-digit NAICS categories but have been matched to corresponding 6-digit NAICS industry codes. The change reported for each occupation to the year 2014 is a percent of growth or decline as estimated by the Bureau of Labor Statistics. The abbreviation nec stands for 'not elsewhere classified.'

LOCATION BY STATE AND REGIONAL CONCENTRATION

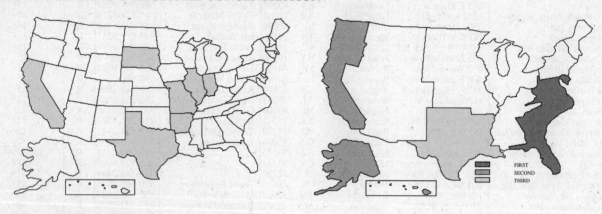

FIRST
SECOND
THIRD

INDUSTRY DATA BY STATE

State	Establishments Total (number)	% of U.S.	Employment Total (number)	% of U.S.	Per Estab.	Payroll Total ($ mil.)	Per Empl. ($)	Sales Total ($ mil.)	% of U.S.	Per Estab. ($)
California	188	13.5	1,798	13.6	10	81.6	45,365	715.6	14.1	3,806,372
Missouri	40	2.9	488	3.7	12	28.0	57,385	464.1	9.1	11,601,525
Illinois	41	2.9	595	4.5	15	28.3	47,560	376.2	7.4	9,176,171
Texas	134	9.6	1,273	9.7	10	53.5	42,006	372.6	7.3	2,780,664
Florida	108	7.8	818	6.2	8	30.7	37,494	245.4	4.8	2,272,083
Indiana	21	1.5	236	1.8	11	10.2	43,203	197.1	3.9	9,386,190
Pennsylvania	67	4.8	596	4.5	9	24.5	41,107	192.7	3.8	2,875,463
North Carolina	38	2.7	326	2.5	9	13.3	40,933	111.4	2.2	2,930,895
Ohio	37	2.7	336	2.6	9	13.4	39,842	103.7	2.0	2,803,270
Wisconsin	17	1.2	259	2.0	15	14.1	54,394	93.7	1.8	5,514,412
Washington	30	2.2	339	2.6	11	13.7	40,404	89.9	1.8	2,995,833
Virginia	25	1.8	255	1.9	10	9.1	35,871	76.4	1.5	3,056,800
Colorado	26	1.9	254	1.9	10	10.1	39,685	59.4	1.2	2,285,077
Arkansas	21	1.5	229	1.7	11	9.8	42,921	53.9	1.1	2,568,429
South Carolina	18	1.3	151	1.1	8	5.5	36,649	53.8	1.1	2,989,611
Michigan	30	2.2	198	1.5	7	8.6	43,444	46.6	0.9	1,554,567
Utah	14	1.0	137	1.0	10	5.1	37,504	34.5	0.7	2,466,571
South Dakota	4	0.3	85	0.6	21	2.7	31,965	27.1	0.5	6,773,000
Connecticut	11	0.8	103	0.8	9	3.9	37,816	23.8	0.5	2,160,727
Oregon	15	1.1	72	0.5	5	2.6	36,236	19.4	0.4	1,296,467
Nevada	7	0.5	48	0.4	7	1.9	38,771	17.8	0.3	2,544,714
Mississippi	13	0.9	59	0.4	5	1.8	30,797	16.9	0.3	1,302,846
Hawaii	8	0.6	42	0.3	5	2.1	49,000	15.3	0.3	1,910,000
Idaho	7	0.5	28	0.2	4	1.0	34,500	8.6	0.2	1,233,000
New Mexico	5	0.4	27	0.2	5	0.9	32,148	8.5	0.2	1,708,200
Maine	5	0.4	19	0.1	4	0.6	31,368	6.2	0.1	1,243,200
Vermont	5	0.4	12	0.1	2	0.4	36,583	4.8	0.1	956,400
New York	73	5.3	500-999	-	-	(D)	-	(D)	-	-
New Jersey	38	2.7	250-499	-	-	(D)	-	(D)	-	-
Georgia	37	2.7	100-249	-	-	(D)	-	(D)	-	-
Arizona	33	2.4	250-499	-	-	(D)	-	(D)	-	-

Continued on next page.

INDUSTRY DATA BY STATE - Continued

State	Establishments		Employment			Payroll		Sales		
	Total (number)	% of U.S.	Total (number)	% of U.S.	Per Estab.	Total ($ mil.)	Per Empl. ($)	Total ($ mil.)	% of U.S.	Per Estab. ($)
Louisiana	32	2.3	100-249	-	-	(D)	-	(D)	-	-
Tennessee	30	2.2	250-499	-	-	(D)	-	(D)	-	-
Maryland	27	1.9	250-499	-	-	(D)	-	(D)	-	-
Massachusetts	26	1.9	100-249	-	-	(D)	-	(D)	-	-
Alabama	22	1.6	100-249	-	-	(D)	-	(D)	-	-
Minnesota	21	1.5	100-249	-	-	(D)	-	(D)	-	-
Kentucky	19	1.4	100-249	-	-	(D)	-	(D)	-	-
Oklahoma	19	1.4	100-249	-	-	(D)	-	(D)	-	-
Kansas	16	1.2	100-249	-	-	(D)	-	(D)	-	-
Iowa	14	1.0	250-499	-	-	(D)	-	(D)	-	-
Nebraska	12	0.9	100-249	-	-	(D)	-	(D)	-	-
Rhode Island	7	0.5	20-99	-	-	(D)	-	(D)	-	-
New Hampshire	6	0.4	20-99	-	-	(D)	-	(D)	-	-
West Virginia	6	0.4	20-99	-	-	(D)	-	(D)	-	-
North Dakota	5	0.4	20-99	-	-	(D)	-	(D)	-	-
Alaska	4	0.3	20-99	-	-	(D)	-	(D)	-	-
Montana	4	0.3	20-99	-	-	(D)	-	(D)	-	-
Delaware	3	0.2	0-19	-	-	(D)	-	(D)	-	-
D.C.	1	0.1	0-19	-	-	(D)	-	(D)	-	-

Source: 2002 *Economic Census*. The states are in descending order of sales or establishments (if sales data are missing for the majority). The symbol (D) appears when data are withheld to prevent disclosure of competitive information. States marked with (D) are sorted by number of establishments. A dash (-) indicates that the data element cannot be calculated. Shaded *states* on the state map indicate those states which have proportionately greater representation in the industry than would be indicated by the states population; the ratio is based on total sales or number of establishments. Shaded *regions* indicate where the industry is regionally most concentrated.

NAICS 423810 - CONSTRUCTION AND MINING (EXCEPT OIL WELL) MACHINERY AND EQUIPMENT MERCHANT WHOLESALERS*

Sales ($ million)

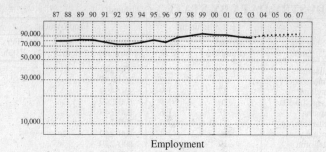

Employment

GENERAL STATISTICS

Year	Establishments (number)	Employment (number)	Payroll ($ million)	Sales ($ million)	Employees per Establishment (number)	Sales per Establishment ($)	Payroll per Employee ($)
1987	4,983	79,720	2,208.6	23,971.0	16.0	4,810,555.9	27,704.5
1988	4,763	80,095	2,391.8	24,400.9 e	16.8	5,123,010.7	29,862.0
1989	4,589	82,280	2,524.7	24,830.7 e	17.9	5,410,917.4	30,684.2
1990	4,644	81,947	2,584.9	25,260.5 e	17.6	5,439,384.2	31,543.6
1991	4,624	77,663	2,431.8	25,690.3 e	16.8	5,555,860.7	31,312.2
1992	5,157	73,518	2,388.7	26,120.2	14.3	5,064,999.0	32,491.4
1993	5,021	73,578	2,548.7	29,841.4 e	14.7	5,943,318.1	34,639.4
1994	4,970	77,135	2,844.2	33,562.5 e	15.5	6,753,018.1	36,873.0
1995	4,987	81,881	3,162.9	37,283.7 e	16.4	7,476,178.1	38,628.0
1996	4,953 e	77,492 e	3,003.9 e	41,004.8 e	15.6 e	8,278,780.5 e	38,764.0 e
1997	5,321	87,611	3,604.6	44,726.0	16.5	8,405,562.9	41,143.2
1998	5,267	91,431	3,945.8	46,327.9 e	17.4	8,795,880.0	43,156.0
1999	5,214	95,928	4,274.3	47,929.8 e	18.4	9,192,520.1	44,557.4
2000	5,152	93,450	4,285.0	49,531.7 e	18.1	9,614,072.2	45,853.9
2001	5,050	93,168	4,304.2	51,133.6 e	18.4	10,125,465.3	46,198.1
2002	5,026	89,111	4,005.3	52,735.5	17.7	10,492,538.8	44,947.3
2003	4,809	86,834	4,180.4	55,639.8 p	18.1	10,747,467.4 p	48,141.9
2004	5,171 p	92,478 p	4,552.9 p	57,889.0 p	17.9 p	11,155,389.6 p	49,800.1 p
2005	5,194 p	93,454 p	4,701.3 p	60,138.1 p	18.0 p	11,563,311.8 p	51,108.0 p
2006	5,216 p	94,429 p	4,849.8 p	62,387.3 p	18.1 p	11,971,233.9 p	52,415.8 p
2007	5,238 p	95,405 p	4,998.2 p	64,636.4 p	18.2 p	12,379,156.1 p	53,723.7 p

Sources: Economic Census of the United States, 1987, 1992, 1997, and 2002. Establishment counts, employment, and payroll are from *County Business Patterns* for non-Census years. Values followed by a 'p' are projections by the editors. Sales data for non-Census years are extrapolations, marked by 'e'. Data are the most recent available at this level of detail.

INDICES OF CHANGE

Year	Establishments (number)	Employment (number)	Payroll ($ million)	Sales ($ million)	Employees per Establishment (number)	Sales per Establishment ($)	Payroll per Employee ($)
1987	99.1	89.5	55.1	45.5	90.4	45.8	61.6
1992	102.6	82.5	59.6	49.5	80.8	48.3	72.3
1993	99.9	82.6	63.6	56.6 e	83.1	56.6	77.1
1994	98.9	86.6	71.0	63.6 e	87.6	64.4	82.0
1995	99.2	91.9	79.0	70.7 e	92.7	71.3	85.9
1996	98.5 e	87.0 e	75.0 e	77.8 e	88.1 e	78.9 e	86.2 e
1997	105.9	98.3	90.0	84.8	93.2	80.1	91.5
1998	104.8	102.6	98.5	87.8 e	98.3	83.8	96.0
1999	103.7	107.7	106.7	90.9 e	104.0	87.6	99.1
2000	102.5	104.9	107.0	93.9 e	102.3	91.6	102.0
2001	100.5	104.6	107.5	97.0 e	104.0	96.5	102.8
2002	100.0	100.0	100.0	100.0	100.0	100.0	100.0
2003	95.7	97.4	104.4	105.5 p	102.0	102.4 p	107.1
2004	102.9 p	103.8 p	113.7 p	109.8 p	101.0 p	106.3 p	110.8 p
2005	103.3 p	104.9 p	117.4 p	114.0 p	101.7 p	110.2 p	113.7 p
2006	103.8 p	106.0 p	121.1 p	118.3 p	102.4 p	114.1 p	116.6 p
2007	104.2 p	107.1 p	124.8 p	122.6 p	103.0 p	118.0 p	119.5 p

Sources: Same as General Statistics. The values shown reflect change from the base year, 2002. Values above 100 mean greater than 2002, values below 100 mean less than 2002, and a value of 100 in the 1987-2001 or 2003-2007 period means same as 2002. Values followed by a 'p' are projections by the editors; 'e' stands for extrapolation. Data are the most recent available at this level of detail.

SELECTED RATIOS

For 2002	Avg. of All Wholesale	Analyzed Industry	Index	For 2002	Avg. of All Wholesale	Analyzed Industry	Index
Employees per Establishment	15	18	119	Sales per Employee	791,325	591,796	75
Payroll per Establishment	626,122	796,916	127	Sales per Establishment	12,012,387	10,492,539	87
Payroll per Employee	41,161	44,947	109	Expenses per Establishment	na	na	na

Sources: Same as General Statistics. The 'Average of All' column, Wholesale or Retail, represents the average of the sector reported for the most recent complete year available. The Index shows the relationship between the Average and the Analyzed Industry. For example, 100 means that they are equal; 500 that the Analyzed Industry is five times the average; 50 means that the Analyzed Industry is half the national average. The abbreviation 'na' is used to show that data are 'not available'.

*Equivalent to SIC 5082.

LEADING COMPANIES   Number shown: **75**   Total sales ($ mil): **11,712**   Total employment (000): **26.3**

Company Name	Address				CEO Name	Phone	Co. Type	Sales ($ mil)	Empl. (000)
Applied Industrial Technologies	PO Box 6925	Cleveland	OH	44101	David L. Pugh	216-426-4000	P	1,517	4.3
McJunkin Corp.	PO Box 513	Charleston	WV	25322	H Barnard Wehrle III	304-348-5211	R	847*	1.6
Holt Cat	PO Box 207916	San Antonio	TX	78220	Peter Holt	210-648-1111	R	648*	1.8
Empire Southwest L.L.C.	PO Box 2985	Phoenix	AZ	85062	Jeff Whiteman	480-633-4300	R	553*	1.0
RDO Equipment Co.	PO Box 7160	Fargo	ND	58103	Ronald D Offutt	701-239-8735	R	534*	1.2
Atlas Lift Truck Rentals	5050 River Rd	Schiller Park	IL	60176	Howard Bernstein	847-678-3450	R	486*	0.2
Scott Truck and Tractor Inc.	PO Box 4948	Monroe	LA	71211	Scott Cumming	318-387-4160	R	450*	1.0
Whayne Supply Co.	PO Box 35900	Louisville	KY	40232	J Pullen	502-774-4441	R	415*	0.5
H and E Equipment Services	11100 Mead Rd	Baton Rouge	LA	70816	John Engquist	225-298-5200	R	414	1.3
Linder Industrial Machinery Co.	PO Box 4589	Plant City	FL	33563	Jeffrey Cox	813-754-2727	R	255*	0.1
Komatsu Equipment Co.	2350 W 1500 S	Salt Lake City	UT	84104	Terry Sheehan	801-972-3660	R	254*	0.1
Peterson Tractor Co.	PO Box 5258	San Leandro	CA	94577	William E Doyle Jr	510-357-6200	R	250*	0.4
Patten Industries Inc.	635 W Lake St	Elmhurst	IL	60126	Byron C Patten Jr	630-279-4400	R	223*	0.6
Stowers Machinery Corp.	PO Box 14802	Knoxville	TN	37914	Harry W Stowers Jr	865-546-1414	R	223*	0.4
H.O. Penn Machinery Inc.	122 Noxon Rd	Poughkeepsie	NY	12603	CE Thomas Cleveland	845-452-1200	R	222*	0.4
Carolina Tractor	PO Box 1095	Charlotte	NC	28201	Russ Fleming	704-596-6700	R	219*	0.3
Arnold Machinery Co.	6024 W Southern	Laveen	AZ	85339	Russ Fleming	602-237-3755	D	205*	0.4
John Fabick Tractor Co.	1 Fabick Dr	Fenton	MO	63026	Doug Fabick	636-343-5900	R	205*	0.6
Beckwith Machinery Company	4565 William Penn	Murrysville	PA	15668	G Beckwith	724-327-1300	R	152*	0.2
Richard O'Brien Co's Inc.	640 W Tennessee	Denver	CO	80223	Richard O'Brien	303-778-8771	R	141*	0.3
Anderson Equipment Co.	PO Box 339	Bridgeville	PA	15017	Judy Anderson	412-343-2300	R	130*	0.4
Cecil I Walker Machinery Co.	PO Box 2427	Charleston	WV	25329	D Walker	304-949-6400	R	129*	0.4
Dom-Ex Inc.	109 Grant St	Hibbing	MN	55746		218-262-6116	R	127*	<0.1
Cleveland Brothers Equipment	5300 Paxton St	Harrisburg	PA	17111	Jay W Cleveland Jr	717-564-2121	R	126*	0.5
Puckett Machinery Co.	PO Box 3170	Jackson	MS	39207	Richard Puckett	601-969-6000	R	124*	0.3
Western Power & Equipment	6407B NE 117th	Vancouver	WA	98662	C Dean McLain	360-253-2346	P	116	0.2
Dean Machinery Co.	1201 W 31st St	Kansas City	MO	64108	Curt Stokes	816-753-5300	R	114*	0.3
Road Machinery Co.	PO Box 4425	Phoenix	AZ	85030	Mike Boze	602-252-7121	R	112*	0.2
Arnold Machinery Co.	PO Box 30020	Salt Lake City	UT	84130	Kayden Bell	801-972-4000	R	110*	0.3
J and M Service Inc.	11532 Anabel Ave	Garden Grove	CA	92843	Mark Sieve	714-530-3325	R	94*	0.1
Briggs Equipment Inc.	PO Box 20807	Greensboro	NC	27420	Dave Bratton	336-292-6921	R	92*	0.3
Dealers Truck Equipment Inc.	PO Box 31435	Shreveport	LA	71108	Raymond Kayser	318-635-7567	R	92*	0.1
FABCO Equipment Inc.	11200 Silver Sprg	Milwaukee	WI	53225	Jere Fabick	414-461-9100	R	89*	0.5
Chindex International Inc.	7201 Wisconsin	Bethesda	MD	20814	Roberta Lipson	301-215-7777	P	88	0.8
M D Moody and Sons Inc.	PO Box 5350	Jacksonville	FL	32247	M Moody	904-737-4401	R	87*	<0.1
Stribling Equipment L.L.C.	PO Box 6038	Jackson	MS	39288	GS Swanson	601-939-1000	R	85*	0.2
Nebraska Machinery Co.	11002 Sapp Bros Dr	Omaha	NE	68138	Dwayne Swanson	402-891-8600	R	82*	0.4
Warren CAT	PO Box 270720	Oklahoma City	OK	73137	James Nelson	405-947-6771	R	81*	0.2
Roland Machinery Co.	PO Box 2879	Springfield	IL	62708	Raymond E Roland	217-789-7711	R	80*	0.2
Halton Co.	PO Box 3377	Portland	OR	97208	Edward H Halton Jr	503-288-6411	S	78*	0.3
Martin Tractor Company Inc.	1737 SW 42nd St	Topeka	KS	66601	Harry Craig Jr	785-266-5770	R	77*	0.2
Southeastern Equipment Inc.	10874 E Pike Rd	Cambridge	OH	43725	William L Baker	740-432-6303	R	74*	0.2
Mi-Jack Products Inc.	3111 W 167th St	Hazel Crest	IL	60429	Michael Lanigan	708-596-5200	R	70*	0.4
F and M Mafco Inc.	PO Box 11013	Cincinnati	OH	45211	Daniel McKenna	513-367-2151	R	63*	0.2
McCann Industries Inc.	543 S Rohlwing Rd	Addison	IL	60101	Richard J McCann	630-627-8700	R	60*	0.2
Pearce Industries Inc.	PO Box 35068	Houston	TX	77235	Louis M Pearce III	713-723-1050	R	57*	0.6
Power Motive Corp.	5000 Vasquez Blvd	Denver	CO	80216	Jay Baugher	303-355-5900	R	55*	0.1
Aquarius Engineering Inc.	7760 W 20th Ave	Hialeah	FL	33016	Israel Garcia	305-824-1324	R	54*	0.1
Michigan CAT	28004 Ctr Oaks Ct	Wixom	MI	48393	John Griffin	248-348-0900	R	54*	0.1
Monroe Tractor and Implement	1001 Lehigh Station	Henrietta	NY	14467	Janet E Felosky	585-334-3867	R	54*	0.2
VLP Holding Co.	PO Box 4915	Kansas City	MO	64120	James W Foreman	816-241-9290	R	50*	0.1
Yukon Equipment Inc.	2020 E 3rd Ave	Anchorage	AK	99501	Maurice Hollowell	907-277-1541	R	50*	<0.1
YANMAR America Corp.	951 Corporate Grove	Buffalo Grove	IL	60089		847-541-1900	R	49*	0.2
American Pecco Corp.	PO Box 670	Millwood	NY	10546	Ronald A Yakin	914-762-0550	R	45*	0.2
Ben Meadows	190 Etowah Ind Ct	Canton	GA	30114	Karl Hube	770-479-3130	R	41*	<0.1
Builders Rental	PO Box 1376	Oklahoma City	OK	73101	John Hessel	405-525-7431	R	41*	<0.1
PSI Sales Inc.	PO Box 488	Theodore	AL	36590	Van Woodham	251-957-2114	R	41*	<0.1
Rankin County Unit System	620 Marquette Rd	Brandon	MS	39042		601-825-8919	R	38*	<0.1
Triad Machinery Inc.	4530 NE 148th Ave	Portland	OR	97230	Kristine Gittins	503-254-5100	R	36*	<0.1
Logan Corp.	PO Box 58	Huntington	WV	25706	CM England III	304-526-4700	R	35*	0.1
Quinn Group Inc.	1300 Abbott St	Salinas	CA	93901		831-758-8463	R	33*	<0.1
Wolverine Tractor & Equipment	PO Box 19336	Detroit	MI	48219	Robert McNutt	248-356-5200	R	33*	0.1
Hub Construction Specialties Inc.	PO Box 1269	San Bernardino	CA	92402	Robert Gogo	909-889-0161	R	31*	<0.1
Theros Equipment Inc.	PO Box 804	Gainesville	VA	20156	William Theros	540-347-3291	R	29*	<0.1
Scott Construction Equipment	PO Box 997	Saint Rose	LA	70087	Jack Fendrick	504-461-0961	R	28*	<0.1
Mine and Mill Supply Co.	2500 S Combee Rd	Lakeland	FL	33801	Wayne Hart	863-665-5601	R	28*	<0.1
ABM Equipment and Supply Inc.	333 2nd St NE	Hopkins	MN	55343	Ron Martens	952-938-5451	R	27*	<0.1
Advance Equipment Co.	1400 Jackson St	Saint Paul	MN	55117	O Haug	651-489-8881	R	27*	<0.1
Advanced Lift Designs Inc.	1000 Brighton St	Union	NJ	07083	Clifford Sneyers	908-624-9555	R	27*	<0.1
Baskin Auto Truck and Tractor	1844 Hwy 51 S	Covington	TN	38019	Donald Baskin	901-476-2626	R	27*	<0.1
Sokkia Corp.	PO Box 726	Olathe	KS	66051	Ed Yamanaka	913-492-4900	R	27*	<0.1
TT Technology Inc.	PO Box 1516	Silver Springs	FL	34489	Aleta Garner	352-622-2077	R	27*	<0.1
Golden West Equipment Inc.	1000 S Euclid St	La Habra	CA	90631	Michael Kennedy	714-879-3850	R	25*	<0.1
Doyle Equipment Co.	PO Box 1840	Cranberry	PA	16066	David M Smail	724-776-3636	R	25*	<0.1
McAllister Equipment Co.	12500 S Cicero Ave	Alsip	IL	60803	Jack Mosier	708-389-7700	R	25*	0.1

Source: *Ward's Business Directory of U.S. Private and Public Companies*, Volumes 1 and 2, 2005. The company type code used is as follows: P - Public, R - Private, S - Subsidiary, D - Division, J - Joint Venture, A - Affiliate, G - Group. Sales are in millions of dollars, employees are in thousands. An asterisk (*) indicates an estimated sales volume. The symbol < stands for 'less than'. Company names and addresses are truncated, in some cases, to fit into the available space.

OCCUPATIONS EMPLOYED BY MACHINERY, EQUIPMENT, & SUPPLIES WHOLESALE

Occupation	% of Total 2004	Change to 2014	Occupation	% of Total 2004	Change to 2014
Sales reps, wholesale & manufacturing, exc tech	16.2	9.7	Truck drivers, light or delivery services	2.0	9.7
Mobile heavy equipment mechanics, except engines	5.7	9.7	Industrial machinery mechanics	2.0	9.7
Sales reps, wholesale & manufacturing, tech	3.6	9.6	Order clerks	1.8	-28.7
Laborers & freight, stock, & material movers, hand	3.4	-1.3	Secretaries, except legal, medical, & executive	1.7	-7.7
Shipping, receiving, & traffic clerks	3.4	-0.7	Team assemblers	1.7	9.7
Office clerks, general	3.4	-2.4	Bus & truck mechanics & diesel engine specialists	1.6	9.7
Bookkeeping, accounting, & auditing clerks	3.1	-1.3	First-line supervisors of mechanics	1.5	9.6
General & operations managers	3.0	8.5	First-line supervisors/managers of office workers	1.4	-0.6
Customer service representatives	2.6	12.3	Truck drivers, heavy & tractor-trailer	1.3	9.6
Maintenance & repair workers, general	2.4	9.7	Sales managers	1.3	17.3
Parts salespersons	2.4	-12.3	Machinists	1.3	9.7
First-line supervisors/managers of non-retail sales work	2.3	1.4	Welders, cutters, solderers, & brazers	1.0	9.7
Stock clerks & order fillers	2.2	-16.0	Executive secretaries & administrative assistants	1.0	3.9

Source: Industry-Occupation Matrix, Bureau of Labor Statistics. These data are reported based on 4-digit NAICS categories but have been matched to corresponding 6-digit NAICS industry codes. The change reported for each occupation to the year 2014 is a percent of growth or decline as estimated by the Bureau of Labor Statistics. The abbreviation nec stands for 'not elsewhere classified.'

LOCATION BY STATE AND REGIONAL CONCENTRATION

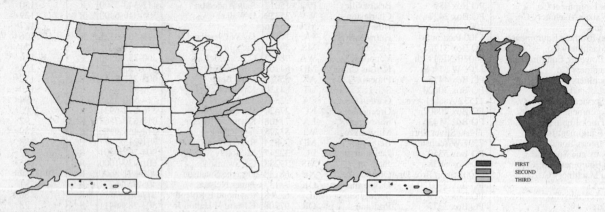

FIRST
SECOND
THIRD

INDUSTRY DATA BY STATE

State	Establishments Total (number)	% of U.S.	Employment Total (number)	% of U.S.	Per Estab.	Payroll Total ($ mil.)	Per Empl. ($)	Sales Total ($ mil.)	% of U.S.	Per Estab. ($)
Illinois	185	3.7	4,080	4.6	22	193.4	47,401	7,778.0	16.3	42,043,368
Texas	396	7.9	6,861	7.7	17	306.4	44,664	3,188.0	6.7	8,050,460
Pennsylvania	246	4.9	4,205	4.7	17	194.2	46,193	3,082.1	6.5	12,528,882
California	368	7.3	5,640	6.4	15	276.0	48,943	2,455.5	5.2	6,672,549
Florida	306	6.1	4,904	5.5	16	203.3	41,461	2,400.9	5.0	7,846,039
Colorado	99	2.0	2,086	2.4	21	96.9	46,458	2,192.0	4.6	22,141,091
North Carolina	141	2.8	3,332	3.8	24	147.5	44,274	1,991.5	4.2	14,124,007
Georgia	185	3.7	2,809	3.2	15	126.3	44,958	1,856.8	3.9	10,036,984
Virginia	179	3.6	2,830	3.2	16	120.2	42,457	1,199.0	2.5	6,698,425
Minnesota	112	2.2	2,159	2.4	19	114.4	52,985	1,119.2	2.4	9,992,643
Tennessee	111	2.2	2,065	2.3	19	89.7	43,440	1,036.9	2.2	9,341,613
Kentucky	143	2.8	2,501	2.8	17	113.0	45,165	992.9	2.1	6,943,329
New York	160	3.2	2,102	2.4	13	103.5	49,255	907.5	1.9	5,671,950
Wisconsin	104	2.1	1,759	2.0	17	84.8	48,214	888.3	1.9	8,541,827
Louisiana	83	1.6	1,478	1.7	18	62.0	41,920	869.2	1.8	10,472,699
Alabama	93	1.8	2,418	2.7	26	109.0	45,071	861.0	1.8	9,258,419
Missouri	127	2.5	2,249	2.5	18	90.3	40,159	805.9	1.7	6,345,921
Indiana	93	1.8	1,717	1.9	18	80.9	47,100	793.2	1.7	8,528,710
West Virginia	103	2.0	2,121	2.4	21	88.4	41,675	772.8	1.6	7,502,485
Arizona	96	1.9	1,942	2.2	20	91.6	47,155	749.8	1.6	7,810,458
Massachusetts	80	1.6	1,424	1.6	18	76.2	53,536	704.5	1.5	8,805,887
Washington	132	2.6	1,570	1.8	12	73.8	47,011	688.1	1.4	5,213,152
Maryland	81	1.6	1,515	1.7	19	68.3	45,075	668.2	1.4	8,249,222
Utah	64	1.3	1,966	2.2	31	86.3	43,891	613.6	1.3	9,588,047
South Carolina	64	1.3	1,364	1.5	21	47.2	34,627	496.9	1.0	7,763,594
Iowa	79	1.6	1,196	1.3	15	50.4	42,151	482.8	1.0	6,111,595
Nevada	59	1.2	1,096	1.2	19	43.4	39,609	434.6	0.9	7,366,661
Oklahoma	70	1.4	1,175	1.3	17	48.9	41,637	400.9	0.8	5,726,700
Kansas	54	1.1	1,112	1.3	21	46.6	41,895	397.3	0.8	7,357,019

Continued on next page.

INDUSTRY DATA BY STATE - Continued

State	Establishments		Employment			Payroll		Sales		
	Total (number)	% of U.S.	Total (number)	% of U.S.	Per Estab.	Total ($ mil.)	Per Empl. ($)	Total ($ mil.)	% of U.S.	Per Estab. ($)
Mississippi	45	0.9	775	0.9	17	33.7	43,535	332.4	0.7	7,386,933
Arkansas	63	1.3	1,005	1.1	16	39.7	39,543	320.0	0.7	5,080,079
Maine	37	0.7	743	0.8	20	33.9	45,668	318.1	0.7	8,596,000
Connecticut	41	0.8	563	0.6	14	32.4	57,515	299.1	0.6	7,295,390
Wyoming	23	0.5	634	0.7	28	34.3	54,038	271.8	0.6	11,817,826
Nebraska	34	0.7	611	0.7	18	30.6	50,113	254.8	0.5	7,493,471
Montana	33	0.7	638	0.7	19	25.7	40,359	239.2	0.5	7,248,606
North Dakota	33	0.7	476	0.5	14	20.6	43,179	209.3	0.4	6,341,667
Idaho	35	0.7	615	0.7	18	26.5	43,093	208.9	0.4	5,967,771
New Hampshire	29	0.6	391	0.4	13	17.5	44,731	195.2	0.4	6,730,862
New Mexico	26	0.5	525	0.6	20	19.1	36,339	183.5	0.4	7,059,346
Alaska	20	0.4	293	0.3	15	16.7	56,993	146.5	0.3	7,323,250
South Dakota	18	0.4	260	0.3	14	10.4	39,996	96.2	0.2	5,342,889
Hawaii	18	0.4	202	0.2	11	7.1	35,381	87.8	0.2	4,879,389
Delaware	14	0.3	136	0.2	10	5.7	42,037	68.2	0.1	4,870,786
Vermont	10	0.2	111	0.1	11	5.1	45,685	65.7	0.1	6,569,000
Ohio	186	3.7	2500-4999	-	-	(D)	-	(D)	-	-
Michigan	138	2.7	1000-2499	-	-	(D)	-	(D)	-	-
New Jersey	106	2.1	1000-2499	-	-	(D)	-	(D)	-	-
Oregon	101	2.0	1000-2499	-	-	(D)	-	(D)	-	-
Rhode Island	11	0.2	100-249	-	-	(D)	-	(D)	-	-
D.C.	1	-	0-19	-	-	(D)	-	(D)	-	-

Source: 2002 *Economic Census*. The states are in descending order of sales or establishments (if sales data are missing for the majority). The symbol (D) appears when data are withheld to prevent disclosure of competitive information. States marked with (D) are sorted by number of establishments. A dash (-) indicates that the data element cannot be calculated. Shaded *states* on the state map indicate those states which have proportionately greater representation in the industry than would be indicated by the states population; the ratio is based on total sales or number of establishments. Shaded *regions* indicate where the industry is regionally most concentrated.

NAICS 423820 - FARM AND GARDEN MACHINERY AND EQUIPMENT MERCHANT WHOLESALERS

Sales ($ million)

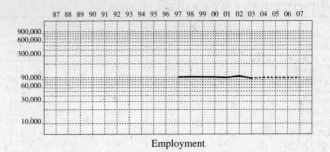

Employment

GENERAL STATISTICS

Year	Establishments (number)	Employment (number)	Payroll ($ million)	Sales ($ million)	Employees per Establishment (number)	Sales per Establishment ($)	Payroll per Employee ($)
1987	-	-	-	-	-	-	-
1988	-	-	-	-	-	-	-
1989	-	-	-	-	-	-	-
1990	-	-	-	-	-	-	-
1991	-	-	-	-	-	-	-
1992	-	-	-	-	-	-	-
1993	-	-	-	-	-	-	-
1994	-	-	-	-	-	-	-
1995	-	-	-	-	-	-	-
1996	-	-	-	-	-	-	-
1997	9,782	101,413	2,860.5	39,713.3	10.4	4,059,834.4	28,206.4
1998	9,582	102,538	2,999.0	40,304.8 e	10.7	4,206,307.7	29,247.7
1999	9,448	102,044	3,099.3	40,896.4 e	10.8	4,328,575.4	30,372.2
2000	9,206	101,374	3,199.4	41,487.9 e	11.0	4,506,617.4	31,560.8
2001	9,086	99,387	3,250.4	42,079.5 e	10.9	4,631,241.5	32,704.3
2002	8,680	107,595	3,494.3	42,671.0	12.4	4,916,013.8	32,476.4
2003	8,578	95,803	3,295.4	43,262.5	11.2	5,014,805.8 p	34,397.2
2004	8,369 p	100,112 p	3,520.6 p	43,854.1 p	11.9 p	5,178,626.9 p	35,189.6 p
2005	8,163 p	99,777 p	3,608.0 p	44,445.6 p	12.1 p	5,342,448.1 p	36,166.8 p
2006	7,956 p	99,442 p	3,695.4 p	45,037.2 p	12.3 p	5,506,269.2 p	37,144.0 p
2007	7,750 p	99,107 p	3,782.7 p	45,628.7 p	12.5 p	5,670,090.4 p	38,121.2 p

Source: *Economic Census of the United States*, 1997 and 2002. Establishment counts, employment, and payroll are from *County Business Patterns* for non-Census years. This is a newly defined industry. Data for prior years are unavailable at the time of publication but may become available over time. Values followed by 'p' are projections by the editors. Sales data for non-Census years are extrapolations, marked by 'e'.

INDICES OF CHANGE

Year	Establishments (number)	Employment (number)	Payroll ($ million)	Sales ($ million)	Employees per Establishment (number)	Sales per Establishment ($)	Payroll per Employee ($)
1987	-	-	-	-	-	-	-
1992	-	-	-	-	-	-	-
1993	-	-	-	-	-	-	-
1994	-	-	-	-	-	-	-
1995	-	-	-	-	-	-	-
1996	-	-	-	-	-	-	-
1997	112.7	94.3	81.9	93.1	83.9	82.6	86.9
1998	110.4	95.3	85.8	94.5 e	86.3	85.6	90.1
1999	108.8	94.8	88.7	95.8 e	87.1	88.1	93.5
2000	106.1	94.2	91.6	97.2 e	88.7	91.7	97.2
2001	104.7	92.4	93.0	98.6 e	87.9	94.2	100.7
2002	100.0	100.0	100.0	100.0	100.0	100.0	100.0
2003	98.8	89.0	94.3	101.4 p	90.1	102.0 p	105.9
2004	96.4 p	93.0 p	100.8 p	102.8 p	95.8 p	105.3 p	108.4 p
2005	94.0 p	92.7 p	103.3 p	104.2 p	97.5 p	108.7 p	111.4 p
2006	91.7 p	92.4 p	105.8 p	105.5 p	99.2 p	112.0 p	114.4 p
2007	89.3 p	92.1 p	108.3 p	106.9 p	100.8 p	115.3 p	117.4 p

Sources: Same as General Statistics. The values shown reflect change from the base year, 2002. Values above 100 mean greater than 2002, values below 100 mean less than 2002, and a value of 100 in the 1987-2001 or 2003-2007 period means same as 2002. Values followed by a 'p' are projections by the editors; 'e' stands for extrapolation. Data are the most recent available at this level of detail.

SELECTED RATIOS

For 2002	Avg. of All Wholesale	Analyzed Industry	Index	For 2002	Avg. of All Wholesale	Analyzed Industry	Index
Employees per Establishment	15	12	83	Sales per Employee	791,325	396,589	50
Payroll per Establishment	626,122	402,569	64	Sales per Establishment	12,012,387	4,916,014	41
Payroll per Employee	41,161	32,476	79	Expenses per Establishment	na	na	na

Sources: Same as General Statistics. The 'Average of All' column, Wholesale or Retail, represents the average of the sector reported for the most recent complete year available. The Index shows the relationship between the Average and the Analyzed Industry. For example, 100 means that they are equal; 500 that the Analyzed Industry is five times the average; 50 means that the Analyzed Industry is half the national average. The abbreviation 'na' is used to show that data are 'not available'.

LEADING COMPANIES   Number shown: **75**   Total sales ($ mil): **12,806**   Total employment (000): **17.8**

Company Name	Address				CEO Name	Phone	Co. Type	Sales ($ mil)	Empl. (000)
Agriliance L.L.C.	PO Box 64089	St. Paul	MN	55164	George Thornton	651-451-5000	J	3,500	3.0
True Value Co.	8600 W Bryn Mawr	Chicago	IL	60631	Bryan R Ableidinger	773-695-5000	R	2,024	2.8
John Taylor Fertilizers Co.	PO Box 15289	Sacramento	CA	95851	Jeffrey Taylor	916-991-4451	R	1,220*	<0.1
Rush Enterprises Inc.	555 IH 35 S, Ste 500	New Braunfels	TX	78130		830-626-5200	P	1,095	1.9
Empire Southwest L.L.C.	PO Box 2985	Phoenix	AZ	85062	Jeff Whiteman	480-633-4300	R	553*	1.0
RDO Equipment Co.	PO Box 7160	Fargo	ND	58103	Ronald D Offutt	701-239-8735	R	534*	1.2
Scott Truck and Tractor Inc.	PO Box 4948	Monroe	LA	71211	Scott Cumming	318-387-4160	R	450*	1.0
Whayne Supply Co.	PO Box 35900	Louisville	KY	40232	J Pullen	502-774-4441	R	415*	0.5
John Fabick Tractor Co.	1 Fabick Dr	Fenton	MO	63026	Doug Fabick	636-343-5900	R	205*	0.6
United Hardware Distributing Co.	5005 Nathan Ln N	Plymouth	MN	55442	David A Heider	763-559-1800	R	144*	0.4
Sun Gro Horticulture Distribution	15831 NE 8th St	Bellevue	WA	98008	Mitch Weaver	425-641-7577	R	136*	<0.1
Timberland Machines	248 Main St	Lancaster	NH	03584		603-788-4738	D	120*	0.3
Arnold Machinery Co.	PO Box 30020	Salt Lake City	UT	84130	Kayden Bell	801-972-4000	R	110*	0.3
Tidewater Companies Inc.	PO Box 1116	Brunswick	GA	31521	Ken S Trowbridge Jr	912-638-7726	R	109*	0.3
Liechty Farm Equipment Inc.	1701 S Defiance	Archbold	OH	43502		419-445-1565	R	103*	<0.1
Hog Inc.	RR 2, Box 8	Greenfield	IL	62044			R	100*	<0.1
Arizona Machinery Group Inc.	11111 W McDowell	Avondale	AZ	85323	Thomas Rosztoczy	623-936-7131	R	93*	<0.1
Jim's Supply Company Inc.	PO Box 668	Bakersfield	CA	93302	Doreen Boylan	661-324-6514	R	85*	0.1
Bucklin Tractor and Implement	PO Box 127	Bucklin	KS	67834		620-826-3271	R	80*	<0.1
Martin Tractor Company Inc.	1737 SW 42nd St	Topeka	KS	66601	Harry Craig Jr	785-266-5770	R	77*	0.2
Underwood Equipment Inc.	PO Box 956	Ottawa	KS	66067	Glen J Underwood	785-242-4400	R	74*	<0.1
Baker Implement Co.	Rt 3 NW	Kennett	MO	63857	Jerry Combs	573-888-4646	R	68*	0.2
Turf Products Corp.	157 Moody Rd	Enfield	CT	06082	F N Zeytoonjian	860-763-3581	R	68*	0.2
Glade and Grove Supply Inc.	PO Drawer 760	Belle Glade	FL	33430	George Cooper	561-996-3095	R	66*	0.2
White's Tractor and Truck Inc.	PO Box 3817	Wilson	NC	27893	D Steve White	252-206-0733	R	62*	0.2
Monroe Tractor and Implement	1001 Lehigh Station	Henrietta	NY	14467	Janet E Felosky	585-334-3867	R	54*	0.2
Dixie Sales Company Inc.	PO Box 1408	Greensboro	NC	27402	James Starmer	336-375-7500	R	50*	0.1
Finch Services Inc.	1127 Littlestown Pke	Westminster	MD	21157	William Finch	410-876-2211	R	42*	0.1
TreeCon Resources Inc.	6004 South US 59	Lufkin	TX	75901	Mike Boatman	936-634-3365	P	41	0.1
Century Supply Corp.	747 E Roosevelt Rd	Lombard	IL	60148	Fred Schmidt	630-889-0800	R	40*	0.3
Carswell Distributing Inc.	PO Box 4193	Winston Salem	NC	27115	William Parsley	336-767-7700	R	39*	<0.1
Barbee-Neuhaus Implement Co.	PO Box 386	Weslaco	TX	78596		956-968-7502	R	36*	<0.1
Simpson Norton Corp.	PO Box 1295	Avondale	AZ	85323	Tom Knect	623-932-5116	R	36*	<0.1
Belarus Tractor International Inc.	7075 W Parkland Ct	Milwaukee	WI	53223	Valery Zakharov	414-355-2000	R	35*	<0.1
Spartan Distributors Inc.	PO Box 246	Sparta	MI	49345	Dawn Johnson	616-887-7301	R	35*	<0.1
Quinn Group Inc.	1300 Abbott St	Salinas	CA	93901		831-758-8463	R	33*	<0.1
Lampson Tractor & Equipment	PO Box 85	Geyserville	CA	95441	Allen Kelly	707-857-3443	R	32*	<0.1
Morrow County Grain Growers	Highway 74	Lexington	OR	97839	Joe McElligott	541-989-8221	R	31*	<0.1
Vetter Equipment Co.	PO Box 226	Audubon	IA	50025		712-563-4219	R	29*	<0.1
Jacobi Sales Inc.	PO Box 67	Palmyra	IN	47164	Brian Jacobi	812-364-6141	R	28*	<0.1
Nelson-Jameson Inc.	PO Box 647	Marshfield	WI	54449	John Nelson	715-387-1151	R	27*	<0.1
Turf Equipment and Supply Inc.	8015 Dorsey Run Rd	Jessup	MD	20794	Lynn Matson	410-799-5575	R	27*	<0.1
Reliable Tractor Inc.	PO Box 808	Tifton	GA	31794	DN Stafford III	229-382-4400	R	26*	<0.1
Arends Brothers Inc.	Route 54 N	Melvin	IL	60952	Kent Arends	217-388-7717	R	25*	0.1
Implement Sales L.L.C.	1574 Stone Ridge Dr	Stone Mountain	GA	30083	Mitch Elkins	770-908-9439	S	25*	<0.1
J-Star Bodco Inc.	801 Janesville Ave	Fort Atkinson	WI	53538		920-563-5521	R	25*	<0.1
Mountainland Supply Co.	1505 W 130 S	Orem	UT	84058	RJ Rasmussen	801-224-6050	R	25*	<0.1
Elite Lawn Irrigation	2667 Product Dr	Rochester Hills	MI	48309	Joseph Lendo	248-852-0088	R	25*	<0.1
Farmers Supply Coop.	PO Box 9009	Greenwood	MS	38930	Clifford Dance	662-453-6341	R	25*	<0.1
Flory Industries Inc.	PO Box 908	Salida	CA	95368	Howard Flory	209-545-1167	R	24*	0.1
Royal Brass and Hose Inc.	PO Box 51468	Knoxville	TN	37950	Garvin Ingram	865-558-0224	R	24*	<0.1
Philadelphia Turf Co.	PO Box 865	Doylestown	PA	18901	Frank Shuman	215-345-7200	R	24*	<0.1
Cnh Inc.	PO Box 3159	Minot	ND	58702		701-858-5500	R	23*	<0.1
M and L Industries Inc.	1210 St Charles St	Houma	LA	70360	Steven Marmande	985-876-2280	R	23*	0.1
Straub International Inc.	PO Box 1606	Great Bend	KS	67530	Ronald Straub	620-792-5256	R	23*	<0.1
Farm-Oyl Company Inc.	2333 Hampden Ave	St. Paul	MN	55114	Robert E Larson	651-646-7571	R	22*	<0.1
Grossenburg Implement Inc.	31341 US Hwy 18	Winner	SD	57580	Barry Grossenburg	605-842-2040	R	22*	<0.1
Yardville Supply Co.	PO Box 8427	Trenton	NJ	08650	George Smith	609-585-5000	R	22*	<0.1
N and S Tractor Co.	PO Box 910	Merced	CA	95341	Arthur Nutcher	209-383-5888	R	21*	<0.1
Capital Ford New Holland Inc.	PO Box 16568	Little Rock	AR	72231	Doug Meyer	501-834-9999	R	21*	<0.1
Blount Greenback Farmers Coop.	1514 W Broadway	Maryville	TN	37801		865-982-2761	R	21*	<0.1
Burks Tractor Company Inc.	3140 Kimberly Rd	Twin Falls	ID	83301	Douglas Burks	208-733-5543	R	21*	<0.1
Dandridge Equipment Inc.	11495 US Hwy 64	Somerville	TN	38068	W Dandridge	901-465-9811	R	21*	<0.1
Lakeside Systems Inc.	PO Box 196	New Holstein	WI	53061	Glenn Lee	920-898-5702	R	20*	<0.1
SMV Industries Inc.	PO Box 1094	Council Bluffs	IA	51502	Rodney Borman	712-366-8040	R	19*	<0.1
Mountain View Equipment Inc.	PO Box 690	Meridian	ID	83680	Randy Stewart	208-888-1593	R	19*	<0.1
Roger Shawn Houck	7887 Wilmington Rd	Oregonia	OH	45054		513-933-0563	R	19*	<0.1
A and M Sales	PO Box 548	Snead	AL	35952	Steve Clowdus	205-466-7163	R	18*	<0.1
Lehman Pipe & Plumbing Supply	PO Box 370417	Miami	FL	33137	Dennis Lehman	305-576-3054	R	18*	<0.1
John Day Co.	POBox 3541	Omaha	NE	68103	John D Fonda	402-455-9000	R	18*	<0.1
Jamestown Implement Inc.	PO Box 1958	Jamestown	ND	58401		701-252-0580	R	17*	<0.1
American Implement Inc.	PO Box 853	Garden City	KS	67846	Duane Koster	620-275-4114	R	17*	<0.1
Painting Machinery	17851 Hwy 13	Wahpeton	ND	58075	William Sprung	701-642-8424	R	17*	<0.1
Polk County Farmers Co-Op	PO Box 47	Rickreall	OR	97371		503-363-2332	R	17*	<0.1
US Fiberglass Inc.	8383 NE Sandy Blvd	Portland	OR	97220		503-252-8348	R	17*	<0.1

Source: Ward's Business Directory of U.S. Private and Public Companies, Volumes 1 and 2, 2005. The company type code used is as follows: P - Public, R - Private, S - Subsidiary, D - Division, J - Joint Venture, A - Affiliate, G - Group. Sales are in millions of dollars, employees are in thousands. An asterisk (*) indicates an estimated sales volume. The symbol < stands for 'less than'. Company names and addresses are truncated, in some cases, to fit into the available space.

OCCUPATIONS EMPLOYED BY FARM & GARDEN MACHINERY & EQUIPMENT WHOLESALE

Occupation	% of Total 2004	Change to 2014	Occupation	% of Total 2004	Change to 2014
Farm equipment mechanics	20.9		Stock clerks & order fillers	1.8	-23.4
Sales reps, wholesale & manufacturing, exc tech	10.1		First-line supervisors/managers of retail sales workers	1.7	-8.0
Parts salespersons	9.0	-20.0	Secretaries, except legal, medical, & executive	1.6	-15.8
Retail salespersons	4.7		Truck drivers, heavy & tractor-trailer	1.6	-0.1
Bookkeeping, accounting, & auditing clerks	4.4	-10.0	Shipping, receiving, & traffic clerks	1.6	-9.6
Office clerks, general	3.3	-11.0	Truck drivers, light or delivery services	1.4	
General & operations managers	3.3	-1.1	Sales reps, wholesale & manufacturing, tech	1.4	.-0.1
First-line supervisors of mechanics	3.0		Customer service representatives	1.3	2.3
Laborers & freight, stock, & material movers, hand	2.6	-10.0	Maintenance & repair workers, general	1.3	-0.1
First-line supervisors/managers of non-retail sales work	1.9	-7.6	First-line supervisors/managers of office workers	1.1	-9.4

Source: Industry-Occupation Matrix, Bureau of Labor Statistics. These data are reported based on 4-digit NAICS categories but have been matched to corresponding 6-digit NAICS industry codes. The change reported for each occupation to the year 2014 is a percent of growth or decline as estimated by the Bureau of Labor Statistics. The abbreviation nec stands for 'not elsewhere classified.'

LOCATION BY STATE AND REGIONAL CONCENTRATION

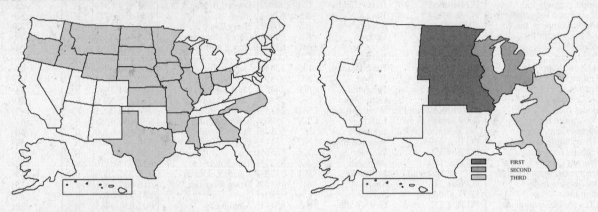

FIRST
SECOND
THIRD

INDUSTRY DATA BY STATE

State	Establishments Total (number)	Establishments % of U.S.	Employment Total (number)	Employment % of U.S.	Employment Per Estab.	Payroll Total ($ mil.)	Payroll Per Empl. ($)	Sales Total ($ mil.)	Sales % of U.S.	Sales Per Estab. ($)
Texas	635	7.3	6,264	6.5	10	197.7	31,563	3,075.8	7.6	4,843,809
California	624	7.2	6,849	7.1	11	248.0	36,203	2,814.5	7.0	4,510,401
Ohio	313	3.6	3,904	4.1	12	129.8	33,238	2,524.7	6.3	8,066,099
Minnesota	376	4.3	4,509	4.7	12	158.7	35,201	2,457.2	6.1	6,535,112
North Carolina	230	2.6	3,188	3.3	14	144.6	45,364	2,364.4	5.9	10,279,930
Georgia	269	3.1	3,125	3.3	12	102.1	32,656	2,270.3	5.6	8,439,788
Missouri	284	3.3	3,309	3.4	12	97.1	29,355	2,216.8	5.5	7,805,532
Illinois	386	4.4	5,087	5.3	13	174.2	34,243	1,927.1	4.8	4,992,575
Iowa	474	5.4	5,630	5.9	12	163.5	29,040	1,821.7	4.5	3,843,251
Wisconsin	353	4.1	4,017	4.2	11	133.9	33,326	1,213.9	3.0	3,438,739
Nebraska	308	3.5	3,652	3.8	12	110.3	30,215	1,117.5	2.8	3,628,399
Indiana	255	2.9	2,886	3.0	11	91.0	31,522	1,106.2	2.7	4,337,976
Florida	318	3.7	2,523	2.6	8	89.4	35,424	1,062.6	2.6	3,341,481
Kansas	260	3.0	3,213	3.3	12	97.6	30,378	990.5	2.5	3,809,681
New York	226	2.6	2,111	2.2	9	70.2	33,268	947.1	2.3	4,190,531
Pennsylvania	269	.3.1	2,752	2.9	10	87.9	31,957	851.4	2.1	3,165,071
Virginia	153	1.8	1,786	1.9	12	55.8	31,223	829.0	2.1	5,418,033
North Dakota	190	2.2	2,151	2.2	11	69.4	32,273	805.7	2.0	4,240,547
Arkansas	195	2.2	2,209	2.3	11	70.2	31,800	777.3	1.9	3,986,015
Tennessee	188	2.2	1,735	1.8	9	52.8	30,420	603.7	1.5	3,211,426
Washington	161	1.8	1,829	1.9	11	60.3	32,993	543.4	1.3	3,375,236
South Dakota	131	1.5	1,541	1.6	12	49.6	32,156	535.5	1.3	4,087,985
Mississippi	147	1.7	1,385	1.4	9	42.5	30,695	486.3	1.2	3,308,007
Oregon	129	1.5	1,405	1.5	11	46.8	33,280	472.1	1.2	3,659,612
Idaho	131	1.5	1,370	1.4	10	44.6	32,518	471.1	1.2	3,596,313
Kentucky	167	1.9	1,356	1.4	8	37.7	27,816	469.3	1.2	2,809,904
Colorado	141	1.6	1,632	1.7	12	53.6	32,873	456.0	1.1	3,233,787
Oklahoma	145	1.7	1,388	1.4	10	39.7	28,572	436.9	1.1	3,013,255
Alabama	168	1.9	1,337	1.4	8	36.5	27,283	411.3	1.0	2,447,964
Louisiana	110	1.3	1,336	1.4	12	38.4	28,711	375.9	0.9	3,417,436
Connecticut	23	0.3	584	0.6	25	26.4	45,178	277.0	0.7	12,043,783
Maryland	55	0.6	698	0.7	13	25.8	36,923	254.6	0.6	4,628,509
Montana	84	1.0	788	0.8	9	24.2	30,745	253.6	0.6	3,019,643

Continued on next page.

INDUSTRY DATA BY STATE - Continued

State	Establishments Total (number)	% of U.S.	Employment Total (number)	% of U.S.	Per Estab.	Payroll Total ($ mil.)	Per Empl. ($)	Sales Total ($ mil.)	% of U.S.	Per Estab. ($)
Utah	59	0.7	891	0.9	15	24.5	27,505	251.4	0.6	4,261,068
South Carolina	94	1.1	773	0.8	8	21.6	27,979	182.3	0.5	1,939,777
Massachusetts	35	0.4	463	0.5	13	20.0	43,270	149.0	0.4	4,257,286
New Mexico	48	0.6	400	0.4	8	10.6	26,585	100.1	0.2	2,085,458
New Hampshire	24	0.3	294	0.3	12	10.4	35,391	80.3	0.2	3,347,167
Wyoming	30	0.3	266	0.3	9	6.3	23,737	79.5	0.2	2,648,633
Vermont	31	0.4	222	0.2	7	6.0	27,189	71.6	0.2	2,308,903
Delaware	19	0.2	240	0.3	13	8.0	33,262	60.8	0.2	3,200,684
Maine	24	0.3	173	0.2	7	4.9	28,098	58.2	0.1	2,425,125
West Virginia	34	0.4	186	0.2	5	3.9	21,000	50.2	0.1	1,475,324
Hawaii	13	0.1	71	0.1	5	3.0	42,803	29.0	0.1	2,232,154
Michigan	201	2.3	1000-2499	-	-	(D)	-	(D)	-	-
New Jersey	84	1.0	500-999	-	-	(D)	-	(D)	-	-
Arizona	81	0.9	1000-2499	-	-	(D)	-	(D)	-	-
Nevada	25	0.3	100-249	-	-	(D)	-	(D)	-	-
Rhode Island	7	0.1	20-99	-	-	(D)	-	(D)	-	-
Alaska	2	-	0-19	-	-	(D)	-	(D)	-	-
D.C.	1	-	20-99	-	-	(D)	-	(D)	-	-

Source: 2002 *Economic Census*. The states are in descending order of sales or establishments (if sales data are missing for the majority). The symbol (D) appears when data are withheld to prevent disclosure of competitive information. States marked with (D) are sorted by number of establishments. A dash (-) indicates that the data element cannot be calculated. Shaded *states* on the state map indicate those states which have proportionately greater representation in the industry than would be indicated by the states population; the ratio is based on total sales or number of establishments. Shaded *regions* indicate where the industry is regionally most concentrated.

NAICS 423830 - INDUSTRIAL MACHINERY AND EQUIPMENT MERCHANT WHOLESALERS

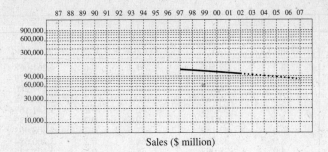

Sales ($ million)

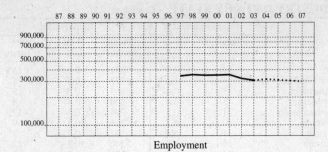

Employment

GENERAL STATISTICS

Year	Establishments (number)	Employment (number)	Payroll ($ million)	Sales ($ million)	Employees per Establishment (number)	Sales per Establishment ($)	Payroll per Employee ($)
1987	-	-	-	-	-	-	-
1988	-	-	-	-	-	-	-
1989	-	-	-	-	-	-	-
1990	-	-	-	-	-	-	-
1991	-	-	-	-	-	-	-
1992	-	-	-	-	-	-	-
1993	-	-	-	-	-	-	-
1994	-	-	-	-	-	-	-
1995	-	-	-	-	-	-	-
1996	-	-	-	-	-	-	-
1997	35,674	342,008	14,167.7	139,947.0	9.6	3,922,941.1	41,425.1
1998	35,479	353,232	15,377.5	134,503.3 e	10.0	3,791,069.1	43,533.7
1999	34,947	347,881	15,534.3	129,059.7 e	10.0	3,693,011.7	44,654.1
2000	34,089	349,093	16,406.3	123,616.0 e	10.2	3,626,273.0	46,996.8
2001	33,098	352,561	16,364.3	118,172.4 e	10.7	3,570,377.7	46,415.4
2002	31,104	320,749	14,901.6	112,728.7	10.3	3,624,250.9	46,458.8
2003	29,719	305,882	14,482.7	107,285.0 p	10.3	3,482,427.5 p	47,347.2
2004	29,378 p	314,677 p	15,436.8 p	101,841.4 p	10.6 p	3,418,934.3 p	48,887.0 p
2005	28,361 p	308,654 p	15,466.2 p	96,397.7 p	10.8 p	3,355,441.0 p	49,793.3 p
2006	27,345 p	302,630 p	15,495.6 p	90,954.1 p	10.9 p	3,291,947.7 p	50,699.6 p
2007	26,328 p	296,606 p	15,525.0 p	85,510.4 p	11.0 p	3,228,454.5 p	51,606.0 p

Source: Economic Census of the United States, 1997 and 2002. Establishment counts, employment, and payroll are from *County Business Patterns* for non-Census years. This is a newly defined industry. Data for prior years are unavailable at the time of publication but may become available over time. Values followed by 'p' are projections by the editors. Sales data for non-Census years are extrapolations, marked by 'e'.

INDICES OF CHANGE

Year	Establishments (number)	Employment (number)	Payroll ($ million)	Sales ($ million)	Employees per Establishment (number)	Sales per Establishment ($)	Payroll per Employee ($)
1987	-	-	-	-	-	-	-
1992	-	-	-	-	-	-	-
1993	-	-	-	-	-	-	-
1994	-	-	-	-	-	-	-
1995	-	-	-	-	-	-	-
1996	-	-	-	-	-	-	-
1997	114.7	106.6	95.1	124.1	93.2	108.2	89.2
1998	114.1	110.1	103.2	119.3 e	97.1	104.6	93.7
1999	112.4	108.5	104.2	114.5 e	97.1	101.9	96.1
2000	109.6	108.8	110.1	109.7 e	99.0	100.1	101.2
2001	106.4	109.9	109.8	104.8 e	103.9	98.5	99.9
2002	100.0	100.0	100.0	100.0	100.0	100.0	100.0
2003	95.5	95.4	97.2	95.2 p	99.9	96.1 p	101.9
2004	94.5 p	98.1 p	103.6 p	90.3 p	103.3 p	94.3 p	105.2 p
2005	91.2 p	96.2 p	103.8 p	85.5 p	104.5 p	92.6 p	107.2 p
2006	87.9 p	94.4 p	104.0 p	80.7 p	105.6 p	90.8 p	109.1 p
2007	84.6 p	92.5 p	104.0 p	75.9 p	106.8 p	89.1 p	111.1 p

Sources: Same as General Statistics. The values shown reflect change from the base year, 2002. Values above 100 mean greater than 2002, values below 100 mean less than 2002, and a value of 100 in the 1987-2001 or 2003-2007 period means same as 2002. Values followed by a 'p' are projections by the editors; 'e' stands for extrapolation. Data are the most recent available at this level of detail.

SELECTED RATIOS

For 2002	Avg. of All Wholesale	Analyzed Industry	Index	For 2002	Avg. of All Wholesale	Analyzed Industry	Index
Employees per Establishment	15	10	69	Sales per Employee	791,325	351,455	44
Payroll per Establishment	626,122	479,090	77	Sales per Establishment	12,012,387	3,624,251	30
Payroll per Employee	41,161	46,459	113	Expenses per Establishment	na	na	na

Sources: Same as General Statistics. The 'Average of All' column, Wholesale or Retail, represents the average of the sector reported for the most recent complete year available. The Index shows the relationship between the Average and the Analyzed Industry. For example, 100 means that they are equal; 500 that the Analyzed Industry is five times the average; 50 means that the Analyzed Industry is half the national average. The abbreviation 'na' is used to show that data are 'not available'.

LEADING COMPANIES   Number shown: **75**   Total sales ($ mil): **41,855**   Total employment (000): **66.6**

Company Name	Address				CEO Name	Phone	Co. Type	Sales ($ mil)	Empl. (000)
W.W. Grainger Inc.	100 Grainger Pkwy	Lake Forest	IL	60045	David W. Grainger	847-535-1000	P	5,050	14.7
WESCO International Inc.	Commerce Court	Pittsburgh	PA	15219	Ron Haley	412-454-2200	P	3,741	5.3
Unisource Worldwide Inc.	6600 Gov Lk	Norcross	GA	30071	Allan Dragone	770-447-9000	S	3,701*	8.0
LL Building Products Inc.	1361 Alps Rd	Wayne	NJ	07470		973-628-3000	R	3,661*	<0.1
Dichtomatik North America	1087 Park Pl	Shakopee	MN	55379	John Rice	952-894-8400	R	2,080*	<0.1
International Seal Company Inc.	14B Sunset Way	Henderson	NV	89014	Orville Marvick	702-433-8433	R	2,080*	<0.1
Airgas Inc.	259 N R-Chester	Radnor	PA	19087	Peter M McCausland	610-687-5253	P	1,896	9.7
American Builders & Contractors	PO Box 838	Beloit	WI	53511	Kenneth A Hendricks	608-362-7777	R	1,520*	3.5
Hawthorne Machinery Inc.	PO Box 120708	San Diego	CA	92112	Tom J Hawthorne	858-674-7000	R	1,371*	0.6
Stewart & Stevenson Services Inc.	2707 N Loop W	Houston	TX	77008	Max Lukens	713-868-7700	P	1,176	3.3
McJunkin Corp.	PO Box 513	Charleston	WV	25322	H Barnard Wehrle III	304-348-5211	R	847*	1.6
Tractor and Equipment Co.	1835 Harnish Blvd	Billings	MT	59101	John J Harnish	406-656-0202	R	747*	0.9
Baldor Electric Co.	PO Box 2400	Fort Smith	AR	72901		479-646-4711	P	648	0.7
Sanderson Ford Trucks	6400 N 51st Ave	Glendale	AZ	85301	David Kimoly	623-842-8787	R	628*	0.5
Koyo Corp.	PO Box 45028	Westlake	OH	44145	Tsutomu Nemoto	440-835-1000	D	564*	0.2
Noland Co.	80 29th St	Newport News	VA	23607	Lloyd U Noland III	757-928-9000	P	548	1.3
Walter Meier Holdings Corp.	PO Box 1349	Auburn	WA	98071		253-351-6000	S	519*	<0.1
Wisconsin Lift Truck Corp.	3125 Intertech Dr	Brookfield	WI	53045	Otto J Wolter	262-781-8010	R	514*	0.6
Atlas Lift Truck Rentals	5050 River Rd	Schiller Park	IL	60176	Howard Bernstein	847-678-3450	R	486*	0.2
Warren Power and Machinery L.P.	PO Box 60662	Midland	TX	79711	Richard Folger	432-563-1863	R	460*	0.2
Morrison Industries Inc.	PO Box P	Grand Rapids	MI	49501	Richard Morrison	616-361-2673	R	452*	0.5
Makino Inc.	7680 Innovation	Mason	OH	45040	Donald Lane	513-573-7200	R	415*	0.2
Petroleum Service Co.	PO Box 454	Wilkes Barre	PA	18703	RW Simms	570-822-1151	R	380*	0.1
Gaspro	PO Box 30707	Honolulu	HI	96820		808-842-2222	S	320*	0.1
Atlas Copco Comptec Inc.	46 School Rd	Voorheesville	NY	12186		518-765-3344	S	296*	0.2
Global Power Equipment Group	6120 S Yale	Tulsa	OK	74136	Al Brousseau	918-488-0828	P	264	0.9
Cherry Relays Inc.	6800 Orngthrpe	Buena Park	CA	90620	Kirby Ku	714-523-0266	R	260*	0.6
Modern Line Products Co.	PO Box 110	Indianola	MS	38751		662-887-4151	R	260*	0.6
Barloworld USA	PO Box 410050	Charlotte	NC	28241	Ken Brown	704-587-1003	S	241*	1.1
Interstate Co's Inc.	2601 E 80th St	Bloomington	MN	55425	Jeffrey Caswell	952-854-2044	R	240*	<0.1
Merriam-Graves Corp.	806 River Rd	Charlestown	NH	03603	Donald Wakeman	603-542-8768	R	237*	0.3
Patten Power Systems Inc.	615 W Lake St	Elmhurst	IL	60126	Byron Patten	630-530-2200	R	237*	0.1
Riekes Equipment Co.	6703 L St	Omaha	NE	68117	Duncan Murphy	402-593-1181	R	227*	<0.1
Valley Welders Supply Inc.	320 N 11th St	Billings	MT	59103	Ron Adkins	406-256-3330	R	227*	<0.1
H.O. Penn Machinery Inc.	122 Noxon Rd	Poughkeepsie	NY	12603	CE Thomas Cleveland	845-452-1200	R	222*	0.4
Greystar Corp.	10375 Richmond	Houston	TX	77042	David Patton	713-953-7007	R	217*	0.5
Roberts Oxygen Company Inc.	17011 Railroad St	Gaithersburg	MD	20877		301-253-5665	R	217*	0.5
Scott Industrial Systems Inc.	PO Box 1387	Dayton	OH	45401	Randall Scott	937-233-8146	R	211*	<0.1
Tomen America Inc.	1285 Av Americas	New York	NY	10019	T Yano	212-397-4600	S	210*	<0.1
Production Tool Supply	PO Box 987	Warren	MI	48089	Larry Wolfe	586-755-5258	R	202*	0.6
Devco Corp.	PO Box 176	Wyckoff	NJ	07481	William Durnan	201-848-8444	R	195*	0.5
Parts Now! L.L.C.	3517 W Beltline	Madison	WI	53713		608-276-8688	R	185*	0.3
Kelly Tractor Co.	8255 NW 58th St	Miami	FL	33166	L Patrick Kelly	305-592-5360	R	180*	0.6
Arbor Handling Services Inc.	2380 Maryland Rd	Willow Grove	PA	19090		215-657-2700	R	179*	<0.1
A. Biederman Inc.	1425 Grand Central	Glendale	CA	91201		818-246-8431	S	168*	<0.1
Sundyne Corp.	14845 W 64th Ave	Arvada	CO	80007		303-425-0800	S	168*	1.0
DXP Enterprises Inc.	7272 Pinemont	Houston	TX	77040	David R Little	713-996-4700	P	161	0.5
Mitutoyo America Corp.	965 Corporate Blvd	Aurora	IL	60504	Noel Ryan	630-820-9666	R	151*	0.2
Stiles Machinery Inc.	3965 44th St SE	Grand Rapids	MI	49512	Peter Kleinschmidt	616-698-7500	R	146*	0.2
Samsung Opto-Electronics Am.	40 Seaview Dr	Secaucus	NJ	07094	JW Ahn	201-902-0347	R	145*	<0.1
Hydraulic Controls Inc.	4700 San Pablo Ave	Emeryville	CA	94608	Richard A Cotter	510-658-8300	R	144*	0.2
Illinois Auto Electric Co.	700 Enterprise St	Aurora	IL	60504	H Bruce Sirotek	630-862-3300	R	144*	0.2
Drago Supply Company Inc.	740 Houston Ave	Port Arthur	TX	77640	Joseph P Drago	409-983-4911	R	139*	0.2
Lift Parts Manufacturing Co.	99 Barron Blvd	Grayslake	IL	60030	Hans Anger	847-223-8989	R	130*	0.3
C and H Distributors Inc.	PO Box 14770	Milwaukee	WI	53214		414-443-1700	R	125*	0.4
DoAll Co.	254 Laurel Ave	Des Plaines	IL	60016	Michael Wilkie	847-824-1122	R	124*	0.1
Bobst Group USA Inc.	146 Harrison Ave	Roseland	NJ	07068	Phillipe Michel	973-226-8000	R	120*	<0.1
FCx Performance Inc.	3000 E 14th Ave	Columbus	OH	43219	Charlie Simon	614-324-6050	S	119*	0.2
MBM Corp.	PO Box 40249	Charleston	SC	29423	William Golde	843-552-2700	R	115*	<0.1
Schmidt Group Inc.	PO Box 25189	Greenville	SC	29616	Carl V Schmidt	864-288-9460	R	113*	<0.1
Arnold Machinery Co.	PO Box 30020	Salt Lake City	UT	84130	Kayden Bell	801-972-4000	R	110*	0.3
Hawkins Inc.	3100 E Hennepin	Minneapolis	MN	55413	John R Hawkins	612-331-6910	P	107	0.2
GoIndustry Michael Fox Intern.	11425 Cronhill Dr	Owings Mills	MD	21117	David S Fox	410-654-7500	D	100*	<0.1
Staubli Corp. Prevost Div.	PO Box 189	Duncan	SC	29334		864-433-1980	D	96*	0.1
Argo International Corp.	140 Franklin St	New York	NY	10013	John Santacroce	212-431-1700	R	90*	0.3
Prime Time Thermographics Inc.	1505 W 10th Pl	Tempe	AZ	85281	Mike Matchinsky	480-829-8890	R	90*	<0.1
Associated Packaging Inc.	435 Calvert Dr	Gallatin	TN	37066	Joe R Smith	615-452-2131	R	86*	0.1
Airgas Rutland Tool & Supply Inc.	PO Box 997	Whittier	CA	90608	Glen Irving	562-566-5000	S	84*	0.4
Picanol of America Inc.	1801 Rutherford Rd	Greenville	SC	29609	James C Thomas	864-288-5475	S	84*	0.3
Kenworth of Tennessee Inc.	550 Spence Ln	Nashville	TN	37210	Lester Turner Jr	615-366-5454	R	83*	0.3
Rogers Machinery Company Inc.	PO Box 23279	Portland	OR	97281	Walt Novak	503-639-6151	R	82*	0.2
Coast Counties Truck & Equip.	PO Box 757	San Jose	CA	95106	Robert Archer	408-453-5510	R	82*	0.1
United States Strong Tool Co.	1251 E 286th St	Cleveland	OH	44132	Cedric Beckett	216-289-2450	R	81*	0.1
Utility Manufacturing	PO Box 1299	City of Industry	CA	91749		626-965-1541	R	80*	0.2
Ace Tool Co.	7337 Bryan Dairy	Largo	FL	33777		727-544-6114	S	78*	0.3

Source: Ward's Business Directory of U.S. Private and Public Companies, Volumes 1 and 2, 2005. The company type code used is as follows: P - Public, R - Private, S - Subsidiary, D - Division, J - Joint Venture, A - Affiliate, G - Group. Sales are in millions of dollars, employees are in thousands. An asterisk (*) indicates an estimated sales volume. The symbol < stands for 'less than'. Company names and addresses are truncated, in some cases, to fit into the available space.

OCCUPATIONS EMPLOYED BY MACHINERY, EQUIPMENT, & SUPPLIES WHOLESALE

Occupation	% of Total 2004	Change to 2014	Occupation	% of Total 2004	Change to 2014
Sales reps, wholesale & manufacturing, exc tech	16.2	9.7	Truck drivers, light or delivery services	2.0	9.7
Mobile heavy equipment mechanics, except engines	5.7	9.7	Industrial machinery mechanics	2.0	9.7
Sales reps, wholesale & manufacturing, tech	3.6	9.6	Order clerks	1.8	-28.7
Laborers & freight, stock, & material movers, hand	3.4	-1.3	Secretaries, except legal, medical, & executive	1.7	-7.7
Shipping, receiving, & traffic clerks	3.4	-0.7	Team assemblers	1.7	9.7
Office clerks, general	3.4	-2.4	Bus & truck mechanics & diesel engine specialists	1.6	9.7
Bookkeeping, accounting, & auditing clerks	3.1	-1.3	First-line supervisors of mechanics	1.5	9.6
General & operations managers	3.0	8.5	First-line supervisors/managers of office workers	1.4	-0.6
Customer service representatives	2.6	12.3	Truck drivers, heavy & tractor-trailer	1.3	9.6
Maintenance & repair workers, general	2.4	9.7	Sales managers	1.3	17.3
Parts salespersons	2.4	-12.3	Machinists	1.3	9.7
First-line supervisors/managers of non-retail sales work	2.3	1.4	Welders, cutters, solderers, & brazers	1.0	9.7
Stock clerks & order fillers	2.2	-16.0	Executive secretaries & administrative assistants	1.0	3.9

Source: Industry-Occupation Matrix, Bureau of Labor Statistics. These data are reported based on 4-digit NAICS categories but have been matched to corresponding 6-digit NAICS industry codes. The change reported for each occupation to the year 2014 is a percent of growth or decline as estimated by the Bureau of Labor Statistics. The abbreviation nec stands for 'not elsewhere classified.'

LOCATION BY STATE AND REGIONAL CONCENTRATION

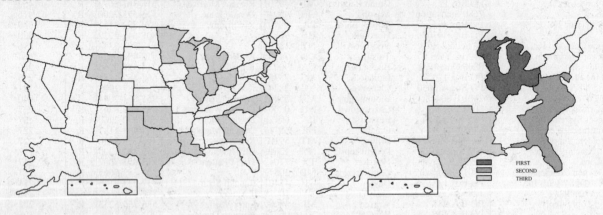

FIRST
SECOND
THIRD

INDUSTRY DATA BY STATE

State	Establishments Total (number)	% of U.S.	Employment Total (number)	% of U.S.	Per Estab.	Payroll Total ($ mil.)	Per Empl. ($)	Sales Total ($ mil.)	% of U.S.	Per Estab. ($)
Texas	3,406	10.9	34,562	10.8	10	1,539.0	44,530	13,023.1	11.5	3,823,583
California	3,057	9.8	29,317	9.2	10	1,325.9	45,227	10,165.6	8.9	3,325,363
Illinois	1,847	5.9	23,426	7.3	13	1,217.7	51,979	9,513.8	8.4	5,150,964
Michigan	1,452	4.6	14,900	4.7	10	723.3	48,541	6,072.1	5.3	4,181,884
Ohio	1,680	5.4	17,801	5.6	11	793.1	44,555	5,733.5	5.0	3,412,781
Georgia	959	3.1	13,522	4.2	14	679.5	50,251	5,280.6	4.6	5,506,339
Pennsylvania	1,327	4.2	14,615	4.6	11	686.3	46,962	5,278.6	4.6	3,977,852
New York	1,328	4.2	11,067	3.5	8	535.8	48,419	4,629.8	4.1	3,486,298
New Jersey	1,045	3.3	10,614	3.3	10	555.8	52,366	4,124.0	3.6	3,946,425
North Carolina	1,018	3.3	11,948	3.7	12	556.0	46,531	4,080.3	3.6	4,008,194
Indiana	774	2.5	7,904	2.5	10	339.0	42,884	3,642.8	3.2	4,706,504
Louisiana	770	2.5	9,815	3.1	13	431.9	44,000	3,043.8	2.7	3,952,982
Massachusetts	624	2.0	7,443	2.3	12	414.1	55,635	2,631.0	2.3	4,216,420
Wisconsin	746	2.4	7,654	2.4	10	343.5	44,879	2,629.6	2.3	3,524,948
Minnesota	570	1.8	6,386	2.0	11	310.6	48,631	2,433.8	2.1	4,269,879
Missouri	590	1.9	6,972	2.2	12	295.5	42,386	2,295.8	2.0	3,891,232
Washington	565	1.8	5,326	1.7	9	248.2	46,595	2,001.5	1.8	3,542,462
Tennessee	606	1.9	6,170	1.9	10	259.2	42,002	1,828.9	1.6	3,017,975
Connecticut	443	1.4	4,586	1.4	10	233.8	50,974	1,762.9	1.6	3,979,413
Virginia	488	1.6	5,281	1.7	11	266.7	50,494	1,637.8	1.4	3,356,225
Oklahoma	592	1.9	5,102	1.6	9	193.7	37,958	1,453.7	1.3	2,455,657
Kentucky	365	1.2	4,243	1.3	12	175.6	41,388	1,446.8	1.3	3,963,959
South Carolina	452	1.4	3,832	1.2	8	166.7	43,515	1,279.1	1.1	2,829,783
Alabama	460	1.5	4,067	1.3	9	164.6	40,472	1,233.1	1.1	2,680,689
Colorado	425	1.4	3,697	1.2	9	182.1	49,247	1,167.4	1.0	2,746,911
Maryland	312	1.0	3,434	1.1	11	157.4	45,831	1,091.6	1.0	3,498,756
Oregon	364	1.2	3,745	1.2	10	164.0	43,783	1,032.5	0.9	2,836,602
Kansas	339	1.1	2,956	0.9	9	118.9	40,227	928.7	0.8	2,739,522
Iowa	261	0.8	2,671	0.8	10	101.0	37,796	713.7	0.6	2,734,571

Continued on next page.

INDUSTRY DATA BY STATE - Continued

State	Establishments		Employment			Payroll		Sales		
	Total (number)	% of U.S.	Total (number)	% of U.S.	Per Estab.	Total ($ mil.)	Per Empl. ($)	Total ($ mil.)	% of U.S.	Per Estab. ($)
Utah	255	0.8	2,259	0.7	9	93.3	41,317	672.7	0.6	2,637,867
New Mexico	187	0.6	1,669	0.5	9	81.1	48,613	593.3	0.5	3,172,471
Arkansas	267	0.9	2,320	0.7	9	79.0	34,039	543.6	0.5	2,035,981
Wyoming	145	0.5	1,332	0.4	9	56.3	42,245	461.4	0.4	3,182,090
New Hampshire	165	0.5	1,255	0.4	8	57.5	45,838	415.7	0.4	2,519,115
Mississippi	193	0.6	1,669	0.5	9	60.4	36,215	405.0	0.4	2,098,472
Idaho	110	0.4	1,069	0.3	10	54.9	51,390	372.6	0.3	3,387,127
Rhode Island	101	0.3	1,018	0.3	10	46.9	46,056	364.8	0.3	3,611,465
Nebraska	146	0.5	1,455	0.5	10	56.7	38,966	346.0	0.3	2,369,664
West Virginia	140	0.4	1,374	0.4	10	47.8	34,793	328.0	0.3	2,343,064
Nevada	113	0.4	949	0.3	8	36.1	38,012	264.7	0.2	2,342,292
Maine	94	0.3	920	0.3	10	41.6	45,202	255.5	0.2	2,717,862
Alaska	61	0.2	548	0.2	9	32.0	58,378	254.1	0.2	4,166,049
South Dakota	45	0.1	864	0.3	19	23.3	26,962	176.1	0.2	3,913,867
Vermont	40	0.1	455	0.1	11	29.6	65,075	162.0	0.1	4,049,825
Delaware	69	0.2	539	0.2	8	20.5	37,991	137.9	0.1	1,998,391
Hawaii	49	0.2	462	0.1	9	16.8	36,340	119.4	0.1	2,435,755
North Dakota	74	0.2	511	0.2	7	16.6	32,462	110.3	0.1	1,490,541
Montana	69	0.2	371	0.1	5	12.3	33,264	82.1	0.1	1,190,507
Florida	1,722	5.5	10K-24999	-	-	(D)	-	(D)	-	-
Arizona	357	1.1	2500-4999	-	-	(D)	-	(D)	-	-
D.C.	5	-	0-19	-	-	(D)	-	(D)	-	-

Source: 2002 *Economic Census*. The states are in descending order of sales or establishments (if sales data are missing for the majority). The symbol (D) appears when data are withheld to prevent disclosure of competitive information. States marked with (D) are sorted by number of establishments. A dash (-) indicates that the data element cannot be calculated. Shaded *states* on the state map indicate those states which have proportionately greater representation in the industry than would be indicated by the states population; the ratio is based on total sales or number of establishments. Shaded *regions* indicate where the industry is regionally most concentrated.

NAICS 423840 - INDUSTRIAL SUPPLIES MERCHANT WHOLESALERS

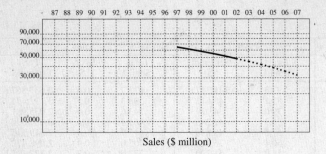

Sales ($ million)

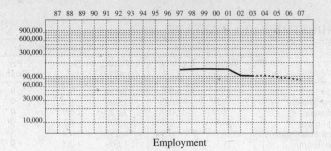

Employment

GENERAL STATISTICS

Year	Establishments (number)	Employment (number)	Payroll ($ million)	Sales ($ million)	Employees per Establishment (number)	Sales per Establishment ($)	Payroll per Employee ($)
1987	-	-	-	-	-	-	-
1988	-	-	-	-	-	-	-
1989	-	-	-	-	-	-	-
1990	-	-	-	-	-	-	-
1991	-	-	-	-	-	-	-
1992	-	-	-	-	-	-	-
1993	-	-	-	-	-	-	-
1994	-	-	-	-	-	-	-
1995	-	-	-	-	-	-	-
1996	-	-	-	-	-	-	-
1997	15,055	140,735	5,240.8	64,861.3	9.3	4,308,289.6	37,238.8
1998	14,982	144,706	5,627.8	61,586.5 e	9.7	4,110,696.8	38,891.3
1999	15,152	146,666	5,859.4	58,311.6 e	9.7	3,848,443.8	39,950.6
2000	14,880	145,730	6,047.6	55,036.8 e	9.8	3,698,708.3	41,498.6
2001	14,723	144,668	5,931.1	51,761.9 e	9.8	3,515,719.6	40,998.1
2002	10,751	105,327	4,359.8	48,487.1	9.8	4,510,008.4	41,393.0
2003	11,008	102,924	4,523.5	45,212.3 p	9.3	3,906,037.1 p	43,949.6
2004	10,788 p	105,224 p	4,710.5 p	41,937.4 p	9.7 p	3,879,577.9 p	44,300.4 p
2005	10,037 p	98,289 p	4,545.7 p	38,662.6 p	9.7 p	3,853,118.6 p	45,235.6 p
2006	9,286 p	91,353 p	4,380.8 p	35,387.7 p	9.7 p	3,826,659.4 p	46,170.7 p
2007	8,535 p	84,418 p	4,215.9 p	32,112.9 p	9.7 p	3,800,200.2 p	47,105.8 p

Source: *Economic Census of the United States*, 1997 and 2002. Establishment counts, employment, and payroll are from *County Business Patterns* for non-Census years. This is a newly defined industry. Data for prior years are unavailable at the time of publication but may become available over time. Values followed by 'p' are projections by the editors. Sales data for non-Census years are extrapolations, marked by 'e'.

INDICES OF CHANGE

Year	Establishments (number)	Employment (number)	Payroll ($ million)	Sales ($ million)	Employees per Establishment (number)	Sales per Establishment ($)	Payroll per Employee ($)
1987	-	-	-	-	-	-	-
1992	-	-	-	-	-	-	-
1993	-	-	-	-	-	-	-
1994	-	-	-	-	-	-	-
1995	-	-	-	-	-	-	-
1996	-	-	-	-	-	-	-
1997	140.0	133.6	120.2	133.8	94.9	95.5	90.0
1998	139.4	137.4	129.1	127.0 e	99.0	91.1	94.0
1999	140.9	139.2	134.4	120.3 e	99.0	85.3	96.5
2000	138.4	138.4	138.7	113.5 e	100.0	82.0	100.3
2001	136.9	137.4	136.0	106.8 e	100.0	78.0	99.0
2002	100.0	100.0	100.0	100.0	100.0	100.0	100.0
2003	102.4	97.7	103.8	93.2 p	95.4	86.6 p	106.2
2004	100.3 p	99.9 p	108.0 p	86.5 p	99.0 p	86.0 p	107.0 p
2005	93.4 p	93.3 p	104.3 p	79.7 p	99.1 p	85.4 p	109.3 p
2006	86.4 p	86.7 p	100.5 p	73.0 p	99.3 p	84.8 p	111.5 p
2007	79.4 p	80.1 p	96.7 p	66.2 p	99.5 p	84.3 p	113.8 p

Sources: Same as General Statistics. The values shown reflect change from the base year, 2002. Values above 100 mean greater than 2002, values below 100 mean less than 2002, and a value of 100 in the 1987-2001 or 2003-2007 period means same as 2002. Values followed by a 'p' are projections by the editors; 'e' stands for extrapolation. Data are the most recent available at this level of detail.

SELECTED RATIOS

For 2002	Avg. of All Wholesale	Analyzed Industry	Index	For 2002	Avg. of All Wholesale	Analyzed Industry	Index
Employees per Establishment	15	10	66	Sales per Employee	791,325	460,348	58
Payroll per Establishment	626,122	405,525	65	Sales per Establishment	12,012,387	4,510,008	38
Payroll per Employee	41,161	41,393	101	Expenses per Establishment	na	na	na

Sources: Same as General Statistics. The 'Average of All' column, Wholesale or Retail, represents the average of the sector reported for the most recent complete year available. The Index shows the relationship between the Average and the Analyzed Industry. For example, 100 means that they are equal; 500 that the Analyzed Industry is five times the average; 50 means that the Analyzed Industry is half the national average. The abbreviation 'na' is used to show that data are 'not available'.

LEADING COMPANIES   Number shown: 75   Total sales ($ mil): 28,061   Total employment (000): 68.7

Company Name	Address				CEO Name	Phone	Co. Type	Sales ($ mil)	Empl. (000)
Genuine Parts Co.	2999 Circle 75 Pkwy	Atlanta	GA	30339	Thomas C. Gallagher	770-953-1700	P	9,097	30.8
WESCO International Inc.	Commerce Court	Pittsburgh	PA	15219	Ron Haley	412-454-2200	P	3,741	5.3
Unisource Worldwide Inc.	6600 Gov Lk	Norcross	GA	30071	Allan Dragone	770-447-9000	S	3,701*	8.0
Motion Industries Inc.	PO Box 1477	Birmingham	AL	35201		205-956-1122	S	2,250	5.0
Cameron and Barkley Co.	PO Box 118007	Charleston	SC	29423	James R Warren	843-745-2400	R	1,078*	2.6
Kaman Corp.	PO Box 1	Bloomfield	CT	06002		860-243-7100	P	895	3.5
H. Muehlstein and Company Inc.	800 Connecticut Ave	Norwalk	CT	06854	J Kevin Donohue	203-855-6000	R	875*	0.4
McJunkin Corp.	PO Box 513	Charleston	WV	25322	H Barnard Wehrle III	304-348-5211	R	847*	1.6
Industrial Distribution Group Inc.	950 E Paces Ferry	Atlanta	GA	30326	Richard M Seigel	770-949-2100	P	483	1.3
Tyco Valves and Controls	9700 W Gulf Bank	Houston	TX	77040	Tom Pickett	713-466-1176	D	479*	0.5
Lawson Products Inc.	1666 E Touhy Ave	Des Plaines	IL	60018	Jeffrey B Belford	847-827-9666	P	420	0.0
Alamo Iron Works Inc.	PO Box 231	San Antonio	TX	78291	Anthony Koch	210-223-6161	R	319*	0.4
Production Tool Supply	PO Box 987	Warren	MI	48089	Larry Wolfe	586-755-5258	R	202*	0.6
Flowers Auto Parts Co.	PO Box 1118	Hickory	NC	28601	Bobby Flowers	828-322-5414	R	182*	0.1
Miller Bearings Inc.	17 S Westmoreland	Orlando	FL	32805	Craig Faber	407-425-9078	R	164*	0.1
Drago Supply Company Inc.	740 Houston Ave	Port Arthur	TX	77640	Joseph P Drago	409-983-4911	R	139*	0.2
Nissho Iwai American Corp.	1211 Av Americas	New York	NY	10036	Teruo Matsumura	212-704-6500	S	130*	0.1
C and H Distributors Inc.	PO Box 14770	Milwaukee	WI	53214		414-443-1700	R	125*	0.4
DoAll Co.	254 Laurel Ave	Des Plaines	IL	60016	Michael Wilkie	847-824-1122	R	124*	0.1
IBT Inc.	PO Box 2982	Schuylkl Hvn	KS	66201	Stephen R Cloud	913-677-3151	R	123*	0.4
Schmidt Group Inc.	PO Box 25189	Greenville	SC	29616	Carl V Schmidt	864-288-9460	R	113*	<0.1
Columbia Pipe and Supply	1120 W Pershing Rd	Chicago	IL	60609	William D Arenberg	773-927-6600	R	112*	0.3
Norwood Promotional Products	2 N Market St	Indianapolis	IN	46204	Thomas B Roller	317-275-2500	R	100*	1.0
Trumbull Industries Inc.	PO Box 30	Warren	OH	44482	Murray Miller	330-393-6624	R	87*	0.3
Associated Packaging Inc.	435 Calvert Dr	Gallatin	TN	37066	Joe R Smith	615-452-2131	R	86*	0.1
United States Strong Tool Co.	1251 E 286th St	Cleveland	OH	44132	Cedric Beckett	216-289-2450	S	81*	0.1
Bearing and Drives Inc.	PO Box 4325	Macon	GA	31208	Andrew H Nations	478-746-7623	R	72*	0.2
Ilapak Inc.	105 Pheasant Run	Newtown	PA	18940	Andrew Axberg	215-579-2900	R	72*	<0.1
Medal Distributing Co.	330 Vine Ave	Sharon	PA	16146	Dominic Preggi	724-342-6839	D	65*	<0.1
Continental Glass	841 W Cermak Rd	Chicago	IL	60608	Richard Giesen	312-666-2050	R	61*	0.1
RAK Industries	10 Deep Rock Rd	Rochester	NY	14624	Michael Kaufman	585-235-9010	R	61*	0.1
Sun Devil Fire Equipment Inc.	2211 S 3rd Dr	Phoenix	AZ	85003	Randy Simmers	623-245-0636	R	60*	<0.1
Black and Co.	PO Box 1160	Decatur	IL	62525	Jeffrey S Black	217-428-4424	R	58*	0.1
Mid-States Supply Company Inc.	1716 Guinotte Ave	Kansas City	MO	64120	Milton Brown	816-842-4290	R	57*	0.2
Zy-Tech Global Industries	10600 Corporate Dr	Stafford	TX	77477	Ray Baker	281-565-1010	R	57*	0.1
Crown Packaging International	8919 Colorado St	Merrillville	IN	46410	Dennis Tilles	219-738-1000	R	54*	0.2
Pacific Pipe Company Inc.	PO Box 23711	Oakland	CA	94623		510-452-0122	R	54*	<0.1
Industrial Supply Solutions Inc.	804 Julian Rd	Salisbury	NC	28147	Frank Carmazzi	704-636-4241	R	53	0.2
Duncan Equipment Co.	3450 S MacArthur	Oklahoma City	OK	73179	David Ragland	405-688-2300	R	52*	0.2
General Tool and Supply Co.	2705 NW Nicolai St	Portland	OR	97210		503-226-3411	R	50*	0.1
Abatix Corp.	8201 Eastpoint Dr	Dallas	TX	75227	Terry W Shaver	214-381-0322	P	49	0.1
East West Industrial Engineering	PO Box 7983	Ann Arbor	MI	48107	Dilip Mullick	734-971-6265	R	49*	0.1
Vegas Fastener Manufacturing	4315 W Oquendo Rd	Las Vegas	NV	89118		702-651-9222	R	49*	0.1
Industrial Supply Company Inc.	PO Box 30600	Salt Lake City	UT	84115	Philip Thompson III	801-484-8644	R	47*	0.1
Persinger Supply Co.	PO Box 188	Prichard	WV	25555	Bernice Deskins	304-486-5401	R	46*	<0.1
T.F. Hudgins Inc.	PO Box 920946	Houston	TX	77292	Ted Edwards	713-682-3651	R	45*	<0.1
Nalpac Enterprises Limited Inc.	1111 E Eight Mile	Ferndale	MI	48220	Ralph Caplan	248-541-1140	R	44*	<0.1
Newman's Inc.	1300 Gazin St	Houston	TX	77020	Steve Mines	713-675-8631	S	43*	0.2
Apache Hose and Belting Inc.	PO Box 1719	Cedar Rapids	IA	52406	Steve Crain	319-365-0471	R	42*	0.2
Mitchell Rubber Products Inc.	10220 San Sevaine	Mira Loma	CA	91752	Mark Mitchell	951-681-5655	R	42*	0.4
United Central Supply	PO Box 8300	Bristol	VA	24203	Jim Tate	276-466-0511	R	42*	0.2
Machine and Welding Supply Co.	PO Box 1708	Dunn	NC	28335	Emmett C Aldredge Jr	910-892-4016	R	40*	0.2
O. Berk Co.	3 Milltown Ct	Union	NJ	07083	Marc M Gaelen	908-851-9500	R	40*	0.1
F.B. Wright Co.	PO Box 770	Dearborn	MI	48121	William J Reno	313-843-8250	R	39*	0.1
Hubbard Industrial Supply Co.	901 W 2nd St	Flint	MI	48502	Robert Fuller	810-234-8681	R	39*	<0.1
Indiana Supply Corp.	3835 E 21st St	Indianapolis	IN	46218	Dave Draga	317-359-5451	R	37*	<0.1
Vellano Brothers Inc.	7 Hemlock St	Latham	NY	12110	Joseph Vellano	518-785-5537	R	35*	<0.1
New England Controls Inc.	PO Box 446	Mansfield	MA	02048	Ronald Hayden	508-339-5522	R	34*	<0.1
Industrial Supply	PO Box 6356	Richmond	VA	23230		757-855-1071	R	34*	0.1
Macomb Pipe and Supply Inc.	34400 Mound Rd	Sterling Heights	MI	48310	William McGivern	586-274-4100	R	33*	<0.1
Cross Sales and Engineering Co.	PO Box 18508	Greensboro	NC	27419	William S Cross III	336-856-6000	R	33*	0.2
Distribution International	PO Box 23847	Houston	TX	77228		713-428-3900	R	33*	<0.1
Metric & Multistandard	120 Old Saw Mill	Hawthorne	NY	10532	Joseph Voves	914-769-5020	R	32*	<0.1
California Industrial Rubber Inc.	2732 S Cherry Ave	Fresno	CA	93706	Larry T Cane	559-485-1487	R	32*	<0.1
Cornerstone Controls Inc.	7251 E Kemper Rd	Cincinnati	OH	45249	Casey Coleman	513-489-2500	R	32*	0.1
Midvale Industries Inc.	6310 Knox Ind Dr	St. Louis	MO	63139		314-647-5604	R	32*	<0.1
Eastern Iowa Supply Inc.	4625 6th St SW	Cedar Rapids	IA	52404	Mary Dimmer-Oakley	319-366-8993	R	32*	<0.1
Schmidt's Wholesale Inc.	PO Box 5100	Monticello	NY	12701	Gary Schmidt	845-794-5900	R	31*	<0.1
Transply Inc.	1005 Vogelsong Rd	York	PA	17404	Ray Gross	717-767-1005	R	30*	<0.1
Ropak Northwest Inc.	2108 B St NW A110	Auburn	WA	98001	David Williams	253-872-0900	S	29*	<0.1
W.L. Halsey Company Inc.	PO Box 6485	Huntsville	AL	35824		256-772-9691	R	29*	0.1
Reid Tool Supply Co.	2265 Black Creek	Muskegon	MI	49444	Paul Reid	231-777-3951	R	28*	<0.1
Schermerhorn Brothers Co.	PO Box 668	Lombard	IL	60148		630-627-9860	R	28*	<0.1
Mill Supply Corp.	PO Box 12216	Salem	OR	97309	Steve Zahradnik	503-585-7411	R	26*	<0.1
Zuckerman-Honickman Inc.	191 S Gulph Rd	King of Prussia	PA	19406	Benjamin Zuckerman	610-962-0100	R	26*	<0.1

Source: Ward's Business Directory of U.S. Private and Public Companies, Volumes 1 and 2, 2005. The company type code used is as follows: P - Public, R - Private, S - Subsidiary, D - Division, J - Joint Venture, A - Affiliate, G - Group. Sales are in millions of dollars, employees are in thousands. An asterisk (*) indicates an estimated sales volume. The symbol < stands for 'less than'. Company names and addresses are truncated, in some cases, to fit into the available space.

OCCUPATIONS EMPLOYED BY MACHINERY, EQUIPMENT, & SUPPLIES WHOLESALE

Occupation	% of Total 2004	Change to 2014	Occupation	% of Total 2004	Change to 2014
Sales reps, wholesale & manufacturing, exc tech	16.2	9.7	Truck drivers, light or delivery services	2.0	9.7
Mobile heavy equipment mechanics, except engines	5.7	9.7	Industrial machinery mechanics	2.0	9.7
Sales reps, wholesale & manufacturing, tech	3.6	9.6	Order clerks	1.8	-28.7
Laborers & freight, stock, & material movers, hand	3.4	-1.3	Secretaries, except legal, medical, & executive	1.7	-7.7
Shipping, receiving, & traffic clerks	3.4	-0.7	Team assemblers	1.7	9.7
Office clerks, general	3.4	-2.4	Bus & truck mechanics & diesel engine specialists	1.6	9.7
Bookkeeping, accounting, & auditing clerks	3.1	-1.3	First-line supervisors of mechanics	1.5	9.6
General & operations managers	3.0	8.5	First-line supervisors/managers of office workers	1.4	-0.6
Customer service representatives	2.6	12.3	Truck drivers, heavy & tractor-trailer	1.3	9.6
Maintenance & repair workers, general	2.4	9.7	Sales managers	1.3	17.3
Parts salespersons	2.4	-12.3	Machinists	1.3	9.7
First-line supervisors/managers of non-retail sales work	2.3	1.4	Welders, cutters, solderers, & brazers	1.0	9.7
Stock clerks & order fillers	2.2	-16.0	Executive secretaries & administrative assistants	1.0	3.9

Source: Industry-Occupation Matrix, Bureau of Labor Statistics. These data are reported based on 4-digit NAICS categories but have been matched to corresponding 6-digit NAICS industry codes. The change reported for each occupation to the year 2014 is a percent of growth or decline as estimated by the Bureau of Labor Statistics. The abbreviation nec stands for 'not elsewhere classified.'

LOCATION BY STATE AND REGIONAL CONCENTRATION

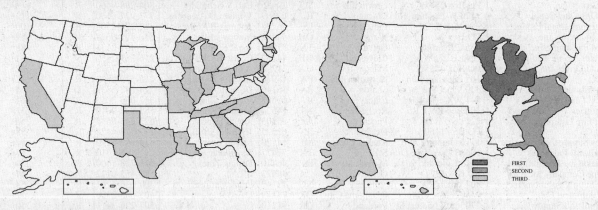

FIRST
SECOND
THIRD

INDUSTRY DATA BY STATE

State	Establishments Total (number)	% of U.S.	Employment Total (number)	% of U.S.	Per Estab.	Payroll Total ($ mil.)	Per Empl. ($)	Sales Total ($ mil.)	% of U.S.	Per Estab. ($)
California	1,211	10.9	11,120	10.3	9	469.6	42,227	7,303.8	14.2	6,031,191
Texas	992	9.0	9,622	8.9	10	416.7	43,312	4,912.5	9.6	4,952,087
Georgia	391	3.5	4,047	3.8	10	181.8	44,929	3,466.3	6.7	8,865,330
Michigan	429	3.9	4,960	4.6	12	220.4	44,432	3,438.3	6.7	8,014,641
Pennsylvania	497	4.5	5,031	4.7	10	230.4	45,795	2,964.3	5.8	5,964,310
Ohio	579	5.2	6,668	6.2	12	272.3	40,831	2,959.3	5.8	5,110,969
New Jersey	399	3.6	4,140	3.8	10	195.7	47,259	2,764.9	5.4	6,929,697
Illinois	640	5.8	7,208	6.7	11	315.0	43,697	2,703.4	5.3	4,224,105
New York	515	4.7	6,125	5.7	12	266.5	43,511	1,790.8	3.5	3,477,231
North Carolina	345	3.1	3,852	3.6	11	138.6	35,980	1,669.5	3.2	4,839,180
Massachusetts	197	1.8	1,971	1.8	10	106.6	54,071	1,432.4	2.8	7,271,096
Florida	530	4.8	3,501	3.3	7	129.8	37,068	1,370.0	2.7	2,584,928
Missouri	229	2.1	1,896	1.8	8	73.5	38,754	1,358.0	2.6	5,930,262
Tennessee	238	2.2	2,687	2.5	11	106.0	39,443	1,266.1	2.5	5,319,819
Indiana	257	2.3	2,664	2.5	10	103.4	38,806	1,227.6	2.4	4,776,591
Wisconsin	239	2.2	2,842	2.6	12	110.6	38,905	1,049.5	2.0	4,391,360
Louisiana	271	2.4	2,887	2.7	11	107.5	37,239	909.6	1.8	3,356,446
Washington	208	1.9	1,909	1.8	9	67.9	35,587	721.5	1.4	3,468,865
Alabama	228	2.1	2,353	2.2	10	84.8	36,020	640.5	1.2	2,809,171
South Carolina	172	1.6	1,653	1.5	10	64.0	38,705	534.4	1.0	3,106,977
Kentucky	151	1.4	1,547	1.4	10	55.8	36,098	512.2	1.0	3,392,166
Virginia	163	1.5	1,528	1.4	9	62.5	40,911	481.1	0.9	2,951,534
Oklahoma	176	1.6	1,486	1.4	8	54.5	36,673	447.3	0.9	2,541,540
Connecticut	140	1.3	1,057	1.0	8	50.2	47,539	427.1	0.8	3,050,657
Oregon	172	1.6	1,270	1.2	7	54.6	42,994	407.3	0.8	2,367,948
Colorado	166	1.5	1,458	1.4	9	56.8	38,973	369.5	0.7	2,225,892
Iowa	112	1.0	839	0.8	7	29.8	35,522	335.4	0.7	2,994,679
Maryland	120	1.1	911	0.8	8	37.9	41,614	278.9	0.5	2,324,042
Arkansas	123	1.1	1,008	0.9	8	34.3	34,057	278.2	0.5	2,261,715

Continued on next page.

INDUSTRY DATA BY STATE - Continued

State	Establishments Total (number)	Establishments % of U.S.	Employment Total (number)	Employment % of U.S.	Employment Per Estab.	Payroll Total ($ mil.)	Payroll Per Empl. ($)	Sales Total ($ mil.)	Sales % of U.S.	Sales Per Estab. ($)
Nebraska	50	0.5	662	0.6	13	25.2	38,091	226.4	0.4	4,528,120
West Virginia	64	0.6	822	0.8	13	25.1	30,568	224.3	0.4	3,505,125
Mississippi	77	0.7	601	0.6	8	20.8	34,621	177.3	0.3	2,301,961
Utah	72	0.7	532	0.5	7	20.3	38,150	171.3	0.3	2,379,000
Nevada	62	0.6	416	0.4	7	16.0	38,351	169.5	0.3	2,734,000
New Hampshire	46	0.4	342	0.3	7	12.8	37,427	92.5	0.2	2,010,674
Rhode Island	38	0.3	360	0.3	9	14.9	41,297	90.5	0.2	2,380,579
Maine	34	0.3	275	0.3	8	12.4	44,909	84.4	0.2	2,483,294
New Mexico	51	0.5	313	0.3	6	11.6	37,054	79.9	0.2	1,566,882
South Dakota	11	0.1	73	0.1	7	3.6	49,493	74.3	0.1	6,750,818
Alaska	21	0.2	137	0.1	7	5.6	40,606	50.7	0.1	2,412,762
Hawaii	22	0.2	204	0.2	9	6.3	30,995	46.2	0.1	2,099,545
Montana	31	0.3	195	0.2	6	5.8	29,846	45.9	0.1	1,479,968
Wyoming	33	0.3	149	0.1	5	6.0	40,322	42.3	0.1	1,281,970
Minnesota	199	1.8	1000-2499	-	-	(D)	-	(D)	-	-
Arizona	137	1.2	500-999	-	-	(D)	-	(D)	-	-
Kansas	108	1.0	500-999	-	-	(D)	-	(D)	-	-
Idaho	42	0.4	100-249	-	-	(D)	-	(D)	-	-
Delaware	31	0.3	100-249	-	-	(D)	-	(D)	-	-
North Dakota	26	0.2	100-249	-	-	(D)	-	(D)	-	-
Vermont	14	0.1	20-99	-	-	(D)	-	(D)	-	-
D.C.	4	-	20-99	-	-	(D)	-	(D)	-	-

Source: 2002 *Economic Census*. The states are in descending order of sales or establishments (if sales data are missing for the majority). The symbol (D) appears when data are withheld to prevent disclosure of competitive information. States marked with (D) are sorted by number of establishments. A dash (-) indicates that the data element cannot be calculated. Shaded *states* on the state map indicate those states which have proportionately greater representation in the industry than would be indicated by the states population; the ratio is based on total sales or number of establishments. Shaded *regions* indicate where the industry is regionally most concentrated.

NAICS 423850 - SERVICE ESTABLISHMENT EQUIPMENT AND SUPPLIES MERCHANT WHOLESALERS

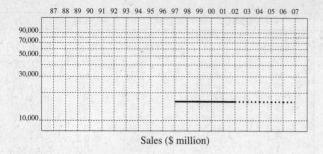

Sales ($ million)

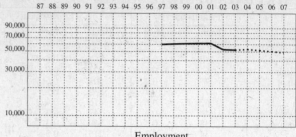

Employment

GENERAL STATISTICS

Year	Establishments (number)	Employment (number)	Payroll ($ million)	Sales ($ million)	Employees per Establishment (number)	Sales per Establishment ($)	Payroll per Employee ($)
1987	-	-	-	-	-	-	-
1988	-	-	-	-	-	-	-
1989	-	-	-	-	-	-	-
1990	-	-	-	-	-	-	-
1991	-	-	-	-	-	-	-
1992	-	-	-	-	-	-	-
1993	-	-	-	-	-	-	-
1994	-	-	-	-	-	-	-
1995	-	-	-	-	-	-	-
1996	-	-	-	-	-	-	-
1997	6,808	59,878	1,804.6	16,038.5	8.8	2,355,831.4	30,137.9
1998	6,765	60,564	1,944.7	16,025.4 e	9.0	2,368,863.3	32,109.8
1999	6,738	61,153	2,056.2	16,012.2 e	9.1	2,376,405.5	33,623.9
2000	6,548	61,407	2,159.6	15,999.1 e	9.4	2,443,353.7	35,168.9
2001	6,426	61,700	2,283.2	15,985.9 e	9.6	2,487,696.9	37,005.6
2002	5,594	52,804	1,902.0	15,972.8	9.4	2,855,345.0	36,020.0
2003	5,183	52,245	2,009.1	15,959.7 p	10.1	2,773,351.0 p	38,455.1
2004	5,219 p	53,126 p	2,130.6 p	15,946.5 p	10.1 p	2,856,808.6 p	39,810.7 p
2005	4,950 p	51,773 p	2,157.6 p	15,933.4 p	10.3 p	2,940,266.2 p	41,101.9 p
2006	4,681 p	50,420 p	2,184.6 p	15,920.2 p	10.4 p	3,023,723.9 p	42,393.1 p
2007	4,412 p	49,068 p	2,211.5 p	15,907.1 p	10.6 p	3,107,181.5 p	43,684.3 p

Source: *Economic Census of the United States*, 1997 and 2002. Establishment counts, employment, and payroll are from *County Business Patterns* for non-Census years. This is a newly defined industry. Data for prior years are unavailable at the time of publication but may become available over time. Values followed by 'p' are projections by the editors. Sales data for non-Census years are extrapolations, marked by 'e'.

INDICES OF CHANGE

Year	Establishments (number)	Employment (number)	Payroll ($ million)	Sales ($ million)	Employees per Establishment (number)	Sales per Establishment ($)	Payroll per Employee ($)
1987	-	-	-	-	-	-	-
1992	-	-	-	-	-	-	-
1993	-	-	-	-	-	-	-
1994	-	-	-	-	-	-	-
1995	-	-	-	-	-	-	-
1996	-	-	-	-	-	-	-
1997	121.7	113.4	94.9	100.4	93.6	82.5	83.7
1998	120.9	114.7	102.2	100.3 e	95.7	83.0	89.1
1999	120.5	115.8	108.1	100.2 e	96.8	83.2	93.3
2000	117.1	116.3	113.5	100.2 e	100.0	85.6	97.6
2001	114.9	116.8	120.0	100.1 e	102.1	87.1	102.7
2002	100.0	100.0	100.0	100.0	100.0	100.0	100.0
2003	92.7	98.9	105.6	99.9 p	107.2	97.1 p	106.8
2004	93.3 p	100.6 p	112.0 p	99.8 p	107.2 p	100.1 p	110.5 p
2005	88.5 p	98.0 p	113.4 p	99.8 p	109.1 p	103.0 p	114.1 p
2006	83.7 p	95.5 p	114.9 p	99.7 p	111.1 p	105.9 p	117.7 p
2007	78.9 p	92.9 p	116.3 p	99.6 p	113.0 p	108.8 p	121.3 p

Sources: Same as General Statistics. The values shown reflect change from the base year, 2002. Values above 100 mean greater than 2002, values below 100 mean less than 2002, and a value of 100 in the 1987-2001 or 2003-2007 period means same as 2002. Values followed by a 'p' are projections by the editors; 'e' stands for extrapolation. Data are the most recent available at this level of detail.

SELECTED RATIOS

For 2002	Avg. of All Wholesale	Analyzed Industry	Index	For 2002	Avg. of All Wholesale	Analyzed Industry	Index
Employees per Establishment	15	9	63	Sales per Employee	791,325	302,492	38
Payroll per Establishment	626,122	340,007	54	Sales per Establishment	12,012,387	2,855,345	24
Payroll per Employee	41,161	36,020	88	Expenses per Establishment	na	na	na

Sources: Same as General Statistics. The 'Average of All' column, Wholesale or Retail, represents the average of the sector reported for the most recent complete year available. The Index shows the relationship between the Average and the Analyzed Industry. For example, 100 means that they are equal; 500 that the Analyzed Industry is five times the average; 50 means that the Analyzed Industry is half the national average. The abbreviation 'na' is used to show that data are 'not available'.

LEADING COMPANIES   Number shown: **75**   Total sales ($ mil): **6,721**   Total employment (000): **18.0**

Company Name	Address				CEO Name	Phone	Co. Type	Sales ($ mil)	Empl. (000)
Unisource Worldwide Inc.	6600 Gov Lk	Norcross	GA	30071	Allan Dragone	770-447-9000	S	3,701*	8.0
Edward Don and Co.	2500 S Harlem Ave	North Riverside	IL	60546	Steve Don	708-442-9400	R	379*	1.2
Clark Foodservice Inc.	950 Arthur Ave	Elk Grove Vill.	IL	60007	Donald J Hindman	847-956-1730	R	310*	0.8
Horizon	5214 S 30th St	Phoenix	AZ	85040	Bill Hayes	602-276-7700	R	213*	0.4
W.S. Lee and Sons Inc.	PO Box 1631	Altoona	PA	16603	Robert Lee	814-696-3535	R	160*	0.3
Unisource Midwest Inc.	PO Box 597	Columbus	OH	43216		614-251-7000	S	125*	0.3
Happ Controls Inc.	106 Garlisch Dr	Elk Grove Vill.	IL	60007	Tom Happ	847-593-6130	S	98*	0.3
Aerial Company Inc.	PO Box 197	Marinette	WI	54143	Ryan Hmielewski	715-735-9323	R	75*	0.4
Emiliani Enterprises	735 Rahway Ave	Union	NJ	07083	Don Emiliani	908-964-6340	R	71*	0.3
Mikara Corp.	3109 Louisiana N	Minneapolis	MN	55427	Michael P Hicks	763-546-9500	R	65*	0.2
Singer Equipment Company Inc.	PO Box 13668	Reading	PA	19612	Fred Singer	610-929-8000	R	56*	0.3
HP Products Corp.	4220 Saquaro Trail	Indianapolis	IN	46268	Donald Ames Shuel	317-298-9950	R	54*	0.3
Chocola Cleaning Materials Inc.	1314 N Larch St	Lansing	MI	48906	Robert Corwin	517-372-9330	R	51*	0.2
Muster Associates Inc.	PO Box 160	Calhoun	KY	42327	John Muster	270-273-3619	R	50*	<0.1
Kaiser Wholesale Inc.	PO Box 1115	New Albany	IN	47150	JR Kaiser	812-945-2651	R	50*	<0.1
PBI Market Equipment Inc.	PO Box 6097	Signal Hill	CA	90755	Tom L Everson	562-595-4785	R	50*	<0.1
Impact Products L.L.C.	2840 Centennial Rd	Toledo	OH	43617	John Harbal	419-841-2891	R	43*	0.2
Paper Mart	5361 Alexander	Cty-Commerce	CA	90040	Rosemary Martin	323-726-8200	R	40*	<0.1
Institutional Wholesale Co.	535 Dry Valley Rd	Cookeville	TN	38506	Jimmy W Mackie	931-537-4000	R	38*	0.1
Wabash National Trailer Centers	3700 N Cage Blvd	Pharr	TX	78577		956-781-8070	R	38*	<0.1
Ro-Vic Inc.	PO Box 1140	Manchester	CT	06045	R Parrott Jr	860-646-3322	R	36*	0.1
Natural Choice	5700 Buckingham	Culver City	CA	90230	Dana Bashor	310-342-5300	R	35*	0.1
Industrial Soap Co.	722 S Vandeventer	St. Louis	MO	63110	Mark Shapiro	314-241-6363	R	35*	0.1
Marlin Industries	PO Box 11642	Philadelphia	PA	19116	Nancy Brownstein	215-671-1540	R	35*	0.1
M. Conley Co.	1312 4th St SE	Canton	OH	44701	Richard D Conley	330-456-8243	R	32*	0.1
National Tanning Supply	2701 N Farmers Mkt	Springfield	IL	62707	David Orlikowski	217-585-4200	R	31*	<0.1
Mutual Trading Company Inc.	431 Crocker St	Los Angeles	CA	90013	N Kanai	213-626-9458	R	30*	1.0
Bermil Industries Corp	461 Doughty Blvd	Inwood	NY	11096	Marc Stern	516-371-4400	R	29*	<0.1
Maly's Inc.	4555 Danvers Dr SE	Grand Rapids	MI	49512	Michael Maly	616-942-0060	R	28*	0.1
Paramount Restaurant Supply	101 Main St	Warren	RI	02885	David Friedman	401-247-6500	R	26*	<0.1
Glover Wholesale Inc.	5427 Armour Rd	Columbus	GA	31908	David Harris	706-322-7376	R	25*	<0.1
Kenway Distributors Inc.	PO Box 9347	Louisville	KY	40209	James W Crutcher	502-367-2201	R	24*	<0.1
Corachem Inc.	83 Ambrogio Dr	Gurnee	IL	60031	Raymond Kloss	847-336-0060	R	23*	<0.1
Adams-Burch Inc.	1901 Stanford Ct	Hyattsville	MD	20785	Dan W Blaylock	301-341-1600	R	23*	0.1
Coast Wide Supply Company Inc.	PO Box 84203	Seattle	WA	98124	W Watkinson	206-624-1225	R	21*	<0.1
Crane Interiors Inc.	PO Box 459	Woodbury	TN	37190	Thomas Evans	615-563-4800	R	20*	0.2
Equipment Concentration Site	1750 Ontario Ave	Watertown	NY	13602		315-772-6675	R	20*	<0.1
American Industrial Supply	519 Potrero Ave	San Francisco	CA	94110	George Herbst	415-826-1144	R	20*	<0.1
Columbus Paper Company Inc.	PO Box 6369	Columbus	GA	31917	Michael Greenblatt	706-689-1361	R	20*	<0.1
San Joaquin Supply Company Inc.	PO Box 2458	Fresno	CA	93745		559-265-7020	R	20*	<0.1
Warren Fire Equipment Inc.	6880 Tod Ave SW	Warren	OH	44481	Robert Malone	330-824-3523	R	20*	<0.1
All Valley Washer Service Inc.	15008 Delano St	Van Nuys	CA	91411	Ron Feinstein	818-787-1100	R	20*	<0.1
Dennis Paper and Food Service	216 Thatcher St	Bangor	ME	04401	Ronald Dennis	207-947-0321	R	20*	<0.1
Kranz Inc.	2200 DeKoven Ave	Racine	WI	53403	Jeff Neubauer	262-638-2200	R	19*	<0.1
Independent Salon Resource Inc.	7301 114th Ave	Largo	FL	33773	James Cheek	727-548-4420	R	19*	<0.1
Holt Paper and Chemical Inc.	PO Box 3197	Salisbury	MD	21802	John Holt	410-742-7577	R	18*	<0.1
LTP Products and Services Inc.	PO Box 486	Concordville	PA	19331	Peter Annunziato	610-459-2701	R	18*	<0.1
Bauman Paper Company Inc.	PO Box 13022	Lexington	KY	40512	FW Baumann Jr	859-252-8891	R	17*	<0.1
McShane Enterprises Inc.	PO Box 1046	East Brunswick	NJ	08816	David R McShane	732-254-3100	R	17*	<0.1
A and A Chemical Products	PO Box 3786	Augusta	GA	30914	Calvin Agner	706-733-1995	R	16*	<0.1
Armstrong McCall Inc.	5538 N 7th St	Phoenix	AZ	85014	Chris Rendazzo	602-277-5481	R	16*	<0.1
Fitch Dustdown Company Inc.	2201 Russell St	Baltimore	MD	21230	Raymond Kirsner	410-539-1953	R	16*	<0.1
Jefferson Supply Co.	PO Box 7446	Charlottesville	VA	22906	Ralph Hathaway	434-977-8244	R	16*	<0.1
Sitex Corp.	PO Box 38	Henderson	KY	42419	Wes Sights	270-827-3537	R	14*	0.2
Omaha Compound Co.	2001 Nicholas St	Omaha	NE	68102	Justin Manvitz	402-346-7117	R	14*	<0.1
Alpha and Omega Janitorial Sups	4013 Clay Ave Ste C	Fort Worth	TX	76117	Douglas Reichert	817-656-8450	R	14*	<0.1
Ana Molinari	52 S Palm Ave	Sarasota	FL	34236	Ana Molinari	941-365-1415	R	14*	<0.1
Beauty Craft Supply & Equipment	11110 Bren Rd W	Hopkins	MN	55343	Maximillio Wexler	952-935-4420	R	14*	<0.1
Blackburn Building Services	132 Cross Rd	Waterford	CT	06385	Steve Blackburn	860-447-2000	R	14*	<0.1
Crown Sanitary Supply Inc.	5553 Anglers Ave	Fort Lauderdale	FL	33312	Mark Finkelstein	954-987-7546	R	14*	<0.1
Dvs Shoe Company Inc.	955 Francisco St	Torrance	CA	90502	Kevin Dunlap	310-715-8300	R	14*	<0.1
G and H Service Corp.	W7934 Prospect Rd	Beaver Dam	WI	53916	Don Geddeis	920-885-6996	R	14*	<0.1
Olla Beauty Supply Inc.	76 Bergen Tpke	Little Ferry	NJ	07643	Steve Di Vito	201-440-6300	R	14*	<0.1
R and R Professsional Moving Inc.	832 St Elizabeth Dr	San Jose	CA	95150	Les Gudger	408-286-0548	R	14*	<0.1
Eagle Maintenance & Janitorial	6130 N Capitol	Washington	DC	20011	Richard Tynes	202-291-0200	R	14*	0.6
Zesco Products Inc.	PO Box 6157	Indianapolis	IN	46206	Clark Zoll	317-269-9300	R	14*	<0.1
Foss North America Inc.	7682 Executive Dr	Eden Prairie	MN	55344	Robert Wang	952-974-9892	R	13*	<0.1
Benedict Refrigeration Service Inc.	PO Box 3008	Eau Claire	WI	54702	Timothy Benedict	715-834-3191	R	12*	<0.1
Pellerin Laundry Machinery Sales	PO Box 1137	Kenner	LA	70063	Curtis Pellerin	504-467-9593	R	12*	<0.1
Midwest Chemical and Supply Inc.	340 E 56th Ave	Denver	CO	80216	Marc Bell	303-293-2122	R	12*	<0.1
Siya Inc.	7825 Somerset Blvd	Paramount	CA	90723	Sudhir Mundhra	562-633-3002	R	12*	<0.1
BDF Laundry Management	2430 Enterprise Dr	Saint Paul	MN	55120	David Demarsh	952-854-2500	R	11*	<0.1
Furniture Works	415 Camp Wisdom	Duncanville	TX	75116	Darell Gilbert	972-283-1464	R	11*	<0.1
Grupo Deco California Corp.	8545 Rosecrans Ave	Paramount	CA	90723	Leon Cooper	323-869-9934	R	11*	<0.1
Jinny Beauty Supply Company Inc.	3505 N Kimball Ave	Chicago	IL	60618	Tae Jhin	773-588-7200	R	11*	<0.1

Source: *Ward's Business Directory of U.S. Private and Public Companies*, Volumes 1 and 2, 2005. The company type code used is as follows: P - Public, R - Private, S - Subsidiary, D - Division, J - Joint Venture, A - Affiliate, G - Group. Sales are in millions of dollars, employees are in thousands. An asterisk (*) indicates an estimated sales volume. The symbol < stands for 'less than'. Company names and addresses are truncated, in some cases, to fit into the available space.

OCCUPATIONS EMPLOYED BY MACHINERY, EQUIPMENT, & SUPPLIES WHOLESALE

Occupation	% of Total 2004	Change to 2014	Occupation	% of Total 2004	Change to 2014
Sales reps, wholesale & manufacturing, exc tech	16.2	9.7	Truck drivers, light or delivery services	2.0	9.7
Mobile heavy equipment mechanics, except engines	5.7	9.7	Industrial machinery mechanics	2.0	9.7
Sales reps, wholesale & manufacturing, tech	3.6	9.6	Order clerks	1.8	-28.7
Laborers & freight, stock, & material movers, hand	3.4	-1.3	Secretaries, except legal, medical, & executive	1.7	-7.7
Shipping, receiving, & traffic clerks	3.4	-0.7	Team assemblers	1.7	9.7
Office clerks, general	3.4	-2.4	Bus & truck mechanics & diesel engine specialists	1.6	9.7
Bookkeeping, accounting, & auditing clerks	3.1	-1.3	First-line supervisors of mechanics	1.5	9.6
General & operations managers	3.0	8.5	First-line supervisors/managers of office workers	1.4	-0.6
Customer service representatives	2.6	12.3	Truck drivers, heavy & tractor-trailer	1.3	9.6
Maintenance & repair workers, general	2.4	9.7	Sales managers	1.3	17.3
Parts salespersons	2.4	-12.3	Machinists	1.3	9.7
First-line supervisors/managers of non-retail sales work	2.3	1.4	Welders, cutters, solderers, & brazers	1.0	9.7
Stock clerks & order fillers	2.2	-16.0	Executive secretaries & administrative assistants	1.0	3.9

Source: Industry-Occupation Matrix, Bureau of Labor Statistics. These data are reported based on 4-digit NAICS categories but have been matched to corresponding 6-digit NAICS industry codes. The change reported for each occupation to the year 2014 is a percent of growth or decline as estimated by the Bureau of Labor Statistics. The abbreviation nec stands for 'not elsewhere classified.'

LOCATION BY STATE AND REGIONAL CONCENTRATION

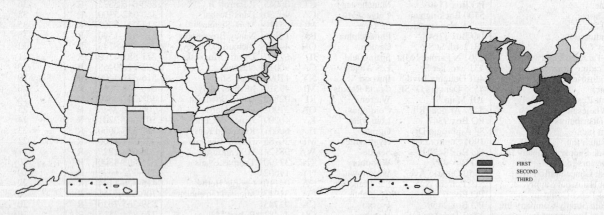

INDUSTRY DATA BY STATE

State	Establishments Total (number)	% of U.S.	Employment Total (number)	% of U.S.	Per Estab.	Payroll Total ($ mil.)	Per Empl. ($)	Sales Total ($ mil.)	% of U.S.	Per Estab. ($)
California	531	9.4	7,606	13.7	14	276.7	36,379	1,866.6	11.1	3,515,254
Texas	379	6.7	3,680	6.6	10	122.7	33,339	1,281.6	7.6	3,381,451
New York	388	6.9	3,750	6.8	10	143.4	38,252	932.0	5.6	2,402,113
Arkansas	62	1.1	399	0.7	6	12.9	32,298	732.4	4.4	11,813,435
New Jersey	194	3.4	2,320	4.2	12	95.7	41,232	704.7	4.2	3,632,216
Pennsylvania	256	4.5	2,364	4.3	9	78.7	33,293	661.1	3.9	2,582,312
Georgia	189	3.3	1,517	2.7	8	50.4	33,222	532.3	3.2	2,816,206
North Carolina	156	2.8	1,318	2.4	8	48.7	36,966	521.2	3.1	3,340,878
Indiana	121	2.1	1,326	2.4	11	62.2	46,878	515.0	3.1	4,256,033
Colorado	107	1.9	928	1.7	9	44.6	48,111	514.7	3.1	4,810,421
Massachusetts	108	1.9	1,314	2.4	12	53.8	40,955	423.0	2.5	3,917,000
Maryland	114	2.0	1,352	2.4	12	47.2	34,905	339.8	2.0	2,980,368
Connecticut	56	1.0	771	1.4	14	36.0	46,668	326.2	1.9	5,825,661
Missouri	146	2.6	1,449	2.6	10	45.7	31,552	255.7	1.5	1,751,712
Wisconsin	109	1.9	1,320	2.4	12	36.5	27,659	251.5	1.5	2,307,404
Washington	125	2.2	938	1.7	8	31.6	33,689	212.6	1.3	1,701,120
Tennessee	129	2.3	897	1.6	7	30.4	33,902	210.1	1.3	1,628,798
Louisiana	104	1.8	979	1.8	9	29.5	30,129	209.0	1.2	2,009,712
South Carolina	90	1.6	829	1.5	9	24.8	29,960	204.2	1.2	2,269,256
Virginia	122	2.2	753	1.4	6	24.2	32,205	191.8	1.1	1,572,475
Alabama	74	1.3	814	1.5	11	25.5	31,350	182.5	1.1	2,465,878
Utah	50	0.9	484	0.9	10	18.4	37,977	150.9	0.9	3,017,540
Oklahoma	63	1.1	497	0.9	8	14.1	28,439	93.9	0.6	1,491,127
Nebraska	26	0.5	452	0.8	17	12.7	28,139	89.9	0.5	3,459,538
Iowa	52	0.9	374	0.7	7	10.6	28,465	66.7	0.4	1,282,635
Rhode Island	27	0.5	198	0.4	7	7.2	36,530	60.4	0.4	2,236,926
North Dakota	21	0.4	207	0.4	10	7.0	33,981	59.5	0.4	2,833,333
Mississippi	42	0.7	353	0.6	8	9.6	27,125	58.5	0.3	1,393,643
Maine	28	0.5	181	0.3	6	6.0	33,055	42.4	0.3	1,513,893

Continued on next page.

INDUSTRY DATA BY STATE - Continued

State	Establishments		Employment			Payroll		Sales		
	Total (number)	% of U.S.	Total (number)	% of U.S.	Per Estab.	Total ($ mil.)	Per Empl. ($)	Total ($ mil.)	% of U.S.	Per Estab. ($)
Alaska	14	0.2	122	0.2	9	4.8	38,992	28.4	0.2	2,027,357
Vermont	9	0.2	110	0.2	12	2.9	26,591	23.9	0.1	2,650,333
Florida	385	6.8	1000-2499	-	-	(D)	-	(D)	-	-
Illinois	280	4.9	2500-4999	-	-	(D)	-	(D)	-	-
Ohio	223	3.9	1000-2499	-	-	(D)	-	(D)	-	-
Michigan	182	3.2	1000-2499	-	-	(D)	-	(D)	-	-
Arizona	110	1.9	500-999	-	-	(D)	-	(D)	-	-
Minnesota	89	1.6	500-999	-	-	(D)	-	(D)	-	-
Kentucky	80	1.4	500-999	-	-	(D)	-	(D)	-	-
Kansas	79	1.4	500-999	-	-	(D)	-	(D)	-	-
Oregon	73	1.3	500-999	-	-	(D)	-	(D)	-	-
Nevada	51	0.9	250-499	-	-	(D)	-	(D)	-	-
New Mexico	36	0.6	100-249	-	-	(D)	-	(D)	-	-
Idaho	35	0.6	100-249	-	-	(D)	-	(D)	-	-
West Virginia	28	0.5	250-499	-	-	(D)	-	(D)	-	-
New Hampshire	22	0.4	100-249	-	-	(D)	-	(D)	-	-
Montana	21	0.4	20-99	-	-	(D)	-	(D)	-	-
South Dakota	21	0.4	100-249	-	-	(D)	-	(D)	-	-
Delaware	20	0.4	100-249	-	-	(D)	-	(D)	-	-
Hawaii	17	0.3	100-249	-	-	(D)	-	(D)	-	-
D.C.	9	0.2	20-99	-	-	(D)	-	(D)	-	-
Wyoming	7	0.1	20-99	-	-	(D)	-	(D)	-	-

Source: 2002 *Economic Census*. The states are in descending order of sales or establishments (if sales data are missing for the majority). The symbol (D) appears when data are withheld to prevent disclosure of competitive information. States marked with (D) are sorted by number of establishments. A dash (-) indicates that the data element cannot be calculated. Shaded *states* on the state map indicate those states which have proportionately greater representation in the industry than would be indicated by the states population; the ratio is based on total sales or number of establishments. Shaded *regions* indicate where the industry is regionally most concentrated.

NAICS 423860 - TRANSPORTATION EQUIPMENT AND SUPPLIES (EXCEPT MOTOR VEHICLE) MERCHANT WHOLESALERS

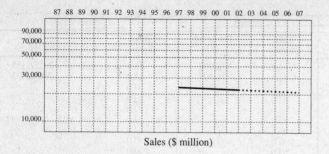

Sales ($ million)

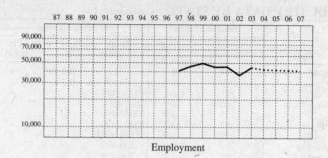

Employment

GENERAL STATISTICS

Year	Establishments (number)	Employment (number)	Payroll ($ million)	Sales ($ million)	Employees per Establishment (number)	Sales per Establishment ($)	Payroll per Employee ($)
1987	-	-	-	-	-	-	-
1988	-	-	-	-	-	-	-
1989	-	-	-	-	-	-	-
1990	-	-	-	-	-	-	-
1991	-	-	-	-	-	-	-
1992	-	-	-	-	-	-	-
1993	-	-	-	-	-	-	-
1994	-	-	-	-	-	-	-
1995	-	-	-	-	-	-	-
1996	-	-	-	-	-	-	-
1997	4,003	40,905	1,723.6	23,682.3	10.2	5,916,137.9	42,136.7
1998	3,991	45,901	2,150.8	23,424.6 e	11.5	5,869,346.0	46,857.4
1999	3,924	49,660	2,338.3	23,166.8 e	12.7	5,903,878.7	47,086.2
2000	3,867	45,159	2,080.4	22,909.1 e	11.7	5,924,251.4	46,068.6
2001	3,730	45,520	2,126.3	22,651.3 e	12.2	6,072,745.3	46,711.5
2002	3,051	36,912	1,728.3	22,393.6	12.1	7,339,757.5	46,822.2
2003	2,926	44,678	2,329.1	22,135.9 p	15.3	6,945,886.3 p	52,130.3
2004	2,884 p	42,562 p	2,176.6 p	21,878.1 p	14.5 p	7,167,276.8 p	51,049.8 p
2005	2,694 p	42,177 p	2,203.7 p	21,620.4 p	15.1 p	7,388,667.3 p	52,104.6 p
2006	2,505 p	41,791 p	2,230.8 p	21,362.6 p	15.6 p	7,610,057.9 p	53,159.4 p
2007	2,315 p	41,405 p	2,258.0 p	21,104.9 p	16.2 p	7,831,448.4 p	54,214.3 p

Source: Economic Census of the United States, 1997 and 2002. Establishment counts, employment, and payroll are from County Business Patterns for non-Census years. This is a newly defined industry. Data for prior years are unavailable at the time of publication but may become available over time. Values followed by 'p' are projections by the editors. Sales data for non-Census years are extrapolations, marked by 'e'.

INDICES OF CHANGE

Year	Establishments (number)	Employment (number)	Payroll ($ million)	Sales ($ million)	Employees per Establishment (number)	Sales per Establishment ($)	Payroll per Employee ($)
1987	-	-	-	-	-	-	-
1992	-	-	-	-	-	-	-
1993	-	-	-	-	-	-	-
1994	-	-	-	-	-	-	-
1995	-	-	-	-	-	-	-
1996	-	-	-	-	-	-	-
1997	131.2	110.8	99.7	105.8	84.3	80.6	90.0
1998	130.8	124.4	124.4	104.6 e	95.0	80.0	100.1
1999	128.6	134.5	135.3	103.5 e	105.0	80.4	100.6
2000	126.7	122.3	120.4	102.3 e	96.7	80.7	98.4
2001	122.3	123.3	123.0	101.2 e	100.8	82.7	99.8
2002	100.0	100.0	100.0	100.0	100.0	100.0	100.0
2003	95.9	121.0	134.8	98.8 p	126.2	94.6 p	111.3
2004	94.5 p	115.3 p	125.9 p	97.7 p	119.9 p	97.7 p	109.0 p
2005	88.3 p	114.3 p	127.5 p	96.5 p	124.6 p	100.7 p	111.3 p
2006	82.1 p	113.2 p	129.1 p	95.4 p	129.3 p	103.7 p	113.5 p
2007	75.9 p	112.2 p	130.6 p	94.2 p	134.0 p	106.7 p	115.8 p

Sources: Same as General Statistics. The values shown reflect change from the base year, 2002. Values above 100 mean greater than 2002, values below 100 mean less than 2002, and a value of 100 in the 1987-2001 or 2003-2007 period means same as 2002. Values followed by a 'p' are projections by the editors; 'e' stands for extrapolation. Data are the most recent available at this level of detail.

SELECTED RATIOS

For 2002	Avg. of All Wholesale	Analyzed Industry	Index	For 2002	Avg. of All Wholesale	Analyzed Industry	Index
Employees per Establishment	15	12	81	Sales per Employee	791,325	606,675	77
Payroll per Establishment	626,122	566,470	90	Sales per Establishment	12,012,387	7,339,757	61
Payroll per Employee	41,161	46,822	114	Expenses per Establishment	na	na	na

Sources: Same as General Statistics. The 'Average of All' column, Wholesale or Retail, represents the average of the sector reported for the most recent complete year available. The Index shows the relationship between the Average and the Analyzed Industry. For example, 100 means that they are equal; 500 that the Analyzed Industry is five times the average; 50 means that the Analyzed Industry is half the national average. The abbreviation 'na' is used to show that data are 'not available'.

LEADING COMPANIES   Number shown: **75**   Total sales ($ mil): **23,297**   Total employment (000): **50.3**

Company Name	Address				CEO Name	Phone	Co. Type	Sales ($ mil)	Empl. (000)
Allied Automotive Group	160 Clairemont Ave	Decatur	GA	30030	Hugh E. Sawyer	404-371-0379	S	10,413*	5.0
US Airways Group Inc.	2345 Crystal Dr	Arlington	VA	22227		703-872-7000	P	7,117	29.5
Stewart & Stevenson Services Inc.	2707 N Loop W	Houston	TX	77008	Max Lukens	713-868-7700	P	1,176	3.3
AAR Corp.	One AAR Pl	Wood Dale	IL	60191	Ira A Eichner	630-227-2000	P	652	2.3
TIMCO Aviation Services Inc.	623 Radar Rd	Greensboro	NC	27410		336-668-4410	P	242	3.4
H.O. Penn Machinery Inc.	122 Noxon Rd	Poughkeepsie	NY	12603	CE Thomas Cleveland	845-452-1200	R	222*	0.4
International Lease Finance Corp.	1999 Av of the Stars	Los Angeles	CA	90067	Steven F Udvar-Hazy	310-788-1999	S	194*	0.1
Kansas City Aviation Center Inc	PO Box 1850	Olathe	KS	66063		913-782-0530	R	179*	<0.1
A. Biederman Inc.	1425 Grand Central	Glendale	CA	91201		818-246-8431	S	168*	<0.1
Medart Inc. (Fenton, Missouri)	124 Manufacturers	Arnold	MO	63010	J Michael Medart	636-282-2300	R	161*	<0.1
Carl F. Ewig Inc.	910 Oak Tree Rd	South Plainfield	NJ	07080	Thomas Ewig	908-756-6222	R	148*	<0.1
Wiggins Airways Inc.	1 Garside Way	Manchester	NH	03103	David Ladd	603-629-9191	R	118*	0.2
Fisheries Supply Co.	1900 N Northlake	Seattle	WA	98103	Carl Sutter	206-632-4462	R	116*	<0.1
Dealers Truck Equipment Inc.	PO Box 31435	Shreveport	LA	71108	Raymond Kayser	318-635-7567	R	92*	0.1
Saab Aircraft of America Inc.	21300 Ridgetop Cir	Sterling	VA	20166	Marty Schultz	703-406-7200	S	92*	<0.1
M7 Aerospace L.P.	10823 NE Entrance	San Antonio	TX	78216	Harold Williams	210-824-9421	R	91*	0.8
Argo International Corp.	140 Franklin St	New York	NY	10013	John Santacroce	212-431-1700	R	90*	0.3
Elliott Aviation Inc.	PO Box 100	Moline	IL	61266	Wynn Elliott	309-799-3183	R	80*	0.4
Miner Enterprises Inc.	PO Box 471	Geneva	IL	60134	Kris Jurasek	630-232-3000	R	79*	0.1
Hawker Pacific Aerospace	11240 Sherman Way	Sun Valley	CA	91352	Richard Fortner	818-765-6201	R	79*	0.5
Halton Co.	PO Box 3377	Portland	OR	97208	Edward H Halton Jr	503-288-6411	S	78*	0.3
ASC International Inc.	PO Box 200728	Arlington	TX	76006	Ollin Taylor	817-640-1300	R	77*	<0.1
Eurojet US Ltd.	PO Box 5 Ste B	Big Sandy	TX	75755	Paul Kroiss	903-769-9838	R	68*	0.1
Holloway-Houston Inc.	5833 Armour Dr	Houston	TX	77020	Charles Chapman	713-674-5631	R	68*	0.1
Willis Lease Finance Corp.	2320 Marinship Way	Sausalito	CA	94965		415-331-5281	P	62	<0.1
Lewis Marine Supply Inc.	PO Box 21107	Fort Lauderdale	FL	33335	Steven Lewis	954-523-4371	R	61*	0.1
Yingling Aircraft Inc.	PO Box 9248	Wichita	KS	67277	Lynn Nichos	316-943-3246	R	59*	<0.1
Paxton Company Inc.	PO Box 12103	Norfolk	VA	23502	Guy Beale Jr	757-853-6781	R	53*	<0.1
Elder Equipment Leasing of WY	663 Cir Dr	Casper	WY	82601	Bruce McGrath	307-265-0450	R	53*	<0.1
Honeywell Hardware Product	875 W Elliot Rd	Tempe	AZ	85284		602-365-7700	D	50*	0.2
Aero Toy Store L.L.C.	1710 W Cypress	Fort Lauderdale	FL	33309	Morris Shirazipour	954-771-1795	R	45*	<0.1
Bizjet Intern. Sales & Support Inc.	3515 N Sheridan Rd	Tulsa	OK	74115	Bernd Kowalewski	918-832-7733	R	45*	0.3
UPS Supply Chain Soloutions	2275 Newlands Dr E	Fernley	NV	89408		775-575-3700	R	42*	<0.1
Aas Amjet Inc.	13945 SW 139th Ct	Miami	FL	33186	Anton Khoury	305-256-0678	R	40*	<0.1
Hill Aircraft and Leasing Corp.	3948 Aviation Cir	Atlanta	GA	30336	Guy Hill	404-691-3330	R	40*	<0.1
Alamo Aircraft Ltd.	PO Box 37343	San Antonio	TX	78237	Jesse E Wulfe	210-434-5577	R	38*	<0.1
Atlantic Track and Turnout Co.	270 Broad St	Bloomfield	NJ	07003	Peter Hughes	973-748-5885	R	38*	<0.1
Calfland Traders Inc.	1301 Rail Head Blvd	Naples	FL	34110	Calvin Carter	239-598-3130	R	38*	<0.1
Hammerhead Aviation L.L.C.	1915 N Marshall 13	El Cajon	CA	92020	Robert Veronneau	619-562-6602	R	37*	<0.1
Tracer Corp.	1600 W Cornell St	Milwaukee	WI	53209	William Morales	414-875-1234	R	36*	<0.1
ZF Industries Inc.	3131 SW 42nd St	Fort Lauderdale	FL	33312		954-581-4043	R	34*	<0.1
Western Aircraft Inc.	4300 S Kennedy St	Boise	ID	83704	Al Hilde Jr	208-338-1800	S	34*	0.2
Asi Holding Inc.	1701B Clint Moore	Boca Raton	FL	33487	Bill Gray	561-241-9599	R	34*	<0.1
Phoenix Aerospace Inc.	PO Box 8744	Kansas City	MO	64114	William Sutherland	816-333-3400	R	31*	<0.1
Unical Aviation Inc.	4775 Irwindale Ave	Baldwin Park	CA	91706	Han Tan	626-962-7343	R	31*	<0.1
Aerodynamics Inc.	PO Box 270100	Waterford	MI	48327	Cheryl L Bush	248-666-3500	R	30*	0.2
Jilco Industries Inc.	PO Box 12	Kidron	OH	44636	Ken Stoltzfus	330-698-0280	R	28*	<0.1
Summit Aviation Inc.	PO Box 258	Middletown	DE	19709	Finn Neilsen	302-834-5400	R	28*	0.1
Med-Craft Inc.	2450 NW 110th Ave	Miami	FL	33172	Mario Duenas	305-594-7444	R	28*	<0.1
Williams and Wells Co.	100 State St	Moonachie	NJ	07074	Stuart Margolin	201-440-1800	R	26*	<0.1
Golf Car Supply	3587 Clover Ln	New Castle	PA	16105	John Lockley	724-658-1741	R	25*	<0.1
International Turbine Service	PO Box 36199	Dallas	TX	75235		214-353-6700	R	25*	<0.1
Summit Radio Corp.	PO Box 276	Teaneck	NJ	07666	Donald Levi	201-837-3644	R	25*	<0.1
Africair Inc.	PO Box 165139	Miami	FL	33116	Bruce Fullerton	305-255-6973	R	22*	<0.1
Wencor West Inc.	PO Box 514	Springville	UT	84663		801-489-2000	R	21*	0.1
Van Bortel Aircraft Inc.	4900 S Collins St	Arlington	TX	76018	Howard Van Bortel	817-468-7788	R	21*	<0.1
Air Frame Mfg and Supply Inc.	26135 Technology	Valencia	CA	91355	Ryuji Kurihara	661-257-7728	R	20*	<0.1
Industry-Railway Suppliers Inc.	811 Golf Ln	Bensenville	IL	60106	Ron Hobbs	630-766-5708	R	20*	<0.1
Pacific Cornetta Inc.	25999 Canyon Crk	Wilsonville	OR	97070	Ching Liu	503-582-8787	R	20*	<0.1
All Nippon Airways Company Ltd.	1251 Av Americas	New York	NY	10020		212-840-3700	R	18*	<0.1
Avio-Diepen Inc.	561 Arpt S Pkwy	Atlanta	GA	30349	Vincent Van Campen	770-996-6430	R	18*	<0.1
HC Merchandisers Inc.	19844 Quiroz Ct	Walnut	CA	91789	Thomas Osborne	909-598-0509	R	18*	<0.1
Charlotte Aircraft Corp.	PO Box 25555	Charlotte	NC	28229	Harold Caldwell	704-537-0212	R	17*	<0.1
Intern. Airline Support Group Inc.	1954 Arpt Rd	Atlanta	GA	30341	Alexius A Dyer III	770-455-7575	R	17	<0.1
Wamco Inc.	11555 Coley River	Fountain Valley	CA	92708	Chris Matthews	714-545-5560	R	17*	<0.1
Executive Aviation Services Inc.	8298 NW 56th St	Miami	FL	33166	Julian Pinder	305-477-1915	R	16*	<0.1
Aeroparts Mfg and Repair Inc.	431 Rio Rancho NE	Rio Rancho	NM	87124	Dean Leavengood	505-891-6600	R	16*	0.1
Aircraft Instrument and Radio Inc.	PO Box 9487	Wichita	KS	67277	Martin Potash	316-945-0445	R	15*	<0.1
Edwards Technical Sales Inc.	613 S Camellia 4	Fort Valley	GA	31030	Jim Edwards	478-825-0751	R	15*	<0.1
First Wave Inc.	5440 S 101st E Ave	Tulsa	OK	74146	Edward Clark	918-622-0007	R	15*	<0.1
GA Telesis Turbine Technology	5400 NW 35th Ave	Fort Lauderdale	FL	33309		954-676-3111	R	15*	<0.1
Inter-State Enterprises Co.	164 Ricci Ave	Walnut	CA	91789	Steven Limb	909-444-1266	R	15*	<0.1
Roberts Aircraft Company Nevada	1715 N Pinal Ave	Casa Grande	AZ	85222		520-836-3333	R	15*	<0.1
Seattle Aero L.L.C.	12410 SE 32nd St	Bellevue	WA	98005	Lindsay Eberts	425-643-4220	R	15*	<0.1
Associated Aircraft Supply Inc.	PO Box 35788	Dallas	TX	75235		214-331-4381	R	15*	<0.1

Source: Ward's Business Directory of U.S. Private and Public Companies, Volumes 1 and 2, 2005. The company type code used is as follows: P - Public, R - Private, S - Subsidiary, D - Division, J - Joint Venture, A - Affiliate, G - Group. Sales are in millions of dollars, employees are in thousands. An asterisk (*) indicates an estimated sales volume. The symbol < stands for 'less than'. Company names and addresses are truncated, in some cases, to fit into the available space.

OCCUPATIONS EMPLOYED BY MACHINERY, EQUIPMENT, & SUPPLIES WHOLESALE

Occupation	% of Total 2004	Change to 2014	Occupation	% of Total 2004	Change to 2014
Sales reps, wholesale & manufacturing, exc tech	16.2	9.7	Truck drivers, light or delivery services	2.0	9.7
Mobile heavy equipment mechanics, except engines	5.7	9.7	Industrial machinery mechanics	2.0	9.7
Sales reps, wholesale & manufacturing, tech	3.6	9.6	Order clerks	1.8	-28.7
Laborers & freight, stock, & material movers, hand	3.4	-1.3	Secretaries, except legal, medical, & executive	1.7	-7.7
Shipping, receiving, & traffic clerks	3.4	-0.7	Team assemblers	1.7	9.7
Office clerks, general	3.4	-2.4	Bus & truck mechanics & diesel engine specialists	1.6	9.7
Bookkeeping, accounting, & auditing clerks	3.1	-1.3	First-line supervisors of mechanics	1.5	9.6
General & operations managers	3.0	8.5	First-line supervisors/managers of office workers	1.4	-0.6
Customer service representatives	2.6	12.3	Truck drivers, heavy & tractor-trailer	1.3	9.6
Maintenance & repair workers, general	2.4	9.7	Sales managers	1.3	17.3
Parts salespersons	2.4	-12.3	Machinists	1.3	9.7
First-line supervisors/managers of non-retail sales work	2.3	1.4	Welders, cutters, solderers, & brazers	1.0	9.7
Stock clerks & order fillers	2.2	-16.0	Executive secretaries & administrative assistants	1.0	3.9

Source: Industry-Occupation Matrix, Bureau of Labor Statistics. These data are reported based on 4-digit NAICS categories but have been matched to corresponding 6-digit NAICS industry codes. The change reported for each occupation to the year 2014 is a percent of growth or decline as estimated by the Bureau of Labor Statistics. The abbreviation nec stands for 'not elsewhere classified.'

LOCATION BY STATE AND REGIONAL CONCENTRATION

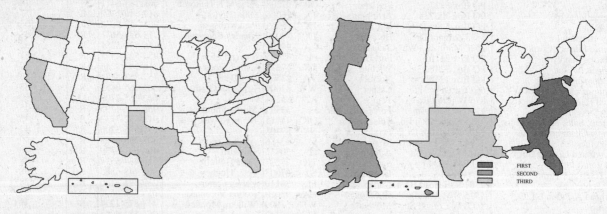

FIRST
SECOND
THIRD

INDUSTRY DATA BY STATE

State	Establishments Total (number)	% of U.S.	Employment Total (number)	% of U.S.	Per Estab.	Payroll Total ($ mil.)	Per Empl. ($)	Sales Total ($ mil.)	% of U.S.	Per Estab. ($)
Texas	296	9.6	4,147	10.9	14	218.2	52,625	4,310.3	15.2	14,561,784
California	459	14.9	4,956	13.1	11	239.1	48,247	3,609.4	12.8	7,863,538
Florida	626	20.4	5,253	13.9	8	227.6	43,330	2,275.5	8.0	3,634,968
New Jersey	105	3.4	1,537	4.1	15	80.5	52,356	2,071.5	7.3	19,728,590
Ohio	58	1.9	823	2.2	14	32.1	38,993	1,116.7	3.9	19,252,707
Washington	142	4.6	1,805	4.8	13	93.5	51,776	1,111.2	3.9	7,825,134
New York	144	4.7	1,415	3.7	10	70.6	49,907	934.1	3.3	6,486,944
Georgia	77	2.5	655	1.7	9	31.1	47,487	568.4	2.0	7,381,247
Connecticut	58	1.9	1,139	3.0	20	65.5	57,511	490.4	1.7	8,455,621
Virginia	61	2.0	781	2.1	13	45.8	58,631	440.9	1.6	7,227,984
Tennessee	49	1.6	982	2.6	20	40.1	40,879	398.5	1.4	8,132,429
Louisiana	74	2.4	1,107	2.9	15	46.0	41,546	319.4	1.1	4,316,014
Pennsylvania	52	1.7	524	1.4	10	23.9	45,531	287.0	1.0	5,518,865
Maryland	44	1.4	891	2.3	20	27.0	30,290	235.5	0.8	5,352,273
Wisconsin	23	0.7	479	1.3	21	27.7	57,923	233.1	0.8	10,133,739
South Carolina	27	0.9	373	1.0	14	17.7	47,426	191.3	0.7	7,085,741
Missouri	49	1.6	429	1.1	9	14.5	33,869	188.3	0.7	3,842,612
Alabama	22	0.7	219	0.6	10	7.4	33,936	166.9	0.6	7,587,136
Colorado	30	1.0	208	0.5	7	8.6	41,418	159.5	0.6	5,315,133
Oregon	42	1.4	346	0.9	8	13.9	40,124	110.3	0.4	2,625,119
North Carolina	53	1.7	315	0.8	6	13.1	41,562	106.1	0.4	2,002,057
Oklahoma	53	1.7	358	0.9	7	14.9	41,480	99.8	0.4	1,883,396
Indiana	32	1.0	156	0.4	5	6.5	41,500	94.1	0.3	2,940,750
Utah	16	0.5	349	0.9	22	12.7	36,401	85.4	0.3	5,339,500
Massachusetts	28	0.9	270	0.7	10	12.1	44,830	76.9	0.3	2,745,893
Iowa	16	0.5	175	0.5	11	8.2	46,869	72.3	0.3	4,518,062
Arkansas	18	0.6	171	0.5	10	4.9	28,491	38.1	0.1	2,115,500
Maine	13	0.4	111	0.3	9	4.2	38,171	22.0	0.1	1,690,385
Nebraska	10	0.3	34	0.1	3	1.3	39,029	18.1	0.1	1,811,900

Continued on next page.

INDUSTRY DATA BY STATE - Continued

State	Establishments Total (number)	% of U.S.	Employment Total (number)	% of U.S.	Per Estab.	Payroll Total ($ mil.)	Per Empl. ($)	Sales Total ($ mil.)	% of U.S.	Per Estab. ($)
Mississippi	9	0.3	34	0.1	4	0.9	27,618	8.5	-	947,444
Illinois	95	3.1	1000-2499	-	-	(D)	-	(D)	-	-
Michigan	57	1.9	1000-2499	-	-	(D)	-	(D)	-	-
Arizona	53	1.7	500-999	-	-	(D)	-	(D)	-	-
Kansas	53	1.7	2500-4999	-	-	(D)	-	(D)	-	-
Minnesota	25	0.8	100-249	-	-	(D)	-	(D)	-	-
New Hampshire	19	0.6	20-99	-	-	(D)	-	(D)	-	-
Nevada	18	0.6	100-249	-	-	(D)	-	(D)	-	-
Kentucky	11	0.4	100-249	-	-	(D)	-	(D)	-	-
Rhode Island	10	0.3	20-99	-	-	(D)	-	(D)	-	-
Idaho	9	0.3	20-99	-	-	(D)	-	(D)	-	-
Alaska	6	0.2	20-99	-	-	(D)	-	(D)	-	-
Montana	5	0.2	20-99	-	-	(D)	-	(D)	-	-
Delaware	3	0.1	0-19	-	-	(D)	-	(D)	-	-
D.C.	3	0.1	0-19	-	-	(D)	-	(D)	-	-
Hawaii	3	0.1	20-99	-	-	(D)	-	(D)	-	-
New Mexico	3	0.1	0-19	-	-	(D)	-	(D)	-	-
Vermont	3	0.1	20-99	-	-	(D)	-	(D)	-	-
West Virginia	3	0.1	100-249	-	-	(D)	-	(D)	-	-
North Dakota	2	0.1	0-19	-	-	(D)	-	(D)	-	-
South Dakota	2	0.1	0-19	-	-	(D)	-	(D)	-	-
Wyoming	2	0.1	0-19	-	-	(D)	-	(D)	-	-

Source: 2002 *Economic Census*. The states are in descending order of sales or establishments (if sales data are missing for the majority). The symbol (D) appears when data are withheld to prevent disclosure of competitive information. States marked with (D) are sorted by number of establishments. A dash (-) indicates that the data element cannot be calculated. Shaded *states* on the state map indicate those states which have proportionately greater representation in the industry than would be indicated by the states population; the ratio is based on total sales or number of establishments. Shaded *regions* indicate where the industry is regionally most concentrated.

NAICS 423910 - SPORTING AND RECREATIONAL GOODS AND SUPPLIES MERCHANT WHOLESALERS*

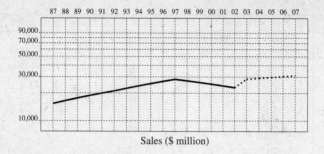

Sales ($ million)

Employment

GENERAL STATISTICS

Year	Establishments (number)	Employment (number)	Payroll ($ million)	Sales ($ million)	Employees per Establishment (number)	Sales per Establishment ($)	Payroll per Employee ($)
1987	4,922	45,625	957.2	15,359.4	9.3	3,120,560.7	20,979.7
1988	4,575	45,352	1,058.3	16,504.5 e	9.9	3,607,541.0	23,335.2
1989	4,195	43,610	1,106.6	17,649.6 e	10.4	4,207,294.4	25,374.9
1990	4,242	46,518	1,165.3	18,794.6 e	11.0	4,430,598.8	25,050.5
1991	4,290	44,480	1,198.9	19,939.7 e	10.4	4,647,948.7	26,953.7
1992	5,530	52,269	1,405.1	21,084.8	9.5	3,812,802.9	26,882.1
1993	5,702	53,646	1,489.1	22,514.6 e	9.4	3,948,544.4	27,757.9
1994	5,730	56,056	1,623.8	23,944.4 e	9.8	4,178,778.4	28,967.5
1995	5,745	60,790	1,748.6	25,374.1 e	10.6	4,416,727.6	28,764.6
1996	5,786 e	58,410 e	1,741.4 e	26,803.9 e	10.1 e	4,632,544.1 e	29,813.4 e
1997	6,080	59,861	1,897.1	28,233.7	9.8	4,643,700.7	31,691.8
1998	6,194	57,666	1,918.9	27,181.0 e	9.3	4,388,275.8	33,276.1
1999	6,179	55,508	1,959.9	26,128.3 e	9.0	4,228,558.0	35,308.4
2000	6,221	57,625	2,139.7	25,075.5 e	9.3	4,030,789.3	37,130.6
2001	6,085	57,716	2,204.7	24,022.8 e	9.5	3,947,875.1	38,198.8
2002	5,476	51,250	1,898.1	22,970.1	9.4	4,194,685.9	37,036.1
2003	5,554	51,540	2,042.6	28,352.8 p	9.3	4,419,864.4 p	39,630.6
2004	6,389 p	59,522 p	2,316.7 p	29,029.7 p	9.3 p	4,451,339.5 p	40,151.0 p
2005	6,494 p	60,267 p	2,394.0 p	29,706.7 p	9.2 p	4,482,814.5 p	41,238.6 p
2006	6,600 p	61,011 p	2,471.3 p	30,383.6 p	9.2 p	4,514,289.5 p	42,326.3 p
2007	6,705 p	61,756 p	2,548.6 p	31,060.5 p	9.1 p	4,545,764.6 p	43,414.0 p

Sources: *Economic Census of the United States*, 1987, 1992, 1997, and 2002. Establishment counts, employment, and payroll are from *County Business Patterns* for non-Census years. Values followed by a 'p' are projections by the editors. Sales data for non-Census years are extrapolations, marked by 'e'. Data are the most recent available at this level of detail.

INDICES OF CHANGE

Year	Establishments (number)	Employment (number)	Payroll ($ million)	Sales ($ million)	Employees per Establishment (number)	Sales per Establishment ($)	Payroll per Employee ($)
1987	89.9	89.0	50.4	66.9	98.9	74.4	56.6
1992	101.0	102.0	74.0	91.8	101.1	90.9	72.6
1993	104.1	104.7	78.5	98.0 e	100.0	94.1	74.9
1994	104.6	109.4	85.5	104.2 e	104.3	99.6	78.2
1995	104.9	118.6	92.1	110.5 e	112.8	105.3	77.7
1996	105.7 e	114.0 e	91.7 e	116.7 e	107.4 e	110.4 e	80.5 e
1997	111.0	116.8	99.9	122.9	104.3	110.7	85.6
1998	113.1	112.5	101.1	118.3 e	98.9	104.6	89.8
1999	112.8	108.3	103.3	113.7 e	95.7	100.8	95.3
2000	113.6	112.4	112.7	109.2 e	98.9	96.1	100.3
2001	111.1	112.6	116.2	104.6 e	101.1	94.1	103.1
2002	100.0	100.0	100.0	100.0	100.0	100.0	100.0
2003	101.4	100.6	107.6	123.4 p	98.7	105.4 p	107.0
2004	116.7 p	116.1 p	122.1 p	126.4 p	98.5 p	106.1 p	108.4 p
2005	118.6 p	117.6 p	126.1 p	129.3 p	98.0 p	106.9 p	111.3 p
2006	120.5 p	119.0 p	130.2 p	132.3 p	97.4 p	107.6 p	114.3 p
2007	122.4 p	120.5 p	134.3 p	135.2 p	96.8 p	108.4 p	117.2 p

Sources: Same as General Statistics. The values shown reflect change from the base year, 2002. Values above 100 mean greater than 2002, values below 100 mean less than 2002, and a value of 100 in the 1987-2001 or 2003-2007 period means same as 2002. Values followed by a 'p' are projections by the editors; 'e' stands for extrapolation. Data are the most recent available at this level of detail.

SELECTED RATIOS

For 2002	Avg. of All Wholesale	Analyzed Industry	Index	For 2002	Avg. of All Wholesale	Analyzed Industry	Index
Employees per Establishment	15	9	63	Sales per Employee	791,325	448,197	57
Payroll per Establishment	626,122	346,622	55	Sales per Establishment	12,012,387	4,194,686	35
Payroll per Employee	41,161	37,036	90	Expenses per Establishment	na	na	na

Sources: Same as General Statistics. The 'Average of All' column, Wholesale or Retail, represents the reverage of the sector reported for the most recent complete year available. The Index shows the relationship between the Average and the Analyzed Industry. For example, 100 means that they are equal; 500 that the Analyzed Industry is five times the average; 50 means that the Analyzed Industry is half the national average. The abbreviation 'na' is used to show that data are 'not available'.

*Equivalent to SIC 5091.

LEADING COMPANIES   Number shown: **75**   Total sales ($ mil): **6,096**   Total employment (000): **17.8**

Company Name	Address			CEO Name	Phone	Co. Type	Sales ($ mil)	Empl. (000)
SCP Pool Corp.	109 Northpark Blvd	Covington	LA	70433		504-892-5521	P	1,311	2.7
Central Garden and Pet Co.	1340 Treat Blvd	Walnut Creek	CA	94597	William E Brown	925-948-4000	P	1,270	4.4
Gander Mountain Co.	4567 American W	Bloomington	MN	55437	Mark R Baker	952-830-8700	P	489	4.0
Browning & Winchester Firearms	1 Browning Pl	Morgan	UT	84050	Charles Guevremont	801-876-2711	R	375*	0.2
Spalding Holdings Corp.	425 Meadow St	Chicopee	MA	01021	James R Craigie	413-536-1200	R	287*	1.0
AcuSport Corp.	1 Hunter Pl	Bellefontaine	OH	43311	William L Fraim	937-593-7010	R	213*	0.3
United Hardware Distributing Co.	5005 Nathan Ln N	Plymouth	MN	55442	David A Heider	763-559-1800	R	144*	0.4
Smith and Wesson Corp.	PO Box 2208	Springfield	MA	01102	Roy Cuny		S	133*	1.0
Bass Pro Shop	5900 Sugarloaf	Lawrenceville	GA	30043		678-847-5500	R	100*	0.2
Pacific Cycle L.L.C. Roadmaster	PO Box 344	Olney	IL	62450	Byron Smith	618-393-2991	D	100*	0.2
Ross Bicycles USA Ltd.	51 Executive Blvd	Farmingdale	NY	11735	Alan Goldmeier	631-249-6000	S	81*	<0.1
RSR Wholesale Guns Inc.	PO Box 4300	Winter Park	FL	32793	Bob Steger	407-677-1000	R	66*	0.2
Pool Water Products Inc.	PO Box 17359	Irvine	CA	92623	Dean Allred	949-756-1666	R	65*	<0.1
Head/Penn Racquet Sports	306 S 45th Ave	Phoenix	AZ	85043	Gregg Weida	602-269-1492	R	53*	0.4
Faber Brothers Inc.	4141 S Pulaski	Chicago	IL	60632	Wayne J Koslowski	773-376-9300	R	50*	0.2
Branch Brook Co.	370 Hwy 36	Hazlet	NJ	07730	Kevin Ventrice	732-787-2700	R	50*	<0.1
Lucky Coin	1525 Airline Dr	Metairie	LA	70001	John Georges	504-835-3232	R	50*	0.1
Shimano American Corp.	PO Box 19615	Irvine	CA	92618	Yoshizo Shimano	949-951-5003	R	46*	0.1
Maurice Sporting Goods	1825 Shermer Rd	Northbrook	IL	60062		847-715-1249	R	37*	<0.1
G. Joannou Cycle Company Inc.	151 Ludlow Ave	Northvale	NJ	07647	Madeline Joannou	201-768-9050	R	36*	<0.1
Raleigh America	6004 S 190th St	Kent	WA	98032	William Austin	253-395-1100	R	35*	<0.1
California Pools	1660 S Alma School	Mesa	AZ	85210	Joan Smith	480-345-0005	R	32*	<0.1
Envirotech International Inc.	734 Greenview Dr	Grand Prairie	TX	75050	Susan Money	972-647-4733	R	32*	<0.1
Regent Sports Corp.	PO Box 11357	Hauppauge	NY	11788	Carl Farra	631-234-2800	R	32*	<0.1
Longstreth Sporting Goods	PO Box 475	Parker Ford	PA	19457	Barbara Longstreth	610-495-7022	R	30*	<0.1
Retail Distributors Inc.	45 Bartlett St	Marlborough	MA	01752	Raymond Wysocki	508-229-7779	R	29*	<0.1
Camfour Inc.	65 Westfield Ind Pk	Westfield	MA	01085	Mike Brown	413-564-2300	R	29*	<0.1
VF Grace Inc.	PO Box 200728	Anchorage	AK	99520	Charles Rush	907-272-6431	R	28*	<0.1
General Pool & S.p.A. Supply Inc.	11285 Sunco Dr	Rancho Cordova	CA	95742	Philip Gelhaus	916-853-2400	R	27*	<0.1
West Barcelona Inc.	10210 Old Katy Rd	Houston	TX	77043	Sam Barcelona	713-464-8313	R	27*	<0.1
Winmark Corp.	4200 Dahlberg Dr	Minneapolis	MN	55422	Stephen M Briggs	612-520-8500	P	27	0.1
2nd Swing Inc.	5810 Baker Rd	Minnetonka	MN	55345	Stanley A Bodine	952-345-3700	R	26	0.1
Hansen's Surfboards Inc.	1105 S Coast 101	Encinitas	CA	92024	Don Hansen	760-753-6595	R	26*	<0.1
Kubic Marketing Inc.	225 S Aviation Blvd	El Segundo	CA	90245	Bob Sayre	310-297-1600	R	25*	<0.1
Nassau Pools Construction Inc.	3420 Westview Dr	Naples	FL	34104	Thomas Threlkeld	239-643-0990	R	25*	<0.1
Robert Mucha Jr A	3 Pauline Cir	Southwick	MA	01077	Robert Mucha	413-569-5488	R	25*	<0.1
Steen Armament Research Inc.	PO Box 98	Stirling	NJ	07980	Charles Steen	908-647-3800	R	25*	<0.1
Rand Intern. Leisure Products Ltd.	51 Executive Blvd	Farmingdale	NY	11735	Allen Goldmeier	631-249-6000	R	24*	<0.1
Advanced Outdoors Inc.	PO Box 127	Hamlin	TX	79520	Joel Euton	325-576-2144	R	23*	<0.1
Kelly's Sports Ltd.	897 S Matlack St	West Chester	PA	19382	Alvy Kelly	610-436-5458	R	22*	<0.1
Walter Craig Inc.	PO Box 547	Selma	AL	36702		334-875-7935	R	22*	<0.1
Ace Cleaners & Reconditioners	PO Box 775	Washington	PA	15301	William Homnick	724-225-8710	R	21*	<0.1
New Hermes Inc.	2200 Northmont	Duluth	GA	30096		770-623-9697	R	21*	0.1
Pan Osprey Inc.	504 W Mission Ave	Escondido	CA	92025		760-739-5890	R	21*	<0.1
Cover Sports USA	5744 Woodland Ave	Philadelphia	PA	19143	Ronald Niffenbaum	215-724-3582	R	20*	<0.1
Kinsey Outdoors Inc.	1658 Steel Way	Mount Joy	PA	17552	Rick Kinsey	717-653-5524	R	20*	<0.1
Mass Movement	3131 E Maria St	Compton	CA	90221		310-635-5658	R	20*	<0.1
New Hankey Company Inc.	61 Turtle Creek Dr	Jupiter	FL	33469	Hurley Hankey	561-746-0061	R	20*	<0.1
Fuji American Advanced Sports	118 Bauer Dr	Oakland	NJ	07436	Pat Cunnane	201-337-1700	R	19*	<0.1
Hans Johnsen Co.	8901 Chancellor	Dallas	TX	75247	Howard H Johnsen	214-879-1515	R	19*	<0.1
Roller Derby Skate Corp.	401 Zion Hill Rd	Atglen	PA	19310	Edwin Seltzer	610-593-6931	R	19*	<0.1
Golden Shield Trading Inc.	PO Box 50	Chino	CA	91708	Monica Liu	562-946-3455	R	19*	<0.1
FBF Inc.	1925 N Macarthur	Oklahoma City	OK	73127		405-789-0530	R	18*	<0.1
Southbend Sporting Goods Inc.	1910 Techny Rd	Northbrook	IL	60062	Jory Katlin	847-715-1400	R	17*	<0.1
Tyr Sport Inc.	PO Box 1930	Huntington Bch	CA	92647	Steve Furniss	714-897-0799	R	17*	<0.1
Rose Industries Inc.	16742 Stagg St	Van Nuys	CA	91406	Ronald Rose	818-988-2823	R	16*	<0.1
Keys Fitness Products Inc.	4009 Distribution	Garland	TX	75041	Tim W Chen	214-340-8888	R	16*	<0.1
Bangers L.P.	PO Box 1685	Birmingham	AL	35201	Rick Bestwick	205-324-8915	R	16*	<0.1
Petzl America Inc.	PO Box 160447	Clearfield	UT	84016	Mark Rasmussen	801-327-3805	R	16*	<0.1
Champro Sports Equipment	3600 Jarvis Ave	Skokie	IL	60076	Wilson Hunt	847-676-3170	R	15*	<0.1
Bliss Murski Sales Inc.	9212 Chancellor	Dallas	TX	75247	Matthew Breeding	214-637-0979	R	15*	<0.1
Bollinger Industries Inc.	602 Fountain Pkwy	Grand Prairie	TX	75050	Bob Bollinger	972-343-1000	R	15*	<0.1
Boss International	3440 Wilshire Blvd	Los Angeles	CA	90010	Steve Chong	213-382-7799	R	15*	<0.1
Dave Bang Associates Inc.	PO Box 8760	Mesa	AZ	85214	Wayne Anderson	480-892-2266	R	15*	<0.1
Exercare Corp.	5227 W 137th St	Cleveland	OH	44142	Brian Massie	216-362-7373	R	15*	<0.1
Golfsmith Intern. Holdings Inc.	288 John R Rd	Troy	MI	48083		248-616-1970	R	15*	<0.1
Hudalla Assoc Inc.	801 Jenney Ave SW	Perham	MN	56573	Bruce Hudalla	218-346-2734	R	15*	<0.1
Kiva Designs Inc.	1350 Hayes St	Benicia	CA	94510	Tom Koenig	707-748-1614	R	15*	<0.1
Pacific Golf Accessories Inc.	7865 SW Cirrus Dr	Beaverton	OR	97008	Mark Regalado	503-641-5417	R	15*	<0.1
Quality Pool Supply Co.	5303 W Vienna Rd	Clio	MI	48420	Cary Engelhart	810-686-3010	R	15*	<0.1
Dunkin-Lewis Inc.	2552 Rocky Ridge	Birmingham	AL	35243	Charles Dunkin	205-822-6104	R	14*	<0.1
Tri-County Custom Sports Inc.	1671 Highwood E	Pontiac	MI	48340	Robert Von Bargen	248-335-6600	R	14*	<0.1
Hayden's Sports Center Inc.	1997 Aucutt Rd	Montgomery	IL	60538	Ronald Kruse	630-892-8961	R	13*	<0.1
Sportco Manufacturing Inc.	1661 Aucutt Rd	Montgomery	IL	60538	Eric Withaar	630-897-3033	R	13*	<0.1
Sportsstuff Inc.	11213 E Cir Ste A	Omaha	NE	68137	Leroy Peterson	402-592-9085	R	13*	<0.1

Source: *Ward's Business Directory of U.S. Private and Public Companies*, Volumes 1 and 2, 2005. The company type code used is as follows: P - Public, R - Private, S - Subsidiary, D - Division, J - Joint Venture, A - Affiliate, G - Group. Sales are in millions of dollars, employees are in thousands. An asterisk (*) indicates an estimated sales volume. The symbol < stands for 'less than'. Company names and addresses are truncated, in some cases, to fit into the available space.

OCCUPATIONS EMPLOYED BY MISCELLANEOUS DURABLE GOODS WHOLESALE

Occupation	% of Total 2004	Change to 2014	Occupation	% of Total 2004	Change to 2014
Sales reps, wholesale & manufacturing, exc tech	14.1	17.2	Inspectors, testers, sorters, samplers, & weighers	1.7	11.1
Laborers & freight, stock, & material movers, hand	12.6	5.5	First-line supervisors/managers of non-retail sales work	1.6	8.4
Truck drivers, heavy & tractor-trailer	4.0	17.2	Truck drivers, light or delivery services	1.5	17.2
Office clerks, general	3.5	4.4	Secretaries, except legal, medical, & executive	1.5	-1.3
Shipping, receiving, & traffic clerks	3.4	6.2	Order clerks	1.4	-24.0
Industrial truck & tractor operators	2.9	5.5	First-line supervisors/managers of office workers	1.4	6.2
Bookkeeping, accounting, & auditing clerks	2.9	5.5	Welders, cutters, solderers, & brazers	1.2	17.2
Stock clerks & order fillers	2.7	-10.2	Retail salespersons	1.2	17.2
General & operations managers	2.6	16.0	Accountants & auditors	1.1	17.2
Team assemblers	2.3	17.2	Maintenance & repair workers, general	1.1	17.2
Packers & packagers, hand	2.3	17.2	First-line supervisors/managers of helpers & laborers	1.1	4.5
Customer service representatives	2.3	20.0			

Source: Industry-Occupation Matrix, Bureau of Labor Statistics. These data are reported based on 4-digit NAICS categories but have been matched to corresponding 6-digit NAICS industry codes. The change reported for each occupation to the year 2014 is a percent of growth or decline as estimated by the Bureau of Labor Statistics. The abbreviation nec stands for 'not elsewhere classified.'

LOCATION BY STATE AND REGIONAL CONCENTRATION

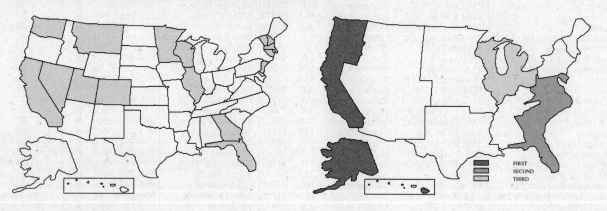

FIRST
SECOND
THIRD

INDUSTRY DATA BY STATE

State	Establishments Total (number)	% of U.S.	Employment Total (number)	% of U.S.	Per Estab.	Payroll Total ($ mil.)	Per Empl. ($)	Sales Total ($ mil.)	% of U.S.	Per Estab. ($)
California	1,036	18.8	9,925	19.2	10	390.3	39,324	4,310.1	18.9	4,160,283
Florida	555	10.1	3,881	7.5	7	146.5	37,756	2,046.8	9.0	3,687,919
Illinois	181	3.3	2,515	4.9	14	110.0	43,754	1,686.8	7.4	9,319,536
Texas	313	5.7	2,217	4.3	7	78.9	35,603	1,034.9	4.5	3,306,409
New Jersey	187	3.4	2,098	4.1	11	94.1	44,833	1,026.4	4.5	5,488,829
New York	285	5.2	2,391	4.6	8	90.8	37,992	1,025.7	4.5	3,599,056
Ohio	175	3.2	2,043	3.9	12	70.0	34,279	842.8	3.7	4,816,051
Washington	176	3.2	2,259	4.4	13	90.1	39,888	840.6	3.7	4,776,170
Wisconsin	98	1.8	1,096	2.1	11	46.2	42,155	827.5	3.6	8,443,867
Georgia	156	2.8	1,586	3.1	10	62.7	39,544	733.7	3.2	4,703,147
Colorado	155	2.8	1,185	2.3	8	44.4	37,464	646.8	2.8	4,172,858
Pennsylvania	163	3.0	1,752	3.4	11	60.2	34,365	618.3	2.7	3,793,503
Massachusetts	123	2.2	1,669	3.2	14	58.9	35,265	586.6	2.6	4,769,309
Minnesota	149	2.7	1,453	2.8	10	50.8	34,954	515.8	2.3	3,461,564
Virginia	82	1.5	953	1.8	12	30.2	31,704	412.5	1.8	5,030,866
North Carolina	124	2.2	1,034	2.0	8	34.3	33,160	379.0	1.7	3,056,847
Alabama	68	1.2	847	1.6	12	25.8	30,407	323.6	1.4	4,759,162
Connecticut	51	0.9	658	1.3	13	25.7	39,064	315.5	1.4	6,185,569
New Hampshire	39	0.7	568	1.1	15	22.8	40,167	297.0	1.3	7,616,205
Missouri	86	1.6	770	1.5	9	24.8	32,235	293.8	1.3	3,416,081
Montana	29	0.5	233	0.4	8	6.5	28,030	280.8	1.2	9,682,690
South Carolina	46	0.8	686	1.3	15	21.6	31,536	277.5	1.2	6,032,239
Vermont	32	0.6	566	1.1	18	20.3	35,779	246.4	1.1	7,699,906
Nevada	50	0.9	528	1.0	11	17.6	33,280	238.8	1.0	4,775,980
Utah	64	1.2	549	1.1	9	18.2	33,109	220.2	1.0	3,440,891
Indiana	82	1.5	668	1.3	8	19.1	28,570	188.7	0.8	2,301,756
Iowa	44	0.8	335	0.6	8	10.7	31,970	177.4	0.8	4,030,795
Tennessee	92	1.7	704	1.4	8	21.0	29,899	167.1	0.7	1,816,315
Louisiana	54	1.0	425	0.8	8	10.5	24,633	133.6	0.6	2,474,611
Kansas	41	0.7	315	0.6	8	9.8	31,162	124.4	0.5	3,033,805
Kentucky	46	0.8	339	0.7	7	10.1	29,823	96.8	0.4	2,103,500

Continued on next page.

INDUSTRY DATA BY STATE - Continued

| State | Establishments | | Employment | | | Payroll | | Sales | | |
	Total (number)	% of U.S.	Total (number)	% of U.S.	Per Estab.	Total ($ mil.)	Per Empl. ($)	Total ($ mil.)	% of U.S.	Per Estab. ($)
Arkansas	36	0.7	216	0.4	6	8.9	41,208	87.3	0.4	2,424,194
Maine	33	0.6	169	0.3	5	4.2	24,692	43.4	0.2	1,314,182
Nebraska	22	0.4	152	0.3	7	4.6	30,257	39.2	0.2	1,780,773
Mississippi	23	0.4	115	0.2	5	3.3	28,383	33.2	0.1	1,441,522
New Mexico	19	0.3	136	0.3	7	3.6	26,669	30.5	0.1	1,606,053
Alaska	8	0.1	63	0.1	8	2.1	32,825	28.5	0.1	3,558,375
North Dakota	8	0.1	74	0.1	9	2.2	29,608	16.2	0.1	2,025,875
West Virginia	20	0.4	83	0.2	4	2.5	29,759	16.1	0.1	803,050
Wyoming	10	0.2	31	0.1	3	0.5	15,032	3.7	-	373,000
Michigan	144	2.6	1000-2499	-	-	(D)	-	(D)	-	-
Oregon	109	2.0	1000-2499	-	-	(D)	-	(D)	-	-
Arizona	88	1.6	500-999	-	-	(D)	-	(D)	-	-
Maryland	70	1.3	500-999	-	-	(D)	-	(D)	-	-
Oklahoma	40	0.7	100-249	-	-	(D)	-	(D)	-	-
Hawaii	34	0.6	100-249	-	-	(D)	-	(D)	-	-
Idaho	34	0.6	250-499	-	-	(D)	-	(D)	-	-
Rhode Island	17	0.3	20-99	-	-	(D)	-	(D)	-	-
Delaware	12	0.2	20-99	-	-	(D)	-	(D)	-	-
South Dakota	7	0.1	20-99	-	-	(D)	-	(D)	-	-
D.C.	1	-	0-19	-	-	(D)	-	(D)	-	-

Source: 2002 *Economic Census*. The states are in descending order of sales or establishments (if sales data are missing for the majority). The symbol (D) appears when data are withheld to prevent disclosure of competitive information. States marked with (D) are sorted by number of establishments. A dash (-) indicates that the data element cannot be calculated. Shaded *states* on the state map indicate those states which have proportionately greater representation in the industry than would be indicated by the states population; the ratio is based on total sales or number of establishments. Shaded *regions* indicate where the industry is regionally most concentrated.

NAICS 423920 - TOY AND HOBBY GOODS AND SUPPLIES MERCHANT WHOLESALERS*

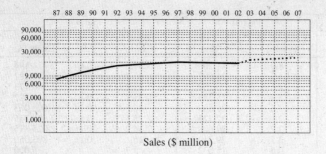

Sales ($ million)

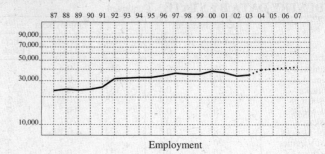

Employment

GENERAL STATISTICS

Year	Establishments (number)	Employment (number)	Payroll ($ million)	Sales ($ million)	Employees per Establishment (number)	Sales per Establishment ($)	Payroll per Employee ($)
1987	2,424	23,455	508.2	8,539.8	9.7	3,523,019.8	21,667.0
1988	2,221	24,226	557.8	10,190.3 e	10.9	4,588,158.5	23,024.8
1989	2,049	23,779	590.5	11,840.7 e	11.6	5,778,770.1	24,832.8
1990	2,123	24,291	637.7	13,491.2 e	11.4	6,354,781.0	26,252.5
1991	2,136	25,664	660.2	15,141.7 e	12.0	7,088,810.9	25,724.8
1992	2,738	31,685	941.9	16,792.2	11.6	6,133,016.8	29,727.0
1993	2,770	32,141	948.2	17,467.0 e	11.6	6,305,776.2	29,501.3
1994	2,751	32,646	970.0	18,141.7 e	11.9	6,594,583.8	29,712.7
1995	2,767	32,715	1,010.7	18,816.5 e	11.8	6,800,325.3	30,894.1
1996	2,810 e	34,242 e	1,055.9 e	19,491.2 e	12.2 e	6,936,370.1 e	30,836.4 e
1997	3,229	36,337	1,229.1	20,166.0	11.3	6,245,277.2	33,825.0
1998	3,186	35,588	1,327.8	19,946.1 e	11.2	6,260,539.9	37,310.3
1999	3,158	35,505	1,329.0	19,726.2 e	11.2	6,246,409.1	37,431.3
2000	3,140	38,325	1,477.7	19,506.2 e	12.2	6,212,178.3	38,556.4
2001	3,025	36,890	1,483.2	19,286.3 e	12.2	6,375,643.0	40,207.1
2002	2,874	33,961	1,388.9	19,066.4	11.8	6,634,098.8	40,896.9
2003	2,786	34,898	1,519.0	22,648.5 p	12.5	7,011,816.9 p	43,526.1
2004	3,264 p	39,703 p	1,653.7 p	23,345.3 p	12.3 p	7,115,576.5 p	43,755.0 p
2005	3,325 p	40,608 p	1,722.2 p	24,042.1 p	12.4 p	7,219,336.1 p	45,061.6 p
2006	3,386 p	41,514 p	1,790.7 p	24,738.9 p	12.5 p	7,323,095.8 p	46,368.2 p
2007	3,447 p	42,420 p	1,859.2 p	25,435.7 p	12.5 p	7,426,855.4 p	47,674.8 p

Sources: Economic Census of the United States, 1987, 1992, 1997, and 2002. Establishment counts, employment, and payroll are from County Business Patterns for non-Census years. Values followed by a 'p' are projections by the editors. Sales data for non-Census years are extrapolations, marked by 'e'. Data are the most recent available at this level of detail.

INDICES OF CHANGE

Year	Establishments (number)	Employment (number)	Payroll ($ million)	Sales ($ million)	Employees per Establishment (number)	Sales per Establishment ($)	Payroll per Employee ($)
1987	84.3	69.1	36.6	44.8	82.2	53.1	53.0
1992	95.3	93.3	67.8	88.1	98.3	92.4	72.7
1993	96.4	94.6	68.3	91.6 e	98.3	95.1	72.1
1994	95.7	96.1	69.8	95.2 e	100.8	99.4	72.7
1995	96.3	96.3	72.8	98.7 e	100.0	102.5	75.5
1996	97.8 e	100.8 e	76.0 e	102.2 e	103.4 e	104.6 e	75.4 e
1997	112.4	107.0	88.5	105.8	95.8	94.1	82.7
1998	110.9	104.8	95.6	104.6 e	94.9	94.4	91.2
1999	109.9	104.5	95.7	103.5 e	94.9	94.2	91.5
2000	109.3	112.9	106.4	102.3 e	103.4	93.6	94.3
2001	105.3	108.6	106.8	101.2 e	103.4	96.1	98.3
2002	100.0	100.0	100.0	100.0	100.0	100.0	100.0
2003	96.9	102.8	109.4	118.8 p	106.2	105.7 p	106.4
2004	113.6 p	116.9 p	119.1 p	122.4 p	104.2 p	107.3 p	107.0 p
2005	115.7 p	119.6 p	124.0 p	126.1 p	104.9 p	108.8 p	110.2 p
2006	117.8 p	122.2 p	128.9 p	129.8 p	105.5 p	110.4 p	113.4 p
2007	119.9 p	124.9 p	133.9 p	133.4 p	106.2 p	111.9 p	116.6 p

Sources: Same as General Statistics. The values shown reflect change from the base year, 2002. Values above 100 mean greater than 2002, values below 100 mean less than 2002, and a value of 100 in the 1987-2001 or 2003-2007 period means same as 2002. Values followed by a 'p' are projections by the editors; 'e' stands for extrapolation. Data are the most recent available at this level of detail.

SELECTED RATIOS

For 2002	Avg. of All Wholesale	Analyzed Industry	Index	For 2002	Avg. of All Wholesale	Analyzed Industry	Index
Employees per Establishment	15	12	79	Sales per Employee	791,325	561,420	71
Payroll per Establishment	626,122	483,264	77	Sales per Establishment	12,012,387	6,634,099	55
Payroll per Employee	41,161	40,897	99	Expenses per Establishment	na	na	na

Sources: Same as General Statistics. The 'Average of All' column, Wholesale or Retail, represents the average of the sector reported for the most recent complete year available. The Index shows the relationship between the Average and the Analyzed Industry. For example, 100 means that they are equal; 500 that the Analyzed Industry is five times the average; 50 means that the Analyzed Industry is half the national average. The abbreviation 'na' is used to show that data are 'not available'.

*Equivalent to SIC 5092.

LEADING COMPANIES   Number shown: **52**   Total sales ($ mil): **3,881**   Total employment (000): **5.6**

Company Name	Address				CEO Name	Phone	Co. Type	Sales ($ mil)	Empl. (000)
Great Planes Model Distributors	PO Box 9021	Champaign	IL	61826	Wayne Hemming	217-398-6300	R	1,683*	0.8
RC2 Corp.	1111 W 22nd St	Oak Brook	IL	60523	Bob Dods	630-573-7200	P	381	0.6
Darice Inc.	13000 Darice Pkwy	Strongsville	OH	44149	Mike Catan	440-238-9150	R	365*	1.0
ABC International Traders Inc.	16730 Schoenborn	North Hills	CA	91343	Isaac Larian	818-894-2525	R	225*	<0.1
Progressive Balloons Inc.	PO Box 850	Saint Peters	MO	63376	Judy Burns	636-240-0444	R	118*	0.2
RC2 Racing Champions Ertl Inc.	PO Box 500	Dyersville	IA	52040		563-875-2000	R	88*	0.2
Ammar's Inc.	710 S College Ave	Bluefield	VA	24605	Keleel A Ammar Jr	276-322-4686	R	85*	0.9
Star Sales Company Inc.	PO Box 1503	Knoxville	TN	37901	Neil Foster	865-524-0771	R	69*	0.1
Playmobil USA Inc.	PO Box 877	Dayton	NJ	08810		609-395-5566	R	47*	<0.1
Hobby Products International Inc.	70 Icon	El Toro	CA	92610	Tatsuro Watanabe	949-753-1099	R	42*	<0.1
Goffa International Corp.	39 Noll St	Brooklyn	NY	11206	Douglas Song	718-361-8883	R	35*	<0.1
Atlantic Bingo Supply Inc.	1700 Midway Rd	Odenton	MD	21113	Larry Weinstein	410-551-2200	R	32*	<0.1
Welcome Industrial Corporation	71 E Industry Ct	Deer Park	NY	11729	Tony Lin	631-242-5556	R	30*	0.1
Brewer Sewing Supplies Co.	3800 W 42nd St	Chicago	IL	60632	Jerry Smith	773-247-2121	R	29*	<0.1
TNT Fireworks	5401 W Skelly Dr	Tulsa	OK	74107		918-446-4441	R	29*	<0.1
Retail Distributors Inc.	45 Bartlett St	Marlborough	MA	01752	Raymond Wysocki	508-229-7779	R	29*	<0.1
Food Market Merchandising Inc.	6401 W 106th St	Minneapolis	MN	55438	Jon Tollefson	952-894-0110	R	28*	<0.1
Twin Hills Collectables L.L.C.	70 Hickory Rd	Hickory	KY	42051		270-856-2277	R	28*	<0.1
Shepher Distributors & Sales Corp.	2300 Linden Blvd	Brooklyn	NY	11208	Hal Monchik	718-649-2525	R	27*	<0.1
Continental Automotive Accesso	205 Troup St	Dublin	GA	31021	Sam Jacobson	478-272-4525	R	27*	<0.1
Consigned Sales Inc.	12105 Grandview	Grandview	MO	64030	Evan Palmer	816-761-8500	R	26*	<0.1
Zapf Creation Inc.	4901 Vineland Rd	Orlando	FL	32811		407-351-7702	R	25*	<0.1
Carimex International Trading Inc.	4601 S Soto St	Los Angeles	CA	90058	Andy Yoon	323-582-8333	R	23*	<0.1
Mod-Ad Agency Inc.	8300 Tonnelle Ave	North Bergen	NJ	07047	Peter Winston	201-662-8500	R	23*	<0.1
Petting Zoo Inc.	120 Langley Rd N	Glen Burnie	MD	21060	John Lizewski	410-760-9792	R	23*	<0.1
Top Line Distributing Inc.	2950 San Pablo Ave	Berkeley	CA	94702	Michael Sloan	510-845-9851	R	23*	<0.1
Middle America Management Inc.	9640 Owensmouth	Chatsworth	CA	91311	Al Bloom	818-349-8700	R	23*	<0.1
Pan De Vida Inc.	PO Box 2369	Montclair	CA	91763	Ruben Ulloa	909-510-5200	R	22*	<0.1
Wm. K. Walthers Inc.	5601 W Florist Ave	Milwaukee	WI	53218	Philip Walthers	414-527-0770	R	22*	0.2
Advance Novelty Inc.	PO Box 846	Findlay	OH	45839	Thomas Heimann	419-424-0363	R	20*	<0.1
Manley Toy Direct L.L.C.	1800 N 9th St	Indianola	IA	50125	Samson Chan	515-961-5935	R	20*	<0.1
International Playthings Inc.	75 D Lackawanna	Parsippany	NJ	07054	Ted Kiesewetter	973-316-2500	R	20*	<0.1
Craftex Wholesale Distributors	7215 Ashcroft Dr	Houston	TX	77081		713-771-6691	R	15*	<0.1
Fun Adventures Inc.	1930 Lansdown Dr	Carrollton	TX	75010	Alan Putter	972-394-8359	R	15*	<0.1
Kipp Brothers Inc.	PO Box 781080	Indianapolis	IN	46278	Bob Glenn	317-814-1475	R	14*	<0.1
Big Bear Fireworks Inc.	8139 Elder Creek Rd	Sacramento	CA	95824	Bruce Zoldan	916-388-1479	R	14*	<0.1
Hico Helium and Balloons	PO Box 1665	Powder Springs	GA	30127		770-439-7454	R	14*	<0.1
Investacard	600 Irwin St	San Rafael	CA	94901	David Shawn	415-559-8777	R	14*	<0.1
Frank Moran and Sons Inc.	1404 Rome Rd	Baltimore	MD	21227	Frank Moran	410-242-6233	R	13*	<0.1
Boley Corp.	2022 Violet St	Los Angeles	CA	90021	Ronald Wong	213-688-8802	R	12*	<0.1
Fun Equipment Sales Inc.	4332 Tejasco	San Antonio	TX	78218	Bill Rutledge	210-822-4386	R	12*	<0.1
Quality Accents Inc.	707 N Main St	Mishawaka	IN	46545	Marlene Hollencamp	574-254-1600	R	12*	<0.1
Siya Inc.	7825 Somerset Blvd	Paramount	CA	90723	Sudhir Mundhra	562-633-3002	R	12*	<0.1
Young Forever Inc.	9868 Sandalfoot	Boca Raton	FL	33428	Steve Rosenthal	561-994-5556	R	12*	<0.1
Nikko America Inc.	2801 Summit Ave	Plano	TX	75074	Yugi Hatori	972-422-0838	R	11*	<0.1
Lou Davis Wholesale	N3211 Hwy H	Lake Geneva	WI	53147	Fred Koermer	262-248-2000	R	10*	<0.1
E.Z. Gregory Inc.	PO Box 44268	Madison	WI	53744	Gary Hermanson	608-271-2324	R	10*	<0.1
Carol School Supply Inc.	17928 Union Tpke	Flushing	NY	11366	Carol Pick	718-380-4203	R	9*	<0.1
Toy Wonders Inc.	234 Moonachie Rd	Moonachie	NJ	07074	Samuel Su	201-229-1700	R	8*	<0.1
Bel Air Tool Corp.	110 Byfield St	Warwick	RI	02888	Steven Alviti	401-781-4408	R	3*	<0.1
Bingo Cactus Supply Inc.	3210 E Roeser Rd	Phoenix	AZ	85040	Sam Whitlock	602-268-2848	R	3*	<0.1
St Louis Crafts Inc.	7606 Idaho Ave	Saint Louis	MO	63111	Edward Nussbaumer	314-638-0038	R	1*	<0.1

Source: Ward's *Business Directory of U.S. Private and Public Companies*, Volumes 1 and 2, 2005. The company type code used is as follows: P - Public, R - Private, S - Subsidiary, D - Division, J - Joint Venture, A - Affiliate, G - Group. Sales are in millions of dollars, employees are in thousands. An asterisk (*) indicates an estimated sales volume. The symbol < stands for 'less than'. Company names and addresses are truncated, in some cases, to fit into the available space.

OCCUPATIONS EMPLOYED BY MISCELLANEOUS DURABLE GOODS WHOLESALE

Occupation	% of Total 2004	Change to 2014	Occupation	% of Total 2004	Change to 2014
Sales reps, wholesale & manufacturing, exc tech	14.1	17.2	Inspectors, testers, sorters, samplers, & weighers	1.7	11.1
Laborers & freight, stock, & material movers, hand	12.6	5.5	First-line supervisors/managers of non-retail sales work	1.6	8.4
Truck drivers, heavy & tractor-trailer	4.0	17.2	Truck drivers, light or delivery services	1.5	17.2
Office clerks, general	3.5	4.4	Secretaries, except legal, medical, & executive	1.5	-1.3
Shipping, receiving, & traffic clerks	3.4	6.2	Order clerks	1.4	-24.0
Industrial truck & tractor operators	2.9	5.5	First-line supervisors/managers of office workers	1.4	6.2
Bookkeeping, accounting, & auditing clerks	2.9	5.5	Welders, cutters, solderers, & brazers	1.2	17.2
Stock clerks & order fillers	2.7	-10.2	Retail salespersons	1.2	17.2
General & operations managers	2.6	16.0	Accountants & auditors	1.1	17.2
Team assemblers	2.3	17.2	Maintenance & repair workers, general	1.1	17.2
Packers & packagers, hand	2.3	17.2	First-line supervisors/managers of helpers & laborers	1.1	4.5
Customer service representatives	2.3	20.0			

Source: *Industry-Occupation Matrix*, Bureau of Labor Statistics. These data are reported based on 4-digit NAICS categories but have been matched to corresponding 6-digit NAICS industry codes. The change reported for each occupation to the year 2014 is a percent of growth or decline as estimated by the Bureau of Labor Statistics. The abbreviation nec stands for 'not elsewhere classified.'

LOCATION BY STATE AND REGIONAL CONCENTRATION

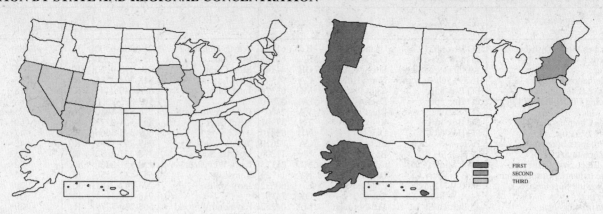

INDUSTRY DATA BY STATE

State	Establishments Total (number)	% of U.S.	Employment Total (number)	% of U.S.	Per Estab.	Payroll Total ($ mil.)	Per Empl. ($)	Sales Total ($ mil.)	% of U.S.	Per Estab. ($)
California	758	26.3	9,281	27.2	12	399.1	43,005	7,058.3	36.8	9,311,739
Illinois	135	4.7	2,960	8.7	22	119.3	40,298	1,189.5	6.2	8,811,015
Texas	159	5.5	1,769	5.2	11	70.3	39,764	874.7	4.6	5,501,497
Pennsylvania	88	3.0	1,371	4.0	16	55.8	40,694	441.7	2.3	5,019,102
Florida	202	7.0	1,406	4.1	7	40.7	28,928	360.0	1.9	1,781,965
Arizona	39	1.4	301	0.9	8	11.5	38,163	299.8	1.6	7,687,359
Iowa	20	0.7	470	1.4	23	22.2	47,262	237.5	1.2	11,876,500
Ohio	91	3.2	1,207	3.5	13	37.3	30,915	233.1	1.2	2,561,604
Utah	33	1.1	659	1.9	20	16.3	24,737	211.1	1.1	6,397,000
Virginia	36	1.2	473	1.4	13	17.0	35,975	209.3	1.1	5,814,194
Wisconsin	45	1.6	534	1.6	12	18.1	33,912	174.5	0.9	3,878,311
Oregon	36	1.2	225	0.7	6	8.3	36,964	161.4	0.8	4,482,417
Missouri	48	1.7	477	1.4	10	16.7	35,107	153.5	0.8	3,197,417
Nevada	28	1.0	258	0.8	9	8.4	32,496	125.2	0.7	4,470,929
Georgia	57	2.0	359	1.1	6	13.5	37,621	120.6	0.6	2,115,982
Indiana	48	1.7	353	1.0	7	11.4	32,275	107.7	0.6	2,244,458
North Carolina	40	1.4	205	0.6	5	8.9	43,200	90.7	0.5	2,266,400
Alabama	14	0.5	369	1.1	26	7.6	20,599	56.1	0.3	4,009,857
Kentucky	18	0.6	122	0.4	7	3.7	30,000	35.0	0.2	1,944,167
South Carolina	19	0.7	148	0.4	8	3.0	19,932	28.7	0.1	1,510,211
Hawaii	15	0.5	89	0.3	6	2.4	26,652	26.3	0.1	1,755,667
Nebraska	11	0.4	92	0.3	8	3.4	36,554	20.6	0.1	1,868,364
Vermont	7	0.2	89	0.3	13	3.0	33,449	19.1	0.1	2,730,000
Louisiana	16	0.6	103	0.3	6	2.5	23,893	17.4	0.1	1,088,938
Arkansas	5	0.2	38	0.1	8	1.1	28,684	10.7	0.1	2,130,200
New Mexico	8	0.3	24	0.1	3	0.6	26,458	10.1	0.1	1,258,625
South Dakota	6	0.2	66	0.2	11	1.8	27,727	7.6	-	1,262,000
West Virginia	8	0.3	56	0.2	7	1.0	17,089	7.0	-	873,625
Maine	5	0.2	17	-	3	0.5	28,941	2.4	-	471,000
New York	281	9.7	2500-4999	-	-	(D)	-	(D)	-	-
New Jersey	149	5.2	1000-2499	-	-	(D)	-	(D)	-	-
Washington	84	2.9	1000-2499	-	-	(D)	-	(D)	-	-
Minnesota	51	1.8	250-499	-	-	(D)	-	(D)	-	-
Colorado	47	1.6	100-249	-	-	(D)	-	(D)	-	-
Michigan	44	1.5	250-499	-	-	(D)	-	(D)	-	-
Massachusetts	41	1.4	250-499	-	-	(D)	-	(D)	-	-
Connecticut	32	1.1	250-499	-	-	(D)	-	(D)	-	-
Maryland	29	1.0	500-999	-	-	(D)	-	(D)	-	-
Tennessee	27	0.9	100-249	-	-	(D)	-	(D)	-	-
Kansas	23	0.8	100-249	-	-	(D)	-	(D)	-	-
Rhode Island	17	0.6	20-99	-	-	(D)	-	(D)	-	-
New Hampshire	15	0.5	100-249	-	-	(D)	-	(D)	-	-
Oklahoma	14	0.5	100-249	-	-	(D)	-	(D)	-	-
Idaho	7	0.2	20-99	-	-	(D)	-	(D)	-	-
Mississippi	7	0.2	20-99	-	-	(D)	-	(D)	-	-
Montana	7	0.2	0-19	-	-	(D)	-	(D)	-	-
Alaska	5	0.2	20-99	-	-	(D)	-	(D)	-	-
Delaware	4	0.1	0-19	-	-	(D)	-	(D)	-	-
North Dakota	4	0.1	20-99	-	-	(D)	-	(D)	-	-
Wyoming	3	0.1	20-99	-	-	(D)	-	(D)	-	-

Source: 2002 *Economic Census*. The states are in descending order of sales or establishments (if sales data are missing for the majority). The symbol (D) appears when data are withheld to prevent disclosure of competitive information. States marked with (D) are sorted by number of establishments. A dash (-) indicates that the data element cannot be calculated. Shaded *states* on the state map indicate those states which have proportionally greater representation in the industry than would be indicated by the states population; the ratio is based on total sales or number of establishments. Shaded *regions* indicate where the industry is regionally most concentrated.

NAICS 423930 - RECYCLABLE MATERIAL MERCHANT WHOLESALERS*

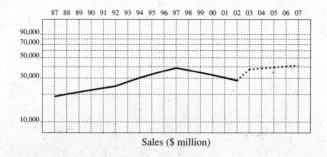

Sales ($ million)

Employment

GENERAL STATISTICS

Year	Establishments (number)	Employment (number)	Payroll ($ million)	Sales ($ million)	Employees per Establishment (number)	Sales per Establishment ($)	Payroll per Employee ($)
1987	8,716	85,762	1,624.1	18,904.3	9.8	2,168,919.2	18,937.3
1988	8,248	93,158	2,153.3	20,015.8 e	11.3	2,426,745.9	23,114.5
1989	8,139	99,304	2,328.5	21,127.4 e	12.2	2,595,822.6	23,448.2
1990	8,628	102,179	2,389.8	22,238.9 e	11.8	2,577,526.7	23,388.4
1991	9,058	105,709	2,401.7	23,350.5 e	11.7	2,577,887.0	22,719.9
1992	8,928	98,005	2,269.1	24,462.0	11.0	2,739,919.4	23,152.9
1993	9,073	100,172	2,414.7	27,319.3 e	11.0	3,011,054.8	24,105.5
1994	9,079	102,395	2,668.8	30,176.7 e	11.3	3,323,791.2	26,063.8
1995	9,541	115,866	3,218.0	33,034.0 e	12.1	3,462,320.5	27,773.5
1996	9,321 e	111,981 e	3,058.5 e	35,891.4 e	12.0 e	3,850,595.4 e	27,312.7 e
1997	9,088	114,992	3,229.1	38,748.7	12.7	4,263,721.4	28,081.1
1998	8,972	113,243	3,185.6	36,640.4 e	12.6	4,083,858.7	28,130.7
1999	8,459	102,260	3,040.1	34,532.1 e	12.1	4,082,286.3	29,729.1
2000	8,267	103,108	3,302.7	32,423.7 e	12.5	3,922,068.5	32,031.2
2001	8,002	99,109	3,132.0	30,315.4 e	12.4	3,788,480.4	31,602.0
2002	7,145	82,433	2,637.5	28,207.1	11.5	3,947,809.7	31,995.7
2003	6,969	83,113	2,833.4	37,353.9 p	11.9	4,468,118.1 p	34,091.1
2004	7,986 p	100,275 p	3,355.9 p	38,385.3 p	12.5 p	4,605,376.0 p	34,033.4 p
2005	7,922 p	100,222 p	3,428.9 p	39,416.7 p	12.6 p	4,742,634.0 p	34,836.6 p
2006	7,857 p	100,169 p	3,501.9 p	40,448.2 p	12.7 p	4,879,892.0 p	35,639.8 p
2007	7,793 p	100,116 p	3,574.8 p	41,479.6 p	12.7 p	5,017,149.9 p	36,443.0 p

Sources: *Economic Census of the United States*, 1987, 1992, 1997, and 2002. Establishment counts, employment, and payroll are from *County Business Patterns* for non-Census years. Values followed by a 'p' are projections by the editors. Sales data for non-Census years are extrapolations, marked by 'e'. Data are the most recent available at this level of detail.

INDICES OF CHANGE

Year	Establishments (number)	Employment (number)	Payroll ($ million)	Sales ($ million)	Employees per Establishment (number)	Sales per Establishment ($)	Payroll per Employee ($)
1987	122.0	104.0	61.6	67.0	85.2	54.9	59.2
1992	125.0	118.9	86.0	86.7	95.7	69.4	72.4
1993	127.0	121.5	91.6	96.9 e	95.7	76.3	75.3
1994	127.1	124.2	101.2	107.0 e	98.3	84.2	81.5
1995	133.5	140.6	122.0	117.1 e	105.2	87.7	86.8
1996	130.5 e	135.8 e	116.0 e	127.2 e	104.3 e	97.5 e	85.4 e
1997	127.2	139.5	122.4	137.4	110.4	108.0	87.8
1998	125.6	137.4	120.8	129.9 e	109.6	103.4	87.9
1999	118.4	124.1	115.3	122.4 e	105.2	103.4	92.9
2000	115.7	125.1	125.2	114.9 e	108.7	99.3	100.1
2001	112.0	120.2	118.7	107.5 e	107.8	96.0	98.8
2002	100.0	100.0	100.0	100.0	100.0	100.0	100.0
2003	97.5	100.8	107.4	132.4 p	103.7	113.2 p	106.5
2004	111.8 p	121.6 p	127.2 p	136.1 p	108.7 p	116.7 p	106.4 p
2005	110.9 p	121.6 p	130.0 p	139.7 p	109.4 p	120.1 p	108.9 p
2006	110.0 p	121.5 p	132.8 p	143.4 p	110.1 p	123.6 p	111.4 p
2007	109.1 p	121.5 p	135.5 p	147.1 p	110.9 p	127.1 p	113.9 p

Sources: Same as General Statistics. The values shown reflect change from the base year, 2002. Values above 100 mean greater than 2002, values below 100 mean less than 2002, and a value of 100 in the 1987-2001 or 2003-2007 period means same as 2002. Values followed by a 'p' are projections by the editors; 'e' stands for extrapolation. Data are the most recent available at this level of detail.

SELECTED RATIOS

For 2002	Avg. of All Wholesale	Analyzed Industry	Index	For 2002	Avg. of All Wholesale	Analyzed Industry	Index
Employees per Establishment	15	12	77	Sales per Employee	791,325	342,182	43
Payroll per Establishment	626,122	369,139	59	Sales per Establishment	12,012,387	3,947,810	33
Payroll per Employee	41,161	31,996	78	Expenses per Establishment	na	na	na

Sources: Same as General Statistics. The 'Average of All' column, Wholesale or Retail, represents the average of the sector reported for the most recent complete year available. The Index shows the relationship between the Average and the Analyzed Industry. For example, 100 means that they are equal; 500 that the Analyzed Industry is five times the average; 50 means that the Analyzed Industry is half the national average. The abbreviation 'na' is used to show that data are 'not available'.

LEADING COMPANIES   Number shown: **75**   Total sales ($ mil): **21,432**   Total employment (000): **64.9**

Company Name	Address				CEO Name	Phone	Co. Type	Sales ($ mil)	Empl. (000)
Tribune Co.	435 N Michigan	Chicago	IL	60611	D. J. Fitzsimmons	312-222-9100	P	5,726	23.8
Commercial Metals Co.	7800 Stemmons	Dallas	TX	75247		214-689-4300	P	4,768	10.6
Houchens Industries Inc.	PO Box 90009	Bowling Green	KY	42102	Jim Gipson	270-843-3252	R	2,005	9.2
Wellman Inc.	595 Shrewsbury Ave	Shrewsbury	NJ	07702	Thomas M Duff	732-212-3300	P	1,305	1.9
Philip Services Corp.	5151 San Felipe	Houston	TX	77056	Robert L Knauss	713-623-8777	R	1,119	8.6
Metal Management Inc.	500 N Dearborn St	Chicago	IL	60610	Daniel W Dienst	312-645-0700	P	1,083	1.5
Tube City L.L.C.	PO Box 2000	Glassport	PA	15045	Michael Coslov	412-678-6141	R	1,006*	0.9
OmniSource Corp.	1610 N Calhoun St	Fort Wayne	IN	46808	Daniel M Rifkin	219-422-5541	R	750	1.4
Hugo Neu-Proler Corp.	901 New Dock St	Terminal Island	CA	90731	Jeffrey Neu	310-831-0281	R	549*	0.3
Basic Fibres Inc.	6019 S Manhattan Pl	Los Angeles	CA	90047	Robert Berg	323-753-3491	R	465*	1.0
PSC Metals Inc.	20521 Chagrin Blvd	Beachwood	OH	44122	Benjamin Elemker	330-484-7610	S	216*	0.6
Federal International Inc.	7935 Clayton Rd	St. Louis	MO	63117	Melvin L Lefkowitz	314-721-3377	R	210*	0.4
Harmon Associates Corp.	2 Jericho Plz	Jericho	NY	11753	Simon Davies	516-997-3400	R	178*	<0.1
New England Recycling Inc.	61 Taylor Reed Pl	Stamford	CT	06906	Michael Ferro	203-324-4090	R	118*	<0.1
Alter Trading Corp.	689 Craig Rd	St. Louis	MO	63141	Keith Rhodes	314-872-2400	R	112*	0.3
Southern Holdings Inc.	4801 Florida Ave	New Orleans	LA	70126	Joel Dupre	504-944-3371	R	109*	0.2
Metalsco Inc.	11775 Borman	St. Louis	MO	63141	Sheldon Tauben	314-997-5200	R	107*	<0.1
Jack Engle and Co.	PO Box 01705	Los Angeles	CA	90001	Alan Engle	323-589-8111	R	106*	<0.1
Potential Industries Inc.	922 E E St	Wilmington	CA	90744	Tony Fan	310-549-5901	R	72*	0.1
Allan Co.	14618 Arrow Hwy	Baldwin Park	CA	91706	Steve Young	626-962-4047	R	69*	0.2
ACC Recycling Corp.	1190 20th St N	St. Petersburg	FL	33713	Michael Accomando	727-896-9600	R	65*	<0.1
Inland Waters Pollution Control	2021 S Schaefer	Detroit	MI	48217	Robert Williams	313-841-5800	R	60*	0.3
Ambit Pacific Recycling Inc.	16222 S Figueroa St	Gardena	CA	90247	Roy Able	310-538-3798	R	58*	<0.1
Minkin Chandler Corp.	13501 Sanders Ave	Detroit	MI	48217	Phillip S Minkin	313-843-5900	R	46*	0.1
Atlas Metal and Iron Corp.	PO Box 5428	Denver	CO	80217	Donald Rosen	303-825-7166	R	45*	<0.1
Energy Answers Corp.	79 N Pearl St	Albany	NY	12207	Patrick F Mahoney	518-434-1227	R	45*	0.1
Metro Recycling Company Inc.	2424 Beekman St	Cincinnati	OH	45214	Chuck Francis	513-251-1800	R	45*	<0.1
Appliance Recycling Centers	7400 Excelsior Blvd	Minneapolis	MN	55426	Edward R Cameron	952-930-9000	P	44	0.2
Phillip Metals Inc.	PO Box 1182	Nashville	TN	37202	Robert Knauss	615-271-3300	R	43*	0.2
Metro Metals Northwest	5611 NE Columbia	Portland	OR	97218	Victor Winkler	503-287-8861	R	41*	<0.1
Allied Vista Inc.	2828 Nagle St	Dallas	TX	75220	Tom Lyon	214-366-3800	R	40*	<0.1
Atlas Mill Supply	PO Box 1530	Los Angeles	CA	90001	Dana Raffle	323-589-8992	R	36*	0.1
Lionetti Associates	450 S Front St	Elizabeth	NJ	07202		908-820-8800	R	36*	<0.1
Green Team of San Jose	1333 Oakland Rd	San Jose	CA	95112	Paul Nelson	408-283-8500	R	34*	<0.1
Western Pacific Pulp and Paper	9333 Stewrt & Gry	Downey	CA	90241	Kevin Duncombe	562-803-4401	R	33*	<0.1
Aadlen Brothers Auto Wrecking	11590 Tuxford St	Sun Valley	CA	91352	Sam Adlen	818-504-1091	R	28*	<0.1
EKCO Metals	2777 E Washington	Los Angeles	CA	90023	Ely Keenberg	323-264-1615	R	28*	<0.1
Rapid Processing L.L.C.	860 Humboldt St	Brooklyn	NY	11222	Cosimo Tristani	718-349-7555	R	27*	<0.1
Smelter Service Corp.	PO Box 432	Mount Pleasant	TN	38474	Jim Barrier	931-379-7765	R	26*	<0.1
Sustainable Resources L.L.C.	1850 N Courtenay	Merritt Island	FL	32953	Paul Bemis	321-453-1040	R	25*	<0.1
Winston Brothers	13200 Mount Elliott	Detroit	MI	48212	Julian Winston	313-891-1380	R	25*	<0.1
Bay Bridge Enterprises L.L.C.	PO Box 7596	Chesapeake	VA	23324		757-543-2066	R	23*	<0.1
State Line Scrap Company Inc.	PO Box 3029	Attleboro	MA	02703	David Bourque	508-399-8300	R	23*	<0.1
Carolina Recycling Group L.L.C.	PO Box 578	Lyman	SC	29365	James Knight	864-233-2747	R	23*	<0.1
Fox Integrated Technologies Inc.	686 N King Rd	San Jose	CA	95133	Robert J Fox	408-929-4369	R	23*	<0.1
Waste Management of Iowa Inc.	PO Box AX	Des Moines	IA	50303	Curtis Hill	515-265-5267	S	23*	0.1
Arizona Recycling Corp.	400 S 15th Ave	Phoenix	AZ	85007	Sal Bova	602-258-5323	R	19*	<0.1
Vista Fibers	2828 Nagle St	Dallas	TX	75220	Tom Lyon	214-366-3800	S	19*	<0.1
Consumers Scrap Recycling Inc.	PO Box 4227	Detroit	MI	48204	Norbert Wierszewski	313-491-8200	R	18*	<0.1
Shredded Products Corp.	700 Commerce Rd	Rocky Mount	VA	24151	Donald G Smith	540-489-7599	S	18*	<0.1
Appertain Corp.	PO Box 1010	Pulaski	TN	38478	Rod Wells	931-363-8284	R	18*	<0.1
M Hiller and Son Inc.	1133 Manhattan Ave	Brooklyn	NY	11222	Leonard Hiller	718-383-2833	R	18*	<0.1
Midnight Auto Recycling L.L.C.	407 E 9th St	San Bernardino	CA	92410		909-889-6800	R	18*	<0.1
Newman Auto Recyclers Inc.	2700 Newman Rd	Mobile	AL	36695	Lon Lindquist	251-639-7447	R	18*	<0.1
Riverside Scrap Iron & Metal	PO Box 5288	Riverside	CA	92517	Daniel Frankel	951-686-2120	P	18*	<0.1
Youngstown Iron and Metal Inc.	100 Division St Ext	Youngstown	OH	44510	Martin Wilhelm	330-743-9000	R	18*	<0.1
Standard Iron and Metal Inc.	4525 San Leandro St	Oakland	CA	94601	Jason Allen	510-535-0222	R	16*	<0.1
Great Lakes Waste Services Inc.	5400 Cogswell Rd	Wayne	MI	48184		734-729-8200	S	15*	0.2
A and S of Modesto Inc.	PO Box 955	Castroville	CA	95012	Stanley Silva	831-633-3379	R	14*	<0.1
Harding Metals Inc.	PO Box 418	Northwood	NH	03261	JJ Harding	603-942-5573	R	14*	<0.1
Circosta Iron and Metal Inc.	1801 Evans Ave	San Francisco	CA	94124	Nick Circosta	415-282-8568	R	14*	<0.1
Midwest Iron and Metal Inc.	PO Box 70	Hutchinson	KS	67504	Roger Crispin	620-662-0551	R	14*	<0.1
North State Recycling	PO Box 720350	Redding	CA	96099	William Short	530-243-4780	R	14*	<0.1
Riverside Scrap	Leesville Ave	Avenel	NJ	07001	Raymond Muir	732-381-3355	R	14*	<0.1
Ace Metal Co.	720 W 23rd St	National City	CA	91950	Donald Humphries	619-635-8787	R	13*	<0.1
Fiber Resources Unlimited Inc.	3833 Bancroft Dr	Spring Valley	CA	91977	John Dalton	619-462-0098	R	11*	<0.1
Mid-City Iron and Metal Corp.	2104 E 15th St	Los Angeles	CA	90021	George Adams	213-747-4281	R	11*	<0.1
Southside Recycling Inc.	PO Box 25447	St. Louis	MO	63125	Tim Jansen	314-631-3400	R	11*	<0.1
American Independent Paper Mills	15 S Depot Plz	Tarrytown	NY	10591	Peter Baselice	914-631-8285	R	11*	<0.1
American Metal Recycling Inc.	11150 Redwood Ave	Fontana	CA	92337	Todd Rubin	909-823-3135	R	11*	<0.1
Bayou City Auction Pool	1802 Breezin Ct	Spring	TX	77380		281-362-1514	R	11*	<0.1
Brooklyn Resources Recovery	741 Rockaway Pkwy	Brooklyn	NY	11236	Robert Rosselli	718-531-6606	R	11*	<0.1
Samuel Frank Metal Company Inc.	600 W Ave	Rochester	NY	14611	Robert Frank	585-328-8040	R	11*	<0.1
Middleman Iron and Metal Co.	5300 Vine St	Cincinnati	OH	45217	Ira Moskwoitz	513-242-0022	R	10*	<0.1
Shadowhawk Inc.	1200 W Struck Ave	Orange	CA	92867	Richard Krueger	714-744-3323	R	10*	<0.1

Source: Ward's Business Directory of U.S. Private and Public Companies, Volumes 1 and 2, 2005. The company type code used is as follows: P - Public, R - Private, S - Subsidiary, D - Division, J - Joint Venture, A - Affiliate, G - Group. Sales are in millions of dollars, employees are in thousands. An asterisk (*) indicates an estimated sales volume. The symbol < stands for 'less than'. Company names and addresses are truncated, in some cases, to fit into the available space.

OCCUPATIONS EMPLOYED BY MISCELLANEOUS DURABLE GOODS WHOLESALE

Occupation	% of Total 2004	Change to 2014	Occupation	% of Total 2004	Change to 2014
Sales reps, wholesale & manufacturing, exc tech	14.1	17.2	Inspectors, testers, sorters, samplers, & weighers	1.7	11.1
Laborers & freight, stock, & material movers, hand	12.6	5.5	First-line supervisors/managers of non-retail sales work	1.6	8.4
Truck drivers, heavy & tractor-trailer	4.0	17.2	Truck drivers, light or delivery services	1.5	17.2
Office clerks, general	3.5	4.4	Secretaries, except legal, medical, & executive	1.5	-1.3
Shipping, receiving, & traffic clerks	3.4	6.2	Order clerks	1.4	-24.0
Industrial truck & tractor operators	2.9	5.5	First-line supervisors/managers of office workers	1.4	6.2
Bookkeeping, accounting, & auditing clerks	2.9	5.5	Welders, cutters, solderers, & brazers	1.2	17.2
Stock clerks & order fillers	2.7	-10.2	Retail salespersons	1.2	17.2
General & operations managers	2.6	16.0	Accountants & auditors	1.1	17.2
Team assemblers	2.3	17.2	Maintenance & repair workers, general	1.1	17.2
Packers & packagers, hand	2.3	17.2	First-line supervisors/managers of helpers & laborers	1.1	4.5
Customer service representatives	2.3	20.0			

Source: Industry-Occupation Matrix, Bureau of Labor Statistics. These data are reported based on 4-digit NAICS categories but have been matched to corresponding 6-digit NAICS industry codes. The change reported for each occupation to the year 2014 is a percent of growth or decline as estimated by the Bureau of Labor Statistics. The abbreviation nec stands for 'not elsewhere classified.'

LOCATION BY STATE AND REGIONAL CONCENTRATION

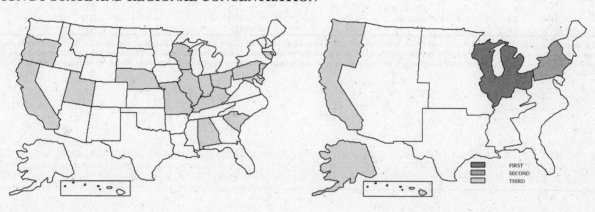

INDUSTRY DATA BY STATE

State	Establishments Total (number)	% of U.S.	Employment Total (number)	% of U.S.	Per Estab.	Payroll Total ($ mil.)	Per Empl. ($)	Sales Total ($ mil.)	% of U.S.	Per Estab. ($)
California	851	12.0	10,567	12.7	12	328.7	31,102	3,579.5	12.5	4,206,282
Pennsylvania	397	5.6	4,435	5.3	11	143.4	32,339	2,338.5	8.2	5,890,418
Ohio	419	5.9	5,273	6.4	13	183.7	34,834	2,217.7	7.8	5,292,742
Texas	472	6.6	6,682	8.1	14	185.5	27,760	1,883.6	6.6	3,990,617
Illinois	387	5.5	4,110	5.0	11	144.1	35,053	1,841.4	6.4	4,758,075
New York	455	6.4	6,108	7.4	13	192.0	31,442	1,606.5	5.6	3,530,835
Missouri	152	2.1	1,769	2.1	12	61.8	34,946	1,430.4	5.0	9,410,645
Michigan	258	3.6	2,935	3.5	11	114.6	39,048	1,043.3	3.7	4,043,674
New Jersey	279	3.9	3,263	3.9	12	118.7	36,377	984.4	3.4	3,528,186
Indiana	190	2.7	2,800	3.4	15	100.8	35,989	933.6	3.3	4,913,889
Florida	296	4.2	2,598	3.1	9	78.8	30,346	815.5	2.9	2,755,017
Wisconsin	171	2.4	2,387	2.9	14	82.1	34,375	782.3	2.7	4,574,807
Georgia	177	2.5	2,089	2.5	12	62.9	30,087	691.1	2.4	3,904,469
South Carolina	104	1.5	1,495	1.8	14	39.6	26,478	581.6	2.0	5,592,260
Connecticut	68	1.0	1,097	1.3	16	43.3	39,497	574.2	2.0	8,444,059
Maryland	94	1.3	1,339	1.6	14	48.3	36,046	567.7	2.0	6,039,691
Alabama	134	1.9	1,401	1.7	10	39.1	27,894	558.5	2.0	4,167,948
North Carolina	203	2.9	2,361	2.8	12	76.5	32,391	521.6	1.8	2,569,330
Oregon	101	1.4	1,525	1.8	15	53.5	35,072	516.4	1.8	5,112,673
Kentucky	115	1.6	1,302	1.6	11	38.7	29,702	491.4	1.7	4,272,687
Tennessee	133	1.9	1,587	1.9	12	45.3	28,561	458.1	1.6	3,444,594
Washington	147	2.1	1,508	1.8	10	51.1	33,910	420.1	1.5	2,857,537
Massachusetts	154	2.2	1,520	1.8	10	56.7	37,327	418.1	1.5	2,714,682
Minnesota	132	1.9	1,206	1.5	9	43.2	35,780	385.2	1.3	2,918,439
Virginia	114	1.6	1,643	2.0	14	49.3	30,018	322.6	1.1	2,829,947
Louisiana	65	0.9	813	1.0	13	22.1	27,133	299.0	1.0	4,599,415
Utah	55	0.8	539	0.7	10	15.7	29,065	286.1	1.0	5,202,655
Iowa	131	1.8	1,276	1.5	10	33.2	26,024	243.8	0.9	1,860,916
Nebraska	59	0.8	344	0.4	6	10.0	29,020	210.5	0.7	3,567,085
Colorado	78	1.1	913	1.1	12	30.4	33,254	201.4	0.7	2,582,397
Arkansas	71	1.0	639	0.8	9	18.0	28,108	178.2	0.6	2,510,352

Continued on next page.

INDUSTRY DATA BY STATE - Continued

State	Establishments		Employment			Payroll		Sales		
	Total (number)	% of U.S.	Total (number)	% of U.S.	Per Estab.	Total ($ mil.)	Per Empl. ($)	Total ($ mil.)	% of U.S.	Per Estab. ($)
Kansas	75	1.1	575	0.7	8	15.6	27,063	132.7	0.5	1,769,853
West Virginia	53	0.7	406	0.5	8	7.7	18,941	125.3	0.4	2,364,962
Mississippi	61	0.9	474	0.6	8	12.8	26,987	116.6	0.4	1,911,721
Oklahoma	66	0.9	649	0.8	10	16.2	25,020	114.4	0.4	1,733,212
Maine	36	0.5	337	0.4	9	10.3	30,469	108.1	0.4	3,002,556
Idaho	34	0.5	277	0.3	8	7.8	28,054	75.2	0.3	2,213,176
New Hampshire	27	0.4	225	0.3	8	9.5	42,271	59.4	0.2	2,198,185
Nevada	30	0.4	246	0.3	8	7.5	30,480	39.3	0.1	1,309,467
South Dakota	24	0.3	171	0.2	7	4.1	23,883	39.0	0.1	1,626,583
New Mexico	28	0.4	213	0.3	8	5.3	24,883	34.2	0.1	1,222,107
Hawaii	22	0.3	201	0.2	9	4.6	22,682	33.4	0.1	1,518,818
North Dakota	20	0.3	209	0.3	10	5.6	26,876	30.1	0.1	1,503,200
Montana	15	0.2	134	0.2	9	3.8	28,142	25.7	0.1	1,710,133
Vermont	12	0.2	46	0.1	4	1.1	24,652	10.5	-	873,333
Wyoming	9	0.1	60	0.1	7	1.2	20,100	10.4	-	1,159,778
Arizona	69	1.0	500-999	-	-	(D)	-	(D)	-	-
Rhode Island	30	0.4	250-499	-	-	(D)	-	(D)	-	-
Delaware	19	0.3	100-249	-	-	(D)	-	(D)	-	-
Alaska	4	0.1	20-99	-	-	(D)	-	(D)	-	-
D.C.	2	-	0-19	-	-	(D)	-	(D)	-	-

Source: 2002 *Economic Census*. The states are in descending order of sales or establishments (if sales data are missing for the majority). The symbol (D) appears when data are withheld to prevent disclosure of competitive information. States marked with (D) are sorted by number of establishments. A dash (-) indicates that the data element cannot be calculated. Shaded *states* on the state map indicate those states which have proportionately greater representation in the industry than would be indicated by the states population; the ratio is based on total sales or number of establishments. Shaded *regions* indicate where the industry is regionally most concentrated.

NAICS 423940 - JEWELRY, WATCH, PRECIOUS STONE, AND PRECIOUS METAL MERCHANT WHOLESALERS*

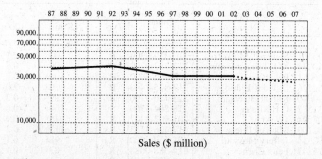

Sales ($ million)

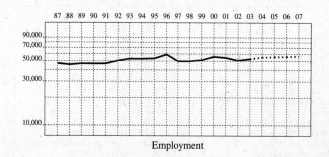

Employment

GENERAL STATISTICS

Year	Establishments (number)	Employment (number)	Payroll ($ million)	Sales ($ million)	Employees per Establishment (number)	Sales per Establishment ($)	Payroll per Employee ($)
1987	6,927	47,062	1,093.0	38,581.6	6.8	5,569,741.6	23,224.7
1988	6,430	45,546	1,196.2	39,126.5 e	7.1	6,084,992.2	26,263.6
1989	6,187	46,734	1,240.2	39,671.4 e	7.6	6,412,057.5	26,537.4
1990	6,347	46,605	1,281.6	40,216.2 e	7.3	6,336,253.3	27,499.2
1991	6,292	46,764	1,299.7	40,761.1 e	7.4	6,478,242.2	27,792.7
1992	7,421	50,452	1,467.7	41,306.0	6.8	5,566,096.2	29,091.0
1993	7,567	52,904	1,495.0	39,524.5 e	7.0	5,223,272.1	28,258.7
1994	7,645	52,850	1,532.6	37,743.0 e	6.9	4,936,952.3	28,999.1
1995	7,670	53,330	1,584.5	35,961.6 e	7.0	4,688,605.0	29,711.2
1996	8,263 e	58,968 e	1,772.6 e	34,180.1 e	7.1 e	4,136,524.3 e	30,060.4 e
1997	7,689	49,820	1,702.8	32,398.6	6.5	4,213,629.9	34,179.0
1998	7,987	49,789	1,765.3	32,405.9 e	6.2	4,057,335.7	35,455.6
1999	8,126	51,289	1,890.1	32,413.3 e	6.3	3,988,835.8	36,852.0
2000	8,355	55,854	2,102.8	32,420.6 e	6.7	3,880,385.4	37,647.7
2001	8,215	54,408	2,080.3	32,428.0 e	6.6	3,947,408.4	38,235.3
2002	8,317	50,845	1,922.0	32,435.3	6.1	3,899,879.8	37,801.2
2003	8,404	52,744	2,099.4	30,722.1 p	6.3	3,350,901.5 p	39,803.6
2004	8,780 p	55,150 p	2,196.9 p	30,060.2 p	6.2 p	3,161,153.1 p	40,492.4 p
2005	8,920 p	55,618 p	2,261.0 p	29,398.3 p	6.1 p	2,971,404.7 p	41,479.1 p
2006	9,060 p	56,086 p	2,325.2 p	28,736.4 p	6.1 p	2,781,656.2 p	42,465.8 p
2007	9,200 p	56,554 p	2,389.4 p	28,074.5 p	6.0 p	2,591,907.8 p	43,452.4 p

Sources: Economic Census of the United States, 1987, 1992, 1997, and 2002. Establishment counts, employment, and payroll are from County Business Patterns for non-Census years. Values followed by a 'p' are projections by the editors. Sales data for non-Census years are extrapolations, marked by 'e'. Data are the most recent available at this level of detail.

INDICES OF CHANGE

Year	Establishments (number)	Employment (number)	Payroll ($ million)	Sales ($ million)	Employees per Establishment (number)	Sales per Establishment ($)	Payroll per Employee ($)
1987	83.3	92.6	56.9	118.9	111.5	142.8	61.4
1992	89.2	99.2	76.4	127.3	111.5	142.7	77.0
1993	91.0	104.0	77.8	121.9 e	114.8	133.9	74.8
1994	91.9	103.9	79.7	116.4 e	113.1	126.6	76.7
1995	92.2	104.9	82.4	110.9 e	114.8	120.2	78.6
1996	99.4 e	116.0 e	92.2 e	105.4 e	116.4 e	106.1 e	79.5 e
1997	92.4	98.0	88.6	99.9	106.6	108.0	90.4
1998	96.0	97.9	91.8	99.9 e	101.6	104.0	93.8
1999	97.7	100.9	98.3	99.9 e	103.3	102.3	97.5
2000	100.5	109.9	109.4	100.0 e	109.8	99.5	99.6
2001	98.8	107.0	108.2	100.0 e	108.2	101.2	101.1
2002	100.0	100.0	100.0	100.0	100.0	100.0	100.0
2003	101.0	103.7	109.2	94.7 p	102.9	85.9 p	105.3
2004	105.6 p	108.5 p	114.3 p	92.7 p	101.7 p	81.1 p	107.1 p
2005	107.3 p	109.4 p	117.6 p	90.6 p	100.6 p	76.2 p	109.7 p
2006	108.9 p	110.3 p	121.0 p	88.6 p	99.5 p	71.3 p	112.3 p
2007	110.6 p	111.2 p	124.3 p	86.6 p	98.4 p	66.5 p	114.9 p

Sources: Same as General Statistics. The values shown reflect change from the base year, 2002. Values above 100 mean greater than 2002, values below 100 mean less than 2002, and a value of 100 in the 1987-2001 or 2003-2007 period means same as 2002. Values followed by a 'p' are projections by the editors; 'e' stands for extrapolation. Data are the most recent available at this level of detail.

SELECTED RATIOS

For 2002	Avg. of All Wholesale	Analyzed Industry	Index	For 2002	Avg. of All Wholesale	Analyzed Industry	Index
Employees per Establishment	15	6	41	Sales per Employee	791,325	637,925	81
Payroll per Establishment	626,122	231,093	37	Sales per Establishment	12,012,387	3,899,880	32
Payroll per Employee	41,161	37,801	92	Expenses per Establishment	na	na	na

Sources: Same as General Statistics. The 'Average of All' column, Wholesale or Retail, represents the average of the sector reported for the most recent complete year available. The Index shows the relationship between the Average and the Analyzed Industry. For example, 100 means that they are equal; 500 that the Analyzed Industry is five times the average; 50 means that the Analyzed Industry is half the national average. The abbreviation 'na' is used to show that data are 'not available'.

*Equivalent to SIC 5094.

LEADING COMPANIES   Number shown: 75   Total sales ($ mil): 80,519   Total employment (000): 29.4

Company Name	Address				CEO Name	Phone	Co. Type	Sales ($ mil)	Empl. (000)
Loews Corp.	667 Madison Ave	New York	NY	10021		212-521-2000	P	73,750	22.0
A-Mark Financial Corp.	100 Wilshire Blvd	Santa Monica	CA	90401	Steven C Markoff	310-319-0200	R	2,800	0.1
M. Fabrikant and Sons Inc.	1 Rockefeller Plz	New York	NY	10020	M Fabrikant Fortgang	212-757-0790	R	900	0.8
Gerson Company Inc.	1450 S Lone Elm Rd	Olathe	KS	66061	Peter Gerson	913-262-7400	R	404*	0.2
K's Merchandise Mart Inc.	3103 N Charles St	Decatur	IL	62526	David K Eldridge	217-875-1440	R	320*	2.0
SunCoast Merchandise Corp.	6315 Bandini Blvd	Los Angeles	CA	90040	Kumar Bhavnani	323-720-9700	R	199*	0.2
Bulova Corp.	1 Bulova Ave	Woodside	NY	11377	C Hoffman	718-204-3300	S	164	0.6
Samsung Opto-Electronics Am.	40 Seaview Dr	Secaucus	NJ	07094	JW Ahn	201-902-0347	R	145*	<0.1
Gordon Brothers Corp.	40 Broad St, 11th Fl	Boston	MA	02109	Michael Frieze	617-426-3233	R	117*	0.2
Speidel Inc.	25 Fairmount Ave	East Providence	RI	02914	Jeffery Mossotti	401-519-2000	R	98*	0.1
Prime Art and Jewel	2930 N Stemmons	Dallas	TX	75247	Felix Chen	214-688-0088	R	83*	0.1
Frank Mastoloni and Sons Inc.	608 5th Ave	New York	NY	10020	Francis J Mastoloni Sr	212-757-7278	R	71*	<0.1
Arts Elegance Inc.	739 E Walnut St	Pasadena	CA	91101	Art Mikaelian	626-405-1522	R	69*	0.1
Star Sales Company Inc.	PO Box 1503	Knoxville	TN	37901	Neil Foster	865-524-0771	R	69*	0.1
Aurea Jewelry Creations L.L.C.	516 5th Ave Fl 5	New York	NY	10036		212-398-3456	R	55*	<0.1
DM Merchandising Inc.	4210 Trans World	Schiller Park	IL	60176	David Marks	847-671-5850	R	52*	<0.1
Bennett Brothers Inc.	30 E Adams St	Chicago	IL	60603	GK Bennett	312-263-4800	R	50*	0.1
Citra Trading Corp.	590 Fifth Ave	New York	NY	10036	Ari Chitrik	212-354-1000	R	44*	<0.1
Jewel Craft of Utah	245 N 1000 W	Clearfield	UT	84015	Nancy Gardner	801-773-2968	R	41*	<0.1
Synergy Gold Group Inc.	3100 47th Ave Ste 5	Long Island City	NY	11101	Gary McMullan	718-472-9600	R	41*	<0.1
Leo Wolleman Inc.	45 W 45th St Fl 10	New York	NY	10036	Todd Wolleman	212-840-1881	R	37*	<0.1
Black Forest Originals-Grandfather	1116 S Oak St	La Crescent	MN	55947	Allan Mc Cormick	507-895-1000	R	34*	<0.1
Memox Corp.	10 E 38th St	New York	NY	10016	Paul Perlmutter	212-696-1870	R	30*	<0.1
Swiss Watch International Inc.	101 S State Rd 7	Hollywood	FL	33023	Lior Ben Shmuel	954-985-3827	R	28	<0.1
Capital Diamond Importers Inc.	517 R1 S Ste 2100	Iselin	NJ	08830		732-750-5010	R	28*	<0.1
Helby Import Co.	37 Hayward Ave	Carteret	NJ	07008	Lawrence Weiss	732-969-5300	R	28*	<0.1
Precious Gems and Jewels	8207 Styers Ct	Laurel	MD	20723	Candice Jones	301-604-7203	R	28*	<0.1
DGSE Companies Inc.	2817 Forest Ln	Dallas	TX	75234	William H Oyster	972-484-3662	P	26	<0.1
Pisani Enterprises Inc.	350 Ocean Ave	San Francisco	CA	94112	Gerald Pisani	415-861-6616	R	25*	<0.1
Boutique Trims Inc.	21200 Pontiac Trl	South Lyon	MI	48178	Kevin Williams	248-437-2017	R	24*	<0.1
Jewels Connection	510 W 6th St	Los Angeles	CA	90014	Daniel Golshirazin	213-689-1332	R	24*	<0.1
Maurice Lacroix U S A Inc.	17835 Ventura Blvd	Encino	CA	91316	Robert Siragusa	818-609-8686	R	24*	<0.1
Michal Golan Inc.	409 W 44th St	New York	NY	10036	Michal Golan	212-541-5998	R	24*	<0.1
RS Co.	PO Box 611	Huntsville	AL	35804	Ron Scott	256-533-9762	R	24*	<0.1
Stella Golden Inc.	250 Spring St 7N103	Atlanta	GA	30303	Jay Eun	404-525-4324	R	24*	<0.1
1928 Jewelry Co.	PO Box 7761	Burbank	CA	91510	Melvyn Bernie	818-841-1928	R	24*	0.3
Corporate Presence Inc.	19 W 21st St	New York	NY	10010	Jeffrey Sehgal	212-989-6446	R	21*	<0.1
GA Heaton Co.	6595 Hwy 49 N	Mariposa	CA	95338	Jerry Heaton	209-377-8227	R	21*	<0.1
Luna Bianca USA Inc.	3409 NW 9th Ave	Fort Lauderdale	FL	33309	Fabrizio Volpino	954-563-2438	R	21*	<0.1
Mar-Ner Numismatics Ltd.	550 W Old Country	Hicksville	NY	11801	Roger Gardner	631-474-1100	R	21*	<0.1
Matagorda Ventures Inc.	800 W S Houston N	Houston	TX	77024	Ron Doohaluk	713-973-7925	R	21*	<0.1
Time Service Inc.	245 23rd St	Toledo	OH	43624	David Perlmetter	419-241-4181	R	20*	0.5
Los Altos Trophy Inc.	10731 Walker St A	Cypress	CA	90630	Beverly Rubin	714-252-5350	R	19*	<0.1
Rosenthal Jewelers Supply Corp.	42 NE 25th St	Miami	FL	33137	Daisy Adouth	305-573-6866	R	19*	<0.1
Audemars Piguet	40 E 57th St	New York	NY	10022	Francios Venahmias	212-758-8400	R	18*	<0.1
Major World Wide Ltd.	19706 53rd Ave	Fresh Meadows	NY	11365	Arthur Rosenberg	718-224-7023	R	18*	<0.1
B and M Imports Inc.	12 E 46th St Fl 4	New York	NY	10017	Mois Medine	212-986-5700	R	17*	<0.1
Fashion Trends Inc.	PO Box 4070	Spanaway	WA	98387	Al Ruskin	253-847-1924	R	17*	<0.1
La Vie Parisienne Inc.	1918 Main St	Santa Monica	CA	90405	Catherine Popesco	310-392-8428	R	17*	<0.1
Vision, Solutions, Impact L.L.C.	2 Harbour Pl	Portsmouth	NH	03801		603-422-7761	R	17*	<0.1
Bally Bead Company Inc.	2304 Ridge Rd	Rockwall	TX	75087	Ward Hudspeth	972-771-4515	R	16*	<0.1
Jewelry Corner Inc.	1201 E Elizabeth St	Brownsville	TX	78520	Chander Buxani	956-544-1786	R	16*	<0.1
Swiss Tech	3 Mason	Irvine	CA			949-458-4200	R	16*	<0.1
Carolina Time Equipment Inc.	PO Box 18158	Charlotte	NC	28218	Henry Allen	704-536-2700	R	15*	<0.1
Evvtex Company Inc.	579 5th Rm 1626	New York	NY	10017	David Zadeh	212-754-2626	R	15*	<0.1
Just Diamonds	702 Colorado St	Austin	TX	78701	Jimmy Williams	512-476-0011	R	15*	<0.1
Denver Merchandise Mart	451 E 58th Ave	Denver	CO	80216	Darrell Hare	303-292-6278	R	15*	<0.1
Esslinger and Company Inc.	1165 Medallion Dr	Saint Paul	MN	55120	Patricia Liquard	651-452-7180	R	14*	<0.1
Cliff Weil Inc.	PO Box 427	Mechanicsville	VA	23116	Alvin B Hutzler II	804-746-1321	R	14*	<0.1
Baroni Designs Inc.	1049 Samoa Blvd	Arcata	CA	95521	Sarah Baroni	707-822-8067	R	14*	<0.1
CTE Systems Inc.	565 W Lambert Rd	Brea	CA	92821	Kathleen Albers		R	14*	<0.1
Golden Grove Trading Inc.	854 W Gldn Grove	Covina	CA	91722	Werner Schulz	626-331-7233	R	14*	<0.1
Jewelry Manufacturers Outlet Inc.	86 Yonkers Ave	Tuckahoe	NY	10707	Steven Ruggiero	914-395-1744	R	14*	<0.1
Killer Beads & Everything Else	PO Box 18797	Panama City	FL	32417	C Mc Laughlin	850-234-6361	R	14*	<0.1
Lauremer Limited Inc.	127 S Broadway	Nyack	NY	10960	Ann Kozlowski		R	14*	<0.1
M Geller Ltd.	29 E Madison St	Chicago	IL	60602	Mark Geller	312-984-1041	R	14*	<0.1
Ming Fung Jewelry Corp.	49 W 45th St	New York	NY	10036		212-997-7552	R	14*	<0.1
Net Products Solutions	12970 Branford St	Pacoima	CA	91331		818-877-4405	R	14*	<0.1
North Star	PO Box 18506	Kansas City	MO	64133	William Ehlers	816-353-1001	R	14*	<0.1
Santa Fe Jewelers	1513 5th St	Santa Fe	NM	87505	Steve Chancellor	505-988-9157	R	14*	<0.1
Security Gold Exchange Inc.	104 Mill St	Grass Valley	CA	95945	Bruce Franklin	530-272-1810	R	14*	<0.1
SKF International Inc.	15 W 37th St Fl 7	New York	NY	10018	Sam Koumi	212-719-9094	R	14*	<0.1
Downey Creations L.L.C.	2265 Executive Dr	Indianapolis	IN	46241	David Downey	317-248-9888	R	12*	<0.1
Bijoux Terner Partnership	6950 NW 77th Ct	Miami	FL	33166	Salomon Terner	305-266-9000	R	11*	<0.1
Chef's Warehouse	7002 F St	Omaha	NE	68117	Tom Schrack	402-339-8900	R	10*	<0.1

Source: Ward's Business Directory of U.S. Private and Public Companies, Volumes 1 and 2, 2005. The company type code used is as follows: P - Public, R - Private, S - Subsidiary, D - Division, J - Joint Venture, A - Affiliate, G - Group. Sales are in millions of dollars, employees are in thousands. An asterisk (*) indicates an estimated sales volume. The symbol < stands for 'less than'. Company names and addresses are truncated, in some cases, to fit into the available space.

OCCUPATIONS EMPLOYED BY MISCELLANEOUS DURABLE GOODS WHOLESALE

Occupation	% of Total 2004	Change to 2014	Occupation	% of Total 2004	Change to 2014
Sales reps, wholesale & manufacturing, exc tech	14.1	17.2	Inspectors, testers, sorters, samplers, & weighers	1.7	11.1
Laborers & freight, stock, & material movers, hand	12.6	5.5	First-line supervisors/managers of non-retail sales work	1.6	8.4
Truck drivers, heavy & tractor-trailer	4.0	17.2	Truck drivers, light or delivery services	1.5	17.2
Office clerks, general	3.5	4.4	Secretaries, except legal, medical, & executive	1.5	-1.3
Shipping, receiving, & traffic clerks	3.4	6.2	Order clerks	1.4	-24.0
Industrial truck & tractor operators	2.9	5.5	First-line supervisors/managers of office workers	1.4	6.2
Bookkeeping, accounting, & auditing clerks	2.9	5.5	Welders, cutters, solderers, & brazers	1.2	17.2
Stock clerks & order fillers	2.7	-10.2	Retail salespersons	1.2	17.2
General & operations managers	2.6	16.0	Accountants & auditors	1.1	17.2
Team assemblers	2.3	17.2	Maintenance & repair workers, general	1.1	17.2
Packers & packagers, hand	2.3	17.2	First-line supervisors/managers of helpers & laborers	1.1	4.5
Customer service representatives	2.3	20.0			

Source: Industry-Occupation Matrix, Bureau of Labor Statistics. These data are reported based on 4-digit NAICS categories but have been matched to corresponding 6-digit NAICS industry codes. The change reported for each occupation to the year 2014 is a percent of growth or decline as estimated by the Bureau of Labor Statistics. The abbreviation nec stands for 'not elsewhere classified.'

LOCATION BY STATE AND REGIONAL CONCENTRATION

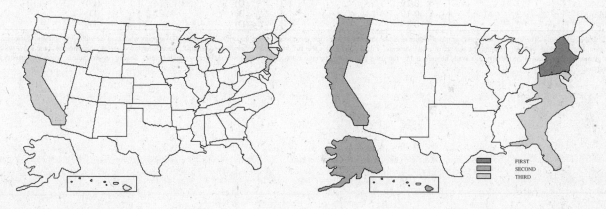

FIRST
SECOND
THIRD

INDUSTRY DATA BY STATE

State	Establishments Total (number)	% of U.S.	Employment Total (number)	% of U.S.	Per Estab.	Payroll Total ($ mil.)	Per Empl. ($)	Sales Total ($ mil.)	% of U.S.	Per Estab. ($)
New York	2,905	35.0	17,093	34.1	6	713.1	41,719	14,777.0	44.7	5,086,763
California	1,503	18.1	7,404	14.8	5	268.8	36,302	6,540.3	19.8	4,351,511
Texas	451	5.4	4,307	8.6	10	169.2	39,291	1,686.8	5.1	3,740,102
New Jersey	283	3.4	2,101	4.2	7	110.8	52,723	1,570.3	4.8	5,548,781
Illinois	285	3.4	2,126	4.2	7	76.4	35,925	872.5	2.6	3,061,561
Michigan	92	1.1	673	1.3	7	27.3	40,547	481.0	1.5	5,228,109
Pennsylvania	158	1.9	972	1.9	6	34.8	35,838	472.4	1.4	2,990,089
Ohio	137	1.7	1,057	2.1	8	32.4	30,633	411.7	1.2	3,005,438
Minnesota	65	0.8	389	0.8	6	14.0	36,031	161.5	0.5	2,485,215
New Mexico	68	0.8	723	1.4	11	23.6	32,656	161.1	0.5	2,369,662
Virginia	61	0.7	332	0.7	5	12.4	37,497	124.2	0.4	2,036,787
Indiana	44	0.5	364	0.7	8	9.5	26,179	108.4	0.3	2,464,250
Oregon	34	0.4	113	0.2	3	2.8	24,354	104.6	0.3	3,075,500
North Carolina	81	1.0	358	0.7	4	10.1	28,302	75.2	0.2	927,827
Louisiana	34	0.4	175	0.3	5	3.8	21,760	71.5	0.2	2,103,471
Colorado	87	1.0	251	0.5	3	6.6	26,207	62.0	0.2	712,701
Wisconsin	45	0.5	315	0.6	7	8.6	27,194	59.2	0.2	1,315,356
Nevada	32	0.4	297	0.6	9	10.8	36,316	57.1	0.2	1,784,781
Tennessee	66	0.8	237	0.5	4	7.9	33,266	49.2	0.1	745,788
New Hampshire	21	0.3	99	0.2	5	4.1	41,182	45.8	0.1	2,180,619
Kentucky	31	0.4	192	0.4	6	5.0	25,870	35.4	0.1	1,140,613
Alabama	34	0.4	183	0.4	5	4.1	22,601	34.8	0.1	1,022,176
South Dakota	18	0.2	244	0.5	14	10.1	41,492	33.4	0.1	1,854,333
Oklahoma	21	0.3	98	0.2	5	3.0	30,837	24.2	0.1	1,150,000
South Carolina	32	0.4	151	0.3	5	3.0	19,861	21.1	0.1	658,156
Kansas	26	0.3	85	0.2	3	3.0	35,318	20.3	0.1	780,000
Vermont	10	0.1	38	0.1	4	1.1	30,184	10.2	-	1,024,200
Montana	11	0.1	16	-	1	0.4	23,187	9.7	-	881,182
Maine	13	0.2	67	0.1	5	1.4	20,537	8.1	-	622,154
Mississippi	14	0.2	40	0.1	3	1.0	23,875	6.8	-	485,429
Alaska	4	-	18	-	5	0.7	40,000	2.8	-	696,500

Continued on next page.

INDUSTRY DATA BY STATE - Continued

State	Establishments Total (number)	% of U.S.	Employment Total (number)	% of U.S.	Per Estab.	Payroll Total ($ mil.)	Per Empl. ($)	Sales Total ($ mil.)	% of U.S.	Per Estab. ($)
Idaho	9	0.1	22	-	2	0.3	14,227	1.8	-	202,000
Nebraska	8	0.1	26	0.1	3	0.3	12,308	1.7	-	210,125
West Virginia	5	0.1	19	-	4	0.2	9,579	1.2	-	249,200
Florida	650	7.8	2500-4999	-	-	(D)	-	(D)	-	-
Georgia	187	2.3	500-999	-	-	(D)	-	(D)	-	-
Rhode Island	132	1.6	1000-2499	-	-	(D)	-	(D)	-	-
Massachusetts	108	1.3	500-999	-	-	(D)	-	(D)	-	-
Arizona	106	1.3	500-999	-	-	(D)	-	(D)	-	-
Hawaii	78	0.9	250-499	-	-	(D)	-	(D)	-	-
Washington	73	0.9	250-499	-	-	(D)	-	(D)	-	-
Missouri	68	0.8	250-499	-	-	(D)	-	(D)	-	-
Maryland	57	0.7	100-249	-	-	(D)	-	(D)	-	-
Connecticut	52	0.6	500-999	-	-	(D)	-	(D)	-	-
Utah	41	0.5	250-499	-	-	(D)	-	(D)	-	-
Arkansas	19	0.2	100-249	-	-	(D)	-	(D)	-	-
Iowa	18	0.2	20-99	-	-	(D)	-	(D)	-	-
Delaware	5	0.1	0-19	-	-	(D)	-	(D)	-	-
D.C.	3	-	0-19	-	-	(D)	-	(D)	-	-
North Dakota	2	-	0-19	-	-	(D)	-	(D)	-	-
Wyoming	2	-	0-19	-	-	(D)	-	(D)	-	-

Source: 2002 Economic Census. The states are in descending order of sales or establishments (if sales data are missing for the majority). The symbol (D) appears when data are withheld to prevent disclosure of competitive information. States marked with (D) are sorted by number of establishments. A dash (-) indicates that the data element cannot be calculated. Shaded *states* on the state map indicate those states which have proportionately greater representation in the industry than would be indicated by the states population; the ratio is based on total sales or number of establishments. Shaded *regions* indicate where the industry is regionally most concentrated.

NAICS 424110 - PRINTING AND WRITING PAPER MERCHANT WHOLESALERS*

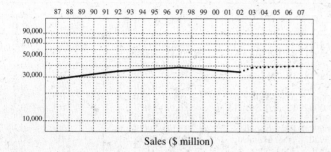

Sales ($ million)

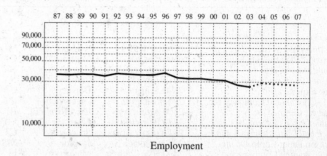

Employment

GENERAL STATISTICS

Year	Establishments (number)	Employment (number)	Payroll ($ million)	Sales ($ million)	Employees per Establishment (number)	Sales per Establishment ($)	Payroll per Employee ($)
1987	2,074	35,900	1,100.1	28,530.6	17.3	13,756,316.3	30,643.5
1988	2,005	35,461	1,193.4	29,802.1 e	17.7	14,863,890.3	33,653.9
1989	1,969	35,999	1,301.7	31,073.5 e	18.3	15,781,361.1	36,159.3
1990	1,924	35,922	1,337.0	32,344.9 e	18.7	16,811,278.6	37,219.5
1991	1,851	34,460	1,274.3	33,616.3 e	18.6	18,161,156.1	36,979.1
1992	2,561	36,646	1,387.3	34,887.8	14.3	13,622,725.5	37,856.8
1993	2,472	36,010	1,388.9	35,589.7 e	14.6	14,397,127.8	38,569.8
1994	2,379	35,479	1,396.8	36,291.7 e	14.9	15,255,023.1	39,369.8
1995	2,335	35,447	1,622.9	36,993.6 e	15.2	15,843,083.5	45,783.8
1996	2,436 e	37,239 e	1,624.7 e	37,695.6 e	15.3 e	15,474,384.2 e	43,629.0 e
1997	2,309	33,135	1,547.3	38,397.5	14.4	16,629,493.3	46,696.8
1998	2,262	32,418	1,630.4	37,600.9 e	14.3	16,622,855.9	50,293.0
1999	2,215	32,512	1,610.9	36,804.3 e	14.7	16,615,936.8	49,547.9
2000	2,104	31,475	1,717.2	36,007.7 e	15.0	17,113,925.9	54,556.5
2001	2,018	31,024	1,712.3	35,211.1 e	15.4	17,448,513.4	55,193.1
2002	1,843	27,767	1,523.2	34,414.5	15.1	18,673,087.4	54,856.5
2003	1,725	26,532	1,528.5	38,521.9 p	15.4	17,671,102.1 p	57,608.1
2004	2,092 p	29,201 p	1,745.1 p	38,971.1 p	14.0 p	17,859,833.5 p	58,884.5 p
2005	2,086 p	28,698 p	1,776.3 p	39,420.3 p	13.7 p	18,048,564.9 p	60,534.3 p
2006	2,080 p	28,194 p	1,807.5 p	39,869.5 p	13.5 p	18,237,296.3 p	62,184.1 p
2007	2,074 p	27,691 p	1,838.7 p	40,318.7 p	13.3 p	18,426,027.8 p	63,833.9 p

Sources: Economic Census of the United States, 1987, 1992, 1997, and 2002. Establishment counts, employment, and payroll are from *County Business Patterns* for non-Census years. Values followed by a 'p' are projections by the editors. Sales data for non-Census years are extrapolations, marked by 'e'. Data are the most recent available at this level of detail.

INDICES OF CHANGE

Year	Establishments (number)	Employment (number)	Payroll ($ million)	Sales ($ million)	Employees per Establishment (number)	Sales per Establishment ($)	Payroll per Employee ($)
1987	112.5	129.3	72.2	82.9	114.6	73.7	55.9
1992	139.0	132.0	91.1	101.4	94.7	73.0	69.0
1993	134.1	129.7	91.2	103.4 e	96.7	77.1	70.3
1994	129.1	127.8	91.7	105.5 e	98.7	81.7	71.8
1995	126.7	127.7	106.5	107.5 e	100.7	84.8	83.5
1996	132.2 e	134.1 e	106.7 e	109.5 e	101.3 e	82.9 e	79.5 e
1997	125.3	119.3	101.6	111.6	95.4	89.1	85.1
1998	122.7	116.8	107.0	109.3 e	94.7	89.0	91.7
1999	120.2	117.1	105.8	106.9 e	97.4	89.0	90.3
2000	114.2	113.4	112.7	104.6 e	99.3	91.7	99.5
2001	109.5	111.7	112.4	102.3 e	102.0	93.4	100.6
2002	100.0	100.0	100.0	100.0	100.0	100.0	100.0
2003	93.6	95.6	100.3	111.9 p	101.9	94.6 p	105.0
2004	113.5 p	105.2 p	114.6 p	113.2 p	92.4 p	95.6 p	107.3 p
2005	113.2 p	103.4 p	116.6 p	114.5 p	91.1 p	96.7 p	110.4 p
2006	112.9 p	101.5 p	118.7 p	115.9 p	89.7 p	97.7 p	113.4 p
2007	112.5 p	99.7 p	120.7 p	117.2 p	88.3 p	98.7 p	116.4 p

Sources: Same as General Statistics. The values shown reflect change from the base year, 2002. Values above 100 mean greater than 2002, values below 100 mean less than 2002, and a value of 100 in the 1987-2001 or 2003-2007 period means same as 2002. Values followed by a 'p' are projections by the editors; 'e' stands for extrapolation. Data are the most recent available at this level of detail.

SELECTED RATIOS

For 2002	Avg. of All Wholesale	Analyzed Industry	Index	For 2002	Avg. of All Wholesale	Analyzed Industry	Index
Employees per Establishment	15	15	101	Sales per Employee	791,325	1,239,403	157
Payroll per Establishment	626,122	826,479	132	Sales per Establishment	12,012,387	18,673,087	155
Payroll per Employee	41,161	54,856	133	Expenses per Establishment	na	na	na

Sources: Same as General Statistics. The 'Average of All' column, Wholesale or Retail, represents the average of the sector reported for the most recent complete year available. The Index shows the relationship between the Average and the Analyzed Industry. For example, 100 means that they are equal; 500 that the Analyzed Industry is five times the average; 50 means that the Analyzed Industry is half the national average. The abbreviation 'na' is used to show that data are 'not available'.

*Equivalent to SIC 5111.

LEADING COMPANIES   Number shown: **38**   Total sales ($ mil): **12,628**   Total employment (000): **30.4**

Company Name	Address				CEO Name	Phone	Co. Type	Sales ($ mil)	Empl. (000)
Hallmark Cards Inc.	PO Box 419580	Kansas City	MO	64141		816-274-5111	R	4,300	18.0
Unisource Worldwide Inc.	6600 Gov Lk	Norcross	GA	30071	Allan Dragone	770-447-9000	S	3,701*	8.0
Gould Paper Corp.	11 Madison Ave	New York	NY	10010	Harry E Gould, Jr	212-301-0000	R	1,125	0.4
Maines Paper and Food Service	101 Broome	Conklin	NY	13748	Chris Mellon	607-779-1200	R	650*	0.8
Kirk Expedx	7500 Amigos Ave	Downey	CA	90242		562-803-0550	R	394*	0.2
A.T. Clayton and Company Inc.	2 Pickwick Plz	Greenwich	CT	06830	Mark Valley Jr	203-861-1190	R	316*	<0.1
Bradner Central Co.	2300 Arthur Ave	Elk Grove Vill.	IL	60007	Richard S Bull	847-290-8485	R	316*	0.2
Frank Parsons Paper Co.	2270 Beaver Rd	Landover	MD	20785	Arthur Keleher	301-386-4700	R	222*	0.3
Price and Pierce International Inc.	281 Tresser Blvd	Stamford	CT	06901	Peter Napoli	203-328-2000	R	200*	<0.1
Jackson Paper Company Inc.	197 N Gallatin St	Jackson	MS	39203	Noel Machost	601-360-9620	R	141*	0.2
Perez Trading Company Inc.	3490 NW 125th St	Miami	FL	33167	John Perez	305-769-0761	R	131*	0.2
Unisource Midwest Inc.	PO Box 597	Columbus	OH	43216		614-251-7000	S	125*	0.3
Marquardt and Company Inc.	161 Av Americas	New York	NY	10013		212-645-7200	R	114*	<0.1
Chris Cam Corp.	808 W Cherokee St	Sioux Falls	SD	57104	Dempster Christenson	605-336-1190	R	111*	0.1
Prime Time Thermographics Inc.	1505 W 10th Pl	Tempe	AZ	85281	Mike Matchinsky	480-829-8890	R	90*	<0.1
Anchor Paper Co.	480 Broadway St	St. Paul	MN	55101	Linda Hartinger	651-298-1311	R	77*	0.1
West Coast Paper Co.	1011 Western Ave	Seattle	WA	98104	Frederick J Stabbert	253-850-1800	R	77*	0.2
Heritage Paper Company Inc.	4011 Morton St	Jacksonville	FL	32217	Robert F Purser Sr	904-737-6603	R	74*	<0.1
Unique Binders Inc.	3550 Lee Hill Dr	Fredericksburg	VA	22408	Sandra Lane	540-374-1828	R	47*	<0.1
CTI Paper Company Inc.	1545 Corp. Center	Sun Prairie	WI	53590	Dan King	608-834-9900	R	43*	<0.1
Hudson Valley Paper Co.	PO Box 1988	Albany	NY	12201	ST Jones III	518-471-5111	R	40*	<0.1
Pacon Corp.	PO Box 7170	Appleton	WI	54912	James Schmitz	920-830-5050	R	40*	0.1
Newell Paper Co.	PO Box 631	Meridian	MS	39301	Tommy Galyean	601-693-1783	D	38*	<0.1
Quality Quick Bindery Services	855 Hwy 169 N	Minneapolis	MN	55441	Theresa Selander	763-541-0627	R	37*	<0.1
Economy Paper of Rochester	1175 Main St E	Rochester	NY	14609	Robert Cherry	585-482-5340	R	34*	<0.1
Websource	161 Av Americas	New York	NY	10013	Matt Dawley	212-255-1600	D	25*	<0.1
Heartland Paper Co.	808 W Cherokee St	Sioux Falls	SD	57104	Dempster Christenson	605-336-1190	D	22*	0.1
Paper Corporation of the U.S.	161 Av Americas	New York	NY	10013		212-645-5900	S	22*	<0.1
BCT International Inc.	3000 NE 30th Pl	Fort Lauderdale	FL	33306		954-563-1224	R	20	<0.1
Holt Paper and Chemical Inc.	PO Box 3197	Salisbury	MD	21802	John Holt	410-742-7577	R	18*	<0.1
HA and Friend Company Inc.	1535 Lewis Ave	Zion	IL	60099	Richard Friend	847-746-1248	R	16*	<0.1
Shorr Packaging	PO Box 6800	Aurora	IL	60598		630-978-1000	R	14*	<0.1
Millcraft Paper Co. Cincinnati Div.	8710 Global Way	West Chester	OH	45069		513-942-4100	D	12*	<0.1
Carrier Envelope Co.	939 Lee St	Elk Grove Vill.	IL	60007	Robert Rogers	847-427-8200	R	11*	<0.1
EH Walker Supply Company Inc.	45 Derwood Cir	Rockville	MD	20850	Edgar Walker	301-738-6500	R	10*	<0.1
Sioux City Stationery Inc.	PO Box 9000	Sioux City	IA	51102	Charles Wolfe	712-277-7000	R	9*	<0.1
360 Services International	12623 Newburgh Rd	Livonia	MI	48150	Kenneth A Pickl II	734-591-9360	R	6*	<0.1
U.S. Printing Supply Co.	1618 Forbes Ave	Pittsburgh	PA	15219	John Micklege	412-566-2244	R	2*	<0.1

Source: *Ward's Business Directory of U.S. Private and Public Companies*, Volumes 1 and 2, 2005. The company type code used is as follows: P - Public, R - Private, S - Subsidiary, D - Division, J - Joint Venture, A - Affiliate, G - Group. Sales are in millions of dollars, employees are in thousands. An asterisk (*) indicates an estimated sales volume. The symbol < stands for 'less than'. Company names and addresses are truncated, in some cases, to fit into the available space.

OCCUPATIONS EMPLOYED BY PAPER & PAPER PRODUCT WHOLESALE

Occupation	% of Total 2004	Change to 2014	Occupation	% of Total 2004	Change to 2014
Sales reps, wholesale & manufacturing, exc tech	19.4	9.6	First-line supervisors/managers of office workers	1.8	-0.7
Laborers & freight, stock, & material movers, hand	5.8	-1.4	Order clerks	1.8	-28.8
Stock clerks & order fillers	5.6	-16.1	Team assemblers	1.7	9.6
Customer service representatives	5.4	12.2	Retail salespersons	1.6	9.6
Shipping, receiving, & traffic clerks	4.8	-0.8	First-line supervisors/managers of non-retail sales work	1.6	1.3
Truck drivers, light or delivery services	4.0	9.6	Packaging & filling machine operators & tenders	1.5	3.7
Bookkeeping, accounting, & auditing clerks	3.8	-1.4	Wholesale & retail buyers, except farm products	1.4	3.6
Truck drivers, heavy & tractor-trailer	3.4	9.6	Packers & packagers, hand	1.2	9.6
Industrial truck & tractor operators	3.0	9.6	Secretaries, except legal, medical, & executive	1.1	-7.8
Office clerks, general	2.9	-2.5	Demonstrators & product promoters	1.1	5.5
General & operations managers	2.2	8.4	Sales reps, wholesale & manufacturing, tech	1.1	9.6

Source: *Industry-Occupation Matrix*, Bureau of Labor Statistics. These data are reported based on 4-digit NAICS categories but have been matched to corresponding 6-digit NAICS industry codes. The change reported for each occupation to the year 2014 is a percent of growth or decline as estimated by the Bureau of Labor Statistics. The abbreviation nec stands for 'not elsewhere classified.'

LOCATION BY STATE AND REGIONAL CONCENTRATION

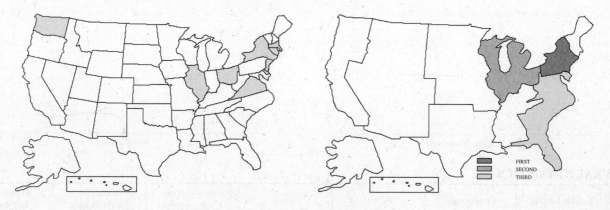

FIRST
SECOND
THIRD

INDUSTRY DATA BY STATE

State	Establishments Total (number)	Establishments % of U.S.	Employment Total (number)	Employment % of U.S.	Employment Per Estab.	Payroll Total ($ mil.)	Payroll Per Empl. ($)	Sales Total ($ mil.)	Sales % of U.S.	Sales Per Estab. ($)
New York	148	8.0	1,816	6.5	12	120.6	66,417	5,375.9	15.6	36,323,932
Illinois	122	6.6	1,891	6.8	15	119.2	63,015	4,375.9	12.7	35,867,795
California	221	12.0	2,896	10.3	13	165.4	57,104	2,588.0	7.5	11,710,575
Ohio	100	5.4	2,332	8.3	23	117.8	50,534	2,286.1	6.6	22,860,650
Washington	31	1.7	745	2.7	24	42.7	57,266	1,763.8	5.1	56,898,065
Connecticut	42	2.3	760	2.7	18	64.5	84,929	1,658.8	4.8	39,495,476
Texas	151	8.2	2,109	7.5	14	95.9	45,485	1,522.5	4.4	10,082,921
New Jersey	103	5.6	1,324	4.7	13	80.1	60,495	1,422.7	4.1	13,812,767
Pennsylvania	86	4.7	1,004	3.6	12	62.0	61,749	1,266.6	3.7	14,728,279
Massachusetts	47	2.6	591	2.1	13	37.0	62,631	1,002.4	2.9	21,326,702
Virginia	30	1.6	489	1.7	16	24.7	50,438	957.4	2.8	31,913,033
Florida	113	6.1	1,314	4.7	12	68.3	51,945	946.5	2.7	8,376,363
North Carolina	36	2.0	959	3.4	27	45.5	47,421	725.9	2.1	20,163,194
Michigan	46	2.5	610	2.2	13	33.6	55,072	675.9	2.0	14,693,848
Wisconsin	46	2.5	700	2.5	15	39.1	55,859	662.0	1.9	14,391,609
Oregon	28	1.5	424	1.5	15	21.3	50,264	351.1	1.0	12,537,929
Kentucky	15	0.8	379	1.4	25	18.5	48,910	339.2	1.0	22,614,600
Tennessee	34	1.8	499	1.8	15	22.8	45,776	323.9	0.9	9,527,618
Indiana	22	1.2	300	1.1	14	14.4	48,103	223.4	0.6	10,154,273
Iowa	16	0.9	333	1.2	21	18.7	56,075	218.1	0.6	13,629,500
Oklahoma	20	1.1	177	0.6	9	8.5	47,881	136.5	0.4	6,825,800
Alabama	23	1.3	252	0.9	11	10.5	41,595	115.7	0.3	5,031,826
Louisiana	14	0.8	328	1.2	23	14.4	43,976	108.3	0.3	7,735,857
Arkansas	7	0.4	111	0.4	16	5.4	48,703	80.2	0.2	11,450,857
South Carolina	16	0.9	135	0.5	8	5.8	43,244	69.8	0.2	4,359,625
Nevada	12	0.7	104	0.4	9	4.3	41,269	64.0	0.2	5,336,917
Nebraska	6	0.3	109	0.4	18	4.3	39,394	51.0	0.1	8,507,667
Hawaii	5	0.3	84	0.3	17	4.1	48,702	44.8	0.1	8,953,800
Mississippi	6	0.3	149	0.5	25	5.2	35,087	35.8	0.1	5,968,833
New Mexico	8	0.4	73	0.3	9	2.4	32,877	20.6	0.1	2,581,250
Montana	6	0.3	42	0.2	7	2.0	46,619	14.0	-	2,336,500
Georgia	64	3.5	500-999	-	-	(D)	-	(D)	-	-
Minnesota	37	2.0	500-999	-	-	(D)	-	(D)	-	-
Missouri	36	2.0	500-999	-	-	(D)	-	(D)	-	-
Colorado	25	1.4	250-499	-	-	(D)	-	(D)	-	-
Maryland	25	1.4	250-499	-	-	(D)	-	(D)	-	-
Arizona	22	1.2	250-499	-	-	(D)	-	(D)	-	-
Kansas	22	1.2	500-999	-	-	(D)	-	(D)	-	-
Utah	13	0.7	250-499	-	-	(D)	-	(D)	-	-
Rhode Island	8	0.4	100-249	-	-	(D)	-	(D)	-	-
New Hampshire	5	0.3	20-99	-	-	(D)	-	(D)	-	-
Maine	4	0.2	20-99	-	-	(D)	-	(D)	-	-
Delaware	3	0.2	20-99	-	-	(D)	-	(D)	-	-
Idaho	3	0.2	20-99	-	-	(D)	-	(D)	-	-
North Dakota	3	0.2	0-19	-	-	(D)	-	(D)	-	-
Alaska	2	0.1	20-99	-	-	(D)	-	(D)	-	-
South Dakota	2	0.1	0-19	-	-	(D)	-	(D)	-	-
Vermont	2	0.1	0-19	-	-	(D)	-	(D)	-	-
Wyoming	2	0.1	0-19	-	-	(D)	-	(D)	-	-
West Virginia	1	0.1	0-19	-	-	(D)	-	(D)	-	-

Source: 2002 *Economic Census*. The states are in descending order of sales or establishments (if sales data are missing for the majority). The symbol (D) appears when data are withheld to prevent disclosure of competitive information. States marked with (D) are sorted by number of establishments. A dash (-) indicates that the data element cannot be calculated. Shaded *states* on the state map indicate those states which have proportionately greater representation in the industry than would be indicated by the states population; the ratio is based on total sales or number of establishments. Shaded *regions* indicate where the industry is regionally most concentrated.

NAICS 424120 - STATIONERY AND OFFICE SUPPLIES MERCHANT WHOLESALERS

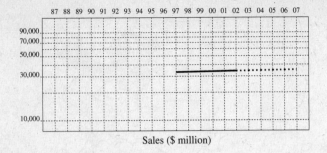

Sales ($ million)

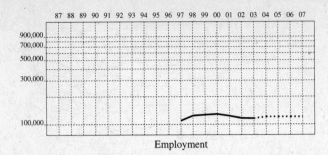

Employment

GENERAL STATISTICS

Year	Establishments (number)	Employment (number)	Payroll ($ million)	Sales ($ million)	Employees per Establishment (number)	Sales per Establishment ($)	Payroll per Employee ($)
1987	-	-	-	-	-	-	-
1988	-	-	-	-	-	-	-
1989	-	-	-	-	-	-	-
1990	-	-	-	-	-	-	-
1991	-	-	-	-	-	-	-
1992	-	-	-	-	-	-	-
1993	-	-	-	-	-	-	-
1994	-	-	-	-	-	-	-
1995	-	-	-	-	-	-	-
1996	-	-	-	-	-	-	-
1997	8,046	109,766	3,308.2	33,271.0	13.6	4,135,098.2	30,138.7
1998	8,099	124,408	3,680.4	33,462.5 e	15.4	4,131,685.4	29,583.3
1999	7,864	127,087	3,733.3	33,654.0 e	16.2	4,279,506.6	29,375.9
2000	7,623	129,198	3,919.2	33,845.6 e	16.9	4,439,926.5	30,334.9
2001	7,323	123,458	3,877.5	34,037.1 e	16.9	4,647,969.4	31,407.2
2002	6,773	116,559	3,582.7	34,228.6	17.2	5,053,683.7	30,737.2
2003	6,665	115,963	3,725.2	34,420.1 p	17.4	5,078,198.3 p	32,124.0
2004	6,437 p	120,815 p	3,860.9 p	34,611.6 p	18.5 p	5,258,261.1 p	31,999.5 p
2005	6,175 p	120,788 p	3,903.7 p	34,803.2 p	19.0 p	5,438,324.0 p	32,367.2 p
2006	5,913 p	120,762 p	3,946.6 p	34,994.7 p	19.6 p	5,618,386.8 p	32,734.9 p
2007	5,651 p	120,736 p	3,989.4 p	35,186.2 p	20.2 p	5,798,449.7 p	33,102.5 p

Source: *Economic Census of the United States*, 1997 and 2002. Establishment counts, employment, and payroll are from *County Business Patterns* for non-Census years. This is a newly defined industry. Data for prior years are unavailable at the time of publication but may become available over time. Values followed by 'p' are projections by the editors. Sales data for non-Census years are extrapolations, marked by 'e'.

INDICES OF CHANGE

Year	Establishments (number)	Employment (number)	Payroll ($ million)	Sales ($ million)	Employees per Establishment (number)	Sales per Establishment ($)	Payroll per Employee ($)
1987	-	-	-	-	-	-	-
1992	-	-	-	-	-	-	-
1993	-	-	-	-	-	-	-
1994	-	-	-	-	-	-	-
1995	-	-	-	-	-	-	-
1996	-	-	-	-	-	-	-
1997	118.8	94.2	92.3	97.2	79.1	81.8	98.1
1998	119.6	106.7	102.7	97.8 e	89.5	81.8	96.2
1999	116.1	109.0	104.2	98.3 e	94.2	84.7	95.6
2000	112.5	110.8	109.4	98.9 e	98.3	87.9	98.7
2001	108.1	105.9	108.2	99.4 e	98.3	92.0	102.2
2002	100.0	100.0	100.0	100.0	100.0	100.0	100.0
2003	98.4	99.5	104.0	100.6 p	101.2	100.5 p	104.5
2004	95.0 p	103.7 p	107.8 p	101.1 p	107.4 p	104.0 p	104.1 p
2005	91.2 p	103.6 p	109.0 p	101.7 p	110.6 p	107.6 p	105.3 p
2006	87.3 p	103.6 p	110.2 p	102.2 p	113.9 p	111.2 p	106.5 p
2007	83.4 p	103.6 p	111.4 p	102.8 p	117.2 p	114.7 p	107.7 p

Sources: Same as General Statistics. The values shown reflect change from the base year, 2002. Values above 100 mean greater than 2002, values below 100 mean less than 2002, and a value of 100 in the 1987-2001 or 2003-2007 period means same as 2002. Values followed by a 'p' are projections by the editors; 'e' stands for extrapolation. Data are the most recent available at this level of detail.

SELECTED RATIOS

For 2002	Avg. of All Wholesale	Analyzed Industry	Index	For 2002	Avg. of All Wholesale	Analyzed Industry	Index
Employees per Establishment	15	17	115	Sales per Employee	791,325	293,659	37
Payroll per Establishment	626,122	528,968	84	Sales per Establishment	12,012,387	5,053,684	42
Payroll per Employee	41,161	30,737	75	Expenses per Establishment	na	na	na

Sources: Same as General Statistics. The 'Average of All' column, Wholesale or Retail, represents the average of the sector reported for the most recent complete year available. The Index shows the relationship between the Average and the Analyzed Industry. For example, 100 means that they are equal; 500 that the Analyzed Industry is five times the average; 50 means that the Analyzed Industry is half the national average. The abbreviation 'na' is used to show that data are 'not available'.

LEADING COMPANIES Number shown: **75** Total sales ($ mil): **22,493** Total employment (000): **56.3**

Company Name	Address				CEO Name	Phone	Co. Type	Sales ($ mil)	Empl. (000)
Genuine Parts Co.	2999 Circle 75 Pkwy	Atlanta	GA	30339	Thomas C. Gallagher	770-953-1700	P	9,097	30.8
United Stationers Inc.	2200 E Golf Rd	Des Plaines	IL	60016	Richard W Gochnauer	847-699-5000	P	4,000	5.7
National Pen Corp.	16885 Del Campo	San Diego	CA	92127	Thomas Liguori	858-675-3000	R	2,410*	0.2
Viking Office Products Inc.	950 W 190th St	Torrance	CA	90502	Irwin Helford	310-225-4500	S	1,295*	2.8
Daisytek Inc.	1025 Central Expwy	Allen	TX	75013	Dale Booth	972-881-4700	S	1,000*	0.3
School Specialty Inc.	PO Box 1579	Appleton	WI	54912		920-734-5712	P	907	2.8
S.P. Richards Co.	PO Box 1266	Smyrna	GA	30081	Dean Beacham	770-436-6881	S	601*	2.1
Servco Pacific Inc.	PO Box 2788	Honolulu	HI	96803	Mark H Fukunaga	808-521-6511	S	307*	0.9
Nashua Corp.	PO Box 2002	Nashua	NH	03061	Andrew B Albert	603-880-2323	P	289	0.0
Thomas Nelson Inc.	PO Box 141000	Nashville	TN	37214	Michael S Hyatt	615-889-9000	P	223	0.6
Frank Parsons Paper Co.	2270 Beaver Rd	Landover	MD	20785	Arthur Keleher	301-386-4700	R	222*	0.3
Nebraska Book Company Inc.	4700 S 19th St	Lincoln	NE	68501	Mark Oppegard	402-421-7300	R	214*	2.1
Office Depot Inc. Bus Serv	3366 E Willow St	Signal Hill	CA	90755		562-490-1000	D	149*	0.9
A.T. Cross Co.	1 Albion Rd	Lincoln	RI	02865	Russell A Boss	401-333-1200	P	125	0.9
Champion Industries Inc.	PO Box 2968	Huntington	WV	25728	Toney K Adkins	304-528-2700	P	122	0.8
Cuna Mutual Business Services	PO Box 431	Madison	WI	53701	Barry Jolette	608-231-4000	S	111*	0.4
TAB Products Co.	935 Lakeview Pky	Vernon Hills	IL	60061	John Boustead	847-968-5400	R	104	0.7
Atomicbox Inc.	125 Lena Dr	Aurora	OH	44202	Thomas Bianco	330-995-6110	R	103*	0.1
American Product Distributors Inc.	8227 Arrowridge	Charlotte	NC	28273	Don Black	704-522-9411	R	102	<0.1
Koval Marketing Inc.	11208 47th Ave W	Mukilteo	WA	98275	Roy Koval	425-347-4249	R	100*	<0.1
C.M. Paula Co.	6049 Hi-Tek Ct	Mason	OH	45040	Greg Ionna	513-336-3100	R	70*	0.1
Lindenmeyr Munroe	30 Hub Dr	Melville	NY	11747		631-293-0505	S	61*	<0.1
Offtech Inc.	30 Upton Dr	Wilmington	MA	01887	Stephen Albano	978-988-0700	R	54*	0.2
Supply Room Companies Inc.	14140 N Washington	Ashland	VA	23005	Yancey S Jones	804-412-1200	R	53*	0.6
PLUS Vision Corp. of America	9610 SW Sunshine	Beaverton	OR	97005	Tsutomo Oishi	503-748-8700	S	45*	<0.1
Ennis Tag and Label Co.	PO Box D	Wolfe City	TX	75496		903-496-2244	D	44*	0.2
Hudson Valley Paper Co.	PO Box 1988	Albany	NY	12201	ST Jones III	518-471-5111	R	40*	<0.1
Paper Mart	5361 Alexander	Cty-Commerce	CA	90040	Rosemary Martin	323-726-8200	R	40*	<0.1
Harbor Packaging Inc.	13100 Danielson St	Poway	CA	92064	Jim Sorenson	858-513-1800	R	34*	0.2
Source 4	4721 Starkey Rd	Roanoke	VA	24014		540-989-6848	R	33*	0.3
Graphic Systems Inc.	6972 Appling Farms	Memphis	TN	38133	Dennis B Kopcial	901-937-5500	R	27*	<0.1
Arctic Office Machine Inc.	PO Box 100083	Anchorage	AK	99510	William Borchardt	907-276-2322	R	27*	0.1
General Binding Corp.	5700 Old Orchard	Skokie	IL	60077		847-965-0600	R	26*	<0.1
Source Management Inc.	2460 W 26th Ave	Denver	CO	80211		303-964-8100	R	22*	<0.1
New Hermes Inc.	2200 Northmont	Duluth	GA	30096		770-623-9697	R	21*	0.1
Digitek Computer Products Inc.	44258 Mercure Cir	Dulles	VA	20166	Paul Martorana	703-421-8300	R	18*	<0.1
Liberty Business Forms	3230 E Main Ave	Spokane	WA	99202	Willy Schumacher	509-536-0515	R	17*	<0.1
HA and Friend Company Inc.	1535 Lewis Ave	Zion	IL	60099	Richard Friend	847-746-1248	R	16*	<0.1
Marimon Business Systems Inc.	7300 Gessner Dr	Houston	TX	77040	Yolanda Marimon	713-856-2000	R	15*	0.1
Yasutomo and Company Inc.	490 Eccles Ave	S. San Francisco	CA	94080	Daniel Egusa	650-737-8888	R	15*	<0.1
Acroprint Time Recorder Co.	5640 Departure Dr	Raleigh	NC	27616	Glenn Robbins	919-872-5800	R	14*	0.1
Cliff Weil Inc.	PO Box 427	Mechanicsville	VA	23116	Alvin B Hutzler II	804-746-1321	R	14*	<0.1
Zebra Pen Corp.	105 Northfield Ave	Edison	NJ	08837	Clem Restaino	732-225-6310	S	14*	<0.1
Office World Inc.	PO Box 89	Lima	OH	45802	Mark Kitson	419-991-4694	R	13*	<0.1
Learning Labs Inc.	PO Box 1419	Calhoun	GA	30703	David Richardson	706-629-4624	R	13*	<0.1
Office Service Co.	1009 Tuckerton Ct	Reading	PA	19605	Jeffery Barbour	610-926-9850	R	13*	<0.1
Carter Paper and Packaging Inc.	PO Box 1349	Peoria	IL	61654	Billie H Carter	309-637-7711	R	12*	<0.1
Louisiana Office Products	PO Box 23851	New Orleans	LA	70183	Frank Giovingo	504-733-9650	R	12*	<0.1
MassEnvelopePlus Co.	30 Cobble Hill Rd	Somerville	MA	02143		617-623-8000	R	12*	<0.1
Printpal Inc.	PO Box 5655	Central Point	OR	97502	Mark Comish	541-282-8479	R	12*	<0.1
BT Office Products	8501 W Side Ave	North Bergen	NJ	07047		201-662-4100	R	11*	<0.1
Carrier Envelope Co.	939 Lee St	Elk Grove Vill.	IL	60007	Robert Rogers	847-427-8200	R	11*	<0.1
American Office Machines Inc.	PO Box 9429	Metairie	LA	70055	John Manzella	504-833-1964	R	10*	<0.1
E.Z. Gregory Inc.	PO Box 44268	Madison	WI	53744	Gary Hermanson	608-271-2324	R	10*	<0.1
Fishman Supply Co.	PO Box 750279	Petaluma	CA	94975	Leland Fishman	707-763-8161	R	10*	<0.1
Sioux City Stationery Inc.	PO Box 9000	Sioux City	IA	51102	Charles Wolfe	712-277-7000	R	9*	<0.1
Charles Ritter Co.	PO Box 215	Mansfield	OH	44901	Kenneth Pepper	419-522-1911	R	9*	<0.1
Southwestern Stationery & Bank	PO Box 18697	Oklahoma City	OK	73154	Robert Allee	405-525-9411	R	9*	<0.1
American Binding Company Inc.	PO Box 829	Kaysville	UT	84037	Calvin Barlow	801-927-3020	R	8*	<0.1
BDB Service and Supply Inc.	6215 14th Ave	Brooklyn	NY	11219	Albert Brauner	718-241-6716	R	8*	<0.1
Brannon and Walsh Inc.	146 W Broadway St	Owatonna	MN	55060	Lisa McGinnis	507-451-6670	R	8*	<0.1
Brittain Merchandising	PO Box 449	Lawton	OK	73502	LD Brittain	580-355-4430	R	8*	<0.1
Eatonform Inc.	2280 Arbor Blvd	Dayton	OH	45439	Richard Mullen	937-298-3406	R	8*	<0.1
Metro Office Products Inc.	4605 Compass Pt	Belcamp	MD	21017	Minh Sheridan	410-297-6666	R	8*	<0.1
Tab of Northeast Florida Inc.	PO Box 551467	Jacksonville	FL	32255	Candice Bobeck	904-398-3600	R	8*	<0.1
Transition Products Inc.	3040 Riverside Dr	Columbus	OH	43221	Jeff Trotier	614-488-6000	R	8*	<0.1
Drexel Technologies Inc.	10840 W 86th St	Lenexa	KS	66214	Deron Taylor	913-371-4430	R	8*	<0.1
Mountainland Business Systems	180 W 2950 S	Salt Lake City	UT	84115	Ralph Diamond	801-487-8508	R	8*	<0.1
Matt Parrott and Sons Co.	PO Box 660	Waterloo	IA	50704	David Buck	319-234-4621	R	7*	<0.1
Northern Stationers Inc.	502 W Washington	Marquette	MI	49855	Denise Bouschor	906-228-7702	R	7*	<0.1
Accurate Office Supply Inc.	PO Box 1032	Caldwell	NJ	07007	Hadar Sieradsky	973-808-1670	R	6*	<0.1
GBS Corp.	4807 Rockside Rd	Independence	OH	44131		216-447-1625	S	6*	<0.1
MCPc Inc.	PO Box 636	Spokane	WA	99201	Brion Potter	509-624-9101	R	6*	<0.1
Progressive Business Equipment	11466 Schenk Dr	Maryland H.	MO	63043	Gerald Clark	314-298-2887	R	6*	<0.1
Sierra Office Supplies and Printing	9950 Horn Rd Ste 5	Sacramento	CA	95827	Michael Kipp	916-369-0491	R	6*	<0.1

Source: Ward's Business Directory of U.S. Private and Public Companies, Volumes 1 and 2, 2005. The company type code used is as follows: P - Public, R - Private, S - Subsidiary, D - Division, J - Joint Venture, A - Affiliate, G - Group. Sales are in millions of dollars, employees are in thousands. An asterisk (*) indicates an estimated sales volume. The symbol < stands for 'less than'. Company names and addresses are truncated, in some cases, to fit into the available space.

OCCUPATIONS EMPLOYED BY PAPER & PAPER PRODUCT WHOLESALE

Occupation	% of Total 2004	Change to 2014	Occupation	% of Total 2004	Change to 2014
Sales reps, wholesale & manufacturing, exc tech	19.4	9.6	First-line supervisors/managers of office workers	1.8	-0.7
Laborers & freight, stock, & material movers, hand	5.8	-1.4	Order clerks	1.8	-28.8
Stock clerks & order fillers	5.6	-16.1	Team assemblers	1.7	9.6
Customer service representatives	5.4	12.2	Retail salespersons	1.6	9.6
Shipping, receiving, & traffic clerks	4.8	-0.8	First-line supervisors/managers of non-retail sales work	1.6	1.3
Truck drivers, light or delivery services	4.0	9.6	Packaging & filling machine operators & tenders	1.5	3.7
Bookkeeping, accounting, & auditing clerks	3.8	-1.4	Wholesale & retail buyers, except farm products	1.4	3.6
Truck drivers, heavy & tractor-trailer	3.4	9.6	Packers & packagers, hand	1.2	9.6
Industrial truck & tractor operators	3.0	9.6	Secretaries, except legal, medical, & executive	1.1	-7.8
Office clerks, general	2.9	-2.5	Demonstrators & product promoters	1.1	5.5
General & operations managers	2.2	8.4	Sales reps, wholesale & manufacturing, tech	1.1	9.6

Source: Industry-Occupation Matrix, Bureau of Labor Statistics. These data are reported based on 4-digit NAICS categories but have been matched to corresponding 6-digit NAICS industry codes. The change reported for each occupation to the year 2014 is a percent of growth or decline as estimated by the Bureau of Labor Statistics. The abbreviation nec stands for 'not elsewhere classified.'

LOCATION BY STATE AND REGIONAL CONCENTRATION

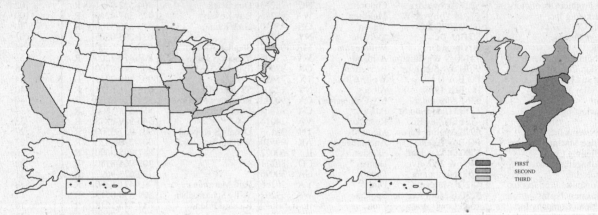

FIRST
SECOND
THIRD

INDUSTRY DATA BY STATE

State	Establishments Total (number)	% of U.S.	Employment Total (number)	% of U.S.	Per Estab.	Payroll Total ($ mil.)	Per Empl. ($)	Sales Total ($ mil.)	% of U.S.	Per Estab. ($)
California	832	12.1	14,228	12.3	17	455.5	32,013	4,293.0	12.5	5,159,868
Missouri	147	2.1	17,697	15.3	120	257.3	14,540	3,509.0	10.2	23,871,027
Illinois	378	5.5	9,892	8.6	26	338.5	34,219	3,292.7	9.6	8,710,815
New Jersey	317	4.6	7,382	6.4	23	224.3	30,386	2,220.0	6.4	7,003,309
Texas	469	6.8	7,819	6.8	17	221.8	28,372	2,139.7	6.2	4,562,360
Ohio	311	4.5	5,849	5.1	19	191.1	32,667	1,745.8	5.1	5,613,624
New York	572	8.3	4,893	4.2	9	197.2	40,309	1,676.2	4.9	2,930,491
Michigan	217	3.2	3,873	3.4	18	130.8	33,765	1,195.9	3.5	5,511,235
Pennsylvania	288	4.2	3,355	2.9	12	138.9	41,412	1,166.2	3.4	4,049,365
Florida	404	5.9	3,387	2.9	8	126.9	37,477	1,152.3	3.3	2,852,139
Massachusetts	137	2.0	2,212	1.9	16	96.8	43,776	1,105.3	3.2	8,067,650
North Carolina	196	2.8	2,364	2.0	12	93.2	39,416	896.9	2.6	4,576,087
Minnesota	134	1.9	2,431	2.1	18	103.6	42,634	784.1	2.3	5,851,612
Tennessee	133	1.9	2,013	1.7	15	73.6	36,578	679.9	2.0	5,112,293
Colorado	130	1.9	1,553	1.3	12	62.5	40,233	617.7	1.8	4,751,792
Washington	127	1.8	1,706	1.5	13	60.6	35,546	535.4	1.6	4,215,921
Virginia	143	2.1	1,551	1.3	11	66.6	42,946	489.3	1.4	3,421,699
Indiana	120	1.7	1,305	1.1	11	47.1	36,087	462.3	1.3	3,852,300
Arizona	108	1.6	1,182	1.0	11	42.8	36,198	417.1	1.2	3,861,583
Kansas	88	1.3	919	0.8	10	35.6	38,783	361.6	1.0	4,109,148
Connecticut	88	1.3	1,130	1.0	13	47.5	41,991	313.5	0.9	3,562,716
Oregon	79	1.1	876	0.8	11	33.1	37,840	310.0	0.9	3,924,544
Wisconsin	102	1.5	1,098	1.0	11	40.2	36,650	299.7	0.9	2,938,265
Kentucky	73	1.1	670	0.6	9	20.7	30,848	291.2	0.8	3,988,959
Louisiana	85	1.2	1,031	0.9	12	30.6	29,727	261.0	0.8	3,070,800
Oklahoma	79	1.1	576	0.5	7	19.8	34,380	208.2	0.6	2,635,266
Utah	60	0.9	491	0.4	8	17.2	35,051	201.6	0.6	3,360,400
Alabama	94	1.4	810	0.7	9	23.6	29,107	178.8	0.5	1,901,660
South Carolina	80	1.2	562	0.5	7	20.3	36,121	157.7	0.5	1,971,788
Iowa	75	1.1	727	0.6	10	23.4	32,151	147.3	0.4	1,964,293
Idaho	24	0.3	443	0.4	18	18.7	42,124	136.3	0.4	5,679,000

Continued on next page.

INDUSTRY DATA BY STATE - Continued

State	Establishments Total (number)	% of U.S.	Employment Total (number)	% of U.S.	Per Estab.	Payroll Total ($ mil.)	Per Empl. ($)	Sales Total ($ mil.)	% of U.S.	Per Estab. ($)
Nevada	33	0.5	368	0.3	11	14.1	38,253	106.3	0.3	3,220,030
Hawaii	47	0.7	381	0.3	8	14.9	39,045	101.2	0.3	2,152,745
Arkansas	45	0.7	404	0.4	9	13.6	33,621	88.3	0.3	1,962,933
Nebraska	38	0.6	360	0.3	9	12.8	35,694	76.5	0.2	2,013,947
Mississippi	49	0.7	306	0.3	6	8.5	27,660	54.8	0.2	1,117,673
New Mexico	34	0.5	244	0.2	7	7.9	32,582	53.0	0.2	1,558,353
Montana	25	0.4	127	0.1	5	4.1	31,921	29.4	0.1	1,174,720
South Dakota	17	0.2	107	0.1	6	1.7	16,280	15.6	-	916,941
North Dakota	14	0.2	57	-	4	1.7	30,088	12.9	-	918,071
Wyoming	7	0.1	27	-	4	0.6	23,037	4.8	-	688,857
Georgia	208	3.0	5K-9999	-	-	(D)	-	(D)	-	-
Maryland	125	1.8	1000-2499	-	-	(D)	-	(D)	-	-
New Hampshire	34	0.5	250-499	-	-	(D)	-	(D)	-	-
Maine	27	0.4	250-499	-	-	(D)	-	(D)	-	-
West Virginia	25	0.4	100-249	-	-	(D)	-	(D)	-	-
Rhode Island	20	0.3	20-99	-	-	(D)	-	(D)	-	-
Vermont	18	0.3	100-249	-	-	(D)	-	(D)	-	-
Delaware	13	0.2	20-99	-	-	(D)	-	(D)	-	-
Alaska	9	0.1	100-249	-	-	(D)	-	(D)	-	-
D.C.	9	0.1	20-99	-	-	(D)	-	(D)	-	-

Source: 2002 *Economic Census*. The states are in descending order of sales or establishments (if sales data are missing for the majority). The symbol (D) appears when data are withheld to prevent disclosure of competitive information. States marked with (D) are sorted by number of establishments. A dash (-) indicates that the data element cannot be calculated. Shaded *states* on the state map indicate those states which have proportionately greater representation in the industry than would be indicated by the states population; the ratio is based on total sales or number of establishments. Shaded *regions* indicate where the industry is regionally most concentrated.

NAICS 424130 - INDUSTRIAL AND PERSONAL SERVICE PAPER MERCHANT WHOLESALERS*

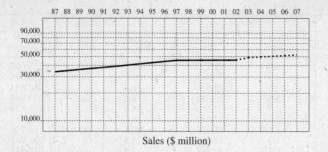

Sales ($ million)

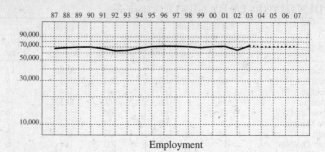

Employment

GENERAL STATISTICS

Year	Establishments (number)	Employment (number)	Payroll ($ million)	Sales ($ million)	Employees per Establishment (number)	Sales per Establishment ($)	Payroll per Employee ($)
1987	4,956	67,142	1,798.5	34,027.7	13.5	6,865,960.5	26,786.5
1988	4,728	68,543	2,021.3	35,028.4 e	14.5	7,408,714.0	29,489.5
1989	4,583	69,539	2,121.2	36,029.1 e	15.2	7,861,466.3	30,503.7
1990	4,667	69,718	2,227.5	37,029.8 e	14.9	7,934,390.4	31,950.1
1991	4,619	67,215	2,176.5	38,030.6 e	14.6	8,233,513.7	32,381.2
1992	5,293	63,567	2,115.5	39,031.3	12.0	7,374,135.7	33,279.8
1993	5,242	64,092	2,126.4	40,303.8 e	12.2	7,688,630.3	33,177.3
1994	5,388	67,972	2,368.0	41,576.4 e	12.6	7,716,481.1	34,837.9
1995	5,466	70,805	2,675.1	42,848.9 e	13.0	7,839,169.4	37,781.2
1996	5,469 e	71,715 e	2,667.7 e	44,121.5 e	13.1 e	8,067,562.6 e	37,198.6 e
1997	5,493	71,449	2,874.7	45,394.0	13.0	8,263,972.3	40,234.3
1998	5,502	70,681	2,992.9	45,465.7 e	12.8	8,263,489.6	42,343.8
1999	5,289	68,989	2,987.7	45,537.4 e	13.0	8,609,839.3	43,306.9
2000	5,193	70,862	3,232.2	45,609.2 e	13.6	8,782,815.3	45,612.7
2001	5,089	71,412	3,290.4	45,680.9 e	14.0	8,976,396.1	46,076.7
2002	4,664	64,661	2,929.5	45,752.6	13.9	9,809,734.1	45,305.5
2003	4,474	72,421	3,530.1	48,752.8 p	16.2	9,189,377.6 p	48,744.0
2004	5,181 p	70,610 p	3,476.8 p	49,624.7 p	13.7 p	9,316,831.8 p	49,401.1 p
2005	5,194 p	70,804 p	3,574.7 p	50,496.6 p	13.7 p	9,444,286.0 p	50,713.6 p
2006	5,207 p	70,997 p	3,672.5 p	51,368.5 p	13.7 p	9,571,740.2 p	52,026.1 p
2007	5,220 p	71,191 p	3,770.4 p	52,240.4 p	13.7 p	9,699,194.3 p	53,338.6 p

Sources: Economic Census of the United States, 1987, 1992, 1997, and 2002. Establishment counts, employment, and payroll are from County Business Patterns for non-Census years. Values followed by a 'p' are projections by the editors. Sales data for non-Census years are extrapolations, marked by 'e'. Data are the most recent available at this level of detail.

INDICES OF CHANGE

Year	Establishments (number)	Employment (number)	Payroll ($ million)	Sales ($ million)	Employees per Establishment (number)	Sales per Establishment ($)	Payroll per Employee ($)
1987	106.3	103.8	61.4	74.4	97.1	70.0	59.1
1992	113.5	98.3	72.2	85.3	86.3	75.2	73.5
1993	112.4	99.1	72.6	88.1 e	87.8	78.4	73.2
1994	115.5	105.1	80.8	90.9 e	90.6	78.7	76.9
1995	117.2	109.5	91.3	93.7 e	93.5	79.9	83.4
1996	117.3 e	110.9 e	91.1 e	96.4 e	94.2 e	82.2 e	82.1 e
1997	117.8	110.5	98.1	99.2	93.5	84.2	88.8
1998	118.0	109.3	102.2	99.4 e	92.1	84.2	93.5
1999	113.4	106.7	102.0	99.5 e	93.5	87.8	95.6
2000	111.3	109.6	110.3	99.7 e	97.8	89.5	100.7
2001	109.1	110.4	112.3	99.8 e	100.7	91.5	101.7
2002	100.0	100.0	100.0	100.0	100.0	100.0	100.0
2003	95.9	112.0	120.5	106.6 p	116.5	93.7 p	107.6
2004	111.1 p	109.2 p	118.7 p	108.5 p	98.5 p	95.0 p	109.0 p
2005	111.4 p	109.5 p	122.0 p	110.4 p	98.5 p	96.3 p	111.9 p
2006	111.6 p	109.8 p	125.4 p	112.3 p	98.5 p	97.6 p	114.8 p
2007	111.9 p	110.1 p	128.7 p	114.2 p	98.6 p	98.9 p	117.7 p

Sources: Same as General Statistics. The values shown reflect change from the base year, 2002. Values above 100 mean greater than 2002, values below 100 mean less than 2002, and a value of 100 in the 1987-2001 or 2003-2007 period means same as 2002. Values followed by a 'p' are projections by the editors; 'e' stands for extrapolation. Data are the most recent available at this level of detail.

SELECTED RATIOS

For 2002	Avg. of All Wholesale	Analyzed Industry	Index	For 2002	Avg. of All Wholesale	Analyzed Industry	Index
Employees per Establishment	15	14	93	Sales per Employee	791,325	707,576	89
Payroll per Establishment	626,122	628,109	100	Sales per Establishment	12,012,387	9,809,734	82
Payroll per Employee	41,161	45,306	110	Expenses per Establishment	na	na	na

Sources: Same as General Statistics. The 'Average of All' column, Wholesale or Retail, represents the average of the sector reported for the most recent complete year available. The Index shows the relationship between the Average and the Analyzed Industry. For example, 100 means that they are equal; 500 that the Analyzed Industry is five times the average; 50 means that the Analyzed Industry is half the national average. The abbreviation 'na' is used to show that data are 'not available'.

*Equivalent to SIC 5113.

LEADING COMPANIES   Number shown: **75**   Total sales ($ mil): **18,047**   Total employment (000): **16.9**

Company Name	Address				CEO Name	Phone	Co. Type	Sales ($ mil)	Empl. (000)
Marubeni America Corp.	450 Lexington Ave	New York	NY	10017	Kazuhiko Sakamoto	212-450-0100	S	8,050*	0.2
Unisource Worldwide Inc.	6600 Gov Lk	Norcross	GA	30071	Allan Dragone	770-447-9000	S	3,701*	8.0
Central National-Gottesman Inc.	3 Manhattanville Rd	Purchase	NY	10577	Kenneth L Wallach	914-696-9000	R	2,300	1.0
Maines Paper and Food Service	101 Broome	Conklin	NY	13748	Chris Mellon	607-779-1200	R	650*	0.8
Clark Foodservice Inc.	950 Arthur Ave	Elk Grove Vill.	IL	60007	Donald J Hindman	847-956-1730	R	310*	0.8
Taymark	4875 White Bear	White Bear Lake	MN	55110	Paul Griffiths	651-426-1667	R	236*	0.4
Pollock Paper and Packaging Co.	PO Box 660005	Dallas	TX	75266	Lonnie Pollock	972-263-0205	R	175*	0.3
Jackson Paper Company Inc.	197 N Gallatin St	Jackson	MS	39203	Noel Machost	601-360-9620	R	141*	0.2
Perez Trading Company Inc.	3490 NW 125th St	Miami	FL	33167	John Perez	305-769-0761	R	131*	0.2
Acme Paper and Supply Inc.	8229 Sandy Ct	Savage	MD	20763		410-792-2333	R	114*	0.2
Chris Cam Corp.	808 W Cherokee St	Sioux Falls	SD	57104	Dempster Christenson	605-336-1190	R	111*	0.1
Albert H. Notini and Sons Inc.	PO Box 299	Lowell	MA	01853	Alex Turshette	978-459-7151	R	105*	0.2
Boelter Companies Inc.	11100 Silver Sprgs	Milwaukee	WI	53225	FW Boelter	414-461-3400	R	87*	0.3
Bunzl New Jersey Inc.	PO Box 668	Dayton	NJ	08810	Paul Lorenzini	732-821-7000	D	80*	0.3
Anchor Paper Co.	480 Broadway St	St. Paul	MN	55101	Linda Hartinger	651-298-1311	R	77*	0.1
West Coast Paper Co.	1011 Western Ave	Seattle	WA	98104	Frederick J Stabbert	253-850-1800	R	77*	0.1
Heritage Paper Company Inc.	4011 Morton St	Jacksonville	FL	32217	Robert F Purser Sr	904-737-6603	R	74*	<0.1
Golden State Containers Inc.	6817 E Acco St	Los Angeles	CA	90040		323-887-4266	R	66*	0.1
BUNZL New England	180 Shrewsbury St	West Boylston	MA	01583	Paul Lorenzini	508-835-6021	D	62*	<0.1
Lindenmeyr Munroe	30 Hub Dr	Melville	NY	11747		631-293-0505	S	61*	<0.1
Pacific Packaging Products Inc.	PO Box 697	Wilmington	MA	01887		978-657-9100	R	60*	0.2
Ernest Paper Products Inc.	5777 Smithway St	Commerce	CA	90040	Timothy G Wilson	323-583-6561	R	57*	0.2
International Forest Products Corp.	1 Patriot Pl	Foxboro	MA	02035	Dan Kraft	508-698-4600	R	51*	<0.1
Connecticut Container Corp.	455 Sackett Point Rd	North Haven	CT	06473	Harry Perkins	203-248-2161	R	50*	0.2
Republic Tobacco L.P.	2301 Ravine Way	Glenview	IL	60025	Donald Levin	847-832-9700	R	50*	0.3
Mooney General Paper Co.	1451 Chestnut Ave	Hillside	NJ	07205	Gary Riemer	973-926-3800	R	49*	<0.1
Forman Inc.	2036 Lord Baltimore	Windsor Mill	MD	21244	JJ Mucha	410-298-7500	R	48*	<0.1
Unique Binders Inc.	3550 Lee Hill Dr	Fredericksburg	VA	22408	Sandra Lane	540-374-1828	R	47*	<0.1
Paper Products Company Inc.	36 Terminal Way	Pittsburgh	PA	15219	Dan Lackner	412-481-6200	R	45*	<0.1
CL Smith Company Inc.	1311 S 39th St	Saint Louis	MO	63110	Clarence Smith	314-771-1202	R	40*	<0.1
Hudson Valley Paper Co.	PO Box 1988	Albany	NY	12201	ST Jones III	518-471-5111	R	40*	<0.1
Paper Mart	5361 Alexander	Cty-Commerce	CA	90040	Rosemary Martin	323-726-8200	R	40*	<0.1
Newell Paper Co.	PO Box 631	Meridian	MS	39301	Tommy Galyean	601-693-1783	D	38*	<0.1
Peninsular Paper Company Inc.	PO Box 1197	Tampa	FL	33610	Richard S Clarke Sr	813-621-3091	R	38*	<0.1
Leon Korol Co.	2050 E Devon Ave	Elk Grove Vill.	IL	60007	Steve Korol	847-956-1616	R	37*	<0.1
Quality Quick Bindery Services	855 Hwy 169 N	Minneapolis	MN	55441	Theresa Selander	763-541-0627	R	37*	<0.1
Economy Paper of Rochester	1175 Main St E	Rochester	NY	14609	Robert Cherry	585-482-5340	R	34*	<0.1
Dacotah Paper Co.	3940 15th Ave NW	Fargo	ND	58108	Matthew Mohr	701-281-1734	R	32*	<0.1
M. Conley Co.	1312 4th St SE	Canton	OH	44701	Richard D Conley	330-456-8243	R	32*	0.1
Fulton Paper Company Inc.	6255 Boat Rock	Atlanta	GA	30336	William N Hirsch	404-629-3600	R	30*	0.1
W.L. Halsey Company Inc.	PO Box 6485	Huntsville	AL	35824		256-772-9691	R	29*	0.1
Primepak Co.	133 Cedar Ln	Teaneck	NJ	07666	William Poppe	201-836-5060	R	28*	<0.1
Brenmar Company Inc.	8523 S 117th St	La Vista	NE	68128	Marlene Hytrek	402-592-3303	R	25*	<0.1
Cottingham Paper Co.	PO Box 163579	Columbus	OH	43216	Richard S Cottingham	614-294-6444	R	25*	<0.1
M and R International Inc.	200 Connecticut Ave	Norwalk	CT	06854	Pedro Belez	203-523-5800	R	25*	<0.1
Garland C. Norris Co.	PO Box 28	Apex	NC	27502	JA King	919-387-1059	R	24*	<0.1
Bradley Industries Inc.	524 Ctr Rd	Frankfort	IL	60423	Stephen Bradley	815-469-2314	R	21*	<0.1
Continental Glass and Plastic Inc.	841 W Cermak Rd	Chicago	IL	60608	Richard A Giesen	312-666-2050	R	21*	0.1
Ferguson Supply and Box Mfg Inc.	2500 Cindy Ln	Charlotte	NC	28269	Paige Burgess	704-597-0310	R	20*	0.1
United States Box Corp.	1296 McCarter Hwy	Newark	NJ	07104	Alan Kossoff	973-481-2000	R	20*	<0.1
Huff United Paper Co.	4101 Sarellen Rd	Richmond	VA	23231	Paul Burns	804-226-1936	S	20*	<0.1
United States Container Corp.	PO Box 58544	Los Angeles	CA	90058	Jeffrey Levine	323-589-1000	R	20*	<0.1
Bauman Paper Company Inc.	PO Box 13022	Lexington	KY	40512	FW Baumann Jr	859-252-8891	R	17*	<0.1
K. Yamada Distributors Ltd.	2949 Koapaka St	Honolulu	HI	96819	Gil Yamada	808-836-3221	R	17*	<0.1
Noble Gift Packaging	170 Gregg St	Lodi	NJ	07644	Moses Gancfried	201-909-8100	R	17*	<0.1
Pacific Koast Graphics Inc.	1251 Maulhardt Ave	Oxnard	CA	93030	Meg Roughan	805-278-6648	R	17*	<0.1
A.J. Schrafel Paper Corp.	PO Box 20788	Floral Park	NY	11002	Alfred J Schrafel	516-437-1700	R	16*	<0.1
Butler Wholesale Products	PO Box 308	Adams	MA	01220	George Askin	413-743-3885	R	16*	<0.1
HA and Friend Company Inc.	1535 Lewis Ave	Zion	IL	60099	Richard Friend	847-746-1248	R	16*	<0.1
Mansfield Paper Company Inc.	PO Box 1070	West Springfield	MA	01090	R Scott Parent	413-781-2000	R	16*	<0.1
Northwest Cheese Distributors Inc.	PO Box 882943	San Francisco	CA	94188	Herb Brosowsky	415-822-5088	R	15*	<0.1
Food Source Inc.	653 Swedesford Rd	Frazer	PA	19355	Pete Schaffer	610-540-0300	R	15*	<0.1
Arkansas Packaging Products Inc.	PO Box 16202	Little Rock	AR	72231	Carl Peterson	501-945-1400	R	15*	<0.1
Shorr Packaging	PO Box 6800	Aurora	IL	60598		630-978-1000	R	14*	<0.1
Mautino Distributing Company	500 N Richard St	Spring Valley	IL	61362	Tony Mautino	815-664-4311	R	13*	<0.1
Servants Inc.	PO Box 848	Jasper	IN	47547		812-634-2201	R	12*	<0.1
Best Way City Wholesalers Inc.	1320 Zerega Ave	Bronx	NY	10462	Paul D Sarlo	718-597-7473	R	12*	<0.1
Carter Paper and Packaging Inc.	PO Box 1349	Peoria	IL	61654	Billie H Carter	309-637-7711	R	12*	<0.1
Sks Bottle and Packaging Inc.	PO Box 1017	Clifton Park	NY	12065	Paul Horan	518-899-7488	R	12*	<0.1
American Paper Towel Co.	10 Industrial Rd	Carlstadt	NJ	07072	Larry Shapiro		R	10*	<0.1
Franklin Cigar and Tobacco Inc.	PO Box 1151	Franklin	LA	70538	Keith A Landen	337-828-3208	R	10*	<0.1
Chef's Warehouse	7002 F St	Omaha	NE	68117	Tom Schrack	402-339-8900	R	10*	<0.1
Fishman Supply Co.	PO Box 750279	Petaluma	CA	94975	Leland Fishman	707-763-8161	R	10*	<0.1
Automatic Bakery Machine Inc.	PO Box 3093	Newport Beach	CA	92659	John Malabisi	949-642-0844	R	8*	<0.1
Bancroft Paper of Jackson Inc.	3880 Bullard St	Jackson	MS	39209	Fredrick Bancroft	601-948-1000	R	6*	<0.1

Source: Ward's Business Directory of U.S. Private and Public Companies, Volumes 1 and 2, 2005. The company type code used is as follows: P - Public, R - Private, S - Subsidiary, D - Division, J - Joint Venture, A - Affiliate, G - Group. Sales are in millions of dollars, employees are in thousands. An asterisk (*) indicates an estimated sales volume. The symbol < stands for 'less than'. Company names and addresses are truncated, in some cases, to fit into the available space.

OCCUPATIONS EMPLOYED BY PAPER & PAPER PRODUCT WHOLESALE

Occupation	% of Total 2004	Change to 2014	Occupation	% of Total 2004	Change to 2014
Sales reps, wholesale & manufacturing, exc tech	19.4	9.6	First-line supervisors/managers of office workers	1.8	-0.7
Laborers & freight, stock, & material movers, hand	5.8	-1.4	Order clerks	1.8	-28.8
Stock clerks & order fillers	5.6	-16.1	Team assemblers	1.7	9.6
Customer service representatives	5.4	12.2	Retail salespersons	1.6	9.6
Shipping, receiving, & traffic clerks	4.8	-0.8	First-line supervisors/managers of non-retail sales work	1.6	1.3
Truck drivers, light or delivery services	4.0	9.6	Packaging & filling machine operators & tenders	1.5	3.7
Bookkeeping, accounting, & auditing clerks	3.8	-1.4	Wholesale & retail buyers, except farm products	1.4	3.6
Truck drivers, heavy & tractor-trailer	3.4	9.6	Packers & packagers, hand	1.2	9.6
Industrial truck & tractor operators	3.0	9.6	Secretaries, except legal, medical, & executive	1.1	-7.8
Office clerks, general	2.9	-2.5	Demonstrators & product promoters	1.1	5.5
General & operations managers	2.2	8.4	Sales reps, wholesale & manufacturing, tech	1.1	9.6

Source: Industry-Occupation Matrix, Bureau of Labor Statistics. These data are reported based on 4-digit NAICS categories but have been matched to corresponding 6-digit NAICS industry codes. The change reported for each occupation to the year 2014 is a percent of growth or decline as estimated by the Bureau of Labor Statistics. The abbreviation nec stands for 'not elsewhere classified.'

LOCATION BY STATE AND REGIONAL CONCENTRATION

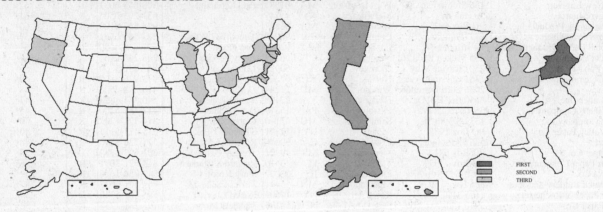

FIRST
SECOND
THIRD

INDUSTRY DATA BY STATE

State	Establishments Total (number)	% of U.S.	Employment Total (number)	% of U.S.	Per Estab.	Payroll Total ($ mil.)	Per Empl. ($)	Sales Total ($ mil.)	% of U.S.	Per Estab. ($)
Illinois	332	7.1	4,755	7.2	14	261.2	54,921	5,168.0	11.4	15,566,367
California	623	13.3	8,245	12.6	13	391.0	47,423	5,021.2	11.0	8,059,644
Ohio	200	4.3	4,113	6.3	21	177.1	43,055	4,080.0	9.0	20,400,095
Georgia	153	3.3	2,525	3.8	17	139.9	55,421	3,825.6	8.4	25,004,203
New York	470	10.1	6,268	9.6	13	261.1	41,660	3,606.8	7.9	7,673,989
Connecticut	88	1.9	1,232	1.9	14	100.6	81,642	2,470.7	5.4	28,076,227
Massachusetts	132	2.8	2,839	4.3	22	143.5	50,554	2,246.1	4.9	17,016,121
Wisconsin	87	1.9	2,053	3.1	24	102.5	49,923	2,110.9	4.6	24,263,287
New Jersey	267	5.7	3,183	4.9	12	170.9	53,683	2,034.5	4.5	7,619,738
Texas	262	5.6	3,069	4.7	12	118.4	38,594	1,621.1	3.6	6,187,382
Pennsylvania	191	4.1	2,674	4.1	14	127.3	47,610	1,435.7	3.2	7,516,613
Maryland	66	1.4	1,347	2.1	20	70.0	51,976	1,403.0	3.1	21,257,697
Florida	285	6.1	3,494	5.3	12	121.7	34,832	1,343.0	3.0	4,712,260
North Carolina	133	2.8	1,982	3.0	15	80.3	40,501	794.2	1.7	5,971,474
Washington	102	2.2	1,317	2.0	13	57.1	43,372	721.6	1.6	7,074,373
Oregon	59	1.3	754	1.1	13	42.1	55,842	639.6	1.4	10,840,203
Virginia	58	1.2	890	1.4	15	39.6	44,457	639.0	1.4	11,016,603
Tennessee	79	1.7	1,043	1.6	13	48.2	46,190	612.4	1.3	7,751,468
South Carolina	68	1.5	701	1.1	10	26.8	38,278	416.2	0.9	6,121,250
Alabama	48	1.0	960	1.5	20	36.5	37,991	402.0	0.9	8,375,417
Indiana	80	1.7	1,132	1.7	14	43.3	38,231	380.3	0.8	4,754,313
Oklahoma	40	0.9	623	0.9	16	22.9	36,801	243.8	0.5	6,095,375
Kentucky	29	0.6	562	0.9	19	23.2	41,212	234.6	0.5	8,091,069
Louisiana	51	1.1	560	0.9	11	18.7	33,420	211.8	0.5	4,152,039
Arkansas	42	0.9	969	1.5	23	28.0	28,901	166.5	0.4	3,963,167
New Hampshire	17	0.4	236	0.4	14	12.0	50,648	138.6	0.3	8,151,000
Hawaii	31	0.7	388	0.6	13	11.6	29,992	112.7	0.2	3,635,194
Mississippi	23	0.5	312	0.5	14	9.9	31,603	82.3	0.2	3,580,261
Iowa	26	0.6	198	0.3	8	8.9	44,773	76.8	0.2	2,952,000
Nebraska	12	0.3	146	0.2	12	6.2	42,377	69.0	0.2	5,749,083
New Mexico	14	0.3	162	0.2	12	5.4	33,284	56.1	0.1	4,004,429

Continued on next page.

INDUSTRY DATA BY STATE - Continued

State	Establishments Total (number)	% of U.S.	Employment Total (number)	% of U.S.	Per Estab.	Payroll Total ($ mil.)	Per Empl. ($)	Sales Total ($ mil.)	% of U.S.	Per Estab. ($)
Vermont	6	0.1	109	0.2	18	5.2	47,862	54.0	0.1	8,995,667
Nevada	24	0.5	110	0.2	5	3.9	35,509	44.1	0.1	1,837,917
Delaware	7	0.1	54	0.1	8	2.1	39,074	11.2	-	1,603,286
Montana	4	0.1	36	0.1	9	1.0	28,889	9.2	-	2,296,000
Michigan	119	2.5	1000-2499	-	-	(D)	-	(D)	-	-
Missouri	93	2.0	1000-2499	-	-	(D)	-	(D)	-	-
Minnesota	88	1.9	500-999	-	-	(D)	-	(D)	-	-
Colorado	80	1.7	500-999	-	-	(D)	-	(D)	-	-
Arizona	52	1.1	500-999	-	-	(D)	-	(D)	-	-
Kansas	39	0.8	250-499	-	-	(D)	-	(D)	-	-
Utah	22	0.5	250-499	-	-	(D)	-	(D)	-	-
Maine	15	0.3	100-249	-	-	(D)	-	(D)	-	-
Rhode Island	15	0.3	100-249	-	-	(D)	-	(D)	-	-
West Virginia	13	0.3	100-249	-	-	(D)	-	(D)	-	-
Alaska	7	0.1	20-99	-	-	(D)	-	(D)	-	-
Idaho	5	0.1	20-99	-	-	(D)	-	(D)	-	-
South Dakota	5	0.1	100-249	-	-	(D)	-	(D)	-	-
North Dakota	4	0.1	100-249	-	-	(D)	-	(D)	-	-
D.C.	3	0.1	0-19	-	-	(D)	-	(D)	-	-

Source: 2002 *Economic Census*. The states are in descending order of sales or establishments (if sales data are missing for the majority). The symbol (D) appears when data are withheld to prevent disclosure of competitive information. States marked with (D) are sorted by number of establishments. A dash (-) indicates that the data element cannot be calculated. Shaded *states* on the state map indicate those states which have proportionately greater representation in the industry than would be indicated by the states population; the ratio is based on total sales or number of establishments. Shaded *regions* indicate where the industry is regionally most concentrated.

NAICS 424210 - DRUGS AND DRUGGISTS' SUNDRIES MERCHANT WHOLESALERS*

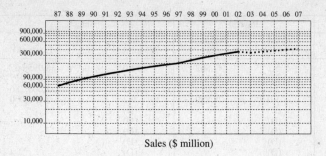

Sales ($ million)

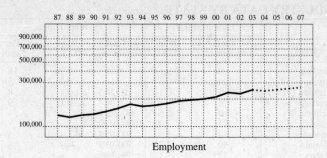

Employment

GENERAL STATISTICS

Year	Establishments (number)	Employment (number)	Payroll ($ million)	Sales ($ million)	Employees per Establishment (number)	Sales per Establishment ($)	Payroll per Employee ($)
1987	4,912	133,102	2,967.8	64,280.1	27.1	13,086,339.6	22,297.2
1988	4,737	126,350	3,395.0	77,337.1 e	26.7	16,326,176.9	26,869.8
1989	4,730	133,325	3,674.0	90,394.2 e	28.2	19,110,824.5	27,556.7
1990	5,185	136,291	4,179.5	103,451.2 e	26.3	19,952,015.4	30,666.0
1991	5,247	145,964	4,775.7	116,508.3 e	27.8	22,204,745.6	32,718.3
1992	6,070	158,167	5,380.0	129,565.3	26.1	21,345,189.5	34,014.7
1993	6,362	175,433	6,466.0	144,281.8 e	27.6	22,678,685.9	36,857.4
1994	6,587	166,130	6,438.2	158,998.3 e	25.2	24,138,196.4	38,754.0
1995	6,891	170,587	7,160.0	173,714.8 e	24.8	25,208,939.2	41,972.7
1996	6,857 e	178,374 e	7,085.0 e	188,431.3 e	26.0 e	27,480,137.1 e	39,719.9 e
1997	8,053	190,127	8,394.9	203,147.8	23.6	25,226,350.4	44,154.2
1998	8,121	194,862	9,319.9	235,168.9 e	24.0	28,958,120.9	47,828.2
1999	7,510	199,759	10,054.9	267,190.0 e	26.6	35,577,896.1	50,335.2
2000	7,418	210,418	11,979.9	299,211.1 e	28.4	40,335,818.3	56,933.9
2001	7,189	234,917	13,695.6	331,232.2 e	32.7	46,074,864.4	58,299.7
2002	7,762	228,221	12,796.7	363,253.3	29.4	46,798,930.7	56,071.5
2003	7,672	251,697	16,575.5	345,405.0 p	32.8	44,015,004.3 p	65,854.8
2004	8,489 p	244,828 p	14,768.0 p	364,377.9 p	29.1 p	45,998,363.4 p	63,791.5 p
2005	8,705 p	252,203 p	15,530.8 p	383,305.8 p	29.3 p	47,981,722.5 p	66,233.0 p
2006	8,921 p	259,578 p	16,293.7 p	402,323.7 p	29.5 p	49,965,081.6 p	68,674.6 p
2007	9,136 p	266,953 p	17,056.6 p	421,296.6 p	29.7 p	51,948,440.7 p	71,116.1 p

Sources: Economic Census of the United States, 1987, 1992, 1997, and 2002. Establishment counts, employment, and payroll are from *County Business Patterns* for non-Census years. Values followed by a 'p' are projections by the editors. Sales data for non-Census years are extrapolations, marked by 'e'. Data are the most recent available at this level of detail.

INDICES OF CHANGE

Year	Establishments (number)	Employment (number)	Payroll ($ million)	Sales ($ million)	Employees per Establishment (number)	Sales per Establishment ($)	Payroll per Employee ($)
1987	63.3	58.3	23.2	17.7	92.2	28.0	39.8
1992	78.2	69.3	42.0	35.7	88.8	45.6	60.7
1993	82.0	76.9	50.5	39.7 e	93.9	48.5	65.7
1994	84.9	72.8	50.3	43.8 e	85.7	51.6	69.1
1995	88.8	74.7	56.0	47.8 e	84.4	53.9	74.9
1996	88.3 e	78.2 e	55.4 e	51.9 e	88.4 e	58.7 e	70.8 e
1997	103.7	83.3	65.6	55.9	80.3	53.9	78.7
1998	104.6	85.4	72.8	64.7 e	81.6	61.9	85.3
1999	96.8	87.5	78.6	73.6 e	90.5	76.0	89.8
2000	95.6	92.2	93.6	82.4 e	96.6	86.2	101.5
2001	92.6	102.9	107.0	91.2 e	111.2	98.5	104.0
2002	100.0	100.0	100.0	100.0	100.0	100.0	100.0
2003	98.8	110.3	129.5	95.1 p	111.6	94.1 p	117.4
2004	109.4 p	107.3 p	115.4 p	100.3 p	99.0 p	98.3 p	113.8 p
2005	112.1 p	110.5 p	121.4 p	105.5 p	99.7 p	102.5 p	118.1 p
2006	114.9 p	113.7 p	127.3 p	110.8 p	100.4 p	106.8 p	122.5 p
2007	117.7 p	117.0 p	133.3 p	116.0 p	101.1 p	111.0 p	126.8 p

*Sources: Same as General Statistics. The values shown reflect change from the base year, 2002. Values above 100 mean greater than 2002, values below 100 mean less than 2002, and a value of 100 in the 1987-2001 or 2003-2007 period means same as 2002. Values followed by a 'p' are projections by the editors; 'e' stands for extrapolation. Data are the most recent available at this level of detail.

SELECTED RATIOS

For 2002	Avg. of All Wholesale	Analyzed Industry	Index	For 2002	Avg. of All Wholesale	Analyzed Industry	Index
Employees per Establishment	15	29	197	Sales per Employee	791,325	1,591,673	201
Payroll per Establishment	626,122	1,648,634	263	Sales per Establishment	12,012,387	46,798,931	390
Payroll per Employee	41,161	56,072	136	Expenses per Establishment	na	na	na

*Sources: Same as General Statistics. The 'Average of All' column, Wholesale or Retail, represents the average of the sector reported for the most recent complete year available. The Index shows the relationship between the Average and the Analyzed Industry. For example, 100 means that they are equal; 500 that the Analyzed Industry is five times the average; 50 means that the Analyzed Industry is half the national average. The abbreviation 'na' is used to show that data are 'not available'.

*Equivalent to SIC 5122.

LEADING COMPANIES   Number shown: **75**   Total sales ($ mil): **363,766**   Total employment (000): **450.6**

Company Name	Address				CEO Name	Phone	Co. Type	Sales ($ mil)	Empl. (000)
McKesson HBOC Inc.	1 Post St	San Francisco	CA	94104	John H. Hammergren	415-983-8300	P	69,506	24.0
Cardinal Health Inc.	7000 Cardinal Pl	Dublin	OH	43017		614-757-5000	P	65,053	55.0
Pfizer Inc.	235 E 42nd St	New York	NY	10017		212-573-2323	P	52,516	122.0
AmerisourceBergen Corp.	PO Box 959	Valley Forge	PA	19482		610-727-7000	P	48,871	14.0
Cardinal Distribution L.P.	7000 Cardinal Pl	Dublin	OH	43017	Robert Walter	614-757-5000	S	27,600*	40.0
SUPERVALU Inc.	11840 Valley View	Eden Prairie	MN	55344		952-828-4000	P	20,205	55.2
Eli Lilly and Co.	Lilly Corporate Ctr	Indianapolis	IN	46285		317-276-2000	P	13,858	46.0
Bindley Western Industries Inc.	7000 Cardinal Pl	Dublin	OH	43017	Robert Walter	614-757-5000	S	8,510*	1.4
Schering-Plough Corp.	1 Giralda Farms	Madison	NJ	07940		973-822-7000	P	8,272	30.5
Rexall Sundown Inc.	6111 Broken Snd	Boca Raton	FL	33487			S	6,328*	1.3
Owens and Minor Inc.	PO Box 27626	Glen Allen	VA	23060		804-747-9794	P	4,525	3.4
Omnicare Inc.	1600 RiverCenter II	Covington	KY	41011		859-392-3300	P	4,120	12.9
Kinray Inc.	35 10th Ave	Whitestone	NY	11357	Stewart Rahr	718-767-1234	R	3,333*	0.8
Eby-Brown Co.	PO Box 3067	Naperville	IL	60566		630-778-2800	R	3,200	2.1
D and K Healthcare Resources Inc.	8235 Forsyth Blvd	St. Louis	MO	63105	J Hord Armstrong III	314-727-3485	P	2,541	0.8
Quality King Distributors Inc.	2060 9th Ave	Ronkonkoma	NY	11779	Bernard Nussdorf	631-737-5555	R	2,300	0.9
Mary Kay Inc.	PO Box 799045	Dallas	TX	75379	David B Holl	972-687-6300	R	1,800*	3.6
Nu Skin International Inc.	75 W Center St	Provo	UT	84601	Lori Bush	801-345-1000	S	1,633*	1.6
Priority Healthcare Corp.	250 Technology Pk	Lake Mary	FL	32746	William Bindley	407-804-6700	P	1,462	0.8
QK Healthcare Inc.	2060 9th Ave	Ronkonkoma	NY	11779	Glenn Nussdorf	631-439-2000	S	1,461*	0.1
Purity Wholesale Grocers Inc.	5400 Broken Sound	Boca Raton	FL	33487	Jeff Levitetz	561-994-9360	R	1,450	0.4
F. Dohmen Co.	PO Box 9	Germantown	WI	53022	John Dohmen	262-255-0022	R	1,368	0.5
Herbalife International Inc.	1800 Century Pk, E.	Los Angeles	CA	90067	Peter M Castleman	310-410-9600	S	1,337*	2.6
Grocers Supply Co. Inc.	PO Box 14200	Houston	TX	77221	Max Levit	713-747-5000	R	1,182*	2.0
PharMerica Inc.	175 Kelsey Ln	Tampa	FL	33619	David Weidner	813-626-7788	S	1,143*	7.5
Nu Skin Enterprises Inc.	1 Nu Skin Plz	Provo	UT	84601	M Truman Hunt	801-345-1000	P	987	7.2
AMCON Distributing Co.	7405 Irvington Rd	Omaha	NE	68122	Kathleen M Evans	402-331-3727	P	824	1.0
Elizabeth Arden Inc.	14100 NW 60th Ave	Miami Lakes	FL	33014	E Scott Beattie	305-818-8000	P	814	2.2
Affiliated Foods Inc.	PO Box 30300	Amarillo	TX	79120	George Langford	806-372-3851	R	790*	1.1
Darby Group Companies Inc.	865 Merrick Ave	Westbury	NY	11590	Carl Ashkin	516-683-1800	R	670*	1.4
Helen of Troy Ltd.	1 Helen of Troy Plz	El Paso	TX	79912		915-225-8000	P	475	0.7
Florida Infusion Services Inc.	1053 Progress Ct	Palm Harbor	FL	34683	Rudy Ciccarello		R	440	<0.1
McQueary Brothers Drug Co.	PO Box 5955	Springfield	MO	65801	Fred McQueary	417-869-2577	R	439*	<0.1
JM Smith Corp.	PO Box 1779	Spartanburg	SC	29304	William Cobb	864-542-9419	R	400*	0.7
Imperial Trading Co.	PO Box 23508	New Orleans	LA	70183	John Georges	504-733-1400	R	389*	0.3
Imperial Distributors Inc.	33 Sword St	Auburn	MA	01501	Michael Sleeper	508-756-5156	R	383*	0.5
DrugMax Inc.	312 Farmington Ave	Farmington	CT	06032	William L LaGamba	860-676-1222	P	214	<0.1
E Com Ventures Inc.	251 International	Sunrise	FL	33325	Michael W Katz	954-335-9100	P	213	1.3
Cost-U-Less Inc.	3633 136th Pl SE	Bellevue	WA	98006	David A Enger	425-945-0213	P	209	0.6
Anderson Wholesale Co.	PO Box 69	Muskogee	OK	74402	John P Gilliam	918-682-5568	R	198*	0.2
SST Corp.	PO Box 1649	Clifton	NJ	07012	George H Turner II	973-473-4300	R	175*	<0.1
Helen of Troy Texas Corp.	1 Helen of Troy Plz	El Paso	TX	79912	Gerald J Rubin	915-225-8000	S	167*	0.3
Gary Farn Ltd.	249 Pepes Farm Rd	Milford	CT	06460	Allison Farn	203-878-8900	R	154*	<0.1
Classic Fragrances Ltd.	132 W 36th St	New York	NY	10011	William Shnipper	212-929-2266	R	136*	<0.1
PRN Pharmaceutical Services Inc.	8351 Rockville Rd	Indianapolis	IN	46234	Caroline Copen	317-273-1552	S	120*	0.2
Midwest Veterinary Supply Inc.	11965 Larc Ind Blvd	Burnsville	MN	55337	Guy Flickinger	952-894-4350	R	115*	0.2
VIVA Life Science Inc.	1239 Victoria St	Costa Mesa	CA	92627	David Fan	949-645-6100	R	113*	0.1
North Carolina Mutual Wholesale	PO Box 411	Durham	NC	27702	David Moody	919-596-2151	R	102*	0.1
Merle Norman Cosmetics Inc.	9130 Bellanca Ave	Los Angeles	CA	90045	Arthur Armstrong	310-641-3000	R	98*	0.3
Reliv' International Inc.	PO Box 405	Chesterfield	MO	63006	Robert L Montgomery	636-537-9715	P	97	0.0
Richards Products Inc.	1461 SW 32nd Ave	Pompano Beach	FL	33069		954-978-0313	R	97*	<0.1
Cardinal Health Specialty Services	401 Mason Rd	La Vergne	TN	37086			S	90*	0.1
Bradley Pharmaceuticals Inc.	383 Route 46 W	Fairfield	NJ	07004	Daniel Glassman	973-882-1505	P	75	0.3
Mason Distributors	5105 NW 159th St	Miami Lakes	FL	33015	Sonia Rodriguez	305-624-5557	R	74*	<0.1
Janco Distributors Inc.	901 Motor Pkwy	Hauppauge	NY	11788	Jules Ertman	631-273-7100	R	73*	<0.1
Miami-Luken Inc.	265 S Pioneer Blvd	Springboro	OH	45066	William M Powers, Jr	513-743-7775	R	73*	<0.1
Natrol Inc.	21411 Prairie St	Chatsworth	CA	91311	Elliott Balbert	818-739-6000	P	73	0.3
Nutrition Now Inc.	6350 NE Campus Dr	Vancouver	WA	98661	Martin Rifkin	360-737-6800	R	68*	<0.1
Chemins Company Inc.	PO Box 2498	Co Springs	CO	80901	James R Cameron	719-579-9650	R	66*	0.2
Experimental Applied Sciences	PO Box 277	Golden	CO	80402	David Lumley	303-384-0080	R	66*	0.3
Mikara Corp.	3109 Louisiana N	Minneapolis	MN	55427	Michael P Hicks	763-546-9500	R	65*	0.2
Humco Holding Group Inc.	7400 Alumax Dr	Texarkana	TX	75501	Greg Pulido	903-831-7808	R	61*	0.1
Apothecary Products Inc.	11750 12th Ave S	Burnsville	MN	55337	John Creel	952-890-1940	R	60*	0.2
Model Imperial Fine Fragrances	1061 SW 30th Ave	Deerfield Beach	FL	33442	Stephen Nussdors	954-418-0097	S	56*	<0.1
ivpcare Inc.	7164 Technology Dr	Frisco	TX	75034	Von L Best	214-387-3500	R	54*	<0.1
ITG-MEDEV Inc.	PO Box 320297	San Francisco	CA	94132	Alan Dishman	415-753-9989	R	49*	<0.1
Reliv' World Corp.	PO Box 405	Chesterfield	MO	63006	Robert L Montgomery	636-537-9715	S	48*	0.2
Somerset Pharmaceuticals Inc.	2202 N Westshore	Tampa	FL	33607	Melvin Sharoky MD	813-288-0040	J	46*	<0.1
Idaho Candy Co.	PO Box 1217	Boise	ID	83701	Dave Wagers	208-342-5505	R	42*	<0.1
Albert Guarnieri Company Inc.	PO Box 927	Warren	OH	44483	A Guarnieri III	330-394-5636	R	41*	<0.1
Integrative Therapeutics Inc.	9725 SW Commerce	Wilsonville	OR	97070		503-582-8386	R	41*	<0.1
Caswell-Massey Company Ltd.	121 Fieldcrest Ave	Edison	NJ	08837	Anne Robinson	732-225-2181	R	40*	<0.1
Sportpharma USA Inc.	1915 Mark Ct	Concord	CA	94520	Robert Walls	925-686-1451	R	40*	<0.1
ADH Health Products Inc.	PO Box 420	Congers	NY	10920	Balram Advani	845-268-0027	R	38*	<0.1
Digital Angel Corp.	490 Villuame Ave	South Saint Paul	MN	55075	Kevin McGrath	651-455-1621	P	37	0.2

Source: Ward's Business Directory of U.S. Private and Public Companies, Volumes 1 and 2, 2005. The company type code used is as follows: P - Public, R - Private, S - Subsidiary, D - Division, J - Joint Venture, A - Affiliate, G - Group. Sales are in millions of dollars, employees are in thousands. An asterisk (*) indicates an estimated sales volume. The symbol < stands for 'less than'. Company names and addresses are truncated, in some cases, to fit into the available space.

OCCUPATIONS EMPLOYED BY DRUGS, & DRUGGISTS' SUNDRIES WHOLESALE

Occupation	% of Total 2004	Change to 2014	Occupation	% of Total 2004	Change to 2014
Sales reps, wholesale & manufacturing, tech	19.7	20.4	First-line supervisors/managers of non-retail sales work	1.8	11.3
Sales reps, wholesale & manufacturing, exc tech	9.6	20.4	Truck drivers, light or delivery services	1.7	20.4
Stock clerks & order fillers	6.9	-7.8	First-line supervisors/managers of office workers	1.5	9.1
Laborers & freight, stock, & material movers, hand	4.4	8.3	Accountants & auditors	1.5	20.4
Customer service representatives	3.6	23.2	Executive secretaries & administrative assistants	1.5	14.1
Shipping, receiving, & traffic clerks	3.2	9.0	Office clerks, general	1.4	7.1
Packers & packagers, hand	2.5	20.4	Packaging & filling machine operators & tenders	1.4	13.9
Bookkeeping, accounting, & auditing clerks	2.5	8.3	Sales managers	1.4	21.1
Pharmacy technicians	2.3	59.9	Order clerks	1.2	-21.8
Pharmacists	1.8	29.1	Team assemblers	1.1	20.3
General & operations managers	1.8	19.2			

Source: Industry-Occupation Matrix, Bureau of Labor Statistics. These data are reported based on 4-digit NAICS categories but have been matched to corresponding 6-digit NAICS industry codes. The change reported for each occupation to the year 2014 is a percent of growth or decline as estimated by the Bureau of Labor Statistics. The abbreviation nec stands for 'not elsewhere classified.'

LOCATION BY STATE AND REGIONAL CONCENTRATION

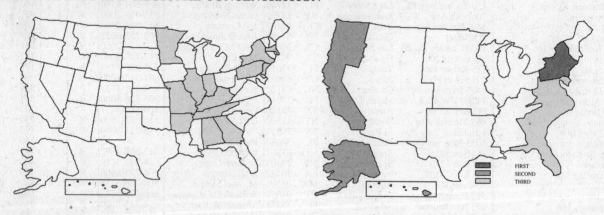

FIRST
SECOND
THIRD

INDUSTRY DATA BY STATE

State	Establishments Total (number)	% of U.S.	Employment Total (number)	% of U.S.	Per Estab.	Payroll Total ($ mil.)	Per Empl. ($)	Sales Total ($ mil.)	% of U.S.	Per Estab. ($)
New York	754	9.8	25,206	10.8	33	1,537.5	60,996	44,137.2	11.4	58,537,408
California	1,282	16.6	28,277	12.1	22	1,836.9	64,961	34,136.8	8.8	26,627,754
New Jersey	576	7.5	32,340	13.8	56	2,391.8	73,958	30,796.9	8.0	53,466,806
Illinois	272	3.5	14,556	6.2	54	903.8	62,093	28,886.9	7.5	106,201,743
Pennsylvania	264	3.4	13,725	5.9	52	775.3	56,485	27,067.2	7.0	102,527,341
Texas	532	6.9	15,885	6.8	30	886.0	55,776	25,549.0	6.6	48,024,391
Indiana	97	1.3	3,360	1.4	35	136.9	40,745	16,954.7	4.4	174,791,186
Florida	734	9.5	11,297	4.8	15	551.5	48,819	16,052.0	4.1	21,869,218
Tennessee	119	1.5	4,833	2.1	41	202.3	41,861	13,608.6	3.5	114,358,361
Georgia	190	2.5	6,780	2.9	36	403.8	59,564	13,469.1	3.5	70,889,795
Massachusetts	123	1.6	8,733	3.7	71	596.1	68,258	12,747.5	3.3	103,637,894
Missouri	146	1.9	2,934	1.3	20	141.2	48,113	12,480.4	3.2	85,482,507
Ohio	187	2.4	5,832	2.5	31	272.6	46,737	10,958.8	2.8	58,603,086
Michigan	132	1.7	2,796	1.2	21	112.9	40,376	7,981.7	2.1	60,467,242
Minnesota	96	1.2	2,633	1.1	27	137.2	52,107	7,413.5	1.9	77,224,448
Alabama	85	1.1	2,333	1.0	27	106.7	45,751	6,945.2	1.8	81,708,718
Wisconsin	99	1.3	2,779	1.2	28	138.5	49,849	6,504.1	1.7	65,698,253
North Carolina	184	2.4	4,105	1.8	22	201.7	49,129	6,362.6	1.6	34,579,277
Washington	146	1.9	2,284	1.0	16	118.5	51,871	6,336.1	1.6	43,398,089
Kentucky	88	1.1	3,432	1.5	39	159.4	46,432	6,112.6	1.6	69,461,511
Louisiana	93	1.2	1,792	0.8	19	68.9	38,470	4,730.2	1.2	50,861,978
Arkansas	51	0.7	2,178	0.9	43	90.6	41,585	4,417.2	1.1	86,611,000
Oklahoma	77	1.0	1,520	0.6	20	45.4	29,849	3,686.3	1.0	47,873,948
Virginia	103	1.3	1,745	0.7	17	72.5	41,553	3,419.5	0.9	33,198,699
Connecticut	101	1.3	4,528	1.9	45	416.9	92,061	3,252.7	0.8	32,205,139
Maryland	106	1.4	2,682	1.1	25	143.7	53,578	2,956.9	0.8	27,895,057
Colorado	124	1.6	1,631	0.7	13	71.6	43,920	2,589.5	0.7	20,883,411
Utah	99	1.3	2,460	1.1	25	114.9	46,692	2,313.3	0.6	23,366,384
Kansas	60	0.8	1,323	0.6	22	58.3	44,054	1,217.3	0.3	20,288,167
Mississippi	57	0.7	601	0.3	11	24.3	40,393	1,202.7	0.3	21,100,860
Oregon	83	1.1	983	0.4	12	33.4	34,000	1,182.2	0.3	14,243,952
South Carolina	62	0.8	797	0.3	13	34.3	43,014	1,052.2	0.3	16,971,323
Hawaii	54	0.7	750	0.3	14	23.9	31,893	867.1	0.2	16,057,370

Continued on next page.

INDUSTRY DATA BY STATE - Continued

State	Establishments Total (number)	% of U.S.	Employment Total (number)	% of U.S.	Per Estab.	Payroll Total ($ mil.)	Per Empl. ($)	Sales Total ($ mil.)	% of U.S.	Per Estab. ($)
Iowa	45	0.6	894	0.4	20	40.5	45,338	835.6	0.2	18,568,556
Nevada	101	1.3	1,175	0.5	12	48.5	41,271	461.5	0.1	4,569,267
Idaho	22	0.3	366	0.2	17	10.3	28,060	256.9	0.1	11,678,136
New Hampshire	18	0.2	280	0.1	16	12.4	44,289	232.7	0.1	12,925,611
South Dakota	14	0.2	233	0.1	17	5.5	23,773	222.5	0.1	15,892,857
North Dakota	18	0.2	222	0.1	12	7.0	31,514	202.6	0.1	11,253,778
Montana	27	0.3	220	0.1	8	7.6	34,714	161.0	-	5,963,815
Vermont	10	0.1	298	0.1	30	12.6	42,450	158.9	-	15,894,200
Wyoming	14	0.2	117	0.1	8	4.9	42,103	49.2	-	3,512,571
Arizona	136	1.8	2500-4999	-	-	(D)	-	(D)	-	-
Nebraska	32	0.4	500-999	-	-	(D)	-	(D)	-	-
New Mexico	26	0.3	250-499	-	-	(D)	-	(D)	-	-
Delaware	22	0.3	5K-9999	-	-	(D)	-	(D)	-	-
West Virginia	20	0.3	500-999	-	-	(D)	-	(D)	-	-
Rhode Island	18	0.2	100-249	-	-	(D)	-	(D)	-	-
Maine	13	0.2	100-249	-	-	(D)	-	(D)	-	-
Alaska	12	0.2	100-249	-	-	(D)	-	(D)	-	-
D.C.	5	0.1	20-99	-	-	(D)	-	(D)	-	-

Source: 2002 *Economic Census.* The states are in descending order of sales or establishments (if sales data are missing for the majority). The symbol (D) appears when data are withheld to prevent disclosure of competitive information. States marked with (D) are sorted by number of establishments. A dash (-) indicates that the data element cannot be calculated. Shaded *states* on the state map indicate those states which have proportionately greater representation in the industry than would be indicated by the states population; the ratio is based on total sales or number of establishments. Shaded *regions* indicate where the industry is regionally most concentrated.

NAICS 424310 - PIECE GOODS, NOTIONS, AND OTHER DRY GOODS MERCHANT WHOLESALERS

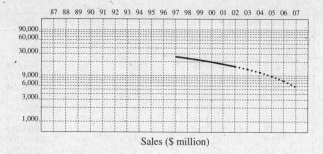

Sales ($ million)

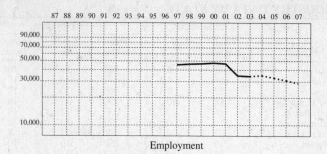

Employment

GENERAL STATISTICS

Year	Establishments (number)	Employment (number)	Payroll ($ million)	Sales ($ million)	Employees per Establishment (number)	Sales per Establishment ($)	Payroll per Employee ($)
1987	-	-	-	-	-	-	-
1988	-	-	-	-	-	-	-
1989	-	-	-	-	-	-	-
1990	-	-	-	-	-	-	-
1991	-	-	-	-	-	-	-
1992	-	-	-	-	-	-	-
1993	-	-	-	-	-	-	-
1994	-	-	-	-	-	-	-
1995	-	-	-	-	-	-	-
1996	-	-	-	-	-	-	-
1997	5,666	45,435	1,611.4	25,776.9	8.0	4,549,399.9	35,466.1
1998	5,739	46,315	1,721.9	23,771.8 e	8.1	4,142,146.7	37,178.0
1999	5,853	46,711	1,788.8	21,766.7 e	8.0	3,718,889.5	38,295.0
2000	5,802	47,544	1,879.6	19,761.5 e	8.2	3,405,987.6	39,534.3
2001	5,668	46,755	1,861.2	17,756.4 e	8.2	3,132,748.8	39,807.1
2002	4,405	34,596	1,367.4	15,751.3	7.9	3,575,777.5	39,524.8
2003	4,288	34,158	1,424.0	13,746.2 p	8.0	2,933,237.6 p	41,689.7
2004	4,348 p	34,898 p	1,493.7 p	11,741.1 p	8.0 p	2,698,688.8 p	42,338.8 p
2005	4,098 p	32,855 p	1,450.9 p	9,735.9 p	8.0 p	2,464,140.0 p	43,227.2 p
2006	3,849 p	30,811 p	1,408.0 p	7,730.8 p	8.0 p	2,229,591.2 p	44,115.7 p
2007	3,599 p	28,767 p	1,365.2 p	5,725.7 p	8.0 p	1,995,042.4 p	45,004.1 p

Source: Economic Census of the United States, 1997 and 2002. Establishment counts, employment, and payroll are from *County Business Patterns* for non-Census years. This is a newly defined industry. Data for prior years are unavailable at the time of publication but may become available over time. Values followed by 'p' are projections by the editors. Sales data for non-Census years are extrapolations, marked by 'e'.

INDICES OF CHANGE

Year	Establishments (number)	Employment (number)	Payroll ($ million)	Sales ($ million)	Employees per Establishment (number)	Sales per Establishment ($)	Payroll per Employee ($)
1987	-	-	-	-	-	-	-
1992	-	-	-	-	-	-	-
1993	-	-	-	-	-	-	-
1994	-	-	-	-	-	-	-
1995	-	-	-	-	-	-	-
1996	-	-	-	-	-	-	-
1997	128.6	131.3	117.8	163.6	101.3	127.2	89.7
1998	130.3	133.9	125.9	150.9 e	102.5	115.8	94.1
1999	132.9	135.0	130.8	138.2 e	101.3	104.0	96.9
2000	131.7	137.4	137.5	125.5 e	103.8	95.3	100.0
2001	128.7	135.1	136.1	112.7 e	103.8	87.6	100.7
2002	100.0	100.0	100.0	100.0	100.0	100.0	100.0
2003	97.3	98.7	104.1	87.3 p	100.8	82.0 p	105.5
2004	98.7 p	100.9 p	109.2 p	74.5 p	101.4 p	75.5 p	107.1 p
2005	93.0 p	95.0 p	106.1 p	61.8 p	101.2 p	68.9 p	109.4 p
2006	87.4 p	89.1 p	103.0 p	49.1 p	101.1 p	62.4 p	111.6 p
2007	81.7 p	83.2 p	99.8 p	36.4 p	101.0 p	55.8 p	113.9 p

Sources: Same as General Statistics. The values shown reflect change from the base year, 2002. Values above 100 mean greater than 2002, values below 100 mean less than 2002, and a value of 100 in the 1987-2001 or 2003-2007 period means same as 2002. Values followed by a 'p' are projections by the editors; 'e' stands for extrapolation. Data are the most recent available at this level of detail.

SELECTED RATIOS

For 2002	Avg. of All Wholesale	Analyzed Industry	Index	For 2002	Avg. of All Wholesale	Analyzed Industry	Index
Employees per Establishment	15	8	53	Sales per Employee	791,325	455,293	58
Payroll per Establishment	626,122	310,420	50	Sales per Establishment	12,012,387	3,575,778	30
Payroll per Employee	41,161	39,525	96	Expenses per Establishment	na	na	na

Sources: Same as General Statistics. The 'Average of All' column, Wholesale or Retail, represents the average of the sector reported for the most recent complete year available. The Index shows the relationship between the Average and the Analyzed Industry. For example, 100 means that they are equal; 500 that the Analyzed Industry is five times the average; 50 means that the Analyzed Industry is half the national average. The abbreviation 'na' is used to show that data are 'not available'.

LEADING COMPANIES   Number shown: **47**   Total sales ($ mil): **11,574**   Total employment (000): **14.8**

Company Name	Address				CEO Name	Phone	Co. Type	Sales ($ mil)	Empl. (000)
Marubeni America Corp.	450 Lexington Ave	New York	NY	10017	Kazuhiko Sakamoto	212-450-0100	S	8,050*	0.2
Barrow Industries Inc	3 Edgewater Dr	Norwood	MA	02062	Stephen Y Barrow	781-440-2666	R	479*	0.3
Helen of Troy Ltd.	1 Helen of Troy Plz	El Paso	TX	79912		915-225-8000	P	475	0.7
Hancock Fabrics Inc.	3406 W Main St	Tupelo	MS	38801	Jane F Aggers	662-842-2834	P	427	6.4
Peachtree Fabrics Inc.	1400 English St NW	Atlanta	GA	30318	Steve Dutson Jr	404-351-5400	R	330*	0.2
Tomen America Inc.	1285 Av Americas	New York	NY	10019	T Yano	212-397-4600	S	210*	<0.1
Delta Apparel Inc.	2750 Premiere Pky	Duluth	GA	30097	Robert W Humphreys	678-775-6900	P	208	4.5
Helen of Troy Texas Corp.	1 Helen of Troy Plz	El Paso	TX	79912	Gerald J Rubin	915-225-8000	S	167*	0.3
Fabricut Inc.	PO Box 470490	Tulsa	OK	74147	David Finer	918-622-7700	R	150*	0.3
Schott International Inc.	2850 Gilchrist Rd	Akron	OH	44305	John C Schott	330-773-7851	R	78*	<0.1
E.E. Schenck Co.	6000 N Cutter Cir	Portland	OR	97208	SG Gray	503-284-4124	R	73*	<0.1
Elna USA	1760 Gilsinn Ln	Fenton	MO	63026	Ken Tacony	636-349-3000	D	73*	<0.1
ATD-American Co.	111-149 Greenwood	Wyncote	PA	19095	Jerome Zaslow	215-576-1380	R	65*	0.1
Burrows Co.	PO Box 747	Wheeling	IL	60090	George J Burrows	847-537-7300	R	61*	0.3
Daewoo International Corp.	85 Challenger Rd	Ridgefield Park	NJ	07660	Young Nam	201-229-4500	R	56*	<0.1
Tag-It Pacific Inc.	21900 Burbank	Woodland Hills	CA	91367	Colin Dyne	818-444-4100	P	55	0.2
Arthur Sanderson & Sons	285 Grand	Englewood	NJ	07631	David Walker	201-894-8400	R	52*	0.1
Heritage Lace Inc.	PO Box 328	Pella	IA	50219	Mark De Cook	641-628-4949	R	52*	0.1
Hoffman California Fabrics	25792 Obrero Dr	Mission Viejo	CA	92691	Philip Hoffman	949-770-2922	R	39*	<0.1
Soltex International Inc.	50 Commerce Ctr	Greenville	SC	29615		864-234-0322	D	38*	<0.1
C and F Enterprises	819 Blue Crab Rd	Newport News	VA	23606	Carol S Fang	757-873-5688	R	31*	0.1
Charter Fabrics Inc.	1430 Broadway	New York	NY	10018	Robert Murello	212-391-8110	R	31*	<0.1
Levcor International Inc.	1065 Av Americas	New York	NY	10018	Robert A Levison	212-354-8500	P	31	0.2
Atlas Textile Company Inc.	PO Box 1821	Los Angeles	CA	90041	Benjamin Kaye	323-588-8700	R	30*	<0.1
Brewer Sewing Supplies Co.	3800 W 42nd St	Chicago	IL	60632	Jerry Smith	773-247-2121	R	29*	<0.1
Beckenstein Men's Fabrics Inc.	257 W 39th St	New York	NY	10018	Neal Boyarsky	212-475-6666	R	29*	<0.1
Mg's Original Products Co.	13618 SE 272nd Ct	Kent	WA	98042	Richard Gradwohl	253-631-1911	R	24*	<0.1
Acme Linen Co.	5136 E Triggs St	Los Angeles	CA	90022	Sam Benzonsky	323-266-4000	R	18*	<0.1
Jim Thompson Silk Co.	1694 Chantilly Dr	Atlanta	GA	30324	Mavis Cahoon	404-325-5004	R	18*	<0.1
Miroglio Textiles U.S.A. Inc.	1430 Broadway, Fl 6	New York	NY	10018	Frank Iovino	212-382-2020	R	18*	<0.1
United Drug Service Inc.	5345 Fulton Ind SW	Atlanta	GA	30336		404-344-1625	R	15*	<0.1
MBR Industries Inc.	3201 NW 116th St	Miami	FL	33167	Bernard Pomeranc	305-769-1000	R	15*	<0.1
Ehrlich, Gress and Co.	51 E 42nd St	New York	NY	10017	Scott Gress	212-499-9500	R	15*	<0.1
Glick Textiles Inc.	2327 Southwest Fwy	Houston	TX	77098	George Levon	713-942-8585	R	15*	<0.1
Logantex Inc.	70 W 36th St	New York	NY	10018	Armand J Vella	212-221-3900	R	15*	<0.1
Kabat Textile Corp.	247 W 37th St	New York	NY	10018	Arthur Adelman	212-398-0011	R	14*	<0.1
Jacobson Capital Services Inc.	150 Croton Ave	Peekskill	NY	10566	Alvin Jacobson	914-736-0600	R	13*	<0.1
Princess Fabrics Inc.	242 W 36th St	New York	NY	10018	Steve Prince	212-354-9393	R	13*	<0.1
Industrial Rubber and Supply Inc.	PO Box 2276	Tacoma	WA	98401	Scott Smallings	253-922-1148	R	10*	<0.1
Mayar Silk Inc.	15 W 36th St, Fl 5	New York	NY	10018	Dan Korn	212-564-1380	R	9*	<0.1
Houles USA Inc.	8584 Melrose Ave	Los Angeles	CA	90069	Pierre Houles	310-652-6171	R	8*	<0.1
Martha Pullen Company Inc.	149 Old Big Cove	Brownsboro	AL	35741		256-533-9586	R	8*	<0.1
A. Frank and Sons Inc.	1501 Guilford Ave	Baltimore	MD	21202	Samuel L Frank	410-727-6260	R	7*	<0.1
DesignCraft Fabric Corp.	2230 N Ridge Dr	Glenview	IL	60025	Mark Weiner	847-904-7000	R	6*	<0.1
John Kaldor Fabricmaker USA	469 7th Ave	New York	NY	10018	John Kaldor	212-629-9260	R	6*	<0.1
Wesco Fabrics Inc.	PO Box 16604	Denver	CO	80216	Marla Gentry	303-388-4101	R	4*	<0.1
Shepherd Products Co.	8080 Moorsbridge	Kalamazoo	MI	49024	Joel M Shepherd III	269-324-3017	R	3*	<0.1

Source: Ward's Business Directory of U.S. Private and Public Companies, Volumes 1 and 2, 2005. The company type code used is as follows: P - Public, R - Private, S - Subsidiary, D - Division, J - Joint Venture, A - Affiliate, G - Group. Sales are in millions of dollars, employees are in thousands. An asterisk (*) indicates an estimated sales volume. The symbol < stands for 'less than'. Company names and addresses are truncated, in some cases, to fit into the available space.

OCCUPATIONS EMPLOYED BY APPAREL, PIECE GOODS, & NOTIONS WHOLESALE

Occupation	% of Total 2004	Change to 2014	Occupation	% of Total 2004	Change to 2014
Sales reps, wholesale & manufacturing, exc tech	15.5	4.0	Wholesale & retail buyers, except farm products	1.9	-1.6
Laborers & freight, stock, & material movers, hand	10.6	-6.4	First-line supervisors/managers of non-retail sales work	1.9	-3.8
Shipping, receiving, & traffic clerks	5.5	-5.8	Order clerks	1.8	-32.4
Stock clerks & order fillers	5.4	-20.3	First-line supervisors/managers of office workers	1.6	-5.7
Retail salespersons	3.9	4.0	Sewing machine operators	1.6	4.0
Packers & packagers, hand	3.8	4.0	Inspectors, testers, sorters, samplers, & weighers	1.4	-1.5
Customer service representatives	3.5	6.5	Accountants & auditors	1.3	4.0
Office clerks, general	3.5	-7.4	Secretaries, except legal, medical, & executive	1.3	-12.5
Fashion designers	2.8	33.9	Production, planning, & expediting clerks	1.1	2.9
Bookkeeping, accounting, & auditing clerks	2.5	-6.4	Industrial truck & tractor operators	1.0	4.0
General & operations managers	2.3	2.9			

Source: Industry-Occupation Matrix, Bureau of Labor Statistics. These data are reported based on 4-digit NAICS categories but have been matched to corresponding 6-digit NAICS industry codes. The change reported for each occupation to the year 2014 is a percent of growth or decline as estimated by the Bureau of Labor Statistics. The abbreviation nec stands for 'not elsewhere classified.'

LOCATION BY STATE AND REGIONAL CONCENTRATION

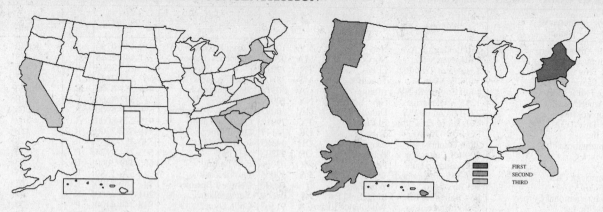

INDUSTRY DATA BY STATE

State	Establishments Total (number)	% of U.S.	Employment Total (number)	% of U.S.	Per Estab.	Payroll Total ($ mil.)	Per Empl. ($)	Sales Total ($ mil.)	% of U.S.	Per Estab. ($)
New York	1,164	26.4	8,956	25.8	8	431.4	48,164	5,182.5	31.6	4,452,302
California	1,116	25.3	7,395	21.3	7	256.3	34,663	3,422.3	20.9	3,066,535
North Carolina	187	4.2	2,258	6.5	12	97.4	43,141	1,391.4	8.5	7,440,401
Georgia	115	2.6	1,337	3.8	12	54.4	40,687	792.0	4.8	6,886,783
New Jersey	261	5.9	1,771	5.1	7	75.4	42,569	716.0	4.4	2,743,333
Texas	160	3.6	1,595	4.6	10	51.6	32,357	673.3	4.1	4,208,275
Florida	239	5.4	1,152	3.3	5	40.2	34,880	409.6	2.5	1,713,937
Pennsylvania	98	2.2	810	2.3	8	32.6	40,274	304.6	1.9	3,108,184
South Carolina	68	1.5	760	2.2	11	27.5	36,249	263.8	1.6	3,879,368
Ohio	54	1.2	456	1.3	8	17.9	39,193	187.4	1.1	3,470,352
Missouri	54	1.2	502	1.4	9	18.2	36,331	157.2	1.0	2,910,963
Arizona	38	0.9	242	0.7	6	7.7	31,645	140.0	0.9	3,683,711
Tennessee	31	0.7	205	0.6	7	7.9	38,307	130.0	0.8	4,192,161
Colorado	49	1.1	421	1.2	9	14.3	33,903	76.9	0.5	1,570,265
Oregon	29	0.7	284	0.8	10	7.9	27,894	74.1	0.5	2,554,759
Virginia	43	1.0	237	0.7	6	8.2	34,451	67.5	0.4	1,569,721
Hawaii	21	0.5	187	0.5	9	6.4	34,310	56.9	0.3	2,709,381
Alabama	24	0.5	211	0.6	9	6.2	29,242	53.8	0.3	2,242,167
Wisconsin	18	0.4	84	0.2	5	2.7	31,774	15.5	0.1	858,944
Kentucky	7	0.2	67	0.2	10	1.8	27,164	14.6	0.1	2,092,000
Utah	17	0.4	60	0.2	4	1.6	27,500	13.5	0.1	796,353
Nevada	9	0.2	37	0.1	4	1.2	32,946	11.8	0.1	1,307,889
Vermont	4	0.1	61	0.2	15	1.6	25,787	9.8	0.1	2,442,750
New Mexico	6	0.1	31	0.1	5	0.8	26,581	5.1	-	857,833
New Hampshire	6	0.1	10	-	2	0.2	20,100	2.2	-	370,000
Montana	4	0.1	13	-	3	0.2	13,846	0.8	-	201,250
South Dakota	4	0.1	5	-	1	0.1	11,600	0.4	-	88,000
Illinois	132	3.0	1000-2499	-	-	(D)	-	(D)	-	-
Massachusetts	80	1.8	500-999	-	-	(D)	-	(D)	-	-
Michigan	52	1.2	500-999	-	-	(D)	-	(D)	-	-
Washington	51	1.2	250-499	-	-	(D)	-	(D)	-	-
Minnesota	38	0.9	250-499	-	-	(D)	-	(D)	-	-
Mississippi	29	0.7	250-499	-	-	(D)	-	(D)	-	-
Indiana	27	0.6	250-499	-	-	(D)	-	(D)	-	-
Maryland	24	0.5	100-249	-	-	(D)	-	(D)	-	-
Oklahoma	21	0.5	250-499	-	-	(D)	-	(D)	-	-
Rhode Island	21	0.5	250-499	-	-	(D)	-	(D)	-	-
Connecticut	19	0.4	100-249	-	-	(D)	-	(D)	-	-
Louisiana	17	0.4	250-499	-	-	(D)	-	(D)	-	-
Kansas	14	0.3	20-99	-	-	(D)	-	(D)	-	-
Arkansas	13	0.3	20-99	-	-	(D)	-	(D)	-	-
Iowa	12	0.3	100-249	-	-	(D)	-	(D)	-	-
D.C.	11	0.2	20-99	-	-	(D)	-	(D)	-	-
Nebraska	8	0.2	20-99	-	-	(D)	-	(D)	-	-
Delaware	6	0.1	20-99	-	-	(D)	-	(D)	-	-
West Virginia	6	0.1	0-19	-	-	(D)	-	(D)	-	-
Maine	4	0.1	0-19	-	-	(D)	-	(D)	-	-
Idaho	2	-	0-19	-	-	(D)	-	(D)	-	-
North Dakota	2	-	0-19	-	-	(D)	-	(D)	-	-
Alaska	1	-	0-19	-	-	(D)	-	(D)	-	-
Wyoming	1	-	0-19	-	-	(D)	-	(D)	-	-

Source: 2002 *Economic Census*. The states are in descending order of sales or establishments (if sales data are missing for the majority). The symbol (D) appears when data are withheld to prevent disclosure of competitive information. States marked with (D) are sorted by number of establishments. A dash (-) indicates that the data element cannot be calculated. Shaded *states* on the state map indicate those states which have proportionately greater representation in the industry than would be indicated by the states population; the ratio is based on total sales or number of establishments. Shaded *regions* indicate where the industry is regionally most concentrated.

NAICS 424320 - MEN'S AND BOYS' CLOTHING AND FURNISHINGS MERCHANT WHOLESALERS*

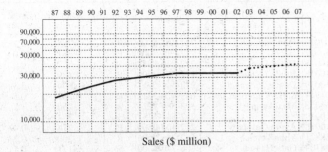

Sales ($ million)

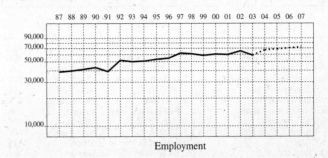

Employment

GENERAL STATISTICS

Year	Establishments (number)	Employment (number)	Payroll ($ million)	Sales ($ million)	Employees per Establishment (number)	Sales per Establishment ($)	Payroll per Employee ($)
1987	3,311	38,773	939.4	18,235.0	11.7	5,507,399.6	24,228.2
1988	2,954	39,894	1,047.5	20,220.5 e	13.5	6,845,125.3	26,257.1
1989	2,760	41,393	1,169.4	22,206.1 e	15.0	8,045,688.4	28,251.2
1990	2,765	43,271	1,194.9	24,191.6 e	15.6	8,749,222.4	27,614.3
1991	2,658	39,150	1,172.8	26,177.2 e	14.7	9,848,457.5	29,956.6
1992	4,620	51,908	1,527.2	28,162.7	11.2	6,095,822.5	29,421.3
1993	4,368	50,000	1,530.2	29,202.2 e	11.4	6,685,485.3	30,604.0
1994	4,312	50,764	1,607.9	30,241.7 e	11.8	7,013,381.3	31,674.0
1995	4,136	53,310	1,675.9	31,281.3 e	12.9	7,563,177.0	31,436.9
1996	4,285 e	54,889 e	1,772.1 e	32,320.8 e	12.8 e	7,542,777.1 e	32,285.2 e
1997	5,006	62,253	2,166.2	33,360.3	12.4	6,664,063.1	34,796.7
1998	4,894	61,105	2,249.5	33,348.9 e	12.5	6,814,250.1	36,813.7
1999	4,769	58,641	2,172.8	33,337.6 e	12.3	6,990,476.0	37,052.6
2000	4,628	60,632	2,383.0	33,326.2 e	13.1	7,200,998.3	39,302.8
2001	4,465	59,912	2,330.2	33,314.9 e	13.4	7,461,334.8	38,893.0
2002	4,473	65,580	2,388.8	33,303.5	14.7	7,445,450.5	36,425.7
2003	4,317	58,904	2,442.8	37,482.8 p	13.6	7,238,126.8 p	41,470.8
2004	5,118 p	67,220 p	2,676.0 p	38,493.8 p	13.1 p	7,233,251.2 p	41,358.7 p
2005	5,237 p	68,869 p	2,778.8 p	39,504.8 p	13.1 p	7,228,375.7 p	42,317.0 p
2006	5,357 p	70,519 p	2,881.5 p	40,515.8 p	13.1 p	7,223,500.1 p	43,275.3 p
2007	5,476 p	72,168 p	2,984.3 p	41,526.8 p	13.1 p	7,218,624.5 p	44,233.5 p

Sources: Economic Census of the United States, 1987, 1992, 1997, and 2002. Establishment counts, employment, and payroll are from *County Business Patterns* for non-Census years. Values followed by a 'p' are projections by the editors. Sales data for non-Census years are extrapolations, marked by 'e'. Data are the most recent available at this level of detail.

INDICES OF CHANGE

Year	Establishments (number)	Employment (number)	Payroll ($ million)	Sales ($ million)	Employees per Establishment (number)	Sales per Establishment ($)	Payroll per Employee ($)
1987	74.0	59.1	39.3	54.8	79.6	74.0	66.5
1992	103.3	79.2	63.9	84.6	76.2	81.9	80.8
1993	97.7	76.2	64.1	87.7 e	77.6	89.8	84.0
1994	96.4	77.4	67.3	90.8 e	80.3	94.2	87.0
1995	92.5	81.3	70.2	93.9 e	87.8	101.6	86.3
1996	95.8 e	83.7 e	74.2 e	97.0 e	87.1 e	101.3 e	88.6 e
1997	111.9	94.9	90.7	100.2	84.4	89.5	95.5
1998	109.4	93.2	94.2	100.1 e	85.0	91.5	101.1
1999	106.6	89.4	91.0	100.1 e	83.7	93.9	101.7
2000	103.5	92.5	99.8	100.1 e	89.1	96.7	107.9
2001	99.8	91.4	97.5	100.0 e	91.2	100.2	106.8
2002	100.0	100.0	100.0	100.0	100.0	100.0	100.0
2003	96.5	89.8	102.3	112.5 p	92.8	97.2 p	113.9
2004	114.4 p	102.5 p	112.0 p	115.6 p	89.0 p	97.1 p	113.5 p
2005	117.1 p	105.0 p	116.3 p	118.6 p	89.0 p	97.1 p	116.2 p
2006	119.8 p	107.5 p	120.6 p	121.7 p	88.9 p	97.0 p	118.8 p
2007	122.4 p	110.0 p	124.9 p	124.7 p	88.9 p	97.0 p	121.4 p

Sources: Same as General Statistics. The values shown reflect change from the base year, 2002. Values above 100 mean greater than 2002, values below 100 mean less than 2002, and a value of 100 in the 1987-2001 or 2003-2007 period means same as 2002. Values followed by a 'p' are projections by the editors; 'e' stands for extrapolation. Data are the most recent available at this level of detail.

SELECTED RATIOS

For 2002	Avg. of All Wholesale	Analyzed Industry	Index	For 2002	Avg. of All Wholesale	Analyzed Industry	Index
Employees per Establishment	15	15	98	Sales per Employee	791,325	507,830	64
Payroll per Establishment	626,122	534,049	85	Sales per Establishment	12,012,387	7,445,450	62
Payroll per Employee	41,161	36,426	88	Expenses per Establishment	na	na	na

Sources: Same as General Statistics. The 'Average of All' column, Wholesale or Retail, represents the average of the sector reported for the most recent complete year available. The Index shows the relationship between the Average and the Analyzed Industry. For example, 100 means that they are equal; 500 that the Analyzed Industry is five times the average; 50 means that the Analyzed Industry is half the national average. The abbreviation 'na' is used to show that data are 'not available'.

*Equivalent to SIC 5136.

LEADING COMPANIES   Number shown: **40**   Total sales ($ mil): **12,562**   Total employment (000): **40.6**

Company Name	Address				CEO Name	Phone	Co. Type	Sales ($ mil)	Empl. (000)
Reebok International Ltd.	100 Tech Center	Stoughton	MA	02072	Paul Fireman	781-401-5000	P	3,785	9.1
Polo Ralph Lauren Corp.	650 Madison Ave	New York	NY	10022		212-318-7000	P	2,381	13.0
Tommy Hilfiger USA Inc.	25 W 39th St, Fl 11	New York	NY	10018	David Dyer	212-840-8888	S	1,877	0.0
Phillips-Van Heusen Corp.	200 Madison Ave	New York	NY	10016	Bruce J Klatsky	212-381-3500	P	1,439	9.0
Nautica Enterprises Inc.	40 W 57th St	New York	NY	10019	Denise V Seegal	212-541-5757	S	694*	3.3
American Fashion Inc.	642 Arizona St	Chula Vista	CA	91911	Steve Kurtzman	619-426-1212	R	282*	0.5
BCBG Max Azria Group	2761 Fruitland Ave	Vernon	CA	90058	Max Azrie	323-589-2224	R	250*	1.2
Nautica International Inc.	40 West 57th St	New York	NY	10019		212-541-5757	S	234*	0.2
G-III Apparel Group Ltd.	512 7th Ave	New York	NY	10018	Aaron Goldfarb	212-403-0500	P	214	0.4
Block Corp.	901 Main St S	Amory	MS	38821	Mike Turcich	662-256-2606	R	200*	0.3
Pacific Trail Inc.	1700 Westlake N	Seattle	WA	98109	Gary Hansen	206-270-5300	S	171*	0.1
Royce Hosiery L.L.C.	PO Box 497	Martinsburg	WV	25402		304-263-8961	R	157*	0.3
Amerex Group Inc.	350 5th Ave	New York	NY	10118	Glenn Palmer	212-967-3000	R	148*	0.3
Broder Brothers Co.	45555 Port St	Plymouth	MI	48170	Vince Tyra	734-454-4800	R	145*	0.3
Alba-Waldensian Inc.	PO Box 100	Valdese	NC	28690	Lee N Mortersen	828-879-6500	S	75*	0.8
Everlast Worldwide Inc.	1350 Broadway	New York	NY	10018	George Q Horowitz	212-239-0990	P	58	0.2
Grandoe Corp.	PO Box 713	Gloversville	NY	12078	Eric Friedman	518-725-8641	R	54*	0.3
Scope Imports Inc.	8020 Blankenship	Houston	TX	77055	Allan Finkelman	713-688-0077	R	50*	<0.1
Wise El Santo Company Inc.	PO Box 8360	St. Louis	MO	63132	Rudolph L Wise	314-428-3100	R	50*	0.1
Sutton Group	1407 Brdway Fl 30	New York	NY	10018	Sam Sutton	212-391-6900	R	38*	<0.1
Kubic Marketing Inc.	225 S Aviation Blvd	El Segundo	CA	90245	Bob Sayre	310-297-1600	R	25*	<0.1
Jim's Formal Wear Co.	1 Tuxedo Park	Trenton	IL	62293	Gary Davis	618-224-9211	R	22*	0.3
Kolon America Inc.	525 7th Ave	New York	NY	10118	Lee Woong-Yeul	646-366-1430	R	22*	<0.1
Robin International USA Inc.	32 W 33rd St	New York	NY	10001	Howard Davidson	212-967-6800	R	19*	<0.1
Berne Apparel Inc.	PO Box 387	New Haven	IN	46774	Ronald Nussbaum	260-469-3136	R	17*	<0.1
Tyr Sport Inc.	PO Box 1930	Huntington Bch	CA	92647	Steve Furniss	714-897-0799	R	17*	<0.1
Ameri-Tech Distributing Inc.	5201 El Paso Dr	El Paso	TX	79905	Alfred Fernandez	915-772-9871	R	16*	0.1
Gateway CDI	909 N 20th St	Saint Louis	MO	63106	Chuck Fandos	314-535-1888	R	14*	0.2
Heyman Corp.	375 N Fairway Dr	Vernon Hills	IL	60061	Lawrence Heyman	847-247-0909	R	14*	0.1
Global Technology Group Ltd.	206 E 38th St Fl 2	New York	NY	10016	Simas Velonskis	212-490-2186	R	14*	<0.1
Zeiger Enterprises Inc.	621 Prospect St	Trenton	NJ	08618	Shelly Zeiger	609-394-1000	R	13*	<0.1
Ocean Pacific Apparel Corp.	3 Studebaker	Irvine	CA	92618	Dick Baker	949-580-1888	R	12*	<0.1
Gem-Dandy Inc.	PO Box 657	Madison	NC	27025		336-548-9624	R	11*	<0.1
Julius Kraft Company Inc.	PO Box 918	Auburn	NY	13021	Kim Vorreuter	315-252-7251	R	11*	<0.1
Cmn Inc.	14015 24 Mile Rd	Shelby	MI	48315	Mikulas Kuzdak	586-677-7954	R	11*	<0.1
Cotton Scrubs and Co.	1370 Welsh Rd	North Wales	PA	19454	Bob Shoenfeld	215-643-9666	R	10*	0.2
Queens City LaCrosse Co.	625 Washington Ave	Bridgeville	PA	15017	Gary Neft	412-257-4120	R	4*	<0.1
Larry Pokras	7351 Heil Ave Ste L	Huntington Bch	CA	92647	Lawrance Pokras	714-841-3838	R	3*	<0.1
International Waters	989 Av Americas	New York	NY	10018	Chandresh Mehta	212-564-3099	D	3*	<0.1
Foremost Athletic Apparel	1307 E Maple Rd	Troy	MI	48083	John G Levy	248-689-3850	R	1*	<0.1

Source: *Ward's Business Directory of U.S. Private and Public Companies*, Volumes 1 and 2, 2005. The company type code used is as follows: P - Public, R - Private, S - Subsidiary, D - Division, J - Joint Venture, A - Affiliate, G - Group. Sales are in millions of dollars, employees are in thousands. An asterisk (*) indicates an estimated sales volume. The symbol < stands for 'less than'. Company names and addresses are truncated, in some cases, to fit into the available space.

OCCUPATIONS EMPLOYED BY APPAREL, PIECE GOODS, & NOTIONS WHOLESALE

Occupation	% of Total 2004	Change to 2014	Occupation	% of Total 2004	Change to 2014
Sales reps, wholesale & manufacturing, exc tech	15.5	4.0	Wholesale & retail buyers, except farm products	1.9	-1.6
Laborers & freight, stock, & material movers, hand	10.6	-6.4	First-line supervisors/managers of non-retail sales work	1.9	-3.8
Shipping, receiving, & traffic clerks	5.5	-5.8	Order clerks	1.8	-32.4
Stock clerks & order fillers	5.4	-20.3	First-line supervisors/managers of office workers	1.6	-5.7
Retail salespersons	3.9	4.0	Sewing machine operators	1.6	4.0
Packers & packagers, hand	3.8	4.0	Inspectors, testers, sorters, samplers, & weighers	1.4	-1.5
Customer service representatives	3.5	6.5	Accountants & auditors	1.3	4.0
Office clerks, general	3.5	-7.4	Secretaries, except legal, medical, & executive	1.3	-12.5
Fashion designers	2.8	33.9	Production, planning, & expediting clerks	1.1	2.9
Bookkeeping, accounting, & auditing clerks	2.5	-6.4	Industrial truck & tractor operators	1.0	4.0
General & operations managers	2.3	2.9			

Source: *Industry-Occupation Matrix*, Bureau of Labor Statistics. These data are reported based on 4-digit NAICS categories but have been matched to corresponding 6-digit NAICS industry codes. The change reported for each occupation to the year 2014 is a percent of growth or decline as estimated by the Bureau of Labor Statistics. The abbreviation nec stands for 'not elsewhere classified.'

LOCATION BY STATE AND REGIONAL CONCENTRATION

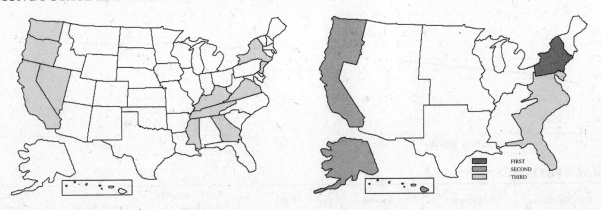

INDUSTRY DATA BY STATE

State	Establishments Total (number)	% of U.S.	Employment Total (number)	% of U.S.	Per Estab.	Payroll Total ($ mil.)	Per Empl. ($)	Sales Total ($ mil.)	% of U.S.	Per Estab. ($)
New York	894	20.0	9,771	14.8	11	483.2	49,449	6,992.1	20.5	7,821,122
California	999	22.3	10,822	16.4	11	377.1	34,845	4,851.0	14.2	4,855,862
New Jersey	272	6.1	4,184	6.3	15	226.6	54,148	2,545.0	7.5	9,356,665
Kentucky	28	0.6	639	1.0	23	18.4	28,746	1,582.3	4.6	56,512,071
Virginia	69	1.5	2,555	3.9	37	66.6	26,072	1,532.3	4.5	22,206,928
Texas	228	5.1	3,639	5.5	16	126.3	34,702	1,416.3	4.2	6,212,013
Tennessee	64	1.4	1,807	2.7	28	50.2	27,778	1,267.0	3.7	19,796,203
Florida	269	6.0	3,574	5.4	13	115.0	32,164	1,243.0	3.7	4,620,944
Pennsylvania	114	2.5	2,365	3.6	21	91.0	38,457	1,227.5	3.6	10,767,614
Georgia	140	3.1	1,951	2.9	14	67.1	34,384	1,056.3	3.1	7,545,293
Washington	77	1.7	2,145	3.2	28	73.7	34,364	983.9	2.9	12,777,351
North Carolina	113	2.5	2,081	3.1	18	59.6	28,618	851.0	2.5	7,530,628
Oregon	35	0.8	684	1.0	20	37.2	54,415	632.9	1.9	18,082,314
Ohio	88	2.0	1,627	2.5	18	54.5	33,501	579.8	1.7	6,588,557
Mississippi	20	0.4	537	0.8	27	13.1	24,387	482.1	1.4	24,103,000
Colorado	68	1.5	741	1.1	11	32.1	43,321	330.5	1.0	4,860,544
South Carolina	40	0.9	807	1.2	20	18.2	22,511	329.0	1.0	8,225,425
Nevada	24	0.5	589	0.9	25	24.0	40,723	247.9	0.7	10,327,125
Maryland	51	1.1	879	1.3	17	35.3	40,117	190.0	0.6	3,725,647
Wisconsin	39	0.9	717	1.1	18	21.7	30,213	184.6	0.5	4,732,718
Kansas	29	0.6	458	0.7	16	12.7	27,657	133.6	0.4	4,605,828
Indiana	47	1.1	451	0.7	10	10.7	23,736	122.4	0.4	2,605,043
Hawaii	49	1.1	371	0.6	8	10.6	28,660	111.1	0.3	2,266,959
Louisiana	31	0.7	330	0.5	11	8.0	24,152	68.9	0.2	2,223,032
Vermont	10	0.2	293	0.4	29	12.7	43,338	60.8	0.2	6,083,600
Oklahoma	18	0.4	144	0.2	8	3.9	27,028	44.8	0.1	2,489,056
Iowa	21	0.5	307	0.5	15	6.9	22,573	32.6	0.1	1,553,381
Montana	12	0.3	62	0.1	5	2.4	38,016	29.4	0.1	2,446,167
Idaho	13	0.3	101	0.2	8	2.5	25,050	27.9	0.1	2,146,538
New Hampshire	12	0.3	137	0.2	11	4.0	29,314	25.3	0.1	2,110,000
New Mexico	9	0.2	27	-	3	0.7	26,148	3.9	-	429,000
North Dakota	3	0.1	19	-	6	0.2	11,000	0.8	-	256,000
Illinois	120	2.7	1000-2499	-	-	(D)	-	(D)	-	-
Massachusetts	68	1.5	500-999	-	-	(D)	-	(D)	-	-
Michigan	64	1.4	1000-2499	-	-	(D)	-	(D)	-	-
Minnesota	58	1.3	500-999	-	-	(D)	-	(D)	-	-
Arizona	52	1.2	250-499	-	-	(D)	-	(D)	-	-
Missouri	51	1.1	1000-2499	-	-	(D)	-	(D)	-	-
Connecticut	43	1.0	250-499	-	-	(D)	-	(D)	-	-
Alabama	38	0.8	2500-4999	-	-	(D)	-	(D)	-	-
Utah	35	0.8	250-499	-	-	(D)	-	(D)	-	-
Arkansas	13	0.3	500-999	-	-	(D)	-	(D)	-	-
Delaware	9	0.2	20-99	-	-	(D)	-	(D)	-	-
West Virginia	9	0.2	20-99	-	-	(D)	-	(D)	-	-
Maine	6	0.1	20-99	-	-	(D)	-	(D)	-	-
Nebraska	6	0.1	20-99	-	-	(D)	-	(D)	-	-
Rhode Island	6	0.1	20-99	-	-	(D)	-	(D)	-	-
D.C.	4	0.1	20-99	-	-	(D)	-	(D)	-	-
Alaska	2	-	0-19	-	-	(D)	-	(D)	-	-
South Dakota	1	-	0-19	-	-	(D)	-	(D)	-	-
Wyoming	1	-	0-19	-	-	(D)	-	(D)	-	-

Source: 2002 *Economic Census*. The states are in descending order of sales or establishments (if sales data are missing for the majority). The symbol (D) appears when data are withheld to prevent disclosure of competitive information. States marked with (D) are sorted by number of establishments. A dash (-) indicates that the data element cannot be calculated. Shaded *states* on the state map indicate those states which have proportionately greater representation in the industry than would be indicated by the states population; the ratio is based on total sales or number of establishments. Shaded *regions* indicate where the industry is regionally most concentrated.

NAICS 424330 - WOMEN'S, CHILDREN'S, AND INFANTS' CLOTHING AND ACCESSORIES MERCHANT WHOLESALERS*

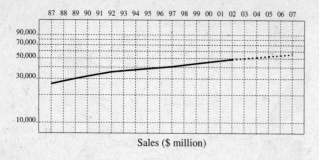

Sales ($ million)

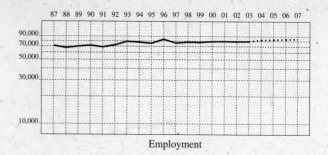

Employment

GENERAL STATISTICS

Year	Establishments (number)	Employment (number)	Payroll ($ million)	Sales ($ million)	Employees per Establishment (number)	Sales per Establishment ($)	Payroll per Employee ($)
1987	6,234	71,059	1,708.6	26,280.2	11.4	4,215,624.0	24,044.8
1988	5,538	67,385	1,799.4	28,123.3 e	12.2	5,078,241.2	26,703.3
1989	5,146	69,935	1,932.9	29,966.5 e	13.6	5,823,260.8	27,638.5
1990	5,194	71,639	2,070.7	31,809.6 e	13.8	6,124,297.3	28,904.6
1991	5,088	68,742	2,097.6	33,652.8 e	13.5	6,614,150.9	30,514.1
1992	7,581	72,485	2,384.5	35,495.9	9.6	4,682,218.7	32,896.5
1993	7,449	79,200	2,480.1	36,517.4 e	10.6	4,902,322.5	31,314.4
1994	7,446	77,736	2,548.0	37,538.9 e	10.4	5,041,485.4	32,777.6
1995	7,082	75,634	2,534.5	38,560.5 e	10.7	5,444,860.2	33,510.1
1996	7,496 e	83,717 e	2,857.7 e	39,582.0 e	11.2 e	5,280,416.2 e	34,135.2 e
1997	8,217	76,256	2,799.5	40,603.5	9.3	4,941,402.0	36,711.9
1998	8,263	78,116	2,953.8	42,236.0 e	9.5	5,111,455.9	37,813.0
1999	7,912	77,609	2,989.6	43,868.4 e	9.8	5,544,542.5	38,521.3
2000	7,824	79,373	3,212.9	45,500.9 e	10.1	5,815,552.1	40,478.6
2001	7,583	79,595	3,348.3	47,133.3 e	10.5	6,215,658.7	42,066.9
2002	7,182	79,158	3,578.8	48,765.8	11.0	6,790,002.8	45,210.8
2003	6,975	79,531	3,770.0	49,847.9 p	11.4	5,981,771.1 p	47,403.3
2004	8,280 p	82,317 p	3,740.2 p	51,259.2 p	9.7 p	6,041,203.7 p	46,209.8 p
2005	8,427 p	83,051 p	3,861.2 p	52,670.4 p	9.6 p	6,100,636.4 p	47,483.8 p
2006	8,575 p	83,784 p	3,982.2 p	54,081.7 p	9.4 p	6,160,069.1 p	48,757.8 p
2007	8,722 p	84,518 p	4,103.2 p	55,493.0 p	9.3 p	6,219,501.8 p	50,031.8 p

Sources: Economic Census of the United States, 1987, 1992, 1997, and 2002. Establishment counts, employment, and payroll are from County Business Patterns for non-Census years. Values followed by a 'p' are projections by the editors. Sales data for non-Census years are extrapolations, marked by 'e'. Data are the most recent available at this level of detail.

INDICES OF CHANGE

Year	Establishments (number)	Employment (number)	Payroll ($ million)	Sales ($ million)	Employees per Establishment (number)	Sales per Establishment ($)	Payroll per Employee ($)
1987	86.8	89.8	47.7	53.9	103.6	62.1	53.2
1992	105.6	91.6	66.6	72.8	87.3	69.0	72.8
1993	103.7	100.1	69.3	74.9 e	96.4	72.2	69.3
1994	103.7	98.2	71.2	77.0 e	94.5	74.2	72.5
1995	98.6	95.5	70.8	79.1 e	97.3	80.2	74.1
1996	104.4 e	105.8 e	79.9 e	81.2 e	101.8 e	77.8 e	75.5 e
1997	114.4	96.3	78.2	83.3	84.5	72.8	81.2
1998	115.1	98.7	82.5	86.6 e	86.4	75.3	83.6
1999	110.2	98.0	83.5	90.0 e	89.1	81.7	85.2
2000	108.9	100.3	89.8	93.3 e	91.8	85.6	89.5
2001	105.6	100.6	93.6	96.7 e	95.5	91.5	93.0
2002	100.0	100.0	100.0	100.0	100.0	100.0	100.0
2003	97.1	100.5	105.3	102.2 p	103.7	88.1 p	104.8
2004	115.3 p	104.0 p	104.5 p	105.1 p	88.3 p	89.0 p	102.2 p
2005	117.3 p	104.9 p	107.9 p	108.0 p	87.0 p	89.8 p	105.0 p
2006	119.4 p	105.8 p	111.3 p	110.9 p	85.6 p	90.7 p	107.8 p
2007	121.4 p	106.8 p	114.7 p	113.8 p	84.2 p	91.6 p	110.7 p

Sources: Same as General Statistics. The values shown reflect change from the base year, 2002. Values above 100 mean greater than 2002, values below 100 mean less than 2002, and a value of 100 in the 1987-2001 or 2003-2007 period means same as 2002. Values followed by a 'p' are projections by the editors; 'e' stands for extrapolation. Data are the most recent available at this level of detail.

SELECTED RATIOS

For 2002	Avg. of All Wholesale	Analyzed Industry	Index	For 2002	Avg. of All Wholesale	Analyzed Industry	Index
Employees per Establishment	15	11	74	Sales per Employee	791,325	616,056	78
Payroll per Establishment	626,122	498,301	80	Sales per Establishment	12,012,387	6,790,003	57
Payroll per Employee	41,161	45,211	110	Expenses per Establishment	na	na	na

Sources: Same as General Statistics. The 'Average of All' column, Wholesale or Retail, represents the average of the sector reported for the most recent complete year available. The Index shows the relationship between the Average and the Analyzed Industry. For example, 100 means that they are equal; 500 that the Analyzed Industry is five times the average; 50 means that the Analyzed Industry is half the national average. The abbreviation 'na' is used to show that data are 'not available'.

*Equivalent to SIC 5137.

LEADING COMPANIES   Number shown: **40**   Total sales ($ mil): **24,210**   Total employment (000): **147.8**

Company Name	Address				CEO Name	Phone	Co. Type	Sales ($ mil)	Empl. (000)
May Department Stores Co.	611 Olive St	St. Louis	MO	63101		314-342-6300	P	14,441	110.0
Reebok International Ltd.	100 Tech Center	Stoughton	MA	02072	Paul Fireman	781-401-5000	P	3,785	9.1
Polo Ralph Lauren Corp.	650 Madison Ave	New York	NY	10022		212-318-7000	P	2,381	13.0
Phillips-Van Heusen Corp.	200 Madison Ave	New York	NY	10016	Bruce J Klatsky	212-381-3500	P	1,439	9.0
Syms Corp.	1 Syms Way	Secaucus	NJ	07094		201-902-9600	P	284	1.8
BCBG Max Azria Group	2761 Fruitland Ave	Vernon	CA	90058	Max Azrie	323-589-2224	R	250*	1.2
G-III Apparel Group Ltd.	512 7th Ave	New York	NY	10018	Aaron Goldfarb	212-403-0500	P	214	0.4
Pacific Trail Inc.	1700 Westlake N	Seattle	WA	98109	Gary Hansen	206-270-5300	S	171*	0.1
Royce Hosiery L.L.C.	PO Box 497	Martinsburg	WV	25402		304-263-8961	R	157*	0.3
Amerex Group Inc.	350 5th Ave	New York	NY	10118	Glenn Palmer	212-967-3000	R	148*	0.3
Broder Brothers Co.	45555 Port St	Plymouth	MI	48170	Vince Tyra	734-454-4800	R	145*	0.3
Delta Galil USA	500 Plz Dr Ste 200	Secaucus	NJ	07094	Norton Sloan	201-392-8929	R	113*	0.2
Cayset Fashions Ltd.	111 Port Jersey Blvd	Jersey City	NJ	07305	Richard Selman	201-432-3839	R	77*	0.1
Everlast Worldwide Inc.	1350 Broadway	New York	NY	10018	George Q Horowitz	212-239-0990	P	58	0.2
Asia Easyfine Ltd.	431 E Tioga St	Philadelphia	PA	19134	Peter Sheintoch	215-739-0200	R	56*	0.1
Grandoe Corp.	PO Box 713	Gloversville	NY	12078	Eric Friedman	518-725-8641	R	54*	0.3
Movie Star Inc.	1115 Broadway	New York	NY	10010	Melvyn Knigin	212-684-3400	P	54	0.3
French Toast	100 W 33rd St	New York	NY	10001	Samuel Gindi	212-594-4740	R	40*	<0.1
Sutton Group	1407 Brdway Fl 30	New York	NY	10018	Sam Sutton	212-391-6900	R	38*	<0.1
Nitches Inc.	10280 Santa Fe	San Diego	CA	92121	Paul M Wyandt	858-625-2633	P	32	<0.1
Celebrity International Inc.	100 W 33rd St	New York	NY	10001	Morris Matalon	212-279-1616	R	27*	<0.1
North Shore Sportswear Inc.	50 Dickson St	Glen Cove	NY	11542	Stephen Bass	516-671-4390	R	25*	<0.1
Topsville Inc.	11800 NW 102nd	Medley	FL	33178	Mark Nitzberg	305-883-8677	S	23*	<0.1
Robin International USA Inc.	32 W 33rd St	New York	NY	10001	Howard Davidson	212-967-6800	R	19*	<0.1
Inter-Pacific Corp.	2257 Colby Ave	Los Angeles	CA	90064	Frank Arnsteine	310-473-7591	R	18*	<0.1
G and A Trading Co.	13260 Temple Ave	City of Industry	CA	91746	Roger Yang	626-961-6006	R	16*	<0.1
Accessory Exchange L.L.C.	1 E 33rd St Fl 6	New York	NY	10016		212-931-5000	R	16*	<0.1
Alfa Travelgear Inc.	1538 Knowles Ave	Los Angeles	CA	90063	Kin Ng	323-981-8686	R	15*	<0.1
M. Foster Associates Inc.	PO Box 420468	Dallas	TX	75342	Bonnye N Sherman	214-631-7732	R	15*	<0.1
Heyman Corp.	375 N Fairway Dr	Vernon Hills	IL	60061	Lawrence Heyman	847-247-0909	R	14*	0.1
Global Technology Group Ltd.	206 E 38th St Fl 2	New York	NY	10016	Simas Velonskis	212-490-2186	R	14*	<0.1
Tahari Ltd.	16 Bleeker St	Millburn	NJ	07041	Elie Tahari	973-258-1777	R	13*	0.2
Zeiger Enterprises Inc.	621 Prospect St	Trenton	NJ	08618	Shelly Zeiger	609-394-1000	R	13*	<0.1
Ocean Pacific Apparel Corp.	3 Studebaker	Irvine	CA	92618	Dick Baker	949-580-1888	R	12*	<0.1
Cmn Inc.	14015 24 Mile Rd	Shelby	MI	48315	Mikulas Kuzdak	586-677-7954	R	11*	<0.1
Cotton Scrubs and Co.	1370 Welsh Rd	North Wales	PA	19454	Bob Shoenfeld	215-643-9666	R	10*	0.2
Accesories That Matter	320 5th Ave	New York	NY	10001	Roy Kean	212-947-3012	R	4*	<0.1
Queens City LaCrosse Co.	625 Washington Ave	Bridgeville	PA	15017	Gary Neft	412-257-4120	R	4*	<0.1
International Waters	989 Av Americas	New York	NY	10018	Chandresh Mehta	212-564-3099	D	3*	<0.1
Foremost Athletic Apparel	1307 E Maple Rd	Troy	MI	48083	John G Levy	248-689-3850	R	1*	<0.1

Source: Ward's Business Directory of U.S. Private and Public Companies, Volumes 1 and 2, 2005. The company type code used is as follows: P - Public, R - Private, S - Subsidiary, D - Division, J - Joint Venture, A - Affiliate, G - Group. Sales are in millions of dollars, employees are in thousands. An asterisk (*) indicates an estimated sales volume. The symbol < stands for 'less than'. Company names and addresses are truncated, in some cases, to fit into the available space.

OCCUPATIONS EMPLOYED BY APPAREL, PIECE GOODS, & NOTIONS WHOLESALE

Occupation	% of Total 2004	Change to 2014	Occupation	% of Total 2004	Change to 2014
Sales reps, wholesale & manufacturing, exc tech	15.5	4.0	Wholesale & retail buyers, except farm products	1.9	-1.6
Laborers & freight, stock, & material movers, hand	10.6	-6.4	First-line supervisors/managers of non-retail sales work	1.9	-3.8
Shipping, receiving, & traffic clerks	5.5	-5.8	Order clerks	1.8	-32.4
Stock clerks & order fillers	5.4	-20.3	First-line supervisors/managers of office workers	1.6	-5.7
Retail salespersons	3.9	4.0	Sewing machine operators	1.6	4.0
Packers & packagers, hand	3.8	4.0	Inspectors, testers, sorters, samplers, & weighers	1.4	-1.5
Customer service representatives	3.5	6.5	Accountants & auditors	1.3	4.0
Office clerks, general	3.5	-7.4	Secretaries, except legal, medical, & executive	1.3	-12.5
Fashion designers	2.8	33.9	Production, planning, & expediting clerks	1.1	2.9
Bookkeeping, accounting, & auditing clerks	2.5	-6.4	Industrial truck & tractor operators	1.0	4.0
General & operations managers	2.3	2.9			

Source: Industry-Occupation Matrix, Bureau of Labor Statistics. These data are reported based on 4-digit NAICS categories but have been matched to corresponding 6-digit NAICS industry codes. The change reported for each occupation to the year 2014 is a percent of growth or decline as estimated by the Bureau of Labor Statistics. The abbreviation nec stands for 'not elsewhere classified.'

LOCATION BY STATE AND REGIONAL CONCENTRATION

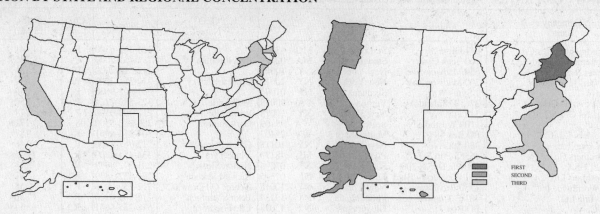

INDUSTRY DATA BY STATE

State	Establishments Total (number)	Establishments % of U.S.	Employment Total (number)	Employment % of U.S.	Employment Per Estab.	Payroll Total ($ mil.)	Payroll Per Empl. ($)	Sales Total ($ mil.)	Sales % of U.S.	Sales Per Estab. ($)
New York	2,323	32.5	31,390	39.6	14	1,828.7	58,258	24,711.0	52.8	10,637,529
California	1,865	26.1	18,957	23.9	10	643.8	33,963	7,568.7	16.2	4,058,280
New Jersey	381	5.3	7,554	9.5	20	356.5	47,195	4,110.2	8.8	10,787,940
Massachusetts	110	1.5	1,449	1.8	13	75.2	51,916	1,987.2	4.2	18,065,500
Florida	562	7.9	2,867	3.6	5	84.0	29,306	1,834.9	3.9	3,264,996
Texas	299	4.2	2,813	3.6	9	86.1	30,604	865.1	1.8	2,893,201
North Carolina	95	1.3	1,027	1.3	11	33.9	32,966	858.9	1.8	9,041,126
Pennsylvania	126	1.8	1,296	1.6	10	46.9	36,188	515.8	1.1	4,093,579
Ohio	67	0.9	2,143	2.7	32	72.5	33,820	507.4	1.1	7,573,373
Kentucky	18	0.3	308	0.4	17	9.6	31,185	363.4	0.8	20,190,167
South Carolina	45	0.6	595	0.8	13	16.9	28,329	306.1	0.7	6,801,622
Colorado	71	1.0	385	0.5	5	16.3	42,283	188.8	0.4	2,659,113
Washington	64	0.9	313	0.4	5	12.2	39,006	139.5	0.3	2,178,984
Rhode Island	14	0.2	129	0.2	9	6.4	49,814	121.3	0.3	8,664,786
Tennessee	54	0.8	331	0.4	6	6.0	18,106	107.6	0.2	1,993,167
Minnesota	46	0.6	368	0.5	8	17.9	48,720	101.6	0.2	2,207,826
Virginia	49	0.7	202	0.3	4	5.6	27,851	80.8	0.2	1,648,143
Nevada	28	0.4	214	0.3	8	5.2	24,355	71.0	0.2	2,537,000
Louisiana	26	0.4	356	0.4	14	7.4	20,851	69.5	0.1	2,672,500
Alabama	30	0.4	173	0.2	6	4.0	23,341	65.6	0.1	2,185,033
Oregon	30	0.4	140	0.2	5	6.9	49,521	59.6	0.1	1,987,833
Wisconsin	27	0.4	161	0.2	6	4.5	27,839	56.5	0.1	2,091,556
Indiana	28	0.4	237	0.3	8	6.7	28,097	50.0	0.1	1,784,357
Utah	27	0.4	179	0.2	7	6.3	35,229	41.1	0.1	1,523,556
Hawaii	48	0.7	150	0.2	3	4.3	28,613	35.6	0.1	741,375
Vermont	8	0.1	98	0.1	12	3.3	33,888	20.1	-	2,508,625
Wyoming	6	0.1	44	0.1	7	1.3	29,295	10.6	-	1,763,833
New Hampshire	16	0.2	57	0.1	4	1.4	24,246	9.2	-	577,062
Idaho	5	0.1	22	-	4	0.3	13,636	2.3	-	468,000
Illinois	167	2.3	1000-2499	-	-	(D)	-	(D)	-	-
Georgia	134	1.9	500-999	-	-	(D)	-	(D)	-	-
Michigan	51	0.7	100-249	-	-	(D)	-	(D)	-	-
Arizona	49	0.7	250-499	-	-	(D)	-	(D)	-	-
Missouri	47	0.7	250-499	-	-	(D)	-	(D)	-	-
Connecticut	46	0.6	500-999	-	-	(D)	-	(D)	-	-
Maryland	46	0.6	250-499	-	-	(D)	-	(D)	-	-
Arkansas	19	0.3	20-99	-	-	(D)	-	(D)	-	-
Oklahoma	17	0.2	20-99	-	-	(D)	-	(D)	-	-
Mississippi	13	0.2	20-99	-	-	(D)	-	(D)	-	-
Delaware	12	0.2	100-249	-	-	(D)	-	(D)	-	-
Nebraska	12	0.2	100-249	-	-	(D)	-	(D)	-	-
Kansas	10	0.1	100-249	-	-	(D)	-	(D)	-	-
Maine	10	0.1	20-99	-	-	(D)	-	(D)	-	-
D.C.	9	0.1	20-99	-	-	(D)	-	(D)	-	-
Iowa	8	0.1	20-99	-	-	(D)	-	(D)	-	-
Montana	7	0.1	0-19	-	-	(D)	-	(D)	-	-
New Mexico	7	0.1	0-19	-	-	(D)	-	(D)	-	-
South Dakota	4	0.1	0-19	-	-	(D)	-	(D)	-	-
Alaska	3	-	0-19	-	-	(D)	-	(D)	-	-
North Dakota	3	-	0-19	-	-	(D)	-	(D)	-	-
West Virginia	2	-	20-99	-	-	(D)	-	(D)	-	-

Source: 2002 *Economic Census*. The states are in descending order of sales or establishments (if sales data are missing for the majority). The symbol (D) appears when data are withheld to prevent disclosure of competitive information. States marked with (D) are sorted by number of establishments. A dash (-) indicates that the data element cannot be calculated. Shaded *states* on the state map indicate those states which have proportionately greater representation in the industry than would be indicated by the states population; the ratio is based on total sales or number of establishments. Shaded *regions* indicate where the industry is regionally most concentrated.

NAICS 424340 - FOOTWEAR MERCHANT WHOLESALERS*

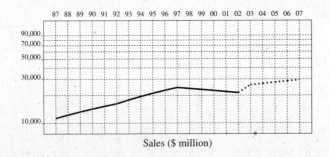

Sales ($ million)

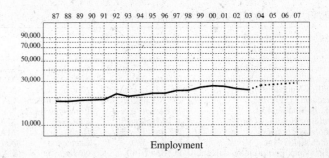

Employment

GENERAL STATISTICS

Year	Establishments (number)	Employment (number)	Payroll ($ million)	Sales ($ million)	Employees per Establishment (number)	Sales per Establishment ($)	Payroll per Employee ($)
1987	1,694	18,179	588.3	11,293.1	10.7	6,666,528.9	32,361.5
1988	1,535	18,103	610.3	12,284.9 e	11.8	8,003,192.2	33,712.6
1989	1,415	18,554	629.5	13,276.8 e	13.1	9,382,897.5	33,928.0
1990	1,386	18,775	702.6	14,268.7 e	13.5	10,294,877.3	37,422.1
1991	1,327	18,934	738.6	15,260.5 e	14.3	11,500,000.0	39,009.2
1992	1,712	21,826	880.2	16,252.4	12.7	9,493,224.3	40,328.0
1993	1,659	20,516	853.7	17,874.7 e	12.4	10,774,382.2	41,611.4
1994	1,665	21,191	947.1	19,496.9 e	12.7	11,709,849.8	44,693.5
1995	1,609	22,105	1,009.6	21,119.2 e	13.7	13,125,668.1	45,672.9
1996	1,629 e	22,101 e	1,027.0 e	22,741.4 e	13.6 e	13,960,343.8 e	46,468.5 e
1997	1,818	23,630	1,182.5	24,363.7	13.0	13,401,375.1	50,042.3
1998	1,745	23,748	1,339.8	23,758.0 e	13.6	13,614,911.2	56,417.4
1999	1,750	25,688	1,409.7	23,152.3 e	14.7	13,229,908.6	54,877.8
2000	1,773	26,592	1,473.0	22,546.7 e	15.0	12,716,672.3	55,391.4
2001	1,755	26,170	1,498.7	21,941.0 e	14.9	12,501,982.9	57,269.0
2002	1,728	24,753	1,301.6	21,335.3	14.3	12,346,817.1	52,583.5
2003	1,727	24,025	1,425.8	25,989.7 p	13.9	14,571,342.5 p	59,345.9
2004	1,812 p	26,862 p	1,596.8 p	26,834.3 p	14.9 p	14,942,069.3 p	61,572.1 p
2005	1,831 p	27,396 p	1,659.1 p	27,678.9 p	15.1 p	15,312,796.1 p	63,308.0 p
2006	1,849 p	27,930 p	1,721.3 p	28,523.5 p	15.2 p	15,683,523.0 p	65,043.9 p
2007	1,868 p	28,465 p	1,783.6 p	29,368.2 p	15.4 p	16,054,249.8 p	66,779.8 p

Sources: Economic Census of the United States, 1987, 1992, 1997, and 2002. Establishment counts, employment, and payroll are from *County Business Patterns* for non-Census years. Values followed by a 'p' are projections by the editors. Sales data for non-Census years are extrapolations, marked by 'e'. Data are the most recent available at this level of detail.

INDICES OF CHANGE

Year	Establishments (number)	Employment (number)	Payroll ($ million)	Sales ($ million)	Employees per Establishment (number)	Sales per Establishment ($)	Payroll per Employee ($)
1987	98.0	73.4	45.2	52.9	74.8	54.0	61.5
1992	99.1	88.2	67.6	76.2	88.8	76.9	76.7
1993	96.0	82.9	65.6	83.8 e	86.7	87.3	79.1
1994	96.4	85.6	72.8	91.4 e	88.8	94.8	85.0
1995	93.1	89.3	77.6	99.0 e	95.8	106.3	86.9
1996	94.3 e	89.3 e	78.9 e	106.6 e	95.1 e	113.1 e	88.4 e
1997	105.2	95.5	90.8	114.2	90.9	108.5	95.2
1998	101.0	95.9	102.9	111.4 e	95.1	110.3	107.3
1999	101.3	103.8	108.3	108.5 e	102.8	107.2	104.4
2000	102.6	107.4	113.2	105.7 e	104.9	103.0	105.3
2001	101.6	105.7	115.1	102.8 e	104.2	101.3	108.9
2002	100.0	100.0	100.0	100.0	100.0	100.0	100.0
2003	99.9	97.1	109.5	121.8 p	97.3	118.0 p	112.9
2004	104.8 p	108.5 p	122.7 p	125.8 p	104.2 p	121.0 p	117.1 p
2005	105.9 p	110.7 p	127.5 p	129.7 p	105.4 p	124.0 p	120.4 p
2006	107.0 p	112.8 p	132.2 p	133.7 p	106.6 p	127.0 p	123.7 p
2007	108.1 p	115.0 p	137.0 p	137.7 p	107.7 p	130.0 p	127.0 p

Sources: Same as General Statistics. The values shown reflect change from the base year, 2002. Values above 100 mean greater than 2002, values below 100 mean less than 2002, and a value of 100 in the 1987-2001 or 2003-2007 period means same as 2002. Values followed by a 'p' are projections by the editors; 'e' stands for extrapolation. Data are the most recent available at this level of detail.

SELECTED RATIOS

For 2002	Avg. of All Wholesale	Analyzed Industry	Index	For 2002	Avg. of All Wholesale	Analyzed Industry	Index
Employees per Establishment	15	14	96	Sales per Employee	791,325	861,928	109
Payroll per Establishment	626,122	753,241	120	Sales per Establishment	12,012,387	12,346,817	103
Payroll per Employee	41,161	52,584	128	Expenses per Establishment	na	na	na

Sources: Same as General Statistics. The 'Average of All' column, Wholesale or Retail, represents the average of the sector reported for the most recent complete year available. The Index shows the relationship between the Average and the Analyzed Industry. For example, 100 means that they are equal; 500 that the Analyzed Industry is five times the average; 50 means that the Analyzed Industry is half the national average. The abbreviation 'na' is used to show that data are 'not available'.

*Equivalent to SIC 5139.

LEADING COMPANIES   Number shown: **27**   Total sales ($ mil): **10,129**   Total employment (000): **37.1**

Company Name	Address				CEO Name	Phone	Co. Type	Sales ($ mil)	Empl. (000)
Reebok International Ltd.	100 Tech Center	Stoughton	MA	02072	Paul Fireman	781-401-5000	P	3,785	9.1
Brown Shoe Company Inc.	PO Box 29	St. Louis	MO	63166	Ronald A Fromm	314-854-4000	P	1,832	11.6
Phillips-Van Heusen Corp.	200 Madison Ave	New York	NY	10016	Bruce J Klatsky	212-381-3500	P	1,439	9.0
Skechers U.S.A. Inc.	228 Manhattan Bch	Manhattan Bch	CA	90266	Michael Greenberg	310-318-3100	P	920	2.6
Steven Madden Ltd.	16 Barnett Ave	Long Island City	NY	11104	Jamieson A Karson	718-446-1800	P	338	1.5
Spalding Holdings Corp.	425 Meadow St	Chicopee	MA	01021	James R Craigie	413-536-1200	R	287*	1.0
Mootsies Tootsies	PO Box 37	Boston	MA	02137	Mark J Cocozza	617-364-5090	S	225	0.1
Ballet Makers Inc.	PO Box 580	Exeter	NH	03833		603-772-5966	R	219*	0.2
Birkenstock Footprint Sandals Inc.	PO Box 6140	Novato	CA	94948	Margot Fraser	415-892-4200	R	189*	0.3
Hi-Tec Sports USA Inc.	4801 Stoddard Rd	Modesto	CA	95356	Paul Brooks	209-545-1111	R	188*	0.5
Jimlar Corp.	160 Great Neck Rd	Great Neck	NY	11021	Frank Vigonola	516-829-1717	R	137*	0.1
Candie's Inc.	215 W 40th St	New York	NY	10018	Neil Cole	212-730-0030	P	131	0.2
Jack Schwartz Shoes Inc.	155 Av Americas	New York	NY	10013	Bernard Schwartz	212-691-4700	R	116*	<0.1
Eastland Shoe Corp.	4 Meetinghouse Rd	Freeport	ME	04032	James Klein	207-865-6314	R	80*	<0.1
Wolff Shoe Co.	1705 L Williams	Fenton	MO	63026	Gary Wolff	636-343-7770	R	76*	<0.1
D. Myers and Sons Inc.	4311 Erdman Ave	Baltimore	MD	21213	E Carey Ries	410-522-7500	R	34*	<0.1
Kubic Marketing Inc.	225 S Aviation Blvd	El Segundo	CA	90245	Bob Sayre	310-297-1600	R	25*	<0.1
Impo International Inc.	PO Box 639	Santa Maria	CA	93456	Erik Keeler	805-922-7753	R	19*	<0.1
Inter-Pacific Corp.	2257 Colby Ave	Los Angeles	CA	90064	Frank Arnsteine	310-473-7591	R	18*	<0.1
Micromall USA Inc.	7 Cumberland Xing	Smyrna	GA	30080	Terry Asfaw	678-305-0135	R	16*	<0.1
Dvs Shoe Company Inc.	955 Francisco St	Torrance	CA	90502	Kevin Dunlap	310-715-8300	R	14*	<0.1
Super Shoe Stores Inc.	PO Box 239	Cumberland	MD	21502	Terry Tierney	301-759-4300	R	14*	0.2
Zeiger Enterprises Inc.	621 Prospect St	Trenton	NJ	08618	Shelly Zeiger	609-394-1000	R	13*	<0.1
Hickory Brands Inc.	PO Box 429	Hickory	NC	28603	Nissan Joseph	828-322-2600	R	9*	<0.1
Badorf Shoe Company Inc.	PO Box 367	Lititz	PA	17543	Duane Gingerich	717-626-8521	R	3*	<0.1
Foremost Athletic Apparel	1307 E Maple Rd	Troy	MI	48083	John G Levy	248-689-3850	R	1*	<0.1
AirBoss Polymer Products Corp.	200 Veterans Blvd	South Haven	MI	49090	Jerry VanVlack	269-637-2181	R	1*	<0.1

Source: Ward's Business Directory of U.S. Private and Public Companies, Volumes 1 and 2, 2005. The company type code used is as follows: P - Public, R - Private, S - Subsidiary, D - Division, J - Joint Venture, A - Affiliate, G - Group. Sales are in millions of dollars, employees are in thousands. An asterisk (*) indicates an estimated sales volume. The symbol < stands for 'less than'. Company names and addresses are truncated, in some cases, to fit into the available space.

OCCUPATIONS EMPLOYED BY APPAREL, PIECE GOODS, & NOTIONS WHOLESALE

Occupation	% of Total 2004	Change to 2014	Occupation	% of Total 2004	Change to 2014
Sales reps, wholesale & manufacturing, exc tech	15.5	4.0	Wholesale & retail buyers, except farm products	1.9	-1.6
Laborers & freight, stock, & material movers, hand	10.6	-6.4	First-line supervisors/managers of non-retail sales work	1.9	-3.8
Shipping, receiving, & traffic clerks	5.5	-5.8	Order clerks	1.8	-32.4
Stock clerks & order fillers	5.4	-20.3	First-line supervisors/managers of office workers	1.6	-5.7
Retail salespersons	3.9	4.0	Sewing machine operators	1.6	4.0
Packers & packagers, hand	3.8	4.0	Inspectors, testers, sorters, samplers, & weighers	1.4	-1.5
Customer service representatives	3.5	6.5	Accountants & auditors	1.3	4.0
Office clerks, general	3.5	-7.4	Secretaries, except legal, medical, & executive	1.3	-12.5
Fashion designers	2.8	33.9	Production, planning, & expediting clerks	1.1	2.9
Bookkeeping, accounting, & auditing clerks	2.5	-6.4	Industrial truck & tractor operators	1.0	4.0
General & operations managers	2.3	2.9			

Source: Industry-Occupation Matrix, Bureau of Labor Statistics. These data are reported based on 4-digit NAICS categories but have been matched to corresponding 6-digit NAICS industry codes. The change reported for each occupation to the year 2014 is a percent of growth or decline as estimated by the Bureau of Labor Statistics. The abbreviation nec stands for 'not elsewhere classified.'

LOCATION BY STATE AND REGIONAL CONCENTRATION

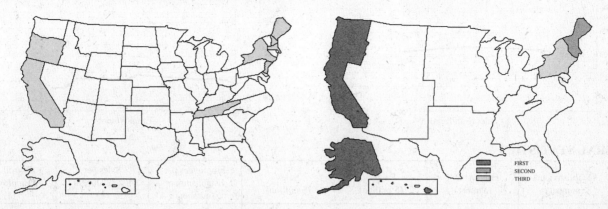

INDUSTRY DATA BY STATE

State	Establishments Total (number)	% of U.S.	Employment Total (number)	% of U.S.	Per Estab.	Payroll Total ($ mil.)	Per Empl. ($)	Sales Total ($ mil.)	% of U.S.	Per Estab. ($)
Massachusetts	59	3.4	4,252	15.8	72	218.1	51,285	3,655.6	17.3	61,958,729
California	453	26.3	4,532	16.8	10	250.5	55,284	3,575.7	17.0	7,893,444
Oregon	16	0.9	2,318	8.6	145	95.6	41,256	3,117.6	14.8	194,848,625
New York	297	17.2	4,010	14.9	14	197.8	49,329	2,201.6	10.4	7,412,808
New Jersey	95	5.5	1,605	6.0	17	67.8	42,268	1,261.1	6.0	13,275,158
New Hampshire	18	1.0	1,589	5.9	88	126.0	79,305	915.7	4.3	50,872,167
Florida	207	12.0	1,473	5.5	7	70.2	47,637	907.1	4.3	4,382,043
Tennessee	27	1.6	723	2.7	27	32.1	44,400	745.2	3.5	27,598,926
Pennsylvania	50	2.9	613	2.3	12	35.1	57,259	343.6	1.6	6,871,900
Maine	16	0.9	589	2.2	37	28.7	48,722	318.2	1.5	19,887,625
Maryland	9	0.5	217	0.8	24	14.6	67,373	273.8	1.3	30,421,556
Texas	92	5.3	484	1.8	5	14.9	30,876	218.1	1.0	2,370,489
North Carolina	28	1.6	373	1.4	13	14.4	38,574	216.4	1.0	7,729,750
Wisconsin	17	1.0	409	1.5	24	21.9	53,626	205.2	1.0	12,072,765
Colorado	19	1.1	312	1.2	16	16.8	53,859	158.3	0.8	8,330,316
Virginia	16	0.9	182	0.7	11	12.7	69,989	88.3	0.4	5,519,875
Ohio	12	0.7	35	0.1	3	1.8	52,429	39.3	0.2	3,271,333
Nevada	10	0.6	47	0.2	5	1.8	38,234	33.9	0.2	3,385,300
Vermont	5	0.3	40	0.1	8	1.4	34,875	23.7	0.1	4,733,600
Kentucky	10	0.6	58	0.2	6	0.9	15,448	9.2	-	917,900
Utah	5	0.3	48	0.2	10	1.0	20,667	8.7	-	1,739,400
Hawaii	11	0.6	31	0.1	3	0.8	25,258	5.4	-	488,091
South Carolina	8	0.5	22	0.1	3	0.7	31,273	4.0	-	501,125
Illinois	31	1.8	100-249	-	-	(D)	-	(D)	-	-
Missouri	31	1.8	1000-2499	-	-	(D)	-	(D)	-	-
Georgia	29	1.7	100-249	-	-	(D)	-	(D)	-	-
Washington	24	1.4	250-499	-	-	(D)	-	(D)	-	-
Michigan	21	1.2	250-499	-	-	(D)	-	(D)	-	-
Alabama	18	1.0	100-249	-	-	(D)	-	(D)	-	-
Indiana	13	0.8	20-99	-	-	(D)	-	(D)	-	-
Minnesota	13	0.8	20-99	-	-	(D)	-	(D)	-	-
Arizona	12	0.7	20-99	-	-	(D)	-	(D)	-	-
Connecticut	10	0.6	100-249	-	-	(D)	-	(D)	-	-
Arkansas	7	0.4	20-99	-	-	(D)	-	(D)	-	-
Delaware	5	0.3	20-99	-	-	(D)	-	(D)	-	-
Kansas	5	0.3	0-19	-	-	(D)	-	(D)	-	-
Louisiana	4	0.2	20-99	-	-	(D)	-	(D)	-	-
Mississippi	4	0.2	20-99	-	-	(D)	-	(D)	-	-
D.C.	3	0.2	0-19	-	-	(D)	-	(D)	-	-
Iowa	3	0.2	20-99	-	-	(D)	-	(D)	-	-
Rhode Island	3	0.2	0-19	-	-	(D)	-	(D)	-	-
Idaho	2	0.1	0-19	-	-	(D)	-	(D)	-	-
Oklahoma	2	0.1	0-19	-	-	(D)	-	(D)	-	-
Montana	1	0.1	0-19	-	-	(D)	-	(D)	-	-
Nebraska	1	0.1	0-19	-	-	(D)	-	(D)	-	-
New Mexico	1	0.1	20-99	-	-	(D)	-	(D)	-	-
North Dakota	1	0.1	20-99	-	-	(D)	-	(D)	-	-
West Virginia	1	0.1	0-19	-	-	(D)	-	(D)	-	-

Source: 2002 *Economic Census.* The states are in descending order of sales or establishments (if sales data are missing for the majority). The symbol (D) appears when data are withheld to prevent disclosure of competitive information. States marked with (D) are sorted by number of establishments. A dash (-) indicates that the data element cannot be calculated. Shaded *states* on the state map indicate those states which have proportionately greater representation in the industry than would be indicated by the states population; the ratio is based on total sales or number of establishments. Shaded *regions* indicate where the industry is regionally most concentrated.

NAICS 424410 - GENERAL LINE GROCERY MERCHANT WHOLESALERS*

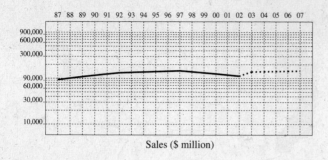

Sales ($ million)

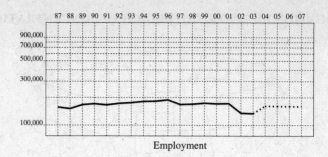

Employment

GENERAL STATISTICS

Year	Establishments (number)	Employment (number)	Payroll ($ million)	Sales ($ million)	Employees per Establishment (number)	Sales per Establishment ($)	Payroll per Employee ($)
1987	4,368	157,191	3,702.5	93,215.2	36.0	21,340,476.2	23,554.1
1988	3,998	151,514	3,920.1	101,092.7 e	37.9	25,285,817.9	25,872.9
1989	3,738	167,220	4,358.7	108,970.2 e	44.7	29,152,006.4	26,065.7
1990	3,751	171,302	4,574.1	116,847.6 e	45.7	31,151,053.1	26,702.0
1991	3,653	166,525	4,663.1	124,725.1 e	45.6	34,143,197.4	28,002.4
1992	4,528	172,827	5,025.8	132,602.6	38.2	29,285,026.5	29,079.9
1993	4,412	175,974	5,216.3	135,419.9 e	39.9	30,693,540.3	29,642.4
1994	4,653	181,304	5,572.0	138,237.3 e	39.0	29,709,284.3	30,732.9
1995	4,545	182,444	5,645.9	141,054.6 e	40.1	31,035,115.5	30,945.9
1996	4,463 e	188,415 e	5,930.0 e	143,872.0 e	42.2 e	32,236,612.1 e	31,473.1 e
1997	4,138	168,190	5,541.0	146,689.3	40.6	35,449,323.3	32,944.9
1998	4,296	169,768	5,892.3	139,857.7 e	39.5	32,555,335.2	34,708.0
1999	4,163	173,722	6,284.4	133,026.1 e	41.7	31,954,393.5	36,175.0
2000	4,036	171,229	6,480.9	126,194.6 e	42.4	31,267,234.9	37,849.4
2001	3,993	172,432	7,149.0	119,363.0 e	43.2	29,893,057.9	41,459.9
2002	3,212	135,562	5,506.7	112,531.4	42.2	35,034,682.4	40,621.3
2003	3,377	134,048	5,613.2	139,192.0 p	39.7	34,654,963.4 p	41,874.4
2004	3,860 p	161,420 p	6,741.8 p	140,761.0 p	41.7 p	35,127,707.9 p	42,250.8 p
2005	3,836 p	160,795 p	6,895.6 p	142,329.9 p	41.8 p	35,600,452.4 p	43,365.5 p
2006	3,812 p	160,171 p	7,049.5 p	143,898.8 p	41.8 p	36,073,197.0 p	44,480.3 p
2007	3,788 p	159,547 p	7,203.3 p	145,467.7 p	41.9 p	36,545,941.5 p	45,595.0 p

Sources: Economic Census of the United States, 1987, 1992, 1997, and 2002. Establishment counts, employment, and payroll are from County Business Patterns for non-Census years. Values followed by a 'p' are projections by the editors. Sales data for non-Census years are extrapolations, marked by 'e'. Data are the most recent available at this level of detail.

INDICES OF CHANGE

Year	Establishments (number)	Employment (number)	Payroll ($ million)	Sales ($ million)	Employees per Establishment (number)	Sales per Establishment ($)	Payroll per Employee ($)
1987	136.0	116.0	67.2	82.8	85.3	60.9	58.0
1992	141.0	127.5	91.3	117.8	90.5	83.6	71.6
1993	137.4	129.8	94.7	120.3 e	94.5	87.6	73.0
1994	144.9	133.7	101.2	122.8 e	92.4	84.8	75.7
1995	141.5	134.6	102.5	125.3 e	95.0	88.6	76.2
1996	138.9 e	139.0 e	107.7 e	127.9 e	100.0 e	92.0 e	77.5 e
1997	128.8	124.1	100.6	130.4	96.2	101.2	81.1
1998	133.7	125.2	107.0	124.3 e	93.6	92.9	85.4
1999	129.6	128.1	114.1	118.2 e	98.8	91.2	89.1
2000	125.7	126.3	117.7	112.1 e	100.5	89.2	93.2
2001	124.3	127.2	129.8	106.1 e	102.4	85.3	102.1
2002	100.0	100.0	100.0	100.0	100.0	100.0	100.0
2003	105.1	98.9	101.9	123.7 p	94.1	98.9 p	103.1
2004	120.2 p	119.1 p	122.4 p	125.1 p	98.8 p	100.3 p	104.0 p
2005	119.4 p	118.6 p	125.2 p	126.5 p	99.0 p	101.6 p	106.8 p
2006	118.7 p	118.2 p	128.0 p	127.9 p	99.1 p	103.0 p	109.5 p
2007	117.9 p	117.7 p	130.8 p	129.3 p	99.3 p	104.3 p	112.2 p

Sources: Same as General Statistics. The values shown reflect change from the base year, 2002. Values above 100 mean greater than 2002, values below 100 mean less than 2002, and a value of 100 in the 1987-2001 or 2003-2007 period means same as 2002. Values followed by a 'p' are projections by the editors; 'e' stands for extrapolation. Data are the most recent available at this level of detail.

SELECTED RATIOS

For 2002	Avg. of All Wholesale	Analyzed Industry	Index	For 2002	Avg. of All Wholesale	Analyzed Industry	Index
Employees per Establishment	15	42	282	Sales per Employee	791,325	830,110	105
Payroll per Establishment	626,122	1,714,415	274	Sales per Establishment	12,012,387	35,034,682	292
Payroll per Employee	41,161	40,621	99	Expenses per Establishment	na	na	na

Sources: Same as General Statistics. The 'Average of All' column, Wholesale or Retail, represents the average of the sector reported for the most recent complete year available. The Index shows the relationship between the Average and the Analyzed Industry. For example, 100 means that they are equal; 500 that the Analyzed Industry is five times the average; 50 means that the Analyzed Industry is half the national average. The abbreviation 'na' is used to show that data are 'not available'.

*Equivalent to SIC 5141.

LEADING COMPANIES

Number shown: **75** Total sales ($ mil): **204,420** Total employment (000): **346.6**

Company Name	Address				CEO Name	Phone	Co. Type	Sales ($ mil)	Empl. (000)
SYSCO Corp.	1390 Enclave Pkwy	Houston	TX	77077		281-584-1390	P	29,335	47.0
SUPERVALU Inc.	11840 Valley View	Eden Prairie	MN	55344		952-828-4000	P	20,205	55.2
Fleming Companies Inc.	PO Box 299013	Lewisville	TX	75029	Archie R Dykes	972-906-8000	P	15,503	33.0
C and S Wholesale Grocers Inc.	PO Box 821	Brattleboro	VT	05302	Edward Albertian	802-257-4371	R	13,000	12.0
McLane Company Inc.	4747 McLane Pkwy	Temple	TX	76504	Grady Rosier	254-771-7500	S	12,672*	14.5
Advantage Sales & Marketing	19100 Von Karman	Irvine	CA	92612	Sonny King	949-797-2900	R	12,501*	12.0
BJ's Wholesale Club Inc.	PO Box 9601	Natick	MA	01760		508-651-7400	P	7,220	18.5
Performance Food Group Co.	12500 W Creek	Richmond	VA	23238	Robert C Sledd	804-484-7700	P	6,149	11.0
Tree of Life Inc.	PO Box 410	St. Augustine	FL	32085	Richard A Thorne	904-940-2100	S	6,010*	5.3
Associated Grocers Inc.	PO Box 3763	Seattle	WA	98124	Robert P Hermanns	206-762-2100	R	4,845*	1.0
Roundy's Inc.	23000 Roundy Dr	Pewaukee	WI	53072		262-953-7999	S	4,777	21.9
Nash Finch Co.	PO Box 355	Minneapolis	MN	55440	Ron Marshall	952-832-0534	P	3,897	8.7
Gordon Food Service Inc.	PO Box 1787	Grand Rapids	MI	49501	Daniel Gordon	616-530-7000	R	3,450	6.4
Eastern Region of Supervalu	PO Box 26967	Richmond	VA	23261	Jeff Noddle	804-746-6000	R	3,412*	5.9
Eby-Brown Co.	PO Box 3067	Naperville	IL	60566		630-778-2800	R	3,200	2.1
H.T. Hackney Co.	PO Box 238	Knoxville	TN	37901	William B Sansom	865-546-1291	R	3,100	3.5
Unified Western Grocers Inc.	PO Box 513396	Los Angeles	CA	90051	Louis A Amen	323-264-5200	R	3,040	2.9
Services Group of America Inc.	4025 Delridge SW	Seattle	WA	98106	Thomas J Stewart	206-933-5000	R	2,200	3.5
Spartan Stores Inc.	PO Box 8700	Grand Rapids	MI	49518		616-878-2000	P	2,055	6.9
Dallas Market Center Ltd.	2100 Stemmons Fwy	Dallas	TX	75207	Bill Winsor	214-655-6100	R	1,973*	0.4
Smart and Final Stores Corp.	600 Citadel Dr	Los Angeles	CA	90040	Ross E Roeder	323-869-7500	S	1,959*	5.8
SYSCO Food Services	PO Box 248	Indianapolis	IN	46206	Walter C Mills	317-291-2020	S	1,957*	0.4
Federated Group Inc.	3025 W Salt Creek	Arlington H.	IL	60005	David C Dougherty	847-577-1200	R	1,938*	0.4
Smart and Final Inc.	PO Box 512377	Los Angeles	CA	90051		323-869-7500	P	1,730	5.1
Dot Foods Inc.	PO Box 192	Mount Sterling	IL	62353		217-773-4411	R	1,573	2.2
U.R.M. Stores Inc.	PO Box 3365	Spokane	WA	99220	Dean Sonnenberg	509-467-2620	R	1,563*	2.0
Di Giorgio Corp.	380 Middlesex Ave	Carteret	NJ	07008	Stephen R Bokser	732-541-5555	R	1,544	1.2
GSC Enterprises Inc.	PO Box 638	Sulphur Springs	TX	75483		903-885-0829	R	1,500*	2.0
Associated Wholesalers Inc.	PO Box 67	Robesonia	PA	19551	J Christopher Michael	610-693-3161	R	1,483*	1.4
Topco Associates Inc.	7711 Gross Point Rd	Skokie	IL	60077	Steven Lauer	847-676-3030	R	1,455*	0.3
Purity Wholesale Grocers Inc.	5400 Broken Sound	Boca Raton	FL	33487	Jeff Levitetz	561-994-9360	R	1,450	0.4
Shamrock Foods Co.	2540 N 29th Ave	Phoenix	AZ	85009		602-233-6400	R	1,354	2.3
Grocers Supply Co. Inc.	PO Box 14200	Houston	TX	77221	Max Levit	713-747-5000	R	1,182*	2.0
Ben E. Keith Co.	PO Box 2628	Fort Worth	TX	76113	Howard Hallam	817-877-5700	R	1,173*	2.3
SUPERVALU Champaign	PO Box 9008	Champaign	IL	61826		217-384-2800	S	1,000*	0.9
Affiliated Foods Southwest Inc.	PO Box 3627	Little Rock	AR	72203	Jerry W Davis	501-455-3590	R	982*	0.9
International MultiFoods Corp.	PO Box 2942	Minneapolis	MN	55402	Gary E Costley	952-594-3300	S	908	2.2
Associated Food Stores Inc.	PO Box 30430	Salt Lake City	UT	84130	Richard A Parkinson	801-973-4400	R	907*	1.4
Sysco Food Serv San Francisco	5900 Stewart Ave	Fremont	CA	94537	Thomas Lankford	510-226-3000	S	901*	0.8
Bozzuto's Inc.	275 Schoolhouse Rd	Cheshire	CT	06410	Michael A Bozzuto	203-272-3511	R	900	1.0
AMCON Distributing Co.	7405 Irvington Rd	Omaha	NE	68122	Kathleen M Evans	402-331-3727	P	824	1.0
Dairy Maid Foods Inc.	2540 N 29th Ave	Phoenix	AZ	85009		602-233-6400	D	808*	0.2
Affiliated Foods Inc.	PO Box 30300	Amarillo	TX	79120	George Langford	806-372-3851	R	790*	1.1
American Seaway Foods Inc.	5300 Richmond Rd	Cleveland	OH	44146	Anthony C Rego	216-292-7000	S	741*	0.7
Certified Grocers Midwest Inc.	1 Certified Dr	Hodgkins	IL	60525	Ken Koester	708-579-2100	R	730*	2.1
Merchants Grocery Co.	PO Box 1268	Culpeper	VA	22701	Elvin V Smythers	540-825-0786	R	726*	0.2
Piggly Wiggly Carolina Inc.	PO Box 118047	Charleston	SC	29423	Joseph T Newton III	843-554-9880	R	700*	5.0
Affiliated Foods Midwest	PO Box 1067	Norfolk	NE	68702	Martin Arter	402-371-0555	R	687*	0.6
Maines Paper and Food Service	101 Broome	Conklin	NY	13748	Chris Mellon	607-779-1200	R	650*	0.8
Grocery Supply Co.	9300 E Billy the Kid	El Paso	TX	79907		915-858-1053	S	624*	1.5
Sysco Food Services of Houston	PO Box 15316	Houston	TX	77220	Keith Miller	713-672-8080	S	579*	0.8
S and D Coffee Inc.	PO Box 1628	Concord	NC	28026	Alan Davis	704-782-3121	R	551*	0.6
Cross Mark	5100 Legacy Dr	Plano	TX	75024	David Baxley	469-814-1000	R	530*	0.5
Sysco Food Services of Kansas	PO Box 820	Olathe	KS	66061	Thomas E Lankford	913-829-5555	D	521*	0.8
Fresh Brands Distributing Inc.	PO Box 419	Sheboygan	WI	53082	Elwood F Winn	920-457-4433	S	502*	1.8
Western Family Foods Inc.	PO Box 4057	Portland	OR	97208	Ronald King	503-639-6300	R	500*	<0.1
Hallsmith-Sysco Food Services	380 S Worcester St	Norton	MA	02766	Thaire Bryant	508-285-6361	S	491*	1.2
Robert Orr-Sysco Food Services	PO Box 305137	Nashville	TN	37230	Nick K Taras	615-350-7100	S	490*	1.1
Camellia Food Stores Inc.	1300 Diamond Sprgs	Virginia Beach	VA	23455	Edward G Dery	757-855-3371	R	470*	0.8
Krasdale Foods Inc.	65 W Red Oak Ln	White Plains	NY	10604	Charles A Krasne	914-694-6400	R	459*	0.6
Sysco Food Services-Jacksonville	PO Box 37045	Jacksonville	FL	32236	Walter R Rudisiler	904-786-2600	S	449*	0.6
Sysco Food Services of Baraboo	910 South Blvd	Baraboo	WI	53913	Thomas Lankford	608-356-8711	D	444*	0.7
McCabe's Quality Foods Inc.	17600 S Rafael	Portland	OR	97230	Joe Kematz	503-256-4770	R	438*	<0.1
Institutional Sales Associates	PO Box 8938	Houston	TX	77249	Ron Koska	713-692-7213	R	424*	<0.1
US FoodService Inc. Carolina Div.	125 Fort Mill Pkwy	Fort Mill	SC	29715	Dan Harris	803-802-6000	S	421*	1.0
Boddie-Noell Enterprises Inc.	PO Box 1908	Rocky Mount	NC	27802	Willaim L Boddie	252-937-2000	R	420*	12.0
Associated Grocers of the South	PO Box 11044	Birmingham	AL	35202	Gerald Totoritis	205-808-4838	R	413*	0.5
AJC International Inc.	5188 Roswell NW	Atlanta	GA	30342	Gerald L Allison	404-252-6750	R	400*	0.2
Imperial Trading Co.	PO Box 23508	New Orleans	LA	70183	John Georges	504-733-1400	R	389*	0.3
Farm Boy Meats Inc.	PO Box 996	Evansville	IN	47706	Robert J Bonenberger	812-425-5231	R	388*	<0.1
Lankford-Sysco Food Services Inc.	PO Box 477	Pocomoke City	MD	21851	Thomas Lankford	410-677-5555	S	385*	0.7
Central Grocers Co-op Inc.	11100 Belmont Ave	Franklin Park	IL	60131	Joe Caccamo	847-451-0660	R	380*	0.3
Nobel/Sysco Food Services Co.	PO Box 5566	Denver	CO	80217	Chris DeWitt	303-458-4000	S	378*	0.9
Kehe Food Distributors Inc.	900 N Schmidt Rd	Romeoville	IL	60446	Jerry Kehe	815-886-0700	R	359*	0.7
Laurel Grocery Company Inc.	PO Box 4100	London	KY	40743	James K Buchanan	606-878-6601	R	356*	0.7

Source: Ward's Business Directory of U.S. Private and Public Companies, Volumes 1 and 2, 2005. The company type code used is as follows: P - Public, R - Private, S - Subsidiary, D - Division, J - Joint Venture, A - Affiliate, G - Group. Sales are in millions of dollars, employees are in thousands. An asterisk (*) indicates an estimated sales volume. The symbol < stands for 'less than'. Company names and addresses are truncated, in some cases, to fit into the available space.

OCCUPATIONS EMPLOYED BY GROCERY & RELATED PRODUCTS WHOLESALE

Occupation	% of Total 2004	Change to 2014	Occupation	% of Total 2004	Change to 2014
Sales reps, wholesale & manufacturing, exc tech	12.7	10.6	Office clerks, general	1.9	-1.6
Laborers & freight, stock, & material movers, hand	11.0	-0.5	Bookkeeping, accounting, & auditing clerks	1.7	-0.5
Driver/sales workers	9.0	10.4	General & operations managers	1.5	9.4
Truck drivers, heavy & tractor-trailer	9.0	10.4	First-line supervisors/managers of non-retail sales work	1.5	2.2
Truck drivers, light or delivery services	5.0	10.4	Customer service representatives	1.5	13.2
Stock clerks & order fillers	4.4	-15.3	Wholesale & retail buyers, except farm products	1.2	4.5
Industrial truck & tractor operators	4.0	-0.5	First-line supervisors/managers of transporation workers	1.1	10.6
Packers & packagers, hand	2.8	10.6	Maintenance & repair workers, general	1.0	10.6
Shipping, receiving, & traffic clerks	2.1	0.1	First-line supervisors/managers of office workers	1.0	0.2
Packaging & filling machine operators & tenders	2.0	-5.8			

Source: Industry-Occupation Matrix, Bureau of Labor Statistics. These data are reported based on 4-digit NAICS categories but have been matched to corresponding 6-digit NAICS industry codes. The change reported for each occupation to the year 2014 is a percent of growth or decline as estimated by the Bureau of Labor Statistics. The abbreviation nec stands for 'not elsewhere classified.'

LOCATION BY STATE AND REGIONAL CONCENTRATION

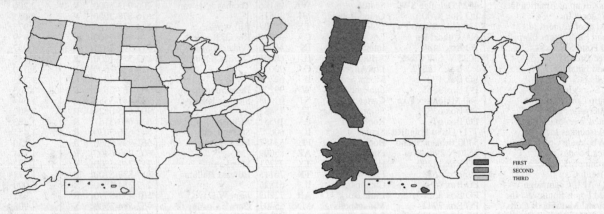

FIRST
SECOND
THIRD

INDUSTRY DATA BY STATE

State	Establishments Total (number)	% of U.S.	Employment Total (number)	% of U.S.	Per Estab.	Payroll Total ($ mil.)	Per Empl. ($)	Sales Total ($ mil.)	% of U.S.	Per Estab. ($)
Illinois	149	4.7	8,055	6.0	54	315.6	39,176	11,241.9	9.7	75,448,705
California	464	14.5	11,899	8.9	26	496.6	41,732	8,724.8	7.6	18,803,494
Texas	190	5.9	9,690	7.3	51	376.6	38,869	7,381.8	6.4	38,851,789
Minnesota	42	1.3	3,656	2.7	87	174.9	47,830	6,773.3	5.9	161,268,024
Ohio	101	3.2	5,144	3.9	51	212.9	41,393	5,206.3	4.5	51,547,683
Florida	263	8.2	6,737	5.0	26	284.4	42,220	4,661.6	4.0	17,724,764
New York	354	11.0	6,727	5.0	19	277.7	41,283	4,483.1	3.9	12,664,088
Wisconsin	40	1.2	4,741	3.5	119	191.8	40,456	4,297.5	3.7	107,437,850
Michigan	96	3.0	3,977	3.0	41	214.9	54,033	4,254.2	3.7	44,314,698
Pennsylvania	121	3.8	6,288	4.7	52	266.6	42,399	4,142.7	3.6	34,237,264
Georgia	98	3.1	3,186	2.4	33	125.0	39,236	3,650.3	3.2	37,248,000
Maryland	70	2.2	4,322	3.2	62	178.3	41,247	3,022.9	2.6	43,184,043
Alabama	32	1.0	3,385	2.5	106	126.9	37,494	2,930.6	2.5	91,582,125
Virginia	60	1.9	3,004	2.2	50	124.0	41,272	2,779.0	2.4	46,316,000
Kansas	15	0.5	2,393	1.8	160	101.1	42,236	2,621.1	2.3	174,741,533
North Carolina	68	2.1	3,444	2.6	51	130.8	37,984	2,614.7	2.3	38,452,162
Washington	70	2.2	3,793	2.8	54	172.7	45,534	2,519.4	2.2	35,991,914
Missouri	47	1.5	1,346	1.0	29	55.8	41,479	2,015.5	1.7	42,883,000
Arkansas	26	0.8	1,393	1.0	54	48.6	34,919	1,948.8	1.7	74,955,692
Tennessee	44	1.4	2,716	2.0	62	104.0	38,275	1,909.7	1.7	43,402,364
Nebraska	18	0.6	1,938	1.5	108	66.9	34,512	1,879.9	1.6	104,440,222
Massachusetts	92	2.9	2,968	2.2	32	121.0	40,755	1,874.4	1.6	20,374,130
Indiana	41	1.3	2,582	1.9	63	92.4	35,777	1,666.9	1.4	40,655,902
Oregon	34	1.1	1,344	1.0	40	57.9	43,093	1,653.7	1.4	48,638,559
Utah	24	0.7	2,062	1.5	86	72.8	35,287	1,453.3	1.3	60,555,833
Maine	12	0.4	1,072	0.8	89	49.2	45,921	1,415.5	1.2	117,958,833
Mississippi	17	0.5	1,478	1.1	87	52.6	35,604	1,335.5	1.2	78,556,882
Louisiana	43	1.3	2,062	1.5	48	69.4	33,678	1,274.3	1.1	29,634,512
Oklahoma	24	0.7	1,965	1.5	82	75.3	38,324	1,223.3	1.1	50,972,125
Kentucky	26	0.8	1,403	1.1	54	51.2	36,466	1,125.9	1.0	43,305,500
South Carolina	29	0.9	1,681	1.3	58	68.7	40,881	956.6	0.8	32,987,310
Connecticut	36	1.1	1,027	0.8	29	51.6	50,209	895.0	0.8	24,861,333
Colorado	44	1.4	1,555	1.2	35	65.7	42,277	849.0	0.7	19,296,341

Continued on next page.

INDUSTRY DATA BY STATE - Continued

State	Establishments		Employment			Payroll		Sales		
	Total (number)	% of U.S.	Total (number)	% of U.S.	Per Estab.	Total ($ mil.)	Per Empl. ($)	Total ($ mil.)	% of U.S.	Per Estab. ($)
North Dakota	10	0.3	1,026	0.8	103	35.8	34,857	814.1	0.7	81,405,500
Hawaii	41	1.3	559	0.4	14	17.7	31,678	493.1	0.4	12,027,146
Montana	9	0.3	565	0.4	63	19.8	34,965	492.0	0.4	54,670,222
New Mexico	14	0.4	790	0.6	56	34.5	43,651	393.2	0.3	28,088,214
Iowa	15	0.5	819	0.6	55	29.2	35,668	368.9	0.3	24,595,200
Nevada	28	0.9	444	0.3	16	22.2	50,110	234.2	0.2	8,365,750
Idaho	9	0.3	494	0.4	55	15.2	30,763	210.9	0.2	23,429,333
West Virginia	11	0.3	322	0.2	29	10.7	33,329	147.5	0.1	13,410,636
Alaska	14	0.4	172	0.1	12	5.1	29,814	58.7	0.1	4,191,857
New Jersey	143	4.5	5K-9999	-	-	(D)	-	(D)	-	-
Arizona	58	1.8	1000-2499	-	-	(D)	-	(D)	-	-
D.C.	15	0.5	100-249	-	-	(D)	-	(D)	-	-
Rhode Island	15	0.5	250-499	-	-	(D)	-	(D)	-	-
New Hampshire	9	0.3	20-99	-	-	(D)	-	(D)	-	-
Vermont	9	0.3	1000-2499	-	-	(D)	-	(D)	-	-
Delaware	8	0.2	100-249	-	-	(D)	-	(D)	-	-
South Dakota	4	0.1	100-249	-	-	(D)	-	(D)	-	-
Wyoming	2	0.1	0-19	-	-	(D)	-	(D)	-	-

Source: 2002 *Economic Census*. The states are in descending order of sales or establishments (if sales data are missing for the majority). The symbol (D) appears when data are withheld to prevent disclosure of competitive information. States marked with (D) are sorted by number of establishments. A dash (-) indicates that the data element cannot be calculated. Shaded *states* on the state map indicate those states which have proportionately greater representation in the industry than would be indicated by the states population; the ratio is based on total sales or number of establishments. Shaded *regions* indicate where the industry is regionally most concentrated.

NAICS 424420 - PACKAGED FROZEN FOOD MERCHANT WHOLESALERS*

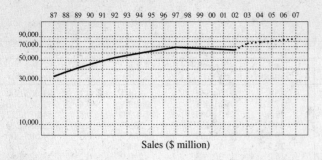

87 88 89 90 91 92 93 94 95 96 97 98 99 00 01 02 03 04 05 06 07

Sales ($ million)

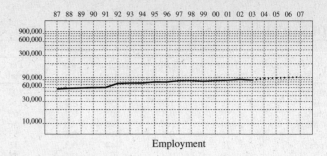

87 88 89 90 91 92 93 94 95 96 97 98 99 00 01 02 03 04 05 06 07

Employment

GENERAL STATISTICS

Year	Establishments (number)	Employment (number)	Payroll ($ million)	Sales ($ million)	Employees per Establishment (number)	Sales per Establishment ($)	Payroll per Employee ($)
1987	2,835	56,199	1,281.1	33,263.6	19.8	11,733,192.2	22,795.8
1988	2,671	58,028	1,413.7	37,262.1 e	21.7	13,950,617.7	24,362.4
1989	2,538	59,007	1,492.8	41,260.6 e	23.2	16,257,131.6	25,298.7
1990	2,438	59,865	1,588.7	45,259.0 e	24.6	18,563,986.9	26,538.0
1991	2,358	60,351	1,653.6	49,257.5 e	25.6	20,889,525.0	27,399.7
1992	3,468	73,755	2,113.9	53,256.0	21.3	15,356,401.4	28,661.1
1993	3,247	75,075	2,184.6	56,427.8 e	23.1	17,378,441.6	29,098.9
1994	3,054	75,345	2,304.1	59,599.5 e	24.7	19,515,225.9	30,580.7
1995	2,911	79,675	2,422.1	62,771.3 e	27.4	21,563,483.3	30,399.7
1996	3,083 e	79,462 e	2,461.4 e	65,943.0 e	25.8 e	21,389,231.3 e	30,975.8 e
1997	3,838	85,067	2,800.3	69,114.8	22.2	18,008,025.0	32,918.8
1998	3,677	85,491	3,015.1	68,202.0 e	23.3	18,548,267.6	35,268.0
1999	3,588	82,915	2,989.1	67,289.2 e	23.1	18,753,946.5	36,050.2
2000	3,509	85,680	3,224.3	66,376.3 e	24.4	18,916,027.4	37,631.8
2001	3,390	87,251	3,328.7	65,463.5 e	25.7	19,310,772.9	38,151.2
2002	3,625	91,448	3,540.2	64,550.7	25.2	17,807,089.7	38,712.7
2003	3,569	88,038	3,636.1	76,007.2 p	24.7	20,530,059.3 p	41,301.3
2004	3,821 p	96,114 p	3,813.7 p	78,292.6 p	25.5 p	20,828,144.4 p	41,321.8 p
2005	3,894 p	98,410 p	3,966.5 p	80,578.1 p	25.7 p	21,126,229.6 p	42,408.9 p
2006	3,967 p	100,706 p	4,119.3 p	82,863.5 p	25.8 p	21,424,314.8 p	43,496.0 p
2007	4,040 p	103,002 p	4,272.1 p	85,148.9 p	26.0 p	21,722,399.9 p	44,583.1 p

Sources: *Economic Census of the United States*, 1987, 1992, 1997, and 2002. Establishment counts, employment, and payroll are from *County Business Patterns* for non-Census years. Values followed by a 'p' are projections by the editors. Sales data for non-Census years are extrapolations, marked by 'e'. Data are the most recent available at this level of detail.

INDICES OF CHANGE

Year	Establishments (number)	Employment (number)	Payroll ($ million)	Sales ($ million)	Employees per Establishment (number)	Sales per Establishment ($)	Payroll per Employee ($)
1987	78.2	61.5	36.2	51.5	78.6	65.9	58.9
1992	95.7	80.7	59.7	82.5	84.5	86.2	74.0
1993	89.6	82.1	61.7	87.4 e	91.7	97.6	75.2
1994	84.2	82.4	65.1	92.3 e	98.0	109.6	79.0
1995	80.3	87.1	68.4	97.2 e	108.7	121.1	78.5
1996	85.0 e	86.9 e	69.5 e	102.2 e	102.4 e	120.1 e	80.0 e
1997	105.9	93.0	79.1	107.1	88.1	101.1	85.0
1998	101.4	93.5	85.2	105.7 e	92.5	104.2	91.1
1999	99.0	90.7	84.4	104.2 e	91.7	105.3	93.1
2000	96.8	93.7	91.1	102.8 e	96.8	106.2	97.2
2001	93.5	95.4	94.0	101.4 e	102.0	108.4	98.5
2002	100.0	100.0	100.0	100.0	100.0	100.0	100.0
2003	98.5	96.3	102.7	117.7 p	97.9	115.3 p	106.7
2004	105.4 p	105.1 p	107.7 p	121.3 p	101.1 p	117.0 p	106.7 p
2005	107.4 p	107.6 p	112.0 p	124.8 p	101.8 p	118.6 p	109.5 p
2006	109.4 p	110.1 p	116.4 p	128.4 p	102.5 p	120.3 p	112.4 p
2007	111.5 p	112.6 p	120.7 p	131.9 p	103.2 p	122.0 p	115.2 p

Sources: Same as General Statistics. The values shown reflect change from the base year, 2002. Values above 100 mean greater than 2002, values below 100 mean less than 2002, and a value of 100 in the 1987-2001 or 2003-2007 period means same as 2002. Values followed by a 'p' are projections by the editors; 'e' stands for extrapolation. Data are the most recent available at this level of detail.

SELECTED RATIOS

For 2002	Avg. of All Wholesale	Analyzed Industry	Index	For 2002	Avg. of All Wholesale	Analyzed Industry	Index
Employees per Establishment	15	25	169	Sales per Employee	791,325	705,873	89
Payroll per Establishment	626,122	976,607	156	Sales per Establishment	12,012,387	17,807,090	148
Payroll per Employee	41,161	38,713	94	Expenses per Establishment	na	na	na

Sources: Same as General Statistics. The 'Average of All' column, Wholesale or Retail, represents the average of the sector reported for the most recent complete year available. The Index shows the relationship between the Average and the Analyzed Industry. For example, 100 means that they are equal; 500 that the Analyzed Industry is five times the average; 50 means that the Analyzed Industry is half the national average. The abbreviation 'na' is used to show that data are 'not available'.

*Equivalent to SIC 5142.

LEADING COMPANIES   Number shown: **75**   Total sales ($ mil): **70,934**   Total employment (000): **90.5**

Company Name	Address				CEO Name	Phone	Co. Type	Sales ($ mil)	Empl. (000)
SYSCO Corp.	1390 Enclave Pkwy	Houston	TX	77077		281-584-1390	P	29,335	47.0
Advantage Sales & Marketing	19100 Von Karman	Irvine	CA	92612	Sonny King	949-797-2900	R	12,501*	12.0
Performance Food Group Co.	12500 W Creek	Richmond	VA	23238	Robert C Sledd	804-484-7700	P	6,149	11.0
Associated Grocers Inc.	PO Box 3763	Seattle	WA	98124	Robert P Hermanns	206-762-2100	R	4,845*	1.0
H.T. Hackney Co.	PO Box 238	Knoxville	TN	37901	William B Sansom	865-546-1291	R	3,100	3.5
Unified Western Grocers Inc.	PO Box 513396	Los Angeles	CA	90051	Louis A Amen	323-264-5200	R	3,040	2.9
Purity Wholesale Grocers Inc.	5400 Broken Sound	Boca Raton	FL	33487	Jeff Levitetz	561-994-9360	R	1,450	0.4
Shamrock Foods Co.	2540 N 29th Ave	Phoenix	AZ	85009		602-233-6400	R	1,354	2.3
VIP Foodservice	PO Box 517	Kahului	HI	96733	Nelson Okumura	808-877-5055	R	1,032*	0.1
Sunkist Growers Inc.	PO Box 7888	Van Nuys	CA	91409	Jeffrey D Gargiulo	818-986-4800	R	942	0.4
Bozzuto's Inc.	275 Schoolhouse Rd	Cheshire	CT	06410	Michael A Bozzuto	203-272-3511	R	900	1.0
Sherwood Food Distributors	18615 Sherwood	Detroit	MI	48234	J Lawrence Tushman	313-366-3100	R	762	0.7
Institutional Sales Associates	PO Box 8938	Houston	TX	77249	Ron Koska	713-692-7213	R	424*	<0.1
Norpac Food Sales	4350 SW Galewood	Lake Oswego	OR	97035	Mike Woods	503-635-9311	R	400*	<0.1
Burris Foods Inc.	PO Box 219	Milford	DE	19963	Robert D Burris	302-422-4531	R	379*	1.0
FoodSalesWest Inc.	5880 W Las Posita	Pleasanton	CA	94588	Dave Lyons	925-460-0630	R	355*	<0.1
Southeast Frozen Food Co.	18770 NE 6th Ave	Miami	FL	33179	John Robinson	305-652-4622	R	337*	0.5
Sunfresh Inc.	PO Box 400	Royal City	WA	99357	Randy Niessner	509-346-9223	R	320*	0.1
Clark Foodservice Inc.	950 Arthur Ave	Elk Grove Vill.	IL	60007	Donald J Hindman	847-956-1730	R	310*	0.8
Glazier Foods Co.	11303 Antoine	Houston	TX	77066	Thomas A Glazier	713-869-6411	R	223*	0.4
Atalanta Corp.	1 Atalanta Plz	Elizabeth	NJ	07206	George Gellert	908-351-8000	R	208*	0.1
Harker's Distribution Inc.	PO Box 1308	Le Mars	IA	51031	Ron Geiger	712-546-8171	R	202*	0.8
Acosta Sales Co.	6600 Corp. Center	Jacksonville	FL	32216	Gary Chartrand	904-281-9800	R	179*	0.3
W.S. Lee and Sons Inc.	PO Box 1631	Altoona	PA	16603	Robert Lee	814-696-3535	R	160*	0.3
Troyer Foods Inc.	PO Box 608	Goshen	IN	46527	Paris Ball-Miller	574-533-0302	R	150*	0.2
Sysco Food Service of Jamestown	2063 Allen St Ext	Falconer	NY	14733	Vernon E Wetmore Jr	716-665-5620	D	140*	0.3
J.M. Sealts Co.	PO Box 300	Lima	OH	45802	Larry Easterday	419-224-8075	R	127*	<0.1
Lincoln Provision Inc.	824 W 38th Pl	Chicago	IL	60609		773-254-2400	R	108*	0.1
Scariano Brothers L.L.C.	PO Box 26009	New Orleans	LA	70186	Jack Scariano	504-246-6600	R	108*	0.1
Logan International II L.L.C.	PO Box 1000	Boardman	OR	97818	Dennis Logan	541-481-3070	R	103*	0.1
Bratt-Foster Inc.	306 Lakeside Rd	Syracuse	NY	13209	John L Foster	315-488-3840	R	89*	<0.1
FreshPoint Southern California	5301 Rivergrade Rd	Irwindale	CA	91706	Verne Lusby	626-813-5600	D	80*	0.3
Plee-Zing Inc.	1640 Pleasant Rd	Glenview	IL	60025	Don Donakowski	847-998-0200	R	72*	<0.1
Wilcox Frozen Foods Inc.	2200 Oakdale Ave	San Francisco	CA	94124	Robert C Smith	415-282-4116	R	62*	<0.1
J. Kings Food Service Profession.	700 Furrows Rd	Holtsville	NY	11742	John King	631-289-8401	R	60*	0.2
Rainsweet	PO Box 6109	Salem	OR	97304	George Crispin	503-363-4293	R	59*	0.2
Sidari's Italian Foods	3820 Lakeside E	Cleveland	OH	44114	Joe Sidari	216-431-3344	R	56*	<0.1
Kaelbel Wholesale Inc.	2501 SW 31st St	Fort Lauderdale	FL	33312	Eddie Kaelbel	954-797-7789	R	52*	<0.1
Summit Import Corp.	100 Summit Pl	Jersey City	NJ	07305	Whiting Wu	201-985-9800	R	52*	0.1
Will Poultry Company Inc.	PO Box 1146	Buffalo	NY	14240	Donald Will	716-853-2000	R	51*	0.1
Cirelli Foods Inc.	30 Commerce Blvd	Middleboro	MA	02346	Chuck Dillon	508-947-8778	R	42*	0.1
Buzz Products Inc.	4818 Kanawha E	Charleston	WV	25306	Dickinson Gould	304-925-4781	R	40*	<0.1
Advantage Food Marketing Corp.	PO Box 367	Roslyn Heights	NY	11577	Charlie Mastropaolo	516-625-2600	R	35*	<0.1
Becker Food Company Inc.	4160 N Washington	Milwaukee	WI	53212	Stephen S Becker	414-964-5353	R	35*	<0.1
Rainbow Inc.	98-715 Kuahao Pl	Pearl City	HI	96782	William Prideaux	808-487-6455	R	35*	<0.1
Tusco Grocers Inc.	PO Box 240	Dennison	OH	44621	Gregory W Kimble	740-922-2223	R	35*	<0.1
DBB Marketing Co.	155 Sansome St	San Francisco	CA	94104	Douglas Clendenning	415-956-7860	R	30*	<0.1
Louis Foehrkolb Inc.	7901 Oceano Ave	Jessup	MD	20794	Louis Foehrkolb	410-799-4260	R	29*	<0.1
Pocahontas Foods USA Inc.	PO Box 9729	Richmond	VA	23228	Steve Push	804-262-8614	S	28*	0.1
Roberts Foods Inc.	1615 W Jefferson St	Springfield	IL	62702	Dean Robert Jr	217-793-2633	S	25*	<0.1
Flanders Provision Company Inc.	PO Box 720	Waycross	GA	31502	Chris Huff	912-283-5191	R	21*	<0.1
Bakery DeFrance	603 Dover Rd Ste 6	Rockville	MD	20850	Joe Asseily	301-762-8770	R	20*	0.2
Alabama Food Group Inc.	PO Drawer 1207	Alexander City	AL	35011	Hugh A Neighbors III	256-234-5071	R	18*	<0.1
Consolidated Poultry and Egg Co.	426 St Paul Ave	Memphis	TN	38126	James J Skefos	901-526-7392	R	18*	<0.1
Schwans Sales	7751 N Hartman Ln	Tucson	AZ	85743		520-744-8843	R	17*	<0.1
Harvest Farms Inc.	45000 Yucca Ave	Lancaster	CA	93534	George Callas	661-945-3636	R	17*	<0.1
Butler Wholesale Products	PO Box 308	Adams	MA	01220	George Askin	413-743-3885	R	16*	<0.1
James Calvetti Meats Inc.	4240 S Morgan St	Chicago	IL	60609	James C Calvetti	773-927-9242	R	16*	<0.1
Moore Food Distributors Inc.	9910 Page Blvd	St. Louis	MO	63132	Al Moore	314-426-1300	R	16*	<0.1
Food Source Inc.	653 Swedesford Rd	Frazer	PA	19355	Pete Schaffer	610-540-0300	R	15*	<0.1
William George Company Inc.	1002 Mize St	Lufkin	TX	75904	Randy George	936-634-7738	R	15*	0.2
Leelanau Fruit Co.	2900 S W Bay Shore	Suttons Bay	MI	49682	Glen LaCross	231-271-3514	R	13*	0.1
Brown's Ice Cream Co.	2929 University SE	Minneapolis	MN	55414	Tim Nelson	612-378-1075	R	12*	<0.1
Rogers Brothers Wholesale Inc.	460 E Brooks St	Galesburg	IL	61401	Frank Rogers	309-342-2127	R	11*	<0.1
Wilson Foods Company L.L.C.	1811 W 1700 S	Salt Lake City	UT	84104		801-972-5633	R	11*	0.2
Amigo's Mexican Foods Inc.	1202 E Poplar St	Deming	NM	88030	Barbara Orquiz	505-546-6841	R	11*	<0.1
Francis-Mustoe and Co.	1440 N Harbor Blvd	Fullerton	CA	92835	Claude Jones	714-992-6710	R	10*	<0.1
John E. Koerner and Company Inc.	PO Box 10218	New Orleans	LA	70181	Tim Koerner	504-734-1100	R	10*	<0.1
Kewaskum Frozen Foods Inc.	PO Box 510	Kewaskum	WI	53040	Robert Beisbier	262-626-2181	R	9*	<0.1
Paris Foods Corp.	1632 Carman St	Camden	NJ	08105	Richard Marks	856-964-0915	R	9*	<0.1
Muffin Town	17 Walden St	Winthrop	MA	02152	John Anderson	617-846-1565	R	8*	<0.1
J. Weil and Co.	5907 Clinton St	Boise	ID	83704	Gene Tippits	208-377-0590	R	8*	<0.1
Lone Elm Sales Inc.	9695 N Van Dyne	Van Dyne	WI	54979	Glen Dedow	920-688-2338	R	8*	<0.1
Hipp Wholesale Foods Inc.	PO Box 207	Gothenburg	NE	69138	Belva M Hipp	308-537-7500	R	7*	<0.1
Hoban Foods Inc.	1599 E Warren Ave	Detroit	MI	48207	Donald VanTiem	313-833-1500	R	7*	<0.1

Source: Ward's Business Directory of U.S. Private and Public Companies, Volumes 1 and 2, 2005. The company type code used is as follows: P - Public, R - Private, S - Subsidiary, D - Division, J - Joint Venture, A - Affiliate, G - Group. Sales are in millions of dollars, employees are in thousands. An asterisk (*) indicates an estimated sales volume. The symbol < stands for 'less than'. Company names and addresses are truncated, in some cases, to fit into the available space.

OCCUPATIONS EMPLOYED BY GROCERY & RELATED PRODUCTS WHOLESALE

Occupation	% of Total 2004	Change to 2014	Occupation	% of Total 2004	Change to 2014
Sales reps, wholesale & manufacturing, exc tech	12.7	10.6	Office clerks, general	1.9	-1.6
Laborers & freight, stock, & material movers, hand	11.0	-0.5	Bookkeeping, accounting, & auditing clerks	1.7	-0.5
Driver/sales workers	9.0	10.4	General & operations managers	1.5	9.4
Truck drivers, heavy & tractor-trailer	9.0	10.4	First-line supervisors/managers of non-retail sales work	1.5	2.2
Truck drivers, light or delivery services	5.0	10.4	Customer service representatives	1.5	13.2
Stock clerks & order fillers	4.4	-15.3	Wholesale & retail buyers, except farm products	1.2	4.5
Industrial truck & tractor operators	4.0	-0.5	First-line supervisors/managers of transporation workers	1.1	10.6
Packers & packagers, hand	2.8	10.6	Maintenance & repair workers, general	1.0	10.6
Shipping, receiving, & traffic clerks	2.1	0.1	First-line supervisors/managers of office workers	1.0	0.2
Packaging & filling machine operators & tenders	2.0	-5.8			

Source: Industry-Occupation Matrix, Bureau of Labor Statistics. These data are reported based on 4-digit NAICS categories but have been matched to corresponding 6-digit NAICS industry codes. The change reported for each occupation to the year 2014 is a percent of growth or decline as estimated by the Bureau of Labor Statistics. The abbreviation nec stands for 'not elsewhere classified.'

LOCATION BY STATE AND REGIONAL CONCENTRATION

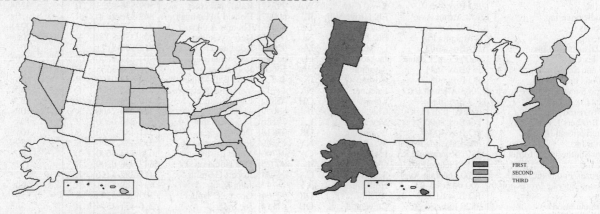

FIRST
SECOND
THIRD

INDUSTRY DATA BY STATE

State	Establishments Total (number)	% of U.S.	Employment Total (number)	% of U.S.	Per Estab.	Payroll Total ($ mil.)	Per Empl. ($)	Sales Total ($ mil.)	% of U.S.	Per Estab. ($)
California	549	15.1	11,389	12.0	21	425.9	37,397	9,235.8	14.0	16,822,945
Florida	304	8.4	6,425	6.8	21	253.2	39,409	5,193.6	7.9	17,084,115
New York	326	9.0	4,770	5.0	15	168.4	35,298	3,262.6	4.9	10,008,080
New Jersey	155	4.3	3,547	3.7	23	166.7	46,984	3,200.0	4.8	20,644,955
Texas	212	5.8	4,952	5.2	23	193.4	39,062	3,066.3	4.6	14,463,825
Washington	165	4.5	1,939	2.0	12	87.4	45,095	3,064.8	4.6	18,574,648
Illinois	177	4.9	3,768	4.0	21	179.7	47,693	2,785.4	4.2	15,736,853
Pennsylvania	127	3.5	4,101	4.3	32	152.8	37,252	2,495.3	3.8	19,647,850
Georgia	97	2.7	3,446	3.6	36	144.0	41,796	2,447.4	3.7	25,230,412
Massachusetts	111	3.1	2,579	2.7	23	114.2	44,287	2,335.1	3.5	21,036,766
Nebraska	22	0.6	1,378	1.5	63	72.6	52,705	2,128.3	3.2	96,740,364
Tennessee	54	1.5	2,847	3.0	53	121.3	42,604	2,108.6	3.2	39,047,907
Ohio	86	2.4	3,100	3.3	36	124.5	40,162	1,965.6	3.0	22,855,826
Minnesota	58	1.6	2,238	2.4	39	100.3	44,813	1,859.8	2.8	32,065,310
Wisconsin	61	1.7	2,748	2.9	45	112.3	40,878	1,606.5	2.4	26,336,689
Colorado	52	1.4	3,115	3.3	60	93.6	30,040	1,508.9	2.3	29,016,904
North Carolina	64	1.8	2,500	2.6	39	69.6	27,830	1,379.6	2.1	21,556,625
Missouri	70	1.9	2,980	3.1	43	109.6	36,776	1,306.2	2.0	18,659,514
Maryland	60	1.7	1,182	1.2	20	43.3	36,620	1,175.3	1.8	19,587,933
Michigan	91	2.5	1,561	1.6	17	59.3	37,967	1,138.8	1.7	12,514,165
Virginia	53	1.5	1,463	1.5	28	52.4	35,846	1,112.5	1.7	20,989,717
Louisiana	81	2.2	1,895	2.0	23	57.5	30,333	896.9	1.4	11,072,444
Oklahoma	32	0.9	2,452	2.6	77	69.8	28,465	891.6	1.3	27,861,625
South Carolina	23	0.6	871	0.9	38	33.9	38,954	721.1	1.1	31,354,174
Kansas	27	0.7	1,220	1.3	45	42.8	35,049	717.4	1.1	26,571,741
Kentucky	28	0.8	1,379	1.5	49	50.1	36,315	697.8	1.1	24,922,286
Hawaii	66	1.8	1,450	1.5	22	46.1	31,783	696.9	1.1	10,559,606
Arizona	43	1.2	1,304	1.4	30	25.4	19,441	670.2	1.0	15,585,000
Connecticut	37	1.0	481	0.5	13	24.3	50,530	639.8	1.0	17,291,189
Oregon	43	1.2	1,585	1.7	37	48.6	30,657	623.1	0.9	14,491,023
Mississippi	26	0.7	987	1.0	38	39.2	39,732	547.2	0.8	21,045,577
Nevada	28	0.8	849	0.9	30	37.8	44,544	522.2	0.8	18,649,893
Iowa	28	0.8	1,154	1.2	41	38.1	33,038	373.1	0.6	13,324,536

Continued on next page.

INDUSTRY DATA BY STATE - Continued

State	Establishments Total (number)	% of U.S.	Employment Total (number)	% of U.S.	Per Estab.	Payroll Total ($ mil.)	Per Empl. ($)	Sales Total ($ mil.)	% of U.S.	Per Estab. ($)
Maine	24	0.7	901	0.9	38	28.0	31,099	353.5	0.5	14,729,917
New Mexico	14	0.4	427	0.5	30	13.0	30,473	152.0	0.2	10,854,000
Idaho	15	0.4	334	0.4	22	7.1	21,225	70.3	0.1	4,684,467
Alaska	14	0.4	83	0.1	6	2.8	33,747	25.4	-	1,814,071
West Virginia	6	0.2	104	0.1	17	2.3	22,433	23.6	-	3,933,667
Montana	9	0.2	25	-	3	0.7	28,840	19.3	-	2,148,000
Indiana	49	1.4	1000-2499	-	-	(D)	-	(D)	-	-
Alabama	33	0.9	500-999	-	-	(D)	-	(D)	-	-
Arkansas	28	0.8	500-999	-	-	(D)	-	(D)	-	-
Rhode Island	25	0.7	250-499	-	-	(D)	-	(D)	-	-
New Hampshire	18	0.5	100-249	-	-	(D)	-	(D)	-	-
Utah	14	0.4	500-999	-	-	(D)	-	(D)	-	-
Delaware	6	0.2	100-249	-	-	(D)	-	(D)	-	-
Vermont	6	0.2	100-249	-	-	(D)	-	(D)	-	-
South Dakota	5	0.1	500-999	-	-	(D)	-	(D)	-	-
D.C.	3	0.1	0-19	-	-	(D)	-	(D)	-	-
North Dakota	3	0.1	250-499	-	-	(D)	-	(D)	-	-
Wyoming	1	-	0-19	-	-	(D)	-	(D)	-	-

Source: 2002 *Economic Census*. The states are in descending order of sales or establishments (if sales data are missing for the majority). The symbol (D) appears when data are withheld to prevent disclosure of competitive information. States marked with (D) are sorted by number of establishments. A dash (-) indicates that the data element cannot be calculated. Shaded *states* on the state map indicate those states which have proportionately greater representation in the industry than would be indicated by the states population; the ratio is based on total sales or number of establishments. Shaded *regions* indicate where the industry is regionally most concentrated.

NAICS 424430 - DAIRY PRODUCT (EXCEPT DRIED OR CANNED) MERCHANT WHOLESALERS*

Sales ($ million)

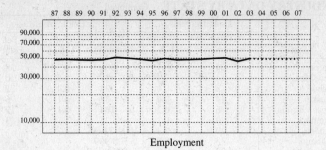

Employment

GENERAL STATISTICS

Year	Establishments (number)	Employment (number)	Payroll ($ million)	Sales ($ million)	Employees per Establishment (number)	Sales per Establishment ($)	Payroll per Employee ($)
1987	3,743	48,038	1,097.1	26,926.6	12.8	7,193,855.2	22,838.2
1988	3,455	48,488	1,191.8	28,606.1 e	14.0	8,279,623.7	24,579.3
1989	3,245	47,830	1,190.9	30,285.6 e	14.7	9,333,004.6	24,898.6
1990	3,192	47,432	1,240.8	31,965.1 e	14.9	10,014,129.1	26,159.6
1991	3,132	48,016	1,330.8	33,644.6 e	15.3	10,742,209.5	27,715.8
1992	3,378	50,975	1,469.9	35,324.1	15.1	10,457,104.8	28,835.7
1993	3,191	49,924	1,531.9	35,178.2 e	15.6	11,024,193.0	30,684.6
1994	3,024	48,542	1,576.9	35,032.4 e	16.1	11,584,788.4	32,485.3
1995	2,873	46,817	1,523.3	34,886.5 e	16.3	12,142,882.0	32,537.3
1996	2,899 e	49,384 e	1,645.0 e	34,740.7 e	17.0 e	11,983,684.0 e	33,310.4 e
1997	2,862	47,742	1,637.1	34,594.8	16.7	12,087,631.0	34,290.6
1998	2,794	48,096	1,764.9	35,058.7 e	17.2	12,547,866.9	36,695.4
1999	2,769	48,499	1,832.2	35,522.7 e	17.5	12,828,703.5	37,778.1
2000	2,741	49,578	1,890.9	35,986.6 e	18.1	13,129,011.3	38,139.6
2001	2,741	50,239	2,001.1	36,450.6 e	18.3	13,298,270.7	39,832.3
2002	2,550	45,939	1,874.4	36,914.5	18.0	14,476,274.5	40,801.9
2003	2,478	49,371	2,140.6	38,211.4 p	19.9	14,642,636.3 p	43,358.4
2004	2,437 p	48,696 p	2,123.1 p	38,728.0 p	19.4 p	15,033,510.9 p	43,652.9 p
2005	2,374 p	48,715 p	2,182.9 p	39,244.7 p	19.8 p	15,424,385.5 p	44,876.1 p
2006	2,310 p	48,734 p	2,242.7 p	39,761.3 p	20.1 p	15,815,260.2 p	46,099.4 p
2007	2,247 p	48,753 p	2,302.5 p	40,278.0 p	20.5 p	16,206,134.8 p	47,322.7 p

Sources: *Economic Census of the United States*, 1987, 1992, 1997, and 2002. Establishment counts, employment, and payroll are from *County Business Patterns* for non-Census years. Values followed by a 'p' are projections by the editors. Sales data for non-Census years are extrapolations, marked by 'e'. Data are the most recent available at this level of detail.

INDICES OF CHANGE

Year	Establishments (number)	Employment (number)	Payroll ($ million)	Sales ($ million)	Employees per Establishment (number)	Sales per Establishment ($)	Payroll per Employee ($)
1987	146.8	104.6	58.5	72.9	71.1	49.7	56.0
1992	132.5	111.0	78.4	95.7	83.9	72.2	70.7
1993	125.1	108.7	81.7	95.3 e	86.7	76.2	75.2
1994	118.6	105.7	84.1	94.9 e	89.4	80.0	79.6
1995	112.7	101.9	81.3	94.5 e	90.6	83.9	79.7
1996	113.7 e	107.5 e	87.8 e	94.1 e	94.4 e	82.8 e	81.6 e
1997	112.2	103.9	87.3	93.7	92.8	83.5	84.0
1998	109.6	104.7	94.2	95.0 e	95.6	86.7	89.9
1999	108.6	105.6	97.7	96.2 e	97.2	88.6	92.6
2000	107.5	107.9	100.9	97.5 e	100.6	90.7	93.5
2001	107.5	109.4	106.8	98.7 e	101.7	91.9	97.6
2002	100.0	100.0	100.0	100.0	100.0	100.0	100.0
2003	97.2	107.5	114.2	103.5 p	110.7	101.1 p	106.3
2004	95.6 p	106.0 p	113.3 p	104.9 p	107.9 p	103.8 p	107.0 p
2005	93.1 p	106.0 p	116.5 p	106.3 p	109.9 p	106.5 p	110.0 p
2006	90.6 p	106.1 p	119.7 p	107.7 p	111.8 p	109.2 p	113.0 p
2007	88.1 p	106.1 p	122.8 p	109.1 p	113.7 p	111.9 p	116.0 p

Sources: Same as General Statistics. The values shown reflect change from the base year, 2002. Values above 100 mean greater than 2002, values below 100 mean less than 2002, and a value of 100 in the 1987-2001 or 2003-2007 period means same as 2002. Values followed by a 'p' are projections by the editors; 'e' stands for extrapolation. Data are the most recent available at this level of detail.

SELECTED RATIOS

For 2002	Avg. of All Wholesale	Analyzed Industry	Index	For 2002	Avg. of All Wholesale	Analyzed Industry	Index
Employees per Establishment	15	18	121	Sales per Employee	791,325	803,555	102
Payroll per Establishment	626,122	735,059	117	Sales per Establishment	12,012,387	14,476,275	121
Payroll per Employee	41,161	40,802	99	Expenses per Establishment	na	na	na

Sources: Same as General Statistics. The 'Average of All' column, Wholesale or Retail, represents the average of the sector reported for the most recent complete year available. The Index shows the relationship between the Average and the Analyzed Industry. For example, 100 means that they are equal; 500 that the Analyzed Industry is five times the average; 50 means that the Analyzed Industry is half the national average. The abbreviation 'na' is used to show that data are 'not available'.

*Equivalent to SIC 5143.

LEADING COMPANIES   Number shown: **54**   Total sales ($ mil): **9,903**   Total employment (000): **10.7**

Company Name	Address				CEO Name	Phone	Co. Type	Sales ($ mil)	Empl. (000)
Melody Farms Inc.	31111 Industrial Rd	Livonia	MI	48150	Rodney George	734-525-4000	R	2,335*	0.5
Purity Wholesale Grocers Inc.	5400 Broken Sound	Boca Raton	FL	33487	Jeff Levitetz	561-994-9360	R	1,450	0.4
Shamrock Foods Co.	2540 N 29th Ave	Phoenix	AZ	85009		602-233-6400	R	1,354	2.3
Dairylea Cooperative Inc.	PO Box 4844	Syracuse	NY	13221	Clyde Rutherford	315-433-0100	R	881*	0.3
Associated Milk Producers Inc.	PO Box 455	New Ulm	MN	56073	Paul Toft	507-354-8295	R	876*	1.7
Affiliated Foods Inc.	PO Box 30300	Amarillo	TX	79120	George Langford	806-372-3851	R	790*	1.1
Burris Foods Inc.	PO Box 219	Milford	DE	19963	Robert D Burris	302-422-4531	R	379*	1.0
Dairy Fresh Products Co.	601 Rockefeller Ave	Ontario	CA	91761	Jim DeKeyser	909-975-1019	S	232*	0.5
Atalanta Corp.	1 Atalanta Plz	Elizabeth	NJ	07206	George Gellert	908-351-8000	R	208*	0.1
W.S. Lee and Sons Inc.	PO Box 1631	Altoona	PA	16603	Robert Lee	814-696-3535	R	160*	0.3
Grassland Dairy Products Inc.	PO Box 160	Greenwood	WI	54437		715-267-6182	R	158*	0.2
Tony's Fine Foods	PO Box 1501	W. Sacramento	CA	95605	Karl Berger	916-374-4150	R	119*	0.4
M.E. Franks Inc.	175 Strafford Ave	Wayne	PA	19087	Donald W Street	610-989-9688	R	117*	<0.1
Clover-Stornetta Farms Inc.	PO Box 750369	Petaluma	CA	94975	Dan Benedetti	707-778-8448	R	84*	0.2
Dairy Fresh Food Inc.	21405 Trolley Ind	Taylor	MI	48180	Alan Must	313-295-6300	R	80*	0.2
Lincoln Poultry and Egg Co.	2005 M St	Lincoln	NE	68510	Richard Evnen	402-477-3757	R	63*	0.2
J. Kings Food Service Profession.	700 Furrows Rd	Holtsville	NY	11742	John King	631-289-8401	R	60*	0.2
Inland Northwest Dairies L.L.C.	PO Box 7310	Spokane	WA	99207		509-489-8600	R	38*	0.1
Reilly Dairy and Food Co.	PO Box 19217	Tampa	FL	33686	Gerald Reilly	813-839-8458	R	36*	<0.1
Tusco Grocers Inc.	PO Box 240	Dennison	OH	44621	Gregory W Kimble	740-922-2223	R	35*	<0.1
Pint Size Corp.	99-1287 Waiua Pl	Aiea	HI	96701		808-487-0030	R	32*	0.1
Zanios Foods Inc.	PO Box 27730	Albuquerque	NM	87125	Jim Zanios	505-831-1411	R	32*	0.1
Philly's Famous Water Ice Inc.	1102 N 28th St	Tampa	FL	33605	Alex Plotkin	813-353-8645	R	31*	0.1
Omaha Beef Company Inc.	PO Box 339	Danbury	CT	06813	Brian Street	203-748-2651	R	26*	<0.1
Elgin Dairy Foods Inc.	3707 W Harrison St	Chicago	IL	60624	Ed Gignac	773-722-7100	R	23*	<0.1
Minster Farmers Cooperative	PO Box 100	Minster	OH	45865	Dale Meyer	419-628-2367	R	20*	<0.1
Roney Oatman Inc.	735 Prairie St	Aurora	IL	60506		708-344-9200	R	19*	<0.1
Superior Dairies Inc.	1411 Holmes St	Saginaw	MI	48602	James Reis	989-792-1234	R	19*	<0.1
Cedar Crest Specialties Inc.	PO Box 260	Cedarburg	WI	53012	Kenneth Kohlwey	262-377-7252	R	17*	<0.1
Mike Hudson Distributing Inc.	PO Box 808033	Petaluma	CA	94975		707-763-7388	R	17*	<0.1
Salvati Foods Inc.	595 S Broadway	Hicksville	NY	11801	Andrew Benzoni	516-932-8300	R	16*	<0.1
Northwest Cheese Distributors Inc.	PO Box 882943	San Francisco	CA	94188	Herb Brosowsky	415-822-5088	R	15*	<0.1
Axelrod Foods Inc.	PO Box 795	Paterson	NJ	07533		973-684-0600	S	15*	<0.1
Prairie Farms Dairy Inc. Ice Cream	PO Box 19766	St. Louis	MO	63144		314-962-2550	D	14*	<0.1
Middlefield Cheese	PO Box 757	Middlefield	OH	44062	John Rothenbuhler	440-632-5228	R	14*	<0.1
Brown's Ice Cream Co.	2929 University SE	Minneapolis	MN	55414	Tim Nelson	612-378-1075	R	12*	<0.1
Great West Egg Industries	2183 E 11th St	Los Angeles	CA	90021	Seymour Teichner	213-626-7538	R	10*	<0.1
Cold Spring Cooperative Creamery	301 1st St S	Cold Spring	MN	56320	Dave Regnier	320-685-8651	R	10*	<0.1
Abbott's Premium Ice Cream Inc.	PO Box 411	Center Conway	NH	03813	Charles S Marshall	603-356-2344	R	9*	<0.1
Asael Farr and Sons Co.	PO Box 1167	Ogden	UT	84402		801-393-8629	R	9*	<0.1
Farmers Cooperative Dairy Inc.	104 Rotery Dr	West Hazleton	PA	18202		570-453-0203	D	9*	<0.1
John R. White Company Inc.	PO Box 10043	Birmingham	AL	35202	Donald Patton	205-595-8381	R	9*	<0.1
Sunrise AG Cooperative	PO Box 458	Buckman	MN	56317	Ron Grittner	320-468-6433	R	9*	<0.1
Wenzel Farm Sausage	500 E 29th St	Marshfield	WI	54449	H Wenzel	715-387-1218	R	9*	<0.1
Dairy-Mix Inc.	3020 46th Ave N	St. Petersburg	FL	33714	Edward J Coryn	727-525-6101	R	8*	<0.1
Lone Elm Sales Inc.	9695 N Van Dyne	Van Dyne	WI	54979	Glen Dedow	920-688-2338	R	8*	<0.1
Hoban Foods Inc.	1599 E Warren Ave	Detroit	MI	48207	Donald VanTiem	313-833-1500	R	7*	<0.1
Wades Dairy Inc.	1316 Barnum Ave	Bridgeport	CT	06610	Douglas H Wade Jr	203-579-9233	R	7*	<0.1
Gordon Food Company Inc.	PO Box 41534	Memphis	TN	38174	Michael Gordon	901-454-4100	R	6*	<0.1
Getchell Brothers Inc.	PO Box 8	Brewer	ME	04412	Doug Farnham	207-989-7335	R	5*	<0.1
R.J. Rous Inc.	4366 W Ogden Ave	Chicago	IL	60623	Rudolph J Rous	773-521-3663	R	5*	<0.1
H.C. Davis Company Inc.	PO Box 346	Bridgeville	DE	19933	HC Davis	302-337-7001	R	3*	<0.1
Cutrufellos Creamery Inc.	1390 Barnum Ave	Stratford	CT	06497	Trent D'Eramo	203-378-2651	R	2*	<0.1
Granger Farmers Cooperative	Rte 1	Harmony	MN	55939	Benjamin Phillips	507-772-4433	R	1*	<0.1

Source: Ward's Business Directory of U.S. Private and Public Companies, Volumes 1 and 2, 2005. The company type code used is as follows: P - Public, R - Private, S - Subsidiary, D - Division, J - Joint Venture, A - Affiliate, G - Group. Sales are in millions of dollars, employees are in thousands. An asterisk (*) indicates an estimated sales volume. The symbol < stands for 'less than'. Company names and addresses are truncated, in some cases, to fit into the available space.

OCCUPATIONS EMPLOYED BY GROCERY & RELATED PRODUCTS WHOLESALE

Occupation	% of Total 2004	Change to 2014	Occupation	% of Total 2004	Change to 2014
Sales reps, wholesale & manufacturing, exc tech	12.7	10.6	Office clerks, general	1.9	-1.6
Laborers & freight, stock, & material movers, hand	11.0	-0.5	Bookkeeping, accounting, & auditing clerks	1.7	-0.5
Driver/sales workers	9.0	10.4	General & operations managers	1.5	9.4
Truck drivers, heavy & tractor-trailer	9.0	10.4	First-line supervisors/managers of non-retail sales work	1.5	2.2
Truck drivers, light or delivery services	5.0	10.4	Customer service representatives	1.5	13.2
Stock clerks & order fillers	4.4	-15.3	Wholesale & retail buyers, except farm products	1.2	4.5
Industrial truck & tractor operators	4.0	-0.5	First-line supervisors/managers of transporation workers	1.1	10.6
Packers & packagers, hand	2.8	10.6	Maintenance & repair workers, general	1.0	10.6
Shipping, receiving, & traffic clerks	2.1	0.1	First-line supervisors/managers of office workers	1.0	0.2
Packaging & filling machine operators & tenders	2.0	-5.8			

Source: Industry-Occupation Matrix, Bureau of Labor Statistics. These data are reported based on 4-digit NAICS categories but have been matched to corresponding 6-digit NAICS industry codes. The change reported for each occupation to the year 2014 is a percent of growth or decline as estimated by the Bureau of Labor Statistics. The abbreviation nec stands for 'not elsewhere classified.'

LOCATION BY STATE AND REGIONAL CONCENTRATION

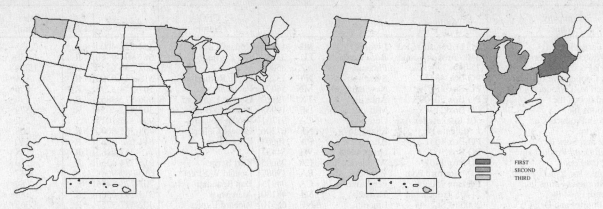

INDUSTRY DATA BY STATE

State	Establishments Total (number)	% of U.S.	Employment Total (number)	% of U.S.	Per Estab.	Payroll Total ($ mil.)	Per Empl. ($)	Sales Total ($ mil.)	% of U.S.	Per Estab. ($)
New Jersey	127	5.0	3,277	7.0	26	133.7	40,793	3,983.7	10.6	31,367,874
California	333	13.0	5,328	11.4	16	196.9	36,961	3,317.4	8.8	9,962,282
New York	316	12.3	4,109	8.8	13	161.4	39,275	3,156.6	8.4	9,989,351
Massachusetts	44	1.7	1,514	3.2	34	72.8	48,057	2,840.7	7.6	64,561,318
Wisconsin	119	4.6	3,196	6.8	27	109.6	34,304	2,344.1	6.3	19,698,454
Illinois	147	5.7	2,090	4.5	14	85.0	40,676	2,147.8	5.7	14,610,714
Pennsylvania	108	4.2	1,655	3.5	15	69.5	41,968	1,924.7	5.1	17,821,037
Minnesota	62	2.4	841	1.8	14	36.4	43,256	1,607.8	4.3	25,932,274
Washington	56	2.2	1,187	2.5	21	37.6	31,714	1,500.9	4.0	26,801,554
Florida	145	5.7	1,811	3.9	12	64.7	35,722	1,210.0	3.2	8,344,552
Michigan	81	3.2	1,587	3.4	20	66.4	41,831	1,086.9	2.9	13,418,432
Texas	113	4.4	1,819	3.9	16	59.4	32,657	1,067.9	2.8	9,450,690
Virginia	34	1.3	597	1.3	18	21.6	36,263	903.6	2.4	26,577,118
Arizona	40	1.6	615	1.3	15	21.0	34,213	562.9	1.5	14,072,050
Missouri	51	2.0	856	1.8	17	43.8	51,164	555.4	1.5	10,890,275
Vermont	8	0.3	143	0.3	18	5.7	39,748	409.5	1.1	51,183,000
Connecticut	24	0.9	546	1.2	23	24.4	44,692	384.0	1.0	16,001,167
North Carolina	65	2.5	899	1.9	14	29.4	32,648	368.1	1.0	5,663,062
Georgia	47	1.8	721	1.5	15	21.4	29,667	363.6	1.0	7,735,894
Indiana	38	1.5	474	1.0	12	15.6	32,899	277.0	0.7	7,289,474
Utah	24	0.9	496	1.1	21	13.9	28,123	229.6	0.6	9,565,583
Iowa	24	0.9	414	0.9	17	17.9	43,234	187.8	0.5	7,825,625
Tennessee	32	1.2	535	1.1	17	14.1	26,350	181.3	0.5	5,665,969
Nebraska	12	0.5	158	0.3	13	5.8	36,418	159.8	0.4	13,317,417
Kentucky	46	1.8	478	1.0	10	15.9	33,262	150.6	0.4	3,273,783
Idaho	15	0.6	117	0.3	8	2.6	22,581	127.2	0.3	8,478,800
Kansas	28	1.1	178	0.4	6	6.3	35,124	95.8	0.3	3,423,071
Nevada	20	0.8	214	0.5	11	7.8	36,444	88.3	0.2	4,415,700
New Mexico	10	0.4	120	0.3	12	4.0	33,650	80.6	0.2	8,061,200
New Hampshire	12	0.5	109	0.2	9	4.0	37,119	54.0	0.1	4,499,500
Hawaii	13	0.5	171	0.4	13	5.1	29,813	53.3	0.1	4,102,538
Maine	14	0.5	105	0.2	8	4.2	40,152	53.0	0.1	3,787,357
Mississippi	18	0.7	134	0.3	7	3.3	24,440	41.0	0.1	2,277,278
North Dakota	19	0.7	49	0.1	3	1.5	29,959	25.8	0.1	1,358,526
Montana	11	0.4	53	0.1	5	1.1	21,566	15.7	-	1,424,909
Wyoming	9	0.4	42	0.1	5	1.1	27,262	11.9	-	1,322,556
South Dakota	6	0.2	8	-	1	0.3	33,375	2.8	-	463,000
Ohio	68	2.7	5K-9999	-	-	(D)	-	(D)	-	-
Alabama	32	1.2	250-499	-	-	(D)	-	(D)	-	-
South Carolina	31	1.2	250-499	-	-	(D)	-	(D)	-	-
Colorado	30	1.2	1000-2499	-	-	(D)	-	(D)	-	-
Maryland	29	1.1	250-499	-	-	(D)	-	(D)	-	-
Louisiana	24	0.9	100-249	-	-	(D)	-	(D)	-	-
Oregon	22	0.9	250-499	-	-	(D)	-	(D)	-	-
Oklahoma	21	0.8	100-249	-	-	(D)	-	(D)	-	-
Arkansas	16	0.6	100-249	-	-	(D)	-	(D)	-	-
West Virginia	8	0.3	100-249	-	-	(D)	-	(D)	-	-
D.C.	5	0.2	20-99	-	-	(D)	-	(D)	-	-
Alaska	4	0.2	20-99	-	-	(D)	-	(D)	-	-
Rhode Island	3	0.1	20-99	-	-	(D)	-	(D)	-	-

Source: 2002 *Economic Census*. The states are in descending order of sales or establishments (if sales data are missing for the majority). The symbol (D) appears when data are withheld to prevent disclosure of competitive information. States marked with (D) are sorted by number of establishments. A dash (-) indicates that the data element cannot be calculated. Shaded *states* on the state map indicate those states which have proportionately greater representation in the industry than would be indicated by the states population; the ratio is based on total sales or number of establishments. Shaded *regions* indicate where the industry is regionally most concentrated.

NAICS 424440 - POULTRY AND POULTRY PRODUCT MERCHANT WHOLESALERS*

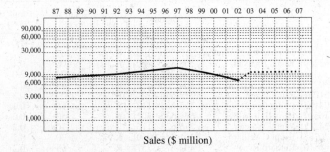

Sales ($ million)

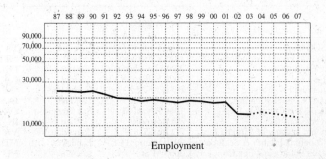

Employment

GENERAL STATISTICS

Year	Establishments (number)	Employment (number)	Payroll ($ million)	Sales ($ million)	Employees per Establishment (number)	Sales per Establishment ($)	Payroll per Employee ($)
1987	1,372	23,850	405.5	8,553.7	17.4	6,234,475.2	17,002.1
1988	1,298	23,720	438.3	8,866.6 e	18.3	6,830,970.7	18,478.1
1989	1,207	23,169	445.3	9,179.5 e	19.2	7,605,219.6	19,219.6
1990	1,152	23,765	477.9	9,492.4 e	20.6	8,239,930.6	20,109.4
1991	1,118	21,903	476.4	9,805.3 e	19.6	8,770,393.6	21,750.4
1992	1,224	19,916	444.3	10,118.2	16.3	8,266,503.3	22,308.7
1993	1,141	19,672	448.9	10,856.5 e	17.2	9,514,899.2	22,819.2
1994	1,069	18,488	433.3	11,594.8 e	17.3	10,846,398.5	23,436.8
1995	1,019	19,091	448.8	12,333.0 e	18.7	12,103,042.2	23,508.5
1996	968 e	18,459 e	481.4 e	13,071.3 e	19.1 e	13,503,409.1 e	26,079.4 e
1997	1,040	17,792	490.6	13,809.6	17.1	13,278,461.5	27,574.2
1998	1,016	18,661	533.4	12,512.8 e	18.4	12,315,728.3	28,583.7
1999	975	18,352	542.0	11,216.0 e	18.8	11,503,548.7	29,533.6
2000	937	17,612	537.8	9,919.1 e	18.8	10,586,061.9	30,536.6
2001	960	17,975	577.3	8,622.3 e	18.7	8,981,583.3	32,115.5
2002	749	13,367	394.0	7,325.5	17.8	9,780,373.8	29,475.6
2003	738	13,203	423.1	11,040.3 p	17.9	12,477,657.2 p	32,044.4
2004	772 p	14,029 p	505.4 p	11,109.2 p	18.2 p	12,781,197.8 p	33,554.7 p
2005	740 p	13,438 p	509.3 p	11,178.1 p	18.1 p	13,084,738.3 p	34,507.9 p
2006	708 p	12,846 p	513.2 p	11,247.0 p	18.1 p	13,388,278.9 p	35,461.2 p
2007	676 p	12,255 p	517.1 p	11,315.8 p	18.1 p	13,691,819.5 p	36,414.5 p

Sources: Economic Census of the United States, 1987, 1992, 1997, and 2002. Establishment counts, employment, and payroll are from County Business Patterns for non-Census years. Values followed by a 'p' are projections by the editors. Sales data for non-Census years are extrapolations, marked by 'e'. Data are the most recent available at this level of detail.

INDICES OF CHANGE

Year	Establishments (number)	Employment (number)	Payroll ($ million)	Sales ($ million)	Employees per Establishment (number)	Sales per Establishment ($)	Payroll per Employee ($)
1987	183.2	178.4	102.9	116.8	97.8	63.7	57.7
1992	163.4	149.0	112.8	138.1	91.6	84.5	75.7
1993	152.3	147.2	113.9	148.2 e	96.6	97.3	77.4
1994	142.7	138.3	110.0	158.3 e	97.2	110.9	79.5
1995	136.0	142.8	113.9	168.4 e	105.1	123.7	79.8
1996	129.2 e	138.1 e	122.2 e	178.4 e	107.3 e	138.1 e	88.5 e
1997	138.9	133.1	124.5	188.5	96.1	135.8	93.5
1998	135.6	139.6	135.4	170.8 e	103.4	125.9	97.0
1999	130.2	137.3	137.6	153.1 e	105.6	117.6	100.2
2000	125.1	131.8	136.5	135.4 e	105.6	108.2	103.6
2001	128.2	134.5	146.5	117.7 e	105.1	91.8	109.0
2002	100.0	100.0	100.0	100.0	100.0	100.0	100.0
2003	98.5	98.8	107.4	150.7 p	100.5	127.6 p	108.7
2004	103.0 p	105.0 p	128.3 p	151.7 p	102.0 p	130.7 p	113.8 p
2005	98.8 p	100.5 p	129.3 p	152.6 p	101.9 p	133.8 p	117.1 p
2006	94.5 p	96.1 p	130.2 p	153.5 p	101.8 p	136.9 p	120.3 p
2007	90.3 p	91.7 p	131.2 p	154.5 p	101.7 p	140.0 p	123.5 p

Sources: Same as General Statistics. The values shown reflect change from the base year, 2002. Values above 100 mean greater than 2002, values below 100 mean less than 2002, and a value of 100 in the 1987-2001 or 2003-2007 period means same as 2002. Values followed by a 'p' are projections by the editors; 'e' stands for extrapolation. Data are the most recent available at this level of detail.

SELECTED RATIOS

For 2002	Avg. of All Wholesale	Analyzed Industry	Index	For 2002	Avg. of All Wholesale	Analyzed Industry	Index
Employees per Establishment	15	18	119	Sales per Employee	791,325	548,029	69
Payroll per Establishment	626,122	526,035	84	Sales per Establishment	12,012,387	9,780,374	81
Payroll per Employee	41,161	29,476	72	Expenses per Establishment	na	na	na

Sources: Same as General Statistics. The 'Average of All' column, Wholesale or Retail, represents the average of the sector reported for the most recent complete year available. The Index shows the relationship between the Average and the Analyzed Industry. For example, 100 means that they are equal; 500 that the Analyzed Industry is five times the average; 50 means that the Analyzed Industry is half the national average. The abbreviation 'na' is used to show that data are 'not available'.

*Equivalent to SIC 5144.

LEADING COMPANIES   Number shown: 25   Total sales ($ mil): 32,094   Total employment (000): 52.5

Company Name	Address				CEO Name	Phone	Co. Type	Sales ($ mil)	Empl. (000)
SYSCO Corp.	1390 Enclave Pkwy	Houston	TX	77077		281-584-1390	P	29,335	47.0
Sherwood Food Distributors	18615 Sherwood	Detroit	MI	48234	J Lawrence Tushman	313-366-3100	R	762	0.7
Agar Supply Inc.	225 John Hancock	Taunton	MA	02780	Karen Bressler	508-821-2060	R	400*	0.4
Cagle's Inc.	2000 Hills Ave NW	Atlanta	GA	30318	J Douglas Cagle	404-355-2820	P	304	2.0
Sutherland Foodservice Inc.	PO Box 786	Forest Park	GA	30298	Gene Sutherland, Sr	404-366-8550	R	248*	0.2
Harker's Distribution Inc.	PO Box 1308	Le Mars	IA	51031	Ron Geiger	712-546-8171	R	202*	0.8
United Meat Company Inc.	1040 Bryant St	San Francisco	CA	94103	Philip Gee Jr	415-864-2118	R	195*	<0.1
Troyer Foods Inc.	PO Box 608	Goshen	IN	46527	Paris Ball-Miller	574-533-0302	R	150*	0.2
Dutt and Wagner of Virginia Inc.	PO Box 518	Abingdon	VA	24212	Peggy Wagner	276-628-2116	R	70*	0.2
Metropolitan Poultry & Seafood	1920 Stanford Ct	Landover	MD	20785	Brian C Willard	301-772-0060	R	70*	0.2
Lincoln Poultry and Egg Co.	2005 M St	Lincoln	NE	68510	Richard Evnen	402-477-3757	R	63*	0.2
J. Kings Food Service Profession.	700 Furrows Rd	Holtsville	NY	11742	John King	631-289-8401	R	60*	0.2
Will Poultry Company Inc.	PO Box 1146	Buffalo	NY	14240	Donald Will	716-853-2000	R	51*	0.1
Vallet Food Service Inc.	1230 E 12th St	Dubuque	IA	52001	Edward G White	563-588-2347	R	41*	<0.1
Zanios Foods Inc.	PO Box 27730	Albuquerque	NM	87125	Jim Zanios	505-831-1411	R	32*	0.1
Jawd Associates Inc.	Hunts Pt Coop	Bronx	NY	10474	Robert Corazza	212-589-2000	R	25*	<0.1
Roberts Foods Inc.	1615 W Jefferson St	Springfield	IL	62702	Dean Robert Jr	217-793-2633	S	25*	<0.1
Consolidated Poultry and Egg Co.	426 St Paul Ave	Memphis	TN	38126	James J Skefos	901-526-7392	R	18*	<0.1
Feather Crest Farms Inc.	14374 E SH 21	Bryan	TX	77808	Bryan Barrett	979-589-2576	R	14*	<0.1
Goetz & Sons Western Meat	1220 Hewitt Ave	Everett	WA	98201	Jim Horton	425-252-1151	R	7*	<0.1
Intra-Coastal Packing Inc.	3222 S Military Trl	Lake Worth	FL	33463	Gerald Duthler	561-964-6020	R	7*	<0.1
Liberty Gold Fruit Co.	PO Box 2187	S. San Francisco	CA	94083	Harry Battat	650-583-4700	R	5*	<0.1
Barber's Poultry Inc.	PO Box 363	Broomfield	CO	80038	David R Barber	303-466-7338	R	4*	<0.1
Norbest Inc.	PO Box 1000	Midvale	UT	84047	Steven R Jensen	801-566-5656	R	3*	<0.1
Joseph Trenk and Sons	171 Thomas St	Newark	NJ	07114	David Trenk	973-589-5778	R	2*	<0.1

Source: *Ward's Business Directory of U.S. Private and Public Companies*, Volumes 1 and 2, 2005. The company type code used is as follows: P - Public, R - Private, S - Subsidiary, D - Division, J - Joint Venture, A - Affiliate, G - Group. Sales are in millions of dollars, employees are in thousands. An asterisk (*) indicates an estimated sales volume. The symbol < stands for 'less than'. Company names and addresses are truncated, in some cases, to fit into the available space.

OCCUPATIONS EMPLOYED BY GROCERY & RELATED PRODUCTS WHOLESALE

Occupation	% of Total 2004	Change to 2014	Occupation	% of Total 2004	Change to 2014
Sales reps, wholesale & manufacturing, exc tech	12.7	10.6	Office clerks, general	1.9	-1.6
Laborers & freight, stock, & material movers, hand	11.0	-0.5	Bookkeeping, accounting, & auditing clerks	1.7	-0.5
Driver/sales workers	9.0	10.4	General & operations managers	1.5	9.4
Truck drivers, heavy & tractor-trailer	9.0	10.4	First-line supervisors/managers of non-retail sales work	1.5	2.2
Truck drivers, light or delivery services	5.0	10.4	Customer service representatives	1.5	13.2
Stock clerks & order fillers	4.4	-15.3	Wholesale & retail buyers, except farm products	1.2	4.5
Industrial truck & tractor operators	4.0	-0.5	First-line supervisors/managers of transporation workers	1.1	10.6
Packers & packagers, hand	2.8	10.6	Maintenance & repair workers, general	1.0	10.6
Shipping, receiving, & traffic clerks	2.1	0.1	First-line supervisors/managers of office workers	1.0	0.2
Packaging & filling machine operators & tenders	2.0	-5.8			

Source: *Industry-Occupation Matrix*, Bureau of Labor Statistics. These data are reported based on 4-digit NAICS categories but have been matched to corresponding 6-digit NAICS industry codes. The change reported for each occupation to the year 2014 is a percent of growth or decline as estimated by the Bureau of Labor Statistics. The abbreviation nec stands for 'not elsewhere classified.'

LOCATION BY STATE AND REGIONAL CONCENTRATION

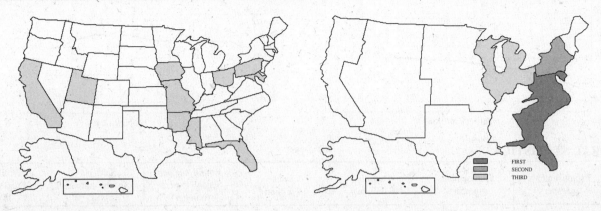

FIRST
SECOND
THIRD

INDUSTRY DATA BY STATE

State	Establishments Total (number)	% of U.S.	Employment Total (number)	% of U.S.	Per Estab.	Payroll Total ($ mil.)	Per Empl. ($)	Sales Total ($ mil.)	% of U.S.	Per Estab. ($)
California	91	12.2	2,504	18.2	28	64.1	25,603	1,007.1	12.5	11,066,758
Arkansas	19	2.5	555	4.0	29	19.4	35,029	769.2	9.5	40,486,526
New York	69	9.2	653	4.7	9	20.4	31,213	507.3	6.3	7,351,739
Florida	36	4.8	789	5.7	22	22.2	28,191	489.6	6.1	13,600,306
Texas	44	5.9	958	7.0	22	24.4	25,502	427.5	5.3	9,715,045
Pennsylvania	39	5.2	803	5.8	21	22.8	28,453	424.1	5.3	10,873,846
Ohio	33	4.4	1,220	8.9	37	29.7	24,309	406.7	5.0	12,324,394
Missouri	19	2.5	249	1.8	13	8.9	35,663	293.2	3.6	15,433,947
Maryland	18	2.4	496	3.6	28	20.9	42,175	290.9	3.6	16,160,333
Georgia	40	5.3	613	4.5	15	15.3	24,883	205.4	2.5	5,134,975
Mississippi	14	1.9	122	0.9	9	4.8	39,205	194.4	2.4	13,888,429
New Jersey	28	3.7	318	2.3	11	10.6	33,292	191.7	2.4	6,846,250
Utah	8	1.1	107	0.8	13	3.8	35,972	149.7	1.9	18,716,750
Iowa	8	1.1	216	1.6	27	4.7	21,810	136.5	1.7	17,057,375
Alabama	12	1.6	150	1.1	13	5.0	33,167	128.4	1.6	10,703,167
North Carolina	25	3.3	290	2.1	12	8.1	27,897	108.2	1.3	4,326,240
Connecticut	6	0.8	135	1.0	23	5.5	40,393	98.4	1.2	16,404,000
Tennessee	14	1.9	126	0.9	9	4.7	37,635	87.3	1.1	6,236,929
Colorado	9	1.2	141	1.0	16	4.8	33,908	76.0	0.9	8,441,889
Indiana	12	1.6	168	1.2	14	5.1	30,244	69.5	0.9	5,791,083
Virginia	12	1.6	214	1.6	18	6.6	31,005	58.9	0.7	4,907,250
Wisconsin	15	2.0	235	1.7	16	5.6	23,834	57.5	0.7	3,834,533
South Carolina	8	1.1	108	0.8	14	3.8	35,083	41.4	0.5	5,171,625
Michigan	11	1.5	50	0.4	5	1.5	29,180	31.9	0.4	2,902,727
Oklahoma	6	0.8	39	0.3	7	1.1	27,051	24.7	0.3	4,111,000
Hawaii	5	0.7	73	0.5	15	1.8	25,233	16.7	0.2	3,349,400
Louisiana	4	0.5	18	0.1	5	0.5	27,111	9.1	0.1	2,275,000
Illinois	44	5.9	500-999	-	-	(D)	-	(D)	-	-
Massachusetts	20	2.7	250-499	-	-	(D)	-	(D)	-	-
Minnesota	13	1.7	100-249	-	-	(D)	-	(D)	-	-
Kentucky	9	1.2	20-99	-	-	(D)	-	(D)	-	-
Washington	9	1.2	100-249	-	-	(D)	-	(D)	-	-
Arizona	6	0.8	20-99	-	-	(D)	-	(D)	-	-
Nevada	5	0.7	20-99	-	-	(D)	-	(D)	-	-
New Hampshire	5	0.7	250-499	-	-	(D)	-	(D)	-	-
Rhode Island	5	0.7	20-99	-	-	(D)	-	(D)	-	-
Oregon	4	0.5	100-249	-	-	(D)	-	(D)	-	-
Delaware	3	0.4	0-19	-	-	(D)	-	(D)	-	-
D.C.	3	0.4	0-19	-	-	(D)	-	(D)	-	-
Idaho	2	0.3	0-19	-	-	(D)	-	(D)	-	-
Kansas	2	0.3	0-19	-	-	(D)	-	(D)	-	-
Maine	2	0.3	20-99	-	-	(D)	-	(D)	-	-
Nebraska	2	0.3	0-19	-	-	(D)	-	(D)	-	-
New Mexico	2	0.3	20-99	-	-	(D)	-	(D)	-	-
Vermont	2	0.3	0-19	-	-	(D)	-	(D)	-	-
West Virginia	2	0.3	20-99	-	-	(D)	-	(D)	-	-
Montana	1	0.1	0-19	-	-	(D)	-	(D)	-	-
North Dakota	1	0.1	0-19	-	-	(D)	-	(D)	-	-
South Dakota	1	0.1	0-19	-	-	(D)	-	(D)	-	-

Source: 2002 Economic Census. The states are in descending order of sales or establishments (if sales data are missing for the majority). The symbol (D) appears when data are withheld to prevent disclosure of competitive information. States marked with (D) are sorted by number of establishments. A dash (-) indicates that the data element cannot be calculated. Shaded *states* on the state map indicate those states which have proportionately greater representation in the industry than would be indicated by the states population; the ratio is based on total sales or number of establishments. Shaded *regions* indicate where the industry is regionally most concentrated.

NAICS 424450 - CONFECTIONERY MERCHANT WHOLESALERS*

Sales ($ million)

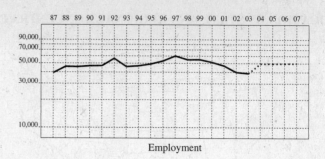

Employment

GENERAL STATISTICS

Year	Establishments (number)	Employment (number)	Payroll ($ million)	Sales ($ million)	Employees per Establishment (number)	Sales per Establishment ($)	Payroll per Employee ($)
1987	2,818	39,271	828.6	13,952.0	13.9	4,951,029.1	21,099.5
1988	2,620	45,978	1,071.9	15,522.7 e	17.5	5,924,694.7	23,313.3
1989	2,514	45,696	1,115.2	17,093.4 e	18.2	6,799,284.0	24,404.8
1990	2,505	46,704	1,218.9	18,664.0 e	18.6	7,450,698.6	26,098.4
1991	2,454	46,899	1,263.3	20,234.7 e	19.1	8,245,599.0	26,936.6
1992	2,693	56,322	1,203.5	21,805.4	20.9	8,097,066.5	21,368.2
1993	2,548	45,891	1,182.4	22,878.3 e	18.0	8,978,924.6	25,765.4
1994	2,541	46,847	1,256.3	23,951.2 e	18.4	9,425,895.3	26,817.1
1995	2,464	49,075	1,330.9	25,024.1 e	19.9	10,155,884.7	27,119.7
1996	2,541 e	52,979 e	1,436.3 e	26,097.0 e	20.8 e	10,270,366.0 e	27,110.7 e
1997	2,621	60,010	1,835.2	27,169.9	22.9	10,366,234.3	30,581.6
1998	2,499	54,639	1,464.1	27,641.8 e	21.9	11,061,136.5	26,795.9
1999	2,473	54,870	1,540.1	28,113.7 e	22.2	11,368,241.0	28,068.2
2000	2,397	51,332	1,735.4	28,585.5 e	21.4	11,925,548.6	33,807.3
2001	2,381	46,929	1,680.8	29,057.4 e	19.7	12,203,872.3	35,816.7
2002	2,283	39,964	1,240.2	29,529.3	17.5	12,934,428.4	31,032.9
2003	2,335	38,831	1,268.7	32,338.4 e	16.6	13,493,506.5 p	32,672.6
2004	2,336 p	49,384 p	1,643.6 p	33,383.2 p	20.9 p	13,976,868.3 p	33,849.9 p
2005	2,317 p	49,497 p	1,678.0 p	34,428.1 p	21.0 p	14,460,230.1 p	34,546.9 p
2006	2,297 p	49,610 p	1,712.4 p	35,472.9 p	21.2 p	14,943,591.9 p	35,243.9 p
2007	2,278 p	49,723 p	1,746.9 p	36,517.7 p	21.4 p	15,426,953.6 p	35,940.9 p

Sources: Economic Census of the United States, 1987, 1992, 1997, and 2002. Establishment counts, employment, and payroll are from *County Business Patterns* for non-Census years. Values followed by a 'p' are projections by the editors. Sales data for non-Census years are extrapolations, marked by 'e'. Data are the most recent available at this level of detail.

INDICES OF CHANGE

Year	Establishments (number)	Employment (number)	Payroll ($ million)	Sales ($ million)	Employees per Establishment (number)	Sales per Establishment ($)	Payroll per Employee ($)
1987	123.4	98.3	66.8	47.2	79.4	38.3	68.0
1992	118.0	140.9	97.0	73.8	119.4	62.6	68.9
1993	111.6	114.8	95.3	77.5 e	102.9	69.4	83.0
1994	111.3	117.2	101.3	81.1 e	105.1	72.9	86.4
1995	107.9	122.8	107.3	84.7 e	113.7	78.5	87.4
1996	111.3 e	132.6 e	115.8 e	88.4 e	118.9 e	79.4 e	87.4 e
1997	114.8	150.2	148.0	92.0	130.9	80.1	98.5
1998	109.5	136.7	118.1	93.6 e	125.1	85.5	86.3
1999	108.3	137.3	124.2	95.2 e	126.9	87.9	90.4
2000	105.0	128.4	139.9	96.8 e	122.3	92.2	108.9
2001	104.3	117.4	135.5	98.4 e	112.6	94.4	115.4
2002	100.0	100.0	100.0	100.0	100.0	100.0	100.0
2003	102.3	97.2	102.3	109.5 p	95.0	104.3 p	105.3
2004	102.3 p	123.6 p	132.5 p	113.1 p	119.2 p	108.1 p	109.1 p
2005	101.5 p	123.9 p	135.3 p	116.6 p	120.2 p	111.8 p	111.3 p
2006	100.6 p	124.1 p	138.1 p	120.1 p	121.3 p	115.5 p	113.6 p
2007	99.8 p	124.4 p	140.9 p	123.7 p	122.3 p	119.3 p	115.8 p

*Sources: Same as General Statistics. The values shown reflect change from the base year, 2002. Values above 100 mean greater than 2002, values below 100 mean less than 2002, and a value of 100 in the 1987-2001 or 2003-2007 period means same as 2002. Values followed by a 'p' are projections by the editors; 'e' stands for extrapolation. Data are the most recent available at this level of detail.

SELECTED RATIOS

For 2002	Avg. of All Wholesale	Analyzed Industry	Index	For 2002	Avg. of All Wholesale	Analyzed Industry	Index
Employees per Establishment	15	18	117	Sales per Employee	791,325	738,898	93
Payroll per Establishment	626,122	543,233	87	Sales per Establishment	12,012,387	12,934,428	108
Payroll per Employee	41,161	31,033	75	Expenses per Establishment	na	na	na

*Sources: Same as General Statistics. The 'Average of All' column, Wholesale or Retail, represents the average of the sector reported for the most recent complete year available. The Index shows the relationship between the Average and the Analyzed Industry. For example, 100 means that they are equal; 500 that the Analyzed Industry is five times the average; 50 means that the Analyzed Industry is half the national average. The abbreviation 'na' is used to show that data are 'not available'.

*Equivalent to SIC 5145.

LEADING COMPANIES Number shown: **58** Total sales ($ mil): **9,447** Total employment (000): **39.4**

Company Name	Address				CEO Name	Phone	Co. Type	Sales ($ mil)	Empl. (000)
Eby-Brown Co.	PO Box 3067	Naperville	IL	60566		630-778-2800	R	3,200	2.1
Universal Corp.	PO Box 25099	Richmond	VA	23260	Henry H Harrell	804-359-9311	P	2,271	30.0
Grocers Supply Co. Inc.	PO Box 14200	Houston	TX	77221	Max Levit	713-747-5000	R	1,182*	2.0
Grocery Supply Co.	9300 E Billy the Kid	El Paso	TX	79907		915-858-1053	S	624*	1.5
Torn and Glasser Inc.	PO Box 21823	Los Angeles	CA	90021	Robert Glasser	213-627-6496	R	291*	<0.1
Farner-Bocken Co.	1751 Hwy 30 E	Carroll	IA	51401	John Norgaard	712-792-3503	R	259*	0.5
J.T. Davenport and Sons Inc.	PO Box 1105	Sanford	NC	27330	John T Davenport Jr	919-774-9444	R	214*	0.3
Albert H. Notini and Sons Inc.	PO Box 299	Lowell	MA	01853	Alex Turshette	978-459-7151	R	105*	0.2
Bunn Capitol Co.	PO Box 4227	Springfield	IL	62708	Robert H Bunn	217-529-5401	R	90*	0.3
Safier's Inc.	8700 Harvard Ave	Cleveland	OH	44105		216-341-8700	R	88*	<0.1
MLO Products Inc.	2351 N Watney Way	Fairfield	CA	94533	Doug Williamson	707-399-2500	R	84*	0.2
Mound City Industries Inc.	1315 Cherokee St	St. Louis	MO	63118	Robert L Krekeler	314-773-5200	R	70*	<0.1
Poore Brothers Inc.	3500 S La Cometa	Goodyear	AZ	85338	Thomas W Freeze	623-932-6200	P	69	0.3
Los Angeles Nut House	1601 E Olympic	Los Angeles	CA	90021	Don Present	213-623-2541	R	66*	<0.1
R.H. Barringer Distributing Inc.	1620 Fairfax Rd	Greensboro	NC	27407	Mark Craig	336-854-0555	R	62*	0.2
Louisville Pecan Company Inc.	PO Box 38	Louisville	AL	36048	Homer Henson	334-266-5388	R	59*	<0.1
Kaiser Wholesale Inc.	PO Box 1115	New Albany	IN	47150	JR Kaiser	812-945-2651	R	50*	<0.1
Idaho Candy Co.	PO Box 1217	Boise	ID	83701	Dave Wagers	208-342-5505	R	42*	<0.1
Albert Guarnieri Company Inc.	PO Box 927	Warren	OH	44483	A Guarnieri III	330-394-5636	R	41*	<0.1
Fritz Company Inc.	1912 Hastings Ave	Newport	MN	55055	Elizabeth Hoekstra	651-459-9751	R	40*	0.1
Score Acquisitions Corp.	200 Corporate Dr	Blauvelt	NY	10913	Scott Semel	845-353-1251	R	40	<0.1
Hammons Products Company Inc.	PO Box 140	Stockton	MO	65785	Brian Hammons	417-276-5181	R	38*	0.1
SWD Corp.	PO Box 340	Lima	OH	45802	Carl Berger	419-227-2436	R	35*	<0.1
Pine Lesser and Sons Inc.	PO Box 1807	Clifton	NJ	07015	Allan G Lesser	973-478-3310	R	32*	<0.1
Edmiston Brothers Inc.	PO Box 371	Crockett	TX	75835	AC Rainn	936-544-2118	R	29*	<0.1
Keilson-Dayton Co.	PO Box 1457	Dayton	OH	45401	GT Wellinghoff	937-236-1070	R	29*	<0.1
Montano Cigarettes, Candy	290 Boston Post Rd	Milford	CT	06460	Gary Montano	203-877-0341	R	29*	<0.1
Albert's Organics Inc.	PO Box 624	Bridgeport	NJ	08014	Barclay Hope	856-241-9090	R	26*	<0.1
National Cinema Supply Corp.	14499 N Dale Mabry	Tampa	FL	33618	Barney Bailey	813-962-2772	R	26*	<0.1
Wiemuth and Son Company Inc.	PO Box 3128	Terre Haute	IN	47803	Robert A Wiemuth	812-232-3384	R	20*	<0.1
Blackburn-Russell Company Inc.	PO Box 157	Bedford	PA	15522	Robert B Blackburn	814-623-5181	R	18*	<0.1
A.W. Marshall Co.	PO Box 16127	Salt Lake City	UT	84116	Bill Marshall	801-328-4713	R	17*	<0.1
Prince of Peace Enterprises Inc.	3536 Arden Rd	Hayward	CA	94545	Kenneth Yeung	510-887-1899	R	17*	<0.1
Queen City Wholesale Inc.	PO Box 1083	Sioux Falls	SD	57101	Bill Wehrkamp	605-336-3215	R	16*	<0.1
J. Sosnick and Son Inc.	258 Littlefield Ave	S. San Francisco	CA	94080	Jeffrey Sosnick	650-952-2226	P	15*	<0.1
Doster Warehouse Inc.	933 Ashley St	Rochelle	GA	31079	Jack Chastain	229-365-2469	R	15*	<0.1
Sparkle Flavors	3701 Shell St	El Paso	TX	79901	David Nieves	915-592-2639	R	13*	<0.1
Honor Snack L.L.C.	2034 B S Alex Rd	West Carrollton	OH	45449		937-847-9800	R	11*	<0.1
Franklin Cigar and Tobacco Inc.	PO Box 1151	Franklin	LA	70538	Keith A Landen	337-828-3208	R	10*	<0.1
John F. Trompeter Co.	637 E Main St	Louisville	KY	40202		502-585-5852	R	10*	<0.1
Lavin Candy Company Inc.	4989 S Catherine St	Plattsburgh	NY	12901	Irvin C Reid	518-563-4630	R	10*	<0.1
Quality Candy Shoppes/Buddy	PO Box 070581	Milwaukee	WI	53207	Margaret Gile	414-483-4500	R	10	0.3
City Beverage	1105 E Lafayette St	Bloomington	IL	61704	Robert R Wombacher	309-662-1373	R	9*	<0.1
Miller Distributing Inc.	PO Box 6	Saint Clair	PA	17970	W Miller	570-429-1191	R	9*	<0.1
S.N.A.C.C. Distributing Co.	2105 Central Ave	Cincinnati	OH	45214	Gary Krummen	513-723-1777	R	8*	<0.1
Eagle Wholesale L.P.	PO Box 742	Tyler	TX	75710	Gordon Atkins	903-592-4321	R	6*	<0.1
Huser-Paul Company Inc.	3636 Illinois Rd	Fort Wayne	IN	46804		260-432-0557	R	6*	<0.1
Tidewater Wholesalers Inc.	708 W Constance Rd	Suffolk	VA	23434	John Orange	757-539-3261	R	6*	<0.1
Laymon Candy Company Inc.	276 Commercial Rd	San Bernardino	CA	92408	Kenneth Laymon	909-825-4408	R	6*	<0.1
F.B. McFadden Wholesale Inc.	415 Railroad Ave	Rock Springs	WY	82901	EH McFadden	307-362-5441	R	5*	<0.1
John Hayes and Sons	PO Box 6184	Wolcott	CT	06716	John F Hayes III	203-879-4616	R	5*	<0.1
Helen Grace Chocolates Inc.	2369 E Pacifica Pl	Compton	CA	90220	Robert Hadraft	310-638-8400	R	5*	<0.1
Blankinship Distributors Inc.	1905 Vine St	Kansas City	MO	64108	G L Blankinship	816-842-6825	R	3*	<0.1
Felknor International Inc.	PO Box 715	Monon	IN	47959	Jim McIntyre	219-253-6615	R	2*	<0.1
Pape Pecan House	PO Box 1281	Seguin	TX	78156	Kenneth Pape	830-379-7442	R	1*	<0.1
Bronson Syrup Company Inc.	1650 Locust Ave	Bohemia	NY	11716	Steven Goldstein	631-563-1177	R	1*	<0.1
Bucky Bairdo's Inc.	103 E Silverspring	Milwaukee	WI	53217	David Baird	414-332-9007	R	1*	<0.1
Euro American Trading-Merchants	37 Centennial St	Collegeville	PA	19426	Robert D Moyer	610-454-0854	R	1*	<0.1

Source: Ward's Business Directory of U.S. Private and Public Companies, Volumes 1 and 2, 2005. The company type code used is as follows: P - Public, R - Private, S - Subsidiary, D - Division, J - Joint Venture, A - Affiliate, G - Group. Sales are in millions of dollars, employees are in thousands. An asterisk (*) indicates an estimated sales volume. The symbol < stands for 'less than'. Company names and addresses are truncated, in some cases, to fit into the available space.

OCCUPATIONS EMPLOYED BY GROCERY & RELATED PRODUCTS WHOLESALE

Occupation	% of Total 2004	Change to 2014	Occupation	% of Total 2004	Change to 2014
Sales reps, wholesale & manufacturing, exc tech	12.7	10.6	Office clerks, general	1.9	-1.6
Laborers & freight, stock, & material movers, hand	11.0	-0.5	Bookkeeping, accounting, & auditing clerks	1.7	-0.5
Driver/sales workers	9.0	10.4	General & operations managers	1.5	9.4
Truck drivers, heavy & tractor-trailer	9.0	10.4	First-line supervisors/managers of non-retail sales work	1.5	2.2
Truck drivers, light or delivery services	5.0	10.4	Customer service representatives	1.5	13.2
Stock clerks & order fillers	4.4	-15.3	Wholesale & retail buyers, except farm products	1.2	4.5
Industrial truck & tractor operators	4.0	-0.5	First-line supervisors/managers of transporation workers	1.1	10.6
Packers & packagers, hand	2.8	10.6	Maintenance & repair workers, general	1.0	10.6
Shipping, receiving, & traffic clerks	2.1	0.1	First-line supervisors/managers of office workers	1.0	0.2
Packaging & filling machine operators & tenders	2.0	-5.8			

Source: Industry-Occupation Matrix, Bureau of Labor Statistics. These data are reported based on 4-digit NAICS categories but have been matched to corresponding 6-digit NAICS industry codes. The change reported for each occupation to the year 2014 is a percent of growth or decline as estimated by the Bureau of Labor Statistics. The abbreviation nec stands for 'not elsewhere classified.'

LOCATION BY STATE AND REGIONAL CONCENTRATION

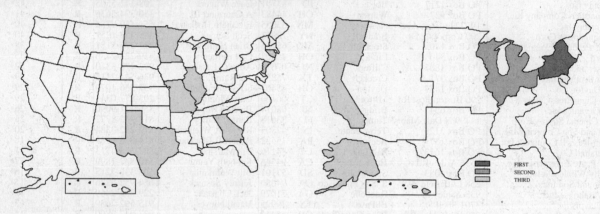

FIRST
SECOND
THIRD

INDUSTRY DATA BY STATE

State	Establishments Total (number)	% of U.S.	Employment Total (number)	% of U.S.	Per Estab.	Payroll Total ($ mil.)	Per Empl. ($)	Sales Total ($ mil.)	% of U.S.	Per Estab. ($)
New Jersey	132	5.7	4,391	11.3	33	221.4	50,413	7,102.9	22.2	53,809,485
California	274	11.9	5,315	13.7	19	153.6	28,896	3,809.9	11.9	13,904,602
Illinois	124	5.4	2,585	6.6	21	88.8	34,367	3,791.4	11.8	30,575,871
Texas	137	5.9	2,710	7.0	20	78.5	28,963	2,444.9	7.6	17,846,241
New York	228	9.9	2,811	7.2	12	85.7	30,491	1,552.5	4.9	6,809,237
Georgia	61	2.6	1,338	3.4	22	40.5	30,279	1,152.7	3.6	18,897,311
Ohio	81	3.5	1,452	3.7	18	45.9	31,595	1,137.3	3.6	14,040,765
Florida	122	5.3	1,480	3.8	12	41.9	28,283	922.2	2.9	7,558,844
North Carolina	49	2.1	1,238	3.2	25	33.1	26,725	845.1	2.6	17,247,694
Pennsylvania	99	4.3	1,770	4.5	18	58.0	32,786	836.1	2.6	8,445,677
Missouri	46	2.0	1,354	3.5	29	39.4	29,111	803.5	2.5	17,467,283
Michigan	81	3.5	1,207	3.1	15	31.1	25,787	746.2	2.3	9,212,272
Minnesota	45	2.0	627	1.6	14	20.6	32,839	565.5	1.8	12,566,867
Massachusetts	51	2.2	780	2.0	15	21.7	27,814	534.2	1.7	10,474,647
Washington	51	2.2	403	1.0	8	11.9	29,526	434.1	1.4	8,511,098
Connecticut	32	1.4	543	1.4	17	19.0	35,028	413.2	1.3	12,912,062
Virginia	50	2.2	824	2.1	16	28.0	33,972	402.0	1.3	8,039,720
Colorado	34	1.5	536	1.4	16	15.4	28,800	365.6	1.1	10,753,971
Tennessee	38	1.6	517	1.3	14	15.2	29,484	354.3	1.1	9,324,368
Wisconsin	52	2.3	733	1.9	14	20.1	27,486	287.3	0.9	5,525,942
South Carolina	20	0.9	279	0.7	14	7.6	27,194	271.0	0.8	13,547,800
Kansas	15	0.7	216	0.6	14	6.7	31,231	268.9	0.8	17,929,600
Alabama	36	1.6	613	1.6	17	22.9	37,356	260.3	0.8	7,229,389
Arizona	25	1.1	296	0.8	12	10.4	35,189	243.9	0.8	9,757,080
Oregon	21	0.9	256	0.7	12	7.6	29,551	225.8	0.7	10,752,667
Louisiana	36	1.6	429	1.1	12	10.0	23,263	204.1	0.6	5,668,111
Indiana	66	2.9	568	1.5	9	14.2	24,958	185.4	0.6	2,809,152
Oklahoma	18	0.8	203	0.5	11	5.4	26,443	169.9	0.5	9,439,278
Kentucky	28	1.2	383	1.0	14	13.4	34,859	161.5	0.5	5,767,000
North Dakota	6	0.3	189	0.5	32	6.2	32,698	131.5	0.4	21,913,500
Arkansas	17	0.7	109	0.3	6	3.8	34,505	128.7	0.4	7,572,412
Hawaii	34	1.5	440	1.1	13	10.5	23,839	122.0	0.4	3,587,353
West Virginia	13	0.6	150	0.4	12	3.6	23,933	108.0	0.3	8,309,769

Continued on next page.

INDUSTRY DATA BY STATE - Continued

State	Establishments		Employment			Payroll		Sales		
	Total (number)	% of U.S.	Total (number)	% of U.S.	Per Estab.	Total ($ mil.)	Per Empl. ($)	Total ($ mil.)	% of U.S.	Per Estab. ($)
Nevada	20	0.9	232	0.6	12	6.4	27,530	82.6	0.3	4,130,150
Mississippi	27	1.2	193	0.5	7	4.6	23,705	80.3	0.3	2,974,185
Idaho	6	0.3	78	0.2	13	2.1	27,256	75.5	0.2	12,588,000
Utah	16	0.7	69	0.2	4	3.0	44,072	74.3	0.2	4,646,562
Alaska	7	0.3	101	0.3	14	3.6	35,683	45.1	0.1	6,442,571
Nebraska	17	0.7	61	0.2	4	1.2	19,311	18.7	0.1	1,101,235
Vermont	4	0.2	26	0.1	7	0.5	19,385	2.9	-	729,500
Wyoming	3	0.1	5	-	2	0.1	21,400	1.0	-	324,333
Montana	4	0.2	3	-	1	-	15,667	0.6	-	139,500
Maryland	26	1.1	500-999	-	-	(D)	-	(D)	-	-
Iowa	13	0.6	250-499	-	-	(D)	-	(D)	-	-
New Hampshire	10	0.4	100-249	-	-	(D)	-	(D)	-	-
New Mexico	9	0.4	100-249	-	-	(D)	-	(D)	-	-
Rhode Island	9	0.4	20-99	-	-	(D)	-	(D)	-	-
Delaware	5	0.2	20-99	-	-	(D)	-	(D)	-	-
Maine	5	0.2	100-249	-	-	(D)	-	(D)	-	-
South Dakota	3	0.1	20-99	-	-	(D)	-	(D)	-	-
D.C.	1	-	0-19	-	-	(D)	-	(D)	-	-

Source: 2002 *Economic Census*. The states are in descending order of sales or establishments (if sales data are missing for the majority). The symbol (D) appears when data are withheld to prevent disclosure of competitive information. States marked with (D) are sorted by number of establishments. A dash (-) indicates that the data element cannot be calculated. Shaded *states* on the state map indicate those states which have proportionately greater representation in the industry than would be indicated by the states population; the ratio is based on total sales or number of establishments. Shaded *regions* indicate where the industry is regionally most concentrated.

NAICS 424460 - FISH AND SEAFOOD MERCHANT WHOLESALERS*

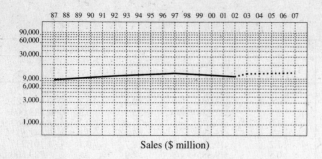

Sales ($ million)

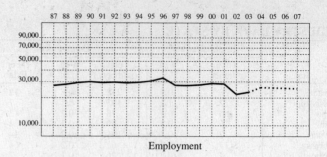

Employment

GENERAL STATISTICS

Year	Establishments (number)	Employment (number)	Payroll ($ million)	Sales ($ million)	Employees per Establishment (number)	Sales per Establishment ($)	Payroll per Employee ($)
1987	2,745	27,233	473.4	9,386.5	9.9	3,419,490.0	17,383.3
1988	2,618	28,058	536.7	9,805.5 e	10.7	3,745,416.3	19,128.2
1989	2,587	29,333	571.3	10,224.4 e	11.3	3,952,222.7	19,476.4
1990	2,606	30,028	603.4	10,643.3 e	11.5	4,084,152.0	20,094.6
1991	2,584	29,280	611.3	11,062.2 e	11.3	4,281,037.2	20,877.7
1992	3,100	29,651	591.3	11,481.2	9.6	3,703,612.9	19,942.0
1993	3,168	29,094	613.2	11,818.1 e	9.2	3,730,460.9	21,076.5
1994	3,223	29,511	648.7	12,155.0 e	9.2	3,771,331.1	21,981.6
1995	3,168	30,545	702.0	12,492.0 e	9.6	3,943,181.8	22,982.5
1996	3,287 e	32,961 e	747.1 e	12,828.9 e	10.0 e	3,902,920.6 e	22,666.2 e
1997	2,960	27,402	684.4	13,165.8	9.3	4,447,905.4	24,976.3
1998	3,070	27,234	736.1	12,772.2 e	8.9	4,160,312.7	27,028.7
1999	3,048	27,706	797.3	12,378.5 e	9.1	4,061,194.2	28,777.2
2000	2,992	28,710	854.6	11,984.9 e	9.6	4,005,641.7	29,768.3
2001	2,980	28,405	882.2	11,591.2 e	9.5	3,889,677.9	31,059.0
2002	2,494	21,903	676.7	11,197.6	8.8	4,489,815.6	30,895.3
2003	2,456	23,091	743.5	12,925.8 p	9.4	4,247,734.5 p	32,197.8
2004	2,943 p	25,997 p	844.3 p	13,086.3 p	8.8 p	4,279,906.4 p	32,520.4 p
2005	2,949 p	25,747 p	863.2 p	13,246.7 p	8.7 p	4,312,078.3 p	33,452.0 p
2006	2,955 p	25,498 p	882.0 p	13,407.2 p	8.5 p	4,344,250.2 p	34,383.6 p
2007	2,962 p	25,248 p	900.8 p	13,567.7 p	8.4 p	4,376,422.1 p	35,315.2 p

Sources: Economic Census of the United States, 1987, 1992, 1997, and 2002. Establishment counts, employment, and payroll are from County Business Patterns for non-Census years. Values followed by a 'p' are projections by the editors. Sales data for non-Census years are extrapolations, marked by 'e'. Data are the most recent available at this level of detail.

INDICES OF CHANGE

Year	Establishments (number)	Employment (number)	Payroll ($ million)	Sales ($ million)	Employees per Establishment (number)	Sales per Establishment ($)	Payroll per Employee ($)
1987	110.1	124.3	70.0	83.8	112.5	76.2	56.3
1992	124.3	135.4	87.4	102.5	109.1	82.5	64.5
1993	127.0	132.8	90.6	105.5 e	104.5	83.1	68.2
1994	129.2	134.7	95.9	108.6 e	104.5	84.0	71.1
1995	127.0	139.5	103.7	111.6 e	109.1	87.8	74.4
1996	131.8 e	150.5 e	110.4 e	114.6 e	113.6 e	86.9 e	73.4 e
1997	118.7	125.1	101.1	117.6	105.7	99.1	80.8
1998	123.1	124.3	108.8	114.1 e	101.1	92.7	87.5
1999	122.2	126.5	117.8	110.5 e	103.4	90.5	93.1
2000	120.0	131.1	126.3	107.0 e	109.1	89.2	96.4
2001	119.5	129.7	130.4	103.5 e	108.0	86.6	100.5
2002	100.0	100.0	100.0	100.0	100.0	100.0	100.0
2003	98.5	105.4	109.9	115.4 p	106.8	94.6 p	104.2
2004	118.0 p	118.7 p	124.8 p	116.9 p	99.7 p	95.3 p	105.3 p
2005	118.3 p	117.6 p	127.6 p	118.3 p	98.3 p	96.0 p	108.3 p
2006	118.5 p	116.4 p	130.3 p	119.7 p	97.0 p	96.8 p	111.3 p
2007	118.7 p	115.3 p	133.1 p	121.2 p	95.7 p	97.5 p	114.3 p

Sources: Same as General Statistics. The values shown reflect change from the base year, 2002. Values above 100 mean greater than 2002, values below 100 mean less than 2002, and a value of 100 in the 1987-2001 or 2003-2007 period means same as 2002. Values followed by a 'p' are projections by the editors; 'e' stands for extrapolation. Data are the most recent available at this level of detail.

SELECTED RATIOS

For 2002	Avg. of All Wholesale	Analyzed Industry	Index	For 2002	Avg. of All Wholesale	Analyzed Industry	Index
Employees per Establishment	15	9	59	Sales per Employee	791,325	511,236	65
Payroll per Establishment	626,122	271,331	43	Sales per Establishment	12,012,387	4,489,816	37
Payroll per Employee	41,161	30,895	75	Expenses per Establishment	na	na	na

Sources: Same as General Statistics. The 'Average of All' column, Wholesale or Retail, represents the average of the sector reported for the most recent complete year available. The Index shows the relationship between the Average and the Analyzed Industry. For example, 100 means that they are equal; 500 that the Analyzed Industry is five times the average; 50 means that the Analyzed Industry is half the national average. The abbreviation 'na' is used to show that data are 'not available'.

*Equivalent to SIC 5146.

LEADING COMPANIES　　Number shown: **51**　　Total sales ($ mil): **33,126**　　Total employment (000): **52.7**

Company Name	Address				CEO Name	Phone	Co. Type	Sales ($ mil)	Empl. (000)
SYSCO Corp.	1390 Enclave Pkwy	Houston	TX	77077		281-584-1390	P	29,335	47.0
Shamrock Foods Co.	2540 N 29th Ave	Phoenix	AZ	85009		602-233-6400	R	1,354	2.3
Agar Supply Inc.	225 John Hancock	Taunton	MA	02780	Karen Bressler	508-821-2060	R	400*	0.4
Empress International Ltd.	10 Harbor Park Dr	Port Washington	NY	11050	Tim McLellan	516-621-5900	S	252*	<0.1
Inland Seafood Corp.	1222 Menlo Dr	Atlanta	GA	30318	Joel Knox	404-350-5850	R	230*	0.3
Atalanta Corp.	1 Atalanta Plz	Elizabeth	NJ	07206	George Gellert	908-351-8000	R	208*	0.1
Dole and Bailey Inc.	PO Box 2405	Woburn	MA	01888	DM Matheson	781-935-1234	R	196*	0.2
Troyer Foods Inc.	PO Box 608	Goshen	IN	46527	Paris Ball-Miller	574-533-0302	R	150*	0.2
Ore-Cal Corp.	634 S Crocker St	Los Angeles	CA	90021	William Shinbane	213-680-9540	R	97*	0.2
Clark Seafood Company Inc.	4401 Clark St	Pascagoula	MS	39567	Philip Horn	228-762-4511	R	70*	0.1
Metropolitan Poultry & Seafood	1920 Stanford Ct	Landover	MD	20785	Brian C Willard	301-772-0060	R	70*	0.2
Joe Patti Seafood Co.	PO Box 12567	Pensacola	FL	32591		850-432-3315	R	64*	<0.1
North Landing Corp.	610 Brighton Rd	Clifton	NJ	07012	Bragi Henningsson	973-249-5300	R	54*	<0.1
Kaelbel Wholesale Inc.	2501 SW 31st St	Fort Lauderdale	FL	33312	Eddie Kaelbel	954-797-7789	R	52*	<0.1
Will Poultry Company Inc.	PO Box 1146	Buffalo	NY	14240	Donald Will	716-853-2000	R	51*	0.1
Progressive Companies Inc.	PO Box B	Spirit Lake	IA	51360	Larry Stoller	712-336-1750	R	50*	<0.1
Ocean Gold Seafoods Inc.	PO Box 1104	Westport	WA	98595	Dennis Rydman	360-268-9286	R	44*	0.2
Caleb Haley and Company Inc.	14 Fulton Fish Mkt	New York	NY	10038	Neal Smith	212-732-7474	R	44*	<0.1
Becker Food Company Inc.	4160 N Washington	Milwaukee	WI	53212	Stephen S Becker	414-964-5353	R	35*	<0.1
Slade Gorton and Company Inc.	225 Southampton St	Boston	MA	02118	Michael C Gorton	617-442-5800	R	34*	0.2
Floribbean Wholesale Inc.	5151 NW 17th St	Margate	FL	33063	Mike Black	954-968-4091	R	32*	<0.1
Zanios Foods Inc.	PO Box 27730	Albuquerque	NM	87125	Jim Zanios	505-831-1411	R	32*	0.1
Louis Foehrkolb Inc.	7901 Oceano Ave	Jessup	MD	20794	Louis Foehrkolb	410-799-4260	R	29*	<0.1
Bayou Caddy Fisheries Inc.	5200 Shipyard Rd	Lakeshore	MS	39558	Joseph Cure	228-467-4332	R	23*	<0.1
East Coast Seafood Intern. Inc.	PO Box 790	Lynn	MA	01903	Michael Tourkistas	781-593-1737	R	23*	<0.1
Ipswich Shellfish Company Inc.	PO Box 550	Ipswich	MA	01938	George Pappas	978-356-4371	R	20*	<0.1
Morley Sales Company Inc.	119 N 2nd St	Geneva	IL	60134	Gary R Slavik	630-845-8750	R	20*	<0.1
Borstein Seafood Inc.	PO Box 188	Bellingham	WA	98227	Myer Bornstein	360-734-7990	R	19*	0.3
Mar-Lees L.L.C.	110 H Melville	New Bedford	MA	02740	John Lees	508-991-6026	R	17*	0.1
Okuhara Foods Inc.	881 N King St	Honolulu	HI	96817	James Okuhara	808-848-0581	R	15*	<0.1
L.N. White and Company Inc.	225 W 34th St	New York	NY	10122	David White	212-239-7474	R	12*	<0.1
Tennessee Shell Co.	PO Box 609	Camden	TN	38320		731-584-7747	R	12*	<0.1
Catfish Wholesale Inc.	PO Box 759	Abbeville	LA	70511	James Rich	337-643-6700	R	10*	<0.1
Goetz & Sons Western Meat	1220 Hewitt Ave	Everett	WA	98201	Jim Horton	425-252-1151	R	7*	<0.1
Sierra Seafood Co.	PO Box 235	Oakhurst	CA	93644	Joe Sweat	559-683-3479	R	7*	<0.1
Quinault Pride Seafoods	PO Box 217	Taholah	WA	98587		360-276-4431	R	7*	<0.1
L.D. Amory and Company Inc.	PO Box 518	Hampton	VA	23669		757-722-1915	R	6*	<0.1
O.W. and B.S. Look Company Inc.	PO Box 504	Jonesport	ME	04649	B Sid Look	207-497-5672	R	6*	<0.1
Liberty Gold Fruit Co.	PO Box 2187	S. San Francisco	CA	94083	Harry Battat	650-583-4700	R	5*	<0.1
Water Street Seafood Inc.	PO Box 121	Apalachicola	FL	32329	Steven Rash	850-653-8902	R	4*	<0.1
Amende and Schultz Corp.	PO Box 788	South Pasadena	CA	91031	Terry Schultz	323-682-3806	R	4*	<0.1
Mazzetta Co.	P O Box 1126	Highland Park	IL	60035	Tom Mazzetta	847-433-1150	R	4*	<0.1
Starboard Inc.	1714 East Blvd	Charlotte	NC	28203	Ronald H Wrenn	704-334-1677	R	4*	<0.1
Turner New Zealand Inc.	PO Box 8919	Newport Beach	CA	92658	Noel Turner	949-622-6181	R	4*	<0.1
Mount Pleasant Seafood Co.	1 Seafood Dr	Mount Pleasant	SC	29464	Rial Fitch	843-884-4122	R	3*	<0.1
Ocean Crest Seafoods Inc.	PO Box 1183	Gloucester	MA	01930	Leonard Parco	978-281-0232	R	3*	<0.1
B and B Fisheries Inc.	715 E Int Spdwy	Daytona Beach	FL	32118	Raymond Flippo	386-252-6542	R	2*	<0.1
Marvin Hayes Fish Co.	256 W Lakeview Dr	Hornbeak	TN	38232	Jan Dyer	731-538-2166	R	2*	<0.1
Mendocino Sea Vegetable Co.	PO Box 455	Philo	CA	95466	John Lewallen		R	2*	<0.1
Chesapeake Seafood Caterers	1216 S Talbot St	Saint Michaels	MD	21663	Glenn Higgins	410-745-5056	R	1*	<0.1
Walter Meier Inc.	12555 W Wirth St	Brookfield	WI	53005		262-783-7100	R	1*	<0.1

Source: Ward's Business Directory of U.S. Private and Public Companies, Volumes 1 and 2, 2005. The company type code used is as follows: P - Public, R - Private, S - Subsidiary, D - Division, J - Joint Venture, A - Affiliate, G - Group. Sales are in millions of dollars, employees are in thousands. An asterisk (*) indicates an estimated sales volume. The symbol < stands for 'less than'. Company names and addresses are truncated, in some cases, to fit into the available space.

OCCUPATIONS EMPLOYED BY GROCERY & RELATED PRODUCTS WHOLESALE

Occupation	% of Total 2004	Change to 2014	Occupation	% of Total 2004	Change to 2014
Sales reps, wholesale & manufacturing, exc tech	12.7	10.6	Office clerks, general	1.9	-1.6
Laborers & freight, stock, & material movers, hand	11.0	-0.5	Bookkeeping, accounting, & auditing clerks	1.7	-0.5
Driver/sales workers	9.0	10.4	General & operations managers	1.5	9.4
Truck drivers, heavy & tractor-trailer	9.0	10.4	First-line supervisors/managers of non-retail sales work	1.5	2.2
Truck drivers, light or delivery services	5.0	10.4	Customer service representatives	1.5	13.2
Stock clerks & order fillers	4.4	-15.3	Wholesale & retail buyers, except farm products	1.2	4.5
Industrial truck & tractor operators	4.0	-0.5	First-line supervisors/managers of transporation workers	1.1	10.6
Packers & packagers, hand	2.8	10.6	Maintenance & repair workers, general	1.0	10.6
Shipping, receiving, & traffic clerks	2.1	0.1	First-line supervisors/managers of office workers	1.0	0.2
Packaging & filling machine operators & tenders	2.0	-5.8			

Source: Industry-Occupation Matrix, Bureau of Labor Statistics. These data are reported based on 4-digit NAICS categories but have been matched to corresponding 6-digit NAICS industry codes. The change reported for each occupation to the year 2014 is a percent of growth or decline as estimated by the Bureau of Labor Statistics. The abbreviation nec stands for 'not elsewhere classified.'

LOCATION BY STATE AND REGIONAL CONCENTRATION

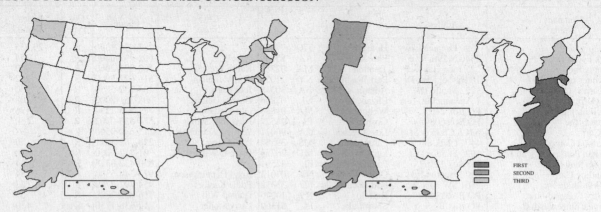

FIRST
SECOND
THIRD

INDUSTRY DATA BY STATE

State	Establishments Total (number)	% of U.S.	Employment Total (number)	% of U.S.	Per Estab.	Payroll Total ($ mil.)	Per Empl. ($)	Sales Total ($ mil.)	% of U.S.	Per Estab. ($)
California	289	11.5	3,820	17.0	13	115.0	30,113	1,622.6	13.6	5,614,460
New York	298	11.8	2,119	9.4	7	71.3	33,664	1,235.8	10.4	4,146,956
Massachusetts	168	6.7	1,839	8.2	11	74.7	40,630	1,179.6	9.9	7,021,601
Florida	303	12.0	1,708	7.6	6	51.3	30,053	1,112.9	9.3	3,672,937
Washington	127	5.0	1,044	4.6	8	40.1	38,457	1,008.7	8.5	7,942,559
Rhode Island	35	1.4	338	1.5	10	12.7	37,450	620.3	5.2	17,724,200
Maine	181	7.2	1,008	4.5	6	27.9	27,634	546.4	4.6	3,018,597
Georgia	42	1.7	583	2.6	14	26.7	45,722	542.5	4.5	12,916,286
New Jersey	93	3.7	1,051	4.7	11	36.1	34,382	530.9	4.4	5,709,108
Texas	103	4.1	946	4.2	9	26.0	27,475	492.4	4.1	4,780,816
Louisiana	135	5.4	1,082	4.8	8	19.1	17,690	331.8	2.8	2,457,407
Maryland	65	2.6	751	3.3	12	25.3	33,690	320.1	2.7	4,924,431
Pennsylvania	47	1.9	567	2.5	12	20.7	36,587	262.8	2.2	5,592,511
Virginia	89	3.5	811	3.6	9	17.6	21,670	189.7	1.6	2,131,955
North Carolina	71	2.8	669	3.0	9	14.7	21,906	179.2	1.5	2,523,676
Connecticut	20	0.8	132	0.6	7	6.4	48,538	126.1	1.1	6,305,850
Hawaii	40	1.6	360	1.6	9	10.1	28,156	121.1	1.0	3,027,825
Colorado	11	0.4	256	1.1	23	9.1	35,559	76.7	0.6	6,971,364
Alaska	77	3.1	160	0.7	2	6.2	38,725	67.4	0.6	874,675
Alabama	32	1.3	479	2.1	15	5.6	11,620	54.5	0.5	1,702,156
Mississippi	24	1.0	142	0.6	6	3.0	20,930	53.1	0.4	2,213,250
South Carolina	24	1.0	181	0.8	8	3.6	19,978	46.1	0.4	1,919,208
Oregon	27	1.1	142	0.6	5	4.7	33,254	45.7	0.4	1,690,926
Michigan	23	0.9	148	0.7	6	3.3	22,473	39.9	0.3	1,734,652
Nevada	14	0.6	56	0.2	4	2.7	49,071	36.6	0.3	2,611,214
Tennessee	13	0.5	96	0.4	7	1.9	19,615	31.1	0.3	2,389,231
Wisconsin	11	0.4	101	0.4	9	2.5	25,040	29.0	0.2	2,636,636
Illinois	41	1.6	500-999	-	-	(D)	-	(D)	-	-
New Hampshire	14	0.6	20-99	-	-	(D)	-	(D)	-	-
Arizona	12	0.5	100-249	-	-	(D)	-	(D)	-	-
Minnesota	12	0.5	100-249	-	-	(D)	-	(D)	-	-
Ohio	12	0.5	100-249	-	-	(D)	-	(D)	-	-
Kentucky	9	0.4	100-249	-	-	(D)	-	(D)	-	-
Missouri	9	0.4	20-99	-	-	(D)	-	(D)	-	-
Delaware	6	0.2	20-99	-	-	(D)	-	(D)	-	-
Indiana	4	0.2	100-249	-	-	(D)	-	(D)	-	-
Nebraska	4	0.2	20-99	-	-	(D)	-	(D)	-	-
New Mexico	4	0.2	0-19	-	-	(D)	-	(D)	-	-
Utah	4	0.2	20-99	-	-	(D)	-	(D)	-	-
Vermont	4	0.2	20-99	-	-	(D)	-	(D)	-	-
Arkansas	3	0.1	0-19	-	-	(D)	-	(D)	-	-
Kansas	3	0.1	20-99	-	-	(D)	-	(D)	-	-
D.C.	2	0.1	20-99	-	-	(D)	-	(D)	-	-
Idaho	2	0.1	0-19	-	-	(D)	-	(D)	-	-
Iowa	2	0.1	0-19	-	-	(D)	-	(D)	-	-
South Dakota	2	0.1	0-19	-	-	(D)	-	(D)	-	-
Montana	1	-	0-19	-	-	(D)	-	(D)	-	-
Oklahoma	1	-	0-19	-	-	(D)	-	(D)	-	-
West Virginia	1	-	0-19	-	-	(D)	-	(D)	-	-
Wyoming	1	-	0-19	-	-	(D)	-	(D)	-	-

Source: 2002 *Economic Census*. The states are in descending order of sales or establishments (if sales data are missing for the majority). The symbol (D) appears when data are withheld to prevent disclosure of competitive information. States marked with (D) are sorted by number of establishments. A dash (-) indicates that the data element cannot be calculated. Shaded *states* on the state map indicate those states which have proportionately greater representation in the industry than would be indicated by the states population; the ratio is based on total sales or number of establishments. Shaded *regions* indicate where the industry is regionally most concentrated.

NAICS 424470 - MEAT AND MEAT PRODUCT MERCHANT WHOLESALERS

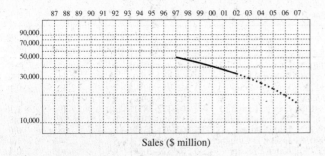

Sales ($ million)

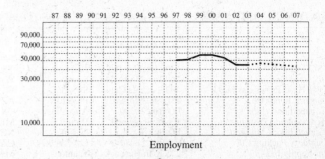

Employment

GENERAL STATISTICS

Year	Establishments (number)	Employment (number)	Payroll ($ million)	Sales ($ million)	Employees per Establishment (number)	Sales per Establishment ($)	Payroll per Employee ($)
1987	-	-	-	-	-	-	-
1988	-	-	-	-	-	-	-
1989	-	-	-	-	-	-	-
1990	-	-	-	-	-	-	-
1991	-	-	-	-	-	-	-
1992	-	-	-	-	-	-	-
1993	-	-	-	-	-	-	-
1994	-	-	-	-	-	-	-
1995	-	-	-	-	-	-	-
1996	-	-	-	-	-	-	-
1997	3,557	50,256	1,490.9	51,326.4	14.1	14,429,687.9	29,666.1
1998	3,480	50,997	1,601.2	47,786.9 e	14.7	13,731,873.6	31,397.9
1999	3,423	57,172	1,850.3	44,247.4 e	16.7	12,926,508.9	32,363.7
2000	3,353	57,312	1,885.8	40,708.0 e	17.1	12,140,757.5	32,904.4
2001	3,305	53,407	1,811.5	37,168.5 e	16.2	11,246,136.2	33,918.4
2002	2,889	44,704	1,565.2	33,629.0	15.5	11,640,360.0	35,012.5
2003	2,804	44,597	1,636.5	30,089.5 p	15.9	10,466,927.0 p	36,695.3
2004	2,750 p	46,445 p	1,738.2 p	26,550.0 p	16.7 p	9,832,938.4 p	37,404.3 p
2005	2,623 p	45,255 p	1,749.8 p	23,010.6 p	16.9 p	9,198,949.7 p	38,471.1 p
2006	2,496 p	44,065 p	1,761.5 p	19,471.1 p	17.1 p	8,564,961.0 p	39,538.0 p
2007	2,369 p	42,874 p	1,773.1 p	15,931.6 p	17.4 p	7,930,972.4 p	40,604.8 p

Source: *Economic Census of the United States*, 1997 and 2002. Establishment counts, employment, and payroll are from *County Business Patterns* for non-Census years. This is a newly defined industry. Data for prior years are unavailable at the time of publication but may become available over time. Values followed by 'p' are projections by the editors. Sales data for non-Census years are extrapolations, marked by 'e'.

INDICES OF CHANGE

Year	Establishments (number)	Employment (number)	Payroll ($ million)	Sales ($ million)	Employees per Establishment (number)	Sales per Establishment ($)	Payroll per Employee ($)
1987	-	-	-	-	-	-	-
1992	-	-	-	-	-	-	-
1993	-	-	-	-	-	-	-
1994	-	-	-	-	-	-	-
1995	-	-	-	-	-	-	-
1996	-	-	-	-	-	-	-
1997	123.1	112.4	95.3	152.6	91.0	124.0	84.7
1998	120.5	114.1	102.3	142.1 e	94.8	118.0	89.7
1999	118.5	127.9	118.2	131.6 e	107.7	111.0	92.4
2000	116.1	128.2	120.5	121.1 e	110.3	104.3	94.0
2001	114.4	119.5	115.7	110.5 e	104.5	96.6	96.9
2002	100.0	100.0	100.0	100.0	100.0	100.0	100.0
2003	97.1	99.8	104.6	89.5 p	102.6	89.9 p	104.8
2004	95.2 p	103.9 p	111.1 p	78.9 p	107.6 p	84.5 p	106.8 p
2005	90.8 p	101.2 p	111.8 p	68.4 p	109.1 p	79.0 p	109.9 p
2006	86.4 p	98.6 p	112.5 p	57.9 p	110.6 p	73.6 p	112.9 p
2007	82.0 p	95.9 p	113.3 p	47.4 p	112.1 p	68.1 p	116.0 p

Sources: Same as General Statistics. The values shown reflect change from the base year, 2002. Values above 100 mean greater than 2002, values below 100 mean less than 2002, and a value of 100 in the 1987-2001 or 2003-2007 period means same as 2002. Values followed by a 'p' are projections by the editors; 'e' stands for extrapolation. Data are the most recent available at this level of detail.

SELECTED RATIOS

For 2002	Avg. of All Wholesale	Analyzed Industry	Index	For 2002	Avg. of All Wholesale	Analyzed Industry	Index
Employees per Establishment	15	15	104	Sales per Employee	791,325	752,259	95
Payroll per Establishment	626,122	541,779	87	Sales per Establishment	12,012,387	11,640,360	97
Payroll per Employee	41,161	35,013	85	Expenses per Establishment	na	na	na

Sources: Same as General Statistics. The 'Average of All' column, Wholesale or Retail, represents the average of the sector reported for the most recent complete year available. The Index shows the relationship between the Average and the Analyzed Industry. For example, 100 means that they are equal; 500 that the Analyzed Industry is five times the average; 50 means that the Analyzed Industry is half the national average. The abbreviation 'na' is used to show that data are 'not available'.

LEADING COMPANIES   Number shown: 66   Total sales ($ mil): 44,346   Total employment (000): 60.1

Company Name	Address				CEO Name	Phone	Co. Type	Sales ($ mil)	Empl. (000)
SYSCO Corp.	1390 Enclave Pkwy	Houston	TX	77077		281-584-1390	P	29,335	47.0
Associated Grocers Inc.	PO Box 3763	Seattle	WA	98124	Robert P Hermanns	206-762-2100	R	4,845*	1.0
Boar's Head Provisions Inc.	400 Sarasota Quay	Sarasota	FL	34236	Van Ayvazain	941-955-0994	R	2,382*	0.1
Shamrock Foods Co.	2540 N 29th Ave	Phoenix	AZ	85009		602-233-6400	R	1,354	2.3
Affiliated Foods Inc.	PO Box 30300	Amarillo	TX	79120	George Langford	806-372-3851	R	790*	1.1
Sherwood Food Distributors	18615 Sherwood	Detroit	MI	48234	J Lawrence Tushman	313-366-3100	R	762	0.7
Affiliated Foods Midwest	PO Box 1067	Norfolk	NE	68702	Martin Arter	402-371-0555	R	687*	0.6
Clougherty Packing Co.	PO Box 58870	Los Angeles	CA	90058	Joseph D Clougherty	323-583-4621	S	446*	1.4
Agar Supply Inc.	225 John Hancock	Taunton	MA	02780	Karen Bressler	508-821-2060	R	400*	0.4
Great Western Meats Inc.	PO Box 568366	Orlando	FL	32856	Greg Vorhees	407-841-4270	R	316*	<0.1
Cagle's Inc.	2000 Hills Ave NW	Atlanta	GA	30318	J Douglas Cagle	404-355-2820	P	304	2.0
Atalanta Corp.	1 Atalanta Plz	Elizabeth	NJ	07206	George Gellert	908-351-8000	R	208*	0.1
Dole and Bailey Inc.	PO Box 2405	Woburn	MA	01888	DM Matheson	781-935-1234	R	196*	0.2
United Meat Company Inc.	1040 Bryant St	San Francisco	CA	94103	Philip Gee Jr	415-864-2118	R	195*	<0.1
Pancho's Management Inc.	2855 Lamb Pl	Memphis	TN	38118	Brenda O'Brien	901-362-9691	R	174*	0.2
Earp Distribution	6550 Kansas Ave	Kansas City	KS	66111	Donald C Earp	913-287-3311	R	160*	0.2
Troyer Foods Inc.	PO Box 608	Goshen	IN	46527	Paris Ball-Miller	574-533-0302	R	150*	0.2
Interstate Meat Distributors Inc.	PO Box 298	Clackamas	OR	97015	Jerry Meng	503-656-0633	R	135*	0.1
Midamar Corp.	PO Box 218	Cedar Rapids	IA	52406	Bill Aossey	319-362-3711	R	128*	<0.1
Tony's Fine Foods	PO Box 1501	W. Sacramento	CA	95605	Karl Berger	916-374-4150	R	119*	0.4
Waco Meat Service Inc.	PO Box 7249	Waco	TX	76714	Dana Harrell	254-772-5644	R	117*	<0.1
Lincoln Provision Inc.	824 W 38th Pl	Chicago	IL	60609		773-254-2400	R	108*	0.1
Scariano Brothers L.L.C.	PO Box 26009	New Orleans	LA	70186	Jack Scariano	504-246-6600	R	108*	0.1
J and B Meats Corp.	PO Box 69	Coal Valley	IL	61240	Jeff Jobe	309-799-7341	R	107*	0.1
Fontanini Meats	911 W 37th Pl	Chicago	IL	60609	Eugene Fontanini	773-890-0600	R	85*	0.3
J. Kings Food Service Profession.	700 Furrows Rd	Holtsville	NY	11742	John King	631-289-8401	R	60*	0.2
Will Poultry Company Inc.	PO Box 1146	Buffalo	NY	14240	Donald Will	716-853-2000	R	51*	0.1
HPC Foodservice	205 Enterprise Dr	Bristol	CT	06010		860-583-3908	R	50*	<0.1
Poston Packing of Florence Inc.	5810 Pamplico Hwy	Florence	SC	29505	Aubrey Poston	843-662-1376	R	50*	<0.1
Lionel Lavallee Company Inc.	PO Box 229	Haverhill	MA	01831	Leonard Lavallee	978-374-6391	R	39*	<0.1
Tusco Grocers Inc.	PO Box 240	Dennison	OH	44621	Gregory W Kimble	740-922-2223	R	35*	<0.1
Calihan Pork Processors Inc.	PO Box 1155	Peoria	IL	61653	Louis Landon	309-674-9175	R	32*	<0.1
Zanios Foods Inc.	PO Box 27730	Albuquerque	NM	87125	Jim Zanios	505-831-1411	R	32*	0.1
Dutch Prime Foods Inc.	PO Box 660	Long Branch	NJ	07740	Bernard Kennedy	732-222-0910	R	31*	<0.1
Hill Meat Co.	PO Box 1066	Pendleton	OR	97801	Jim Cheney	541-276-7621	R	28*	0.1
Omaha Beef Company Inc.	PO Box 339	Danbury	CT	06813	Brian Street	203-748-2651	R	26*	<0.1
Southern Provision Company Inc.	1944 Rossville Ave	Chattanooga	TN	37408	Scott McHenry	423-267-3894	R	22*	<0.1
St. James Gourmet Inc.	105 Bi County Blvd	Farmingdale	NY	11735	Brian Weiner	631-454-4896	S	20*	<0.1
D'Artagnan Inc.	280 Wilson Ave	Newark	NJ	07105	George Faison		R	19*	<0.1
Deen Meats and Cooked Foods	PO Box 4155	Fort Worth	TX	76164	Danny Deen	817-335-2257	R	19*	<0.1
Consolidated Poultry and Egg Co.	426 St Paul Ave	Memphis	TN	38126	James J Skefos	901-526-7392	R	18*	<0.1
Mike Hudson Distributing Inc.	PO Box 808033	Petaluma	CA	94975		707-763-7388	R	17*	<0.1
James Calvetti Meats Inc.	4240 S Morgan St	Chicago	IL	60609	James C Calvetti	773-927-9242	R	16*	<0.1
Moore Food Distributors Inc.	9910 Page Blvd	St. Louis	MO	63132	Al Moore	314-426-1300	R	16*	<0.1
Salem Packing Co.	PO Box 131	Salem	NJ	08079	Sam Bonaccurso	856-935-1206	R	12*	<0.1
Diggs Packing Co.	1207 Rogers St	Columbia	MO	65201		573-449-2995	R	11*	<0.1
Rogers Brothers Wholesale Inc.	460 E Brooks St	Galesburg	IL	61401	Frank Rogers	309-342-2127	R	11*	<0.1
Great River Food	19355 San Jose Ave	City of Industry	CA	91748	Derek Lee	909-595-8831	R	10*	<0.1
Heinkel's Packing Company Inc.	PO Box 2134	Decatur	IL	62524	Miles Wright	217-428-4401	R	10*	<0.1
Weber Processing Plant Inc.	725 N Jackson St	Cuba City	WI	53807	Lee Weber	608-744-2159	R	10*	<0.1
Habbersett Sausage Inc.	PO Box 146	Folcroft	PA	19032		610-532-9973	S	9*	<0.1
Caughman's Meat Plant Inc.	PO Box 457	Lexington	SC	29071	Ronnie Caughman	803-356-3216	R	9*	<0.1
Wenzel Farm Sausage	500 E 29th St	Marshfield	WI	54449	H Wenzel	715-387-1218	R	9*	<0.1
Tyler Meat Co.	PO Box 9296	Toledo	OH	43697	Jerry Jaffe	419-244-6200	R	7*	<0.1
J and G Food Products Inc.	1631 Auburn St	Columbia	SC	29204	William Allawos	803-256-1608	R	7*	<0.1
Montana Quality Foods	PO Box 1408	Miles City	MT	59301	John Munsell	406-232-0690	R	7*	<0.1
Boyle Meat Co.	1638 St Louis Ave	Kansas City	MO	64101	Christy Chester	816-842-5852	R	6*	<0.1
Gordon Food Company Inc.	PO Box 41534	Memphis	TN	38174	Michael Gordon	901-454-4100	R	6*	<0.1
Lisbon Sausage Company Inc.	PO Box 2028	New Bedford	MA	02741	Antonio Rodrigues	508-993-7645	R	5*	<0.1
City Market Inc.	PO Box 729	Grand Junction	CO	81502	Phylis Norris	970-241-0750	S	5*	<0.1
Troutman Brothers	PO Box 73	Klingerstown	PA	17941		570-425-2341	R	5*	<0.1
Dayton Meat Products Inc.	102 Montezuma St	Malcom	IA	50157	Bill Dayton	641-528-3420	R	5*	<0.1
Natural Meat Specialties	2065 Rockhurst	Co Springs	CO	80918	Dave Johnston	719-548-1735	R	4*	<0.1
Siemer's Distributing Co.	1400 Commerce Dr	New Lexington	OH	43764	Joseph Siemer	740-342-3230	R	4*	<0.1
Transmudo Company Inc.	999 Brickell Ave	Miami	FL	33131	Alberto J Senosiain	305-539-1205	R	2*	<0.1
Amato International Inc.	407 Lincoln Rd	Miami	FL	33139	Claudette Touzard	305-674-1001	R	1*	<0.1

Source: Ward's Business Directory of U.S. Private and Public Companies, Volumes 1 and 2, 2005. The company type code used is as follows: P - Public, R - Private, S - Subsidiary, D - Division, J - Joint Venture, A - Affiliate, G - Group. Sales are in millions of dollars, employees are in thousands. An asterisk (*) indicates an estimated sales volume. The symbol < stands for 'less than'. Company names and addresses are truncated, in some cases, to fit into the available space.

OCCUPATIONS EMPLOYED BY GROCERY & RELATED PRODUCTS WHOLESALE

Occupation	% of Total 2004	Change to 2014	Occupation	% of Total 2004	Change to 2014
Sales reps, wholesale & manufacturing, exc tech	12.7	10.6	Office clerks, general	1.9	-1.6
Laborers & freight, stock, & material movers, hand	11.0	-0.5	Bookkeeping, accounting, & auditing clerks	1.7	-0.5
Driver/sales workers	9.0	10.4	General & operations managers	1.5	9.4
Truck drivers, heavy & tractor-trailer	9.0	10.4	First-line supervisors/managers of non-retail sales work	1.5	2.2
Truck drivers, light or delivery services	5.0	10.4	Customer service representatives	1.5	13.2
Stock clerks & order fillers	4.4	-15.3	Wholesale & retail buyers, except farm products	1.2	4.5
Industrial truck & tractor operators	4.0	-0.5	First-line supervisors/managers of transporation workers	1.1	10.6
Packers & packagers, hand	2.8	10.6	Maintenance & repair workers, general	1.0	10.6
Shipping, receiving, & traffic clerks	2.1	0.1	First-line supervisors/managers of office workers	1.0	0.2
Packaging & filling machine operators & tenders	2.0	-5.8			

Source: Industry-Occupation Matrix, Bureau of Labor Statistics. These data are reported based on 4-digit NAICS categories but have been matched to corresponding 6-digit NAICS industry codes. The change reported for each occupation to the year 2014 is a percent of growth or decline as estimated by the Bureau of Labor Statistics. The abbreviation nec stands for 'not elsewhere classified.'

LOCATION BY STATE AND REGIONAL CONCENTRATION

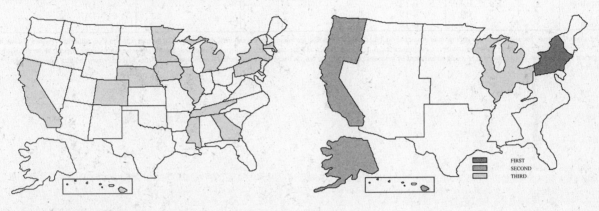

FIRST
SECOND
THIRD

INDUSTRY DATA BY STATE

State	Establishments Total (number)	Establishments % of U.S.	Employment Total (number)	Employment % of U.S.	Employment Per Estab.	Payroll Total ($ mil.)	Payroll Per Empl. ($)	Sales Total ($ mil.)	Sales % of U.S.	Sales Per Estab. ($)
California	401	13.8	7,604	16.9	19	249.9	32,860	5,184.7	15.2	12,929,431
New York	506	17.4	5,131	11.4	10	181.7	35,421	3,847.4	11.2	7,603,626
Texas	179	6.1	3,462	7.7	19	97.1	28,055	2,331.8	6.8	13,026,966
Pennsylvania	109	3.7	1,851	4.1	17	70.9	38,307	2,309.9	6.8	21,191,670
Georgia	55	1.9	1,667	3.7	30	63.5	38,114	2,127.1	6.2	38,673,927
Illinois	212	7.3	2,908	6.5	14	118.5	40,733	2,034.9	5.9	9,598,392
Colorado	45	1.5	599	1.3	13	22.2	37,000	1,489.5	4.4	33,100,422
Ohio	70	2.4	1,338	3.0	19	61.9	46,257	1,370.2	4.0	19,573,857
Michigan	98	3.4	1,603	3.6	16	59.3	36,989	1,320.7	3.9	13,476,980
Florida	151	5.2	2,078	4.6	14	73.7	35,462	1,272.6	3.7	8,428,033
Minnesota	59	2.0	1,119	2.5	19	46.3	41,340	852.6	2.5	14,451,339
Massachusetts	61	2.1	1,072	2.4	18	51.7	48,202	844.5	2.5	13,845,049
Tennessee	31	1.1	759	1.7	24	26.4	34,843	753.3	2.2	24,300,806
Missouri	49	1.7	934	2.1	19	30.0	32,066	628.6	1.8	12,829,327
Iowa	30	1.0	818	1.8	27	22.0	26,846	626.6	1.8	20,886,367
Washington	62	2.1	631	1.4	10	24.8	39,252	510.7	1.5	8,237,226
Mississippi	19	0.7	229	0.5	12	10.7	46,707	425.1	1.2	22,372,632
Virginia	35	1.2	656	1.5	19	19.9	30,331	381.6	1.1	10,903,200
Oregon	28	1.0	438	1.0	16	15.3	34,986	335.3	1.0	11,976,679
North Carolina	45	1.5	746	1.7	17	21.4	28,721	331.1	1.0	7,357,822
Nebraska	14	0.5	250	0.6	18	11.2	44,852	326.7	1.0	23,336,571
Louisiana	36	1.2	712	1.6	20	18.8	26,360	296.8	0.9	8,243,167
Indiana	32	1.1	503	1.1	16	16.6	33,042	288.4	0.8	9,011,906
Wisconsin	45	1.5	656	1.5	15	19.5	29,660	263.8	0.8	5,863,156
Maryland	25	0.9	515	1.1	21	18.5	35,973	256.2	0.7	10,246,520
Connecticut	31	1.1	485	1.1	16	19.5	40,186	247.8	0.7	7,994,645
Kentucky	29	1.0	545	1.2	19	15.0	27,528	184.1	0.5	6,349,966
Nevada	13	0.4	201	0.4	15	7.5	37,100	167.2	0.5	12,859,692
Arkansas	13	0.4	305	0.7	23	8.4	27,587	165.3	0.5	12,717,846
Hawaii	18	0.6	356	0.8	20	9.0	25,205	154.5	0.5	8,582,778
Kansas	15	0.5	150	0.3	10	4.3	28,600	90.4	0.3	6,029,267
Alabama	20	0.7	199	0.4	10	6.6	33,266	79.9	0.2	3,993,700
South Carolina	25	0.9	186	0.4	7	5.0	27,000	77.4	0.2	3,097,280

Continued on next page.

INDUSTRY DATA BY STATE - Continued

State	Establishments		Employment			Payroll		Sales		
	Total (number)	% of U.S.	Total (number)	% of U.S.	Per Estab.	Total ($ mil.)	Per Empl. ($)	Total ($ mil.)	% of U.S.	Per Estab. ($)
Oklahoma	12	0.4	106	0.2	9	2.4	22,934	39.7	0.1	3,311,833
Alaska	6	0.2	56	0.1	9	2.3	40,214	39.4	0.1	6,570,167
New Mexico	15	0.5	97	0.2	6	1.5	15,485	38.2	0.1	2,549,600
Montana	9	0.3	61	0.1	7	1.7	27,525	31.5	0.1	3,504,000
Vermont	10	0.3	75	0.2	8	1.9	24,800	18.7	0.1	1,870,400
South Dakota	6	0.2	9	-	2	0.2	21,889	1.4	-	226,833
New Jersey	188	6.5	1000-2499	-	-	(D)	-	(D)	-	-
Arizona	37	1.3	500-999	-	-	(D)	-	(D)	-	-
Utah	17	0.6	100-249	-	-	(D)	-	(D)	-	-
Rhode Island	12	0.4	100-249	-	-	(D)	-	(D)	-	-
Delaware	7	0.2	20-99	-	-	(D)	-	(D)	-	-
D.C.	7	0.2	100-249	-	-	(D)	-	(D)	-	-
Idaho	6	0.2	20-99	-	-	(D)	-	(D)	-	-
Maine	6	0.2	100-249	-	-	(D)	-	(D)	-	-
West Virginia	5	0.2	20-99	-	-	(D)	-	(D)	-	-
New Hampshire	4	0.1	0-19	-	-	(D)	-	(D)	-	-
Wyoming	3	0.1	0-19	-	-	(D)	-	(D)	-	-
North Dakota	2	0.1	0-19	-	-	(D)	-	(D)	-	-

Source: 2002 *Economic Census*. The states are in descending order of sales or establishments (if sales data are missing for the majority). The symbol (D) appears when data are withheld to prevent disclosure of competitive information. States marked with (D) are sorted by number of establishments. A dash (-) indicates that the data element cannot be calculated. Shaded *states* on the state map indicate those states which have proportionately greater representation in the industry than would be indicated by the states population; the ratio is based on total sales or number of establishments. Shaded *regions* indicate where the industry is regionally most concentrated.

NAICS 424480 - FRESH FRUIT AND VEGETABLE MERCHANT WHOLESALERS*

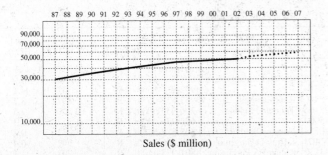

Sales ($ million)

Employment

GENERAL STATISTICS

Year	Establishments (number)	Employment (number)	Payroll ($ million)	Sales ($ million)	Employees per Establishment (number)	Sales per Establishment ($)	Payroll per Employee ($)
1987	5,838	98,870	1,810.6	30,449.7	16.9	5,215,776.0	18,312.9
1988	5,411	100,388	1,971.3	32,062.3 e	18.6	5,925,392.7	19,636.8
1989	5,075	98,514	2,037.2	33,674.8 e	19.4	6,635,428.6	20,679.3
1990	4,980	92,682	2,099.5	35,287.3 e	18.6	7,085,803.2	22,652.7
1991	4,848	89,811	2,098.6	36,899.8 e	18.5	7,611,344.9	23,366.8
1992	6,003	101,372	2,372.1	38,512.3	16.9	6,415,508.9	23,400.0
1993	5,770	101,764	2,488.7	40,078.0 e	17.6	6,945,927.2	24,455.6
1994	5,662	105,908	2,629.0	41,643.7 e	18.7	7,354,945.2	24,823.4
1995	5,422	107,572	2,713.5	43,209.4 e	19.8	7,969,273.3	25,225.0
1996	5,460 e	105,495 e	2,785.6 e	44,775.1 e	19.3 e	8,200,567.8 e	26,405.0 e
1997	6,121	109,771	3,021.2	46,340.8	17.9	7,570,789.1	27,522.8
1998	5,979	105,047	3,190.1	47,018.5 e	17.6	7,863,937.1	30,368.3
1999	5,880	106,582	3,285.1	47,696.2 e	18.1	8,111,591.8	30,822.3
2000	5,829	108,650	3,539.9	48,373.8 e	18.6	8,298,823.1	32,580.4
2001	5,753	113,100	3,753.3	49,051.5 e	19.7	8,526,250.7	33,185.6
2002	5,376	110,578	3,569.9	49,729.2	20.6	9,250,223.2	32,284.0
2003	5,253	104,632	3,649.1	52,913.3 p	19.9	9,108,600.1 p	34,875.6
2004	5,743 p	111,922 p	3,908.6 p	54,250.1 p	19.5 p	9,305,335.6 p	35,420.8 p
2005	5,763 p	112,849 p	4,035.6 p	55,587.0 p	19.7 p	9,502,071.0 p	36,411.4 p
2006	5,782 p	113,777 p	4,162.6 p	56,923.8 p	19.8 p	9,698,806.4 p	37,401.9 p
2007	5,802 p	114,705 p	4,289.6 p	58,260.7 p	19.9 p	9,895,541.9 p	38,392.5 p

Sources: Economic Census of the United States, 1987, 1992, 1997, and 2002. Establishment counts, employment, and payroll are from *County Business Patterns* for non-Census years. Values followed by a 'p' are projections by the editors. Sales data for non-Census years are extrapolations, marked by 'e'. Data are the most recent available at this level of detail.

INDICES OF CHANGE

Year	Establishments (number)	Employment (number)	Payroll ($ million)	Sales ($ million)	Employees per Establishment (number)	Sales per Establishment ($)	Payroll per Employee ($)
1987	108.6	89.4	50.7	61.2	82.0	56.4	56.7
1992	111.7	91.7	66.4	77.4	82.0	69.4	72.5
1993	107.3	92.0	69.7	80.6 e	85.4	75.1	75.8
1994	105.3	95.8	73.6	83.7 e	90.8	79.5	76.9
1995	100.9	97.3	76.0	86.9 e	96.1	86.2	78.1
1996	101.6 e	95.4 e	78.0 e	90.0 e	93.7 e	88.7 e	81.8 e
1997	113.9	99.3	84.6	93.2	86.9	81.8	85.3
1998	111.2	95.0	89.4	94.5 e	85.4	85.0	94.1
1999	109.4	96.4	92.0	95.9 e	87.9	87.7	95.5
2000	108.4	98.3	99.2	97.3 e	90.3	89.7	100.9
2001	107.0	102.3	105.1	98.6 e	95.6	92.2	102.8
2002	100.0	100.0	100.0	100.0	100.0	100.0	100.0
2003	97.7	94.6	102.2	106.4 p	96.7	98.5 p	108.0
2004	106.8 p	101.2 p	109.5 p	109.1 p	94.9 p	100.6 p	109.7 p
2005	107.2 p	102.1 p	113.0 p	111.8 p	95.4 p	102.7 p	112.8 p
2006	107.6 p	102.9 p	116.6 p	114.5 p	95.9 p	104.8 p	115.9 p
2007	107.9 p	103.7 p	120.2 p	117.2 p	96.4 p	107.0 p	118.9 p

Sources: Same as General Statistics. The values shown reflect change from the base year, 2002. Values above 100 mean greater than 2002, values below 100 mean less than 2002, and a value of 100 in the 1987-2001 or 2003-2007 period means same as 2002. Values followed by a 'p' are projections by the editors; 'e' stands for extrapolation. Data are the most recent available at this level of detail.

SELECTED RATIOS

For 2002	Avg. of All Wholesale	Analyzed Industry	Index	For 2002	Avg. of All Wholesale	Analyzed Industry	Index
Employees per Establishment	15	21	138	Sales per Employee	791,325	449,721	57
Payroll per Establishment	626,122	664,044	106	Sales per Establishment	12,012,387	9,250,223	77
Payroll per Employee	41,161	32,284	78	Expenses per Establishment	na	na	na

Sources: Same as General Statistics. The 'Average of All' column, Wholesale or Retail, represents the average of the sector reported for the most recent complete year available. The Index shows the relationship between the Average and the Analyzed Industry. For example, 100 means that they are equal; 500 that the Analyzed Industry is five times the average; 50 means that the Analyzed Industry is half the national average. The abbreviation 'na' is used to show that data are 'not available'.

*Equivalent to SIC 5148.

LEADING COMPANIES   Number shown: 75   Total sales ($ mil): 57,791   Total employment (000): 94.3

Company Name	Address				CEO Name	Phone	Co. Type	Sales ($ mil)	Empl. (000)
SYSCO Corp.	1390 Enclave Pkwy	Houston	TX	77077		281-584-1390	P	29,335	47.0
Performance Food Group Co.	12500 W Creek	Richmond	VA	23238	Robert C Sledd	804-484-7700	P	6,149	11.0
C.H. Robinson Worldwide Inc.	8100 Mitchell Rd	Eden Prairie	MN	55344		952-937-8500	P	4,342	4.1
Nash Finch Co.	PO Box 355	Minneapolis	MN	55440	Ron Marshall	952-832-0534	P	3,897	8.7
Services Group of America Inc.	4025 Delridge SW	Seattle	WA	98106	Thomas J Stewart	206-933-5000	R	2,200	3.5
Shamrock Foods Co.	2540 N 29th Ave	Phoenix	AZ	85009		602-233-6400	R	1,354	2.3
VIP Foodservice	PO Box 517	Kahului	HI	96733	Nelson Okumura	808-877-5055	R	1,032*	0.1
Sunkist Growers Inc.	PO Box 7888	Van Nuys	CA	91409	Jeffrey D Gargiulo	818-986-4800	R	942	0.4
Associated Food Stores Inc.	PO Box 30430	Salt Lake City	UT	84130	Richard A Parkinson	801-973-4400	R	907*	1.4
JC Produce Inc.	PO Box 1027	W. Sacramento	CA	95691		916-372-4050	R	887*	0.3
FreshPoint Inc.	1390 Enclave Pkwy	Houston	TX	77077	Brian M Sturgeon	281-584-1390	S	732*	2.5
Affiliated Foods Midwest	PO Box 1067	Norfolk	NE	68702	Martin Arter	402-371-0555	R	687*	0.6
R.D. Offutt Co.	PO Box 7160	Fargo	ND	58106	Ronald D Offutt	701-237-6062	R	575*	2.0
DiMare Florida	PO Box 11128	Tampa	FL	33680		813-238-7981	D	479*	0.2
Riviana Foods Inc.	PO Box 2636	Houston	TX	77252	Frank A Godchaux III	713-529-3251	S	396	2.8
Sunfresh Inc.	PO Box 400	Royal City	WA	99357	Randy Niessner	509-346-9223	R	320*	0.1
Produce Supply Express	4411 S Grove Rd	Spokane	WA	99224	John Hutchins	509-838-7006	R	255*	<0.1
DNE World Fruit Sales Inc.	1900 Old Dixie Hwy	Fort Pierce	FL	34946	Greg Nelson	772-465-1110	S	236*	<0.1
Tripifoods Inc.	PO Box 1107	Buffalo	NY	14240	CJ Tripi	716-853-7400	R	218*	0.3
Bland Farms Inc.	PO Box 2299	Reidsville	GA	30453	Delbert Bland	912-654-1426	R	209*	<0.1
Sanson Co.	3716 Croton Ave	Cleveland	OH	44115	Jeffrey Sanson	216-431-8560	R	207*	<0.1
Magi Inc.	PO Box 157	Brewster	WA	98812		509-689-2511	R	194*	0.3
Pancho's Management Inc.	2855 Lamb Pl	Memphis	TN	38118	Brenda O'Brien	901-362-9691	R	174*	0.2
Red's Market Inc.	8807 Exchange Dr	Orlando	FL	32809	Robert Gordon	407-857-3930	S	169*	0.3
Inland Fruit Co.	300 N Frontage Rd	Wapato	WA	98951	Susan Putman	509-877-2126	R	111*	0.5
Costa Fruit and Produce Co.	18 Bunker Hill Ind	Charlestown	MA	02129	Manuel R Costa	617-241-8007	R	105*	0.2
H. Smith Packing Corp.	55 N St, Ste C	Presque Isle	ME	04769	Greogory Smith	207-764-4540	R	103*	<0.1
Paramount Export Co.	175 Filbert St	Oakland	CA	94607	Nick Kukulan	510-839-0150	R	98*	0.1
John H. Burrows Inc.	PO Box 604	Sparks	NV	89431	John H Burrows	775-358-2442	R	82*	0.2
FreshPoint Southern California	5301 Rivergrade Rd	Irwindale	CA	91706	Verne Lusby	626-813-5600	D	80*	0.3
Veronica Foods Co.	PO Box 2225	Oakland	CA	94621	Michael Bradley	510-535-6833	R	78*	<0.1
Hickenbottom and Sons Inc.	301 Warehouse Ave	Sunnyside	WA	98944	Jerry Hickenbottom	509-837-4100	R	65*	<0.1
S.K.H. Management Co.	PO Box 1500	Lititz	PA	17543	Paul W Stauffer	717-626-4771	R	57*	1.0
Jac Vandenberg Inc.	100 Corporate Blvd	Yonkers	NY	10701	David Schiro	914-964-5900	R	56*	<0.1
Lee Ray-Tarantino Company Inc.	PO Box 2408	S. San Francisco	CA	94083	Paul Tarantino	650-871-4323	S	55*	0.1
Progressive Produce Co.	5790 Peachtree St	Commerce	CA	90040	James K Leimkuhler	323-890-8100	R	50*	0.1
Nor-Cal Produce Inc.	PO Box 980188	W. Sacramento	CA	95798	Dan Achondo	916-373-0830	R	47*	0.1
Community Suffolk Inc.	304 2nd St	Everett	MA	02149	Joe Piazza	617-389-5200	R	44*	<0.1
Jackson Produce Co.	3226 McKelvey Rd	Bridgeton	MO	63044	Gerald Jackson	314-291-1080	R	43*	<0.1
Earth Brothers Ltd.	PO Box 188	Proctorsville	VT	05153	Steve Birge	802-226-7480	R	42*	0.1
Oneonta Trading Corp.	PO Box 549	Wenatchee	WA	98807	Dalton Thomas	509-663-2631	R	42*	0.1
Muir-Roberts Company Inc.	PO Box 328	Salt Lake City	UT	84110	Phillip R Muir	801-363-7695	R	41*	<0.1
Vanguard International Inc.	22605 SE 56th St	Issaquah	WA	98029	Craig Stauffer	425-557-8250	R	38*	<0.1
Del Monte Fresh Produce	14 Stuart Dr	Kankakee	IL	60901	Warren Ouwenga	815-936-7400	R	36*	<0.1
D'Arrigo Brothers	105 New England	Chelsea	MA	02150	Peter A D'Arrigo, Jr	617-884-1800	R	35*	<0.1
Father's Produce Inc.	3 Bethlehem Ct	Delmar	NY	12054	Harold Father	518-463-2297	R	33*	<0.1
General Produce Company Ltd.	PO Box 308	Sacramento	CA	95812	Daniel Chan	916-441-6431	R	32*	0.3
A. Sam Farm Inc.	PO Box 591	Dunkirk	NY	14048	Charles Sam	716-366-6666	R	31*	0.1
Chiquita Fresh, North America	3403 Macintosh Rd	Fort Lauderdale	FL	33316	Cyrus F Freldhelm Jr	513-784-8935	R	31*	0.1
DiMare Brothers Inc.	84 N England	Chelsea	MA	02150		617-889-3800	R	31*	0.1
Federal Fruit and Produce Co.	1890 E 58th Ave	Denver	CO	80216	Stan Kouba	303-292-1303	R	30*	<0.1
Frieda's Inc.	4465 Corp. Center	Los Alamitos	CA	90720	Frieda Caplan	714-826-6100	R	30*	0.1
Mission Produce Inc.	PO Box 5267	Oxnard	CA	93031	Steve Barnard	805-981-3650	R	28*	0.1
Albert's Organics Inc.	PO Box 624	Bridgeport	NJ	08014	Barclay Hope	856-241-9090	R	26*	<0.1
Roberts Foods Inc.	1615 W Jefferson St	Springfield	IL	62702	Dean Robert Jr	217-793-2633	S	25*	<0.1
J. Hellman Produce Inc.	1601 E Olympic	Los Angeles	CA	90021	Bryce Hellman	213-243-9105	R	23*	<0.1
Hollar and Greene Produce Co.	PO Box 3500	Boone	NC	28607	Dale Greene	828-264-2177	R	21*	<0.1
Van Solkema Produce Inc.	PO Box 308	Byron Center	MI	49315	Jerry Van Solkema	616-878-1508	R	21*	<0.1
Diamond Fruit Growers	PO Box 185	Odell	OR	97044	Ronald K Girardelli	541-354-5300	R	20*	0.2
Alabama Food Group Inc.	PO Drawer 1207	Alexander City	AL	35011	Hugh A Neighbors III	256-234-5071	R	18*	<0.1
Meyer Tomatoes	PO Box 606	King City	CA	93930	RL Meyer	831-385-4047	R	18*	0.5
Moody Creek Produce Inc.	PO Box 329	Sugar City	ID	83448	Bart Webster	208-356-9447	R	16*	<0.1
Moore Food Distributors Inc.	9910 Page Blvd	St. Louis	MO	63132	Al Moore	314-426-1300	R	16*	<0.1
William George Company Inc.	1002 Mize St	Lufkin	TX	75904	Randy George	936-634-7738	R	15*	0.2
Edwards Fruit Co.	PO Box 1687	Lakeland	FL	33802	David L Edwards	863-682-2022	R	14*	<0.1
Sparkle Flavors	3701 Shell St	El Paso	TX	79925	David Nieves	915-592-2639	R	13*	<0.1
John Livacich Produce Inc.	PO Box 70209	Riverside	CA	92513	John Livacich	909-734-6060	R	13*	<0.1
Blue Star Growers Inc.	100 Blue Star Way	Cashmere	WA	98815	Terry Twitchell	509-782-2922	R	12*	0.3
Rogers Brothers Wholesale Inc.	460 E Brooks St	Galesburg	IL	61401	Frank Rogers	309-342-2127	R	11*	<0.1
Ritchey Produce Company Inc.	PO Box 1416	Zanesville	OH	43702	Nadim Ritchey	740-454-0545	R	10*	<0.1
Great West Egg Industries	2183 E 11th St	Los Angeles	CA	90021	Seymour Teichner	213-626-7538	R	10*	<0.1
A.J. Rinella and Company Inc.	Brdway Menands	Albany	NY	12204	Peter Rinella	518-465-4581	R	10*	<0.1
Natural Energy Unlimited Inc.	108 Royal St	New Orleans	LA	70130	Ruthann Menutis	504-525-6887	S	10*	0.3
Casey Woodwyk Inc.	PO Box 9	Hudsonville	MI	49426	Jim Woodwyk	616-669-1700	R	9*	<0.1
Brown Brothers Produce Co.	9647 Idot Shed Rd	Nashville	IL	62263	John Brown	618-327-8154	R	9*	<0.1

Source: Ward's Business Directory of U.S. Private and Public Companies, Volumes 1 and 2, 2005. The company type code used is as follows: P - Public, R - Private, S - Subsidiary, D - Division, J - Joint Venture, A - Affiliate, G - Group. Sales are in millions of dollars, employees are in thousands. An asterisk (*) indicates an estimated sales volume. The symbol < stands for 'less than'. Company names and addresses are truncated, in some cases, to fit into the available space.

OCCUPATIONS EMPLOYED BY GROCERY & RELATED PRODUCTS WHOLESALE

Occupation	% of Total 2004	Change to 2014	Occupation	% of Total 2004	Change to 2014
Sales reps, wholesale & manufacturing, exc tech	12.7	10.6	Office clerks, general	1.9	-1.6
Laborers & freight, stock, & material movers, hand	11.0	-0.5	Bookkeeping, accounting, & auditing clerks	1.7	-0.5
Driver/sales workers	9.0	10.4	General & operations managers	1.5	9.4
Truck drivers, heavy & tractor-trailer	9.0	10.4	First-line supervisors/managers of non-retail sales work	1.5	2.2
Truck drivers, light or delivery services	5.0	10.4	Customer service representatives	1.5	13.2
Stock clerks & order fillers	4.4	-15.3	Wholesale & retail buyers, except farm products	1.2	4.5
Industrial truck & tractor operators	4.0	-0.5	First-line supervisors/managers of transporation workers	1.1	10.6
Packers & packagers, hand	2.8	10.6	Maintenance & repair workers, general	1.0	10.6
Shipping, receiving, & traffic clerks	2.1	0.1	First-line supervisors/managers of office workers	1.0	0.2
Packaging & filling machine operators & tenders	2.0	-5.8			

Source: Industry-Occupation Matrix, Bureau of Labor Statistics. These data are reported based on 4-digit NAICS categories but have been matched to corresponding 6-digit NAICS industry codes. The change reported for each occupation to the year 2014 is a percent of growth or decline as estimated by the Bureau of Labor Statistics. The abbreviation nec stands for 'not elsewhere classified.'

LOCATION BY STATE AND REGIONAL CONCENTRATION

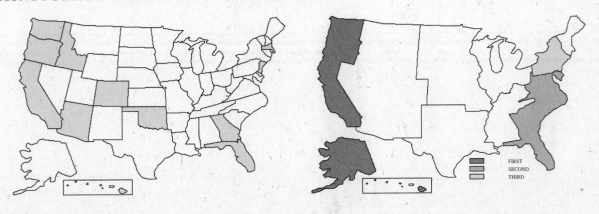

FIRST
SECOND
THIRD

INDUSTRY DATA BY STATE

State	Establishments Total (number)	% of U.S.	Employment Total (number)	% of U.S.	Per Estab.	Payroll Total ($ mil.)	Per Empl. ($)	Sales Total ($ mil.)	% of U.S.	Per Estab. ($)
California	1,106	20.5	26,091	23.6	24	989.4	37,920	15,795.6	31.8	14,281,765
Florida	566	10.5	11,800	10.7	21	293.2	24,847	3,888.7	7.8	6,870,565
New York	523	9.7	5,812	5.3	11	224.6	38,637	3,304.3	6.7	6,317,946
Texas	338	6.3	7,733	7.0	23	214.5	27,739	2,842.1	5.7	8,408,589
New Jersey	221	4.1	2,543	2.3	12	106.3	41,820	2,032.8	4.1	9,198,281
Pennsylvania	228	4.2	4,145	3.7	18	145.8	35,169	1,970.4	4.0	8,642,110
Washington	171	3.2	6,563	5.9	38	177.5	27,048	1,946.2	3.9	11,381,544
Illinois	200	3.7	2,258	2.0	11	104.8	46,391	1,367.3	2.8	6,836,740
Massachusetts	151	2.8	2,371	2.1	16	106.9	45,071	1,365.9	2.7	9,045,940
Georgia	143	2.6	3,373	3.1	24	103.4	30,650	1,361.6	2.7	9,521,741
Arizona	158	2.9	4,784	4.3	30	87.8	18,343	1,356.0	2.7	8,582,411
Ohio	134	2.5	3,011	2.7	22	111.8	37,125	1,320.6	2.7	9,855,149
Michigan	150	2.8	1,849	1.7	12	63.3	34,243	938.6	1.9	6,257,493
Idaho	58	1.1	2,525	2.3	44	46.4	18,382	855.6	1.7	14,751,086
Maryland	71	1.3	1,907	1.7	27	68.6	35,954	808.9	1.6	11,392,859
Minnesota	68	1.3	1,542	1.4	23	64.7	41,986	789.6	1.6	11,611,485
Oregon	90	1.7	2,728	2.5	30	77.8	28,504	736.8	1.5	8,186,556
Colorado	77	1.4	2,140	1.9	28	60.0	28,043	705.4	1.4	9,161,091
Oklahoma	43	0.8	815	0.7	19	21.4	26,202	636.8	1.3	14,810,209
North Carolina	87	1.6	1,633	1.5	19	41.6	25,454	505.2	1.0	5,807,241
Indiana	35	0.6	1,186	1.1	34	45.3	38,212	469.1	0.9	13,403,400
Wisconsin	56	1.0	1,070	1.0	19	36.0	33,688	445.9	0.9	7,962,964
Tennessee	65	1.2	1,571	1.4	24	52.9	33,682	431.9	0.9	6,644,015
Connecticut	41	0.8	699	0.6	17	25.8	36,864	357.1	0.7	8,709,341
Missouri	58	1.1	677	0.6	12	25.6	37,826	341.2	0.7	5,882,086
Hawaii	51	0.9	824	0.7	16	23.1	28,076	234.9	0.5	4,606,490
Virginia	62	1.1	1,089	1.0	18	28.3	25,946	229.8	0.5	3,707,097
Kentucky	45	0.8	694	0.6	15	20.9	30,146	220.1	0.4	4,892,044
Louisiana	41	0.8	945	0.9	23	24.2	25,579	216.8	0.4	5,286,951
Arkansas	19	0.4	273	0.2	14	9.4	34,260	177.0	0.4	9,314,316
Nevada	20	0.4	622	0.6	31	18.8	30,289	168.6	0.3	8,432,200
Alabama	31	0.6	473	0.4	15	14.3	30,258	168.4	0.3	5,433,290
South Carolina	39	0.7	434	0.4	11	12.0	27,604	167.7	0.3	4,300,256

Continued on next page.

INDUSTRY DATA BY STATE - Continued

State	Establishments		Employment			Payroll		Sales		
	Total (number)	% of U.S.	Total (number)	% of U.S.	Per Estab.	Total ($ mil.)	Per Empl. ($)	Total ($ mil.)	% of U.S.	Per Estab. ($)
Kansas	26	0.5	358	0.3	14	13.8	38,492	158.4	0.3	6,090,423
Iowa	17	0.3	395	0.4	23	14.7	37,089	151.3	0.3	8,902,353
Utah	27	0.5	280	0.3	10	9.4	33,732	148.2	0.3	5,487,074
Maine	29	0.5	271	0.2	9	8.3	30,668	133.8	0.3	4,613,207
West Virginia	19	0.4	629	0.6	33	13.0	20,704	124.9	0.3	6,571,684
New Mexico	23	0.4	258	0.2	11	8.8	33,926	91.5	0.2	3,979,522
Mississippi	23	0.4	274	0.2	12	6.7	24,518	75.9	0.2	3,301,217
North Dakota	12	0.2	242	0.2	20	4.1	17,050	69.1	0.1	5,759,417
Vermont	6	0.1	208	0.2	35	5.7	27,625	36.9	0.1	6,142,333
Alaska	5	0.1	79	0.1	16	3.7	46,633	27.1	0.1	5,413,600
Nebraska	6	0.1	202	0.2	34	4.0	19,713	25.8	0.1	4,301,000
New Hampshire	9	0.2	119	0.1	13	3.1	26,378	23.3	-	2,590,222
Wyoming	3	0.1	19	-	6	0.4	22,947	3.8	-	1,267,333
Rhode Island	17	0.3	100-249	-	-	(D)	-	(D)	-	-
D.C.	13	0.2	250-499	-	-	(D)	-	(D)	-	-
Delaware	7	0.1	20-99	-	-	(D)	-	(D)	-	-
Montana	6	0.1	250-499	-	-	(D)	-	(D)	-	-
South Dakota	3	0.1	20-99	-	-	(D)	-	(D)	-	-

Source: 2002 *Economic Census*. The states are in descending order of sales or establishments (if sales data are missing for the majority). The symbol (D) appears when data are withheld to prevent disclosure of competitive information. States marked with (D) are sorted by number of establishments. A dash (-) indicates that the data element cannot be calculated. Shaded *states* on the state map indicate those states which have proportionately greater representation in the industry than would be indicated by the states population; the ratio is based on total sales or number of establishments. Shaded *regions* indicate where the industry is regionally most concentrated.

NAICS 424490 - OTHER GROCERY AND RELATED PRODUCTS MERCHANT WHOLESALERS

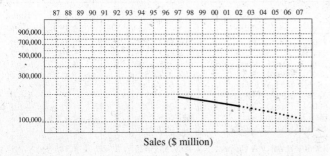

Sales ($ million)

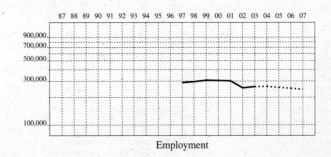

Employment

GENERAL STATISTICS

Year	Establishments (number)	Employment (number)	Payroll ($ million)	Sales ($ million)	Employees per Establishment (number)	Sales per Establishment ($)	Payroll per Employee ($)
1987	-	-	-	-	-	-	-
1988	-	-	-	-	-	-	-
1989	-	-	-	-	-	-	-
1990	-	-	-	-	-	-	-
1991	-	-	-	-	-	-	-
1992	-	-	-	-	-	-	-
1993	-	-	-	-	-	-	-
1994	-	-	-	-	-	-	-
1995	-	-	-	-	-	-	-
1996	-	-	-	-	-	-	-
1997	14,623	288,689	9,277.5	186,758.7	19.7	12,771,572.2	32,136.7
1998	14,607	295,821	10,127.7	178,876.7 e	20.3	12,245,957.4	34,235.9
1999	14,249	306,357	10,950.3	170,994.7 e	21.5	12,000,470.2	35,743.6
2000	13,927	304,421	11,418.7	163,112.7 e	21.9	11,711,976.7	37,509.7
2001	13,703	301,333	11,771.6	155,230.7 e	22.0	11,328,227.4	39,065.0
2002	12,345	253,076	9,167.6	147,348.7	20.5	11,935,901.2	36,224.7
2003	12,234	260,806	10,184.3	139,466.7 p	21.3	11,277,013.7 p	39,049.4
2004	11,922 p	262,334 p	10,645.6 p	131,584.7 p	21.9 p	11,070,726.8 p	40,286.0 p
2005	11,485 p	256,114 p	10,703.5 p	123,702.7 p	22.1 p	10,864,440.0 p	41,287.3 p
2006	11,048 p	249,894 p	10,761.4 p	115,820.7 p	22.3 p	10,658,153.2 p	42,288.6 p
2007	10,610 p	243,674 p	10,819.3 p	107,938.7 p	22.5 p	10,451,866.4 p	43,290.0 p

Source: Economic Census of the United States, 1997 and 2002. Establishment counts, employment, and payroll are from County Business Patterns for non-Census years. This is a newly defined industry. Data for prior years are unavailable at the time of publication but may become available over time. Values followed by 'p' are projections by the editors. Sales data for non-Census years are extrapolations, marked by 'e'.

INDICES OF CHANGE

Year	Establishments (number)	Employment (number)	Payroll ($ million)	Sales ($ million)	Employees per Establishment (number)	Sales per Establishment ($)	Payroll per Employee ($)
1987	-	-	-	-	-	-	-
1992	-	-	-	-	-	-	-
1993	-	-	-	-	-	-	-
1994	-	-	-	-	-	-	-
1995	-	-	-	-	-	-	-
1996	-	-	-	-	-	-	-
1997	118.5	114.1	101.2	126.7	96.1	107.0	88.7
1998	118.3	116.9	110.5	121.4 e	99.0	102.6	94.5
1999	115.4	121.1	119.4	116.0 e	104.9	100.5	98.7
2000	112.8	120.3	124.6	110.7 e	106.8	98.1	103.5
2001	111.0	119.1	128.4	105.3 e	107.3	94.9	107.8
2002	100.0	100.0	100.0	100.0	100.0	100.0	100.0
2003	99.1	103.1	111.1	94.7 p	104.0	94.5 p	107.8
2004	96.6 p	103.7 p	116.1 p	89.3 p	106.6 p	92.8 p	111.2 p
2005	93.0 p	101.2 p	116.8 p	84.0 p	107.6 p	91.0 p	114.0 p
2006	89.5 p	98.7 p	117.4 p	78.6 p	108.6 p	89.3 p	116.7 p
2007	85.9 p	96.3 p	118.0 p	73.3 p	109.6 p	87.6 p	119.5 p

Sources: Same as General Statistics. The values shown reflect change from the base year, 2002. Values above 100 mean greater than 2002, values below 100 mean less than 2002, and a value of 100 in the 1987-2001 or 2003-2007 period means same as 2002. Values followed by 'p' are projections by the editors; 'e' stands for extrapolation. Data are the most recent available at this level of detail.

SELECTED RATIOS

For 2002	Avg. of All Wholesale	Analyzed Industry	Index	For 2002	Avg. of All Wholesale	Analyzed Industry	Index
Employees per Establishment	15	21	137	Sales per Employee	791,325	582,231	74
Payroll per Establishment	626,122	742,616	119	Sales per Establishment	12,012,387	11,935,901	99
Payroll per Employee	41,161	36,225	88	Expenses per Establishment	na	na	na

Sources: Same as General Statistics. The 'Average of All' column, Wholesale or Retail, represents the average of the sector reported for the most recent complete year available. The Index shows the relationship between the Average and the Analyzed Industry. For example, 100 means that they are equal; 500 that the Analyzed Industry is five times the average; 50 means that the Analyzed Industry is half the national average. The abbreviation 'na' is used to show that data are 'not available'.

LEADING COMPANIES   Number shown: **75**   Total sales ($ mil): **66,922**   Total employment (000): **222.2**

Company Name	Address				CEO Name	Phone	Co. Type	Sales ($ mil)	Empl. (000)
SYSCO Corp.	1390 Enclave Pkwy	Houston	TX	77077		281-584-1390	P	29,335	47.0
Starbucks Corp.	PO Box 34067	Seattle	WA	98124		206-447-1575	P	5,294	96.7
M.B.M. Corp.	PO Box 800	Rocky Mount	NC	27802	Jerry L Wordsworth	919-985-7200	R	4,744	3.5
Coors Brewing Co.	PO Box 2991	Golden	CO	80401	Peter H Coors	303-279-6565	S	2,410	5.4
Melody Farms Inc.	31111 Industrial Rd	Livonia	MI	48150	Rodney George	734-525-4000	R	2,335*	0.5
Universal Corp.	PO Box 25099	Richmond	VA	23260	Henry H Harrell	804-359-9311	P	2,271	30.0
Distribution Plus Inc.	825 Green Bay Rd	Wilmette	IL	60091	Dan O'Connell	847-256-8289	R	1,712*	1.0
Topco Associates Inc.	7711 Gross Point Rd	Skokie	IL	60077	Steven Lauer	847-676-3030	R	1,455*	0.3
National Distributing Company	PO Box 44127	Atlanta	GA	30336	Charlie Andrews	404-696-9440	R	1,360*	2.5
Shamrock Foods Co.	2540 N 29th Ave	Phoenix	AZ	85009		602-233-6400	R	1,354	2.3
Dial Corp.	15501 N Dial Blvd	Scottsdale	AZ	85260	Bradley A Casper	480-754-3425	S	1,345	2.5
Honickman Affiliates	8275 Rte 130	Pennsauken	NJ	08110	Harold Honickman	856-665-6200	R	983*	5.0
Sunkist Growers Inc.	PO Box 7888	Van Nuys	CA	91409	Jeffrey D Gargiulo	818-986-4800	R	942	0.4
Bozzuto's Inc.	275 Schoolhouse Rd	Cheshire	CT	06410	Michael A Bozzuto	203-272-3511	R	900	1.0
Bakemark West	7351 Crider Ave	Pico Rivera	CA	90660	Joe Castor	562-949-1054	R	618*	0.2
S and D Coffee Inc.	PO Box 1628	Concord	NC	28026	Alan Davis	704-782-3121	R	551*	0.6
Challenge Dairy Products Inc.	PO Box 2369	Dublin	CA	94568	John Whetten	925-828-6160	R	524*	<0.1
National Beverage Corp.	1 N University Dr	Fort Lauderdale	FL	33324	Joseph G Caporella	954-581-0922	P	512	1.5
Fresh Brands Distributing Inc.	PO Box 419	Sheboygan	WI	53082	Elwood F Winn	920-457-4433	S	502*	1.8
Phoenix Coca-Cola Bottling Co.	PO Box 20008	Phoenix	AZ	85036		480-831-0400	D	410*	1.0
Gold Coast Beverage Distributors	3325 NW 70th Ave	Miami	FL	33122	Art Friedman	305-591-9800	R	405*	0.7
Norpac Food Sales	4350 SW Galewood	Lake Oswego	OR	97035	Mike Woods	503-635-9311	R	400*	<0.1
Riviana Foods Inc.	PO Box 2636	Houston	TX	77252	Frank A Godchaux III	713-529-3251	S	396	2.8
Kehe Food Distributors Inc.	900 N Schmidt Rd	Romeoville	IL	60446	Jerry Kehe	815-886-0700	R	359*	0.7
Torn and Glasser Inc.	PO Box 21823	Los Angeles	CA	90021	Robert Glasser	213-627-6496	R	291*	<0.1
Weider Nutrition International Inc.	2002 S 5070 W	Salt Lake City	UT	84104		801-975-5000	P	258	0.7
Dairy Fresh Products Co.	601 Rockefeller Ave	Ontario	CA	91761	Jim DeKeyser	909-975-1019	S	232*	0.5
H and H Meat Products Inc.	PO Box 358	Mercedes	TX	78570	Liborio Hinojosa	956-565-6363	R	210*	1.0
Dole and Bailey Inc.	PO Box 2405	Woburn	MA	01888	DM Matheson	781-935-1234	R	196*	0.2
High Grade Beverage	PO Box 7092	N. Brunswick	NJ	08902	Joseph DeMarco	732-821-7600	R	192*	0.4
Polar Corp.	PO Box 15011	Worcester	MA	01615	Ralph Crowley	508-753-4300	R	191*	0.7
Jordanos Inc.	550 S Patterson Ave	Santa Barbara	CA	93111	Peter Jordano	805-964-0611	R	188*	0.5
Columbia Distributing Co.	6840 N Cutter Cir	Portland	OR	97217	Edward L Maletis	503-289-9600	R	176*	0.6
JFC International Inc.	540 Forbes Blvd	S. San Francisco	CA	94080	Hiroyuka Enomoto	650-873-8400	S	166*	0.1
C.C. Clark Inc.	PO Box 966	Starkville	MS	39760		662-323-4317	R	148*	0.8
Peet's Coffee and Tea Inc.	PO Box 12509	Berkeley	CA	94712	Patrick J O'Dea	510-594-2100	P	146	2.1
Kalil Bottling Company Inc.	4045 S 38th St	Phoenix	AZ	85040		602-437-0900	R	137*	0.2
Atlantic Premium Brands Ltd.	1033 Skokie Blvd	Northbrook	IL	60062	Thomas M Dalton	847-412-6200	P	130	0.5
Mounthood Beverage Co.	3601 NW Yeon Ave	Portland	OR	97210	Richard Lytle	503-274-9990	R	130*	0.6
Noble Americas Corp.	333 Ludlow St	Stamford	CT	06902	Vicente Del Castillo	203-324-8555	R	129*	<0.1
Dr Pepper & Seven Up Bottling	950 Stelzer Rd	Columbus	OH	43219		614-237-4201	D	128*	0.3
Imperial Commodities Corp.	17 Battery Pl	New York	NY	10004	John Morley	212-837-9400	S	128*	<0.1
Gate City Beverage Distributors	2505 Steel St	San Bernardino	CA	92408	Leona Aronoff	909-799-1600	R	127*	0.4
Canteen Service Co.	5695 W River NE	Belmont	MI	49306	Fred Tiggleman	616-785-2500	S	120*	0.8
Tony's Fine Foods	PO Box 1501	W. Sacramento	CA	95605	Karl Berger	916-374-4150	R	119*	0.4
Crest Beverage Co.	PO Box 26640	San Diego	CA	92121	Steve S Sourapas	858-566-1800	R	115*	0.2
Pepsi-Cola General Bottlers	PO Box 1596	South Bend	IN	46634		219-234-1311	D	113*	<0.1
Crystal Bottling Company Inc.	575 Display Way	Sacramento	CA	95838	Hayes Johnson	916-568-3300	S	107*	<0.1
7-Up Corp.	400 Hosmer Ave	Modesto	CA	95351	John Varni	209-521-1777	R	107*	<0.1
Minges Bottling Group	PO Box 520	Ayden	NC	28513	Jeff Minges	252-746-9705	R	101*	0.2
Paramount Export Co.	175 Filbert St	Oakland	CA	94607	Nick Kukulan	510-839-0150	R	98*	<0.1
Reliv' International Inc.	PO Box 405	Chesterfield	MO	63006	Robert L Montgomery	636-537-9715	P	97	0.0
L and E Bottling Company Inc.	PO Box 11159	Olympia	WA	98508	Brian Charneski	360-357-3812	R	91*	<0.1
Schiff's Restaurant Service Inc.	3410 N Main Ave	Scranton	PA	18508		570-343-1294	R	86*	0.1
MLO Products Inc.	2351 N Watney Way	Fairfield	CA	94533	Doug Williamson	707-399-2500	R	84*	0.2
Bruno Scheidt Inc.	71 W 23rd St	New York	NY	10010	Charles E Scheidt	212-741-8290	R	83*	<0.1
North Shore Bottling Company	1900 Linden Blvd	Brooklyn	NY	11207	Marilyn Miller	718-272-8900	R	82*	0.1
Bi Rite Foodservice Distributors	123 S Hill Dr	Brisbane	CA	94005	Steve Barulich	415-656-0254	S	80*	0.2
Buffalo Rock Co. Gadsden Div.	PO Box 2307	Gadsden	AL	35903	James C Lee, III	256-492-8400	D	78*	0.2
Veronica Foods Co.	PO Box 2225	Oakland	CA	94621	Michael Bradley	510-535-6833	R	78*	<0.1
Pepsi-Cola Bottling Co.	PO Box 165	Springville	UT	84663	Kelly Clay	801-491-3366	R	69*	0.1
Southern Beverage Company Inc.	1939 Davis Johnson	Richland	MS	39218	Theo Costas	601-969-5550	R	65*	0.1
Coffee Beanery Limited Inc.	3429 Pierson Pl	Flushing	MI	48433	Joanne Shaw	810-733-1020	R	62*	0.1
Essex Grain Products Inc.	9 Lee Blvd	Frazer	PA	19355	Alice Bierer	610-647-3800	R	60*	<0.1
Ira Higdon Grocery Company Inc.	PO Box 488	Cairo	GA	39828	Larry Higdon	229-377-1272	R	59*	<0.1
Pepsi-Cola Batavia Bottling Corp.	319 W Main St	Batavia	NY	14020	R W Houseknecht Jr	585-343-7479	R	59*	0.1
Jim L. Shetakis Distributing Co.	PO Box 14987	Las Vegas	NV	89114	Lloyd Meher	702-735-8985	R	58*	0.2
Odom Corp.	20415 72nd Ave S	Kent	WA	98032	John P Odom	253-437-3000	R	58*	0.5
Rolf's Patisserie Inc.	4343 W Touhy Ave	Lincolnwood	IL	60712	Lloyd Culbertson	847-675-6565	R	56*	<0.1
Novamex	1477 Lomaland Dr	El Paso	TX	79935	Luis Fernandez	915-594-1618	R	56*	0.2
Golden Brand Bottling Inc.	2225 Jerrold Ave	San Francisco	CA	94124	Jim Molakides	415-643-9900	R	54*	0.2
Vermont Pure Holdings Ltd.	PO Box 536	Williston	VT	05495	Henry E Baker	802-860-1126	P	53	0.3
Caravan Trading Co.	33300 Western Ave	Union City	CA	94587	Joseph Maroun	510-487-2600	R	52*	0.4
Summit Import Corp.	100 Summit Pl	Jersey City	NJ	07305	Whiting Wu	201-985-9200	R	52*	0.1
Jarritos Distributors	1477 Lomaland Dr	El Paso	TX	79935		915-594-1618	S	51*	0.1

Source: Ward's Business Directory of U.S. Private and Public Companies, Volumes 1 and 2, 2005. The company type code used is as follows: P - Public, R - Private, S - Subsidiary, D - Division, J - Joint Venture, A - Affiliate, G - Group. Sales are in millions of dollars, employees are in thousands. An asterisk (*) indicates an estimated sales volume. The symbol < stands for 'less than'. Company names and addresses are truncated, in some cases, to fit into the available space.

OCCUPATIONS EMPLOYED BY GROCERY & RELATED PRODUCTS WHOLESALE

Occupation	% of Total 2004	Change to 2014	Occupation	% of Total 2004	Change to 2014
Sales reps, wholesale & manufacturing, exc tech	12.7	10.6	Office clerks, general	1.9	-1.6
Laborers & freight, stock, & material movers, hand	11.0	-0.5	Bookkeeping, accounting, & auditing clerks	1.7	-0.5
Driver/sales workers	9.0	10.4	General & operations managers	1.5	9.4
Truck drivers, heavy & tractor-trailer	9.0	10.4	First-line supervisors/managers of non-retail sales work	1.5	2.2
Truck drivers, light or delivery services	5.0	10.4	Customer service representatives	1.5	13.2
Stock clerks & order fillers	4.4	-15.3	Wholesale & retail buyers, except farm products	1.2	4.5
Industrial truck & tractor operators	4.0	-0.5	First-line supervisors/managers of transporation workers	1.1	10.6
Packers & packagers, hand	2.8	10.6	Maintenance & repair workers, general	1.0	10.6
Shipping, receiving, & traffic clerks	2.1	0.1	First-line supervisors/managers of office workers	1.0	0.2
Packaging & filling machine operators & tenders	2.0	-5.8			

Source: Industry-Occupation Matrix, Bureau of Labor Statistics. These data are reported based on 4-digit NAICS categories but have been matched to corresponding 6-digit NAICS industry codes. The change reported for each occupation to the year 2014 is a percent of growth or decline as estimated by the Bureau of Labor Statistics. The abbreviation nec stands for 'not elsewhere classified.'

LOCATION BY STATE AND REGIONAL CONCENTRATION

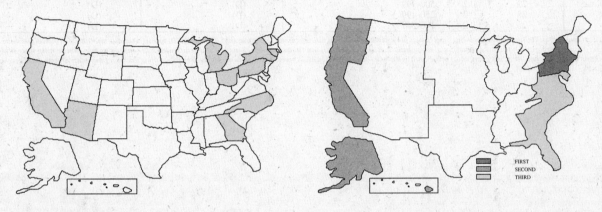

FIRST
SECOND
THIRD

INDUSTRY DATA BY STATE

State	Establishments Total (number)	% of U.S.	Employment Total (number)	% of U.S.	Per Estab.	Payroll Total ($ mil.)	Per Empl. ($)	Sales Total ($ mil.)	% of U.S.	Per Estab. ($)
California	1,890	15.3	34,635	13.6	18	1,341.3	38,728	20,530.3	13.1	10,862,611
New York	1,474	11.9	21,788	8.5	15	822.5	37,751	18,457.1	11.8	12,521,807
Pennsylvania	445	3.6	10,702	4.2	24	402.9	37,643	8,446.3	5.4	18,980,366
Texas	654	5.3	13,717	5.4	21	472.1	34,420	8,297.6	5.3	12,687,411
Ohio	358	2.9	9,880	3.9	28	344.4	34,856	7,849.9	5.0	21,926,994
Florida	814	6.6	11,306	4.4	14	395.7	34,996	6,785.3	4.3	8,335,799
Michigan	361	2.9	10,845	4.2	30	422.0	38,911	6,314.1	4.0	17,490,449
Georgia	290	2.3	6,469	2.5	22	236.5	36,562	5,650.4	3.6	19,484,124
North Carolina	259	2.1	8,700	3.4	34	298.2	34,281	4,478.5	2.9	17,291,502
Connecticut	175	1.4	5,703	2.2	33	251.5	44,100	4,289.2	2.7	24,509,623
Arizona	221	1.8	4,254	1.7	19	157.4	37,011	3,842.0	2.5	17,384,480
Virginia	196	1.6	5,133	2.0	26	195.5	38,078	2,995.8	1.9	15,284,607
Tennessee	156	1.3	4,674	1.8	30	176.4	37,739	2,530.4	1.6	16,220,622
Wisconsin	210	1.7	5,100	2.0	24	170.4	33,414	2,085.8	1.3	9,932,490
Alabama	123	1.0	3,536	1.4	29	113.2	32,010	1,081.3	0.7	8,791,146
Mississippi	79	0.6	2,235	0.9	28	66.8	29,889	599.0	0.4	7,581,949
Maine	71	0.6	1,206	0.5	17	37.7	31,226	414.5	0.3	5,838,366
New Mexico	81	0.7	1,214	0.5	15	39.2	32,282	367.6	0.2	4,538,198
Rhode Island	34	0.3	779	0.3	23	27.1	34,734	298.1	0.2	8,767,971
Hawaii	98	0.8	1,293	0.5	13	36.6	28,294	271.3	0.2	2,767,888
Vermont	49	0.4	651	0.3	13	20.8	31,900	188.1	0.1	3,837,980
Wyoming	35	0.3	456	0.2	13	12.6	27,724	97.9	0.1	2,796,400
New Jersey	606	4.9	10K-24999	-	-	(D)	-	(D)	-	-
Illinois	508	4.1	10K-24999	-	-	(D)	-	(D)	-	-
Washington	286	2.3	5K-9999	-	-	(D)	-	(D)	-	-
Massachusetts	262	2.1	5K-9999	-	-	(D)	-	(D)	-	-
Missouri	239	1.9	2500-4999	-	-	(D)	-	(D)	-	-
Maryland	197	1.6	5K-9999	-	-	(D)	-	(D)	-	-
Minnesota	196	1.6	2500-4999	-	-	(D)	-	(D)	-	-
Colorado	190	1.5	2500-4999	-	-	(D)	-	(D)	-	-
Oregon	190	1.5	2500-4999	-	-	(D)	-	(D)	-	-
Indiana	179	1.4	5K-9999	-	-	(D)	-	(D)	-	-
Louisiana	158	1.3	2500-4999	-	-	(D)	-	(D)	-	-

Continued on next page.

INDUSTRY DATA BY STATE - Continued

State	Establishments Total (number)	% of U.S.	Employment Total (number)	% of U.S.	Per Estab.	Payroll Total ($ mil.)	Per Empl. ($)	Sales Total ($ mil.)	% of U.S.	Per Estab. ($)
Utah	116	0.9	1000-2499	-	-	(D)	-	(D)	-	-
South Carolina	113	0.9	2500-4999	-	-	(D)	-	(D)	-	-
Kansas	110	0.9	2500-4999	-	-	(D)	-	(D)	-	-
Oklahoma	106	0.9	1000-2499	-	-	(D)	-	(D)	-	-
Kentucky	105	0.8	2500-4999	-	-	(D)	-	(D)	-	-
Arkansas	104	0.8	1000-2499	-	-	(D)	-	(D)	-	-
Iowa	95	0.8	1000-2499	-	-	(D)	-	(D)	-	-
Nevada	80	0.6	1000-2499	-	-	(D)	-	(D)	-	-
Nebraska	71	0.6	1000-2499	-	-	(D)	-	(D)	-	-
New Hampshire	67	0.5	1000-2499	-	-	(D)	-	(D)	-	-
Idaho	65	0.5	1000-2499	-	-	(D)	-	(D)	-	-
Montana	55	0.4	500-999	-	-	(D)	-	(D)	-	-
West Virginia	53	0.4	1000-2499	-	-	(D)	-	(D)	-	-
Delaware	35	0.3	250-499	-	-	(D)	-	(D)	-	-
North Dakota	34	0.3	500-999	-	-	(D)	-	(D)	-	-
South Dakota	29	0.2	500-999	-	-	(D)	-	(D)	-	-
Alaska	28	0.2	250-499	-	-	(D)	-	(D)	-	-
D.C.	23	0.2	100-249	-	-	(D)	-	(D)	-	-

Source: 2002 *Economic Census*. The states are in descending order of sales or establishments (if sales data are missing for the majority). The symbol (D) appears when data are withheld to prevent disclosure of competitive information. States marked with (D) are sorted by number of establishments. A dash (-) indicates that the data element cannot be calculated. Shaded *states* on the state map indicate those states which have proportionately greater representation in the industry than would be indicated by the states population; the ratio is based on total sales or number of establishments. Shaded *regions* indicate where the industry is regionally most concentrated.

NAICS 424510 - GRAIN AND FIELD BEAN MERCHANT WHOLESALERS*

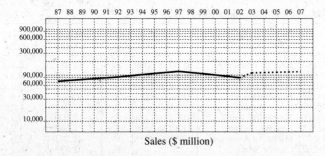

Sales ($ million)

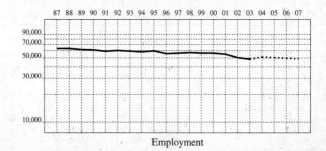

Employment

GENERAL STATISTICS

Year	Establishments (number)	Employment (number)	Payroll ($ million)	Sales ($ million)	Employees per Establishment (number)	Sales per Establishment ($)	Payroll per Employee ($)
1987	8,155	63,272	1,273.0	73,511.5	7.8	9,014,285.7	20,119.5
1988	7,871	63,283	1,345.7	76,989.9 e	8.0	9,781,463.6	21,264.8
1989	7,660	61,644	1,351.1	80,468.3 e	8.0	10,505,000.0	21,917.8
1990	7,426	61,082	1,375.5	83,946.8 e	8.2	11,304,443.8	22,518.9
1991	7,180	59,011	1,365.9	87,425.2 e	8.2	12,176,211.7	23,146.5
1992	7,444	60,243	1,446.2	90,903.6	8.1	12,211,660.4	24,006.1
1993	7,185	59,195	1,436.1	96,785.4 e	8.2	13,470,480.2	24,260.5
1994	6,960	58,117	1,478.7	102,667.2 e	8.4	14,751,034.5	25,443.5
1995	6,815	59,692	1,587.0	108,549.0 e	8.8	15,927,953.0	26,586.5
1996	6,622 e	55,652 e	1,522.4 e	114,430.8 e	8.4 e	17,280,398.7 e	27,355.7 e
1997	6,569	56,368	1,642.9	120,312.6	8.6	18,315,207.8	29,146.0
1998	6,304	57,138	1,715.7	113,768.6 e	9.1	18,047,049.5	30,027.3
1999	6,197	56,523	1,750.5	107,224.6 e	9.1	17,302,662.6	30,969.7
2000	6,077	56,407	1,783.1	100,680.6 e	9.3	16,567,484.0	31,611.4
2001	5,890	54,945	1,812.1	94,136.6 e	9.3	15,982,444.8	32,980.3
2002	5,390	50,398	1,694.6	87,592.6	9.4	16,250,946.2	33,624.4
2003	5,134	48,486	1,733.5	111,914.9 p	9.4	19,231,223.3 p	35,752.0
2004	5,262 p	51,127 p	1,850.8 p	113,762.3 p	9.6 p	19,810,714.8 p	35,582.4 p
2005	5,095 p	50,394 p	1,884.5 p	115,609.7 p	9.7 p	20,390,206.3 p	36,524.7 p
2006	4,929 p	49,660 p	1,918.2 p	117,457.1 p	9.8 p	20,969,697.8 p	37,467.0 p
2007	4,763 p	48,926 p	1,951.8 p	119,304.5 p	9.9 p	21,549,189.4 p	38,409.3 p

Sources: *Economic Census of the United States*, 1987, 1992, 1997, and 2002. Establishment counts, employment, and payroll are from *County Business Patterns* for non-Census years. Values followed by a 'p' are projections by the editors. Sales data for non-Census years are extrapolations, marked by 'e'. Data are the most recent available at this level of detail.

INDICES OF CHANGE

Year	Establishments (number)	Employment (number)	Payroll ($ million)	Sales ($ million)	Employees per Establishment (number)	Sales per Establishment ($)	Payroll per Employee ($)
1987	151.3	125.5	75.1	83.9	83.0	55.5	59.8
1992	138.1	119.5	85.3	103.8	86.2	75.1	71.4
1993	133.3	117.5	84.7	110.5 e	87.2	82.9	72.2
1994	129.1	115.3	87.3	117.2 e	89.4	90.8	75.7
1995	126.4	118.4	93.7	123.9 e	93.6	98.0	79.1
1996	122.9 e	110.4 e	89.8 e	130.6 e	89.4 e	106.3 e	81.4 e
1997	121.9	111.8	96.9	137.4	91.5	112.7	86.7
1998	117.0	113.4	101.2	129.9 e	96.8	111.1	89.3
1999	115.0	112.2	103.3	122.4 e	96.8	106.5	92.1
2000	112.7	111.9	105.2	114.9 e	98.9	101.9	94.0
2001	109.3	109.0	106.9	107.5 e	98.9	98.3	98.1
2002	100.0	100.0	100.0	100.0	100.0	100.0	100.0
2003	95.3	96.2	102.3	127.8 p	100.5	118.3 p	106.3
2004	97.6 p	101.4 p	109.2 p	129.9 p	101.8 p	121.9 p	105.8 p
2005	94.5 p	100.0 p	111.2 p	132.0 p	103.0 p	125.5 p	108.6 p
2006	91.4 p	98.5 p	113.2 p	134.1 p	104.1 p	129.0 p	111.4 p
2007	88.4 p	97.1 p	115.2 p	136.2 p	105.2 p	132.6 p	114.2 p

Sources: Same as General Statistics. The values shown reflect change from the base year, 2002. Values above 100 mean greater than 2002, values below 100 mean less than 2002, and a value of 100 in the 1987-2001 or 2003-2007 period means same as 2002. Values followed by a 'p' are projections by the editors; 'e' stands for extrapolation. Data are the most recent available at this level of detail.

SELECTED RATIOS

For 2002	Avg. of All Wholesale	Analyzed Industry	Index	For 2002	Avg. of All Wholesale	Analyzed Industry	Index
Employees per Establishment	15	9	63	Sales per Employee	791,325	1,738,017	220
Payroll per Establishment	626,122	314,397	50	Sales per Establishment	12,012,387	16,250,946	135
Payroll per Employee	41,161	33,624	82	Expenses per Establishment	na	na	na

Sources: Same as General Statistics. The 'Average of All' column, Wholesale or Retail, represents the average of the sector reported for the most recent complete year available. The Index shows the relationship between the Average and the Analyzed Industry. For example, 100 means that they are equal; 500 that the Analyzed Industry is five times the average; 50 means that the Analyzed Industry is half the national average. The abbreviation 'na' is used to show that data are 'not available'.

*Equivalent to SIC 5153.

LEADING COMPANIES   Number shown: **75**   Total sales ($ mil): **31,624**   Total employment (000): **30.5**

Company Name	Address				CEO Name	Phone	Co. Type	Sales ($ mil)	Empl. (000)
CHS Inc.	PO Box 64089	St. Paul	MN	55164	John D. Johnson	651-355-6000	P	11,051	6.8
Seaboard Corp.	PO Box 2972	Schuylkl Hvn	KS	66201	H Harry Bresky	913-676-8800	P	2,684	9.5
Leprino Foods Co.	PO Box 173400	Denver	CO	80217	Wesley J Allan	303-480-2600	R	2,500*	3.3
DeBruce Grain Inc.	PO Box 34621	Kansas City	MO	64117	Paul DeBruce	816-421-8182	R	2,018	0.4
CGB Enterprises Inc.	PO Box 249	Mandeville	LA	70470	Kevin Adams	985-867-3500	R	2,012*	1.0
Scoular Co.	9401 Indian Creek	Overland Park	KS	66210	Marshall E Faith	913-338-1474	R	2,000	0.3
ADM Grain	4666 Faries Pkwy	Decatur	IL	62525	Lew Batchelder	217-424-5200	S	1,662*	1.2
Andersons Inc.	PO Box 119	Maumee	OH	43537	Michael J Anderson	419-893-5050	P	1,247	2.9
Countrymark Cooperative Inc.	225 SE St, Ste 144	Indianapolis	IN	46202	Charlie Smith		R	1,083*	0.9
Frontier Cooperative Co.	PO Box 379	David City	NE	68632		402-367-3019	R	593*	0.1
Johnson Cooperative Grain Co.	PO Box 280	Johnson	KS	67855	Steve Arnold	620-492-6210	R	336*	<0.1
Torn and Glasser Inc.	PO Box 21823	Los Angeles	CA	90021	Robert Glasser	213-627-6496	R	291*	<0.1
Aurora Cooperative Elevator Co.	PO Box 209	Aurora	NE	68818	George Hohwieler	402-694-2106	R	249*	<0.1
Demeter Inc.	PO Box 668	Fowler	IN	47944	Donald Brouillette	765-884-9320	R	210*	0.1
Wheeler Brothers Grain Inc.	PO Box 29	Watonga	OK	73772	Mike Mahoney	580-623-7223	R	180*	0.1
Ag Partners L.L.C.	PO Box 38	Albert City	IA	50510	Troy Upah	712-843-2291	J	175*	0.1
Universal Cooperative Inc.	1300 Corp Ctr	Eagan	MN	55121	Terry Bohman	651-239-1000	R	167*	0.3
Effingham Equity	PO Box 488	Effingham	IL	62401		217-342-4101	R	155*	0.4
Chaffee Lynchburg Farmers	5048 156 R Ave SE	Leonard	ND	58052		701-645-2391	R	149*	<0.1
MaxYield Coop.	PO Box 49	West Bend	IA	50597		515-887-7211	R	125*	<0.1
Madison Farmers Elevator Co.	PO Box 228	Madison	SD	57042		605-256-4584	R	119*	<0.1
Perryton Equity Exchange	PO Box 889	Perryton	TX	79070	Doug Mitchell	806-435-4016	R	110*	0.1
Wilco Farmers	PO Box 258	Mount Angel	OR	97362	Michael Jamison	503-845-6122	R	100*	<0.1
JaGee Corp.	PO Box 9600	Fort Worth	TX	76147	Richard F Garvey	817-335-5881	R	95*	0.3
Cooperative Elevator Co.	PO Box 619	Pigeon	MI	48755	Pat Anderson	989-453-4500	R	86*	0.2
DeLong Company Inc.	PO Box 552	Clinton	WI	53525	David D DeLong	608-676-2255	R	80*	0.1
Farmers Britt Co-Op	PO Box 156	Britt	IA	50423	Ron Eisenman	641-843-3878	R	79*	<0.1
Sunrise Cooperative Inc.	82 Townsend Ave	Norwalk	OH	44857		419-668-3336	R	77*	<0.1
New Vision Coop.	PO Box 877	Worthington	MN	56187	Ron Jorgenson	507-376-4113	R	73*	<0.1
Farmers Elevator Co.	434 1st St	Chappell	NE	69129		308-874-2245	R	64*	0.1
Metamora Grain	PO Box G	Metamora	OH	43540		419-644-4711	R	63*	<0.1
AgriPride F.S. Inc.	PO Box 329	Nashville	IL	62263	Randy Newcomb	618-327-3046	R	62*	0.1
Lucky Farmers Inc.	PO Box 217	Woodville	OH	43469	James Eckel	419-849-2711	R	62*	<0.1
Ag-Valley Co-op.	PO Box 68	Edison	NE	68936	David Brown	308-927-3681	R	60*	<0.1
Interstate Commodities Inc.	PO Box 607	Troy	NY	12180	Victor A Oberting Jr	518-272-7212	R	60*	<0.1
Battle Creek Farmers Cooperative	PO Box 10	Battle Creek	NE	68715			R	58*	<0.1
Sunray Coop.	PO Box 430	Sunray	TX	79086		806-948-4121	R	56*	<0.1
Michigan Agricultural	PO Box 96	Blissfield	MI	49228	Harmon Geers	517-486-2171	R	55*	<0.1
Alliance Grain Co.	PO Box 546	Gibson City	IL	60936		217-784-4284	R	53*	<0.1
Gulf Pacific Rice Company Inc.	12010 Taylor Rd	Houston	TX	77041	Fred Brenchkman	713-464-0606	R	50*	<0.1
Ludlow Cooperative Elevator Inc.	PO Box 155	Ludlow	IL	60949		217-396-4111	R	50*	<0.1
Farmers Elevator Co.	10955 N St	Waverly	IL	62692		217-965-4004	R	50*	<0.1
Agrisource Inc.	PO Box 1000	Burley	ID	83318		208-678-2286	R	48*	<0.1
Farmers Cooperative Association	105 Jackson St	Jackson	MN	56143	Steve Glidden	507-847-4160	R	47*	<0.1
Fasco Mills Company Inc.	PO Box 170	Mendota	IL	61342	Curt Zimmerman	815-539-7491	R	47*	<0.1
Fessenden Cooperative Association	PO Box 126	Fessenden	ND	58438		701-547-3291	R	46*	<0.1
Spokane Seed Co.	PO Box 11007	Spokane	WA	99211	Peter Johnstone	509-535-3671	R	46*	<0.1
Andale Farmers Cooperative Inc.	PO Box 18	Andale	KS	67001		316-444-2141	R	45*	<0.1
East Central Iowa Cooperative	PO Box 300	Hudson	IA	50643		319-988-3257	R	45*	<0.1
Mountain View Coop.	110 Main St W	Dutton	MT	59433		406-476-3411	R	45*	<0.1
AGP Grain Cooperative	770 County Rd DD	Farwell	TX	79325		806-825-2565	R	43*	<0.1
Colusa Elevator Company Inc.	PO Box 26	Colusa	IL	62329	Donald P Griffiths Sr	217-755-4221	R	43*	<0.1
Anthony Farmers Cooperative	PO Box 111	Anthony	KS	67003	Jerry Miller	620-842-5181	R	42*	<0.1
Farmers Cooperative Association	PO Box 127	Brule	NE	69127	Tom Struckman	308-287-2304	R	39*	<0.1
Frontier FS Coop.	PO Box 359	Jefferson	WI	53549	Perry Goetsch	920-674-7000	R	38*	<0.1
Heartland Co-op	PO Box 73	Trumbull	NE	68980		402-743-2381	P	38*	<0.1
Farmers Cooperative Co.	304 Ellsworth St	Dows	IA	50071		515-852-4136	R	36*	<0.1
Frontier Trading Inc.	PO Box 460	Roff	OK	74865	Gene Garrett	580-456-7732	R	34*	<0.1
V.H.. Associates Inc.	PO Box 380	Cerro Gordo	IL	61818	Roger Oliver	217-677-2131	R	34*	<0.1
Deshler Farmers Elevator Co.	PO Box 226	Deshler	OH	43516		419-278-3015	R	34*	<0.1
Rolling Hills Fs Inc.	PO Box 191	Winterset	IA	50273		515-462-2644	R	34*	<0.1
Trinidad Benham Corp.	PO Box 378007	Denver	CO	80237	Carl Hartman	303-220-1400	R	34*	<0.1
Ottawa Cooperative Association	PO Box 680	Ottawa	KS	66067		785-242-5170	R	32*	<0.1
Morrow County Grain Growers	Highway 74	Lexington	OR	97839	Joe McElligott	541-989-8221	R	31*	<0.1
Great Bend Cooperative	PO Box 68	Great Bend	KS	67530	Eric Batman	620-793-3531	R	29*	<0.1
Cooperative Agricultural Services	415 W 2nd St	Oakley	KS	67748		785-672-3300	R	28*	<0.1
Jackson-Jennings Farm Bureau	PO Box 304	Seymour	IN	47274		812-522-4911	R	28*	<0.1
Arizona Grain Inc.	PO Box 11188	Casa Grande	AZ	85230	John Skelley	520-836-8228	R	27*	<0.1
Farmers Cooperative Co.	PO Box 127	Brookings	SD	57006		605-692-6216	R	27*	<0.1
Gateway Co-Op	PO Box 125	Galva	IL	61434		309-932-2081	R	27*	<0.1
Trainor Grain and Supply Co.	13201 N 2753 East	Forrest	IL	61741		815-832-5512	R	27*	<0.1
Coshocton Grain Co.	PO Box 606	Coshocton	OH	43812	Rhoda Crown	740-622-0941	R	26*	<0.1
Town And Country Coop.	107 Railroad St	LaGrange	OH	44050		440-355-5641	R	26*	<0.1
Lawrence County Exchange	PO Box 487	Moulton	AL	35650	Gene Pickens	256-974-6126	R	25*	<0.1
Nomura and Company Inc.	40 Broderick Rd	Burlingame	CA	94010	George Okamoto	650-692-5457	R	25*	<0.1

Source: Ward's Business Directory of U.S. Private and Public Companies, Volumes 1 and 2, 2005. The company type code used is as follows: P - Public, R - Private, S - Subsidiary, D - Division, J - Joint Venture, A - Affiliate, G - Group. Sales are in millions of dollars, employees are in thousands. An asterisk (*) indicates an estimated sales volume. The symbol < stands for 'less than'. Company names and addresses are truncated, in some cases, to fit into the available space.

OCCUPATIONS EMPLOYED BY FARM-PRODUCT RAW MATERIAL WHOLESALE

Occupation	% of Total 2004	Change to 2014	Occupation	% of Total 2004	Change to 2014
Laborers & freight, stock, & material movers, hand	14.7	-30.3	Secretaries, except legal, medical, & executive	1.6	-34.9
Farmworkers, farm & ranch animals	9.1	-22.9	Farmworkers & laborers, crop, nursery, & greenhouse	1.6	-22.6
Truck drivers, heavy & tractor-trailer	6.9	-22.6	Agricultural workers, nec	1.5	-22.5
Office clerks, general	4.9	-31.1	First-line supervisors/managers of transporation workers	1.4	-22.6
Bookkeeping, accounting, & auditing clerks	4.7	-30.3	First-line supervisors/managers of office workers	1.4	-29.9
Conveyor operators & tenders	4.6	-22.6	Billing & posting clerks & machine operators	1.3	-34.9
Sales reps, wholesale & manufacturing, exc tech	4.4	-22.6	Industrial truck & tractor operators	1.2	-22.6
Graders & sorters, agricultural products	4.4	-23.8	Agricultural equipment operators	1.2	-22.6
General & operations managers	3.0	-23.4	Maintenance & repair workers, general	1.2	-22.6
Purchasing agents & buyers, farm products	2.8	-22.6	First-line supervisors/managers of helpers & laborers	1.1	-22.5
Truck drivers, light or delivery services	1.9	-22.6	Weighers, measurers, checkers, & samplers	1.1	-38.1

Source: Industry-Occupation Matrix, Bureau of Labor Statistics. These data are reported based on 4-digit NAICS categories but have been matched to corresponding 6-digit NAICS industry codes. The change reported for each occupation to the year 2014 is a percent of growth or decline as estimated by the Bureau of Labor Statistics. The abbreviation nec stands for 'not elsewhere classified.'

LOCATION BY STATE AND REGIONAL CONCENTRATION

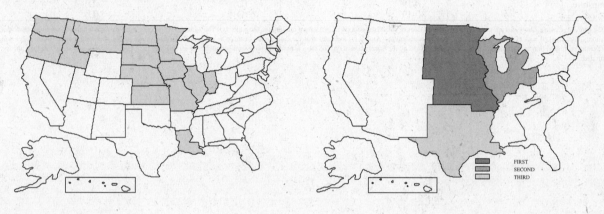

FIRST
SECOND
THIRD

INDUSTRY DATA BY STATE

State	Establishments Total (number)	% of U.S.	Employment Total (number)	% of U.S.	Per Estab.	Payroll Total ($ mil.)	Per Empl. ($)	Sales Total ($ mil.)	% of U.S.	Per Estab. ($)
Illinois	660	12.2	5,321	10.6	8	183.5	34,490	11,120.2	13.0	16,848,779
Louisiana	61	1.1	1,355	2.7	22	55.3	40,824	8,245.0	9.6	135,163,902
Iowa	579	10.7	6,361	12.7	11	204.6	32,171	6,692.8	7.8	11,559,299
Missouri	205	3.8	2,497	5.0	12	79.8	31,953	6,173.5	7.2	30,114,741
Kansas	493	9.1	4,188	8.3	8	129.1	30,830	6,117.6	7.1	12,409,000
Minnesota	297	5.5	3,633	7.2	12	142.4	39,187	5,471.6	6.4	18,422,960
Nebraska	348	6.4	3,356	6.7	10	95.1	28,331	4,035.1	4.7	11,595,132
Texas	288	5.3	2,410	4.8	8	70.0	29,037	3,032.7	3.5	10,530,094
Oregon	58	1.1	646	1.3	11	28.3	43,789	2,419.6	2.8	41,717,069
Indiana	218	4.0	1,825	3.6	8	66.6	36,504	2,397.7	2.8	10,998,550
North Dakota	270	5.0	2,007	4.0	7	66.6	33,186	2,185.0	2.6	8,092,726
Ohio	212	3.9	1,954	3.9	9	65.2	33,388	2,116.0	2.5	9,980,915
Washington	153	2.8	907	1.8	6	33.0	36,354	1,858.7	2.2	12,148,294
South Dakota	176	3.3	1,356	2.7	8	45.6	33,594	1,600.6	1.9	9,094,085
California	166	3.1	1,586	3.2	10	56.8	35,820	1,473.9	1.7	8,878,614
Florida	46	0.8	219	0.4	5	9.6	43,776	1,113.0	1.3	24,195,609
Kentucky	45	0.8	627	1.2	14	14.7	23,431	1,087.2	1.3	24,159,044
Tennessee	43	0.8	533	1.1	12	18.3	34,278	977.9	1.1	22,742,023
Montana	82	1.5	344	0.7	4	10.3	30,073	903.9	1.1	11,023,073
Wisconsin	68	1.3	819	1.6	12	28.1	34,368	797.7	0.9	11,731,456
Colorado	107	2.0	888	1.8	8	29.9	33,617	753.9	0.9	7,046,009
Oklahoma	111	2.0	1,018	2.0	9	28.9	28,433	713.6	0.8	6,429,243
Idaho	103	1.9	1,106	2.2	11	31.8	28,780	647.6	0.8	6,286,922
Arkansas	68	1.3	783	1.6	12	25.8	32,935	617.5	0.7	9,080,632
Pennsylvania	35	0.6	580	1.2	17	12.7	21,928	298.5	0.3	8,529,200
Mississippi	37	0.7	273	0.5	7	8.7	31,875	288.8	0.3	7,806,027
Virginia	24	0.4	144	0.3	6	5.7	39,757	257.1	0.3	10,714,083
North Carolina	68	1.3	430	0.9	6	10.7	24,805	243.6	0.3	3,582,441
Georgia	42	0.8	190	0.4	5	5.9	30,995	144.6	0.2	3,442,571
Maryland	20	0.4	115	0.2	6	4.1	35,670	98.5	0.1	4,923,200
Utah	17	0.3	76	0.2	4	2.1	27,289	60.1	0.1	3,534,235

Continued on next page.

INDUSTRY DATA BY STATE - Continued

State	Establishments Total (number)	% of U.S.	Employment Total (number)	% of U.S.	Per Estab.	Payroll Total ($ mil.)	Per Empl. ($)	Sales Total ($ mil.)	% of U.S.	Per Estab. ($)
South Carolina	26	0.5	99	0.2	4	2.8	27,990	52.9	0.1	2,033,538
Delaware	11	0.2	48	0.1	4	1.3	27,021	50.2	0.1	4,564,364
Alabama	10	0.2	48	0.1	5	1.4	29,958	13.8	-	1,377,000
Wyoming	9	0.2	32	0.1	4	1.0	30,625	12.7	-	1,410,444
Nevada	4	0.1	10	-	3	0.2	21,100	3.0	-	740,750
Michigan	98	1.8	500-999	-	-	(D)	-	(D)	-	-
New York	79	1.5	500-999	-	-	(D)	-	(D)	-	-
New Jersey	27	0.5	100-249	-	-	(D)	-	(D)	-	-
Arizona	21	0.4	100-249	-	-	(D)	-	(D)	-	-
Maine	7	0.1	20-99	-	-	(D)	-	(D)	-	-
Massachusetts	6	0.1	0-19	-	-	(D)	-	(D)	-	-
New Mexico	5	0.1	20-99	-	-	(D)	-	(D)	-	-
Connecticut	3	0.1	250-499	-	-	(D)	-	(D)	-	-
Vermont	3	0.1	20-99	-	-	(D)	-	(D)	-	-
Hawaii	2	-	0-19	-	-	(D)	-	(D)	-	-
West Virginia	2	-	0-19	-	-	(D)	-	(D)	-	-
New Hampshire	1	-	0-19	-	-	(D)	-	(D)	-	-
Rhode Island	1	-	0-19	-	-	(D)	-	(D)	-	-

Source: 2002 *Economic Census*. The states are in descending order of sales or establishments (if sales data are missing for the majority). The symbol (D) appears when data are withheld to prevent disclosure of competitive information. States marked with (D) are sorted by number of establishments. A dash (-) indicates that the data element cannot be calculated. Shaded *states* on the state map indicate those states which have proportionately greater representation in the industry than would be indicated by the states population; the ratio is based on total sales or number of establishments. Shaded *regions* indicate where the industry is regionally most concentrated.

NAICS 424520 - LIVESTOCK MERCHANT WHOLESALERS*

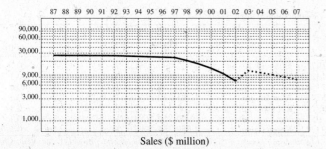

Sales ($ million)

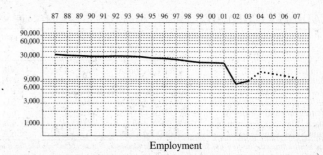

Employment

GENERAL STATISTICS

Year	Establishments (number)	Employment (number)	Payroll ($ million)	Sales ($ million)	Employees per Establishment (number)	Sales per Establishment ($)	Payroll per Employee ($)
1987	2,592	34,510	237.6	26,725.8	13.3	10,310,879.6	6,885.0
1988	2,433	33,147	252.0	26,665.7 e	13.6	10,960,008.2	7,602.5
1989	2,332	32,530	252.5	26,605.6 e	13.9	11,408,919.4	7,762.1
1990	2,301	31,578	258.9	26,545.5 e	13.7	11,536,505.9	8,198.7
1991	2,255	31,567	260.0	26,485.4 e	14.0	11,745,188.5	8,236.4
1992	2,316	32,034	254.8	26,425.3	13.8	11,409,887.7	7,954.0
1993	2,368	31,852	265.7	25,959.9 e	13.5	10,962,795.6	8,341.7
1994	2,372	31,127	270.2	25,494.6 e	13.1	10,748,145.0	8,680.6
1995	2,239	29,176	262.2	25,029.2 e	13.0	11,178,740.5	8,986.8
1996	2,059 e	28,551 e	269.1 e	24,563.9 e	13.9 e	11,930,014.6 e	9,425.2 e
1997	2,090	27,182	260.2	24,098.5	13.0	11,530,382.8	9,572.5
1998	2,043	25,116	255.7	20,759.4 e	12.3	10,161,223.7	10,180.8
1999	1,960	23,453	254.6	17,420.3 e	12.0	8,887,887.8	10,855.8
2000	1,905	23,170	280.8	14,081.1 e	12.2	7,391,674.5	12,121.0
2001	1,879	22,736	278.0	10,742.0 e	12.1	5,716,881.3	12,227.3
2002	1,106	7,934	115.1	7,402.9	7.2	6,693,399.6	14,507.2
2003	1,094	9,311	145.0	12,523.9 p	8.5	7,690,744.3 p	15,575.7
2004	1,443 p	14,763 p	213.1 p	11,386.9 p	10.0 p	7,400,151.4 p	13,902.8 p
2005	1,372 p	13,430 p	209.5 p	10,250.0 p	9.7 p	7,109,558.6 p	14,355.3 p
2006	1,302 p	12,096 p	205.9 p	9,113.0 p	9.5 p	6,818,965.8 p	14,807.8 p
2007	1,231 p	10,763 p	202.3 p	7,976.1 p	9.2 p	6,528,372.9 p	15,260.3 p

Sources: Economic Census of the United States, 1987, 1992, 1997, and 2002. Establishment counts, employment, and payroll are from *County Business Patterns* for non-Census years. Values followed by a 'p' are projections by the editors. Sales data for non-Census years are extrapolations, marked by 'e'. Data are the most recent available at this level of detail.

INDICES OF CHANGE

Year	Establishments (number)	Employment (number)	Payroll ($ million)	Sales ($ million)	Employees per Establishment (number)	Sales per Establishment ($)	Payroll per Employee ($)
1987	234.4	435.0	206.4	361.0	184.7	154.0	47.5
1992	209.4	403.8	221.4	357.0	191.7	170.5	54.8
1993	214.1	401.5	230.8	350.7 e	187.5	163.8	57.5
1994	214.5	392.3	234.8	344.4 e	181.9	160.6	59.8
1995	202.4	367.7	227.8	338.1 e	180.6	167.0	61.9
1996	186.2 e	359.9 e	233.8 e	331.8 e	193.1 e	178.2 e	65.0 e
1997	189.0	342.6	226.1	325.5	180.6	172.3	66.0
1998	184.7	316.6	222.2	280.4 e	170.8	151.8	70.2
1999	177.2	295.6	221.2	235.3 e	166.7	132.8	74.8
2000	172.2	292.0	244.0	190.2 e	169.4	110.4	83.6
2001	169.9	286.6	241.5	145.1 e	168.1	85.4	84.3
2002	100.0	100.0	100.0	100.0	100.0	100.0	100.0
2003	98.9	117.4	126.0	169.2 p	118.2	114.9 p	107.4
2004	130.5 p	186.1 p	185.1 p	153.8 p	139.1 p	110.6 p	95.8 p
2005	124.1 p	169.3 p	182.0 p	138.5 p	135.3 p	106.2 p	99.0 p
2006	117.7 p	152.5 p	178.9 p	123.1 p	131.4 p	101.9 p	102.1 p
2007	111.3 p	135.7 p	175.7 p	107.7 p	127.5 p	97.5 p	105.2 p

*Sources: Same as General Statistics. The values shown reflect change from the base year, 2002. Values above 100 mean greater than 2002, values below 100 mean less than 2002, and a value of 100 in the 1987-2001 or 2003-2007 period means same as 2002. Values followed by a 'p' are projections by the editors; 'e' stands for extrapolation. Data are the most recent available at this level of detail.

SELECTED RATIOS

For 2002	Avg. of All Wholesale	Analyzed Industry	Index	For 2002	Avg. of All Wholesale	Analyzed Industry	Index
Employees per Establishment	15	7	48	Sales per Employee	791,325	933,060	118
Payroll per Establishment	626,122	104,069	17	Sales per Establishment	12,012,387	6,693,400	56
Payroll per Employee	41,161	14,507	35	Expenses per Establishment	na	na	na

Sources: Same as General Statistics. The 'Average of All' column, Wholesale or Retail, represents the average of the sector reported for the most recent complete year available. The Index shows the relationship between the Average and the Analyzed Industry. For example, 100 means that they are equal; 500 that the Analyzed Industry is five times the average; 50 means that the Analyzed Industry is half the national average. The abbreviation 'na' is used to show that data are 'not available'.

*Equivalent to SIC 5154.

LEADING COMPANIES   Number shown: **7**   Total sales ($ mil): **458**   Total employment (000): **0.3**

Company Name	Address				CEO Name	Phone	Co. Type	Sales ($ mil)	Empl. (000)
Prairie Livestock L.L.C.	PO Drawer 636	West Point	MS	39773	James D. Bryan	662-494-5651	R	260*	<0.1
United Producers Inc.	PO Box 29800	Columbus	OH	43229	W Dennis Bolling	614-890-6666	R	104*	<0.1
Vintage Sales Stables Inc.	3451 Lincoln Hwy E	Paradise	PA	17562		717-768-8204	R	59*	<0.1
Bales Continental Commission Co.	PO Box 1337	Huron	SD	57350	Alan Bales	605-352-8682	R	25*	<0.1
El Toro Land and Cattle Co.	PO Box G	Heber	CA	92249	Robert Odell	760-352-6312	R	6*	<0.1
Haskell Livestock Auction Inc.	PO Box 146	Haskell	TX	79521	Joe Tate	940-864-2624	R	2*	<0.1
Visalia Sales Yard Inc.	29660 Rd 152	Visalia	CA	93292	Karen Green	559-734-9092	R	2*	<0.1

Source: Ward's Business Directory of U.S. Private and Public Companies, Volumes 1 and 2, 2005. The company type code used is as follows: P - Public, R - Private, S - Subsidiary, D - Division, J - Joint Venture, A - Affiliate, G - Group. Sales are in millions of dollars, employees are in thousands. An asterisk (*) indicates an estimated sales volume. The symbol < stands for 'less than'. Company names and addresses are truncated, in some cases, to fit into the available space.

OCCUPATIONS EMPLOYED BY FARM-PRODUCT RAW MATERIAL WHOLESALE

Occupation	% of Total 2004	Change to 2014	Occupation	% of Total 2004	Change to 2014
Laborers & freight, stock, & material movers, hand	14.7	-30.3	Secretaries, except legal, medical, & executive	1.6	-34.9
Farmworkers, farm & ranch animals	9.1	-22.9	Farmworkers & laborers, crop, nursery, & greenhouse	1.6	-22.6
Truck drivers, heavy & tractor-trailer	6.9	-22.6	Agricultural workers, nec	1.5	-22.5
Office clerks, general	4.9	-31.1	First-line supervisors/managers of transporation workers	1.4	-22.6
Bookkeeping, accounting, & auditing clerks	4.7	-30.3	First-line supervisors/managers of office workers	1.4	-29.9
Conveyor operators & tenders	4.6	-22.6	Billing & posting clerks & machine operators	1.3	-34.9
Sales reps, wholesale & manufacturing, exc tech	4.4	-22.6	Industrial truck & tractor operators	1.2	-22.6
Graders & sorters, agricultural products	4.4	-23.8	Agricultural equipment operators	1.2	-22.6
General & operations managers	3.0	-23.4	Maintenance & repair workers, general	1.2	-22.6
Purchasing agents & buyers, farm products	2.8	-22.6	First-line supervisors/managers of helpers & laborers	1.1	-22.5
Truck drivers, light or delivery services	1.9	-22.6	Weighers, measurers, checkers, & samplers	1.1	-38.1

Source: Industry-Occupation Matrix, Bureau of Labor Statistics. These data are reported based on 4-digit NAICS categories but have been matched to corresponding 6-digit NAICS industry codes. The change reported for each occupation to the year 2014 is a percent of growth or decline as estimated by the Bureau of Labor Statistics. The abbreviation nec stands for 'not elsewhere classified.'

LOCATION BY STATE AND REGIONAL CONCENTRATION

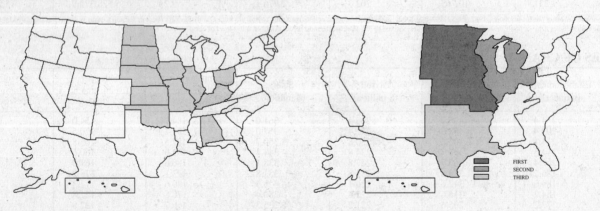

INDUSTRY DATA BY STATE

State	Establishments Total (number)	% of U.S.	Employment Total (number)	% of U.S.	Per Estab.	Payroll Total ($ mil.)	Per Empl. ($)	Sales Total ($ mil.)	% of U.S.	Per Estab. ($)
Missouri	56	5.1	438	5.6	8	6.2	14,226	985.3	13.9	17,594,214
Iowa	119	10.8	738	9.4	6	17.8	24,141	675.5	9.5	5,676,664
Texas	117	10.6	1,006	12.8	9	11.6	11,541	441.9	6.2	3,776,624
Illinois	72	6.5	296	3.8	4	7.2	24,436	427.4	6.0	5,935,653
Ohio	34	3.1	236	3.0	7	5.9	25,038	424.8	6.0	12,494,794
Kentucky	24	2.2	163	2.1	7	2.4	14,472	219.7	3.1	9,155,958
California	47	4.3	157	2.0	3	5.1	32,427	198.2	2.8	4,216,319
North Carolina	19	1.7	202	2.6	11	3.7	18,302	171.1	2.4	9,004,421
Alabama	21	1.9	262	3.3	12	3.2	12,328	156.4	2.2	7,446,619
Tennessee	31	2.8	241	3.1	8	2.7	11,054	131.5	1.9	4,243,129

Continued on next page.

INDUSTRY DATA BY STATE - Continued

State	Establishments Total (number)	Establishments % of U.S.	Employment Total (number)	Employment % of U.S.	Employment Per Estab.	Payroll Total ($ mil.)	Payroll Per Empl. ($)	Sales Total ($ mil.)	Sales % of U.S.	Sales Per Estab. ($)
Wisconsin	37	3.4	167	2.1	5	2.8	16,922	112.3	1.6	3,035,595
Nebraska	31	2.8	422	5.4	14	3.4	8,073	105.8	1.5	3,412,032
Oklahoma	34	3.1	320	4.1	9	2.8	8,719	104.5	1.5	3,073,441
Pennsylvania	25	2.3	155	2.0	6	2.3	14,568	97.0	1.4	3,878,040
Kansas	30	2.7	366	4.7	12	3.5	9,500	69.9	1.0	2,329,367
Florida	17	1.5	46	0.6	3	1.0	21,304	59.7	0.8	3,513,706
North Dakota	13	1.2	156	2.0	12	1.6	10,558	54.8	0.8	4,217,923
Georgia	17	1.5	81	1.0	5	1.1	13,605	54.2	0.8	3,187,529
South Dakota	27	2.5	236	3.0	9	2.4	10,364	53.3	0.8	1,974,444
New York	20	1.8	99	1.3	5	1.6	15,768	34.5	0.5	1,722,800
Virginia	20	1.8	101	1.3	5	1.0	9,752	33.6	0.5	1,680,950
South Carolina	13	1.2	80	1.0	6	1.1	13,275	33.6	0.5	2,583,462
Oregon	6	0.5	41	0.5	7	0.4	9,049	20.1	0.3	3,347,000
Colorado	9	0.8	104	1.3	12	1.0	9,740	15.4	0.2	1,709,333
Washington	7	0.6	66	0.8	9	0.8	11,939	8.0	0.1	1,136,000
Minnesota	57	5.2	100-249	-	-	(D)	-	(D)	-	-
Indiana	44	4.0	100-249	-	-	(D)	-	(D)	-	-
Michigan	20	1.8	100-249	-	-	(D)	-	(D)	-	-
Mississippi	16	1.5	250-499	-	-	(D)	-	(D)	-	-
Arizona	15	1.4	100-249	-	-	(D)	-	(D)	-	-
Montana	13	1.2	100-249	-	-	(D)	-	(D)	-	-
Arkansas	12	1.1	100-249	-	-	(D)	-	(D)	-	-
New Mexico	11	1.0	100-249	-	-	(D)	-	(D)	-	-
Louisiana	10	0.9	20-99	-	-	(D)	-	(D)	-	-
New Jersey	9	0.8	20-99	-	-	(D)	-	(D)	-	-
West Virginia	9	0.8	20-99	-	-	(D)	-	(D)	-	-
Idaho	6	0.5	20-99	-	-	(D)	-	(D)	-	-
Massachusetts	6	0.5	20-99	-	-	(D)	-	(D)	-	-
Vermont	6	0.5	20-99	-	-	(D)	-	(D)	-	-
Utah	5	0.5	20-99	-	-	(D)	-	(D)	-	-
Maryland	4	0.4	0-19	-	-	(D)	-	(D)	-	-
Wyoming	3	0.3	0-19	-	-	(D)	-	(D)	-	-
Connecticut	2	0.2	0-19	-	-	(D)	-	(D)	-	-
Nevada	2	0.2	20-99	-	-	(D)	-	(D)	-	-
Delaware	1	0.1	0-19	-	-	(D)	-	(D)	-	-
Maine	1	0.1	0-19	-	-	(D)	-	(D)	-	-
New Hampshire	1	0.1	0-19	-	-	(D)	-	(D)	-	-
Rhode Island	1	0.1	0-19	-	-	(D)	-	(D)	-	-

Source: 2002 *Economic Census*. The states are in descending order of sales or establishments (if sales data are missing for the majority). The symbol (D) appears when data are withheld to prevent disclosure of competitive information. States marked with (D) are sorted by number of establishments. A dash (-) indicates that the data element cannot be calculated. Shaded *states* on the state map indicate those states which have proportionately greater representation in the industry than would be indicated by the states population; the ratio is based on total sales or number of establishments. Shaded *regions* indicate where the industry is regionally most concentrated.

NAICS 424590 - OTHER FARM PRODUCT RAW MATERIAL MERCHANT WHOLESALERS*

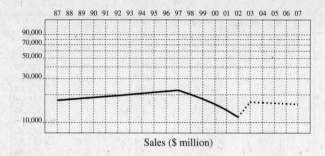

Sales ($ million)

Employment

GENERAL STATISTICS

Year	Establishments (number)	Employment (number)	Payroll ($ million)	Sales ($ million)	Employees per Establishment (number)	Sales per Establishment ($)	Payroll per Employee ($)
1987	1,830	18,944	336.4	17,368.9	10.4	9,491,202.2	17,757.6
1988	1,698	16,759	334.7	17,803.2 e	9.9	10,484,805.7	19,971.4
1989	1,611	15,455	338.0	18,237.5 e	9.6	11,320,608.3	21,869.9
1990	1,573	15,582	359.7	18,671.8 e	9.9	11,870,184.4	23,084.3
1991	1,558	14,896	364.2	19,106.2 e	9.6	12,263,286.3	24,449.5
1992	1,791	16,433	399.4	19,540.5	9.2	10,910,385.3	24,304.8
1993	1,828	15,371	408.4	20,107.4 e	8.4	10,999,671.8	26,569.5
1994	1,717	14,688	394.2	20,674.4 e	8.6	12,041,001.7	26,838.2
1995	1,699	14,971	400.0	21,241.3 e	8.8	12,502,236.6	26,718.3
1996	1,716 e	14,115 e	421.7 e	21,808.3 e	8.2 e	12,708,799.5 e	29,876.0 e
1997	1,684	13,971	402.9	22,375.2	8.3	13,286,935.9	28,838.3
1998	1,693	13,139	405.7	20,191.1 e	7.8	11,926,225.6	30,877.5
1999	1,603	12,243	390.9	18,007.0 e	7.6	11,233,312.5	31,928.4
2000	1,564	12,410	419.4	15,822.9 e	7.9	10,116,943.7	33,798.9
2001	1,517	12,866	463.8	13,638.8 e	8.5	8,990,639.4	36,048.9
2002	1,048	7,418	284.6	11,454.7	7.1	10,930,057.3	38,366.1
2003	1,031	7,462	342.5	16,653.6 p	7.2	11,295,999.2 p	45,901.0
2004	1,334 p	9,237 p	400.1 p	16,436.0 p	7.0 p	11,293,496.9 p	40,785.9 p
2005	1,305 p	8,716 p	402.3 p	16,218.5 p	6.8 p	11,290,994.6 p	42,133.4 p
2006	1,275 p	8,196 p	404.5 p	16,000.9 p	6.6 p	11,288,492.4 p	43,480.9 p
2007	1,246 p	7,675 p	406.7 p	15,783.3 p	6.5 p	11,285,990.1 p	44,828.3 p

Sources: Economic Census of the United States, 1987, 1992, 1997, and 2002. Establishment counts, employment, and payroll are from *County Business Patterns* for non-Census years. Values followed by a 'p' are projections by the editors. Sales data for non-Census years are extrapolations, marked by 'e'. Data are the most recent available at this level of detail.

INDICES OF CHANGE

Year	Establishments (number)	Employment (number)	Payroll ($ million)	Sales ($ million)	Employees per Establishment (number)	Sales per Establishment ($)	Payroll per Employee ($)
1987	174.6	255.4	118.2	151.6	146.5	86.8	46.3
1992	170.9	221.5	140.3	170.6	129.6	99.8	63.3
1993	174.4	207.2	143.5	175.5 e	118.3	100.6	69.3
1994	163.8	198.0	138.5	180.5 e	121.1	110.2	70.0
1995	162.1	201.8	140.5	185.4 e	123.9	114.4	69.6
1996	163.7 e	190.3 e	148.2 e	190.4 e	115.5 e	116.3 e	77.9 e
1997	160.7	188.3	141.6	195.3	116.9	121.6	75.2
1998	161.5	177.1	142.6	176.3 e	109.9	109.1	80.5
1999	153.0	165.0	137.4	157.2 e	107.0	102.8	83.2
2000	149.2	167.3	147.4	138.1 e	111.3	92.6	88.1
2001	144.8	173.4	163.0	119.1 e	119.7	82.3	94.0
2002	100.0	100.0	100.0	100.0	100.0	100.0	100.0
2003	98.4	100.6	120.3	145.4 p	101.9	103.3 p	119.6
2004	127.3 p	124.5 p	140.6 p	143.5 p	98.7 p	103.3 p	106.3 p
2005	124.5 p	117.5 p	141.4 p	141.6 p	96.2 p	103.3 p	109.8 p
2006	121.7 p	110.5 p	142.1 p	139.7 p	93.6 p	103.3 p	113.3 p
2007	118.9 p	103.5 p	142.9 p	137.8 p	91.0 p	103.3 p	116.8 p

Sources: Same as General Statistics. The values shown reflect change from the base year, 2002. Values above 100 mean greater than 2002, values below 100 mean less than 2002, and a value of 100 in the 1987-2001 or 2003-2007 period means same as 2002. Values followed by a 'p' are projections by the editors; 'e' stands for extrapolation. Data are the most recent available at this level of detail.

SELECTED RATIOS

For 2002	Avg. of All Wholesale	Analyzed Industry	Index	For 2002	Avg. of All Wholesale	Analyzed Industry	Index
Employees per Establishment	15	7	47	Sales per Employee	791,325	1,544,176	195
Payroll per Establishment	626,122	271,565	43	Sales per Establishment	12,012,387	10,930,057	91
Payroll per Employee	41,161	38,366	93	Expenses per Establishment	na	na	na

Sources: Same as General Statistics. The 'Average of All' column, Wholesale or Retail, represents the average of the sector reported for the most recent complete year available. The Index shows the relationship between the Average and the Analyzed Industry. For example, 100 means that they are equal; 500 that the Analyzed Industry is five times the average; 50 means that the Analyzed Industry is half the national average. The abbreviation 'na' is used to show that data are 'not available'.

*Equivalent to SIC 5159.

LEADING COMPANIES   Number shown: **18**   Total sales ($ mil): **6,595**   Total employment (000): **35.7**

Company Name	Address				CEO Name	Phone	Co. Type	Sales ($ mil)	Empl. (000)
Universal Corp.	PO Box 25099	Richmond	VA	23260	Henry H. Harrell	804-359-9311	P	2,271	30.0
DeBruce Grain Inc.	PO Box 34621	Kansas City	MO	64117	Paul DeBruce	816-421-8182	R	2,018	0.4
Standard Commercial Corp.	PO Box 450	Wilson	NC	27894	Robert E Harrison	252-291-5507	P	780	3.8
Calcot Ltd.	PO Box 259	Bakersfield	CA	93302	Robert W Norris	661-327-5961	R	435*	<0.1
Hail and Cotton Inc.	PO Box 638	Springfield	TN	37172	Daryl Smith	615-384-9576	R	235*	0.1
Staplcotn Cooperative Association	PO Box 547	Greenwood	MS	38935	Woods E Eastland	662-453-6231	R	189*	0.2
Birdsong Corp.	PO Box 1400	Suffolk	VA	23439	George Birdsong	757-539-3456	R	180*	0.5
Hog Inc.	RR 2, Box 8	Greenfield	IL	62044			R	100*	<0.1
McClesky Mills Inc.	197 Rhodes St	Smithville	GA	31787	Jerry M Chandler	229-434-6920	R	95*	0.1
S. Shamash and Sons	42 W 39th St	New York	NY	10018	Kevin Kiley	212-840-3111	R	94*	0.1
Commodity Specialists Co.	400 S 4th St	Minneapolis	MN	55415	Philip J Lindau	612-330-9889	R	70*	0.1
Louisville Pecan Company Inc.	PO Box 38	Louisville	AL	36048	Homer Henson	334-266-5388	R	59*	<0.1
International AG Commodities Inc.	PO Box 696	Clements	CA	95227	Randy Lush	916-775-1381	R	23*	<0.1
A.M. Bickley Inc.	PO Box 91	Marshallville	GA	31057		478-967-2291	R	15*	<0.1
Damascus Peanut Co.	PO Box 526	Arlington	GA	39841	Johnny Phillips	229-725-4230	R	12*	<0.1
Jirdon Agri Chemicals Inc.	PO Box 516	Morrill	NE	69358	William L Siegel	308-247-2126	R	12*	<0.1
Red Mile Inc.	PO Box 420	Lexington	KY	40588	A M Chuddy	859-255-0752	R	4*	<0.1
Wonalancet Co.	1130 Senoia Rd	Tyrone	GA	30290	James J Dunn	770-774-2820	R	2*	<0.1

Source: *Ward's Business Directory of U.S. Private and Public Companies*, Volumes 1 and 2, 2005. The company type code used is as follows: P - Public, R - Private, S - Subsidiary, D - Division, J - Joint Venture, A - Affiliate, G - Group. Sales are in millions of dollars, employees are in thousands. An asterisk (*) indicates an estimated sales volume. The symbol < stands for 'less than'. Company names and addresses are truncated, in some cases, to fit into the available space.

OCCUPATIONS EMPLOYED BY FARM-PRODUCT RAW MATERIAL WHOLESALE

Occupation	% of Total 2004	Change to 2014	Occupation	% of Total 2004	Change to 2014
Laborers & freight, stock, & material movers, hand	14.7	-30.3	Secretaries, except legal, medical, & executive	1.6	-34.9
Farmworkers, farm & ranch animals	9.1	-22.9	Farmworkers & laborers, crop, nursery, & greenhouse	1.6	-22.6
Truck drivers, heavy & tractor-trailer	6.9	-22.6	Agricultural workers, nec	1.5	-22.5
Office clerks, general	4.9	-31.1	First-line supervisors/managers of transporation workers	1.4	-22.6
Bookkeeping, accounting, & auditing clerks	4.7	-30.3	First-line supervisors/managers of office workers	1.4	-29.9
Conveyor operators & tenders	4.6	-22.6	Billing & posting clerks & machine operators	1.3	-34.9
Sales reps, wholesale & manufacturing, exc tech	4.4	-22.6	Industrial truck & tractor operators	1.2	-22.6
Graders & sorters, agricultural products	4.4	-23.8	Agricultural equipment operators	1.2	-22.6
General & operations managers	3.0	-23.4	Maintenance & repair workers, general	1.2	-22.6
Purchasing agents & buyers, farm products	2.8	-22.6	First-line supervisors/managers of helpers & laborers	1.1	-22.5
Truck drivers, light or delivery services	1.9	-22.6	Weighers, measurers, checkers, & samplers	1.1	-38.1

Source: *Industry-Occupation Matrix*, Bureau of Labor Statistics. These data are reported based on 4-digit NAICS categories but have been matched to corresponding 6-digit NAICS industry codes. The change reported for each occupation to the year 2014 is a percent of growth or decline as estimated by the Bureau of Labor Statistics. The abbreviation nec stands for 'not elsewhere classified.'

LOCATION BY STATE AND REGIONAL CONCENTRATION

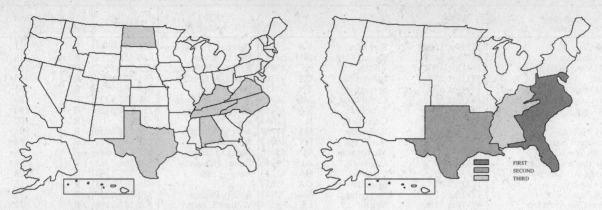

INDUSTRY DATA BY STATE

State	Establishments Total (number)	% of U.S.	Employment Total (number)	% of U.S.	Per Estab.	Payroll Total ($ mil.)	Per Empl. ($)	Sales Total ($ mil.)	% of U.S.	Per Estab. ($)
Tennessee	39	3.7	515	7.7	13	23.0	44,631	1,959.4	18.3	50,241,897
Texas	134	12.8	954	14.2	7	32.8	34,379	1,582.6	14.8	11,810,724
California	107	10.2	755	11.2	7	31.1	41,213	1,212.2	11.3	11,329,364
North Carolina	66	6.3	451	6.7	7	16.7	36,925	643.6	6.0	9,751,894
Virginia	29	2.8	299	4.4	10	26.0	86,960	529.5	4.9	18,257,000
Alabama	35	3.3	361	5.4	10	10.0	27,665	277.6	2.6	7,930,086
Kentucky	53	5.1	427	6.4	8	9.1	21,255	260.1	2.4	4,907,811
Pennsylvania	20	1.9	123	1.8	6	5.8	47,407	206.4	1.9	10,319,000
Georgia	69	6.6	309	4.6	4	7.5	24,320	160.8	1.5	2,331,087
Florida	53	5.1	318	4.7	6	12.0	37,651	92.2	0.9	1,738,792
Illinois	23	2.2	107	1.6	5	2.9	26,963	69.6	0.6	3,027,174
Wisconsin	20	1.9	139	2.1	7	4.6	33,345	64.0	0.6	3,201,550
South Carolina	21	2.0	49	0.7	2	1.6	32,837	62.3	0.6	2,964,762
Iowa	10	1.0	57	0.8	6	1.7	30,035	51.6	0.5	5,160,900
Ohio	11	1.0	72	1.1	7	2.5	35,069	39.8	0.4	3,616,818
North Dakota	4	0.4	19	0.3	5	0.6	32,632	29.5	0.3	7,382,500
Colorado	11	1.0	55	0.8	5	1.4	25,091	26.4	0.2	2,398,091
Missouri	14	1.3	135	2.0	10	3.3	24,600	23.2	0.2	1,654,143
Nebraska	6	0.6	45	0.7	8	0.9	20,822	21.5	0.2	3,591,333
Oklahoma	12	1.1	44	0.7	4	1.4	31,273	20.4	0.2	1,695,917
South Dakota	5	0.5	18	0.3	4	0.6	35,167	15.1	0.1	3,027,400
Washington	12	1.1	40	0.6	3	0.9	23,425	13.9	0.1	1,161,333
Oregon	8	0.8	42	0.6	5	0.7	17,095	10.0	0.1	1,252,625
Kansas	6	0.6	11	0.2	2	0.3	31,091	4.4	-	726,667
New York	95	9.1	250-499	-	-	(D)	-	(D)	-	-
New Jersey	25	2.4	100-249	-	-	(D)	-	(D)	-	-
Louisiana	18	1.7	100-249	-	-	(D)	-	(D)	-	-
Massachusetts	17	1.6	100-249	-	-	(D)	-	(D)	-	-
Mississippi	16	1.5	100-249	-	-	(D)	-	(D)	-	-
Minnesota	15	1.4	20-99	-	-	(D)	-	(D)	-	-
Michigan	14	1.3	20-99	-	-	(D)	-	(D)	-	-
Arkansas	12	1.1	20-99	-	-	(D)	-	(D)	-	-
Connecticut	11	1.0	20-99	-	-	(D)	-	(D)	-	-
Arizona	8	0.8	20-99	-	-	(D)	-	(D)	-	-
Maine	7	0.7	20-99	-	-	(D)	-	(D)	-	-
New Mexico	7	0.7	0-19	-	-	(D)	-	(D)	-	-
Idaho	6	0.6	20-99	-	-	(D)	-	(D)	-	-
Maryland	6	0.6	0-19	-	-	(D)	-	(D)	-	-
Indiana	5	0.5	0-19	-	-	(D)	-	(D)	-	-
Montana	5	0.5	0-19	-	-	(D)	-	(D)	-	-
Rhode Island	4	0.4	0-19	-	-	(D)	-	(D)	-	-
New Hampshire	3	0.3	0-19	-	-	(D)	-	(D)	-	-
Nevada	2	0.2	0-19	-	-	(D)	-	(D)	-	-
Hawaii	1	0.1	0-19	-	-	(D)	-	(D)	-	-
Utah	1	0.1	0-19	-	-	(D)	-	(D)	-	-
West Virginia	1	0.1	0-19	-	-	(D)	-	(D)	-	-
Wyoming	1	0.1	0-19	-	-	(D)	-	(D)	-	-

Source: 2002 *Economic Census*. The states are in descending order of sales or establishments (if sales data are missing for the majority). The symbol (D) appears when data are withheld to prevent disclosure of competitive information. States marked with (D) are sorted by number of establishments. A dash (-) indicates that the data element cannot be calculated. Shaded *states* on the state map indicate those states which have proportionately greater representation in the industry than would be indicated by the states population; the ratio is based on total sales or number of establishments. Shaded *regions* indicate where the industry is regionally most concentrated.

NAICS 424610 - PLASTICS MATERIALS AND BASIC FORMS AND SHAPES MERCHANT WHOLESALERS*

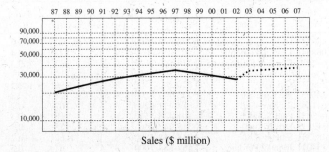

Sales ($ million)

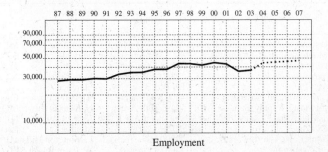

Employment

GENERAL STATISTICS

Year	Establishments (number)	Employment (number)	Payroll ($ million)	Sales ($ million)	Employees per Establishment (number)	Sales per Establishment ($)	Payroll per Employee ($)
1987	2,744	28,453	788.4	20,307.5	10.4	7,400,692.4	27,708.9
1988	2,660	29,227	863.4	21,960.8 e	11.0	8,255,939.8	29,541.2
1989	2,511	29,227	926.8	23,614.0 e	11.6	9,404,221.4	31,710.4
1990	2,522	30,153	973.4	25,267.3 e	12.0	10,018,755.0	32,282.0
1991	2,581	29,898	999.1	26,920.5 e	11.6	10,430,259.6	33,417.0
1992	3,490	33,459	1,160.9	28,573.8	9.6	8,187,335.2	34,696.2
1993	3,509	34,936	1,225.4	29,897.7 e	10.0	8,520,290.7	35,075.6
1994	3,524	35,112	1,293.7	31,221.6 e	10.0	8,859,704.9	36,845.0
1995	3,603	37,855	1,431.4	32,545.5 e	10.5	9,032,889.3	37,812.7
1996	3,765 e	37,868 e	1,460.9 e	33,869.4 e	10.1 e	8,995,856.6 e	38,578.7 e
1997	4,349	43,680	1,743.7	35,193.3	10.0	8,092,274.1	39,919.9
1998	4,258	43,497	1,832.7	33,718.9 e	10.2	7,918,962.0	42,133.9
1999	4,158	41,990	1,838.1	32,244.6 e	10.1	7,754,829.2	43,774.7
2000	4,038	44,576	2,054.6	30,770.2 e	11.0	7,620,163.4	46,091.2
2001	3,908	43,116	1,951.5	29,295.9 e	11.0	7,496,381.8	45,261.7
2002	3,433	35,904	1,642.9	27,821.5	10.5	8,104,136.3	45,758.1
2003	3,387	36,829	1,734.7	34,495.2 p	10.9	7,808,579.8 p	47,100.6
2004	4,255 p	44,338 p	2,094.4 p	35,147.4 p	10.3 p	7,726,554.7 p	49,001.3 p
2005	4,346 p	45,240 p	2,170.8 p	35,799.6 p	10.3 p	7,644,529.6 p	50,212.5 p
2006	4,437 p	46,142 p	2,247.1 p	36,451.9 p	10.3 p	7,562,504.5 p	51,423.7 p
2007	4,527 p	47,044 p	2,323.5 p	37,104.1 p	10.3 p	7,480,479.4 p	52,634.9 p

Sources: Economic Census of the United States, 1987, 1992, 1997, and 2002. Establishment counts, employment, and payroll are from County Business Patterns for non-Census years. Values followed by a 'p' are projections by the editors. Sales data for non-Census years are extrapolations, marked by 'e'. Data are the most recent available at this level of detail.

INDICES OF CHANGE

Year	Establishments (number)	Employment (number)	Payroll ($ million)	Sales ($ million)	Employees per Establishment (number)	Sales per Establishment ($)	Payroll per Employee ($)
1987	79.9	79.2	48.0	73.0	99.0	91.3	60.6
1992	101.7	93.2	70.7	102.7	91.4	101.0	75.8
1993	102.2	97.3	74.6	107.5 e	95.2	105.1	76.7
1994	102.7	97.8	78.7	112.2 e	95.2	109.3	80.5
1995	105.0	105.4	87.1	117.0 e	100.0	111.5	82.6
1996	109.7 e	105.5 e	88.9 e	121.7 e	96.2 e	111.0 e	84.3 e
1997	126.7	121.7	106.1	126.5	95.2	99.9	87.2
1998	124.0	121.1	111.6	121.2 e	97.1	97.7	92.1
1999	121.1	117.0	111.9	115.9 e	96.2	95.7	95.7
2000	117.6	124.2	125.1	110.6 e	104.8	94.0	100.7
2001	113.8	120.1	118.8	105.3 e	104.8	92.5	98.9
2002	100.0	100.0	100.0	100.0	100.0	100.0	100.0
2003	98.7	102.6	105.6	124.0 p	103.6	96.4 p	102.9
2004	123.9 p	123.5 p	127.5 p	126.3 p	98.5 p	95.3 p	107.1 p
2005	126.6 p	126.0 p	132.1 p	128.7 p	98.2 p	94.3 p	109.7 p
2006	129.2 p	128.5 p	136.8 p	131.0 p	97.9 p	93.3 p	112.4 p
2007	131.9 p	131.0 p	141.4 p	133.4 p	97.6 p	92.3 p	115.0 p

Sources: Same as General Statistics. The values shown reflect change from the base year, 2002. Values above 100 mean greater than 2002, values below 100 mean less than 2002, and a value of 100 in the 1987-2001 or 2003-2007 period means same as 2002. Values followed by a 'p' are projections by the editors; 'e' stands for extrapolation. Data are the most recent available at this level of detail.

SELECTED RATIOS

For 2002	Avg. of All Wholesale	Analyzed Industry	Index	For 2002	Avg. of All Wholesale	Analyzed Industry	Index
Employees per Establishment	15	10	70	Sales per Employee	791,325	774,886	98
Payroll per Establishment	626,122	478,561	76	Sales per Establishment	12,012,387	8,104,136	67
Payroll per Employee	41,161	45,758	111	Expenses per Establishment	na	na	na

Sources: Same as General Statistics. The 'Average of All' column, Wholesale or Retail, represents the average of the sector reported for the most recent complete year available. The Index shows the relationship between the Average and the Analyzed Industry. For example, 100 means that they are equal; 500 that the Analyzed Industry is five times the average; 50 means that the Analyzed Industry is half the national average. The abbreviation 'na' is used to show that data are 'not available'.

*Equivalent to SIC 5162.

LEADING COMPANIES   Number shown: 52   Total sales ($ mil): 48,657   Total employment (000): 4.0

Company Name	Address			CEO Name	Phone	Co. Type	Sales ($ mil)	Empl. (000)
ThyssenKrupp Materials N.A. Inc.	22355 W 11 Mile Rd	Southfield	MI 48034	Hans-Erich Forster	248-233-5600	S	45,632*	0.2
H. Muehlstein and Company Inc.	800 Connecticut Ave	Norwalk	CT 06854	J Kevin Donohue	203-855-6000	R	875*	0.4
TricorBraun	460 N Lindbergh	St. Louis	MO 63141	Kenneth Kranzberg	314-569-3633	R	323*	0.3
Tomen America Inc.	1285 Av Americas	New York	NY 10019	T Yano	212-397-4600	S	210*	<0.1
Tarkett Inc.	PO Box 354	Florence	AL 35631	Jack Lee	610-266-5500	R	196*	<0.1
Solvay Advanced Polymers	4500 McGinnis	Alpharetta	GA 30005	Joe Greulich	770-772-8200	R	171*	0.2
Regal Plastic Supply Co.	111 E 10th Ave	N. Kansas City	MO 64116	Richard Cull	816-421-6290	R	162*	0.2
Rapid Industrial Plastics Inc.	13 Linden Ave E	Jersey City	NJ 07305	Paul Sirotkin	201-433-5500	R	150*	<0.1
Abell Corp.	PO Box 8056	Monroe	LA 71211	Dixon Abell	318-343-7565	R	125*	0.2
CalsonicKansei North America	27000 Hills Tech Ct	Farmington Hills	MI 48331	Shizuo Kato	248-848-4800	S	62*	0.2
Laird Plastics Inc.	1400 Centrepark	W. Palm Beach	FL 33401	John W Perdiue	561-684-7000	S	61*	0.5
FFR Inc.	28900 Fountain	Cleveland	OH 44139	Gerald A Conway	440-505-6919	R	54*	0.2
Mooney General Paper Co.	1451 Chestnut Ave	Hillside	NJ 07205	Gary Riemer	973-926-3800	R	49*	<0.1
Paper Products Company Inc.	36 Terminal Way	Pittsburgh	PA 15219	Dan Lackner	412-481-6200	R	45*	<0.1
Forrer Supply Company Inc.	PO Box 220	Germantown	WI 53022	Steve Forrer	262-255-3030	R	38*	<0.1
Mid America Lining Co.	PO Box 458	Union City	TN 38281	Mike Joslin	731-885-8888	R	34*	<0.1
Port Plastics Inc.	16750 Chestnut St	City of Industry	CA 91747	N Palmer	626-333-7678	R	31*	0.1
Outwater Plastics Industries Inc.	PO Box 403	Wood Ridge	NJ 07075	Peter Kessler	973-340-1040	R	31*	0.1
Federal Plastics Corp.	715 S Ave E	Cranford	NJ 07016	Peter Triano	908-272-5800	R	27*	<0.1
Major-Prime Plastics Inc.	PO Box 6240	Villa Park	IL 60181	John Hadley	630-834-9400	R	26*	<0.1
Ohio Valley Supply Co.	3512 Spring Grove	Cincinnati	OH 45223	Kenneth Shear	513-681-8300	R	25*	<0.1
General Rubber & Plastics Of	PO Box 17204	Louisville	KY 40217	Westman Burnett	502-635-2605	R	23*	<0.1
Hardin Tubular Sales Inc.	PO Box 374	Victoria	TX 77902	Doc Hardin	361-573-2252	R	21*	<0.1
NMC Group Inc.	2755 Thompson Crk	Pomona	CA 91767	Douglas Stephen	909-451-2280	R	21*	<0.1
How-Mac Manufacturing Inc.	720 Puget Ave A	Sedro Woolley	WA 98284	Joel Howard	360-855-2649	R	20*	<0.1
Paramount Can Company Inc.	16430 Phoebe Ave	La Mirada	CA 90638	Jack Gample	714-562-8410	R	20*	<0.1
Advanced Plastics Inc.	7360 Cockrill Bend	Nashville	TN 37209	Roy Abner	615-350-6500	R	20*	<0.1
Erdmann Corp.	PO Box 1269	Louisville	KY 40201	James Smith	502-584-1271	R	20*	<0.1
Lainiere De Picardie Inc.	180 Wheeler Ct	Langhorne	PA 19047	John Huss	215-702-9090	R	19*	<0.1
Jatco Inc.	725 Zwissig Way	Union City	CA 94587	Paul Appelblom	510-487-0888	R	19*	0.2
Rex Pipe and Supply Co.	10311 Berea Rd	Cleveland	OH 44102	Joseph Cleary	216-651-1900	R	14*	<0.1
Modern Plastics Inc.	PO Box 3974	Bridgeport	CT 06605	Bing Carbone	203-333-3128	R	13*	<0.1
Thermoplastic Services Inc.	PO Box 1024	Dequincy	LA 70633	Ashley Wade	337-786-7022	R	10*	<0.1
Norplex Inc.	PO Box 814	Auburn	WA 98071	Ralph Schley	253-735-3431	R	10*	<0.1
AIA Plastics Inc.	290 E 56th Ave	Denver	CO 80216	Jim Donaldson	303-296-9696	R	10*	<0.1
State Seal Co.	4135 E Wood St	Phoenix	AZ 85040		602-437-1532	R	10*	<0.1
Bradley Supply Company Inc.	PO Box 29096	Chicago	IL 60629		773-434-7400	R	10*	<0.1
Scott Industries of KY L.L.C.	6701 Cane Run Rd	Louisville	KY 40258	Marco Maccaferri	502-933-6060	R	9*	<0.1
Prime Alliance Inc.	1803 Hull Ave	Des Moines	IA 50309	Tom Irvine	515-264-4110	R	9*	<0.1
Fiber Systems Inc.	521 Kiser St	Dayton	OH 45404	Ted Morton	937-222-9017	R	9*	<0.1
Prince Rubber and Plastics Inc.	137 Arthur St	Buffalo	NY 14207	Tom Hanshar	716-877-7400	R	8*	<0.1
Beck Packaging Corp.	PO Box 20250	Lehigh Valley	PA 18002	Irwin Beck	610-264-0551	R	6*	<0.1
Corr Tech Inc.	4545 Homestead Rd	Houston	TX 77028	Doris Gottesman	713-674-7887	R	6*	<0.1
CPD Industries	4665 State St	Montclair	CA 91763	Carlos Hurtado	909-613-1999	R	6*	<0.1
Allpak Co.	1010 Lake St	Oak Park	IL 60301	Bert Levy	708-383-7200	R	4*	<0.1
Marine Specialty Company Inc.	PO Box 1388	Mobile	AL 36633	Tom Kelly	251-432-0581	R	3*	<0.1
PlastiFab Inc.	1425 Palomares St	La Verne	CA 91750	Robert Lincoln	909-596-1927	R	3*	<0.1
Prestige Packaging Inc.	6190 Regency Pkwy	Norcross	GA 30071	Michael A Griffin	770-448-1422	R	3*	<0.1
Isco Inc.	6360 Fiesta Dr	Columbus	OH 43235	Brian Amerine	614-792-2206	R	1*	<0.1
American Renolit Corp.	135 Algonquin	Whippany	NJ 07981	David Mittiga	973-386-9200	R	1*	<0.1
Aztec Supply Co.	977 North Enterprise	Orange	CA 92867	Eric Berge	714-771-6580	R	1*	<0.1
Sun Pacific Industries	748 S Stimson Ave	City of Industry	CA 91745		626-855-9048	R	1*	<0.1

Source: Ward's Business Directory of U.S. Private and Public Companies, Volumes 1 and 2, 2005. The company type code used is as follows: P - Public, R - Private, S - Subsidiary, D - Division, J - Joint Venture, A - Affiliate, G - Group. Sales are in millions of dollars, employees are in thousands. An asterisk (*) indicates an estimated sales volume. The symbol < stands for 'less than'. Company names and addresses are truncated, in some cases, to fit into the available space.

OCCUPATIONS EMPLOYED BY CHEMICAL & ALLIED PRODUCTS WHOLESALE

Occupation	% of Total 2004	Change to 2014	Occupation	% of Total 2004	Change to 2014
Sales reps, wholesale & manufacturing, exc tech	11.9	15.3	Bookkeeping, accounting, & auditing clerks	2.1	3.7
Sales reps, wholesale & manufacturing, tech	6.8	15.3	Executive secretaries & administrative assistants	1.8	9.2
Truck drivers, heavy & tractor-trailer	6.4	15.3	First-line supervisors/managers of production workers	1.7	15.3
Laborers & freight, stock, & material movers, hand	5.8	3.7	Maintenance & repair workers, general	1.7	15.3
General & operations managers	3.3	14.1	Secretaries, except legal, medical, & executive	1.6	-3.0
Truck drivers, light or delivery services	3.3	15.3	First-line supervisors/managers of office workers	1.5	4.5
Office clerks, general	3.2	2.6	Petroleum pump system operators, refinery operators	1.4	15.2
Customer service representatives	3.1	18.0	Stock clerks & order fillers	1.2	-11.7
Packaging & filling machine operators & tenders	3.0	9.1	Sales managers	1.2	16.0
Team assemblers	2.8	15.3	Order clerks	1.1	-25.0
Industrial truck & tractor operators	2.6	15.3	Chemical equipment operators & tenders	1.0	15.2
Shipping, receiving, & traffic clerks	2.4	4.4	Accountants & auditors	1.0	15.3
First-line supervisors/managers of non-retail sales work	2.1	6.6			

Source: Industry-Occupation Matrix, Bureau of Labor Statistics. These data are reported based on 4-digit NAICS categories but have been matched to corresponding 6-digit NAICS industry codes. The change reported for each occupation to the year 2014 is a percent of growth or decline as estimated by the Bureau of Labor Statistics. The abbreviation nec stands for 'not elsewhere classified.'

LOCATION BY STATE AND REGIONAL CONCENTRATION

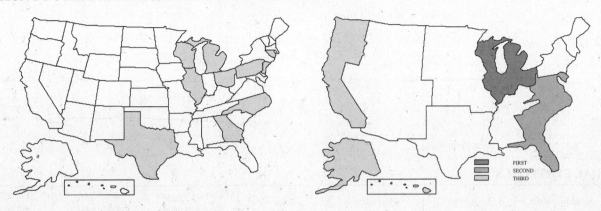

INDUSTRY DATA BY STATE

State	Establishments Total (number)	% of U.S.	Employment Total (number)	% of U.S.	Per Estab.	Payroll Total ($ mil.)	Per Empl. ($)	Sales Total ($ mil.)	% of U.S.	Per Estab. ($)
North Carolina	97	2.8	2,100	5.8	22	91.8	43,701	3,982.2	13.8	41,053,206
Texas	277	8.1	2,920	8.0	11	133.7	45,795	3,173.5	11.0	11,456,628
Michigan	144	4.2	1,922	5.3	13	118.4	61,589	2,996.0	10.4	20,805,243
California	460	13.4	4,108	11.3	9	183.7	44,723	2,415.3	8.4	5,250,707
Illinois	209	6.1	2,006	5.5	10	96.3	48,004	1,814.9	6.3	8,683,665
New York	214	6.2	1,688	4.6	8	97.1	57,496	1,789.1	6.2	8,360,379
New Jersey	194	5.6	1,954	5.4	10	98.6	50,446	1,515.6	5.3	7,812,222
Pennsylvania	138	4.0	2,109	5.8	15	120.2	57,008	1,487.4	5.2	10,778,500
Ohio	186	5.4	2,831	7.8	15	107.8	38,096	1,345.1	4.7	7,231,790
Georgia	124	3.6	1,037	2.8	8	55.5	53,552	930.7	3.2	7,505,903
Connecticut	57	1.7	722	2.0	13	42.5	58,902	793.3	2.8	13,916,930
Wisconsin	65	1.9	1,242	3.4	19	59.9	48,200	638.7	2.2	9,826,385
Massachusetts	99	2.9	1,014	2.8	10	48.6	47,955	527.4	1.8	5,327,202
Minnesota	58	1.7	676	1.9	12	32.2	47,652	496.1	1.7	8,552,638
Indiana	75	2.2	887	2.4	12	33.8	38,103	374.6	1.3	4,994,413
Colorado	49	1.4	467	1.3	10	19.5	41,818	358.9	1.2	7,323,571
Alabama	30	0.9	808	2.2	27	40.1	49,615	340.7	1.2	11,356,133
Washington	56	1.6	486	1.3	9	18.4	37,936	330.4	1.1	5,899,107
Missouri	70	2.0	597	1.6	9	26.8	44,946	274.9	1.0	3,927,214
Tennessee	54	1.6	477	1.3	9	17.5	36,713	177.2	0.6	3,281,870
South Carolina	37	1.1	393	1.1	11	15.6	39,639	153.2	0.5	4,141,189
Kansas	32	0.9	369	1.0	12	14.2	38,442	142.6	0.5	4,455,750
Oregon	40	1.2	382	1.0	10	14.0	36,534	142.2	0.5	3,554,650
Kentucky	27	0.8	406	1.1	15	13.7	33,667	127.4	0.4	4,718,741
Mississippi	18	0.5	190	0.5	11	6.0	31,374	112.2	0.4	6,233,667
Virginia	37	1.1	250	0.7	7	11.1	44,316	101.3	0.4	2,738,838
Iowa	19	0.6	186	0.5	10	7.6	40,634	96.6	0.3	5,081,895
Louisiana	33	1.0	292	0.8	9	9.7	33,264	84.7	0.3	2,565,364
Utah	35	1.0	254	0.7	7	8.4	33,224	84.2	0.3	2,404,857
Oklahoma	31	0.9	256	0.7	8	7.2	28,266	63.1	0.2	2,036,903
Rhode Island	16	0.5	82	0.2	5	3.4	41,280	54.8	0.2	3,424,500
Maine	9	0.3	104	0.3	12	5.7	55,135	50.8	0.2	5,643,333
West Virginia	8	0.2	114	0.3	14	3.2	28,167	22.4	0.1	2,803,875
New Mexico	12	0.3	60	0.2	5	2.2	37,067	19.9	0.1	1,656,833
Nevada	18	0.5	80	0.2	4	2.9	36,700	17.0	0.1	944,278
Hawaii	8	0.2	74	0.2	9	3.2	42,716	15.7	0.1	1,963,875
North Dakota	6	0.2	44	0.1	7	1.5	33,841	9.1	-	1,523,833
Wyoming	4	0.1	7	-	2	0.2	31,286	3.5	-	873,500
Florida	240	7.0	1000-2499	-	-	(D)	-	(D)	-	-
Arizona	44	1.3	250-499	-	-	(D)	-	(D)	-	-
Maryland	29	0.8	100-249	-	-	(D)	-	(D)	-	-
New Hampshire	23	0.7	100-249	-	-	(D)	-	(D)	-	-
Arkansas	16	0.5	100-249	-	-	(D)	-	(D)	-	-
Nebraska	14	0.4	100-249	-	-	(D)	-	(D)	-	-
Delaware	11	0.3	100-249	-	-	(D)	-	(D)	-	-
Idaho	4	0.1	0-19	-	-	(D)	-	(D)	-	-
South Dakota	3	0.1	0-19	-	-	(D)	-	(D)	-	-
Vermont	3	0.1	20-99	-	-	(D)	-	(D)	-	-
Alaska	2	0.1	20-99	-	-	(D)	-	(D)	-	-
Montana	1	-	0-19	-	-	(D)	-	(D)	-	-

Source: 2002 *Economic Census*. The states are in descending order of sales or establishments (if sales data are missing for the majority). The symbol (D) appears when data are withheld to prevent disclosure of competitive information. States marked with (D) are sorted by number of establishments. A dash (-) indicates that the data element cannot be calculated. Shaded *states* on the state map indicate those states which have proportionately greater representation in the industry than would be indicated by the states population; the ratio is based on total sales or number of establishments. Shaded *regions* indicate where the industry is regionally most concentrated.

NAICS 424690 - OTHER CHEMICAL AND ALLIED PRODUCTS MERCHANT WHOLESALERS*

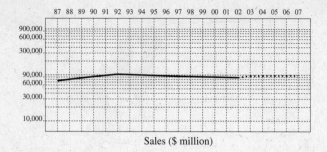

Sales ($ million)

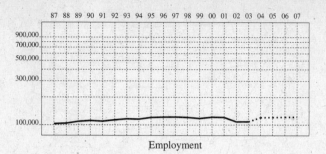

Employment

GENERAL STATISTICS

Year	Establishments (number)	Employment (number)	Payroll ($ million)	Sales ($ million)	Employees per Establishment (number)	Sales per Establishment ($)	Payroll per Employee ($)
1987	9,961	102,989	3,058.4	74,312.2 e	10.3	7,460,315.2	29,696.4
1988	9,389	104,206	3,444.1	80,229.2 e	11.1	8,545,020.8	33,050.9
1989	9,045	109,177	3,758.1	86,146.2 e	12.1	9,524,179.1	34,422.1
1990	9,014	111,448	4,028.7	92,063.3 e	12.4	10,213,368.1	36,148.7
1991	9,230	109,727	3,997.5	97,980.3 e	11.9	10,615,417.1	36,431.3
1992	10,703	113,551	4,434.7	103,897.4	10.6	9,707,315.7	39,054.7
1993	10,653	116,544	4,712.6	101,864.0 e	10.9	9,562,001.3	40,436.2
1994	10,695	115,680	4,729.6	99,830.5 e	10.8	9,334,315.1	40,885.2
1995	10,733	120,698	5,197.3	97,797.1 e	11.2	9,111,814.0	43,060.4
1996	10,928 e	121,732 e	5,378.5 e	95,763.6 e	11.1 e	8,763,140.6 e	44,183.1 e
1997	11,571	122,088	5,497.7	93,730.2	10.6	8,100,440.8	45,030.6
1998	11,530	120,929	5,727.8	92,597.1 e	10.5	8,030,971.4	47,365.0
1999	11,252	117,834	5,859.9	91,464.0 e	10.5	8,128,688.2	49,730.1
2000	11,255	121,824	6,196.7	90,330.9 e	10.8	8,025,846.3	50,865.6
2001	11,911	121,143	6,300.4	89,197.8 e	10.2	7,488,691.1	52,007.6
2002	11,117	108,487	5,830.0	88,064.7	9.8	7,921,624.5	53,739.2
2003	9,695	108,806	5,839.7	95,387.6 p	11.2	7,898,309.3 p	53,670.6
2004	11,636 p	120,519 p	6,674.4 p	95,762.1 p	10.3 p	7,794,190.2 p	56,302.8 p
2005	11,761 p	121,185 p	6,867.0 p	96,136.6 p	10.3 p	7,690,071.1 p	57,788.9 p
2006	11,886 p	121,851 p	7,059.6 p	96,511.1 p	10.2 p	7,585,951.9 p	59,275.0 p
2007	12,011 p	122,518 p	7,252.3 p	96,885.6 p	10.1 p	7,481,832.8 p	60,761.1 p

Sources: Economic Census of the United States, 1987, 1992, 1997, and 2002. Establishment counts, employment, and payroll are from *County Business Patterns* for non-Census years. Values followed by a 'p' are projections by the editors. Sales data for non-Census years are extrapolations, marked by 'e'. Data are the most recent available at this level of detail.

INDICES OF CHANGE

Year	Establishments (number)	Employment (number)	Payroll ($ million)	Sales ($ million)	Employees per Establishment (number)	Sales per Establishment ($)	Payroll per Employee ($)
1987	89.6	94.9	52.5	84.4	105.1	94.2	55.3
1992	96.3	104.7	76.1	118.0	108.2	122.5	72.7
1993	95.8	107.4	80.8	115.7 e	111.2	120.7	75.2
1994	96.2	106.6	81.1	113.4 e	110.2	117.8	76.1
1995	96.5	111.3	89.1	111.1 e	114.3	115.0	80.1
1996	98.3 e	112.2 e	92.3 e	108.7 e	113.3 e	110.6 e	82.2 e
1997	104.1	112.5	94.3	106.4	108.2	102.3	83.8
1998	103.7	111.5	98.2	105.1 e	107.1	101.4	88.1
1999	101.2	108.6	100.5	103.9 e	107.1	102.6	92.5
2000	101.2	112.3	106.3	102.6 e	110.2	101.3	94.7
2001	107.1	111.7	108.1	101.3 e	104.1	94.5	96.8
2002	100.0	100.0	100.0	100.0	100.0	100.0	100.0
2003	87.2	100.3	100.2	108.3 p	114.5	99.7 p	99.9
2004	104.7 p	111.1 p	114.5 p	108.7 p	105.5 p	98.4 p	104.8 p
2005	105.8 p	111.7 p	117.8 p	109.2 p	104.8 p	97.1 p	107.5 p
2006	106.9 p	112.3 p	121.1 p	109.6 p	104.1 p	95.8 p	110.3 p
2007	108.0 p	112.9 p	124.4 p	110.0 p	103.5 p	94.4 p	113.1 p

Sources: Same as General Statistics. The values shown reflect change from the base year, 2002. Values above 100 mean greater than 2002, values below 100 mean less than 2002, and a value of 100 in the 1987-2001 or 2003-2007 period means same as 2002. Values followed by a 'p' are projections by the editors; 'e' stands for extrapolation. Data are the most recent available at this level of detail.

SELECTED RATIOS

For 2002	Avg. of All Wholesale	Analyzed Industry	Index	For 2002	Avg. of All Wholesale	Analyzed Industry	Index
Employees per Establishment	15	10	65	Sales per Employee	791,325	811,753	103
Payroll per Establishment	626,122	524,422	84	Sales per Establishment	12,012,387	7,921,625	66
Payroll per Employee	41,161	53,739	131	Expenses per Establishment	na	na	na

Sources: Same as General Statistics. The 'Average of All' column, Wholesale or Retail, represents the average of the sector reported for the most recent complete year available. The Index shows the relationship between the Average and the Analyzed Industry. For example, 100 means that they are equal; 500 that the Analyzed Industry is five times the average; 50 means that the Analyzed Industry is half the national average. The abbreviation 'na' is used to show that data are 'not available'.

*Equivalent to SIC 5169.

LEADING COMPANIES Number shown: **75** Total sales ($ mil): **194,704** Total employment (000): **110.4**

Company Name	Address				CEO Name	Phone	Co. Type	Sales ($ mil)	Empl. (000)
ChevronTexaco Corp.	6001 Bollinger Cyn	San Ramon	CA	94583		925-845-1000	P	155,300	56.0
Chevron Products Company Inc.	6001 Bollinger Cyn	San Ramon	CA	94583	David Reeves	925-842-3232	R	15,300*	8.9
Brenntag Great Lakes L.L.C.	PO Box 444	Butler	WI	53007	James Holcomb	262-252-3550	R	3,290*	0.1
Brenntag Mid-South Inc.	PO Box 20	Henderson	KY	42419	Rodger Gilbert	270-827-4509	R	3,290*	<0.1
Univar USA Inc.	PO Box 34325	Seattle	WA	98124	Darwin H Simpson	425-889-3400	S	2,346	3.5
Acuity Brands Inc.	1170 Peachtree	Atlanta	GA	30309	John K Morgan	404-853-1400	P	2,104	11.0
Wacker Chemical Corp.	3301 Sutton Rd	Adrian	MI	49221	Dirk Funke	517-264-8500	S	2,029*	0.5
Airgas Inc.	259 N R-Chester	Radnor	PA	19087	Peter M McCausland	610-687-5253	P	1,896	9.7
Sigma-Aldrich Corp.	3050 Spruce St	St. Louis	MO	63103	David R Harvey	314-771-5765	P	1,409	6.1
CHEMCENTRAL Corp.	PO Box 730	Bedford Park	IL	60499	John R Yanney	708-594-7000	R	900	1.0
Seegott Inc.	10235 Philipp Pkwy	Streetsboro	OH	44241	Paul L Seegott	330-528-0808	R	422*	0.1
Lawson Products Inc.	1666 E Touhy Ave	Des Plaines	IL	60018	Jeffrey B Belford	847-827-9666	P	420	0.0
Chemed Corp.	2600 Chemed Ctr	Cincinnati	OH	45202	Edward L Hutton	513-762-6900	P	309	3.4
Aceto Corp.	1 Hollow Ln	Lake Success	NY	11042	Leonard S Schwartz	516-627-6000	P	298	0.3
McCall Oil and Chemical Co.	826 5480 NW Front	Portland	OR	97210	Bob McCall	503-221-6400	R	278*	0.1
Waxie Sanitary Supply	9353 Waxie Way	San Diego	CA	92123	Charles Wax	858-292-8111	R	253*	0.5
JLM Industries Inc.	8675 Hidden River	Tampa	FL	33637	John L Macdonald	813-632-3300	R	242	0.2
Merriam-Graves Corp.	806 River Rd	Charlestown	NH	03603	Donald Wakeman	603-542-8768	R	237*	0.3
Tomen America Inc.	1285 Av Americas	New York	NY	10019	T Yano	212-397-4600	S	210*	<0.1
THP United Enterprises Inc.	PO Box 1991	Milwaukee	WI	53201		262-523-6500	R	187*	2.0
Holston Gases Inc.	PO Box 27248	Knoxville	TN	37927	Robert Anders	865-573-1917	R	183*	0.2
Federal Process Corp.	4620 Richmond Rd	Cleveland	OH	44128	Jon Outcalt	216-464-6440	R	179*	<0.1
SST Corp.	PO Box 1649	Clifton	NJ	07012	George H Turner II	973-473-4300	R	175*	<0.1
Mays Chemical Company Inc.	5611 E 71st St	Indianapolis	IN	46220	William G Mays	317-842-8722	R	167	0.2
Universal Cooperative Inc.	1300 Corp Ctr	Eagan	MN	55121	Terry Bohman	651-239-1000	R	167*	0.3
Brandt Technologies Inc.	231 W Grand Ave	Bensenville	IL	60106	T R Brandt	630-787-1800	R	159*	<0.1
Ellsworth Corp.	W222 Cheaney N	Germantown	WI	53022	Paul Ellsworth	262-253-8600	R	155*	<0.1
Valley National Gases Inc.	200 W Beau St	Washington	PA	15301	James P Hart	724-228-3000	P	154	0.6
Nissho Iwai American Corp.	1211 Av Americas	New York	NY	10036	Teruo Matsumura	212-704-6500	S	130*	0.1
Bruker Biospin Corp.	15 Fortune Dr	Billerica	MA	01821	Frank Laukien	978-667-9580	R	122*	0.2
Kraft Chemical Co.	1975 N Hawthorne	Melrose Park	IL	60160	Betsy Liberman	708-345-5200	R	122*	<0.1
EMCO Chemical Distributors Inc.	PO Box 1030	North Chicago	IL	60064		847-689-2200	R	120*	0.2
Coastal Chemical Company L.L.C.	PO Box 820	Abbeville	LA	70511	Randy King	337-898-0001	S	105*	0.3
American Product Distributors Inc.	8227 Arrowridge	Charlotte	NC	28273	Don Black	704-522-9411	R	102	<0.1
Chem Rite Industries L.L.C.	19725 W Edgewood	Lannon	WI	53046	Ronald Whitt	262-255-3880	R	102*	0.1
Data2 Corp.	222 Turner Blvd	Saint Peters	MO	63376	Jack Delo	636-278-8888	R	81*	0.1
NuCo2 Inc.	2800 SE Market Pl	Stuart	FL	34997	M E DeDomenico	561-221-1754	P	81	0.5
Meherrin Agricultural & Chemical	PO Box 200	Severn	NC	27877	Bill McKeown	252-585-1744	R	75*	0.2
Ecolab Inc. Food & Beverage Div.	370 N Wabasha St	St. Paul	MN	55102		651-293-2233	D	74*	0.5
Ulrich Chemical Inc.	3111 N Post Rd	Indianapolis	IN	46226	Edward M Pitkin	317-898-8632	R	73*	0.2
Los Angeles Chemical Inc.	4545 Ardine St	South Gate	CA	90280	Jeff Wulff	323-832-5000	R	70*	0.2
Louisiana Chemical Equipment	PO Box 65064	Baton Rouge	LA	70896	Alvin Rotenberg	225-923-3602	R	69*	<0.1
P.F.G. Lester Company Inc.	PO Box 340	Lebanon	TN	37088		615-444-2963	S	64*	0.2
BUNZL New England	180 Shrewsbury St	West Boylston	MA	01583	Paul Lorenzini	508-835-6021	D	62*	<0.1
LCI Ltd.	PO Box 49000	Jacksonvl Bch	FL	32240		904-241-1200	R	62*	<0.1
Tulstar Products Inc.	5510 S Lewis Ave	Tulsa	OK	74105	Mark Nagle	918-749-9060	R	62*	0.1
Humco Holding Group Inc.	7400 Alumax Dr	Texarkana	TX	75501	Greg Pulido	903-831-7808	R	61*	0.1
Tekra Corp.	16700 W Lincoln	New Berlin	WI	53151		262-784-5533	R	59*	0.1
Lotepro Corp.	115 Stevens Ave	Valhalla	NY	10595	Hans Kistenmacher	914-747-3500	S	55*	<0.1
Kanematsu U.S.A. Inc.	114 W 47th St	New York	NY	10036	M Shimojima	212-704-9400	S	52*	<0.1
Gallard-Schlesinger Industries Inc.	245 Newtown Rd	Plainview	NY	11803	Jelle Westra	516-683-6900	S	48*	<0.1
Texas Molecular L.P.	PO Box 1914	Deer Park	TX	77536	Casey Borowski	281-930-2525	R	44*	0.1
KMG Chemicals Inc.	10611 Harwin Dr	Houston	TX	77036	J Neal Butler	713-988-9252	P	44	0.1
LaRoche Industries Inc.	1100 Johnson	Atlanta	GA	30342	Harold Ingalls	404-851-0300	R	41*	<0.1
Machine and Welding Supply Co.	PO Box 1708	Dunn	NC	28335	Emmett C Aldredge Jr	910-892-4016	R	40*	0.2
Sierra Chemical Co.	PO Box 50730	Sparks	NV	89435	Stanley Kinder	775-358-0888	R	40*	<0.1
US Filter Corp.	2600 S 17th Ave	Broadview	IL	60155		708-345-7290	R	39*	<0.1
Granitize Products Inc.	PO Box 2306	South Gate	CA	90280	Betty Raymondo	562-923-5438	R	38*	<0.1
Peninsular Paper Company Inc.	PO Box 1197	Tampa	FL	33610	Richard S Clarke Sr	813-621-3091	R	38*	<0.1
Delta Colours Inc.	2005 Newpt Plc	Lawrenceville	GA	30043	Shawn Hays	770-277-8819	R	36*	<0.1
Fitz Chem Corp.	450 E Devon	Itasca	IL	60143	Robert C Becker	630-941-0410	R	36*	<0.1
Industrial Soap Co.	722 S Vandeventer	St. Louis	MO	63110	Mark Shapiro	314-241-6363	R	35*	0.1
Buckeye Rubber and Packing Co.	23940 Mercantile Rd	Cleveland	OH	44122	Edward Klemm	216-464-8900	R	34*	<0.1
Economy Paper of Rochester	1175 Main St E	Rochester	NY	14609	Robert Cherry	585-482-5340	R	34*	<0.1
Hill Brothers Chemical Co.	1675 N Main St	Orange	CA	92867	Ronald R Hill	714-998-8800	R	33*	<0.1
Apache Nitrogen Products Inc.	PO Box 700	Benson	AZ	85602	Robert Cashdollar	520-720-2217	R	30*	<0.1
Ideal Chemical and Supply Co.	4025 Air Park St	Memphis	TN	38118	Sam Block Jr	901-363-7720	R	29*	0.1
Monson Co's Inc.	154 Pioneer Park	Leominster	MA	01453	Charles Walkovich	978-534-1425	R	27*	<0.1
Phoenix Products Co.	55 Container Dr	Terryville	CT	06786	John Haase	860-589-7502	R	27*	<0.1
Maine OXY-Acetylene Supply Co.	22 Albiston Way	Auburn	ME	04210	Dan Guerin	207-784-5788	R	26*	<0.1
Thomas Scientific	PO Box 99	Swedesboro	NJ	08085	G Wesner	856-467-2000	R	26*	0.1
Topmost Chemical and Paper	PO Box 18913	Memphis	TN	38188	A Proffer	901-363-7278	R	26*	<0.1
A. Daigger and Company Inc.	620 Lakeview Pkwy	Vernon Hills	IL	60061	Jim Woldenberg	847-816-5060	R	25*	<0.1
Automotive International Inc.	11308 Tamarco Dr	Cincinnati	OH	45242	Richard Hallberg Jr	513-489-7883	R	25*	<0.1
G.J. Chemical Company Inc.	370-376 Adams St	Newark	NJ	07114	Diane Colonna	973-589-1450	R	25*	<0.1

Source: Ward's Business Directory of U.S. Private and Public Companies, Volumes 1 and 2, 2005. The company type code used is as follows: P - Public, R - Private, S - Subsidiary, D - Division, J - Joint Venture, A - Affiliate, G - Group. Sales are in millions of dollars, employees are in thousands. An asterisk (*) indicates an estimated sales volume. The symbol < stands for 'less than'. Company names and addresses are truncated, in some cases, to fit into the available space.

OCCUPATIONS EMPLOYED BY CHEMICAL & ALLIED PRODUCTS WHOLESALE

Occupation	% of Total 2004	Change to 2014	Occupation	% of Total 2004	Change to 2014
Sales reps, wholesale & manufacturing, exc tech	11.9	15.3	Bookkeeping, accounting, & auditing clerks	2.1	3.7
Sales reps, wholesale & manufacturing, tech	6.8	15.3	Executive secretaries & administrative assistants	1.8	9.2
Truck drivers, heavy & tractor-trailer	6.4	15.3	First-line supervisors/managers of production workers	1.7	15.3
Laborers & freight, stock, & material movers, hand	5.8	3.7	Maintenance & repair workers, general	1.7	15.3
General & operations managers	3.3	14.1	Secretaries, except legal, medical, & executive	1.6	-3.0
Truck drivers, light or delivery services	3.3	15.3	First-line supervisors/managers of office workers	1.5	4.5
Office clerks, general	3.2	2.6	Petroleum pump system operators, refinery operators	1.4	15.2
Customer service representatives	3.1	18.0	Stock clerks & order fillers	1.2	-11.7
Packaging & filling machine operators & tenders	3.0	9.1	Sales managers	1.2	16.0
Team assemblers	2.8	15.3	Order clerks	1.1	-25.0
Industrial truck & tractor operators	2.6	15.3	Chemical equipment operators & tenders	1.0	15.2
Shipping, receiving, & traffic clerks	2.4	4.4	Accountants & auditors	1.0	15.3
First-line supervisors/managers of non-retail sales work	2.1	6.6			

Source: Industry-Occupation Matrix, Bureau of Labor Statistics. These data are reported based on 4-digit NAICS categories but have been matched to corresponding 6-digit NAICS industry codes. The change reported for each occupation to the year 2014 is a percent of growth or decline as estimated by the Bureau of Labor Statistics. The abbreviation nec stands for 'not elsewhere classified.'

LOCATION BY STATE AND REGIONAL CONCENTRATION

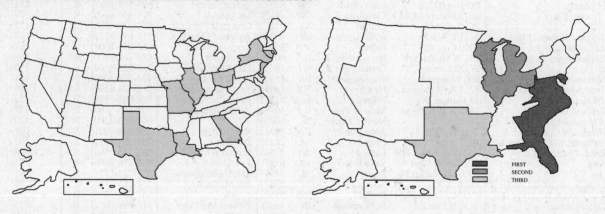

FIRST
SECOND
THIRD

INDUSTRY DATA BY STATE

State	Establishments Total (number)	% of U.S.	Employment Total (number)	% of U.S.	Per Estab.	Payroll Total ($ mil.)	Per Empl. ($)	Sales Total ($ mil.)	% of U.S.	Per Estab. ($)
Texas	1,176	10.5	10,249	9.8	9	556.0	54,245	11,618.6	13.4	9,879,753
New York	620	5.6	5,641	5.4	9	347.9	61,673	8,303.3	9.6	13,392,360
New Jersey	539	4.8	5,263	5.0	10	318.2	60,463	5,768.3	6.6	10,701,902
Georgia	461	4.1	5,404	5.2	12	269.1	49,799	5,578.6	6.4	12,100,991
California	1,041	9.3	9,152	8.7	9	462.2	50,503	4,997.6	5.8	4,800,736
Illinois	525	4.7	5,834	5.6	11	308.2	52,834	4,565.7	5.3	8,696,512
Ohio	492	4.4	5,287	5.0	11	260.7	49,301	4,405.2	5.1	8,953,717
Pennsylvania	449	4.0	5,388	5.1	12	285.4	52,977	3,760.5	4.3	8,375,187
Connecticut	148	1.3	2,013	1.9	14	116.4	57,823	2,163.0	2.5	14,614,892
Louisiana	248	2.2	2,901	2.8	12	159.8	55,087	2,118.5	2.4	8,542,359
North Carolina	365	3.3	3,490	3.3	10	176.9	50,685	2,080.2	2.4	5,699,082
Missouri	241	2.2	2,744	2.6	11	116.8	42,580	2,034.1	2.3	8,440,290
Michigan	311	2.8	2,772	2.6	9	167.0	60,236	1,537.9	1.8	4,944,952
Minnesota	221	2.0	2,107	2.0	10	108.6	51,542	1,444.6	1.7	6,536,606
Indiana	255	2.3	2,578	2.5	10	123.5	47,892	1,345.0	1.6	5,274,639
Wisconsin	227	2.0	2,356	2.2	10	107.7	45,710	1,148.0	1.3	5,057,485
Tennessee	212	1.9	2,303	2.2	11	114.0	49,512	1,045.6	1.2	4,931,976
Alabama	138	1.2	999	1.0	7	47.7	47,706	1,021.2	1.2	7,399,935
Oregon	126	1.1	814	0.8	6	34.0	41,732	850.3	1.0	6,748,238
South Carolina	179	1.6	1,267	1.2	7	58.3	46,049	799.7	0.9	4,467,492
Virginia	189	1.7	1,405	1.3	7	64.9	46,183	737.2	0.8	3,900,661
Washington	188	1.7	1,407	1.3	7	68.3	48,539	694.9	0.8	3,696,016
Kansas	110	1.0	871	0.8	8	42.8	49,191	673.7	0.8	6,124,836
Colorado	171	1.5	1,102	1.1	6	56.8	51,536	621.0	0.7	3,631,684
Kentucky	107	1.0	1,224	1.2	11	48.8	39,850	557.1	0.6	5,206,131
Oklahoma	162	1.5	906	0.9	6	42.0	46,375	544.9	0.6	3,363,543
Mississippi	75	0.7	948	0.9	13	72.6	76,541	349.8	0.4	4,664,453
Utah	94	0.8	854	0.8	9	35.7	41,854	308.2	0.4	3,278,702
Iowa	83	0.7	540	0.5	7	22.2	41,194	229.7	0.3	2,767,771
Rhode Island	45	0.4	510	0.5	11	23.0	45,102	220.8	0.3	4,907,333
New Mexico	73	0.7	460	0.4	6	20.4	44,272	196.9	0.2	2,697,836

Continued on next page.

INDUSTRY DATA BY STATE - Continued

State	Establishments		Employment			Payroll		Sales		
	Total (number)	% of U.S.	Total (number)	% of U.S.	Per Estab.	Total ($ mil.)	Per Empl. ($)	Total ($ mil.)	% of U.S.	Per Estab. ($)
Hawaii	32	0.3	414	0.4	13	19.5	46,988	137.6	0.2	4,298,938
Wyoming	48	0.4	286	0.3	6	15.6	54,486	114.0	0.1	2,375,021
Nevada	51	0.5	332	0.3	7	13.9	41,774	88.5	0.1	1,735,529
Maine	29	0.3	270	0.3	9	9.7	35,830	85.5	0.1	2,947,655
North Dakota	33	0.3	198	0.2	6	8.0	40,308	67.2	0.1	2,037,394
Florida	692	6.2	2500-4999	-	-	(D)	-	(D)	-	-
Massachusetts	190	1.7	1000-2499	-	-	(D)	-	(D)	-	-
Arizona	179	1.6	1000-2499	-	-	(D)	-	(D)	-	-
Maryland	162	1.5	1000-2499	-	-	(D)	-	(D)	-	-
Arkansas	97	0.9	500-999	-	-	(D)	-	(D)	-	-
New Hampshire	65	0.6	250-499	-	-	(D)	-	(D)	-	-
West Virginia	61	0.5	500-999	-	-	(D)	-	(D)	-	-
Idaho	53	0.5	100-249	-	-	(D)	-	(D)	-	-
Nebraska	51	0.5	250-499	-	-	(D)	-	(D)	-	-
Delaware	40	0.4	2500-4999	-	-	(D)	-	(D)	-	-
Montana	28	0.3	100-249	-	-	(D)	-	(D)	-	-
Vermont	25	0.2	20-99	-	-	(D)	-	(D)	-	-
South Dakota	24	0.2	100-249	-	-	(D)	-	(D)	-	-
Alaska	23	0.2	100-249	-	-	(D)	-	(D)	-	-
D.C.	4	-	20-99	-	-	(D)	-	(D)	-	-

Source: 2002 *Economic Census*. The states are in descending order of sales or establishments (if sales data are missing for the majority). The symbol (D) appears when data are withheld to prevent disclosure of competitive information. States marked with (D) are sorted by number of establishments. A dash (-) indicates that the data element cannot be calculated. Shaded *states* on the state map indicate those states which have proportionately greater representation in the industry than would be indicated by the states population; the ratio is based on total sales or number of establishments. Shaded *regions* indicate where the industry is regionally most concentrated.

NAICS 424710 - PETROLEUM BULK STATIONS AND TERMINALS

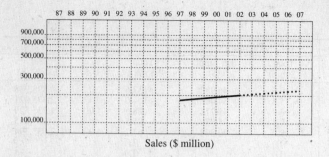

Sales ($ million)

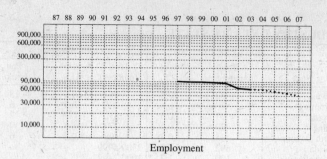

Employment

GENERAL STATISTICS

Year	Establishments (number)	Employment (number)	Payroll ($ million)	Sales ($ million)	Employees per Establishment (number)	Sales per Establishment ($)	Payroll per Employee ($)
1987	-	-	-	-	-	-	-
1988	-	-	-	-	-	-	-
1989	-	-	-	-	-	-	-
1990	-	-	-	-	-	-	-
1991	-	-	-	-	-	-	-
1992	-	-	-	-	-	-	-
1993	-	-	-	-	-	-	-
1994	-	-	-	-	-	-	-
1995	-	-	-	-	-	-	-
1996	-	-	-	-	-	-	-
1997	7,690	102,489	3,165.9	176,719.2	13.3	22,980,390.1	30,890.1
1998	7,503	99,466	3,305.4	181,742.6 e	13.3	24,222,652.3	33,231.5
1999	7,500	99,286	3,448.6	186,765.9 e	13.2	24,902,122.7	34,734.0
2000	7,203	97,236	3,600.0	191,789.3 e	13.5	26,626,305.7	37,023.5
2001	7,020	94,034	3,731.9	196,812.6 e	13.4	28,035,988.6	39,686.7
2002	4,776	72,919	2,956.9	201,836.0	15.3	42,260,469.0	40,550.5
2003	4,689	69,537	2,938.7	206,859.4 p	14.8	39,127,780.1 p	42,260.3
2004	4,492 p	68,252 p	3,150.3 p	211,882.7 p	15.1 p	42,258,196.8 p	44,582.6 p
2005	3,959 p	62,638 p	3,111.2 p	216,906.1 p	15.4 p	45,388,613.6 p	46,500.5 p
2006	3,425 p	57,023 p	3,072.0 p	221,929.4 p	15.7 p	48,519,030.3 p	48,418.4 p
2007	2,892 p	51,409 p	3,032.9 p	226,952.8 p	16.0 p	51,649,447.1 p	50,336.3 p

Source: *Economic Census of the United States*, 1997 and 2002. Establishment counts, employment, and payroll are from *County Business Patterns* for non-Census years. This is a newly defined industry. Data for prior years are unavailable at the time of publication but may become available over time. Values followed by 'p' are projections by the editors. Sales data for non-Census years are extrapolations, marked by 'e'.

INDICES OF CHANGE

Year	Establishments (number)	Employment (number)	Payroll ($ million)	Sales ($ million)	Employees per Establishment (number)	Sales per Establishment ($)	Payroll per Employee ($)
1987	-	-	-	-	-	-	-
1992	-	-	-	-	-	-	-
1993	-	-	-	-	-	-	-
1994	-	-	-	-	-	-	-
1995	-	-	-	-	-	-	-
1996	-	-	-	-	-	-	-
1997	161.0	140.6	107.1	87.6	86.9	54.4	76.2
1998	157.1	136.4	111.8	90.0 e	86.9	57.3	82.0
1999	157.0	136.2	116.6	92.5 e	86.3	58.9	85.7
2000	150.8	133.3	121.7	95.0 e	88.2	63.0	91.3
2001	147.0	129.0	126.2	97.5 e	87.6	66.3	97.9
2002	100.0	100.0	100.0	100.0	100.0	100.0	100.0
2003	98.2	95.4	99.4	102.5 p	96.9	92.6 p	104.2
2004	94.1 p	93.6 p	106.5 p	105.0 p	98.6 p	100.0 p	109.9 p
2005	82.9 p	85.9 p	105.2 p	107.5 p	100.7 p	107.4 p	114.7 p
2006	71.7 p	78.2 p	103.9 p	110.0 p	102.7 p	114.8 p	119.4 p
2007	60.5 p	70.5 p	102.6 p	112.4 p	104.8 p	122.2 p	124.1 p

Sources: Same as General Statistics. The values shown reflect change from the base year, 2002. Values above 100 mean greater than 2002, values below 100 mean less than 2002, and a value of 100 in the 1987-2001 or 2003-2007 period means same as 2002. Values followed by a 'p' are projections by the editors; 'e' stands for extrapolation. Data are the most recent available at this level of detail.

SELECTED RATIOS

For 2002	Avg. of All Wholesale	Analyzed Industry	Index	For 2002	Avg. of All Wholesale	Analyzed Industry	Index
Employees per Establishment	15	15	102	Sales per Employee	791,325	2,767,948	350
Payroll per Establishment	626,122	619,116	99	Sales per Establishment	12,012,387	42,260,469	352
Payroll per Employee	41,161	40,550	99	Expenses per Establishment	na	na	na

Sources: Same as General Statistics. The 'Average of All' column, Wholesale or Retail, represents the average of the sector reported for the most recent complete year available. The Index shows the relationship between the Average and the Analyzed Industry. For example, 100 means that they are equal; 500 that the Analyzed Industry is five times the average; 50 means that the Analyzed Industry is half the national average. The abbreviation 'na' is used to show that data are 'not available'.

LEADING COMPANIES   Number shown: **75**   Total sales ($ mil): **39,978**   Total employment (000): **27.4**

Company Name	Address				CEO Name	Phone	Co. Type	Sales ($ mil)	Empl. (000)
Amerada Hess Corp.	1185 Av Americas	New York	NY	10036		212-997-8500	P	16,733	11.5
TEPPCO Partners L.P.	PO Box 2521	Houston	TX	77252		713-759-3636	P	5,958	1.1
Sunoco Logistics Partners L.P.	10 Penn Ctr	Philadelphia	PA	19103	John G Drosdick	215-977-3000	P	3,465	1.1
RaceTrac Petroleum Inc.	PO Box 105035	Atlanta	GA	30348	Carl E Bolch, Jr	770-431-7600	R	2,771	4.7
Adams Resources and Energy Inc.	4400 Post Oak	Houston	TX	77027	K S Adams Jr	713-881-3600	P	2,069	0.7
Axel Johnson Inc.	300 Atlantic St	Stamford	CT	06901	Antonia Johnson	203-326-5200	S	1,907*	<0.1
Truman Arnold Companies Inc.	PO Box 1481	Texarkana	TX	75504	Gregory Arnold	903-794-3835	R	1,205	0.5
RKA Petroleum Companies Inc.	28340 Wick Rd	Romulus	MI	48174	Roger L Alberti	734-946-2199	R	1,124*	0.1
Kaneb Pipe Line Partners L.P.	2435 N Central Expy	Richardson	TX	75080		972-699-4062	P	648	0.0
Progressive Farmers Coop.	1221 Grant St	De Pere	WI	54115	Frank Hutjens	920-336-6449	R	473*	<0.1
Englefield Oil Co.	447 James Pkwy	Heath	OH	43056	Ben Englefield	740-928-8215	R	300*	1.5
Olympian Co.	999 Bayhill Dr	San Bruno	CA	94066	Fred Bertetta	650-873-8200	R	293*	0.3
McCall Oil and Chemical Co.	826 5480 NW Front	Portland	OR	97210	Bob McCall	503-221-6400	R	278*	0.1
Jacobus Energy Inc.	11815 W Bradley Rd	Milwaukee	WI	53224	CD Jacobus	414-359-0700	R	198*	0.3
Oxbow Corp.	1601 Forum Pl	W. Palm Beach	FL	33401	William I Koch	561-697-4300	R	192*	0.3
Midland 66 Oil Company Inc.	1612 Garden City	Midland	TX	79701	Randall Stevens	432-682-9404	R	166*	<0.1
NOCO Energy Corp.	2440 Sheridan Dr	Tonawanda	NY	14150	Jim Newman	716-833-6626	R	164*	0.6
Petroleum Marketers Inc.	3000 Ogden Rd	Roanoke	VA	24014	Ron Hare	540-772-4700	R	151*	0.7
Beck Suppliers Inc.	PO Box 808	Fremont	OH	43420	Douglas L Beck	419-332-5527	R	140*	0.3
Bauer Built Inc.	PO Box 248	Durand	WI	54736	Jerry M Bauer	715-672-4295	R	137*	0.5
Service Oil Inc.	1718 Main Ave E	West Fargo	ND	58078	Steven D Lenthe	701-277-1050	R	132*	0.2
District Petroleum Products Inc.	1814 River Rd	Huron	OH	44839	Scott Stipp	419-433-8373	R	131*	0.2
Jardine Petroleum Co.	PO Box 510170	North Salt Lake	UT	84054	Steve Moore	801-397-8300	R	120*	0.1
Stuarts' Petroleum Corp.	11 E 4th St	Bakersfield	CA	93307	John Stuart, Sr	661-325-6320	R	112*	<0.1
Julian W. Perkins Inc.	40657 Butternut	Elyria	OH	44035	P Brine	440-458-5125	R	82*	<0.1
Powell Distributing Company Inc.	PO Box 17160	Portland	OR	97217	L Powell Jr	503-289-5558	R	80*	<0.1
G and M Oil Company Inc.	HC 84, Box 6	Barbourville	KY	40906	Jerry Garland	606-546-3909	R	75*	0.2
Reeder Distributors Inc.	5450 Wilbarger St	Fort Worth	TX	76119	Gary M Reeder	817-429-5957	R	49*	<0.1
Luther P. Miller Inc.	PO Box 714	Somerset	PA	15501	Troy Miller	814-445-6569	R	44*	<0.1
Johnson Oil Company of Gaylord	PO Box 629	Gaylord	MI	49734	Dale E Johnson	989-732-2451	R	42*	<0.1
Frontier FS Coop.	PO Box 359	Jefferson	WI	53549	Perry Goetsch	920-674-7000	R	38*	<0.1
Etna Oil Company Inc.	PO Box 429	Ottawa	IL	61350	Rocky Cioni	815-434-0353	R	36*	<0.1
Illini F.S. Inc.	1509 E University St	Urbana	IL	61802	John Reifsteck	217-384-8300	R	36*	0.1
FOF Inc.	471 N Curtis Rd	Boise	ID	83706	Marla Gardner	208-377-0024	R	35*	<0.1
Curry Oil Company Inc.	1450 S Main St	London	KY	40741	Joe Curry	606-864-5119	R	31*	0.2
G and B Oil Company Inc.	PO Box 811	Elkin	NC	28621	Jeffery C Eidson	336-835-3607	R	30*	0.1
River Country Coop.	1080 W River St	Chippewa Falls	WI	54729		715-723-2828	R	29*	0.2
Yoder Oil Company Inc.	PO Box 1097	Elkhart	IN	46515	Kent J Yoder	574-264-2107	R	28*	<0.1
Colvard Oil Company Inc.	317 S Jefferson Ave	West Jefferson	NC	28694	Larry Dollar		R	25*	<0.1
Ampride	200 Sd Hwy 44	Chancellor	SD	57015		605-647-2700	R	24*	<0.1
Barney Holland Oil Co.	PO Box 1260	Fort Worth	TX	76101	Barney B Holland Jr	817-834-6600	R	24*	<0.1
H.C. Lewis Oil Co.	PO Box 649	Welch	WV	24801	HC Lewis Jr	304-436-2148	R	23*	<0.1
Newark Farmers Grain Co.	PO Box 398	Newark	IL	60541		815-695-5141	R	22*	<0.1
Jefferson City Oil Company Inc.	PO Box 576	Jefferson City	MO	65102	John Kolb	573-634-2025	R	21*	<0.1
Central Iowa Coop.	PO Box 190	Jewell	IA	50130	Kevin Larson	515-827-5431	R	20*	<0.1
Home Oil Co.	PO Box 608	Osceola	AR	72370	JL Price, Jr	870-563-6573	R	18*	<0.1
Central Co-op	245 SE 18th St	Owatonna	MN	55060	Dave Seykora	507-451-1230	R	17*	<0.1
Acorn Petroleum Inc.	76 S Sierra Madre St	Co Springs	CO	80903	Harlan Ochs	719-634-8874	R	16*	<0.1
East Jordan Cooperative Co.	PO Box 377	East Jordan	MI	49727		231-536-2275	R	16*	<0.1
Farmers Union Oil of Kenmare	PO Box 726	Kenmare	ND	58746		701-385-4277	R	16*	<0.1
Local Oil Company of Anoka Inc.	PO Box 517	Anoka	MN	55303	Leonard Dehn	763-421-4923	R	15*	0.1
Lyon County Cooperative Oil Co.	1100 E Main St	Marshall	MN	56258		507-532-9686	R	15*	<0.1
Plains Equity Exchange	PO Box 157	Plains	KS	67869	Vonn Richardson	620-563-7269	R	14*	<0.1
Black Oil Company Inc.	PO Box 159	Monticello	UT	84535	J Burton Black	435-587-2215	R	13*	<0.1
Fapp Brothers Petroleum Inc.	9915 S 148th St	Omaha	NE	68138	Bernie Raiter	402-895-2202	R	13*	<0.1
Porter Oil Company Inc.	306 S Motel Blvd	Las Cruces	NM	88005	Martin Porter	505-524-8666	R	13*	<0.1
Cooperative Gas and Oil Inc.	PO Box 137	Sioux Center	IA	51250	Roger Fedders	712-722-2501	R	11*	<0.1
McCracken Oil and Propane Co.	2010 S Main St	Wake Forest	NC	27588	Jay Cates	919-556-9018	R	11*	0.1
Northern Lakes Co-op Inc.	PO Box 985	Hayward	WI	54843		715-634-4841	R	11*	0.2
Lakeside Oil Company Inc.	555 W Brown Deer	Milwaukee	WI	53217	William Elliott	414-540-4000	R	10*	<0.1
Wooten Oil Co.	PO Box 1277	Goldsboro	NC	27533	SD Wooten Jr	919-734-1357	R	10*	<0.1
Rockbridge Farmers Coop.	645 Waddell St	Lexington	VA	24450		540-463-7381	R	9*	<0.1
Cowboy Oil Co.	PO Box L	Pocatello	ID	83201	DG Geisler	208-232-7814	R	8*	<0.1
E.O. Habhegger Company Inc.	460 Penn St	Yeadon	PA	19050	Kenneth T Hagman	610-622-1977	R	8*	<0.1
Kohler Oil and Propane Co.	4130 Main St	Brown City	MI	48416	Robert Kohler	810-346-2820	R	8*	<0.1
Northern Coop Services	107 W Main St	Lake Mills	IA	50450	Wayne Trenhaile	641-592-0011	R	8*	<0.1
C and S Inc.	300 W 1st St	Portales	NM	88130	Mike Stratton	505-356-4496	R	7*	<0.1
Farmers Union Cooperative Oil Co.	PO Box 1018	Luverne	MN	56156		507-283-9571	R	7*	<0.1
Reece Oil Co.	PO Box 3195	Terre Haute	IN	47803	Jack Reece	812-232-6621	R	7*	<0.1
Thaler Oil Company Inc.	310 S Main St	Chippewa Falls	WI	54729	Steve Thaler	715-723-2822	R	7*	<0.1
Bemidji Cooperative Association	PO Box 980	Bemidji	MN	56619	R Lewis	218-751-4260	R	6*	<0.1
G.A. Sadowsky and Son Inc.	PO Drawer D	Dickinson	ND	58601	AG Sadowsky	701-225-2713	R	6*	<0.1
Glover Oil Company Inc.	3109 S Main St	Melbourne	FL	32903	JH Glover	321-723-3953	R	6*	<0.1
St. Martin Oil and Gas Inc.	2040 Terr Hwy	St. Martinville	LA	70582	Jimmy Poirier	337-394-3163	R	6*	<0.1
A and W Oil Company Inc.	PO Box 180100	Fort Smith	AR	72918	Brad Arterbury	479-646-0595	R	5*	<0.1

Source: *Ward's Business Directory of U.S. Private and Public Companies*, Volumes 1 and 2, 2005. The company type code used is as follows: P - Public, R - Private, S - Subsidiary, D - Division, J - Joint Venture, A - Affiliate, G - Group. Sales are in millions of dollars, employees are in thousands. An asterisk (*) indicates an estimated sales volume. The symbol < stands for 'less than'. Company names and addresses are truncated, in some cases, to fit into the available space.

OCCUPATIONS EMPLOYED BY PETROLEUM & PETROLEUM PRODUCTS WHOLESALE

Occupation	% of Total 2004	Change to 2014	Occupation	% of Total 2004	Change to 2014
Truck drivers, heavy & tractor-trailer	19.5	-27.2	First-line supervisors/managers of transporation workers	1.7	-27.2
Cashiers, except gaming	8.3	-34.5	Billing & posting clerks & machine operators	1.5	-38.8
Sales reps, wholesale & manufacturing, exc tech	7.2	-27.2	First-line supervisors/managers of office workers	1.5	-34.1
Truck drivers, light or delivery services	5.2	-27.2	Retail salespersons	1.4	-27.2
Bookkeeping, accounting, & auditing clerks	4.2	-34.5	First-line supervisors/managers of retail sales workers	1.4	-33.1
Office clerks, general	3.7	-35.3	First-line supervisors/managers of non-retail sales work	1.3	-32.7
General & operations managers	3.5	-28.0	Accountants & auditors	1.2	-27.2
Laborers & freight, stock, & material movers, hand	3.0	-34.5	Bus & truck mechanics & diesel engine specialists	1.1	-27.3
Maintenance & repair workers, general	2.5	-27.2	Dispatchers, except police, fire, & ambulance	1.0	-34.6
Driver/sales workers	2.0	-27.2	Sales reps, wholesale & manufacturing, tech	1.0	-27.2
Secretaries, except legal, medical, & executive	1.8	-38.8	Customer service representatives	1.0	-25.6
Service station attendants	1.8	-34.7			

Source: Industry-Occupation Matrix, Bureau of Labor Statistics. These data are reported based on 4-digit NAICS categories but have been matched to corresponding 6-digit NAICS industry codes. The change reported for each occupation to the year 2014 is a percent of growth or decline as estimated by the Bureau of Labor Statistics. The abbreviation nec stands for 'not elsewhere classified.'

LOCATION BY STATE AND REGIONAL CONCENTRATION

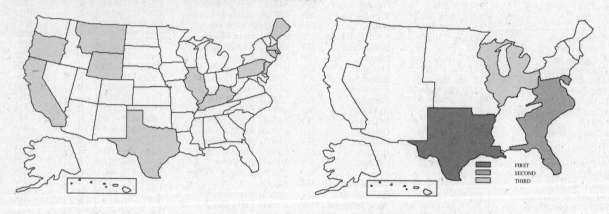

FIRST
SECOND
THIRD

INDUSTRY DATA BY STATE

State	Establishments Total (number)	% of U.S.	Employment Total (number)	% of U.S.	Per Estab.	Payroll Total ($ mil.)	Per Empl. ($)	Sales Total ($ mil.)	% of U.S.	Per Estab. ($)
Texas	488	10.1	7,092	10.1	15	395.1	55,706	37,809.8	18.0	77,479,125
California	317	6.6	5,649	8.1	18	268.1	47,466	25,801.3	12.3	81,392,132
Illinois	166	3.4	2,778	4.0	17	136.5	49,151	16,846.6	8.0	101,485,633
Connecticut	34	0.7	1,065	1.5	31	93.1	87,445	10,807.4	5.1	317,863,765
Pennsylvania	163	3.4	2,912	4.2	18	132.5	45,505	10,297.5	4.9	63,174,957
Florida	203	4.2	2,691	3.8	13	116.3	43,203	10,271.2	4.9	50,596,828
New York	175	3.6	2,219	3.2	13	98.2	44,269	7,756.6	3.7	44,323,309
Ohio	126	2.6	1,969	2.8	16	85.3	43,297	7,733.2	3.7	61,374,643
New Jersey	96	2.0	1,692	2.4	18	87.0	51,425	7,006.3	3.3	72,981,896
Massachusetts	68	1.4	1,555	2.2	23	76.5	49,216	6,168.9	2.9	90,719,265
Georgia	187	3.9	2,287	3.3	12	86.0	37,592	5,304.4	2.5	28,365,824
Washington	82	1.7	1,275	1.8	16	46.2	36,243	3,636.5	1.7	44,346,976
Tennessee	133	2.8	1,708	2.4	13	53.8	31,506	3,327.4	1.6	25,017,744
Indiana	113	2.3	1,469	2.1	13	52.2	35,555	3,261.3	1.6	28,861,363
Oregon	74	1.5	1,537	2.2	21	46.8	30,418	3,138.2	1.5	42,408,459
Louisiana	192	4.0	2,367	3.4	12	82.8	34,963	3,122.5	1.5	16,263,245
Kentucky	113	2.3	2,035	2.9	18	60.0	29,490	3,113.3	1.5	27,551,381
Wisconsin	85	1.8	1,117	1.6	13	43.1	38,565	2,957.0	1.4	34,788,412
Virginia	103	2.1	1,641	2.3	16	52.7	32,102	2,915.8	1.4	28,308,854
North Carolina	144	3.0	2,122	3.0	15	64.0	30,142	2,804.9	1.3	19,478,306
Oklahoma	101	2.1	1,096	1.6	11	36.1	32,930	2,364.8	1.1	23,414,307
Minnesota	89	1.8	1,145	1.6	13	35.6	31,081	2,083.4	1.0	23,408,764
Alabama	129	2.7	1,354	1.9	10	42.5	31,382	1,969.1	0.9	15,264,442
Maryland	39	0.8	578	0.8	15	25.4	43,976	1,520.6	0.7	38,990,513
Missouri	115	2.4	1,244	1.8	11	40.6	32,598	1,462.8	0.7	12,719,722
Utah	48	1.0	914	1.3	19	26.0	28,447	1,404.6	0.7	29,262,312
Arkansas	123	2.5	1,657	2.4	13	38.2	23,025	1,322.0	0.6	10,748,244
Mississippi	103	2.1	1,409	2.0	14	38.1	27,008	1,195.0	0.6	11,602,262
Colorado	84	1.7	1,336	1.9	16	46.7	34,925	1,188.5	0.6	14,148,274
Wyoming	45	0.9	418	0.6	9	12.3	29,490	1,065.0	0.5	23,665,800
Kansas	79	1.6	951	1.4	12	27.9	29,299	1,030.9	0.5	13,049,190

Continued on next page.

INDUSTRY DATA BY STATE - Continued

State	Establishments		Employment			Payroll		Sales		
	Total (number)	% of U.S.	Total (number)	% of U.S.	Per Estab.	Total ($ mil.)	Per Empl. ($)	Total ($ mil.)	% of U.S.	Per Estab. ($)
South Carolina	84	1.7	894	1.3	11	28.3	31,600	1,007.1	0.5	11,988,976
Maine	25	0.5	571	0.8	23	19.3	33,867	1,002.5	0.5	40,099,680
Iowa	101	2.1	1,082	1.5	11	28.8	26,615	998.9	0.5	9,889,782
New Mexico	60	1.2	757	1.1	13	20.6	27,157	944.9	0.4	15,748,417
Montana	59	1.2	851	1.2	14	21.3	25,060	893.0	0.4	15,135,356
Rhode Island	14	0.3	246	0.4	18	9.3	37,606	656.2	0.3	46,868,286
New Hampshire	16	0.3	288	0.4	18	10.0	34,802	654.0	0.3	40,874,500
Nebraska	51	1.1	531	0.8	10	15.1	28,395	618.4	0.3	12,125,745
Alaska	41	0.8	413	0.6	10	18.9	45,697	429.1	0.2	10,466,659
West Virginia	39	0.8	430	0.6	11	13.4	31,172	417.0	0.2	10,692,000
North Dakota	36	0.7	390	0.6	11	10.1	25,969	373.4	0.2	10,372,611
South Dakota	31	0.6	538	0.8	17	15.0	27,885	373.0	0.2	12,033,581
Vermont	11	0.2	218	0.3	20	7.7	35,514	332.7	0.2	30,241,182
Idaho	31	0.6	357	0.5	12	9.8	27,459	252.3	0.1	8,139,968
Nevada	21	0.4	211	0.3	10	8.4	40,019	247.3	0.1	11,777,714
Michigan	122	2.5	1000-2499	-	-	(D)	-	(D)	-	-
Arizona	51	1.1	1000-2499	-	-	(D)	-	(D)	-	-
Hawaii	18	0.4	100-249	-	-	(D)	-	(D)	-	-
Delaware	6	0.1	20-99	-	-	(D)	-	(D)	-	-
D.C.	2	-	0-19	-	-	(D)	-	(D)	-	-

Source: 2002 Economic Census. The states are in descending order of sales or establishments (if sales data are missing for the majority). The symbol (D) appears when data are withheld to prevent disclosure of competitive information. States marked with (D) are sorted by number of establishments. A dash (-) indicates that the data element cannot be calculated. Shaded states on the state map indicate those states which have proportionately greater representation in the industry than would be indicated by the states population; the ratio is based on total sales or number of establishments. Shaded regions indicate where the industry is regionally most concentrated.

NAICS 424720 - PETROLEUM AND PETROLEUM PRODUCTS MERCHANT WHOLESALERS (EXCEPT BULK STATIONS AND TERMINALS)*

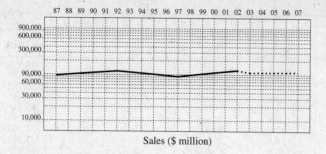

Sales ($ million)

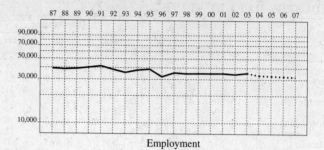

Employment

GENERAL STATISTICS

Year	Establishments (number)	Employment (number)	Payroll ($ million)	Sales ($ million)	Employees per Establishment (number)	Sales per Establishment ($)	Payroll per Employee ($)
1987	4,373	39,265	968.4	95,218.5	9.0	21,774,182.5	24,663.2
1988	3,976	38,525	1,036.0	99,991.5 e	9.7	25,148,767.6	26,891.6
1989	3,826	39,040	1,071.4	104,764.5 e	10.2	27,382,253.0	27,443.6
1990	3,835	40,257	1,155.2	109,537.5 e	10.5	28,562,581.5	28,695.6
1991	3,895	41,705	1,237.9	114,310.5 e	10.7	29,348,010.3	29,682.3
1992	3,962	38,297	1,219.9	119,083.5	9.7	30,056,410.9	31,853.7
1993	3,879	35,459	1,203.5	113,447.7 e	9.1	29,246,635.7	33,940.6
1994	3,864	37,663	1,344.1	107,812.0 e	9.7	27,901,656.3	35,687.5
1995	3,824	38,608	1,410.7	102,176.2 e	10.1	26,719,717.6	36,539.1
1996	3,146 e	32,022 e	1,274.6 e	96,540.5 e	10.2 e	30,686,745.1 e	39,803.9 e
1997	3,607	35,340	1,314.0	90,904.7	9.8	25,202,301.1	37,181.7
1998	3,747	34,598	1,452.0	97,559.8 e	9.2	26,036,765.4	41,967.7
1999	3,660	34,766	1,469.5	104,214.8 e	9.5	28,473,994.5	42,268.3
2000	3,459	34,754	1,622.8	110,869.9 e	10.0	32,052,581.7	46,695.0
2001	3,355	34,866	1,847.3	117,524.9 e	10.4	35,029,788.4	52,981.4
2002	3,185	34,107	1,481.4	124,180.0	10.7	38,989,011.0	43,433.9
2003	3,013	35,204	1,723.5	111,347.4 p	11.7	33,824,977.1 p	48,958.0
2004	3,154 p	33,189 p	1,738.5 p	111,887.2 p	10.5 p	34,402,831.8 p	51,202.1 p
2005	3,095 p	32,795 p	1,782.4 p	112,427.1 p	10.6 p	34,980,686.4 p	52,782.1 p
2006	3,036 p	32,401 p	1,826.4 p	112,966.9 p	10.6 p	35,558,541.0 p	54,362.2 p
2007	2,978 p	32,007 p	1,870.3 p	113,506.8 p	10.7 p	36,136,395.7 p	55,942.3 p

Sources: Economic Census of the United States, 1987, 1992, 1997, and 2002. Establishment counts, employment, and payroll are from County Business Patterns for non-Census years. Values followed by a 'p' are projections by the editors. Sales data for non-Census years are extrapolations, marked by 'e'. Data are the most recent available at this level of detail.

INDICES OF CHANGE

Year	Establishments (number)	Employment (number)	Payroll ($ million)	Sales ($ million)	Employees per Establishment (number)	Sales per Establishment ($)	Payroll per Employee ($)
1987	137.3	115.1	65.4	76.7	84.1	55.8	56.8
1992	124.4	112.3	82.3	95.9	90.7	77.1	73.3
1993	121.8	104.0	81.2	91.4 e	85.0	75.0	78.1
1994	121.3	110.4	90.7	86.8 e	90.7	71.6	82.2
1995	120.1	113.2	95.2	82.3 e	94.4	68.5	84.1
1996	98.8 e	93.9 e	86.0 e	77.7 e	95.3 e	78.7 e	91.6 e
1997	113.2	103.6	88.7	73.2	91.6	64.6	85.6
1998	117.6	101.4	98.0	78.6 e	86.0	66.8	96.6
1999	114.9	101.9	99.2	83.9 e	88.8	73.0	97.3
2000	108.6	101.9	109.5	89.3 e	93.5	82.2	107.5
2001	105.3	102.2	124.7	94.6 e	97.2	89.8	122.0
2002	100.0	100.0	100.0	100.0	100.0	100.0	100.0
2003	94.6	103.2	116.3	89.7 p	109.2	86.8 p	112.7
2004	99.0 p	97.3 p	117.4 p	90.1 p	98.3 p	88.2 p	117.9 p
2005	97.2 p	96.2 p	120.3 p	90.5 p	98.8 p	89.7 p	121.5 p
2006	95.3 p	95.0 p	123.3 p	91.0 p	99.3 p	91.2 p	125.2 p
2007	93.5 p	93.8 p	126.3 p	91.4 p	99.8 p	92.7 p	128.8 p

Sources: Same as General Statistics. The values shown reflect change from the base year, 2002. Values above 100 mean greater than 2002, values below 100 mean less than 2002, and a value of 100 in the 1987-2001 or 2003-2007 period means same as 2002. Values followed by a 'p' are projections by the editors; 'e' stands for extrapolation. Data are the most recent available at this level of detail.

SELECTED RATIOS

For 2002	Avg. of All Wholesale	Analyzed Industry	Index	For 2002	Avg. of All Wholesale	Analyzed Industry	Index
Employees per Establishment	15	11	72	Sales per Employee	791,325	3,640,895	460
Payroll per Establishment	626,122	465,118	74	Sales per Establishment	12,012,387	38,989,011	325
Payroll per Employee	41,161	43,434	106	Expenses per Establishment	na	na	na

Sources: Same as General Statistics. The 'Average of All' column, Wholesale or Retail, represents the average of the sector reported for the most recent complete year available. The Index shows the relationship between the Average and the Analyzed Industry. For example, 100 means that they are equal; 500 that the Analyzed Industry is five times the average; 50 means that the Analyzed Industry is half the national average. The abbreviation 'na' is used to show that data are 'not available'.

*Equivalent to SIC 5172.

LEADING COMPANIES　Number shown: **75**　Total sales ($ mil): **257,837**　Total employment (000): **127.1**

Company Name	Address				CEO Name	Phone	Co. Type	Sales ($ mil)	Empl. (000)
ChevronTexaco Corp.	6001 Bollinger Cyn	San Ramon	CA	94583		925-845-1000	P	155,300	56.0
Sunoco Inc.	10 Penn Center	Philadelphia	PA	19103	John G Drosdick	215-977-3000	P	25,508	14.9
Chevron Products Company Inc.	6001 Bollinger Cyn	San Ramon	CA	94583	David Reeves	925-842-3232	R	15,300*	8.9
Flying J Inc.	PO Box 678	Brigham City	UT	84302	J Phillip Adams	801-624-1000	R	7,500	12.5
Castrol North America Holdings	1500 Valley Rd	Wayne	NJ	07470	Mike Dearden	973-633-2200	S	7,489*	2.0
World Fuel Services Corp.	9800 NW 41st St	Miami	FL	33178	Michael J Kasbar	305-428-8000	P	5,635	0.4
Transammonia Inc.	350 Park Ave	New York	NY	10022	Ronald P Stanton	212-223-3200	R	3,967	0.3
Dead River Co.	PO Box 1427	Bangor	ME	04402	P Andrews Nixon	207-947-8641	R	3,749*	1.0
Gulf Oil L.P.	PO Box 9151	Chelsea	MA	02150	Gary Kaneb	617-889-9000	R	3,600	0.4
Frontier Oil Corp.	10000 Mem Dr	Houston	TX	77024	James R Gibbs	713-688-9600	P	2,862	0.7
RaceTrac Petroleum Inc.	PO Box 105035	Atlanta	GA	30348	Carl E Bolch, Jr	770-431-7600	R	2,771	4.7
Giant Industries Inc.	PO Box 12999	Scottsdale	AZ	85267	Morgan Gust	480-585-8888	P	2,512	2.4
Wallis Oil Co.	106 E Washington	Cuba	MO	65453	Lynn Wallis	573-885-2277	R	2,318*	0.7
Axel Johnson Inc.	300 Atlantic St	Stamford	CT	06901	Antonia Johnson	203-326-5200	S	1,907*	<0.1
Ever-Ready Oil Co.	PO Box 25845	Albuquerque	NM	87125	Charles L Ochs	505-842-6121	R	1,481*	0.3
Ferrellgas Partners L.P.	1 Liberty Plz	Liberty	MO	64068	James E Ferrell	816-792-1600	P	1,379	4.3
RKA Petroleum Companies Inc.	28340 Wick Rd	Romulus	MI	48174	Roger L Alberti	734-946-2199	R	1,124*	0.1
Delgasco Inc.	3617 Lexington Rd	Winchester	KY	40391	Glen Jennings	859-744-6171	S	1,063*	0.2
Kaneb Services L.L.C.	2435 N Central Expy	Richardson	TX	75080	John R Barnes	972-699-4041	P	1,055	1.1
US Oil Company Inc.	PO Box 25	Combined Locks	WI	54113		920-739-6101	R	980*	0.4
Agway Energy Products	PO Box 4933	Syracuse	NY	13221	Michael R Hopsicker	315-449-7380	S	645*	1.7
Quality Oil Company L.L.C.	PO Box 2736	Winston Salem	NC	27102	Graham Bennett	336-722-3441	R	470*	0.6
Trans-Tec Services Inc.	2 Greenwich	Greenwich	CT	06830	Paul H Stebbins	203-863-0001	S	429*	<0.1
Kiel Brothers Oil Co.	3801 Tupelo Dr	Columbus	IN	47202	Gregory Pence	812-342-5700	R	394*	1.8
Mercury Air Group Inc.	5456 McConnell	Los Angeles	CA	90066	Joseph A Czyzyk	310-827-2737	P	385	1.0
Petroleum Service Co.	PO Box 454	Wilkes Barre	PA	18703	RW Simms	570-822-1151	R	380*	0.1
Johnson Cooperative Grain Co.	PO Box 280	Johnson	KS	67855	Steve Arnold	620-492-6210	R	336*	<0.1
Gaspro	PO Box 30707	Honolulu	HI	96820		808-842-2222	S	320*	0.1
Consumer Cooperative Oil Co.	PO Box 668	Sauk City	WI	53583	DeLorman Enge	608-643-3301	R	319*	<0.1
Green Valley Acquisition Co.	477 E Beaver Ave	State College	PA	16801	Henry D Sahakian	814-234-6000	R	296	2.5
McCall Oil and Chemical Co.	826 5480 NW Front	Portland	OR	97210	Bob McCall	503-221-6400	R	278*	0.1
Castle Oil Corp.	500 Mamaroneck	Harrison	NY	10528	Michael Romita	914-381-6600	R	266*	0.3
Paraco Gas Corp.	2975 Westchester	Purchase	NY	10577	Joe Armentano	914-696-4427	R	238*	0.1
Heritage FS Inc.	PO Box 339	Gilman	IL	60938		815-265-4751	R	232*	<0.1
Keystops Inc.	PO Box 2809	Franklin	KY	42135	Lester Key	270-586-8283	R	225*	0.2
Chesapeake Utilities Corp.	909 Silver Lake	Dover	DE	19904	Ralph J Adkins	302-734-6799	P	221	0.5
Vesco Oil Corp.	PO Box 525	Southfield	MI	48037	Donald Epstein	248-557-1600	R	216*	0.3
Webber Oil Co.	PO Box 929	Bangor	ME	04402	Larry Mahaney	207-942-5501	R	203*	0.2
Whitaker Oil Co.	1557 Marietta NW	Atlanta	GA	30318	Bart Whitaker III	404-355-8220	R	195*	<0.1
Gull Industries Inc.	PO Box 24687	Seattle	WA	98124	Douglas L True	206-624-5900	R	191*	0.1
Romanelli and Son Inc.	PO Box 544	Lindenhurst	NY	11757	Marty Romanelli	631-956-1201	R	191*	<0.1
Iowa Oil Co.	PO Box 712	Dubuque	IA	52004	Brian Enke	563-672-3663	R	187*	0.2
Federal Process Corp.	4620 Richmond Rd	Cleveland	OH	44128	Jon Outcalt	216-464-6440	R	179*	<0.1
Penn Octane Corp.	77-530 Enfield Ln	Palm Desert	CA	92211	Jerome B Richter	760-772-9080	P	178	<0.1
Miller Oil Co.	1000 E City Hall	Norfolk	VA	23504	Jeffery G Miller	757-623-1682	R	176*	0.5
Missouri Petroleum Products	1620 Woodson Rd	St. Louis	MO	63114	Gene R Allen	314-991-2180	S	176*	0.2
Ag Partners L.L.C.	PO Box 38	Albert City	IA	50510	Troy Upah	712-843-2291	J	175*	0.1
Gresham Petroleum Co.	PO Box 690	Indianola	MS	38751	Bill McPherson	662-887-2160	R	167*	<0.1
NOCO Energy Corp.	2440 Sheridan Dr	Tonawanda	NY	14150	Jim Newman	716-833-6626	R	164*	0.6
Effingham Equity	PO Box 488	Effingham	IL	62401		217-342-4101	R	155*	0.4
Valley National Gases Inc.	200 W Beau St	Washington	PA	15301	James P Hart	724-228-3000	P	154	0.6
Beck Suppliers Inc.	PO Box 808	Fremont	OH	43420	Douglas L Beck	419-332-5527	R	140*	0.5
Eden Oil Company Inc.	124 N Fieldcrest Rd	Eden	NC	27288	Ried Teague	336-635-3311	R	133*	<0.1
Northville Industries Corp.	25 Melville Park Rd	Melville	NY	11747	Jay Bernstein	631-293-4700	R	123*	<0.1
Rex Oil Company Inc.	PO Box 1050	Thomasville	NC	27360	Harold S Kennedy	336-472-3000	R	112*	<0.1
Perryton Equity Exchange	PO Box 889	Perryton	TX	79070	Doug Mitchell	806-435-4016	R	110*	0.1
Continental Resources of Illinois	PO Box 749	Mount Vernon	IL	62864	Richard Straeter	618-242-1717	R	108*	<0.1
Kimber Petroleum Corp.	545 Martinsville Rd	Liberty Corner	NJ	07938	WS Kimber Jr	908-903-9600	R	102*	0.2
Wilco Farmers	PO Box 258	Mount Angel	OR	97362	Michael Jamison	503-845-6122	R	100*	<0.1
Carson Oil Company Inc.	PO Box 10948	Portland	OR	97296	JA Carson	503-224-8500	R	96*	0.3
Condon Oil Company Inc.	PO Box 184	Ripon	WI	54971	Kent B Bauman	920-748-3186	R	95*	0.3
Streicher Mobile Fueling Inc.	800 W Cypress	Fort Lauderdale	FL	33309	Richard E Galthright	954-308-4200	P	90	0.2
Menomonie Farmers Union Coop.	PO Box 438	Menomonie	WI	54751	Gerry Hoag	715-232-6200	R	89*	0.1
Surner Heating Company Inc.	60 Shumway St	Amherst	MA	01002	Bruce Montue	413-253-5999	R	86*	<0.1
Drake Petroleum Company Inc.	PO Box 866	N Grsvnrdl	CT	06255	Warren Alpert	860-935-5200	S	83*	0.1
Halron Oil Company Inc.	PO Box 2188	Green Bay	WI	54306		920-437-0466	R	83*	0.1
Powell Distributing Company Inc.	PO Box 17160	Portland	OR	97217	L Powell Jr	503-289-5558	R	80*	0.1
Patterson Oil Co.	PO Box 898	Torrington	CT	06790	Barry Patterson	860-489-9271	R	79*	<0.1
J and H Oil Co.	PO Box 9464	Wyoming	MI	49509	Jerry Hop	616-534-2181	R	75*	0.4
Joseph F. Boente Sons Inc.	PO Box 288	Carlinville	IL	62626	Larry Boente	217-854-3164	R	75*	<0.1
Silco Oil Co.	181 E 56th Ave	Denver	CO	80216	Sue Vanderburg	303-292-0500	R	70*	0.4
Jax USA	W129 Washngtn N	Menomonee Fls	WI	53051	Eric Peter	262-781-8850	R	68*	<0.1
MIFCO	9009 Ctr St	Manassas	VA	20110		703-368-3121	R	68*	0.1
Global Companies L.L.C.	800 South St	Waltham	MA	02454	Alfred Slifka	781-894-8800	R	66*	0.2
Arnold Owens Inc.	PO Box 3697	Bloomington	IL	61702	Michael Owens	309-828-7750	R	64*	0.3

Source: Ward's Business Directory of U.S. Private and Public Companies, Volumes 1 and 2, 2005. The company type code used is as follows: P - Public, R - Private, S - Subsidiary, D - Division, J - Joint Venture, A - Affiliate, G - Group. Sales are in millions of dollars, employees are in thousands. An asterisk (*) indicates an estimated sales volume. The symbol < stands for 'less than'. Company names and addresses are truncated, in some cases, to fit into the available space.

OCCUPATIONS EMPLOYED BY PETROLEUM & PETROLEUM PRODUCTS WHOLESALE

Occupation	% of Total 2004	Change to 2014	Occupation	% of Total 2004	Change to 2014
Truck drivers, heavy & tractor-trailer	19.5	-27.2	First-line supervisors/managers of transporation workers	1.7	-27.2
Cashiers, except gaming	8.3	-34.5	Billing & posting clerks & machine operators	1.5	-38.8
Sales reps, wholesale & manufacturing, exc tech	7.2	-27.2	First-line supervisors/managers of office workers	1.5	-34.1
Truck drivers, light or delivery services	5.2	-27.2	Retail salespersons	1.4	-27.2
Bookkeeping, accounting, & auditing clerks	4.2	-34.5	First-line supervisors/managers of retail sales workers	1.4	-33.1
Office clerks, general	3.7	-35.3	First-line supervisors/managers of non-retail sales work	1.3	-32.7
General & operations managers	3.5	-28.0	Accountants & auditors	1.2	-27.2
Laborers & freight, stock, & material movers, hand	3.0	-34.5	Bus & truck mechanics & diesel engine specialists	1.1	-27.3
Maintenance & repair workers, general	2.5	-27.2	Dispatchers, except police, fire, & ambulance	1.0	-34.6
Driver/sales workers	2.0	-27.2	Sales reps, wholesale & manufacturing, tech	1.0	-27.2
Secretaries, except legal, medical, & executive	1.8	-38.8	Customer service representatives	1.0	-25.6
Service station attendants	1.8	-34.7			

Source: Industry-Occupation Matrix, Bureau of Labor Statistics. These data are reported based on 4-digit NAICS categories but have been matched to corresponding 6-digit NAICS industry codes. The change reported for each occupation to the year 2014 is a percent of growth or decline as estimated by the Bureau of Labor Statistics. The abbreviation nec stands for 'not elsewhere classified.'

LOCATION BY STATE AND REGIONAL CONCENTRATION

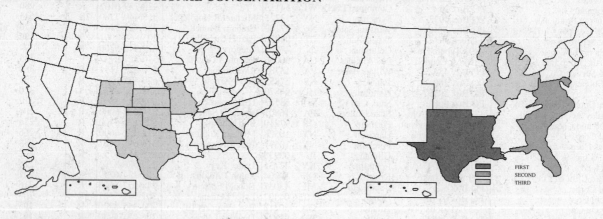

INDUSTRY DATA BY STATE

State	Establishments Total (number)	% of U.S.	Employment Total (number)	% of U.S.	Per Estab.	Payroll Total ($ mil.)	Per Empl. ($)	Sales Total ($ mil.)	% of U.S.	Per Estab. ($)
Texas	397	12.3	5,157	14.8	13	283.4	54,947	39,193.3	35.2	98,723,776
Georgia	113	3.5	1,230	3.5	11	60.0	48,820	10,065.8	9.0	89,078,168
California	238	7.4	3,120	9.0	13	160.9	51,563	6,598.2	5.9	27,723,387
Missouri	63	2.0	738	2.1	12	41.2	55,764	4,245.5	3.8	67,388,095
New York	155	4.8	1,664	4.8	11	75.8	45,530	4,201.9	3.8	27,109,226
Colorado	47	1.5	639	1.8	14	25.2	39,495	3,535.3	3.2	75,219,000
Florida	155	4.8	1,282	3.7	8	44.2	34,458	2,195.2	2.0	14,162,413
Kansas	59	1.8	395	1.1	7	19.0	48,086	1,947.4	1.8	33,006,576
Minnesota	65	2.0	552	1.6	8	21.4	38,848	1,920.5	1.7	29,545,508
Oklahoma	106	3.3	937	2.7	9	34.9	37,260	1,803.5	1.6	17,014,151
Illinois	127	3.9	1,993	5.7	16	46.7	23,441	1,670.5	1.5	13,153,512
North Carolina	97	3.0	686	2.0	7	30.5	44,485	1,332.7	1.2	13,738,732
Pennsylvania	90	2.8	1,359	3.9	15	53.1	39,109	1,280.0	1.2	14,221,933
Ohio	102	3.2	758	2.2	7	30.4	40,135	1,261.0	1.1	12,362,931
Wisconsin	67	2.1	419	1.2	6	15.9	37,876	1,175.6	1.1	17,545,582
Maryland	25	0.8	239	0.7	10	11.9	49,711	1,109.3	1.0	44,370,480
Tennessee	71	2.2	524	1.5	7	18.5	35,317	1,054.2	0.9	14,848,183
Arkansas	45	1.4	578	1.7	13	21.9	37,969	1,005.4	0.9	22,343,289
Virginia	60	1.9	521	1.5	9	19.6	37,608	865.7	0.8	14,428,433
Kentucky	58	1.8	810	2.3	14	38.5	47,544	862.6	0.8	14,872,879
Alabama	85	2.6	967	2.8	11	26.3	27,206	775.0	0.7	9,117,706
Louisiana	72	2.2	641	1.8	9	20.4	31,899	747.4	0.7	10,380,931
Washington	46	1.4	591	1.7	13	22.7	38,462	682.9	0.6	14,846,391
Indiana	66	2.1	536	1.5	8	21.9	40,791	674.1	0.6	10,213,182
Mississippi	45	1.4	436	1.3	10	13.8	31,661	480.3	0.4	10,672,689
Oregon	34	1.1	404	1.2	12	14.6	36,196	422.0	0.4	12,413,088
Iowa	47	1.5	376	1.1	8	10.2	27,223	410.6	0.4	8,737,128
Nevada	22	0.7	215	0.6	10	7.1	32,828	385.8	0.3	17,536,045
South Carolina	59	1.8	452	1.3	8	14.0	30,934	324.9	0.3	5,506,424
West Virginia	28	0.9	298	0.9	11	8.1	27,315	313.0	0.3	11,178,286
Nebraska	29	0.9	358	1.0	12	7.8	21,726	201.3	0.2	6,940,655

Continued on next page.

INDUSTRY DATA BY STATE - Continued

State	Establishments		Employment			Payroll		Sales		
	Total (number)	% of U.S.	Total (number)	% of U.S.	Per Estab.	Total ($ mil.)	Per Empl. ($)	Total ($ mil.)	% of U.S.	Per Estab. ($)
Idaho	22	0.7	280	0.8	13	9.1	32,621	174.7	0.2	7,941,955
North Dakota	25	0.8	167	0.5	7	4.2	25,024	153.4	0.1	6,134,160
Montana	20	0.6	65	0.2	3	2.0	30,431	113.4	0.1	5,668,850
Utah	25	0.8	181	0.5	7	4.8	26,536	104.1	0.1	4,162,400
New Mexico	25	0.8	240	0.7	10	6.6	27,454	87.9	0.1	3,517,400
Wyoming	11	0.3	69	0.2	6	2.6	37,174	62.5	0.1	5,684,545
South Dakota	16	0.5	92	0.3	6	2.0	21,337	54.1	-	3,379,125
Vermont	5	0.2	32	0.1	6	1.1	34,750	38.5	-	7,694,400
Alaska	8	0.2	61	0.2	8	2.2	35,557	14.8	-	1,849,750
New Jersey	110	3.4	1000-2499	-	-	(D)	-	(D)	-	-
Michigan	85	2.6	500-999	-	-	(D)	-	(D)	-	-
Massachusetts	56	1.7	250-499	-	-	(D)	-	(D)	-	-
Connecticut	37	1.2	250-499	-	-	(D)	-	(D)	-	-
Arizona	36	1.1	250-499	-	-	(D)	-	(D)	-	-
Delaware	16	0.5	20-99	-	-	(D)	-	(D)	-	-
Maine	16	0.5	100-249	-	-	(D)	-	(D)	-	-
New Hampshire	12	0.4	20-99	-	-	(D)	-	(D)	-	-
Rhode Island	9	0.3	100-249	-	-	(D)	-	(D)	-	-
Hawaii	7	0.2	20-99	-	-	(D)	-	(D)	-	-
D.C.	2	0.1	20-99	-	-	(D)	-	(D)	-	-

Source: 2002 Economic Census. The states are in descending order of sales or establishments (if sales data are missing for the majority). The symbol (D) appears when data are withheld to prevent disclosure of competitive information. States marked with (D) are sorted by number of establishments. A dash (-) indicates that the data element cannot be calculated. Shaded *states* on the state map indicate those states which have proportionately greater representation in the industry than would be indicated by the states population; the ratio is based on total sales or number of establishments. Shaded *regions* indicate where the industry is regionally most concentrated.

NAICS 424810 - BEER AND ALE MERCHANT WHOLESALERS*

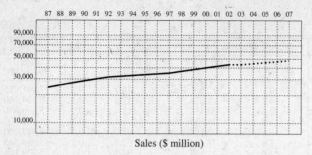

Sales ($ million)

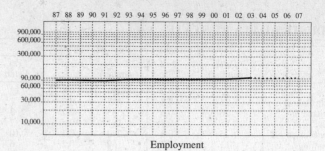

Employment

GENERAL STATISTICS

Year	Establishments (number)	Employment (number)	Payroll ($ million)	Sales ($ million)	Employees per Establishment (number)	Sales per Establishment ($)	Payroll per Employee ($)
1987	3,934	90,091	2,314.7	24,288.0	22.9	6,173,868.8	25,692.9
1988	3,775	90,852	2,496.3	25,751.0 e	24.1	6,821,457.0	27,476.6
1989	3,545	89,762	2,480.7	27,214.1 e	25.3	7,676,756.0	27,636.4
1990	3,406	89,177	2,595.5	28,677.1 e	26.2	8,419,583.1	29,105.0
1991	3,284	88,880	2,680.0	30,140.2 e	27.1	9,177,892.8	30,153.0
1992	3,403	91,086	2,851.8	31,603.2	26.8	9,286,864.5	31,308.9
1993	3,298	94,076	2,960.6	32,282.0 e	28.5	9,788,356.6	31,470.3
1994	3,211	94,902	3,055.6	32,960.8 e	29.6	10,264,964.2	32,197.4
1995	3,123	95,892	3,130.3	33,639.6 e	30.7	10,771,565.8	32,644.0
1996	2,864 e	94,361 e	3,217.7 e	34,318.4 e	32.9 e	11,982,681.6 e	34,099.9 e
1997	3,013	96,284	3,308.6	34,997.2	32.0	11,615,399.9	34,362.9
1998	2,957	95,440	3,450.0	36,669.6 e	32.3	12,400,960.4	36,148.4
1999	2,876	96,252	3,574.8	38,342.1 e	33.5	13,331,738.5	37,140.0
2000	2,788	97,379	3,741.1	40,014.5 e	34.9	14,352,410.3	38,417.6
2001	2,713	97,580	3,867.1	41,687.0 e	36.0	15,365,632.1	39,629.8
2002	2,566	100,629	4,072.3	43,359.4	39.2	16,897,661.7	40,468.5
2003	2,462	104,491	4,208.9	43,377.7 p	42.4	16,281,318.3 p	40,279.7
2004	2,420 p	101,552 p	4,201.8 p	44,540.2 p	40.2 p	16,914,945.5 p	41,726.4 p
2005	2,341 p	102,331 p	4,315.6 p	45,702.6 p	41.2 p	17,548,572.7 p	42,648.8 p
2006	2,262 p	103,110 p	4,429.5 p	46,865.1 p	42.2 p	18,182,199.9 p	43,571.1 p
2007	2,183 p	103,890 p	4,543.4 p	48,027.6 p	43.3 p	18,815,827.1 p	44,493.5 p

Sources: *Economic Census of the United States*, 1987, 1992, 1997, and 2002. Establishment counts, employment, and payroll are from *County Business Patterns* for non-Census years. Values followed by a 'p' are projections by the editors. Sales data for non-Census years are extrapolations, marked by 'e'. Data are the most recent available at this level of detail.

INDICES OF CHANGE

Year	Establishments (number)	Employment (number)	Payroll ($ million)	Sales ($ million)	Employees per Establishment (number)	Sales per Establishment ($)	Payroll per Employee ($)
1987	153.3	89.5	56.8	56.0	58.4	36.5	63.5
1992	132.6	90.5	70.0	72.9	68.4	55.0	77.4
1993	128.5	93.5	72.7	74.5 e	72.7	57.9	77.8
1994	125.1	94.3	75.0	76.0 e	75.5	60.7	79.6
1995	121.7	95.3	76.9	77.6 e	78.3	63.7	80.7
1996	111.6 e	93.8 e	79.0 e	79.1 e	83.9 e	70.9 e	84.3 e
1997	117.4	95.7	81.2	80.7	81.6	68.7	84.9
1998	115.2	94.8	84.7	84.6 e	82.4	73.4	89.3
1999	112.1	95.7	87.8	88.4 e	85.5	78.9	91.8
2000	108.7	96.8	91.9	92.3 e	89.0	84.9	94.9
2001	105.7	97.0	95.0	96.1 e	91.8	90.9	97.9
2002	100.0	100.0	100.0	100.0	100.0	100.0	100.0
2003	95.9	103.8	103.4	100.0 p	108.3	96.4 p	99.5
2004	94.3 p	100.9 p	103.2 p	102.7 p	102.5 p	100.1 p	103.1 p
2005	91.2 p	101.7 p	106.0 p	105.4 p	105.1 p	103.9 p	105.4 p
2006	88.2 p	102.5 p	108.8 p	108.1 p	107.7 p	107.6 p	107.7 p
2007	85.1 p	103.2 p	111.6 p	110.8 p	110.4 p	111.4 p	109.9 p

Sources: Same as General Statistics. The values shown reflect change from the base year, 2002. Values above 100 mean greater than 2002, values below 100 mean less than 2002, and a value of 100 in the 1987-2001 or 2003-2007 period means same as 2002. Values followed by a 'p' are projections by the editors; 'e' stands for extrapolation. Data are the most recent available at this level of detail.

SELECTED RATIOS

For 2002	Avg. of All Wholesale	Analyzed Industry	Index	For 2002	Avg. of All Wholesale	Analyzed Industry	Index
Employees per Establishment	15	39	262	Sales per Employee	791,325	430,884	54
Payroll per Establishment	626,122	1,587,023	253	Sales per Establishment	12,012,387	16,897,662	141
Payroll per Employee	41,161	40,468	98	Expenses per Establishment	na	na	na

Sources: Same as General Statistics. The 'Average of All' column, Wholesale or Retail, represents the average of the sector reported for the most recent complete year available. The Index shows the relationship between the Average and the Analyzed Industry. For example, 100 means that they are equal; 500 that the Analyzed Industry is five times the average; 50 means that the Analyzed Industry is half the national average. The abbreviation 'na' is used to show that data are 'not available'.

*Equivalent to SIC 5181.

LEADING COMPANIES   Number shown: 75   Total sales ($ mil): 26,587   Total employment (000): 57.6

Company Name	Address				CEO Name	Phone	Co. Type	Sales ($ mil)	Empl. (000)
Anheuser-Busch Inc.	1 Busch Pl	St. Louis	MO	63118	Patrick T. Stokes	314-577-2000	S	9,710*	23.3
Southern Wine & Spirits	1600 NW 163rd St	Miami	FL	33169	Harvey R Chaplin	305-625-4171	R	5,400	8.0
Glazer's Wholesale Drug Inc.	PO Box 809013	Dallas	TX	75380	Jerry Cargill	972-702-0900	R	2,200	5.5
Young's Market Company L.L.C.	2164 N Batavia St	Orange	CA	92865	Charles Andrews	714-283-4933	R	1,400	1.8
National Distributing Company	PO Box 44127	Atlanta	GA	30336	Charlie Andrews	404-696-9440	R	1,360*	2.5
Ben E. Keith Co.	PO Box 2628	Fort Worth	TX	76113	Howard Hallam	817-877-5700	R	1,173*	2.3
General Beverage Sales Co.	PO Box 44326	Madison	WI	53744	Daniel Weinstein	608-271-1234	R	421*	0.5
Gold Coast Beverage Distributors	3325 NW 70th Ave	Miami	FL	33122	Art Friedman	305-591-9800	R	405*	0.7
Labatt USA Inc.	101 Marritt 7	Norwalk	CT	06856		203-750-6600	R	300*	0.5
High Grade Beverage	PO Box 7092	N. Brunswick	NJ	08902	Joseph DeMarco	732-821-7600	R	192*	0.4
Jordanos Inc.	550 S Patterson Ave	Santa Barbara	CA	93111	Peter Jordano	805-964-0611	R	188*	0.5
Clare Rose Inc.	72 Clare Rose Blvd	Patchogue	NY	11772	Lisa Rose	631-475-1840	R	180	0.3
Columbia Distributing Co.	6840 N Cutter Cir	Portland	OR	97217	Edward L Maletis	503-289-9600	R	176*	0.6
Western Distributing Co.	PO Box 5542	Denver	CO	80217	Vieri Gaines	303-388-5755	R	160*	0.7
Atlanta Beverage Co.	PO Box 44008	Atlanta	GA	30336	C Mark Pirrung	404-699-6700	R	158*	0.4
Mounthood Beverage Co.	3601 NW Yeon Ave	Portland	OR	97210	Richard Lytle	503-274-9990	R	130*	0.6
Gate City Beverage Distributors	2505 Steel St	San Bernardino	CA	92408	Leona Aronoff	909-799-1600	R	127*	0.4
Powers Distributing Company Inc.	3700 Giddings Rd	Orion	MI	48359	Jerry Powers	248-393-3700	R	118*	0.3
Crest Beverage Co.	PO Box 26640	San Diego	CA	92121	Steve S Sourapas	858-566-1800	R	115*	0.2
DET Distributing Co.	301 Great Circle Rd	Nashville	TN	37228	Fred Dettwiler	615-244-4113	R	112*	0.2
Wisconsin Distributors Inc.	900 Progress Way	Sun Prairie	WI	53590	Pierre McCormick	608-834-2337	R	108*	0.1
Budco of San Antonio Inc.	PO Box 937	San Antonio	TX	78294	Berkley V Dawson	210-225-3044	R	107*	0.3
General Wholesale Co.	1271-A Tacoma Dr	Atlanta	GA	30318	William D Young Sr	404-351-3626	R	107*	0.3
Nevada Beverage Co.	PO Box 93538	Las Vegas	NV	89119	Pat Clark	702-739-9474	R	89*	0.3
D. Canale Beverages Inc.	45 E H Crump W	Memphis	TN	38106	Christopher W Canale	901-948-4543	R	87*	0.2
B. Olinde and Sons Company Inc.	9536 Airline Hwy	Baton Rouge	LA	70815	JB Olinde	225-926-3380	R	71*	0.2
General Distributing Co.	PO Box 221210	Salt Lake City	UT	84122	Micheal P Brennan	801-531-7895	R	71*	0.1
Great Dane Pub and Brewery	123 E Doty St	Madison	WI	53703	Elliot Butler	608-284-0000	R	69*	0.1
R.H. Barringer Distributing Inc.	1620 Fairfax Rd	Greensboro	NC	27407	Mark Craig	336-854-0555	R	62*	0.2
William Thies and Sons Inc.	791 Pk of Com	Boca Raton	FL	33487	Dennis Thies	561-237-1400	R	62*	0.2
Odom Corp.	20415 72nd Ave S	Kent	WA	98032	John P Odom	253-437-3000	R	58*	0.5
Beauchamp Distributing Co.	1911 S Santa Fe Ave	Compton	CA	90221	Patrick L Beauchamp	310-639-5320	R	58	0.2
Golden Brand Bottling Inc.	2225 Jerrold Ave	San Francisco	CA	94124	Jim Molakides	415-643-9900	R	54*	0.2
Better Brands of Atlanta Inc.	755 NW Jefferson St	Atlanta	GA	30318		404-872-4731	R	53*	0.2
Grey Eagle Distributors Inc.	2340 Millpark Dr	Maryland H.	MO	63043	Jerry Clinton	314-429-9100	R	52*	0.2
N.K.S. Distributors Inc.	PO Box 758	New Castle	DE	19720	James V Tigani Jr	302-322-1811	R	52*	0.2
Giglio Distributing Co.	PO Box 4046	Beaumont	TX	77704	JC Giglio	409-838-1654	R	51*	0.2
Pacific Beverage Company Inc.	5305 Ekwil St	Santa Barbara	CA	93111	Peter Jordano	805-964-0611	S	51*	0.2
Frank B. Fuhrer Wholesale Co.	3100 E Carson St	Pittsburgh	PA	15203	David Fuhrer	412-488-8844	R	50*	0.2
Muller Inc.	2800 Grant Ave	Philadelphia	PA	19114	John Janosko	215-676-7575	R	49*	0.2
Coastal Beverage Company Inc.	301 Harley Rd	Wilmington	NC	28405	Lewis T Nunnelee III	910-799-3011	R	48*	0.2
Standard Beverage Corp.	PO Box 968	Wichita	KS	67201	L Rudd	316-838-7707	R	48*	0.2
Buck Distributing Company Inc.	PO Box 1490	Upper Marlboro	MD	20773	Betty J Buck	301-952-0400	R	45*	0.1
Hartford Distributors Inc.	PO Box 8400	Manchester	CT	06040	Ross Hollander	860-643-2337	R	45*	0.2
Hubert Distributors Inc.	1200 Auburn Rd	Pontiac	MI	48342	Alice J Gustafson	248-858-2340	R	43*	0.1
McLaughlin and Moran Inc.	PO Box 20217	Cranston	RI	02920	Terence Moran	401-463-5454	R	43*	0.1
H. Dennert Distributing Corp.	351 Wilmer Ave	Cincinnati	OH	45226	Ronald J Plattner	513-871-7272	R	42*	0.1
Pyramid Breweries Inc.	91 S Ryl Brougham	Seattle	WA	98134	George Hancock	206-682-8322	P	40	0.4
Kramer Beverage Company Inc.	PO Box 470	Hammonton	NJ	08037	Charles W Kramer	609-704-7000	R	40*	0.1
Tri County Beverage Co.	14301 Prospect Ave	Dearborn	MI	48126	Walter Wolpin	313-584-7100	R	40*	0.1
Beloit Beverage Company Inc.	4059 W Bradley Rd	Milwaukee	WI	53209	Don Morello	414-362-5000	R	39*	0.1
Quality Beverage Inc.	PO Box 671	Taunton	MA	02780	Conrad Wetterau	508-822-6200	R	37*	0.1
Markstein Beverage Co.	PO Box 6902	San Marcos	CA	92079	Ken Markstein	760-744-9004	R	36*	0.1
Moon Distributors Inc.	2800 Vance St	Little Rock	AR	72206	Harry Hastings	501-375-8291	R	36*	0.1
Northern Distributing Co.	PO Box 315	Glens Falls	NY	12801	Maureen E Ireland	518-792-3112	R	36*	0.1
Superior Distributing Co.	1045 S Caldwell	Tiffin	OH	44883	Kris Klepper	419-447-7756	R	36*	<0.1
Wayne Densch Inc.	2900 W 1st St	Sanford	FL	32771	Leonard Williams	407-323-5600	R	36*	0.1
Burke Beverages Inc.	536 East Ave	La Grange	IL	60525	Kevin Burke	708-579-0333	R	35*	0.1
Capital Beverage Co.	2424 Del Monte St	W. Sacramento	CA	95691	Kenneth Adamson	916-371-8164	R	35*	0.1
Delaware Importers Inc.	PO Box 271	New Castle	DE	19720	EJ Stegemeier	302-656-4487	R	35*	0.1
Bob Hall Inc.	5600 SE Crane Hwy	Upper Marlboro	MD	20772	Evalina S Mitchell	301-627-1900	R	30*	0.1
Greene Beverage Company Inc.	PO Box 1699	Tuscaloosa	AL	35403	Spencer Burchfield	205-345-6950	R	30*	<0.1
House of Schwan Inc.	PO Box 782950	Wichita	KS	67278	Barry Schwan	316-636-9100	R	30*	<0.1
Maple City Ice Co.	371 Cleveland Rd	Norwalk	OH	44857		419-668-2531	R	30*	<0.1
Skokie Valley Beverage Co.	199 Shepard Ave	Wheeling	IL	60090	William P Schimang	847-541-1500	R	30*	<0.1
Commercial Distributing Co.	PO Box 1476	Westfield	MA	01086	Richard C Placek	413-562-9691	R	29*	<0.1
Capital Beverage Corp.	700 Columbia St	Brooklyn	NY	11231	Carmine N Stella	718-488-8500	P	28	<0.1
High Life Sales Co.	1325 N Topping Ave	Kansas City	MO	64120	Steve Mos	816-483-3700	R	27*	0.1
Clarke Distributors Inc.	PO Box 624	Keene	NH	03431	Jeffery A Clarke	603-352-0344	R	26*	0.1
Lake Beverage Corp.	900 John St	West Henrietta	NY	14586	Hank Schroeder	585-427-0090	R	26*	<0.1
Cunningham Wholesale Inc.	PO Box 32651	Charlotte	NC	28232	T E Cunningham	704-392-8371	R	25*	<0.1
Classic City Beverages Inc.	530 Calhoun Dr	Athens	GA	30603	Robert L O'Rear	706-353-1650	R	24*	<0.1
Goody-Goody Liquor Store Inc.	10301 Harry Hines	Dallas	TX	75220	Joe Jansen	214-350-5806	R	24*	0.2
Wasatch Brew Pub	PO Box 459	Park City	UT	84060	Greg Schirf	435-645-9500	R	24*	<0.1
Crown Beer Distributors Inc.	PO Box 1255	Wall	NJ	07719	Paul Rapisardi	732-223-9100	R	23*	<0.1

Source: Ward's Business Directory of U.S. Private and Public Companies, Volumes 1 and 2, 2005. The company type code used is as follows: P - Public, R - Private, S - Subsidiary, D - Division, J - Joint Venture, A - Affiliate, G - Group. Sales are in millions of dollars, employees are in thousands. An asterisk (*) indicates an estimated sales volume. The symbol < stands for 'less than'. Company names and addresses are truncated, in some cases, to fit into the available space.

OCCUPATIONS EMPLOYED BY BEER, WINE, & DISTILLED ALCOHOLIC BEVERAGE WHOLESALE

Occupation	% of Total 2004	Change to 2014	Occupation	% of Total 2004	Change to 2014
Sales reps, wholesale & manufacturing, exc tech	23.3	11.9	General & operations managers	2.1	10.7
Truck drivers, heavy & tractor-trailer	9.1	11.9	Sales managers	2.1	12.6
Laborers & freight, stock, & material movers, hand	8.7	0.7	First-line supervisors/managers of transporation workers	1.7	11.9
Driver/sales workers	8.1	11.6	Office clerks, general	1.7	-0.4
Truck drivers, light or delivery services	5.9	11.8	Bookkeeping, accounting, & auditing clerks	1.5	0.7
Industrial truck & tractor operators	5.7	0.7	Shipping, receiving, & traffic clerks	1.1	1.3
First-line supervisors/managers of non-retail sales work	4.1	3.4	Executive secretaries & administrative assistants	1.1	6.1
Merchandise displayers & window trimmers	2.2	11.5	Demonstrators & product promoters	1.1	7.6
Stock clerks & order fillers	2.2	-14.3	First-line supervisors/managers of helpers & laborers	1.0	11.9

Source: Industry-Occupation Matrix, Bureau of Labor Statistics. These data are reported based on 4-digit NAICS categories but have been matched to corresponding 6-digit NAICS industry codes. The change reported for each occupation to the year 2014 is a percent of growth or decline as estimated by the Bureau of Labor Statistics. The abbreviation nec stands for 'not elsewhere classified.'

LOCATION BY STATE AND REGIONAL CONCENTRATION

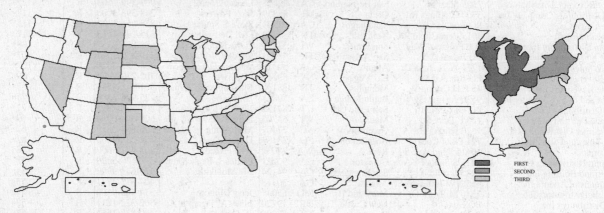

INDUSTRY DATA BY STATE

State	Establishments Total (number)	% of U.S.	Employment Total (number)	% of U.S.	Per Estab.	Payroll Total ($ mil.)	Per Empl. ($)	Sales Total ($ mil.)	% of U.S.	Per Estab. ($)
Texas	168	6.6	9,605	9.5	57	389.0	40,496	5,260.0	11.9	31,309,714
California	203	7.9	10,180	10.1	50	408.4	40,118	4,573.1	10.3	22,527,635
New York	194	7.6	6,226	6.2	32	275.9	44,314	2,870.5	6.5	14,796,314
Illinois	114	4.5	3,941	3.9	35	199.3	50,583	2,814.9	6.3	24,691,877
Florida	89	3.5	5,935	5.9	67	242.5	40,852	2,577.4	5.8	28,959,135
Connecticut	23	0.9	1,475	1.5	64	99.1	67,161	1,899.6	4.3	82,592,826
Ohio	89	3.5	3,847	3.8	43	171.5	44,579	1,566.9	3.5	17,605,978
Pennsylvania	174	6.8	3,322	3.3	19	132.4	39,846	1,513.3	3.4	8,696,851
Michigan	103	4.0	3,831	3.8	37	157.1	41,000	1,317.2	3.0	12,788,563
Georgia	52	2.0	2,925	2.9	56	116.1	39,708	1,250.3	2.8	24,043,519
North Carolina	61	2.4	2,931	2.9	48	101.4	34,586	1,047.5	2.4	17,172,656
New Jersey	51	2.0	1,856	1.8	36	96.4	51,958	988.9	2.2	19,389,294
Colorado	49	1.9	2,004	2.0	41	80.0	39,926	947.9	2.1	19,344,347
Virginia	61	2.4	2,668	2.6	44	108.2	40,555	931.5	2.1	15,270,836
Wisconsin	84	3.3	2,705	2.7	32	103.8	38,359	924.1	2.1	11,001,679
Massachusetts	39	1.5	1,750	1.7	45	82.1	46,934	808.1	1.8	20,720,359
Washington	56	2.2	2,528	2.5	45	92.2	36,462	776.6	1.8	13,867,482
Missouri	62	2.4	1,945	1.9	31	80.0	41,122	756.5	1.7	12,202,145
Indiana	49	1.9	1,611	1.6	33	61.1	37,899	702.6	1.6	14,338,163
Louisiana	38	1.5	2,052	2.0	54	67.9	33,089	699.8	1.6	18,416,711
Tennessee	35	1.4	2,030	2.0	58	88.9	43,803	683.0	1.5	19,515,171
South Carolina	30	1.2	1,719	1.7	57	63.8	37,098	672.1	1.5	22,403,533
Maryland	38	1.5	1,583	1.6	42	68.0	42,930	658.4	1.5	17,325,289
Minnesota	66	2.6	1,563	1.5	24	67.4	43,116	621.8	1.4	9,420,818
Alabama	34	1.3	1,601	1.6	47	50.3	31,426	552.6	1.2	16,252,088
Oregon	50	2.0	1,444	1.4	29	51.6	35,715	444.0	1.0	8,879,580
Oklahoma	42	1.6	1,124	1.1	27	36.4	32,351	438.7	1.0	10,445,238
Kentucky	31	1.2	1,085	1.1	35	42.0	38,681	436.0	1.0	14,065,032
Mississippi	35	1.4	1,292	1.3	37	42.8	33,131	414.1	0.9	11,832,314
Iowa	40	1.6	1,176	1.2	29	47.8	40,656	398.5	0.9	9,962,400
Nevada	21	0.8	1,006	1.0	48	41.1	40,840	376.5	0.8	17,927,095
Kansas	41	1.6	930	0.9	23	35.3	37,961	323.9	0.7	7,899,805
New Mexico	22	0.9	761	0.8	35	25.6	33,706	313.9	0.7	14,268,545

Continued on next page.

INDUSTRY DATA BY STATE - Continued

State	Establishments		Employment			Payroll		Sales		
	Total (number)	% of U.S.	Total (number)	% of U.S.	Per Estab.	Total ($ mil.)	Per Empl. ($)	Total ($ mil.)	% of U.S.	Per Estab. ($)
Arkansas	32	1.2	824	0.8	26	27.7	33,635	302.9	0.7	9,465,875
New Hampshire	11	0.4	662	0.7	60	31.8	48,106	275.8	0.6	25,072,091
Maine	11	0.4	643	0.6	58	24.2	37,616	238.4	0.5	21,671,636
Nebraska	30	1.2	506	0.5	17	19.8	39,200	232.8	0.5	7,760,100
Montana	29	1.1	764	0.8	26	22.4	29,267	210.0	0.5	7,242,483
Utah	13	0.5	559	0.6	43	20.9	37,426	198.1	0.4	15,237,923
Idaho	23	0.9	617	0.6	27	18.8	30,527	162.5	0.4	7,065,130
Delaware	9	0.4	279	0.3	31	13.3	47,502	133.7	0.3	14,851,111
Vermont	8	0.3	469	0.5	59	18.3	39,094	133.1	0.3	16,631,375
South Dakota	15	0.6	346	0.3	23	12.1	34,884	125.8	0.3	8,388,733
Rhode Island	7	0.3	267	0.3	38	12.0	44,944	124.5	0.3	17,782,000
North Dakota	19	0.7	302	0.3	16	11.5	38,086	104.2	0.2	5,482,421
Wyoming	22	0.9	193	0.2	9	7.1	36,606	75.0	0.2	3,409,364
West Virginia	37	1.4	500-999	-	-	(D)	-	(D)	-	-
Arizona	26	1.0	1000-2499	-	-	(D)	-	(D)	-	-
Hawaii	12	0.5	500-999	-	-	(D)	-	(D)	-	-
Alaska	7	0.3	250-499	-	-	(D)	-	(D)	-	-
D.C.	6	0.2	100-249	-	-	(D)	-	(D)	-	-

Source: 2002 *Economic Census*. The states are in descending order of sales or establishments (if sales data are missing for the majority): The symbol (D) appears when data are withheld to prevent disclosure of competitive information. States marked with (D) are sorted by number of establishments. A dash (-) indicates that the data element cannot be calculated. Shaded *states* on the state map indicate those states which have proportionately greater representation in the industry than would be indicated by the states population; the ratio is based on total sales or number of establishments. Shaded *regions* indicate where the industry is regionally most concentrated.

NAICS 424820 - WINE AND DISTILLED ALCOHOLIC BEVERAGE MERCHANT WHOLESALERS*

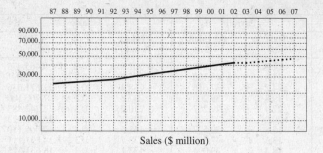

Sales ($ million)

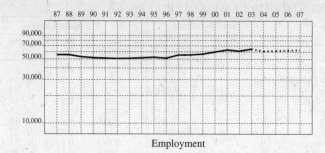

Employment

GENERAL STATISTICS

Year	Establishments (number)	Employment (number)	Payroll ($ million)	Sales ($ million)	Employees per Establishment (number)	Sales per Establishment ($)	Payroll per Employee ($)
1987	1,901	55,719	1,534.7	25,144.6	29.3	13,227,038.4	27,543.6
1988	1,801	55,706	1,630.3	25,692.5 e	30.9	14,265,685.7	29,266.1
1989	1,697	52,946	1,618.6	26,240.4 e	31.2	15,462,816.7	30,570.8
1990	1,653	51,782	1,692.8	26,788.3 e	31.3	16,205,868.1	32,690.9
1991	1,596	51,182	1,739.9	27,336.2 e	32.1	17,127,944.9	33,994.4
1992	1,856	50,735	1,817.8	27,884.1	27.3	15,023,760.8	35,829.3
1993	1,757	51,027	1,904.2	29,248.5 e	29.0	16,646,841.2	37,317.5
1994	1,779	51,684	1,947.3	30,612.9 e	29.1	17,207,925.8	37,677.0
1995	1,783	52,481	2,043.9	31,977.2 e	29.4	17,934,492.4	38,945.5
1996	1,719 e	51,270 e	2,073.5 e	33,341.6 e	29.8 e	19,395,927.9 e	40,442.8 e
1997	1,837	55,393	2,358.5	34,706.0	30.2	18,892,759.9	42,577.6
1998	1,837	55,568	2,490.1	36,284.0 e	30.2	19,751,769.2	44,811.8
1999	1,844	56,717	2,755.1	37,862.0 e	30.8	20,532,538.0	48,576.3
2000	1,842	59,880	3,021.0	39,440.0 e	32.5	21,411,509.2	50,450.6
2001	1,853	63,050	3,263.3	41,018.0 e	34.0	22,135,995.7	51,757.5
2002	1,838	61,258	3,192.0	42,596.0	33.3	23,175,190.4	52,107.5
2003	1,847	64,475	3,508.8	42,463.9 p	34.9	23,057,348.4 p	54,420.4
2004	1,851 p	60,970 p	3,380.7 p	43,664.2 p	32.9 p	23,649,403.6 p	55,735.2 p
2005	1,858 p	61,595 p	3,504.1 p	44,864.6 p	33.1 p	24,241,458.8 p	57,424.9 p
2006	1,865 p	62,220 p	3,627.5 p	46,065.0 p	33.4 p	24,833,514.0 p	59,114.5 p
2007	1,871 p	62,845 p	3,750.9 p	47,265.3 p	33.6 p	25,425,569.3 p	60,804.2 p

Sources: *Economic Census of the United States*, 1987, 1992, 1997, and 2002. Establishment counts, employment, and payroll are from *County Business Patterns* for non-Census years. Values followed by a 'p' are projections by the editors. Sales data for non-Census years are extrapolations, marked by 'e'. Data are the most recent available at this level of detail.

INDICES OF CHANGE

Year	Establishments (number)	Employment (number)	Payroll ($ million)	Sales ($ million)	Employees per Establishment (number)	Sales per Establishment ($)	Payroll per Employee ($)
1987	103.4	91.0	48.1	59.0	88.0	57.1	52.9
1992	101.0	82.8	56.9	65.5	82.0	64.8	68.8
1993	95.6	83.3	59.7	68.7 e	87.1	71.8	71.6
1994	96.8	84.4	61.0	71.9 e	87.4	74.3	72.3
1995	97.0	85.7	64.0	75.1 e	88.3	77.4	74.7
1996	93.5 e	83.7 e	65.0 e	78.3 e	89.5 e	83.7 e	77.6 e
1997	99.9	90.4	73.9	81.5	90.7	81.5	81.7
1998	99.9	90.7	78.0	85.2 e	90.7	85.2	86.0
1999	100.3	92.6	86.3	88.9 e	92.5	88.6	93.2
2000	100.2	97.8	94.6	92.6 e	97.6	92.4	96.8
2001	100.8	102.9	102.2	96.3 e	102.1	95.5	99.3
2002	100.0	100.0	100.0	100.0	100.0	100.0	100.0
2003	100.5	105.3	109.9	99.7 p	104.8	99.5 p	104.4
2004	100.7 p	99.5 p	105.9 p	102.5 p	98.8 p	102.0 p	107.0 p
2005	101.1 p	100.6 p	109.8 p	105.3 p	99.5 p	104.6 p	110.2 p
2006	101.4 p	101.6 p	113.6 p	108.1 p	100.2 p	107.2 p	113.4 p
2007	101.8 p	102.6 p	117.5 p	111.0 p	100.8 p	109.7 p	116.7 p

Sources: Same as General Statistics. The values shown reflect change from the base year, 2002. Values above 100 mean greater than 2002, values below 100 mean less than 2002, and a value of 100 in the 1987-2001 or 2003-2007 period means same as 2002. Values followed by a 'p' are projections by the editors; 'e' stands for extrapolation. Data are the most recent available at this level of detail.

SELECTED RATIOS

For 2002	Avg. of All Wholesale	Analyzed Industry	Index	For 2002	Avg. of All Wholesale	Analyzed Industry	Index
Employees per Establishment	15	33	223	Sales per Employee	791,325	695,354	88
Payroll per Establishment	626,122	1,736,670	277	Sales per Establishment	12,012,387	23,175,190	193
Payroll per Employee	41,161	52,107	127	Expenses per Establishment	na	na	na

Sources: Same as General Statistics. The 'Average of All' column, Wholesale or Retail, represents the average of the sector reported for the most recent complete year available. The Index shows the relationship between the Average and the Analyzed Industry. For example, 100 means that they are equal; 500 that the Analyzed Industry is five times the average; 50 means that the Analyzed Industry is half the national average. The abbreviation 'na' is used to show that data are 'not available'.

*Equivalent to SIC 5182.

LEADING COMPANIES Number shown: **65**   Total sales ($ mil): **16,453**   Total employment (000): **31.3**

Company Name	Address				CEO Name	Phone	Co. Type	Sales ($ mil)	Empl. (000)
Southern Wine & Spirits	1600 NW 163rd St	Miami	FL	33169	Harvey R. Chaplin	305-625-4171	R	5,400	8.0
Glazer's Wholesale Drug Inc.	PO Box 809013	Dallas	TX	75380	Jerry Cargill	972-702-0900	R	2,200	5.5
Young's Market Company L.L.C.	2164 N Batavia St	Orange	CA	92865	Charles Andrews	714-283-4933	R	1,400	1.8
National Distributing Company	PO Box 44127	Atlanta	GA	30336	Charlie Andrews	404-696-9440	R	1,360*	2.5
Block Distributing Company Inc.	6511 Tri County	Schertz	TX	78154	Eddie Block	210-224-7531	R	1,191*	0.4
Charmer Industries Inc.	50 48th St, Ste 19	Astoria	NY	11105	Steven M Drucker	718-726-2500	S	785*	1.5
Commonwealth Wine and Spirits	2300 Stanley Gault	Louisville	KY	40223	Vertner Smith III	502-254-8600	R	504*	0.2
Central European Distribution	1343 Main St	Sarasota	FL	34236	William V Carey	941-330-1558	P	429	1.9
General Beverage Sales Co.	PO Box 44326	Madison	WI	53744	Daniel Weinstein	608-271-1234	R	421*	0.5
Johnson Brothers Co.	1999 Shepard Rd	Saint Paul	MN	55116		651-649-5800	R	344*	1.1
Cost-U-Less Inc.	3633 136th Pl SE	Bellevue	WA	98006	David A Enger	425-945-0213	P	209	0.6
Columbia Distributing Co.	6840 N Cutter Cir	Portland	OR	97217	Edward L Maletis	503-289-9600	R	176*	0.6
Western Distributing Co.	PO Box 5542	Denver	CO	80217	Vieri Gaines	303-388-5755	R	160*	0.7
Major Brands Inc.	550 E 13th Ave	Kansas City	MO	64116	Robert Epstein	816-221-1070	R	153*	0.5
Mounthood Beverage Co.	3601 NW Yeon Ave	Portland	OR	97210	Richard Lytle	503-274-9990	R	130*	0.6
R and R Marketing L.L.C.	10 Patton Dr	West Caldwell	NJ	07006	Howard Jacobs	973-228-5100	R	126*	0.3
General Wholesale Co.	1271-A Tacoma Dr	Atlanta	GA	30318	William D Young Sr	404-351-3626	R	107*	0.3
RH Phillips-Hogue	26836 County 12A	Esparto	CA	95627	John Giguiere	530-662-3215	R	102*	0.3
Olinger Distributing Co.	5337 W 78th St	Indianapolis	IN	46268	Jim Oliver	317-876-1188	D	100*	0.4
D. Canale Beverages Inc.	45 E H Crump W	Memphis	TN	38106	Christopher W Canale	901-948-4543	R	87*	0.2
Badger Liquor Company Inc.	850 S Morris St	Fond du Lac	WI	54935	Ronald Sadoff	920-923-8160	R	58*	0.2
Odom Corp.	20415 72nd Ave S	Kent	WA	98032	John P Odom	253-437-3000	R	58*	0.5
Better Brands of Atlanta Inc.	755 NW Jefferson St	Atlanta	GA	30318		404-872-4731	R	53*	0.2
N.K.S. Distributors Inc.	PO Box 758	New Castle	DE	19720	James V Tigani Jr	302-322-1811	R	52*	0.2
Giglio Distributing Co.	PO Box 4046	Beaumont	TX	77704	JC Giglio	409-838-1654	R	51*	0.2
Windsor Vineyards	PO Box 368	Windsor	CA	95492	Kate Langford	707-836-5000	R	51*	0.2
Edison Liquor Corp.	PO Box 609	Brookfield	WI	53008	Dick Deutsch	262-821-0600	S	50*	0.1
Standard Beverage Corp.	PO Box 968	Wichita	KS	67201	L Rudd	316-838-7707	R	48*	0.2
Kramer Beverage Company Inc.	PO Box 470	Hammonton	NJ	08037	Charles W Kramer	609-704-7000	R	40*	0.1
Markstein Beverage Co.	PO Box 6902	San Marcos	CA	92079	Ken Markstein	760-744-9004	R	36*	0.1
Moon Distributors Inc.	2800 Vance St	Little Rock	AR	72206	Harry Hastings	501-375-8291	R	36*	0.1
Capital Beverage Co.	2424 Del Monte St	W. Sacramento	CA	95691	Kenneth Adamson	916-371-8164	R	35*	0.1
Delaware Importers Inc.	PO Box 271	New Castle	DE	19720	EJ Stegemeier	302-656-4487	R	35*	0.1
Sebastiani Vineyards	389 4th St E	Sonoma	CA	95476	Mary Cuneo	707-938-5532	R	34*	0.1
Commercial Distributing Co.	PO Box 1476	Westfield	MA	01086	Richard C Placek	413-562-9691	R	29*	<0.1
Brownforman Wines	4040 Civic Ctr Dr	San Rafael	CA	94903	Owsley Brown	415-444-7400	S	25*	<0.1
Goody-Goody Liquor Store Inc.	10301 Harry Hines	Dallas	TX	75220	Joe Jansen	214-350-5806	R	24*	0.2
J.W. Costello Beverage & S.W.	4370 S Valley View	Las Vegas	NV	89102	JW Costello	702-876-4000	R	23*	<0.1
Henry A. Fox Sales Co.	4494 36th St SE	Grand Rapids	MI	49512	Henry A Fox Jr	616-949-1210	R	21*	0.1
Fine Wine Brokers Inc.	4621 N Lincoln Ave	Chicago	IL	60625	Phil Bernstein		R	20*	<0.1
Savannah Distributing Inc.	PO Box 1388	Savannah	GA	31402	Henry Monsees	912-233-1167	R	20*	<0.1
Silver State Liquor and Wine	325 E Nugget Ave	Sparks	NV	89431		775-331-3400	S	20*	<0.1
Sterling Distributing Co.	4433 S 96th St	Omaha	NE	68127	Gene Pace	402-339-2300	R	20*	<0.1
Koerner Distributors Inc.	10074 Samuel Rd	Carterville	IL	62918	Paul Koerner	618-985-3767	R	19*	<0.1
Nackard, Fred Wholesale Liquor	PO Box 2182	Prescott	AZ	86302		928-445-7200	R	19*	<0.1
Ed Phillips and Sons Co.	PO Box 9095	Fargo	ND	58106		701-277-1499	S	16*	<0.1
V. Santoni and Co.	PO Box 1236	Woodland	CA	95776	Chuck Santoni	530-666-4447	R	16*	<0.1
Federal Wine and Liquor Co.	PO Box 519	Kearny	NJ	07032	Richard Leventhal	973-624-6444	S	15*	<0.1
J. Sosnick and Son Inc.	258 Littlefield Ave	S. San Francisco	CA	94080	Jeffrey Sosnick	650-952-2226	R	15*	<0.1
Vintwood International Ltd.	40 Prospect St	Huntington	NY	11743	Frank A Gentile	631-424-9777	R	15*	<0.1
Knapp Vineyard Winery	2770 County Rd 128	Romulus	NY	14541	Gene Pierce	607-869-9271	R	14*	<0.1
Mautino Distributing Company	500 N Richard St	Spring Valley	IL	61362	Tony Mautino	815-664-4311	R	13*	<0.1
Major Brands-Columbia	1502 Bus Loop 70W	Columbia	MO	65202		573-443-3169	D	12*	<0.1
Maggiore Wholesale	2927 Harrisburg N E	Canton	OH	44705	S V Maggiore Jr	330-454-7913	R	11*	<0.1
Pike Distributors Inc.	PO Box 465	Newberry	MI	49868	Stanley J Ketviris II	906-293-8611	R	11*	<0.1
Dwan and Company Inc.	PO Box 96	Torrington	CT	06790	William J Sweetman	860-489-3149	R	10*	<0.1
Rochester Liquor Corp.	155 Paragon Dr	Rochester	NY	14624		585-349-7700	S	10*	<0.1
City Beverage	1105 E Lafayette St	Bloomington	IL	61704	Robert R Wombacher	309-662-1373	R	9*	<0.1
Blach Distributing Co.	131 Main St	Elko	NV	89803	Patrick Blach	775-738-5147	R	8*	<0.1
Iron City Distributing Inc.	2670 Commercial	Mingo Junction	OH	43938	Michael Bellas	740-598-4171	S	5*	<0.1
Chatham Imports Inc.	257 Park Ave S	New York	NY	10010	Jo Magliocco	212-473-1100	R	4*	<0.1
877 Spirits Inc.	770 Middleneck Rd	Great Neck	NY	11024	Harvey Shofsky	516-504-8000	R	3*	<0.1
Winesellers Ltd.	9933 N Lawler Ave	Skokie	IL	60077	Yale Sager	847-679-0121	R	3*	<0.1
Boisset U.S.A.	650 5th St, Ste 403	San Francisco	CA	94107	Jean-Charles Boisset	415-979-0630	R	2*	<0.1
Erwin Distributing Co.	530 Monocacy Blvd	Frederick	MD	21701	Frank L Erwin	301-662-0372	R	1*	<0.1

Source: Ward's Business Directory of U.S. Private and Public Companies, Volumes 1 and 2, 2005. The company type code used is as follows: P - Public, R - Private, S - Subsidiary, D - Division, J - Joint Venture, A - Affiliate, G - Group. Sales are in millions of dollars, employees are in thousands. An asterisk (*) indicates an estimated sales volume. The symbol < stands for 'less than'. Company names and addresses are truncated, in some cases, to fit into the available space.

OCCUPATIONS EMPLOYED BY BEER, WINE, & DISTILLED ALCOHOLIC BEVERAGE WHOLESALE

Occupation	% of Total 2004	Change to 2014	Occupation	% of Total 2004	Change to 2014
Sales reps, wholesale & manufacturing, exc tech	23.3	11.9	General & operations managers	2.1	10.7
Truck drivers, heavy & tractor-trailer	9.1	11.9	Sales managers	2.1	12.6
Laborers & freight, stock, & material movers, hand	8.7	0.7	First-line supervisors/managers of transporation workers	1.7	11.9
Driver/sales workers	8.1	11.6	Office clerks, general	1.7	-0.4
Truck drivers, light or delivery services	5.9	11.8	Bookkeeping, accounting, & auditing clerks	1.5	0.7
Industrial truck & tractor operators	5.7	0.7	Shipping, receiving, & traffic clerks	1.1	1.3
First-line supervisors/managers of non-retail sales work	4.1	3.4	Executive secretaries & administrative assistants	1.1	6.1
Merchandise displayers & window trimmers	2.2	11.5	Demonstrators & product promoters	1.1	7.6
Stock clerks & order fillers	2.2	-14.3	First-line supervisors/managers of helpers & laborers	1.0	11.9

Source: Industry-Occupation Matrix, Bureau of Labor Statistics. These data are reported based on 4-digit NAICS categories but have been matched to corresponding 6-digit NAICS industry codes. The change reported for each occupation to the year 2014 is a percent of growth or decline as estimated by the Bureau of Labor Statistics. The abbreviation nec stands for 'not elsewhere classified.'

LOCATION BY STATE AND REGIONAL CONCENTRATION

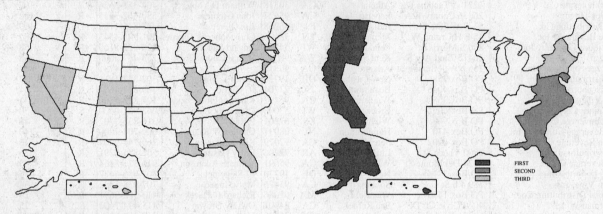

FIRST
SECOND
THIRD

INDUSTRY DATA BY STATE

State	Establishments Total (number)	% of U.S.	Employment Total (number)	% of U.S.	Per Estab.	Payroll Total ($ mil.)	Per Empl. ($)	Sales Total ($ mil.)	% of U.S.	Per Estab. ($)
California	308	17.4	8,663	14.0	28	533.7	61,610	7,497.9	17.4	24,343,935
New York	178	10.1	5,723	9.3	32	381.4	66,649	6,182.7	14.3	34,734,017
Florida	107	6.0	5,537	9.0	52	307.7	55,565	3,768.0	8.7	35,215,336
Illinois	83	4.7	4,556	7.4	55	211.7	46,473	3,140.2	7.3	37,834,253
Texas	96	5.4	3,650	5.9	38	162.5	44,509	2,324.6	5.4	24,214,562
Massachusetts	45	2.5	1,947	3.2	43	112.2	57,635	1,805.8	4.2	40,128,956
New Jersey	65	3.7	2,507	4.1	39	158.3	63,133	1,667.9	3.9	25,659,262
Georgia	48	2.7	2,040	3.3	43	113.6	55,695	1,346.1	3.1	28,044,375
Colorado	38	2.1	1,365	2.2	36	69.0	50,555	1,133.4	2.6	29,827,500
Ohio	38	2.1	1,393	2.3	37	54.7	39,277	984.3	2.3	25,902,632
Maryland	45	2.5	1,154	1.9	26	53.9	46,688	798.3	1.8	17,740,889
Louisiana	25	1.4	1,641	2.7	66	65.6	39,972	790.6	1.8	31,624,600
Minnesota	33	1.9	992	1.6	30	53.6	53,987	753.6	1.7	22,835,485
Wisconsin	30	1.7	1,353	2.2	45	58.9	43,512	610.5	1.4	20,350,533
Virginia	43	2.4	1,193	1.9	28	53.7	45,009	582.2	1.3	13,540,605
Nevada	15	0.8	814	1.3	54	58.6	71,985	556.6	1.3	37,105,000
Missouri	24	1.4	1,049	1.7	44	44.2	42,133	535.6	1.2	22,315,208
South Carolina	19	1.1	897	1.5	47	39.1	43,603	456.0	1.1	23,997,579
North Carolina	61	3.4	1,525	2.5	25	55.0	36,086	432.6	1.0	7,091,541
Tennessee	21	1.2	729	1.2	35	40.3	55,244	414.7	1.0	19,745,905
Kansas	14	0.8	549	0.9	39	20.5	37,257	367.0	0.8	26,211,857
Kentucky	15	0.8	475	0.8	32	22.9	48,196	298.6	0.7	19,905,667
Hawaii	16	0.9	427	0.7	27	21.6	50,546	270.2	0.6	16,887,000
Oklahoma	16	0.9	324	0.5	20	12.1	37,306	269.8	0.6	16,859,625
Oregon	32	1.8	792	1.3	25	31.0	39,177	250.1	0.6	7,815,844
Alabama	28	1.6	775	1.3	28	31.6	40,726	240.0	0.6	8,572,250
D.C.	14	0.8	381	0.6	27	18.9	49,604	198.8	0.5	14,201,571
Pennsylvania	47	2.7	503	0.8	11	20.6	40,950	194.4	0.4	4,137,064
Rhode Island	14	0.8	271	0.4	19	12.6	46,399	192.2	0.4	13,728,357
Arkansas	6	0.3	330	0.5	55	12.7	38,345	164.5	0.4	27,413,500
Nebraska	5	0.3	291	0.5	58	11.6	39,983	128.0	0.3	25,591,400
Iowa	16	0.9	282	0.5	18	9.1	32,170	86.2	0.2	5,385,187
Maine	6	0.3	134	0.2	22	5.1	38,358	80.4	0.2	13,406,500

Continued on next page.

INDUSTRY DATA BY STATE - Continued

State	Establishments Total (number)	% of U.S.	Employment Total (number)	% of U.S.	Per Estab.	Payroll Total ($ mil.)	Per Empl. ($)	Sales Total ($ mil.)	% of U.S.	Per Estab. ($)
Idaho	10	0.6	168	0.3	17	5.9	35,018	44.4	0.1	4,436,000
Vermont	3	0.2	127	0.2	42	7.0	55,386	31.3	0.1	10,438,333
Montana	5	0.3	21	-	4	0.4	20,048	6.5	-	1,306,800
New Hampshire	5	0.3	12	-	2	0.4	34,250	2.6	-	510,600
Michigan	41	2.3	1000-2499	-	-	(D)	-	(D)	-	-
Washington	39	2.2	1000-2499	-	-	(D)	-	(D)	-	-
Connecticut	32	1.8	1000-2499	-	-	(D)	-	(D)	-	-
Arizona	19	1.1	1000-2499	-	-	(D)	-	(D)	-	-
Indiana	15	0.8	500-999	-	-	(D)	-	(D)	-	-
New Mexico	12	0.7	250-499	-	-	(D)	-	(D)	-	-
West Virginia	10	0.6	100-249	-	-	(D)	-	(D)	-	-
Delaware	6	0.3	100-249	-	-	(D)	-	(D)	-	-
Mississippi	6	0.3	100-249	-	-	(D)	-	(D)	-	-
South Dakota	6	0.3	100-249	-	-	(D)	-	(D)	-	-
North Dakota	4	0.2	100-249	-	-	(D)	-	(D)	-	-
Alaska	3	0.2	100-249	-	-	(D)	-	(D)	-	-
Utah	2	0.1	20-99	-	-	(D)	-	(D)	-	-
Wyoming	2	0.1	20-99	-	-	(D)	-	(D)	-	-

Source: 2002 Economic Census. The states are in descending order of sales or establishments (if sales data are missing for the majority). The symbol (D) appears when data are withheld to prevent disclosure of competitive information. States marked with (D) are sorted by number of establishments. A dash (-) indicates that the data element cannot be calculated. Shaded states on the state map indicate those states which have proportionately greater representation in the industry than would be indicated by the states population; the ratio is based on total sales or number of establishments. Shaded regions indicate where the industry is regionally most concentrated.

NAICS 424910 - FARM SUPPLIES MERCHANT WHOLESALERS

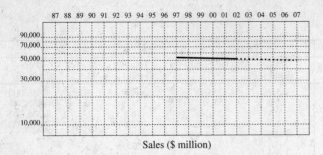

Sales ($ million)

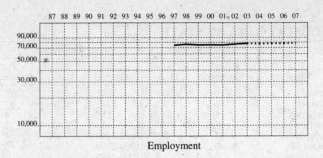

Employment

GENERAL STATISTICS

Year	Establishments (number)	Employment (number)	Payroll ($ million)	Sales ($ million)	Employees per Establishment (number)	Sales per Establishment ($)	Payroll per Employee ($)
1987	-	-	-	-	-	-	-
1988	-	-	-	-	-	-	-
1989	-	-	-	-	-	-	-
1990	-	-	-	-	-	-	-
1991	-	-	-	-	-	-	-
1992	-	-	-	-	-	-	-
1993	-	-	-	-	-	-	-
1994	-	-	-	-	-	-	-
1995	-	-	-	-	-	-	-
1996	-	-	-	-	-	-	-
1997	7,378	74,508	2,562.5	53,634.3	10.1	7,269,490.4	34,392.3
1998	7,425	76,223	2,595.9	53,222.6 e	10.3	7,168,024.2	34,056.6
1999	7,313	75,012	2,611.5	52,810.9 e	10.3	7,221,504.2	34,814.4
2000	7,158	75,258	2,732.4	52,399.1 e	10.5	7,320,360.4	36,306.7
2001	6,885	74,868	2,798.2	51,987.4 e	10.9	7,550,823.5	37,375.7
2002	7,392	76,587	2,855.3	51,575.7	10.4	6,977,232.1	37,281.8
2003	7,628	77,780	3,062.7	51,164.0 p	10.2	7,229,835.4 p	39,376.7
2004	7,348 p	77,234 p	3,060.7 p	50,752.3 p	10.5 p	7,223,720.1 p	39,652.7 p
2005	7,357 p	77,605 p	3,139.5 p	50,340.5 p	10.6 p	7,217,604.7 p	40,508.6 p
2006	7,366 p	77,977 p	3,218.3 p	49,928.8 p	10.6 p	7,211,489.4 p	41,364.5 p
2007	7,375 p	78,348 p	3,297.0 p	49,517.1 p	10.7 p	7,205,374.0 p	42,220.4 p

Source: *Economic Census of the United States*, 1997 and 2002. Establishment counts, employment, and payroll are from *County Business Patterns* for non-Census years. This is a newly defined industry. Data for prior years are unavailable at the time of publication but may become available over time. Values followed by 'p' are projections by the editors. Sales data for non-Census years are extrapolations, marked by 'e'.

INDICES OF CHANGE

Year	Establishments (number)	Employment (number)	Payroll ($ million)	Sales ($ million)	Employees per Establishment (number)	Sales per Establishment ($)	Payroll per Employee ($)
1987	-	-	-	-	-	-	-
1992	-	-	-	-	-	-	-
1993	-	-	-	-	-	-	-
1994	-	-	-	-	-	-	-
1995	-	-	-	-	-	-	-
1996	-	-	-	-	-	-	-
1997	99.8	97.3	89.7	104.0	97.1	104.2	92.2
1998	100.4	99.5	90.9	103.2 e	99.0	102.7	91.3
1999	98.9	97.9	91.5	102.4 e	99.0	103.5	93.4
2000	96.8	98.3	95.7	101.6 e	101.0	104.9	97.4
2001	93.1	97.8	98.0	100.8 e	104.8	108.2	100.3
2002	100.0	100.0	100.0	100.0	100.0	100.0	100.0
2003	103.2	101.6	107.3	99.2 p	98.0	103.6 p	105.6
2004	99.4 p	100.8 p	107.2 p	98.4 p	101.4 p	103.5 p	106.4 p
2005	99.5 p	101.3 p	110.0 p	97.6 p	101.7 p	103.4 p	108.7 p
2006	99.7 p	101.8 p	112.7 p	96.8 p	102.1 p	103.4 p	111.0 p
2007	99.8 p	102.3 p	115.5 p	96.0 p	102.5 p	103.3 p	113.2 p

Sources: Same as General Statistics. The values shown reflect change from the base year, 2002. Values above 100 mean greater than 2002, values below 100 mean less than 2002, and a value of 100 in the 1987-2001 or 2003-2007 period means same as 2002. Values followed by a 'p' are projections by the editors; 'e' stands for extrapolation. Data are the most recent available at this level of detail.

SELECTED RATIOS

For 2002	Avg. of All Wholesale	Analyzed Industry	Index	For 2002	Avg. of All Wholesale	Analyzed Industry	Index
Employees per Establishment	15	10	69	Sales per Employee	791,325	673,426	85
Payroll per Establishment	626,122	386,269	62	Sales per Establishment	12,012,387	6,977,232	58
Payroll per Employee	41,161	37,282	91	Expenses per Establishment	na	na	na

Sources: Same as General Statistics. The 'Average of All' column, Wholesale or Retail, represents the average of the sector reported for the most recent complete year available. The Index shows the relationship between the Average and the Analyzed Industry. For example, 100 means that they are equal; 500 that the Analyzed Industry is five times the average; 50 means that the Analyzed Industry is half the national average. The abbreviation 'na' is used to show that data are 'not available'.

LEADING COMPANIES   Number shown: **75'**   Total sales ($ mil): **27,596**   Total employment (000): **30.9**

Company Name	Address				CEO Name	Phone	Co. Type	Sales ($ mil)	Empl. (000)
Transammonia Inc.	350 Park Ave	New York	NY	10022	Ronald P. Stanton	212-223-3200	R	3,967	0.3
Agriliance L.L.C.	PO Box 64089	St. Paul	MN	55164	George Thornton	651-451-5000	J	3,500	3.0
Scoular Co.	9401 Indian Creek	Overland Park	KS	66210	Marshall E Faith	913-338-1474	R	2,000	0.3
ADM Grain	4666 Faries Pkwy	Decatur	IL	62525	Lew Batchelder	217-424-5200	S	1,662*	1.2
Southern States Cooperative Inc.	PO Box 26234	Richmond	VA	23260	Tom Scribner	804-281-1000	R	1,516	5.7
Wilbur-Ellis Co.	345 California St	San Francisco	CA	94104		415-772-4000	R	1,366	2.3
Central Garden and Pet Co.	1340 Treat Blvd	Walnut Creek	CA	94597	William E Brown	925-948-4000	P	1,270	4.4
Andersons Inc.	PO Box 119	Maumee	OH	43537	Michael J Anderson	419-893-5050	P	1,247	2.9
North Pacific Group Inc.	PO Box 3915	Portland	OR	97208		503-231-1166	R	1,227	0.8
John Taylor Fertilizers Co.	PO Box 15289	Sacramento	CA	95851	Jeffrey Taylor	916-991-4451	R	1,220*	<0.1
Countrymark Cooperative Inc.	225 SE St, Ste 144	Indianapolis	IN	46202	Charlie Smith		R	1,083*	0.9
MFA Inc.	125 Lexington Ave	Sweet Springs	MO	65351		660-335-6355	D	760*	<0.1
Royster-Clark Inc.	1251 Av Americas	New York	NY	10020	Francis P Jenkins, Jr	212-332-2965	R	746*	2.6
Frontier Cooperative Co.	PO Box 379	David City	NE	68632		402-367-3019	R	593*	0.1
Progressive Farmers Coop.	1221 Grant St	De Pere	WI	54115	Frank Hutjens	920-336-6449	R	473*	<0.1
Johnson Cooperative Grain Co.	PO Box 280	Johnson	KS	67855	Steve Arnold	620-492-6210	R	336*	<0.1
Heritage FS Inc.	PO Box 339	Gilman	IL	60938		815-265-4751	R	232*	<0.1
Horizon	5214 S 30th St	Phoenix	AZ	85040	Bill Hayes	602-276-7700	R	213*	0.4
Watonwan Farm Services	PO Box 68	Truman	MN	56088	Ed Bosanko		R	208*	0.3
Ag Services of America Inc.	PO Box 668	Cedar Falls	IA	50613	Henry C Jungling Jr	319-277-0261	S	198	0.2
Wheeler Brothers Grain Inc.	PO Box 29	Watonga	OK	73772	Mike Mahoney	580-623-7223	R	180*	0.1
Ag Partners L.L.C.	PO Box 38	Albert City	IA	50510	Troy Upah	712-843-2291	J	175*	0.1
A.L. Gilbert Co.	PO Box 38	Oakdale	CA	95361	Robert T Gilbert	209-847-1721	R	158*	0.2
Estes Inc.	PO Box 8287	Wichita Falls	TX	76307		940-766-0163	R	144*	<0.1
Fruit Growers Supply Co.	14130 Riverside Dr	Sherman Oaks	CA	91423	Nazir Khan	818-986-6480	R	135*	0.2
Noble Americas Corp.	333 Ludlow St	Stamford	CT	06902	Vicente Del Castillo	203-324-8555	R	129*	<0.1
Abell Corp.	PO Box 8056	Monroe	LA	71211	Dixon Abell	318-343-7565	R	125*	0.2
Madison Farmers Elevator Co.	PO Box 228	Madison	SD	57042		605-256-4584	R	119*	<0.1
Perryton Equity Exchange	PO Box 889	Perryton	TX	79070	Doug Mitchell	806-435-4016	R	110*	0.1
Wilco Farmers	PO Box 258	Mount Angel	OR	97362	Michael Jamison	503-845-6122	R	100*	<0.1
Menomonie Farmers Union Coop.	PO Box 438	Menomonie	WI	54751	Gerry Hoag	715-232-6200	R	89*	0.1
Dairyland Seed Company Inc.	PO Box 958	West Bend	WI	53095	Steven Strachota	262-338-0163	R	88*	0.1
Shipman Elevator Co.	PO Box 349	Shipman	IL	62685		618-729-3228	R	85*	0.1
DeLong Company Inc.	PO Box 552	Clinton	WI	53525	David D DeLong	608-676-2255	R	80*	0.1
Farmers Britt Co-Op	PO Box 156	Britt	IA	50423	Ron Eisenman	641-843-3878	R	79*	<0.1
Frenchman Valley Farmer's	PO Box 578	Imperial	NE	69033	Max Kaiser	308-882-3200	R	78*	0.2
Minn-Kota Ag Products Inc.	PO Box 175	Breckenridge	MN	56520	George M Schuler III	218-643-8464	R	78*	<0.1
New Vision Coop.	PO Box 877	Worthington	MN	56187	Ron Jorgenson	507-376-4113	R	73*	<0.1
Greenway Co-Operative Service	PO Box 6878	Rochester	MN	55903		507-289-4086	R	67*	<0.1
Gibson Farmers Coop.	PO Box 497	Trenton	TN	38382	Larry Cochran	731-855-1896	R	65*	<0.1
Metamora Grain	PO Box G	Metamora	OH	43540		419-644-4711	R	63*	<0.1
Osborne Distributing Company	PO Box 2100	Vernon	TX	76385	Lloyd Osborne	940-552-7711	R	63*	0.1
AgriPride F.S. Inc.	PO Box 329	Nashville	IL	62263	Randy Newcomb	618-327-3046	R	62*	0.1
Lucky Farmers Inc.	PO Box 217	Woodville	OH	43469	James Eckel	419-849-2711	R	62*	0.1
Ag-Valley Co-op.	PO Box 68	Edison	NE	68936	David Brown	308-927-3681	R	60*	<0.1
California Ammonia Co.	PO Box 280	French Camp	CA	95231		209-982-1000	R	59*	<0.1
Battle Creek Farmers Cooperative	PO Box 10	Battle Creek	NE	68715			R	58*	<0.1
S.K.H. Management Co.	PO Box 1500	Lititz	PA	17543	Paul W Stauffer	717-626-4771	R	57*	1.0
Sunray Coop.	PO Box 430	Sunray	TX	79086		806-948-4121	R	56*	<0.1
Stanislaus Farm Supply Co.	624 E Service Rd	Modesto	CA	95358	Anselmo Bettencourt	209-538-7070	R	50*	<0.1
Farmers Cooperative Association	428 Barnes Ave	Alva	OK	73717	Randy Schwerdtfeger	580-327-3854	R	49*	<0.1
Agrisource Inc.	PO Box 1000	Burley	ID	83318		208-678-2286	R	48*	<0.1
Farmers Cooperative Association	105 Jackson St	Jackson	MN	56143	Steve Glidden	507-847-4160	R	47*	<0.1
Fasco Mills Company Inc.	PO Box 170	Mendota	IL	61342	Curt Zimmerman	815-539-7491	R	47*	<0.1
Fessenden Cooperative Association	PO Box 126	Fessenden	ND	58438		701-547-3291	R	46*	<0.1
East Central Iowa Cooperative	PO Box 300	Hudson	IA	50643		319-988-3257	R	45*	<0.1
Mountain View Coop.	110 Main St W	Dutton	MT	59433		406-476-3411	R	45*	<0.1
Moyer and Son Inc.	PO Box 64198	Souderton	PA	18964	John Moyer	215-723-6000	R	45*	0.3
Northwest Wholesale Inc.	PO Box 1649	Wenatchee	WA	98807		509-662-2141	R	45*	<0.1
AGP Grain Cooperative	770 County Rd DD	Farwell	TX	79325		806-825-2565	R	43*	<0.1
Boettcher Enterprises Inc.	PO Box 486	Beloit	KS	67420	Jerry Boettcher	785-738-5781	R	43*	<0.1
Country Pride Cooperative	648 W 2nd St	Winner	SD	57580	Carl Dickinson	605-842-2711	R	43*	0.2
New Horizon FS Inc.	PO Box 31	Tipton	IA	52772	Robert Hartman	563-886-2104	R	43*	0.1
Twomey Co.	PO Box 158	Smithshire	IL	61478	J Craig Twomey	309-325-7100	R	43*	<0.1
Anthony Farmers Cooperative	PO Box 111	Anthony	KS	67003	Jerry Miller	620-842-5181	R	42*	<0.1
American Pride Coop.	55 W Bromley Ln	Brighton	CO	80601	Al Shivley	303-659-1230	R	39*	0.2
Frontier FS Coop.	PO Box 359	Jefferson	WI	53549	Perry Goetsch	920-674-7000	R	38*	<0.1
Heartland Co-op	PO Box 73	Trumbull	NE	68980		402-743-2381	R	38*	<0.1
Kettle-Lakes Coop.	PO Box 305	Random Lake	WI	53075		920-994-4316	R	38*	<0.1
Farmers Cooperative Co.	304 Ellsworth St	Dows	IA	50071		515-852-4136	R	36*	<0.1
Illini F.S. Inc.	1509 E University St	Urbana	IL	61802	John Reifsteck	217-384-8300	R	36*	0.1
Frontier Trading Inc.	PO Box 460	Roff	OK	74865	Gene Garrett	580-456-7732	R	34*	<0.1
V.H. Associates Inc.	PO Box 380	Cerro Gordo	IL	61818	Roger Oliver	217-677-2131	R	34*	<0.1
Agland Co-Op Inc.	364 Lisbon St	Canfield	OH	44406		330-533-5551	R	33*	0.1
Wright and Wilhelmy Inc.	11005 E St	Omaha	NE	68137	Darcy Michalek	402-593-0600	R	33*	<0.1

Source: Ward's Business Directory of U.S. Private and Public Companies, Volumes 1 and 2, 2005. The company type code used is as follows: P - Public, R - Private, S - Subsidiary, D - Division, J - Joint Venture, A - Affiliate, G - Group. Sales are in millions of dollars, employees are in thousands. An asterisk (*) indicates an estimated sales volume. The symbol < stands for 'less than'. Company names and addresses are truncated, in some cases, to fit into the available space.

OCCUPATIONS EMPLOYED BY MISCELLANEOUS NONDURABLE GOODS WHOLESALE

Occupation	% of Total 2004	Change to 2014	Occupation	% of Total 2004	Change to 2014
Sales reps, wholesale & manufacturing, exc tech	12.9	11.6	Customer service representatives	2.2	14.3
Laborers & freight, stock, & material movers, hand	9.3	- 0.5	Retail salespersons	2.2	11.6
Truck drivers, light or delivery services	5.6	11.3	Driver/sales workers	2.0	11.2
Stock clerks & order fillers	5.2	-14.5	Team assemblers	1.7	11.6
Truck drivers, heavy & tractor-trailer	4.0	11.6	Industrial truck & tractor operators	1.6	11.6
Shipping, receiving, & traffic clerks	3.6	1.1	First-line supervisors/managers of office workers	1.5	1.2
Farmworkers & laborers, crop, nursery, & greenhouse	3.3	11.3	First-line supervisors/managers of non-retail sales work	1.5	3.2
Office clerks, general	2.8	-0.6	Sales reps, wholesale & manufacturing, tech	1.4	11.6
Bookkeeping, accounting, & auditing clerks	2.8	0.5	Secretaries, except legal, medical, & executive	1.4	-6.0
Packers & packagers, hand	2.7	11.6	Cashiers, except gaming	1.3	0.5
General & operations managers	2.3	10.5	Order clerks	1.3	-27.7

Source: Industry-Occupation Matrix, Bureau of Labor Statistics. These data are reported based on 4-digit NAICS categories but have been matched to corresponding 6-digit NAICS industry codes. The change reported for each occupation to the year 2014 is a percent of growth or decline as estimated by the Bureau of Labor Statistics. The abbreviation nec stands for 'not elsewhere classified.'

LOCATION BY STATE AND REGIONAL CONCENTRATION

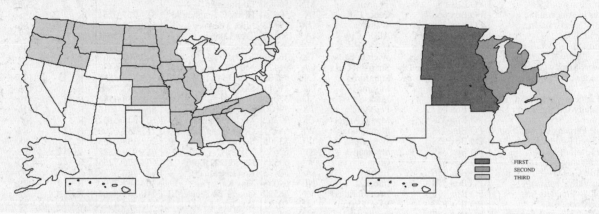

INDUSTRY DATA BY STATE

State	Establishments Total (number)	% of U.S.	Employment Total (number)	% of U.S.	Per Estab.	Payroll Total ($ mil.)	Per Empl. ($)	Sales Total ($ mil.)	% of U.S.	Per Estab. ($)
Illinois	485	6.3	5,404	6.9	11	221.4	40,965	5,494.1	10.2	11,327,946
California	626	8.1	8,862	11.2	14	371.4	41,912	4,912.1	9.1	7,846,859
Iowa	409	5.3	5,129	6.5	13	193.0	37,637	3,973.0	7.4	9,713,861
New York	208	2.7	1,579	2.0	8	70.9	44,877	2,889.9	5.4	13,893,837
Tennessee	123	1.6	2,008	2.5	16	88.0	43,835	2,733.6	5.1	22,224,146
Florida	368	4.8	2,742	3.5	7	100.6	36,693	2,510.4	4.7	6,821,842
Georgia	281	3.7	2,645	3.4	9	88.6	33,481	2,029.3	3.8	7,221,804
Minnesota	304	4.0	2,684	3.4	9	99.4	37,031	1,989.0	3.7	6,542,862
Michigan	153	2.0	1,681	2.1	11	75.6	44,982	1,911.0	3.6	12,490,118
Texas	506	6.6	3,975	5.0	8	129.9	32,684	1,887.0	3.5	3,729,279
Kansas	197	2.6	1,865	2.4	9	62.9	33,746	1,836.8	3.4	9,323,914
Nebraska	247	3.2	2,443	3.1	10	86.1	35,235	1,824.9	3.4	7,388,178
North Carolina	193	2.5	2,648	3.4	14	133.9	50,584	1,754.2	3.3	9,089,067
Missouri	258	3.4	3,024	3.8	12	103.9	34,356	1,645.2	3.1	6,376,605
Ohio	275	3.6	2,652	3.4	10	108.4	40,862	1,331.0	2.5	4,839,822
Washington	214	2.8	2,125	2.7	10	73.5	34,600	1,211.8	2.3	5,662,762
Indiana	302	3.9	2,568	3.3	9	83.3	32,427	1,200.0	2.2	3,973,533
Pennsylvania	195	2.5	2,361	3.0	12	76.9	32,554	1,131.2	2.1	5,801,179
Wisconsin	228	3.0	2,248	2.9	10	81.0	36,015	959.2	1.8	4,207,066
Arkansas	132	1.7	1,469	1.9	11	46.1	31,395	785.7	1.5	5,952,636
Oregon	128	1.7	1,545	2.0	12	52.5	33,992	778.9	1.4	6,085,461
New Jersey	101	1.3	1,148	1.5	11	47.4	41,249	765.1	1.4	7,575,317
Colorado	112	1.5	913	1.2	8	31.9	34,900	718.2	1.3	6,412,500
Idaho	138	1.8	1,738	2.2	13	59.4	34,190	682.8	1.3	4,948,058
North Dakota	104	1.4	867	1.1	8	29.4	33,943	586.9	1.1	5,643,375
Mississippi	105	1.4	1,353	1.7	13	38.1	28,141	584.6	1.1	5,567,724
Alabama	91	1.2	959	1.2	11	30.6	31,954	552.4	1.0	6,069,802
Kentucky	143	1.9	1,427	1.8	10	39.1	27,416	535.8	1.0	3,746,741
Oklahoma	122	1.6	764	1.0	6	23.3	30,503	480.4	0.9	3,937,967
Louisiana	115	1.5	1,120	1.4	10	36.2	32,339	469.4	0.9	4,082,122
South Dakota	111	1.4	808	1.0	7	25.7	31,771	461.9	0.9	4,161,189

Continued on next page.

INDUSTRY DATA BY STATE - Continued

State	Establishments		Employment			Payroll		Sales		
	Total (number)	% of U.S.	Total (number)	% of U.S.	Per Estab.	Total ($ mil.)	Per Empl. ($)	Total ($ mil.)	% of U.S.	Per Estab. ($)
Virginia	104	1.4	1,135	1.4	11	36.2	31,901	437.5	0.8	4,206,904
Maryland	59	0.8	741	0.9	13	29.7	40,069	322.3	0.6	5,462,169
Massachusetts	52	0.7	588	0.7	11	23.1	39,347	316.0	0.6	6,077,615
South Carolina	94	1.2	681	0.9	7	20.8	30,526	300.4	0.6	3,195,691
Montana	69	0.9	466	0.6	7	12.1	26,017	195.2	0.4	2,829,391
Hawaii	20	0.3	327	0.4	16	13.1	40,214	173.0	0.3	8,651,300
Utah	31	0.4	214	0.3	7	7.8	36,252	96.4	0.2	3,110,935
New Mexico	32	0.4	194	0.2	6	5.5	28,397	74.0	0.1	2,313,594
Vermont	19	0.2	114	0.1	6	4.5	39,465	65.1	0.1	3,424,895
Nevada	21	0.3	101	0.1	5	3.6	35,416	52.1	0.1	2,480,286
Maine	18	0.2	115	0.1	6	3.8	33,391	42.5	0.1	2,360,278
Arizona	84	1.1	500-999	-	-	(D)	-	(D)	-	-
Connecticut	36	0.5	250-499	-	-	(D)	-	(D)	-	-
Delaware	21	0.3	100-249	-	-	(D)	-	(D)	-	-
New Hampshire	14	0.2	20-99	-	-	(D)	-	(D)	-	-
West Virginia	14	0.2	20-99	-	-	(D)	-	(D)	-	-
Wyoming	14	0.2	20-99	-	-	(D)	-	(D)	-	-
Rhode Island	10	0.1	20-99	-	-	(D)	-	(D)	-	-
Alaska	1	-	0-19	-	-	(D)	-	(D)	-	-
D.C.	1	-	0-19	-	-	(D)	-	(D)	-	-

Source: 2002 *Economic Census*. The states are in descending order of sales or establishments (if sales data are missing for the majority). The symbol (D) appears when data are withheld to prevent disclosure of competitive information. States marked with (D) are sorted by number of establishments. A dash (-) indicates that the data element cannot be calculated. Shaded *states* on the state map indicate those states which have proportionately greater representation in the industry than would be indicated by the states population; the ratio is based on total sales or number of establishments. Shaded *regions* indicate where the industry is regionally most concentrated.

NAICS 424920 - BOOK, PERIODICAL AND NEWSPAPER MERCHANT WHOLESALERS*

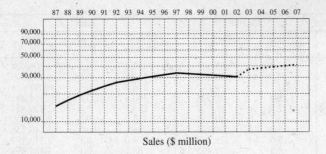

Sales ($ million)

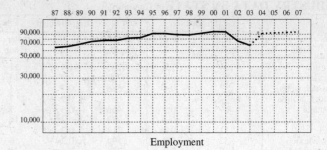

Employment

GENERAL STATISTICS

Year	Establishments (number)	Employment (number)	Payroll ($ million)	Sales ($ million)	Employees per Establishment (number)	Sales per Establishment ($)	Payroll per Employee ($)
1987	3,935	64,837	1,367.9	14,695.6	16.5	3,734,587.0	21,097.5
1988	3,822	66,446	1,448.5	17,070.2 e	17.4	4,466,300.4	21,799.7
1989	3,621	70,297	1,654.0	19,444.9 e	19.4	5,370,035.9	23,528.7
1990	3,699	75,355	1,909.8	21,819.5 e	20.4	5,898,756.4	25,344.0
1991	3,827	77,392	1,955.5	24,194.2 e	20.2	6,321,975.4	25,267.5
1992	4,205	77,392	2,044.2	26,568.8	18.4	6,318,382.9	26,413.6
1993	4,220	81,794	2,293.8	27,981.1 e	19.4	6,630,592.4	28,043.6
1994	4,233	82,834	2,324.2	29,393.4 e	19.6	6,943,869.6	28,058.5
1995	4,351	91,746	2,643.1	30,805.7 e	21.1	7,080,142.5	28,808.9
1996	4,374 e	91,607 e	2,722.0 e	32,218.0 e	20.9	7,365,797.9 e	29,713.9 e
1997	4,265	89,309	2,618.1	33,630.3	20.9	7,885,181.7	29,315.1
1998	4,195	88,774	2,835.2	33,004.3 e	21.2	7,867,537.5	31,937.3
1999	4,105	92,201	3,287.8	32,378.3 e	22.5	7,887,537.1	35,659.0
2000	3,998	96,303	3,624.9	31,752.4 e	24.1	7,942,061.0	37,640.7
2001	3,883	95,795	3,428.2	31,126.4 e	24.7	8,016,064.9	35,786.4
2002	3,466	76,129	2,406.5	30,500.4	22.0	8,799,884.6	31,610.8
2003	3,308	68,329	2,393.3	36,802.9 p	20.7	9,149,450.8 p	35,026.6
2004	3,902 p	91,943 p	3,355.1 p	37,922.5 p	23.6 p	9,427,851.5 p	37,447.4 p
2005	3,894 p	93,096 p	3,460.2 p	39,042.1 p	23.9 p	9,706,252.3 p	38,372.6 p
2006	3,887 p	94,250 p	3,565.3 p	40,161.7 p	24.3 p	9,984,653.1 p	39,297.7 p
2007	3,879 p	95,403 p	3,670.4 p	41,281.2 p	24.6 p	10,263,053.8 p	40,222.9 p

Sources: Economic Census of the United States, 1987, 1992, 1997, and 2002. Establishment counts, employment, and payroll are from *County Business Patterns* for non-Census years. Values followed by a 'p' are projections by the editors. Sales data for non-Census years are extrapolations, marked by 'e'. Data are the most recent available at this level of detail.

INDICES OF CHANGE

Year	Establishments (number)	Employment (number)	Payroll ($ million)	Sales ($ million)	Employees per Establishment (number)	Sales per Establishment ($)	Payroll per Employee ($)
1987	113.5	85.2	56.8	48.2	75.0	42.4	66.7
1992	121.3	101.7	84.9	87.1	83.6	71.8	83.6
1993	121.8	107.4	95.3	91.7 e	88.2	75.3	88.7
1994	122.1	108.8	96.6	96.4 e	89.1	78.9	88.8
1995	125.5	120.5	109.8	101.0 e	95.9	80.5	91.1
1996	126.2 e	120.3 e	113.1 e	105.6 e	95.0 e	83.7 e	94.0 e
1997	123.1	117.3	108.8	110.3	95.0	89.6	92.7
1998	121.0	116.6	117.8	108.2 e	96.4	89.4	101.0
1999	118.4	121.1	136.6	106.2 e	102.3	89.6	112.8
2000	115.3	126.5	150.6	104.1 e	109.5	90.3	119.1
2001	112.0	125.8	142.5	102.1 e	112.3	91.1	113.2
2002	100.0	100.0	100.0	100.0	100.0	100.0	100.0
2003	95.4	89.8	99.5	120.7 p	93.9	104.0 p	110.8
2004	112.6 p	120.8 p	139.4 p	124.3 p	107.2 p	107.1 p	118.5 p
2005	112.4 p	122.3 p	143.8 p	128.0 p	108.7 p	110.3 p	121.4 p
2006	112.1 p	123.8 p	148.2 p	131.7 p	110.3 p	113.5 p	124.3 p
2007	111.9 p	125.3 p	152.5 p	135.3 p	111.8 p	116.6 p	127.2 p

*Sources: Same as General Statistics. The values shown reflect change from the base year, 2002. Values above 100 mean greater than 2002, values below 100 mean less than 2002, and a value of 100 in the 1987-2001 or 2003-2007 period means same as 2002. Values followed by a 'p' are projections by the editors; 'e' stands for extrapolation. Data are the most recent available at this level of detail.

SELECTED RATIOS

For 2002	Avg. of All Wholesale	Analyzed Industry	Index	For 2002	Avg. of All Wholesale	Analyzed Industry	Index
Employees per Establishment	15	22	147	Sales per Employee	791,325	400,641	51
Payroll per Establishment	626,122	694,316	111	Sales per Establishment	12,012,387	8,799,885	73
Payroll per Employee	41,161	31,611	77	Expenses per Establishment	na	na	na

*Sources: Same as General Statistics. The 'Average of All' column, Wholesale or Retail, represents the average of the sector reported for the most recent complete year available. The Index shows the relationship between the Average and the Analyzed Industry. For example, 100 means that they are equal; 500 that the Analyzed Industry is five times the average; 50 means that the Analyzed Industry is half the national average. The abbreviation 'na' is used to show that data are 'not available'.

*Equivalent to SIC 5192.

LEADING COMPANIES   Number shown: **33**   Total sales ($ mil): **15,591**   Total employment (000): **39.6**

Company Name	Address				CEO Name	Phone	Co. Type	Sales ($ mil)	Empl. (000)
Express-Times	PO Box 391	Easton	PA	18044		610-258-7171	R	7,095*	0.4
Ingram Industries Inc.	PO Box 23049	Nashville	TN	37202	Martha R Ingram	615-298-8200	R	2,195*	6.7
Follett Corp.	2233 West St	River Grove	IL	60171	R Mark Litzinger	708-583-2000	R	1,899	10.0
Anderson News Co.	6016 Brookvale Ln	Knoxville	TN	37919	Charles Anderson	865-584-9765	R	1,127*	7.0
Advanced Marketing Services Inc.	5880 Oberlin Dr	San Diego	CA	92121	Bob Bartlett	858-457-2500	P	912	1.5
Chas. Levy Circulating Co.	1200 N N Branch	Chicago	IL	60622	Carol G Kloster	312-440-4400	R	775*	6.5
Levy Home Entertainment L.L.C.	4201 Raymond Dr	Hillside	IL	60162		708-547-4400	D	285*	1.7
MBS Textbook Exchange Inc.	2711 W Ash St	Columbia	MO	65203	Bob Pugh	573-445-2243	R	216*	0.9
Nebraska Book Company Inc.	4700 S 19th St	Lincoln	NE	68501	Mark Oppegard	402-421-7300	R	214*	2.1
Blackwell's Book Services	6024 Jean Rd	Lake Oswego	OR	97035	Daniel P Halloran	503-684-1140	S	144*	0.4
Recording For The Blind	20 Roszel Rd	Princeton	NJ	08540	John Kelly	609-452-0606	R	131*	0.2
Spring Arbor Distribution Inc.	1 Ingram Blvd	La Vergne	TN	37086	Janet McDonald		R	107*	0.5
PMG International Inc.	1011 N Frio St	San Antonio	TX	78207	Bill Salomon	210-226-6820	R	83*	0.3
Blackwell's Delaware Inc.	6024 SW Jean Rd	Lake Oswego	OR	97035	Philip Blackwell	503-684-1140	R	77*	0.3
Publishers Group West Inc.	1700 4th St	Berkeley	CA	94710	Rich Freese	510-528-1444	S	68*	0.2
Distribution Systems of America	235 Pinelawn Rd	Melville	NY	11747		631-843-4000	S	47*	0.2
P.B.D. Inc.	1650 Bluegrass Lks	Alpharetta	GA	30004	James E Dockter	770-442-8633	R	46*	0.2
Whitaker House Publishing	30 Hunt Valley Cir	New Kensington	PA	15068	Robert Whitaker	724-334-7000	R	32*	0.1
Bookpeople Inc.	7900 Edgewater Dr	Oakland	CA	94621	Gene Taback	510-632-4700	R	30*	<0.1
Morehouse Continuum	PO Box 1321	Harrisburg	PA	17105	Ken Quigley	717-541-8130	R	25*	<0.1
Regina Press	PO Box 608	Melville	NY	11747	George Malhame	631-694-8600	R	20*	<0.1
Bookmasters Inc.	PO Box 2139	Mansfield	OH	44905	Ray Sevin	419-589-5100	R	12*	<0.1
Media That Delivers	8132 N 87th Pl	Scottsdale	AZ	85258	Michael Dee	480-460-5203	R	9*	<0.1
United Learning Inc.	1560 Sherman Ave	Evanston	IL	60201	Joel Altschul	847-328-6700	R	9*	<0.1
Southeastern Family Publishers	2201 Cantu Ct	Sarasota	FL	34232	Valarie Headsburg	941-377-6908	R	8*	<0.1
Mountain West Printing	1150 W Custer Pl	Denver	CO	80223	Martin Walker	303-744-3313	R	7*	<0.1
Ashgate Publishing Co.	2252 Ridge Rd	Brookfield	VT	05036	Nigel Farrow	802-276-3162	R	6*	<0.1
Booklegger	PO Box 2626	Grass Valley	CA	95945	Robert Kraut	530-272-1556	R	4*	<0.1
Kenney Communications Inc.	1215 Spruce Ave	Orlando	FL	32824	Barbara Kenney	407-859-3113	R	3*	<0.1
BookWorld Services Inc.	1933 Whitfield Pk	Sarasota	FL	34243	Ron T Smith	941-758-8094	R	2*	<0.1
Mendocino Sea Vegetable Co.	PO Box 455	Philo	CA	95466	John Lewallen		R	2*	<0.1
Beeman Jorgensen Inc.	7510 Allisonville	Indianapolis	IN	46250	Brett Johnson	317-841-7677	R	1*	<0.1
Mississippi Safety Services Inc.	PO Box 1379	Clinton	MS	39060	John Brodbeck	601-924-7815	R	1*	<0.1

Source: Ward's Business Directory of U.S. Private and Public Companies, Volumes 1 and 2, 2005. The company type code used is as follows: P - Public, R - Private, S - Subsidiary, D - Division, J - Joint Venture, A - Affiliate, G - Group. Sales are in millions of dollars, employees are in thousands. An asterisk (*) indicates an estimated sales volume. The symbol < stands for 'less than'. Company names and addresses are truncated, in some cases, to fit into the available space.

OCCUPATIONS EMPLOYED BY MISCELLANEOUS NONDURABLE GOODS WHOLESALE

Occupation	% of Total 2004	Change to 2014	Occupation	% of Total 2004	Change to 2014
Sales reps, wholesale & manufacturing, exc tech	12.9	11.6	Customer service representatives	2.2	14.3
Laborers & freight, stock, & material movers, hand	9.3	0.5	Retail salespersons	2.2	11.6
Truck drivers, light or delivery services	5.6	11.3	Driver/sales workers	2.0	11.2
Stock clerks & order fillers	5.2	-14.5	Team assemblers	1.7	11.6
Truck drivers, heavy & tractor-trailer	4.0	11.6	Industrial truck & tractor operators	1.6	11.6
Shipping, receiving, & traffic clerks	3.6	1.1	First-line supervisors/managers of office workers	1.5	1.2
Farmworkers & laborers, crop, nursery, & greenhouse	3.3	11.3	First-line supervisors/managers of non-retail sales work	1.5	3.2
Office clerks, general	2.8	-0.6	Sales reps, wholesale & manufacturing, tech	1.4	11.6
Bookkeeping, accounting, & auditing clerks	2.8	0.5	Secretaries, except legal, medical, & executive	1.4	-6.0
Packers & packagers, hand	2.7	11.6	Cashiers, except gaming	1.3	0.5
General & operations managers	2.3	10.5	Order clerks	1.3	-27.7

Source: Industry-Occupation Matrix, Bureau of Labor Statistics. These data are reported based on 4-digit NAICS categories but have been matched to corresponding 6-digit NAICS industry codes. The change reported for each occupation to the year 2014 is a percent of growth or decline as estimated by the Bureau of Labor Statistics. The abbreviation nec stands for 'not elsewhere classified.'

LOCATION BY STATE AND REGIONAL CONCENTRATION

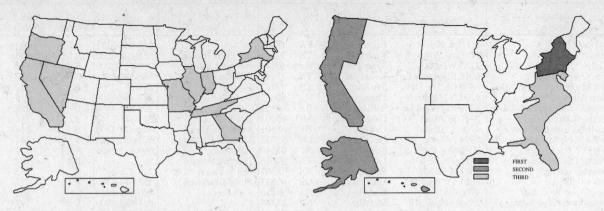

INDUSTRY DATA BY STATE

State	Establishments Total (number)	% of U.S.	Employment Total (number)	% of U.S.	Per Estab.	Payroll Total ($ mil.)	Per Empl. ($)	Sales Total ($ mil.)	% of U.S.	Per Estab. ($)
Illinois	202	5.8	12,318	16.2	61	358.3	29,084	4,752.9	15.4	23,529,050
California	446	12.9	8,327	10.9	19	302.8	36,358	4,124.8	13.4	9,248,330
New York	380	11.0	4,725	6.2	12	225.7	47,768	3,393.4	11.0	8,930,087
Tennessee	87	2.5	4,003	5.3	46	129.4	32,322	1,431.2	4.6	16,450,069
Texas	198	5.7	2,878	3.8	15	96.4	33,482	1,402.9	4.5	7,085,465
Indiana	55	1.6	1,649	2.2	30	40.9	24,802	1,086.2	3.5	19,748,927
Georgia	102	2.9	1,948	2.6	19	73.7	37,834	982.8	3.2	9,634,882
Pennsylvania	153	4.4	3,695	4.9	24	93.7	25,358	930.4	3.0	6,081,320
Florida	196	5.7	2,661	3.5	14	72.1	27,078	827.3	2.7	4,221,163
Missouri	55	1.6	2,519	3.3	46	82.2	32,649	756.8	2.4	13,760,691
Massachusetts	105	3.0	2,158	2.8	21	61.8	28,661	718.4	2.3	6,842,362
Ohio	104	3.0	2,621	3.4	25	67.4	25,723	587.4	1.9	5,648,077
Virginia	75	2.2	1,041	1.4	14	35.2	33,846	504.7	1.6	6,729,840
Maryland	72	2.1	858	1.1	12	29.7	34,563	482.0	1.6	6,693,819
Alabama	37	1.1	1,221	1.6	33	28.8	23,589	444.8	1.4	12,022,216
Oregon	46	1.3	1,333	1.8	29	33.5	25,125	444.5	1.4	9,663,587
Colorado	53	1.5	1,028	1.4	19	27.3	26,535	386.0	1.2	7,282,075
Minnesota	82	2.4	2,433	3.2	30	84.0	34,536	363.7	1.2	4,435,915
Michigan	92	2.7	1,020	1.3	11	33.0	32,363	321.3	1.0	3,492,728
Washington	100	2.9	951	1.3	10	32.2	33,879	297.0	1.0	2,969,500
North Carolina	71	2.0	631	0.8	9	19.8	31,390	257.6	0.8	3,627,521
Nevada	23	0.7	658	0.9	29	17.9	27,208	224.7	0.7	9,770,957
Utah	44	1.3	457	0.6	10	15.2	33,179	213.9	0.7	4,861,477
Wisconsin	58	1.7	954	1.3	16	26.0	27,270	153.1	0.5	2,640,000
Iowa	22	0.6	701	0.9	32	17.2	24,499	151.6	0.5	6,890,409
Louisiana	32	0.9	478	0.6	15	12.5	26,123	141.5	0.5	4,420,750
Oklahoma	33	1.0	456	0.6	14	11.4	24,890	126.9	0.4	3,845,091
Kentucky	28	0.8	589	0.8	21	17.6	29,862	124.7	0.4	4,453,286
Nebraska	17	0.5	461	0.6	27	12.5	27,200	115.8	0.4	6,813,765
Vermont	14	0.4	212	0.3	15	5.7	26,693	42.6	0.1	3,042,214
Hawaii	19	0.5	196	0.3	10	4.8	24,658	37.0	0.1	1,949,474
Mississippi	13	0.4	127	0.2	10	3.3	26,323	36.2	0.1	2,785,231
Maine	19	0.5	128	0.2	7	3.3	25,977	25.7	0.1	1,350,737
North Dakota	8	0.2	80	0.1	10	2.1	25,788	13.2	-	1,653,625
Wyoming	6	0.2	28	-	5	0.4	15,286	2.8	-	460,833
Idaho	4	0.1	18	-	5	0.4	21,222	1.2	-	301,250
New Jersey	140	4.0	2500-4999	-	-	(D)	-	(D)	-	-
Arizona	62	1.8	500-999	-	-	(D)	-	(D)	-	-
Connecticut	50	1.4	1000-2499	-	-	(D)	-	(D)	-	-
South Carolina	32	0.9	250-499	-	-	(D)	-	(D)	-	-
Kansas	27	0.8	250-499	-	-	(D)	-	(D)	-	-
New Hampshire	21	0.6	250-499	-	-	(D)	-	(D)	-	-
Arkansas	19	0.5	250-499	-	-	(D)	-	(D)	-	-
West Virginia	15	0.4	100-249	-	-	(D)	-	(D)	-	-
New Mexico	13	0.4	100-249	-	-	(D)	-	(D)	-	-
Montana	8	0.2	100-249	-	-	(D)	-	(D)	-	-
D.C.	7	0.2	250-499	-	-	(D)	-	(D)	-	-
Delaware	6	0.2	1000-2499	-	-	(D)	-	(D)	-	-
South Dakota	6	0.2	20-99	-	-	(D)	-	(D)	-	-
Rhode Island	5	0.1	0-19	-	-	(D)	-	(D)	-	-
Alaska	2	0.1	20-99	-	-	(D)	-	(D)	-	-

Source: 2002 *Economic Census*. The states are in descending order of sales or establishments (if sales data are missing for the majority). The symbol (D) appears when data are withheld to prevent disclosure of competitive information. States marked with (D) are sorted by number of establishments. A dash (-) indicates that the data element cannot be calculated. Shaded *states* on the state map indicate those states which have proportionately greater representation in the industry than would be indicated by the states population; the ratio is based on total sales or number of establishments. Shaded *regions* indicate where the industry is regionally most concentrated.

NAICS 424930 - FLOWER, NURSERY STOCK, AND FLORISTS' SUPPLIES MERCHANT WHOLESALERS

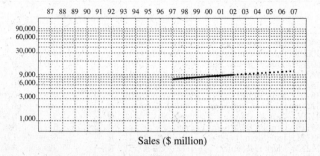

Sales ($ million)

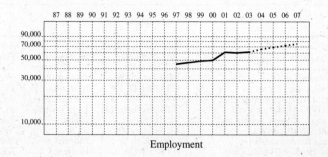

Employment

GENERAL STATISTICS

Year	Establishments (number)	Employment (number)	Payroll ($ million)	Sales ($ million)	Employees per Establishment (number)	Sales per Establishment ($)	Payroll per Employee ($)
1987	-	-	-	-	-	-	-
1988	-	-	-	-	-	-	-
1989	-	-	-	-	-	-	-
1990	-	-	-	-	-	-	-
1991	-	-	-	-	-	-	-
1992	-	-	-	-	-	-	-
1993	-	-	-	-	-	-	-
1994	-	-	-	-	-	-	-
1995	-	-	-	-	-	-	-
1996	-	-	-	-	-	-	-
1997	3,900	44,939	1,026.8	8,002.8	11.5	2,052,000.0	22,848.8
1998	3,935	46,742	1,126.1	8,406.7 e	11.9	2,136,401.5	24,091.8
1999	4,034	48,621	1,227.4	8,810.7 e	12.1	2,184,105.1	25,244.2
2000	4,104	49,657	1,333.4	9,214.6 e	12.1	2,245,277.8	26,852.1
2001	4,598	60,890	1,607.7	9,618.6 e	13.2	2,091,900.8	26,403.4
2002	4,816	60,010	1,580.2	10,022.5	12.5	2,081,083.9	26,332.3
2003	4,796	61,298	1,602.7	10,426.4 p	12.8	2,139,103.9 p	26,146.0
2004	5,028 p	65,720 p	1,788.6 p	10,830.4 p	13.2 p	2,141,192.1 p	27,635.8 p
2005	5,207 p	68,858 p	1,896.4 p	11,234.3 p	13.4 p	2,143,280.4 p	28,190.5 p
2006	5,386 p	71,997 p	2,004.1 p	11,638.3 p	13.6 p	2,145,368.7 p	28,745.2 p
2007	5,565 p	75,136 p	2,111.8 p	12,042.2 p	13.8 p	2,147,457.0 p	29,299.9 p

Source: Economic Census of the United States, 1997 and 2002. Establishment counts, employment, and payroll are from County Business Patterns for non-Census years. This is a newly defined industry. Data for prior years are unavailable at the time of publication but may become available over time. Values followed by 'p' are projections by the editors. Sales data for non-Census years are extrapolations, marked by 'e'.

INDICES OF CHANGE

Year	Establishments (number)	Employment (number)	Payroll ($ million)	Sales ($ million)	Employees per Establishment (number)	Sales per Establishment ($)	Payroll per Employee ($)
1987	-	-	-	-	-	-	-
1992	-	-	-	-	-	-	-
1993	-	-	-	-	-	-	-
1994	-	-	-	-	-	-	-
1995	-	-	-	-	-	-	-
1996	-	-	-	-	-	-	-
1997	81.0	74.9	65.0	79.8	92.0	98.6	86.8
1998	81.7	77.9	71.3	83.9 e	95.2	102.7	91.5
1999	83.8	81.0	77.7	87.9 e	96.8	105.0	95.9
2000	85.2	82.7	84.4	91.9 e	96.8	107.9	102.0
2001	95.5	101.5	101.7	96.0 e	105.6	100.5	100.3
2002	100.0	100.0	100.0	100.0	100.0	100.0	100.0
2003	99.6	102.1	101.4	104.0 p	102.2	102.8 p	99.3
2004	104.4 p	109.5 p	113.2 p	108.1 p	105.4 p	102.9 p	105.0 p
2005	108.1 p	114.7 p	120.0 p	112.1 p	107.2 p	103.0 p	107.1 p
2006	111.8 p	120.0 p	126.8 p	116.1 p	108.9 p	103.1 p	109.2 p
2007	115.6 p	125.2 p	133.6 p	120.2 p	110.7 p	103.2 p	111.3 p

Sources: Same as General Statistics. The values shown reflect change from the base year, 2002. Values above 100 mean greater than 2002, values below 100 mean less than 2002, and a value of 100 in the 1987-2001 or 2003-2007 period means same as 2002. Values followed by a 'p' are projections by the editors; 'e' stands for extrapolation. Data are the most recent available at this level of detail.

SELECTED RATIOS

For 2002	Avg. of All Wholesale	Analyzed Industry	Index	For 2002	Avg. of All Wholesale	Analyzed Industry	Index
Employees per Establishment	15	12	83	Sales per Employee	791,325	167,014	21
Payroll per Establishment	626,122	328,115	52	Sales per Establishment	12,012,387	2,081,084	17
Payroll per Employee	41,161	26,332	64	Expenses per Establishment	na	na	na

Sources: Same as General Statistics. The 'Average of All' column, Wholesale or Retail, represents the average of the sector reported for the most recent complete year available. The Index shows the relationship between the Average and the Analyzed Industry. For example, 100 means that they are equal; 500 that the Analyzed Industry is five times the average; 50 means that the Analyzed Industry is half the national average. The abbreviation 'na' is used to show that data are 'not available'.

LEADING COMPANIES   Number shown: 30   Total sales ($ mil): 1,408   Total employment (000): 6.5

Company Name	Address				CEO Name	Phone	Co. Type	Sales ($ mil)	Empl. (000)
Gerson Company Inc.	1450 S Lone Elm Rd	Olathe	KS	66061	Peter Gerson	913-262-7400	R	404*	0.2
John Deere Landscapes	5610 McGinnis	Alpharetta	GA	30005	Dave Werning	770-442-8881	D	150*	0.5
Ball Horticultural Co.	622 Town Rd	West Chicago	IL	60185	Anna Caroline Ball	630-231-3600	R	90*	0.5
Manatee Fruit Co.	1320 33rd St W	Palmetto	FL	34221	WH Preston	941-722-2871	R	79*	0.3
Pursley Turf Farms	9115 58th Dr E	Bradenton	FL	34202		941-722-4547	R	63*	<0.1
Knud Nielsen Company Inc.	PO Box 746	Evergreen	AL	36401	John Smith	251-578-2900	R	61*	0.3
NAPCO Marketing Corp.	7800 Bayberry Rd	Jacksonville	FL	32256	David M Bailys	904-737-8500	R	58*	<0.1
L and L Nursery Supply Inc.	5350 G St	Chino	CA	91708	Tom Medhurst	909-591-0461	R	52*	0.3
Bailey Nurseries Inc.	1325 Bailey Rd	St. Paul	MN	55119	Gordon Bailey, Jr	651-459-9744	R	51*	0.4
Stein Garden and Gifts	5400 S 27th St	Milwaukee	WI	53221	Jack Stein	414-761-5404	R	50*	1.0
Bay Houston Towing Co.	PO Box 3006	Houston	TX	77253	Mark E Kuebler	713-529-3755	R	38*	0.4
Greenleaf Wholesale Florists	PO Box 537	Brighton	CO	80601	Scott Kitayama	303-659-8000	R	37*	0.3
Roy Houff and Co.	6200 S Oak	Chicago	IL	60638	Scott Stecker	773-586-8118	R	37*	0.2
Metrolina Greenhouses Inc.	16400 H Concord	Huntersville	NC	28078	Tom Van Wingerden	704-875-1371	R	28*	0.3
New England Pottery Co.	1000 Washington St	Foxboro	MA	02035	Lawrence D Gitlitz	508-543-7700	S	27*	0.2
Mahoney's Rocky Ledge Farm	242 Cambridge St	Winchester	MA	01890	Paul Mahoney	781-729-5900	R	25*	0.3
Boutique Trims Inc.	21200 Pontiac Trl	South Lyon	MI	48178	Kevin Williams	248-437-2017	R	24*	<0.1
Valley Crest Tree Co.	24121 Ventura Blvd	Calabasas	CA	91302	Robert L Crudup, Jr	818-737-2600	S	22*	0.4
Arty Imports Inc.	1300 Wycliff Ave	Dallas	TX	75207		214-741-1289	R	21*	<0.1
Rott-Keller Supply Co.	PO Box 390	Fargo	ND	58107	Herb F Rott Jr	701-235-0563	R	19*	<0.1
Mid American Growers	Rte 89	Granville	IL	61326	N Vanwingerden	815-339-6831	R	11*	0.2
Universal American Flowers	6610 Anderson Rd	Tampa	FL	33634	Herbert Jordan	813-885-6936	R	11*	0.1
Zieger and Sons Inc.	6215 Ardleigh St	Philadelphia	PA	19138	PC Zieger	215-438-7060	R	10*	<0.1
JR Johnson Supply Inc.	2582 Long Lake Rd	Roseville	MN	55113	John Johnson	651-636-1330	R	9*	0.1
Olsen Distributing Co.	969 N Pepper Rd	Barrington	IL	60010	Robert Olsen	847-381-9333	R	8*	<0.1
Silk and Morgan Inc.	33866 Woodward	Birmingham	MI	48009	Dale Morgan		R	7*	<0.1
Green-Tek Inc.	407 N Main St	Edgerton	WI	53534	Linda Bracha	608-884-9454	R	6*	<0.1
FW Ritter Sons Co.	PO Box 45	S. Rockwood	MI	48179	Fred Ritter	734-379-9622	R	6*	<0.1
Village Green Inc.	4303 Miller Rd	Wilmington	DE	19802	Scott Weiler	302-764-2234	R	2*	<0.1
International Decoratives Inc.	PO Box 777	Valley Center	CA	92082	RE Russell	760-749-2682	R	1	<0.1

Source: *Ward's Business Directory of U.S. Private and Public Companies*, Volumes 1 and 2, 2005. The company type code used is as follows: P - Public, R - Private, S - Subsidiary, D - Division, J - Joint Venture, A - Affiliate, G - Group. Sales are in millions of dollars, employees are in thousands. An asterisk (*) indicates an estimated sales volume. The symbol < stands for 'less than'. Company names and addresses are truncated, in some cases, to fit into the available space.

OCCUPATIONS EMPLOYED BY MISCELLANEOUS NONDURABLE GOODS WHOLESALE

Occupation	% of Total 2004	Change to 2014	Occupation	% of Total 2004	Change to 2014
Sales reps, wholesale & manufacturing, exc tech	12.9	11.6	Customer service representatives	2.2	14.3
Laborers & freight, stock, & material movers, hand	9.3	0.5	Retail salespersons	2.2	11.6
Truck drivers, light or delivery services	5.6	11.3	Driver/sales workers	2.0	11.2
Stock clerks & order fillers	5.2	-14.5	Team assemblers	1.7	11.6
Truck drivers, heavy & tractor-trailer	4.0	11.6	Industrial truck & tractor operators	1.6	11.6
Shipping, receiving, & traffic clerks	3.6	1.1	First-line supervisors/managers of office workers	1.5	1.2
Farmworkers & laborers, crop, nursery, & greenhouse	3.3	11.3	First-line supervisors/managers of non-retail sales work	1.5	3.2
Office clerks, general	2.8	-0.6	Sales reps, wholesale & manufacturing, tech	1.4	11.6
Bookkeeping, accounting, & auditing clerks	2.8	0.5	Secretaries, except legal, medical, & executive	1.4	-6.0
Packers & packagers, hand	2.7	11.6	Cashiers, except gaming	1.3	0.5
General & operations managers	2.3	10.5	Order clerks	1.3	-27.7

Source: *Industry-Occupation Matrix*, Bureau of Labor Statistics. These data are reported based on 4-digit NAICS categories but have been matched to corresponding 6-digit NAICS industry codes. The change reported for each occupation to the year 2014 is a percent of growth or decline as estimated by the Bureau of Labor Statistics. The abbreviation nec stands for 'not elsewhere classified.'

LOCATION BY STATE AND REGIONAL CONCENTRATION

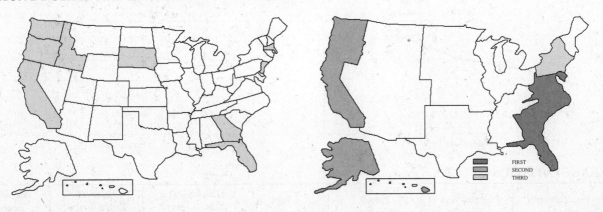

INDUSTRY DATA BY STATE

State	Establishments Total (number)	% of U.S.	Employment Total (number)	% of U.S.	Per Estab.	Payroll Total ($ mil.)	Per Empl. ($)	Sales Total ($ mil.)	% of U.S.	Per Estab. ($)
Florida	688	14.2	7,866	13.1	11	219.3	27,877	1,764.4	17.6	2,564,592
California	758	15.6	10,924	18.2	14	280.3	25,662	1,667.4	16.6	2,199,744
New York	296	6.1	2,767	4.6	9	94.4	34,101	605.4	6.0	2,045,213
New Jersey	164	3.4	2,503	4.2	15	84.0	33,545	587.3	5.9	3,581,226
Texas	368	7.6	4,215	7.0	11	99.9	23,713	559.1	5.6	1,519,236
Illinois	176	3.6	2,696	4.5	15	84.1	31,202	435.7	4.3	2,475,341
Pennsylvania	148	3.0	2,178	3.6	15	55.3	25,384	334.8	3.3	2,261,838
Ohio	152	3.1	2,089	3.5	14	61.1	29,267	334.7	3.3	2,202,132
Georgia	156	3.2	1,753	2.9	11	49.7	28,331	320.9	3.2	2,056,737
Washington	136	2.8	1,463	2.4	11	43.9	29,992	277.5	2.8	2,040,375
Michigan	128	2.6	1,340	2.2	10	37.2	27,784	268.5	2.7	2,097,492
Massachusetts	84	1.7	1,268	2.1	15	41.6	32,793	246.7	2.5	2,936,893
Oregon	85	1.8	870	1.5	10	20.4	23,405	163.3	1.6	1,921,200
Minnesota	74	1.5	969	1.6	13	26.1	26,956	158.6	1.6	2,143,838
North Carolina	131	2.7	1,048	1.7	8	25.4	24,226	154.2	1.5	1,177,084
Wisconsin	71	1.5	886	1.5	12	22.9	25,805	142.1	1.4	2,001,423
Colorado	65	1.3	803	1.3	12	22.1	27,461	133.1	1.3	2,047,585
Tennessee	93	1.9	852	1.4	9	20.8	24,360	131.3	1.3	1,411,409
Missouri	70	1.4	985	1.6	14	22.0	22,321	122.3	1.2	1,747,243
Alabama	58	1.2	1,076	1.8	19	17.9	16,609	118.3	1.2	2,039,655
Indiana	80	1.6	883	1.5	11	20.1	22,729	115.2	1.1	1,440,137
South Carolina	69	1.4	1,030	1.7	15	21.8	21,201	113.9	1.1	1,650,188
Mississippi	38	0.8	538	0.9	14	10.7	19,970	104.4	1.0	2,748,526
Virginia	60	1.2	803	1.3	13	16.2	20,233	78.7	0.8	1,312,433
Idaho	18	0.4	256	0.4	14	9.3	36,219	74.0	0.7	4,109,833
South Dakota	11	0.2	292	0.5	27	7.7	26,305	61.1	0.6	5,552,182
Oklahoma	46	0.9	416	0.7	9	9.4	22,654	60.4	0.6	1,313,283
Louisiana	50	1.0	472	0.8	9	8.2	17,362	47.2	0.5	943,180
Kentucky	46	0.9	348	0.6	8	8.1	23,336	46.4	0.5	1,008,783
Iowa	29	0.6	271	0.5	9	5.5	20,203	39.4	0.4	1,359,931
Hawaii	44	0.9	422	0.7	10	8.0	18,960	38.0	0.4	863,545
Kansas	26	0.5	216	0.4	8	5.1	23,792	35.6	0.4	1,367,808
Arkansas	34	0.7	255	0.4	8	5.3	20,643	31.0	0.3	910,882
Utah	30	0.6	268	0.4	9	5.4	20,183	28.3	0.3	944,533
Vermont	12	0.2	88	0.1	7	3.1	34,943	21.5	0.2	1,789,833
Nebraska	15	0.3	159	0.3	11	3.4	21,239	21.1	0.2	1,405,667
Nevada	19	0.4	103	0.2	5	2.8	27,573	17.6	0.2	927,947
Montana	11	0.2	91	0.2	8	2.0	22,505	17.1	0.2	1,554,182
Alaska	9	0.2	88	0.1	10	1.0	11,739	5.1	0.1	563,889
North Dakota	7	0.1	29	-	4	0.3	11,310	2.8	-	404,286
Arizona	86	1.8	1000-2499	-	-	(D)	-	(D)	-	-
Maryland	69	1.4	1000-2499	-	-	(D)	-	(D)	-	-
Connecticut	50	1.0	500-999	-	-	(D)	-	(D)	-	-
New Hampshire	18	0.4	100-249	-	-	(D)	-	(D)	-	-
New Mexico	17	0.4	20-99	-	-	(D)	-	(D)	-	-
West Virginia	15	0.3	100-249	-	-	(D)	-	(D)	-	-
Maine	13	0.3	20-99	-	-	(D)	-	(D)	-	-
Delaware	9	0.2	100-249	-	-	(D)	-	(D)	-	-
D.C.	9	0.2	100-249	-	-	(D)	-	(D)	-	-
Rhode Island	8	0.2	100-249	-	-	(D)	-	(D)	-	-
Wyoming	5	0.1	0-19	-	-	(D)	-	(D)	-	-

Source: 2002 Economic Census. The states are in descending order of sales or establishments (if sales data are missing for the majority). The symbol (D) appears when data are withheld to prevent disclosure of competitive information. States marked with (D) are sorted by number of establishments. A dash (-) indicates that the data element cannot be calculated. Shaded states on the state map indicate those states which have proportionately greater representation in the industry than would be indicated by the states population; the ratio is based on total sales or number of establishments. Shaded regions indicate where the industry is regionally most concentrated.

NAICS 424940 - TOBACCO AND TOBACCO PRODUCT MERCHANT WHOLESALERS*

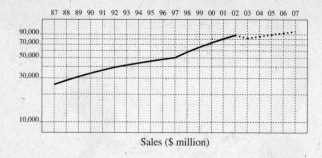

Sales ($ million)

Employment

GENERAL STATISTICS

Year	Establishments (number)	Employment (number)	Payroll ($ million)	Sales ($ million)	Employees per Establishment (number)	Sales per Establishment ($)	Payroll per Employee ($)
1987	1,813	42,672	784.9	25,465.0	23.5	14,045,780.5	18,393.8
1988	1,702	42,092	858.3	28,219.9 e	24.7	16,580,434.8	20,391.0
1989	1,577	42,975	919.2	30,974.8 e	27.3	19,641,598.0	21,389.2
1990	1,522	43,073	986.5	33,729.6 e	28.3	22,161,366.6	22,903.0
1991	1,421	42,522	1,030.1	36,484.5 e	29.9	25,675,228.7	24,225.1
1992	1,702	50,345	1,272.2	39,239.4	29.6	23,054,876.6	25,269.6
1993	1,620	51,459	1,347.1	41,445.3 e	31.8	25,583,518.5	26,178.1
1994	1,564	53,802	1,425.4	43,651.2 e	34.4	27,909,974.4	26,493.4
1995	1,496	54,226	1,424.4	45,857.0 e	36.2	30,653,074.9	26,267.8
1996	1,456 e	54,876 e	1,496.9 e	48,062.9 e	37.7 e	33,010,233.5 e	27,277.9 e
1997	1,561	57,046	1,589.7	50,268.8	36.5	32,202,946.8	27,867.0
1998	1,573	55,531	1,656.3	57,857.0 e	35.3	36,781,309.6	29,826.6
1999	1,548	56,328	1,764.0	65,445.2 e	36.4	42,277,261.0	31,316.6
2000	1,539	57,802	1,898.9	73,033.4 e	37.6	47,455,100.7	32,851.5
2001	1,520	57,261	1,951.0	80,621.6 e	37.7	53,040,526.3	34,072.2
2002	1,636	58,609	1,982.2	88,209.8	35.8	53,917,970.7	33,820.7
2003	1,595	59,810	2,100.0	81,751.5 p	37.5	52,843,972.4 p	35,110.7
2004	1,522 p	62,712 p	2,185.7 p	85,571.0 p	40.8 p	55,355,092.7 p	36,092.5 p
2005	1,516 p	63,925 p	2,268.5 p	89,390.6 p	41.6 p	57,866,212.9 p	37,072.4 p
2006	1,510 p	65,139 p	2,351.3 p	93,210.1 p	42.5 p	60,377,333.2 p	38,052.2 p
2007	1,504 p	66,352 p	2,434.1 p	97,029.7 p	43.4 p	62,888,453.5 p	39,032.1 p

Sources: *Economic Census of the United States*, 1987, 1992, 1997, and 2002. Establishment counts, employment, and payroll are from *County Business Patterns* for non-Census years. Values followed by a 'p' are projections by the editors. Sales data for non-Census years are extrapolations, marked by 'e'. Data are the most recent available at this level of detail.

INDICES OF CHANGE

Year	Establishments (number)	Employment (number)	Payroll ($ million)	Sales ($ million)	Employees per Establishment (number)	Sales per Establishment ($)	Payroll per Employee ($)
1987	110.8	72.8	39.6	28.9	65.6	26.1	54.4
1992	104.0	85.9	64.2	44.5	82.7	42.8	74.7
1993	99.0	87.8	68.0	47.0 e	88.8	47.4	77.4
1994	95.6	91.8	71.9	49.5 e	96.1	51.8	78.3
1995	91.4	92.5	71.9	52.0 e	101.1	56.9	77.7
1996	89.0 e	93.6 e	75.5 e	54.5 e	105.3 e	61.2 e	80.7 e
1997	95.4	97.3	80.2	57.0	102.0	59.7	82.4
1998	96.1	94.7	83.6	65.6 e	98.6	68.2	88.2
1999	94.6	96.1	89.0	74.2 e	101.7	78.4	92.6
2000	94.1	98.6	95.8	82.8 e	105.0	88.0	97.1
2001	92.9	97.7	98.4	91.4 e	105.3	98.4	100.7
2002	100.0	100.0	100.0	100.0	100.0	100.0	100.0
2003	97.5	102.0	105.9	92.7 p	104.7	98.0 p	103.8
2004	93.1 p	107.0 p	110.3 p	97.0 p	113.9 p	102.7 p	106.7 p
2005	92.7 p	109.1 p	114.4 p	101.3 p	116.3 p	107.3 p	109.6 p
2006	92.3 p	111.1 p	118.6 p	105.7 p	118.7 p	112.0 p	112.5 p
2007	91.9 p	113.2 p	122.8 p	110.0 p	121.2 p	116.6 p	115.4 p

Sources: Same as General Statistics. The values shown reflect change from the base year, 2002. Values above 100 mean greater than 2002, values below 100 mean less than 2002, and a value of 100 in the 1987-2001 or 2003-2007 period means same as 2002. Values followed by a 'p' are projections by the editors; 'e' stands for extrapolation. Data are the most recent available at this level of detail.

SELECTED RATIOS

For 2002	Avg. of All Wholesale	Analyzed Industry	Index	For 2002	Avg. of All Wholesale	Analyzed Industry	Index
Employees per Establishment	15	36	240	Sales per Employee	791,325	1,505,056	190
Payroll per Establishment	626,122	1,211,614	194	Sales per Establishment	12,012,387	53,917,971	449
Payroll per Employee	41,161	33,821	82	Expenses per Establishment	na	na	na

Sources: Same as General Statistics. The 'Average of All' column, Wholesale or Retail, represents the average of the sector reported for the most recent complete year available. The Index shows the relationship between the Average and the Analyzed Industry. For example, 100 means that they are equal; 500 that the Analyzed Industry is five times the average; 50 means that the Analyzed Industry is half the national average. The abbreviation 'na' is used to show that data are 'not available'.

*Equivalent to SIC 5194.

LEADING COMPANIES   Number shown: **39**   Total sales ($ mil): **9,041**   Total employment (000): **14.3**

Company Name	Address				CEO Name	Phone	Co. Type	Sales ($ mil)	Empl. (000)
Eby-Brown Co.	PO Box 3067	Naperville	IL	60566		630-778-2800	R	3,200	2.1
GSC Enterprises Inc.	PO Box 638	Sulphur Springs	TX	75483	Steven B Daniels	903-885-0829	R	1,500*	2.0
DIMON Inc.	512 Bridge St	Danville	VA	24541	Steven B Daniels	434-792-7511	P	835	4.1
AMCON Distributing Co.	7405 Irvington Rd	Omaha	NE	68122	Kathleen M Evans	402-331-3727	P	824	1.0
Grocery Supply Co.	9300 E Billy the Kid	El Paso	TX	79907		915-858-1053	S	624*	1.5
Imperial Trading Co.	PO Box 23508	New Orleans	LA	70183	John Georges	504-733-1400	R	389*	0.3
800-JR Cigar Inc.	2589 Eric Ln	Burlington	NC	27215	Lewis Rothman	973-884-9555	R	317*	1.1
Farner-Bocken Co.	1751 Hwy 30 E	Carroll	IA	51401	John Norgaard	712-792-3503	R	259*	0.5
J.T. Davenport and Sons Inc.	PO Box 1105	Sanford	NC	27330	John T Davenport Jr	919-774-9444	R	214*	0.3
Albert H. Notini and Sons Inc.	PO Box 299	Lowell	MA	01853	Alex Turshette	978-459-7151	R	105*	0.2
Safier's Inc.	8700 Harvard Ave	Cleveland	OH	44105		216-341-8700	R	88*	<0.1
Mound City Industries Inc.	1315 Cherokee St	St. Louis	MO	63118	Robert L Krekeler	314-773-5200	R	70*	<0.1
Kaiser Wholesale Inc.	PO Box 1115	New Albany	IN	47150	JR Kaiser	812-945-2651	R	50*	<0.1
Republic Tobacco L.P.	2301 Ravine Way	Glenview	IL	60025	Donald Levin	847-832-9700	R	50*	0.3
JC Newman Cigar Co.	PO Box 2030	Tampa	FL	33601	Eric Newman	813-248-2124	R	48*	0.1
Axton Candy and Tobacco Co.	PO Box 32219	Louisville	KY	40232	Tommy Chappell	502-634-8000	R	48*	<0.1
Idaho Candy Co.	PO Box 1217	Boise	ID	83701	Dave Wagers	208-342-5505	R	42*	<0.1
Albert Guarnieri Company Inc.	PO Box 927	Warren	OH	44483	A Guarnieri III	330-394-5636	R	41*	<0.1
Fritz Company Inc.	1912 Hastings Ave	Newport	MN	55055	Elizabeth Hoekstra	651-459-9751	R	40*	0.1
SWD Corp.	PO Box 340	Lima	OH	45802	Carl Berger	419-227-2436	R	35*	<0.1
Pine Lesser and Sons Inc.	PO Box 1807	Clifton	NJ	07015	Allan G Lesser	973-478-3310	R	32*	<0.1
Edmiston Brothers Inc.	PO Box 371	Crockett	TX	75835	AC Rainn	936-544-2118	R	29*	<0.1
Keilson-Dayton Co.	PO Box 1457	Dayton	OH	45401	GT Wellinghoff	937-236-1070	R	29*	<0.1
Montano Cigarettes, Candy	290 Boston Post Rd	Milford	CT	06460	Gary Montano	203-877-0341	R	29*	<0.1
Wiemuth and Son Company Inc.	PO Box 3128	Terre Haute	IN	47803	Robert A Wiemuth	812-232-3384	R	20*	<0.1
Blackburn-Russell Company Inc.	PO Box 157	Bedford	PA	15522	Robert B Blackburn	814-623-5181	R	18*	<0.1
A.W. Marshall Co.	PO Box 16127	Salt Lake City	UT	84116	Bill Marshall	801-328-4713	R	17*	<0.1
Queen City Wholesale Inc.	PO Box 1083	Sioux Falls	SD	57101	Bill Wehrkamp	605-336-3215	R	16*	<0.1
Franklin Cigar and Tobacco Inc.	PO Box 1151	Franklin	LA	70538	Keith A Landen	337-828-3208	R	10*	<0.1
John F. Trompeter Co.	637 E Main St	Louisville	KY	40202		502-585-5852	R	10*	<0.1
Lavin Candy Company Inc.	4989 S Catherine St	Plattsburgh	NY	12901	Irvin C Reid	518-563-4630	R	10*	<0.1
Miller Distributing Inc.	PO Box 6	Saint Clair	PA	17970	W Miller	570-429-1191	R	9*	<0.1
Eagle Wholesale L.P.	PO Box 742	Tyler	TX	75710	Gordon Atkins	903-592-4321	R	6*	<0.1
Huser-Paul Company Inc.	3636 Illinois Rd	Fort Wayne	IN	46804		260-432-0557	R	6*	<0.1
Tidewater Wholesalers Inc.	708 W Constance Rd	Suffolk	VA	23434	John Orange	757-539-3261	R	6*	<0.1
Adams Apple Distributing L.P.	2301 Ravine Way	Glenview	IL	60025	Ellis Levin	847-832-9900	R	5*	<0.1
F.B. McFadden Wholesale Inc.	415 Railroad Ave	Rock Springs	WY	82901	EH McFadden	307-362-5441	R	5*	<0.1
Valley Vending Service Inc.	PO Box 506	Martins Ferry	OH	43935		740-633-3303	R	4*	<0.1
Evolve One Inc.	1000 Clint Moore	Boca Raton	FL	33487	Irwin Horowitz	561-988-0819	P	1	<0.1

Source: Ward's Business Directory of U.S. Private and Public Companies, Volumes 1 and 2, 2005. The company type code used is as follows: P - Public, R - Private, S - Subsidiary, D - Division, J - Joint Venture, A - Affiliate, G - Group. Sales are in millions of dollars, employees are in thousands. An asterisk (*) indicates an estimated sales volume. The symbol < stands for 'less than'. Company names and addresses are truncated, in some cases, to fit into the available space.

OCCUPATIONS EMPLOYED BY MISCELLANEOUS NONDURABLE GOODS WHOLESALE

Occupation	% of Total 2004	Change to 2014	Occupation	% of Total 2004	Change to 2014
Sales reps, wholesale & manufacturing, exc tech	12.9	11.6	Customer service representatives	2.2	14.3
Laborers & freight, stock, & material movers, hand	9.3	0.5	Retail salespersons	2.2	11.6
Truck drivers, light or delivery services	5.6	11.3	Driver/sales workers	2.0	11.2
Stock clerks & order fillers	5.2	-14.5	Team assemblers	1.7	11.6
Truck drivers, heavy & tractor-trailer	4.0	11.6	Industrial truck & tractor operators	1.6	11.6
Shipping, receiving, & traffic clerks	3.6	1.1	First-line supervisors/managers of office workers	1.5	1.2
Farmworkers & laborers, crop, nursery, & greenhouse	3.3	11.3	First-line supervisors/managers of non-retail sales work	1.5	3.2
Office clerks, general	2.8	-0.6	Sales reps, wholesale & manufacturing, tech	1.4	11.6
Bookkeeping, accounting, & auditing clerks	2.8	0.5	Secretaries, except legal, medical, & executive	1.4	-6.0
Packers & packagers, hand	2.7	11.6	Cashiers, except gaming	1.3	0.5
General & operations managers	2.3	10.5	Order clerks	1.3	-27.7

Source: Industry-Occupation Matrix, Bureau of Labor Statistics. These data are reported based on 4-digit NAICS categories but have been matched to corresponding 6-digit NAICS industry codes. The change reported for each occupation to the year 2014 is a percent of growth or decline as estimated by the Bureau of Labor Statistics. The abbreviation nec stands for 'not elsewhere classified.'

LOCATION BY STATE AND REGIONAL CONCENTRATION

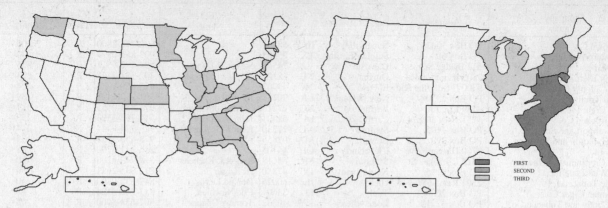

INDUSTRY DATA BY STATE

State	Establishments Total (number)	% of U.S.	Employment Total (number)	% of U.S.	Per Estab.	Payroll Total ($ mil.)	Per Empl. ($)	Sales Total ($ mil.)	% of U.S.	Per Estab. ($)
Kentucky	48	3.0	4,409	7.5	92	173.7	39,405	6,163.0	7.3	128,395,042
California	99	6.1	3,888	6.6	39	137.3	35,312	5,424.4	6.4	54,791,475
New York	168	10.4	3,567	6.1	21	124.5	34,913	5,028.4	5.9	29,930,673
Texas	75	4.6	3,517	6.0	47	120.5	34,256	4,665.7	5.5	62,209,307
Florida	158	9.8	3,443	5.8	22	107.6	31,246	4,549.3	5.4	28,792,835
North Carolina	58	3.6	3,443	5.8	59	114.1	33,144	4,372.3	5.2	75,384,672
Illinois	49	3.0	2,465	4.2	50	89.8	36,443	3,893.6	4.6	79,460,816
Pennsylvania	90	5.6	2,327	4.0	26	73.1	31,416	3,852.4	4.5	42,804,744
Ohio	70	4.3	1,743	3.0	25	54.4	31,196	3,684.5	4.3	52,635,614
Georgia	38	2.3	2,000	3.4	53	72.8	36,422	3,586.4	4.2	94,378,579
New Jersey	84	5.2	1,253	2.1	15	52.1	41,610	3,378.3	4.0	40,217,857
Michigan	56	3.5	1,229	2.1	22	43.5	35,395	2,849.7	3.4	50,887,482
Massachusetts	26	1.6	1,102	1.9	42	60.2	54,665	2,834.1	3.3	109,002,962
Indiana	32	2.0	1,494	2.5	47	45.0	30,141	2,509.2	3.0	78,413,344
Virginia	39	2.4	1,857	3.2	48	69.4	37,370	2,274.3	2.7	58,316,487
Minnesota	28	1.7	1,204	2.0	43	47.5	39,492	2,201.2	2.6	78,615,357
Louisiana	33	2.0	1,357	2.3	41	42.9	31,604	2,023.6	2.4	61,322,061
Colorado	15	0.9	1,084	1.8	72	38.2	35,197	1,970.7	2.3	131,381,933
Washington	26	1.6	986	1.7	38	34.8	35,292	1,806.1	2.1	69,465,885
Wisconsin	35	2.2	1,409	2.4	40	40.3	28,603	1,635.2	1.9	46,719,486
Alabama	21	1.3	1,339	2.3	64	40.1	29,921	1,570.0	1.9	74,762,381
Tennessee	35	2.2	1,213	2.1	35	40.7	33,590	1,433.0	1.7	40,941,971
Mississippi	23	1.4	1,283	2.2	56	39.0	30,389	1,290.0	1.5	56,085,348
Missouri	24	1.5	782	1.3	33	28.8	36,790	1,210.0	1.4	50,418,375
Kansas	15	0.9	366	0.6	24	13.0	35,495	947.9	1.1	63,193,733
Oklahoma	21	1.3	692	1.2	33	19.8	28,568	678.4	0.8	32,305,762
Arkansas	20	1.2	691	1.2	35	17.5	25,398	604.4	0.7	30,217,950
Oregon	10	0.6	460	0.8	46	14.3	31,009	572.2	0.7	57,218,600
South Carolina	37	2.3	613	1.0	17	17.1	27,910	488.2	0.6	13,195,838
West Virginia	16	1.0	425	0.7	27	13.3	31,407	475.3	0.6	29,705,438
Nevada	18	1.1	254	0.4	14	8.2	32,362	377.9	0.4	20,992,611
Idaho	9	0.6	217	0.4	24	5.3	24,429	216.5	0.3	24,059,222
Utah	4	0.2	193	0.3	48	6.2	31,964	196.7	0.2	49,169,750
Vermont	6	0.4	243	0.4	41	7.0	28,860	187.9	0.2	31,312,167
North Dakota	6	0.4	223	0.4	37	5.7	25,502	121.2	0.1	20,196,667
Montana	10	0.6	155	0.3	15	5.0	32,142	88.0	0.1	8,802,500
Hawaii	9	0.6	93	0.2	10	2.6	28,011	81.2	0.1	9,017,778
South Dakota	5	0.3	112	0.2	22	2.8	24,688	59.6	0.1	11,910,600
Wyoming	9	0.6	85	0.1	9	1.8	21,176	47.6	0.1	5,293,333
Connecticut	19	1.2	1000-2499	-	-	(D)	-	(D)	-	-
Arizona	13	0.8	500-999	-	-	(D)	-	(D)	-	-
Maryland	13	0.8	500-999	-	-	(D)	-	(D)	-	-
Nebraska	11	0.7	250-499	-	-	(D)	-	(D)	-	-
Iowa	8	0.5	500-999	-	-	(D)	-	(D)	-	-
New Hampshire	8	0.5	500-999	-	-	(D)	-	(D)	-	-
New Mexico	8	0.5	250-499	-	-	(D)	-	(D)	-	-
Delaware	6	0.4	20-99	-	-	(D)	-	(D)	-	-
Rhode Island	4	0.2	20-99	-	-	(D)	-	(D)	-	-
Maine	2	0.1	250-499	-	-	(D)	-	(D)	-	-
D.C.	1	0.1	100-249	-	-	(D)	-	(D)	-	-

Source: 2002 *Economic Census*. The states are in descending order of sales or establishments (if sales data are missing for the majority). The symbol (D) appears when data are withheld to prevent disclosure of competitive information. States marked with (D) are sorted by number of establishments. A dash (-) indicates that the data element cannot be calculated. Shaded *states* on the state map indicate those states which have proportionately greater representation in the industry than would be indicated by the states population; the ratio is based on total sales or number of establishments. Shaded *regions* indicate where the industry is regionally most concentrated.

NAICS 424950 - PAINT, VARNISH, AND SUPPLIES MERCHANT WHOLESALERS*

87 88 89 90 91 92 93 94 95 96 97 98 99 00 01 02 03 04 05 06 07

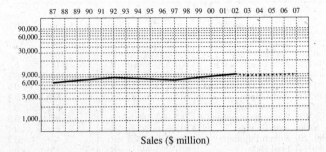

Sales ($ million)

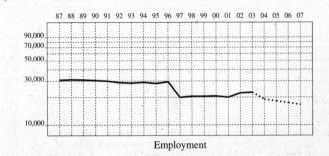

Employment

GENERAL STATISTICS

Year	Establishments (number)	Employment (number)	Payroll ($ million)	Sales ($ million)	Employees per Establishment (number)	Sales per Establishment ($)	Payroll per Employee ($)
1987	3,657	30,780	660.3	6,701.8	8.4	1,832,595.0	21,452.2
1988	3,468	31,085	706.6	7,085.7 e	9.0	2,043,166.1	22,731.2
1989	3,460	30,917	720.6	7,469.5 e	8.9	2,158,815.0	23,307.6
1990	3,438	30,472	742.6	7,853.3 e	8.9	2,284,264.1	24,369.9
1991	3,415	29,948	759.0	8,237.2 e	8.8	2,412,064.4	25,343.9
1992	3,539	28,862	781.6	8,621.0	8.2	2,435,998.9	27,080.6
1993	3,465	28,493	799.5	8,398.9 e	8.2	2,423,925.0	28,059.5
1994	3,544	29,051	858.3	8,176.8 e	8.2	2,307,223.5	29,544.6
1995	3,348	28,198	855.2	7,954.7 e	8.4	2,375,955.8	30,328.4
1996	3,422 e	29,442 e	898.0 e	7,732.6 e	8.6	2,259,672.7 e	30,500.6 e
1997	2,192	19,917	676.4	7,510.5	9.1	3,426,323.0	33,960.9
1998	2,219	20,466	749.4	8,015.4 e	9.2	3,612,176.7	36,616.8
1999	2,186	20,470	758.5	8,520.3 e	9.4	3,897,685.3	37,054.2
2000	2,179	20,619	810.2	9,025.3 e	9.5	4,141,927.5	39,295.5
2001	2,093	19,970	798.3	9,530.2 e	9.5	4,553,358.8	39,977.2
2002	2,311	22,280	908.4	10,035.1	9.6	4,342,319.3	40,772.0
2003	2,299	22,598	977.5	9,373.9 p	9.8	4,400,989.2 p	43,256.2
2004	1,962 p	18,992 p	889.9 p	9,514.4 p	9.6 p	4,576,785.9 p	43,823.0 p
2005	1,852 p	18,203 p	900.8 p	9,655.0 p	9.7 p	4,752,582.7 p	45,204.3 p
2006	1,742 p	17,414 p	911.7 p	9,795.5 p	9.7 p	4,928,379.4 p	46,585.6 p
2007	1,631 p	16,625 p	922.7 p	9,936.0 p	9.8 p	5,104,176.1 p	47,966.9 p

Sources: Economic Census of the United States, 1987, 1992, 1997, and 2002. Establishment counts, employment, and payroll are from *County Business Patterns* for non-Census years. Values followed by a 'p' are projections by the editors. Sales data for non-Census years are extrapolations, marked by 'e'. Data are the most recent available at this level of detail.

INDICES OF CHANGE

Year	Establishments (number)	Employment (number)	Payroll ($ million)	Sales ($ million)	Employees per Establishment (number)	Sales per Establishment ($)	Payroll per Employee ($)
1987	158.2	138.2	72.7	66.8	87.5	42.2	52.6
1992	153.1	129.5	86.0	85.9	85.4	56.1	66.4
1993	149.9	127.9	88.0	83.7 e	85.4	55.8	68.8
1994	153.4	130.4	94.5	81.5 e	85.4	53.1	72.5
1995	144.9	126.6	94.1	79.3 e	87.5	54.7	74.4
1996	148.1 e	132.1 e	98.9 e	77.1 e	89.6 e	52.0 e	74.8 e
1997	94.9	89.4	74.5	74.8	94.8	78.9	83.3
1998	96.0	91.9	82.5	79.9 e	95.8	83.2	89.8
1999	94.6	91.9	83.5	84.9 e	97.9	89.8	90.9
2000	94.3	92.5	89.2	89.9 e	99.0	95.4	96.4
2001	90.6	89.6	87.9	95.0 e	99.0	104.9	98.1
2002	100.0	100.0	100.0	100.0	100.0	100.0	100.0
2003	99.5	101.4	107.6	93.4 p	102.4	101.4 p	106.1
2004	84.9 p	85.2 p	98.0 p	94.8 p	99.8 p	105.4 p	107.5 p
2005	80.1 p	81.7 p	99.2 p	96.2 p	100.6 p	109.4 p	110.9 p
2006	75.4 p	78.2 p	100.4 p	97.6 p	101.4 p	113.5 p	114.3 p
2007	70.6 p	74.6 p	101.6 p	99.0 p	102.1 p	117.5 p	117.6 p

Sources: Same as General Statistics. The values shown reflect change from the base year, 2002. Values above 100 mean greater than 2002, values below 100 mean less than 2002, and a value of 100 in the 1987-2001 or 2003-2007 period means same as 2002. Values followed by a 'p' are projections by the editors; 'e' stands for extrapolation. Data are the most recent available at this level of detail.

SELECTED RATIOS

For 2002	Avg. of All Wholesale	Analyzed Industry	Index	For 2002	Avg. of All Wholesale	Analyzed Industry	Index
Employees per Establishment	15	10	65	Sales per Employee	791,325	450,408	57
Payroll per Establishment	626,122	393,077	63	Sales per Establishment	12,012,387	4,342,319	36
Payroll per Employee	41,161	40,772	99	Expenses per Establishment	na	na	na

Sources: Same as General Statistics. The 'Average of All' column, Wholesale or Retail, represents the average of the sector reported for the most recent complete year available. The Index shows the relationship between the Average and the Analyzed Industry. For example, 100 means that they are equal; 500 that the Analyzed Industry is five times the average; 50 means that the Analyzed Industry is half the national average. The abbreviation 'na' is used to show that data are 'not available'.

*Equivalent to SIC 5198.

LEADING COMPANIES   Number shown: 24   Total sales ($ mil): 7,280   Total employment (000): 30.4

Company Name	Address				CEO Name	Phone	Co. Type	Sales ($ mil)	Empl. (000)
Menard Inc.	4777 Menard Dr	Eau Claire	WI	54703	John R. Menard, Jr.	715-876-5911	R	6,065*	27.0
FinishMaster Inc.	54 Monument Cir	Indianapolis	IN	46204	Andre B Lacy	317-237-3678	P	386	1.5
Seabrook Wallcoverings Inc.	1325 Farmville Rd	Memphis	TN	38122	James Seabrook Jr	901-320-3500	R	118*	0.2
Atomicbox Inc.	125 Lena Dr	Aurora	OH	44202	Thomas Bianco	330-995-6110	R	103*	0.1
Emery Waterhouse Co.	PO Box 659	Portland	ME	04104	Charles Hildrein Jr	207-775-2371	R	90*	0.3
G and T Industries Inc.	PO Box 8098	Grand Rapids	MI	49518	Kim Gilpin	616-452-8611	R	69*	0.1
Mattos Inc.	4501 Beech Rd	Temple Hills	MD	20748	John A Mattos	301-423-1142	R	67*	0.1
Brewster Wallcovering Co.	67 Pacella Park Dr	Randolph	MA	02368	Kenneth Grandberg	781-963-4800	R	66*	0.3
Murco Wall Products Inc.	2032 N Commerce	Fort Worth	TX	76106	Joan Benton	817-626-1987	R	54*	0.1
HPM Building Supply	380 Kanoelehua Ave	Hilo	HI	96720	Robert Fujimoto	808-934-4266	R	47*	0.2
Colonial Building Supply L.L.C.	PO Box 459	Centerville	UT	84014	Fred Hale	801-295-9471	R	45*	<0.1
Fargo Glass and Paint Co.	1801 7th Ave N	Fargo	ND	58102	Gerald Lovell	701-235-4441	R	42*	0.1
Lansco Colors	305 W Grand Ave	Montvale	NJ	07645	Donald Greenwald	201-307-5995	R	19*	<0.1
Terrace Supply Co.	710 N Addison Rd	Villa Park	IL	60181	Gary Lichtenheld	630-530-1000	R	17*	<0.1
Sun-Rys Distributing Corp.	RR 1 Box 337	Moline	IL	61265	Gregory Mosley	309-799-7091	R	17*	<0.1
Teknol Inc.	PO Box 13387	Dayton	OH	45413	Kent Von Behran	937-890-6547	R	17*	<0.1
ISCO Corp.	1225 Cottman Ave	Philadelphia	PA	19111	Erwin Raichle	215-742-6200	R	12*	<0.1
FinishMaster Automotive	4259 40th St SE	Grand Rapids	MI	49512		616-949-7604	R	10*	<0.1
Painters Supply Company Inc.	3701 S Santa Fe Dr	Englewood	CO	80110	Francis Heckendorf	303-762-1606	R	9*	<0.1
California Car Color	1411 Industrial Rd	San Carlos	CA	94070	Gerald Stimple	650-592-2605	R	9*	<0.1
Easton Wholesale Company Inc.	PO Box 839	Easton	MD	21601	Thomas Cover	410-822-0600	R	8*	<0.1
Flamemaster Corp.	PO Box 1458	Sun Valley	CA	91353	Joseph Mazin	818-982-1650	P	5	<0.1
RAE Products and Chemical Inc.	11630 S Cicero Ave	Alsip	IL	60803	Donna Gurenberg	708-396-1984	R	2*	<0.1
Paint Supply Co.	2528 W Pembroke	Hampton	VA	23661	Robert Wood	757-247-6651	R	1*	<0.1

Source: *Ward's Business Directory of U.S. Private and Public Companies*, Volumes 1 and 2, 2005. The company type code used is as follows: P - Public, R - Private, S - Subsidiary, D - Division, J - Joint Venture, A - Affiliate, G - Group. Sales are in millions of dollars, employees are in thousands. An asterisk (*) indicates an estimated sales volume. The symbol < stands for 'less than'. Company names and addresses are truncated, in some cases, to fit into the available space.

OCCUPATIONS EMPLOYED BY MISCELLANEOUS NONDURABLE GOODS WHOLESALE

Occupation	% of Total 2004	Change to 2014	Occupation	% of Total 2004	Change to 2014
Sales reps, wholesale & manufacturing, exc tech	12.9	11.6	Customer service representatives	2.2	14.3
Laborers & freight, stock, & material movers, hand	9.3	0.5	Retail salespersons	2.2	11.6
Truck drivers, light or delivery services	5.6	11.3	Driver/sales workers	2.0	11.2
Stock clerks & order fillers	5.2	-14.5	Team assemblers	1.7	11.6
Truck drivers, heavy & tractor-trailer	4.0	11.6	Industrial truck & tractor operators	1.6	11.6
Shipping, receiving, & traffic clerks	3.6	1.1	First-line supervisors/managers of office workers	1.5	1.2
Farmworkers & laborers, crop, nursery, & greenhouse	3.3	11.3	First-line supervisors/managers of non-retail sales work	1.5	3.2
Office clerks, general	2.8	-0.6	Sales reps, wholesale & manufacturing, tech	1.4	11.6
Bookkeeping, accounting, & auditing clerks	2.8	0.5	Secretaries, except legal, medical, & executive	1.4	-6.0
Packers & packagers, hand	2.7	11.6	Cashiers, except gaming	1.3	0.5
General & operations managers	2.3	10.5	Order clerks	1.3	-27.7

Source: *Industry-Occupation Matrix*, Bureau of Labor Statistics. These data are reported based on 4-digit NAICS categories but have been matched to corresponding 6-digit NAICS industry codes. The change reported for each occupation to the year 2014 is a percent of growth or decline as estimated by the Bureau of Labor Statistics. The abbreviation nec stands for 'not elsewhere classified.'

LOCATION BY STATE AND REGIONAL CONCENTRATION

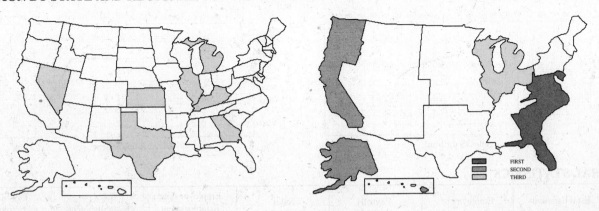

INDUSTRY DATA BY STATE

State	Establishments Total (number)	Establishments % of U.S.	Employment Total (number)	Employment % of U.S.	Employment Per Estab.	Payroll Total ($ mil.)	Payroll Per Empl. ($)	Sales Total ($ mil.)	Sales % of U.S.	Sales Per Estab. ($)
Michigan	52	2.2	1,284	5.7	25	71.3	55,565	855.7	8.5	16,455,115
California	275	11.9	2,663	11.9	10	119.3	44,801	819.0	8.1	2,978,320
Texas	210	9.1	1,943	8.7	9	72.5	37,335	773.4	7.7	3,682,643
Illinois	86	3.7	978	4.4	11	46.0	47,039	623.7	6.2	7,252,360
Georgia	84	3.6	598	2.7	7	24.0	40,060	523.2	5.2	6,228,679
Ohio	96	4.2	1,242	5.6	13	50.5	40,672	431.0	4.3	4,489,438
Pennsylvania	101	4.4	1,203	5.4	12	47.8	39,768	385.1	3.8	3,812,653
New York	122	5.3	1,211	5.4	10	47.8	39,460	335.4	3.3	2,749,205
Florida	207	9.0	1,259	5.6	6	40.5	32,156	304.9	3.0	1,472,923
Kentucky	31	1.3	499	2.2	16	21.8	43,703	209.2	2.1	6,748,097
Massachusetts	49	2.1	774	3.5	16	34.9	45,083	203.2	2.0	4,147,245
Indiana	59	2.6	623	2.8	11	18.9	30,268	179.6	1.8	3,043,475
North Carolina	71	3.1	552	2.5	8	17.0	30,842	177.1	1.8	2,493,986
Nevada	16	0.7	197	0.9	12	7.7	38,893	129.3	1.3	8,079,313
Washington	61	2.6	429	1.9	7	16.5	38,520	124.4	1.2	2,039,721
Kansas	19	0.8	272	1.2	14	11.3	41,710	108.3	1.1	5,700,737
Missouri	53	2.3	308	1.4	6	9.3	30,045	89.6	0.9	1,690,358
Tennessee	40	1.7	308	1.4	8	10.0	32,386	87.0	0.9	2,175,075
Virginia	49	2.1	338	1.5	7	11.6	34,204	83.6	0.8	1,705,898
Oregon	29	1.3	273	1.2	9	9.7	35,388	74.3	0.7	2,563,724
Louisiana	47	2.0	286	1.3	6	9.9	34,769	72.6	0.7	1,545,383
Wisconsin	42	1.8	318	1.4	8	10.3	32,531	72.0	0.7	1,714,976
South Carolina	33	1.4	220	1.0	7	6.0	27,159	65.3	0.6	1,977,970
Alabama	34	1.5	194	0.9	6	5.6	28,701	45.8	0.5	1,345,706
Oklahoma	27	1.2	184	0.8	7	5.4	29,223	41.8	0.4	1,547,407
Iowa	14	0.6	93	0.4	7	2.5	26,946	17.8	0.2	1,268,286
Mississippi	10	0.4	70	0.3	7	2.2	30,757	16.2	0.2	1,615,400
Idaho	9	0.4	62	0.3	7	1.6	25,113	10.2	0.1	1,129,111
Wyoming	3	0.1	5	-	2	0.1	19,800	1.2	-	385,667
New Jersey	80	3.5	1000-2499	-	-	(D)	-	(D)	-	-
Maryland	53	2.3	250-499	-	-	(D)	-	(D)	-	-
Arizona	46	2.0	250-499	-	-	(D)	-	(D)	-	-
Minnesota	36	1.6	500-999	-	-	(D)	-	(D)	-	-
Colorado	35	1.5	250-499	-	-	(D)	-	(D)	-	-
Utah	22	1.0	250-499	-	-	(D)	-	(D)	-	-
Connecticut	17	0.7	100-249	-	-	(D)	-	(D)	-	-
New Mexico	14	0.6	20-99	-	-	(D)	-	(D)	-	-
Nebraska	13	0.6	20-99	-	-	(D)	-	(D)	-	-
Arkansas	11	0.5	100-249	-	-	(D)	-	(D)	-	-
Hawaii	10	0.4	20-99	-	-	(D)	-	(D)	-	-
Delaware	8	0.3	100-249	-	-	(D)	-	(D)	-	-
North Dakota	7	0.3	20-99	-	-	(D)	-	(D)	-	-
West Virginia	7	0.3	20-99	-	-	(D)	-	(D)	-	-
Maine	5	0.2	20-99	-	-	(D)	-	(D)	-	-
New Hampshire	4	0.2	0-19	-	-	(D)	-	(D)	-	-
Rhode Island	4	0.2	20-99	-	-	(D)	-	(D)	-	-
Vermont	4	0.2	20-99	-	-	(D)	-	(D)	-	-
Montana	3	0.1	20-99	-	-	(D)	-	(D)	-	-
South Dakota	2	0.1	0-19	-	-	(D)	-	(D)	-	-
Alaska	1	-	20-99	-	-	(D)	-	(D)	-	-
D.C.	1	-	0-19	-	-	(D)	-	(D)	-	-

Source: 2002 Economic Census. The states are in descending order of sales or establishments (if sales data are missing for the majority). The symbol (D) appears when data are withheld to prevent disclosure of competitive information. States marked with (D) are sorted by number of establishments. A dash (-) indicates that the data element cannot be calculated. Shaded *states* on the state map indicate those states which have proportionately greater representation in the industry than would be indicated by the states population; the ratio is based on total sales or number of establishments. Shaded *regions* indicate where the industry is regionally most concentrated.

NAICS 424990 - OTHER MISCELLANEOUS NONDURABLE GOODS MERCHANT WHOLESALERS

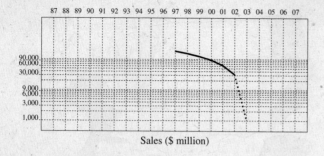

Sales ($ million)

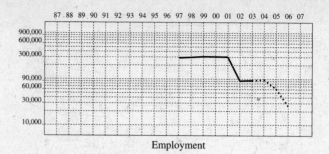

Employment

GENERAL STATISTICS

Year	Establishments (number)	Employment (number)	Payroll ($ million)	Sales ($ million)	Employees per Establishment (number)	Sales per Establishment ($)	Payroll per Employee ($)
1987	-	-	-	-	-	-	-
1988	-	-	-	-	-	-	-
1989	-	-	-	-	-	-	-
1990	-	-	-	-	-	-	-
1991	-	-	-	-	-	-	-
1992	-	-	-	-	-	-	-
1993	-	-	-	-	-	-	-
1994	-	-	-	-	-	-	-
1995	-	-	-	-	-	-	-
1996	-	-	-	-	-	-	-
1997	14,623	288,689	9,277.5	186,758.7	20	12,771,572	32,137
1998	14,607	295,821	10,127.7	155,807.4 e	20	10,666,623	34,236
1999	14,249	306,357	10,950.3	124,856.0 e	22	8,762,441	35,744
2000	13,927	304,421	11,418.7	93,904.7 e	22	6,742,635	37,510
2001	13,703	301,333	11,771.6	62,953.3 e	22	4,594,128	39,065
2002	13,652	91,494	3,166.3	32,002.0	7	2,344,127	34,607
2003	13,793	93,352	3,295.2	1,050.7 p	7	409,469 p	35,299
2004	13,373 p	97,397 p	4,137.0 p		8 p		37,449 p
2005	13,196 p	61,694 p	3,028.1 p		5 p		37,933 p
2006	13,019 p	25,991 p	1,919.3 p		3 p		38,417 p
2007	12,843 p		810.4 p		1 p		38,901 p

Source: *Economic Census of the United States*, 1997 and 2002. Establishment counts, employment, and payroll are from *County Business Patterns* for non-Census years. This is a newly defined industry. Data for prior years are unavailable at the time of publication but may become available over time. Values followed by 'p' are projections by the editors. Sales data for non-Census years are extrapolations, marked by 'e'.

INDICES OF CHANGE

Year	Establishments (number)	Employment (number)	Payroll ($ million)	Sales ($ million)	Employees per Establishment (number)	Sales per Establishment ($)	Payroll per Employee ($)
1987	-	-	-	-	-	-	-
1992	-	-	-	-	-	-	-
1993	-	-	-	-	-	-	-
1994	-	-	-	-	-	-	-
1995	-	-	-	-	-	-	-
1996	-	-	-	-	-	-	-
1997	107.1	315.5	293.0	583.6	293.9	544.8	92.9
1998	107.0	323.3	319.9	486.9 e	302.9	455.0	98.9
1999	104.4	334.8	345.8	390.2 e	320.8	373.8	103.3
2000	102.0	332.7	360.6	293.4 e	326.8	287.6	108.4
2001	100.4	329.3	371.8	196.7 e	328.3	196.0	112.9
2002	100.0	100.0	100.0	100.0	100.0	100.0	100.0
2003	101.0	102.0	104.1	3.3 p	101.0	17.5 p	102.0
2004	98.0 p	106.5 p	130.7 p		113.8 p		108.2 p
2005	96.7 p	67.4 p	95.6 p		78.9 p		109.6 p
2006	95.4 p	28.4 p	60.6 p		44.0 p		111.0 p
2007	94.1 p		25.6 p		9.1 p		112.4 p

Sources: Same as General Statistics. The values shown reflect change from the base year, 2002. Values above 100 mean greater than 2002, values below 100 mean less than 2002, and a value of 100 in the 1987-2001 or 2003-2007 period means same as 2002. Values followed by a 'p' are projections by the editors; 'e' stands for extrapolation. Data are the most recent available at this level of detail.

SELECTED RATIOS

For 2002	Avg. of All Retail	Analyzed Industry	Index	For 2002	Avg. of All Retail	Analyzed Industry	Index
Employees per Establishment	17	7	40	Sales per Employee	174,682	349,772	200
Payroll per Establishment	333,445	231,929	70	Sales per Establishment	3,332,269	2,344,125	70
Payroll per Employee	20,311	34,607	170	Expenses per Establishment	na	na	na

Sources: Same as General Statistics. The 'Average of All' column, Wholesale or Retail, represents the average of the sector reported for the most recent complete year available. The Index shows the relationship between the Average and the Analyzed Industry. For example, 100 means that they are equal; 500 that the Analyzed Industry is five times the average; 50 means that the Analyzed Industry is half the national average. The abbreviation 'na' is used to show that data are 'not available'.

LEADING COMPANIES   Number shown: **75**   Total sales ($ mil): **20,182**   Total employment (000): **46.9**

Company Name	Address				CEO Name	Phone	Co. Type	Sales ($ mil)	Empl. (000)
Marubeni America Corp.	450 Lexington Ave	New York	NY	10017	Kazuhiko Sakamoto	212-450-0100	S	8,050*	0.2
Universal Corp.	PO Box 25099	Richmond	VA	23260	Henry H Harrell	804-359-9311	P	2,271	30.0
Golden State Foods Corp.	18301 Von Karman	Irvine	CA	92612		949-252-2000	S	2,000	2.5
FUJIFILM Medical Systems USA	419 W Ave	Stamford	CT	06902	Takuski Nasu	203-324-2000	S	1,446*	0.2
Central Garden and Pet Co.	1340 Treat Blvd	Walnut Creek	CA	94597	William E Brown	925-948-4000	P	1,270	4.4
Goodall Rubber Co.	790 Birney Hwy	Aston	PA	19014	Terry Taylor	610-361-0800	S	1,223*	<0.1
Darby Group Companies Inc.	865 Merrick Ave	Westbury	NY	11590	Carl Ashkin	516-683-1800	R	670*	1.4
Taymark	4875 White Bear	White Bear Lake	MN	55110	Paul Griffiths	651-426-1667	R	236*	0.4
Roman Inc.	555 Lawrence Ave	Roselle	IL	60172	Ronald Jedlinski	630-529-3000	R	199*	0.2
Imperial Commodities Corp.	17 Battery Pl	New York	NY	10004	John Morley	212-837-9400	S	128*	<0.1
A.T. Cross Co.	1 Albion Rd	Lincoln	RI	02865	Russell A Boss	401-333-1200	P	125	0.9
Boyds Collection Ltd.	350 South St	McSherrystown	PA	17344		717-633-9898	P	113	0.4
Spring Arbor Distribution Inc.	1 Ingram Blvd	La Vergne	TN	37086	Janet McDonald		R	107*	0.5
Northeast Mississippi Coca-Cola	PO Box 966	Starkville	MS	39760	Harold Clark	662-338-3400	S	102*	0.2
Koval Marketing Inc.	11208 47th Ave W	Mukilteo	WA	98275	Roy Koval	425-347-4249	R	100*	<0.1
Ultralife Batteries Inc.	2000 Technology	Newark	NY	14513	John D Kavazanjian	315-332-7100	P	98	0.9
Worldwide Retail Exchange L.L.C.	625 N Washington	Alexandria	VA	22314	Colin Dyer	703-234-5100	R	85*	0.1
Lewis-Goetz and Company Inc.	PO Box 895	Coraopolis	PA	15108		412-341-7100	R	84*	<0.1
Kurt S. Adler Inc.	1107 Broadway	New York	NY	10010	Kurt S Adler	212-924-0900	R	80*	0.2
PQ Acquisition Company Inc.	1 Maplewood Dr	Hazleton	PA	18201		570-384-5555	S	76*	<0.1
C.M. Paula Co.	6049 Hi-Tek Ct	Mason	OH	45040	Greg Ionna	513-336-3100	R	70*	0.1
Buxton Acquisition Inc.	PO Box 1650	Springfield	MA	01102	Russell Whiteford	413-734-5900	R	69*	0.1
Sullivans	3101 N 4th Ave	Sioux Falls	SD	57117	Marian Sullivan	605-339-4274	R	69*	<0.1
NAPCO Marketing Corp.	7800 Bayberry Rd	Jacksonville	FL	32256	David M Bailys	904-737-8500	R	58*	<0.1
Greene Rubber Company Inc.	20 Cross St	Woburn	MA	01801	John Connors	781-937-9909	R	55*	<0.1
FFR Inc.	28900 Fountain	Cleveland	OH	44139	Gerald A Conway	440-505-6919	R	54*	0.2
Specialized Products Co.	1100 S Kimball Ave	Southlake	TX	76092	Pete Smith	817-329-6647	R	50*	0.1
Wise El Santo Company Inc.	PO Box 8360	St. Louis	MO	63132	Rudolph L Wise	314-428-3100	R	50*	0.1
Specialty Merchandise Corp.	9447 De Soto Ave	Chatsworth	CA	91311	Mark Schwartz	818-998-3300	R	48*	0.3
Leather Factory Inc.	3847 E Loop 820 S	Fort Worth	TX	76119	Ronald C Morgan	817-496-4414	P	46	0.3
Accents Unlimited Inc.	5205 W Donges Bay	Mequon	WI	53092	Ron Creten	262-242-5205	R	45*	<0.1
Hair U Wear	5900 Equitable Rd	Kansas City	MO	64120	Michael Napolitano	816-231-3700	R	44*	<0.1
Moore Brothers Inc.	PO Box 1108	Cheraw	SC	29520	Jim Crawford III	843-537-5211	R	43*	<0.1
United Pacific Pet L.L.C.	12060 Cabernet Dr	Fontana	CA	92337	Maureen Costello	909-360-8550	R	43*	<0.1
Foam Products of San Antonio Inc.	1119 N Mesquite St	San Antonio	TX	78202		210-228-0033	R	42*	<0.1
Maxim Lighting International	13280 Amar Rd	City of Industry	CA	91746	Jacob Sperling	626-964-7500	R	42*	<0.1
L.W. Barrett Company Inc.	PO Box 19430	Denver	CO	80219	Dennis Vick	303-934-5755	R	40*	<0.1
Alaska Mill and Feed	PO Box 101246	Anchorage	AK	99510	Ken Sherwood	907-279-4519	R	38*	<0.1
Alvin and Company Inc.	PO Box 188	Windsor	CT	06095	Scott Shoham	860-243-8991	R	38*	0.2
Hopkins Distribution Company Inc.	PO Box 70206	Reno	NV	89570	Robert Hopkins	775-829-4440	R	35*	<0.1
Foam Factory and Upholstery Inc.	22800 Hall Rd	Clinton Twp.	MI	48036	S Baladomente	586-627-3626	R	35*	<0.1
Buckeye Rubber and Packing Co.	23940 Mercantile Rd	Cleveland	OH	44122	Edward Klemm	216-464-8900	R	34*	<0.1
Trinidad Benham Corp.	PO Box 378007	Denver	CO	80237	Carl Hartman	303-220-1400	R	34*	<0.1
Boss Holdings Inc.	221 W 1st St	Kewanee	IL	61443	G Louis Graziadio III	309-852-2131	P	33	0.1
Rust Wholesale Company Inc.	PO Box 230	Greensburg	IN	47240		812-663-7394	R	33*	<0.1
M. Conley Co.	1312 4th St SE	Canton	OH	44701	Richard D Conley	330-456-8243	R	32*	0.1
Hanna's Candle Co.	PO Box 3647	Fayetteville	AR	72702	Bert Hanna	479-443-5467	R	32*	0.3
Educational Development Corp.	PO Box 470663	Tulsa	OK	74146	Randall W White	918-622-4522	P	30	<0.1
Laguna Clay Co.	14400 Lomitas Ave	City of Industry	CA	91746	Jonathan Brooks	626-330-0631	R	30*	<0.1
Nelson-Jameson Inc.	PO Box 647	Marshfield	WI	54449	John Nelson	715-387-1151	R	27*	<0.1
New England Pottery Co.	1000 Washington St	Foxboro	MA	02035	Lawrence D Gitlitz	508-543-7700	S	27*	0.2
AC World of Products	1410 Queenscastle	Charleston	SC	29414	Alisia Dulaney	843-763-8083	R	27*	<0.1
Claymore Sieck Co.	311 E Chase St	Baltimore	MD	21202	Jeff Gilliams	410-685-4660	R	26*	<0.1
Whatcom Farmers Co-Op	PO Box 611	Lynden	WA	98264		360-354-2108	R	24*	<0.1
Recycled Wood Products	1313 E Philip Blvd	Pomona	CA	91766	Chris Kiralla	909-868-6882	R	22*	<0.1
Robert J Matthews Company Inc.	PO Box 9101	Canton	OH	44711	J Matthews	330-834-3000	R	22*	<0.1
W.P. Ballard and Co.	PO Box 12246	Birmingham	AL	35202	John Beeler Jr	205-251-7272	R	21*	<0.1
Whitney Design Inc.	13213 Corp Exchg	Bridgeton	MO	63044	James Glenn	314-428-5657	R	21*	<0.1
Corporate Presence Inc.	19 W 21st St	New York	NY	10010	Jeffrey Sehgal	212-989-6446	R	21*	<0.1
Major World Wide Ltd.	19706 53rd Ave	Fresh Meadows	NY	11365	Arthur Rosenberg	718-224-7023	R	18*	<0.1
Fashion Trends Inc.	PO Box 4070	Spanaway	WA	98387	Al Ruskin	253-847-1924	R	17*	<0.1
Til-Mar Inc.	PO Box 941	Shelby	NC	28151	James Martin	704-484-3051	R	17*	<0.1
CJ Zone Manufacturing Co.	2025 S Vandeventer	Saint Louis	MO	63110	Charles Zone	314-771-7107	R	15*	0.1
Gateway CDI	909 N 20th St	Saint Louis	MO	63106	Chuck Fandos	314-535-1888	R	14*	0.2
Cliff Weil Inc.	PO Box 427	Mechanicsville	VA	23116	Alvin B Hutzler II	804-746-1321	R	14*	<0.1
Bethany Lowe Designs Inc.	16655 County 16	Osco	IL	61274	Bethany Lowe	309-944-6214	R	14*	<0.1
MG Novelty Company Inc.	300 N Macarthur	Oklahoma City	OK	73127	Michael Dillon	405-948-1234	R	14*	<0.1
Huckleberry People Inc.	1021 Waverly St	Missoula	MT	59802	Lois Richardson	406-721-6024	R	13*	<0.1
Falcon Industries Inc.	212 W Hanover Rd	Graham	NC	27253	RW Miller	336-229-1048	R	12*	<0.1
Julius Kraft Company Inc.	PO Box 918	Auburn	NY	13021	Kim Vorreuter	315-252-7251	R	11*	<0.1
Duroc USA	PO Box 351208	Los Angeles	CA	90035	Albert Tor	323-278-1111	R	11*	<0.1
GE Richards Graphic Supplies Inc.	5320 S Laburnum	Richmond	VA	23231		804-328-2557	R	11*	<0.1
Lou Davis Wholesale	N3211 Hwy H	Lake Geneva	WI	53147	Fred Koermer	262-248-2000	R	10*	<0.1
Housechem Inc.	25 Industrial Park	Waldwick	NJ	07463	Manfred Riegg	201-445-8808	R	10*	<0.1
Charles River BRF Inc.	305 Almeda-Genoa	Houston	TX	77047	Raj Bhalla	713-433-5846	S	9*	<0.1

Source: Ward's Business Directory of U.S. Private and Public Companies, Volumes 1 and 2, 2005. The company type code used is as follows: P - Public, R - Private, S - Subsidiary, D - Division, J - Joint Venture, A - Affiliate, G - Group. Sales are in millions of dollars, employees are in thousands. An asterisk (*) indicates an estimated sales volume. The symbol < stands for 'less than'. Company names and addresses are truncated, in some cases, to fit into the available space.

OCCUPATIONS EMPLOYED BY MISCELLANEOUS NONDURABLE GOODS WHOLESALE

Occupation	% of Total 2004	Change to 2014	Occupation	% of Total 2004	Change to 2014
Sales reps, wholesale & manufacturing, exc tech	12.9	11.6	Customer service representatives	2.2	14.3
Laborers & freight, stock, & material movers, hand	9.3	0.5	Retail salespersons	2.2	11.6
Truck drivers, light or delivery services	5.6	11.3	Driver/sales workers	2.0	11.2
Stock clerks & order fillers	5.2	-14.5	Team assemblers	1.7	11.6
Truck drivers, heavy & tractor-trailer	4.0	11.6	Industrial truck & tractor operators	1.6	11.6
Shipping, receiving, & traffic clerks	3.6	1.1	First-line supervisors/managers of office workers	1.5	1.2
Farmworkers & laborers, crop, nursery, & greenhouse	3.3	11.3	First-line supervisors/managers of non-retail sales work	1.5	3.2
Office clerks, general	2.8	-0.6	Sales reps, wholesale & manufacturing, tech	1.4	11.6
Bookkeeping, accounting, & auditing clerks	2.8	0.5	Secretaries, except legal, medical, & executive	1.4	-6.0
Packers & packagers, hand	2.7	11.6	Cashiers, except gaming	1.3	0.5
General & operations managers	2.3	10.5	Order clerks	1.3	-27.7

Source: Industry-Occupation Matrix, Bureau of Labor Statistics. These data are reported based on 4-digit NAICS categories but have been matched to corresponding 6-digit NAICS industry codes. The change reported for each occupation to the year 2014 is a percent of growth or decline as estimated by the Bureau of Labor Statistics. The abbreviation nec stands for 'not elsewhere classified.'

LOCATION BY STATE AND REGIONAL CONCENTRATION

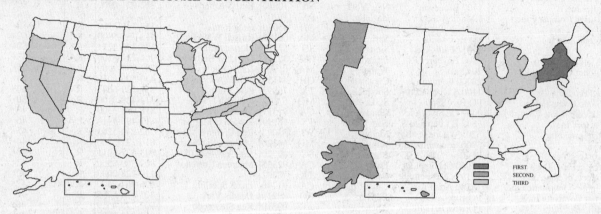

FIRST
SECOND
THIRD

INDUSTRY DATA BY STATE

State	Establishments Total (number)	% of U.S.	Employment Total (number)	% of U.S.	Per Estab.	Payroll Total ($ mil.)	Per Empl. ($)	Sales Total ($ mil.)	% of U.S.	Per Estab. ($)
California	2,840	20.8	19,336	21.1	7	636.0	32,892	5,376.2	16.8	1,893,029
New York	1,616	11.8	8,539	9.3	5	362.6	42,470	5,106.7	16.0	3,160,069
Texas	832	6.1	5,508	6.0	7	172.0	31,221	1,835.4	5.7	2,206,043
Illinois	537	3.9	4,945	5.4	9	186.4	37,687	1,670.6	5.2	3,110,957
Florida	1,288	9.4	5,387	5.9	4	151.9	28,202	1,612.0	5.0	1,251,575
Pennsylvania	409	3.0	3,777	4.1	9	137.7	36,462	1,345.9	4.2	3,290,817
Ohio	367	2.7	3,148	3.4	9	106.3	33,766	1,174.7	3.7	3,200,807
North Carolina	328	2.4	2,182	2.4	7	116.9	53,569	1,020.8	3.2	3,112,308
Tennessee	161	1.2	2,193	2.4	14	72.2	32,907	1,001.4	3.1	6,220,124
Michigan	257	1.9	1,732	1.9	7	61.0	35,193	892.5	2.8	3,472,860
Wisconsin	150	1.1	1,672	1.8	11	60.0	35,884	820.1	2.6	5,467,427
Oregon	163	1.2	1,103	1.2	7	37.6	34,130	437.5	1.4	2,684,258
Virginia	187	1.4	1,541	1.7	8	47.6	30,888	408.0	1.3	2,181,561
Missouri	194	1.4	1,776	1.9	9	52.2	29,381	402.8	1.3	2,076,196
Nevada	128	0.9	852	0.9	7	24.6	28,910	248.7	0.8	1,942,906
Oklahoma	88	0.6	716	0.8	8	16.7	23,367	132.2	0.4	1,502,068
Kentucky	85	0.6	527	0.6	6	14.0	26,639	125.6	0.4	1,478,059
Louisiana	134	1.0	745	0.8	6	18.3	24,603	117.4	0.4	876,284
Alabama	109	0.8	540	0.6	5	13.2	24,435	110.0	0.3	1,009,450
Rhode Island	40	0.3	291	0.3	7	11.6	40,027	91.7	0.3	2,293,500
New Mexico	62	0.5	206	0.2	3	4.9	24,019	40.3	0.1	650,710
Montana	37	0.3	187	0.2	5	3.6	19,070	23.4	0.1	633,730
Idaho	45	0.3	182	0.2	4	4.3	23,357	23.2	0.1	514,533
New Jersey	631	4.6	2500-4999	-	-	(D)	-	(D)	-	-
Georgia	397	2.9	1000-2499	-	-	(D)	-	(D)	-	-
Washington	285	2.1	1000-2499	-	-	(D)	-	(D)	-	-
Massachusetts	268	2.0	1000-2499	-	-	(D)	-	(D)	-	-
Minnesota	259	1.9	1000-2499	-	-	(D)	-	(D)	-	-
Arizona	191	1.4	500-999	-	-	(D)	-	(D)	-	-
Colorado	190	1.4	1000-2499	-	-	(D)	-	(D)	-	-
Maryland	166	1.2	1000-2499	-	-	(D)	-	(D)	-	-

Continued on next page.

INDUSTRY DATA BY STATE - Continued

State	Establishments		Employment			Payroll		Sales		
	Total (number)	% of U.S.	Total (number)	% of U.S.	Per Estab.	Total ($ mil.)	Per Empl. ($)	Total ($ mil.)	% of U.S.	Per Estab. ($)
Indiana	157	1.2	1000-2499	-	-	(D)	-	(D)	-	-
Connecticut	133	1.0	1000-2499	-	-	(D)	-	(D)	-	-
South Carolina	127	0.9	500-999	-	-	(D)	-	(D)	-	-
Hawaii	89	0.7	500-999	-	-	(D)	-	(D)	-	-
Utah	89	0.7	500-999	-	-	(D)	-	(D)	-	-
Kansas	85	0.6	500-999	-	-	(D)	-	(D)	-	-
Iowa	84	0.6	500-999	-	-	(D)	-	(D)	-	-
Arkansas	83	0.6	250-499	-	-	(D)	-	(D)	-	-
Maine	55	0.4	250-499	-	-	(D)	-	(D)	-	-
Mississippi	52	0.4	250-499	-	-	(D)	-	(D)	-	-
Nebraska	44	0.3	250-499	-	-	(D)	-	(D)	-	-
New Hampshire	32	0.2	100-249	-	-	(D)	-	(D)	-	-
Delaware	31	0.2	100-249	-	-	(D)	-	(D)	-	-
West Virginia	30	0.2	100-249	-	-	(D)	-	(D)	-	-
D.C.	23	0.2	100-249	-	-	(D)	-	(D)	-	-
Vermont	23	0.2	100-249	-	-	(D)	-	(D)	-	-
South Dakota	21	0.2	100-249	-	-	(D)	-	(D)	-	-
Alaska	20	0.1	100-249	-	-	(D)	-	(D)	-	-
Wyoming	16	0.1	20-99	-	-	(D)	-	(D)	-	-
North Dakota	14	0.1	20-99	-	-	(D)	-	(D)	-	-

Source: 2002 *Economic Census*. The states are in descending order of sales or establishments (if sales data are missing for the majority). The symbol (D) appears when data are withheld to prevent disclosure of competitive information. States marked with (D) are sorted by number of establishments. A dash (-) indicates that the data element cannot be calculated. Shaded *states* on the state map indicate those states which have proportionately greater representation in the industry than would be indicated by the states population; the ratio is based on total sales or number of establishments. Shaded *regions* indicate where the industry is regionally most concentrated.

NAICS 441110 - NEW CAR DEALERS*

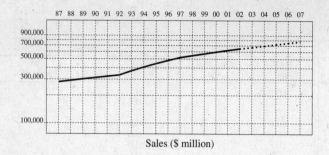

Sales ($ million)

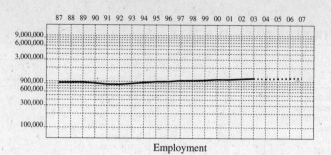

Employment

GENERAL STATISTICS

Year	Establishments (number)	Employment (number)	Payroll ($ million)	Sales ($ million)	Employees per Establishment (number)	Sales per Establishment ($)	Payroll per Employee ($)
1987	28,320	939,929	22,205.0	280,529.2	33	9,905,692	23,624
1988	27,382	952,524	24,463.7	291,183.7 e	35	10,634,128	25,683
1989	26,745	959,731	24,076.4	301,838.1 e	36	11,285,777	25,087
1990	26,132	917,207	23,919.1	312,492.5 e	35	11,958,231	26,078
1991	25,785	865,341	23,059.7	323,146.9 e	34	12,532,360	26,648
1992	24,380	860,139	24,421.3	333,801.4	35	13,691,608	28,392
1993	24,561	898,983	27,563.7	370,835.5 e	37	15,098,551	30,661
1994	24,130	949,438	30,685.7	407,869.6 e	39	16,903,009	32,320
1995	24,230	990,767	32,425.3	444,903.6 e	41	18,361,684	32,728
1996	24,138 e	997,735 e	32,257.5 e	481,937.7 e	41 e	19,965,933 e	32,331 e
1997	25,897	1,046,243	35,202.8	518,971.8	40	20,039,843	33,647
1998	26,216	1,049,618	38,856.5	544,775.8 e	40	20,780,278	37,020
1999	26,117	1,070,428	42,321.7	570,579.7 e	41	21,847,062	39,537
2000	26,225	1,111,848	44,768.3	596,383.7 e	42	22,741,036	40,265
2001	26,444	1,112,471	46,915.5	622,187.6 e	42	23,528,499	42,172
2002	26,672	1,146,478	46,231.4	647,991.6	43	24,294,826	40,325
2003	26,707	1,174,545	49,201.3	668,406.4 p	44	25,898,140 p	41,890
2004	25,673 p	1,153,786 p	49,919.7 p	695,208.4 p	45 p	26,933,446 p	43,998 p
2005	25,649 p	1,170,590 p	51,750.2 p	722,010.4 p	45 p	27,968,753 p	45,237 p
2006	25,626 p	1,187,394 p	53,580.7 p	748,812.4 p	46 p	29,004,060 p	46,476 p
2007	25,602 p	1,204,197 p	55,411.1 p	775,614.4 p	47 p	30,039,367 p	47,715 p

Sources: Economic Census of the United States, 1987, 1992, 1997, and 2002. Establishment counts, employment, and payroll are from *County Business Patterns* for non-Census years. Values followed by a 'p' are projections by the editors. Sales data for non-Census years are extrapolations, marked by 'e'. Data are the most recent available at this level of detail.

INDICES OF CHANGE

Year	Establishments (number)	Employment (number)	Payroll ($ million)	Sales ($ million)	Employees per Establishment (number)	Sales per Establishment ($)	Payroll per Employee ($)
1987	106.2	82.0	48.0	43.3	77.2	40.8	58.6
1992	91.4	75.0	52.8	51.5	82.1	56.4	70.4
1993	92.1	78.4	59.6	57.2 e	85.1	62.1	76.0
1994	90.5	82.8	66.4	62.9 e	91.4	69.6	80.1
1995	90.8	86.4	70.1	68.7 e	95.2	75.6	81.2
1996	90.5 e	87.0 e	69.8 e	74.4 e	96.1 e	82.2 e	80.2 e
1997	97.1	91.3	76.1	80.1	94.0	82.5	83.4
1998	98.3	91.6	84.0	84.1 e	93.1	85.5	91.8
1999	97.9	93.4	91.5	88.1 e	95.4	89.9	98.0
2000	98.3	97.0	96.8	92.0 e	98.6	93.6	99.9
2001	99.1	97.0	101.5	96.0 e	97.9	96.8	104.6
2002	100.0	100.0	100.0	100.0	100.0	100.0	100.0
2003	100.1	102.4	106.4	103.2 p	102.3	106.6 p	103.9
2004	96.3 p	100.6 p	108.0 p	107.3 p	104.0 p	110.9 p	109.1 p
2005	96.2 p	102.1 p	111.9 p	111.4 p	105.6 p	115.1 p	112.2 p
2006	96.1 p	103.6 p	115.9 p	115.6 p	107.1 p	119.4 p	115.3 p
2007	96.0 p	105.0 p	119.9 p	119.7 p	108.7 p	123.6 p	118.3 p

*Sources: Same as General Statistics. The values shown reflect change from the base year, 2002. Values above 100 mean greater than 2002, values below 100 mean less than 2002, and a value of 100 in the 1987-2001 or 2003-2007 period means same as 2002. Values followed by a 'p' are projections by the editors; 'e' stands for extrapolation. Data are the most recent available at this level of detail.

SELECTED RATIOS

For 2002	Avg. of All Retail	Analyzed Industry	Index	For 2002	Avg. of All Retail	Analyzed Industry	Index
Employees per Establishment	17	43	254	Sales per Employee	174,682	565,202	324
Payroll per Establishment	333,445	1,733,331	520	Sales per Establishment	3,332,269	24,294,826	729
Payroll per Employee	20,311	40,325	199	Expenses per Establishment	na	na	na

*Sources: Same as General Statistics. The 'Average of All' column, Wholesale or Retail, represents the average of the sector reported for the most recent complete year available. The Index shows the relationship between the Average and the Analyzed Industry. For example, 100 means that they are equal; 500 that the Analyzed Industry is five times the average; 50 means that the Analyzed Industry is half the national average. The abbreviation 'na' is used to show that data are 'not available'.

*Equivalent to SIC 5511.

LEADING COMPANIES   Number shown: **75**   Total sales ($ mil): **110,902**   Total employment (000): **136.6**

Company Name	Address				CEO Name	Phone	Co. Type	Sales ($ mil)	Empl. (000)
AutoNation Inc.	110 SE 6th St	Fort Lauderdale	FL	33301	Dan Agnew	954-769-6000	P	19,425	27.0
Ricart Chrysler Plymouth	465 S Hamilton Rd	Columbus	OH	43227	Fred Ricart		R	12,000*	1.0
UnitedAuto Group Inc.	13400 Outer Dr W	Detroit	MI	48239	Samuel X Difeo Jr	313-592-7311	P	9,886	13.0
JM Family Enterprises Inc.	100 Jim Moran Blvd	Deerfield Beach	FL	33442	Colin Brown	954-429-2000	R	7,700	3.7
Sonic Automotive Inc.	PO 18747	Charlotte	NC	28212	Jeffrey C Rachor	704-532-3320	P	7,395	11.3
Group 1 Automotive Inc.	950 Echo Ln	Houston	TX	77024	Earl J Hesterberg	713-647-5700	P	5,435	7.4
Asbury Automotive Group Inc.	3 Landmark Sq	Stamford	CT	06901	Kenneth B Gilman	203-356-4400	P	5,301	8.0
VT Inc.	Po Box 795	Schuylkl Hvn	KS	66201	Cecil L Van Tuyl	913-432-6400	R	4,300*	6.0
Lithia Motors Inc.	360 E Jackson St	Medford	OR	97501	Sidney B DeBoer	541-776-6899	P	2,746	5.1
Larry H. Miller Group	9350 S 150 E	Sandy	UT	84070	Karen G Miller	801-563-4100	R	2,550*	6.0
Hendrick Automotive Group	PO Box 18649	Charlotte	NC	28218	Jim Perkins	704-568-5550	R	2,300	4.7
Holman Enterprises	PO Box 1400	Pennsauken	NJ	08109	Joseph S Holman	856-663-5200	R	2,043*	2.6
Jordan Automotive Group	609 E Jefferson Blvd	Mishawaka	IN	46545	Craig Kapson	574-259-1981	R	2,000*	0.2
Don Massey Cadillac Inc.	40475 Ann Arbor Rd	Plymouth	MI	48170	Donald E Massey	734-453-7500	S	1,000*	1.5
Lou Fusz Automotive Network	9245 N Lindbergh	St. Louis	MO	63141	Lou Fusz Jr	314-994-1500	R	966*	1.1
Jeff Wyler Dealer Group	829 Eastgate S Dr	Cincinnati	OH	45245	Jeff Wyler	513-752-7450	R	882*	1.0
Herb Chambers Cos.	259 McGrath Hwy	Somerville	MA	02145	Herbert G Chambers	617-666-8333	R	800*	1.0
Beaudry Motor Co.	4600 E 2nd St	Tucson	AZ	85711	Bob Beaudry	520-748-1000	R	795*	0.9
Courtesy Acura Isuzu	7590 S Broadway	Littleton	CO	80122	Terry Dixon	303-795-7800	R	791*	1.1
Galpin Motors Inc.	15505 Roscoe Blvd	North Hills	CA	91343	Bert Boeckmann	818-787-3800	R	769*	0.9
Prestige Automotive Group	G-7401 Clio Rd	Mount Morris	MI	48458	Gregory Jackson	810-686-2310	R	767	0.4
Richardson and Partners	8601 Lomas NE	Albuquerque	NM	87112	Kenneth Blewett	505-292-0000	R	723*	0.8
Bob Rohrman Auto Group	701 Sagamore Pkwy	Lafayette	IN	47905	Bob Rohrman	765-448-1000	R	648*	0.9
Tuttle-Click Automotive Group	43 Auto Center Dr	Irvine	CA	92618	Robert H Tuttle		R	647*	1.4
Ricart Automotive	PO Box 27130	Columbus	OH	43227	Rhett C Ricart	614-836-5321	R	644*	1.0
Rosenthal Automotive Cos.	1100 S Glebe Rd	Arlington	VA	22204	Robert M Rosenthal	703-553-4300	S	644*	1.6
Jim Koons Management Co.	2000 Chain Bridge	Vienna	VA	22182	James E Koons	703-356-0400	R	642*	1.4
Sanderson Ford Trucks	6400 N 51st Ave	Glendale	AZ	85301	David Kimoly	623-842-8787	R	628*	0.5
David McDavid Auto Group	3700 Arpt Fwy	Irving	TX	75062	David McDavid Jr	972-790-6020	S	596*	1.1
Pacifico Group	6701 Essington Ave	Philadelphia	PA	19153	Kerry Pacifico	215-492-1700	R	570*	0.4
Ancira Enterprises Inc.	PO Box 29719	San Antonio	TX	78229	Ernesto Ancira Jr	210-681-4900	R	569*	0.7
Warnock Automotive Group Inc.	PO Box 346	East Hanover	NJ	07936	Michael Critchley	973-884-2100	R	538*	0.5
Ourisman Automotive Enterprises	4400 Branch Ave	Marlow Heights	MD	20748	John Ourisman	301-423-4000	R	522*	1.0
Braman Management Association	2060 Biscayne Blvd	Miami	FL	33137	Norman Braman	305-576-1889	R	500*	0.8
Spitzer Management Inc.	150 E Bridge St	Elyria	OH	44035	Alan Spitzer	440-323-4671	R	500*	1.0
Toresco Enterprises Inc.	170 Rte 22 E	Springfield	NJ	07081	Donald Toresco	973-467-2900	R	498	0.7
Lupient Automotive Group	7100 Wayzata Blvd	Golden Valley	MN	55426	James Lupient	763-546-2222	R	494*	1.0
Coggin Automotive Corp.	PO Box 1649	Jacksonville	FL	32201	Luther Coggin	904-992-4110	R	475*	1.0
Saab Cars USA Inc.	4405-A International	Norcross	GA	30093	Peter Augustsson	770-279-0100	R	450*	0.2
Sanderson Ford Inc.	6400 N 51st Ave	Glendale	AZ	85301	David Kimmerle	623-842-8600	R	440*	0.5
Curry Corp.	727 Central Ave	Scarsdale	NY	10583	Bernard F Curry Jr	914-723-9200	R	439*	0.5
Martin Automotive Group Inc.	2211 Scottsville Rd	Bowling Green	KY	42104	Cornelius A Martin	270-842-6323	R	435	0.7
Scott-McRae Automotive Group	701 Riverside Park	Jacksonville	FL	32204	Henry H Graham Jr	904-354-4000	R	430*	0.7
Cherry Creek Dodge Inc.	2727 S Havana St	Aurora	CO	80014	Sidney B DeBoer	303-751-1104	S	414*	0.1
Kelley Automotive Group Inc.	633 Ave of Autos	Fort Wayne	IN	46804	Jim Kelley	260-434-4750	R	405*	1.2
Major Automotive Companies Inc.	43-40 Northern Blvd	Long Island City	NY	11101	Bruce Bendell	718-937-3700	P	380	0.5
S. Woods Enterprises Inc.	PO Box 76037	Tampa	FL	33675	Sanford L Woods	813-620-4300	R	332	0.4
Gunn Chevrolet Inc.	12602 IH-35 N	San Antonio	TX	78233		210-599-5000	R	329*	0.7
Burt Automotive Network	5200 S Broadway	Englewood	CO	80110	Lloyd Chavez	303-761-0333	R	319*	1.2
Fletcher Jones Management Group	175 E Reno, Ste C-6	Las Vegas	NV	89119	Fletcher Jones Jr	702-739-9800	R	315*	0.6
Champion Ford Gulf Freeway	12227 Gulf Fwy	Houston	TX	77034	Bob Zweig	713-371-4300	R	308*	0.4
Servco Pacific Inc.	PO Box 2788	Honolulu	HI	96803	Mark H Fukunaga	808-521-6511	S	307*	0.9
Arrow Truck Sales Inc.	3200 Manchester	Kansas City	MO	64129	Ed Justis	816-923-5000	R	300*	0.3
Barrier Motors Inc.	11950 Bellv Rdmnd	Bellevue	WA	98005		425-455-8535	R	300*	0.3
Western Truck Parts & Equipment	1441 Richards Blvd	Sacramento	CA	95814	James Coles	916-441-6151	R	300*	0.1
Harrell-Swatty Cos.	6 Concourse Pky NE	Atlanta	GA	30328	H Steve Harrell, Sr	770-969-0204	R	287	0.4
CarsDirect.com	909 Sepulveda Blvd	El Segundo	CA	90245	Robert N Brisco		R	286*	0.4
Ancira Winton Chevrolet Inc.	6111 Bandera Rd	San Antonio	TX	78238	Ernesto Ancira Jr	210-681-4900	S	285*	0.3
Guaranty Chevrolet-Pontiac	PO Box 279	Junction City	OR	97448	Shannon Nill	541-998-2333	R	278*	0.5
Truck Country of Rockford Inc.	10785 Hwy 61 S	Rockford	IL	61109	Jack McCoy	815-398-9455	S	278*	1.0
Hometown Auto Retailers Inc.	774 Straits Tpke	Watertown	CT	06795		860-945-6900	P	265	0.4
Damerow Beaverton Ford	12325 SW Canyon	Beaverton	OR	97005		503-644-1131	R	265*	0.3
Midway Ford Truck Center Inc.	PO Box 12656	Kansas City	MO	64116	Donald C Ahnger	816-455-3000	R	260*	0.3
Jim Click Ford Inc.	PO Box 12399	Tucson	AZ	85732	Jim Click	520-747-2000	R	256*	0.9
Automanage Inc.	5726 Dixie Hwy	Fairfield	OH	45014		513-874-8797	R	254*	0.4
S and C Ford	2001 Market St	San Francisco	CA	94114	Ray P Siotto	415-861-6000	R	250*	0.2
Gwatney Cos.	2000 Covington Pike	Memphis	TN	38128	Russell Gwatney	901-387-2000	R	247*	0.3
Ted Britt Ford	11165 Main St	Fairfax	VA	22030	Gardner Britt	703-591-8484	R	246*	0.3
Joe Myers Ford Inc.	16634 Northwest	Houston	TX	77040	Terry Luker		R	233*	0.5
Family Automotive Group Inc.	33396 Capistrano	SJ Bautista	CA	92675	Raymond Dixon	949-493-4100	R	227	0.3
John Sullivan Dealerships	700 Automall Dr	Roseville	CA	95661	John Sullivan	916-782-1243	R	225*	0.3
Boyland Auto Group Inc.	710 W Marine Dr	Astoria	OR	97103	Dorian S Boyland	503-325-6411	R	222	0.4
Buz Post Pontiac/GMC Inc.	PO Box 1568	Arlington	TX	76010	Buz Post	817-467-1234	R	220*	0.3
Salinas Valley Ford Sales Inc.	1100 Auto Center	Salinas	CA	93907	Ronald W Frieberg	831-444-4444	R	220*	0.3
Lawrence Marshall Chevrolet	900 Business 290 N	Hempstead	TX	77445	Ray Childress	979-826-2411	R	207*	0.3

Source: Ward's Business Directory of U.S. Private and Public Companies, Volumes 1 and 2, 2005. The company type code used is as follows: P - Public, R - Private, S - Subsidiary, D - Division, J - Joint Venture, A - Affiliate, G - Group. Sales are in millions of dollars, employees are in thousands. An asterisk (*) indicates an estimated sales volume. The symbol < stands for 'less than'. Company names and addresses are truncated, in some cases, to fit into the available space.

OCCUPATIONS EMPLOYED BY AUTOMOBILE DEALERS

Occupation	% of Total 2004	Change to 2014	Occupation	% of Total 2004	Change to 2014
Retail salespersons	21.5	17.7	General & operations managers	2.2	16.5
Automotive service technicians & mechanics	18.1	17.7	Cashiers, except gaming	1.8	6.0
Cleaners of vehicles & equipment	6.4	6.7	Sales managers	1.7	26.0
Parts salespersons	5.3	-5.8	Truck drivers, light or delivery services	1.5	18.0
First-line supervisors/managers of retail sales workers	4.1	8.3	First-line supervisors/managers of office workers	1.2	6.7
Automotive body & related repairers	3.4	3.2	Laborers & freight, stock, & material movers, hand	1.1	6.0
Office clerks, general	2.9	4.8	Helpers-Installation, maintenance, & repair workers	1.1	17.7
First-line supervisors of mechanics	2.8	17.7	Receptionists & information clerks	1.1	12.2
Bookkeeping, accounting, & auditing clerks	2.8	6.0	Customer service representatives	1.1	20.6
Counter & rental clerks	2.4	23.6	Switchboard operators, including answering service	1.1	-11.7

Source: Industry-Occupation Matrix, Bureau of Labor Statistics. These data are reported based on 4-digit NAICS categories but have been matched to corresponding 6-digit NAICS industry codes. The change reported for each occupation to the year 2014 is a percent of growth or decline as estimated by the Bureau of Labor Statistics. The abbreviation nec stands for 'not elsewhere classified.'

LOCATION BY STATE AND REGIONAL CONCENTRATION

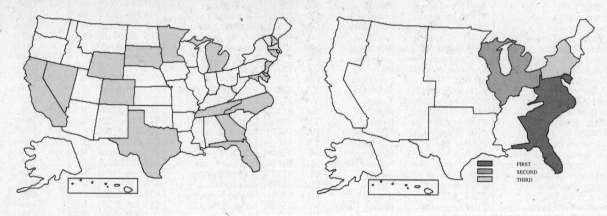

INDUSTRY DATA BY STATE

State	Establishments Total (number)	Establishments % of U.S.	Employment Total (number)	Employment % of U.S.	Employment Per Estab.	Payroll Total ($ mil.)	Payroll Per Empl. ($)	Sales Total ($ mil.)	Sales % of U.S.	Sales Per Estab. ($)
California	2,255	8.5	130,858	11.4	58	6,078.4	46,450	79,799.6	12.4	35,387,865
Texas	1,663	6.2	91,104	8.0	55	3,697.4	40,585	54,260.5	8.4	32,628,079
Florida	1,341	5.0	71,148	6.2	53	2,951.8	41,488	43,431.3	6.7	32,387,233
New York	1,421	5.3	50,252	4.4	35	2,156.6	42,915	31,478.7	4.9	22,152,526
Illinois	1,197	4.5	48,646	4.3	41	1,999.6	41,105	27,621.1	4.3	23,075,312
Pennsylvania	1,518	5.7	53,998	4.7	36	1,952.9	36,167	27,282.8	4.2	17,972,879
Michigan	958	3.6	39,529	3.5	41	1,735.9	43,914	26,555.3	4.1	27,719,531
Ohio	1,148	4.3	47,360	4.1	41	1,757.6	37,111	24,831.8	3.8	21,630,498
New Jersey	789	3.0	32,636	2.9	41	1,556.8	47,701	23,154.5	3.6	29,346,622
Georgia	783	2.9	35,420	3.1	45	1,445.4	40,808	20,141.8	3.1	25,723,861
North Carolina	930	3.5	33,779	3.0	36	1,295.1	38,340	18,879.5	2.9	20,300,575
Virginia	639	2.4	31,546	2.8	49	1,290.1	40,895	16,125.5	2.5	25,235,576
Massachusetts	594	2.2	25,853	2.3	44	1,140.3	44,108	14,783.1	2.3	24,887,387
Maryland	406	1.5	26,268	2.3	65	1,102.5	41,971	13,944.0	2.2	34,344,719
Indiana	663	2.5	24,126	2.1	36	881.2	36,524	13,188.4	2.0	19,892,062
Missouri	626	2.3	24,147	2.1	39	942.8	39,045	13,025.9	2.0	20,808,072
Tennessee	604	2.3	24,329	2.1	40	938.0	38,553	12,732.7	2.0	21,080,679
Wisconsin	686	2.6	25,665	2.2	37	879.1	34,251	12,231.1	1.9	17,829,643
Minnesota	573	2.1	22,370	2.0	39	832.0	37,195	11,858.6	1.8	20,695,560
Colorado	367	1.4	19,347	1.7	53	869.6	44,948	11,738.2	1.8	31,984,210
Washington	491	1.8	22,512	2.0	46	954.2	42,384	11,588.2	1.8	23,601,301
Alabama	430	1.6	16,724	1.5	39	590.4	35,304	9,164.3	1.4	21,312,286
Louisiana	362	1.4	17,130	1.5	47	624.1	36,431	8,897.4	1.4	24,578,503
Connecticut	421	1.6	15,532	1.4	37	703.7	45,309	8,693.2	1.3	20,648,922
South Carolina	441	1.7	14,492	1.3	33	552.9	38,151	7,988.2	1.2	18,113,918
Oklahoma	394	1.5	13,629	1.2	35	472.8	34,691	7,403.9	1.1	18,791,538
Oregon	363	1.4	14,268	1.2	39	558.4	39,136	7,244.4	1.1	19,957,017
Kentucky	422	1.6	15,075	1.3	36	513.2	34,042	7,164.9	1.1	16,978,495
Iowa	454	1.7	13,421	1.2	30	450.7	33,584	6,162.1	1.0	13,572,885
Kansas	347	1.3	10,422	0.9	30	389.1	37,333	5,377.1	0.8	15,496,006
Arkansas	330	1.2	9,128	0.8	28	312.6	34,249	5,300.1	0.8	16,060,961
Nevada	120	0.4	9,380	0.8	78	417.9	44,554	5,274.0	0.8	43,949,708
Mississippi	295	1.1	9,393	0.8	32	321.1	34,183	4,905.9	0.8	16,630,214

Continued on next page.

INDUSTRY DATA BY STATE - Continued

State	Establishments		Employment			Payroll		Sales		
	Total (number)	% of U.S.	Total (number)	% of U.S.	Per Estab.	Total ($ mil.)	Per Empl. ($)	Total ($ mil.)	% of U.S.	Per Estab. ($)
Utah	215	0.8	8,688	0.8	40	310.7	35,757	4,550.1	0.7	21,163,079
New Hampshire	204	0.8	7,224	0.6	35	298.4	41,303	4,157.5	0.6	20,379,750
Nebraska	269	1.0	7,653	0.7	28	271.1	35,428	4,007.9	0.6	14,899,130
New Mexico	178	0.7	7,181	0.6	40	269.1	37,476	3,688.2	0.6	20,719,972
West Virginia	227	0.9	6,575	0.6	29	205.8	31,308	3,303.5	0.5	14,553,057
Maine	177	0.7	5,775	0.5	33	211.7	36,652	2,779.4	0.4	15,703,068
Idaho	158	0.6	5,258	0.5	33	192.1	36,536	2,580.3	0.4	16,330,861
Delaware	81	0.3	4,278	0.4	53	163.1	38,133	2,238.9	0.3	27,640,284
Hawaii	76	0.3	4,060	0.4	53	166.8	41,075	2,169.4	0.3	28,544,092
Rhode Island	92	0.3	3,561	0.3	39	146.1	41,036	2,106.1	0.3	22,892,196
Montana	158	0.6	4,364	0.4	28	127.9	29,312	1,912.6	0.3	12,105,171
South Dakota	140	0.5	3,660	0.3	26	122.9	33,570	1,778.3	0.3	12,702,321
North Dakota	117	0.4	3,711	0.3	32	113.9	30,696	1,600.2	0.2	13,677,111
Vermont	111	0.4	2,998	0.3	27	110.2	36,769	1,501.7	0.2	13,528,432
Alaska	47	0.2	2,375	0.2	51	101.3	42,637	1,236.6	0.2	26,311,553
Wyoming	74	0.3	2,322	0.2	31	78.9	34,000	1,121.2	0.2	15,151,500
Arizona	309	1.2	10K-24999	-	-	(D)	-	(D)	-	-
D.C.	6	-	100-249	-	-	(D)	-	(D)	-	-

Source: 2002 *Economic Census*. The states are in descending order of sales or establishments (if sales data are missing for the majority). The symbol (D) appears when data are withheld to prevent disclosure of competitive information. States marked with (D) are sorted by number of establishments. A dash (-) indicates that the data element cannot be calculated. Shaded *states* on the state map indicate those states which have proportionately greater representation in the industry than would be indicated by the states population; the ratio is based on total sales or number of establishments. Shaded *regions* indicate where the industry is regionally most concentrated.

NAICS 441120 - USED CAR DEALERS*

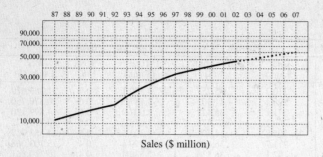

Sales ($ million)

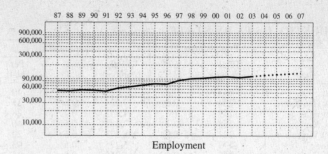

Employment

GENERAL STATISTICS

Year	Establishments (number)	Employment (number)	Payroll ($ million)	Sales ($ million)	Employees per Establishment (number)	Sales per Establishment ($)	Payroll per Employee ($)
1987	14,948	55,494	808.8	10,848.7	4	725,763	14,574
1988	13,781	54,407	899.4	11,885.2 e	4	862,434	16,531
1989	14,819	56,888	950.0	12,921.8 e	4	871,975	16,699
1990	14,283	56,125	968.9	13,958.3 e	4	977,267	17,263
1991	14,656	53,952	962.1	14,994.8 e	4	1,023,117	17,833
1992	18,672	62,793	1,131.8	16,031.3	3	858,574	18,024
1993	19,281	67,392	1,319.0	19,761.1 e	4	1,024,900	19,572
1994	19,569	72,847	1,504.7	23,491.0 e	4	1,200,419	20,656
1995	19,656	78,303	1,676.5	27,220.8 e	4	1,384,860	21,410
1996	20,047 e	76,714 e	1,577.4 e	30,950.7 e	4 e	1,543,907 e	20,562 e
1997	23,340	92,752	2,197.4	34,680.5	4	1,485,883	23,691
1998	23,651	101,761	2,577.9	37,334.8 e	4	1,578,570	25,333
1999	23,998	104,753	2,859.6	39,989.0 e	4	1,666,347	27,298
2000	24,653	110,256	3,068.4	42,643.3 e	5	1,729,739	27,830
2001	25,188	112,948	3,246.0	45,297.5 e	5	1,798,377	28,739
2002	25,008	108,430	2,981.5	47,951.8	4	1,917,457	27,497
2003	25,571	115,140	3,220.7	49,860.6 p	5	1,971,174 p	27,972
2004	27,534 p	121,756 p	3,465.5 p	52,565.0 p	5 p	2,051,242 p	30,167 p
2005	28,363 p	126,258 p	3,641.7 p	55,269.5 p	5 p	2,131,309 p	31,091 p
2006	29,193 p	130,761 p	3,817.9 p	57,974.0 p	5 p	2,211,377 p	32,015 p
2007	30,023 p	135,263 p	3,994.1 p	60,678.5 p	5 p	2,291,444 p	32,939 p

Sources: Economic Census of the United States, 1987, 1992, 1997, and 2002. Establishment counts, employment, and payroll are from County Business Patterns for non-Census years. Values followed by a 'p' are projections by the editors. Sales data for non-Census years are extrapolations, marked by 'e'. Data are the most recent available at this level of detail.

INDICES OF CHANGE

Year	Establishments (number)	Employment (number)	Payroll ($ million)	Sales ($ million)	Employees per Establishment (number)	Sales per Establishment ($)	Payroll per Employee ($)
1987	59.8	51.2	27.1	22.6	85.3	37.9	53.0
1992	74.7	57.9	38.0	33.4	78.4	44.8	65.6
1993	77.1	62.2	44.2	41.2 e	80.7	53.5	71.2
1994	78.3	67.2	50.5	49.0 e	85.3	62.6	75.1
1995	78.6	72.2	56.2	56.8 e	92.3	72.2	77.9
1996	80.2 e	70.7 e	52.9 e	64.5 e	87.6 e	80.5 e	74.8 e
1997	93.3	85.5	73.7	72.3	92.3	77.5	86.2
1998	94.6	93.8	86.5	77.9 e	99.2	82.3	92.1
1999	96.0	96.6	95.9	83.4 e	101.5	86.9	99.3
2000	98.6	101.7	102.9	88.9 e	103.8	90.2	101.2
2001	100.7	104.2	108.9	94.5 e	103.8	93.8	104.5
2002	100.0	100.0	100.0	100.0	100.0	100.0	100.0
2003	102.3	106.2	108.0	104.0 p	103.9	102.8 p	101.7
2004	110.1 p	112.3 p	116.2 p	109.6 p	104.0 p	107.0 p	109.7 p
2005	113.4 p	116.4 p	122.1 p	115.3 p	105.3 p	111.2 p	113.1 p
2006	116.7 p	120.6 p	128.1 p	120.9 p	106.6 p	115.3 p	116.4 p
2007	120.1 p	124.7 p	134.0 p	126.5 p	108.0 p	119.5 p	119.8 p

Sources: Same as General Statistics. The values shown reflect change from the base year, 2002. Values above 100 mean greater than 2002, values below 100 mean less than 2002, and a value of 100 in the 1987-2001 or 2003-2007 period means same as 2002. Values followed by a 'p' are projections by the editors; 'e' stands for extrapolation. Data are the most recent available at this level of detail.

SELECTED RATIOS

For 2002	Avg. of All Retail	Analyzed Industry	Index	For 2002	Avg. of All Retail	Analyzed Industry	Index
Employees per Establishment	17	4	26	Sales per Employee	174,682	442,237	253
Payroll per Establishment	333,445	119,221	36	Sales per Establishment	3,332,269	1,917,457	58
Payroll per Employee	20,311	27,497	135	Expenses per Establishment	na	na	na

Sources: Same as General Statistics. The 'Average of All' column, Wholesale or Retail, represents the average of the sector reported for the most recent complete year available. The Index shows the relationship between the Average and the Analyzed Industry. For example, 100 means that they are equal; 500 that the Analyzed Industry is five times the average; 50 means that the Analyzed Industry is half the national average. The abbreviation 'na' is used to show that data are 'not available'.

*Equivalent to SIC 5521.

LEADING COMPANIES   Number shown: **18**   Total sales ($ mil): **5,085**   Total employment (000): **10.5**

Company Name	Address				CEO Name	Phone	Co. Type	Sales ($ mil)	Empl. (000)
CarMax Inc.	4900 Cox Rd	Glen Allen	VA	23060	Austin Ligon	804-747-0422	P	4,598	9.7
Metro Salvage	825 Rankin Rd	Houston	TX	77073	John Nichols	281-821-2300	R	88*	<0.1
Freightliner of Hartford Inc.	222 Roberts St	East Hartford	CT	06108	Lindy Bigliazzi	860-289-0201	R	82*	<0.1
Alan Young Buick-GMC Truck	7724 NE Loop 820	N Richland Hls	TX	76180	Alan J Young	817-589-3300	R	41	<0.1
David Taylor Cadillac Co.	PO Box 36428	Houston	TX	77236	David W Taylor Jr	713-777-7151	R	39*	0.2
Sport Truck USA-Coldwater Inc.	647 E Chicago St	Coldwater	MI	49036	Shawn Avra	517-278-5557	R	34*	<0.1
Pye's Auto Sales Inc.	6303 Fm 1960 Rd W	Humble	TX	77338	Sidney Pye	281-446-1515	R	33*	<0.1
Dunlo Motors Inc.	5241 W Broadway	Minneapolis	MN	55429	Andrew Duncanson	763-533-0594	R	31*	<0.1
NE Penna Salvage Company Inc.	PO Box 596	Pittston	PA	18640	Jean Conlon	570-654-1709	R	30*	<0.1
Autohaus of Minneapolis Inc.	7705 42nd Ave N	Minneapolis	MN	55427	Thomas Boettcher	763-535-5700	R	28*	<0.1
B and G Auto Sales Inc.	PO Box 590	Colton	CA	92324	Shirley Chadwick	909-825-1173	R	25*	<0.1
Delaware Public Auto Auction	2323 N Dupont	New Castle	DE	19720	Doug Powell	302-656-0500	R	25*	<0.1
Elliff Motors Inc.	1307 W Harrison St	Harlingen	TX	78550	Bill Elliff	956-423-3434	R	14*	<0.1
National Auto Credit Inc.	555 Madison Ave	New York	NY	10022	James J McNamara	212-644-1400	P	7	<0.1
Manhiem Keystone Public Auto	488 Firehouse Rd	Grantville	PA	17028		717-469-7900	R	5*	<0.1
Chet's Wrecking & Auto Parts Inc.	1735 Page Blvd	Springfield	MA	01104	Kenneth Bousquet	413-543-3247	R	4*	<0.1
Harbor Auto Liquidators	17800 S Vermont	Gardena	CA	90248	Lewis Canfield	714-934-8310	R	2*	<0.1
Homeland Security Network Inc.	PO Box 1678	Frisco	TX	75034	Charles Norman	214-618-6400	P	1	<0.1

Source: *Ward's Business Directory of U.S. Private and Public Companies*, Volumes 1 and 2, 2005. The company type code used is as follows: P - Public, R - Private, S - Subsidiary, D - Division, J - Joint Venture, A - Affiliate, G - Group. Sales are in millions of dollars, employees are in thousands. An asterisk (*) indicates an estimated sales volume. The symbol < stands for 'less than'. Company names and addresses are truncated, in some cases, to fit into the available space.

OCCUPATIONS EMPLOYED BY AUTOMOBILE DEALERS

Occupation	% of Total 2004	Change to 2014	Occupation	% of Total 2004	Change to 2014
Retail salespersons	21.5	17.7	General & operations managers	2.2	16.5
Automotive service technicians & mechanics	18.1	17.7	Cashiers, except gaming	1.8	6.0
Cleaners of vehicles & equipment	6.4	6.7	Sales managers	1.7	26.0
Parts salespersons	5.3	-5.8	Truck drivers, light or delivery services	1.5	18.0
First-line supervisors/managers of retail sales workers	4.1	8.3	First-line supervisors/managers of office workers	1.2	6.7
Automotive body & related repairers	3.4	3.2	Laborers & freight, stock, & material movers, hand	1.1	6.0
Office clerks, general	2.9	4.8	Helpers-Installation, maintenance, & repair workers	1.1	17.7
First-line supervisors of mechanics	2.8	17.7	Receptionists & information clerks	1.1	12.2
Bookkeeping, accounting, & auditing clerks	2.8	6.0	Customer service representatives	1.1	20.6
Counter & rental clerks	2.4	23.6	Switchboard operators, including answering service	1.1	-11.7

Source: *Industry-Occupation Matrix*, Bureau of Labor Statistics. These data are reported based on 4-digit NAICS categories but have been matched to corresponding 6-digit NAICS industry codes. The change reported for each occupation to the year 2014 is a percent of growth or decline as estimated by the Bureau of Labor Statistics. The abbreviation nec stands for 'not elsewhere classified.'

LOCATION BY STATE AND REGIONAL CONCENTRATION

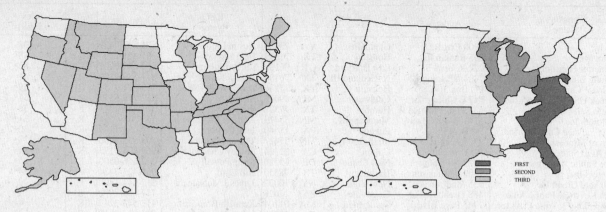

INDUSTRY DATA BY STATE

State	Establishments Total (number)	Establishments % of U.S.	Employment Total (number)	Employment % of U.S.	Employment Per Estab.	Payroll Total ($ mil.)	Payroll Per Empl. ($)	Sales Total ($ mil.)	Sales % of U.S.	Sales Per Estab. ($)
Texas	2,193	8.8	10,557	9.7	5	310.1	29,372	4,928.2	10.2	2,247,233
California	1,537	6.1	7,914	7.3	5	230.3	29,103	3,675.3	7.6	2,391,185
Florida	1,669	6.7	6,893	6.3	4	189.5	27,497	3,200.7	6.7	1,917,726
Pennsylvania	1,188	4.7	5,123	4.7	4	134.1	26,175	2,180.3	4.5	1,835,277
Ohio	1,039	4.1	4,655	4.3	4	126.2	27,111	1,999.7	4.2	1,924,675
North Carolina	1,084	4.3	4,212	3.9	4	110.2	26,171	1,786.2	3.7	1,647,793
Illinois	819	3.3	4,096	3.8	5	113.4	27,676	1,735.7	3.6	2,119,333
New York	1,097	4.4	3,513	3.2	3	97.2	27,673	1,734.0	3.6	1,580,674
Virginia	775	3.1	3,985	3.7	5	120.5	30,243	1,705.9	3.5	2,201,185
Georgia	840	3.4	3,436	3.2	4	94.0	27,350	1,573.7	3.3	1,873,495
Indiana	831	3.3	3,525	3.2	4	93.1	26,413	1,527.0	3.2	1,837,549
Tennessee	688	2.7	3,025	2.8	4	76.1	25,146	1,302.1	2.7	1,892,517
Michigan	680	2.7	2,578	2.4	4	70.6	27,394	1,190.3	2.5	1,750,371
Missouri	702	2.8	2,684	2.5	4	67.0	24,977	1,090.8	2.3	1,553,832
Wisconsin	552	2.2	2,601	2.4	5	69.3	26,636	1,069.0	2.2	1,936,621
Alabama	632	2.5	2,422	2.2	4	58.0	23,960	1,021.0	2.1	1,615,487
Massachusetts	495	2.0	1,884	1.7	4	59.9	31,792	993.4	2.1	2,006,820
New Jersey	525	2.1	1,864	1.7	4	53.2	28,550	988.5	2.1	1,882,781
Kentucky	490	2.0	2,076	1.9	4	56.6	27,252	972.0	2.0	1,983,671
Washington	503	2.0	2,604	2.4	5	72.1	27,671	947.2	2.0	1,883,119
Colorado	400	1.6	1,886	1.7	5	65.9	34,918	884.9	1.8	2,212,228
South Carolina	529	2.1	2,108	1.9	4	52.4	24,848	873.7	1.8	1,651,567
Utah	250	1.0	1,500	1.4	6	39.9	26,586	806.2	1.7	3,224,632
Arkansas	400	1.6	1,587	1.5	4	38.7	24,379	703.8	1.5	1,759,460
Minnesota	391	1.6	1,429	1.3	4	37.0	25,923	668.2	1.4	1,708,877
Oklahoma	363	1.4	1,519	1.4	4	40.2	26,446	652.7	1.4	1,797,970
Oregon	303	1.2	1,275	1.2	4	40.1	31,473	586.9	1.2	1,936,825
Maryland	269	1.1	1,366	1.3	5	40.8	29,847	571.0	1.2	2,122,784
Kansas	313	1.2	1,134	1.0	4	27.5	24,282	473.9	1.0	1,514,160
Mississippi	357	1.4	1,153	1.1	3	27.1	23,516	472.7	1.0	1,324,227
Iowa	333	1.3	1,281	1.2	4	29.9	23,364	468.0	1.0	1,405,378
Louisiana	272	1.1	1,247	1.1	5	26.1	20,909	430.5	0.9	1,582,710
Nevada	123	0.5	987	0.9	8	29.6	29,989	382.5	0.8	3,109,943
Nebraska	242	1.0	818	0.8	3	21.4	26,150	367.1	0.8	1,516,789
Connecticut	231	0.9	982	0.9	4	29.4	29,915	352.6	0.7	1,526,277
New Hampshire	157	0.6	869	0.8	6	29.8	34,274	343.9	0.7	2,190,452
Idaho	154	0.6	814	0.7	5	23.5	28,834	336.8	0.7	2,187,117
New Mexico	168	0.7	658	0.6	4	18.2	27,585	324.6	0.7	1,931,875
West Virginia	214	0.9	622	0.6	3	14.2	22,793	280.9	0.6	1,312,654
Maine	183	0.7	909	0.8	5	17.6	19,399	257.9	0.5	1,409,235
Montana	125	0.5	573	0.5	5	13.7	23,869	239.7	0.5	1,917,848
South Dakota	97	0.4	459	0.4	5	12.5	27,192	216.1	0.4	2,227,907
Rhode Island	134	0.5	491	0.5	4	15.1	30,819	182.5	0.4	1,361,843
Delaware	94	0.4	472	0.4	5	13.8	29,150	159.0	0.3	1,691,468
Alaska	35	0.1	309	0.3	9	10.8	34,848	149.3	0.3	4,264,314
Vermont	95	0.4	380	0.3	4	10.7	28,118	133.3	0.3	1,402,905
Wyoming	49	0.2	199	0.2	4	5.3	26,789	109.5	0.2	2,234,653
Hawaii	31	0.1	180	0.2	6	6.5	36,350	91.7	0.2	2,959,000
North Dakota	68	0.3	247	0.2	4	4.6	18,684	82.4	0.2	1,212,029
Arizona	330	1.3	1000-2499	-	-	(D)	-	(D)	-	-
D.C.	12	-	20-99	-	-	(D)	-	(D)	-	-

Source: 2002 *Economic Census*. The states are in descending order of sales or establishments (if sales data are missing for the majority). The symbol (D) appears when data are withheld to prevent disclosure of competitive information. States marked with (D) are sorted by number of establishments. A dash (-) indicates that the data element cannot be calculated. Shaded *states* on the state map indicate those states which have proportionately greater representation in the industry than would be indicated by the states population; the ratio is based on total sales or number of establishments. Shaded *regions* indicate where the industry is regionally most concentrated.

NAICS 441210 - RECREATIONAL VEHICLE DEALERS*

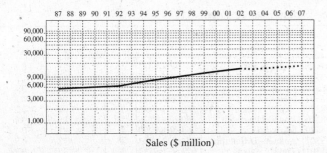

Sales ($ million)

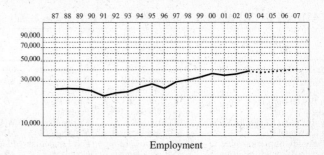

Employment

GENERAL STATISTICS

Year	Establishments (number)	Employment (number)	Payroll ($ million)	Sales ($ million)	Employees per Establishment (number)	Sales per Establishment ($)	Payroll per Employee ($)
1987	3,006	24,621	437.4	5,538.5	8	1,842,482	17,765
1988	2,815	24,991	497.4	5,693.5 e	9	2,022,558	19,903
1989	2,700	24,742	483.5	5,848.6 e	9	2,166,148	19,542
1990	2,711	23,523	480.1	6,003.7 e	9	2,214,570	20,410
1991	2,656	20,718	458.5	6,158.7 e	8	2,318,788	22,130
1992	2,826	22,304	514.3	6,313.8	8	2,234,183	23,059
1993	2,840	23,028	571.2	7,065.0 e	8	2,487,676	24,805
1994	2,850	25,593	662.4	7,816.2 e	9	2,742,526	25,882
1995	2,867	27,923	714.3	8,567.3 e	10	2,988,246	25,581
1996	2,803 e	25,024 e	686.5 e	9,318.5 e	9 e	3,324,474 e	27,434 e
1997	3,014	29,463	814.0	10,069.7	10	3,340,975	27,628
1998	3,012	30,999	962.8	11,050.4 e	10	3,668,801	31,059
1999	3,039	33,272	1,090.0	12,031.2 e	11	3,958,921	32,760
2000	3,114	36,376	1,146.5	13,011.9 e	12	4,178,513	31,519
2001	3,134	34,829	1,143.0	13,992.6 e	11	4,464,780	32,817
2002	3,088	35,932	1,240.9	14,973.4	12	4,848,883	34,535
2003	3,064	38,578	1,421.5	14,503.2 p	13	4,705,411 p	36,848
2004	3,121 p	37,208 p	1,329.7 p	15,154.6 p	12 p	4,900,146 p	36,922 p
2005	3,144 p	38,192 p	1,390.3 p	15,806.1 p	12 p	5,094,882 p	38,059 p
2006	3,167 p	39,176 p	1,451.0 p	16,457.5 p	12 p	5,289,618 p	39,197 p
2007	3,190 p	40,161 p	1,511.7 p	17,109.0 p	13 p	5,484,353 p	40,334 p

Sources: *Economic Census of the United States*, 1987, 1992, 1997, and 2002. Establishment counts, employment, and payroll are from *County Business Patterns* for non-Census years. Values followed by a 'p' are projections by the editors. Sales data for non-Census years are extrapolations, marked by 'e'. Data are the most recent available at this level of detail.

INDICES OF CHANGE

Year	Establishments (number)	Employment (number)	Payroll ($ million)	Sales ($ million)	Employees per Establishment (number)	Sales per Establishment ($)	Payroll per Employee ($)
1987	97.3	68.5	35.2	37.0	70.5	38.0	51.4
1992	91.5	62.1	41.4	42.2	67.9	46.1	66.8
1993	92.0	64.1	46.0	47.2 e	69.6	51.3	71.8
1994	92.3	71.2	53.4	52.2 e	77.3	56.6	74.9
1995	92.8	77.7	57.6	57.2 e	83.4	61.6	74.1
1996	90.8 e	69.6 e	55.3 e	62.2 e	76.5 e	68.6 e	79.4 e
1997	97.6	82.0	65.6	67.3	84.2	68.9	80.0
1998	97.5	86.3	77.6	73.8 e	88.5	75.7	89.9
1999	98.4	92.6	87.8	80.4 e	93.7	81.6	94.9
2000	100.8	101.2	92.4	86.9 e	100.5	86.2	91.3
2001	101.5	96.9	92.1	93.5 e	95.4	92.1	95.0
2002	100.0	100.0	100.0	100.0	100.0	100.0	100.0
2003	99.2	107.4	114.6	96.9 p	108.2	97.0 p	106.7
2004	101.1 p	103.5 p	107.2 p	101.2 p	102.8 p	101.1 p	106.9 p
2005	101.8 p	106.3 p	112.0 p	105.6 p	104.9 p	105.1 p	110.2 p
2006	102.6 p	109.0 p	116.9 p	109.9 p	107.1 p	109.1 p	113.5 p
2007	103.3 p	111.8 p	121.8 p	114.3 p	109.3 p	113.1 p	116.8 p

Sources: Same as General Statistics. The values shown reflect change from the base year, 2002. Values above 100 mean greater than 2002, values below 100 mean less than 2002, and a value of 100 in the 1987-2001 or 2003-2007 period means same as 2002. Values followed by a 'p' are projections by the editors; 'e' stands for extrapolation. Data are the most recent available at this level of detail.

SELECTED RATIOS

For 2002	Avg. of All Retail	Analyzed Industry	Index	For 2002	Avg. of All Retail	Analyzed Industry	Index
Employees per Establishment	17	12	69	Sales per Employee	174,682	416,714	239
Payroll per Establishment	333,445	401,848	121	Sales per Establishment	3,332,269	4,848,883	146
Payroll per Employee	20,311	34,535	170	Expenses per Establishment	na	na	na

Sources: Same as General Statistics. The 'Average of All' column, Wholesale or Retail, represents the average of the sector reported for the most recent complete year available. The Index shows the relationship between the Average and the Analyzed Industry. For example, 100 means that they are equal; 500 that the Analyzed Industry is five times the average; 50 means that the Analyzed Industry is half the national average. The abbreviation 'na' is used to show that data are 'not available'.

*Equivalent to SIC 5561.

LEADING COMPANIES   Number shown: **19**   Total sales ($ mil): **1,237**   Total employment (000): **3.7**

Company Name	Address				CEO Name	Phone	Co. Type	Sales ($ mil)	Empl. (000)
Guaranty Chevrolet-Pontiac	PO Box 279	Junction City	OR	97448	Shannon Nill	541-998-2333	R	278*	0.5
Camping World Inc.	PO Box 90018	Bowling Green	KY	42102	Mark Boggess	270-781-2718	R	206*	1.3
Cruise America Inc.	11 W Hampton Ave	Mesa	AZ	85210	Robert A Smalley	480-464-7300	R	131*	0.4
Van Boxtel Ford Inc.	PO Box 11567	Green Bay	WI	54307	Fred Koehne	920-499-3131	R	106*	0.2
Poulsbo RV Inc.	19705 Viking NW	Poulsbo	WA	98370	Ken Wakazuru	360-697-4445	R	100*	0.2
Roy Robinson Chevrolet Subaru	PO Box 168	Marysville	WA	98270	Roy Robinson	360-659-6236	R	88*	0.1
Iten Chevrolet Co.	6701 Brooklyn Blvd	Minneapolis	MN	55429	Marty Iten	763-561-9220	R	81*	0.1
Holiday R.V. Superstores Inc.	200 E Broward	Fort Lauderdale	FL	33301	Anthony D Borzillo	954-522-9903	P	78	0.2
Glendale Automotive Group	4510 W Glendale	Glendale	AZ	85301	Tim F Corwin	623-931-9111	R	32*	<0.1
La Mesa RV Center Inc.	7430 Copley Park Pl	San Diego	CA	92111	James R Kimbrell	858-874-8000	R	32*	0.3
Robert Crist and Company RV	2025 E Main St	Mesa	AZ	85213	Paul Skogebo	480-834-9410	R	25*	<0.1
Blaine Jensen & Sons RV Centers	780 N 900 W	Kaysville	UT	84037	Craig Jensen	801-544-4298	R	14*	<0.1
Mies Equipment Inc.	PO Box 436	Watkins	MN	55389	Steve Mies	320-764-5310	R	12*	<0.1
RL Ryerson Company Inc.	N58W14500 Shawn	Menomonee Fls	WI	53051	John Eimerman	262-252-2000	R	12*	<0.1
Dean's RV Superstore Inc.	9955 E 21st St	Tulsa	OK	74129	Randy Coy	918-664-3333	R	11*	<0.1
Reines R.V. Center Inc.	10850 Balls Ford Rd	Manassas	VA	20109	Lindsey Reines	703-392-1100	R	8*	<0.1
Wheeler's Las Vegas RV	13175 Las Vegas S	Las Vegas	NV	89124	Andy Wheeler	702-896-9000	S	8*	<0.1
Brd Supply Inc.	52571 Commerce Ct	Bristol	IN	46507	Ron Dempster	574-848-4256	R	7*	<0.1
Charlie's RV & Camping Center	10100 Liberty Rd	Randallstown	MD	21133	Charles Widerman	410-655-5200	R	7*	<0.1

Source: Ward's Business Directory of U.S. Private and Public Companies, Volumes 1 and 2, 2005. The company type code used is as follows: P - Public, R - Private, S - Subsidiary, D - Division, J - Joint Venture, A - Affiliate, G - Group. Sales are in millions of dollars, employees are in thousands. An asterisk (*) indicates an estimated sales volume. The symbol < stands for 'less than'. Company names and addresses are truncated, in some cases, to fit into the available space.

OCCUPATIONS EMPLOYED BY OTHER MOTOR VEHICLE DEALERS

Occupation	% of Total 2004	Change to 2014	Occupation	% of Total 2004	Change to 2014
Retail salespersons	20.8	21.4	First-line supervisors of mechanics	2.8	21.4
Motorcycle mechanics	9.0	15.8	Cashiers, except gaming	2.0	9.2
Parts salespersons	8.1	-2.9	Laborers & freight, stock, & material movers, hand	1.8	9.2
Recreational vehicle service technicians	5.6	21.4	Helpers-Installation, maintenance, & repair workers	1.6	21.4
Motorboat mechanics	5.5	21.4	Secretaries, except legal, medical, & executive	1.4	2.1
First-line supervisors/managers of retail sales workers	4.6	11.6	Counter & rental clerks	1.4	27.4
General & operations managers	3.4	20.1	Automotive service technicians & mechanics	1.1	21.4
Bookkeeping, accounting, & auditing clerks	3.2	9.2	Shipping, receiving, & traffic clerks	1.1	9.9
Office clerks, general	3.2	8.0	Janitors & cleaners, except maids	1.1	21.4
Cleaners of vehicles & equipment	3.1	8.6			

Source: Industry-Occupation Matrix, Bureau of Labor Statistics. These data are reported based on 4-digit NAICS categories but have been matched to corresponding 6-digit NAICS industry codes. The change reported for each occupation to the year 2014 is a percent of growth or decline as estimated by the Bureau of Labor Statistics. The abbreviation nec stands for 'not elsewhere classified.'

LOCATION BY STATE AND REGIONAL CONCENTRATION

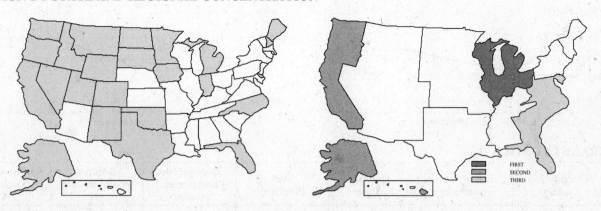

FIRST
SECOND
THIRD

INDUSTRY DATA BY STATE

State	Establishments Total (number)	% of U.S.	Employment Total (number)	% of U.S.	Per Estab.	Payroll Total ($ mil.)	Per Empl. ($)	Sales Total ($ mil.)	% of U.S.	Per Estab. ($)
California	326	10.6	5,141	14.6	16	200.4	38,990	2,130.4	14.4	6,535,031
Florida	192	6.2	2,391	6.8	12	91.0	38,043	1,497.5	10.1	7,799,380
Texas	215	7.0	2,512	7.1	12	82.9	32,986	1,037.8	7.0	4,826,940
Michigan	158	5.1	1,517	4.3	10	54.8	36,132	640.3	4.3	4,052,715
Oregon	94	3.1	1,273	3.6	14	51.4	40,376	639.2	4.3	6,800,404
Washington	94	3.1	1,332	3.8	14	48.3	36,252	550.6	3.7	5,857,053
New York	131	4.3	1,337	3.8	10	45.1	33,751	501.6	3.4	3,829,008
Indiana	75	2.4	1,116	3.2	15	40.3	36,101	460.7	3.1	6,143,027
Ohio	114	3.7	1,165	3.3	10	37.7	32,354	439.0	3.0	3,851,000
Pennsylvania	109	3.5	1,039	2.9	10	31.7	30,487	416.9	2.8	3,824,743
North Carolina	66	2.1	836	2.4	13	28.4	33,990	393.5	2.7	5,962,061
Colorado	73	2.4	849	2.4	12	32.6	38,360	356.9	2.4	4,889,507
Nevada	33	1.1	633	1.8	19	29.9	47,300	315.1	2.1	9,547,758
Illinois	91	3.0	836	2.4	9	27.7	33,102	311.3	2.1	3,421,385
Minnesota	85	2.8	754	2.1	9	25.5	33,775	305.4	2.1	3,593,282
Tennessee	46	1.5	540	1.5	12	20.8	38,594	275.9	1.9	5,998,174
Georgia	60	1.9	655	1.9	11	22.3	34,073	274.3	1.8	4,571,650
Wisconsin	96	3.1	788	2.2	8	21.3	27,036	265.4	1.8	2,764,896
Missouri	62	2.0	695	2.0	11	21.6	31,027	222.0	1.5	3,581,387
Alabama	38	1.2	340	1.0	9	11.2	33,044	188.6	1.3	4,962,132
Oklahoma	43	1.4	515	1.5	12	14.1	27,447	188.4	1.3	4,381,116
Iowa	53	1.7	414	1.2	8	13.0	31,413	186.5	1.3	3,519,094
Louisiana	42	1.4	475	1.3	11	13.3	28,059	174.8	1.2	4,161,143
Utah	50	1.6	440	1.2	9	15.7	35,670	173.5	1.2	3,469,760
Massachusetts	30	1.0	468	1.3	16	18.1	38,647	171.6	1.2	5,720,900
Idaho	59	1.9	542	1.5	9	15.8	29,098	163.5	1.1	2,770,949
Virginia	46	1.5	405	1.1	9	14.0	34,662	148.8	1.0	3,235,478
South Carolina	34	1.1	330	0.9	10	10.8	32,615	136.1	0.9	4,004,000
New Jersey	34	1.1	417	1.2	12	14.5	34,832	135.5	0.9	3,985,471
New Hampshire	26	0.8	320	0.9	12	13.3	41,606	129.6	0.9	4,984,192
New Mexico	38	1.2	407	1.2	11	12.2	30,034	128.3	0.9	3,376,526
Montana	30	1.0	381	1.1	13	9.9	26,013	122.6	0.8	4,085,667
Maryland	23	0.7	262	0.7	11	9.2	35,004	120.4	0.8	5,235,304
Arkansas	43	1.4	333	0.9	8	9.0	27,138	118.2	0.8	2,748,558
Mississippi	31	1.0	294	0.8	9	10.4	35,395	115.3	0.8	3,718,290
Kentucky	33	1.1	280	0.8	8	8.7	31,121	101.7	0.7	3,082,394
Kansas	40	1.3	289	0.8	7	6.6	22,945	77.9	0.5	1,946,625
Maine	26	0.8	179	0.5	7	5.7	31,592	74.5	0.5	2,863,577
South Dakota	20	0.6	194	0.6	10	6.0	30,933	66.9	0.5	3,346,950
North Dakota	18	0.6	154	0.4	9	5.3	34,292	65.4	0.4	3,632,944
Connecticut	18	0.6	164	0.5	9	6.5	39,860	60.0	0.4	3,335,278
West Virginia	20	0.6	173	0.5	9	5.3	30,578	53.8	0.4	2,692,150
Nebraska	17	0.6	168	0.5	10	5.5	32,732	48.5	0.3	2,853,824
Alaska	12	0.4	129	0.4	11	5.1	39,147	46.6	0.3	3,882,750
Wyoming	20	0.6	115	0.3	6	3.0	26,339	43.2	0.3	2,157,700
Delaware	10	0.3	115	0.3	11	3.3	29,096	37.5	0.3	3,750,000
Vermont	11	0.4	114	0.3	10	3.5	31,079	33.2	0.2	3,020,273
Arizona	90	2.9	1000-2499	-	-	(D)	-	(D)	-	-
Rhode Island	3	0.1	20-99	-	-	(D)	-	(D)	-	-
Hawaii	2	0.1	0-19	-	-	(D)	-	(D)	-	-

Source: 2002 *Economic Census*. The states are in descending order of sales or establishments (if sales data are missing for the majority). The symbol (D) appears when data are withheld to prevent disclosure of competitive information. States marked with (D) are sorted by number of establishments. A dash (-) indicates that the data element cannot be calculated. Shaded *states* on the state map indicate those states which have proportionally greater representation in the industry than would be indicated by the states population; the ratio is based on total sales or number of establishments. Shaded *regions* indicate where the industry is regionally most concentrated.

NAICS 441221 - MOTORCYCLE DEALERS*

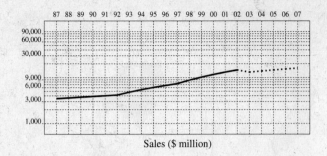

Sales ($ million)

Employment

GENERAL STATISTICS

Year	Establishments (number)	Employment (number)	Payroll ($ million)	Sales ($ million)	Employees per Establishment (number)	Sales per Establishment ($)	Payroll per Employee ($)
1987	4,197	27,070	381.8	3,475.4	6	828,068	14,104
1988	3,835	24,941	388.8	3,612.8 e	7	942,060	15,589
1989	3,527	22,949	379.6	3,750.3 e	7	1,063,312	16,541
1990	3,457	22,283	392.1	3,887.8 e	6	1,124,617	17,596
1991	3,386	21,349	405.1	4,025.2 e	6	1,188,777	18,975
1992	3,585	22,184	427.2	4,162.7	6	1,161,144	19,257
1993	3,601	23,212	482.4	4,804.0 e	6	1,334,074	20,782
1994	3,605	24,984	547.4	5,445.3 e	7	1,510,485	21,910
1995	3,622	27,322	623.6	6,086.7 e	8	1,680,480	22,824
1996	3,189 e	23,071 e	545.9 e	6,728.0 e	7 e	2,109,752 e	23,662 e
1997	3,635	29,026	712.1	7,369.3	8	2,027,318	24,533
1998	3,736	30,401	835.0	8,831.0 e	8	2,363,749	27,466
1999	3,814	33,050	975.7	10,292.6 e	9	2,698,646	29,522
2000	3,968	38,005	1,175.5	11,754.3 e	10	2,962,274	30,930
2001	4,271	43,249	1,366.2	13,216.0 e	10	3,094,350	31,589
2002	4,581	46,440	1,415.1	14,677.6	10	3,204,025	30,472
2003	5,159	54,725	1,769.4	13,190.6 p	11	3,252,404 p	32,332
2004	4,313 p	44,662 p	1,462.1 p	13,918.0 p	10 p	3,419,649 p	34,072 p
2005	4,367 p	46,263 p	1,540.7 p	14,645.4 p	11 p	3,586,894 p	35,256 p
2006	4,420 p	47,864 p	1,619.3 p	15,372.8 p	11 p	3,754,140 p	36,440 p
2007	4,473 p	49,466 p	1,698.0 p	16,100.3 p	11 p	3,921,385 p	37,624 p

Sources: Economic Census of the United States, 1987, 1992, 1997, and 2002. Establishment counts, employment, and payroll are from *County Business Patterns* for non-Census years. Values followed by a 'p' are projections by the editors. Sales data for non-Census years are extrapolations, marked by 'e'. Data are the most recent available at this level of detail.

INDICES OF CHANGE

Year	Establishments (number)	Employment (number)	Payroll ($ million)	Sales ($ million)	Employees per Establishment (number)	Sales per Establishment ($)	Payroll per Employee ($)
1987	91.6	58.3	27.0	23.7	63.1	25.8	46.3
1992	78.3	47.8	30.2	28.4	61.2	36.2	63.2
1993	78.6	50.0	34.1	32.7 e	63.1	41.6	68.2
1994	78.7	53.8	38.7	37.1 e	68.1	47.1	71.9
1995	79.1	58.8	44.1	41.5 e	74.0	52.4	74.9
1996	69.6 e	49.7 e	38.6 e	45.8 e	71.0 e	65.8 e	77.7 e
1997	79.3	62.5	50.3	50.2	78.9	63.3	80.5
1998	81.6	65.5	59.0	60.2 e	79.9	73.8	90.1
1999	83.3	71.2	68.9	70.1 e	85.8	84.2	96.9
2000	86.6	81.8	83.1	80.1 e	94.7	92.5	101.5
2001	93.2	93.1	96.5	90.0 e	99.6	96.6	103.7
2002	100.0	100.0	100.0	100.0	100.0	100.0	100.0
2003	112.6	117.8	125.0	89.9 p	104.6	101.5 p	106.1
2004	94.2 p	96.2 p	103.3 p	94.8 p	101.5 p	106.7 p	111.8 p
2005	95.3 p	99.6 p	108.9 p	99.8 p	104.3 p	111.9 p	115.7 p
2006	96.5 p	103.1 p	114.4 p	104.7 p	107.1 p	117.2 p	119.6 p
2007	97.6 p	106.5 p	120.0 p	109.7 p	109.8 p	122.4 p	123.5 p

Sources: Same as General Statistics. The values shown reflect change from the base year, 2002. Values above 100 mean greater than 2002, values below 100 mean less than 2002, and a value of 100 in the 1987-2001 or 2003-2007 period means same as 2002. Values followed by a 'p' are projections by the editors; 'e' stands for extrapolation. Data are the most recent available at this level of detail.

SELECTED RATIOS

For 2002	Avg. of All Retail	Analyzed Industry	Index	For 2002	Avg. of All Retail	Analyzed Industry	Index
Employees per Establishment	17	10	60	Sales per Employee	174,682	316,056	181
Payroll per Establishment	333,445	308,909	93	Sales per Establishment	3,332,269	3,204,025	96
Payroll per Employee	20,311	30,472	150	Expenses per Establishment	na	na	na

Sources: Same as General Statistics. The 'Average of All' column, Wholesale or Retail, represents the average of the sector reported for the most recent complete year available. The Index shows the relationship between the Average and the Analyzed Industry. For example, 100 means that they are equal; 500 that the Analyzed Industry is five times the average; 50 means that the Analyzed Industry is half the national average. The abbreviation 'na' is used to show that data are 'not available'.

*Equivalent to SIC 5571.

LEADING COMPANIES   Number shown: **12**   Total sales ($ mil): **582**   Total employment (000): **1.0**

Company Name	Address				CEO Name	Phone	Co. Type	Sales ($ mil)	Empl. (000)
Family Automotive Group Inc.	33396 Capistrano	SJ Bautista	CA	92675	Raymond Dixon	949-493-4100	R	227	0.3
Riva World	3671 N Dixie Hwy	Pompano Beach	FL	33064	Steve Bamdas	305-451-3320	R	88*	<0.1
BMW of San Francisco	1675 Howard St	San Francisco	CA	94103	Henry Schmitt	415-863-9000	R	79*	0.2
Kolbe Cycle Sales	22123 Ventura Blvd	Woodland Hills	CA	91364	Andrew R Kolbe	818-348-7865	R	58*	0.1
Destination Harley-Davidson	2302 Pacific Hwy E	Tacoma	WA	98424	Ed Wallace	253-922-3700	R	34*	<0.1
Dudley Perkins Co.	66 Page St	San Francisco	CA	94102	Tom Perkins	415-703-9494	R	28*	<0.1
White Brothers Inc.	24845 Corbit Pl	Yorba Linda	CA	92887	Tom White	714-692-3404	R	25	0.1
Hopf Equipment Inc.	506 E 19th St	Huntingburg	IN	47542	Charles Hopf	812-683-2763	R	14*	<0.1
Metro Kawasaki	PO Box 7179	Jackson	MS	39282	R Deviney	601-373-9531	R	10*	<0.1
Unkefer Homer Farm Equipment	PO Box 87	Minerva	OH	44657	Homer Unkefer	330-868-6419	R	10*	<0.1
North Country Harley-Davidson	3099 N Belfast Ave	Augusta	ME	04330	Calvin Reynolds	207-622-7994	R	8*	<0.1
Stoneridge Motorsports L.L.C.	975 S 12th W	Rexburg	ID	83440	Kenneth Burt	208-356-9251	R	1*	<0.1

Source: *Ward's Business Directory of U.S. Private and Public Companies*, Volumes 1 and 2, 2005. The company type code used is as follows: P - Public, R - Private, S - Subsidiary, D - Division, J - Joint Venture, A - Affiliate, G - Group. Sales are in millions of dollars, employees are in thousands. An asterisk (*) indicates an estimated sales volume. The symbol < stands for 'less than'. Company names and addresses are truncated, in some cases, to fit into the available space.

OCCUPATIONS EMPLOYED BY OTHER MOTOR VEHICLE DEALERS

Occupation	% of Total 2004	Change to 2014	Occupation	% of Total 2004	Change to 2014
Retail salespersons	20.8	21.4	First-line supervisors of mechanics	2.8	21.4
Motorcycle mechanics	9.0	15.8	Cashiers, except gaming	2.0	9.2
Parts salespersons	8.1	-2.9	Laborers & freight, stock, & material movers, hand	1.8	9.2
Recreational vehicle service technicians	5.6	21.4	Helpers-Installation, maintenance, & repair workers	1.6	21.4
Motorboat mechanics	5.5	21.4	Secretaries, except legal, medical, & executive	1.4	2.1
First-line supervisors/managers of retail sales workers	4.6	11.6	Counter & rental clerks	1.4	27.4
General & operations managers	3.4	20.1	Automotive service technicians & mechanics	1.1	21.4
Bookkeeping, accounting, & auditing clerks	3.2	9.2	Shipping, receiving, & traffic clerks	1.1	9.9
Office clerks, general	3.2	8.0	Janitors & cleaners, except maids	1.1	21.4
Cleaners of vehicles & equipment	3.1	8.6			

Source: *Industry-Occupation Matrix*, Bureau of Labor Statistics. These data are reported based on 4-digit NAICS categories but have been matched to corresponding 6-digit NAICS industry codes. The change reported for each occupation to the year 2014 is a percent of growth or decline as estimated by the Bureau of Labor Statistics. The abbreviation nec stands for 'not elsewhere classified.'

LOCATION BY STATE AND REGIONAL CONCENTRATION

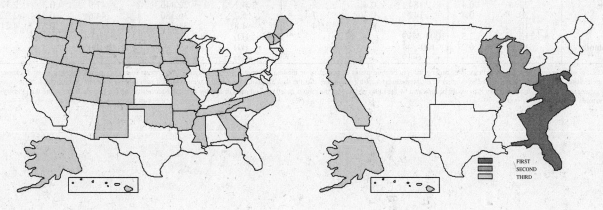

FIRST
SECOND
THIRD

INDUSTRY DATA BY STATE

State	Establishments Total (number)	% of U.S.	Employment Total (number)	% of U.S.	Per Estab.	Payroll Total ($ mil.)	Per Empl. ($)	Sales Total ($ mil.)	% of U.S.	Per Estab. ($)
California	531	10.8	5,983	11.9	11	200.5	33,513	1,804.9	11.3	3,399,034
Texas	280	5.7	3,161	6.3	11	102.0	32,264	1,015.4	6.4	3,626,454
Florida	259	5.3	2,471	4.9	10	81.6	33,034	787.3	4.9	3,039,938
Pennsylvania	218	4.5	2,297	4.6	11	63.0	27,436	721.6	4.5	3,310,289
Ohio	195	4.0	2,141	4.3	11	59.9	27,964	714.3	4.5	3,663,041
Illinois	166	3.4	1,968	3.9	12	60.0	30,509	604.3	3.8	3,640,193
New York	205	4.2	1,676	3.3	8	47.6	28,399	575.1	3.6	2,805,151

Continued on next page.

INDUSTRY DATA BY STATE - Continued

State	Establishments Total (number)	% of U.S.	Employment Total (number)	% of U.S.	Per Estab.	Payroll Total ($ mil.)	Per Empl. ($)	Sales Total ($ mil.)	% of U.S.	Per Estab. ($)
North Carolina	189	3.9	1,843	3.7	10	53.1	28,800	540.9	3.4	2,861,788
Michigan	155	3.2	1,613	3.2	10	50.9	31,536	526.8	3.3	3,398,877
Wisconsin	152	3.1	1,591	3.2	10	50.1	31,519	522.6	3.3	3,438,368
Colorado	97	2.0	1,404	2.8	14	46.1	32,812	434.0	2.7	4,474,216
Georgia	137	2.8	1,314	2.6	10	40.1	30,516	425.1	2.7	3,102,839
Indiana	127	2.6	1,294	2.6	10	38.4	29,653	402.0	2.5	3,165,362
Minnesota	112	2.3	1,294	2.6	12	40.0	30,883	400.2	2.5	3,573,161
Missouri	116	2.4	1,159	2.3	10	31.6	27,257	372.8	2.3	3,213,836
Virginia	116	2.4	1,266	2.5	11	37.5	29,618	366.5	2.3	3,159,069
Washington	109	2.2	1,227	2.4	11	39.0	31,748	356.2	2.2	3,267,523
Tennessee	113	2.3	1,080	2.2	10	33.2	30,780	347.8	2.2	3,077,575
New Jersey	89	1.8	862	1.7	10	30.4	35,311	299.0	1.9	3,359,461
Massachusetts	71	1.4	803	1.6	11	26.5	32,978	265.4	1.7	3,737,986
Iowa	82	1.7	699	1.4	9	19.7	28,152	244.9	1.5	2,986,829
Alabama	73	1.5	693	1.4	9	19.3	27,843	225.8	1.4	3,092,877
Oregon	79	1.6	691	1.4	9	19.6	28,389	224.1	1.4	2,836,506
Maryland	56	1.1	735	1.5	13	22.2	30,158	219.8	1.4	3,925,786
South Carolina	73	1.5	594	1.2	8	16.2	27,219	210.9	1.3	2,889,205
Oklahoma	67	1.4	550	1.1	8	14.3	25,976	209.2	1.3	3,121,806
New Hampshire	52	1.1	552	1.1	11	20.6	37,404	206.5	1.3	3,971,865
Louisiana	67	1.4	650	1.3	10	18.2	27,940	204.5	1.3	3,052,866
Kentucky	70	1.4	666	1.3	10	14.6	21,908	203.6	1.3	2,908,057
Utah	63	1.3	584	1.2	9	16.3	27,827	190.1	1.2	3,017,683
Arkansas	62	1.3	479	1.0	8	14.4	30,163	181.3	1.1	2,924,645
Mississippi	55	1.1	429	0.9	8	11.1	25,762	170.5	1.1	3,099,527
West Virginia	47	1.0	465	0.9	10	11.5	24,690	164.5	1.0	3,499,851
Connecticut	52	1.1	459	0.9	9	18.6	40,455	161.0	1.0	3,096,038
Nevada	41	0.8	517	1.0	13	15.3	29,582	149.2	0.9	3,639,098
New Mexico	45	0.9	422	0.8	9	13.3	31,547	126.1	0.8	2,803,067
Maine	40	0.8	310	0.6	8	9.2	29,603	122.3	0.8	3,057,675
Kansas	52	1.1	426	0.8	8	11.0	25,725	119.3	0.7	2,293,808
Idaho	48	1.0	348	0.7	7	8.9	25,468	103.9	0.7	2,165,604
Montana	39	0.8	341	0.7	9	8.5	25,015	103.5	0.6	2,654,667
Nebraska	39	0.8	295	0.6	8	8.3	28,200	93.9	0.6	2,406,410
South Dakota	25	0.5	230	0.5	9	6.8	29,757	82.1	0.5	3,282,320
Hawaii	18	0.4	189	0.4	10	6.6	35,079	73.7	0.5	4,097,111
Delaware	15	0.3	276	0.5	18	9.6	34,797	71.6	0.4	4,773,067
North Dakota	25	0.5	174	0.3	7	4.2	23,943	55.4	0.3	2,216,680
Wyoming	22	0.4	184	0.4	8	4.1	22,446	47.9	0.3	2,178,636
Vermont	20	0.4	142	0.3	7	5.2	36,380	44.6	0.3	2,228,900
Alaska	10	0.2	138	0.3	14	4.8	34,478	42.1	0.3	4,210,200
Arizona	113	2.3	1000-2499	-	-	(D)	-	(D)	-	-
Rhode Island	10	0.2	100-249	-	-	(D)	-	(D)	-	-
D.C.	1	-	0-19	-	-	(D)	-	(D)	-	-

Source: 2002 *Economic Census*. The states are in descending order of sales or establishments (if sales data are missing for the majority). The symbol (D) appears when data are withheld to prevent disclosure of competitive information. States marked with (D) are sorted by number of establishments. A dash (-) indicates that the data element cannot be calculated. Shaded *states* on the state map indicate those states which have proportionately greater representation in the industry than would be indicated by the states population; the ratio is based on total sales or number of establishments. Shaded *regions* indicate where the industry is regionally most concentrated.

NAICS 441222 - BOAT DEALERS*

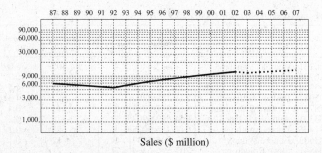

Sales ($ million)

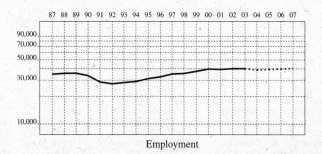

Employment

GENERAL STATISTICS

Year	Establishments (number)	Employment (number)	Payroll ($ million)	Sales ($ million)	Employees per Establishment (number)	Sales per Establishment ($)	Payroll per Employee ($)
1987	5,174	34,875	620.3	6,824.2	7	1,318,941	17,786
1988	4,862	35,653	689.8	6,566.7 e	7	1,350,617	19,348
1989	4,631	35,756	673.0	6,309.3 e	8	1,362,406	18,822
1990	4,645	33,696	629.0	6,051.9 e	7	1,302,885	18,667
1991	4,541	28,573	564.7	5,794.5 e	6	1,276,041	19,763
1992	4,773	27,282	558.0	5,537.1	6	1,160,088	20,453
1993	4,758	28,162	599.0	6,216.5 e	6	1,306,536	21,270
1994	4,778	28,925	664.3	6,895.9 e	6	1,443,261	22,966
1995	4,775	31,240	713.8	7,575.4 e	7	1,586,471	22,849
1996	4,925 e	32,669 e	744.8 e	8,254.8 e	7 e	1,676,101 e	22,798 e
1997	5,262	35,134	839.3	8,934.2	7	1,697,872	23,888
1998	5,219	35,574	930.7	9,626.8 e	7	1,844,559	26,162
1999	5,284	37,560	1,036.7	10,319.3 e	7	1,952,935	27,601
2000	5,289	39,772	1,138.9	11,011.9 e	8	2,082,031	28,636
2001	5,301	39,405	1,128.9	11,704.4 e	7	2,207,964	28,648
2002	5,500	40,169	1,166.0	12,397.0	7	2,253,995	29,027
2003	5,567	40,148	1,242.0	11,765.3 e	7	2,199,646 e	30,936
2004	5,465 p	38,901 p	1,198.5 p	12,193.4 p	7 p	2,268,555 p	30,903 p
2005	5,515 p	39,402 p	1,240.5 p	12,621.5 p	7 p	2,337,464 p	31,725 p
2006	5,564 p	39,904 p	1,282.6 p	13,049.6 p	7 p	2,406,373 p	32,547 p
2007	5,614 p	40,405 p	1,324.6 p	13,477.8 p	7 p	2,475,282 p	33,369 p

Sources: Economic Census of the United States, 1987, 1992, 1997, and 2002. Establishment counts, employment, and payroll are from *County Business Patterns* for non-Census years. Values followed by a 'p' are projections by the editors. Sales data for non-Census years are extrapolations, marked by 'e'. Data are the most recent available at this level of detail.

INDICES OF CHANGE

Year	Establishments (number)	Employment (number)	Payroll ($ million)	Sales ($ million)	Employees per Establishment (number)	Sales per Establishment ($)	Payroll per Employee ($)
1987	94.1	86.8	53.2	55.0	91.7	58.5	61.3
1992	86.8	67.9	47.9	44.7	78.0	51.5	70.5
1993	86.5	70.1	51.4	50.1 e	80.8	58.0	73.3
1994	86.9	72.0	57.0	55.6 e	83.5	64.0	79.1
1995	86.8	77.8	61.2	61.1 e	89.0	70.4	78.7
1996	89.5 e	81.3 e	63.9 e	66.6 e	90.4 e	74.4 e	78.5 e
1997	95.7	87.5	72.0	72.1	91.7	75.3	82.3
1998	94.9	88.6	79.8	77.7 e	93.1	81.8	90.1
1999	96.1	93.5	88.9	83.2 e	97.2	86.6	95.1
2000	96.2	99.0	97.7	88.8 e	102.7	92.4	98.7
2001	96.4	98.1	96.8	94.4 e	101.3	98.0	98.7
2002	100.0	100.0	100.0	100.0	100.0	100.0	100.0
2003	101.2	99.9	106.5	94.9 p	98.7	97.6 p	106.6
2004	99.4 p	96.8 p	102.8 p	98.4 p	97.1 p	100.6 p	106.5 p
2005	100.3 p	98.1 p	106.4 p	101.8 p	97.5 p	103.7 p	109.3 p
2006	101.2 p	99.3 p	110.0 p	105.3 p	97.9 p	106.8 p	112.1 p
2007	102.1 p	100.6 p	113.6 p	108.7 p	98.3 p	109.8 p	115.0 p

Sources: Same as General Statistics. The values shown reflect change from the base year, 2002. Values above 100 mean greater than 2002, values below 100 mean less than 2002, and a value of 100 in the 1987-2001 or 2003-2007 period means same as 2002. Values followed by a 'p' are projections by the editors; 'e' stands for extrapolation. Data are the most recent available at this level of detail.

SELECTED RATIOS

For 2002	Avg. of All Retail	Analyzed Industry	Index	For 2002	Avg. of All Retail	Analyzed Industry	Index
Employees per Establishment	17	7	43	Sales per Employee	174,682	308,620	177
Payroll per Establishment	333,445	211,994	64	Sales per Establishment	3,332,269	2,253,995	68
Payroll per Employee	20,311	29,027	143	Expenses per Establishment	na	na	na

Sources: Same as General Statistics. The 'Average of All' column, Wholesale or Retail, represents the average of the sector reported for the most recent complete year available. The Index shows the relationship between the Average and the Analyzed Industry. For example, 100 means that they are equal; 500 that the Analyzed Industry is five times the average; 50 means that the Analyzed Industry is half the national average. The abbreviation 'na' is used to show that data are 'not available'.

*Equivalent to SIC 5551.

LEADING COMPANIES   Number shown: **12**   Total sales ($ mil): **7,161**   Total employment (000): **23.3**

Company Name	Address				CEO Name	Phone	Co. Type	Sales ($ mil)	Empl. (000)
VT Inc.	Po Box 795	Schuylkl Hvn	KS	66201	Cecil L. Van Tuyl	913-432-6400	R	4,300*	6.0
Ritz Camera Centers Inc.	6711 Ritz Way	Beltsville	MD	20705	David M Ritz	301-419-0000	R	1,135	10.7
MarineMax Inc.	18167 US 19 Hwy N	Clearwater	FL	33764		727-531-1700	P	762	1.5
West Marine Inc.	PO Box 50070	Watsonville	CA	95077	Richard E Everett	831-728-2700	P	682	4.3
Travis Boats and Motors Inc.	12116 Jekel Cir	Austin	TX	78727	Richard S Birnbaum	512-347-8787	S	141	0.4
Holiday RV Superstores Inc.	200 E Broward	Fort Lauderdale	FL	33301	Anthony D Borzillo	954-522-9903	P	78	0.2
Boat Center Inc.	49 Douglas St	Savannah	GA	31406	Darryl Smith	912-355-0025	R	25*	<0.1
Wilcox Bait and Tackle Inc.	9501 Jefferson Ave	Newport News	VA	23605	Elmore Wilcox	757-595-5537	R	12*	<0.1
Manset Marine Supply Co.	PO Box 709	Rockland	ME	04841	Steve Rodstrome	207-596-6464	R	11*	<0.1
D and R Boats Inc.	271 Rte 22	Green Brook	NJ	08812	Robert Barone	732-968-2600	R	7*	<0.1
Navatek Ltd.	PO Box 29816	Honolulu	HI	96820	Steven Loui	808-531-7001	S	7*	<0.1
Boulder Outdoor Center Inc.	2707 Spruce St	Boulder	CO	80302	Eric Bader	303-444-8420	R	1*	<0.1

Source: *Ward's Business Directory of U.S. Private and Public Companies*, Volumes 1 and 2, 2005. The company type code used is as follows: P - Public, R - Private, S - Subsidiary, D - Division, J - Joint Venture, A - Affiliate, G - Group. Sales are in millions of dollars, employees are in thousands. An asterisk (*) indicates an estimated sales volume. The symbol < stands for 'less than'. Company names and addresses are truncated, in some cases, to fit into the available space.

OCCUPATIONS EMPLOYED BY OTHER MOTOR VEHICLE DEALERS

Occupation	% of Total 2004	Change to 2014	Occupation	% of Total 2004	Change to 2014
Retail salespersons	20.8	21.4	First-line supervisors of mechanics	2.8	21.4
Motorcycle mechanics	9.0	15.8	Cashiers, except gaming	2.0	9.2
Parts salespersons	8.1	-2.9	Laborers & freight, stock, & material movers, hand	1.8	9.2
Recreational vehicle service technicians	5.6	21.4	Helpers-Installation, maintenance, & repair workers	1.6	21.4
Motorboat mechanics	5.5	21.4	Secretaries, except legal, medical, & executive	1.4	2.1
First-line supervisors/managers of retail sales workers	4.6	11.6	Counter & rental clerks	1.4	27.4
General & operations managers	3.4	20.1	Automotive service technicians & mechanics	1.1	21.4
Bookkeeping, accounting, & auditing clerks	3.2	9.2	Shipping, receiving, & traffic clerks	1.1	9.9
Office clerks, general	3.2	8.0	Janitors & cleaners, except maids	1.1	21.4
Cleaners of vehicles & equipment	3.1	8.6			

Source: *Industry-Occupation Matrix*, Bureau of Labor Statistics. These data are reported based on 4-digit NAICS categories but have been matched to corresponding 6-digit NAICS industry codes. The change reported for each occupation to the year 2014 is a percent of growth or decline as estimated by the Bureau of Labor Statistics. The abbreviation nec stands for 'not elsewhere classified.'

LOCATION BY STATE AND REGIONAL CONCENTRATION

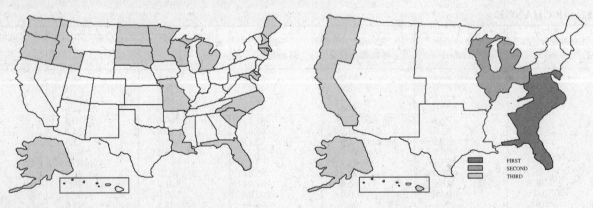

INDUSTRY DATA BY STATE

State	Establishments		Employment			Payroll		Sales		
	Total (number)	% of U.S.	Total (number)	% of U.S.	Per Estab.	Total ($ mil.)	Per Empl. ($)	Total ($ mil.)	% of U.S.	Per Estab. ($)
Florida	916	16.6	5,971	15.0	7	167.2	28,006	2,218.9	18.0	2,422,361
California	364	6.6	3,292	8.2	9	97.9	29,728	988.2	8.0	2,714,802
Texas	287	5.2	2,161	5.4	8	64.5	29,858	642.4	5.2	2,238,328
New York	276	5.0	1,897	4.8	7	60.2	31,755	625.7	5.1	2,267,033
Michigan	238	4.3	1,715	4.3	7	51.9	30,292	562.4	4.6	2,362,979
Maryland	158	2.9	1,356	3.4	9	42.7	31,497	507.5	4.1	3,211,956
Washington	201	3.6	1,303	3.3	6	40.3	30,965	395.2	3.2	1,965,945

Continued on next page.

INDUSTRY DATA BY STATE - Continued

State	Establishments Total (number)	% of U.S.	Employment Total (number)	% of U.S.	Per Estab.	Payroll Total ($ mil.)	Per Empl. ($)	Sales Total ($ mil.)	% of U.S.	Per Estab. ($)
Minnesota	165	3.0	1,320	3.3	8	39.2	29,673	390.1	3.2	2,364,406
Wisconsin	162	2.9	1,378	3.5	9	38.3	27,798	387.9	3.1	2,394,383
Massachusetts	132	2.4	1,045	2.6	8	37.9	36,222	381.3	3.1	2,888,955
New Jersey	161	2.9	1,169	2.9	7	36.1	30,869	368.3	3.0	2,287,857
Missouri	135	2.4	1,247	3.1	9	32.8	26,280	367.2	3.0	2,720,015
North Carolina	176	3.2	1,174	2.9	7	31.9	27,149	355.6	2.9	2,020,642
Ohio	147	2.7	1,050	2.6	7	30.5	29,084	342.6	2.8	2,330,837
Illinois	125	2.3	973	2.4	8	26.8	27,570	271.3	2.2	2,170,048
Virginia	108	2.0	830	2.1	8	25.2	30,311	265.5	2.1	2,458,361
Connecticut	97	1.8	677	1.7	7	24.6	36,341	236.0	1.9	2,433,361
Louisiana	119	2.2	955	2.4	8	23.1	24,232	235.6	1.9	1,979,773
Georgia	122	2.2	875	2.2	7	23.2	26,517	232.5	1.9	1,905,746
South Carolina	128	2.3	890	2.2	7	23.6	26,528	231.2	1.9	1,806,062
Tennessee	97	1.8	560	1.4	6	17.8	31,775	201.4	1.6	2,076,680
Indiana	101	1.8	781	2.0	8	22.1	28,273	201.3	1.6	1,992,733
Oregon	74	1.3	495	1.2	7	15.0	30,240	173.2	1.4	2,340,716
Alabama	96	1.7	496	1.2	5	12.4	25,054	163.4	1.3	1,702,115
Pennsylvania	96	1.7	616	1.5	6	14.6	23,714	145.0	1.2	1,510,740
Maine	71	1.3	494	1.2	7	12.6	25,522	118.8	1.0	1,672,873
Oklahoma	69	1.2	445	1.1	6	11.1	24,917	112.0	0.9	1,623,333
Kentucky	65	1.2	412	1.0	6	9.2	22,408	104.3	0.8	1,604,569
New Hampshire	38	0.7	408	1.0	11	12.1	29,664	95.3	0.8	2,508,842
Arkansas	57	1.0	322	0.8	6	8.2	25,323	90.6	0.7	1,590,263
Rhode Island	47	0.9	309	0.8	7	8.8	28,612	81.6	0.7	1,735,213
Iowa	56	1.0	272	0.7	5	7.8	28,757	79.6	0.6	1,421,732
Alaska	39	0.7	266	0.7	7	7.8	29,357	73.1	0.6	1,874,000
Mississippi	53	1.0	289	0.7	5	6.8	23,651	72.3	0.6	1,364,830
Colorado	32	0.6	285	0.7	9	7.8	27,302	70.5	0.6	2,203,406
Delaware	27	0.5	324	0.8	12	9.0	27,707	69.6	0.6	2,577,000
Utah	28	0.5	189	0.5	7	5.2	27,598	58.0	0.5	2,070,607
Idaho	25	0.5	199	0.5	8	5.9	29,477	55.9	0.5	2,234,040
North Dakota	16	0.3	147	0.4	9	4.4	30,163	46.4	0.4	2,897,625
Nebraska	24	0.4	142	0.4	6	3.9	27,268	41.8	0.3	1,740,917
Nevada	15	0.3	138	0.3	9	4.7	33,812	40.8	0.3	2,720,667
South Dakota	18	0.3	116	0.3	6	3.1	26,431	36.1	0.3	2,002,944
Kansas	26	0.5	147	0.4	6	3.9	26,272	33.6	0.3	1,292,346
Montana	18	0.3	66	0.2	4	1.5	23,273	22.8	0.2	1,265,278
West Virginia	19	0.3	110	0.3	6	2.1	19,236	21.2	0.2	1,114,684
Vermont	16	0.3	75	0.2	5	1.8	24,547	16.3	0.1	1,016,000
Wyoming	4	0.1	27	0.1	7	0.6	20,630	7.5	0.1	1,886,500
New Mexico	10	0.2	34	0.1	3	0.8	23,912	6.4	0.1	638,200
Arizona	53	1.0	250-499	-	-	(D)	-	(D)	-	-
Hawaii	15	0.3	100-249	-	-	(D)	-	(D)	-	-
D.C.	1	-	0-19	-	-	(D)	-	(D)	-	-

Source: 2002 *Economic Census*. The states are in descending order of sales or establishments (if sales data are missing for the majority). The symbol (D) appears when data are withheld to prevent disclosure of competitive information. States marked with (D) are sorted by number of establishments. A dash (-) indicates that the data element cannot be calculated. Shaded *states* on the state map indicate those states which have proportionately greater representation in the industry than would be indicated by the states population; the ratio is based on total sales or number of establishments. Shaded *regions* indicate where the industry is regionally most concentrated.

NAICS 441229 - ALL OTHER MOTOR VEHICLE DEALERS*

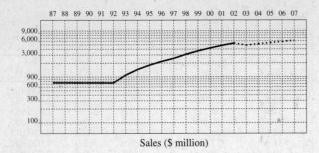

Sales ($ million)

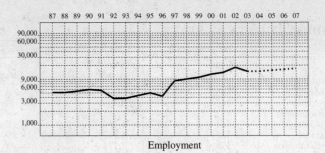

Employment

GENERAL STATISTICS

Year	Establishments (number)	Employment (number)	Payroll ($ million)	Sales ($ million)	Employees per Establishment (number)	Sales per Establishment ($)	Payroll per Employee ($)
1987	852	5,094	82.7	743.7	6	872,887	16,235
1988	822	5,105	100.4	742.2 e	6	902,920	19,667
1989	813	5,441	109.0	740.7 e	7	911,070	20,033
1990	890	5,922	117.9	739.2 e	7	830,562	19,909
1991	906	5,636	113.4	737.7 e	6	814,238	20,121
1992	829	3,762	71.5	736.2	5	888,058	19,006
1993	869	3,811	78.0	1,092.4 e	4	1,257,077	20,467
1994	936	4,357	95.0	1,448.6 e	5	1,547,650	21,804
1995	1,005	4,982	111.6	1,804.9 e	5	1,795,920	22,401
1996	964 e	4,225 e	97.0 e	2,161.1 e	4 e	2,241,805 e	22,959 e
1997	1,678	9,145	204.6	2,517.3	5	1,500,179	22,373
1998	1,894	10,089	241.7	3,087.9 e	5	1,630,338	23,957
1999	1,944	10,945	292.1	3,658.4 e	6	1,881,904	26,688
2000	2,143	12,780	371.5	4,229.0 e	6	1,973,394	29,066
2001	2,216	13,951	388.2	4,799.5 e	6	2,165,859	27,824
2002	2,536	17,960	488.6	5,370.1	7	2,117,549	27,204
2003	2,432	14,722	433.6	4,859.4 p	6	2,310,858 p	29,450
2004	2,462 p	14,800 p	419.3 p	5,176.6 p	6 p	2,411,169 p	29,446 p
2005	2,580 p	15,543 p	443.6 p	5,493.8 p	6 p	2,511,480 p	30,174 p
2006	2,698 p	16,285 p	468.0 p	5,811.0 p	6 p	2,611,791 p	30,902 p
2007	2,817 p	17,028 p	492.4 p	6,128.2 p	6 p	2,712,102 p	31,630 p

Sources: *Economic Census of the United States*, 1987, 1992, 1997, and 2002. Establishment counts, employment, and payroll are from *County Business Patterns* for non-Census years. Values followed by a 'p' are projections by the editors. Sales data for non-Census years are extrapolations, marked by 'e'. Data are the most recent available at this level of detail.

INDICES OF CHANGE

Year	Establishments (number)	Employment (number)	Payroll ($ million)	Sales ($ million)	Employees per Establishment (number)	Sales per Establishment ($)	Payroll per Employee ($)
1987	33.6	28.4	16.9	13.8	84.7	41.2	59.7
1992	32.7	20.9	14.6	13.7	63.5	41.9	69.9
1993	34.3	21.2	16.0	20.3 e	62.1	59.4	75.2
1994	36.9	24.3	19.4	27.0 e	66.4	73.1	80.1
1995	39.6	27.7	22.8	33.6 e	70.6	84.8	82.3
1996	38.0 e	23.5 e	19.9 e	40.2 e	62.1 e	105.9 e	84.4 e
1997	66.2	50.9	41.9	46.9	76.2	70.8	82.2
1998	74.7	56.2	49.5	57.5 e	74.8	77.0	88.1
1999	76.7	60.9	59.8	68.1 e	79.1	88.9	98.1
2000	84.5	71.2	76.0	78.8 e	84.7	93.2	106.8
2001	87.4	77.7	79.5	89.4 e	89.0	102.3	102.3
2002	100.0	100.0	100.0	100.0	100.0	100.0	100.0
2003	95.9	82.0	88.7	90.5 p	85.5	109.1 p	108.3
2004	97.1 p	82.4 p	85.8 p	96.4 p	80.9 p	113.9 p	108.2 p
2005	101.7 p	86.5 p	90.8 p	102.3 p	81.0 p	118.6 p	110.9 p
2006	106.4 p	90.7 p	95.8 p	108.2 p	81.1 p	123.3 p	113.6 p
2007	111.1 p	94.8 p	100.8 p	114.1 p	81.2 p	128.1 p	116.3 p

Sources: Same as General Statistics. The values shown reflect change from the base year, 2002. Values above 100 mean greater than 2002, values below 100 mean less than 2002, and a value of 100 in the 1987-2001 or 2003-2007 period means same as 2002. Values followed by a 'p' are projections by the editors; 'e' stands for extrapolation. Data are the most recent available at this level of detail.

SELECTED RATIOS

For 2002	Avg. of All Retail	Analyzed Industry	Index	For 2002	Avg. of All Retail	Analyzed Industry	Index
Employees per Establishment	17	7	42	Sales per Employee	174,682	299,004	171
Payroll per Establishment	333,445	192,661	58	Sales per Establishment	3,332,269	2,117,549	64
Payroll per Employee	20,311	27,204	134	Expenses per Establishment	na	na	na

Sources: Same as General Statistics. The 'Average of All' column, Wholesale or Retail, represents the average of the sector reported for the most recent complete year available. The Index shows the relationship between the Average and the Analyzed Industry. For example, 100 means that they are equal; 500 that the Analyzed Industry is five times the average; 50 means that the Analyzed Industry is half the national average. The abbreviation 'na' is used to show that data are 'not available'.

*Equivalent to SIC 5599.

LEADING COMPANIES   Number shown: **31**   Total sales ($ mil): **9,306**   Total employment (000): **14.0**

Company Name	Address				CEO Name	Phone	Co. Type	Sales ($ mil)	Empl. (000)
Group 1 Automotive Inc.	950 Echo Ln	Houston	TX	77024	Earl J. Hesterberg	713-647-5700	P	5,435	7.4
Rush Enterprises Inc.	555 IH 35 S, Ste 500	New Braunfels	TX	78130		830-626-5200	P	1,095	1.9
Thompson Lift Truck Co.	PO Box 10367	Birmingham	AL	35202	Mike Thompson	205-849-3658	R	819*	1.3
Hitchcock Automotive Resources	PO Box 8610	City of Industry	CA	91748	F E Hitchcock Jr	626-839-8400	R	665*	0.8
Family Automotive Group Inc.	33396 Capistrano	SJ Bautista	CA	92675	Raymond Dixon	949-493-4100	R	227	0.3
Wiggins Airways Inc.	1 Garside Way	Manchester	NH	03103	David Ladd	603-629-9191	R	118*	0.2
Van Boxtel Ford Inc.	PO Box 11567	Green Bay	WI	54307	Fred Koehne	920-499-3131	R	106*	0.2
Family Ford Sales Inc.	1602 Florence Blvd	Florence	AL	35630		256-764-3351	R	96	0.1
Corley's Auto Sales Inc.	1870 W Santa Fe	Grants	NM	87020	Eddie B Corley, Sr	505-285-4595	R	88	0.2
Greater Rockford Auto Auction	5937 Sandy Hollow	Rockford	IL	61109	Dwight Clark	815-874-7800	R	88*	<0.1
Motor Power Equipment Co.	PO Box 80030	Billings	MT	59108	Bruce Sunwall	406-252-5651	R	73*	<0.1
Ewald's Mayfair Chrysler	2201 N Mayfair Rd	Milwaukee	WI	53222		414-258-5000	R	62*	0.1
Cummins Intermountain Inc.	PO Box 25428	Salt Lake City	UT	84125	Lorin K Pugh	801-355-6500	S	60*	0.3
Sun State Intern. Trucks L.L.C.	6020 Adamo Dr	Tampa	FL	33619		813-621-1331	R	60	0.2
Stevens Aviation Inc.	600 Delaware	Greenville	SC	29605		864-678-6000	R	49*	0.3
Aero Toy Store L.L.C.	1710 W Cypress	Fort Lauderdale	FL	33309	Morris Shirazipour	954-771-1795	R	45*	<0.1
North Coast Nissan Inc.	7168 Pearl Rd	Cleveland	OH	44130	Jacob Studor	440-884-7800	R	38*	<0.1
Corporate Fleet Services	5400 Arpt Dr	Charlotte	NC	28208	Tom McCune	704-359-0007	R	29*	<0.1
Reliable Tractor Inc.	PO Box 808	Tifton	GA	31794	DN Stafford III	229-382-4400	R	26*	<0.1
M and L Industries Inc.	1210 St Charles St	Houma	LA	70360	Steven Marmande	985-876-2280	R	23*	0.1
Bowlin Travel Centers Inc.	150 Louisiana NE	Albuquerque	NM	87108	Michael L Bowlin	505-266-5985	P	22	0.2
Jersey Shore Peterbilt Inc.	PO Box 729	Clarksburg	NJ	08510	William Demidowitz	609-259-5950	R	15*	<0.1
Muncie Aviation Co.	PO Box 1169	Muncie	IN	47308	Otto Arrington	765-289-7141	R	15*	<0.1
Capital Aviation Instrument Corp.	10503 Observation	Manassas	VA	20110	Pat Colgan	703-369-0500	R	12*	<0.1
International Furniture	1516 E Reelfoot Ave	Union City	TN	38261	W O Neal	731-885-6471	R	9*	<0.1
La Pine Truck Sales Inc.	3131 E Royalton Rd	Cleveland	OH	44147	Mel Morris	440-526-6363	R	8*	<0.1
AV Automotive L.L.C.	3100 Jefferson Davis	Arlington	VA	22202		703-684-8500	R	7*	<0.1
Kamp Implement Co.	PO Box 629	Belgrade	MT	59714	Tom J Kamp	406-388-4295	R	6*	<0.1
Kermit K. Kistler Inc.	7886 Kings Hwy	New Tripoli	PA	18066	Ronald Kistler	610-298-2011	R	6*	<0.1
Meridian Jet Prop Inc.	3796 Vest Mill Rd	Winston Salem	NC	27103	William D Gardner	336-765-5454	S	3*	<0.1
Stoneridge Motorsports L.L.C.	975 S 12th W	Rexburg	ID	83440	Kenneth Burt	208-356-9251	R	1*	<0.1

Source: Ward's Business Directory of U.S. Private and Public Companies, Volumes 1 and 2, 2005. The company type code used is as follows: P - Public, R - Private, S - Subsidiary, D - Division, J - Joint Venture, A - Affiliate, G - Group. Sales are in millions of dollars, employees are in thousands. An asterisk (*) indicates an estimated sales volume. The symbol < stands for 'less than'. Company names and addresses are truncated, in some cases, to fit into the available space.

OCCUPATIONS EMPLOYED BY OTHER MOTOR VEHICLE DEALERS

Occupation	% of Total 2004	Change to 2014	Occupation	% of Total 2004	Change to 2014
Retail salespersons	20.8	21.4	First-line supervisors of mechanics	2.8	21.4
Motorcycle mechanics	9.0	15.8	Cashiers, except gaming	2.0	9.2
Parts salespersons	8.1	-2.9	Laborers & freight, stock, & material movers, hand	1.8	9.2
Recreational vehicle service technicians	5.6	21.4	Helpers-Installation, maintenance, & repair workers	1.6	21.4
Motorboat mechanics	5.5	21.4	Secretaries, except legal, medical, & executive	1.4	2.1
First-line supervisors/managers of retail sales workers	4.6	11.6	Counter & rental clerks	1.4	27.4
General & operations managers	3.4	20.1	Automotive service technicians & mechanics	1.1	21.4
Bookkeeping, accounting, & auditing clerks	3.2	9.2	Shipping, receiving, & traffic clerks	1.1	9.9
Office clerks, general	3.2	8.0	Janitors & cleaners, except maids	1.1	21.4
Cleaners of vehicles & equipment	3.1	8.6			

Source: Industry-Occupation Matrix, Bureau of Labor Statistics. These data are reported based on 4-digit NAICS categories but have been matched to corresponding 6-digit NAICS industry codes. The change reported for each occupation to the year 2014 is a percent of growth or decline as estimated by the Bureau of Labor Statistics. The abbreviation nec stands for 'not elsewhere classified.'

LOCATION BY STATE AND REGIONAL CONCENTRATION

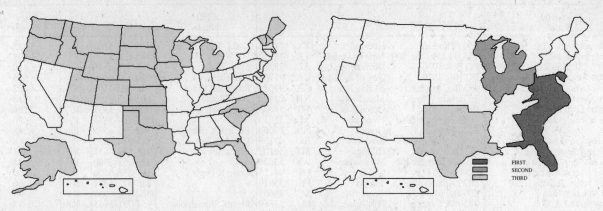

INDUSTRY DATA BY STATE

State	Establishments Total (number)	% of U.S.	Employment Total (number)	% of U.S.	Per Estab.	Payroll Total ($ mil.)	Per Empl. ($)	Sales Total ($ mil.)	% of U.S.	Per Estab. ($)
Florida	204	9.2	1,157	8.4	6	31.0	26,790	417.1	10.5	2,044,760
Texas	194	8.8	1,200	8.7	6	31.4	26,128	341.3	8.6	1,759,124
California	156	7.1	1,334	9.6	9	34.9	26,131	333.2	8.4	2,135,692
Michigan	91	4.1	524	3.8	6	13.6	25,874	156.6	4.0	1,720,396
North Carolina	65	2.9	317	2.3	5	9.3	29,328	149.6	3.8	2,301,292
South Carolina	46	2.1	740	5.3	16	13.4	18,055	141.3	3.6	3,071,478
Colorado	58	2.6	291	2.1	5	9.5	32,718	139.6	3.5	2,406,052
Minnesota	75	3.4	475	3.4	6	11.6	24,322	139.4	3.5	1,858,067
Idaho	33	1.5	335	2.4	10	10.8	32,275	122.8	3.1	3,720,182
Ohio	71	3.2	391	2.8	6	13.0	33,353	118.8	3.0	1,672,761
Washington	55	2.5	555	4.0	10	20.7	37,301	116.4	2.9	2,115,836
New York	87	3.9	391	2.8	4	9.1	23,171	110.5	2.8	1,270,207
Illinois	63	2.9	380	2.7	6	11.6	30,463	107.2	2.7	1,701,127
Wisconsin	61	2.8	358	2.6	6	8.0	22,218	90.4	2.3	1,481,836
Utah	26	1.2	254	1.8	10	6.9	27,138	82.6	2.1	3,176,846
Indiana	44	2.0	351	2.5	8	8.8	24,969	80.1	2.0	1,819,773
Missouri	38	1.7	242	1.7	6	6.8	28,281	69.9	1.8	1,839,632
Kansas	25	1.1	205	1.5	8	5.8	28,298	69.7	1.8	2,789,160
New Jersey	30	1.4	236	1.7	8	11.3	47,835	66.7	1.7	2,223,400
Maine	36	1.6	219	1.6	6	5.1	23,201	61.3	1.6	1,703,889
Oregon	43	1.9	196	1.4	5	5.4	27,388	61.2	1.5	1,423,349
Iowa	42	1.9	239	1.7	6	6.5	27,276	60.1	1.5	1,430,833
Alabama	42	1.9	159	1.1	4	4.2	26,283	59.8	1.5	1,423,024
New Hampshire	24	1.1	188	1.4	8	5.6	29,766	57.7	1.5	2,403,917
Pennsylvania	48	2.2	304	2.2	6	6.0	19,645	57.4	1.5	1,196,458
Kentucky	38	1.7	179	1.3	5	4.3	24,229	53.3	1.3	1,402,184
Oklahoma	38	1.7	163	1.2	4	4.7	28,969	53.3	1.3	1,401,605
Georgia	53	2.4	210	1.5	4	5.2	24,890	52.6	1.3	992,811
Louisiana	39	1.8	224	1.6	6	5.6	24,964	51.5	1.3	1,321,590
Massachusetts	25	1.1	176	1.3	7	4.7	26,449	50.9	1.3	2,035,600
Tennessee	31	1.4	150	1.1	5	4.1	27,273	42.7	1.1	1,376,290
Alaska	22	1.0	152	1.1	7	4.0	26,263	41.5	1.0	1,888,045
Maryland	26	1.2	124	0.9	5	5.3	42,718	40.8	1.0	1,567,500
Vermont	20	0.9	145	1.0	7	4.1	28,221	38.6	1.0	1,931,400
Nebraska	13	0.6	79	0.6	6	2.3	28,772	34.9	0.9	2,684,538
Montana	21	1.0	138	1.0	7	2.7	19,406	33.6	0.8	1,597,762
Mississippi	24	1.1	93	0.7	4	2.0	21,548	25.6	0.6	1,068,375
Arkansas	27	1.2	78	0.6	3	1.5	19,449	21.8	0.6	809,222
Connecticut	16	0.7	89	0.6	6	2.6	29,382	21.1	0.5	1,319,563
North Dakota	17	0.8	72	0.5	4	1.3	18,375	19.8	0.5	1,166,353
Wyoming	16	0.7	55	0.4	3	1.4	25,255	18.4	0.5	1,150,813
South Dakota	11	0.5	78	0.6	7	1.6	20,936	16.7	0.4	1,518,273
Virginia	20	0.9	59	0.4	3	1.3	21,763	15.8	0.4	789,450
New Mexico	10	0.5	64	0.5	6	1.9	30,203	14.3	0.4	1,427,500
Nevada	18	0.8	88	0.6	5	1.6	18,125	14.1	0.4	781,667
Delaware	6	0.3	33	0.2	6	1.4	42,242	12.1	0.3	2,024,833
West Virginia	7	0.3	37	0.3	5	0.9	24,297	8.8	0.2	1,253,714
Arizona	45	2.0	250-499	-	-	(D)	-	(D)	-	-
Rhode Island	6	0.3	20-99	-	-	(D)	-	(D)	-	-
D.C.	2	0.1	0-19	-	-	(D)	-	(D)	-	-
Hawaii	1	-	0-19	-	-	(D)	-	(D)	-	-

Source: 2002 *Economic Census*. The states are in descending order of sales or establishments (if sales data are missing for the majority). The symbol (D) appears when data are withheld to prevent disclosure of competitive information. States marked with (D) are sorted by number of establishments. A dash (-) indicates that the data element cannot be calculated. Shaded *states* on the state map indicate those states which have proportionately greater representation in the industry than would be indicated by the states population; the ratio is based on total sales or number of establishments. Shaded *regions* indicate where the industry is regionally most concentrated.

NAICS 441310 - AUTOMOTIVE PARTS AND ACCESSORIES STORES

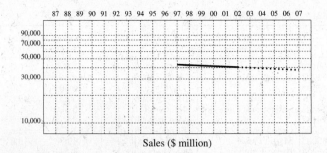

Sales ($ million)

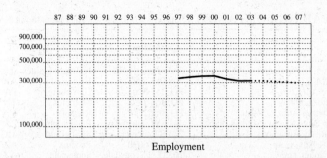

Employment

GENERAL STATISTICS

Year	Establishments (number)	Employment (number)	Payroll ($ million)	Sales ($ million)	Employees per Establishment (number)	Sales per Establishment ($)	Payroll per Employee ($)
1987	-	-	-	-	-	-	-
1988	-	-	-	-	-	-	-
1989	-	-	-	-	-	-	-
1990	-	-	-	-	-	-	-
1991	-	-	-	-	-	-	-
1992	-	-	-	-	-	-	-
1993	-	-	-	-	-	-	-
1994	-	-	-	-	-	-	-
1995	-	-	-	-	-	-	-
1996	-	-	-	-	-	-	-
1997	42,519	334,556	6,718.2	43,165.7	8	1,015,210	20,081
1998	41,873	345,416	7,228.4	42,607.1 e	8	1,017,531	20,927
1999	41,869	353,602	7,447.0	42,048.5 e	8	1,004,287	21,060
2000	41,084	355,342	7,828.0	41,489.9 e	9	1,009,879	22,029
2001	40,766	328,832	7,870.6	40,931.2 e	8	1,004,054	23,935
2002	40,116	313,272	6,949.5	40,372.6	8	1,006,397	22,184
2003	39,492	314,266	7,182.1	39,814.0 p	8	1,001,669 p	22,854
2004	39,146 p	313,623 p	7,497.3 p	39,255.4 p	8 p	999,415 p	23,825 p
2005	38,657 p	308,268 p	7,542.2 p	38,696.8 p	8 p	997,161 p	24,315 p
2006	38,167 p	302,913 p	7,587.1 p	38,138.2 p	8 p	994,906 p	24,804 p
2007	37,678 p	297,559 p	7,632.1 p	37,579.6 p	8 p	992,652 p	25,294 p

Source: Economic Census of the United States, 1997 and 2002. Establishment counts, employment, and payroll are from *County Business Patterns* for non-Census years. This is a newly defined industry. Data for prior years are unavailable at the time of publication but may become available over time. Values followed by 'p' are projections by the editors. Sales data for non-Census years are extrapolations, marked by 'e'.

INDICES OF CHANGE

Year	Establishments (number)	Employment (number)	Payroll ($ million)	Sales ($ million)	Employees per Establishment (number)	Sales per Establishment ($)	Payroll per Employee ($)
1987	-	-	-	-	-	-	-
1992	-	-	-	-	-	-	-
1993	-	-	-	-	-	-	-
1994	-	-	-	-	-	-	-
1995	-	-	-	-	-	-	-
1996	-	-	-	-	-	-	-
1997	106.0	106.8	96.7	106.9	101.2	100.9	90.5
1998	104.4	110.3	104.0	105.5 e	105.0	101.1	94.3
1999	104.4	112.9	107.2	104.2 e	107.6	99.8	94.9
2000	102.4	113.4	112.6	102.8 e	110.1	100.3	99.3
2001	101.6	105.0	113.3	101.4 e	103.7	99.8	107.9
2002	100.0	100.0	100.0	100.0	100.0	100.0	100.0
2003	98.4	100.3	103.3	98.6 p	101.9	99.5 p	103.0
2004	97.6 p	100.1 p	107.9 p	97.2 p	102.6 p	99.3 p	107.4 p
2005	96.4 p	98.4 p	108.5 p	95.8 p	102.1 p	99.1 p	109.6 p
2006	95.1 p	96.7 p	109.2 p	94.5 p	101.7 p	98.9 p	111.8 p
2007	93.9 p	95.0 p	109.8 p	93.1 p	101.3 p	98.6 p	114.0 p

Sources: Same as General Statistics. The values shown reflect change from the base year, 2002. Values above 100 mean greater than 2002, values below 100 mean less than 2002, and a value of 100 in the 1987-2001 or 2003-2007 period means same as 2002. Values followed by a 'p' are projections by the editors; 'e' stands for extrapolation. Data are the most recent available at this level of detail.

SELECTED RATIOS

For 2002	Avg of All Retail	Analyzed Industry	Index	For 2002	Avg. of All Retail	Analyzed Industry	Index
Employees per Establishment	17	8	46	Sales per Employee	174,682	128,874	74
Payroll per Establishment	333,445	173,235	52	Sales per Establishment	3,332,269	1,006,397	30
Payroll per Employee	20,311	22,184	109	Expenses per Establishment	na	na	na

Sources: Same as General Statistics. The 'Average of All' column, Wholesale or Retail, represents the average of the sector reported for the most recent complete year available. The Index shows the relationship between the Average and the Analyzed Industry. For example, 100 means that they are equal; 500 that the Analyzed Industry is five times the average; 50 means that the Analyzed Industry is half the national average. The abbreviation 'na' is used to show that data are 'not available'.

LEADING COMPANIES   Number shown: **75**   Total sales ($ mil): **98,521**   Total employment (000): **517.7**

Company Name	Address				CEO Name	Phone	Co. Type	Sales ($ mil)	Empl. (000)
Sears, Roebuck and Co.	3333 Beverly Rd	Hoffman Estates	IL	60179		847-286-2500	D	36,099	250.0
SAM'S Club	608 SW 8th St	Bentonville	AR	72712	Kevin Turner	479-273-4000	D	24,801*	36.0
Rite Aid Corp.	PO Box 3165	Harrisburg	PA	17105		717-761-2633	P	16,600	75.0
AutoZone Inc.	PO Box 2198	Memphis	TN	38101		901-495-6500	P	5,637	49.0
Advance Auto Parts Inc.	PO Box 2710	Roanoke	VA	24001	Lawrence P Castellini	540-362-4911	P	3,800	35.0
Pep Boys-Manny, Moe and Jack	3111 W Allegheny	Philadelphia	PA	19132		215-430-9000	P	2,273	21.3
O'Reilly Automotive Inc.	233 S Patterson Ave	Springfield	MO	65802	Greg Henslee	417-862-6708	P	1,721	15.6
CSK Auto Corp.	PO Box 6030	Phoenix	AZ	85005	Martin Fraser	602-265-9200	P	1,578	13.6
Discount Tire Co.	20225 N Scottsdale	Scottsdale	AZ	85254	Bruce T Halle	480-606-6000	R	1,541	9.5
MarineMax Inc.	18167 US 19 Hwy N	Clearwater	FL	33764		727-531-1700	P	762	1.5
WheelWorks	120 Cam Real	Belmont	CA	94002		650-592-3200	R	249*	0.4
CSK Holdings Group Inc.	PO Box 6030	Phoenix	AZ	85012	Martin Fraser	602-265-9200	R	235*	0.5
Lithia of Sioux Falls	4200 W 12th St	Sioux Falls	SD	57107		605-336-1700	S	201*	0.2
Legacy Automotive Inc.	413 Industrial Blvd	McDonough	GA	30253	Emanuel D Jones	770-914-2800	R	172	0.3
Ewald Automotive Group Inc.	36833 E Wisconsin	Oconomowoc	WI	53066	Emil Ewald	262-567-5555	R	165*	0.5
Travis Boats and Motors Inc.	12116 Jekel Cir	Austin	TX	78727	Richard S Birnbaum	512-347-8787	S	141	0.4
Team Schierl Cos.	PO Box 308	Stevens Point	WI	54481	William Schierl	715-345-5060	R	133*	0.6
District Petroleum Products Inc.	1814 River Rd	Huron	OH	44839	Scott Stipp	419-433-8373	R	131*	0.2
Big O Tires Inc.	12650 E Briarwood	Englewood	CO	80112	John Adams	303-728-5500	S	125*	0.5
Rose City Chevrolet Inc.	8150 N Lombard	Portland	OR	97203	Jock Schowalter	503-286-1641	R	106*	0.1
Martin Cadillac Company Inc.	12101 W Olympic	Los Angeles	CA	90064	Dana R Martin	310-820-3611	R	98*	0.2
Midwest Auto Parts	2565 Kasota Ave	St. Paul	MN	55108	Herb Lohse	651-644-6448	R	95*	0.8
Vista Ford	21501 Ventura Blvd	Woodland Hills	CA	91364	Steve Shuken	818-884-7600	R	89*	0.2
Big 10 Tire Co.	3938A Government	Mobile	AL	36693	Don Kennemer	251-666-9938	R	87*	0.8
Capitol Chevrolet Inc.	PO Box 36	Montgomery	AL	36101	Phil Marshall	334-272-8700	R	80*	0.2
Mike Daugherty Chevrolet Inc.	2449 Fulton Ave	Sacramento	CA	95825	Michael D Daugherty	916-482-1600	R	80*	0.2
Red River Motor Co.	221 Traffic St	Bossier City	LA	71171	James N Fritze	318-742-3411	R	79*	0.1
Atwood Distributing Inc.	2717 N Van Buren	Enid	OK	73703	G Atwood	580-233-3702	R	66*	0.9
Peerless Tyre Co.	5000 Kingston St	Denver	CO	80239	Samuel E Forbes	303-371-4300	R	62*	0.3
Allied Oil and Supply Inc.	PO Box 3687	Omaha	NE	68103	RC Heinson	402-344-4343	R	60*	0.2
Rhode Island Mack Sales and Serv	1 Mack Dr	Avon	MA	02322		508-559-0771	R	56*	<0.1
Barry Bunker Chevrolet Cadillac	1307 N Wabash Ave	Marion	IN	46952	Barry Bunker	765-664-1275	R	54*	<0.1
Gwatney Chevrolet-Geo	2000 Covington Pike	Memphis	TN	38128	Russell Gwatney	901-387-2000	S	54*	0.1
Shamrock Ford Lincoln Mercury	829 Tecumseh Rd	Clinton	MI	49236	Jeffrey L Shamberger	517-456-7414	R	52	<0.1
Palmetto Ford Inc.	PO Box 31820	Charleston	SC	29417	Graham Eubank	843-571-3673	R	50*	0.1
Jett Racing and Sales Inc.	1301 Lincoln St	Laredo	TX	78040	Wolf Hofman	956-722-3102	R	46*	<0.1
John Rogin Buick Inc.	30500 Plymouth Rd	Livonia	MI	48150	John Rogin	734-525-0900	R	45*	<0.1
Boggus Ford	PO Box 2318	McAllen	TX	78502	Bob Boggus	956-686-7411	R	44*	0.1
Kenworth of Dayton	7740 Ctr Point 70	Dayton	OH	45424		937-235-2589	R	44*	<0.1
Technicar Inc.	450 Commerce Blvd	Oldsmar	FL	34677	Jim Duffy	813-855-0022	R	42*	0.2
Schottenstein Stores Corp	3251 Westerville Rd	Columbus	OH	43224		614-471-4711	D	40*	0.3
Year One Inc.	P O Box 521	Braselton	GA	30517	Kevin King	770-493-6568	R	39*	0.2
Vogler Motor Company Inc.	PO Box 2946	Carbondale	IL	62901	Frank Black	618-457-8135	R	37*	<0.1
Watson Truck and Supply Inc.	PO Box 10	Hobbs	NM	88240	Charley R Smith	505-397-2411	R	36*	0.2
Jack Williams Tire Company Inc.	PO Box 3655	Scranton	PA	18505	William C Williams	570-457-5000	R	35*	0.4
Dow Chevrolet Oldsmobile Inc.	PO Box 6	Mineola	TX	75773	Ed Dow	903-569-2621	R	33*	<0.1
Dick Gidron Ford Inc.	2030 E Tremont Ave	Bronx	NY	10462	Richard Gidron	718-409-4400	R	31*	<0.1
Mid-Tenn Ford Truck Sales Inc.	1319 Foster Ave	Nashville	TN	37210	WE Boyte	615-259-2050	R	31*	<0.1
Murray's Bargain Center	27207 Plymouth Rd	Detroit	MI	48239	Lou Mancini	313-937-8360	R	31*	0.2
Melton Motors Inc.	15100 Eureka Rd	Southgate	MI	48195	George Melton	734-283-2600	R	29*	<0.1
Benny's Inc.	340 Waterman Ave	Esmond	RI	02917		401-231-1000	R	27*	0.3
Heritage Ford Lincoln Mercury	1115 E Spring St	Cookeville	TN	38501	Jamie Vegara	931-526-3325	R	27*	<0.1
Ewald's Hartford Ford Lincoln	5788 Hwy 60 E	Hartford	WI	53027		262-673-9400	D	23*	<0.1
Winfield Consumer Products Inc.	PO Box 839	Winfield	KS	67156	Robert D Tyler	620-221-2268	R	22*	0.1
Hedahls Parts Plus	PO Box 1038	Bismarck	ND	58502	Richard Hedahl	701-223-8393	R	21*	0.2
Blount Greenback Farmers Coop.	1514 W Broadway	Maryville	TN	37801		865-982-2761	R	21*	<0.1
US Auto Parts Network Inc.	17150 Margay Ave	Carson	CA	90746	Mehran Nia	310-719-8666	R	20*	<0.1
E Auto Parts Inc.	10441 Alta Dr	Jacksonville	FL	32226	Ben Hakimian	904-757-1975	R	19*	<0.1
Cooling Systems Specialists	100 Rte 46	Totowa	NJ	07512	Brian Drost	201-794-7595	R	18*	<0.1
Factory Motor Parts Inc.	PO Box 24301	Seattle	WA	98124		425-251-8614	R	18*	<0.1
Bookcliff Auto Parts Inc.	PO Box 4858	Grand Junction	CO	81502	Mike Akens	970-242-2077	R	17*	<0.1
Maryland Truck Parts Inc.	29376 Matthewstwn	Easton	MD	21601	Mark Hardisty	410-822-5752	R	17*	<0.1
Jersey Shore Peterbilt Inc.	PO Box 729	Clarksburg	NJ	08510	William Demidowitz	609-259-5950	R	15*	<0.1
API Autobody Products Inc.	133 S Monroe St	Butler	PA	16001		814-226-7340	R	15*	<0.1
Ideal Automotive & Truck	6560 Powerline Rd	Fort Lauderdale	FL	33309	Daniel Cramer	954-493-9800	R	15*	<0.1
Campbell Supply Company Inc.	1526 N Ind Ave	Sioux Falls	SD	57104	David Campbell	605-331-5470	R	14*	0.2
Distributors Warehouse Inc.	PO Box 7239	Paducah	KY	42002	Steve Korte	270-442-8201	R	14*	<0.1
Mid America Motors Inc.	6041 N Lindbergh	Hazelwood	MO	63042	Kevin A Maher	314-731-1800	R	14*	<0.1
GM Auto Recycling Inc.	3486 Recycle Rd	Rancho Cordova	CA	95742	Darren Moore	916-631-8844	R	14*	<0.1
Falls Auto Parts and Supplies Inc.	N89W16688 Grant	Menomonee Fls	WI	53051		262-251-0400	R	14*	<0.1
Auto Trim Designs	2506 Phyllis Ln	Billings	MT	59102	Steve Zabawa	406-656-3947	R	13*	<0.1
Idaho Truck Specialties L.L.C.	600 N Eagle Rd	Meridian	ID	83642		208-887-7788	R	13*	<0.1
AW Imported Auto Parts Inc.	52 State Rte 35 S	Eatontown	NJ	07724	Arnold Wenzel	732-542-5600	R	13*	<0.1
Ace Drive Products & Servics Inc.	520 York St	Elizabeth	NJ	07201	David Giladi	908-820-4343	R	12*	<0.1
A1 Radiator Repair Inc.	875 E 2nd St	Reno	NV	89502	Kenneth Zeal	775-322-0191	R	12*	<0.1

Source: *Ward's Business Directory of U.S. Private and Public Companies*, Volumes 1 and 2, 2005. The company type code used is as follows: P - Public, R - Private, S - Subsidiary, D - Division, J - Joint Venture, A - Affiliate, G - Group. Sales are in millions of dollars, employees are in thousands. An asterisk (*) indicates an estimated sales volume. The symbol < stands for 'less than'. Company names and addresses are truncated, in some cases, to fit into the available space.

OCCUPATIONS EMPLOYED BY AUTOMOTIVE PARTS, ACCESSORIES, & TIRE STORES

Occupation	% of Total 2004	Change to 2014	Occupation	% of Total 2004	Change to 2014
Parts salespersons	13.8	-6.1	Laborers & freight, stock, & material movers, hand	2.3	5.6
Tire repairers & changers	12.5	5.5	Sales reps, wholesale & manufacturing, exc tech	2.0	17.3
Retail salespersons	11.6	17.3	Counter & rental clerks	2.0	23.2
Automotive service technicians & mechanics	11.6	17.3	Bookkeeping, accounting, & auditing clerks	1.9	5.6
Truck drivers, light or delivery services	7.4	17.2	Stock clerks & order fillers	1.9	-10.1
First-line supervisors/managers of retail sales workers	6.5	8.0	Cashiers, except gaming	1.9	5.6
First-line supervisors of mechanics	3.2	17.3	Office clerks, general	1.9	4.4
General & operations managers	2.4	16.1			

Source: *Industry-Occupation Matrix*, Bureau of Labor Statistics. These data are reported based on 4-digit NAICS categories but have been matched to corresponding 6-digit NAICS industry codes. The change reported for each occupation to the year 2014 is a percent of growth or decline as estimated by the Bureau of Labor Statistics. The abbreviation nec stands for 'not elsewhere classified.'

LOCATION BY STATE AND REGIONAL CONCENTRATION

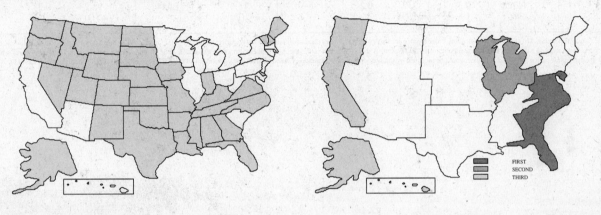

INDUSTRY DATA BY STATE

State	Establishments Total (number)	% of U.S.	Employment Total (number)	% of U.S.	Per Estab.	Payroll Total ($ mil.)	Per Empl. ($)	Sales Total ($ mil.)	% of U.S.	Per Estab. ($)
California	3,985	10.1	35,139	11.5	9	805.7	22,930	4,656.7	11.9	1,168,551
Texas	3,061	7.8	24,902	8.2	8	562.2	22,576	3,522.1	9.0	1,150,624
Florida	2,168	5.5	16,440	5.4	8	345.6	21,021	2,117.8	5.4	976,828
New York	1,719	4.4	12,672	4.2	7	279.3	22,037	1,600.6	4.1	931,136
Pennsylvania	1,637	4.2	12,761	4.2	8	257.7	20,195	1,523.3	3.9	930,557
Ohio	1,494	3.8	12,064	4.0	8	260.1	21,563	1,477.0	3.8	988,649
Michigan	1,421	3.6	10,491	3.4	7	249.3	23,764	1,423.7	3.6	1,001,935
Illinois	1,283	3.3	10,402	3.4	8	238.9	22,968	1,317.1	3.4	1,026,604
North Carolina	1,335	3.4	10,304	3.4	8	203.6	19,762	1,280.5	3.3	959,205
Georgia	1,200	3.0	9,556	3.1	8	194.4	20,346	1,217.7	3.1	1,014,752
Virginia	1,034	2.6	8,668	2.8	8	181.2	20,904	1,038.3	2.7	1,004,132
Tennessee	964	2.4	7,802	2.6	8	161.4	20,693	958.7	2.4	994,503
Indiana	958	2.4	7,696	2.5	8	164.2	21,335	937.8	2.4	978,863
Washington	874	2.2	6,961	2.3	8	169.2	24,311	911.7	2.3	1,043,127
Missouri	986	2.5	7,215	2.4	7	158.4	21,954	911.1	2.3	924,015
New Jersey	824	2.1	6,885	2.3	8	160.6	23,321	876.9	2.2	1,064,159
Colorado	627	1.6	5,217	1.7	8	124.2	23,803	705.6	1.8	1,125,282
Alabama	873	2.2	5,491	1.8	6	109.4	19,929	690.6	1.8	791,097
Minnesota	788	2.0	5,613	1.8	7	123.0	21,905	684.1	1.7	868,098
Louisiana	764	1.9	5,501	1.8	7	115.8	21,045	678.5	1.7	888,034
Massachusetts	679	1.7	5,235	1.7	8	127.3	24,309	663.5	1.7	977,214
Kentucky	735	1.9	5,173	1.7	7	102.9	19,896	646.0	1.7	878,907
Maryland	543	1.4	5,041	1.7	9	116.0	23,015	640.5	1.6	1,179,630
Wisconsin	808	2.0	5,248	1.7	6	115.1	21,936	637.7	1.6	789,203
Oklahoma	601	1.5	4,029	1.3	7	87.6	21,748	575.6	1.5	957,742
South Carolina	645	1.6	4,783	1.6	7	89.0	18,614	565.0	1.4	876,034
Oregon	561	1.4	4,116	1.4	7	97.8	23,766	535.1	1.4	953,756
Iowa	600	1.5	4,031	1.3	7	84.8	21,036	482.4	1.2	804,073
Mississippi	571	1.4	3,662	1.2	6	75.7	20,658	454.5	1.2	795,937
Arkansas	591	1.5	3,606	1.2	6	72.8	20,182	445.9	1.1	754,470
Kansas	568	1.4	3,300	1.1	6	72.3	21,922	444.4	1.1	782,428
Connecticut	384	1.0	3,300	1.1	9	81.3	24,624	406.3	1.0	1,058,177
Utah	293	0.7	2,634	0.9	9	59.9	22,733	336.9	0.9	1,149,976
Nebraska	355	0.9	2,207	0.7	6	47.7	21,635	284.7	0.7	801,851
New Mexico	274	0.7	2,252	0.7	8	47.0	20,865	282.0	0.7	1,029,226

Continued on next page.

INDUSTRY DATA BY STATE - Continued

State	Establishments		Employment			Payroll		Sales		
	Total (number)	% of U.S.	Total (number)	% of U.S.	Per Estab.	Total ($ mil.)	Per Empl. ($)	Total ($ mil.)	% of U.S.	Per Estab. ($)
Nevada	223	0.6	2,168	0.7	10	47.3	21,804	278.2	0.7	1,247,556
West Virginia	327	0.8	2,188	0.7	7	37.8	17,276	264.5	0.7	808,890
Maine	269	0.7	1,831	0.6	7	42.6	23,287	243.6	0.6	905,695
New Hampshire	234	0.6	1,841	0.6	8	42.5	23,109	243.2	0.6	1,039,269
Montana	231	0.6	1,480	0.5	6	34.1	23,018	209.2	0.5	905,697
Idaho	246	0.6	1,616	0.5	7	35.3	21,848	199.8	0.5	812,037
Alaska	112	0.3	893	0.3	8	24.9	27,907	154.5	0.4	1,379,437
Hawaii	143	0.4	1,029	0.3	7	22.1	21,524	142.3	0.4	995,168
North Dakota	150	0.4	933	0.3	6	21.0	22,521	117.2	0.3	781,053
South Dakota	142	0.4	877	0.3	6	19.3	21,973	107.3	0.3	755,958
Delaware	102	0.3	916	0.3	9	18.1	19,749	104.0	0.3	1,019,598
Rhode Island	99	0.3	771	0.3	8	18.2	23,625	98.5	0.3	994,535
Vermont	122	0.3	778	0.3	6	19.0	24,451	98.2	0.3	805,311
Wyoming	117	0.3	717	0.2	6	15.4	21,424	98.2	0.3	839,026
Arizona	698	1.8	5K-9999	-	-	(D)	-	(D)	-	-
D.C.	23	0.1	100-249	-	-	(D)	-	(D)	-	-

Source: 2002 Economic Census. The states are in descending order of sales or establishments (if sales data are missing for the majority). The symbol (D) appears when data are withheld to prevent disclosure of competitive information. States marked with (D) are sorted by number of establishments. A dash (-) indicates that the data element cannot be calculated. Shaded *states* on the state map indicate those states which have proportionately greater representation in the industry than would be indicated by the states population; the ratio is based on total sales or number of establishments. Shaded *regions* indicate where the industry is regionally most concentrated.

NAICS 441320 - TIRE DEALERS

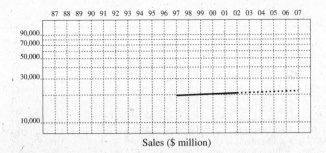

Sales ($ million)

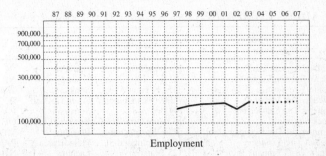

Employment

GENERAL STATISTICS

Year	Establishments (number)	Employment (number)	Payroll ($ million)	Sales ($ million)	Employees per Establishment (number)	Sales per Establishment ($)	Payroll per Employee ($)
1987	-	-	-	-	-	-	-
1988	-	-	-	-	-	-	-
1989	-	-	-	-	-	-	-
1990	-	-	-	-	-	-	-
1991	-	-	-	-	-	-	-
1992	-	-	-	-	-	-	-
1993	-	-	-	-	-	-	-
1994	-	-	-	-	-	-	-
1995	-	-	-	-	-	-	-
1996	-	-	-	-	-	-	-
1997	17,288	142,644	3,550.7	19,659.3	8	1,137,164	24,892
1998	17,758	153,338	3,917.5	19,889.0 e	9	1,120,000	25,548
1999	17,790	160,055	4,194.6	20,118.6 e	9	1,130,895	26,207
2000	17,988	161,914	4,376.7	20,348.3 e	9	1,131,215	27,031
2001	18,408	164,533	4,561.0	20,578.0 e	9	1,117,881	27,721
2002	17,579	141,647	4,047.7	20,807.6	8	1,183,663	28,576
2003	18,997	169,034	4,914.4	21,037.3 p	9	1,159,449 p	29,074
2004	18,742 p	164,776 p	4,897.2 p	21,266.9 p	9 p	1,165,919 p	29,880 p
2005	18,935 p	166,928 p	5,065.7 p	21,496.6 p	9 p	1,172,389 p	30,599 p
2006	19,127 p	169,081 p	5,234.2 p	21,726.3 p	9 p	1,178,859 p	31,317 p
2007	19,319 p	171,233 p	5,402.7 p	21,955.9 p	9 p	1,185,329 p	32,035 p

Source: *Economic Census of the United States*, 1997 and 2002. Establishment counts, employment, and payroll are from *County Business Patterns* for non-Census years. This is a newly defined industry. Data for prior years are unavailable at the time of publication but may become available over time. Values followed by 'p' are projections by the editors. Sales data for non-Census years are extrapolations, marked by 'e'.

INDICES OF CHANGE

Year	Establishments (number)	Employment (number)	Payroll ($ million)	Sales ($ million)	Employees per Establishment (number)	Sales per Establishment ($)	Payroll per Employee ($)
1987	-	-	-	-	-	-	-
1992	-	-	-	-	-	-	-
1993	-	-	-	-	-	-	-
1994	-	-	-	-	-	-	-
1995	-	-	-	-	-	-	-
1996	-	-	-	-	-	-	-
1997	98.3	100.7	87.7	94.5	103.0	96.1	87.1
1998	101.0	108.3	96.8	95.6 e	106.7	94.6	89.4
1999	101.2	113.0	103.6	96.7 e	111.7	95.5	91.7
2000	102.3	114.3	108.1	97.8 e	111.7	95.6	94.6
2001	104.7	116.2	112.7	98.9 e	110.5	94.4	97.0
2002	100.0	100.0	100.0	100.0	100.0	100.0	100.0
2003	108.1	119.3	121.4	101.1 p	110.4	98.0 p	101.7
2004	106.6 p	116.3 p	121.0 p	102.2 p	108.8 p	98.5 p	104.6 p
2005	107.7 p	117.8 p	125.2 p	103.3 p	109.1 p	99.0 p	107.1 p
2006	108.8 p	119.4 p	129.3 p	104.4 p	109.3 p	99.6 p	109.6 p
2007	109.9 p	120.9 p	133.5 p	105.5 p	109.6 p	100.1 p	112.1 p

Sources: Same as General Statistics. The values shown reflect change from the base year, 2002. Values above 100 mean greater than 2002, values below 100 mean less than 2002, and a value of 100 in the 1987-2001 or 2003-2007 period means same as 2002. Values followed by a 'p' are projections by the editors; 'e' stands for extrapolation. Data are the most recent available at this level of detail.

SELECTED RATIOS

For 2002	Avg. of All Retail	Analyzed Industry	Index	For 2002	Avg. of All Retail	Analyzed Industry	Index
Employees per Establishment	17	8	48	Sales per Employee	174,682	146,898	84
Payroll per Establishment	333,445	230,255	69	Sales per Establishment	3,332,269	1,183,663	36
Payroll per Employee	20,311	28,576	141	Expenses per Establishment	na	na	na

Sources: Same as General Statistics. The 'Average of All' column, Wholesale or Retail, represents the average of the sector reported for the most recent complete year available. The Index shows the relationship between the Average and the Analyzed Industry. For example, 100 means that they are equal; 500 that the Analyzed Industry is five times the average; 50 means that the Analyzed Industry is half the national average. The abbreviation 'na' is used to show that data are 'not available'.

LEADING COMPANIES   Number shown: **12**   Total sales ($ mil): **336**   Total employment (000): **0.3**

Company Name	Address				CEO Name	Phone	Co. Type	Sales ($ mil)	Empl. (000)
Midland-Impact L.L.P.	PO Box 560	Danville	IN	46122	Greg Gore	317-745-4491	R	230*	<0.1
L & W Service Center Inc.	PO Box 190	Kearney	NE	68848	Marc Loescher	308-237-2185	R	15*	<0.1
Alpine Tire Service of Spokane	3534 E Trent Ave	Spokane	WA	99202	Kermit Yochum	509-535-0261	R	13*	<0.1
Chicago Tire Inc.	16001 Van Drunen	South Holland	IL	60473	John Wagner	708-331-8980	R	11*	<0.1
Walter's Tire Service Inc.	PO Box 348	Somerset	PA	15501	James Walters	814-445-4124	R	11*	<0.1
Speck Sales Inc.	17746 N Dixie Hwy	Bowling Green	OH	43402	Esther Speck	419-353-8312	R	10*	<0.1
Commercial Tire Company Inc.	5790 Washington	Elkridge	MD	21075	Jesse Albright	410-796-4330	R	10*	<0.1
General Tire Service	3375 Richmond St	Philadelphia	PA	19134	John Morrone	215-425-9980	R	10*	<0.1
Salta's Tire Company Inc.	125 Water St	Laconia	NH	03246	William Salta	603-524-9030	R	8*	<0.1
Van Kleeck's Tire Inc.	PO Box 617	Lake Katrine	NY	12449	Clayton Van Kleeck	845-382-1292	R	8*	<0.1
Phelps Tire Co.	PO Box 24968	Seattle	WA	98124	Norval Phelps	206-622-8977	R	5*	<0.1
Crosstown Used Auto Parts	218 Pascal St N	Saint Paul	MN	55104	Clyde Payne	612-861-3020	R	4*	<0.1

Source: Ward's Business Directory of U.S. Private and Public Companies, Volumes 1 and 2, 2005. The company type code used is as follows: P - Public, R - Private, S - Subsidiary, D - Division, J - Joint Venture, A - Affiliate, G - Group. Sales are in millions of dollars, employees are in thousands. An asterisk (*) indicates an estimated sales volume. The symbol < stands for 'less than'. Company names and addresses are truncated, in some cases, to fit into the available space.

OCCUPATIONS EMPLOYED BY AUTOMOTIVE PARTS, ACCESSORIES, & TIRE STORES

Occupation	% of Total 2004	Change to 2014	Occupation	% of Total 2004	Change to 2014
Parts salespersons	13.8	-6.1	Laborers & freight, stock, & material movers, hand	2.3	5.6
Tire repairers & changers	12.5	5.5	Sales reps, wholesale & manufacturing, exc tech	2.0	17.3
Retail salespersons	11.6	17.3	Counter & rental clerks	2.0	23.2
Automotive service technicians & mechanics	11.6	17.3	Bookkeeping, accounting, & auditing clerks	1.9	5.6
Truck drivers, light or delivery services	7.4	17.2	Stock clerks & order fillers	1.9	-10.1
First-line supervisors/managers of retail sales workers	6.5	8.0	Cashiers, except gaming	1.9	5.6
First-line supervisors of mechanics	3.2	17.3	Office clerks, general	1.9	4.4
General & operations managers	2.4	16.1			

Source: Industry-Occupation Matrix, Bureau of Labor Statistics. These data are reported based on 4-digit NAICS categories but have been matched to corresponding 6-digit NAICS industry codes. The change reported for each occupation to the year 2014 is a percent of growth or decline as estimated by the Bureau of Labor Statistics. The abbreviation nec stands for 'not elsewhere classified.'

LOCATION BY STATE AND REGIONAL CONCENTRATION

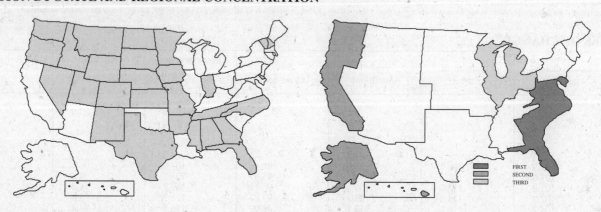

FIRST
SECOND
THIRD

INDUSTRY DATA BY STATE

State	Establishments		Employment			Payroll		Sales		
	Total (number)	% of U.S.	Total (number)	% of U.S.	Per Estab.	Total ($ mil.)	Per Empl. ($)	Total ($ mil.)	% of U.S.	Per Estab. ($)
California	2,071	11.3	16,396	11.0	8	485.7	29,621	2,533.3	11.7	1,223,224
Texas	1,426	7.8	11,905	8.0	8	315.1	26,470	1,682.6	7.8	1,179,909
Florida	1,164	6.4	8,380	5.6	7	263.2	31,408	1,220.1	5.6	1,048,164
Ohio	701	3.8	5,719	3.8	8	163.8	28,636	866.9	4.0	1,236,603
Pennsylvania	651	3.6	5,577	3.7	9	155.6	27,904	854.5	4.0	1,312,550
Georgia	754	4.1	5,844	3.9	8	169.0	28,918	766.2	3.5	1,016,176
North Carolina	744	4.1	5,471	3.7	7	153.6	28,072	728.4	3.4	979,086
Michigan	533	2.9	3,986	2.7	7	108.1	27,117	719.5	3.3	1,349,880
New York	623	3.4	4,701	3.2	8	139.8	29,747	708.5	3.3	1,137,244

Continued on next page.

INDUSTRY DATA BY STATE - Continued

State	Establishments Total (number)	Establishments % of U.S.	Employment Total (number)	Employment % of U.S.	Employment Per Estab.	Payroll Total ($ mil.)	Payroll Per Empl. ($)	Sales Total ($ mil.)	Sales % of U.S.	Sales Per Estab. ($)
Illinois	581	3.2	5,322	3.6	9	144.0	27,063	664.7	3.1	1,144,081
Washington	385	2.1	4,395	3.0	11	139.1	31,659	656.4	3.0	1,705,036
Missouri	495	2.7	4,118	2.8	8	110.1	26,728	588.6	2.7	1,189,162
Indiana	400	2.2	3,756	2.5	9	104.6	27,851	550.6	2.5	1,376,600
Oregon	288	1.6	3,409	2.3	12	111.8	32,787	536.2	2.5	1,861,972
Virginia	463	2.5	3,937	2.6	9	120.5	30,614	511.8	2.4	1,105,441
Colorado	320	1.8	2,922	2.0	9	85.7	29,323	445.7	2.1	1,392,922
Tennessee	431	2.4	3,106	2.1	7	87.1	28,057	428.4	2.0	994,065
New Jersey	372	2.0	2,722	1.8	7	91.7	33,671	425.4	2.0	1,143,427
Minnesota	272	1.5	2,682	1.8	10	77.3	28,825	393.2	1.8	1,445,449
Alabama	459	2.5	3,102	2.1	7	79.8	25,738	391.3	1.8	852,458
Massachusetts	259	1.4	2,267	1.5	9	73.6	32,468	380.1	1.8	1,467,490
Wisconsin	259	1.4	2,301	1.5	9	69.2	30,080	352.9	1.6	1,362,490
Maryland	265	1.5	2,303	1.5	9	82.1	35,655	351.7	1.6	1,327,306
Louisiana	333	1.8	2,590	1.7	8	66.8	25,802	328.2	1.5	985,652
Kentucky	318	1.7	2,379	1.6	7	60.5	25,449	303.8	1.4	955,324
Iowa	259	1.4	1,993	1.3	8	54.6	27,379	285.0	1.3	1,100,544
South Carolina	341	1.9	2,266	1.5	7	59.9	26,420	283.9	1.3	832,633
Kansas	241	1.3	1,789	1.2	7	48.2	26,925	239.3	1.1	992,913
Connecticut	162	0.9	1,501	1.0	9	47.6	31,698	236.9	1.1	1,462,475
Mississippi	278	1.5	1,801	1.2	6	45.7	25,356	236.3	1.1	850,147
Idaho	145	0.8	1,495	1.0	10	44.0	29,454	232.1	1.1	1,600,683
Utah	185	1.0	1,741	1.2	9	48.5	27,831	231.9	1.1	1,253,486
Arkansas	273	1.5	1,750	1.2	6	43.1	24,618	231.0	1.1	846,278
Oklahoma	255	1.4	1,853	1.2	7	44.7	24,132	230.8	1.1	905,255
Nebraska	167	0.9	1,242	0.8	7	35.7	28,721	199.1	0.9	1,192,180
Nevada	108	0.6	1,013	0.7	9	29.9	29,496	174.3	0.8	1,614,185
New Mexico	128	0.7	1,198	0.8	9	31.4	26,179	160.4	0.7	1,253,492
West Virginia	149	0.8	1,048	0.7	7	24.9	23,770	155.9	0.7	1,046,631
Montana	121	0.7	904	0.6	7	23.9	26,475	136.2	0.6	1,125,645
New Hampshire	87	0.5	673	0.5	8	20.1	29,819	121.6	0.6	1,397,379
North Dakota	60	0.3	603	0.4	10	17.6	29,207	102.0	0.5	1,700,283
Maine	63	0.3	601	0.4	10	16.8	27,872	92.3	0.4	1,464,540
South Dakota	70	0.4	564	0.4	8	15.2	26,954	90.9	0.4	1,299,014
Wyoming	69	0.4	490	0.3	7	11.6	23,622	64.3	0.3	931,870
Vermont	40	0.2	287	0.2	7	9.3	32,307	59.2	0.3	1,479,975
Delaware	42	0.2	421	0.3	10	12.8	30,439	59.0	0.3	1,405,857
Hawaii	50	0.3	434	0.3	9	13.4	30,972	55.9	0.3	1,117,080
Rhode Island	38	0.2	300	0.2	8	9.7	32,490	50.7	0.2	1,335,026
Alaska	25	0.1	302	0.2	12	9.4	31,139	48.0	0.2	1,919,560
Arizona	328	1.8	2500-4999	-	-	(D)	-	(D)	-	-
D.C.	6	-	20-99	-	-	(D)	-	(D)	-	-

Source: 2002 *Economic Census*. The states are in descending order of sales or establishments (if sales data are missing for the majority). The symbol (D) appears when data are withheld to prevent disclosure of competitive information. States marked with (D) are sorted by number of establishments. A dash (-) indicates that the data element cannot be calculated. Shaded *states* on the state map indicate those states which have proportionately greater representation in the industry than would be indicated by the states population; the ratio is based on total sales or number of establishments. Shaded *regions* indicate where the industry is regionally most concentrated.

NAICS 442110 - FURNITURE STORES

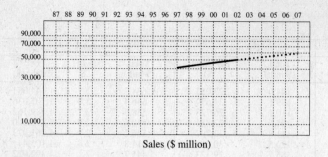

Sales ($ million)

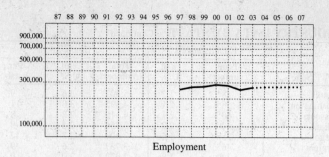

Employment

GENERAL STATISTICS

Year	Establishments (number)	Employment (number)	Payroll ($ million)	Sales ($ million)	Employees per Establishment (number)	Sales per Establishment ($)	Payroll per Employee ($)
1987	-	-	-	-	-	-	-
1988	-	-	-	-	-	-	-
1989	-	-	-	-	-	-	-
1990	-	-	-	-	-	-	-
1991	-	-	-	-	-	-	-
1992	-	-	-	-	-	-	-
1993	-	-	-	-	-	-	-
1994	-	-	-	-	-	-	-
1995	-	-	-	-	-	-	-
1996	-	-	-	-	-	-	-
1997	29,461	251,300	5,619.6	40,968.3	9	1,390,594	22,362
1998	29,707	267,013	6,395.3	42,792.7 e	9	1,440,491	23,951
1999	29,574	270,455	6,966.9	44,617.0 e	9	1,508,657	25,760
2000	29,720	284,060	7,472.7	46,441.4 e	10	1,562,631	26,307
2001	29,920	278,231	7,467.8	48,265.8 e	9	1,613,161	26,840
2002	28,126	250,240	6,940.4	50,090.1	9	1,780,919	27,735
2003	28,318	264,889	7,368.0	51,914.5 p	9	1,801,770 p	27,815
2004	28,369 p	268,741 p	7,866.7 p	53,738.9 p	9 p	1,873,873 p	29,397 p
2005	28,146 p	269,276 p	8,110.8 p	55,563.2 p	10 p	1,945,976 p	30,290 p
2006	27,923 p	269,812 p	8,355.0 p	57,387.6 p	10 p	2,018,079 p	31,183 p
2007	27,700 p	270,348 p	8,599.1 p	59,212.0 p	10 p	2,090,182 p	32,076 p

Source: Economic Census of the United States, 1997 and 2002. Establishment counts, employment, and payroll are from *County Business Patterns* for non-Census years. This is a newly defined industry. Data for prior years are unavailable at the time of publication but may become available over time. Values followed by 'p' are projections by the editors. Sales data for non-Census years are extrapolations, marked by 'e'.

INDICES OF CHANGE

Year	Establishments (number)	Employment (number)	Payroll ($ million)	Sales ($ million)	Employees per Establishment (number)	Sales per Establishment ($)	Payroll per Employee ($)
1987	-	-	-	-	-	-	-
1992	-	-	-	-	-	-	-
1993	-	-	-	-	-	-	-
1994	-	-	-	-	-	-	-
1995	-	-	-	-	-	-	-
1996	-	-	-	-	-	-	-
1997	104.7	100.4	81.0	81.8	95.5	78.1	80.6
1998	105.6	106.7	92.1	85.4 e	101.2	80.9	86.4
1999	105.1	108.1	100.4	89.1 e	102.3	84.7	92.9
2000	105.7	113.5	107.7	92.7 e	107.9	87.7	94.9
2001	106.4	111.2	107.6	96.4 e	104.5	90.6	96.8
2002	100.0	100.0	100.0	100.0	100.0	100.0	100.0
2003	100.7	105.9	106.2	103.6 p	105.1	101.2 p	100.3
2004	100.9 p	107.4 p	113.3 p	107.3 p	106.5 p	105.2 p	106.0 p
2005	100.1 p	107.6 p	116.9 p	110.9 p	107.5 p	109.3 p	109.2 p
2006	99.3 p	107.8 p	120.4 p	114.6 p	108.5 p	113.3 p	112.4 p
2007	98.5 p	108.0 p	123.9 p	118.2 p	109.5 p	117.4 p	115.7 p

Sources: Same as General Statistics. The values shown reflect change from the base year, 2002. Values above 100 mean greater than 2002, values below 100 mean less than 2002, and a value of 100 in the 1987-2001 or 2003-2007 period means same as 2002. Values followed by a 'p' are projections by the editors; 'e' stands for extrapolation. Data are the most recent available at this level of detail.

SELECTED RATIOS

For 2002	Avg. of All Retail	Analyzed Industry	Index	For 2002	Avg. of All Retail	Analyzed Industry	Index
Employees per Establishment	17	9	52	Sales per Employee	174,682	200,168	115
Payroll per Establishment	333,445	246,760	74	Sales per Establishment	3,332,269	1,780,919	53
Payroll per Employee	20,311	27,735	137	Expenses per Establishment	na	na	na

Sources: Same as General Statistics. The 'Average of All' column, Wholesale or Retail, represents the average of the sector reported for the most recent complete year available. The Index shows the relationship between the Average and the Analyzed Industry. For example, 100 means that they are equal; 500 that the Analyzed Industry is five times the average; 50 means that the Analyzed Industry is half the national average. The abbreviation 'na' is used to show that data are 'not available'.

LEADING COMPANIES Number shown: **75** Total sales ($ mil): **43,710** Total employment (000): **215.5**

Company Name	Address				CEO Name	Phone	Co. Type	Sales ($ mil)	Empl. (000)
Staples Inc.	PO Box 9328	Framingham	MA	01702		508-253-5000	P	14,448	65.1
Office Depot Inc.	2200 Germantown	Delray Beach	FL	33445	Charles E Brown	561-266-4800	P	13,565	46.0
Pier 1 Imports Inc.	301 Commerce St	Fort Worth	TX	76102	Marvin J Girouard	817-252-8000	P	1,898	17.6
Rooms To Go Inc.	11540 Hwy 92 E	Seffner	FL	33584	Jeffrey Seaman	813-623-5400	R	1,400	5.7
Ethan Allen Interiors Inc.	PO Box 1966	Danbury	CT	06813		203-743-8000	P	955	6.6
Pier 1 Imports (U.S.) Inc.	301 Commerce St	Fort Worth	TX	76102	Marvin J Girouard	817-878-8000	S	811*	9.4
Cost Plus Inc.	200 4th St	Oakland	CA	94607	Murray H Dashe	510-893-7300	P	802	5.5
Farmers Furniture Company Inc.	1851 Telfair St	Dublin	GA	31021	Greg Glass	478-275-3150	S	780*	1.3
Aaron Rents Inc.	309 Paces Ferry	Atlanta	GA	30305	R C Loudermilk Jr	404-231-0011	P	767	5.4
Haverty Furniture Companies Inc.	780 Johnson Ferry	Atlanta	GA	30342		404-443-2900	P	745	4.2
Value City Furniture Div.	1800 Moler Rd	Columbus	OH	43207	Jay L Schottenstein	614-221-9200	D	680*	4.9
Elder-Beerman Stores Corp.	PO Box 1448	Dayton	OH	45401	Byron L Bergren	937-296-2700	S	671	6.1
Bombay Company Inc.	PO Box 161009	Fort Worth	TX	76161	James D Carreker	817-347-8200	P	596	5.5
Levitz Furniture Inc.	7887 N Federal Hwy	Boca Raton	FL	33487	Alan Rosenberg	561-994-6006	S	500	2.5
Art Van Furniture Inc.	6500 E 14 Mile Rd	Warren	MI	48092	Art Van Elslander	586-939-0800	R	455*	3.0
American Television & Appliance	2404 W Beltline	Madison	WI	53713	Douglas Reuhl	608-271-1000	R	350*	1.8
CORT Furniture Rental Corp.	11250 Waples Mill	Fairfax	VA	22030	Paul N Arnold	703-968-8500	S	350*	2.8
Heilig-Meyers Co.	12501 Patterson Ave	Richmond	VA	23233		804-784-7500	P	324	0.0
Rowe Companies	1650 Tysons Blvd	McLean	VA	22102	Gerald M Birnbach	703-847-8670	P	295	2.6
Wickes Furniture Company Inc.	1100 Lombard Ave	Lombard	IL	60148	Howard Flavin		R	250*	2.5
Raymour & Flanigan Furniture Co.	PO Box 220	Liverpool	NY	13088	Neil Goldberg	315-453-2500	R	204*	3.0
Nebraska Furniture Mart Inc.	PO Box 3000	Omaha	NE	68103	Ron Blumkins	402-255-6327	S	180*	1.2
Goodman's Inc.	PO Box 13289	Phoenix	AZ	85002	Adam Goodman	602-263-1110	R	178*	0.1
Vermont Country Store	5650 Main St	Manchester Ctr	VT	05255	Lyman Orton	802-362-8460	R	167*	1.0
BKM Total Office of California	1201 Bell Ave	Tustin	CA	92780	Bill Kohots	714-566-1400	D	152*	1.0
Porter of Racine	301 6th St	Racine	WI	53403	HR Waters	262-633-6363	R	139*	0.1
Marlo Furniture Company Inc.	725 Rockville Pike	Rockville	MD	20852	Neal Glickfield	301-738-9595	R	138*	0.7
Leath Furniture Inc.	4370 Peachtree N E	Atlanta	GA	30319	Ronald D Phillips	404-848-0880	R	118*	0.8
Grand Home Furnishings	4235 Electric Rd SW	Roanoke	VA	24014	George B Cartledge Jr	540-774-7004	R	100*	0.8
U.S. Home Systems Inc.	750 121 Bypass	Lewisville	TX	75067		214-488-6300	P	89	0.7
Schewel Furniture Company Inc.	PO Box 1600	Lynchburg	VA	24505	Jack Schewel	434-845-2326	R	86*	0.7
Granite Furniture Company Inc.	1050 E 2100 S	Salt Lake City	UT	84106	Jim Taggart	801-486-3333	R	82*	0.4
Marsh Pottery L.L.C.	3775 Av Carolinas	Fort Mill	SC	29708	Tim Marsh	803-548-7075	R	77*	0.2
Miskelly Furniture	101 Arpt Rd	Jackson	MS	39208	Howard L Miskelly Jr	601-939-6288	R	76*	0.3
B. Olinde and Sons Company Inc.	9536 Airline Hwy	Baton Rouge	LA	70815	JB Olinde	225-926-3380	R	71*	0.2
El Dorado Furniture Co.	4200 NW 167th St	Miami	FL	33054	Manuel Capo	305-624-2400	R	70*	0.3
Georgia Lighting	530 14th St	Atlanta	GA	30318	Robert Nardelli	404-875-4754	S	66*	0.2
Steinhafels Inc.	W231 N1013 164	Waukesha	WI	53186	Gary Steinhafel	262-436-4600	R	66*	0.4
Sam Levitz Furniture Co.	3430 E 36th St	Tucson	AZ	85713	Sam R Levitz	520-624-7443	R	62*	0.5
Appliance Depot and More	425 E Macewen Dr	Osprey	FL	34229		941-966-0725	R	57*	<0.1
Plunkett Furniture Co.	2500 W Golf Rd	Hoffman Estates	IL	60194	Hugh Plunkett	847-843-9000	R	54*	0.4
Big Sandy Furniture Inc.	45 Cty Rd 407	South Point	OH	45680	John C Stewart Jr	740-894-4242	R	48*	0.3
DeKalb Office Environments	1320 Ridgeland Pky	Alpharetta	GA	30004	John R Rasper	770-360-0200	R	41*	0.1
Cabot House Inc.	16 Walnut St	Haverhill	MA	01830	Robert Bendeston	978-374-4705	R	40*	0.2
Loth Mbi Inc.	3574 E Kemper Rd	Cincinnati	OH	45241	J B Buse	513-554-4900	R	40*	0.1
R.H. Kuhn Co.	55th St & A V R R	Pittsburgh	PA	15201	Michael R Kuhn	412-784-1250	R	38*	0.3
Weir's Furniture Village	PO Box 600125	Dallas	TX	75360	Dan Weir	214-528-0321	R	38*	0.2
Stevens Office Interiors	1449 Erie Blvd E	Syracuse	NY	13201	Thomas Maugeri	315-479-5595	R	37*	<0.1
Lack Valley Stores Ltd.	1300 San Patricia St	Pharr	TX	78577	Lee Aaronson	956-702-3361	R	35*	0.3
Grand Furniture Discount Stores	1305 Baker Rd	Virginia Beach	VA	23455	Steve Stein	757-460-3800	R	32*	0.4
Carol House Furniture Inc.	2332 Millpark Dr	Maryland H.	MO	63043	Brook Dubman	314-427-4200	R	30*	0.1
Scott Rice of Kansas City Inc.	PO Box 419380	Kansas City	MO	64141	Ed Wills	913-888-7600	R	29*	0.1
Olum's of Binghamton Inc.	3701 Vestal Pkwy E	Vestal	NY	13850	Gilbert S Rouff	607-729-5775	R	28*	0.2
LFD Inc.	725 E Esperanza St	McAllen	TX	78501	Greg Thrash	956-686-2271	R	26*	0.3
Desks Inc.	1385 S Santa Fe Dr	Denver	CO	80223	Jay Stark	303-777-8880	R	25*	<0.1
Office Pavilion Inc.	6807 Portwest Dr	Houston	TX	77024	Steve Marnoy	713-803-0000	S	25*	<0.1
Mazer's Discount Home Centers	41st St 2nd Ave S	Birmingham	AL	35222	JB Mazer	205-591-6565	R	24*	0.2
Arenson Office Furnishings Inc.	1115 Broadway Fl 6	New York	NY	10010	Lawrence Tuck	212-633-2400	R	23*	0.1
Baker's Furniture and Accessories	1036 S Jupiter	Garland	TX	75040	James Baker	972-494-4688	R	21*	0.1
Gorman's Gallery Inc.	29145 Telegraph Rd	Southfield	MI	48034	Bernard D Moray	248-353-9880	R	21*	0.1
LA-Z Recliner Shop Inc.	724 Hoffman St	Hammond	IN	46327	Chuck Forcey	219-937-3360	R	21*	0.1
Seattle Office Furniture L.L.C.	3035 1st Ave	Seattle	WA	98121	Cheryl Thompson	206-728-5710	R	21*	<0.1
Hinson Galleries Inc.	1208-24 13th Ave	Columbus	GA	31901	Robert Hinson	706-327-3671	R	20*	<0.1
Kilgore's Clear Lake Lumber Co.	PO Box 1099	League City	TX	77574	W Lawther	281-332-9351	R	19*	<0.1
Chase Lumber and Fuel Inc.	PO Box 45	Sun Prairie	WI	53590	David Chase	608-837-5101	R	19*	<0.1
Discount City Home Center	1301 E Main St	Havelock	NC	28532	Robert Hill	252-447-1880	R	18*	<0.1
Electronic Office Systems	107 Fairfield Rd	Fairfield	NJ	07004	Andrew W Ritshel	973-808-0100	R	18*	<0.1
Smulekoff Furniture Company Inc.	PO Box 74090	Cedar Rapids	IA	52407	Ann Lipsky	319-362-2181	R	16*	0.1
Brandon House Furniture Co.	1100 S University	Little Rock	AR	72204	Benton Brandon	501-663-1400	R	15*	0.1
Hurwitz-Mintz Furniture Co.	227 Chartres St	New Orleans	LA	70130		504-568-9555	R	15*	0.1
Universal Furniture House Inc.	1600 Westbank	Harvey	LA	70058	CJ Dawson		R	12*	0.2
Kittle's Home Furnishings	8600 Allisonville Rd	Indianapolis	IN	46250		317-849-5300	R	11*	<0.1
Pete Moore Appliance Inc.	1613-1615 W State	Bristol	VA	24201	Clarise Senter	276-466-8197	R	11*	<0.1
H and H Service Stores Inc.	4990 Altama Ave	Brunswick	GA	31525	William Brunson	912-265-8100	R	11*	<0.1
International Furniture	1516 E Reelfoot Ave	Union City	TN	38261	W O Neal	731-885-6471	R	9*	<0.1

Source: Ward's Business Directory of U.S. Private and Public Companies, Volumes 1 and 2, 2005. The company type code used is as follows: P - Public, R - Private, S - Subsidiary, D - Division, J - Joint Venture, A - Affiliate, G - Group. Sales are in millions of dollars, employees are in thousands. An asterisk (*) indicates an estimated sales volume. The symbol < stands for 'less than'. Company names and addresses are truncated, in some cases, to fit into the available space.

OCCUPATIONS EMPLOYED BY FURNITURE STORES

Occupation	% of Total 2004	Change to 2014	Occupation	% of Total 2004	Change to 2014
Retail salespersons	36.6	17.2	Cashiers, except gaming	2.4	5.5
Truck drivers, light or delivery services	8.7	17.0	Stock clerks & order fillers	2.2	-10.2
Laborers & freight, stock, & material movers, hand	7.8	5.5	Interior designers	2.0	3.2
First-line supervisors/managers of retail sales workers	5.7	7.8	Customer service representatives	2.0	20.0
Office clerks, general	3.3	4.3	Shipping, receiving, & traffic clerks	1.9	6.1
Bookkeeping, accounting, & auditing clerks	2.5	5.5	Sales reps, wholesale & manufacturing, exc tech	1.2	17.2
General & operations managers	2.5	16.0	First-line supervisors/managers of office workers	1.2	6.2

Source: Industry-Occupation Matrix, Bureau of Labor Statistics. These data are reported based on 4-digit NAICS categories but have been matched to corresponding 6-digit NAICS industry codes. The change reported for each occupation to the year 2014 is a percent of growth or decline as estimated by the Bureau of Labor Statistics. The abbreviation nec stands for 'not elsewhere classified.'

LOCATION BY STATE AND REGIONAL CONCENTRATION

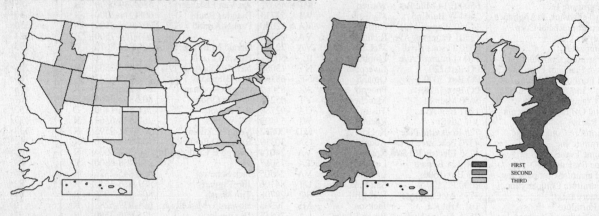

FIRST
SECOND
THIRD

INDUSTRY DATA BY STATE

State	Establishments Total (number)	% of U.S.	Employment Total (number)	% of U.S.	Per Estab.	Payroll Total ($ mil.)	Per Empl. ($)	Sales Total ($ mil.)	% of U.S.	Per Estab. ($)
California	3,066	10.9	24,910	10.0	8	772.3	31,002	5,968.6	11.9	1,946,721
Florida	2,085	7.4	15,857	6.3	8	479.1	30,215	3,868.7	7.7	1,855,514
Texas	1,962	6.9	17,881	7.2	9	500.1	27,966	3,623.8	7.2	1,846,978
New York	1,775	6.3	13,516	5.4	8	404.8	29,947	3,112.7	6.2	1,753,661
Pennsylvania	1,137	4.0	10,497	4.2	9	272.6	25,972	2,000.4	4.0	1,759,373
North Carolina	1,144	4.1	10,373	4.2	9	265.0	25,542	1,966.1	3.9	1,718,581
New Jersey	944	3.3	8,057	3.2	9	241.1	29,919	1,964.7	3.9	2,081,267
Ohio	996	3.5	9,995	4.0	10	276.0	27,618	1,906.7	3.8	1,914,379
Illinois	1,047	3.7	9,098	3.6	9	247.5	27,200	1,878.9	3.7	1,794,575
Michigan	803	2.8	10,021	4.0	12	254.3	25,382	1,761.8	3.5	2,194,067
Virginia	764	2.7	8,135	3.3	11	229.2	28,171	1,610.5	3.2	2,108,026
Georgia	1,033	3.7	8,202	3.3	8	213.1	25,979	1,609.4	3.2	1,557,984
Massachusetts	526	1.9	5,712	2.3	11	197.2	34,528	1,235.6	2.5	2,349,084
Maryland	471	1.7	5,230	2.1	11	157.1	30,043	1,064.3	2.1	2,259,764
Colorado	458	1.6	4,438	1.8	10	150.6	33,941	990.8	2.0	2,163,317
Minnesota	449	1.6	5,068	2.0	11	140.5	27,729	956.5	1.9	2,130,330
Washington	530	1.9	4,535	1.8	9	127.2	28,059	930.4	1.9	1,755,549
Indiana	598	2.1	5,099	2.0	9	129.2	25,336	878.0	1.7	1,468,234
Tennessee	575	2.0	4,538	1.8	8	126.7	27,912	869.6	1.7	1,512,423
Wisconsin	481	1.7	4,583	1.8	10	116.5	25,426	786.1	1.6	1,634,341
Missouri	537	1.9	4,386	1.8	8	112.8	25,709	777.8	1.5	1,448,408
Connecticut	363	1.3	3,030	1.2	8	97.4	32,142	700.5	1.4	1,929,620
Louisiana	435	1.5	4,258	1.7	10	98.0	23,023	652.1	1.3	1,499,182
Alabama	606	2.1	4,250	1.7	7	97.1	22,844	629.1	1.3	1,038,087
South Carolina	580	2.1	4,075	1.6	7	97.2	23,853	611.3	1.2	1,053,971
Utah	219	0.8	2,889	1.2	13	80.0	27,686	580.7	1.2	2,651,484
Kentucky	413	1.5	3,338	1.3	8	76.8	23,020	559.3	1.1	1,354,291
Oregon	379	1.3	2,691	1.1	7	74.4	27,637	496.4	1.0	1,309,884
Iowa	300	1.1	2,795	1.1	9	66.6	23,819	471.4	0.9	1,571,350
Nevada	180	0.6	2,566	1.0	14	66.2	25,818	454.8	0.9	2,526,589
Oklahoma	293	1.0	2,971	1.2	10	67.6	22,752	446.1	0.9	1,522,430
Nebraska	135	0.5	2,133	0.9	16	51.8	24,280	426.5	0.8	3,159,274
Kansas	270	1.0	2,114	0.8	8	53.2	25,159	384.6	0.8	1,424,426
Arkansas	335	1.2	2,431	1.0	7	55.2	22,710	367.2	0.7	1,096,027
Mississippi	323	1.1	2,579	1.0	8	58.5	22,673	347.6	0.7	1,076,170

Continued on next page.

INDUSTRY DATA BY STATE - Continued

State	Establishments		Employment			Payroll		Sales		
	Total (number)	% of U.S.	Total (number)	% of U.S.	Per Estab.	Total ($ mil.)	Per Empl. ($)	Total ($ mil.)	% of U.S.	Per Estab. ($)
New Mexico	185	0.7	1,930	0.8	10	37.8	19,594	293.6	0.6	1,586,822
New Hampshire	157	0.6	1,317	0.5	8	42.7	32,412	281.5	0.6	1,793,019
Delaware	108	0.4	1,460	0.6	14	44.6	30,579	280.8	0.6	2,599,574
Idaho	138	0.5	1,336	0.5	10	33.9	25,374	240.8	0.5	1,745,043
West Virginia	173	0.6	1,332	0.5	8	31.5	23,645	220.8	0.4	1,276,428
Montana	113	0.4	927	0.4	8	20.0	21,621	150.9	0.3	1,335,027
Hawaii	76	0.3	592	0.2	8	18.2	30,742	139.1	0.3	1,830,671
Maine	118	0.4	922	0.4	8	22.4	24,325	137.9	0.3	1,168,763
South Dakota	81	0.3	762	0.3	9	18.8	24,734	133.6	0.3	1,649,198
Rhode Island	71	0.3	516	0.2	7	13.1	25,452	120.7	0.2	1,700,634
Alaska	38	0.1	305	0.1	8	9.1	29,816	75.3	0.1	1,981,211
North Dakota	62	0.2	570	0.2	9	11.2	19,611	73.3	0.1	1,182,613
Vermont	63	0.2	409	0.2	6	11.1	27,068	71.2	0.1	1,130,000
Wyoming	61	0.2	384	0.2	6	8.5	22,167	60.1	0.1	984,492
Arizona	549	1.9	2500-4999	-	-	(D)	-	(D)	-	-
D.C.	39	0.1	100-249	-	-	(D)	-	(D)	-	-

Source: 2002 *Economic Census*. The states are in descending order of sales or establishments (if sales data are missing for the majority). The symbol (D) appears when data are withheld to prevent disclosure of competitive information. States marked with (D) are sorted by number of establishments. A dash (-) indicates that the data element cannot be calculated. Shaded *states* on the state map indicate those states which have proportionately greater representation in the industry than would be indicated by the states population; the ratio is based on total sales or number of establishments. Shaded *regions* indicate where the industry is regionally most concentrated.

NAICS 442210 - FLOOR COVERING STORES

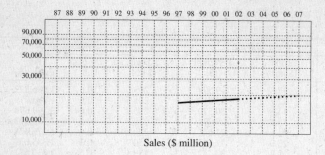

Sales ($ million)

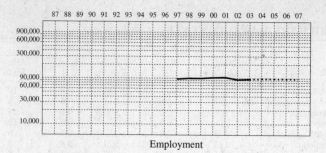

Employment

GENERAL STATISTICS

Year	Establishments (number)	Employment (number)	Payroll ($ million)	Sales ($ million)	Employees per Establishment (number)	Sales per Establishment ($)	Payroll per Employee ($)
1987	-	-	-	-	-	-	-
1988	-	-	-	-	-	-	-
1989	-	-	-	-	-	-	-
1990	-	-	-	-	-	-	-
1991	-	-	-	-	-	-	-
1992	-	-	-	-	-	-	-
1993	-	-	-	-	-	-	-
1994	-	-	-	-	-	-	-
1995	-	-	-	-	-	-	-
1996	-	-	-	-	-	-	-
1997	16,603	96,186	2,458.2	16,471.8	6	992,098	25,557
1998	15,956	99,920	2,740.1	16,821.0 e	6	1,054,210	27,423
1999	15,720	99,683	2,969.9	17,170.1 e	6	1,092,248	29,793
2000	15,845	103,479	3,171.9	17,519.3 e	7	1,105,668	30,652
2001	16,127	105,106	3,294.1	17,868.5 e	7	1,107,986	31,341
2002	15,262	93,513	2,885.4	18,217.7	6	1,193,661	30,856
2003	15,037	95,532	3,016.0	18,566.8 p	6	1,209,235 p	31,571
2004	14,982 p	97,724 p	3,260.6 p	18,916.0 p	6 p	1,243,023 p	33,378 p
2005	14,779 p	97,390 p	3,342.3 p	19,265.2 p	7 p	1,276,811 p	34,323 p
2006	14,576 p	97,056 p	3,424.0 p	19,614.3 p	7 p	1,310,598 p	35,268 p
2007	14,373 p	96,722 p	3,505.8 p	19,963.5 p	7 p	1,344,386 p	36,213 p

Source: Economic Census of the United States, 1997 and 2002. Establishment counts, employment, and payroll are from County Business Patterns for non-Census years. This is a newly defined industry. Data for prior years are unavailable at the time of publication but may become available over time. Values followed by 'p' are projections by the editors. Sales data for non-Census years are extrapolations, marked by 'e'.

INDICES OF CHANGE

Year	Establishments (number)	Employment (number)	Payroll ($ million)	Sales ($ million)	Employees per Establishment (number)	Sales per Establishment ($)	Payroll per Employee ($)
1987	-	-	-	-	-	-	-
1992	-	-	-	-	-	-	-
1993	-	-	-	-	-	-	-
1994	-	-	-	-	-	-	-
1995	-	-	-	-	-	-	-
1996	-	-	-	-	-	-	-
1997	108.8	102.9	85.2	90.4	94.7	83.1	82.8
1998	104.5	106.9	95.0	92.3 e	102.8	88.3	88.9
1999	103.0	106.6	102.9	94.2 e	102.8	91.5	96.6
2000	103.8	110.7	109.9	96.2 e	106.1	92.6	99.3
2001	105.7	112.4	114.2	98.1 e	106.1	92.8	101.6
2002	100.0	100.0	100.0	100.0	100.0	100.0	100.0
2003	98.5	102.2	104.5	101.9 p	103.7	101.3 p	102.3
2004	98.2 p	104.5 p	113.0 p	103.8 p	105.8 p	104.1 p	108.2 p
2005	96.8 p	104.1 p	115.8 p	105.8 p	106.7 p	107.0 p	111.2 p
2006	95.5 p	103.8 p	118.7 p	107.7 p	107.6 p	109.8 p	114.3 p
2007	94.2 p	103.4 p	121.5 p	109.6 p	108.5 p	112.6 p	117.4 p

Sources: Same as General Statistics. The values shown reflect change from the base year, 2002. Values above 100 mean greater than 2002, values below 100 mean less than 2002, and a value of 100 in the 1987-2001 or 2003-2007 period means same as 2002. Values followed by a 'p' are projections by the editors; 'e' stands for extrapolation. Data are the most recent available at this level of detail.

SELECTED RATIOS

For 2002	Avg. of All Retail	Analyzed Industry	Index	For 2002	Avg. of All Retail	Analyzed Industry	Index
Employees per Establishment	17	6	36	Sales per Employee	174,682	194,814	112
Payroll per Establishment	333,445	189,060	57	Sales per Establishment	3,332,269	1,193,661	36
Payroll per Employee	20,311	30,856	152	Expenses per Establishment	na	na	na

Sources: Same as General Statistics. The 'Average of All' column, Wholesale or Retail, represents the average of the sector reported for the most recent complete year available. The Index shows the relationship between the Average and the Analyzed Industry. For example, 100 means that they are equal; 500 that the Analyzed Industry is five times the average; 50 means that the Analyzed Industry is half the national average. The abbreviation 'na' is used to show that data are 'not available'.

LEADING COMPANIES   Number shown: **38**   Total sales ($ mil): **958**   Total employment (000): **3.2**

Company Name	Address				CEO Name	Phone	Co. Type	Sales ($ mil)	Empl. (000)
Heilig-Meyers Co.	12501 Patterson Ave	Richmond	VA	23233		804-784-7500	P	324	0.0
Granite Furniture Company Inc.	1050 E 2100 S	Salt Lake City	UT	84106	Jim Taggart	801-486-3333	R	82*	0.4
ABC Carpet Company Inc.	888 Broadway	New York	NY	10003	Jerome Weinrib	212-473-3000	R	73*	0.5
Steinhafels Inc.	W231 N1013 164	Waukesha	WI	53186	Gary Steinhafel	262-436-4600	R	66*	0.4
Hagopian and Sons Inc.	14000 W 8 Mile Rd	Oak Park	MI	48237	Edmond Hagopian	248-546-7847	R	54*	0.2
Plunkett Furniture Co.	2500 W Golf Rd	Hoffman Estates	IL	60194	Hugh Plunkett	847-843-9000	R	54*	0.4
MMM Carpets Unlimited Inc.	3100 Molinero St	Santa Clara	CA	95054	Victor Molinaro	408-988-4661	R	29*	0.2
Larson Distributing Company Inc.	PO Box 16189	Denver	CO	80216	John L Larson Jr	303-296-7253	R	25*	<0.1
Blackton Inc.	1714 Alden Rd	Orlando	FL	32803	Michael Blackton	407-898-2661	R	19*	<0.1
Midwest Floor Coverings	PO Box 65768	Salt Lake City	UT	84165	John Parrish	801-972-1125	R	18*	<0.1
Brandon House Furniture Co.	1100 S University	Little Rock	AR	72204	Benton Brandon	501-663-1400	R	15*	0.1
Cloud Carpet and Draperies Inc.	4699 Industrial Rd	Las Vegas	NV	89103	Roy Shelton	702-798-0798	R	15*	0.1
Croft Lumber Company Inc.	PO Box 190	Sayre	PA	18840	Warren Croft	570-888-2364	R	14*	<0.1
Miller's Interiors Inc.	PO Box 1116	Lynnwood	WA	98046	William W Miller	425-743-3213	R	14*	<0.1
AGA John Inc.	8687 Melrose Ave	Los Angeles	CA	90069	Jerry Illoulian	310-657-0890	R	14*	<0.1
Modern Builders Supply Inc.	PO Box 1287	Mountain View	AR	72560	Buddy Bolin	870-269-3808	R	14*	<0.1
J B'S Factory Carpet	3100 22nd Ave N	Saint Petersburg	FL	33713	John Boukalis	727-322-5757	R	11*	<0.1
Vartan Pedian and Sons	6535 N Lincoln Ave	Lincolnwood	IL	60712	Tim Dillon	847-675-9111	R	10*	<0.1
Old Dominion Floor Company Inc.	3350 Speeks Dr	Midlothian	VA	23112	John Jones	804-674-0315	R	9*	<0.1
Miller's Carpet One	500 W Basin Rd	New Castle	DE	19720	Andrew L Miller	302-322-5452	R	8*	<0.1
Creative Flooring Design Inc.	PO Box 3905	Sedona	AZ	86340	David Harvey	928-204-5542	R	8*	<0.1
Designer's Choice Unlimited Inc.	17041 A Commerce	Fort Myers	FL	33912	Robert Gallagher	239-267-2383	R	8*	<0.1
Olson Floor Covering Inc.	PO Box 607	Wausau	WI	54402	Galen Olson	715-359-9221	R	7*	<0.1
Concorde Flooring Systems Inc.	31 E 32nd St	New York	NY	10016	David Numark	212-685-1300	R	7*	<0.1
Torkan Inc.	245 E 72nd St	New York	NY	10021	Torkan Maham	212-779-9247	R	6*	<0.1
Carpet Co-Op	897 S Soderquist Rd	Turlock	CA	95380	Jeff Jaggers	209-632-9451	R	6*	<0.1
Closson's Co.	10100 Montgomery	Cincinnati	OH	45242		513-762-5500	R	6*	<0.1
Hopkins Furniture & Floor	2323 Hwy 67	Festus	MO	63028	Nick Hopkins	636-937-2400	R	6*	<0.1
Mehdi Dilmaghani Inc.	540 Central	Scarsdale	NY	10583	Dennis Dilmaghani	914-472-1700	R	6*	<0.1
New York Carpets	1225 S State College	Anaheim	CA	92806		714-778-3585	R	6*	<0.1
Bricks and Tiles Unlimited	9030 Aero St	San Antonio	TX	78217	Carlos Cardin	210-828-0011	R	6*	<0.1
O'Krent Floor Covering Co.	2075 N Loop 1604 E	San Antonio	TX	78232	Sam O'Krent	210-227-7387	R	5*	<0.1
Williams Furniture & Design	2248 State Rd 44	N Smyrna Bch	FL	32168	Dale Williams	386-428-4349	R	4*	<0.1
HW Rivett Flooring	2300 Broadway	Sacramento	CA	95818	Ron Reich	916-455-2637	R	3*	<0.1
Romans Interiors Inc.	PO Box 648	Harlingen	TX	78551	Steven Romans	956-428-8141	R	3*	<0.1
CHC Inc.	8 W Main St	Plano	IL	60545	Mike Turner	630-552-3400	R	2*	<0.1
Brasure's Pest Control Inc.	PO Box 1100	Selbyville	DE	19975	Carroll Brasure	302-436-8140	R	2*	<0.1
Champion Cleaning Systems Inc.	3010 Poplar Rd	Sharpsburg	GA	30277	Joel Reets	770-253-6070	R	1*	<0.1

Source: *Ward's Business Directory of U.S. Private and Public Companies*, Volumes 1 and 2, 2005. The company type code used is as follows: P - Public, R - Private, S - Subsidiary, D - Division, J - Joint Venture, A - Affiliate, G - Group. Sales are in millions of dollars, employees are in thousands. An asterisk (*) indicates an estimated sales volume. The symbol < stands for 'less than'. Company names and addresses are truncated, in some cases, to fit into the available space.

OCCUPATIONS EMPLOYED BY HOME FURNISHINGS STORES

Occupation	% of Total 2004	Change to 2014	Occupation	% of Total 2004	Change to 2014
Retail salespersons	38.7	22.8	General & operations managers	2.1	21.5
First-line supervisors/managers of retail sales workers	6.7	13.0	Shipping, receiving, & traffic clerks	2.0	11.2
Cashiers, except gaming	6.7	10.5	Assemblers & fabricators, nec	1.5	13.6
Carpet installers	4.5	10.5	Sales reps, wholesale & manufacturing, exc tech	1.4	22.8
Stock clerks & order fillers	4.3	-6.0	Customer service representatives	1.3	25.7
Laborers & freight, stock, & material movers, hand	3.4	10.5	Floor layers, except carpet, wood, & hard tiles	1.3	22.8
Office clerks, general	2.7	9.3	Secretaries, except legal, medical, & executive	1.1	3.3
Bookkeeping, accounting, & auditing clerks	2.4	10.5	Truck drivers, light or delivery services	1.0	22.8

Source: *Industry-Occupation Matrix*, Bureau of Labor Statistics. These data are reported based on 4-digit NAICS categories but have been matched to corresponding 6-digit NAICS industry codes. The change reported for each occupation to the year 2014 is a percent of growth or decline as estimated by the Bureau of Labor Statistics. The abbreviation nec stands for 'not elsewhere classified.'

LOCATION BY STATE AND REGIONAL CONCENTRATION

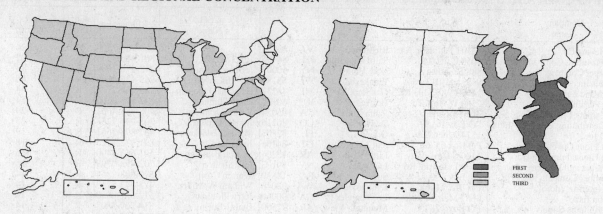

INDUSTRY DATA BY STATE

State	Establishments Total (number)	% of U.S.	Employment Total (number)	% of U.S.	Per Estab.	Payroll Total ($ mil.)	Per Empl. ($)	Sales Total ($ mil.)	% of U.S.	Per Estab. ($)
California	1,517	9.9	11,335	12.1	7	381.1	33,620	2,192.9	12.0	1,445,553
Texas	889	5.8	5,199	5.5	6	165.8	31,892	1,227.0	6.7	1,380,232
Florida	958	6.3	4,786	5.1	5	145.7	30,443	1,108.1	6.1	1,156,714
Illinois	633	4.1	4,585	4.9	7	160.8	35,078	927.4	5.1	1,465,093
New York	877	5.7	4,760	5.1	5	153.4	32,229	850.9	4.7	970,235
Georgia	496	3.2	3,092	3.3	6	101.0	32,679	758.9	4.2	1,530,071
Ohio	668	4.4	4,077	4.4	6	118.0	28,953	757.2	4.2	1,133,554
Michigan	524	3.4	3,700	3.9	7	119.4	32,272	710.5	3.9	1,355,983
Pennsylvania	622	4.1	3,731	4.0	6	111.1	29,771	649.6	3.6	1,044,392
North Carolina	487	3.2	2,703	2.9	6	78.2	28,913	534.2	2.9	1,096,852
Virginia	450	2.9	2,691	2.9	6	87.9	32,663	501.6	2.8	1,114,578
Minnesota	343	2.2	2,218	2.4	6	70.9	31,972	482.9	2.7	1,408,017
New Jersey	433	2.8	2,318	2.5	5	78.1	33,696	479.7	2.6	1,107,841
Washington	353	2.3	2,326	2.5	7	71.9	30,921	450.4	2.5	1,275,989
Wisconsin	376	2.5	2,561	2.7	7	76.7	29,947	445.4	2.4	1,184,492
Maryland	314	2.1	1,964	2.1	6	64.8	33,016	412.9	2.3	1,314,882
Massachusetts	347	2.3	2,091	2.2	6	73.2	35,006	412.7	2.3	1,189,378
Indiana	388	2.5	2,319	2.5	6	63.3	27,305	404.5	2.2	1,042,572
Colorado	280	1.8	1,816	1.9	6	63.9	35,180	399.1	2.2	1,425,300
Missouri	322	2.1	1,978	2.1	6	57.0	28,810	351.4	1.9	1,091,183
Tennessee	282	1.8	1,485	1.6	5	42.6	28,672	299.5	1.6	1,062,152
Oregon	218	1.4	1,555	1.7	7	45.0	28,965	294.0	1.6	1,348,491
Kentucky	243	1.6	1,375	1.5	6	33.7	24,473	232.2	1.3	955,519
Alabama	253	1.7	1,335	1.4	5	34.3	25,692	228.7	1.3	903,787
South Carolina	231	1.5	1,128	1.2	5	30.1	26,684	214.3	1.2	927,844
Louisiana	209	1.4	1,222	1.3	6	31.3	25,573	194.7	1.1	931,593
Iowa	198	1.3	1,209	1.3	6	34.2	28,256	189.6	1.0	957,369
Kansas	175	1.1	1,222	1.3	7	35.0	28,675	188.4	1.0	1,076,583
Nevada	94	0.6	1,056	1.1	11	29.5	27,950	187.7	1.0	1,997,319
Connecticut	198	1.3	859	0.9	4	29.7	34,601	180.0	1.0	909,040
Oklahoma	168	1.1	906	1.0	5	23.6	26,022	160.8	0.9	957,065
Utah	134	0.9	752	0.8	6	20.6	27,445	159.6	0.9	1,191,306
Arkansas	138	0.9	644	0.7	5	17.3	26,811	120.4	0.7	872,261
Idaho	98	0.6	592	0.6	6	14.5	24,556	111.3	0.6	1,135,592
New Mexico	107	0.7	621	0.7	6	16.1	25,990	103.8	0.6	970,290
Mississippi	137	0.9	645	0.7	5	16.5	25,629	103.8	0.6	757,416
New Hampshire	98	0.6	498	0.5	5	16.8	33,653	100.3	0.6	1,023,214
Nebraska	94	0.6	668	0.7	7	17.8	26,669	95.2	0.5	1,013,202
Montana	83	0.5	404	0.4	5	11.9	29,562	78.1	0.4	941,145
Delaware	52	0.3	424	0.5	8	14.3	33,611	76.6	0.4	1,473,712
West Virginia	104	0.7	536	0.6	5	11.5	21,368	73.1	0.4	702,644
Maine	83	0.5	347	0.4	4	8.7	25,043	64.3	0.4	774,458
North Dakota	49	0.3	415	0.4	8	10.1	24,335	59.8	0.3	1,220,469
Hawaii	42	0.3	312	0.3	7	9.5	30,500	54.3	0.3	1,292,286
Rhode Island	59	0.4	254	0.3	4	7.8	30,697	45.6	0.3	773,508
Alaska	42	0.3	222	0.2	5	7.3	32,721	45.4	0.2	1,081,000
South Dakota	46	0.3	245	0.3	5	6.0	24,616	42.9	0.2	933,348
Vermont	50	0.3	255	0.3	5	7.0	27,416	40.1	0.2	802,720
Wyoming	49	0.3	208	0.2	4	5.2	25,139	39.3	0.2	801,776
Arizona	269	1.8	1000-2499	-	-	(D)	-	(D)	-	-
D.C.	10	0.1	20-99	-	-	(D)	-	(D)	-	-

Source: 2002 Economic Census. The states are in descending order of sales or establishments (if sales data are missing for the majority). The symbol (D) appears when data are withheld to prevent disclosure of competitive information. States marked with (D) are sorted by number of establishments. A dash (-) indicates that the data element cannot be calculated. Shaded *states* on the state map indicate those states which have proportionately greater representation in the industry than would be indicated by the states population; the ratio is based on total sales or number of establishments. Shaded *regions* indicate where the industry is regionally most concentrated.

NAICS 442291 - WINDOW TREATMENT STORES

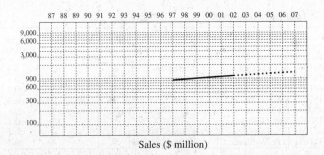

Sales ($ million)

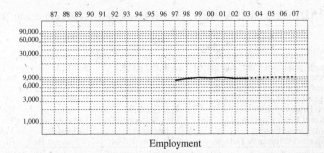

Employment

GENERAL STATISTICS

Year	Establishments (number)	Employment (number)	Payroll ($ million)	Sales ($ million)	Employees per Establishment (number)	Sales per Establishment ($)	Payroll per Employee ($)
1987	-	-	-	-	-	-	-
1988	-	-	-	-	-	-	-
1989	-	-	-	-	-	-	-
1990	-	-	-	-	-	-	-
1991	-	-	-	-	-	-	-
1992	-	-	-	-	-	-	-
1993	-	-	-	-	-	-	-
1994	-	-	-	-	-	-	-
1995	-	-	-	-	-	-	-
1996	-	-	-	-	-	-	-
1997	2,126	8,548	148.6	915.3	4	430,527	17,384
1998	2,203	9,333	176.9	962.3 e	4	436,804	18,954
1999	2,292	9,894	210.0	1,009.3 e	4	440,339	21,225
2000	2,318	9,689	204.5	1,056.2 e	4	455,667	21,107
2001	2,335	9,955	226.2	1,103.2 e	4	472,469	22,722
2002	2,171	9,349	195.3	1,150.2	4	529,799	20,895
2003	2,285	9,381	208.1	1,197.2 p	4	522,802 p	22,188
2004	2,312 p	9,820 p	228.8 p	1,244.2 p	4 p	540,479 p	23,466 p
2005	2,329 p	9,913 p	237.0 p	1,291.1 p	4 p	558,155 p	24,173 p
2006	2,345 p	10,005 p	245.3 p	1,338.1 p	4 p	575,832 p	24,880 p
2007	2,361 p	10,098 p	253.6 p	1,385.1 p	4 p	593,509 p	25,587 p

Source: Economic Census of the United States, 1997 and 2002. Establishment counts, employment, and payroll are from *County Business Patterns* for non-Census years. This is a newly defined industry. Data for prior years are unavailable at the time of publication but may become available over time. Values followed by 'p' are projections by the editors. Sales data for non-Census years are extrapolations, marked by 'e'.

INDICES OF CHANGE

Year	Establishments (number)	Employment (number)	Payroll ($ million)	Sales ($ million)	Employees per Establishment (number)	Sales per Establishment ($)	Payroll per Employee ($)
1987	-	-	-	-	-	-	-
1992	-	-	-	-	-	-	-
1993	-	-	-	-	-	-	-
1994	-	-	-	-	-	-	-
1995	-	-	-	-	-	-	-
1996	-	-	-	-	-	-	-
1997	97.9	91.4	76.1	79.6	92.9	81.3	83.2
1998	101.5	99.8	90.6	83.7 e	97.5	82.4	90.7
1999	105.6	105.8	107.5	87.7 e	99.9	83.1	101.6
2000	106.8	103.6	104.7	91.8 e	97.5	86.0	101.0
2001	107.6	106.5	115.8	95.9 e	99.9	89.2	108.7
2002	100.0	100.0	100.0	100.0	100.0	100.0	100.0
2003	105.3	100.3	106.6	104.1 p	95.3	98.7 p	106.2
2004	106.5 p	105.0 p	117.1 p	108.2 p	99.3 p	102.0 p	112.3 p
2005	107.3 p	106.0 p	121.3 p	112.3 p	99.8 p	105.4 p	115.7 p
2006	108.0 p	107.0 p	125.6 p	116.3 p	100.2 p	108.7 p	119.1 p
2007	108.8 p	108.0 p	129.8 p	120.4 p	100.6 p	112.0 p	122.5 p

*Sources: Same as General Statistics. The values shown reflect change from the base year, 2002. Values above 100 mean greater than 2002, values below 100 mean less than 2002, and a value of 100 in the 1987-2001 or 2003-2007 period means same as 2002. Values followed by a 'p' are projections by the editors; 'e' stands for extrapolation. Data are the most recent available at this level of detail.

SELECTED RATIOS

For 2002	Avg. of All Retail	Analyzed Industry	Index	For 2002	Avg. of All Retail	Analyzed Industry	Index
Employees per Establishment	17	4	25	Sales per Employee	174,682	123,028	70
Payroll per Establishment	333,445	89,980	27	Sales per Establishment	3,332,269	529,799	16
Payroll per Employee	20,311	20,895	103	Expenses per Establishment	na	na	na

*Sources: Same as General Statistics. The 'Average of All' column, Wholesale or Retail, represents the average of the sector reported for the most recent complete year available. The Index shows the relationship between the Average and the Analyzed Industry. For example, 100 means that they are equal; 500 that the Analyzed Industry is five times the average; 50 means that the Analyzed Industry is half the national average. The abbreviation 'na' is used to show that data are 'not available'.

LEADING COMPANIES   Number shown: **8**   Total sales ($ mil): **182**   Total employment (000): **1.2**

Company Name	Address				CEO Name	Phone	Co. Type	Sales ($ mil)	Empl. (000)
Granite Furniture Company Inc.	1050 E 2100 S	Salt Lake City	UT	84106	Jim Taggart	801-486-3333	R	82*	0.4
Fabric Place	136 Howard St	Framingham	MA	01701		508-872-4888	R	57*	0.5
Cloud Carpet and Draperies Inc.	4699 Industrial Rd	Las Vegas	NV	89103	Roy Shelton	702-798-0798	R	15*	0.1
Allied Realty Co.	PO Box 1700	Huntington	WV	25717	L Polan III	304-525-9125	R	9*	0.1
Aero Drapery Corp.	3525 State Rd 32 W	Westfield	IN	46074	Ed Mullins	317-896-2521	R	5*	<0.1
O'Krent Floor Covering Co.	2075 N Loop 1604 E	San Antonio	TX	78232	Sam O'Krent	210-227-7387	R	5*	<0.1
Home Decor Outlet	18 Pocasset St	Fall River	MA	02721	Eric De Silva	508-823-5141	R	4*	<0.1
Williams Furniture & Design	2248 State Rd 44	N Smyrna Bch	FL	32168	Dale Williams	386-428-4349	R	4*	<0.1

Source: *Ward's Business Directory of U.S. Private and Public Companies*, Volumes 1 and 2, 2005. The company type code used is as follows: P - Public, R - Private, S - Subsidiary, D - Division, J - Joint Venture, A - Affiliate, G - Group. Sales are in millions of dollars, employees are in thousands. An asterisk (*) indicates an estimated sales volume. The symbol < stands for 'less than'. Company names and addresses are truncated, in some cases, to fit into the available space.

OCCUPATIONS EMPLOYED BY HOME FURNISHINGS STORES

Occupation	% of Total 2004	Change to 2014	Occupation	% of Total 2004	Change to 2014
Retail salespersons	38.7	22.8	General & operations managers	2.1	21.5
First-line supervisors/managers of retail sales workers	6.7	13.0	Shipping, receiving, & traffic clerks	2.0	11.2
Cashiers, except gaming	6.7	10.5	Assemblers & fabricators, nec	1.5	13.6
Carpet installers	4.5	10.5	Sales reps, wholesale & manufacturing, exc tech	1.4	22.8
Stock clerks & order fillers	4.3	-6.0	Customer service representatives	1.3	25.7
Laborers & freight, stock, & material movers, hand	3.4	10.5	Floor layers, except carpet, wood, & hard tiles	1.3	22.8
Office clerks, general	2.7	9.3	Secretaries, except legal, medical, & executive	1.1	3.3
Bookkeeping, accounting, & auditing clerks	2.4	10.5	Truck drivers, light or delivery services	1.0	22.8

Source: *Industry-Occupation Matrix*, Bureau of Labor Statistics. These data are reported based on 4-digit NAICS categories but have been matched to corresponding 6-digit NAICS industry codes. The change reported for each occupation to the year 2014 is a percent of growth or decline as estimated by the Bureau of Labor Statistics. The abbreviation nec stands for 'not elsewhere classified.'

LOCATION BY STATE AND REGIONAL CONCENTRATION

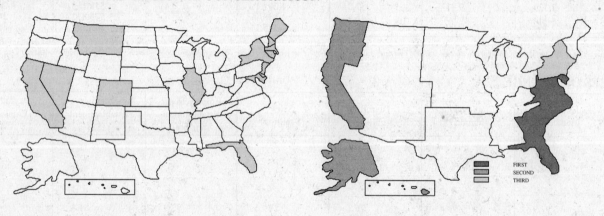

INDUSTRY DATA BY STATE

State	Establishments Total (number)	Establishments % of U.S.	Employment Total (number)	Employment % of U.S.	Employment Per Estab.	Payroll Total ($ mil.)	Payroll Per Empl. ($)	Sales Total ($ mil.)	Sales % of U.S.	Sales Per Estab. ($)
California	299	13.8	1,497	16.6	5	29.3	19,603	197.5	17.5	660,656
Florida	259	12.0	879	9.7	3	18.4	20,884	106.2	9.4	409,938
New York	169	7.8	728	8.1	4	16.9	23,202	95.4	8.5	564,722
New Jersey	103	4.8	546	6.0	5	11.9	21,885	75.2	6.7	730,291
Texas	132	6.1	657	7.3	5	14.6	22,193	73.9	6.6	559,705
Illinois	100	4.6	359	4.0	4	8.9	24,652	52.8	4.7	528,120
Massachusetts	71	3.3	356	3.9	5	7.6	21,301	45.4	4.0	639,423
Pennsylvania	70	3.2	391	4.3	6	7.4	18,852	43.6	3.9	622,857
Michigan	57	2.6	271	3.0	5	6.0	21,974	34.3	3.0	601,158
Colorado	59	2.7	229	2.5	4	5.0	21,729	30.9	2.7	523,712
Maryland	33	1.5	152	1.7	5	4.3	28,296	24.8	2.2	752,152
Connecticut	34	1.6	147	1.6	4	3.5	24,054	22.7	2.0	666,794
Georgia	44	2.0	157	1.7	4	3.6	23,191	20.7	1.8	470,886

Continued on next page.

INDUSTRY DATA BY STATE - Continued

State	Establishments Total (number)	% of U.S.	Employment Total (number)	% of U.S.	Per Estab.	Payroll Total ($ mil.)	Per Empl. ($)	Sales Total ($ mil.)	% of U.S.	Per Estab. ($)
Virginia	50	2.3	160	1.8	3	3.2	19,737	20.6	1.8	411,220
Ohio	44	2.0	183	2.0	4	4.0	22,011	20.5	1.8	464,773
North Carolina	55	2.5	245	2.7	4	4.3	17,649	18.9	1.7	343,782
Washington	38	1.8	144	1.6	4	3.3	22,743	17.9	1.6	470,632
Nevada	24	1.1	102	1.1	4	2.5	24,549	16.9	1.5	704,083
Minnesota	23	1.1	118	1.3	5	2.8	24,034	14.2	1.3	615,609
South Carolina	39	1.8	111	1.2	3	2.3	20,586	12.3	1.1	316,359
Wisconsin	30	1.4	96	1.1	3	1.9	19,677	10.0	0.9	334,500
Missouri	27	1.2	85	0.9	3	1.5	18,035	9.4	0.8	349,963
Indiana	33	1.5	102	1.1	3	1.7	16,892	9.0	0.8	273,242
Maine	12	0.6	55	0.6	5	1.4	25,818	8.8	0.8	730,000
Tennessee	32	1.5	98	1.1	3	1.8	18,439	8.6	0.8	268,000
Louisiana	22	1.0	75	0.8	3	1.5	20,653	8.5	0.8	388,455
Utah	17	0.8	62	0.7	4	1.2	19,677	8.3	0.7	489,000
Oregon	24	1.1	58	0.6	2	1.0	16,517	8.2	0.7	340,875
Kentucky	16	0.7	67	0.7	4	1.2	17,985	7.8	0.7	484,875
Alabama	24	1.1	77	0.9	3	1.1	13,727	7.2	0.6	300,792
Delaware	10	0.5	37	0.4	4	0.7	18,541	7.1	0.6	708,000
Iowa	21	1.0	75	0.8	4	1.6	21,747	5.8	0.5	278,381
New Hampshire	11	0.5	40	0.4	4	0.7	16,850	5.1	0.5	468,091
Kansas	14	0.6	90	1.0	6	1.2	13,611	5.1	0.5	367,000
Arkansas	10	0.5	39	0.4	4	0.8	21,564	4.8	0.4	475,700
Idaho	7	0.3	26	0.3	4	0.7	25,500	4.1	0.4	583,857
Montana	9	0.4	26	0.3	3	0.4	14,269	4.1	0.4	452,778
Nebraska	11	0.5	38	0.4	3	0.9	23,053	4.0	0.4	366,455
Oklahoma	16	0.7	38	0.4	2	0.6	16,105	4.0	0.4	250,813
Mississippi	11	0.5	27	0.3	2	0.4	15,630	3.6	0.3	324,182
New Mexico	12	0.6	28	0.3	2	0.4	13,036	3.0	0.3	249,000
Hawaii	5	0.2	19	0.2	4	0.3	14,632	2.1	0.2	416,600
Wyoming	4	0.2	11	0.1	3	0.1	11,273	0.8	0.1	201,000
North Dakota	5	0.2	15	0.2	3	0.1	9,200	0.8	0.1	155,200
Arizona	56	2.6	100-249	-	-	(D)	-	(D)	-	-
Rhode Island	12	0.6	20-99	-	-	(D)	-	(D)	-	-
Vermont	3	0.1	20-99	-	-	(D)	-	(D)	-	-
West Virginia	3	0.1	0-19	-	-	(D)	-	(D)	-	-
Alaska	1	-	0-19	-	-	(D)	-	(D)	-	-
D.C.	1	-	0-19	-	-	(D)	-	(D)	-	-
South Dakota	1	-	0-19	-	-	(D)	-	(D)	-	-

Source: 2002 *Economic Census*. The states are in descending order of sales or establishments (if sales data are missing for the majority). The symbol (D) appears when data are withheld to prevent disclosure of competitive information. States marked with (D) are sorted by number of establishments. A dash (-) indicates that the data element cannot be calculated. Shaded *states* on the state map indicate those states which have proportionately greater representation in the industry than would be indicated by the states population; the ratio is based on total sales or number of establishments. Shaded *regions* indicate where the industry is regionally most concentrated.

NAICS 442299 - ALL OTHER HOME FURNISHINGS STORES

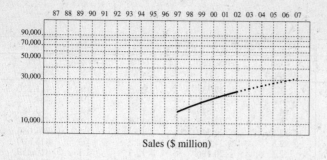

Sales ($ million)

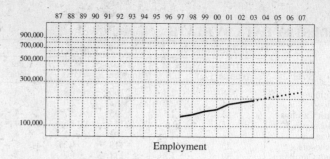

Employment

GENERAL STATISTICS

Year	Establishments (number)	Employment (number)	Payroll ($ million)	Sales ($ million)	Employees per Establishment (number)	Sales per Establishment ($)	Payroll per Employee ($)
1987	-	-		-	-	-	
1988	-	-		-	-	-	
1989	-	-		-	-	-	-
1990	-	-		-	-	-	-
1991	-	-		-	-	-	-
1992	-	-		-	-	-	-
1993	-	-		-	-	-	-
1994	-	-		-	-	-	-
1995	-	-		-	-	-	-
1996	-	-		-	-	-	-
1997	16,535	126,811	1,733.1	13,335.4	8	806,495	13,667
1998	16,535	133,433	1,965.0	15,114.8 e	8	914,111	14,726
1999	16,672	145,310	2,260.9	16,894.2 e	9	1,013,330	15,559
2000	16,959	151,956	2,507.0	18,673.7 e	9	1,101,107	16,498
2001	17,384	174,026	2,656.0	20,453.1 e	10	1,176,547	15,262
2002	19,482	182,913	2,861.9	22,232.5	9	1,141,182	15,646
2003	19,753	190,915	3,079.3	24,011.9 p	10	1,280,314 p	16,129
2004	19,940 p	203,622 p	3,327.2 p	25,791.4 p	10 p	1,353,129 p	16,631 p
2005	20,521 p	215,050 p	3,549.7 p	27,570.8 p	11 p	1,425,944 p	16,950 p
2006	21,101 p	226,478 p	3,772.1 p	29,350.2 p	11 p	1,498,759 p	17,269 p
2007	21,682 p	237,906 p	3,994.5 p	31,129.6 p	11 p	1,571,573 p	17,588 p

Source: Economic Census of the United States, 1997 and 2002. Establishment counts, employment, and payroll are from *County Business Patterns* for non-Census years. This is a newly defined industry. Data for prior years are unavailable at the time of publication but may become available over time. Values followed by 'p' are projections by the editors. Sales data for non-Census years are extrapolations, marked by 'e'.

INDICES OF CHANGE

Year	Establishments (number)	Employment (number)	Payroll ($ million)	Sales ($ million)	Employees per Establishment (number)	Sales per Establishment ($)	Payroll per Employee ($)
1987	-	-		-	-	-	-
1992	-	-	-	-	-	-	-
1993	-	-	-	-	-	-	-
1994	-	-		-	-	-	-
1995	-	-		-	-	-	-
1996	-	-		-	-	-	-
1997	84.9	69.3	60.6	60.0	82.0	70.7	87.3
1998	84.9	72.9	68.7	68.0 e	86.3	80.1	94.1
1999	85.6	79.4	79.0	76.0 e	92.7	88.8	99.4
2000	87.0	83.1	87.6	84.0 e	95.9	96.5	105.4
2001	89.2	95.1	92.8	92.0 e	106.5	103.1	97.5
2002	100.0	100.0	100.0	100.0	100.0	100.0	100.0
2003	101.4	104.4	107.6	108.0 p	102.9	112.2 p	103.1
2004	102.4 p	111.3 p	116.3 p	116.0 p	110.1 p	118.6 p	106.3 p
2005	105.3 p	117.6 p	124.0 p	124.0 p	113.8 p	125.0 p	108.3 p
2006	108.3 p	123.8 p	131.8 p	132.0 p	117.5 p	131.3 p	110.4 p
2007	111.3 p	130.1 p	139.6 p	140.0 p	121.2 p	137.7 p	112.4 p

Sources: Same as General Statistics. The values shown reflect change from the base year, 2002. Values above 100 mean greater than 2002, values below 100 mean less than 2002, and a value of 100 in the 1987-2001 or 2003-2007 period means same as 2002. Values followed by a 'p' are projections by the editors; 'e' stands for extrapolation. Data are the most recent available at this level of detail.

SELECTED RATIOS

For 2002	Avg. of All Retail	Analyzed Industry	Index	For 2002	Avg. of All Retail	Analyzed Industry	Index
Employees per Establishment	17	9	55	Sales per Employee	174,682	121,547	70
Payroll per Establishment	333,445	146,901	44	Sales per Establishment	3,332,269	1,141,182	34
Payroll per Employee	20,311	15,646	77	Expenses per Establishment	na	na	na

Sources: Same as General Statistics. The 'Average of All' column, Wholesale or Retail, represents the average of the sector reported for the most recent complete year available. The Index shows the relationship between the Average and the Analyzed Industry. For example, 100 means that they are equal; 500 that the Analyzed Industry is five times the average; 50 means that the Analyzed Industry is half the national average. The abbreviation 'na' is used to show that data are 'not available'.

LEADING COMPANIES

Number shown: **55**   Total sales ($ mil): **57,225**   Total employment (000): **203.6**

Company Name	Address				CEO Name	Phone	Co. Type	Sales ($ mil)	Empl. (000)
Morgan Crucible Company PLC	3102 Old Savannah	Augusta	GA	30906		706-796-4200	R	34,492*	14.5
Dollar General Corp.	100 Mission Ridge	Goodlettsville	TN	37072	David A Perdue Jr	615-855-4000	P	6,870	57.8
Bed Bath and Beyond Inc.	650 Liberty Ave	Union	NJ	07083	Warren Eisenberg	908-688-0888	P	4,478	29.0
Linens 'n Things Inc.	6 Brighton Rd	Clifton	NJ	07015	Norman Axelrod	973-778-1300	P	2,661	17.2
Williams-Sonoma Inc.	3250 Van Ness Ave	San Francisco	CA	94109	W Howard Lester	415-421-7900	P	2,609	36.0
Pier 1 Imports Inc.	301 Commerce St	Fort Worth	TX	76102	Marvin J Girouard	817-252-8000	P	1,898	17.6
Pier 1 Imports (U.S.) Inc.	301 Commerce St	Fort Worth	TX	76102	Marvin J Girouard	817-878-8000	S	811*	9.4
Cost Plus Inc.	200 4th St	Oakland	CA	94607	Murray H Dashe	510-893-7300	P	802	5.5
Garden Ridge Corp.	19411 Atrium Pl	Houston	TX	77084	John Rice	281-579-7901	R	521*	5.0
California Acrylic Industries Inc.	1462 E 9th St	Pomona	CA	91766	Casie Lloyd	909-623-8781	R	439*	1.3
Fortunoff Fine Jewelry	PO Box 1550	Westbury	NY	11590	Helene Fortunoff	516-832-9000	R	230*	2.3
Nebraska Furniture Mart Inc.	PO Box 3000	Omaha	NE	68103	Ron Blumkins	402-255-6327	S	180*	1.2
Vermont Country Store	5650 Main St	Manchester Ctr	VT	05255	Lyman Orton	802-362-8460	R	167*	1.0
Lamps Plus Inc.	20250 Plummer St	Chatsworth	CA	91311	Dennis Swanson	818-886-5267	R	135*	0.9
Marsh Pottery L.L.C.	3775 Av Carolinas	Fort Mill	SC	29708	Tim Marsh	803-548-7075	R	77*	0.2
3 Day Blinds Inc.	2220 E Cerritos Ave	Anaheim	CA	92806	Jim Buch	714-634-4600	R	70*	1.2
Gross Electric Inc.	PO Box 352377	Toledo	OH	43635	Laurie Gross	419-537-1818	R	58*	<0.1
Market Antiques	1227 Slocum St	Dallas	TX	75207		214-748-6684	R	53*	0.1
Ostrow Co.	PO Box 10550	Rock Hill	SC	29731	Joel J Ostrow	803-324-4284	R	53*	0.6
Jett Racing and Sales Inc.	1301 Lincoln St	Laredo	TX	78040	Wolf Hofman	956-722-3102	R	46*	<0.1
Allure Home Creation Inc.	85 Fulton St	Boonton	NJ	07005	Stanley Ho	973-402-8888	R	42*	<0.1
Janovic Plaza Inc.	30-35 Thomson Ave	Long Island City	NY	11101	Paul Renn	718-392-3999	R	40*	0.3
Schottenstein Stores Corp	3251 Westerville Rd	Columbus	OH	43224		614-471-4711	D	40*	0.3
Morton Mfg and Trade Inc.	1440 E Cedar St	Ontario	CA	91761	WEI Ding	909-923-5818	R	32*	0.1
LB Electric Supply Company Inc.	5202 New Utrecht	Brooklyn	NY	11219	Carol Lifton	718-438-9010	R	31*	<0.1
Albert S. Smyth Company Inc.	2020 York Rd	L Timonium	MD	21093	Leonard G Getschel	410-252-6666	R	31*	0.2
Bering Home Center Inc.	6102 Westheimer Rd	Houston	TX	77057	Norman J Bering II	713-785-6400	R	31*	0.2
Saturday Knight Ltd.	2100 Section Rd	Cincinnati	OH	45237	Franklin Kling	513-641-1400	R	28*	0.2
Benny's Inc.	340 Waterman Ave	Esmond	RI	02917		401-231-1000	R	27*	0.3
Buck Stoves	PO Box 69	Spruce Pine	NC	28777	Robert Bailey	828-765-6144	R	25*	0.1
Partitions and Accessories Co.	1220 S Pasadena	Mesa	AZ	85210	Sandra Borelli	480-969-6606	R	21*	<0.1
Kitchen Etc. Inc.	32 Industrial Dr	Exeter	NH	03833	Robert Camp	603-772-1904	R	17*	0.2
Standale Lumber and Supply Co.	4100 Lk Mich Drv	Grand Rapids	MI	49504	K L Holtvluwer Jr	616-453-8207	R	17*	<0.1
Jackson's Lemmon Avenue Pottery	6950 Lemmon Ave	Dallas	TX	75209	Robert Jackson	214-350-9200	R	15*	<0.1
Brandon House Furniture Co.	1100 S University	Little Rock	AR	72204	Benton Brandon	501-663-1400	R	15*	0.1
Progressive Lighting Inc.	2420 Tech Center	Lawrenceville	GA	30043	Terry McMIllian	770-476-8537	R	15*	0.1
Chesapeake Knife and Tool	9385-G Gerwig Ln	Columbia	MD	21046	Melvin Herman	301-621-8164	R	14*	<0.1
Sanders Gallery	4334 Central Ave	Hot Springs	AR	71913		501-525-2420	R	14*	<0.1
Golden Grove Trading Inc.	854 W Gldn Grove	Covina	CA	91722	Werner Schulz	626-331-7233	R	14*	<0.1
Fairfax Kitchen and Bath Inc.	14325 Willard Rd	Chantilly	VA	20151	Hamid Sharifi	703-817-1977	R	14*	<0.1
Classic Lighting Inc.	PO Box 2052	Stafford	TX	77497	Bryant Dussetschleger	281-494-0300	R	13*	<0.1
Debbie Supply Inc.	453 W Commercial	East Rochester	NY	14445	Mark Barbero	585-586-8069	R	11*	<0.1
Pier 19 Inc.	506 E Happy Valley	Cave City	KY	42127	Rodney Williams	270-773-2025	R	11*	<0.1
Function Junction Inc.	4763 Johnson Dr	Mission	KS	66205	Steve Eberman	913-384-4700	R	10*	<0.1
Fostoria Factory Outlet Co.	769 National Rd	Wheeling	WV	26003	David G Gerlach Jr	304-233-3035	S	9*	<0.1
Platypus Inc.	32A Jefferson Plz	Princeton	NJ	08540	Jeffrey Schulman	732-274-9500	R	9*	<0.1
Rabideaux's Sausage Kitchen Inc.	105 Hwy 165	Iowa	LA	70647	Joseph Daigle	337-582-3184	R	7*	<0.1
Supply House Inc.	7204 NW 79th Ter	Miami	FL	33166	Fernando Figueira	305-883-2131	R	6*	<0.1
Home Decor Outlet	18 Pocasset St	Fall River	MA	02721	Eric De Silva	508-823-5141	R	4*	<0.1
Windham House Inc.	41 Northern Blvd	Greenvale	NY	11548	Megan Deroulet	516-621-7722	R	3*	<0.1
Arrelle Fine Linens Inc.	445 N Wells St	Chicago	IL	60610	Robert Rosenberg	312-321-3696	R	2*	<0.1
Brooke Pottery Inc.	223 N Kentucky Ave	Lakeland	FL	33801	Gloria Brooke	863-688-6844	R	2*	<0.1
Flooring America	402 Hope Mills Rd	Fayetteville	NC	28304	Harold Brewington	910-424-1778	D	2*	<0.1
Villeroy and Boch USA Inc.	5275 Spring Valley	Dallas	TX	75240	David Guthrie	972-503-9090	R	2*	<0.1
Jacquelynn's China Matching	219 N Milwaukee	Milwaukee	WI	53202	Jacquelynn G Ives	414-272-8880	R	1	<0.1

Source: *Ward's Business Directory of U.S. Private and Public Companies*, Volumes 1 and 2, 2005. The company type code used is as follows: P - Public, R - Private, S - Subsidiary, D - Division, J - Joint Venture, A - Affiliate, G - Group. Sales are in millions of dollars, employees are in thousands. An asterisk (*) indicates an estimated sales volume. The symbol < stands for 'less than'. Company names and addresses are truncated, in some cases, to fit into the available space.

OCCUPATIONS EMPLOYED BY HOME FURNISHINGS STORES

Occupation	% of Total 2004	Change to 2014	Occupation	% of Total 2004	Change to 2014
Retail salespersons	38.7	22.8	General & operations managers	2.1	21.5
First-line supervisors/managers of retail sales workers	6.7	13.0	Shipping, receiving, & traffic clerks	2.0	11.2
Cashiers, except gaming	6.7	10.5	Assemblers & fabricators, nec	1.5	13.6
Carpet installers	4.5	10.5	Sales reps, wholesale & manufacturing, exc tech	1.4	22.8
Stock clerks & order fillers	4.3	-6.0	Customer service representatives	1.3	25.7
Laborers & freight, stock, & material movers, hand	3.4	10.5	Floor layers, except carpet, wood, & hard tiles	1.3	22.8
Office clerks, general	2.7	9.3	Secretaries, except legal, medical, & executive	1.1	3.3
Bookkeeping, accounting, & auditing clerks	2.4	10.5	Truck drivers, light or delivery services	1.0	22.8

Source: *Industry-Occupation Matrix*, Bureau of Labor Statistics. These data are reported based on 4-digit NAICS categories but have been matched to corresponding 6-digit NAICS industry codes. The change reported for each occupation to the year 2014 is a percent of growth or decline as estimated by the Bureau of Labor Statistics. The abbreviation nec stands for 'not elsewhere classified.'

LOCATION BY STATE AND REGIONAL CONCENTRATION

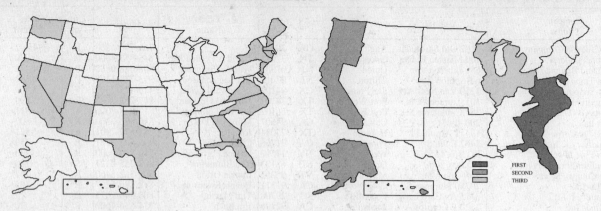

INDUSTRY DATA BY STATE

State	Establishments		Employment			Payroll		Sales		
	Total (number)	% of U.S.	Total (number)	% of U.S.	Per Estab.	Total ($ mil.)	Per Empl. ($)	Total ($ mil.)	% of U.S.	Per Estab. ($)
California	2,300	11.8	25,193	13.8	11	398.6	15,822	3,246.1	14.6	1,411,327
New York	1,180	6.0	11,842	6.5	10	223.1	18,842	1,743.7	7.8	1,477,684
Texas	1,270	6.5	13,934	7.6	11	211.4	15,168	1,654.5	7.4	1,302,773
Florida	1,436	7.4	12,512	6.9	9	200.7	16,041	1,653.0	7.4	1,151,122
New Jersey	602	3.1	7,584	4.2	13	128.3	16,918	1,062.5	4.8	1,764,914
Illinois	698	3.6	8,537	4.7	12	128.9	15,104	984.0	4.4	1,409,719
Massachusetts	539	2.8	6,641	3.6	12	109.5	16,489	902.0	4.1	1,673,484
Georgia	680	3.5	6,423	3.5	9	97.2	15,139	726.6	3.3	1,068,568
Pennsylvania	696	3.6	6,057	3.3	9	89.0	14,688	708.6	3.2	1,018,116
Virginia	600	3.1	6,069	3.3	10	84.9	13,988	687.2	3.1	1,145,287
Ohio	593	3.0	5,543	3.0	9	79.6	14,366	605.2	2.7	1,020,540
North Carolina	659	3.4	5,343	2.9	8	78.2	14,643	591.5	2.7	897,627
Michigan	586	3.0	4,846	2.7	8	76.9	15,875	564.7	2.5	963,676
Washington	507	2.6	4,207	2.3	8	69.8	16,591	508.1	2.3	1,002,199
Connecticut	319	1.6	3,459	1.9	11	61.2	17,691	502.1	2.3	1,573,915
Colorado	501	2.6	4,329	2.4	9	66.0	15,251	493.1	2.2	984,319
Maryland	334	1.7	3,287	1.8	10	54.5	16,579	427.8	1.9	1,280,707
Tennessee	387	2.0	3,459	1.9	9	53.7	15,537	410.2	1.8	1,059,866
Missouri	377	1.9	3,452	1.9	9	50.9	14,746	360.3	1.6	955,716
Arizona	335	1.7	2,893	1.6	9	43.0	14,860	360.1	1.6	1,074,896
Minnesota	364	1.9	3,625	2.0	10	51.1	14,102	357.5	1.6	982,091
South Carolina	342	1.8	2,375	1.3	7	36.4	15,314	292.9	1.3	856,471
Indiana	385	2.0	2,764	1.5	7	40.2	14,534	281.8	1.3	731,899
Alabama	354	1.8	2,575	1.4	7	34.9	13,553	271.7	1.2	767,441
Wisconsin	319	1.6	2,536	1.4	8	38.9	15,356	268.5	1.2	841,690
Oregon	281	1.4	1,946	1.1	7	29.5	15,177	229.9	1.0	818,274
Louisiana	252	1.3	1,917	1.1	8	24.5	12,794	219.3	1.0	870,313
Kentucky	217	1.1	1,759	1.0	8	23.8	13,522	193.2	0.9	890,484
New Hampshire	137	0.7	1,139	0.6	8	20.3	17,795	167.1	0.8	1,219,380
Kansas	176	0.9	1,512	0.8	9	19.1	12,620	153.5	0.7	871,994
Nevada	142	0.7	1,127	0.6	8	18.1	16,103	151.1	0.7	1,064,169
Oklahoma	167	0.9	1,385	0.8	8	17.4	12,528	145.1	0.7	868,892
Utah	153	0.8	1,396	0.8	9	18.6	13,340	128.7	0.6	840,856
Maine	152	0.8	836	0.5	6	14.8	17,743	119.8	0.5	787,888
Arkansas	170	0.9	948	0.5	6	15.0	15,825	117.1	0.5	688,541
Delaware	79	0.4	846	0.5	11	14.0	16,541	110.2	0.5	1,395,013
Iowa	158	0.8	1,004	0.6	6	13.3	13,296	96.0	0.4	607,367
Mississippi	165	0.8	948	0.5	6	12.2	12,858	92.0	0.4	557,418
New Mexico	140	0.7	848	0.5	6	13.5	15,973	91.5	0.4	653,550
Hawaii	66	0.3	517	0.3	8	11.0	21,280	63.2	0.3	957,758
Nebraska	88	0.5	567	0.3	6	7.2	12,653	58.4	0.3	663,932
Idaho	88	0.5	494	0.3	6	7.4	15,016	57.6	0.3	654,830
Montana	86	0.4	367	0.2	4	5.1	13,880	38.6	0.2	449,360
North Dakota	40	0.2	220	0.1	6	3.0	13,500	21.7	0.1	542,325
Wyoming	32	0.2	102	0.1	3	1.3	13,137	9.1	-	284,219
Rhode Island	86	0.4	1000-2499	-	-	(D)	-	(D)	-	-
Vermont	80	0.4	500-999	-	-	(D)	-	(D)	-	-
West Virginia	59	0.3	250-499	-	-	(D)	-	(D)	-	-
D.C.	57	0.3	500-999	-	-	(D)	-	(D)	-	-
Alaska	39	0.2	100-249	-	-	(D)	-	(D)	-	-
South Dakota	34	0.2	100-249	-	-	(D)	-	(D)	-	-

Source: 2002 *Economic Census*. The states are in descending order of sales or establishments (if sales data are missing for the majority). The symbol (D) appears when data are withheld to prevent disclosure of competitive information. States marked with (D) are sorted by number of establishments. A dash (-) indicates that the data element cannot be calculated. Shaded *states* on the state map indicate those states which have proportionately greater representation in the industry than would be indicated by the states population; the ratio is based on total sales or number of establishments. Shaded *regions* indicate where the industry is regionally most concentrated.

NAICS 443111 - HOUSEHOLD APPLIANCE STORES

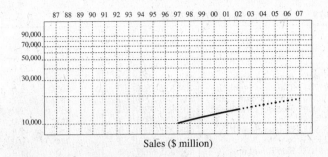

Sales ($ million)

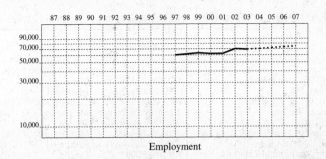

Employment

GENERAL STATISTICS

Year	Establishments (number)	Employment (number)	Payroll ($ million)	Sales ($ million)	Employees per Establishment (number)	Sales per Establishment ($)	Payroll per Employee ($)
1987	-	-	-	-	-	-	-
1988	-	-	-	-	-	-	-
1989	-	-	-	-	-	-	-
1990	-	-	-	-	-	-	-
1991	-	-	-	-	-	-	-
1992	-	-	-	-	-	-	-
1993	-	-	-	-	-	-	-
1994	-	-	-	-	-	-	-
1995	-	-	-	-	-	-	-
1996	-	-	-	-	-	-	-
1997	10,484	60,220	1,217.5	10,082.9	6	961,742	20,217
1998	10,319	61,694	1,333.8	10,901.4 e	6	1,056,436	21,620
1999	10,044	63,350	1,424.6	11,719.8 e	6	1,166,848	22,488
2000	9,828	62,186	1,481.7	12,538.3 e	6	1,275,771	23,828
2001	9,872	62,372	1,542.7	13,356.7 e	6	1,352,992	24,734
2002	10,326	70,122	1,794.8	14,175.2	7	1,372,768	25,595
2003	10,013	69,183	1,842.7	14,993.7 p	7	1,503,132 p	26,635
2004	9,902 p	70,271 p	1,936.2 p	15,812.1 p	7 p	1,590,381 p	27,795 p
2005	9,846 p	71,798 p	2,040.3 p	16,630.6 p	7 p	1,677,630 p	28,847 p
2006	9,790 p	73,325 p	2,144.5 p	17,449.0 p	7 p	1,764,880 p	29,899 p
2007	9,734 p	74,853 p	2,248.6 p	18,267.5 p	8 p	1,852,129 p	30,951 p

Source: Economic Census of the United States, 1997 and 2002. Establishment counts, employment, and payroll are from *County Business Patterns* for non-Census years. This is a newly defined industry. Data for prior years are unavailable at the time of publication but may become available over time. Values followed by 'p' are projections by the editors. Sales data for non-Census years are extrapolations, marked by 'e'.

INDICES OF CHANGE

Year	Establishments (number)	Employment (number)	Payroll ($ million)	Sales ($ million)	Employees per Establishment (number)	Sales per Establishment ($)	Payroll per Employee ($)
1987	-	-	-	-	-	-	-
1992	-	-	-	-	-	-	-
1993	-	-	-	-	-	-	-
1994	-	-	-	-	-	-	-
1995	-	-	-	-	-	-	-
1996	-	-	-	-	-	-	-
1997	101.5	85.9	67.8	71.1	83.9	70.1	79.0
1998	99.9	88.0	74.3	76.9 e	88.4	77.0	84.5
1999	97.3	90.3	79.4	82.7 e	92.8	85.0	87.9
2000	95.2	88.7	82.6	88.5 e	92.8	92.9	93.1
2001	95.6	88.9	86.0	94.2 e	92.8	98.6	96.6
2002	100.0	100.0	100.0	100.0	100.0	100.0	100.0
2003	97.0	98.7	102.7	105.8 p	101.7	109.5 p	104.1
2004	95.9 p	100.2 p	107.9 p	111.5 p	104.2 p	115.9 p	108.6 p
2005	95.4 p	102.4 p	113.7 p	117.3 p	106.9 p	122.2 p	112.7 p
2006	94.8 p	104.6 p	119.5 p	123.1 p	109.6 p	128.6 p	116.8 p
2007	94.3 p	106.7 p	125.3 p	128.9 p	112.4 p	134.9 p	120.9 p

Sources: Same as General Statistics. The values shown reflect change from the base year, 2002. Values above 100 mean greater than 2002, values below 100 mean less than 2002, and a value of 100 in the 1987-2001 or 2003-2007 period means same as 2002. Values followed by a 'p' are projections by the editors; 'e' stands for extrapolation. Data are the most recent available at this level of detail.

SELECTED RATIOS

For 2002	Avg. of All Retail	Analyzed Industry	Index	For 2002	Avg. of All Retail	Analyzed Industry	Index
Employees per Establishment	17	7	40	Sales per Employee	174,682	202,151	116
Payroll per Establishment	333,445	173,811	52	Sales per Establishment	3,332,269	1,372,768	41
Payroll per Employee	20,311	25,595	126	Expenses per Establishment	na	na	na

Sources: Same as General Statistics. The 'Average of All' column, Wholesale or Retail, represents the average of the sector reported for the most recent complete year available. The Index shows the relationship between the Average and the Analyzed Industry. For example, 100 means that they are equal; 500 that the Analyzed Industry is five times the average; 50 means that the Analyzed Industry is half the national average. The abbreviation 'na' is used to show that data are 'not available'.

LEADING COMPANIES   Number shown: **58**   Total sales ($ mil): **68,078**   Total employment (000): **229.8**

Company Name	Address				CEO Name	Phone	Co. Type	Sales ($ mil)	Empl. (000)
Lowe's Companies Inc.	PO Box 1111	N. Wilkesboro	NC	28656		336-658-4000	P	36,464	123.0
Best Buy Company Inc.	PO Box 9312	Minneapolis	MN	55440	Bradbury Anderson	612-291-1000	P	27,400	90.0
Conn's Inc.	3295 College St	Beaumont	TX	77701	Thomas J Frank Sr	409-832-1696	P	567	2.0
H.H. Gregg Appliances	4151 E 96th St	Indianapolis	IN	46240	Jerry Throgmartin	317-848-8710	R	480*	2.2
Brookstone Inc.	1 Innovation Way	Merrimack	NH	03054	Michael F Anthony	603-880-9500	P	434	2.9
REX Stores Corp.	2875 Needmore Rd	Dayton	OH	45414		937-276-3931	P	417	1.0
American Television & Appliance	2404 W Beltline	Madison	WI	53713	Douglas Reuhl	608-271-1000	R	350*	1.8
Heilig-Meyers Co.	12501 Patterson Ave	Richmond	VA	23233		804-784-7500	P	324	0.0
Nebraska Furniture Mart Inc.	PO Box 3000	Omaha	NE	68103	Ron Blumkins	402-255-6327	S	180*	1.2
Pieratt's Inc.	110 S Mount Tabor	Lexington	KY	40517	Bruce W Pieratt	859-268-6200	R	121*	<0.1
Barbeques Galore Inc.	10 Orchard Rd	Lake Forest	CA	92630	Michael Lindblad	949-597-2400	S	102*	0.6
Grand Home Furnishings	4235 Electric Rd SW	Roanoke	VA	24014	George B Cartledge Jr	540-774-7004	R	100*	0.8
Avanti Products Inc.	10880 NW 30th St	Miami	FL	33172	Richard Ladd	305-592-7834	R	87*	<0.1
McQueeny-Lock Co.	520 W Pennway	Kansas City	MO	64108	Mike McQueeny	816-842-3503	R	84*	<0.1
BGE Home Products & Services	7161 Columbia	Columbia	MD	21046	Bill Munn	410-720-6600	S	79*	0.5
B. Olinde and Sons Company Inc.	9536 Airline Hwy	Baton Rouge	LA	70815	JB Olinde	225-926-3380	R	71*	0.2
Standard Companies Inc.	1535 Kalamazoo SE	Grand Rapids	MI	49507	T O Rottschafer	616-243-3653	R	58*	0.2
Appliance Depot and More	425 E Macewen Dr	Osprey	FL	34229		941-966-0725	R	57*	<0.1
Mercury BE L.L.C.	3255 Saco St	Los Angeles	CA	90058	Nassir Ebrahimi	323-588-4700	R	55*	<0.1
Wholesale Supply Group Inc.	PO Box 4080	Cleveland	TN	37320	Lloyd D Rogers	423-478-1191	R	50*	0.3
Big Sandy Furniture Inc.	45 Cty Rd 407	South Point	OH	45680	John C Stewart Jr	740-894-4242	R	48*	0.3
Excalibur Electronics Inc.	13755 SW 119th	Miami	FL	33186	Shane Samole	305-477-8080	R	46*	<0.1
Crystal Promotions Inc.	1820 S Grand Ave	Los Angeles	CA	90015	Arsalan Dokhanian	213-744-0700	R	44*	<0.1
Baillio's Warehouse Showroom	5301 Menaul NE	Albuquerque	NM	87110	Jack Baillio	505-883-7511	R	41*	0.1
Corner Distributors Inc.	3940 Merritt Ave	Bronx	NY	10466	Francis Vegliante	718-798-1500	R	40*	<0.1
Olum's of Binghamton Inc.	3701 Vestal Pkwy E	Vestal	NY	13850	Gilbert S Rouff	607-729-5775	R	28*	0.2
Benny's Inc.	340 Waterman Ave	Esmond	RI	02917		401-231-1000	R	27*	0.3
LFD Inc.	725 E Esperanza St	McAllen	TX	78501	Greg Thrash	956-686-2271	R	26*	0.3
Southern L.P. Gas Inc.	PO Box 1010	De Queen	AR	71832	Lu Gray	870-642-2234	R	26*	<0.1
Coast Wide Supply Company Inc.	PO Box 84203	Seattle	WA	98124	W Watkinson	206-624-1225	R	21*	<0.1
Adray Appliance & Photo Center	20219 Carlysle	Dearborn	MI	48124	Debra Adray	313-274-9500	R	20*	0.1
W-D Bryant and Son Inc.	372 S 5th St	Williamsburg	KY	40769	Lee Bryant	606-549-2385	R	19*	<0.1
Edelsteins Better Furniture Inc.	PO Box 3369	Brownsville	TX	78523	Ruben Edelstein	956-542-5605	R	17*	0.3
L & W Service Center Inc.	PO Box 190	Kearney	NE	68848	Marc Loescher	308-237-2185	R	15*	<0.1
Gas Inc.	77 Jefferson Pkwy	Newnan	GA	30263		770-502-8800	R	14*	0.1
Peerless Water Treatment	12201 Minnetonka	Hopkins	MN	55305	Gary Capone	952-938-1880	R	14*	<0.1
Fairfax Kitchen and Bath Inc.	14325 Willard Rd	Chantilly	VA	20151	Hamid Sharifi	703-817-1977	R	14*	<0.1
Modern Builders Supply Inc.	PO Box 1287	Mountain View	AR	72560	Buddy Bolin	870-269-3808	R	14*	<0.1
Universal Furniture House Inc.	1600 Westbank	Harvey	LA	70058	CJ Dawson		R	12*	0.2
DeSears Appliances Inc.	6430 14th St W	Bradenton	FL	34207	John Rice	941-751-7525	R	11*	0.1
Pete Moore Appliance Inc.	1643-1615 W State	Bristol	VA	24201	Clarise Senter	276-466-8197	R	11*	0.1
H and H Service Stores Inc.	4990 Altama Ave	Brunswick	GA	31525	William Brunson	912-265-8100	R	11*	<0.1
Guaranteed Foods Inc.	7700 Wedd Street	Overland Park	KS	66204	Thomas G Williams	913-248-8778	R	10*	<0.1
Washing Equipment of Texas Ltd.	PO Box 200066	San Antonio	TX	78220	Bob Lye	210-662-9744	R	10*	<0.1
International Furniture	1516 E Reelfoot Ave	Union City	TN	38261	W O Neal	731-885-6471	R	9*	<0.1
Cook's Inc.	1100 Washington	Grand Haven	MI	49417	Greg E Cook	616-842-0180	R	7*	<0.1
McDaniels Sales Co.	16839 S US Hwy 27	Lansing	MI	48906	Donald Jessup	517-482-0748	R	6*	<0.1
Klinginsmith TV and Appliance	1812 E 9th St	Trenton	MO	64683	Jacob Klinginsmith	660-359-5947	R	6*	<0.1
Richard, P.C. and Son Long Island	111 Old Country Rd	Carle Place	NY	11514		516-294-2900	R	5*	<0.1
Culligan Water Conditioning Inc.	6901 E 38th St	Indianapolis	IN	46226		317-925-6484	S	5*	<0.1
RW Bowman Corp.	3861 N Main St	Las Cruces	NM	88012	Robert Bowman	505-523-3933	R	4*	<0.1
Eklund Appliance and TV	1007 Central Av W	Great Falls	MT	59404	Calvin Eklund	406-761-3430	R	4*	<0.1
Western Natural Gas Co.	2960 Strickland St	Jacksonville	FL	32254	Henry C Baker	904-387-3511	R	4*	<0.1
Dobbs, Arvin John	131 N Main St	Blythe	CA	92225	Arvin Dobbs	760-922-4111	R	4*	<0.1
Eckert TV and Appliances	15712 Willets Point	Whitestone	NY	11357	Bernard Eckert	718-746-8438	R	3*	<0.1
Ralph's Power Sewing Machine	PO Box 11307	Denver	CO	80211	Raul Badillo	303-455-6831	P	2*	<0.1
Superior-Deshler Inc.	207 S Maple St	Davenport	NE	68335	Dennis Schardt	402-364-2125	R	1*	<0.1
Quality Maintenance Enterprises	PO Box 3043	Missoula	MT	59806		406-251-3402	R	1*	<0.1

Source: *Ward's Business Directory of U.S. Private and Public Companies*, Volumes 1 and 2, 2005. The company type code used is as follows: P - Public, R - Private, S - Subsidiary, D - Division, J - Joint Venture, A - Affiliate, G - Group. Sales are in millions of dollars, employees are in thousands. An asterisk (*) indicates an estimated sales volume. The symbol < stands for 'less than'. Company names and addresses are truncated, in some cases, to fit into the available space.

OCCUPATIONS EMPLOYED BY ELECTRONICS & APPLIANCE STORES

Occupation	% of Total 2004	Change to 2014	Occupation	% of Total 2004	Change to 2014
Retail salespersons	33.8	23.3	Office clerks, general	2.1	10.1
Cashiers, except gaming	5.7	11.1	Truck drivers, light or delivery services	2.1	23.1
First-line supervisors/managers of retail sales workers	5.6	13.5	Computer support specialists	1.8	24.5
Computer, automated teller, & office machine repairers	3.9	12.0	Bookkeeping, accounting, & auditing clerks	1.7	11.2
Customer service representatives	3.5	26.4	Shipping, receiving, & traffic clerks	1.6	12.0
Home appliance repairers	2.7	-5.6	Laborers & freight, stock, & material movers, hand	1.6	10.9
Stock clerks & order fillers	2.7	-5.5	Sales representatives, services, nec	1.2	24.0
Electronic home entertainment installers & repairers	2.3	10.8	Sales reps, wholesale & manufacturing, tech	1.2	24.1
General & operations managers	2.1	22.4	First-line supervisors of mechanics	1.0	23.6

Source: *Industry-Occupation Matrix*, Bureau of Labor Statistics. These data are reported based on 4-digit NAICS categories but have been matched to corresponding 6-digit NAICS industry codes. The change reported for each occupation to the year 2014 is a percent of growth or decline as estimated by the Bureau of Labor Statistics. The abbreviation nec stands for 'not elsewhere classified.'

LOCATION BY STATE AND REGIONAL CONCENTRATION

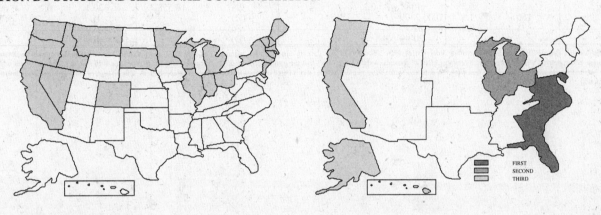

FIRST
SECOND
THIRD

INDUSTRY DATA BY STATE

State	Establishments Total (number)	% of U.S.	Employment Total (number)	% of U.S.	Per Estab.	Payroll Total ($ mil.)	Per Empl. ($)	Sales Total ($ mil.)	% of U.S.	Per Estab. ($)
California	896	8.7	6,648	9.6	7	198.6	29,877	1,692.3	12.2	1,888,713
New York	604	5.8	3,948	5.7	7	124.3	31,475	1,339.3	9.6	2,217,406
Texas	631	6.1	4,692	6.8	7	110.0	23,434	887.7	6.4	1,406,775
Illinois	393	3.8	3,408	4.9	9	113.5	33,295	733.6	5.3	1,866,613
Ohio	383	3.7	3,664	5.3	10	90.7	24,742	710.7	5.1	1,855,483
Michigan	360	3.5	4,229	6.1	12	89.9	21,264	698.8	5.0	1,941,197
New Jersey	272	2.6	1,725	2.5	6	57.1	33,082	556.3	4.0	2,045,195
Florida	528	5.1	2,442	3.5	5	70.7	28,957	523.8	3.8	991,992
Indiana	281	2.7	2,218	3.2	8	49.9	22,509	440.7	3.2	1,568,317
Pennsylvania	442	4.3	2,471	3.6	6	56.7	22,935	415.2	3.0	939,362
Massachusetts	218	2.1	1,551	2.2	7	44.5	28,670	344.6	2.5	1,580,697
Minnesota	255	2.5	1,812	2.6	7	47.7	26,322	318.8	2.3	1,250,098
Washington	250	2.4	1,759	2.5	7	51.0	28,999	315.6	2.3	1,262,344
North Carolina	310	3.0	1,686	2.4	5	41.4	24,579	292.5	2.1	943,419
Wisconsin	256	2.5	1,663	2.4	6	41.4	24,884	288.1	2.1	1,125,309
Connecticut	134	1.3	1,056	1.5	8	35.7	33,787	276.2	2.0	2,061,067
Tennessee	226	2.2	1,490	2.2	7	34.3	23,042	246.8	1.8	1,092,097
Virginia	260	2.5	1,322	1.9	5	31.1	23,560	227.5	1.6	874,888
Missouri	279	2.7	1,373	2.0	5	29.8	21,737	223.8	1.6	802,208
Oregon	172	1.7	1,108	1.6	6	29.9	26,997	221.5	1.6	1,287,558
Colorado	169	1.6	1,200	1.7	7	31.2	25,992	217.8	1.6	1,288,988
Georgia	238	2.3	1,492	2.2	6	30.9	20,743	208.8	1.5	877,403
Louisiana	151	1.5	1,082	1.6	7	27.5	25,411	202.1	1.5	1,338,702
Maryland	144	1.4	918	1.3	6	25.9	28,179	189.5	1.4	1,316,188
Kentucky	174	1.7	1,134	1.6	7	26.6	23,499	187.5	1.3	1,077,552
Oklahoma	164	1.6	843	1.2	5	16.8	19,881	151.6	1.1	924,445
Iowa	218	2.1	1,194	1.7	5	22.4	18,734	149.4	1.1	685,202
South Carolina	178	1.7	767	1.1	4	18.2	23,691	139.7	1.0	784,933
Alabama	188	1.8	826	1.2	4	17.0	20,547	128.1	0.9	681,277
Montana	65	0.6	494	0.7	8	10.7	21,745	118.5	0.9	1,823,246
Kansas	164	1.6	826	1.2	5	16.9	20,448	118.2	0.8	720,482
New Hampshire	66	0.6	427	0.6	6	16.7	39,213	117.5	0.8	1,780,939
Arkansas	135	1.3	592	0.9	4	12.0	20,198	101.9	0.7	754,681

Continued on next page.

INDUSTRY DATA BY STATE - Continued

State	Establishments Total (number)	% of U.S.	Employment Total (number)	% of U.S.	Per Estab.	Payroll Total ($ mil.)	Per Empl. ($)	Sales Total ($ mil.)	% of U.S.	Per Estab. ($)
Utah	94	0.9	543	0.8	6	13.0	23,947	96.4	0.7	1,025,309
Mississippi	130	1.3	801	1.2	6	15.1	18,908	94.6	0.7	727,431
Nevada	57	0.6	477	0.7	8	11.3	23,784	82.7	0.6	1,451,158
New Mexico	65	0.6	507	0.7	8	11.0	21,771	79.1	0.6	1,216,877
Nebraska	90	0.9	473	0.7	5	9.0	18,939	68.2	0.5	758,256
Maine	65	0.6	393	0.6	6	9.0	22,858	64.1	0.5	986,723
Idaho	83	0.8	386	0.6	5	7.6	19,733	63.1	0.5	760,036
Rhode Island	39	0.4	200	0.3	5	5.7	28,435	53.7	0.4	1,376,615
South Dakota	64	0.6	405	0.6	6	7.8	19,262	52.4	0.4	819,516
Vermont	42	0.4	247	0.4	6	6.4	25,830	42.7	0.3	1,017,429
West Virginia	71	0.7	360	0.5	5	6.1	16,889	41.1	0.3	579,141
Delaware	38	0.4	226	0.3	6	6.4	28,487	37.2	0.3	978,605
Hawaii	34	0.3	138	0.2	4	3.6	26,413	29.2	0.2	857,353
North Dakota	41	0.4	213	0.3	5	3.9	18,216	25.5	0.2	622,073
Wyoming	33	0.3	138	0.2	4	2.6	18,558	20.1	0.1	609,394
Arizona	156	1.5	1000-2499	-	-	(D)	-	(D)	-	-
Alaska	21	0.2	20-99	-	-	(D)	-	(D)	-	-
D.C.	3	-	20-99	-	-	(D)	-	(D)	-	-

Source: 2002 *Economic Census*. The states are in descending order of sales or establishments (if sales data are missing for the majority). The symbol (D) appears when data are withheld to prevent disclosure of competitive information. States marked with (D) are sorted by number of establishments. A dash (-) indicates that the data element cannot be calculated. Shaded *states* on the state map indicate those states which have proportionately greater representation in the industry than would be indicated by the states population; the ratio is based on total sales or number of establishments. Shaded *regions* indicate where the industry is regionally most concentrated.

NAICS 443112 - RADIO, TELEVISION, AND OTHER ELECTRONICS STORES

Sales ($ million)

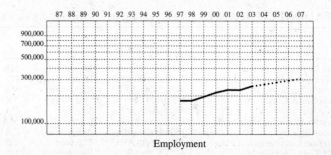

Employment

GENERAL STATISTICS

Year	Establishments (number)	Employment (number)	Payroll ($ million)	Sales ($ million)	Employees per Establishment (number)	Sales per Establishment ($)	Payroll per Employee ($)
1987	-	-	-	-	-	-	-
1988	-	-	-	-	-	-	-
1989	-	-	-	-	-	-	-
1990	-	-	-	-	-	-	-
1991	-	-	-	-	-	-	-
1992	-	-	-	-	-	-	-
1993	-	-	-	-	-	-	-
1994	-	-	-	-	-	-	-
1995	-	-	-	-	-	-	-
1996	-	-	-	-	-	-	-
1997	18,305	176,813	3,244.8	32,168.1	10	1,757,339	18,352
1998	18,498	176,740	3,800.3	35,508.1 e	10	1,919,564	21,502
1999	18,997	195,092	4,510.1	38,848.1 e	10	2,044,960	23,118
2000	19,787	216,693	5,131.4	42,188.1 e	11	2,132,112	23,680
2001	21,724	232,233	5,736.6	45,528.1 e	11	2,095,751	24,702
2002	23,521	231,194	5,365.7	48,868.1	10	2,077,637	23,208
2003	24,664	254,625	6,073.1	52,208.1 p	10	2,226,281 p	23,851
2004	25,335 p	266,125 p	6,672.0 p	55,548.1 p	11 p	2,289,629 p	25,701 p
2005	26,473 p	279,678 p	7,130.6 p	58,888.1 p	11 p	2,352,978 p	26,469 p
2006	27,610 p	293,231 p	7,589.3 p	62,228.1 p	11 p	2,416,327 p	27,236 p
2007	28,748 p	306,784 p	8,047.9 p	65,568.1 p	11 p	2,479,675 p	28,004 p

Source: *Economic Census of the United States*, 1997 and 2002. Establishment counts, employment, and payroll are from *County Business Patterns* for non-Census years. This is a newly defined industry. Data for prior years are unavailable at the time of publication but may become available over time. Values followed by 'p' are projections by the editors. Sales data for non-Census years are extrapolations, marked by 'e'.

INDICES OF CHANGE

Year	Establishments (number)	Employment (number)	Payroll ($ million)	Sales ($ million)	Employees per Establishment (number)	Sales per Establishment ($)	Payroll per Employee ($)
1987	-	-	-	-	-	-	-
1992	-	-	-	-	-	-	-
1993	-	-	-	-	-	-	-
1994	-	-	-	-	-	-	-
1995	-	-	-	-	-	-	-
1996	-	-	-	-	-	-	-
1997	77.8	76.5	60.5	65.8	98.7	84.6	79.1
1998	78.6	76.4	70.8	72.7 e	97.7	92.4	92.6
1999	80.8	84.4	84.1	79.5 e	104.8	98.4	99.6
2000	84.1	93.7	95.6	86.3 e	111.9	102.6	102.0
2001	92.4	100.4	106.9	93.2 e	108.9	100.9	106.4
2002	100.0	100.0	100.0	100.0	100.0	100.0	100.0
2003	104.9	110.1	113.2	106.8 p	105.0	107.2 p	102.8
2004	107.7 p	115.1 p	124.3 p	113.7 p	107.8 p	110.2 p	110.7 p
2005	112.5 p	121.0 p	132.9 p	120.5 p	108.8 p	113.3 p	114.0 p
2006	117.4 p	126.8 p	141.4 p	127.3 p	109.8 p	116.3 p	117.4 p
2007	122.2 p	132.7 p	150.0 p	134.2 p	110.8 p	119.4 p	120.7 p

Sources: Same as General Statistics. The values shown reflect change from the base year, 2002. Values above 100 mean greater than 2002, values below 100 mean less than 2002, and a value of 100 in the 1987-2001 or 2003-2007 period means same as 2002. Values followed by a 'p' are projections by the editors; 'e' stands for extrapolation. Data are the most recent available at this level of detail.

SELECTED RATIOS

For 2002	Avg. of All Retail	Analyzed Industry	Index	For 2002	Avg. of All Retail	Analyzed Industry	Index
Employees per Establishment	17	10	58	Sales per Employee	174,682	211,373	121
Payroll per Establishment	333,445	228,122	68	Sales per Establishment	3,332,269	2,077,637	62
Payroll per Employee	20,311	23,208	114	Expenses per Establishment	na	na	na

Sources: Same as General Statistics. The 'Average of All' column, Wholesale or Retail, represents the average of the sector reported for the most recent complete year available. The Index shows the relationship between the Average and the Analyzed Industry. For example, 100 means that they are equal; 500 that the Analyzed Industry is five times the average; 50 means that the Analyzed Industry is half the national average. The abbreviation 'na' is used to show that data are 'not available'.

LEADING COMPANIES   Number shown: **75**   Total sales ($ mil): **64,108**   Total employment (000): **247.0**

Company Name	Address				CEO Name	Phone	Co. Type	Sales ($ mil)	Empl. (000)
Best Buy Company Inc.	PO Box 9312	Minneapolis	MN	55440	Bradbury Anderson	612-291-1000	P	27,400	90.0
Office Depot Inc.	2200 Germantown	Delray Beach	FL	33445	Charles E Brown	561-266-4800	P	13,565	46.0
Circuit City Stores Inc.	9950 Mayland Dr	Richmond	VA	23233		804-527-4000	P	9,745	42.3
RadioShack Corp.	PO Box 17180	Fort Worth	TX	76102	David J Edmondson	817-415-3700	P	4,842	39.5
Fry's Electronics Inc.	600 E Brokaw Rd	San Jose	CA	95112	John Fry	408-487-4500	R	2,265*	6.0
Tweeter Home Entertainment	40 Pequot Way	Canton	MA	02021	Samuel Bloomberg	781-830-3000	P	778	3.6
Good Guys Inc.	1600 Harbor Bay	Alameda	CA	94502	Thomas F Herman	510-747-6000	S	750	2.7
Ultimate Electronics Inc.	321 W 84th Ave	Thornton	CO	80260	Mark Wattles	303-412-2500	P	713	3.5
H.H. Gregg Appliances	4151 E 96th St	Indianapolis	IN	46240	Jerry Throgmartin	317-848-8710	R	480*	2.2
REX Stores Corp.	2875 Needmore Rd	Dayton	OH	45414		937-276-3931	P	417	1.0
American Television & Appliance	2404 W Beltline	Madison	WI	53713	Douglas Reuhl	608-271-1000	R	350*	1.8
Heilig-Meyers Co.	12501 Patterson Ave	Richmond	VA	23233		804-784-7500	P	324	0.0
ABC Appliance Inc.	PO Box 436001	Pontiac	MI	48343	Gordon Hartunian	248-335-4222	R	277*	1.8
Columbia Audio-Video Inc.	1741 2nd St	Highland Park	IL	60035	Gary Rozak	847-433-6010	R	212*	0.1
Nebraska Furniture Mart Inc.	PO Box 3000	Omaha	NE	68103	Ron Blumkins	402-255-6327	S	180*	1.2
Paul's TV - King of Big Screen	500 N Harbor Blvd	La Habra	CA	90631	Paul Goldenberg	562-697-6751	R	155*	<0.1
Pieratt's Inc.	110 S Mount Tabor	Lexington	KY	40517	Bruce W Pieratt	859-268-6200	R	121*	<0.1
North American Telecom Services	2894 O Washingtn	Canonsburg	PA	15317		724-941-2900	R	102*	0.5
Crutchfield Corp.	1 Crutchfield Park	Charlottesville	VA	22911	Bill Crutchfield	434-817-1000	R	88*	0.5
Granite Furniture Company Inc.	1050 E 2100 S	Salt Lake City	UT	84106	Jim Taggart	801-486-3333	R	82*	0.4
Queen City TV & Appliance	2430 I-85 S	Charlotte	NC	28208	Woodrow Player Jr	704-391-6000	R	59*	0.2
Mercury BE L.L.C.	3255 Saco St	Los Angeles	CA	90058	Nassir Ebrahimi	323-588-4700	R	55*	<0.1
Saint Elizabeth Home Medical	PO Box 30550	Lincoln	NE	68503	Robert Lanik	402-464-8755	R	51*	0.1
Foreign Trade Corp.	130 W Cochran St	Simi Valley	CA	93065	Ramin Rostami	818-428-2000	R	49*	<0.1
Harvey Electronics Inc.	205 Chubb Ave	Lyndhurst	NJ	07071	Franklin C Karp	201-842-0078	P	43	0.2
Audio Ethics Inc.	8200 Arrowridge	Charlotte	NC	28273	Donnie Haulk		R	42*	<0.1
Ed Kellum and Son Appliance Co.	4533 Cole Ave	Dallas	TX	75205	Ed Kellum	214-526-1717	R	42*	0.1
Dailey & Wells Communications	3440 E Houston St	San Antonio	TX	78219	Richard Wells	210-893-6500	R	42*	<0.1
Audiovisual Inc.	6721 Bury Dr	Eden Prairie	MN	55346	Joe Stoebner	952-949-3700	R	41*	0.1
Baillio's Warehouse Showroom	5301 Menaul NE	Albuquerque	NM	87110	Jack Baillio	505-883-7511	R	41*	0.1
Northern Video Systems Inc.	4465 Granite Dr	Rocklin	CA	95677	Mark Haney	916-630-4700	R	35*	<0.1
Mobile Line Communications	24280 Swartz Dr	Lake Forest	CA	92630	Dennis Curtis	949-580-2500	R	33*	<0.1
Arjay Telecom	23215 Hawthorne	Torrance	CA	90505	Arun Bhumitra	310-791-3300	R	31*	0.2
Circuit City	855 E Birch St	Brea	CA	92821		714-256-2140	R	29*	0.2
Primetv L.L.C.	125 Murray Hill Rd	Southern Pines	NC	28387	David Hagen	910-693-1555	R	27*	0.1
Aero-Tech Communications Inc.	24280 Sherwood	Center Line	MI	48015	Billie Bowmer	586-757-0301	R	26*	<0.1
Consumers Marine Electronics Inc.	PO Box 1319	Belmar	NJ	07719	Philip Perricone	732-681-9025	R	25*	<0.1
Atlantic Business Communications	4319 35th St, Ste 2	Orlando	FL	32811	Joel Botbol	407-872-1170	R	25*	<0.1
Michael L Merrill and Associates	1400 W Lambert Rd	Brea	CA	92821	Michael Merrill	714-256-2206	R	25*	<0.1
A1 Wireless USA Inc.	3940 30th St	Long Island City	NY	11101	Patricia Sinha		R	24*	0.1
Inkley's Inc.	6711 Ritz Way	Beltsville	MD	20705	David Ritz		S	24*	<0.1
J.J.R. Enterprises Inc.	10491 Placerville	Sacramento	CA	95827	Dan Reilly	916-363-2666	R	22*	0.1
Matter of Fax	105 Harrison Ave	Harrison	NJ	07029	Jonathan Sheldon	973-482-3700	R	21*	<0.1
Americom Telecommunications	3005 Vanguard Dr	Memphis	TN	38131	Jeff Patrick	901-346-2255	R	20*	<0.1
Entrepreneurial Ventures Inc.	590 Division St	Campbell	CA	95008	Dennis Webb	408-866-8255	R	20*	<0.1
Hillcrest Hi-Fidelity	4488 Spring Valley	Dallas	TX	75244	Michael Gallant	972-716-9900	R	20*	<0.1
Professional Audio Design Inc.	357 Liberty St	Rockland	MA	02370	David Malekpour	781-982-2600	R	19*	<0.1
Broadcasters General Store Inc.	2480 SE 52nd St	Ocala	FL	34480	David Kerstin	352-622-7700	R	18*	<0.1
Derby Computer Superstore	PO Box 576	East Moline	IL	61244	Alan Derbyshire	309-755-2662	R	17*	<0.1
Edelsteins Better Furniture Inc.	PO Box 3369	Brownsville	TX	78523	Ruben Edelstein	956-542-5605	R	17*	0.3
Markey's Audio-Visual Inc.	2909 S Meridian St	Indianapolis	IN	46225	Kevin Markey	317-783-1155	R	17*	0.2
Heritage Communications Inc.	2402 Wildwood Ave	N. Little Rock	AR	72120	Terri Mitchel	501-835-1182	R	16*	<0.1
Times Communications Systems	PO Box 1119	Oak Island	NC	28465	John Vereen	910-278-9567	R	16*	<0.1
Freedom Wireless Inc.	160 Alameda Plz	Butler	PA	16001	Daron Rogers	724-284-6033	R	15*	<0.1
L & W Service Center Inc.	PO Box 190	Kearney	NE	68848	Marc Loescher	308-237-2185	P	15*	<0.1
NTELOS	500 Summers St 300	Charleston	WV	25301		304-353-8900	R	15*	<0.1
Dalbec Audio Lab	58 King St	Troy	NY	12180	Richard Dalbec	518-272-7098	R	14*	<0.1
Tri Electronics Inc.	PO Box 4310	Hammond	IN	46324	James V Donovan	219-931-6850	R	14*	<0.1
American Satellite & Entertain.	40 Terrill Pk	Concord	NH	03301	Todd Toler	603-228-8815	R	14*	<0.1
Authorized Cellular	15835 Hall Rd	Macomb	MI	48044	David Gagnon	586-566-8555	R	13*	<0.1
Crimson Tech Inc.	107 Providence St	Putnam	CT	06260		860-928-3353	R	13*	<0.1
Cyracom International Inc.	7330 N Oracle Rd	Tucson	AZ	85704	Kenneth Anders	520-745-9447	R	13*	<0.1
Amerilink Marketing Corp.	435 E Main St	Greenwood	IN	46143	Jeff Brummett	317-883-3320	R	13*	<0.1
Brazos Cellular Communications	104 N Ave E	Olney	TX	76374		940-873-5100	R	12*	<0.1
Sound of Market Street	15 S 11th St, 2nd Fl	Philadelphia	PA	19107		215-925-3150	R	12*	<0.1
Cellular Connection	845 Broad Ripple	Indianapolis	IN	46220		317-466-0980	R	12*	<0.1
Cell-Direct	409 Campus St	Kissimmee	FL	34747	Jonhn Bencie	407-390-1999	R	11*	<0.1
DeSears Appliances Inc.	6430 14th St W	Bradenton	FL	34207	John Rice	941-751-7525	R	11*	0.1
H and H Service Stores Inc.	4990 Altama Ave	Brunswick	GA	31525	William Brunson	912-265-8100	R	11*	<0.1
Champaign Telephone Co.	1300 S Neil St	Champaign	IL	61820	Mike Hosier	217-359-4282	R	10*	<0.1
Cavin's Inc.	PO Box 31848	Raleigh	NC	27622	Dusty Milner	919-781-1220	R	10*	<0.1
Agape Home Healthcare Inc.	24 N St	Randolph	MA	02368	Delphine Feldman	617-926-5009	R	10*	<0.1
Cellular Connections	305 W Main St	Kelso	WA	98626	Ken Merrell	360-577-0601	R	10*	<0.1
Global Mart	PO Box 743	Logan	UT	84323	Bret Peterson	435-755-9266	R	10*	<0.1
Indiana Paging Network Inc.	6745 W Johnson Rd	Laporte	IN	46350	William Eisele	219-874-5000	R	10*	<0.1

Source: Ward's Business Directory of U.S. Private and Public Companies, Volumes 1 and 2, 2005. The company type code used is as follows: P - Public, R - Private, S - Subsidiary, D - Division, J - Joint Venture, A - Affiliate, G - Group. Sales are in millions of dollars, employees are in thousands. An asterisk (*) indicates an estimated sales volume. The symbol < stands for 'less than'. Company names and addresses are truncated, in some cases, to fit into the available space.

OCCUPATIONS EMPLOYED BY ELECTRONICS & APPLIANCE STORES

Occupation	% of Total 2004	Change to 2014	Occupation	% of Total 2004	Change to 2014
Retail salespersons	33.8	23.3	Office clerks, general	2.1	10.1
Cashiers, except gaming	5.7	11.1	Truck drivers, light or delivery services	2.1	23.1
First-line supervisors/managers of retail sales workers	5.6	13.5	Computer support specialists	1.8	24.5
Computer, automated teller, & office machine repairers	3.9	12.0	Bookkeeping, accounting, & auditing clerks	1.7	11.2
Customer service representatives	3.5	26.4	Shipping, receiving, & traffic clerks	1.6	12.0
Home appliance repairers	2.7	-5.6	Laborers & freight, stock, & material movers, hand	1.6	10.9
Stock clerks & order fillers	2.7	-5.5	Sales representatives, services, nec	1.2	24.0
Electronic home entertainment installers & repairers	2.3	10.8	Sales reps, wholesale & manufacturing, tech	1.2	24.1
General & operations managers	2.1	22.4	First-line supervisors of mechanics	1.0	23.6

Source: Industry-Occupation Matrix, Bureau of Labor Statistics. These data are reported based on 4-digit NAICS categories but have been matched to corresponding 6-digit NAICS industry codes. The change reported for each occupation to the year 2014 is a percent of growth or decline as estimated by the Bureau of Labor Statistics. The abbreviation nec stands for 'not elsewhere classified.'

LOCATION BY STATE AND REGIONAL CONCENTRATION

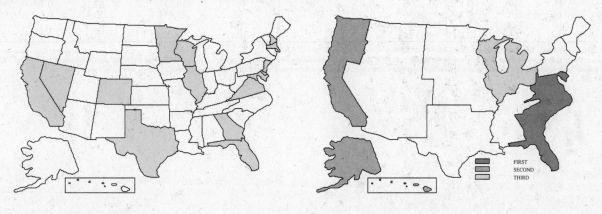

FIRST
SECOND
THIRD

INDUSTRY DATA BY STATE

State	Establishments Total (number)	Establishments % of U.S.	Employment Total (number)	Employment % of U.S.	Employment Per Estab.	Payroll Total ($ mil.)	Payroll Per Empl. ($)	Sales Total ($ mil.)	Sales % of U.S.	Sales Per Estab. ($)
California	2,920	12.4	31,782	13.9	11	831.7	26,169	7,372.8	15.2	2,524,927
Texas	1,734	7.4	17,086	7.5	10	388.3	22,724	3,625.2	7.5	2,090,649
Florida	1,562	6.6	14,868	6.5	10	345.3	23,223	3,613.3	7.5	2,313,261
New York	1,854	7.9	13,993	6.1	8	336.7	24,064	3,091.0	6.4	1,667,190
Illinois	1,084	4.6	11,711	5.1	11	264.4	22,574	2,521.1	5.2	2,325,715
Pennsylvania	904	3.8	8,557	3.8	9	191.6	22,394	1,760.8	3.6	1,947,742
New Jersey	734	3.1	7,327	3.2	10	179.3	24,474	1,707.4	3.5	2,326,191
Michigan	852	3.6	8,416	3.7	10	184.8	21,958	1,684.0	3.5	1,976,500
Ohio	863	3.7	8,421	3.7	10	172.5	20,490	1,634.5	3.4	1,893,957
Virginia	702	3.0	8,078	3.5	12	177.3	21,948	1,492.0	3.1	2,125,352
Georgia	756	3.2	7,164	3.1	9	168.4	23,513	1,483.1	3.1	1,961,708
Minnesota	351	1.5	5,165	2.3	15	113.8	22,034	1,277.3	2.6	3,639,040
Massachusetts	468	2.0	5,433	2.4	12	131.3	24,168	1,210.9	2.5	2,587,449
North Carolina	637	2.7	5,931	2.6	9	131.0	22,080	1,140.2	2.4	1,789,953
Maryland	381	1.6	4,747	2.1	12	112.3	23,650	1,056.7	2.2	2,773,446
Wisconsin	373	1.6	4,782	2.1	13	112.8	23,590	980.9	2.0	2,629,799
Missouri	507	2.2	4,680	2.1	9	103.4	22,091	976.5	2.0	1,926,089
Indiana	537	2.3	4,683	2.1	9	104.8	22,385	944.9	2.0	1,759,624
Colorado	389	1.7	4,281	1.9	11	96.2	22,463	919.8	1.9	2,364,622
Washington	398	1.7	4,041	1.8	10	102.5	25,365	915.4	1.9	2,299,942
Tennessee	450	1.9	3,480	1.5	8	81.9	23,540	678.9	1.4	1,508,729
Connecticut	264	1.1	2,695	1.2	10	64.7	23,996	568.8	1.2	2,154,568
Oregon	284	1.2	2,440	1.1	9	57.9	23,711	510.4	1.1	1,797,243
South Carolina	307	1.3	2,584	1.1	8	53.0	20,509	483.0	1.0	1,573,378
Alabama	330	1.4	2,565	1.1	8	60.8	23,700	478.9	1.0	1,451,352
Louisiana	286	1.2	2,433	1.1	9	51.8	21,280	468.3	1.0	1,637,311
Nevada	219	0.9	2,078	0.9	9	47.6	22,913	447.5	0.9	2,043,388
Kentucky	294	1.2	2,214	1.0	8	44.1	19,938	404.7	0.8	1,376,602
Kansas	233	1.0	2,069	0.9	9	43.6	21,088	391.0	0.8	1,678,185
New Hampshire	128	0.5	1,670	0.7	13	36.8	22,042	379.1	0.8	2,961,531
Oklahoma	292	1.2	2,327	1.0	8	48.3	20,746	367.2	0.8	1,257,387
Iowa	258	1.1	2,215	1.0	9	45.8	20,658	362.9	0.7	1,406,415
Utah	174	0.7	1,265	0.6	7	31.5	24,919	270.5	0.6	1,554,661

Continued on next page.

INDUSTRY DATA BY STATE - Continued

State	Establishments Total (number)	% of U.S.	Employment Total (number)	% of U.S.	Per Estab.	Payroll Total ($ mil.)	Per Empl. ($)	Sales Total ($ mil.)	% of U.S.	Per Estab. ($)
Arkansas	235	1.0	1,729	0.8	7	32.0	18,532	262.0	0.5	1,114,847
Delaware	67	0.3	1,333	0.6	20	23.3	17,473	232.4	0.5	3,468,582
Mississippi	191	0.8	1,117	0.5	6	24.5	21,919	218.8	0.5	1,145,560
New Mexico	120	0.5	1,114	0.5	9	23.0	20,626	217.6	0.4	1,813,717
Nebraska	116	0.5	1,177	0.5	10	23.1	19,649	203.1	0.4	1,750,974
Maine	90	0.4	727	0.3	8	16.6	22,777	149.6	0.3	1,662,567
Idaho	125	0.5	809	0.4	6	20.1	24,803	142.7	0.3	1,141,688
West Virginia	114	0.5	699	0.3	6	15.7	22,486	134.4	0.3	1,179,061
Hawaii	86	0.4	661	0.3	8	14.8	22,464	125.3	0.3	1,457,198
Rhode Island	81	0.3	622	0.3	8	14.8	23,826	122.0	0.3	1,505,938
North Dakota	65	0.3	626	0.3	10	12.1	19,350	107.4	0.2	1,651,646
Montana	89	0.4	586	0.3	7	12.0	20,432	106.4	0.2	1,195,371
South Dakota	70	0.3	534	0.2	8	11.8	22,180	98.4	0.2	1,406,000
Vermont	48	0.2	409	0.2	9	8.9	21,775	80.6	0.2	1,680,021
Alaska	32	0.1	206	0.1	6	7.5	36,631	62.1	0.1	1,941,906
Wyoming	57	0.2	356	0.2	6	7.8	21,947	50.4	0.1	883,474
Arizona	393	1.7	2500-4999	-	-	(D)	-	(D)	-	-
D.C.	32	0.1	100-249	-	-	(D)	-	(D)	-	-

Source: 2002 *Economic Census*. The states are in descending order of sales or establishments (if sales data are missing for the majority). The symbol (D) appears when data are withheld to prevent disclosure of competitive information. States marked with (D) are sorted by number of establishments. A dash (-) indicates that the data element cannot be calculated. Shaded *states* on the state map indicate those states which have proportionately greater representation in the industry than would be indicated by the states population; the ratio is based on total sales or number of establishments. Shaded *regions* indicate where the industry is regionally most concentrated.

NAICS 443120 - COMPUTER AND SOFTWARE STORES

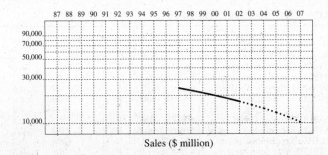

Sales ($ million)

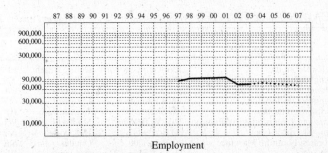

Employment

GENERAL STATISTICS

Year	Establishments (number)	Employment (number)	Payroll ($ million)	Sales ($ million)	Employees per Establishment (number)	Sales per Establishment ($)	Payroll per Employee ($)
1987	-	-	-	-	-	-	-
1988	-	-	-	-	-	-	-
1989	-	-	-	-	-	-	-
1990	-	-	-	-	-	-	-
1991	-	-	-	-	-	-	-
1992	-	-	-	-	-	-	-
1993	-	-	-	-	-	-	-
1994	-	-	-	-	-	-	-
1995	-	-	-	-	-	-	-
1996	-	-	-	-	-	-	-
1997	11,741	90,501	2,277.8	24,058.7	8	2,049,118	25,169
1998	13,233	103,433	3,050.1	22,673.1 e	8	1,713,378	29,489
1999	13,046	105,061	3,238.1	21,287.6 e	8	1,631,731	30,821
2000	12,889	106,213	4,187.4	19,902.0 e	8	1,544,107	39,425
2001	13,069	109,025	3,866.9	18,516.4 e	8	1,416,821	35,468
2002	10,133	75,277	1,897.1	17,130.9	7	1,690,602	25,201
2003	10,456	76,734	1,996.2	15,745.3 p	7	1,397,305 p	26,014
2004	10,648 p	81,799 p	2,570.2 p	14,359.7 p	8 p	1,318,166 p	30,028 p
2005	10,290 p	78,455 p	2,480.1 p	12,974.2 p	8 p	1,239,026 p	29,978 p
2006	9,931 p	75,110 p	2,390.0 p	11,588.6 p	7 p	1,159,887 p	29,928 p
2007	9,573 p	71,765 p	2,300.0 p	10,203.0 p	7 p	1,080,747 p	29,879 p

Source: *Economic Census of the United States*, 1997 and 2002. Establishment counts, employment, and payroll are from *County Business Patterns* for non-Census years. This is a newly defined industry. Data for prior years are unavailable at the time of publication but may become available over time. Values followed by 'p' are projections by the editors. Sales data for non-Census years are extrapolations, marked by 'e'.

INDICES OF CHANGE

Year	Establishments (number)	Employment (number)	Payroll ($ million)	Sales ($ million)	Employees per Establishment (number)	Sales per Establishment ($)	Payroll per Employee ($)
1987	-	-	-	-	-	-	-
1992	-	-	-	-	-	-	-
1993	-	-	-	-	-	-	-
1994	-	-	-	-	-	-	-
1995	-	-	-	-	-	-	-
1996	-	-	-	-	-	-	-
1997	115.9	120.2	120.1	140.4	103.6	121.2	99.9
1998	130.6	137.4	160.8	132.4 e	105.0	101.3	117.0
1999	128.7	139.6	170.7	124.3 e	109.0	96.5	122.3
2000	127.2	141.1	220.7	116.2 e	110.4	91.3	156.4
2001	129.0	144.8	203.8	108.1 e	111.7	83.8	140.7
2002	100.0	100.0	100.0	100.0	100.0	100.0	100.0
2003	103.2	101.9	105.2	91.9 p	98.8	82.7 p	103.2
2004	105.1 p	108.7 p	135.5 p	83.8 p	102.4 p	78.0 p	119.2 p
2005	101.5 p	104.2 p	130.7 p	75.7 p	101.6 p	73.3 p	119.0 p
2006	98.0 p	99.8 p	126.0 p	67.6 p	100.8 p	68.6 p	118.8 p
2007	94.5 p	95.3 p	121.2 p	59.6 p	100.0 p	63.9 p	118.6 p

Sources: Same as General Statistics. The values shown reflect change from the base year, 2002. Values above 100 mean greater than 2002, values below 100 mean less than 2002, and a value of 100 in the 1987-2001 or 2003-2007 period means same as 2002. Values followed by a 'p' are projections by the editors; 'e' stands for extrapolation. Data are the most recent available at this level of detail.

SELECTED RATIOS

For 2002	Avg. of All Retail	Analyzed Industry	Index	For 2002	Avg. of All Retail	Analyzed Industry	Index
Employees per Establishment	17	7	44	Sales per Employee	174,682	227,571	130
Payroll per Establishment	333,445	187,218	56	Sales per Establishment	3,332,269	1,690,602	51
Payroll per Employee	20,311	25,201	124	Expenses per Establishment	na	na	na

Sources: Same as General Statistics. The 'Average of All' column, Wholesale or Retail, represents the average of the sector reported for the most recent complete year available. The Index shows the relationship between the Average and the Analyzed Industry. For example, 100 means that they are equal; 500 that the Analyzed Industry is five times the average; 50 means that the Analyzed Industry is half the national average. The abbreviation 'na' is used to show that data are 'not available'.

LEADING COMPANIES Number shown: **75** Total sales ($ mil): **22,637** Total employment (000): **81.0**

Company Name	Address				CEO Name	Phone	Co. Type	Sales ($ mil)	Empl. (000)
Office Depot Inc.	2200 Germantown	Delray Beach	FL	33445	Charles E. Brown	561-266-4800	P	13,565	46.0
CompUSA Inc.	14951 N Dallas Pky	Dallas	TX	75254	Lawrence Mondry	972-982-4000	S	4,700	19.7
Electronics Boutique Inc.	931 S Matlack St	West Chester	PA	19382	Jeffrey W Griffiths	610-430-8100	S	1,334*	4.6
Computer Factory Inc.	399A Executive	Elmsford	NY	10523	Jay Gottlieb	914-347-5000	R	364*	1.0
Quill Computer Div.	100 Shelter Rd	Lincolnshire	IL	60069			D	352*	1.2
American Television & Appliance	2404 W Beltline	Madison	WI	53713	Douglas Reuhl	608-271-1000	R	350*	1.8
Sam Ash Music Corp.	PO Box 9047	Hicksville	NY	11802	Richard Ash	516-932-6400	R	233*	0.7
Nebraska Furniture Mart Inc.	PO Box 3000	Omaha	NE	68103	Ron Blumkins	402-255-6327	S	180*	1.2
Print Inc.	11255 Kirkland Way	Kirkland	WA	98033	Doug Johnson	425-822-6130	R	70*	0.3
Central Computer Systems Inc.	3777 Stevens Creek	Santa Clara	CA	95051	Saul Yeung	408-248-5888	R	66*	<0.1
Computer Tech	1140 Cypress Station	Houston	TX	77090	Ming Chung	281-444-0242	R	58*	0.2
MTM Technologies Inc.	850 Canal St	Stamford	CT	06902	Francis J Alfano	203-975-3700	P	52	0.2
K-Mac Enterprises Inc.	PO Box 6538	Fort Smith	AR	72906	Brent McGruder	479-646-2053	R	48*	0.2
Jade Systems Corp.	39-40 24th St	Long Island City	NY	11101	Ken Wasmer	718-392-2908	R	46*	<0.1
Dinastia International Corp.	402 W Calton Rd	Laredo	TX	78041	Patrick Wong	956-791-1000	R	42*	<0.1
Quality Imaging Products	1 Marconi, Ste A	Irvine	CA	92618	Paul Mcdonnel	949-855-6364	R	42*	0.2
Baillio's Warehouse Showroom	5301 Menaul NE	Albuquerque	NM	87110	Jack Baillio	505-883-7511	R	41*	0.1
Leadertech Systems of Chicago	210 Mittel Dr	Wood Dale	IL	60191	Leechin Su	630-238-9988	R	40*	<0.1
Peopleclick Inc.	2 Hannover Sq	Raleigh	NC	27601	James Buchanan	919-645-2800	R	36*	0.3
Dakota Collectibles	2000 Schafer St	Bismarck	ND	58501	George Westphal	701-255-2409	R	35*	<0.1
Resource One Computer Systems	1159 Dublin Rd	Columbus	OH	43215	Stampp Corbin	614-485-4800	R	31*	<0.1
Sears Home Services Group	8440 S Hardy Dr	Tempe	AZ	85284		480-893-8477	R	31*	0.3
TransNet Corp.	45 Columbia Rd	Somerville	NJ	08876	Steven J Wilk	908-253-0500	P	31	0.2
Rigel Computer Systems Inc.	8045 W Chester Pke	Upper Darby	PA	19082	Murray Gorson	610-853-4806	R	30*	<0.1
Integrated Components Source	1740 Emerson Ave	Oxnard	CA	93033	Thomas Justus	805-822-5100	R	29*	<0.1
Proactive Net Inc.	2055 Laurelwood Rd	Santa Clara	CA	95054	Ajay Singh	408-454-4500	R	28*	0.1
STL Technology Partners	PO Box 1899	Bloomington	IL	61702	Kathryn Norman	309-661-7851	R	28*	0.1
Communications Plus	1449 Fairmont Rd	Morgantown	WV	26501	Charles Moore	304-983-8642	R	28*	<0.1
Databazaar	12070 Miramar	Hollywood	FL	33025	Anindya Seal	954-843-0483	R	27*	<0.1
Argo Data Resources Inc.	12770 Coit Rd	Dallas	TX	75251		972-866-3300	R	27*	0.2
Odama Systems Inc.	1147 Stanford St	Santa Monica	CA	90403	J Odama	310-829-3806	R	25*	<0.1
PC Professional Inc.	1615 Webster St	Oakland	CA	94612	Daniel Sanguinetti	510-465-5700	R	25*	<0.1
Encore Development Inc.	5210 Belfort Rd	Jacksonville	FL	32256	Bob Leonard	904-245-7500	R	23*	<0.1
American Computer & Electronics	704 Quince Orchard	Gaithersburg	MD	20878		301-258-9850	R	21*	<0.1
Complete Computing Inc.	400 W 7th St	Little Rock	AR	72201	Dan Harpool	501-372-3379	R	21*	<0.1
Centurian Surplus Inc.	375 Tennant Ave	Morgan Hill	CA	95037	Jorge Lovato	408-778-2001	R	21*	<0.1
Financial Profiles Inc.	18818 Teller	Irvine	CA	92612			S	20*	0.1
Surplus Sourcing Group Inc.	21029 Itasca St	Chatsworth	CA	91311	Tony Shah	818-407-0200	R	19*	<0.1
Xerxes Computer Corp.	5735 Shakopee	Bloomington	MN	55437	David A Duhaime	952-936-9280	R	19*	<0.1
Derby Computer Superstore	PO Box 576	East Moline	IL	61244	Alan Derbyshire	309-755-2662	R	17*	<0.1
Actimize Inc.	350 5th Ave	New York	NY	10118	Reuven Battat	212-643-4600	R	17*	<0.1
ATX II L.L.C.	7305 Commercial	Fort Pierce	FL	34951	Steve Willett	772-467-8777	R	17*	<0.1
Mdserve Inc.	4800 Sugar Grove	Stafford	TX	77477		281-295-1500	R	17*	<0.1
Fishtech Solutions Inc.	10021 W 299th St	Louisburg	KS	66053	Charles Fisher	913-837-4216	R	17*	<0.1
Micromall USA Inc.	7 Cumberland Xing	Smyrna	GA	30080	Terry Asfaw	678-305-0135	R	16*	<0.1
Syscom Co.	1 Centerpointe Dr	La Palma	CA	90623	Han Sung	714-228-2220	R	16*	<0.1
Onquest Technologies Inc.	8915 NW 27th St	Miami	FL	33172	Frank Puentes	305-594-3034	R	16*	<0.1
Multiview Corp.	500 Edgewater Dr	Wakefield	MA	01880		781-245-2700	R	15*	<0.1
Acc Systems Inc.	1 Robert Ln	Glen Head	NY	11545	Louis Addonisio	516-674-0191	R	15*	<0.1
Century Computer Corp.	PO Box 310629	Detroit	MI	48231	Rob Remdenok	313-965-0460	R	15*	<0.1
Britannia Inc.	1616 Directors Row	Fort Wayne	IN	46808	Peter Harrison	260-482-6321	R	14*	<0.1
CCB Inc.	1902 Hoquiam	Renton	WA	98059		425-271-9818	R	14*	<0.1
Garland, Harwood	16861 Foothill Blvd	Fontana	CA	92335		909-349-2250	R	14*	<0.1
Homeseekerscom Inc.	6490 S McCarran	Reno	NV	89509		775-827-6886	R	14*	<0.1
Information Networks Inc.	21 Charles St	Westport	CT	06880	Robert Sloat	203-226-3367	R	14*	<0.1
Lee Yang Computers	2404 Rodeo Dr	Austin	TX	78727		512-775-1361	R	14*	<0.1
MacCenter	3343 W Commercial	Fort Lauderdale	FL	33309	Michael France	954-486-5500	R	14*	<0.1
Micro Strategies Inc.	PO Box 1139	Denville	NJ	07834	Anthony Bongiovanni	973-625-7721	R	14*	<0.1
NietoCom	6 N Chantsong Cir	Spring	TX	77382		281-362-7218	R	14*	<0.1
Ems Computing Inc.	3401 NW 98th St	Gainesville	FL	32606	Eric Stockton	352-374-9881	R	14*	<0.1
Technoland Inc.	1050 Stewart Dr	Sunnyvale	CA	94085	Tom Singleton		R	13*	<0.1
International Micro Systems Inc.	2741 E Belt Line Rd	Carrollton	TX	75006	Sid Saber	972-416-4000	R	13*	<0.1
1-Rex Inc.	PO Box 1230	Fort Worth	TX	76101	Rex Akers	817-531-8992	R	13*	0.1
Eastern Computer Exchange Inc.	105 Cascade Blvd	Milford	CT	06460	Barry Williams	203-877-4334	R	13*	<0.1
Learning Center	PO Box 339	Seneca	PA	16346	Lee Richey	814-677-2447	R	13*	<0.1
Minimax Corp.	930 Blue Gentian Rd	Saint Paul	MN	55121	Corey Maple	651-251-3005	R	13*	<0.1
Gold Circuit Inc.	210 S Beck Ave	Chandler	AZ	85226	James Greenberg	480-829-0404	R	12*	<0.1
Manhattan Information Systems	228 E 45th St Fl 6	New York	NY	10017	Anthony Candido	212-557-0123	R	12*	<0.1
AMT Datasouth Corp.	4765 Calle Quetzal	Camarillo	CA	93012		805-388-5799	R	12*	<0.1
Harmony Computers & Electronics	1801 Flatbush Ave	Brooklyn	NY	11210			R	12*	<0.1
Jadtec Computer Group	1520 W Yale Ave	Orange	CA	92867	John A Dieball	714-637-2900	R	12*	<0.1
Winners Circle Systems	2930 Shattuck	Berkeley	CA	94705	Andy Jong	510-845-4814	R	12*	<0.1
Printpal Inc.	PO Box 5655	Central Point	OR	97502	Mark Comish	541-282-8479	R	12*	<0.1
Workshare Technology Inc.	208 Utah St	San Francisco	CA	94103	Joe Fantuzzi	415-975-3855	R	11*	<0.1
Adtech Computers	1571 E Whitmore	Ceres	CA	95307	James Lawson	209-541-1111	R	11*	<0.1

Source: Ward's Business Directory of U.S. Private and Public Companies, Volumes 1 and 2, 2005. The company type code used is as follows: P - Public, R - Private, S - Subsidiary, D - Division, J - Joint Venture, A - Affiliate, G - Group. Sales are in millions of dollars, employees are in thousands. An asterisk (*) indicates an estimated sales volume. The symbol < stands for 'less than'. Company names and addresses are truncated, in some cases, to fit into the available space.

OCCUPATIONS EMPLOYED BY ELECTRONICS & APPLIANCE STORES

Occupation	% of Total 2004	Change to 2014	Occupation	% of Total 2004	Change to 2014
Retail salespersons	33.8	23.3	Office clerks, general	2.1	10.1
Cashiers, except gaming	5.7	11.1	Truck drivers, light or delivery services	2.1	23.1
First-line supervisors/managers of retail sales workers	5.6	13.5	Computer support specialists	1.8	24.5
Computer, automated teller, & office machine repairers	3.9	12.0	Bookkeeping, accounting, & auditing clerks	1.7	11.2
Customer service representatives	3.5	26.4	Shipping, receiving, & traffic clerks	1.6	12.0
Home appliance repairers	2.7	-5.6	Laborers & freight, stock, & material movers, hand	1.6	10.9
Stock clerks & order fillers	2.7	-5.5	Sales representatives, services, nec	1.2	24.0
Electronic home entertainment installers & repairers	2.3	10.8	Sales reps, wholesale & manufacturing, tech	1.2	24.1
General & operations managers	2.1	22.4	First-line supervisors of mechanics	1.0	23.6

Source: Industry-Occupation Matrix, Bureau of Labor Statistics. These data are reported based on 4-digit NAICS categories but have been matched to corresponding 6-digit NAICS industry codes. The change reported for each occupation to the year 2014 is a percent of growth or decline as estimated by the Bureau of Labor Statistics. The abbreviation nec stands for 'not elsewhere classified.'

LOCATION BY STATE AND REGIONAL CONCENTRATION

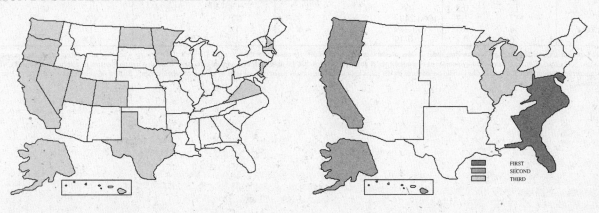

FIRST
SECOND
THIRD

INDUSTRY DATA BY STATE

State	Establishments Total (number)	% of U.S.	Employment Total (number)	% of U.S.	Per Estab.	Payroll Total ($ mil.)	Per Empl. ($)	Sales Total ($ mil.)	% of U.S.	Per Estab. ($)
California	1,325	13.1	13,365	18.1	10	361.5	27,049	3,709.9	22.2	2,799,959
Texas	737	7.3	6,145	8.3	8	150.2	24,444	1,503.6	9.0	2,040,221
Florida	681	6.7	3,948	5.3	6	101.4	25,677	868.9	5.2	1,275,903
New York	558	5.5	3,474	4.7	6	86.2	24,826	863.0	5.2	1,546,681
Ohio	408	4.0	2,932	4.0	7	64.8	22,105	612.0	3.7	1,499,988
Illinois	384	3.8	2,536	3.4	7	57.0	22,479	534.7	3.2	1,392,326
New Jersey	350	3.5	2,302	3.1	7	57.8	25,095	527.5	3.2	1,507,071
Massachusetts	232	2.3	1,987	2.7	9	68.1	34,297	515.9	3.1	2,223,586
Virginia	292	2.9	2,536	3.4	9	63.7	25,100	509.4	3.1	1,744,486
Pennsylvania	395	3.9	2,810	3.8	7	58.2	20,713	480.6	2.9	1,216,792
Michigan	308	3.0	2,205	3.0	7	54.4	24,658	439.7	2.6	1,427,633
Georgia	308	3.0	2,052	2.8	7	56.6	27,595	409.9	2.5	1,330,692
Washington	254	2.5	1,882	2.5	7	47.7	25,338	408.4	2.4	1,607,850
Oregon	160	1.6	1,150	1.6	7	30.4	26,437	317.3	1.9	1,982,869
Maryland	204	2.0	1,369	1.9	7	34.8	25,387	315.1	1.9	1,544,569
Colorado	185	1.8	1,480	2.0	8	37.0	25,026	313.0	1.9	1,692,103
North Carolina	281	2.8	1,586	2.1	6	38.8	24,452	303.0	1.8	1,078,295
Minnesota	192	1.9	1,438	1.9	7	35.4	24,598	297.1	1.8	1,547,620
Missouri	202	2.0	1,244	1.7	6	31.8	25,565	265.5	1.6	1,314,149
Tennessee	172	1.7	1,052	1.4	6	24.9	23,637	224.4	1.3	1,304,855
Wisconsin	185	1.8	1,141	1.5	6	27.5	24,099	221.6	1.3	1,197,859
Indiana	212	2.1	1,547	2.1	7	32.8	21,183	214.3	1.3	1,010,887
Utah	113	1.1	872	1.2	8	19.0	21,823	192.5	1.2	1,703,920
Connecticut	111	1.1	804	1.1	7	22.1	27,439	192.4	1.2	1,733,045
Louisiana	127	1.3	776	1.0	6	16.4	21,120	146.3	0.9	1,152,346
Kansas	105	1.0	733	1.0	7	16.0	21,793	145.8	0.9	1,388,762
Alabama	143	1.4	876	1.2	6	19.1	21,836	141.7	0.8	990,895
Nevada	88	0.9	608	0.8	7	15.1	24,811	137.6	0.8	1,563,773
Hawaii	39	0.4	457	0.6	12	9.5	20,770	128.9	0.8	3,303,846
Kentucky	126	1.2	743	1.0	6	15.6	21,039	121.6	0.7	964,992
Oklahoma	120	1.2	629	0.9	5	12.2	19,450	116.4	0.7	970,192
New Hampshire	72	0.7	495	0.7	7	11.5	23,299	108.7	0.7	1,509,903
South Carolina	122	1.2	689	0.9	6	14.3	20,713	100.9	0.6	826,787

Continued on next page.

INDUSTRY DATA BY STATE - Continued

State	Establishments Total (number)	Establishments % of U.S.	Employment Total (number)	Employment % of U.S.	Employment Per Estab.	Payroll Total ($ mil.)	Payroll Per Empl. ($)	Sales Total ($ mil.)	Sales % of U.S.	Sales Per Estab. ($)
Iowa	108	1.1	533	0.7	5	10.4	19,589	89.1	0.5	825,074
New Mexico	58	0.6	405	0.5	7	9.6	23,593	86.8	0.5	1,496,397
Nebraska	61	0.6	407	0.6	7	8.8	21,720	75.2	0.5	1,232,033
Arkansas	81	0.8	454	0.6	6	10.6	23,313	74.6	0.4	920,593
Alaska	31	0.3	267	0.4	9	6.6	24,873	70.8	0.4	2,282,452
Delaware	30	0.3	209	0.3	7	6.2	29,464	65.9	0.4	2,196,833
Idaho	53	0.5	334	0.5	6	7.0	20,832	55.7	0.3	1,051,208
Mississippi	62	0.6	326	0.4	5	8.0	24,558	54.6	0.3	881,194
North Dakota	40	0.4	272	0.4	7	5.9	21,603	52.9	0.3	1,322,825
Rhode Island	24	0.2	183	0.2	8	5.1	27,896	48.7	0.3	2,030,958
Montana	42	0.4	257	0.3	6	5.2	20,109	40.1	0.2	955,286
West Virginia	52	0.5	242	0.3	5	3.9	16,182	33.6	0.2	647,000
Maine	44	0.4	130	0.2	3	2.9	22,062	25.7	0.2	584,955
Wyoming	23	0.2	96	0.1	4	1.6	16,719	12.4	0.1	540,087
Vermont	17	0.2	68	0.1	4	1.5	21,824	10.2	0.1	599,706
Arizona	177	1.7	1000-2499	-	-	(D)	-	(D)	-	-
South Dakota	34	0.3	100-249	-	-	(D)	-	(D)	-	-
D.C.	6	0.1	0-19	-	-	(D)	-	(D)	-	-

Source: 2002 *Economic Census*. The states are in descending order of sales or establishments (if sales data are missing for the majority). The symbol (D) appears when data are withheld to prevent disclosure of competitive information. States marked with (D) are sorted by number of establishments. A dash (-) indicates that the data element cannot be calculated. Shaded *states* on the state map indicate those states which have proportionately greater representation in the industry than would be indicated by the states population; the ratio is based on total sales or number of establishments. Shaded *regions* indicate where the industry is regionally most concentrated.

NAICS 443130 - CAMERA AND PHOTOGRAPHIC SUPPLIES STORES*

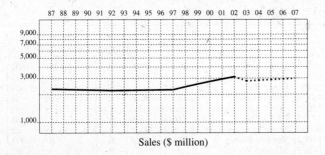

Sales ($ million)

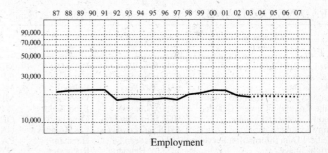

Employment

GENERAL STATISTICS

Year	Establishments (number)	Employment (number)	Payroll ($ million)	Sales ($ million)	Employees per Establishment (number)	Sales per Establishment ($)	Payroll per Employee ($)
1987	3,791	21,425	276.0	2,294.0	6	605,117	12,882
1988	3,618	22,043	314.4	2,276.7 e	6	629,270	14,263
1989	3,591	22,181	330.8	2,259.4 e	6	629,184	14,914
1990	3,594	22,481	353.5	2,242.1 e	6	623,845	15,724
1991	3,613	22,495	354.6	2,224.8 e	6	615,776	15,763
1992	3,012	17,407	285.4	2,207.5	6	732,902	16,396
1993	3,035	17,965	296.8	2,216.3 e	6	730,247	16,521
1994	2,958	17,704	297.0	2,225.2 e	6	752,265	16,776
1995	2,935	17,792	302.2	2,234.0 e	6	761,158	16,985
1996	2,815 e	18,213 e	334.7 e	2,242.9 e	7 e	796,767 e	18,377 e
1997	2,843	17,508	324.0	2,251.7	6	792,015	18,506
1998	3,156	20,009	390.0	2,422.4 e	6	767,567	19,491
1999	3,080	20,761	400.1	2,593.2 e	7	841,942	19,272
2000	3,088	22,229	436.1	2,763.9 e	7	895,052	19,617
2001	3,082	22,106	447.1	2,934.7 e	7	952,194	20,224
2002	2,762	19,420	423.4	3,105.4	7	1,124,331	21,803
2003	2,613	18,779	429.7	2,795.0 p	7	996,104 p	22,884
2004	2,640 p	19,131 p	434.1 p	2,840.8 p	7 p	1,023,222 p	22,370 p
2005	2,583 p	19,031 p	443.2 p	2,886.5 p	7 p	1,050,340 p	22,892 p
2006	2,526 p	18,931 p	452.2 p	2,932.3 p	7 p	1,077,458 p	23,414 p
2007	2,469 p	18,831 p	461.3 p	2,978.1 p	7 p	1,104,576 p	23,936 p

Sources: *Economic Census of the United States*, 1987, 1992, 1997, and 2002. Establishment counts, employment, and payroll are from *County Business Patterns* for non-Census years. Values followed by a 'p' are projections by the editors. Sales data for non-Census years are extrapolations, marked by 'e'. Data are the most recent available at this level of detail.

INDICES OF CHANGE

Year	Establishments (number)	Employment (number)	Payroll ($ million)	Sales ($ million)	Employees per Establishment (number)	Sales per Establishment ($)	Payroll per Employee ($)
1987	137.3	110.3	65.2	73.9	81.1	53.8	59.1
1992	109.1	89.6	67.4	71.1	82.5	65.2	75.2
1993	109.9	92.5	70.1	71.4 e	83.9	64.9	75.8
1994	107.1	91.2	70.1	71.7 e	85.3	66.9	76.9
1995	106.3	91.6	71.4	71.9 e	86.8	67.7	77.9
1996	101.9 e	93.8 e	79.0 e	72.2 e	92.4 e	70.9 e	84.3 e
1997	102.9	90.2	76.5	72.5	88.2	70.4	84.9
1998	114.3	103.0	92.1	78.0 e	89.6	68.3	89.4
1999	111.5	106.9	94.5	83.5 e	95.3	74.9	88.4
2000	111.8	114.5	103.0	89.0 e	102.4	79.6	90.0
2001	111.6	113.8	105.6	94.5 e	102.4	84.7	92.8
2002	100.0	100.0	100.0	100.0	100.0	100.0	100.0
2003	94.6	96.7	101.5	90.0 p	102.2	88.6 p	105.0
2004	95.6 p	98.5 p	102.5 p	91.5 p	101.4 p	91.0 p	102.6 p
2005	93.5 p	98.0 p	104.7 p	93.0 p	102.6 p	93.4 p	105.0 p
2006	91.5 p	97.5 p	106.8 p	94.4 p	103.7 p	95.8 p	107.4 p
2007	89.4 p	97.0 p	108.9 p	95.9 p	104.9 p	98.2 p	109.8 p

Sources: Same as General Statistics. The values shown reflect change from the base year, 2002. Values above 100 mean greater than 2002, values below 100 mean less than 2002, and a value of 100 in the 1987-2001 or 2003-2007 period means same as 2002. Values followed by a 'p' are projections by the editors; 'e' stands for extrapolation. Data are the most recent available at this level of detail.

SELECTED RATIOS

For 2002	Avg. of All Retail	Analyzed Industry	Index	For 2002	Avg. of All Retail	Analyzed Industry	Index
Employees per Establishment	17	7	41	Sales per Employee	174,682	159,907	92
Payroll per Establishment	333,445	153,303	46	Sales per Establishment	3,332,269	1,124,331	34
Payroll per Employee	20,311	21,803	107	Expenses per Establishment	na	na	na

Sources: Same as General Statistics. The 'Average of All' column, Wholesale or Retail, represents the average of the sector reported for the most recent complete year available. The Index shows the relationship between the Average and the Analyzed Industry. For example, 100 means that they are equal; 500 that the Analyzed Industry is five times the average; 50 means that the Analyzed Industry is half the national average. The abbreviation 'na' is used to show that data are 'not available'.

*Equivalent to SIC 5946.

LEADING COMPANIES   Number shown: **15**   Total sales ($ mil): **1,275**   Total employment (000): **11.5**

Company Name	Address				CEO Name	Phone	Co. Type	Sales ($ mil)	Empl. (000)
Ritz Camera Centers Inc.	6711 Ritz Way	Beltsville	MD	20705	David M. Ritz	301-419-0000	R	1,135	10.7
Waterhouse nc.	670 Queen St	Honolulu	HI	96813	Edwin Wong	808-592-4800	R	36*	0.4
Inkley's Inc.	6711 Ritz Way	Beltsville	MD	20705	David Ritz		S	24*	<0.1
Adray Appliance & Photo Center	20219 Carlysle	Dearborn	MI	48124	Debra Adray	313-274-9500	R	20*	0.1
Mike Crivello's Camera Centers	18110 Bluemnd	Brookfield	WI	53045	Sebastian Crivello	262-782-4303	R	17*	<0.1
Dodd Camera and Video	2077 East 30th St	Cleveland	OH	44115	RL Greiner	216-361-6800	R	12*	<0.1
Samy's Camera Inc.	431 S Fairfax Ave	Los Angeles	CA	90036	Samy Kamienowizz	323-938-2420	R	8*	<0.1
Medical Data Information Services	417 Caredean Dr	Horsham	PA	19044	Stephen Fosnot	215-672-9367	R	6*	<0.1
Wright Images	3333 W Henrietta	Rochester	NY	14623	Michael Wright		R	5*	<0.1
Alan Gordon Enterprises Inc.	5625 Melrose Ave	Hollywood	CA	90038	G Loucks	323-466-3561	R	4*	<0.1
Hoag Enterprises Inc.	PO Box 4406	Springfield	MO	65808	Charles Hoag	417-883-8300	R	3*	<0.1
Dixie Color Lab L.L.C.	510 S Highland St	Memphis	TN	38111	Britt Woodward	901-458-1818	R	2*	<0.1
Harold Tymer Company Inc.	1601 Broadway St	Vancouver	WA	98663	Bill Tymer	360-696-0859	R	2*	<0.1
Broadway Photo Video Retail	777 Bloomfield Ave	Caldwell	NJ	07006	Vicky Feinsilver	973-226-1313	R	2*	<0.1
Klein Camera and Hi-Fi Inc.	44 Main St	Westport	CT	06880	Robert Hertzel	203-227-6980	R	1*	<0.1

Source: *Ward's Business Directory of U.S. Private and Public Companies*, Volumes 1 and 2, 2005. The company type code used is as follows: P - Public, R - Private, S - Subsidiary, D - Division, J - Joint Venture, A - Affiliate, G - Group. Sales are in millions of dollars, employees are in thousands. An asterisk (*) indicates an estimated sales volume. The symbol < stands for 'less than'. Company names and addresses are truncated, in some cases, to fit into the available space.

OCCUPATIONS EMPLOYED BY ELECTRONICS & APPLIANCE STORES

Occupation	% of Total 2004	Change to 2014	Occupation	% of Total 2004	Change to 2014
Retail salespersons	33.8	23.3	Office clerks, general	2.1	10.1
Cashiers, except gaming	5.7	11.1	Truck drivers, light or delivery services	2.1	23.1
First-line supervisors/managers of retail sales workers	5.6	13.5	Computer support specialists	1.8	24.5
Computer, automated teller, & office machine repairers	3.9	12.0	Bookkeeping, accounting, & auditing clerks	1.7	11.2
Customer service representatives	3.5	26.4	Shipping, receiving, & traffic clerks	1.6	12.0
Home appliance repairers	2.7	-5.6	Laborers & freight, stock, & material movers, hand	1.6	10.9
Stock clerks & order fillers	2.7	-5.5	Sales representatives, services, nec	1.2	24.0
Electronic home entertainment installers & repairers	2.3	10.8	Sales reps, wholesale & manufacturing, tech	1.2	24.1
General & operations managers	2.1	22.4	First-line supervisors of mechanics	1.0	23.6

Source: *Industry-Occupation Matrix*, Bureau of Labor Statistics. These data are reported based on 4-digit NAICS categories but have been matched to corresponding 6-digit NAICS industry codes. The change reported for each occupation to the year 2014 is a percent of growth or decline as estimated by the Bureau of Labor Statistics. The abbreviation nec stands for 'not elsewhere classified.'

LOCATION BY STATE AND REGIONAL CONCENTRATION

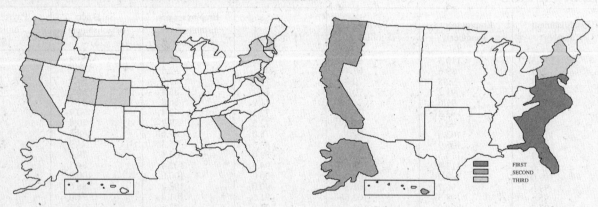

INDUSTRY DATA BY STATE

State	Establishments Total (number)	% of U.S.	Employment Total (number)	% of U.S.	Per Estab.	Payroll Total ($ mil.)	Per Empl. ($)	Sales Total ($ mil.)	% of U.S.	Per Estab. ($)
New York	228	8.2	1,766	8.9	8	61.1	34,603	857.5	27.2	3,761,004
California	376	13.5	2,459	12.5	7	61.4	24,967	411.4	13.0	1,094,263
Texas	149	5.4	911	4.6	6	20.8	22,777	129.6	4.1	869,591
Pennsylvania	156	5.6	1,075	5.4	7	20.0	18,608	121.3	3.8	777,673

Continued on next page.

INDUSTRY DATA BY STATE - Continued

State	Establishments Total (number)	% of U.S.	Employment Total (number)	% of U.S.	Per Estab.	Payroll Total ($ mil.)	Per Empl. ($)	Sales Total ($ mil.)	% of U.S.	Per Estab. ($)
Florida	144	5.2	816	4.1	6	17.6	21,544	115.0	3.6	798,528
Illinois	124	4.5	953	4.8	8	18.4	19,343	113.7	3.6	917,194
Georgia	113	4.1	873	4.4	8	20.0	22,885	101.0	3.2	893,735
Ohio	115	4.1	934	4.7	8	14.6	15,615	98.0	3.1	852,252
Minnesota	75	2.7	934	4.7	12	15.6	16,687	86.5	2.7	1,153,240
Massachusetts	83	3.0	636	3.2	8	13.9	21,863	86.0	2.7	1,036,723
Washington	78	2.8	505	2.6	6	11.8	23,416	80.1	2.5	1,027,436
Michigan	69	2.5	532	2.7	8	10.9	20,534	76.0	2.4	1,101,174
Maryland	64	2.3	539	2.7	8	11.1	20,531	73.7	2.3	1,152,203
Colorado	56	2.0	534	2.7	10	13.3	24,869	69.1	2.2	1,233,250
Virginia	94	3.4	596	3.0	6	10.4	17,468	66.3	2.1	705,234
New Jersey	88	3.2	466	2.4	5	9.9	21,165	58.1	1.8	659,977
Indiana	41	1.5	306	1.5	7	7.5	24,402	51.8	1.6	1,262,415
North Carolina	58	2.1	428	2.2	7	7.9	18,451	47.2	1.5	813,431
Utah	30	1.1	288	1.5	10	5.8	19,972	41.6	1.3	1,386,167
Oregon	65	2.3	308	1.6	5	5.6	18,039	40.6	1.3	624,600
Tennessee	35	1.3	259	1.3	7	5.1	19,815	35.3	1.1	1,008,771
Missouri	37	1.3	309	1.6	8	6.2	19,951	30.8	1.0	832,297
Connecticut	44	1.6	267	1.4	6	5.2	19,532	30.8	1.0	699,114
Wisconsin	36	1.3	249	1.3	7	4.2	17,012	24.3	0.8	675,722
Louisiana	31	1.1	214	1.1	7	4.4	20,612	21.6	0.7	696,000
New Hampshire	27	1.0	164	0.8	6	3.4	20,890	21.1	0.7	782,481
Alabama	28	1.0	196	1.0	7	3.8	19,408	19.6	0.6	701,000
South Carolina	37	1.3	194	1.0	5	3.3	16,866	17.0	0.5	459,514
Kansas	24	0.9	165	0.8	7	3.3	19,927	16.3	0.5	677,625
Delaware	10	0.4	115	0.6	11	2.4	21,252	15.1	0.5	1,513,300
Oklahoma	10	0.4	84	0.4	8	2.4	28,631	15.1	0.5	1,512,800
Iowa	26	0.9	177	0.9	7	2.4	13,723	15.1	0.5	579,115
Nevada	18	0.6	146	0.7	8	3.6	24,795	14.4	0.5	801,444
New Mexico	20	0.7	102	0.5	5	2.4	23,314	12.4	0.4	618,250
Kentucky	17	0.6	128	0.6	8	2.5	19,547	11.4	0.4	672,941
Idaho	15	0.5	87	0.4	6	1.9	21,609	9.5	0.3	634,733
Nebraska	11	0.4	81	0.4	7	1.5	19,037	9.3	0.3	845,818
Hawaii	12	0.4	76	0.4	6	1.3	17,158	7.5	0.2	626,500
Rhode Island	10	0.4	60	0.3	6	1.1	19,100	7.4	0.2	737,900
Vermont	9	0.3	60	0.3	7	1.0	15,867	6.3	0.2	700,333
Maine	12	0.4	62	0.3	5	1.1	17,371	5.6	0.2	470,583
West Virginia	8	0.3	56	0.3	7	0.9	16,804	5.0	0.2	626,250
Mississippi	6	0.2	48	0.2	8	1.0	21,563	4.6	0.1	763,167
North Dakota	6	0.2	56	0.3	9	0.9	15,250	4.2	0.1	705,000
Montana	5	0.2	28	0.1	6	0.6	19,929	3.5	0.1	709,200
Arkansas	5	0.2	27	0.1	5	0.5	18,556	2.7	0.1	530,000
Wyoming	5	0.2	18	0.1	4	0.3	16,222	1.9	0.1	382,600
Arizona	39	1.4	250-499	-	-	(D)	-	(D)	-	-
D.C.	19	0.7	100-249	-	-	(D)	-	(D)	-	-
Alaska	7	0.3	20-99	-	-	(D)	-	(D)	-	-
South Dakota	4	0.1	0-19	-	-	(D)	-	(D)	-	-

Source: 2002 *Economic Census*. The states are in descending order of sales or establishments (if sales data are missing for the majority). The symbol (D) appears when data are withheld to prevent disclosure of competitive information. States marked with (D) are sorted by number of establishments. A dash (-) indicates that the data element cannot be calculated. Shaded *states* on the state map indicate those states which have proportionately greater representation in the industry than would be indicated by the states population; the ratio is based on total sales or number of establishments. Shaded *regions* indicate where the industry is regionally most concentrated.

NAICS 444100 - BUILDING MATERIAL AND SUPPLY DEALERS

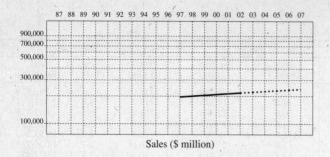

Sales ($ million)

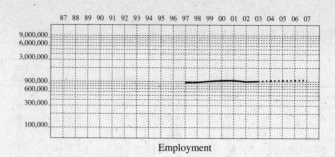

Employment

GENERAL STATISTICS

Year	Establishments (number)	Employment (number)	Payroll ($ million)	Sales ($ million)	Employees per Establishment (number)	Sales per Establishment ($)	Payroll per Employee ($)
1987	-	-	-	-	-	-	-
1988	-	-	-	-	-	-	-
1989	-	-	-	-	-	-	-
1990	-	-	-	-	-	-	-
1991	-	-	-	-	-	-	-
1992	-	-	-	-	-	-	-
1993	-	-	-	-	-	-	-
1994	-	-	-	-	-	-	-
1995	-	-	-	-	-	-	-
1996	-	-	-	-	-	-	-
1997	71,916	952,296	22,313.1	195,888.2	13	2,723,847	23,431
1998	71,482	963,535	24,255.8	200,170.6 e	13	2,800,293	25,174
1999	71,238	1,012,190	26,376.1	204,452.9 e	14	2,869,998	26,058
2000	70,931	1,055,242	28,421.7	208,735.3 e	15	2,942,794	26,934
2001	71,851	1,062,400	30,336.8	213,017.7 e	15	2,964,714	28,555
2002	67,472	995,037	26,462.2	217,300.0	15	3,220,595	26,594
2003	66,890	1,014,414	27,755.9	221,582.4 p	15	3,225,353 p	27,361
2004	67,042 p	1,050,669 p	30,089.0 p	225,864.7 p	16 p	3,312,490 p	28,748 p
2005	66,239 p	1,061,368 p	30,971.2 p	230,147.1 p	16 p	3,399,628 p	29,360 p
2006	65,436 p	1,072,067 p	31,853.4 p	234,429.5 p	16 p	3,486,765 p	29,972 p
2007	64,633 p	1,082,765 p	32,735.6 p	238,711.8 p	17 p	3,573,902 p	30,583 p

Source: Economic Census of the United States, 1997 and 2002. Establishment counts, employment, and payroll are from *County Business Patterns* for non-Census years. This is a newly defined industry. Data for prior years are unavailable at the time of publication but may become available over time. Values followed by 'p' are projections by the editors. Sales data for non-Census years are extrapolations, marked by 'e'.

INDICES OF CHANGE

Year	Establishments (number)	Employment (number)	Payroll ($ million)	Sales ($ million)	Employees per Establishment (number)	Sales per Establishment ($)	Payroll per Employee ($)
1987	-	-	-	-	-	-	-
1992	-	-	-	-	-	-	-
1993	-	-	-	-	-	-	-
1994	-	-	-	-	-	-	-
1995	-	-	-	-	-	-	-
1996	-	-	-	-	-	-	-
1997	106.6	95.7	84.3	90.1	89.8	84.6	88.1
1998	105.9	96.8	91.7	92.1 e	91.4	86.9	94.7
1999	105.6	101.7	99.7	94.1 e	96.3	89.1	98.0
2000	105.1	106.1	107.4	96.1 e	100.9	91.4	101.3
2001	106.5	106.8	114.6	98.0 e	100.3	92.1	107.4
2002	100.0	100.0	100.0	100.0	100.0	100.0	100.0
2003	99.1	101.9	104.9	102.0 p	102.8	100.1 p	102.9
2004	99.4 p	105.6 p	113.7 p	103.9 p	106.0 p	102.9 p	108.1 p
2005	98.2 p	106.7 p	117.0 p	105.9 p	108.1 p	105.6 p	110.4 p
2006	97.0 p	107.7 p	120.4 p	107.9 p	110.3 p	108.3 p	112.7 p
2007	95.8 p	108.8 p	123.7 p	109.9 p	112.4 p	111.0 p	115.0 p

Sources: Same as General Statistics. The values shown reflect change from the base year, 2002. Values above 100 mean greater than 2002, values below 100 mean less than 2002, and a value of 100 in the 1987-2001 or 2003-2007 period means same as 2002. Values followed by a 'p' are projections by the editors; 'e' stands for extrapolation. Data are the most recent available at this level of detail.

SELECTED RATIOS

For 2002	Avg. of All Retail	Analyzed Industry	Index	For 2002	Avg. of All Retail	Analyzed Industry	Index
Employees per Establishment	17	15	87	Sales per Employee	174,682	218,384	125
Payroll per Establishment	333,445	392,195	118	Sales per Establishment	3,332,269	3,220,595	97
Payroll per Employee	20,311	26,594	131	Expenses per Establishment	na	na	na

Sources: Same as General Statistics. The 'Average of All' column, Wholesale or Retail, represents the average of the sector reported for the most recent complete year available. The Index shows the relationship between the Average and the Analyzed Industry. For example, 100 means that they are equal; 500 that the Analyzed Industry is five times the average; 50 means that the Analyzed Industry is half the national average. The abbreviation 'na' is used to show that data are 'not available'.

LEADING COMPANIES   Number shown: **75**   Total sales ($ mil): **158,498**   Total employment (000): **726.4**

Company Name	Address				CEO Name	Phone	Co. Type	Sales ($ mil)	Empl. (000)
Home Depot Inc.	2455 Paces Ferry Rd	Atlanta	GA	30339		770-433-8211	P	64,806	300.0
Lowe's Companies Inc.	PO Box 1111	N. Wilkesboro	NC	28656		336-658-4000	P	36,464	123.0
Kmart Corp.	3100 W Big Beaver	Troy	MI	48084		248-643-1000	D	17,072	158.0
Sherwin-Williams Co.	PO Box 6027	Cleveland	OH	44101	C M Connor	216-566-2000	P	6,114	25.8
Menard Inc.	4777 Menard Dr	Eau Claire	WI	54703	John R Menard, Jr	715-876-5911	R	6,065*	27.0
Collins and Aikman Corp.	250 Stephenson	Troy	MI	48083		248-824-2500	P	3,984	23.9
Stock Building Supply Holdings	PO Box 58515	Raleigh	NC	27658	Fenton N Hord	919-431-1000	S	3,580	10.0
Do It Best Corp.	PO Box 868	Fort Wayne	IN	46801	Steve Hawkinson	260-748-5300	R	2,727	1.4
84 Lumber Co.	PO Box 8484	Eighty Four	PA	15330	Joseph A Hardy	724-228-8820	R	2,538	6.8
Building Materials Holding Corp.	4 Embarcadero Ctr	San Francisco	CA	94111	Robert E Mellor	415-627-9100	P	2,092	12.0
Lanoga Corp.	PO Box 97040	Redmond	WA	98073	Paul Brewer	425-883-4125	R	1,952	8.0
Dan Incorporated Oregon	PO Box 2200	Oregon City	OR	97045	Craig T Danielson	503-655-9141	R	1,345*	0.3
Andersons Inc.	PO Box 119	Maumee	OH	43537	Michael J Anderson	419-893-5050	P	1,247	2.9
Foxworth-Galbraith Lumber Co.	17111 Waterview	Dallas	TX	75252	JC Galbraith	972-437-6100	R	641*	2.5
Wickes Lumber	706 N Deerpath Dr	Vernon Hills	IL	60061	Barry Segal	847-367-3400	D	578	2.0
Forks Prairie Mart Inc.	PO Box 1429	Forks	WA	98331	Bert W Paul	360-374-6161	R	471*	<0.1
Kelly-Moore Paint Company Inc.	PO Box 3016	San Carlos	CA	94070	Herb Giffins	650-592-8337	R	325*	0.3
United Building Centers	125 W 5th St	Winona	MN	55987	Dale Kukowski	507-452-2361	D	300*	2.4
Central Michigan Lumber Co.	500 E Steel St	St. Johns	MI	48879	Daniel Rogers	989-224-1257	R	262*	0.9
M.L. McDonald Sales Inc.	PO Box 315	Watertown	MA	02472	Kevin ODonnell	617-923-0900	R	236*	0.2
Edward Hines Lumber Co.	1000 Corp. Grove	Buffalo Grove	IL	60089	Edward Hines	847-353-7700	R	220*	0.1
H and S Hardware	5416 Preston Hwy	Louisville	KY	40213	Stanley Soswksy	502-969-1337	R	210*	0.1
Dunn Edwards Corp.	4885 E 52nd Pl	Los Angeles	CA	90040	Ken Edwards	323-771-3330	R	208*	1.5
Scherer Brothers Lumber Co.	9410 73rd Ave N	Brooklyn Park	MN	55428	Peter L Scherer	612-379-9633	R	202*	0.8
Wolohan Lumber Co.	PO Box 3235	Saginaw	MI	48605		989-793-4532	R	197*	0.7
Lampert Yards Inc.	1850 Como Ave	St. Paul	MN	55108	Daniel L Fesler	651-695-3600	R	182*	0.5
Great Plains Companies Inc.	One Carlson Pkwy	Plymouth	MN	55447	Michael R Wigley	763-258-0110	R	179*	0.2
K and A Lumber Company Inc.	1001 W Mowry Dr	Homestead	FL	33030	Richard Jackson II	305-245-5312	R	179*	0.1
Orchard Supply Hardware Stores	125 N Milpitas Blvd	Milpitas	CA	95035		408-945-9555	S	177*	<0.1
National Home Centers Inc.	PO Box 789	Springdale	AR	72765	Danny R Funderburg	479-756-1700	R	175*	0.8
National Lumber Co.	PO Box 32	Mansfield	MA	02048	Steven Kaitz	508-339-8020	R	175	0.4
Scheels All Sports Inc.	3202 13th S Ave	Fargo	ND	58106	Steve D Scheel	701-298-2918	R	167*	2.0
Alexander Lumber Co.	PO Box 831	Aurora	IL	60507	Walter Alexander	630-844-5123	R	161*	<0.1
Magnolia Steel Company Inc.	PO Box 5007	Meridian	MS	39302	Cecil Crowe	601-693-4301	R	149*	0.2
Central Valley Builders Supply	1100 Vintage Ave	St. Helena	CA	94574	Kathleen Patterson	707-963-3622	R	134*	0.2
Wille Electric Supply Co.	PO Box 3246	Modesto	CA	95353	LR Robinson III	209-527-6800	R	131*	<0.1
E.C. Barton and Co.	PO Box 4040	Jonesboro	AR	72403	Niel Crowson	870-932-6673	R	125*	0.5
H.W. Jenkins Lumber Co.	PO Box 18347	Memphis	TN	38181	HW Jenkins Jr	901-363-7641	R	114*	0.1
Leaman Building Materials L.P.	PO Box 80	Thompsons	TX	77481	Mick McKirahan	281-238-1100	R	102*	0.5
Williams Kitchen and Bath	658 Richmond	Grand Rapids	MI	49504	James Williams	616-456-1613	R	97*	0.5
Justin Industries Inc.	PO Box 548	Fort Worth	TX	76101	Randy Watson	817-336-5125	S	96*	1.7
Hirshfield's Inc.	725 2nd Ave N	Minneapolis	MN	55405	Hans Hirshfield	612-377-3910	R	93*	0.5
Interceramic Inc.	2333 S Jupiter Rd	Garland	TX	75041	Victor Almeida	214-503-5500	S	85*	0.2
Vidalia Naval Stores Co.	PO Box 1659	Vidalia	GA	30475	Hugh Peterson Jr	912-537-8964	R	85*	0.3
McLendon Hardware Inc.	440 Rainer Ave S	Renton	WA	98055	Gail McLendon	425-235-3555	R	84*	0.5
McQueeny-Lock Co.	520 W Pennway	Kansas City	MO	64108	Mike McQueeny	816-842-3503	R	84*	<0.1
Spahn and Rose Lumber Co.	PO Box 149	Dubuque	IA	52004	J Hannan	563-582-3606	R	83*	<0.1
Collins Pine Company Inc.	1618 SW 1st Ave	Portland	OR	97201	Eric Schooler	503-227-1219	R	82*	<0.1
Lezzer Lumber Inc.	PO Box 217	Curwensville	PA	16833	M Lezzer	814-236-0220	R	81*	0.3
Busy Beaver Building Centers Inc.	3130 William Pitt	Pittsburgh	PA	15238	Charles Bender	412-828-2323	R	79*	0.4
Vaughan and Sons Inc.	PO Box 17258	San Antonio	TX	78217	Curtis T Vaughan III	210-590-9300	R	79*	0.3
Martin Tractor Company Inc.	1737 SW 42nd St	Topeka	KS	66601	Harry Craig Jr	785-266-5770	R	77*	0.2
Pechin Shopping Village	PO Box 340	Dunbar	PA	15431	Sullivan D'Amico	724-277-4251	R	73*	0.4
Jewett-Cameron Trading Ltd.	PO Box 1010	North Plains	OR	97133	Donald M Boone	503-647-0110	P	71	<0.1
Ro-Mac Lumber and Supply Inc.	700 E Main St	Leesburg	FL	34748	HD Robuck Jr	352-787-4545	R	70*	0.3
Smede-Son Steel and Supply Inc.	12584 Inkster Rd	Redford	MI	48239	Albert Huyser	313-937-8300	R	68*	<0.1
N. Siperstein Inc.	415 Montgomery St	Jersey City	NJ	07302	Steven Siperstein	201-333-2215	R	67*	0.3
Atwood Distributing Inc.	2717 N Van Buren	Enid	OK	73703	G Atwood	580-233-3702	R	66*	0.9
Riverhead Building Supply Corp.	1093 Pulaski St	Riverhead	NY	11901	Edgar Goodale	631-727-1400	R	66*	0.3
Cleveland Wrecking Co.	628 E Edna Pl	Covina	CA	91723	Jim Sheridan	626-967-9799	R	64*	0.6
Western Products Inc.	117 23rd St N	Fargo	ND	58102	Michael J Bullinger	701-293-5310	R	64*	0.1
Zeeland Lumber and Supply Inc.	146 E Washington	Zeeland	MI	49464	H Van Den Bosch	616-772-2119	R	64*	0.1
F.E. Wheaton Lumber Co.	204 W Wheaton Ave	Yorkville	IL	60560	Jeff Brown	630-553-8300	R	63*	0.2
Wilson Lumber Company Inc.	4818 Meridian St	Huntsville	AL	35811	Ken J Wilson	256-852-7411	R	62*	0.2
R.P. Lumber Company Inc.	514 E Vandalia St	Edwardsville	IL	62025	Robert Plummer	618-656-1514	R	60*	0.4
Lummus Supply Co.	1554 Bolton Rd NW	Atlanta	GA	30331	WL Lummus	404-794-1501	R	59*	0.2
Scotty's Inc.	5300 N Recker Hwy	Winter Haven	FL	33880	Thomas E Morris		R	59*	0.5
Standard Companies Inc.	1535 Kalamazoo SE	Grand Rapids	MI	49507	T O Rottschafer	616-243-3653	R	58*	0.2
Gilcrest/Jewett Lumber Co.	PO Box 1000	Waukee	IA	50263	Phillip S Worth	515-280-7200	R	57*	0.2
T.H. Rogers Lumber Co.	PO Box 5770	Edmond	OK	73083	John M Kennedy	405-330-2181	R	57*	0.2
Millard Lumber Inc.	PO Box 45445	Omaha	NE	68145	G Richard Russell	402-896-2800	R	55*	0.2
Nickerson Lumber Co.	PO Box 99	Orleans	MA	02653	Joshua A Nickerson Jr	508-255-0200	R	54*	0.3
Atlas Tubular L.P.	1710 S Hwy 77	Robstown	TX	78380	John Hubbard	361-387-7505	R	50*	<0.1
National Lumber Co.	24595 Groesbeck	Warren	MI	48089	James Rosenthal	586-775-8200	R	50*	0.1
Wholesale Supply Group Inc.	PO Box 4080	Cleveland	TN	37320	Lloyd D Rogers	423-478-1191	R	50*	0.3

Source: Ward's Business Directory of U.S. Private and Public Companies, Volumes 1 and 2, 2005. The company type code used is as follows: P - Public, R - Private, S - Subsidiary, D - Division, J - Joint Venture, A - Affiliate, G - Group. Sales are in millions of dollars, employees are in thousands. An asterisk (*) indicates an estimated sales volume. The symbol < stands for 'less than'. Company names and addresses are truncated, in some cases, to fit into the available space.

OCCUPATIONS EMPLOYED BY BUILDING MATERIAL & SUPPLIES DEALERS

Occupation	% of Total 2004	Change to 2014	Occupation	% of Total 2004	Change to 2014
Retail salespersons	34.5	20.9	Sales reps, wholesale & manufacturing, exc tech	2.8	20.9
Cashiers, except gaming	11.7	8.8	Shipping, receiving, & traffic clerks	2.4	9.5
First-line supervisors/managers of retail sales workers	6.7	11.3	General & operations managers	2.0	19.7
Laborers & freight, stock, & material movers, hand	5.8	8.8	Truck drivers, heavy & tractor-trailer	1.7	20.8
Industrial truck & tractor operators	5.0	8.8	Bookkeeping, accounting, & auditing clerks	1.5	8.8
Stock clerks & order fillers	3.6	-7.4	Office clerks, general	1.3	7.6
Truck drivers, light or delivery services	3.2	20.8			

Source: Industry-Occupation Matrix, Bureau of Labor Statistics. These data are reported based on 4-digit NAICS categories but have been matched to corresponding 6-digit NAICS industry codes. The change reported for each occupation to the year 2014 is a percent of growth or decline as estimated by the Bureau of Labor Statistics. The abbreviation nec stands for 'not elsewhere classified.'

LOCATION BY STATE AND REGIONAL CONCENTRATION

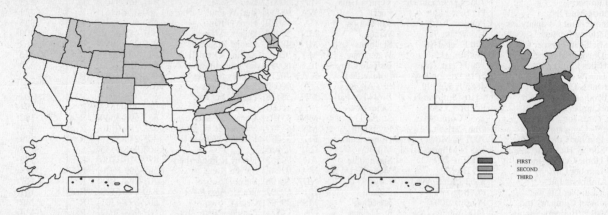

FIRST
SECOND
THIRD

INDUSTRY DATA BY STATE

State	Establishments Total (number)	% of U.S.	Employment Total (number)	% of U.S.	Per Estab.	Payroll Total ($ mil.)	Per Empl. ($)	Sales Total ($ mil.)	% of U.S.	Per Estab. ($)
Texas	4,068	6.1	66,977	6.8	16	1,691.3	25,252	14,375.6	6.7	3,533,814
California	5,606	8.3	54,476	5.5	10	1,646.6	30,226	12,528.7	5.8	2,234,869
New York	4,049	6.0	53,387	5.4	13	1,502.3	28,140	12,096.4	5.6	2,987,497
Illinois	2,661	4.0	43,161	4.4	16	1,165.4	27,000	9,349.2	4.3	3,513,411
Pennsylvania	2,880	4.3	39,523	4.0	14	995.4	25,186	8,208.7	3.8	2,850,253
Ohio	2,773	4.1	39,519	4.0	14	974.2	24,651	7,957.5	3.7	2,869,631
Georgia	1,948	2.9	32,918	3.3	17	896.5	27,235	7,450.3	3.5	3,824,569
Virginia	1,459	2.2	25,353	2.6	17	666.5	26,291	5,897.0	2.7	4,041,793
Massachusetts	1,468	2.2	23,261	2.4	16	763.0	32,801	5,734.5	2.7	3,906,305
Florida	3,798	5.7	24,559	2.5	6	722.3	29,410	5,210.4	2.4	1,371,876
Indiana	1,685	2.5	24,540	2.5	15	599.5	24,428	4,892.9	2.3	2,903,772
Minnesota	1,623	2.4	21,787	2.2	13	581.3	26,681	4,804.7	2.2	2,960,375
Michigan	2,706	4.0	22,504	2.3	8	662.6	29,444	4,745.7	2.2	1,753,782
Tennessee	1,502	2.2	20,691	2.1	14	540.2	26,106	4,482.9	2.1	2,984,646
Washington	1,372	2.0	20,354	2.1	15	594.7	29,217	4,345.8	2.0	3,167,503
Missouri	1,676	2.5	22,477	2.3	13	534.3	23,771	4,294.3	2.0	2,562,223
Colorado	1,195	1.8	19,169	1.9	16	528.4	27,565	4,104.1	1.9	3,434,391
North Carolina	2,215	3.3	16,738	1.7	8	507.7	30,333	3,904.5	1.8	1,762,772
New Jersey	1,796	2.7	15,244	1.5	8	555.9	36,469	3,644.7	1.7	2,029,360
Alabama	1,145	1.7	15,338	1.6	13	352.9	23,007	3,026.1	1.4	2,642,871
Kentucky	1,143	1.7	14,143	1.4	12	351.8	24,873	2,942.9	1.4	2,574,675
Wisconsin	1,589	2.4	15,601	1.6	10	426.1	27,315	2,917.0	1.4	1,835,768
Louisiana	1,082	1.6	14,391	1.5	13	327.9	22,785	2,900.8	1.3	2,680,970
Oregon	958	1.4	11,141	1.1	12	318.8	28,612	2,497.0	1.2	2,606,439
Iowa	1,108	1.6	11,746	1.2	11	281.6	23,977	2,330.9	1.1	2,103,661
Maryland	985	1.5	8,302	0.8	8	300.3	36,177	2,141.8	1.0	2,174,389
Connecticut	849	1.3	7,674	0.8	9	296.0	38,576	2,080.2	1.0	2,450,234
Oklahoma	873	1.3	10,501	1.1	12	244.6	23,290	2,041.3	0.9	2,338,288
South Carolina	1,115	1.7	8,386	0.8	8	250.6	29,884	1,816.7	0.8	1,629,312
Kansas	852	1.3	9,378	0.9	11	223.2	23,797	1,732.2	0.8	2,033,102
Arkansas	781	1.2	8,475	0.9	11	197.5	23,309	1,720.7	0.8	2,203,137
Mississippi	748	1.1	8,735	0.9	12	201.1	23,027	1,710.9	0.8	2,287,238
New Hampshire	482	0.7	7,086	0.7	15	218.7	30,869	1,661.5	0.8	3,447,104
Nebraska	684	1.0	7,470	0.8	11	184.6	24,708	1,418.0	0.7	2,073,069
West Virginia	498	0.7	6,176	0.6	12	141.7	22,950	1,236.6	0.6	2,483,078
New Mexico	449	0.7	5,866	0.6	13	144.0	24,552	1,164.4	0.5	2,593,236
Idaho	502	0.7	5,670	0.6	11	141.9	25,019	1,161.9	0.5	2,314,468

Continued on next page.

INDUSTRY DATA BY STATE - Continued

State	Establishments		Employment			Payroll		Sales		
	Total (number)	% of U.S.	Total (number)	% of U.S.	Per Estab.	Total ($ mil.)	Per Empl. ($)	Total ($ mil.)	% of U.S.	Per Estab. ($)
Utah	538	0.8	4,765	0.5	9	141.0	29,588	1,063.1	0.5	1,975,968
Maine	493	0.7	3,935	0.4	8	111.4	28,320	883.6	0.4	1,792,201
Montana	474	0.7	4,191	0.4	9	97.9	23,358	815.9	0.4	1,721,241
Nevada	375	0.6	3,118	0.3	8	104.0	33,346	725.0	0.3	1,933,331
Hawaii	210	0.3	3,262	0.3	16	83.2	25,506	690.6	0.3	3,288,643
South Dakota	358	0.5	3,197	0.3	9	73.0	22,839	674.7	0.3	1,884,721
Rhode Island	213	0.3	2,573	0.3	12	84.2	32,717	653.3	0.3	3,067,188
Vermont	292	0.4	2,796	0.3	10	81.3	29,082	638.5	0.3	2,186,777
Delaware	222	0.3	2,105	0.2	9	66.5	31,596	494.9	0.2	2,229,342
Alaska	182	0.3	2,170	0.2	12	68.7	31,678	473.7	0.2	2,602,665
Wyoming	220	0.3	2,044	0.2	9	52.1	25,502	396.1	0.2	1,800,232
North Dakota	300	0.4	1,812	0.2	6	39.0	21,503	291.5	0.1	971,693
Arizona	941	1.4	2,416	0.2	3	45.1	18,675	260.9	0.1	277,275
D.C.	49	0.1	64	-	1	1.7	25,984	15.2	-	309,776

Source: 2002 *Economic Census*. The states are in descending order of sales or establishments (if sales data are missing for the majority). The symbol (D) appears when data are withheld to prevent disclosure of competitive information. States marked with (D) are sorted by number of establishments. A dash (-) indicates that the data element cannot be calculated. Shaded *states* on the state map indicate those states which have proportionately greater representation in the industry than would be indicated by the states population; the ratio is based on total sales or number of establishments. Shaded *regions* indicate where the industry is regionally most concentrated.

NAICS 444210 - OUTDOOR POWER EQUIPMENT STORES

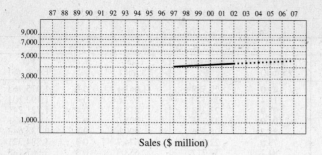

Sales ($ million)

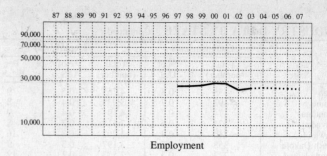

Employment

GENERAL STATISTICS

Year	Establishments (number)	Employment (number)	Payroll ($ million)	Sales ($ million)	Employees per Establishment (number)	Sales per Establishment ($)	Payroll per Employee ($)
1987	-	-	-	-	-	-	-
1988	-	-	-	-	-	-	-
1989	-	-	-	-	-	-	-
1990	-	-	-	-	-	-	-
1991	-	-	-	-	-	-	-
1992	-	-	-	-	-	-	-
1993	-	-	-	-	-	-	-
1994	-	-	-	-	-	-	-
1995	-	-	-	-	-	-	-
1996	-	-	-	-	-	-	-
1997	4,769	26,479	535.5	4,069.2	6	853,261	20,224
1998	4,769	26,580	582.6	4,136.2 e	6	867,310	21,919
1999	4,624	27,032	627.5	4,203.2 e	6	908,997	23,213
2000	4,558	28,606	678.3	4,270.2 e	6	936,859	23,711
2001	4,514	28,436	711.7	4,337.2 e	6	960,834	25,027
2002	4,386	24,293	590.4	4,404.2	6	1,004,151	24,301
2003	4,325	25,270	658.7	4,471.2 p	6	1,028,191 p	26,068
2004	4,248 p	25,700 p	693.4 p	4,538.2 p	6 p	1,058,559 p	26,939 p
2005	4,169 p	25,457 p	710.2 p	4,605.2 p	6 p	1,088,927 p	27,800 p
2006	4,090 p	25,214 p	727.0 p	4,672.2 p	6 p	1,119,295 p	28,661 p
2007	4,012 p	24,972 p	743.7 p	4,739.2 p	6 p	1,149,663 p	29,523 p

Source: *Economic Census of the United States*, 1997 and 2002. Establishment counts, employment, and payroll are from *County Business Patterns* for non-Census years. This is a newly defined industry. Data for prior years are unavailable at the time of publication but may become available over time. Values followed by 'p' are projections by the editors. Sales data for non-Census years are extrapolations, marked by 'e'.

INDICES OF CHANGE

Year	Establishments (number)	Employment (number)	Payroll ($ million)	Sales ($ million)	Employees per Establishment (number)	Sales per Establishment ($)	Payroll per Employee ($)
1987	-	-	-	-	-	-	-
1992	-	-	-	-	-	-	-
1993	-	-	-	-	-	-	-
1994	-	-	-	-	-	-	-
1995	-	-	-	-	-	-	-
1996	-	-	-	-	-	-	-
1997	108.7	109.0	90.7	92.4	101.1	85.0	83.2
1998	108.7	109.4	98.7	93.9 e	101.1	86.4	90.2
1999	105.4	111.3	106.3	95.4 e	104.7	90.5	95.5
2000	103.9	117.8	114.9	97.0 e	113.7	93.3	97.6
2001	102.9	117.1	120.6	98.5 e	113.7	95.7	103.0
2002	100.0	100.0	100.0	100.0	100.0	100.0	100.0
2003	98.6	104.0	111.6	101.5 p	105.5	102.4 p	107.3
2004	96.9 p	105.8 p	117.5 p	103.0 p	108.6 p	105.4 p	110.9 p
2005	95.1 p	104.8 p	120.3 p	104.6 p	109.3 p	108.4 p	114.4 p
2006	93.3 p	103.8 p	123.1 p	106.1 p	110.0 p	111.5 p	117.9 p
2007	91.5 p	102.8 p	126.0 p	107.6 p	110.7 p	114.5 p	121.5 p

Sources: Same as General Statistics. The values shown reflect change from the base year, 2002. Values above 100 mean greater than 2002, values below 100 mean less than 2002, and a value of 100 in the 1987-2001 or 2003-2007 period means same as 2002. Values followed by a 'p' are projections by the editors; 'e' stands for extrapolation. Data are the most recent available at this level of detail.

SELECTED RATIOS

For 2002	Avg. of All Retail	Analyzed Industry	Index	For 2002	Avg. of All Retail	Analyzed Industry	Index
Employees per Establishment	17	6	33	Sales per Employee	174,682	181,295	104
Payroll per Establishment	333,445	134,599	40	Sales per Establishment	3,332,269	1,004,151	30
Payroll per Employee	20,311	24,301	120	Expenses per Establishment	na	na	na

Sources: Same as General Statistics. The 'Average of All' column, Wholesale or Retail, represents the average of the sector reported for the most recent complete year available. The Index shows the relationship between the Average and the Analyzed Industry. For example, 100 means that they are equal; 500 that the Analyzed Industry is five times the average; 50 means that the Analyzed Industry is half the national average. The abbreviation 'na' is used to show that data are 'not available'.

LEADING COMPANIES   Number shown: 19   Total sales ($ mil): 228   Total employment (000): 0.5

Company Name	Address				CEO Name	Phone	Co. Type	Sales ($ mil)	Empl. (000)
Finch Services Inc.	1127 Littlestown Pke	Westminster	MD	21157	William Finch	410-876-2211	R	42*	0.1
D and G Equipment Inc.	2525 E Grand River	Williamston	MI	48895		517-655-4606	R	18*	<0.1
Walpole Feed and Supply Co.	PO Box 1723	Okeechobee	FL	34973	Edward Walpole	863-763-6905	R	15*	<0.1
AG-Power Inc.	6301 W University	Mc Kinney	TX	75071	Jack Radke	972-542-0301	R	13*	<0.1
WF Miller Turf & Industrial	PO Box 605	Novi	MI	48376	Mark Vogler	248-349-4100	R	13*	<0.1
Stevenson Tractor Inc.	1792 S Military Hwy	Chesapeake	VA	23320		757-420-4220	R	12*	<0.1
Umberger's of Fontana Inc.	1067 Horseshoe Pke	Lebanon	PA	17042	Donald Umberger	717-867-5161	R	12*	<0.1
Morton Equipment Co.	PO Box 1056	Levelland	TX	79336	Barry Armes	806-894-7343	R	11*	<0.1
Homestead Lawn and Tractor Co.	3529 Apd 40	Cleveland	TN	37311	Neil Groothuis	423-559-1958	R	10*	<0.1
Mount Horeb Implement Inc.	1650 US 18 & 151	Mount Horeb	WI	53572	Michael Mc Nall	608-437-5501	R	10*	<0.1
PL Rohrer and Bro Inc.	PO Box 250	Smoketown	PA	17576	Earl Rohrer	717-299-2571	R	10*	<0.1
Porter Henderson Implement Co.	3993 Tractor Trl	San Angelo	TX	76905	Joe Henderson	325-653-4541	R	10*	<0.1
Walkers Farm and Garden Inc.	PO Box 315	Union	MI	49130	Bradley Walker	269-641-5841	R	10*	<0.1
D and D Equipment Company Inc.	PO Box 31	Chilton	WI	53014	Stephen Dvorak	920-849-9304	R	10*	<0.1
Titan Machinery L.L.C.	3401 32nd Ave SW	Fargo	ND	58103	Peter Christianson	701-235-3171	R	10*	<0.1
Glencoe Equipment Inc.	2910 9th St E	Glencoe	MN	55336	Curt Weber	320-864-5571	R	8*	<0.1
Rosy Brothers Inc.	5727 Dryden Rd	Dryden	MI	48428	Steven Roszczewski	810-796-3770	R	8*	<0.1
Big John Manufacturing Inc.	PO Box 456	Osmond	NE	68765	James Fritz	402-748-3860	R	4*	<0.1
Bill's Service Center Inc.	509 Sonderen St	O Fallon	MO	63366	Theresa Williams	636-240-1255	R	2*	<0.1

Source: Ward's Business Directory of U.S. Private and Public Companies, Volumes 1 and 2, 2005. The company type code used is as follows: P - Public, R - Private, S - Subsidiary, D - Division, J - Joint Venture, A - Affiliate, G - Group. Sales are in millions of dollars, employees are in thousands. An asterisk (*) indicates an estimated sales volume. The symbol < stands for 'less than'. Company names and addresses are truncated, in some cases, to fit into the available space.

OCCUPATIONS EMPLOYED BY LAWN & GARDEN EQUIPMENT & SUPPLIES STORES

Occupation	% of Total 2004	Change to 2014	Occupation	% of Total 2004	Change to 2014
Retail salespersons	20.0	17.6	Truck drivers, heavy & tractor-trailer	2.4	17.6
Cashiers, except gaming	8.7	5.8	General & operations managers	2.3	16.4
Landscaping & groundskeeping workers	7.5	18.6	Sales reps, wholesale & manufacturing, exc tech	2.1	17.6
Laborers & freight, stock, & material movers, hand	7.1	5.8	Office clerks, general	2.1	4.7
Farmworkers & laborers, crop, nursery, & greenhouse	6.9	17.4	Stock clerks & order fillers	2.0	-9.9
Outdoor power equipment & other small engine mechanics	5.2	17.6	Parts salespersons	1.5	-6.1
First-line supervisors/managers of retail sales workers	4.6	8.2	Maintenance & repair workers, general	1.0	17.6
Truck drivers, light or delivery services	2.5	17.6	Floral designers	1.0	17.3
Bookkeeping, accounting, & auditing clerks	2.5	5.8			

Source: Industry-Occupation Matrix, Bureau of Labor Statistics. These data are reported based on 4-digit NAICS categories but have been matched to corresponding 6-digit NAICS industry codes. The change reported for each occupation to the year 2014 is a percent of growth or decline as estimated by the Bureau of Labor Statistics. The abbreviation nec stands for 'not elsewhere classified.'

LOCATION BY STATE AND REGIONAL CONCENTRATION

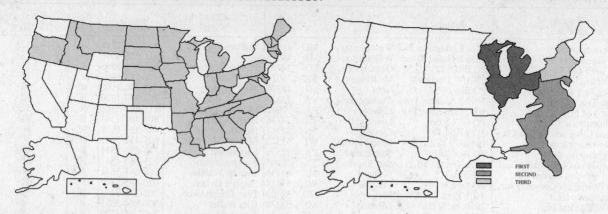

INDUSTRY DATA BY STATE

State	Establishments Total (number)	% of U.S.	Employment Total (number)	% of U.S.	Per Estab.	Payroll Total ($ mil.)	Per Empl. ($)	Sales Total ($ mil.)	% of U.S.	Per Estab. ($)
New York	250	5.7	1,474	6.0	6	39.3	26,692	304.1	6.7	1,216,216
Pennsylvania	277	6.3	1,482	6.0	5	32.9	22,228	259.3	5.7	936,170
Michigan	198	4.5	1,128	4.6	6	29.9	26,535	236.5	5.2	1,194,348
Texas	221	5.0	1,450	5.9	7	35.7	24,606	234.6	5.2	1,061,407
Florida	241	5.5	1,239	5.0	5	31.1	25,109	222.2	4.9	922,000
Ohio	221	5.0	1,376	5.6	6	33.2	24,153	216.2	4.8	978,339
Indiana	192	4.3	1,121	4.5	6	26.3	23,430	197.4	4.4	1,028,375
North Carolina	184	4.2	1,036	4.2	6	24.6	23,733	179.3	4.0	974,630
California	212	4.8	1,051	4.3	5	26.2	24,951	175.8	3.9	829,151
Illinois	153	3.5	917	3.7	6	22.6	24,622	161.8	3.6	1,057,497
Georgia	150	3.4	785	3.2	5	19.0	24,247	137.3	3.0	915,287
Missouri	115	2.6	691	2.8	6	16.4	23,722	124.2	2.7	1,080,183
Virginia	122	2.8	805	3.3	7	17.5	21,757	118.5	2.6	971,123
Massachusetts	102	2.3	614	2.5	6	18.1	29,487	117.0	2.6	1,147,235
Maryland	62	1.4	561	2.3	9	15.7	27,913	107.7	2.4	1,737,177
Wisconsin	138	3.1	621	2.5	5	14.4	23,192	107.0	2.4	775,138
Minnesota	99	2.2	522	2.1	5	13.2	25,257	106.5	2.4	1,075,525
Tennessee	91	2.1	541	2.2	6	13.1	24,301	98.1	2.2	1,078,187
Washington	76	1.7	465	1.9	6	14.0	30,112	89.5	2.0	1,177,566
Iowa	94	2.1	400	1.6	4	8.4	21,063	89.3	2.0	950,521
Louisiana	77	1.7	496	2.0	6	10.5	21,109	87.6	1.9	1,137,078
New Jersey	99	2.2	480	1.9	5	12.7	26,515	87.0	1.9	879,283
Kentucky	77	1.7	461	1.9	6	9.4	20,295	81.8	1.8	1,062,571
South Carolina	88	2.0	413	1.7	5	9.6	23,329	78.9	1.7	896,727
Alabama	102	2.3	422	1.7	4	8.8	20,744	78.7	1.7	771,088
Connecticut	82	1.9	415	1.7	5	11.7	28,241	77.6	1.7	946,329
Arkansas	56	1.3	300	1.2	5	7.0	23,483	72.7	1.6	1,297,964
Maine	47	1.1	266	1.1	6	6.4	24,192	65.2	1.4	1,388,000
Oregon	63	1.4	373	1.5	6	10.1	27,029	63.0	1.4	1,000,683
Kansas	50	1.1	289	1.2	6	7.3	25,308	55.5	1.2	1,110,860
Oklahoma	56	1.3	305	1.2	5	7.0	22,990	53.5	1.2	954,536
Mississippi	62	1.4	280	1.1	5	5.5	19,539	53.1	1.2	856,726
New Hampshire	40	0.9	226	0.9	6	5.9	26,035	44.0	1.0	1,099,200
Arizona	35	0.8	212	0.9	6	6.9	32,604	42.5	0.9	1,212,857
Vermont	31	0.7	165	0.7	5	3.9	23,436	34.2	0.8	1,101,871
Nebraska	33	0.7	190	0.8	6	4.0	21,100	33.8	0.7	1,025,333
Colorado	34	0.8	150	0.6	4	4.1	27,400	30.3	0.7	889,912
Utah	33	0.7	183	0.7	6	4.3	23,311	28.7	0.6	870,818
Delaware	18	0.4	96	0.4	5	2.9	30,687	28.4	0.6	1,577,500
South Dakota	13	0.3	111	0.4	9	2.4	21,405	22.5	0.5	1,731,462
West Virginia	23	0.5	88	0.4	4	2.1	24,273	22.4	0.5	973,174
Idaho	31	0.7	124	0.5	4	2.7	21,669	21.2	0.5	683,871
Montana	13	0.3	80	0.3	6	1.5	18,725	18.3	0.4	1,408,308
North Dakota	8	0.2	66	0.3	8	1.3	19,636	12.6	0.3	1,576,250
Rhode Island	16	0.4	60	0.2	4	1.6	26,517	12.3	0.3	768,188
Nevada	12	0.3	78	0.3	7	1.6	20,962	10.8	0.2	899,417
Hawaii	5	0.1	43	0.2	9	1.4	32,116	9.4	0.2	1,873,800
New Mexico	9	0.2	49	0.2	5	0.9	18,878	5.5	0.1	606,000
Alaska	3	0.1	19	0.1	6	0.5	24,526	3.0	0.1	1,000,000
Wyoming	7	0.2	6	-	1	0.1	12,667	0.8	-	110,286

Source: 2002 *Economic Census.* The states are in descending order of sales or establishments (if sales data are missing for the majority). The symbol (D) appears when data are withheld to prevent disclosure of competitive information. States marked with (D) are sorted by number of establishments. A dash (-) indicates that the data element cannot be calculated. Shaded *states* on the state map indicate those states which have proportionately greater representation in the industry than would be indicated by the states population; the ratio is based on total sales or number of establishments. Shaded *regions* indicate where the industry is regionally most concentrated.

NAICS 444220 - NURSERY, GARDEN CENTER, AND FARM SUPPLY STORES

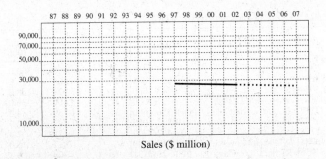

Sales ($ million)

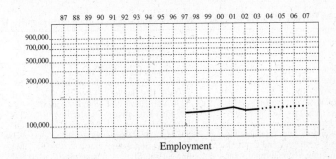

Employment

GENERAL STATISTICS

Year	Establishments (number)	Employment (number)	Payroll ($ million)	Sales ($ million)	Employees per Establishment (number)	Sales per Establishment ($)	Payroll per Employee ($)
1987	-	-	-	-	-	-	-
1988	-	-	-	-	-	-	-
1989	-	-	-	-	-	-	-
1990	-	-	-	-	-	-	-
1991	-	-	-	-	-	-	-
1992	-	-	-	-	-	-	-
1993	-	-	-	-	-	-	-
1994	-	-	-	-	-	-	-
1995	-	-	-	-	-	-	-
1996	-	-	-	-	-	-	-
1997	16,432	139,137	2,760.3	27,608.7	9	1,680,179	19,839
1998	16,510	141,046	2,937.5	27,396.8 e	9	1,659,407	20,827
1999	16,431	144,474	3,176.1	27,184.9 e	9	1,654,490	21,984
2000	16,459	151,539	3,350.3	26,973.0 e	9	1,638,801	22,108
2001	17,770	158,290	3,652.8	26,761.1 e	9	1,505,973	23,076
2002	16,679	146,856	3,178.6	26,549.2	9	1,591,777	21,644
2003	16,533	150,088	3,380.8	26,337.4 p	9	1,529,971 p	22,525
2004	16,971 p	155,674 p	3,608.1 p	26,125.5 p	9 p	1,503,742 p	23,256 p
2005	17,041 p	157,756 p	3,708.8 p	25,913.6 p	9 p	1,477,514 p	23,641 p
2006	17,112 p	159,838 p	3,809.5 p	25,701.7 p	9 p	1,451,285 p	24,026 p
2007	17,183 p	161,919 p	3,910.3 p	25,489.8 p	9 p	1,425,057 p	24,412 p

Source: Economic Census of the United States, 1997 and 2002. Establishment counts, employment, and payroll are from *County Business Patterns* for non-Census years. This is a newly defined industry. Data for prior years are unavailable at the time of publication but may become available over time. Values followed by 'p' are projections by the editors. Sales data for non-Census years are extrapolations, marked by 'e'.

INDICES OF CHANGE

Year	Establishments (number)	Employment (number)	Payroll ($ million)	Sales ($ million)	Employees per Establishment (number)	Sales per Establishment ($)	Payroll per Employee ($)
1987	-	-	-	-	-	-	-
1992	-	-	-	-	-	-	-
1993	-	-	-	-	-	-	-
1994	-	-	-	-	-	-	-
1995	-	-	-	-	-	-	-
1996	-	-	-	-	-	-	-
1997	98.5	94.7	86.8	104.0	96.5	105.6	91.7
1998	99.0	96.0	92.4	103.2 e	96.5	104.2	96.2
1999	98.5	98.4	99.9	102.4 e	99.9	103.9	101.6
2000	98.7	103.2	105.4	101.6 e	104.5	103.0	102.1
2001	106.5	107.8	114.9	100.8 e	101.1	94.6	106.6
2002	100.0	100.0	100.0	100.0	100.0	100.0	100.0
2003	99.1	102.2	106.4	99.2 p	103.1	96.1 p	104.1
2004	101.7 p	106.0 p	113.5 p	98.4 p	104.2 p	94.5 p	107.4 p
2005	102.2 p	107.4 p	116.7 p	97.6 p	105.2 p	92.8 p	109.2 p
2006	102.6 p	108.8 p	119.8 p	96.8 p	106.2 p	91.2 p	111.0 p
2007	103.0 p	110.3 p	123.0 p	96.0 p	107.2 p	89.5 p	112.8 p

Sources: Same as General Statistics. The values shown reflect change from the base year, 2002. Values above 100 mean greater than 2002, values below 100 mean less than 2002, and a value of 100 in the 1987-2001 or 2003-2007 period means same as 2002. Values followed by a 'p' are projections by the editors; 'e' stands for extrapolation. Data are the most recent available at this level of detail.

SELECTED RATIOS

For 2002	Avg. of All Retail	Analyzed Industry	Index	For 2002	Avg. of All Retail	Analyzed Industry	Index
Employees per Establishment	17	9	52	Sales per Employee	174,682	180,784	103
Payroll per Establishment	333,445	190,576	57	Sales per Establishment	3,332,269	1,591,777	48
Payroll per Employee	20,311	21,644	107	Expenses per Establishment	na	na	na

Sources: Same as General Statistics. The 'Average of All' column, Wholesale or Retail, represents the average of the sector reported for the most recent complete year available. The Index shows the relationship between the Average and the Analyzed Industry. For example, 100 means that they are equal; 500 that the Analyzed Industry is five times the average; 50 means that the Analyzed Industry is half the national average. The abbreviation 'na' is used to show that data are 'not available'.

LEADING COMPANIES   Number shown: 60   Total sales ($ mil): 127,923   Total employment (000): 644.7

Company Name	Address				CEO Name	Phone	Co. Type	Sales ($ mil)	Empl. (000)
Home Depot Inc.	2455 Paces Ferry Rd	Atlanta	GA	30339		770-433-8211	P	64,806	300.0
Lowe's Companies Inc.	PO Box 1111	N. Wilkesboro	NC	28656		336-658-4000	P	36,464	123.0
Kmart Corp.	3100 W Big Beaver	Troy	MI	48084		248-643-1000	D	17,072	158.0
Williams-Sonoma Inc.	3250 Van Ness Ave	San Francisco	CA	94109	W Howard Lester	415-421-7900	P	2,609	36.0
Tractor Supply Co.	320 Plus Park Blvd	Nashville	TN	37217	Joseph Scarlett	615-366-4600	P	1,739	4.2
Andersons Inc.	PO Box 119	Maumee	OH	43537	Michael J Anderson	419-893-5050	P	1,247	2.9
Foodarama Supermarkets Inc.	922 Hwy 33, Bldg 6	Freehold	NJ	07728		732-462-4700	P	1,175	7.4
Frank's Nursery and Crafts Inc.	580 Kirts Suite 300	Troy	MI	48084	Walter Spokowski	248-712-7000	S	317	5.0
J.W. Jung Seed Company Inc.	335 S High St	Randolph	WI	53956	Richard J Zondag	920-326-3121	R	300*	0.3
Heritage FS Inc.	PO Box 339	Gilman	IL	60938		815-265-4751	R	232*	<0.1
Horizon	5214 S 30th St	Phoenix	AZ	85040	Bill Hayes	602-276-7700	R	213*	0.4
Orchard Supply Hardware Stores	125 N Milpitas Blvd	Milpitas	CA	95035		408-945-9555	S	177*	<0.1
Z.V. Pate Inc.	PO Box 159	Laurel Hill	NC	28351	David L Burns	910-462-2122	R	176*	0.9
Treeland Nursery Co.	23475 Long Valley	Woodland Hills	CA	91367	John Boething	818-883-1222	R	112*	0.8
George W. Park Seed Inc.	1 Parkton Ave	Greenwood	SC	29647	Karen Park Jennings	864-223-8555	R	103*	0.2
Menomonie Farmers Union Coop.	PO Box 438	Menomonie	WI	54751	Gerry Hoag	715-232-6200	R	89*	0.1
Busy Beaver Building Centers Inc.	3130 William Pitt	Pittsburgh	PA	15238	Charles Bender	412-828-2323	R	79*	0.4
Hinsdale Nurseries Inc.	7200 S Madison St	Hinsdale	IL	60521	Richard Theidel	630-323-1411	R	72*	0.1
Gibson Farmers Coop.	PO Box 497	Trenton	TN	38382	Larry Cochran	731-855-1896	R	65*	<0.1
Pursley Turf Farms	9115 58th Dr E	Bradenton	FL	34202		941-722-4547	R	63*	<0.1
S.K.H. Management Co.	PO Box 1500	Lititz	PA	17543	Paul W Stauffer	717-626-4771	R	57*	1.0
Stanislaus Farm Supply Co.	624 E Service Rd	Modesto	CA	95358	Anselmo Bettencourt	209-538-7070	R	50*	<0.1
Stein Garden and Gifts	5400 S 27th St	Milwaukee	WI	53221	Jack Stein	414-761-5404	R	50*	1.0
Calloway's Nursery Inc.	4200 Arpt Fwy	Fort Worth	TX	76117	James C Estill	817-222-1122	P	48	0.3
Barnes Nursery Inc.	3511 Cleveland Rd	Huron	OH	44839	Robert W Barnes	419-433-5525	R	48*	0.2
Anchor Lumber Company Inc.	1505 1st Ave	Silvis	IL	61282	James McGehee	309-792-0050	R	42*	<0.1
Griffin Land and Nurseries Inc.	1 Rockefeller Plz	New York	NY	10020	Edgar M Cullman	212-218-7910	P	41	0.2
Alaska Mill and Feed	PO Box 101246	Anchorage	AK	99510	Ken Sherwood	907-279-4519	R	38*	<0.1
Bay Houston Towing Co.	PO Box 3006	Houston	TX	77253	Mark E Kuebler	713-529-3755	R	38*	0.4
Kettle-Lakes Coop.	PO Box 305	Random Lake	WI	53075		920-994-4316	R	38*	<0.1
JM McConkey and Company Inc.	PO Box 1690	Sumner	WA	98390	Ed McConkey	253-863-8111	R	36*	<0.1
Danco Prairie FS Coop.	5371 Farmco Dr	Madison	WI	53704	Kevin Lins	608-241-4181	R	30*	<0.1
Jacobi Sales Inc.	PO Box 67	Palmyra	IN	47164	Brian Jacobi	812-364-6141	R	28*	<0.1
Big Horn Cooperative Market	PO Box 591	Greybull	WY	82426	Darrel Horton	307-765-2061	R	26*	0.1
Mahoney's Rocky Ledge Farm	242 Cambridge St	Winchester	MA	01890	Paul Mahoney	781-729-5900	R	25*	0.3
Recycled Wood Products	1313 E Philip Blvd	Pomona	CA	91766	Chris Kiralla	909-868-6882	R	22*	<0.1
Revels Tractor Company Inc.	PO Box 339	Fuquay Varina	NC	27526	Charles Revels Jr	919-552-5697	R	16*	<0.1
Jackson's Lemmon Avenue Pottery	6950 Lemmon Ave	Dallas	TX	75209	Robert Jackson	214-350-9200	R	15*	<0.1
Mid-Wood Inc.	111 E Gypsy Ln	Bowling Green	OH	43402		419-352-5231	R	14*	<0.1
Northampton Farm Bureau	300 Bushkill St	Tatamy	PA	18085		610-258-2871	R	14*	<0.1
Plains Equity Exchange	PO Box 157	Plains	KS	67869	Vonn Richardson	620-563-7269	R	14*	<0.1
McMinn Loudan Farmers Coop.	PO	Athens	TN	37303		423-745-0443	R	13*	<0.1
Jirdon Agri Chemicals Inc.	PO Box 516	Morrill	NE	69358	William L Siegel	308-247-2126	R	12*	<0.1
Ionatron Inc.	3590 E Columbia St	Tucson	AZ	85714	Thomas C Dearmin	520-628-7415	P	11	0.2
PL Rohrer and Bro Inc.	PO Box 250	Smoketown	PA	17576	Earl Rohrer	717-299-2571	R	10*	<0.1
Farmers Union Oil of Valley City	151 9th Ave NW	Valley City	ND	58072		701-845-0812	R	10*	<0.1
Triple D Equipment Inc.	2820 Firehouse Rd	Deland	FL	32720	C Delong	386-734-2119	R	10*	<0.1
Rockbridge Farmers Coop.	645 Waddell St	Lexington	VA	24450		540-463-7381	R	9*	<0.1
Zamaroni Quarry Inc.	3500 Petaluma Hill	Santa Rosa	CA	95404	Louie Zamaroni	707-543-8400	R	9*	<0.1
South Florida Ford New Holland	1995 NE 8th St	Homestead	FL	33033	Jose Cardenal	305-247-1321	R	8*	<0.1
Western Cooperative Co.	PO Drawer H	Alliance	NE	69301	Mark Thompson	308-762-3112	R	6*	<0.1
Memphis New Holland Inc.	3849 New Getwell	Memphis	TN	38118	David Sax	901-362-9200	R	5*	<0.1
White's Old Mill Garden Center	3133 Old Mill Rd	Chesapeake	VA	23323	Norman White	757-487-2300	R	5*	<0.1
Chambers Farm and Garden	PO Box 548	Cullman	AL	35056	Tim Chambers	256-734-3892	R	4*	<0.1
Coos Grange Supply Co.	1085 S 2nd St	Coos Bay	OR	97420		541-267-7051	R	4*	<0.1
Benton County Coop.	PO Box 278	Ashland	MS	38603	Bobby Thompson	662-224-8933	R	2*	<0.1
Veldheer Tulip Garden Inc.	12755 Quincy St	Holland	MI	49424	Jim Veldheer	616-399-1900	R	2*	<0.1
Cactus Sands Nursery & Garden	1533 Hwy 17 S	N. Myrtle Beach	SC	29582	Jack Bonner	843-272-5314	R	1*	<0.1
Ninth Street Flowers Ltd.	411 E 9th St	New York	NY	10009	Elizabeth Ryan	212-995-1111	R	1*	<0.1
Better Stones and Masonry Supply	200 Tolland St	East Hartford	CT	06108	William Smallwood	860-289-1414	R	1*	<0.1

Source: Ward's Business Directory of U.S. Private and Public Companies, Volumes 1 and 2, 2005. The company type code used is as follows: P - Public, R - Private, S - Subsidiary, D - Division, J - Joint Venture, A - Affiliate, G - Group. Sales are in millions of dollars, employees are in thousands. An asterisk (*) indicates an estimated sales volume. The symbol < stands for 'less than'. Company names and addresses are truncated, in some cases, to fit into the available space.

OCCUPATIONS EMPLOYED BY LAWN & GARDEN EQUIPMENT & SUPPLIES STORES

Occupation	% of Total 2004	Change to 2014	Occupation	% of Total 2004	Change to 2014
Retail salespersons	20.0	17.6	Truck drivers, heavy & tractor-trailer	2.4	17.6
Cashiers, except gaming	8.7	5.8	General & operations managers	2.3	16.4
Landscaping & groundskeeping workers	7.5	18.6	Sales reps, wholesale & manufacturing, exc tech	2.1	17.6
Laborers & freight, stock, & material movers, hand	7.1	5.8	Office clerks, general	2.1	4.7
Farmworkers & laborers, crop, nursery, & greenhouse	6.9	17.4	Stock clerks & order fillers	2.0	-9.9
Outdoor power equipment & other small engine mechanics	5.2	17.6	Parts salespersons	1.5	-6.1
First-line supervisors/managers of retail sales workers	4.6	8.2	Maintenance & repair workers, general	1.0	17.6
Truck drivers, light or delivery services	2.5	17.6	Floral designers	1.0	17.3
Bookkeeping, accounting, & auditing clerks	2.5	5.8			

Source: Industry-Occupation Matrix, Bureau of Labor Statistics. These data are reported based on 4-digit NAICS categories but have been matched to corresponding 6-digit NAICS industry codes. The change reported for each occupation to the year 2014 is a percent of growth or decline as estimated by the Bureau of Labor Statistics. The abbreviation nec stands for 'not elsewhere classified.'

LOCATION BY STATE AND REGIONAL CONCENTRATION

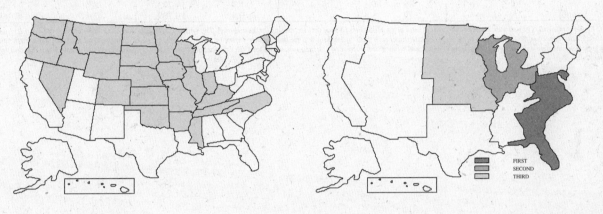

INDUSTRY DATA BY STATE

State	Establishments Total (number)	% of U.S.	Employment Total (number)	% of U.S.	Per Estab.	Payroll Total ($ mil.)	Per Empl. ($)	Sales Total ($ mil.)	% of U.S.	Per Estab. ($)
California	1,191	7.1	12,052	8.2	10	306.3	25,417	2,089.4	7.9	1,754,348
Texas	1,243	7.4	10,705	7.3	9	192.2	17,957	1,618.9	6.1	1,302,416
Illinois	640	3.8	6,664	4.5	10	170.4	25,567	1,409.3	5.3	2,202,002
Iowa	503	3.0	4,054	2.8	8	108.7	26,824	1,298.9	4.9	2,582,227
Minnesota	509	3.0	4,594	3.1	9	106.9	23,271	1,206.4	4.6	2,370,096
Ohio	675	4.0	6,381	4.4	9	125.1	19,607	1,019.6	3.9	1,510,502
Missouri	565	3.4	4,785	3.3	8	96.6	20,195	940.5	3.6	1,664,634
Wisconsin	435	2.6	4,981	3.4	11	117.5	23,594	937.2	3.5	2,154,568
New York	625	3.7	5,342	3.6	9	126.3	23,636	850.7	3.2	1,361,083
Michigan	517	3.1	4,292	2.9	8	97.4	22,691	816.9	3.1	1,580,033
Indiana	476	2.8	4,258	2.9	9	90.0	21,126	797.1	3.0	1,674,475
North Carolina	578	3.5	4,059	2.8	7	81.0	19,948	787.2	3.0	1,361,884
Pennsylvania	682	4.1	5,383	3.7	8	109.0	20,244	769.5	2.9	1,128,306
Tennessee	395	2.4	4,237	2.9	11	82.9	19,563	730.6	2.8	1,849,666
Washington	431	2.6	4,064	2.8	9	97.5	23,981	679.4	2.6	1,576,237
Nebraska	305	1.8	2,514	1.7	8	61.8	24,582	672.4	2.5	2,204,649
Virginia	444	2.7	4,631	3.2	10	94.0	20,298	655.1	2.5	1,475,509
Kentucky	362	2.2	3,185	2.2	9	66.2	20,799	616.7	2.3	1,703,597
Florida	624	3.7	4,079	2.8	7	76.1	18,653	572.6	2.2	917,559
Georgia	443	2.7	3,926	2.7	9	74.4	18,947	568.7	2.2	1,283,822
Kansas	281	1.7	2,465	1.7	9	50.1	20,309	530.3	2.0	1,887,342
Mississippi	215	1.3	1,564	1.1	7	31.8	20,343	466.2	1.8	2,168,205
Colorado	263	1.6	3,012	2.1	11	67.5	22,397	427.4	1.6	1,625,202
Alabama	351	2.1	2,046	1.4	6	37.6	18,379	413.1	1.6	1,176,832
Oklahoma	271	1.6	2,129	1.5	8	37.8	17,777	402.6	1.5	1,485,601
Arkansas	258	1.5	1,915	1.3	7	40.1	20,964	385.2	1.5	1,493,050
Oregon	267	1.6	2,434	1.7	9	48.6	19,955	382.5	1.4	1,432,697
North Dakota	124	0.7	1,130	0.8	9	26.3	23,240	371.0	1.4	2,991,879
New Jersey	357	2.1	2,688	1.8	8	64.5	24,003	369.3	1.4	1,034,457
Maryland	214	1.3	2,763	1.9	13	61.9	22,414	342.5	1.3	1,600,579
Louisiana	258	1.5	2,045	1.4	8	37.9	18,551	338.7	1.3	1,312,740
South Dakota	152	0.9	1,205	0.8	8	28.1	23,344	333.6	1.3	2,194,447
Massachusetts	258	1.5	2,066	1.4	8	54.8	26,519	288.8	1.1	1,119,221
Idaho	128	0.8	1,296	0.9	10	29.9	23,104	277.4	1.1	2,167,109
Arizona	206	1.2	2,188	1.5	11	45.1	20,627	265.7	1.0	1,289,985

Continued on next page.

INDUSTRY DATA BY STATE - Continued

State	Establishments Total (number)	% of U.S.	Employment Total (number)	% of U.S.	Per Estab.	Payroll Total ($ mil.)	Per Empl. ($)	Sales Total ($ mil.)	% of U.S.	Per Estab. ($)
Montana	125	0.7	1,064	0.7	9	23.0	21,597	248.0	0.9	1,983,640
Connecticut	190	1.1	2,001	1.4	11	44.7	22,334	234.0	0.9	1,231,684
South Carolina	284	1.7	1,634	1.1	6	28.9	17,704	229.1	0.9	806,743
Utah	109	0.7	1,152	0.8	11	21.9	19,006	172.9	0.7	1,585,844
Nevada	72	0.4	924	0.6	13	21.2	22,903	153.8	0.6	2,136,125
West Virginia	111	0.7	711	0.5	6	12.1	17,046	115.6	0.4	1,041,811
New Mexico	92	0.6	734	0.5	8	12.2	16,553	102.7	0.4	1,116,054
Wyoming	62	0.4	425	0.3	7	8.9	20,944	102.2	0.4	1,648,935
New Hampshire	106	0.6	678	0.5	6	16.0	23,552	97.7	0.4	921,896
Vermont	62	0.4	470	0.3	8	11.6	24,600	84.7	0.3	1,365,887
Maine	95	0.6	620	0.4	7	12.4	19,937	76.6	0.3	805,789
Delaware	50	0.3	396	0.3	8	9.0	22,780	60.8	0.2	1,216,140
Hawaii	40	0.2	300	0.2	8	6.3	21,080	48.5	0.2	1,211,575
Rhode Island	36	0.2	238	0.2	7	5.8	24,315	34.1	0.1	948,389
Alaska	20	0.1	86	0.1	4	1.7	19,733	8.4	-	422,500
D.C.	3	-	19	-	6	0.4	19,789	2.1	-	691,333

Source: 2002 *Economic Census*. The states are in descending order of sales or establishments (if sales data are missing for the majority). The symbol (D) appears when data are withheld to prevent disclosure of competitive information. States marked with (D) are sorted by number of establishments. A dash (-) indicates that the data element cannot be calculated. Shaded *states* on the state map indicate those states which have proportionately greater representation in the industry than would be indicated by the states population; the ratio is based on total sales or number of establishments. Shaded *regions* indicate where the industry is regionally most concentrated.

NAICS 445110 - SUPERMARKETS AND OTHER GROCERY (EXCEPT CONVENIENCE) STORES

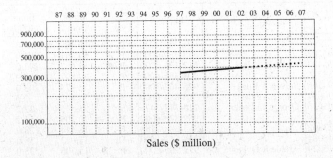

Sales ($ million)

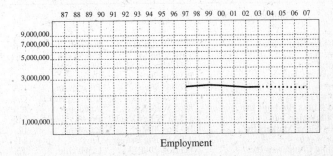

Employment

GENERAL STATISTICS

Year	Establishments (number)	Employment (number)	Payroll ($ million)	Sales ($ million)	Employees per Establishment (number)	Sales per Establishment ($)	Payroll per Employee ($)
1987	-	-	-	-	-	-	-
1988	-	-	-	-	-	-	-
1989	-	-	-	-	-	-	-
1990	-	-	-	-	-	-	-
1991	-	-	-	-	-	-	-
1992	-	-	-	-	-	-	-
1993	-	-	-	-	-	-	-
1994	-	-	-	-	-	-	-
1995	-	-	-	-	-	-	-
1996	-	-	-	-	-	-	-
1997	69,461	2,489,721	35,827.8	351,402.7	36	5,058,993	14,390
1998	68,521	2,532,977	37,985.8	359,977.0 e	37	5,253,529	14,996
1999	69,004	2,583,957	39,938.7	368,551.4 e	37	5,341,015	15,456
2000	68,779	2,543,527	41,795.0	377,125.7 e	37	5,483,153	16,432
2001	68,797	2,487,338	42,341.5	385,700.1 e	36	5,606,351	17,023
2002	66,092	2,432,487	42,742.0	394,274.4	37	5,965,540	17,571
2003	67,039	2,444,364	43,735.4	402,848.8 p	36	6,024,764 p	17,892
2004	66,480 p	2,440,100 p	45,714.9 p	411,423.1 p	37 p	6,188,573 p	18,712 p
2005	66,040 p	2,424,612 p	46,987.7 p	419,997.5 p	37 p	6,352,383 p	19,327 p
2006	65,600 p	2,409,124 p	48,260.4 p	428,571.8 p	37 p	6,516,192 p	19,942 p
2007	65,159 p	2,393,636 p	49,533.2 p	437,146.2 p	37 p	6,680,002 p	20,557 p

Source: Economic Census of the United States, 1997 and 2002. Establishment counts, employment, and payroll are from *County Business Patterns* for non-Census years. This is a newly defined industry. Data for prior years are unavailable at the time of publication but may become available over time. Values followed by 'p' are projections by the editors. Sales data for non-Census years are extrapolations, marked by 'e'.

INDICES OF CHANGE

Year	Establishments (number)	Employment (number)	Payroll ($ million)	Sales ($ million)	Employees per Establishment (number)	Sales per Establishment ($)	Payroll per Employee ($)
1987	-	-	-	-	-	-	-
1992	-	-	-	-	-	-	-
1993	-	-	-	-	-	-	-
1994	-	-	-	-	-	-	-
1995	-	-	-	-	-	-	-
1996	-	-	-	-	-	-	-
1997	105.1	102.4	83.8	89.1	97.3	84.8	81.9
1998	103.7	104.1	88.9	91.3 e	100.5	88.1	85.3
1999	104.4	106.2	93.4	93.5 e	101.6	89.5	88.0
2000	104.1	104.6	97.8	95.7 e	100.5	91.9	93.5
2001	104.1	102.3	99.1	97.8 e	98.4	94.0	96.9
2002	100.0	100.0	100.0	100.0	100.0	100.0	100.0
2003	101.4	100.5	102.3	102.2 p	99.1	101.0 p	101.8
2004	100.6 p	100.3 p	107.0 p	104.3 p	99.8 p	103.7 p	106.5 p
2005	99.9 p	99.7 p	109.9 p	106.5 p	99.8 p	106.5 p	110.0 p
2006	99.3 p	99.0 p	112.9 p	108.7 p	99.9 p	109.2 p	113.5 p
2007	98.6 p	98.4 p	115.9 p	110.9 p	99.9 p	112.0 p	117.0 p

Sources: Same as General Statistics. The values shown reflect change from the base year, 2002. Values above 100 mean greater than 2002, values below 100 mean less than 2002, and a value of 100 in the 1987-2001 or 2003-2007 period means same as 2002. Values followed by a 'p' are projections by the editors; 'e' stands for extrapolation. Data are the most recent available at this level of detail.

SELECTED RATIOS

For 2002	Avg. of All Retail	Analyzed Industry	Index	For 2002	Avg. of All Retail	Analyzed Industry	Index
Employees per Establishment	17	37	217	Sales per Employee	174,682	162,087	93
Payroll per Establishment	333,445	646,705	194	Sales per Establishment	3,332,269	5,965,540	179
Payroll per Employee	20,311	17,571	87	Expenses per Establishment	na	na	na

Sources: Same as General Statistics. The 'Average of All' column, Wholesale or Retail, represents the average of the sector reported for the most recent complete year available. The Index shows the relationship between the Average and the Analyzed Industry. For example, 100 means that they are equal; 500 that the Analyzed Industry is five times the average; 50 means that the Analyzed Industry is half the national average. The abbreviation 'na' is used to show that data are 'not available'.

LEADING COMPANIES   Number shown: **75**   Total sales ($ mil): **811,787**   Total employment (000): **17,503.2**

Company Name	Address				CEO Name	Phone	Co. Type	Sales ($ mil)	Empl. (000)
Wal-Mart Stores Inc.	702 SW 8th St	Bentonville	AR	72716		501-273-4000	P	288,189	15,000.0
Kroger Co.	1014 Vine St	Cincinnati	OH	45202		513-762-4000	P	53,791	288.0
Target Corp.	1000 Nicollet Mall	Minneapolis	MN	55403	Linda L Ahlers	612-304-6073	P	45,682	273.0
Albertson's Inc.	PO Box 20	Boise	ID	83726		208-395-6200	P	39,897	200.0
Safeway Inc.	PO Box 99	Pleasanton	CA	94566	Steven A Burd	925-467-3000	P	35,823	208.0
Ralphs Grocery Co.	PO Box 54143	Los Angeles	CA	90054	John Burgon	310-884-9000	S	34,402*	30.0
Food 4 Less Holdings Inc.	8065 Watt Ave	Antelope	CA	95626	George Golleher	916-348-3425	S	25,515*	22.2
SUPERVALU Inc.	11840 Valley View	Eden Prairie	MN	55344		952-828-4000	P	20,205	55.2
Publix Super Markets Inc.	PO Box 407	Lakeland	FL	33802		863-688-1188	R	18,554	128.0
Kmart Corp.	3100 W Big Beaver	Troy	MI	48084		248-643-1000	D	17,072	158.0
Fleming Companies Inc.	PO Box 299013	Lewisville	TX	75029	Archie R Dykes	972-906-8000	P	15,503	33.0
Winn-Dixie Stores Inc.	PO Box B	Jacksonville	FL	32203		904-783-5000	P	12,633	113.0
Meijer Great Lakes L.P.	2929 Walker NW	Grand Rapids	MI	49544	Paul Boyer	616-453-6711	R	11,900*	70.0
Great Atlantic and Pacific Tea Inc.	PO Box 418	Montvale	NJ	07645	Christian W E Haub	201-573-9700	P	10,812	74.0
H.E. Butt Grocery Co.	PO Box 839999	San Antonio	TX	78283	Charles C Butt	210-938-8000	R	10,733*	56.0
Rosauer's Supermarkets Inc.	PO Box 9000	Spokane	WA	99209	Jeff Philipps	509-326-8900	R	9,422*	1.8
Food Lion L.L.C.	PO Box 1330	Salisbury	NC	28145	Rick Anicetti	704-633-8250	S	8,099*	73.0
BJ's Wholesale Club Inc.	PO Box 9601	Natick	MA	01760		508-651-7400	P	7,220	18.5
Scolari's Food and Drug Co.	PO Box 5070	Reno	NV	89513	Joey Scolari	775-331-7700	R	6,733*	1.3
Giant Food Inc.	6400 Sheriff Rd	Landover	MD	20785	Mark Smith	301-341-4100	S	5,289*	35.0
Giant Eagle Inc.	101 Kappa Dr	Pittsburgh	PA	15238	Raymond Burgo	412-963-6200	R	5,200	36.0
Four B Corp.	5300 Speaker Rd	Kansas City	KS	66106	John Ball	913-299-3447	R	4,633*	4.0
Hy-Vee Inc.	5820 Westown Pky	W. Des Moines	IA	50266	Richard N Jurgens	515-267-2800	R	4,600	47.0
Shaw's Supermarkets Inc.	PO Box 600	East Bridgewater	MA	02333	Nicola DeFelice	508-313-4000	S	4,537*	30.7
QuikTrip Corp.	PO Box 3475	Tulsa	OK	74101	Chester Cadieux	918-615-7700	R	4,051	7.0
Pathmark Stores Inc.	200 Milik St	Carteret	NJ	07008	James L Moody Jr	732-499-3000	P	3,991	26.0
Nash Finch Co.	PO Box 355	Minneapolis	MN	55440	Ron Marshall	952-832-0534	P	3,897	8.7
Whole Foods Market Inc.	601 N Lamar Blvd	Austin	TX	78703		512-477-4455	P	3,865	32.1
Falley's Inc.	3120 S Kansas Ave	Topeka	KS	66611	Stan Edde	785-267-1501	R	3,720*	<0.1
Wegmans Food Markets Inc.	PO Box 30844	Rochester	NY	14603	Colleen Wegman	716-328-2550	R	3,600	32.0
Stater Bros. Markets	21700 Barton Rd	Colton	CA	92324	Jack H Brown	909-783-5000	S	3,596*	14.5
Pantry Inc.	PO Box 1410	Sanford	NC	27331	Byron E Allumbaugh	919-774-6700	P	3,493	9.8
Gordon Food Service Inc.	PO Box 1787	Grand Rapids	MI	49501	Daniel Gordon	616-530-7000	R	3,450	6.4
Hannaford Brothers Co.	PO Box 1000	Portland	ME	04104	Ronald C Hodge	207-883-2911	S	3,239*	23.0
Raley's Inc.	PO Box 15618	Sacramento	CA	95852	William J Coyne	916-373-3333	R	3,200	16.2
Better Val-U Supermarkets Inc.	663 Norwich Rd	Plainfield	CT	06374	Frank Bokoff	860-564-7681	R	3,167*	0.6
Ruddick Corp.	301 S Tryon St	Charlotte	NC	28202	Alan T Dickson	704-372-5404	P	2,869	18.2
Tops Markets Inc.	PO Box 1027	Buffalo	NY	14240	Max Henderson	716-635-5000	S	2,744*	21.0
Harris Teeter Inc.	701 Crestdale Dr	Matthews	NC	28104	Fred J Morganthall II	704-844-3100	S	2,582	15.3
Golub Corp.	501 Duanesburg Rd	Schenectady	NY	12306	Lewis Golub	518-355-5000	R	2,540	22.0
Giant Industries Inc.	PO Box 12999	Scottsdale	AZ	85267	Morgan Gust	480-585-8888	P	2,512	2.4
Casey's General Stores Inc.	1 Convenience Blvd	Ankeny	IA	50021		515-965-6100	P	2,368	14.6
Jay C Food Stores	PO Box 1004	Seymour	IN	47274	James McCoy	812-522-1374	D	2,356*	2.0
Wawa Inc.	260 W Baltimore	Wawa	PA	19063		610-358-8000	R	2,332*	13.0
Wallis Oil Co.	106 E Washington	Cuba	MO	65453	Lynn Wallis	573-885-2277	R	2,318*	0.7
Schnuck Markets Inc.	PO Box 46928	St. Louis	MO	63146		314-994-9900	R	2,200	16.5
Save Mart Supermarkets	PO Box 4278	Modesto	CA	95352	Robert M Piccinini	209-577-1600	R	2,194	9.4
WinCo Foods Inc.	PO Box 5756	Boise	ID	83705		208-377-0110	R	2,139	7.5
Ingles Markets Inc.	PO Box 6676	Asheville	NC	28816		828-669-2941	P	2,137	14.7
Weis Markets Inc.	PO Box 471	Sunbury	PA	17801	Norman S Rich	570-286-4571	P	2,098	18.6
Cumberland Farms Inc.	777 Dedham St	Canton	MA	02021	Lilly Haseotes Bentas	781-828-4900	R	2,007*	7.0
Houchens Industries Inc.	PO Box 90009	Bowling Green	KY	42102	Jim Gipson	270-843-3252	R	2,005	9.2
Smart and Final Stores Corp.	600 Citadel Dr	Los Angeles	CA	90040	Ross E Roeder	323-869-7500	S	1,959*	5.8
DeMoulas Super Markets Inc.	875 East St	Tewksbury	MA	01876	Julien Lacourse	978-851-8000	R	1,930*	12.9
Highland Park Market Inc.	317 Highland St	Manchester	CT	06040	Timothy J Devanney	860-646-4277	R	1,898*	0.4
King Soopers Inc.	65 Tejon St	Denver	CO	80223	Russ Dispense	303-778-3100	S	1,895*	14.5
Bashas' Inc.	PO Box 488	Chandler	AZ	85244	Eddie Basha Jr	480-895-9350	R	1,800	13.8
Bruno's Supermarkets Inc.	PO Box 2486	Birmingham	AL	35201	Dean Cohagen	205-940-9400	S	1,744*	14.5
Brookshire Grocery Co.	PO Box 1411	Tyler	TX	75710	Bruce G Brookshire	903-534-3000	R	1,740*	12.0
Smart and Final Inc.	PO Box 512377	Los Angeles	CA	90051		323-869-7500	P	1,730	5.1
Crown Central Petroleum Corp.	PO Box 1168	Baltimore	MD	21203		410-539-7400	S	1,700*	2.6
Marsh Supermarkets Inc.	9800 Crosspoint	Indianapolis	IN	46256	Don E Marsh	317-594-2100	P	1,654	14.3
Todd Holding Co.	2313 17th St	Greeley	CO	80631	Mick Todd	970-352-4980	R	1,616*	0.3
Kash N' Karry Food Stores Inc.	6401 Harney Rd	Tampa	FL	33610		813-620-1139	S	1,516*	11.0
Brookshire Brothers Ltd.	PO Box 1688	Lufkin	TX	75902	Bruce Brookshire	936-634-8155	R	1,500*	12.0
Minyard Food Stores Inc.	PO Box 518	Coppell	TX	75019	Bob Minyard	972-393-8700	R	1,500	6.7
Dan Incorporated Oregon	PO Box 2200	Oregon City	OR	97045	Craig T Danielson	503-655-9141	R	1,345*	0.3
Shopper's Food Warehouse Corp.	4600 Forbes Blvd	Lanham	MD	20706	William J White	301-306-8600	S	1,288*	7.0
Holiday Companies Inc.	PO Box 1224	Minneapolis	MN	55440	Ronald A Erickson	952-830-8700	R	1,250	6.0
Big Y Foods Inc.	PO Box 7840	Springfield	MA	01102	Donald H D'Amour	413-784-0600	R	1,210	8.6
Foodarama Supermarkets Inc.	922 Hwy 33, Bldg 6	Freehold	NJ	07728		732-462-4700	P	1,175	7.4
Quality Food Centers Inc.	10116 NE 8th St	Bellevue	WA	98004	Darrell Webb	425-455-3761	S	1,110*	6.5
K-Va-T Food Stores Inc.	PO Box 1158	Abingdon	VA	24211		276-628-5503	R	1,063	9.3
Fiesta Mart Inc.	5235 Katy Fwy	Houston	TX	77007	Louis Katopodis	713-869-5060	R	1,050	7.5
SUPERVALU Champaign	PO Box 9008	Champaign	IL	61826		217-384-2800	S	1,000*	0.9

Source: Ward's Business Directory of U.S. Private and Public Companies, Volumes 1 and 2, 2005. The company type code used is as follows: P - Public, R - Private, S - Subsidiary, D - Division, J - Joint Venture, A - Affiliate, G - Group. Sales are in millions of dollars, employees are in thousands. An asterisk (*) indicates an estimated sales volume. The symbol < stands for 'less than'. Company names and addresses are truncated, in some cases, to fit into the available space.

OCCUPATIONS EMPLOYED BY GROCERY STORES

Occupation	% of Total 2004	Change to 2014	Occupation	% of Total 2004	Change to 2014
Cashiers, except gaming	33.7	-2.6	Customer service representatives	2.4	24.6
Stock clerks & order fillers	15.2	-6.7	Retail salespersons	1.9	21.8
Packers & packagers, hand	8.0	11.0	Laborers & freight, stock, & material movers, hand	1.9	9.6
First-line supervisors/managers of retail sales workers	5.3	12.0	Bakers	1.8	21.7
Food preparation workers	4.2	21.8	General & operations managers	1.3	20.5
Combined food preparation & serving workers	4.0	15.1	Counter attendants	1.1	10.1
Butchers & meat cutters	3.6	9.6			

Source: *Industry-Occupation Matrix*, Bureau of Labor Statistics. These data are reported based on 4-digit NAICS categories but have been matched to corresponding 6-digit NAICS industry codes. The change reported for each occupation to the year 2014 is a percent of growth or decline as estimated by the Bureau of Labor Statistics. The abbreviation nec stands for 'not elsewhere classified.'

LOCATION BY STATE AND REGIONAL CONCENTRATION

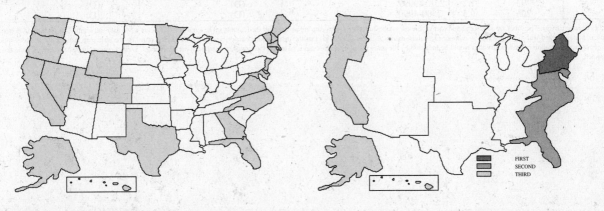

FIRST
SECOND
THIRD

INDUSTRY DATA BY STATE

State	Establishments Total (number)	% of U.S.	Employment Total (number)	% of U.S.	Per Estab.	Payroll Total ($ mil.)	Per Empl. ($)	Sales Total ($ mil.)	% of U.S.	Per Estab. ($)
California	7,690	11.6	252,589	10.4	33	6,258.6	24,778	54,112.7	13.7	7,036,756
Texas	3,915	5.9	162,358	6.7	41	2,874.6	17,705	28,701.3	7.3	7,331,113
Florida	3,398	5.1	178,711	7.3	53	2,771.1	15,506	24,700.7	6.2	7,269,191
New York	7,526	11.4	155,038	6.4	21	2,654.3	17,120	24,573.0	6.2	3,265,075
Pennsylvania	2,787	4.2	122,560	5.0	44	1,823.3	14,876	17,113.2	4.3	6,140,368
Illinois	2,750	4.2	75,338	3.1	27	1,313.9	17,440	16,181.6	4.1	5,884,216
Ohio	2,329	3.5	102,543	4.2	44	1,614.2	15,741	15,364.7	3.9	6,597,119
New Jersey	2,363	3.6	81,388	3.3	34	1,667.1	20,483	14,710.2	3.7	6,225,236
Georgia	1,820	2.8	84,833	3.5	47	1,234.5	14,552	11,566.8	2.9	6,355,361
North Carolina	1,939	2.9	72,515	3.0	37	1,101.6	15,191	11,504.4	2.9	5,933,155
Michigan	2,413	3.6	75,058	3.1	31	1,204.1	16,042	10,688.2	2.7	4,429,435
Massachusetts	1,252	1.9	67,959	2.8	54	1,217.1	17,909	10,636.3	2.7	8,495,457
Virginia	1,556	2.4	60,214	2.5	39	1,059.4	17,594	10,384.4	2.6	6,673,772
Washington	1,478	2.2	52,129	2.1	35	1,134.2	21,757	9,843.8	2.5	6,660,190
Maryland	1,091	1.6	47,803	2.0	44	1,019.5	21,328	8,704.1	2.2	7,978,052
Wisconsin	1,122	1.7	51,151	2.1	46	723.5	14,145	7,466.2	1.9	6,654,360
Minnesota	984	1.5	47,286	1.9	48	752.9	15,923	7,260.5	1.8	7,378,608
Colorado	763	1.2	37,120	1.5	49	902.1	24,302	7,179.1	1.8	9,409,005
Tennessee	1,379	2.1	46,291	1.9	34	649.7	14,035	6,612.3	1.7	4,795,001
Indiana	1,121	1.7	45,429	1.9	41	650.9	14,327	6,477.5	1.6	5,778,368
Missouri	1,141	1.7	43,405	1.8	38	705.4	16,252	6,458.5	1.6	5,660,372
Connecticut	775	1.2	36,403	1.5	47	751.3	20,637	6,226.3	1.6	8,033,968
Alabama	1,019	1.5	35,585	1.5	35	531.4	14,932	5,409.3	1.4	5,308,485
South Carolina	940	1.4	38,167	1.6	41	537.8	14,092	5,377.2	1.4	5,720,384
Oregon	850	1.3	30,529	1.3	36	587.0	19,229	5,290.4	1.3	6,223,949
Louisiana	1,292	2.0	37,538	1.5	29	501.1	13,348	4,830.5	1.2	3,738,783
Kentucky	1,031	1.6	34,256	1.4	33	471.1	13,753	4,794.2	1.2	4,650,029
Iowa	684	1.0	33,432	1.4	49	474.6	14,196	3,984.7	1.0	5,825,586
Kansas	570	0.9	24,119	1.0	42	352.6	14,618	3,306.4	0.8	5,800,695
Nevada	360	0.5	17,483	0.7	49	394.8	22,582	3,257.3	0.8	9,048,139
Utah	350	0.5	20,742	0.9	59	330.5	15,935	2,997.3	0.8	8,563,740
Oklahoma	738	1.1	22,437	0.9	30	315.2	14,048	2,986.0	0.8	4,046,112
New Hampshire	294	0.4	17,450	0.7	59	271.3	15,547	2,807.9	0.7	9,550,639
Mississippi	746	1.1	19,518	0.8	26	262.7	13,461	2,501.8	0.6	3,353,563
Arkansas	705	1.1	18,020	0.7	26	238.6	13,243	2,401.7	0.6	3,406,610
Maine	388	0.6	15,062	0.6	39	235.5	15,634	2,390.9	0.6	6,162,113
Nebraska	486	0.7	17,822	0.7	37	239.5	13,438	2,197.8	0.6	4,522,177

Continued on next page.

INDUSTRY DATA BY STATE - Continued

State	Establishments Total (number)	% of U.S.	Employment Total (number)	% of U.S.	Per Estab.	Payroll Total ($ mil.)	Per Empl. ($)	Sales Total ($ mil.)	% of U.S.	Per Estab. ($)
West Virginia	512	0.8	15,865	0.7	31	186.7	11,766	1,968.6	0.5	3,844,953
Hawaii	316	0.5	8,998	0.4	28	183.9	20,440	1,809.7	0.5	5,726,848
New Mexico	288	0.4	11,673	0.5	41	215.0	18,419	1,797.0	0.5	6,239,517
Idaho	296	0.4	10,555	0.4	36	187.4	17,753	1,737.2	0.4	5,868,872
Rhode Island	208	0.3	9,012	0.4	43	162.9	18,081	1,544.8	0.4	7,427,106
Montana	296	0.4	8,199	0.3	28	137.2	16,738	1,247.4	0.3	4,214,034
Delaware	144	0.2	6,813	0.3	47	130.8	19,200	1,179.1	0.3	8,188,181
Vermont	272	0.4	8,366	0.3	31	124.6	14,896	1,143.6	0.3	4,204,294
Alaska	217	0.3	6,229	0.3	29	128.3	20,600	1,093.5	0.3	5,039,267
South Dakota	247	0.4	7,925	0.3	32	104.5	13,187	936.5	0.2	3,791,700
North Dakota	201	0.3	6,189	0.3	31	75.3	12,171	793.7	0.2	3,948,796
Wyoming	110	0.2	4,271	0.2	39	77.5	18,149	672.5	0.2	6,114,045
Arizona	793	1.2	25K-49999	-	-	(D)	-	(D)	-	-
D.C.	205	0.3	2500-4999	-	-	(D)	-	(D)	-	-

Source: 2002 *Economic Census*. The states are in descending order of sales or establishments (if sales data are missing for the majority). The symbol (D) appears when data are withheld to prevent disclosure of competitive information. States marked with (D) are sorted by number of establishments. A dash (-) indicates that the data element cannot be calculated. Shaded *states* on the state map indicate those states which have proportionately greater representation in the industry than would be indicated by the states population; the ratio is based on total sales or number of establishments. Shaded *regions* indicate where the industry is regionally most concentrated.

NAICS 445120 - CONVENIENCE STORES

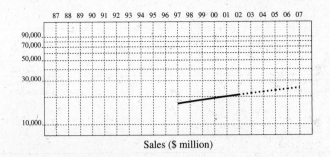

Sales ($ million)

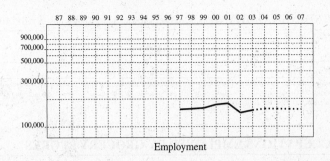

Employment

GENERAL STATISTICS

Year	Establishments (number)	Employment (number)	Payroll ($ million)	Sales ($ million)	Employees per Establishment (number)	Sales per Establishment ($)	Payroll per Employee ($)
1987	-	-	-	-	-	-	-
1988	-	-	-	-	-	-	-
1989	-	-	-	-	-	-	-
1990	-	-	-	-	-	-	-
1991	-	-	-	-	-	-	-
1992	-	-	-	-	-	-	-
1993	-	-	-	-	-	-	-
1994	-	-	-	-	-	-	-
1995	-	-	-	-	-	-	-
1996	-	-	-	-	-	-	-
1997	27,081	153,887	1,598.4	16,847.8	6	622,126	10,387
1998	27,676	156,041	1,762.0	17,661.2 e	6	638,141	11,292
1999	28,427	159,280	1,929.7	18,474.6 e	6	649,896	12,115
2000	29,496	173,341	2,176.9	19,288.0 e	6	653,918	12,559
2001	30,560	178,466	2,291.6	20,101.4 e	6	657,767	12,840
2002	29,422	141,240	1,832.1	20,914.8	5	710,855	12,972
2003	29,925	150,363	1,987.5	21,728.2 p	5	706,105 p	13,218
2004	30,963 p	155,947 p	2,178.3 p	22,541.5 p	5 p	720,578 p	13,995 p
2005	31,469 p	155,198 p	2,237.9 p	23,354.9 p	5 p	735,050 p	14,444 p
2006	31,975 p	154,448 p	2,297.5 p	24,168.3 p	5 p	749,523 p	14,893 p
2007	32,480 p	153,698 p	2,357.1 p	24,981.7 p	5 p	763,996 p	15,342 p

Source: Economic Census of the United States, 1997 and 2002. Establishment counts, employment, and payroll are from *County Business Patterns* for non-Census years. This is a newly defined industry. Data for prior years are unavailable at the time of publication but may become available over time. Values followed by 'p' are projections by the editors. Sales data for non-Census years are extrapolations, marked by 'e'.

INDICES OF CHANGE

Year	Establishments (number)	Employment (number)	Payroll ($ million)	Sales ($ million)	Employees per Establishment (number)	Sales per Establishment ($)	Payroll per Employee ($)
1987	-	-	-	-	-	-	-
1992	-	-	-	-	-	-	-
1993	-	-	-	-	-	-	-
1994	-	-	-	-	-	-	-
1995	-	-	-	-	-	-	-
1996	-	-	-	-	-	-	-
1997	92.0	109.0	87.2	80.6	118.7	87.5	80.1
1998	94.1	110.5	96.2	84.4 e	116.7	89.8	87.0
1999	96.6	112.8	105.3	88.3 e	116.7	91.4	93.4
2000	100.3	122.7	118.8	92.2 e	122.9	92.0	96.8
2001	103.9	126.4	125.1	96.1 e	120.8	92.5	99.0
2002	100.0	100.0	100.0	100.0	100.0	100.0	100.0
2003	101.7	106.5	108.5	103.9 p	104.7	99.3 p	101.9
2004	105.2 p	110.4 p	118.9 p	107.8 p	104.2 p	101.4 p	107.9 p
2005	107.0 p	109.9 p	122.1 p	111.7 p	101.6 p	103.4 p	111.3 p
2006	108.7 p	109.4 p	125.4 p	115.6 p	99.1 p	105.4 p	114.8 p
2007	110.4 p	108.8 p	128.7 p	119.4 p	96.5 p	107.5 p	118.3 p

Sources: Same as General Statistics. The values shown reflect change from the base year, 2002. Values above 100 mean greater than 2002, values below 100 mean less than 2002, and a value of 100 in the 1987-2001 or 2003-2007 period means same as 2002. Values followed by a 'p' are projections by the editors; 'e' stands for extrapolation. Data are the most recent available at this level of detail.

SELECTED RATIOS

For 2002	Avg. of All Retail	Analyzed Industry	Index	For 2002	Avg. of All Retail	Analyzed Industry	Index
Employees per Establishment	17	5	28	Sales per Employee	174,682	148,080	85
Payroll per Establishment	333,445	62,271	19	Sales per Establishment	3,332,269	710,855	21
Payroll per Employee	20,311	12,972	64	Expenses per Establishment	na	na	na

Sources: Same as General Statistics. The 'Average of All' column, Wholesale or Retail, represents the average of the sector reported for the most recent complete year available. The Index shows the relationship between the Average and the Analyzed Industry. For example, 100 means that they are equal; 500 that the Analyzed Industry is five times the average; 50 means that the Analyzed Industry is half the national average. The abbreviation 'na' is used to show that data are 'not available'.

2081

LEADING COMPANIES Number shown: **1** Total sales ($ mil): **10** Total employment (000): **0.0**

Company Name	Address				CEO Name	Phone	Co. Type	Sales ($ mil)	Empl. (000)
Perry Dell Farms	90 Indian Rock Dam	York	PA	17403		717-741-3485	R	10*	<0.1

Source: Ward's Business Directory of U.S. Private and Public Companies, Volumes 1 and 2, 2005. The company type code used is as follows: P - Public, R - Private, S - Subsidiary, D - Division, J - Joint Venture, A - Affiliate, G - Group. Sales are in millions of dollars, employees are in thousands. An asterisk (*) indicates an estimated sales volume. The symbol < stands for 'less than'. Company names and addresses are truncated, in some cases, to fit into the available space.

OCCUPATIONS EMPLOYED BY GROCERY STORES

Occupation	% of Total 2004	Change to 2014	Occupation	% of Total 2004	Change to 2014
Cashiers, except gaming	33.7	-2.6	Customer service representatives	2.4	24.6
Stock clerks & order fillers	15.2	-6.7	Retail salespersons	1.9	21.8
Packers & packagers, hand	8.0	11.0	Laborers & freight, stock, & material movers, hand	1.9	9.6
First-line supervisors/managers of retail sales workers	5.3	12.0	Bakers	1.8	21.7
Food preparation workers	4.2	21.8	General & operations managers	1.3	20.5
Combined food preparation & serving workers	4.0	15.1	Counter attendants	1.1	10.1
Butchers & meat cutters	3.6	9.6			

Source: Industry-Occupation Matrix, Bureau of Labor Statistics. These data are reported based on 4-digit NAICS categories but have been matched to corresponding 6-digit NAICS industry codes. The change reported for each occupation to the year 2014 is a percent of growth or decline as estimated by the Bureau of Labor Statistics. The abbreviation nec stands for 'not elsewhere classified.'

LOCATION BY STATE AND REGIONAL CONCENTRATION

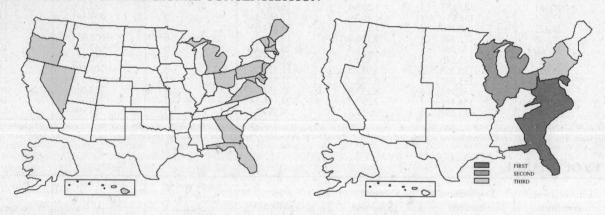

FIRST
SECOND
THIRD

INDUSTRY DATA BY STATE

State	Establishments Total (number)	% of U.S.	Employment Total (number)	% of U.S.	Per Estab.	Payroll Total ($ mil.)	Per Empl. ($)	Sales Total ($ mil.)	% of U.S.	Per Estab. ($)
California	2,238	7.7	11,056	8.0	5	148.8	13,457	1,843.8	9.0	823,842
New Jersey	1,561	5.3	9,996	7.2	6	160.6	16,066	1,713.1	8.4	1,097,410
Pennsylvania	1,112	3.8	8,794	6.4	8	118.6	13,486	1,336.4	6.6	1,201,808
Texas	2,328	8.0	6,667	4.8	3	83.7	12,548	1,267.4	6.2	544,418
New York	1,943	6.7	9,268	6.7	5	120.9	13,046	1,170.8	5.7	602,561
Florida	2,289	7.8	6,505	4.7	3	87.7	13,483	1,148.7	5.6	501,833
Michigan	1,588	5.4	7,606	5.5	5	91.8	12,075	1,073.0	5.3	675,715
Ohio	1,601	5.5	8,177	5.9	5	93.9	11,479	980.1	4.8	612,169
Massachusetts	1,271	4.4	6,174	4.5	5	93.0	15,057	904.7	4.4	711,814
Virginia	1,073	3.7	7,376	5.3	7	89.5	12,129	781.1	3.8	727,920
Illinois	1,019	3.5	6,031	4.4	6	67.4	11,176	701.1	3.4	688,052
Maryland	699	2.4	4,594	3.3	7	64.7	14,089	596.5	2.9	853,336
Georgia	1,013	3.5	2,580	1.9	3	33.7	13,057	562.4	2.8	555,228
North Carolina	836	2.9	2,667	1.9	3	33.4	12,523	495.8	2.4	593,026
Oregon	603	2.1	3,166	2.3	5	41.5	13,110	400.1	2.0	663,434
Washington	575	2.0	2,362	1.7	4	30.8	13,057	379.8	1.9	660,487
Missouri	385	1.3	2,033	1.5	5	26.5	13,028	309.3	1.5	803,465
Hawaii	183	0.6	1,753	1.3	10	31.5	17,979	299.3	1.5	1,635,568
Tennessee	527	1.8	1,775	1.3	3	22.2	12,481	290.0	1.4	550,273
Louisiana	501	1.7	1,933	1.4	4	20.6	10,669	268.4	1.3	535,776
Alabama	436	1.5	1,494	1.1	3	16.6	11,096	261.5	1.3	599,874
Indiana	310	1.1	2,122	1.5	7	25.1	11,835	260.8	1.3	841,184

Continued on next page.

INDUSTRY DATA BY STATE - Continued

State	Establishments		Employment			Payroll		Sales		
	Total (number)	% of U.S.	Total (number)	% of U.S.	Per Estab.	Total ($ mil.)	Per Empl. ($)	Total ($ mil.)	% of U.S.	Per Estab. ($)
South Carolina	422	1.4	1,570	1.1	4	19.3	12,297	253.9	1.2	601,607
Kentucky	333	1.1	1,724	1.2	5	19.6	11,397	251.1	1.2	754,018
New Hampshire	266	0.9	1,262	0.9	5	16.1	12,752	217.7	1.1	818,515
Maine	350	1.2	1,923	1.4	5	21.3	11,093	205.6	1.0	587,434
Nevada	218	0.7	1,260	0.9	6	18.3	14,539	195.1	1.0	895,083
Oklahoma	359	1.2	1,287	0.9	4	12.3	9,561	179.0	0.9	498,577
Delaware	110	0.4	957	0.7	9	14.0	14,627	173.9	0.9	1,581,236
Connecticut	334	1.1	1,101	0.8	3	15.2	13,843	162.0	0.8	484,955
Minnesota	247	0.8	1,173	0.8	5	12.4	10,600	157.7	0.8	638,611
Mississippi	309	1.1	1,270	0.9	4	12.6	9,952	148.6	0.7	480,913
Colorado	192	0.7	1,220	0.9	6	16.4	13,417	145.5	0.7	757,693
West Virginia	222	0.8	1,077	0.8	5	10.2	9,509	125.2	0.6	564,005
Arkansas	172	0.6	870	0.6	5	8.0	9,208	120.6	0.6	701,436
Wisconsin	195	0.7	678	0.5	3	7.8	11,437	114.6	0.6	587,456
Rhode Island	152	0.5	476	0.3	3	6.3	13,294	85.1	0.4	560,125
New Mexico	126	0.4	864	0.6	7	10.8	12,543	82.9	0.4	657,794
Vermont	134	0.5	820	0.6	6	9.2	11,255	82.2	0.4	613,261
Iowa	118	0.4	686	0.5	6	6.2	9,077	77.6	0.4	657,534
Kansas	120	0.4	495	0.4	4	5.6	11,335	76.1	0.4	633,825
Utah	89	0.3	587	0.4	7	6.5	11,135	65.5	0.3	735,899
Nebraska	71	0.2	411	0.3	6	4.0	9,781	51.6	0.3	727,155
Idaho	67	0.2	353	0.3	5	3.5	9,853	49.2	0.2	734,418
South Dakota	45	0.2	159	0.1	4	2.1	13,195	27.2	0.1	603,733
Alaska	31	0.1	177	0.1	6	2.5	14,249	20.0	0.1	645,290
Montana	43	0.1	136	0.1	3	1.4	10,051	19.2	0.1	445,512
Wyoming	17	0.1	80	0.1	5	0.8	9,913	7.4	-	437,941
North Dakota	4	-	17	-	4	0.2	14,353	3.2	-	789,500
Arizona	301	1.0	1000-2499	-	-	(D)	-	(D)	-	-
D.C.	74	0.3	250-499	-	-	(D)	-	(D)	-	-

Source: 2002 *Economic Census*. The states are in descending order of sales or establishments (if sales data are missing for the majority). The symbol (D) appears when data are withheld to prevent disclosure of competitive information. States marked with (D) are sorted by number of establishments. A dash (-) indicates that the data element cannot be calculated. Shaded *states* on the state map indicate those states which have proportionately greater representation in the industry than would be indicated by the states population; the ratio is based on total sales or number of establishments. Shaded *regions* indicate where the industry is regionally most concentrated.

NAICS 445210 - MEAT MARKETS

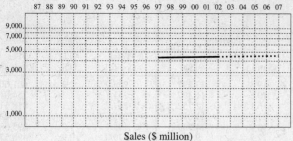

Sales ($ million)

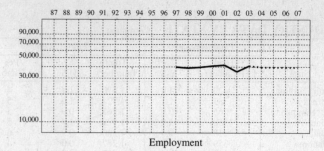

Employment

GENERAL STATISTICS

Year	Establishments (number)	Employment (number)	Payroll ($ million)	Sales ($ million)	Employees per Establishment (number)	Sales per Establishment ($)	Payroll per Employee ($)
1987	-	-	-	-	-	-	-
1988	-	-	-	-	-	-	-
1989	-	-	-	-	-	-	-
1990	-	-	-	-	-	-	-
1991	-	-	-	-	-	-	-
1992	-	-	-	-	-	-	-
1993	-	-	-	-	-	-	-
1994	-	-	-	-	-	-	-
1995	-	-	-	-	-	-	-
1996	-	-	-	-	-	-	-
1997	7,214	39,866	544.4	4,347.0	6	602,578	13,656
1998	6,615	38,886	564.4	4,367.5 e	6	660,241	14,514
1999	6,516	39,664	593.9	4,388.0 e	6	673,418	14,973
2000	6,517	41,010	643.3	4,408.5 e	6	676,460	15,687
2001	6,599	41,924	695.6	4,429.0 e	6	671,160	16,593
2002	5,847	35,524	572.9	4,449.5	6	760,985	16,127
2003	5,902	41,039	629.7	4,470.0 p	7	756,923 p	15,344
2004	5,689 p	39,567 p	659.8 p	4,490.5 p	7 p	780,576 p	16,686 p
2005	5,496 p	39,533 p	673.2 p	4,511.0 p	7 p	804,228 p	17,040 p
2006	5,304 p	39,499 p	686.6 p	4,531.5 p	7 p	827,880 p	17,394 p
2007	5,111 p	39,466 p	700.0 p	4,552.0 p	7 p	851,533 p	17,748 p

Source: *Economic Census of the United States*, 1997 and 2002. Establishment counts, employment, and payroll are from *County Business Patterns* for non-Census years. This is a newly defined industry. Data for prior years are unavailable at the time of publication but may become available over time. Values followed by 'p' are projections by the editors. Sales data for non-Census years are extrapolations, marked by 'e'.

INDICES OF CHANGE

Year	Establishments (number)	Employment (number)	Payroll ($ million)	Sales ($ million)	Employees per Establishment (number)	Sales per Establishment ($)	Payroll per Employee ($)
1987	-	-	-	-	-	-	-
1992	-	-	-	-	-	-	-
1993	-	-	-	-	-	-	-
1994	-	-	-	-	-	-	-
1995	-	-	-	-	-	-	-
1996	-	-	-	-	-	-	-
1997	123.4	112.2	95.0	97.7	90.5	79.2	84.7
1998	113.1	109.5	98.5	98.2 e	97.1	86.8	90.0
1999	111.4	111.7	103.7	98.6 e	100.4	88.5	92.8
2000	111.5	115.4	112.3	99.1 e	103.7	88.9	97.3
2001	112.9	118.0	121.4	99.5 e	105.3	88.2	102.9
2002	100.0	100.0	100.0	100.0	100.0	100.0	100.0
2003	100.9	115.5	109.9	100.5 p	114.4	99.5 p	95.1
2004	97.3 p	111.4 p	115.2 p	100.9 p	113.4 p	102.6 p	103.5 p
2005	94.0 p	111.3 p	117.5 p	101.4 p	116.4 p	105.7 p	105.7 p
2006	90.7 p	111.2 p	119.8 p	101.8 p	119.3 p	108.8 p	107.9 p
2007	87.4 p	111.1 p	122.2 p	102.3 p	122.3 p	111.9 p	110.0 p

Sources: Same as General Statistics. The values shown reflect change from the base year, 2002. Values above 100 mean greater than 2002, values below 100 mean less than 2002, and a value of 100 in the 1987-2001 or 2003-2007 period means same as 2002. Values followed by a 'p' are projections by the editors; 'e' stands for extrapolation. Data are the most recent available at this level of detail.

SELECTED RATIOS

For 2002	Avg. of All Retail	Analyzed Industry	Index	For 2002	Avg. of All Retail	Analyzed Industry	Index
Employees per Establishment	17	6	36	Sales per Employee	174,682	125,253	72
Payroll per Establishment	333,445	97,983	29	Sales per Establishment	3,332,269	760,985	23
Payroll per Employee	20,311	16,127	79	Expenses per Establishment	na	na	na

Sources: Same as General Statistics. The 'Average of All' column, Wholesale or Retail, represents the average of the sector reported for the most recent complete year available. The Index shows the relationship between the Average and the Analyzed Industry. For example, 100 means that they are equal; 500 that the Analyzed Industry is five times the average; 50 means that the Analyzed Industry is half the national average. The abbreviation 'na' is used to show that data are 'not available'.

LEADING COMPANIES   Number shown: **19**   Total sales ($ mil): **206**   Total employment (000): **0.8**

Company Name	Address				CEO Name	Phone	Co. Type	Sales ($ mil)	Empl. (000)
Spec's Family Partner's	2410 Smith St	Houston	TX	77006	John Rydman	713-526-8787	R	80*	0.3
Dewig Brothers Packing Inc.	PO Box 186	Haubstadt	IN	47639	Thomas Dewig	812-768-6208	R	17*	<0.1
Abe's French Market Foods	3935 Ryan St	Lake Charles	LA	70605	Mark Abraham	337-477-5499	R	14*	<0.1
Weber Processing Plant Inc.	725 N Jackson St	Cuba City	WI	53807	Lee Weber	608-744-2159	R	10*	<0.1
Kewaskum Frozen Foods Inc.	PO Box 510	Kewaskum	WI	53040	Robert Beisbier	262-626-2181	R	9*	<0.1
Cable Meat Center	PO Box 527	Marlow	OK	73055	Tom Wheat	580-658-6646	R	9*	<0.1
Caughman's Meat Plant Inc.	PO Box 457	Lexington	SC	29071	Ronnie Caughman	803-356-3216	R	9*	<0.1
Manley Meats Inc.	302 S 400 E	Decatur	IN	46733	Roger Manley	260-592-7313	R	7*	<0.1
Rabideaux's Sausage Kitchen Inc.	105 Hwy 165	Iowa	LA	70647	Joseph Daigle	337-582-3184	R	7*	<0.1
L.D. Amory and Company Inc.	PO Box 518	Hampton	VA	23669		757-722-1915	R	6*	<0.1
Bavaria Sausage Kitchen Inc.	6317 Nesbitt Rd	Madison	WI	53719	Fred Voll	608-845-6691	R	6*	<0.1
Kasper's Meat Market Inc.	119 E Post Office St	Weimar	TX	78962	Maurice Kasper	979-725-8227	R	6*	<0.1
McDonald's Meats Inc.	PO Box 117	Clear Lake	MN	55319	David McDonald	320-743-2311	R	6*	<0.1
Lee Williams Meats Inc.	3002 131st St	Toledo	OH	43611	Barry Williams	419-729-3893	R	6*	<0.1
Lewright Meats Inc.	108 N Iowa Ave	Eagle Grove	IA	50533	Paul Bubeck	515-448-4286	R	5*	<0.1
Stockton Poultry Market	PO Box 2129	Stockton	CA	95201	John Luu	209-466-9503	R	5*	<0.1
Brandon Meats and Sausage Inc.	PO Box 382	Brandon	WI	53919	Alan Feucht	920-346-2227	R	3*	<0.1
Mount Pleasant Seafood Co.	1 Seafood Dr	Mount Pleasant	SC	29464	Rial Fitch	843-884-4122	R	3*	<0.1
YS and CH Enterprises Inc.	PO Box 17223	Honolulu	HI	96817	Ronald L Kim	808-845-0447	R	1*	<0.1

Source: *Ward's Business Directory of U.S. Private and Public Companies*, Volumes 1 and 2, 2005. The company type code used is as follows: P - Public, R - Private, S - Subsidiary, D - Division, J - Joint Venture, A - Affiliate, G - Group. Sales are in millions of dollars, employees are in thousands. An asterisk (*) indicates an estimated sales volume. The symbol < stands for 'less than'. Company names and addresses are truncated, in some cases, to fit into the available space.

OCCUPATIONS EMPLOYED BY SPECIALTY FOOD STORES

Occupation	% of Total 2004	Change to 2014	Occupation	% of Total 2004	Change to 2014
Cashiers, except gaming	15.5	7.3	Sales reps, wholesale & manufacturing, exc tech	2.6	19.2
Retail salespersons	10.0	19.2	Packers & packagers, hand	2.4	19.2
Combined food preparation & serving workers	5.2	19.2	Truck drivers, heavy & tractor-trailer	2.0	19.2
Butchers & meat cutters	4.8	7.3	Meat, poultry, & fish cutters & trimmers	1.9	19.2
Food preparation workers	4.4	19.2	General & operations managers	1.8	18.0
Driver/sales workers	4.4	19.0	Bakers	1.7	19.0
Stock clerks & order fillers	4.0	-8.7	First-line supervisors/managers of food service workers	1.4	19.2
Laborers & freight, stock, & material movers, hand	3.9	7.3	Bookkeeping, accounting, & auditing clerks	1.4	7.3
First-line supervisors/managers of retail sales workers	3.9	9.6	Office clerks, general	1.4	6.1
Truck drivers, light or delivery services	3.7	19.2	Packaging & filling machine operators & tenders	1.0	12.8
Counter attendants	3.3	19.2			

Source: *Industry-Occupation Matrix*, Bureau of Labor Statistics. These data are reported based on 4-digit NAICS categories but have been matched to corresponding 6-digit NAICS industry codes. The change reported for each occupation to the year 2014 is a percent of growth or decline as estimated by the Bureau of Labor Statistics. The abbreviation nec stands for 'not elsewhere classified.'

INDUSTRY DATA BY STATE

State-level data are not available.

NAICS 445220 - FISH AND SEAFOOD MARKETS

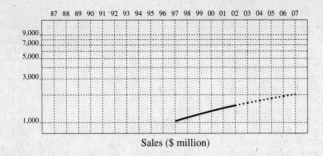

Sales ($ million)

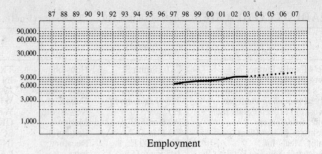

Employment

GENERAL STATISTICS

Year	Establishments (number)	Employment (number)	Payroll ($ million)	Sales ($ million)	Employees per Establishment (number)	Sales per Establishment ($)	Payroll per Employee ($)
1987	-	-	-	-	-	-	-
1988	-	-	-	-	-	-	-
1989	-	-	-	-	-	-	-
1990	-	-	-	-	-	-	-
1991	-	-	-	-	-	-	-
1992	-	-	-	-	-	-	-
1993	-	-	-	-	-	-	-
1994	-	-	-	-	-	-	-
1995	-	-	-	-	-	-	-
1996	-	-	-	-	-	-	-
1997	1,634	7,120	101.9	1,037.6	4	635,006	14,312
1998	1,772	7,855	121.5	1,136.7 e	4	641,503	15,468
1999	1,807	8,299	137.7	1,235.9 e	5	683,944	16,592
2000	1,853	8,458	137.3	1,335.0 e	5	720,469	16,234
2001	1,940	8,990	149.3	1,434.2 e	5	739,264	16,609
2002	2,047	10,261	184.0	1,533.3	5	749,055	17,928
2003	2,125	10,346	186.1	1,632.5 p	5	784,879 p	17,986
2004	2,191 p	10,930 p	201.0 p	1,731.6 p	5 p	810,595 p	18,727 p
2005	2,268 p	11,472 p	214.9 p	1,830.7 p	5 p	836,311 p	19,297 p
2006	2,345 p	12,014 p	228.8 p	1,929.9 p	5 p	862,027 p	19,867 p
2007	2,422 p	12,557 p	242.7 p	2,029.0 p	5 p	887,743 p	20,437 p

Source: Economic Census of the United States, 1997 and 2002. Establishment counts, employment, and payroll are from *County Business Patterns* for non-Census years. This is a newly defined industry. Data for prior years are unavailable at the time of publication but may become available over time. Values followed by 'p' are projections by the editors. Sales data for non-Census years are extrapolations, marked by 'e'.

INDICES OF CHANGE

Year	Establishments (number)	Employment (number)	Payroll ($ million)	Sales ($ million)	Employees per Establishment (number)	Sales per Establishment ($)	Payroll per Employee ($)
1987	-	-	-	-	-	-	-
1992	-	-	-	-	-	-	-
1993	-	-	-	-	-	-	-
1994	-	-	-	-	-	-	-
1995	-	-	-	-	-	-	-
1996	-	-	-	-	-	-	-
1997	79.8	69.4	55.4	67.7	87.8	84.8	79.8
1998	86.6	76.6	66.0	74.1 e	87.8	85.6	86.3
1999	88.3	80.9	74.9	80.6 e	91.8	91.3	92.6
2000	90.5	82.4	74.6	87.1 e	91.8	96.2	90.6
2001	94.8	87.6	81.2	93.5 e	91.8	98.7	92.6
2002	100.0	100.0	100.0	100.0	100.0	100.0	100.0
2003	103.8	100.8	101.2	106.5 p	97.1	104.8 p	100.3
2004	107.0 p	106.5 p	109.3 p	112.9 p	100.1 p	108.2 p	104.5 p
2005	110.8 p	111.8 p	116.8 p	119.4 p	101.9 p	111.6 p	107.6 p
2006	114.5 p	117.1 p	124.4 p	125.9 p	103.8 p	115.1 p	110.8 p
2007	118.3 p	122.4 p	131.9 p	132.3 p	105.7 p	118.5 p	114.0 p

Sources: Same as General Statistics. The values shown reflect change from the base year, 2002. Values above 100 mean greater than 2002, values below 100 mean less than 2002, and a value of 100 in the 1987-2001 or 2003-2007 period means same as 2002. Values followed by a 'p' are projections by the editors; 'e' stands for extrapolation. Data are the most recent available at this level of detail.

SELECTED RATIOS

For 2002	Avg. of All Retail	Analyzed Industry	Index	For 2002	Avg. of All Retail	Analyzed Industry	Index
Employees per Establishment	17	5	30	Sales per Employee	174,682	149,431	86
Payroll per Establishment	333,445	89,866	27	Sales per Establishment	3,332,269	749,055	22
Payroll per Employee	20,311	17,928	88	Expenses per Establishment	na	na	na

Sources: Same as General Statistics. The 'Average of All' column, Wholesale or Retail, represents the average of the sector reported for the most recent complete year available. The Index shows the relationship between the Average and the Analyzed Industry. For example, 100 means that they are equal; 500 that the Analyzed Industry is five times the average; 50 means that the Analyzed Industry is half the national average. The abbreviation 'na' is used to show that data are 'not available'.

LEADING COMPANIES　　Number shown: **5**　　Total sales ($ mil): **60**　　Total employment (000): **0.3**

Company Name	Address				CEO Name	Phone	Co. Type	Sales ($ mil)	Empl. (000)
Tony's Seafood Ltd.	5215 Plank Rd	Baton Rouge	LA	70805	William Pizzolato	225-357-9669	R	42*	0.2
Quinault Pride Seafoods	PO Box 217	Taholah	WA	98587		360-276-4431	R	7*	<0.1
Chesapeake Bay Packing L.L.C.	800 Terminal Ave	Newport News	VA	23607		757-244-8440	R	6*	<0.1
Captain Faunce Seafood Inc.	PO Box 397	Montross	VA	22520	Joseph Howeth	804-493-8690	R	3*	<0.1
Taku Store	550 S Franklin St	Juneau	AK	99801	Giovanni Gallizio	907-463-4617	R	3*	<0.1

Source: Ward's Business Directory of U.S. Private and Public Companies, Volumes 1 and 2, 2005. The company type code used is as follows: P - Public, R - Private, S - Subsidiary, D - Division, J - Joint Venture, A - Affiliate, G - Group. Sales are in millions of dollars, employees are in thousands. An asterisk (*) indicates an estimated sales volume. The symbol < stands for 'less than'. Company names and addresses are truncated, in some cases, to fit into the available space.

OCCUPATIONS EMPLOYED BY SPECIALTY FOOD STORES

Occupation	% of Total 2004	Change to 2014	Occupation	% of Total 2004	Change to 2014
Cashiers, except gaming	15.5	7.3	Sales reps, wholesale & manufacturing, exc tech	2.6	19.2
Retail salespersons	10.0	19.2	Packers & packagers, hand	2.4	19.2
Combined food preparation & serving workers	5.2	19.2	Truck drivers, heavy & tractor-trailer	2.0	19.2
Butchers & meat cutters	4.8	7.3	Meat, poultry, & fish cutters & trimmers	1.9	19.2
Food preparation workers	4.4	19.2	General & operations managers	1.8	18.0
Driver/sales workers	4.4	19.0	Bakers	1.7	19.0
Stock clerks & order fillers	4.0	-8.7	First-line supervisors/managers of food service workers	1.4	19.2
Laborers & freight, stock, & material movers, hand	3.9	7.3	Bookkeeping, accounting, & auditing clerks	1.4	7.3
First-line supervisors/managers of retail sales workers	3.9	9.6	Office clerks, general	1.4	6.1
Truck drivers, light or delivery services	3.7	19.2	Packaging & filling machine operators & tenders	1.0	12.8
Counter attendants	3.3	19.2			

Source: Industry-Occupation Matrix, Bureau of Labor Statistics. These data are reported based on 4-digit NAICS categories but have been matched to corresponding 6-digit NAICS industry codes. The change reported for each occupation to the year 2014 is a percent of growth or decline as estimated by the Bureau of Labor Statistics. The abbreviation nec stands for 'not elsewhere classified.'

INDUSTRY DATA BY STATE

State-level data are not available.

NAICS 445230 - FRUIT AND VEGETABLE MARKETS*

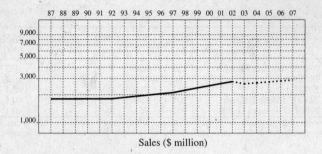

Sales ($ million)

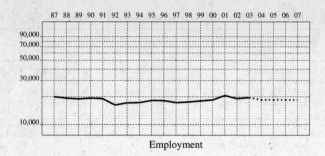

Employment

GENERAL STATISTICS

Year	Establishments (number)	Employment (number)	Payroll ($ million)	Sales ($ million)	Employees per Establishment (number)	Sales per Establishment ($)	Payroll per Employee ($)
1987	3,271	20,013	185.9	1,802.2	6	550,963	9,289
1988	3,001	19,290	199.0	1,803.6 e	6	601,000	10,316
1989	2,854	18,948	206.5	1,805.0 e	7	632,446	10,898
1990	2,942	19,312	223.3	1,806.5 e	7	614,038	11,563
1991	3,145	19,076	243.7	1,807.9 e	6	574,849	12,775
1992	2,971	16,258	198.5	1,809.3	6	608,987	12,209
1993	3,092	17,166	233.1	1,868.8 e	6	604,398	13,579
1994	3,108	17,268	228.9	1,928.3 e	6	620,431	13,256
1995	3,103	18,227	249.5	1,987.8 e	6	640,606	13,689
1996	3,024 e	18,153 e	257.0 e	2,047.3 e	6 e	677,017 e	14,157 e
1997	3,179	17,251	237.0	2,106.8	5	662,724	13,738
1998	3,206	17,522	256.0	2,239.8 e	6	698,624	14,610
1999	3,166	18,011	273.2	2,372.8 e	6	749,455	15,168
2000	3,204	18,451	295.0	2,505.8 e	6	782,073	15,989
2001	3,382	20,615	374.5	2,638.7 e	6	780,233	18,166
2002	3,239	19,094	316.9	2,771.7	6	855,738	16,596
2003	3,292	19,572	342.3	2,622.8 p	6	805,092 p	17,490
2004	3,287 p	18,514 p	337.3 p	2,686.5 p	6 p	821,474 p	17,998 p
2005	3,304 p	18,518 p	346.5 p	2,750.2 p	6 p	837,855 p	18,472 p
2006	3,322 p	18,521 p	355.8 p	2,813.9 p	6 p	854,237 p	18,946 p
2007	3,340 p	18,525 p	365.0 p	2,877.5 p	6 p	870,619 p	19,420 p

Sources: *Economic Census of the United States*, 1987, 1992, 1997, and 2002. Establishment counts, employment, and payroll are from *County Business Patterns* for non-Census years. Values followed by a 'p' are projections by the editors. Sales data for non-Census years are extrapolations, marked by 'e'. Data are the most recent available at this level of detail.

INDICES OF CHANGE

Year	Establishments (number)	Employment (number)	Payroll ($ million)	Sales ($ million)	Employees per Establishment (number)	Sales per Establishment ($)	Payroll per Employee ($)
1987	101.0	104.8	58.7	65.0	103.5	64.4	56.0
1992	91.7	85.1	62.6	65.3	93.3	71.2	73.6
1993	95.5	89.9	73.6	67.4 e	95.0	70.6	81.8
1994	96.0	90.4	72.2	69.6 e	95.0	72.5	79.9
1995	95.8	95.5	78.7	71.7 e	100.1	74.9	82.5
1996	93.4 e	95.1 e	81.1 e	73.9 e	101.8 e	79.1 e	85.3 e
1997	98.1	90.3	74.8	76.0	91.6	77.4	82.8
1998	99.0	91.8	80.8	80.8 e	93.3	81.6	88.0
1999	97.7	94.3	86.2	85.6 e	96.7	87.6	91.4
2000	98.9	96.6	93.1	90.4 e	98.4	91.4	96.3
2001	104.4	108.0	118.2	95.2 e	103.5	91.2	109.5
2002	100.0	100.0	100.0	100.0	100.0	100.0	100.0
2003	101.6	102.5	108.0	94.6 p	100.9	94.1 p	105.4
2004	101.5 p	97.0 p	106.4 p	96.9 p	95.5 p	96.0 p	108.5 p
2005	102.0 p	97.0 p	109.4 p	99.2 p	95.0 p	97.9 p	111.3 p
2006	102.6 p	97.0 p	112.3 p	101.5 p	94.4 p	99.8 p	114.2 p
2007	103.1 p	97.0 p	115.2 p	103.8 p	93.9 p	101.7 p	117.0 p

Sources: Same as General Statistics. The values shown reflect change from the base year, 2002. Values above 100 mean greater than 2002, values below 100 mean less than 2002, and a value of 100 in the 1987-2001 or 2003-2007 period means same as 2002. Values followed by a 'p' are projections by the editors; 'e' stands for extrapolation. Data are the most recent available at this level of detail.

SELECTED RATIOS

For 2002	Avg. of All Retail	Analyzed Industry	Index	For 2002	Avg. of All Retail	Analyzed Industry	Index
Employees per Establishment	17	6	35	Sales per Employee	174,682	145,163	83
Payroll per Establishment	333,445	97,833	29	Sales per Establishment	3,332,269	855,738	26
Payroll per Employee	20,311	16,596	82	Expenses per Establishment	na	na	na

Sources: Same as General Statistics. The 'Average of All' column, Wholesale or Retail, represents the average of the sector reported for the most recent complete year available. The Index shows the relationship between the Average and the Analyzed Industry. For example, 100 means that they are equal; 500 that the Analyzed Industry is five times the average; 50 means that the Analyzed Industry is half the national average. The abbreviation 'na' is used to show that data are 'not available'.

*Equivalent to SIC 5431.

LEADING COMPANIES　Number shown: **4**　Total sales ($ mil): **3,950**　Total employment (000): **9.0**

Company Name	Address				CEO Name	Phone	Co. Type	Sales ($ mil)	Empl. (000)
Nash Finch Co.	PO Box 355	Minneapolis	MN	55440	Ron Marshall	952-832-0534	P	3,897	8.7
Earth Brothers Ltd.	PO Box 188	Proctorsville	VT	05153	Steve Birge	802-226-7480	R	42*	0.1
Mixon Fruit Farms Inc.	2712 26th Ave E	Bradenton	FL	34208	WP Mixon Jr	941-748-5829	R	6*	0.1
Springdale Farm Market Inc.	1638 Springdale Rd	Cherry Hill	NJ	08003	Mary Jarvis	856-424-8674	R	5*	<0.1

Source: *Ward's Business Directory of U.S. Private and Public Companies*, Volumes 1 and 2, 2005. The company type code used is as follows: P - Public, R - Private, S - Subsidiary, D - Division, J - Joint Venture, A - Affiliate, G - Group. Sales are in millions of dollars, employees are in thousands. An asterisk (*) indicates an estimated sales volume. The symbol < stands for 'less than'. Company names and addresses are truncated, in some cases, to fit into the available space.

OCCUPATIONS EMPLOYED BY SPECIALTY FOOD STORES

Occupation	% of Total 2004	Change to 2014	Occupation	% of Total 2004	Change to 2014
Cashiers, except gaming	15.5	7.3	Sales reps, wholesale & manufacturing, exc tech	2.6	19.2
Retail salespersons	10.0	19.2	Packers & packagers, hand	2.4	19.2
Combined food preparation & serving workers	5.2	19.2	Truck drivers, heavy & tractor-trailer	2.0	19.2
Butchers & meat cutters	4.8	7.3	Meat, poultry, & fish cutters & trimmers	1.9	19.2
Food preparation workers	4.4	19.2	General & operations managers	1.8	18.0
Driver/sales workers	4.4	19.0	Bakers	1.7	19.0
Stock clerks & order fillers	4.0	-8.7	First-line supervisors/managers of food service workers	1.4	19.2
Laborers & freight, stock, & material movers, hand	3.9	7.3	Bookkeeping, accounting, & auditing clerks	1.4	7.3
First-line supervisors/managers of retail sales workers	3.9	9.6	Office clerks, general	1.4	6.1
Truck drivers, light or delivery services	3.7	19.2	Packaging & filling machine operators & tenders	1.0	12.8
Counter attendants	3.3	19.2			

Source: *Industry-Occupation Matrix*, Bureau of Labor Statistics. These data are reported based on 4-digit NAICS categories but have been matched to corresponding 6-digit NAICS industry codes. The change reported for each occupation to the year 2014 is a percent of growth or decline as estimated by the Bureau of Labor Statistics. The abbreviation nec stands for 'not elsewhere classified.'

INDUSTRY DATA BY STATE

State-level data are not available.

NAICS 445291 - BAKED GOODS STORES

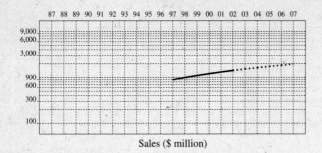

Sales ($ million)

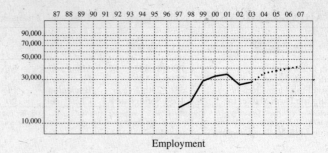

Employment

GENERAL STATISTICS

Year	Establishments (number)	Employment (number)	Payroll ($ million)	Sales ($ million)	Employees per Establishment (number)	Sales per Establishment ($)	Payroll per Employee ($)
1987	-	-	-	-	-	-	-
1988	-	-	-	-	-	-	-
1989	-	-	-	-	-	-	-
1990	-	-	-	-	-	-	-
1991	-	-	-	-	-	-	-
1992	-	-	-	-	-	-	-
1993	-	-	-	-	-	-	-
1994	-	-	-	-	-	-	-
1995	-	-	-	-	-	-	-
1996	-	-	-	-	-	-	-
1997	2,790	14,810	191.0	890.3	5	319,104	12,897
1998	3,334	17,244	249.7	995.8 *e*	5	298,690	14,480
1999	4,924	29,001	548.5	1,101.4 *e*	6	223,673	18,913
2000	5,451	32,736	609.8	1,206.9 *e*	6	221,408	18,628
2001	5,728	34,380	645.0	1,312.4 *e*	6	229,125	18,761
2002	4,485	26,285	497.9	1,418.0	6	316,157	18,942
2003	4,942	28,135	514.6	1,523.5 *p*	6	245,457 *p*	18,290
2004	5,888 *p*	35,147 *p*	688.6 *p*	1,629.0 *p*	6 *p*	239,008 *p*	20,837 *p*
2005	6,230 *p*	37,412 *p*	744.4 *p*	1,734.6 *p*	6 *p*	232,560 *p*	21,729 *p*
2006	6,571 *p*	39,678 *p*	800.3 *p*	1,840.1 *p*	6 *p*	226,111 *p*	22,620 *p*
2007	6,912 *p*	41,943 *p*	856.1 *p*	1,945.6 *p*	6 *p*	219,663 *p*	23,511 *p*

Source: *Economic Census of the United States*, 1997 and 2002. Establishment counts, employment, and payroll are from *County Business Patterns* for non-Census years. This is a newly defined industry. Data for prior years are unavailable at the time of publication but may become available over time. Values followed by 'p' are projections by the editors. Sales data for non-Census years are extrapolations, marked by 'e'.

INDICES OF CHANGE

Year	Establishments (number)	Employment (number)	Payroll ($ million)	Sales ($ million)	Employees per Establishment (number)	Sales per Establishment ($)	Payroll per Employee ($)
1987	-	-	-	-	-	-	-
1992	-	-	-	-	-	-	-
1993	-	-	-	-	-	-	-
1994	-	-	-	-	-	-	-
1995	-	-	-	-	-	-	-
1996	-	-	-	-	-	-	-
1997	62.2	56.3	38.4	62.8	90.4	100.9	68.1
1998	74.3	65.6	50.2	70.2 *e*	88.7	94.5	76.4
1999	109.8	110.3	110.2	77.7 *e*	100.7	70.7	99.8
2000	121.5	124.5	122.5	85.1 *e*	102.4	70.0	98.3
2001	127.7	130.8	129.5	92.6 *e*	102.4	72.5	99.0
2002	100.0	100.0	100.0	100.0	100.0	100.0	100.0
2003	110.2	107.0	103.4	107.4 *p*	97.1	77.6 *p*	96.6
2004	131.3 *p*	133.7 *p*	138.3 *p*	114.9 *p*	103.7 *p*	75.6 *p*	110.0 *p*
2005	138.9 *p*	142.3 *p*	149.5 *p*	122.3 *p*	105.3 *p*	73.6 *p*	114.7 *p*
2006	146.5 *p*	151.0 *p*	160.7 *p*	129.8 *p*	106.9 *p*	71.5 *p*	119.4 *p*
2007	154.1 *p*	159.6 *p*	172.0 *p*	137.2 *p*	108.5 *p*	69.5 *p*	124.1 *p*

Sources: Same as General Statistics. The values shown reflect change from the base year, 2002. Values above 100 mean greater than 2002, values below 100 mean less than 2002, and a value of 100 in the 1987-2001 or 2003-2007 period means same as 2002. Values followed by a 'p' are projections by the editors; 'e' stands for extrapolation. Data are the most recent available at this level of detail.

SELECTED RATIOS

For 2002	Avg. of All Retail	Analyzed Industry	Index	For 2002	Avg. of All Retail	Analyzed Industry	Index
Employees per Establishment	17	6	35	Sales per Employee	174,682	53,946	31
Payroll per Establishment	333,445	111,012	33	Sales per Establishment	3,332,269	316,157	9
Payroll per Employee	20,311	18,942	93	Expenses per Establishment	na	na	na

Sources: Same as General Statistics. The 'Average of All' column, Wholesale or Retail, represents the average of the sector reported for the most recent complete year available. The Index shows the relationship between the Average and the Analyzed Industry. For example, 100 means that they are equal; 500 that the Analyzed Industry is five times the average; 50 means that the Analyzed Industry is half the national average. The abbreviation 'na' is used to show that data are 'not available'.

LEADING COMPANIES   Number shown: **49**   Total sales ($ mil): **226**   Total employment (000): **1.9**

Company Name	Address				CEO Name	Phone	Co. Type	Sales ($ mil)	Empl. (000)
Maple Donuts Inc.	3455 E Market St	York	PA	17402	Charles Burnside	717-757-7826	R	33*	0.2
Alessi Bakeries	2909 W Cypress St	Tampa	FL	33609	Phillip Alessi	813-871-2286	R	16*	<0.1
George Weston Bakeries	6361 Topaz Ct	Fort Myers	FL	33912		239-277-9646	R	13*	0.1
Doughnut Peddler	3659 E Southern	Mesa	AZ	85206	Steve Smith	480-985-1038	R	9*	<0.1
Twin City Bagels Inc.	130 Hardman Ave S	South Saint Paul	MN	55075	Shimon Harosh	651-554-0200	R	9*	<0.1
Huber Orchard and Winery Inc.	19816 Huber Rd	Borden	IN	47106	Greg Huber	812-923-9813	R	9*	<0.1
Scholars Inn Bakehouse	125 N College Ave	Bloomington	IN	47404		812-331-6029	R	8*	<0.1
Jaciva's Inc.	4733 SE Hawthorne	Portland	OR	97215	Jacob Elmer	503-234-8115	R	7*	<0.1
Burke's Bakery	121 W Main St	Danville	KY	40422	Joe Burke	859-236-5661	R	5*	<0.1
Holts Bakery Inc.	101 Sellers St	Douglas	GA	31533		912-384-2202	R	5*	<0.1
Pettit's Pastry Inc.	502 N 16th St	Omaha	NE	68102	Brett Pettit	402-345-1111	R	5*	<0.1
Sugar Plum Bakery	1353 Laskin Rd	Virginia Beach	VA	23451		757-422-3913	R	5*	<0.1
Wedemeyer Bakery Inc.	314 Harbor Way	S. San Francisco	CA	94080	Larry Strain	650-873-1000	R	5*	<0.1
Sweetheart Bakery Inc.	19200 Kelly Rd	Detroit	MI	48225		313-839-6330	R	5*	<0.1
Pastian's Bakery	3320 2nd St NW	Albuquerque	NM	87107	Cheryl Pastians	505-345-7773	R	5*	<0.1
Los Bagels Inc.	1085 I St	Arcata	CA	95521	Dennis Rael	707-822-3150	R	5*	<0.1
Kretchmar Bakery Inc.	664 3rd St	Beaver	PA	15009	Henry Kretchmar	724-774-2324	R	4*	<0.1
Leonard's Bakery Ltd.	933 Kapahulu Ave	Honolulu	HI	96816	Frank Rego	808-737-5591	R	4*	<0.1
Millburn Bagel Inc.	321 Millburn Ave	Millburn	NJ	07041	Martin Wayne	973-379-1099	R	4*	<0.1
Stahl's Bakery Inc.	51021 Washington	New Baltimore	MI	48047	Joseph Stabile	586-716-8500	R	4*	<0.1
Provence Breads	PO Box 23946	Nashville	TN	37202	Terry Hall	615-386-0363	R	4*	<0.1
Chompie's	3202 E Greenway	Phoenix	AZ	85032	Louis Borenstein	602-971-8010	R	3*	0.1
Almira's Bakery	2635 169th St	Hammond	IN	46323		219-844-4334	R	3*	<0.1
Bagatelle Bakery Inc.	1425 N Pershing St	Wichita	KS	67208	Naji Toubia	316-684-5662	R	3*	<0.1
Dusek's Bakery Inc.	223 Central Ave N	Faribault	MN	55021	Marylee Becker	507-334-6495	R	3*	<0.1
Nantucket Bake Shop Inc.	PO Box 539	Nantucket	MA	02554	David Bradt	508-228-2797	R	3*	<0.1
Weiman's Bakery Inc.	127 N 17th St	Richmond	VA	23219	Morton Weiman	804-644-7412	R	3*	<0.1
Tripoli Bakery Inc.	104 Common St	Lawrence	MA	01840	Rosario Zappella	978-682-7754	R	3*	<0.1
Bent's Cookie Factory	7 Pleasant St	Milton	MA	02186	Eugene Pierotti	617-698-5945	R	3*	<0.1
Schneider's Bakery Inc.	6 S State St	Westerville	OH	43081	Jeff Hamler	614-882-6611	R	3*	<0.1
Del Buono Bakery Inc.	319 Black Horse Pke	Haddon Heights	NJ	08035	Nino Del Buono	856-546-9585	R	3*	<0.1
Dilusso Baking	1135 NW Galveston	Bend	OR	97701	Nick Lapham	541-383-8155	R	3*	<0.1
Edgar's Old Style Bakery	3439 Colonnade	Birmingham	AL	35243	Dottie Smith	205-968-0150	R	3*	<0.1
Einstein Bagels Inc.	27365 Woodward	Berkley	MI	48072		248-545-9888	R	3*	<0.1
Flour Shop Bakery and Pizza	1727 W John Beers	Stevensville	MI	49127	Klaus Nixdorf	269-429-3259	R	3*	<0.1
Joan and Gary's Original Bagel	1496 Reisterstown	Pikesville	MD	21208	Gary Van Hoven	410-484-9102	R	3*	<0.1
Norcia Bakery	624 Belden Ave NE	Canton	OH	44704	Donald Horne	330-454-1077	R	3*	<0.1
Bread and Co.	4105 Hillsboro Rd	Nashville	TN	37215	Ann Clay	615-292-7323	R	3*	<0.1
Missouri Baking Co.	2027 Edwards St	Saint Louis	MO	63110	Chris Gambaro	314-773-6566	R	2*	<0.1
Rolling Pin Pastry Company Inc.	3218 W Galbraith	Cincinnati	OH	45239	R Hanes	513-741-7517	R	2*	<0.1
Meadowbrook Orchards Inc.	209 Chace Hill Rd	Sterling	MA	01564	David Chandler	978-365-7617	R	2*	<0.1
Rosemark Bakery Inc.	258 Snelling Ave S	Saint Paul	MN	55105	Carol Rosemark	651-698-3838	R	2*	<0.1
BLF Enterprises Inc.	445 S State St	Westerville	OH	43081	Bruce Fowler	614-899-6100	R	1*	<0.1
Daube's Bakery Inc.	1310 5th Pl NW	Rochester	MN	55901	Cynthia Daube	507-289-3095	R	1*	<0.1
Dunkin' Donuts	283 Providence St	West Warwick	RI	02893		401-822-2434	R	1*	<0.1
Mozzicato Pastry & Bake Shop	329 Franklin Ave	Hartford	CT	06114	Gisella Mozzicato	860-296-0426	R	1*	<0.1
Kennedy's Bakery Inc.	PO Box 396	Cambridge	OH	43725	Bob Kennedy	740-432-2301	R	1*	<0.1
Ro Do Company Inc.	3509 Maccorkle SE	Charleston	WV	25304	Amy Vickers	304-925-4261	R	1*	<0.1
Herman's Bakery and Coffee Shop	130 Main St S	Cambridge	MN	55008	Herman Oestreich	763-689-1515	R	1*	<0.1

Source: Ward's Business Directory of U.S. Private and Public Companies, Volumes 1 and 2, 2005. The company type code used is as follows: P - Public, R - Private, S - Subsidiary, D - Division, J - Joint Venture, A - Affiliate, G - Group. Sales are in millions of dollars, employees are in thousands. An asterisk (*) indicates an estimated sales volume. The symbol < stands for 'less than'. Company names and addresses are truncated, in some cases, to fit into the available space.

OCCUPATIONS EMPLOYED BY SPECIALTY FOOD STORES

Occupation	% of Total 2004	Change to 2014	Occupation	% of Total 2004	Change to 2014
Cashiers, except gaming	15.5	7.3	Sales reps, wholesale & manufacturing, exc tech	2.6	19.2
Retail salespersons	10.0	19.2	Packers & packagers, hand	2.4	19.2
Combined food preparation & serving workers	5.2	19.2	Truck drivers, heavy & tractor-trailer	2.0	19.2
Butchers & meat cutters	4.8	7.3	Meat, poultry, & fish cutters & trimmers	1.9	19.2
Food preparation workers	4.4	19.2	General & operations managers	1.8	18.0
Driver/sales workers	4.4	19.0	Bakers	1.7	19.0
Stock clerks & order fillers	4.0	-8.7	First-line supervisors/managers of food service workers	1.4	19.2
Laborers & freight, stock, & material movers, hand	3.9	7.3	Bookkeeping, accounting, & auditing clerks	1.4	7.3
First-line supervisors/managers of retail sales workers	3.9	9.6	Office clerks, general	1.4	6.1
Truck drivers, light or delivery services	3.7	19.2	Packaging & filling machine operators & tenders	1.0	12.8
Counter attendants	3.3	19.2			

Source: Industry-Occupation Matrix, Bureau of Labor Statistics. These data are reported based on 4-digit NAICS categories but have been matched to corresponding 6-digit NAICS industry codes. The change reported for each occupation to the year 2014 is a percent of growth or decline as estimated by the Bureau of Labor Statistics. The abbreviation nec stands for 'not elsewhere classified.'

INDUSTRY DATA BY STATE

State-level data are not available.

NAICS 445292 - CONFECTIONERY AND NUT STORES

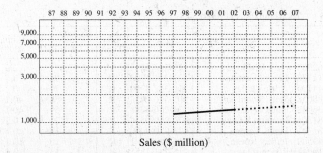

Sales ($ million)

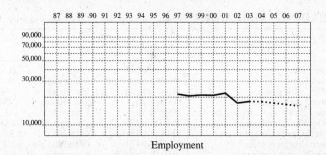

Employment

GENERAL STATISTICS

Year	Establishments (number)	Employment (number)	Payroll ($ million)	Sales ($ million)	Employees per Establishment (number)	Sales per Establishment ($)	Payroll per Employee ($)
1987	-	-	-	-	-	-	-
1988	-	-	-	-	-	-	-
1989	-	-	-	-	-	-	-
1990	-	-	-	-	-	-	-
1991	-	-	-	-	-	-	-
1992	-	-	-	-	-	-	-
1993	-	-	-	-	-	-	-
1994	-	-	-	-	-	-	-
1995	-	-	-	-	-	-	-
1996	-	-	-	-	-	-	-
1997	3,684	21,578	190.8	1,227.9	6	333,306	8,842
1998	3,826	20,638	213.3	1,255.2 e	5	328,058	10,335
1999	3,885	21,079	225.7	1,282.4 e	5	330,090	10,707
2000	3,961	20,938	248.6	1,309.7 e	5	330,637	11,873
2001	3,839	22,140	253.2	1,336.9 e	6	348,242	11,437
2002	3,437	17,284	211.0	1,364.2	5	396,902	12,207
2003	3,523	17,949	221.5	1,391.4 p	5	382,447 p	12,340
2004	3,550 p	17,867 p	239.9 p	1,418.7 p	5 p	393,278 p	13,244 p
2005	3,503 p	17,277 p	244.0 p	1,445.9 p	5 p	404,109 p	13,779 p
2006	3,456 p	16,686 p	248.1 p	1,473.2 p	5 p	414,940 p	14,313 p
2007	3,410 p	16,096 p	252.2 p	1,500.4 p	5 p	425,771 p	14,848 p

Source: *Economic Census of the United States*, 1997 and 2002. Establishment counts, employment, and payroll are from *County Business Patterns* for non-Census years. This is a newly defined industry. Data for prior years are unavailable at the time of publication but may become available over time. Values followed by 'p' are projections by the editors. Sales data for non-Census years are extrapolations, marked by 'e'.

INDICES OF CHANGE

Year	Establishments (number)	Employment (number)	Payroll ($ million)	Sales ($ million)	Employees per Establishment (number)	Sales per Establishment ($)	Payroll per Employee ($)
1987	-	-	-	-	-	-	-
1992	-	-	-	-	-	-	-
1993	-	-	-	-	-	-	-
1994	-	-	-	-	-	-	-
1995	-	-	-	-	-	-	-
1996	-	-	-	-	-	-	-
1997	107.2	124.8	90.4	90.0	117.3	84.0	72.4
1998	111.3	119.4	101.1	92.0 e	107.4	82.7	84.7
1999	113.0	122.0	107.0	94.0 e	107.4	83.2	87.7
2000	115.2	121.1	117.8	96.0 e	105.4	83.3	97.3
2001	111.7	128.1	120.0	98.0 e	115.3	87.7	93.7
2002	100.0	100.0	100.0	100.0	100.0	100.0	100.0
2003	102.5	103.8	105.0	102.0 p	101.3	96.4 p	101.1
2004	103.3 p	103.4 p	113.7 p	104.0 p	99.9 p	99.1 p	108.5 p
2005	101.9 p	100.0 p	115.6 p	106.0 p	97.9 p	101.8 p	112.9 p
2006	100.6 p	96.5 p	117.6 p	108.0 p	96.0 p	104.5 p	117.3 p
2007	99.2 p	93.1 p	119.5 p	110.0 p	94.0 p	107.3 p	121.6 p

Sources: Same as General Statistics. The values shown reflect change from the base year, 2002. Values above 100 mean greater than 2002, values below 100 mean less than 2002, and a value of 100 in the 1987-2001 or 2003-2007 period means same as 2002. Values followed by a 'p' are projections by the editors; 'e' stands for extrapolation. Data are the most recent available at this level of detail.

SELECTED RATIOS

For 2002	Avg. of All Retail	Analyzed Industry	Index	For 2002	Avg. of All Retail	Analyzed Industry	Index
Employees per Establishment	17	5	30	Sales per Employee	174,682	78,926	45
Payroll per Establishment	333,445	61,386	18	Sales per Establishment	3,332,269	396,902	12
Payroll per Employee	20,311	12,207	60	Expenses per Establishment	na	na	na

Sources: Same as General Statistics. The 'Average of All' column, Wholesale or Retail, represents the average of the sector reported for the most recent complete year available. The Index shows the relationship between the Average and the Analyzed Industry. For example, 100 means that they are equal; 500 that the Analyzed Industry is five times the average; 50 means that the Analyzed Industry is half the national average. The abbreviation 'na' is used to show that data are 'not available'.

LEADING COMPANIES   Number shown: **26**   Total sales ($ mil): **956**   Total employment (000): **4.1**

Company Name	Address				CEO Name	Phone	Co. Type	Sales ($ mil)	Empl. (000)
Kirlins Inc.	PO Box 3097	Quincy	IL	62305	Gary Kirlin	217-224-8953	S	477*	2.0
Lanco Corp.	350 Wireless Blvd	Hauppauge	NY	11788	Brian Landow	631-231-2300	R	96*	0.4
Malley's Chocolates	13400 Brookpark Rd	Cleveland	OH	44135	Adele Malley	216-362-8700	R	77*	0.2
Stahmann Farms Inc.	PO Box 70	San Miguel	NM	88058	Sally Stahmann	505-526-2453	R	68*	<0.1
Louisville Pecan Company Inc.	PO Box 38	Louisville	AL	36048	Homer Henson	334-266-5388	R	59*	<0.1
Rocky Mtn Chocolate Factory	265 Turner Dr	Durango	CO	81303	Franklin E Crail	970-259-0554	P	21	0.2
Cerreta Candy Company Inc.	5345 W Glendale	Glendale	AZ	85301	James Cerreta	623-930-9000	R	19*	<0.1
Koeze Company Inc.	PO Box 9470	Grand Rapids	MI	49509	Jeffrey Koeze	616-724-2601	R	15*	<0.1
Bucks County Coffee Co.	2250 W Cabot Blvd	Langhorne	PA	19047	Rodger Owen	215-741-1855	R	13*	0.4
Beerntsen's Confectionery Inc.	108 N 8th St	Manitowoc	WI	54220	Dean Schadrie	920-684-9616	R	12*	<0.1
Dinstuhl's Candies	5280 Pleasant View	Memphis	TN	38134	Jack Rice	901-377-2639	R	12*	<0.1
Hoffman's Chocolate Shoppe	5190 Lake Worth Rd	Greenacres	FL	33463	Fred Meltzer	561-967-2213	R	12*	<0.1
Philadelphia Candies Inc.	1546 E State St	Hermitage	PA	16148	Spyros Macris	724-981-6341	R	11*	<0.1
Quality Candy Shoppes/Buddy	PO Box 070581	Milwaukee	WI	53207	Margaret Gile	414-483-4500	R	10*	0.3
Bitterman Family Confections	PO Box 410227	Kansas City	MO	64141	Alan Bitterman	816-531-3107	R	8*	<0.1
Fort Fudge Shop Inc.	PO Box 340	Mackinaw City	MI	49701	Robert Heilman	231-436-8931	R	8*	<0.1
Harbor Sweets Inc.	85 Leavitt St	Salem	MA	01970	Phyllis LeBlanc	978-745-7648	R	7*	<0.1
Jaciva's Inc.	4733 SE Hawthorne	Portland	OR	97215	Jacob Elmer	503-234-8115	R	7*	<0.1
Faroh Candies Inc.	6890 Pearl Rd	Middleburg H.	OH	44130	George Faroh	440-842-4070	R	6*	<0.1
Zahars Inc.	4803 Liberty Ave	Vermilion	OH	44089	Rhonda Zahars	440-967-6318	R	6*	<0.1
Abbott's Candy and Gifts	48 E Walnut St	Hagerstown	IN	47346	Suanna Goodnight	765-489-4442	R	5*	<0.1
Schenone Specialty Foods Inc.	PO Box 730	Clements	CA	95227		209-759-3340	R	3	<0.1
Truan's Candies Inc.	13716 Tireman St	Detroit	MI	48228	Mark Truan	313-584-3400	R	2*	<0.1
Pape Pecan House	PO Box 1281	Seguin	TX	78156	Kenneth Pape	830-379-7442	R	1*	<0.1
Bucky Bairdo's Inc.	103 E Silverspring	Milwaukee	WI	53217	David Baird	414-332-9007	R	1*	<0.1
Candy Express Franchising Inc.	10480 Patuxent	Columbia	MD	21044	David Rosenberg	410-964-5500	R	1*	<0.1

Source: Ward's Business Directory of U.S. Private and Public Companies, Volumes 1 and 2, 2005. The company type code used is as follows: P - Public, R - Private, S - Subsidiary, D - Division, J - Joint Venture, A - Affiliate, G - Group. Sales are in millions of dollars, employees are in thousands. An asterisk (*) indicates an estimated sales volume. The symbol < stands for 'less than'. Company names and addresses are truncated, in some cases, to fit into the available space.

OCCUPATIONS EMPLOYED BY SPECIALTY FOOD STORES

Occupation	% of Total 2004	Change to 2014	Occupation	% of Total 2004	Change to 2014
Cashiers, except gaming	15.5	7.3	Sales reps, wholesale & manufacturing, exc tech	2.6	19.2
Retail salespersons	10.0	19.2	Packers & packagers, hand	2.4	19.2
Combined food preparation & serving workers	5.2	19.2	Truck drivers, heavy & tractor-trailer	2.0	19.2
Butchers & meat cutters	4.8	7.3	Meat, poultry, & fish cutters & trimmers	1.9	19.2
Food preparation workers	4.4	19.2	General & operations managers	1.8	18.0
Driver/sales workers	4.4	19.0	Bakers	1.7	19.0
Stock clerks & order fillers	4.0	-8.7	First-line supervisors/managers of food service workers	1.4	19.2
Laborers & freight, stock, & material movers, hand	3.9	7.3	Bookkeeping, accounting, & auditing clerks	1.4	7.3
First-line supervisors/managers of retail sales workers	3.9	9.6	Office clerks, general	1.4	6.1
Truck drivers, light or delivery services	3.7	19.2	Packaging & filling machine operators & tenders	1.0	12.8
Counter attendants	3.3	19.2			

Source: Industry-Occupation Matrix, Bureau of Labor Statistics. These data are reported based on 4-digit NAICS categories but have been matched to corresponding 6-digit NAICS industry codes. The change reported for each occupation to the year 2014 is a percent of growth or decline as estimated by the Bureau of Labor Statistics. The abbreviation nec stands for 'not elsewhere classified.'

INDUSTRY DATA BY STATE

State-level data are not available.

NAICS 445299 - ALL OTHER SPECIALTY FOOD STORES

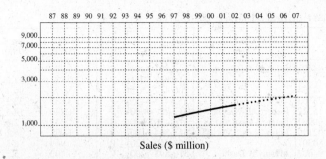

Sales ($ million)

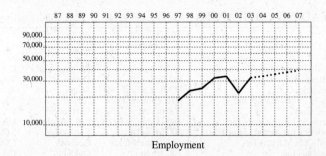

Employment

GENERAL STATISTICS

Year	Establishments (number)	Employment (number)	Payroll ($ million)	Sales ($ million)	Employees per Establishment (number)	Sales per Establishment ($)	Payroll per Employee ($)
1987	-	-	-	-	-	-	-
1988	-	-	-	-	-	-	-
1989	-	-	-	-	-	-	-
1990	-	-	-	-	-	-	-
1991	-	-	-	-	-	-	-
1992	-	-	-	-	-	-	-
1993	-	-	-	-	-	-	-
1994	-	-	-	-	-	-	-
1995	-	-	-	-	-	-	-
1996	-	-	-	-	-	-	-
1997	3,872	18,206	190.5	1,220.3	5	315,160	10,464
1998	4,840	23,379	281.3	1,306.1 e	5	269,859	12,032
1999	5,628	24,804	331.4	1,391.9 e	4	247,324	13,361
2000	6,767	32,262	424.0	1,477.8 e	5	218,377	13,142
2001	6,721	33,736	432.1	1,563.6 e	5	232,640	12,808
2002	5,451	21,953	276.8	1,649.4	4	302,586	12,608
2003	6,693	32,564	490.8	1,735.2 p	5	243,977 p	15,072
2004	7,250 p	33,723 p	488.5 p	1,821.0 p	5 p	238,164 p	14,844 p
2005	7,635 p	35,478 p	523.9 p	1,906.9 p	5 p	232,350 p	15,360 p
2006	8,020 p	37,234 p	559.4 p	1,992.7 p	5 p	226,536 p	15,875 p
2007	8,405 p	38,989 p	594.8 p	2,078.5 p	5 p	220,723 p	16,390 p

Source: Economic Census of the United States, 1997 and 2002. Establishment counts, employment, and payroll are from *County Business Patterns* for non-Census years. This is a newly defined industry. Data for prior years are unavailable at the time of publication but may become available over time. Values followed by 'p' are projections by the editors. Sales data for non-Census years are extrapolations, marked by 'e'.

INDICES OF CHANGE

Year	Establishments (number)	Employment (number)	Payroll ($ million)	Sales ($ million)	Employees per Establishment (number)	Sales per Establishment ($)	Payroll per Employee ($)
1987	-	-	-	-	-	-	-
1992	-	-	-	-	-	-	-
1993	-	-	-	-	-	-	-
1994	-	-	-	-	-	-	-
1995	-	-	-	-	-	-	-
1996	-	-	-	-	-	-	-
1997	71.0	82.9	68.8	74.0	116.7	104.2	83.0
1998	88.8	106.5	101.6	79.2 e	119.2	89.2	95,4
1999	103.2	113.0	119.7	84.4 e	109.3	81.7	106.0
2000	124.1	147.0	153.2	89.6 e	119.2	72.2	104.2
2001	123.3	153.7	156.1	94.8 e	124.2	76.9	101.6
2002	100.0	100.0	100.0	100.0	100.0	100.0	100.0
2003	122.8	148.3	177.3	105.2 p	120.8	80.6 p	119.5
2004	133.0 p	153.6 p	176.5 p	110.4 p	114.0 p	78.7 p	117.7 p
2005	140.1 p	161.6 p	189.3 p	115.6 p	113.6 p	76.8 p	121.8 p
2006	147.1 p	169.6 p	202.1 p	120.8 p	113.2 p	74.9 p	125.9 p
2007	154.2 p	177.6 p	214.9 p	126.0 p	112.8 p	72.9 p	130.0 p

Sources: Same as General Statistics. The values shown reflect change from the base year, 2002. Values above 100 mean greater than 2002, values below 100 mean less than 2002, and a value of 100 in the 1987-2001 or 2003-2007 period means same as 2002. Values followed by a 'p' are projections by the editors; 'e' stands for extrapolation. Data are the most recent available at this level of detail.

SELECTED RATIOS

For 2002	Avg. of All Retail	Analyzed Industry	Index	For 2002	Avg. of All Retail	Analyzed Industry	Index
Employees per Establishment	17	4	24	Sales per Employee	174,682	75,133	43
Payroll per Establishment	333,445	50,776	15	Sales per Establishment	3,332,269	302,586	9
Payroll per Employee	20,311	12,608	62	Expenses per Establishment	na	na	na

Sources: Same as General Statistics. The 'Average of All' column, Wholesale or Retail, represents the average of the sector reported for the most recent complete year available. The Index shows the relationship between the Average and the Analyzed Industry. For example, 100 means that they are equal; 500 that the Analyzed Industry is five times the average; 50 means that the Analyzed Industry is half the national average. The abbreviation 'na' is used to show that data are 'not available'.

LEADING COMPANIES　　Number shown: **42**　　Total sales ($ mil): **42,384**　　Total employment (000): **202.8**

Company Name	Address				CEO Name	Phone	Co. Type	Sales ($ mil)	Empl. (000)
Whole Foods Market S Pacific	15315 Magnolia	Sherman Oaks	CA	91403	Michael Besancon	818-501-8484	S	15,755*	4.0
7-Eleven Inc.	PO Box 711	Dallas	TX	75221		214-828-7011	P	10,882	31.0
Starbucks Corp.	PO Box 34067	Seattle	WA	98124		206-447-1575	P	5,294	96.7
Whole Foods Market Inc.	601 N Lamar Blvd	Austin	TX	78703		512-477-4455	P	3,865	32.1
GNC Corp.	300 6th Ave	Pittsburgh	PA	15222	Robert J DiNicola	412-288-4600	S	1,430	14.3
Herbalife International Inc.	1800 Century Pk, E	Los Angeles	CA	90067	Peter M Castleman	310-410-9600	S	1,337*	2.6
Modern Continental Companies	600 Mem Dr	Cambridge	MA	02139	Lelio "Les" Marino	617-864-6300	R	1,098	4.2
Wild Oats Markets Inc.	3375 Mitchell Ln	Boulder	CO	80301		303-440-5220	P	969	8.3
Cost Plus Inc.	200 4th St	Oakland	CA	94607	Murray H Dashe	510-893-7300	P	802	5.5
Heritage Dairy Stores Inc.	376 Jessup Rd	Thorofare	NJ	08086	Harold R Heritage	856-845-2855	R	165*	0.4
Team Schierl Cos.	PO Box 308	Stevens Point	WI	54481	William Schierl	715-345-5060	R	133*	0.6
Miller and Holmes Inc.	2311 O'Neil Rd	Hudson	WI	54016	Jerry Peterson	715-377-1730	R	103*	0.3
Gold Standard Enterprises Inc.	5100 W Dumpster	Skokie	IL	60077	Michael Binstein	847-674-4200	R	72*	0.3
Frontier Equity Exchange	PO Box 998	Goodland	KS	67735	Ned Smith	785-899-3681	R	62*	<0.1
Turner Dairy Farms Inc.	1049 Jefferson Rd	Pittsburgh	PA	15235		412-372-2211	R	61*	0.2
Diedrich Coffee Inc.	28 Executive Pk	Irvine	CA	92614	Paul C Heeschen	949-260-1600	P	55	0.8
Masotta Variety and Deli	307 Main St	Woburn	MA	01801	Catino Masotta	781-935-2648	R	51*	<0.1
Belmont Springs Water Inc.	36 Country Club Ln	Belmont	MA	02478		617-489-4752	S	32*	0.2
Medifast Inc.	11445 Cronhill Dr	Owings Mills	MD	21117	Bradley T MacDonald	410-581-8042	P	25	0.1
V Sattui Winery	1111 White Ln	Saint Helena	CA	94574	Tom Davies	707-963-7774	R	24*	<0.1
Homestead Dairies Inc.	PO Box 428	Massena	NY	13662	David Squires	315-769-2456	R	17*	<0.1
Northwest Cheese Distributors Inc.	PO Box 882943	San Francisco	CA	94188	Herb Brosowsky	415-822-5088	R	15*	<0.1
Grafton Village Cheese Co.	PO Box 87	Grafton	VT	05146	Stephan Morse	802-843-2221	R	14*	<0.1
Middlefield Cheese	PO Box 757	Middlefield	OH	44062	John Rothenbuhler	440-632-5228	R	14*	<0.1
Dixie Chili Inc.	733 Monmouth St	Newport	KY	41071	Panny Sarakatsannis	859-291-5337	R	14*	<0.1
Bucks County Coffee Co.	2250 W Cabot Blvd	Langhorne	PA	19047	Rodger Owen	215-741-1855	R	13*	0.4
Pittsburgh Snax and Nut Inc.	2517 Penn Ave 19	Pittsburgh	PA	15235	Richard Cuneo	412-391-4444	R	11*	<0.1
Amigo's Mexican Foods Inc.	1202 E Poplar St	Deming	NM	88030	Barbara Orquiz	505-546-6841	R	11*	<0.1
Pastaworks	3735 SE Hawthorne	Portland	OR	97214	Peter DeGarmo	503-232-1010	R	9*	<0.1
Krohn Dairy Store	N2915 County AB	Luxemburg	WI	54217	Mike Sipple	920-845-2901	R	7*	0.1
Simon's Specialty Cheese Inc.	PO Box 223	Little Chute	WI	54140		920-788-6311	R	7*	0.1
Deters Dairy	PO Box 3216	Quincy	IL	62305	Norma Weiman	217-223-5484	R	7*	<0.1
Valley Dairy	3200 Graham Ave	Windber	PA	15963		814-467-5537	R	6*	<0.1
Mangia Italiano	3145 S Grand Blvd	Saint Louis	MO	63118	David Burmeister	314-664-8585	R	6*	<0.1
Amir Foods Inc.	4422 Mayfield Rd	South Euclid	OH	44121	Butch Rassi	216-291-1800	R	5*	<0.1
Turner New Zealand Inc.	PO Box 8919	Newport Beach	CA	92658	Noel Turner	949-622-6181	R	4*	<0.1
Plaza Bakery Haagen Dazs	56 E San Francisco	Santa Fe	NM	87501	Fred Libby	505-988-3858	R	3*	<0.1
Adventure in Food Trading Inc.	84 Montgomery St	Albany	NY	12207	Joseph R Messina	518-436-7603	R	2*	<0.1
Atlanta Bread Co.	4100 Pelham Rd	Greenville	SC	29615		864-627-4300	R	2*	<0.1
Daybreak Coffee Roasters Inc.	2377 Main St, Ste 3	Glastonbury	CT	06033	Thomas Clarke	860-657-4466	R	1*	<0.1
Rita's Italian Ice	640 E Penn Ave	Lebanon	PA	17042	Jim Plummer	717-306-4217	R	1*	<0.1
Pape Pecan House	PO Box 1281	Seguin	TX	78156	Kenneth Pape	830-379-7442	R	1*	<0.1

Source: Ward's Business Directory of U.S. Private and Public Companies, Volumes 1 and 2, 2005. The company type code used is as follows: P - Public, R - Private, S - Subsidiary, D - Division, J - Joint Venture, A - Affiliate, G - Group. Sales are in millions of dollars, employees are in thousands. An asterisk (*) indicates an estimated sales volume. The symbol < stands for 'less than'. Company names and addresses are truncated, in some cases, to fit into the available space.

OCCUPATIONS EMPLOYED BY SPECIALTY FOOD STORES

Occupation	% of Total 2004	Change to 2014	Occupation	% of Total 2004	Change to 2014
Cashiers, except gaming	15.5	7.3	Sales reps, wholesale & manufacturing, exc tech	2.6	19.2
Retail salespersons	10.0	19.2	Packers & packagers, hand	2.4	19.2
Combined food preparation & serving workers	5.2	19.2	Truck drivers, heavy & tractor-trailer	2.0	19.2
Butchers & meat cutters	4.8	7.3	Meat, poultry, & fish cutters & trimmers	1.9	19.2
Food preparation workers	4.4	19.2	General & operations managers	1.8	18.0
Driver/sales workers	4.4	19.0	Bakers	1.7	19.0
Stock clerks & order fillers	4.0	-8.7	First-line supervisors/managers of food service workers	1.4	19.2
Laborers & freight, stock, & material movers, hand	3.9	7.3	Bookkeeping, accounting, & auditing clerks	1.4	7.3
First-line supervisors/managers of retail sales workers	3.9	9.6	Office clerks, general	1.4	6.1
Truck drivers, light or delivery services	3.7	19.2	Packaging & filling machine operators & tenders	1.0	12.8
Counter attendants	3.3	19.2			

Source: Industry-Occupation Matrix, Bureau of Labor Statistics. These data are reported based on 4-digit NAICS categories but have been matched to corresponding 6-digit NAICS industry codes. The change reported for each occupation to the year 2014 is a percent of growth or decline as estimated by the Bureau of Labor Statistics. The abbreviation nec stands for 'not elsewhere classified.'

INDUSTRY DATA BY STATE

State-level data are not available.

NAICS 445310 - BEER, WINE, AND LIQUOR STORES*

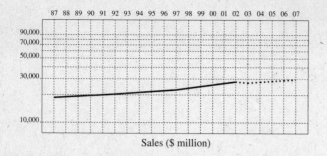

Sales ($ million)

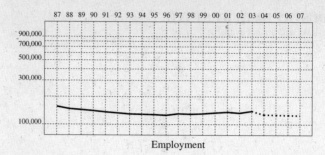

Employment

GENERAL STATISTICS

Year	Establishments (number)	Employment (number)	Payroll ($ million)	Sales ($ million)	Employees per Establishment (number)	Sales per Establishment ($)	Payroll per Employee ($)
1987-	35,194	156,519	1,454.3	18,597.0	4	528,414	9,292
1988	31,934	147,807	1,516.7	18,941.4 e	5	593,142	10,261
1989	31,655	144,234	1,543.8	19,285.8 e	5	609,250	10,703
1990	30,823	140,548	1,551.1	19,630.2 e	5	636,869	11,036
1991	30,623	136,206	1,577.7	19,974.7 e	4	652,278	11,583
1992	31,386	132,989	1,522.8	20,319.1	4	647,394	11,451
1993	30,249	129,617	1,552.9	20,792.1 e	4	687,365	11,981
1994	29,544	128,727	1,594.5	21,265.1 e	4	719,777	12,387
1995	28,952	127,708	1,612.9	21,738.1 e	4	750,832	12,630
1996	29,053 e	125,767 e	1,690.0 e	22,211.1 e	4 e	764,503 e	13,438 e
1997	29,613	130,635	1,699.3	22,684.1	4	766,018	13,008
1998	27,862	129,102	1,820.5	23,699.4 e	5	850,600	14,101
1999	28,149	130,568	1,941.1	24,714.7 e	5	877,996	14,867
2000	28,463	133,687	2,065.5	25,730.0 e	5	903,981	15,450
2001	28,695	136,212	2,153.9	26,745.3 e	5	932,055	15,813
2002	28,881	133,097	2,069.1	27,760.6	5	961,207	15,546
2003	29,141	139,449	2,245.4	27,107.8 p	5	974,528 p	16,102
2004	27,331 p	127,586 p	2,164.6 p	27,693.4 p	5 p	1,001,813 p	16,635 p
2005	27,033 p	126,711 p	2,211.5 p	28,278.9 p	5 p	1,029,098 p	17,048 p
2006	26,735 p	125,835 p	2,258.5 p	28,864.5 p	5 p	1,056,383 p	17,460 p
2007	26,437 p	124,960 p	2,305.5 p	29,450.0 p	5 p	1,083,668 p	17,873 p

Sources: *Economic Census of the United States*, 1987, 1992, 1997, and 2002. Establishment counts, employment, and payroll are from *County Business Patterns* for non-Census years. Values followed by a 'p' are projections by the editors. Sales data for non-Census years are extrapolations, marked by 'e'. Data are the most recent available at this level of detail.

INDICES OF CHANGE

Year	Establishments (number)	Employment (number)	Payroll ($ million)	Sales ($ million)	Employees per Establishment (number)	Sales per Establishment ($)	Payroll per Employee ($)
1987	121.9	117.6	70.3	67.0	95.5	55.0	59.8
1992	108.7	99.9	73.6	73.2	91.1	67.4	73.7
1993	104.7	97.4	75.1	74.9 e	93.3	71.5	77.1
1994	102.3	96.7	77.1	76.6 e	95.5	74.9	79.7
1995	100.2	96.0	78.0	78.3 e	95.5	78.1	81.2
1996	100.6 e	94.5 e	81.7 e	80.0 e	93.3 e	79.5 e	86.4 e
1997	102.5	98.2	82.1	81.7	95.5	79.7	83.7
1998	96.5	97.0	88.0	85.4 e	99.8	88.5	90.7
1999	97.5	98.1	93.8	89.0 e	99.8	91.3	95.6
2000	98.6	100.4	99.8	92.7 e	102.0	94.0	99.4
2001	99.4	102.3	104.1	96.3 e	102.0	97.0	101.7
2002	100.0	100.0	100.0	100.0	100.0	100.0	100.0
2003	100.9	104.8	108.5	97.6 p	103.8	101.4 p	103.6
2004	94.6 p	95.9 p	104.6 p	99.8 p	100.8 p	104.2 p	107.0 p
2005	93.6 p	95.2 p	106.9 p	101.9 p	101.1 p	107.1 p	109.7 p
2006	92.6 p	94.5 p	109.2 p	104.0 p	101.5 p	109.9 p	112.3 p
2007	91.5 p	93.9 p	111.4 p	106.1 p	101.8 p	112.7 p	115.0 p

Sources: Same as General Statistics. The values shown reflect change from the base year, 2002. Values above 100 mean greater than 2002, values below 100 mean less than 2002, and a value of 100 in the 1987-2001 or 2003-2007 period means same as 2002. Values followed by a 'p' are projections by the editors; 'e' stands for extrapolation. Data are the most recent available at this level of detail.

SELECTED RATIOS

For 2002	Avg. of All Retail	Analyzed Industry	Index	For 2002	Avg. of All Retail	Analyzed Industry	Index
Employees per Establishment	17	5	27	Sales per Employee	174,682	208,574	119
Payroll per Establishment	333,445	71,641	21	Sales per Establishment	3,332,269	961,207	29
Payroll per Employee	20,311	15,546	77	Expenses per Establishment	na	na	na

Sources: Same as General Statistics. The 'Average of All' column, Wholesale or Retail, represents the average of the sector reported for the most recent complete year available. The Index shows the relationship between the Average and the Analyzed Industry. For example, 100 means that they are equal; 500 that the Analyzed Industry is five times the average; 50 means that the Analyzed Industry is half the national average. The abbreviation 'na' is used to show that data are 'not available'.

*Equivalent to SIC 5921.

LEADING COMPANIES   Number shown: **30**   Total sales ($ mil): **4,586**   Total employment (000): **25.7**

Company Name	Address				CEO Name	Phone	Co. Type	Sales ($ mil)	Empl. (000)
Foodarama Supermarkets Inc.	922 Hwy 33, Bldg 6	Freehold	NJ	07728		732-462-4700	P	1,175	7.4
Village Super Market Inc.	PO Box 7812	Edison	NJ	08818		973-467-2200	P	958	4.3
Trader Joe's Co.	PO Box 5049	Monrovia	CA	91017	Dan Bane	626-441-1177	R	900*	4.5
Coborn's Inc.	PO Box 6146	St. Cloud	MN	56302	Don Wetter	320-252-4222	R	434	4.0
21st Amendments Inc.	1158 W 86th St	Indianapolis	IN	46260	James A James	317-846-1678	R	197*	0.1
ABC Fine Wine and Spirits	PO Box 593688	Orlando	FL	32859	Charles E Bailes III	407-851-0000	R	193*	1.7
Spec's Family Partner's	2410 Smith St	Houston	TX	77006	John Rydman	713-526-8787	R	80*	0.3
Gold Standard Enterprises Inc.	5100 W Dumpster	Skokie	IL	60077	Michael Binstein	847-674-4200	R	72*	0.3
Wente Family Estates	5565 Tesla Rd	Livermore	CA	94550	Carolyn Wente	925-456-2300	R	70*	0.3
David Briggs Enterprises Inc.	701 Metairie Rd	Metairie	LA	70005	David A Briggs Jr	504-831-9415	R	59*	0.5
Total Beverage Corp.	11325 7 Locks Rd	Potomac	MD	20854	David Trone	301-795-1080	R	54*	0.2
North Coast Brewing Company	455 N Main St	Fort Bragg	CA	95437	Mark Ruedrich	707-964-2739	R	53*	0.1
Flanigan's Enterprises Inc.	5059 NE 18th Ave	Fort Lauderdale	FL	33334	James G Flanigan	954-377-1961	P	46	0.8
Martin Wine's Ltd.	3827 Baronne St	New Orleans	LA	70115		504-899-7411	R	39*	0.3
Sunday River Brewing Inc.	PO Box 847	Bethel	ME	04217	Grant Wilson	207-824-4253	R	32*	<0.1
Thrifty Discount Liquor and Wines	3238 Barksdale Blvd	Bossier City	LA	71112	Roland P Toups	318-742-3240	R	30*	0.1
Estes Park Brewery Inc.	PO Box 2136	Estes Park	CO	80517	Tyler Lemirande	970-586-5421	R	27*	<0.1
Navarro Vineyards	PO Box 47	Philo	CA	95466	Ted Bennett	707-895-3686	R	25*	<0.1
Goody-Goody Liquor Store Inc.	10301 Harry Hines	Dallas	TX	75220	Joe Jansen	214-350-5806	R	24*	0.2
V Sattui Winery	1111 White Ln	Saint Helena	CA	94574	Tom Davies	707-963-7774	R	24*	<0.1
Vicente Foods Inc.	12027 San Vicente	Los Angeles	CA	90049		310-472-5215	R	18*	0.1
Cedar Brewing Company Inc.	500 Blairs Ferry NE	Cedar Rapids	IA	52402	Rebecca Mumau	319-378-9090	R	16*	<0.1
Old Market Pub and Brewery	6959 Multnomah	Portland	OR	97223	Andrew Bigley	503-244-0450	R	13*	<0.1
Red Newt Cellars Inc.	3675 Tichenor Rd	Hector	NY	14841	David Whiting	607-546-4100	R	12*	<0.1
Kings Liquor Inc.	6659 Camp Bowie	Fort Worth	TX	76116	Jack Labovitz	817-732-8091	R	9*	<0.1
Gainey Vineyard	PO Box 910	Santa Ynez	CA	93460	Daniel Gainey	805-688-0558	R	9*	<0.1
Foss Co.	1224 Washington	Golden	CO	80401	Robert Lowry	303-279-3373	R	6*	<0.1
Little Hills Winery Gift Shop	710 S Main St	Saint Charles	MO	63301		636-925-2609	R	6*	<0.1
Williamsville Brewery Ltd.	1911 W Main St	Richmond	VA	23220	Robert Cabaniss	804-355-8580	R	5*	<0.1
Players Lounge	1605 SW 13th St	Gainesville	FL	32608	James Gagnon	352-378-5933	R	2*	<0.1

Source: Ward's Business Directory of U.S. Private and Public Companies, Volumes 1 and 2, 2005. The company type code used is as follows: P - Public, R - Private, S - Subsidiary, D - Division, J - Joint Venture, A - Affiliate, G - Group. Sales are in millions of dollars, employees are in thousands. An asterisk (*) indicates an estimated sales volume. The symbol < stands for 'less than'. Company names and addresses are truncated, in some cases, to fit into the available space.

OCCUPATIONS EMPLOYED BY BEER, WINE, & LIQUOR STORES

Occupation	% of Total 2004	Change to 2014	Occupation	% of Total 2004	Change to 2014
Cashiers, except gaming	42.4	-1.3	General & operations managers	2.1	8.6
Retail salespersons	13.5	9.7	Driver/sales workers	1.8	9.7
First-line supervisors/managers of retail sales workers	9.3	0.9	Truck drivers, light or delivery services	1.8	9.7
Stock clerks & order fillers	7.1	-16.0	Bookkeeping, accounting, & auditing clerks	1.5	-1.2
Sales reps, wholesale & manufacturing, exc tech	3.5	9.7	Truck drivers, heavy & tractor-trailer	1.5	9.7
Laborers & freight, stock, & material movers, hand	2.3	-1.3			

Source: Industry-Occupation Matrix, Bureau of Labor Statistics. These data are reported based on 4-digit NAICS categories but have been matched to corresponding 6-digit NAICS industry codes. The change reported for each occupation to the year 2014 is a percent of growth or decline as estimated by the Bureau of Labor Statistics. The abbreviation nec stands for 'not elsewhere classified.'

LOCATION BY STATE AND REGIONAL CONCENTRATION

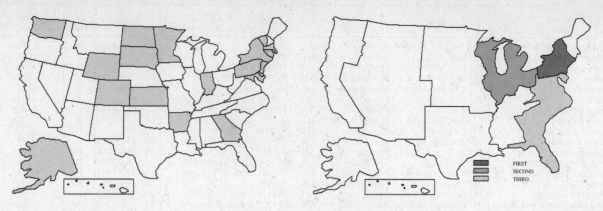

INDUSTRY DATA BY STATE

State	Establishments Total (number)	% of U.S.	Employment Total (number)	% of U.S.	Per Estab.	Payroll Total ($ mil.)	Per Empl. ($)	Sales Total ($ mil.)	% of U.S.	Per Estab. ($)
California	3,236	11.2	10,156	7.6	3	163.4	16,093	2,278.8	8.1	704,190
Pennsylvania	1,697	5.9	7,716	5.8	5	150.5	19,500	2,228.9	7.9	1,313,414
New York	2,211	7.6	8,334	6.3	4	159.6	19,151	2,040.5	7.2	922,901
New Jersey	1,687	5.8	8,525	6.4	5	144.2	16,915	1,988.2	7.0	1,178,527
Texas	1,515	5.2	6,933	5.2	5	112.4	16,217	1,730.7	6.1	1,142,408
Massachusetts	1,311	4.5	8,700	6.5	7	142.6	16,388	1,633.2	5.8	1,245,790
Illinois	1,186	4.1	6,143	4.6	5	98.0	15,949	1,192.4	4.2	1,005,381
Florida	1,081	3.7	4,663	3.5	4	73.4	15,741	1,026.9	3.6	949,935
Minnesota	912	3.1	6,719	5.1	7	84.6	12,588	997.8	3.5	1,094,068
Colorado	1,017	3.5	4,580	3.4	5	70.4	15,379	997.4	3.5	980,719
Maryland	1,063	3.7	5,835	4.4	5	93.8	16,067	961.0	3.4	904,072
Michigan	1,158	4.0	4,716	3.5	4	61.1	12,947	867.5	3.1	749,143
Georgia	757	2.6	3,573	2.7	5	57.3	16,048	798.9	2.8	1,055,338
Washington	421	1.5	1,685	1.3	4	33.2	19,699	704.1	2.5	1,672,542
Indiana	845	2.9	4,560	3.4	5	58.1	12,746	690.6	2.4	817,264
Ohio	907	3.1	4,438	3.3	5	52.4	11,804	687.5	2.4	758,031
Connecticut	684	2.4	2,653	2.0	4	47.5	17,921	656.4	2.3	959,654
Virginia	305	1.1	1,889	1.4	6	30.5	16,158	475.9	1.7	1,560,216
North Carolina	452	1.6	1,998	1.5	4	38.3	19,173	469.0	1.7	1,037,553
Tennessee	471	1.6	2,011	1.5	4	32.3	16,061	405.1	1.4	860,163
Kentucky	390	1.3	2,123	1.6	5	29.6	13,963	392.6	1.4	1,006,662
Wisconsin	437	1.5	2,267	1.7	5	26.1	11,508	386.2	1.4	883,851
Kansas	539	1.9	2,113	1.6	4	19.3	9,144	370.7	1.3	687,776
Alabama	308	1.1	1,061	0.8	3	18.4	17,346	319.6	1.1	1,037,740
Arkansas	337	1.2	1,524	1.1	5	20.8	13,652	315.4	1.1	935,887
South Carolina	365	1.3	1,110	0.8	3	16.5	14,879	306.0	1.1	838,375
Oregon	198	0.7	711	0.5	4	9.9	13,862	268.0	0.9	1,353,505
Missouri	379	1.3	1,457	1.1	4	19.7	13,518	246.0	0.9	649,169
Delaware	221	0.8	978	0.7	4	15.7	16,038	232.9	0.8	1,054,045
Rhode Island	216	0.7	1,046	0.8	5	16.7	15,919	212.2	0.8	982,352
Oklahoma	291	1.0	1,019	0.8	4	9.7	9,542	176.8	0.6	607,574
Mississippi	289	1.0	827	0.6	3	10.1	12,158	165.3	0.6	572,048
Louisiana	170	0.6	893	0.7	5	15.2	17,054	153.8	0.5	904,882
Alaska	95	0.3	502	0.4	5	9.7	19,235	110.4	0.4	1,162,600
New Mexico	119	0.4	974	0.7	8	11.0	11,254	105.1	0.4	883,277
Nevada	75	0.3	434	0.3	6	7.8	17,968	103.3	0.4	1,377,080
Nebraska	185	0.6	685	0.5	4	6.9	10,089	101.2	0.4	547,108
Wyoming	113	0.4	834	0.6	7	8.8	10,508	88.4	0.3	782,106
Vermont	117	0.4	437	0.3	4	8.8	20,151	88.1	0.3	752,786
North Dakota	103	0.4	731	0.5	7	7.1	9,647	85.8	0.3	833,369
South Dakota	124	0.4	718	0.5	6	6.8	9,446	84.4	0.3	680,847
Iowa	129	0.4	670	0.5	5	7.1	10,542	83.1	0.3	644,512
Maine	58	0.2	288	0.2	5	5.2	18,014	72.6	0.3	1,251,879
Montana	70	0.2	287	0.2	4	3.5	12,066	65.6	0.2	937,371
West Virginia	56	0.2	254	0.2	5	3.3	13,020	43.8	0.2	782,196
Hawaii	61	0.2	202	0.2	3	2.7	13,252	37.1	0.1	608,836
Arizona	194	0.7	500-999	-	-	(D)	-	(D)	-	-
D.C.	174	0.6	500-999	-	-	(D)	-	(D)	-	-
New Hampshire	85	0.3	500-999	-	-	(D)	-	(D)	-	-
Idaho	78	0.3	250-499	-	-	(D)	-	(D)	-	-
Utah	65	0.2	250-499	-	-	(D)	-	(D)	-	-

Source: 2002 *Economic Census*. The states are in descending order of sales or establishments (if sales data are missing for the majority). The symbol (D) appears when data are withheld to prevent disclosure of competitive information. States marked with (D) are sorted by number of establishments. A dash (-) indicates that the data element cannot be calculated. Shaded *states* on the state map indicate those states which have proportionately greater representation in the industry than would be indicated by the states population; the ratio is based on total sales or number of establishments. Shaded *regions* indicate where the industry is regionally most concentrated.

NAICS 446110 - PHARMACIES AND DRUG STORES*

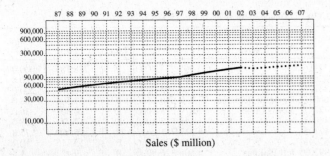

Sales ($ million)

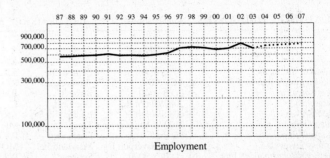

Employment

GENERAL STATISTICS

Year	Establishments (number)	Employment (number)	Payroll ($ million)	Sales ($ million)	Employees per Establishment (number)	Sales per Establishment ($)	Payroll per Employee ($)
1987	52,181	573,692	6,476.4	53,824.5	11	1,031,496	11,289
1988	50,774	576,979	7,032.7	58,557.1 e	11	1,153,289	12,189
1989	50,625	587,551	7,615.2	63,289.7 e	12	1,250,167	12,961
1990	49,956	593,202	8,254.3	68,022.3 e	12	1,361,644	13,915
1991	49,113	609,088	8,952.0	72,755.0 e	12	1,481,380	14,697
1992	48,142	587,943	9,060.3	77,487.6	12	1,609,563	15,410
1993	47,146	590,407	9,431.7	81,716.3 e	13	1,733,260	15,975
1994	45,676	583,486	9,718.0	85,944.9 e	13	1,881,621	16,655
1995	44,550	599,139	10,110.3	90,173.6 e	13	2,024,099	16,875
1996	45,865 e	624,408 e	10,731.7 e	94,402.2 e	14 e	2,058,262 e	17,187 e
1997	43,615	703,752	11,587.5	98,630.9	16	2,261,399	16,465
1998	42,563	722,779	12,010.8	110,026.3 e	17	2,585,023	16,617
1999	41,846	709,175	13,395.9	121,421.7 e	17	2,901,633	18,889
2000	40,617	680,251	14,543.0	132,817.1 e	17	3,269,989	21,379
2001	40,026	699,160	15,484.0	144,212.6 e	18	3,602,972	22,147
2002	40,530	792,982	15,763.9	155,608.0	20	3,839,328	19,879
2003	39,433	699,949	16,010.3	147,987.8 p	18	3,654,614 p	22,874
2004	38,024 p	746,837 p	16,422.2 p	154,303.3 p	19 p	3,834,236 p	22,542 p
2005	37,199 p	758,356 p	17,030.0 p	160,618.9 p	20 p	4,013,859 p	23,182 p
2006	36,374 p	769,874 p	17,637.9 p	166,934.4 p	20 p	4,193,482 p	23,821 p
2007	35,549 p	781,392 p	18,245.7 p	173,250.0 p	21 p	4,373,105 p	24,460 p

Sources: Economic Census of the United States, 1987, 1992, 1997, and 2002. Establishment counts, employment, and payroll are from *County Business Patterns* for non-Census years. Values followed by a 'p' are projections by the editors. Sales data for non-Census years are extrapolations, marked by 'e'. Data are the most recent available at this level of detail.

INDICES OF CHANGE

Year	Establishments (number)	Employment (number)	Payroll ($ million)	Sales ($ million)	Employees per Establishment (number)	Sales per Establishment ($)	Payroll per Employee ($)
1987	128.7	72.3	41.1	34.6	56.2	26.9	56.8
1992	118.8	74.1	57.5	49.8	62.4	41.9	77.5
1993	116.3	74.5	59.8	52.5 e	63.9	45.1	80.4
1994	112.7	73.6	61.6	55.2 e	65.4	49.0	83.8
1995	109.9	75.6	64.1	57.9 e	68.5	52.7	84.9
1996	113.2 e	78.7 e	68.1 e	60.7 e	69.5 e	53.6 e	86.5 e
1997	107.6	88.7	73.5	63.4	82.3	58.9	82.8
1998	105.0	91.1	76.2	70.7 e	86.9	67.3	83.6
1999	103.2	89.4	85.0	78.0 e	86.4	75.6	95.0
2000	100.2	85.8	92.3	85.4 e	85.4	85.2	107.5
2001	98.8	88.2	98.2	92.7 e	89.4	93.8	111.4
2002	100.0	100.0	100.0	100.0	100.0	100.0	100.0
2003	97.3	88.3	101.6	95.1 p	90.7	95.2 p	115.1
2004	93.8 p	94.2 p	104.2 p	99.2 p	97.2 p	99.9 p	113.4 p
2005	91.8 p	95.6 p	108.0 p	103.2 p	99.9 p	104.5 p	116.6 p
2006	89.7 p	97.1 p	111.9 p	107.3 p	102.5 p	109.2 p	119.8 p
2007	87.7 p	98.5 p	115.7 p	111.3 p	105.2 p	113.9 p	123.0 p

Sources: Same as General Statistics. The values shown reflect change from the base year, 2002. Values above 100 mean greater than 2002, values below 100 mean less than 2002, and a value of 100 in the 1987-2001 or 2003-2007 period means same as 2002. Values followed by a 'p' are projections by the editors; 'e' stands for extrapolation. Data are the most recent available at this level of detail.

SELECTED RATIOS

For 2002	Avg. of All Retail	Analyzed Industry	Index	For 2002	Avg. of All Retail	Analyzed Industry	Index
Employees per Establishment	17	20	115	Sales per Employee	174,682	196,231	112
Payroll per Establishment	333,445	388,944	117	Sales per Establishment	3,332,269	3,839,328	115
Payroll per Employee	20,311	19,879	98	Expenses per Establishment	na	na	na

Sources: Same as General Statistics. The 'Average of All' column, Wholesale or Retail, represents the average of the sector reported for the most recent complete year available. The Index shows the relationship between the Average and the Analyzed Industry. For example, 100 means that they are equal; 500 that the Analyzed Industry is five times the average; 50 means that the Analyzed Industry is half the national average. The abbreviation 'na' is used to show that data are 'not available'.

*Equivalent to SIC 5912.

LEADING COMPANIES Number shown: 73   Total sales ($ mil): **533,139**   Total employment (000): **15,985.1**

Company Name	Address				CEO Name	Phone	Co. Type	Sales ($ mil)	Empl. (000)
Wal-Mart Stores Inc.	702 SW 8th St	Bentonville	AR	72716		501-273-4000	P	288,189	15,000.0
CVS Pharmacy Inc.	1 CVS Dr	Woonsocket	RI	02895	Thomas Ryan	401-765-1500	S	50,947*	110.0
Albertson's Inc.	PO Box 20	Boise	ID	83726		208-395-6200	P	39,897	200.0
Walgreen Co.	200 Wilmot Rd	Deerfield	IL	60015	David W Bernauer	847-940-2500	P	37,508	163.0
SAM'S Club	608 SW 8th St	Bentonville	AR	72712	Kevin Turner	479-273-4000	D	24,801*	36.0
Kmart Corp.	3100 W Big Beaver	Troy	MI	48084		248-643-1000	D	17,072	158.0
Rite Aid Corp.	PO Box 3165	Harrisburg	PA	17105		717-761-2633	P	16,600	75.0
Express Scripts Inc.	13900 Riverport Dr	Maryland H.	MO	63043		314-770-1666	P	15,115	10.7
Rosauer's Supermarkets Inc.	PO Box 9000	Spokane	WA	99209	Jeff Philipps	509-326-8900	R	9,422*	1.8
Giant Food Inc.	6400 Sheriff Rd	Landover	MD	20785	Mark Smith	301-341-4100	S	5,289*	35.0
Longs Drug Stores Corp.	PO Box 5222	Walnut Creek	CA	94596	Warren F Bryant	925-937-1170	P	4,530	22.2
Hannaford Brothers Co.	PO Box 1000	Portland	ME	04104	Ronald C Hodge	207-883-2911	S	3,239*	23.0
Raley's Inc.	PO Box 15618	Sacramento	CA	95852	William J Coyne	916-373-3333	R	3,200	16.2
Longs Drug Stores California Inc.	141 N Civic Dr	Walnut Creek	CA	94596		925-937-1170	S	3,156*	15.5
Beverly Enterprises Inc.	1000 Beverly Way	Fort Smith	AR	72919	William R Floyd	501-201-2000	P	1,989	36.3
Mariner Health Care, Inc.	1 Ravinia Dr	Atlanta	GA	30346	Victor L Lund	678-443-7000	R	1,715	35.0
Duane Reade Inc.	440 Ninth Ave	New York	NY	10001	Anthony J Cuti	212-273-5700	R	1,384	6.1
Dan Incorporated Oregon	PO Box 2200	Oregon City	OR	97045	Craig T Danielson	503-655-9141	R	1,345*	0.3
Fred's Inc.	4300 New Getwell	Memphis	TN	38118	Michael J Hayes	901-365-8880	P	1,303	9.0
SUPERVALU Champaign	PO Box 9008	Champaign	IL	61826		217-384-2800	S	1,000*	0.9
NCS HealthCare Inc.	3201 Enterprise Pky	Beachwood	OH	44122	Kevin B Shaw	216-514-3350	S	646*	2.5
Snyder's Drug Stores Inc.	14525 Hwy 7	Minnetonka	MN	55345	Daryl A Katz	952-935-5441	S	600*	5.0
Haggen Inc.	PO Box 9704	Bellingham	WA	98227		360-733-8720	R	583*	3.5
Chronimed Inc.	10900 Red Circle Dr	Minnetonka	MN	55343	Henry F Blissenbach	952-979-3600	P	560	0.4
Discount Drug Mart Inc.	211 Commerce Dr	Medina	OH	44256	Parviz Boodjeh	330-725-2340	R	533*	2.8
Coborn's Inc.	PO Box 6146	St. Cloud	MN	56302	Don Wetter	320-252-4222	R	434	4.0
Macey's Inc.	9075 Sandy Pkwy	Sandy	UT	84070	Dick King	801-561-5400	S	364*	2.0
Enesco Group Inc.	225 Windsor Dr	Itasca	IL	60143		630-875-5300	P	269	1.3
drugstore.com inc.	13920 SE Eastgate	Bellevue	WA	98005		425-372-3200	P	246	0.5
Happy Harry's Inc.	326 Ruthar Dr	Newark	DE	19711	Alan B Levin	302-366-0335	R	200*	1.6
Bartell Drug Co.	4727 Denver Ave S	Seattle	WA	98134	George D Bartell	206-763-2626	R	170*	1.7
Navarro Discount Pharmacies	5959 NW 37th Ave	Miami	FL	33142	Jose Navarro	305-633-3000	R	139*	0.9
Thrifty Drug Stores	6901 E Fish Lake	Maple Grove	MN	55369	Robert Narveson	763-513-4370	R	112*	1.0
May's Drug Stores Inc.	1437 S Boulder	Tulsa	OK	74119	Gerald Heller	918-592-6297	R	96*	0.8
Lewis Drug Inc.	2701 S Minnesota	Sioux Falls	SD	57105	Mark E Griffin	605-367-2000	R	68*	0.8
Nyer Medical Group Inc.	1292 Hammond St	Bangor	ME	04401	Samuel Nyer	207-942-5273	P	62	0.2
ivpcare Inc.	7164 Technology Dr	Frisco	TX	75034	Von L Best	214-387-3500	R	54*	0.1
Park Pharmacy Corp.	10711 Preston Rd	Dallas	TX	75230	James C Rambin	214-692-9921	P	54	0.2
Astrup Drug Inc.	PO Box 658	Austin	MN	55912	Leonard B Astrup	507-433-7447	R	30*	0.3
Parkway Drugs Inc.	7366 N Lincoln Ave	Lincolnwood	IL	60645	Edward Fox	847-673-2424	R	25*	0.1
Hemophilia Health Services Inc.	6820 Charlotte Pike	Nashville	TN	37209	Kyle J Callahan	615-352-2500	S	20*	0.1
Allen's of Hastings Inc.	PO Box 987	Hastings	NE	68901	Robert M Allen	402-463-5633	R	16*	0.2
Jim Myers Drug Inc.	3325 University E	Tuscaloosa	AL	35404	Roger Meyers	205-556-3800	R	14*	<0.1
Rinderer's Drug Stores Inc.	1053 Cave Sprgs Rd	St. Peters	MO	63376	Matt Carlisle	636-928-3957	R	14*	<0.1
Colonial Surgical Supply Inc.	1812 1/2 N Vermont	Los Angeles	CA	90027	Mike Saleh	323-666-4044	R	13*	<0.1
Degen-Berglund Inc.	4000 M Coulee	La Crosse	WI	54601	Dan Reckase	608-775-8500	R	11*	0.1
Wall Drug Store Inc.	510 Main St	Wall	SD	57790	Richard J Hustead	605-279-2175	R	11*	0.2
Community Surgical Supply	PO Box 4686	Toms River	NJ	08754	Phillip Fried	732-349-2990	R	11*	<0.1
Northwest Hills Pharmacy/Florist	3910 Far W Blvd	Austin	TX	78731	Tom Sansing	512-345-3712	R	10*	<0.1
People's Pharmacy Inc.	4018 N Lamar Blvd	Austin	TX	78756	Bill Swail	512-459-9090	R	10*	<0.1
Crosby's Drugs Inc.	2609 N High St	Columbus	OH	43202	Jerome M Cohen	614-263-9424	R	6*	<0.1
Foss Co.	1224 Washington	Golden	CO	80401	Robert Lowry	303-279-3373	R	6*	<0.1
Abington Pharmacy Inc.	1460 Old York Rd	Abington	PA	19001		215-884-2767	R	5*	<0.1
Halpin's Pharmacy Inc.	11406 E Sprague	Spokane	WA	99206	Rick Erickson	509-928-9500	R	5*	<0.1
King's Peachtree Battle Drugs	2345 Peachtree Rd	Atlanta	GA	30305	J Stephen Anderson	404-233-2101	R	5*	<0.1
Standard Drug Co.	1 Westbury Sq	St. Charles	MO	63301	Gerald W Roberts	636-946-6557	R	5*	<0.1
Lincoln Pharmacy	232 North Ave	Millvale	PA	15209	Jennifer Cohen	412-821-2379	R	4*	<0.1
Richmond Apothecaries Inc.	5001 W Broad St	Richmond	VA	23230	Daniel A Herbert	804-285-8055	R	4*	<0.1
Vertical Health Solutions Inc.	6925 112th Circle N	Largo	FL	33773	Brian T Nugent	727-548-8345	P	3	<0.1
Keasling's Drug Store	1414 Main St	Keokuk	IA	52632	H Wesley Brown	319-524-5436	R	3*	<0.1
Strathmore Pharmacy Inc.	1181 N McHenry Rd	Buffalo Grove	IL	60089	Jeffrey D Lundgren	847-541-1191	R	3*	<0.1
Vetline Inc.	425 John Deere Rd	Fort Collins	CO	80524	Kenneth A Larson	970-484-1900	R	3*	<0.1
Carver Hardware Inc.	PO Box 427	Muscatine	IA	52761	Roy Carver Jr	319-263-2261	R	2*	<0.1
Consumer Discount Drug Store	6542 Hollywood	Hollywood	CA	90028	Ted N Turner	323-461-3606	R	2*	<0.1
Cambridge Chemists Inc.	21 E 65th St	New York	NY	10021	Joseph Policar	212-734-5678	R	1*	<0.1
Campbell's Pharmacy	PO Box 382	Adamsville	AL	35005	Dennis Campbell	205-674-3566	R	1*	<0.1
CompuScription Inc.	1123 N Dunton Ave	Arlington H.	IL	60004	John Fischer	847-392-6593	R	1*	<0.1
Hesselberg Drug Co.	3660 Vista Ave	St. Louis	MO	63110	Ben Hesselberg	314-771-2900	R	1*	<0.1
Low Cost Healthcare of Indiana	4076 S Keystone	Indianapolis	IN	46227	Terry Cole	317-787-7205	R	1*	<0.1
Medicine Shop	110 Main St	Park Ridge	IL	60068	Maria Costas	847-698-3323	R	1*	<0.1
Post Oak Pharmacy Inc.	5018 San Felipe St	Houston	TX	77056	Bruce Gingrich	713-621-1560	R	1*	<0.1
Simple Wisdom Inc.	775 S Graham St	Memphis	TN	38111	Mary Ann Davis	901-458-4686	R	1*	<0.1
Teasley Drug	PO Box 120	Gravette	AR	72736	Ron Teasley	479-787-5966	R	1*	<0.1

Source: Ward's Business Directory of U.S. Private and Public Companies, Volumes 1 and 2, 2005. The company type code used is as follows: P - Public, R - Private, S - Subsidiary, D - Division, J - Joint Venture, A - Affiliate, G - Group. Sales are in millions of dollars, employees are in thousands. An asterisk (*) indicates an estimated sales volume. The symbol < stands for 'less than'. Company names and addresses are truncated, in some cases, to fit into the available space.

OCCUPATIONS EMPLOYED BY PHARMACIES & DRUG STORES

Occupation	% of Total 2004	Change to 2014	Occupation	% of Total 2004	Change to 2014
Cashiers, except gaming	30.0	9.0	Pharmacy aides	4.8	14.6
Pharmacy technicians	20.3	21.1	Retail salespersons	3.7	21.1
Pharmacists	14.5	18.5	General & operations managers	3.7	19.8
First-line supervisors/managers of retail sales workers	5.2	11.4	Truck drivers, light or delivery services	1.3	21.1
Stock clerks & order fillers	5.0	-7.2	Photographic processing machine operators	1.2	-39.5

Source: *Industry-Occupation Matrix*, Bureau of Labor Statistics. These data are reported based on 4-digit NAICS categories but have been matched to corresponding 6-digit NAICS industry codes. The change reported for each occupation to the year 2014 is a percent of growth or decline as estimated by the Bureau of Labor Statistics. The abbreviation nec stands for 'not elsewhere classified.'

LOCATION BY STATE AND REGIONAL CONCENTRATION

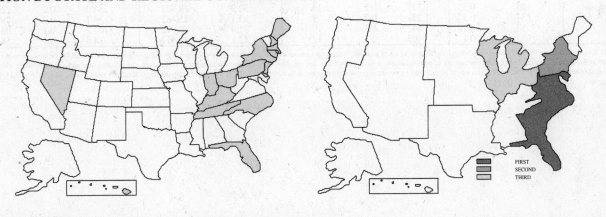

FIRST
SECOND
THIRD

INDUSTRY DATA BY STATE

State	Establishments Total (number)	% of U.S.	Employment Total (number)	% of U.S.	Per Estab.	Payroll Total ($ mil.)	Per Empl. ($)	Sales Total ($ mil.)	% of U.S.	Per Estab. ($)
California	4,011	10.0	86,779	11.1	22	2,298.2	26,484	17,635.8	11.5	4,396,861
New York	3,500	8.7	57,377	7.3	16	1,134.6	19,774	14,229.1	9.3	4,065,470
Florida	2,289	5.7	57,334	7.3	25	1,078.2	18,805	10,304.4	6.7	4,501,691
Pennsylvania	2,196	5.5	38,510	4.9	18	695.4	18,058	8,161.7	5.3	3,716,617
Texas	2,305	5.7	44,983	5.7	20	859.5	19,108	7,827.7	5.1	3,395,949
Ohio	1,622	4.0	36,715	4.7	23	610.2	16,621	6,815.1	4.4	4,201,685
Illinois	1,497	3.7	39,548	5.0	26	722.8	18,276	6,285.6	4.1	4,198,823
New Jersey	1,477	3.7	28,953	3.7	20	519.6	17,946	6,281.7	4.1	4,253,004
Michigan	1,504	3.7	28,178	3.6	19	528.6	18,760	5,743.0	3.7	3,818,474
Massachusetts	916	2.3	29,615	3.8	32	425.9	14,380	5,140.7	3.3	5,612,106
North Carolina	1,303	3.2	22,141	2.8	17	419.7	18,957	4,929.6	3.2	3,783,273
Georgia	1,282	3.2	19,330	2.5	15	357.6	18,502	3,829.1	2.5	2,986,855
Tennessee	979	2.4	18,435	2.4	19	359.3	19,488	3,792.5	2.5	3,873,892
Indiana	824	2.0	18,945	2.4	23	343.6	18,139	3,566.8	2.3	4,328,697
Virginia	954	2.4	17,728	2.3	19	313.1	17,661	3,502.9	2.3	3,671,843
Missouri	742	1.8	15,126	1.9	20	310.2	20,507	2,867.3	1.9	3,864,221
Maryland	700	1.7	12,341	1.6	18	236.9	19,195	2,801.5	1.8	4,002,080
Wisconsin	752	1.9	16,296	2.1	22	320.9	19,691	2,704.9	1.8	3,596,920
Connecticut	504	1.3	13,954	1.8	28	229.2	16,428	2,659.1	1.7	5,276,036
Louisiana	841	2.1	12,579	1.6	15	256.3	20,375	2,443.9	1.6	2,905,954
Alabama	879	2.2	10,984	1.4	12	220.0	20,034	2,382.8	1.5	2,710,769
Kentucky	744	1.8	10,989	1.4	15	232.5	21,154	2,382.2	1.5	3,201,858
Washington	644	1.6	11,173	1.4	17	272.8	24,416	2,294.0	1.5	3,562,039
Minnesota	605	1.5	13,358	1.7	22	233.9	17,509	2,251.2	1.5	3,721,038
South Carolina	649	1.6	9,377	1.2	14	165.6	17,659	2,150.3	1.4	3,313,259
Arizona	432	1.1	13,243	1.7	31	268.5	20,276	2,082.6	1.4	4,820,935
Oklahoma	590	1.5	8,321	1.1	14	164.1	19,719	1,540.7	1.0	2,611,397
Mississippi	597	1.5	6,793	0.9	11	144.4	21,253	1,424.4	0.9	2,385,925
Iowa	480	1.2	7,945	1.0	17	163.9	20,632	1,300.7	0.8	2,709,750
Colorado	342	0.9	7,562	1.0	22	140.0	18,514	1,161.2	0.8	3,395,462
West Virginia	349	0.9	4,619	0.6	13	98.7	21,360	1,139.6	0.7	3,265,341
Kansas	408	1.0	6,165	0.8	15	147.4	23,915	1,100.0	0.7	2,695,988
Arkansas	532	1.3	5,394	0.7	10	117.6	21,802	1,059.2	0.7	1,990,987
Oregon	348	0.9	5,777	0.7	17	143.1	24,773	1,059.0	0.7	3,043,221
Rhode Island	164	0.4	5,556	0.7	34	77.6	13,967	988.5	0.6	6,027,555
Nevada	206	0.5	5,247	0.7	25	118.9	22,666	896.1	0.6	4,350,184
Nebraska	286	0.7	5,424	0.7	19	102.1	18,830	862.9	0.6	3,017,049

Continued on next page.

INDUSTRY DATA BY STATE - Continued

State	Establishments		Employment			Payroll		Sales		
	Total (number)	% of U.S.	Total (number)	% of U.S.	Per Estab.	Total ($ mil.)	Per Empl. ($)	Total ($ mil.)	% of U.S.	Per Estab. ($)
Hawaii	113	0.3	3,835	0.5	34	79.1	20,630	841.7	0.5	7,448,584
New Hampshire	174	0.4	4,015	0.5	23	71.8	17,887	759.1	0.5	4,362,632
Maine	195	0.5	2,804	0.4	14	67.4	24,036	693.0	0.5	3,554,051
New Mexico	158	0.4	3,917	0.5	25	73.5	18,769	653.1	0.4	4,133,848
Delaware	128	0.3	2,732	0.3	21	59.8	21,876	604.7	0.4	4,724,367
Utah	176	0.4	2,079	0.3	12	48.1	23,145	414.5	0.3	2,355,165
D.C.	83	0.2	2,079	0.3	25	31.8	15,304	393.8	0.3	4,744,072
Vermont	109	0.3	1,539	0.2	14	37.5	24,383	373.6	0.2	3,427,798
Idaho	140	0.3	2,042	0.3	15	46.5	22,758	352.7	0.2	2,518,943
North Dakota	157	0.4	1,646	0.2	10	43.2	26,237	348.1	0.2	2,216,949
South Dakota	128	0.3	1,737	0.2	14	32.9	18,921	284.2	0.2	2,220,633
Montana	134	0.3	1,221	0.2	9	31.1	25,467	239.7	0.2	1,789,134
Wyoming	53	0.1	547	0.1	10	11.4	20,912	107.7	0.1	2,031,358
Alaska	33	0.1	405	0.1	12	12.8	31,617	84.6	0.1	2,564,606

Source: 2002 *Economic Census*. The states are in descending order of sales or establishments (if sales data are missing for the majority). The symbol (D) appears when data are withheld to prevent disclosure of competitive information. States marked with (D) are sorted by number of establishments. A dash (-) indicates that the data element cannot be calculated. Shaded *states* on the state map indicate those states which have proportionately greater representation in the industry than would be indicated by the states population; the ratio is based on total sales or number of establishments. Shaded *regions* indicate where the industry is regionally most concentrated.

NAICS 446120 - COSMETICS, BEAUTY SUPPLIES, AND PERFUME STORES

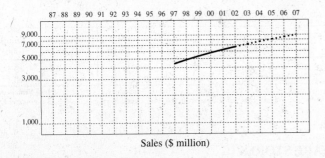

Sales ($ million)

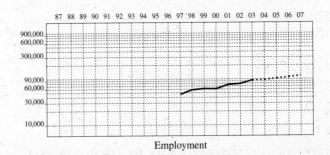

Employment

GENERAL STATISTICS

Year	Establishments (number)	Employment (number)	Payroll ($ million)	Sales ($ million)	Employees per Establishment (number)	Sales per Establishment ($)	Payroll per Employee ($)
1987	-	-	-	-	-	-	-
1988	-	-	-	-	-	-	-
1989	-	-	-	-	-	-	-
1990	-	-	-	-	-	-	-
1991	-	-	-	-	-	-	-
1992	-	-	-	-	-	-	-
1993	-	-	-	-	-	-	-
1994	-	-	-	-	-	-	-
1995	-	-	-	-	-	-	-
1996	-	-	-	-	-	-	-
1997	9,014	46,527	603.6	4,419.0	5	490,237	12,973
1998	9,518	58,171	695.1	4,875.3 e	6	512,218	11,949
1999	9,587	61,771	759.0	5,331.6 e	6	556,126	12,287
2000	9,615	61,237	842.4	5,787.9 e	6	601,963	13,757
2001	10,630	75,658	1,054.1	6,244.2 e	7	587,410	13,933
2002	10,786	78,859	974.0	6,700.5	7	621,218	12,351
2003	11,938	94,730	1,274.9	7,156.8 p	8	654,161 p	13,458
2004	11,920 p	96,689 p	1,295.7 p	7,613.0 p	8 p	680,627 p	13,516 p
2005	12,361 p	103,828 p	1,398.0 p	8,069.3 p	9 p	707,093 p	13,655 p
2006	12,802 p	110,966 p	1,500.4 p	8,525.6 p	9 p	733,559 p	13,795 p
2007	13,243 p	118,104 p	1,602.8 p	8,981.9 p	9 p	760,025 p	13,934 p

Source: *Economic Census of the United States*, 1997 and 2002. Establishment counts, employment, and payroll are from *County Business Patterns* for non-Census years. This is a newly defined industry. Data for prior years are unavailable at the time of publication but may become available over time. Values followed by 'p' are projections by the editors. Sales data for non-Census years are extrapolations, marked by 'e'.

INDICES OF CHANGE

Year	Establishments (number)	Employment (number)	Payroll ($ million)	Sales ($ million)	Employees per Establishment (number)	Sales per Establishment ($)	Payroll per Employee ($)
1987	-	-	-	-	-	-	-
1992	-	-	-	-	-	-	-
1993	-	-	-	-	-	-	-
1994	-	-	-	-	-	-	-
1995	-	-	-	-	-	-	-
1996	-	-	-	-	-	-	-
1997	83.6	59.0	62.0	66.0	71.1	78.9	105.0
1998	88.2	73.8	71.4	72.8 e	83.4	82.5	96.7
1999	88.9	78.3	77.9	79.6 e	87.5	89.5	99.5
2000	89.1	77.7	86.5	86.4 e	87.5	96.9	111.4
2001	98.6	95.9	108.2	93.2 e	97.1	94.6	112.8
2002	100.0	100.0	100.0	100.0	100.0	100.0	100.0
2003	110.7	120.1	130.9	106.8 p	108.5	105.3 p	109.0
2004	110.5 p	122.6 p	133.0 p	113.6 p	112.9 p	109.6 p	109.4 p
2005	114.6 p	131.7 p	143.5 p	120.4 p	118.4 p	113.8 p	110.6 p
2006	118.7 p	140.7 p	154.1 p	127.2 p	124.0 p	118.1 p	111.7 p
2007	122.8 p	149.8 p	164.6 p	134.0 p	129.5 p	122.3 p	112.8 p

Sources: Same as General Statistics. The values shown reflect change from the base year, 2002. Values above 100 mean greater than 2002, values below 100 mean less than 2002, and a value of 100 in the 1987-2001 or 2003-2007 period means same as 2002. Values followed by a 'p' are projections by the editors; 'e' stands for extrapolation. Data are the most recent available at this level of detail.

SELECTED RATIOS

For 2002	Avg. of All Retail	Analyzed Industry	Index	For 2002	Avg. of All Retail	Analyzed Industry	Index
Employees per Establishment	17	7	43	Sales per Employee	174,682	84,968	49
Payroll per Establishment	333,445	90,300	27	Sales per Establishment	3,332,269	621,218	19
Payroll per Employee	20,311	12,351	61	Expenses per Establishment	na	na	na

Sources: Same as General Statistics. The 'Average of All' column, Wholesale or Retail, represents the average of the sector reported for the most recent complete year available. The Index shows the relationship between the Average and the Analyzed Industry. For example, 100 means that they are equal; 500 that the Analyzed Industry is five times the average; 50 means that the Analyzed Industry is half the national average. The abbreviation 'na' is used to show that data are 'not available'.

LEADING COMPANIES   Number shown: **2**   Total sales ($ mil): **49**   Total employment (000): **0.1**

Company Name	Address				CEO Name	Phone	Co. Type	Sales ($ mil)	Empl. (000)
Jett Racing and Sales Inc.	1301 Lincoln St	Laredo	TX	78040	Wolf Hofman	956-722-3102	R	46*	<0.1
Beauty Towne Inc.	147 Delta Dr	Pittsburgh	PA	15238	M Deligotti	412-963-9871	R	3*	<0.1

Source: Ward's Business Directory of U.S. Private and Public Companies, Volumes 1 and 2, 2005. The company type code used is as follows: P - Public, R - Private, S - Subsidiary, D - Division, J - Joint Venture, A - Affiliate, G - Group. Sales are in millions of dollars, employees are in thousands. An asterisk (*) indicates an estimated sales volume. The symbol < stands for 'less than'. Company names and addresses are truncated, in some cases, to fit into the available space.

OCCUPATIONS EMPLOYED BY HEALTH & PERSONAL CARE STORES

Occupation	% of Total 2004	Change to 2014	Occupation	% of Total 2004	Change to 2014
Retail salespersons	32.6	32.4	Stock clerks & order fillers	2.0	-1.4
Cashiers, except gaming	10.4	19.2	General & operations managers	1.8	31.0
Opticians, dispensing	8.2	12.5	Receptionists & information clerks	1.7	26.1
First-line supervisors/managers of retail sales workers	7.5	21.8	Bookkeeping, accounting, & auditing clerks	1.5	19.2
Ophthalmic laboratory technicians	2.9	2.2	Optometrists	1.2	14.2
Sales reps, wholesale & manufacturing, exc tech	2.8	32.4	Truck drivers, light or delivery services	1.1	32.4
Customer service representatives	2.3	35.6	Laborers & freight, stock, & material movers, hand	1.0	19.2
Office clerks, general	2.2	17.8			

Source: Industry-Occupation Matrix, Bureau of Labor Statistics. These data are reported based on 4-digit NAICS categories but have been matched to corresponding 6-digit NAICS industry codes. The change reported for each occupation to the year 2014 is a percent of growth or decline as estimated by the Bureau of Labor Statistics. The abbreviation nec stands for 'not elsewhere classified.'

LOCATION BY STATE AND REGIONAL CONCENTRATION

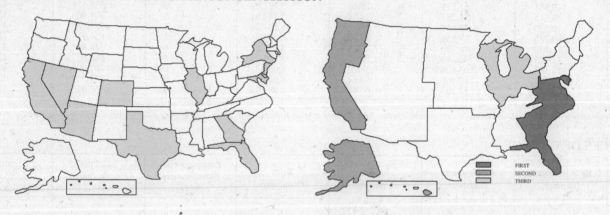

INDUSTRY DATA BY STATE

State	Establishments Total (number)	% of U.S.	Employment Total (number)	% of U.S.	Per Estab.	Payroll Total ($ mil.)	Per Empl. ($)	Sales Total ($ mil.)	% of U.S.	Per Estab. ($)
California	1,392	12.9	8,876	11.7	6	130.3	14,678	876.7	14.0	629,819
Texas	890	8.2	6,371	8.4	7	77.6	12,174	562.1	8.9	631,611
New York	775	7.2	5,063	6.7	7	78.8	15,567	537.2	8.6	693,124
Florida	815	7.5	4,465	5.9	5	59.1	13,232	443.5	7.1	544,139
Illinois	472	4.4	4,234	5.6	9	51.4	12,147	356.1	5.7	754,496
Ohio	401	3.7	2,781	3.7	7	34.6	12,450	235.0	3.7	585,998
Pennsylvania	366	3.4	3,316	4.4	9	32.4	9,769	226.6	3.6	619,008
Georgia	438	4.1	2,709	3.6	6	31.2	11,528	217.1	3.5	495,648
New Jersey	337	3.1	2,191	2.9	7	27.9	12,715	199.8	3.2	592,899
Michigan	354	3.3	2,431	3.2	7	26.1	10,740	188.7	3.0	533,116
North Carolina	330	3.1	2,177	2.9	7	24.2	11,096	158.1	2.5	478,979
Virginia	269	2.5	1,724	2.3	6	18.7	10,861	146.7	2.3	545,204
Maryland	251	2.3	1,799	2.4	7	20.2	11,203	139.7	2.2	556,598
Arizona	185	1.7	1,697	2.2	9	21.2	12,467	138.4	2.2	748,081
Massachusetts	198	1.8	1,540	2.0	8	21.3	13,827	128.5	2.0	648,995
Colorado	181	1.7	1,761	2.3	10	19.2	10,876	117.4	1.9	648,597
Indiana	214	2.0	1,636	2.2	8	16.4	10,034	114.6	1.8	535,407
Tennessee	242	2.2	1,442	1.9	6	16.8	11,619	108.9	1.7	450,070
Missouri	190	1.8	1,527	2.0	8	17.4	11,378	103.0	1.6	541,926

Continued on next page.

INDUSTRY DATA BY STATE - Continued

State	Establishments Total (number)	% of U.S.	Employment Total (number)	% of U.S.	Per Estab.	Payroll Total ($ mil.)	Per Empl. ($)	Sales Total ($ mil.)	% of U.S.	Per Estab. ($)
Nevada	104	1.0	904	1.2	9	12.7	14,012	89.2	1.4	857,644
Louisiana	183	1.7	1,195	1.6	7	12.8	10,736	88.0	1.4	481,093
Alabama	215	2.0	1,089	1.4	5	11.9	10,972	87.9	1.4	408,637
Washington	174	1.6	1,066	1.4	6	12.8	11,977	80.5	1.3	462,851
Minnesota	121	1.1	1,339	1.8	11	12.2	9,096	79.2	1.3	654,942
Connecticut	116	1.1	842	1.1	7	11.6	13,721	76.0	1.2	655,534
Wisconsin	121	1.1	1,172	1.5	10	10.5	8,934	69.9	1.1	577,727
Oklahoma	160	1.5	1,167	1.5	7	11.7	10,015	69.8	1.1	435,969
South Carolina	178	1.6	964	1.3	5	10.2	10,561	69.2	1.1	388,826
Kentucky	130	1.2	1,029	1.4	8	9.3	9,083	66.9	1.1	514,262
Kansas	84	0.8	878	1.2	10	9.8	11,114	51.0	0.8	607,464
Mississippi	124	1.1	715	0.9	6	6.2	8,620	47.3	0.8	381,065
Oregon	93	0.9	521	0.7	6	6.9	13,319	42.4	0.7	455,527
Arkansas	103	1.0	570	0.8	6	5.5	9,614	39.3	0.6	381,233
Utah	72	0.7	559	0.7	8	5.3	9,513	38.3	0.6	531,861
Iowa	68	0.6	664	0.9	10	5.6	8,452	35.8	0.6	526,971
Nebraska	47	0.4	440	0.6	9	4.3	9,814	26.7	0.4	567,596
New Hampshire	36	0.3	275	0.4	8	4.1	14,953	24.5	0.4	679,306
New Mexico	54	0.5	325	0.4	6	4.0	12,182	24.0	0.4	443,907
Delaware	32	0.3	247	0.3	8	2.9	11,684	22.9	0.4	715,406
Hawaii	31	0.3	178	0.2	6	3.3	18,371	22.5	0.4	724,258
West Virginia	40	0.4	318	0.4	8	2.8	8,679	21.3	0.3	533,075
D.C.	31	0.3	203	0.3	7	3.4	16,788	19.4	0.3	625,387
Maine	27	0.3	231	0.3	9	2.2	9,524	15.8	0.3	584,741
Idaho	30	0.3	254	0.3	8	2.2	8,732	15.2	0.2	507,067
Rhode Island	24	0.2	153	0.2	6	2.0	13,065	13.5	0.2	561,375
Montana	28	0.3	185	0.2	7	1.6	8,676	10.3	0.2	368,536
North Dakota	17	0.2	182	0.2	11	1.3	7,055	8.8	0.1	519,941
South Dakota	15	0.1	134	0.2	9	1.1	8,015	8.2	0.1	548,133
Alaska	10	0.1	95	0.1	10	2.5	26,232	6.9	0.1	688,600
Vermont	12	0.1	101	0.1	8	1.0	10,089	6.6	0.1	553,917
Wyoming	16	0.1	101	0.1	6	1.0	10,267	6.3	0.1	391,000

Source: 2002 *Economic Census*. The states are in descending order of sales or establishments (if sales data are missing for the majority). The symbol (D) appears when data are withheld to prevent disclosure of competitive information. States marked with (D) are sorted by number of establishments. A dash (-) indicates that the data element cannot be calculated. Shaded *states* on the state map indicate those states which have proportionately greater representation in the industry than would be indicated by the states population; the ratio is based on total sales or number of establishments. Shaded *regions* indicate where the industry is regionally most concentrated.

NAICS 446130 - OPTICAL GOODS STORES

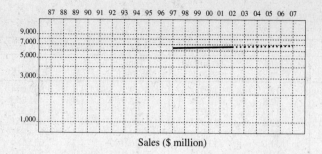

Sales ($ million)

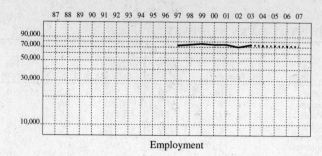

Employment

GENERAL STATISTICS

Year	Establishments (number)	Employment (number)	Payroll ($ million)	Sales ($ million)	Employees per Establishment (number)	Sales per Establishment ($)	Payroll per Employee ($)
1987	-	-	-	-	-	-	-
1988	-	-	-	-	-	-	-
1989	-	-	-	-	-	-	-
1990	-	-	-	-	-	-	-
1991	-	-	-	-	-	-	-
1992	-	-	-	-	-	-	-
1993	-	-	-	-	-	-	-
1994	-	-	-	-	-	-	-
1995	-	-	-	-	-	-	-
1996	-	-	-	-	-	-	-
1997	15,192	73,049	1,401.2	6,432.1	5	423,387	19,182
1998	14,722	74,367	1,600.7	6,475.6 e	5	439,859	21,524
1999	14,673	76,074	1,632.6	6,519.1 e	5	444,294	21,461
2000	14,281	74,426	1,696.6	6,562.6 e	5	459,536	22,796
2001	14,006	74,617	1,679.1	6,606.1 e	5	471,665	22,503
2002	13,031	70,156	1,629.8	6,649.7	5	510,295	23,230
2003	12,889	73,946	1,673.9	6,693.2 p	6	512,692 p	22,637
2004	12,548 p	72,778 p	1,748.1 p	6,736.7 p	6 p	528,269 p	24,022 p
2005	12,157 p	72,521 p	1,781.0 p	6,780.2 p	6 p	543,846 p	24,551 p
2006	11,765 p	72,265 p	1,814.0 p	6,823.7 p	6 p	559,423 p	25,081 p
2007	11,374 p	72,008 p	1,847.0 p	6,867.2 p	6 p	575,000 p	25,610 p

Source: Economic Census of the United States, 1997 and 2002. Establishment counts, employment, and payroll are from County Business Patterns for non-Census years. This is a newly defined industry. Data for prior years are unavailable at the time of publication but may become available over time. Values followed by 'p' are projections by the editors. Sales data for non-Census years are extrapolations, marked by 'e'.

INDICES OF CHANGE

Year	Establishments (number)	Employment (number)	Payroll ($ million)	Sales ($ million)	Employees per Establishment (number)	Sales per Establishment ($)	Payroll per Employee ($)
1987	-	-	-	-	-	-	-
1992	-	-	-	-	-	-	-
1993	-	-	-	-	-	-	-
1994	-	-	-	-	-	-	-
1995	-	-	-	-	-	-	-
1996	-	-	-	-	-	-	-
1997	116.6	104.1	86.0	96.7	89.2	83.0	82.6
1998	113.0	106.0	98.2	97.4 e	94.7	86.2	92.7
1999	112.6	108.4	100.2	98.0 e	96.6	87.1	92.4
2000	109.6	106.1	104.1	98.7 e	96.6	90.1	98.1
2001	107.5	106.4	103.0	99.3 e	98.4	92.4	96.9
2002	100.0	100.0	100.0	100.0	100.0	100.0	100.0
2003	98.9	105.4	102.7	100.7 p	106.6	100.5 p	97.4
2004	96.3 p	103.7 p	107.3 p	101.3 p	106.7 p	103.5 p	103.4 p
2005	93.3 p	103.4 p	109.3 p	102.0 p	109.0 p	106.6 p	105.7 p
2006	90.3 p	103.0 p	111.3 p	102.6 p	111.3 p	109.6 p	108.0 p
2007	87.3 p	102.6 p	113.3 p	103.3 p	113.6 p	112.7 p	110.2 p

Sources: Same as General Statistics. The values shown reflect change from the base year, 2002. Values above 100 mean greater than 2002, values below 100 mean less than 2002, and a value of 100 in the 1987-2001 or 2003-2007 period means same as 2002. Values followed by a 'p' are projections by the editors; 'e' stands for extrapolation. Data are the most recent available at this level of detail.

SELECTED RATIOS

For 2002	Avg. of All Retail	Analyzed Industry	Index	For 2002	Avg. of All Retail	Analyzed Industry	Index
Employees per Establishment	17	5	32	Sales per Employee	174,682	94,784	54
Payroll per Establishment	333,445	125,068	38	Sales per Establishment	3,332,269	510,295	15
Payroll per Employee	20,311	23,230	114	Expenses per Establishment	na	na	na

Sources: Same as General Statistics. The 'Average of All' column, Wholesale or Retail, represents the average of the sector reported for the most recent complete year available. The Index shows the relationship between the Average and the Analyzed Industry. For example, 100 means that they are equal; 500 that the Analyzed Industry is five times the average; 50 means that the Analyzed Industry is half the national average. The abbreviation 'na' is used to show that data are 'not available'.

LEADING COMPANIES   Number shown: **11**   Total sales ($ mil): **37,922**   Total employment (000): **267.6**

Company Name	Address				CEO Name	Phone	Co. Type	Sales ($ mil)	Empl. (000)
Sears, Roebuck and Co.	3333 Beverly Rd	Hoffman Estates	IL	60179		847-286-2500	D	36,099	250.0
Cole National Corp.	1925 Enterprise Pky	Twinsburg	OH	44087		330-486-3100	S	1,202	13.7
National Vision Inc.	296 Grayson Hwy	Lawrenceville	GA	30045	L Reade Fahs	770-822-3600	P	243	2.7
1-800 CONTACTS Inc.	66 E Wadsworth	Draper	UT	84020	Brian W Bethers	801-924-9800	P	187	0.8
Lombart Instruments U.S.	5358 Robin Hood	Norfolk	VA	23513	Kenneth Lombart	757-853-8888	R	125*	0.1
Dr Bizer's Visionworld	516 E Lewis & Clark	Clarksville	IN	47129	Mark Lynn	812-282-2020	R	25*	<0.1
Emerging Vision Inc.	100 Q Roosevelt	Garden City	NY	11530	Alan Cohen	516-390-2100	P	14	0.1
Eye Med	401 Meridian St N	Huntsville	AL	35801		256-533-7300	R	13*	<0.1
Sunland Optical Company Inc.	1156 Barranca Dr	El Paso	TX	79935	Tony Lich	915-591-9483	R	9*	<0.1
San Luis Obisbo Eye Assoc A ME	234 Heather Ct Ste 1	Templeton	CA	93465		805-434-5970	R	2*	<0.1
EYE DRx	1255 Broad St	Bloomfield	NJ	07003	Dywane Carter	973-338-7575	R	2*	<0.1

Source: Ward's Business Directory of U.S. Private and Public Companies, Volumes 1 and 2, 2005. The company type code used is as follows: P - Public, R - Private, S - Subsidiary, D - Division, J - Joint Venture, A - Affiliate, G - Group. Sales are in millions of dollars, employees are in thousands. An asterisk (*) indicates an estimated sales volume. The symbol < stands for 'less than'. Company names and addresses are truncated, in some cases, to fit into the available space.

OCCUPATIONS EMPLOYED BY HEALTH & PERSONAL CARE STORES

Occupation	% of Total 2004	Change to 2014	Occupation	% of Total 2004	Change to 2014
Retail salespersons	32.6	32.4	Stock clerks & order fillers	2.0	1.4
Cashiers, except gaming	10.4	19.2	General & operations managers	1.8	31.0
Opticians, dispensing	8.2	12.5	Receptionists & information clerks	1.7	26.1
First-line supervisors/managers of retail sales workers	7.5	21.8	Bookkeeping, accounting, & auditing clerks	1.5	19.2
Ophthalmic laboratory technicians	2.9	2.2	Optometrists	1.2	14.2
Sales reps, wholesale & manufacturing, exc tech	2.8	32.4	Truck drivers, light or delivery services	1.1	32.4
Customer service representatives	2.3	35.6	Laborers & freight, stock, & material movers, hand	1.0	19.2
Office clerks, general	2.2	17.8			

Source: Industry-Occupation Matrix, Bureau of Labor Statistics. These data are reported based on 4-digit NAICS categories but have been matched to corresponding 6-digit NAICS industry codes. The change reported for each occupation to the year 2014 is a percent of growth or decline as estimated by the Bureau of Labor Statistics. The abbreviation nec stands for 'not elsewhere classified.'

LOCATION BY STATE AND REGIONAL CONCENTRATION

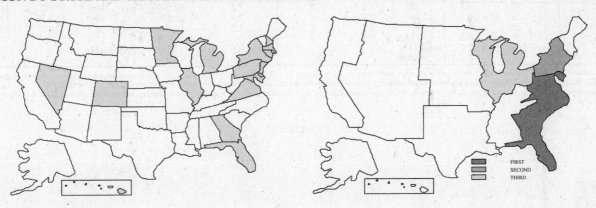

INDUSTRY DATA BY STATE

State	Establishments Total (number)	% of U.S.	Employment Total (number)	% of U.S.	Per Estab.	Payroll Total ($ mil.)	Per Empl. ($)	Sales Total ($ mil.)	% of U.S.	Per Estab. ($)
New York	1,206	9.3	6,478	9.2	5	171.3	26,441	650.0	9.8	538,984
California	1,027	7.9	6,179	8.8	6	151.1	24,459	610.3	9.2	594,216
Florida	1,067	8.2	5,497	7.8	5	117.5	21,369	483.5	7.3	453,165
Texas	922	7.1	4,766	6.8	5	98.7	20,711	452.0	6.8	490,240
Pennsylvania	704	5.4	3,428	4.9	5	78.7	22,963	324.5	4.9	460,911
Illinois	528	4.1	3,630	5.2	7	76.2	20,986	310.6	4.7	588,297
Michigan	449	3.4	2,723	3.9	6	78.3	28,755	274.1	4.1	610,361
Ohio	545	4.2	2,669	3.8	5	62.3	23,344	259.8	3.9	476,670
New Jersey	497	3.8	2,359	3.4	5	66.6	28,214	255.8	3.8	514,656
Georgia	346	2.7	2,104	3.0	6	46.9	22,291	201.4	3.0	582,220

Continued on next page.

INDUSTRY DATA BY STATE - Continued

State	Establishments Total (number)	% of U.S.	Employment Total (number)	% of U.S.	Per Estab.	Payroll Total ($ mil.)	Per Empl. ($)	Sales Total ($ mil.)	% of U.S.	Per Estab. ($)
Virginia	361	2.8	2,012	2.9	6	50.1	24,922	198.0	3.0	548,352
Maryland	338	2.6	1,839	2.6	5	45.1	24,545	185.3	2.8	548,275
Massachusetts	310	2.4	1,620	2.3	5	41.5	25,629	160.9	2.4	519,165
Colorado	292	2.2	1,416	2.0	5	31.2	22,061	140.0	2.1	479,418
North Carolina	289	2.2	1,540	2.2	5	34.6	22,496	136.9	2.1	473,765
Minnesota	263	2.0	1,447	2.1	6	33.5	23,123	135.7	2.0	515,977
Missouri	250	1.9	1,434	2.0	6	32.7	22,778	127.1	1.9	508,248
Washington	257	2.0	1,203	1.7	5	28.0	23,283	124.6	1.9	484,914
Wisconsin	238	1.8	1,327	1.9	6	28.0	21,081	117.2	1.8	492,328
Indiana	219	1.7	1,404	2.0	6	28.9	20,570	114.8	1.7	524,114
Connecticut	190	1.5	1,086	1.5	6	30.3	27,883	112.0	1.7	589,305
Tennessee	201	1.5	1,222	1.7	6	25.7	21,029	107.5	1.6	534,706
Louisiana	182	1.4	982	1.4	5	18.2	18,546	79.4	1.2	436,368
South Carolina	176	1.4	882	1.3	5	18.6	21,070	76.8	1.2	436,085
Oregon	163	1.3	736	1.0	5	17.2	23,319	72.7	1.1	446,000
Alabama	167	1.3	816	1.2	5	16.2	19,904	68.4	1.0	409,323
Kentucky	101	0.8	680	1.0	7	14.3	21,034	67.4	1.0	667,079
Nevada	83	0.6	468	0.7	6	12.0	25,551	57.5	0.9	692,325
Iowa	139	1.1	635	0.9	5	13.2	20,764	56.1	0.8	403,633
Kansas	122	0.9	555	0.8	5	11.1	20,031	49.4	0.7	404,754
Oklahoma	112	0.9	592	0.8	5	11.4	19,338	49.3	0.7	440,536
Utah	113	0.9	564	0.8	5	11.5	20,388	48.1	0.7	426,027
New Mexico	91	0.7	441	0.6	5	7.8	17,673	35.4	0.5	389,066
New Hampshire	64	0.5	357	0.5	6	8.5	23,936	35.0	0.5	546,438
Mississippi	89	0.7	400	0.6	4	7.8	19,520	33.4	0.5	375,247
Nebraska	81	0.6	423	0.6	5	8.4	19,849	33.2	0.5	409,346
Hawaii	73	0.6	338	0.5	5	6.6	19,657	33.1	0.5	453,110
West Virginia	71	0.5	355	0.5	5	6.6	18,614	30.0	0.5	422,437
Delaware	43	0.3	253	0.4	6	5.5	21,609	23.1	0.3	536,605
Maine	49	0.4	211	0.3	4	4.6	21,706	19.1	0.3	389,959
Arkansas	46	0.4	221	0.3	5	4.1	18,661	17.8	0.3	387,457
Idaho	43	0.3	189	0.3	4	3.7	19,820	17.6	0.3	409,395
Rhode Island	42	0.3	161	0.2	4	4.0	25,112	16.7	0.3	397,881
North Dakota	38	0.3	183	0.3	5	3.4	18,831	15.2	0.2	398,842
Alaska	32	0.2	139	0.2	4	3.6	26,014	14.9	0.2	464,781
Montana	36	0.3	168	0.2	5	3.5	20,595	14.8	0.2	412,167
Vermont	29	0.2	107	0.2	4	2.8	25,879	10.7	0.2	370,379
South Dakota	29	0.2	125	0.2	4	2.2	17,480	10.3	0.2	356,345
Wyoming	20	0.2	83	0.1	4	1.6	19,157	7.0	0.1	350,350
Arizona	263	2.0	1000-2499	-	-	(D)	-	(D)	-	-
D.C.	41	0.3	250-499	-	-	(D)	-	(D)	-	-

Source: 2002 Economic Census. The states are in descending order of sales or establishments (if sales data are missing for the majority). The symbol (D) appears when data are withheld to prevent disclosure of competitive information. States marked with (D) are sorted by number of establishments. A dash (-) indicates that the data element cannot be calculated. Shaded *states* on the state map indicate those states which have proportionally greater representation in the industry than would be indicated by the states population; the ratio is based on total sales or number of establishments. Shaded *regions* indicate where the industry is regionally most concentrated.

NAICS 446191 - FOOD (HEALTH) SUPPLEMENT STORES

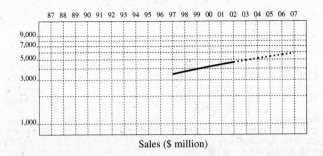

Sales ($ million)

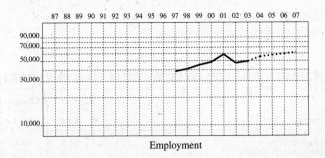

Employment

GENERAL STATISTICS

Year	Establishments (number)	Employment (number)	Payroll ($ million)	Sales ($ million)	Employees per Establishment (number)	Sales per Establishment ($)	Payroll per Employee ($)
1987	-	-	-	-	-	-	-
1988	-	-	-	-	-	-	-
1989	-	-	-	-	-	-	-
1990	-	-	-	-	-	-	-
1991	-	-	-	-	-	-	-
1992	-	-	-	-	-	-	-
1993	-	-	-	-	-	-	-
1994	-	-	-	-	-	-	-
1995	-	-	-	-	-	-	-
1996	-	-	-	-	-	-	-
1997	7,404	38,537	485.0	3,488.6	5	471,178	12,585
1998	7,932	40,941	560.1	3,726.3 e	5	469,784	13,681
1999	8,384	45,149	601.6	3,964.1 e	5	472,813	13,325
2000	8,655	48,547	705.4	4,201.8 e	6	485,476	14,529
2001	9,027	58,868	790.6	4,439.5 e	7	491,805	13,430
2002	9,525	47,321	696.7	4,677.3	5	491,050	14,723
2003	9,547	49,528	792.3	4,915.0	5	498,159 p	15,998
2004	10,105 p	55,478 p	859.4 p	5,152.7 p	6 p	503,248 p	15,814 p
2005	10,471 p	57,601 p	908.9 p	5,390.4 p	6 p	508,336 p	16,258 p
2006	10,837 p	59,724 p	958.3 p	5,628.2 p	6 p	513,424 p	16,701 p
2007	11,204 p	61,847 p	1,007.7 p	5,865.9 p	6 p	518,512 p	17,145 p

Source: *Economic Census of the United States*, 1997 and 2002. Establishment counts, employment, and payroll are from *County Business Patterns* for non-Census years. This is a newly defined industry. Data for prior years are unavailable at the time of publication but may become available over time. Values followed by 'p' are projections by the editors. Sales data for non-Census years are extrapolations, marked by 'e'.

INDICES OF CHANGE

Year	Establishments (number)	Employment (number)	Payroll ($ million)	Sales ($ million)	Employees per Establishment (number)	Sales per Establishment ($)	Payroll per Employee ($)
1987	-	-	-	-	-	-	-
1992	-	-	-	-	-	-	-
1993	-	-	-	-	-	-	-
1994	-	-	-	-	-	-	-
1995	-	-	-	-	-	-	-
1996	-	-	-	-	-	-	-
1997	77.7	81.4	69.6	74.6	104.7	96.0	85.5
1998	83.3	86.5	80.4	79.7 e	104.7	95.7	92.9
1999	88.0	95.4	86.4	84.8 e	108.7	96.3	90.5
2000	90.9	102.6	101.2	89.8 e	112.7	98.9	98.7
2001	94.8	124.4	113.5	94.9 e	130.8	100.2	91.2
2002	100.0	100.0	100.0	100.0	100.0	100.0	100.0
2003	100.2	104.7	113.7	105.1 p	104.4	101.4 p	108.7
2004	106.1 p	117.2 p	123.4 p	110.2 p	111.2 p	102.5 p	107.4 p
2005	109.9 p	121.7 p	130.5 p	115.2 p	111.6 p	103.5 p	110.4 p
2006	113.8 p	126.2 p	137.5 p	120.3 p	112.0 p	104.6 p	113.4 p
2007	117.6 p	130.7 p	144.6 p	125.4 p	112.4 p	105.6 p	116.5 p

Sources: Same as General Statistics. The values shown reflect change from the base year, 2002. Values above 100 mean greater than 2002, values below 100 mean less than 2002, and a value of 100 in the 1987-2001 or 2003-2007 period means same as 2002. Values followed by a 'p' are projections by the editors; 'e' stands for extrapolation. Data are the most recent available at this level of detail.

SELECTED RATIOS

For 2002	Avg. of All Retail	Analyzed Industry	Index	For 2002	Avg. of All Retail	Analyzed Industry	Index
Employees per Establishment	17	5	29	Sales per Employee	174,682	98,841	57
Payroll per Establishment	333,445	73,144	22	Sales per Establishment	3,332,269	491,050	15
Payroll per Employee	20,311	14,723	72	Expenses per Establishment	na	na	na

Sources: Same as General Statistics. The 'Average of All' column, Wholesale or Retail, represents the average of the sector reported for the most recent complete year available. The Index shows the relationship between the Average and the Analyzed Industry. For example, 100 means that they are equal; 500 that the Analyzed Industry is five times the average; 50 means that the Analyzed Industry is half the national average. The abbreviation 'na' is used to show that data are 'not available'.

LEADING COMPANIES

No company data available for this industry.

OCCUPATIONS EMPLOYED BY HEALTH & PERSONAL CARE STORES

Occupation	% of Total 2004	Change to 2014	Occupation	% of Total 2004	Change to 2014
Retail salespersons	32.6	32.4	Stock clerks & order fillers	2.0	1.4
Cashiers, except gaming	10.4	19.2	General & operations managers	1.8	31.0
Opticians, dispensing	8.2	12.5	Receptionists & information clerks	1.7	26.1
First-line supervisors/managers of retail sales workers	7.5	21.8	Bookkeeping, accounting, & auditing clerks	1.5	19.2
Ophthalmic laboratory technicians	2.9	2.2	Optometrists	1.2	14.2
Sales reps, wholesale & manufacturing, exc tech	2.8	32.4	Truck drivers, light or delivery services	1.1	32.4
Customer service representatives	2.3	35.6	Laborers & freight, stock, & material movers, hand	1.0	19.2
Office clerks, general	2.2	17.8			

Source: *Industry-Occupation Matrix*, Bureau of Labor Statistics. These data are reported based on 4-digit NAICS categories but have been matched to corresponding 6-digit NAICS industry codes. The change reported for each occupation to the year 2014 is a percent of growth or decline as estimated by the Bureau of Labor Statistics. The abbreviation nec stands for 'not elsewhere classified.'

LOCATION BY STATE AND REGIONAL CONCENTRATION

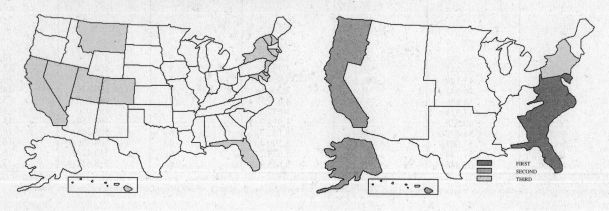

FIRST
SECOND
THIRD

INDUSTRY DATA BY STATE

State	Establishments Total (number)	% of U.S.	Employment Total (number)	% of U.S.	Per Estab.	Payroll Total ($ mil.)	Per Empl. ($)	Sales Total ($ mil.)	% of U.S.	Per Estab. ($)
California	1,124	11.8	6,358	13.6	6	111.9	17,601	769.5	16.5	684,578
Florida	861	9.0	4,065	8.7	5	62.3	15,318	425.3	9.1	493,969
New York	673	7.1	3,536	7.5	5	57.3	16,218	419.6	9.0	623,404
Texas	643	6.7	2,953	6.3	5	42.0	14,218	281.7	6.1	438,084
Pennsylvania	420	4.4	2,039	4.3	5	27.2	13,346	190.6	4.1	453,888
New Jersey	332	3.5	1,454	3.1	4	24.2	16,631	181.6	3.9	547,060
Illinois	361	3.8	1,652	3.5	5	26.5	16,044	170.3	3.7	471,803
Colorado	211	2.2	1,114	2.4	5	18.1	16,266	147.2	3.2	697,611
Ohio	332	3.5	1,762	3.8	5	22.1	12,555	139.9	3.0	421,527
Michigan	277	2.9	1,461	3.1	5	21.7	14,887	134.6	2.9	486,014
Georgia	310	3.3	1,275	2.7	4	17.5	13,696	113.9	2.4	367,484
North Carolina	246	2.6	1,270	2.7	5	16.9	13,289	108.3	2.3	440,232
Virginia	262	2.8	1,199	2.6	5	15.6	13,032	100.6	2.2	383,885
Massachusetts	184	1.9	1,047	2.2	6	16.7	15,904	97.2	2.1	528,370
Washington	226	2.4	1,086	2.3	5	17.4	15,994	93.6	2.0	414,310
Maryland	165	1.7	937	2.0	6	12.9	13,764	92.2	2.0	558,824
Connecticut	111	1.2	633	1.3	6	10.5	16,633	71.6	1.5	645,027
Indiana	178	1.9	851	1.8	5	10.7	12,623	68.2	1.5	382,949
South Carolina	106	1.1	678	1.4	6	9.3	13,673	58.9	1.3	555,915
Minnesota	154	1.6	794	1.7	5	10.2	12,843	55.6	1.2	361,143
Missouri	166	1.7	789	1.7	5	8.3	10,515	53.9	1.2	324,572
Tennessee	159	1.7	623	1.3	4	8.4	13,536	52.6	1.1	330,635
Nevada	99	1.0	397	0.8	4	6.6	16,736	47.0	1.0	474,465
Oregon	113	1.2	515	1.1	5	7.3	14,171	46.1	1.0	407,982
Wisconsin	150	1.6	564	1.2	4	6.8	12,046	44.4	1.0	296,200
Hawaii	55	0.6	392	0.8	7	6.2	15,712	42.3	0.9	769,945
Louisiana	117	1.2	561	1.2	5	6.3	11,171	41.8	0.9	357,214
Kentucky	100	1.0	577	1.2	6	6.8	11,778	40.5	0.9	405,070

Continued on next page.

INDUSTRY DATA BY STATE - Continued

State	Establishments Total (number)	% of U.S.	Employment Total (number)	% of U.S.	Per Estab.	Payroll Total ($ mil.)	Per Empl. ($)	Sales Total ($ mil.)	% of U.S.	Per Estab. ($)
Alabama	111	1.2	450	1.0	4	5.6	12,433	40.1	0.9	361,180
Utah	90	0.9	443	0.9	5	5.3	11,944	38.9	0.8	432,589
Oklahoma	112	1.2	478	1.0	4	5.6	11,741	37.8	0.8	337,607
Iowa	82	0.9	366	0.8	4	3.9	10,691	29.1	0.6	354,573
Kansas	88	0.9	337	0.7	4	3.9	11,677	26.2	0.6	297,693
Arkansas	64	0.7	324	0.7	5	4.3	13,167	25.4	0.5	396,750
New Mexico	68	0.7	267	0.6	4	4.0	14,861	23.5	0.5	346,265
New Hampshire	53	0.6	238	0.5	4	3.7	15,735	22.3	0.5	420,943
Nebraska	52	0.5	243	0.5	5	3.1	12,749	20.6	0.4	396,635
Montana	45	0.5	249	0.5	6	3.2	12,783	20.1	0.4	447,756
Maine	35	0.4	212	0.5	6	3.1	14,703	19.5	0.4	557,971
Mississippi	62	0.7	251	0.5	4	3.1	12,442	19.1	0.4	307,274
Vermont	32	0.3	234	0.5	7	2.9	12,530	17.9	0.4	560,719
Delaware	29	0.3	139	0.3	5	2.2	16,122	16.2	0.3	557,552
Idaho	50	0.5	202	0.4	4	1.8	8,718	14.9	0.3	298,840
Rhode Island	31	0.3	124	0.3	4	2.1	16,952	13.9	0.3	449,839
West Virginia	55	0.6	182	0.4	3	2.1	11,709	12.4	0.3	225,764
Alaska	20	0.2	108	0.2	5	1.6	15,241	9.6	0.2	481,150
South Dakota	23	0.2	116	0.2	5	1.0	8,612	7.3	0.2	318,696
North Dakota	19	0.2	78	0.2	4	0.8	9,949	6.7	0.1	354,684
Wyoming	22	0.2	60	0.1	3	0.6	10,050	4.7	0.1	211,455
Arizona	225	2.4	1000-2499	-	-	(D)	-	(D)	-	-
D.C.	23	0.2	20-99	-	-	(D)	-	(D)	-	-

Source: 2002 Economic Census. The states are in descending order of sales or establishments (if sales data are missing for the majority). The symbol (D) appears when data are withheld to prevent disclosure of competitive information. States marked with (D) are sorted by number of establishments. A dash (-) indicates that the data element cannot be calculated. Shaded states on the state map indicate those states which have proportionately greater representation in the industry than would be indicated by the states population; the ratio is based on total sales or number of establishments. Shaded regions indicate where the industry is regionally most concentrated.

NAICS 446199 - ALL OTHER HEALTH AND PERSONAL CARE STORES

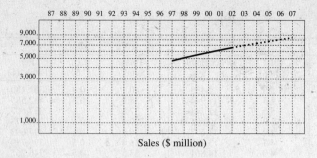

Sales ($ million)

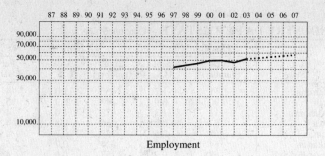

Employment

GENERAL STATISTICS

Year	Establishments (number)	Employment (number)	Payroll ($ million)	Sales ($ million)	Employees per Establishment (number)	Sales per Establishment ($)	Payroll per Employee ($)
1987	-	-	-	-	-	-	-
1988	-	-	-	-	-	-	-
1989	-	-	-	-	-	-	-
1990	-	-	-	-	-	-	-
1991	-	-	-	-	-	-	-
1992	-	-	-	-	-	-	-
1993	-	-	-	-	-	-	-
1994	-	-	-	-	-	-	-
1995	-	-	-	-	-	-	-
1996	-	-	-	-	-	-	-
1997	7,716	41,829	1,113.3	4,730.3	5	613,051	26,616
1998	7,983	43,962	1,258.8	5,101.3 e	6	639,022	28,634
1999	7,902	46,076	1,371.1	5,472.3 e	6	692,524	29,757
2000	8,021	49,435	1,493.8	5,843.3 e	6	728,504	30,217
2001	8,209	49,769	1,626.9	6,214.3 e	6	757,016	32,688
2002	8,101	47,231	1,511.8	6,585.4	6	812,906	32,009
2003	8,640	51,710	1,764.4	6,956.4 p	6	846,094 p	34,121
2004	8,555 p	52,841 p	1,836.5 p	7,327.4 p	6 p	885,787 p	35,177 p
2005	8,674 p	54,265 p	1,933.4 p	7,698.4 p	6 p	925,479 p	36,327 p
2006	8,792 p	55,689 p	2,030.4 p	8,069.4 p	6 p	965,172 p	37,477 p
2007	8,910 p	57,113 p	2,127.4 p	8,440.4 p	7 p	1,004,864 p	38,627 p

Source: *Economic Census of the United States*, 1997 and 2002. Establishment counts, employment, and payroll are from *County Business Patterns* for non-Census years. This is a newly defined industry. Data for prior years are unavailable at the time of publication but may become available over time. Values followed by 'p' are projections by the editors. Sales data for non-Census years are extrapolations, marked by 'e'.

INDICES OF CHANGE

Year	Establishments (number)	Employment (number)	Payroll ($ million)	Sales ($ million)	Employees per Establishment (number)	Sales per Establishment ($)	Payroll per Employee ($)
1987	-	-	-	-	-	-	-
1992	-	-	-	-	-	-	-
1993	-	-	-	-	-	-	-
1994	-	-	-	-	-	-	-
1995	-	-	-	-	-	-	-
1996	-	-	-	-	-	-	-
1997	95.2	88.6	73.6	71.8	92.6	75.4	83.1
1998	98.5	93.1	83.3	77.5 e	94.3	78.6	89.5
1999	97.5	97.6	90.7	83.1 e	99.5	85.2	93.0
2000	99.0	104.7	98.8	88.7 e	106.3	89.6	94.4
2001	101.3	105.4	107.6	94.4 e	104.6	93.1	102.1
2002	100.0	100.0	100.0	100.0	100.0	100.0	100.0
2003	106.7	109.5	116.7	105.6 p	102.7	104.1 p	106.6
2004	105.6 p	111.9 p	121.5 p	111.3 p	106.7 p	109.0 p	109.9 p
2005	107.1 p	114.9 p	127.9 p	116.9 p	108.3 p	113.8 p	113.5 p
2006	108.5 p	117.9 p	134.3 p	122.5 p	110.0 p	118.7 p	117.1 p
2007	110.0 p	120.9 p	140.7 p	128.2 p	111.7 p	123.6 p	120.7 p

Sources: Same as General Statistics. The values shown reflect change from the base year, 2002. Values above 100 mean greater than 2002, values below 100 mean less than 2002, and a value of 100 in the 1987-2001 or 2003-2007 period means same as 2002. Values followed by a 'p' are projections by the editors; 'e' stands for extrapolation. Data are the most recent available at this level of detail.

SELECTED RATIOS

For 2002	Avg. of All Retail	Analyzed Industry	Index	For 2002	Avg. of All Retail	Analyzed Industry	Index
Employees per Establishment	17	6	34	Sales per Employee	174,682	139,429	80
Payroll per Establishment	333,445	186,622	56	Sales per Establishment	3,332,269	812,906	24
Payroll per Employee	20,311	32,009	158	Expenses per Establishment	na	na	na

Sources: Same as General Statistics. The 'Average of All' column, Wholesale or Retail, represents the average of the sector reported for the most recent complete year available. The Index shows the relationship between the Average and the Analyzed Industry. For example, 100 means that they are equal; 500 that the Analyzed Industry is five times the average; 50 means that the Analyzed Industry is half the national average. The abbreviation 'na' is used to show that data are 'not available'.

LEADING COMPANIES   Number shown: **16**   Total sales ($ mil): **177**   Total employment (000): **0.6**

Company Name	Address				CEO Name	Phone	Co. Type	Sales ($ mil)	Empl. (000)
Mercury Medical	PO Box 20000	Saint Petersburg	FL	33742	Stanley Pangalakis	727-573-0088	R	51*	0.1
Hemocue Inc.	40 Empire Dr	Lake Forest	CA	92630		949-859-2630	R	26*	<0.1
Extended Care Support Inc.	1900 7th St	Richmond	CA	94801	James Cassin	510-233-7332	R	15*	<0.1
Maxi-Aids Inc.	PO Box 3209	Farmingdale	NY	11735	Harold Zaretsky	631-752-0521	R	14*	<0.1
Central Medical Equipment Co.	3517 Walnut St	Harrisburg	PA	17109	F Luft	717-657-2100	R	14*	<0.1
Carlton J Enterprises L.L.C.	3715 Hawkins St NE	Albuquerque	NM	87109		505-344-9933	R	10*	<0.1
Adorno Rogers Technology Inc.	PO Box 81557	Austin	TX	78708	Jack Jacobs	512-474-7267	R	9*	<0.1
BioMeridian International Inc.	12411 S 265 W	Draper	UT	84020	Jacob Carter	801-501-7516	R	7*	<0.1
Fletcher's Medical Supplies Inc.	1080 Edgewood S	Jacksonville	FL	32205	David Fletcher	904-387-4481	R	6*	<0.1
Home Care Service Inc.	PO Box 4397	Metuchen	NJ	08840	Ron Gellis	732-906-9201	R	6*	<0.1
Lifeline Lifetech	8040 S Madison St	Burr Ridge	IL	60527	Cork Farkas	630-455-2122	R	4*	<0.1
Apache OXY-Med Inc.	962 E Isabella Ave	Mesa	AZ	85204		480-926-0133	R	3*	<0.1
Homedeq Inc.	7311 Ardmore St	Houston	TX	77054	A Kennedy	713-748-6225	R	3*	<0.1
Coral Medical Home Equipment	PO Box 9720	Tavernier	FL	33070	Cleveland West	305-744-0258	R	3*	<0.1
Home Care Equipment Inc.	1135 Lester St	Poplar Bluff	MO	63901	Deidre Lawson	573-686-3720	R	3*	<0.1
Oklahoma Respiratory Care Inc.	623 N Porter Ave	Norman	OK	73071	Aaron Barnes	405-360-4405	R	2*	<0.1

Source: Ward's Business Directory of U.S. Private and Public Companies, Volumes 1 and 2, 2005. The company type code used is as follows: P - Public, R - Private, S - Subsidiary, D - Division, J - Joint Venture, A - Affiliate, G - Group. Sales are in millions of dollars, employees are in thousands. An asterisk (*) indicates an estimated sales volume. The symbol < stands for 'less than'. Company names and addresses are truncated, in some cases, to fit into the available space.

OCCUPATIONS EMPLOYED BY HEALTH & PERSONAL CARE STORES

Occupation	% of Total 2004	Change to 2014	Occupation	% of Total 2004	Change to 2014
Retail salespersons	32.6	32.4	Stock clerks & order fillers	2.0	1.4
Cashiers, except gaming	10.4	19.2	General & operations managers	1.8	31.0
Opticians, dispensing	8.2	12.5	Receptionists & information clerks	1.7	26.1
First-line supervisors/managers of retail sales workers	7.5	21.8	Bookkeeping, accounting, & auditing clerks	1.5	19.2
Ophthalmic laboratory technicians	2.9	2.2	Optometrists	1.2	14.2
Sales reps, wholesale & manufacturing, exc tech	2.8	32.4	Truck drivers, light or delivery services	1.1	32.4
Customer service representatives	2.3	35.6	Laborers & freight, stock, & material movers, hand	1.0	19.2
Office clerks, general	2.2	17.8			

Source: Industry-Occupation Matrix, Bureau of Labor Statistics. These data are reported based on 4-digit NAICS categories but have been matched to corresponding 6-digit NAICS industry codes. The change reported for each occupation to the year 2014 is a percent of growth or decline as estimated by the Bureau of Labor Statistics. The abbreviation nec stands for 'not elsewhere classified.'

LOCATION BY STATE AND REGIONAL CONCENTRATION

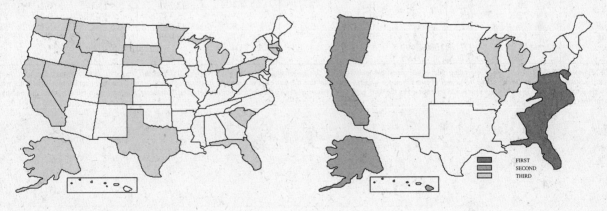

INDUSTRY DATA BY STATE

State	Establishments Total (number)	Establishments % of U.S.	Employment Total (number)	Employment % of U.S.	Employment Per Estab.	Payroll Total ($ mil.)	Payroll Per Empl. ($)	Sales Total ($ mil.)	Sales % of U.S.	Sales Per Estab. ($)
California	899	11.0	5,349	11.1	6	177.8	33,245	852.0	12.9	947,754
Texas	628	7.7	3,709	7.7	6	119.3	32,158	539.3	8.2	858,683
Florida	788	9.6	3,481	7.2	4	117.9	33,875	491.2	7.4	623,391
New York	494	6.0	3,166	6.6	6	106.5	33,654	432.2	6.5	874,943
Ohio	384	4.7	2,687	5.6	7	85.5	31,835	360.0	5.4	937,513

Continued on next page.

INDUSTRY DATA BY STATE - Continued

State	Establishments Total (number)	% of U.S.	Employment Total (number)	% of U.S.	Per Estab.	Payroll Total ($ mil.)	Per Empl. ($)	Sales Total ($ mil.)	% of U.S.	Per Estab. ($)
Pennsylvania	349	4.3	2,359	4.9	7	79.0	33,500	319.8	4.8	916,372
Michigan	277	3.4	1,977	4.1	7	70.5	35,646	281.1	4.2	1,014,632
Illinois	300	3.7	1,606	3.3	5	47.8	29,734	188.7	2.9	628,940
Washington	197	2.4	1,171	2.4	6	39.0	33,326	179.8	2.7	912,640
Massachusetts	170	2.1	1,159	2.4	7	44.6	38,487	177.3	2.7	1,042,718
New Jersey	223	2.7	1,118	2.3	5	38.1	34,117	169.5	2.6	759,942
North Carolina	256	3.1	1,306	2.7	5	38.1	29,190	152.3	2.3	594,988
Georgia	205	2.5	985	2.0	5	30.5	30,933	141.1	2.1	688,234
Minnesota	136	1.7	978	2.0	7	32.3	33,045	129.3	2.0	950,699
Tennessee	143	1.7	948	2.0	7	30.4	32,079	122.8	1.9	858,895
Missouri	165	2.0	968	2.0	6	29.2	30,130	116.8	1.8	707,933
Virginia	170	2.1	855	1.8	5	29.0	33,964	111.9	1.7	658,076
Indiana	163	2.0	997	2.1	6	30.6	30,703	111.0	1.7	680,945
Wisconsin	108	1.3	728	1.5	7	23.6	32,456	108.7	1.6	1,006,435
Colorado	110	1.3	711	1.5	6	25.3	35,513	105.8	1.6	962,164
Alabama	150	1.8	990	2.1	7	25.8	26,020	105.8	1.6	705,007
Connecticut	94	1.1	578	1.2	6	22.0	38,035	99.1	1.5	1,054,383
South Carolina	135	1.6	717	1.5	5	20.4	28,442	98.3	1.5	728,089
Louisiana	142	1.7	705	1.5	5	20.9	29,715	96.1	1.5	676,761
Kentucky	147	1.8	778	1.6	5	22.3	28,654	89.9	1.4	611,878
Maryland	132	1.6	588	1.2	4	20.5	34,903	86.7	1.3	657,076
Oregon	101	1.2	606	1.3	6	18.1	29,889	73.9	1.1	731,267
Iowa	90	1.1	528	1.1	6	15.1	28,517	63.0	1.0	699,856
Nevada	50	0.6	370	0.8	7	11.9	32,197	57.8	0.9	1,156,800
Kansas	96	1.2	559	1.2	6	15.9	28,354	57.2	0.9	595,479
Oklahoma	97	1.2	451	0.9	5	11.9	26,377	55.3	0.8	570,546
Mississippi	75	0.9	387	0.8	5	11.4	29,532	51.0	0.8	680,533
Idaho	47	0.6	297	0.6	6	7.8	26,337	46.1	0.7	981,894
Rhode Island	35	0.4	275	0.6	8	9.9	35,989	43.9	0.7	1,253,343
West Virginia	68	0.8	402	0.8	6	10.1	25,030	42.4	0.6	623,471
Arkansas	49	0.6	220	0.5	4	6.4	29,268	38.2	0.6	779,429
New Mexico	46	0.6	295	0.6	6	8.9	30,119	35.9	0.5	780,022
South Dakota	24	0.3	126	0.3	5	5.1	40,532	34.7	0.5	1,447,167
Utah	64	0.8	255	0.5	4	7.1	28,004	33.7	0.5	526,547
Nebraska	54	0.7	214	0.4	4	5.8	27,019	30.2	0.5	558,852
Montana	31	0.4	456	0.9	15	8.8	19,274	29.8	0.4	959,871
New Hampshire	43	0.5	182	0.4	4	7.5	41,132	23.7	0.4	551,070
Hawaii	23	0.3	172	0.4	7	5.0	28,953	21.7	0.3	942,348
Alaska	14	0.2	109	0.2	8	4.3	39,908	16.6	0.3	1,183,714
North Dakota	14	0.2	130	0.3	9	4.0	30,469	15.3	0.2	1,091,071
Vermont	20	0.2	136	0.3	7	4.4	32,235	15.1	0.2	755,100
Maine	22	0.3	92	0.2	4	2.3	25,337	11.3	0.2	511,864
Delaware	16	0.2	76	0.2	5	1.8	23,882	9.4	0.1	585,313
Wyoming	12	0.1	27	0.1	2	0.7	26,926	4.0	0.1	334,333
Arizona	141	1.7	1000-2499	-	-	(D)	-	(D)	-	-
D.C.	7	0.1	20-99	-	-	(D)	-	(D)	-	-

Source: 2002 *Economic Census*. The states are in descending order of sales or establishments (if sales data are missing for the majority). The symbol (D) appears when data are withheld to prevent disclosure of competitive information. States marked with (D) are sorted by number of establishments. A dash (-) indicates that the data element cannot be calculated. Shaded *states* on the state map indicate those states which have proportionately greater representation in the industry than would be indicated by the states population; the ratio is based on total sales or number of establishments. Shaded *regions* indicate where the industry is regionally most concentrated.

NAICS 447110 - GASOLINE STATIONS WITH CONVENIENCE STORES

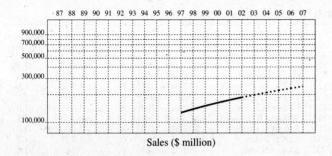

Sales ($ million)

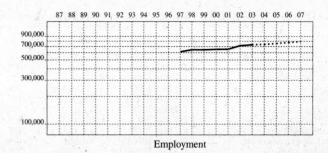

Employment

GENERAL STATISTICS

Year	Establishments (number)	Employment (number)	Payroll ($ million)	Sales ($ million)	Employees per Establishment (number)	Sales per Establishment ($)	Payroll per Employee ($)
1987	-	-	-	-	-	-	-
1988	-	-	-	-	-	-	-
1989	-	-	-	-	-	-	-
1990	-	-	-	-	-	-	-
1991	-	-	-	-	-	-	-
1992	-	-	-	-	-	-	-
1993	-	-	-	-	-	-	-
1994	-	-	-	-	-	-	-
1995	-	-	-	-	-	-	-
1996	-	-	-	-	-	-	-
1997	81,684	613,957	7,228.6	127,609.1	8	1,562,229	11,774
1998	82,184	646,958	7,990.1	139,393.3 e	8	1,696,112	12,350
1999	81,486	645,931	8,446.2	151,177.4 e	8	1,855,257	13,076
2000	80,512	653,279	8,925.8	162,961.6 e	8	2,024,066	13,663
2001	81,171	655,433	9,018.5	174,745.8 e	8	2,152,810	13,759
2002	92,979	716,012	9,997.6	186,530.0	8	2,006,151	13,963
2003	92,705	733,040	10,566.1	198,314.1 p	8	2,258,623 p	14,414
2004	92,437 p	738,496 p	10,967.5 p	210,098.3 p	8 p	2,366,009 p	14,976 p
2005	94,378 p	756,526 p	11,489.0 p	221,882.5 p	8 p	2,473,395 p	15,398 p
2006	96,318 p	774,557 p	12,010.4 p	233,666.6 p	8 p	2,580,781 p	15,821 p
2007	98,259 p	792,588 p	12,531.8 p	245,450.8 p	8 p	2,688,168 p	16,243 p

Source: Economic Census of the United States, 1997 and 2002. Establishment counts, employment, and payroll are from County Business Patterns for non-Census years. This is a newly defined industry. Data for prior years are unavailable at the time of publication but may become available over time. Values followed by 'p' are projections by the editors. Sales data for non-Census years are extrapolations, marked by 'e'.

INDICES OF CHANGE

Year	Establishments (number)	Employment (number)	Payroll ($ million)	Sales ($ million)	Employees per Establishment (number)	Sales per Establishment ($)	Payroll per Employee ($)
1987	-	-	-	-	-	-	-
1992	-	-	-	-	-	-	-
1993	-	-	-	-	-	-	-
1994	-	-	-	-	-	-	-
1995	-	-	-	-	-	-	-
1996	-	-	-	-	-	-	-
1997	87.9	85.7	72.3	68.4	97.4	77.9	84.3
1998	88.4	90.4	79.9	74.7 e	102.6	84.5	88.5
1999	87.6	90.2	84.5	81.0 e	102.6	92.5	93.6
2000	86.6	91.2	89.3	87.4 e	105.2	100.9	97.9
2001	87.3	91.5	90.2	93.7 e	105.2	107.3	98.5
2002	100.0	100.0	100.0	100.0	100.0	100.0	100.0
2003	99.7	102.4	105.7	106.3 p	102.7	112.6 p	103.2
2004	99.4 p	103.1 p	109.7 p	112.6 p	104.1 p	117.9 p	107.3 p
2005	101.5 p	105.7 p	114.9 p	119.0 p	104.6 p	123.3 p	110.3 p
2006	103.6 p	108.2 p	120.1 p	125.3 p	105.1 p	128.6 p	113.3 p
2007	105.7 p	110.7 p	125.3 p	131.6 p	105.6 p	134.0 p	116.3 p

Sources: Same as General Statistics. The values shown reflect change from the base year, 2002. Values above 100 mean greater than 2002, values below 100 mean less than 2002, and a value of 100 in the 1987-2001 or 2003-2007 period means same as 2002. Values followed by a 'p' are projections by the editors; 'e' stands for extrapolation. Data are the most recent available at this level of detail.

SELECTED RATIOS

For 2002	Avg. of All Retail	Analyzed Industry	Index	For 2002	Avg. of All Retail	Analyzed Industry	Index
Employees per Establishment	17	8	45	Sales per Employee	174,682	260,512	149
Payroll per Establishment	333,445	107,526	32	Sales per Establishment	3,332,269	2,006,151	60
Payroll per Employee	20,311	13,963	69	Expenses per Establishment	na	na	na

Sources: Same as General Statistics. The 'Average of All' column, Wholesale or Retail, represents the average of the sector reported for the most recent complete year available. The Index shows the relationship between the Average and the Analyzed Industry. For example, 100 means that they are equal; 500 that the Analyzed Industry is five times the average; 50 means that the Analyzed Industry is half the national average. The abbreviation 'na' is used to show that data are 'not available'.

LEADING COMPANIES   Number shown: **75**   Total sales ($ mil): **363,451**   Total employment (000): **216.3**

Company Name	Address				CEO Name	Phone	Co. Type	Sales ($ mil)	Empl. (000)
Exxon Mobil Corp.	5959 Las Colinas	Irving	TX	75039		972-444-1000	P	298,027	92.5
CITGO Petroleum Corp.	PO Box 3758	Tulsa	OK	74102	Aires Barreto	918-495-4000	S	10,428*	4.3
Murphy Oil Corp.	PO Box 7000	El Dorado	AR	71731	Claiborne P Deming	870-862-6411	P	8,360	4.8
Flying J Inc.	PO Box 678	Brigham City	UT	84302	J Phillip Adams	801-624-1000	R	7,500	12.5
QuikTrip Corp.	PO Box 3475	Tulsa	OK	74101	Chester Cadieux	918-615-7700	R	4,051	7.0
H.T. Hackney Co.	PO Box 238	Knoxville	TN	37901	William B Sansom	865-546-1291	R	3,100	3.5
Sinclair Oil Corp.	PO Box 30825	Salt Lake City	UT	84130	Robert E Holding	801-524-2700	R	2,900	7.0
RaceTrac Petroleum Inc.	PO Box 105035	Atlanta	GA	30348	Carl E Bolch, Jr	770-431-7600	R	2,771	4.7
Giant Industries Inc.	PO Box 12999	Scottsdale	AZ	85267	Morgan Gust	480-585-8888	P	2,512	2.4
Casey's General Stores Inc.	1 Convenience Blvd	Ankeny	IA	50021		515-965-6100	P	2,368	14.6
Wawa Inc.	260 W Baltimore	Wawa	PA	19063		610-358-8000	R	2,332*	13.0
Sheetz Inc.	5700 6th Ave	Altoona	PA	16602		814-946-3611	R	2,300	9.9
GROWMARK Inc.	PO Box 2500	Bloomington	IL	61702	William Davisson	309-557-6000	R	2,080	0.6
Cumberland Farms Inc.	777 Dedham St	Canton	MA	02021	Lilly Haseotes Bentas	781-828-4900	R	2,007*	7.0
Love's Travel Stops & Country	PO Box 26210	Oklahoma City	OK	73126	Greg Love	405-751-9000	R	1,900	3.5
Crown Central Petroleum Corp.	PO Box 1168	Baltimore	MD	21203		410-539-7400	S	1,700*	2.6
Petro Stopping Centers L.P.	PO Box 26808	El Paso	TX	79926	Jack A Cardwell, Sr	915-779-4711	S	1,307	4.2
Holiday Companies Inc.	PO Box 1224	Minneapolis	MN	55440	Ronald A Erickson	952-830-8700	R	1,250	6.0
US Oil Company Inc.	PO Box 25	Combined Locks	WI	54113		920-739-6101	R	980*	0.4
Maverik Country Stores Inc.	PO Box 8008	Afton	WY	83110	Michael Call	307-885-3861	R	375*	2.5
Englefield Oil Co.	447 James Pkwy	Heath	OH	43056	Ben Englefield	740-928-8215	R	300*	1.5
Green Valley Acquisition Co.	477 E Beaver Ave	State College	PA	16801	Henry D Sahakian	814-234-6000	R	296	2.5
Olympian Co.	999 Bayhill Dr	San Bruno	CA	94066	Fred Bertetta	650-873-8200	R	293*	0.3
Jaco Oil Co.	3101 State Rd	Bakersfield	CA	93308	Tom J Jamison	661-393-7000	R	242*	0.4
Time Oil Co.	PO Box 24447	Seattle	WA	98124	H Roger Holliday	206-285-2400	R	236*	0.2
Heritage FS Inc.	PO Box 339	Gilman	IL	60938		815-265-4751	R	232*	<0.1
Keystops Inc.	PO Box 2809	Franklin	KY	42135	Lester Key	270-586-8283	R	225*	0.2
Shirley Oil and Supply Inc.	PO Box 17	Mc Lean	IL	61754	Chuck Beeler	309-874-2323	R	212*	0.5
Watonwan Farm Services	PO Box 68	Truman	MN	56088	Ed Bosanko		R	208*	0.3
Gull Industries Inc.	PO Box 24687	Seattle	WA	98124	Douglas L True	206-624-5900	R	191*	0.1
Gibbs Oil Co.	PO Box 9151	Chelsea	MA	02150	Gary Kaneb	617-887-3200	S	174*	0.4
Gas America Services Inc.	2700 W Main St	Greenfield	IN	46140	Stephanie White	317-468-2515	R	170*	0.6
Kocolene Marketing L.L.C.	PO Box 448	Seymour	IN	47274	Robert R Myers	812-522-2224	R	169*	0.4
NOCO Energy Corp.	2440 Sheridan Dr	Tonawanda	NY	14150	Jim Newman	716-833-6626	R	164*	0.6
Service Oil Inc.	1718 Main Ave E	West Fargo	ND	58078	Steven D Lenthe	701-277-1050	R	132*	0.2
District Petroleum Products Inc.	1814 River Rd	Huron	OH	44839	Scott Stipp	419-433-8373	R	131*	0.2
Premium Oil Co.	2005 S 300 W	Salt Lake City	UT	84115	Paul S Callister	801-487-4721	R	104*	0.1
Miller and Holmes Inc.	2311 O'Neil Rd	Hudson	WI	54016	Jerry Peterson	715-377-1730	R	103*	0.3
Carson Oil Company Inc.	PO Box 10948	Portland	OR	97296	JA Carson	503-224-8500	R	96*	0.3
Condon Oil Company Inc.	PO Box 184	Ripon	WI	54971	Kent B Bauman	920-748-3186	R	95*	0.3
Halron Oil Company Inc.	PO Box 2188	Green Bay	WI	54306		920-437-0466	R	83*	0.1
Imperial Company Inc.	5115 E Pickard Rd	Mount Pleasant	MI	48858	David Johnson	989-773-9921	R	76*	0.4
J and H Oil Co.	PO Box 9464	Wyoming	MI	49509	Jerry Hop	616-534-2181	R	75*	0.4
Joseph F. Boente Sons Inc.	PO Box 288	Carlinville	IL	62626	Larry Boente	217-854-3164	R	75*	<0.1
Silco Oil Co.	181 E 56th Ave	Denver	CO	80216	Sue Vanderburg	303-292-0500	R	70*	0.4
Arnold Owens Inc.	PO Box 3697	Bloomington	IL	61702	Michael Owens	309-828-7750	R	64*	0.3
Peerless Tyre Co.	5000 Kingston St	Denver	CO	80239	Samuel E Forbes	303-371-4300	R	62*	0.3
Ag-Valley Co-op.	PO Box 68	Edison	NE	68936	David Brown	308-927-3681	R	60*	<0.1
Humboldt Petroleum Inc.	PO Box 131	Eureka	CA	95502	Robert Wotherspoon	707-443-3069	R	56*	0.1
Rite Way Oil and Gas Inc.	PO Box 27049	Omaha	NE	68127	Rex E Ekwall	402-331-6400	R	56*	0.2
Campbell Oil Company Inc.	PO Box 907	Massillon	OH	44648	Brian Burrow	330-343-7031	R	48*	<0.1
Quik Stop Markets Inc.	4567 Enterprise St	Fremont	CA	94538	Van Tarver	510-657-8500	S	47*	<0.1
Schmuckal Oil Co.	1516 Barlow St	Traverse City	MI	49686	Arthur Schmuckal	231-946-2800	R	45*	0.3
Agriland F.S. Inc.	PO Box 680	Harlan	IA	51537	Lud Buman	712-755-5141	S	40*	<0.1
Farmers Union Oil Co.	600 Hwy 2 W	Devils Lake	ND	58301	Terry Borstad	701-662-4014	R	40*	<0.1
American Pride Coop.	55 W Bromley Ln	Brighton	CO	80601	Al Shivley	303-659-1230	R	39*	0.2
Monte Vista Cooperative Inc.	1601 E Hwy 160	Monte Vista	CO	81144	Mike Spearmen	719-852-5181	R	38*	<0.1
Southwest Energy Distributors Inc.	415 N Grant Ave	Odessa	TX	79761	Clay Wood	432-332-1301	R	38*	0.1
FOF Inc.	471 N Curtis Rd	Boise	ID	83706	Marla Gardner	208-377-0024	R	35*	<0.1
Door County Cooperative Inc.	92 E Maple St	Sturgeon Bay	WI	54235	Randall Seiler	920-743-6555	R	32*	<0.1
Great Bend Cooperative	PO Box 68	Great Bend	KS	67530	Eric Batman	620-793-3531	R	29*	<0.1
Cooperative Agricultural Services	415 W 2nd St	Oakley	KS	67748		785-672-3300	R	28*	<0.1
FFP Operating Partners L.P.	2801 Glenda Ave	Fort Worth	TX	76117	Robert J Byrnes	817-838-4700	S	28*	0.1
Yoder Oil Company Inc.	PO Box 1097	Elkhart	IN	46515	Kent J Yoder	574-264-2107	R	28*	<0.1
Town And Country Coop.	107 Railroad St	LaGrange	OH	44050		440-355-5641	R	26*	<0.1
Urwiler Oil and Fertilizer Inc.	301 Hwy 15 E	Laurel	NE	68745	Greg Urwiler	402-256-3177	R	25*	<0.1
Ampride	200 Sd Hwy 44	Chancellor	SD	57015		605-647-2700	R	24*	<0.1
Bowlin Travel Centers Inc.	150 Louisiana NE	Albuquerque	NM	87108	Michael L Bowlin	505-266-5985	P	22	0.2
Bay Oil Co.	3914 Hwy 3	Dickinson	TX	77539	Link C Smith	281-337-4671	R	21*	0.1
Cannon Oil Corp.	PO Drawer 6307	Dothan	AL	36302	Frank Weathers	334-794-2776	R	21*	0.1
Farmers Union Oil Co.	PO Box 219	Ellendale	ND	58436	Kevin Brokaw	701-349-3280	R	21*	<0.1
Newsom Oil Company Inc.	1503 W 10th St	Roanoke Rapids	NC	27870	David J Newsom	252-537-3587	S	21*	0.1
Sublette Cooperative Inc.	PO Box 340	Sublette	KS	67877		620-675-2297	R	20*	<0.1
Friends Enterprises	PO Box 2708	Morgan City	LA	70381	John O'Neill	985-384-1610	R	19*	<0.1
Gay Johnson's Inc.	PO Box 1829	Grand Junction	CO	81502	Bert Johnson	970-242-3021	R	19*	<0.1

Source: Ward's Business Directory of U.S. Private and Public Companies, Volumes 1 and 2, 2005. The company type code used is as follows: P - Public, R - Private, S - Subsidiary, D - Division, J - Joint Venture, A - Affiliate, G - Group. Sales are in millions of dollars, employees are in thousands. An asterisk (*) indicates an estimated sales volume. The symbol < stands for 'less than'. Company names and addresses are truncated, in some cases, to fit into the available space.

OCCUPATIONS EMPLOYED BY GASOLINE STATIONS

Occupation	% of Total 2004	Change to 2014	Occupation	% of Total 2004	Change to 2014
Cashiers, except gaming	61.3	-4.0	General & operations managers	1.2	5.6
First-line supervisors/managers of retail sales workers	9.7	-1.8	Cooks, short order	1.2	-3.9
Service station attendants	3.6	-14.6	Stock clerks & order fillers	1.1	-18.3
Combined food preparation & serving workers	2.7	11.8	Food preparation workers	1.1	6.7
Automotive service technicians & mechanics	2.5	-4.0	Bookkeeping, accounting, & auditing clerks	1.1	-4.0
Retail salespersons	1.9	6.7	Janitors & cleaners, except maids	1.0	6.7
Waiters & waitresses	1.4	6.7	Cleaners of vehicles & equipment	1.0	-9.4
Cooks, fast food	1.3	6.7			

Source: *Industry-Occupation Matrix*, Bureau of Labor Statistics. These data are reported based on 4-digit NAICS categories but have been matched to corresponding 6-digit NAICS industry codes. The change reported for each occupation to the year 2014 is a percent of growth or decline as estimated by the Bureau of Labor Statistics. The abbreviation nec stands for 'not elsewhere classified.'

LOCATION BY STATE AND REGIONAL CONCENTRATION

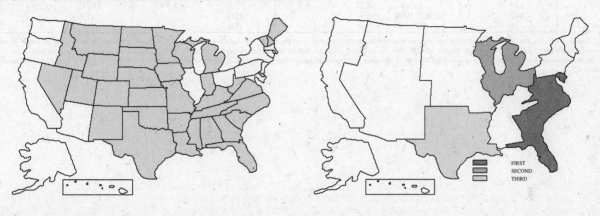

INDUSTRY DATA BY STATE

State	Establishments Total (number)	% of U.S.	Employment Total (number)	% of U.S.	Per Estab.	Payroll Total ($ mil.)	Per Empl. ($)	Sales Total ($ mil.)	% of U.S.	Per Estab. ($)
Texas	9,143	9.8	61,343	8.5	7	863.9	14,083	16,544.1	8.9	1,809,486
California	5,768	6.2	46,459	6.4	8	724.4	15,592	16,480.6	8.8	2,857,253
Florida	5,676	6.1	39,429	5.5	7	595.8	15,111	11,749.4	6.3	2,070,019
Ohio	3,537	3.8	29,670	4.1	8	429.8	14,486	8,070.5	4.3	2,281,735
Illinois	3,280	3.5	26,135	3.6	8	359.4	13,751	7,216.2	3.9	2,200,049
Michigan	3,402	3.6	23,312	3.2	7	317.4	13,614	7,150.5	3.8	2,101,840
Pennsylvania	2,996	3.2	29,002	4.0	10	367.8	12,683	6,884.8	3.7	2,297,984
Georgia	4,050	4.3	24,686	3.4	6	365.9	14,821	6,871.2	3.7	1,696,584
North Carolina	4,081	4.4	25,082	3.5	6	362.2	14,440	6,710.0	3.6	1,644,208
New York	3,252	3.5	24,215	3.4	7	344.3	14,220	6,300.4	3.4	1,937,379
Virginia	2,912	3.1	24,457	3.4	8	350.5	14,330	5,838.5	3.1	2,004,965
Missouri	2,446	2.6	20,439	2.8	8	284.0	13,896	5,281.2	2.8	2,159,137
Indiana	2,354	2.5	19,828	2.7	8	274.3	13,836	4,884.9	2.6	2,075,159
Wisconsin	2,235	2.4	20,023	2.8	9	261.9	13,078	4,805.1	2.6	2,149,946
Minnesota	2,078	2.2	22,059	3.1	11	298.9	13,551	4,625.0	2.5	2,225,710
Tennessee	2,892	3.1	18,377	2.5	6	248.8	13,541	4,428.7	2.4	1,531,373
South Carolina	2,163	2.3	15,747	2.2	7	225.3	14,305	3,846.5	2.1	1,778,328
Alabama	2,613	2.8	14,386	2.0	6	194.4	13,516	3,532.6	1.9	1,351,941
Washington	1,727	1.8	12,923	1.8	7	188.7	14,603	3,459.3	1.9	2,003,094
Louisiana	2,133	2.3	15,885	2.2	7	196.8	12,387	3,405.0	1.8	1,596,338
Kentucky	1,958	2.1	16,444	2.3	8	199.2	12,116	3,347.1	1.8	1,709,448
Colorado	1,454	1.6	12,311	1.7	8	179.1	14,547	3,125.4	1.7	2,149,487
Iowa	1,581	1.7	14,790	2.0	9	181.1	12,242	2,757.6	1.5	1,744,201
Maryland	1,087	1.2	9,684	1.3	9	148.2	15,304	2,740.7	1.5	2,521,320
Oklahoma	1,676	1.8	11,776	1.6	7	147.6	12,537	2,738.6	1.5	1,634,026
Massachusetts	1,104	1.2	8,242	1.1	7	132.4	16,060	2,620.1	1.4	2,373,241
Mississippi	1,692	1.8	11,599	1.6	7	149.1	12,856	2,393.4	1.3	1,414,567
Arkansas	1,390	1.5	10,907	1.5	8	123.2	11,297	2,165.0	1.2	1,557,568
Kansas	1,110	1.2	8,457	1.2	8	113.5	13,416	2,077.4	1.1	1,871,507
New Jersey	692	0.7	6,652	0.9	10	101.1	15,206	1,775.8	1.0	2,566,172
Connecticut	706	0.8	4,561	0.6	6	84.0	18,422	1,760.5	0.9	2,493,680
West Virginia	986	1.1	8,489	1.2	9	97.9	11,533	1,737.7	0.9	1,762,368
Utah	775	0.8	8,107	1.1	10	100.3	12,378	1,718.7	0.9	2,217,705
Nevada	571	0.6	5,523	0.8	10	86.1	15,597	1,479.5	0.8	2,591,117
New Mexico	726	0.8	5,604	0.8	8	76.4	13,625	1,366.5	0.7	1,882,167

Continued on next page.

INDUSTRY DATA BY STATE - Continued

State	Establishments Total (number)	% of U.S.	Employment Total (number)	% of U.S.	Per Estab.	Payroll Total ($ mil.)	Per Empl. ($)	Sales Total ($ mil.)	% of U.S.	Per Estab. ($)
Nebraska	814	0.9	6,426	0.9	8	81.8	12,727	1,321.6	0.7	1,623,596
Oregon	607	0.6	6,704	0.9	11	82.6	12,315	1,182.5	0.6	1,948,145
Maine	671	0.7	5,826	0.8	9	75.8	13,008	1,180.2	0.6	1,758,826
New Hampshire	459	0.5	3,953	0.5	9	61.6	15,595	1,047.5	0.6	2,282,137
Idaho	533	0.6	4,149	0.6	8	53.3	12,843	953.8	0.5	1,789,417
South Dakota	505	0.5	4,792	0.7	9	57.0	11,897	825.4	0.4	1,634,497
Montana	406	0.4	3,645	0.5	9	45.6	12,509	824.7	0.4	2,031,251
Vermont	368	0.4	3,023	0.4	8	43.5	14,406	640.6	0.3	1,740,845
Hawaii	217	0.2	2,292	0.3	11	35.1	15,296	568.6	0.3	2,620,143
North Dakota	309	0.3	3,056	0.4	10	38.5	12,592	532.3	0.3	1,722,731
Delaware	223	0.2	1,872	0.3	8	29.4	15,679	498.9	0.3	2,237,377
Rhode Island	235	0.3	1,575	0.2	7	23.3	14,770	469.5	0.3	1,997,787
Wyoming	270	0.3	2,149	0.3	8	28.3	13,186	456.1	0.2	1,689,204
Alaska	145	0.2	1,211	0.2	8	22.8	18,817	348.0	0.2	2,399,821
Arizona	1,647	1.8	10K-24999	-	-	(D)	-	(D)	-	-
D.C.	36	-	250-499	-	-	(D)	-	(D)	-	-

Source: 2002 *Economic Census*. The states are in descending order of sales or establishments (if sales data are missing for the majority). The symbol (D) appears when data are withheld to prevent disclosure of competitive information. States marked with (D) are sorted by number of establishments. A dash (-) indicates that the data element cannot be calculated. Shaded *states* on the state map indicate those states which have proportionately greater representation in the industry than would be indicated by the states population; the ratio is based on total sales or number of establishments. Shaded *regions* indicate where the industry is regionally most concentrated.

NAICS 447190 - OTHER GASOLINE STATIONS

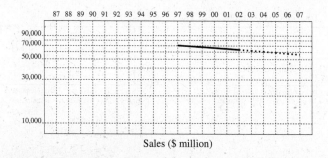

Sales ($ million)

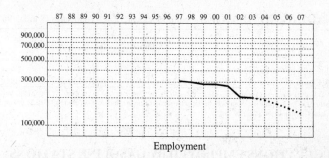

Employment

GENERAL STATISTICS

Year	Establishments (number)	Employment (number)	Payroll ($ million)	Sales ($ million)	Employees per Establishment (number)	Sales per Establishment ($)	Payroll per Employee ($)
1987	-	-	-	-	-	-	-
1988	-	-	-	-	-	-	-
1989	-	-	-	-	-	-	-
1990	-	-	-	-	-	-	-
1991	-	-	-	-	-	-	-
1992	-	-	-	-	-	-	-
1993	-	-	-	-	-	-	-
1994	-	-	-	-	-	-	-
1995	-	-	-	-	-	-	-
1996	-	-	-	-	-	-	-
1997	45,205	308,105	4,253.5	70,556.7	7	1,560,816	13,805
1998	41,710	299,447	4,339.6	69,142.4 e	7	1,657,693	14,492
1999	39,609	284,103	4,379.1	67,728.1 e	7	1,709,916	15,414
2000	39,136	283,804	4,396.0	66,313.8 e	7	1,694,444	15,490
2001	37,721	271,851	4,437.2	64,899.4 e	7	1,720,512	16,322
2002	27,923	206,769	3,670.2	63,485.1	7	2,273,578	17,750
2003	26,759	203,452	3,725.7	62,070.8 p	8	2,143,172 p	18,313
2004	24,752 p	192,281 p	3,762.4 p	60,656.5 p	8 p	2,249,938 p	18,933 p
2005	21,723 p	174,010 p	3,660.2 p	59,242.2 p	8 p	2,356,703 p	19,681 p
2006	18,695 p	155,740 p	3,557.9 p	57,827.9 p	8 p	2,463,469 p	20,429 p
2007	15,666 p	137,470 p	3,455.6 p	56,413.5 p	8 p	2,570,234 p	21,177 p

Source: *Economic Census of the United States*, 1997 and 2002. Establishment counts, employment, and payroll are from *County Business Patterns* for non-Census years. This is a newly defined industry. Data for prior years are unavailable at the time of publication but may become available over time. Values followed by 'p' are projections by the editors. Sales data for non-Census years are extrapolations, marked by 'e'.

INDICES OF CHANGE

Year	Establishments (number)	Employment (number)	Payroll ($ million)	Sales ($ million)	Employees per Establishment (number)	Sales per Establishment ($)	Payroll per Employee ($)
1987	-	-	-	-	-	-	-
1992	-	-	-	-	-	-	-
1993	-	-	-	-	-	-	-
1994	-	-	-	-	-	-	-
1995	-	-	-	-	-	-	-
1996	-	-	-	-	-	-	-
1997	161.9	149.0	115.9	111.1	91.8	68.7	77.8
1998	149.4	144.8	118.2	108.9 e	97.2	72.9	81.6
1999	141.9	137.4	119.3	106.7 e	97.2	75.2	86.8
2000	140.2	137.3	119.8	104.5 e	98.6	74.5	87.3
2001	135.1	131.5	120.9	102.2 e	97.2	75.7	92.0
2002	100.0	100.0	100.0	100.0	100.0	100.0	100.0
2003	95.8	98.4	101.5	97.8 p	102.7	94.3 p	103.2
2004	88.6 p	93.0 p	102.5 p	95.5 p	103.3 p	99.0 p	106.7 p
2005	77.8 p	84.2 p	99.7 p	93.3 p	104.6 p	103.7 p	110.9 p
2006	67.0 p	75.3 p	96.9 p	91.1 p	106.0 p	108.4 p	115.1 p
2007	56.1 p	66.5 p	94.2 p	88.9 p	107.3 p	113.0 p	119.3 p

Sources: Same as General Statistics. The values shown reflect change from the base year, 2002. Values above 100 mean greater than 2002, values below 100 mean less than 2002, and a value of 100 in the 1987-2001 or 2003-2007 period means same as 2002. Values followed by a 'p' are projections by the editors; 'e' stands for extrapolation. Data are the most recent available at this level of detail.

SELECTED RATIOS

For 2002	Avg. of All Retail	Analyzed Industry	Index	For 2002	Avg. of All Retail	Analyzed Industry	Index
Employees per Establishment	17	7	44	Sales per Employee	174,682	307,034	176
Payroll per Establishment	333,445	131,438	39	Sales per Establishment	3,332,269	2,273,578	68
Payroll per Employee	20,311	17,750	87	Expenses per Establishment	na	na	na

Sources: Same as General Statistics. The 'Average of All' column, Wholesale or Retail, represents the average of the sector reported for the most recent complete year available. The Index shows the relationship between the Average and the Analyzed Industry. For example, 100 means that they are equal; 500 that the Analyzed Industry is five times the average; 50 means that the Analyzed Industry is half the national average. The abbreviation 'na' is used to show that data are 'not available'.

LEADING COMPANIES   Number shown: **2**   Total sales ($ mil): **96**   Total employment (000): **0.1**

Company Name	Address				CEO Name	Phone	Co. Type	Sales ($ mil)	Empl. (000)
Farmers Britt Co-Op	PO Box 156	Britt	IA	50423	Ron Eisenman	641-843-3878	R	79*	<0.1
Polk County Farmers Co-Op	PO Box 47	Rickreall	OR	97371		503-363-2332	R	17*	<0.1

Source: Ward's Business Directory of U.S. Private and Public Companies, Volumes 1 and 2, 2005. The company type code used is as follows: P - Public, R - Private, S - Subsidiary, D - Division, J - Joint Venture, A - Affiliate, G - Group. Sales are in millions of dollars, employees are in thousands. An asterisk (*) indicates an estimated sales volume. The symbol < stands for 'less than'. Company names and addresses are truncated, in some cases, to fit into the available space.

OCCUPATIONS EMPLOYED BY GASOLINE STATIONS

Occupation	% of Total 2004	Change to 2014	Occupation	% of Total 2004	Change to 2014
Cashiers, except gaming	61.3	-4.0	General & operations managers	1.2	5.6
First-line supervisors/managers of retail sales workers	9.7	-1.8	Cooks, short order	1.2	-3.9
Service station attendants	3.6	-14.6	Stock clerks & order fillers	1.1	-18.3
Combined food preparation & serving workers	2.7	11.8	Food preparation workers	1.1	6.7
Automotive service technicians & mechanics	2.5	-4.0	Bookkeeping, accounting, & auditing clerks	1.1	-4.0
Retail salespersons	1.9	6.7	Janitors & cleaners, except maids	1.0	6.7
Waiters & waitresses	1.4	6.7	Cleaners of vehicles & equipment	1.0	-9.4
Cooks, fast food	1.3	6.7			

Source: Industry-Occupation Matrix, Bureau of Labor Statistics. These data are reported based on 4-digit NAICS categories but have been matched to corresponding 6-digit NAICS industry codes. The change reported for each occupation to the year 2014 is a percent of growth or decline as estimated by the Bureau of Labor Statistics. The abbreviation nec stands for 'not elsewhere classified.'

LOCATION BY STATE AND REGIONAL CONCENTRATION

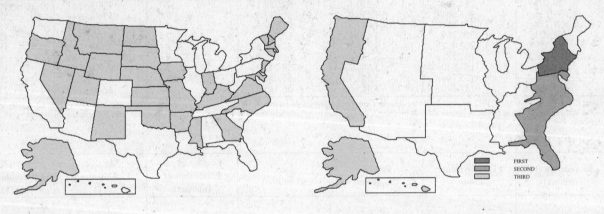

FIRST
SECOND
THIRD

INDUSTRY DATA BY STATE

State	Establishments Total (number)	% of U.S.	Employment Total (number)	% of U.S.	Per Estab.	Payroll Total ($ mil.)	Per Empl. ($)	Sales Total ($ mil.)	% of U.S.	Per Estab. ($)
California	2,482	8.9	18,237	8.9	7	325.3	17,837	6,940.5	11.1	2,796,334
Texas	1,467	5.3	11,770	5.7	8	207.3	17,614	3,784.5	6.1	2,579,777
New Jersey	2,057	7.4	9,483	4.6	5	175.9	18,550	3,297.5	5.3	1,603,069
New York	2,195	7.9	10,067	4.9	5	185.1	18,382	3,220.7	5.2	1,467,295
Pennsylvania	1,480	5.3	10,801	5.3	7	180.8	16,743	2,791.7	4.5	1,886,295
Ohio	923	3.3	8,145	4.0	9	145.2	17,828	2,375.9	3.8	2,574,078
Indiana	550	2.0	5,868	2.9	11	103.6	17,651	2,147.1	3.4	3,903,905
Virginia	711	2.6	6,499	3.2	9	126.0	19,380	2,047.7	3.3	2,879,979
Georgia	645	2.3	5,446	2.7	8	97.0	17,815	1,928.8	3.1	2,990,363
Massachusetts	1,229	4.4	6,386	3.1	5	128.6	20,138	1,879.2	3.0	1,529,043
Florida	868	3.1	5,335	2.6	6	95.7	17,929	1,742.2	2.8	2,007,166
Illinois	873	3.1	6,056	3.0	7	106.8	17,629	1,683.6	2.7	1,928,495
North Carolina	737	2.7	4,497	2.2	6	98.0	21,790	1,657.1	2.7	2,248,463
Missouri	690	2.5	5,645	2.8	8	97.1	17,207	1,606.3	2.6	2,327,938
Michigan	799	2.9	5,133	2.5	6	93.2	18,161	1,578.6	2.5	1,975,728
Maryland	648	2.3	4,822	2.4	7	87.9	18,230	1,418.8	2.3	2,189,491
Oregon	539	1.9	5,212	2.5	10	82.6	15,844	1,302.1	2.1	2,415,683
Kentucky	485	1.7	3,845	1.9	8	60.6	15,762	1,246.3	2.0	2,569,699
Wisconsin	432	1.6	3,655	1.8	8	63.3	17,308	1,154.5	1.9	2,672,493

Continued on next page.

INDUSTRY DATA BY STATE - Continued

State	Establishments		Employment			Payroll		Sales		
	Total (number)	% of U.S.	Total (number)	% of U.S.	Per Estab.	Total ($ mil.)	Per Empl. ($)	Total ($ mil.)	% of U.S.	Per Estab. ($)
Tennessee	447	1.6	3,664	1.8	8	67.1	18,301	1,124.1	1.8	2,514,834
Oklahoma	344	1.2	2,993	1.5	9	47.6	15,904	1,019.1	1.6	2,962,515
Louisiana	412	1.5	4,398	2.1	11	63.8	14,501	914.8	1.5	2,220,502
Minnesota	527	1.9	4,286	2.1	8	70.5	16,441	896.6	1.4	1,701,381
Iowa	416	1.5	3,631	1.8	9	58.6	16,137	896.5	1.4	2,154,959
Arkansas	305	1.1	2,777	1.4	9	45.4	16,340	856.8	1.4	2,809,210
Mississippi	317	1.1	2,831	1.4	9	42.9	15,160	835.3	1.3	2,634,984
Connecticut	513	1.8	2,979	1.5	6	63.0	21,133	824.0	1.3	1,606,292
South Carolina	313	1.1	2,408	1.2	8	41.9	17,412	791.0	1.3	2,527,208
Washington	377	1.4	2,931	1.4	8	55.5	18,930	775.1	1.2	2,055,851
Alabama	365	1.3	2,719	1.3	7	44.8	16,469	771.6	1.2	2,114,066
Nebraska	302	1.1	2,734	1.3	9	48.2	17,632	764.5	1.2	2,531,517
New Mexico	232	0.8	2,471	1.2	11	39.0	15,783	730.1	1.2	3,147,009
Colorado	272	1.0	2,390	1.2	9	45.7	19,108	706.3	1.1	2,596,640
Kansas	354	1.3	2,476	1.2	7	40.7	16,440	608.3	1.0	1,718,263
Wyoming	131	0.5	1,852	0.9	14	33.9	18,321	589.6	0.9	4,501,092
North Dakota	187	0.7	1,851	0.9	10	31.0	16,761	481.0	0.8	2,572,209
Utah	109	0.4	1,383	0.7	13	21.9	15,841	478.5	0.8	4,390,321
Nevada	100	0.4	1,784	0.9	18	31.1	17,446	461.5	0.7	4,615,430
Idaho	130	0.5	1,459	0.7	11	22.8	15,615	444.7	0.7	3,420,892
Montana	191	0.7	1,515	0.7	8	21.4	14,101	395.6	0.6	2,071,000
West Virginia	226	0.8	1,427	0.7	6	23.0	16,091	330.2	0.5	1,460,978
Maine	222	0.8	1,494	0.7	7	23.6	15,799	319.8	0.5	1,440,482
New Hampshire	165	0.6	1,050	0.5	6	22.0	20,936	303.1	0.5	1,836,848
South Dakota	173	0.6	1,096	0.5	6	17.6	16,097	298.7	0.5	1,726,792
Hawaii	107	0.4	1,151	0.6	11	18.1	15,700	209.8	0.3	1,961,028
Rhode Island	158	0.6	703	0.3	4	15.1	21,531	186.3	0.3	1,179,063
Alaska	84	0.3	622	0.3	7	12.6	20,198	163.9	0.3	1,950,595
Vermont	111	0.4	829	0.4	7	14.7	17,725	157.1	0.3	1,415,009
Delaware	89	0.3	498	0.2	6	8.8	17,735	139.1	0.2	1,563,427
Arizona	219	0.8	2500-4999	-	-	(D)	-	(D)	-	-
D.C.	47	0.2	250-499	-	-	(D)	-	(D)	-	-

Source: 2002 *Economic Census*. The states are in descending order of sales or establishments (if sales data are missing for the majority). The symbol (D) appears when data are withheld to prevent disclosure of competitive information. States marked with (D) are sorted by number of establishments. A dash (-) indicates that the data element cannot be calculated. Shaded *states* on the state map indicate those states which have proportionately greater representation in the industry than would be indicated by the states population; the ratio is based on total sales or number of establishments. Shaded *regions* indicate where the industry is regionally most concentrated.

NAICS 448110 - MEN'S CLOTHING STORES

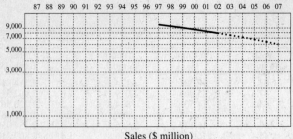

Sales ($ million)

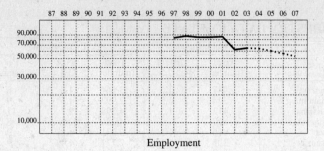

Employment

GENERAL STATISTICS

Year	Establishments (number)	Employment (number)	Payroll ($ million)	Sales ($ million)	Employees per Establishment (number)	Sales per Establishment ($)	Payroll per Employee ($)
1987	-	-	-	-	-	-	-
1988	-	-	-	-	-	-	-
1989	-	-	-	-	-	-	-
1990	-	-	-	-	-	-	-
1991	-	-	-	-	-	-	-
1992	-	-	-	-	-	-	-
1993	-	-	-	-	-	-	-
1994	-	-	-	-	-	-	-
1995	-	-	-	-	-	-	-
1996	-	-	-	-	-	-	-
1997	12,143	83,581	1,325.2	9,864.6	7	812,369	15,855
1998	11,861	87,447	1,434.7	9,477.7 e	7	799,067	16,406
1999	11,445	84,890	1,481.0	9,090.9 e	7	794,309	17,446
2000	10,670	84,973	1,594.8	8,704.0 e	8	815,746	18,768
2001	10,732	86,192	1,551.3	8,317.1 e	8	774,985	17,998
2002	9,428	62,246	1,274.2	7,930.3	7	841,141	20,471
2003	9,189	64,728	1,303.3	7,543.4 p	7	815,575 p	20,135
2004	8,718 p	64,057 p	1,378.3 p	7,156.6 p	7 p	818,233 p	21,228 p
2005	8,202 p	60,283 p	1,367.0 p	6,769.7 p	7 p	820,892 p	21,997 p
2006	7,687 p	56,510 p	1,355.7 p	6,382.8 p	7 p	823,550 p	22,765 p
2007	7,171 p	52,736 p	1,344.4 p	5,996.0 p	7 p	826,209 p	23,534 p

Source: *Economic Census of the United States*, 1997 and 2002. Establishment counts, employment, and payroll are from *County Business Patterns* for non-Census years. This is a newly defined industry. Data for prior years are unavailable at the time of publication but may become available over time. Values followed by 'p' are projections by the editors. Sales data for non-Census years are extrapolations, marked by 'e'.

INDICES OF CHANGE

Year	Establishments (number)	Employment (number)	Payroll ($ million)	Sales ($ million)	Employees per Establishment (number)	Sales per Establishment ($)	Payroll per Employee ($)
1987	-	-	-	-	-	-	-
1992	-	-	-	-	-	-	-
1993	-	-	-	-	-	-	-
1994	-	-	-	-	-	-	-
1995	-	-	-	-	-	-	-
1996	-	-	-	-	-	-	-
1997	128.8	134.3	104.0	124.4	104.5	96.6	77.5
1998	125.8	140.5	112.6	119.5 e	112.1	95.0	80.1
1999	121.4	136.4	116.2	114.6 e	112.1	94.4	85.2
2000	113.2	136.5	125.2	109.8 e	121.2	97.0	91.7
2001	113.8	138.5	121.7	104.9 e	121.2	92.1	87.9
2002	100.0	100.0	100.0	100.0	100.0	100.0	100.0
2003	97.5	104.0	102.3	95.1 p	106.7	97.0 p	98.4
2004	92.5 p	102.9 p	108.2 p	90.2 p	109.9 p	97.3 p	103.7 p
2005	87.0 p	96.8 p	107.3 p	85.4 p	109.6 p	97.6 p	107.5 p
2006	81.5 p	90.8 p	106.4 p	80.5 p	109.3 p	97.9 p	111.2 p
2007	76.1 p	84.7 p	105.5 p	75.6 p	109.0 p	98.2 p	115.0 p

Sources: Same as General Statistics. The values shown reflect change from the base year, 2002. Values above 100 mean greater than 2002, values below 100 mean less than 2002, and a value of 100 in the 1987-2001 or 2003-2007 period means same as 2002. Values followed by a 'p' are projections by the editors; 'e' stands for extrapolation. Data are the most recent available at this level of detail.

SELECTED RATIOS

For 2002	Avg. of All Retail	Analyzed Industry	Index	For 2002	Avg. of All Retail	Analyzed Industry	Index
Employees per Establishment	17	7	39	Sales per Employee	174,682	127,402	73
Payroll per Establishment	333,445	135,152	41	Sales per Establishment	3,332,269	841,141	25
Payroll per Employee	20,311	20,471	101	Expenses per Establishment	na	na	na

Sources: Same as General Statistics. The 'Average of All' column, Wholesale or Retail, represents the average of the sector reported for the most recent complete year available. The Index shows the relationship between the Average and the Analyzed Industry. For example, 100 means that they are equal; 500 that the Analyzed Industry is five times the average; 50 means that the Analyzed Industry is half the national average. The abbreviation 'na' is used to show that data are 'not available'.

LEADING COMPANIES   Number shown: **35**   Total sales ($ mil): **37,622**   Total employment (000): **274.9**

Company Name	Address				CEO Name	Phone	Co. Type	Sales ($ mil)	Empl. (000)
Limited Brands Inc.	PO Box 16000	Columbus	OH	43216	Deborah Fine	614-415-7000	P	8,934	98.9
Nordstrom Inc.	1617 6th Ave	Seattle	WA	98101	Jim Bromley	206-628-2111	P	6,492	52.0
Old Navy	2 Folsom St	San Francisco	CA	94105	Jenny J Ming	650-952-4400	S	5,804	8.0
Neiman Marcus Group Inc.	1618 Main St	Dallas	TX	75201		214-741-6911	P	3,546	15.7
Charming Shoppes Inc.	450 Winks Ln	Bensalem	PA	19020	Dorrit J Bern	215-245-9100	P	2,286	25.0
Phillips-Van Heusen Corp.	200 Madison Ave	New York	NY	10016	Bruce J Klatsky	212-381-3500	P	1,439	9.0
Men's Wearhouse Inc.	5803 Glenmont Dr	Houston	TX	77081	Charles Bresler PhD	713-592-7200	P	1,393	12.3
Pacific Sunwear of California Inc.	PO Box 68042	Anaheim	CA	92817		714-414-4000	P	1,230	12.2
Urban Outfitters Inc.	1809 Walnut St	Philadelphia	PA	19103	Richard A Hayne	215-564-2313	P	828	4.6
Guess Inc.	1444 S Alameda St	Los Angeles	CA	90021	Carlos E Alberini	213-765-3100	P	729	4.8
Nautica Enterprises Inc.	40 W 57th St	New York	NY	10019	Denise V Seegal	212-541-5757	S	694*	3.3
Hot Topic Inc.	18305 San Jose Ave	City of Industry	CA	91748	Gerald Cook	626-839-4681	P	657	6.8
Hartmarx Corp.	101 N Wacker Dr	Chicago	IL	60606	Elbert O Hand	312-372-6300	P	586	0.0
Maurices Inc.	105 W Superior St	Duluth	MN	55802	R Brenninkmeyer	218-727-8431	R	510*	3.5
Buckle Inc.	PO Box 1480	Kearney	NE	68848	Daniel J Hirschfeld	308-236-8491	P	423	5.8
Jos. A. Bank Clothiers Inc.	PO Box 1000	Hampstead	MD	21074	Andrew A Giordano	410-239-2700	P	372	1.9
Harold's Stores Inc.	5919 Maple Ave	Dallas	TX	75235		214-366-0600	P	360	0.8
Deb Shops Inc.	9401 Blue Grass Rd	Philadelphia	PA	19114	Marvin Rounick	215-676-6000	P	304	3.6
Syms Corp.	1 Syms Way	Secaucus	NJ	07094		201-902-9600	P	284	1.8
Long Rap Inc.	1420 Wisconsin NW	Washington	DC	20007	Chuck Rendelman	202-337-6610	R	188*	0.4
Conway Stores Inc.	11 W 34th St	New York	NY	10001	Abie Cowen	212-967-5300	R	181*	1.2
S and K Famous Brands Inc.	PO Box 31800	Richmond	VA	23294	Stewart M Kasen	804-346-2500	P	176	2.1
Rochester Big & Tall Clothing	625 Howard St	San Francisco	CA	94105	Robert L Sockolov	415-536-4181	R	55*	0.3
Fine's	1164 Azalea Garden	Norfolk	VA	23502	Mitchell Fine	757-857-6013	S	24*	0.2
Sharpe Dry Goods Co.	PO Box 328	Checotah	OK	74426	Louis Sharpe IV	918-473-2233	R	24*	0.2
Paul Stuart Inc.	Madison Ave & 45th	New York	NY	10017	Clifford Grodd	212-682-0320	R	22*	0.2
Miltons Inc.	250 Granite St	Braintree	MA	02184	Dana Katz	781-848-1880	R	21*	0.2
Mossimo Inc.	2016 Broadway	Santa Monica	CA	90404	Mossimo Giannulli	310-460-0040	P	20	<0.1
Burtons Inc.	800 Frederick St	Cumberland	MD	21502	RW Burton	301-777-3866	R	9*	<0.1
Norton Ditto Inc.	2425 W Alabama	Houston	TX	77027	Richard Hite	713-688-9800	R	9*	<0.1
Fashion World Inc.	420 N Rodeo Dr	Beverly Hills	CA	90210	Bijan Pakzad	310-273-6544	R	6*	<0.1
Rubenstein Brothers Inc.	102 St Charles Ave	New Orleans	LA	70130	David Rubenstein	504-581-6666	R	6*	<0.1
Cappelli Straworld Inc.	5450 NW 82nd Ave	Miami	FL	33166	Bonnie Rubel	305-597-7180	R	5*	<0.1
Steven-Windsor Inc.	6535 Arlington Blvd	Falls Church	VA	22042		703-533-1337	R	4*	<0.1
J. Altis Ltd.	3072 Stony Point Rd	Richmond	VA	23235	James Altis	804-272-7731	R	1*	<0.1

Source: Ward's Business Directory of U.S. Private and Public Companies, Volumes 1 and 2, 2005. The company type code used is as follows: P - Public, R - Private, S - Subsidiary, D - Division, J - Joint Venture, A - Affiliate, G - Group. Sales are in millions of dollars and employees are in thousands. An asterisk (*) indicates an estimated sales volume. The symbol < stands for 'less than'. Company names and addresses are truncated, in some cases, to fit into the available space.

OCCUPATIONS EMPLOYED BY CLOTHING STORES

Occupation	% of Total 2004	Change to 2014	Occupation	% of Total 2004	Change to 2014
Retail salespersons	61.6	14.4	General & operations managers	1.6	13.2
First-line supervisors/managers of retail sales workers	11.1	5.2	Shipping, receiving, & traffic clerks	1.1	3.6
Cashiers, except gaming	10.0	2.9	Tailors, dressmakers, & custom sewers	1.0	14.3
Stock clerks & order fillers	3.1	-12.4			

Source: Industry-Occupation Matrix, Bureau of Labor Statistics. These data are reported based on 4-digit NAICS categories but have been matched to corresponding 6-digit NAICS industry codes. The change reported for each occupation to the year 2014 is a percent of growth or decline as estimated by the Bureau of Labor Statistics. The abbreviation nec stands for 'not elsewhere classified.'

LOCATION BY STATE AND REGIONAL CONCENTRATION

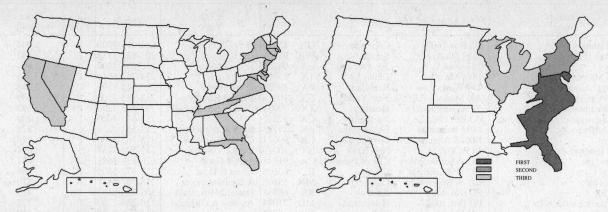

INDUSTRY DATA BY STATE

State	Establishments Total (number)	% of U.S.	Employment Total (number)	% of U.S.	Per Estab.	Payroll Total ($ mil.)	Per Empl. ($)	Sales Total ($ mil.)	% of U.S.	Per Estab. ($)
New York	1,015	10.8	6,900	11.1	7	152.5	22,107	1,045.8	13.2	1,030,329
California	1,072	11.4	7,100	11.4	7	157.0	22,113	984.0	12.4	917,870
Texas	523	5.5	3,914	6.3	7	79.9	20,421	494.6	6.2	945,616
New Jersey	430	4.6	3,128	5.0	7	60.8	19,440	435.7	5.5	1,013,200
Florida	595	6.3	3,395	5.5	6	68.8	20,276	426.5	5.4	716,739
Pennsylvania	426	4.5	2,817	4.5	7	60.8	21,575	353.8	4.5	830,519
Illinois	445	4.7	2,918	4.7	7	57.7	19,769	351.4	4.4	789,748
Virginia	360	3.8	2,582	4.1	7	43.7	16,916	297.8	3.8	827,250
Georgia	310	3.3	1,956	3.1	6	39.8	20,358	269.2	3.4	868,406
Michigan	318	3.4	2,141	3.4	7	44.2	20,656	268.7	3.4	844,814
Ohio	364	3.9	2,479	4.0	7	43.4	17,503	256.8	3.2	705,552
Massachusetts	218	2.3	1,545	2.5	7	35.7	23,098	214.8	2.7	985,459
Maryland	198	2.1	1,337	2.1	7	27.9	20,859	205.0	2.6	1,035,354
North Carolina	292	3.1	1,801	2.9	6	34.3	19,058	204.2	2.6	699,154
Tennessee	198	2.1	1,405	2.3	7	29.0	20,637	164.5	2.1	830,717
Connecticut	125	1.3	995	1.6	8	35.2	35,369	162.9	2.1	1,302,848
Missouri	140	1.5	964	1.5	7	18.9	19,613	123.7	1.6	883,464
Indiana	161	1.7	1,009	1.6	6	17.1	16,952	113.0	1.4	701,745
Louisiana	151	1.6	1,045	1.7	7	18.5	17,675	112.5	1.4	745,298
Colorado	126	1.3	738	1.2	6	18.5	25,112	104.7	1.3	830,937
South Carolina	176	1.9	947	1.5	5	15.7	16,556	102.1	1.3	580,074
Washington	118	1.3	759	1.2	6	18.1	23,908	96.7	1.2	819,780
Minnesota	129	1.4	855	1.4	7	16.1	18,855	96.2	1.2	745,566
Alabama	153	1.6	862	1.4	6	15.2	17,668	90.8	1.1	593,784
Wisconsin	142	1.5	799	1.3	6	15.4	19,335	86.2	1.1	606,979
Arizona	109	1.2	652	1.0	6	13.1	20,112	76.2	1.0	699,257
Nevada	64	0.7	478	0.8	7	12.1	25,264	65.8	0.8	1,028,016
Iowa	112	1.2	694	1.1	6	11.7	16,837	65.5	0.8	584,554
Kentucky	84	0.9	479	0.8	6	8.0	16,737	50.8	0.6	604,357
Kansas	57	0.6	383	0.6	7	7.3	19,164	49.8	0.6	873,333
Mississippi	83	0.9	513	0.8	6	7.4	14,409	48.4	0.6	583,446
Oklahoma	57	0.6	475	0.8	8	8.3	17,549	46.7	0.6	820,123
Oregon	75	0.8	437	0.7	6	9.1	20,881	43.6	0.6	580,720
Utah	65	0.7	430	0.7	7	7.7	17,812	41.5	0.5	638,892
Nebraska	58	0.6	399	0.6	7	8.5	21,363	40.5	0.5	697,569
D.C.	42	0.4	265	0.4	6	6.9	26,008	38.9	0.5	925,524
Arkansas	63	0.7	363	0.6	6	5.9	16,171	34.0	0.4	540,333
Hawaii	55	0.6	308	0.5	6	5.5	17,769	32.9	0.4	598,345
Maine	32	0.3	233	0.4	7	3.8	16,476	28.6	0.4	894,531
Delaware	27	0.3	225	0.4	8	4.0	17,671	26.6	0.3	984,185
New Hampshire	35	0.4	229	0.4	7	4.8	20,948	25.4	0.3	724,457
New Mexico	37	0.4	175	0.3	5	3.5	19,880	22.1	0.3	597,568
Rhode Island	39	0.4	157	0.3	4	3.3	20,732	20.5	0.3	524,872
Alaska	18	0.2	122	0.2	7	2.7	22,352	19.1	0.2	1,063,611
West Virginia	29	0.3	209	0.3	7	3.4	16,431	17.9	0.2	615,621
South Dakota	24	0.3	164	0.3	7	2.7	16,366	15.2	0.2	633,167
Idaho	26	0.3	125	0.2	5	2.0	15,888	10.5	0.1	403,000
Vermont	18	0.2	89	0.1	5	1.7	19,449	10.1	0.1	560,000
North Dakota	14	0.1	73	0.1	5	1.5	21,110	8.1	0.1	577,786
Wyoming	12	0.1	75	0.1	6	1.7	22,813	7.9	0.1	660,583
Montana	17	0.2	80	0.1	5	1.3	16,287	6.8	0.1	401,059

Source: 2002 *Economic Census*. The states are in descending order of sales or establishments (if sales data are missing for the majority). The symbol (D) appears when data are withheld to prevent disclosure of competitive information. States marked with (D) are sorted by number of establishments. A dash (-) indicates that the data element cannot be calculated. Shaded *states* on the state map indicate those states which have proportionately greater representation in the industry than would be indicated by the states population; the ratio is based on total sales or number of establishments. Shaded *regions* indicate where the industry is regionally most concentrated.

NAICS 448120 - WOMEN'S CLOTHING STORES*

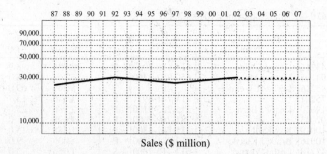

Sales ($ million)

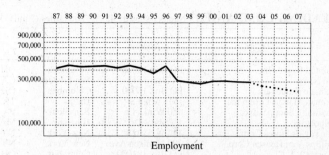

Employment

GENERAL STATISTICS

Year	Establishments (number)	Employment (number)	Payroll ($ million)	Sales ($ million)	Employees per Establishment (number)	Sales per Establishment ($)	Payroll per Employee ($)
1987	52,304	418,972	3,150.3	25,867.6	8	494,563	7,519
1988	52,758	450,551	3,728.2	26,959.3 e	9	510,999	8,275
1989	50,142	434,326	3,810.9	28,051.1 e	9	559,433	8,774
1990	50,175	438,983	4,013.6	29,142.8 e	9	580,823	9,143
1991	48,845	444,580	4,043.8	30,234.6 e	9	618,991	9,096
1992	50,174	423,022	3,690.3	31,326.3	8	624,353	8,724
1993	50,236	448,696	4,193.1	30,512.6 e	9	607,385	9,345
1994	47,715	419,793	4,124.8	29,698.9 e	9	622,423	9,826
1995	42,204	369,816	3,547.9	28,885.1 e	9	684,416	9,594
1996	49,179 e	444,420 e	4,361.4 e	28,071.4 e	9 e	570,801 e	9,814 e
1997	39,672	305,685	3,365.8	27,257.7	8	687,077	11,011
1998	37,442	294,304	3,516.3	28,065.5 e	8	749,572	11,948
1999	36,154	283,872	3,734.9	28,873.2 e	8	798,618	13,157
2000	35,633	302,491	3,893.3	29,681.0 e	9	832,964	12,871
2001	35,564	304,645	4,044.8	30,488.8 e	9	857,294	13,277
2002	33,984	298,809	3,872.7	31,296.6	9	920,921	12,961
2003	32,554	295,732	3,982.5	30,265.2 p	9	883,116 p	13,467
2004	31,494 p	269,356 p	3,944.7 p	30,411.1 p	9 p	908,184 p	13,943 p
2005	30,126 p	257,594 p	3,957.7 p	30,556.9 p	9 p	933,252 p	14,323 p
2006	28,758 p	245,832 p	3,970.7 p	30,702.7 p	9 p	958,319 p	14,704 p
2007	27,390 p	234,069 p	3,983.7 p	30,848.5 p	9 p	983,387 p	15,084 p

Sources: *Economic Census of the United States*, 1987, 1992, 1997, and 2002. Establishment counts, employment, and payroll are from *County Business Patterns* for non-Census years. Values followed by a 'p' are projections by the editors. Sales data for non-Census years are extrapolations, marked by 'e'. Data are the most recent available at this level of detail.

INDICES OF CHANGE

Year	Establishments (number)	Employment (number)	Payroll ($ million)	Sales ($ million)	Employees per Establishment (number)	Sales per Establishment ($)	Payroll per Employee ($)
1987	153.9	140.2	81.3	82.7	91.0	53.7	58.0
1992	147.6	141.6	95.3	100.1	95.5	67.8	67.3
1993	147.8	150.2	108.3	97.5 e	101.2	66.0	72.1
1994	140.4	140.5	106.5	94.9 e	100.1	67.6	75.8
1995	124.2	123.8	91.6	92.3 e	100.1	74.3	74.0
1996	144.7 e	148.7 e	112.6 e	89.7 e	102.4 e	62.0 e	75.7 e
1997	116.7	102.3	86.9	87.1	87.6	74.6	85.0
1998	110.2	98.5	90.8	89.7 e	89.8	81.4	92.2
1999	106.4	95.0	96.4	92.3 e	89.8	86.7	101.5
2000	104.9	101.2	100.5	94.8 e	96.7	90.4	99.3
2001	104.6	102.0	104.4	97.4 e	97.8	93.1	102.4
2002	100.0	100.0	100.0	100.0	100.0	100.0	100.0
2003	95.8	99.0	102.8	96.7 p	103.3	95.9 p	103.9
2004	92.7 p	90.1 p	101.9 p	97.2 p	97.4 p	98.6 p	107.6 p
2005	88.6 p	86.2 p	102.2 p	97.6 p	97.4 p	101.3 p	110.5 p
2006	84.6 p	82.3 p	102.5 p	98.1 p	97.4 p	104.1 p	113.5 p
2007	80.6 p	78.3 p	102.9 p	98.6 p	97.5 p	106.8 p	116.4 p

Sources: Same as General Statistics. The values shown reflect change from the base year, 2002. Values above 100 mean greater than 2002, values below 100 mean less than 2002, and a value of 100 in the 1987-2001 or 2003-2007 period means same as 2002. Values followed by a 'p' are projections by the editors; 'e' stands for extrapolation. Data are the most recent available at this level of detail.

SELECTED RATIOS

For 2002	Avg. of All Retail	Analyzed Industry	Index	For 2002	Avg. of All Retail	Analyzed Industry	Index
Employees per Establishment	17	9	52	Sales per Employee	174,682	104,738	60
Payroll per Establishment	333,445	113,958	34	Sales per Establishment	3,332,269	920,921	28
Payroll per Employee	20,311	12,961	64	Expenses per Establishment	na	na	na

Sources: Same as General Statistics. The 'Average of All' column, Wholesale or Retail, represents the average of the sector reported for the most recent complete year available. The Index shows the relationship between the Average and the Analyzed Industry. For example, 100 means that they are equal; 500 that the Analyzed Industry is five times the average; 50 means that the Analyzed Industry is half the national average. The abbreviation 'na' is used to show that data are 'not available'.

*Equivalent to SIC 5621.

LEADING COMPANIES   Number shown: **45**   Total sales ($ mil): **42,676**   Total employment (000): **350.3**

Company Name	Address				CEO Name	Phone	Co. Type	Sales ($ mil)	Empl. (000)
Limited Brands Inc.	PO Box 16000	Columbus	OH	43216	Deborah Fine	614-415-7000	P	8,934	98.9
Old Navy	2 Folsom St	San Francisco	CA	94105	Jenny J Ming	650-952-4400	S	5,804	8.0
Intimate Brands Inc.	PO Box 16000	Columbus	OH	43216	Leslie H Wexner		S	5,367	69.0
Neiman Marcus Group Inc.	1618 Main St	Dallas	TX	75201		214-741-6911	P	3,546	15.7
Charming Shoppes Inc.	450 Winks Ln	Bensalem	PA	19020	Dorrit J Bern	215-245-9100	P	2,286	25.0
Talbots Inc.	1 Talbots Dr	Hingham	MA	02043		781-749-7600	P	1,698	11.0
AnnTaylor Stores Corp.	142 W 57th St	New York	NY	10019	Kay Krill	212-541-3300	P	1,588	13.0
Phillips-Van Heusen Corp.	200 Madison Ave	New York	NY	10016	Bruce J Klatsky	212-381-3500	P	1,439	9.0
Express L.L.C.	PO Box 181000	Columbus	OH	43218	Leslie Wexner	614-415-7000	S	1,356*	3.0
Pacific Sunwear of California Inc.	PO Box 68042	Anaheim	CA	92817		714-414-4000	P	1,230	12.2
Urban Outfitters Inc.	1809 Walnut St	Philadelphia	PA	19103	Richard A Hayne	215-564-2313	P	828	4.6
Chico's FAS Inc.	11215 Metro Pky	Fort Myers	FL	33912	Scott A Edmonds	941-277-6200	P	769	7.1
Dress Barn Inc.	30 Dunnigan Dr	Suffern	NY	10901	David R Jaffe	845-369-4500	P	755	8.5
Cato Corp.	PO Box 34216	Charlotte	NC	28234	John P Derham Cato	704-554-8510	P	747	9.1
Guess Inc.	1444 S Alameda St	Los Angeles	CA	90021	Carlos E Alberini	213-765-3100	P	729	4.8
Charlotte Russe Holding Inc.	4645 Morena Blvd	San Diego	CA	92117		858-587-1500	P	539	6.5
Maurices Inc.	105 W Superior St	Duluth	MN	55802	R Brenninkmeyer	218-727-8431	R	510*	3.5
Mothers Work Inc.	456 N 5th St	Philadelphia	PA	19123	Dan W Matthias	215-873-2200	P	492	5.0
Wet Seal Inc.	26972 Burbank	Foothill Ranch	CA	92610		949-583-9029	P	439	6.7
Buckle Inc.	PO Box 1480	Kearney	NE	68848	Daniel J Hirschfeld	308-236-8491	P	423	5.8
United Retail Group Inc.	365 W Passaic St	Rochelle Park	NJ	07662	Raphael Benaroya	201-845-0880	P	399	5.2
Loehmann's Holdings Inc.	2500 Halsey St	Bronx	NY	10461	William J Fox	718-409-2000	S	365	1.8
Harold's Stores Inc.	5919 Maple Ave	Dallas	TX	75235		214-366-0600	P	360	0.8
One Price Clothing Stores Inc.	PO Box 2487	Spartanburg	SC	29304	John Disa	864-433-8888	P	332	3.9
Deb Shops Inc.	9401 Blue Grass Rd	Philadelphia	PA	19114	Marvin Rounick	215-676-6000	P	304	3.6
Catherines Stores Corp.	3742 Lamar Ave	Memphis	TN	38118	Diane Paccioone	901-363-3900	S	290*	1.7
Clothestime Inc.	5325 E Hunter Ave	Anaheim	CA	92807	David A Sepjal	714-779-5881	R	290*	2.1
Cache Inc.	1440 Broadway	New York	NY	10018		212-575-3200	P	247	2.1
Long Rap Inc.	1420 Wisconsin NW	Washington	DC	20007	Chuck Rendelman	202-337-6610	R	188*	0.4
Silver Fox Inc.	1207 3rd St S, Ste 7	Naples	FL	34102	Hank Greenburg	941-262-7598	R	103*	0.1
Georgiou Studio	808 Brannan St	San Francisco	CA	94103	George Georgiou	415-554-8000	R	57*	<0.1
Bedford Fair Industries	51 Weaver St, Ste 2	Greenwich	CT	06831	Steve Whiteman	203-629-2020	S	53*	<0.1
Lillie Rubin Affiliates Inc.	1440 Broadway, Fl 5	New York	NY	10018		212-575-3200	S	45*	0.8
Henri Bendel Inc.	712 5th Ave	New York	NY	10019		212-247-1100	S	39*	0.2
Sharpe Dry Goods Co.	PO Box 328	Checotah	OK	74426	Louis Sharpe IV	918-473-2233	R	24*	0.2
Sealfons Inc.	410 Springfield Ave	Summit	NJ	07901	Bert Model	908-277-1777	R	23*	0.3
Paul Stuart Inc.	Madison Ave & 45th	New York	NY	10017	Clifford Grodd	212-682-0320	R	22*	0.2
Cargo Landing Inc.	153 W Orangethorpe	Placentia	CA	92870	Loretta Brister	714-524-1301	R	15*	0.2
Griffin 88 Store Inc.	PO Box 88	Polkton	NC	28135	Todd Griffin	704-272-8021	R	15*	0.1
Lady Grace Stores Inc.	PO Box 128	Malden	MA	02148	Steve Berson	781-322-1721	R	15*	0.2
Cappelli Straworld Inc.	5450 NW 82nd Ave	Miami	FL	33166	Bonnie Rubel	305-597-7180	R	5*	<0.1
Bringing Up Baby Inc.	2415 Wilshire Blvd	Santa Monica	CA	90403	Corky Harvey	310-826-5774	R	2*	<0.1
Coplon's	6235 River Rd	Richmond	VA	23229	Hank Greenburg	804-288-3699	R	2*	<0.1
CHW Corp.	300 Delaware Ave	Wilmington	DE	19801	Michael Moore	302-427-5933	S	1*	<0.1
Emeralds to Coconuts Inc.	2730 N Henderson	Dallas	TX	75206	Lulie M Scott	214-823-3620	R	1*	<0.1

Source: Ward's Business Directory of U.S. Private and Public Companies, Volumes 1 and 2, 2005. The company type code used is as follows: P - Public, R - Private, S - Subsidiary, D - Division, J - Joint Venture, A - Affiliate, G - Group. Sales are in millions of dollars, employees are in thousands. An asterisk (*) indicates an estimated sales volume. The symbol < stands for 'less than'. Company names and addresses are truncated, in some cases, to fit into the available space.

OCCUPATIONS EMPLOYED BY CLOTHING STORES

Occupation	% of Total 2004	Change to 2014	Occupation	% of Total 2004	Change to 2014
Retail salespersons	61.6	14.4	General & operations managers	1.6	13.2
First-line supervisors/managers of retail sales workers	11.1	5.2	Shipping, receiving, & traffic clerks	1.1	3.6
Cashiers, except gaming	10.0	2.9	Tailors, dressmakers, & custom sewers	1.0	14.3
Stock clerks & order fillers	3.1	-12.4			

Source: Industry-Occupation Matrix, Bureau of Labor Statistics. These data are reported based on 4-digit NAICS categories but have been matched to corresponding 6-digit NAICS industry codes. The change reported for each occupation to the year 2014 is a percent of growth or decline as estimated by the Bureau of Labor Statistics. The abbreviation nec stands for 'not elsewhere classified.'

LOCATION BY STATE AND REGIONAL CONCENTRATION

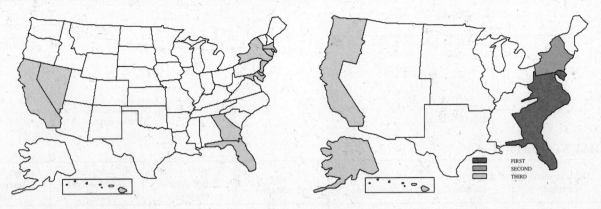

FIRST
SECOND
THIRD

INDUSTRY DATA BY STATE

State	Establishments		Employment			Payroll		Sales		
	Total (number)	% of U.S.	Total (number)	% of U.S.	Per Estab.	Total ($ mil.)	Per Empl. ($)	Total ($ mil.)	% of U.S.	Per Estab. ($)
New York	3,017	8.9	29,023	9.9	10	477.5	16,451	4,013.9	13.1	1,330,414
California	3,933	11.6	35,720	12.2	9	499.8	13,993	3,988.4	13.0	1,014,091
Florida	2,641	7.8	20,805	7.1	8	284.8	13,691	2,242.8	7.3	849,234
Texas	2,368	7.0	20,663	7.0	9	259.3	12,547	2,082.3	6.8	879,337
New Jersey	1,379	4.1	13,992	4.8	10	189.5	13,545	1,578.2	5.2	1,144,440
Illinois	1,438	4.2	13,657	4.6	9	170.9	12,511	1,353.4	4.4	941,180
Pennsylvania	1,345	4.0	12,975	4.4	10	154.2	11,885	1,279.2	4.2	951,103
Massachusetts	871	2.6	8,577	2.9	10	124.3	14,491	967.3	3.2	1,110,574
Michigan	1,101	3.2	9,715	3.3	9	113.0	11,635	931.9	3.0	846,382
Ohio	1,075	3.2	10,226	3.5	10	112.9	11,036	921.8	3.0	857,499
Georgia	1,130	3.3	9,491	3.2	8	115.5	12,171	893.9	2.9	791,054
Virginia	869	2.6	7,979	2.7	9	96.9	12,143	778.3	2.5	895,626
North Carolina	1,125	3.3	8,537	2.9	8	94.8	11,110	762.5	2.5	677,791
Maryland	636	1.9	6,699	2.3	11	78.0	11,642	638.2	2.1	1,003,483
Tennessee	677	2.0	5,608	1.9	8	60.9	10,861	485.8	1.6	717,513
Connecticut	502	1.5	4,508	1.5	9	62.0	13,742	485.7	1.6	967,454
Missouri	597	1.8	5,132	1.7	9	59.4	11,580	481.0	1.6	805,658
Minnesota	563	1.7	5,100	1.7	9	60.7	11,904	469.2	1.5	833,336
Louisiana	538	1.6	4,629	1.6	9	50.0	10,810	435.7	1.4	809,786
Indiana	586	1.7	4,869	1.7	8	53.0	10,884	434.8	1.4	741,922
South Carolina	619	1.8	4,492	1.5	7	51.5	11,454	425.6	1.4	687,595
Colorado	491	1.4	3,465	1.2	7	49.4	14,261	373.2	1.2	760,143
Wisconsin	493	1.5	3,970	1.4	8	42.4	10,677	344.0	1.1	697,819
Washington	484	1.4	3,702	1.3	8	46.7	12,622	340.9	1.1	704,279
Alabama	535	1.6	3,751	1.3	7	41.2	10,986	337.8	1.1	631,490
Nevada	215	0.6	1,968	0.7	9	34.2	17,384	284.6	0.9	1,323,549
Kentucky	360	1.1	2,816	1.0	8	28.4	10,073	254.4	0.8	706,786
Mississippi	368	1.1	2,254	0.8	6	24.2	10,739	219.3	0.7	595,832
Oregon	308	0.9	2,042	0.7	7	29.7	14,541	213.8	0.7	694,195
Oklahoma	282	0.8	2,319	0.8	8	28.1	12,096	212.7	0.7	754,404
Kansas	246	0.7	1,908	0.6	8	21.3	11,182	185.1	0.6	752,569
Arkansas	291	0.9	1,898	0.6	7	22.2	11,697	181.2	0.6	622,725
Iowa	304	0.9	2,091	0.7	7	20.3	9,711	167.1	0.5	549,543
Hawaii	206	0.6	1,685	0.6	8	21.3	12,665	162.4	0.5	788,131
New Hampshire	160	0.5	1,307	0.4	8	15.4	11,800	130.3	0.4	814,656
Rhode Island	142	0.4	1,165	0.4	8	16.3	13,979	128.6	0.4	905,521
Utah	168	0.5	1,468	0.5	9	15.3	10,393	116.9	0.4	695,964
Delaware	126	0.4	1,110	0.4	9	13.3	11,940	110.6	0.4	877,635
Nebraska	180	0.5	1,300	0.4	7	13.5	10,412	106.4	0.3	590,978
New Mexico	177	0.5	1,048	0.4	6	11.7	11,205	92.9	0.3	524,689
West Virginia	148	0.4	990	0.3	7	10.2	10,318	87.5	0.3	591,270
Maine	124	0.4	819	0.3	7	10.4	12,756	82.0	0.3	661,347
Idaho	105	0.3	713	0.2	7	8.2	11,496	62.0	0.2	590,676
Vermont	100	0.3	593	0.2	6	8.2	13,823	59.3	0.2	593,420
North Dakota	69	0.2	589	0.2	9	5.6	9,545	45.5	0.1	659,304
South Dakota	78	0.2	534	0.2	7	5.0	9,440	42.9	0.1	550,256
Montana	90	0.3	504	0.2	6	4.7	9,401	37.5	0.1	416,678
Alaska	39	0.1	251	0.1	6	3.8	15,211	28.7	0.1	735,077
Wyoming	58	0.2	263	0.1	5	3.2	12,141	28.1	0.1	485,328
Arizona	503	1.5	2500-4999	-	-	(D)	-	(D)	-	-
D.C.	95	0.3	500-999	-	-	(D)	-	(D)	-	-

Source: 2002 Economic Census. The states are in descending order of sales or establishments (if sales data are missing for the majority). The symbol (D) appears when data are withheld to prevent disclosure of competitive information. States marked with (D) are sorted by number of establishments. A dash (-) indicates that the data element cannot be calculated. Shaded states on the state map indicate those states which have proportionately greater representation in the industry than would be indicated by the states population; the ratio is based on total sales or number of establishments. Shaded regions indicate where the industry is regionally most concentrated.

NAICS 448130 - CHILDREN'S AND INFANTS' CLOTHING STORES*

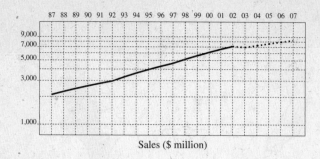

Sales ($ million)

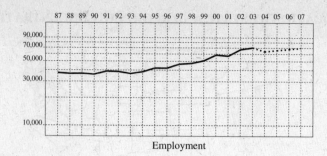

Employment

GENERAL STATISTICS

Year	Establishments (number)	Employment (number)	Payroll ($ million)	Sales ($ million)	Employees per Establishment (number)	Sales per Establishment ($)	Payroll per Employee ($)
1987	6,146	37,284	244.9	2,101.5	6	341,930	6,569
1988	5,786	36,566	272.7	2,272.5 e	6	392,758	7,458
1989	5,528	36,702	288.3	2,443.6 e	7	442,040	7,855
1990	5,592	35,867	306.0	2,614.6 e	6	467,561	8,531
1991	5,694	38,881	324.5	2,785.6 e	7	489,217	8,346
1992	5,637	38,509	323.0	2,956.7	7	524,517	8,388
1993	5,377	36,558	335.1	3,293.0 e	7	612,423	9,166
1994	5,264	38,368	359.6	3,629.2 e	7	689,438	9,372
1995	5,125	42,125	392.5	3,965.5 e	8	773,756	9,318
1996	5,362 e	42,068 e	397.4 e	4,301.7 e	8 e	802,257 e	9,447 e
1997	5,115	46,520	474.4	4,638.0	9	906,745	10,198
1998	5,165	47,442	533.6	5,132.5 e	9	993,699	11,247
1999	5,333	50,686	582.7	5,626.9 e	10	1,055,112	11,496
2000	5,647	58,608	675.4	6,121.4 e	10	1,084,003	11,523
2001	5,724	57,076	726.2	6,615.8 e	10	1,155,804	12,723
2002	6,568	67,148	787.9	7,110.3	10	1,082,563	11,734
2003	6,457	70,220	828.0	6,942.5 p	11	1,231,801 p	11,791
2004	5,754 p	63,812 p	786.7 p	7,276.9 p	11 p	1,289,853 p	12,786 p
2005	5,769 p	65,801 p	822.8 p	7,611.2 p	11 p	1,347,904 p	13,127 p
2006	5,784 p	67,789 p	858.9 p	7,945.6 p	12 p	1,405,956 p	13,468 p
2007	5,799 p	69,777 p	895.0 p	8,279.9 p	12 p	1,464,007 p	13,810 p

Sources: Economic Census of the United States, 1987, 1992, 1997, and 2002. Establishment counts, employment, and payroll are from *County Business Patterns* for non-Census years. Values followed by a 'p' are projections by the editors. Sales data for non-Census years are extrapolations, marked by 'e'. Data are the most recent available at this level of detail.

INDICES OF CHANGE

Year	Establishments (number)	Employment (number)	Payroll ($ million)	Sales ($ million)	Employees per Establishment (number)	Sales per Establishment ($)	Payroll per Employee ($)
1987	93.6	55.5	31.1	29.6	59.7	31.6	56.0
1992	85.8	57.3	41.0	41.6	66.5	48.5	71.5
1993	81.9	54.4	42.5	46.3 e	66.5	56.6	78.1
1994	80.1	57.1	45.6	51.0 e	71.4	63.7	79.9
1995	78.0	62.7	49.8	55.8 e	80.2	71.5	79.4
1996	81.6 e	62.6 e	50.4 e	60.5 e	76.3 e	74.1 e	80.5 e
1997	77.9	69.3	60.2	65.2	89.0	83.8	86.9
1998	78.6	70.7	67.7	72.2 e	90.0	91.8	95.8
1999	81.2	75.5	74.0	79.1 e	92.9	97.5	98.0
2000	86.0	87.3	85.7	86.1 e	101.7	100.1	98.2
2001	87.1	85.0	92.2	93.0 e	97.8	106.8	108.4
2002	100.0	100.0	100.0	100.0	100.0	100.0	100.0
2003	98.3	104.6	105.1	97.6 p	106.4	113.8 p	100.5
2004	87.6 p	95.0 p	99.8 p	102.3 p	107.5 p	119.1 p	109.0 p
2005	87.8 p	98.0 p	104.4 p	107.0 p	110.6 p	124.5 p	111.9 p
2006	88.1 p	101.0 p	109.0 p	111.7 p	113.7 p	129.9 p	114.8 p
2007	88.3 p	103.9 p	113.6 p	116.5 p	116.8 p	135.2 p	117.7 p

Sources: Same as General Statistics. The values shown reflect change from the base year, 2002. Values above 100 mean greater than 2002, values below 100 mean less than 2002, and a value of 100 in the 1987-2001 or 2003-2007 period means same as 2002. Values followed by a 'p' are projections by the editors; 'e' stands for extrapolation. Data are the most recent available at this level of detail.

SELECTED RATIOS

For 2002	Avg. of All Retail	Analyzed Industry	Index	For 2002	Avg. of All Retail	Analyzed Industry	Index
Employees per Establishment	17	10	60	Sales per Employee	174,682	105,890	61
Payroll per Establishment	333,445	119,968	36	Sales per Establishment	3,332,269	1,082,563	32
Payroll per Employee	20,311	11,734	58	Expenses per Establishment	na	na	na

Sources: Same as General Statistics. The 'Average of All' column, Wholesale or Retail, represents the average of the sector reported for the most recent complete year available. The Index shows the relationship between the Average and the Analyzed Industry. For example, 100 means that they are equal; 500 that the Analyzed Industry is five times the average; 50 means that the Analyzed Industry is half the national average. The abbreviation 'na' is used to show that data are 'not available'.

*Equivalent to SIC 5641.

LEADING COMPANIES   Number shown: **12**   Total sales ($ mil): **21,384**   Total employment (000): **137.3**

Company Name	Address				CEO Name	Phone	Co. Type	Sales ($ mil)	Empl. (000)
Toys 'R' Us Inc.	1 Geoffrey Way	Wayne	NJ	07470	John Barbour	973-617-3500	P	11,566	65.0
Babies 'R' Us	461 From Rd	Paramus	NJ	07652	Richard Markee	212-262-7800	D	3,874*	5.0
Charming Shoppes Inc.	450 Winks Ln	Bensalem	PA	19020	Dorrit J Bern	215-245-9100	P	2,286	25.0
Children's Place Retail Stores Inc.	915 Secaucus Rd	Secaucus	NJ	07094	Ezra Dabah	201-558-2400	P	1,157	11.1
Too Inc.	8323 Walton Pkwy	New Albany	OH	43054	Sally A Boyer	614-775-3500	P	676	9.6
Gymboree Corp.	500 Howard St	San Francisco	CA	94005	Lisa M Harper	415-278-7000	P	583	9.3
Children's Books and Toys Inc.	460 E Swedesford	Wayne	PA	19087	Fred Kayne	610-292-6600	P	460	3.2
OshKosh B'Gosh Inc.	PO Box 300	Oshkosh	WI	54901	Douglas W Hyde	920-231-8800	P	399	4.7
One Price Clothing Stores Inc.	PO Box 2487	Spartanburg	SC	29304	John Disa	864-433-8888	P	332	3.9
Winmark Corp.	4200 Dahlberg Dr	Minneapolis	MN	55422	Stephen M Briggs	612-520-8500	P	27	0.1
Sealfons Inc.	410 Springfield Ave	Summit	NJ	07901	Bert Model	908-277-1777	R	23*	0.3
Cotton Tails Inc.	4560 Poplar Ave	Memphis	TN	38117	Mickie Brugge	901-685-8417	R	1*	<0.1

Source: *Ward's Business Directory of U.S. Private and Public Companies*, Volumes 1 and 2, 2005. The company type code used is as follows: P - Public, R - Private, S - Subsidiary, D - Division, J - Joint Venture, A - Affiliate, G - Group. Sales are in millions of dollars, employees are in thousands. An asterisk (*) indicates an estimated sales volume. The symbol < stands for 'less than'. Company names and addresses are truncated, in some cases, to fit into the available space.

OCCUPATIONS EMPLOYED BY CLOTHING STORES

Occupation	% of Total 2004	Change to 2014	Occupation	% of Total 2004	Change to 2014
Retail salespersons	61.6	14.4	General & operations managers	1.6	13.2
First-line supervisors/managers of retail sales workers	11.1	5.2	Shipping, receiving, & traffic clerks	1.1	3.6
Cashiers, except gaming	10.0	2.9	Tailors, dressmakers, & custom sewers	1.0	14.3
Stock clerks & order fillers	3.1	-12.4			

Source: *Industry-Occupation Matrix*, Bureau of Labor Statistics. These data are reported based on 4-digit NAICS categories but have been matched to corresponding 6-digit NAICS industry codes. The change reported for each occupation to the year 2014 is a percent of growth or decline as estimated by the Bureau of Labor Statistics. The abbreviation nec stands for 'not elsewhere classified.'

LOCATION BY STATE AND REGIONAL CONCENTRATION

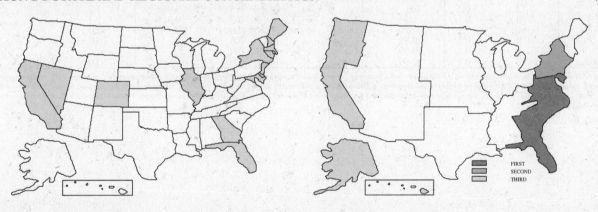

FIRST
SECOND
THIRD

INDUSTRY DATA BY STATE

State	Establishments Total (number)	Establishments % of U.S.	Employment Total (number)	Employment % of U.S.	Employment Per Estab.	Payroll Total ($ mil.)	Payroll Per Empl. ($)	Sales Total ($ mil.)	Sales % of U.S.	Sales Per Estab. ($)
New York	639	9.7	7,941	11.9	12	112.5	14,173	932.3	13.2	1,458,984
California	769	11.7	7,749	11.6	10	99.7	12,871	896.6	12.7	1,165,913
New Jersey	320	4.9	4,293	6.4	13	57.6	13,421	519.2	7.3	1,622,612
Texas	463	7.1	4,209	6.3	9	48.0	11,404	449.8	6.4	971,579
Florida	414	6.3	3,845	5.7	9	47.3	12,294	420.7	5.9	1,016,169
Illinois	283	4.3	3,136	4.7	11	35.5	11,329	328.8	4.6	1,161,996
Pennsylvania	279	4.3	3,244	4.8	12	35.5	10,955	324.4	4.6	1,162,573
Massachusetts	198	3.0	2,175	3.2	11	27.6	12,675	252.4	3.6	1,274,884
Ohio	212	3.2	2,462	3.7	12	26.1	10,582	246.9	3.5	1,164,538
Michigan	199	3.0	2,179	3.3	11	22.5	10,346	220.2	3.1	1,106,467
Georgia	218	3.3	2,010	3.0	9	21.0	10,426	198.1	2.8	908,757
Virginia	168	2.6	1,678	2.5	10	18.7	11,157	178.5	2.5	1,062,393
Maryland	137	2.1	1,575	2.4	11	17.8	11,295	161.4	2.3	1,178,073

Continued on next page.

INDUSTRY DATA BY STATE - Continued

State	Establishments Total (number)	% of U.S.	Employment Total (number)	% of U.S.	Per Estab.	Payroll Total ($ mil.)	Per Empl. ($)	Sales Total ($ mil.)	% of U.S.	Per Estab. ($)
North Carolina	165	2.5	1,637	2.4	10	15.3	9,354	150.6	2.1	912,491
Connecticut	120	1.8	1,387	2.1	12	16.3	11,727	144.2	2.0	1,201,425
Tennessee	143	2.2	1,384	2.1	10	14.2	10,285	131.1	1.9	916,671
Missouri	137	2.1	1,383	2.1	10	14.0	10,127	124.0	1.8	905,044
Indiana	107	1.6	1,130	1.7	11	11.6	10,291	110.4	1.6	1,031,804
Colorado	99	1.5	875	1.3	9	10.8	12,362	102.1	1.4	1,031,131
Minnesota	88	1.3	1,125	1.7	13	11.4	10,102	97.6	1.4	1,109,409
Washington	102	1.6	836	1.2	8	9.6	11,475	85.9	1.2	842,422
South Carolina	107	1.6	823	1.2	8	9.0	10,978	79.7	1.1	744,486
Alabama	124	1.9	866	1.3	7	8.2	9,462	72.9	1.0	588,298
Wisconsin	87	1.3	857	1.3	10	8.1	9,510	69.0	1.0	793,517
Louisiana	112	1.7	786	1.2	7	8.0	10,139	67.5	1.0	602,482
Oregon	75	1.1	582	0.9	8	7.4	12,749	67.4	1.0	898,080
Kentucky	81	1.2	545	0.8	7	5.6	10,218	53.4	0.8	659,790
Utah	63	1.0	601	0.9	10	6.0	9,930	49.8	0.7	790,302
Oklahoma	47	0.7	534	0.8	11	4.3	7,998	44.7	0.6	950,660
Kansas	43	0.7	503	0.8	12	4.7	9,431	44.3	0.6	1,030,349
Nevada	32	0.5	290	0.4	9	3.9	13,469	40.8	0.6	1,274,781
Delaware	23	0.4	308	0.5	13	3.3	10,750	40.3	0.6	1,752,826
New Hampshire	43	0.7	364	0.5	8	4.2	11,599	38.9	0.5	904,860
Maine	30	0.5	315	0.5	10	4.0	12,825	37.4	0.5	1,245,867
Rhode Island	25	0.4	286	0.4	11	3.9	13,776	33.7	0.5	1,348,320
Iowa	40	0.6	408	0.6	10	3.7	9,113	32.5	0.5	812,375
Mississippi	68	1.0	416	0.6	6	3.8	9,147	31.6	0.4	464,809
Arkansas	50	0.8	277	0.4	6	2.4	8,520	20.9	0.3	417,440
Hawaii	23	0.4	179	0.3	8	2.1	11,486	19.4	0.3	842,391
Nebraska	24	0.4	245	0.4	10	2.1	8,604	17.0	0.2	706,750
New Mexico	22	0.3	173	0.3	8	2.2	12,555	15.5	0.2	703,273
Vermont	23	0.4	165	0.2	7	1.7	10,570	13.6	0.2	590,348
West Virginia	12	0.2	67	0.1	6	0.7	10,687	8.4	0.1	702,917
Idaho	12	0.2	81	0.1	7	0.8	10,284	7.5	0.1	627,500
South Dakota	9	0.1	68	0.1	8	0.5	7,574	4.9	0.1	541,778
Montana	13	0.2	51	0.1	4	0.5	9,078	3.3	-	253,846
Wyoming	6	0.1	22	-	4	0.2	9,318	1.4	-	226,833
Arizona	80	1.2	500-999	-	-	(D)	-	(D)	-	-
Alaska	9	0.1	20-99	-	-	(D)	-	(D)	-	-
D.C.	9	0.1	20-99	-	-	(D)	-	(D)	-	-
North Dakota	6	0.1	20-99	-	-	(D)	-	(D)	-	-

Source: 2002 *Economic Census*. The states are in descending order of sales or establishments (if sales data are missing for the majority). The symbol (D) appears when data are withheld to prevent disclosure of competitive information. States marked with (D) are sorted by number of establishments. A dash (-) indicates that the data element cannot be calculated. Shaded *states* on the state map indicate those states which have proportionately greater representation in the industry than would be indicated by the states population; the ratio is based on total sales or number of establishments. Shaded *regions* indicate where the industry is regionally most concentrated.

NAICS 448140 - FAMILY CLOTHING STORES*

87 88 89 90 91 92 93 94 95 96 97 98 99 00 01 02 03 04 05 06 07

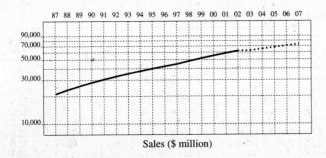

Sales ($ million)

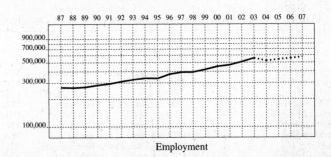

Employment

GENERAL STATISTICS

Year	Establishments (number)	Employment (number)	Payroll ($ million)	Sales ($ million)	Employees per Establishment (number)	Sales per Establishment ($)	Payroll per Employee ($)
1987	18,443	267,719	2,362.4	21,117.1	15	1,144,993	8,824
1988	17,786	265,267	2,498.1	23,451.1 e	15	1,318,515	9,417
1989	17,288	269,490	2,714.6	25,785.1 e	16	1,491,503	10,073
1990	17,796	282,608	2,954.6	28,119.1 e	16	1,580,080	10,455
1991	17,955	292,890	3,038.3	30,453.1 e	16	1,696,079	10,374
1992	19,452	309,516	3,468.9	32,787.1	16	1,685,539	11,208
1993	19,417	325,123	3,626.0	35,188.9 e	17	1,812,273	11,153
1994	19,522	338,331	3,924.2	37,590.7 e	17	1,925,556	11,599
1995	19,044	336,476	3,974.1	39,992.5 e	18	2,100,005	11,811
1996	21,105 e	374,080 e	4,337.0 e	42,394.3 e	18 e	2,008,732 e	11,594 e
1997	20,450	392,269	4,797.1	44,796.1	19	2,190,518	12,229
1998	20,832	393,741	5,195.9	48,255.1 e	19	2,316,393	13,196
1999	20,901	419,754	5,654.5	51,714.1 e	20	2,474,239	13,471
2000	20,627	453,088	5,918.3	55,173.1 e	22	2,674,798	13,062
2001	21,774	469,949	6,452.3	58,632.1 e	22	2,692,755	13,730
2002	24,407	509,094	7,248.8	62,091.0	21	2,543,985	14,239
2003	24,065	557,323	7,715.1	62,549.5 p	23	2,822,805 p	13,843
2004	23,403 p	522,651 p	7,369.2 p	65,220.5 p	23 p	2,922,136 p	14,635 p
2005	23,776 p	539,830 p	7,692.0 p	67,891.5 p	23 p	3,021,466 p	14,952 p
2006	24,148 p	557,009 p	8,014.9 p	70,562.5 p	24 p	3,120,796 p	15,269 p
2007	24,520 p	574,188 p	8,337.7 p	73,233.4 p	24 p	3,220,127 p	15,586 p

Sources: *Economic Census of the United States*, 1987, 1992, 1997, and 2002. Establishment counts, employment, and payroll are from *County Business Patterns* for non-Census years. Values followed by a 'p' are projections by the editors. Sales data for non-Census years are extrapolations, marked by 'e'. Data are the most recent available at this level of detail.

INDICES OF CHANGE

Year	Establishments (number)	Employment (number)	Payroll ($ million)	Sales ($ million)	Employees per Establishment (number)	Sales per Establishment ($)	Payroll per Employee ($)
1987	75.6	52.6	32.6	34.0	69.5	45.0	62.0
1992	79.7	60.8	47.9	52.8	76.2	66.3	78.7
1993	79.6	63.9	50.0	56.7 e	80.1	71.2	78.3
1994	80.0	66.5	54.1	60.5 e	82.9	75.7	81.5
1995	78.0	66.1	54.8	64.4 e	84.9	82.5	82.9
1996	86.5 e	73.5 e	59.8 e	68.3 e	84.9 e	79.0 e	81.4 e
1997	83.8	77.1	66.2	72.1	92.0	86.1	85.9
1998	85.4	77.3	71.7	77.7 e	90.6	91.1	92.7
1999	85.6	82.5	78.0	83.3 e	96.4	97.3	94.6
2000	84.5	89.0	81.6	88.9 e	105.5	105.1	91.7
2001	89.2	92.3	89.0	94.4 e	103.6	105.8	96.4
2002	100.0	100.0	100.0	100.0	100.0	100.0	100.0
2003	98.6	109.5	106.4	100.7 p	111.0	111.0 p	97.2
2004	95.9 p	102.7 p	101.7 p	105.0 p	108.8 p	114.9 p	102.8 p
2005	97.4 p	106.0 p	106.1 p	109.3 p	111.3 p	118.8 p	105.0 p
2006	98.9 p	109.4 p	110.6 p	113.6 p	113.7 p	122.7 p	107.2 p
2007	100.5 p	112.8 p	115.0 p	117.9 p	116.1 p	126.6 p	109.5 p

Sources: Same as General Statistics. The values shown reflect change from the base year, 2002. Values above 100 mean greater than 2002, values below 100 mean less than 2002, and a value of 100 in the 1987-2001 or 2003-2007 period means same as 2002. Values followed by a 'p' are projections by the editors; 'e' stands for extrapolation. Data are the most recent available at this level of detail.

SELECTED RATIOS

For 2002	Avg. of All Retail	Analyzed Industry	Index	For 2002	Avg. of All Retail	Analyzed Industry	Index
Employees per Establishment	17	21	123	Sales per Employee	174,682	121,964	70
Payroll per Establishment	333,445	296,997	89	Sales per Establishment	3,332,269	2,543,985	76
Payroll per Employee	20,311	14,239	70	Expenses per Establishment	na	na	na

Sources: Same as General Statistics. The 'Average of All' column, Wholesale or Retail, represents the average of the sector reported for the most recent complete year available. The Index shows the relationship between the Average and the Analyzed Industry. For example, 100 means that they are equal; 500 that the Analyzed Industry is five times the average; 50 means that the Analyzed Industry is half the national average. The abbreviation 'na' is used to show that data are 'not available'.

*Equivalent to SIC 5651.

LEADING COMPANIES   Number shown: 36   Total sales ($ mil): 153,064   Total employment (000): 1,208.8

Company Name	Address				CEO Name	Phone	Co. Type	Sales ($ mil)	Empl. (000)
Target Corp.	1000 Nicollet Mall	Minneapolis	MN	55403	Linda L. Ahlers	612-304-6073	P	45,682	273.0
Kmart Corp.	3100 W Big Beaver	Troy	MI	48084		248-643-1000	D	17,072	158.0
Gap Inc.	2 Folsom St	San Francisco	CA	94105		415-952-4400	P	16,267	150.0
TJX Companies Inc.	770 Cochituate Rd	Framingham	MA	01701	Arnold S Barron	508-390-1000	P	14,914	112.7
Limited Brands Inc.	PO Box 16000	Columbus	OH	43216	Deborah Fine	614-415-7000	P	8,934	98.9
Dollar General Corp.	100 Mission Ridge	Goodlettsville	TN	37072	David A Perdue Jr	615-855-4000	P	6,870	57.8
Nordstrom Inc.	1617 6th Ave	Seattle	WA	98101	Jim Bromley	206-628-2111	P	6,492	52.0
Saks Inc.	750 Lakeshore Pkwy	Birmingham	AL	35211	Andrew Jennings	205-940-4000	P	6,437	52.0
Foot Locker Inc.	112 W 34th St	New York	NY	10120		212-720-3700	P	5,355	40.3
Ross Stores Inc.	8333 Central Ave	Newark	CA	94560	Michael Balmuth	510-505-4400	P	3,786	26.6
Burlington Coat Factory	1830 Rte 130	Burlington	NJ	08016		609-387-7800	P	2,878	24.0
Polo Ralph Lauren Corp.	650 Madison Ave	New York	NY	10022		212-318-7000	P	2,381	13.0
Abercrombie and Fitch Co.	6301 Fitch Path	New Albany	OH	43054	Michael S Jeffries	614-283-6500	P	2,021	30.2
Pier 1 Imports Inc.	301 Commerce St	Fort Worth	TX	76102	Marvin J Girouard	817-252-8000	P	1,898	17.6
American Eagle Outfitters Inc.	PO Box 788	Warrendale	PA	15086	James V O'Donnell	724-776-4857	P	1,881	13.9
Lands' End Inc.	2 Lands' End Ln	Dodgeville	WI	53595	Gary C Comer	608-935-9341	S	1,600	10.0
Stein Mart Inc.	1200 Riverplace	Jacksonville	FL	32207	Michael D Fisher	904-346-1500	P	1,355	14.0
Stage Stores Inc.	10201 Main St	Houston	TX	77025		713-667-5601	P	1,244	12.8
Goody's Family Clothing Inc.	PO Box 22000	Knoxville	TN	37933	Robert M Goodfriend	865-966-2000	P	1,227	10.0
Urban Outfitters Inc.	1809 Walnut St	Philadelphia	PA	19103	Richard A Hayne	215-564-2313	P	828	4.6
Pier 1 Imports (U.S.) Inc.	301 Commerce St	Fort Worth	TX	76102	Marvin J Girouard	817-878-8000	S	811*	9.4
Recreational Equipment Inc.	6750 S 228th St	Kent	WA	98032	Dennis Madsen	253-395-3780	R	735	7.0
Factory 2-U Stores Inc.	4000 Ruffin Rd	San Diego	CA	92123	Norman G Plotkin	858-627-1800	P	493	3.5
Casual Male Retail Group Inc.	555 Turnpike St	Canton	MA	02021		781-828-9300	P	429	3.9
Buckle Inc.	PO Box 1480	Kearney	NE	68848	Daniel J Hirschfeld	308-236-8491	P	423	5.8
Syms Corp.	1 Syms Way	Secaucus	NJ	07094		201-902-9600	P	284	1.8
Crescent Retail J.V.	500 Crescent Ct	Dallas	TX	75201	Crawford Brock	214-871-3600	S	253*	0.1
Hamrick's Inc.	742 Peachoid Rd	Gaffney	SC	29341	Barry Hamrick	864-489-6095	R	220*	2.5
Big Dog Holdings Inc.	121 Gray Ave	Santa Barbara	CA	93101	Andrew D Feshbach	805-963-8727	P	104	1.4
Coopers Inc.	11205 Montgmry	Albuquerque	NM	87111	Carrie McDermott	505-296-8344	R	52*	0.5
Ron Jon Surf Shop	3850 S Banana River	Cocoa Beach	FL	32931	Ed Moriarty	321-799-8888	R	49*	0.4
Glik Stores	3248 Nameoki Rd	Granite City	IL	62040	Jeffrey W Glik	618-876-6717	R	34*	0.5
Dawahare's Inc.	1845 Alexandria Dr	Lexington	KY	40504	Harding Dawahare	859-278-0422	R	20*	0.2
Bob's Stores Inc.	160 Corporate Ct	Meriden	CT	06450	David Farrell	203-235-5775	S	18*	0.2
Foursome Inc.	841 E Lake St	Wayzata	MN	55391	Gordon Engel	952-473-4667	R	10*	<0.1
Foss Co.	1224 Washington	Golden	CO	80401	Robert Lowry	303-279-3373	R	6*	<0.1

Source: *Ward's Business Directory of U.S. Private and Public Companies*, Volumes 1 and 2, 2005. The company type code used is as follows: P - Public, R - Private, S - Subsidiary, D - Division, J - Joint Venture, A - Affiliate, G - Group. Sales are in millions of dollars, employees are in thousands. An asterisk (*) indicates an estimated sales volume. The symbol < stands for 'less than'. Company names and addresses are truncated, in some cases, to fit into the available space.

OCCUPATIONS EMPLOYED BY CLOTHING STORES

Occupation	% of Total 2004	Change to 2014	Occupation	% of Total 2004	Change to 2014
Retail salespersons	61.6	14.4	General & operations managers	1.6	13.2
First-line supervisors/managers of retail sales workers	11.1	5.2	Shipping, receiving, & traffic clerks	1.1	3.6
Cashiers, except gaming	10.0	2.9	Tailors, dressmakers, & custom sewers	1.0	14.3
Stock clerks & order fillers	3.1	-12.4			

Source: *Industry-Occupation Matrix*, Bureau of Labor Statistics. These data are reported based on 4-digit NAICS categories but have been matched to corresponding 6-digit NAICS industry codes. The change reported for each occupation to the year 2014 is a percent of growth or decline as estimated by the Bureau of Labor Statistics. The abbreviation nec stands for 'not elsewhere classified.'

LOCATION BY STATE AND REGIONAL CONCENTRATION

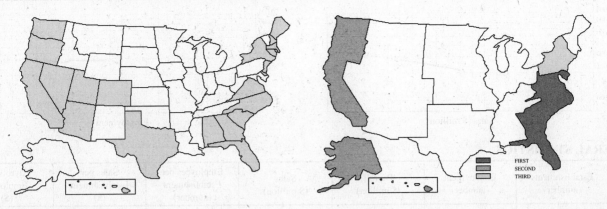

INDUSTRY DATA BY STATE

State	Establishments Total (number)	Establishments % of U.S.	Employment Total (number)	Employment % of U.S.	Employment Per Estab.	Payroll Total ($ mil.)	Payroll Per Empl. ($)	Sales Total ($ mil.)	Sales % of U.S.	Sales Per Estab. ($)
California	2,774	11.3	66,452	12.7	24	1,242.2	18,693	9,417.0	14.7	3,394,725
New York	1,669	6.8	39,615	7.6	24	621.1	15,678	5,531.2	8.7	3,314,072
Texas	1,896	7.7	39,476	7.6	21	504.9	12,789	4,593.3	7.2	2,422,619
Florida	1,839	7.5	32,780	6.3	18	468.1	14,281	4,376.4	6.9	2,379,786
Illinois	851	3.5	22,188	4.2	26	330.8	14,907	2,620.0	4.1	3,078,697
New Jersey	741	3.0	17,284	3.3	23	267.6	15,481	2,305.3	3.6	3,111,067
Pennsylvania	911	3.7	20,694	4.0	23	249.6	12,060	2,300.8	3.6	2,525,621
Massachusetts	635	2.6	17,419	3.3	27	238.7	13,703	2,181.6	3.4	3,435,539
Georgia	775	3.2	17,180	3.3	22	224.2	13,048	1,987.9	3.1	2,565,040
Michigan	749	3.1	15,878	3.0	21	211.1	13,294	1,720.9	2.7	2,297,618
North Carolina	767	3.1	15,460	3.0	20	183.9	11,892	1,719.9	2.7	2,242,404
Ohio	717	2.9	16,335	3.1	23	193.3	11,834	1,697.1	2.7	2,366,930
Virginia	576	2.3	13,395	2.6	23	191.7	14,313	1,662.6	2.6	2,886,380
Washington	456	1.9	11,913	2.3	26	224.5	18,844	1,544.1	2.4	3,386,178
Tennessee	492	2.0	10,262	2.0	21	120.4	11,734	1,215.8	1.9	2,471,061
Maryland	425	1.7	9,981	1.9	23	150.8	15,112	1,198.5	1.9	2,820,087
Alabama	477	1.9	9,094	1.7	19	118.3	13,004	1,089.1	1.7	2,283,161
Arizona	456	1.9	8,553	1.6	19	127.0	14,846	1,078.9	1.7	2,366,068
Connecticut	313	1.3	8,186	1.6	26	116.9	14,276	1,059.8	1.7	3,385,923
Minnesota	401	1.6	9,040	1.7	23	115.7	12,796	985.9	1.5	2,458,703
Indiana	413	1.7	9,744	1.9	24	112.3	11,523	974.3	1.5	2,359,092
South Carolina	483	2.0	7,980	1.5	17	99.0	12,403	956.1	1.5	1,979,600
Oregon	309	1.3	6,976	1.3	23	123.9	17,760	916.5	1.4	2,965,942
Colorado	446	1.8	8,009	1.5	18	117.1	14,624	888.5	1.4	1,992,175
Missouri	420	1.7	7,529	1.4	18	94.6	12,566	840.4	1.3	2,000,967
Louisiana	364	1.5	6,756	1.3	19	72.3	10,704	720.3	1.1	1,978,959
Wisconsin	349	1.4	6,626	1.3	19	72.1	10,888	681.7	1.1	1,953,404
Kentucky	299	1.2	5,985	1.1	20	65.3	10,909	656.6	1.0	2,195,896
Nevada	228	0.9	3,895	0.7	17	76.2	19,558	628.1	1.0	2,754,825
Oklahoma	348	1.4	5,683	1.1	16	61.2	10,777	551.2	0.9	1,583,848
Hawaii	231	0.9	3,958	0.8	17	63.2	15,964	521.0	0.8	2,255,268
Utah	228	0.9	5,253	1.0	23	66.0	12,573	491.0	0.8	2,153,373
Iowa	237	1.0	4,611	0.9	19	52.0	11,270	449.0	0.7	1,894,574
Mississippi	300	1.2	4,098	0.8	14	45.5	11,108	444.7	0.7	1,482,443
Arkansas	246	1.0	4,315	0.8	18	45.2	10,483	439.2	0.7	1,785,350
Kansas	234	1.0	4,428	0.8	19	54.4	12,280	429.1	0.7	1,833,641
New Hampshire	157	0.6	3,287	0.6	21	38.7	11,760	408.9	0.6	2,604,395
Maine	129	0.5	2,932	0.6	23	43.3	14,766	403.9	0.6	3,130,984
New Mexico	197	0.8	2,626	0.5	13	31.6	12,019	298.5	0.5	1,515,142
Rhode Island	86	0.4	1,878	0.4	22	32.8	17,454	273.3	0.4	3,177,593
Nebraska	145	0.6	2,582	0.5	18	28.9	11,191	250.9	0.4	1,730,634
Delaware	96	0.4	1,684	0.3	18	22.8	13,535	239.1	0.4	2,490,177
West Virginia	84	0.3	1,820	0.3	22	18.3	10,063	207.7	0.3	2,472,226
Idaho	121	0.5	1,701	0.3	14	19.5	11,463	171.5	0.3	1,417,744
Alaska	46	0.2	901	0.2	20	18.7	20,784	134.8	0.2	2,930,109
Montana	120	0.5	1,333	0.3	11	15.4	11,587	133.7	0.2	1,114,083
D.C.	45	0.2	1,073	0.2	24	13.9	12,949	123.1	0.2	2,735,578
Vermont	75	0.3	1,117	0.2	15	13.7	12,282	119.1	0.2	1,588,413
North Dakota	65	0.3	844	0.2	13	8.0	9,531	86.2	0.1	1,326,508
South Dakota	57	0.2	894	0.2	16	8.9	9,954	78.7	0.1	1,381,035
Wyoming	61	0.2	461	0.1	8	5.7	12,267	48.9	0.1	801,869

Source: 2002 *Economic Census*. The states are in descending order of sales or establishments (if sales data are missing for the majority). The symbol (D) appears when data are withheld to prevent disclosure of competitive information. States marked with (D) are sorted by number of establishments. A dash (-) indicates that the data element cannot be calculated. Shaded *states* on the state map indicate those states which have proportionately greater representation in the industry than would be indicated by the states population; the ratio is based on total sales or number of establishments. Shaded *regions* indicate where the industry is regionally most concentrated.

NAICS 448150 - CLOTHING ACCESSORIES STORES

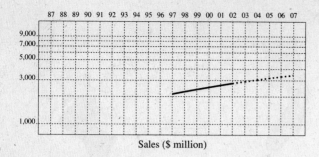

Sales ($ million)

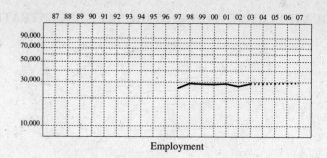

Employment

GENERAL STATISTICS

Year	Establishments (number)	Employment (number)	Payroll ($ million)	Sales ($ million)	Employees per Establishment (number)	Sales per Establishment ($)	Payroll per Employee ($)
1987	-	-	-	-	-	-	-
1988	-	-	-	-	-	-	-
1989	-	-	-	-	-	-	-
1990	-	-	-	-	-	-	-
1991	-	-	-	-	-	-	-
1992	-	-	-	-	-	-	-
1993	-	-	-	-	-	-	-
1994	-	-	-	-	-	-	-
1995	-	-	-	-	-	-	-
1996	-	-	-	-	-	-	-
1997	5,860	25,754	313.8	2,132.3	4	363,874	12,185
1998	5,781	29,088	368.6	2,262.8 e	5	391,419	12,672
1999	5,529	28,628	391.5	2,393.3 e	5	432,861	13,675
2000	5,661	28,463	400.2	2,523.8 e	5	445,819	14,062
2001	5,860	28,860	420.1	2,654.3 e	5	452,948	14,557
2002	5,855	27,014	471.9	2,784.8	5	475,623	17,468
2003	6,172	28,966	550.8	2,915.3 p	5	502,720 p	19,014
2004	6,019 p	28,928 p	551.8 p	3,045.8 p	5 p	524,328 p	19,228 p
2005	6,070 p	29,132 p	585.6 p	3,176.3 p	5 p	545,937 p	20,334 p
2006	6,120 p	29,336 p	619.4 p	3,306.7 p	5 p	567,545 p	21,439 p
2007	6,171 p	29,540 p	653.2 p	3,437.2 p	5 p	589,153 p	22,545 p

Source: Economic Census of the United States, 1997 and 2002. Establishment counts, employment, and payroll are from *County Business Patterns* for non-Census years. This is a newly defined industry. Data for prior years are unavailable at the time of publication but may become available over time. Values followed by 'p' are projections by the editors. Sales data for non-Census years are extrapolations, marked by 'e'.

INDICES OF CHANGE

Year	Establishments (number)	Employment (number)	Payroll ($ million)	Sales ($ million)	Employees per Establishment (number)	Sales per Establishment ($)	Payroll per Employee ($)
1987	-	-	-	-	-	-	-
1992	-	-	-	-	-	-	-
1993	-	-	-	-	-	-	-
1994	-	-	-	-	-	-	-
1995	-	-	-	-	-	-	-
1996	-	-	-	-	-	-	-
1997	100.1	95.3	66.5	76.6	95.4	76.5	69.8
1998	98.7	107.7	78.1	81.3 e	108.4	82.3	72.5
1999	94.4	106.0	83.0	85.9 e	112.7	91.0	78.3
2000	96.7	105.4	84.8	90.6 e	108.4	93.7	80.5
2001	100.1	106.8	89.0	95.3 e	106.2	95.2	83.3
2002	100.0	100.0	100.0	100.0	100.0	100.0	100.0
2003	105.4	107.2	116.7	104.7 p	101.7	105.7 p	108.8
2004	102.8 p	107.1 p	116.9 p	109.4 p	104.1 p	110.2 p	110.1 p
2005	103.7 p	107.8 p	124.1 p	114.1 p	103.9 p	114.8 p	116.4 p
2006	104.5 p	108.6 p	131.3 p	118.7 p	103.8 p	119.3 p	122.7 p
2007	105.4 p	109.4 p	138.4 p	123.4 p	103.6 p	123.9 p	129.1 p

Sources: Same as General Statistics. The values shown reflect change from the base year, 2002. Values above 100 mean greater than 2002, values below 100 mean less than 2002, and a value of 100 in the 1987-2001 or 2003-2007 period means same as 2002. Values followed by a 'p' are projections by the editors; 'e' stands for extrapolation. Data are the most recent available at this level of detail.

SELECTED RATIOS

For 2002	Avg. of All Retail	Analyzed Industry	Index	For 2002	Avg. of All Retail	Analyzed Industry	Index
Employees per Establishment	17	5	27	Sales per Employee	174,682	103,086	59
Payroll per Establishment	333,445	80,596	24	Sales per Establishment	3,332,269	475,623	14
Payroll per Employee	20,311	17,468	86	Expenses per Establishment	na	na	na

Sources: Same as General Statistics. The 'Average of All' column, Wholesale or Retail, represents the average of the sector reported for the most recent complete year available. The Index shows the relationship between the Average and the Analyzed Industry. For example, 100 means that they are equal; 500 that the Analyzed Industry is five times the average; 50 means that the Analyzed Industry is half the national average. The abbreviation 'na' is used to show that data are 'not available'.

LEADING COMPANIES   Number shown: 30   Total sales ($ mil): 19,068   Total employment (000): 195.2

Company Name	Address				CEO Name	Phone	Co. Type	Sales ($ mil)	Empl. (000)
Intimate Brands Inc.	PO Box 16000	Columbus	OH	43216	Leslie H. Wexner		S	5,367	69.0
Cintas Corp.	PO Box 625737	Cincinnati	OH	45262	R T (Dick) Farmer	513-459-1200	P	2,814	28.3
Victoria's Secret Stores Inc.	4 Limited Pkwy, E	Reynoldsburg	OH	43068	Grace Nichols	614-577-7000	S	2,647	29.0
Lands' End Inc.	2 Lands' End Ln	Dodgeville	WI	53595	Gary C Comer	608-935-9341	S	1,600	10.0
Claire's Stores Inc.	3 SW 129th Ave	Pembroke Pines	FL	33027		954-433-3900	P	1,133	16.0
Finish Line Inc.	3308 N Mitthoeffer	Indianapolis	IN	46235	Alan H Cohen	317-899-1022	P	986	12.1
Aeropostale Inc.	112 W 34th St	New York	NY	10120		646-485-5398	P	735	6.1
Hot Topic Inc.	18305 San Jose Ave	City of Industry	CA	91748	Gerald Cook	626-839-4681	P	657	6.8
Kenneth Cole Productions Inc.	603 W 50th St	New York	NY	10019	Paul Blum	212-265-1500	P	468	2.0
One Price Clothing Stores Inc.	PO Box 2487	Spartanburg	SC	29304	John Disa	864-433-8888	P	332	3.9
Rush Communications of NY Inc.	512 Fashion Ave	New York	NY	10018	Russell Simmons	212-840-9399	R	320	0.2
Syms Corp.	1 Syms Way	Secaucus	NJ	07094		201-902-9600	P	284	1.8
Cache Inc.	1440 Broadway	New York	NY	10018		212-575-3200	P	247	2.1
Long Rap Inc.	1420 Wisconsin NW	Washington	DC	20007	Chuck Rendelman	202-337-6610	R	188*	0.4
Sheplers Inc.	6501 W Kellogg	Wichita	KS	67209	Mike Annop	316-946-3838	R	183*	1.2
Conway Stores Inc.	11 W 34th St	New York	NY	10001	Abie Cowen	212-967-5300	R	181*	1.2
Cavender's Boot City	3308 E Pioneer Pwy	Arlington	TX	76010	James Cavender	817-633-2324	R	168*	0.8
Bakers Footwear Group Inc.	2815 Scott Ave	St. Louis	MO	63103	Michele A Bergerac	314-621-0699	P	150	0.6
Swim 'N Sport	2396 NW 96th Ave	Miami	FL	33172	Mark Sidel	305-593-5071	R	138*	0.1
A and E Stores Inc.	1000 Huyler St	Teterboro	NJ	07608	Alan A Ades	201-393-0600	R	125*	1.5
Big Dog Holdings Inc.	121 Gray Ave	Santa Barbara	CA	93101	Andrew D Feshbach	805-963-8727	P	104	1.4
Silver Fox Inc.	1207 3rd St S, Ste 7	Naples	FL	34102	Hank Greenburg	941-262-7598	R	103*	0.1
Georgiou Studio	808 Brannan St	San Francisco	CA	94103	George Georgiou	415-554-8000	R	57*	<0.1
Mitchell's Management Corp.	4444 Shackleford Rd	Norcross	GA	30093	Bob Huth	770-448-8381	R	50*	0.5
Island Water Sports Inc.	1985 NE 2nd St	Deerfield Beach	FL	33441	Lucinda Cottrell	954-427-5665	R	17*	<0.1
Frederick's of Hollywood Inc.	6608 Hollywood	Los Angeles	CA	90028	Linda LoRe	323-466-5151	R	6*	0.1
Queens City LaCrosse Co.	625 Washington Ave	Bridgeville	PA	15017	Gary Neft	412-257-4120	R	4*	<0.1
Coplon's	6235 River Rd	Richmond	VA	23229	Hank Greenburg	804-288-3699	R	2*	<0.1
Bakers Jewelry and Gifts	PO Box 11065	Norfolk	VA	23517	Theodore Baker	757-625-2529	R	1*	<0.1
Fabulous Furs	601 Madison Ave	Covington	KY	41011	Donna Salyers	859-291-3300	R	1*	<0.1

Source: *Ward's Business Directory of U.S. Private and Public Companies*, Volumes 1 and 2, 2005. The company type code used is as follows: P - Public, R - Private, S - Subsidiary, D - Division, J - Joint Venture, A - Affiliate, G - Group. Sales are in millions of dollars, employees are in thousands. An asterisk (*) indicates an estimated sales volume. The symbol < stands for 'less than'. Company names and addresses are truncated, in some cases, to fit into the available space.

OCCUPATIONS EMPLOYED BY CLOTHING STORES

Occupation	% of Total 2004	Change to 2014	Occupation	% of Total 2004	Change to 2014
Retail salespersons	61.6	14.4	General & operations managers	1.6	13.2
First-line supervisors/managers of retail sales workers	11.1	5.2	Shipping, receiving, & traffic clerks	1.1	3.6
Cashiers, except gaming	10.0	2.9	Tailors, dressmakers, & custom sewers	1.0	14.3
Stock clerks & order fillers	3.1	-12.4			

Source: *Industry-Occupation Matrix*, Bureau of Labor Statistics. These data are reported based on 4-digit NAICS categories but have been matched to corresponding 6-digit NAICS industry codes. The change reported for each occupation to the year 2014 is a percent of growth or decline as estimated by the Bureau of Labor Statistics. The abbreviation nec stands for 'not elsewhere classified.'

LOCATION BY STATE AND REGIONAL CONCENTRATION

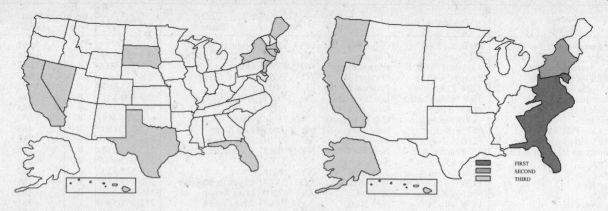

INDUSTRY DATA BY STATE

State	Establishments Total (number)	% of U.S.	Employment Total (number)	% of U.S.	Per Estab.	Payroll Total ($ mil.)	Per Empl. ($)	Sales Total ($ mil.)	% of U.S.	Per Estab. ($)
New York	531	9.1	2,894	10.9	5	84.4	29,172	438.9	16.1	826,561
California	649	11.2	3,195	12.0	5	56.3	17,633	346.5	12.7	533,851
Texas	447	7.7	1,917	7.2	4	37.8	19,696	216.5	7.9	484,284
Florida	442	7.6	1,941	7.3	4	31.5	16,216	191.7	7.0	433,774
Hawaii	74	1.3	531	2.0	7	12.9	24,252	119.3	4.4	1,612,770
Illinois	245	4.2	1,205	4.5	5	22.8	18,890	115.5	4.2	471,616
Pennsylvania	222	3.8	982	3.7	4	13.6	13,894	97.1	3.6	437,360
New Jersey	203	3.5	832	3.1	4	13.8	16,629	84.1	3.1	414,069
Massachusetts	153	2.6	835	3.1	5	14.4	17,229	78.1	2.9	510,170
Ohio	188	3.2	793	3.0	4	10.4	13,140	65.4	2.4	347,862
Michigan	158	2.7	653	2.4	4	9.6	14,677	62.8	2.3	397,500
Virginia	163	2.8	685	2.6	4	10.2	14,854	58.8	2.2	360,785
Georgia	150	2.6	655	2.5	4	9.2	13,988	56.5	2.1	376,533
Nevada	51	0.9	325	1.2	6	8.0	24,578	50.8	1.9	996,471
North Carolina	143	2.5	565	2.1	4	8.0	14,149	47.3	1.7	330,476
Maryland	119	2.0	561	2.1	5	7.4	13,235	46.3	1.7	389,319
Tennessee	119	2.0	470	1.8	4	6.3	13,417	40.9	1.5	343,378
Missouri	109	1.9	456	1.7	4	6.4	14,048	39.3	1.4	360,661
Indiana	99	1.7	445	1.7	4	6.0	13,501	38.6	1.4	390,354
Washington	99	1.7	489	1.8	5	6.3	12,791	36.4	1.3	367,949
Minnesota	101	1.7	474	1.8	5	6.3	13,289	36.2	1.3	357,990
Colorado	97	1.7	399	1.5	4	6.8	17,073	36.1	1.3	372,134
Connecticut	63	1.1	364	1.4	6	5.6	15,376	36.0	1.3	571,190
South Carolina	99	1.7	405	1.5	4	5.5	13,514	35.2	1.3	355,253
Wisconsin	80	1.4	382	1.4	5	5.1	13,241	33.2	1.2	414,438
Louisiana	97	1.7	329	1.2	3	4.2	12,666	25.8	0.9	265,701
Oregon	63	1.1	281	1.1	4	3.7	13,285	24.9	0.9	394,460
Alabama	87	1.5	290	1.1	3	3.8	12,969	23.6	0.9	270,874
Iowa	61	1.0	293	1.1	5	3.4	11,437	16.9	0.6	277,016
Kentucky	52	0.9	222	0.8	4	2.8	12,622	15.4	0.6	296,731
New Mexico	38	0.7	158	0.6	4	2.7	16,816	14.9	0.5	393,158
Maine	20	0.3	84	0.3	4	1.8	21,774	14.9	0.5	744,550
Kansas	46	0.8	195	0.7	4	2.5	13,015	13.7	0.5	298,761
Utah	47	0.8	210	0.8	4	2.3	11,038	12.9	0.5	275,277
Oklahoma	43	0.7	189	0.7	4	2.1	11,270	12.7	0.5	294,302
Arkansas	46	0.8	157	0.6	3	1.8	11,389	10.9	0.4	236,870
Mississippi	54	0.9	177	0.7	3	2.2	12,209	10.8	0.4	200,667
Delaware	19	0.3	105	0.4	6	1.6	15,029	9.8	0.4	517,368
New Hampshire	27	0.5	131	0.5	5	2.2	16,977	9.5	0.3	350,185
Rhode Island	19	0.3	108	0.4	6	1.5	14,102	9.2	0.3	481,947
Nebraska	37	0.6	168	0.6	5	1.9	11,488	9.1	0.3	245,838
West Virginia	24	0.4	95	0.4	4	1.3	13,958	7.3	0.3	302,250
South Dakota	23	0.4	114	0.4	5	1.5	12,807	6.9	0.3	298,130
Vermont	14	0.2	84	0.3	6	1.4	17,250	6.7	0.2	477,857
Idaho	22	0.4	82	0.3	4	0.9	11,317	4.9	0.2	224,091
Montana	17	0.3	69	0.3	4	1.0	13,841	4.7	0.2	279,294
Wyoming	8	0.1	29	0.1	4	0.3	9,241	1.7	0.1	212,125
Arizona	98	1.7	250-499	-	-	(D)	-	(D)	-	-
D.C.	18	0.3	20-99	-	-	(D)	-	(D)	-	-
Alaska	15	0.3	20-99	-	-	(D)	-	(D)	-	-
North Dakota	11	0.2	20-99	-	-	(D)	-	(D)	-	-

Source: 2002 *Economic Census*. The states are in descending order of sales or establishments (if sales data are missing for the majority). The symbol (D) appears when data are withheld to prevent disclosure of competitive information. States marked with (D) are sorted by number of establishments. A dash (-) indicates that the data element cannot be calculated. Shaded *states* on the state map indicate those which have proportionately greater representation in the industry than would be indicated by the states population; the ratio is based on total sales or number of establishments. Shaded *regions* indicate where the industry is regionally most concentrated.

NAICS 448190 - OTHER CLOTHING STORES

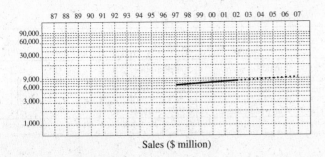

Sales ($ million)

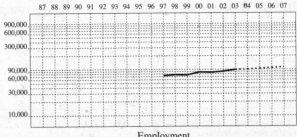

Employment

GENERAL STATISTICS

Year	Establishments (number)	Employment (number)	Payroll ($ million)	Sales ($ million)	Employees per Establishment (number)	Sales per Establishment ($)	Payroll per Employee ($)
1987	-	-	-	-	-	-	-
1988	-	-	-	-	-	-	-
1989	-	-	-	-	-	-	-
1990	-	-	-	-	-	-	-
1991	-	-	-	-	-	-	-
1992	-	-	-	-	-	-	-
1993	-	-	-	-	-	-	-
1994	-	-	-	-	-	-	-
1995	-	-	-	-	-	-	-
1996	-	-	-	-	-	-	-
1997	11,500	74,121	948.7	7,229.4	6	628,644	12,799
1998	11,748	76,899	1,067.9	7,571.3 e	7	644,480	13,887
1999	11,677	75,994	1,129.5	7,913.3 e	7	677,682	14,863
2000	11,751	87,776	1,235.6	8,255.2 e	8	702,514	14,077
2001	12,057	86,530	1,324.3	8,597.2 e	7	713,046	15,305
2002	10,581	90,922	1,259.6	8,939.1	9	844,829	13,853
2003	12,053	99,355	1,521.1	9,281.1 p	8	833,012 p	15,310
2004	11,582 p	100,840 p	1,540.3 p	9,623.0 p	9 p	870,482 p	15,429 p
2005	11,571 p	104,922 p	1,622.3 p	9,965.0 p	9 p	907,952 p	15,711 p
2006	11,561 p	109,003 p	1,704.3 p	10,306.9 p	10 p	945,422 p	15,993 p
2007	11,550 p	113,085 p	1,786.2 p	10,648.9 p	10 p	982,892 p	16,276 p

Source: *Economic Census of the United States*, 1997 and 2002. Establishment counts, employment, and payroll are from *County Business Patterns* for non-Census years. This is a newly defined industry. Data for prior years are unavailable at the time of publication but may become available over time. Values followed by 'p' are projections by the editors. Sales data for non-Census years are extrapolations, marked by 'e'.

INDICES OF CHANGE

Year	Establishments (number)	Employment (number)	Payroll ($ million)	Sales ($ million)	Employees per Establishment (number)	Sales per Establishment ($)	Payroll per Employee ($)
1987	-	-	-	-	-	-	-
1992	-	-	-	-	-	-	-
1993	-	-	-	-	-	-	-
1994	-	-	-	-	-	-	-
1995	-	-	-	-	-	-	-
1996	-	-	-	-	-	-	-
1997	108.7	81.5	75.3	80.9	74.5	74.4	92.4
1998	111.0	84.6	84.8	84.7 e	75.6	76.3	100.2
1999	110.4	83.6	89.7	88.5 e	75.6	80.2	107.3
2000	111.1	96.5	98.1	92.3 e	87.3	83.2	101.6
2001	113.9	95.2	105.1	96.2 e	83.8	84.4	110.5
2002	100.0	100.0	100.0	100.0	100.0	100.0	100.0
2003	113.9	109.3	120.8	103.8 p	95.9	98.6 p	110.5
2004	109.5 p	110.9 p	122.3 p	107.7 p	102.0 p	103.0 p	111.4 p
2005	109.4 p	115.4 p	128.8 p	111.5 p	106.3 p	107.5 p	113.4 p
2006	109.3 p	119.9 p	135.3 p	115.3 p	110.7 p	111.9 p	115.4 p
2007	109.2 p	124.4 p	141.8 p	119.1 p	115.0 p	116.3 p	117.5 p

Sources: Same as General Statistics. The values shown reflect change from the base year, 2002. Values above 100 mean greater than 2002, values below 100 mean less than 2002, and a value of 100 in the 1987-2001 or 2003-2007 period means same as 2002. Values followed by a 'p' are projections by the editors; 'e' stands for extrapolation. Data are the most recent available at this level of detail.

SELECTED RATIOS

For 2002	Avg. of All Retail	Analyzed Industry	Index	For 2002	Avg. of All Retail	Analyzed Industry	Index
Employees per Establishment	17	9	51	Sales per Employee	174,682	98,317	56
Payroll per Establishment	333,445	119,039	36	Sales per Establishment	3,332,269	844,829	25
Payroll per Employee	20,311	13,853	68	Expenses per Establishment	na	na	na

Sources: Same as General Statistics. The 'Average of All' column, Wholesale or Retail, represents the average of the sector reported for the most recent complete year available. The Index shows the relationship between the Average and the Analyzed Industry. For example, 100 means that they are equal; 500 that the Analyzed Industry is five times the average; 50 means that the Analyzed Industry is half the national average. The abbreviation 'na' is used to show that data are 'not available'.

2139

LEADING COMPANIES　Number shown: 5　Total sales ($ mil): 35　Total employment (000): 0.2

Company Name	Address				CEO Name	Phone	Co. Type	Sales ($ mil)	Empl. (000)
Bluewater Rubber and Gasket	1802 Engineers Rd	Belle Chasse	LA	70037	Ronald Labauve	504-392-3001	R	15*	<0.1
Nirve Sports Ltd.	18401 Bandilier Cir	Fountain Valley	CA	92708	Danilo Bond	714-593-8301	R	10*	<0.1
Human-i-Tees Inc.	400 Columbus Ave	Valhalla	NY	10595	Lori Genaro	914-745-1000	R	5*	<0.1
Peachtree Industries Inc.	PO Box 1367	Andrews	NC	28901	Fred Ripper	828-321-3290	R	4*	<0.1
Krell Development	5N373 Andrene Ln	Itasca	IL	60143	Wally Maschuga	630-773-0164	R	2*	<0.1

Source: Ward's Business Directory of U.S. Private and Public Companies, Volumes 1 and 2, 2005. The company type code used is as follows: P - Public, R - Private, S - Subsidiary, D - Division, J - Joint Venture, A - Affiliate, G - Group. Sales are in millions of dollars, employees are in thousands. An asterisk (*) indicates an estimated sales volume. The symbol < stands for 'less than'. Company names and addresses are truncated, in some cases, to fit into the available space.

OCCUPATIONS EMPLOYED BY CLOTHING STORES

Occupation	% of Total 2004	Change to 2014	Occupation	% of Total 2004	Change to 2014
Retail salespersons	61.6	14.4	General & operations managers	1.6	13.2
First-line supervisors/managers of retail sales workers	11.1	5.2	Shipping, receiving, & traffic clerks	1.1	3.6
Cashiers, except gaming	10.0	2.9	Tailors, dressmakers, & custom sewers	1.0	14.3
Stock clerks & order fillers	3.1	-12.4			

Source: Industry-Occupation Matrix, Bureau of Labor Statistics. These data are reported based on 4-digit NAICS categories but have been matched to corresponding 6-digit NAICS industry codes. The change reported for each occupation to the year 2014 is a percent of growth or decline as estimated by the Bureau of Labor Statistics. The abbreviation nec stands for 'not elsewhere classified.'

LOCATION BY STATE AND REGIONAL CONCENTRATION

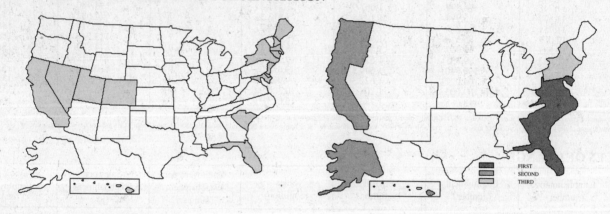

FIRST
SECOND
THIRD

INDUSTRY DATA BY STATE

State	Establishments		Employment			Payroll		Sales		
	Total (number)	% of U.S.	Total (number)	% of U.S.	Per Estab.	Total ($ mil.)	Per Empl. ($)	Total ($ mil.)	% of U.S.	Per Estab. ($)
California	1,230	11.5	11,179	12.3	9	166.5	14,893	1,060.6	13.3	862,240
New York	842	7.9	6,804	7.5	8	117.3	17,237	727.4	9.1	863,950
Florida	918	8.6	7,035	7.8	8	102.5	14,565	644.5	8.1	702,044
Texas	671	6.3	5,642	6.2	8	75.3	13,348	467.0	5.9	695,963
New Jersey	401	3.8	3,354	3.7	8	52.5	15,645	348.3	4.4	868,554
Illinois	414	3.9	3,723	4.1	9	56.3	15,118	335.9	4.2	811,408
Pennsylvania	413	3.9	3,870	4.3	9	54.2	14,018	328.2	4.1	794,651
Massachusetts	268	2.5	2,449	2.7	9	39.4	16,108	259.0	3.3	966,448
Ohio	345	3.2	3,242	3.6	9	41.6	12,842	256.6	3.2	743,907
Michigan	332	3.1	2,936	3.2	9	40.0	13,622	238.4	3.0	718,181
Virginia	233	2.2	2,606	2.9	11	30.6	11,738	202.1	2.5	867,511
North Carolina	294	2.8	2,482	2.7	8	30.2	12,150	195.2	2.5	663,820
Georgia	264	2.5	2,256	2.5	9	28.9	12,825	193.7	2.4	733,720
Colorado	269	2.5	2,007	2.2	7	33.2	16,521	188.0	2.4	698,732
Maryland	192	1.8	1,943	2.1	10	27.4	14,080	174.0	2.2	906,193
South Carolina	230	2.2	1,689	1.9	7	21.6	12,786	151.6	1.9	659,235
Tennessee	202	1.9	1,743	1.9	9	23.4	13,413	143.5	1.8	710,173
Minnesota	158	1.5	1,638	1.8	10	22.4	13,702	127.7	1.6	807,994
Missouri	203	1.9	1,531	1.7	8	19.7	12,849	124.1	1.6	611,562
Washington	196	1.8	1,476	1.6	8	21.4	14,507	122.0	1.5	622,582

Continued on next page.

INDUSTRY DATA BY STATE - Continued

State	Establishments		Employment			Payroll		Sales		
	Total (number)	% of U.S.	Total (number)	% of U.S.	Per Estab.	Total ($ mil.)	Per Empl. ($)	Total ($ mil.)	% of U.S.	Per Estab. ($)
Wisconsin	184	1.7	1,803	2.0	10	20.2	11,188	119.9	1.5	651,837
Arizona	160	1.5	1,516	1.7	9	19.0	12,535	119.7	1.5	748,363
Indiana	182	1.7	1,534	1.7	8	20.2	13,194	115.0	1.4	631,951
Louisiana	176	1.7	1,534	1.7	9	16.7	10,872	114.8	1.4	651,994
Connecticut	128	1.2	1,178	1.3	9	17.7	15,025	105.6	1.3	825,266
Alabama	154	1.4	1,211	1.3	8	14.4	11,909	100.5	1.3	652,351
Hawaii	130	1.2	839	0.9	6	12.3	14,694	90.5	1.1	696,123
Oregon	133	1.2	832	0.9	6	11.7	14,094	79.1	1.0	594,714
Nevada	87	0.8	841	0.9	10	12.9	15,284	78.7	1.0	904,747
Kentucky	122	1.1	974	1.1	8	11.0	11,283	70.7	0.9	579,664
Utah	84	0.8	763	0.8	9	9.3	12,225	61.0	0.8	726,738
Iowa	108	1.0	1,005	1.1	9	10.8	10,764	58.4	0.7	541,120
Kansas	87	0.8	777	0.9	9	9.1	11,753	57.4	0.7	660,287
Mississippi	81	0.8	546	0.6	7	6.9	12,593	45.3	0.6	559,395
Oklahoma	78	0.7	664	0.7	9	8.1	12,261	44.0	0.6	564,167
New Hampshire	51	0.5	502	0.6	10	6.7	13,337	41.5	0.5	813,333
Maine	59	0.6	338	0.4	6	5.2	15,254	38.0	0.5	644,186
Delaware	42	0.4	357	0.4	9	5.1	14,272	34.5	0.4	821,476
Arkansas	66	0.6	448	0.5	7	4.3	9,565	34.0	0.4	515,727
New Mexico	67	0.6	438	0.5	7	5.7	12,998	33.8	0.4	505,164
Nebraska	69	0.6	564	0.6	8	5.6	9,913	33.1	0.4	479,507
D.C.	19	0.2	252	0.3	13	4.8	19,052	27.5	0.3	1,447,579
Rhode Island	42	0.4	268	0.3	6	3.7	13,694	25.9	0.3	616,548
West Virginia	39	0.4	383	0.4	10	4.3	11,298	24.0	0.3	615,769
Idaho	42	0.4	340	0.4	8	4.3	12,671	23.0	0.3	548,119
Montana	36	0.3	231	0.3	6	2.7	11,584	18.5	0.2	514,250
Alaska	24	0.2	102	0.1	4	3.3	32,833	18.0	0.2	749,458
Vermont	28	0.3	224	0.2	8	2.5	10,982	16.0	0.2	571,750
South Dakota	36	0.3	222	0.2	6	2.3	10,437	15.1	0.2	419,472
North Dakota	34	0.3	224	0.2	7	2.3	10,161	13.5	0.2	397,176
Wyoming	32	0.3	102	0.1	3	1.7	16,627	10.8	0.1	338,187

Source: 2002 *Economic Census*. The states are in descending order of sales or establishments (if sales data are missing for the majority). The symbol (D) appears when data are withheld to prevent disclosure of competitive information. States marked with (D) are sorted by number of establishments. A dash (-) indicates that the data element cannot be calculated. Shaded *states* on the state map indicate those states which have proportionately greater representation in the industry than would be indicated by the states population; the ratio is based on total sales or number of establishments. Shaded *regions* indicate where the industry is regionally most concentrated.

NAICS 448210 - SHOE STORES*

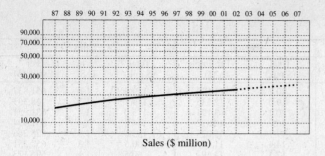

Sales ($ million)

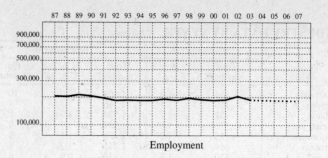

Employment

GENERAL STATISTICS

Year	Establishments (number)	Employment (number)	Payroll ($ million)	Sales ($ million)	Employees per Establishment (number)	Sales per Establishment ($)	Payroll per Employee ($)
1987	39,488	205,237	1,880.5	14,410.8	5	364,941	9,163
1988	38,525	203,202	2,035.3	15,105.3 e	5	392,091	10,016
1989	38,350	212,868	2,078.3	15,799.8 e	6	411,990	9,763
1990	37,450	206,199	2,152.4	16,494.3 e	6	440,435	10,439
1991	36,479	196,250	2,111.7	17,188.9 e	5	471,200	10,760
1992	37,206	184,415	2,184.5	17,883.4	5	480,659	11,846
1993	35,224	186,227	2,184.0	18,415.4 e	5	522,808	11,728
1994	34,795	184,533	2,236.2	18,947.4 e	5	544,544	12,118
1995	33,049	184,833	2,207.3	19,479.3 e	6	589,407	11,942
1996	34,846 e	191,267 e	2,366.3 e	20,011.3 e	6 e	574,278 e	12,372 e
1997	31,399	185,803	2,348.6	20,543.3	6	654,266	12,640
1998	29,602	195,502	2,472.5	21,034.1 e	7	710,565	12,647
1999	30,042	188,875	2,608.5	21,525.0 e	6	716,497	13,811
2000	29,664	185,076	2,611.2	22,015.8 e	6	742,174	14,109
2001	28,175	187,624	2,698.9	22,506.7 e	7	798,818	14,384
2002	28,388	204,825	2,676.1	22,997.5	7	810,115	13,065
2003	27,352	187,975	2,835.2	23,825.0 p	7	836,855 p	15,083
2004	26,380 p	185,318 p	2,807.8 p	24,390.0 p	7 p	867,479 p	15,011 p
2005	25,586 p	184,400 p	2,860.3 p	24,955.0 p	7 p	898,104 p	15,333 p
2006	24,791 p	183,483 p	2,912.9 p	25,520.0 p	7 p	928,728 p	15,655 p
2007	23,997 p	182,566 p	2,965.5 p	26,085.0 p	7 p	959,352 p	15,978 p

Sources: *Economic Census of the United States*, 1987, 1992, 1997, and 2002. Establishment counts, employment, and payroll are from *County Business Patterns* for non-Census years. Values followed by a 'p' are projections by the editors. Sales data for non-Census years are extrapolations, marked by 'e'. Data are the most recent available at this level of detail.

INDICES OF CHANGE

Year	Establishments (number)	Employment (number)	Payroll ($ million)	Sales ($ million)	Employees per Establishment (number)	Sales per Establishment ($)	Payroll per Employee ($)
1987	139.1	100.2	70.3	62.7	72.1	45.0	70.1
1992	131.1	90.0	81.6	77.8	69.3	59.3	90.7
1993	124.1	90.9	81.6	80.1 e	73.5	64.5	89.8
1994	122.6	90.1	83.6	82.4 e	73.5	67.2	92.8
1995	116.4	90.2	82.5	84.7 e	77.6	72.8	91.4
1996	122.7 e	93.4 e	88.4 e	87.0 e	76.2	70.9 e	94.7 e
1997	110.6	90.7	87.8	89.3	81.8	80.8	96.7
1998	104.3	95.4	92.4	91.5 e	91.5	87.7	96.8
1999	105.8	92.2	97.5	93.6 e	87.3	88.4	105.7
2000	104.5	90.4	97.6	95.7 e	85.9	91.6	108.0
2001	99.2	91.6	100.9	97.9 e	92.9	98.6	110.1
2002	100.0	100.0	100.0	100.0	100.0	100.0	100.0
2003	96.4	91.8	105.9	103.6 p	95.2	103.3 p	115.4
2004	92.9 p	90.5 p	104.9 p	106.1 p	95.4 p	107.1 p	114.9 p
2005	90.1 p	90.0 p	106.9 p	108.5 p	97.0 p	110.9 p	117.4 p
2006	87.3 p	89.6 p	108.8 p	111.0 p	98.6 p	114.6 p	119.8 p
2007	84.5 p	89.1 p	110.8 p	113.4 p	100.1 p	118.4 p	122.3 p

Sources: Same as General Statistics. The values shown reflect change from the base year, 2002. Values above 100 mean greater than 2002, values below 100 mean less than 2002, and a value of 100 in the 1987-2001 or 2003-2007 period means same as 2002. Values followed by a 'p' are projections by the editors; 'e' stands for extrapolation. Data are the most recent available at this level of detail.

SELECTED RATIOS

For 2002	Avg. of All Retail	Analyzed Industry	Index	For 2002	Avg. of All Retail	Analyzed Industry	Index
Employees per Establishment	17	7	43	Sales per Employee	174,682	112,279	64
Payroll per Establishment	333,445	94,269	28	Sales per Establishment	3,332,269	810,115	24
Payroll per Employee	20,311	13,065	64	Expenses per Establishment	na	na	na

Sources: Same as General Statistics. The 'Average of All' column, Wholesale or Retail, represents the average of the sector reported for the most recent complete year available. The Index shows the relationship between the Average and the Analyzed Industry. For example, 100 means that they are equal; 500 that the Analyzed Industry is five times the average; 50 means that the Analyzed Industry is half the national average. The abbreviation 'na' is used to show that data are 'not available'.

*Equivalent to SIC 5661.

LEADING COMPANIES   Number shown: **28**   Total sales ($ mil): **45,414**   Total employment (000): **292.3**

Company Name	Address				CEO Name	Phone	Co. Type	Sales ($ mil)	Empl. (000)
May Department Stores Co.	611 Olive St	St. Louis	MO	63101		314-342-6300	P	14,441	110.0
Nike Inc.	1 Bowerman Dr	Beaverton	OR	97005		503-641-6453	P	12,253	24.7
Foot Locker Inc.	112 W 34th St	New York	NY	10120		212-720-3700	P	5,355	40.3
Payless ShoeSource Inc.	3231 SE 6th Ave	Topeka	KS	66607	Steven J Douglass	785-233-5171	P	2,660	30.0
Footstar Inc.	933 MacArthur Blvd	Mahwah	NJ	07430	Dale W Hilpert	201-934-2000	P	1,973	21.1
Brown Shoe Company Inc.	PO Box 29	St. Louis	MO	63166	Ronald A Fromm	314-854-4000	P	1,832	11.6
Phillips-Van Heusen Corp.	200 Madison Ave	New York	NY	10016	Bruce J Klatsky	212-381-3500	P	1,439	9.0
Genesco Inc.	PO Box 731	Nashville	TN	37202		615-367-7000	P	837	6.2
DSW Inc.	4150 E 5th Ave	Columbus	OH	43219	Jay L Shottenstein	614-237-7100	S	791	4.6
Elder-Beerman Stores Corp.	PO Box 1448	Dayton	OH	45401	Byron L Bergren	937-296-2700	S	671	6.1
Shoe Carnival Inc.	8233 Baumgart Rd	Evansville	IN	47725		812-867-6471	P	590	3.8
Stride Rite Corp.	PO Box 9191	Lexington	MA	02420	David M Chamberlain	617-824-6000	P	558	2.5
Just for Feet	90 McKee Dr	Mahwah	NJ	07430	Shawn Neville	201-760-5000	S	536*	15.0
Kenneth Cole Productions Inc.	603 W 50th St	New York	NY	10019	Paul Blum	212-265-1500	P	468	2.0
Steven Madden Ltd.	16 Barnett Ave	Long Island City	NY	11104	Jamieson A Karson	718-446-1800	P	338	1.5
Cavender's Boot City	3308 E Pioneer Pwy	Arlington	TX	76010	James Cavender	817-633-2324	R	168*	0.8
Bakers Footwear Group Inc.	2815 Scott Ave	St. Louis	MO	63103	Michele A Bergerac	314-621-0699	P	150	0.6
Eurostar Inc.	13425 S Figueroa St	Los Angeles	CA	90061	Eric Alon	310-715-9300	R	102*	0.5
Shoe Pavilion Inc.	1380 Fitzgerald Dr	Pinole	CA	94564	Dmitry Beinus	510-222-4405	P	84	0.5
Tradehome Shoe Stores Inc.	8300 97th St S	Cottage Grove	MN	55016	Patrick Teal	651-459-8600	R	52*	0.5
Steve's Shoes Inc.	11333 Strang Line	Lenexa	KS	66215	Michael G Yeager	913-469-5535	R	25*	0.4
Sharpe Dry Goods Co.	PO Box 328	Checotah	OK	74426	Louis Sharpe IV	918-473-2233	R	24*	0.2
Bob's Stores Inc.	160 Corporate Ct	Meriden	CT	06450	David Farrell	203-235-5775	S	18*	0.2
Super Shoe Stores Inc.	PO Box 239	Cumberland	MD	21502	Terry Tierney	301-759-4300	R	14*	0.2
Foursome Inc.	841 E Lake St	Wayzata	MN	55391	Gordon Engel	952-473-4667	R	10*	<0.1
RunTex Inc.	422 W Riverside Dr	Austin	TX	78704	Paul Carrozza	512-472-3254	R	9*	<0.1
Van Hoecks Shoes	95 Monroe Ctr NW	Grand Rapids	MI	49503	Greg Clarin	616-456-6923	R	8*	<0.1
Rubenstein Brothers Inc.	102 St Charles Ave	New Orleans	LA	70130	David Rubenstein	504-581-6666	R	6*	<0.1

Source: *Ward's Business Directory of U.S. Private and Public Companies*, Volumes 1 and 2, 2005. The company type code used is as follows: P - Public, R - Private, S - Subsidiary, D - Division, J - Joint Venture, A - Affiliate, G - Group. Sales are in millions of dollars, employees are in thousands. An asterisk (*) indicates an estimated sales volume. The symbol < stands for 'less than'. Company names and addresses are truncated, in some cases, to fit into the available space.

OCCUPATIONS EMPLOYED BY SHOE STORES

Occupation	% of Total 2004	Change to 2014	Occupation	% of Total 2004	Change to 2014
Retail salespersons	68.6	4.8	Stock clerks & order fillers	2.1	-19.7
First-line supervisors/managers of retail sales workers	15.5	-3.5	General & operations managers	1.6	3.8
Cashiers, except gaming	6.1	-5.6			

Source: *Industry-Occupation Matrix*, Bureau of Labor Statistics. These data are reported based on 4-digit NAICS categories but have been matched to corresponding 6-digit NAICS industry codes. The change reported for each occupation to the year 2014 is a percent of growth or decline as estimated by the Bureau of Labor Statistics. The abbreviation nec stands for 'not elsewhere classified.'

LOCATION BY STATE AND REGIONAL CONCENTRATION

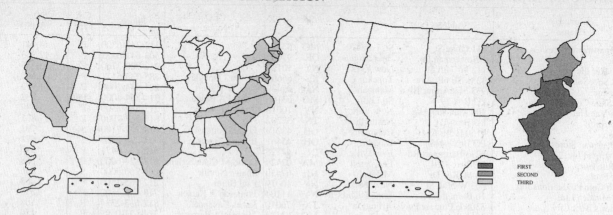

INDUSTRY DATA BY STATE

State	Establishments Total (number)	% of U.S.	Employment Total (number)	% of U.S.	Per Estab.	Payroll Total ($ mil.)	Per Empl. ($)	Sales Total ($ mil.)	% of U.S.	Per Estab. ($)
California	3,193	11.2	22,641	11.0	7	341.4	15,080	2,789.8	12.2	873,725
New York	2,292	8.0	16,076	7.8	7	253.1	15,745	2,182.6	9.5	952,268
Texas	1,969	6.9	15,616	7.6	8	193.4	12,382	1,735.5	7.6	881,409
Florida	1,970	6.9	13,892	6.8	7	182.5	13,135	1,638.4	7.1	831,691
Pennsylvania	1,361	4.8	9,320	4.5	7	117.0	12,551	1,075.9	4.7	790,504
Illinois	1,252	4.4	9,059	4.4	7	125.3	13,831	1,027.3	4.5	820,555
New Jersey	1,194	4.2	8,119	4.0	7	110.3	13,583	967.5	4.2	810,260
Ohio	1,135	4.0	8,000	3.9	7	89.6	11,206	783.0	3.4	689,900
Georgia	906	3.2	7,735	3.8	9	91.0	11,768	762.7	3.3	841,820
Michigan	974	3.4	6,609	3.2	7	87.3	13,211	714.3	3.1	733,370
North Carolina	790	2.8	6,995	3.4	9	76.9	10,994	642.7	2.8	813,605
Virginia	745	2.6	6,126	3.0	8	70.4	11,499	634.4	2.8	851,495
Massachusetts	681	2.4	5,079	2.5	7	73.2	14,411	583.8	2.5	857,341
Maryland	626	2.2	5,144	2.5	8	61.0	11,866	580.7	2.5	927,688
Tennessee	611	2.1	4,619	2.3	8	53.7	11,616	462.9	2.0	757,619
Indiana	544	1.9	4,073	2.0	7	47.1	11,559	414.5	1.8	762,007
Missouri	552	1.9	3,679	1.8	7	46.7	12,685	398.8	1.7	722,426
Louisiana	425	1.5	3,409	1.7	8	36.3	10,637	341.5	1.5	803,544
South Carolina	428	1.5	3,336	1.6	8	38.8	11,634	335.7	1.5	784,341
Wisconsin	448	1.6	3,256	1.6	7	43.9	13,487	328.4	1.4	733,031
Colorado	410	1.4	2,831	1.4	7	37.8	13,359	309.5	1.3	754,924
Minnesota	425	1.5	2,757	1.3	6	37.2	13,507	297.3	1.3	699,555
Connecticut	318	1.1	2,392	1.2	8	35.8	14,962	294.4	1.3	925,692
Alabama	393	1.4	3,079	1.5	8	33.2	10,781	290.7	1.3	739,613
Washington	434	1.5	2,573	1.3	6	36.1	14,041	289.3	1.3	666,645
Nevada	233	0.8	1,753	0.9	8	27.8	15,856	242.0	1.1	1,038,549
Kentucky	361	1.3	2,429	1.2	7	27.5	11,308	240.3	1.0	665,753
Oregon	257	0.9	1,677	0.8	7	25.1	14,968	213.7	0.9	831,568
Mississippi	265	0.9	1,856	0.9	7	19.8	10,689	180.9	0.8	682,823
Oklahoma	281	1.0	1,947	0.9	7	21.2	10,897	169.2	0.7	602,117
Kansas	237	0.8	1,650	0.8	7	19.2	11,627	161.3	0.7	680,675
Iowa	265	0.9	1,651	0.8	6	17.9	10,871	143.6	0.6	541,891
New Hampshire	178	0.6	1,238	0.6	7	16.9	13,617	136.9	0.6	769,247
Arkansas	221	0.8	1,443	0.7	7	16.3	11,268	133.4	0.6	603,638
Hawaii	118	0.4	947	0.5	8	14.2	14,947	131.6	0.6	1,115,254
Utah	203	0.7	1,150	0.6	6	13.6	11,822	113.7	0.5	560,049
New Mexico	165	0.6	999	0.5	6	13.2	13,187	106.5	0.5	645,727
Delaware	102	0.4	749	0.4	7	10.1	13,526	103.1	0.4	1,011,127
West Virginia	150	0.5	927	0.5	6	10.3	11,076	92.0	0.4	613,513
Nebraska	173	0.6	992	0.5	6	11.8	11,905	90.5	0.4	522,838
Maine	129	0.5	644	0.3	5	10.3	15,918	84.7	0.4	656,217
Rhode Island	82	0.3	519	0.3	6	8.4	16,129	62.3	0.3	759,366
Vermont	74	0.3	475	0.2	6	7.5	15,842	50.8	0.2	686,270
Idaho	110	0.4	562	0.3	5	6.3	11,269	49.9	0.2	453,418
Montana	74	0.3	358	0.2	5	4.2	11,852	34.1	0.1	460,500
South Dakota	72	0.3	378	0.2	5	4.3	11,341	33.6	0.1	467,111
Alaska	35	0.1	184	0.1	5	3.1	16,951	27.4	0.1	783,714
North Dakota	60	0.2	279	0.1	5	3.3	11,789	24.1	0.1	401,950
Wyoming	46	0.2	197	0.1	4	2.3	11,807	21.1	0.1	459,087
Arizona	467	1.6	2500-4999	-	-	(D)	-	(D)	-	-
D.C.	65	0.2	500-999	-	-	(D)	-	(D)	-	-

Source: 2002 *Economic Census*. The states are in descending order of sales or establishments (if sales data are missing for the majority). The symbol (D) appears when data are withheld to prevent disclosure of competitive information. States marked with (D) are sorted by number of establishments. A dash (-) indicates that the data element cannot be calculated. Shaded *states* on the state map indicate those states which have proportionately greater representation in the industry than would be indicated by the states population; the ratio is based on total sales or number of establishments. Shaded *regions* indicate where the industry is regionally most concentrated.

NAICS 448310 - JEWELRY STORES*

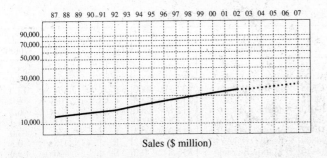

Sales ($ million)

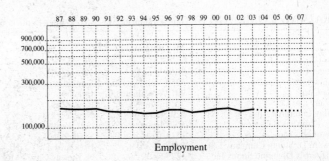

Employment

GENERAL STATISTICS

Year	Establishments (number)	Employment (number)	Payroll ($ million)	Sales ($ million)	Employees per Establishment (number)	Sales per Establishment ($)	Payroll per Employee ($)
1987	28,050	162,795	1,921.5	11,994.3	6	427,604	11,803
1988	26,951	159,650	2,162.4	12,395.8 e	6	459,938	13,545
1989	27,367	159,444	2,250.2	12,797.4 e	6	467,622	14,113
1990	26,583	160,811	2,322.1	13,198.9 e	6	496,517	14,440
1991	26,399	150,269	2,214.6	13,600.4 e	6	515,186	14,738
1992	28,077	147,888	2,224.4	14,002.0	5	498,700	15,041
1993	27,590	147,687	2,304.6	14,903.9 e	5	540,192	15,605
1994	26,995	141,748	2,427.7	15,805.7 e	5	585,505	17,127
1995	27,487	143,377	2,555.5	16,707.6 e	5	607,836	17,824
1996	28,577 e	154,979 e	2,648.6 e	17,609.4 e	5 e	616,209 e	17,090 e
1997	28,336	154,877	2,836.0	18,511.3	6	653,279	18,311
1998	28,090	144,371	3,029.9	19,446.0 e	5	692,275	20,987
1999	28,552	148,849	3,326.0	20,380.7 e	5	713,809	22,345
2000	29,303	156,383	3,637.7	21,315.4 e	5	727,413	23,262
2001	29,780	159,314	3,651.4	22,250.1 e	5	747,148	22,920
2002	28,537	147,924	3,457.1	23,184.8	5	812,445	23,371
2003	28,527	154,495	3,679.8	23,341.2 p	5	804,887 p	23,818
2004	29,160 p	149,109 p	3,764.5 p	24,115.9 p	5 p	829,273 p	24,979 p
2005	29,294 p	148,717 p	3,877.9 p	24,890.6 p	5 p	853,659 p	25,753 p
2006	29,428 p	148,325 p	3,991.3 p	25,665.3 p	5 p	878,045 p	26,526 p
2007	29,562 p	147,932 p	4,104.7 p	26,439.9 p	5 p	902,432 p	27,299 p

Sources: Economic Census of the United States, 1987, 1992, 1997, and 2002. Establishment counts, employment, and payroll are from County Business Patterns for non-Census years. Values followed by a 'p' are projections by the editors. Sales data for non-Census years are extrapolations, marked by 'e'. Data are the most recent available at this level of detail.

INDICES OF CHANGE

Year	Establishments (number)	Employment (number)	Payroll ($ million)	Sales ($ million)	Employees per Establishment (number)	Sales per Establishment ($)	Payroll per Employee ($)
1987	98.3	110.1	55.6	51.7	111.9	52.6	50.5
1992	98.4	100.0	64.3	60.4	102.2	61.4	64.4
1993	96.7	99.8	66.7	64.3 e	104.2	66.5	66.8
1994	94.6	95.8	70.2	68.2 e	102.2	72.1	73.3
1995	96.3	96.9	73.9	72.1 e	100.3	74.8	76.3
1996	100.1 e	104.8 e	76.6 e	76.0 e	104.2 e	75.8 e	73.1 e
1997	99.3	104.7	82.0	79.8	106.1	80.4	78.4
1998	98.4	97.6	87.6	83.9 e	98.4	85.2	89.8
1999	100.1	100.6	96.2	87.9 e	100.3	87.9	95.6
2000	102.7	105.7	105.2	91.9 e	102.2	89.5	99.5
2001	104.4	107.7	105.6	96.0 e	102.2	92.0	98.1
2002	100.0	100.0	100.0	100.0	100.0	100.0	100.0
2003	100.0	104.4	106.4	100.7 p	104.5	99.1 p	101.9
2004	102.2 p	100.8 p	108.9 p	104.0 p	98.1 p	102.1 p	106.9 p
2005	102.7 p	100.5 p	112.2 p	107.4 p	97.3 p	105.1 p	110.2 p
2006	103.1 p	100.3 p	115.5 p	110.7 p	96.5 p	108.1 p	113.5 p
2007	103.6 p	100.0 p	118.7 p	114.0 p	95.7 p	111.1 p	116.8 p

Sources: Same as General Statistics. The values shown reflect change from the base year, 2002. Values above 100 mean greater than 2002, values below 100 mean less than 2002, and a value of 100 in the 1987-2001 or 2003-2007 period means same as 2002. Values followed by a 'p' are projections by the editors; 'e' stands for extrapolation. Data are the most recent available at this level of detail.

SELECTED RATIOS

For 2002	Avg. of All Retail	Analyzed Industry	Index	For 2002	Avg. of All Retail	Analyzed Industry	Index
Employees per Establishment	17	5	31	Sales per Employee	174,682	156,734	90
Payroll per Establishment	333,445	121,143	36	Sales per Establishment	3,332,269	812,445	24
Payroll per Employee	20,311	23,371	115	Expenses per Establishment	na	na	na

Sources: Same as General Statistics. The 'Average of All' column, Wholesale or Retail, represents the average of the sector reported for the most recent complete year available. The Index shows the relationship between the Average and the Analyzed Industry. For example, 100 means that they are equal; 500 that the Analyzed Industry is five times the average; 50 means that the Analyzed Industry is half the national average. The abbreviation 'na' is used to show that data are 'not available'.

*Equivalent to SIC 5944.

LEADING COMPANIES   Number shown: **39**   Total sales ($ mil): **65,420**   Total employment (000): **384.0**

Company Name	Address				CEO Name	Phone	Co. Type	Sales ($ mil)	Empl. (000)
Kroger Co.	1014 Vine St	Cincinnati	OH	45202		513-762-4000	P	53,791	288.0
Williams-Sonoma Inc.	3250 Van Ness Ave	San Francisco	CA	94109	W Howard Lester	415-421-7900	P	2,609	36.0
Zale Corp.	901 W Walnut Hill	Irving	TX	75038	Robert J DiNicola	972-580-4000	P	2,304	17.0
Tiffany and Co.	727 Fifth Ave	New York	NY	10022		212-755-8000	P	2,205	6.9
Finlay Enterprises Inc.	529 5th Ave	New York	NY	10017	Arthur E Reiner	212-808-2800	P	924	6.2
Pier 1 Imports (U.S.) Inc.	301 Commerce St	Fort Worth	TX	76102	Marvin J Girouard	817-878-8000	S	811*	9.4
Friedman's Inc.	171 Crossroads Pky	Savannah	GA	31422	Douglas D Anderson	912-233-9333	P	436	4.0
Edward D. Sultan Company Ltd.	PO Box 301	Honolulu	HI	96809	Edward D Sultan III	808-833-7772	R	418*	0.3
Helzberg's Diamond Shops Inc.	1825 Swift	N. Kansas City	MO	64116	H Marvin Beasley	816-842-7780	S	400*	3.0
Whitehall Jewellers Inc.	155 N Wacker Dr	Chicago	IL	60606	Lucinda M Baier	312-782-6800	P	334	2.5
Gordon's Div.	901 W Walnut Hill	Irving	TX	75038	Charlene Wuellner	972-580-4000	D	262*	2.8
Fortunoff Fine Jewelry	PO Box 1550	Westbury	NY	11590	Helene Fortunoff	516-832-9000	R	230*	2.3
Samuels Jewelers Inc.	2914 Montopolis Dr	Austin	TX	78741	David B Barr	512-369-1400	P	122	0.9
Piercing Pagoda Inc.	901 W Walnut Hill	Irving	TX	75038	Mary Forte	972-580-4000	S	104*	2.0
Reeds Jewelers Inc.	PO Box 2229	Wilmington	NC	28402		910-350-3100	S	102	0.7
Ben Bridge Jeweler Inc.	PO Box 1908	Seattle	WA	98111	EL Bridge	206-448-8800	S	88*	0.7
Albert S. Smyth Company Inc.	2020 York Rd	L Timonium	MD	21093	Leonard G Getschel	410-252-6666	R	31*	0.2
Murray's Bargain Center	27207 Plymouth Rd	Detroit	MI	48239	Lou Mancini	313-937-8360	R	31*	0.2
DGSE Companies Inc.	2817 Forest Ln	Dallas	TX	75234	William H Oyster	972-484-3662	P	26	<0.1
Matagorda Ventures Inc.	800 W S Houston N	Houston	TX	77024	Ron Doohaluk	713-973-7925	R	21*	<0.1
Harry Winston Inc.	718 5th Ave	New York	NY	10019	Thomas O'Neill	212-245-2000	R	19*	0.1
Johnson Family Diamond Cellar	6280 Sawmill Rd	Dublin	OH	43017	Robert Johnson	614-336-4545	R	19*	0.1
S. Joseph and Sons Inc.	320 6th Ave	Des Moines	IA	50309	William Baum	515-283-1961	R	19*	<0.1
Jewelry Corner Inc.	1201 E Elizabeth St	Brownsville	TX	78520	Chander Buxani	956-544-1786	R	16*	<0.1
Just Diamonds	702 Colorado St	Austin	TX	78701	Jimmy Williams	512-476-0011	R	15*	<0.1
Carlyle and Company Jewelers	PO Box 21768	Greensboro	NC	27420	John K Cohen	336-294-2450	R	15*	0.1
Schwarzschild Jewelers Inc.	PO Box 12517	Richmond	VA	23241	Peter Boone	804-644-1941	R	15*	0.1
Wall Drug Store Inc.	510 Main St	Wall	SD	57790	Richard J Hustead	605-279-2175	R	11*	0.2
Pala International Inc.	912 S Live Oak	Fallbrook	CA	92028	William Larson	760-728-9121	R	10*	<0.1
Tappins Inc.	452 Pompton Ave	Cedar Grove	NJ	07009	Frank F Goodman	973-239-6201	R	7*	<0.1
Las Savell Jewelry Inc.	61 S McLean Blvd	Memphis	TN	38104	Las Savell	901-725-4200	R	5*	<0.1
Medallion Watch L.L.C.	510 2nd St	Lancaster	PA	17603		717-397-3651	R	4*	<0.1
USN Corp.	2121 Av of the Stars	Los Angeles	CA	90067	Terry Washburn		R	4	<0.1
Randolph Jewelers	375 Main St	Placerville	CA	95667	Charles Stephens	530-622-3787	R	3*	<0.1
Collector	912 S Live Oak	Fallbrook	CA	92028	William Larson	760-728-9121	D	2*	<0.1
Hoover's Jewelers Inc.	409 N Dewey	North Platte	NE	69101	Mike Jurado	308-532-0752	R	2*	<0.1
Hughes Rental and Sales Inc.	1611 S Gregg St	Big Spring	TX	79720	James Hughes	432-263-0234	R	2*	<0.1
Sleeping Beauty Turquoise	PO Box 111	Globe	AZ	85502	Monty Nichols	928-425-7625	R	2*	<0.1
Elizabeth Locke Jewels	968 Madison Ave	New York	NY	10021	Irene Kojen	212-744-7878	R	1*	<0.1

Source: *Ward's Business Directory of U.S. Private and Public Companies*, Volumes 1 and 2, 2005. The company type code used is as follows: P - Public, R - Private, S - Subsidiary, D - Division, J - Joint Venture, A - Affiliate, G - Group. Sales are in millions of dollars, employees are in thousands. An asterisk (*) indicates an estimated sales volume. The symbol < stands for 'less than'. Company names and addresses are truncated, in some cases, to fit into the available space.

OCCUPATIONS EMPLOYED BY JEWELRY, LUGGAGE, & LEATHER GOODS STORES

Occupation	% of Total 2004	Change to 2014	Occupation	% of Total 2004	Change to 2014
Retail salespersons	61.2	12.7	Bookkeeping, accounting, & auditing clerks	1.7	1.4
First-line supervisors/managers of retail sales workers	10.6	3.7	General & operations managers	1.6	11.6
Cashiers, except gaming	3.2	1.4	Watch repairers	1.1	-1.1
Office clerks, general	2.2	0.3			

Source: *Industry-Occupation Matrix*, Bureau of Labor Statistics. These data are reported based on 4-digit NAICS categories but have been matched to corresponding 6-digit NAICS industry codes. The change reported for each occupation to the year 2014 is a percent of growth or decline as estimated by the Bureau of Labor Statistics. The abbreviation nec stands for 'not elsewhere classified.'

LOCATION BY STATE AND REGIONAL CONCENTRATION

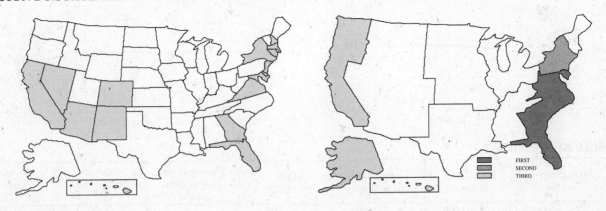

INDUSTRY DATA BY STATE

State	Establishments Total (number)	% of U.S.	Employment Total (number)	% of U.S.	Per Estab.	Payroll Total ($ mil.)	Per Empl. ($)	Sales Total ($ mil.)	% of U.S.	Per Estab. ($)
California	3,203	11.2	15,498	10.4	5	411.3	26,540	2,914.6	12.5	909,954
New York	2,345	8.2	10,341	7.0	4	278.4	26,918	2,121.1	9.1	904,518
Florida	2,361	8.2	9,998	6.7	4	233.5	23,359	1,670.3	7.2	707,447
Texas	1,837	6.4	9,524	6.4	5	222.6	23,368	1,558.1	6.7	848,179
Illinois	1,084	3.8	6,031	4.1	6	142.6	23,637	976.6	4.2	900,964
Pennsylvania	1,254	4.4	6,890	4.6	5	146.7	21,287	927.1	4.0	739,321
New Jersey	1,055	3.7	5,033	3.4	5	123.6	24,561	846.1	3.6	802,025
Ohio	1,057	3.7	6,415	4.3	6	135.4	21,100	843.8	3.6	798,296
Massachusetts	688	2.4	3,855	2.6	6	99.7	25,860	743.2	3.2	1,080,231
Michigan	895	3.1	5,024	3.4	6	119.4	23,762	728.5	3.1	813,934
Georgia	826	2.9	4,392	3.0	5	100.6	22,913	689.4	3.0	834,570
Virginia	773	2.7	4,646	3.1	6	102.6	22,079	667.5	2.9	863,552
North Carolina	902	3.2	4,895	3.3	5	98.8	20,176	569.4	2.4	631,271
Maryland	550	1.9	3,408	2.3	6	84.9	24,920	545.7	2.3	992,098
Indiana	519	1.8	3,139	2.1	6	66.4	21,165	452.6	1.9	872,019
Colorado	485	1.7	2,471	1.7	5	61.6	24,910	417.1	1.8	860,037
Arizona	516	1.8	2,629	1.8	5	65.0	24,728	415.0	1.8	804,234
Washington	512	1.8	2,760	1.9	5	66.9	24,246	408.5	1.8	797,947
Wisconsin	469	1.6	2,815	1.9	6	61.9	21,973	374.3	1.6	798,085
Minnesota	407	1.4	2,573	1.7	6	59.6	23,145	371.9	1.6	913,781
Tennessee	550	1.9	2,897	1.9	5	61.4	21,208	362.7	1.6	659,418
Missouri	477	1.7	2,464	1.7	5	57.3	23,272	355.2	1.5	744,740
Connecticut	354	1.2	1,959	1.3	6	53.8	27,455	350.6	1.5	990,525
Hawaii	380	1.3	2,027	1.4	5	48.5	23,944	344.4	1.5	906,184
Louisiana	414	1.4	2,065	1.4	5	44.0	21,328	286.5	1.2	692,017
South Carolina	482	1.7	2,407	1.6	5	46.0	19,093	276.4	1.2	573,477
Alabama	448	1.6	2,295	1.5	5	44.5	19,376	270.0	1.2	602,592
Nevada	251	0.9	1,532	1.0	6	42.4	27,654	267.3	1.1	1,064,869
Kentucky	359	1.3	1,943	1.3	5	38.0	19,581	245.6	1.1	684,220
Oregon	278	1.0	1,464	1.0	5	31.8	21,742	211.1	0.9	759,525
Oklahoma	255	0.9	1,298	0.9	5	30.9	23,790	190.3	0.8	746,314
Iowa	260	0.9	1,652	1.1	6	33.6	20,340	188.5	0.8	725,023
New Mexico	243	0.8	1,259	0.8	5	26.9	21,380	182.3	0.8	750,284
New Hampshire	145	0.5	907	0.6	6	22.3	24,587	166.2	0.7	1,146,110
Kansas	215	0.8	1,178	0.8	5	25.9	21,946	147.5	0.6	685,828
Arkansas	212	0.7	1,058	0.7	5	23.9	22,543	140.8	0.6	664,137
Mississippi	253	0.9	1,112	0.7	4	20.5	18,462	121.2	0.5	478,866
Utah	171	0.6	999	0.7	6	20.7	20,753	112.6	0.5	658,246
Delaware	102	0.4	565	0.4	6	13.0	23,058	97.1	0.4	952,196
West Virginia	153	0.5	728	0.5	5	14.3	19,585	87.9	0.4	574,242
Maine	101	0.4	510	0.3	5	11.4	22,410	76.2	0.3	754,861
Idaho	91	0.3	453	0.3	5	11.7	25,876	61.9	0.3	679,736
D.C.	52	0.2	253	0.2	5	8.5	33,672	50.5	0.2	970,538
North Dakota	51	0.2	317	0.2	6	6.2	19,675	43.6	0.2	855,039
Montana	91	0.3	368	0.2	4	6.5	17,723	40.4	0.2	443,703
Vermont	50	0.2	245	0.2	5	5.3	21,833	29.5	0.1	589,840
Nebraska	138	0.5	1000-2499	-	-	(D)	-	(D)	-	-
Rhode Island	126	0.4	500-999	-	-	(D)	-	(D)	-	-
Alaska	72	0.3	250-499	-	-	(D)	-	(D)	-	-
South Dakota	69	0.2	250-499	-	-	(D)	-	(D)	-	-
Wyoming	44	0.2	100-249	-	-	(D)	-	(D)	-	-

Source: 2002 *Economic Census*. The states are in descending order of sales or establishments (if sales data are missing for the majority). The symbol (D) appears when data are withheld to prevent disclosure of competitive information. States marked with (D) are sorted by number of establishments. A dash (-) indicates that the data element cannot be calculated. Shaded *states* on the state map indicate those states which have proportionately greater representation in the industry than would be indicated by the states population; the ratio is based on total sales or number of establishments. Shaded *regions* indicate where the industry is regionally most concentrated.

NAICS 448320 - LUGGAGE AND LEATHER GOODS STORES*

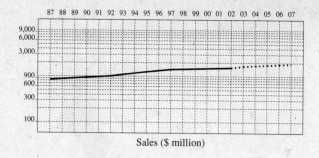

Sales ($ million)

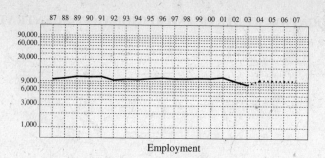

Employment

GENERAL STATISTICS

Year	Establishments (number)	Employment (number)	Payroll ($ million)	Sales ($ million)	Employees per Establishment (number)	Sales per Establishment ($)	Payroll per Employee ($)
1987	2,009	11,033	122.4	839.1	6	417,670	11,094
1988	2,010	11,659	147.4	872.8 e	6	434,229	12,643
1989	2,005	12,644	159.7	906.6 e	6	452,170	12,630
1990	2,054	12,524	164.5	940.3 e	6	457,790	13,135
1991	2,157	12,666	164.9	974.1 e	6	451,599	13,019
1992	1,907	10,684	146.9	1,007.9	6	528,527	13,749
1993	1,901	11,106	157.3	1,091.3 e	6	574,066	14,163
1994	1,921	11,031	165.0	1,174.7 e	6	611,504	14,958
1995	1,944	11,568	179.2	1,258.2 e	6	647,222	15,491
1996	1,975 e	11,920 e	184.5 e	1,341.6 e	6 e	679,291 e	15,478 e
1997	2,126	11,543	187.7	1,425.0	5	670,273	16,261
1998	2,082	11,562	191.9	1,450.9 e	6	696,857	16,598
1999	2,041	11,891	225.6	1,476.7 e	6	723,524	18,972
2000	1,990	11,807	234.0	1,502.6 e	6	755,060	19,818
2001	2,002	12,436	248.2	1,528.4 e	6	763,449	19,962
2002	1,733	10,235	209.1	1,554.3	6	896,874	20,435
2003	1,643	8,633	194.1	1,670.2 p	5	859,610 p	22,487
2004	1,868 p	10,746 p	233.0 p	1,724.4 p	6 p	888,975 p	21,674 p
2005	1,857 p	10,666 p	238.7 p	1,778.7 p	6 p	918,340 p	22,312 p
2006	1,845 p	10,585 p	244.5 p	1,832.9 p	6 p	947,705 p	22,949 p
2007	1,834 p	10,505 p	250.2 p	1,887.2 p	6 p	977,070 p	23,587 p

Sources: *Economic Census of the United States*, 1987, 1992, 1997, and 2002. Establishment counts, employment, and payroll are from *County Business Patterns* for non-Census years. Values followed by a 'p' are projections by the editors. Sales data for non-Census years are extrapolations, marked by 'e'. Data are the most recent available at this level of detail.

INDICES OF CHANGE

Year	Establishments (number)	Employment (number)	Payroll ($ million)	Sales ($ million)	Employees per Establishment (number)	Sales per Establishment ($)	Payroll per Employee ($)
1987	115.9	107.8	58.5	54.0	93.1	46.6	54.3
1992	110.0	104.4	70.2	64.8	94.8	58.9	67.3
1993	109.7	108.5	75.2	70.2 e	98.2	64.0	69.3
1994	110.8	107.8	78.9	75.6 e	96.5	68.2	73.2
1995	112.2	113.0	85.7	81.0 e	101.6	72.2	75.8
1996	114.0 e	116.5 e	88.2 e	86.3 e	101.6 e	75.7 e	75.7 e
1997	122.7	112.8	89.7	91.7	91.4	74.7	79.6
1998	120.1	113.0	91.8	93.3 e	94.8	77.7	81.2
1999	117.8	116.2	107.9	95.0 e	98.2	80.7	92.8
2000	114.8	115.4	111.9	96.7 e	99.9	84.2	97.0
2001	115.5	121.5	118.7	98.3 e	105.0	85.1	97.7
2002	100.0	100.0	100.0	100.0	100.0	100.0	100.0
2003	94.8	84.3	92.8	107.5 p	89.0	95.8 p	110.0
2004	107.8 p	105.0 p	111.4 p	110.9 p	97.0 p	99.1 p	106.1 p
2005	107.1 p	104.2 p	114.1 p	114.4 p	96.8 p	102.4 p	109.2 p
2006	106.5 p	103.4 p	116.9 p	117.9 p	96.7 p	105.7 p	112.3 p
2007	105.8 p	102.6 p	119.6 p	121.4 p	96.5 p	108.9 p	115.4 p

Sources: Same as General Statistics. The values shown reflect change from the base year, 2002. Values above 100 mean greater than 2002, values below 100 mean less than 2002, and a value of 100 in the 1987-2001 or 2003-2007 period means same as 2002. Values followed by a 'p' are projections by the editors; 'e' stands for extrapolation. Data are the most recent available at this level of detail.

SELECTED RATIOS

For 2002	Avg. of All Retail	Analyzed Industry	Index	For 2002	Avg. of All Retail	Analyzed Industry	Index
Employees per Establishment	17	6	35	Sales per Employee	174,682	151,860	87
Payroll per Establishment	333,445	120,686	36	Sales per Establishment	3,332,269	896,874	27
Payroll per Employee	20,311	20,435	101	Expenses per Establishment	na	na	na

Sources: Same as General Statistics. The 'Average of All' column, Wholesale or Retail, represents the average of the sector reported for the most recent complete year available. The Index shows the relationship between the Average and the Analyzed Industry. For example, 100 means that they are equal; 500 that the Analyzed Industry is five times the average; 50 means that the Analyzed Industry is half the national average. The abbreviation 'na' is used to show that data are 'not available'.

*Equivalent to SIC 5948.

LEADING COMPANIES   Number shown: **1**   Total sales ($ mil): **441**   Total employment (000): **4.2**

Company Name	Address			CEO Name	Phone	Co. Type	Sales ($ mil)	Empl. (000)
Wilsons The Leather Experts Inc.	PO Box 1009	Minneapolis	MN 55440		763-391-4000	P	441	4.2

Source: Ward's Business Directory of U.S. Private and Public Companies, Volumes 1 and 2, 2005. The company type code used is as follows: P - Public, R - Private, S - Subsidiary, D - Division, J - Joint Venture, A - Affiliate, G - Group. Sales are in millions of dollars, employees are in thousands. An asterisk (*) indicates an estimated sales volume. The symbol < stands for 'less than'. Company names and addresses are truncated, in some cases, to fit into the available space.

OCCUPATIONS EMPLOYED BY JEWELRY, LUGGAGE, & LEATHER GOODS STORES

Occupation	% of Total 2004	Change to 2014	Occupation	% of Total 2004	Change to 2014
Retail salespersons	61.2	12.7	Bookkeeping, accounting, & auditing clerks	1.7	1.4
First-line supervisors/managers of retail sales workers	10.6	3.7	General & operations managers	1.6	11.6
Cashiers, except gaming	3.2	1.4	Watch repairers	1.1	-1.1
Office clerks, general	2.2	0.3			

Source: Industry-Occupation Matrix, Bureau of Labor Statistics. These data are reported based on 4-digit NAICS categories but have been matched to corresponding 6-digit NAICS industry codes. The change reported for each occupation to the year 2014 is a percent of growth or decline as estimated by the Bureau of Labor Statistics. The abbreviation nec stands for 'not elsewhere classified.'

LOCATION BY STATE AND REGIONAL CONCENTRATION

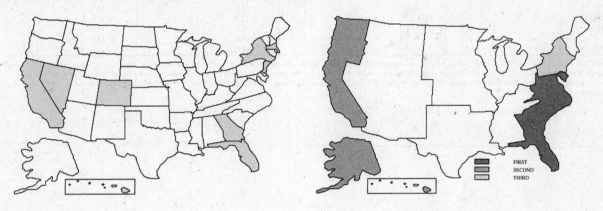

INDUSTRY DATA BY STATE

State	Establishments Total (number)	% of U.S.	Employment Total (number)	% of U.S.	Per Estab.	Payroll Total ($ mil.)	Per Empl. ($)	Sales Total ($ mil.)	% of U.S.	Per Estab. ($)
New York	181	10.5	1,134	11.1	6	35.8	31,563	275.3	17.8	1,521,199
California	244	14.1	1,463	14.3	6	32.2	22,013	263.8	17.1	1,081,164
Florida	180	10.4	940	9.2	5	16.6	17,671	126.1	8.2	700,750
Texas	101	5.8	698	6.8	7	12.5	17,908	102.7	6.7	1,016,743
Hawaii	22	1.3	279	2.7	13	10.3	36,896	84.7	5.5	3,848,364
Nevada	34	2.0	278	2.7	8	7.4	26,529	72.0	4.7	2,117,029
New Jersey	59	3.4	386	3.8	7	7.6	19,715	60.9	3.9	1,032,356
Pennsylvania	65	3.8	393	3.8	6	7.4	18,735	50.4	3.3	775,554
Georgia	61	3.5	394	3.9	6	6.8	17,350	43.2	2.8	708,525
Illinois	66	3.8	334	3.3	5	6.8	20,251	42.4	2.7	642,758
Massachusetts	52	3.0	266	2.6	5	5.9	22,132	41.0	2.7	788,981
Ohio	46	2.7	277	2.7	6	4.5	16,152	35.1	2.3	763,500
Michigan	66	3.8	326	3.2	5	4.7	14,276	32.1	2.1	485,833
Virginia	37	2.1	189	1.8	5	3.7	19,439	27.4	1.8	739,973
Colorado	40	2.3	198	1.9	5	3.8	19,005	24.8	1.6	619,300
North Carolina	30	1.7	184	1.8	6	3.0	16,255	20.3	1.3	675,467
Maryland	35	2.0	279	2.7	8	3.5	12,613	19.6	1.3	559,829
Missouri	30	1.7	180	1.8	6	2.6	14,467	18.0	1.2	600,167
Washington	33	1.9	152	1.5	5	2.5	16,493	16.8	1.1	508,000
Minnesota	26	1.5	176	1.7	7	3.2	18,415	16.0	1.0	613,654
Oregon	16	0.9	118	1.2	7	2.4	20,449	13.7	0.9	855,000
Louisiana	22	1.3	113	1.1	5	1.9	16,398	13.0	0.8	592,682
Connecticut	22	1.3	88	0.9	4	1.9	21,886	11.7	0.8	529,591
Tennessee	25	1.4	138	1.3	6	2.1	15,145	11.4	0.7	454,600

Continued on next page.

INDUSTRY DATA BY STATE - Continued

State	Establishments Total (number)	Establishments % of U.S.	Employment Total (number)	Employment % of U.S.	Employment Per Estab.	Payroll Total ($ mil.)	Payroll Per Empl. ($)	Sales Total ($ mil.)	Sales % of U.S.	Sales Per Estab. ($)
Indiana	22	1.3	108	1.1	5	1.8	16,500	10.5	0.7	476,955
South Carolina	23	1.3	150	1.5	7	1.9	12,493	9.3	0.6	404,261
Wisconsin	16	0.9	85	0.8	5	1.1	13,282	7.1	0.5	442,313
Utah	9	0.5	73	0.7	8	1.7	23,438	6.9	0.4	768,556
New Mexico	12	0.7	70	0.7	6	0.9	13,314	5.8	0.4	479,500
Kentucky	7	0.4	57	0.6	8	1.2	21,105	5.7	0.4	819,000
Kansas	9	0.5	61	0.6	7	0.9	14,377	5.4	0.3	599,000
New Hampshire	10	0.6	23	0.2	2	0.5	22,652	4.8	0.3	482,600
Maine	12	0.7	56	0.5	5	0.8	14,214	4.4	0.3	368,417
Oklahoma	10	0.6	56	0.5	6	0.6	10,446	4.3	0.3	427,600
Alabama	8	0.5	43	0.4	5	0.6	13,907	4.2	0.3	523,500
Vermont	6	0.3	29	0.3	5	0.6	20,517	3.8	0.2	639,500
West Virginia	7	0.4	38	0.4	5	0.4	11,605	3.4	0.2	482,429
Iowa	8	0.5	50	0.5	6	0.5	10,180	3.3	0.2	417,000
Delaware	5	0.3	29	0.3	6	0.5	18,586	2.9	0.2	583,800
Arkansas	6	0.3	26	0.3	4	0.4	14,385	1.7	0.1	276,167
Mississippi	4	0.2	13	0.1	3	0.2	14,462	1.4	0.1	352,500
Montana	3	0.2	4	-	1	0.1	19,750	0.8	0.1	280,000
Idaho	3	0.2	11	0.1	4	0.1	11,182	0.8	-	253,667
Arizona	37	2.1	100-249	-	-	(D)	-	(D)	-	-
D.C.	10	0.6	20-99	-	-	(D)	-	(D)	-	-
Nebraska	4	0.2	0-19	-	-	(D)	-	(D)	-	-
Rhode Island	4	0.2	0-19	-	-	(D)	-	(D)	-	-
Wyoming	2	0.1	0-19	-	-	(D)	-	(D)	-	-
Alaska	1	0.1	0-19	-	-	(D)	-	(D)	-	-
South Dakota	1	0.1	0-19	-	-	(D)	-	(D)	-	-

Source: 2002 *Economic Census*. The states are in descending order of sales or establishments (if sales data are missing for the majority). The symbol (D) appears when data are withheld to prevent disclosure of competitive information. States marked with (D) are sorted by number of establishments. A dash (-) indicates that the data element cannot be calculated. Shaded *states* on the state map indicate those states which have proportionately greater representation in the industry than would be indicated by the states population; the ratio is based on total sales or number of establishments. Shaded *regions* indicate where the industry is regionally most concentrated.

NAICS 451110 - SPORTING GOODS STORES

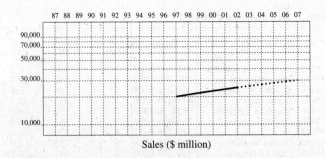

Sales ($ million)

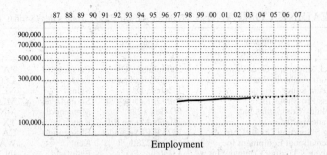

Employment

GENERAL STATISTICS

Year	Establishments (number)	Employment (number)	Payroll ($ million)	Sales ($ million)	Employees per Establishment (number)	Sales per Establishment ($)	Payroll per Employee ($)
1987	-	-	-	-	-	-	-
1988	-	-	-	-	-	-	-
1989	-	-	-	-	-	-	-
1990	-	-	-	-	-	-	-
1991	-	-	-	-	-	-	-
1992	-	-	-	-	-	-	-
1993	-	-	-	-	-	-	-
1994	-	-	-	-	-	-	-
1995	-	-	-	-	-	-	-
1996	-	-	-	-	-	-	-
1997	24,424	176,190	2,387.9	20,043.3	7	820,640	13,553
1998	24,138	181,408	2,652.7	21,039.3 e	8	871,627	14,623
1999	23,140	181,739	2,752.9	22,035.3 e	8	952,262	15,148
2000	22,611	184,964	2,948.3	23,031.4 e	8	1,018,591	15,940
2001	22,468	189,494	3,062.1	24,027.4 e	8	1,069,405	16,159
2002	22,193	187,693	3,015.8	25,023.4	8	1,127,536	16,068
2003	22,410	191,777	3,212.8	26,019.4 p	9	1,196,091 p	16,753
2004	21,540 p	194,336 p	3,363.2 p	27,015.4 p	9 p	1,258,781 p	17,392 p
2005	21,161 p	196,732 p	3,488.6 p	28,011.5 p	9 p	1,321,471 p	17,874 p
2006	20,783 p	199,128 p	3,614.0 p	29,007.5 p	9 p	1,384,161 p	18,356 p
2007	20,404 p	201,524 p	3,739.3 p	30,003.5 p	10 p	1,446,851 p	18,839 p

Source: Economic Census of the United States, 1997 and 2002. Establishment counts, employment, and payroll are from County Business Patterns for non-Census years. This is a newly defined industry. Data for prior years are unavailable at the time of publication but may become available over time. Values followed by 'p' are projections by the editors. Sales data for non-Census years are extrapolations, marked by 'e'.

INDICES OF CHANGE

Year	Establishments (number)	Employment (number)	Payroll ($ million)	Sales ($ million)	Employees per Establishment (number)	Sales per Establishment ($)	Payroll per Employee ($)
1987	-	-	-	-	-	-	-
1992	-	-	-	-	-	-	-
1993	-	-	-	-	-	-	-
1994	-	-	-	-	-	-	-
1995	-	-	-	-	-	-	-
1996	-	-	-	-	-	-	-
1997	110.1	93.9	79.2	80.1	85.1	72.8	84.3
1998	108.8	96.7	88.0	84.1 e	88.7	77.3	91.0
1999	104.3	96.8	91.3	88.1 e	93.4	84.5	94.3
2000	101.9	98.5	97.8	92.0 e	97.0	90.3	99.2
2001	101.2	101.0	101.5	96.0 e	99.3	94.8	100.6
2002	100.0	100.0	100.0	100.0	100.0	100.0	100.0
2003	101.0	102.2	106.5	104.0 p	101.2	106.1 p	104.3
2004	97.1 p	103.5 p	111.5 p	108.0 p	105.9 p	111.6 p	108.2 p
2005	95.4 p	104.8 p	115.7 p	111.9 p	108.7 p	117.2 p	111.2 p
2006	93.6 p	106.1 p	119.8 p	115.9 p	111.4 p	122.8 p	114.2 p
2007	91.9 p	107.4 p	124.0 p	119.9 p	114.1 p	128.3 p	117.2 p

Sources: Same as General Statistics. The values shown reflect change from the base year, 2002. Values above 100 mean greater than 2002, values below 100 mean less than 2002, and a value of 100 in the 1987-2001 or 2003-2007 period means same as 2002. Values followed by a 'p' are projections by the editors; 'e' stands for extrapolation. Data are the most recent available at this level of detail.

SELECTED RATIOS

For 2002	Avg. of All Retail	Analyzed Industry	Index	For 2002	Avg. of All Retail	Analyzed Industry	Index
Employees per Establishment	17	8	50	Sales per Employee	174,682	133,321	76
Payroll per Establishment	333,445	135,890	41	Sales per Establishment	3,332,269	1,127,536	34
Payroll per Employee	20,311	16,068	79	Expenses per Establishment	na	na	na

Sources: Same as General Statistics. The 'Average of All' column, Wholesale or Retail, represents the average of the sector reported for the most recent complete year available. The Index shows the relationship between the Average and the Analyzed Industry. For example, 100 means that they are equal; 500 that the Analyzed Industry is five times the average; 50 means that the Analyzed Industry is half the national average. The abbreviation 'na' is used to show that data are 'not available'.

LEADING COMPANIES   Number shown: **52**   Total sales ($ mil): **13,298**   Total employment (000): **77.7**

Company Name	Address				CEO Name	Phone	Co. Type	Sales ($ mil)	Empl. (000)
Dick's Sporting Goods Inc.	200 Industry Dr	Pittsburgh	PA	15275	William J. Colombo	412-809-0100	P	2,109	7.5
Sports Authority Inc.	1050 W Hampden	Englewood	CO	80110	Martin Hanaka	303-200-5050	P	1,760	17.0
Cabela's Inc.	1 Cabela Dr	Sidney	NE	69160	Richard N Cabela	308-254-5505	P	1,556	7.8
Bass Pro Shops Inc.	2500 E Kearney St	Springfield	MO	65898	James Hagale	417-873-5000	R	1,422*	10.7
Holiday Companies Inc.	PO Box 1224	Minneapolis	MN	55440	Ronald A Erickson	952-830-8700	R	1,250	6.0
Academy Ltd.	1800 N Mason Rd	Katy	TX	77449	David Gochman	281-646-5200	R	863*	6.0
Big 5 Sporting Goods Corp.	2525 E El Segundo	El Segundo	CA	90245		310-536-0611	P	779	0.0
Recreational Equipment Inc.	6750 S 228th St	Kent	WA	98032	Dennis Madsen	253-395-3780	R	735	7.0
Galyan's Trading Company Inc.	1 Galyans Pky	Plainfield	IN	46168	Edwin J Holman	317-532-0200	S	691	6.1
Hibbett Sporting Goods Inc.	451 Industrial Ln	Birmingham	AL	35211	Michael J Newsome	205-942-4292	P	378	0.0
Spalding Holdings Corp.	425 Meadow St	Chicopee	MA	01021	James R Craigie	413-536-1200	R	287*	1.0
Sport Chalet Inc.	1 Sport Chalet Dr	La Canada	CA	91011	Craig L Levra	818-949-5300	P	264	2.7
Sportsman's Guide Inc.	411 Farwell Ave	South St. Paul	MN	55075	Gregory R Binkley	651-451-3030	P	233	0.7
Scheels All Sports Inc.	3202 13th S Ave	Fargo	ND	58106	Steve D Scheel	701-298-2918	R	167*	2.0
Saucony Inc.	PO Box 6046	Peabody	MA	01960	John H Fisher	978-532-9000	P	166	0.3
Performance Inc.	PO Box 2741	Chapel Hill	NC	27514	Gary Snook	919-933-9113	R	87*	0.6
Pro Golf Discount Inc.	13405 SE 30th St	Bellevue	WA	98005	Randy Silver	425-401-0388	S	50*	0.1
Ron Jon Surf Shop	3850 S Banana River	Cocoa Beach	FL	32931	Ed Moriarty	321-799-8888	R	49*	0.4
Fotoball USA Inc.	6740 Cobra Way	San Diego	CA	92121	Scott P Dickey	858-909-9900	R	44*	0.1
Aspen Sports Inc.	408 E Cooper Ave	Aspen	CO	81611	Ernest Frywald	970-925-6331	R	43*	0.1
U.S. Fitness Products	5912 Oleander Dr	Wilmington	NC	28403	Bill Martin	910-790-2029	R	42*	<0.1
Kevin Inc.	PO Box 904	Kittery	ME	03904	Kevin Adams	207-439-2700	R	40*	0.3
Kelly's Sports Ltd.	897 S Matlack St	West Chester	PA	19382	Alvy Kelly	610-436-5458	R	22*	<0.1
Cole Sport Ski Shops	PO Box 3509	Park City	UT	84060	Gary E Cole	435-649-4800	R	22*	<0.1
Walter Craig Inc.	PO Box 547	Selma	AL	36702		334-875-7935	R	22*	<0.1
Numrich Gun Parts Corp.	226 Williams Ln	West Hurley	NY	12491	Gregory M Jenks		R	21*	0.1
Island Water Sports Inc.	1985 NE 2nd St	Deerfield Beach	FL	33441	Lucinda Cottrell	954-427-5665	R	17*	<0.1
Golfsmith Intern. Holdings Inc.	288 John R Rd	Troy	MI	48083		248-616-1970	R	15*	<0.1
Bacharach-Rasin Company Inc.	802 Gleneagles Ct	Baltimore	MD	21286	Christopher Hutchins	410-825-6747	R	12*	<0.1
Golf Galaxy	950 E Gilford Rd	Schaumburg	IL	60173		847-882-3828	R	12*	<0.1
Laux Sporting Goods Inc.	25 Pineview Dr	Amherst	NY	14228	David Laux	716-691-3367	R	12*	<0.1
Lew Horton Distributing Inc.	PO Box 5023	Westborough	MA	01581	Lewis Horton	508-366-7400	R	12*	<0.1
Wilcox Bait and Tackle Inc.	9501 Jefferson Ave	Newport News	VA	23605	Elmore Wilcox	757-595-5537	R	12*	<0.1
Mel Cottons Sporting Goods	1266 W San Carlos	San Jose	CA	95126	Steve Zehring	408-287-5994	R	11*	0.1
Athletic Supply of California	PO Box 690400	Stockton	CA	95269	Maureen Grogan	209-952-1887	R	10*	<0.1
Temple's Sporting Goods	1524 6th Ave	Moline	IL	61265	Robert Norton	309-764-8313	R	10*	<0.1
I and I Sports Supply Co.	19751 Figueroa St	Carson	CA	90745	Alan Iba	310-715-6800	R	10*	<0.1
Las Vegas Golf and Tennis Inc.	780 Brookline Trace	Alpharetta	GA	30022	Tom Hurford		R	8*	<0.1
Allanti Cycling Co.	144 Franklin Rd	Brentwood	TN	37027	Kerry Roberts	615-373-4700	R	6*	<0.1
Foss Co.	1224 Washington	Golden	CO	80401	Robert Lowry	303-279-3373	R	6*	<0.1
World Cycling Productions Inc.	2225 University W	Saint Paul	MN	55114	Timothy Grady	651-644-5200	R	6*	<0.1
AARCEE Party Rentals Inc.	3501 Hwy 100 S	Minneapolis	MN	55416	Richard Nelson	952-922-7233	R	5*	<0.1
Dive Shop Inc.	999 S Yates Rd	Memphis	TN	38119	Doug McNeese	901-763-3483	R	5*	<0.1
Vegas Golf Inc.	4860 W Desert Inn	Las Vegas	NV	89102	Lance Cangey	702-873-8077	R	5*	<0.1
US Underwater Services Inc.	PO Box 1311	Joshua	TX	76058	Michael Erinakes	817-447-7321	R	4*	<0.1
Ranger Joe's International	4030 Victory Dr	Columbus	GA	31903		706-689-3455	R	3*	<0.1
Carter's Shooting Center Inc.	6231 Treschwig Rd	Spring	TX	77373	William O Carter	281-443-8393	R	3*	<0.1
Two Creeks Ski Shop Snowmass	PO Box 1248	Aspen	CO	81612	Pat O Donnell	970-923-8740	R	3*	<0.1
Dakota Fence Co.	PO Box 62	Bismarck	ND	58502		701-223-0828	R	3*	<0.1
Blue Ridge Arsenal Inc.	14725 Flint Lee Rd	Chantilly	VA	20151	Earl Curtis	703-818-0230	R	1*	<0.1
Hall's Diving Center & Career	1994 Overseas Hwy	Marathon	FL	33050	Robert Brayman	305-743-5929	R	1*	<0.1
Lahaina Divers Inc.	143 Dickenson St	Lahaina	HI	96761	Greg Howeth	808-667-7496	R	1*	<0.1

Source: *Ward's Business Directory of U.S. Private and Public Companies*, Volumes 1 and 2, 2005. The company type code used is as follows: P - Public, R - Private, S - Subsidiary, D - Division, J - Joint Venture, A - Affiliate, G - Group. Sales are in millions of dollars, employees are in thousands. An asterisk (*) indicates an estimated sales volume. The symbol < stands for 'less than'. Company names and addresses are truncated, in some cases, to fit into the available space.

OCCUPATIONS EMPLOYED BY SPORTING GOODS STORES

Occupation	% of Total 2004	Change to 2014	Occupation	% of Total 2004	Change to 2014
Retail salespersons	51.6	24.6	Bookkeeping, accounting, & auditing clerks	1.9	12.1
Cashiers, except gaming	9.6	12.1	Shipping, receiving, & traffic clerks	1.8	12.8
First-line supervisors/managers of retail sales workers	8.5	14.6	Stock clerks & order fillers	1.4	-4.6
Bicycle repairers	3.4	14.4	Office clerks, general	1.3	10.9
General & operations managers	2.0	23.3	Sales reps, wholesale & manufacturing, exc tech	1.1	24.6

Source: *Industry-Occupation Matrix*, Bureau of Labor Statistics. These data are reported based on 4-digit NAICS categories but have been matched to corresponding 6-digit NAICS industry codes. The change reported for each occupation to the year 2014 is a percent of growth or decline as estimated by the Bureau of Labor Statistics. The abbreviation nec stands for 'not elsewhere classified.'

LOCATION BY STATE AND REGIONAL CONCENTRATION

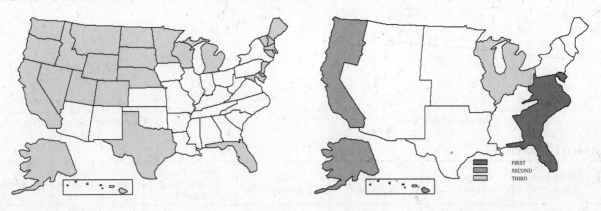

INDUSTRY DATA BY STATE

State	Establishments		Employment			Payroll		Sales		
	Total (number)	% of U.S.	Total (number)	% of U.S.	Per Estab.	Total ($ mil.)	Per Empl. ($)	Total ($ mil.)	% of U.S.	Per Estab. ($)
California	2,430	10.9	25,079	13.3	10	405.2	16,159	3,303.9	13.2	1,359,645
Texas	1,147	5.2	11,331	6.0	10	191.2	16,877	1,855.0	7.4	1,617,227
New York	1,171	5.3	9,881	5.3	8	169.3	17,132	1,527.3	6.1	1,304,303
Florida	1,369	6.2	9,068	4.8	7	159.7	17,615	1,321.8	5.3	965,516
Michigan	896	4.0	8,378	4.5	9	129.4	15,441	1,080.9	4.3	1,206,346
Pennsylvania	940	4.2	7,596	4.0	8	105.5	13,893	999.4	4.0	1,063,163
Illinois	827	3.7	6,845	3.6	8	111.1	16,234	921.3	3.7	1,114,047
Colorado	786	3.5	7,595	4.0	10	116.1	15,293	871.3	3.5	1,108,504
New Jersey	607	2.7	4,956	2.6	8	93.0	18,772	812.5	3.2	1,338,565
Ohio	784	3.5	6,419	3.4	8	96.1	14,967	802.1	3.2	1,023,133
Minnesota	565	2.5	6,415	3.4	11	91.4	14,251	784.2	3.1	1,388,019
Washington	597	2.7	5,296	2.8	9	89.2	16,844	695.6	2.8	1,165,166
Massachusetts	590	2.7	4,518	2.4	8	77.3	17,118	613.3	2.5	1,039,564
Georgia	522	2.3	4,288	2.3	8	73.9	17,242	612.9	2.5	1,174,048
North Carolina	624	2.8	4,391	2.3	7	67.6	15,387	539.1	2.2	864,000
Virginia	507	2.3	4,198	2.2	8	70.6	16,808	538.0	2.2	1,061,061
Wisconsin	543	2.4	4,488	2.4	8	64.5	14,382	523.0	2.1	963,223
Maryland	377	1.7	3,706	2.0	10	58.7	15,852	506.8	2.0	1,344,379
Oregon	404	1.8	3,719	2.0	9	62.2	16,717	481.9	1.9	1,192,829
Missouri	419	1.9	3,720	2.0	9	56.9	15,288	449.1	1.8	1,071,905
Indiana	481	2.2	3,246	1.7	7	50.1	15,424	388.5	1.6	807,665
Connecticut	322	1.4	2,367	1.3	7	43.2	18,256	352.6	1.4	1,094,972
Tennessee	364	1.6	2,726	1.4	7	45.3	16,624	347.8	1.4	955,467
Utah	259	1.2	3,054	1.6	12	41.7	13,648	334.5	1.3	1,291,444
Alabama	316	1.4	1,871	1.0	6	28.9	15,455	256.6	1.0	812,180
Louisiana	227	1.0	1,606	0.9	7	26.2	16,335	250.5	1.0	1,103,335
South Carolina	293	1.3	1,802	1.0	6	31.2	17,295	249.8	1.0	852,512
Kentucky	269	1.2	1,853	1.0	7	27.4	14,807	246.0	1.0	914,487
New Hampshire	214	1.0	1,843	1.0	9	31.0	16,805	227.0	0.9	1,060,790
Idaho	223	1.0	1,899	1.0	9	26.4	13,895	210.8	0.8	945,170
Kansas	197	0.9	1,545	0.8	8	27.6	17,840	209.3	0.8	1,062,624
Oklahoma	200	0.9	1,387	0.7	7	21.5	15,529	191.2	0.8	955,850
Iowa	247	1.1	1,823	1.0	7	26.4	14,473	189.8	0.8	768,482
Nevada	147	0.7	1,489	0.8	10	24.8	16,674	184.2	0.7	1,252,830
Montana	188	0.8	1,567	0.8	8	22.6	14,425	172.2	0.7	915,819
Nebraska	140	0.6	1,572	0.8	11	24.5	15,574	170.6	0.7	1,218,314
Maine	166	0.7	1,297	0.7	8	21.4	16,483	154.5	0.6	930,699
Arkansas	237	1.1	1,106	0.6	5	16.4	14,799	135.6	0.5	571,966
Mississippi	176	0.8	1,000	0.5	6	15.5	15,486	131.6	0.5	747,807
Hawaii	129	0.6	1,073	0.6	8	16.5	15,404	128.2	0.5	993,473
New Mexico	156	0.7	1,059	0.6	7	15.3	14,455	118.4	0.5	759,173
Vermont	147	0.7	1,174	0.6	8	16.7	14,185	114.9	0.5	781,905
South Dakota	93	0.4	913	0.5	10	14.0	15,372	101.9	0.4	1,095,258
Alaska	98	0.4	592	0.3	6	11.7	19,775	96.7	0.4	986,888
Delaware	83	0.4	604	0.3	7	10.5	17,301	96.2	0.4	1,158,494
North Dakota	50	0.2	730	0.4	15	10.9	14,941	79.9	0.3	1,597,200
Rhode Island	85	0.4	507	0.3	6	9.6	18,874	72.5	0.3	853,353
Wyoming	108	0.5	622	0.3	6	9.1	14,558	64.1	0.3	593,389
West Virginia	127	0.6	576	0.3	5	7.9	13,764	63.7	0.3	501,583
Arizona	380	1.7	2500-4999	-	-	(D)	-	(D)	-	-
D.C.	12	0.1	100-249	-	-	(D)	-	(D)	-	-

Source: 2002 *Economic Census*. The states are in descending order of sales or establishments (if sales data are missing for the majority). The symbol (D) appears when data are withheld to prevent disclosure of competitive information. States marked with (D) are sorted by number of establishments. A dash (-) indicates that the data element cannot be calculated. Shaded *states* on the state map indicate those states which have proportionately greater representation in the industry than would be indicated by the states population; the ratio is based on total sales or number of establishments. Shaded *regions* indicate where the industry is regionally most concentrated.

NAICS 451120 - HOBBY, TOY, AND GAME STORES*

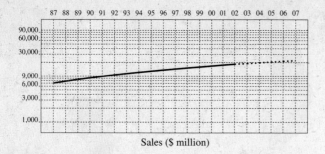

Sales ($ million)

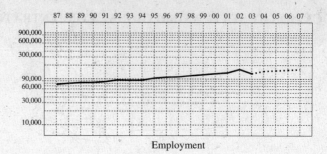

Employment

GENERAL STATISTICS

Year	Establishments (number)	Employment (number)	Payroll ($ million)	Sales ($ million)	Employees per Establishment (number)	Sales per Establishment ($)	Payroll per Employee ($)
1987	9,629	75,932	613.9	7,031.4	8	730,232	8,085
1988	9,213	79,867	714.8	7,750.5 e	9	841,257	8,950
1989	9,036	82,830	778.5	8,469.7 e	9	937,329	9,399
1990	9,378	83,121	834.0	9,188.9 e	9	979,836	10,034
1991	9,629	86,947	895.9	9,908.1 e	9	1,028,985	10,304
1992	10,860	94,804	991.9	10,627.3	9	978,573	10,463
1993	10,678	93,379	1,027.3	11,379.5 e	9	1,065,696	11,001
1994	10,402	93,976	1,127.1	12,131.7 e	9	1,166,285	11,994
1995	10,347	103,960	1,190.0	12,883.9 e	10	1,245,182	11,447
1996	10,970 e	109,346 e	1,249.6 e	13,636.1 e	10 e	1,243,036 e	11,428 e
1997	10,824	111,757	1,368.6	14,388.3	10	1,329,296	12,246
1998	10,921	118,584	1,581.9	15,188.5 e	11	1,390,764	13,340
1999	10,789	124,806	1,686.0	15,988.8 e	12	1,481,950	13,509
2000	10,911	131,456	1,775.3	16,789.0 e	12	1,538,722	13,505
2001	10,783	137,147	1,894.0	17,589.2 e	13	1,631,199	13,810
2002	12,467	163,137	2,009.8	18,389.5	13	1,475,050	12,320
2003	10,274	131,480	1,801.2	19,012.2 p	13	1,659,873 p	13,699
2004	11,560 p	148,452 p	2,054.5 p	19,768.5 p	13 p	1,714,980 p	14,495 p
2005	11,687 p	153,035 p	2,142.0 p	20,524.8 p	13 p	1,770,087 p	14,828 p
2006	11,814 p	157,618 p	2,229.5 p	21,281.1 p	14 p	1,825,194 p	15,161 p
2007	11,941 p	162,200 p	2,317.0 p	22,037.4 p	14 p	1,880,302 p	15,493 p

Sources: Economic Census of the United States, 1987, 1992, 1997, and 2002. Establishment counts, employment, and payroll are from *County Business Patterns* for non-Census years. Values followed by a 'p' are projections by the editors. Sales data for non-Census years are extrapolations, marked by 'e'. Data are the most recent available at this level of detail.

INDICES OF CHANGE

Year	Establishments (number)	Employment (number)	Payroll ($ million)	Sales ($ million)	Employees per Establishment (number)	Sales per Establishment ($)	Payroll per Employee ($)
1987	77.2	46.5	30.5	38.2	60.4	49.5	65.6
1992	87.1	58.1	49.4	57.8	66.5	66.3	84.9
1993	85.7	57.2	51.1	61.9 e	66.5	72.2	89.3
1994	83.4	57.6	56.1	66.0 e	68.8	79.1	97.4
1995	83.0	63.7	59.2	70.1 e	76.4	84.4	92.9
1996	88.0 e	67.0 e	62.2 e	74.2 e	76.4 e	84.3 e	92.8 e
1997	86.8	68.5	68.1	78.2	78.7	90.1	99.4
1998	87.6	72.7	78.7	82.6 e	83.3	94.3	108.3
1999	86.5	76.5	83.9	86.9 e	88.6	100.5	109.7
2000	87.5	80.6	88.3	91.3 e	91.7	104.3	109.6
2001	86.5	84.1	94.2	95.6 e	97.1	110.6	112.1
2002	100.0	100.0	100.0	100.0	100.0	100.0	100.0
2003	82.4	80.6	89.6	103.4 p	97.8	112.5 p	111.2
2004	92.7 p	91.0 p	102.2 p	107.5 p	99.5 p	116.3 p	117.7 p
2005	93.7 p	93.8 p	106.6 p	111.6 p	101.9 p	120.0 p	120.4 p
2006	94.8 p	96.6 p	110.9 p	115.7 p	104.3 p	123.7 p	123.1 p
2007	95.8 p	99.4 p	115.3 p	119.8 p	106.7 p	127.5 p	125.8 p

Sources: Same as General Statistics. The values shown reflect change from the base year, 2002. Values above 100 mean greater than 2002, values below 100 mean less than 2002, and a value of 100 in the 1987-2001 or 2003-2007 period means same as 2002. Values followed by a 'p' are projections by the editors; 'e' stands for extrapolation. Data are the most recent available at this level of detail.

SELECTED RATIOS

For 2002	Avg. of All Retail	Analyzed Industry	Index	For 2002	Avg. of All Retail	Analyzed Industry	Index
Employees per Establishment	17	13	77	Sales per Employee	174,682	112,724	65
Payroll per Establishment	333,445	161,211	48	Sales per Establishment	3,332,269	1,475,050	44
Payroll per Employee	20,311	12,320	61	Expenses per Establishment	na	na	na

Sources: Same as General Statistics. The 'Average of All' column, Wholesale or Retail, represents the average of the sector reported for the most recent complete year available. The Index shows the relationship between the Average and the Analyzed Industry. For example, 100 means that they are equal; 500 that the Analyzed Industry is five times the average; 50 means that the Analyzed Industry is half the national average. The abbreviation 'na' is used to show that data are 'not available'.

*Equivalent to SIC 5945.

LEADING COMPANIES Number shown: **19**   Total sales ($ mil): **18,926**   Total employment (000): **142.4**

Company Name	Address				CEO Name	Phone	Co. Type	Sales ($ mil)	Empl. (000)
Toys 'R' Us Inc.	1 Geoffrey Way	Wayne	NJ	07470	John Barbour	973-617-3500	P	11,566	65.0
Michaels Stores Inc.	PO Box 619566	Dallas	TX	75261		972-409-1300	P	3,393	38.8
KB Holdings L.L.C.	100 West St	Pittsfield	MA	01201	Michael L Glazer	413-496-3000	S	1,500*	15.0
Hobby Lobby Stores Inc.	7707 SW 44th St	Oklahoma City	OK	73179	David Green	405-745-1100	R	1,297	15.0
Brookstone Inc.	1 Innovation Way	Merrimack	NH	03054	Michael F Anthony	603-880-9500	P	434	2.9
A.C. Moore Inc.	500 University Ct	Blackwood	NJ	08012	Lawrence Fine	856-228-6700	S	276*	1.0
Paradies Shops Inc.	5950 Fulton Ind SW	Atlanta	GA	30336	Dick Dickson	404-344-7905	R	135*	1.5
Rag Shops Inc.	111 Wagaraw Rd	Hawthorne	NJ	07506	Ronald S Staffieri	973-423-1303	S	116	1.4
Paper Warehouse Inc.	7630 Excelsior Blvd	Minneapolis	MN	55426	Yale T Dolginow	952-936-1000	P	75	0.9
Fabric Place	136 Howard St	Framingham	MA	01701		508-872-4888	R	57*	0.5
Mary Maxim Inc.	PO Box 5019	Port Huron	MI	48061	Larry McPhedrain	810-987-2000	R	31*	0.2
Bally Bead Company Inc.	2304 Ridge Rd	Rockwall	TX	75087	Ward Hudspeth	972-771-4515	R	16*	<0.1
Quality Accents Inc.	707 N Main St	Mishawaka	IN	46545	Marlene Hollencamp	574-254-1600	R	12*	<0.1
Carol School Supply Inc.	17928 Union Tpke	Flushing	NY	11366	Carol Pick	718-380-4203	R	9*	<0.1
Toys and Treasures International	1706 S Western Ave	Sioux Falls	SD	57105	Sharon Busch	605-339-2226	R	4*	<0.1
Broadway Photo Video Retail	777 Bloomfield Ave	Caldwell	NJ	07006	Vicky Feinsilver	973-226-1313	R	2*	<0.1
Huckleberry Press L.L.C.	PO Box 51772	Durham	NC	27717	Noreen Woltz		R	2*	<0.1
Total Identity Corp.	1007 N Federal	Fort Lauderdale	FL	33304	Matthew P Dwyer		P	1	<0.1
St Louis Crafts Inc.	7606 Idaho Ave	Saint Louis	MO	63111	Edward Nussbaumer	314-638-0038	R	1*	<0.1

Source: Ward's Business Directory of U.S. Private and Public Companies, Volumes 1 and 2, 2005. The company type code used is as follows: P - Public, R - Private, S - Subsidiary, D - Division, J - Joint Venture, A - Affiliate, G - Group. Sales are in millions of dollars, employees are in thousands. An asterisk (*) indicates an estimated sales volume. The symbol < stands for 'less than'. Company names and addresses are truncated, in some cases, to fit into the available space.

OCCUPATIONS EMPLOYED BY HOBBY, TOY, SEWING, & MUSICAL INSTRUMENT STORES

Occupation	% of Total 2004	Change to 2014	Occupation	% of Total 2004	Change to 2014
Retail salespersons	42.2	19.1	Musical instrument repairers & tuners	1.6	7.0
Cashiers, except gaming	23.6	7.2	Self-enrichment education teachers	1.4	19.0
First-line supervisors/managers of retail sales workers	8.3	9.6	Office clerks, general	1.3	6.0
Stock clerks & order fillers	2.3	-8.8	Shipping, receiving, & traffic clerks	1.1	7.8
General & operations managers	1.7	17.9	Customer service representatives	1.1	21.9
Laborers & freight, stock, & material movers, hand	1.6	7.2	Bookkeeping, accounting, & auditing clerks	1.1	7.2

Source: Industry-Occupation Matrix, Bureau of Labor Statistics. These data are reported based on 4-digit NAICS categories but have been matched to corresponding 6-digit NAICS industry codes. The change reported for each occupation to the year 2014 is a percent of growth or decline as estimated by the Bureau of Labor Statistics. The abbreviation nec stands for 'not elsewhere classified.'

LOCATION BY STATE AND REGIONAL CONCENTRATION

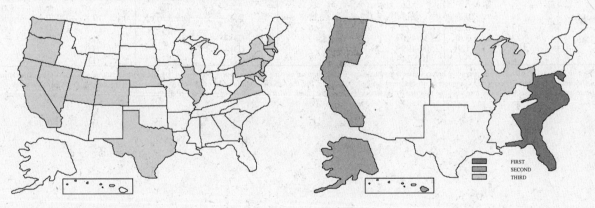

FIRST
SECOND
THIRD

INDUSTRY DATA BY STATE

State	Establishments Total (number)	% of U.S.	Employment Total (number)	% of U.S.	Per Estab.	Payroll Total ($ mil.)	Per Empl. ($)	Sales Total ($ mil.)	% of U.S.	Per Estab. ($)
California	1,159	11.2	17,020	11.7	15	222.7	13,086	1,986.7	12.3	1,714,190
New York	635	6.1	8,387	5.8	13	129.2	15,406	1,299.0	8.0	2,045,605
Texas	597	5.7	9,848	6.8	16	125.1	12,707	1,142.3	7.1	1,913,370
New Jersey	406	3.9	5,825	4.0	14	85.3	14,638	836.6	5.2	2,060,591

Continued on next page.

INDUSTRY DATA BY STATE - Continued

State	Establishments Total (number)	% of U.S.	Employment Total (number)	% of U.S.	Per Estab.	Payroll Total ($ mil.)	Per Empl. ($)	Sales Total ($ mil.)	% of U.S.	Per Estab. ($)
Florida	539	5.2	7,546	5.2	14	86.0	11,393	824.6	5.1	1,529,946
Pennsylvania	473	4.6	6,883	4.7	15	82.8	12,029	810.5	5.0	1,713,510
Illinois	451	4.3	6,849	4.7	15	85.9	12,547	799.3	4.9	1,772,395
Ohio	421	4.1	6,089	4.2	14	70.4	11,559	638.8	3.9	1,517,380
Massachusetts	277	2.7	4,379	3.0	16	59.1	13,504	497.2	3.1	1,795,018
Virginia	304	2.9	4,746	3.3	16	55.6	11,707	469.7	2.9	1,545,056
Maryland	202	1.9	3,569	2.5	18	45.8	12,836	433.8	2.7	2,147,376
Georgia	238	2.3	3,773	2.6	16	43.4	11,496	372.3	2.3	1,564,420
North Carolina	280	2.7	3,371	2.3	12	41.4	12,273	355.7	2.2	1,270,196
Washington	328	3.2	3,545	2.4	11	46.1	13,011	350.9	2.2	1,069,869
Colorado	244	2.3	2,998	2.1	12	38.8	12,951	331.9	2.0	1,360,057
Indiana	239	2.3	3,054	2.1	13	34.0	11,147	312.2	1.9	1,306,142
Missouri	224	2.2	2,932	2.0	13	32.7	11,154	298.4	1.8	1,332,348
Connecticut	172	1.7	2,242	1.5	13	31.7	14,153	285.5	1.8	1,659,797
Wisconsin	243	2.3	2,980	2.1	12	30.3	10,184	260.4	1.6	1,071,564
Tennessee	210	2.0	2,600	1.8	12	28.5	10,967	253.0	1.6	1,204,881
Minnesota	187	1.8	2,941	2.0	16	29.5	10,019	237.4	1.5	1,269,465
Oregon	186	1.8	2,062	1.4	11	25.6	12,437	202.6	1.3	1,089,258
Louisiana	117	1.1	1,965	1.4	17	20.6	10,503	185.3	1.1	1,584,060
Oklahoma	107	1.0	1,581	1.1	15	18.0	11,399	162.5	1.0	1,518,364
Kansas	97	0.9	1,559	1.1	16	17.2	11,024	153.3	0.9	1,580,320
Alabama	107	1.0	1,383	1.0	13	16.1	11,625	147.8	0.9	1,381,355
New Hampshire	98	0.9	1,232	0.8	13	15.2	12,307	146.9	0.9	1,498,796
Utah	115	1.1	1,811	1.2	16	17.2	9,518	144.9	0.9	1,259,652
South Carolina	133	1.3	1,586	1.1	12	15.7	9,916	141.1	0.9	1,061,008
Iowa	118	1.1	1,498	1.0	13	15.1	10,055	136.3	0.8	1,155,178
Kentucky	99	1.0	1,338	0.9	14	15.3	11,463	134.3	0.8	1,356,283
Nebraska	74	0.7	931	0.6	13	10.7	11,463	112.7	0.7	1,522,419
Nevada	77	0.7	989	0.7	13	13.1	13,241	109.6	0.7	1,423,506
Arkansas	61	0.6	958	0.7	16	10.5	10,950	94.1	0.6	1,541,984
Delaware	35	0.3	507	0.3	14	7.8	15,327	81.9	0.5	2,339,086
New Mexico	58	0.6	757	0.5	13	9.3	12,239	79.8	0.5	1,375,845
Hawaii	58	0.6	520	0.4	9	7.3	13,952	69.9	0.4	1,204,931
Mississippi	48	0.5	773	0.5	16	7.4	9,512	69.9	0.4	1,455,479
West Virginia	41	0.4	680	0.5	17	6.6	9,675	64.9	0.4	1,581,902
Idaho	66	0.6	789	0.5	12	7.5	9,451	60.1	0.4	910,591
Maine	58	0.6	505	0.3	9	6.1	12,004	54.5	0.3	939,034
Rhode Island	50	0.5	460	0.3	9	6.1	13,283	51.4	0.3	1,027,220
Alaska	35	0.3	300	0.2	9	4.2	13,883	39.4	0.2	1,126,600
Montana	53	0.5	439	0.3	8	6.3	14,276	37.9	0.2	714,887
South Dakota	32	0.3	401	0.3	13	3.8	9,524	34.8	0.2	1,087,219
Vermont	23	0.2	244	0.2	11	2.5	10,078	23.5	0.1	1,020,478
North Dakota	24	0.2	262	0.2	11	2.4	9,126	19.8	0.1	825,667
Wyoming	17	0.2	105	0.1	6	1.3	12,543	11.5	0.1	677,235
Michigan	372	3.6	2500-4999	-	-	(D)	-	(D)	-	-
Arizona	195	1.9	2500-4999	-	-	(D)	-	(D)	-	-
D.C.	9	0.1	100-249	-	-	(D)	-	(D)	-	-

Source: 2002 *Economic Census*. The states are in descending order of sales or establishments (if sales data are missing for the majority). The symbol (D) appears when data are withheld to prevent disclosure of competitive information. States marked with (D) are sorted by number of establishments. A dash (-) indicates that the data element cannot be calculated. Shaded *states* on the state map indicate those states which have proportionately greater representation in the industry than would be indicated by the states population; the ratio is based on total sales or number of establishments. Shaded *regions* indicate where the industry is regionally most concentrated.

NAICS 451130 - SEWING, NEEDLEWORK, AND PIECE GOODS STORES

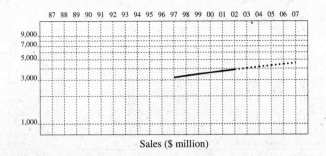

Sales ($ million)

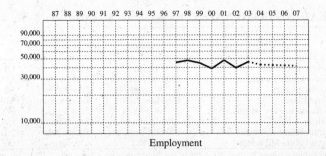

Employment

GENERAL STATISTICS

Year	Establishments (number)	Employment (number)	Payroll ($ million)	Sales ($ million)	Employees per Establishment (number)	Sales per Establishment ($)	Payroll per Employee ($)
1987	-	-	-	-	-	-	-
1988	-	-	-	-	-	-	-
1989	-	-	-	-	-	-	-
1990	-	-	-	-	-	-	-
1991	-	-	-	-	-	-	-
1992	-	-	-	-	-	-	-
1993	-	-	-	-	-	-	-
1994	-	-	-	-	-	-	-
1995	-	-	-	-	-	-	-
1996	-	-	-	-	-	-	-
1997	6,590	45,351	494.8	3,182.9	7	482,989	10,911
1998	6,217	47,784	499.3	3,324.7 e	8	534,773	10,449
1999	5,888	44,797	521.2	3,466.5 e	8	588,735	11,635
2000	5,695	38,952	507.2	3,608.3 e	7	633,583	13,020
2001	5,543	47,960	602.3	3,750.0 e	9	676,536	12,557
2002	5,413	39,606	525.1	3,891.8	7	718,977	13,257
2003	5,513	46,029	564.5	4,033.6 p	8	770,940 p	12,265
2004	5,096 p	42,760 p	579.5 p	4,175.4 p	8 p	818,085 p	13,528 p
2005	4,911 p	42,361 p	591.7 p	4,317.2 p	8 p	865,230 p	13,906 p
2006	4,726 p	41,963 p	603.9 p	4,459.0 p	9 p	912,375 p	14,285 p
2007	4,541 p	41,564 p	616.1 p	4,600.7 p	9 p	959,520 p	14,664 p

Source: Economic Census of the United States, 1997 and 2002. Establishment counts, employment, and payroll are from *County Business Patterns* for non-Census years. This is a newly defined industry. Data for prior years are unavailable at the time of publication but may become available over time. Values followed by 'p' are projections by the editors. Sales data for non-Census years are extrapolations, marked by 'e'.

INDICES OF CHANGE

Year	Establishments (number)	Employment (number)	Payroll ($ million)	Sales ($ million)	Employees per Establishment (number)	Sales per Establishment ($)	Payroll per Employee ($)
1987	-	-	-	-	-	-	-
1992	-	-	-	-	-	-	-
1993	-	-	-	-	-	-	-
1994	-	-	-	-	-	-	-
1995	-	-	-	-	-	-	-
1996	-	-	-	-	-	-	-
1997	121.7	114.5	94.2	81.8	94.3	67.2	82.3
1998	114.9	120.6	95.1	85.4 e	105.2	74.4	78.8
1999	108.8	113.1	99.3	89.1 e	103.9	81.9	87.8
2000	105.2	98.3	96.6	92.7 e	92.9	88.1	98.2
2001	102.4	121.1	114.7	96.4 e	118.9	94.1	94.7
2002	100.0	100.0	100.0	100.0	100.0	100.0	100.0
2003	101.8	116.2	107.5	103.6 p	114.1	107.2 p	92.5
2004	94.2 p	108.0 p	110.4 p	107.3 p	113.3 p	113.8 p	102.0 p
2005	90.7 p	107.0 p	112.7 p	110.9 p	115.6 p	120.3 p	104.9 p
2006	87.3 p	106.0 p	115.0 p	114.6 p	117.9 p	126.9 p	107.8 p
2007	83.9 p	104.9 p	117.3 p	118.2 p	120.2 p	133.5 p	110.6 p

Sources: Same as General Statistics. The values shown reflect change from the base year, 2002. Values above 100 mean greater than 2002, values below 100 mean less than 2002, and a value of 100 in the 1987-2001 or 2003-2007 period means same as 2002. Values followed by a 'p' are projections by the editors; 'e' stands for extrapolation. Data are the most recent available at this level of detail.

SELECTED RATIOS

For 2002	Avg. of All Retail	Analyzed Industry	Index	For 2002	Avg. of All Retail	Analyzed Industry	Index
Employees per Establishment	17	7	43	Sales per Employee	174,682	98,263	56
Payroll per Establishment	333,445	97,000	29	Sales per Establishment	3,332,269	718,977	22
Payroll per Employee	20,311	13,257	65	Expenses per Establishment	na	na	na

Sources: Same as General Statistics. The 'Average of All' column, Wholesale or Retail, represents the average of the sector reported for the most recent complete year available. The Index shows the relationship between the Average and the Analyzed Industry. For example, 100 means that they are equal; 500 that the Analyzed Industry is five times the average; 50 means that the Analyzed Industry is half the national average. The abbreviation 'na' is used to show that data are 'not available'.

LEADING COMPANIES   Number shown: **8**   Total sales ($ mil): **2,462**   Total employment (000): **30.1**

Company Name	Address				CEO Name	Phone	Co. Type	Sales ($ mil)	Empl. (000)
Jo-Ann Stores Inc.	5555 Darrow Rd	Hudson	OH	44236		330-656-2600	P	1,812	21.7
Hancock Fabrics Inc.	3406 W Main St	Tupelo	MS	38801	Jane F Aggers	662-842-2834	P	427	6.4
Rag Shops Inc.	111 Wagaraw Rd	Hawthorne	NJ	07506	Ronald S Staffieri	973-423-1303	S	116	1.4
Fabric Place	136 Howard St	Framingham	MA	01701		508-872-4888	R	57*	0.5
Beckenstein Men's Fabrics Inc.	257 W 39th St	New York	NY	10018	Neal Boyarsky	212-475-6666	R	29*	<0.1
Quilt In A Day	1955 Diamond St	San Marcos	CA	92069	Eleanor Burns	760-591-0929	R	8*	<0.1
Martha Pullen Company Inc.	149 Old Big Cove	Brownsboro	AL	35741		256-533-9586	R	8*	<0.1
Home Fabric Mills Inc.	PO Box 888	Cheshire	CT	06410	Glenda Kirby	203-272-3529	R	6*	<0.1

Source: Ward's Business Directory of U.S. Private and Public Companies, Volumes 1 and 2, 2005. The company type code used is as follows: P - Public, R - Private, S - Subsidiary, D - Division, J - Joint Venture, A - Affiliate, G - Group. Sales are in millions of dollars, employees are in thousands. An asterisk (*) indicates an estimated sales volume. The symbol < stands for 'less than'. Company names and addresses are truncated, in some cases, to fit into the available space.

OCCUPATIONS EMPLOYED BY HOBBY, TOY, SEWING, & MUSICAL INSTRUMENT STORES

Occupation	% of Total 2004	Change to 2014	Occupation	% of Total 2004	Change to 2014
Retail salespersons	42.2	19.1	Musical instrument repairers & tuners	1.6	7.0
Cashiers, except gaming	23.6	7.2	Self-enrichment education teachers	1.4	19.0
First-line supervisors/managers of retail sales workers	8.3	9.6	Office clerks, general	1.3	6.0
Stock clerks & order fillers	2.3	-8.8	Shipping, receiving, & traffic clerks	1.1	7.8
General & operations managers	1.7	17.9	Customer service representatives	1.1	21.9
Laborers & freight, stock, & material movers, hand	1.6	7.2	Bookkeeping, accounting, & auditing clerks	1.1	7.2

Source: Industry-Occupation Matrix, Bureau of Labor Statistics. These data are reported based on 4-digit NAICS categories but have been matched to corresponding 6-digit NAICS industry codes. The change reported for each occupation to the year 2014 is a percent of growth or decline as estimated by the Bureau of Labor Statistics. The abbreviation nec stands for 'not elsewhere classified.'

LOCATION BY STATE AND REGIONAL CONCENTRATION

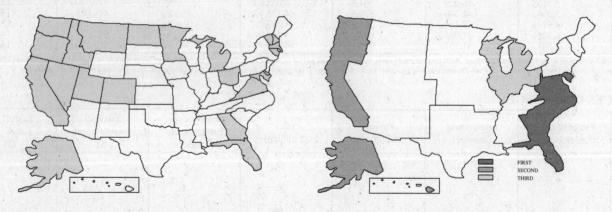

INDUSTRY DATA BY STATE

State	Establishments Total (number)	% of U.S.	Employment Total (number)	% of U.S.	Per Estab.	Payroll Total ($ mil.)	Per Empl. ($)	Sales Total ($ mil.)	% of U.S.	Per Estab. ($)
California	614	11.3	5,056	12.6	8	74.8	14,799	544.5	13.9	886,831
New York	339	6.2	2,369	5.9	7	38.8	16,390	258.3	6.6	762,044
Texas	336	6.2	2,415	6.0	7	30.6	12,658	236.6	6.0	704,143
Florida	307	5.7	1,803	4.5	6	27.5	15,258	221.2	5.7	720,664
Michigan	212	3.9	1,987	5.0	9	24.0	12,093	198.4	5.1	935,840
Ohio	221	4.1	1,721	4.3	8	20.5	11,895	176.9	4.5	800,593
Illinois	210	3.9	1,599	4.0	8	19.3	12,059	145.2	3.7	691,576
Washington	178	3.3	1,406	3.5	8	17.0	12,080	140.2	3.6	787,511
Pennsylvania	196	3.6	1,261	3.1	6	14.8	11,764	128.3	3.3	654,811
Minnesota	138	2.5	1,390	3.5	10	15.1	10,865	119.9	3.1	868,754
Virginia	155	2.9	1,237	3.1	8	16.7	13,462	113.1	2.9	729,994
Georgia	133	2.5	1,028	2.6	8	17.3	16,789	112.4	2.9	845,120
Massachusetts	123	2.3	984	2.5	8	16.1	16,351	109.9	2.8	893,122
Maryland	95	1.8	1,015	2.5	11	14.6	14,425	103.7	2.7	1,091,632
Oregon	107	2.0	1,055	2.6	10	12.7	11,994	86.5	2.2	807,981

Continued on next page.

INDUSTRY DATA BY STATE - Continued

State	Establishments Total (number)	% of U.S.	Employment Total (number)	% of U.S.	Per Estab.	Payroll Total ($ mil.)	Per Empl. ($)	Sales Total ($ mil.)	% of U.S.	Per Estab. ($)
North Carolina	141	2.6	918	2.3	7	13.7	14,919	80.9	2.1	573,830
Indiana	123	2.3	802	2.0	7	9.3	11,600	76.3	2.0	620,366
Connecticut	72	1.3	552	1.4	8	11.2	20,259	75.9	1.9	1,053,556
New Jersey	104	1.9	642	1.6	6	9.7	15,174	71.9	1.8	691,721
Wisconsin	135	2.5	925	2.3	7	8.9	9,623	71.0	1.8	526,000
Colorado	95	1.8	807	2.0	8	10.3	12,782	63.6	1.6	669,421
Tennessee	106	2.0	729	1.8	7	9.7	13,244	61.9	1.6	584,085
Missouri	93	1.7	653	1.6	7	7.4	11,368	54.6	1.4	587,538
Utah	82	1.5	612	1.5	7	6.5	10,592	50.6	1.3	616,634
Louisiana	63	1.2	468	1.2	7	5.9	12,690	39.4	1.0	625,095
Alabama	75	1.4	466	1.2	6	6.0	12,921	38.1	1.0	508,173
Kansas	75	1.4	456	1.1	6	4.8	10,564	36.4	0.9	484,827
Iowa	87	1.6	477	1.2	5	4.1	8,669	34.7	0.9	398,678
Nevada	35	0.6	284	0.7	8	4.1	14,472	31.8	0.8	909,171
South Carolina	77	1.4	495	1.2	6	5.8	11,725	31.2	0.8	405,571
Oklahoma	56	1.0	408	1.0	7	4.5	10,926	31.0	0.8	554,286
Kentucky	54	1.0	387	1.0	7	4.7	12,209	30.6	0.8	566,500
New Hampshire	40	0.7	250	0.6	6	4.0	16,052	28.2	0.7	706,150
Idaho	43	0.8	266	0.7	6	2.5	9,372	24.1	0.6	560,814
Montana	40	0.7	251	0.6	6	2.0	7,869	18.8	0.5	469,725
Alaska	25	0.5	151	0.4	6	1.8	11,921	18.5	0.5	740,720
Nebraska	41	0.8	270	0.7	7	2.3	8,422	17.6	0.5	429,512
Arkansas	42	0.8	264	0.7	6	3.1	11,705	17.5	0.4	415,571
Maine	35	0.6	169	0.4	5	2.1	12,420	17.0	0.4	485,343
New Mexico	37	0.7	172	0.4	5	1.9	11,326	16.1	0.4	434,649
Mississippi	37	0.7	217	0.5	6	2.8	12,737	14.6	0.4	393,973
Vermont	24	0.4	115	0.3	5	1.8	15,583	13.7	0.4	571,000
Delaware	13	0.2	108	0.3	8	1.4	12,889	12.1	0.3	929,077
North Dakota	21	0.4	155	0.4	7	1.5	9,542	11.6	0.3	551,429
West Virginia	23	0.4	110	0.3	5	1.5	13,282	9.8	0.3	427,043
South Dakota	18	0.3	87	0.2	5	1.0	11,586	8.1	0.2	449,278
Wyoming	28	0.5	99	0.2	4	0.8	8,071	5.8	0.1	207,357
Hawaii	10	0.2	72	0.2	7	0.9	12,792	4.8	0.1	475,100
Arizona	92	1.7	500-999	-	-	(D)	-	(D)	-	-
Rhode Island	14	0.3	100-249	-	-	(D)	-	(D)	-	-
D.C.	7	0.1	20-99	-	-	(D)	-	(D)	-	-

Source: 2002 *Economic Census*. The states are in descending order of sales or establishments (if sales data are missing for the majority). The symbol (D) appears when data are withheld to prevent disclosure of competitive information. States marked with (D) are sorted by number of establishments. A dash (-) indicates that the data element cannot be calculated. Shaded *states* on the state map indicate those states which have proportionately greater representation in the industry than would be indicated by the states population; the ratio is based on total sales or number of establishments. Shaded *regions* indicate where the industry is regionally most concentrated.

NAICS 451140 - MUSICAL INSTRUMENT AND SUPPLIES STORES*

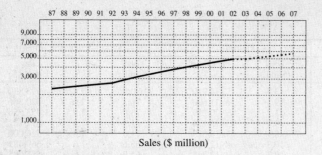

Sales ($ million)

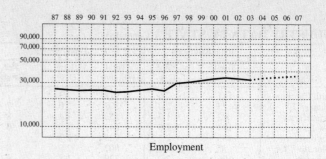

Employment

GENERAL STATISTICS

Year	Establishments (number)	Employment (number)	Payroll ($ million)	Sales ($ million)	Employees per Establishment (number)	Sales per Establishment ($)	Payroll per Employee ($)
1987	4,690	25,748	351.9	2,321.2	6	494,925	13,667
1988	4,406	25,133	383.2	2,393.9 e	6	543,327	15,247
1989	4,224	24,660	386.1	2,466.7 e	6	583,972	15,657
1990	4,253	24,854	404.6	2,539.4 e	6	597,084	16,279
1991	4,270	24,853	410.8	2,612.1 e	6	611,733	16,529
1992	4,149	23,605	402.6	2,684.8	6	647,096	17,056
1993	4,142	23,979	429.0	2,908.0 e	6	702,076	17,891
1994	4,138	24,916	462.9	3,131.2 e	6	756,694	18,578
1995	4,097	25,749	501.2	3,354.3 e	6	818,721	19,465
1996	3,976 e	24,562 e	491.4 e	3,577.5 e	6 e	899,774 e	20,007 e
1997	4,477	29,675	567.4	3,800.7	7	848,939	19,121
1998	4,505	30,498	655.8	4,027.8 e	7	894,082	21,503
1999	4,429	31,761	700.1	4,255.0 e	7	960,709	22,043
2000	4,391	33,211	752.7	4,482.1 e	8	1,020,752	22,665
2001	4,358	34,142	765.9	4,709.3 e	8	1,080,601	22,433
2002	4,462	33,338	737.5	4,936.4	7	1,106,320	22,120
2003	4,417	32,396	752.7	4,945.8 p	7	1,133,844 p	23,235
2004	4,359 p	33,754 p	801.7 p	5,129.1 p	8 p	1,174,834 p	24,247 p
2005	4,364 p	34,413 p	830.9 p	5,312.4 p	8 p	1,215,824 p	24,826 p
2006	4,368 p	35,071 p	860.2 p	5,495.7 p	8 p	1,256,815 p	25,406 p
2007	4,373 p	35,730 p	889.4 p	5,679.0 p	8 p	1,297,805 p	25,986 p

Sources: Economic Census of the United States, 1987, 1992, 1997, and 2002. Establishment counts, employment, and payroll are from County Business Patterns for non-Census years. Values followed by a 'p' are projections by the editors. Sales data for non-Census years are extrapolations, marked by 'e'. Data are the most recent available at this level of detail.

INDICES OF CHANGE

Year	Establishments (number)	Employment (number)	Payroll ($ million)	Sales ($ million)	Employees per Establishment (number)	Sales per Establishment ($)	Payroll per Employee ($)
1987	105.1	77.2	47.7	47.0	73.6	44.7	61.8
1992	93.0	70.8	54.6	54.4	76.3	58.5	77.1
1993	92.8	71.9	58.2	58.9 e	77.6	63.5	80.9
1994	92.7	74.7	62.8	63.4 e	80.3	68.4	84.0
1995	91.8	77.2	68.0	68.0 e	84.3	74.0	88.0
1996	89.1 e	73.7 e	66.6 e	72.5 e	83.0 e	81.3 e	90.4 e
1997	100.3	89.0	76.9	77.0	88.3	76.7	86.4
1998	101.0	91.5	88.9	81.6 e	91.0	80.8	97.2
1999	99.3	95.3	94.9	86.2 e	96.4	86.8	99.6
2000	98.4	99.6	102.1	90.8 e	101.7	92.3	102.5
2001	97.7	102.4	103.9	95.4 e	104.4	97.7	101.4
2002	100.0	100.0	100.0	100.0	100.0	100.0	100.0
2003	99.0	97.2	102.1	100.2 p	98.2	102.5 p	105.0
2004	97.7 p	101.2 p	108.7 p	103.9 p	103.5 p	106.2 p	109.6 p
2005	97.8 p	103.2 p	112.7 p	107.6 p	105.4 p	109.9 p	112.2 p
2006	97.9 p	105.2 p	116.6 p	111.3 p	107.3 p	113.6 p	114.9 p
2007	98.0 p	107.2 p	120.6 p	115.0 p	109.3 p	117.3 p	117.5 p

Sources: Same as General Statistics. The values shown reflect change from the base year, 2002. Values above 100 mean greater than 2002, values below 100 mean less than 2002, and a value of 100 in the 1987-2001 or 2003-2007 period means same as 2002. Values followed by a 'p' are projections by the editors; 'e' stands for extrapolation. Data are the most recent available at this level of detail.

SELECTED RATIOS

For 2002	Avg. of All Retail	Analyzed Industry	Index	For 2002	Avg. of All Retail	Analyzed Industry	Index
Employees per Establishment	17	7	44	Sales per Employee	174,682	148,071	85
Payroll per Establishment	333,445	165,274	50	Sales per Establishment	3,332,269	1,106,320	33
Payroll per Employee	20,311	22,120	109	Expenses per Establishment	na	na	na

Sources: Same as General Statistics. The 'Average of All' column, Wholesale or Retail, represents the average of the sector reported for the most recent complete year available. The Index shows the relationship between the Average and the Analyzed Industry. For example, 100 means that they are equal; 500 that the Analyzed Industry is five times the average; 50 means that the Analyzed Industry is half the national average. The abbreviation 'na' is used to show that data are 'not available'.

*Equivalent to SIC 5736.

LEADING COMPANIES   Number shown: **19**   Total sales ($ mil): **2,036**   Total employment (000): **9.4**

Company Name	Address				CEO Name	Phone	Co. Type	Sales ($ mil)	Empl. (000)
Guitar Center Inc.	5795 Lindero	Westlake Village	CA	91362	Marty Albertson	818-735-8800	P	1,513	6.4
Sam Ash Music Corp.	PO Box 9047	Hicksville	NY	11802	Richard Ash	516-932-6400	R	233*	0.7
Baldwin Piano Inc.	309 Plus Park Blvd	Nashville	TN	37217	Henry E Juszkiewicz	615-871-4500	S	86*	1.5
Cascio Music Company Inc.	13819 W National	New Berlin	WI	53151	Michael Cascio	262-786-6249	R	77*	0.1
J.W. Pepper and Son Inc.	2480 Industrial Blvd	Paoli	PA	19301	Greg Burtch	610-648-0500	R	26*	0.1
Sherman, Clay and Co.	1111 Bayhill Dr	San Bruno	CA	94066	Fred Concklin	650-952-2300	R	22*	0.1
Washington Music Sales Center	11151 Viers Mill Rd	Wheaton	MD	20902		301-946-8808	R	21*	<0.1
Manny's Music	156 W 48th St	New York	NY	10036		212-819-0576	R	16*	<0.1
Edwin F Kalmus Company Inc.	PO Box 5011	Boca Raton	FL	33431	Leon Galison	561-241-6340	R	11*	<0.1
Piano and Organ Distributors Inc.	2403 New Raleigh	Durham	NC	27703	Bill Boyce	919-596-2105	R	6*	<0.1
Candyman Ltd.	851 St Michael's Dr	Santa Fe	NM	87501		505-983-9309	R	5*	<0.1
Howren Music Co.	9814 Monroe Rd	Charlotte	NC	28209	Gregory J Howren	704-847-4255	R	5*	<0.1
Day Music Co.	5516 SE Foster Rd	Portland	OR	97206	Robert C Day	503-775-4351	R	3*	<0.1
E.E. Forbes and Sons Piano Inc.	3048 Montgomery	Homewood	AL	35209	French Forbes Jr	205-879-4154	R	3*	<0.1
Jeffers Handbell Supply Inc.	455 Western Ln	Irmo	SC	29063	Connie Jeffers	803-781-0555	R	2*	<0.1
Matt Umanov Guitars	273 Bleecker St	New York	NY	10014	Matt Umanov	212-675-2157	R	2*	<0.1
Paragon Music Center Inc.	2119 W Hillsboro	Tampa	FL	33603	Dick Rumore	813-876-3459	R	2*	<0.1
West L.A. Music	11345 Santa Monica	Los Angeles	CA	90025	Don Griffin	310-477-1945	R	2*	<0.1
Consignment Music	4040 Park Ave	Memphis	TN	38111	Joe Nathan	901-458-2094	R	1*	<0.1

Source: *Ward's Business Directory of U.S. Private and Public Companies*, Volumes 1 and 2, 2005. The company type code used is as follows: P - Public, R - Private, S - Subsidiary, D - Division, J - Joint Venture, A - Affiliate, G - Group. Sales are in millions of dollars, employees are in thousands. An asterisk (*) indicates an estimated sales volume. The symbol < stands for 'less than'. Company names and addresses are truncated, in some cases, to fit into the available space.

OCCUPATIONS EMPLOYED BY HOBBY, TOY, SEWING, & MUSICAL INSTRUMENT STORES

Occupation	% of Total 2004	Change to 2014	Occupation	% of Total 2004	Change to 2014
Retail salespersons	42.2	19.1	Musical instrument repairers & tuners	1.6	7.0
Cashiers, except gaming	23.6	7.2	Self-enrichment education teachers	1.4	19.0
First-line supervisors/managers of retail sales workers	8.3	9.6	Office clerks, general	1.3	6.0
Stock clerks & order fillers	2.3	-8.8	Shipping, receiving, & traffic clerks	1.1	7.8
General & operations managers	1.7	17.9	Customer service representatives	1.1	21.9
Laborers & freight, stock, & material movers, hand	1.6	7.2	Bookkeeping, accounting, & auditing clerks	1.1	7.2

Source: *Industry-Occupation Matrix*, Bureau of Labor Statistics. These data are reported based on 4-digit NAICS categories but have been matched to corresponding 6-digit NAICS industry codes. The change reported for each occupation to the year 2014 is a percent of growth or decline as estimated by the Bureau of Labor Statistics. The abbreviation nec stands for 'not elsewhere classified.'

LOCATION BY STATE AND REGIONAL CONCENTRATION

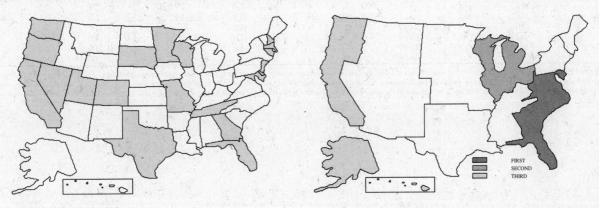

INDUSTRY DATA BY STATE

State	Establishments Total (number)	% of U.S.	Employment Total (number)	% of U.S.	Per Estab.	Payroll Total ($ mil.)	Per Empl. ($)	Sales Total ($ mil.)	% of U.S.	Per Estab. ($)
California	482	10.7	3,866	11.4	8	90.9	23,505	692.6	13.8	1,436,878
Texas	260	5.8	2,502	7.4	10	62.6	25,019	403.6	8.1	1,552,250
New York	243	5.4	1,642	4.8	7	38.0	23,121	314.2	6.3	1,293,123
Florida	258	5.8	1,781	5.3	7	39.0	21,894	279.0	5.6	1,081,450

Continued on next page.

INDUSTRY DATA BY STATE - Continued

State	Establishments Total (number)	% of U.S.	Employment Total (number)	% of U.S.	Per Estab.	Payroll Total ($ mil.)	Per Empl. ($)	Sales Total ($ mil.)	% of U.S.	Per Estab. ($)
Illinois	201	4.5	1,558	4.6	8	32.0	20,566	223.1	4.5	1,109,821
Ohio	201	4.5	1,412	4.2	7	27.4	19,427	191.3	3.8	951,900
New Jersey	106	2.4	1,155	3.4	11	26.2	22,716	189.9	3.8	1,791,528
Pennsylvania	184	4.1	1,298	3.8	7	26.6	20,489	186.3	3.7	1,012,516
Massachusetts	112	2.5	1,089	3.2	10	27.2	24,933	166.8	3.3	1,489,482
Maryland	81	1.8	857	2.5	11	19.3	22,505	143.2	2.9	1,768,494
Georgia	115	2.6	963	2.8	8	20.3	21,091	135.7	2.7	1,180,104
North Carolina	140	3.1	904	2.7	6	20.4	22,533	130.0	2.6	928,336
Washington	135	3.0	868	2.6	6	18.4	21,169	124.8	2.5	924,444
Virginia	122	2.7	947	2.8	8	16.1	17,041	124.2	2.5	1,018,262
Minnesota	92	2.1	767	2.3	8	17.9	23,394	113.8	2.3	1,236,674
Wisconsin	91	2.0	987	2.9	11	21.2	21,501	107.9	2.2	1,185,802
Missouri	117	2.6	782	2.3	7	18.3	23,451	104.0	2.1	888,513
Tennessee	104	2.3	638	1.9	6	14.0	21,884	100.5	2.0	965,962
Colorado	87	1.9	736	2.2	8	15.3	20,855	100.2	2.0	1,152,149
Indiana	109	2.4	804	2.4	7	16.0	19,930	97.1	1.9	891,211
Connecticut	59	1.3	384	1.1	7	9.5	24,690	63.6	1.3	1,078,627
Oregon	77	1.7	425	1.3	6	10.0	23,624	59.9	1.2	778,403
Utah	59	1.3	463	1.4	8	9.9	21,397	58.4	1.2	989,254
Iowa	63	1.4	499	1.5	8	12.2	24,491	57.1	1.1	905,873
Alabama	63	1.4	435	1.3	7	9.3	21,423	54.2	1.1	860,587
Louisiana	61	1.4	343	1.0	6	7.1	20,665	50.0	1.0	819,311
Kansas	57	1.3	426	1.3	7	8.9	20,866	46.2	0.9	810,281
Kentucky	61	1.4	310	0.9	5	7.2	23,106	46.0	0.9	753,967
Oklahoma	54	1.2	327	1.0	6	7.1	21,786	45.2	0.9	836,926
South Carolina	59	1.3	356	1.0	6	8.8	24,666	44.3	0.9	750,763
Nevada	24	0.5	245	0.7	10	5.3	21,612	39.1	0.8	1,629,917
Nebraska	37	0.8	286	0.8	8	4.2	14,601	27.0	0.5	730,514
New Hampshire	25	0.6	147	0.4	6	4.8	32,354	24.4	0.5	977,680
Arkansas	44	1.0	166	0.5	4	3.4	20,361	23.7	0.5	538,977
Mississippi	36	0.8	209	0.6	6	3.8	18,134	23.1	0.5	640,361
New Mexico	35	0.8	179	0.5	5	3.2	17,872	21.1	0.4	602,600
West Virginia	30	0.7	154	0.5	5	2.7	17,831	19.4	0.4	645,433
Idaho	30	0.7	171	0.5	6	3.4	19,877	18.4	0.4	613,733
Hawaii	21	0.5	117	0.3	6	2.1	18,111	16.4	0.3	782,143
Delaware	12	0.3	91	0.3	8	2.8	31,110	14.6	0.3	1,216,333
South Dakota	20	0.4	131	0.4	7	2.4	18,351	13.7	0.3	683,500
Montana	22	0.5	105	0.3	5	2.1	19,600	13.0	0.3	592,227
North Dakota	14	0.3	124	0.4	9	2.2	17,823	10.5	0.2	748,786
Alaska	16	0.4	67	0.2	4	1.4	20,552	10.2	0.2	634,500
Maine	16	0.4	64	0.2	4	1.5	23,328	8.9	0.2	553,313
Vermont	13	0.3	47	0.1	4	1.4	29,830	7.8	0.2	602,077
Wyoming	7	0.2	31	0.1	4	0.4	14,226	2.9	0.1	410,857
Michigan	130	2.9	1000-2499	-	-	(D)	-	(D)	-	-
Arizona	82	1.8	500-999	-	-	(D)	-	(D)	-	-
Rhode Island	13	0.3	20-99	-	-	(D)	-	(D)	-	-
D.C.	4	0.1	0-19	-	-	(D)	-	(D)	-	-

Source: 2002 *Economic Census*. The states are in descending order of sales or establishments (if sales data are missing for the majority). The symbol (D) appears when data are withheld to prevent disclosure of competitive information. States marked with (D) are sorted by number of establishments. A dash (-) indicates that the data element cannot be calculated. Shaded *states* on the state map indicate those states which have proportionately greater representation in the industry than would be indicated by the states population; the ratio is based on total sales or number of establishments. Shaded *regions* indicate where the industry is regionally most concentrated.

NAICS 451211 - BOOK STORES*

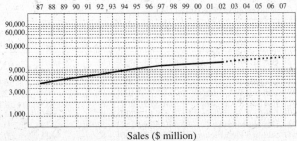

Sales ($ million)

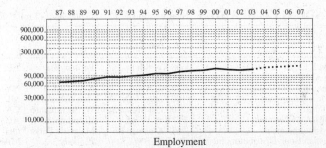

Employment

GENERAL STATISTICS

Year	Establishments (number)	Employment (number)	Payroll ($ million)	Sales ($ million)	Employees per Establishment (number)	Sales per Establishment ($)	Payroll per Employee ($)
1987	11,076	72,334	581.4	5,115.5	7	461,854	8,038
1988	10,628	74,705	654.9	5,695.4 e	7	535,886	8,766
1989	11,529	77,716	729.3	6,275.3 e	7	544,306	9,384
1990	11,722	86,077	826.3	6,855.1 e	7	584,806	9,600
1991	12,272	93,696	920.3	7,435.0 e	8	605,851	9,822
1992	12,887	92,480	928.0	8,014.9	7	621,937	10,035
1993	13,499	98,592	1,023.1	8,886.9 e	7	658,338	10,377
1994	13,520	102,380	1,105.4	9,759.0 e	8	721,819	10,797
1995	13,403	110,890	1,260.0	10,631.0 e	8	793,181	11,363
1996	13,964 e	110,215 e	1,213.6 e	11,503.1 e	8 e	823,768 e	11,011 e
1997	12,363	121,473	1,447.3	12,375.1	10	1,000,979	11,915
1998	12,151	127,184	1,566.2	12,809.8 e	10	1,054,218	12,314
1999	11,957	130,396	1,641.7	13,244.5 e	11	1,107,679	12,590
2000	11,662	141,515	1,743.3	13,679.2 e	12	1,172,974	12,319
2001	11,559	134,432	1,838.0	14,113.9 e	12	1,221,034	13,673
2002	10,898	130,861	1,737.6	14,548.6	12	1,334,983	13,278
2003	11,036	135,479	1,748.8	15,784.3 p	12	1,318,057 p	12,909
2004	12,040 p	148,413 p	1,981.3 p	16,457.9 p	13 p	1,375,743 p	13,961 p
2005	12,031 p	152,874 p	2,064.4 p	17,131.4 p	13 p	1,433,429 p	14,283 p
2006	12,021 p	157,336 p	2,147.5 p	17,805.0 p	13 p	1,491,115 p	14,604 p
2007	12,012 p	161,797 p	2,230.7 p	18,478.6 p	14 p	1,548,801 p	14,925 p

Sources: Economic Census of the United States, 1987, 1992, 1997, and 2002. Establishment counts, employment, and payroll are from *County Business Patterns* for non-Census years. Values followed by a 'p' are projections by the editors. Sales data for non-Census years are extrapolations, marked by 'e'. Data are the most recent available at this level of detail.

INDICES OF CHANGE

Year	Establishments (number)	Employment (number)	Payroll ($ million)	Sales ($ million)	Employees per Establishment (number)	Sales per Establishment ($)	Payroll per Employee ($)
1987	101.6	55.3	33.5	35.2	54.1	34.6	60.5
1992	118.3	70.7	53.4	55.1	60.0	46.6	75.6
1993	123.9	75.3	58.9	61.1 e	60.8	49.3	78.2
1994	124.1	78.2	63.6	67.1 e	63.3	54.1	81.3
1995	123.0	84.7	72.5	73.1 e	69.1	59.4	85.6
1996	128.1 e	84.2 e	69.8 e	79.1 e	65.8 e	61.7 e	82.9 e
1997	113.4	92.8	83.3	85.1	81.6	75.0	89.7
1998	111.5	97.2	90.1	88.0 e	87.4	79.0	92.7
1999	109.7	99.6	94.5	91.0 e	90.8	83.0	94.8
2000	107.0	108.1	100.3	94.0 e	100.8	87.9	92.8
2001	106.1	102.7	105.8	97.0 e	96.6	91.5	103.0
2002	100.0	100.0	100.0	100.0	100.0	100.0	100.0
2003	101.3	103.5	100.6	108.5 p	102.2	98.7 p	97.2
2004	110.5 p	113.4 p	114.0 p	113.1 p	104.7 p	103.1 p	105.1 p
2005	110.4 p	116.8 p	118.8 p	117.8 p	108.0 p	107.4 p	107.6 p
2006	110.3 p	120.2 p	123.6 p	122.4 p	111.4 p	111.7 p	110.0 p
2007	110.2 p	123.6 p	128.4 p	127.0 p	114.7 p	116.0 p	112.4 p

Sources: Same as General Statistics. The values shown reflect change from the base year, 2002. Values above 100 mean greater than 2002, values below 100 mean less than 2002, and a value of 100 in the 1987-2001 or 2003-2007 period means same as 2002. Values followed by a 'p' are projections by the editors; 'e' stands for extrapolation. Data are the most recent available at this level of detail.

SELECTED RATIOS

For 2002	Avg. of All Retail	Analyzed Industry	Index	For 2002	Avg. of All Retail	Analyzed Industry	Index
Employees per Establishment	17	12	71	Sales per Employee	174,682	111,176	64
Payroll per Establishment	333,445	159,440	48	Sales per Establishment	3,332,269	1,334,983	40
Payroll per Employee	20,311	13,278	65	Expenses per Establishment	na	na	na

Sources: Same as General Statistics. The 'Average of All' column, Wholesale or Retail, represents the average of the sector reported for the most recent complete year available. The Index shows the relationship between the Average and the Analyzed Industry. For example, 100 means that they are equal; 500 that the Analyzed Industry is five times the average; 50 means that the Analyzed Industry is half the national average. The abbreviation 'na' is used to show that data are 'not available'.

*Equivalent to SIC 5942.

LEADING COMPANIES   Number shown: **22**   Total sales ($ mil): **52,340**   Total employment (000): **211.2**

Company Name	Address				CEO Name	Phone	Co. Type	Sales ($ mil)	Empl. (000)
SAM'S Club	608 SW 8th St	Bentonville	AR	72712	Kevin Turner	479-273-4000	D	24,801*	36.0
Rite Aid Corp.	PO Box 3165	Harrisburg	PA	17105		717-761-2633	P	16,600	75.0
Barnes and Noble Inc.	122 5th Ave	New York	NY	10011	Leonard Riggio	212-633-3300	P	4,874	56.0
Borders Group Inc.	100 Phoenix Dr	Ann Arbor	MI	48108	Vincent E Altruda	734-477-1100	P	3,903	32.3
MTS Inc.	2500 Del Monte St	W. Sacramento	CA	95691	E Allen Rodriguez	916-373-2502	R	983	4.8
Books-A-Million Inc.	PO Box 19768	Birmingham	AL	35219	Clyde B Anderson	205-942-3737	P	475	4.8
ASM International	9639 Kinsman Rd	Materials Park	OH	44073	Donald Muzyka	440-338-5151	R	179*	0.1
Christian Book Distributors Inc.	PO Box 7000	Peabody	MA	01961	Stephen Hendrickson	978-977-5060	R	121*	0.5
Shakespeare and Co.	939 Lexington Ave	New York	NY	10021	Steve Carlin	212-570-0201	R	69*	<0.1
Voertman's	1314 W Hickory	Denton	TX	76201		940-387-1313	R	55*	<0.1
University Book Store Inc.	4326 University NE	Seattle	WA	98105		206-634-3400	R	49*	0.3
Elliott Bay Book Co.	101 S Main St	Seattle	WA	98104		206-624-6600	R	46*	<0.1
Books Inc.	160 Folsom St	San Francisco	CA	94105	Michael Tucker	415-442-0982	R	45*	0.2
Powell's Books Inc.	7 NW 9th Ave	Portland	OR	97209	Michael Powell	503-228-4651	R	38*	0.5
University Cooperative Society Inc.	2244 Guadalupe St	Austin	TX	78705	George Mitchell	512-476-7211	R	24*	0.1
Little Professor Book Center	PO Box 3'160	Ann Arbor	MI	48103	John Glazer		R	23*	<0.1
ARE Press Inc.	PO Box 595	Virginia Beach	VA	23451	Charles Cayce	757-428-3588	R	21*	<0.1
21st Century Christian	PO Box 40526	Nashville	TN	37204	Barry Brewer	615-383-3842	R	12*	<0.1
Wall Drug Store Inc.	510 Main St	Wall	SD	57790	Richard J Hustead	605-279-2175	R	11*	0.2
Watermark Books	4701 E Douglas	Wichita	KS	67218		316-682-1181	R	8*	<0.1
Total Identity Corp.	1007 N Federal	Fort Lauderdale	FL	33304	Matthew P Dwyer		P	1	<0.1
Art Hacker Books Inc.	45 W 57th St Fl 5	New York	NY	10019	Seymour Hacker	212-688-7600	R	1*	<0.1

Source: *Ward's Business Directory of U.S. Private and Public Companies*, Volumes 1 and 2, 2005. The company type code used is as follows: P - Public, R - Private, S - Subsidiary, D - Division, J - Joint Venture, A - Affiliate, G - Group. Sales are in millions of dollars, employees are in thousands. An asterisk (*) indicates an estimated sales volume. The symbol < stands for 'less than'. Company names and addresses are truncated, in some cases, to fit into the available space.

OCCUPATIONS EMPLOYED BY BOOK, PERIODICAL, & MUSIC STORES

Occupation	% of Total 2004	Change to 2014	Occupation	% of Total 2004	Change to 2014
Retail salespersons	41.4	18.9	General & operations managers	1.6	17.7
Cashiers, except gaming	22.8	7.0	Bookkeeping, accounting, & auditing clerks	1.2	7.0
First-line supervisors/managers of retail sales workers	9.8	9.4	Counter attendants	1.1	18.9
Stock clerks & order fillers	3.3	-8.9	Wholesale & retail buyers, except farm products	1.1	12.4
Shipping, receiving, & traffic clerks	1.9	7.6	Laborers & freight, stock, & material movers, hand	1.0	7.0
Combined food preparation & serving workers	1.6	18.9	Sales reps, wholesale & manufacturing, exc tech	1.0	18.9

Source: *Industry-Occupation Matrix*, Bureau of Labor Statistics. These data are reported based on 4-digit NAICS categories but have been matched to corresponding 6-digit NAICS industry codes. The change reported for each occupation to the year 2014 is a percent of growth or decline as estimated by the Bureau of Labor Statistics. The abbreviation nec stands for 'not elsewhere classified.'

LOCATION BY STATE AND REGIONAL CONCENTRATION

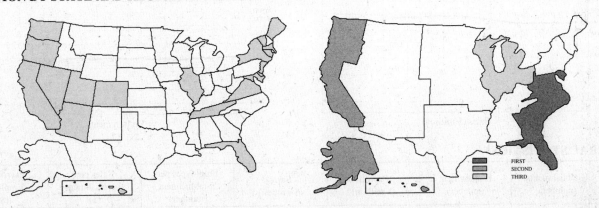

FIRST
SECOND
THIRD

INDUSTRY DATA BY STATE

State	Establishments Total (number)	% of U.S.	Employment Total (number)	% of U.S.	Per Estab.	Payroll Total ($ mil.)	Per Empl. ($)	Sales Total ($ mil.)	% of U.S.	Per Estab. ($)
California	1,183	10.9	19,407	14.5	16	259.5	13,374	1,995.5	13.2	1,686,828
New York	610	5.6	8,304	6.2	14	125.1	15,064	1,119.3	7.4	1,834,918
Texas	640	5.9	7,989	6.0	12	104.5	13,075	977.4	6.5	1,527,164
Florida	555	5.1	6,925	5.2	12	91.2	13,165	832.4	5.5	1,499,849
Illinois	435	4.0	6,481	4.9	15	87.4	13,488	692.6	4.6	1,592,122
Pennsylvania	460	4.2	5,656	4.2	12	77.8	13,754	666.1	4.4	1,447,993
Michigan	379	3.5	4,995	3.7	13	66.1	13,243	537.6	3.6	1,418,414
Massachusetts	296	2.7	3,978	3.0	13	61.3	15,405	521.1	3.5	1,760,611
Virginia	351	3.2	4,515	3.4	13	55.7	12,346	515.4	3.4	1,468,299
Ohio	397	3.7	4,848	3.6	12	58.8	12,133	508.6	3.4	1,281,033
New Jersey	268	2.5	3,537	2.6	13	49.5	13,982	480.3	3.2	1,792,198
Georgia	345	3.2	3,339	2.5	10	45.5	13,627	392.6	2.6	1,137,887
Washington	303	2.8	3,238	2.4	11	45.1	13,925	368.4	2.4	1,215,845
North Carolina	337	3.1	3,473	2.6	10	42.9	12,350	349.1	2.3	1,035,985
Maryland	189	1.7	2,653	2.0	14	34.4	12,962	313.3	2.1	1,657,503
Tennessee	248	2.3	2,907	2.2	12	37.3	12,834	311.4	2.1	1,255,589
Indiana	225	2.1	2,742	2.1	12	32.5	11,860	294.3	2.0	1,308,213
Colorado	207	1.9	2,508	1.9	12	33.6	13,404	284.8	1.9	1,375,681
Connecticut	145	1.3	1,899	1.4	13	28.5	15,004	248.5	1.6	1,713,821
Oregon	193	1.8	2,142	1.6	11	31.4	14,655	247.9	1.6	1,284,311
Arizona	204	1.9	1,893	1.4	9	26.8	14,162	243.2	1.6	1,192,363
Missouri	225	2.1	2,068	1.5	9	25.4	12,263	231.8	1.5	1,030,182
Wisconsin	221	2.0	2,408	1.8	11	27.5	11,426	228.5	1.5	1,033,738
South Carolina	151	1.4	1,546	1.2	10	18.3	11,858	173.3	1.2	1,147,517
Louisiana	151	1.4	1,589	1.2	11	19.2	12,077	170.2	1.1	1,127,311
Alabama	182	1.7	1,928	1.4	11	21.7	11,267	170.0	1.1	934,291
Kentucky	144	1.3	1,506	1.1	10	18.3	12,127	160.8	1.1	1,116,590
Kansas	115	1.1	1,435	1.1	12	17.2	12,014	138.9	0.9	1,207,452
Oklahoma	114	1.0	1,153	0.9	10	14.1	12,264	130.0	0.9	1,140,368
Utah	111	1.0	1,279	1.0	12	15.3	11,998	124.5	0.8	1,121,514
Iowa	124	1.1	1,298	1.0	10	13.9	10,706	119.4	0.8	962,629
D.C.	52	0.5	922	0.7	18	14.2	15,412	105.5	0.7	2,028,577
Nevada	62	0.6	704	0.5	11	10.2	14,544	94.6	0.6	1,525,210
Arkansas	103	0.9	850	0.6	8	10.2	11,951	91.0	0.6	883,612
Hawaii	50	0.5	749	0.6	15	13.2	17,609	87.3	0.6	1,746,580
Maine	82	0.8	674	0.5	8	9.2	13,687	73.9	0.5	901,268
New Mexico	89	0.8	686	0.5	8	9.8	14,316	70.5	0.5	792,124
West Virginia	82	0.8	546	0.4	7	6.3	11,625	67.2	0.4	819,598
Delaware	39	0.4	432	0.3	11	6.6	15,343	60.0	0.4	1,539,256
Vermont	54	0.5	448	0.3	8	6.0	13,295	44.2	0.3	818,481
Alaska	56	0.5	311	0.2	6	4.7	15,129	37.1	0.2	662,875
Minnesota	191	1.8	1000-2499	-	-	(D)	-	(D)	-	-
Mississippi	89	0.8	500-999	-	-	(D)	-	(D)	-	-
New Hampshire	77	0.7	500-999	-	-	(D)	-	(D)	-	-
Nebraska	75	0.7	500-999	-	-	(D)	-	(D)	-	-
Montana	61	0.6	500-999	-	-	(D)	-	(D)	-	-
Idaho	56	0.5	500-999	-	-	(D)	-	(D)	-	-
Wyoming	50	0.5	100-249	-	-	(D)	-	(D)	-	-
Rhode Island	38	0.3	250-499	-	-	(D)	-	(D)	-	-
North Dakota	25	0.2	250-499	-	-	(D)	-	(D)	-	-
South Dakota	21	0.2	100-249	-	-	(D)	-	(D)	-	-

Source: 2002 *Economic Census*. The states are in descending order of sales or establishments (if sales data are missing for the majority). The symbol (D) appears when data are withheld to prevent disclosure of competitive information. States marked with (D) are sorted by number of establishments. A dash (-) indicates that the data element cannot be calculated. Shaded *states* on the state map indicate those states which have proportionately greater representation in the industry than would be indicated by the states population; the ratio is based on total sales or number of establishments. Shaded *regions* indicate where the industry is regionally most concentrated.

NAICS 451212 - NEWS DEALERS AND NEWSSTANDS*

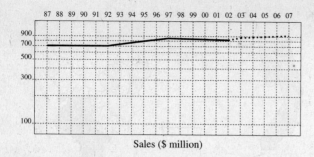

Sales ($ million)

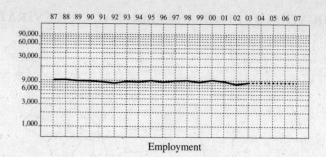

Employment

GENERAL STATISTICS

Year	Establishments (number)	Employment (number)	Payroll ($ million)	Sales ($ million)	Employees per Establishment (number)	Sales per Establishment ($)	Payroll per Employee ($)
1987	2,198	10,149	90.2	703.2	5	319,927	8,888
1988	2,078	10,252	93.6	703.4 e	5	338,499	9,130
1989	1,967	9,718	90.4	703.6 e	5	357,702	9,302
1990	1,982	9,663	95.5	703.8 e	5	355,096	9,883
1991	2,022	9,208	94.2	704.1 e	5	348,220	10,230
1992	2,260	8,696	91.1	704.3	4	311,637	10,476
1993	2,362	9,490	100.8	734.2 e	4	310,838	10,622
1994	2,310	9,247	102.7	764.1 e	4	330,779	11,106
1995	2,286	9,911	117.5	794.0 e	4	347,332	11,856
1996	2,254 e	9,263 e	110.3 e	823.9 e	4 e	365,528 e	11,908 e
1997	2,313	9,770	119.3	853.8	4	369,131	12,211
1998	2,230	9,963	137.3	847.5 e	5	380,042	13,781
1999	2,108	9,194	123.8	841.2 e	4	399,045	13,465
2000	2,031	10,151	153.2	834.9 e	5	411,068	15,094
2001	2,040	9,553	152.2	828.6 e	5	406,163	15,935
2002	1,853	8,274	115.1	822.3	4	443,749	13,907
2003	1,751	8,976	126.6	874.7 p	5	417,302 p	14,101
2004	2,024 p	9,114 p	143.5 p	886.7 p	5 p	423,788 p	15,578 p
2005	2,013 p	9,071 p	146.9 p	898.7 p	5 p	430,274 p	15,990 p
2006	2,003 p	9,028 p	150.4 p	910.7 p	5 p	436,759 p	16,401 p
2007	1,992 p	8,985 p	153.8 p	922.6 p	5 p	443,245 p	16,813 p

Sources: *Economic Census of the United States*, 1987, 1992, 1997, and 2002. Establishment counts, employment, and payroll are from *County Business Patterns* for non-Census years. Values followed by a 'p' are projections by the editors. Sales data for non-Census years are extrapolations, marked by 'e'. Data are the most recent available at this level of detail.

INDICES OF CHANGE

Year	Establishments (number)	Employment (number)	Payroll ($ million)	Sales ($ million)	Employees per Establishment (number)	Sales per Establishment ($)	Payroll per Employee ($)
1987	118.6	122.7	78.4	85.5	103.0	72.1	63.9
1992	122.0	105.1	79.2	85.7	85.1	70.2	75.3
1993	127.5	114.7	87.6	89.3 e	89.6	70.0	76.4
1994	124.7	111.8	89.3	92.9 e	89.6	74.5	79.9
1995	123.4	119.8	102.1	96.6 e	96.3	78.3	85.2
1996	121.6 e	112.0 e	95.9 e	100.2 e	91.8 e	82.4 e	85.6 e
1997	124.8	118.1	103.7	103.8	94.1	83.2	87.8
1998	120.3	120.4	119.3	103.1 e	100.8	85.6	99.1
1999	113.8	111.1	107.6	102.3 e	98.5	89.9	96.8
2000	109.6	122.7	133.1	101.5 e	112.0	92.6	108.5
2001	110.1	115.5	132.3	100.8 e	105.3	91.5	114.6
2002	100.0	100.0	100.0	100.0	100.0	100.0	100.0
2003	94.5	108.5	110.0	106.4 p	114.8	94.0 p	101.4
2004	109.2 p	110.1 p	124.7 p	107.8 p	101.9 p	95.5 p	112.0 p
2005	108.6 p	109.6 p	127.7 p	109.3 p	102.0 p	97.0 p	115.0 p
2006	108.1 p	109.1 p	130.7 p	110.7 p	102.1 p	98.4 p	117.9 p
2007	107.5 p	108.6 p	133.7 p	112.2 p	102.3 p	99.9 p	120.9 p

Sources: Same as General Statistics. The values shown reflect change from the base year, 2002. Values above 100 mean greater than 2002, values below 100 mean less than 2002, and a value of 100 in the 1987-2001 or 2003-2007 period means same as 2002. Values followed by a 'p' are projections by the editors; 'e' stands for extrapolation. Data are the most recent available at this level of detail.

SELECTED RATIOS

For 2002	Avg. of All Retail	Analyzed Industry	Index	For 2002	Avg. of All Retail	Analyzed Industry	Index
Employees per Establishment	17	4	26	Sales per Employee	174,682	99,380	57
Payroll per Establishment	333,445	62,098	19	Sales per Establishment	3,332,269	443,749	13
Payroll per Employee	20,311	13,907	68	Expenses per Establishment	na	na	na

Sources: Same as General Statistics. The 'Average of All' column, Wholesale or Retail, represents the average of the sector reported for the most recent complete year available. The Index shows the relationship between the Average and the Analyzed Industry. For example, 100 means that they are equal; 500 that the Analyzed Industry is five times the average; 50 means that the Analyzed Industry is half the national average. The abbreviation 'na' is used to show that data are 'not available'.

*Equivalent to SIC 5994.

LEADING COMPANIES Number shown: 1   Total sales ($ mil): 2   Total employment (000): 0.0

Company Name	Address				CEO Name	Phone	Co. Type	Sales ($ mil)	Empl. (000)
Healy News Store Inc.	231 Robinson St	Wakefield	RI	02879	Freeman A. Healy Jr.	401-789-9566	R	2*	<0.1

Source: Ward's Business Directory of U.S. Private and Public Companies, Volumes 1 and 2, 2005. The company type code used is as follows: P - Public, R - Private, S - Subsidiary, D - Division, J - Joint Venture, A - Affiliate, G - Group. Sales are in millions of dollars, employees are in thousands. An asterisk (*) indicates an estimated sales volume. The symbol < stands for 'less than'. Company names and addresses are truncated, in some cases, to fit into the available space.

OCCUPATIONS EMPLOYED BY BOOK, PERIODICAL, & MUSIC STORES

Occupation	% of Total 2004	Change to 2014	Occupation	% of Total 2004	Change to 2014
Retail salespersons	41.4	18.9	General & operations managers	1.6	17.7
Cashiers, except gaming	22.8	7.0	Bookkeeping, accounting, & auditing clerks	1.2	7.0
First-line supervisors/managers of retail sales workers	9.8	9.4	Counter attendants	1.1	18.9
Stock clerks & order fillers	3.3	-8.9	Wholesale & retail buyers, except farm products	1.1	12.4
Shipping, receiving, & traffic clerks	1.9	7.6	Laborers & freight, stock, & material movers, hand	1.0	7.0
Combined food preparation & serving workers	1.6	18.9	Sales reps, wholesale & manufacturing, exc tech	1.0	18.9

Source: Industry-Occupation Matrix, Bureau of Labor Statistics. These data are reported based on 4-digit NAICS categories but have been matched to corresponding 6-digit NAICS industry codes. The change reported for each occupation to the year 2014 is a percent of growth or decline as estimated by the Bureau of Labor Statistics. The abbreviation nec stands for 'not elsewhere classified.'

LOCATION BY STATE AND REGIONAL CONCENTRATION

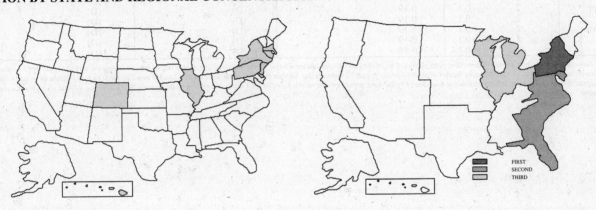

FIRST
SECOND
THIRD

INDUSTRY DATA BY STATE

State	Establishments		Employment			Payroll		Sales		
	Total (number)	% of U.S.	Total (number)	% of U.S.	Per Estab.	Total ($ mil.)	Per Empl. ($)	Total ($ mil.)	% of U.S.	Per Estab. ($)
New York	595	32.2	1,759	22.3	3	24.9	14,148	220.9	27.3	371,198
California	139	7.5	991	12.5	7	12.7	12,857	72.1	8.9	518,360
New Jersey	151	8.2	642	8.1	4	9.2	14,343	68.9	8.5	456,146
Pennsylvania	141	7.6	541	6.8	4	6.6	12,283	50.0	6.2	354,518
Illinois	100	5.4	350	4.4	4	5.3	15,226	46.8	5.8	467,650
Massachusetts	71	3.8	449	5.7	6	6.3	13,962	43.1	5.3	607,437
Florida	57	3.1	393	5.0	7	6.1	15,522	40.6	5.0	711,982
Texas	51	2.8	233	2.9	5	4.8	20,545	28.9	3.6	566,922
Ohio	58	3.1	273	3.5	5	4.2	15,282	22.4	2.8	385,914
Virginia	37	2.0	170	2.2	5	2.2	12,976	15.5	1.9	418,027
Connecticut	33	1.8	118	1.5	4	1.9	15,839	15.3	1.9	462,909
Georgia	25	1.4	192	2.4	8	2.1	11,078	14.5	1.8	581,240
Colorado	17	0.9	133	1.7	8	2.4	17,752	14.3	1.8	839,059
Maryland	36	1.9	152	1.9	4	2.0	13,007	11.4	1.4	315,389
Delaware	13	0.7	53	0.7	4	0.9	16,245	10.4	1.3	803,769
Hawaii	6	0.3	92	1.2	15	1.8	19,630	9.4	1.2	1,570,000
Indiana	23	1.2	73	0.9	3	0.8	11,301	8.8	1.1	384,304
Kentucky	7	0.4	64	0.8	9	1.3	20,156	7.8	1.0	1,110,571
Missouri	22	1.2	94	1.2	4	1.4	15,404	7.6	0.9	346,318
Washington	23	1.2	77	1.0	3	0.9	12,143	7.1	0.9	307,261
North Carolina	25	1.4	92	1.2	4	1.0	10,413	5.5	0.7	221,960
South Carolina	9	0.5	62	0.8	7	0.6	9,952	5.5	0.7	609,444

Continued on next page.

2167

INDUSTRY DATA BY STATE - Continued

State	Establishments Total (number)	% of U.S.	Employment Total (number)	% of U.S.	Per Estab.	Payroll Total ($ mil.)	Per Empl. ($)	Sales Total ($ mil.)	% of U.S.	Per Estab. ($)
Wisconsin	10	0.5	48	0.6	5	0.5	11,063	4.7	0.6	474,800
Louisiana	8	0.4	27	0.3	3	0.3	10,815	3.0	0.4	368,750
Oregon	9	0.5	22	0.3	2	0.3	14,136	2.6	0.3	290,444
Iowa	9	0.5	45	0.6	5	0.6	12,333	2.5	0.3	279,889
Alabama	8	0.4	40	0.5	5	0.5	12,125	2.0	0.2	250,375
Maine	7	0.4	33	0.4	5	0.3	9,970	1.9	0.2	270,143
Nevada	6	0.3	16	0.2	3	0.2	15,313	1.8	0.2	294,000
West Virginia	9	0.5	32	0.4	4	0.3	10,906	1.5	0.2	171,333
Kansas	12	0.6	29	0.4	2	0.4	12,103	1.5	0.2	127,333
Utah	5	0.3	17	0.2	3	0.3	16,412	1.5	0.2	294,000
Oklahoma	4	0.2	10	0.1	3	0.1	9,900	1.4	0.2	348,000
New Mexico	7	0.4	16	0.2	2	0.1	8,750	1.4	0.2	195,571
Arkansas	4	0.2	11	0.1	3	0.1	8,182	0.9	0.1	226,250
Tennessee	4	0.2	6	0.1	2	0.1	10,500	0.8	0.1	188,500
Vermont	3	0.2	8	0.1	3	0.1	11,750	0.5	0.1	151,667
Michigan	28	1.5	100-249	-	-	(D)	-	(D)	-	-
D.C.	21	1.1	20-99	-	-	(D)	-	(D)	-	-
Arizona	15	0.8	20-99	-	-	(D)	-	(D)	-	-
Minnesota	13	0.7	20-99	-	-	(D)	-	(D)	-	-
New Hampshire	7	0.4	20-99	-	-	(D)	-	(D)	-	-
South Dakota	5	0.3	20-99	-	-	(D)	-	(D)	-	-
Rhode Island	4	0.2	20-99	-	-	(D)	-	(D)	-	-
Idaho	2	0.1	0-19	-	-	(D)	-	(D)	-	-
Mississippi	2	0.1	0-19	-	-	(D)	-	(D)	-	-
Montana	2	0.1	0-19	-	-	(D)	-	(D)	-	-
North Dakota	2	0.1	0-19	-	-	(D)	-	(D)	-	-
Nebraska	1	0.1	0-19	-	-	(D)	-	(D)	-	-
Wyoming	1	0.1	0-19	-	-	(D)	-	(D)	-	-

Source: 2002 Economic Census. The states are in descending order of sales or establishments (if sales data are missing for the majority). The symbol (D) appears when data are withheld to prevent disclosure of competitive information. States marked with (D) are sorted by number of establishments. A dash (-) indicates that the data element cannot be calculated. Shaded states on the state map indicate those states which have proportionately greater representation in the industry than would be indicated by the states population; the ratio is based on total sales or number of establishments. Shaded regions indicate where the industry is regionally most concentrated.

NAICS 451220 - PRERECORDED TAPE, COMPACT DISC, AND RECORD STORES*

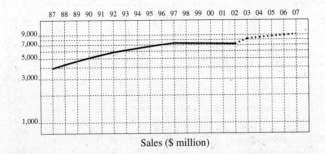

Sales ($ million)

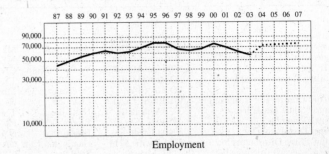

Employment

GENERAL STATISTICS

Year	Establishments (number)	Employment (number)	Payroll ($ million)	Sales ($ million)	Employees per Establishment (number)	Sales per Establishment ($)	Payroll per Employee ($)
1987	6,272	44,408	371.7	3,930.4	7	626,658	8,370
1988	6,295	49,783	435.3	4,316.4 e	8	685,687	8,744
1989	6,444	55,165	499.7	4,702.3 e	9	729,718	9,058
1990	7,146	60,123	550.2	5,088.3 e	8	712,049	9,151
1991	7,588	64,077	617.9	5,474.3 e	8	721,442	9,643
1992	7,924	60,438	592.5	5,860.2	8	739,551	9,803
1993	8,242	62,601	643.5	6,161.5 e	8	747,573	10,279
1994	8,714	69,209	716.9	6,462.8 e	8	741,657	10,359
1995	8,842	77,894	774.3	6,764.2 e	9	765,008	9,940
1996	9,322 e	77,695 e	810.1 e	7,065.5 e	8 e	757,938 e	10,427 e
1997	8,158	66,623	728.0	7,366.8	8	903,015	10,927
1998	7,950	64,347	801.0	7,331.8 e	8	922,240	12,448
1999	7,763	67,180	821.7	7,296.8 e	9	939,948	12,231
2000	7,720	75,988	884.9	7,261.8 e	10	940,651	11,645
2001	7,702	69,533	907.1	7,226.8 e	9	938,306	13,045
2002	6,974	62,310	737.8	7,191.8	9	1,031,236	11,840
2003	6,443	56,859	709.7	8,198.1 p	9	1,006,435 p	12,482
2004	8,009 p	72,459 p	917.2 p	8,430.9 p	9 p	1,029,967 p	13,051 p
2005	8,053 p	73,423 p	943.3 p	8,663.8 p	9 p	1,053,498 p	13,322 p
2006	8,096 p	74,387 p	969.4 p	8,896.6 p	9 p	1,077,030 p	13,594 p
2007	8,140 p	75,352 p	995.5 p	9,129.5 p	9 p	1,100,561 p	13,865 p

Sources: *Economic Census of the United States*, 1987, 1992, 1997, and 2002. Establishment counts, employment, and payroll are from *County Business Patterns* for non-Census years. Values followed by a 'p' are projections by the editors. Sales data for non-Census years are extrapolations, marked by 'e'. Data are the most recent available at this level of detail.

INDICES OF CHANGE

Year	Establishments (number)	Employment (number)	Payroll ($ million)	Sales ($ million)	Employees per Establishment (number)	Sales per Establishment ($)	Payroll per Employee ($)
1987	89.9	71.3	50.4	54.7	79.5	60.8	70.7
1992	113.6	97.0	80.3	81.5	85.1	71.7	82.8
1993	118.2	100.5	87.2	85.7 e	85.1	72.5	86.8
1994	124.9	111.1	97.2	89.9 e	88.4	71.9	87.5
1995	126.8	125.0	105.0	94.1 e	98.5	74.2	84.0
1996	133.7 e	124.7 e	109.8 e	98.2 e	92.9 e	73.5 e	88.1 e
1997	117.0	106.9	98.7	102.4	91.8	87.6	92.3
1998	114.0	103.3	108.6	101.9 e	90.7	89.4	105.1
1999	111.3	107.8	111.4	101.5 e	97.4	91.1	103.3
2000	110.7	122.0	119.9	101.0 e	109.7	91.2	98.3
2001	110.4	111.6	123.0	100.5 e	100.7	91.0	110.2
2002	100.0	100.0	100.0	100.0	100.0	100.0	100.0
2003	92.4	91.3	96.2	114.0 p	98.8	97.6 p	105.4
2004	114.8 p	116.3 p	124.3 p	117.2 p	102.2 p	99.9 p	110.2 p
2005	115.5 p	117.8 p	127.9 p	120.5 p	103.1 p	102.2 p	112.5 p
2006	116.1 p	119.4 p	131.4 p	123.7 p	104.1 p	104.4 p	114.8 p
2007	116.7 p	120.9 p	134.9 p	126.9 p	105.0 p	106.7 p	117.1 p

Sources: Same as General Statistics. The values shown reflect change from the base year, 2002. Values above 100 mean greater than 2002, values below 100 mean less than 2002, and a value of 100 in the 1987-2001 or 2003-2007 period means same as 2002. Values followed by a 'p' are projections by the editors; 'e' stands for extrapolation. Data are the most recent available at this level of detail.

SELECTED RATIOS

For 2002	Avg. of All Retail	Analyzed Industry	Index	For 2002	Avg. of All Retail	Analyzed Industry	Index
Employees per Establishment	17	9	53	Sales per Employee	174,682	115,420	66
Payroll per Establishment	333,445	105,788	32	Sales per Establishment	3,332,269	1,031,236	31
Payroll per Employee	20,311	11,840	58	Expenses per Establishment	na	na	na

Sources: Same as General Statistics. The 'Average of All' column, Wholesale or Retail, represents the average of the sector reported for the most recent complete year available. The Index shows the relationship between the Average and the Analyzed Industry. For example, 100 means that they are equal; 500 that the Analyzed Industry is five times the average; 50 means that the Analyzed Industry is half the national average. The abbreviation 'na' is used to show that data are 'not available'.

*Equivalent to SIC 5735.

LEADING COMPANIES   Number shown: 17   Total sales ($ mil): 7,587   Total employment (000): 57.2

Company Name	Address				CEO Name	Phone	Co. Type	Sales ($ mil)	Empl. (000)
Borders Group Inc.	100 Phoenix Dr	Ann Arbor	MI	48108	Vincent E. Altruda	734-477-1100	P	3,903	32.3
Trans World Entertainment Corp.	38 Corporate Cir	Albany	NY	12203	Robert J Higgins	518-452-1242	P	1,331	8.2
MTS Inc.	2500 Del Monte St	W. Sacramento	CA	95691	E Allen Rodriguez	916-373-2502	R	983	4.8
Hastings Entertainment Inc.	PO Box 35350	Amarillo	TX	79120		806-351-2300	P	508	6.8
Coborn's Inc.	PO Box 6146	St. Cloud	MN	56302	Don Wetter	320-252-4222	R	434	4.0
Record Exchange of Roanoke Inc.	916 Bridle Path Ln	Charlotte	NC	28211	Don Rosenberg	704-364-1784	R	122*	<0.1
Central South Music Inc.	3730 Vulcan Dr	Nashville	TN	37211	Randall Davidson	615-833-5960	R	84*	0.7
Visual Sound Inc.	485 Park Way	Broomall	PA	19008	John Bogosian	610-544-8700	R	66*	<0.1
Corner Distributors Inc.	3940 Merritt Ave	Bronx	NY	10466	Francis Vegliante	718-798-1500	R	40*	<0.1
Prajin 1 Stop Distributors Inc.	5701 Pacific 5711	Huntington Park	CA	90255	Antonio Prajin	323-588-9323	R	38*	<0.1
Disco Azteca Distributors Inc.	417 E Main St	Stockton	CA	95202	Jose Sanchez	209-462-1389	R	33*	<0.1
Music Millenium Inc.	3158 E Burnside St	Portland	OR	97214	Terry Courier	503-231-8943	R	16*	<0.1
Sound of Market Street	15 S 11th St, 2nd Fl	Philadelphia	PA	19107		215-925-3150	R	12*	<0.1
Crow's Nest Music	2108 Plainfield Rd	Crest Hill	IL	60435	Floyd Crow	815-725-9196	R	6*	<0.1
TW Inc.	40 Carmans Rd	Massapequa	NY	11758		516-795-1900	R	6*	<0.1
Candyman Ltd.	851 St Michael's Dr	Santa Fe	NM	87501		505-983-9309	R	5*	<0.1
George's Music Room	3915 W Roosevelt	Chicago	IL	60624	George Daniels	773-762-8910	R	1*	<0.1

Source: Ward's Business Directory of U.S. Private and Public Companies, Volumes 1 and 2, 2005. The company type code used is as follows: P - Public, R - Private, S - Subsidiary, D - Division, J - Joint Venture, A - Affiliate, G - Group. Sales are in millions of dollars, employees are in thousands. An asterisk (*) indicates an estimated sales volume. The symbol < stands for 'less than'. Company names and addresses are truncated, in some cases, to fit into the available space.

OCCUPATIONS EMPLOYED BY BOOK, PERIODICAL, & MUSIC STORES

Occupation	% of Total 2004	Change to 2014	Occupation	% of Total 2004	Change to 2014
Retail salespersons	41.4	18.9	General & operations managers	1.6	17.7
Cashiers, except gaming	22.8	7.0	Bookkeeping, accounting, & auditing clerks	1.2	7.0
First-line supervisors/managers of retail sales workers	9.8	9.4	Counter attendants	1.1	18.9
Stock clerks & order fillers	3.3	-8.9	Wholesale & retail buyers, except farm products	1.1	12.4
Shipping, receiving, & traffic clerks	1.9	7.6	Laborers & freight, stock, & material movers, hand	1.0	7.0
Combined food preparation & serving workers	1.6	18.9	Sales reps, wholesale & manufacturing, exc tech	1.0	18.9

Source: Industry-Occupation Matrix, Bureau of Labor Statistics. These data are reported based on 4-digit NAICS categories but have been matched to corresponding 6-digit NAICS industry codes. The change reported for each occupation to the year 2014 is a percent of growth or decline as estimated by the Bureau of Labor Statistics. The abbreviation nec stands for 'not elsewhere classified.'

LOCATION BY STATE AND REGIONAL CONCENTRATION

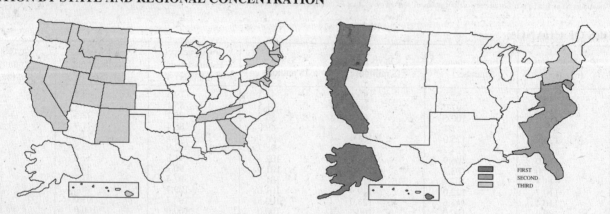

FIRST
SECOND
THIRD

INDUSTRY DATA BY STATE

State	Establishments Total (number)	% of U.S.	Employment Total (number)	% of U.S.	Per Estab.	Payroll Total ($ mil.)	Per Empl. ($)	Sales Total ($ mil.)	% of U.S.	Per Estab. ($)
California	931	13.3	9,120	14.6	10	122.8	13,464	1,193.7	16.5	1,282,158
New York	579	8.3	4,939	7.9	9	62.2	12,587	660.4	9.1	1,140,636
Texas	418	6.0	4,523	7.2	11	52.7	11,658	499.4	6.9	1,194,644
Florida	339	4.9	2,454	3.9	7	30.7	12,520	307.6	4.3	907,504
Pennsylvania	313	4.5	2,604	4.2	8	28.9	11,086	302.9	4.2	967,652
Ohio	295	4.2	2,825	4.5	10	29.8	10,533	275.6	3.8	934,349

Continued on next page.

INDUSTRY DATA BY STATE - Continued

State	Establishments Total (number)	% of U.S.	Employment Total (number)	% of U.S.	Per Estab.	Payroll Total ($ mil.)	Per Empl. ($)	Sales Total ($ mil.)	% of U.S.	Per Estab. ($)
Massachusetts	186	2.7	1,827	2.9	10	22.8	12,500	271.6	3.8	1,460,306
Illinois	307	4.4	2,576	4.1	8	30.3	11,761	257.6	3.6	839,065
New Jersey	249	3.6	1,701	2.7	7	22.4	13,183	232.0	3.2	931,562
Georgia	188	2.7	1,686	2.7	9	19.4	11,535	194.5	2.7	1,034,468
Virginia	167	2.4	1,455	2.3	9	17.5	12,005	168.8	2.3	1,010,820
Colorado	124	1.8	1,404	2.2	11	16.4	11,679	163.8	2.3	1,320,815
North Carolina	184	2.6	1,623	2.6	9	18.3	11,245	161.9	2.2	879,641
Washington	160	2.3	1,340	2.1	8	17.0	12,704	158.6	2.2	991,344
Tennessee	160	2.3	1,372	2.2	9	16.6	12,071	149.2	2.1	932,550
Maryland	150	2.1	1,295	2.1	9	14.1	10,916	145.8	2.0	972,273
Connecticut	107	1.5	981	1.6	9	11.7	11,931	130.4	1.8	1,218,701
Missouri	113	1.6	1,177	1.9	10	12.0	10,203	101.9	1.4	902,177
Indiana	143	2.0	1,077	1.7	8	10.9	10,134	97.8	1.4	684,203
Wisconsin	118	1.7	894	1.4	8	10.0	11,227	87.3	1.2	739,508
Minnesota	100	1.4	895	1.4	9	10.8	12,061	84.4	1.2	844,280
Utah	57	0.8	717	1.1	13	7.0	9,812	82.8	1.1	1,452,509
Oklahoma	53	0.8	778	1.2	15	8.5	10,865	80.5	1.1	1,519,396
Louisiana	108	1.5	741	1.2	7	8.2	11,046	80.1	1.1	741,861
Oregon	97	1.4	692	1.1	7	9.8	14,188	78.8	1.1	811,866
New Mexico	41	0.6	782	1.2	19	8.1	10,414	77.6	1.1	1,891,829
Kentucky	82	1.2	623	1.0	8	6.7	10,790	67.3	0.9	820,805
Alabama	83	1.2	601	1.0	7	6.3	10,527	65.7	0.9	791,675
South Carolina	84	1.2	633	1.0	8	7.6	11,927	64.1	0.9	762,631
Kansas	69	1.0	836	1.3	12	8.4	9,993	63.3	0.9	917,551
Nevada	46	0.7	407	0.6	9	4.9	11,988	56.9	0.8	1,237,043
New Hampshire	45	0.6	329	0.5	7	4.1	12,444	53.2	0.7	1,183,156
Arkansas	34	0.5	538	0.9	16	5.1	9,546	47.6	0.7	1,400,618
Iowa	62	0.9	491	0.8	8	5.5	11,130	46.6	0.6	751,806
Hawaii	56	0.8	312	0.5	6	4.2	13,433	43.9	0.6	783,589
Idaho	37	0.5	476	0.8	13	4.8	10,011	40.4	0.6	1,092,973
Mississippi	58	0.8	347	0.6	6	4.1	11,677	38.8	0.5	668,690
Montana	30	0.4	397	0.6	13	4.0	9,997	35.2	0.5	1,173,767
Rhode Island	44	0.6	265	0.4	6	3.6	13,642	35.1	0.5	798,614
Nebraska	33	0.5	375	0.6	11	3.3	8,931	28.8	0.4	871,424
Maine	32	0.5	179	0.3	6	2.1	11,520	26.7	0.4	833,344
West Virginia	33	0.5	236	0.4	7	2.8	11,775	26.2	0.4	793,061
Delaware	23	0.3	153	0.2	7	1.8	11,810	20.2	0.3	876,696
Vermont	18	0.3	120	0.2	7	1.6	13,542	14.6	0.2	810,278
Wyoming	11	0.2	171	0.3	16	1.5	8,678	14.6	0.2	1,324,909
North Dakota	19	0.3	141	0.2	7	1.4	10,156	13.9	0.2	733,053
South Dakota	23	0.3	144	0.2	6	1.8	12,354	13.2	0.2	573,304
Alaska	17	0.2	114	0.2	7	1.1	9,772	12.5	0.2	733,118
Michigan	224	3.2	1000-2499	-	-	(D)	-	(D)	-	-
Arizona	105	1.5	1000-2499	-	-	(D)	-	(D)	-	-
D.C.	32	0.5	250-499	-	-	(D)	-	(D)	-	-

Source: 2002 *Economic Census*. The states are in descending order of sales or establishments (if sales data are missing for the majority). The symbol (D) appears when data are withheld to prevent disclosure of competitive information. States marked with (D) are sorted by number of establishments. A dash (-) indicates that the data element cannot be calculated. Shaded *states* on the state map indicate those states which have proportionately greater representation in the industry than would be indicated by the states population; the ratio is based on total sales or number of establishments. Shaded *regions* indicate where the industry is regionally most concentrated.

NAICS 452111 - DEPARTMENT STORES (EXCEPT DISCOUNT DEPARTMENT STORES)

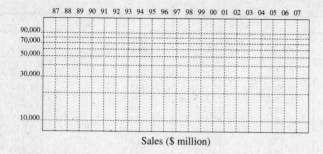

Sales ($ million)

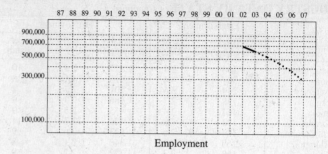

Employment

GENERAL STATISTICS

Year	Establishments (number)	Employment (number)	Payroll ($ million)	Sales ($ million)	Employees per Establishment (number)	Sales per Establishment ($)	Payroll per Employee ($)
1987	-	-	-	-	-	-	-
1988	-	-	-	-	-	-	-
1989	-	-	-	-	-	-	-
1990	-	-	-	-	-	-	-
1991	-	-	-	-	-	-	-
1992	-	-	-	-	-	-	-
1993	-	-	-	-	-	-	-
1994	-	-	-	-	-	-	-
1995	-	-	-	-	-	-	-
1996	-	-	-	-	-	-	-
1997	-	-	-	-	-	-	-
1998	-	-	-	-	-	-	-
1999	-	-	-	-	-	-	-
2000	-	-	-	-	-	-	-
2001	-	-	-	-	-	-	-
2002	3,938	689,270	11,149.6	89,849.8	175	22,816,105	16,176
2003	3,867	610,543	10,310.3	-	158	-	16,887
2004	3,796 p	531,816 p	9,471.1 p	-	141 p	-	17,598 p
2005	3,725 p	453,089 p	8,631.9 p	-	124 p	-	18,310 p
2006	3,654 p	374,362 p	7,792.6 p	-	106 p	-	19,021 p
2007	3,583 p	295,635 p	6,953.4 p	-	89 p	-	19,732 p

Source: *Economic Census of the United States*, 2002. Establishment counts, employment, and payroll are from *County Business Patterns* for non-Census years. This is a newly defined industry. Data for prior years are unavailable at the time of publication but may become available over time. Values followed by 'p' are projections by the editors. Sales data for non-Census years are extrapolations, marked by 'e'.

INDICES OF CHANGE

Year	Establishments (number)	Employment (number)	Payroll ($ million)	Sales ($ million)	Employees per Establishment (number)	Sales per Establishment ($)	Payroll per Employee ($)
1987	-	-	-	-	-	-	-
1992	-	-	-	-	-	-	-
1993	-	-	-	-	-	-	-
1994	-	-	-	-	-	-	-
1995	-	-	-	-	-	-	-
1996	-	-	-	-	-	-	-
1997	-	-	-	-	-	-	-
1998	-	-	-	-	-	-	-
1999	-	-	-	-	-	-	-
2000	-	-	-	-	-	-	-
2001	-	-	-	-	-	-	-
2002	100.0	100.0	100.0	100.0	100.0	100.0	100.0
2003	98.2	88.6	92.5	-	90.2	-	104.4
2004	96.4 p	77.2 p	84.9 p	-	80.4 p	-	108.8 p
2005	94.6 p	65.7 p	77.4 p	-	70.6 p	-	113.2 p
2006	92.8 p	54.3 p	69.9 p	-	60.8 p	-	117.6 p
2007	91.0 p	42.9 p	62.4 p	-	51.0 p	-	122.0 p

Sources: Same as General Statistics. The values shown reflect change from the base year, 2002. Values above 100 mean greater than 2002, values below 100 mean less than 2002, and a value of 100 in the 2003-2007 period means same as 2002. Values followed by a 'p' are projections by the editors; 'e' stands for extrapolation. Data are the most recent available at this level of detail.

SELECTED RATIOS

For 2002	Avg. of All Retail	Analyzed Industry	Index	For 2002	Avg. of All Retail	Analyzed Industry	Index
Employees per Establishment	17	175	1,033	Sales per Employee	174,682	130,355	75
Payroll per Establishment	333,445	2,831,280	849	Sales per Establishment	3,332,269	22,816,105	685
Payroll per Employee	20,311	16,176	80	Expenses per Establishment	na	na	na

Sources: Same as General Statistics. The 'Average of All' column, Wholesale or Retail, represents the average of the sector reported for the most recent complete year available. The Index shows the relationship between the Average and the Analyzed Industry. For example, 100 means that they are equal; 500 that the Analyzed Industry is five times the average; 50 means that the Analyzed Industry is half the national average. The abbreviation 'na' is used to show that data are 'not available'.

LEADING COMPANIES Number shown: **43** Total sales ($ mil): **615,884** Total employment (000): **16,673.8**

Company Name	Address				CEO Name	Phone	Co. Type	Sales ($ mil)	Empl. (000)
Wal-Mart Stores Inc.	702 SW 8th St	Bentonville	AR	72716		501-273-4000	P	288,189	15,000.0
Foley's	1110 Main St	Houston	TX	77002	Andrew P Pickman	713-405-7033	D	99,626*	20.0
Target Corp.	1000 Nicollet Mall	Minneapolis	MN	55403	Linda L Ahlers	612-304-6073	P	45,682	273.0
Sears, Roebuck and Co.	3333 Beverly Rd	Hoffman Estates	IL	60179		847-286-2500	D	36,099	250.0
Target Stores Inc.	1000 Nicollet Mall	Minneapolis	MN	55403	Gregg Steinhafel	612-304-6073	D	29,961*	245.0
J.C. Penney Company Inc.	6501 Legacy Dr	Plano	TX	75024		972-431-1000	P	17,786	250.0
Federated Department Stores Inc.	7 W Seventh St	Cincinnati	OH	45202		513-579-7758	P	15,630	111.0
May Department Stores Co.	611 Olive St	St. Louis	MO	63101		314-342-6300	P	14,441	·110.0
Gordmans	12100 W Center Rd	Omaha	NE	68144	Jeffrey J Gordman	402-691-4000	R	13,815*	2.8
Kohl's Corp.	N54 Woodale W	Menomonee Fls	WI	53051	William S Kellogg	414-783-5800	P	11,701	100.0
Dillard's Inc.	PO Box 486	Little Rock	AR	72203	Alex Dillard	501-376-5200	P	7,530	53.6
Nordstrom Inc.	1617 6th Ave	Seattle	WA	98101	Jim Bromley	206-628-2111	P	6,492	52.0
Kohl's Department Stores Inc.	N56 Ridgewood W	Menomonee Fls	WI	53051	Larry Montgomery	262-703-7000	S	4,557*	43.0
Mervyn's	22301 Foothill Blvd	Hayward	CA	94541	Diane L Neal	510-727-3000	S	4,038*	32.0
Neiman Marcus Group Inc.	1618 Main St	Dallas	TX	75201		214-741-6911	P	3,546	15.7
ShopKo Stores Inc.	PO Box 19060	Green Bay	WI	54307		920-497-2211	P	3,167	19.0
Belk Inc.	2801 W Tyvola Rd	Charlotte	NC	28217	John M Belk	704-357-1000	R	2,265	17.2
Rich's/Lazarus/Goldsmith's	223 Perimeter Center	Atlanta	GA	30346	David L Nichols	770-913-4000	S	1,907*	15.0
Robinsons-May	6150 Laurel Canyon	N. Hollywood	CA	91606	John Dunham	818-766-4111	S	1,643*	11.0
Gilmore Brothers Inc.	143 S Kalamazoo	Kalamazoo	MI	49007	Steven Phillips	269-345-3541	R	1,493*	0.3
Bon-Ton Stores Inc.	PO Box 2821	York	PA	17405	Byron Bergren	717-757-7660	P	1,310	13.5
Meier and Frank	6160 Laural Canyon	N Hollywood	CA	91606	Crieg Israel	818-508-5226	D	1,062*	5.0
Boscov's Department Stores Inc.	PO Box 4116	Reading	PA	19606		610-779-2000	R	1,051	11.0
Peebles Inc.	1 Peebles St	South Hill	VA	23970	Michael F Moorman	434-447-5200	S	748*	4.0
Elder-Beerman Stores Corp.	PO Box 1448	Dayton	OH	45401	Byron L Bergren	937-296-2700	S	671	6.1
Gottschalks Inc.	PO Box 28920	Fresno	CA	93720	James R Famalette	559-434-4800	P	668	5.8
Filene's Basement Corp.	12 Gill St, Ste 1600	Woburn	MA	01801	Mark Shulman	617-348-7000	S	183*	1.5
Von Maur Inc.	6565 Brady St	Davenport	IA	52806	Charles R von Maur	563-388-2200	R	113*	1.2
Troutman's Emporium	PO Box 5467	Eugene	OR	97405	Dallas Troutman	541-746-9611	R	111*	1.5
B.C. Moore and Sons Inc.	PO Drawer 72	Wadesboro	NC	28170	James C Crawford Jr	704-694-2171	R	97*	1.3
Mansour's Inc.	PO Box 1349	LaGrange	GA	30241	Alfred Mansour Jr	706-884-7305	R	40*	0.4
Schottenstein Stores Corp	3251 Westerville Rd	Columbus	OH	43224		614-471-4711	D	40*	0.3
Halls Merchandising Inc.	200 E 25th St	Kansas City	MO	64108	Robert Leitstein	816-274-8111	S	39*	0.4
Jenss Department Stores Inc.	4001 Maple Rd	Amherst	NY	14221	L Dautch	716-837-1100	R	35*	0.3
U.S. Factory Outlets Inc.	7 Penn Plz	New York	NY	10001	Frederic K Raiff	212-563-3650	R	35*	0.3
Ralph's Foods	501 N Carol Malone	Grayson	KY	41143	Tim Forth	606-474-5522	S	26*	<0.1
Popular Dry Goods Co.	119 Bridge St	Las Vegas	NM	87701		505-425-7272	R	20*	<0.1
Allen's of Hastings Inc.	PO Box 987	Hastings	NE	68901	Robert M Allen	402-463-5633	R	16*	0.2
Silverman Brothers Inc.	6601 Harvard Ave	Cleveland	OH	44105	Alan Silverman		R	14*	0.2
Langston Co.	PO Box 83138	Oklahoma City	OK	73148	M Barber	405-235-9536	R	12*	0.1
Rozier Mercantile Co.	PO Box 150	Perryville	MO	63775	James Lottes	573-547-6521	R	12*	<0.1
Northern Lakes Co-op Inc.	PO Box 985	Hayward	WI	54843		715-634-4841	R	11*	0.2
Annie Sez	40-50 Broad St	Bloomfield	NJ	07003		973-743-3300	D	4*	<0.1

Source: Ward's Business Directory of U.S. Private and Public Companies, Volumes 1 and 2, 2005. The company type code used is as follows: P - Public, R - Private, S - Subsidiary, D - Division, J - Joint Venture, A - Affiliate, G - Group. Sales are in millions of dollars, employees are in thousands. An asterisk (*) indicates an estimated sales volume. The symbol < stands for 'less than'. Company names and addresses are truncated, in some cases, to fit into the available space.

OCCUPATIONS EMPLOYED BY DEPARTMENT STORES

Occupation	% of Total 2004	Change to 2014	Occupation	% of Total 2004	Change to 2014
Retail salespersons	38.6	13.8	Shipping, receiving, & traffic clerks	2.5	6.6
Stock clerks & order fillers	15.5	0.2	First-line supervisors/managers of office workers	1.6	6.7
Cashiers, except gaming	13.7	6.0	Customer service representatives	1.6	20.5
First-line supervisors/managers of retail sales workers	3.0	8.4	Security guards	1.2	-5.8

Source: Industry-Occupation Matrix, Bureau of Labor Statistics. These data are reported based on 4-digit NAICS categories but have been matched to corresponding 6-digit NAICS industry codes. The change reported for each occupation to the year 2014 is a percent of growth or decline as estimated by the Bureau of Labor Statistics. The abbreviation nec stands for 'not elsewhere classified.'

LOCATION BY STATE AND REGIONAL CONCENTRATION

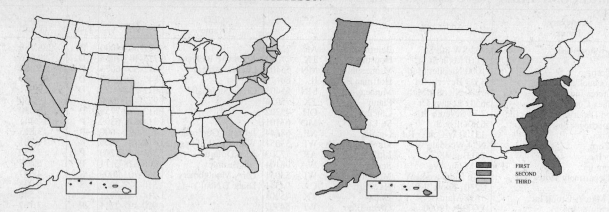

INDUSTRY DATA BY STATE

State	Establishments Total (number)	% of U.S.	Employment Total (number)	% of U.S.	Per Estab.	Payroll Total ($ mil.)	Per Empl. ($)	Sales Total ($ mil.)	% of U.S.	Per Estab. ($)
California	444	12.0	83,195	12.4	187	1,438.3	17,288	12,500.0	14.4	28,153,180
Texas	286	7.7	50,347	7.5	176	855.9	17,000	6,972.5	8.0	24,379,294
New York	179	4.8	45,248	6.8	253	849.5	18,773	6,575.6	7.6	36,735,223
Florida	237	6.4	43,255	6.5	183	740.9	17,129	5,732.0	6.6	24,185,814
Pennsylvania	194	5.2	36,110	5.4	186	533.8	14,782	4,189.1	4.8	21,593,093
Illinois	140	3.8	28,046	4.2	200	479.3	17,091	3,906.9	4.5	27,906,493
New Jersey	91	2.5	22,360	3.3	246	419.6	18,764	3,328.6	3.8	36,577,791
Ohio	172	4.6	30,627	4.6	178	443.3	14,473	3,293.8	3.8	19,149,988
Virginia	111	3.0	20,896	3.1	188	299.0	14,308	2,407.7	2.8	21,691,108
Georgia	113	3.0	18,739	2.8	166	300.4	16,030	2,327.4	2.7	20,596,558
Massachusetts	67	1.8	15,684	2.3	234	274.9	17,528	2,131.5	2.5	31,813,687
North Carolina	124	3.3	18,179	2.7	147	250.4	13,771	2,024.8	2.3	16,328,766
Maryland	76	2.1	16,714	2.5	220	219.6	13,136	1,870.2	2.2	24,607,947
Washington	79	2.1	12,737	1.9	161	235.9	18,518	1,739.4	2.0	22,018,304
Tennessee	86	2.3	13,546	2.0	158	205.0	15,131	1,537.3	1.8	17,875,012
Missouri	66	1.8	12,825	1.9	194	185.6	14,470	1,500.5	1.7	22,734,758
Minnesota	63	1.7	13,059	2.0	207	196.4	15,041	1,480.3	1.7	23,496,714
Indiana	79	2.1	12,472	1.9	158	171.1	13,715	1,429.1	1.6	18,090,367
Wisconsin	76	2.1	10,254	1.5	135	159.2	15,530	1,294.2	1.5	17,028,671
Colorado	66	1.8	10,524	1.6	159	167.7	15,936	1,287.3	1.5	19,503,879
Louisiana	56	1.5	9,528	1.4	170	145.6	15,278	1,223.7	1.4	21,850,911
Connecticut	39	1.1	8,841	1.3	227	144.4	16,328	1,087.9	1.3	27,896,051
South Carolina	61	1.6	8,299	1.2	136	118.9	14,327	920.6	1.1	15,091,754
Kentucky	46	1.2	7,466	1.1	162	113.0	15,132	919.2	1.1	19,982,935
Nevada	32	0.9	5,295	0.8	165	99.6	18,811	823.2	0.9	25,724,594
Oregon	36	1.0	5,785	0.9	161	97.5	16,861	799.1	0.9	22,196,611
Oklahoma	40	1.1	6,079	0.9	152	93.6	15,398	748.8	0.9	18,720,575
Kansas	34	0.9	5,810	0.9	171	86.5	14,893	700.7	0.8	20,609,294
Iowa	47	1.3	5,432	0.8	116	81.0	14,918	665.4	0.8	14,157,723
Mississippi	36	1.0	4,643	0.7	129	73.8	15,888	607.4	0.7	16,872,722
New Hampshire	22	0.6	4,193	0.6	191	66.7	15,911	545.8	0.6	24,808,636
Arkansas	21	0.6	4,210	0.6	200	62.9	14,951	511.6	0.6	24,359,762
Utah	31	0.8	4,635	0.7	150	66.1	14,255	509.1	0.6	16,421,355
Delaware	16	0.4	3,687	0.6	230	54.6	14,800	450.5	0.5	28,156,375
West Virginia	28	0.8	3,520	0.5	126	48.3	13,713	421.5	0.5	15,052,393
Nebraska	26	0.7	3,251	0.5	125	48.9	15,035	388.6	0.4	14,945,115
Idaho	23	0.6	2,529	0.4	110	38.6	15,251	310.1	0.4	13,482,174
Maine	13	0.4	1,976	0.3	152	29.1	14,745	256.7	0.3	19,743,615
North Dakota	15	0.4	2,043	0.3	136	27.0	13,238	235.8	0.3	15,718,067
Rhode Island	8	0.2	1,694	0.3	212	29.5	17,420	230.5	0.3	28,816,125
Montana	17	0.5	1,594	0.2	94	25.4	15,907	201.1	0.2	11,827,941
South Dakota	10	0.3	1,254	0.2	125	19.4	15,509	169.6	0.2	16,961,900
Vermont	6	0.2	689	0.1	115	11.3	16,422	111.3	0.1	18,551,833
Michigan	108	2.9	10K-24999	-	-	(D)	-	(D)	-	-
Arizona	72	1.9	10K-24999	-	-	(D)	-	(D)	-	-
Alabama	55	1.5	5K-9999	-	-	(D)	-	(D)	-	-
New Mexico	25	0.7	2500-4999	-	-	(D)	-	(D)	-	-
Hawaii	19	0.5	2500-4999	-	-	(D)	-	(D)	-	-
Wyoming	7	0.2	500-999	-	-	(D)	-	(D)	-	-
Alaska	4	0.1	500-999	-	-	(D)	-	(D)	-	-
D.C.	3	0.1	500-999	-	-	(D)	-	(D)	-	-

Source: 2002 *Economic Census*. The states are in descending order of sales or establishments (if sales data are missing for the majority). The symbol (D) appears when data are withheld to prevent disclosure of competitive information. States marked with (D) are sorted by number of establishments. A dash (-) indicates that the data element cannot be calculated. Shaded *states* on the state map indicate those states which have proportionately greater representation in the industry than would be indicated by the states population; the ratio is based on total sales or number of establishments. Shaded *regions* indicate where the industry is regionally most concentrated.

NAICS 452112 - DISCOUNT DEPARTMENT STORES

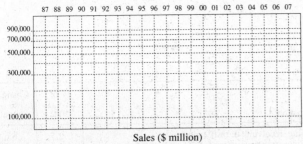

Sales ($ million)

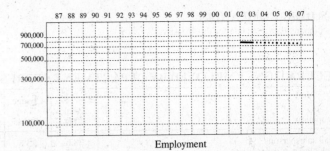

Employment

GENERAL STATISTICS

Year	Establishments (number)	Employment (number)	Payroll ($ million)	Sales ($ million)	Employees per Establishment (number)	Sales per Establishment ($)	Payroll per Employee ($)
1987	-	-	-	-	-	-	-
1988	-	-	-	-	-	-	-
1989	-	-	-	-	-	-	-
1990	-	-	-	-	-	-	-
1991	-	-	-	-	-	-	-
1992	-	-	-	-	-	-	-
1993	-	-	-	-	-	-	-
1994	-	-	-	-	-	-	-
1995	-	-	-	-	-	-	-
1996	-	-	-	-	-	-	-
1997	-	-	-	-	-	-	-
1998	-	-	-	-	-	-	-
1999	-	-	-	-	-	-	-
2000	-	-	-	-	-	-	-
2001	-	-	-	-	-	-	-
2002	5,690	764,714	12,630.2	134,166.2	134	23,579,290	16,516
2003	5,499	758,066	13,229.2	-	138	-	17,451
2004	5,308 p	751,418 p	13,828.2 p	-	141 p	-	18,386 p
2005	5,117 p	744,770 p	14,427.1 p	-	145 p	-	19,321 p
2006	4,926 p	738,122 p	15,026.1 p	-	148 p	-	20,256 p
2007	4,735 p	731,474 p	15,625.1 p	-	152 p	-	21,191 p

Source: *Economic Census of the United States*, 2002. Establishment counts, employment, and payroll are from *County Business Patterns* for non-Census years. This is a newly defined industry. Data for prior years are unavailable at the time of publication but may become available over time. Values followed by 'p' are projections by the editors. Sales data for non-Census years are extrapolations, marked by 'e'.

INDICES OF CHANGE

Year	Establishments (number)	Employment (number)	Payroll ($ million)	Sales ($ million)	Employees per Establishment (number)	Sales per Establishment ($)	Payroll per Employee ($)
1987	-	-	-	-	-	-	-
1992	-	-	-	-	-	-	-
1993	-	-	-	-	-	-	-
1994	-	-	-	-	-	-	-
1995	-	-	-	-	-	-	-
1996	-	-	-	-	-	-	-
1997	-	-	-	-	-	-	-
1998	-	-	-	-	-	-	-
1999	-	-	-	-	-	-	-
2000	-	-	-	-	-	-	-
2001	-	-	-	-	-	-	-
2002	100.0	100.0	100.0	100.0	100.0	100.0	100.0
2003	96.6	99.1	104.7	-	102.6	-	105.7
2004	93.3 p	98.3 p	109.5 p	-	105.1 p	-	111.3 p
2005	89.9 p	97.4 p	114.2 p	-	107.7 p	-	117.0 p
2006	86.6 p	96.5 p	119.0 p	-	110.3 p	-	122.6 p
2007	83.2 p	95.7 p	123.7 p	-	112.9 p	-	128.3 p

Sources: Same as General Statistics. The values shown reflect change from the base year, 2002. Values above 100 mean greater than 2002, values below 100 mean less than 2002, and a value of 100 in the 2003-2007 period means same as 2002. Values followed by a 'p' are projections by the editors; 'e' stands for extrapolation. Data are the most recent available at this level of detail.

SELECTED RATIOS

For 2002	Avg. of All Retail	Analyzed Industry	Index	For 2002	Avg. of All Retail	Analyzed Industry	Index
Employees per Establishment	17	134	793	Sales per Employee	174,682	175,446	100
Payroll per Establishment	333,445	2,219,721	666	Sales per Establishment	3,332,269	23,579,290	708
Payroll per Employee	20,311	16,516	81	Expenses per Establishment	na	na	na

Sources: Same as General Statistics. The 'Average of All' column, Wholesale or Retail, represents the average of the sector reported for the most recent complete year available. The Index shows the relationship between the Average and the Analyzed Industry. For example, 100 means that they are equal; 500 that the Analyzed Industry is five times the average; 50 means that the Analyzed Industry is half the national average. The abbreviation 'na' is used to show that data are 'not available'.

LEADING COMPANIES

No company data available for this industry.

OCCUPATIONS EMPLOYED BY DEPARTMENT STORES

Occupation	% of Total 2004	Change to 2014	Occupation	% of Total 2004	Change to 2014
Retail salespersons	38.6	13.8	Shipping, receiving, & traffic clerks	2.5	6.6
Stock clerks & order fillers	15.5	0.2	First-line supervisors/managers of office workers	1.6	6.7
Cashiers, except gaming	13.7	6.0	Customer service representatives	1.6	20.5
First-line supervisors/managers of retail sales workers	3.0	8.4	Security guards	1.2	-5.8

Source: Industry-Occupation Matrix, Bureau of Labor Statistics. These data are reported based on 4-digit NAICS categories but have been matched to corresponding 6-digit NAICS industry codes. The change reported for each occupation to the year 2014 is a percent of growth or decline as estimated by the Bureau of Labor Statistics. The abbreviation nec stands for 'not elsewhere classified.'

LOCATION BY STATE AND REGIONAL CONCENTRATION

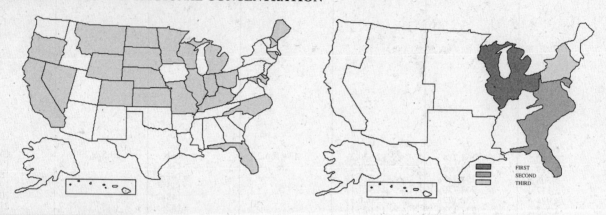

FIRST
SECOND
THIRD

INDUSTRY DATA BY STATE

State	Establishments Total (number)	% of U.S.	Employment Total (number)	% of U.S.	Per Estab.	Payroll Total ($ mil.)	Per Empl. ($)	Sales Total ($ mil.)	% of U.S.	Per Estab. ($)
California	469	8.3	83,254	10.9	178	1,546.4	18,575	16,673.3	12.5	35,550,838
Illinois	324	5.7	46,103	6.0	142	697.1	15,120	7,762.5	5.8	23,958,485
Florida	283	5.0	39,839	5.2	141	688.0	17,269	7,065.3	5.3	24,965,615
Texas	320	5.7	40,184	5.3	126	663.6	16,514	6,980.5	5.2	21,813,987
Ohio	285	5.0	37,411	4.9	131	596.0	15,930	6,638.5	5.0	23,292,895
Pennsylvania	306	5.4	34,506	4.5	113	535.9	15,532	5,981.0	4.5	19,545,712
New York	274	4.8	32,662	4.3	119	537.3	16,451	5,850.6	4.4	21,352,661
Michigan	243	4.3	32,840	4.3	135	522.6	15,913	5,503.1	4.1	22,646,568
Wisconsin	201	3.6	28,449	3.7	142	417.0	14,657	4,534.5	3.4	22,559,831
Minnesota	159	2.8	25,070	3.3	158	395.5	15,776	4,314.6	3.2	27,135,987
New Jersey	150	2.7	20,574	2.7	137	351.2	17,068	4,007.2	3.0	26,714,353
North Carolina	152	2.7	21,272	2.8	140	349.9	16,448	3,621.2	2.7	23,823,921
Maryland	130	2.3	19,517	2.6	150	315.8	16,181	3,525.8	2.6	27,121,331
Georgia	161	2.8	21,066	2.8	131	335.8	15,940	3,359.8	2.5	20,868,106
Indiana	155	2.7	19,979	2.6	129	296.9	14,858	3,238.4	2.4	20,892,781
Missouri	146	2.6	19,556	2.6	134	304.7	15,579	3,101.3	2.3	21,242,014
Virginia	128	2.3	16,628	2.2	130	273.2	16,427	3,066.8	2.3	23,959,727
Massachusetts	132	2.3	15,508	2.0	117	301.5	19,439	3,032.7	2.3	22,974,773
Washington	97	1.7	14,385	1.9	148	266.1	18,495	2,716.1	2.0	28,000,825
Tennessee	108	1.9	13,766	1.8	127	231.4	16,810	2,343.0	1.7	21,694,194
Kentucky	96	1.7	12,422	1.6	129	198.1	15,950	2,073.6	1.5	21,600,063
Colorado	76	1.3	10,353	1.4	136	178.9	17,280	1,890.6	1.4	24,876,105
Connecticut	82	1.5	9,628	1.3	117	170.0	17,659	1,778.6	1.3	21,690,841
Oregon	58	1.0	8,104	1.1	140	152.3	18,790	1,545.8	1.2	26,651,793
Iowa	88	1.6	9,560	1.3	109	143.8	15,045	1,526.3	1.1	17,344,659
Kansas	62	1.1	8,530	1.1	138	136.5	16,000	1,339.4	1.0	21,602,645
New Hampshire	56	1.0	6,313	0.8	113	123.1	19,501	1,318.3	1.0	23,541,071
South Carolina	70	1.2	7,929	1.0	113	133.9	16,889	1,302.8	1.0	18,611,557
Oklahoma	72	1.3	8,358	1.1	116	124.8	14,933	1,255.0	0.9	17,430,542
Nevada	38	0.7	6,288	0.8	165	118.6	18,866	1,181.1	0.9	31,082,605
Louisiana	64	1.1	7,759	1.0	121	123.2	15,878	1,161.8	0.9	18,153,328
Nebraska	48	0.8	5,999	0.8	125	87.4	14,561	927.0	0.7	19,312,437

Continued on next page.

INDUSTRY DATA BY STATE - Continued

State	Establishments		Employment			Payroll		Sales		
	Total (number)	% of U.S.	Total (number)	% of U.S.	Per Estab.	Total ($ mil.)	Per Empl. ($)	Total ($ mil.)	% of U.S.	Per Estab. ($)
Utah	49	0.9	5,546	0.7	113	93.6	16,878	924.8	0.7	18,873,143
Arkansas	51	0.9	6,030	0.8	118	93.5	15,512	901.8	0.7	17,681,471
West Virginia	41	0.7	4,748	0.6	116	74.6	15,709	800.2	0.6	19,518,098
Maine	47	0.8	4,690	0.6	100	74.9	15,973	783.6	0.6	16,671,979
New Mexico	30	0.5	3,818	0.5	127	63.6	16,662	684.5	0.5	22,816,800
North Dakota	22	0.4	3,400	0.4	155	53.0	15,579	644.3	0.5	29,284,636
Mississippi	36	0.6	4,319	0.6	120	63.6	14,725	601.7	0.4	16,713,361
South Dakota	30	0.5	3,632	0.5	121	53.6	14,763	584.0	0.4	19,466,133
Delaware	21	0.4	2,704	0.4	129	44.3	16,402	532.7	0.4	25,366,619
Montana	27	0.5	3,087	0.4	114	49.5	16,040	527.2	0.4	19,525,296
Idaho	29	0.5	3,132	0.4	108	47.0	15,008	503.8	0.4	17,373,655
Rhode Island	22	0.4	2,534	0.3	115	40.3	15,918	402.2	0.3	18,282,773
Wyoming	13	0.2	1,389	0.2	107	25.1	18,082	255.0	0.2	19,616,692
Vermont	19	0.3	1,614	0.2	85	24.1	14,911	251.1	0.2	13,218,211
Arizona	88	1.6	10K-24999	-	-	(D)	-	(D)	-	-
Alabama	71	1.3	5K-9999	-	-	(D)	-	(D)	-	-
Hawaii	13	0.2	2500-4999	-	-	(D)	-	(D)	-	-
Alaska	7	0.1	1000-2499	-	-	(D)	-	(D)	-	-
D.C.	1		100-249	-	-	(D)	-	(D)	-	-

Source: 2002 *Economic Census.* The states are in descending order of sales or establishments (if sales data are missing for the majority). The symbol (D) appears when data are withheld to prevent disclosure of competitive information. States marked with (D) are sorted by number of establishments. A dash (-) indicates that the data element cannot be calculated. Shaded *states* on the state map indicate those states which have proportionately greater representation in the industry than would be indicated by the states population; the ratio is based on total sales or number of establishments. Shaded *regions* indicate where the industry is regionally most concentrated.

NAICS 452910 - WAREHOUSE CLUBS AND SUPERCENTERS

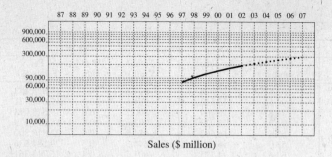

Sales ($ million)

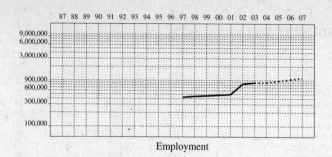

Employment

GENERAL STATISTICS

Year	Establishments (number)	Employment (number)	Payroll ($ million)	Sales ($ million)	Employees per Establishment (number)	Sales per Establishment ($)	Payroll per Employee ($)
1987	-	-	-	-	-	-	-
1988	-	-	-	-	-	-	-
1989	-	-	-	-	-	-	-
1990	-	-	-	-	-	-	-
1991	-	-	-	-	-	-	-
1992	-	-	-	-	-	-	-
1993	-	-	-	-	-	-	-
1994	-	-	-	-	-	-	-
1995	-	-	-	-	-	-	-
1996	-	-	-	-	-	-	-
1997	1,530	428,357	5,862.6	81,918.8	280	53,541,699	13,686
1998	1,788	449,645	7,021.7	103,458.9 e	251	57,862,922	15,616
1999	1,840	461,992	7,915.2	124,999.0 e	251	67,934,244	17,133
2000	1,968	477,521	8,736.6	146,539.1 e	243	74,460,932	18,296
2001	2,051	495,230	9,330.9	168,079.2 e	242	81,949,887	18,841
2002	2,915	837,200	15,847.1	189,619.3	287	65,049,510	18,929
2003	3,047	889,932	17,299.8	211,159.4 p	292	80,432,530 p	19,440
2004	3,165 p	890,421 p	17,913.2 p	232,699.5 p	278 p	84,327,576 p	21,076 p
2005	3,416 p	968,745 p	19,819.5 p	254,239.6 p	281 p	88,222,623 p	21,990 p
2006	3,666 p	1,047,070 p	21,725.9 p	275,779.7 p	285 p	92,117,670 p	22,904 p
2007	3,917 p	1,125,394 p	23,632.3 p	297,319.8 p	288 p	96,012,717 p	23,819 p

Source: Economic Census of the United States, 1997 and 2002. Establishment counts, employment, and payroll are from *County Business Patterns* for non-Census years. This is a newly defined industry. Data for prior years are unavailable at the time of publication but may become available over time. Values followed by 'p' are projections by the editors. Sales data for non-Census years are extrapolations, marked by 'e'.

INDICES OF CHANGE

Year	Establishments (number)	Employment (number)	Payroll ($ million)	Sales ($ million)	Employees per Establishment (number)	Sales per Establishment ($)	Payroll per Employee ($)
1987	-	-	-	-	-	-	-
1992	-	-	-	-	-	-	-
1993	-	-	-	-	-	-	-
1994	-	-	-	-	-	-	-
1995	-	-	-	-	-	-	-
1996	-	-	-	-	-	-	-
1997	52.5	51.2	37.0	43.2	97.5	82.3	72.3
1998	61.3	53.7	44.3	54.6 e	87.6	89.0	82.5
1999	63.1	55.2	49.9	65.9 e	87.4	104.4	90.5
2000	67.5	57.0	55.1	77.3 e	84.5	114.5	96.7
2001	70.4	59.2	58.9	88.6 e	84.1	126.0	99.5
2002	100.0	100.0	100.0	100.0	100.0	100.0	100.0
2003	104.5	106.3	109.2	111.4 p	101.7	123.6 p	102.7
2004	108.6 p	106.4 p	113.0 p	122.7 p	96.7 p	129.6 p	111.3 p
2005	117.2 p	115.7 p	125.1 p	134.1 p	97.9 p	135.6 p	116.2 p
2006	125.8 p	125.1 p	137.1 p	145.4 p	99.1 p	141.6 p	121.0 p
2007	134.4 p	134.4 p	149.1 p	156.8 p	100.4 p	147.6 p	125.8 p

Sources: Same as General Statistics. The values shown reflect change from the base year, 2002. Values above 100 mean greater than 2002, values below 100 mean less than 2002, and a value of 100 in the 1987-2001 or 2003-2007 period means same as 2002. Values followed by a 'p' are projections by the editors; 'e' stands for extrapolation. Data are the most recent available at this level of detail.

SELECTED RATIOS

For 2002	Avg. of All Retail	Analyzed Industry	Index	For 2002	Avg. of All Retail	Analyzed Industry	Index
Employees per Establishment	17	287	1,694	Sales per Employee	174,682	226,492	130
Payroll per Establishment	333,445	5,436,398	1,630	Sales per Establishment	3,332,269	65,049,510	1,952
Payroll per Employee	20,311	18,929	93	Expenses per Establishment	na	na	na

Sources: Same as General Statistics. The 'Average of All' column, Wholesale or Retail, represents the average of the sector reported for the most recent complete year available. The Index shows the relationship between the Average and the Analyzed Industry. For example, 100 means that they are equal; 500 that the Analyzed Industry is five times the average; 50 means that the Analyzed Industry is half the national average. The abbreviation 'na' is used to show that data are 'not available'.

LEADING COMPANIES   Number shown: **35**   Total sales ($ mil): **358,264**   Total employment (000): **15,398.8**

Company Name	Address			CEO Name	Phone	Co. Type	Sales ($ mil)	Empl. (000)
Wal-Mart Stores Inc.	702 SW 8th St	Bentonville	AR 72716		501-273-4000	P	288,189	15,000.0
Target Corp.	1000 Nicollet Mall	Minneapolis	MN 55403	Linda L Ahlers	612-304-6073	P	45,682	273.0
Meijer Great Lakes L.P.	2929 Walker NW	Grand Rapids	MI 49544	Paul Boyer	616-453-6711	R	11,900*	70.0
BJ's Wholesale Club Inc.	PO Box 9601	Natick	MA 01760		508-651-7400	P	7,220	18.5
Fred's Inc.	4300 New Getwell	Memphis	TN 38118	Michael J Hayes	901-365-8880	P	1,303	9.0
Cost Plus Inc.	200 4th St	Oakland	CA 94607	Murray H Dashe	510-893-7300	P	802	5.5
Garden Ridge Corp.	19411 Atrium Pl	Houston	TX 77084	John Rice	281-579-7901	R	521*	5.0
Marden Discount Store Inc.	184 College Ave	Waterville	ME 04901	Harold Marden	207-873-6111	R	442*	0.9
Alloy Inc.	151 W 26th St	New York	NY 10001	Matthew C Diamond	212-244-4307	P	403	4.0
K's Merchandise Mart Inc.	3103 N Charles St	Decatur	IL 62526	David K Eldridge	217-875-1440	R	320*	2.0
Green Valley Acquisition Co.	477 E Beaver Ave	State College	PA 16801	Henry D Sahakian	814-234-6000	R	296	2.5
Odd Job Stores Inc.	200 Helen St	South Plainfield	NJ 07080	Sam Friedland	908-222-1000	R	234	2.2
Z.V. Pate Inc.	PO Box 159	Laurel Hill	NC 28351	David L Burns	910-462-2122	R	176*	0.9
G.I. Joe's Inc.	9805 SW Boeckman	Wilsonville	OR 97070	Norm Daniels	503-682-2242	R	124*	1.0
Grand Home Furnishings	4235 Electric Rd SW	Roanoke	VA 24014	George B Cartledge Jr	540-774-7004	R	100*	0.8
Ammar's Inc.	710 S College Ave	Bluefield	VA 24605	Keleel A Ammar Jr	276-322-4686	R	85*	0.9
Kugler Oil Co.	PO Box 1748	McCook	NE 69001	Diane Kugler	308-345-2280	R	69*	0.2
Atwood Distributing Inc.	2717 N Van Buren	Enid	OK 73703	G Atwood	580-233-3702	R	66*	0.9
University Book Store Inc.	4326 University NE	Seattle	WA 98105		206-634-3400	R	49*	0.3
Thruway Food Market & Shopping	78 Oak St	Walden	NY 12586	Arthur Concors	845-778-3535	R	39*	0.4
Danco Prairie FS Coop.	5371 Farmco Dr	Madison	WI 53704	Kevin Lins	608-241-4181	R	30*	<0.1
Four Seasons Cooperative	PO Box 148	Britton	SD 57430		605-448-2231	R	28*	<0.1
Hammer and Wikan Inc.	PO Box 249	Petersburg	AK 99833	Gainhart Samuelson	907-772-4811	R	28*	<0.1
Mazer's Discount Home Centers	41st St 2nd Ave S	Birmingham	AL 35222	JB Mazer	205-591-6565	R	24*	0.2
University Cooperative Society Inc.	2244 Guadalupe St	Austin	TX 78705	George Mitchell	512-476-7211	R	24*	0.1
Richards Brothers Supermarket Inc.	PO Box 866	Mountain Grove	MO 65711	Wells E Richards	417-926-4168	R	23*	<0.1
Friends Enterprises	PO Box 2708	Morgan City	LA 70381	John O'Neill	985-384-1610	R	19*	<0.1
Mid-Wood Inc.	111 E Gypsy Ln	Bowling Green	OH 43402		419-352-5231	R	14*	<0.1
Pierre Part Store Inc.	PO Box 10	Pierre Part	LA 70339	Logi J Guillot	985-252-6261	R	13*	<0.1
Cooperative Sampo Corp.	Box 220	Menahga	MN 56464		218-564-4534	R	11*	<0.1
Sutton Cooperative Grain Co.	PO Box 368	Sutton	NE 68979	Bruce Trautman	402-773-5531	R	10*	<0.1
Kikiktagruk Inupiat Corp.	PO Box 1050	Kotzebue	AK 99752	Chris Lethin	907-442-3165	R	8*	<0.1
Kane Industries Corp.	1250 Graves Ave	Oxnard	CA 93030	Alan S Gordon	805-988-3904	R	6*	<0.1
Schaeperkoetter Store Inc.	PO Box 37	Mount Sterling	MO 65062	I R Schaeperkoetter	573-943-6321	R	5*	<0.1
Harold L. Keay and Son	56 Main St	Albion	ME 04910	Kevin G Keay	207-437-2540	R	2*	<0.1

Source: *Ward's Business Directory of U.S. Private and Public Companies*, Volumes 1 and 2, 2005. The company type code used is as follows: P - Public, R - Private, S - Subsidiary, D - Division, J - Joint Venture, A - Affiliate, G - Group. Sales are in millions of dollars, employees are in thousands. An asterisk (*) indicates an estimated sales volume. The symbol < stands for 'less than'. Company names and addresses are truncated, in some cases, to fit into the available space.

OCCUPATIONS EMPLOYED BY OTHER GENERAL MERCHANDISE STORES

Occupation	% of Total 2004	Change to 2014	Occupation	% of Total 2004	Change to 2014
Retail salespersons	26.1	19.4	First-line supervisors/managers of office workers	2.0	8.1
Cashiers, except gaming	21.2	7.4	Packers & packagers, hand	1.7	19.4
Stock clerks & order fillers	11.6	-8.5	Janitors & cleaners, except maids	1.7	19.4
First-line supervisors/managers of retail sales workers	4.7	9.8	Shipping, receiving, & traffic clerks	1.4	8.1
Customer service representatives	2.3	22.1			

Source: *Industry-Occupation Matrix*, Bureau of Labor Statistics. These data are reported based on 4-digit NAICS categories but have been matched to corresponding 6-digit NAICS industry codes. The change reported for each occupation to the year 2014 is a percent of growth or decline as estimated by the Bureau of Labor Statistics. The abbreviation nec stands for 'not elsewhere classified.'

LOCATION BY STATE AND REGIONAL CONCENTRATION

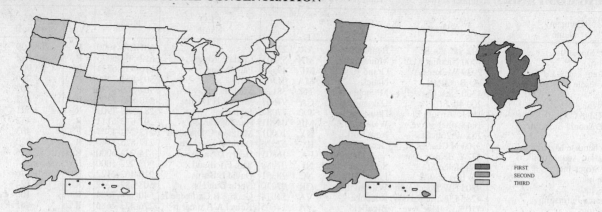

INDUSTRY DATA BY STATE

State	Establishments Total (number)	% of U.S.	Employment Total (number)	% of U.S.	Per Estab.	Payroll Total ($ mil.)	Per Empl. ($)	Sales Total ($ mil.)	% of U.S.	Per Estab. ($)
Ohio	131	4.5	33,711	4.1	257	539.5	16,004	6,638.1	3.5	50,672,824
Indiana	102	3.5	34,466	4.1	338	552.3	16,025	6,190.0	3.2	60,686,549
Virginia	88	3.0	25,655	3.1	292	499.4	19,467	6,187.1	3.2	70,307,716
Washington	92	3.2	20,529	2.5	223	483.5	23,550	5,631.8	2.9	61,215,402
New York	88	3.0	16,500	2.0	188	358.2	21,708	5,563.5	2.9	63,221,466
Illinois	87	3.0	23,513	2.8	270	424.6	18,060	5,331.5	2.8	61,281,540
Oregon	118	4.1	19,359	2.3	164	405.1	20,927	4,430.2	2.3	37,544,119
Colorado	60	2.1	15,974	1.9	266	349.6	21,886	4,117.2	2.2	68,619,967
New Jersey	33	1.1	4,765	0.6	144	122.0	25,603	2,312.7	1.2	70,082,939
Utah	39	1.3	9,623	1.2	247	187.5	19,488	2,187.4	1.1	56,088,103
Maryland	32	1.1	5,694	0.7	178	125.7	22,073	1,876.4	1.0	58,637,563
Massachusetts	25	0.9	3,767	0.5	151	84.5	22,441	1,538.9	0.8	61,556,000
Alaska	19	0.7	4,617	0.6	243	104.9	22,720	1,296.6	0.7	68,240,684
Connecticut	19	0.7	3,246	0.4	171	73.8	22,730	1,114.6	0.6	58,665,526
New Hampshire	15	0.5	2,780	0.3	185	58.6	21,064	862.3	0.5	57,488,333
Delaware	6	0.2	1,631	0.2	272	31.0	19,026	437.8	0.2	72,964,667
Texas	285	9.8	50K-99999	-	-	(D)	-	(D)	-	-
Florida	167	5.7	50K-99999	-	-	(D)	-	(D)	-	-
Michigan	142	4.9	50K-99999	-	-	(D)	-	(D)	-	-
California	132	4.5	25K-49999	-	-	(D)	-	(D)	-	-
Georgia	101	3.5	25K-49999	-	-	(D)	-	(D)	-	-
North Carolina	91	3.1	25K-49999	-	-	(D)	-	(D)	-	-
Pennsylvania	87	3.0	10K-24999	-	-	(D)	-	(D)	-	-
Tennessee	81	2.8	25K-49999	-	-	(D)	-	(D)	-	-
Missouri	80	2.7	25K-49999	-	-	(D)	-	(D)	-	-
Alabama	72	2.5	25K-49999	-	-	(D)	-	(D)	-	-
Louisiana	67	2.3	25K-49999	-	-	(D)	-	(D)	-	-
Arizona	60	2.1	10K-24999	-	-	(D)	-	(D)	-	-
Kentucky	58	2.0	10K-24999	-	-	(D)	-	(D)	-	-
South Carolina	54	1.9	10K-24999	-	-	(D)	-	(D)	-	-
Oklahoma	52	1.8	10K-24999	-	-	(D)	-	(D)	-	-
Mississippi	51	1.8	10K-24999	-	-	(D)	-	(D)	-	-
Arkansas	50	1.7	10K-24999	-	-	(D)	-	(D)	-	-
Iowa	40	1.4	10K-24999	-	-	(D)	-	(D)	-	-
Kansas	37	1.3	10K-24999	-	-	(D)	-	(D)	-	-
Wisconsin	37	1.3	5K-9999	-	-	(D)	-	(D)	-	-
Minnesota	35	1.2	5K-9999	-	-	(D)	-	(D)	-	-
New Mexico	26	0.9	5K-9999	-	-	(D)	-	(D)	-	-
West Virginia	26	0.9	5K-9999	-	-	(D)	-	(D)	-	-
Idaho	25	0.9	5K-9999	-	-	(D)	-	(D)	-	-
Nebraska	20	0.7	5K-9999	-	-	(D)	-	(D)	-	-
Nevada	20	0.7	5K-9999	-	-	(D)	-	(D)	-	-
Maine	14	0.5	2500-4999	-	-	(D)	-	(D)	-	-
Montana	11	0.4	2500-4999	-	-	(D)	-	(D)	-	-
Hawaii	10	0.3	1000-2499	-	-	(D)	-	(D)	-	-
Wyoming	9	0.3	2500-4999	-	-	(D)	-	(D)	-	-
South Dakota	8	0.3	1000-2499	-	-	(D)	-	(D)	-	-
Rhode Island	6	0.2	500-999	-	-	(D)	-	(D)	-	-
North Dakota	3	0.1	500-999	-	-	(D)	-	(D)	-	-
Vermont	1	-	100-249	-	-	(D)	-	(D)	-	-

Source: 2002 Economic Census. The states are in descending order of sales or establishments (if sales data are missing for the majority). The symbol (D) appears when data are withheld to prevent disclosure of competitive information. States marked with (D) are sorted by number of establishments. A dash (-) indicates that the data element cannot be calculated. Shaded states on the state map indicate those states which have proportionately greater representation in the industry than would be indicated by the states population; the ratio is based on total sales or number of establishments. Shaded regions indicate where the industry is regionally most concentrated.

NAICS 452990 - ALL OTHER GENERAL MERCHANDISE STORES

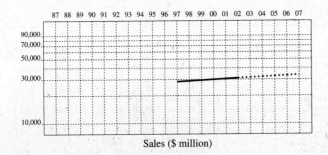

Sales ($ million)

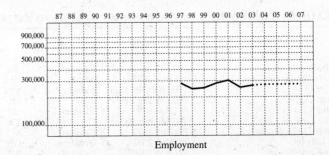

Employment

GENERAL STATISTICS

Year	Establishments (number)	Employment (number)	Payroll ($ million)	Sales ($ million)	Employees per Establishment (number)	Sales per Establishment ($)	Payroll per Employee ($)
1987	-	-	-	-	-	-	-
1988	-	-	-	-	-	-	-
1989	-	-	-	-	-	-	-
1990	-	-	-	-	-	-	-
1991	-	-	-	-	-	-	-
1992	-	-	-	-	-	-	-
1993	-	-	-	-	-	-	-
1994	-	-	-	-	-	-	-
1995	-	-	-	-	-	-	-
1996	-	-	-	-	-	-	-
1997	24,275	283,606	2,925.1	28,417.5	12	1,170,649	10,314
1998	24,424	245,949	3,142.1	28,939.7 e	10	1,184,888	12,775
1999	25,756	251,555	3,322.9	29,461.9 e	10	1,143,885	13,209
2000	27,243	282,734	3,828.7	29,984.1 e	10	1,100,617	13,542
2001	28,744	303,411	4,276.2	30,506.3 e	11	1,061,311	14,094
2002	28,364	253,752	3,255.4	31,028.5	9	1,093,941	12,829
2003	29,545	266,639	3,766.7	31,550.7 p	9	1,046,128 p	14,126
2004	30,718 p	272,030 p	4,031.7 p	32,072.9 p	9 p	1,023,341 p	14,760 p
2005	31,671 p	272,621 p	4,164.0 p	32,595.2 p	8 p	1,000,554 p	15,204 p
2006	32,624 p	273,213 p	4,296.3 p	33,117.4 p	8 p	977,767 p	15,648 p
2007	33,577 p	273,804 p	4,428.6 p	33,639.6 p	8 p	954,981 p	16,092 p

Source: *Economic Census of the United States,* 1997 and 2002. Establishment counts, employment, and payroll are from *County Business Patterns* for non-Census years. This is a newly defined industry. Data for prior years are unavailable at the time of publication but may become available over time. Values followed by 'p' are projections by the editors. Sales data for non-Census years are extrapolations, marked by 'e'.

INDICES OF CHANGE

Year	Establishments (number)	Employment (number)	Payroll ($ million)	Sales ($ million)	Employees per Establishment (number)	Sales per Establishment ($)	Payroll per Employee ($)
1987	-	-	-	-	-	-	-
1992	-	-	-	-	-	-	-
1993	-	-	-	-	-	-	-
1994	-	-	-	-	-	-	-
1995	-	-	-	-	-	-	-
1996	-	-	-	-	-	-	-
1997	85.6	111.8	89.9	91.6	130.8	107.0	80.4
1998	86.1	96.9	96.5	93.3 e	112.9	108.3	99.6
1999	90.8	99.1	102.1	95.0 e	109.5	104.6	103.0
2000	96.0	111.4	117.6	96.6 e	116.2	100.6	105.6
2001	101.3	119.6	131.4	98.3 e	118.5	97.0	109.9
2002	100.0	100.0	100.0	100.0	100.0	100.0	100.0
2003	104.2	105.1	115.7	101.7 p	100.9	95.6 p	110.1
2004	108.3 p	107.2 p	123.8 p	103.4 p	97.5 p	93.5 p	115.0 p
2005	111.7 p	107.4 p	127.9 p	105.0 p	93.7 p	91.5 p	118.5 p
2006	115.0 p	107.7 p	132.0 p	106.7 p	89.9 p	89.4 p	122.0 p
2007	118.4 p	107.9 p	136.0 p	108.4 p	86.1 p	87.3 p	125.4 p

Sources: Same as General Statistics. The values shown reflect change from the base year, 2002. Values above 100 mean greater than 2002, values below 100 mean less than 2002, and a value of 100 in the 1987-2001 or 2003-2007 period means same as 2002. Values followed by a 'p' are projections by the editors; 'e' stands for extrapolation. Data are the most recent available at this level of detail.

SELECTED RATIOS

For 2002	Avg. of All Retail	Analyzed Industry	Index	For 2002	Avg. of All Retail	Analyzed Industry	Index
Employees per Establishment	17	9	53	Sales per Employee	174,682	122,279	70
Payroll per Establishment	333,445	114,773	34	Sales per Establishment	3,332,269	1,093,941	33
Payroll per Employee	20,311	12,829	63	Expenses per Establishment	na	na	na

Sources: Same as General Statistics. The 'Average of All' column, Wholesale or Retail, represents the average of the sector reported for the most recent complete year available. The Index shows the relationship between the Average and the Analyzed Industry. For example, 100 means that they are equal; 500 that the Analyzed Industry is five times the average; 50 means that the Analyzed Industry is half the national average. The abbreviation 'na' is used to show that data are 'not available'.

LEADING COMPANIES

Number shown: **29**   Total sales ($ mil): **443,317**   Total employment (000): **15,817.3**

Company Name	Address				CEO Name	Phone	Co. Type	Sales ($ mil)	Empl. (000)
Wal-Mart Stores Inc.	702 SW 8th St	Bentonville	AR	72716		501-273-4000	P	288,189	15,000.0
Costco Wholesale Corp.	PO Box 34331	Seattle	WA	98124	Jeffrey H Brotman	425-313-8100	P	47,146	110.0
Target Corp.	1000 Nicollet Mall	Minneapolis	MN	55403	Linda L Ahlers	612-304-6073	P	45,682	273.0
Kmart Corp.	3100 W Big Beaver	Troy	MI	48084		248-643-1000	D	17,072	158.0
Flying J Inc.	PO Box 678	Brigham City	UT	84302	J Phillip Adams	801-624-1000	R	7,500	12.5
Dollar General Corp.	100 Mission Ridge	Goodlettsville	TN	37072	David A Perdue Jr	615-855-4000	P	6,870	57.8
Family Dollar Stores Inc.	PO Box 1017	Charlotte	NC	28201	R David Alexander Jr	704-847-6961	P	5,282	39.0
Big Lots Inc.	PO Box 28512	Columbus	OH	43228		614-278-6800	P	4,375	47.2
ShopKo Stores Inc.	PO Box 19060	Green Bay	WI	54307		920-497-2211	P	3,167	19.0
Dollar Tree Stores Inc.	PO Box 2500	Norfolk	VA	23501	Macon F Brock	757-321-5000	P	3,126	28.7
RaceTrac Petroleum Inc.	PO Box 105035	Atlanta	GA	30348	Carl E Bolch, Jr	770-431-7600	R	2,771	4.7
Retail Ventures Inc.	3241 Westerville Rd	Columbus	OH	43224		614-471-4722	P	2,594	18.4
Sheetz Inc.	5700 6th Ave	Altoona	PA	16602		814-946-3611	R	2,300	9.9
Love's Travel Stops & Country	PO Box 26210	Oklahoma City	OK	73126	Greg Love	405-751-9000	R	1,900	3.5
Petro Stopping Centers L.P.	PO Box 26808	El Paso	TX	79926	Jack A Cardwell, Sr	915-779-4711	S	1,307	4.2
Fred's Inc.	4300 New Getwell	Memphis	TN	38118	Michael J Hayes	901-365-8800	P	1,303	9.0
Tuesday Morning Corp.	6250 LBJ Fwy	Dallas	TX	75240	B D Chereskin	972-387-3562	P	898	7.8
99 Cents Only Stores	4000 Union Pacific	Commerce	CA	90023	Jeff Gold	323-980-8145	P	863	7.6
Duckwall-Alco Stores Inc.	401 Cottage St	Abilene	KS	67410		785-263-3350	P	433	5.3
BUY.COM Inc.	85 Enterprise Dr	Aliso Viejo	CA	92656	Scott A Blum	949-389-2000	R	291	0.1
Pechin Shopping Village	PO Box 340	Dunbar	PA	15431	Sullivan D'Amico	724-277-4251	R	73*	0.4
Masotta Variety and Deli	307 Main St	Woburn	MA	01801	Catino Masotta	781-935-2648	R	51*	<0.1
99 Cent Stuff L.L.C.	1801 Clint Moore	Boca Raton	FL	33487	R Zimmerman	561-999-9815	P	47	0.4
Oklahoma Goodwill Industries Inc.	410 SW 3rd St	Oklahoma City	OK	73109	Linda Saleski	405-236-4451	R	37*	0.4
Greetings and Readings Inc.	809 Taylor Ave	Towson	MD	21286	Steve Baum	410-825-4225	R	12*	0.2
Richloom Fabrics Corp.	261 5th Ave	New York	NY	10016	Fred Richman	212-685-5400	R	10*	0.1
Uniway of Augusta Inc.	PO Box 211044	Augusta	GA	30917	Jimmy Carter	706-860-1151	R	9*	<0.1
Belleville Scale Co.	PO Box 15	Belleville	NJ	07109	James Colleton	973-759-4487	R	8*	<0.1
Ranger Joe's International	4030 Victory Dr	Columbus	GA	31903		706-689-3455	R	3*	<0.1

Source: *Ward's Business Directory of U.S. Private and Public Companies*, Volumes 1 and 2, 2005. The company type code used is as follows: P - Public, R - Private, S - Subsidiary, D - Division, J - Joint Venture, A - Affiliate, G - Group. Sales are in millions of dollars, employees are in thousands. An asterisk (*) indicates an estimated sales volume. The symbol < stands for 'less than'. Company names and addresses are truncated, in some cases, to fit into the available space.

OCCUPATIONS EMPLOYED BY OTHER GENERAL MERCHANDISE STORES

Occupation	% of Total 2004	Change to 2014	Occupation	% of Total 2004	Change to 2014
Retail salespersons	26.1	19.4	First-line supervisors/managers of office workers	2.0	8.1
Cashiers, except gaming	21.2	7.4	Packers & packagers, hand	1.7	19.4
Stock clerks & order fillers	11.6	-8.5	Janitors & cleaners, except maids	1.7	19.4
First-line supervisors/managers of retail sales workers	4.7	9.8	Shipping, receiving, & traffic clerks	1.4	8.1
Customer service representatives	2.3	22.1			

Source: *Industry-Occupation Matrix*, Bureau of Labor Statistics. These data are reported based on 4-digit NAICS categories but have been matched to corresponding 6-digit NAICS industry codes. The change reported for each occupation to the year 2014 is a percent of growth or decline as estimated by the Bureau of Labor Statistics. The abbreviation nec stands for 'not elsewhere classified.'

LOCATION BY STATE AND REGIONAL CONCENTRATION

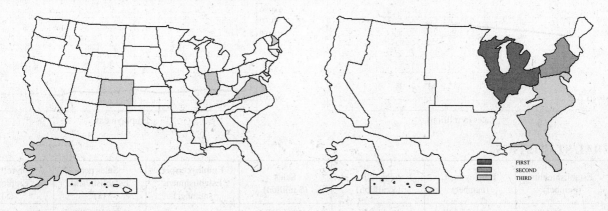

FIRST
SECOND
THIRD

INDUSTRY DATA BY STATE

State	Establishments Total (number)	% of U.S.	Employment Total (number)	% of U.S.	Per Estab.	Payroll Total ($ mil.)	Per Empl. ($)	Sales Total ($ mil.)	% of U.S.	Per Estab. ($)
New York	1,835	6.4	13,957	5.3	8	212.2	15,200	1,739.2	5.2	947,774
Illinois	1,031	3.6	10,703	4.1	10	144.7	13,523	1,438.5	4.3	1,395,254
Ohio	1,218	4.3	11,599	4.4	10	149.0	12,846	1,420.4	4.3	1,166,154
Virginia	892	3.1	7,391	2.8	8	95.0	12,859	904.3	2.7	1,013,761
Indiana	706	2.5	6,783	2.6	10	84.8	12,499	856.8	2.6	1,213,550
New Jersey	706	2.5	5,698	2.2	8	85.8	15,061	734.3	2.2	1,040,067
Colorado	220	0.8	3,366	1.3	15	49.5	14,698	498.8	1.5	2,267,300
Maryland	422	1.5	3,711	1.4	9	53.9	14,515	494.5	1.5	1,171,744
Massachusetts	370	1.3	3,912	1.5	11	59.2	15,136	436.8	1.3	1,180,611
Washington	246	0.9	2,621	1.0	11	40.5	15,463	319.9	1.0	1,300,415
Oregon	184	0.6	1,894	0.7	10	26.9	14,191	252.0	0.8	1,369,739
Utah	119	0.4	2,052	0.8	17	26.1	12,739	216.4	0.7	1,818,731
Connecticut	208	0.7	1,617	0.6	8	23.3	14,403	201.5	0.6	968,846
New Hampshire	151	0.5	1,516	0.6	10	18.4	12,151	161.2	0.5	1,067,464
Alaska	74	0.3	975	0.4	13	18.0	18,510	139.5	0.4	1,885,554
Delaware	100	0.4	949	0.4	9	11.9	12,502	108.4	0.3	1,083,550
Texas	2,447	8.6	10K-24999	-	-	(D)	-	(D)	-	-
Florida	1,510	5.3	10K-24999	-	-	(D)	-	(D)	-	-
California	1,467	5.2	10K-24999	-	-	(D)	-	(D)	-	-
Pennsylvania	1,301	4.6	10K-24999	-	-	(D)	-	(D)	-	-
North Carolina	1,268	4.5	10K-24999	-	-	(D)	-	(D)	-	-
Georgia	1,189	4.2	5K-9999	-	-	(D)	-	(D)	-	-
Michigan	957	3.4	5K-9999	-	-	(D)	-	(D)	-	-
Tennessee	903	3.2	5K-9999	-	-	(D)	-	(D)	-	-
Alabama	868	3.1	5K-9999	-	-	(D)	-	(D)	-	-
Missouri	734	2.6	5K-9999	-	-	(D)	-	(D)	-	-
Kentucky	684	2.4	5K-9999	-	-	(D)	-	(D)	-	-
Louisiana	684	2.4	5K-9999	-	-	(D)	-	(D)	-	-
South Carolina	677	2.4	5K-9999	-	-	(D)	-	(D)	-	-
Mississippi	667	2.3	5K-9999	-	-	(D)	-	(D)	-	-
Oklahoma	564	2.0	2500-4999	-	-	(D)	-	(D)	-	-
Arkansas	559	2.0	2500-4999	-	-	(D)	-	(D)	-	-
Wisconsin	387	1.4	5K-9999	-	-	(D)	-	(D)	-	-
Iowa	381	1.3	2500-4999	-	-	(D)	-	(D)	-	-
Kansas	364	1.3	2500-4999	-	-	(D)	-	(D)	-	-
West Virginia	342	1.2	2500-4999	-	-	(D)	-	(D)	-	-
Arizona	341	1.2	2500-4999	-	-	(D)	-	(D)	-	-
Minnesota	340	1.2	2500-4999	-	-	(D)	-	(D)	-	-
Nebraska	228	0.8	1000-2499	-	-	(D)	-	(D)	-	-
Maine	204	0.7	1000-2499	-	-	(D)	-	(D)	-	-
New Mexico	173	0.6	1000-2499	-	-	(D)	-	(D)	-	-
Idaho	124	0.4	1000-2499	-	-	(D)	-	(D)	-	-
Nevada	90	0.3	1000-2499	-	-	(D)	-	(D)	-	-
South Dakota	85	0.3	500-999	-	-	(D)	-	(D)	-	-
Vermont	84	0.3	500-999	-	-	(D)	-	(D)	-	-
Montana	78	0.3	500-999	-	-	(D)	-	(D)	-	-
Rhode Island	72	0.3	1000-2499	-	-	(D)	-	(D)	-	-
Hawaii	65	0.2	1000-2499	-	-	(D)	-	(D)	-	-
Wyoming	56	0.2	250-499	-	-	(D)	-	(D)	-	-
North Dakota	51	0.2	500-999	-	-	(D)	-	(D)	-	-
D.C.	30	0.1	100-249	-	-	(D)	-	(D)	-	-

Source: 2002 *Economic Census*. The states are in descending order of sales or establishments (if sales data are missing for the majority). The symbol (D) appears when data are withheld to prevent disclosure of competitive information. States marked with (D) are sorted by number of establishments. A dash (-) indicates that the data element cannot be calculated. Shaded *states* on the state map indicate those states which have proportionately greater representation in the industry than would be indicated by the states population; the ratio is based on total sales or number of establishments. Shaded *regions* indicate where the industry is regionally most concentrated.

NAICS 453110 - FLORISTS*

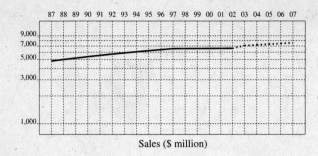

Sales ($ million)

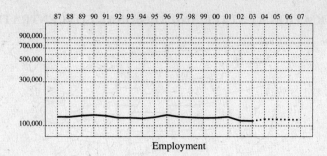

Employment

GENERAL STATISTICS

Year	Establishments (number)	Employment (number)	Payroll ($ million)	Sales ($ million)	Employees per Establishment (number)	Sales per Establishment ($)	Payroll per Employee ($)
1987	26,683	125,048	1,019.3	4,810.4	5	180,280	8,151
1988	25,284	124,874	1,110.3	4,992.1e	5	197,441	8,891
1989	25,859	128,691	1,173.6	5,173.9e	5	200,081	9,120
1990	25,784	130,936	1,219.0	5,355.7e	5	207,714	9,310
1991	26,537	128,547	1,222.7	5,537.5e	5	208,671	9,512
1992	27,341	122,114	1,207.3	5,719.2	5	209,180	9,887
1993	27,204	122,083	1,236.8	5,886.4e	5	216,380	10,131
1994	26,757	120,354	1,270.8	6,053.6e	5	226,244	10,559
1995	26,403	123,628	1,321.1	6,220.7e	5	235,606	10,686
1996	27,691e	131,093e	1,416.6e	6,387.9e	5e	230,685e	10,806e
1997	26,200	125,195	1,396.4	6,555.1	5	250,195	11,154
1998	25,617	123,223	1,468.5	6,563.6e	5	256,219	11,917
1999	24,798	121,783	1,537.6	6,572.0e	5	265,023	12,626
2000	24,197	122,224	1,584.1	6,580.5e	5	271,956	12,961
2001	23,870	125,116	1,643.8	6,589.0e	5	276,037	13,138
2002	22,753	113,929	1,489.1	6,597.5	5	289,960	13,070
2003	22,022	113,270	1,471.9	7,062.4p	5	289,649p	12,994
2004	23,645p	118,302p	1,636.7p	7,190.4p	5p	296,360p	13,771p
2005	23,430p	117,707p	1,669.6p	7,318.4p	5p	303,071p	14,093p
2006	23,214p	117,112p	1,702.5p	7,446.3p	5p	309,782p	14,415p
2007	22,998p	116,518p	1,735.4p	7,574.3p	5p	316,493p	14,736p

Sources: Economic Census of the United States, 1987, 1992, 1997, and 2002. Establishment counts, employment, and payroll are from County Business Patterns for non-Census years. Values followed by a 'p' are projections by the editors. Sales data for non-Census years are extrapolations, marked by 'e'. Data are the most recent available at this level of detail.

INDICES OF CHANGE

Year	Establishments (number)	Employment (number)	Payroll ($ million)	Sales ($ million)	Employees per Establishment (number)	Sales per Establishment	Payroll per Employee ($)
1987	117.3	109.8	68.5	72.9	93.9	62.2	62.4
1992	120.2	107.2	81.1	86.7	89.9	72.1	75.6
1993	119.6	107.2	83.1	89.2e	89.9	74.6	77.5
1994	117.6	105.6	85.3	91.8e	89.9	78.0	80.8
1995	116.0	108.5	88.7	94.3e	93.9	81.3	81.8
1996	121.7e	115.1e	95.1e	96.8e	93.9e	79.6e	82.7e
1997	115.1	109.9	93.8	99.4	95.9	86.3	85.3
1998	112.6	108.2	98.6	99.5e	95.9	88.4	91.2
1999	109.0	106.9	103.3	99.6e	97.9	91.4	96.6
2000	106.3	107.3	106.4	99.7e	101.9	93.8	99.2
2001	104.9	109.8	110.4	99.9e	103.9	95.2	100.5
2002	100.0	100.0	100.0	100.0	100.0	100.0	100.0
2003	96.8	99.4	98.8	107.0p	102.7	99.9p	99.4
2004	103.9p	103.8p	109.9p	109.0p	100.1p	102.2p	105.4p
2005	103.0p	103.3p	112.1p	110.9p	100.5p	104.5p	107.8p
2006	102.0p	102.8p	114.3p	112.9p	100.8p	106.8p	110.3p
2007	101.1p	102.3p	116.5p	114.8p	101.2p	109.2p	112.7p

Sources: Same as General Statistics. The values shown reflect change from the base year, 2002. Values above 100 mean greater than 2002, values below 100 mean less than 2002, and a value of 100 in the 1987-2001 or 2003-2007 period means same as 2002. Values followed by a 'p' are projections by the editors; 'e' stands for extrapolation. Data are the most recent available at this level of detail.

SELECTED RATIOS

For 2002	Avg. of All Retail	Analyzed Industry	Index	For 2002	Avg. of All Retail	Analyzed Industry	Index
Employees per Establishment	17	5	30	Sales per Employee	174,682	57,909	33
Payroll per Establishment	333,445	65,446	20	Sales per Establishment	3,332,269	289,960	9
Payroll per Employee	20,311	13,070	64	Expenses per Establishment	na	na	na

Sources: Same as General Statistics. The 'Average of All' column, Wholesale or Retail, represents the average of the sector reported for the most recent complete year available. The Index shows the relationship between the Average and the Analyzed Industry. For example, 100 means that they are equal; 500 that the Analyzed Industry is five times the average; 50 means that the Analyzed Industry is half the national average. The abbreviation 'na' is used to show that data are 'not available'.

*Equivalent to SIC 5992.

LEADING COMPANIES   Number shown: **17**   Total sales ($ mil): **4,278**   Total employment (000): **19.5**

Company Name	Address				CEO Name	Phone	Co. Type	Sales ($ mil)	Empl. (000)
Marsh Supermarkets Inc.	9800 Crosspoint	Indianapolis	IN	46256	Don E. Marsh	317-594-2100	P	1,654	14.3
Cactus and Tropicals Inc.	2735 S 2000 E	Salt Lake City	UT	84109	Lorraine Miller	801-485-2542	R	1,470*	<0.1
1-800-Flowers.com Inc.	1600 Stewart Ave	Westbury	NY	11590	C G McCann	516-237-6000	P	604	2.5
FTD Group Inc.	3113 Woodcreek Dr	Downers Grove	IL	60515	Michael Soenen	630-719-7800	P	397	0.9
Stein Garden and Gifts	5400 S 27th St	Milwaukee	WI	53221	Jack Stein	414-761-5404	R	50*	1.0
Amlings Flowerland	540 W Ogden Ave	Hinsdale	IL	60521	Carl Hayes	630-850-5000	R	33*	0.4
Lloyd's Florist	8118 Preston Hwy	Louisville	KY	40219	Mike Gattie	502-968-5428	R	30*	<0.1
Northwest Hills Pharmacy/Florist	3910 Far W Blvd	Austin	TX	78731	Tom Sansing	512-345-3712	R	10*	<0.1
Strossner's Bakery Inc.	21 Roper Mountain	Greenville	SC	29607	Richard Strossner	864-233-2990	R	7*	<0.1
Springdale Farm Market Inc.	1638 Springdale Rd	Cherry Hill	NJ	08003	Mary Jarvis	856-424-8674	R	5*	<0.1
Decorative Decor Inc.	PO Box 3830	Wichita	KS	67201	Ron Doty	316-265-0801	R	4*	<0.1
Ronsley Inc.	501 W Huron St	Chicago	IL	60610	Michael Leventhal	312-649-0707	R	4*	<0.1
Tillie's Flower Shop	3701 E Harry	Wichita	KS	67218	Kenneth Denton	316-687-0630	R	4*	<0.1
Sonoma Flower Co.	6683 Sonoma Hwy	Santa Rosa	CA	95409	E Farmer-Bowers	707-539-2000	R	2*	<0.1
Plant Sitters Inc.	1401 W River Rd	Minneapolis	MN	55411	Joann Hilton	612-340-9157	R	2*	<0.1
Village Green Inc.	4303 Miller Rd	Wilmington	DE	19802	Scott Weiler	302-764-2234	R	2*	<0.1
Freda's Fancy Florist Antiques Inc.	11517 Main St	Louisville	KY	40243	Freda Chapman	502-245-3174	R	1*	<0.1

Source: *Ward's Business Directory of U.S. Private and Public Companies*, Volumes 1 and 2, 2005. The company type code used is as follows: P - Public, R - Private, S - Subsidiary, D - Division, J - Joint Venture, A - Affiliate, G - Group. Sales are in millions of dollars, employees are in thousands. An asterisk (*) indicates an estimated sales volume. The symbol < stands for 'less than'. Company names and addresses are truncated, in some cases, to fit into the available space.

OCCUPATIONS EMPLOYED BY FLORISTS

Occupation	% of Total 2004	Change to 2014	Occupation	% of Total 2004	Change to 2014
Floral designers	42.1	11.8	Office clerks, general	2.0	-0.4
Retail salespersons	16.2	11.9	Driver/sales workers	1.8	11.9
Truck drivers, light or delivery services	14.1	11.8	Farmworkers & laborers, crop, nursery, & greenhouse	1.7	11.9
Cashiers, except gaming	5.0	0.7	General & operations managers	1.4	10.7
First-line supervisors/managers of retail sales workers	3.0	2.9	Laborers & freight, stock, & material movers, hand	1.3	0.7
Bookkeeping, accounting, & auditing clerks	2.5	0.7	Order clerks	1.1	-27.3

Source: *Industry-Occupation Matrix*, Bureau of Labor Statistics. These data are reported based on 4-digit NAICS categories but have been matched to corresponding 6-digit NAICS industry codes. The change reported for each occupation to the year 2014 is a percent of growth or decline as estimated by the Bureau of Labor Statistics. The abbreviation nec stands for 'not elsewhere classified.'

LOCATION BY STATE AND REGIONAL CONCENTRATION

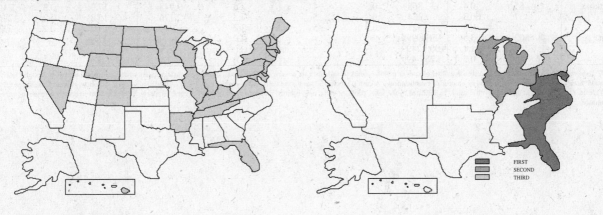

INDUSTRY DATA BY STATE

State	Establishments		Employment			Payroll		Sales		
	Total (number)	% of U.S.	Total (number)	% of U.S.	Per Estab.	Total ($ mil.)	Per Empl. ($)	Total ($ mil.)	% of U.S.	Per Estab. ($)
California	1,943	8.5	9,821	8.6	5	130.9	13,326	640.5	9.7	329,632
New York	1,501	6.6	6,414	5.6	4	107.3	16,727	514.6	7.8	342,853
Texas	1,467	6.4	6,573	5.8	4	88.3	13,438	411.4	6.2	280,446
Florida	1,164	5.1	5,738	5.0	5	77.1	13,444	352.6	5.3	302,891
Illinois	985	4.3	5,836	5.1	6	79.6	13,648	327.4	4.9	332,420
Pennsylvania	1,110	4.9	5,772	5.1	5	74.4	12,887	319.7	4.8	288,025

Continued on next page.

INDUSTRY DATA BY STATE - Continued

State	Establishments Total (number)	% of U.S.	Employment Total (number)	% of U.S.	Per Estab.	Payroll Total ($ mil.)	Per Empl. ($)	Sales Total ($ mil.)	% of U.S.	Per Estab. ($)
Ohio	958	4.2	5,388	4.7	6	65.8	12,221	278.3	4.2	290,548
New Jersey	771	3.4	3,464	3.0	4	52.9	15,259	241.4	3.6	313,057
Massachusetts	597	2.6	2,788	2.4	5	46.8	16,781	207.8	3.1	348,045
Virginia	603	2.7	3,438	3.0	6	47.8	13,892	181.8	2.7	301,436
Minnesota	459	2.0	3,217	2.8	7	36.7	11,411	176.7	2.7	384,919
Georgia	665	2.9	2,901	2.5	4	38.9	13,395	173.2	2.6	260,412
North Carolina	687	3.0	2,911	2.5	4	37.4	12,848	165.1	2.5	240,351
Indiana	567	2.5	3,318	2.9	6	38.3	11,541	158.7	2.4	279,974
Tennessee	526	2.3	2,309	2.0	4	30.8	13,349	139.1	2.1	264,420
Maryland	364	1.6	2,515	2.2	7	37.5	14,930	134.3	2.0	368,874
Wisconsin	478	2.1	2,873	2.5	6	30.9	10,764	132.4	2.0	276,973
Missouri	515	2.3	2,538	2.2	5	32.8	12,920	130.2	2.0	252,862
Colorado	352	1.5	1,817	1.6	5	25.0	13,781	109.7	1.7	311,526
Washington	416	1.8	1,930	1.7	5	24.4	12,620	105.5	1.6	253,704
Connecticut	286	1.3	1,594	1.4	6	23.4	14,680	101.0	1.5	353,045
Kentucky	386	1.7	1,892	1.7	5	22.4	11,820	99.3	1.5	257,321
Alabama	406	1.8	1,601	1.4	4	18.1	11,307	88.4	1.3	217,616
Louisiana	332	1.5	1,437	1.3	4	17.6	12,230	76.8	1.2	231,202
Oklahoma	342	1.5	1,563	1.4	5	16.1	10,326	74.4	1.1	217,658
South Carolina	345	1.5	1,321	1.2	4	15.9	12,073	72.8	1.1	211,072
Iowa	330	1.5	1,595	1.4	5	14.5	9,061	67.9	1.0	205,739
Arkansas	312	1.4	1,288	1.1	4	14.8	11,455	64.0	1.0	205,103
Mississippi	290	1.3	1,143	1.0	4	13.0	11,375	62.2	0.9	214,624
Oregon	251	1.1	1,278	1.1	5	14.4	11,250	60.4	0.9	240,801
Kansas	272	1.2	1,284	1.1	5	12.8	9,968	58.7	0.9	215,625
West Virginia	213	0.9	950	0.8	4	10.3	10,816	46.4	0.7	218,042
New Hampshire	140	0.6	828	0.7	6	10.6	12,768	43.2	0.7	308,571
Utah	143	0.6	722	0.6	5	8.2	11,294	39.7	0.6	277,755
Nebraska	178	0.8	833	0.7	5	8.7	10,442	39.1	0.6	219,708
Hawaii	100	0.4	545	0.5	5	7.5	13,690	38.8	0.6	388,100
Nevada	115	0.5	600	0.5	5	8.3	13,908	37.5	0.6	326,270
Maine	154	0.7	679	0.6	4	7.8	11,490	36.1	0.5	234,532
New Mexico	132	0.6	613	0.5	5	6.8	11,121	31.9	0.5	241,727
Delaware	73	0.3	512	0.4	7	7.6	14,871	29.5	0.4	404,164
Rhode Island	112	0.5	459	0.4	4	6.3	13,771	28.5	0.4	254,652
Idaho	116	0.5	570	0.5	5	5.0	8,802	26.9	0.4	231,750
Montana	103	0.5	482	0.4	5	5.8	12,052	24.0	0.4	232,942
South Dakota	104	0.5	429	0.4	4	4.3	9,960	19.8	0.3	190,288
Vermont	78	0.3	321	0.3	4	4.2	12,938	18.9	0.3	242,654
North Dakota	85	0.4	365	0.3	4	3.6	9,948	17.9	0.3	210,059
Alaska	57	0.3	284	0.2	5	3.5	12,176	15.8	0.2	276,965
Wyoming	65	0.3	321	0.3	5	3.2	9,960	15.2	0.2	233,262
Michigan	802	3.5	5K-9999	-	-	(D)	-	(D)	-	-
Arizona	257	1.1	1000-2499	-	-	(D)	-	(D)	-	-
D.C.	43	0.2	250-499	-	-	(D)	-	(D)	-	-

Source: 2002 *Economic Census*. The states are in descending order of sales or establishments (if sales data are missing for the majority). The symbol (D) appears when data are withheld to prevent disclosure of competitive information. States marked with (D) are sorted by number of establishments. A dash (-) indicates that the data element cannot be calculated. Shaded *states* on the state map indicate those states which have proportionately greater representation in the industry than would be indicated by the states population; the ratio is based on total sales or number of establishments. Shaded *regions* indicate where the industry is regionally most concentrated.

NAICS 453210 - OFFICE SUPPLIES AND STATIONERY STORES

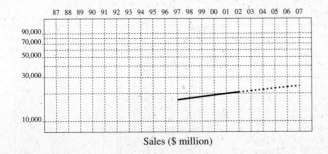

Sales ($ million)

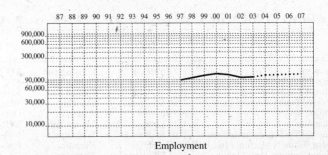

Employment

GENERAL STATISTICS

Year	Establishments (number)	Employment (number)	Payroll ($ million)	Sales ($ million)	Employees per Establishment (number)	Sales per Establishment ($)	Payroll per Employee ($)
1987	-	-	-	-	-	-	-
1988	-	-	-	-	-	-	-
1989	-	-	-	-	-	-	-
1990	-	-	-	-	-	-	-
1991	-	-	-	-	-	-	-
1992	-	-	-	-	-	-	-
1993	-	-	-	-	-	-	-
1994	-	-	-	-	-	-	-
1995	-	-	-	-	-	-	-
1996	-	-	-	-	-	-	-
1997	7,330	98,121	1,580.7	17,075.7	13	2,329,563	16,110
1998	7,728	110,227	1,990.6	17,783.7 e	14	2,301,204	18,059
1999	8,415	124,063	2,415.5	18,491.7 e	15	2,197,470	19,470
2000	8,617	134,941	2,702.1	19,199.7 e	16	2,228,120	20,024
2001	8,787	127,922	2,685.7	19,907.7 e	15	2,265,587	20,995
2002	8,574	111,381	2,217.5	20,615.7	13	2,404,446	19,909
2003	8,840	113,729	2,315.6	21,323.7 p	13	2,317,553 p	20,361
2004	9,269 p	124,768 p	2,690.9 p	22,031.7 p	13 p	2,326,073 p	21,844 p
2005	9,505 p	126,660 p	2,795.5 p	22,739.7 p	13 p	2,334,594 p	22,486 p
2006	9,740 p	128,553 p	2,900.1 p	23,447.7 p	13 p	2,343,114 p	23,128 p
2007	9,976 p	130,445 p	3,004.7 p	24,155.7 p	13 p	2,351,634 p	23,770 p

Source: Economic Census of the United States, 1997 and 2002. Establishment counts, employment, and payroll are from *County Business Patterns* for non-Census years. This is a newly defined industry. Data for prior years are unavailable at the time of publication but may become available over time. Values followed by 'p' are projections by the editors. Sales data for non-Census years are extrapolations, marked by 'e'.

INDICES OF CHANGE

Year	Establishments (number)	Employment (number)	Payroll ($ million)	Sales ($ million)	Employees per Establishment (number)	Sales per Establishment ($)	Payroll per Employee ($)
1987	-	-	-	-	-	-	-
1992	-	-	-	-	-	-	-
1993	-	-	-	-	-	-	-
1994	-	-	-	-	-	-	-
1995	-	-	-	-	-	-	-
1996	-	-	-	-	-	-	-
1997	85.5	88.1	71.3	82.8	103.2	96.9	80.9
1998	90.1	99.0	89.8	86.3 e	110.1	95.7	90.7
1999	98.1	111.4	108.9	89.7 e	113.2	91.4	97.8
2000	100.5	121.2	121.9	93.1 e	120.9	92.7	100.6
2001	102.5	114.9	121.1	96.6 e	112.4	94.2	105.5
2002	100.0	100.0	100.0	100.0	100.0	100.0	100.0
2003	103.1	102.1	104.4	103.4 p	99.0	96.4 p	102.3
2004	108.1 p	112.0 p	121.4 p	106.9 p	103.6 p	96.7 p	109.7 p
2005	110.9 p	113.7 p	126.1 p	110.3 p	102.4 p	97.1 p	112.9 p
2006	113.6 p	115.4 p	130.8 p	113.7 p	101.3 p	97.4 p	116.2 p
2007	116.3 p	117.1 p	135.5 p	117.2 p	100.1 p	97.8 p	119.4 p

Sources: Same as General Statistics. The values shown reflect change from the base year, 2002. Values above 100 mean greater than 2002, values below 100 mean less than 2002, and a value of 100 in the 1987-2001 or 2003-2007 period means same as 2002. Values followed by a 'p' are projections by the editors; 'e' stands for extrapolation. Data are the most recent available at this level of detail.

SELECTED RATIOS

For 2002	Avg. of All Retail	Analyzed Industry	Index	For 2002	Avg. of All Retail	Analyzed Industry	Index
Employees per Establishment	17	13	77	Sales per Employee	174,682	185,092	106
Payroll per Establishment	333,445	258,628	78	Sales per Establishment	3,332,269	2,404,446	72
Payroll per Employee	20,311	19,909	98	Expenses per Establishment	na	na	na

Sources: Same as General Statistics. The 'Average of All' column, Wholesale or Retail, represents the average of the sector reported for the most recent complete year available. The Index shows the relationship between the Average and the Analyzed Industry. For example, 100 means that they are equal; 500 that the Analyzed Industry is five times the average; 50 means that the Analyzed Industry is half the national average. The abbreviation 'na' is used to show that data are 'not available'.

LEADING COMPANIES   Number shown: **57**   Total sales ($ mil): **33,015**   Total employment (000): **134.2**

Company Name	Address				CEO Name	Phone	Co. Type	Sales ($ mil)	Empl. (000)
Staples Inc.	PO Box 9328	Framingham	MA	01702		508-253-5000	P	14,448	65.1
Office Depot Inc.	2200 Germantown	Delray Beach	FL	33445	Charles E Brown	561-266-4800	P	13,565	46.0
Hallmark Cards Inc.	PO Box 419580	Kansas City	MO	64141		816-274-5111	R	4,300	18.0
Nebraska Book Company Inc.	4700 S 19th St	Lincoln	NE	68501	Mark Oppegard	402-421-7300	R	214*	2.1
ComDoc Inc.	PO Box 908	Akron	OH	44309	Larry Frank	330-899-8000	R	74*	0.4
Kaplan Co.	1310 Lewisvl Clmns	Lewisville	NC	27023	Hal Kaplan	336-766-7374	R	53*	0.3
American Trading & Production	1100 Stafford St	Washington	MO	63090		636-239-2781	D	42*	0.5
Golden Business Machines Inc.	PO Box 1700	Kingston	PA	18704	Carol Douds	570-288-7554	R	30*	<0.1
Imaging Supplies Depot Inc.	1631 S Sinclair St	Anaheim	CA	92806	Paul Doan	714-978-7291	R	19*	<0.1
Cartridge Family Inc.	229 Brannan	San Francisco	CA	94107	Nate Laskin	415-495-1311	R	18*	<0.1
Payless Office Supply Inc.	PO Box 390157	Omaha	NE	68139	James Matgen	402-891-6210	R	14*	<0.1
Flo-Tech L.L.C.	699 Middle St	Middletown	CT	06457		860-613-3333	R	13*	<0.1
David Martin Inc.	1600 Browns Lane	Jonesboro	AR	72401	David Martin	870-972-0180	R	13*	<0.1
Gold Circuit Inc.	210 S Beck Ave	Chandler	AZ	85226	James Greenberg	480-829-0404	R	12*	<0.1
Business World Inc.	PO Box 34165	Little Rock	AR	72203	Jerry Carlisle	501-378-7797	R	12*	<0.1
S and S Blue Ridge Copiers Inc.	PO Box 866	Salem	VA	24153	Paul Story	540-389-4400	R	11*	<0.1
SBP Image Solutions	2290 Grissom Dr	Saint Louis	MO	63146	Richard Shea	314-567-0087	R	11*	<0.1
Sav-On Discount Office Supplies	PO Box 1657	Fort Worth	TX	76101	Dennis George	817-568-5200	R	10*	0.4
Today's Office Inc.	3157 W Sunset	Springdale	AR	72762		479-751-5861	R	10*	<0.1
Calvert-McBride Printing Co.	PO Box 6337	Fort Smith	AR	72906	William D Calvert	479-646-8311	R	9*	<0.1
Carol School Supply Inc.	17928 Union Tpke	Flushing	NY	11366	Carol Pick	718-380-4203	R	9*	<0.1
American Binding Company Inc.	PO Box 829	Kaysville	UT	84037	Calvin Barlow	801-927-3020	R	8*	<0.1
Office Connection Inc.	8584 Venice Blvd	Los Angeles	CA	90034	Ezekiel Guerra	310-838-5818	R	8*	<0.1
Northern Stationers Inc.	502 W Washington	Marquette	MI	49855	Denise Bouschor	906-228-7702	R	7*	<0.1
Document Imaging Systems Corp.	1520 Washington	Saint Louis	MO	63103	Bonnie Bodkin	314-436-2800	R	6*	<0.1
Caxton Printers Ltd.	312 Main St	Caldwell	ID	83605	David Gipson	208-459-7421	R	6*	<0.1
Logan Business Machines Inc.	417 NE US 24 B	Topeka	KS	66608	Hal Logan	785-233-1102	R	6*	<0.1
Mayes Printing Co.	PO Box 1952	Pensacola	FL	32591	John Phelps	850-477-1111	R	5*	<0.1
Kernersville News	PO Box 337	Kernersville	NC	27285	John Owensby	336-993-2161	R	5*	<0.1
Arkansas Copier Center Inc.	PO Box 192464	Little Rock	AR	72219	Ralph Thompson	501-562-8297	R	5*	<0.1
Phoenix L.L.C.	PO Box 8406	Evansville	IN	47716	Bill Jergens	812-422-1888	R	4*	<0.1
Business Machines Systems Inc.	6101 S Shackleford	Little Rock	AR	72204	Richard Crews	501-375-8380	R	4*	<0.1
Cook's Inc.	807 S Broadway St	Watertown	SD	57201	Merlin Jeitz	605-886-5892	R	4*	<0.1
Advanced Business Concepts	504 Main St	Coshocton	OH	43812	Donald Padgett	740-622-7115	R	4*	<0.1
Perdue Company Inc.	PO Box 6696	Pine Bluff	AR	71611	D Rudder	870-534-2610	R	4*	<0.1
Memphis Communications Corp.	PO Box 770389	Memphis	TN	38177	Dean Berry	901-725-9271	R	3*	<0.1
NSC Diversified	9677 Page Ave	Saint Louis	MO	63132	Marge Zemenick	314-428-6637	R	3*	<0.1
Sara Mana Business Products Inc.	1618 Barber Rd	Sarasota	FL	34240	Mick Dean	941-379-9999	R	3*	<0.1
Palson's Inc.	184 Main St	Worcester	MA	01608	Judy Palson	508-756-8376	R	3*	<0.1
Paper Place	4130 N Marshall	Scottsdale	AZ	85251	Betsy Hendricks	480-941-2858	R	3*	<0.1
Story-Wright Inc.	PO Box 900	Tyler	TX	75710		903-595-1991	R	3*	<0.1
Ponder's Inc.	117 N Madison St	Thomasville	GA	31792	William Ponder	229-226-3341	R	3*	<0.1
Lephart Imaging Systems Inc.	3880 Kettering Blvd	Dayton	OH	45439	Robert Von Derau	937-294-4410	R	3*	<0.1
Key Print Shop Inc.	PO Box 966	Dodge City	KS	67801	Paul Kornechuk	620-227-2101	R	3*	<0.1
Firmin's Office City	PO Box 951	Texarkana	TX	75504	Charles Firmin	903-793-5566	R	3*	<0.1
Ace Reprographic Service Inc.	74 E 30th St	Paterson	NJ	07514	Arthur Scialla	973-684-5945	R	2*	<0.1
Acme Copy Corp.	218 S Wabash Ave	Chicago	IL	60604	Susan Bredfeldt	312-922-6742	R	2*	<0.1
Quality Printing & Office Supply	PO Box 1765	Mobile	AL	36633	Thomas Sykes	251-479-3587	R	2*	<0.1
Sault Printing Company Inc.	PO Box 323	SJ Capistrano	MI	49783	Ronald Maleport	906-632-3369	R	2*	<0.1
Community Support Resource	3124 Zebulon Rd	Rocky Mount	NC	27804		252-972-2200	R	2*	<0.1
Paperwork Co.	11 E Dawes Ave	Bixby	OK	74008	Tom Daniels	918-369-1014	R	2*	<0.1
Greer Citizen Inc.	PO Box 70	Greer	SC	29652	Leland Burch	864-877-2076	R	2*	<0.1
G.C. Office Supply	2224 Stringtown Rd	Grove City	OH	43123	Ann Keil	614-875-2363	R	2*	<0.1
Stuart's of Eldorado Inc.	3213 Northwest Ave	El Dorado	AR	71730	Richard Stuart	870-862-3484	R	2*	<0.1
Sweet Dreams Enterprises	117 E 14th St, Fl 1	New York	NY	10003	Roger Young	212-260-3486	R	2*	<0.1
Bellia Office Products Inc.	1047 N Broad St	Woodbury	NJ	08096	Tom Bellia	856-845-2234	R	1*	<0.1
Diana Dee's Stationery	2060 Huntington Dr	San Marino	CA	91108	Diana Doi	626-289-1062	R	1*	<0.1

Source: Ward's Business Directory of U.S. Private and Public Companies, Volumes 1 and 2, 2005. The company type code used is as follows: P - Public, R - Private, S - Subsidiary, D - Division, J - Joint Venture, A - Affiliate, G - Group. Sales are in millions of dollars, employees are in thousands. An asterisk (*) indicates an estimated sales volume. The symbol < stands for 'less than'. Company names and addresses are truncated, in some cases, to fit into the available space.

OCCUPATIONS EMPLOYED BY OFFICE SUPPLIES, STATIONERY, & GIFT STORES

Occupation	% of Total 2004	Change to 2014	Occupation	% of Total 2004	Change to 2014
Retail salespersons	35.2	17.1	Customer service representatives	1.9	19.9
Cashiers, except gaming	19.9	5.4	Shipping, receiving, & traffic clerks	1.8	6.0
First-line supervisors/managers of retail sales workers	7.4	7.8	Bookkeeping, accounting, & auditing clerks	1.7	5.4
Stock clerks & order fillers	3.7	-10.3	Truck drivers, light or delivery services	1.4	17.1
Computer, automated teller, & office machine repairers	3.0	5.4	Office clerks, general	1.2	4.2
Sales reps, wholesale & manufacturing, exc tech	2.7	17.1	Sales & related workers, nec	1.1	17.1
General & operations managers	2.0	15.9	Laborers & freight, stock, & material movers, hand	1.0	5.4

Source: Industry-Occupation Matrix, Bureau of Labor Statistics. These data are reported based on 4-digit NAICS categories but have been matched to corresponding 6-digit NAICS industry codes. The change reported for each occupation to the year 2014 is a percent of growth or decline as estimated by the Bureau of Labor Statistics. The abbreviation nec stands for 'not elsewhere classified.'

LOCATION BY STATE AND REGIONAL CONCENTRATION

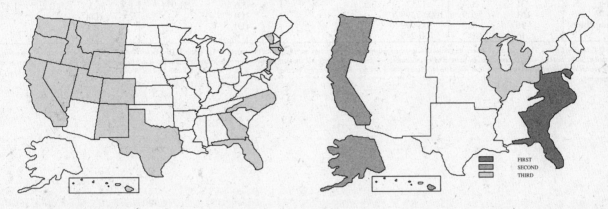

FIRST
SECOND
THIRD

INDUSTRY DATA BY STATE

State	Establishments Total (number)	Establishments % of U.S.	Employment Total (number)	Employment % of U.S.	Employment Per Estab.	Payroll Total ($ mil.)	Payroll Per Empl. ($)	Sales Total ($ mil.)	Sales % of U.S.	Sales Per Estab. ($)
California	1,066	12.5	14,654	13.2	14	305.1	20,823	2,881.0	14.0	2,702,671
Texas	665	7.8	7,993	7.2	12	171.1	21,403	1,504.9	7.3	2,263,075
Florida	513	6.0	6,702	6.0	13	146.1	21,794	1,490.8	7.2	2,906,029
New York	617	7.2	6,880	6.2	11	136.7	19,872	1,317.8	6.4	2,135,793
Ohio	316	3.7	4,753	4.3	15	90.8	19,109	806.4	3.9	2,551,810
Pennsylvania	301	3.5	4,114	3.7	14	75.0	18,242	754.3	3.7	2,506,136
New Jersey	281	3.3	3,431	3.1	12	70.2	20,474	719.4	3.5	2,560,117
Illinois	348	4.1	4,292	3.9	12	81.1	18,885	717.4	3.5	2,061,385
Georgia	258	3.0	3,647	3.3	14	74.1	20,331	672.8	3.3	2,607,593
Michigan	269	3.1	3,599	3.2	13	67.2	18,662	613.0	3.0	2,278,911
North Carolina	248	2.9	3,233	2.9	13	60.6	18,741	563.8	2.7	2,273,460
Virginia	215	2.5	2,743	2.5	13	52.4	19,097	508.8	2.5	2,366,451
Massachusetts	162	1.9	2,635	2.4	16	52.3	19,855	497.8	2.4	3,072,710
Washington	208	2.4	2,598	2.3	12	56.7	21,843	489.1	2.4	2,351,317
Indiana	175	2.0	2,515	2.3	14	48.6	19,316	424.9	2.1	2,427,829
Colorado	187	2.2	2,234	2.0	12	46.0	20,575	409.3	2.0	2,188,743
Maryland	123	1.4	1,900	1.7	15	37.1	19,550	391.9	1.9	3,186,000
Tennessee	172	2.0	2,148	1.9	12	40.1	18,680	359.7	1.7	2,091,453
Missouri	171	2.0	2,065	1.9	12	40.2	19,448	351.9	1.7	2,057,637
Louisiana	140	1.6	1,582	1.4	11	35.7	22,571	317.7	1.5	2,269,329
Wisconsin	119	1.4	1,909	1.7	16	32.4	16,993	313.6	1.5	2,635,504
Connecticut	101	1.2	1,595	1.4	16	30.6	19,216	299.5	1.5	2,965,307
Oregon	127	1.5	1,563	1.4	12	30.4	19,477	298.3	1.4	2,348,976
Minnesota	131	1.5	1,883	1.7	14	30.5	16,215	281.0	1.4	2,145,321
South Carolina	105	1.2	1,385	1.2	13	26.9	19,424	263.5	1.3	2,510,000
Alabama	126	1.5	1,468	1.3	12	27.7	18,894	256.3	1.2	2,034,135
Kentucky	95	1.1	1,361	1.2	14	26.2	19,241	224.1	1.1	2,358,884
Oklahoma	105	1.2	1,335	1.2	13	26.0	19,450	221.9	1.1	2,113,429
Nevada	73	0.9	1,011	0.9	14	21.1	20,916	189.9	0.9	2,600,932
Utah	97	1.1	1,203	1.1	12	21.0	17,477	187.6	0.9	1,934,134
Kansas	90	1.1	1,075	1.0	12	21.2	19,748	176.3	0.9	1,958,867
Iowa	88	1.0	1,062	1.0	12	19.0	17,916	159.6	0.8	1,814,148
New Mexico	70	0.8	960	0.9	14	19.3	20,059	151.3	0.7	2,160,971
Mississippi	73	0.9	822	0.7	11	17.2	20,894	142.1	0.7	1,946,452
Arkansas	77	0.9	734	0.7	10	14.8	20,127	129.2	0.6	1,678,117

Continued on next page.

INDUSTRY DATA BY STATE - Continued

State	Establishments Total (number)	% of U.S.	Employment Total (number)	% of U.S.	Per Estab.	Payroll Total ($ mil.)	Per Empl. ($)	Sales Total ($ mil.)	% of U.S.	Per Estab. ($)
Hawaii	37	0.4	695	0.6	19	16.9	24,252	127.6	0.6	3,449,243
Idaho	55	0.6	747	0.7	14	13.1	17,497	116.4	0.6	2,117,273
Nebraska	52	0.6	700	0.6	13	14.7	20,929	111.7	0.5	2,147,231
West Virginia	49	0.6	562	0.5	11	10.5	18,751	92.5	0.4	1,887,061
Maine	28	0.3	421	0.4	15	7.0	16,563	83.8	0.4	2,991,071
Montana	40	0.5	437	0.4	11	8.3	19,034	77.4	0.4	1,935,575
Vermont	21	0.2	321	0.3	15	7.2	22,399	75.4	0.4	3,591,048
Delaware	22	0.3	324	0.3	15	5.9	18,299	68.1	0.3	3,094,455
Rhode Island	24	0.3	322	0.3	13	6.1	18,882	60.7	0.3	2,528,958
North Dakota	22	0.3	269	0.2	12	5.1	18,833	51.3	0.2	2,333,818
Alaska	24	0.3	231	0.2	10	4.9	21,260	42.1	0.2	1,754,042
South Dakota	21	0.2	226	0.2	11	4.1	18,124	41.5	0.2	1,978,190
Wyoming	31	0.4	257	0.2	8	5.6	21,911	36.3	0.2	1,172,065
Arizona	161	1.9	1000-2499	-	-	(D)	-	(D)	-	-
New Hampshire	46	0.5	500-999	-	-	(D)	-	(D)	-	-
D.C.	16	0.2	100-249	-	-	(D)	-	(D)	-	-

Source: 2002 *Economic Census*. The states are in descending order of sales or establishments (if sales data are missing for the majority). The symbol (D) appears when data are withheld to prevent disclosure of competitive information. States marked with (D) are sorted by number of establishments. A dash (-) indicates that the data element cannot be calculated. Shaded *states* on the state map indicate those states which have proportionately greater representation in the industry than would be indicated by the states population; the ratio is based on total sales or number of establishments. Shaded *regions* indicate where the industry is regionally most concentrated.

NAICS 453220 - GIFT, NOVELTY, AND SOUVENIR STORES*

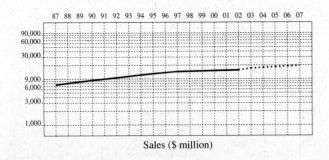

Sales ($ million)

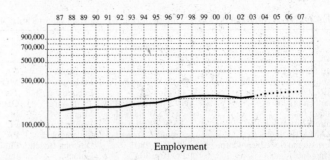

Employment

GENERAL STATISTICS

Year	Establishments (number)	Employment (number)	Payroll ($ million)	Sales ($ million)	Employees per Establishment (number)	Sales per Establishment ($)	Payroll per Employee ($)
1987	32,245	150,730	1,054.7	7,459.2	5	231,329	6,997
1988	30,203	157,163	1,222.8	8,078.1 e	5	267,460	7,781
1989	28,833	159,455	1,319.4	8,696.9 e	6	301,630	8,274
1990	29,455	164,265	1,393.7	9,315.8 e	6	316,272	8,485
1991	29,642	163,067	1,431.2	9,934.7 e	6	335,156	8,777
1992	34,647	164,311	1,466.9	10,553.5	5	304,601	8,928
1993	34,120	174,261	1,594.7	11,342.3 e	5	332,424	9,151
1994	34,402	179,249	1,675.9	12,131.0 e	5	352,625	9,350
1995	33,788	181,154	1,783.8	12,919.8 e	5	382,378	9,847
1996	36,315 e	193,469 e	1,853.6 e	13,708.5 e	5 e	377,489 e	9,581 e
1997	37,285	208,371	2,056.7	14,497.3	6	388,824	9,870
1998	36,603	213,964	2,281.3	14,722.2 e	6	402,212	10,662
1999	35,167	214,739	2,426.2	14,947.1 e	6	425,031	11,298
2000	34,399	214,613	2,544.1	15,171.9 e	6	441,057	11,854
2001	33,678	210,627	2,541.6	15,396.8 e	6	457,177	12,067
2002	35,785	202,285	2,378.3	15,621.7	6	436,543	11,757
2003	34,287	210,030	2,576.9	17,163.6 p	6	473,419 p	12,269
2004	36,787 p	225,407 p	2,760.6 p	17,752.7 p	6 p	486,820 p	12,613 p
2005	37,144 p	229,787 p	2,860.8 p	18,341.9 p	6 p	500,221 p	12,923 p
2006	37,500 p	234,167 p	2,961.0 p	18,931.0 p	6 p	513,621 p	13,233 p
2007	37,856 p	238,548 p	3,061.1 p	19,520.1 p	6 p	527,022 p	13,543 p

Sources: Economic Census of the United States, 1987, 1992, 1997, and 2002. Establishment counts, employment, and payroll are from *County Business Patterns* for non-Census years. Values followed by a 'p' are projections by the editors. Sales data for non-Census years are extrapolations, marked by 'e'. Data are the most recent available at this level of detail.

INDICES OF CHANGE

Year	Establishments (number)	Employment (number)	Payroll ($ million)	Sales ($ million)	Employees per Establishment (number)	Sales per Establishment ($)	Payroll per Employee ($)
1987	90.1	74.5	44.3	47.7	83.1	53.0	59.5
1992	96.8	81.2	61.7	67.6	83.1	69.8	75.9
1993	95.3	86.1	67.1	72.6 e	90.2	76.1	77.8
1994	96.1	88.6	70.5	77.7 e	92.0	80.8	79.5
1995	94.4	89.6	75.0	82.7 e	95.5	87.6	83.8
1996	101.5 e	95.6 e	77.9 e	87.8 e	93.8 e	86.5 e	81.5 e
1997	104.2	103.0	86.5	92.8	99.1	89.1	84.0
1998	102.3	105.8	95.9	94.2 e	102.6	92.1	90.7
1999	98.3	106.2	102.0	95.7 e	107.9	97.4	96.1
2000	96.1	106.1	107.0	97.1 e	109.7	101.0	100.8
2001	94.1	104.1	106.9	98.6 e	111.4	104.7	102.6
2002	100.0	100.0	100.0	100.0	100.0	100.0	100.0
2003	95.8	103.8	108.4	109.9 p	108.4	108.4 p	104.4
2004	102.8 p	111.4 p	116.1 p	113.6 p	109.2 p	111.5 p	107.3 p
2005	103.8 p	113.6 p	120.3 p	117.4 p	110.4 p	114.6 p	109.9 p
2006	104.8 p	115.8 p	124.5 p	121.2 p	111.7 p	117.7 p	112.6 p
2007	105.8 p	117.9 p	128.7 p	125.0 p	113.0 p	120.7 p	115.2 p

Sources: Same as General Statistics. The values shown reflect change from the base year, 2002. Values above 100 mean greater than 2002, values below 100 mean less than 2002, and a value of 100 in the 1987-2001 or 2003-2007 period means same as 2002. Values followed by a 'p' are projections by the editors; 'e' stands for extrapolation. Data are the most recent available at this level of detail.

SELECTED RATIOS

For 2002	Avg. of All Retail	Analyzed Industry	Index	For 2002	Avg. of All Retail	Analyzed Industry	Index
Employees per Establishment	17	6	33	Sales per Employee	174,682	77,226	44
Payroll per Establishment	333,445	66,460	20	Sales per Establishment	3,332,269	436,543	13
Payroll per Employee	20,311	11,757	58	Expenses per Establishment	na	na	na

Sources: Same as General Statistics. The 'Average of All' column, Wholesale or Retail, represents the average of the sector reported for the most recent complete year available. The Index shows the relationship between the Average and the Analyzed Industry. For example, 100 means that they are equal; 500 that the Analyzed Industry is five times the average; 50 means that the Analyzed Industry is half the national average. The abbreviation 'na' is used to show that data are 'not available'.

*Equivalent to SIC 5947.

LEADING COMPANIES   Number shown: **61**   Total sales ($ mil): **41,357**   Total employment (000): **231.5**

Company Name	Address			CEO Name	Phone	Co. Type	Sales ($ mil)	Empl. (000)
Walt Disney Co.	500 S Buena Vista	Burbank	CA 91521	Andy Bird	818-560-1000	P	30,752	114.0
Discovery Communications Inc.	7700 Wisconsin Ave	Bethesda	MD 20814	John S Hendricks	301-986-0444	J	1,717	2.0
CBRL Group Inc.	PO Box 787	Lebanon	TN 37088	Dan W Evins	615-444-5533	P	1,435	69.2
Cole National Corp.	1925 Enterprise Pky	Twinsburg	OH 44087		330-486-3100	S	1,202	13.7
Arango Inc.	7519 SW 88th St	Miami	FL 33156		305-661-4229	R	1,180*	<0.1
Claire's Stores Inc.	3 SW 129th Ave	Pembroke Pines	FL 33027		954-433-3900	P	1,133	16.0
ARAMARK Sports	Aramark Tower	Philadelphia	PA 19107	Norm Miller	215-238-3435	S	700*	0.7
International Speedway Corp.	PO Box 2801	Daytona Beach	FL 32120	James C France	386-254-2700	P	648	1.0
Kirlins Inc.	PO Box 3097	Quincy	IL 62305	Gary Kirlin	217-224-8953	S	477*	2.0
Brookstone Inc.	1 Innovation Way	Merrimack	NH 03054	Michael F Anthony	603-880-9500	P	434	2.9
Speedway Motorsports Inc.	PO Box 600	Concord	NC 28026		704-455-3239	P	404	0.9
Enesco Group Inc.	225 Windsor Dr	Itasca	IL 60143		630-875-5300	P	269	1.3
CA One Services Inc.	40 Fountain Plaza	Buffalo	NY 14202	Nick Biello	716-858-5000	S	254*	2.9
Paradies Shops Inc.	5950 Fulton Ind SW	Atlanta	GA 30336	Dick Dickson	404-344-7905	R	135*	1.5
DFS Group Ltd.	525 Market St	San Francisco	CA 94105	Brian Gencrick	415-977-2700	R	127*	0.4
Voertman's	1314 W Hickory	Denton	TX 76201		940-387-1313	R	55*	<0.1
Jett Racing and Sales Inc.	1301 Lincoln St	Laredo	TX 78040	Wolf Hofman	956-722-3102	R	46*	<0.1
Waterhouse nc.	670 Queen St	Honolulu	HI 96813	Edwin Wong	808-592-4800	R	36*	0.4
Estes Park Brewery Inc.	PO Box 2136	Estes Park	CO 80517	Tyler Lemirande	970-586-5421	R	27*	<0.1
Anthony's Seafood Group	5232 Lovelock	San Diego	CA 92110	Richard A Ghio	619-291-7254	R	26*	0.5
Pisani Enterprises Inc.	350 Ocean Ave	San Francisco	CA 94112	Gerald Pisani	415-861-6616	R	25*	<0.1
CelebrateExpress.com Inc.	11220-120th NE	Kirkland	WA 98033	John Hancock	425-250-1064	R	23*	0.3
Index Notion Company Inc.	887 W Carmel Dr	Carmel	IN 46032	James G Sinclair	317-573-3990	R	23*	0.2
Sprecher Brewing Company Inc.	701 W Glendale Ave	Glendale	WI 53209	Randal Sprecher	414-964-7837	R	16*	<0.1
Wendell August Forge Inc.	PO Box 109	Grove City	PA 16127	Will Knecht	724-458-8360	R	16*	<0.1
War Eagle Mill Inc.	11045 War Eagle Rd	Rogers	AR 72756	Zoe Caywood	479-789-5343	R	16*	<0.1
Bethany Lowe Designs Inc.	16655 County 16	Osco	IL 61274	Bethany Lowe	309-944-6214	R	14*	<0.1
Pierre Part Store Inc.	PO Box 10	Pierre Part	LA 70339	Logi J Guillot	985-252-6261	R	13*	<0.1
Wall Drug Store Inc.	510 Main St	Wall	SD 57790	Richard J Hustead	605-279-2175	R	11*	0.2
Yessick's Design Center	1926 Gunbarrel Rd	Chattanooga	TN 37421	Marsha Yessicks	423-892-1785	R	11*	<0.1
Ninja Jump Inc.	3233 N S Fernando	Los Angeles	CA 90065	R Gourchounian	323-255-5418	R	9*	<0.1
Cold Hollow Cider Mill	PO Box 420	Wappingrs Fls	VT 05677	Gayle Brown	802-244-8771	R	9*	<0.1
Kellerhaus Inc.	PO Box 5337	Laconia	NH 03247	Jeffrey Potter	603-366-4466	R	9*	<0.1
Chittenden Cider Mill	1580 Dorset St	S. Burlington	VT 05403	Bob Chittenden	802-862-4602	R	9*	<0.1
Alpine Wurst and Meathouse Inc.	RR 4 Box 155	Honesdale	PA 18431	Klaus Eifert	570-253-5899	R	9*	<0.1
Twin Hills Collectables L.L.C.	70 Hickory Rd	Hickory	KY 42051	Steve Halsell	270-856-2277	R	7*	<0.1
Crystalix Group International Inc.	5275 S Arville St	Las Vegas	NV 89118	Douglas E Lee	702-740-4616	P	6	<0.1
M and W Sales Inc.	PO Box 758	Belmont	MS 38827	James Mc Dowell	662-454-9419	R	6*	<0.1
Clines Corners Operating Co.	1 Yacht Club Dr	Clines Corners	NM 87070	CC Blair	505-472-5488	R	6*	<0.1
Fun Kingdom Amusements L.L.C.	16120 Foxmoor Dr	Little Rock	AR 72206	Scott Penington	501-888-5653	R	6*	<0.1
Little Hills Winery Gift Shop	710 S Main St	Saint Charles	MO 63301		636-925-2609	R	6*	<0.1
Glendale Assn For Retarded	6512 San Fernando	Glendale	CA 91201	Richard Slavett	818-242-2434	R	5*	0.1
Springdale Farm Market Inc.	1638 Springdale Rd	Cherry Hill	NJ 08003	Mary Jarvis	856-424-8674	R	5*	<0.1
Lakeridge Winery and Vineyards	19239 US Hwy 27	Clermont	FL 34711	C Cox	352-394-8627	R	4*	<0.1
Shell Factory Museum Inc.	2787 N Tamiami	Fort Myers	FL 33903		239-995-2141	R	4*	<0.1
Country Mill Farms L.L.C.	4648 Otto Rd	Charlotte	MI 48813	Bernard Tennes	517-543-1019	R	4*	<0.1
Eventrentals	13930 Willard Rd	Chantilly	VA 20151	David Painter	703-378-2255	R	3*	<0.1
Glass Etc.	4135 La Vista Rd	Tucker	GA 30084	Ed Sutter	770-493-7936	R	3*	<0.1
Party People Limited Inc.	5740 N 7th St	Phoenix	AZ 85014	David Shaw	602-264-7770	R	3*	<0.1
Consumer Marketing Group Inc.	5515 Vista Meadow	Dallas	TX 75248	Mark Lafferty	972-713-7980	R	3*	<0.1
Rebel Party Rents	4215 Bertsos Dr	Las Vegas	NV 89103	Sam Emerson	702-252-0152	R	3*	<0.1
Lesley Roy Designs L.L.C.	845 Whalley Ave	New Haven	CT 06515	Lesley Roy	203-389-7410	R	2*	<0.1
Abbey Party Rents of San Diego	6969 Corte Santa Fe	San Diego	CA 92121	Richard Cutting	858-597-0201	R	2*	<0.1
Balloonatics Inc.	180 Dillon Ave	Campbell	CA 95008	Connie Curry	408-866-8206	R	2*	<0.1
Party Bazaar	9600 N May Ave	Oklahoma City	OK 73120	Betty Sain	405-751-5510	R	2*	<0.1
Golden Gate Marketing	261 Sunridge Way	Vacaville	CA 95688	Sandy Freethy	707-451-4056	R	2*	<0.1
Fort Bragg Rent All Inc.	PO Box 911	Fort Bragg	CA 95437	Holly Kuchar	707-964-6661	R	2*	<0.1
Visitor Information Center	2688 E Mission Bay	San Diego	CA 92109	Theodore Jardine	619-276-8200	R	2*	<0.1
Best Regards Inc.	4901 Morena Blvd	San Diego	CA 92117	Mike McCarron	858-685-5840	R	1*	<0.1
Diana Dee's Stationery	2060 Huntington Dr	San Marino	CA 91108	Diana Doi	626-289-1062	R	1*	<0.1
Lane's Bakery and Gifts Inc.	448 S Park St	Madison	WI 53715	Jerry Lane	608-256-6645	R	1*	<0.1

Source: *Ward's Business Directory of U.S. Private and Public Companies*, Volumes 1 and 2, 2005. The company type code used is as follows: P - Public, R - Private, S - Subsidiary, D - Division, J - Joint Venture, A - Affiliate, G - Group. Sales are in millions of dollars, employees are in thousands. An asterisk (*) indicates an estimated sales volume. The symbol < stands for 'less than'. Company names and addresses are truncated, in some cases, to fit into the available space.

OCCUPATIONS EMPLOYED BY OFFICE SUPPLIES, STATIONERY, & GIFT STORES

Occupation	% of Total 2004	Change to 2014	Occupation	% of Total 2004	Change to 2014
Retail salespersons	35.2	17.1	Customer service representatives	1.9	19.9
Cashiers, except gaming	19.9	5.4	Shipping, receiving, & traffic clerks	1.8	6.0
First-line supervisors/managers of retail sales workers	7.4	7.8	Bookkeeping, accounting, & auditing clerks	1.7	5.4
Stock clerks & order fillers	3.7	-10.3	Truck drivers, light or delivery services	1.4	17.1
Computer, automated teller, & office machine repairers	3.0	5.4	Office clerks, general	1.2	4.2
Sales reps, wholesale & manufacturing, exc tech	2.7	17.1	Sales & related workers, nec	1.1	17.1
General & operations managers	2.0	15.9	Laborers & freight, stock, & material movers, hand	1.0	5.4

Source: *Industry-Occupation Matrix*, Bureau of Labor Statistics. These data are reported based on 4-digit NAICS categories but have been matched to corresponding 6-digit NAICS industry codes. The change reported for each occupation to the year 2014 is a percent of growth or decline as estimated by the Bureau of Labor Statistics. The abbreviation nec stands for 'not elsewhere classified.'

LOCATION BY STATE AND REGIONAL CONCENTRATION

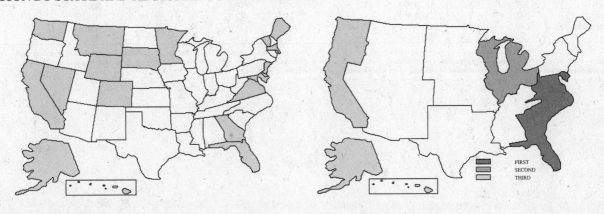

FIRST
SECOND
THIRD

INDUSTRY DATA BY STATE

State	Establishments Total (number)	% of U.S.	Employment Total (number)	% of U.S.	Per Estab.	Payroll Total ($ mil.)	Per Empl. ($)	Sales Total ($ mil.)	% of U.S.	Per Estab. ($)
California	3,641	10.2	22,413	10.8	6	299.2	13,351	1,962.9	12.3	539,114
New York	2,397	6.7	11,900	5.8	5	157.8	13,261	1,137.1	7.1	474,405
Florida	2,193	6.1	13,101	6.3	6	155.9	11,902	1,107.6	6.9	505,052
Texas	2,142	6.0	12,134	5.9	6	142.8	11,772	916.9	5.7	428,058
Pennsylvania	1,563	4.4	9,776	4.7	6	104.9	10,729	691.9	4.3	442,687
Illinois	1,394	3.9	9,418	4.6	7	97.9	10,397	686.1	4.3	492,206
Ohio	1,321	3.7	8,245	4.0	6	85.8	10,411	555.8	3.5	420,717
New Jersey	1,072	3.0	6,500	3.1	6	81.3	12,505	554.2	3.5	516,937
Georgia	828	2.3	5,333	2.6	6	60.2	11,283	446.6	2.8	539,419
Virginia	946	2.6	5,783	2.8	6	68.0	11,761	426.7	2.7	451,060
Massachusetts	882	2.5	5,291	2.6	6	70.9	13,398	420.8	2.6	477,084
North Carolina	1,032	2.9	5,513	2.7	5	62.8	11,399	402.4	2.5	389,949
Minnesota	813	2.3	5,184	2.5	6	57.6	11,104	353.9	2.2	435,261
Washington	842	2.4	4,352	2.1	5	57.8	13,278	343.3	2.1	407,779
Indiana	745	2.1	4,929	2.4	7	50.2	10,176	317.3	2.0	425,842
Maryland	614	1.7	4,299	2.1	7	48.9	11,372	316.4	2.0	515,350
Colorado	782	2.2	4,075	2.0	5	47.7	11,704	299.9	1.9	383,519
Missouri	745	2.1	4,370	2.1	6	48.7	11,154	294.0	1.8	394,626
Tennessee	707	2.0	3,501	1.7	5	44.3	12,667	284.8	1.8	402,801
Wisconsin	845	2.4	4,409	2.1	5	43.5	9,865	275.6	1.7	326,155
Nevada	363	1.0	2,520	1.2	7	38.1	15,132	261.5	1.6	720,347
Hawaii	390	1.1	1,937	0.9	5	27.5	14,192	221.3	1.4	567,374
Louisiana	475	1.3	2,851	1.4	6	31.5	11,046	214.8	1.3	452,116
South Carolina	557	1.6	2,767	1.3	5	33.6	12,153	206.9	1.3	371,479
Connecticut	382	1.1	2,557	1.2	7	31.6	12,369	194.8	1.2	510,058
Oregon	506	1.4	2,365	1.1	5	28.8	12,189	177.6	1.1	351,040
Alabama	438	1.2	2,164	1.0	5	22.7	10,512	146.2	0.9	333,822
Iowa	475	1.3	2,706	1.3	6	22.5	8,303	143.4	0.9	301,935
Kentucky	414	1.2	2,113	1.0	5	19.6	9,299	133.5	0.8	322,572
Kansas	371	1.0	2,141	1.0	6	19.9	9,306	128.9	0.8	347,547
Oklahoma	383	1.1	1,966	1.0	5	19.1	9,703	124.9	0.8	326,211
Alaska	202	0.6	781	0.4	4	16.7	21,392	116.1	0.7	574,822
Utah	269	0.8	1,511	0.7	6	17.6	11,622	113.0	0.7	420,249
Arkansas	327	0.9	1,819	0.9	6	16.4	9,042	96.3	0.6	294,532
Maine	329	0.9	1,105	0.5	3	14.6	13,206	92.2	0.6	280,198

Continued on next page.

INDUSTRY DATA BY STATE - Continued

State	Establishments Total (number)	% of U.S.	Employment Total (number)	% of U.S.	Per Estab.	Payroll Total ($ mil.)	Per Empl. ($)	Sales Total ($ mil.)	% of U.S.	Per Estab. ($)
New Mexico	265	0.7	1,268	0.6	5	16.0	12,623	91.7	0.6	345,951
Nebraska	249	0.7	1,535	0.7	6	15.1	9,812	89.1	0.6	357,831
Mississippi	261	0.7	1,303	0.6	5	12.4	9,490	86.6	0.5	331,950
Montana	200	0.6	904	0.4	5	15.7	17,329	83.7	0.5	418,520
Rhode Island	149	0.4	896	0.4	6	11.2	12,538	67.3	0.4	451,879
West Virginia	190	0.5	961	0.5	5	8.4	8,790	59.1	0.4	310,826
South Dakota	161	0.4	787	0.4	5	9.0	11,394	58.7	0.4	364,571
Vermont	146	0.4	731	0.4	5	9.7	13,224	56.9	0.4	389,993
Delaware	113	0.3	763	0.4	7	7.9	10,317	53.7	0.3	475,257
Idaho	157	0.4	719	0.3	5	6.8	9,451	44.1	0.3	281,057
North Dakota	100	0.3	635	0.3	6	6.6	10,367	36.0	0.2	360,420
Wyoming	106	0.3	391	0.2	4	5.3	13,517	34.9	0.2	329,443
Michigan	1,297	3.6	5K-9999	-	-	(D)	-	(D)	-	-
Arizona	648	1.8	2500-4999	-	-	(D)	-	(D)	-	-
New Hampshire	273	0.8	1000-2499	-	-	(D)	-	(D)	-	-
D.C.	95	0.3	250-499	-	-	(D)	-	(D)	-	-

Source: 2002 *Economic Census*. The states are in descending order of sales or establishments (if sales data are missing for the majority). The symbol (D) appears when data are withheld to prevent disclosure of competitive information. States marked with (D) are sorted by number of establishments. A dash (-) indicates that the data element cannot be calculated. Shaded *states* on the state map indicate those states which have proportionately greater representation in the industry than would be indicated by the states population; the ratio is based on total sales or number of establishments. Shaded *regions* indicate where the industry is regionally most concentrated.

NAICS 453310 - USED MERCHANDISE STORES

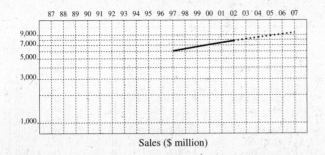

Sales ($ million)

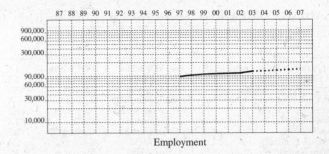

Employment

GENERAL STATISTICS

Year	Establishments (number)	Employment (number)	Payroll ($ million)	Sales ($ million)	Employees per Establishment (number)	Sales per Establishment ($)	Payroll per Employee ($)
1987	-	-	-	-	-	-	-
1988	-	-	-	-	-	-	-
1989	-	-	-	-	-	-	-
1990	-	-	-	-	-	-	-
1991	-	-	-	-	-	-	-
1992	-	-	-	-	-	-	-
1993	-	-	-	-	-	-	-
1994	-	-	-	-	-	-	-
1995	-	-	-	-	-	-	-
1996	-	-	-	-	-	-	-
1997	17,990	97,965	1,203.6	6,043.6	5	335,942	12,286
1998	18,210	105,350	1,387.3	6,393.0 e	6	351,073	13,168
1999	18,037	110,496	1,524.8	6,742.5 e	6	373,814	13,800
2000	17,480	113,837	1,625.1	7,091.9 e	7	405,717	14,276
2001	17,436	115,719	1,698.7	7,441.4 e	7	426,782	14,680
2002	18,207	117,776	1,734.0	7,790.8	6	427,902	14,723
2003	17,872	128,664	1,898.8	8,140.2 p	7	458,754 p	14,758
2004	17,753 p	130,283 p	2,003.6 p	8,489.7 p	7 p	479,292 p	15,585 p
2005	17,719 p	134,646 p	2,109.1 p	8,839.1 p	8 p	499,830 p	15,992 p
2006	17,684 p	139,009 p	2,214.5 p	9,188.6 p	8 p	520,368 p	16,400 p
2007	17,650 p	143,373 p	2,320.0 p	9,538.0 p	8 p	540,906 p	16,807 p

Source: *Economic Census of the United States*, 1997 and 2002. Establishment counts, employment, and payroll are from *County Business Patterns* for non-Census years. This is a newly defined industry. Data for prior years are unavailable at the time of publication but may become available over time. Values followed by 'p' are projections by the editors. Sales data for non-Census years are extrapolations, marked by 'e'.

INDICES OF CHANGE

Year	Establishments (number)	Employment (number)	Payroll ($ million)	Sales ($ million)	Employees per Establishment (number)	Sales per Establishment ($)	Payroll per Employee ($)
1987	-	-	-	-	-	-	-
1992	-	-	-	-	-	-	-
1993	-	-	-	-	-	-	-
1994	-	-	-	-	-	-	-
1995	-	-	-	-	-	-	-
1996	-	-	-	-	-	-	-
1997	98.8	83.2	69.4	77.6	83.5	78.5	83.4
1998	100.0	89.4	80.0	82.1 e	89.7	82.0	89.4
1999	99.1	93.8	87.9	86.5 e	94.3	87.4	93.7
2000	96.0	96.7	93.7	91.0 e	100.5	94.8	97.0
2001	95.8	98.3	98.0	95.5 e	102.0	99.7	99.7
2002	100.0	100.0	100.0	100.0	100.0	100.0	100.0
2003	98.2	109.2	109.5	104.5 p	111.3	107.2 p	100.2
2004	97.5 p	110.6 p	115.5 p	109.0 p	113.3 p	112.0 p	105.9 p
2005	97.3 p	114.3 p	121.6 p	113.5 p	117.3 p	116.8 p	108.6 p
2006	97.1 p	118.0 p	127.7 p	117.9 p	121.3 p	121.6 p	111.4 p
2007	96.9 p	121.7 p	133.8 p	122.4 p	125.3 p	126.4 p	114.2 p

Sources: Same as General Statistics. The values shown reflect change from the base year, 2002. Values above 100 mean greater than 2002, values below 100 mean less than 2002, and a value of 100 in the 1987-2001 or 2003-2007 period means same as 2002. Values followed by a 'p' are projections by the editors; 'e' stands for extrapolation. Data are the most recent available at this level of detail.

SELECTED RATIOS

For 2002	Avg. of All Retail	Analyzed Industry	Index	For 2002	Avg. of All Retail	Analyzed Industry	Index
Employees per Establishment	17	6	38	Sales per Employee	174,682	66,149	38
Payroll per Establishment	333,445	95,238	29	Sales per Establishment	3,332,269	427,902	13
Payroll per Employee	20,311	14,723	72	Expenses per Establishment	na	na	na

Sources: Same as General Statistics. The 'Average of All' column, Wholesale or Retail, represents the average of the sector reported for the most recent complete year available. The Index shows the relationship between the Average and the Analyzed Industry. For example, 100 means that they are equal; 500 that the Analyzed Industry is five times the average; 50 means that the Analyzed Industry is half the national average. The abbreviation 'na' is used to show that data are 'not available'.

LEADING COMPANIES   Number shown: 23   Total sales ($ mil): 1,349   Total employment (000): 11.6

Company Name	Address				CEO Name	Phone	Co. Type	Sales ($ mil)	Empl. (000)
Cash America International Inc.	1600 W 7th St	Fort Worth	TX	76102	Jack R. Daugherty	817-335-1100	P	469	3.8
EZCORP Inc.	1901 Capital Pky	Austin	TX	78746		512-314-3400	P	228	2.4
Nebraska Book Company Inc.	4700 S 19th St	Lincoln	NE	68501	Mark Oppegard	402-421-7300	R	214*	2.1
First Cash Financial Services Inc.	690 E Lamar Blvd	Arlington	TX	76011	Phillip Powell	817-460-3947	P	180	1.5
Shakespeare and Co.	939 Lexington Ave	New York	NY	10021	Steve Carlin	212-570-0201	R	69*	<0.1
Market Antiques	1227 Slocum St	Dallas	TX	75207		214-748-6684	R	53*	0.1
DAK's	1 Courthouse Sq	Carthage	NC	28327	Archie Kelly	910-947-2541	R	26*	<0.1
Goodwill Industries	1080 N 7th St	San Jose	CA	95112	Frank Kent	408-998-5774	R	25*	0.4
Buffalo Exchange	PO Box 40488	Tucson	AZ	85717	Kerstin Block	520-622-2711	R	21*	0.3
Goodwill Industries Grand Rapids	3035 Prairie St SW	Grandville	MI	49418	Phillip Weaver	616-532-4200	R	10*	0.2
Skinner Inc.	357 Main St	Bolton	MA	01740	Karen M Keane	978-779-6241	R	9*	<0.1
Sunrise Enterprises of Roseburg	1950 Mulholland	Roseburg	OR	97470		541-673-0195	R	9*	0.2
Skyway Technology Group Inc.	5014 Tampa W Blvd	Tampa	FL	33634	Byron Norrie	813-249-0101	R	6*	<0.1
Closson's Co.	10100 Montgomery	Cincinnati	OH	45242		513-762-5500	R	6*	<0.1
Midwest Copier Exchange Inc.	3300 Washington St	Waukegan	IL	60085	Edward Spriegel		R	6*	<0.1
W Terr of The Salvation Army	PO Box 24054	Oakland	CA	94623		510-451-4514	R	5*	0.1
Best Collateral Inc.	12 Harbor Dr	Novato	CA	94945	Robert Verhoeff	415-893-7610	R	4*	<0.1
Eisner Associates Inc.	516 N Ave E	Westfield	NJ	07090		908-233-6585	R	3*	<0.1
Didier Aaron Inc.	32 E 67th St	New York	NY	10021	Herve Aaron	212-988-5248	R	2*	<0.1
Total Identity Corp.	1007 N Federal	Fort Lauderdale	FL	33304	Matthew P Dwyer		P	1	<0.1
Millionair Club Charity Inc.	2515 Western Ave	Seattle	WA	98121		206-728-5627	R	1*	<0.1
Boss Unlimited	18 S Broadway	Denver	CO	80209	Ronald Wright	303-871-0373	R	1*	<0.1
Maverick Machinery Company Inc.	PO Box 661	Atkinson	IL	61235	WR Ellenwood	309-936-7731	R	1*	<0.1

Source: Ward's Business Directory of U.S. Private and Public Companies, Volumes 1 and 2, 2005. The company type code used is as follows: P - Public, R - Private, S - Subsidiary, D - Division, J - Joint Venture, A - Affiliate, G - Group. Sales are in millions of dollars, employees are in thousands. An asterisk (*) indicates an estimated sales volume. The symbol < stands for 'less than'. Company names and addresses are truncated, in some cases, to fit into the available space.

OCCUPATIONS EMPLOYED BY USED MERCHANDISE STORES

Occupation	% of Total 2004	Change to 2014	Occupation	% of Total 2004	Change to 2014
Retail salespersons	35.8	43.0	Truck drivers, light or delivery services	2.8	43.0
Cashiers, except gaming	17.0	28.7	Shipping, receiving, & traffic clerks	1.7	29.5
First-line supervisors/managers of retail sales workers	7.6	31.6	Office clerks, general	1.7	27.2
Laborers & freight, stock, & material movers, hand	7.5	28.7	General & operations managers	1.6	41.5
Stock clerks & order fillers	6.9	9.5	Bookkeeping, accounting, & auditing clerks	1.2	28.6

Source: Industry-Occupation Matrix, Bureau of Labor Statistics. These data are reported based on 4-digit NAICS categories but have been matched to corresponding 6-digit NAICS industry codes. The change reported for each occupation to the year 2014 is a percent of growth or decline as estimated by the Bureau of Labor Statistics. The abbreviation nec stands for 'not elsewhere classified.'

LOCATION BY STATE AND REGIONAL CONCENTRATION

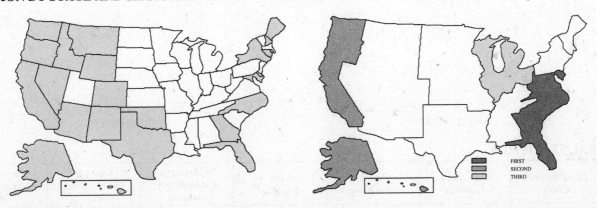

INDUSTRY DATA BY STATE

State	Establishments Total (number)	% of U.S.	Employment Total (number)	% of U.S.	Per Estab.	Payroll Total ($ mil.)	Per Empl. ($)	Sales Total ($ mil.)	% of U.S.	Per Estab. ($)
California	1,938	10.7	15,156	13.0	8	250.5	16,530	1,097.5	14.1	566,303
New York	956	5.3	4,296	3.7	4	101.1	23,540	569.0	7.3	595,215
Texas	1,235	6.8	8,794	7.5	7	125.4	14,265	568.3	7.3	460,190
Florida	1,277	7.0	6,325	5.4	5	92.6	14,634	486.8	6.3	381,169
Illinois	610	3.4	4,128	3.5	7	63.9	15,490	278.9	3.6	457,211
Ohio	630	3.5	4,803	4.1	8	66.5	13,842	268.4	3.5	426,010
Washington	582	3.2	4,615	4.0	8	68.8	14,917	265.7	3.4	456,598
Pennsylvania	640	3.5	4,610	4.0	7	61.3	13,289	241.1	3.1	376,700
Georgia	537	3.0	2,861	2.5	5	42.7	14,922	219.1	2.8	408,095
North Carolina	564	3.1	3,368	2.9	6	47.3	14,054	210.0	2.7	372,342
Arizona	345	1.9	3,433	2.9	10	50.3	14,647	209.3	2.7	606,548
Virginia	522	2.9	3,386	2.9	6	47.1	13,923	193.2	2.5	370,084
Oregon	427	2.4	3,065	2.6	7	48.4	15,778	189.1	2.4	442,859
Maryland	310	1.7	2,804	2.4	9	45.4	16,205	180.4	2.3	581,887
Colorado	400	2.2	2,841	2.4	7	41.7	14,691	171.7	2.2	429,287
Massachusetts	365	2.0	1,852	1.6	5	33.7	18,178	155.1	2.0	424,929
Indiana	401	2.2	3,055	2.6	8	38.2	12,503	152.2	2.0	379,559
Missouri	477	2.6	2,447	2.1	5	31.3	12,808	147.9	1.9	310,025
Wisconsin	342	1.9	2,795	2.4	8	36.9	13,210	137.7	1.8	402,541
Tennessee	407	2.2	1,968	1.7	5	26.0	13,197	135.8	1.7	333,585
Minnesota	303	1.7	2,377	2.0	8	30.8	12,952	133.1	1.7	439,429
Alabama	305	1.7	1,975	1.7	6	27.5	13,916	126.5	1.6	414,816
Connecticut	240	1.3	1,162	1.0	5	23.1	19,897	125.9	1.6	524,608
Louisiana	234	1.3	1,719	1.5	7	27.7	16,134	125.3	1.6	535,342
Oklahoma	284	1.6	1,602	1.4	6	21.7	13,575	102.1	1.3	359,366
New Jersey	265	1.5	1,345	1.2	5	21.2	15,752	100.7	1.3	379,943
South Carolina	293	1.6	1,479	1.3	5	22.2	14,999	99.6	1.3	339,918
Kentucky	282	1.6	1,691	1.5	6	21.5	12,730	93.9	1.2	333,032
Iowa	296	1.6	1,512	1.3	5	16.9	11,191	73.0	0.9	246,787
Nevada	106	0.6	860	0.7	8	14.1	16,394	63.8	0.8	601,434
Kansas	234	1.3	1,311	1.1	6	16.2	12,322	60.4	0.8	257,996
New Mexico	121	0.7	689	0.6	6	11.6	16,893	54.6	0.7	451,595
Maine	123	0.7	495	0.4	4	6.9	13,937	50.2	0.6	407,902
Arkansas	186	1.0	625	0.5	3	9.2	14,648	46.4	0.6	249,484
Mississippi	167	0.9	889	0.8	5	10.4	11,687	46.0	0.6	275,749
New Hampshire	113	0.6	534	0.5	5	7.6	14,240	41.3	0.5	365,920
Nebraska	146	0.8	969	0.8	7	11.4	11,721	40.8	0.5	279,445
Idaho	116	0.6	673	0.6	6	9.9	14,685	39.7	0.5	342,569
Hawaii	68	0.4	451	0.4	7	8.5	18,785	36.9	0.5	542,324
Montana	108	0.6	677	0.6	6	7.2	10,687	30.2	0.4	279,630
Rhode Island	76	0.4	538	0.5	7	7.0	13,032	28.1	0.4	370,118
Utah	72	0.4	460	0.4	6	7.1	15,346	28.0	0.4	389,014
West Virginia	100	0.6	434	0.4	4	5.3	12,129	21.5	0.3	214,630
Delaware	55	0.3	430	0.4	8	5.3	12,284	21.4	0.3	388,218
Alaska	48	0.3	362	0.3	8	6.8	18,729	21.3	0.3	443,375
South Dakota	89	0.5	401	0.3	5	4.3	10,768	19.0	0.2	213,348
Vermont	74	0.4	257	0.2	3	3.3	12,712	17.7	0.2	239,014
Wyoming	55	0.3	258	0.2	5	3.2	12,314	15.9	0.2	288,618
North Dakota	37	0.2	272	0.2	7	2.8	10,478	9.5	0.1	255,973
Michigan	524	2.9	2500-4999	-	-	(D)	-	(D)	-	-
D.C.	47	0.3	250-499	-	-	(D)	-	(D)	-	-

Source: 2002 *Economic Census*. The states are in descending order of sales or establishments (if sales data are missing for the majority). The symbol (D) appears when data are withheld to prevent disclosure of competitive information. States marked with (D) are sorted by number of establishments. A dash (-) indicates that the data element cannot be calculated. Shaded *states* on the state map indicate those states which have proportionately greater representation in the industry than would be indicated by the states population; the ratio is based on total sales or number of establishments. Shaded *regions* indicate where the industry is regionally most concentrated.

NAICS 453910 - PET AND PET SUPPLIES STORES

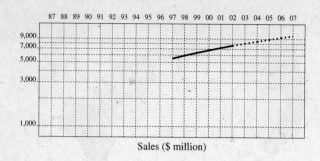

Sales ($ million)

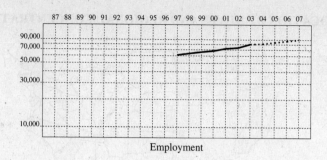

Employment

GENERAL STATISTICS

Year	Establishments (number)	Employment (number)	Payroll ($ million)	Sales ($ million)	Employees per Establishment (number)	Sales per Establishment ($)	Payroll per Employee ($)
1987	-	-	-	-	-	-	-
1988	-	-	-	-	-	-	-
1989	-	-	-	-	-	-	-
1990	-	-	-	-	-	-	-
1991	-	-	-	-	-	-	-
1992	-	-	-	-	-	-	-
1993	-	-	-	-	-	-	-
1994	-	-	-	-	-	-	-
1995	-	-	-	-	-	-	-
1996	-	-	-	-	-	-	-
1997	8,318	61,192	709.1	5,492.7	7	660,339	11,588
1998	8,455	63,645	801.3	5,920.2 e	8	700,200	12,590
1999	8,213	66,075	880.0	6,347.7 e	8	772,883	13,318
2000	8,138	67,967	947.8	6,775.2 e	8	832,536	13,945
2001	7,945	72,120	1,010.8	7,202.7 e	9	906,566	14,016
2002	7,629	73,543	1,025.2	7,630.2	10	1,000,152	13,940
2003	7,671	80,456	1,179.6	8,057.7 p	10	1,049,895 p	14,661
2004	7,501 p	81,233 p	1,220.5 p	8,485.1 p	11 p	1,117,832 p	15,239 p
2005	7,363 p	84,220 p	1,291.6 p	8,912.6 p	11 p	1,185,770 p	15,690 p
2006	7,225 p	87,207 p	1,362.7 p	9,340.1 p	12 p	1,253,708 p	16,140 p
2007	7,087 p	90,194 p	1,433.7 p	9,767.6 p	12 p	1,321,645 p	16,591 p

Source: Economic Census of the United States, 1997 and 2002. Establishment counts, employment, and payroll are from *County Business Patterns* for non-Census years. This is a newly defined industry. Data for prior years are unavailable at the time of publication but may become available over time. Values followed by 'p' are projections by the editors. Sales data for non-Census years are extrapolations, marked by 'e'.

INDICES OF CHANGE

Year	Establishments (number)	Employment (number)	Payroll ($ million)	Sales ($ million)	Employees per Establishment (number)	Sales per Establishment ($)	Payroll per Employee ($)
1987	-	-	-	-	-	-	-
1992	-	-	-	-	-	-	-
1993	-	-	-	-	-	-	-
1994	-	-	-	-	-	-	-
1995	-	-	-	-	-	-	-
1996	-	-	-	-	-	-	-
1997	109.0	83.2	69.2	72.0	76.8	66.0	83.1
1998	110.8	86.5	78.2	77.6 e	77.8	70.0	90.3
1999	107.7	89.8	85.8	83.2 e	83.0	77.3	95.5
2000	106.7	92.4	92.5	88.8 e	87.1	83.2	100.0
2001	104.1	98.1	98.6	94.4 e	94.4	90.6	100.6
2002	100.0	100.0	100.0	100.0	100.0	100.0	100.0
2003	100.6	109.4	115.1	105.6 p	108.8	105.0 p	105.2
2004	98.3 p	110.5 p	119.1 p	111.2 p	111.4 p	111.8 p	109.3 p
2005	96.5 p	114.5 p	126.0 p	116.8 p	116.8 p	118.6 p	112.6 p
2006	94.7 p	118.6 p	132.9 p	122.4 p	122.3 p	125.4 p	115.8 p
2007	92.9 p	122.6 p	139.9 p	128.0 p	127.7 p	132.1 p	119.0 p

Sources: Same as General Statistics. The values shown reflect change from the base year, 2002. Values above 100 mean greater than 2002, values below 100 mean less than 2002, and a value of 100 in the 1987-2001 or 2003-2007 period means same as 2002. Values followed by a 'p' are projections by the editors; 'e' stands for extrapolation. Data are the most recent available at this level of detail.

SELECTED RATIOS

For 2002	Avg. of All Retail	Analyzed Industry	Index	For 2002	Avg. of All Retail	Analyzed Industry	Index
Employees per Establishment	17	10	57	Sales per Employee	174,682	103,751	59
Payroll per Establishment	333,445	134,376	40	Sales per Establishment	3,332,269	1,000,152	30
Payroll per Employee	20,311	13,940	69	Expenses per Establishment	na	na	na

Sources: Same as General Statistics. The 'Average of All' column, Wholesale or Retail, represents the average of the sector reported for the most recent complete year available. The Index shows the relationship between the Average and the Analyzed Industry. For example, 100 means that they are equal; 500 that the Analyzed Industry is five times the average; 50 means that the Analyzed Industry is half the national average. The abbreviation 'na' is used to show that data are 'not available'.

LEADING COMPANIES   Number shown: 5   Total sales ($ mil): 98   Total employment (000): 0.2

Company Name	Address				CEO Name	Phone	Co. Type	Sales ($ mil)	Empl. (000)
Alaska Mill and Feed	PO Box 101246	Anchorage	AK	99510	Ken Sherwood	907-279-4519	R	38*	<0.1
Burkmann Feeds L.L.C.	100 Georgetown Ln	Glasgow	KY	42141		270-651-8000	R	29*	<0.1
RMC Inc	PO Box 1109	Harrisonburg	VA	22803	Jack Reich	540-434-5333	D	20*	<0.1
Pratt Feed and Supply Co.	5237 W Glendale	Glendale	AZ	85301	Dan Pratt	623-939-3326	R	8*	<0.1
Aquarium Environments Inc.	6955 Greenville Ave	Dallas	TX	75231	Roger Degregori	214-369-9086	R	2*	<0.1

Source: Ward's Business Directory of U.S. Private and Public Companies, Volumes 1 and 2, 2005. The company type code used is as follows: P - Public, R - Private, S - Subsidiary, D - Division, J - Joint Venture, A - Affiliate, G - Group. Sales are in millions of dollars, employees are in thousands. An asterisk (*) indicates an estimated sales volume. The symbol < stands for 'less than'. Company names and addresses are truncated, in some cases, to fit into the available space.

OCCUPATIONS EMPLOYED BY OTHER MISCELLANEOUS STORE RETAILERS

Occupation	% of Total 2004	Change to 2014	Occupation	% of Total 2004	Change to 2014
Retail salespersons	33.8	29.1	Office clerks, general	2.0	14.9
Cashiers, except gaming	11.6	16.2	Sales reps, wholesale & manufacturing, exc tech	2.0	29.1
First-line supervisors/managers of retail sales workers	7.4	18.8	Bookkeeping, accounting, & auditing clerks	1.9	16.2
Nonfarm animal caretakers	3.7	28.7	Assemblers & fabricators, nec	1.6	19.4
Stock clerks & order fillers	3.1	-1.1	Shipping, receiving, & traffic clerks	1.5	16.9
Manufactured building & mobile home installers	2.1	16.2	Installation, maintenance, & repair workers, nec	1.3	29.1
General & operations managers	2.1	27.8	Truck drivers, light or delivery services	1.2	29.1
Laborers & freight, stock, & material movers, hand	2.1	16.2	Secretaries, except legal, medical, & executive	1.2	8.6

Source: Industry-Occupation Matrix, Bureau of Labor Statistics. These data are reported based on 4-digit NAICS categories but have been matched to corresponding 6-digit NAICS industry codes. The change reported for each occupation to the year 2014 is a percent of growth or decline as estimated by the Bureau of Labor Statistics. The abbreviation nec stands for 'not elsewhere classified.'

LOCATION BY STATE AND REGIONAL CONCENTRATION

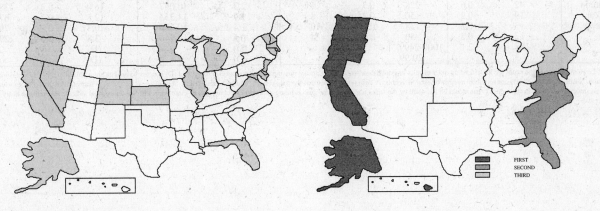

INDUSTRY DATA BY STATE

State	Establishments Total (number)	% of U.S.	Employment Total (number)	% of U.S.	Per Estab.	Payroll Total ($ mil.)	Per Empl. ($)	Sales Total ($ mil.)	% of U.S.	Per Estab. ($)
California	1,060	13.9	10,242	13.9	10	152.6	14,901	1,211.8	16.0	1,143,238
Texas	378	5.0	4,573	6.2	12	67.4	14,749	494.6	6.5	1,308,463
Florida	545	7.1	4,072	5.5	7	63.0	15,468	418.9	5.5	768,712
New York	582	7.6	4,039	5.5	7	52.8	13,083	411.2	5.4	706,503
Illinois	309	4.1	3,348	4.6	11	45.7	13,655	351.6	4.6	1,137,964
Pennsylvania	351	4.6	3,631	4.9	10	45.9	12,654	338.0	4.5	963,020
Michigan	271	3.6	2,881	3.9	11	38.1	13,230	300.9	4.0	1,110,188
New Jersey	273	3.6	2,326	3.2	9	37.0	15,889	276.8	3.6	1,013,824
Ohio	301	3.9	3,379	4.6	11	42.8	12,655	260.5	3.4	865,551
Colorado	188	2.5	1,991	2.7	11	29.6	14,869	224.7	3.0	1,195,064
Washington	200	2.6	1,907	2.6	10	29.2	15,298	211.9	2.8	1,059,555
Virginia	170	2.2	2,083	2.8	12	28.5	13,699	207.3	2.7	1,219,647
Maryland	160	2.1	1,978	2.7	12	27.2	13,734	197.4	2.6	1,233,700
Massachusetts	171	2.2	1,869	2.5	11	27.7	14,798	191.2	2.5	1,117,883
Georgia	187	2.5	1,884	2.6	10	26.3	13,955	190.6	2.5	1,019,278
Minnesota	157	2.1	1,880	2.6	12	22.4	11,914	158.4	2.1	1,009,159

Continued on next page.

INDUSTRY DATA BY STATE - Continued

State	Establishments Total (number)	Establishments % of U.S.	Employment Total (number)	Employment % of U.S.	Employment Per Estab.	Payroll Total ($ mil.)	Payroll Per Empl. ($)	Sales Total ($ mil.)	Sales % of U.S.	Sales Per Estab. ($)
North Carolina	182	2.4	1,573	2.1	9	21.5	13,687	156.4	2.1	859,604
Indiana	160	2.1	1,652	2.2	10	20.9	12,656	154.1	2.0	963,031
Wisconsin	143	1.9	1,587	2.2	11	18.8	11,859	142.5	1.9	996,301
Missouri	135	1.8	1,238	1.7	9	16.2	13,111	121.5	1.6	900,037
Oregon	131	1.7	1,038	1.4	8	14.2	13,684	120.8	1.6	921,924
Connecticut	114	1.5	1,134	1.5	10	16.4	14,430	117.8	1.6	1,033,763
Tennessee	117	1.5	1,094	1.5	9	15.6	14,245	107.4	1.4	917,821
Nevada	61	0.8	783	1.1	13	12.5	15,995	84.1	1.1	1,378,049
Kansas	73	1.0	732	1.0	10	9.4	12,872	72.2	1.0	988,575
Kentucky	74	1.0	709	1.0	10	9.3	13,059	69.0	0.9	932,595
South Carolina	96	1.3	623	0.8	6	8.5	13,706	66.9	0.9	697,073
New Hampshire	62	0.8	708	1.0	11	9.5	13,369	66.8	0.9	1,077,161
Oklahoma	59	0.8	536	0.7	9	8.5	15,918	62.1	0.8	1,053,203
Louisiana	78	1.0	602	0.8	8	8.1	13,502	58.7	0.8	753,038
Utah	51	0.7	596	0.8	12	7.6	12,799	52.7	0.7	1,034,196
Iowa	65	0.9	486	0.7	7	5.8	11,922	46.7	0.6	718,600
New Mexico	42	0.6	429	0.6	10	5.4	12,613	45.7	0.6	1,088,833
Rhode Island	37	0.5	310	0.4	8	4.2	13,519	45.1	0.6	1,217,730
Alabama	61	0.8	474	0.6	8	5.9	12,426	36.8	0.5	602,721
Nebraska	45	0.6	371	0.5	8	4.1	11,178	34.2	0.5	760,956
Delaware	37	0.5	365	0.5	10	5.2	14,378	33.3	0.4	899,514
Hawaii	35	0.5	316	0.4	9	4.8	15,247	32.9	0.4	939,400
Arkansas	46	0.6	287	0.4	6	3.6	12,683	30.5	0.4	662,478
Mississippi	30	0.4	249	0.3	8	3.1	12,337	27.3	0.4	908,700
Maine	46	0.6	245	0.3	5	3.4	14,069	25.1	0.3	546,326
Idaho	26	0.3	214	0.3	8	3.2	14,925	23.4	0.3	901,308
Alaska	21	0.3	170	0.2	8	3.2	18,941	22.4	0.3	1,068,571
Vermont	23	0.3	166	0.2	7	2.5	14,922	19.1	0.3	831,826
Montana	25	0.3	206	0.3	8	2.3	11,238	17.3	0.2	692,120
West Virginia	42	0.6	228	0.3	5	2.3	10,057	16.0	0.2	381,214
South Dakota	19	0.2	150	0.2	8	1.7	11,353	12.8	0.2	675,684
North Dakota	13	0.2	133	0.2	10	1.4	10,684	10.3	0.1	795,923
Wyoming	13	0.2	50	0.1	4	0.5	10,940	3.8	0.1	294,385
Arizona	158	2.1	1000-2499	-	-	(D)	-	(D)	-	-
D.C.	3	-	20-99	-	-	(D)	-	(D)	-	-

Source: 2002 *Economic Census*. The states are in descending order of sales or establishments (if sales data are missing for the majority). The symbol (D) appears when data are withheld to prevent disclosure of competitive information. States marked with (D) are sorted by number of establishments. A dash (-) indicates that the data element cannot be calculated. Shaded *states* on the state map indicate those states which have proportionately greater representation in the industry than would be indicated by the states population; the ratio is based on total sales or number of establishments. Shaded *regions* indicate where the industry is regionally most concentrated.

NAICS 453920 - ART DEALERS

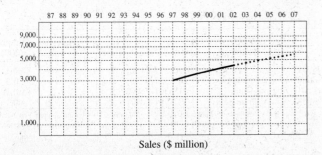

Sales ($ million)

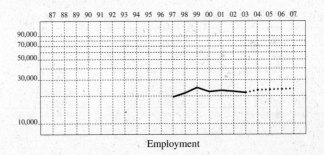

Employment

GENERAL STATISTICS

Year	Establishments (number)	Employment (number)	Payroll ($ million)	Sales ($ million)	Employees per Establishment (number)	Sales per Establishment ($)	Payroll per Employee ($)
1987	-	-	-	-	-	-	-
1988	-	-	-	-	-	-	-
1989	-	-	-	-	-	-	-
1990	-	-	-	-	-	-	-
1991	-	-	-	-	-	-	-
1992	-	-	-	-	-	-	-
1993	-	-	-	-	-	-	-
1994	-	-	-	-	-	-	-
1995	-	-	-	-	-	-	-
1996	-	-	-	-	-	-	-
1997	5,698	19,510	401.2	3,000.8	3	526,641	20,564
1998	5,948	21,506	521.1	3,272.0 e	4	550,101	24,230
1999	5,921	24,707	598.4	3,543.2 e	4	598,412	24,220
2000	5,971	22,284	602.0	3,814.4 e	4	638,821	27,015
2001	6,162	22,988	602.4	4,085.6 e	4	663,031	26,206
2002	6,294	22,419	669.1	4,356.8	4	692,215	29,846
2003	6,304	21,747	628.8	4,628.0 p	3	732,244 p	28,915
2004	6,436 p	23,140 p	715.1 p	4,899.2 p	4 p	766,732 p	31,324 p
2005	6,534 p	23,383 p	750.2 p	5,170.4 p	4 p	801,219 p	32,691 p
2006	6,632 p	23,627 p	785.3 p	5,441.6 p	4 p	835,707 p	34,058 p
2007	6,730 p	23,870 p	820.4 p	5,712.8 p	4 p	870,195 p	35,424 p

Source: *Economic Census of the United States*, 1997 and 2002. Establishment counts, employment, and payroll are from *County Business Patterns* for non-Census years. This is a newly defined industry. Data for prior years are unavailable at the time of publication but may become available over time. Values followed by 'p' are projections by the editors. Sales data for non-Census years are extrapolations, marked by 'e'.

INDICES OF CHANGE

Year	Establishments (number)	Employment (number)	Payroll ($ million)	Sales ($ million)	Employees per Establishment (number)	Sales per Establishment ($)	Payroll per Employee ($)
1987	-	-	-	-	-	-	-
1992	-	-	-	-	-	-	-
1993	-	-	-	-	-	-	-
1994	-	-	-	-	-	-	-
1995	-	-	-	-	-	-	-
1996	-	-	-	-	-	-	-
1997	90.5	87.0	60.0	68.9	95.5	76.1	68.9
1998	94.5	95.9	77.9	75.1 e	101.1	79.5	81.2
1999	94.1	110.2	89.4	81.3 e	117.9	86.4	81.1
2000	94.9	99.4	90.0	87.6 e	103.9	92.3	90.5
2001	97.9	102.5	90.0	93.8 e	103.9	95.8	87.8
2002	100.0	100.0	100.0	100.0	100.0	100.0	100.0
2003	100.2	97.0	94.0	106.2 p	96.8	105.8 p	96.9
2004	102.2 p	103.2 p	106.9 p	112.4 p	101.0 p	110.8 p	105.0 p
2005	103.8 p	104.3 p	112.1 p	118.7 p	100.6 p	115.7 p	109.5 p
2006	105.4 p	105.4 p	117.4 p	124.9 p	100.2 p	120.7 p	114.1 p
2007	106.9 p	106.5 p	122.6 p	131.1 p	99.7 p	125.7 p	118.7 p

Sources: Same as General Statistics. The values shown reflect change from the base year, 2002. Values above 100 mean greater than 2002, values below 100 mean less than 2002, and a value of 100 in the 1987-2001 or 2003-2007 period means same as 2002. Values followed by a 'p' are projections by the editors; 'e' stands for extrapolation. Data are the most recent available at this level of detail.

SELECTED RATIOS

For 2002	Avg. of All Retail	Analyzed Industry	Index	For 2002	Avg. of All Retail	Analyzed Industry	Index
Employees per Establishment	17	4	21	Sales per Employee	174,682	194,335	111
Payroll per Establishment	333,445	106,310	32	Sales per Establishment	3,332,269	692,215	21
Payroll per Employee	20,311	29,846	147	Expenses per Establishment	na	na	na

Sources: Same as General Statistics. The 'Average of All' column, Wholesale or Retail, represents the average of the sector reported for the most recent complete year available. The Index shows the relationship between the Average and the Analyzed Industry. For example, 100 means that they are equal; 500 that the Analyzed Industry is five times the average; 50 means that the Analyzed Industry is half the national average. The abbreviation 'na' is used to show that data are 'not available'.

LEADING COMPANIES　Number shown: **4**　　Total sales ($ mil): **39**　　Total employment (000): **0.2**

Company Name	Address				CEO Name	Phone	Co. Type	Sales ($ mil)	Empl. (000)
Inst For Develop Human Being	PO Box 370	Nevada City	CA	95959		530-272-0180	R	19*	<0.1
Picture Galleries Inc.	PO Box 1000	Meridian	ID	83680	Lance Saunders	208-321-9500	R	14*	0.2
Segye Times Inc.	3842 9th St	Long Island City	NY	11101	Inseung Chun	718-361-2600	R	3*	<0.1
Crystal Art Gallery	3359 E 50th St	Los Angeles	CA	90058	Randy Greenberg	323-581-6617	R	3*	<0.1

Source: *Ward's Business Directory of U.S. Private and Public Companies*, Volumes 1 and 2, 2005. The company type code used is as follows: P - Public, R - Private, S - Subsidiary, D - Division, J - Joint Venture, A - Affiliate, G - Group. Sales are in millions of dollars, employees are in thousands. An asterisk (*) indicates an estimated sales volume. The symbol < stands for 'less than'. Company names and addresses are truncated, in some cases, to fit into the available space.

OCCUPATIONS EMPLOYED BY OTHER MISCELLANEOUS STORE RETAILERS

Occupation	% of Total 2004	Change to 2014	Occupation	% of Total 2004	Change to 2014
Retail salespersons	33.8	29.1	Office clerks, general	2.0	14.9
Cashiers, except gaming	11.6	16.2	Sales reps, wholesale & manufacturing, exc tech	2.0	29.1
First-line supervisors/managers of retail sales workers	7.4	18.8	Bookkeeping, accounting, & auditing clerks	1.9	16.2
Nonfarm animal caretakers	3.7	28.7	Assemblers & fabricators, nec	1.6	19.4
Stock clerks & order fillers	3.1	-1.1	Shipping, receiving, & traffic clerks	1.5	16.9
Manufactured building & mobile home installers	2.1	16.2	Installation, maintenance, & repair workers, nec	1.3	29.1
General & operations managers	2.1	27.8	Truck drivers, light or delivery services	1.2	29.1
Laborers & freight, stock, & material movers, hand	2.1	16.2	Secretaries, except legal, medical, & executive	1.2	8.6

Source: *Industry-Occupation Matrix*, Bureau of Labor Statistics. These data are reported based on 4-digit NAICS categories but have been matched to corresponding 6-digit NAICS industry codes. The change reported for each occupation to the year 2014 is a percent of growth or decline as estimated by the Bureau of Labor Statistics. The abbreviation nec stands for 'not elsewhere classified.'

LOCATION BY STATE AND REGIONAL CONCENTRATION

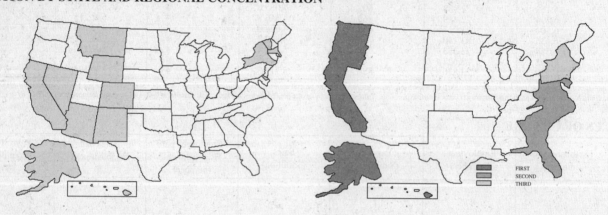

FIRST
SECOND
THIRD

INDUSTRY DATA BY STATE

State	Establishments		Employment			Payroll		Sales		
	Total (number)	% of U.S.	Total (number)	% of U.S.	Per Estab.	Total ($ mil.)	Per Empl. ($)	Total ($ mil.)	% of U.S.	Per Estab. ($)
New York	663	10.5	3,067	14.0	5	211.1	68,838	1,487.5	35.1	2,243,544
California	846	13.4	2,898	13.2	3	80.7	27,852	573.8	13.5	678,310
Florida	473	7.5	1,486	6.8	3	32.7	22,005	208.0	4.9	439,799
New Mexico	193	3.0	619	2.8	3	18.6	30,021	143.5	3.4	743,399
Illinois	199	3.1	739	3.4	4	17.8	24,118	139.3	3.3	699,899
Michigan	173	2.7	701	3.2	4	18.1	25,879	134.6	3.2	777,936
Arizona	204	3.2	723	3.3	4	16.4	22,716	113.7	2.7	557,505
Texas	281	4.4	933	4.3	3	17.9	19,179	113.1	2.7	402,520
Colorado	199	3.1	732	3.3	4	16.5	22,564	109.5	2.6	550,211
Massachusetts	195	3.1	546	2.5	3	15.6	28,509	107.3	2.5	550,097
Delaware	25	0.4	127	0.6	5	2.6	20,228	78.6	1.9	3,143,080
Pennsylvania	181	2.9	704	3.2	4	14.0	19,939	66.7	1.6	368,729
Hawaii	96	1.5	494	2.3	5	12.8	25,895	63.2	1.5	658,542
Nevada	59	0.9	269	1.2	5	10.2	38,030	53.8	1.3	912,712
Washington	162	2.6	462	2.1	3	9.2	19,874	53.2	1.3	328,179
Georgia	146	2.3	472	2.2	3	10.0	21,125	51.4	1.2	351,925
New Jersey	137	2.2	350	1.6	3	7.1	20,426	44.5	1.1	324,876

Continued on next page.

INDUSTRY DATA BY STATE - Continued

State	Establishments Total (number)	Establishments % of U.S.	Employment Total (number)	Employment % of U.S.	Employment Per Estab.	Payroll Total ($ mil.)	Payroll Per Empl. ($)	Sales Total ($ mil.)	Sales % of U.S.	Sales Per Estab. ($)
Louisiana	78	1.2	264	1.2	3	6.7	25,235	43.7	1.0	559,897
North Carolina	151	2.4	397	1.8	3	7.4	18,710	43.6	1.0	289,020
Oregon	111	1.8	417	1.9	4	7.4	17,681	42.0	1.0	378,252
Virginia	140	2.2	449	2.0	3	7.9	17,679	38.8	0.9	276,907
Wisconsin	139	2.2	498	2.3	4	6.7	13,454	38.7	0.9	278,698
Maryland	104	1.6	354	1.6	3	8.1	22,791	38.6	0.9	371,615
South Carolina	102	1.6	343	1.6	3	6.5	18,845	38.1	0.9	373,922
Minnesota	109	1.7	348	1.6	3	6.5	18,621	35.5	0.8	326,046
Ohio	129	2.0	467	2.1	4	7.4	15,752	32.6	0.8	252,961
Missouri	69	1.1	204	0.9	3	4.1	20,255	31.1	0.7	450,971
Tennessee	80	1.3	262	1.2	3	4.5	17,344	30.6	0.7	382,438
Connecticut	62	1.0	149	0.7	2	3.4	23,094	29.4	0.7	473,403
Wyoming	42	0.7	118	0.5	3	3.6	30,305	25.2	0.6	601,119
Utah	64	1.0	262	1.2	4	4.6	17,714	23.0	0.5	359,094
Montana	60	0.9	135	0.6	2	2.6	19,022	18.4	0.4	306,817
Alaska	52	0.8	123	0.6	2	3.2	25,984	17.0	0.4	327,346
Vermont	33	0.5	110	0.5	3	2.0	17,809	14.1	0.3	428,364
Maine	51	0.8	77	0.4	2	1.8	23,078	14.1	0.3	276,373
Alabama	50	0.8	182	0.8	4	2.7	14,791	14.0	0.3	279,340
Iowa	58	0.9	187	0.9	3	2.8	15,182	13.8	0.3	237,069
Idaho	32	0.5	141	0.6	4	2.1	15,220	13.7	0.3	426,969
Indiana	60	0.9	167	0.8	3	2.7	16,251	12.9	0.3	214,667
Kentucky	45	0.7	142	0.6	3	2.0	14,099	10.5	0.2	233,933
Nebraska	31	0.5	125	0.6	4	1.9	14,872	9.9	0.2	320,548
Oklahoma	35	0.6	75	0.3	2	1.0	13,667	8.3	0.2	236,400
Kansas	32	0.5	115	0.5	4	1.7	14,817	8.2	0.2	257,188
New Hampshire	24	0.4	73	0.3	3	1.2	16,849	6.9	0.2	288,125
Arkansas	33	0.5	73	0.3	2	1.4	19,562	6.3	0.1	192,212
South Dakota	23	0.4	89	0.4	4	1.1	12,899	5.2	0.1	226,783
Mississippi	20	0.3	61	0.3	3	0.8	12,344	4.8	0.1	240,650
West Virginia	14	0.2	37	0.2	3	0.5	14,000	2.8	0.1	200,143
North Dakota	7	0.1	8	-	1	0.1	10,375	0.8	-	112,714
D.C.	34	0.5	20-99	-	-	(D)	-	(D)	-	-
Rhode Island	22	0.3	20-99	-	-	(D)	-	(D)	-	-

Source: 2002 *Economic Census.* The states are in descending order of sales or establishments (if sales data are missing for the majority). The symbol (D) appears when data are withheld to prevent disclosure of competitive information. States marked with (D) are sorted by number of establishments. A dash (-) indicates that the data element cannot be calculated. Shaded *states* on the state map indicate those states which have proportionately greater representation in the industry than would be indicated by the states population; the ratio is based on total sales or number of establishments. Shaded *regions* indicate where the industry is regionally most concentrated.

NAICS 453930 - MANUFACTURED (MOBILE) HOME DEALERS*

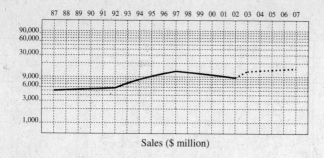

Sales ($ million)

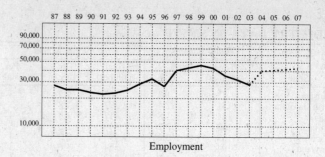

Employment

GENERAL STATISTICS

Year	Establishments (number)	Employment (number)	Payroll ($ million)	Sales ($ million)	Employees per Establishment (number)	Sales per Establishment ($)	Payroll per Employee ($)
1987	5,053	27,486	445.1	5,015.4	5	992,559	16,194
1988	4,545	24,711	456.0	5,154.8 e	5	1,134,169	18,453
1989	4,404	24,717	447.5	5,294.1 e	6	1,202,112	18,105
1990	4,162	23,053	445.7	5,433.5 e	6	1,305,502	19,334
1991	4,054	22,197	420.0	5,572.8 e	6	1,374,642	18,921
1992	4,053	22,814	478.2	5,712.1	6	1,409,351	20,961
1993	4,146	24,561	605.4	7,239.2 e	6	1,746,069	24,649
1994	4,294	28,632	785.7	8,766.3 e	7	2,041,523	27,441
1995	4,501	32,584	911.5	10,293.3 e	7	2,286,892	27,974
1996	3,998 e	27,017 e	726.4 e	11,820.4 e	7 e	2,956,578 e	26,887 e
1997	5,485	40,401	1,122.7	13,347.5	7	2,433,455	27,789
1998	5,723	43,231	1,342.1	12,591.1 e	8	2,200,092	31,045
1999	5,951	46,195	1,370.5	11,834.8 e	8	1,988,700	29,668
2000	6,156	43,101	1,270.6	11,078.4 e	7	1,799,607	29,480
2001	5,865	35,519	1,043.8	10,322.0 e	6	1,759,934	29,386
2002	5,551	32,142	888.1	9,565.6	6	1,723,228	27,630
2003	5,069	28,383	863.9	13,180.6 p	6	2,354,548 p	30,436
2004	5,785 p	40,063 p	1,274.4 p	13,708.9 p	7 p	2,423,065 p	33,246 p
2005	5,885 p	41,072 p	1,327.0 p	14,237.2 p	7 p	2,491,583 p	34,167 p
2006	5,985 p	42,081 p	1,379.6 p	14,765.5 p	7 p	2,560,100 p	35,087 p
2007	6,085 p	43,089 p	1,432.1 p	15,293.8 p	7 p	2,628,617 p	36,008 p

Sources: Economic Census of the United States, 1987, 1992, 1997, and 2002. Establishment counts, employment, and payroll are from County Business Patterns for non-Census years. Values followed by a 'p' are projections by the editors. Sales data for non-Census years are extrapolations, marked by 'e'. Data are the most recent available at this level of detail.

INDICES OF CHANGE

Year	Establishments (number)	Employment (number)	Payroll ($ million)	Sales ($ million)	Employees per Establishment (number)	Sales per Establishment ($)	Payroll per Employee ($)
1987	91.0	85.5	50.1	52.4	93.3	57.6	58.6
1992	73.0	71.0	53.8	59.7	96.7	81.8	75.9
1993	74.7	76.4	68.2	75.7 e	101.9	101.3	89.2
1994	77.4	89.1	88.5	91.6 e	115.7	118.5	99.3
1995	81.1	101.4	102.6	107.6 e	124.3	132.7	101.2
1996	72.0 e	84.1 e	81.8 e	123.6 e	117.4 e	171.6 e	97.3 e
1997	98.8	125.7	126.4	139.5	127.8	141.2	100.6
1998	103.1	134.5	151.1	131.6 e	131.3	127.7	112.4
1999	107.2	143.7	154.3	123.7 e	134.7	115.4	107.4
2000	110.9	134.1	143.1	115.8 e	120.9	104.4	106.7
2001	105.7	110.5	117.5	107.9 e	105.3	102.1	106.4
2002	100.0	100.0	100.0	100.0	100.0	100.0	100.0
2003	91.3	88.3	97.3	137.8 p	96.7	136.6 p	110.2
2004	104.2 p	124.6 p	143.5 p	143.3 p	121.2 p	140.6 p	120.3 p
2005	106.0 p	127.8 p	149.4 p	148.8 p	122.6 p	144.6 p	123.7 p
2006	107.8 p	130.9 p	155.3 p	154.4 p	124.0 p	148.6 p	127.0 p
2007	109.6 p	134.1 p	161.3 p	159.9 p	125.4 p	152.5 p	130.3 p

Sources: Same as General Statistics. The values shown reflect change from the base year, 2002. Values above 100 mean greater than 2002, values below 100 mean less than 2002, and a value of 100 in the 1987-2001 or 2003-2007 period means same as 2002. Values followed by a 'p' are projections by the editors; 'e' stands for extrapolation. Data are the most recent available at this level of detail.

SELECTED RATIOS

For 2002	Avg. of All Retail	Analyzed Industry	Index	For 2002	Avg. of All Retail	Analyzed Industry	Index
Employees per Establishment	17	6	34	Sales per Employee	174,682	297,606	170
Payroll per Establishment	333,445	159,985	48	Sales per Establishment	3,332,269	1,723,228	52
Payroll per Employee	20,311	27,630	136	Expenses per Establishment	na	na	na

Sources: Same as General Statistics. The 'Average of All' column, Wholesale or Retail, represents the average of the sector reported for the most recent complete year available. The Index shows the relationship between the Average and the Analyzed Industry. For example, 100 means that they are equal; 500 that the Analyzed Industry is five times the average; 50 means that the Analyzed Industry is half the national average. The abbreviation 'na' is used to show that data are 'not available'.

*Equivalent to SIC 5271.

LEADING COMPANIES   Number shown: **4**   Total sales ($ mil): **423**   Total employment (000): **5.3**

Company Name	Address				CEO Name	Phone	Co. Type	Sales ($ mil)	Empl. (000)
Reorganized Sale OKWD Inc.	7800 McCloud Rd	Greensboro	NC	27409	Myles E. Standish	336-664-2400	S	398	5.2
George R. Pierce Inc.	PO Box 80708	Billings	MT	59107	Ron Pierce	406-655-8000	R	12*	<0.1
Mobile Home Stuff Store Inc.	N6446 Rlg Mdws	Fond du Lac	WI	54937	Anthony Widowsky	920-923-0098	R	7*	<0.1
Frontier Homes Inc.	412 Main St	Summersville	WV	26651	Fred Fogleman	304-872-3271	R	6*	<0.1

Source: Ward's Business Directory of U.S. Private and Public Companies, Volumes 1 and 2, 2005. The company type code used is as follows: P - Public, R - Private, S - Subsidiary, D - Division, J - Joint Venture, A - Affiliate, G - Group. Sales are in millions of dollars, employees are in thousands. An asterisk (*) indicates an estimated sales volume. The symbol < stands for 'less than'. Company names and addresses are truncated, in some cases, to fit into the available space.

OCCUPATIONS EMPLOYED BY OTHER MISCELLANEOUS STORE RETAILERS

Occupation	% of Total 2004	Change to 2014	Occupation	% of Total 2004	Change to 2014
Retail salespersons	33.8	29.1	Office clerks, general	2.0	14.9
Cashiers, except gaming	11.6	16.2	Sales reps, wholesale & manufacturing, exc tech	2.0	29.1
First-line supervisors/managers of retail sales workers	7.4	18.8	Bookkeeping, accounting, & auditing clerks	1.9	16.2
Nonfarm animal caretakers	3.7	28.7	Assemblers & fabricators, nec	1.6	19.4
Stock clerks & order fillers	3.1	-1.1	Shipping, receiving, & traffic clerks	1.5	16.9
Manufactured building & mobile home installers	2.1	16.2	Installation, maintenance, & repair workers, nec	1.3	29.1
General & operations managers	2.1	27.8	Truck drivers, light or delivery services	1.2	29.1
Laborers & freight, stock, & material movers, hand	2.1	16.2	Secretaries, except legal, medical, & executive	1.2	8.6

Source: Industry-Occupation Matrix, Bureau of Labor Statistics. These data are reported based on 4-digit NAICS categories but have been matched to corresponding 6-digit NAICS industry codes. The change reported for each occupation to the year 2014 is a percent of growth or decline as estimated by the Bureau of Labor Statistics. The abbreviation nec stands for 'not elsewhere classified.'

LOCATION BY STATE AND REGIONAL CONCENTRATION

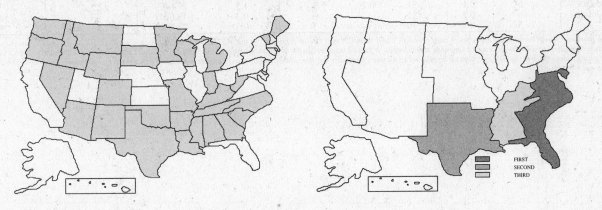

FIRST
SECOND
THIRD

INDUSTRY DATA BY STATE

State	Establishments Total (number)	% of U.S.	Employment Total (number)	% of U.S.	Per Estab.	Payroll Total ($ mil.)	Per Empl. ($)	Sales Total ($ mil.)	% of U.S.	Per Estab. ($)
North Carolina	518	9.3	2,694	8.4	5	80.7	29,945	916.7	9.6	1,769,770
Texas	533	9.6	3,286	10.3	6	84.2	25,637	870.3	9.2	1,632,835
Florida	310	5.6	1,482	4.6	5	37.7	25,427	487.6	5.1	1,572,971
Georgia	261	4.7	1,689	5.3	6	38.2	22,606	456.3	4.8	1,748,138
Michigan	231	4.2	1,496	4.7	6	42.4	28,356	454.1	4.8	1,965,719
California	166	3.0	949	3.0	6	30.5	32,153	435.8	4.6	2,625,193
South Carolina	271	4.9	1,368	4.3	5	39.0	28,534	403.0	4.2	1,487,207
Tennessee	209	3.8	1,194	3.7	6	35.3	29,529	342.2	3.6	1,637,211
Arizona	180	3.2	731	2.3	4	20.0	27,338	301.8	3.2	1,676,561
Kentucky	172	3.1	1,129	3.5	7	28.3	25,082	289.6	3.0	1,683,855
Ohio	152	2.7	1,042	3.3	7	28.2	27,099	284.9	3.0	1,874,237
Louisiana	123	2.2	728	2.3	6	22.0	30,187	266.6	2.8	2,167,463
Pennsylvania	151	2.7	1,037	3.2	7	29.5	28,442	258.5	2.7	1,712,205
Missouri	152	2.7	941	2.9	6	23.2	24,628	232.9	2.4	1,532,559
Alabama	188	3.4	709	2.2	4	18.4	25,942	231.1	2.4	1,229,112
Virginia	136	2.4	780	2.4	6	25.6	32,778	228.2	2.4	1,678,081
Washington	123	2.2	728	2.3	6	22.4	30,757	227.0	2.4	1,845,512

Continued on next page.

INDUSTRY DATA BY STATE - Continued

State	Establishments		Employment			Payroll		Sales		
	Total (number)	% of U.S.	Total (number)	% of U.S.	Per Estab.	Total ($ mil.)	Per Empl. ($)	Total ($ mil.)	% of U.S.	Per Estab. ($)
Indiana	143	2.6	879	2.7	6	24.2	27,578	224.5	2.4	1,569,846
New York	133	2.4	827	2.6	6	22.8	27,522	221.5	2.3	1,665,083
Wisconsin	88	1.6	595	1.9	7	19.2	32,306	190.0	2.0	2,159,102
Minnesota	67	1.2	515	1.6	8	18.9	36,637	176.0	1.9	2,626,746
Oklahoma	85	1.5	689	2.2	8	15.9	23,096	169.9	1.8	1,999,412
Colorado	94	1.7	479	1.5	5	12.5	26,157	165.0	1.7	1,755,532
Oregon	82	1.5	410	1.3	5	12.4	30,305	162.2	1.7	1,978,183
Arkansas	104	1.9	576	1.8	6	13.3	23,024	151.4	1.6	1,456,058
West Virginia	82	1.5	701	2.2	9	17.3	24,656	141.5	1.5	1,725,598
Mississippi	131	2.4	619	1.9	5	15.9	25,724	137.3	1.4	1,048,435
New Mexico	95	1.7	480	1.5	5	12.0	25,029	135.0	1.4	1,421,063
Maine	44	0.8	301	0.9	7	10.3	34,342	126.4	1.3	2,873,523
Illinois	80	1.4	410	1.3	5	10.5	25,585	117.3	1.2	1,466,862
Kansas	53	1.0	313	1.0	6	9.1	28,971	74.6	0.8	1,407,698
Nevada	40	0.7	198	0.6	5	5.2	26,379	68.1	0.7	1,703,350
Delaware	27	0.5	231	0.7	9	6.6	28,615	67.4	0.7	2,497,000
Idaho	41	0.7	183	0.6	4	5.3	28,732	62.0	0.7	1,512,634
Montana	36	0.6	209	0.7	6	5.3	25,512	57.9	0.6	1,609,194
Iowa	34	0.6	245	0.8	7	8.1	33,004	57.0	0.6	1,676,882
South Dakota	23	0.4	162	0.5	7	4.7	28,858	42.4	0.4	1,843,174
Nebraska	33	0.6	224	0.7	7	4.8	21,549	41.1	0.4	1,246,455
Wyoming	24	0.4	126	0.4	5	3.4	26,603	40.8	0.4	1,700,750
New Hampshire	21	0.4	86	0.3	4	3.3	38,151	37.8	0.4	1,798,048
Maryland	24	0.4	127	0.4	5	3.5	27,268	30.7	0.3	1,277,125
Vermont	14	0.3	108	0.3	8	3.4	31,565	29.9	0.3	2,139,143
Utah	30	0.5	98	0.3	3	2.5	25,816	29.5	0.3	983,433
New Jersey	12	0.2	46	0.1	4	1.6	35,609	28.0	0.3	2,331,083
North Dakota	22	0.4	137	0.4	6	2.9	21,270	19.1	0.2	870,364
Massachusetts	6	0.1	51	0.2	9	1.5	29,647	12.5	0.1	2,075,667
Connecticut	6	0.1	15	-	3	0.3	18,667	3.3	-	545,833
Alaska	3	0.1	10	-	3	0.3	28,800	2.4	-	795,000

Source: 2002 Economic Census. The states are in descending order of sales or establishments (if sales data are missing for the majority). The symbol (D) appears when data are withheld to prevent disclosure of competitive information. States marked with (D) are sorted by number of establishments. A dash (-) indicates that the data element cannot be calculated. Shaded states on the state map indicate those states which have proportionately greater representation in the industry than would be indicated by the states population; the ratio is based on total sales or number of establishments. Shaded regions indicate where the industry is regionally most concentrated.

NAICS 453991 - TOBACCO STORES*

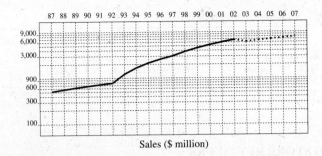

Sales ($ million)

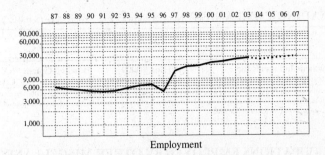

Employment

GENERAL STATISTICS

Year	Establishments (number)	Employment (number)	Payroll ($ million)	Sales ($ million)	Employees per Establishment (number)	Sales per Establishment ($)	Payroll per Employee ($)
1987	1,948	6,736	57.2	518.1	4	265,965	8,492
1988	1,683	6,175	57.6	570.9 e	4	339,216	9,328
1989	1,515	5,913	55.4	623.6 e	4	411,617	9,369
1990	1,440	5,484	55.4	676.4 e	4	469,722	10,102
1991	1,388	5,343	58.7	729.1 e	4	525,288	10,986
1992	1,477	5,530	61.8	781.8	4	529,316	11,175
1993	1,551	6,296	77.3	1,239.1 e	4	798,904	12,278
1994	1,655	7,146	91.5	1,696.4 e	4	1,025,015	12,804
1995	1,840	7,536	106.8	2,153.8 e	4	1,170,544	14,172
1996	1,270 e	5,302 e	77.6 e	2,611.1 e	4 e	2,055,984 e	14,636 e
1997	3,884	14,880	213.4	3,068.4	4	790,010	14,341
1998	4,514	18,503	269.4	3,811.0 e	4	844,264	14,560
1999	4,775	19,178	293.5	4,553.6 e	4	953,637	15,304
2000	5,483	22,357	352.3	5,296.2 e	4	965,936	15,759
2001	5,313	23,713	358.0	6,038.8 e	5	1,136,614	15,097
2002	6,296	26,426	397.3	6,781.4	4	1,077,103	15,034
2003	6,323	28,053	430.0	6,183.2 p	4	1,340,434 p	15,329
2004	6,107 p	26,145 p	408.4 p	6,608.1 p	4 p	1,399,903 p	17,075 p
2005	6,443 p	27,647 p	434.1 p	7,032.9 p	4 p	1,459,373 p	17,542 p
2006	6,780 p	29,150 p	459.8 p	7,457.8 p	4 p	1,518,842 p	18,009 p
2007	7,116 p	30,652 p	485.5 p	7,882.7 p	5 p	1,578,311 p	18,477 p

Sources: Economic Census of the United States, 1987, 1992, 1997, and 2002. Establishment counts, employment, and payroll are from *County Business Patterns* for non-Census years. Values followed by a 'p' are projections by the editors. Sales data for non-Census years are extrapolations, marked by 'e'. Data are the most recent available at this level of detail.

INDICES OF CHANGE

Year	Establishments (number)	Employment (number)	Payroll ($ million)	Sales ($ million)	Employees per Establishment (number)	Sales per Establishment ($)	Payroll per Employee ($)
1987	30.9	25.5	14.4	7.6	83.4	24.7	56.5
1992	23.5	20.9	15.6	11.5	88.2	49.1	74.3
1993	24.6	23.8	19.5	18.3 e	97.7	74.2	81.7
1994	26.3	27.0	23.0	25.0 e	102.4	95.2	85.2
1995	29.2	28.5	26.9	31.8 e	97.7	108.7	94.3
1996	20.2 e	20.1 e	19.5 e	38.5 e	100.1 e	190.9 e	97.4 e
1997	61.7	56.3	53.7	45.2	90.5	73.3	95.4
1998	71.7	70.0	67.8	56.2 e	97.7	78.4	96.8
1999	75.8	72.6	73.9	67.1 e	95.3	88.5	101.8
2000	87.1	84.6	88.7	78.1 e	97.7	89.7	104.8
2001	84.4	89.7	90.1	89.0 e	107.2	105.5	100.4
2002	100.0	100.0	100.0	100.0	100.0	100.0	100.0
2003	100.4	106.2	108.2	91.2 p	105.7	124.4 p	102.0
2004	97.0 p	98.9 p	102.8 p	97.4 p	104.8 p	130.0 p	113.6 p
2005	102.3 p	104.6 p	109.3 p	103.7 p	105.8 p	135.5 p	116.7 p
2006	107.7 p	110.3 p	115.7 p	110.0 p	106.8 p	141.0 p	119.8 p
2007	113.0 p	116.0 p	122.2 p	116.2 p	107.8 p	146.5 p	122.9 p

Sources: Same as General Statistics. The values shown reflect change from the base year, 2002. Values above 100 mean greater than 2002, values below 100 mean less than 2002, and a value of 100 in the 1987-2001 or 2003-2007 period means same as 2002. Values followed by a 'p' are projections by the editors; 'e' stands for extrapolation. Data are the most recent available at this level of detail.

SELECTED RATIOS

For 2002	Avg. of All Retail	Analyzed Industry	Index	For 2002	Avg. of All Retail	Analyzed Industry	Index
Employees per Establishment	17	4	25	Sales per Employee	174,682	256,620	147
Payroll per Establishment	333,445	63,101	19	Sales per Establishment	3,332,269	1,077,103	32
Payroll per Employee	20,311	15,034	74	Expenses per Establishment	na	na	na

Sources: Same as General Statistics. The 'Average of All' column, Wholesale or Retail, represents the average of the sector reported for the most recent complete year available. The Index shows the relationship between the Average and the Analyzed Industry. For example, 100 means that they are equal; 500 that the Analyzed Industry is five times the average; 50 means that the Analyzed Industry is half the national average. The abbreviation 'na' is used to show that data are 'not available'.

*Equivalent to SIC 5993.

LEADING COMPANIES   Number shown: 2   Total sales ($ mil): **2,019**   Total employment (000): **9.3**

Company Name	Address				CEO Name	Phone	Co. Type	Sales ($ mil)	Empl. (000)
Houchens Industries Inc.	PO Box 90009	Bowling Green	KY	42102	Jim Gipson	270-843-3252	R	2,005	9.2
Patton Music Company Inc.	811 Kearney Ave	Modesto	CA	95350	James B Reed	209-529-6500	R	14*	0.1

Source: *Ward's Business Directory of U.S. Private and Public Companies*, Volumes 1 and 2, 2005. The company type code used is as follows: P - Public, R - Private, S - Subsidiary, D - Division, J - Joint Venture, A - Affiliate, G - Group. Sales are in millions of dollars, employees are in thousands. An asterisk (*) indicates an estimated sales volume. The symbol < stands for 'less than'. Company names and addresses are truncated, in some cases, to fit into the available space.

OCCUPATIONS EMPLOYED BY OTHER MISCELLANEOUS STORE RETAILERS

Occupation	% of Total 2004	Change to 2014	Occupation	% of Total 2004	Change to 2014
Retail salespersons	33.8	29.1	Office clerks, general	2.0	14.9
Cashiers, except gaming	11.6	16.2	Sales reps, wholesale & manufacturing, exc tech	2.0	29.1
First-line supervisors/managers of retail sales workers	7.4	18.8	Bookkeeping, accounting, & auditing clerks	1.9	16.2
Nonfarm animal caretakers	3.7	28.7	Assemblers & fabricators, nec	1.6	19.4
Stock clerks & order fillers	3.1	-1.1	Shipping, receiving, & traffic clerks	1.5	16.9
Manufactured building & mobile home installers	2.1	16.2	Installation, maintenance, & repair workers, nec	1.3	29.1
General & operations managers	2.1	27.8	Truck drivers, light or delivery services	1.2	29.1
Laborers & freight, stock, & material movers, hand	2.1	16.2	Secretaries, except legal, medical, & executive	1.2	8.6

Source: *Industry-Occupation Matrix*, Bureau of Labor Statistics. These data are reported based on 4-digit NAICS categories but have been matched to corresponding 6-digit NAICS industry codes. The change reported for each occupation to the year 2014 is a percent of growth or decline as estimated by the Bureau of Labor Statistics. The abbreviation nec stands for 'not elsewhere classified.'

INDUSTRY DATA BY STATE

State-level data are not available.

NAICS 453998 - ALL OTHER MISCELLANEOUS STORE RETAILERS (EXCEPT TOBACCO STORES)

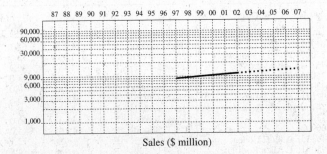

Sales ($ million)

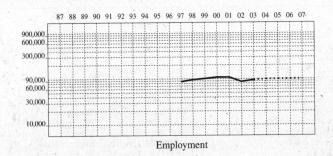

Employment

GENERAL STATISTICS

Year	Establishments (number)	Employment (number)	Payroll ($ million)	Sales ($ million)	Employees per Establishment (number)	Sales per Establishment ($)	Payroll per Employee ($)
1987	-	-	-	-	-	-	-
1988	-	-	-	-	-	-	-
1989	-	-	-	-	-	-	-
1990	-	-	-	-	-	-	-
1991	-	-	-	-	-	-	-
1992	-	-	-	-	-	-	-
1993	-	-	-	-	-	-	-
1994	-	-	-	-	-	-	-
1995	-	-	-	-	-	-	-
1996	-	-	-	-	-	-	-
1997	17,648	87,351	1,481.7	9,028.0	5	511,559	16,963
1998	19,621	96,242	1,793.4	9,543.4 e	5	486,386	18,634
1999	19,969	101,588	1,986.7	10,058.8 e	5	503,719	19,556
2000	20,602	108,337	2,199.2	10,574.1 e	5	513,258	20,300
2001	20,255	107,870	2,293.0	11,089.5 e	5	547,496	21,257
2002	18,210	86,937	1,954.3	11,604.9	5	637,282	22,480
2003	19,256	94,949	2,162.6	12,120.3 p	5	615,432 p	22,776
2004	19,693 p	99,106 p	2,363.1 p	12,635.7 p	5 p	638,903 p	24,114 p
2005	19,774 p	99,480 p	2,458.5 p	13,151.1 p	5 p	662,374 p	25,072 p
2006	19,856 p	99,853 p	2,553.9 p	13,666.4 p	5 p	685,845 p	26,031 p
2007	19,938 p	100,227 p	2,649.3 p	14,181.8 p	5 p	709,316 p	26,989 p

Source: Economic Census of the United States, 1997 and 2002. Establishment counts, employment, and payroll are from *County Business Patterns* for non-Census years. This is a newly defined industry. Data for prior years are unavailable at the time of publication but may become available over time. Values followed by 'p' are projections by the editors. Sales data for non-Census years are extrapolations, marked by 'e'.

INDICES OF CHANGE

Year	Establishments (number)	Employment (number)	Payroll ($ million)	Sales ($ million)	Employees per Establishment (number)	Sales per Establishment ($)	Payroll per Employee ($)
1987	-	-	-	-	-	-	-
1992	-	-	-	-	-	-	-
1993	-	-	-	-	-	-	-
1994	-	-	-	-	-	-	-
1995	-	-	-	-	-	-	-
1996	-	-	-	-	-	-	-
1997	96.9	100.5	75.8	77.8	102.6	80.3	75.5
1998	107.7	110.7	91.8	82.2 e	102.6	76.3	82.9
1999	109.7	116.9	101.7	86.7 e	106.8	79.0	87.0
2000	113.1	124.6	112.5	91.1 e	111.0	80.5	90.3
2001	111.2	124.1	117.3	95.6 e	111.0	85.9	94.6
2002	100.0	100.0	100.0	100.0	100.0	100.0	100.0
2003	105.7	109.2	110.7	104.4 p	103.3	96.6 p	101.3
2004	108.1 p	114.0 p	120.9 p	108.9 p	105.5 p	100.3 p	107.3 p
2005	108.6 p	114.4 p	125.8 p	113.3 p	105.5 p	103.9 p	111.5 p
2006	109.0 p	114.9 p	130.7 p	117.8 p	105.5 p	107.6 p	115.8 p
2007	109.5 p	115.3 p	135.6 p	122.2 p	105.6 p	111.3 p	120.1 p

Sources: Same as General Statistics. The values shown reflect change from the base year, 2002. Values above 100 mean greater than 2002, values below 100 mean less than 2002, and a value of 100 in the 1987-2001 or 2003-2007 period means same as 2002. Values followed by a 'p' are projections by the editors; 'e' stands for extrapolation. Data are the most recent available at this level of detail.

SELECTED RATIOS

For 2002	Avg. of All Retail	Analyzed Industry	Index	For 2002	Avg. of All Retail	Analyzed Industry	Index
Employees per Establishment	17	5	28	Sales per Employee	174,682	133,486	76
Payroll per Establishment	333,445	107,322	32	Sales per Establishment	3,332,269	637,282	19
Payroll per Employee	20,311	22,480	111	Expenses per Establishment	na	na	na

Sources: Same as General Statistics. The 'Average of All' column, Wholesale or Retail, represents the average of the sector reported for the most recent complete year available. The Index shows the relationship between the Average and the Analyzed Industry. For example, 100 means that they are equal; 500 that the Analyzed Industry is five times the average; 50 means that the Analyzed Industry is half the national average. The abbreviation 'na' is used to show that data are 'not available'.

LEADING COMPANIES   Number shown: **75**   Total sales ($ mil): **37,948**   Total employment (000): **176.2**

Company Name	Address				CEO Name	Phone	Co. Type	Sales ($ mil)	Empl. (000)
Staples Inc.	PO Box 9328	Framingham	MA	01702		508-253-5000	P	14,448	65.1
PETsMART Inc.	19601 N 27th Ave	Phoenix	AZ	85027	Philip L Francis	623-580-6100	P	3,363	13.5
Energy Transfer Partners L.P.	2838 Woodside St	Dallas	TX	75204	Ray C Davis	918-492-7272	P	2,482	2.9
CellStar Corp.	1730 Briercroft Ct	Carrollton	TX	75006	Robert A Kaiser	972-466-5000	P	1,793	1.0
Bath and Body Works Inc.	7 Limited Pkwy, E	Reynoldsburg	OH	43068		614-856-6000	S	1,781	0.0
Petco Animal Supplies Inc.	9125 Rehco Rd	San Diego	CA	92121	Brian Devine	858-453-7845	P	1,654	15.3
Scientifics	60 Pearce Ave	Tonawanda	NY	14150	Randy Burkard	716-874-9091	R	1,223*	0.3
Claire's Stores Inc.	3 SW 129th Ave	Pembroke Pines	FL	33027		954-433-3900	P	1,133	16.0
Petro Holdings Inc.	2187 Atlantic St	Stamford	CT	06902		203-325-5400	S	1,105	3.0
Finish Line Inc.	3308 N Mitthoeffer	Indianapolis	IN	46235	Alan H Cohen	317-899-1022	P	986	12.1
MTS Inc.	2500 Del Monte St	W. Sacramento	CA	95691	E Allen Rodriguez	916-373-2502	R	983	4.8
Yankee Candle Company Inc.	PO Box 110	South Deerfield	MA	01373	Harlan M Kent	413-665-8306	P	554	4.2
CellStar Ltd.	2080 McDaniel Dr	Carrollton	TX	75006	James L Johnson		S	518*	1.0
Party City Corp.	400 Commons Way	Rockaway	NJ	07866	Ralph D Dillon	973-983-0888	P	516	4.5
Children's Books and Toys Inc.	460 E Swedesford	Wayne	PA	19087	Fred Kayne	610-292-6600	P	460	3.2
Restoration Hardware Inc.	15 Koch Rd, Ste J	Corte Madera	CA	94925	Gary G Friedman	415-924-1005	P	439	3.5
Brookstone Inc.	1 Innovation Way	Merrimack	NH	03054	Michael F Anthony	603-880-9500	P	434	2.9
A.C. Moore Arts and Crafts Inc.	500 University Crt	Blackwood	NJ	08012	Lawrence H Fine	856-228-6700	P	434	4.8
CPI Corp.	1706 Washington	St. Louis	MO	63103		314-231-1575	P	302	7.3
Overstock.com Inc.	6322 South 3000 E	Salt Lake City	UT	84121	Patrick M Byrne	801-947-3100	P	239	0.3
Midland-Impact L.L.P.	PO Box 560	Danville	IN	46122	Greg Gore	317-745-4491	R	230*	<0.1
E Com Ventures Inc.	251 International	Sunrise	FL	33325	Michael W Katz	954-335-9100	P	213	1.3
Anthony and Sylvan Pools Corp.	6690 Beta Dr	Mayfield Village	OH	44143		440-720-3301	P	181	0.5
Imperial Auto Auction	PO Box 2156	Lakeland	FL	33806		863-688-8458	R	125*	0.1
A.I. Friedman	44 W 18th St	New York	NY	10011	Jim White	212-243-9000	R	115*	0.2
RTKL International Ltd.	901 S Bond St	Baltimore	MD	21231	David C Hudson	410-528-8600	S	115*	0.9
Brass Eagle Inc.	PO Box 1956	Rogers	AR	72757		479-464-8700	S	105	0.3
Duty Free Americas Inc.	6100 Hollywood	Hollywood	FL	33024		954-986-7700	S	100*	0.4
Providence Home Services	1310 NE 44th Ave	Portland	OR	97213		503-215-4664	R	97*	0.7
Hickory Tech Corp.	PO Box 3248	Mankato	MN	56002	Myrita P Craig	507-387-1151	P	93	0.4
Briggs Equipment Inc.	PO Box 20807	Greensboro	NC	27420	Dave Bratton	336-292-6921	R	92*	0.3
Shasta Industries Inc.	6031 N 16th St	Phoenix	AZ	85016	Edward Ast	602-532-3750	R	87*	0.7
Littleton Coin Company Inc.	1309 Mount Eustis	Littleton	NH	03561	David Sundman	603-444-3571	R	84*	0.4
Star Lumbers New Home	902 E Indianapolis	Wichita	KS	67211		316-269-0481	R	71*	0.1
Pass Pets Ltd.	65 Centre Pt	St. Charles	MO	63304	Jeff Parks	636-447-7900	R	67*	0.2
HearUSA Inc.	1250 Northpoint Pky	W. Palm Beach	FL	33407	Paul A Brown	561-478-8770	P	66	0.5
Shultz Foods Co.	PO Box 993	Hanover	PA	17331	Dave Humbert	717-637-5931	R	66*	0.3
Hollywood Media Corp.	2255 Glades Rd	Boca Raton	FL	33431		561-998-8000	P	65	0.2
Ace Mart Restaurant Supply Co.	PO Box 18100	San Antonio	TX	78218	Bud Gustafson	210-323-4400	R	55*	0.3
Source Inc.	14060 Proton Rd	Dallas	TX	75244	David Potter		R	54*	0.3
Philadelphia Bourse Inc.	4601 Forbes Blvd	Lanham Seabrk	MD	20706	John Hozik	301-731-0811	R	53*	0.1
Greco and Sons Inc.	280 S Westgate Dr	Carol Stream	IL	60188	Edwardo Greco	630-668-1000	R	46*	0.1
Industrial Truck Sales & Service	4100 Randleman Rd	Greensboro	NC	27406	Deeny Boyce	336-275-9121	R	45*	0.2
PHONEXTRA INC.	15 Gardner Rd	Fairfield	NJ	07004	John Negri	973-808-7000	R	43*	0.2
Raleigh Mine & Industrial Supply	PO Box 72	Mount Hope	WV	25880	S Smith	304-877-5503	R	42*	<0.1
Brooks Tractor Inc.	PO Box 9	Sun Prairie	WI	53590	Lewis P Brooks	608-837-5141	R	39*	<0.1
Bingham Cooperative Inc.	PO Box 887	Blackfoot	ID	83221	Mike Jensen	208-785-3440	R	36*	<0.1
Foam Factory and Upholstery Inc.	22800 Hall Rd	Clinton Twp.	MI	48036	S Baladomente	586-627-3626	R	35*	<0.1
Norton Metal Inc.	1350 Lawson Rd	Fort Worth	TX	76131	Larry Dunlap	817-232-0404	R	34*	<0.1
Western Reserve Farm Co-Op	PO Box 339	Middlefield	OH	44062	Michael Eastlake	440-632-0271	R	34*	<0.1
Envirotech International Inc.	734 Greenview Dr	Grand Prairie	TX	75050	Susan Money	972-647-4733	R	32*	<0.1
Successories Inc.	2520 Diehl Rd	Aurora	IL	60504	John C Carroll	630-820-7200	R	32	0.1
Wynn Fire & Rescue Equipment	PO Box 1585	Corbin	KY	40702	Charles Wynn	606-523-9269	R	31*	<0.1
Wild Birds Unlimited Inc.	11711 N College	Carmel	IN	46032	James Carpenter	317-571-7100	R	31*	<0.1
Floral Supply Syndicate	PO Box 1305	Camarillo	CA	93010		805-389-1141	R	30*	0.1
Wright and McGill Co.	PO Box 16011	Denver	CO	80216	John Jilling	303-321-1481	R	30*	0.3
Communications Plus	1449 Fairmont Rd	Morgantown	WV	26501	Charles Moore	304-983-8642	R	28*	<0.1
Hall, Bruce Corp.	PO Box 707	Cooperstown	NY	13326	Gregory Hall	607-547-9961	R	26*	<0.1
Goldfarb Electric Supply Inc.	PO Box 3319	Charleston	WV	25333	Bruce Goldfarb	304-342-2153	R	25*	<0.1
Chicago Communications Service	200 Spangler	Elmhurst	IL	60126		630-832-3311	R	25*	<0.1
Daniel Smith Artist Materials	4150 1st Ave S	Seattle	WA	98134	John Cogley	206-223-9599	R	25	0.1
Wabash Valley Services Co.	909 N Court St	Grayville	IL	62844	Jim Stevens	618-375-2311	R	25*	<0.1
Pisani Enterprises Inc.	350 Ocean Ave	San Francisco	CA	94112	Gerald Pisani	415-861-6616	R	25*	<0.1
Avidex Industries L.L.C.	14949 NE 40th St	Redmond	WA	98052		206-763-7711	R	23*	<0.1
Vitacost Holdings Inc.	2049 High Ridge Rd	Boynton Beach	FL	33426	Wayne Gorsek	561-752-8888	R	23	<0.1
Partitions and Accessories Co.	1220 S Pasadena	Mesa	AZ	85210	Sandra Borelli	480-969-6606	R	21*	<0.1
Farmers Supply Association Inc.	16240 Hwy 14 E	Harrisburg	AR	72432	Roger Tohlner	870-578-2468	R	21*	<0.1
AC Installations By Rusher Inc.	19626 Normandie	Torrance	CA	90502	George Rusher	310-323-7201	R	21*	<0.1
Mar-Ner Numismatics Ltd.	550 W Old Country	Hicksville	NY	11801	Roger Gardner	631-474-1100	R	21*	<0.1
Quickbeam Systems Inc.	4201 Yale Blvd NE	Albuquerque	NM	87107	Gary Mathews	505-345-9230	R	20*	<0.1
Cutting Edge Audio Group L.L.C.	290 Division St	San Francisco	CA	94103		415-487-2323	R	20*	<0.1
Modern Development Co.	3333 W Coast Hwy	Newport Beach	CA	92663		949-646-6400	R	20*	0.2
Kilgore's Clear Lake Lumber Co.	PO Box 1099	League City	TX	77574	W Lawther	281-332-9351	R	19*	<0.1
Los Altos Trophy Inc.	10731 Walker St A	Cypress	CA	90630	Beverly Rubin	714-252-5350	R	19*	<0.1
Technuity Inc.	6024 W 79th St	Indianapolis	IN	46278	Dean Petruzzi	317-872-8111	R	19*	<0.1

Source: Ward's Business Directory of U.S. Private and Public Companies, Volumes 1 and 2, 2005. The company type code used is as follows: P - Public, R - Private, S - Subsidiary, D - Division, J - Joint Venture, A - Affiliate, G - Group. Sales are in millions of dollars, employees are in thousands. An asterisk (*) indicates an estimated sales volume. The symbol < stands for 'less than'. Company names and addresses are truncated, in some cases, to fit into the available space.

OCCUPATIONS EMPLOYED BY OTHER MISCELLANEOUS STORE RETAILERS

Occupation	% of Total 2004	Change to 2014	Occupation	% of Total 2004	Change to 2014
Retail salespersons	33.8	29.1	Office clerks, general	2.0	14.9
Cashiers, except gaming	11.6	16.2	Sales reps, wholesale & manufacturing, exc tech	2.0	29.1
First-line supervisors/managers of retail sales workers	7.4	18.8	Bookkeeping, accounting, & auditing clerks	1.9	16.2
Nonfarm animal caretakers	3.7	28.7	Assemblers & fabricators, nec	1.6	19.4
Stock clerks & order fillers	3.1	-1.1	Shipping, receiving, & traffic clerks	1.5	16.9
Manufactured building & mobile home installers	2.1	16.2	Installation, maintenance, & repair workers, nec	1.3	29.1
General & operations managers	2.1	27.8	Truck drivers, light or delivery services	1.2	29.1
Laborers & freight, stock, & material movers, hand	2.1	16.2	Secretaries, except legal, medical, & executive	1.2	8.6

Source: *Industry-Occupation Matrix*, Bureau of Labor Statistics. These data are reported based on 4-digit NAICS categories but have been matched to corresponding 6-digit NAICS industry codes. The change reported for each occupation to the year 2014 is a percent of growth or decline as estimated by the Bureau of Labor Statistics. The abbreviation nec stands for 'not elsewhere classified.'

INDUSTRY DATA BY STATE

State-level data are not available.

NAICS 454113 - MAIL-ORDER HOUSES

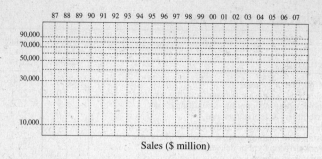

Sales ($ million)

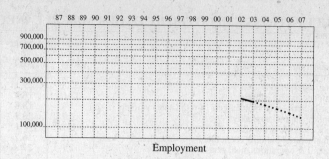

Employment

GENERAL STATISTICS

Year	Establishments (number)	Employment (number)	Payroll ($ million)	Sales ($ million)	Employees per Establishment (number)	Sales per Establishment ($)	Payroll per Employee ($)
1987	-	-	-	-	-	-	-
1988	-	-	-	-	-	-	-
1989	-	-	-	-	-	-	-
1990	-	-	-	-	-	-	-
1991	-	-	-	-	-	-	-
1992	-	-	-	-	-	-	-
1993	-	-	-	-	-	-	-
1994	-	-	-	-	-	-	-
1995	-	-	-	-	-	-	-
1996	-	-	-	-	-	-	-
1997	-	-	-	-	-	-	-
1998	-	-	-	-	-	-	-
1999	-	-	-	-	-	-	-
2000	-	-	-	-	-	-	-
2001	-	-	-	-	-	-	-
2002	10,261	211,884	6,698.1	95,343.4	21	9,291,826	31,612
2003	7,736	195,844	6,759.1	-	25	-	34,513
2004	5,211 p	179,804 p	6,820.2 p	-	30 p	-	37,414 p
2005	2,686 p	163,764 p	6,881.2 p	-	35 p	-	40,315 p
2006	161 p	147,724 p	6,942.3 p	-	39 p	-	43,215 p
2007		131,684 p	7,003.3 p	-	44 p	-	46,116 p

Source: Economic Census of the United States, 2002. Establishment counts, employment, and payroll are from *County Business Patterns* for non-Census years. This is a newly defined industry. Data for prior years are unavailable at the time of publication but may become available over time. Values followed by 'p' are projections by the editors. Sales data for non-Census years are extrapolations, marked by 'e'.

INDICES OF CHANGE

Year	Establishments (number)	Employment (number)	Payroll ($ million)	Sales ($ million)	Employees per Establishment (number)	Sales per Establishment ($)	Payroll per Employee ($)
1987	-	-	-	-	-	-	-
1992	-	-	-	-	-	-	-
1993	-	-	-	-	-	-	-
1994	-	-	-	-	-	-	-
1995	-	-	-	-	-	-	-
1996	-	-	-	-	-	-	-
1997	-	-	-	-	-	-	-
1998	-	-	-	-	-	-	-
1999	-	-	-	-	-	-	-
2000	-	-	-	-	-	-	-
2001	-	-	-	-	-	-	-
2002	100.0	100.0	100.0	100.0	100.0	100.0	100.0
2003	75.4	92.4	100.9	-	122.6	-	109.2
2004	50.8 p	84.9 p	101.8 p	-	145.2 p	-	118.4 p
2005	26.2 p	77.3 p	102.7 p	-	167.8 p	-	127.5 p
2006	1.6 p	69.7 p	103.6 p	-	190.4 p	-	136.7 p
2007		62.1 p	104.6 p	-	213.0 p	-	145.9 p

Sources: Same as General Statistics. The values shown reflect change from the base year, 2002. Values above 100 mean greater than 2002, values below 100 mean less than 2002, and a value of 100 in the 2003-2007 period means same as 2002. Values followed by a 'p' are projections by the editors; 'e' stands for extrapolation. Data are the most recent available at this level of detail.

SELECTED RATIOS

For 2002	Avg. of All Retail	Analyzed Industry	Index	For 2002	Avg. of All Retail	Analyzed Industry	Index
Employees per Establishment	17	21	122	Sales per Employee	174,682	449,979	258
Payroll per Establishment	333,445	652,772	196	Sales per Establishment	3,332,269	9,291,826	279
Payroll per Employee	20,311	31,612	156	Expenses per Establishment	na	na	na

Sources: Same as General Statistics. The 'Average of All' column, Wholesale or Retail, represents the average of the sector reported for the most recent complete year available. The Index shows the relationship between the Average and the Analyzed Industry. For example, 100 means that they are equal; 500 that the Analyzed Industry is five times the average; 50 means that the Analyzed Industry is half the national average. The abbreviation 'na' is used to show that data are 'not available'.

LEADING COMPANIES   Number shown: **75**   Total sales ($ mil): **381,297**   Total employment (000): **1,775.5**

Company Name	Address				CEO Name	Phone	Co. Type	Sales ($ mil)	Empl. (000)
Dell Inc.	1 Dell Way	Round Rock	TX	78682	Michael S. Dell	512-728-4737	P	49,205	55.2
Target Corp.	1000 Nicollet Mall	Minneapolis	MN	55403	Linda L Ahlers	612-304-6073	P	45,682	273.0
Sears, Roebuck and Co.	3333 Beverly Rd	Hoffman Estates	IL	60179		847-286-2500	D	36,099	250.0
Medco Health Solutions Inc.	100 Parsons Pond Dr	Franklin Lakes	NJ	07417	Bryan D Birch	201-269-6400	P	35,352	13.0
CVS Corp.	1 CVS Dr	Woonsocket	RI	02895		401-765-1500	P	30,594	100.0
Comcast Corp.	1500 Market St	Philadelphia	PA	19102		215-665-1700	P	20,307	68.0
J.C. Penney Company Inc.	6501 Legacy Dr	Plano	TX	75024		972-431-1000	P	17,786	250.0
Federated Department Stores Inc.	7 W Seventh St	Cincinnati	OH	45202		513-579-7758	P	15,630	111.0
Limited Brands Inc.	PO Box 16000	Columbus	OH	43216	Deborah Fine	614-415-7000	P	8,934	98.9
Amazon.com Inc.	PO Box 81226	Seattle	WA	98108	Jeffrey P Bezos	206-266-1000	P	6,920	9.0
Rexall Sundown Inc.	6111 Broken Snd	Boca Raton	FL	33487			S	6,328*	1.3
IAC/InterActiveCorp.	152 W 57th St	New York	NY	10019	Barry Diller	212-314-7300	P	6,193	26.0
CDW Corp.	200 N Milwaukee	Vernon Hills	IL	60061	John A Edwardson	847-465-6000	P	5,738	2.9
Intimate Brands Inc.	PO Box 16000	Columbus	OH	43216	Leslie H Wexner		S	5,367	69.0
Foot Locker Inc.	112 W 34th St	New York	NY	10120		212-720-3700	P	5,355	40.3
Barnes and Noble Inc.	122 5th Ave	New York	NY	10011	Leonard Riggio	212-633-3300	P	4,874	56.0
QVC Inc.	Studio Park	West Chester	PA	19380	Douglas Briggs	484-701-1000	S	4,800	15.0
CompUSA Inc.	14951 N Dallas Pky	Dallas	TX	75254	Lawrence Mondry	972-982-4000	S	4,700	19.7
Corporate Express Inc.	1 Environmental	Broomfield	CO	80021	Michael Cate	303-664-2000	S	4,210*	10.8
Gateway Inc.	143003 Gateway Pl	Poway	CA	92064		858-848-3401	P	3,650	7.4
Insight Enterprises Inc.	1305 W Auto Dr	Tempe	AZ	85284	Richard Fennessy	480-902-1001	P	3,083	4.0
Williams-Sonoma Inc.	3250 Van Ness Ave	San Francisco	CA	94109	W Howard Lester	415-421-7900	P	2,609	36.0
Blue Chip Stamps	PO Box 831	Pasadena	CA	91102	Bob Bird	626-585-6714	S	2,588*	<0.1
Reader's Digest Association Inc.	Readers Digest Rd	Pleasantville	NY	10570		914-238-1000	P	2,389	4.3
Fry's Electronics Inc.	600 E Brokaw Rd	San Jose	CA	95112	John Fry	408-487-4500	R	2,265*	6.0
HSN L.P.	1 HSN Dr	St. Petersburg	FL	33729	Thomas J McInerney	727-872-1000	S	2,200*	4.5
Micro Warehouse Inc.	535 Connecticut Ave	Norwalk	CT	06854		203-899-4000	R	2,000	2.7
Beverly Enterprises Inc.	1000 Beverly Way	Fort Smith	AR	72959	William R Floyd	501-201-2000	P	1,989	36.3
Systemax Inc.	11 Harbor Pk Dr	Port Washington	NY	11050	Richard Leeds	516-608-7000	P	1,928	3.1
Follett Corp.	2233 West St	River Grove	IL	60171	R Mark Litzinger	708-583-2000	R	1,899	10.0
Mary Kay Inc.	PO Box 799045	Dallas	TX	75379	David B Holl	972-687-6300	R	1,800*	3.6
Sports Authority Inc.	1050 W Hampden	Englewood	CO	80110	Martin Hanaka	303-200-5050	P	1,760	17.0
Talbots Inc.	1 Talbots Dr	Hingham	MA	02043		781-749-7600	P	1,698	11.0
Fingerhut Companies Inc.	PO Box 1250	St. Cloud	MN	56395			S	1,694*	10.0
Lands' End Inc.	2 Lands' End Ln	Dodgeville	WI	53595	Gary C Comer	608-935-9341	S	1,600	10.0
Miles Kimball Co.	PO Box 3600	Oshkosh	WI	54901	Mike Muoio	920-231-3800	S	1,567*	0.7
Cabela's Inc.	1 Cabela Dr	Sidney	NE	69160	Richard N Cabela	308-254-5505	R	1,556	7.8
Discount Tire Co.	20225 N Scottsdale	Scottsdale	AZ	85254	Bruce T Halle	480-606-6000	R	1,541	9.5
KB Holdings L.L.C.	100 West St	Pittsfield	MA	01201	Michael L Glazer	413-496-3000	S	1,500*	15.0
Bass Pro Shops Inc.	2500 E Kearney St	Springfield	MO	65898	James Hagale	417-873-5000	R	1,422*	10.7
L.L. Bean Inc.	15 Casco St	Freeport	ME	04033	Leon A Gorman	207-865-4761	R	1,410	3.8
PC Connection Inc.	730 Milford Rd	Merrimack	NH	03054	Patricia Gallup	603-683-2000	P	1,354	1.4
Trans World Entertainment Corp.	38 Corporate Cir	Albany	NY	12203	Robert J Higgins	518-452-1242	P	1,331	8.2
Brylane Inc.	463 7th Ave	New York	NY	10018		212-613-9500	S	1,328*	6.4
America's Collectibles Network	10001 Kingston Pike	Knoxville	TN	37922	F Robert Hall	865-692-6000	R	1,301*	1.3
Scientifics	60 Pearce Ave	Tonawanda	NY	14150	Randy Burkard	716-874-9091	R	1,223*	0.3
PC Mall Inc.	2555 W 190th St	Torrance	CA	90504	Frank F Khulusi	310-354-5600	P	1,157	1.4
Claire's Stores Inc.	3 SW 129th Ave	Pembroke Pines	FL	33027		954-433-3900	P	1,133	16.0
Checks Unlimited	PO Box 19000	Co Springs	CO	80935	Steve Berry	719-531-2555	S	1,101*	1.0
Longaberger Co.	1500 E Main St	Newark	OH	43055	Tami Longaberger	740-322-5900	R	1,012*	7.3
Recreational Equipment Inc.	6750 S 228th St	Kent	WA	98032	Dennis Madsen	253-395-3780	R	735	7.0
Patagonia Inc.	259 W Santa Clara	Ventura	CA	93001	Yvon Chouinard	805-643-8616	S	721*	0.3
West Marine Inc.	PO Box 50070	Watsonville	CA	95077	Richard E Everett	831-728-2700	P	682	4.3
Sharper Image Corp.	650 Davis St	San Francisco	CA	94111	Richard Thalheimer	415-445-6000	P	647	2.4
Charles Keath	PO Box 310709	Boca Raton	FL	33431	Michael Tiernan	561-241-1700	R	635*	0.3
ValueVision Media Inc.	6740 Shady Oak Rd	Eden Prairie	MN	55344	Marshall S Geller	952-943-6000	P	617	1.0
Blair Corp.	220 Hickory St	Warren	PA	16366	Craig N Johnson	814-723-3600	P	582	2.6
Standex International Corp.	6 Manor Pky	Salem	NH	03079	Roger L Fix	603-893-9701	P	577	5.2
Chronimed Inc.	10900 Red Circle Dr	Minnetonka	MN	55343	Henry F Blissenbach	952-979-3600	P	560	0.4
Black Box Corp.	1000 Park Dr	Lawrence	PA	15055	Frederick C Young	724-746-5500	P	520	2.8
Coldwater Creek Inc.	1 Coldwater Creek	Sandpoint	ID	83864		208-263-2266	P	519	3.4
Zones Inc.	1102 15th St SW	Auburn	WA	98001		235-205-3000	P	496	0.5
Children's Books and Toys Inc.	460 E Swedesford	Wayne	PA	19087	Fred Kayne	610-292-6600	P	460	3.2
Brookstone Inc.	1 Innovation Way	Merrimack	NH	03054	Michael F Anthony	603-880-9500	P	434	2.9
PolyMedica Corp.	11 State St	Woburn	MA	01801	Patrick T Ryan	781-933-2020	P	420	1.7
Hanover Direct Inc.	115 River Rd	Edgewater	NJ	07020	Wayne P Garten	201-863-7300	P	415	1.9
McMaster-Carr Supply Co.	Box 4355	Chicago	IL	60680	JA Delaney	630-834-9600	R	413*	1.0
J. Jill Group Inc.	4 Batterymarch Park	Quincy	MA	02169	Gordon R Cooke	617-376-4300	P	377	2.6
Jos. A. Bank Clothiers Inc.	PO Box 1000	Hampstead	MD	21074	Andrew A Giordano	410-239-2700	P	372	1.9
Harold's Stores Inc.	5919 Maple Ave	Dallas	TX	75235		214-366-0600	P	360	0.8
American Girl LLC	8400 Fairway Pl	Middleton	WI	53562	Ellen L Brothers	608 836 4848	S	350*	1.4
Wal-Mart.com USA L.L.C.	7000 Marina Blvd	Brisbane	CA	94005	John Fleming	650-837-5000	S	327*	0.3
Digi-Key Inc.	701 Brooks Ave S	Thief River Falls	MN	56701	Mark Larson		R	325*	1.3
J.W. Jung Seed Company Inc.	335 S High St	Randolph	WI	53956	Richard J Zondag	920-326-3121	R	300*	0.3
BUY.COM Inc.	85 Enterprise Dr	Aliso Viejo	CA	92656	Scott A Blum	949-389-2000	R	291	0.1

Source: *Ward's Business Directory of U.S. Private and Public Companies*, Volumes 1 and 2, 2005. The company type code used is as follows: P - Public, R - Private, S - Subsidiary, D - Division, J - Joint Venture, A - Affiliate, G - Group. Sales are in millions of dollars, employees are in thousands. An asterisk (*) indicates an estimated sales volume. The symbol < stands for 'less than'. Company names and addresses are truncated, in some cases, to fit into the available space.

OCCUPATIONS EMPLOYED BY ELECTRONIC SHOPPING & MAIL-ORDER HOUSES

Occupation	% of Total 2004	Change to 2014	Occupation	% of Total 2004	Change to 2014
Customer service representatives	15.7	40.8	Sales reps, wholesale & manufacturing, exc tech	2.2	37.6
Order clerks	11.6	26.8	Bookkeeping, accounting, & auditing clerks	1.6	23.9
Stock clerks & order fillers	5.0	5.4	General & operations managers	1.5	36.2
Telemarketers	4.7	1.4	Mail clerks & mail machine operators, except postal	1.3	-29.5
Retail salespersons	4.2	37.6	Computer programmers	1.3	12.3
Shipping, receiving, & traffic clerks	4.1	24.6	Wholesale & retail buyers, except farm products	1.3	30.1
Packers & packagers, hand	4.0	37.6	Data entry keyers	1.2	5.6
Laborers & freight, stock, & material movers, hand	2.8	23.9	Pharmacy technicians	1.1	68.8
Office clerks, general	2.3	22.5	Sales & related workers, nec	1.1	37.6
First-line supervisors/managers of office workers	2.2	24.8	Pharmacists	1.0	52.1

Source: Industry-Occupation Matrix, Bureau of Labor Statistics. These data are reported based on 4-digit NAICS categories but have been matched to corresponding 6-digit NAICS industry codes. The change reported for each occupation to the year 2014 is a percent of growth or decline as estimated by the Bureau of Labor Statistics. The abbreviation nec stands for 'not elsewhere classified.'

LOCATION BY STATE AND REGIONAL CONCENTRATION

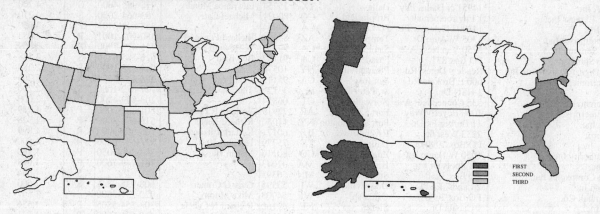

INDUSTRY DATA BY STATE

State	Establishments Total (number)	% of U.S.	Employment Total (number)	% of U.S.	Per Estab.	Payroll Total ($ mil.)	Per Empl. ($)	Sales Total ($ mil.)	% of U.S.	Per Estab. ($)
California	1,516	14.7	21,282	9.9	14	749.8	35,231	8,691.7	9.1	5,733,296
Illinois	440	4.3	12,417	5.8	28	500.6	40,312	8,248.2	8.6	18,745,959
Pennsylvania	414	4.0	15,635	7.3	38	558.9	35,749	7,865.2	8.2	18,998,022
Texas	525	5.1	7,952	3.7	15	262.8	33,052	7,732.4	8.1	14,728,451
Florida	793	7.7	15,910	7.4	20	492.7	30,967	6,129.2	6.4	7,729,153
Ohio	362	3.5	11,722	5.4	32	318.4	27,164	5,367.8	5.6	14,828,273
New Jersey	339	3.3	7,815	3.6	23	252.6	32,321	5,263.3	5.5	15,525,826
New York	892	8.6	11,564	5.4	13	427.4	36,960	4,256.5	4.4	4,771,872
Wisconsin	208	2.0	13,157	6.1	63	377.5	28,692	3,393.9	3.5	16,316,808
Indiana	141	1.4	7,777	3.6	55	220.0	28,292	2,987.5	3.1	21,187,652
Nevada	102	1.0	3,138	1.5	31	90.7	28,911	2,981.5	3.1	29,230,382
Missouri	191	1.9	6,218	2.9	33	147.2	23,671	2,294.9	2.4	12,015,236
Massachusetts	235	2.3	5,778	2.7	25	166.4	28,793	2,184.1	2.3	9,293,868
Connecticut	186	1.8	4,208	2.0	23	167.2	39,735	2,089.3	2.2	11,232,640
Minnesota	248	2.4	5,947	2.8	24	215.0	36,147	2,022.2	2.1	8,153,831
Virginia	225	2.2	6,210	2.9	28	156.1	25,138	1,930.3	2.0	8,579,160
Washington	262	2.5	4,753	2.2	18	130.6	27,476	1,722.8	1.8	6,575,748
North Carolina	248	2.4	5,088	2.4	21	141.3	27,767	1,512.2	1.6	6,097,552
Tennessee	176	1.7	3,598	1.7	20	121.0	33,633	1,408.6	1.5	8,003,557
Georgia	288	2.8	3,986	1.9	14	128.9	32,339	1,352.5	1.4	4,696,181
Nebraska	60	0.6	3,595	1.7	60	77.4	21,532	1,306.3	1.4	21,772,233
New Hampshire	89	0.9	1,948	0.9	22	78.2	40,132	1,116.5	1.2	12,544,910
Maryland	189	1.8	2,370	1.1	13	82.5	34,804	1,004.1	1.0	5,312,926
New Mexico	68	0.7	1,287	0.6	19	36.1	28,061	935.0	1.0	13,749,382
Utah	117	1.1	1,790	0.8	15	43.4	24,237	905.2	0.9	7,736,393
Oregon	176	1.7	1,883	0.9	11	58.8	31,202	870.1	0.9	4,943,483
Alabama	86	0.8	1,671	0.8	19	52.3	31,296	856.5	0.9	9,959,407
Colorado	219	2.1	3,492	1.6	16	100.3	28,714	743.1	0.8	3,393,233
Maine	71	0.7	2,218	1.0	31	45.1	20,315	722.1	0.8	10,170,662
Kentucky	108	1.0	1,771	0.8	16	49.7	28,080	453.1	0.5	4,195,259
West Virginia	34	0.3	867	0.4	25	23.7	27,366	403.3	0.4	11,862,206
Louisiana	63	0.6	510	0.2	8	18.5	36,339	387.7	0.4	6,153,889
Iowa	99	1.0	1,445	0.7	15	33.2	23,006	347.2	0.4	3,506,768

Continued on next page.

INDUSTRY DATA BY STATE - Continued

State	Establishments		Employment			Payroll		Sales		
	Total (number)	% of U.S.	Total (number)	% of U.S.	Per Estab.	Total ($ mil.)	Per Empl. ($)	Total ($ mil.)	% of U.S.	Per Estab. ($)
Kansas	97	0.9	925	0.4	10	23.4	25,255	318.7	0.3	3,285,082
Vermont	56	0.5	894	0.4	16	30.0	33,586	258.8	0.3	4,620,893
South Carolina	81	0.8	949	0.4	12	25.4	26,717	180.7	0.2	2,230,580
Wyoming	22	0.2	541	0.3	25	13.7	25,375	147.7	0.2	6,712,318
Delaware	30	0.3	275	0.1	9	9.6	34,898	134.2	0.1	4,472,467
Oklahoma	73	0.7	514	0.2	7	14.9	29,018	127.0	0.1	1,739,452
Hawaii	21	0.2	122	0.1	6	2.9	24,025	43.2	-	2,059,000
Idaho	47	0.5	260	0.1	6	5.0	19,185	41.9	-	891,085
Mississippi	39	0.4	209	0.1	5	4.5	21,301	35.9	-	920,769
Montana	32	0.3	106	-	3	1.9	18,311	22.6	-	707,188
Alaska	13	0.1	92	-	7	2.2	24,098	18.3	-	1,407,077
Michigan	255	2.5	2500-4999	-	-	(D)	-	(D)	-	-
Arizona	223	2.2	2500-4999	-	-	(D)	-	(D)	-	-
Arkansas	57	0.6	500-999	-	-	(D)	-	(D)	-	-
Rhode Island	43	0.4	500-999	-	-	(D)	-	(D)	-	-
South Dakota	26	0.3	2500-4999	-	-	(D)	-	(D)	-	-
D.C.	16	0.2	100-249	-	-	(D)	-	(D)	-	-
North Dakota	16	0.2	250-499	-	-	(D)	-	(D)	-	-

Source: 2002 *Economic Census*. The states are in descending order of sales or establishments (if sales data are missing for the majority). The symbol (D) appears when data are withheld to prevent disclosure of competitive information. States marked with (D) are sorted by number of establishments. A dash (-) indicates that the data element cannot be calculated. Shaded *states* on the state map indicate those states which have proportionately greater representation in the industry than would be indicated by the states population; the ratio is based on total sales or number of establishments. Shaded *regions* indicate where the industry is regionally most concentrated.

NAICS 454210 - VENDING MACHINE OPERATORS*

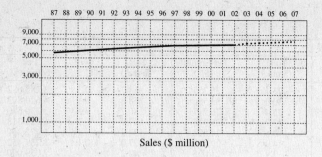

Sales ($ million)

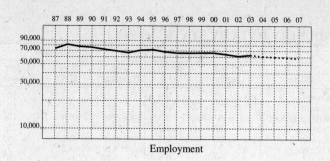

Employment

GENERAL STATISTICS

Year	Establishments (number)	Employment (number)	Payroll ($ million)	Sales ($ million)	Employees per Establishment (number)	Sales per Establishment ($)	Payroll per Employee ($)
1987	5,302	73,652	1,090.2	5,692.3	14	1,073,614	14,802
1988	4,983	81,739	1,232.3	5,819.8 e	16	1,167,931	15,076
1989	4,873	77,537	1,250.6	5,947.4 e	16	1,220,480	16,129
1990	5,144	76,130	1,258.9	6,075.0 e	15	1,180,988	16,536
1991	5,298	72,526	1,242.2	6,202.5 e	14	1,170,725	17,128
1992	6,391	69,628	1,232.0	6,330.1	11	990,471	17,694
1993	5,881	66,651	1,227.1	6,441.0 e	11	1,095,222	18,411
1994	5,975	71,046	1,323.9	6,551.9 e	12	1,096,552	18,634
1995	6,124	72,054	1,378.1	6,662.7 e	12	1,087,965	19,126
1996	5,872 e	68,350 e	1,399.6 e	6,773.6 e	12 e	1,153,542 e	20,477 e
1997	7,070	66,348	1,333.4	6,884.5	9	973,762	20,097
1998	6,381	66,324	1,428.0	6,913.0 e	10	1,083,371	21,531
1999	6,251	66,614	1,479.9	6,941.5 e	11	1,110,459	22,216
2000	6,155	66,657	1,510.2	6,970.0 e	11	1,132,407	22,657
2001	6,004	64,266	1,501.0	6,998.5 e	11	1,165,632	23,355
2002	5,945	61,317	1,391.6	7,026.9	10	1,181,992	22,695
2003	5,613	62,907	1,420.6	7,304.9 p	11	1,111,114 p	22,582
2004	6,437 p	60,968 p	1,519.3 p	7,398.0 p	9 p	1,110,325 p	24,360 p
2005	6,504 p	60,005 p	1,539.8 p	7,491.0 p	9 p	1,109,537 p	24,916 p
2006	6,570 p	59,043 p	1,560.2 p	7,584.0 p	9 p	1,108,748 p	25,471 p
2007	6,637 p	58,080 p	1,580.7 p	7,677.0 p	8 p	1,107,959 p	26,027 p

Sources: *Economic Census of the United States*, 1987, 1992, 1997, and 2002. Establishment counts, employment, and payroll are from *County Business Patterns* for non-Census years. Values followed by a 'p' are projections by the editors. Sales data for non-Census years are extrapolations, marked by 'e'. Data are the most recent available at this level of detail.

INDICES OF CHANGE

Year	Establishments (number)	Employment (number)	Payroll ($ million)	Sales ($ million)	Employees per Establishment (number)	Sales per Establishment ($)	Payroll per Employee ($)
1987	89.2	120.1	78.3	81.0	134.8	90.8	65.2
1992	107.5	113.6	88.5	90.1	105.7	83.8	78.0
1993	98.9	108.7	88.2	91.7 e	109.6	92.7	81.1
1994	100.5	115.9	95.1	93.2 e	115.4	92.8	82.1
1995	103.0	117.5	99.0	94.8 e	114.4	92.0	84.3
1996	98.8 e	111.5 e	100.6 e	96.4 e	112.5 e	97.6 e	90.2 e
1997	118.9	108.2	95.8	98.0	91.1	82.4	88.6
1998	107.3	108.2	102.6	98.4 e	100.8	91.7	94.9
1999	105.1	108.6	106.3	98.8 e	103.7	93.9	97.9
2000	103.5	108.7	108.5	99.2 e	104.7	95.8	99.8
2001	101.0	104.8	107.9	99.6 e	103.7	98.6	102.9
2002	100.0	100.0	100.0	100.0	100.0	100.0	100.0
2003	94.4	102.6	102.1	104.0 p	108.7	94.0 p	99.5
2004	108.3 p	99.4 p	109.2 p	105.3 p	88.9 p	93.9 p	107.3 p
2005	109.4 p	97.9 p	110.7 p	106.6 p	85.7 p	93.9 p	109.8 p
2006	110.5 p	96.3 p	112.1 p	107.9 p	82.6 p	93.8 p	112.2 p
2007	111.6 p	94.7 p	113.6 p	109.3 p	79.4 p	93.7 p	114.7 p

Sources: Same as General Statistics. The values shown reflect change from the base year, 2002. Values above 100 mean greater than 2002, values below 100 mean less than 2002, and a value of 100 in the 1987-2001 or 2003-2007 period means same as 2002. Values followed by a 'p' are projections by the editors; 'e' stands for extrapolation. Data are the most recent available at this level of detail.

SELECTED RATIOS

For 2002	Avg. of All Retail	Analyzed Industry	Index	For 2002	Avg. of All Retail	Analyzed Industry	Index
Employees per Establishment	17	10	61	Sales per Employee	174,682	114,600	66
Payroll per Establishment	333,445	234,074	70	Sales per Establishment	3,332,269	1,181,992	35
Payroll per Employee	20,311	22,695	112	Expenses per Establishment	na	na	na

Sources: Same as General Statistics. The 'Average of All' column, Wholesale or Retail, represents the average of the sector reported for the most recent complete year available. The Index shows the relationship between the Average and the Analyzed Industry. For example, 100 means that they are equal; 500 that the Analyzed Industry is five times the average; 50 means that the Analyzed Industry is half the national average. The abbreviation 'na' is used to show that data are 'not available'.

*Equivalent to SIC 5962.

LEADING COMPANIES   Number shown: **23**   Total sales ($ mil): **5,634**   Total employment (000): **3.8**

Company Name	Address				CEO Name	Phone	Co. Type	Sales ($ mil)	Empl. (000)
Compass Group USA Inc	2400 Yorkmont Rd	Charlotte	NC	28217	Gary Green	704-329-4000	D	4,997*	0.9
Nutrition Inc.	PO Box 328	West Newton	PA	15089	Edward Caswell	724-872-7887	R	199*	<0.1
Canteen Service Co.	5695 W River NE	Belmont	MI	49306	Fred Tiggleman	616-785-2500	S	120*	0.8
Glacier Water Services Inc.	1385 Park Center Dr	Vista	CA	92081	Brian H McInerney	760-560-1111	P	72	0.3
Ace Coffee Bar Inc.	601 E Lake St	Streamwood	IL	60107	Bernard Cavitt	630-233-2800	R	41*	0.6
Natural Choice	5700 Buckingham	Culver City	CA	90230	Dana Bashor	310-342-5300	R	35*	0.1
Protel Inc.	4150 Kidron Rd	Lakeland	FL	33811	Regis Mellon	863-644-5505	S	29*	<0.1
Calderon Brothers Vending Inc.	PO Box 29099	Indianapolis	IN	46229	Steven Calderon	317-899-1234	R	28	0.2
Nackard, Fred Wholesale Liquor	PO Box 2182	Prescott	AZ	86302		928-445-7200	R	19*	<0.1
Konop Companies Inc.	1725 Industrial Dr	Green Bay	WI	54302	Thomas J Konop	920-468-8517	R	18*	0.2
Advanced Vending Systems Inc.	PO Box 987	Ringgold	GA	30736	Eddy Logan	706-866-6044	R	14	0.1
Patton Music Company Inc.	811 Kearney Ave	Modesto	CA	95350	James B Reed	209-529-6500	R	14*	0.1
Vend-Omack Sales Inc.	PO Box 382	Morrison	IL	61270	Stanley Domack	815-772-4035	R	13*	<0.1
Shealy Sales and Vending Inc.	PO Box 4926	Columbia	SC	29240	G Shealy	803-754-9101	R	9*	<0.1
Food Services Inc.	PO Box 670	Opp	AL	36467	James Weeks	334-493-4505	R	5*	<0.1
Quality Co's Inc.	1491 Quality Way	Tallahassee	FL	32303	David Pulsifer	850-576-2865	R	5*	<0.1
Vend-A-Snack of Clarksdale Inc.	PO Box 638	Clarksdale	MS	38614	Cal Edlin	662-627-9691	R	4*	<0.1
Manhill Food Service	1771 Auburn Rd	Seneca Falls	NY	13148	Jack Hilimire	315-568-8303	R	3*	<0.1
Vacationland Vendors Inc.	PO Box 177	Wisconsin Dells	WI	53965	David Gussel	608-254-8515	R	3*	<0.1
South Peninsula Sales Inc.	3801 Charter	San Jose	CA	95136	Marsha Micik	408-978-3588	R	2*	<0.1
Terminal Amusement Co.	301 W Clinton Ave	Oaklyn	NJ	08107	George Hamilton Jr	856-854-2100	R	2*	<0.1
Five Star Food Services	6001 Century Oaks	Chattanooga	TN	37416		423-490-4428	R	2*	<0.1
Coffee-Serv Inc.	1452 Southwind	Dresher	PA	19025	Jack Kirshner	215-848-8400	R	2*	<0.1

Source: *Ward's Business Directory of U.S. Private and Public Companies*, Volumes 1 and 2, 2005. The company type code used is as follows: P - Public, R - Private, S - Subsidiary, D - Division, J - Joint Venture, A - Affiliate, G - Group. Sales are in millions of dollars, employees are in thousands. An asterisk (*) indicates an estimated sales volume. The symbol < stands for 'less than'. Company names and addresses are truncated, in some cases, to fit into the available space.

OCCUPATIONS EMPLOYED BY VENDING MACHINE OPERATORS

Occupation	% of Total 2004	Change to 2014	Occupation	% of Total 2004	Change to 2014
Coin, vending, & amusement machine servicers	20.1	-5.4	Bookkeeping, accounting, & auditing clerks	2.2	-5.4
Driver/sales workers	19.9	4.7	Food preparation & serving related workers, nec	2.1	0.6
Food preparation workers	5.1	5.1	Laborers & freight, stock, & material movers, hand	2.0	-5.4
Combined food preparation & serving workers	4.4	5.1	Sales reps, wholesale & manufacturing, exc tech	1.8	5.0
Truck drivers, light or delivery services	4.4	5.1	First-line supervisors/managers of transporation workers	1.8	5.1
Office clerks, general	3.1	-6.5	First-line supervisors of mechanics	1.7	5.1
Counter attendants	3.0	5.1	Maintenance & repair workers, general	1.3	5.0
General & operations managers	2.5	4.0	First-line supervisors/managers of office workers	1.3	-4.8
First-line supervisors/managers of food service workers	2.3	5.1	Secretaries, except legal, medical, & executive	1.2	-11.6
Cashiers, except gaming	2.2	-5.4	Cooks, institution & cafeteria	1.2	5.0

Source: *Industry-Occupation Matrix*, Bureau of Labor Statistics. These data are reported based on 4-digit NAICS categories but have been matched to corresponding 6-digit NAICS industry codes. The change reported for each occupation to the year 2014 is a percent of growth or decline as estimated by the Bureau of Labor Statistics. The abbreviation nec stands for 'not elsewhere classified.'

LOCATION BY STATE AND REGIONAL CONCENTRATION

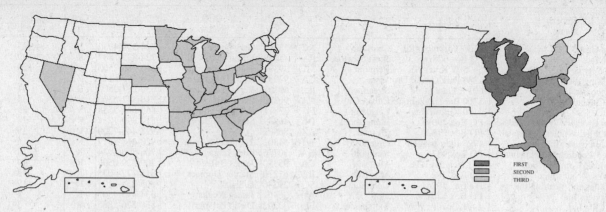

FIRST
SECOND
THIRD

INDUSTRY DATA BY STATE

State	Establishments Total (number)	% of U.S.	Employment Total (number)	% of U.S.	Per Estab.	Payroll Total ($ mil.)	Per Empl. ($)	Sales Total ($ mil.)	% of U.S.	Per Estab. ($)
Ohio	344	5.8	6,476	10.7	19	126.5	19,541	519.6	7.4	1,510,375
California	412	7.0	3,710	6.1	9	96.7	26,066	496.6	7.0	1,205,371
North Carolina	180	3.0	2,764	4.6	15	64.6	23,388	474.3	6.7	2,635,006
New York	342	5.8	2,932	4.8	9	75.2	25,647	453.2	6.4	1,325,064
Illinois	315	5.3	3,565	5.9	11	85.3	23,930	398.7	5.7	1,265,790
Texas	425	7.2	3,172	5.2	7	71.9	22,659	395.4	5.6	930,238
Pennsylvania	295	5.0	3,680	6.1	12	80.6	21,910	380.3	5.4	1,289,027
Michigan	196	3.3	2,342	3.9	12	61.9	26,444	285.0	4.0	1,454,051
Georgia	158	2.7	2,138	3.5	14	49.3	23,037	239.5	3.4	1,515,728
Florida	383	6.5	1,943	3.2	5	43.7	22,482	234.5	3.3	612,146
Indiana	164	2.8	2,176	3.6	13	50.0	22,980	232.1	3.3	1,415,220
Wisconsin	130	2.2	1,880	3.1	14	46.9	24,933	224.9	3.2	1,729,969
Tennessee	219	3.7	2,053	3.4	9	45.1	21,980	216.2	3.1	987,032
Missouri	176	3.0	1,735	2.9	10	40.1	23,101	194.0	2.8	1,102,227
Maryland	112	1.9	1,163	1.9	10	35.8	30,819	188.3	2.7	1,681,402
Minnesota	156	2.6	1,477	2.4	9	34.7	23,520	182.7	2.6	1,171,186
Virginia	130	2.2	1,283	2.1	10	28.4	22,126	151.0	2.1	1,161,277
Massachusetts	111	1.9	1,098	1.8	10	31.6	28,811	144.5	2.0	1,301,523
Kentucky	102	1.7	1,414	2.3	14	29.3	20,700	139.8	2.0	1,370,333
New Jersey	147	2.5	873	1.4	6	25.1	28,740	129.5	1.8	880,993
South Carolina	77	1.3	1,573	2.6	20	29.0	18,420	113.7	1.6	1,476,403
Alabama	101	1.7	930	1.5	9	20.1	21,663	104.1	1.5	1,030,545
Washington	79	1.3	567	0.9	7	15.9	28,115	79.3	1.1	1,004,241
Colorado	99	1.7	702	1.2	7	16.4	23,322	76.8	1.1	776,091
Arkansas	59	1.0	776	1.3	13	13.6	17,530	74.3	1.1	1,259,475
Delaware	17	0.3	357	0.6	21	9.2	25,720	71.9	1.0	4,226,647
Iowa	79	1.3	672	1.1	9	12.9	19,176	69.2	1.0	875,823
Kansas	61	1.0	473	0.8	8	11.9	25,053	65.4	0.9	1,071,508
Oregon	60	1.0	519	0.9	9	13.3	25,559	65.2	0.9	1,087,417
Connecticut	51	0.9	612	1.0	12	15.1	24,716	61.4	0.9	1,203,333
Nebraska	40	0.7	657	1.1	16	11.6	17,703	60.2	0.9	1,504,850
Louisiana	60	1.0	571	0.9	10	10.7	18,665	54.1	0.8	901,400
Nevada	40	0.7	314	0.5	8	8.4	26,879	47.5	0.7	1,186,925
Oklahoma	93	1.6	481	0.8	5	8.7	18,012	45.2	0.6	485,656
Mississippi	49	0.8	442	0.7	9	8.3	18,781	43.3	0.6	883,388
West Virginia	75	1.3	395	0.7	5	6.1	15,532	34.5	0.5	460,667
Utah	38	0.6	276	0.5	7	5.9	21,464	33.9	0.5	893,184
Maine	26	0.4	397	0.7	15	8.0	20,111	31.2	0.4	1,201,231
Idaho	28	0.5	168	0.3	6	3.6	21,661	19.8	0.3	706,214
New Hampshire	28	0.5	142	0.2	5	3.9	27,528	17.1	0.2	612,250
New Mexico	29	0.5	146	0.2	5	3.2	21,719	16.9	0.2	583,310
Vermont	12	0.2	148	0.2	12	3.4	22,838	16.7	0.2	1,390,000
Alaska	9	0.2	99	0.2	11	3.0	30,131	15.3	0.2	1,704,444
South Dakota	21	0.4	100	0.2	5	2.0	19,800	11.1	0.2	529,619
North Dakota	11	0.2	95	0.2	9	2.0	20,842	10.7	0.2	973,182
Hawaii	22	0.4	90	0.1	4	1.3	14,433	6.5	0.1	294,182
Montana	11	0.2	60	0.1	5	1.0	17,000	5.3	0.1	477,364
Wyoming	11	0.2	35	0.1	3	0.6	17,286	4.0	0.1	367,455
Arizona	114	1.9	500-999	-	-	(D)	-	(D)	-	-
Rhode Island	20	0.3	100-249	-	-	(D)	-	(D)	-	-
D.C.	4	0.1	20-99	-	-	(D)	-	(D)	-	-

Source: 2002 *Economic Census*. The states are in descending order of sales or establishments (if sales data are missing for the majority). The symbol (D) appears when data are withheld to prevent disclosure of competitive information. States marked with (D) are sorted by number of establishments. A dash (-) indicates that the data element cannot be calculated. Shaded *states* on the state map indicate those states which have proportionately greater representation in the industry than would be indicated by the states population; the ratio is based on total sales or number of establishments. Shaded *regions* indicate where the industry is regionally most concentrated.

NAICS 454311 - HEATING OIL DEALERS

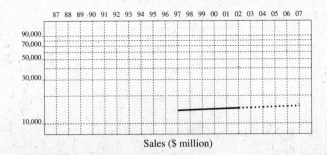

Sales ($ million)

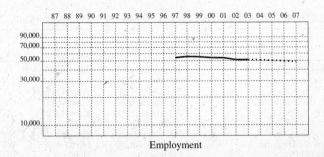

Employment

GENERAL STATISTICS

Year	Establishments (number)	Employment (number)	Payroll ($ million)	Sales ($ million)	Employees per Establishment (number)	Sales per Establishment ($)	Payroll per Employee ($)
1987	-	-	-	-	-	-	-
1988	-	-	-	-	-	-	-
1989	-	-	-	-	-	-	-
1990	-	-	-	-	-	-	-
1991	-	-	-	-	-	-	-
1992	-	-	-	-	-	-	-
1993	-	-	-	-	-	-	-
1994	-	-	-	-	-	-	-
1995	-	-	-	-	-	-	-
1996	-	-	-	-	-	-	-
1997	5,657	54,106	1,527.9	13,866.8	10	2,451,264	28,239
1998	5,577	55,588	1,618.8	14,023.4 e	10	2,514,509	29,121
1999	5,422	55,196	1,665.0	14,180.0 e	10	2,615,277	30,165
2000	5,248	53,936	1,722.8	14,336.6 e	10	2,731,830	31,942
2001	5,110	53,761	1,818.6	14,493.3 e	10	2,836,255	33,828
2002	4,681	51,246	1,730.2	14,649.9	11	3,129,647	33,762
2003	4,612	51,226	1,840.5	14,806.5 p	11	3,160,501 p	35,929
2004	4,438 p	50,900 p	1,891.1 p	14,963.1 p	11 p	3,288,321 p	37,000 p
2005	4,251 p	50,230 p	1,938.1 p	15,119.7 p	12 p	3,416,141 p	38,287 p
2006	4,064 p	49,560 p	1,985.0 p	15,276.3 p	12 p	3,543,961 p	39,573 p
2007	3,877 p	48,890 p	2,031.9 p	15,433.0 p	12 p	3,671,782 p	40,859 p

Source: Economic Census of the United States, 1997 and 2002. Establishment counts, employment, and payroll are from County Business Patterns for non-Census years. This is a newly defined industry. Data for prior years are unavailable at the time of publication but may become available over time. Values followed by 'p' are projections by the editors. Sales data for non-Census years are extrapolations, marked by 'e'.

INDICES OF CHANGE

Year	Establishments (number)	Employment (number)	Payroll ($ million)	Sales ($ million)	Employees per Establishment (number)	Sales per Establishment ($)	Payroll per Employee ($)
1987	-	-	-	-	-	-	-
1992	-	-	-	-	-	-	-
1993	-	-	-	-	-	-	-
1994	-	-	-	-	-	-	-
1995	-	-	-	-	-	-	-
1996	-	-	-	-	-	-	-
1997	120.9	105.6	88.3	94.7	87.7	78.3	83.6
1998	119.1	108.5	93.6	95.7 e	91.3	80.3	86.3
1999	115.8	107.7	96.2	96.8 e	93.2	83.6	89.3
2000	112.1	105.2	99.6	97.9 e	94.1	87.3	94.6
2001	109.2	104.9	105.1	98.9 e	95.9	90.6	100.2
2002	100.0	100.0	100.0	100.0	100.0	100.0	100.0
2003	98.5	100.0	106.4	101.1 p	101.5	101.0 p	106.4
2004	94.8 p	99.3 p	109.3 p	102.1 p	103.6 p	105.1 p	109.6 p
2005	90.8 p	98.0 p	112.0 p	103.2 p	105.8 p	109.2 p	113.4 p
2006	86.8 p	96.7 p	114.7 p	104.3 p	108.0 p	113.2 p	117.2 p
2007	82.8 p	95.4 p	117.4 p	105.3 p	110.1 p	117.3 p	121.0 p

Sources: Same as General Statistics. The values shown reflect change from the base year, 2002. Values above 100 mean greater than 2002, values below 100 mean less than 2002, and a value of 100 in the 1987-2001 or 2003-2007 period means same as 2002. Values followed by a 'p' are projections by the editors; 'e' stands for extrapolation. Data are the most recent available at this level of detail.

SELECTED RATIOS

For 2002	Avg. of All Retail	Analyzed Industry	Index	For 2002	Avg. of All Retail	Analyzed Industry	Index
Employees per Establishment	17	11	65	Sales per Employee	174,682	285,874	164
Payroll per Establishment	333,445	369,618	111	Sales per Establishment	3,332,269	3,129,647	94
Payroll per Employee	20,311	33,762	166	Expenses per Establishment	na	na	na

Sources: Same as General Statistics. The 'Average of All' column, Wholesale or Retail, represents the average of the sector reported for the most recent complete year available. The Index shows the relationship between the Average and the Analyzed Industry. For example, 100 means that they are equal; 500 that the Analyzed Industry is five times the average; 50 means that the Analyzed Industry is half the national average. The abbreviation 'na' is used to show that data are 'not available'.

LEADING COMPANIES   Number shown: 57   Total sales ($ mil): 72,794   Total employment (000): 35.6

Company Name	Address				CEO Name	Phone	Co. Type	Sales ($ mil)	Empl. (000)
Valero Energy Corp.	1 Valero Wy	San Antonio	TX	78249		210-345-2000	P	54,619	20.0
Tesoro Petroleum Corp.	300 Concord Plaza	San Antonio	TX	78216		210-828-8484	P	12,262	3.6
CH Energy Group Inc.	284 South Ave	Poughkeepsie	NY	12601		845-452-2000	P	1,300	0.9
Petro Holdings Inc.	2187 Atlantic St	Stamford	CT	06902		203-325-5400	S	1,105	3.0
Inergy L.P.	2 Brush Creek Blvd	Kansas City	MO	64111		816-842-8181	P	482	1.1
Quality Oil Company L.L.C.	PO Box 2736	Winston Salem	NC	27102	Graham Bennett	336-722-3441	R	470*	0.6
Castle Oil Corp.	500 Mamaroneck	Harrison	NY	10528	Michael Romita	914-381-6600	R	266*	0.3
Jacobus Energy Inc.	11815 W Bradley Rd	Milwaukee	WI	53224	CD Jacobus	414-359-0700	R	198*	0.3
Iowa Oil Co.	PO Box 712	Dubuque	IA	52004	Brian Enke	563-672-3663	R	187*	0.2
NOCO Energy Corp.	2440 Sheridan Dr	Tonawanda	NY	14150	Jim Newman	716-833-6626	R	164*	0.6
Petroleum Marketers Inc.	3000 Ogden Rd	Roanoke	VA	24014	Ron Hare	540-772-4700	R	151*	0.7
Team Schierl Cos.	PO Box 308	Stevens Point	WI	54481	William Schierl	715-345-5060	R	133*	0.6
Irving Oil Corp.	190 Commerce Way	Portsmouth	NH	03801	Arthur Irving	603-559-8736	R	92*	0.1
Patterson Oil Co.	PO Box 898	Torrington	CT	06790	Barry Patterson	860-489-9271	R	79*	<0.1
Able Oil Co.	PO Box 630	Rockaway	NJ	07866	Chris Westad	973-625-1012	S	73*	<0.1
Kugler Oil Co.	PO Box 1748	McCook	NE	69001	Diane Kugler	308-345-2280	R	69*	0.2
MIFCO	9009 Ctr St	Manassas	VA	20110		703-368-3121	R	68*	<0.1
Global Companies L.L.C.	800 South St	Waltham	MA	02454	Alfred Slifka	781-894-8800	R	66*	0.2
Farmers Elevator Co.	434 1st St	Chappell	NE	69129		308-874-2245	R	64*	0.1
Norbert E. Mitchell Company Inc.	PO Box 186	Danbury	CT	06813		203-744-0600	R	62*	0.1
Kingston Oil Supply Corp.	PO Box 760	Port Ewen	NY	12466	Leo Lebowitz	845-331-0770	S	60*	0.2
Amos Post Div.	PO Box 351	Catskill	NY	12414		518-943-3500	D	58*	<0.1
Forward Corp.	PO Box 549	Standish	MI	48658	Terry McTaggart	989-846-4501	R	57*	0.6
Farmers Union Cooperative	47018 S Dakota 46	Beresford	SD	57004		605-957-4141	R	52*	<0.1
Schmuckal Oil Co.	1516 Barlow St	Traverse City	MI	49686	Arthur Schmuckal	231-946-2800	R	45*	0.3
Able Energy Inc.	198 Green Pond Rd	Rockaway	NJ	07866	Timothy Harrington	973-625-1012	P	43	<0.1
Johnson Oil Company of Gaylord	PO Box 629	Gaylord	MI	49734	Dale E Johnson	989-732-2451	R	42*	<0.1
J.W. Pierson Co.	89 Dodd St	East Orange	NJ	07019	James Pierson	973-673-5000	R	39*	<0.1
Woodruff Energy Co.	PO Box 777	Bridgeton	NJ	08302	Robert A Woodruff Sr	856-455-1111	R	38*	<0.1
Riggins Inc.	3938 S Main Rd	Vineland	NJ	08360	Paul Riggins	856-825-7600	R	34*	<0.1
Frontier F.S. Cooperative	16119 Hwy 81 W	Darlington	WI	53530	Perry Goetsch	608-776-4600	S	32*	<0.1
LaForgia Fuel Oil Co.	1640 McDonald Ave	Brooklyn	NY	11230	Frank LaForgia	718-627-5100	R	31*	<0.1
Lehigh Oil Co.	410 Bank St	New London	CT	06320		860-887-3525	R	31*	<0.1
Robison Oil Corp.	500 Executive Blvd	Elmsford	NY	10523	Fran Singer	914-345-5700	R	30*	0.2
Four Seasons Cooperative	PO Box 148	Britton	SD	57430		605-448-2231	R	28*	<0.1
Hall, Bruce Corp.	PO Box 707	Cooperstown	NY	13326	Gregory Hall	607-547-9961	R	26*	<0.1
Northeast Coop.	445 S Main St	West Point	NE	68788		402-372-5303	R	25*	<0.1
Daigle Oil Co.	PO Box 328	Fort Kent	ME	04743	Richard Daigle	207-834-5027	R	21*	0.2
Larsen Cooperative Company Inc.	Box 37	Larsen	WI	54947		920-836-2113	R	21*	<0.1
Valley Oil Division	36 Brownstone Ave	Portland	CT	06480		860-342-3500	D	19*	<0.1
New Horizons Supply Cooperative	770 Lincoln Ave	Fennimore	WI	53809	Dean Roth	608-822-3217	R	16*	<0.1
Lawes Coal Company Inc.	PO Box 258	Shrewsbury	NJ	07702	Donald E Lawes Jr	732-741-6300	R	15*	<0.1
Local Oil Company of Anoka Inc.	PO Box 517	Anoka	MN	55303	Leonard Dehn	763-421-4923	R	15*	0.1
Lyon County Cooperative Oil Co.	1100 E Main St	Marshall	MN	56258		507-532-9686	R	15*	<0.1
Northampton Farm Bureau	300 Bushkill St	Tatamy	PA	18085		610-258-2871	R	14*	<0.1
Blanchardville Cooperative Oil	401 S Main St	Blanchardville	WI	53516	David Erickson	608-523-4294	R	11*	<0.1
Pickelner Fuel Company Inc.	210 Locust St	Williamsport	PA	17701	William Pickelner	570-323-9488	R	10*	<0.1
Holcomb Fuel Company Inc.	PO Box 486	Newtown	CT	06470	Ed Miller	203-426-5804	R	9*	<0.1
Rockbridge Farmers Coop.	645 Waddell St	Lexington	VA	24450		540-463-7381	R	9*	<0.1
Jet Fuel Oil Co.	PO Box 819	Saint Petersburg	FL	33731	Anthony Lineberger	727-824-8909	R	8*	<0.1
Kennedy Oil Company Inc.	1203 Courtesy Rd	High Point	NC	27260	Harold R Ridge	336-885-5184	R	6*	<0.1
Wilson of Wallingford Inc.	221 Rogers Ln	Wallingford	PA	19086	David O'Connell	610-566-7600	R	6*	<0.1
Ackner Fuels Inc.	2692 NY 43	Averill Park	NY	12018	Harry Ackner	518-674-3812	R	5*	<0.1
Chula Farmers Cooperative	PO Box 10	Chula	MO	64635	Steve Smith	660-639-3125	R	4*	<0.1
Rose Brick and Materials Inc.	918 Oliver Plow Ct	South Bend	IN	46601	R Harwood	574-234-2133	R	4*	<0.1
A.J. Petrunis Inc.	173 Water St	Bridgeton	NJ	08302	Michael Petrunis	856-451-7558	R	2*	<0.1
C and P Oil Inc.	PO Box 157	Millersburg	IN	46543	Ted Groff	574-642-3823	R	2*	<0.1

Source: Ward's Business Directory of U.S. Private and Public Companies, Volumes 1 and 2, 2005. The company type code used is as follows: P - Public, R - Private, S - Subsidiary, D - Division, J - Joint Venture, A - Affiliate, G - Group. Sales are in millions of dollars, employees are in thousands. An asterisk (*) indicates an estimated sales volume. The symbol < stands for 'less than'. Company names and addresses are truncated, in some cases, to fit into the available space.

OCCUPATIONS EMPLOYED BY DIRECT SELLING ESTABLISHMENTS

Occupation	% of Total 2004	Change to 2014	Occupation	% of Total 2004	Change to 2014
Truck drivers, heavy & tractor-trailer	12.8	1.6	Sales reps, wholesale & manufacturing, exc tech	2.5	1.6
Heating, air conditioning, & refrigeration mechanics	8.1	1.6	Laborers & freight, stock, & material movers, hand	2.5	-8.5
Driver/sales workers	8.0	0.9	Secretaries, except legal, medical, & executive	2.5	-14.5
Telemarketers	6.4	-22.4	First-line supervisors/managers of transporation workers	2.1	1.6
Truck drivers, light or delivery services	5.7	1.6	First-line supervisors/managers of retail sales workers	1.7	-6.5
Office clerks, general	4.2	-9.5	First-line supervisors/managers of office workers	1.6	-7.8
Customer service representatives	4.1	4.1	First-line supervisors of mechanics	1.3	1.6
Cashiers, except gaming	3.7	-8.5	Maintenance & repair workers, general	1.2	1.6
Retail salespersons	3.5	1.6	Installation, maintenance, & repair workers, nec	1.1	1.6
General & operations managers	3.3	0.6	Billing & posting clerks & machine operators	1.0	-14.4
Bookkeeping, accounting, & auditing clerks	2.7	-8.5			

Source: Industry-Occupation Matrix, Bureau of Labor Statistics. These data are reported based on 4-digit NAICS categories but have been matched to corresponding 6-digit NAICS industry codes. The change reported for each occupation to the year 2014 is a percent of growth or decline as estimated by the Bureau of Labor Statistics. The abbreviation nec stands for 'not elsewhere classified.'

LOCATION BY STATE AND REGIONAL CONCENTRATION

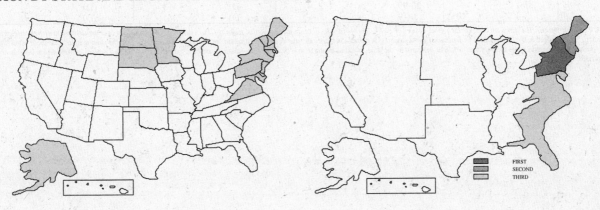

FIRST
SECOND
THIRD

INDUSTRY DATA BY STATE

State	Establishments Total (number)	% of U.S.	Employment Total (number)	% of U.S.	Per Estab.	Payroll Total ($ mil.)	Per Empl. ($)	Sales Total ($ mil.)	% of U.S.	Per Estab. ($)
New York	788	16.9	9,666	19.3	12	375.1	38,809	2,693.8	18.9	3,418,532
Pennsylvania	559	12.0	6,334	12.6	11	201.7	31,844	1,715.6	12.0	3,069,091
Massachusetts	527	11.3	5,175	10.3	10	199.6	38,570	1,189.7	8.3	2,257,562
Connecticut	334	7.1	4,198	8.4	13	174.8	41,630	940.7	6.6	2,816,560
New Jersey	295	6.3	3,306	6.6	11	126.3	38,214	791.0	5.5	2,681,227
Maine	260	5.6	2,956	5.9	11	82.7	27,975	774.3	5.4	2,978,104
Maryland	100	2.1	2,041	4.1	20	67.1	32,854	701.8	4.9	7,017,790
Virginia	180	3.9	2,057	4.1	11	61.8	30,034	504.6	3.5	2,803,339
New Hampshire	122	2.6	1,837	3.7	15	65.4	35,593	444.9	3.1	3,646,803
Michigan	88	1.9	573	1.1	7	15.2	26,489	277.1	1.9	3,149,352
Texas	38	0.8	234	0.5	6	8.1	34,816	265.3	1.9	6,981,053
Vermont	79	1.7	1,010	2.0	13	33.8	33,515	263.6	1.8	3,336,987
Minnesota	80	1.7	643	1.3	8	15.5	24,087	253.8	1.8	3,172,625
Alaska	60	1.3	628	1.3	10	23.3	37,102	218.4	1.5	3,639,333
Washington	57	1.2	650	1.3	11	24.2	37,183	218.0	1.5	3,823,772
Wisconsin	87	1.9	590	1.2	7	14.9	25,210	187.5	1.3	2,154,989
California	37	0.8	261	0.5	7	9.3	35,808	186.5	1.3	5,041,568
Oregon	28	0.6	291	0.6	10	9.2	31,526	156.1	1.1	5,574,929
Illinois	44	0.9	466	0.9	11	10.4	22,320	141.5	1.0	3,216,659
Indiana	49	1.0	383	0.8	8	10.9	28,337	115.0	0.8	2,347,735
Alabama	11	0.2	264	0.5	24	5.9	22,246	95.4	0.7	8,671,909
Nebraska	18	0.4	169	0.3	9	4.5	26,651	85.6	0.6	4,754,889
South Dakota	26	0.6	193	0.4	7	3.8	19,881	80.7	0.6	3,103,192
West Virginia	20	0.4	213	0.4	11	6.1	28,437	78.4	0.5	3,919,250
North Dakota	40	0.9	253	0.5	6	4.1	16,162	71.1	0.5	1,778,350
Missouri	25	0.5	153	0.3	6	4.2	27,693	69.4	0.5	2,775,840
Iowa	34	0.7	210	0.4	6	5.2	24,538	65.3	0.5	1,920,324
Delaware	27	0.6	266	0.5	10	9.8	36,722	62.7	0.4	2,321,778
Idaho	39	0.8	143	0.3	4	3.4	23,923	62.7	0.4	1,606,564
South Carolina	45	1.0	185	0.4	4	4.2	22,557	42.8	0.3	951,667
Tennessee	10	0.2	65	0.1	7	2.1	32,708	34.3	0.2	3,428,800
Mississippi	11	0.2	100	0.2	9	1.6	16,400	29.2	0.2	2,658,364
Montana	8	0.2	55	0.1	7	0.9	17,218	11.7	0.1	1,463,875

Continued on next page.

INDUSTRY DATA BY STATE - Continued

	Establishments		Employment			Payroll		Sales		
State	Total (number)	% of U.S.	Total (number)	% of U.S.	Per Estab.	Total ($ mil.)	Per Empl. ($)	Total ($ mil.)	% of U.S.	Per Estab. ($)
Louisiana	7	0.1	39	0.1	6	1.4	36,513	9.8	0.1	1,394,571
North Carolina	182	3.9	1000-2499	-	-	(D)	-	(D)	-	-
Ohio	113	2.4	500-999	-	-	(D)	-	(D)	-	-
Rhode Island	93	2.0	1000-2499	-	-	(D)	-	(D)	-	-
Florida	35	0.7	250-499	-	-	(D)	-	(D)	-	-
Kansas	20	0.4	100-249	-	-	(D)	-	(D)	-	-
Kentucky	18	0.4	100-249	-	-	(D)	-	(D)	-	-
Colorado	14	0.3	20-99	-	-	(D)	-	(D)	-	-
Oklahoma	14	0.3	100-249	-	-	(D)	-	(D)	-	-
New Mexico	13	0.3	20-99	-	-	(D)	-	(D)	-	-
Georgia	10	0.2	20-99	-	-	(D)	-	(D)	-	-
Nevada	8	0.2	100-249	-	-	(D)	-	(D)	-	-
Wyoming	7	0.1	20-99	-	-	(D)	-	(D)	-	-
Arkansas	6	0.1	100-249	-	-	(D)	-	(D)	-	-
Arizona	2	-	20-99	-	-	(D)	-	(D)	-	-
D.C.	2	-	0-19	-	-	(D)	-	(D)	-	-
Hawaii	1	-	20-99	-	-	(D)	-	(D)	-	-
Utah	1	-	0-19	-	-	(D)	-	(D)	-	-

Source: 2002 *Economic Census*. The states are in descending order of sales or establishments (if sales data are missing for the majority). The symbol (D) appears when data are withheld to prevent disclosure of competitive information. States marked with (D) are sorted by number of establishments. A dash (-) indicates that the data element cannot be calculated. Shaded *states* on the state map indicate those states which have proportionately greater representation in the industry than would be indicated by the states population; the ratio is based on total sales or number of establishments. Shaded *regions* indicate where the industry is regionally most concentrated.

NAICS 454312 - LIQUEFIED PETROLEUM GAS (BOTTLED GAS) DEALERS

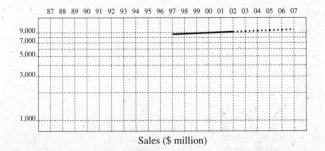

Sales ($ million)

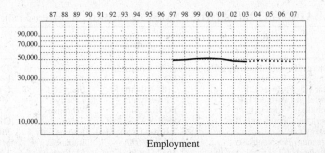

Employment

GENERAL STATISTICS

Year	Establishments (number)	Employment (number)	Payroll ($ million)	Sales ($ million)	Employees per Establishment (number)	Sales per Establishment ($)	Payroll per Employee ($)
1987	-	-	-	-	-	-	-
1988	-	-	-	-	-	-	-
1989	-	-	-	-	-	-	-
1990	-	-	-	-	-	-	-
1991	-	-	-	-	-	-	-
1992	-	-	-	-	-	-	-
1993	-	-	-	-	-	-	-
1994	-	-	-	-	-	-	-
1995	-	-	-	-	-	-	-
1996	-	-	-	-	-	-	-
1997	6,623	48,889	1,216.0	8,657.3	7	1,307,157	24,873
1998	6,627	49,532	1,297.3	8,765.8 e	8	1,322,746	26,191
1999	6,497	51,023	1,314.7	8,874.4 e	8	1,365,919	25,767
2000	6,274	51,382	1,394.4	8,982.9 e	8	1,431,769	27,138
2001	6,210	50,593	1,465.7	9,091.5 e	8	1,464,003	28,970
2002	6,178	47,974	1,388.4	9,200.0	8	1,489,154	28,941
2003	5,835	47,211	1,398.7	9,308.5 p	8	1,536,752 p	29,627
2004	5,814 p	48,289 p	1,479.5 p	9,417.1 p	8 p	1,576,741 p	30,639 p
2005	5,687 p	47,983 p	1,511.0 p	9,525.6 p	8 p	1,616,730 p	31,459 p
2006	5,560 p	47,676 p	1,542.5 p	9,634.2 p	8 p	1,656,718 p	32,279 p
2007	5,433 p	47,370 p	1,573.9 p	9,742.7 p	9 p	1,696,707 p	33,099 p

Source: Economic Census of the United States, 1997 and 2002. Establishment counts, employment, and payroll are from County Business Patterns for non-Census years. This is a newly defined industry. Data for prior years are unavailable at the time of publication but may become available over time. Values followed by 'p' are projections by the editors. Sales data for non-Census years are extrapolations, marked by 'e'.

INDICES OF CHANGE

Year	Establishments (number)	Employment (number)	Payroll ($ million)	Sales ($ million)	Employees per Establishment (number)	Sales per Establishment ($)	Payroll per Employee ($)
1987	-	-	-	-	-	-	-
1992	-	-	-	-	-	-	-
1993	-	-	-	-	-	-	-
1994	-	-	-	-	-	-	-
1995	-	-	-	-	-	-	-
1996	-	-	-	-	-	-	-
1997	107.2	101.9	87.6	94.1	95.3	87.8	85.9
1998	107.3	103.2	93.4	95.3 e	96.6	88.8	90.5
1999	105.2	106.4	94.7	96.5 e	101.7	91.7	89.0
2000	101.6	107.1	100.4	97.6 e	105.6	96.1	93.8
2001	100.5	105.5	105.6	98.8 e	104.3	98.3	100.1
2002	100.0	100.0	100.0	100.0	100.0	100.0	100.0
2003	94.4	98.4	100.7	101.2 p	104.2	103.2 p	102.4
2004	94.1 p	100.7 p	106.6 p	102.4 p	106.3 p	105.9 p	105.9 p
2005	92.0 p	100.0 p	108.8 p	103.5 p	107.5 p	108.6 p	108.7 p
2006	90.0 p	99.4 p	111.1 p	104.7 p	108.8 p	111.3 p	111.5 p
2007	87.9 p	98.7 p	113.4 p	105.9 p	110.1 p	113.9 p	114.4 p

Sources: Same as General Statistics. The values shown reflect change from the base year, 2002. Values above 100 mean greater than 2002, values below 100 mean less than 2002, and a value of 100 in the 1987-2001 or 2003-2007 period means same as 2002. Values followed by a 'p' are projections by the editors; 'e' stands for extrapolation. Data are the most recent available at this level of detail.

SELECTED RATIOS

For 2002	Avg. of All Retail	Analyzed Industry	Index	For 2002	Avg. of All Retail	Analyzed Industry	Index
Employees per Establishment	17	8	46	Sales per Employee	174,682	191,770	110
Payroll per Establishment	333,445	224,733	67	Sales per Establishment	3,332,269	1,489,154	45
Payroll per Employee	20,311	28,941	142	Expenses per Establishment	na	na	na

Sources: Same as General Statistics. The 'Average of All' column, Wholesale or Retail, represents the average of the sector reported for the most recent complete year available. The Index shows the relationship between the Average and the Analyzed Industry. For example, 100 means that they are equal; 500 that the Analyzed Industry is five times the average; 50 means that the Analyzed Industry is half the national average. The abbreviation 'na' is used to show that data are 'not available'.

LEADING COMPANIES   Number shown: **50**   Total sales ($ mil): **10,962**   Total employment (000): **26.8**

Company Name	Address				CEO Name	Phone	Co. Type	Sales ($ mil)	Empl. (000)
Energy Transfer Partners L.P.	2838 Woodside St	Dallas	TX	75204	Ray C. Davis	918-492-7272	P	2,482	2.9
AmeriGas Partners L.P.	PO Box 965	Valley Forge	PA	19482	Eugene V N Bissell	610-337-7000	P	1,776	6.1
Star Gas Partners L.P.	2187 Atlantic St	Stamford	CT	06902	Joseph P Cavanaugh	203-328-7300	P	1,454	4.2
Ferrellgas Partners L.P.	1 Liberty Plz	Liberty	MO	64068	James E Ferrell	816-792-1600	P	1,379	4.3
Suburban Propane L.P.	PO Box 206	Whippany	NJ	07981	Mark A Alexander	973-887-5300	S	1,307	3.0
Heritage Operating L.P.	8801 S Yale Ave	Tulsa	OK	74137	H Michael Krimbill	918-492-7272	S	716*	2.4
Inergy L.P.	2 Brush Creek Blvd	Kansas City	MO	64111		816-842-8181	P	482	1.1
Gresham Petroleum Co.	PO Box 690	Indianola	MS	38751	Bill McPherson	662-887-2160	R	167*	<0.1
Midland 66 Oil Company Inc.	1612 Garden City	Midland	TX	79701	Randall Stevens	432-682-9404	R	166*	<0.1
Martin Midstream Partners L.P.	4200 Stone Rd	Kilgore	TX	75662	Ruben Martin	903-983-6200	J	163*	0.3
North Central Cooperative Inc.	PO Box 299	Wabash	IN	46992	Darrell Smith	260-563-8381	R	106*	<0.1
Patterson Oil Co.	PO Box 898	Torrington	CT	06790	Barry Patterson	860-489-9271	R	79*	<0.1
Carolane Propane Gas Inc.	339 S Main St	Lexington	NC	27292		336-249-8981	R	57*	0.1
Roanoke Gas Co.	PO Box 13007	Roanoke	VA	24030		540-777-4427	S	57*	0.2
All Star Gas Corp.	PO Box 303	Lebanon	MO	65536	Paul Lindsey	417-532-3103	R	41*	0.3
Como Oil Company Inc.	PO Box 16108	Duluth	MN	55816	Tony Sega	218-722-6666	R	40*	0.1
Monte Vista Cooperative Inc.	1601 E Hwy 160	Monte Vista	CO	81144	Mike Spearmen	719-852-5181	R	38*	<0.1
ADA Coca-Cola & Dr Pepper	PO Box 1671	ADA	OK	74821	Frank Crabtree	580-332-0257	R	34*	<0.1
Jenkins Gas and Oil Company Inc.	PO Box 156	Pollocksville	NC	28573	John Mattocks	252-224-8911	R	33*	0.2
Frontier F.S. Cooperative	16119 Hwy 81 W	Darlington	WI	53530	Perry Goetsch	608-776-4600	S	32*	<0.1
Cooperative Agricultural Services	415 W 2nd St	Oakley	KS	67748		785-672-3300	R	28*	<0.1
Four Seasons Cooperative	PO Box 148	Britton	SD	57430		605-448-2231	R	28*	<0.1
Maine OXY-Acetylene Supply Co.	22 Albiston Way	Auburn	ME	04210	Dan Guerin	207-784-5788	R	26*	<0.1
Southern L.P. Gas Inc.	PO Box 1010	De Queen	AR	71832	Lu Gray	870-642-2234	R	26*	<0.1
Highland Propane Co.	PO Box 13007	Roanoke	VA	24030		540-343-7928	S	23*	<0.1
Farmers Union Oil Co.	PO Box 219	Ellendale	ND	58436	Kevin Brokaw	701-349-3280	R	21*	<0.1
Home Oil Co.	PO Box 608	Osceola	AR	72370	JL Price, Jr	870-563-6573	R	18*	<0.1
Sharp Energy Inc.	648 Ocean Hwy	Pocomoke City	MD	21851	Jerry West	410-957-0422	S	18*	0.1
WELSCO Inc.	PO Box 1058	N. Little Rock	AR	72115	Angela Harrison	501-771-1204	R	16*	<0.1
Mutual Liquid Gas & Equipment	17117 S Broadway	Gardena	CA	90248	MS Moore	323-321-3771	R	15*	<0.1
Central Oil of Virginia Corp.	PO Box 587	Rocky Mount	VA	24151		540-483-5342	R	14*	<0.1
Farmers Elevator and Supply Co.	301 E Market St	Morrison	IL	61270	Doug Vandernyde	815-772-4029	R	14*	<0.1
Gas Inc.	77 Jefferson Pkwy	Newnan	GA	30263		770-502-8800	R	14*	0.1
Litter Industries Inc.	PO Box 297	Chillicothe	OH	45601	Robert E Litter	740-773-2196	R	13*	0.1
Farmers Union Oil of Valley City	151 9th Ave NW	Valley City	ND	58072		701-845-0812	R	10*	<0.1
Fueltec United Inc.	707 N Main St	S. Hutchinson	KS	67505		620-663-6300	R	10*	<0.1
Pickelner Fuel Company Inc.	210 Locust St	Williamsport	PA	17701	William Pickelner	570-323-9488	R	10*	<0.1
TriCounty Farm Service Inc.	PO Box 367	Jerseyville	IL	62052	Ross Prough	618-498-5534	R	9*	<0.1
Apollo Propane Inc.	2680 Viking Ln	Dayton	OH	45439	Walter Fritzsche	937-298-0300	R	6*	<0.1
Glaser Gas Inc.	PO Box 38	Calhan	CO	80808	Edward Glaser	719-347-2338	R	5*	<0.1
Range Cooperatives Inc.	102 S Hoover Rd	Virginia	MN	55792	John Briski	218-741-7393	R	5*	<0.1
Bob Loyd L.P. Gas Co.	PO Box 367	Winters	TX	79567	Doug Wheat	325-754-4555	R	4*	<0.1
TenBrook Sales Inc.	700 S Berkley Rd	Kokomo	IN	46901		765-459-3141	R	4*	<0.1
Western Natural Gas Co.	2960 Strickland St	Jacksonville	FL	32254	Henry C Baker	904-387-3511	R	4*	<0.1
Stem Brothers Inc.	PO Box T	Milford	NJ	08848	Richard Stem	908-995-4825	R	3*	<0.1
Butane Power and Equipment Co.	507 N Beverly St	Casper	WY	82609	Thomas S Lankford	307-234-8985	R	2*	<0.1
Fowler Bottle Gas Service Inc.	PO Box 192	Fowler	IN	47944	Earnest L Hutchins	765-884-0250	R	2*	<0.1
Raymond Oil Co.	PO Box 142	Huron	SD	57350	EH Erling	605-352-8711	R	2*	<0.1
Peoples Gas and Oil Company Inc.	209 N Patterson St	Maxton	NC	28364	James L McNair	910-844-3124	R	1*	<0.1
Superior-Deshler Inc.	207 S Maple St	Davenport	NE	68335	Dennis Schardt	402-364-2125	R	1*	<0.1

Source: Ward's Business Directory of U.S. Private and Public Companies, Volumes 1 and 2, 2005. The company type code used is as follows: P - Public, R - Private, S - Subsidiary, D - Division, J - Joint Venture, A - Affiliate, G - Group. Sales are in millions of dollars, employees are in thousands. An asterisk (*) indicates an estimated sales volume. The symbol < stands for 'less than'. Company names and addresses are truncated, in some cases, to fit into the available space.

OCCUPATIONS EMPLOYED BY DIRECT SELLING ESTABLISHMENTS

Occupation	% of Total 2004	Change to 2014	Occupation	% of Total 2004	Change to 2014
Truck drivers, heavy & tractor-trailer	12.8	1.6	Sales reps, wholesale & manufacturing, exc tech	2.5	1.6
Heating, air conditioning, & refrigeration mechanics	8.1	1.6	Laborers & freight, stock, & material movers, hand	2.5	-8.5
Driver/sales workers	8.0	0.9	Secretaries, except legal, medical, & executive	2.5	-14.5
Telemarketers	6.4	-22.4	First-line supervisors/managers of transporation workers	2.1	1.6
Truck drivers, light or delivery services	5.7	1.6	First-line supervisors/managers of retail sales workers	1.7	-6.5
Office clerks, general	4.2	-9.5	First-line supervisors/managers of office workers	1.6	-7.8
Customer service representatives	4.1	4.1	First-line supervisors of mechanics	1.3	1.6
Cashiers, except gaming	3.7	-8.5	Maintenance & repair workers, general	1.2	1.6
Retail salespersons	3.5	1.6	Installation, maintenance, & repair workers, nec	1.1	1.6
General & operations managers	3.3	0.6	Billing & posting clerks & machine operators	1.0	-14.4
Bookkeeping, accounting, & auditing clerks	2.7	-8.5			

Source: Industry-Occupation Matrix, Bureau of Labor Statistics. These data are reported based on 4-digit NAICS categories but have been matched to corresponding 6-digit NAICS industry codes. The change reported for each occupation to the year 2014 is a percent of growth or decline as estimated by the Bureau of Labor Statistics. The abbreviation nec stands for 'not elsewhere classified.'

LOCATION BY STATE AND REGIONAL CONCENTRATION

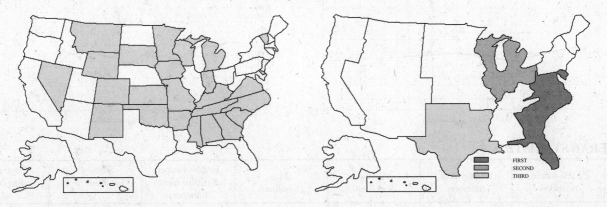

FIRST
SECOND
THIRD

INDUSTRY DATA BY STATE

State	Establishments Total (number)	% of U.S.	Employment Total (number)	% of U.S.	Per Estab.	Payroll Total ($ mil.)	Per Empl. ($)	Sales Total ($ mil.)	% of U.S.	Per Estab. ($)
California	300	4.8	2,818	5.9	9	92.0	32,647	709.4	7.6	2,364,587
Michigan	277	4.5	2,101	4.4	8	68.9	32,775	554.8	6.0	2,002,953
Texas	487	7.9	3,141	6.6	6	82.7	26,323	516.7	5.6	1,061,012
North Carolina	323	5.2	2,748	5.7	9	77.4	28,169	480.5	5.2	1,487,508
Florida	278	4.5	2,439	5.1	9	69.8	28,634	401.4	4.3	1,443,773
Pennsylvania	164	2.6	1,805	3.8	11	54.6	30,232	373.6	4.0	2,277,768
Ohio	173	2.8	1,571	3.3	9	48.4	30,796	354.1	3.8	2,046,936
New York	180	2.9	1,796	3.7	10	61.5	34,229	344.9	3.7	1,916,333
Missouri	309	5.0	1,666	3.5	5	41.8	25,077	303.0	3.3	980,602
Georgia	274	4.4	1,980	4.1	7	53.4	26,969	302.6	3.3	1,104,449
Wisconsin	198	3.2	1,470	3.1	7	40.4	27,457	300.9	3.2	1,519,530
Indiana	174	2.8	1,418	3.0	8	42.5	30,001	295.5	3.2	1,698,293
Illinois	195	3.1	1,230	2.6	6	37.9	30,774	286.1	3.1	1,467,005
Minnesota	155	2.5	1,149	2.4	7	30.1	26,228	259.2	2.8	1,672,303
Virginia	117	1.9	1,323	2.8	11	36.9	27,862	256.2	2.8	2,189,402
Alabama	232	3.7	1,597	3.3	7	43.3	27,098	247.6	2.7	1,067,375
Tennessee	154	2.5	1,295	2.7	8	30.2	23,312	227.5	2.4	1,477,039
Colorado	116	1.9	822	1.7	7	27.7	33,713	203.1	2.2	1,751,147
Arkansas	168	2.7	1,021	2.1	6	25.3	24,761	174.6	1.9	1,039,256
Mississippi	157	2.5	1,165	2.4	7	31.4	26,991	174.4	1.9	1,111,006
South Carolina	132	2.1	1,115	2.3	8	28.7	25,766	163.3	1.8	1,237,265
Iowa	134	2.2	773	1.6	6	19.1	24,718	158.8	1.7	1,185,313
Kentucky	123	2.0	786	1.6	6	21.3	27,162	151.2	1.6	1,229,114
Massachusetts	61	1.0	747	1.6	12	29.3	39,258	148.7	1.6	2,437,033
Washington	87	1.4	606	1.3	7	18.2	30,015	139.9	1.5	1,607,885
Oklahoma	158	2.5	889	1.9	6	21.1	23,717	131.0	1.4	829,215
Maryland	48	0.8	700	1.5	15	21.4	30,584	124.1	1.3	2,585,938
New Mexico	106	1.7	698	1.5	7	16.2	23,152	115.8	1.2	1,092,170
Kansas	93	1.5	489	1.0	5	12.5	25,636	106.8	1.2	1,148,355
Connecticut	42	0.7	693	1.4	16	24.1	34,719	105.4	1.1	2,508,595
Arizona	63	1.0	530	1.1	8	15.1	28,464	94.4	1.0	1,497,635
Louisiana	87	1.4	580	1.2	7	13.1	22,586	78.6	0.8	903,736
Vermont	46	0.7	455	0.9	10	14.0	30,767	76.6	0.8	1,664,500
Delaware	23	0.4	322	0.7	14	11.8	36,534	58.5	0.6	2,543,435
Nevada	42	0.7	304	0.6	7	8.1	26,651	57.7	0.6	1,374,119
Montana	54	0.9	277	0.6	5	6.6	23,845	51.8	0.6	958,519
South Dakota	47	0.8	245	0.5	5	5.9	24,220	47.4	0.5	1,007,553
West Virginia	29	0.5	244	0.5	8	5.6	22,828	47.1	0.5	1,622,966
Utah	34	0.5	202	0.4	6	4.9	24,342	46.5	0.5	1,368,265
Maine	35	0.6	247	0.5	7	6.6	26,680	40.0	0.4	1,143,400
Wyoming	41	0.7	165	0.3	4	4.4	26,491	32.1	0.3	782,610
North Dakota	18	0.3	73	0.2	4	1.6	22,425	19.8	0.2	1,100,389
Nebraska	58	0.9	250-499	-	-	(D)	-	(D)	-	-
Oregon	49	0.8	250-499	-	-	(D)	-	(D)	-	-
New Jersey	48	0.8	250-499	-	-	(D)	-	(D)	-	-
Idaho	46	0.7	250-499	-	-	(D)	-	(D)	-	-
New Hampshire	30	0.5	500-999	-	-	(D)	-	(D)	-	-
Alaska	18	0.3	20-99	-	-	(D)	-	(D)	-	-
Rhode Island	11	0.2	100-249	-	-	(D)	-	(D)	-	-
Hawaii	9	0.1	100-249	-	-	(D)	-	(D)	-	-

Source: 2002 *Economic Census*. The states are in descending order of sales or establishments (if sales data are missing for the majority). The symbol (D) appears when data are withheld to prevent disclosure of competitive information. States marked with (D) are sorted by number of establishments. A dash (-) indicates that the data element cannot be calculated. Shaded *states* on the state map indicate those states which have proportionately greater representation in the industry than would be indicated by the states population; the ratio is based on total sales or number of establishments. Shaded *regions* indicate where the industry is regionally most concentrated.

NAICS 454319 - OTHER FUEL DEALERS*

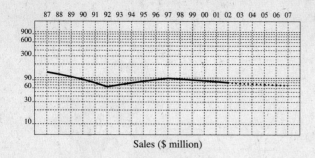

Sales ($ million)

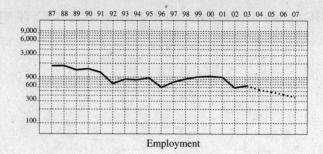

Employment

GENERAL STATISTICS

Year	Establishments (number)	Employment (number)	Payroll ($ million)	Sales ($ million)	Employees per Establishment (number)	Sales per Establishment ($)	Payroll per Employee ($)
1987	549	1,762	18.8	134.8	3	245,537	10,670
1988	497	1,770	26.0	120.6 e	4	242,656	14,689
1989	427	1,437	21.4	106.5 e	3	249,415	14,892
1990	397	1,520	21.3	92.3 e	4	232,494	14,013
1991	394	1,277	19.9	78.2 e	3	198,477	15,583
1992	297	719	9.0	64.0	2	215,488	12,517
1993	311	899	14.4	70.8 e	3	227,653	16,018
1994	309	876	15.1	77.6 e	3	251,133	17,237
1995	278	961	17.2	84.5 e	4	303,957	17,898
1996	219 e	600 e	12.6 e	91.3 e	3 e	416,895 e	21,000 e
1997	252	783	11.4	98.1	3	389,286	14,559
1998	303	913	17.6	94.4 e	3	311,535	19,277
1999	285	1,015	19.5	90.7 e	4	318,211	19,212
2000	298	1,042	26.0	87.0 e	4	291,896	24,989
2001	280	997	27.4	83.3 e	4	297,429	27,472
2002	230	591	10.9	79.6	3	345,978	18,467
2003	230	654	12.6	76.0 p	3	355,357 p	19,271
2004	185 p	538 p	15.9 p	74.2 p	3 p	363,795 p	23,279 p
2005	169 p	481 p	15.8 p	72.5 p	3 p	372,234 p	23,919 p
2006	154 p	425 p	15.6 p	70.7 p	3 p	380,673 p	24,559 p
2007	138 p	368 p	15.4 p	69.0 p	3 p	389,112 p	25,200 p

Sources: Economic Census of the United States, 1987, 1992, 1997, and 2002. Establishment counts, employment, and payroll are from *County Business Patterns* for non-Census years. Values followed by a 'p' are projections by the editors. Sales data for non-Census years are extrapolations, marked by 'e'. Data are the most recent available at this level of detail.

INDICES OF CHANGE

Year	Establishments (number)	Employment (number)	Payroll ($ million)	Sales ($ million)	Employees per Establishment (number)	Sales per Establishment ($)	Payroll per Employee ($)
1987	238.7	298.1	172.3	169.4	124.5	71.0	57.8
1992	129.1	121.7	82.5	80.4	93.4	62.3	67.8
1993	135.2	152.1	131.9	89.0 e	112.9	65.8	86.7
1994	134.3	148.2	138.4	97.5 e	109.0	72.6	93.3
1995	120.9	162.6	157.6	106.2 e	136.2	87.9	96.9
1996	95.2 e	101.5 e	115.4 e	114.7 e	105.1 e	120.5 e	113.7 e
1997	109.6	132.5	104.5	123.3	120.6	112.5	78.8
1998	131.7	154.5	161.3	118.6 e	116.8	90.0	104.4
1999	123.9	171.7	178.7	114.0 e	140.1	92.0	104.0
2000	129.6	176.3	238.2	109.3 e	136.2	84.4	135.3
2001	121.7	168.7	251.1	104.7 e	140.1	86.0	148.8
2002	100.0	100.0	100.0	100.0	100.0	100.0	100.0
2003	100.0	110.7	115.5	95.5 p	110.7	102.7 p	104.4
2004	80.5 p	91.0 p	146.1 p	93.3 p	117.2 p	105.1 p	126.1 p
2005	73.6 p	81.4 p	144.3 p	91.1 p	116.6 p	107.6 p	129.5 p
2006	66.8 p	71.9 p	142.5 p	88.9 p	116.0 p	110.0 p	133.0 p
2007	59.9 p	62.3 p	140.7 p	86.7 p	115.3 p	112.5 p	136.5 p

Sources: Same as General Statistics. The values shown reflect change from the base year, 2002. Values above 100 mean greater than 2002, values below 100 mean less than 2002, and a value of 100 in the 1987-2001 or 2003-2007 period means same as 2002. Values followed by a 'p' are projections by the editors; 'e' stands for extrapolation. Data are the most recent available at this level of detail.

SELECTED RATIOS

For 2002	Avg. of All Retail	Analyzed Industry	Index	For 2002	Avg. of All Retail	Analyzed Industry	Index
Employees per Establishment	17	3	15	Sales per Employee	174,682	134,645	77
Payroll per Establishment	333,445	47,452	14	Sales per Establishment	3,332,269	345,978	10
Payroll per Employee	20,311	18,467	91	Expenses per Establishment	na	na	na

Sources: Same as General Statistics. The 'Average of All' column, Wholesale or Retail, represents the average of the sector reported for the most recent complete year available. The Index shows the relationship between the Average and the Analyzed Industry. For example, 100 means that they are equal; 500 that the Analyzed Industry is five times the average; 50 means that the Analyzed Industry is half the national average. The abbreviation 'na' is used to show that data are 'not available'.

*Equivalent to SIC 5989.

LEADING COMPANIES   Number shown: 5   Total sales ($ mil): 1,469   Total employment (000): 3.3

Company Name	Address				CEO Name	Phone	Co. Type	Sales ($ mil)	Empl. (000)
Petro Holdings Inc.	2187 Atlantic St	Stamford	CT	06902		203-325-5400	S	1,105	3.0
Time Oil Co.	PO Box 24447	Seattle	WA	98124	H Roger Holliday	206-285-2400	R	236*	0.2
Refron Inc.	38-18 33rd St	Long Island City	NY	11101	Jay Kestenbaum	718-392-8002	R	90*	<0.1
Nobles County Cooperative Oil Co.	1200 2nd Ave	Worthington	MN	56187	Billy Gordon	507-376-3104	R	32*	<0.1
Western Cooperative Co.	PO Drawer H	Alliance	NE	69301	Mark Thompson	308-762-3112	R	6*	<0.1

Source: Ward's Business Directory of U.S. Private and Public Companies, Volumes 1 and 2, 2005. The company type code used is as follows: P - Public, R - Private, S - Subsidiary, D - Division, J - Joint Venture, A - Affiliate, G - Group. Sales are in millions of dollars, employees are in thousands. An asterisk (*) indicates an estimated sales volume. The symbol < stands for 'less than'. Company names and addresses are truncated, in some cases, to fit into the available space.

OCCUPATIONS EMPLOYED BY DIRECT SELLING ESTABLISHMENTS

Occupation	% of Total 2004	Change to 2014	Occupation	% of Total 2004	Change to 2014
Truck drivers, heavy & tractor-trailer	12.8	1.6	Sales reps, wholesale & manufacturing, exc tech	2.5	1.6
Heating, air conditioning, & refrigeration mechanics	8.1	1.6	Laborers & freight, stock, & material movers, hand	2.5	-8.5
Driver/sales workers	8.0	0.9	Secretaries, except legal, medical, & executive	2.5	-14.5
Telemarketers	6.4	-22.4	First-line supervisors/managers of transporation workers	2.1	1.6
Truck drivers, light or delivery services	5.7	1.6	First-line supervisors/managers of retail sales workers	1.7	-6.5
Office clerks, general	4.2	-9.5	First-line supervisors/managers of office workers	1.6	-7.8
Customer service representatives	4.1	4.1	First-line supervisors of mechanics	1.3	1.6
Cashiers, except gaming	3.7	-8.5	Maintenance & repair workers, general	1.2	1.6
Retail salespersons	3.5	1.6	Installation, maintenance, & repair workers, nec	1.1	1.6
General & operations managers	3.3	0.6	Billing & posting clerks & machine operators	1.0	-14.4
Bookkeeping, accounting, & auditing clerks	2.7	-8.5			

Source: Industry-Occupation Matrix, Bureau of Labor Statistics. These data are reported based on 4-digit NAICS categories but have been matched to corresponding 6-digit NAICS industry codes. The change reported for each occupation to the year 2014 is a percent of growth or decline as estimated by the Bureau of Labor Statistics. The abbreviation nec stands for 'not elsewhere classified.'

LOCATION BY STATE AND REGIONAL CONCENTRATION

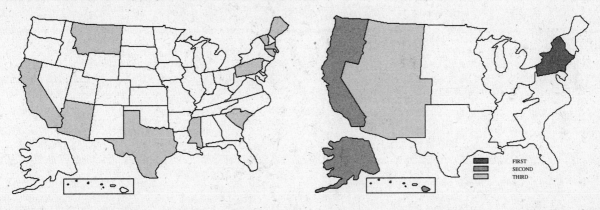

FIRST
SECOND
THIRD

INDUSTRY DATA BY STATE

State	Establishments Total (number)	% of U.S.	Employment Total (number)	% of U.S.	Per Estab.	Payroll Total ($ mil.)	Per Empl. ($)	Sales Total ($ mil.)	% of U.S.	Per Estab. ($)
Pennsylvania	33	16.2	105	20.2	3	2.0	18,819	14.0	21.7	422,909
California	36	17.6	123	23.7	3	2.0	16,114	11.0	17.1	305,361
Texas	9	4.4	37	7.1	4	0.9	24,027	7.0	10.9	775,667
New York	15	7.4	42	8.1	3	0.6	13,167	4.1	6.4	274,067
Maine	5	2.5	17	3.3	3	0.3	20,118	2.6	4.1	525,600
Arizona	7	3.4	18	3.5*	3	0.3	19,333	2.3	3.6	333,143
Connecticut	4	2.0	6	1.2	2	0.2	26,500	2.1	3.3	536,750
Mississippi	3	1.5	10	1.9	3	0.2	18,600	2.0	3.1	655,667
Illinois	8	3.9	16	3.1	2	0.4	22,375	1.9	3.0	238,750
Massachusetts	4	2.0	5	1.0	1	0.2	46,200	1.6	2.5	396,750
South Carolina	4	2.0	7	1.3	2	0.2	22,000	1.5	2.4	378,750
Virginia	7	3.4	15	2.9	2	0.2	13,467	1.1	1.7	159,286
Vermont	4	2.0	7	1.3	2	0.1	13,000	0.8	1.3	208,500
Washington	6	2.9	4	0.8	1	0.1	17,000	0.7	1.2	123,667

Continued on next page.

INDUSTRY DATA BY STATE - Continued

State	Establishments Total (number)	% of U.S.	Employment Total (number)	% of U.S.	Per Estab.	Payroll Total ($ mil.)	Per Empl. ($)	Sales Total ($ mil.)	% of U.S.	Per Estab. ($)
Maryland	4	2.0	14	2.7	4	0.1	7,857	0.7	1.1	170,000
Montana	3	1.5	13	2.5	4	0.2	13,000	0.6	1.0	210,667
Wisconsin	3	1.5	2	0.4	1	-	9,000	0.4	0.7	149,333
Minnesota	3	1.5	5	1.0	2	-	9,800	0.4	0.7	146,667
West Virginia	3	1.5	2	0.4	1	-	23,000	0.4	0.6	135,667
Tennessee	4	2.0	3	0.6	1	-	11,333	0.3	0.5	80,750
Utah	6	2.9	0-19	-	-	(D)	-	(D)	-	-
Colorado	3	1.5	0-19	-	-	(D)	-	(D)	-	-
New Mexico	3	1.5	0-19	-	-	(D)	-	(D)	-	-
Oregon	3	1.5	0-19	-	-	(D)	-	(D)	-	-
Florida	2	1.0	0-19	-	-	(D)	-	(D)	-	-
Georgia	2	1.0	0-19	-	-	(D)	-	(D)	-	-
Idaho	2	1.0	0-19	-	-	(D)	-	(D)	-	-
Nevada	2	1.0	0-19	-	-	(D)	-	(D)	-	-
New Hampshire	2	1.0	0-19	-	-	(D)	-	(D)	-	-
New Jersey	2	1.0	0-19	-	-	(D)	-	(D)	-	-
Ohio	2	1.0	0-19	-	-	(D)	-	(D)	-	-
Oklahoma	2	1.0	0-19	-	-	(D)	-	(D)	-	-
Alaska	1	0.5	0-19	-	-	(D)	-	(D)	-	-
Arkansas	1	0.5	0-19	-	-	(D)	-	(D)	-	-
Kansas	1	0.5	0-19	-	-	(D)	-	(D)	-	-
Kentucky	1	0.5	0-19	-	-	(D)	-	(D)	-	-
Nebraska	1	0.5	0-19	-	-	(D)	-	(D)	-	-
North Carolina	1	0.5	0-19	-	-	(D)	-	(D)	-	-
Rhode Island	1	0.5	0-19	-	-	(D)	-	(D)	-	-
Wyoming	1	0.5	0-19	-	-	(D)	-	(D)	-	-

Source: 2002 *Economic Census*. The states are in descending order of sales or establishments (if sales data are missing for the majority). The symbol (D) appears when data are withheld to prevent disclosure of competitive information. States marked with (D) are sorted by number of establishments. A dash (-) indicates that the data element cannot be calculated. Shaded *states* on the state map indicate those states which have proportionately greater representation in the industry than would be indicated by the states population; the ratio is based on total sales or number of establishments. Shaded *regions* indicate where the industry is regionally most concentrated.

NAICS 454390 - OTHER DIRECT SELLING ESTABLISHMENTS

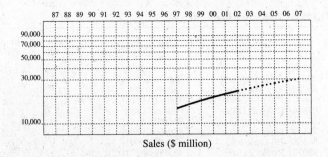

Sales ($ million)

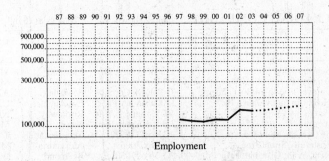

Employment

GENERAL STATISTICS

Year	Establishments (number)	Employment (number)	Payroll ($ million)	Sales ($ million)	Employees per Establishment (number)	Sales per Establishment ($)	Payroll per Employee ($)
1987	-	-	-	-	-	-	-
1988	-	-	-	-	-	-	-
1989	-	-	-	-	-	-	-
1990	-	-	-	-	-	-	-
1991	-	-	-	-	-	-	-
1992	-	-	-	-	-	-	-
1993	-	-	-	-	-	-	-
1994	-	-	-	-	-	-	-
1995	-	-	-	-	-	-	-
1996	-	-	-	-	8	-	-
1997	14,867	117,461	2,491.2	14,581.6	8	980,803	21,209
1998	14,607	113,059	2,597.5	16,141.5 e	8	1,105,050	22,975
1999	14,477	110,901	2,755.8	17,701.3 e	8	1,222,722	24,849
2000	14,973	116,816	2,988.6	19,261.2 e	8	1,286,396	25,584
2001	14,232	115,750	3,082.6	20,821.1 e	8	1,462,977	26,632
2002	22,416	148,702	3,776.2	22,381.0	7	998,436	25,394
2003	21,740	144,971	4,079.4	23,940.8 p	7	1,298,626 p	28,139
2004	21,901 p	146,618 p	4,174.3 p	25,500.7 p	7 p	1,333,644 p	28,885 p
2005	23,186 p	152,284 p	4,440.3 p	27,060.6 p	7 p	1,368,661 p	29,864 p
2006	24,471 p	157,951 p	4,706.3 p	28,620.4 p	6 p	1,403,679 p	30,843 p
2007	25,757 p	163,618 p	4,972.4 p	30,180.3 p	6 p	1,438,697 p	31,822 p

Source: *Economic Census of the United States*, 1997 and 2002. Establishment counts, employment, and payroll are from *County Business Patterns* for non-Census years. This is a newly defined industry. Data for prior years are unavailable at the time of publication but may become available over time. Values followed by 'p' are projections by the editors. Sales data for non-Census years are extrapolations, marked by 'e'.

INDICES OF CHANGE

Year	Establishments (number)	Employment (number)	Payroll ($ million)	Sales ($ million)	Employees per Establishment (number)	Sales per Establishment ($)	Payroll per Employee ($)
1987	-	-	-	-	-	-	-
1992	-	-	-	-	-	-	-
1993	-	-	-	-	-	-	-
1994	-	-	-	-	-	-	-
1995	-	-	-	-	-	-	-
1996	-	-	-	-	-	-	-
1997	66.3	79.0	66.0	65.2	119.1	98.2	83.5
1998	65.2	76.0	68.8	72.1 e	116.1	110.7	90.5
1999	64.6	74.6	73.0	79.1 e	116.1	122.5	97.9
2000	66.8	78.6	79.1	86.1 e	117.6	128.8	100.7
2001	63.5	77.8	81.6	93.0 e	122.1	146.5	104.9
2002	100.0	100.0	100.0	100.0	100.0	100.0	100.0
2003	97.0	97.5	108.0	107.0 p	100.5	130.1 p	110.8
2004	97.7 p	98.6 p	110.5 p	113.9 p	101.4 p	133.6 p	113.7 p
2005	103.4 p	102.4 p	117.6 p	120.9 p	98.5 p	137.1 p	117.6 p
2006	109.2 p	106.2 p	124.6 p	127.9 p	95.5 p	140.6 p	121.5 p
2007	114.9 p	110.0 p	131.7 p	134.8 p	92.6 p	144.1 p	125.3 p

Sources: Same as General Statistics. The values shown reflect change from the base year, 2002. Values above 100 mean greater than 2002, values below 100 mean less than 2002, and a value of 100 in the 1987-2001 or 2003-2007 period means same as 2002. Values followed by a 'p' are projections by the editors; 'e' stands for extrapolation. Data are the most recent available at this level of detail.

SELECTED RATIOS

For 2002	Avg. of All Retail	Analyzed Industry	Index	For 2002	Avg. of All Retail	Analyzed Industry	Index
Employees per Establishment	17	7	39	Sales per Employee	174,682	150,509	86
Payroll per Establishment	333,445	168,459	51	Sales per Establishment	3,332,269	998,436	30
Payroll per Employee	20,311	25,394	125	Expenses per Establishment	na	na	na

Sources: Same as General Statistics. The 'Average of All' column, Wholesale or Retail, represents the average of the sector reported for the most recent complete year available. The Index shows the relationship between the Average and the Analyzed Industry. For example, 100 means that they are equal; 500 that the Analyzed Industry is five times the average; 50 means that the Analyzed Industry is half the national average. The abbreviation 'na' is used to show that data are 'not available'.

LEADING COMPANIES   Number shown: **22**   Total sales ($ mil): **11,145**   Total employment (000): **45.0**

Company Name	Address				CEO Name	Phone	Co. Type	Sales ($ mil)	Empl. (000)
Schwan Food Co.	115 W College Dr	Marshall	MN	56258		507-532-3274	R	3,700*	24.0
Amway Corp.	PO Box 513	Ada	MI	49301	Doug DeVos	616-787-6000	S	2,443*	6.0
Forever Living Products Intern.	7501 E McCormick	Scottsdale	AZ	85258	Rex Maughan	480-998-8888	R	2,012	4.1
Herbalife International Inc.	1800 Century Pk, E	Los Angeles	CA	90067	Peter M Castleman	310-410-9600	S	1,337*	2.6
Party City Corp.	400 Commons Way	Rockaway	NJ	07866	Ralph D Dillon	973-983-0888	P	516	4.5
Inergy L.P.	2 Brush Creek Blvd	Kansas City	MO	64111		816-842-8181	P	482	1.1
SCOOTER Store Inc.	PO Box 310709	New Braunfels	TX	78132	Doug Harrison	830-608-9200	R	319	1.5
Tastefully Simple Inc.	PO Box 3006	Alexandria	MN	56308	Jill Blashack	320-763-0695	R	97	0.3
Rena-Ware Distributors Inc.	PO Box 97050	Redmond	WA	98073	Russel Zylstra	425-881-6171	R	53*	<0.1
Bluefly Inc.	42 W 39th St	New York	NY	10018	Alan Kane	212-944-8000	P	38	<0.1
UndercoverWear Inc.	30 Commerce Way	Tewksbury	MA	01876	Walter J James	978-851-8580	R	35*	<0.1
Belmont Springs Water Inc.	36 Country Club Ln	Belmont	MA	02478		617-489-4752	S	32*	0.2
Geerlings and Wade Inc.	960 Turnpike St	Canton	MA	02021	Huib E Geerlings	781-821-4152	P	28	<0.1
Sparkletts D S Waters L.P.	3302 W Earll Dr	Phoenix	AZ	85017		602-415-3201	R	17*	0.1
Howe Coffee Co.	PO Box 269	Grove City	PA	16127	Ernest May	724-458-9410	R	13*	0.1
Pro-Cut International L.L.C.	10 Technology Dr 4	West Lebanon	NH	03784		603-298-5200	R	7*	<0.1
Rich-United Corp.	PO Box 4999	Sanford	FL	32772	Brent Adamson	407-322-3663	R	4*	<0.1
Jordan Group	PO Box 090045	Milwaukee	WI	53209	Lawrence Jordan	414-431-0100	R	4*	<0.1
C and S Enterprises Inc.	1801 Commerce Ct	Columbia	MO	65202	Bill Schulz	573-874-6147	R	3*	<0.1
Brevard Water Conditioning Inc.	PO Box 9307	Daytona Beach	FL	32120	Michael Carey	386-274-5036	R	2*	<0.1
tradeair.com Inc.	1600 W Cornell	Milwaukee	WI	53209	Bill Morales	414-875-2188	R	2*	<0.1
Tupperware U.S. Inc.	PO Box 2353	Orlando	FL	32802	Alan D Kennedy	407-847-3111	S	1*	<0.1

Source: Ward's Business Directory of U.S. Private and Public Companies, Volumes 1 and 2, 2005. The company type code used is as follows: P - Public, R - Private, S - Subsidiary, D - Division, J - Joint Venture, A - Affiliate, G - Group. Sales are in millions of dollars, employees are in thousands. An asterisk (*) indicates an estimated sales volume. The symbol < stands for 'less than'. Company names and addresses are truncated, in some cases, to fit into the available space.

OCCUPATIONS EMPLOYED BY DIRECT SELLING ESTABLISHMENTS

Occupation	% of Total 2004	Change to 2014	Occupation	% of Total 2004	Change to 2014
Truck drivers, heavy & tractor-trailer	12.8	1.6	Sales reps, wholesale & manufacturing, exc tech	2.5	1.6
Heating, air conditioning, & refrigeration mechanics	8.1	1.6	Laborers & freight, stock, & material movers, hand	2.5	-8.5
Driver/sales workers	8.0	0.9	Secretaries, except legal, medical, & executive	2.5	-14.5
Telemarketers	6.4	-22.4	First-line supervisors/managers of transporation workers	2.1	1.6
Truck drivers, light or delivery services	5.7	1.6	First-line supervisors/managers of retail sales workers	1.7	-6.5
Office clerks, general	4.2	-9.5	First-line supervisors/managers of office workers	1.6	-7.8
Customer service representatives	4.1	4.1	First-line supervisors of mechanics	1.3	1.6
Cashiers, except gaming	3.7	-8.5	Maintenance & repair workers, general	1.2	1.6
Retail salespersons	3.5	1.6	Installation, maintenance, & repair workers, nec	1.1	1.6
General & operations managers	3.3	0.6	Billing & posting clerks & machine operators	1.0	-14.4
Bookkeeping, accounting, & auditing clerks	2.7	-8.5			

Source: Industry-Occupation Matrix, Bureau of Labor Statistics. These data are reported based on 4-digit NAICS categories but have been matched to corresponding 6-digit NAICS industry codes. The change reported for each occupation to the year 2014 is a percent of growth or decline as estimated by the Bureau of Labor Statistics. The abbreviation nec stands for 'not elsewhere classified.'

LOCATION BY STATE AND REGIONAL CONCENTRATION

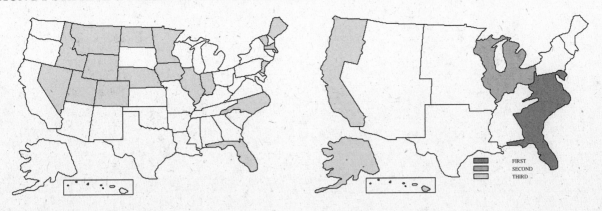

FIRST
SECOND
THIRD

INDUSTRY DATA BY STATE

State	Establishments		Employment			Payroll		Sales		
	Total (number)	% of U.S.	Total (number)	% of U.S.	Per Estab.	Total ($ mil.)	Per Empl. ($)	Total ($ mil.)	% of U.S.	Per Estab. ($)
California	2,170	9.9	16,359	11.4	8	455.8	27,865	2,475.1	11.5	1,140,593
Illinois	1,010	4.6	8,720	6.1	9	250.3	28,705	1,883.3	8.8	1,864,652
New York	1,366	6.2	8,460	5.9	6	240.4	28,420	1,486.8	6.9	1,088,438
Texas	1,375	6.2	9,246	6.5	7	236.1	25,534	1,221.9	5.7	888,633
Florida	1,598	7.3	8,471	5.9	5	202.9	23,947	1,152.2	5.4	721,023
Pennsylvania	888	4.0	6,630	4.6	7	174.8	26,367	915.4	4.3	1,030,832
New Jersey	640	2.9	4,388	3.1	7	133.2	30,355	848.1	3.9	1,325,133
Minnesota	571	2.6	4,254	3.0	7	129.8	30,513	698.6	3.3	1,223,545
Ohio	778	3.5	4,969	3.5	6	130.6	26,293	669.1	3.1	859,990
Massachusetts	458	2.1	3,692	2.6	8	117.4	31,804	663.6	3.1	1,448,952
Indiana	559	2.5	3,921	2.7	7	93.5	23,850	620.7	2.9	1,110,449
Michigan	692	3.1	4,338	3.0	6	111.9	25,787	594.0	2.8	858,447
North Carolina	590	2.7	3,618	2.5	6	79.3	21,912	577.6	2.7	979,007
Iowa	358	1.6	2,240	1.6	6	55.9	24,956	489.9	2.3	1,368,508
Virginia	563	2.6	3,866	2.7	7	82.2	21,251	434.2	2.0	771,176
Georgia	526	2.4	3,171	2.2	6	74.5	23,505	432.3	2.0	821,825
Missouri	533	2.4	3,008	2.1	6	81.3	27,026	429.3	2.0	805,379
Wisconsin	515	2.3	2,791	2.0	5	73.6	26,360	413.3	1.9	802,548
Maryland	450	2.0	2,962	2.1	7	86.8	29,299	397.5	1.9	883,256
Washington	568	2.6	3,194	2.2	6	76.2	23,850	387.3	1.8	681,886
Colorado	492	2.2	3,190	2.2	6	69.3	21,717	373.3	1.7	758,646
Nebraska	230	1.0	1,543	1.1	7	33.2	21,505	355.1	1.7	1,544,087
Louisiana	307	1.4	2,222	1.6	7	54.4	24,499	333.5	1.6	1,086,173
Tennessee	351	1.6	2,276	1.6	6	48.2	21,188	300.4	1.4	855,912
Utah	232	1.1	2,132	1.5	9	43.1	20,238	259.2	1.2	1,117,405
Oregon	338	1.5	1,542	1.1	5	34.7	22,532	217.1	1.0	642,447
Oklahoma	247	1.1	1,562	1.1	6	36.2	23,198	211.3	1.0	855,607
Alabama	264	1.2	1,268	0.9	5	24.4	19,230	205.7	1.0	778,985
Nevada	190	0.9	1,301	0.9	7	36.8	28,263	194.6	0.9	1,024,216
Kentucky	271	1.2	1,598	1.1	6	34.0	21,250	194.1	0.9	716,277
South Carolina	309	1.4	1,691	1.2	5	35.2	20,832	185.8	0.9	601,375
Connecticut	194	0.9	1,388	1.0	7	36.3	26,177	183.1	0.9	943,655
Kansas	289	1.3	1,457	1.0	5	33.3	22,845	178.4	0.8	617,190
Arkansas	178	0.8	780	0.5	4	17.0	21,840	111.1	0.5	624,360
Maine	121	0.5	821	0.6	7	18.8	22,843	105.3	0.5	870,612
North Dakota	112	0.5	620	0.4	6	15.1	24,282	99.7	0.5	890,446
Idaho	152	0.7	727	0.5	5	17.8	24,476	99.2	0.5	652,395
New Mexico	132	0.6	799	0.6	6	18.0	22,527	92.8	0.4	702,955
Montana	132	0.6	688	0.5	5	12.5	18,147	87.1	0.4	660,098
Mississippi	165	0.7	907	0.6	5	15.5	17,067	83.1	0.4	503,382
New Hampshire	91	0.4	575	0.4	6	14.0	24,355	74.2	0.3	815,901
Vermont	79	0.4	360	0.3	5	10.6	29,400	69.1	0.3	874,835
West Virginia	94	0.4	496	0.3	5	11.0	22,252	57.3	0.3	609,862
Hawaii	81	0.4	450	0.3	6	8.5	18,780	50.8	0.2	627,333
Delaware	67	0.3	361	0.3	5	7.7	21,224	40.5	0.2	604,060
Wyoming	60	0.3	344	0.2	6	7.0	20,384	38.4	0.2	639,450
Alaska	48	0.2	153	0.1	3	2.7	17,804	19.1	0.1	397,500
Arizona	380	1.7	1000-2499	-	-	(D)	-	(D)	-	-
South Dakota	114	0.5	500-999	-	-	(D)	-	(D)	-	-
Rhode Island	63	0.3	250-499	-	-	(D)	-	(D)	-	-
D.C.	20	0.1	100-249	-	-	(D)	-	(D)	-	-

Source: 2002 *Economic Census*. The states are in descending order of sales or establishments (if sales data are missing for the majority). The symbol (D) appears when data are withheld to prevent disclosure of competitive information. States marked with (D) are sorted by number of establishments. A dash (-) indicates that the data element cannot be calculated. Shaded *states* on the state map indicate those states which have proportionately greater representation in the industry than would be indicated by the states population; the ratio is based on total sales or number of establishments. Shaded *regions* indicate where the industry is regionally most concentrated.

Indexes

NAICS INDEX

PRODUCT/ACTIVITY INDEX

COMPANY INDEX

NAICS INDEX

The NAICS Index shows industries sorted by the *Annual Survey of Manufactures'* NAICS number and then by name. Roman numerals refer to volume numbers. Volume designations are followed by page references. The abbreviation nec stands for 'not elsewhere classified.'

Food Manufacturing

311111 - Dog and Cat Food Manufacturing, p. I-3
311119 - Animal Food Manufacturing, nec, p. I-8
31121M - Flour Milling and Malt Manufacturing, p. I-14
311221 - Wet Corn Milling, p. I-21
311225 - Fats and Oils Refining and Blending, p. I-25
31122N - Soybean and Other Oilseed Processing, p. I-30
311230 - Breakfast Cereal Manufacturing, p. I-35
311313 - Beet Sugar Manufacturing, p. I-39
31131N - Sugar Cane Mills and Refining, p. I-43
311320 - Chocolate and Confectionery Manufacturing from Cacao Beans, p. I-47
311330 - Confectionery Manufacturing from Purchased Chocolate, p. I-51
311340 - Nonchocolate Confectionery Manufacturing, p. I-56
31141M - Frozen Food Manufacturing, p. I-61
31142M - Fruit and Vegetable Canning, Pickling, and Drying, p. I-67
311513 - Cheese Manufacturing, p. I-75
311514 - Dry, Condensed, and Evaporated Dairy Product Manufacturing, p. I-80
31151N - Fluid Milk and Butter Manufacturing, p. I-85
311520 - Ice Cream and Frozen Dessert Manufacturing, p. I-91
311615 - Poultry Processing, p. I-96
31161N - Animal (Except Poultry) Slaughtering and Processing, p. I-101
31171M - Seafood Product Preparation and Packaging, p. I-109
31181M - Bread and Bakery Product Manufacturing, p. I-115
31182M - Cookie, Cracker, and Pasta Manufacturing, p. I-123
311830 - Tortilla Manufacturing, p. I-132
31191M - Snack Food Manufacturing, p. I-136
311920 - Coffee and Tea Manufacturing, p. I-142
311930 - Flavoring Syrup and Concentrate Manufacturing, p. I 146
31194M - Seasoning and Dressing Manufacturing, p. I-151
31199M - Food Manufacturing, nec, p. I-157

Beverage & Tobacco Products

31211M - Soft Drink and Ice Manufacturing, p. I-164
312120 - Breweries, p. I-171
312130 - Wineries, p. I-176
312140 - Distilleries, p. I-180
312210 - Tobacco Steaming and Redrying, p. I-184
31222M - Tobacco Product Manufacturing, p. I-187

Textile Mills

31311M - Fiber, Yarn, and Thread Mills, p. I-191
313210 - Broadwoven Fabric Mills, p. I-197
31322M - Narrow Fabric Mills and Schiffli Machine Embroidery, p. I-202
313230 - Nonwoven Fabric Mills, p. I-207
31324M - Knit Fabric Mills, p. I-212
31331M - Textile and Fabric Finishing Mills, p. I-217
313320 - Fabric Coating Mills, p. I-223

Textile Mill Products

314110 - Carpet and Rug Mills, p. I-228
31412M - Curtain and Linen Mills, p. I-233
31491M - Textile Bag and Canvas Mills, p. I-238
314991 - Rope, Cordage, and Twine Mills, p. I-243
314992 - Tire Cord and Tire Fabric Mills, p. I-247
314999 - Textile Product Mills, nec, p. I-250

Apparel Manufacturing

31511M - Hosiery and Sock Mills, p. I-255
31519M - Apparel Knitting Mills, nec, p. I-261
31521M - Cut and Sew Apparel Contractors, p. I-266
31522M - Men's and Boys' Cut and Sew Apparel Manufacturing, p. I-271
31523M - Women's and Girls' Cut and Sew Apparel Manufacturing, p. I-278
31529M - Cut and Sew Apparel Manufacturing, nec, p. I-284
31599M - Apparel Accessories and Other Apparel Manufacturing, p. I-289

Leather & Allied Products

316110 - Leather and Hide Tanning and Finishing, p. I-295
31621M - Footwear Manufacturing, p. I-299
31699M - Leather and Allied Product Manufacturing, nec, p. I-305

Wood Products Manufacturing

32111M - Sawmills and Wood Preservation, p. I-311
321219 - Reconstituted Wood Product Manufacturing, p. I-318
32121N - Veneer and Plywood Manufacturing, p. I-323
32121P - Engineered Wood Product Manufacturing, p. I-328
32191M - Millwork, p. I-333
321920 - Wood Container and Pallet Manufacturing, p. I-342
321991 - Manufactured Home (Mobile Home) Manufacturing, p. I-347
321992 - Prefabricated Wood Building Manufacturing, p. I-352
321999 - Wood Product Manufacturing, nec, p. I-357

Paper Manufacturing

322110 - Pulp Mills, p. I-362
32212M - Paper and Newsprint Mills, p. I-367
322130 - Paperboard Mills, p. I-373
32221M - Paperboard Container Manufacturing, p. I-378
32222N - Coated and Laminated Paper and Packaging Manufacturing, p. I-387
32222P - Coated, Uncoated and Multiwall Bag and Packaging Manufacturing, p. I-394
32223M - Stationery Product Manufacturing, p. I-402
322291 - Sanitary Paper Product Manufacturing, p. I-410
322299 - Converted Paper Product Manufacturing, nec, p. I-414

Printing & Related Support

32311M - Printing, p. I-419
32312M - Support Activities for Printing, p. I-435

Petroleum & Coal Products

324110 - Petroleum Refineries, p. I-442
324121 - Asphalt Paving Mixture and Block Manufacturing, p. I-447
324122 - Asphalt Shingle and Coating Materials Manufacturing, p. I-452
324191 - Petroleum Lubricating Oil and Grease Manufacturing, p. I-457
324199 - Petroleum and Coal Products Manufacturing, nec, p. I-462
325110 - Petrochemical Manufacturing, p. I-466
325120 - Industrial Gas Manufacturing, p. I-470
32513M - Synthetic Dye and Pigment Manufacturing, p. I-474
325181 - Alkalies and Chlorine Manufacturing, p. I-479
325182 - Carbon Black Manufacturing, p. I-483
325188 - Basic Inorganic Chemical Manufacturing, nec, p. I-487
32519M - Basic Organic Chemical Manufacturing, nec, p. I-492
325211 - Plastics Material and Resin Manufacturing, p. I-499
325212 - Synthetic Rubber Manufacturing, p. I-504
32522M - Artificial and Synthetic Fibers and Filaments Manufacturing, p. I-509
325311 - Nitrogenous Fertilizer Manufacturing, p. I-515
325312 - Phosphatic Fertilizer Manufacturing, p. I-519
325314 - Fertilizer (Mixing Only) Manufacturing, p. I-523
325320 - Pesticide and Other Agricultural Chemical Manufacturing, p. I-528
325411 - Medicinal and Botanical Manufacturing, p. I-533
325412 - Pharmaceutical Preparation Manufacturing, p. I-538
325413 - In-vitro Diagnostic Substance Manufacturing, p. I-543
325414 - Biological Product (Except Diagnostic) Manufacturing, p. I-548
325510 - Paint and Coating Manufacturing, p. I-553
325520 - Adhesive Manufacturing, p. I-559
32561M - Soap and Cleaning Compound Manufacturing, p. I-565
325620 - Toilet Preparation Manufacturing, p. I-574
325910 - Printing Ink Manufacturing, p. I-579
325920 - Explosives Manufacturing, p. I-584
325991 - Custom Compounding of Purchased Resins, p. I-588
32599N - Chemical Product and Preparation Manufacturing, nec, p. I-594

Plastics & Rubber

326111 - Plastics Bag Manufacturing, p. I-602
326112 - Plastics Packaging Film and Sheet Manufacturing, p. I-608
326113 - Unlaminated Plastics Film and Sheet (Except Packaging) Manufacturing, p. I-614
326121 - Unsupported Plastics Profile Shape Manufacturing, p. I-620
326122 - Plastics Pipe and Pipe Fitting Manufacturing, p. I-625
326130 - Laminated Plastics Plate, Sheet, and Shape Manufacturing, p. I-630
326140 - Polystyrene Foam Product Manufacturing, p. I-635
326150 - Urethane and Other Foam Product (Except Polystyrene) Manufacturing, p. I-640
326160 - Plastics Bottle Manufacturing, p. I-645
32619M - Plastics Product Manufacturing, p. I-650
32621M - Tire Manufacturing, p. I-659
326220 - Rubber and Plastics Hoses and Belting Manufacturing, p. I-664
32629M - Rubber Product Manufacturing, nec, p. I-669

Nonmetallic Mineral Products

327111 - Vitreous China Plumbing Fixture and China and Earthenware Bathroom Accessories Manufacturing, p. I-676
327112 - Vitreous China, Fine Earthenware, and Other Pottery Product Manufacturing, p. I-680
327113 - Porcelain Electrical Supply Manufacturing, p. I-685
327121 - Brick and Structural Clay Tile Manufacturing, p. I-690
327122 - Ceramic Wall and Floor Tile Manufacturing, p. I-694
327123 - Structural Clay Product Manufacturing, nec, p. I-698
32712N - Refractory Manufacturing, p. I-702
327211 - Flat Glass Manufacturing, p. I-708
327212 - Pressed and Blown Glass and Glassware Manufacturing, nec, p. I-712
327213 - Glass Container Manufacturing, p. I-717
327215 - Glass Product Manufacturing Made of Purchased Glass, p. I-721
327310 - Cement Manufacturing, p. I-726
327320 - Ready-mix Concrete Manufacturing, p. I-731
32733M - Concrete Pipe, Brick, and Block Manufacturing, p. I-736
327390 - Concrete Product Manufacturing, nec, p. I-742
327410 - Lime Manufacturing, p. I-747
327420 - Gypsum Product Manufacturing, p. I-751
327910 - Abrasive Product Manufacturing, p. I-755
327991 - Cut Stone and Stone Product Manufacturing, p. I-761
327992 - Ground or Treated Mineral and Earth Manufacturing, p. I-766
327993 - Mineral Wool Manufacturing, p. I-770
327999 - Nonmetallic Mineral Product Manufacturing, nec, p. I-775

Primary Metals Manufacturing

33111M - Iron and Steel Mills and Ferroalloy Manufacturing, p. I-779
331210 - Iron and Steel Pipe and Tube Manufacturing from Purchased Steel, p. I-787
33122M - Rolling and Drawing of Purchased Steel, p. I-792
331311 - Alumina Refining, p. I-799
331312 - Primary Aluminum Production, p. I-802
331314 - Secondary Smelting and Alloying of Aluminum, p. I-806
331316 - Aluminum Extruded Product Manufacturing, p. I-810
33131N - Aluminum Rolling and Drawing, p. I-815
331411 - Primary Smelting and Refining of Copper, p. I-821
331419 - Primary Smelting and Refining of Nonferrous Metal (Except Copper and Aluminum), p. I-824
33142M - Copper Rolling, Drawing, Extruding, and Alloying, p. I-829
33149M - Nonferrous Metal (Except Copper and Aluminum) Rolling, Drawing, Extruding, and Alloying, p. I-836
33151M - Ferrous Metal Foundries, p. I-844
33152N - Aluminum Foundries, p. I-851
33152P - Nonaluminum Foundries, p. I-856

Fabricated Metal Products

332114 - Custom Roll Forming, p. I-862
332117 - Powder Metallurgy Parts Manufacturing, p. I-866
33211N - Forging, p. I-871
33211P - Crown, Closure and Metal Stamping Manufacturing, p. I-878
33221N - Cutlery, Kitchen Utensil, Pot and Pan Manufacturing, p. II-885
33221P - Hand Tool and Saw Blade Manufacturing, p. II-891
33231M - Plate Work and Fabricated Structural Product Manufacturing, p. II-898
33232M - Ornamental, Sheet and Architectural Metal Work Manufacturing, p. II-907
332410 - Power Boiler and Heat Exchanger Manufacturing, p. II-917
332420 - Metal Tank (Heavy Gauge) Manufacturing, p. II-922
33243M - Metal Can, Box, and Other Metal Container (Light Gauge) Manufacturing, p. II-927
332510 - Hardware Manufacturing, p. II-932
33261M - Spring and Wire Product Manufacturing, p. II-938
332710 - Machine Shops, p. II-944
332721 - Precision Tuned Product Manufacturing, p. II-951
332722 - Bolt, Nut, Screw, Rivet, and Washer Manufacturing, p. II-957
33281M - Coating, Engraving, Heat Treating, and Allied Activities, p. II-963
332913 - Plumbing Fixture Fitting and Trim Manufacturing, p. II-973

Numbers following p. or pp. are page references. Roman numerals indicate volume numbers. Page references are to the starting pages of NAICS industries.

33291N - Valves and Fittings Manufacturing, Non-plumbing, p. II-979

332991 - Ball and Roller Bearing Manufacturing, p. II-987

332992 - Small Arms Ammunition Manufacturing, p. II-992

332993 - Ammunition (Except Small Arms) Manufacturing, p. II-996

332994 - Small Arms Manufacturing, p. II-1000

332995 - Ordnance and Accessories Manufacturing, nec, p. II-1004

332996 - Fabricated Pipe and Pipe Fitting Manufacturing, p. II-1008

33299N - Fabricated Metal Products Manufacturing, nec, p. II-1013

Machinery Manufacturing

333111 - Farm Machinery and Equipment Manufacturing, p. II-1022

333112 - Lawn and Garden Tractor and Home Lawn and Garden Equipment Manufacturing, p. II-1027

333120 - Construction Machinery Manufacturing, p. II-1032

33313M - Mining and Oil and Gas Field Machinery Manufacturing, p. II-1038

333210 - Sawmill and Woodworking Machinery Manufacturing, p. II-1045

333220 - Plastics and Rubber Industry Machinery Manufacturing, p. II-1050

333295 - Semiconductor Machinery Manufacturing, p. II-1055

33329N - Machinery Manufacturing, nec, p. II-1060

333313 - Office Machinery Manufacturing, p. II-1076

333314 - Optical Instrument and Lens Manufacturing, p. II-1081

333315 - Photographic and Photocopying Equipment Manufacturing, p. II-1086

33331N - Commercial and Service Industry Machinery Manufacturing, nec, p. II-1091

333414 - Heating Equipment (Except Warm Air Furnaces) Manufacturing, p. II-1100

333415 - Air-conditioning and Warm Air Heating Equipment and Commercial and Industrial Refrigeration Equipment Manufacturing, p. II-1105

33341N - Ventilation Equipment Manufacturing, p. II-1111

333511 - Industrial Mold Manufacturing, p. II-1118

333512 - Machine Tool (Metal Cutting Types) Manufacturing, p. II-1123

333513 - Machine Tool (Metal Forming Types) Manufacturing, p. II-1128

333514 - Special Die and Tool, Die Set, Jig, and Fixture Manufacturing, p. II-1133

333515 - Cutting Tool and Machine Tool Accessory Manufacturing, p. II-1139

333516 - Rolling Mill Machinery and Equipment Manufacturing, p. II-1146

333518 - Metalworking Machinery Manufacturing, nec, p. II-1151

333611 - Turbine and Turbine Generator Set Unit Manufacturing, p. II-1156

333612 - Speed Changer, Industrial High-speed Drive, and Gear Manufacturing, p. II-1161

333613 - Mechanical Power Transmission Equipment Manufacturing, p. II-1167

333618 - Engine Equipment Manufacturing, nec, p. II-1172

333911 - Pump and Pumping Equipment Manufacturing, p. II-1178

333912 - Air and Gas Compressor Manufacturing, p. II-1183

333913 - Measuring and Dispensing Pump Manufacturing, p. II-1188

33392M - Material Handling Equipment Manufacturing, p. II-1193

333991 - Power-driven Hand Tool Manufacturing, p. II-1206

333993 - Packaging Machinery Manufacturing, p. II-1211

333994 - Industrial Process Furnace and Oven Manufacturing, p. II-1216

33399N - Fluid Power Equipment Manufacturing, p. II-1221

33399P - General Purpose Machinery Manufacturing, nec, p. II-1228

Computers & Electronics

334111 - Electronic Computer Manufacturing, p. II-1237

334112 - Computer Storage Device Manufacturing, p. II-1242

334113 - Computer Terminal Manufacturing, p. II-1247

334119 - Computer Peripheral Equipment Manufacturing, nec, p. II-1251

334210 - Telephone Apparatus Manufacturing, p. II-1256

334220 - Radio and Television Broadcasting and Wireless Communications Equipment Manufacturing, p. II-1261

334290 - Communications Equipment Manufacturing, nec, p. II-1266

334310 - Audio and Video Equipment Manufacturing, p. II-1271

334411 - Electron Tube Manufacturing, p. II-1276

334412 - Bare Printed Circuit Board Manufacturing, p. II-1281

334413 - Semiconductor and Related Device Manufacturing, p. II-1286

334414 - Electronic Capacitor Manufacturing, p. II-1291

334415 - Electronic Resistor Manufacturing, p. II-1296

334416 - Electronic Coil, Transformer, and Other Inductor Manufacturing, p. II-1301

334417 - Electronic Connector Manufacturing, p. II-1306

334418 - Printed Circuit Assembly (Electronic Assembly) Manufacturing, p. II-1311

334419 - Electronic Component Manufacturing, nec, p. II-1316

334510 - Electromedical and Electrotherapeutic Apparatus Manufacturing, p. II-1321

334511 - Search, Detection, Navigation, Guidance, Aeronautical, and Nautical System and Instrument Manufacturing, p. II-1326

334512 - Automatic Environmental Controls for Residential, Commercial, and Appliance Use, p. II-1331

334513 - Instruments and Related Products for Measuring, Displaying and Controlling Industrial Process Variables, p. II-1336

334514 - Totalizing Fluid Meter and Counting Device Manufacturing, p. II-1341

334515 - Instrument Manufacturing for Measuring and Testing Electricity and Electrical Signals, p. II-1346

334516 - Analytical Laboratory Instrument Manufacturing, p. II-1351

334517 - Irradiation Apparatus Manufacturing, p. II-1356

334518 - Watch, Clock, and Parts Manufacturing, p. II-1361

334519 - Measuring and Controlling Device Manufacturing, nec, p. II-1366

334611 - Software Reproducing, p. II-1371

334612 - Prerecorded Compact Disc (Except Software), Tape, and Record Reproducing, p. II-1375

334613 - Magnetic and Optical Recording Media Manufacturing, p. II-1380

Electrical Equipment

335110 - Electric Lamp Bulb and Parts Manufacturing, p. II-1385

33512M - Lighting Fixture Manufacturing, p. II-1389

33521M - Small Electrical Appliance Manufacturing, p. II-1396

335221 - Household Cooking Appliance Manufacturing, p. II-1403

335222 - Household Refrigerator and Home Freezer Manufacturing, p. II-1408

335224 - Household Laundry Equipment Manufacturing, p. II-1412

335228 - Major Household Appliance Manufacturing, nec, p. II-1416

335311 - Power, Distribution, and Specialty Transformer Manufacturing, p. II-1420

335312 - Motor and Generator Manufacturing, p. II-1426

335313 - Switchgear and Switchboard Apparatus Manufacturing, p. II-1431

335314 - Relay and Industrial Control Manufacturing, p. II-1436

335911 - Storage Battery Manufacturing, p. II-1441

335912 - Primary Battery Manufacturing, p. II-1446

33592M - Communication and Energy Wire and Cable Manufacturing, p. II-1450

33593M - Wiring Device Manufacturing, p. II-1456

335991 - Carbon and Graphite Product Manufacturing, p. II-1462

335999 - Electrical Equipment and Component Manufacturing, nec, p. II-1467

Transportation Equipment

336111 - Automobile Manufacturing, p. II-1472

336112 - Light Truck and Utility Vehicle Manufacturing, p. II-1477

Numbers following p. or pp. are page references. Roman numerals indicate volume numbers. Page references are to the starting pages of NAICS industries.

2237

336120 - Heavy Duty Truck Manufacturing, p. II-1481

336211 - Motor Vehicle Body and Trailer Manufacturing, p. II-1485

336212 - Truck Trailer Manufacturing, p. II-1490

336213 - Motor Home Manufacturing, p. II-1495

336214 - Travel Trailer and Camper Manufacturing, p. II-1499

33631M - Motor Vehicle Gasoline Engine and Engine Parts Manufacturing, p. II-1504

33632M - Motor Vehicle Electrical and Electronic Equipment Manufacturing, p. II-1511

336330 - Motor Vehicle Steering and Suspension Component (Except Spring) Manufacturing, p. II-1518

336340 - Motor Vehicle Brake System Manufacturing, p. II-1523

336350 - Motor Vehicle Transmission and Power Train Parts Manufacturing, p. II-1529

336360 - Motor Vehicle Seating and Interior Trim Manufacturing, p. II-1535

336370 - Motor Vehicle Metal Stamping, p. II-1540

336391 - Motor Vehicle Air-conditioning Manufacturing, p. II-1545

336399 - Motor Vehicle Parts Manufacturing, nec, p. II-1550

336411 - Aircraft Manufacturing, p. II-1556

336412 - Aircraft Engine and Engine Parts Manufacturing, p. II-1561

336413 - Aircraft Parts and Auxiliary Equipment Manufacturing, nec, p. II-1566

336414 - Guided Missile and Space Vehicle Manufacturing, p. II-1571

336415 - Guided Missile and Space Vehicle Propulsion Unit and Propulsion Unit Parts Manufacturing, p. II-1575

336419 - Guided Missile and Space Vehicle Parts and Auxiliary Equipment Manufacturing, nec, p. II-1579

336510 - Railroad Rolling Stock Manufacturing, p. II-1583

336611 - Ship Building and Repairing, p. II-1588

336612 - Boat Building, p. II-1593

336991 - Motorcycle, Bicycle, and Parts Manufacturing, p. II-1598

336992 - Military Armored Vehicle, Tank, and Tank Component Manufacturing, p. II-1602

336999 - Transportation Equipment Manufacturing, nec, p. II-1606

Furniture & Related Products

337110 - Wood Kitchen Cabinet and Counter Top Manufacturing, p. II-1610

337121 - Upholstered Household Furniture Manufacturing, p. II-1615

337122 - Nonupholstered Wood Household Furniture Manufacturing, p. II-1620

337127 - Institutional Furniture Manufacturing, p. II-1626

33712N - Household Nonupholstered Furniture, nec, p. II-1631

337212 - Custom Architectural Woodwork and Millwork Manufacturing, p. II-1638

337215 - Showcase, Partition, Shelving, and Locker Manufacturing, p. II-1643

33721N - Office Furniture Manufacturing, p. II-1649

337910 - Mattress Manufacturing, p. II-1656

337920 - Blind and Shade Manufacturing, p. II-1661

Miscellaneous Manufacturing

339111 - Laboratory Apparatus and Furniture Manufacturing, p. II-1665

339112 - Surgical and Medical Instrument Manufacturing, p. II-1670

339113 - Surgical Appliance and Supplies Manufacturing, p. II-1675

339114 - Dental Equipment and Supplies Manufacturing, p. II-1681

339115 - Ophthalmic Goods Manufacturing, p. II-1686

339116 - Dental Laboratories, p. II-1691

33991M - Jewelry and Silverware Manufacturing, p. II-1695

339920 - Sporting and Athletic Goods Manufacturing, p. II-1701

33993M - Doll, Toy, and Game Manufacturing, p. II-1707

33994M - Office Supplies (Except Paper) Manufacturing, p. II-1713

339950 - Sign Manufacturing, p. II-1719

339991 - Gasket, Packing, and Sealing Device Manufacturing, p. II-1724

339992 - Musical Instrument Manufacturing, p. II-1730

339993 - Fastener, Button, Needle, and Pin Manufacturing, p. II-1734

339994 - Broom, Brush, and Mop Manufacturing, p. II-1739

339995 - Burial Casket Manufacturing, p. II-1744

339999 - Miscellaneous Manufacturing, nec, p. II-1748

Wholesale Trade, Durable Goods

423110 - Automobile and Other Motor Vehicle Merchant Wholesalers, p. III-1757

423120 - Motor Vehicle Supplies and New Parts Merchant Wholesalers, p. III-1761

423130 - Tire and Tube Merchant Wholesalers, p. III-1765

423140 - Motor Vehicle Parts (Used) Merchant Wholesalers, p. III-1769

423210 - Furniture Merchant Wholesalers, p. III-1773

423220 - Home Furnishing Merchant Wholesalers, p. III-1777

423310 - Lumber, Plywood, Millwork, and Wood Panel Merchant Wholesalers, p. III-1781

423320 - Brick, Stone, and Related Construction Material Merchant Wholesalers, p. III-1785

423330 - Roofing, Siding, and Insulation Material Merchant Wholesalers, p. III-1789

423390 - Other Construction Material Merchant Wholesalers, p. III-1793

423410 - Photographic Equipment and Supplies Merchant Wholesalers, p. III-1797

423420 - Office Equipment Merchant Wholesalers, p. III-1800

423430 - Computer and Computer Peripheral Equipment and Software Merchant Wholesalers, p. III-1804

423440 - Other Commercial Equipment Merchant Wholesalers, p. III-1808

423450 - Medical, Dental, and Hospital Equipment and Supplies Merchant Wholesalers, p. III-1812

423460 - Ophthalmic Goods Merchant Wholesalers, p. III-1816

423490 - Other Professional Equipment and Supplies Merchant Wholesalers, p. III-1819

423510 - Metal Service Centers and Other Metal Merchant Wholesalers, p. III-1823

423520 - Coal and Other Mineral and Ore Merchant Wholesalers, p. III-1827

423610 - Electrical Apparatus and Equipment, Wiring Supplies, and Related Equipment Merchant Wholesalers, p. III-1830

423620 - Electrical and Electronic Appliance, Television and Radio Set Merchant Wholesalers, p. III-1834

423690 - Other Electronic Parts and Equipment Merchant Wholesalers, p. III-1838

423710 - Hardware Merchant Wholesalers, p. III-1842

423720 - Plumbing and Heating Equipment and Supplies (Hydronics) Merchant Wholesalers, p. III-1846

423730 - Warm Air Heating and Air-conditioning Equipment and Supplies Merchant Wholesalers, p. III-1850

423740 - Refrigeration Equipment and Supplies Merchant Wholesalers, p. III-1854

423810 - Construction and Mining (Except Oil Well) Machinery and Equipment Merchant Wholesalers, p. III-1858

423820 - Farm and Garden Machinery and Equipment Merchant Wholesalers, p. III-1862

423830 - Industrial Machinery and Equipment Merchant Wholesalers, p. III-1866

423840 - Industrial Supplies Merchant Wholesalers, p. III-1870

423850 - Service Establishment Equipment and Supplies Merchant Wholesalers, p. III-1874

423860 - Transportation Equipment and Supplies (Except Motor Vehicle) Merchant Wholesalers, p. III-1878

423910 - Sporting and Recreational Goods and Supplies Merchant Wholesalers, p. III-1882

423920 - Toy and Hobby Goods and Supplies Merchant Wholesalers, p. III-1886

423930 - Recyclable Material Merchant Wholesalers, p. III-1889

423940 - Jewelry, Watch, Precious Stone, and Precious Metal Merchant Wholesalers, p. III-1893

Wholesale Trade, Nondurables

424110 - Printing and Writing Paper Merchant Wholesalers, p. III-1897

424120 - Stationary and Office Supplies Merchant Wholesalers, p. III-1900

Numbers following p. or pp. are page references. Roman numerals indicate volume numbers. Page references are to the starting pages of NAICS industries.

424130 - Industrial and Personal Service Paper Merchant Wholesalers, p. III-1904

424210 - Drugs and Druggists' Sundries Merchant Wholesalers, p. III-1908

424310 - Piece Goods, Notions, and Other Dry Goods Merchant Wholesalers, p. III-1912

424320 - Men's and Boys' Clothing and Furnishings Merchant Wholesalers, p. III-1915

424330 - Women's, Children's, and Infants' Clothing and Accessories Merchant Wholesalers, p. III-1918

424340 - Footwear Merchant Wholesalers, p. III-1921

424410 - General Line Grocery Merchant Wholesalers, p. III-1924

424420 - Packaged Frozen Food Merchant Wholesalers, p. III-1928

424430 - Dairy Product (Except Dried or Canned) Merchant Wholesalers, p. III-1932

424440 - Poultry and Poultry Product Merchant Wholesalers, p. III-1935

424450 - Confectionery Merchant Wholesalers, p. III-1938

424460 - Fish and Seafood Merchant Wholesalers, p. III-1942

424470 - Meat and Meat Product Merchant Wholesalers, p. III-1945

424480 - Fresh Fruit and Vegetable Merchant Wholesalers, p. III-1949

424490 - Other Grocery and Related Products Merchant Wholesalers, p. III-1953

424510 - Grain and Field Bean Merchant Wholesalers, p. III-1957

424520 - Livestock Merchant Wholesalers, p. III-1961

424590 - Other Farm Product Raw Material Merchant Wholesalers, p. III-1964

424610 - Plastics Materials and Basic Forms and Shapes Merchant Wholesalers, p. III-1967

424690 - Other Chemical and Allied Products Merchant Wholesalers, p. III-1970

424710 - Petroleum Bulk Stations and Terminals, p. III-1974

424720 - Petroleum and Petroleum Products Merchant Wholesalers (Except Bulk Stations and Terminals), p. III-1978

424810 - Beer and Ale Merchant Wholesalers, p. III-1982

424820 - Wine and Distilled Alcoholic Beverage Merchant Wholesalers, p. III-1986

424910 - Farm Supplies Merchant Wholesalers, p. III-1990

424920 - Book, Periodical and Newspaper Merchant Wholesalers, p. III-1994

424930 - Flower, Nursery Stock, and Florists' Supplies Merchant Wholesalers, p. III-1997

424940 - Tobacco and Tobacco Product Merchant Wholesalers, p. III-2000

424950 - Paint, Varnish, and Supplies Merchant Wholesalers, p. III-2003

424990 - Other Miscellaneous Nondurable Goods Merchant Wholesalers, p. III-2006

Retail Trade

Motor Vehicle & Parts Dealers

441110 - New Car Dealers, p. III-2010

441120 - Used Car Dealers, p. III-2014

441210 - Recreational Vehicle Dealers, p. III-2017

441221 - Motorcycle Dealers, p. III-2020

441222 - Boat Dealers, p. III-2023

441229 - All Other Motor Vehicle Dealers, p. III-2026

441310 - Automotive Parts and Accessories Stores, p. III-2029

441320 - Tire Dealers, p. III-2033

Furniture & Home Furnishings Stores

442110 - Furniture Stores, p. III-2036

442210 - Floor Covering Stores, p. III-2040

442291 - Window Treatment Stores, p. III-2043

442299 - All Other Home Furnishings Stores, p. III-2046

Electronics & Appliance Stores

443111 - Household Appliance Stores, p. III-2049

443112 - Radio, Television, and Other Electronics Stores, p. III-2053

443120 - Computer and Software Stores, p. III-2057

443130 - Camera and Photographic Supplies Stores, p. III-2061

Building Materials & Garden Dealers

444100 - Building Material and Supply Dealers, p. III-2064

444210 - Outdoor Power Equipment Stores, p. III-2068

444220 - Nursery, Garden Center, and Farm Supply Stores, p. III-2071

Food & Beverage Stores

445110 - Supermarkets and Other Grocery (Except Convenience) Stores, p. III-2075

445120 - Convenience Stores, p. III-2079

445210 - Meat Markets, p. III-2082

445220 - Fish and Seafood Markets, p. III-2084

445230 - Fruit and Vegetable Markets, p. III-2086

445291 - Baked Goods Stores, p. III-2088

445292 - Confectionery and Nut Stores, p. III-2091

445299 - All Other Specialty Food Stores, p. III-2093

445310 - Beer, Wine, and Liquor Stores, p. III-2096

Health & Personal Care Stores

446110 - Pharmacies and Drug Stores, p. III-2099

446120 - Cosmetics, Beauty Supplies, and Perfume Stores, p. III-2103

446130 - Optical Goods Stores, p. III-2106

446191 - Food (Health) Supplement Stores, p. III-2109

446199 - All Other Health and Personal Care Stores, p. III-2112

Gasoline Stations

447110 - Gasoline Stations With Convenience Stores, p. III-2115

447190 - Other Gasoline Stations, p. III-2119

Clothing Stores

448110 - Men's Clothing Stores, p. III-2122

448120 - Women's Clothing Stores, p. III-2125

448130 - Children's and Infants' Clothing Stores, p. III-2128

448140 - Family Clothing Stores, p. III-2131

448150 - Clothing Accessories Stores, p. III-2134

448190 - Other Clothing Stores, p. III-2137

448210 - Shoe Stores, p. III-2140

448310 - Jewelry Stores, p. III-2143

448320 - Luggage and Leather Goods Stores, p. III-2146

Sporting Goods, Hobby, Books, & Music

451110 - Sporting Goods Stores, p. III-2149

451120 - Hobby, Toy, and Game Stores, p. III-2152

451130 - Sewing, Needlework, and Piece Goods Stores, p. III-2155

451140 - Musical Instrument and Supplies Stores, p. III-2158

451211 - Book Stores, p. III-2161

451212 - News Dealers and Newsstands, p. III-2164

451220 - Prerecorded Tape, Compact Disc, and Record Stores, p. III-2167

General Merchandise Stores

452111 - Department Stores (Except Discount Department Stores), p. III-2170

452112 - Discount Department Stores, p. III-2173

452910 - Warehouse Clubs and Supercenters, p. III-2176

452990 - All Other General Merchandise Stores, p. III-2179

Miscellaneous Store Retailers

453110 - Florists, p. III-2182

453210 - Office Supplies and Stationery Stores, p. III-2185

453220 - Gift, Novelty, and Souvenir Stores, p. III-2189

453310 - Used Merchandise Stores, p. III-2193

453910 - Pet and Pet Supplies Stores, p. III-2196

453920 - Art Dealers, p. III-2199

453930 - Manufactured (Mobile) Home Dealers, p. III-2202

453991 - Tobacco Stores, p. III-2205

Numbers following p. or pp. are page references. Roman numerals indicate volume numbers. Page references are to the starting pages of NAICS industries.

2239

NAICS Index

453998 - All Other Miscellaneous Store Retailers (Except Tobacco Stores), p. III-2207

454113 - Mail-order Houses, p. III-2210

454210 - Vending Machine Operators, p. III-2214

454311 - Heating Oil Dealers, p. III-2217

454312 - Liquefied Petroleum Gas (Bottled Gas) Dealers, p. III-2221

454319 - Other Fuel Dealers, p. III-2224

454390 - Other Direct Selling Establishments, p. III-2227

Alphabetic Index

Abrasive Product Manufacturing (NAICS 327910), p. I-755

Adhesive Manufacturing (NAICS 325520), p. I-559

Air and Gas Compressor Manufacturing (NAICS 333912), p. II-1183

Air-conditioning and Warm Air Heating Equipment and Commercial and Industrial Refrigeration Equipment Manufacturing (NAICS 333415), p. II-1105

Aircraft Engine and Engine Parts Manufacturing (NAICS 336412), p. II-1561

Aircraft Manufacturing (NAICS 336411), p. II-1556

Aircraft Parts and Auxiliary Equipment Manufacturing, nec (NAICS 336413), p. II-1566

Alkalies and Chlorine Manufacturing (NAICS 325181), p. I-479

All Other General Merchandise Stores (NAICS 452990), p. III-2179

All Other Health and Personal Care Stores (NAICS 446199), p. III-2112

All Other Home Furnishings Stores (NAICS 442299), p. III-2046

All Other Miscellaneous Store Retailers (Except Tobacco Stores) (NAICS 453998), p. III-2207

All Other Motor Vehicle Dealers (NAICS 441229), p. III-2026

All Other Specialty Food Stores (NAICS 445299), p. III-2093

Alumina Refining (NAICS 331311), p. I-799

Aluminum Extruded Product Manufacturing (NAICS 331316), p. I-810

Aluminum Foundries (NAICS 33152N), p. I-851

Aluminum Rolling and Drawing (NAICS 33131N), p. I-815

Ammunition (Except Small Arms) Manufacturing (NAICS 332993), p. II-996

Analytical Laboratory Instrument Manufacturing (NAICS 334516), p. II-1351

Animal (Except Poultry) Slaughtering and Processing (NAICS 31161N), p. I-101

Animal Food Manufacturing, nec (NAICS 311119), p. I-8

Apparel Accessories and Other Apparel Manufacturing (NAICS 31599M), p. I-289

Apparel Knitting Mills, nec (NAICS 31519M), p. I-261

Art Dealers (NAICS 453920), p. III-2199

Artificial and Synthetic Fibers and Filaments Manufacturing (NAICS 32522M), p. I-509

Asphalt Paving Mixture and Block Manufacturing (NAICS 324121), p. I-447

Asphalt Shingle and Coating Materials Manufacturing (NAICS 324122), p. I-452

Audio and Video Equipment Manufacturing (NAICS 334310), p. II-1271

Automatic Environmental Controls for Residential, Commercial, and Appliance Use (NAICS 334512), p. II-1331

Automobile and Other Motor Vehicle Merchant Wholesalers (NAICS 423110), p. III-1757

Automobile Manufacturing (NAICS 336111), p. II-1472

Automotive Parts and Accessories Stores (NAICS 441310), p. III-2029

Baked Goods Stores (NAICS 445291), p. III-2088

Ball and Roller Bearing Manufacturing (NAICS 332991), p. II-987

Bare Printed Circuit Board Manufacturing (NAICS 334412), p. II-1281

Basic Inorganic Chemical Manufacturing, nec (NAICS 325188), p. I-487

Basic Organic Chemical Manufacturing, nec (NAICS 32519M), p. I-492

Beer and Ale Merchant Wholesalers (NAICS 424810), p. III-1982

Beer, Wine, and Liquor Stores (NAICS 445310), p. III-2096

Beet Sugar Manufacturing (NAICS 311313), p. I-39

Biological Product (Except Diagnostic) Manufacturing (NAICS 325414), p. I-548

Blind and Shade Manufacturing (NAICS 337920), p. II-1661

Boat Building (NAICS 336612), p. II-1593

Boat Dealers (NAICS 441222), p. III-2023

Bolt, Nut, Screw, Rivet, and Washer Manufacturing (NAICS 332722), p. II-957

Book Stores (NAICS 451211), p. III-2161

Book, Periodical and Newspaper Merchant Wholesalers (NAICS 424920), p. III-1994

Bread and Bakery Product Manufacturing (NAICS 31181M), p. I-115

Breakfast Cereal Manufacturing (NAICS 311230), p. I-35

Breweries (NAICS 312120), p. I-171

Brick and Structural Clay Tile Manufacturing (NAICS 327121), p. I-690

Brick, Stone, and Related Construction Material Merchant Wholesalers (NAICS 423320), p. III-1785

Broadwoven Fabric Mills (NAICS 313210), p. I-197

Broom, Brush, and Mop Manufacturing (NAICS 339994), p. II-1739

Building Material and Supply Dealers (NAICS 444100), p. III-2064

Burial Casket Manufacturing (NAICS 339995), p. II-1744

Camera and Photographic Supplies Stores (NAICS 443130), p. III-2061

Carbon and Graphite Product Manufacturing (NAICS 335991), p. II-1462

Carbon Black Manufacturing (NAICS 325182), p. I-483

Carpet and Rug Mills (NAICS 314110), p. I-228

Cement Manufacturing (NAICS 327310), p. I-726

Ceramic Wall and Floor Tile Manufacturing (NAICS 327122), p. I-694

Cheese Manufacturing (NAICS 311513), p. I-75

Chemical Product and Preparation Manufacturing, nec (NAICS 32599N), p. I-594

Children's and Infants' Clothing Stores (NAICS 448130), p. III-2128

Chocolate and Confectionery Manufacturing from Cacao Beans (NAICS 311320), p. I-47

Clothing Accessories Stores (NAICS 448150), p. III-2134

Coal and Other Mineral and Ore Merchant Wholesalers (NAICS 423520), p. III-1827

Coated and Laminated Paper and Packaging Manufacturing (NAICS 32222N), p. I-387

Coated, Uncoated and Multiwall Bag and Packaging Manufacturing (NAICS 32222P), p. I-394

Coating, Engraving, Heat Treating, and Allied Activities (NAICS 33281M), p. II-963

Coffee and Tea Manufacturing (NAICS 311920), p. I-142

Commercial and Service Industry Machinery Manufacturing, nec (NAICS 33331N), p. II-1091

Communication and Energy Wire and Cable Manufacturing (NAICS 33592M), p. II-1450

Communications Equipment Manufacturing, nec (NAICS 334290), p. II-1266

Computer and Computer Peripheral Equipment and Software Merchant Wholesalers (NAICS 423430), p. III-1804

Computer and Software Stores (NAICS 443120), p. III-2057

Computer Peripheral Equipment Manufacturing, nec (NAICS 334119), p. II-1251

Computer Storage Device Manufacturing (NAICS 334112), p. II-1242

Computer Terminal Manufacturing (NAICS 334113), p. II-1247

Concrete Pipe, Brick, and Block Manufacturing (NAICS 32733M), p. I-736

Concrete Product Manufacturing, nec (NAICS 327390), p. I-742

Confectionery and Nut Stores (NAICS 445292), p. III-2091

Confectionery Manufacturing from Purchased Chocolate (NAICS 311330), p. I-51

Confectionery Merchant Wholesalers (NAICS 424450), p. III-1938

Construction and Mining (Except Oil Well) Machinery and Equipment Merchant Wholesalers (NAICS 423810), p. III-1858

Construction Machinery Manufacturing (NAICS 333120), p. II-1032

Convenience Stores (NAICS 445120), p. III-2079

Converted Paper Product Manufacturing, nec (NAICS 322299), p. I-414

Cookie, Cracker, and Pasta Manufacturing (NAICS 31182M), p. I-123

Copper Rolling, Drawing, Extruding, and Alloying (NAICS 33142M), p. I-829

Cosmetics, Beauty Supplies, and Perfume Stores (NAICS 446120), p. III-2103

Crown, Closure and Metal Stamping Manufacturing (NAICS 33211P), p. I-878

Curtain and Linen Mills (NAICS 31412M), p. I-233

Custom Architectural Woodwork and Millwork Manufacturing (NAICS 337212), p. II-1638

Numbers following p. or pp. are page references. Roman numerals indicate volume numbers. Page references are to the starting pages of NAICS industries.

2240

Custom Compounding of Purchased Resins (NAICS 325991), p. I-588

Custom Roll Forming (NAICS 332114), p. I-862

Cut and Sew Apparel Contractors (NAICS 31521M), p. I-266

Cut and Sew Apparel Manufacturing, nec (NAICS 31529M), p. I-284

Cut Stone and Stone Product Manufacturing (NAICS 327991), p. I-761

Cutlery, Kitchen Utensil, Pot and Pan Manufacturing (NAICS 33221N), p. II-885

Cutting Tool and Machine Tool Accessory Manufacturing (NAICS 333515), p. II-1139

Dairy Product (Except Dried or Canned) Merchant Wholesalers (NAICS 424430), p. III-1932

Dental Equipment and Supplies Manufacturing (NAICS 339114), p. II-1681

Dental Laboratories (NAICS 339116), p. II-1691

Department Stores (Except Discount Department Stores) (NAICS 452111), p. III-2170

Discount Department Stores (NAICS 452112), p. III-2173

Distilleries (NAICS 312140), p. I-180

Dog and Cat Food Manufacturing (NAICS 311111), p. I-3

Doll, Toy, and Game Manufacturing (NAICS 33993M), p. II-1707

Drugs and Druggists' Sundries Merchant Wholesalers (NAICS 424210), p. III-1908

Dry, Condensed, and Evaporated Dairy Product Manufacturing (NAICS 311514), p. I-80

Electric Lamp Bulb and Parts Manufacturing (NAICS 335110), p. II-1385

Electrical and Electronic Appliance, Television and Radio Set Merchant Wholesalers (NAICS 423620), p. III-1834

Electrical Apparatus and Equipment, Wiring Supplies, and Related Equipment Merchant Wholesalers (NAICS 423610), p. III-1830

Electrical Equipment and Component Manufacturing, nec (NAICS 335999), p. II-1467

Electromedical and Electrotherapeutic Apparatus Manufacturing (NAICS 334510), p. II-1321

Electron Tube Manufacturing (NAICS 334411), p. II-1276

Electronic Capacitor Manufacturing (NAICS 334414), p. II-1291

Electronic Coil, Transformer, and Other Inductor Manufacturing (NAICS 334416), p. II-1301

Electronic Component Manufacturing, nec (NAICS 334419), p. II-1316

Electronic Computer Manufacturing (NAICS 334111), p. II-1237

Electronic Connector Manufacturing (NAICS 334417), p. II-1306

Electronic Resistor Manufacturing (NAICS 334415), p. II-1296

Engine Equipment Manufacturing, nec (NAICS 333618), p. II-1172

Engineered Wood Product Manufacturing (NAICS 32121P), p. I-328

Explosives Manufacturing (NAICS 325920), p. I-584

Fabric Coating Mills (NAICS 313320), p. I-223

Fabricated Metal Products Manufacturing, nec (NAICS 33299N), p. II-1013

Fabricated Pipe and Pipe Fitting Manufacturing (NAICS 332996), p. II-1008

Family Clothing Stores (NAICS 448140), p. III-2131

Farm and Garden Machinery and Equipment Merchant Wholesalers (NAICS 423820), p. III-1862

Farm Machinery and Equipment Manufacturing (NAICS 333111), p. II-1022

Farm Supplies Merchant Wholesalers (NAICS 424910), p. III-1990

Fastener, Button, Needle, and Pin Manufacturing (NAICS 339993), p. II-1734

Fats and Oils Refining and Blending (NAICS 311225), p. I-25

Ferrous Metal Foundries (NAICS 33151M), p. I-844

Fertilizer (mixing Only) Manufacturing (NAICS 325314), p. I-523

Fiber, Yarn, and Thread Mills (NAICS 31311M), p. I-191

Fish and Seafood Markets (NAICS 445220), p. III-2084

Fish and Seafood Merchant Wholesalers (NAICS 424460), p. III-1942

Flat Glass Manufacturing (NAICS 327211), p. I-708

Flavoring Syrup and Concentrate Manufacturing (NAICS 311930), p. I-146

Floor Covering Stores (NAICS 442210), p. III-2040

Florists (NAICS 453110), p. III-2182

Flour Milling and Malt Manufacturing (NAICS 31121M), p. I-14

Flower, Nursery Stock, and Florists' Supplies Merchant Wholesalers (NAICS 424930), p. III-1997

Fluid Milk and Butter Manufacturing (NAICS 31151N), p. I-85

Fluid Power Equipment Manufacturing (NAICS 33399N), p. II-1221

Food (Health) Supplement Stores (NAICS 446191), p. III-2109

Food Manufacturing, nec (NAICS 31199M), p. I-157

Footwear Manufacturing (NAICS 31621M), p. I-299

Footwear Merchant Wholesalers (NAICS 424340), p. III-1921

Forging (NAICS 33211N), p. I-871

Fresh Fruit and Vegetable Merchant Wholesalers (NAICS 424480), p. III-1949

Frozen Food Manufacturing (NAICS 31141M), p. I-61

Fruit and Vegetable Canning, Pickling, and Drying (NAICS 31142M), p. I-67

Fruit and Vegetable Markets (NAICS 445230), p. III-2086

Furniture Merchant Wholesalers (NAICS 423210), p. III-1773

Furniture Stores (NAICS 442110), p. III-2036

Gasket, Packing, and Sealing Device Manufacturing (NAICS 339991), p. II-1724

Gasoline Stations With Convenience Stores (NAICS 447110), p. III-2115

General Line Grocery Merchant Wholesalers (NAICS 424410), p. III-1924

General Purpose Machinery Manufacturing, nec (NAICS 33399P), p. II-1228

Gift, Novelty, and Souvenir Stores (NAICS 453220), p. III-2189

Glass Container Manufacturing (NAICS 327213), p. I-717

Glass Product Manufacturing Made of Purchased Glass (NAICS 327215), p. I-721

Grain and Field Bean Merchant Wholesalers (NAICS 424510), p. III-1957

Ground or Treated Mineral and Earth Manufacturing (NAICS 327992), p. I-766

Guided Missile and Space Vehicle Manufacturing (NAICS 336414), p. II-1571

Guided Missile and Space Vehicle Parts and Auxiliary Equipment Manufacturing, nec (NAICS 336419), p. II-1579

Guided Missile and Space Vehicle Propulsion Unit and Propulsion Unit Parts Manufacturing (NAICS 336415), p. II-1575

Gypsum Product Manufacturing (NAICS 327420), p. I-751

Hand Tool and Saw Blade Manufacturing (NAICS 33221P), p. II-891

Hardware Manufacturing (NAICS 332510), p. II-932

Hardware Merchant Wholesalers (NAICS 423710), p. III-1842

Heating Equipment (Except Warm Air Furnaces) Manufacturing (NAICS 333414), p. II-1100

Heating Oil Dealers (NAICS 454311), p. III-2217

Heavy Duty Truck Manufacturing (NAICS 336120), p. II-1481

Hobby, Toy, and Game Stores (NAICS 451120), p. III-2152

Home Furnishing Merchant Wholesalers (NAICS 423220), p. III-1777

Hosiery and Sock Mills (NAICS 31511M), p. I-255

Household Appliance Stores (NAICS 443111), p. III-2049

Household Cooking Appliance Manufacturing (NAICS 335221), p. II-1403

Household Laundry Equipment Manufacturing (NAICS 335224), p. II-1412

Household Nonupholstered Furniture, nec (NAICS 33712N), p. II-1631

Household Refrigerator and Home Freezer Manufacturing (NAICS 335222), p. II-1408

Ice Cream and Frozen Dessert Manufacturing (NAICS 311520), p. I-91

In-vitro Diagnostic Substance Manufacturing (NAICS 325413), p. I-543

Industrial and Personal Service Paper Merchant Wholesalers (NAICS 424130), p. III-1904

Industrial Gas Manufacturing (NAICS 325120), p. I-470

Industrial Machinery and Equipment Merchant Wholesalers (NAICS 423830), p. III-1866

Industrial Mold Manufacturing (NAICS 333511), p. II-1118

Industrial Process Furnace and Oven Manufacturing (NAICS 333994), p. II-1216

Industrial Supplies Merchant Wholesalers (NAICS 423840), p. III-1870

Institutional Furniture Manufacturing (NAICS 337127), p. II-1626

Instrument Manufacturing for Measuring and Testing Electricity and Electrical Signals (NAICS 334515), p. II-1346

Instruments and Related Products for Measuring, Displaying and Controlling Industrial Process Variables (NAICS 334513), p. II-1336

Numbers following p. or pp. are page references. Roman numerals indicate volume numbers. Page references are to the starting pages of NAICS industries.

2241

Iron and Steel Mills and Ferroalloy Manufacturing (NAICS 33111M), p. I-779

Iron and Steel Pipe and Tube Manufacturing from Purchased Steel (NAICS 331210), p. I-787

Irradiation Apparatus Manufacturing (NAICS 334517), p. II-1356

Jewelry and Silverware Manufacturing (NAICS 33991M), p. II-1695

Jewelry Stores (NAICS 448310), p. III-2143

Jewelry, Watch, Precious Stone, and Precious Metal Merchant Wholesalers (NAICS 423940), p. III-1893

Knit Fabric Mills (NAICS 31324M), p. I-212

Laboratory Apparatus and Furniture Manufacturing (NAICS 339111), p. II-1665

Laminated Plastics Plate, Sheet, and Shape Manufacturing (NAICS 326130), p. I-630

Lawn and Garden Tractor and Home Lawn and Garden Equipment Manufacturing (NAICS 333112), p. II-1027

Leather and Allied Product Manufacturing, nec (NAICS 31699M), p. I-305

Leather and Hide Tanning and Finishing (NAICS 316110), p. I-295

Light Truck and Utility Vehicle Manufacturing (NAICS 336112), p. II-1477

Lighting Fixture Manufacturing (NAICS 33512M), p. II-1389

Lime Manufacturing (NAICS 327410), p. I-747

Liquefied Petroleum Gas (Bottled Gas) Dealers (NAICS 454312), p. III-2221

Livestock Merchant Wholesalers (NAICS 424520), p. III-1961

Luggage and Leather Goods Stores (NAICS 448320), p. III-2146

Lumber, Plywood, Millwork, and Wood Panel Merchant Wholesalers (NAICS 423310), p. III-1781

Machine Shops (NAICS 332710), p. II-944

Machine Tool (metal Cutting Types) Manufacturing (NAICS 333512), p. II-1123

Machine Tool (metal Forming Types) Manufacturing (NAICS 333513), p. II-1128

Machinery Manufacturing, nec (NAICS 33329N), p. II-1060

Magnetic and Optical Recording Media Manufacturing (NAICS 334613), p. II-1380

Mail-order Houses (NAICS 454113), p. III-2210

Major Household Appliance Manufacturing, nec (NAICS 335228), p. II-1416

Manufactured (Mobile) Home Dealers (NAICS 453930), p. III-2202

Manufactured Home (Mobile Home) Manufacturing (NAICS 321991), p. I-347

Material Handling Equipment Manufacturing (NAICS 33392M), p. II-1193

Mattress Manufacturing (NAICS 337910), p. II-1656

Measuring and Controlling Device Manufacturing, nec (NAICS 334519), p. II-1366

Measuring and Dispensing Pump Manufacturing (NAICS 333913), p. II-1188

Meat and Meat Product Merchant Wholesalers (NAICS 424470), p. III-1945

Meat Markets (NAICS 445210), p. III-2082

Mechanical Power Transmission Equipment Manufacturing (NAICS 333613), p. II-1167

Medical, Dental, and Hospital Equipment and Supplies Merchant Wholesalers (NAICS 423450), p. III-1812

Medicinal and Botanical Manufacturing (NAICS 325411), p. I-533

Men's and Boys' Clothing and Furnishings Merchant Wholesalers (NAICS 424320), p. III-1915

Men's and Boys' Cut and Sew Apparel Manufacturing (NAICS 31522M), p. I-271

Men's Clothing Stores (NAICS 448110), p. III-2122

Metal Can, Box, and Other Metal Container (Light Gauge) Manufacturing (NAICS 33243M), p. II-927

Metal Service Centers and Other Metal Merchant Wholesalers (NAICS 423510), p. III-1823

Metal Tank (Heavy Gauge) Manufacturing (NAICS 332420), p. II-922

Metalworking Machinery Manufacturing, nec (NAICS 333518), p. II-1151

Military Armored Vehicle, Tank, and Tank Component Manufacturing (NAICS 336992), p. II-1602

Millwork (NAICS 32191M), p. I-333

Mineral Wool Manufacturing (NAICS 327993), p. I-770

Mining and Oil and Gas Field Machinery Manufacturing (NAICS 33313M), p. II-1038

Miscellaneous Manufacturing, nec (NAICS 339999), p. II-1748

Motor and Generator Manufacturing (NAICS 335312), p. II-1426

Motor Home Manufacturing (NAICS 336213), p. II-1495

Motor Vehicle Air-conditioning Manufacturing (NAICS 336391), p. II-1545

Motor Vehicle Body and Trailer Manufacturing (NAICS 336211), p. II-1485

Motor Vehicle Brake System Manufacturing (NAICS 336340), p. II-1523

Motor Vehicle Electrical and Electronic Equipment Manufacturing (NAICS 33632M), p. II-1511

Motor Vehicle Gasoline Engine and Engine Parts Manufacturing (NAICS 33631M), p. II-1504

Motor Vehicle Metal Stamping (NAICS 336370), p. II-1540

Motor Vehicle Parts (Used) Merchant Wholesalers (NAICS 423140), p. III-1769

Motor Vehicle Parts Manufacturing, nec (NAICS 336399), p. II-1550

Motor Vehicle Seating and Interior Trim Manufacturing (NAICS 336360), p. II-1535

Motor Vehicle Steering and Suspension Component (Except Spring) Manufacturing (NAICS 336330), p. II-1518

Motor Vehicle Supplies and New Parts Merchant Wholesalers (NAICS 423120), p. III-1761

Motor Vehicle Transmission and Power Train Parts Manufacturing (NAICS 336350), p. II-1529

Motorcycle Dealers (NAICS 441221), p. III-2020

Motorcycle, Bicycle, and Parts Manufacturing (NAICS 336991), p. II-1598

Musical Instrument and Supplies Stores (NAICS 451140), p. III-2158

Musical Instrument Manufacturing (NAICS 339992), p. II-1730

Narrow Fabric Mills and Schiffli Machine Embroidery (NAICS 31322M), p. I-202

New Car Dealers (NAICS 441110), p. III-2010

News Dealers and Newsstands (NAICS 451212), p. III-2164

Nitrogenous Fertilizer Manufacturing (NAICS 325311), p. I-515

Nonaluminum Foundries (NAICS 33152P), p. I-856

Nonchocolate Confectionery Manufacturing (NAICS 311340), p. I-56

Nonferrous Metal (Except Copper and Aluminum) Rolling, Drawing, Extruding, and Alloying (NAICS 33149M), p. I-836

Nonmetallic Mineral Product Manufacturing, nec (NAICS 327999), p. I-775

Nonupholstered Wood Household Furniture Manufacturing (NAICS 337122), p. II-1620

Nonwoven Fabric Mills (NAICS 313230), p. I-207

Nursery, Garden Center, and Farm Supply Stores (NAICS 444220), p. III-2071

Office Equipment Merchant Wholesalers (NAICS 423420), p. III-1800

Office Furniture Manufacturing (NAICS 33721N), p. II-1649

Office Machinery Manufacturing (NAICS 333313), p. II-1076

Office Supplies (Except Paper) Manufacturing (NAICS 33994M), p. II-1713

Office Supplies and Stationery Stores (NAICS 453210), p. III-2185

Ophthalmic Goods Manufacturing (NAICS 339115), p. II-1686

Ophthalmic Goods Merchant Wholesalers (NAICS 423460), p. III-1816

Optical Goods Stores (NAICS 446130), p. III-2106

Optical Instrument and Lens Manufacturing (NAICS 333314), p. II-1081

Ordnance and Accessories Manufacturing, nec (NAICS 332995), p. II-1004

Ornamental, Sheet and Architectural Metal Work Manufacturing (NAICS 33232M), p. II-907

Other Chemical and Allied Products Merchant Wholesalers (NAICS 424690), p. III-1970

Other Clothing Stores (NAICS 448190), p. III-2137

Other Commercial Equipment Merchant Wholesalers (NAICS 423440), p. III-1808

Other Construction Material Merchant Wholesalers (NAICS 423390), p. III-1793

Other Direct Selling Establishments (NAICS 454390), p. III-2227

Other Electronic Parts and Equipment Merchant Wholesalers (NAICS 423690), p. III-1838

Other Farm Product Raw Material Merchant Wholesalers (NAICS 424590), p. III-1964

Other Fuel Dealers (NAICS 454319), p. III-2224

Other Gasoline Stations (NAICS 447190), p. III-2119

Other Grocery and Related Products Merchant Wholesalers (NAICS 424490), p. III-1953

Other Miscellaneous Nondurable Goods Merchant Wholesalers (NAICS 424990), p. III-2006

Other Professional Equipment and Supplies Merchant Wholesalers (NAICS 423490), p. III-1819

Outdoor Power Equipment Stores (NAICS 444210), p. III-2068

Packaged Frozen Food Merchant Wholesalers (NAICS 424420), p. III-1928

Numbers following p. or pp. are page references. Roman numerals indicate volume numbers. Page references are to the starting pages of NAICS industries.

Packaging Machinery Manufacturing (NAICS 333993), p. II-1211

Paint and Coating Manufacturing (NAICS 325510), p. I-553

Paint, Varnish, and Supplies Merchant Wholesalers (NAICS 424950), p. III-2003

Paper and Newsprint Mills (NAICS 32212M), p. I-367

Paperboard Container Manufacturing (NAICS 32221M), p. I-378

Paperboard Mills (NAICS 322130), p. I-373

Pesticide and Other Agricultural Chemical Manufacturing (NAICS 325320), p. I-528

Pet and Pet Supplies Stores (NAICS 453910), p. III-2196

Petrochemical Manufacturing (NAICS 325110), p. I-466

Petroleum and Coal Products Manufacturing, nec (NAICS 324199), p. I-462

Petroleum and Petroleum Products Merchant Wholesalers (Except Bulk Stations and Terminals) (NAICS 424720), p. III-1978

Petroleum Bulk Stations and Terminals (NAICS 424710), p. III-1974

Petroleum Lubricating Oil and Grease Manufacturing (NAICS 324191), p. I-457

Petroleum Refineries (NAICS 324110), p. I-442

Pharmaceutical Preparation Manufacturing (NAICS 325412), p. I-538

Pharmacies and Drug Stores (NAICS 446110), p. III-2099

Phosphatic Fertilizer Manufacturing (NAICS 325312), p. I-519

Photographic and Photocopying Equipment Manufacturing (NAICS 333315), p. II-1086

Photographic Equipment and Supplies Merchant Wholesalers (NAICS 423410), p. III-1797

Piece Goods, Notions, and Other Dry Goods Merchant Wholesalers (NAICS 424310), p. III-1912

Plastics and Rubber Industry Machinery Manufacturing (NAICS 333220), p. II-1050

Plastics Bag Manufacturing (NAICS 326111), p. I-602

Plastics Bottle Manufacturing (NAICS 326160), p. I-645

Plastics Material and Resin Manufacturing (NAICS 325211), p. I-499

Plastics Materials and Basic Forms and Shapes Merchant Wholesalers (NAICS 424610), p. III-1967

Plastics Packaging Film and Sheet Manufacturing (NAICS 326112), p. I-608

Plastics Pipe and Pipe Fitting Manufacturing (NAICS 326122), p. I-625

Plastics Product Manufacturing (NAICS 32619M), p. I-650

Plate Work and Fabricated Structural Product Manufacturing (NAICS 33231M), p. II-898

Plumbing and Heating Equipment and Supplies (Hydronics) Merchant Wholesalers (NAICS 423720), p. III-1846

Plumbing Fixture Fitting and Trim Manufacturing (NAICS 332913), p. II-973

Polystyrene Foam Product Manufacturing (NAICS 326140), p. I-635

Porcelain Electrical Supply Manufacturing (NAICS 327113), p. I-685

Poultry and Poultry Product Merchant Wholesalers (NAICS 424440), p. III-1935

Poultry Processing (NAICS 311615), p. I-96

Powder Metallurgy Parts Manufacturing (NAICS 332117), p. I-866

Power Boiler and Heat Exchanger Manufacturing (NAICS 332410), p. II-917

Power, Distribution, and Specialty Transformer Manufacturing (NAICS 335311), p. II-1420

Power-driven Hand Tool Manufacturing (NAICS 333991), p. II-1206

Precision Tuned Product Manufacturing (NAICS 332721), p. II-951

Prefabricated Wood Building Manufacturing (NAICS 321992), p. I-352

Prerecorded Compact Disc (Except Software), Tape, and Record Reproducing (NAICS 334612), p. II-1375

Prerecorded Tape, Compact Disc, and Record Stores (NAICS 451220), p. III-2167

Pressed and Blown Glass and Glassware Manufacturing, nec (NAICS 327212), p. I-712

Primary Aluminum Production (NAICS 331312), p. I-802

Primary Battery Manufacturing (NAICS 335912), p. II-1446

Primary Smelting and Refining of Copper (NAICS 331411), p. I-821

Primary Smelting and Refining of Nonferrous Metal (Except Copper and Aluminum) (NAICS 331419), p. I-824

Printed Circuit Assembly (Electronic Assembly) Manufacturing (NAICS 334418), p. II-1311

Printing (NAICS 32311M), p. I-419

Printing and Writing Paper Merchant Wholesalers (NAICS 424110), p. III-1897

Printing Ink Manufacturing (NAICS 325910), p. I-579

Pulp Mills (NAICS 322110), p. I-362

Pump and Pumping Equipment Manufacturing (NAICS 333911), p. II-1178

Radio and Television Broadcasting and Wireless Communications Equipment Manufacturing (NAICS 334220), p. II-1261

Radio, Television, and Other Electronics Stores (NAICS 443112), p. III-2053

Railroad Rolling Stock Manufacturing (NAICS 336510), p. II-1583

Ready-mix Concrete Manufacturing (NAICS 327320), p. I-731

Reconstituted Wood Product Manufacturing (NAICS 321219), p. I-318

Recreational Vehicle Dealers (NAICS 441210), p. III-2017

Recyclable Material Merchant Wholesalers (NAICS 423930), p. III-1889

Refractory Manufacturing (NAICS 32712N), p. I-702

Refrigeration Equipment and Supplies Merchant Wholesalers (NAICS 423740), p. III-1854

Relay and Industrial Control Manufacturing (NAICS 335314), p. II-1436

Rolling and Drawing of Purchased Steel (NAICS 33122M), p. I-792

Rolling Mill Machinery and Equipment Manufacturing (NAICS 333516), p. II-1146

Roofing, Siding, and Insulation Material Merchant Wholesalers (NAICS 423330), p. III-1789

Rope, Cordage, and Twine Mills (NAICS 314991), p. I-243

Rubber and Plastics Hoses and Belting Manufacturing (NAICS 326220), p. I-664

Rubber Product Manufacturing, nec (NAICS 32629M), p. I-669

Sanitary Paper Product Manufacturing (NAICS 322291), p. I-410

Sawmill and Woodworking Machinery Manufacturing (NAICS 333210), p. II-1045

Sawmills and Wood Preservation (NAICS 32111M), p. I-311

Seafood Product Preparation and Packaging (NAICS 31171M), p. I-109

Search, Detection, Navigation, Guidance, Aeronautical, and Nautical System and Instrument Manufacturing (NAICS 334511), p. II-1326

Seasoning and Dressing Manufacturing (NAICS 31194M), p. I-151

Secondary Smelting and Alloying of Aluminum (NAICS 331314), p. I-806

Semiconductor and Related Device Manufacturing (NAICS 334413), p. II-1286

Semiconductor Machinery Manufacturing (NAICS 333295), p. II-1055

Service Establishment Equipment and Supplies Merchant Wholesalers (NAICS 423850), p. III-1874

Sewing, Needlework, and Piece Goods Stores (NAICS 451130), p. III-2155

Ship Building and Repairing (NAICS 336611), p. II-1588

Shoe Stores (NAICS 448210), p. III-2140

Showcase, Partition, Shelving, and Locker Manufacturing (NAICS 337215), p. II-1643

Sign Manufacturing (NAICS 339950), p. II-1719

Small Arms Ammunition Manufacturing (NAICS 332992), p. II-992

Small Arms Manufacturing (NAICS 332994), p. II-1000

Small Electrical Appliance Manufacturing (NAICS 33521M), p. II-1396

Snack Food Manufacturing (NAICS 31191M), p. I-136

Soap and Cleaning Compound Manufacturing (NAICS 32561M), p. I-565

Soft Drink and Ice Manufacturing (NAICS 31211M), p. I-164

Software Reproducing (NAICS 334611), p. II-1371

Soybean and Other Oilseed Processing (NAICS 31122N), p. I-30

Special Die and Tool, Die Set, Jig, and Fixture Manufacturing (NAICS 333514), p. II-1133

Speed Changer, Industrial High-speed Drive, and Gear Manufacturing (NAICS 333612), p. II-1161

Sporting and Athletic Goods Manufacturing (NAICS 339920), p. II-1701

Sporting and Recreational Goods and Supplies Merchant Wholesalers (NAICS 423910), p. III-1882

Sporting Goods Stores (NAICS 451110), p. III-2149

Spring and Wire Product Manufacturing (NAICS 33261M), p. II-938

Numbers following p. or pp. are page references. Roman numerals indicate volume numbers. Page references are to the starting pages of NAICS industries.

2243

Stationary and Office Supplies Merchant Wholesalers (NAICS 424120), p. III-1900

Stationery Product Manufacturing (NAICS 32223M), p. I-402

Storage Battery Manufacturing (NAICS 335911), p. II-1441

Structural Clay Product Manufacturing, nec (NAICS 327123), p. I-698

Sugar Cane Mills and Refining (NAICS 31131N), p. I-43

Supermarkets and Other Grocery (Except Convenience) Stores (NAICS 445110), p. III-2075

Support Activities for Printing (NAICS 32312M), p. I-435

Surgical and Medical Instrument Manufacturing (NAICS 339112), p. II-1670

Surgical Appliance and Supplies Manufacturing (NAICS 339113), p. II-1675

Switchgear and Switchboard Apparatus Manufacturing (NAICS 335313), p. II-1431

Synthetic Dye and Pigment Manufacturing (NAICS 32513M), p. I-474

Synthetic Rubber Manufacturing (NAICS 325212), p. I-504

Telephone Apparatus Manufacturing (NAICS 334210), p. II-1256

Textile and Fabric Finishing Mills (NAICS 31331M), p. I-217

Textile Bag and Canvas Mills (NAICS 31491M), p. I-238

Textile Product Mills, nec (NAICS 314999), p. I-250

Tire and Tube Merchant Wholesalers (NAICS 423130), p. III-1765

Tire Cord and Tire Fabric Mills (NAICS 314992), p. I-247

Tire Dealers (NAICS 441320), p. III-2033

Tire Manufacturing (NAICS 32621M), p. I-659

Tobacco and Tobacco Product Merchant Wholesalers (NAICS 424940), p. III-2000

Tobacco Product Manufacturing (NAICS 31222M), p. I-187

Tobacco Steaming and Redrying (NAICS 312210), p. I-184

Tobacco Stores (NAICS 453991), p. III-2205

Toilet Preparation Manufacturing (NAICS 325620), p. I-574

Tortilla Manufacturing (NAICS 311830), p. I-132

Totalizing Fluid Meter and Counting Device Manufacturing (NAICS 334514), p. II-1341

Toy and Hobby Goods and Supplies Merchant Wholesalers (NAICS 423920), p. III-1886

Transportation Equipment and Supplies (Except Motor Vehicle) Merchant Wholesalers (NAICS 423860), p. III-1878

Transportation Equipment Manufacturing, nec (NAICS 336999), p. II-1606

Travel Trailer and Camper Manufacturing (NAICS 336214), p. II-1499

Truck Trailer Manufacturing (NAICS 336212), p. II-1490

Turbine and Turbine Generator Set Unit Manufacturing (NAICS 333611), p. II-1156

Unlaminated Plastics Film and Sheet (Except Packaging) Manufacturing (NAICS 326113), p. I-614

Unsupported Plastics Profile Shape Manufacturing (NAICS 326121), p. I-620

Upholstered Household Furniture Manufacturing (NAICS 337121), p. II-1615

Urethane and Other Foam Product (Except Polystyrene) Manufacturing (NAICS 326150), p. I-640

Used Car Dealers (NAICS 441120), p. III-2014

Used Merchandise Stores (NAICS 453310), p. III-2193

Valves and Fittings Manufacturing, Nonplumbing (NAICS 33291N), p. II-979

Vending Machine Operators (NAICS 454210), p. III-2214

Veneer and Plywood Manufacturing (NAICS 32121N), p. I-323

Ventilation Equipment Manufacturing (NAICS 33341N), p. II-1111

Vitreous China Plumbing Fixture and China and Earthenware Bathroom Accessories Manufacturing (NAICS 327111), p. I-676

Vitreous China, Fine Earthenware, and Other Pottery Product Manufacturing (NAICS 327112), p. I-680

Warehouse Clubs and Supercenters (NAICS 452910), p. III-2176

Warm Air Heating and Air-conditioning Equipment and Supplies Merchant Wholesalers (NAICS 423730), p. III-1850

Watch, Clock, and Parts Manufacturing (NAICS 334518), p. II-1361

Wet Corn Milling (NAICS 311221), p. I-21

Window Treatment Stores (NAICS 442291), p. III-2043

Wine and Distilled Alcoholic Beverage Merchant Wholesalers (NAICS 424820), p. III-1986

Wineries (NAICS 312130), p. I-176

Wiring Device Manufacturing (NAICS 33593M), p. II-1456

Women's and Girls' Cut and Sew Apparel Manufacturing (NAICS 31523M), p. I-278

Women's Clothing Stores (NAICS 448120), p. III-2125

Women's, Children's, and Infants' Clothing and Accessories Merchant Wholesalers (NAICS 424330), p. III-1918

Wood Container and Pallet Manufacturing (NAICS 321920), p. I-342

Wood Kitchen Cabinet and Counter Top Manufacturing (NAICS 337110), p. II-1610

Wood Product Manufacturing, nec (NAICS 321999), p. I-357

Numbers following p. or pp. are page references. Roman numerals indicate volume numbers. Page references are to the starting pages of NAICS industries.

PRODUCT/ACTIVITY INDEX

This index holds references to more than 7,900 product categories and commercial activities. All references are to page numbers, by volume. Pages refer to the starting page of the industry that produces the product or carries on the activity. The Roman numerals indicate volumes, arabic numbers are pages within the volumes.

Abattoirs, p. I-101
Abrasion testing machines, p. II-1366
Abrasive points
— dental, p. II-1681
Abrasive products, p. I-755
Abrasives, p. III-1870
ABS resins, p. I-499
Absorbent paper stock, p. I-367
Absorbers (gas), p. II-922
Absorption analyzers, p. II-1336
Acceleration indicators, p. II-1326
Accelerators (chemical), p. I-492
Accelerometers, p. II-1366
Accordions, p. II-1730
Accounting machines, p. III-1800
Accumulators (pressure vessel), p. II-922
Acetal resins, p. I-499
Acetaldehyde, p. I-492
Acetate fibers and filaments, p. I-509
Acetate of lime, p. I-492
Acetate spun yarns, p. I-191
Acetates, p. I-492
Acetic acid, p. I-492
Acetic anhydride, p. I-492
Acetin, p. I-492
Acetone, p. I-492
Acetylene, p. I-470
Acetylene cylinders, p. II-922
Acetylsalicylic acid, p. I-533
Acid dyes, p. I-474
Acid esters, p. I-492
Acid oils, p. I-442
Acidity instruments, p. II-1336
Acidity measuring equipment, p. II-1351
Acidophilus milk, p. I-85
Acids, pp. I-492, III-1970
Acoustical suspension systems, p. II-907
Acrolein, p. I-492
Acrylate rubber, p. I-504
Acrylate-butadiene rubber, p. I-504
Acrylic and modacrylic filament, p. I-191
Acrylic fibers and filaments, p. I-509
Acrylic film and unlaminated sheet, p. I-614
Acrylic resins, p. I-499
Acrylic rubber, p. I-504
Acrylic spun yarns, p. I-191
Acrylonitrile, p. I-492

Acrylonitrile fibers and filaments, p. I-509
Actinometers (meteorological), p. II-1366
Action figures, p. II-1707
Activated carbon or charcoal, p. I-594
Actuators (fluid power), p. II-1221
Acyclic hydrocarbons, p. I-466
Adding machines, p. II-1076
Additives (gasoline), p. I-594
Address lists flexographic, p. I-419
Address lists gravure, p. I-419
Address lists lithographic, p. I-419
Address lists printing, p. I-419
Address lists screen printing, p. I-419
Addressing machines, p. III-1800
Adhesive tape, p. I-387
— medical, p. II-1675
Adhesives, p. I-559
Adhesives and sealants, p. III-1970
Adipic acid, p. I-492
Adipic acid esters or amines, p. I-492
Adiponitrile, p. I-492
Adobe bricks, p. I-698
Adrenal derivatives, p. I-533
Adrenal medicinal preparations, p. I-538
Advertising materials, p. I-419
Aerial cameras, p. II-1086
Aerial work platforms, p. II-1193
Aeronautical equipment, p. III-1878
Aeronautical systems, p. II-1326
Aerosol can filling, p. I-594
Aerosol cans, p. II-927
Aerosol packaging services, p. I-594
Aerosol valves, p. II-979
After-shave preparations, p. I-574
Aftercoolers, p. II-917
Agar culture media, p. I-548
Agar-agar grinding, p. I-533
Aggregate spreaders, p. II-1032
Aggressins, p. I-548
Agricultural chemicals, p. III-1990
Agricultural handtools, p. II-891
Agricultural implements, p. III-1862
Agricultural lime, p. I-747
Agricultural limestone, p. III-1990
Agricultural machinery and equipment, p. III-1862
Agricultural magazines, p. I-419
Air bag assemblies, p. II-1550

Air boat building, p. II-1593
Air brake systems, p. II-1523
Air cargo containers, p. II-927
Air circuit breakers, p. II-1431
Air compressors, p. II-1183
Air cowls, p. II-907
Air filters, p. II-1550
Air flow controllers, p. II-1331
Air laid nonwoven fabrics, p. I-207
Air pollution control equipment, p. III-1850
Air purification equipment, pp. II-1111, 1396
Air receiver tanks, p. II-922
Air scrubbing systems, p. II-1111
Air traffic control radar, p. II-1326
Air washers, p. II-1111
Air-conditioners, pp. II-1105, 1545, III-1834
Air-conditioning and heating units, p. II-1105
Air-conditioning compressors, p. II-1105
Air-conditioning condensers, p. II-1105
Air-conditioning equipment, pp. II-1105, III-1850
Aircraft, pp. II-1556, III-1878
Aircraft and automotive wire, pp. I-829, 836
Aircraft artillery, p. II-1004
Aircraft assemblies, p. II-1566
Aircraft auxiliary parts, p. II-1566
Aircraft carrier catapults, p. II-1228
Aircraft control surface assemblies, p. II-1566
Aircraft conversions, p. II-1556
Aircraft dealers, p. III-2026
Aircraft engine and engine parts, p. II-1561
Aircraft engine cradles, p. II-1193
Aircraft engine instruments, p. II-1366
Aircraft engine overhauling, p. II-1561
Aircraft engine rebuilding, p. II-1561
Aircraft engines and parts, p. III-1878
Aircraft equipment, p. III-1878
Aircraft flight instruments, p. II-1326
Aircraft fuselage, p. II-1566
Aircraft hardware, p. II-932
Aircraft lighting fixtures, p. II-1511
Aircraft loading hoists, p. II-1193
Aircraft overhauling, p. II-1556
Aircraft propellers and parts, p. II-1566
Aircraft rebuilding, p. II-1556
Aircraft seats, p. II-1535
Aircraft tie down strap assemblies, p. I-250
Aircraft tire, p. I-659

Aircraft turbines, p. II-1561

Aircurtains, p. II-1111

Airframe assemblies, pp. II-1566, 1579

Airframe equipment instruments, p. II-1326

Airfreshners, p. I-565

Airlocks, p. II-898

Airport lighting transformers, p. II-1420

Airspeed instruments, p. II-1326

Alarm apparatus, p. III-1830

Alarm clocks, p. II-1361

Alarm systems and equipment, p. II-1266

Albums, pp. I-419, III-1900

Alcohol, p. III-1970

Alcoholic beverages, pp. I-176, 180, III-1982, 1986

Aldehydes, p. I-492

Ale, p. III-1982

Ale brewing, p. I-171

Alfalfa, pp. I-8, III-1990

Alfalfa for animals, p. I-8

Alfalfa meal, p. I-8

Alginates, p. I-492

Alginic acid, p. I-492

Alidades (surveying), p. II-1366

Alignment equipment (vehicle), p. II-1091

Aliphatics, pp. I-442, 466

Alkalies, pp. I-479, III-1970

Alkaline cell primary batteries, p. II-1446

Alkaline cell storage batteries, p. II-1441

Alkaline manganese primary batteries, p. II-1446

Alkyd resins, p. I-499

Alkylates, p. I-442

All-terrain vehicles, pp. II-1606, III-1757, 2020

Allergenic extracts, p. I-548

Allergens, p. I-548

Alloy steel castings, p. I-844

Allyl resins, p. I-499

Almanac binding, p. I-435

Almanacs, p. I-419

Almond pastes, p. I-157

Alternator and generator testers, p. II-1346

Alternators and generators, p. II-1511

Altimeters, p. II-1326

Alumina, p. I-799

Alumina fused refractories, p. I-702

Alumina porcelain insulators, p. I-685

Aluminous refractory cement, p. I-702

Aluminum alloys, pp. I-802, 806

Aluminum bar, p. I-810

Aluminum billet, p. I-806

Aluminum cans, p. II-927

Aluminum castings, p. I-851

Aluminum chloride, p. I-487

Aluminum compounds, p. I-487

Aluminum die-casting foundries, p. I-851

Aluminum die-castings, p. I-851

Aluminum extrusion ingot, p. I-806

Aluminum flakes, p. I-806

Aluminum foil, p. I-815

Aluminum forgings, p. I-871

Aluminum foundries, p. I-851

Aluminum freezer foil, p. II-1013

Aluminum hydroxide, p. I-487

Aluminum ingot, pp. I-802, 806

Aluminum ladders, p. II-1013

Aluminum oxide, p. I-799

Aluminum oxide (fused) abrasives, p. I-755

Aluminum pipe, p. I-810

Aluminum plate, p. I-815

Aluminum recovery, p. I-806

Aluminum rod, p. I-810

Aluminum shapes, p. I-802

Aluminum sheet, p. I-815

Aluminum smelting, p. I-806

Aluminum sulfate, p. I-487

Aluminum tube, p. I-810

Aluminum tube blooms, p. I-810

Aluminum welded tube, p. I-815

Alums, p. I-487

Amalgamators, p. II-1038

Amalgams (dental), p. II-1681

Amatols, p. I-584

Ambulance bodies, p. II-1495

Ambulances, pp. II-1485, III-1757

Amino acid analyzers, p. II-1351

Amino resins, p. I-499

Amino-aldehyde resins, p. I-499

Aminoanthraquinone, p. I-492

Aminoazobenzene, p. I-492

Aminoazotoluene, p. I-492

Aminophenol, p. I-492

Ammonia, pp. I-515, 565, III-1970, 1990

Ammonium chloride, p. I-487

Ammonium compounds, p. I-487

Ammonium hydroxide, p. I-487

Ammonium molybdate, p. I-487

Ammonium nitrate, p. I-515

Ammonium perchlorate, p. I-487

Ammonium phosphates, p. I-519

Ammonium sulfate, p. I-515

Ammonium thiosulfate, p. I-487

Ammunition, pp. II-992, 996

Ammunition boxes, pp. I-342, II-927

Ammunition carts, pp. II-1000, 1004

Ampere-hour meters, p. II-1346

Amphetamines, p. I-533

Amplifiers, pp. II-1261, 1271, 1467

Amusement machines, p. II-1748

Amusement park equipment, p. III-1874

Amyl acetate, p. I-492

Analgesic preparations, p. I-538

Analog computers, p. II-1237

Analytical instruments, p. III-1819

Andirons, p. II-1013

Anesthesia apparatus, p. II-1670

Anesthetic preparations, p. I-538

Anesthetics, p. I-533

Angiourographic diagnostic preparations, p. I-538

Angle rings, p. II-1139

Angle valves, p. II-979

Angle-of-attack instrumentation, p. II-1326

Angle-of-yaw instrumentation, p. II-1326

Angles (iron), p. II-1013

Anhydrous ammonia, p. I-515

Anhydrous butterfat, p. I-85

Anidex fibers and filaments, p. I-509

Aniline, p. I-492

Animal black, p. I-483

Animal fats, p. I-101

Animal feed mills, pp. I-3, 8

Animal feeds, pp. I-3, 8, III-1990

Animal fibers, p. I-191

Animal hair, p. III-1964

Animal oil rendering, p. I-101

Animal traps, p. II-1013

Animal-drawn vehicles, p. II-1606

Anise oil, p. I-594

Anklets, p. I-255

Annato extract, p. I-492

Annealing vats, p. II-922

Annular ball bearings, p. II-987

Annunciators, p. II-1336

Anodizing equipment, p. II-1060

Anodizing metals, p. II-963

Answering machines, p. III-1834

Ant poisons, p. I-528

Antacid preparations, p. I-538

Antennas, p. III-1838

— satellite, p. II-1261

— transmitting and receiving, p. II-1261

Anthelmintic preparations, p. I-538

Anthracene, p. I-492

Anthraquinone dyes, p. I-474

Antiaircraft artillery, p. II-1004

Antibacterial preparations, p. I-538

Antibiotic preparations, p. I-538

Antibiotics, pp. I-533, III-1908

Anticholinergics, p. I-533

Anticonvulsants, p. I-533

Antidepressant preparations, p. I-538

Antidepressants, p. I-533

Antifreeze, p. III-1970

Antifreeze preparations, p. I-594

Antigens, p. I-548

Antihistamine preparations, p. I-538

Antimony, p. I-824

Antimony based pigments, p. I-474

Antimony oxide, p. I-487

Antineoplastic preparations, p. I-538

Antiperspirants, p. I-574

Antipyretic preparations, p. I-538

Antique auto dealers, p. III-2014

Antique book, p. III-1994

Antique furniture, p. III-1773

Antique homefurnishing, p. III-1777

Antique houseware, p. III-1777

Antique jewelry, p. III-1893

Antique shops, p. III-2193

Antiscald bath and shower valves, p. II-973

Antiscaling compounds, p. I-594

Antiseptic preparations, p. I-538

Antiseptics, p. III-1908

Antiserums, p. I-548

Antispasmodic preparations, p. I-538

Antisubmarine projectors, p. II-1004

Antitank rocket launchers, p. II-1004

Antitoxins, p. I-548

Antivenoms, p. I-548

Apothecaries, p. III-2099

Apparatus wire and cord, p. I-836

Apparatus wire or cord, pp. I-815, 829

Apparel, pp. I-266, III-2122, 2125, 2128, 2134, 2193

— fillings, p. I-250

— findings, p. I-289

— fur, pp. I-266, 284

— trimmings, p. III-1912

Numbers following p. or pp. are page references. Roman numerals indicate volume numbers. Page references are to the starting pages of the industries that produce the product or carry out the activity.

— trimmings and findings, p. I-266
— webbings, p. I-202
Applejack distilling, p. I-176
Appliance controls, p. II-1331
Appliance cords, p. II-1467
Appliance hardware, p. II-932
Appliance regulators, p. II-1331
Appliance timers, p. II-1361
Appliances, pp. III-2049, 2193
— gas, p. III-1846
— household, p. III-1834
— surgical, p. III-1812
Applicators
— wood, p. I-357
Appointment books and refills, p. I-419
Aprons, pp. I-266, 271, 278, 289, 305
— machinery, p. I-305
Aquarium accessories, p. II-1013
Aquariums, p. I-721
Arbor presses, p. II-1128
Arbors, p. II-1139
Arc lamps (therapeutic), p. II-1321
Arc lighting fixtures, p. II-1389
Arc-welding equipment, p. II-1228
Arc-welding transformers, p. II-1420
Arch supports, p. II-1675
Archery equipment, pp. II-1701, III-1882
Architect's equipment, p. III-1819
Architectural block, p. I-736
Architectural coatings, p. I-553
Architectural metalwork, pp. II-907, III-1793
Architectural sculptures, pp. I-680, 761
Architectural terra cotta, p. I-698
Architectural wall panels, p. I-742
Architectural woodwork, p. II-1638
Arctics, p. I-299
Area and sports luminaries, p. II-1389
Argon, p. I-470
Arm bands, pp. I-266, 289
Armature relays, p. II-1436
Armatures, p. II-1426
Armor plate, p. I-779
Armored cable, p. I-829
Armored military vehicles, p. II-1602
Aromatic chemicals, p. III-1970
Arrestors and coils, p. II-1456
Arsenate insecticides, p. I-528
Arsenates, p. I-487
Arsenic based pigments, p. I-474
Arsenic compounds, p. I-487
Arsenite insecticides, p. I-528
Arsenites, p. I-487
Art auctions, p. III-2199
Art dealers, p. III-2199
Art galleries retailing art, p. III-2199
Art goods, p. I-751
Art prints, p. I-419
Art supplies, p. III-2207
Artichokes, p. I-67
Artificial flower arrangements, p. II-1748
Artificial flowers, p. III-1997
Artificial limbs, p. II-1675
Artillery devices, p. II-996
Artist's paint, p. II-1713
Artist's supplies, p. II-1713

Ascorbic acid, p. I-533
Ascots, pp. I-266, 289
Ashtrays, pp. I-680, 712, 721
Asphalt and asphaltic materials, p. I-442
Asphalt paper, p. I-367
Asphalt paving blocks, p. I-447
Asphalt paving mixtures, pp. I-442, 447
Asphalt road compounds, p. I-447
Asphalt roofing cements, p. I-452
Asphalt roofing coatings, p. I-452
Asphalt roofing construction machinery, p. II-1032
Asphalt roofing shingles, p. III-1789
Asphalt saturated boards, p. I-452
Asphalt saturated mats and felts, p. I-452
Asphalt shingles, p. I-452
Assembly machines, p. II-1151
Astringent preparations, p. I-538
Athletic clothing, pp. I-261, 266, 271, 278
Athletic equipment, p. III-2149
Athletic footwear, p. III-1921
Athletic goods, pp. II-1701, III-1882
Athletic shoes, pp. I-299, III-2140
Athletic socks, p. I-255
Athletic uniforms, pp. I-266, 284, III-1882
Atlases, p. I-419
ATM's, p. II-1251
Atom smashers, p. II-1467
Atomizers, p. II-1748
Atropine and derivatives, p. I-533
Attache cases, p. I-305
Attic fans, p. II-1111
Auction houses, p. III-2207
Auction markets
— horses and mules, p. III-1964
— livestock, p. III-1961
— tobacco, p. III-1964
Audio cabinets, p. II-1631
Audio equipment, pp. III-1834, 2053
Audiofrequency oscillators, p. II-1346
Audiological equipment, p. II-1321
Audiometers, p. II-1346
Audiotapes, pp. II-1380, III-1838
Augers, pp. II-891, 1032, 1038
Auto body shop supplies, p. III-1761
Auto supplies, p. III-2029
Autoclaves
— dental, p. II-1681
— industrial, p. II-922
— laboratory, p. II-1665
Autogiros, p. II-1556
Automated blood and body fluid analyzers, p. II-1321
Automatic, p. II-979
Automatic chemical analyzers, p. II-1351
Automatic merchandising machine operators, p. III-2214
Automatic screw machines, p. II-1123
Automatic teller machines, pp. II-1251, III-1800
Automatic transmissions, p. II-1529
Automobile service station equipment, p. III-1761
Automobiles, p. III-1757
— accessories, p. III-1761
    antennas, p. II-1261
— auctions, p. III-1757
— bodies, p. II-1485
— children's, p. II-1707

— dealers, pp. III-2010, 2014
— glass, p. III-1761
— hardware, p. II-932
— lifts, p. II-1193
— parts dealers, p. III-2029
— polishes and cleaners, p. I-565
— radio receivers, p. II-1271
— seat covers, p. II-1535
— seat frames, p. II-1013
— skid chains, p. II-938
— storage batteries, p. II-1441
— suspension springs, p. II-938
— transporter trailers, pp. II-1490, 1499
— trimmings, p. II-1535
Automotive air-conditioners, p. III-1850
Automotive audio equipment, p. III-2029
Automotive chemicals, p. III-1970
Automotive diagnostic equipment, p. II-1346
Automotive electrical switches, p. II-1456
Automotive emissions testing equipment, p. II-1366
Automotive harness and ignition sets, p. II-1511
Automotive light bulbs, p. II-1385
Automotive lighting fixtures, p. II-1511
Automotive or aircraft wire and cable, p. I-815
Automotive parts, pp. III-1761, 2029
Automotive radios, p. III-1834
Automotive steering assemblies, p. II-1518
Automotive suspensions, p. II-1518
Automotive theft alarm systems, p. II-1266
Automotive tire dealers, p. III-2033
Autophones, p. II-1730
Autotransformers, p. II-1420
Autotransformers for switchboards, p. II-1420
Aviation fuels, p. I-442
Awls, p. II-891
Awnings, pp. I-650, II-907, III-1793
Awnings and canopies, p. I-238
Axes, p. II-891
Axle bearings, p. II-1529
Axles, p. I-779
Azides explosives, p. I-584
Azine dyes, p. I-474
Azo dyes, p. I-474
Azobenzene, p. I-492
Baby clothing, pp. III-1918, 2128
Baby foods, pp. I-67, III-1953
Baby formula, p. I-80
Baby furniture, p. III-1773
Baby powder and baby oil, p. I-574
Baby scales, p. II-1228
Backflow preventors, p. II-973
Backhoes, p. II-1032
Bacon, p. I-101
Bacterial vaccines, p. I-548
Bacterins, p. I-548
Badges, pp. I-250, 650, II-1013
Badminton equipment, p. II-1701
Baffles, p. II-898
Bag filling machines, p. II-1211
Bag leather, p. I-295
Bagels, p. I-115
Bags, pp. I-191, 238, 250, 305, 394, 602, II-1701, III-1904
Bags and bagging fabrics, p. I-212
Bait, pp. II-1701, III-1882

Numbers following p. or pp. are page references. Roman numerals indicate volume numbers. Page references are to the starting pages of the industries that produce the product or carry out the activity.

2247

Baked beans, p. I-67
Baked goods, pp. I-115, III-2088
Baked ham, p. III-2082
Bakeries, p. I-115
Bakers' service apparel, pp. I-266, 271, 278
Bakery machinery and equipment, pp. II-1060, III-1866
Bakery ovens, p. II-1060
Bakery products, pp. I-115, 123, III-1928, 1953
Baking chocolate, pp. I-47, 51
Baking powder, p. I-157
Balances, p. II-1228
Balances and scales, pp. II-1665, III-1808, 1819
Balancing equipment, p. II-1091
Balcony railings, p. II-907
Bale throwers, p. II-1022
Bale ties, p. II-938
Balers (farm), p. II-1022
Baling machinery, p. II-1228
Ball bearings, p. II-987
Ball joints, p. II-1167
Ball point pens, p. II-1713
Ball valves, p. II-979
Ballasts, p. II-1420
Ballet slippers, p. I-299
Balloon shops, p. III-2189
Balloons, pp. I-650, 669
Balls
— rubber, p. II-1707
— sport, p. II-1701
— steel, p. I-779
Band uniforms, pp. I-266, 284
Bandages, p. III-1908
Bandages and dressings, p. II-1675
Bandeaux, pp. I-266, 278
Bandsaws, p. II-1045
Banjos, p. II-1730
Bank and turn indicators, p. II-1326
Bank chests, p. II-1013
Bank fixtures, p. II-907
Banners, p. I-250
Bannisters, p. II-907
Baptismal fonts, p. I-761
Bar mill machinery, p. II-1146
Bar soaps, p. I-565
Barbecue sauce, p. I-67
Barbecues, p. II-1403
Barbed wire, pp. I-792, II-938
Barber shop equipment, p. III-1874
Barber's scissors, p. II-885
Barbers' service apparel, pp. I-266, 271
Barbiturates, pp. I-533, 538
Barbituric acid, p. I-533
Barge sections, p. II-898
Barges, p. II-1588
Barium compounds, p. I-487
Barium diagnostic substances, p. I-538
Barium hydroxide, p. I-487
Barley
— feed, p. I-8
— flour, p. I-14
— malt, p. I-14
Barn stanchions and standards, p. II-907
Barographs, p. II-1366
Barometers, p. II-1366

Barometric condensers, p. II-917
Barrel heading and staves, p. I-342
Barrels
— gun, pp. II-1000, 1004
— metal, p. II-927
— new and reconditioned, p. III-1870
— wood, coopered, p. I-342
Barricades, p. II-1013
Bars, p. I-821
— iron, p. I-779
— metal, p. III-1823
— reinforcing, p. II-898
— steel, pp. I-779, 792
Barytes based pigments, p. I-474
Baseball caps, pp. I-266, 289
Baseball equipment, pp. II-1701, III-1882
Baseball uniforms, pp. I-266, 284
Baseboard heaters, p. III-1850
Baseboard heating equipment, p. II-1100
Baseboards, pp. I-333, II-907
Basketball equipment, p. II-1701
Basketball uniforms, pp. I-266, 284
Baskets, pp. I-342, 792, II-938
Bassinets, p. II-1631
Bassoons, p. II-1730
Bath fans, p. II-1396
Bath mats, pp. I-228, 669
Bath salts, p. I-574
Bath shops, p. III-2046
Bathing caps, p. I-289
Bathing suits, pp. I-261, 266, 271, 278, 284
Bathrobes, pp. I-261, 266, 271, 278, 284
Bathroom accessories, pp. I-650, 676, III-1777
Bathroom fixtures, p. II-1013
Bathroom scales, p. II-1228
Bathroom vanities, p. II-1610
Bathtubs, pp. I-650, II-1013
Batteries, pp. II-1441, 1446, III-1761, 1830
Batters (prepared), pp. I-14, 123
Battery chargers, p. II-1467
Battery testers, p. II-1346
Batting, p. I-250
Bauxite brick, p. I-702
Bay oil, p. I-594
Bazaars, p. III-2227
BB guns, p. II-1000
BB shot, p. II-992
Beach sandals, p. I-299
Beach umbrellas, p. II-1748
Beachwear, pp. I-261, 266, 271, 278, 284
Beader machines, p. II-1128
Beaming machinery for yarn, p. II-1060
Beaming yarn, p. I-191
Beams (wood), p. I-311
Beans
— baked, p. I-67
— dry, p. III-1957
Bearing pullers, p. II-891
Bearings, pp. II-987, 1167, 1504, III-1870
Beauty parlor equipment, p. III-1874
Beauty preparations, p. III-1908
Beauty supplies, pp. III-1908, 2103
Bed frames, p. II-1620
Bedcoverings, p. II-1396
Bedjackets, pp. I-266, 278

Bedroom furniture, p. II-1620
Beds, pp. II-1620, 1631
— hospital, pp. II-1665, III-1812
— sleep-system ensembles, p. II-1656
— wood dormitory, p. II-1620
— wood hotel, p. II-1620
Bedsets, pp. I-212, 233
Bedspreads, pp. I-212, 233
Beef, p. I-101
Beef carcasses, p. I-101
Beef stew, p. I-101
Beekeeping supplies, p. III-1990
Beer, pp. III-1982, 2096
Beer bottles, p. I-717
Beer brewing, p. I-171
Beer cans, p. II-927
Beer cooling and dispensing equipment, p. II-1105
Beer kegs, p. II-927
Beeswax polishes and waxes, p. I-565
Beet pulp, p. I-39
Beet sugar refining, p. I-39
Belladonna preparations, p. I-538
Bellows, pp. II-1013, 1228
Bells
— electric, p. II-1467
— musical, p. II-1730
Belt and buckle assembly kits, p. III-1912
Belt conveyor systems, p. II-1193
Belt laces, p. I-305
Belting, p. I-250
Belting butts, p. I-295
Belting
— fabrics, p. I-202
— industrial, p. III-1870
— leather, p. I-295
— machinery, p. I-305
— rubber, p. I-664
Belts
— apparel, pp. I-266, 289
— conveyor, p. II-938
— drying, p. II-938
— leather safety, p. I-305
— machine gun, pp. II-1000, 1004
— money, pp. I-266, 289
Benches
— laboratory, p. II-1665
— park, p. II-1626
— public building, p. II-1626
— work, p. II-1626
Bending and forming machines, p. II-1128
Bends (pipe), p. II-1008
Bentwood (steam bent) products, p. I-357
Benzaldehyde, p. I-492
Benzene, pp. I-442, 466
Benzene hexachloride insecticides, p. I-528
Benzoic acid, p. I-492
Berries, pp. I-67, III-1949
Berry crates, p. I-342
Berry cups, p. I-342
Berry harvesting machines, p. II-1022
Beryllia porcelain insulators, p. I-685
Beryllium castings, p. I-856
Beryllium die-castings, p. I-856
Beryllium oxide, p. I-487
Beryllium refining, p. I-824

Numbers following p. or pp. are page references. Roman numerals indicate volume numbers. Page references are to the starting pages of the industries that produce the product or carry out the activity.

Beta-ray irradiation equipment, p. II-1356
Betatrons, p. II-1467
Beverage bases, pp. I-146, III-1953
Beverage bottling machinery, p. III-1866
Beverage concentrates, p. III-1953
Beverage containers, p. I-717
Beverage coolers, p. III-1854
Beverage flavorings, p. I-146
Beverage syrups, p. I-146
Beverages
— alcoholic, p. III-1982
— beer, etc., pp. I-171
— bottled water, p. I-164
— dietary, p. I-80
— fruit and vegetable, pp. I-67, 164
— liquors, p. I-180
— milk based, p. I-85
— soft drink, p. I-164
— wine, spirits, pp. III-1986
— wines and brandies, p. I-176
Bias bindings, pp. I-202, 250
Bibs, p. I-266
Bibs and aprons, pp. I-266, 289
Bicycle pumps, p. II-1183
Bicycles, pp. II-1598, III-1757, 1882, 2020, 2149,
  2193
Bidets, p. I-676
Billboards, p. II-1719
Billet mill machinery, p. II-1146
Billets (steel), p. I-779
Billfolds, p. I-305
Billiard equipment, pp. II-1701, III-1882
Binder's board, p. I-373
Binders (looseleaf), p. III-1900
Bindery machinery, p. II-1060
Binding equipment, p. II-1076
Binocular cases, p. I-305
Binoculars, pp. II-1081, III-1816
Bins
— fabricated metal plate work, p. II-898
— metal, p. II-927
— storage, p. III-1793
Biohazard protective clothing, p. II-1675
Biologicals and allied products, p. III-1908
Bird feed, p. I-8
Birth control devices, p. I-669
Birth control pills, p. I-538
Biscuits, p. I-115
Bismuth refining, p. I-824
Bits and knives for metalworking, p. II-1139
Bits
— drill, metalworking, pp. II-1139
— edge tool, woodworking, pp. II-891
— rock drills, pp. II-1032, 1038
Black pigments, p. I-474
Black plate, p. III-1823
Blackboards, pp. I-761, II-1713, III-1819
Blackplate, p. I-779
Blacksmith's aprons, p. I-305
Blackstrap invert, p. I-43
Blackstrap molasses, p. I-43
Blades, p. III-1842
— graders, p. II-1032
— knife, p. II-885

— razor, p. III-1908
— saw, p. II-891
Blanc fixe, p. I-474
Blank cartridges, p. II-992
Blank tapes, pp. II-1380, III-1838
Blankbooks, pp. I-419, III-1900
Blanket bags, p. I-238
Blankets, pp. I-207, 233, III-1777
Blankets and bedspreads, p. I-197
Blankets
— electric, pp. II-1396, III-1834
Blanks
— cutting tool, p. II-1139
— light bulbs, p. I-712
— ophthalmic lens, pp. I-712, 721
— wood, p. I-333
Blast furnaces, p. I-779
Blasting accessories, p. I-584
Blasting powders, p. I-584
Bleacher seating, p. II-1626
Bleaches, pp. I-565, III-1970
Blended flour, p. I-14
Blenders, p. II-1396
Blimps, p. II-1556
Blinds, pp. I-1661, III-1777
Blister copper, p. I-821
Block and tackle, p. II-1193
Block ice, p. I-164
Blocks
— asphalt paving, p. I-447
— concrete and cinder, p. I-736
— fire clay, p. I-702
— glass, p. I-712
— tackle, wood, pp. I-357
— tailors' pressing wood, p. I-357
Blood bank process equipment, p. II-1351
Blood derivative diagnostic substances, p. I-543
Blood derivatives, pp. I-548, III-1908
Blood fractions, p. I-548
Blood glucose test kits, p. I-543
Blood plasma, p. III-1908
Blood pressure apparatus, p. II-1670
Blood testing apparatus, p. II-1665
Blood transfusion apparatus, p. II-1670
Blooming and slabbing mill machinery, p. II-1146
Blooms (steel), p. I-779
Blouses, pp. I-261, 266, 278, 284
Blow dryers, p. II-1396
Blow molding machinery for plastics, p. II-1050
Blow torches, p. II-891
Blower filter units, p. II-1111
Blowers
— forage, p. II-1022
— industrial, p. III-1866
— leaf, p. II-1027
Blueprint equipment, p. II-1086
Blueprinting equipment, p. III-1800
Blushes
— face, p. I-574
Board
— bagasse, p. I-318
— gypsum, p. I-751
— particle, p. I-318

Boards
— asphalt saturated, p. I-452
— bulletin, wood and cork, pp. I-357
— wood, pp. I-311, 333, 357
Boat and ship lighting fixtures, p. II-1511
Boat dealers, p. III-2023
Boat lifts, p. II-1193
Boat sections, p. II-898
Boat trailers, pp. II-1490, 1499, III-2023
Boats, pp. I-650, II-1593, III-1878, 1882
Bobbin blocks and blanks, p. I-333
Bobbins, pp. I-378, II-1060
Bobsleds, p. II-1701
Body stockings, pp. I-261, 266, 278
Bofors guns, p. II-1004
Boiler casings, p. II-917
Boiler controls, p. II-1336
Boiler couplings and drains, p. II-979
Boiler gauge cocks, p. II-979
Boiler tubes, p. I-787
Boilers, pp. II-917, 1100, III-1846
Bologna, p. I-101
Bolts, pp. I-650, II-957
Bomb lifts, p. II-1193
Bombcluster adapters, p. II-996
Bombs, p. II-996
Bond paper, pp. I-367, 402
Bonded-fiber fabrics, p. I-207
Bone black, p. I-483
Bone china, p. I-680
Bone drills, p. II-1670
Bone meal, p. I-8
Bone novelties, p. II-1748
Bone plates and screws, p. II-1670
Bone rongeurs, p. II-1670
Book ends, p. II-1013
Book paper, pp. I-367, 387
Bookbinder's leather, p. I-295
Bookbinding machines, p. II-1060
Bookcases, pp. II-1620, 1631, 1649
Bookkeeping machines, p. III-1800
Books, pp. I-419, III-1900, 1994, 2161, 2193
Boomerangs, p. II-1701
Boosters (voltage), p. II-1420
Boosters and bursters (artillery), p. II-996
Boot and shoe cut stock and findings, pp. I-305,
  III-1874
Boot and shoe lasts, p. I-357
Boot making and repairing machinery, p. II-1060
Boots, pp. I-299, III-1921
Borax, p. I-487
Bordeaux mixture insecticides, p. I-528
Boric acid, p. I-487
Boring machines, p. II-1123
Boron compounds, p. I-487
Borosilicate, p. I-487
Botanical extract preparations, p. I-538
Botanical insecticides, p. I-528
Botanicals, p. III-1908
Bottle caps, pp. I-650, 878
Bottle corks, p. I-357
Bottle covers, p. I-357
Bottle warmers, p. II-1396
Bottle washing systems, p. II-1211
Bottled gas, p. III-2221

Numbers following p. or pp. are page references. Roman numerals indicate volume numbers. Page references are to the starting pages of the industries that produce the product or carry out the activity.

Product/Activity Index

2249

Bottled water, pp. III-1953, 2227
Bottles, pp. I-717, III-1870
— plastics, p. I-645
— vacuum, p. II-927
— waste, p. III-1889
Bottling flavored water, p. I-164
Bottling machinery, p. II-1211
Bottling machinery and equipment, p. III-1866
Boudoir lamp fixtures, p. II-1389
Bouillon, p. I-67
Boulets, p. I-462
Bovine semen, p. III-1964
Bow ties, pp. I-266, 289
Bowling center furniture, p. II-1626
Bowling equipment, pp. III-1882, 2149
Bowling pin blanks, p. I-333
Bowling pin machines, p. II-1701
Bowls, pp. I-357, 650
Bows, p. I-250
— archery, p. II-1701
— shoe, leather, pp. I-305
Box cleats, p. I-342
Box lumber, p. I-342
Box lunches, p. I-157
Box shook, p. I-342
Box springs, p. II-1656
Box toes, p. I-305
Boxed beef, p. I-101
Boxed meat produced, p. I-101
Boxes
— cigar, wood and part wood, pp. I-342
— corrugated and solid fiber, p. I-378
— electrical wiring, p. II-1456
— folding, p. I-378
— hat, p. I-305
— industrial, p. III-1870
— jewelry, p. I-342
— leather, p. I-305
— light gauge metal, p. II-927
— paperboard, p. III-1904
— sanitary food, p. I-378
— setup, p. I-378
— shipping, p. I-378
— truck, p. II-1485
— waste, p. III-1889
— wood, p. I-342
Boxing equipment, p. II-1701
Boxspring frames, p. II-1643
Boys' socks, p. I-255
Bra-slips, pp. I-266, 278
Bracelets, p. II-1695
Brackets, pp. I-333, II-932, 938
Brads, p. III-1842
— iron or steel, p. I-792
— metal, p. II-938
Braiding machinery for textiles, p. II-1060
Brake caliper assemblies, p. II-1523
Brake cylinders, p. II-1523
Brake discs (rotor), p. II-1523
Brake drums, p. II-1523
Brake fluid
— synthetic, p. I-594
Brake fluids
— petroleum, p. I-457
Brake hose assemblies, p. II-1523

Brake linings, p. II-1523
Brake pads and shoes, p. II-1523
Brake service equipment, p. II-1091
Brakes and clutches, pp. II-1167, 1436
Brakes and parts, pp. II-1523, 1583
Brakes
— electromagnetic, p. II-1436
— press, metalworking, pp. II-1128
Bran, p. I-14
Branding irons, p. II-1713
Brandy and brandy spirits, p. III-1986
Brandy distilling, p. I-176
Brass die-castings, p. I-856
Brass foundries, p. I-856
Brass goods (plumbing), p. III-1846
Brass polishes, p. I-565
Brass products, p. I-829
Brassieres, pp. I-266, 278
Brasswork, p. II-907
Braziers, p. II-1403
Brazilwood extract, p. I-492
Brazing, p. II-963
Bread and bread-type roll mixes, p. I-123
Bread and bread-type rolls, p. I-115
Bread crumbs, p. I-157
Bread machines, p. II-1396
Bread slicing machinery, p. II-1060
Bread wrapping machines, p. II-1211
Breakers
— coal, p. II-1038
— vacuum, plumbing, pp. II-979
Breakfast bars
— nonchocolate covered, p. I-56
Breakfast cereals, pp. I-35, III-1953
Breechings (metal plate), p. II-898
Breweries, p. I-171
Brewers' malt, p. I-14
Brewers' pitch, p. I-492
Brewers' rice, p. I-14
Brewers' yeast, p. III-1953
Brewery machinery, p. II-1060
Bricks, pp. I-690, III-1785
— adobe, p. I-698
— clay refractory, p. I-702
— concrete, p. I-736
— glass, pp. I-712, 721
— nonclay refractory, p. I-702
Bridal dresses or gowns, pp. I-266, 278
Bridal gown shops, p. III-2137
Bridge and gate lifting machinery, p. II-1228
Bridge sections, p. II-898
Bridges, pp. II-1346, 1691
Bridle leather, p. I-295
Briefcases, p. I-305
Briefs, pp. I-266, 284
— underwear, pp. I-261, 266, 271, 278
Briquettes, p. I-462
Bristles, p. III-1964
Bristols board stock, p. I-373
Bristols paper stock, p. I-367
Broaches, p. II-1139
Broaching machines, p. II-1123
Broadcast equipment, p. II-1261
Broadcasting equipment, p. III-1838
Broadwoven fabrics, p. I-197

Broadwoven fabrics finishing, p. I-217
Brocades weaving, p. I-197
Bromine, p. I-487
Bromochloromethane, p. I-492
Bronchoscopes, pp. II-1321, 1670
Bronze die-castings, p. I-856
Bronze foundries, p. I-856
Bronze printing inks, p. I-579
Bronze products, p. I-829
Broomcorn, p. III-1964
Brooms, pp. II-1739, III-1777
Broth, p. I-67
Brown beet sugar refining, p. I-39
Brown sugar, pp. I-39, 43
Brucine, p. I-533
Brush blocks
— carbon or molded graphite, p. II-1462
— wood, turned and shaped, pp. I-333
Brushes and brush stock contacts, p. II-1462
Brushes
— artists', p. II-1713
— household and industrial, p. II-1739
— paint, p. II-1739
— rubber, p. I-669
Brushing machines, p. II-1123
Brushplates, p. II-1462
Bubble bath preparations, p. I-574
Bubble packaging materials, p. I-650
Bucket and scarifier teeth, p. II-1032
Buckets
— elevator or conveyor, p. II-1193
— excavating, p. II-1032
— wood, coopered, pp. I-342
Buckles, p. II-1734
Buckwheat flour, p. I-14
Buffets (furniture), p. II-1620
Buffing and polishing machines, p. II-1123
Buffing and polishing wheels, p. I-755
Buffing compounds, p. I-565
Buffing machines, p. II-1206
Builder's hardware, p. II-932
Building blocks, p. III-1785
Building board, p. III-1781
Building controls, p. II-1331
Building materials, pp. I-650, III-1793
Building panels, p. I-650
Building paper, p. III-1793
Building paper stock, p. I-367
Building stone, p. III-1785
Building tile, p. I-690
Buildings
— mobile, p. I-347
— prefabricated, pp. I-352, II-898, III-1781, 1793
Built-up mica, p. I-775
Bulbs, p. II-1385
Bulgur (flour), p. I-14
Bulk gasoline, p. III-1974
Bulk storage tanks, p. II-922
Bulldozers, p. II-1032
Bullet jackets, p. II-992
Bulletin boards, p. I-357
Bulletproof vests, p. II-1675
Bumpers, p. II-1550
Bundling machinery, p. II-1076
Bungs (wood), p. I-357

Numbers following p. or pp. are page references. Roman numerals indicate volume numbers. Page references are to the starting pages of the industries that produce the product or carry out the activity.

Bunsen burners, p. II-1665
Buntings, pp. I-266, 284
Buoyancy instruments, p. II-1336
Buoys, pp. I-357, II-898
Burglar alarm systems and equipment, p. II-1266
Burial caskets, pp. II-1744, III-1874
Burial garments, pp. I-266, 284
Burial vaults, pp. I-742, 761, II-1744
Burner ignition transformers, p. II-1420
Burners
— fuel oil and distillate oil, p. III-1846
— heating, p. II-1100
Burnishing machines, p. II-1123
Burnt wood articles, p. I-357
Burnt-out laces, p. I-250
Bus bar structures, p. II-1431
Bus bars, p. II-1456
Bus bodies, p. II-1485
Buses, pp. II-1481, 1583, III-1757
Bushings
— plain, p. II-1167
— plastics, p. I-650
— wood, p. I-357
Business directories, p. I-419
Business forms, p. I-419
Business machines and equipment, p. III-1800
Butadiene, pp. I-466, 492
Butadiene copolymers, pp. I-499, 504
Butadiene rubber, p. I-504
Butane, p. I-466
Butcher knives, p. II-885
Butcher shops, p. III-2082
Butter, pp. I-85, III-1932
Butter processing machinery, p. II-1060
Butter
— creamery and whey, p. I-85
Butterfly valves, p. II-979
Buttermilk, p. I-85
Button cells (battery), p. II-1446
Buttonhole and eyelet machinery, p. II-1060
Buttons, pp. II-1695, 1734
Butyl acetate, p. I-492
Butyl rubber, p. I-504
Butylene, pp. I-442, 466
C-clamps, p. II-891
Cabin cruisers, p. II-1593
Cabinet hardware, p. II-932
Cabinets, pp. II-1631, 1649
— kitchen, p. II-1610
— kitchen, built in, pp. III-1781
— kitchen, free standing, pp. III-1773
— metal, p. II-1631
— metal household, p. II-1631
— metal, radio and TV, pp. II-1631
— wood household, p. II-1620
— wood office, p. II-1649
Cable decoders, p. II-1261
Cable TV equipment, p. II-1261
Cable
— copper, p. I-829
— iron or steel, p. I-792
— nonferrous, p. II-1450
— noninsulated wire, p. II-938
— wire, p. III-1823

Cabs
— agricultural machinery, p. II-1022
— construction machinery, p. II-1032
— industrial trucks, p. II-1193
— trucks, vans, pp. II-1477
Caddy carts, p. II-1701
Cadmium, p. I-824
Cafeteria fixtures, p. II-1643
Cafeteria furniture, p. II-1626
Caffeine and derivatives, p. I-533
Caftans, pp. I-266, 271, 278, 284
Cages, p. II-938
Caissons, p. II-922
Cake, p. I-115
Cake frosting, p. I-157
Cake frosting mixes, p. I-157
Cake mixes, p. I-123
Cake ornaments, p. I-56
Cake
— frozen, p. I-115
Calcimines, pp. I-553, III-2003
Calcium carbide, p. I-487
Calcium citrate, p. I-492
Calcium hydroxide, p. I-747
Calcium hypochlorite, p. I-487
Calcium inorganic compounds, p. I-487
Calcium organic compounds, p. I-492
Calcium oxalate, p. I-492
Calcium oxide, p. I-747
Calculators, pp. II-1076, III-1800
Calendar shops, p. III-2207
Calendars, p. I-419
Calendering machinery for textiles, p. II-1060
Calf high sheer hosiery, p. I-255
Calipers (brake), p. II-1523
Calipers and dividers, p. II-891
Calliopes (steam organs), p. II-1730
Camcorders, p. II-1271
Camelback, pp. I-659, II-1050
Camera bags, p. I-305
Camera equipment, p. III-1797
Camera lenses, p. II-1081
Camera shops, p. III-2061
Cameras, pp. II-1086, 1261
Camisoles, pp. I-266, 278
Camp furniture
— metal, p. II-1631
— reed and rattan, p. II-1631
— wood, p. II-1620
Camper dealers
— recreational, p. III-2017
Camper units (trucks), p. II-1499
Camphor
— natural, p. I-492
— synthetic, p. I-492
Camping equipment, p. III-1882
Camping trailers, p. III-1757
Camping trailers and chassis, p. II-1499
Cams, p. II-1139
Can forming machines, p. II-1128
Can keys, p. II-938
Can lids and ends, p. II-927
Can openers, pp. II-891, 1396
Canceling machinery (postal), p. II-1076
Candied fruits and fruit peel, p. I-56

Candles, pp. II-1748, III-2207
Candy, pp. I-47, 51, 56, III-1938, 2091
Candy bars, pp. I-47, 56
Cane sugar, pp. I-43, III-1953
Cane syrup, p. I-43
Canes, pp. II-1013, 1748
Canisters (ammo), p. II-996
Canned food, p. III-1953
Canned meats, p. I-101
Canned nuts, p. I-136
Canning machinery, p. II-1211
Canning supplies, p. III-1870
Cannons, p. II-1004
Cannulae, p. II-1670
Canola oil, pp. I-25, 30
Canopies
— sheet metal, p. II-907
Cans
— aluminum, p. II-927
— metal, p. II-927
— steel, p. II-927
Cants
— resawed (lumber), p. I-333
Canvas
— artist's, p. II-1713
— bags, p. I-238
— board, p. II-1713
— products, p. I-238
— shoes, p. I-299
Capacitors, pp. II-1291, 1467, III-1838
Capes, pp. I-266, 278
— fur, pp. I-266, 284
— waterproof, p. I-284
Capping machinery, p. II-1211
Caprolactam, p. I-492
Caps, pp. I-261, 266, 289
— academic, pp. I-266, 284
— blasting, p. I-584
— bomb, p. II-996
— fur, p. I-284
— heel and toe, leather, pp. I-305
— leather, p. I-284
— pick-up truck, p. II-1499
— toy pistol, p. I-594
Capsules (gelatin), p. I-594
Car alarms, p. II-1266
Car bodies, p. II-1485
Car seals, p. II-1013
Car seats, p. II-1631
Car stereos, p. II-1271
Car wash equipment, p. III-1874
Car wheels, p. I-779
Carbides, p. I-487
Carbines, p. II-1000
Carbinol, p. I-492
Carbohydrate plastics, p. I-499
Carbon (activated), p. I-594
Carbon arc lamps, p. II-1321
Carbon black, pp. I-483, III-1970
Carbon brick, p. I-702
Carbon compounds
— inorganic, p. I-487
— organic, p. I-492
Carbon dioxide, p. I-470
Carbon disulfide, p. I-487

Carbon electrodes, p. II-1462

Carbon monoxide detectors, pp. II-1266, III-1838

Carbon paper, p. II-1713

Carbon specialties

— aerospace, p. II-1462

— electrical, p. II-1462

— mechanical, p. II-1462

Carbon tetrachloride, p. I-492

Carbonated drinks, p. I-164

Carbonic acid, p. I-487

Carbonizing equipment, p. II-1060

Carbons

— electric, p. II-1462

— lighting, p. II-1462

Carburetor cleaners, p. I-594

Carburetors, p. II-1504

Card cases, pp. I-305, II-1695

Card shops, p. III-2189

Card tables, pp. II-1620, 1631

Cardboard, pp. I-373, 394, III-1904

Carded nonwoven fabrics, p. I-207

Carded yarn, p. I-191

Cardiac preparations, p. I-538

Carding machinery, p. II-1060

Cardiodynameter, p. II-1321

Cardiographs, p. II-1321

Cardiophones, p. II-1321

Cardioscope, p. II-1321

Cardiotachometer, p. II-1321

Cards, p. I-419

— die-cut, p. I-414

— die-cut office supply, p. I-402

— greeting, p. III-1900

Cargo ship building, p. II-1588

Carnival equipment, p. III-1874

Carnival park rides, p. II-1091

Carnival shooting galleries, p. II-1091

Carousel conveyors, p. II-1193

Carousels, p. II-1091

Carpenter's handtools, p. II-891

Carpet, pp. I-228, III-1777, 2040

Carpet cleaning equipment, pp. II-1091, 1396

Carpet linings, p. I-197

Carpet paddings, p. I-207

Carpet spinning, p. I-191

Carpet sweepers, p. II-1091

Carports

— prefabricated, p. II-898

Carriages

— baby, p. II-1707

— doll, p. II-1707

Carrier equipment, p. II-1256

Carrots, p. I-157

Cars

— electric, p. II-1472

— mining, p. II-1038

Carton filling machinery, p. II-1211

Cartons, p. III-1904

— egg, molded pulp, pp. I-414

— folding, p. I-378

— milk, p. I-378

Cartridge cases, p. II-992

Cartridge shapes, p. I-829

Cartridge toner, p. III-1900

Cartridges, pp. II-992, 1206

Carts

— caddy, p. II-1701

— grocery, p. II-1193

— lawn and garden, p. II-1027

Carving sets, p. II-885

Carwashing machinery, p. II-1091

Case leather, p. I-295

Casein, p. I-80

— fibers and filaments, p. I-509

— plastics, p. I-499

Casements, p. II-907

Cases

— jewelry, p. I-305

— jewelry, precious metal, pp. II-1695

— luggage, p. I-305

— musical instrument, p. I-305

— shipping, wood, wirebound, pp. I-342

— wood packing, p. I-342

— wood shipping, p. I-342

Cash boxes, p. II-927

Cash registers, pp. II-1076, III-1800

Casings

— metal, pp. II-898, 907

— sausage, p. I-620

Caskets

— burial, pp. II-1744, III-1874

— hardware, p. II-932

Casks, p. I-342

Casseroles, p. II-1396

Cassette tapes, p. II-1375

Cast iron pipe, p. III-1823

Cast stone, p. I-742

Casters, p. II-932

Castings, pp. I-844, 851, 856

Castor oil, p. I-30

Cat food, p. I-3

Cat litter, p. I-594

CAT Scanners, p. II-1356

Catalogs, p. I-419

Catalogs of collections, p. I-419

Catalytic converters, p. II-1550

Catapult guns, p. II-1004

Cathartic preparations, p. I-538

Catheters, p. II-1670

Cathode ray tubes (CRT), p. II-1276

Cathodic protection equipment, p. II-1467

Catsup, p. I-67

Cattle, p. III-1961

Cattle feeding and watering equipment, p. II-1022

Cattle feeds, p. I-8

Caulking

— compounds, p. I-559

— guns, p. II-891

— materials, p. III-1970

Caustic potash, p. I-479

Caustic soda, pp. I-479, III-1970

CB radios, p. II-1261

CD-ROMs

— drives, p. II-1242

— software, p. II-1371

Cedar chests, p. II-1620

Cedar oil, p. I-594

Ceiling fans, p. II-1396

Ceiling lighting, p. II-1389

Ceiling lumber, pp. I-311, 333

Ceilometers, p. II-1366

Cellophane film or sheet, p. I-509

Cellophane tape, p. III-1900

Cellos and parts, p. II-1730

Cellular telephones, pp. II-1261, III-1838, 2053

Cellulose acetate, pp. I-492, 499

Cellulose nitrate resins, p. I-499

Cellulose propionate resins, p. I-499

Cellulose xanthate, p. I-499

Cellulosic fibers, p. I-509

Cellulosic film, p. I-614

Cellulosic yarn, p. I-509

Cement, pp. I-726, III-1785

— clay refractory, p. I-702

— clinker, p. I-726

— Keene's, p. I-751

— kilns, p. II-1060

— rubber, p. I-559

Cement-making machinery, p. III-1866

Cements

— asphalt roofing, p. I-452

— dental, p. II-1681

Cemetery memorial dealers, p. III-2207

Centering machines, p. II-1123

Central heating equipment, p. III-1850

Central nervous system stimulants, p. I-538

Central office and switching equipment, p. II-1256

Central vacuuming systems, pp. II-1091, 1396

Central-mixed concrete, p. I-731

Centrifugal pumps, p. II-1178

Centrifuges, p. II-1228

Cephalosporin, p. I-533

Ceramic colors, p. I-474

Ceramic construction materials, p. III-1785

Ceramic fiber, p. I-775

Ceramic kilns and furnaces, p. II-1216

Ceramic tile, p. I-694

Cereal grain flour, p. I-14

Cereal grain germ, p. I-14

Cereal products, p. III-1953

Cerium salts, p. I-487

Cervical collars, p. II-1675

Cesium and cesium compounds, p. I-487

Cetyl alcohol, p. I-492

Chafing dishes, p. II-1396

Chain, p. II-938

Chain fittings, p. II-1013

Chain hoists, p. II-1193

Chain ladders, p. II-907

Chain link fencing, pp. I-792, II-938

Chains, p. II-938

— power transmission, p. II-1167

— precious metal, p. II-1695

— surveyor's, p. II-1366

Chainsaw blades, p. II-891

Chainsaws, pp. II-1206, III-1866

Chairs, pp. II-1620, 1649

— barber and beauty, p. II-1626

— cane, p. II-1631

— dentist's, p. II-1681

— glides, p. II-1643

— metal household, p. II-1631

— portable folding, p. II-1626

— seats, p. II-1643

— springs, p. II-1615

— stacking, p. II-1626
— upholstered, p. II-1615
— wood, p. II-1649
Chalk, p. II-1713
Chalkboards, p. II-1713
Chambrays weaving, p. I-197
Chamfering machines, p. II-1123
Chamois, p. I-295
Champagne, p. I-176
Chandeliers, p. II-1389
Change making machines, p. II-1091
Channel black, p. I-483
Charcoal, p. I-492
— activated, p. I-594
— briquettes, p. I-492
Chasers, p. II-1139
Chasing metals, p. II-963
Chassis, p. II-1472
— heavy truck, p. II-1481
— light truck, p. II-1477
— motor vehicle, p. III-1757
Chauffeurs' hats and caps, pp. I-266, 289
Check handling machines, p. III-1800
Check valves, p. II-979
Check writing machines, p. II-1076
Checkbooks, p. I-419
— covers, pp. I-305, II-1695
Checkers and checkerboards, p. II-1707
Cheese, pp. I-75, III-1932
— confections, p. III-1938
— cottage, p. I-85
— curls and puffs, p. I-136
— imitation, p. I-75
— natural, p. I-75
— processing machinery, p. II-1060
— salad dressing, p. I-151
— spreads, p. I-75
Cheesecloths, p. I-197
Chemical additives, p. III-1970
Chemical finishing, p. I-217
Chemical gases, p. III-1970
Chemical kilns, p. II-1060
Chemical machinery, p. III-1866
Chemical milling machines, p. II-1123
Chemical processing machinery, p. II-1060
Chemical stoneware, p. I-680
Chemical toilets, p. I-650
Chemicals, pp. III-1970, 1990
Chemises, pp. I-261, 266, 278
Chessmen and chessboards, p. II-1707
Chestnut extract, p. I-492
Chests
— safe deposit, p. II-1013
— tool, p. I-342
Chewing gum, pp. I-56, III-1938
Chewing gum machinery, p. II-1060
Chewing tobacco, pp. I-187, III-2000
Chicken and chicken products, p. III-1935
Chicken brooders, p. II-1022
Chicken coops, pp. I 342, 352
Chicken feeders, p. II-1022
Chicken feeds, p. I-8
Chicken netting, p. II-938

Chickens
— processing, p. I-96
— slaughtering, p. I-96
Chicks, p. III-1964
Children's clothing, p. III-1918
Children's shoes, p. I-299
Children's socks, p. I-255
Children's vehicles, p. III-1886
Chili con carne, p. I-67
Chili pepper or powder, p. I-151
Chili sauce, p. I-67
Chimes, pp. II-1467, 1730
Chimney caps, p. I-742
China closets, p. II-1620
China cooking ware, p. I-680
China tableware, p. I-680
Chinaware, pp. III-1777, 1808, 2046
Chinese foods canning, p. I-67
Chinese noodles, p. I-157
Chintzes weaving, p. I-197
Chip placement machinery, p. II-1060
Chipboard, pp. I-318, 373, 394
Chipper mills, p. I-311
Chippers, p. II-1027
— portable, commercial, pp. II-1032
— stationary, p. II-1060
Chips, p. III-1938
Chisels, pp. II-891, 1206
Chloral, p. I-492
Chlordane insecticides, p. I-528
Chloride of lime, p. I-487
Chlorinated rubber, p. I-504
Chlorine, p. I-479
Chlorine compounds, p. I-487
Chlorine dioxide, p. I-487
Chloroacetic acid, p. I-492
Chlorobenzene, p. I-492
Chlorodifluoromethane, p. I-470
Chlorofluorocarbon gases, p. I-470
Chloroform, p. I-492
Chloronaphthalene, p. I-492
Chlorophenol, p. I-492
Chloropicrin, p. I-492
Chloroprene rubber, p. I-504
Chlorosulfonated polyethylenes, p. I-504
Chlorosulfonic acid, p. I-487
Chlorotoluene, p. I-492
Chocolate, pp. I-47, 51, III-1953
Chocolate milk, p. I-85
Chocolate processing machinery, p. II-1060
Chocolate
— bars, p. I-47
— candy, p. III-1938
— coatings, p. I-51
— confectionery, p. I-47
— covered candy bars, p. I-51
— granola bars, p. I-51
Chokes for electronic circuitry, p. II-1301
Cholera serums, p. I-548
Cholinesterse inhibitors, p. I-528
Chop suey
— frozen, p. I-61
Chow mein
— frozen, p. I-61
Chowders, p. I-109

Christmas tree assemblies (oil field), p. II-1038
Christmas tree lighting sets, p. II-1389
Christmas tree ornaments, pp. I-712, 721, II-1748
Christmas trees, pp. II-1748, III-2227
Chromatographic instruments, p. II-1351
Chromatographs, p. II-1336
Chrome pigments, p. I-474
Chrome plating, p. II-963
Chromic acid, p. I-487
Chromium, p. I-824
— compounds, p. I-487
— oxide, p. I-487
— salts, p. I-487
Chronographs, p. II-1361
Chronometers, p. II-1361
Chronoscopes, p. II-1351
Chucking machines, p. II-1123
Chucks, p. II-1139
Church furniture, p. II-1626
Church supplies, p. III-1819
Chutes, p. II-898
Cider, p. I-151
— presses, p. II-1060
— vinegar, p. I-151
Cigar and cigarette holders, p. I-650
Cigar boxes, p. I-342
Cigar cases, pp. I-305, II-1695
Cigarette cases, pp. I-305, II-1695
Cigarette holders, p. II-1748
Cigarette lighter flints, p. II-1748
Cigarette lighters, p. II-1748
Cigarette making machinery, p. II-1060
Cigarette paper, pp. I-367, 414
Cigarette stands, pp. III-2205, 2227
Cigarette tow, p. I-509
Cigarette vending machines, p. II-1091
Cigarettes, pp. I-187, III-2000
Cigars, pp. I-187, III-2000, 2205
Cinchona and derivatives, p. I-533
Cinder block (clinker), p. I-736
Circuit board making machinery, p. II-1060
Circuit boards, pp. II-1281, III-1838
Circuit breakers, pp. II-1431, III-1830
Circuit testers, p. II-1346
Circuits, p. III-1838
Circular, p. I-212
Circular knitting machinery, p. II-1060
Circular saws, pp. II-1045, 1206
Citizens band radios, p. II-1261
Citral, p. I-492
Citrates, p. I-492
Citric acid, p. I-492
Citronella oil, p. I-594
Citronellal, p. I-492
Citrus pulp, pp. I-8, 61
Clamps, p. II-1139
— surgical, p. II-1670
Clarinets, p. II-1730
Clasps
— shoe (leather), p. I-305
Clay
— construction materials, p. III-1785
— modeling, p. II-1713
— refractories, p. I-702
— statuary, p. I-680

Numbers following p. or pp. are page references. Roman numerals indicate volume numbers. Page references are to the starting pages of the industries that produce the product or carry out the activity.

Product/Activity Index

2253

Clayworking and tempering machinery, p. II-1060
Clean room suits, p. II-1675
Cleaners, p. II-1396
Cleaning compounds, p. III-1970
Cleaning equipment
— ultrasonic, p. II-1467
Cleaning machinery
— mining, p. II-1038
Cleavers, p. II-885
Clerical vestments, pp. I-261, 266, 284
Climbing shoes, p. I-299
Clipboards, p. I-357
Clippers
— animal, p. II-891
— fingernail, p. II-885
Clips
— gun, pp. II-1000, 1004
Clock materials and parts, p. II-1361
Clock radios, p. II-1271
Clock shops, p. III-2143
Clock springs, p. II-1361
Clocks, pp. II-1361, III-1893
Closed circuit TV equipment, p. II-1261
Closures, pp. I-878, III-1904
Cloth, p. I-755
— spreading machinery, p. II-1060
— winding reels, p. I-357
— woven wire, p. II-938
Clothes dryer controls, p. II-1331
Clothes dryers (clothes horses), p. I-357
Clothes hangers, p. I-650
Clothespins, pp. I-357, 650
Clothing, pp. III-1915, 1918, 2122, 2125, 2128, 2131, 2193
Clothing accessories, p. III-1918
Clothing
— doll, p. II-1707
— fur, pp. I-266, 284
— leather or sheep-lined, pp. I-266, 284
— water resistant, pp. I-266, 271, 278, 284
— water-repellent, pp. I-266, 271, 278, 284
— waterproof, pp. I-266, 284
Cloths, p. II-1739
— dusting and polishing, p. I-565
Clove oil, p. I-594
Clubs (sport), p. II-1701
Clutches and brakes, p. II-1167
Coagulation diagnostic substances, pp. I-538, 543
Coal, p. III-1827
— breakers, cutters, and pulverizers, pp. II-1038
— chutes, p. II-907
— conveyors, p. II-1193
— tar distillates, p. I-492
— tar paving materials, p. I-447
— tar products, p. III-1970
— tar resins, p. I-499
Coat hangers, p. II-938
Coat linings (fur), pp. I-266, 284
Coat trimmings, pp. I-266, 289
Coatings
— chocolate, p. I-47
Coats, pp. I-266, 271, 278, 284, III-2137
— artificial leather, pp. I-266, 284
— fur, pp. I-266, 284
— leather, pp. I-266, 284

— nontailored service apparel, pp. I-266, 271, 278
— tailored, pp. I-271, 278
— waterproof, pp. I-266, 289
Coaxial cable, pp. I-815, III-1830
— copper, p. I-829
— nonferrous, pp. I-836, II-1450
Coaxial connectors, p. II-1306
Cobalt, p. I-824
Cobalt 60, p. I-487
Cobalt chloride, p. I-487
Cobalt compounds, p. I-487
Cobalt sulfate, p. I-487
Cocaine and derivatives, p. I-533
Cocks (plumbing), p. II-973
Cocktail mixes, p. I-157
Cocktails, p. III-1986
Cocoa, p. I-47
— beans, p. III-1964
— butter, p. I-47
— powdered, p. I-51
Coconut
— desiccated and shredded, p. I-157
— oil, pp. I-25, 30
Cod liver oil, pp. I-109, 533
Codeine and derivatives, p. I-533
Coding machinery, p. II-1211
Coffee, pp. I-142, III-1953, 2093
— blended, p. I-142
— concentrates, p. I-142
— extracts, p. I-142
— filters, p. I-414
— flavoring and syrups, p. I-142
— iced, p. I-164
— instant, p. I-142
— makers, pp. II-1091, 1396
— roasting machinery, p. II-1060
— substitute, p. I-142
— tables, p. II-1620
Coil winding machinery, p. II-1151
Coils
— ignition, p. II-1511
— motors and generators, p. II-1426
— pipe, p. II-1008
Coin counting machinery, p. II-1076
Coin purses, pp. I-305, II-1695
Coin sorting machines, p. III-1800
Coin wrapping machines, p. II-1076
Coin-operated devices
— amusement, p. II-1748
— gambling, p. II-1748
— jukeboxes, p. II-1271
— music and vending, p. III-1808
— vending, p. II-1091
Coins, pp. II-1695, III-1893
Coke, p. III-1827
— petroleum, p. I-442
— products, pp. I-462, 779
Cold cathode fluorescent lamp tubes, p. II-1385
Cold forgings, p. I-871
Cold remedies, p. I-538
Cold rolling mill machinery, p. II-1146
Cold rolling steel shapes, p. I-792
Cold storage machinery, p. III-1854
Cole slaw, p. I-157
Collagen sausage casings, p. I-101

Collapsible tubes, p. II-927
Collar and cuff sets, pp. I-261, 266, 278
Collar leather, p. I-295
Collars, p. II-1139
— collar pads, p. I-305
— dog, p. I-305
— shaft for power, p. II-1167
Collating machinery, pp. II-1060, 1076
Collectible gift shops, p. III-2189
Collector rings, p. II-1426
Collector's items, p. III-2207
Collets, p. II-1139
Colognes, pp. I-574, III-1908
Colonscopes, p. II-1321
Color pigments, p. I-474
Color separation services, p. I-435
Colorimeters, p. II-1351
Coloring books, p. III-1886
Colostomy appliances, p. II-1675
Columns
— architectural, p. I-751
— fractionating, p. II-922
— porch, wood, pp. I-333
Comb cases, pp. I-305, II-1695
Combines, p. II-1022
Combing machinery, p. II-1060
Combs
— metal, p. II-1013
— plastics, p. I-650
— rubber, p. I-669
Combustion control instruments, p. II-1336
Comforters, p. I-233
Comic books, p. I-419
Commercial bakeries, p. I-115
Communication wafer, p. I-115
Communications equipment, pp. II-1261, III-1838
Communications headgear, p. II-1256
Communications wire or cable, pp. I-815, 829, 836, II-1450
Communion wafer, p. I-115
Commutators, p. II-1426
Compact disc players, p. II-1271
Compact discs, pp. II-1371, 1375, 1380
Compacts
— precious metal, p. II-1695
— solid leather, p. I-305
Compasses, pp. II-1326, 1366
Compost, p. I-523
Compressed gas cylinder valves, p. II-979
Compressed gases, pp. I-470, III-1970
Compression molding machinery for plastics, p. II-1050
Compression packings, p. II-1724
Compressors, pp. II-1183, 1545, III-1850, 1854, 1866
Computers, pp. II-1237, III-1804, 2057
— boards, pp. III-1804, 1838
— chips, p. III-1838
— equipment, p. III-2057
— forms, p. I-419
— furniture, pp. II-1620, 1631
— i/o equipment, p. II-1251
— media, p. II-1380
— paper, pp. I-402, III-1900
— peripherals, p. III-1804
— printer cartridges, p. I-594
— printers, p. III-1804

Numbers following p. or pp. are page references. Roman numerals indicate volume numbers. Page references are to the starting pages of the industries that produce the product or carry out the activity.

2254

— servers, p. II-1237
— software, p. III-1804
— terminals, p. II-1247
Concentrates
— drink, p. I-146
— flavoring, p. I-146
— frozen fruit juice, p. I-61
— metallic, p. III-1827
Concentration machinery, p. II-1038
Concrete
— additives, pp. I-594, III-1970
— batch plants, p. I-731
— building products, p. III-1785
— dry mixture, p. I-775
— finishing machinery, p. II-1032
— forms, p. II-907
— furniture, p. I-742
— gunning equipment, p. II-1032
— mixing machinery, p. II-1032
— processing equipment, p. III-1858
— products, p. I-742
— products machinery, p. II-1060
— re-bars, pp. II-898, III-1823
— reinforcing mesh, p. II-938
— tanks, p. I-742
Condensed milk, p. I-80
Condensed milk machinery, p. II-1060
Condensed whey, p. I-80
Condenser boxes, p. II-917
Condensers, p. II-1467
— electronic, pp. II-1291, III-1838
— steam, p. II-917
— synchronous, p. II-1426
Condensing units, pp. III-1850, 1854, 1866
Condoms, p. I-669
Conductor connectors, p. II-1456
Conduit, p. II-1456
— concrete, p. I-736
— vitrified clay, p. I-698
— welded and lock joint, p. I-787
Cones, p. I-378
— ice cream, p. I-123
— pyrometric, p. I-680
Confectioner's sugar, pp. I-39, 43
Confectionery, pp. I-56, III-1938, 2091
— chocolate, p. I-47
— machinery, p. II-1060
Confetti, p. I-414
Connecting rods, p. II-1504
Connectors and terminals, p. II-1456
Connectors
— electric cord, p. II-1456
— electronic, pp. II-1306, III-1838
— power, p. II-1431
— solderless, p. II-1456
— twist on wire, p. II-1456
Constant velocity joints, p. II-1529
Construction
— adhesives, p. I-559
— machinery, pp. II-1032, III-1858
— materials, p. III-1830
— paper, pp. I-367, 402
— tractors, p. II-1032
Consumer electronics, pp. III-1834, 2053
Consumption meters, p. II-1341

Contact lenses, pp. II-1686, III-1816
Contacts (electrical), pp. II-1456, 1462
Container board stock, p. I-373
Container ships, p. II-1588
Containers, p. III-1904
— air cargo, p. II-927
— foil, p. II-1013
— glass, p. I-717
— industrial, p. III-1870
— lmetal, p. II-927
— wood, p. I-342
Contraceptive preparations, p. I-538
Control devices
— circuits, p. II-1436
— electric, p. II-1436
— industrial, p. II-1436
— panels, p. II-1431
— process, p. II-1336
— relays, p. II-1436
— revolution and timing, p. II-1341
— speed, p. II-1436
— street light, p. II-1266
— transformers, p. II-1420
— valves, p. II-979
Convalescent supplies, p. III-2112
Convection ovens, p. II-1403
Convenience food, pp. III-2079, 2115
Converters (phase and rotary), p. II-1426
Convertible sofas, p. II-1615
Convertible tops for vehicles, p. II-1550
Conveying equipment, pp. III-1862, 1866
Conveyor belts, p. I-664
Conveyors, p. II-1193
Cooked meats, p. I-101
Cookie dough, p. I-123
Cookies, pp. I-123, III-1953
— filled, p. I-123
Cooking
— appliances, p. II-1396
— chocolate, p. I-47
— equipment, pp. II-1091, III-1808, 1834, 1846
— oils, p. III-1953
— utensils, pp. I-712, 844, II-885, III-1777
— ware, pp. I-680, 712, 721
Coolers, pp. I-635, 650, II-1105
Cooling towers, p. II-1105
Cooperage, pp. I-342, III-1870
Coopered tubs, p. I-342
Copper, pp. I-821, 829
— alloys, pp. I-821, 829
— base pigments, p. I-474
— castings, p. I-856
— chloride, p. I-487
— cleaners, p. I-565
— compounds, p. I-487
— die-castings, p. I-856
— foil, pp. I-829, II-1013
— forgings, p. I-871
— iodide, p. I-487
— powder, p. I-829
— products, p. I-829
— shapes, pp. I-821, 829
— sulfate, p. I-487
Copying machines, p. III-1800
Cord, p. I-243

Cord sets, pp. I-815, 829, 836
Cord
— connectors, electric, pp. II-1456
— tire, p. I-247
Cordage, pp. I-243, II-1060, III-1870
Cordite explosives, p. I-584
Cordless telephones, p. II-1256
Cords and braids, p. I-202
Corduroys, p. I-197
Core baking ovens, p. II-1216
Core drills, p. II-1038
Cores, p. I-378
— bullet, p. II-992
— sand foundry, p. II-1013
Cork, pp. I-357, III-1870
Corks (bottle), p. I-357
Corn breakfast foods, p. I-35
Corn chips, pp. I-136, III-1938
Corn confections, p. I-56
Corn cribs, p. I-352
Corn dextrin, p. I-21
Corn flour, p. I-14
Corn gluten
— feed, p. I-21
— meal, p. I-21
Corn heads for combines, p. II-1022
Corn meal, p. I-14
Corn oil, pp. I-21, 25
— cake and meal, p. I-21
Corn pickers and shellers, p. II-1022
Corn poppers, pp. II-1091, 1396
Corn popping machinery, p. II-1060
Corn remover pads, p. II-1675
Corn starch, p. I-21
Corn sweeteners, p. I-21
Corn syrups, p. I-157
Corn
— malt, p. I-14
Corneal microscopes, p. II-1670
Corned meats, p. I-101
Cornets, p. II-1730
Cornices, pp. I-333, II-907
Cornmeal
— edible, p. III-1953
Corrals
— metal, p. II-907
Correction fluids, p. I-594
Corrugated boxes, p. I-378
Corrugated pads, p. I-378
Corrugated paper, p. I-378
Corselets, pp. I-266, 278
Corsets, pp. I-266, 278
— surgical, p. II-1675
Cortisone, p. I-533
Cosmetics, pp. III-1908, 2103
— bags, pp. I-305, II-1695
— creams, p. I-574
Costume jewelry, pp. II-1695, III-1893, 2134
Costume shops, p. III-2137
Costumes, pp. I-266, 284
Cots, pp. II 1620, 1631
— springs, p. II-1615
Cottage cheese, p. I-85
Cotter pins, p. II-957

Numbers following p. or pp. are page references. Roman numerals indicate volume numbers. Page references are to the starting pages of the industries that produce the product or carry out the activity.

Cotton
— applicators, p. II-1675
— balers and presses, p. II-1022
— balls, absorbent, pp. II-1675
— battings, p. I-250
— cordage spun yarns, p. I-191
— fabrics, pp. I-197, 202
— fiber paper stock, p. I-367
— ginning machinery, p. II-1022
— harvesting machinery, p. II-1022
— raw, p. III-1964
— spun yarns, p. I-191
— thread, p. I-191
Cottonseed oil, pp. I-25, 30
Couch springs, p. II-1615
Couches, p. II-1615
Cough drops, pp. I-56, 538
Coulometric analyzers, pp. II-1336, 1351
Coumarin, p. I-492
Coumarone-indene resins, p. I-499
Count rate meters, p. II-1366
Counter type registers, p. II-1341
Counter units, p. II-1643
Counterbores, pp. II-891, 1139
Countermeasure sets, p. II-1326
Counters, pp. I-305, II-1341
— revolution, p. II-1341
Countersinks, p. II-1139
Countertops, pp. I-650, 761, II-1610, 1643
Counting devices, p. II-1341
Couplings
— hose, p. II-979
— pipe, p. II-1008
— power transmission, p. II-1167
Coveralls, pp. I-266, 271, 278
Covers, p. I-238
— annealing, p. II-898
— bottle and demijohn, p. I-357
— floating, p. II-898
Cowls
— sheet metal, p. II-907
Crab traps, p. II-938
Cracker making machinery, p. II-1060
Crackers, p. I-123
Cradle assembly machinery, p. II-1151
Cradles, p. II-1620
Craft kits, pp. II-1707, III-1886
Craft supplies, p. III-2152
Crane controls, p. II-1436
Cranes, pp. II-1032, 1193, III-1858, 1866
Crankcase additives, p. I-594
Crankshaft assemblies, p. II-1504
Crankshaft grinding machines, p. II-1123
Crates, p. I-342
Crayons, p. II-1713
Cream, pp. I-80, 85, III-1932
Cream of tartar, p. I-492
Cream separators, pp. II-1022, 1060
Cream stations, p. III-1932
Creamery butter, p. I-85
Creamery products, pp. III-1932, 1953
Credit cards, pp. I-419, 650
Cremating ovens, p. II-1228
Creosote, p. I-492
Crepe paper, p. I-414

Cresol resins, p. I-499
Cresols, p. I-492
Cresylic acids, p. I-492
Crew socks, p. I-255
Cribs, pp. II-1620, 1631
Crochet spun yarns, p. I-191
Crochet ware, p. I-250
Crock pots, p. II-1396
Crockery, p. I-680
Croissants, p. I-115
Crop driers, p. II-1022
Crop preparation machinery, p. III-1862
Crops (riding), p. I-305
Croquet sets, p. II-1701
Cross valves, p. II-979
Croutons, p. I-115
Crowns, pp. I-878, III-1870
CRTs, p. II-1276
Crucibles, p. I-702
Crude oil, pp. I-442, III-1974, 1978
Cruise controls, p. II-1511
Crullers, p. I-115
Crushed stone, p. III-1785
Crushing machinery, pp. II-1032, 1038
Crutches, pp. II-1675, III-1812
Cryogenic tanks, p. II-922
Crystallized fruits, p. I-56
Crystals
— electronic, p. II-1316
CT/CAT scanners, p. II-1356
Cubicles, p. II-1431
Cuff links, pp. II-1695, 1734
Culottes, pp. I-266, 278
Cultivators, pp. II-1022, 1027, III-1862
Culture media, p. I-548
Cultured marble, p. I-650
Cultured stone, p. I-650
Culvert pipe, p. I-736
Culverts, pp. II-898, 907
Cumene, pp. I-442, 466
Cummerbunds, pp. I-266, 289
Cupolas, p. II-898
Cups, pp. I-414, 635, 650, III-1777, 1904
Curbing, p. I-761
Cured fish, p. III-1942
Cured hides, p. I-101
Cured meats, p. I-101
Curios, p. III-2189
Curlers, p. I-669
Curling irons, p. II-1396
Currency machinery, pp. II-1076, III-1800
Current limiting reactors, p. II-1420
Current measuring equipment, p. II-1346
Current taps, p. II-1456
Current-carrying devices, p. III-1830
Curtain or drapery fixtures, p. II-1661
Curtain rods and fittings, p. II-1661
Curtain stretchers, p. I-357
Curtain walls, p. II-907
Curtains, pp. I-212, III-1777
Curtains and draperies, pp. I-197, 233, III-2043
Cushion springs, p. II-1615
Cushions, pp. I-233, 640
Custard, p. I-91
Cut glass, p. I-721

Cut-off machines, p. II-1123
Cutlery, pp. II-885, 1695, III-1842
Cutouts (switch and fuse), p. II-1456
Cutters
— coal, p. II-1038
— glass, p. II-891
— metal milling, p. II-1139
Cutting dies, pp. II-891, 1133
Cutting instruments (dental), p. II-1681
Cutting machines, p. II-1123
Cutting oils, pp. I-457, 594
Cyanides, p. I-487
Cyclic aromatic hydrocarbons, pp. I-442, 466
Cyclic crudes, pp. I-492, III-1970
Cyclo rubber, p. I-504
Cyclohexane, p. I-492
Cyclones, p. II-898
Cyclopentane, p. I-492
Cyclopropane, p. I-492
Cyclopropane medicinal preparations, p. I-538
Cycloterpenes, p. I-492
Cyclotrons, p. II-1467
Cylinder boring machines, p. II-1123
Cylinder heads, p. II-1504
Cylinder pipe, p. I-736
Cylinder wire cloth, p. II-938
Cylinders
— fluid power, p. II-1221
— gun, pp. II-1000, 1004
— master brake, p. II-1523
— pressure, p. II-922
Cymbals, p. II-1730
Cystoscopes, pp. II-1321, 1670
Cytology and histology substances, p. I-543
Dairy cattle feeds, p. I-8
Dairy depots, p. III-1932
Dairy food canning, p. I-80
Dairy products, pp. III-1932, 1953, 2093
Dam gates, p. II-898
Damper operators, p. II-1331
Dampers, p. II-907
Darning thread, p. I-191
Dart guns, p. II-1000
Darts and dart games, p. II-1707
Data communications equipment, p. II-1256
Data loggers, p. II-1336
Data processing machines, p. III-1804
Date stamps (hand), p. II-1713
Dates, pp. I-56, 67
Dating devices, p. II-1361
Davits, p. II-1193
DDT, p. I-528
Dead bolts, p. II-932
Deburring machines, p. II-1123
Decade boxes, p. II-1346
Decahydronaphthalene, p. I-492
Deep-fat fryers, pp. II-1091, 1396
Defibrilators, p. II-1321
Defluorinated phosphates, p. I-519
Defoamers, p. I-594
Defoliants, p. I-528
Degreasing preparations, pp. I-565, 594
Dehumidifiers, pp. II-1105, 1396
Dehydrated milk, p. I-80
Deicing preparations, p. I-594

Numbers following p. or pp. are page references. Roman numerals indicate volume numbers. Page references are to the starting pages of the industries that produce the product or carry out the activity.

Deinking plants, p. I-362
Delicatessen scales, p. II-1228
Delicatessens, pp. III-2075, 2082
Delivery cases, p. II-938
Demand meters, p. II-1346
Demountable cargo containers, p. II-1490
Denatured alcohol, p. I-492
Denims weaving, p. I-197
Densified wood, p. I-318
Densitometers, pp. II-1086, 1351
Density and specific gravity instruments, p. II-1336
Dental alloys for amalgams, p. II-1681
Dental chairs, pp. II-1681, III-1812
Dental equipment, pp. II-1681, III-1812
Dental floss, p. I-574
Dental glues and cements, p. II-1681
Dental hand instruments, p. II-1681
Dental impression materials, p. II-1681
Dental instrument delivery systems, p. II-1681
Dental laboratories, p. II-1691
Dental laboratory equipment, p. II-1681
Dental wax, p. II-1681
Dentifrices, pp. I-565, III-1908
Dentists' supplies, p. III-1812
Denture adhesives, p. I-574
Denture cleaners, p. I-574
Denture materials, p. II-1681
Dentures, p. II-1691
Deodorants, pp. I-565, 574, III-1908, 1970
Depilatory preparations, p. I-574
Depth charge projectors, p. II-1004
Depth charges, p. II-996
Dermatological preparations, p. I-538
Derricks, p. II-1038
Desalination kits, p. I-594
Desiccants, p. I-766
Desk fans, p. II-1396
Desk lamps, p. II-1389
Desk sets, p. I-305
Desks, pp. II-1620, 1649
Desserts
— dairy, p. III-1932
— frozen, p. I-91
— frozen bakery, p. I-115
Detergents, pp. I-565, III-1970
Detonators, pp. I-584, II-996
Deuterium oxide, p. I-487
Developers (photo), p. I-594
Developing equipment, p. II-1086
Dextrin, p. I-21
Dextrin glues, p. I-559
Diagnostic biological preparations, p. I-538
Diagnostic equipment, pp. II-1321, III-1812
Diagnostic reagents, p. III-1908
Diagnostic substances, p. I-543
Diagnostics, p. III-1908
Dialysis equipment, p. II-1321
Diammonium phosphates, p. I-519
Diamond cloths, p. II-938
Diamond dies, p. II-1133
Diamond dressing wheels, p. I-755
Diamonds, pp. III-1870, 1893
Diaper covers, pp. I-266, 284
Diapers, pp. I-250, 367, 410, III-1904, 1918
Diaphragms, p. I-669

Diaries, p. I-419
Diathermy apparatus, p. II-1321
Diathermy units, p. II-1321
Diazo, p. I-594
Dichlorodifluoromethane, p. I-470
Dichromates, p. I-487
Dickeys, pp. I-266, 278
Dictating machines, pp. II-1076, III-1800
Dictionaries, p. I-419
Dictionary binding, p. I-435
Dicyandiamine resins, p. I-499
Die sets, p. II-1133
Die sinking machines, p. II-1123
Die-casting dies, p. II-1118
Die-casting machines, p. II-1128
Die-castings, pp. I-851, 856
Die-cut paper, pp. I-402, 414
Dielectric heating equipment, p. II-1216
Dies and die holders, p. II-1133
Dies and taps, p. II-1139
Dies
— cutting, p. II-891
— metalworking, p. II-1133
— plastics forming, p. II-1133
— steel rule, pp. II-891, 1133
Diesel engines, p. II-1172
Diesel fuels, p. I-442
Dietary drinks, p. I-80
Diethylcyclohexane, p. I-492
Diethylene glycol, p. I-492
Digesters (industrial), p. II-922
Digestive system preparations, p. I-538
Digital cameras, p. II-1251
Digital computers, p. II-1237
Digital displays, p. II-1336
Digital panel meters, p. II-1346
Digital printing presses, p. II-1060
Digital test equipment, p. II-1346
Digital video disc players, p. II-1271
Digitalis medicinal preparations, p. I-538
Digitoxin, p. I-533
Diisocyanate resins, p. I-499
Dimension lumber, pp. I-311, 333
Dimension stock, p. I-333
Dimension stone, p. I-761
Dimethyl divinyl acetylene, p. I-492
Dimethylhydrazine, p. I-492
Dimmer switches, p. II-1456
Dinette sets, p. II-1631
Dinghies, p. I-669
Dinners (frozen), pp. I-61, 109, III-1928
Dinnerware, pp. I-635, 650
Diode and transistor testers, p. II-1346
Diodes, pp. II-1286, III-1838
Diphenylamine, p. I-492
Dips, pp. I-151, 528
— cheese based, p. I-75
— sour cream based, p. I-85
Directories, p. I-419
Discount coupon books, p. I-419
Dishcloths, p. I-212
Dishes, pp. I-357, 680, II-1707, III-1777, 1904
Dishwasher detergents, p. I-565
Dishwashers, pp. II-1416, III-1834
Dishwashing equipment, p. III-1808

Dishwashing machines, pp. II-1091, 1416
Disinfectants, p. I-565
Disk and ring springs, p. II-938
Disk drives, pp. II-1242, III-1804
Diskettes, pp. II-1380, III-1838
Dispensing pumps, p. II-1188
Disperse dyes, p. I-474
Dispersions (pigment), p. I-553
Display cases, pp. II-1105, 1643, III-1808, 1854
Display instruments, p. II-1336
Displays, p. II-1719
Distance measuring equipment, p. II-1326
Distillation ovens, p. II-1216
Distilled alcoholic beverages, p. III-1986
Distilled water, p. I-594
Distiller's malt, p. I-14
Distillery machinery, p. III-1866
Distilling equipment, p. II-1060
Distortion meters, p. II-1346
Distribution boards, p. II-1431
Distribution cutouts, p. II-1431
Distribution transformers, p. II-1420
Distributor caps, p. II-1511
Distributors (engine), p. II-1511
Ditchers and trenchers, p. II-1032
Diuretics, p. I-538
Diving equipment, p. III-2149
Dodecene, p. I-466
Dog food, p. I-3
Dog furnishings, p. I-305
Doilies, p. I-414
Doll carriages, p. II-1707
Doll clothing, p. II-1707
Dollar stores, p. III-2179
Dollies, p. II-1193
Dolls, pp. II-1707, III-1886
Dolomite, p. I-747
Dolomitic lime, p. I-747
Door and jamb assemblies, p. II-907
Door frames and sash, pp. I-333, II-907
Door hoods, p. II-907
Door jambs, p. I-333
Door locks, p. II-932
Door openers, pp. II-932, 1467
Door shutters, p. I-333
Door trim, p. I-333
Door units, p. I-333
Doormats, pp. I-228, 650, 669
Doors, pp. I-333, 650, 721, II-907, 1013, III-1781
Dopes, p. I-553
Dories, p. II-1593
Dosimetry devices, p. II-1366
Dough mixing machinery, p. II-1060
Doughnuts, p. I-115
Doughs, pp. I-14, 123, III-1928
Dovetailing machines, p. II-1045
Dowel pins, p. II-957
Dowels, p. I-357
Down-filled clothing, pp. I-266, 271, 278, 284
Downspouts, p. II-907
Draft gauges, p. II-1336
Drafting instruments, pp. II-1366, III-1819
Drafting materials, p. II-1713
Drafting tables, pp. II-1626, III-1819
Draglines, p. II-1032

Dragon's blood, p. I-492

Drags
— farm, p. II-1022
— road construction, p. II-1032

Drain cocks, p. II-973

Drain pipe cleaners, p. I-565

Drain plugs, p. II-1013

Drain tile, p. I-698

Drainboards, p. II-1610

Draperies, pp. I-233, III-1777

Drapes (surgical), p. II-1675

Draw bench machines, p. II-1151

Drawers, pp. I-261, 266, 271, 278

Drawing inks, p. I-594

Drawing machinery for textiles, p. II-1060

Drawing tables, p. II-1626

Drawknives, p. II-891

Dredge building, p. II-1588

Dredging machinery, p. II-1032

Dress gloves, pp. I-261, 266, 289

Dress shoes, p. I-299

Dress shops, p. III-2137

Dress trimmings, pp. I-266, 289

Dressers, pp. II-1620, 1631

Dresses, pp. I-261, 266, 278, 284, III-1918

Dressing, p. I-295

Dressing gowns, pp. I-266, 278

Dressing hides, p. I-295

Dressing tables, pp. II-1620, 1631

Dressings, pp. II-1675, III-1812

Dried foods, p. III-1953

Dried meats, p. I-101

Driers
— paint, and varnish, pp. I-553
— photographic, pp. I-594, II-1086

Driftmeters, p. II-1326

Drill bits, pp. II-891, 1139

Drill presses, pp. II-1045, 1123

Drill stands, p. II-1013

Drilling equipment, p. II-1038

Drilling machines, p. II-1123

Drilling mud, pp. I-594, III-1970

Drilling platforms, p. II-1588

Drilling rigs, p. II-1038

Drills, pp. II-891, 1038, 1206, 1681

Drinking fountains, pp. I-650, 676, II-1013, 1105

Drive chains, p. II-1167

Drive shafts, p. II-1529

Drop forgings, p. I-871

Drop hammers, p. II-1128

Drug proprietaries, p. III-1908

Drug stores, p. III-2099

Druggists' sundries, p. III-1908

Drugs, p. III-1908

Drum cradles, p. II-1193

Drums, pp. I-342, 650, II-927, III-1870

Drums (musical), p. II-1730

Dry beans, p. III-1957

Dry cell batteries, p. II-1446

Dry cells, p. II-1446

Dry ice, pp. I-470, III-1970

Dry milk, p. I-80

Dry milk processing machinery, p. II-1060

Dry milk products and mixtures, p. I-80

Dry milk products for animal feed, p. I-80

Dry mix concrete, p. I-775

Dry mixes, p. I-123

Dry pasta, p. I-123

Dry shavers, p. II-1396

Drycleaning equipment, pp. II-1091, 1412, III-1874

Drycleaning preparations, p. I-565

Drydocks, p. II-1588

Dryers, pp. II-1091, 1412, 1665, III-1834

Drying kilns, p. II-1060

Drying machinery, p. II-1060

Drywall supplies, p. III-1785

Ducks, p. I-96

Ducks weaving, p. I-197

Duct tape, p. I-387

Ductile iron castings, p. I-844

Ducting, p. II-898

Ducts, pp. II-907, 1431

Dumbbells, p. II-1701

Dumbwaiters, p. II-1193

Dump trailer, p. II-1490

Dump-truck lifting mechanisms, p. II-1485

Dumpers (mining car), p. II-1038

Dungarees, pp. I-266, 271, 278, 284

Duplex receptacles, p. II-1456

Duplicating inks, p. I-579

Duplicating machines, p. II-1123

Durum flour, p. I-14

Dust and fume collecting equipment, p. II-1111

Dust cloths, p. I-250

Dust collection equipment, p. III-1850

Dusters, pp. I-266, 278
— farm, p. II-1022

DVD players, p. II-1271

Dwellings (prefab), p. II-898

Dye preparations, p. I-594

Dyeing machinery, p. II-1060

Dyes, pp. I-474, 492, III-1970

Dynamite, p. I-584

Dynamometers, p. II-1366

Dynamos, p. II-1426

Dynamotors, p. II-1426

Earth station communications equipment, p. II-1261

Earthenware
— articles, coarse, pp. I-680
— semivitreous, p. I-680

Earthworm food and bedding, p. I-8

Easels, p. II-1713

Eating utensils, p. III-1904

Eaves, p. II-907

Ecclesiastical statuary, pp. I-680, 751, 761, 775

Ecclesiastical ware, p. II-1013

Economizers, p. II-917

Edge tools, p. II-891

Editing equipment (movie), p. II-1086

Effervescent salts, p. I-538

Egg cases, p. I-342

Egg cookers, p. II-1396

Egg noodles, pp. I-123, 157

Egg substitutes, p. I-157

Eggnog, pp. I-80, 85, 180

Eggs, pp. I-157, III-1935

Elapsed time meters, p. II-1346

Elastic fabrics, pp. I-197, 202

Elastic hosiery (orthopedic), p. II-1675

Elastomeric fibers and filaments, p. I-509

Elastomers, pp. I-499, 504

Electric air cleaner controls, p. II-1331

Electric autos, p. II-1472

Electric bells, p. II-1467

Electric blankets, pp. II-1396, III-1834

Electric comfort heating equipment, p. II-1396

Electric controllers, p. II-1336

Electric fence chargers, p. II-1467

Electric furnace transformers, p. II-1420

Electric heat proportioning controls, p. II-1331

Electric lamp bulb parts, p. II-1385

Electric lamps, p. II-1385

Electric light bulbs, p. II-1385

Electric motors, p. III-1830

Electric musical instruments, p. II-1730

Electric outboard motors, p. II-1172

Electric space heater controls, p. II-1331

Electric space heaters, p. II-1396

Electrical ignition cable, p. II-1511

Electrical metallic tube (EMTs), p. II-1456

Electrical network analyzers, p. II-1346

Electrical power measuring equipment, p. II-1346

Electrical signs, pp. II-1719, III-1808

Electricity measuring instruments, p. II-1346

Electricity testing equipment, p. II-1346

Electrocardiographs, p. II-1321

Electrochemical generators, p. II-1467

Electrochemical milling machines, p. II-1123

Electrode discharge metal cutting machines, p. II-1123

Electrode holders, p. II-1228

Electrodes, pp. II-1228, 1336, 1385, 1462

Electroencephalographs, p. II-1321

Electrogastrograph, p. II-1321

Electrohydraulic servo valves, p. II-979

Electrolyte diagnostic substances, p. I-538

Electrolytic conductivity instruments, pp. II-1336, 1351

Electrolytic metal cutting machines, p. II-1123

Electromagnetic flowmeters, p. II-1336

Electromechanical counters, p. II-1341

Electromedical diagnostic equipment, p. II-1321

Electromedical equipment, pp. II-1321, III-1812

Electromedical therapy equipment, p. II-1321

Electrometallurical ferroalloy, p. I-779

Electromyographs, p. II-1321

Electron beam welding equipment, p. II-1228

Electron linear accelerators, p. II-1467

Electron microprobes, p. II-1351

Electron microscopes, p. II-1351

Electron paramagnetic spin-type apparatus, p. II-1351

Electron tube machinery, p. II-1060

Electron tube parts, pp. I-712, 721, II-1276

Electron tube test equipment, p. II-1346

Electron tubes, p. II-1276

Electron-discharge metal cutting machines, p. II-1123

Electronic games, p. III-1886

Electronic guidance systems and equipment, p. II-1326

Electronic parts, p. III-1838

Electronic test equipment, p. II-1346

Electronic totalizing counters, p. II-1341

Electronic toys, p. II-1707

Electronic tubes, p. III-1838

Electrophoresis instruments, p. II-1351

Electroplating machinery and equipment, p. II-1060
Electrostatic particle accelerators, p. II-1467
Electrostatic precipitation equipment, p. II-1111
Electrotherapeutic apparatus, p. II-1321
Electrotherapeutic lamp bulbs, p. II-1385
Electrotherapy units, p. II-1321
Electrotype plate preparation services, p. I-435
Electrotyping machinery, p. II-1060
Elemental analyzers, p. II-1351
Elevator guide rails, p. II-907
Elevators, pp. II-1193, III-1866
Embalming fluids, p. I-594
Embossing stamps, p. II-1713
Embroideries, p. I-202
Embroidery kits, p. I-1707
Embroidery machinery, p. II-1060
Embroidery products, p. III-1912
Embroidery spun yarns, p. I-191
Embroidery thread, p. I-191
Emergency lighting, p. II-1389
Emulsifiers, p. I-565
Enamel paints, p. I-553
Enameling ovens, p. II-1216
Enamels, p. III-2003
— dental, p. II-1681
Encyclopedias, p. I-419
End tables, pp. II-1620, 1631
Endocrine products, p. I-533
Endocrine substances, p. III-1908
Endoscopic equipment, p. II-1321
Endrin insecticides, p. I-528
Energy cutoff controls, p. II-1331
Energy measuring equipment, p. II-1346
Energy wire or cable, pp. I-815, 829, 836
Engine block assemblies, p. II-1504
Engine degreasers, p. I-594
Engine starting fluids, p. I-594
Engine testing equipment, p. III-1761
Engine valves, p. II-1504
Engineers' equipment, p. III-1819
Engines, pp. II-1504, III-1761
— aircraft, pp. II-1561, III-1878
— diesel, p. II-1172
— diesel locomotive, p. II-1172
— internal combustion, pp. II-1172, III-1866
— marine, p. III-1878
— natural gas, p. II-1172
Engraver's handtools, p. II-891
Engraving machinery, p. III-1866
Enlargers (photo), p. II-1086
Ensemble dresses, pp. I-261, 266, 278
Envelope making machinery, p. II-1060
Envelope paper, p. III-1897
Envelopes, pp. I-402, III-1900
Environmental control systems, p. II-1331
Enzyme and isoenzyme substances, p. I-543
Enzyme proteins, pp. I-492, 533
Eosin dyes, p. I-474
Ephedrine and derivatives, p. I-533
Epichlorohydrin bisphenol, p. I-499
Epichlorohydrin diphenol, p. I-499
Epichlorohydrin elastomers, p. I-504
Epoxy adhesives, p. I-559
Epoxy coatings, p. I-553
Epoxy resins, p. I-499

Erasers, p. I-669
Ergot alkaloids, p. I-533
Escalators, pp. II-1193, III-1866
Essential oils, pp. I-492, 594, III-1970
Ester gum, p. I-499
Esters, p. I-492
Etching equipment, p. II-1055
Etching metals, p. II-963
Ethane, p. I-466
Ethanol, p. I-492
Ethyl acetate, p. I-492
Ethyl alcohol, pp. I-180, 492, III-1986
Ethyl butyrate, p. I-492
Ethyl cellulose, p. I-492
Ethyl chloride, p. I-492
Ethyl ether, p. I-492
Ethyl formate, p. I-492
Ethyl nitrite, p. I-492
Ethyl perhydrophenanthrene, p. I-492
Ethylbenzene, p. I-466
Ethylcellulose plastics, p. I-499
Ethylene, pp. I-442, 466
Ethylene glycol, p. I-492
Ethylene glycol ether, p. I-492
Ethylene oxide, p. I-492
Ethylene-propylene rubber, p. I-504
Ethylene-propylene-nonconjugated diene, p. I-504
Ethylene-vinyl acetate resins, p. I-499
Eucalyptus oil, p. I-594
Evaporated milk, p. I-80
Evaporation meters, p. II-1366
Evaporative condensers, p. II-1105
Excavating machinery, p. III-1858
Excavators, p. II-1032
Excelsior, p. I-357
Exchangers (heat), p. II-917
Exciter assemblies, p. II-1426
Exercise equipment, p. III-2149
Exercise machines, p. II-1701
Exhaust and tail pipes, p. II-1550
Exhaust fans, p. II-1111
Exhaust systems, p. II-1550
Expansion joints, p. II-898
Explosives, pp. I-584, III-1970
Exposure meters, p. II-1086
Extension cords, p. II-1467
Extension ladders, p. I-357
Extension planks, p. I-357
Exterior wood shutters, p. I-333
Exterminating chemicals, p. I-528
Extracts
— coffee, p. I-142
— dyeing and tanning, p. I-492
— food, p. I-151
— malt, p. I-151
— tea, p. I-142
Extruded rubber goods, p. I-669
Extruding machinery, pp. II-1050, 1060, 1128
Extrusion billet, p. I-815
Extrusion dies, p. II-1133
Extrusion ingot, pp. I-802, 815
Eye and ear preparations, p. I-538
Eye examining instruments, p. II-1670
Eye make-up, p. I-574
Eyeglass cases, p. I-305

Eyeglass frames, p. II-1686
Eyeglasses, p. III-1816
Eyelets
— metal, p. II-1734
Eyes
— glass and plastics, p. II-1686
Fabric shops, p. III-2155
Fabric softeners, p. I-565
Fabrics, pp. I-197, 202, 207, 212, 217, 247, II-938, III-1912
Face creams, p. I-574
Face plates, p. II-1456
Facial tissue, pp. I-367, 410, III-1904
Facing machines, p. II-1123
Facsimile equipment, p. II-1256
Facsimile machines, p. III-1838
Facsimile toner cartridges, p. I-594
Fan belts, p. I-664
Fan controls, p. II-1331
Fans, pp. II-1111, 1396, 1511, III-1834, 1866
Fare collection equipment, p. II-1341
Farina, pp. I-14, 35
Farm buildings, pp. I-352, II-898
Farm machinery, p. III-1862
Farm storage tanks, p. II-922
Farm supplies, p. III-1990
Farm tractors and attachments, p. II-1022
Farm wagons, p. II-1022
Farm-type conveyers, p. II-1193
Fasteners, pp. II-1734, III-1842
Fathometers, p. II-1326
Fatigue testing machines, p. II-1366
Fats
— animal, p. I-101
Fatty acids, p. I-492
Fatty alcohols, p. I-492
Faucet handles, p. I-676
Faucets, p. II-973
Feather dusters, p. II-1748
Feather-filled clothing, pp. I-266, 271, 278, 284
Feathers, pp. II-1748, III-1964
Feed additives, p. III-1990
Feed bags, p. I-238
Feed bags for horses, p. I-305
Feed concentrates, p. I-8
Feed premixes, p. I-8
Feed processing equipment, p. II-1022
Feed supplements, pp. I-3, 8
Feeder voltage regulators, p. II-1420
Feeders (animal), p. III-1862
Feeders (mineral), p. II-1038
Feeds, pp. III-1990, 2071
— animal, p. I-8
— dog and cat, p. I-3
— specialty, p. I-8
Feldspar, p. I-766
Felt tip markers, p. II-1713
Felts, pp. I-197, 207, 367
Fence gates, p. I-792
Fence posts, p. I-779
Fences and gates, p. II-907
Fencing, pp. I-357, II-938, III-1781, 1793
Fencing equipment (sport), p. II-1701
Fermentation equipment, p. II-1060
Fermention tanks, p. II-922

Numbers following p. or pp. are page references. Roman numerals indicate volume numbers. Page references are to the starting pages of the industries that produce the product or carry out the activity.

Product/Activity Index

Ferric chloride, p. I-487
Ferric oxide, p. I-487
Ferric oxide pigments, p. I-474
Ferris wheels, p. II-1091
Ferroalloys, pp. I-779, III-1823
Ferrochromium, p. I-779
Ferrocyanides, p. I-487
Ferromanganese, p. I-779
Ferromolybdenum, p. I-779
Ferrophosphorus, p. I-779
Ferrosilicon, p. I-779
Ferrotitanium, p. I-779
Ferrotungsten, p. I-779
Ferrous forgings, p. I-871
Ferrous metals, p. III-1823
Ferrovanadium, p. I-779
Ferryboat building, p. II-1588
Fertilizers, pp. I-515, 519, 523, III-1990
Fertilizing machinery, p. II-1022
Fever remedies, p. I-538
Fiber cans, pp. I-378, III-1904
Fiber drums, p. I-378
Fiber furniture, p. II-1631
Fiber glasses, p. I-202
Fiber optic cable, p. II-1450
Fiber optic connectors, p. II-1306
Fiber spools, p. I-378
Fiber tubes, p. I-378
Fiberboard, pp. I-318, III-1781
Fiberglass
— building materials, p. III-1793
— fabrics, pp. I-197, III-1912
— insulation, p. I-770
Fibers, pp. I-712, II-1462, III-1964, 1970
Fibers and filaments, p. I-509
Fiction books, p. I-419
Field artillery, p. II-1004
Field jackets, pp. I-266, 271
Field strength measuring equipment, p. II-1346
Fifth wheel assemblies, p. II-1485
Filaments (bulb), p. II-1385
File cards and folders, p. III-1900
File folders, p. I-402
Files, p. II-1139
— handheld, p. II-891
Filing cabinets, p. II-1649
Filing machines, p. II-1123
Fillers, p. I-553
Filling, p. I-250
Fillings
— cake or pie, p. I-157
Film
— developing equipment, pp. II-1086, III-1797
— photographic, p. III-1797
— plastics, pp. I-608, 614
— sensitized, p. I-594
Filter papers, p. III-1904
Filters, p. II-1550
— air-conditioner, p. II-1111
— electronic component, p. II-1316
— furnace, p. II-1111
— industrial, p. II-1228
— paper, p. I-414
Fin assemblies, p. II-996
Financial magazines, p. I-419

Findings
— boot and shoe, p. I-305
— jeweler's, p. II-1695
— suit and coat, pp. I-266, 289
Fine paper, p. III-1897
Finger joint lumber, p. I-328
Finishing, p. I-228
Finishing agents, p. I-565
Finishing leather, p. I-295
Finishing machinery for textile, p. II-1060
Fire detection and alarm systems, p. II-1266
Fire detector systems, p. II-1366
Fire doors, p. II-907
Fire escapes, p. II-907
Fire extinguisher chemicals, pp. I-594, III-1970
Fire extinguishers, p. II-1748
Fire hose, p. I-250
Fire hydrant valves, p. II-979
Fire hydrants, p. II-979
Fire retardant chemicals, p. I-594
Firearms, pp. II-1000, III-1882
Fireboat building, p. II-1588
Firebrick, p. I-702
Firefighters' uniforms, pp. I-266, 271, 278
Firefighting equipment, p. III-1874
Firefighting suits, p. II-1675
Fireplace fixtures, p. II-1013
Fireplace inserts, p. II-1100
Fireplace logs, p. II-1389
Fireplaces, p. III-1846
Firewood, pp. I-357, III-2224
Fireworks, pp. I-594, III-1886
Fireworks shops, p. III-2207
Firkins and kits, p. I-342
First-aid kits, pp. II-1675, III-1812
First-aid supplies, p. III-1908
Fish, pp. I-109, III-1942
Fish and marine animal oils, p. I-109
Fish and seafood chowder, p. I-109
Fish egg bait canning, p. I-109
Fish finders, p. II-1326
Fish food for feeding fish, p. I-8
Fish freezing, p. I-109
Fish liver oils, p. I-533
Fish markets, p. III-2084
Fish meal, p. I-109
Fish wire, p. II-891
Fish
— canned, p. III-1953
— canned and cured, p. I-109
— fresh or frozen, p. I-109
— fresh prepared, p. I-109
— packaged frozen, p. III-1928
Fishing boats, p. II-1588
Fishing equipment, p. III-1882
Fishing knives, p. II-885
Fishing nets, p. I-250
Fishing supplies, p. III-2149
Fishing tackle, p. II-1701
Fitness equipment, p. III-1882
Fittings
— pipe, pp. I-625, 844
— unions, p. I-625
— valves, p. III-1846
Fixers (photo), p. I-594

Fixtures, pp. II-1643, 1661, III-1808
— lighting, p. III-1830
Flagpoles, pp. I-357, II-907
Flags, pp. I-250, III-2207
Flagstones cutting, p. I-761
Flakeboard, p. I-318
Flame photometers, p. II-1351
Flame safety controls, p. II-1331
Flame throwers, p. II-1004
Flange facing machines, p. II-1123
Flange units, p. II-987
Flanges, p. II-979
Flannel shirts, pp. I-266, 271, 278, 284
Flannels, p. I-197
Flares, p. I-594
Flash apparatus, p. II-1086
Flash bulbs, p. II-1385
Flashlight batteries, p. II-1446
Flashlight bulb, p. II-1385
Flashlights, pp. II-1389, III-1830
Flat bright steel strip, p. I-792
Flat glass, pp. I-708, III-1793
Flat panel displays, p. II-1251
Flat springs, p. II-938
Flatbed trailers, p. II-1490
Flatware, pp. II-885, III-1777, 1893
Flavored milk drinks, p. I-85
Flavoring concentrates, p. I-146
Flavoring extracts, pp. I-151, III-1953
Flavoring materials, p. I-492
Flavoring pastes, p. I-146
Flax spun yarns, p. I-191
Flaxseed oil, pp. I-25, 30
Flea markets, pp. III-2193, 2227
Flea powders or sprays, p. I-528
Fleshers (leather), p. I-295
Flexible metal hose and tubing, p. II-1013
Flexible packaging, pp. I-387, 394
Flexible wiring boards, p. II-1281
Flexographic inks, p. I-579
Flexographic printing, p. I-419
Flexographic printing presses, p. II-1060
Flies (fishing), p. II-1701
Flight and navigation sensors, p. II-1326
Flight recorders, p. II-1326
Flight simulation machinery, p. II-1091
Flints, p. II-1748
Flitches, p. I-311
Float controls, p. II-1331
Flood gates, p. II-898
Floodlights, p. II-1389
Floor baseboards, p. I-333
Floor coverings, pp. I-650, III-1777, 2040
Floor jacks, p. II-898
Floor lamps, p. II-1389
Floor maintenance equipment, p. III-1874
Floor mats, p. I-669
Floor polishes and waxes, p. I-565
Floor posts, p. II-898
Floor sanding machines, p. II-1091
Floor scrubbing machines, p. II-1396
Floor standing fans, p. II-1396
Floor tile, p. I-694
Floor trusses, p. I-328
Floor waxers, p. II-1396

Numbers following p. or pp. are page references. Roman numerals indicate volume numbers. Page references are to the starting pages of the industries that produce the product or carry out the activity.

Flooring, pp. I-311, 333, II-907, III-1781
Floppy disk drives, p. II-1242
Florist's supplies, p. III-1997
Florists, p. III-2182
Florists' articles, p. I-680
Flotation machinery, p. II-1038
Flour, pp. I-14, 123, 357, III-1953
Flour bags, p. I-238
Flour milling machinery, p. II-1060
Flour mixes, p. I-14
Flow actuated switches, p. II-1436
Flow instruments, p. II-1336
Flower boxes, p. I-751
Flower bulbs, p. III-1990
Flower pots, p. I-680
Flower shops, pp. III-2182, 2207
Flowers, pp. II-1748, III-1997
Flue lining, p. I-698
Flue pipe and linings, p. III-1785
Flues, p. II-907
Fluid power actuators, p. II-1221
Fluid power aircraft subassemblies, p. II-979
Fluid power cylinders, p. II-1221
Fluid power hose assemblies, p. II-979
Fluid power motors, p. II-1221
Fluid power pumps, p. II-1221
Fluid power valves and hose fittings, p. II-979
Fluid-power transmission equipment, p. III-1866
Fluidic devices, p. II-1336
Flumes, pp. II-898, 907
Fluoboric acid, p. I-487
Fluorescent ballasts, p. II-1420
Fluorescent dyes, p. I-474
Fluorescent lamp tubes, p. II-1385
Fluorescent lighting, pp. II-1389, 1420
Fluorinated hydrocarbon gases, p. I-470
Fluorine, p. I-487
Fluoro rubbers, p. I-504
Fluoro-polymer resins, p. I-499
Fluorocarbon derivative rubbers, p. I-504
Fluorocarbon fibers and filaments, p. I-509
Fluorocarbon gases, p. I-470
Fluorohydrocarbon resins, p. I-499
Fluoroscopes, p. II-1356
Fluoroscopic X-ray apparatus, p. II-1356
Fluroescent lamp electrodes, p. II-1385
Flush tanks, p. II-1013
Flush valves, p. II-973
Flutes and parts, p. II-1730
Fluxes, p. I-594
Fly sprays, p. I-528
Fly swatters, p. II-1013
Flytraps, p. II-1389
Flywheels and ring gears, p. II-1504
Foam plastics, pp. I-640, III-1967
Foam polystyrene, p. I-635
Foil, p. II-1013
— aluminum, p. I-815
— bags, p. I-394
— containers, p. II-1013
— copper, p. I-829
— gold, p. I-836
— nickel, p. I-836
— sheet, p. I-394
— silver, p. I-836

Folders, p. III-1900
Folding boxboard stock, p. I-373
Folding boxes, p. I-378
Folding paper and paperboard containers, p. I-378
Food, pp. III-2075, 2109
Food processing machinery, p. III-1866
Food service equipment, p. III-1808
Food warming equipment, p. II-1091
Food waste disposal units, p. II-1416
Food
— carts, p. II-1606
— choppers, p. II-1060
— coloring, pp. I-151, 474
— containers, pp. I-378, 414, 635
— dehydrating equipment, p. II-1060
— extracts, p. I-151
— mixers, p. II-1396
— packaging, p. I-717
— packaging machinery, p. II-1211
— storage bags, p. I-602
— trays, p. I-414
Foot appliances (orthopedic), p. II-1675
Football equipment, pp. II-1701, III-1882
Footholds, p. I-299
Footies, p. I-255
Footwear, pp. I-299, III-1921, 2149
Footwear parts, pp. I-650, 669
Forceps, p. II-1670
Forestry machinery, p. III-1858
Forging machinery, p. II-1128
Forgings, pp. I-779, 871
Forklift trucks, p. III-1866
Forklifts, p. II-1193
Forks, pp. II-885, 891
Formal jackets, pp. I-266, 271
Formaldehyde, p. I-492
Formalin, p. I-492
Formic acid, p. I-492
Forming machines, p. II-1128
Forms handling machines, p. III-1800
Forms
— concrete, p. II-907
— paper, p. III-1900
— rubber products, p. I-680
— shoe display, p. I-357
Fortified wines, p. I-176
Foundation garments, pp. I-266, 278
Foundry casting molds, p. II-1118
Foundry core oil, p. I-594
Foundry cores, p. II-1013
Foundry machinery and equipment, p. III-1866
Foundry pattern making, p. II-1013
Foundry products, p. III-1823
Fountain fruits and syrups, p. III-1938
Fountain lighting fixtures, p. II-1389
Fountain pens, p. II-1713
Fountains, p. II-1013
— drinking, pp. II-1013, III-1846, 1854
— plaster of paris, p. I-751
— refrigerated drinking, p. II-1105
Fourdrinier machinery, p. II-1060
Fourdrinier wire cloth, p. II-938
Fractional horsepower motors, p. II-1426
Fractionating equipment, p. II-1060
Frame alignment equipment, p. II-1091

Frames and pictures, p. III-1777
Frames
— canvases, p. II-1713
— door and window, pp. I-333, II-907
— ophthalmic, p. III-1816
— textile machinery, p. II-1060
Freeze-dried food, p. I-67
Freezers, pp. II-1408, III-1834
Freezing equipment, p. II-1105
French fries, p. I-61
French toast, p. I-61
Frequency converters, p. II-1426
Frequency meters, p. II-1346
Frequency synthesizers, p. II-1346
Fresh fish, p. III-1942
Fresh fruits, p. III-1949
Fresh meats, p. III-1945
Fresh poultry, p. III-1935
Fresh seafood, p. III-1942
Fretted instruments, p. II-1730
Frit, p. I-553
Frogs (iron or steel), p. I-779
Frost protection machinery, p. III-1862
Frosting, p. I-157
Frozen ades, p. I-61
Frozen bread, p. I-115
Frozen cake, p. I-115
Frozen citrus pulp, p. I-61
Frozen custard, p. I-91
Frozen desserts, p. I-91
Frozen dinners, p. I-61
Frozen doughs, p. I-123
Frozen fish, p. III-1942
Frozen food bags, p. I-602
Frozen food entrees, p. I-61
Frozen foods, p. III-1928
Frozen fruit, p. I-61
Frozen meat pies, p. I-101
Frozen meats, pp. III-1945, 2082
Frozen pizza, p. I-61
Frozen pot pies, p. I-61
Frozen poultry, p. III-1935
Frozen rice dishes, p. I-61
Frozen seafood, p. III-1942
Frozen side dishes, p. I-61
Frozen soups, p. I-61
Frozen waffles, p. I-61
Fruit and vegetable stands, p. III-2086
Fruit baskets, p. I-342
Fruit brining, p. I-67
Fruit butters, p. I-67
Fruit crates, p. I-342
Fruit drinks, p. I-164
Fruit extracts, p. I-151
Fruit flour, p. I-14
Fruit harvesting machines, p. II-1022
Fruit juice, pp. I-61, 67
Fruit peel products, p. I-56
Fruit pickling, p. I-67
Fruit pie fillings, p. I-67
Fruit pops, p. I-91
Fruit stands, pp. III-2086, 2227
Fruit syrups, p. I-146
Fruits, p. I-56

Fruits and vegetables, p. I-67
— artificial, p. I-650
Fruits
— artificial, pp. I-712, 721, II-1748
— canned, pp. I-67, III-1953
— fresh, p. III-1949
— frozen, pp. I-61, III-1928
Fryers (kitchen), p. II-1396
Fudge, pp. I-47, 51, 56
Fuel bladders, p. I-669
Fuel briquettes or boulets, p. I-462
Fuel cells, pp. II-1286, 1467
Fuel densitometers, p, II-1366
Fuel injection systems, p. II-1504
Fuel mixture indicators, p. II-1366
Fuel oil, pp. III-1978, 2217
Fuel oil bulk terminals, p. III-1974
Fuel oils, p. I-442
Fuel propellants, pp. I-487, 492
Fuel pumps, pp. I-1504, 1511
Fuel system instruments, p. II-1366
Fuel totalizers, p. II-1366
Fuels, pp. I-442, III-1827
Fuelwood, p. I-311
Fuller's earth, p. I-766
Fumigating chambers, p. II-898
Function generators, p. II-1346
Funds transfer devices, p. II-1251
Fungicides, p. I-528
Fur accessories and trimings, pp. I-266, 284
Fur apparel, pp. I-266, 284, III-2137
Fur clothing, pp. I-266, 284, III-1918
Fur cuttings and scraps, p. III-1889
Fur plates and trimmings, pp. I-266, 284
Fur stripping, p. I-295
Furnace black, p. I-483
Furnace casings, p. II-907
Furnace filters, p. II-1111
Furnace flues, p. II-907
Furnaces, pp. II-1100, 1216, III-1846
— dental laboratory, p. II-1681
— drying, p. II-1216
— floor and wall, p. II-1100
— industrial, p. II-1216
— industrial process, p. III-1866
— laboratory, p. II-1665
— warm air, pp. II-1105, III-1850
Furnishings, pp. III-1915, 1918, 2134
Furniture, pp. II-1631, 1649, III-1773, 2036, 2193
— cut stone, p. I-761
— dimension stock, p. I-333
— factory, p. II-1626
— frames, p. II-1643
— hardware, p. II-932
— hospital, p. II-1665
— household, p. II-1615
— inlays, p. I-357
— institutional, p. II-1626
— laboratory, p. II-1665
— office, p. II-1649
— outdoor, pp. II-1620, 1631
— parts, pp. II-1643, III-1773
— polishes and waxes, p. I-565
— public building, p. II-1626
— restaurant, p. II-1626

— springs, p. II-938
— squares, p. I-333
— tops, p. I-721
— trimmings, p. I-250
— unassembled, p. II-1620
— unfinished, p. II-1620
— wood, p. II-1620
Furriers, p. III-2137
Furring channels, p. II-907
Furs
— dressed, p. I-295
— raw, p. III-1964
Fuse clips, p. II-1431
Fuse cutouts, p. II-1456
Fuse mountings, p. II-1431
Fuses, pp. II-1431, III-1830
— ammunition, p. II-996
Fustic wood extract, p. I-492
Futon frames, p. II-1620
Gaitors, p. I-299
Galleries (art), p. III-2199
Galoshes, p. I-299
Galvanizing machinery, p. II-1146
Galvanometers, pp. II-1346, 1366
Gambier extract, p. I-492
Game software, p. III-1804
Games, pp. II-1707, III-1886, 2152
— coin-operated, p. II-1748
— computer software, p. II-1371
Gamma ray equipment, p. II-1356
Garage door openers, p. II-1467
Garage doors, pp. I-333, II-907
Garages, pp. I-352, II-898
Garbage cans, p. II-927
Garbage disposals, pp. II-1091, 1416, III-1808, 1834
Garbage incinerators, pp. I-742, II-1216
Garbage truck bodies, p. II-1485
Garden centers, p. III-2071
Garden furniture, pp. I-742, 761, II-1620
Garden hose, p. I-664
Garden machinery, pp. II-1027, III-1862
Garden pottery, p. I-680
Garden power equipment, p. III-2068
Garden supplies, p. III-1990
Garden umbrellas, p. II-1748
Garment hangers, p. I-357
Garment leather, p. I-295
Garment storage bags, p. I-238
Garments
— leather, pp. I-266, 284
— oiling, p. I-223
Garnetting machinery, p. II-1060
Garter belts, pp. I-266, 278
Garters, pp. I-266, 278
Gas analyzers, pp. II-1336, 1351
Gas and liquid analysis instruments, p. II-1336
Gas burner automatic controls, p. II-1331
Gas burners, p. II-1100
Gas chromatographic instruments, pp. II-1336, 1351
Gas fireplaces, pp. II-1100, III-1846
Gas flow instrumentation, p. II-1336
Gas generating machinery, p. II-1228
Gas hot water heaters, p. III-1846
Gas leak detectors, p. II-1366
Gas lighting fixtures, p. II-1389

Gas liquefying machinery, p. II-1060
Gas masks, p. II-1675
Gas ranges, pp. II-1091, 1403, III-1846
Gas separating machinery, p. II-1228
Gas space heaters, p. II-1100
Gas storage tanks, p. II-922
Gas tanks, p. II-1550
Gas turbine generator sets, p. II-1156
Gas turbines, pp. II-1156, 1561
Gas valves, p. II-979
Gas welding equipment, p. II-1228
Gas welding rods, p. II-1228
Gas well machinery, p. II-1038
Gas-oil burners, p. II-1100
Gases, pp. I-470, III-1970
Gaskets, pp. II-1724, III-1870
Gasmeters, p. II-1341
Gasoline, pp. I-442, III-1978
Gasoline bulk terminals, p. III-1974
Gasoline dispensing meters, p. II-1341
Gasoline engine parts, pp. I-1504, 1561
Gasoline engines, pp. II-1172, 1504, 1561
Gasoline marketing equipment, p. III-1761
Gasoline measuring and dispensing pumps, p. II-1188
Gasoline service station equipment, p. III-1761
Gastroscopes, pp. II-1321, 1670
Gate and bridge lifting machinery, p. II-1228
Gate valves, p. II-979
Gates, p. II-907
Gauge blocks, p. II-891
Gauges, pp. II-1336, 1341
— machinists', pp. II-891, 1081
— pressure-temperature, p. II-1341
Gauze, p. III-1908
— surgical, pp. I-197, II-1675
Gavels, p. I-357
Gear cutting machines, p. II-1123
Gear pullers, p. II-891
Gear rolling machines, p. II-1128
Gearmotors, p. II-1161
Gears, pp. II-1161, 1529
Geese, p. I-96
Geiger counters, p. II-1366
Gelatin, pp. III-1953, 1970
Gelatin capsules, p. I-594
Gelatin desserts, p. I-157
Gelatin for cooking, p. I-157
Gem stone processing machinery, p. II-1060
Gem stones, p. III-1893
Generating apparatus, pp. II-1228, 1426, 1511
Generator controls, p. II-1431
Generator sets, pp. II-1156, 1426
Generator voltage regulators, p. II-1420
Generators, pp. II-1426, 1511, III-1761, 1769
Generators sets, p. II-1426
Generators
— electrical, p. III-1830
— smoke, p. II-1004
— X-ray, p. II-1356
Geodesic domes, p. I-352
Geophysical instruments, p. II-1366
Geraniol, p. I-492
Germanium refining, p. I-824
Gift shops, p. III-2189
Gift wrap, pp. I-387, III-1900

Numbers following p. or pp. are page references. Roman numerals indicate volume numbers. Page references are to the starting pages of the industries that produce the product or carry out the activity.

Girders (concrete), p. I-742
Girdles, pp. I-261, 266, 278
Girls' hosiery, p. I-255
Girls' socks, p. I-255
Glandular derivatives, p. I-533
Glandular medicinals, p. I-538
Glass, p. I-712
Glass cleaners, p. I-565
Glass fabrics, p. I-202
Glass fiber, p. I-712
Glass making machinery, p. II-1060
Glass packaging containers, p. I-717
Glass products, pp. I-712, 721
Glass scrap, p. III-1889
Glass
— automotive, pp. I-712, 721, III-1761
— plate, pp. I-708, III-1793
Glasses (field, opera), pp. II-1081
Glasshouse refractories, p. I-702
Glassine wrapping paper, pp. I-367, 414
Glassware, pp. I-712, 721, III-1777, 1812, 2046
Glauber's salt, p. I-487
Glaziers' putty, p. I-553
Glide slope instrumentation, p. II-1326
Gliders, p. II-1556
Global positioning systems, p. II-1261
Globe covers and maps, p. I-419
Globe valves, p. II-979
Globes (geographical), p. II-1748
Glove leather, p. I-295
Glove linings, pp. I-266, 284, 289
Gloves, pp. III-1915, 1918
— knit, p. I-261
— leather, pp. I-266, 289
— plastics, p. I-650
— rubber, p. II-1675
— sport, p. II-1701
Glow lamp bulbs, p. II-1385
Glue (dental), p. II-1681
Glues, pp. I-559, III-1970
Gluten, p. I-21
Glycerin, pp. I-492, 565
Glycosides, p. I-533
Goats, p. III-1961
Gocarts, pp. II-1606, 1707, III-1882
Goggles, p. II-1686
Gold, pp. I-836, II-963
— bullion, p. I-824
— foil, pp. I-836, II-1013
— printing inks, p. I-579
Golf carts, pp. II-1606, III-1878, 1882, 2026
Golf equipment, p. III-1882
Golf pro shops, p. III-2149
Golf shoes, p. I-299
Golfing equipment, p. II-1701
Gongs, p. II-1467
Gouges (wood), p. II-891
Gourmet food, p. III-2093
Governors
— diesel engine, p. II-1172
— engine, p. II-1504
— gasoline engine, p. II-1172
— steam, p. II-1156

Gowns, pp. I-266, 284
— formal, pp. I-266, 278
— hospital, pp. I-266, 284
— wedding, pp. I-266, 278
GPS systems, p. II-1261
Grader attachments, p. II-1032
Graders, p. II-1032
Grading machinery, pp. II-1022, 1060
Gradual switches (pneumatic), p. II-1331
Graduation caps and gowns, pp. I-266, 284
Graham flour, p. I-14
Graham wafers, p. I-123
Grain, p. III-1957
Grain alcohol, pp. I-180, 492
Grain drills, p. II-1022
Grain measures, p. I-357
Grain milling machinery, p. II-1060
Grain mills, pp. I-8, 14, 35
Grain stackers, p. II-1022
Granola, p. I-35
Granola bars, pp. I-47, 51, 56
Granulated sugar, pp. I-39, 43
Granulator and pelletizer, p. II-1050
Grapefruit oil, p. I-594
Grapes, p. I-67
Graphic arts plates, p. I-594
Graphic recording meters, p. II-1346
Graphite, p. I-766
Graphite electrodes, p. II-1462
Graphite specialties, p. II-1462
Grass mowing equipment, pp. II-891, 1022, 1027
Gratings, pp. II-907, 1081
Gravure inks, p. I-579
Gravure printing presses, p. II-1060
Gravy canning, p. I-67
Gravy mixes, p. I-151
Grease seals, p. II-1724
Greases
— inedible, p. I-25
— lubricating, pp. I-457, 594
Greenhouses, p. II-898
Greeting cards, pp. I-419, III-1900, 2189
Grenade launchers, p. II-1000
Grenades, p. II-996
Griddles and grills, p. II-1396
Grilles and grillwork, pp. II-907, 938
Grillwork, p. II-907
Grinders, p. II-1206
Grinding balls, p. I-755
Grinding machines, p. II-1123
Grinding oils, p. I-457
Grinding spices, p. I-151
Grinding wheels, p. I-755
Grips and handles, p. I-669
Groceries, p. III-1924
Grocers' bags and sacks, p. I-394
Grocery bags, p. I-602
Grocery carts, p. II-1193
Grocery stores, p. III-2075
Grommets, pp. I-669, III-1870
Ground clamps, p. II-1456
Ground fault circuit interrupters, p. II-1456
Groundwood paper, pp. I-367, 387, III-1897
Groundwood paper products, p. I-367
Groundwood pulp, p. I-362

Grow light fixtures, p. II-1389
Guardrails, p. II-907
Guards
— bannisters, p. II-907
— wire, p. II-938
Guided missiles and space vehicles, pp. II-1575, 1579, III-1878
Guides
— street maps, p. I-419
Guitars, p. II-1730
Gum and wood chemicals, pp. I-492, III-1970
Gummed paper products, p. I-387
Gummed tapes, pp. III-1900, 1904
Gun barrels, pp. II-1000, 1004
Gun effect devices, p. II-1286
Gun forgings, pp. I-779, 871
Gun magazines, pp. II-1000, 1004
Gun shops, p. III-2149
Gun sights, p. II-1081
Gun springs, p. II-938
Gun stocks, p. I-333
Gun trigger locks, p. II-932
Gun turrets, p. II-1004
Gunpowder, p. I-584
Guns, pp. II-1000, 1004
— BB and pellet, p. II-1000
— caulking, p. II-891
— sporting, p. III-1882
Gunsmith shops, p. III-2149
Gutters, pp. I-650, 862, II-907, III-1789
Gymnasium equipment, p. II-1701
Gynecological supplies, p. II-1675
Gypsum
— building products, pp. I-751, III-1793
— products, p. I-751
Gyrocompasses, p. II-1326
Gyrogimbals, p. II-1326
Gyroscopes, p. II-1326
Hair accessories, p. III-1912
Hair care products, p. I-669
Hair clippers, pp. II-885, 891, 1022, 1396
Hair coloring, p. I-574
Hair curlers, pp. II-1013, 1396
Hair driers, p. II-1396
Hair dryers, pp. II-1091, III-1834
Hair nets, p. II-1748
Hair preparations, pp. I-574, III-1874, 1908
Hair sprays, p. I-574
Hairbrushes, p. II-1739
Hairpieces, p. II-1748
Hairpins, pp. I-669, II-1734
Hairsprings, p. II-938
Hall effect devices, p. II-1286
Halloware, p. II-1695
Halogen light bulbs, p. II-1385
Halogenated hydrocarbon derivatives, p. I-492
Halvah, p. I-56
Hammer forgings, p. I-871
Hammer mill machinery, pp. II-1032, 1038
Hammers
— handtools, p. II-891
— piano, p. II-1730
— wood, meat, pp. I-357
Hammocks, pp. I-250, II-1620, 1631
Hampers (laundry), pp. I-650, II-907, 1631

Hams, p. I-101
— canned, p. I-101
— poultry, p. I-96
— preserved, p. I-101
Hand dryers, p. II-1091
Hand held computers, p. II-1237
Hand lotions, p. I-574
Hand soaps, p. I-565
Hand stamps, p. II-1361
Hand trucks, p. II-1193
Handbag leather, p. I-295
Handbags, pp. I-305, II-1695, III-1918, 2134
Handcuffs, p. II-1013
Handkerchiefs, pp. I-266, 289, 410
Handle blanks, p. I-333
Handles, pp. I-305, 357, 650, 676, II-1013
Handtools, p. III-1842
— machinists' precision, pp. II-891, III-1866
— motor vehicle mechanics', pp. II-891, III-1761
— power-driven, p. II-1206
Hang gliders, p. II-1556
Hangar doors, p. II-907
Hangers (garment), p. I-357
Hard candies, p. I-56
Hard disk drives, p. II-1242
Hard drive media, p. II-1380
Hard fiber fabrics, p. I-197
Hard fiber spun yarns, p. I-191
Hard fiber thread, p. I-191
Hard hats, p. II-1675
Hardboard, p. I-318
Hardness testing equipment, p. II-1366
Hardware, p. III-1842
— motor vehicle, p. III-1761
— plastics, p. I-650
Hardwood
— dimension lumber, p. I-333
— distillates, p. I-492
— plywood composites, p. I-323
— veneer or plywood, p. I-323
Harmonicas, p. II-1730
Harness
— assemblies, p. II-1316
— equipment, p. III-1990
— leather, p. I-295
— parts, p. II-1013
Harnesses (dog), p. I-305
Harps, p. II-1730
Harpsichords, p. II-1730
Harrows, p. II-1022
Harvest straw hats, p. I-289
Harvesting machinery, pp. II-1022, III-1862
Hassock fans, p. II-1396
Hat blocks, p. II-1748
Hat bodies, pp. I-266, 289
Hat findings, pp. I-266, 289
Hat linings and trimmings, pp. I-266, 289
Hatchets, p. II-891
Hats, pp. I-261, 266, 289, 414, III-1915, 1918, 2134
— cloth, pp. I-266, 289
— fur, pp. I-266, 284
— leather, pp. I-266, 284
— trimmed, pp. I-266, 289
Hay, pp. I-8, III-1990
Hay balers and presses, p. II-1022

Haying machinery, pp. II-1022, III-1862
Head rice, p. I-14
Headbands, pp. I-266, 289
Headboards, p. II-1620
Heading (barrel), p. I-342
Heads-up displays, p. II-1326
Health and beauty aids, p. III-2099
Health foods, pp. III-1949, 1953
Health lamp bulbs, p. II-1385
Hearing aids, pp. II-1321, III-1812, 2112
Hearse bodies, p. II-1485
Heart-lung machines, p. II-1321
Heat exchangers, p. II-917
Heat pumps, pp. II-1105, III-1850
Heat shields, p. II-1462
Heaters, p. II-1105
— portable, pp. II-1396, III-1834
— space, p. II-1100
— swimming pool, p. II-1100
— tape, p. II-1396
Heating boilers, p. III-1846
Heating equipment, pp. II-1100, 1105, III-1846, 1850
Heating oils, pp. I-442, III-2217
Heating pads, p. II-1396
Heating regulators, p. II-1331
Heating units, pp. II-1100, 1396
Heavy water, p. I-487
Hedge shears, p. II-891
Hedge trimmers, p. II-1027
Heel caps, p. I-305
Heel lifts, p. I-305
Heels (shoe), pp. I-305, 357
Helical springs, p. II-938
Helicopters, p. II-1556
Helium, p. I-470
Helmets, p. II-1675
Hematology diagnostic substances, pp. I-538, 543
Hematology instruments, p. II-1351
Hematology products, p. I-548
Hemlock extract, p. I-492
Hemp bags, p. I-191
Hemp ropes, p. I-191
Hemp spun yarns, p. I-191
Heptanes, p. I-466
Heptenes, p. I-466
Herbicides, p. I-528
Heterocyclic chemicals, p. I-492
Hexadecanol, p. I-492
Hexamethylenediamine, p. I-492
Hexamethylenetetramine, p. I-492
Hexanol, p. I-492
Hides, pp. I-295, III-1964
High chairs, p. II-1620
High fructose corn syrup, p. I-21
High intensity lamp bulbs, p. II-1385
Highway bridge sections, p. II-898
Highway guardrails, p. II-907
Highway line marking machinery, p. II-1032
Hinges, p. II-932
Hitches (trailer), p. II-1550
HIV test kits, p. I-543
Hobby shops, p. III-2152
Hobbyhorses, p. II-1707
Hobbyists' supplies, p. III-1886
Hobs, p. II-1139

Hockey equipment, pp. II-1701, III-1882
Hockey skates, p. II-1701
Hoes, p. II-891
Hog feeding equipment, p. II-1022
Hogs, p. III-1961
Hogsheads, p. I-342
Hoists, pp. II-1193, III-1761, 1866
Holepunchers, pp. II-1076, 1713
Holloware, p. II-1013
Holsters, p. I-305
Homefurnishings, pp. III-1777, 2046
Hominy, p. I-67
Hominy grits, pp. I-14, 35
Homogenizing machinery, p. II-1060
Honey, p. III-1953
Honing and lapping machines, p. II-1123
Honing heads, p. II-1139
Hoods
— industrial, p. II-898
— range, pp. II-907, 1396
Hook and eye fasteners, p. II-1734
Hook and eye latches, p. II-957
Hook and loop fastener fabric, p. I-202
Hooks, p. II-957
— fishing, p. II-1701
— handtools, p. II-891
— metal screw, p. II-957
Hoops, pp. I-342, 779, II-1013
Hop extract, pp. I-151, III-1953
Hopper feed devices, p. II-1139
Hoppers, pp. II-898, 927
Hops, p. III-1964
Horizon situation instrumentation, p. II-1326
Hormone diagnostic substances, p. I-543
Hormone preparations, p. I-538
Hormones and derivatives, p. I-533
Horse bits, p. II-1013
Horse boots and muzzles, p. I-305
Horse trailers, pp. II-1490, 1499
Horsemeat, pp. I-3, 101
Horseradish, pp. I-67, 151
Horses, p. III-1964
Horseshoe nails, p. I-792
Horseshoes, p. I-871
Hose
— clamps, p. II-957
— couplings, p. II-979
— fabrics, p. I-202
— flexible metal, p. II-1013
— industrial, p. III-1870
Hoses, p. I-664
Hosiery, pp. I-255, III-1915, 1918, 2137
Hosiery machines, p. II-1060
Hosiery
— orthopedic, p. II-1675
— sheer, p. I-255
Hospital apparel, pp. I-266, 271, 278
Hospital beds, pp. II-1665, III-1812
Hospital equipment, p. III-1812
Hospital furniture, pp. II-1665, III-1812
Hot dogs, pp. I-96, 101
Hot forgings, p. I-871
Hot strip mill machinery, p. II-1146
Hot tubs, pp. I-342, 650, III-1882, 2207
Hot water bottles, p. I-669

Numbers following p. or pp. are page references. Roman numerals indicate volume numbers. Page references are to the starting pages of the industries that produce the product or carry out the activity.

Hot water heaters, p. II-1416
Hotel equipment, p. III-1808
Hotel furniture, p. III-1773
Hotel tableware, p. I-680
Hotplates, pp. II-1091, 1396
House slippers, p. I-299
Housecoats, pp. I-261, 266, 278, 284
Housedresses, pp. I-266, 278
Houses (prefab), pp. I-347, 352, II-898
Housewares, pp. III-1777, 1834, 2046
Hovercraft, p. II-1593
Howitzers, p. II-1004
Hubs (wood), p. I-357
Hulling machinery, p. II-1022
Humidifiers, pp. II-1396, III-1834, 1850
Humidifying equipment, p. II-1105
Humidistats, p. II-1331
Humidity controls, p. II-1331
Humidity instruments, pp. II-1336, 1366
Hunting dress, pp. I-266, 271
Hunting equipment, p. III-1882
Hunting knives, p. II-885
Hybrid computers, p. II-1237
Hybrid integrated circuits, p. II-1286
Hydrated lime, p. I-747
Hydraulic aircraft subassemblies, p. II-979
Hydraulic cylinders, p. II-1221
Hydraulic fluids, pp. I-442, 457, 594
Hydraulic hose fittings, p. II-979
Hydraulic hoses, p. I-664
Hydraulic power transmissions, p. III-1866
Hydraulic pumps, pp. II-1221, III-1866
Hydraulic slave cylinders, p. II-1523
Hydraulic turbine generators, p. II-1156
Hydraulic turbines, p. II-1156
Hydraulic valves, p. II-979
Hydrazine, p. I-487
Hydrochloric acid, p. I-487
Hydrocyanic acid, p. I-487
Hydrofluoric acid, p. I-487
Hydrofluosilicic acid, p. I-487
Hydrogen, p. I-470
Hydrogen peroxide, p. I-487
Hydrogen sulfide, p. I-487
Hydrometers, pp. II-1336, 1366
Hydronic circulator control, p. II-1331
Hydronic heating equipment, pp. II-1100, III-1846
Hydronic limit controls, p. II-1331
Hydrophones, p. II-1326
Hydroquinone, p. I-492
Hydrostatic drives, p. II-1221
Hydrostatic transmissions, p. II-1221
Hydrosulfites, p. I-487
Hydrotherapy equipment, p. II-1675
Hygrometers, pp. II-1336, 1366
Hygrothermographs, p. II-1366
Hypnotic drugs, p. I-533
Hypochlorites, p. I-487
Hypodermic needles and syringes, p. II-1670
Hypophosphites, p. I-487
I-joists, p. I-328
Ice, p. I-164
Ice bank controls, p. II-1331
Ice boxes, p. II-1408
Ice buckets, pp. I-635, 640, 650

Ice chests, pp. I-635, 640, 650, II-927
Ice cream, pp. I-91, III-1932, 2093
— cones, pp. I-123, III-1953
— machinery, p. II-1060
— mix, p. I-80
— specialties, p. I-91
— vending machines, p. II-1091
Ice crushers, pp. II-1228, 1396
Ice maker controls, p. II-1331
Ice milk, p. I-91
— mix, p. I-80
— specialties, p. I-91
Ice skates, p. II-1701
Ice wine, p. I-176
Ice
— dry, pp. I-470, III-1970
Ice-making machinery, pp. II-1105, III-1854
Iced coffee, p. I-164
Iced tea, p. I-164
Ices and sherbets, p. I-91
Identification plates, p. II-1013
Identity recorders, p. III-1797
Igniters (ammunition), p. II-996
Ignition controls, p. II-1331
Ignition points, p. II-1511
Ignition testing instruments, p. II-1346
Ignition wiring harness, p. II-1511
Illuminated indoor lighting, p. II-1389
Images
— small gypsum, p. I-751
— small papier-mache, p. I-775
Immersion heaters, p. II-1396
Immunology instruments, p. II-1351
Impact wrenches, p. II-1206
Impedance measuring equipment, p. II-1346
Impeller and counter driven flow meters, p. II-1341
Implants (surgical), p. II-1675
Impression material (dental), p. II-1681
In-built thermostats, p. II-1331
In-vitro diagnostic substances, p. I-543
In-vivo diagnostic substances, p. I-538
Incandescent filament lamp bulbs, p. II-1385
Incense, p. I-594
Incinerator control systems, p. II-1331
Incinerators, pp. I-742, II-1216
Incubators
— infant, p. II-1675
— laboratory, p. II-1665
— poultry, p. II-1022
Indelible inks, p. I-594
Indexing tables, p. II-1139
India inks, p. I-594
Indium chloride, p. I-487
Induction heating equipment, p. II-1216
Inductors (electronic), p. II-1301
Industrial belting reinforcement, p. I-247
Industrial chemicals, p. III-1970
Industrial gases, pp. I-470, III-1970
Industrial scales, p. II-1228
Inedible products, p. I-101
Inertial navigation systems, p. II-1326
Infant cereals, p. I-35
Infant incubators, p. II-1675
Infant's formulas, p. I-80
Infant's shoes, p. I-299

Infants outerwear, p. I-284
Infants' apparel, p. I-284
Infants' clothing, p. III-1918
Infrared analytical instruments, p. II-1351
Infrared homing systems, p. II-1326
Infrared instruments, p. II-1336
Infrared lamp bulbs, p. II-1385
Infrared lamp fixtures, p. II-1389
Infrared ovens, p. II-1216
Infrared sensors, p. II-1286
Ingot, pp. I-779, 802, 815, 824, 836, III-1823, 1893
Inhalation therapy equipment, p. II-1670
Inhalators, p. II-1670
Inhibitors, p. I-594
Injection molding machinery, p. II-1050
Ink, p. III-1900
Ink eradicators, p. I-565
Inked ribbons, pp. II-1713, III-1900
Inkjet cartridges, p. I-579
Inkjet inks, p. I-579
Inks, pp. I-579, 594, III-1870
Inner soles, p. I-305
Inner tubes, p. I-659
Innerspring cushions, p. II-1656
Inorganic chemicals, p. III-1970
Inorganic pigments, p. I-474
Input/output equipment, p. II-1251
Insect lamps, p. II-1389
Insect screening, p. II-938
Insecticides, p. I-528
Inserts, p. II-1139
Instant coffee, p. I-142
Instant hot cereals, p. I-35
Instant printing, p. I-419
Instant tea, p. I-142
Institutional furniture, p. II-1626
Institutional lighting fixtures, p. II-1389
Instrument control panels, p. II-1511
Instrument landing instrumentation, p. II-1326
Instrument lenses, p. II-1081
Instrument panels, p. II-1341
Instrument shunts, p. II-1346
Instrument springs, p. II-938
Instrument transformers, p. II-1420
Instruments, pp. II-1326, 1346, 1670, 1730, III-1819, 1866
Insulated wire, pp. I-815, 829, III-1830
Insulating batts, pp. I-414, 770
Insulating firebrick, p. I-702
Insulating glass, pp. I-708, 721
Insulating materials, p. I-357
Insulating oils, p. I-594
Insulation and cushioning, pp. I-635, 640
Insulation board, p. I-318
Insulation materials, p. III-1789
Insulators, pp. I-685, 712, 721, II-1456, III-1830
Insulin, pp. I-533, 538
Intaglio printing, p. I-419
Integrated circuits, p. III-1838
Integrated microcircuits, p. II-1286
Integrated-circuit testers, p. II-1346
Integrating electricity meters, p. II-1346
Integrating meters, p. II-1341
Intercom systems and equipment, p. II-1266
Intercooler shells, p. II-917

Numbers following p. or pp. are page references. Roman numerals indicate volume numbers. Page references are to the starting pages of the industries that produce the product or carry out the activity.

2265

Interferometers, p. II-1081
Interlinings, p. I-266
Internal combustion engine analyzers, p. II-1346
Internal combustion engines, pp. II-1172, 1504, 1561, III-1866
Intra ocular lenses, p. II-1675
Intrauterine devices, p. II-1675
Intravenous solutions, p. I-538
Invert sugar, p. I-43
Inverters, pp. II-1426, 1467
Investment castings, pp. I-844, 851, 856
Iodides, p. I-487
Iodinated diagnostic substances, p. I-538
Iodine, p. I-487
Ion chambers, p. II-1366
Ion exchange resins, p. I-499
Ionomer resins, p. I-499
Ionone, p. I-492
Iridium bar, p. I-836
Iridium refining, p. I-824
Iron, p. I-779
Iron based pigments, p. I-474
Iron castings, p. I-844
Iron compounds, p. I-487
Iron forgings, p. I-871
Iron foundries, p. I-844
Iron lungs, p. II-1675
Iron sinter, p. I-779
Iron sulphate, p. I-487
Ironers and mangles, p. II-1412
Ironing boards, pp. I-357, II-1013
Irons, p. II-1396
Irradiation apparatus and tubes, p. II-1356
Irradiation equipment, p. II-1356
Irrigation equipment, pp. II-1022, III-1862
Irrigation pipe, pp. I-736, II-907
Isobutane, p. I-466
Isobutene, p. I-466
Isobutylene polymer resins, p. I-499
Isobutylene-isoprene rubber, p. I-504
Isocyanate rubber, p. I-504
Isocyanates, p. I-492
Isolation transformers, p. II-1420
Isoprene, p. I-466
Isopropyl alcohol, p. I-492
Italian foods, p. I-67
IV apparatus, p. II-1670
Jack hammers, p. II-1032
Jackets, pp. I-261, 266, 271, 278, 284, 305, II-898, 992
Jacks, pp. II-891, 1228
Jacquard card cutting machinery, p. II-1060
Jalousies, p. II-907
Janitorial chemicals, p. III-1970
Janitorial equipment, p. III-1874
Japanning ovens, p. II-1216
Japans, p. I-553
Jars, pp. I-650, 717
Jean-cut casual slacks, pp. I-266, 271, 278
Jeans, pp. I-266, 278, 284
Jellies, pp. I-67, III-1953
Jelly candies, p. I-56
Jerseys, pp. I-261, 266, 271, 278
Jet fuels, p. I-442
Jet propulsion engines, p. II-1561

Jet propulsion projectiles, p. II-996
Jewel settings and mountings, p. II-1695
Jeweler's findings, p. II-1695
Jeweler's handtools, p. II-891
Jewelers' findings, p. III-1893
Jewelry, pp. II-1695, III-1893, 2134, 2143
Jigs, p. II-1133
Jigsaws, pp. II-1045, 1206
Job stampings, p. II-1540
Jogging machines, p. II-1701
Jogging suits, pp. I-261, 266, 271, 278, 284
Joint compounds, pp. I-559, 751
Jointers, p. II-1045
Joints, pp. II-1167, 1529, 1566
Joists, pp. II-898, 907
Joystick devices, p. II-1251
Jugs, pp. I-635, 640, II-927
Juice extractors, pp. II-1060, 1396
Juice pops, p. I-91
Juices, pp. I-61, 67, III-1928, 1953
Jukeboxes, p. II-1271
Jumpsuits, pp. I-266, 278
Junction boxes, p. II-1456
Jute bags, p. I-197
Jute piece goods, p. III-1912
Juvenile furniture, pp. II-1615, 1620, 1631
Juvenile magazines, p. I-419
Kaolin, p. I-766
Keene's cement, p. I-751
Kegs, p. I-342
Kelp meal and pellets, p. I-8
Kelvin bridges, p. II-1346
Kerosene, p. I-442
Kerosene space heaters, p. II-1100
Ketchup, p. I-67
Ketone compounds, p. I-492
Kettles, p. II-922
Key blanks, p. II-932
Key cases, pp. I-305, II-1695
Key cutting machines, p. II-1123
Key rings, p. II-938
Keyboards, pp. II-1251, 1730
Keyless entry systems, p. II-1511
Keys and locks, p. III-1842
Keysets, p. II-1256
Kiln furniture, p. I-702
Kilns, pp. II-1060, 1216, III-1866
Kinematic test equipment, p. II-1366
Kit car bodies, p. II-1485
Kitchen appliances, p. III-1834
Kitchen articles, p. I-680
Kitchen cabinets, pp. II-1610, III-1781
Kitchen chairs, pp. II-1620, 1631
Kitchen cutlery, p. II-885
Kitchen degreasers, p. I-565
Kitchen furniture, pp. II-1620, 1631
Kitchen utensils, pp. I-650, II-885, III-1777, 1808
Kitchenware, pp. I-357, 680, III-2046
Kites, p. II-1707
Klystron tubes, p. II-1276
Knapsacks, p. I-238
Knickers, pp. I-266, 271, 278, 284
Knickknack shelves, p. II-1620
Knife blades, p. II-885
Knife blanks, p. II-885

Knife switches, p. II-1431
Knishes, p. I-115
Knit gloves, pp. I-261, 266, 289
Knitting machinery, p. II-1060
Knives, pp. II-885, 891, 1139, 1396, 1670, III-1842, 1904
Knobs, pp. I-357, II-1730
Knot tying machinery, p. II-1060
Knurling machines, p. II-1128
Kraft liner board, p. I-373
Kraft paper stock, p. I-367
Label making equipment, p. II-1713
Labeling, p. II-1211
Labels, p. III-1912
Laboratory animal feed, p. I-8
Laboratory centrifuges, p. II-1665
Laboratory coats, pp. I-266, 271, 278
Laboratory distilling apparatus, p. II-1665
Laboratory equipment, pp. II-1665, III-1812, 1819
Laboratory evaporation apparatus, p. II-1665
Laboratory freezers, p. II-1665
Laboratory furniture, p. II-1665
Laboratory glassware, pp. I-712, 721
Laboratory instruments, pp. II-1081, 1351
Laboratory sample preparation apparatus, p. II-1665
Laboratory testing instruments, p. II-1346
Lace, pp. I-212, 250
Lace leather, p. I-295
Lace making machinery, p. II-1060
Lace products, p. I-212
Laces, pp. I-202, 305
Lacquering ovens, p. II-1216
Lacquers, pp. I-553, III-2003
Lactic acid, p. I-492
Lactose, p. I-80
Ladder jacks, pp. I-357, II-1013
Ladder rounds or rungs, p. I-333
Ladders, pp. I-357, 650, II-907, 1013, III-1866
Ladle bails, p. II-898
Ladles, p. II-898
Lager brewing, p. I-171
Lakes, p. I-474
Lamb, p. I-101
Lamb carcasses, p. I-101
Laminated aluminum foil, p. II-1013
Laminated glass, pp. I-708, 721
Laminated plastics plate, p. I-630
Laminated structural wood members, p. I-328
Laminated veneer lumber, p. I-328
Laminating foil, p. I-394
Laminating metals, p. II-963
Lamp ballasts, p. II-1420
Lamp bases, p. I-680
Lamp black, p. I-483
Lamp bulb parts, p. II-1385
Lamp bulbs and tubes, p. II-1385
Lamp frames, p. II-938
Lamp holders, p. II-1456
Lamp shade frames, p. II-1013
Lamp shades, pp. I-650, 712, 721, II-1389
Lamp shops, p. III-2046
Lamp sockets, p. II-1456
Lamps, pp. II-1356, 1389, III-1777
Land preparation machinery, pp. II-1032, III-1858, 1862

Numbers following p. or pp. are page references. Roman numerals indicate volume numbers. Page references are to the starting pages of the industries that produce the product or carry out the activity.

2266

Landing mats, p. II-898
Lanterns, p. II-1389
Lapidary work, p. II-1695
Laptop computers, p. II-1237
Lard, pp. I-101, III-1945
Laser boring, p. II-1123
Laser diodes, p. II-1286
Laser disks, p. II-1375
Laser equipment, p. II-1321
Laser systems, p. II-1321
Laser welding equipment, p. II-1228
Lashes, p. I-305
Last sole patterns, p. I-357
Latex foam rubber, p. I-669
Latex paint, p. I-553
Latex rubber, p. I-504
Lath, pp. I-318, 333, 751, II-898
Lathes, pp. II-1045, 1123
Lathmills, p. I-333
Latigo leather, p. I-295
Laundry bags, p. I-238
Laundry bluing, p. I-565
Laundry equipment, p. II-1412
Laundry extractors, p. II-1091
Laundry hampers, pp. II-927, 1631
Laundry machinery, pp. II-1091, III-1834, 1874
Laundry nets, p. I-250
Laundry pressing machines, p. II-1091
Laundry soap, pp. I-565, III-1970
Laundry tubs, pp. I-650, II-1013
Lauric acid esters and amines, p. I-492
Lavatories, pp. I-676, II-1013
Lawn and garden equipment, p. II-1027
Lawn care supplies, p. III-1990
Lawn edgers, pp. II-891, 1027
Lawn furniture, pp. II-1620, 1631
Lawn hose nozzles, p. II-979
Lawn maintenance machinery, p. III-1862
Lawn power equipment, p. III-2068
Lawn supplies, p. III-2071
Lawnmowers, pp. II-891, 1022, 1027, III-1862
Laxative preparations, p. I-538
LCD screen units, p. II-1316
Lead, p. I-766
Lead acid storage batteries, p. II-1441
Lead and lead alloy bar, p. I-836
Lead based pigments, p. I-474
Lead castings, p. I-856
Lead die-castings, p. I-856
Lead foil, p. II-1013
Lead oxides, p. I-487
Lead pigments, p. I-474
Lead rolling, p. I-836
Lead silicate, p. I-487
Lead smelting, p. I-824
Lead-in wires, p. II-1385
Leaf, p. II-1013
Leaf blowers, p. II-1027
Leaf skimmers and rakes, p. II-891
Leaf springs, p. II-938
Leaf tobacco, p. III-1964
Leak detectors, p. II-1366
Leashes, p. I-305
Leather, p. I-223
Leather tanning, p. I-295

Leather upper athletic footwear, p. I-299
Leather welting, p. I-305
Leather working machinery, p. II-1060
Leather
— apparel, pp. I-266, 284
— belting, p. I-305
— clothing, pp. I-266, 284
— coats, p. III-2137
— coloring, p. I-295
— converters, p. I-295
— cut stock, pp. I-305, III-1921
— footwear, p. I-299
— gloves, pp. I-266, 289, II-1701
— goods, pp. I-305, III-2146
— handbags and purses, p. I-305
— house slippers, p. I-299
— luggage, p. I-305
Leatherboard, pp. I-373, 394
Lecithin, pp. I-25, 30
LEDs, p. II-1286
Leggings, pp. I-266, 278, 284, 305
Leggins, p. I-278
Lemon oil, p. I-594
Lens blanks, pp. I-650, 712, 721, III-1816
Lens hoods, p. II-1086
Lens mounts, p. II-1686
Lenses, pp. II-1081, 1686
Leotards, pp. I-261, 266, 278
Letter folding, p. II-1076
Letter pins, p. II-1139
Letterpress inks, p. I-579
Letterpress printing presses, p. II-1060
Letters, p. I-402
Letters for signs, p. II-1719
Level and bulk measuring instruments, p. II-1336
Level gauges, p. II-1366
Levels, p. II-891
Levels and tapes, p. II-1366
Licorice candy, p. I-56
Lids, p. I-878
Lids and ends, p. II-927
Lie detectors, p. II-1366
Life preservers, p. II-1675
Life rafts, pp. I-650, 669
Lift trucks, p. III-1866
Lifts, p. I-305
Light bulb and tube, p. II-1060
Light bulbs, pp. II-1385, III-1830
Light emitting diodes, p. II-1286
Light meters, p. II-1086
Light rail cars, p. II-1583
Light utility trucks, pp. II-1477, III-2010, 2014
Lighter fluids, p. I-594
Lighters, pp. II-1695, 1748
Lighting carbons, p. II-1462
Lighting fixtures, pp. II-1389, III-1830
Lighting transformers, p. II-1420
Lightning arrestors and coils, p. II-1456
Lightning protection equipment, p. II-1456
Lignin plastics, p. I-499
Limbs, p. II-1675
Lime, pp. III-1785, 1990
Lime oil, p. I-594
Lime production, p. I-747
Lime-sulfur fungicides, p. I-528

Limit controls, p. II-1331
Limited price variety stores, p. III-2179
Lindane pesticides, p. I-528
Line voltage regulators, p. II-1420
Linear accelerators, p. II-1467
Linear ball bearings, p. II-987
Linear counters, p. II-1341
Linear esters fibers and filaments, p. I-509
Linear roller bearings, p. II-987
Linens, pp. I-233, III-1777, 2046
Liner brick and plates, p. I-698
Liners, p. II-898
Lingerie, pp. I-266, 278, III-1918, 2137
Lining leather, p. I-295
Linings, pp. I-250, 266, 289, 305, II-1013
Links, pp. II-1000, 1004
Linoleic acid esters and amines, p. I-492
Linoleum floor coverings, p. I-650
Linotype machines, p. II-1060
Linseed oil, pp. I-25, 30
Lintels, p. I-742
Lip balms, p. I-538
Lipsticks, p. I-574
Liquefied gases, p. III-1970
Liquefied petroleum gas, pp. I-442, II-922, III-1974, 1978, 2221
Liquid air, p. I-470
Liquid analysis instruments, p. II-1336
Liquid beet syrup, p. I-39
Liquid chromatographic instruments, p. II-1351
Liquid concentration instruments, p. II-1336
Liquid flow meters, p. II-1341
Liquid level controls, p. II-1331
Liquid level instruments, p. II-1336
Liquid oxygen tanks, p. II-922
Liquid sugar, pp. I-39, 43
Liquor, pp. I-47, 51
Liquor stores, p. III-2096
Liquors, pp. I-176, 180, III-1986
List finders and roledex address files, p. II-1713
Litharge, p. I-474
Lithium batteries, p. II-1446
Lithium compounds, p. I-487
Lithographic inks, p. I-579
Lithographic printing, p. I-419
Lithographic printing presses, p. II-1060
Lithopone, p. I-474
Lithotripters, p. II-1321
Livens projectors, p. II-1004
Livestock, pp. III-1961, 1964
Livestock auction markets, pp. III-1961, 1964
Livestock feeds, pp. I-8, III-1990
Living room furniture, pp. II-1615, 1620, 1631
Loaded computer boards, pp. II-1311, III-1804
Loaders, p. II-1032
Loading machines, p. II-1038
Local area network equipment, p. II-1256
Lock washers, p. II-957
Lockers, pp. II-1105, 1643, III-1808, 1854
Locks, pp. II-932, 1091, III-1842
Locksmith equipment, p. III-1874
Locomotive and rail car light fixtures, p. II-1511
Locomotive cranes, p. II-1193
Locomotive diesel engines, p. II-1172
Locomotives, pp. II-1583, III-1878

Numbers following p. or pp. are page references. Roman numerals indicate volume numbers. Page references are to the starting pages of the industries that produce the product or carry out the activity.

2267

Log cabins, p. I-352
Log debarking machinery, pp. II-1032, 1060
Log splitters, pp. II-1032, 1060
Logging equipment, p. III-1858
Logging trailers, p. II-1490
Logic circuit testers, p. II-1346
Logs, p. II-1100
Logwood extract, p. I-492
Loom bobbins, p. II-1060
Loom reeds, p. II-1060
Looms for textiles, p. II-1060
Loopers for textiles, p. II-1060
Looseleaf binders, p. III-1900
Looseleaf binders and devices, p. I-419
Looseleaf fillers and paper, pp. I-367, 402
Lotions, p. I-574
Loudspeakers, p. II-1271
Lounging robes and dressing gowns, pp. I-261, 266, 271, 278, 284
Loupes, p. II-1081
Louver windows, pp. I-333, II-907
Louvers, p. II-907
Lozenges, p. I-56
Lubricating oils and greases, pp. I-442, 457, 594, III-1974, 1978
Lubrication systems, p. II-1583
Luggage, pp. I-305, III-2146
— hardware, p. II-932
— linings, p. I-250
— racks, p. II-1550
Lugs and connectors, pp. II-1456, III-1830
Lumber, pp. I-311, 328, 333, 357, III-1781
Luminous panel ceilings, p. II-1389
Luminous tube transformers, p. II-1420
Lunch boxes, p. II-927
Luncheon meat, pp. I-96, 101
Lye, p. I-565
Macaroni, pp. I-123, 157, III-1953
Machetes, p. II-891
Machine bases, p. II-1013
Machine guards, p. II-907
Machine gun belts, pp. II-1000, 1004
Machine guns, pp. II-1000, 1004
Machine keys, p. II-957
Machine knives, pp. II-891, 1139
Machine shops, p. II-944
Machine tool attachments, p. II-1139
Machine tool transformers, p. II-1420
Machine tools, pp. II-1123, 1128, III-1866
Machinists' measuring tools, pp. II-891, III-1866
Machmeters, p. II-1326
Mackinaws, pp. I-266, 271, 278, 284
Magazine racks, p. II-1620
Magazine stands, p. III-2164
Magazines, p. III-1994
Magazines and periodicals, p. I-419
Magic supplies, p. III-2152
Magnesia, p. I-533
Magnesia refractory cement, p. I-702
Magnesite, p. I-766
Magnesium and magnesium alloy bar, p. I-836
Magnesium carbonate, p. I-487
Magnesium castings, p. I-856
Magnesium chloride, p. I-487
Magnesium compounds, p. I-487

Magnesium die-castings, p. I-856
Magnesium foil, pp. I-836, II-1013
Magnesium refining, p. I-824
Magnesium rolling, p. I-836
Magnet wire, pp. I-815, 829, 836
Magnetic and optical media, p. II-1380
Magnetic counters, p. II-1341
Magnetic flow meters, p. II-1336
Magnetic forming machines, p. II-1128
Magnetic ink recognition devices, p. II-1251
Magnetic recording media for tapes, p. II-1380
Magnetic resonance imaging apparatus, p. II-1351
Magnetic resonance imaging equipment, p. II-1321
Magnetic tapes, pp. II-1380, III-1838
Magnetic/optical storage units, p. II-1242
Magnetometers, p. II-1366
Magnetron tubes, p. II-1276
Magnets, pp. I-685, II-1013
Magnifiers, p. II-1686
Magnifying glasses, p. II-1081
Magnifying instruments, p. II-1081
Mail carrier cases, p. II-1643
Mail chutes, p. II-907
Mail handling machinery, p. II-1076
Mailboxes, p. II-927
Mailing cases, p. I-378
Mailing machines, p. III-1800
Mainframe computers, p. II-1237
Make-up, p. I-574
Malacca furniture, p. II-1631
Malathion, p. I-528
Maleic anhydride, p. I-492
Mallets, pp. I-357, II-891
Malonic dinitrile, p. I-492
Malt, pp. I-14, III-1953
Malt milling machinery, p. II-1060
Malt
— extract, pp. I-151, III-1953
— flour, p. I-14
— liquor, p. I-171
— sprouts, p. I-14
Malted milk, p. I-80
Maltodextrins, p. I-21
Man-made fibers, p. III-1970
Mandolins, p. II-1730
Mandrels, p. II-1139
Manganese dioxide, p. I-487
Manganese metal ferroalloys, p. I-779
Mangrove extract, p. I-492
Manhole covers, p. I-844
Manicure preparations, p. I-574
Manifolds, pp. II-1008, 1504
Manila folders, p. I-402
Manmade cellulosic fibers, p. I-509
Manmade fabrics, pp. I-197, 202
Manmade fiber, p. I-509
Manmade fiber thread, p. I-191
Manmade staple spun yarns, p. I-191
Mannequins, pp. II-1748, III-1808
Mannitol hexanitrate explosives, p. I-584
Manometers, p. II-1336
Manufactured, p. III-1793
Manufactured (mobile) buildings, p. I-347
Manufactured (mobile) classrooms, p. I-347
Manufactured (mobile) homes, pp. I-347, III-2202

Maps, pp. I-419, III-1994
Marbles, p. II-1707
Margaric acid, p. I-492
Margarine, pp. I-21, 25, III-1953
Margarine-butter blends, p. I-25
Marine and navy auxiliary controls, p. II-1436
Marine engines, p. II-1172
Marine hardware, p. II-932
Marine horns, p. II-1013
Marine paints, p. I-553
Marine power boilers, p. II-917
Marine radio equipment, p. II-1261
Marine service stations, p. III-2119
Marine storage batteries, p. II-1441
Marine supplies, pp. III-1878, 1882
Marine supply dealers, p. III-2023
Marionettes, p. II-1748
Marker boards, p. II-1713
Marking devices, pp. II-1713, III-1900
Marking machines, p. II-1151
Marmalade, p. I-67
Marquetry, p. I-357
Marshmallow creme, p. I-56
Marshmallows, p. I-56
Marzipan, p. I-56
Maser, p. II-1467
Mashers, p. I-357
Masking tape, p. I-387
Mason's handtools, p. II-891
Mason's materials, p. III-1785
Mass spectrometers, p. II-1351
Mass spectroscopy instrumentation, p. II-1351
Massage machines, p. II-1396
Mastics, p. III-1970
Masts, p. I-357
Matches and match books, p. I-594
Materials handling machinery, p. III-1866
Maternity bras and corsets, pp. I-266, 278
Maternity shops, p. III-2125
Mats and matting, p. II-938
Mattocks, p. II-891
Mattress protectors, p. I-669
Mattress springs and spring units, p. II-938
Mattresses, pp. I-650, 669, II-1656, III-1773, 2036
Matzo baking, p. I-115
Mauls, pp. I-357, II-891
Mayonnaise, p. I-151
Meal, pp. I-8, 14
Measuring and testing equipment, p. III-1866
Measuring attachments, p. II-1139
Measuring instruments, pp. II-1336, 1346
Measuring tools, p. II-891
Measuring wheels, p. II-1341
Meat and bone meal and tankage, p. I-101
Meat canning, pp. I-3, 67, 96, 101
Meat extracts, p. I-101
Meat grinders, p. II-1060
Meat markets, p. III-2082
Meat products, pp. I-3, 96
Meat products canning, p. I-101
Meats, pp. I-101, III-1928, 1945, 1953
Meats and meat products, p. III-1945
Mechanic's creepers, p. II-1193
Mechanic's hand soaps and pastes, p. I-565
Mechanic's handtools, p. II-891

Numbers following p. or pp. are page references. Roman numerals indicate volume numbers. Page references are to the starting pages of the industries that produce the product or carry out the activity.

2268

Mechanic's tools, p. III-1761
Mechanical leather, p. I-295
Mechanical measuring instruments, p. II-1336
Mechanical pencil refills, p. II-1713
Mechanical pencils, p. II-1713
Mechanical power transmission supplies, p. III-1870
Mechanical rubber goods, pp. I-669, III-1870
Mechanisms, p. II-1361
Mechanisms for coin-operated machines, p. II-1091
Medical cleaning equipment, p. II-1321
Medical equipment, p. III-1812
Medical furniture, p. III-1812
Medical glassware, pp. I-712, 721, III-1812
Medical instruments, p. III-1812
Medical radiation therapy equipment, p. II-1356
Medical service apparel, pp. I-266, 271, 278
Medical sundries, p. III-1908
Medical supplies, p. III-1812
Medical thermometers, p. II-1670
Medical ultrasound equipment, p. II-1321
Medicinal chemicals, p. I-533
Medicine cabinets, pp. II-1610, 1631
Medium density fiberboard, p. I-318
Melamine resins, p. I-499
Melt blown nonwoven fabrics, p. I-207
Melton jackets, pp. I-266, 271, 278, 284
Memory boards, p. II-1311
Men's and boys' clothing, p. III-1915
Men's and boys' furnishings, p. III-1915
Men's socks, p. I-255
Mercerizing machinery, p. II-1060
Merchandise bags, p. I-602
Merchandising machines, p. III-1808
Mercuric oxide batteries, p. II-1446
Mercury arc rectifiers, p. II-1467
Mercury chloride, p. I-487
Mercury compounds, p. I-487
Mercury fulminate explosives, p. I-584
Mercury halide lamp bulbs, p. II-1385
Mercury oxide, p. I-487
Mesh, pp. I-779, 792, 815, 829, 836, II-938
Metabolite diagnostic substances, p. I-538
Metal cans, p. II-927
Metal casting machinery and equipment, p. II-1060
Metal cutting machine tools, p. II-1123
Metal cutting saw blades, p. II-891
Metal cyanides, p. III-1970
Metal deposit forming machines, p. II-1128
Metal detectors, p. II-1366
Metal fabric and mesh safety gloves, p. II-1675
Metal foil containers, p. II-1013
Metal forming machine tools, p. II-1128
Metal framed furniture, p. II-1615
Metal hand stamps, p. II-1713
Metal melting furnaces, p. II-1216
Metal motor vehicle body parts stamping, p. II-1540
Metal oxide silicon devices, p. II-1286
Metal polishes, p. I-565
Metal powder and flake, pp. I-779, 792, 806, 829, 836
Metal products, p. III-1823
Metal scrap and waste, p. III-1889
Metal stampings, p. I-878
Metallic concentrates, p. III-1827
Metallic pigments, p. I-474
Metallic soap, p. I-492

Metals, pp. III-1823, 1893
Metals sales offices, p. III-1823
Metals service centers, p. III-1823
Metalworking lathes, p. II-1123
Metalworking machinery, p. III-1866
Meteorologic tracking systems, p. II-1366
Meteorological instruments, p. II-1366
Metering devices, p. II-1341
Metering panels, p. II-1431
Meters, pp. II-1336, 1341, 1346, III-1830, 1866, 1874
Methoxychlor insecticides, p. I-528
Methyl acetone, p. I-492
Methyl acrylate resins, p. I-499
Methyl alcohol, p. I-492
Methyl cellulose resins, p. I-499
Methyl chloride, p. I-492
Methyl methacrylate resins, p. I-499
Methyl perhydrofluorine, p. I-492
Methyl salicylate, p. I-492
Methyl violet toners, p. I-474
Methylamine, p. I-492
Methylene chloride, p. I-492
Mexican foods, p. I-61
Mexican foods canning, p. I-67
Mica, p. I-775
Micro and macro premixes, p. I-8
Micro-lithography equipment, p. II-1055
Microbiology instruments, p. II-1351
Microcomputers, p. II-1237
Microcontroller chip, p. II-1286
Microfiche equipment, p. II-1086
Microfilm equipment, pp. II-1086, III-1800
Micrometers, p. II-891
Microphones, p. II-1271
Microprobes, p. II-1351
Microprocessor chip, p. II-1286
Microscopes, pp. II-1081, 1351
Microwave communications equipment, p. II-1261
Microwave components, p. II-1316
Microwave ovens, pp. II-1091, 1403
Microwave test equipment, p. II-1346
Microwaveware, p. I-650
Military dress uniforms, pp. I-266, 271, 278
Military insignia, pp. I-250, II-1013
Military vehicles, p. III-1878
Milk, pp. I-80, 85, III-1932, 1953
Milk based drinks, pp. I-80, 85
Milk carton board, pp. I-373, 394
Milk drink, p. I-85
Milk pasteurizing, p. I-85
Milk processing, pp. I-85, II-1060
Milk substitutes, p. I-85
Milking machinery, p. III-1862
Milking machines, p. II-1022
Milkshake mixes, p. I-80
Mill menders, p. I-250
Mill supplies, p. III-1870
Millinery, pp. I-266, 289, III-1918
Millinery supplies, p. III-1912
Millinery trimmings, pp. I-266, 289
Milling machines, p. II-1123
Milling rice, p. I-14
Millwork, pp. I-311, II-1638, III-1781
Mine conveyors, p. II-1193
Mine props, p. I-311

Mine ties, p. I-311
Miner's lamps, p. II-1389
Mineral colors and pigments, p. I-474
Mineral feed supplements, pp. I-3, 8
Mineral processing machinery, p. II-1038
Mineral supplements, pp. I-3, 8, III-1990
Mineral wool insulation, p. I-770
Mineral wool products, p. I-770
Minerals, p. III-1827
Mines, p. II-996
Mini-mills, p. I-779
Miniblinds, p. II-1661
Minicomputers, p. II-1237
Mining cars, p. II-1038
Mining locomotives, p. II-1583
Mining machinery, pp. III-1858, 1866
Minivans, p. II-1477
Mirrors, pp. I-721, II-1081, III-1761, 1777
Missile warheads, p. II-996
Miter boxes, p. II-891
Mittens, pp. I-261, 266, 289
Mix, p. I-80
Mixed drinks, p. I-180
Mixers, p. II-1032
Mixes, pp. I-14, 123, III-1953
Mobile homes, pp. I-347, III-2202
Moccasins, p. I-299
Modacrylic fibers and filaments, p. I-509
Modacrylic spun yarns, p. I-191
Model kits, pp. II-1707, III-1886
Model railroad, p. II-1707
Modeling clay, p. II-1713
Models, pp. II-1707, 1748
Modems, pp. II-1256, III-1838
Modular furniture, p. II-1649
Mohair, p. III-1964
Mohair yarn, p. I-191
Moisture analyzers, p. II-1351
Moisture meters, p. II-1336
Molasses, pp. I-39, 43, III-1953
Molded packings and seals, p. II-1724
Molded pulp products, p. I-414
Molding, p. III-1781
Moldings, p. I-333
Moldings and trim, p. II-1540
Molds, pp. I-844, II-1118
— casting, p. II-1118
— forming, p. II-1118
— plastics and rubber, p. II-1118
— steel ingots, p. I-844
Molybdenum, p. I-836
Molybdenum silicon ferroalloys, p. I-779
Money chests, p. II-1013
Monitors, p. II-1251
Monochlorodifluoromethane, p. I-470
Monochrometers, p. II-1351
Monolithic integrated circuits, p. II-1286
Monomethylparaminophenol sulfate, p. I-492
Monorail systems, p. II-1193
Monosodium glutamate, p. I-492
Monuments and grave markers, p. I-761
Mop wringers, p. II-1091
Mopeds, pp. II-1598, III-1757, 2020
Mops, p. II-1739
Mordant dyes, p. I-474

Mordants, p. I-565

Morphine and derivatives, p. I-533

Mortar, p. I-702

Mortar mixers, p. II-1032

Mortar shells, p. II-996

Mortars, pp. I-702, II-1004

Mortisers, p. II-1045

Mosaic tile, p. I-694

Moth repellants, p. I-528

Mother boards, p. III-1804

Motion picture cameras, pp. II-1086, III-1797

Motion picture film, p. I-594

Motion picture projectors, p. II-1086

Motor bike dealers, p. III-2020

Motor control accessories, p. II-1436

Motor control centers, p. II-1436

Motor controls, pp. II-1436, III-1830

Motor generator sets, pp. II-1156, 1426

Motor home dealers, p. III-2017

Motor homes, pp. II-1477, 1481, 1495, III-1757

Motor oils, pp. I-457, 594

Motor scooters, pp. II-1598, III-2020

Motor starters, p. II-1436

Motor truck scales, p. II-1228

Motor vehicles, p. III-1757

Motorboats, p. II-1593

Motorcycle dealers, p. III-2020

Motorcycle parts, pp. III-1761, 2020

Motorcycles, pp. II-1598, III-1757

Motors

— electric, pp. II-1426, III-1830

— fluid power, p. II-1221

— gear, p. II-1161

— outboard, pp. II-1172, III-1882

— starter, p. II-1511

Mouse devices, p. II-1251

Mouthpieces (music), p. II-1730

Mouthwashes, p. I-538, 574

Movements (clock), p. II-1361

MRI imaging equipment, p. II-1321

Mucilage adhesives, p. I-559

Mufflers, pp. I-261, 266, 289, II-1550, III-1761

Mulch, p. III-1990

Mulchers, p. II-1027

Mules, p. III-1964

Multimeters, p. II-1346

Multiplex equipment, p. II-1256

Muscle relaxants, p. I-538

Mushrooms, p. I-67

Music books, p. I-419

Music boxes, p. II-1748

Music rolls, p. II-1730

Music stores, pp. III-2158, 2167, 2193

Musical instrument accessories, p. II-1730

Musical instrument cases, p. I-305

Musical instruments, pp. II-1707, 1730

Mustard, p. I-151

Myrobalans extract, p. I-492

N-methylpiperazine, p. I-533

N-type rubber, p. I-504

Nail guns, p. II-1206

Nail heading machines, p. II-1128

Nail polish remover, p. I-574

Nail polishes, p. I-574

Nailers and staplers, p. II-1206

Nails, pp. I-792, 815, 836, II-938, III-1823

Name plate blanks, pp. II-1013, 1719

Napalm, p. I-594

Naphtha, pp. I-442, 492

Naphthalene, p. I-492

Naphthalenesulfonic acid, p. I-492

Naphthenic acid soaps, p. I-492

Naphthenic acids, pp. I-442, 492

Naphthol, p. I-492

Naphtholsulfonic acids, p. I-492

Napkins, pp. I-233, 367, 410, III-1777, 1904

Narrow fabrics, p. I-202

Natural fiber, p. I-191

Natural fiber fabrics, pp. I-197, 202

Natural fiber yarns, p. I-191

Natural gas engines, p. II-1172

Natural nonfood coloring, p. I-492

Nautical systems, p. II-1326

Naval artillery, p. II-1004

Naval ship building, p. II-1588

Naval stores, p. I-492

Navigational instruments, pp. II-1326, III-1838, 1878

Near beer brewing, p. I-171

Neatsfoot oil rendering, p. I-101

Neckpieces

— fur, pp. I-266, 284

Neckties, pp. I-261, 266, 289, III-1915

Neckwear, pp. I-261, 266, 289, III-2134

Needle roller bearings, p. II-987

Needlecraft, p. III-2155

Needles, pp. II-1060, 1734, III-1912

— hypodermic and suture, p. II-1670

— phonograph, p. II-1316

Negligees, pp. I-261, 266, 278

Neon, p. I-470

Neon signs, p. II-1719

Neoprene, p. I-504

Nephelometers, p. II-1351

Nephoscopes, p. II-1366

Net and lace making machinery, p. II-1060

Net goods, p. III-1912

Netting, pp. I-197, 212, 650, II-938

Neutral spirits, pp. I-180, III-1986

Neutron activation analysis instruments, p. II-1351

Newel posts, p. I-333

News dealers, p. III-2164

Newsletters, p. I-419

Newspaper agencies, p. III-1994

Newspaper inserting equipment, p. II-1060

Newspapers, p. I-419, III-1994

Newsprint, pp. I-367, III-1897

Newsstands, p. III-2164

Nibs, p. II-1713

Nickel, pp. I-824, 836

Nickel alloy die-castings, p. I-856

Nickel ammonium sulfate, p. I-487

Nickel cadmium storage batteries, p. II-1441

Nickel carbonate, p. I-487

Nickel castings, p. I-856

Nickel compounds, p. I-487

Nickel die-castings, p. I-856

Nickel foil, p. II-1013

Nickel sulfate, p. I-487

Nicotine and derivatives, p. I-533

Nicotine insecticides, p. I-528

Night stands, p. II-1620

Nightgowns, pp. I-261, 266, 271, 278, 284

Nightshirts, pp. I-261, 266, 271, 278, 284

Nightwear, pp. I-261, 266, 271, 278, 284, III-1915

Niobium, p. I-824

Nipples (metal), p. II-1008

Nipples and teething rings, p. I-669

Nitrated hydrocarbon derivatives, p. I-492

Nitric acid, p. I-515

Nitrile rubber, p. I-504

Nitrile-butadiene rubber, p. I-504

Nitrile-chloroprene rubbers, p. I-504

Nitroaniline, p. I-492

Nitrobenzene, p. I-492

Nitrocellulose, p. I-499

Nitrocellulose explosives, p. I-584

Nitrocellulose fibers, p. I-509

Nitrogen, p. I-470

Nitrogenous fertilizers, pp. I-515, 523

Nitroglycerin explosives, p. I-584

Nitrophenol, p. I-492

Nitrosated hydrocarbons, p. I-492

Nitroso dyes, p. I-474

Nitrostarch explosives, p. I-584

Nitrous ether, p. I-492

Nitrous oxide, p. I-470

Noise protectors, p. II-1675

Nonalcoholic beer, p. I-171

Nonalcoholic wines, p. I-176

Nonclay refractories, p. I-702

Nondairy creamers, pp. I-80, 85

Nonene, p. I-466

Nonfat dry milk, p. I-80

Nonferrous, p. I-856

Nonferrous alloys, p. I-836

Nonferrous metal, p. I-824

Nonferrous metal shapes, p. I-836

Nonferrous metals, pp. I-824, 836, 856, III-1823

Nonferrous wire, p. I-836

Nonprescription drugs, pp. I-538, III-1908

Nonstick metal cooking utensils, p. II-885

Nonwoven fabric tapes, p. I-207

Nonwoven fabrics, p. I-207

Nonwoven felts, p. I-207

Noodle mixes, pp. I-67, 123, 157

Noodles, pp. I-123, 157

Nose and ear plugs, p. II-1675

Notebook computers, p. II-1237

Notebooks, pp. I-402, III-1900

Novelties, pp. I-305, 357, II-1013, 1695, 1748, III-2189

Nozzles

— aerosol spray, p. I-650

— fire fighting, p. II-979

— lawn hose, p. II-979

Nuclear application valves, p. II-979

Nuclear fuels, p. I-487

Nuclear instrument modules, p. II-1366

Nuclear irradiation equipment, p. II-1356

Nuclear medicine, p. I-538

Nuclear reactor control rod drive mechanisms, p. II-917

Nuclear reactor steam supply systems, p. II-917

Nuclear reactors, p. II-917

Nuclear shielding, p. II-898

Numbers following p. or pp. are page references. Roman numerals indicate volume numbers. Page references are to the starting pages of the industries that produce the product or carry out the activity.

Nuclear waste casks, p. II-922
Numerical controls, p. II-1436
Numerically controlled machine tools, p. II-1123
Nursery furniture, pp. II-1620, 1631
Nursery stock, p. III-1997
Nut rods, pp. I-779, 792
Nut shellers, p. II-1022
Nuts, pp. I-136, III-1938
— chocolate covered, pp. I-47, 51
— covered, p. I-56
— metal, p. II-957
— unprocessed, p. III-1964
Nylon fibers and filaments, p. I-509
Nylon hosiery, p. I-255
Nylon resins, p. I-499
Nylon spun yarns, p. I-191
Nylon thread, p. I-191
Nylon yarn, p. I-191
Nylons, p. I-255
Oak extract, p. I-492
Oars, p. I-357
Oat flour, p. I-14
Oatmeal, p. I-35
Oats
— breakfast, p. I-35
— rolled, p. I-35
Oboes, p. II-1730
Ocarinas, p. II-1730
Ocher pigments, p. I-474
Octophones, p. II-1730
Oerlikon guns, p. II-1004
Off-highway tracked vehicles, p. II-1606
Off-highway trucks, p. II-1032
Office equipment, p. III-1800
Office furniture, pp. II-1649, III-1773, 2036
Office machines, p. III-1800
Office paper, pp. I-367, 402
Office supplies, pp. I-402, III-1900, 2185
Offset inks, p. I-579
Offset printing, p. I-419
Offset printing presses, p. II-1060
Ohmmeters, p. II-1346
Oil, p. I-442
Oil and gas drilling machinery, p. II-1038
Oil and gas offshore platforms, p. II-1588
Oil kernels, p. III-1964
Oil measuring and dispensing pumps, p. II-1188
Oil nuts, p. III-1964
Oil well machinery, p. III-1866
Oil well pumps, p. II-1178
Oil well supplies, p. III-1866
Oil
— additives, pp. I-442, 594, III-1970
— animal, p. I-101
— burners, pp. II-1100, III-1846
— corn, p. I-21
— drilling muds, p. III-1970
— filters, pp. II-1550, III-1761
— olive, p. I-25
— petroleum, pp. III-1974, 1978
— seals, p. II-1724
— storage tanks, p. II-922
— vegetable stearin, p. I-25
— waste, p. III-1889
Oil-based additives, p. I-462

Oilcloth, p. I-223
Oils, pp. I-492, 533, 594
— cooking and salad, p. III-1953
— fuel, p. I-442
— lubricating, p. I-457
— lubricating petroleum, p. I-457
— lubricating, synthetic, pp. I-594
— soluble, p. I-565
— wood, p. I-492
Oilseed machinery, p. II-1060
Oilseeds, p. III-1964
Olefin fibers, p. I-509
Olefins, p. I-466
Oleic acid, p. I-492
Oleic acid esters, p. I-492
Oleum, p. I-487
Olive oil, pp. I-25, 30
Olives, p. I-67
Omnibearing instrumentation, p. II-1326
Onions pickled, p. I-67
Opera hats, pp. I-266, 289
Operating room tables, p. II-1665
Ophthalmic agents, p. I-533
Ophthalmic goods, p. III-1816
Ophthalmic instruments, p. II-1670
Ophthalmometers and ophthalmoscopes, p. II-1670
Opium, p. I-533
Optical disk drives, p. II-1242
Optical goods, pp. III-1816, 2106
Optical gun sighting instruments, p. II-1081
Optical instruments, p. II-1081
Optical lens machinery, p. II-1060
Optical readers and scanners, p. II-1251
Optical test and inspection equipment, p. II-1081
Optoelectronic devices, p. II-1286
Optometers, p. II-1670
Optometric equipment, p. III-1816
Oral contraceptives, p. I-538
Orange oil, p. I-594
Ore concentrates, p. III-1827
Ore crushing machinery, p. II-1038
Ores, p. III-1827
Organic chemicals, p. III-1970
Organic fibers and filaments, p. I-509
Organic pigments, p. I-474
Organizers for closets etc., p. I-650
Organo-inorganic compound, p. I-492
Organo-phosphate insecticides, p. I-528
Oriented strandboard, p. I-318
Ornamental ironwork, p. III-1793
Ornamental metalwork, p. II-907
Ornamental plaster work, p. I-751
Ornamental woodwork, p. I-333
Ornaments
— Christmas tree, pp. I-712, 721, II-1389, 1748
Orris oil, p. I-594
Orthodichlorobenzene, p. I-492
Orthodontic appliances, pp. II-1681, 1691
Orthopedic devices, p. II-1675
Orthopedic equipment, p. III-1812
Orthopedic hosiery, p. II-1675
Orthopedic plaster, p. I-751
Orthopedic shoes, pp. I-299, II-1675, III-2140
Oscillators, p. II-1346
Oscilloscopes, p. II-1346

Osmometers, p. II-1351
Ossein, p. I-594
Otoscopes, p. II-1321
Ottomans, p. II-1615
Outboard motor dealers, p. III-2023
Outboard motors, pp. II-1172, III-1882
Outdoor furniture, p. III-1773
Outdoor sporting equipment, p. III-2149
Outerwear, pp. III-1915, 1918
Outlet boxes, p. II-1456
Outlets, p. II-1456
Oven cleaners, p. I-565
Oven controls, p. II-1331
Ovens, p. III-1846
— bakery, p. II-1060
— commercial, pp. II-1091, III-1808
— household, pp. II-1403, III-1834
— industrial, pp. II-1216, III-1866
— laboratory, p. II-1665
— portable, pp. II-1396, 1403
Ovenware, pp. I-712, 721
Overall jackets, pp. I-266, 271
Overalls, pp. I-266, 271
Overcoats, pp. I-266, 271, 278
Overhead conveyors, p. II-1193
Overhead projectors, pp. II-1086, 1251
Overhead traveling cranes, p. II-1193
Overshoes, p. I-299
Oxalates, p. I-492
Oxalic acid, p. I-492
Oxial mechanical face seals, p. II-1724
Oxygen, p. I-470
Oxygen tents, p. II-1670
Ozone machines, p. II-1091
Pacemakers, p. II-1321
Pacifiers, p. I-669
Packaging, pp. I-640, 650
— film, p. I-608
— machinery, p. II-1211
— material, p. III-1870
Packer's fluids, p. I-594
Packing cases, p. I-342
Packing crates, p. I-342
Packing machinery, p. III-1866
Packing materials, p. III-1870
Pacs, p. I-299
Padded envelopes, p. I-402
Padding and wadding, p. I-250
Paddings
— apparel, p. III-1912
Paddles, p. I-357
Padlocks, p. II-932
Pads and protectors, p. I-233
Pads
— corrugated and solid fiberboard, p. I-378
— desk, p. I-402
— excelsior, p. I-357
— incontinent and bed, p. I-410
— rattan, p. I-357
— scouring, p. II-1013
Pagers, p. II-1261
Pails
— coopered wood, p. I-342
— plastics, p. I-650

Numbers following p. or pp. are page references. Roman numerals indicate volume numbers. Page references are to the starting pages of the industries that produce the product or carry out the activity.

Product/Activity Index

2271

— plywood, p. I-342
— wood, p. I-342
Paint and varnish removers, p. I-553
Paint baking and drying ovens, p. II-1216
Paint rollers, pp. II-1739, III-2003
Paint spray guns, p. II-1206
Paint sprayers, p. II-1183
Paint sticks, pp. I-357, 650, II-1013
Paint thinners, p. I-553
Paintbrush cleaners, p. I-553
Paintbrushes, pp. II-1739, III-2003
Painter's supplies, p. III-2003
Paints, pp. I-553, III-2003
— artist's, p. II-1713
— emulsion, p. I-553
— oil and alkyd, p. I-553
Pajamas, pp. I-261, 266, 271, 278, 284
Palettes, p. II-1713
Pallet containers, p. I-342
Pallet movers, p. II-1193
Pallet or skid jacks, p. II-1193
Pallet parts, pp. I-342, II-1013
Pallets, pp. I-342, 378, II-1013
Pallets and skids, p. III-1866
Palm-kernel oil, pp. I-25, 30
Palmitic acid, p. I-492
Pamphlets, pp. I-419, 435, III-1994
Panama hats, pp. I-266, 289
Pancake mixes, p. I-123
Pancake syrups, p. I-157
Pancakes (frozen), p. I-61
Panel work (wood), p. I-333
Paneling, p. III-1781
Panels
— generator control and metering, p. II-1431
— hardwood plywood, p. I-323
— prefabricated metal building, p. II-898
— prefabricated wood building, p. I-352
— softwood plywood, p. I-323
Panties, pp. I-261, 266, 278, 284
Pants, pp. I-266, 278, 284
Pants outfits, pp. I-266, 278
Pants
— athletic, pp. I-261, 266, 271, 278, 284
— dress, pp. I-266, 271
— leather, pp. I-266, 284
— outerwear, p. I-261
— rubber, p. I-284
— sweat, pp. I-266, 271, 278, 284
— vulcanized rubber, p. I-284
— waterproof outerwear, pp. I-266, 284
— work, pp. I-266, 271
Pantsuits, pp. I-266, 278, 284
Panty girdles, p. I-278
Panty hose, p. I-255
Paper, pp. I-367, 755, III-1897, 1904
Paper and pulp machinery, p. III-1866
Paper bag machinery, p. II-1060
Paper bags, pp. I-394, III-1904
Paper clips, pp. I-792, II-938
Paper cups, p. I-378
Paper cutters, p. II-1713
Paper dishes, pp. I-378, 414
Paper dresses, pp. I-266, 278
Paper fabrics, pp. I-197, 202

Paper machine wire cloth, p. II-938
Paper making machinery, p. II-1060
Paper mills, p. I-367
Paper napkins, p. I-410
Paper novelties, p. I-414
Paper plates, p. I-378
Paper products, pp. I-402, 414
Paper shells, p. II-992
Paper stock, p. I-367
Paper towels, pp. I-367, 410
Paper yarn, p. I-191
Paper
— asphalt, p. I-367
— building, p. III-1793
— carbon, p. II-1713
— corrugated, p. I-378
— newsprint, p. I-367
— office, p. III-1900
— photographic, p. I-594
— scrap, p. III-1889
— stencil, p. II-1713
Paperboard, pp. I-373, 394, III-1904
Paperboard machinery, p. II-1060
Paperboard mills, p. I-373
Paperboard products, p. I-373
Papier-mache statuary, p. I-775
Parachutes, p. I-250
Paraffin waxes, p. I-442
Paraffins, p. I-466
Parallel strand lumber, p. I-328
Pararosaniline dyes, p. I-474
Parasols, p. II-1748
Parathion insecticides, p. I-528
Parcel post scales, p. II-1228
Parchment leather, p. I-295
Paris green insecticides, p. I-528
Parking meters, p. II-1341
Parquet flooring, p. I-333
Particle accelerators, p. II-1467
Particle beam excitation instruments, p. II-1351
Particle size analyzers, p. II-1351
Particleboard, pp. I-318, III-1781
Partitions, pp. II-1643, III-1808
— corrugated and solid fiber, p. I-378
— freestanding, p. II-1643
— metal, p. II-907
Passenger ships, p. II-1588
Pasta
— dry, p. I-123
— fresh, p. I-157
— machinery, p. II-1060
— mixes, p. I-157
Paste, pp. I-792, 806, 829
— adhesive, p. I-559
— fruit and vegetable, p. I-67
— iron or steel, p. I-779
— nonferrous metals, p. I-836
Pasteurizing equipment, p. II-1060
Pastrami, p. I-101
Pastries, pp. I-115, 123
Pastry boards, p. I-357
Patent leather, p. I-295
Patent medicine preparations, p. I-538
Patient monitoring equipment, pp. II-1321, III-1812

Patrol boat building, p. II-1588
Patterns, pp. II-1013, III-1866
— shoe, pp. II-1748, III-1874
Paving blocks, pp. I-447, 736
Paving brick, p. I-690
Paving machinery, p. II-1032
PBX equipment, p. II-1256
Peanut butter, p. I-136
Peanuts
— cake, p. I-30
— combines, p. II-1022
— oil, p. I-25
— roasting machines, p. II-1060
Pearl drilling, p. II-1695
Pearl essence pigment, p. I-474
Pearlitic castings, p. I-844
Pearls, pp. II-1695, III-1893
Peat pots, p. I-775
Pectin, p. I-151
Pedometers, p. II-1341
Pegs (leather shoes), p. I-305
Pellet guns, p. II-1000
Pellet mills, p. II-1038
Pellets (air rifle and pistol), p. II-992
Pelts, pp. I-295, III-1964
Pelvimeters, p. II-1670
Pen refills, p. II-1713
Pencil leads, p. II-1713
Pencil sharpeners, p. II-1713
Pencil slats, p. I-357
Pencils, pp. II-1713, III-1900
Pendant lamps, p. II-1389
Penetrants, p. I-565
Penetrating fluids, p. I-594
Penicillin, pp. I-533, 538
Pens, pp. II-1713, III-1900
Penstocks, p. II-898
Pentachlorophenol, p. I-492
Pentaerythritol, p. I-492
Pentanes, p. I-466
Pentenes, p. I-466
Pentolite explosives, p. I-584
Pepper, p. I-151
Peppermint oil, p. I-594
Percales, p. I-197
Perchloric acid, p. I-487
Perchloroethylene, p. I-492
Percolators, p. II-1396
Percussion caps, p. II-992
Percussion instruments, p. II-1730
Perfumes, pp. I-492, 574, III-1908, 2103
Periodicals, pp. I-419, III-1994
Peripheral controller boards, p. II-1311
Peripheral equipment (computer), p. III-1804
Periscopes, p. II-1081
Perlite, p. I-766
Peroxides, pp. I-487, 492
Persian orange lake, p. I-474
Personal computers, p. II-1237
Pesticides, pp. I-528, III-1970, 1990
Pet food, pp. I-3, 8, III-1953
PET scanners, p. II-1321
Petrochemicals, p. I-442

Numbers following p. or pp. are page references. Roman numerals indicate volume numbers. Page references are to the starting pages of the industries that produce the product or carry out the activity.

Petroleum, p. III-1978
— coke, p. I-442
— jelly, pp. I-442, 462
— lubricating oils, pp. I-442, 457
— polymer resins, p. I-499
— refineries, p. I-442
— refining machinery, p. II-1060
— storage tanks, p. II-922
— waxes, p. I-462
Pets
— shops, p. III-2196
— supplies, p. III-2196
Pews, p. II-1626
Pewter ware, p. II-1695
Pharmaceuticals, pp. I-538, III-1908, 2099
Phase angle meters, p. II-1346
Phase converters, p. II-1426
Phenol, p. I-492
Phenolic resins, p. I-499
Phenoxy resins, p. I-499
Phonocardiographs, p. II-1321
Phonograph records, p. II-1375
Phonographs, p. III-1808
Phosgene, p. I-492
Phosphatic fertilizers, pp. I-519, 523
Phosphomolybdic acid lakes and toners, p. I-474
Phosphoric acid, pp. I-492, 519
Phosphorus compounds, p. I-487
Phosphorus oxychloride, p. I-487
Phosphotungstic acid lakes and toners, p. I-474
Photo albums, pp. I-419, III-1900
Photo finishing equipment, p. III-1797
Photocopy supplies, p. III-1900
Photocopying
— machines, p. II-1086
— toners, p. I-594
Photoelectric cells, p. II-1286
Photoengraving machinery, p. II-1060
Photoflash bulbs, p. II-1385
Photoflash equipment, p. II-1086
Photograph folders, p. I-414
Photography
— chemicals, p. I-594
— equipment, pp. II-1086, III-1797
— film, p. I-594
— lenses, p. II-1081
— plastics, p. I-614
— supplies, p. III-2061
Photomask blanks (glass), p. I-712
Photomasks, p. I-594
Photometers, p. II-1351
Photonexcitation analyzers, p. II-1351
Photosensitized paper, p. I-594
Phototypesetting services, p. I-435
Photovoltaic devices, p. II-1286
Phthalate acid, p. I-492
Phthalic alkyd resins, p. I-499
Phthalic anhydride, pp. I-492, 499
Phthalocyanine pigments, p. I-474
Physiotherapy equipment, p. II-1670
Physostigmine and derivatives, p. I-533
Pianos
— hardware, p. II-932
— parts, p. II-1730
— stores, p. III-2158

Piccolos and parts, p. II-1730
Pick-up trucks, p. II-1477
Pickled fruits, p. I-67
Picklers (metal), p. II-1146
Pickles, p. I-67
Picks, p. II-891
Pickup canopies, p. II-1499
Picnic jugs, p. I-650
Picric acid explosives, p. I-584
Picture frames, p. III-2046
Pie crust shells, p. I-123
Piece goods, pp. III-1912, 2155
Pies, pp. I-115, III-1928
Piezoelectric crystals, p. II-1316
Piezoelectric devices, p. II-1316
Pig iron, pp. I-779, III-1823
Pig's feet, p. I-101
Pigments, pp. I-474, III-2003
Pile fabrics, p. I-212
Pile shells, pp. II-898, 907
Pile-driving equipment, p. II-1032
Pilings
— foundation, p. I-311
— iron or steel, p. I-779
— round wood, p. I-311
— wood, p. I-311
Pillow blocks, p. II-987
Pillowcases, p. I-233
Pillows, p. I-233
Pinball machines, p. II-1748
Pine oil, p. I-492
Pinene, p. I-492
Pins, p. II-1734
Pins and brooches, p. II-1695
Pipe, pp. I-787, 810
Pipe and pipe fittings, pp. I-844, II-1008
Pipe and tube mill machinery, p. II-1146
Pipe bannisters (metal), p. II-907
Pipe organs, p. II-1730
Pipe tobacco, pp. I-187, III-2000
Pipe
— aluminum, p. I-810
— bits and stems (tobacco), p. I-669
— brass, p. I-829
— cleaners, p. II-1748
— concrete, p. I-736
— couplings, pp. I-844, II-1008
— cutting machines, p. II-1123
— fabricated metal plate, p. II-898
— fabricating, p. II-1008
— fittings, p. I-625
— guards (metal), p. II-907
— hangers, p. II-1013
— headers, p. II-1008
— iron or steel, p. I-779
— metal, p. III-1823
— nonferrous metals, p. I-836
— railings (metal), p. II-907
— rigid plastics, p. I-625
— sealing compounds, p. I-559
— sheet metal, p. II-907
Pipeline machinery, p. III-1866
Pipes
— smoking, p. II-1748
Pistols, p. II-1000

Pistons, pp. II-1504, III-1866
Pitch, pp. I-452, 492
Pitometers, p. II-1366
Pituitary gland derivatives, p. I-533
Pituitary gland preparations, p. I-538
Pizza doughs, p. I-123
Pizzas, pp. I-61, 157, III-1928, 1953
Placemats, p. I-233
Planar cable connectors, p. II-1306
Planers
— bituminous, p. II-1032
— handheld, p. II-1206
— metalworking, p. II-1123
— woodworking, p. II-1045
Planes (handheld), p. II-891
Planing mills, p. I-333
Plant foods, pp. I-515, 519
Plant growth regulants, p. I-528
Planting machinery
— farm, pp. II-1022, III-1862
Plasma jet spray machines, p. II-1128
Plasma process cutting machines, p. II-1123
Plasma welding equipment, p. II-1228
Plasmas, p. I-548
— blood, p. III-1908
Plaster, pp. I-751, III-1785
Plaster and plasterboard, p. I-751
Plasticizers, pp. I-492, III-1967
Plastics, p. II-1631
— bags, p. III-1904
— film, p. I-614
— foam, pp. III-1870, 1904
— gowns, pp. I-266, 284
— industry machinery, p. III-1866
— materials, p. III-1967
— rainwear, pp. I-266, 284
— resins, pp. I-588, III-1967
— scrap, p. III-1889
— shapes, p. III-1967
— wood fillers, p. I-553
— working machinery, p. II-1050
Plastisol
— coating compounds, p. I-553
Plate glass, p. III-1793
Plate rolling mill machinery, p. II-1146
Plate work, p. II-898
Plate
— aluminum, p. I-815
— copper and copper alloy, p. I-829
— iron or steel, p. I-779
— laminated plastics, p. I-630
— nonferrous metals, p. I-836
Plated metal cutlery, pp. II-885, III-1893
Plated metal flatware, p. II-885
Plated ware, p. II-1013
Plates, p. II-1456
— molded pulp, p. I-414
— polystyrene foam, p. I-635
Platinum, pp. I-824, 836
Platinum foil and leaf, p. II-1013
Playground equipment, p. III-1882
Playing cards, p. III-1886
Playpens, pp. II-1620, 1631
Playsuits, pp. I-266, 278, 284
Pleasure boats, pp. II-1593, III-1882

Numbers following p. or pp. are page references. Roman numerals indicate volume numbers. Page references are to the starting pages of the industries that produce the product or carry out the activity.

Product/Activity Index

2273

Pliers, p. II-891
Plinth blocks, p. I-736
Plotters, p. II-1251
Plows, pp. II-1022, III-1862
— construction, p. II-1032
Plug valves, p. II-979
Plugs
— electric cord, p. II-1456
— magnetic metal drain, p. II-1013
— wood, p. I-357
Plumber's brass goods, p. III-1846
Plumber's handtools, p. II-891
Plumber's putty, p. I-559
Plumbing and heating valves, pp. II-979, III-1846
Plumbing
— equipment, p. III-1846
— fittings, p. II-973
— fixtures, pp. I-650, 676, II-1013, III-1846
— supplies, p. III-1846
Plywood, pp. I-323, III-1781
Pneumatic aircraft subassemblies, p. II-979
Pneumatic controllers, p. II-1336
Pneumatic cylinders, p. II-1221
Pneumatic hoses, pp. I-664, II-979
Pneumatic pumps, pp. II-1221, III-1866
Pneumatic relays, p. II-1331
Pneumatic tube conveyors, p. II-1193
Pneumatic valves, p. II-979
Pocket folders, p. I-402
Pocket knives, p. II-885
Pocketbooks, p. II-1695
Pockets, p. I-266
Point of sale terminals, pp. II-1251, III-1800
Pointing devices, p. II-1251
Pointing furs, p. I-284
Points (dental), p. II-1681
Polariscopes, p. II-1351
Polarizers, p. II-1351
Polarographic equipment, p. II-1351
Pole line hardware, p. III-1830
Poles
— concrete, p. I-742
— metal, p. III-1823
— wood, p. I-311
Police
— caps and hats, pp. I-266, 289
— dress uniforms, pp. I-271, 278
— supplies, p. III-2207
— uniforms, p. I-266
Polished rice, p. I-14
Polishers (handheld), p. II-1206
Polishes, pp. I-565, III-1970
Polishing machines, p. II-1123
Polishing preparations, p. I-565
Polishing wheels, p. I-755
Pollution control equipment, pp. III-1850, 1866
Polo shirts, pp. I-261, 266, 271, 278
Polyacrylonitrile resins, p. I-499
Polyamide resins, p. I-499
Polycarbonate resins, p. I-499
Polyester
— fibers, p. I-509
— resins, p. I-499
— spun yarns, p. I-191
— thread, p. I-191

Polyethylene, pp. I-499, 504, 614
Polyethylene terephthalate (PET), pp. I-499, 509
Polygraph machines, p. II-1366
Polyhexamethylenediamine adipamide resins,
    p. I-499
Polyhydric alcohols, p. I-492
Polyisobutylene resins, p. I-499
Polyisobutylene rubber, p. I-504
Polymethacrylate resins, p. I-499
Polymethylene rubber, p. I-504
Polyolefin fibers and filaments, p. I-509
Polypropylene, pp. I-191, 499, 614
Polystyrene, pp. I-499, 635
Polysulfide rubber, p. I-504
Polytetrafluoroethylene resins, p. I-499
Polyurethane, pp. I-499, 553, 640
Polyvinyl alcohol resins, p. I-499
Polyvinyl chloride (PVC) resins, p. I-499
Polyvinyl ester fibers and filaments, p. I-509
Polyvinyl film, p. I-614
Polyvinyl resins, p. I-499
Polyvinylidene chloride, p. I-509
Ponchos, pp. I-266, 284
Pop (soda), p. I-164
Popcorn, pp. I-56, 136, 157, III-1938
— balls, p. I-56
— poppers, p. II-1396
Porcelain, pp. I-680, 685
Porch furniture, p. II-1620
Porch shades, p. II-1661
Porch swings, p. II-1631
Porch work, p. I-333
Pork, p. I-101
Pork and beans (canning), p. I-67
Pork carcasses, p. I-101
Pork rinds, p. I-136
Porter, p. III-1982
Position emission tomography scanners, p. II-1321
Position indicators, p. II-1326
Positive crankcase ventilation valves, p. II-1504
Positive displacement meters, p. II-1341
Post hole diggers, pp. II-891, 1032
Post office scales, p. II-1228
Postage meters, pp. II-1076, III-1800
Postage stamp vending machines, p. II-1091
Postal service lock boxes, p. II-1643
Postcards, pp. I-419, III-1900
Posters, p. I-419
Posts
— concrete, p. I-742
— wood, p. I-311
Pot pies, p. I-61
Potassic fertilizers, p. I-523
Potassium, pp. I-487, 492
Potassium aluminum sulfate, p. I-487
Potassium bichromate and chromate, p. I-487
Potassium bitartrate, p. I-492
Potassium bromide, p. I-487
Potassium carbonate, p. I-479
Potassium chlorate, p. I-487
Potassium chloride, p. I-487
Potassium cyanide, p. I-487
Potassium hydroxide, p. I-479
Potassium hypochlorate, p. I-487
Potassium iodide, p. I-487

Potassium nitrate, p. I-487
Potassium permanganate, p. I-487
Potassium salts, p. I-487
Potassium sulfate, p. I-487
Potato chips, pp. I-136, III-1938
Potato diggers, p. II-1022
Potato flour, p. I-14
Potato mashers, p. II-885
Potato mixes, p. I-157
Potato products, p. I-67
Potato starches, p. I-21
Potato sticks, p. I-136
Potatoes, p. I-157
Potentiometric instruments, pp. II-1336, 1346
Potpourri, p. II-1748
Pots, p. II-922
Pots and pans, p. II-885
Pots
— glass-house, p. I-702
Potted meats, p. I-101
Pottery products, p. I-680
Potting soil, p. I-523
Poultry, pp. I-96, III-1935
— brooders, p. II-1022
— canned, p. III-1953
— dealers, p. III-2082
— equipment, p. III-1862
— feeds, p. I-8
— live and dressed, p. III-1935
— netting, p. II-938
— packaged frozen, p. III-1928
Powder, pp. I-574, 792, 806, 829
Powder puffs, p. I-250
Powder
— baking, p. I-157
— coatings, p. I-553
— iron or steel, p. I-779
— metal forming presses, p. II-1128
— nonferrous metals, p. I-836
Powdered drink mixes, p. I-157
Powdered milk, p. I-80
Prayer shawls, pp. I-261, 266, 284
Pre-recorded tapes, p. II-1375
Precast concrete
— block, p. I-736
— pipe, p. I-736
— products, p. I-742
Precious metals, pp. I-824, III-1893
Precious metals (shapes), p. I-836
Precious stones, p. III-1893
Precision tools, p. II-891
Prefabricated buildings, pp. I-352, II-898, III-1781,
    1793
Prefabricated homes, pp. I-352, II-898
Pregnancy test kits, p. I-543
Prepared flour mixes, pp. I-14, 123
Prepared foods, pp. III-1928, 1932, 1953
Prepared meals, p. I-157
Prepared sauces, p. I-151
Prepress services, p. I-435
Prescription drugs, p. III-1908
Preserves, p. I-67
Presoaks, p. I-565
Press brakes, p. II-1128
Press forgings, p. I-871

Numbers following p. or pp. are page references. Roman numerals indicate volume numbers. Page references are to the starting pages of the industries that produce the product or carry out the activity.

Pressed and molded pulp goods, p. III-1904
Pressed felts, p. I-207
Pressed logs of sawdust, p. I-357
Presses, pp. II-1045, 1060, 1128
— farm, p. II-1022
— metal baling, p. II-1228
— printing, p. II-1060
Pressing blocks (tailor's), p. I-357
Pressure control valves, p. II-979
Pressure controllers, p. II-1331
Pressure cookers, p. II-885
Pressure gauges, p. II-1336
Pressure instruments, p. II-1336
Pressure pipe, p. I-736
Pressure sensitive paper, p. I-387
Pressure transducers, p. II-1366
Pressure treated lumber, p. I-311
Pressurestats, p. II-1331
Prestressed concrete, pp. I-736, 742
Pretzels, pp. I-115, 136, III-1928, 1953
Prime mover generator sets, p. II-1426
Primers, pp. I-553, II-996
Print shops
— digital, p. I-419
— engraving, p. I-419
— flexographic, p. I-419
— gravure, p. I-419
— letterpress, p. I-419
— lithographic (offset), p. I-419
— quick, p. I-419
— screen, p. I-419
Printed circuit assemblies, p. II-1311
Printed circuit boards, pp. II-1281, 1311, III-1838
Printed circuit laminates, p. II-1316
Printers
— computer, pp. II-1251, III-1804
Printing inks, pp. I-579, III-1870
Printing machinery for textiles, p. II-1060
Printing paper, pp. III-1897, 1900
Printing plate engraving machinery, p. II-1060
Printing plates, p. II-1060
Printing press rollers, p. II-1060
Printing presses, p. II-1060
Printing trade machinery, p. III-1866
Printing
— digital, p. I-419
— flexographic, p. I-419
— gravure, p. I-419
— letterpress, p. I-419
— lithographic, p. I-419
— photo-offset, p. I-419
— quick, p. I-419
— screen, p. I-419
Prisms (optical), p. II-1081
Prison beds, p. III-1626
Private branch exchange equipment, p. II-1256
Pro shops, p. III-2149
Probes
— electric medical, p. II-1321
— surgical, p. II-1670
Procaine and derivatives, p. I-533
Process control instruments, p. II-1336
Produce (fresh), p. III-1949
Produce markets, p. III-2086
Produce stands, pp. III-2086, 2227

Production counters, p. II-1341
Profile shapes, pp. I-620, 630
Programmers, p. II-1336
Projectiles, p. II-996
Projection equipment, pp. II-1086, III-1797
Projection lenses, p. II-1081
Projection screens, p. II-1086
Projection TVs, p. II-1271
Projectors, p. II-1004
Propane, pp. I-442, III-1974
Propeller straightening presses, p. II-1151
Propellers, p. II-1013
Prophylactics, p. I-669
Propulsion units, p. II-1575
Propylcarbinol, p. I-492
Propylene, pp. I-442, 466
Propylene glycol, p. I-492
Propylene resins, p. I-499
Prosthetic appliances, pp. II-1675, III-1812
Prosthetics, p. III-2112
Protective footwear, p. I-299
Protectors (sports), p. II-1701
Protein analyzers, p. II-1351
Protein fibers and filaments, p. I-509
Pruners, p. II-891
Prunes (dried), p. I-67
Prussian blue pigments, p. I-474
Public address systems, pp. II-1271, III-1838
Public building furniture, p. III-1773
Pudding pops (frozen), p. I-91
Puddings, p. I-157
Pulleys, pp. I-357, II-1167, 1193
Pulp, pp. I-362, 367, 373, 414
Pulp molding machinery, p. II-1060
Pulse, p. II-1346
Pulse analyzers, p. II-1366
Pumice, pp. I-755, 766
Pumps, pp. I-299, II-1178, 1504, III-1761
Pumps and pumping equipment, p. III-1866
Pumps
— fluid power, p. II-1221
— industrial, p. II-1178
— measuring, p. II-1188
— oil field, p. II-1178
— railroad, p. II-1178
— sump, p. II-1178
Punched felts, p. I-207
Punches, pp. II-891, 1133
Punching machines, p. II-1128
Puppets, p. II-1748
Purlins, p. II-907
Purses, pp. I-305, II-1695
Pushers, p. II-1139
Putty knives, p. II-891
Puzzles, p. II-1886
PVC pipe, p. I-625
Pyrethrin insecticides, p. I-528
Pyrheliometers, p. II-1366
Pyroligneous acids, p. I-492
Pyrometer tubes, p. I-680
Pyrometers, p. II-1336
Pyrometric cones, p. I-680
Pyrophyllite, p. I-766
Pyrotechnics, pp. I-594, II-1000
Pyroxylin, p. I-499

Quarry tiles, p. I-694
Quarrying machinery, pp. II-1038, III-1858
Quartz crystals, p. II-1316
Quebracho extracts, p. I-492
Quercitron extracts, p. I-492
Quick printing, p. I-419
Quicklime, p. I-747
Quilts, p. I-233
Quinine, p. I-533
Rabbit food, p. I-8
Rabbits, p. I-96
Race cars, p. II-1606
Raceways, p. II-1456
Racing forms, p. I-419
Rack and panel connectors, p. II-1306
Rack and pinion assemblies, p. II-1518
Racks, pp. II-898, 938, 1550
Radar
— detectors, p. II-1326
— equipment, p. III-1838
— systems, p. II-1326
— testing instruments, p. II-1346
RADIAC equipment, p. II-1366
Radiation instruments, p. II-1366
Radiation shields, p. II-1675
Radiators, pp. II-1100, 1396, 1550, III-1761
— additives, p. I-594
— hoses, p. I-664
— shields, p. II-907
Radio transmitters, p. II-1261
Radioactive diagnostic substances, p. I-538
Radioactive elements, p. I-487
Radioactive isotopes, p. I-487
Radioactive pharmaceutical isotopes, p. III-1908
Radiofrequency measuring equipment, p. II-1346
Radiofrequency oscillators, p. II-1346
Radios, pp. III-1834, 1838, 2053
— headphones, p. II-1271
— housings, p. I-650
— magnetic instrumentation, p. II-1326
— parts, p. III-1838
— receivers, p. II-1271
— towers, p. II-898
Radium chloride, p. I-487
Radium equipment, p. II-1356
Radium luminous compounds, p. I-487
Rafts, p. I-669
Rags, p. III-1889
Rail bonds, p. II-1456
Rail joints, p. I-779
Rail laying equipment, p. II-1583
Railings, pp. I-333, II-907
Railroad car journal bearings, p. II-1167
Railroad cars, pp. II-1583, III-1878
Railroad crossings, p. I-779
Railroad equipment, p. III-1878
Railroad locomotives, p. II-1583
Railroad models (hobby), p. II-1707
Railroad rolling stock, p. II-1583
Railroad seating, p. II-1535
Railroad signaling equipment, p. II-1266
Railroad ties, p. I-311
Railroad track scales, p. II-1228
Rails, pp. I-357, 779, 815, III-1823
Railway bridges, p. II-898

Railway motors, p. II-1426
Rain gauges, p. II-1366
Raincoats, pp. I-223, 266, 271, 278, 284
Raisins, p. I-67
Rakes, pp. II-891, 1022
Ramie spun yarns, p. I-191
Rands, p. I-305
Range finders, p. II-1086
Range hoods, p. II-1396
Ranges, pp. II-1091, 1403
Rapeseed, pp. I-25, 30
Rapid transit cars, p. II-1583
Rare earth salts, p. I-487
Rare manuscripts, p. III-2193
Rasps, p. II-891
Ratchets, p. II-891
Rate-of-climb instrumentation, p. II-1326
Rattan and rattan goods, pp. I-357, II-1631
Raw beet sugar, p. I-39
Raw farm products, p. III-1964
Rawhide, p. I-295
Rayon fibers and filaments, p. I-509
Rayon
— spun yarns, p. I-191
— thread, p. I-191
Razor blade strip steel, p. I-792
Razor blades, pp. II-885, III-1908
Razors, pp. II-885, 1396, III-1834, 1908
— strops, p. I-305
Reactor containment vessels, p. II-898
Reactors, p. II-917
Readers (microfilm), p. II-1086
Reamers, p. II-1139
Reaming machines, p. II-1123
Receipt books, p. III-1900
Receiver-transmitter units, p. II-1261
Receptacles, pp. II-1456, III-1830
Recessed lighting, p. II-1389
Rechargeable battery packs, p. II-1441
Rechargeable nickel cadmium batteries, p. II-1441
Reclaimed wool processing, p. I-250
Recliners, p. II-1615
Recoil mechanisms, pp. II-1000, 1004
Recoilless rifles, p. II-1004
Reconditioned barrels, p. III-1870
Reconstituted
— wood panels, p. I-318
— wood sheets, p. I-318
Record stores, pp. III-2167, 2193
Recorders, p. III-1834
— oscillographic, p. II-1346
— process control, p. II-1336
Recreational equipment, p. III-1882
Recreational vehicles, pp. III-1757, 2017
Rectifiers, pp. II-1286, 1316, 1467, III-1838
Rectifying equipment, p. II-1060
Recyclable materials, p. III-1889
Red oil, p. I-492
Redox, p. II-1351
Reducers (speed), p. II-1161
Reduction gears, p. II-1161
Reed furniture, p. II-1631
Reed ware, p. I-357
Reeds (musical), p. II-1730

Reels
— fishing, p. II-1701
— metal, p. II-1013
— plastics, p. I-650
— plywood, p. I-357
— wood, p. I-357
Refinery gases, p. I-442
Refinery machinery, p. III-1866
Reflectors, pp. I-650, II-1081, 1389
Refractometers, pp. II-1336, 1351
Refractories, pp. I-702, III-1870
Refractory cement, p. I-702
Refrigerated doughs, p. I-123
Refrigerated lockers, p. II-1105
Refrigerators, pp. II-1408, III-1834, 1854
Regalia, pp. I-266, 284
Registers
— linear tallying, p. II-1341
— metal air, p. II-907
Regulating transformers, p. II-1420
Regulators, p. II-1420
— motor vehicle, p. II-1511
— power, p. II-1431
— voltage, p. III-1830
Reinforcing mesh, p. II-938
Relays, pp. II-1346, 1436, III-1830
Religious books, pp. I-419, III-2161
Religious furniture, pp. II-1626, III-1773
Religious goods, p. III-2207
Religious magazines, p. I-419
Religious supplies, p. III-1819
Relishes, p. I-67
Remote controls, p. II-1266
Repeater and transceiver equipment, p. II-1256
Report covers, p. I-402
Reserpines, p. I-533
Resilient floor coverings, p. I-650
Resins, pp. I-499, III-1967, 1970
Resistance measuring equipment, p. II-1346
Resistance thermometers, p. II-1336
Resistance welding equipment, p. II-1228
Resistors (electronic), pp. II-1296, III-1838
Resolvers, p. II-1426
Resonance instruments, p. II-1351
Resonant reed devices, p. II-1316
Resorcinol, p. I-492
Respiratory analysis equipment, p. II-1321
Respiratory protection masks, p. II-1675
Restaurant equipment, p. III-1808
Restaurant furniture, pp. II-1626, III-1773
Restraints, p. II-1675
Retail scales, p. II-1228
Retarders, p. I-594
Retinoscopes, pp. II-1321, 1670
Retorts, p. II-922
Retractors (medical), p. II-1670
Retreading materials, p. I-659
Revolvers, p. II-1000
Rhenium refining, p. I-824
Rheostats, pp. II-1316, 1436, 1456
Ribbons, pp. I-202, 207, 250, II-1713
— inked, pp. II-1713, III-1900
— textile, p. III-1912
Rice bran, p. I-14
Rice flour, p. I-14

Rice malt, p. I-14
Rice meal, p. I-14
Rice
— breakfast foods, p. I-35
— brewer's, p. I-14
— brown, p. I-14
— mixes, pp. I-14, 67, 157
— polished, p. III-1953
— starches, p. I-21
— unpolished, p. III-1957
Riding clothes, pp. I-266, 271, 278
Riding crops, p. I-305
Rifles, pp. II-1000, 1004
— toy, p. II-1707
Rifling machines, p. II-1123
Rims (auto), p. II-1550
Rings (piston), p. II-1504
Riveting guns, p. II-1206
Riveting machines, p. II-1128
Rivets, p. II-957
Roach poisons, p. I-528
Road construction machinery, p. III-1858
Road oils, pp. I-442, 462
Roasted nuts and seeds, p. I-136
Roasters, p. II-1396
Roasting machinery, p. II-1060
Robes (lounging), pp. I-261, 266, 271, 278, 284
Rock crushing machinery, pp. II-1032, 1038
Rock drill bits, p. II-1038
Rock drills, pp. II-1032, 1038
Rocker arms and parts, p. II-1504
Rockers, p. II-1620
— upholstered, p. II-1615
Rockets
— ammunition, p. II-996
— casings, p. II-898
— engines, pp. II-1561, 1575
— guided missiles, p. II-1571
— launchers, p. II-1004
Rocking horses, p. II-1707
Rod
— aluminum, pp. I-810, 815
— copper and copper alloy, p. I-829
— laminated plastics, p. I-630
— nonferrous metals, p. I-836
— nonrigid plastics, p. I-620
Rodenticides, p. I-528
Rods
— fishing, p. II-1701
— hard rubber, p. I-669
— iron or steel, p. I-779
— metal, p. III-1823
— surveyor's, p. II-1366
Roller bearings, p. II-987
Roller leather, p. I-295
Roller skates, p. II-1701
Rollers
— road construction, p. II-1032
— wood, p. I-357
Rolling doors, p. II-907
Rolling mill machinery, p. II-1146
Rolling mill rolls, pp. I-844, II-1146
Rolling pins, p. I-357
Rolls (rubber), p. I-669
Rolls and buns, p. I-115

Numbers following p. or pp. are page references. Roman numerals indicate volume numbers. Page references are to the starting pages of the industries that produce the product or carry out the activity.

Rompers, pp. I-266, 284
Roof deck, p. II-907
Roof trusses, p. I-328
Roofing, p. I-669
— cements, p. I-452
— coatings, p. I-452
— felts, p. I-452
— materials, pp. III-1781, 1789
— sheet metal, p. II-907
— tile, pp. I-698, 742
Room air-conditioners, pp. II-1105, III-1834
Room dividers, p. II-1620
Room heaters, pp. II-1100, 1396
Room thermostats, p. II-1331
Root removing chemicals, p. I-528
Root starches, p. I-21
Rope fittings, p. II-1013
Ropes, pp. I-243, III-1870
— hemp, p. I-191
— wire, pp. II-938, III-1823
Rosaries, p. II-1695
Rosins, pp. I-492, 499, III-1970
Rotary hoes, p. II-1022
Rotary tillers, p. II-1022
Rotenone insecticides, p. I-528
Rotogravure printing, p. I-419
Rotor retainers and housings, p. II-1426
Rotors, p. II-1426
Rouge (cosmetic), p. I-574
Round stave baskets, p. I-342
Rounds (steel tube), p. I-779
Rounds or rungs (furniture), p. I-333
Routers, p. II-1206
Roving machinery (textiles), p. II-1060
Rowboats, p. II-1593
Rubber and plastics belts and hoses, p. I-664
Rubber bands, p. I-669
Rubber cements, p. I-559
Rubber floor coverings, p. I-650
Rubber goods
— mechanical, pp. I-669, III-1870
— medical, p. III-1908
Rubber processing preparations, p. I-594
Rubber scrap and scrap tires, p. III-1889
Rubber stamps, pp. II-1713, III-1900
Rubber working machinery, p. II-1050
Rubber
— synthetic, p. I-504
— thread, p. I-202
Rug cleaning preparations, p. I-565
Rugs, pp. I-228, III-1777, 2040
Rulers, pp. I-357, 650, II-891
Rules (slide), p. II-1366
Rust inhibitors, pp. I-457, 594
Rust removers, p. I-565
RV dealers, p. III-2017
Rye flour, p. I-14
Rye malt, p. I-14
S-type rubber, p. I-504
Saccharin, p. I-492
Sachet (scented), p. I-574
Sacks, pp. I-394, III-1904
Saddle soaps, p. I-565
Saddle trees (wood), p. I-357

Saddlery, p. III-1990
— leather, p. I-295
— parts, p. II-1013
— stores, p. III-2149
Saddles and parts
— leather, p. I-305
Safes, pp. II-1013, III-1800
Safety belts, p. I-305
Safety fuses, p. I-584
Safety glass, p. I-721
Safety pins, p. II-1734
Safety razor blades, p. II-885
Safflower oil, pp. I-25, 30
Sailboards, p. II-1701
Sailboats, pp. II-1593, III-2023
Sailing ships, p. II-1588
Sails, p. I-238
Sal soda, p. I-479
Salad dressing mixes, pp. I-67, 151
Salad dressings, pp. I-151, III-1953
Salad oils, p. III-1953
Salads, p. I-157
Sales books, pp. I-419, III-1900
Salicylic acid, pp. I-492, 533
Salsa, p. I-67
Salt, p. I-594
— table, pp. I-151, III-1953
Salt substitute, p. I-151
Salted meats, p. I-101
Saltines, p. I-123
Salts
— bath, p. III-1908
— industrial, p. III-1970
Sand, pp. III-1785, 1870
Sand castings, pp. I-851, 856
Sand mixers, p. II-1032
Sandals, p. I-299
— children's, p. I-299
— plastics, p. I-299
— rubber, p. I-299
Sanders (handheld power-driven), p. II-1206
Sanding machines, pp. II-1045, 1091
Sandpaper, p. I-755
Sandpaper making machines, p. II-1060
Sandwich spreads, pp. I-101, 151
Sandwich toasters, p. II-1396
Sandwiches, pp. I-157, III-1953
Sanitary food containers, pp. I-378, III-1904
Sanitary napkins, pp. I-367, 410
Sanitary paper products, pp. I-367, III-1904
Sanitary products, pp. I-367, 410
Sanitary ware, pp. II-1013, III-1846
Saran, p. I-509
Sash
— balance springs, p. II-938
— metal, p. II-907
— wood, p. I-333
Satchels, p. I-305
Satellite antennas, p. II-1261
Satellite equipment, p. II-1261
Satin white pigments, p. I-474
Saturable transformers, p. II-1420
Saturated felts, pp. I-367, 452
Sauce mixes, pp. I-67, 151

Sauces, p. I-151
— meat, p. I-151
— seafood, p. I-151
— tomato, p. I-67
— vegetable, p. I-151
Sauerkraut, p. I-67
Sauna heaters, p. II-1396
Sauna rooms, p. I-352
Sausage, p. I-101
Sausage casings, pp. I-101, 620, III-1953
Saw blades, p. II-891
Sawdust, p. I-311
Sawed lumber, pp. I-311, 333
Sawing machines, p. II-1123
Sawmill equipment, p. II-1045
Sawmill machinery, p. III-1866
Sawmills, p. I-311
Saws, pp. II-891, 1045, 1206
— surgical, p. II-1670
Saxophones, p. II-1730
Scaffolding, p. III-1858
Scaffolds (metal), p. II-907
Scalers (nuclear radiation), p. II-1366
Scales, pp. II-1228, 1665
Scarfing machines, p. II-1045
Scarfing units, p. II-1146
Scarifiers (road), p. II-1032
Scarves, pp. I-261, 266, 289
Scattershields (engine), p. II-1529
Schiffli machinery, pp. I-202, II-1060
Scholarly journals, p. I-419
Scholastic magazines, p. I-419
School books, p. I-419
School buses, pp. II-1485, III-1757
School equipment, p. III-1819
School furniture, pp. II-1626, III-1773
School supplies, p. III-2185
Science kits, p. II-1707
Scientific apparatus, p. I-721
Scientific glassware, pp. I-712, 721
Scientific instruments, p. III-1819
Scientific lab equipment, p. III-1819
Scintillation detectors, p. II-1366
Scissors, pp. II-885, 1396
Scoops, pp. I-357, II-891
Scooters, p. II-1707
Scoreboards, p. II-1719
Scouring cleansers, p. I-565
Scouring pads, p. II-1013
Scrap materials, p. III-1889
Scrapbooks, pp. I-419, III-1900
Scraper loaders, p. II-1038
Scrapers
— construction, p. II-1032
Screen doors, p. II-907
Screen process inks, p. I-579
Screening (window), p. I-650
Screening and sifting machinery, p. II-1228
Screening machinery, pp. II-1032, 1038
Screens
— door and window, pp. I-333, II-907, III-1781
— projection, p. II-1086
Screw and nut slotting machines, p. II-1123
Screw conveyors, p. II-1193
Screw eyes (metal), p. II-957

Numbers following p. or pp. are page references. Roman numerals indicate volume numbers. Page references are to the starting pages of the industries that produce the product or carry out the activity.

2277

Screwdowns and boxes machinery, p. II-1151
Screwdrivers, pp. II-891, 1206
Screwdriving machines, p. II-1151
Screwjacks, p. II-891
Screws (metal), p. II-957
Scuba diving equipment, p. II-1701
Sculptures, pp. I-680, 751
Scythes, p. II-891
Seafood, pp. I-109, III-1942, 2084
— canned, p. III-1953
— fresh prepared, p. I-109
— frozen, p. I-109
— packaged frozen, p. III-1928
Seal presses, p. II-1713
Sealants, p. III-1970
Sealing compounds, p. I-559
Seals, p. III-1870
— grease or oil, p. II-1724
Seam welding equipment, p. II-1228
Search and detection systems, p. II-1326
Searchlights, p. II-1389
Seasonal stores, p. III-2189
Seasoning salt, p. I-151
Seat belts, pp. I-305, II-1535
Seat covers
— auto, p. III-1761
— rattan, p. I-357
Seat cushions, p. I-640
Seats
— railroad, p. II-1535
— toilet, p. I-357
— transportation, p. II-1535
Seaweed processing, p. I-109
Sebacic acid, p. I-492
Second-hand stores, p. III-2193
Security safes, p. III-1800
Security systems, p. III-1830
Sedative preparations, p. I-538
Sedimentary mineral machinery, p. II-1038
Seed bags, p. I-238
Seed packets, p. I-402
Seed snacks, p. I-136
Seed treatment preparations, p. I-528
Seeders, pp. II-1022, 1027
Seeds, pp. III-1938, 1990
Seismographs, p. II-1366
Seismometers, p. II-1366
Seismoscopes, p. II-1366
Selenium, p. I-824
Selenium compounds, p. I-487
Selenium dioxide, p. I-487
Selenium shapes, p. I-836
Semen (bovine), p. III-1964
Semi-finished metal products, p. III-1823
Semi-trailer, p. II-1490
Semiconductors
— battery chargers, p. II-1467
— circuit networks, p. II-1286
— devices, pp. II-1286, III-1838
— dice and wafers, p. II-1286
— machinery, p. II-1055
— making machinery, p. II-1055
— memory chips, p. II-1286
— power supplies, p. II-1467
— test equipment, p. II-1346

Semidiesel engines, p. II-1172
Semisteel foundries, p. I-844
Semolina flour, p. I-14
Sensitized cloth or paper, p. I-594
Sensitometers, p. II-1086
Sentinel (cardiac), p. II-1321
Septic tanks, pp. I-650, II-922, III-1785, 1793
Sequencing controls, p. II-1331
Series capacitors, p. II-1467
Serums, p. I-548
Service apparel, pp. I-266, 271, 278
Service establishment equipment, p. III-1874
Service stations (gasoline), p. III-2119
Serving carts, pp. II-1620, 1631
Servomotors, p. II-1426
Setup boxboard stock, p. I-373
Sewage treatment equipment, p. II-1091
Sewer pipe, pp. I-698, 736, 844
Sewing accessories, p. III-1912
Sewing and mending kits, p. II-1748
Sewing cases, pp. I-305, II-1695
Sewing machines, pp. II-1060, III-1834, 1866, 2049
— cabinets, p. II-1631
Sewing supplies, p. III-2155
Sewing threads, p. I-191
Sextants, pp. II-1326, 1366
Shade pulls, p. II-1661
Shades
— lamp, p. II-1389
— window, p. II-1661
Shakes, p. I-311
Shale (expanded), p. I-766
Shampoos, p. I-574
Shanks (shoe), p. I-305
Shaving brushes, p. II-1739
Shaving machines, p. II-1123
Shaving preparations, pp. I-574, III-1908
Shearing machines, p. II-1128
Shearling, p. I-295
Shears, pp. II-885, 891, 1022, 1206
Sheathing
— asphalt saturated, p. I-452
— paper, p. I-367
Sheaves (power transmission), p. II-1167
Sheep, p. III-1961
Sheep shears, p. II-1022
Sheet, p. I-635
Sheet metal
— forming machines, p. II-1128
— roofing materials, p. III-1789
Sheet music, pp. I-419, III-2158
Sheet pilings, p. I-779
Sheet
— aluminum, p. I-815
— copper, p. I-829
— laminated plastics, p. I-630
— plastics, p. I-614
Sheeting (rubber), p. I-669
Sheets
— steel, p. I-779
— textile, pp. I-197, 233
Shell novelties, p. II-1748
Shell slugs, p. I-779
Shellac, pp. I-553, III-2003
Shellfish, p. I-109

Shells
— artillery, p. II-996
— small arms, p. II-992
Shelving, p. II-1643
— commercial, p. III-1808
— wire, p. II-938
Sherbets, p. I-91
Shims (metal), p. II-1013
Shingle mills, p. I-311
Shingles, pp. I-311, 452, III-1781, 1789
Ship cranes, p. II-1193
Ship furniture, p. II-1626
Ship propellers, p. I-856
Ship repair, p. II-1588
Ship scaling, p. II-1588
Ship sections, p. II-898
Shipboard cable, pp. I-815, 829
Shipping bags, p. I-238
Shipping barrels, p. II-927
Shipping cases, p. I-342
Shipping containers, pp. I-378, III-1870
Shipping crates, p. I-342
Shipping pads, pp. I-635, 640
Shipping pails, p. III-1870
Shipping supplies, p. III-1904
Ships, pp. II-1588, III-1878
Shirts
— outerwear, pp. I-261, 266, 271, 278, 284
— underwear, pp. I-261, 266, 271, 278, 284
Shock absorbers, p. II-1518
Shoe and boot parts, p. I-669
Shoe boxes, p. I-378
Shoe display forms, p. I-357
Shoe kits, p. I-305
Shoe making machinery, pp. II-1060, III-1866
Shoe parts, p. I-650
Shoe polisher, p. II-1396
Shoe polishes, p. I-565
Shoe repair materials, p. III-1874
Shoe soles, p. I-305
Shoe stretchers, p. I-357
Shoe trees, p. I-357
Shoes, pp. I-299, III-1921, 2140
— athletic, p. I-299
— ballet, p. I-299
— children's and infant's, p. I-299
— cleated or spiked, all materials, pp. I-299
— orthopedic, p. III-2140
— orthopedic extension, p. II-1675
— plastics or plastics soled fabric upper, p. I-299
— rubber or rubber soled fabric upper, p. I-299
— sports, p. III-2149
— theatrical, p. I-299
— wooden, p. I-299
Shook, p. I-342
Shop equipment (service station), p. III-1761
Shopping bags, p. III-1904
Shortening, pp. I-25, 30, III-1953
Shorts
— outerwear, pp. I-261, 266, 271, 278, 284
— underwear, pp. I-261, 266, 271
Shot (BB), p. II-992
Shotgun shells, p. II-992
Shotguns, p. II-1000
Shovel loaders, p. II-1032

Numbers following p. or pp. are page references. Roman numerals indicate volume numbers. Page references are to the starting pages of the industries that produce the product or carry out the activity.

Shovels, pp. II-891, 1032
Showcases, pp. II-1105, 1643, III-1808
Showers
— curtains, p. I-233
— heads, p. II-973
— receptors, p. II-1013
— rods, p. II-1013
— sandals, p. I-299
— stalls, pp. I-650, II-1013
Shredders, p. II-1022
Shutters
— door and window, pp. I-333, II-907
— plastics, p. I-650
— wood, p. I-333
Sick room supplies, p. III-2112
Sickles, p. II-891
Siding, pp. I-452, III-1789
— dressed lumber, p. I-311
— plastics, p. I-650
— sheet metal, p. II-907
— wood, p. III-1781
Siding mills, p. I-311
Sienna pigment, p. I-474
Sieves, pp. II-938, 1038, 1060, 1228
Sifting machines, p. II-1060
Sights (telescopic), p. II-1081
Signal and control cable, pp. I-815, 829
Signal generators, p. II-1346
Signal systems, p. III-1830
Signaling transformers, p. II-1420
Signals, p. II-1266
Signs, pp. II-1719, III-1808
Silica gel, p. I-487
Silicofluorides, p. I-487
Silicomanganese ferroalloys, p. I-779
Silicon (ultra high purity), p. I-766
Silicon carbide abrasives, p. I-755
Silicon wafers, p. II-1286
Silicone, p. I-492
— resins, p. I-499
— rubber, p. I-504
Silk
— fabrics, p. I-197
— raw, p. III-1964
— screens, p. II-1060
— spun yarns, p. I-191
— thread, p. I-191
Sills
— concrete, p. I-742
Silos, pp. I-742, II-898
— staves, p. I-333
— stock, p. I-333
Silver, p. I-836
Silver beating, p. II-1013
Silver bromide, p. I-487
Silver bullion, p. I-824
Silver chloride, p. I-487
Silver compounds, p. I-487
Silver foil, pp. I-836, II-1013
Silver nitrate, p. I-487
Silver polishes, p. I-565
Silver refining (primary), p. I-824
Silver shapes, p. I-836
Silverware, p. III-1893
Sine bars, p. II-1139

Sinks, pp. I-650, 676, II-1013
Sirens, p. II-1266
Skateboards, p. II-1701
Skates (ice and roller), p. II-1701
Skelp (iron or steel), p. I-779
Skewers, p. I-357
Ski pants, pp. I-261, 266, 271, 278, 284
Ski suits, pp. I-261, 266, 271, 278, 284
Skids, p. II-1013
Skids and pallets, p. I-342
Skiing equipment, p. III-1882
Skin grafting equipment, p. II-1670
Skins, pp. I-295, III-1964
Skirting (leather), p. I-295
Skirts, pp. I-261, 266, 278, 284
Skis, p. II-1701
Skivers (leather), p. I-295
Skylights, p. II-907
Slacks, pp. I-261, 266, 271, 278, 284
Slag mixers, p. II-1032
Slate products, p. I-761
Slaw (fresh coleslaw), p. I-157
Sledgehammers, p. II-891
Sleds (children's), p. II-1707
Sleeper mechanisms (bed), p. II-1643
Sleeping bags, p. I-250
Sleeves (welder's), p. I-305
Slicing machinery, p. II-1060
Slide fasteners, p. II-1734
Slings (lifting), p. II-938
Slip rings, p. II-1426
Slipcovers, pp. I-233, III-1777
Slipper socks, pp. I-255, 299
Slippers, pp. I-299, III-1921
Slips, pp. I-261, 266, 278
Slot machines, p. II-1748
Slotting machines, p. II-1123
Sludge tables, p. II-1228
Slumped brick, p. I-736
Small arms ammunition, p. II-992
Small game, p. I-96
Smelting machinery, p. III-1866
Smelting ovens, p. II-1216
Smelting pots and retorts, p. II-922
Smoke detectors, pp. II-1266, III-1834
Smoke generators, p. II-1004
Smoked meats, p. I-101
Smokers' supplies, p. III-2205
Smokestacks, p. II-898
Smoking tobacco, p. I-187
Snack machines, p. II-1091
Snap switches, p. II-1456
Snow fence, p. I-357
Snow fence lath, p. I-333
Snow making machinery, p. II-1105
Snow plow attachments, pp. II-1027, 1032
Snow plows, p. III-1858
Snowblowers, pp. II-1027, III-1858, 1862
Snowmobiles, pp. II-1606, III-1757, 2026
Snowshoes, p. II-1701
Snowsuits, pp. I-261, 266, 271, 278, 284
Snuff, pp. I-187, III-2000
Soaps, p. I-565
— dishes, p. I-676
— dispensers, p. II-1013

Social stationery, p. III-1900
Sockets (electric), p. II-1456
Sockets and socket sets, p. II-891
Socks, pp. I-255, 299
Sod harvesting machines, p. II-1022
Soda (pop), p. I-164
Soda ash, p. I-479
Soda bottles, p. I-717
Soda carbonated, p. I-164
Soda crackers, p. I-123
Soda fountain equipment, p. II-1105
Soda fountain fixtures, p. III-1808
Soda fountain syrups, p. I-146
Sodium acetate, p. I-492
Sodium alginate, p. I-492
Sodium aluminate, p. I-487
Sodium aluminum sulfate, p. I-487
Sodium antimoniate, p. I-487
Sodium arsenite, p. I-487
Sodium arsenite insecticides, p. I-528
Sodium benzoate, p. I-492
Sodium bicarbonate, p. I-479
Sodium bichromate and chromate, p. I-487
Sodium borate, p. I-487
Sodium borohydride, p. I-487
Sodium bromide, p. I-487
Sodium carbonate, p. I-479
Sodium chlorate, p. I-487
Sodium chloride pharmaceuticals, p. I-538
Sodium cyanide, p. I-487
Sodium glutamate, p. I-492
Sodium hydrosulfite, p. I-487
Sodium hydroxide, p. I-479
Sodium hypochlorite, p. I-487
Sodium inorganic compounds, p. I-487
Sodium molybdate, p. I-487
Sodium organic compounds, p. I-492
Sodium pentachlorophenate, p. I-492
Sodium perborate, p. I-487
Sodium peroxide, p. I-487
Sodium phosphate, p. I-487
Sodium polyphosphate, p. I-487
Sodium salicylate preparations, p. I-538
Sodium silicate, p. I-487
Sodium silicofluoride, p. I-487
Sodium stannate, p. I-487
Sodium sulfate, p. I-487
Sodium sulfoxalate formaldehyde, p. I-492
Sodium tetraborate, p. I-487
Sodium thiosulfate, p. I-487
Sodium tungstate, p. I-487
Sodium uranate, p. I-487
Sodium vapor lamp bulbs, p. II-1385
Sofa beds, p. II-1615
Sofas, p. II-1615
Soft drinks, pp. I-164, III-1953, 2093
— cans, p. II-927
— concentrates, p. I-146
— vending machines, p. II-1091
Softeners (leather or textile), p. I-565
Software, pp. II-1371, III-1804, 2057
Softwood dimension lumber, p. I-333
Softwood distillates, p. I-492
Softwood plywood composites, p. I-323
Softwood veneer or plywood, p. I-323

Numbers following p. or pp. are page references. Roman numerals indicate volume numbers. Page references are to the starting pages of the industries that produce the product or carry out the activity.

Soil pipe, p. I-844
Soil testing kits, p. I-594
Solar cells, pp. II-1286, III-1838
Solar energy heating equipment, p. II-1100
Solar heating panels, p. III-1846
Solar heating systems, p. II-1100
Solar lighting fixtures, p. II-1389
Solar reflective film, p. III-1789
Solarimeters, p. II-1366
Solder wire, p. I-836
Soldering equipment, p. II-1228
Soldering guns, p. II-891
Soldering tips, p. II-891
Solderless connectors, p. II-1456
Sole leather, p. I-295
Solenoids, p. II-1316
— switches, p. II-1436
— valves, p. II-979
Soles (boot and shoe), p. I-305
Solid fuel propellants, p. I-487
Solvent dyes, p. I-474
Solvents, p. I-442
Sonabuoys, p. II-1326
Sonar equipment, p. III-1838
Sonar fish finders, p. II-1326
Sonar systems, p. II-1326
Soot removing chemicals, p. I-565
Sorbitol, p. I-492
Sorghum flour, p. I-14
Sorghum syrup, p. I-157
Sound insulation, p. III-1789
Soups, pp. I-61, 67, 109, III-1928, 1953
— cans, p. II-927
— mixes, pp. I-67, 157
Sour cream, p. I-85
Souvenirs, p. III-2189
Soy sauce, p. I-151
Soybeans, p. III-1957
— cakes and meal, p. I-30
— cooking oil, p. I-25
— fibers and filaments, p. I-509
— flour and grits, p. I-30
— millfeed, p. I-30
— oil, p. I-30
— plastics, p. I-499
— protein concentrates, p. I-30
— protein isolates, p. I-30
Space capsules, p. II-1579
Space heaters, p. II-1100
Space satellites, p. II-1261
Space simulation chambers, p. II-898
Space suits, p. II-1675
Space vehicle guidance systems, p. II-1326
Space vehicles, p. II-1571
Spades, p. II-891
Spaghetti, pp. I-67, 123, III-1953
Spandex, pp. I-197, 509
Spark plugs, pp. II-1346, 1511
— insulators, p. I-685
Sparkling wine, p. I-176
Spars (wood), p. I-357
Spats (leather), p. I-305
Spatulas, p. I-669
Speaker cabinets, p. II-1631
Speaker systems, p. II-1271

Spearmint oil, p. I-594
Spectrofluorometers, p. II-1351
Spectrographs, p. II-1351
Spectrometers, pp. II-1351, 1366
Spectrophotometers, p. II-1351
Spectrum analyzers, p. II-1346
Speculums, p. II-1670
Speed changers, p. II-1161
Speed reducers, p. II-1161
Speed shops, p. III-2029
Sphygmomanometers, p. II-1670
Spices, pp. I-151, III-1953, 2093
Spiegeleisen ferroalloys, p. I-779
Spigots
— plumbing, p. II-973
— wood, p. I-357
Spike rods, p. I-779
Spikes, pp. I-792, II-938, III-1823
Spindles, p. II-1060
Spinning yarn, p. I-191
Spiral cloth, p. II-938
Spirits (distilled), pp. I-180, III-1986
Spline rolling machines, p. II-1128
Splint baskets, p. I-342
Splints, p. II-1675
Splits (leather), p. I-295
Spokes (wood), p. I-357
Sponges, pp. I-650, 669, II-1013
— iron, p. I-779
Spools, pp. I-357, II-1060
Spoons, p. II-885
Sport coats, pp. I-266, 271, 284
Sport shirts, pp. I-266, 271
Sport utility vehicles, pp. II-1477, III-1757
Sporting goods, pp. II-1701, III-1882, 2149, 2193
Sports clothing, pp. I-261, 266, 271, 278, 284
Sports equipment, p. III-1882
Sports gear, p. III-2149
Sportswear, p. III-1915
Spot removers, p. I-565
Spot welding equipment, p. II-1228
Spotlights, pp. II-1389, 1511
Spouts (metal), p. II-907
Spray painting equipment, pp. III-1866, 2003
Sprayers
— farm, pp. II-1022, III-1862
— manual, p. II-1183
Spreaders
— farm, p. II-1022
— fertilizer, p. III-1862
— lawn and garden, p. II-1027
Spreads
— cheese, p. I-75
Spring pins (metal), p. II-957
Spring washers (metal), p. II-957
Spring winding machines, p. II-1128
Springs
— assembled bed and box, p. II-1656
— clock and watch, p. II-1361
— heavy gauge, p. II-938
— light gauge, p. II-938
— precision, p. II-938
— seat, p. II-938
— steel, p. III-1823

Sprinklers
— agricultural, p. III-1862
— lawn, p. II-979
— systems, pp. II-1228, III-1874
Sprockets (transmission), p. II-1167
Spunbonded fabrics, p. I-207
Squares (carpenters'), p. II-891
Squash equipment, p. II-1701
Stabilizing bars, p. II-1013
Stackers, pp. II-1193, III-1866
Stadium seating, p. II-1626
Stage lighting equipment, p. II-1389
Stained glass, pp. I-708, 721
Stainless steel, pp. I-779, 844
Stains, pp. I-553, III-2003
— biological, p. I-474
Staircases, p. II-907
Stairs, p. II-907
— railings, pp. I-333, II-907
— treads, pp. I-669, II-907
Stairways, p. II-1193
Stairwork, p. I-333
Stakes (surveyor's), p. I-357
Stalk choppers, p. II-1022
Stalls (metal), p. II-907
Stamp pads, pp. I-594, II-1713
Stamping devices, p. II-1713
Stamping machines, p. II-1128
Stampings, p. I-878
Standing wave equipment, p. II-1346
Stands, p. II-1643
Stannic and stannous chloride, p. I-487
Staple removers, p. II-1713
Staplers, pp. II-1206, 1713
Staples, pp. I-792, II-938, III-1842
Starch glues, p. I-559
Starches, pp. I-21, 565
Starters, p. II-1511
Static converters, p. II-1286
Static pressure regulators, p. II-1331
Stationery, pp. I-402, III-1900, 2185
Stators (motor), p. II-1426
Statuary, pp. I-680, 751, 761, 775
Staves (barrel), p. I-342
Stays (leather shoe), p. I-305
Steam condensers, p. II-917
Steam cookers, pp. II-1091, 1396
Steam fittings, p. II-979
Steam heating equipment, p. II-1100
Steam pressure controls, p. II-1331
Steam separating machinery, p. II-1228
Steam tables, p. II-1091
Steam traps, p. II-979
Steam turbines, p. II-1156
Stearic acid, p. I-492
Stearin (animal), p. I-101
Steatite porcelain insulators, p. I-685
Steel, p. III-1823
— balls, p. I-779
— cans, p. II-927
— castings, p. I-844
— forgings, p. I-871
— foundries, p. I-844
— investment foundries, p. I-844
— joists, p. II-898

Numbers following p. or pp. are page references. Roman numerals indicate volume numbers. Page references are to the starting pages of the industries that produce the product or carry out the activity.

2280

— mill products, p. I-779
— railroad car racks, p. II-898
— shot abrasives, p. I-755
Steel wool, pp. II-1013, III-1823
Steepwater concentrate, p. I-21
Steering boxes, p. II-1518
Steering columns, p. II-1518
Steering wheels, p. II-1518
Stemware, pp. I-712, 721
Stencils
— inks, p. I-579
— paper, p. II-1713
Stenography machinery, p. II-1076
Stepladders, pp. I-357, II-1013
Stereorubber, p. I-504
Stereos, pp. III-1834, 2029, 2053
— cabinets, p. II-1631
Sterilizers
— dental, p. II-1681
— hospital and surgical, p. II-1675
— laboratory, p. II-1665
Sterilizing chambers, p. II-898
Steriods, p. I-533
Stethoscopes, p. II-1670
Sticks (sports), p. II-1701
Stilbene dyes, p. I-474
Still gases, p. I-442
Stills, p. II-922
Stitchers and trimmers (book), p. II-1060
Stockings, p. I-255
Stone working machinery, p. II-1060
Stonecutters' handtools, p. II-891
Stones
— beneficiating machinery, p. II-1038
— building, p. III-1785
— cutting saw blades, p. II-891
— precious and semiprecious, p. III-1893
— synthetic, gem, pp. I-775
Stoneware, p. I-680
Stools, pp. II-1620, 1631
Stop valves, p. II-979
Stopcock drains, p. II-973
Stoppers
— cork, p. I-357
— rubber, p. I-669
Storage batteries, pp. II-1441, III-1830
Storage battery chargers, p. II-1426
Storage bins, p. III-1793
Storage devices (computer), p. II-1242
Storage tanks, pp. II-922, III-1823
Store display fixtures, p. II-1643
Store equipment, p. III-1808
Store fixtures, p. III-1808
Store furniture, p. III-1773
Storm doors, pp. I-333, II-907
Stove boards, p. II-907
Stove linings, p. I-698
Stove pipes and flues, p. II-907
Stoves, pp. II-1091, 1403, III-1846
Straddle carriers, p. II-1193
Straight razors, p. II-885
Strainers
— plpeline, p. II-1228
Strandboard
— oriented, p. I-318

Stranded wire, p. II-938
Strap leather, p. I-295
Strappings, p. II-1013
Straps, p. I-305
— watch, pp. I-305, II-1695
Straw, p. III-1990
— baskets, p. I-357
— hats, p. I-289
Street lighting, p. II-1389
Street sweeping equipment, p. III-1858
Streetcars, p. II-1583
Stretch limousines, p. II-1485
Stretchers
— curtain, p. I-357
— medical, p. II-1675
Stretching machines, p. II-1128
Strings, p. I-243
— musical, p. II-1730
Stroboscopes, p. II-1346
Strobotrons, p. II-1385
Strollers (baby), p. II-1707
Strontium, p. I-487
Structural clay tile, pp. I-690, III-1785
Struts (vehicle), p. II-1518
Strychnine and derivatives, p. I-533
Stucco, p. I-775
Stud mills, p. I-311
Studio equipment, p. II-1261
Studs, pp. I-333, II-907
Stuffed toys, p. II-1707
Stuffer (sausage), p. II-1060
Styphnic acid explosives, p. I-584
Styrene, pp. I-442, 466
Styrene resins, p. I-499
Styrene-acrylonitrile resins, p. I-499
Styrene-butadiene rubber, p. I-504
Styrene-chloroprene rubber, p. I-504
Styrene-isoprene rubber, p. I-504
Submachine guns, p. II-1000
Submarine building, p. II-1588
Subpresses (machine tool), p. II-1133
Subscriber loop equipment, p. II-1256
Substation transformers, p. II-1420
Subway cars, pp. II-1583, III-1878
Suction therapy apparatus, p. II-1670
Sugar, pp. I-21, 43
— cane, p. I-43
— confectionery, pp. I-39, 43
— granulated, pp. I-39, 43
— invert, pp. I-39, 43
— liquid, p. I-39
— raw, pp. I-43, III-1964
— refined, pp. I-43, III-1953
— substitutes, pp. I-492, 594
Sugar refining machinery, p. II-1060
Sugarcane mills, p. I-43
Sugarcane refining, p. I-43
Suit trimmings, pp. I-266, 289
Suitcases
— all materials, p. I-305
— metal hardware, p. II-932
Suits, pp. I-261, 266, 284, III-1915
— firefighting, p. II-1675
— nontailored, pp. I-271, 278

— space, p. II-1675
— tailored, pp. I-271, 278
Sulfa drugs, p. I-533
Sulfides and sulfites, p. I-487
Sulfocyanides, p. I-487
Sulfonamides, p. I-533
Sulfur, p. I-487
Sulfur chloride, p. I-487
Sulfur dioxide, p. I-487
Sulfur hexafluoride gas, p. I-487
Sulfur insecticides, p. I-528
Sulfured fruit and vegetables, p. I-67
Sulfuric acid, pp. I-487, III-1970
Sulphonated derivatives, p. I-492
Sumac extract, p. I-492
Sump pumps, p. II-1178
Sunflower seed oil (cake and meal), p. I-30
Sunglasses, pp. II-1686, III-1816, 2106
Sunroofs, p. II-1550
Sunscreen lotions, p. I-574
Sunsuits, p. I-284
Suntan lotions and oils, p. I-574
Superalloys, pp. I-779, 836
Supermarkets, p. III-2075
Superphosphates, p. I-519
Superstores, p. III-2176
Supports
— orthopedic, p. II-1675
Suppositories, p. I-538
Surface active agents, pp. I-565, III-1970
Surface area analyzers, p. II-1351
Surface burner controls, p. II-1331
Surface mining machinery, p. II-1032
Surfboards, p. II-1701
Surge suppressors, p. II-1467
Surgical appliances, p. III-1812
Surgical clamps, p. II-1670
Surgical dressings, p. II-1675
Surgical implants, p. II-1675
Surgical instruments, p. III-1812
Surgical knives, p. II-1670
Surgical staplers, p. II-1670
Surgical supplies, pp. II-1675, III-1812
Surgical support systems, p. II-1321
Surgical towels, p. III-1812
Surimi, p. I-109
Surveying equipment, p. III-1819
Surveying instruments, p. II-1366
Surveyor's stakes, p. I-357
Suspenders, pp. I-266, 289
Sutures
— surgical, p. II-1675
Swaging machines, p. II-1128
Swatters (fly), p. II-1013
Sweat bands, pp. I-261, 266, 284, 295
Sweat pants, pp. I-261, 266, 271, 278, 284
Sweat suits, pp. I-261, 266, 271, 278, 284
Sweaters, pp. I-261, 266, 271, 278, 284
— jackets, pp. I-261, 266, 271, 278, 284
— vests, pp. I-261, 266, 271, 278, 284
Sweatshirts, pp. I-261, 266, 271, 278, 284
Sweep generators, p. II-1346
Sweep oscillators, p. II-1346
Sweepers
— vacuums, p. II-1396

Numbers following p. or pp. are page references. Roman numerals indicate volume numbers. Page references are to the starting pages of the industries that produce the product or carry out the activity.

2281

Product/Activity Index

Sweeping compounds, p. I-565
Sweet yeast goods, p. I-115
Sweetening syrups, p. I-157
Swimming pools, pp. II-1701, III-1882
— covers, p. I-650
— filters, p. II-1091
— heaters, p. II-1100
— lighting, p. II-1389
— preparations, p. I-594
— supplies, p. III-2207
Swimming suits, pp. I-261, 266, 271, 278, 284
Swimwear, pp. III-1915, 1918, 2137
Swine, p. III-1961
Swine feed, p. I-8
Switch boxes, p. II-1456
Switch cutouts, p. II-1456
Switchboards, pp. II-1431, III-1830
Switches, pp. II-1316, 1456
— electric power, p. II-1431
— electrical, p. III-1830
— electronic, p. III-1838
— outlet box mounting, p. II-1456
— pneumatic positioning, p. II-1331
— thermostatic, p. II-1331
Switchgear, p. II-1431
Switching equipment, pp. II-1256, 1431
Swords, p. II-885
Synchronous condensers, p. II-1426
Synchronous motors, p. II-1426
Synchroscopes, p. II-1346
Synthesizers (music), p. II-1730
Synthetic chocolate, p. I-56
Synthetic gem stones, p. I-775
Synthetic rubber, pp. I-504, III-1970
Synthetic sweeteners, p. I-492
Syringes, p. II-1670
Syrup
— beverage, p. I-146
— cane, p. I-43
— chocolate, pp. I-47, 51
— corn, pp. I-21, 157
— flavoring, pp. I-142, 146
— fountain, p. III-1938
— sweetening, p. I-157
Syrups, pp. I-39, 157, III-1953
T-shirts, p. III-2137
— outerwear, pp. I-261, 266, 271, 278, 284
— underwear, pp. I-261, 266, 271, 278, 284
T-squares (drafting), p. II-1366
Table tops, pp. I-761, II-1610
Tablecloths, pp. I-197, 212, 233, 410
Tables, pp. II-1620, 1631, 1649
Tablets, pp. I-367, 402, II-1013
Tableware, pp. I-680, 712, 721, III-1777, 1893, 1904
Tachometer generators, p. II-1346
Tack shops, p. III-2149
Tackle
— blocks, p. I-357
— fishing, p. II-1701
— shops, p. III-2149
Tacks, pp. I-792, II-938, III-1842
Taffrail logs, p. II-1326
Tailors' scissors, p. II-885
Tailors' supplies, p. III-1874
Talc, p. I-766

Talcum powders, p. I-574
Tall oil, p. I-492
Tallow, p. I-101
Tally counters, p. II-1341
Tallying meters, p. II-1341
Tampers (powered), p. II-1032
Tampions guns, p. II-1004
Tank artillery, p. II-1004
Tank bodies, p. II-1485
Tank tops, pp. I-266, 284
— outerwear, pp. I-261, 271, 278
— underwear, pp. I-261, 271, 278
Tank trailer, p. II-1490
Tank truck meters, p. II-1341
Tank trucks, p. II-1485
Tanks
— concrete, p. I-742
— flush, p. I-676
— heavy gauge metal, p. II-922
— military, p. II-1602
— photographic developing, p. II-1086
— storage, pp. I-650, III-1823
— wood, p. I-342
Tannery leather, p. I-295
Tannery machinery, p. II-1060
Tannic acid, p. I-492
Tanning agents, pp. I-487, 492
Tanning extracts, p. I-492
Tantalum, p. I-824
Tape dispensers, p. II-1713
Tape measures, p. II-891
Tape players, pp. II-1271, III-1834
Tape storage units, p. II-1242
Tapes, pp. I-387, 402
— blank, audio and video, pp. III-1838
— cellophane, p. III-1900
— magnetic recording, p. II-1380
— medical adhesive, p. II-1675
— medical and surgical, p. III-1812
— nonwoven fabric, p. I-207
— surveyor's, p. II-1366
— textile, p. III-1912
— varnished and coated, p. I-223
Tapioca, p. I-21
Tapping machines, p. II-1123
Taps (electrical), p. II-1456
Taps (leather shoe), p. I-305
Taps and dies, p. II-1139
Tar, pp. I-442, 492
Tar acid resins, p. I-499
Tar and asphalt paving mixtures, p. I-447
Tar and tar oils, p. I-492
Tar paper, pp. I-367, 452
Tar roofing cements and coatings, p. I-452
Target drones (aircraft), p. II-1556
Targets (aircraft), p. II-1566
Tarpaulins, p. I-238
Tarred felts, p. III-1789
Tartar sauce, p. I-151
Tartaric acid, p. I-492
Tartrates, p. I-492
Taxicabs, p. III-1757
Taxidermy supplies, p. III-1874
Taximeters, p. II-1341
Tea, pp. I-142, 164, III-1953

Tea and coffee, p. III-2093
Tea blending, p. I-142
Teaching machines, pp. II-1091, III-1819
Teakettles, pp. I-712, II-885, 1396
Tear gas, p. I-492
Technetium medicinal preparations, p. I-538
Teddies, pp. I-266, 278
Teeth, pp. II-1681, 1691, III-1812
Telegraph equipment, p. III-1838
Telemetering instruments, p. II-1336
Telephones, pp. II-1256, 1261, III-1838, 2053
— answering machines, pp. II-1256, III-1834
— booths, p. II-1643
— carrier line equipment, p. II-1256
— carrier switching equipment, p. II-1256
— directories, p. I-419
— equipment, p. III-1838
Teleprinters, p. II-1247
Telescopes, p. II-1081
Television (closed-circuit), p. II-1261
Televisions, pp. II-1271, III-1834, 2053
— antennas, p. II-1261
— cabinets, p. II-1631
— cameras, p. III-1797
— housings, p. I-650
— towers, p. II-898
— tubes, p. I-1276
Tellurium, p. I-824
Temperature controls, p. II-1331
Temperature instruments, p. II-1336
Temperature sensors, p. II-1331
Tempered glass, p. I-721
Templates (drafting), p. II-1366
Temples and fronts, p. II-1686
Tennis equipment, p. III-1882
Tennis goods, p. II-1701
Tennis shirts, pp. I-261, 266, 271, 278, 284
Tennis skirts, pp. I-261, 266, 278
Tensile strength testing equipment, p. II-1366
Tent poles, p. I-357
Tents, p. I-238
Terminals and connectors, p. II-1456
Terminals
— computer, p. II-1247
— petroleum, p. III-1974
Termite poisons, p. I-528
Terneplate, pp. I-779, III-1823
Ternes, p. I-779
Terpineol, p. I-492
Terrazzo products, p. I-742
Terrycloth, p. I-197
Tert-butylated bis ether fluid, p. I-492
Tetrachloroethylene, p. I-492
Tetracycline, p. I-533
Tetraethyl lead, p. I-492
Tetryl explosive materials, p. I-584
Textile bags, p. I-238
Textile finishing assistants, p. I-565
Textile finishing machinery, p. II-1060
Textile fire hose, p. I-250
Textile glass fibers, p. I-712
Textile guides (porcelain), p. I-680
Textile leathers, p. I-305
Textile machinery, pp. II-1060, III-1866
Textile printing inks, p. I-579

Numbers following p. or pp. are page references. Roman numerals indicate volume numbers. Page references are to the starting pages of the industries that produce the product or carry out the activity.

Textile printing machinery, p. II-1060
Textile products, pp. I-197, 202, 212, 217
Textile scouring agents, p. I-565
Textile waste, p. III-1889
Textiles, p. III-1912
Texturizing machinery for textiles, p. II-1060
Theater costumes, pp. I-266, 284
Theater equipment, p. III-1797
Theater scenery, p. II-1748
Theater seats, pp. II-1626, III-1773
Theobromine and derivatives, p. I-533
Theodolites, pp. II-1081, 1366
Therapeutic X-ray apparatus, p. II-1356
Therapy equipment, p. III-1812
Thermal analysis instruments, p. II-1351
Thermal conductivity instruments, pp. II-1336, 1351
Thermal insulation, p. I-635
Thermistors, pp. II-1296, 1336
Thermocouples, pp. II-1331, 1336, 1366
Thermoelectric generators, p. II-1467
Thermoform packaging machinery, p. II-1211
Thermoforming machinery for plastics, p. II-1050
Thermogravimetric analyzers, p. II-1351
Thermometers, pp. II-1336, 1366, 1670, III-1812
Thermoplastic resins, p. I-499
Thermosetting plastics, p. I-499
Thermosetting vulcanizable elastomers, p. I-504
Thermostatic traps, p. II-979
Thermostats, pp. II-1331, 1550
Thickness gauging instruments, p. II-1366
Thimbles for wire rope, p. II-1013
Thin film integrated circuits, p. II-1286
Thin layer deposition equipment, p. II-1055
Thiocyanate, p. I-487
Thioglycolic acid, p. I-492
Thiol rubber, p. I-504
Thread, pp. I-191, 669, III-1870, 1912
— cutting dies, p. II-1139
— making machinery, p. II-1060
— rolling machines, p. II-1128
Threading machines, p. II-1123
Through-hole machinery, p. II-1060
Thrust power indicators, p. II-1366
Thrust roller bearings, p. II-987
Thyristors, p. II-1286
Thyroid preparations, p. I-538
Tick powders or sprays, p. I-528
Tie plates (iron or steel), p. I-779
Tie shops, p. III-2134
Tie wires, p. I-792
Ties, pp. I-261, 266, 289
— railroad, pp. I-311, 742
— wood, p. I-311
Tiles
— adhesives, p. I-559
— ceramic wall and floor, p. I-694
— clay (structural), p. I-690
— clay refractory, p. I-702
— cork, p. I-357
— floor, p. I-650
— kilns, p. II-1216
— machinery, p. II-1060
— roofing and drain (clay), p. I-698
— sewer (clay), p. I-698
— structural clay, p. III-1785

Tillers, pp. II-1027, III-1862
Timber, pp. I-311, 328
Time clocks, p. II-1361
Time cycle and controllers, p. II-1336
Time locks, p. II-1361
Time planners/organizers, p. I-419
Time program controls, p. II-1331
Time recording machines, p. III-1800
Time stamps, p. II-1361
Time switches, p. II-1431
Timers, p. II-1361
Timing belts, p. I-664
Timing devices, p. II-1436
Timing gears, p. II-1504
Timing mechanisms, p. II-1361
Timing motors, p. II-1426
Tin, pp. I-824, 836
— compounds, p. I-487
— plate, p. III-1823
— plate cans, p. II-927
— salts, p. I-487
— shapes, p. I-836
Tin base alloys, p. I-824
Tin chloride, p. I-487
Tin foil, p. II-1013
Tin oxide, p. I-487
Tincture of iodine, p. I-538
Tinner's snips, p. II-891
Tinplate, p. I-779
Tinsel, p. II-1748
Tints (hair), p. I-574
Tints and dyes, p. I-594
Tips (leather shoe), p. I-305
Tires, pp. I-659, III-2033
— chains, p. II-938
— cord and fabric, p. I-247
— covers, p. II-1535
— inflators, aerosol, pp. I-594
— making machinery, p. II-1050
— motor vehicle, p. III-1765
— mounting machines, p. II-1091
— plastics, p. I-650
— recapping machinery, pp. II-1050, III-1866
— repair materials, pp. I-659, III-1765
— scrap, p. III-1889
— shredding machinery, p. II-1050
— tubes, p. III-1765
— used, p. III-1765
Tissue paper, pp. I-367, III-1904
Titania porcelain insulators, p. I-685
Titanium, pp. I-824, 836
Titanium castings, p. I-856
Titanium die-castings, p. I-856
Titanium dioxide, p. I-487
Titanium forgings, p. I-871
Titanium pigments, p. I-474
Titanium shapes, p. I-836
Titrimeters, p. II-1351
TNT (trinitrotoluene), p. I-584
Toaster ovens, p. II-1396
Toasters, pp. II-1396, III-1834
Tobacco, pp. III-1964, 2000, 2205
— auctions, p. III-1964
— harvester machines, p. II-1022
— hogsheads, p. I-342

— leaf processing and aging, p. I-184
— pipes, p. II-1748
— pouches, pp. I-305, II-1695
— processing machinery, p. II-1060
— products, pp. I-187, III-2000
— sheeting services, p. I-187
— stemming and redrying, p. I-184
Toboggans, p. II-1701
Toe caps (leather), p. I-305
Toffee, p. I-56
Tofu, pp. I-91, 157
Toggle bolts, p. II-957
Toilet bowl cleaners, p. I-565
Toilet fixtures, pp. I-650, 676, II-1013
Toilet kits and cases, pp. I-305, II-1695
Toilet paper, pp. I-367, 410
Toilet preparations, pp. I-574, III-1908
Toilet seats, p. I-357
Toilet soaps, p. III-1908
Toilet tissue, p. III-1904
Toilet ware, p. II-1013
Toilet water, p. I-574
Toiletries, p. III-1908
Toll switching equipment, p. II-1256
Toluene, pp. I-442, 466
Toluidines, p. I-492
Tomato harvesting machines, p. II-1022
Toner cartridges, pp. I-594, III-1900
— rebuilding, p. I-594
Toners, pp. I-474, 594
Tongue depressors, p. II-1675
Tongues (boot and shoe), p. I-305
Tonometers (medical), p. II-1670
Tool boxes, p. II-927
Tool chests, p. I-342
Tool handles, p. I-357
Tool stands, p. II-1626
Tool steel, p. I-779
Toolholders, p. II-1139
Tools, p. II-1139
— auto, p. III-1761
— dentist's, p. II-1681
— hand, pp. II-891, III-1842
— handheld, pp. II-891, 1206
— machinists', p. III-1866
— woodworking, p. II-891
Toothbrushes, pp. II-1396, 1739, III-1834, 1908
Toothpastes, p. I-565
Toothpicks, p. I-357
Top lifts (boot and shoe), p. I-305
Topcoats, pp. I-266, 271
Toppings, p. III-1953
Tops
— automotive, p. II-1550
Torpedo tubes, p. II-1004
Torpedoes, p. II-996
Torque converters, p. II-1529
Torque motors, p. II-1426
Torsion bars, p. II-938
Torsion testing equipment, p. II-1366
Tortilla chips, p. I-136
Tortillas, p. I-132
Totalizing meters, p. II-1341
Toupees, p. II-1748
Tow targets (aircraft), p. II-1566

Numbers following p. or pp. are page references. Roman numerals indicate volume numbers. Page references are to the starting pages of the industries that produce the product or carry out the activity.

Product/Activity Index

Tow trucks, p. II-1485
Towboats, p. II-1588
Towel bar holders, p. I-676
Towelettes, p. I-574
Towels and washcloths, pp. I-197, 212, 233, III-1777
Towels
— industrial, p. III-1870
— paper, pp. I-367, 410
— surgical, p. III-1812
Towing bars, p. II-1550
Toxoids, p. I-548
Toy furniture, p. II-1707
Toys, pp. II-1707, III-1886, 2152
— doll, p. II-1707
— stuffed, p. II-1707
Tracer igniters, p. II-996
Track and field equipment, p. II-1701
Track lighting fixtures, p. II-1389
Traction apparatus, p. II-1675
Tractors, p. II-1481
Tractors and attachments, pp. II-1022, 1027, 1032
Tractors
— crawler, p. II-1032
— farm and garden, p. III-1862
— highway, p. III-1757
— industrial, pp. II-1193, III-1866
Trade journals, p. I-419
Traffic signals, p. II-1266
Trailer hitches, p. II-1550
Trailer parts, p. III-1761
Trailers, pp. II-1490, 1499
— camping, p. II-1499
— industrial, p. III-1866
— motor vehicle, p. III-1757
Training pants, pp. I-266, 284
Tranquilizer preparations, p. I-538
Transaxles, p. II-1529
Transceivers, p. II-1261
Transcutaneous nerve stimulators, p. II-1321
Transducers, pp. II-1316, 1366
Transformers, p. III-1830
— arc-welding, p. II-1420
— electric power, p. II-1420
— electronic, pp. II-1301, III-1838
— ignition, p. II-1420
— reactor, p. II-1420
Transistor radio batteries, p. II-1446
Transistors, pp. II-1286, III-1838
Transit-mixed concrete, p. I-731
Transits (surveying), p. II-1366
Transmissions
— belting, pp. I-305, 664
— coolers, p. II-1550
— equipment, p. III-1830
— fluids, pp. I-457, 594
— pole and line hardware, p. II-1456
— towers, p. II-898
— vehicular, p. II-1529
— voltage regulators, p. II-1420
Transmitters, pp. II-1336, III-1838
Transplanters (farm), p. II-1022
Transportation equipment, p. III-1878
Transportation equipment seating, p. II-1535

Traps
— animal and fish, p. II-938
— water, p. II-973
Trapshooting equipment, p. III-1882
Trash bags, p. I-602
Trash compactors, pp. II-1091, 1416
Trash containers, p. I-650
Trash racks, p. II-898
Travel guides, p. I-419
Travel trailers, pp. II-1499, III-1757, 2017
Traveling bags, p. I-305
Traveling wave tubes, p. II-1276
Tray trucks (restaurant), p. II-1626
Trays
— carrier (wood), p. I-342
— food, p. I-414
— photographic, p. II-1086
— wire, p. II-938
— wood, p. I-357
Treads
— metal stair, p. II-907
— rubber, p. I-659
Tree nut oils, pp. I-25, 30
Tree shakers, p. II-1022
Trees, p. III-1997
Trellises
— wood, p. I-333
Trenching machines, p. II-1032
Trestle parts, p. I-311
Triacetate fibers, p. I-509
Trichloroethylene, p. I-492
Trichlorophenoxyacetic acid, p. I-492
Tricresyl phosphate, p. I-492
Tricycles, pp. II-1598, 1707
Tridecyl alcohol, p. I-492
Trim and molding, p. II-907
Trim
— metal, p. II-907
— wood, p. I-333
Trimmers, pp. II-891, 1027
Trimmings
— fur, pp. I-266, 284
— leather shoe, p. I-305
Trinitrotoluene (TNT), p. I-584
Triphenyl phosphate, p. I-492
Tripods (camera), p. II-1086
Trocars, p. II-1670
Trombones, p. II-1730
Trophies, pp. II-1013, 1695, III-1893, 2207
Trophy bases, p. I-357
Trouble lights, p. II-1389
Troughs
— elevator, p. II-907
— industrial, p. II-898
Trousers, pp. I-261, 266, 271
— pressers, p. II-1396
Trowels, p. II-891
Truck bodies, p. II-1485
Truck campers, p. II-1499
Truck caps, p. III-2029
Truck concrete mixers, p. I-731
Truck parts, p. III-1761
Truck stops, p. III-2119
Truck tractors, pp. II-1481, 1485, III-1757
Truck trailers, p. III-1757

Trucks, p. II-1481
— industrial, pp. II-1193, III-1866
— light duty, p. II-1477
— off-highway, p. II-1032
— road, p. III-1757
Trumpets, p. II-1730
Trunks, p. I-305
Truss plates, p. II-898
Trusses, p. I-328
Tub and tile cleaners, p. I-565
Tube, pp. I-787, 810
Tube blooms, p. I-810
Tube blooms (aluminum), p. I-810
Tube rolling machinery, p. II-1146
Tube
— aluminum, p. I-810
— iron or steel, p. I-779
— nonrigid plastics, p. I-620
— rounds (iron or steel), p. I-779
— welded (aluminum), p. I-815
Tuberculin, p. I-548
Tubes, p. II-1008
— cathode ray, p. II-1276
— electron, p. II-1276
— electronic, p. III-1838
— klystron, p. II-1276
— X-ray, p. II-1356
Tubing
— copper and copper alloy, p. I-829
— flexible metal, p. II-1013
— mechanical, p. I-787
— metal, p. III-1823
— nonferrous metals, p. I-836
— rubber, p. I-669
— seamless steel, p. I-779
— wrought iron or steel, p. I-779
Tubs
— laundry or bath, p. II-1013
Tufting machinery for textiles, p. II-1060
Tugboats, p. II-1588
Tumblers (plastics), p. I-650
Tungstates, p. I-487
Tungsten carbide powder, p. I-836
Tungsten compounds, p. I-487
Tungsten shapes, p. I-836
Tuning forks, p. II-1730
Tunnel lining, p. II-898
Tunnels, p. II-898
Turbidity instruments, p. II-1336
Turbidometers, p. II-1351
Turbines, pp. II-1156, III-1866, 1878
— flow meters, p. II-1336
— meters, p. II-1341
Turkeys, pp. I-96, III-1935
— feeds, p. I-8
— red oil, p. I-565
Turnbuckles, p. II-957
Turning machines, p. II-1123
Turnings (furniture), p. I-333
Turpentine, pp. I-492, III-1970
Turret lathes, p. II-1123
Turrets (gun), p. II-1004
Tuxedos, p. I-271

Numbers following p. or pp. are page references. Roman numerals indicate volume numbers. Page references are to the starting pages of the industries that produce the product or carry out the activity.

TVs
— sets, p. II-1271
— stands, pp. II-1620, 1631
— stores, p. III-2053
Twines, pp. I-243, III-1870
Twist drills, p. III-1866
Typesetting machinery, p. II-1060
Typewriters, pp. II-1076, III-1800
— paper, p. III-1900
— ribbons, p. II-1713
Ukuleles, p. II-1730
Ultra lights (aircraft), p. II-1556
Ultramarine pigments, p. I-474
Ultrasonics
— boring machines, p. II-1123
— cleaning equipment, p. II-1467
— dental equipment, p. II-1681
— generators, p. II-1467
— medical cleaning equipment, p. II-1675
— medical equipment, p. II-1321
— metal forming machines, p. II-1128
— scanning devices, p. II-1321
— testing equipment, p. II-1366
— welding equipment, p. II-1228
Ultraviolet analytical instruments, p. II-1351
Ultraviolet lamp
— bulbs, p. II-1385
— fixtures, p. II-1389
Umber, p. I-474
Umbrellas, pp. II-1748, III-1915
Uncoated groundwood, p. I-367
Underground mining machinery, p. II-1038
Undertakers' equipment, p. III-1874
Underwater lighting fixtures, p. II-1389
Underwater navigational systems, p. II-1326
Underwear, pp. I-261, 266, 271, 278, 284, III-1915, 1918
— shirts, pp. I-261, 266, 271, 278, 284
— shorts, pp. I-261, 266, 271, 278, 284
Uniforms, pp. III-2137, 2149
— band, pp. I-266, 284
— dress, pp. I-266, 271, 278
— hats and caps, pp. I-266, 289
— nontailored, pp. I-261, 266, 271, 278
— shirts, pp. I-266, 271, 278, 284
— team athletic, pp. I-266, 284
Uninterruptible power supplies, p. II-1467
Union suits, pp. I-261, 266, 271, 278, 284
Unions
— pipe, p. II-979
Unisex clothing, pp. III-1918, 2131
Unit heaters, pp. II-1100, 1396
Unit set forms, p. I-419
Universal joints, pp. II-1167, 1529, 1566
Unleavened bread, p. I-115
Upholstered furniture, p. II-1615
Upholsterers' equipment, p. III-1874
Upholstering filling, p. I-250
Upholstery
— leather, p. I-295
— materials, p. III-2155
  springs, p. II-938
Upper leather, p. I-295
Uppers, p. I-305
Upset forgings, p. I-871

Upsetters, p. II-1128
UPSs, p. II-1467
Uranium oxide, p. I-487
Uranium
— compounds, p. I-487
— enriched, p. I-487
Urea, pp. I-499, 515
Urethane foam products, p. I-640
Urethane rubber, p. I-504
Urinals, pp. I-650, 676, II-1013
Urns, pp. I-751, II-1396
Utility buildings, p. II-898
Utility containers, p. I-650
Utility trailer dealers, p. III-2026
Utility trailers, pp. II-1499, III-1757
V-belts, p. I-664
Vaccines, pp. I-548, III-1908
Vacuum bottles, p. II-927
Vacuum brake boosters, p. II-1523
Vacuum cleaner belts, p. I-664
Vacuum cleaners, pp. II-1091, 1396, III-1834, 2049
Vacuum pumps, pp. II-1183, 1665
Vacuum relays, p. II-1436
Vacuum tanks, p. II-922
Vacuum tube blanks, pp. I-712, 721
Vacuum tubes, p. II-1276
Vacuums
— yard, p. II-1027
Valises, p. I-305
Valonia extract, p. I-492
Valve grinding machines, p. II-1123
Valves, p. III-1870
— engine, p. II-1504
— hydraulic and pneumatic, pp. II-979, III-1866
— industrial, p. II-979
— inline plumbing and heating, p. II-979
— nuclear applications, p. II-979
— plumbing and heating, p. III-1846
— water works, p. II-979
Vamps (leather), p. I-305
Vanillin (synthetic), p. I-492
Vanities, pp. II-1610, 1620, 1631
Vanity cases, p. I-305
Vanity tops, p. II-1610
Vans, pp. II-1477, 1495
Vapor heating controls, p. II-1331
Vapor lamps, p. II-1385
Vapor separating machinery, p. II-1228
Vaporizers, p. II-1396
Variable control instruments, p. II-1336
Variety meats, p. I-101
Varistors, p. II-1296
Varnishes, pp. I-553, III-2003
Vases, pp. I-680, 712, 721, 751
Vat dyes, p. I-474
Vats, pp. II-922, 927
Vaults, pp. II-1013, 1744
VCRs, p. II-1271
Veal, p. I-101
Vegetable alkaloids, p. I-533
Vegetables, pp. I-61, 157, III-1928, 1949
Vehicle scales, p. II-1228
Vehicle stock, p. I-333

Vehicles
— children's, pp. II-1598, 1707, III-1886
— recreational, p. III-1757
Vehicular lighting, p. II-1511
Vellum leather, p. I-295
Velvet, p. I-197
Vending machines, pp. II-1091, III-1808
Veneer and plywood forming machinery, p. II-1045
Veneer baskets, p. I-342
Veneer work, p. I-357
Venetian blinds, pp. I-333, II-1661
Ventilating equipment, p. III-1850
Ventilating fans, p. II-1111
Ventilating kitchen fans, p. II-1396
Ventilation and exhaust fans, p. II-1396
Ventilators, p. II-907
Vermiculite, p. I-766
Vermifuge preparations, p. I-538
Vermilion pigments, p. I-474
Vermouth, p. I-176
Vertical blinds, p. II-1661
Vessels (heavy gauge metal), p. II-922
Vestments
— academic and clerical, pp. I-266, 284
Vests, pp. I-266, 284
— nontailored, pp. I-271, 278
— tailored, pp. I-271, 278
Veterinarians' equipment, p. III-1819
Veterinarians' instruments, p. II-1670
Veterinarians' medicines, p. III-1908
Veterinary medicinal preparations, p. I-538
Vibraphones, p. II-1730
Vibration meters, p. II-1366
Vibrators (concrete), p. II-1032
Video cameras, pp. II-1271, III-1797, 1834
Video cassettes, pp. II-1375, 1380
— recorders, p. II-1271
Video game machines, p. II-1707
Video tapes, pp. II-1375, III-2167
— blank, pp. II-1380, III-1838
Vinegar, p. I-151
Vinyl acetate, p. I-492
Vinyl acetate resins, p. I-499
Vinyl and vinyl copolymer film, p. I-614
Vinyl chloride resins, p. I-499
Vinyl coated fabrics, p. I-223
Vinyl fibers and filaments, p. I-509
Vinyl floor coverings, p. I-650
Vinyl resins, p. I-499
Vinyl siding, p. III-1789
Vinyl upper athletic footwear, p. I-299
Vinylidene chloride fiber, p. I-509
Vinylidene resins, p. I-499
Violas and parts, p. II-1730
Violins and parts, p. II-1730
Viral diagnostic test substances, p. I-543
Virus vaccines, p. I-548
Viscose fibers, p. I-509
Viscosimeters, p. II-1366
Viscosity instruments, p. II-1336
Vises, p. II-891
Vitamin preparations, p. I-538
Vitamins, pp. I-533, III-1908, 2109
Voltage regulators, pp. II-1286, 1420, 1511, III-1830
Voltmeters, p. II-1346

Numbers following p. or pp. are page references. Roman numerals indicate volume numbers. Page references are to the starting pages of the industries that produce the product or carry out the activity.

Voting machines, pp. II-1076, III-1874
Vulcanized fiber products, p. I-378
Vulcanized oils, p. I-504
Vulcanizing machinery, p. II-1050
Wads (ammunition), p. II-992
Wafer processing equipment, p. II-1055
Waferboard, p. I-318
Wafers (semiconductor), p. II-1286
Waffle, p. I-61
Waffle irons, p. II-1396
Wagons
— children's, p. II-1707
— farm, p. II-1022
— lawn and garden, p. II-1027
Wainscots, p. I-333
Walkers (baby), p. II-1707
Walkways (moving), p. II-1193
Wall clocks, p. II-1361
Wall coverings, p. III-2003
Wall lamps, p. II-1389
Wall tile, p. I-694
Wallboard, pp. I-751, III-1781
Wallets, pp. I-305, II-1695
Wallpaper, pp. I-387, III-2003
Wallpaper cleaners, p. I-565
Wardrobe bags, p. I-305
Wardrobes, pp. II-1620, 1631
Warehouse clubs, p. III-2176
Warehouses, p. II-898
Warm air heating equipment, p. III-1850
Warming trays, p. II-1396
Warmup suits, pp. I-261, 266, 271, 278, 284
Warp fabrics, p. I-212
Warping machinery, p. II-1060
Washboards, p. I-357
Washers (aggregate and sand), p. II-1038
Washers (metal), p. II-957
Washing machines, pp. II-1091, 1412
Waste materials, p. III-1889
Wastebaskets, p. I-378
Watch bands, pp. I-305, II-1695
Watch batteries, p. II-1446
Watch crystals, pp. I-650, 721
Watch jewels, p. II-1361
Watch shops, p. III-2143
Watchcases, p. II-1361
Watches and parts, pp. II-1361, III-1893
Water, pp. I-538, II-1105
Water bed frames, pp. II-1620, 1631
Water bed mattresses, p. II-1656
Water closet bowls, p. I-676
Water closets, p. II-1013
Water colors (artist's), p. II-1713
Water coolers, p. III-1854
Water heater controls, p. II-1331
Water heaters, pp. II-1091, 1416, III-1834, 1846
Water hoses, p. I-664
Water leak detectors, p. II-1366
Water pipe (cast iron), p. I-844
Water pulsating devices, p. II-1396
Water purification equipment, p. II-1091
Water quality monitoring systems, p. II-1336
Water softening compounds, p. III-1970
Water softening equipment, pp. II-1091, III-1846
Water tanks, p. II-922

Water traps, p. II-973
Water treatment equipment, pp. II-1091, III-1866, 1874
Water turbines, p. II-1156
Water well drilling machinery, p. II-1038
Water
— artificially carbonated, p. I-164
— bottled, pp. I-164, III-1953, 2093
— distilled, p. I-594
— flavored, p. I-164
Watering cans, p. I-650
Watermeters, p. II-1341
Watt-hour meters, p. II-1346
Wattle extract, p. I-492
Wattmeters, p. II-1346
Waveform measuring equipment, p. II-1346
Wax figures, p. II-1748
Wax removers, p. I-565
Waxed paper, pp. I-387, III-1904
Waxes, pp. I-442, 462, 565, III-1970
Weapons (self-propelled), p. II-1602
Weather stripping, pp. I-250, 333, II-907, III-1789
Weather tracking equipment, p. II-1366
Weather vanes, p. II-1228
Weatherproof wire, pp. I-815, 829
Weaving
— machinery, p. II-1060
Webbing (cane, reed, and rattan), p. I-357
Wedding dresses, pp. I-266, 278
Weeding machines, p. II-1022
Weft fabrics knitting, p. I-212
Welded iron, p. I-792
Welders' aprons, p. I-305
Welders' hoods, p. II-1675
Welders' jackets, p. I-305
Welding equipment, p. II-1228
Welding gases, p. III-1970
Welding machinery, p. III-1866
Welding positioners, p. II-1133
Welding rods, p. I-836
Welding supplies, p. III-1870
Welding wire or rods, p. II-1228
Weldments, p. II-898
Well casings, pp. I-779, 787
Well logging equipment, p. II-1038
Wells (light, sheet metal), pp. II-907
Welting leather, p. I-295
Western wear, p. III-2131
Wet blues, p. I-295
Wet laid nonwoven fabrics, p. I-207
Wet machine board mills, p. I-373
Wet milling corn, p. I-21
Wet suits, p. II-1701
Wetting agents, p. I-565
Wheat bran, p. I-14
Wheat breakfast cereal, p. I-35
Wheat flour, p. I-14
Wheat germ, p. I-14
Wheat malt, p. I-14
Wheatstone bridges, p. II-1346
Wheelbarrows, p. II-1193
Wheelchairs, pp. II-1675, III-1812
Wheels, pp. I-755, II-1550
— abrasive, p. I-755
— car and locomotive, p. I-779

— motor vehicle, p. III-1761
— position indicators, p. II-1326
— pullers, p. II-891
— steering, p. II-1518
Whetstones, p. I-755
Whey, pp. I-75, 80
Whey butter, p. I-85
Whipped topping, pp. I-61, 80, 85
Whippers (household), p. II-1396
Whipping cream, p. I-85
Whips (horse), p. I-305
Whipstocks, p. I-305
Whirlpool baths, pp. II-1675, III-1812
White extender pigments, p. I-474
White metal castings, p. I-856
Whiting, p. I-474
Whole body counters (nuclear), p. II-1366
Wicker furniture, p. II-1631
Wicks, p. I-202
Wide area network equipment, p. II-1256
Wigs, pp. II-1748, III-2134
Willow and willow products, pp. I-357, II-1631
Winches, pp. II-1193, III-1866
Wind direction indicators, p. II-1366
Wind turbines, p. II-1156
Windbreakers, pp. I-266, 271, 278, 284
Winding machinery (textiles), p. II-1060
Windmills, pp. II-1022, 1156
Windows, pp. I-333, II-907
— cleaners, p. I-565
— frames, pp. I-333, 650, II-907, III-1781
— screening, p. II-938
— screens, pp. I-333, II-907
— shade rollers, p. II-1661
— shades, pp. II-1661, III-1777
— treatments, p. III-2043
— trim, p. I-333
— units, p. I-333
Windshield wipers, pp. II-1511, 1550
Windshields, p. I-650
— washer pumps, p. II-1511
Wine coolers, pp. I-176, III-1986
Wineries, p. I-176
Wines, pp. I-176, III-1986, 2096
Wintergreen oil, p. I-594
Wipers (windshield), p. II-1550
Wipes (fabric), p. I-207
Wiping cloths, p. III-1870
Wire, p. III-1823
— armored, p. I-815
— bare, p. I-815
— copper, p. I-829
— flat, rolled strip, pp. I-792
— insulated, pp. I-815, III-1830
— iron or steel, p. I-792
— mechanical, p. I-829
— nonferrous metals, p. I-836
Wire and cable, p. III-1823
Wire and cable insulating machinery, p. II-1060
Wire cages, p. I-792
Wire carts, p. I-792
Wire cloth, pp. I-792, 815, 829, 836
Wire garment hangers, p. I-792
Wire products, pp. I-779, 792
Wire rope, p. III-1823

Numbers following p. or pp. are page references. Roman numerals indicate volume numbers. Page references are to the starting pages of the industries that produce the product or carry out the activity.

Wire rope hoists, p. II-1193
Wire screening, pp. I-815, 836, III-1823
Wiredrawing dies, p. II-1133
Wiredrawing machinery, p. II-1151
Wiring harness, p. II-1511
Wiring supplies, p. III-1830
Witch hazel extract, p. I-492
Women's clothing, p. III-1918
Wood alcohol, p. I-492
Wood burning stoves, p. III-2046
Wood chips, p. I-311
Wood cutting saw blades, p. II-891
Wood distillates, p. I-492
Wood door frames and sash, p. I-333
Wood drying kilns, p. II-1060
Wood fencing, pp. I-311, III-1781
Wood fillers, p. I-553
Wood flooring, pp. I-333, III-1781
Wood flour, p. I-357
Wood framed furniture, p. II-1615
Wood heel blocks, p. I-357
Wood heels (finished), p. I-357
Wood I-joists, p. I-328
Wood moldings, p. I-333
Wood oils, p. I-492
Wood products, p. I-311
Wood pulp, p. I-362
Wood shingles, p. III-1781
Wood shutters, p. I-333
Wood siding, p. III-1781
Wood stoves, p. II-1100
Wood treating preparations, p. III-1970
Wood verneer laminating machines, p. II-1045
Wood window frames and sash, p. I-333
Wood wool (excelsior), p. I-357
Woodenware (kitchen), p. I-357
Woodworking machinery, p. III-1866
Woodworking machines, p. II-1045
Wool and worsted finishing machinery, p. II-1060
Wool
— fabrics, pp. I-197, 202
— raw, p. III-1964
— spun yarn, p. I-191
— tops and noils, pp. I-217, III-1964
— yarns, p. I-191
Worcestershire sauce, p. I-151
Word processing equipment, p. II-1076
Work benches, p. II-1626
Work clothing, p. III-1915
Work coats and jackets, pp. I-266, 271
Work gloves, pp. I-261, 266, 289
Work pants, pp. I-266, 271
Work shirts, pp. I-266, 271
Work shoes, p. I-299
Workstations (computer), p. II-1237
Worsted fabrics, p. I-197
Wrappers
— excelsior, p. I-357
Wrapping, p. II-1211
Wrapping paper, p. III-1904
Wreaths, p. II-1748
Wrenches, pp. II-891, 1206
Writing inks, p. I-594
Writing paper, pp. I-367, 402, III-1900
Wrought iron furniture, p. II-1631

Wrought iron or steel pipe, pp. I-779, II-1008
X-mas tree light bulbs, p. II-1385
X-ray
— apparatus and tubes, p. II-1356
— film and plates (sensitized), p. I-594
— generators, p. II-1356
— irradiation equipment, p. II-1356
— machines and parts, p. III-1812
— tubes, p. II-1356
X-Y recorders, p. II-1346
Xanthone insecticides, p. I-528
Xylene, pp. I-442, 466
Xylophones, p. II-1730
Yachts, pp. II-1588, 1593
Yard goods, p. III-1912
Yard lights, p. II-1389
Yardsticks, pp. I-357, II-891
Yarn, p. I-191
— cellulosic filament, p. I-509
— fiberglass, p. I-712
— noncellulosic, p. I-509
Yarn texturizing machines, p. II-1060
Yearbooks, p. I-419
Yeast, pp. I-157, III-1953
Yogurt, pp. I-80, 85, 91, III-1932
Zein fibers, p. I-509
Zinc, pp. I-824, 836
— compounds, p. I-487
— die-castings, p. I-856
— dust reclaiming, p. I-836
— foil and leaf, p. II-1013
— shapes, p. I-836
Zinc ammonium chloride, p. I-487
Zinc chloride, p. I-487
Zinc hydrosulfite, p. I-487
Zinc oxide, p. I-487
Zinc oxide medicinals, p. I-538
Zinc sulfide, p. I-487
Zipper making machinery, p. II-1060
Zipper tape, p. I-202
Zippers, pp. II-1734, III-1912
Zirconium, p. I-836
Zirconium refining, p. I-824
Zirconium shapes, p. I-836
Zithers, p. II-1730

Numbers following p. or pp. are page references. Roman numerals indicate volume numbers. Page references are to the starting pages of the industries that produce the product or carry out the activity.

COMPANY INDEX

This index shows, in alphabetical order, more than 18,300 companies in *Manufacturing and Distribution USA, 4th Edition*. Organizations may be public or private companies, subsidiaries or divisions of companies, joint ventures or affiliates, or corporate groups. Each company entry is followed by one or more page numbers preceded by a volume number ("I-", "II-", or "III-") in the case of single appearances or the phrase "Vol. I", etc., in the case of multiple appearances. After the page numbers, the NAICS under which the company is listed follows in brackets. Some company names may be abbreviated.

1-800 CONTACTS Inc., pp. Vol. II-1082, Vol. III-2107 [NAICS 333314, 446130]

1-800-Flowers.com Inc., p. III-2183 [NAICS 453110]

1-Rex Inc., p. III-2058 [NAICS 443120]

1928 Jewelry Co., pp. Vol. II-1696, Vol. III-1894 [NAICS 33991M, 423940]

20th Century Fiberglass Inc., p. II-1500 [NAICS 336214]

21st Amendments Inc., p. III-2097 [NAICS 445310]

21st Century Christian, p. III-2162 [NAICS 451211]

21st Century Optics Inc., p. II-1687 [NAICS 339115]

21st Century Technologies Inc., p. II-1749 [NAICS 339999]

2nd Avenue Design, p. II-1632 [NAICS 33712N]

2nd Swing Inc., p. III-1883 [NAICS 423910]

2Wire Inc., p. II-1257 [NAICS 334210]

3-D Service Ltd., p. II-1162 [NAICS 333612]

3 Day Blinds Inc., pp. Vol. II-1662, Vol. III-2047 [NAICS 337920, 442299]

3-V Chemical Corp., p. I-493 [NAICS 32519M]

31 Inc., p. I-660 [NAICS 32621M]

360 Services International, p. III-1898 [NAICS 424110]

3Com Corp., pp. Vol. II-1252, 1257, 1267, 1457 [NAICS 334119, 334210, 334290, 33593M]

3E, p. I-1427 [NAICS 335312]

3M, p. I-756 [NAICS 327910]

3M Co., pp. Vol. I-388, 534, 560, 776, Vol. II-1082, 1322, 1381, 1682 [NAICS 32222N, 325411, 325520, 327999, 333314, 334510, 334613, 339114]

3M Touch Systems, p. II-1272 [NAICS 334310]

3M Visual Systems Div., p. II-1381 [NAICS 334613]

4Life Research L.C., p. I-534 [NAICS 325411]

5 B's Inc., p. I-251 [NAICS 314999]

7-Eleven Inc., p. III-2094 [NAICS 445299]

7-Up Corp., pp. Vol. I-165, Vol. III-1954 [NAICS 31211M, 424490]

80/20 Inc., p. I-811 [NAICS 331316]

800-JR Cigar Inc., p. III-2001 [NAICS 424940]

84 Lumber Co., p. III-2065 [NAICS 444100]

877 Spirits Inc., p. III-1987 [NAICS 424820]

99 Cent Stuff L.L.C., p. III-2180 [NAICS 452990]

99 Cents Only Stores, p. III-2180 [NAICS 452990]

A-1 Babbitt Company Inc., p. I-825 [NAICS 331419]

A-1 Carbide Corp., p. II-1725 [NAICS 339991]

A and A Chemical Products, p. III-1875 [NAICS 423850]

A and A Mechanical Inc., p. III-1851 [NAICS 423730]

A and B Process Systems Corp., pp. Vol. II-980, 1014, 1194, 1337 [NAICS 33291N, 33299N, 33392M, 334513]

A and B Tube Benders Inc., p. II-1524 [NAICS 336340]

A and D Engineering Inc., p. III-1809 [NAICS 423440]

A and E Stores Inc., p. III-2135 [NAICS 448150]

A and H Manufacturing Co., pp. Vol. I-388, 415, Vol. II-1212 [NAICS 32222N, 322299, 333993]

A and H Sportswear Company Inc., pp. Vol. I-272, 279 [NAICS 31522M, 31523M]

A and J Manufacturing L.L.C., p. II-1404 [NAICS 335221]

A and J Technical Supply Co., p. I-660 [NAICS 32621M]

A and J Washroom Accessories, p. II-1189 [NAICS 333913]

A and K Railroad Materials Inc., p. III-1831 [NAICS 423610]

A and L Shielding Inc., p. II-1357 [NAICS 334517]

A and M Sales, p. III-1863 [NAICS 423820]

A and P Recycling Inc., p. I-807 [NAICS 331314]

A and R Auto Salvage Inc., p. III-1770 [NAICS 423140]

A and S of Modesto Inc., p. III-1890 [NAICS 423930]

A and S Tribal Industries, p. I-244 [NAICS 314991]

A and V of The Triad Inc., p. III-1835 [NAICS 423620]

A and W Oil Company Inc., p. III-1975 [NAICS 424710]

A. Biederman Inc., pp. Vol. III-1867, 1879 [NAICS 423830, 423860]

A. Daigger and Company Inc., pp. Vol. III-1820, 1971 [NAICS 423490, 424690]

A-DEC Inc., pp. Vol. II-1222, 1390, 1611, 1682 [NAICS 33399N, 33512M, 337110, 339114]

A Duda and Sons Inc., pp. Vol. I-62, 68 [NAICS 31141M, 31142M]

A. Finkl and Sons Co., pp. Vol. I-872, Vol. II-1134 [NAICS 33211N, 333514]

A. Frank and Sons Inc., p. III-1913 [NAICS 424310]

A Jaffe Sandberg & Sikorski Corp., p. II-1696 [NAICS 33991M]

A Leventhal and Sons Inc., p. III-1813 [NAICS 423450]

A-Line Products Corp., p. I-505 [NAICS 325212]

A-Mark Financial Corp., p. III-1894 [NAICS 423940]

A-One Laminating Corp., p. I-224 [NAICS 313320]

A. Pomerantz and Co., p. III-1774 [NAICS 423210]

A Rifkin Co., p. I-239 [NAICS 31491M]

A-Roo Co., pp. Vol. I-395, 603 [NAICS 32222P, 326111]

A. Sam Farm Inc., p. III-1950 [NAICS 424480]

A Schonbek and Company Inc., p. II-1390 [NAICS 33512M]

A. Schulman Inc., p. I-589 [NAICS 325991]

A Smith Bowman Distillery, p. I-181 [NAICS 312140]

A. Teichert and Son Inc., p. I-732 [NAICS 327320]

A To Z Drying, p. I-529 [NAICS 325320]

A Z-Tech Inc., p. I-830 [NAICS 33142M]

A Zerega's Sons Inc., p. I-124 [NAICS 31182M]

A1 Radiator Repair Inc., p. III-2030 [NAICS 441310]

A1 Wireless USA Inc., p. III-2054 [NAICS 443112]

AAA Glass Corp., p. I-718 [NAICS 327213]

AAA Tire Finishing Equipment, p. I-660 [NAICS 32621M]

Aadlen Brothers Auto Wrecking, p. III-1890 [NAICS 423930]

AAF International, pp. Vol. I-771, Vol. II-1101, 1112, 1229 [NAICS 327993, 333414, 33341N, 33399P]

AAF-McQuay Inc., pp. Vol. II-1101, 1106, 1112, 1217, 1229 [NAICS 333414, 333415, 33341N, 333994, 33399P]

AAI Corp., pp. Vol. II-1005, 1229, 1327, 1337 [NAICS 332995, 33399P, 334511, 334513]

Aakron Rule Corp., p. II-1714 [NAICS 33994M]

AAON Inc., p. II-1106 [NAICS 333415]

Aaper Alcohol and Blaze Products, p. I-493 [NAICS 32519M]

AAR Corp., pp. Vol. II-1194, 1567, Vol. III-1879 [NAICS 33392M, 336413, 423860]

AARCEE Party Rentals Inc., p. III-2150 [NAICS 451110]

Aargus Plastics Inc., p. I-603 [NAICS 326111]

Aarhus United USA Inc., p. I-26 [NAICS 311225]

Aaron and Company Inc., p. III-1851 [NAICS 423730]

Aaron Rents Inc., pp. Vol. II-1616, 1621, 1650, Vol. III-2037 [NAICS 337121, 337122, 33721N, 442110]

Aas Amjet Inc., p. III-1879 [NAICS 423860]

AB and B Auto Parts Inc., p. III-1770 [NAICS 423140]

AB Carter Inc., p. II-1666 [NAICS 339111]

A.B. Dick Co., p. III-1801 [NAICS 423420]

Abarta Inc., p. I-165 [NAICS 31211M]

Abatix Corp., p. III-1871 [NAICS 423840]

Abaxis Inc., p. II-1322 [NAICS 334510]

ABB Air Preheater Inc., p. II-1101 [NAICS 333414]

ABB Automation Analytical Div., p. II-1352 [NAICS 334516]

ABB Optical North America, p. III-1817 [NAICS 423460]

ABB Power T and D Company Inc., pp. Vol. II-1421, 1432 [NAICS 335311, 335313]

ABB SSAC Inc., p. II-1332 [NAICS 334512]

Abbey Party Rents of San Diego, p. III-2190 [NAICS 453220]

Abbott Hospital Products Div., p. II-1671 [NAICS 339112]

Abbott Industries Inc., pp. Vol. I-646, Vol. II-1397 [NAICS 326160, 33521M]

Abbott Laboratories, pp. Vol. I-68, 539, 575, Vol. II-1671 [NAICS 31142M, 325412, 325620, 339112]

Abbott Laboratories Diagnostic, pp. Vol. II-1352, 1671 [NAICS 334516, 339112]

Abbott Laboratories, Ross Products, pp. Vol. I-68, 81, 539 [NAICS 31142M, 311514, 325412]

Abbott's Candy and Gifts, pp. Vol. I-48, Vol. III-2092 [NAICS 311320, 445292]

Abbott's Premium Ice Cream Inc., p. III-1933 [NAICS 424430]

ABC Appliance Inc., p. III-2054 [NAICS 443112]

ABC Battery Company Inc., pp. Vol. II-1442, 1447 [NAICS 335911, 335912]

ABC Carpet Company Inc., p. III-2041 [NAICS 442210]

ABC Fine Wine and Spirits, p. III-2097 [NAICS 445310]

ABC Inc., p. III-1828 [NAICS 423520]

ABC Industries Inc., p. III-1809 [NAICS 423440]

ABC International Traders Inc., pp. Vol. III-1835, 1887 [NAICS 423620, 423920]

ABC Minneapolis L.L.C., p. III-1758 [NAICS 423110]

ABC Salvage Corp., p. I-363 [NAICS 322110]

ABC School Equipment Inc., pp. Vol. II-1087, 1714 [NAICS 333315, 33994M]

ABC Supply, p. III-1790 [NAICS 423330]

ABCO Automation Inc., p. II-1212 [NAICS 333993]

Abco Corp., p. II-1404 [NAICS 335221]

ABCO Laboratories Inc., p. I-534 [NAICS 325411]

ABCO Refrigeration Supply Corp., pp. Vol. III-1851, 1855 [NAICS 423730, 423740]

Abdallah Candies Inc., pp. Vol. I-48, 57 [NAICS 311320, 311340]

Abdite Industries Inc., p. II-1562 [NAICS 336412]

ABE Corp., p. III-1774 [NAICS 423210]

Abe's French Market Foods, p. III-2083 [NAICS 445210]

Abell Corp., pp. Vol. III-1968, 1991 [NAICS 424610, 424910]

Abercrombie and Fitch Co., p. III-2132 [NAICS 448140]

Aberdeen L.L.C., p. II-1238 [NAICS 334111]

Abernathy Co., p. I-566 [NAICS 32561M]

Abgenix Inc., p. I-549 [NAICS 325414]

Abilene Machine Inc., pp. Vol. II-1173, 1505 [NAICS 333618, 33631M]

Abington Pharmacy Inc., p. III-2100 [NAICS 446110]

Able Coil and Electronics Inc., p. II-1297 [NAICS 334415]

Able Energy Inc., pp. Vol. III-1851, 2218 [NAICS 423730, 454311]

Able Manufacturing L.L.C., p. II-1486 [NAICS 336211]

Able Oil Co., p. III-2218 [NAICS 454311]

ABM Equipment and Supply Inc., p. III-1859 [NAICS 423810]

Abraham Technical Services Inc., p. II-1077 [NAICS 333313]

Abrams Instrument Corp., p. II-1362 [NAICS 334518]

Abrisa Glass & Coating, p. I-709 [NAICS 327211]

ABS Alaskan Inc., p. II-1442 [NAICS 335911]

ABS Computer Technologies Inc., p. II-1238 [NAICS 334111]

Abuelita Mexican Food Products, p. I-133 [NAICS 311830]

AC Furniture Company Inc., pp. Vol. II-1616, 1627 [NAICS 337121, 337127]

AC Houston Lumber Co., pp. Vol. I-329, Vol. III-1782, 1794 [NAICS 32121P, 423310, 423390]

AC Installations By Rusher Inc., pp. Vol. III-1851, 2208 [NAICS 423730, 453998]

A.C. Moore Arts and Crafts Inc., p. III-2208 [NAICS 453998]

A.C. Moore Inc., p. III-2153 [NAICS 451120]

AC Technology Corp., p. II-1162 [NAICS 333612]

AC World of Products, p. III-2007 [NAICS 424990]

Academy Ltd., p. III-2150 [NAICS 451110]

Acadia Industries Inc., p. I-603 [NAICS 326111]

Acadia Polymers Corp., pp. Vol. I-670, Vol. II-945 [NAICS 32629M, 332710]

Acambis Inc., p. I-549 [NAICS 325414]

Acar Industries Inc., p. II-1607 [NAICS 336999]

ACC Recycling Corp., p. III-1890 [NAICS 423930]

Acc Systems Inc., p. III-2058 [NAICS 443120]

Accent Fabrics Inc., p. I-203 [NAICS 31322M]

Accent Marble Company Inc., p. I-762 [NAICS 327991]

Accents Unlimited Inc., p. III-2007 [NAICS 424990]

Accesories That Matter, p. III-1919 [NAICS 424330]

Access Battery & Power Systems, p. II-1442 [NAICS 335911]

Access Business Group Nutrilite, p. I-165 [NAICS 31211M]

Accessory Exchange L.L.C., p. III-1919 [NAICS 424330]

ACCO World Corp., pp. Vol. I-379, 420, Vol. II-1077, 1238, 1650 [NAICS 32221M, 32311M, 333313, 334111, 33721N]

Accraply Inc., pp. Vol. II-1061, 1212 [NAICS 33329N, 333993]

Accratronics Seals Corp., p. II-1005 [NAICS 332995]

Accu-Router Inc., p. II-1046 [NAICS 333210]

Accu-Therm Inc., p. II-1101 [NAICS 333414]

Accu-Time Systems Inc., p. II-1362 [NAICS 334518]

Accubuilt Inc., pp. Vol. II-1486, 1607 [NAICS 336211, 336999]

AccuCorp, p. I-147 [NAICS 311930]

Accumed Technologies Inc., p. I-285 [NAICS 31529M]

Accumetric L.L.C., pp. Vol. I-560, Vol. II-1033, 1189, 1432 [NAICS 325520, 333120, 333913, 335313]

Accurate Arms Co., p. I-585 [NAICS 325920]

Accurate Cos., p. I-585 [NAICS 325920]

Accurate Foam Co., p. I-505 [NAICS 325212]

Accurate Measurement Controls, p. II-1342 [NAICS 334514]

Accurate Metal Fabricators Inc., p. II-1312 [NAICS 334418]

Accurate Office Supply Inc., p. III-1901 [NAICS 424120]

Accurate Paper Recycling Inc., p. I-363 [NAICS 322110]

Accurate Transmissions Inc., pp. Vol. II-1512, 1530 [NAICS 33632M, 336350]

Accuride Corp., p. II-1486 [NAICS 336211]

Accusplit Inc., p. II-1362 [NAICS 334518]

Accutrex Clocks, p. II-1362 [NAICS 334518]

ACCUTRONICS Inc., p. II-1238 [NAICS 334111]

ACD Inc., p. II-1157 [NAICS 333611]

Ace Cleaners & Reconditioners, p. III-1883 [NAICS 423910]

Ace Coffee Bar Inc.,.p. III-2215 [NAICS 454210]

Ace Drive Products & Servics Inc., p. III-2030 [NAICS 441310]

Ace Educational Supplies Inc., p. III-1820 [NAICS 423490]

Ace Hardware Corp., pp. Vol. I-554, Vol. III-1843 [NAICS 325510, 423710]

Ace Holdings, p. II-1696 [NAICS 33991M]

Ace Manufacturing and Parts Co., p. II-1530 [NAICS 336350]

Ace Mart Restaurant Supply Co., pp. Vol. III-1831, 1843, 2208 [NAICS 423610, 423710, 453998]

Ace Metal Co., p. III-1890 [NAICS 423930]

Ace Reprographic Service Inc., p. III-2186 [NAICS 453210]

Ace-Tex Enterprises Inc., pp. Vol. I-234, 251 [NAICS 31412M, 314999]

Ace Tool Co., pp. Vol. III-1843, 1867 [NAICS 423710, 423830]

AceCo Precision Mfg Inc., p. II-886 [NAICS 33221N]

Acer America Corp., pp. Vol. II-1238, 1252 [NAICS 334111, 334119]

Aceto Corp., p. III-1971 [NAICS 424690]

Numbers following p. or pp. are page references. Roman numerals indicate volume numbers. Bracketed items indicate industries. Page references are to the starting pages of company tables.

Acetylene Gas Co., p. I-471 [NAICS 325120]

ACG Holdings Inc., p. I-420 [NAICS 32311M]

ACH Food Companies Inc., pp. Vol. I-26, 158 [NAICS 311225, 31199M]

Achieva, p. I-343 [NAICS 321920]

Achilles USA Inc., p. I-615 [NAICS 326113]

Ackner Fuels Inc., p. III-2218 [NAICS 454311]

ACM Products Co., p. I-756 [NAICS 327910]

ACMA Computers Inc., p. II-1238 [NAICS 334111]

Acme Alliance L.L.C., pp. Vol. I-837, 845, 852, 857 [NAICS 33149M, 33151M, 33152N, 33152P]

Acme Boiler Company Inc., p. I-825 [NAICS 331419]

Acme Copy Corp., p. III-2186 [NAICS 453210]

Acme Electric Corp., p. II-1442 [NAICS 335911]

Acme Lawn and Garden Co., pp. Vol. I-529, Vol. II-892 [NAICS 325320, 33221P]

Acme Linen Co., p. III-1913 [NAICS 424310]

Acme-McCrary Corp., p. I-256 [NAICS 31511M]

Acme Mills Co., pp. Vol. I-224, 251 [NAICS 313320, 314999]

Acme Paper and Supply Inc., p. III-1905 [NAICS 424130]

Acme Recording Inc., p. II-1376 [NAICS 334612]

Acme Refrigeration of Baton, pp. Vol. III-1851, 1855 [NAICS 423730, 423740]

Acme Scale, p. III-1820 [NAICS 423490]

Acme Trading Corp., pp. Vol. III-1774, 1778 [NAICS 423210, 423220]

Acme United Corp., pp. Vol. I-358, Vol. II-886, 892 [NAICS 321999, 33221N, 33221P]

Acme Vial and Glass Company, p. I-718 [NAICS 327213]

ACMI Corp., pp. Vol. II-1671, 1749 [NAICS 339112, 339999]

ACO Optical Lab, p. III-1817 [NAICS 423460]

Acor Orthopedic Inc., p. I-300 [NAICS 31621M]

Acorn Petroleum Inc., p. III-1975 [NAICS 424710]

Acorn Products Inc., pp. Vol. I-256, Vol. II-892, 1607 [NAICS 31511M, 33221P, 336999]

Acosta Sales Co., p. III-1929 [NAICS 424420]

ACR Electronics Inc., pp. Vol. II-1386, 1390 [NAICS 335110, 33512M]

ACR Group Inc., pp. Vol. II-1332, Vol. III-1851, 1855 [NAICS 334512, 423730, 423740]

ACR Supply Inc., pp. Vol. III-1851, 1855 [NAICS 423730, 423740]

Acroprint Time Recorder Co., pp. Vol. II-1248, 1362, Vol. III-1901 [NAICS 334113, 334518, 424120]

Acrowood Corp., p. II-1046 [NAICS 333210]

ACT Electronics Inc., p. II-1282 [NAICS 334412]

Actaris, p. II-1342 [NAICS 334514]

Actaris Metering Systems, pp. Vol. II-1342, 1432 [NAICS 334514, 335313]

Acterna Corp., pp. Vol. II-1252, 1257, 1262, 1267, 1272, 1347 [NAICS 334119, 334210, 334220, 334290, 334310, 334515]

Actimize Inc., p. III-2058 [NAICS 443120]

Action Duplication Inc., p. II-1381 [NAICS 334613]

Action Inc., p. I-306 [NAICS 31699M]

Action Manufacturing Inc., pp. Vol. I-585, Vol. II-997, 1005, 1432 [NAICS 325920, 332993, 332995, 335313]

Action Performance Companies, pp. Vol. I-272, 279, 626, 713, Vol. II-1708 [NAICS 31522M, 31523M, 326122, 327212, 33993M]

Action Products Co., p. II-1594 [NAICS 336612]

Action Products International Inc., p. II-1708 [NAICS 33993M]

Active Chemical Systems Inc., p. II-1463 [NAICS 335991]

Acton Research Corp., pp. Vol. I-722, Vol. II-1352 [NAICS 327215, 334516]

Actown-Electrocoil Inc., pp. Vol. II-1302, 1421 [NAICS 334416, 335311]

Actuality Systems Inc., p. II-1248 [NAICS 334113]

Actuant Corp., pp. Vol. II-1140, 1551 [NAICS 333515, 336399]

Acu-Grind Tool Works Inc., pp. Vol. II-892, 945, 1124, 1140 [NAICS 33221P, 332710, 333512, 333515]

Acucote Inc., p. I-415 [NAICS 322299]

Acuity Brands Inc., p. III-1971 [NAICS 424690]

Acupowder International L.L.C., pp. Vol. I-807, 830 [NAICS 331314, 33142M]

AcuSport Corp., p. III-1883 [NAICS 423910]

Acutrack Inc., p. II-1381 [NAICS 334613]

Ad-A-Day Calendar Co., p. I-374 [NAICS 322130]

AD Electronics Inc., p. II-1297 [NAICS 334415]

Ad Industries Inc., p. I-609 [NAICS 326112]

A.D. Wynne Company Inc., p. III-1774 [NAICS 423210]

ADA Coca-Cola & Dr Pepper, p. III-2222 [NAICS 454312]

Adalet, p. I-852 [NAICS 33152N]

Adam Metal Products Co., p. II-1386 [NAICS 335110]

Adams Apple Distributing L.P., p. III-2001 [NAICS 424940]

Adams Building Materials Inc., pp. Vol. I-329, Vol. III-1782 [NAICS 32121P, 423310]

Adams-Burch Inc., p. III-1875 [NAICS 423850]

Adams Fertilizer Equipment, p. II-1023 [NAICS 333111]

Adams Golf Inc., p. II-1702 [NAICS 339920]

Adams Outdoor Advertising L.P., p. II-1720 [NAICS 339950]

Adams Resources and Energy Inc., p. III-1975 [NAICS 424710]

Adams Rite Manufacturing Co., p. II-1332 [NAICS 334512]

Adams Vegetable Oil Inc., p. I-26 [NAICS 311225]

Adaptec Inc., p. II-1252 [NAICS 334119]

Adaptive Electronics, pp. Vol. I-1282, 1347 [NAICS 334412, 334515]

Adaptive Micro Systems Inc., p. II-1720 [NAICS 339950]

Adapto Inc., p. II-952 [NAICS 332721]

ADC Telecommunications Inc., pp. Vol. II-1252, 1257, 1262, 1267, 1317, 1322 [NAICS 334119, 334210, 334220, 334290, 334419, 334510]

Adco Inc., p. I-560 [NAICS 325520]

ADCO Manufacturing, p. II-1212 [NAICS 333993]

ADCOLE Corp., p. II-1580 [NAICS 336419]

Adcolor Screenprinting Inc., p. II-1536 [NAICS 336360]

Addax Inc., p. I-510 [NAICS 32522M]

Addco Inc., p. II-1332 [NAICS 334512]

Addison Machine Engineering Inc., p. II-1147 [NAICS 333516]

Addison McKee Tube Forming, p. II-1147 [NAICS 333516]

Addison Products Co., p. II-1217 [NAICS 333994]

Addvantage Technologies Group, p. II-1077 [NAICS 333313]

ADE Corp., pp. Vol. II-1347, 1367 [NAICS 334515, 334519]

Adele Fashion Knits, p. I-262 [NAICS 31519M]

Adele Knits Inc., pp. Vol. I-213, 234 [NAICS 31324M, 31412M]

Adell Plastics Inc., p. I-589 [NAICS 325991]

Ademco Group, p. II-1267 [NAICS 334290]

ADESA Inc., p. III-1758 [NAICS 423110]

ADESA St Louis, p. III-1758 [NAICS 423110]

Adesta Communications Inc., p. II-1367 [NAICS 334519]

ADH Health Products Inc., p. III-1909 [NAICS 424210]

Adheron Coatings Corp., pp. Vol. I-554, 560 [NAICS 325510, 325520]

Adhesives Research Inc., pp. Vol. I-388, 560, 615, 631 [NAICS 32222N, 325520, 326113, 326130]

Adidas America Inc., pp. Vol. I-272, 279, 300 [NAICS 31522M, 31523M, 31621M]

Adleta Corp., pp. Vol. I-229, Vol. III-1778 [NAICS 314110, 423220]

ADM Cocoa, pp. Vol. I-48, 52 [NAICS 311320, 311330]

ADM Corp., p. I-403 [NAICS 32223M]

ADM Grain, pp. Vol. III-1958, 1991 [NAICS 424510, 424910]

Admanco Inc., pp. Vol. I-239, 306 [NAICS 31491M, 31699M]

AdobeAir Inc., p. II-1106 [NAICS 333415]

Adorn L.L.C., pp. Vol. I-631, Vol. II-1611 [NAICS 326130, 337110]

Adorno Rogers Technology Inc., p. III-2113 [NAICS 446199]

Adray Appliance & Photo Center, pp. Vol. III-2050, 2062 [NAICS 443111, 443130]

Adrian Homes, p. I-353 [NAICS 321992]

Adrian Steel Co., pp. Vol. I-879, Vol. II-1644, 1650 [NAICS 33211P, 337215, 33721N]

ADT Security Services Inc., p. III-1839 [NAICS 423690]

Adtech Computers, p. III-2058 [NAICS 443120]

ADTRAN Inc., pp. Vol. II-1257, 1262, 1432 [NAICS 334210, 334220, 335313]

Adva-Lite Inc., p. II-1447 [NAICS 335912]

Advance Auto Parts Inc., p. III-2030 [NAICS 441310]

Advance Business Systems, p. III-1801 [NAICS 423420]

Advance Carbon Products Inc., p. II-1463 [NAICS 335991]

Advance Composites Inc., p. I-500 [NAICS 325211]

Advance Equipment Co., p. III-1859 [NAICS 423810]

Advance Foam Plastics Inc., p. I-636 [NAICS 326140]

Advance Food Company Inc., pp. Vol. I-102, 158 [NAICS 31161N, 31199M]

Advance Hydraulics Inc., p. II-1157 [NAICS 333611]

Advance Manufacturing Co., p. II-1639 [NAICS 337212]

Advance Manufacturing Inc., p. II-1129 [NAICS 333513]

Advance Novelty Inc., p. III-1887 [NAICS 423920]

Advance Packaging Corp., p. I-379 [NAICS 32221M]

Advance Plastics Unlimited Inc., p. I-646 [NAICS 326160]

Advance Publications Inc., pp. Vol. I-420, 436 [NAICS 32311M, 32312M]

Advance Reproductions Corp., p. II-1087 [NAICS 333315]

Advance Research Chemicals Inc., pp. Vol. I-493, Vol. II-1447 [NAICS 32519M, 335912]

Advance Ross Corp., p. II-1112 [NAICS 33341N]

Advance Transformer Co., pp. Vol. II-1302, 1386, 1421 [NAICS 334416, 335110, 335311]

Advanced Battery Systems Inc., p. II-1442 [NAICS 335911]

Advanced Building Products Inc., p. III-1790 [NAICS 423330]

Advanced Business Concepts, p. III-2186 [NAICS 453210]

Advanced Chemical Co., p. I-825 [NAICS 331419]

Advanced ChemTech Inc., p. I-493 [NAICS 32519M]

Advanced Component, pp. Vol. I-636, 771 [NAICS 326140, 327993]

Advanced Concepts Inc., p. II-1257 [NAICS 334210]

Advanced Containment Systems, p. II-1500 [NAICS 336214]

Advanced Crystal Sciences Inc., p. II-1056 [NAICS 333295]

Advanced Digital Information, p. II-1243 [NAICS 334112]

Advanced Drainage Systems Inc., pp. Vol. I-621, 651 [NAICS 326121, 32619M]

Advanced Electronics Inc., p. II-1312 [NAICS 334418]

Advanced Environmental, p. I-358 [NAICS 321999]

Advanced Fibre Communications, p. II-1257 [NAICS 334210]

Advanced Innovations West L.L.C., p. III-1774 [NAICS 423210]

Advanced Instrument Develop., p. II-1357 [NAICS 334517]

Advanced Internment Systems, p. II-1745 [NAICS 339995]

Advanced Labelworx Inc., p. II-1212 [NAICS 333993]

Advanced Lift Designs Inc., p. III-1859 [NAICS 423810]

Advanced Lighting Technologies, pp. Vol. II-1386, 1390 [NAICS 335110, 33512M]

Advanced Machine & Engineering, pp. Vol. II-958, 1134 [NAICS 332722, 333514]

Advanced Marketing Services Inc., p. III-1995 [NAICS 424920]

Advanced Materials Group Inc., p. I-771 [NAICS 327993]

Advanced Micro Devices Inc., p. II-1287 [NAICS 334413]

Advanced Network Inc., p. III-1809 [NAICS 423440]

Advanced Neuromodulation, pp. Vol. II-1322, 1671 [NAICS 334510, 339112]

Advanced Outdoors Inc., p. III-1883 [NAICS 423910]

Advanced Plastics Inc., p. III-1968 [NAICS 424610]

Advanced Scientifics Inc., p. I-603 [NAICS 326111]

Advanced Silicon Materials L.L.C., p. I-767 [NAICS 327992]

Advanced Technologies Intern., p. III-1805 [NAICS 423430]

Advanced Vending Systems Inc., p. III-2215 [NAICS 454210]

Advanced Ventures In Technology, p. II-1051 [NAICS 333220]

Advantage Engineering Inc., p. II-918 [NAICS 332410]

Advantage Food Marketing Corp., p. III-1929 [NAICS 424420]

Advantage Performance, p. III-1766 [NAICS 423130]

Advantage Sales & Marketing, pp. Vol. III-1925, 1929 [NAICS 424410, 424420]

Advantech Corp., p. II-1238 [NAICS 334111]

Advantek Inc., pp. Vol. II-1014, 1243, 1317 [NAICS 33299N, 334112, 334419]

AdvanTel Inc., p. III-1839 [NAICS 423690]

Advantis Technologies Inc., p. I-595 [NAICS 32599N]

Adventure in Food Trading Inc., p. III-2094 [NAICS 445299]

AE C Solutions, p. II-1362 [NAICS 334518]

A.E. Petsche Company Inc., pp. Vol. I-837, Vol. II-1307, Vol. III-1831 [NAICS 33149M, 334417, 423610]

AE Staley Manufacturing Co., p. I-22 [NAICS 311221]

Aearo Co., p. II-1676 [NAICS 339113]

AEC, pp. Vol. II-1437, 1457, 1512 [NAICS 335314, 33593M, 33632M]

Aerco International Inc., pp. Vol. II-918, 1417 [NAICS 332410, 335228]

Aerial Company Inc., p. III-1875 [NAICS 423850]

Aerial Machine and Tool Corp., p. II-1536 [NAICS 336360]

Aero Drapery Corp., pp. Vol. II-1662, Vol. III-2044 [NAICS 337920, 442291]

Aero Electric Connector Inc., p. II-1307 [NAICS 334417]

Aero Metals Inc., p. I-845 [NAICS 33151M]

Aero-Motive Co., pp. Vol. II-1152, 1650 [NAICS 333518, 33721N]

Aero Propulsion Support Inc., pp. Vol. II-1157, 1562 [NAICS 333611, 336412]

Aero Rubber Company Inc., p. I-665 [NAICS 326220]

Aero Systems Engineering Inc., p. II-1173 [NAICS 333618]

Aero-Tech Communications Inc., p. III-2054 [NAICS 443112]

Aero Toy Store L.L.C., pp. Vol. III-1879, 2027 [NAICS 423860, 441229]

Aero Union Corp., p. II-1486 [NAICS 336211]

AeroControlex Group, pp. Vol. II-1184, 1327, 1332, 1337, 1437 [NAICS 333912, 334511, 334512, 334513, 335314]

Aerodynamics Inc., p. III-1879 [NAICS 423860]

Aeroflex Inc., pp. Vol. II-1287, 1317, 1337, 1468 [NAICS 334413, 334419, 334513, 335999]

Aeroflex Laboratories Inc., p. II-1427 [NAICS 335312]

Aeroflex UTMC Microelectronic, p. II-1580 [NAICS 336419]

Aerojet, pp. Vol. II-1576, 1580 [NAICS 336415, 336419]

Aerojet Fine Chemicals, p. I-475 [NAICS 32513M]

Aeronca Inc., p. II-1580 [NAICS 336419]

Aeroparts Mfg and Repair Inc., p. III-1879 [NAICS 423860]

Aeropostale Inc., p. III-2135 [NAICS 448150]

AEROPRES Corp., p. I-471 [NAICS 325120]

Aeroquip-Vickers Inc., pp. Vol. II-980, 1222, 1229, 1427, 1437, 1551, 1567 [NAICS 33291N, 33399N, 33399P, 335312, 335314, 336399, 336413]

Aerosance Inc., p. II-1562 [NAICS 336412]

Aerospace Display System Inc., p. II-1362 [NAICS 334518]

Aerospace Mfg Technologies Inc., p. I-863 [NAICS 332114]

Aerostar International Inc., pp. Vol. I-198, 670, Vol. II-1557, 1720 [NAICS 313210, 32629M, 336411, 339950]

Aerostructures Corp., pp. Vol. II-1327, 1580 [NAICS 334511, 336419]

Aerotech Inc., pp. Vol. II-1106, 1112, 1427 [NAICS 333415, 33341N, 335312]

Aerothrust Corp., pp. Vol. II-1173, 1562 [NAICS 333618, 336412]

Aerovox Div. P.P.C., p. II-1292 [NAICS 334414]

Aervoe Industries Inc., p. I-458 [NAICS 324191]

AESP Inc., p. II-1307 [NAICS 334417]

Aetna Bearing Co., p. II-988 [NAICS 332991]

Aetna Insulated Wire Co., p. I-837 [NAICS 33149M]

Aetrium Inc., p. II-1352 [NAICS 334516]

AFA Protective Systems Inc., p. III-1831 [NAICS 423610]

AFCO, p. II-1179 [NAICS 333911]

AFCO Industries Inc., pp. Vol. I-803, 811 [NAICS 331312, 331316]

AFCO Metals Inc., p. III-1824 [NAICS 423510]

AFCO Plastic Products, p. I-621 [NAICS 326121]

AFCO Racing Products, p. II-1519 [NAICS 336330]

Affiliated Foods Inc., pp. Vol. III-1909, 1925, 1933, 1946 [NAICS 424210, 424410, 424430, 424470]

Affiliated Foods Midwest, pp. Vol. III-1925, 1946, 1950 [NAICS 424410, 424470, 424480]

Affiliated Foods Southwest Inc., p. III-1925 [NAICS 424410]

AFG Industries Inc., p. I-709 [NAICS 327211]

AFGD Inc., p. III-1794 [NAICS 423390]

AFM Machining Inc., p. II-1576 [NAICS 336415]

AFP Imaging Corp., pp. Vol. II-1087, 1357 [NAICS 333315, 334517]

Africair Inc., p. III-1879 [NAICS 423860]

Ag-Bag International Ltd., p. I-395 [NAICS 32222P]

AG/GRO Fertilizer Company Inc., p. I-520 [NAICS 325312]

AG Partners Cooperative Inc., pp. Vol. I-15, 524 [NAICS 31121M, 325314]

Ag Partners L.L.C., pp. Vol. III-1958, 1979, 1991 [NAICS 424510, 424720, 424910]

Numbers following p. or pp. are page references. Roman numerals indicate volume numbers. Bracketed items indicate industries. Page references are to the starting pages of company tables.

AG-Power Inc., p. III-2069 [NAICS 444210]

Ag Processing Inc., p. I-26 [NAICS 311225]

Ag Services of America Inc., p. III-1991 [NAICS 424910]

Ag-Valley Co-op., pp. Vol. III-1958, 1991, 2116 [NAICS 424510, 424910, 447110]

AGA John Inc., p. III-2041 [NAICS 442210]

Agape Home Healthcare Inc., p. III-2054 [NAICS 443112]

Agar Supply Inc., pp. Vol. III-1936, 1943, 1946 [NAICS 424440, 424460, 424470]

AGC Automotive Americas, pp. Vol. I-709, 722 [NAICS 327211, 327215]

AGC Inc., p. II-1562 [NAICS 336412]

AGCO Corp., p. II-1023 [NAICS 333111]

Agency for Instructional Tech., pp. Vol. III-1805, 1809 [NAICS 423430, 423440]

Agere Systems Inc., pp. Vol. II-1282, 1287, 1317, 1468 [NAICS 334412, 334413, 334419, 335999]

Aggregates Industries, pp. Vol. I-732, 743 [NAICS 327320, 327390]

Agilent Technologies Inc., pp. Vol. II-1262, 1287, 1347, 1352 [NAICS 334220, 334413, 334515, 334516]

Agilysys Inc., pp. Vol. III-1805, 1839 [NAICS 423430, 423690]

Agland Co-Op Inc., p. III-1991 [NAICS 424910]

Agland Inc., pp. Vol. I-9, 524 [NAICS 311119, 325314]

AGM Automotive Inc., p. III-1770 [NAICS 423140]

Agouron Pharmaceuticals Inc., p. I-539 [NAICS 325412]

AGP Grain Cooperative, pp. Vol. III-1958, 1991 [NAICS 424510, 424910]

Agracetus Co., p. I-544 [NAICS 325413]

Agraquest Inc., p. I-529 [NAICS 325320]

Agri-Cel Inc., p. I-636 [NAICS 326140]

Agri-Fab Inc., pp. Vol. I-879, Vol. II-1028 [NAICS 33211P, 333112]

Agri-Mark Inc., pp. Vol. I-76, 86 [NAICS 311513, 31151N]

Agricultural Installations Inc., p. I-480 [NAICS 325181]

Agrifos Fertilizer Inc., pp. Vol. I-488, 520 [NAICS 325188, 325312]

Agriland F.S. Inc., p. III-2116 [NAICS 447110]

Agriliance L.L.C., pp. Vol. I-524, Vol. III-1863, 1991 [NAICS 325314, 423820, 424910]

AgriPride F.S. Inc., pp. Vol. III-1958, 1991 [NAICS 424510, 424910]

Agriprocessors Inc., p. I-97 [NAICS 311615]

Agrisource Inc., pp. Vol. III-1958, 1991 [NAICS 424510, 424910]

Agrium Inc., pp. Vol. I-520, 529 [NAICS 325312, 325320]

Agrium US Inc., p. I-516 [NAICS 325311]

Agusta Aerospace Corp., p. II-1557 [NAICS 336411]

Agway Energy Products, p. III-1979 [NAICS 424720]

AHF-Ducommun, pp. Vol. II-1567, 1580 [NAICS 336413, 336419]

AHI Supply Inc., p. I-727 [NAICS 327310]

Ahresty Wilmington Corp., p. I-852 [NAICS 33152N]

A.I. Friedman, p. III-2208 [NAICS 453998]

AIA Plastics Inc., pp. Vol. I-709, Vol. III-1968 [NAICS 327211; 424610]

Aida-Dayton Technologies Corp., p. II-1129 [NAICS 333513]

Aim Aviation Inc., p. II-1327 [NAICS 334511]

Air Cleaning Technologies Inc., p. III-1851 [NAICS 423730]

Air Cooled Exchangers Inc., p. II-918 [NAICS 332410]

Air Cruisers Company Inc., pp. Vol. I-670, Vol. II-1567, 1676 [NAICS 32629M, 336413, 339113]

Air Cruisers Company Plant 1, pp. Vol. I-272, 670, Vol. II-1317, 1327, 1676 [NAICS 31522M, 32629M, 334419, 334511, 339113]

Air-Flo Manufacturing Inc., p. II-1046 [NAICS 333210]

Air Frame Mfg and Supply Inc., p. III-1879 [NAICS 423860]

Air Guide Corp., p. I-811 [NAICS 331316]

Air Liquide, p. I-471 [NAICS 325120]

Air Methods Corp., pp. Vol. II-908, 1567, 1632 [NAICS 33232M, 336413, 33712N]

Air Products and Chemicals Inc., pp. Vol. I-471, 475, Vol. II-1061 [NAICS 325120, 32513M, 33329N]

Air System Components, p. II-1101 [NAICS 333414]

Air Technical Industries Inc., p. II-886 [NAICS 33221N]

Air Techniques Inc., pp. Vol. II-1184, 1666, 1682 [NAICS 333912, 339111, 339114]

Airborn Inc., p. II-1307 [NAICS 334417]

AirBoss Polymer Products Corp., p. III-1922 [NAICS 424340]

Aircap MTD, pp. Vol. II-892, 1028 [NAICS 33221P, 333112]

Aircom Manufacturing Inc., p. II-1119 [NAICS 333511]

Aircon, p. II-1546 [NAICS 336391]

Aircraft Braking Systems Corp., pp. Vol. I-505, Vol. II-1567 [NAICS 325212, 336413]

Aircraft Instrument and Radio Inc., p. III-1879 [NAICS 423860]

Airdyne Inc., p. II-1184 [NAICS 333912]

Airfloat Systems Inc., p. II-1194 [NAICS 33392M]

Airgas Inc., pp. Vol. I-443, 471, Vol. III-1867, 1971 [NAICS 324110, 325120, 423830, 424690]

Airgas Mid South Inc., pp. Vol. I-471, 560, Vol. II-1229 [NAICS 325120, 325520, 33399P]

Airgas Rutland Tool & Supply Inc., pp. Vol. III-1843, 1867 [NAICS 423710, 423830]

Airgas South, p. I-471 [NAICS 325120]

Airguard Industries Inc., p. II-1112 [NAICS 33341N]

Airlite Synthetics Mfg Inc., p. I-510 [NAICS 32522M]

Airmar Technology Corp., p. II-1124 [NAICS 333512]

Airmec Inc., p. I-505 [NAICS 325212]

Airosol Company Inc., p. I-471 [NAICS 325120]

Airpax Corporation L.L.C., pp. Vol. II-1014, 1432, 1468, 1725 [NAICS 33299N, 335313, 335999, 339991]

Airpot Corp., p. II-1519 [NAICS 336330]

Airshow Inc., pp. Vol. II-1267, 1567 [NAICS 334290, 336413]

Airtex Products L.L.C., p. II-1179 [NAICS 333911]

Airway Industries Inc., p. I-306 [NAICS 31699M]

Airway Sheet Metal Company Inc., p. II-918 [NAICS 332410]

AIRXCEL Inc., pp. Vol. II-1101, 1106, 1546 [NAICS 333414, 333415, 336391]

AIX Media Group, p. II-1381 [NAICS 334613]

A.J. Daw Printing Ink Co., p. I-580 [NAICS 325910]

A.J. Petrunis Inc., p. III-2218 [NAICS 454311]

AJ Plastics Inc., p. II-974 [NAICS 332913]

A.J. Rinella and Company Inc., p. III-1950 [NAICS 424480]

A.J. Schrafel Paper Corp., pp. Vol. I-374, Vol. III-1905 [NAICS 322130, 424130]

Ajax Manufacturing Co., p. II-1129 [NAICS 333513]

AJC International Inc., p. III-1925 [NAICS 424410]

AJD Forest Products L.P., p. I-343 [NAICS 321920]

Ajinomoto Food Ingredients L.L.C., p. I-147 [NAICS 311930]

AJS Controls Inc., p. II-1082 [NAICS 333314]

A.K. Allen Inc., p. II-1124 [NAICS 333512]

AK Steel Holding Corp., pp. Vol. I-780, 793 [NAICS 33111M, 33122M]

A.K.A.P. Inc., p. I-709 [NAICS 327211]

Akcess Pacific Group, p. I-411 [NAICS 322291]

Akdo Intertrade Inc., p. III-1786 [NAICS 423320]

Akers National Roll Co., pp. Vol. I-845, 857 [NAICS 33151M, 33152P]

Akorn Inc., pp. Vol. II-1357, 1687 [NAICS 334517, 339115]

Akro-Mils Corp., p. II-1632 [NAICS 33712N]

Akron Auto Auction Inc., p. III-1758 [NAICS 423110]

Akron Porcelain and Plastics Co., pp. Vol. I-686, 703, 776 [NAICS 327113, 32712N, 327999]

Akron Special Machinery Inc., p. II-1051 [NAICS 333220]

Akzo Nobel Coatings Inc., p. I-554 [NAICS 325510]

Al-Corn Clean Fuel, p. I-493 [NAICS 32519M]

AL Eastmond and Sons Inc., pp. Vol. II-918, 923 [NAICS 332410, 332420]

A.L. Gilbert Co., p. III-1991 [NAICS 424910]

AL-KO Kober Corp., pp. Vol. II-1500, 1530 [NAICS 336214, 336350]

Al Larson Boat Shop, p. II-1589 [NAICS 336611]

AL Schutzman Co., p. I-137 [NAICS 31191M]

Alabama Food Group Inc., pp. Vol. III-1929, 1950 [NAICS 424420, 424480]

Alabama Metal Industries Corp., pp. Vol. I-793, Vol. II-899, 908 [NAICS 33122M, 33231M, 33232M]

Alabama River Newsprint Co., p. I-368 [NAICS 32212M]

Alabama Shipyard Inc., p. II-1589 [NAICS 336611]

Alamac America Knits L.L.C., p. I-213 [NAICS 31324M]

Alamac Knit Fabrics Inc., p. I-213 [NAICS 31324M]

Alamo Aircraft Ltd., p. III-1879 [NAICS 423860]

Alamo Cement Co., p. I-727 [NAICS 327310]

Alamo Foam Inc., p. I-636 [NAICS 326140]

Alamo Group Inc., p. II-1023 [NAICS 333111]

Alamo Iron Works Inc., pp. Vol. II-899, 1491, Vol. III-1824, 1871 [NAICS 33231M, 336212, 423510, 423840]

Alamo Marble Ltd., p. I-762 [NAICS 327991]

Alamo Service Company Inc., p. III-1855 [NAICS 423740]

Numbers following p. or pp. are page references. Roman numerals indicate volume numbers. Bracketed items indicate industries. Page references are to the starting pages of company tables.

2293

Alan Gordon Enterprises Inc., p. III-2062 [NAICS 443130]

Alan Wire Company Inc., pp. Vol. I-830, Vol. II-1451 [NAICS 33142M, 33592M]

Alan Young Buick-GMC Truck, p. III-2015 [NAICS 441120]

Alarama Jewelry Inc., p. II-1696 [NAICS 33991M]

ALARIS Medical Systems Inc., p. II-1671 [NAICS 339112]

Alaron Corp., p. I-807 [NAICS 331314]

Alaska Diesel Electric Inc., p. II-1173 [NAICS 333618]

Alaska Metal Recycling Co., p. I-807 [NAICS 331314]

Alaska Mill and Feed, pp. Vol. I-516, Vol. III-2007, 2072, 2197 [NAICS 325311, 424990, 444220, 453910]

Alaska Ship and Drydock Inc., p. II-1589 [NAICS 336611]

Alaska Wild Berry Products Inc., p. I-48 [NAICS 311320]

Alaskan Brewing L.L.C., p. I-172 [NAICS 312120]

Alaskan Copper Works Alco, pp. Vol. II-1009, 1152 [NAICS 332996, 333518]

Alba-Waldensian Inc., pp. Vol. I-256, 262, Vol. III-1916 [NAICS 31511M, 31519M, 424320]

Albanese Candy and Nut, p. I-48 [NAICS 311320]

Albany Industries Inc., p. II-1616 [NAICS 337121]

Albany International Corp., p. I-198 [NAICS 313210]

Albany International Corp. Mt Vern, p. I-198 [NAICS 313210]

Albany Steel Inc., pp. Vol. II-899, 908, Vol. III-1824 [NAICS 33231M, 33232M, 423510]

Albemarle Boats Inc., p. II-1594 [NAICS 336612]

Albemarle Corp., pp. Vol. I-488, 500 [NAICS 325188, 325211]

Albeni Falls Building Supply Inc., p. III-1790 [NAICS 423330]

Alberox Corp., pp. Vol. I-686, Vol. II-1292 [NAICS 327113, 334414]

Albert Guarnieri Company Inc., pp. Vol. III-1909, 1939, 2001 [NAICS 424210, 424450, 424940]

Albert H. Notini and Sons Inc., pp. Vol. III-1905, 1939, 2001 [NAICS 424130, 424450, 424940]

Albert's Organics Inc., pp. Vol. III-1939, 1950 [NAICS 424450, 424480]

Albert S. Smyth Company Inc., pp. Vol. III-2047, 2144 [NAICS 442299, 448310]

Alberto-Culver Co., pp. Vol. I-68, 575 [NAICS 31142M, 325620]

Albertson's Inc., pp. Vol. III-2076, 2100 [NAICS 445110, 446110]

Albion Industries Inc., pp. Vol. I-660, Vol. II-933, 1014 [NAICS 32621M, 332510, 33299N]

Albis Plastics Corp., p. I-589 [NAICS 325991]

Albright's Mill, p. I-4 [NAICS 311111]

Albuquerque Tortilla Company, p. I-133 [NAICS 311830]

Alcan Composites USA Inc., pp. Vol. I-636, 651, 816, Vol. II-908 [NAICS 326140, 32619M, 33131N, 33232M]

Alcas Corp., p. II-886 [NAICS 33221N]

Alcatel, p. II-1257 [NAICS 334210]

Alco Chemical, p. I-475 [NAICS 32513M]

Alco Industries Inc., pp. Vol. I-524, 529, 621, 670 [NAICS 325314, 325320, 326121, 32629M]

Alco Manufacturing Corp., p. II-952 [NAICS 332721]

Alcoa, pp. Vol. I-811, Vol. II-908 [NAICS 331316, 33232M]

Alcoa Closure Systems Intern., pp. Vol. I-458, 626, 879, Vol. II-1061 [NAICS 324191, 326122, 33211P, 33329N]

Alcoa Inc., pp. Vol. I-803, 837 [NAICS 331312, 33149M]

Alcon, p. II-1322 [NAICS 334510]

Alcon Laboratories Inc., p. I-539 [NAICS 325412]

Alcotec Wire Corp., p. I-816 [NAICS 33131N]

Alden and Ott Printing Ink Co., p. I-580 [NAICS 325910]

Alden O Sherman Company Inc., p. II-1562 [NAICS 336412]

Alden Shoe Co., p. I-300 [NAICS 31621M]

Aldrich Co., p. II-1417 [NAICS 335228]

Alejandro's Tortilla Factory, p. I-133 [NAICS 311830]

Alert Stamping and Mfg Co., p. II-1386 [NAICS 335110]

Alesis Studio Electronics Inc., p. II-1731 [NAICS 339992]

Alessi Bakeries, p. III-2089 [NAICS 445291]

Alex Products Inc., pp. Vol. I-811, Vol. II-1009 [NAICS 331316, 332996]

Alexander Doll Co., p. II-1708 [NAICS 33993M]

Alexander Fabrics Inc., pp. Vol. I-213, 218 [NAICS 31324M, 31331M]

Alexander Global Promotions Inc., p. II-1708 [NAICS 33993M]

Alexander Lumber Co., p. III-2065 [NAICS 444100]

Alfa Leisure Inc., pp. Vol. II-1473, 1500 [NAICS 336111, 336214]

Alfa-Pet Inc., p. I-4 [NAICS 311111]

Alfa Travelgear Inc., p. III-1919 [NAICS 424330]

Alfred Dunner Inc., p. I-279 [NAICS 31523M]

Alfred Nickles Bakery Inc., p. I-116 [NAICS 31181M]

Alfred Paquette, p. I-279 [NAICS 31523M]

Alga Plastics Co., p. I-609 [NAICS 326112]

Algas-SDI International L.L.C., p. I-516 [NAICS 325311]

Alger Corp., p. I-203 [NAICS 31322M]

Alger Manufacturing Company, p. II-952 [NAICS 332721]

Alice Manufacturing Co., p. I-198 [NAICS 313210]

Align Technology Inc., p. II-1682 [NAICS 339114]

Alinabal Inc., pp. Vol. I-631, Vol. II-1168 [NAICS 326130, 333613]

All American-Arkansas Poly Corp., p. I-603 [NAICS 326111]

All American Asphalt, p. III-1786 [NAICS 423320]

All American Lighting Corp., p. II-1404 [NAICS 335221]

All American Packaging, p. I-379 [NAICS 32221M]

All American Pharmaceutical, p. I-534 [NAICS 325411]

All American Poly Corp., p. I-603 [NAICS 326111]

All American Racers Inc., p. II-1473 [NAICS 336111]

All American Semiconductor Inc., p. III-1839 [NAICS 423690]

All Copy Products L.L.C., p. III-1801 [NAICS 423420]

All Nippon Airways Company Ltd., p. III-1879 [NAICS 423860]

All Plastics and Fiberglass Inc., p. I-699 [NAICS 327123]

All Power Battery Inc., p. II-1447 [NAICS 335912]

All Star Gas Corp., p. III-2222 [NAICS 454312]

All-Tech Plastics L.L.C., p. I-621 [NAICS 326121]

All Tile Inc., p. III-1778 [NAICS 423220]

All Trans Parts Incorporated, p. II-1530 [NAICS 336350]

All Valley Washer Service Inc., p. III-1875 [NAICS 423850]

Allan Co., p. III-1890 [NAICS 423930]

Allanti Cycling Co., p. III-2150 [NAICS 451110]

Allegheny Metals and Minerals, p. I-703 [NAICS 32712N]

Allegheny Refrigeration Service, p. III-1855 [NAICS 423740]

Allegheny Technologies Inc., pp. Vol. I-780, Vol. II-899, 1317, 1567 [NAICS 33111M, 33231M, 334419, 336413]

Allegro MicroSystems Inc., p. II-1287 [NAICS 334413]

Allen Canning Co., p. I-68 [NAICS 31142M]

Allen Co., p. I-306 [NAICS 31699M]

Allen Company Inc., p. I-448 [NAICS 324121]

Allen-Edmonds Shoe Corp., p. I-300 [NAICS 31621M]

Allen Extruders Inc., p. I-636 [NAICS 326140]

Allen Foods Inc., p. III-1809 [NAICS 423440]

Allen Organ Co., p. II-1731 [NAICS 339992]

Allen's of Hastings Inc., pp. Vol. III-2100, 2171 [NAICS 446110, 452111]

Allensville Planing Mill Inc., pp. Vol. I-324, 329, 353, 358 [NAICS 32121N, 32121P, 321992, 321999]

Allergan Inc., pp. Vol. I-539, Vol. II-1687 [NAICS 325412, 339115]

Allergy Laboratories Inc., pp. Vol. I-544, 718 [NAICS 325413, 327213]

Alley-Cassetty Brick and Block, p. I-737 [NAICS 32733M]

Alliance Gaming Corp., p. II-1749 [NAICS 339999]

Alliance Grain Co., p. III-1958 [NAICS 424510]

Alliance Metals Inc., pp. Vol. I-816, Vol. III-1824 [NAICS 33131N, 423510]

Alliance Remanufacturing Inc., pp. Vol. II-1173, 1505, 1512 [NAICS 333618, 33631M, 33632M]

Alliance Rubber Co., p. I-670 [NAICS 32629M]

Alliance Systems Ltd., p. III-1805 [NAICS 423430]

Alliance Winding Equipment Inc., p. II-1129 [NAICS 333513]

Alliant Techsystems Inc., pp. Vol. II-997, 1005 [NAICS 332993, 332995]

Allied Aerofoam Products L.L.C., p. I-641 [NAICS 326150]

Allied Aerospace Industries Inc., p. II-1580 [NAICS 336419]

Allied Automotive Group, p. III-1879 [NAICS 423860]

Numbers following p. or pp. are page references. Roman numerals indicate volume numbers. Bracketed items indicate industries. Page references are to the starting pages of company tables.

2294

Allied Building Products Corp., p. III-1794 [NAICS 423390]

Allied Chucker & Engineering Co., p. II-1530 [NAICS 336350]

Allied Components International, p. I-686 [NAICS 327113]

Allied Defense Group Inc., pp. Vol. II-997, 1001, 1005, 1603 [NAICS 332993, 332994, 332995, 336992]

Allied Foam Products Inc., p. I-636 [NAICS 326140]

Allied Foods Inc., p. I-4 [NAICS 311111]

Allied Healthcare Products Inc., p. II-1397 [NAICS 33521M]

Allied Machine & Engineering, pp. Vol. II-1124, 1134, 1140, 1207 [NAICS 333512, 333514, 333515, 333991]

Allied Materials, pp. Vol. I-732, 737, 743 [NAICS 327320, 32733M, 327390]

Allied Mineral Products Inc., p. I-703 [NAICS 32712N]

Allied Motion Technologies Inc., p. II-1347 [NAICS 334515]

Allied Oil and Supply Inc., pp. Vol. III-1766, 2030 [NAICS 423130, 441310]

Allied Pallet Company Inc., p. I-343 [NAICS 321920]

Allied Printing Services Inc., p. I-436 [NAICS 32312M]

Allied Realty Co., p. III-2044 [NAICS 442291]

Allied Systems Company Inc., pp. Vol. II-1033, 1194 [NAICS 333120, 33392M]

Allied Tube and Conduit, p. II-939 [NAICS 33261M]

Allied Universal Corp., pp. Vol. I-480, 488, 516 [NAICS 325181, 325188, 325311]

Allied-Vaughn Div., p. I-262 [NAICS 31519M]

Allied Vision, p. III-1809 [NAICS 423440]

Allied Vista Inc., p. III-1890 [NAICS 423930]

Allied Witan Co., p. I-771 [NAICS 327993]

Allison Abrasives Inc., p. I-756 [NAICS 327910]

Allison-Erwin Co., p. III-1778 [NAICS 423220]

Alloy Die Casting Co., pp. Vol. I-852, 857 [NAICS 33152N, 33152P]

Alloy Inc., p. III-2177 [NAICS 452910]

Alloy Surfaces Co., p. II-1005 [NAICS 332995]

Alloyd Company Inc., pp. Vol. I-609, 651, Vol. II-1212 [NAICS 326112, 32619M, 333993]

Allpak Co., p. III-1968 [NAICS 424610]

Allstar Magnetics Inc., p. I-686 [NAICS 327113]

Allsteel Inc., p. II-1650 [NAICS 33721N]

Alltech Biotechnology Center Inc., pp. Vol. I-9, 493, 595 [NAICS 311119, 32519M, 32599N]

ALLTEL Corp., p. III-1839 [NAICS 423690]

Allteq Industries Inc., p. II-1056 [NAICS 333295]

Alltrista Consumer Products Inc., p. I-358 [NAICS 321999]

Allure Home Creation Inc., pp. Vol. III-1778, 2047 [NAICS 423220, 442299]

Allway Tools Inc., p. II-1740 [NAICS 339994]

Alma Plantation Ltd., p. I-44 [NAICS 31131N]

Alma Products Co., p. II-1512 [NAICS 33632M]

ALMART Enterprises Inc., p. III-1820 [NAICS 423490]

Almco Inc., p. II-1152 [NAICS 333518]

Almira's Bakery, p. III-2089 [NAICS 445291]

Almore Dye House, p. I-218 [NAICS 31331M]

Aloe Commodities Intern. Inc., p. I-534 [NAICS 325411]

Aloha Tofu Factory Inc., p. I-31 [NAICS 31122N]

ALP. Lighting Components Inc., pp. Vol. II-1082, 1386 [NAICS 333314, 335110]

Alpena Auto Electric Inc., p. II-1447 [NAICS 335912]

Alpha and Omega Janitorial Sups, p. III-1875 [NAICS 423850]

Alpha Associates Inc., p. I-771 [NAICS 327993]

Alpha Ceramics Inc., p. I-686 [NAICS 327113]

Alpha-Core Inc., p. I-816 [NAICS 33131N]

Alpha Dyno Nobel, p. I-585 [NAICS 325920]

Alpha Omega Plastics Co., p. I-589 [NAICS 325991]

Alpha Packaging Inc., pp. Vol. I-621, 646 [NAICS 326121, 326160]

Alpha Precision Inc., p. I-709 [NAICS 327211]

Alpha Pro Tech Ltd., p. I-411 [NAICS 322291]

Alpha Systems, pp. Vol. II-1087, 1243 [NAICS 333315, 334112]

Alpha Systems Inc., p. I-560 [NAICS 325520]

Alpha Technologies Group Inc., p. II-1307 [NAICS 334417]

Alpha Technology Corp., pp. Vol. I-857, Vol. II-1119 [NAICS 33152P, 333511]

Alpha Tile Distributors Inc., p. III-1786 [NAICS 423320]

Alpha Wire Co., p. II-1307 [NAICS 334417]

Alphagary Corp., pp. Vol. I-500, 595, 651 [NAICS 325211, 32599N, 32619M]

Alpharma Inc., pp. Vol. I-534, 539 [NAICS 325411, 325412]

Alpine Armoring Inc., p. II-1603 [NAICS 336992]

Alpine Electronics Mfg of America, p. II-1272 [NAICS 334310]

Alpine Group Inc., pp. Vol. I-837, Vol. II-1257, 1567 [NAICS 33149M, 334210, 336413]

Alpine Health Products L.L.C., p. I-534 [NAICS 325411]

Alpine Industries Inc., pp. Vol. II-1112, 1397 [NAICS 33341N, 33521M]

Alpine Tire Service Of Spokane, pp. Vol. III-1766, 2034 [NAICS 423130, 441320]

Alpine Wurst and Meathouse Inc., p. III-2190 [NAICS 453220]

Alpla Inc., p. I-646 [NAICS 326160]

Alro Metals Service Center, p. III-1824 [NAICS 423510]

Alshire International Inc., p. II-1376 [NAICS 334612]

Alstom Power Air Preheater Co., pp. Vol. II-918, 1101, 1106 [NAICS 332410, 333414, 333415]

ALSTOM Power Conversion Inc, pp. Vol. II-1157, 1421, 1427 [NAICS 333611, 335311, 335312]

Alta Computer Services Ltd., p. III-1805 [NAICS 423430]

Altadis U.S.A. Inc., pp. Vol. I-188, 368, 379 [NAICS 31222M, 32212M, 32221M]

Altec Industries Inc., pp. Vol. II-1033, 1194, 1486 [NAICS 333120, 33392M, 336211]

Altech Lansing, pp. Vol. II-1272, 1317 [NAICS 334310, 334419]

Altek Inc., p. II-1119 [NAICS 333511]

Alter Trading Corp., p. III-1890 [NAICS 423930]

Altera Corp., p. II-1287 [NAICS 334413]

Altira Inc., p. I-646 [NAICS 326160]

Altivia Corp., pp. Vol. I-480, 488 [NAICS 325181, 325188]

Altman Stage Lighting Inc., p. II-1386 [NAICS 335110]

Alto Dairy Coop., p. I-76 [NAICS 311513]

Alto Products Corporation AL, pp. Vol. II-1486, 1530 [NAICS 336211, 336350]

Alto-Shaam Inc., p. II-1217 [NAICS 333994]

Altoona-Beasley Mfg Inc., p. II-1173 [NAICS 333618]

Altria Group Inc., pp. Vol. I-36, 68, 76, 102, 143, 172, 188 [NAICS 311230, 31142M, 311513, 31161N, 311920, 312120, 31222M]

Altron Inc., pp. Vol. II-1282, 1312 [NAICS 334412, 334418]

Alturdyne, p. II-1157 [NAICS 333611]

Aluchem Inc., p. I-767 [NAICS 327992]

Aluf Plastics, pp. Vol. I-603, 615 [NAICS 326111, 326113]

Alumacraft Boat Company Inc., pp. Vol. I-811, Vol. II-1594 [NAICS 331316, 336612]

Aluminum Blanking Company Inc., pp. Vol. I-816, 830 [NAICS 33131N, 33142M]

Aluminum Casting & Engineering, pp. Vol. I-224, 852, Vol. II-964, 1134 [NAICS 313320, 33152N, 33281M, 333514]

Aluminum Coil Anodizing Corp., p. I-816 [NAICS 33131N]

Aluminum Precision Products Inc., p. I-872 [NAICS 33211N]

Aluminum Screen Mfg Inc., p. I-811 [NAICS 331316]

Aluminum Shapes L.L.C., p. I-811 [NAICS 331316]

Alvaco Trading Company Inc., p. II-1687 [NAICS 339115]

Alvin and Company Inc., pp. Vol. III-1820, 2007 [NAICS 423490, 424990]

Alvord-Polk Tool Company Inc., p. II-1463 [NAICS 335991]

Alwin Manufacturing Inc., p. II-1189 [NAICS 333913]

A.M. Bickley Inc., p. III-1965 [NAICS 424590]

A.M. Castle and Co., pp. Vol. I-803, Vol. III-1824 [NAICS 331312, 423510]

AM General L.L.C., pp. Vol. II-1194, 1473 [NAICS 33392M, 336111]

AM-Gold Products Inc., p. II-1696 [NAICS 33991M]

AM-Safe Inc., pp. Vol. I-251, Vol. II-1536, 1567 [NAICS 314999, 336360, 336413]

AM Todd Company Inc., p. I-152 [NAICS 31194M]

AMA Plastics, p. II-1134 [NAICS 333514]

AMAK Brake L.L.C., p. II-1524 [NAICS 336340]

Amalga Composites Inc., p. I-621 [NAICS 326121]

Amalgamated Sugar L.L.C., p. I-40 [NAICS 311313]

Amano Cincinnati Inc., p. II-1362 [NAICS 334518]

Amarillo Gear Co., p. II-1162 [NAICS 333612]

Amarillo Hardware Co., pp. Vol. III-1774, 1835, 1843, 1847 [NAICS 423210, 423620, 423710, 423720]

Amarr Garage Doors, p. II-1468 [NAICS 335999]

Amatech Polyccl Inc., p. I-771 [NAICS 327993]

Amato International Inc., p. III-1946 [NAICS 424470]

Amazon.com Inc., p. III-2211 [NAICS 454113]

Numbers following p. or pp. are page references. Roman numerals indicate volume numbers. Bracketed items indicate industries. Page references are to the starting pages of company tables.

2295

Company Index

Ambit Pacific Recycling Inc., p. III-1890 [NAICS 423930]

Amcast Industrial Corp., pp. Vol. I-811, 872, Vol. II-908, 974, 980, 1106 [NAICS 331316, 33211N, 33232M, 332913, 33291N, 333415]

AMCC, p. II-1243 [NAICS 334112]

AMCO Water Metering Systems, pp. Vol. II-1342, 1432 [NAICS 334514, 335313]

Amcon Block and Precast Inc., p. I-737 [NAICS 32733M]

AMCON Distributing Co., pp. Vol. III-1909, 1925, 2001 [NAICS 424210, 424410, 424940]

Amcor Flexibles Healthcare, pp. Vol. I-379, 395, 603, 609, Vol. II-1676 [NAICS 32221M, 32222P, 326111, 326112, 339113]

AMCOR Masonry Products, p. I-737 [NAICS 32733M]

Amende and Schultz Corp., p. III-1943 [NAICS 424460]

Amerada Hess Corp., pp. Vol. I-443, 458, Vol. III-1975 [NAICS 324110, 324191, 424710]

Ameralia Inc., p. I-480 [NAICS 325181]

Amerbelle Textiles L.L.C., pp. Vol. I-218, 224 [NAICS 31331M, 313320]

AmerCable Inc., p. II-1451 [NAICS 33592M]

Amerequip Corp., p. II-1023 [NAICS 333111]

Amerex Group Inc., pp. Vol. III-1916, 1919 [NAICS 424320, 424330]

Amerhart Ltd., p. III-1782 [NAICS 423310]

Ameri Forge Corp., p. I-872 [NAICS 33211N]

Ameri-Tech Distributing Inc., p. III-1916 [NAICS 424320]

Ameriban Inc., p. I-251 [NAICS 314999]

America Citel Inc., p. II-1277 [NAICS 334411]

America's Collectibles Network, p. III-2211 [NAICS 454113]

Americal Corp., p. I-256 [NAICS 31511M]

American Ace L.L.C., p. I-143 [NAICS 311920]

American Acrylic Corp., p. I-631 [NAICS 326130]

American and Efird Inc., pp. Vol. I-192, 218 [NAICS 31311M, 31331M]

American Apparel, pp. Vol. I-267, 279 [NAICS 31521M, 31523M]

American Apparel Inc., pp. Vol. I-272, 279 [NAICS 31522M, 31523M]

American Art Clay Company Inc., pp. Vol. I-475, Vol. II-1714 [NAICS 32513M, 33994M]

American Asphalt Paving Co., p. I-448 [NAICS 324121]

American Auto Accessories Inc., pp. Vol. II-933, 1397 [NAICS 332510, 33521M]

American Automated Engineering, p. II-1572 [NAICS 336414]

American Axle & Mfg Holdings, p. II-1551 [NAICS 336399]

American Bag and Burlap Co., p. I-239 [NAICS 31491M]

American Banknote Corp., p. I-420 [NAICS 32311M]

American Basic Industries Inc., p. II-964 [NAICS 33281M]

American Belt Co., p. I-306 [NAICS 31699M]

American Biltrite Inc., pp. Vol. I-388, 626, 670, 695 [NAICS 32222N, 326122, 32629M, 327122]

American Binding Company Inc., pp. Vol. III-1901, 2186 [NAICS 424120, 453210]

American Bio Curve Soft Lens, p. II-1687 [NAICS 339115]

American Builders & Contractors, pp. Vol. III-1782, 1790, 1843, 1867 [NAICS 423310, 423330, 423710, 423830]

American Buildings Co., pp. Vol. II-899, 908 [NAICS 33231M, 33232M]

American Cable Co., pp. Vol. II-1307, 1312, 1451, 1512 [NAICS 334417, 334418, 33592M, 33632M]

American Capacitor Corp., p. II-1292 [NAICS 334414]

American Carrier Equipment Inc., p. II-1491 [NAICS 336212]

American Cast Iron Pipe Co., pp. Vol. I-780, 845, 857, Vol. II-899, 980 [NAICS 33111M, 33151M, 33152P, 33231M, 33291N]

American Computer & Electronics, p. III-2058 [NAICS 443120]

American Concrete Pipe Inc., p. I-737 [NAICS 32733M]

American Consolidated Industries, p. II-1519 [NAICS 336330]

American Copper and Brass Inc., p. III-1851 [NAICS 423730]

American Corrugated Products Inc., pp. Vol. I-609, 636 [NAICS 326112, 326140]

American Crystal Sugar Co., pp. Vol. I-40, 44 [NAICS 311313, 31131N]

American Decorative Services Inc., pp. Vol. I-224, 388, 415, 631 [NAICS 313320, 32222N, 322299, 326130]

American Dehydrated Foods Inc., p. I-4 [NAICS 311111]

American Dental, p. II-1682 [NAICS 339114]

American Distillation Inc., p. I-493 [NAICS 32519M]

American Drapery Blind & Carpet, p. III-1778 [NAICS 423220]

American Drew, p. II-1621 [NAICS 337122]

American Eagle Outfitters Inc., p. III-2132 [NAICS 448140]

American Electronic Components, pp. Vol. II-1327, 1432 [NAICS 334511, 335313]

American Encoder Repair Service, p. III-1831 [NAICS 423610]

American Essentials Inc., p. I-256 [NAICS 31511M]

American Eurocopter L.L.C., p. II-1557 [NAICS 336411]

American Fabrics Co., pp. Vol. I-208, 213 [NAICS 313230, 31324M]

American Fashion Inc., p. III-1916 [NAICS 424320]

American Fasteners Inc., p. III-1843 [NAICS 423710]

American Felt and Filter Inc., p. I-208 [NAICS 313230]

American Fence Company Inc., p. II-939 [NAICS 33261M]

American Fiber and Finishing Inc., pp. Vol. I-234, 251 [NAICS 31412M, 314999]

American Fiber Resources L.L.C., p. I-363 [NAICS 322110]

American Fish, p. I-110 [NAICS 31171M]

American Flat Glass Distributors, p. III-1794 [NAICS 423390]

American Fluorescent Corp., p. II-1386 [NAICS 335110]

American Foods Group Inc., p. I-102 [NAICS 31161N]

American Frozen Foods Inc., p. I-62 [NAICS 31141M]

American Games Inc., p. I-415 [NAICS 322299]

American Gasket and Rubber Co., p. I-505 [NAICS 325212]

American GFM Corp., p. II-1129 [NAICS 333513]

American Girl LLC, p. III-2211 [NAICS 454113]

American Greenwood Inc., p. II-1735 [NAICS 339993]

American Greetings Corp., pp. Vol. I-379, 388, 415, 420, 681, Vol. II-1720, 1749 [NAICS 32221M, 32222N, 322299, 32311M, 327112, 339950, 339999]

American Harvest Inc., pp. Vol. II-1397, 1404 [NAICS 33521M, 335221]

American Homestar Corp., p. I-353 [NAICS 321992]

American House Spinning Inc., p. I-192 [NAICS 31311M]

American Hydro Corp., pp. Vol. II-1157, 1222 [NAICS 333611, 33399N]

American Identity Now, p. I-251 [NAICS 314999]

American Implement Inc., p. III-1863 [NAICS 423820]

American Independent Paper Mills, p. III-1890 [NAICS 423930]

American Industrial Supply, p. III-1875 [NAICS 423850]

American Inks and Coatings Corp., p. I-580 [NAICS 325910]

American International Industries, pp. Vol. I-575, Vol. II-886 [NAICS 325620, 33221N]

American Iron and Steel Inc., p. I-807 [NAICS 331314]

American Iron-Steel Mfg Co., p. II-1162 [NAICS 333612]

American Ironhorse Motorcycle, p. II-1599 [NAICS 336991]

American Italian Pasta Co., pp. Vol. I-15, 124 [NAICS 31121M, 31182M]

American Leather L.P., p. II-1616 [NAICS 337121]

American Leather Products, p. I-239 [NAICS 31491M]

American Licorice Company Inc., p. I-57 [NAICS 311340]

American Light Bulb Mfg Inc., p. II-1386 [NAICS 335110]

American Locker Group Inc., p. II-1644 [NAICS 337215]

American Manufacturing Co., pp. Vol. I-244, Vol. II-958, 1222, 1437 [NAICS 314991, 332722, 33399N, 335314]

American Maplan Corp., p. II-1051 [NAICS 333220]

American Marazzi Tile Inc., p. I-695 [NAICS 327122]

American-Marsh Pumps, p. II-1023 [NAICS 333111]

American Massage Products Inc., p. II-1657 [NAICS 337910]

American Media Intern. L.L.C., p. II-1376 [NAICS 334612]

Numbers following p. or pp. are page references. Roman numerals indicate volume numbers. Bracketed items indicate industries. Page references are to the starting pages of company tables.

2296

American Medical Sales Inc., p. II-1357 [NAICS 334517]

American Medical Systems, pp. Vol. II-1676, Vol. III-1813 [NAICS 339113, 423450]

American Metal Fibers Inc., p. I-510 [NAICS 32522M]

American Metal Marketing Inc., p. III-1770 [NAICS 423140]

American Metal Recycling Inc., p. III-1890 [NAICS 423930]

American Metalcraft Inc., p. II-886 [NAICS 33221N]

American Meter Co., pp. Vol. II-980, 1342, 1432 [NAICS 33291N, 334514, 335313]

American Micrographics Inc., p. II-1381 [NAICS 334613]

American Modern Metal Corp., pp. Vol. I-803, 811 [NAICS 331312, 331316]

American Modular Systems Inc., p. I-353 [NAICS 321992]

American National Rubber Co., p. I-670 [NAICS 32629M]

American NTN Bearing Mfg Corp., p. II-988 [NAICS 332991]

American of Martinsville, pp. Vol. II-1616, 1627 [NAICS 337121, 337127]

American Office Equipment Inc., p. III-1774 [NAICS 423210]

American Office Machines Inc., p. III-1901 [NAICS 424120]

American Pacific Corp., p. I-475 [NAICS 32513M]

American Panel Corp., p. II-1409 [NAICS 335222]

American Paper Recycling Corp., p. I-363 [NAICS 322110]

American Paper Towel Co., p. III-1905 [NAICS 424130]

American Pavers Mfg Inc., p. I-737 [NAICS 32733M]

American Pecco Corp., pp. Vol. II-1033, Vol. III-1859 [NAICS 333120, 423810]

American Peptide Company Inc., p. I-549 [NAICS 325414]

American Phoenix Inc., p. I-505 [NAICS 325212]

American Piezo Ceramics Inc., p. I-686 [NAICS 327113]

American Plant Food Corp., pp. Vol. I-488, 520, 524 [NAICS 325188, 325312, 325314]

American Plastic Toys Inc., p. II-1708 [NAICS 33993M]

American Power Conversion Corp., pp. Vol. II-1092, 1468 [NAICS 33331N, 335999]

American Pride Coop., pp. Vol. III-1991, 2116 [NAICS 424910, 447110]

American Product Distributors Inc., pp. Vol. III-1901, 1971 [NAICS 424120, 424690]

American Proteins Inc., pp. Vol. I-26, 97 [NAICS 311225, 311615]

American Pulverizer Co., pp. Vol. II-886, 1152 [NAICS 33221N, 333518]

American Quality Products, pp. Vol. I-646, Vol. II-1599 [NAICS 326160, 336991]

American Racing Equipment Inc., p. II-1551 [NAICS 336399]

American Radionic Company Inc., p. II-1292 [NAICS 334414]

American Renolit Corp., p. III-1968 [NAICS 424610]

American Reprographics Co., pp. Vol. I-420, 436 [NAICS 32311M, 32312M]

American Research & Knitting Inc., p. I-213 [NAICS 31324M]

American Ring and Tool Co., p. II-1735 [NAICS 339993]

American Road Machinery Inc., p. II-1028 [NAICS 333112]

American Rubber Products Corp., pp. Vol. I-670, Vol. II-1725 [NAICS 32629M, 339991]

American Safety Utility Corp., p. I-267 [NAICS 31521M]

American Satellite & Entertain., p. III-2054 [NAICS 443112]

American Science & Engineering, p. II-1357 [NAICS 334517]

American Seafoods Group L.L.C., p. I-110 [NAICS 31171M]

American Seating Co., pp. Vol. II-1536, 1627, 1650 [NAICS 336360, 337127, 33721N]

American Seaway Foods Inc., p. III-1925 [NAICS 424410]

American Security Equipment Co., p. II-1267 [NAICS 334290]

American Soy Products Inc., p. I-31 [NAICS 31122N]

American Spring Wire Corp., pp. Vol. I-743, 825, Vol. II-939, 1463 [NAICS 327390, 331419, 33261M, 335991]

American Standard Building, p. I-348 [NAICS 321991]

American Standard Companies, pp. Vol. II-974, 1106, 1551 [NAICS 332913, 333415, 336399]

American Standard Inc., pp. Vol. II-974, 1106, 1486 [NAICS 332913, 333415, 336211]

American Stitchco Inc., p. II-1536 [NAICS 336360]

American Surplus Inc., p. III-1809 [NAICS 423440]

American Suzuki Motor Corp., p. III-1762 [NAICS 423120]

American Tag and Label Corp., p. I-203 [NAICS 31322M]

American Tank and Vessel Inc., p. II-923 [NAICS 332420]

American Tar Co., p. I-453 [NAICS 324122]

American Technical Ceramics, p. II-1292 [NAICS 334414]

American Television & Appliance, pp. Vol. III-2037, 2050, 2054, 2058 [NAICS 442110, 443111, 443112, 443120]

American Textile Co., p. I-218 [NAICS 31331M]

American Thermocraft Corp., p. I-681 [NAICS 327112]

American Thermoplastic Extrusion, p. I-621 [NAICS 326121]

American Tile Supply Inc., p. III-1786 [NAICS 423320]

American Time and Signal Inc., p. II-1362 [NAICS 334518]

American Tire Distributors, p. III-1766 [NAICS 423130]

American Tire Distributors Inc., pp. Vol. III-1762, 1766 [NAICS 423120, 423130]

American Tool and Mold Inc., p. II-1119 [NAICS 333511]

American Torch Tip Company Inc., pp. Vol. I-549, Vol. II-1140 [NAICS 325414, 333515]

American Towing Products, p. II-1500 [NAICS 336214]

American Trading & Production, pp. Vol. I-306, Vol. III-2186 [NAICS 31699M, 453210]

American Trim L.L.C., pp. Vol. I-420, 879, Vol. II-933 [NAICS 32311M, 33211P, 332510]

American Uniform Co., pp. Vol. I-234, 272, 279 [NAICS 31412M, 31522M, 31523M]

American Urethane Inc., p. I-641 [NAICS 326150]

American Velvet Co., p. I-218 [NAICS 31331M]

American Water Heater Co., pp. Vol. II-1101, 1417 [NAICS 333414, 335228]

American Window Concepts, p. III-1778 [NAICS 423220]

American Woodmark Corp., p. I-334 [NAICS 32191M]

American Woolen Co., p. I-234 [NAICS 31412M]

Americana Fabrics, p. I-208 [NAICS 313230]

AmeriCast Technologies Inc., p. I-845 [NAICS 33151M]

Americhem Inc., pp. Vol. I-475, 488, 500, 554 [NAICS 32513M, 325188, 325211, 325510]

Americhem Travel Inc., p. II-1056 [NAICS 333295]

Americom Telecommunications, p. III-2054 [NAICS 443112]

Ameridrives International, pp. Vol. II-1168, 1530 [NAICS 333613, 336350]

AmeriGas Partners L.P., pp. Vol. I-471, Vol. III-2222 [NAICS 325120, 454312]

Amerigon Inc., p. II-1473 [NAICS 336111]

Amerilink Marketing Corp., p. III-2054 [NAICS 443112]

Amerimade Technology Inc., p. II-1056 [NAICS 333295]

Ameriqual Group L.L.C., p. I-158 [NAICS 31199M]

AmerisourceBergen Corp., p. III-1909 [NAICS 424210]

Ameritex Yarn L.L.C., p. I-192 [NAICS 31311M]

Amerityre Corp., p. I-660 [NAICS 32621M]

Ameriwest Industries Inc., p. III-1774 [NAICS 423210]

Amerock Corp., pp. Vol. II-933, 1014 [NAICS 332510, 33299N]

Ameron International Corp., pp. Vol. I-732, 743, 776, 788, Vol. II-899, 964, 1014 [NAICS 327320, 327390, 327999, 331210, 33231M, 33281M, 33299N]

Ames Industrial Supply Co., p. I-505 [NAICS 325212]

Ames International Inc., pp. Vol. I-48, 57 [NAICS 311320, 311340]

Ames Metal Products Co., p. I-825 [NAICS 331419]

Ames Safety Envelope Inc., pp. Vol. I-403, 609 [NAICS 32223M, 326112]

Amesbury Group Inc., p. I-641 [NAICS 326150]

AMETEK Inc., pp. Vol. II-1092, 1112, 1337, 1427 [NAICS 33331N, 33341N, 334513, 335312]

AMETEK Lamb Electric Div, pp. Vol. II-1112, 1427 [NAICS 33341N, 335312]

Ametric, p. I-665 [NAICS 326220]

Amfels Inc., pp. Vol. II-923, 1207, 1589 [NAICS 332420, 333991, 336611]

AMG Industries Corp., pp. Vol. I-807, 837 [NAICS 331314, 33149M]

Amgen Inc., pp. Vol. I-539, 549 [NAICS 325412, 325414]

Amglo Kemlite Laboratories Inc., pp. Vol. II-1277, 1386 [NAICS 334411, 335110]

Amgraph Packaging Inc., pp. Vol. I-603, 609 [NAICS 326111, 326112]

AMI Doduco Inc., pp. Vol. I-837, Vol. II-964 [NAICS 33149M, 33281M]

AMI Inc., p. II-1413 [NAICS 335224]

Amidon Associates Inc., p. III-1831 [NAICS 423610]

Amigo Mobility International Inc., p. II-1607 [NAICS 336999]

Amigo's Mexican Foods Inc., pp. Vol. III-1929, 2094 [NAICS 424420, 445299]

Amigos Canning Company Inc., pp. Vol. I-133, 137 [NAICS 311830, 31191M]

Amir Foods Inc., p. III-2094 [NAICS 445299]

AMIS Holdings Inc., p. II-1287 [NAICS 334413]

Amitron Inc., pp. Vol. II-1282, 1312 [NAICS 334412, 334418]

Amkor Technology Inc., p. II-1287 [NAICS 334413]

Amlings Flowerland, p. III-2183 [NAICS 453110]

Ammar's Inc., pp. Vol. III-1843, 1887, 2177 [NAICS 423710, 423920, 452910]

Amoroso's Baking Co., p. I-116 [NAICS 31181M]

Amos Post Div., p. III-2218 [NAICS 454311]

AMPAC, pp. Vol. I-471, 488, 585 [NAICS 325120, 325188, 325920]

Ampac Packaging L.L.C., pp. Vol. I-603, 609, 615 [NAICS 326111, 326112, 326113]

Ampacet Corp., pp. Vol. I-475, 493 [NAICS 32513M, 32519M]

Amparts International Inc., p. III-1758 [NAICS 423110]

Ampco-Pittsburgh Corp., pp. Vol. II-958, 1112, 1147, 1179, 1302 [NAICS 332722, 33341N, 333516, 333911, 334416]

Ampex Corp., pp. Vol. II-1243, 1262, 1327 [NAICS 334112, 334220, 334511]

Amphenol Corp., pp. Vol. I-837, Vol. II-1082, 1307, 1317, 1457 [NAICS 33149M, 333314, 334417, 334419, 33593M]

Amplas Compounding Inc., p. I-589 [NAICS 325991]

Ampride, pp. Vol. III-1975, 2116 [NAICS 424710, 447110]

Ampro Computers Inc., p. II-1238 [NAICS 334111]

Amscan Holdings Inc., pp. Vol. I-379, 388, 411, 415 [NAICS 32221M, 32222N, 322291, 322299]

Amsco Steel Co., p. II-945 [NAICS 332710]

AMSOIL Inc., pp. Vol. I-458, Vol. II-1112, 1229 [NAICS 324191, 33341N, 33399P]

Amspak, p. I-403 [NAICS 32223M]

Amsted Industries Inc., pp. Vol. I-845, Vol. II-899 [NAICS 33151M, 33231M]

AMT Datasouth Corp., p. III-2058 [NAICS 443120]

AMTEC Precision Products Inc., pp. Vol. II-945, 952 [NAICS 332710, 332721]

Amtech Systems Inc., pp. Vol. II-1217, 1332 [NAICS 333994, 334512]

Amtekco Industries Inc., pp. Vol. II-1014, 1611, 1621, 1627 [NAICS 33299N, 337110, 337122, 337127]

Amtrol Inc., p. II-928 [NAICS 33243M]

Amurol Confections Co., pp. Vol. I-52, 57 [NAICS 311330, 311340]

Amveco Magnetics Inc., p. II-1302 [NAICS 334416]

Amway Corp., p. III-2228 [NAICS 454390]

AMX Corp., p. II-1337 [NAICS 334513]

Amy's Kitchen Inc., p. I-62 [NAICS 31141M]

Ana Molinari, p. III-1875 [NAICS 423850]

Anacomp Inc., pp. Vol. II-1087, 1381 [NAICS 333315, 334613]

ANADIGICS Inc., p. II-1082 [NAICS 333314]

Anaheim Manufacturing Inc., p. II-1417 [NAICS 335228]

Analog Devices Inc., p. II-1287 [NAICS 334413]

Analogic Corp., pp. Vol. II-1252, 1347 [NAICS 334119, 334515]

Analytic Services Inc., p. II-1580 [NAICS 336419]

Anamax Corp., p. I-26 [NAICS 311225]

Anaren Inc., pp. Vol. II-1262, 1337 [NAICS 334220, 334513]

Anaspec Inc., p. I-549 [NAICS 325414]

Anchor Block Company Inc., pp. Vol. I-737, 762 [NAICS 32733M, 327991]

Anchor Brewing Co., p. I-172 [NAICS 312120]

Anchor Coatings of Leesburg Inc., p. I-453 [NAICS 324122]

Anchor Glass Container Corp., p. I-718 [NAICS 327213]

Anchor Group, pp. Vol. I-213, 267, 285 [NAICS 31324M, 31521M, 31529M]

Anchor-Harvey Components, p. I-872 [NAICS 33211N]

Anchor Hocking Specialty Glass, p. I-713 [NAICS 327212]

Anchor Lamina America Inc., p. II-1207 [NAICS 333991]

Anchor Lumber Company Inc., p. III-2072 [NAICS 444220]

Anchor Manufacturing Group, p. II-958 [NAICS 332722]

Anchor Packaging Inc., pp. Vol. I-609, 615 [NAICS 326112, 326113]

Anchor Paper Co., pp. Vol. III-1898, 1905 [NAICS 424110, 424130]

Ancira Enterprises Inc., p. III-2011 [NAICS 441110]

Ancira Winton Chevrolet Inc., p. III-2011 [NAICS 441110]

Anco Products Inc., p. I-771 [NAICS 327993]

Ancra International L.L.C., p. I-244 [NAICS 314991]

Andale Farmers Cooperative Inc., p. III-1958 [NAICS 424510]

Anderol Inc., p. I-458 [NAICS 324191]

Andersen Corp., pp. Vol. I-334, 626, 709, 722 [NAICS 32191M, 326122, 327211, 327215]

Andersen Plastics, p. I-646 [NAICS 326160]

Anderson Bremer Paper Co., p. III-1813 [NAICS 423450]

Anderson Columbia Company Inc., p. I-448 [NAICS 324121]

Anderson Cook Inc., pp. Vol. II-1129, 1140, 1147, 1152 [NAICS 333513, 333515, 333516, 333518]

Anderson Copper and Brass Co., p. II-974 [NAICS 332913]

Anderson Development Inc., pp. Vol. I-453, 493, 554, 595, 722 [NAICS 324122, 32519M, 325510, 32599N, 327215]

Anderson Equipment Co., p. III-1859 [NAICS 423810]

Anderson Erickson Dairy Co., pp. Vol. I-86, 92 [NAICS 31151N, 311520]

Anderson Fabrics Inc., pp. Vol. I-234, 251, Vol. II-1621 [NAICS 31412M, 314999, 337122]

Anderson Forest Products Inc., p. I-343 [NAICS 321920]

Anderson International Corp., p. II-1051 [NAICS 333220]

Anderson News Co., p. III-1995 [NAICS 424920]

Anderson Products Inc., pp. Vol. I-756, Vol. II-1740 [NAICS 327910, 339994]

Anderson-Tully Co., p. I-312 [NAICS 32111M]

Anderson Valley Brewing Inc., p. I-172 [NAICS 312120]

Anderson Wholesale Co., p. III-1909 [NAICS 424210]

Anderson Wood Products Co., p. II-1639 [NAICS 337212]

Andersons Inc., pp. Vol. I-566, 756, Vol. II-1023, Vol. III-1958, 1991, 2065, 2072 [NAICS 32561M, 327910, 333111, 424510, 424910, 444100, 444220]

Andex Industries Inc., p. I-609 [NAICS 326112]

Andin International Inc., p. II-1696 [NAICS 33991M]

Andis Co., pp. Vol. II-886, 1397 [NAICS 33221N, 33521M]

Andrea by Sadek, p. III-1778 [NAICS 423220]

Andrew Corp., pp. Vol. I-837, Vol. II-1317 [NAICS 33149M, 334419]

Andrew Jergens Co., p. I-575 [NAICS 325620]

Andrews Apparel Company Inc., p. I-267 [NAICS 31521M]

Andrews Distributing Inc., p. III-1851 [NAICS 423730]

Andrews Laser Works Corp., p. II-1562 [NAICS 336412]

Android Industries L.L.C., p. II-1749 [NAICS 339999]

Andrx Corp., p. I-539 [NAICS 325412]

Andrzejewski's Marian Church, p. III-1820 [NAICS 423490]

Angell Manufacturing Inc., p. II-1720 [NAICS 339950]

AngioCare Corp., p. II-1322 [NAICS 334510]

Angler Boat Corp., p. II-1594 [NAICS 336612]

Anglers Roslyn Group Ltd., p. II-1714 [NAICS 33994M]

Angstrom Sciences Inc., p. II-1277 [NAICS 334411]

Angus-Palm, pp. Vol. II-1023, 1033, 1194 [NAICS 333111, 333120, 33392M]

Anheuser-Busch Companies Inc., p. II-928 [NAICS 33243M]

Anheuser-Busch Inc., pp. Vol. I-172, Vol. III-1983 [NAICS 312120, 424810]

Anika Therapeutics Inc., p. I-549 [NAICS 325414]

Animal Repellent Inc., p. I-529 [NAICS 325320]

Anita's Mexican Foods Corp., p. I-133 [NAICS 311830]

Anitox Corp., p. I-147 [NAICS 311930]

Numbers following p. or pp. are page references. Roman numerals indicate volume numbers. Bracketed items indicate industries. Page references are to the starting pages of company tables.

2298

Anixter International Inc., p. III-1831 [NAICS 423610]

Annaco Inc., p. I-807 [NAICS 331314]

Annie Sez, p. III-2171 [NAICS 452111]

AnnTaylor Stores Corp., p. III-2126 [NAICS 448120]

Anorad Corp., p. II-1082 [NAICS 333314]

Anpec Industries Inc., p. II-1599 [NAICS 336991]

Anritsu Co., pp. Vol. I-651, Vol. II-1140, 1367 [NAICS 32619M, 333515, 334519]

Ansen Corp., p. II-1282 [NAICS 334412]

Ansewn Shoe Co., p. I-300 [NAICS 31621M]

Ansonia Copper and Brass Inc., pp. Vol. I-822, 830 [NAICS 331411, 33142M]

Anstro Manufacturing Inc., p. II-1524 [NAICS 336340]

Anthony and Sylvan Pools Corp., p. III-2208 [NAICS 453998]

Anthony Farmers Cooperative, pp. Vol. III-1958, 1991 [NAICS 424510, 424910]

Anthony's Seafood Group, p. III-2190 [NAICS 453220]

Antigo Cheese Co., p. I-76 [NAICS 311513]

Antioch Building Materials Co., p. I-732 [NAICS 327320]

Anton Bauer Inc., pp. Vol. II-1087, 1447 [NAICS 333315, 335912]

Anvil Cases Inc., p. I-306 [NAICS 31699M]

A.O. Smith Corp., pp. Vol. II-899, 1417, 1427 [NAICS 33231M, 335228, 335312]

AOC L.L.C., p. I-500 [NAICS 325211]

APAC-Carolina Inc. Barrus Div., p. I-732 [NAICS 327320]

APAC-Florida Inc., p. I-448 [NAICS 324121]

APAC Inc., pp. Vol. I-448, Vol. II-1033 [NAICS 324121, 333120]

APAC-Kansas Inc., p. I-448 [NAICS 324121]

Apache Corp., pp. Vol. I-443, 463 [NAICS 324110, 324199]

Apache Hose and Belting Inc., pp. Vol. I-665, Vol. III-1871 [NAICS 326220, 423840]

Apache Mills Inc., p. I-229 [NAICS 314110]

Apache Nitrogen Products Inc., pp. Vol. I-516, 524, Vol. III-1971 [NAICS 325311, 325314, 424690]

Apache OXY-Med Inc., p. III-2113 [NAICS 446199]

Apex Homes Inc., p. I-353 [NAICS 321992]

Apex Medical Corp., p. I-626 [NAICS 326122]

Apex Mills Corp., p. I-213 [NAICS 31324M]

Apex Molded Products Inc., p. II-1519 [NAICS 336330]

Apex Oil Company Inc., p. I-443 [NAICS 324110]

Apex Plastics, p. I-646 [NAICS 326160]

API Autobody Products Inc., p. III-2030 [NAICS 44131O]

API Delevan, pp. Vol. II-899, 1302, 1437 [NAICS 33231M, 334416, 335314]

Aplix Inc., p. II-958 [NAICS 332722]

APO Health Inc., p. II-1682 [NAICS 339114]

Apogee Enterprises Inc., pp. Vol. I-709, 722, Vol. II-899, 908 [NAICS 327211, 327215, 33231M, 33232M]

Apogent Technologies Inc., pp. Vol. II-1666, 1682 [NAICS 339111, 339114]

Apollo Colors Inc., p. I-475 [NAICS 32513M]

Apollo Distribution, p. III-1835 [NAICS 423620]

Apollo Industries Inc., p. I-529 [NAICS 325320]

Apollo Marble Products Co., p. I-762 [NAICS 327991]

Apollo Propane Inc., p. III-2222 [NAICS 454312]

Apothecary Products Inc., p. III-1909 [NAICS 424210]

Appalachian Brewing Inc., p. I-172 [NAICS 312120]

Appalachian Wood Products Inc., pp. Vol. I-358, Vol. II-1639 [NAICS 321999, 337212]

Apparel Finishing America Inc., p. I-285 [NAICS 31529M]

Apperson Print Management, p. I-403 [NAICS 32223M]

Appertain Corp., p. III-1890 [NAICS 423930]

Apple Computer Inc., pp. Vol. II-1238, 1252 [NAICS 334111, 334119]

Applegate Insulation Mfg Inc., p. I-510 [NAICS 32522M]

Applera Corp., p. II-1352 [NAICS 334516]

Appleton Papers, p. I-388 [NAICS 32222N]

Appliance Depot and More, pp. Vol. III-1835, 2037, 2050 [NAICS 423620, 442110, 443111]

Appliance Factory Outlet, p. III-1835 [NAICS 423620]

Appliance Recycling Centers, p. III-1890 [NAICS 423930]

Applica Inc., pp. Vol. I-306, Vol. II-1397, 1749 [NAICS 31699M, 33521M, 339999]

Application Engineering Corp., pp. Vol. II-918, 1092, 1106, 1229 [NAICS 332410, 33331N, 333415, 33399P]

Applied Aerospace Structures, pp. Vol. II-1567, 1580 [NAICS 336413, 336419]

Applied Art and Technology, p. II-1381 [NAICS 334613]

Applied Biosystems Group, pp. Vol. I-549, Vol. II-1352 [NAICS 325414, 334516]

Applied Biotech Inc., p. I-544 [NAICS 325413]

Applied Ceramics Inc., p. I-686 [NAICS 327113]

Applied Composites Engineering, p. I-510 [NAICS 32522M]

Applied Composites Technology, p. II-1463 [NAICS 335991]

Applied Digital Solutions Inc., pp. Vol. II-1257, Vol. III-1805 [NAICS 334210, 423430]

Applied Extrusion Technologies, pp. Vol. I-615, 626 [NAICS 326113, 326122]

Applied Fiber Telecommunications, p. II-1451 [NAICS 33592M]

Applied Films Corp., pp. Vol. I-722, Vol. II-1061 [NAICS 327215, 33329N]

Applied Imaging Corp., p. I-544 [NAICS 325413]

Applied Industrial Technologies, pp. Vol. II-1222, Vol. III-1859 [NAICS 33399N, 423810]

Applied Innovation Inc., p. II-1432 [NAICS 335313]

Applied Materials Inc., pp. Vol. II-1061, 1092 [NAICS 33329N, 33331N]

Applied Printing Technologies, p. I-436 [NAICS 32312M]

Applied Research Laboratories Inc., p. II-1417 [NAICS 335228]

Applied Sciences Inc., pp. Vol. I-510, Vol. II-1463 [NAICS 32522M, 335991]

Applied Signal Technology Inc., p. II-1262 [NAICS 334220]

Applied Textiles Inc., p. I-218 [NAICS 31331M]

APR Plastic Fabricating Inc., p. I-699 [NAICS 327123]

APR Supply Co., p. III-1847 [NAICS 423720]

APS Petroleum Equipment Inc., p. II-1189 [NAICS 333913]

Apsco International Inc., pp. Vol. II-1282, 1312 [NAICS 334412, 334418]

AptarGroup Inc., pp. Vol. I-626, 879, Vol. II-980, 1014, 1189, 1749 [NAICS 326122, 33211P, 33291N, 33299N, 333913, 339999]

APV Engineered Coatings, p. I-580 [NAICS 325910]

APW Ltd., p. III-1839 [NAICS 423690]

APW Mayville L.L.C., pp. Vol. II-1632, 1650 [NAICS 33712N, 33721N]

APW-Wright Line, pp. Vol. II-1627, 1650 [NAICS 337127, 33721N]

AQS Inc., p. III-1805 [NAICS 423430]

Aqua-Chem Inc., pp. Vol. II-918, 1092, 1101, 1179 [NAICS 332410, 33331N, 333414, 333911]

AquaCell Technologies Inc., p. I-718 [NAICS 327213]

Aquagenix Inc., p. I-529 [NAICS 325320]

Aquaport USA, p. III-1855 [NAICS 423740]

Aquarium Environments Inc., p. III-2197 [NAICS 453910]

Aquarius Engineering Inc., p. III-1859 [NAICS 423810]

Ar-Jay Building Products Inc., p. III-1790 [NAICS 423330]

AR Lintern, p. II-1546 [NAICS 336391]

Araban Coffee Company Inc., p. I-143 [NAICS 311920]

Arachnid Inc., p. II-1708 [NAICS 33993M]

ARAMARK Sports, p. III-2190 [NAICS 453220]

Aranda Tooling Inc., p. II-1541 [NAICS 336370]

Arango Inc., p. III-2190 [NAICS 453220]

Arbill Industries Inc., p. I-218 [NAICS 31331M]

Arbor Handling Services Inc., p. III-1867 [NAICS 423830]

ARC Fasteners Supply Inc., p. III-1843 [NAICS 423710]

ARC Intern. North America Inc., p. III-1778 [NAICS 423220]

Arc Machines Inc., p. II-1162 [NAICS 333612]

ARC Oswego Industries Inc., p. I-285 [NAICS 31529M]

ARC Rubber Inc., p. I-505 [NAICS 325212]

ARC-Tronics Inc., pp. Vol. II-1312, 1451 [NAICS 334418, 33592M]

Arca Xytec Systems Inc., p. I-306 [NAICS 31699M]

Arch Chemicals Inc., pp. Vol. I-388, 566 [NAICS 32222N, 32561M]

Archbold Health Services Inc., p. III-1813 [NAICS 423450]

Archer Daniels Midland Co., pp. Vol. I-9, 15, 22, 26, 48 [NAICS 311119, 31121M, 311221, 311225, 311320]

Archon Vitamin Corp., p. I-534 [NAICS 325411]

Archway Cookies Inc, pp. Vol. I-116, 124 [NAICS 31181M, 31182M]

Archway Mother's Cookies L.L.C., p. I-124 [NAICS 31182M]

Arco Electric Products, p. II-1292 [NAICS 334414]

Arcotronics America Inc., p. II-1292 [NAICS 334414]

Arctic Cat Inc., pp. Vol. I-626, Vol. II-1594, 1607 [NAICS 326122, 336612, 336999]

Arctic Office Machine Inc., pp. Vol. III-1801, 1901 [NAICS 423420, 424120]

Arctic Slope Regional Corp., pp. Vol. I-443, 626 [NAICS 324110, 326122]

Arden Companies, pp. Vol. I-198, 234, 670, Vol. II-1749 [NAICS 313210, 31412M, 32629M, 339999]

Ardisam Inc., p. II-1207 [NAICS 333991]

ARE Inc., p. II-1500 [NAICS 336214]

ARE Press Inc., p. III-2162 [NAICS 451211]

Area Diesel Service Inc., p. II-1562 [NAICS 336412]

Aredco, p. II-1056 [NAICS 333295]

Arena Distributors Inc., p. III-1843 [NAICS 423710]

Arends Brothers Inc., p. III-1863 [NAICS 423820]

Arens Controls Company L.L.C., p. II-1332 [NAICS 334512]

Arenson Office Furnishings Inc., p. III-2037 [NAICS 442110]

Areway Inc., p. I-560 [NAICS 325520]

Argen Corp., p. II-1682 [NAICS 339114]

Argo and Company Inc., p. II-1740 [NAICS 339994]

Argo Data Resources Inc., p. III-2058 [NAICS 443120]

Argo International Corp., pp. Vol. III-1867, 1879 [NAICS 423830, 423860]

Argo Products Co., p. II-1541 [NAICS 336370]

Argo-Tech Corp., p. II-1580 [NAICS 336419]

Argon ST Inc., pp. Vol. II-1267, 1272, 1327, 1347, 1367 [NAICS 334290, 334310, 334511, 334515, 334519]

Argonaut Technologies Inc., p. I-544 [NAICS 325413]

Ariel Corp., p. II-1184 [NAICS 333912]

Aries Industries Inc., p. II-1082 [NAICS 333314]

ARINC Inc., p. II-1580 [NAICS 336419]

Aristo-Craft Inc., p. II-1442 [NAICS 335911]

Aristocrat Stamping and Mfg Inc., p. II-1541 [NAICS 336370]

Aristotle Corp., pp. Vol. I-279, Vol. II-1671 [NAICS 31523M, 339112]

Arizona Auto and Truck Parts Inc., p. III-1770 [NAICS 423140]

Arizona Chemical Company Inc., pp. Vol. I-475, 488 [NAICS 32513M, 325188]

Arizona Grain Inc., p. III-1958 [NAICS 424510]

Arizona Machinery Group Inc., p. III-1863 [NAICS 423820]

Arizona Natural Resources, pp. Vol. I-575, Vol. II-1749 [NAICS 325620, 339999]

Arizona Precision Sheet Metal, p. II-1282 [NAICS 334412]

Arizona Recycling Corp., p. III-1890 [NAICS 423930]

Arizona Wholesale Supply Co., pp. Vol. III-1831, 1835 [NAICS 423610, 423620]

Arjay Telecom, p. III-2054 [NAICS 443112]

Arkansas Aluminum Alloys Inc., pp. Vol. I-803, 816 [NAICS 331312, 33131N]

Arkansas Building Wire Div., pp. Vol. I-816, 830 [NAICS 33131N, 33142M]

Arkansas Copier Center Inc., p. III-2186 [NAICS 453210]

Arkansas Packaging Products Inc., p. III-1905 [NAICS 424130]

Arkansas Steel Associates L.L.C., p. II-1584 [NAICS 336510]

Arkat Nutrition, pp. Vol. I-4, 9 [NAICS 311111, 311119]

Arkwin Industries Inc., p. II-1580 [NAICS 336419]

Arkwright Inc., p. I-615 [NAICS 326113]

Arlington Industries Inc., p. II-1457 [NAICS 33593M]

Armbrust International Ltd., pp. Vol. I-872, Vol. II-1696 [NAICS 33211N, 33991M]

Armitron Corp., p. II-1362 [NAICS 334518]

Armstrong Holdings Inc., pp. Vol. I-626, 651, 695, Vol. II-908, 1616, 1621 [NAICS 326122, 32619M, 327122, 33232M, 337121, 337122]

Armstrong Manufacturing Co., p. II-1046 [NAICS 333210]

Armstrong McCall Inc., p. III-1875 [NAICS 423850]

Arnco Corp., p. II-1082 [NAICS 333314]

Arnold Machinery Co., pp. Vol. III-1859, 1863, 1867 [NAICS 423810, 423820, 423830]

Arnold Motor Supply Co., p. III-1762 [NAICS 423120]

Arnold Owens Inc., pp. Vol. III-1979, 2116 [NAICS 424720, 447110]

Arotech Corp., p. II-1442 [NAICS 335911]

Around The Clock Freightliner, p. III-1758 [NAICS 423110]

ARPAC L.P., p. II-1212 [NAICS 333993]

Array Distribution L.L.C., pp. Vol. III-1805, 1809 [NAICS 423430, 423440]

Array Marketing Group Inc., p. II-1644 [NAICS 337215]

Arrelle Fine Linens Inc., p. III-2047 [NAICS 442299]

Arri Inc., p. III-1798 [NAICS 423410]

Arribas Brothers Company Inc., p. I-713 [NAICS 327212]

Arrington Lumber and Pallet Inc., p. I-343 [NAICS 321920]

ARRIS Group Inc., p. II-1262 [NAICS 334220]

ArrMaz Custom Chemicals, p. I-529 [NAICS 325320]

Arrow Electronics Inc., pp. Vol. III-1831, 1839 [NAICS 423610, 423690]

Arrow Gear Co., p. II-1162 [NAICS 333612]

Arrow Group Industries Inc., pp. Vol. I-353, Vol. II-899 [NAICS 321992, 33231M]

Arrow International Inc., p. II-1671 [NAICS 339112]

Arrow-Piranha, p. II-886 [NAICS 33221N]

Arrow Tru-Line Inc., p. I-863 [NAICS 332114]

Arrow Truck Sales Inc., pp. Vol. III-1758, 2011 [NAICS 423110, 441110]

Arrowhead Conveyor Corp., p. II-923 [NAICS 332420]

Arrowhead Mountain Spring Water, pp. Vol. I-143, 165 [NAICS 311920, 31211M]

Arrowhead Products, p. II-1580 [NAICS 336419]

Art Dreams & Eclectic Art Designs, p. II-1362 [NAICS 334518]

Art Hacker Books Inc., p. III-2162 [NAICS 451211]

Art Leather Manufacturing Co., p. I-306 [NAICS 31699M]

Art Line Inc., p. I-681 [NAICS 327112]

Art Optical Contact Lens Inc., p. II-1687 [NAICS 339115]

Art's Mexican Products Inc., p. I-133 [NAICS 311830]

Art's-Way Manufacturing Inc., p. II-1028 [NAICS 333112]

Art Van Furniture Inc., p. III-2037 [NAICS 442110]

Artco-Bell Corp., p. II-1627 [NAICS 337127]

Artee/Wrapspun Inc., p. I-192 [NAICS 31311M]

Artesa Winery, p. I-177 [NAICS 312130]

Artesyn Technologies Inc., pp. Vol. II-1238, 1252, 1317, 1367 [NAICS 334111, 334119, 334419, 334519]

Artex International Inc., pp. Vol. I-234, 272, 279 [NAICS 31412M, 31522M, 31523M]

Artex Knitting Mills Inc., p. I-262 [NAICS 31519M]

Arthrex Inc., p. II-1671 [NAICS 339112]

ArthroCare Corp., pp. Vol. II-1322, 1671 [NAICS 334510, 339112]

Arthur B Myr Industries Inc., p. II-1740 [NAICS 339994]

Arthur G Russell Company Inc., pp. Vol. II-1152, 1666 [NAICS 333518, 339111]

Arthur Sanderson & Sons, p. III-1913 [NAICS 424310]

Artifacts International, p. II-1632 [NAICS 33712N]

Artlite Office Supply & Furniture, p. III-1774 [NAICS 423210]

Artos Engineering Co., p. II-1152 [NAICS 333518]

Arts Elegance Inc., p. III-1894 [NAICS 423940]

Arty Imports Inc., p. III-1998 [NAICS 424930]

ArvinMeritor Inc., pp. Vol. II-1168, 1427, 1551 [NAICS 333613, 335312, 336399]

AS and E High Energy Systems, p. II-1357 [NAICS 334517]

Asael Farr and Sons Co., p. III-1933 [NAICS 424430]

Asahi Glass America Inc., p. I-709 [NAICS 327211]

Asahi Thermofil Inc., pp. Vol. I-500, 631 [NAICS 325211, 326130]

Asbury Automotive Group Inc., pp. Vol. III-1758, 2011 [NAICS 423110, 441110]

Asbury Graphite Inc., p. II-1463 [NAICS 335991]

Asbury Graphite Mills Inc., p. II-1463 [NAICS 335991]

ASC Capacitors, p. II-1292 [NAICS 334414]

ASC Inc., p. II-933 [NAICS 332510]

ASC International Inc., p. III-1879 [NAICS 423860]

ASC Machine Tools Inc., pp. Vol. II-1129, 1152 [NAICS 333513, 333518]

ASC Systems, p. II-1248 [NAICS 334113]

Ascentra Holdings Inc., p. III-1813 [NAICS 423450]

Aseptico Inc., p. II-1682 [NAICS 339114]

Ash Grove Cement Co., p. I-727 [NAICS 327310]

Ashers Chocolate, pp. Vol. I-52, 57 [NAICS 311330, 311340]

Ashgate Publishing Co., p. III-1995 [NAICS 424920]

Ashgrove Texas L.P., p. I-727 [NAICS 327310]

Ashland Inc., pp. Vol. I-443, 488, 500 [NAICS 324110, 325188, 325211]

Ashley Apparel, p. I-285 [NAICS 31529M]

Ashley F. Ward Inc., pp. Vol. II-952, 1124 [NAICS 332721, 333512]

Ashley Furniture Industries Inc., pp. Vol. II-1616, 1621, 1650 [NAICS 337121, 337122, 33721N]

Ashley Salvage Company Inc., p. I-807 [NAICS 331314]

Ashmore Brothers Inc., p. I-448 [NAICS 324121]

Ashta Chemicals Inc., p. I-480 [NAICS 325181]

Ashtabula Rubber Co., p. II-1119 [NAICS 333511]

Ashworth Inc., pp. Vol. I-272, 290, 300 [NAICS 31522M, 31599M, 31621M]

ASI Corp., p. III-1805 [NAICS 423430]

Asi Holding Inc., pp. Vol. III-1809, 1879 [NAICS 423440, 423860]

Asia Easyfine Ltd., p. III-1919 [NAICS 424330]

AsiRobicon, pp. Vol. II-1162, 1272, 1437, 1468 [NAICS 333612, 334310, 335314, 335999]

ASJ Components Inc., pp. Vol. II-1292, 1297 [NAICS 334414, 334415]

ASM International, p. III-2162 [NAICS 451211]

ASMO North Carolina Inc., p. II-1427 [NAICS 335312]

Aspect Medical Systems Inc., p. II-1322 [NAICS 334510]

Aspect Systems Inc., p. II-1056 [NAICS 333295]

Aspen Furniture L.L.C., p. II-1621 [NAICS 337122]

Aspen Products Inc., pp. Vol. I-395, 415 [NAICS 32222P, 322299]

Aspen Sports Inc., p. III-2150 [NAICS 451110]

Asphalt Construction Company, p. I-737 [NAICS 32733M]

Asphalt Cutbacks Inc., p. I-453 [NAICS 324122]

Asphalt Materials Inc., pp. Vol. I-448, 453, 727 [NAICS 324121, 324122, 327310]

Asq Technology Inc., p. II-1056 [NAICS 333295]

Associated Aircraft Supply Inc., p. III-1879 [NAICS 423860]

Associated Asphalt & Materials, p. III-1786 [NAICS 423320]

Associated Bag Co., p. I-403 [NAICS 32223M]

Associated Dental Laboratory, p. II-1692 [NAICS 339116]

Associated Food Stores Inc,, pp. Vol. III-1925, 1950 [NAICS 424410, 424480]

Associated Grocers Inc., pp. Vol. III-1925, 1929, 1946 [NAICS 424410, 424420, 424470]

Associated Grocers of the South, p. III-1925 [NAICS 424410]

Associated Materials Inc., pp. Vol. I-334, 626, 837 [NAICS 32191M, 326122, 33149M]

Associated Milk Producers Inc., pp. Vol. I-76, 81, 86, 92, Vol. III-1933 [NAICS 311513, 311514, 31151N, 311520, 424430]

Associated Packaging Inc., pp. Vol. III-1867, 1871 [NAICS 423830, 423840]

Associated Pallets Inc., p. I-343 [NAICS 321920]

Associated Rubber Co., pp. Vol. I-505, 660 [NAICS 325212, 32621M]

Associated Wholesalers Inc., p. III-1925 [NAICS 424410]

Associated X-Ray Corp., p. II-1357 [NAICS 334517]

AST Inc., p. II-1212 [NAICS 333993]

Astec Industries Inc., pp. Vol. II-1033, 1039, 1112, 1194 [NAICS 333120, 33313M, 33341N, 33392M]

AstenJohnson Inc., p. I-251 [NAICS 314999]

Astra Products Ltd., p. II-1662 [NAICS 337920]

Astral Industries Inc., p. II-1745 [NAICS 339995]

Astro Air Inc., p. II-918 [NAICS 332410]

Astro-Lounger & Davis Furniture, p. II-1616 [NAICS 337121]

Astro-Med Inc., pp. Vol. I-403, 560, Vol. II-1347, 1714 [NAICS 32223M, 325520, 334515, 33994M]

Astro Shapes Inc., pp. Vol. I-811, Vol. II-964 [NAICS 331316, 33281M]

Astrocosmos Metallurgical Inc, p. III-1824 [NAICS 423510]

Astrokam, p. III-1839 [NAICS 423690]

Astronautics Corporation, pp. Vol. II-1327, 1337 [NAICS 334511, 334513]

Astronics Corp., pp. Vol. II-1390, 1512 [NAICS 33512M, 33632M]

Astrup Drug Inc., p. III-2100 [NAICS 446110]

A.S.V. Inc., p. II-1033 [NAICS 333120]

Asyst Technologies Inc., p. II-1061 [NAICS 33329N]

AT and T Corp., pp. Vol. II-1238, 1257 [NAICS 334111, 334210]

A.T. Clayton and Company Inc., p. III-1898 [NAICS 424110]

A.T. Cross Co., pp. Vol. II-1714, Vol. III-1901, 2007 [NAICS 33994M, 424120, 424990]

Atalanta Corp., pp. Vol. III-1929, 1933, 1943, 1946 [NAICS 424420, 424430, 424460, 424470]

ATC Lighting and Plastics Inc., pp. Vol. I-722, Vol. II-1390, 1486, 1512 [NAICS 327215, 33512M, 336211, 33632M]

ATCO Rubber Products Inc., pp. Vol. I-621, Vol. II-1106 [NAICS 326121, 333415]

ATD-American Co., pp. Vol. III-1774, 1813, 1913 [NAICS 423210, 423450, 424310]

Athana International Inc., p. II-1376 [NAICS 334612]

Athearn Trains, p. II-1708 [NAICS 33993M]

Athletic Supply of California, p. III-2150 [NAICS 451110]

Atkins and Pearce Inc., p. I-198 [NAICS 313210]

Atkinson Candy Co., p. I-57 [NAICS 311340]

Atkinson Milling Co., p. I-15 [NAICS 31121M]

Atlanta Beverage Co., p. III-1983 [NAICS 424810]

Atlanta Bread Co., p. III-2094 [NAICS 445299]

Atlanta Whirlpool Concepts Inc., pp. Vol. I-677, 762 [NAICS 327111, 327991]

Atlantic Bingo Supply Inc., p. III-1887 [NAICS 423920]

Atlantic Business Communications, p. III-2054 [NAICS 443112]

Atlantic Detroit Diesel/Allison Co., pp. Vol. II-1505, 1530 [NAICS 33631M, 336350]

Atlantic Hosiery Outlet, p. I-256 [NAICS 31511M]

Atlantic Marble Company Inc., p. I-762 [NAICS 327991]

Atlantic Medco Inc., p. III-1813 [NAICS 423450]

Atlantic Premium Brands Ltd., p. III-1954 [NAICS 424490]

Atlantic Scale Company Inc., p. III-1809 [NAICS 423440]

Atlantic Spinners Inc., p. I-192 [NAICS 31311M]

Atlantic Tool and Die Inc., p. II-1134 [NAICS 333514]

Atlantic Track and Turnout Co., p. III-1879 [NAICS 423860]

Atlantic Ultraviolet Corp., p. II-1386 [NAICS 335110]

Atlantic Veneer Corp., p. I-324 [NAICS 32121N]

Atlantic Wire Co., p. II-1463 [NAICS 335991]

Atlantic Wood Industries Inc., p. I-312 [NAICS 32111M]

Atlantic Zeiser Co., p. II-1077 [NAICS 333313]

Atlantis Plastics Inc., pp. Vol. I-615, 626 [NAICS 326113, 326122]

Atlas Bolt and Screw Co., p. II-958 [NAICS 332722]

Atlas Copco Comptec Inc., pp. Vol. II-1157, Vol. III-1867 [NAICS 333611, 423830]

Atlas Die L.L.C., pp. Vol. II-892, 1119, 1134, 1714 [NAICS 33221P, 333511, 333514, 33994M]

Atlas Electric Devices Co., p. III-1820 [NAICS 423490]

Atlas Fibre Co., p. I-621 [NAICS 326121]

Atlas Industrial Holdings L.L.C., p. II-1009 [NAICS 332996]

Atlas Lift Truck Rentals, pp. Vol. III-1859, 1867 [NAICS 423810, 423830]

Atlas Material Testing Tech, pp. Vol. II-1352, 1666 [NAICS 334516, 339111]

Atlas Metal and Iron Corp., pp. Vol. I-807, Vol. III-1890 [NAICS 331314, 423930]

Atlas Mill Supply, p. III-1890 [NAICS 423930]

Atlas Minerals and Chemicals Inc., p. I-453 [NAICS 324122]

Atlas Model Railroad Inc., p. II-1708 [NAICS 33993M]

Atlas Peat and Soil Inc., pp. Vol. I-312, 524 [NAICS 32111M, 325314]

Atlas Pen and Pencil Corp., p. II-1714 [NAICS 33994M]

Atlas Pressed Metals, p. I-867 [NAICS 332117]

Atlas Steel Products Co., pp. Vol. I-793, Vol. II-945 [NAICS 33122M, 332710]

Atlas Tag and Label Inc., pp. Vol. I-203, 415 [NAICS 31322M, 322299]

Atlas Textile Company Inc., p. III-1913 [NAICS 424310]

Atlas Tubular L.P., p. III-2065 [NAICS 444100]

Atlas Waste Paper Corp., p. I-363 [NAICS 322110]

Atlaz International Ltd., p. II-1248 [NAICS 334113]

Atmel Corp., p. II-1287 [NAICS 334413]

ATMI Inc., p. I-475 [NAICS 32513M]

ATOFINA Chemicals Inc., pp. Vol. I-480, 488, 549, 566, 595 [NAICS 325181, 325188, 325414, 32561M, 32599N]

Atomergic Chemetals Corp., p. II-1463 [NAICS 335991]

Atomicbox Inc., pp. Vol. III-1843, 1901, 2004 [NAICS 423710, 424120, 424950]

Atotech USA Inc., pp. Vol. I-475, Vol. II-1061 [NAICS 32513M, 33329N]

ATR Supply Co., pp. Vol. III-1847, 1851 [NAICS 423720, 423730]

Atrion Corp., p. I-544 [NAICS 325413]

Atrium Companies Inc., pp. Vol. I-334, 358, 811, Vol. II-908 [NAICS 32191M, 321999, 331316, 33232M]

Atrium Corp., p. I-358 [NAICS 321999]

Atrium Windows and Doors, p. I-722 [NAICS 327215]

Atronix Inc., p. II-1307 [NAICS 334417]

Atsco Products Inc., p. II 1519 [NAICS 336330]

Attala Company Inc., p. I-4 [NAICS 311111]

Attbar Inc., p. II-1594 [NAICS 336612]

Atwater Inc., p. I-510 [NAICS 32522M]

Atwood, p. I-722 [NAICS 327215]

Atwood Distributing Inc., pp. Vol. III-2030, 2065, 2177 [NAICS 441310, 444100, 452910]

ATX II L.L.C., p. III-2058 [NAICS 443120]

Au Bon Pain, p. I-116 [NAICS 31181M]

Auburn Consolidated Industries, p. II-1033 [NAICS 333120]

Auburn Foundry Inc., p. I-845 [NAICS 33151M]

Auburn Gear Inc., pp. Vol. II-928, 1162, 1168, 1530 [NAICS 33243M, 333612, 333613, 336350]

Auction X-Press, p. I-436 [NAICS 32312M]

Audemars Piguet, p. III-1894 [NAICS 423940]

Audio Ethics Inc., p. III-2054 [NAICS 443112]

Audio International Inc., pp. Vol. II-1327, 1567 [NAICS 334511, 336413]

Audio Technica U S Inc., p. III-1839 [NAICS 423690]

Audio-Video Color Corp., pp. Vol. I-379, 388, Vol. II-1376 [NAICS 32221M, 32222N, 334612]

Audio Video Supply Inc., p. III-1813 [NAICS 423450]

AudioDev USA Inc., p. II-1347 [NAICS 334515]

Audiovisual Inc., p. III-2054 [NAICS 443112]

Audiovox Corp., pp. Vol. III-1831, 1835, 1839 [NAICS 423610, 423620, 423690]

Audubon Metals L.L.C., p. I-807 [NAICS 331314]

Auglaize Farmers Cooperative Inc., pp. Vol. I-9, 524 [NAICS 311119, 325314]

August Lotz Company Inc., p. II-1657 [NAICS 337910]

August Schell Brewing Inc., p. I-172 [NAICS 312120]

August Technology Corp., p. II-1082 [NAICS 333314]

Augusta Fiberglass Coatings Inc., p. I-554 [NAICS 325510]

Augusta Sportswear Inc., p. I-239 [NAICS 31491M]

Ault Inc., pp. Vol. II-1421, 1432 [NAICS 335311, 335313]

Aurea Jewelry Creations L.L.C., p. III-1894 [NAICS 423940]

Aurora Casket Company Inc., p. II-1745 [NAICS 339995]

Aurora Cooperative Elevator Co., pp. Vol. I-9, Vol. III-1958 [NAICS 311119, 424510]

Aurora Hardwoods, p. II-1745 [NAICS 339995]

Aurora Textile Finishing Co., p. I-218 [NAICS 31331M]

Austin Powder Co., p. I-585 [NAICS 325920]

Austin Tri-Hawk Automotive Inc., p. II-1541 [NAICS 336370]

Austin/Westran, p. II-1106 [NAICS 333415]

Authorized Cellular, p. III-2054 [NAICS 443112]

Auto Chlor System Inc., p. III-1835 [NAICS 423620]

Auto Crane Co., p. II-1184 [NAICS 333912]

Auto Electric and Battery Inc., p. II-1442 [NAICS 335911]

Auto Meter Products Inc., pp. Vol. I-670, Vol. II-1140, 1337, 1347 [NAICS 32629M, 333515, 334513, 334515]

Auto Recyclers Inc., p. III-1770 [NAICS 423140]

Auto Suture Company U.S.A., p. III-1813 [NAICS 423450]

Auto Trim Designs, p. III-2030 [NAICS 441310]

Autocam Corp., pp. Vol. II-1014, 1092, 1238, 1512, 1671 [NAICS 33299N, 33331N, 334111, 33632M, 339112]

Autocenter Chevrolet Inc., p. III-1770 [NAICS 423140]

Autocrat Inc., pp. Vol. I-143, 147, 152 [NAICS 311920, 311930, 31194M]

Autohaus of Minneapolis Inc., p. III-2015 [NAICS 441120]

Autoliv ASP Inc., p. II-1551 [NAICS 336399]

Automanage Inc., p. III-2011 [NAICS 441110]

Automated Building Components, pp. Vol. I-324, 329, 334 [NAICS 32121N, 32121P, 32191M]

Automated Dynamics, p. II-1463 [NAICS 335991]

Automated Gasket Corp., p. I-374 [NAICS 322130]

Automated Logic Corp., p. II-1332 [NAICS 334512]

Automated Mould Industries Inc., p. II-1134 [NAICS 333514]

Automated Products Inc., pp. Vol. I-329, 353 [NAICS 32121P, 321992]

Automated Systems of Tacoma, p. II-1051 [NAICS 333220]

Automatic Bakery Machine Inc., p. III-1905 [NAICS 424130]

Automatic Feed Co., p. II-1152 [NAICS 333518]

Automatic Handling International, p. II-1147 [NAICS 333516]

Automatic Ice Machine Inc., p. III-1855 [NAICS 423740]

Automatic Machine Products Co., p. II-952 [NAICS 332721]

Automatic Spring Products Corp., p. II-958 [NAICS 332722]

Automotive International Inc., p. III-1971 [NAICS 424690]

Automotive Parts Headquarters, p. III-1762 [NAICS 423120]

Automotive Remanufacturers Inc., pp. Vol. II-1173, 1184, 1505, 1512, 1530 [NAICS 333618, 333912, 33631M, 33632M, 336350]

Automotive Supply Co., p. III-1762 [NAICS 423120]

AutoNation Inc., p. III-2011 [NAICS 441110]

Autosplice Inc., pp. Vol. II-1056, 1307 [NAICS 333295, 334417]

Autotote Lottery Corp., pp. Vol. II-1238, Vol. III-1805 [NAICS 334111, 423430]

Autotronic Controls Corp., p. II-1512 [NAICS 33632M]

Autotronics Inc., p. II-1524 [NAICS 336340]

AutoZone Inc., p. III-2030 [NAICS 441310]

AV Automotive L.L.C., p. III-2027 [NAICS 441229]

Avaho Industries, p. II-1112 [NAICS 33341N]

Avail Medical Products, pp. Vol. I-411, 603 [NAICS 322291, 326111]

Available Plastics Inc., p. II-1632 [NAICS 33712N]

Avant-Garde Technology Inc., p. II-1005 [NAICS 332995]

Avanti, pp. Vol. I-420, 436 [NAICS 32311M, 32312M]

Avanti Linens Inc., p. I-203 [NAICS 31322M]

Avanti Polar Lipids Inc., p. I-493 [NAICS 32519M]

Avanti Products Inc., p. III-2050 [NAICS 443111]

Avatar Corp., pp. Vol. I-26, 458 [NAICS 311225, 324191]

Avcon Industries, p. II-1557 [NAICS 336411]

AVEBE America Inc., pp. Vol. I-22, 158 [NAICS 311221, 31199M]

Avecia Inc., pp. Vol. I-488, 595 [NAICS 325188, 32599N]

Avedis Zildjian Company Inc., p. II-1731 [NAICS 339992]

Avedon Engineering Inc., pp. Vol. I-436, Vol. II-1536 [NAICS 32312M, 336360]

Aventis Pharmaceuticals Inc., p. I-539 [NAICS 325412]

Averitt Hardwoods Intern. Inc., pp. Vol. I-343, 358 [NAICS 321920, 321999]

Avery Dennison Corp., pp. Vol. I-388, 420, 560, 595, Vol. II-1212 [NAICS 32222N, 32311M, 325520, 32599N, 333993]

Avery Weigh-Tronix Inc., p. II-1367 [NAICS 334519]

Aveyard Enterprises Inc., p. III-1770 [NAICS 423140]

AVG Automation Group, pp. Vol. II-1337, 1437 [NAICS 334513, 335314]

Aviall Inc., pp. Vol. II-1092, 1567 [NAICS 33331N, 336413]

Aviat Aircraft Inc., p. II-1557 [NAICS 336411]

Aviation General Inc., p. II-1557 [NAICS 336411]

Avibank Manufacturing Inc., p. II-1735 [NAICS 339993]

Avid Technology Inc., p. II-1272 [NAICS 334310]

Avidex Industries L.L.C., p. III-2208 [NAICS 453998]

Avila's Garden Art, p. I-681 [NAICS 327112]

Avio-Diepen Inc., p. III-1879 [NAICS 423860]

Avis Industrial Corp., pp. Vol. II-1023, 1124, 1194, 1584 [NAICS 333111, 333512, 33392M, 336510]

Avnet Inc., pp. Vol. II-1287, Vol. III-1839 [NAICS 334413, 423690]

Avnet Marketing Services Inc, pp. Vol. III-1805, 1839 [NAICS 423430, 423690]

Avocent Corp., p. II-1252 [NAICS 334119]

Avon Custom Mixing Services Inc., p. I-505 [NAICS 325212]

Avon Products Inc., pp. Vol. I-539, 575 [NAICS 325412, 325620]

Avon Zatec L.L.C., p. II-1087 [NAICS 333315]

Avondale Mills Inc., pp. Vol. I-192, 198 [NAICS 31311M, 313210]

Avtech Corp., p. II-1390 [NAICS 33512M]

Avtron Manufacturing Inc., pp. Vol. II-1297, 1332 [NAICS 334415, 334512]

AVX Corp., pp. Vol. II-1287, 1292, 1307, 1317 [NAICS 334413, 334414, 334417, 334419]

AVX Tantalum Corp., p. II-1292 [NAICS 334414]

AW Chesterton Company Inc., pp. Vol. I-458, 566, Vol. II-1179, 1725 [NAICS 324191, 32561M, 333911, 339991]

AW Co., p. II-1342 [NAICS 334514]

AW Imported Auto Parts Inc., p. III-2030 [NAICS 441310]

A.W. Marshall Co., pp. Vol. III-1939, 2001 [NAICS 424450, 424940]

AW Mercer Inc., pp. Vol. II-928, 1101 [NAICS 33243M, 333414]

Aware Products Inc., p. II-886 [NAICS 33221N]

Awrey Bakeries Inc., pp. Vol. I-116, 124 [NAICS 31181M, 31182M]

Numbers following p. or pp. are page references. Roman numerals indicate volume numbers. Bracketed items indicate industries. Page references are to the starting pages of company tables.

AWS, p. I-343 [NAICS 321920]

Axalto, pp. Vol. I-631, Vol. II-1381 [NAICS 326130, 334613]

Axcelis Technologies Inc., p. II-1061 [NAICS 33329N]

Axel Johnson Inc., pp. Vol. III-1975, 1979 [NAICS 424710, 424720]

Axel Plastics Research Labs, p. I-458 [NAICS 324191]

Axelrod Foods Inc., p. III-1933 [NAICS 424430]

Axiohm Transaction Solutions Inc., p. II-1714 [NAICS 33994M]

Axle Alliance Company L.L.C., p. II-1530 [NAICS 336350]

Axson North America Inc., pp. Vol. I-589, 752 [NAICS 325991, 327420]

AXSYS Technologies Inc., pp. Vol. II-1082, 1297, 1307, 1427, 1437, 1457 [NAICS 333314, 334415, 334417, 335312, 335314, 33593M]

Axton Candy and Tobacco Co., p. III-2001 [NAICS 424940]

AY Manufacturing Ltd., p. I-722 [NAICS 327215]

Ayrshire Electronics, pp. Vol. II-1282, 1312 [NAICS 334412, 334418]

AZ Automotive Corp., pp. Vol. I-879, Vol. II-1541 [NAICS 33211P, 336370]

AZCO Inc., p. II-1432 [NAICS 335313]

Aztec Business Machines Inc., p. III-1801 [NAICS 423420]

Aztec Peroxides Inc., p. I-488 [NAICS 325188]

Aztec Supply Co., p. III-1968 [NAICS 424610]

Azteca Foods Inc., p. I-133 [NAICS 311830]

Azteca Milling Co., p. I-15 [NAICS 31121M]

AZZ Inc., pp. Vol. II-964, 980, 1009, 1390 [NAICS 33281M, 33291N, 332996, 33512M]

B and B Auto Parts Inc., p. III-1770 [NAICS 423140]

B and B Concrete Company Inc., p. II-1536 [NAICS 336360]

B and B Electronics Mfg Co., p. II-1347 [NAICS 334515]

B and B Fisheries Inc., p. III-1943 [NAICS 424460]

B and B Lumber Company Inc., pp. Vol. I-343, 358 [NAICS 321920, 321999]

B and B Tool and Die Inc., p. I-867 [NAICS 332117]

B and C Corp., pp. Vol. I-811, Vol. II-1530 [NAICS 331316, 336350]

B and D Precision Tools Inc., p. II-1662 [NAICS 337920]

B and F System Inc., p. III-1778 [NAICS 423220]

B and G Auto Sales Inc., p. III-2015 [NAICS 441120]

B and G Foods Holdings Corp., p. I-68 [NAICS 31142M]

B and G Manufacturing Inc., p. II-952 [NAICS 332721]

B and H Labeling Systems, p. II-1212 [NAICS 333993]

B and I Fender Trims Inc., p. II-1541 [NAICS 336370]

B and J Seafood L.L.C., p. I-110 [NAICS 31171M]

B and M Imports Inc., p. III-1894 [NAICS 423940]

B and M Machinery Co., p. II-1173 [NAICS 333618]

B Braun Medical Inc, pp. Vol. II-1671, 1676 [NAICS 339112, 339113]

B Frank Inc., p. II-1417 [NAICS 335228]

B. Frank Joy Company Inc., p. III-1782 [NAICS 423310]

B Manischewitz Company L.L.C., p. I-158 [NAICS 31199M]

B Map Core, p. III-1770 [NAICS 423140]

B. Olinde and Sons Company Inc., pp. Vol. III-1983, 2037, 2050 [NAICS 424810, 442110, 443111]

B/T Western Corp., p. III-1758 [NAICS 423110]

B.A. Ballou and Company Inc., p. II-1696 [NAICS 33991M]

B.A. G Corp., p. I-603 [NAICS 326111]

B.A. W Plastics Inc., pp. Vol. I-510, 615 [NAICS 32522M, 326113]

Baader-Brown Manufacturing Co., p. II-1386 [NAICS 335110]

Babbitting Service Inc., p. I-825 [NAICS 331419]

Babcock Lumber Co., pp. Vol. I-312, 324, 334 [NAICS 32111M, 32121N, 32191M]

Babcock Power Inc., pp. Vol. II-918, 1101, 1112, 1157 [NAICS 332410, 333414, 33341N, 333611]

Babies 'R' Us, p. III-2129 [NAICS 448130]

BAC-Brewer Automotive, p. II-1519 [NAICS 336330]

Bacardi Bottling Corp., p. I-181 [NAICS 312140]

Bacharach-Rasin Company Inc., p. III-2150 [NAICS 451110]

Bachman Co., p. I-137 [NAICS 31191M]

Back to Basics Products Inc., p. III-1778 [NAICS 423220]

Bacon Products Corp., p. I-529 [NAICS 325320]

Bacou-Dalloz Americas, p. I-300 [NAICS 31621M]

Badger Corrugating Co., pp. Vol. III-1786, 1790 [NAICS 423320, 423330]

Badger Liquor Company Inc., p. III-1987 [NAICS 424820]

Badger Meter Inc., pp. Vol. II-980, 1337, 1342, 1367, 1432 [NAICS 33291N, 334513, 334514, 334519, 335313]

Badger Paper Mills Inc., pp. Vol. I-368, 415 [NAICS 32212M, 322299]

Badger State Rebuilders Inc., p. II-1442 [NAICS 335911]

Badorf Shoe Company Inc., p. III-1922 [NAICS 424340]

BAE Systems Aerospace, p. II-1327 [NAICS 334511]

BAE SYSTEMS Integrated, pp. Vol. II-1567, 1580 [NAICS 336413, 336419]

BAE Systems Platform Solutions, pp. Vol. II-1337, 1580 [NAICS 334513, 336419]

Bag Makers Inc., pp. Vol. I-395, 603 [NAICS 32222P, 326111]

Bagatelle Bakery Inc., p. III-2089 [NAICS 445291]

Bagcraft Packaging L.L.C., pp. Vol. I-374, 395, 816 [NAICS 322130, 32222P, 33131N]

Bailey Knit Corp., p. I-256 [NAICS 31511M]

Bailey Nurseries Inc., p. III-1998 [NAICS 424930]

Bailey Quarries Inc., p. I-748 [NAICS 327410]

Baillio's Warehouse Showroom, pp. Vol. III-2050, 2054, 2058 [NAICS 443111, 443112, 443120]

Bairnco Corp., pp. Vol. I-505, 554, Vol. II-886, 892, 1282, 1347 [NAICS 325212, 325510, 33221N, 33221P, 334412, 334515]

Bakemark West, pp. Vol. I-158, Vol. III-1954 [NAICS 31199M, 424490]

Baker and Baker Inc., pp. Vol. I-62, 124, 158 [NAICS 31141M, 31182M, 31199M]

Baker Cheese Factory Inc., p. I-76 [NAICS 311513]

Baker Company Inc., p. II-928 [NAICS 33243M]

Baker Furniture, pp. Vol. II-1616, 1621, 1650 [NAICS 337121, 337122, 33721N]

Baker Hosiery Inc., p. I-256 [NAICS 31511M]

Baker Hughes Inc., p. II-1039 [NAICS 33313M]

Baker Implement Co., p. III-1863 [NAICS 423820]

Baker Manufacturing Co., pp. Vol. I-845, Vol. II-1039 [NAICS 33151M, 33313M]

Baker Metal Products Inc., p. I-816 [NAICS 33131N]

Baker Petrolite, p. I-500 [NAICS 325211]

Baker Products, p. II-1046 [NAICS 333210]

Baker Rock Resources, p. I-743 [NAICS 327390]

Baker's Furniture and Accessories, p. III-2037 [NAICS 442110]

Bakers Footwear Group Inc., pp. Vol. III-2135, 2141 [NAICS 448150, 448210]

Bakers Jewelry and Gifts, p. III-2135 [NAICS 448150]

Bakery DeFrance, p. III-1929 [NAICS 424420]

BAL SEAL Engineering Co., pp. Vol. I-554, Vol. II-939, 1725 [NAICS 325510, 33261M, 339991]

Balance Technology Inc., p. II-1666 [NAICS 339111]

Bald Knob Land and Timber Inc., p. I-324 [NAICS 32121N]

Baldor Electric Co., pp. Vol. II-1427, Vol. III-1867 [NAICS 335312, 423830]

Baldwin Piano and Organ Co., p. II-1731 [NAICS 339992]

Baldwin Piano Inc., pp. Vol. II-1731, Vol. III-2159 [NAICS 339992, 451140]

Baldwin Precision Inc., p. II-1046 [NAICS 333210]

Baldwin-Richardson Foods, p. I-147 [NAICS 311930]

Baldwin Richardson Foods Co., p. I-92 [NAICS 311520]

Bale Chevrolet Geo Co., p. III-1762 [NAICS 423120]

Balemaster, p. II-1077 [NAICS 333313]

Bales Continental Commission Co., p. III-1962 [NAICS 424520]

Balimoy Manufacturing, pp. Vol. II-993, 997 [NAICS 332992, 332993]

Balkore Industries Inc., p. II-1342 [NAICS 334514]

Ball Aerospace & Technologies, pp. Vol. II-1317, 1327, 1580 [NAICS 334419, 334511, 336419]

Ball and Prier Tire Inc., p. III-1766 [NAICS 423130]

Ball Corp., pp. Vol. I-626, 879, Vol. II-928, 1257, 1317, 1327, 1580 [NAICS 326122, 33211P, 33243M, 334210, 334419, 334511, 336419]

Ball Horticultural Co., pp. Vol. II-1749, Vol. III-1998 [NAICS 339999, 424930]

Ball Screws and Actuators Inc., p. II-988 [NAICS 332991]

Ballantyne of Omaha Inc., pp. Vol. II-1087, 1272, 1386, 1390, 1627 [NAICS 333315, 334310, 335110, 33512M, 337127]

Ballard Medical Products, p. II-1671 [NAICS 339112]

Ballet Makers Inc., p. III-1922 [NAICS 424340]

Balloonatics Inc., p. III-2190 [NAICS 453220]

Bally Bead Company Inc., pp. Vol. III-1894, 2153 [NAICS 423940, 451120]

Numbers following p. or pp. are page references. Roman numerals indicate volume numbers. Bracketed items indicate industries. Page references are to the starting pages of company tables.

2303

Company Index

Bally Ribbon Mills, pp. Vol. I-198, 203, 251, 788 [NAICS 313210, 31322M, 314999, 331210]

Baltek Corp., p. I-641 [NAICS 326150]

Baltimore Aircoil Company Inc., pp. Vol. II-899, 918, 1106 [NAICS 33231M, 332410, 333415]

Baltimore Spice Inc., pp. Vol. I-147, 152 [NAICS 311930, 31194M]

Bama Co's Inc., pp. Vol. I-62, 116 [NAICS 31141M, 31181M]

Bama Sea Products Inc., p. I-110 [NAICS 31171M]

Bancare Equipment Sales Inc., p. III-1820 [NAICS 423490]

Bancroft Bag Inc., p. I-395 [NAICS 32222P]

Bancroft Paper of Jackson Inc., p. III-1905 [NAICS 424130]

BancTec Inc., p. II-1252 [NAICS 334119]

Band Pro Film-Video Inc., p. III-1798 [NAICS 423610]

Bandag Inc., pp. Vol. I-660, Vol. II-1061 [NAICS 32621M, 33329N]

Bandlock Corp., p. I-589 [NAICS 325991]

Bando Mfg of America Inc., p. I-665 [NAICS 326220]

Bangers L.P., p. III-1883 [NAICS 423910]

Bangor Pipe and Supply Inc., p. III-1851 [NAICS 423730]

Banks Lumber Company Inc., p. I-329 [NAICS 32121P]

Banner Engineering Corp., p. II-1437 [NAICS 335314]

Banner Packaging Inc., pp. Vol. I-615, 641 [NAICS 326113, 326150]

Banta Corp., pp. Vol. I-368, 388, 403, 420, 626 [NAICS 32212M, 32222N, 32223M, 32311M, 326122]

Bar-Lo Carbon Products Inc., p. II-1463 [NAICS 335991]

Bar-S Foods Co., p. I-102 [NAICS 31161N]

Baraboo Candy Co., p. I-48 [NAICS 311320]

Barbara Creations, p. III-1817 [NAICS 423460]

Barbara's Bakery, pp. Vol. I-52, 57 [NAICS 311330, 311340]

Barbara's Bakery Inc., p. I-158 [NAICS 31199M]

Barbee-Neuhaus Implement Co., p. III-1863 [NAICS 423820]

Barbeques Galore Inc., p. III-2050 [NAICS 443111]

Barber Foods, pp. Vol. I-62, 97 [NAICS 31141M, 311615]

Barber Milk Inc., pp. Vol. I-86, 92 [NAICS 31151N, 311520]

Barber's Poultry Inc., p. III-1936 [NAICS 424440]

Barbosa Cabinets Inc., pp. Vol. II-1611, 1650 [NAICS 337110, 33721N]

Barbron Corp., pp. Vol. I-816, Vol. II-974 [NAICS 33131N, 332913]

Barcalounger Corp., pp. Vol. II-1616, 1621 [NAICS 337121, 337122]

Barclay Dean, p. III-1774 [NAICS 423210]

Barco Simulation, p. II-1087 [NAICS 333315]

Bard Manufacturing Company Inc., pp. Vol. II-1101, 1106, 1179 [NAICS 333414, 333415, 333911]

Barden Companies Inc., pp. Vol. III-1758, 1762 [NAICS 423110, 423120]

Barden Corp, pp. Vol. I-879, Vol. II-988, 1014 [NAICS 33211P, 332991, 33299N]

Bardo Custom Blending Inc., p. I-81 [NAICS 311514]

Bardon Enterprises, pp. Vol. II-1611, 1632 [NAICS 337110, 33712N]

Bardons and Oliver Inc., p. II-1147 [NAICS 333516]

Bareman Dairy Inc., p. I-86 [NAICS 31151N]

Bargreen-Ellingson Inc., p. II-1627 [NAICS 337127]

Barker Company Ltd., pp. Vol. II-1106, 1644 [NAICS 333415, 337215]

Barker-Jennings Corp., p. III-1770 [NAICS 423140]

Barker Microfarads Inc., p. II-1292 [NAICS 334414]

Barksdale Inc., pp. Vol. II-980, 1337, 1367, 1457 [NAICS 33291N, 334513, 334519, 33593M]

Barlean's Organic Oils, p. I-26 [NAICS 311225]

Barloworld USA, p. III-1867 [NAICS 423830]

Barnard Manufacturing Inc., p. II-952 [NAICS 332721]

Barnes Aerospace/Advanced, p. II-1562 [NAICS 336412]

Barnes and Noble Inc., pp. Vol. III-2162, 2211 [NAICS 451211, 454113]

Barnes Group Inc., pp. Vol. II-939, 1014, 1567 [NAICS 33261M, 33299N, 336413]

Barnes Nursery Inc., p. III-2072 [NAICS 444220]

Barney Holland Oil Co., p. III-1975 [NAICS 424710]

Barnstead-Thermolyne Corp., pp. Vol. II-1347, 1367, 1386, 1666 [NAICS 334515, 334519, 335110, 339111]

Baron Drawn Steel Corp., pp. Vol. I-793, Vol. II-945, 964, Vol. III-1824 [NAICS 33122M, 332710, 33281M, 423510]

Baron Industries Corp., p. II-1404 [NAICS 335221]

Baroni Designs Inc., p. III-1894 [NAICS 423940]

Barr Animal Foods Inc., p. I-4 [NAICS 311111]

Barr Associates Inc., p. II-1082 [NAICS 333314]

Barr Pharmaceuticals Inc., p. I-539 [NAICS 325412]

Barrel O' Fun, p. I-137 [NAICS 31191M]

Barrelhouse Brewing Co., p. I-172 [NAICS 312120]

Barrett Carpet Mills Inc., p. I-229 [NAICS 314110]

Barrett Trailers Inc., pp. Vol. II-1491, 1500 [NAICS 336212, 336214]

Barretts Minerals Inc., p. I-767 [NAICS 327992]

Barrie House Coffee Company Inc., p. I-143 [NAICS 311920]

Barrier Motors Inc., p. III-2011 [NAICS 441110]

Barron Motor Inc., p. III-1762 [NAICS 423120]

Barron's Wholesale Tire Inc., p. III-1766 [NAICS 423130]

Barrow Industries Inc, p. III-1913 [NAICS 424310]

Barry Bunker Chevrolet Cadillac, p. III-2030 [NAICS 441310]

Barry Optical Laboratory Inc., pp. Vol. I-713, Vol. II-1687 [NAICS 327212, 339115]

Barry-Wehmiller Co's Inc., pp. Vol. I-1061, 1212 [NAICS 33329N, 333993]

Bartell Drug Co., p. III-2100 [NAICS 446110]

Bartell Machinery Systems L.L.C., pp. Vol. II-1051, 1152 [NAICS 333220, 333518]

Barth and Dreyfuss of California, pp. Vol. I-234, Vol. III-1778 [NAICS 31412M, 423220]

Barth Industries Company L.P., pp. Vol. II-1051, 1152 [NAICS 333220, 333518]

Bartlett Corp., p. I-306 [NAICS 31699M]

Barton Inc., pp. Vol. I-172, 181 [NAICS 312120, 312140]

Barton Leasing Inc., p. III-1786 [NAICS 423320]

Barton Nelson Inc., p. I-403 [NAICS 32223M]

Bartow Ethanol of Florida L.C., p. I-181 [NAICS 312140]

Basalite Block, p. I-737 [NAICS 32733M]

Basalite Div., p. I-737 [NAICS 32733M]

Basco Manufacturing Co., p. I-722 [NAICS 327215]

Bascom Maple Farms Inc., p. I-147 [NAICS 311930]

BASF Corp., p. I-595 [NAICS 32599N]

Bashas' Inc., p. III-2076 [NAICS 445110]

Basic American Foods Inc., p. I-68 [NAICS 31142M]

Basic American Metal Products, pp. Vol. II-1129, 1740 [NAICS 333513, 339994]

Basic Fibres Inc., p. III-1890 [NAICS 423930]

Basic Metals Inc., p. I-816 [NAICS 33131N]

Baskin Auto Truck and Tractor, p. III-1859 [NAICS 423810]

Basler Turbo Conversions L.L.C., p. II-1557 [NAICS 336411]

Bass Enterprises Production Inc., pp. Vol. I-484, Vol. II-1463 [NAICS 325182, 335991]

Bass Pro Shop, p. III-1883 [NAICS 423910]

Bass Pro Shops Inc., pp. Vol. II-1594, Vol. III-2150, 2211 [NAICS 336612, 451110, 454113]

Bassett Furniture Industries Inc., pp. Vol. II-1616, 1621, 1657 [NAICS 337121, 337122, 337910]

Bassett Mirror Co., pp. Vol. I-722, Vol. II-1616, 1621, 1632 [NAICS 327215, 337121, 337122, 33712N]

Bates Container Inc., pp. Vol. I-379, 603, Vol. II-1644 [NAICS 32221M, 326111, 337215]

Batesville Casket Company Inc., p. II-1745 [NAICS 339995]

Batesville Tool and Die Inc., pp. Vol. II-1134, 1541 [NAICS 333514, 336370]

Bath and Body Works Inc., p. III-2208 [NAICS 453998]

Bath-TEC Inc., p. I-677 [NAICS 327111]

Batliner Paper Stock Company Inc., pp. Vol. I-363, 374, 415, 609, 615 [NAICS 322110, 322130, 322299, 326112, 326113]

Battat Incorp, p. II-1708 [NAICS 33993M]

Battenfeld Gloucester Engineering, p. II-1051 [NAICS 333220]

Battery Busters Inc., p. II-1442 [NAICS 335911]

Battery Handling Systems Inc., pp. Vol. II-1442, 1447 [NAICS 335911, 335912]

Battery Pros Inc., p. II-1442 [NAICS 335911]

Battery Sales, p. II-1442 [NAICS 335911]

Battery Specialist Co., p. II-1442 [NAICS 335911]

Battery Specialties, pp. Vol. II-1442, 1447 [NAICS 335911, 335912]

Battle Creek Farmers Cooperative, pp. Vol. III-1958, 1991 [NAICS 424510, 424910]

Battle Lumber Company Inc., pp. Vol. I-312, 343 [NAICS 32111M, 321920]

Bauer Built Inc., pp. Vol. III-1762, 1766, 1975 [NAICS 423120, 423130, 424710]

Bauer Compressors Inc., p. II-1184 [NAICS 333912]

Bauerly Companies Inc., pp. Vol. I-448, 732, 737 [NAICS 324121, 327320, 32733M]

Bauman Paper Company Inc., pp. Vol. III-1875, 1905 [NAICS 423850, 424130]

Baume and Mercier, p. II-1362 [NAICS 334518]

Numbers following p. or pp. are page references. Roman numerals indicate volume numbers. Bracketed items indicate industries. Page references are to the starting pages of company tables.

Bausch and Lomb Inc., pp. Vol. I-539, Vol. II-1676, 1682 [NAICS 325412, 339113, 339114]

Bausch & Lomb Inc. Eyewear Div., pp. Vol. II-1082, 1687 [NAICS 333314, 339115]

Bavaria Sausage Kitchen Inc., p. III-2083 [NAICS 445210]

Baxter Healthcare Corp, p. I-539 [NAICS 325412]

Baxter International Inc., pp. Vol. I-549, Vol. II-1671, 1676 [NAICS 325414, 339112, 339113]

Bay Area Labels, pp. Vol. I-403, Vol. II-1720 [NAICS 32223M, 339950]

Bay Bridge Enterprises L.L.C., p. III-1890 [NAICS 423930]

Bay Carbon Inc., p. II-1463 [NAICS 335991]

Bay Cities Container Corp., p. II-1720 [NAICS 339950]

Bay Diesel Corp., p. III-1770 [NAICS 423140]

Bay Foam Inc., pp. Vol. I-609, 636 [NAICS 326112, 326140]

Bay Houston Towing Co., pp. Vol. III-1998, 2072 [NAICS 424930, 444220]

Bay Insulation of Kansas City Inc., p. III-1790 [NAICS 423330]

Bay Microfilm Inc., p. III-1801 [NAICS 423420]

Bay Oil Co., p. III-2116 [NAICS 447110]

Bay Shipbuilding Co., p. II-1589 [NAICS 336611]

Bay State Milling Co., p. I-15 [NAICS 31121M]

Bay State Paper Company Inc., p. I-363 [NAICS 322110]

Bay View Industries, p. I-631 [NAICS 326130]

Bay Zinc Company Inc., p. I-516 [NAICS 325311]

Bayer Environmental Science Inc., p. I-529 [NAICS 325320]

Bayou Caddy Fisheries Inc., p. III-1943 [NAICS 424460]

Bayou City Auction Pool, p. III-1890 [NAICS 423930]

Bayou Co's L.L.C., p. I-788 [NAICS 331210]

Bayou State Oil Corp., p. I-463 [NAICS 324199]

Bayou Steel Corp., p. II-933 [NAICS 332510]

Bayshore Concrete Products Corp., pp. Vol. I-743, Vol. II-899 [NAICS 327390, 33231M]

BBA Fiberweb, pp. Vol. I-218, 500 [NAICS 31331M, 325211]

BBF Printing Solutions Inc., pp. Vol. I-388, 403, 420 [NAICS 32222N, 32223M, 32311M]

BC Industrial Supply Inc., p. III-1820 [NAICS 423490]

B.C. Moore and Sons Inc., p. III-2171 [NAICS 452111]

BC Natural Chicken, p. I-97 [NAICS 311615]

BC Williams, pp. Vol. I-15, 124, 147, 152 [NAICS 31121M, 31182M, 311930, 31194M]

BCBG Max Azria Group, pp. Vol. III-1916, 1919 [NAICS 424320, 424330]

BCT International Inc., pp. Vol. II-1714, Vol. III-1898 [NAICS 33994M, 424110]

BD Accu-Glass, p. I-713 [NAICS 327212]

BD Medical Systems, p. II-1671 [NAICS 339112]

BDB Service and Supply Inc., p. III-1901 [NAICS 424120]

BDF Laundry Management, p. III-1875 [NAICS 423850]

BE Aerospace Inc., p. II-1567 [NAICS 336413]

Beach Manufacturing Inc., pp. Vol. I-722, Vol. II-1536 [NAICS 327215, 336360]

Beacon Container Corp., pp. Vol. I-609, 636 [NAICS 326112, 326140]

Beacon Group Inc., pp. Vol. II-1505, 1580, 1725 [NAICS 33631M, 336419, 339991]

Beacon Journal Publishing Co., p. I-436 [NAICS 32312M]

Beacon Looms Inc., p. I-234 [NAICS 31412M]

Beacon Medical Products L.L.C., p. III-1813 [NAICS 423450]

Beaird Company Ltd., pp. Vol. II-1157, 1584 [NAICS 333611, 336510]

Beall Corp., p. II-1491 [NAICS 336212]

Beall Trailers of Montana Inc., p. II-1491 [NAICS 336212]

Beall Transport Equipment Co., p. II-1491 [NAICS 336212]

Beam Industries, p. II-1397 [NAICS 33521M]

Bear Truss and Components, p. I-329 [NAICS 32121P]

Bearcom Wireless Worldwide Inc., p. III-1839 [NAICS 423690]

Beard Co., p. I-471 [NAICS 325120]

Bearing and Drives Inc., p. III-1871 [NAICS 423840]

Bearing Service of Pennsylvania, pp. Vol. II-988, 1725 [NAICS 332991, 339991]

Bearse Manufacturing Co., p. I-239 [NAICS 31491M]

Beauchamp Distributing Co., p. III-1983 [NAICS 424810]

Beaudry Motor Co., p. III-2011 [NAICS 441110]

Beaulieu Commercial, p. I-229 [NAICS 314110]

Beaulieu of America L.L.C., pp. Vol. I-198, 229 [NAICS 313210, 314110]

Beauti-Vue Products Corp., p. II-1662 [NAICS 337920]

Beauty Craft Supply & Equipment, p. III-1875 [NAICS 423850]

Beauty Towne Inc., p. III-2104 [NAICS 446120]

Beaver Manufacturing Inc., p. I-218 [NAICS 31331M]

Beaver Oil Company Inc., p. I-458 [NAICS 324191]

Beaver Street Brewery, p. I-172 [NAICS 312120]

Beaver Street Fisheries Inc., pp. Vol. I-62, 110 [NAICS 31141M, 31171M]

bebe stores Inc., p. I-290 [NAICS 31599M]

Bechik Products Inc., p. I-244 [NAICS 314991]

Beck Packaging Corp., p. III-1968 [NAICS 424610]

Beck/Picoma, pp. Vol. II-980, 1009 [NAICS 33291N, 332996]

Beck Suppliers Inc., pp. Vol. III-1975, 1979 [NAICS 424710, 424720]

Beckenstein Men's Fabrics Inc., pp. Vol. III-1913, 2156 [NAICS 424310, 451130]

Becker Food Company Inc., pp. Vol. III-1929, 1943 [NAICS 424420, 424460]

Beckett Air Inc., p. II-1101 [NAICS 333414]

Beckett Corp., pp. Vol. II-980, 1179, 1229 [NAICS 33291N, 333911, 33399P]

Beckett Gas Inc., p. II-1101 [NAICS 333414]

Beckman Coulter Inc., p. II-1352 [NAICS 334516]

Beckwith Machinery Company, p. III-1859 [NAICS 423810]

Becon Inc., p. II-1157 [NAICS 333611]

Becromal of America Inc., p. I-816 [NAICS 33131N]

Becton, Dickinson and Co., pp. Vol. I-539, Vol. II-1671, 1676 [NAICS 325412, 339112, 339113]

Bed Bath and Beyond Inc., p. III-2047 [NAICS 442299]

Bedell-Kraus Flexographic, p. I-505 [NAICS 325212]

Bedford Fair Industries, p. III-2126 [NAICS 448120]

Bee Chemical Co., pp. Vol. I-475, 500, 554, 560 [NAICS 32513M, 325211, 325510, 325520]

Bee Electronics Inc., pp. Vol. I-306, 510 [NAICS 31699M, 32522M]

Beef Packers Inc., p. I-102 [NAICS 31161N]

Beeman Jorgensen Inc., p. III-1995 [NAICS 424920]

Beemer Precision Inc., p. I-867 [NAICS 332117]

Beerntsen's Confectionery Inc., p. III-2092 [NAICS 445292]

BEF Corp., p. III-1798 [NAICS 423410]

Begley Lumber Company Inc., p. I-312 [NAICS 32111M]

Begneaud Manufacturing Inc., p. I-816 [NAICS 33131N]

Beheydt's Auto Wrecking, p. III-1770 [NAICS 423140]

Behr Climate Systems Inc., p. II-1546 [NAICS 336391]

Behr Heat Transfer Systems Inc., pp. Vol. II-1101, 1229 [NAICS 333414, 33399P]

Behr Systems Inc., p. II-1184 [NAICS 333912]

BEI Defense Systems Inc., p. II-1572 [NAICS 336414]

BEI Technologies Inc., pp. Vol. II-1317, 1337, 1367, 1671 [NAICS 334419, 334513, 334519, 339112]

Beistle Co., pp. Vol. I-368, 415 [NAICS 32212M, 322299]

Bekaert Corp., pp. Vol. I-248, 780, 793, Vol. II-939 [NAICS 314992, 33111M, 33122M, 33261M]

Bel Air Tool Corp., p. III-1887 [NAICS 423920]

Bel-Art Products Inc., p. II-1666 [NAICS 339111]

Bel Fuse Inc., pp. Vol. II-1257, 1302, 1432 [NAICS 334210, 334416, 335313]

Bel Kaukauna USA Inc., p. I-76 [NAICS 311513]

Bel-Ray Company Inc., p. I-458 [NAICS 324191]

Bel Terr Decorating Inc., p. III-1809 [NAICS 423440]

Belarus Tractor International Inc., p. III-1863 [NAICS 423820]

Belco Crafts Inc., pp. Vol. I-343, Vol. II-1731 [NAICS 321920, 339992]

Belden Tools Inc., p. II-1530 [NAICS 336350]

Belden Wire and Cable Co., pp. Vol. II-1267, Vol. III-1809 [NAICS 334290, 423440]

Belgioioso Cheese Inc., p. I-76 [NAICS 311513]

Belgium Co., p. I-86 [NAICS 31151N]

Belk Inc., p. III-2171 [NAICS 452111]

Belkin Corp., pp. Vol. I-306, Vol. II-1252, 1317, 1421, 1442 [NAICS 31699M, 334119, 334419, 335311, 335911]

Bell Fasteners, p. III-1843 [NAICS 423710]

Bell Flavors and Fragrances Inc., pp. Vol. I-152, 566 [NAICS 31194M, 32561M]

Bell Giro Sport Design Inc., p. II-1599 [NAICS 336991]

Bell Inc., p. I-403 [NAICS 32223M]

Company Index

Numbers following p. or pp. are page references. Roman numerals indicate volume numbers. Bracketed items indicate industries. Page references are to the starting pages of company tables.

2305

Bell Industries Inc., pp. Vol. II-1238, Vol. III-1839, 1847, 1851 [NAICS 334111, 423690, 423720, 423730]

Bell Laboratories Inc., p. I-529 [NAICS 325320]

Bell Manufacturing Company Inc., p. I-203 [NAICS 31322M]

Bell Microproducts Inc., p. III-1839 [NAICS 423690]

Bell Processing Inc., pp. Vol. I-363, 807 [NAICS 322110, 331314]

Bellco Glass Inc., p. I-713 [NAICS 327212]

Belletech Corp., pp. Vol. II-1473, 1749 [NAICS 336111, 339999]

Belleville Scale Co., p. III-2180 [NAICS 452990]

Belleville Shoe Manufacturing Co., p. I-300 [NAICS 31621M]

Belleville Shoe South, p. I-300 [NAICS 31621M]

Bellia Office Products Inc., p. III-2186 [NAICS 453210]

Bellis Steel Company Inc., p. III-1770 [NAICS 423140]

BellSouth Corp., pp. Vol. II-1257, 1267 [NAICS 334210, 334290]

Belmark Inc., pp. Vol. I-379, 388, 609 [NAICS 32221M, 32222N, 326112]

Belmay Company Inc., p. I-493 [NAICS 32519M]

Belmont Springs Water Inc., pp. Vol. III-2094, 2228 [NAICS 445299, 454390]

Beloit Beverage Company Inc., p. III-1983 [NAICS 424810]

Beloit Pattern Works, p. II-1639 [NAICS 337212]

Belt Corporation of America Inc., p. I-665 [NAICS 326220]

Belton Metal Company Inc., p. I-807 [NAICS 331314]

Beltway International L.L.C., p. III-1758 [NAICS 423110]

Belvedere USA Corp., pp. Vol. II-1397, 1611, 1627 [NAICS 33521M, 337110, 337127]

Belvieu Enviromental Fuel, p. I-443 [NAICS 324110]

Bemidji Cooperative Association, p. III-1975 [NAICS 424710]

Bemis Associates Inc., p. I-560 [NAICS 325520]

Bemis Company Inc., pp. Vol. I-388, 626, Vol. II-1212 [NAICS 32222N, 326122, 333993]

Bemis Manufacturing Co., pp. Vol. I-358, 651, Vol. II-908, 1632, 1676 [NAICS 321999, 32619M, 33232M, 33712N, 339113]

Ben Bridge Jeweler Inc., p. III-2144 [NAICS 448310]

Ben E. Keith Co., pp. Vol. III-1925, 1983 [NAICS 424410, 424810]

Ben Hill Griffin Inc., p. I-516 [NAICS 325311]

Ben-Mar Hosiery Inc., p. I-256 [NAICS 31511M]

Ben Meadows, p. III-1859 [NAICS 423810]

Ben Myerson Candy Company Inc., pp. Vol. I-52, 57 [NAICS 311330, 311340]

BenchCraft L.L.C., pp. Vol. II-1616, 1621, 1657 [NAICS 337121, 337122, 337910]

Benchmade Knife Company Inc., p. II-886 [NAICS 33221N]

Benchmark Doors, p. I-699 [NAICS 327123]

Benchmark Electronics Inc., pp. Vol. II-1282, 1317 [NAICS 334412, 334419]

Benco Steel Inc., p. II-945 [NAICS 332710]

Bend Industries Inc., pp. Vol. I-727, 737, 743 [NAICS 327310, 32733M, 327390]

Bendco Machine and Tool Inc., p. II-1147 [NAICS 333516]

Benedict-Miller L.L.C., pp. Vol. II-964, 1092, Vol. III-1824 [NAICS 33281M, 33331N, 423510]

Benedict Refrigeration Service Inc., pp. Vol. III-1855, 1875 [NAICS 423740, 423850]

Beneteau USA Inc., p. II-1594 [NAICS 336612]

Benfield Electric Supply Inc., p. III-1831 [NAICS 423610]

Benham Enterprises Inc., p. III-1855 [NAICS 423740]

Benicia Fabrication & Machine, pp. Vol. II-918, 923 [NAICS 332410, 332420]

Benjamin Moore and Co., pp. Vol. I-500, 554 [NAICS 325211, 325510]

Bennett Brothers Inc., pp. Vol. III-1778, 1894 [NAICS 423220, 423940]

Bennett Pump Co., pp. Vol. II-1077, 1189 [NAICS 333313, 333913]

Benny's Inc., pp. Vol. III-2030, 2047, 2050 [NAICS 441310, 442299, 443111]

Benoist Brothers Supply Inc., pp. Vol. III-1847, 1851 [NAICS 423720, 423730]

Benson Industries Inc., p. I-722 [NAICS 327215]

Benson International, pp. Vol. II-1491, 1500 [NAICS 336212, 336214]

Benson's Inc., p. I-116 [NAICS 31181M]

Bent's Cookie Factory, p. III-2089 [NAICS 445291]

Bentech Manufacturing, p. II-1584 [NAICS 336510]

Bentek Manufacturing Inc., pp. Vol. II-1056, 1332 [NAICS 333295, 334512]

Benteler Automotive, p. II-1541 [NAICS 336370]

Bentley World Packaging Ltd., p. I-343 [NAICS 321920]

Benton County Coop., p. III-2072 [NAICS 444220]

Benton Foundry Inc., p. I-845 [NAICS 33151M]

Bepco Inc., p. II-1524 [NAICS 336340]

Berardi's Fresh Roast Coffee Inc., p. I-143 [NAICS 311920]

Berenfield Containers Inc., p. II-928 [NAICS 33243M]

Beretta USA Corp., p. II-1001 [NAICS 332994]

Bergamot Brass Works Inc., p. II-1735 [NAICS 339993]

Bergey Windpower Company Inc., p. II-1157 [NAICS 333611]

Bergquist Company Inc., pp. Vol. I-670, 713 [NAICS 32629M, 327212]

Bergquist Imports Inc., p. I-681 [NAICS 327112]

Bergson Tire Company Inc., pp. Vol. I-660, Vol. III-1766 [NAICS 32621M, 423130]

Bergstrom Inc., pp. Vol. II-1112, 1546 [NAICS 33341N, 336391]

Bering Home Center Inc., p. III-2047 [NAICS 442299]

Beringer Wine Estates Co., p. I-177 [NAICS 312130]

Berk-Tek A Nexans Co., pp. Vol. I-793, Vol. II-1082, 1451, 1457 [NAICS 33122M, 333314, 33592M, 33593M]

Berkeley Farms Inc., p. I-86 [NAICS 31151N]

Berkline/Benchcraft Holdings Inc., p. II-1616 [NAICS 337121]

Berkshire Corp., p. II-1740 [NAICS 339994]

Berlin and Jones Company Inc., p. I-403 [NAICS 32223M]

Berliss Bearing Co., p. II-988 [NAICS 332991]

Berlyn Extruders Inc., p. II-1051 [NAICS 333220]

Berman Industries Inc., pp. Vol. II-1390, 1468 [NAICS 33512M, 335999]

Bermil Industries Corp, p. III-1875 [NAICS 423850]

Bernafon Inc., p. II-1322 [NAICS 334510]

Bernard Chaus Inc., pp. Vol. I-279, 290 [NAICS 31523M, 31599M]

Berne Apparel Inc., p. III-1916 [NAICS 424320]

Berner Foods Corp., p. I-76 [NAICS 311513]

Bernhard Woodwork Ltd., p. II-1639 [NAICS 337212]

Bernhardt Furniture Company Inc., pp. Vol. II-1616, 1621, 1650 [NAICS 337121, 337122, 33721N]

Berry Contracting Inc., pp. Vol. I-780, Vol. II-899, 923 [NAICS 33111M, 33231M, 332420]

Berry Plastics Corp., p. I-626 [NAICS 326122]

Berryman Products Inc., p. I-458 [NAICS 324191]

Berryville Graphics Inc., pp. Vol. I-420, 436 [NAICS 32311M, 32312M]

Bertch Cabinet Manufacturing Inc., p. II-1611 [NAICS 337110]

Bertram Dental Laboratory, p. II-1692 [NAICS 339116]

Bertram Yacht Inc., pp. Vol. II-1589, 1594 [NAICS 336611, 336612]

Berwick Offray L.L.C., p. II-1536 [NAICS 336360]

Berwick Steel Co., p. III-1824 [NAICS 423510]

Bescor Video Accessories Ltd., p. II-1442 [NAICS 335911]

Besly Products Corp., p. II-1207 [NAICS 333991]

Bess Eaton Donut Flour Inc., p. I-116 [NAICS 31181M]

Besse Forest Products Group, pp. Vol. I-312, 324 [NAICS 32111M, 32121N]

Besser, p. I-737 [NAICS 32733M]

Besser Co., pp. Vol. II-1033, 1147 [NAICS 333120, 333516]

Besser Company Inc., p. II-1033 [NAICS 333120]

Best Access Systems, p. II-933 [NAICS 332510]

Best Brands Corp., p. I-124 [NAICS 31182M]

Best Brands L.L.C., p. I-147 [NAICS 311930]

Best Buy Company Inc., pp. Vol. III-2050, 2054 [NAICS 443111, 443112]

Best Chairs Inc. County Line Div., pp. Vol. II-1616, 1621 [NAICS 337121, 337122]

Best Collateral Inc., p. III-2194 [NAICS 453310]

Best Express Foods Inc., pp. Vol. I-133, 137 [NAICS 311830, 31191M]

Best Foam Fabricators Inc., pp. Vol. I-631, 641 [NAICS 326130, 326150]

Best Image Systems Inc., p. III-1801 [NAICS 423420]

Best Manufacturing, p. I-290 [NAICS 31599M]

Best Manufacturing Inc., p. I-251 [NAICS 314999]

Best Moulding Corp., p. II-1639 [NAICS 337212]

Best Plumbing Tile and Stone, p. III-1847 [NAICS 423720]

Best Products Inc., p. II-1332 [NAICS 334512]

Best Regards Inc., p. III-2190 [NAICS 453220]

Best Way City Wholesalers Inc., p. III-1905 [NAICS 424130]

Bestfoods Foodservice, p. I-147 [NAICS 311930]

BestSweet Inc., pp. Vol. I-52, 57, 534 [NAICS 311330, 311340, 325411]

Numbers following p. or pp. are page references. Roman numerals indicate volume numbers. Bracketed items indicate industries. Page references are to the starting pages of company tables.

Bestt Liebco Corp., p. II-1740 [NAICS 339994]

Beta/Kramer Lighting, p. II-1390 [NAICS 33512M]

Beta Steel Corp., p. I-793 [NAICS 33122M]

Betaseed Inc., p. I-40 [NAICS 311313]

Betatronix Inc., p. II-1297 [NAICS 334415]

Betco Corp., p. I-566 [NAICS 32561M]

Betenbender Manufacturing Inc., p. II-886 [NAICS 33221N]

Beth's Fine Desserts Inc., p. I-124 [NAICS 31182M]

Bethany Lowe Designs Inc., pp. Vol. III-2007, 2190 [NAICS 424990, 453220]

Bethesda Softworks/Media, p. II-1381 [NAICS 334613]

Bethlehem Steel Corp., pp. Vol. I-780, Vol. II-899 [NAICS 33111M, 33231M]

Bettcher Amherst Metal Products, p. II-1541 [NAICS 336370]

Bettcher Industries Inc., p. II-886 [NAICS 33221N]

Better Baked Foods Inc., p. I-137 [NAICS 31191M]

Better Beverages Inc., p. I-147 [NAICS 311930]

Better Beverages Ltd., p. I-165 [NAICS 31211M]

Better Brands of Atlanta Inc., pp. Vol. III-1983, 1987 [NAICS 424810, 424820]

Better Made Snack Foods Inc., p. I-137 [NAICS 31191M]

Better Roads Inc., p. I-448 [NAICS 324121]

Better Stones and Masonry Supply, p. III-2072 [NAICS 444220]

Better Val-U Supermarkets Inc., p. III-2076 [NAICS 445110]

Betts Industries Inc., pp. Vol. I-743, Vol. II-1386, 1491 [NAICS 327390, 335110, 336212]

Betts Spring Co., pp. Vol. II-958, 1486 [NAICS 332722, 336211]

Betty Dain Creations Inc., pp. Vol. II-886, 1740 [NAICS 33221N, 339994]

Betty Machine Company Inc., p. II-952 [NAICS 332721]

Bevans Oyster Company Inc., p. I-110 [NAICS 31171M]

Beverage Capital Corp., p. I-165 [NAICS 31211M]

Beverage Control Inc., p. III-1855 [NAICS 423740]

Beverly Enterprises Inc., pp. Vol. III-2100, 2211 [NAICS 446110, 454113]

Bexar Concrete Works Ltd., p. I-743 [NAICS 327390]

B.F. Goodrich Aerospace, p. II-1557 [NAICS 336411]

BFS, p. I-9 [NAICS 311119]

BFS Retail & Commercial, p. I-660 [NAICS 32621M]

Bg Computer Services Inc., p. II-1248 [NAICS 334113]

BG Products Inc., p. I-458 [NAICS 324191]

BGE Home Products & Services, p. III-2050 [NAICS 443111]

BH Aircraft Company Inc., p. II-1562 [NAICS 336412]

Bh Electronics Inc., pp. Vol. II-1302, 1421 [NAICS 334416, 335311]

BHA Group Holdings Inc., p. II-1112 [NAICS 33341N]

BI Nutraceuticals, p. I-534 [NAICS 325411]

Bi Rite Foodservice Distributors, p. III-1954 [NAICS 424490]

Bianchi International, pp. Vol. I-290, 306, 510 [NAICS 31599M, 31699M, 32522M]

Bibler Brothers Lumber Inc., p. I-312 [NAICS 32111M]

Bickford Broadcast Vehicles, p. II-1478 [NAICS 336112]

Biddeford Blankets L.L.C., pp. Vol. I-192, 234 [NAICS 31311M, 31412M]

Biddle Precision Components Inc., p. II-952 [NAICS 332721]

Biederlack of America Corp., p. I-234 [NAICS 31412M]

Biery Cheese Company Inc., p. I-76 [NAICS 311513]

Biesemeyer Manufacturing Corp., p. II-1046 [NAICS 333210]

Big 10 Tire Co., p. III-2030 [NAICS 441310]

Big 5 Sporting Goods Corp., p. III-2150 [NAICS 451110]

Big Bear Fireworks Inc., p. III-1887 [NAICS 423920]

Big Dog Holdings Inc., pp. Vol. III-2132, 2135 [NAICS 448140, 448150]

Big Gain Inc., p. I-9 [NAICS 311119]

Big Horn Cooperative Market, p. III-2072 [NAICS 444220]

Big John Manufacturing Inc., p. III-2069 [NAICS 444210]

Big Lots Inc., p. III-2180 [NAICS 452990]

Big O Tires Inc., pp. Vol. III-1762, 1766, 2030 [NAICS 423120, 423130, 441310]

Big River Zinc Corp., pp. Vol. I-488, 825, 837, Vol. II-964 [NAICS 325188, 331419, 33149M, 33281M]

Big Sandy Furniture Inc., pp. Vol. III-2037, 2050 [NAICS 442110, 443111]

Big Sky Auto Auction Inc., p. III-1758 [NAICS 423110]

Big Sky Brewing Company Inc., p. I-172 [NAICS 312120]

Big Springs Inc., p. I-165 [NAICS 31211M]

Big Tex Trailer Manufacturing Inc., p. II-1500 [NAICS 336214]

Big V Feeds Inc., pp. Vol. I-4, 9, 15 [NAICS 311111, 311119, 31121M]

Big Y Foods Inc., p. III-2076 [NAICS 445110]

Bigham Insulation and Supply Inc., p. III-1790 [NAICS 423330]

Bijoux Terner Partnership, p. III-1894 [NAICS 423940]

Bike Track Inc., p. II-1599 [NAICS 336991]

Bil-Jac Foods Inc., p. I-4 [NAICS 311111]

Bill's Service Center Inc., p. III-2069 [NAICS 444210]

Bill's Used Auto Parts Inc., p. III-1770 [NAICS 423140]

Billco Manufacturing Inc., p. II-1124 [NAICS 333512]

Billows Electric Supply Co., p. III-1831 [NAICS 423610]

Bilt Best Windows, p. I-722 [NAICS 327215]

Biltrite Corp., p. I-670 [NAICS 32629M]

BINAX Inc., p. I-544 [NAICS 325413]

Bindagraphics Inc., p. I-580 [NAICS 325910]

Bindley Western Industries Inc., p. III-1909 [NAICS 424210]

Bing Group L.L.C., p. III-1762 [NAICS 423120]

Bingham Cooperative Inc., pp. Vol. I-524, Vol. III-2208 [NAICS 325314, 453998]

Bingo Cactus Supply Inc., p. III-1887 [NAICS 423920]

Bintz Restaurant Supply Co., p. III-1809 [NAICS 423440]

Bio-Botanica Inc., p. I-534 [NAICS 325411]

Bio-Lab Inc., pp. Vol. I-595, Vol. II-1092 [NAICS 32599N, 33331N]

Bio-Oregon Inc., p. I-516 [NAICS 325311]

Bio-Rad Laboratories Inc., pp. Vol. I-544, 595, Vol. II-1352 [NAICS 325413, 32599N, 334516]

Bio San Labs Inc., p. I-534 [NAICS 325411]

Bioanalytical Systems Inc., pp. Vol. II-1352, 1666 [NAICS 334516, 339111]

BioControl Systems Inc., p. I-544 [NAICS 325413]

Biocor Animal Health Inc., p. I-549 [NAICS 325414]

Biodex Medical Systems Inc., p. II-1357 [NAICS 334517]

BioForm Medical Inc., p. I-549 [NAICS 325414]

Biogen Idec Inc., p. I-549 [NAICS 325414]

Biogenex Laboratories Inc., p. I-544 [NAICS 325413]

Biokyowa Inc., pp. Vol. I-4, 9 [NAICS 311111, 311119]

Biolase Technology Inc., p. II-1682 [NAICS 339114]

Biolog Inc., p. I-544 [NAICS 325413]

BioMed Co., p. II-1740 [NAICS 339994]

Biomerica Inc., pp. Vol. I-544, Vol. II-1682 [NAICS 325413, 339114]

BioMeridian International Inc., p. III-2113 [NAICS 446199]

Biomet Inc., pp. Vol. II-1671, 1676 [NAICS 339112, 339113]

Biomune Co., pp. Vol. I-549, Vol. II-1671 [NAICS 325414, 339112]

Bioplastics Co., p. I-203 [NAICS 31322M]

Biora Inc., p. III-1809 [NAICS 423440]

Bioscientific Inc., p. I-516 [NAICS 325311]

Biosite Inc., pp. Vol. I-544, Vol. II-1352, 1671 [NAICS 325413, 334516, 339112]

BioSource International Inc., pp. Vol. I-488, 544 [NAICS 325188, 325413]

Biotage Inc., p. II-1352 [NAICS 334516]

Biovail Technologies Ltd., pp. Vol. I-147, Vol. II-1671 [NAICS 311930, 339112]

BioVeris Corp., p. I-544 [NAICS 325413]

Birch Machinery Co., p. II-1051 [NAICS 333220]

Birchcraft Studios, p. II-1696 [NAICS 33991M]

Birchwood Foods, p. I-102 [NAICS 31161N]

Bird Electronic Corp., p. II-1302 [NAICS 334416]

Bird-X Inc., p. I-244 [NAICS 314991]

Birds Eye Foods Inc., pp. Vol. I-62, 68 [NAICS 31141M, 31142M]

Birdsong Corp., p. III-1965 [NAICS 424590]

Birkenstock Footprint Sandals Inc., p. III-1922 [NAICS 424340]

Birmingham Fastener and Supply, p. II-958 [NAICS 332722]

Birmingham Hot Metal Coatings, p. I-703 [NAICS 32712N]

Bisco Inc., p. II-1682 [NAICS 339114]

Bisco Industries Inc., p. III-1843 [NAICS 423710]

Biscomerica Corp., pp. Vol. I-57, 124 [NAICS 311340, 31182M]

Numbers following p. or pp. are page references. Roman numerals indicate volume numbers. Bracketed items indicate industries. Page references are to the starting pages of company tables.

2307

Company Index

Bishop Electronics Corp., p. II-1292 [NAICS 334414]

Bisk Education, p. II-1749 [NAICS 339999]

Bison Building Materials Ltd., pp. Vol. I-312, 334 [NAICS 32111M, 32191M]

Bison Corp., p. I-480 [NAICS 325181]

Bison Gear and Engineering Corp., pp. Vol. II-1162, 1530 [NAICS 333612, 336350]

Bissell Inc., pp. Vol. I-251, 566, Vol. II-908, 1092, 1397 [NAICS 314999, 32561M, 33232M, 33331N, 33521M]

bitMAX L.L.C., p. II-1381 [NAICS 334613]

Bitterman Family Confections, p. III-2092 [NAICS 445292]

Bituminous Roadways Inc., p. I-453 [NAICS 324122]

BIW Cable Systems Inc., p. II-939 [NAICS 33261M]

Bizjet Intern. Sales & Support Inc., pp. Vol. II-1557, Vol. III-1879 [NAICS 336411, 423860]

BJ's Restaurants Inc., p. I-172 [NAICS 312120]

BJ's Wholesale Club Inc., pp. Vol. III-1774, 1835, 1925, 2076, 2177 [NAICS 423210, 423620, 424410, 445110, 452910]

BJ Services Co., p. II-1039 [NAICS 33313M]

BJB Enterprises Inc., p. I-589 [NAICS 325991]

BJK Industries Inc., pp. Vol. I-603, 621 [NAICS 326111, 326121]

Bk Entertainment Inc., pp. Vol. I-374, 403, 415 [NAICS 322130, 32223M, 322299]

BKM Total Office of California, p. III-2037 [NAICS 442110]

Blach Distributing Co., p. III-1987 [NAICS 424820]

Black and Co., p. III-1871 [NAICS 423840]

Black and Decker Corp., pp. Vol. II-1028, 1124, 1207, 1397 [NAICS 333112, 333512, 333991, 33521M]

Black Box Corp., pp. Vol. II-1257, 1262, 1267, 1317, 1427, Vol. III-2211 [NAICS 334210, 334220, 334290, 334419, 335312, 454113]

Black Brothers Co., p. II-1046 [NAICS 333210]

Black Diamond Equipment Ltd., p. I-239 [NAICS 31491M]

Black Forest Originals-Grandfather, p. III-1894 [NAICS 423940]

Black Hills Special Services, pp. Vol. II-1632, 1708 [NAICS 33712N, 33993M]

Black Hills Work Shop & Training, pp. Vol. II-1312, 1749 [NAICS 334418, 339999]

Black Millwork Company Inc., p. I-334 [NAICS 32191M]

Black Oil Company Inc., p. III-1975 [NAICS 424710]

Black Prince Distillery Inc., p. I-181 [NAICS 312140]

Black River Manufacturing Inc., p. II-952 [NAICS 332721]

Blackburn Building Services, p. III-1875 [NAICS 423850]

Blackburn-Russell Company Inc., pp. Vol. III-1939, 2001 [NAICS 424450, 424940]

Blackhawk Foundry & Machine, p. I-845 [NAICS 33151M]

Blacklick Machine Company Inc., p. I-703 [NAICS 32712N]

Blackmer Flow Technologies, p. II-1184 [NAICS 333912]

Blacksheep Inc., pp. Vol. I-306, 636, Vol. II-1023 [NAICS 31699M, 326140, 333111]

Blackton Inc., pp. Vol. III-1778, 2041 [NAICS 423220, 442210]

Blackwell's Book Services, p. III-1995 [NAICS 424920]

Blackwell's Delaware Inc., p. III-1995 [NAICS 424920]

Blaine Jensen & Sons RV Centers, p. III-2018 [NAICS 441210]

Blair Corp., p. III-2211 [NAICS 454113]

Blake's Creamery, p. I-92 [NAICS 311520]

Blakeslee Inc., p. II-1417 [NAICS 335228]

Blakeslee Prestress Inc., p. I-743 [NAICS 327390]

Blanchardville Cooperative Oil, p. III-2218 [NAICS 454311]

Bland Farms Inc., p. III-1950 [NAICS 424480]

Blandin Paper Mill, p. I-388 [NAICS 32222N]

Blankinship Distributors Inc., p. III-1939 [NAICS 424450]

Blaser Die Casting Co., p. I-857 [NAICS 33152P]

Blauer Manufacturing Inc., p. I-267 [NAICS 31521M]

Blazer Industries Inc., p. I-353 [NAICS 321992]

Blendtec Inc., p. II-1397 [NAICS 33521M]

Blenko Glass Company Inc., p. I-681 [NAICS 327112]

Bleyer Industries Inc., p. I-603 [NAICS 326111]

Bleyle Inc., p. I-262 [NAICS 31519M]

BLF Enterprises Inc., p. III-2089 [NAICS 445291]

Blind Maker Inc., p. II-1662 [NAICS 337920]

Blinds and Designs Inc., p. II-1662 [NAICS 337920]

Blish-Mize Co., p. III-1843 [NAICS 423710]

Bliss Murski Sales Inc., p. III-1883 [NAICS 423910]

Blissfield Manufacturing Co., pp. Vol. II-918, 923, 1184, 1603 [NAICS 332410, 332420, 333912, 336992]

Blistex Inc., p. I-575 [NAICS 325620]

Block and Company Inc., p. II-1077 [NAICS 333313]

Block Corp., p. III-1916 [NAICS 424320]

Block Distributing Company Inc., p. III-1987 [NAICS 424820]

Blommer Chocolate Co., pp. Vol. I-48, 52, 86 [NAICS 311320, 311330, 31151N]

Bloom Engineering Company Inc., p. I-771 [NAICS 327993]

Bloomer Candy Co., pp. Vol. I-48, 52 [NAICS 311320, 311330]

Bloomfield Bakers Ltd., p. I-124 [NAICS 31182M]

Bloomsburg Carpet Industries Inc., p. I-229 [NAICS 314110]

Bloomsburg Mills Inc., p. I-198 [NAICS 313210]

Blount Greenback Farmers Coop., pp. Vol. III-1863, 2030 [NAICS 423820, 441310]

Blount Inc, pp. Vol. II-892, 1023 [NAICS 33221P, 333111]

Blount International Inc., pp. Vol. II-892, 933, 988, 993, 997, 1033, 1168, Vol. III-1817 [NAICS 33221P, 332510, 332991, 332992, 332993, 333120, 333613, 423460]

Blue Bell Creameries L.P., p. I-92 [NAICS 311520]

Blue Bird Body Co., p. II-1486 [NAICS 336211]

Blue Bird Corp., pp. Vol. II-1473, 1486 [NAICS 336111, 336211]

Blue Chip Group Inc., p. I-81 [NAICS 311514]

Blue Chip Stamps, pp. Vol. III-1824, 2211 [NAICS 423510, 454113]

Blue Coat Systems Inc., p. II-1243 [NAICS 334112]

Blue Nile Inc., p. II-1696 [NAICS 33991M]

Blue Ridge Arsenal Inc., p. III-2150 [NAICS 451110]

Blue Ridge Farms Inc., pp. Vol. I-62, 158 [NAICS 31141M, 31199M]

Blue Ridge Industrial, p. I-229 [NAICS 314110]

Blue Ridge Metals Corp., p. II-1519 [NAICS 336330]

Blue Ridge Truss and Supply Inc., pp. Vol. I-324, 329 [NAICS 32121N, 32121P]

Blue Seal Feeds Inc., pp. Vol. I-4, 9 [NAICS 311111, 311119]

Blue Star Growers Inc., p. III-1950 [NAICS 424480]

Bluearc Corp., p. II-1243 [NAICS 334112]

Bluebonnet Feeds, pp. Vol. I-4, 9 [NAICS 311111, 311119]

Bluefly Inc., p. III-2228 [NAICS 454390]

Bluewater Rubber and Gasket, p. III-2138 [NAICS 448190]

Bluff Springs Paper Company Ltd., p. I-403 [NAICS 32223M]

Blumenthal Print Works Inc., p. I-218 [NAICS 31331M]

Blyth Inc., p. II-1749 [NAICS 339999]

BMB, pp. Vol. I-251, 306, 510 [NAICS 314999, 31699M, 32522M]

BMC Industries Inc., p. II-1687 [NAICS 339115]

BMW of North America L.L.C., pp. Vol. II-1473, 1599 [NAICS 336111, 336991]

BMW of San Francisco, p. III-2021 [NAICS 441221]

Bnz Materials Inc., p. I-703 [NAICS 32712N]

Boar's Head Provisions Inc., p. III-1946 [NAICS 424470]

Boart Longyear Co., pp. Vol. II-1039, 1140, 1207 [NAICS 33313M, 333515, 333991]

Boat Center Inc., p. III-2024 [NAICS 441222]

Bob Evans Farms Inc., pp. Vol. I-68, 102, 147 [NAICS 31142M, 31161N, 311930]

Bob Hall Inc., p. III-1983 [NAICS 424810]

Bob Loyd L.P. Gas Co., p. III-2222 [NAICS 454312]

Bob Rohrman Auto Group, p. III-2011 [NAICS 441110]

Bob's Space Racers Inc., p. II-1708 [NAICS 33993M]

Bob's Stores Inc., pp. Vol. III-2132, 2141 [NAICS 448140, 448210]

Bob Siemon Designs, p. II-1696 [NAICS 33991M]

Bobcat Co., pp. Vol. II-1023, 1194 [NAICS 333111, 33392M]

Bobs Candies Inc., p. I-52 [NAICS 311330]

Bobst Group USA Inc., p. III-1867 [NAICS 423830]

BOC Edwards, p. II-1184 [NAICS 333912]

Boccard USA Corp., p. II-1009 [NAICS 332996]

Bocchi Laboratories Inc., p. I-575 [NAICS 325620]

Boces Albany, p. III-1805 [NAICS 423430]

Boch Olmsmoblie, p. III-1770 [NAICS 423140]

Boddie-Noell Enterprises Inc., p. III-1925 [NAICS 424410]

Bodine Aluminum Inc., pp. Vol. I-852, 857, Vol. II-964, 1014 [NAICS 33152N, 33152P, 33281M, 33299N]

Numbers following p. or pp. are page references. Roman numerals indicate volume numbers. Bracketed items indicate industries. Page references are to the starting pages of company tables.

Bodine Co., p. II-1386 [NAICS 335110]

Bodine Electric Co., pp. Vol. II-1162, 1427 [NAICS 333612, 335312]

Bodine Electric of Decatur, p. II-1432 [NAICS 335313]

Boehme-Filatex Inc., p. I-458 [NAICS 324191]

Boehringer Ingelheim, p. I-539 [NAICS 325412]

Boehringer Ingelheim Vetmedica, pp. Vol. I-539, Vol. II-1671 [NAICS 325412, 339112]

Boeing Aircraft & Missile Systems, pp. Vol. II-1327, 1468, 1557, 1567, 1580 [NAICS 334511, 335999, 336411, 336413, 336419]

Boeing Co., pp. Vol. II-1557, 1562, 1567, 1572, 1580 [NAICS 336411, 336412, 336413, 336414, 336419]

Boeing Co. Philadelphia, p. II-1557 [NAICS 336411]

Boekel Scientific, p. II-1666 [NAICS 339111]

Boelter Companies Inc., pp. Vol. III-1809, 1905 [NAICS 423440, 424130]

Boettcher Enterprises Inc., p. III-1991 [NAICS 424910]

Boggs Inc., p. I-830 [NAICS 33142M]

Boggus Ford, p. III-2030 [NAICS 441310]

Bohler Uddeholm America Inc., pp. Vol. II-899, Vol. III-1824 [NAICS 33231M, 423510]

Bohn and Dawson Inc., pp. Vol. I-358, Vol. II-1632 [NAICS 321999, 33712N]

Boise Cascade Corp, pp. Vol. I-312, 319, 324, 334 [NAICS 32111M, 321219, 32121N, 32191M]

Boisset U.S.A., p. III-1987 [NAICS 424820]

Bokan Brothers Engine Rebuilders, p. III-1770 [NAICS 423140]

Boley Corp., p. III-1887 [NAICS 423920]

Boll Medical Inc., p. III-1813 [NAICS 423450]

Bollinger Industries Inc., p. III-1883 [NAICS 423910]

Bollinger Shipyards Inc., p. II-1589 [NAICS 336611]

Bollman Hat Co., pp. Vol. I-198, 290 [NAICS 313210, 31599M]

Bollore Inc., p. II-1292 [NAICS 334414]

Bolner's Fiesta Products Inc., p. I-152 [NAICS 31194M]

Bomardier Transportation Systems, p. II-1607 [NAICS 336999]

Bomark Inc., p. I-580 [NAICS 325910]

Bomarko Inc., pp. Vol. I-395, 609, 816 [NAICS 32222P, 326112, 33131N]

Bombardier Aerospace Learjet, pp. Vol. II-1327, 1557 [NAICS 334511, 336411]

Bombardier Aviation Services Inc., p. II-1557 [NAICS 336411]

Bombay Company Inc., p. III-2037 [NAICS 442110]

Bon Secour Fisheries Inc., p. I-110 [NAICS 31171M]

Bon-Ton Stores Inc., p. III-2171 [NAICS 452111]

Bon Tool Co., p. II-1207 [NAICS 333991]

Bona Dent Laboratories Inc., p. II-1682 [NAICS 339114]

Bona Vista Programs Inc., pp. Vol. II-1312, 1735 [NAICS 334418, 339993]

Bond Leather Company Inc., p. I-296 [NAICS 316110]

BondCote Corp., pp. Vol. I-224, 239, 453 [NAICS 313320, 31491M, 324122]

Bonell Manufacturing Co., p. II-1147 [NAICS 333516]

Bongards Creameries, pp. Vol. I-76, 86 [NAICS 311513, 31151N]

Bonham-Haley Mountain States, p. I-48 [NAICS 311320]

Bonide Products Inc., p. I-529 [NAICS 325320]

Bonita Packaging Products Inc., p. I-395 [NAICS 32222P]

Bonnavilla Homes, pp. Vol. I-348, 353 [NAICS 321991, 321992]

Bonnell Industries Inc., p. II-1028 [NAICS 333112]

Bonney Forge Corp., pp. Vol. I-872, Vol. II-952 [NAICS 33211N, 332721]

Book Covers Inc., p. I-374 [NAICS 322130]

Bookcliff Auto Parts Inc., p. III-2030 [NAICS 441310]

Booklegger, p. III-1995 [NAICS 424920]

Bookmasters Inc., p. III-1995 [NAICS 424920]

Bookpeople Inc., p. III-1995 [NAICS 424920]

Books-A-Million Inc., p. III-2162 [NAICS 451211]

Books Inc., p. III-2162 [NAICS 451211]

Books On Tape Inc., p. II-1376 [NAICS 334612]

BookWorld Services Inc., p. III-1995 [NAICS 424920]

Boos Dental Laboratory, p. II-1682 [NAICS 339114]

Boosters Inc., p. I-203 [NAICS 31322M]

Boots & Coots Intern, p. II-1039 [NAICS 33313M]

Bootz Manufacturing Co., p. I-681 [NAICS 327112]

Boral Bricks Inc., p. I-703 [NAICS 32712N]

Borden Chemical Inc., p. I-500 [NAICS 325211]

Borden Milk Products L.P., p. I-86 [NAICS 31151N]

Border Distributing Company Inc., p. III-1770 [NAICS 423140]

Border Foods Inc., pp. Vol. I-62, 68, 76, 158 [NAICS 31141M, 31142M, 311513, 31199M]

Border Steel Inc., pp. Vol. I-793, Vol. II-1014 [NAICS 33122M, 33299N]

Borders Group Inc., pp. Vol. III-2162, 2168 [NAICS 451211, 451220]

Boren Explosives Company Inc., p. I-585 [NAICS 325920]

Borgeson Universal Company Inc., p. II-1530 [NAICS 336350]

BorgWarner Inc., pp. Vol. II-908, 1014, 1551 [NAICS 33232M, 33299N, 336399]

Bornquist Inc., pp. Vol. III-1809, 1847, 1855 [NAICS 423440, 423720, 423740]

Borrell Electric Company Inc., p. II-1421 [NAICS 335311]

Borroughs Corp., pp. Vol. II-1627, 1644, 1650 [NAICS 337127, 337215, 33721N]

Borstein Seafood Inc., p. III-1943 [NAICS 424460]

Bosch Doboy Inc., p. II-1212 [NAICS 333993]

Bosch Rexroth Corp, pp. Vol. II-980, 1162, 1222, 1427, 1437 [NAICS 33291N, 333612, 33399N, 335312, 335314]

Boscov's Department Stores Inc., p. III-2171 [NAICS 452111]

Bose Corp., pp. Vol. II-1262, 1272, 1551 [NAICS 334220, 334310, 336399]

Bosma Industries for the Blind, p. I-285 [NAICS 31529M]

Boss Holdings Inc., p. III-2007 [NAICS 424990]

Boss International, p. III-1883 [NAICS 423910]

Boss Unlimited, p. III-2194 [NAICS 453310]

Bossong Hosiery Mills Inc., p. I-256 [NAICS 31511M]

Bostik Findley Inc., pp. Vol. I-560, 752 [NAICS 325520, 327420]

Boston Acoustics Inc., p. II-1272 [NAICS 334310]

Boston Beer Company Inc., p. I-172 [NAICS 312120]

Boston Scientific Corp., p. II-1671 [NAICS 339112]

Botanical Laboratories Inc., p. I-534 [NAICS 325411]

Bottcher America Corp., p. II-1714 [NAICS 33994M]

Bou-Matic, p. II-1023 [NAICS 333111]

Boulder Outdoor Center Inc., p. III-2024 [NAICS 441222]

Bourdon Forge Company Inc., p. I-872 [NAICS 33211N]

Boutique Trims Inc., pp. Vol. III-1894, 1998 [NAICS 423940, 424930]

Bow Industries of Virginia Inc., p. II-1381 [NAICS 334613]

Bowater Inc., pp. Vol. I-358, 363, 368, 388 [NAICS 321999, 322110, 32212M, 32222N]

Bowater Newsprint Directory Div., p. I-368 [NAICS 32212M]

Bowie Industries Inc., p. II-1028 [NAICS 333112]

Bowles Fluidics Corp., p. II-974 [NAICS 332913]

Bowlin Travel Centers Inc., pp. Vol. III-2027, 2116 [NAICS 441229, 447110]

Bowne and Company Inc., p. I-420 [NAICS 32311M]

Boyd Coffee Co., pp. Vol. I-143, 158 [NAICS 311920, 31199M]

Boyd Industries Inc., p. II-1682 [NAICS 339114]

Boyds Collection Ltd., pp. Vol. II-1708, Vol. III-2007 [NAICS 33993M, 424990]

Boydstun Metal Works Inc., p. II-1491 [NAICS 336212]

Boyer Candy Company Inc., p. I-57 [NAICS 311340]

Boyertown Foundry Co., p. II-918 [NAICS 332410]

Boyland Auto Group Inc., p. III-2011 [NAICS 441110]

Boyle Meat Co., p. III-1946 [NAICS 424470]

Bozzuto's Inc., pp. Vol. III-1925, 1929, 1954 [NAICS 424410, 424420, 424490]

BP Chemicals Inc., pp. Vol. I-493, 500, 722 [NAICS 32519M, 325211, 327215]

BP Industries Inc., p. III-1778 [NAICS 423220]

BP Products Inc., p. II-1404 [NAICS 335221]

BPC Manufacturing, p. II-974 [NAICS 332913]

Bpi By-Product Industries Inc., p. I-703 [NAICS 32712N]

BPI Inc., p. I-703 [NAICS 32712N]

BPS Reprographics Services, p. I-420 [NAICS 32311M]

BPX Films Co., p. I-615 [NAICS 326113]

Bracalente Manufacturing Co., p. II-952 [NAICS 332721]

Bradbury Company Inc., p. II-1147 [NAICS 333516]

Bradco Supply Corp., pp. Vol. III-1782, 1790, 1794 [NAICS 423310, 423330, 423390]

Braden Carco Gearmatic Winch, pp. Vol. I-872, Vol. II-1033 [NAICS 33211N, 333120]

Braden-Sutphin Ink Co., pp. Vol. I-580, Vol. II-1714 [NAICS 325910, 33994M]

Bradford Company Inc., pp. Vol. I-343, 374, 379, 403, 415 [NAICS 321920, 322130, 32221M, 32223M, 322299]

Bradford Industries Inc., pp. Vol. I-224, 510 [NAICS 313320, 32522M]

Bradford White Corp., pp. Vol. II-1217, 1417 [NAICS 333994, 335228]

Bradington-Young L.L.C., p. II-1616 [NAICS 337121]

Bradley Industries Inc., p. III-1905 [NAICS 424130]

Bradley Lifting Corp., p. I-803 [NAICS 331312]

Bradley Pharmaceuticals Inc., p. III-1909 [NAICS 424210]

Bradley-Rogers Corp., p. II-1362 [NAICS 334518]

Bradley Supply Company Inc., p. III-1968 [NAICS 424610]

Bradner Central Co., pp. Vol. I-436, Vol. III-1898 [NAICS 32312M, 424110]

Bradshaw International Inc., p. III-1778 [NAICS 423220]

Brady Corp., pp. Vol. I-388, 560, Vol. II-1749 [NAICS 32222N, 325520, 339999]

Brady Distributing Co., p. III-1809 [NAICS 423440]

Braeburn Alloy Steel, p. I-872 [NAICS 33211N]

Braid Electric Company Inc., pp. Vol. III-1831, 1839 [NAICS 423610, 423690]

Brake Resources Inc., p. II-1524 [NAICS 336340]

Brakebush Brothers Inc., p. I-97 [NAICS 311615]

Brakur Custom Cabinetry Inc., pp. Vol. II-1611, 1632 [NAICS 337110, 33712N]

Braman Management Association, p. III-2011 [NAICS 441110]

Branch Brook Co., pp. Vol. III-1847, 1883 [NAICS 423720, 423910]

Brand-Nu Laboratories Inc., p. I-493 [NAICS 32519M]

Brandon House Furniture Co., pp. Vol. III-2037, 2041, 2047 [NAICS 442110, 442210, 442299]

Brandon Meats and Sausage Inc., p. III-2083 [NAICS 445210]

Brandrud Furniture Inc., p. II-1632 [NAICS 33712N]

Brandt Consolidated Inc., p. I-524 [NAICS 325314]

Brandt Technologies Inc., p. III-1971 [NAICS 424690]

Brandywine Recyclers Inc., pp. Vol. I-363, 807 [NAICS 322110, 331314]

Branko Perforating FWD Inc., p. I-825 [NAICS 331419]

Brannon and Walsh Inc., p. III-1901 [NAICS 424120]

Branson Ultrasonics Corp., p. II-1124 [NAICS 333512]

Brasher's Cascade Auto Auction, p. III-1758 [NAICS 423110]

Brass-Craft Manufacturing Co., pp. Vol. I-780, Vol. II-974, 980, 1092 [NAICS 33111M, 332913, 33291N, 33331N]

Brass Eagle Inc., pp. Vol. II-1749, Vol. III-2208 [NAICS 339999, 453998]

Brasseler USA Manufacturing, p. II-1682 [NAICS 339114]

Brasure's Pest Control Inc., p. III-2041 [NAICS 442210]

Braswell Foods Inc., p. I-4 [NAICS 311111]

Bratt-Foster Inc., p. III-1929 [NAICS 424420]

Brauer Supply Co., p. III-1851 [NAICS 423730]

Braum's Ice Cream & Dairy Stores, pp. Vol. I-86, 92, 102, 116, 158 [NAICS 31151N, 311520, 31161N, 31181M, 31199M]

Braun Corp., pp. Vol. II-1194, 1676 [NAICS 33392M, 339113]

Brave Products Inc., pp. Vol. II-892, 1033 [NAICS 33221P, 333120]

Braxton Culler Inc., p. II-1632 [NAICS 33712N]

Braxton Manufacturing Inc., pp. Vol. II-1580, 1735 [NAICS 336419, 339993]

Brazeway Inc., pp. Vol. I-811, Vol. II-918, 1009, 1106 [NAICS 331316, 332410, 332996, 333415]

Brazos Cellular Communications, p. III-2054 [NAICS 443112]

BRC Rubber and Plastics Inc., pp. Vol. I-670, Vol. II-1725 [NAICS 32629M, 339991]

Brd Supply Inc., p. III-2018 [NAICS 441210]

Bread and Co., p. III-2089 [NAICS 445291]

Breckenridge Material Inc., p. I-732 [NAICS 327320]

Brecon Knitting Mill Inc., p. I-213 [NAICS 31324M]

Brede Exposition Service, p. II-1720 [NAICS 339950]

Bredero Shaw, p. I-554 [NAICS 325510]

Breeder's Choice Pet Foods Inc., p. I-4 [NAICS 311111]

Breeze-Eastern, p. II-1580 [NAICS 336419]

Bremner Inc., p. I-124 [NAICS 31182M]

Bren-Tronics Inc., p. II-1447 [NAICS 335912]

Brenmar Company Inc., p. III-1905 [NAICS 424130]

Brennan Equipment and Mfg Inc., p. I-660 [NAICS 32621M]

Brenner Tank L.L.C., pp. Vol. II-923, 1491 [NAICS 332420, 336212]

Brenner Tool and Die Inc., pp. Vol. II-1119, 1134 [NAICS 333511, 333514]

Brenntag Great Lakes L.L.C., p. III-1971 [NAICS 424690]

Brenntag Mid-South Inc., p. III-1971 [NAICS 424690]

Brenton Engineering Co., p. II-1212 [NAICS 333993]

BRENTS INC., p. I-262 [NAICS 31519M]

Brentwood Benson Music, p. II-1376 [NAICS 334612]

Bretford Manufacturing Co., pp. Vol. II-1272, 1632, 1644, 1650 [NAICS 334310, 33712N, 337215, 33721N]

Breton Industries Inc., pp. Vol. I-203, 224 [NAICS 31322M, 313320]

Brevard Water Conditioning Inc., p. III-2228 [NAICS 454390]

Brewco Inc., p. II-1046 [NAICS 333210]

Brewer's Alley, p. I-172 [NAICS 312120]

Brewer Science Inc., pp. Vol. I-488, 493, Vol. II-1666 [NAICS 325188, 32519M, 339111]

Brewer Sewing Supplies Co., pp. Vol. III-1887, 1913 [NAICS 423920, 424310]

Brewster Wallcovering Co., p. III-2004 [NAICS 424950]

Brian Moore Guitars Inc., p. II-1731 [NAICS 339992]

Briar Knitting Inc., p. I-262 [NAICS 31519M]

Brick & Tile Corporation, p. I-691 [NAICS 327121]

Bricks and Tiles Unlimited, p. III-2041 [NAICS 442210]

Bridgeport Brewing Co., p. I-172 [NAICS 312120]

Bridgeport Fittings Inc., p. II-1307 [NAICS 334417]

Bridgeport Insulated Wire Co., p. I-830 [NAICS 33142M]

Bridgeport Metal Goods Mfg Co., p. II-928 [NAICS 33243M]

Bridgestone Americas Holding Inc., p. I-660 [NAICS 32621M]

Bridgewater Interiors L.L.C., p. II-1627 [NAICS 337127]

bridgeways, p. II-1557 [NAICS 336411]

Bridgford Foods Corp., pp. Vol. I-62, 116 [NAICS 31141M, 31181M]

Bridon American Corp., pp. Vol. II-939, 1657 [NAICS 33261M, 337910]

Bridon Cordage L.L.C., p. I-244 [NAICS 314991]

Briess Malt and Ingredients Co., pp. Vol. I-15, 147 [NAICS 31121M, 311930]

Briggs and Stratton Corp., p. II-1173 [NAICS 333618]

Briggs Corp., p. III-1813 [NAICS 423450]

Briggs Equipment Inc., pp. Vol. III-1859, 2208 [NAICS 423810, 453998]

Briggs Incorporated of Omaha, pp. Vol. III-1847, 1851 [NAICS 423720, 423730]

Brigham's Ice Cream, pp. Vol. I-92, 147 [NAICS 311520, 311930]

Bright Cooperative Inc., p. II-1500 [NAICS 336214]

Bright Image Corp., pp. Vol. II-1332, 1731 [NAICS 334512, 339992]

Brighton-Best Socket Screw Mfg, p. III-1843 [NAICS 423710]

Brightpoint Inc., p. III-1839 [NAICS 423690]

Brilliance Audio Inc., p. II-1376 [NAICS 334612]

Brillion Iron Works Inc., pp. Vol. I-845, Vol. II-1023, 1463 [NAICS 33151M, 333111, 335991]

Brimrose Corporation of America, p. II-1005 [NAICS 332995]

Brin Glass Co., p. III-1794 [NAICS 423390]

Bringing Up Baby Inc., p. III-2126 [NAICS 448120]

Brinkmann Corp., pp. Vol. II-1312, 1327, 1337, 1390 [NAICS 334418, 334511, 334513, 33512M]

Brisk Coffee Co., p. I-143 [NAICS 311920]

Bristol Babcock Inc., pp. Vol. II-1337, 1347, 1437 [NAICS 334513, 334515, 335314]

Bristol Compressors Inc., p. II-1184 [NAICS 333912]

Bristol Farms Inc., p. I-116 [NAICS 31181M]

Bristol-Myers Squibb Co., p. I-539 [NAICS 325412]

Britannia Inc., p. III-2058 [NAICS 443120]

Brite Wood Corp., p. I-631 [NAICS 326130]

Brittain Merchandising, p. III-1901 [NAICS 424120]

Brittany Dyeing and Printing Corp., p. I-218 [NAICS 31331M]

Brittany Fabrics Inc., pp. Vol. I-203, 213 [NAICS 31322M, 31324M]

Britz Fertilizer Inc., p. I-516 [NAICS 325311]

Brix Group Inc., pp. Vol. III-1805, 1839 [NAICS 423430, 423690]

Broadcast Electronics Inc., pp. Vol. II-928, 1243, 1272, 1317, 1381 [NAICS 33243M, 334112, 334310, 334419, 334613]

Broadcaster Press Inc., p. I-420 [NAICS 32311M]

Numbers following p. or pp. are page references. Roman numerals indicate volume numbers. Bracketed items indicate industries. Page references are to the starting pages of company tables.

Broadcasters General Store Inc., pp. Vol. III-1820, 2054 [NAICS 423490, 443112]

Broadcom Corp., p. II-1287 [NAICS 334413]

Broadway Engineering Services, p. II-1056 [NAICS 333295]

Broadway Photo Video Retail, pp. Vol. III-2062, 2153 [NAICS 443130, 451120]

Broadwing Corp., p. II-1257 [NAICS 334210]

Broadxent Inc., p. II-1257 [NAICS 334210]

Broan-Nutone L.L.C., pp. Vol. II-899, 1112, 1397, 1611, 1731 [NAICS 33231M, 33341N, 33521M, 337110, 339992]

Broaster Co., p. II-1404 [NAICS 335221]

Brocade Communications Systems, p. II-1252 [NAICS 334119]

Brock-McVey Co., p. III-1855 [NAICS 423740]

Brockway Pressed Metals Inc., p. I-867 [NAICS 332117]

Brockway-Smith Co., p. III-1782 [NAICS 423310]

Broder Brothers Co., pp. Vol. III-1916, 1919 [NAICS 424320, 424330]

Brodnax Mills Inc., p. I-192 [NAICS 31311M]

Broin Enterprises Inc., p. I-493 [NAICS 32519M]

Broken Arrow Productions Inc., p. II-1381 [NAICS 334613]

Bronner Brothers Inc., pp. Vol. I-575, Vol. II-886 [NAICS 325620, 33221N]

Bronson Precision Products, p. II-952 [NAICS 332721]

Bronson Syrup Company Inc., p. III-1939 [NAICS 424450]

Brooke Pottery Inc., p. III-2047 [NAICS 442299]

Brookfield Engineering, p. II-1332 [NAICS 334512]

Brooklyn Resources Recovery, p. III-1890 [NAICS 423930]

Brooks Automation Inc., pp. Vol. II-1061, 1287 [NAICS 33329N, 334413]

Brooks Brothers Inc., pp. Vol. I-272, 279 [NAICS 31522M, 31523M]

Brooks Food Group Inc., pp. Vol. I-62, 158 [NAICS 31141M, 31199M]

Brooks Instrument, pp. Vol. II-980, 1342, 1347, 1437 [NAICS 33291N, 334514, 334515, 335314]

Brooks Tactical, p. II-1519 [NAICS 336330]

Brooks Tractor Inc., p. III-2208 [NAICS 453998]

Brookshire Brothers Ltd., p. III-2076 [NAICS 445110]

Brookshire Grocery Co., p. III-2076 [NAICS 445110]

Brookstone Inc., pp. Vol. III-2050, 2153, 2190, 2208, 2211 [NAICS 443111, 451120, 453220, 453998, 454113]

Brooktrout Inc., p. II-1282 [NAICS 334412]

Brookville Wood Products Inc., p. I-358 [NAICS 321999]

Bross Construction Co., p. I-732 [NAICS 327320]

Brother International, p. II-1077 [NAICS 333313]

Brother International Corp. (USA), pp. Vol. II-1077, Vol. III-1801, 1835 [NAICS 333313, 423420, 423620]

Brotherhood Winery, p. I-177 [NAICS 312130]

Brothers Optical Laboratory Inc., p. II-1687 [NAICS 339115]

Brown Brothers Produce Co., p. III-1950 [NAICS 424480]

Brown-Forman Corp., pp. Vol. I-177, 181, 343 [NAICS 312130, 312140, 321920]

Brown Industrial Inc., p. II-1051 [NAICS 333220]

Brown Jordan Co., p. II-1632 [NAICS 33712N]

Brown Manufacturing Corp., p. II-1028 [NAICS 333112]

Brown Paper Goods Co., p. I-395 [NAICS 32222P]

Brown Printing Co., p. I-436 [NAICS 32312M]

Brown's Ice Cream Co., pp. Vol. III-1929, 1933 [NAICS 424420, 424430]

Brown Shoe Company Inc., pp. Vol. I-300, 306, Vol. III-1922, 2141 [NAICS 31621M, 31699M, 424340, 448210]

Brownforman Wines, p. III-1987 [NAICS 424820]

Browning & Winchester Firearms, pp. Vol. II-1001, 1005, Vol. III-1883 [NAICS 332994, 332995, 423910]

Brownlee Lighting, p. II-1386 [NAICS 335110]

Brownstone Gallery Ltd., p. III-1778 [NAICS 423220]

Brownwood Furniture, p. II-1657 [NAICS 337910]

Brox Industries Inc., p. I-448 [NAICS 324121]

Broyhill Inc., p. II-1028 [NAICS 333112]

BRP Manufacturing Co., p. I-665 [NAICS 326220]

Bruce Foods Corp., pp. Vol. I-68, 152 [NAICS 31142M, 31194M]

Bruce Fox Inc., p. II-1696 [NAICS 33991M]

Bruce Kreofsky and Sons Inc., p. III-1794 [NAICS 423390]

Bruce Oakley Inc., pp. Vol. I-15, 516, 520 [NAICS 31121M, 325311, 325312]

Bruce Supply Corp., p. III-1847 [NAICS 423720]

Bruckner Truck Sales Inc., p. III-1762 [NAICS 423120]

Brueton Inc., p. I-762 [NAICS 327991]

Brueton Industries Inc., pp. Vol. I-762, Vol. II-1632 [NAICS 327991, 33712N]

Bruewer Woodwork Mfg Co., p. II-1639 [NAICS 337212]

Bruker AXS Inc., p. II-1357 [NAICS 334517]

Bruker Biospin Corp., pp. Vol. II-1322, 1352, Vol. III-1971 [NAICS 334510, 334516, 424690]

Bruker Daltonics Inc., p. II-1352 [NAICS 334516]

Bruker Medical Inc., p. II-1352 [NAICS 334516]

Brumlow Mills Inc., p. I-229 [NAICS 314110]

Bruneel Tire Factory Inc., p. III-1766 [NAICS 423130]

Brunner and Lay Inc., pp. Vol. II-1039, 1207 [NAICS 33313M, 333991]

Brunner International Inc., pp. Vol. II-1140, 1168, 1486, 1524 [NAICS 333515, 333613, 336211, 336340]

Brunner Manufacturing Inc., p. II-958 [NAICS 332722]

Bruno's Supermarkets Inc., p. III-2076 [NAICS 445110]

Bruno Scheidt Inc., p. III-1954 [NAICS 424490]

Brunsell Lumber, pp. Vol. I-329, Vol. II-1611, 1650 [NAICS 32121P, 337110, 33721N]

Brunswick Corp., pp. Vol. II-1173, 1594, 1702 [NAICS 333618, 336612, 339920]

Brush Engineered Materials Inc., pp. Vol. I-822, 825, 837, 857 [NAICS 331411, 331419, 33149M, 33152P]

Bryan Boilers, pp. Vol. II-918, 1417 [NAICS 332410, 335228]

Bryan Foods Inc., p. I-102 [NAICS 31161N]

Bryant-Habegger Co., p. III-1851 [NAICS 423730]

Brylane Inc., p. III-2211 [NAICS 454113]

Bryte Technologies Inc., p. I-510 [NAICS 32522M]

BSN-Jobst Inc., pp. Vol. I-272, Vol. II-1676 [NAICS 31522M, 339113]

BST Systems Inc., p. II-1447 [NAICS 335912]

BT Office Products, p. III-1901 [NAICS 424120]

BTD Manufacturing Inc., p. II-1134 [NAICS 333514]

BTL Industries Inc., p. II-1302 [NAICS 334416]

Buck Company Inc., pp. Vol. I-845, 852, 857 [NAICS 33151M, 33152N, 33152P]

Buck Distributing Company Inc., p. III-1983 [NAICS 424810]

Buck Equipment Inc., p. II-1584 [NAICS 336510]

Buck Knives Inc., pp. Vol. II-886, 892 [NAICS 33221N, 33221P]

Buck Stoves, pp. Vol. II-1101, 1404, 1417, Vol. III-2047 [NAICS 333414, 335221, 335228, 442299]

Buckeye International Inc., p. I-480 [NAICS 325181]

Buckeye Pacific Corp., p. III-1782 [NAICS 423310]

Buckeye Pipe Line Company L.P., p. I-443 [NAICS 324110]

Buckeye Polymers Inc., p. I-589 [NAICS 325991]

Buckeye Rubber and Packing Co., pp. Vol. III-1971, 2007 [NAICS 424690, 424990]

Buckeye Technologies Inc., p. I-510 [NAICS 32522M]

Buckeye Vacuum Cleaner Supply, p. III-1835 [NAICS 423620]

Buckingham-Virginia Slate, pp. Vol. I-453, 762 [NAICS 324122, 327991]

Buckle Inc., pp. Vol. III-2123, 2126, 2132 [NAICS 448110, 448120, 448140]

Buckley Industries Inc., p. I-641 [NAICS 326150]

Buckley Powder Co., p. I-585 [NAICS 325920]

Bucklin Tractor and Implement, p. III-1863 [NAICS 423820]

Buckman Laboratories Inc., p. I-595 [NAICS 32599N]

Bucks County Coffee Co., pp. Vol. III-2092, 2094 [NAICS 445292, 445299]

Bucky Bairdo's Inc., pp. Vol. III-1939, 2092 [NAICS 424450, 445292]

Bucyrus Blades Inc., p. II-1028 [NAICS 333112]

Bucyrus International Inc., p. II-1039 [NAICS 33313M]

Bucyrus Precision Tech Inc., pp. Vol. II-1505, 1530 [NAICS 33631M, 336350]

Bud Industries Inc., pp. Vol. II-928, 1432 [NAICS 33243M, 335313]

Budco of San Antonio Inc., p. III-1983 [NAICS 424810]

Budge Industries L.L.C., p. I-239 [NAICS 31491M]

Budney Industries Inc., pp. Vol. II-1505, 1562 [NAICS 33631M, 336412]

Budnick Converting Inc., p. I-415 [NAICS 322299]

Buechel Stone Corp., p. I-762 [NAICS 327991]

Buehler Ltd., p. II-1666 [NAICS 339111]

Bueno Foods Inc., p. I-133 [NAICS 311830]

Buffalo Air Handling Co., pp. Vol. II-1112, 1217 [NAICS 33341N, 333994]

Buffalo Bill's Brew Pub, p. I-172 [NAICS 312120]

Buffalo Crushed Stone Inc., p. I-448 [NAICS 324121]

Buffalo Exchange, p. III-2194 [NAICS 453310]

Buffalo Games Inc., p. II-1708 [NAICS 33993M]

Buffalo Printers Supply Inc., p. III-1798 [NAICS 423410]

Buffalo Rock Co. Gadsden Div., p. III-1954 [NAICS 424490]

Buffalo Vac L.L.C., p. II-918 [NAICS 332410]

Buffington and Associates Inc., p. III-1847 [NAICS 423720]

Buhrke Industries Inc., p. II-1541 [NAICS 336370]

Buhrman-Pharr Gifts, p. III-1843 [NAICS 423710]

Buick Mine and Mill, p. I-825 [NAICS 331419]

Builders First Source, pp. Vol. I-651, Vol. II-908 [NAICS 32619M, 33232M]

Builders FirstSource Blackstone, pp. Vol. I-334, 651, Vol. II-908 [NAICS 32191M, 32619M, 33232M]

Builders FirstSource Inc., pp. Vol. I-334, 358, 762, Vol. II-1644, Vol. III-1782, 1843 [NAICS 32191M, 321999, 327991, 337215, 423310, 423710]

Builders Firstsource of Jacksonville, pp. Vol. I-329, 334 [NAICS 32121P, 32191M]

Builders General Supply Co., pp. Vol. III-1782, 1786, 1790, 1794 [NAICS 423310, 423320, 423330, 423390]

Builders Rental, p. III-1859 [NAICS 423810]

Building & Industrial Wholesale, p. III-1790 [NAICS 423330]

Building Materials Holding Corp., pp. Vol. III-1794, 2065 [NAICS 423390, 444100]

Building Products Inc., pp. Vol. III-1782, 1790 [NAICS 423310, 423330]

Bulk Lift International Inc., p. I-395 [NAICS 32222P]

Bull HN Information Systems Inc., p. II-1238 [NAICS 334111]

Bull Moose Tube Co., p. I-780 [NAICS 33111M]

Bulldog Battery Corp., p. II-1447 [NAICS 335912]

Bullen Ultrasonics Inc., p. I-686 [NAICS 327113]

Bullet Line Inc., p. I-251 [NAICS 314999]

Bulloch Fertilizer Company Inc., pp. Vol. I-516, 520 [NAICS 325311, 325312]

Bulova Corp., pp. Vol. II-1362, 1432, 1696, Vol. III-1894 [NAICS 334518, 335313, 33991M, 423940]

Bumble Bee Seafoods L.L.C., p. I-110 [NAICS 31171M]

Bumper Specialties Inc., p. I-641 [NAICS 326150]

Bumper To Bumper Autowares, p. III-1770 [NAICS 423140]

Bunge Ltd., pp. Vol. I-68, 516 [NAICS 31142M, 325311]

Bunge Milling Inc., pp. Vol. I-9, 15, 26, 31 [NAICS 311119, 31121M, 311225, 31122N]

Bunge North America, pp. Vol. I-15, 26, 147, 152, 158 [NAICS 31121M, 311225, 311930, 31194M, 31199M]

Bunge North America East, p. I-26 [NAICS 311225]

Bunge North America Inc., pp. Vol. I-15, 26, 147, 152, 158 [NAICS 31121M, 311225, 311930, 31194M, 31199M]

Bunker Hill Cheese Company Inc., p. I-76 [NAICS 311513]

Bunn Capitol Co., p. III-1939 [NAICS 424450]

Bunting Bearings Corp., pp. Vol. I-857, Vol. II-1168 [NAICS 33152P, 333613]

Bunting Inc., p. II-1714 [NAICS 33994M]

Bunzl Extrusion, p. I-631 [NAICS 326130]

Bunzl Extrusion Columbia Inc., p. I-615 [NAICS 326113]

Bunzl Extrusion of Massachusetts, p. I-621 [NAICS 326121]

BUNZL New England, pp. Vol. III-1905, 1971 [NAICS 424130, 424690]

Bunzl New Jersey Inc., p. III-1905 [NAICS 424130]

Burd and Fletcher Co., p. I-379 [NAICS 32221M]

Burdette Dental Laboratory Inc., p. II-1682 [NAICS 339114]

Burge Inc., p. I-480 [NAICS 325181]

Burger Boat Co., p. II-1594 [NAICS 336612]

Burgers Ozark Country Cured, p. I-97 [NAICS 311615]

Burgess-Norton Manufacturing, p. II-1014 [NAICS 33299N]

Burggraf Tire Supply Inc., p. III-1766 [NAICS 423130]

Burke Beverages Inc., p. III-1983 [NAICS 424810]

Burke Hosiery Mills Inc., p. I-256 [NAICS 31511M]

Burke Industries Inc., p. I-670 [NAICS 32629M]

Burke Mills Inc., pp. Vol. I-192, 198, 218 [NAICS 31311M, 313210, 31331M]

Burke's Bakery, p. III-2089 [NAICS 445291]

Burkmann Feeds L.L.C., p. III-2197 [NAICS 453910]

Burks Tractor Company Inc., p. III-1863 [NAICS 423820]

Burlen Corp., p. I-279 [NAICS 31523M]

Burlington Coat Factory, p. III-2132 [NAICS 448140]

Burlington Homes of Maine, pp. Vol. I-348, 353 [NAICS 321991, 321992]

Burlington Industries L.L.C., pp. Vol. I-192, 198, 229 [NAICS 31311M, 313210, 314110]

Burlington Rug Corp., p. I-229 [NAICS 314110]

Burly Corporation, p. II-939 [NAICS 33261M]

Burnes of Boston/Connoisseur, pp. Vol. I-358, Vol. II-1014 [NAICS 321999, 33299N]

Burnett Dairy Co-Operative, p. I-76 [NAICS 311513]

Burnham Holdings Inc., pp. Vol. I-845, Vol. II-899, 1101, 1106, 1217 [NAICS 33151M, 33231M, 333414, 333415, 333994]

Burns Systems, p. II-1417 [NAICS 335228]

Burnside Industries L.L.C., p. II-1541 [NAICS 336370]

Burpee Co., p. II-1189 [NAICS 333913]

Burr Oak Tool and Gauge Inc., pp. Vol. II-918, 1134 [NAICS 332410, 333514]

Burris Foods Inc., pp. Vol. III-1929, 1933 [NAICS 424420, 424430]

Burroughs Ross Colville L.L.C., p. I-343 [NAICS 321920]

Burrows Co., pp. Vol. III-1809, 1813, 1913 [NAICS 423440, 423450, 424310]

Burrows Paper Corp., p. I-368 [NAICS 32212M]

Burt Automotive Network, p. III-2011 [NAICS 441110]

Burton Snowboards, p. II-1702 [NAICS 339920]

Burtons Inc., p. III-2123 [NAICS 448110]

Burtronics Business Systems Inc., p. III-1801 [NAICS 423420]

BUSE Timber and Sales Inc., p. I-358 [NAICS 321999]

Bush Brothers and Co., p. I-158 [NAICS 31199M]

Bush Hog L.L.C., p. II-1023 [NAICS 333111]

Bush Industries Inc., pp. Vol. II-1616, 1621, 1627, 1644, 1650 [NAICS 337121, 337122, 337127, 337215, 33721N]

Business Development Labs Inc., p. I-143 [NAICS 311920]

Business Furniture Corp., p. III-1774 [NAICS 423210]

Business Furniture Inc., p. III-1774 [NAICS 423210]

Business Interiors, p. III-1774 [NAICS 423210]

Business Interiors Northwest Inc., p. III-1774 [NAICS 423210]

Business Machines Systems Inc., p. III-2186 [NAICS 453210]

Business Office Systems Inc., p. III-1774 [NAICS 423210]

Business World Inc., p. III-2186 [NAICS 453210]

Busse Hospital Disposables, p. I-411 [NAICS 322291]

Busy Beaver Building Centers Inc., pp. Vol. III-2065, 2072 [NAICS 444100, 444220]

Butane Power and Equipment Co., p. III-2222 [NAICS 454312]

Butler A-1 Motors, p. III-1770 [NAICS 423140]

Butler Home Products Inc., p. II-1740 [NAICS 339994]

Butler-Johnson Corp., p. III-1794 [NAICS 423390]

Butler Manufacturing Co., pp. Vol. I-353, Vol. II-899 [NAICS 321992, 33231M]

Butler National Corp., p. II-1557 [NAICS 336411]

Butler Paper Recycling Inc., p. I-363 [NAICS 322110]

Butler Wholesale Products, pp. Vol. III-1905, 1929 [NAICS 424130, 424420]

Butter Krust Baking Company Inc., p. I-116 [NAICS 31181M]

Butterball Farms Inc., p. I-86 [NAICS 31151N]

Butternut Mountain Farm, p. I-44 [NAICS 31131N]

Butts Manufacturing Co., p. II-1413 [NAICS 335224]

Buxton Acquisition Inc., p. III-2007 [NAICS 424990]

BUY.COM Inc., pp. Vol. III-2180, 2211 [NAICS 452990, 454113]

Buz Post Pontiac/GMC Inc., p. III-2011 [NAICS 441110]

Buzz Products Inc., p. III-1929 [NAICS 424420]

Buzzi Unicem USA, p. I-727 [NAICS 327310]

BUZZI UNICEM USA Inc., p. I-727 [NAICS 327310]

Buzzi Unicem USA Midwest, p. I-727 [NAICS 327310]

BW Elliott Manufacturing L.L.C., pp. Vol. II-1033, 1168, 1530 [NAICS 333120, 333613, 336350]

BW Johnson Manufacturing Inc., p. I-505 [NAICS 325212]

Bway Corp., p. I-651 [NAICS 32619M]

BWAY Corp., pp. Vol. II-928, 1014 [NAICS 33243M, 33299N]

BWX Technologies Inc., pp. Vol. I-475, Vol. II-1092 [NAICS 32513M, 33331N]

Numbers following p. or pp. are page references. Roman numerals indicate volume numbers. Bracketed items indicate industries. Page references are to the starting pages of company tables.

BWXT Pantex L.L.C., pp. Vol. I-585, Vol. II-1005, 1312, 1572 [NAICS 325920, 332995, 334418, 336414]

Bybee Stone Company Inc., p. I-762 [NAICS 327991]

Bycap Inc., p. II-1292 [NAICS 334414]

Byer California, pp. Vol. I-279, 285, 290 [NAICS 31523M, 31529M, 31599M]

Byrne Dairy Inc., pp. Vol. I-86, 92 [NAICS 31151N, 311520]

Byrne Electrical Specialists, p. II-1312 [NAICS 334418]

Bytheway's Manufacturing Inc., p. II-1662 [NAICS 337920]

C and A Floorcoverings, p. I-229 [NAICS 314110]

C and A Tool Engineering Inc., p. II-1119 [NAICS 333511]

C and D Aerospace Inc., pp. Vol. II-928, 1536, 1567 [NAICS 33243M, 336360, 336413]

C and D Technologies Inc., pp. Vol. II-1442, 1468 [NAICS 335911, 335999]

C and F Enterprises, p. III-1913 [NAICS 424310]

C and F Forge Co., p. I-830 [NAICS 33142M]

C and H Distributors Inc., pp. Vol. I-748, 762, Vol. III-1867, 1871 [NAICS 327410, 327991, 423830, 423840]

C and J Jewelry Company Inc., pp. Vol. II-1696, 1714 [NAICS 33991M, 33994M]

C and L Supply Co., p. III-1835 [NAICS 423620]

C and M Fine Pack Inc., p. I-609 [NAICS 326112]

C and M Mills Inc., p. I-256 [NAICS 31511M]

C and P Oil Inc., p. III-2218 [NAICS 454311]

C and S Enterprises Inc., p. III-2228 [NAICS 454390]

C and S Inc., p. III-1975 [NAICS 424710]

C and S Wholesale Grocers Inc., p. III-1925 [NAICS 424410]

C Brewer Co., p. II-1119 [NAICS 333511]

C-COR Corp., p. II-1262 [NAICS 334220]

C. Cowles and Co., pp. Vol. I-879, Vol. II-964, 1014 [NAICS 33211P, 33281M, 33299N]

C-E Minerals Inc., p. I-703 [NAICS 32712N]

C Fan Company Inc., p. II-1505 [NAICS 33631M]

C. Lee Cook, p. II-1505 [NAICS 33631M]

C-Mor Co., p. II-1662 [NAICS 337920]

C-Tech Industries Inc., pp. Vol. I-566, Vol. II-1092 [NAICS 32561M, 33331N]

C-Thru Ruler Co., p. II-1735 [NAICS 339993]

C.A. International Inc., p. III-1786 [NAICS 423320]

C.A. M Audio Inc., p. III-1798 [NAICS 423410]

CA One Services Inc., p. III-2190 [NAICS 453220]

Cabela's Inc., pp. Vol. III-2150, 2211 [NAICS 451110, 454113]

Cabinet and Bath Supply Inc., p. III-1847 [NAICS 423720]

Cabinetry By Karman, p. II-1611 [NAICS 337110]

Cable Meat Center, p. III-2083 [NAICS 445210]

Cable Mfg and Assembly Inc., p. II-1451 [NAICS 33592M]

Cabot Corp., pp. Vol. I-475, 484, Vol. II-1463 [NAICS 32513M, 325182, 335991]

Cabot Hosiery Mills Inc., p. I-256 [NAICS 31511M]

Cabot House Inc., p. III-2037 [NAICS 442110]

Cabot Microelectronics Corp., p. I-776 [NAICS 327999]

Cache Inc., pp. Vol. III-2126, 2135 [NAICS 448120, 448150]

Cactus and Tropicals Inc., p. III-2183 [NAICS 453110]

Cactus Sands Nursery & Garden, p. III-2072 [NAICS 444220]

Caddock Electronics Inc., p. II-1297 [NAICS 334415]

Cadet Manufacturing Co., p. II-1397 [NAICS 33521M]

Cadillac Coffee Company Inc., p. I-143 [NAICS 311920]

Cadillac Curtain Corp., p. I-234 [NAICS 31412M]

Cadillac Products Packaging Co., p. I-609 [NAICS 326112]

Cadman Inc., p. I-732 [NAICS 327320]

Cadmus Communications Corp., p. I-420 [NAICS 32311M]

Cadmus Specialty Printing, p. I-436 [NAICS 32312M]

Cadmus Specialty Publications, p. I-436 [NAICS 32312M]

Cady Cheese Inc., p. I-76 [NAICS 311513]

CAE Remanufacturing L.L.C., p. II-1546 [NAICS 336391]

Caffall Brothers Forest Products, pp. Vol. I-312, 358 [NAICS 32111M, 321999]

Cagle's Inc., pp. Vol. I-97, Vol. III-1936, 1946 [NAICS 311615, 424440, 424470]

CAI Inc., p. I-580 [NAICS 325910]

Cain and Bultman Inc., pp. Vol. III-1778, 1835 [NAICS 423220, 423620]

Cain Electrical Supply Corp., pp. Vol. II-1468, Vol. III-1831 [NAICS 335999, 423610]

Caitac Garment Processing Inc., pp. Vol. I-272, 279 [NAICS 31522M, 31523M]

Caito Fisheries Inc., p. I-110 [NAICS 31171M]

Cajun Sugar Cooperative Inc., p. I-44 [NAICS 31131N]

Cakebread Cellars, p. I-177 [NAICS 312130]

Cal-Chip Electronics Inc., pp. Vol. I-686, Vol. II-1292, 1297 [NAICS 327113, 334414, 334415]

Cal-Cru, p. I-267 [NAICS 31521M]

Cal-Maine Foods Inc., p. I-97 [NAICS 311615]

Cal Quality Electronics Inc., p. II-1312 [NAICS 334418]

Cal-Steam Supply Inc., p. III-1847 [NAICS 423720]

CalAmp Corp., pp. Vol. II-1262, 1272 [NAICS 334220, 334310]

Calaveras Materials Inc., pp. Vol. I-448, 732 [NAICS 324121, 327320]

Calcar Quarries Inc., p. I-748 [NAICS 327410]

Calcot Ltd., p. III-1965 [NAICS 424590]

Calderon Brothers Vending Inc., p. III-2215 [NAICS 454210]

Caldwell Manufacturing Inc., p. I-811 [NAICS 331316]

Caldwell Tanks Alliance L.L.C., p. II-923 [NAICS 332420]

Caldwell Tanks Inc., p. II-923 [NAICS 332420]

Caleb Haley and Company Inc., p. III-1943 [NAICS 424460]

Calevas Foods, p. I-147 [NAICS 311930]

Calfland Traders Inc., p. III-1879 [NAICS 423860]

Calgon Carbon Corp., pp. Vol. I-475, Vol. II-1463 [NAICS 32513M, 335991]

California Acrylic Industries Inc., p. III-2047 [NAICS 442299]

California Ammonia Co., p. III-1991 [NAICS 424910]

California Automotive Sealing Inc., pp. Vol. I-641, Vol. II-1725 [NAICS 326150, 339991]

California Car Color, p. III-2004 [NAICS 424950]

California Cedar Products Co., pp. Vol. I-358, Vol. II-1714 [NAICS 321999, 33994M]

California Combining Corp., p. I-224 [NAICS 313320]

California Dairies Inc., p. I-86 [NAICS 31151N]

California Hydronics Corp., p. III-1847 [NAICS 423720]

California Industrial Rubber Inc., p. III-1871 [NAICS 423840]

California Magnetics, p. II-1376 [NAICS 334612]

California Micro Devices Corp., pp. Vol. II-1292, 1297 [NAICS 334414, 334415]

California Natural Products, p. I-143 [NAICS 311920]

California Olive Ranch Inc., p. I-26 [NAICS 311225]

California Panel and Veneer Co., p. III-1794 [NAICS 423390]

California Paperboard Corp., p. I-374 [NAICS 322130]

California Pools, p. III-1883 [NAICS 423910]

California Products Corp., p. I-453 [NAICS 324122]

California Ribbon and Carbon Co., p. II-1714 [NAICS 33994M]

California Shellfish Company Inc., p. I-110 [NAICS 31171M]

California Spray Dry Co., p. I-4 [NAICS 311111]

California Steel Industries, pp. Vol. I-780, Vol. II-908 [NAICS 33111M, 33232M]

California Truss Company Inc., p. I-329 [NAICS 32121P]

California Wholesale Material, p. III-1786 [NAICS 423320]

Calihan Pork Processors Inc., p. III-1946 [NAICS 424470]

Callaway Golf Co., p. II-1702 [NAICS 339920]

Callen Die Casting Co., p. I-852 [NAICS 33152N]

Callen Photo Mount Inc., p. II-1087 [NAICS 333315]

Callery Chemical Co., p. I-480 [NAICS 325181]

Callidus Technologies L.L.C., p. II-1217 [NAICS 333994]

Calloway's Nursery Inc., p. III-2072 [NAICS 444220]

Calpine Containers Inc., pp. Vol. I-343, Vol. II-928 [NAICS 321920, 33243M]

Calrepco Inc., p. III-1794 [NAICS 423390]

CalsonicKansei North America, pp. Vol. III-1851, 1968 [NAICS 423730, 424610]

Caltag Laboratory, pp. Vol. I-544, Vol. II-1666 [NAICS 325413, 339111]

Calton Dental Lab, p. II-1692 [NAICS 339116]

Calva Products Company Inc., p. I-81 [NAICS 311514]

Calvary Industries Inc., p. I-458 [NAICS 324191]

Calvert Manufacturing Inc., p. II-1046 [NAICS 333210]

Numbers following p. or pp. are page references. Roman numerals indicate volume numbers. Bracketed items indicate industries. Page references are to the starting pages of company tables.

2313

Company Index

Calvert-McBride Printing Co., p. III-2186 [NAICS 453210]

Cambrex Corp., pp. Vol. I-488, 529, 539, 595 [NAICS 325188, 325320, 325412, 32599N]

Cambria Assn for Blind, p. I-239 [NAICS 31491M]

Cambridge Brewing Company Inc., p. I-172 [NAICS 312120]

Cambridge Chemists Inc., p. III-2100 [NAICS 446110]

Cambridge Engineering Inc., p. II-1217 [NAICS 333994]

Cambridge International Inc., pp. Vol. II-939, 1168 [NAICS 33261M, 333613]

Cambridge Isotope Laboratories, p. I-595 [NAICS 32599N]

Cambridge-Lee Industries Inc., pp. Vol. I-822, 830, 837 [NAICS 331411, 33142M, 33149M]

Cambro Manufacturing Inc., p. I-636 [NAICS 326140]

Camco Manufacturing Inc., pp. Vol. I-251, Vol. III-1762 [NAICS 314999, 423120]

Camcor Inc., p. III-1798 [NAICS 423410]

Cameca Instruments Inc., p. III-1820 [NAICS 423490]

Camellia Food Stores Inc., p. III-1925 [NAICS 424410]

Camera Platforms International, p. II-1473 [NAICS 336111]

Cameron and Barkley Co., pp. Vol. III-1831, 1839, 1871 [NAICS 423610, 423690, 423840]

Cameron Ashley Building Prods, p. III-1790 [NAICS 423330]

Cameron Diversified Products Inc., p. I-867 [NAICS 332117]

Camfour Inc., p. III-1883 [NAICS 423910]

Camillus Western Cutlery Co., p. II-886 [NAICS 33221N]

Camino Real Foods Inc., p. I-62 [NAICS 31141M]

Camp-Hill Corp., p. I-788 [NAICS 331210]

Campbell Concrete & Materials, p. I-732 [NAICS 327320]

Campbell Foundry Co., p. I-845 [NAICS 33151M]

Campbell Oil Company Inc., p. III-2116 [NAICS 447110]

Campbell Rhea Inc., p. II-1666 [NAICS 339111]

Campbell's Pharmacy, p. III-2100 [NAICS 446110]

Campbell Soup Co., pp. Vol. I-62, 68, 116 [NAICS 31141M, 31142M, 31181M]

Campbell Supply Company Inc., p. III-2030 [NAICS 441310]

Camping World Inc., p. III-2018 [NAICS 441210]

Can Corporation of America Inc., p. II-928 [NAICS 33243M]

Canberra Corp., p. I-566 [NAICS 32561M]

Candela Corp., pp. Vol. II-1322, 1671 [NAICS 334510, 339112]

Candie's Inc., pp. Vol. I-300, Vol. III-1922 [NAICS 31621M, 424340]

Candy Express Franchising Inc., p. III-2092 [NAICS 445292]

Candy Flower Aquisition Corp., p. I-48 [NAICS 311320]

Candy Kitchen Shoppes Inc., p. I-57 [NAICS 311340]

Candyman Ltd., pp. Vol. III-2159, 2168 [NAICS 451140, 451220]

Cane Creek Cycling Components, p. II-1599 [NAICS 336991]

Cannon Company Inc., p. III-1855 [NAICS 423740]

Cannon Equipment Inc., pp. Vol. II-939, 1023, 1644 [NAICS 33261M, 333111, 337215]

Cannon Oil Corp., p. III-2116 [NAICS 447110]

Cannon Safe Inc., p. III-1801 [NAICS 423420]

Cannon USA Inc., p. II-1051 [NAICS 333220]

Cannondale Bicycle Corp., pp. Vol. I-272, 290, Vol. II-1599 [NAICS 31522M, 31599M, 336991]

Canon Business Solutions West, p. III-1801 [NAICS 423420]

Canon U.S.A. Inc., pp. Vol. II-1077, 1087, 1252, 1272, 1427 [NAICS 333313, 333315, 334119, 334310, 335312]

Canson Inc., p. II-1714 [NAICS 33994M]

Canteen Service Co., pp. Vol. III-1954, 2215 [NAICS 424490, 454210]

Cantel Medical Corp., p. II-1671 [NAICS 339112]

Cantex Inc., pp. Vol. I-626, Vol. II-1009 [NAICS 326122, 332996]

Canton Drop Forge Inc., pp. Vol. I-837, 872 [NAICS 33149M, 33211N]

Canvas Systems L.L.C., p. III-1805 [NAICS 423430]

Canyon Creek Cabinet Co., pp. Vol. II-1611, 1632, 1650 [NAICS 337110, 33712N, 33721N]

Canyon Eyewear, p. III-1817 [NAICS 423460]

Capax Technologies Inc., p. II-1292 [NAICS 334414]

Capco Inc., pp. Vol. II-993, 997, 1302 [NAICS 332992, 332993, 334416]

Capco Machinery Systems Inc., p. II-1147 [NAICS 333516]

Capcon International Inc., p. II-1292 [NAICS 334414]

Cape Cod Lumber Company Inc., p. II-1611 [NAICS 337110]

Cape Cod Potato Chip Co., p. I-137 [NAICS 31191M]

Cape May Foods Inc., p. I-110 [NAICS 31171M]

Capel Inc., pp. Vol. I-192, 229 [NAICS 31311M, 314110]

Capital Aviation Instrument Corp., p. III-2027 [NAICS 441229]

Capital Beverage Co., pp. Vol. III-1983, 1987 [NAICS 424810, 424820]

Capital Beverage Corp., p. III-1983 [NAICS 424810]

Capital Diamond Importers Inc., p. III-1894 [NAICS 423940]

Capital Ford New Holland Inc., p. III-1863 [NAICS 423820]

Capital-Mercury Apparel Ltd., p. I-272 [NAICS 31522M]

Capital Resin Corp., p. I-488 [NAICS 325188]

Capital Tire Inc., p. III-1766 [NAICS 423130]

Capitol Cement, p. I-727 [NAICS 327310]

Capitol Chevrolet Inc., pp. Vol. III-1762, 2030 [NAICS 423120, 441310]

Capitol Light and Supply Co., p. III-1831 [NAICS 423610]

Capitol Office Solutions Inc., p. III-1801 [NAICS 423420]

Capitol Products Corp., p. I-811 [NAICS 331316]

Capitol Stampings Corp., p. II-1162 [NAICS 333612]

Capitol Technologies Inc., p. II-1129 [NAICS 333513]

Capitol USA L.L.C., p. I-560 [NAICS 325520]

Capitol Welders Supply Inc., p. I-471 [NAICS 325120]

Caplugs L.L.C., p. I-244 [NAICS 314991]

Capo Industries Inc., p. II-1157 [NAICS 333611]

Cappaert Manufactured Housing, p. I-348 [NAICS 321991]

Cappelli Straworld Inc., pp. Vol. III-2123, 2126 [NAICS 448110, 448120]

Capresso Inc., p. III-1835 [NAICS 423620]

Capri Industries Inc., p. I-762 [NAICS 327991]

Capstan Atlantic, p. I-867 [NAICS 332117]

Capstone Turbine Corp., p. II-1157 [NAICS 333611]

Capt Neill's Seafood Inc., p. I-110 [NAICS 31171M]

Captain Faunce Seafood Inc., p. III-2085 [NAICS 445220]

Captive-Aire Systems Inc., p. II-1112 [NAICS 33341N]

Captive Fasteners Corp., p. II-958 [NAICS 332722]

Captive Plastics Inc., pp. Vol. I-646, 651, Vol. II-1119 [NAICS 326160, 32619M, 333511]

Car Brite Inc., p. I-566 [NAICS 32561M]

Car Component Technologies Inc., pp. Vol. II-1014, 1530 [NAICS 33299N, 336350]

Car-Freshner Corp., p. I-566 [NAICS 32561M]

Car-Graph Inc., p. II-1463 [NAICS 335991]

Caraustar Industries Inc., pp. Vol. I-374, 379, 626 [NAICS 322130, 32221M, 326122]

Caravan Trading Co., pp. Vol. I-116, Vol. III-1954 [NAICS 31181M, 424490]

Caravan Trailer L.L.C., p. III-1762 [NAICS 423120]

Carbo Ceramics Inc., pp. Vol. I-681, 776, Vol. II-1039 [NAICS 327112, 327999, 33313M]

Carbon Carbon Advanced, p. II-1463 [NAICS 335991]

Carbone Lorraine North America, pp. Vol. I-686, Vol. II-1432, 1463 [NAICS 327113, 335313, 335991]

Carbone of America Corp., pp. Vol. II-1056, 1463 [NAICS 333295, 335991]

Carbrella L.L.C., p. II-1536 [NAICS 336360]

Carclo Technical Plastics, p. I-651 [NAICS 32619M]

Cardell Kitchen and Bath Cabinets, p. II-1611 [NAICS 337110]

Carder Inc., p. III-1786 [NAICS 423320]

Cardiac Rhythm Management, p. II-1676 [NAICS 339113]

Cardiac Science Inc., p. II-1322 [NAICS 334510]

Cardinal Aluminum Company Inc., p. I-811 [NAICS 331316]

Cardinal CG, p. I-713 [NAICS 327212]

Cardinal Comb & Brush Mfg Corp., p. II-1740 [NAICS 339994]

Cardinal Distribution L.P., pp. Vol. III-1813, 1909 [NAICS 423450, 424210]

Cardinal FG, p. I-709 [NAICS 327211]

Cardinal Health Inc., p. III-1909 [NAICS 424210]

Cardinal Health Specialty Services, p. III-1909 [NAICS 424210]

Cardinal Home Products, p. II-1632 [NAICS 33712N]

Cardinal Homes Inc., p. I-353 [NAICS 321992]

Cardinal Industrial Insulation Inc., p. I-771 [NAICS 327993]

Cardinal Rubber Co., p. I-505 [NAICS 325212]

Cardinal Scale Manufacturing, p. II-1229 [NAICS 33399P]

Cardinal TG, pp. Vol. I-709, 713 [NAICS 327211, 327212]

Cardington Yutaka Technologies, p. II-1530 [NAICS 336350]

Care Plan International Inc., p. I-267 [NAICS 31521M]

Care Rehab & Orthopaedic, p. III-1813 [NAICS 423450]

Cargill Dow L.L.C., p. I-631 [NAICS 326130]

Cargill Dry Corn Ingredients Inc., p. I-15 [NAICS 31121M]

Cargill Inc., pp. Vol. I-22, 26, 97, 102, 780, Vol. II-899 [NAICS 311221, 311225, 311615, 31161N, 33111M, 33231M]

Cargill Juice North America Inc., p. I-152 [NAICS 31194M]

Cargill Malt Inc., p. I-15 [NAICS 31121M]

Cargill Meats Solution Corp., p. I-102 [NAICS 31161N]

Cargill Turkey Products, p. I-97 [NAICS 311615]

Cargo Landing Inc., p. III-2126 [NAICS 448120]

Cargotec Inc., p. III-1794 [NAICS 423390]

Carhartt Inc., p. I-272 [NAICS 31522M]

Carimex International Trading Inc., p. III-1887 [NAICS 423920]

Carl F. Ewig Inc., p. III-1879 [NAICS 423860]

Carl Fischer L.L.C., p. II-1376 [NAICS 334612]

Carl Zeiss Meditec, pp. Vol. II-1322, 1687 [NAICS 334510, 339115]

Carla Corp., p. II-1696 [NAICS 33991M]

Carleton Technologies Inc., p. II-1749 [NAICS 339999]

Carlex Glass Co., p. I-722 [NAICS 327215]

Carlin Combustion Technology, p. II-1101 [NAICS 333414]

Carling Technologies Inc., pp. Vol. II-1427, 1432, 1457, 1468 [NAICS 335312, 335313, 33593M, 335999]

Carlisle and Finch Co., p. II-1386 [NAICS 335110]

Carlisle Companies Inc., pp. Vol. I-626, 670 [NAICS 326122, 32629M]

Carlisle Corp., pp. Vol. I-626, 670, Vol. II-1033, 1061 [NAICS 326122, 32629M, 333120, 33329N]

Carlisle Sanitary Maintenance, p. II-1740 [NAICS 339994]

Carlisle SynTec Inc., pp. Vol. I-453, 560, 595 [NAICS 324122, 325520, 32599N]

Carlisle Tire and Wheel Co., pp. Vol. I-660, Vol. II-1551 [NAICS 32621M, 336399]

Carlton-Bates Co., p. III-1839 [NAICS 423690]

Carlton Co., p. II-1207 [NAICS 333991]

Carlton Forge Works, p. I-872 [NAICS 33211N]

Carlton J Enterprises L.L.C., p. III-2113 [NAICS 446199]

Carlyle and Company Jewelers, p. III-2144 [NAICS 448310]

Carlyle Inc., pp. Vol. II-1451, Vol. III-1820 [NAICS 33592M, 423490]

CarMax Inc., p. III-2015 [NAICS 441120]

Carmeuse Lime, pp. Vol. I-748, 767 [NAICS 327410, 327992]

Carnes Co., p. II-1397 [NAICS 33521M]

Carol House Furniture Inc., p. III-2037 [NAICS 442110]

Carol School Supply Inc., pp. Vol. III-1820, 1887, 2153, 2186 [NAICS 423490, 423920, 451120, 453210]

Carolane Propane Gas Inc., p. III-2222 [NAICS 454312]

Carolina Building Solutions L.L.C., pp. Vol. I-348, 353 [NAICS 321991, 321992]

Carolina By-Products Co., p. I-4 [NAICS 311111]

Carolina Canners Inc., p. I-165 [NAICS 31211M]

Carolina Container Company Inc., p. I-379 [NAICS 32221M]

Carolina Cotton Works Inc., p. I-218 [NAICS 31331M]

Carolina Fashions Inc., p. I-285 [NAICS 31529M]

Carolina Foam Inc., p. I-505 [NAICS 325212]

Carolina Group, p. I-188 [NAICS 31222M]

Carolina Hosiery Mills Inc., p. I-256 [NAICS 31511M]

Carolina Machine Works, p. II-1584 [NAICS 336510]

Carolina Manufacturing Inc., p. I-239 [NAICS 31491M]

Carolina Mills Inc., pp. Vol. I-192, 198, Vol. II-1650 [NAICS 31311M, 313210, 33721N]

Carolina Model Home Corp., p. I-353 [NAICS 321992]

Carolina Narrow Fabric Co., pp. Vol. I-203, 213 [NAICS 31322M, 31324M]

Carolina Recycling Group L.L.C., p. III-1890 [NAICS 423930]

Carolina Skiff L.L.C., p. II-1594 [NAICS 336612]

Carolina Time Equipment Inc., p. III-1894 [NAICS 423940]

Carolina Tractor, pp. Vol. II-1173, Vol. III-1859 [NAICS 333618, 423810]

Carolina Tractor/CAT, pp. Vol. II-1092, 1427 [NAICS 33331N, 335312]

Carolina Visual, p. I-285 [NAICS 31529M]

Carolina Yarn Processors, p. I-218 [NAICS 31331M]

Carondelet Foundry Co., p. I-845 [NAICS 33151M]

Carousel Carpet Mills Inc., p. I-229 [NAICS 314110]

Carpenter Co., pp. Vol. I-198, 208, 500, 510, 641 [NAICS 313210, 313230, 325211, 32522M, 326150]

Carpenter Contractors of America, pp. Vol. I-324, 329 [NAICS 32121N, 32121P]

Carpenter Group, p. II-1033 [NAICS 333120]

Carpenter Technology Corp., p. I-780 [NAICS 33111M]

Carpet Co-Op, p. III-2041 [NAICS 44221O]

Carpet Cushions and Supplies Inc., p. III-1778 [NAICS 423220]

CARQUEST Corp., pp. Vol. III-1762, 1770 [NAICS 423120, 423140]

Carr Corp., p. II-1357 [NAICS 334517]

Carr Lane Manufacturing Co., pp. Vol. II-958, 1124 [NAICS 332722, 333512]

Carr Lowrey Glass Co., pp. Vol. I-709, 713, 718, Vol. II-1119 [NAICS 327211, 327212, 327213, 333511]

Carr Metal Products Inc., p. I-306 [NAICS 31699M]

Carr Supply Inc., p. III-1847 [NAICS 423720]

Carriage Inc., pp. Vol. II-1496, 1500 [NAICS 336213, 336214]

Carrier Access Corp., pp. Vol. II-1257, 1468 [NAICS 334210, 335999]

Carrier Envelope Co., pp. Vol. III-1898, 1901 [NAICS 424110, 424120]

Carrier Transcold of Maine, p. III-1855 [NAICS 423740]

Carrier Transicold of Utah, p. III-1855 [NAICS 423740]

Carris Reels Inc., pp. Vol. I-343, 358, Vol. II-1014 [NAICS 321920, 321999, 33299N]

Carroll's Discount Office Furniture, p. III-1774 [NAICS 423210]

CarsDirect.com, p. III-2011 [NAICS 441110]

Carskadden Optical Co., p. I-709 [NAICS 327211]

Carson-Dellosa Publishing Inc., p. II-1749 [NAICS 339999]

Carson Engineering and Mfg Inc., p. II-1147 [NAICS 333516]

Carson Industries Inc., pp. Vol. I-681, Vol. II-1731 [NAICS 327112, 339992]

Carson Oil Company Inc., pp. Vol. III-1979, 2116 [NAICS 424720, 447110]

Carsons Inc., p. II-1616 [NAICS 337121]

Carstens Inc., p. II-1243 [NAICS 334112]

Carswell Distributing Inc., p. III-1863 [NAICS 423820]

Carter Brothers Manufacturing Inc., p. II-1473 [NAICS 336111]

Carter Grandle, pp. Vol. I-229, 234, 239, Vol. II-1632 [NAICS 314110, 31412M, 31491M, 33712N]

Carter Manufacturing Corp., p. II-1297 [NAICS 334415]

Carter, Moore and Company Inc., p. I-192 [NAICS 31311M]

Carter Paper and Packaging Inc., pp. Vol. III-1901, 1905 [NAICS 424120, 424130]

Carter's Shooting Center Inc., p. III-2150 [NAICS 451110]

Carter-Waters Corp., pp. Vol. III-1786, 1790, 1794 [NAICS 423320, 423330, 423390]

Carton Service Inc., p. I-379 [NAICS 32221M]

Cartridge Actuated Devices Inc., p. I-585 [NAICS 325920]

Cartridge Family Inc., p. III-2186 [NAICS 453210]

Carvel Corp., p. I-92 [NAICS 311520]

Carver Boat Corp., p. II-1594 [NAICS 336612]

Carver Hardware Inc., p. III-2100 [NAICS 446110]

Carvin Guitars, p. II-1731 [NAICS 339992]

Casa Di Bertacchi Corp., p. I-124 [NAICS 31182M]

Casa Valdez Inc., p. I-133 [NAICS 311830]

Cascade Coffee Inc., p. I-143 [NAICS 311920]

Cascade Corp., pp. Vol. II-1014, 1194, 1222 [NAICS 33299N, 33392M, 33399N]

Cascade Designs, p. II-1702 [NAICS 339920]

Cascade Engineering Inc., pp. Vol. I-651, Vol. II-1749 [NAICS 32619M, 339999]

Cascade General Inc., p. II-1589 [NAICS 336611]

Cascade Microtech Inc., pp. Vol. II-1347, 1367 [NAICS 334515, 334519]

Cascade Steel Rolling Mills Inc., p. I-788 [NAICS 331210]

Numbers following p. or pp. are page references. Roman numerals indicate volume numbers. Bracketed items indicate industries. Page references are to the starting pages of company tables.

2315

Cascades Auburn Fiber, p. I-363 [NAICS 322110]

Cascades Tissue Group, pp. Vol. I-368, 411, 415 [NAICS 32212M, 322291, 322299]

Cascio Music Company Inc., p. III-2159 [NAICS 451140]

Case Farms of Ohio Inc., pp. Vol. I-97, 102 [NAICS 311615, 31161N]

Case Parts Co., p. III-1855 [NAICS 423740]

Case Systems Inc., pp. Vol. II-1632, 1666 [NAICS 33712N, 339111]

Casey's General Stores Inc., pp. Vol. III-2076, 2116 [NAICS 445110, 447110]

Casey Tool and Machine Inc., pp. Vol. II-1119, 1134 [NAICS 333511, 333514]

Casey Woodwyk Inc., p. III-1950 [NAICS 424480]

Cash America International Inc., p. III-2194 [NAICS 453310]

Cash Register Sales Inc., p. III-1801 [NAICS 423420]

Cashco Inc., pp. Vol. II-1421, 1432 [NAICS 335311, 335313]

Casio Holdings Inc., p. II-1362 [NAICS 334518]

Casket Shells Inc., p. II-1745 [NAICS 339995]

Cass Clay Creamery Inc., pp. Vol. I-76, 86, 92 [NAICS 311513, 31151N, 311520]

Cass Polymers, p. I-589 [NAICS 325991]

Cast-Crete Corp., pp. Vol. I-743, Vol. II-939 [NAICS 327390, 33261M]

Cast-Rite Corp., p. I-852 [NAICS 33152N]

Cast Technologies Inc., p. I-852 [NAICS 33152N]

Castaic Brick, p. I-691 [NAICS 327121]

Casting Designs Inc., p. I-752 [NAICS 327420]

Castle Industries Inc., p. II-1536 [NAICS 336360]

Castle Oil Corp., pp. Vol. III-1979, 2218 [NAICS 424720, 454311]

Castle Wells Management Inc., p. I-681 [NAICS 327112]

Castleberry Office Furnishings, p. III-1774 [NAICS 423210]

Castleford Tailors Corporation Ltd., p. I-267 [NAICS 31521M]

CastPower L.L.C., p. I-703 [NAICS 32712N]

Castrol Lubricants Div., p. I-458 [NAICS 324191]

Castrol North America Holdings, pp. Vol. I-458, Vol. III-1979 [NAICS 324191, 424720]

Casual Male Retail Group Inc., p. III-2132 [NAICS 448140]

Caswell-Massey Company Ltd., p. III-1909 [NAICS 424210]

Catalina Cylinder, pp. Vol. I-811, Vol. II-928 [NAICS 331316, 33243M]

Catalina Finer Food Corp., p. I-133 [NAICS 311830]

Catalina Lighting Inc., p. II-1390 [NAICS 33512M]

Catalina Yachts Inc., p. II-1594 [NAICS 336612]

Catalyst Manufacturing Services, pp. Vol. II-1282, 1312 [NAICS 334412, 334418]

Catalyst Telecom, p. III-1839 [NAICS 423690]

Catalytic Solutions Inc., p. I-475 [NAICS 32513M]

Catania Spagna Corp., p. I-26 [NAICS 311225]

Catapult Communications Corp., p. II-1347 [NAICS 334515]

Catawba Sox Inc., p. I-256 [NAICS 31511M]

Catawissa Lumber & Specialty Inc., pp. Vol. I-358, Vol. II-1621 [NAICS 321999, 337122]

Catching Fluidpower Inc., p. II-1222 [NAICS 33399N]

Caterpillar Inc., pp. Vol. II-1023, 1033, 1173, 1194 [NAICS 333111, 333120, 333618, 33392M]

Caterpillar Inc. Engines Div., p. II-1173 [NAICS 333618]

Caterpillar Work Tools Inc., pp. Vol. II-1028, 1039, 1168, 1207 [NAICS 333112, 33313M, 333613, 333991]

Catfish Wholesale Inc., p. III-1943 [NAICS 424460]

Cathedral Art Metal Company Inc., p. II-1696 [NAICS 33991M]

Catherines Stores Corp., p. III-2126 [NAICS 448120]

Catholic University of America, p. I-709 [NAICS 327211]

Cato Corp., p. III-2126 [NAICS 448120]

Caughman's Meat Plant Inc., pp. Vol. III-1946, 2083 [NAICS 424470, 445210]

Causeway Lumber Company Inc., p. I-329 [NAICS 32121P]

Cavaform Inc., p. II-1051 [NAICS 333220]

Cavalier Homes Inc., p. I-348 [NAICS 321991]

Cavco Industries Inc., p. I-348 [NAICS 321991]

Cave Quarries Inc., p. I-748 [NAICS 327410]

Cavender's Boot City, pp. Vol. III-2135, 2141 [NAICS 448150, 448210]

Cavin's Inc., p. III-2054 [NAICS 443112]

Caxton Printers Ltd., p. III-2186 [NAICS 453210]

Caye Upholstery L.L.C., pp. Vol. II-1616, 1644 [NAICS 337121, 337215]

Caylor Industrial Sales Inc., p. III-1794 [NAICS 423390]

Caymus Vineyards, p. I-177 [NAICS 312130]

Cayset Fashions Ltd., p. III-1919 [NAICS 424330]

CB & I Howe-Baker Process, pp. Vol. II-923, 1039 [NAICS 332420, 33313M]

CB & I Howe-Baker Process Tech, p. II-1009 [NAICS 332996]

CB and K Supply Inc., p. III-1847 [NAICS 423720]

CBI Laboratories Inc., p. I-575 [NAICS 325620]

CBRL Group Inc., p. III-2190 [NAICS 453220]

CBS Builders Supply, p. I-329 [NAICS 32121P]

C.C. Clark Inc., pp. Vol. I-165, Vol. III-1954 [NAICS 31211M, 424490]

CC Food Inc., p. I-133 [NAICS 311830]

CCB Inc., p. III-2058 [NAICS 443120]

CCI Manufacturing, p. II-1607 [NAICS 336999]

CCI Manufacturing Inc., p. I-762 [NAICS 327991]

CCL Container Corp., p. II-928 [NAICS 33243M]

CCL Custom Manufacturing Inc., pp. Vol. I-539, 566, 575, Vol. II-1749 [NAICS 325412, 32561M, 325620, 339999]

CCP Industries Inc., pp. Vol. I-198, 208, 229, 411, 566 [NAICS 313210, 313230, 314110, 322291, 32561M]

CDL Technology Inc., p. II-1051 [NAICS 333220]

CDP Diamond Products Inc., p. I-756 [NAICS 327910]

CDR Pigments and Dispersions, p. I-580 [NAICS 325910]

CDR Systems Corp., pp. Vol. I-500, 743 [NAICS 325211, 327390]

CDW Corp., p. III-2211 [NAICS 454113]

Ce De Candy Inc., p. I-57 [NAICS 311340]

CEA Technologies Inc., p. II-1119 [NAICS 333511]

Cecil I Walker Machinery Co., p. III-1859 [NAICS 423810]

Cecil Saydah Co., pp. Vol. I-218, Vol. II-1536 [NAICS 31331M, 336360]

CECO Environmental Corp., p. II-1112 [NAICS 33341N]

CECORP, p. II-1248 [NAICS 334113]

Cedar Brewing Company Inc., pp. Vol. I-172, Vol. III-2097 [NAICS 312120, 445310]

Cedar Crest Specialties Inc., p. III-1933 [NAICS 424430]

Cedar River Paper Co., pp. Vol. I-363, 415 [NAICS 322110, 322299]

Cee Sportswear Inc., p. I-279 [NAICS 31523M]

CEI Company Ltd., pp. Vol. II-1512, 1546 [NAICS 33632M, 336391]

CEI Equipment Company Inc., p. II-1491 [NAICS 336212]

Celanese Chemicals - Americas, pp. Vol. I-475, 480 [NAICS 32513M, 325181]

CelebrateExpress.com Inc., p. III-2190 [NAICS 453220]

Celebrity International Inc., p. III-1919 [NAICS 424330]

Celerity Group Inc., p. II-1061 [NAICS 33329N]

Celestial Seasonings Inc., p. I-534 [NAICS 325411]

Celestron International, p. III-1817 [NAICS 423460]

Celgene Corp., p. I-595 [NAICS 32599N]

Celina Aluminum Precision, pp. Vol. II-1222, 1505 [NAICS 33399N, 33631M]

Cell-Direct, p. III-2054 [NAICS 443112]

Cello-Foil Products Inc., pp. Vol. I-395, 603, 609 [NAICS 32222P, 326111, 326112]

Cellotape Inc., pp. Vol. I-403, Vol. II-1720 [NAICS 32223M, 339950]

CellStar Corp., pp. Vol. III-1839, 2208 [NAICS 423690, 453998]

CellStar Ltd., pp. Vol. III-1839, 2208 [NAICS 423690, 453998]

Cellu Tissue Corp., pp. Vol. I-368, 411, 415 [NAICS 32212M, 322291, 322299]

Cellucap Manufacturing, p. I-411 [NAICS 322291]

Cellular Connection, p. III-2054 [NAICS 443112]

Cellular Connections, p. III-2054 [NAICS 443112]

Celsion Corp., p. II-1357 [NAICS 334517]

CEM Corp., pp. Vol. II-1352, 1666 [NAICS 334516, 339111]

Cembell Industries Inc., p. II-918 [NAICS 332410]

Cemex, pp. Vol. I-727, 732 [NAICS 327310, 327320]

Cemex Construction Materials Inc., p. I-732 [NAICS 327320]

Cemline Corp., p. II-1417 [NAICS 335228]

Cempro Inc., p. I-752 [NAICS 327420]

Centech Plastics Inc., p. II-1119 [NAICS 333511]

Center Manufacturing Inc., pp. Vol. I-879, Vol. II-939, 1009, 1749 [NAICS 33211P, 33261M, 332996, 339999]

Centerforce Clutches, p. II-1530 [NAICS 336350]

Centex Corp., pp. Vol. I-732, 752 [NAICS 327320, 327420]

Central Audio Visual Equipment, p. III-1798 [NAICS 423410]

Central Bi-Products Rendering Inc., p. I-9 [NAICS 311119]

Central Builder Supplies, p. III-1790 [NAICS 423330]

Central Can Company Inc., pp. Vol. II-928, 964 [NAICS 33243M, 33281M]

Central Carolina Hosiery Inc., p. I-256 [NAICS 31511M]

Central Co-op, p. III-1975 [NAICS 424710]

Central Coating Company Inc., p. III-1790 [NAICS 423330]

Central Computer Systems Inc., p. III-2058 [NAICS 443120]

Central Dairy and Ice Cream Co., p. I-92 [NAICS 311520]

Central European Distribution, p. III-1987 [NAICS 424820]

Central Garden and Pet Co., pp. Vol. II-1028, Vol. III-1883, 1991, 2007 [NAICS 333112, 423910, 424910, 424990]

Central Grocers Co-op Inc., p. III-1925 [NAICS 424410]

Central Ink Corp., p. I-580 [NAICS 325910]

Central Iowa Coop., p. III-1975 [NAICS 424710]

Central Medical Equipment Co., p. III-2113 [NAICS 446199]

Central Michigan Lumber Co., p. III-2065 [NAICS 444100]

Central Mine Equipment Co., p. II-1207 [NAICS 333991]

Central Missouri Agriservice, pp. Vol. I-9, 524 [NAICS 311119, 325314]

Central Moloney Inc., p. II-1421 [NAICS 335311]

Central National-Gottesman Inc., p. III-1905 [NAICS 424130]

Central Nebraska Tubing, p. I-788 [NAICS 331210]

Central Oil of Virginia Corp., p. III-2222 [NAICS 454312]

Central Optical Laboratories Inc., p. III-1817 [NAICS 423460]

Central Pre-Mix Concrete Inc., pp. Vol. I-448, 732, 737 [NAICS 324121, 327320, 32733M]

Central Resistor Corp., p. II-1297 [NAICS 334415]

Central Rubber and Plastics Inc., p. I-505 [NAICS 325212]

Central South Music Inc., p. III-2168 [NAICS 451220]

Central Sprinkler Co., p. II-1229 [NAICS 33399P]

Central States Business Forms, p. I-403 [NAICS 32223M]

Central Steel and Wire Co., p. III-1824 [NAICS 423510]

Central Stone Co., p. I-762 [NAICS 327991]

Central Textiles Inc., pp. Vol. I-198, 251 [NAICS 313210, 314999]

Central Valley Builders Supply, pp. Vol. III-1782, 2065 [NAICS 423310, 444100]

Central Woodwork Inc., pp. Vol. I-312, 334 [NAICS 32111M, 32191M]

Centricut L.L.C., pp. Vol. II-1124, 1129 [NAICS 333512, 333513]

Centrilift, pp. Vol. I-837, Vol. II-1162, 1179, 1437 [NAICS 33149M, 333612, 333911, 335314]

Centrix Inc., p. II-1682 [NAICS 339114]

Centuri Corp., p. II-1708 [NAICS 33993M]

Centurian Surplus Inc., p. III-2058 [NAICS 443120]

Centurion Wireless Technologies, pp. Vol. II-1262, 1272, 1442 [NAICS 334220, 334310, 335911]

Century Air Conditioning Supply, p. III-1851 [NAICS 423730]

Century Aluminum Co., p. I-816 [NAICS 33131N]

Century Color Inc., p. I-580 [NAICS 325910]

Century Computer Corp., p. III-2058 [NAICS 443120]

Century Manufacturing Inc., pp. Vol. I-681, 709 [NAICS 327112, 327211]

Century Products Inc., p. I-343 [NAICS 321920]

Century Steel L.L.C., pp. Vol. I-793, Vol. II-964, Vol. III-1824 [NAICS 33122M, 33281M, 423510]

Century Supply Corp., p. III-1863 [NAICS 423820]

Century Tubes Inc., pp. Vol. I-788, 830 [NAICS 331210, 33142M]

Cenveo Inc., pp. Vol. I-403, 420 [NAICS 32223M, 32311M]

Cephalon Inc., p. I-539 [NAICS 325412]

Cequent Towing Products, p. II-1607 [NAICS 336999]

Ceradyne Inc., pp. Vol. I-681, 686, Vol. II-1277 [NAICS 327112, 327113, 334411]

Ceramatec Inc., p. I-686 [NAICS 327113]

Ceramic Magnetics Inc., p. I-686 [NAICS 327113]

Ceramic Tech Inc., p. I-686 [NAICS 327113]

Ceramic To Metal Seals Inc., p. I-686 [NAICS 327113]

Ceramics Process Systems Corp., pp. Vol. I-681, 776 [NAICS 327112, 327999]

Ceramo Company Inc., p. I-681 [NAICS 327112]

CeramTec North America, p. I-686 [NAICS 327113]

CerCo L.L.C., pp. Vol. I-686, 703, 776, 800 [NAICS 327113, 32712N, 327999, 331311]

Cereform USA, p. I-124 [NAICS 31182M]

Cerex Advanced Fabrics, pp. Vol. I-198, 208, 510 [NAICS 313210, 313230, 32522M]

Ceridian Corp., p. II-1262 [NAICS 334220]

Cerreta Candy Company Inc., pp. Vol. I-48, 57, Vol. III-2092 [NAICS 311320, 311340, 445292]

Cerro Flow Products Inc., p. I-830 [NAICS 33142M]

Cerro Metal Products Inc., pp. Vol. I-830, 837, 852, 857 [NAICS 33142M, 33149M, 33152N, 33152P]

Cerro Wire and Cable Inc., pp. Vol. I-830, Vol. II-1451 [NAICS 33142M, 33592M]

Cersosimo Lumber Company Inc., p. I-358 [NAICS 321999]

CertainTeed Corp., p. I-453 [NAICS 324122]

Certified Grocers Midwest Inc., p. III-1925 [NAICS 424410]

Certified Slings Inc., p. I-244 [NAICS 314991]

Certified Steel Hamilton, p. II-945 [NAICS 332710]

Certis USA L.L.C., p. II-1028 [NAICS 333112]

Cerus Corp., p. I-549 [NAICS 325414]

Cervitor Kitchens Inc., pp. Vol. II-1404, 1409 [NAICS 335221, 335222]

Ces Computers Inc., p. III-1805 [NAICS 423430]

Cesko Sales Co., p. II-1292 [NAICS 334414]

Cessford Construction Co., p. I-762 [NAICS 327991]

Cessna Aircraft Co., p. II-1557 [NAICS 336411]

Cetek Technologies Inc., p. I-686 [NAICS 327113]

CF Gomma USA Inc., pp. Vol. I-665, Vol. II-952 [NAICS 326220, 332721]

CF Industries Inc., pp. Vol. I-516, 520 [NAICS 325311, 325312]

C.F. Martin and Company Inc., p. II-1731 [NAICS 339992]

CFC International Inc., pp. Vol. I-560, Vol. II-964 [NAICS 325520, 33281M]

CFI of Wisconsin Inc., pp. Vol. I-76, 81 [NAICS 311513, 311514]

CFM, pp. Vol. I-845, Vol. II-1101 [NAICS 33151M, 333414]

CFS Media Services, p. II-1381 [NAICS 334613]

CG Bretting Manufacturing Co., p. II-1212 [NAICS 333993]

CG M Inc., p. I-727 [NAICS 327310]

CGB Enterprises Inc., p. III-1958 [NAICS 424510]

CGI International Inc., p. I-471 [NAICS 325120]

CGR Products Inc., p. II-1119 [NAICS 333511]

CH Energy Group Inc., p. III-2218 [NAICS 454311]

C.H. Robinson Worldwide Inc., p. III-1950 [NAICS 424480]

Chaco Inc., p. I-300 [NAICS 31621M]

Chaffee Lynchburg Farmers, p. III-1958 [NAICS 424510]

Chalk Hill Estate & Winery L.L.C., p. I-177 [NAICS 312130]

Challenge Dairy Products Inc., pp. Vol. I-81, 86, Vol. III-1954 [NAICS 311514, 31151N, 424490]

Challenge Manufacturing Inc., pp. Vol. I-879, Vol. II-1541 [NAICS 33211P, 336370]

Challenge Printing Inc., pp. Vol. I-436, Vol. II-1720 [NAICS 32312M, 339950]

Chalmette Refining L.L.C., pp. Vol. I-443, 488 [NAICS 324110, 325188]

Chalone Wine Group Ltd., p. I-177 [NAICS 312130]

Chambers Belt, p. I-285 [NAICS 31529M]

Chambers Electronics Inc., p. II-1584 [NAICS 336510]

Chambers Farm and Garden, p. III-2072 [NAICS 444220]

Chambersburg Engineering Co., p. II-1129 [NAICS 333513]

Champaign Landmark Inc., pp. Vol. I-9, 524 [NAICS 311119, 325314]

Champaign Telephone Co., p. III-2054 [NAICS 443112]

Champion Cleaning Systems Inc., p. III-2041 [NAICS 442210]

Champion Enterprises Inc., p. I-348 [NAICS 321991]

Champion Ford Gulf Freeway, p. III-2011 [NAICS 441110]

Champion Home Builders Co., pp. Vol. I-353, Vol. II-899 [NAICS 321992, 33231M]

Champion Industries Inc., pp. Vol. I-436, Vol. III-1774, 1901 [NAICS 32312M, 423210, 424120]

Champion Laboratories Inc., p. II-1112 [NAICS 33341N]

Champion Mfg Industries Inc., p. II-1009 [NAICS 332996]

Champion Performance Products, p. I-534 [NAICS 325411]

Champion Technologies Inc, pp. Vol. I-595, Vol. II-1039 [NAICS 32599N, 33313M]

Champion Window Inc., p. I-811 [NAICS 331316]

Champro Sports Equipment, p. III-1883 [NAICS 423910]

Chandler Materials Co., p. I-737 [NAICS 32733M]

Chandler Ready-Mix Inc., p. I-732 [NAICS 327320]

Numbers following p. or pp. are page references. Roman numerals indicate volume numbers. Bracketed items indicate industries. Page references are to the starting pages of company tables.

2317

Chandler Signs L.P., pp. Vol. I-239, Vol. II-1720 [NAICS 31491M, 339950]

Chanel Inc., pp. Vol. I-279, 575 [NAICS 31523M, 325620]

Chaney Enterprises, pp. Vol. I-732, 737 [NAICS 327320, 32733M]

Channel Industries Inc., p. I-686 [NAICS 327113],

Channel Products Inc., pp. Vol. I-686, Vol. II-1327 [NAICS 327113, 334511]

Channell Commercial Corp., p. II-1468 [NAICS 335999]

CHANNELLOCK Inc., p. II-892 [NAICS 33221P]

Chanute Manufacturing, p. II-918 [NAICS 332410]

Chapel Steel Corp., p. II-945 [NAICS 332710]

Chapin, p. II-1184 [NAICS 333912]

Chapin and Bangs Company Inc., p. II-945 [NAICS 332710]

Chapin Watermatics Inc., p. I-665 [NAICS 326220]

Chardon Rubber Co., pp. Vol. I-621, 665, Vol. II-1725 [NAICS 326121, 326220, 339991]

Chariot Eagle Inc., pp. Vol. I-348, 353 [NAICS 321991, 321992]

Charles And Colvard Ltd., p. II-1696 [NAICS 33991M]

Charles Blalock and Sons Inc., pp. Vol. I-448, 727, 737 [NAICS 324121, 327310, 32733M]

Charles C. Hart Seed Co., p. I-516 [NAICS 325311]

Charles D Jones and Company Inc., p. III-1851 [NAICS 423730]

Charles D Owen Mfg Co., p. I-234 [NAICS 31412M]

Charles E Jarrell Contracting Inc., p. II-1129 [NAICS 333513]

Charles Industries Ltd., pp. Vol. II-933, 1257, 1262, 1468 [NAICS 332510, 334210, 334220, 335999]

Charles J Miller Inc., p. I-448 [NAICS 324121]

Charles Jacquin Et Cie Inc., p. I-181 [NAICS 312140]

Charles Keath, p. III-2211 [NAICS 454113]

Charles Machine Works Inc., pp. Vol. II-1033, 1140, 1207, 1367 [NAICS 333120, 333515, 333991, 334519]

Charles Ritter Co., p. III-1901 [NAICS 424120]

Charles River BRF Inc., p. III-2007 [NAICS 424990]

Charles River Laboratories Intern, p. I-549 [NAICS 325414]

Charles Ross and Son Co., p. II-1189 [NAICS 333913]

Charles Sadek Import Inc., p. III-1778 [NAICS 423220]

Charleston Hosiery Inc., pp. Vol. I-272, 279 [NAICS 31522M, 31523M]

Charleston Metal Products Inc., p. II-952 [NAICS 332721]

Charleston Steel and Metal Co., p. I-807 [NAICS 331314]

Charleston Stone Co., p. I-748 [NAICS 327410]

Charlie's RV & Camping Center, p. III-2018 [NAICS 441210]

Charlie's Specialties Inc., p. I-124 [NAICS 31182M]

Charlotte Aircraft Corp., p. III-1879 [NAICS 423860]

Charlotte Pipe and Foundry Co., pp. Vol. I-626, 780, Vol. II-1009 [NAICS 326122, 33111M, 332996]

Charlotte Russe Holding Inc., p. III-2126 [NAICS 448120]

Charlotte Trimming Company Inc., p. I-203 [NAICS 31322M]

Charmac Inc., pp. Vol. II-1500, 1607 [NAICS 336214, 336999]

Charmer Industries Inc., p. III-1987 [NAICS 424820]

Charming Shoppes Inc., pp. Vol. III-2123, 2126, 2129 [NAICS 448110, 448120, 448130]

Chart Cryogenic Systems, p. I-771 [NAICS 327993]

Chart Inc., pp. Vol. II-899, 1317 [NAICS 33231M, 334419]

Chart Industries Inc., pp. Vol. I-780, Vol. II-899, 1106, 1337, 1437 [NAICS 33111M, 33231M, 333415, 334513, 335314]

Charter Fabrics Inc., p. III-1913 [NAICS 424310]

Charter Mfg Inc, pp. Vol. I-780, 793, 803, Vol. II-939, 1505 [NAICS 33111M, 33122M, 331312, 33261M, 33631M]

Charter Steel, p. I-780 [NAICS 33111M]

Chas. Levy Circulating Co., p. III-1995 [NAICS 424920]

Chase Brass and Copper Co., p. I-830 [NAICS 33142M]

Chase Corp., p. II-1390 [NAICS 33512M]

Chase Lumber and Fuel Inc., p. III-2037 [NAICS 442110]

Chase Packaging Inc., pp. Vol. I-239, 374 [NAICS 31491M, 322130]

Chase Products Co., p. I-471 [NAICS 325120]

Chateau Chantal, p. I-177 [NAICS 312130]

Chateau Elan Winery and Resort, p. I-177 [NAICS 312130]

Chateau Montelena Winery, p. I-177 [NAICS 312130]

Chateau St. Jean, p. I-177 [NAICS 312130]

Chatham Borgstena Auto Textile, p. II-1536 [NAICS 336360]

Chatham Brass Company Inc., p. II-974 [NAICS 332913]

Chatham Imports Inc., p. III-1987 [NAICS 424820]

Chatham Steel Corp., p. III-1824 [NAICS 423510]

Chatleff Controls Inc., p. II-1217 [NAICS 333994]

Chattanooga Bakery Inc., p. I-137 [NAICS 31191M]

Chattem Inc., pp. Vol. I-488, 575 [NAICS 325188, 325620]

Chautauqua Hardware Corp., pp. Vol. I-857, Vol. II-952 [NAICS 33152P, 332721]

CHC Inc., p. III-2041 [NAICS 442210]

Check Printers Inc., p. I-403 [NAICS 32223M]

Checker Motors Corp., p. II-1541 [NAICS 336370]

Checkered Flag Corp., p. III-1770 [NAICS 423140]

Checkpoint Systems Inc., p. II-1267 [NAICS 334290]

Checks Unlimited, pp. Vol. I-420, Vol. III-2211 [NAICS 32311M, 454113]

Checon Corp., p. II-1277 [NAICS 334411]

Chef America Inc., p. I-62 [NAICS 31141M]

Chef's Warehouse, pp. Vol. III-1894, 1905 [NAICS 423940, 424130]

Chefmaster Inc., pp. Vol. I-147, 152 [NAICS 311930, 31194M]

Chelsea Building Products Inc., pp. Vol. I-621, 651 [NAICS 326121, 32619M]

Chelsea Clock Company Inc., p. II-1362 [NAICS 334518]

Chelsea Milling Co., p. I-15 [NAICS 31121M]

Chelsea Modular Homes Inc., p. I-353 [NAICS 321992]

Chem Rite Industries L.L.C., p. III-1971 [NAICS 424690]

Chem Tec Equipment Inc., p. II-1342 [NAICS 334514]

Chem-Tech Finishers Inc., p. I-229 [NAICS 314110]

Chem-Trol Inc., p. I-529 [NAICS 325320]

CHEMCENTRAL Corp., p. III-1971 [NAICS 424690]

Chemco Manufacturing Inc., p. II-1184 [NAICS 333912]

ChemDesign Corp., p. I-493 [NAICS 32519M]

Chemed Corp., p. III-1971 [NAICS 424690]

Chemence Inc., p. I-560 [NAICS 325520]

Chemetall Foote Corp., p. I-488 [NAICS 325188]

CHEMetrics Inc., p. I-544 [NAICS 325413]

Chemglass Inc., pp. Vol. I-670, 709, 713, Vol. II-1140 [NAICS 32629M, 327211, 327212, 333515]

Chemical Lime Ltd., pp. Vol. I-727, 748 [NAICS 327310, 327410]

Chemineer Inc., p. II-1666 [NAICS 339111]

Chemins Company Inc., pp. Vol. I-534, Vol. III-1909 [NAICS 325411, 424210]

Chemionics Corp., p. I-589 [NAICS 325991]

Chemmasters, p. I-453 [NAICS 324122]

Chemplex Industries Inc., p. II-1357 [NAICS 334517]

Chemprene Inc., p. I-224 [NAICS 313320]

Chemrock Corp., p. I-767 [NAICS 327992]

Chemtex Print USA Inc., p. I-218 [NAICS 31331M]

Chemtool Inc., pp. Vol. I-458, 566, Vol. II-964 [NAICS 324191, 32561M, 33281M]

ChemTreat Inc., p. I-566 [NAICS 32561M]

Chenango Valley Pet Foods Inc., p. I-4 [NAICS 311111]

Cheney Pulp and Paper Co., p. I-363 [NAICS 322110]

Chernoff Sales Inc., p. III-1855 [NAICS 423740]

Cherokee Aluminum Trailers, p. II-1500 [NAICS 336214]

Cherokee Brick and Tile Co., p. I-691 [NAICS 327121]

Cherokee Hosiery Mills Inc., p. I-256 [NAICS 31511M]

Cherokee Inc., pp. Vol. I-279, 300 [NAICS 31523M, 31621M]

Cherokee Products Inc., p. I-585 [NAICS 325920]

Cherokee Uniforms, p. I-300 [NAICS 31621M]

Cherry Central Co-op Inc., pp. Vol. I-62, 158 [NAICS 31141M, 31199M]

Cherry Creek Dodge Inc., p. III-2011 [NAICS 441110]

Cherry Electrical Products, pp. Vol. II-1347, 1457 [NAICS 334515, 33593M]

Cherry Relays Inc., p. III-1867 [NAICS 423830]

Cherry Valley Tool and Machine, p. II-1524 [NAICS 336340]

Cheryl and Company Inc., p. I-124 [NAICS 31182M]

Chesapeake Bay Packing L.L.C., p. III-2085 [NAICS 445220]

Chesapeake Corp., pp. Vol. I-363, 368, 374, 388 [NAICS 322110, 32212M, 322130, 32222N]

Chesapeake Hardwood Products, p. I-324 [NAICS 32121N]

Chesapeake Knife and Tool, p. III-2047 [NAICS 442299]

Chesapeake Seafood Caterers, p. III-1943 [NAICS 424460]

Chesapeake Utilities Corp., p. III-1979 [NAICS 424720]

Chessco Industries Inc., pp. Vol. I-458, 589 [NAICS 324191, 325991]

Chesterfield Yarn Mills Inc., p. I-192 [NAICS 31311M]

Chestertown Foods Inc., p. I-97 [NAICS 311615]

Chestnut Ridge Foam Inc., pp. Vol. I-234, 641, Vol. II-1657 [NAICS 31412M, 326150, 337910]

Chet's Wrecking & Auto Parts Inc., pp. Vol. III-1770, 2015 [NAICS 423140, 441120]

Chevron Products Co., p. I-443 [NAICS 324110]

Chevron Products Company Inc., pp. Vol. I-443, 595, Vol. III-1971, 1979 [NAICS 324110, 32599N, 424690, 424720]

ChevronTexaco Corp., pp. Vol. I-443, 595, Vol. III-1971, 1979 [NAICS 324110, 32599N, 424690, 424720]

CHF Industries Inc., p. I-234 [NAICS 31412M]

Chicago Communications Service, p. III-2208 [NAICS 453998]

Chicago Extruded Metals Co., pp. Vol. I-830, 857, Vol. II-1134 [NAICS 33142M, 33152P, 333514]

Chicago Faucets, p. II-974 [NAICS 332913]

Chicago Metal Rolled Products, p. I-788 [NAICS 331210]

Chicago Metallic Products Inc., pp. Vol. I-811, Vol. II-886 [NAICS 331316, 33221N]

Chicago Packaging Corp., p. I-374 [NAICS 322130]

Chicago Rivet and Machine Co., pp. Vol. II-958, 1129 [NAICS 332722, 333513]

Chicago Rubber Co., p. I-660 [NAICS 32621M]

Chicago Slitter Company Inc., p. II-1152 [NAICS 333518]

Chicago Steel L.P., pp. Vol. II-945, Vol. III-1824 [NAICS 332710, 423510]

Chicago Textile Corp., p. I-285 [NAICS 31529M]

Chicago Tire Inc., pp. Vol. III-1766, 2034 [NAICS 423130, 441320]

Chicago Tube and Iron Co., p. I-788 [NAICS 331210]

Chico's FAS Inc., p. III-2126 [NAICS 448120]

Chief Automotive Systems Inc., p. II-1607 [NAICS 336999]

Chief Industries Inc., pp. Vol. I-353, Vol. II-899, 928, 1061, 1194 [NAICS 321992, 33231M, 33243M, 33329N, 33392M]

Chilcote Co., p. II-1087 [NAICS 333315]

Child Craft Industries Inc., p. II-1657 [NAICS 337910]

Children's Books and Toys Inc., pp. Vol. II-1708, Vol. III-2129, 2208, 2211 [NAICS 33993M, 448130, 453998, 454113]

Children's Place Retail Stores Inc., p. III-2129 [NAICS 448130]

Chindex International Inc., pp. Vol. III-1813, 1820, 1859 [NAICS 423450, 423490, 423810]

Chippewa Valley Ethanol L.L.P., p. I-493 [NAICS 32519M]

Chiquita Brands International Inc., pp. Vol. I-26, 68 [NAICS 311225, 31142M]

Chiquita Fresh, North America, p. III-1950 [NAICS 424480]

Chiral Technologies Inc., p. III-1820 [NAICS 423490]

Chiron Corp., p. I-539 [NAICS 325412]

Chittenden Cider Mill, p. III-2190 [NAICS 453220]

Chocola Cleaning Materials Inc., p. III-1875 [NAICS 423850]

Chocolate By Design Inc., p. I-48 [NAICS 311320]

Choctaw-Kaul Distribution, p. I-290 [NAICS 31599M]

Choctaw Mfg Enterprises, p. II-1312 [NAICS 334418]

Choice Products USA L.L.C., p. I-57 [NAICS 311340]

Cholestech Corp., pp. Vol. I-544, Vol. II-1322 [NAICS 325413, 334510]

Chompie's, p. III-2089 [NAICS 445291]

Chophouse and Brewery, p. I-172 [NAICS 312120]

Chris Cam Corp., pp. Vol. III-1898, 1905 [NAICS 424110, 424130]

Chris Craft Corp., p. II-1594 [NAICS 336612]

Chris Stone and Associates, p. I-218 [NAICS 31331M]

Chris Stone Inc., p. I-218 [NAICS 31331M]

Christensen Arms, p. II-1001 [NAICS 332994]

Christensen Shipyards Ltd., p. II-1589 [NAICS 336611]

Christian Book Distributors Inc., p. III-2162 [NAICS 451211]

Christian Publications Inc., p. III-1820 [NAICS 423490]

Christie Digital Systems USA Inc., p. II-1087 [NAICS 333315]

Christopher Ranch, p. I-158 [NAICS 31199M]

Christy Concrete Products Inc., pp. Vol. I-651, 743 [NAICS 32619M, 327390]

Christy Refractories L.L.C., pp. Vol. I-686, 703, 771 [NAICS 327113, 32712N, 327993]

Chroma Systems, p. I-229 [NAICS 314110]

Chromalloy Castings Tampa Corp., p. II-1157 [NAICS 333611]

Chromalloy San Diego, p. II-1562 [NAICS 336412]

Chromcraft Revington Inc., pp. Vol. II-1616, 1621, 1650 [NAICS 337121, 337122, 33721N]

Chronimed Inc., pp. Vol. III-2100, 2211 [NAICS 446110, 454113]

Chrono-Log Corp., p. II-1362 [NAICS 334518]

CHS Inc., pp. Vol. I-15, Vol. III-1958 [NAICS 31121M, 424510]

Chudnow Manufacturing Inc., p. II-1189 [NAICS 333913]

Chugach Alaska Corp., pp. Vol. I-110, 312 [NAICS 31171M, 32111M]

Chukar Cherry Company Inc., p. I-48 [NAICS 311320]

Chula Farmers Cooperative, p. III-2218 [NAICS 454311]

Church and Dwight Company Inc., pp. Vol. I-480, 566 [NAICS 325181, 32561M]

Church Chair Industries Inc., pp. Vol. II-1616, 1632 [NAICS 337121, 33712N]

CHW Corp., p. III-2126 [NAICS 448120]

Ciba Specialty Chemicals Corp, pp. Vol. I-493, 595 [NAICS 32519M, 32599N]

CIC International Ltd., pp. Vol. II-993, 997, 1001, 1557, 1603 [NAICS 332992, 332993, 332994, 336411, 336992]

Cicon Engineering Co., pp. Vol. II-1307, 1451 [NAICS 334417, 33592M]

Cidra Corp., p. II-1082 [NAICS 333314]

CIENA Corp., pp. Vol. II-1257, 1267 [NAICS 334210, 334290]

Cignys Bridgeport Facility, p. I-699 [NAICS 327123]

Cignys Saginaw, pp. Vol. II-988, 1530 [NAICS 332991, 336350]

Cinch Connectors, pp. Vol. II-1307, 1457 [NAICS 334417, 33593M]

Cinram Inc., pp. Vol. II-1376, 1381 [NAICS 334612, 334613]

Cintas Corp., pp. Vol. I-272, 279, Vol. II-1676, Vol. III-2135 [NAICS 31522M, 31523M, 339113, 448150]

Ciphergen Biosystems Inc., p. II-1666 [NAICS 339111]

Ciprico Inc., p. II-1243 [NAICS 334112]

Circle Seal Controls Inc., p. II-1580 [NAICS 336419]

CIRCOR International Inc., p. II-980 [NAICS 33291N]

Circosta Iron and Metal Inc., p. III-1890 [NAICS 423930]

Circuit City, p. III-2054 [NAICS 443112]

Circuit City Stores Inc., p. III-2054 [NAICS 443112]

Circuit Components Inc., p. II-1292 [NAICS 334414]

Cirelli Foods Inc., p. III-1929 [NAICS 424420]

Cirrus Design Corp., p. I-1557 [NAICS 336411]

Cirrus Logic Inc., p. II-1257 [NAICS 334210]

Cirtronics Corp., pp. Vol. II-1282, 1312 [NAICS 334412, 334418]

CIS-US Inc., p. I-544 [NAICS 325413]

Cisco Brothers Corporation Inc., p. II-1632 [NAICS 33712N]

Cisco-Linksys L.L.C., p. II-1252 [NAICS 334119]

Cisco Systems Inc., pp. Vol. II-1252, 1257 [NAICS 334119, 334210]

Citation Aluminum, pp. Vol. I-852, 857, Vol. II-945 [NAICS 33152N, 33152P, 332710]

Citation Castings Inc., p. I-845 [NAICS 33151M]

Citation Wisconsin Castings, pp. Vol. I-845, Vol. II-1179, 1505 [NAICS 33151M, 333911, 33631M]

CITCO Operations, p. I-756 [NAICS 327910]

CITGO Asphalt Refining Co., p. I-443 [NAICS 324110]

CITGO Petroleum Corp., pp. Vol. I-443, 448, Vol. III-2116 [NAICS 324110, 324121, 447110]

CitiSteel USA Inc., p. II-980 [NAICS 33291N]

Citra Trading Corp., p. III-1894 [NAICS 423940]

Citrus Publishing Inc., p. I-420 [NAICS 32311M]

City Animation Co., pp. Vol. III-1835, 1839 [NAICS 423620, 423690]

City Beverage, pp. Vol. III-1939, 1987 [NAICS 424450, 424820]

City Carton Recycling Co., p. I-363 [NAICS 322110]

City Ice Co., pp. Vol. I-471, Vol. III-1855 [NAICS 325120, 423740]

City Market Inc., p. III-1946 [NAICS 424470]

Civic Recycling, p. I-363 [NAICS 322110]

CJ Langenfelder and Son Inc., p. III-1786 [NAICS 423320]

Numbers following p. or pp. are page references. Roman numerals indicate volume numbers. Bracketed items indicate industries. Page references are to the starting pages of company tables.

2319

CJ Vitner and Company Inc., pp. Vol. I-124, 137 [NAICS 31182M, 31191M]

CJ Winter Machine Technologies, p. II-1129 [NAICS 333513]

CJ Zone Manufacturing Co., p. III-2007 [NAICS 424990]

CJT Koolcarb Inc., pp. Vol. II-1039, 1140 [NAICS 33313M, 333515]

CK Supply Inc., p. III-1851 [NAICS 423730]

CL Smith Company Inc., pp. Vol. I-646, Vol. III-1905 [NAICS 326160, 424130]

CL Smith Industrial Co., pp. Vol. I-681, 752 [NAICS 327112, 327420]

CLA Inc., p. II-1524 [NAICS 336340]

Clabber Girl Corp., p. I-158 [NAICS 31199M]

Clack Corp., p. II-923 [NAICS 332420]

Clair Brothers Audio Enterprises, p. II-1272 [NAICS 334310]

Claire's Stores Inc., pp. Vol. III-2135, 2190, 2208, 2211 [NAICS 448150, 453220, 453998, 454113]

Claire-Sprayway Inc., pp. Vol. I-471, 529, 566 [NAICS 325120, 325320, 32561M]

Clairex Technologies Inc., p. II-1297 [NAICS 334415]

Clairon Metals Corp., p. II-1134 [NAICS 333514]

Clancy Systems International Inc., p. II-1248 [NAICS 334113]

CLARCOR Inc., pp. Vol. I-379, 776, Vol. II-1129, 1551 [NAICS 32221M, 327999, 333513, 336399]

Clare Rose Inc., p. III-1983 [NAICS 424810]

Clariant Corp., pp. Vol. I-475, 488, 493 [NAICS 32513M, 325188, 32519M]

Clariant Performance Plastics, pp. Vol. I-510, 589 [NAICS 32522M, 325991]

Clarion Bathware, p. II-1028 [NAICS 333112]

Clarion Corporation of America, p. II-1272 [NAICS 334310]

Clarion Sintered Metals Inc., p. I-867 [NAICS 332117]

Clark Companies North America, p. I-300 [NAICS 31621M]

Clark Container Inc., p. I-395 [NAICS 32222P]

Clark Foam Products Corp., p. I-641 [NAICS 326150]

Clark Foodservice Inc., pp. Vol. III-1875, 1905, 1929 [NAICS 423850, 424130, 424420]

Clark Grave Vault Co., p. I-743 [NAICS 327390]

Clark Pacific Inc., pp. Vol. I-743, Vol. III-1786 [NAICS 327390, 423320]

Clark-Reliance Corp., pp. Vol. II-1140, 1222 [NAICS 333515, 33399N]

Clark Seafood Company Inc., p. III-1943 [NAICS 424460]

Clarke Distributors Inc., p. III-1983 [NAICS 424810]

Clarke Electronics Co., p. II-1277 [NAICS 334411]

Clasen Quality Coatings Inc., p. I-48 [NAICS 311320]

Classic City Beverages Inc., p. III-1983 [NAICS 424810]

Classic Coil Company Inc., p. II-1302 [NAICS 334416]

Classic Components Corp., p. III-1805 [NAICS 423430]

Classic Fragrances Ltd., p. III-1909 [NAICS 424210]

Classic Leather Inc., p. II-1616 [NAICS 337121]

Classic Lighting Inc., p. III-2047 [NAICS 442299]

Classic Optical Laboratory Inc., p. II-1687 [NAICS 339115]

Classico Seating, p. II-1632 [NAICS 33712N]

Classy Closets Etc Inc., p. II-1632 [NAICS 33712N]

Clausing Industrial 600 Group Inc., pp. Vol. II-1124, 1140, 1207 [NAICS 333512, 333515, 333991]

Clauss Cutlery, p. II-886 [NAICS 33221N]

Clawson Tank Company Inc., p. I-699 [NAICS 327123]

Claxton Poultry Farms, p. I-9 [NAICS 311119]

Claymore Sieck Co., p. III-2007 [NAICS 424990]

Clayson Knitting Company Inc., p. I-256 [NAICS 31511M]

Clayton Corp., p. II-1189 [NAICS 333913]

Clayton Homes Inc., p. I-348 [NAICS 321991]

Clayton Industries, pp. Vol. II-1157, 1367 [NAICS 333611, 334519]

Clayton Metals Inc., pp. Vol. I-816, 822, 830 [NAICS 33131N, 331411, 33142M]

Clean Earth Environment Group, p. II-1478 [NAICS 336112]

Clean Fuels Technology Inc., p. I-488 [NAICS 325188]

Clean Green Packing Co., p. I-22 [NAICS 311221]

Clean Room Plastics Inc., p. II-1056 [NAICS 333295]

Cleanlook Chemical Corp., p. I-646 [NAICS 326160]

Cleanpak International Inc., pp. Vol. II-1106, 1112, 1390 [NAICS 333415, 33341N, 33512M]

Clear Cube Technology Inc., p. II-1238 [NAICS 334111]

Clear Lam Packaging Inc., pp. Vol. I-388, 395, 609 [NAICS 32222N, 32222P, 326112]

Clear Pack Co., p. I-621 [NAICS 326121]

Clear View Bag Company Inc., p. I-603 [NAICS 326111]

Clearspan Components Inc., pp. Vol. I-329, 353 [NAICS 32121P, 321992]

Clearvision Optical Co., p. III-1820 [NAICS 423490]

Clearwater Mattress Company Inc., p. II-1657 [NAICS 337910]

Cleary Millwork Company Inc., p. III-1782 [NAICS 423310]

Clemco Industries Corp., p. II-1152 [NAICS 333518]

Clement Industries Inc., p. II-1491 [NAICS 336212]

Clements Foods Co., pp. Vol. I-147, 152 [NAICS 311930, 31194M]

Cleveland Brothers Equipment, p. III-1859 [NAICS 423810]

Cleveland Chair Co., p. II-1616 [NAICS 337121]

Cleveland-Cliffs Inc., p. I-837 [NAICS 33149M]

Cleveland Coca-Cola Bottling Co., p. I-165 [NAICS 31211M]

Cleveland Crystals Inc., p. II-1451 [NAICS 33592M]

Cleveland Gear Company Inc., p. II-1162 [NAICS 333612]

Cleveland Hardware and Forging, pp. Vol. I-872, Vol. II-1519, 1607 [NAICS 33211N, 336330, 336999]

Cleveland Motion Control Inc., p. II-1162 [NAICS 333612]

Cleveland Plastic Films, pp. Vol. I-603, 615 [NAICS 326111, 326113]

Cleveland Wrecking Co., pp. Vol. III-1782, 2065 [NAICS 423310, 444100]

Clever Stone Co., p. I-453 [NAICS 324122]

Cliff Weil Inc., pp. Vol. III-1809, 1894, 1901, 2007 [NAICS 423440, 423940, 424120, 424990]

Climate Control Inc., p. II-1184 [NAICS 333912]

Climate Guard Construction, p. III-1790 [NAICS 423330]

Climatic Control Company Inc., p. III-1851 [NAICS 423730]

Climatic Corp., pp. Vol. III-1835, 1851 [NAICS 423620, 423730]

Clines Corners Operating Co., p. III-2190 [NAICS 453220]

Clinical Data Inc., p. II-1352 [NAICS 334516]

Clinical Specialties Inc., p. III-1813 [NAICS 423450]

Clint Williams Co., p. I-137 [NAICS 31191M]

Clinton Machine Company Inc., p. III-1824 [NAICS 423510]

Clips Ltd., p. III-1817 [NAICS 423460]

Clontech Laboratories Inc., p. I-549 [NAICS 325414]

Clopay Plastic Products Co., pp. Vol. I-334, 615 [NAICS 32191M, 326113]

Clorox Co., pp. Vol. I-68, 566, Vol. II-1092 [NAICS 31142M, 32561M, 33331N]

Clos Du Val Wine Company Ltd., p. I-177 [NAICS 312130]

Closet World Inc., p. II-1644 [NAICS 337215]

Closson's Co., pp. Vol. III-2041, 2194 [NAICS 442210, 453310]

Closure Medical Corp., p. I-560 [NAICS 325520]

Clothestime Inc., p. III-2126 [NAICS 448120]

Cloud Carpet and Draperies Inc., pp. Vol. III-2041, 2044 [NAICS 442210, 442291]

Clougherty Packing Co., pp. Vol. I-102, Vol. III-1946 [NAICS 31161N, 424470]

Clover Farms Dairy Company Inc., p. I-86 [NAICS 31151N]

Clover-Stornetta Farms Inc., pp. Vol. I-86, Vol. III-1933 [NAICS 31151N, 424430]

Cloverland/Green Spring Dairy, p. I-86 [NAICS 31151N]

Clow Valve Co., p. I-845 [NAICS 33151M]

Clow Water Systems Co., pp. Vol. I-780, Vol. II-980, 1009 [NAICS 33111M, 33291N, 332996]

Club Monaco, pp. Vol. I-272, 279 [NAICS 31522M, 31523M]

Cly-Del Manufacturing Inc., p. II-1735 [NAICS 339993]

CM Almy, p. I-285 [NAICS 31529M]

C.M. Paula Co., pp. Vol. III-1901, 2007 [NAICS 424120, 424990]

CM Trailers, p. II-1500 [NAICS 336214]

Cmb Components Inc., p. III-1831 [NAICS 423610]

CME Corporation Mitsuba, pp. Vol. II-1112, 1229, 1427, 1468 [NAICS 33341N, 33399P, 335312, 335999]

CMI International Inc., pp. Vol. I-845, 852, Vol. II-1092, 1134 [NAICS 33151M, 33152N, 33331N, 333514]

Cmn Inc., pp. Vol. III-1916, 1919 [NAICS 424320, 424330]

CMP Industries L.L.C., p. II-1682 [NAICS 339114]

CMS Peripherals Inc., p. II-1243 [NAICS 334112]

Numbers following p. or pp. are page references. Roman numerals indicate volume numbers. Bracketed items indicate industries. Page references are to the starting pages of company tables.

2320

CMTEK Intl., pp. Vol. II-1282, 1312 [NAICS 334412, 334418]

CMW Inc., p. I-825 [NAICS 331419]

Cnh Inc., p. III-1863 [NAICS 423820]

CNI Inc., p. I-306 [NAICS 31699M]

CNS Inc., p. II-1322 [NAICS 334510]

CNW Inc., p. II-1696 [NAICS 33991M]

Co-Op Country Farmers Elevator, pp. Vol. I-15, 524 [NAICS 31121M, 325314]

Co-Optical Ltd., p. III-1817 [NAICS 423460]

Coach Inc., p. I-290 [NAICS 31599M]

Coachmen Industries Inc., pp. Vol. I-353, Vol. II-1473, 1496, 1500 [NAICS 321992, 336111, 336213, 336214]

Coast Counties Truck & Equip., pp. Vol. III-1762, 1867 [NAICS 423120, 423830]

Coast Distribution System Inc., p. III-1762 [NAICS 423120]

Coast Engine and Equipment, pp. Vol. II-1173, 1584 [NAICS 333618, 336510]

Coast Foundry and Mfg Co., p. II-974 [NAICS 332913]

Coast to Coast Business Equipment, p. III-1801 [NAICS 423420]

Coast Wide Supply Company Inc., pp. Vol. III-1875, 2050 [NAICS 423850, 443111]

Coastal Aluminum Rolling Mills, p. I-816 [NAICS 33131N]

Coastal Beverage Company Inc., p. III-1983 [NAICS 424810]

Coastal Chemical Company L.L.C., p. III-1971 [NAICS 424690]

Coastal Enterprises of Jacksonville, p. II-1557 [NAICS 336411]

Coastal Lumber Co., p. I-312 [NAICS 32111M]

Coastal Plastics Inc., p. I-589 [NAICS 325991]

Coastal Training Technologies, p. II-1376 [NAICS 334612]

Coaster Company of America, p. III-1774 [NAICS 423210]

Coats Screen Inc., p. I-580 [NAICS 325910]

Coborn's Inc., pp. Vol. I-102, 116, Vol. III-2097, 2100, 2168 [NAICS 31161N, 31181M, 445310, 446110, 451220]

Cobra Electronics Corp., p. II-1262 [NAICS 334220]

Coca-Cola, p. I-165 [NAICS 31211M]

Coca-Cola Bottling Consolidated, p. I-165 [NAICS 31211M]

Coca-Cola Bottling of St. Louis, p. I-165 [NAICS 31211M]

Coca-Cola Co., pp. Vol. I-62, 147, 165 [NAICS 31141M, 311930, 31211M]

Coca-Cola Enterprises Inc., p. I-165 [NAICS 31211M]

Coca-Cola North America, p. I-62 [NAICS 31141M]

Coca-Cola Swire Pacific Holdings, p. I-165 [NAICS 31211M]

Cocalico Biologicals Inc., p. I-549 [NAICS 325414]

Coddington Brewing Co., p. I-172 [NAICS 312120]

Coe Manufacturing Co., p. II-1033 [NAICS 333120]

Coen Company Inc., p. II-1101 [NAICS 333414]

Coeur d'Alene Builders Supply, p. I-329 [NAICS 32121P]

Cofer Brothers Inc., p. III-1794 [NAICS 423390]

Coffee Bean International Inc., p. III-1809 [NAICS 423440]

Coffee Beanery Limited Inc., pp. Vol. I-143, 147, Vol. III-1954 [NAICS 311920, 311930, 424490]

Coffee Holding Company Inc., p. I-143 [NAICS 311920]

Coffee-Serv Inc., p. III-2215 [NAICS 454210]

Coffman Stairs L.L.C., p. I-358 [NAICS 321999]

Coggin Automotive Corp., p. III-2011 [NAICS 441110]

Coghlin Companies Inc., p. II-1432 [NAICS 335313]

Cognex Corp., pp. Vol. II-1238, 1337 [NAICS 334111, 334513]

Coherent Inc., pp. Vol. II-1322, 1468 [NAICS 334510, 335999]

Cohu Inc., pp. Vol. II-1061, 1262, 1347, 1367 [NAICS 33329N, 334220, 334515, 334519]

Coilhose Pneumatics Inc., p. I-665 [NAICS 326220]

Coils Inc., pp. Vol. II-1421, 1512 [NAICS 335311, 33632M]

CoinBank Automated Systems Inc., p. II-1077 [NAICS 333313]

Coinstar Inc., p. II-1077 [NAICS 333313]

Colby Furniture Company Inc., p. II-1657 [NAICS 337910]

Cold Hollow Cider Mill, p. III-2190 [NAICS 453220]

Cold Spring Cooperative Creamery, p. III-1933 [NAICS 424430]

Cold Spring Granite Company Inc., p. I-762 [NAICS 327991]

Coldwater Creek Inc., p. III-2211 [NAICS 454113]

Coldwater Veneer Inc., p. I-324 [NAICS 32121N]

Cole-Haan Holdings Inc., p. I-300 [NAICS 31621M]

Cole National Corp., pp. Vol. II-1687, Vol. III-2107, 2190 [NAICS 339115, 446130, 453220]

Cole Sport Ski Shops, p. III-2150 [NAICS 451110]

Cole Tool and Die Co., p. II-1541 [NAICS 336370]

Coleman Company Inc., pp. Vol. I-290, 641, Vol. II-1390, 1404, 1702 [NAICS 31599M, 326150, 33512M, 335221, 339920]

Coleman Dairy, pp. Vol. I-86, 158, 165 [NAICS 31151N, 31199M, 31211M]

Coleman Powermate Inc., p. II-1427 [NAICS 335312]

Colfor Manufacturing Inc., pp. Vol. I-872, Vol. II-1541 [NAICS 33211N, 336370]

Colfor Mfg Inc. Forging Div., p. I-872 [NAICS 33211N]

Colgate-Palmolive Co., pp. Vol. I-566, 575 [NAICS 32561M, 325620]

Collector, p. III-2144 [NAICS 448310]

Collegedale Casework Inc., p. II-1666 [NAICS 339111]

Collegedale Casework L.L.C., p. II-1666 [NAICS 339111]

Collins and Aikman Corp., pp. Vol. I-198, 224, 229, 415, Vol. II-1551, Vol. III-2065 [NAICS 313210, 313320, 314110, 322299, 336399, 444100]

Collins Industries Inc., pp. Vol. II-1194, 1473, 1486 [NAICS 33392M, 336111, 336211]

Collins Pine Company Inc., pp. Vol. I-312, Vol. III-2065 [NAICS 32111M, 444100]

Colonial Bag Co., p. I-395 [NAICS 32222P]

Colonial Bag Corp., p. I-603 [NAICS 326111]

Colonial Building Supply L.L.C., pp. Vol. III-1786, 2004 [NAICS 423320, 424950]

Colonial Commercial Corp., pp. Vol. III-1843, 1851 [NAICS 423710, 423730]

Colonial Metals Co., p. I-830 [NAICS 33142M]

Colonial Rubber Co., pp. Vol. I-244, 505 [NAICS 314991, 325212]

Colonial Surgical Supply Inc., p. III-2100 [NAICS 446110]

Colonna's Shipyard Inc., p. II-1594 [NAICS 336612]

Colony Hardware Supply Inc., p. III-1843 [NAICS 423710]

Color-Box L.L.C., p. II-1720 [NAICS 339950]

Color Converting L.L.C., p. I-580 [NAICS 325910]

Color Craft Graphic Arts Inc., p. I-374 [NAICS 322130]

Color Masters, p. I-603 [NAICS 326111]

Color Spectrum Inc., p. I-192 [NAICS 31311M]

Color Wheel Paint Mfg Inc., p. I-554 [NAICS 325510]

Colorado Lien Co., p. I-767 [NAICS 327992]

Colorado MEDtech Inc., pp. Vol. II-1322, 1352, 1367 [NAICS 334510, 334516, 334519]

Colorado Serum Company Inc., p. I-549 [NAICS 325414]

Colorado Sweet Gold L.L.C., p. I-22 [NAICS 311221]

Colorcon, p. I-152 [NAICS 31194M]

Colorite Plastics and Polymers, p. I-665 [NAICS 326220]

Colorite Plastics Co., pp. Vol. I-554, 651, 665 [NAICS 325510, 32619M, 326220]

Colormasters L.L.C., p. I-603 [NAICS 326111]

Colortec Inc., p. II-1740 [NAICS 339994]

ColorTree Incorporated of Virginia, p. I-403 [NAICS 32223M]

Colt Reproduction Center Inc., p. II-1372 [NAICS 334611]

Colt's Manufacturing Inc., p. II-1001 [NAICS 332994]

Colter's Restaurants Ltd., p. III-1786 [NAICS 423320]

Columbia Audio-Video Inc., pp. Vol. III-1835, 2054 [NAICS 423620, 443112]

Columbia Distributing Co., pp. Vol. III-1954, 1983, 1987 [NAICS 424490, 424810, 424820]

Columbia Empire Farms Inc., p. I-137 [NAICS 31191M]

Columbia Falls Aluminum L.L.C., p. I-803 [NAICS 331312]

Columbia Farms Inc., p. I-9 [NAICS 311119]

Columbia Forest Products Inc., pp. Vol. I-324, 334 [NAICS 32121N, 32191M]

Columbia Gear Corp., p. II-1162 [NAICS 333612]

Columbia House Co., p. I-272 [NAICS 31522M]

Columbia Lighting Inc., p. II-1390 [NAICS 33512M]

Columbia Machine Inc., p. I-743 [NAICS 327390]

Columbia Pipe and Supply, pp. Vol. II-933, Vol. III-1824, 1871 [NAICS 332510, 423510, 423840]

Columbia Showcase & Cabinet, p. II-1639 [NAICS 337212]

Columbia Sportswear Co., pp. Vol. I-272, 285, 290, 300 [NAICS 31522M, 31529M, 31599M, 31621M]

Columbia Sugar Factory, p. I-44 [NAICS 31131N]

Columbia Ventures Corp., p. I-811 [NAICS 331316]

Numbers following p. or pp. are page references. Roman numerals indicate volume numbers. Bracketed items indicate industries. Page references are to the starting pages of company tables.

2321

Columbia Woodworking Inc., p. II-1639 [NAICS 337212]

Columbiaknit Inc., p. I-262 [NAICS 31519M]

Columbian Tectank, p. II-923 [NAICS 332420]

Columbus Chemical Industries Inc., p. I-544 [NAICS 325413]

Columbus Industries Inc., pp. Vol. I-415, 825, Vol. II-1112 [NAICS 322299, 331419, 33341N]

Columbus Instruments Intern., p. II-1342 [NAICS 334514]

Columbus Lumber L.L.C., p. I-312 [NAICS 32111M]

Columbus McKinnon Corp., pp. Vol. I-872, Vol. II-1033, 1194 [NAICS 33211N, 333120, 33392M]

Columbus Paper Company Inc., p. III-1875 [NAICS 423850]

Columbus Steel Castings Co., pp. Vol. I-845, Vol. II-1584 [NAICS 33151M, 336510]

Columbus Steel Drum, p. II-928 [NAICS 33243M]

Colusa Elevator Company Inc., p. III-1958 [NAICS 424510]

Colvard Oil Company Inc., p. III-1975 [NAICS 424710]

Comair Rotron Inc., p. II-1112 [NAICS 33341N]

Comar Inc., pp. Vol. I-646, 713, 718 [NAICS 326160, 327212, 327213]

Comark Building Systems Inc., p. I-353 [NAICS 321992]

Comau Pico, p. II-1229 [NAICS 33399P]

Combe Inc., pp. Vol. I-566, 575 [NAICS 32561M, 325620]

Comcast Corp., p. III-2211 [NAICS 454113]

Comdata Corp, p. II-1077 [NAICS 333313]

ComDoc Inc., p. III-2186 [NAICS 453210]

Comfortex Corp., p. II-1662 [NAICS 337920]

Command Plastic Corp., pp. Vol. I-603, 609 [NAICS 326111, 326112]

Commander Aircraft Co., p. II-1557 [NAICS 336411]

Commercial Alloys Corp., p. III-1824 [NAICS 423510]

Commercial Brick Corp., p. I-691 [NAICS 327121]

Commercial Creamery Co., p. I-76 [NAICS 311513]

Commercial Distributing Co., pp. Vol. III-1983, 1987 [NAICS 424810, 424820]

Commercial Enameling Co., p. I-681 [NAICS 327112]

Commercial Insulating Glass Co., pp. Vol. I-709, 713 [NAICS 327211, 327212]

Commercial Manufacturing Inc., p. II-1189 [NAICS 333913]

Commercial Metals Co., pp. Vol. I-780, 830, Vol. II-899, Vol. III-1824, 1890 [NAICS 33111M, 33142M, 33231M, 423510, 423930]

Commercial Sewing Inc., pp. Vol. I-239, 285 [NAICS 31491M, 31529M]

Commercial Steel Treating Corp., p. II-964 [NAICS 33281M]

Commercial Tire Company Inc., pp. Vol. III-1766, 2034 [NAICS 423130, 441320]

Commercial Tire of Louisiana Inc., p. III-1766 [NAICS 423130]

Commercial Turf Products Ltd., pp. Vol. II-1023, 1028, 1033, 1184 [NAICS 333111, 333112, 333120, 333912]

Commodity Specialists Co., p. III-1965 [NAICS 424590]

Commodore Machine Inc., p. II-1129 [NAICS 333513]

Commonwealth Supply Inc., p. I-471 [NAICS 325120]

Commonwealth Wine and Spirits, p. III-1987 [NAICS 424820]

CommScope Inc., pp. Vol. I-837, Vol. II-1082, 1262 [NAICS 33149M, 333314, 334220]

Communication Coil Inc., pp. Vol. II-1302, 1421 [NAICS 334416, 335311]

Communications Plus, pp. Vol. III-2058, 2208 [NAICS 443120, 453998]

Communications Systems Inc., p. II-1257 [NAICS 334210]

Communications Test Design Inc., pp. Vol. II-1257, 1267, 1347, 1367 [NAICS 334210, 334290, 334515, 334519]

Community Asphalt Corp., p. I-448 [NAICS 324121]

Community Coffee L.L.C., p. I-143 [NAICS 311920]

Community Light and Sound Inc., p. II-1272 [NAICS 334310]

Community Suffolk Inc., p. III-1950 [NAICS 424480]

Community Support Resource, p. III-2186 [NAICS 453210]

Community Surgical Supply, p. III-2100 [NAICS 446110]

Como Oil Company Inc., p. III-2222 [NAICS 454312]

Comp View Inc., p. III-1798 [NAICS 423410]

Compact Automation Products Inc., p. II-923 [NAICS 332420]

Compact Industries Inc., pp. Vol. I-143, 152 [NAICS 311920, 31194M]

Companion Technologies, p. III-1805 [NAICS 423430]

Compass Aerospace Northwest, p. II-1580 [NAICS 336419]

Compass Group USA Inc, pp. Vol. I-158, Vol. III-2215 [NAICS 31199M, 454210]

Compass Technology of Burlington, p. III-1839 [NAICS 423690]

Compeq International Corp., p. II-1282 [NAICS 334412]

Competition Cams Inc., p. II-1505 [NAICS 33631M]

Compex Corp., p. II-1292 [NAICS 334414]

Compex Technologies Inc., p. II-1322 [NAICS 334510]

Complete Computing Inc., p. III-2058 [NAICS 443120]

Component General Inc., p. II-1297 [NAICS 334415]

Component Parts Machine Inc., p. II-1546 [NAICS 336391]

Composidie Inc., p. II-1134 [NAICS 333514]

Composiflex Inc., pp. Vol. I-631, Vol. II-1357 [NAICS 326130, 334517]

Composites USA, p. I-788 [NAICS 331210]

Comprehensive Video Group, p. III-1798 [NAICS 423410]

Compressed Air Systems Inc., pp. Vol. II-1184, 1584 [NAICS 333912, 336510]

Compression Polymers Corp., p. I-615 [NAICS 326113]

Compressor Systems Inc., p. II-1184 [NAICS 333912]

CompuCom Systems Inc., p. III-1805 [NAICS 423430]

CompuDyne Corp., pp. Vol. II-1267, 1327, 1468 [NAICS 334290, 334511, 335999]

Compugraphics USA Inc., p. II-1056 [NAICS 333295]

CompuLink Corp., p. II-1307 [NAICS 334417]

Compunetix Inc., pp. Vol. II-1257, 1262 [NAICS 334210, 334220]

CompUSA Inc., pp. Vol. III-2058, 2211 [NAICS 443120, 454113]

CompuScription Inc., p. III-2100 [NAICS 446110]

Computer Composition Corp., p. II-1376 [NAICS 334612]

Computer Crafts Inc., p. II-1451 [NAICS 33592M]

Computer Factory Inc., p. III-2058 [NAICS 443120]

Computer Network Technology, pp. Vol. II-1252, 1267 [NAICS 334119, 334290]

Computer Sales International Inc., p. III-1805 [NAICS 423430]

Computer Sciences Corp., p. II-1317 [NAICS 334419]

Computer Tech, p. III-2058 [NAICS 443120]

Computers Now, p. II-1248 [NAICS 334113]

Computers Plus Inc., pp. Vol. II-1238, 1248 [NAICS 334111, 334113]

Computerwise Inc., p. II-1248 [NAICS 334113]

CompX International Inc., pp. Vol. II-886, 892, 1644 [NAICS 33221N, 33221P, 337215]

CompX Regout, p. II-988 [NAICS 332991]

Comtech Telecommunications, p. II-1262 [NAICS 334220]

Comtran Corp., p. I-830 [NAICS 33142M]

Comus International Inc., p. II-1297 [NAICS 334415]

Comverse Technology Inc., pp. Vol. II-1238, 1257, 1337, 1347 [NAICS 334111, 334210, 334513, 334515]

Con-Cise Contact Lens Co., p. II-1687 [NAICS 339115]

Con Sun Food Industries Inc., p. I-92 [NAICS 311520]

Con-Vey Keystone Inc., pp. Vol. II-1046, 1740 [NAICS 333210, 339994]

ConAgra Beef Co., p. I-102 [NAICS 31161N]

ConAgra Foods Inc., pp. Vol. I-9, 15, 62, 76, 97, 102, 524, 529 [NAICS 311119, 31121M, 31141M, 311513, 311615, 31161N, 325314, 325320]

ConAgra Foods Ingredients Co., p. I-152 [NAICS 31194M]

ConArt Inc., pp. Vol. I-737, 762 [NAICS 32733M, 327991]

Concannon Vineyard, p. I-177 [NAICS 312130]

Concentric Systems Inc., p. II-1238 [NAICS 334111]

Concept Electronics Inc., p. II-1362 [NAICS 334518]

Concept Industries Inc., p. I-636 [NAICS 326140]

Concept Packaging Group, pp. Vol. I-379, 636 [NAICS 32221M, 326140]

CONCO Co's, pp. Vol. I-762, Vol. III-1786 [NAICS 327991, 423320]

Concord Camera Corp., p. II-1087 [NAICS 333315]

Concord Fabrics Inc., pp. Vol. I-198, 208 [NAICS 313210, 313230]

Concord Records Inc., p. II-1376 [NAICS 334612]

Concorde Castings Inc., pp. Vol. I-845, 857 [NAICS 33151M, 33152P]

Concorde Flooring Systems Inc., p. III-2041 [NAICS 442210]

Concorde Interspace Battery Corp., p. II-1442 [NAICS 335911]

Concote Corp., pp. Vol. I-403, 641 [NAICS 32223M, 326150]

Concrete Co., pp. Vol. I-732, 743 [NAICS 327320, 327390]

Concrete Sealants Inc., pp. Vol. I-505, Vol. II-1725 [NAICS 325212, 339991]

Concrete Technology Inc., p. I-743 [NAICS 327390]

Concurrent Computer Corp., p. II-1238 [NAICS 334111]

Condenser Products, p. II-1292 [NAICS 334414]

Condon Oil Company Inc., pp. Vol. III-1979, 2116 [NAICS 424720, 447110]

Cone Mills Corp., pp. Vol. I-198, 290, 500 [NAICS 313210, 31599M, 325211]

Conexant Systems Inc., pp. Vol. II-1257, 1282, 1287 [NAICS 334210, 334412, 334413]

Confer Plastics Inc., p. II-1708 [NAICS 33993M]

Confi-Dental Products Inc., p. II-1682 [NAICS 339114]

Confluence Water Sports, p. II-1594 [NAICS 336612]

Conglas, p. I-453 [NAICS 324122]

Congoleum Corp., p. I-651 [NAICS 32619M]

Conicella-Fessler Dental, p. II-1692 [NAICS 339116]

Conitex Sonoco Inc., pp. Vol. I-368, 379, 415 [NAICS 32212M, 32221M, 322299]

Conklin Company Inc., pp. Vol. I-453, 493, 529 [NAICS 324122, 32519M, 325320]

Conley Casting Supply Co., p. I-505 [NAICS 325212]

Conley Corp., p. I-621 [NAICS 326121]

CONMED Corp., pp. Vol. II-1322, 1671, 1676 [NAICS 334510, 339112, 339113]

Conn's Inc., p. III-2050 [NAICS 443111]

Connecticut Coal Inc., p. III-1828 [NAICS 423520]

Connecticut Container Corp., p. III-1905 [NAICS 424130]

Connecticut Stamping & Bending, pp. Vol. I-830, Vol. II-974 [NAICS 33142M, 332913]

Connector Manufacturing Co., p. II-1307 [NAICS 334417]

Connell L.P., pp. Vol. I-837, Vol. II-1134 [NAICS 33149M, 333514]

Connoisseurs Products Corp., p. I-756 [NAICS 327910]

Connor-Winfield Corp., p. II-1347 [NAICS 334515]

Conrad Enterprises Inc., p. II-1482 [NAICS 336120]

Conrad Fafard Inc., p. I-524 [NAICS 325314]

Conrad Industries Inc., pp. Vol. II-1589, 1594 [NAICS 336611, 336612]

Consarc Corp., p. II-1217 [NAICS 333994]

Consigned Sales Inc., p. III-1887 [NAICS 423920]

Consignment Music, p. III-2159 [NAICS 451140]

Consolidated Container Co., p. I-646 [NAICS 326160]

Consolidated Container Inc., p. I-646 [NAICS 326160]

Consolidated Container L.L.C., p. I-646 [NAICS 326160]

Consolidated Converting Co., p. I-415 [NAICS 322299]

Consolidated Diesel Co., p. II-1173 [NAICS 333618]

Consolidated Electrical Distrib., p. III-1831 [NAICS 423610]

Consolidated Engineering Inc., p. II-1217 [NAICS 333994]

Consolidated Fabricators Corp., p. II-928 [NAICS 33243M]

Consolidated Grain and Barge Co., p. I-31 [NAICS 31122N]

Consolidated Graphics Inc., pp. Vol. I-420, 436 [NAICS 32311M, 32312M]

Consolidated Metco Inc., pp. Vol. I-852, Vol. II-899, 1551 [NAICS 33152N, 33231M, 336399]

Consolidated Pac Foundries Inc., pp. Vol. I-845, 857 [NAICS 33151M, 33152P]

Consolidated Pipe and Supply Inc., p. III-1847 [NAICS 423720]

Consolidated Polymer, p. I-621 [NAICS 326121]

Consolidated Poultry and Egg Co., pp. Vol. III-1929, 1936, 1946 [NAICS 424420, 424440, 424470]

Consolidated Purchasing Corp., p. III-1798 [NAICS 423410]

Consolidated Systems Inc., pp. Vol. I-554, Vol. II-933 [NAICS 325510, 332510]

Constar International Inc., p. I-646 [NAICS 326160]

Constellation Brands Inc., p. I-177 [NAICS 312130]

Construction Specialties Inc., p. III-1820 [NAICS 423490]

Construction Trailer Specialists, p. II-1491 [NAICS 336212]

Consultronics Ltd., pp. Vol. II-1238, 1347 [NAICS 334111, 334515]

Consumer Cooperative Oil Co., p. III-1979 [NAICS 424720]

Consumer Discount Drug Store, p. III-2100 [NAICS 446110]

Consumer Marketing Group Inc., p. III-2190 [NAICS 453220]

Consumers Concrete Corp., p. I-732 [NAICS 327320]

Consumers Marine Electronics Inc., p. III-2054 [NAICS 443112]

Consumers Scrap Recycling Inc., p. III-1890 [NAICS 423930]

Container Research Corp., p. II-928 [NAICS 33243M]

Contec Inc., p. I-234 [NAICS 31412M]

Contech Construction Products Inc., pp. Vol. I-780, 811 [NAICS 33111M, 331316]

Contempora Fabrics Inc., p. I-213 [NAICS 31324M]

Contemporary Control Systems, p. II-1297 [NAICS 334415]

Contemporary Cybernetics Group, p. II-1243 [NAICS 334112]

Contender Boats Inc., p. II-1594 [NAICS 336612]

ContiGroup Companies Inc., pp. Vol. I-9, 15, 97, 102, 110 [NAICS 311119, 31121M, 311615, 31161N, 31171M]

Continental AГА, p. II-1184 [NAICS 333912]

Continental Airlines Inc., p. I-68 [NAICS 31142M]

Continental Aluminum Co., p. I-803 [NAICS 331312]

Continental Automotive Accesso, p. III-1887 [NAICS 423920]

Continental Binder & Specialty, p. I-609 [NAICS 326112]

Continental Biomass Industries Inc., p. II-1046 [NAICS 333210]

Continental Carbon Co., p. II-1463 [NAICS 335991]

Continental Cast Stone Mfg Inc., p. I-762 [NAICS 327991]

Continental Culture Specialists, p. I-549 [NAICS 325414]

Continental Diamond Tool Corp., p. I-756 [NAICS 327910]

Continental Disc Corp., pp. Vol. II-980, 1749 [NAICS 33291N, 339999]

Continental Equipment Mfg Inc., p. II-1033 [NAICS 333120]

Continental Glass, p. III-1871 [NAICS 423840]

Continental Glass and Plastic Inc., p. III-1905 [NAICS 424130]

Continental Graphics Corp., p. I-420 [NAICS 32311M]

Continental Jewelry, p. II-1696 [NAICS 33991M]

Continental Machines Inc., pp. Vol. II-1046, 1124, 1179, 1222 [NAICS 333210, 333512, 333911, 33399N]

Continental Materials Corp., pp. Vol. I-732, 743, Vol. II-1106 [NAICS 327320, 327390, 333415]

Continental Mills Inc., p. I-124 [NAICS 31182M]

Continental Office Furniture Corp., p. III-1774 [NAICS 423210]

Continental Plastic Corp., p. I-300 [NAICS 31621M]

Continental Products, pp. Vol. I-603, Vol. II-1023 [NAICS 326111, 333111]

Continental Resources of Illinois, pp. Vol. I-443, Vol. III-1979 [NAICS 324110, 424720]

Continental Rubber Co., p. I-505 [NAICS 325212]

Continental Structural Plastics, p. II-1536 [NAICS 336360]

Continental Tire North America, p. I-660 [NAICS 32621M]

Contour CRC Co., p. II-1147 [NAICS 333516]

Contour Packaging Corp., p. I-646 [NAICS 326160]

Contour Products Inc., p. I-636 [NAICS 326140]

Contractors Heating & Supply Co., p. III-1851 [NAICS 423730]

Contractors Roofing & Supply Inc., p. III-1790 [NAICS 423330]

Contractors Specialties Inc., p. III-1843 [NAICS 423710]

Contractors Steel Company Inc., pp. Vol. II-1009, Vol. III-1824 [NAICS 332996, 423510]

Control Components Inc., p. II-980 [NAICS 33291N]

Controlled Molding Inc., p. II-1051 [NAICS 333220]

Controlotron Corp., p. II-1342 [NAICS 334514]

Controls Engineering Maintenance, p. II-1589 [NAICS 336611]

Converse Inc., pp. Vol. I-272, 290, 300 [NAICS 31522M, 31599M, 31621M]

Converting Inc., p. I-415 [NAICS 322299]

Converto Manufacturing Inc., p. II-1491 [NAICS 336212]

Conway Stores Inc., pp. Vol. III-2123, 2135 [NAICS 448110, 448150]

Conwed Designscape, p. I-319 [NAICS 321219]

Numbers following p. or pp. are page references. Roman numerals indicate volume numbers. Bracketed items indicate industries. Page references are to the starting pages of company tables.

2323

Conwed Plastics, p. I-621 [NAICS 326121]

Cook Inc., pp. Vol. II-1671, 1676 [NAICS 339112, 339113]

Cook's Inc., pp. Vol. III-2050, 2186 [NAICS 443111, 453210]

Cookshack Inc., p. II-1404 [NAICS 335221]

Cookson Electronics Assembly, pp. Vol. I-771, 825, 837, Vol. II-1457 [NAICS 327993, 331419, 33149M, 33593M]

Cookson Precious Metals Div., pp. Vol. I-686, 703, 825 [NAICS 327113, 32712N, 331419]

Cooktek Inc., p. II-1404 [NAICS 335221]

Coolergiant Computers Inc., p. II-1248 [NAICS 334113]

Cooley Inc., p. I-224 [NAICS 313320]

Cooling Systems Specialists, p. III-2030 [NAICS 441310]

Cooper Cameron Corp., pp. Vol. II-980, 1039, 1157, 1173, 1184 [NAICS 33291N, 33313M, 333611, 333618, 333912]

Cooper Classics, p. III-1774 [NAICS 423210]

Cooper Companies Inc., pp. Vol. I-539, Vol. II-1082, 1687 [NAICS 325412, 333314, 339115]

Cooper Electric Supply Co., p. III-1831 [NAICS 423610]

Cooper Hand Tools, p. II-892 [NAICS 33221P]

Cooper Hosiery Mills Inc., pp. Vol. I-256, 290 [NAICS 31511M, 31599M]

Cooper Industries Ltd., pp. Vol. II-892, 933, 1207, 1390, 1421, 1468 [NAICS 33221P, 332510, 333991, 33512M, 335311, 335999]

Cooper Manufacturing Co., p. II-1725 [NAICS 339991]

Cooper Tire and Rubber Co., pp. Vol. I-560, 660, 665, 670, Vol. II-1551 [NAICS 325520, 32621M, 326220, 32629M, 336399]

Cooperative Agricultural Services, pp. Vol. III-1958, 2116, 2222 [NAICS 424510, 447110, 454312]

Cooperative Elevator Co., p. III-1958 [NAICS 424510]

Cooperative Gas and Oil Inc., p. III-1975 [NAICS 424710]

Cooperative Optical Services Inc., p. II-1687 [NAICS 339115]

Cooperative Reserve Supply Inc., pp. Vol. III-1786, 1790 [NAICS 423320, 423330]

Cooperative Sampo Corp., p. III-2177 [NAICS 452910]

Coopers Inc., p. III-2132 [NAICS 448140]

Coors Brewing Co., pp. Vol. I-172, 718, Vol. II-928, Vol. III-1954 [NAICS 312120, 327213, 33243M, 424490]

Coors Energy Co., p. III-1828 [NAICS 423520]

CoorsTek Inc., pp. Vol. I-681, 686, 691, Vol. II-1317 [NAICS 327112, 327113, 327121, 334419]

Coos Grange Supply Co., p. III-2072 [NAICS 444220]

Coosa Steel Corp., p. III-1809 [NAICS 423440]

CoPar Inc., pp. Vol. I-857, Vol. II-1101 [NAICS 33152P, 333414]

Copart Inc., p. III-1758 [NAICS 423110]

Copiers Northwest Inc., p. III-1801 [NAICS 423420]

Copland Inc., p. I-198 [NAICS 313210]

Copley Controls Corp., pp. Vol. II-1262, 1272 [NAICS 334220, 334310]

Coplon's, pp. Vol. III-2126, 2135 [NAICS 448120, 448150]

Copper State Rubber of Arizona, p. I-665 [NAICS 326220]

Copperweld Corp., pp. Vol. I-788, 793 [NAICS 331210, 33122M]

Copperweld Corp. Shelby Div., pp. Vol. I-788, 793, Vol. II-1009 [NAICS 331210, 33122M, 332996]

Copy Systems Inc., p. III-1801 [NAICS 423420]

Copyfax Inc., p. III-1801 [NAICS 423420]

Corachem Inc., p. III-1875 [NAICS 423850]

Coraglass, p. I-722 [NAICS 327215]

Coral Medical Home Equipment, p. III-2113 [NAICS 446199]

Corbett Package Co., p. I-343 [NAICS 321920]

Corbin Saddles Inc., p. II-1599 [NAICS 336991]

Corbitt Manufacturing Inc., p. I-312 [NAICS 32111M]

Cordova Floors and Installation, p. III-1790 [NAICS 423330]

Core Laboratories Inc., pp. Vol. I-458, Vol. II-1302 [NAICS 324191, 334416]

Corey Steel Co., p. I-793 [NAICS 33122M]

Corhart Refractories Corp., p. I-703 [NAICS 32712N]

Corinthian Inc., p. II-1616 [NAICS 337121]

Corinthian Marble Inc., p. I-762 [NAICS 327991]

Corixa Corp., p. I-549 [NAICS 325414]

Corley's Auto Sales Inc., p. III-2027 [NAICS 441229]

Corn Plus, p. I-493 [NAICS 32519M]

Corn Products Development Inc., pp. Vol. I-15, 22, 147 [NAICS 31121M, 311221, 311930]

Corn Products International Inc., p. I-22 [NAICS 311221]

Cornell-Dubilier Electronics Inc., pp. Vol. II-1292, 1302 [NAICS 334414, 334416]

Cornell Industrial Corp., p. II-1046 [NAICS 333210]

Cornell of California Inc., p. I-267 [NAICS 31521M]

Corner Distributors Inc., pp. Vol. III-1835, 2050, 2168 [NAICS 423620, 443111, 451220]

Cornerstone Controls Inc., p. III-1871 [NAICS 423840]

Corning Inc., pp. Vol. I-709, 713, 722, 837, Vol. II-1257, 1427 [NAICS 327211, 327212, 327215, 33149M, 334210, 335312]

Corona Clipper, p. II-1028 [NAICS 333112]

Coronado Stone Products, p. I-762 [NAICS 327991]

Coroplast Inc., pp. Vol. I-500, 609, 615 [NAICS 325211, 326112, 326113]

CoroTech Acquisition Co., p. I-699 [NAICS 327123]

Corporate Environments of GA, p. III-1774 [NAICS 423210]

Corporate Express Inc., p. III-2211 [NAICS 454113]

Corporate Express Office Products, p. III-1774 [NAICS 423210]

Corporate Fleet Services, p. III-2027 [NAICS 441229]

Corporate Presence Inc., pp. Vol. III-1894, 2007 [NAICS 423940, 424990]

Corpus Christi Gasket/Fastener, pp. Vol. II-958, 1725 [NAICS 332722, 339991]

Corr Tech Inc., pp. Vol. III-1820, 1968 [NAICS 423490, 424610]

Correct Construction Inc., p. II-1147 [NAICS 333516]

Correct Craft Inc., p. II-1594 [NAICS 336612]

Correctional Industries, p. II-1720 [NAICS 339950]

Corrections Department, NM, p. II-1740 [NAICS 339994]

Corriher Sand and Stone Inc., p. III-1786 [NAICS 423320]

Corrugated Services Inc., pp. Vol. I-363, 379 [NAICS 322110, 32221M]

Corry Micronics Inc., p. II-1292 [NAICS 334414]

Corry Rubber Corp., pp. Vol. I-665, Vol. II-974 [NAICS 326220, 332913]

Corsican Furniture Inc., pp. Vol. II-1632, 1657 [NAICS 33712N, 337910]

Corsicana Bedding Inc., p. II-1657 [NAICS 337910]

Corsicana Technologies Inc., pp. Vol. I-493, 516 [NAICS 32519M, 325311]

CORT Furniture Rental Corp., p. III-2037 [NAICS 442110]

Cortina Fabrics Inc., pp. Vol. I-192, 213 [NAICS 31311M, 31324M]

Cortland Line Company Inc., p. I-244 [NAICS 314991]

Corydon Stone and Asphalt Inc., pp. Vol. I-453, 748 [NAICS 324122, 327410]

Coshocton Grain Co., p. III-1958 [NAICS 424510]

Cosmic Plastics Inc., p. I-589 [NAICS 325991]

Cosmo Store Services L.L.C., p. III-1843 [NAICS 423710]

Cosmolab Inc., p. I-575 [NAICS 325620]

Cosmopolitan Chemical Div., p. III-1847 [NAICS 423720]

Cospolich Refrigerator Inc., p. II-1409 [NAICS 335222]

Cost Plus Inc., pp. Vol. III-2037, 2047, 2094, 2177 [NAICS 442110, 442299, 445299, 452910]

Cost-U-Less Inc., pp. Vol. III-1909, 1987 [NAICS 424210, 424820]

Costa Fruit and Produce Co., p. III-1950 [NAICS 424480]

Costco Wholesale Corp., p. III-2180 [NAICS 452990]

Costume Gallery, p. I-285 [NAICS 31529M]

Coto Technology Corp., pp. Vol. II-1302, 1512 [NAICS 334416, 33632M]

Cottingham Paper Co., p. III-1905 [NAICS 424130]

Cotton Goods Manufacturing Inc., pp. Vol. I-234, 239, Vol. II-1092, 1229, 1676 [NAICS 31412M, 31491M, 33331N, 33399P, 339113]

Cotton Scrubs and Co., pp. Vol. III-1916, 1919 [NAICS 424320, 424330]

Cotton Tails Inc., p. III-2129 [NAICS 448130]

Cottrell Inc., p. II-1194 [NAICS 33392M]

Cougle's Recycling Inc., p. I-363 [NAICS 322110]

Country Clipper, p. II-1028 [NAICS 333112]

Country Fresh L.L.C., pp. Vol. I-86, 92, 165 [NAICS 31151N, 311520, 31211M]

Country Home Products, pp. Vol. II-1023, 1028 [NAICS 333111, 333112]

Country Mill Farms L.L.C., p. III-2190 [NAICS 453220]

Country Pride Cooperative, p. III-1991 [NAICS 424910]

Country Pure Foods Inc., p. I-165 [NAICS 31211M]

Numbers following p. or pp. are page references. Roman numerals indicate volume numbers. Bracketed items indicate industries. Page references are to the starting pages of company tables.

2324

Country Spring Farmers Co-Op, pp. Vol. I-15, 524 [NAICS 31121M, 325314]

Countrymark Cooperative Inc., pp. Vol. I-9, 516, Vol. III-1958, 1991 [NAICS 311119, 325311, 424510, 424910]

Countrymark Cooperative L.L.P., p. I-443 [NAICS 324110]

County Concrete Corp., pp. Vol. I-732, 737, 743 [NAICS 327320, 32733M, 327390]

County Home Improvement Center, p. III-1794 [NAICS 423390]

Courtesy Acura Isuzu, p. III-2011 [NAICS 441110]

Courtesy Corp., pp. Vol. II-1119, 1134, 1749 [NAICS 333511, 333514, 339999]

Cover Sports USA, p. III-1883 [NAICS 423910]

Covercraft Industries Inc., p. II-1536 [NAICS 336360]

Coverking Inc., p. II-1536 [NAICS 336360]

Covert Manufacturing Inc., p. II-1119 [NAICS 333511]

Covington Detroit Diesel Allison, p. II-1173 [NAICS 333618]

COW Industries Inc., p. II-1152 [NAICS 333518]

Cowboy Oil Co., p. III-1975 [NAICS 424710]

Cowtown Boot Co., p. I-300 [NAICS 31621M]

Cox and Company Inc., p. II-1332 [NAICS 334512]

Cox Automationsystems L.L.C., p. II-1152 [NAICS 333518]

Cox Industries Inc., p. I-312 [NAICS 32111M]

Cox Interior Inc., p. I-358 [NAICS 321999]

Cox Lumber Company Inc., pp. Vol. I-329, 334 [NAICS 32121P, 32191M]

Coyote Vision USA, p. III-1817 [NAICS 423460]

Cozy Harbor Seafood Inc., p. I-110 [NAICS 31171M]

Cozzoli Machine Co., p. II-1212 [NAICS 333993]

CP and P Inc., pp. Vol. I-575, Vol. II-1749 [NAICS 325620, 339999]

CP Flexible Packaging, pp. Vol. I-510, 603, 631 [NAICS 32522M, 326111, 326130]

CP Technologies, p. II-1451 [NAICS 33592M]

CPC Aeroscience, p. I-471 [NAICS 325120]

CPD Industries, p. III-1968 [NAICS 424610]

CPI Corp., p. III-2208 [NAICS 453998]

CPQ Colorchrome Inc., p. III-1798 [NAICS 423410]

CPS Corp., p. I-580 [NAICS 325910]

CPS Products Inc., p. II-1332 [NAICS 334512]

C.R. Bard Inc., pp. Vol. II-1322, 1671, 1676 [NAICS 334510, 339112, 339113]

CR Onsrud Inc., p. II-1046 [NAICS 333210]

CR/T Inc., p. I-580 [NAICS 325910]

Craft-Co Enterprises Inc., p. II-1512 [NAICS 33632M]

Craftech EDM Corp., p. II-1119 [NAICS 333511]

Craftex Wholesale Distributors, p. III-1887 [NAICS 423920]

Craftmade International Inc., p. III-1835 [NAICS 423620]

Craftmaster Furniture Corp., p. II-1616 [NAICS 337121]

Craftsman Tool and Mold Co., p. II-1051 [NAICS 333220]

Craig Technologies Inc., p. II-988 [NAICS 332991]

Crain M-M Sales Inc., p. III-1758 [NAICS 423110]

Cram-A-Lot, p. II-1023 [NAICS 333111]

Cramco Inc., pp. Vol. II-1621, 1632 [NAICS 337122, 33712N]

Cramer Coil and Transformer Co., p. II-1302 [NAICS 334416]

CranBarry Inc., p. I-285 [NAICS 31529M]

Crane America Services Inc., p. II-1194 [NAICS 33392M]

Crane and Company Inc., p. I-368 [NAICS 32212M]

Crane Carrier Co., p. II-1482 [NAICS 336120]

Crane Co., pp. Vol. II-980, 1222, 1317, 1327, 1427, 1551, 1567, 1580, Vol. III-1782 [NAICS 33291N, 33399N, 334419, 334511, 335312, 336399, 336413, 336419, 423310]

Crane Interiors Inc., pp. Vol. II-1594, Vol. III-1875 [NAICS 336612, 423850]

Crane Plastics Manufacturing Ltd., pp. Vol. I-358, 621 [NAICS 321999, 326121]

Crane Technologies Group Inc., pp. Vol. II-1505, 1512, 1599 [NAICS 33631M, 33632M, 336991]

Cranel Inc., p. II-1312 [NAICS 334418]

Cranesville Aggregate Co's Inc., p. III-1786 [NAICS 423320]

Cranesville Block Company Inc., pp. Vol. I-732, 737 [NAICS 327320, 32733M]

Crawford Knitting Company Inc., p. I-256 [NAICS 31511M]

Cray Inc., p. II-1243 [NAICS 334112]

CRC-Evans Pipeline Intern. Inc., pp. Vol. II-1124, 1147 [NAICS 333512, 333516]

Creative Fabricators L.L.C., p. I-22 [NAICS 311221]

Creative Flooring Design Inc., p. III-2041 [NAICS 442210]

Creative Foam Corp., pp. Vol. I-636, 641, 670, Vol. II-1725 [NAICS 326140, 326150, 32629M, 339991]

Creative Foods L.L.C., p. I-26 [NAICS 311225]

Creative Industries, p. I-695 [NAICS 327122]

Creative Precision West Inc., p. II-1519 [NAICS 336330]

Creative Urethanes Inc., p. I-660 [NAICS 32621M]

Creativity For Kids, p. II-1708 [NAICS 33993M]

Credence, p. II-1347 [NAICS 334515]

Credence Systems Corp., p. II-1347 [NAICS 334515]

Cree Inc., p. II-1287 [NAICS 334413]

Creed-Monarch Inc., p. II-952 [NAICS 332721]

Crenlo Inc., p. II-1644 [NAICS 337215]

Cres Cor Corp., p. II-1217 [NAICS 333994]

Crescent Cardboard L.L.C., pp. Vol. I-374, 395 [NAICS 322130, 32222P]

Crescent City Security Inc., p. III-1813 [NAICS 423450]

Crescent Hosiery Mills Inc., p. I-256 [NAICS 31511M]

Crescent Plastics Inc., pp. Vol. I-621, Vol. II-1106 [NAICS 326121, 333415]

Crescent Retail J.V., p. III-2132 [NAICS 448140]

Cresent Enterprises Inc., pp. Vol. II-1621, 1650 [NAICS 337122, 33721N]

Cressona Knit Products Inc., p. I-267 [NAICS 31521M]

Crest Beverage Co., pp. Vol. III-1954, 1983 [NAICS 424490, 424810]

Crest Foods Company Inc., pp. Vol. I-147, 158, 566 [NAICS 311930, 31199M, 32561M]

Crest/Good Manufacturing Co., p. II-974 [NAICS 332913]

Crest Rubber Company Inc., p. I-505 [NAICS 325212]

Crest Steel Corp., p. III-1770 [NAICS 423140]

Crestview Aerospace Corp., pp. Vol. II-1557, 1580 [NAICS 33641-1, 336419]

Crestwood Inc., p. II-1611 [NAICS 337110]

Cretex Companies Inc., pp. Vol. I-743, Vol. II-945 [NAICS 327390, 332710]

Cricket Hosiery Inc., p. I-256 [NAICS 31511M]

Crider Inc., p. I-97 [NAICS 311615]

Cridge Inc., p. I-681 [NAICS 327112]

Crimson Tech Inc., p. III-2054 [NAICS 443112]

Crippen Manufacturing Inc., p. I-756 [NAICS 327910]

Criterion Bell and Specialty Co., pp. Vol. I-203, Vol. II-1731 [NAICS 31322M, 339992]

Criterion Catalyst & Technologies, pp. Vol. I-488, 493 [NAICS 325188, 32519M]

Criterion Machinery Inc., p. II-1147 [NAICS 333516]

Croft L.L.C., p. I-811 [NAICS 331316]

Croft Lumber Company Inc., p. III-2041 [NAICS 442210]

Crom Corp., pp. Vol. I-743, Vol. II-923 [NAICS 327390, 332420]

Crompton Corp., pp. Vol. I-488, 493, 825 [NAICS 325188, 32519M, 331419]

Cromwell Leather Company Inc., p. I-296 [NAICS 316110]

Crosby Group Inc., p. II-933 [NAICS 332510]

Crosby's Drugs Inc., p. III-2100 [NAICS 446110]

Croscill Home Inc., p. I-234 [NAICS 31412M]

Crosible Inc., pp. Vol. I-208, 395 [NAICS 313230, 32222P]

Crosman Corp., pp. Vol. II-1001, 1207 [NAICS 332994, 333991]

Cross Manufacturing Inc., p. II-1222 [NAICS 33399N]

Cross Mark, p. III-1925 [NAICS 424410]

Cross Oil Refining & Marketing, p. I-458 [NAICS 324191]

Cross Sales and Engineering Co., p. III-1871 [NAICS 423840]

Crossroads Ford Truck Sales Inc., pp. Vol. III-1758, 1762 [NAICS 423110, 423120]

Crosstown Used Auto Parts, pp. Vol. III-1770, 2034 [NAICS 423140, 441320]

Crossville Inc., pp. Vol. I-691, 695 [NAICS 327121, 327122]

Crotty Corp., p. II-1725 [NAICS 339991]

Crow's Nest Music, p. III-2168 [NAICS 451220]

Crowder Industries Inc., p. I-343 [NAICS 321920]

Crowley Foods Inc., pp. Vol. I-86, 92 [NAICS 31151N, 311520]

Crown Battery Manufacturing Co., pp. Vol. II-1442, 1447 [NAICS 335911, 335912]

Crown Beer Distributors Inc., p. III-1983 [NAICS 424810]

Crown Candy Corp., pp. Vol. I-52, 57 [NAICS 311330, 311340]

Crown Central Petroleum Corp., pp. Vol. I-443, Vol. III-2076, 2116 [NAICS 324110, 445110, 447110]

Numbers following p. or pp. are page references. Roman numerals indicate volume numbers. Bracketed items indicate industries. Page references are to the starting pages of company tables.

2325

Crown Cork and Seal Inc., pp. Vol. I-626, 879, Vol. II-928, 1229 [NAICS 326122, 33211P, 33243M, 33399P]

Crown Crafts Inc., pp. Vol. I-198, 229, 234 [NAICS 313210, 314110, 31412M]

Crown Equipment Corp., p. II-1194 [NAICS 33392M]

Crown Fence Co., p. I-788 [NAICS 331210]

Crown Group Distributing, p. III-1820 [NAICS 423490]

Crown Group Inc., p. II-964 [NAICS 33281M]

Crown International Inc., pp. Vol. II-1262, 1272 [NAICS 334220, 334310]

Crown Magnetics Inc., p. II-1381 [NAICS 334613]

Crown Optical Co., pp. Vol. I-713, Vol. II-1687 [NAICS 327212, 339115]

Crown Pacific Partners L.P., pp. Vol. I-312, 324, 334 [NAICS 32111M, 32121N, 32191M]

Crown Packaging International, p. III-1871 [NAICS 423840]

Crown Photo Systems Inc., p. II-1087 [NAICS 333315]

Crown Poly Inc., p. I-603 [NAICS 326111]

Crown Remanufacturing Inc., p. II-1512 [NAICS 33632M]

CROWN Risdon, p. I-388 [NAICS 32222N]

Crown Roll Leaf Inc., pp. Vol. I-436, 816 [NAICS 32312M, 33131N]

Crown Sanitary Supply Inc., p. III-1875 [NAICS 423850]

Crown Technology L.L.C., p. I-453 [NAICS 324122]

Crownline Boats Inc., p. II-1594 [NAICS 336612]

CRS Auto Parts Inc., p. III-1770 [NAICS 423140]

CRS Emergency Vehicles Inc., p. II-1607 [NAICS 336999]

Crucible Compaction Metals, p. I-867 [NAICS 332117]

Crucible Specialty Metals, pp. Vol. II-1014, 1124, 1129, 1140 [NAICS 33299N, 333512, 333513, 333515]

Cruise America Inc., p. III-2018 [NAICS 441210]

Crumb Rubber Technology Inc., p. I-665 [NAICS 326220]

Crumrine Manufacturing, p. II-1735 [NAICS 339993]

Crutchfield Corp., p. III-2054 [NAICS 443112]

Cryogenic Industries, p. II-918 [NAICS 332410]

Crystal Art Gallery, p. III-2200 [NAICS 453920]

Crystal Bottling Company Inc., p. III-1954 [NAICS 424490]

Crystal Cream and Butter Co., pp. Vol. I-86, 92 [NAICS 31151N, 311520]

Crystal Farms Inc., pp. Vol. I-9, 158 [NAICS 311119, 31199M]

Crystal Lake Foods, p. I-97 [NAICS 311615]

Crystal Lake Manufacturing Inc., p. II-1740 [NAICS 339994]

Crystal Promotions Inc., pp. Vol. III-1835, 2050 [NAICS 423620, 443111]

Crystal Specialties Inc., p. I-703 [NAICS 32712N]

Crystal Springs Printworks Inc., pp. Vol. I-218, 224 [NAICS 31331M, 313320]

Crystal Window & Door Systems, p. I-722 [NAICS 327215]

Crystalix Group International Inc., p. III-2190 [NAICS 453220]

Crysteel Manufacturing Co., pp. Vol. II-1222, 1486 [NAICS 33399N, 336211]

Crystx Composites, p. I-776 [NAICS 327999]

CS Steen Syrup Mill Inc., p. I-44 [NAICS 31131N]

CSC Laboratories Group, p. II-1687 [NAICS 339115]

CSI Technologies Inc., p. II-1292 [NAICS 334414]

CSK Auto Corp., p. III-2030 [NAICS 441310]

CSK Holdings Group Inc., p. III-2030 [NAICS 441310]

CSM Manufacturing L.L.C., p. II-952 [NAICS 332721]

CSP Inc., p. II-1248 [NAICS 334113]

CSS Industries Inc., pp. Vol. I-415, 420 [NAICS 322299, 32311M]

CTA Acoustics Inc., pp. Vol. I-251, 510, 771 [NAICS 314999, 32522M, 327993]

CTC Parker Automation, p. II-1248 [NAICS 334113]

CTE Systems Inc., p. III-1894 [NAICS 423940]

CTI Paper Company Inc., p. III-1898 [NAICS 424110]

CTL Aerospace Inc., pp. Vol. I-621, 631 [NAICS 326121, 326130]

CTS Corp., pp. Vol. II-1267, 1317, 1567 [NAICS 334290, 334419, 336413]

Cubic Corp., pp. Vol. I-379, Vol. II-1092, 1262, 1327, 1367 [NAICS 32221M, 33331N, 334220, 334511, 334519]

Cucina Classica Italiana Inc., p. I-76 [NAICS 311513]

Cudahy Tanning Co., p. I-296 [NAICS 316110]

Cues Inc., p. II-1087 [NAICS 333315]

Cuisine Solutions Inc., pp. Vol. I-97, 110 [NAICS 311615, 31171M]

Culligan International Co., pp. Vol. I-595, Vol. II-1092, 1189, 1229, 1332 [NAICS 32599N, 33331N, 333913, 33399P, 334512]

Culligan of Greater Kansas City, p. I-165 [NAICS 31211M]

Culligan Water Conditioning Inc., p. III-2050 [NAICS 443111]

Culp Inc., p. I-198 [NAICS 313210]

Culpepper Plastics Corp., p. II-1051 [NAICS 333220]

Cumberland Dairy Inc., p. I-92 [NAICS 311520]

Cumberland Engineering Corp., p. II-1051 [NAICS 333220]

Cumberland Farms Inc., pp. Vol. III-2076, 2116 [NAICS 445110, 447110]

Cumberland Packing Corp., p. I-152 [NAICS 31194M]

Cummings-Moore Graphite Co., p. II-1463 [NAICS 335991]

Cummins-Allison Corp., pp. Vol. II-1014, 1077, 1152, 1342, 1714 [NAICS 33299N, 333313, 333518, 334514, 33994M]

Cummins Inc., pp. Vol. II-1173, 1427, 1512, 1551 [NAICS 333618, 335312, 33632M, 336399]

Cummins Intermountain Inc., p. III-2027 [NAICS 441229]

Cummins Marine, pp. Vol. II-1162, 1173 [NAICS 333612, 333618]

Cuna Mutual Business Services, p. III-1901 [NAICS 424120]

Cunningham Wholesale Inc., p. III-1983 [NAICS 424810]

Cuno Inc., p. II-1229 [NAICS 33399P]

Cupples' J and J Company Inc., p. II-952 [NAICS 332721]

Curbell Inc., pp. Vol. II-1262, 1267, 1322 [NAICS 334220, 334290, 334510]

Current Controls Inc., p. I-686 [NAICS 327113]

Curry Corp., p. III-2011 [NAICS 441110]

Curry Oil Company Inc., p. III-1975 [NAICS 424710]

Curtis Instruments Inc., pp. Vol. I-670, Vol. II-1162, 1337, 1347, 1437 [NAICS 32629M, 333612, 334513, 334515, 335314]

Curtis-Maruyasu America, p. II-1009 [NAICS 332996]

Curtis PMC Inc., p. II-1437 [NAICS 335314]

Curtis Screw Company L.L.C., p. II-952 [NAICS 332721]

Curtis Toledo Inc., pp. Vol. II-1147, 1184 [NAICS 333516, 333912]

Curtis Universal Joint Inc., p. II-1530 [NAICS 336350]

Curtiss-Wright Corp., pp. Vol. II-964, 1092, 1222, 1580 [NAICS 33281M, 33331N, 33399N, 336419]

Curwood Inc., p. I-631 [NAICS 326130]

Cushing and Company Inc., pp. Vol. II-1714, Vol. III-1820 [NAICS 33994M, 423490]

Custom Alloy Sales Inc., p. I-807 [NAICS 331314]

Custom Aluminum Products Inc., p. I-811 [NAICS 331316]

Custom Bilt Metals, p. III-1794 [NAICS 423390]

Custom Bottle of Connecticut Inc., p. I-646 [NAICS 326160]

Custom Building Products Inc., pp. Vol. I-475, 560, 752 [NAICS 32513M, 325520, 327420]

Custom Cable Inc., p. I-830 [NAICS 33142M]

Custom Chrome Mfg Inc., p. II-1599 [NAICS 336991]

Custom Deco, p. I-722 [NAICS 327215]

Custom Direct L.L.C., p. I-420 [NAICS 32311M]

Custom Electronics Inc., p. II-1292 [NAICS 334414]

Custom Engineering Co., p. II-1129 [NAICS 333513]

Custom Eyes Inc., p. II-1687 [NAICS 339115]

Custom Faberkin Inc., p. I-239 [NAICS 31491M]

Custom Fiberglass Molding Inc., p. II-1607 [NAICS 336999]

Custom Glass Distributors Inc., p. III-1794 [NAICS 423390]

Custom Hoists Inc., p. II-1222 [NAICS 33399N]

Custom Marble and Onyx Inc., p. I-762 [NAICS 327991]

Custom Metalcraft Inc., p. II-923 [NAICS 332420]

Custom Packaging Inc., p. II-1720 [NAICS 339950]

Custom Pak Illinois Inc., pp. Vol. I-458, 703 [NAICS 324191, 32712N]

Custom Plastic Developments Inc., p. II-1119 [NAICS 333511]

Custom Plastics Inc., p. I-621 [NAICS 326121]

Custom Rollform Products Inc., p. II-1147 [NAICS 333516]

Custom Sales and Service Inc., pp. Vol. I-348, Vol. II-1478 [NAICS 321991, 336112]

Custom Screens Inc., p. I-218 [NAICS 31331M]

Numbers following p. or pp. are page references. Roman numerals indicate volume numbers. Bracketed items indicate industries. Page references are to the starting pages of company tables.

2326

Custom Service Plastics Inc., p. II-1051 [NAICS 333220]

Customized Structures Inc., p. I-353 [NAICS 321992]

Cutrufellos Creamery Inc., p. III-1933 [NAICS 424430]

Cutter and Buck Inc., pp. Vol. I-272, 290 [NAICS 31522M, 31599M]

Cutting Edge Audio Group L.L.C., p. III-2208 [NAICS 453998]

Cutting Edge Tex Styles L.L.C., p. I-374 [NAICS 322130]

C.V. Source Inc., p. II-1530 [NAICS 336350]

CV Therapeutics Inc., p. I-549 [NAICS 325414]

CVI Business Systems, p. III-1801 [NAICS 423420]

CVS Corp., p. III-2211 [NAICS 454113]

CVS Pharmacy Inc., p. III-2100 [NAICS 446110]

CVS Systems L.P., p. III-1835 [NAICS 423620]

CW Industries Inc., pp. Vol. II-1307, 1451, 1457 [NAICS 334417, 33592M, 33593M]

CW Matthews Contracting Inc., p. I-448 [NAICS 324121]

CWC Industries Inc., p. I-816 [NAICS 33131N]

CWCI Supply Inc., p. III-1790 [NAICS 423330]

Cyanotech Corp., pp. Vol. I-534, 549 [NAICS 325411, 325414]

CyberGuard Corp., p. II-1238 [NAICS 334111]

Cyberonics Inc., p. II-1322 [NAICS 334510]

CyberOptics Corp., pp. Vol. II-1082, 1322, 1468 [NAICS 333314, 334510, 335999]

Cybertouch Inc., p. II-1248 [NAICS 334113]

CYBEX International Inc., p. II-1702 [NAICS 339920]

Cycle Plastics, p. I-395 [NAICS 32222P]

Cycle Systems Inc., pp. Vol. I-363, 807 [NAICS 322110, 331314]

Cyclo Manufacturing Co., p. I-660 [NAICS 32621M]

Cygnus Technologies L.L.C., p. II-1357 [NAICS 334517]

Cymer Inc., pp. Vol. II-1061, 1087, 1468 [NAICS 33329N, 333315, 335999]

Cypress Semiconductor Corp., pp. Vol. II-1257, 1287 [NAICS 334210, 334413]

Cyracom International Inc., p. III-2054 [NAICS 443112]

Cyrk Inc., p. I-420 [NAICS 32311M]

Cytec Industries Inc., pp. Vol. I-475, 488, 500, 510, 560, Vol. II-1468 [NAICS 32513M, 325188, 325211, 32522M, 325520, 335999]

Cytogen Corp., p. I-544 [NAICS 325413]

Cytyc Corp., p. II-1352 [NAICS 334516]

D/A Mid South Inc., p. III-1798 [NAICS 423410]

D'Ambra Construction Inc., p. I-453 [NAICS 324122]

D and D Equipment Company Inc., p. III-2069 [NAICS 444210]

D and D Feed and Farm Supply, pp. Vol. I-15, 524 [NAICS 31121M, 325314]

D and G Equipment Inc., p. III-2069 [NAICS 444210]

D and H Distributing Co., pp. Vol. III-1805, 1835, 1839 [NAICS 423430, 423620, 423690]

D and K Custom Machine Design, pp. Vol. I-615, Vol. II-1124 [NAICS 326113, 333512]

D and K Group Inc., p. I-615 [NAICS 326113]

D and K Healthcare Resources Inc., p. III-1909 [NAICS 424210]

D and N Micro Products Inc., p. II-1357 [NAICS 334517]

D and P Embroidery Company Inc., pp. Vol. I-203, 213 [NAICS 31322M, 31324M]

D and R Boats Inc., p. III-2024 [NAICS 441222]

D and S Manufacturing Inc., pp. Vol. II-1077, 1189 [NAICS 333313, 333913]

D and W Diesel Inc., p. III-1770 [NAICS 423140]

D'Angelo Sandwich Shop, pp. Vol. I-116, 158 [NAICS 31181M, 31199M]

D'Arrigo Brothers, p. III-1950 [NAICS 424480]

D'Artagnan Inc., p. III-1946 [NAICS 424470]

D. Canale Beverages Inc., pp. Vol. III-1983, 1987 [NAICS 424810, 424820]

D. Myers and Sons Inc., p. III-1922 [NAICS 424340]

D'San Corp., p. II-1362 [NAICS 334518]

Da-Lite Screen Company Inc., pp. Vol. II-1087, 1272, 1627, 1644 [NAICS 333315, 334310, 337127, 337215]

Da-Pro Rubber Inc., p. I-670 [NAICS 32629M]

DA Stuart Co., pp. Vol. I-26, 458 [NAICS 311225, 324191]

DAA Draexlmaier Automotive, p. I-306 [NAICS 31699M]

Dab-O-Matic Corp., p. II-1740 [NAICS 339994]

DAC Vision Inc., p. III-1817 [NAICS 423460]

DACCO Inc., pp. Vol. II-1530, 1551 [NAICS 336350, 336399]

Dacor Inc., pp. Vol. II-1397, 1404, 1417 [NAICS 33521M, 335221, 335228]

Dacotah Paper Co., p. III-1905 [NAICS 424130]

DADCO Inc., p. II-1162 [NAICS 333612]

Dade Behring Inc., pp. Vol. I-544, Vol. II-1367, 1671 [NAICS 325413, 334519, 339112]

Dade Truss Company Inc., p. I-329 [NAICS 32121P]

Daewoo International Corp., pp. Vol. III-1762, 1913 [NAICS 423120, 424310]

Dahl-Tech Inc., p. I-646 [NAICS 326160]

Dahlgren and Company Inc., pp. Vol. I-9, 52, 137 [NAICS 311119, 311330, 31191M]

Daigle Oil Co., p. III-2218 [NAICS 454311]

Daiki Corp., p. II-1033 [NAICS 333120]

Daikin America Inc., pp. Vol. I-500, 589 [NAICS 325211, 325991]

Daikin Clutch Corp., p. II-1530 [NAICS 336350]

Dailey & Wells Communications, p. III-2054 [NAICS 443112]

DaimlerChrysler Corp., pp. Vol. II-1473, 1486, 1541, 1551 [NAICS 336111, 336211, 336370, 336399]

Dairy Farmers of America Inc., pp. Vol. I-68, 76, 81, 86 [NAICS 31142M, 311513, 311514, 31151N]

Dairy Fresh Corp., p. I-86 [NAICS 31151N]

Dairy Fresh Corp. Cowarts Div., p. I-86 [NAICS 31151N]

Dairy Fresh Food Inc., p. III-1933 [NAICS 424430]

Dairy Fresh L.L.C., p. I-92 [NAICS 311520]

Dairy Fresh Products Co., pp. Vol. III-1933, 1954 [NAICS 424430, 424490]

Dairy Maid Foods Inc., p. III-1925 [NAICS 424410]

Dairy-Mix Inc., p. III-1933 [NAICS 424430]

Dairyland Seed Company Inc., p. III-1991 [NAICS 424910]

Dairylea Cooperative Inc., p. III-1933 [NAICS 424430]

Dairyman's Supply Co., p. III-1794 [NAICS 423390]

Daisytek Inc., pp. Vol. III-1805, 1901 [NAICS 423430, 424120]

DAK's, p. III-2194 [NAICS 453310]

Dakocytomation Inc., pp. Vol. II-1352, 1666 [NAICS 334516, 339111]

Dakota Collectibles, p. III-2058 [NAICS 443120]

Dakota Creek Industries Inc., p. II-1589 [NAICS 336611]

Dakota Electric Supply Co., p. III-1851 [NAICS 423730]

Dakota Fence Co., p. III-2150 [NAICS 451110]

Dakota Gasification Company Inc., pp. Vol. I-471, 488, 516 [NAICS 325120, 325188, 325311]

Dakota Granite Co., pp. Vol. I-691, 762 [NAICS 327121, 327991]

Dakota Growers Pasta Co., p. I-124 [NAICS 31182M]

Dakota Tribal Industry Inc., p. I-285 [NAICS 31529M]

Daktronics Inc., p. II-1720 [NAICS 339950]

Dal-Tile International Inc., p. I-695 [NAICS 327122]

Dalbec Audio Lab, p. III-2054 [NAICS 443112]

Dalhart R & R Machine Works, p. II-1147 [NAICS 333516]

Dallas Airmotive Inc., pp. Vol. II-1173, 1562 [NAICS 333618, 336412]

Dallas Bias Fabrics, p. I-267 [NAICS 31521M]

Dallas-Fort Worth Roofing Supply, p. III-1790 [NAICS 423330]

Dallas Manufacturing Inc., pp. Vol. I-239, Vol. II-1594, 1749 [NAICS 31491M, 336612, 339999]

Dallas Market Center Ltd., p. III-1925 [NAICS 424410]

Dallas Specialty and Mfg Co., p. II-974 [NAICS 332913]

Dallis Brothers Inc., p. I-143 [NAICS 311920]

Dalton Corp., p. I-845 [NAICS 33151M]

Dalton Enterprises Inc., p. I-589 [NAICS 325991]

Dalton Industries L.L.C., p. II-1147 [NAICS 333516]

Damar Machine Co., p. II-1119 [NAICS 333511]

Damascus Peanut Co., p. III-1965 [NAICS 424590]

Damerow Beaverton Ford, p. III-2011 [NAICS 441110]

Damons Management Inc., p. III-1786 [NAICS 423320]

Damron Corp., p. I-143 [NAICS 311920]

Dan Incorporated Oregon, pp. Vol. III-2065, 2076, 2100 [NAICS 444100, 445110, 446110]

Dan Lewis Enterprises, p. III-1766 [NAICS 423130]

Dan River Inc., pp. Vol. I-198, 234 [NAICS 313210, 31412M]

Dan T Moore Co., p. I-660 [NAICS 32621M]

Dana Corp., pp. Vol. II-1473, 1486, 1551 [NAICS 336111, 336211, 336399]

Dana Corp. Plumley Div., pp. Vol. II-1092, 1725 [NAICS 33331N, 339991]

Dana Coupled Products, pp. Vol. I-670, Vol. II-1009 [NAICS 32629M, 332996]

Dana Kepner Co., pp. Vol. III-1794, 1847 [NAICS 423390, 423720]

Dana Labels Inc., p. I-203 [NAICS 31322M]

Danafilms Inc., p. I-621 [NAICS 326121]

Numbers following p. or pp. are page references. Roman numerals indicate volume numbers. Bracketed items indicate industries. Page references are to the starting pages of company tables.

2327

Danaher Corp., pp. Vol. II-892, 1106, 1140, 1207, 1332, 1342, 1437 [NAICS 33221P, 333415, 333515, 333991, 334512, 334514, 335314]

Danaher Tool Group, p. II-892 [NAICS 33221P]

Dancker, Sellew and Douglas Inc., p. III-1774 [NAICS 423210]

Danco Prairie FS Coop., pp. Vol. III-2072, 2177 [NAICS 444220, 452910]

Dandridge Equipment Inc., p. III-1863 [NAICS 423820]

Dandux, p. II-964 [NAICS 33281M]

Danecraft Inc., p. II-1696 [NAICS 33991M]

Danfoss Inc., p. II-1332 [NAICS 334512]

Danhard Inc., p. II-1546 [NAICS 336391]

Daniel L Bowers Company Inc., p. I-471 [NAICS 325120]

Daniel Measurement & Control, pp. Vol. II-958, 980, 1009, 1337, 1342 [NAICS 332722, 33291N, 332996, 334513, 334514]

Daniel Smith Artist Materials, p. III-2208 [NAICS 453998]

Danisco Inc., p. I-147 [NAICS 311930]

Dannon Company Inc., p. I-86 [NAICS 31151N]

Dantona Industries Inc., p. II-1442 [NAICS 335911]

Danville Metal Stamping Inc., pp. Vol. II-1562, 1567 [NAICS 336412, 336413]

DAP Inc., p. I-560 [NAICS 325520]

DAPCO Industries, pp. Vol. II-1134, 1207 [NAICS 333514, 333991]

Daramic Inc., pp. Vol. I-670, Vol. II-899 [NAICS 32629M, 33231M]

Darby Group Companies Inc., pp. Vol. II-1682, Vol. III-1813, 1909, 2007 [NAICS 339114, 423450, 424210, 424990]

Dare Products Inc., p. I-244 [NAICS 314991]

Darice Inc., p. III-1887 [NAICS 423920]

Dark Dynamite Inc., p. II-1473 [NAICS 336111]

Darling Co., p. I-665 [NAICS 326220]

Darling International Inc., pp. Vol. I-9, 26 [NAICS 311119, 311225]

Darlington Fabrics Corp., pp. Vol. I-203, 213 [NAICS 31322M, 31324N]

Darlington Veneer Company Inc., pp. Vol. I-312, 324 [NAICS 32111M, 32121N]

Darrow Medical Corp., p. III-1813 [NAICS 423450]

Dart Container Corp., pp. Vol. I-626, 641 [NAICS 326122, 326150]

Dartmouth Printing Co., p. I-420 [NAICS 32311M]

Dash Designs Inc., pp. Vol. I-229, Vol. II-1536 [NAICS 314110, 336360]

Data Device Corp., pp. Vol. II-1252, 1267, 1427 [NAICS 334119, 334290, 335312]

Data Financial Business Services, p. III-1820 [NAICS 423490]

Data Label Inc., p. I-415 [NAICS 322299]

Data Management Internationale, p. II-1243 [NAICS 334112]

Data2 Corp., p. III-1971 [NAICS 424690]

Databazaar, p. III-2058 [NAICS 443120]

DataMark Graphics Inc., p. I-203 [NAICS 31322M]

Datametrics Corp., p. II-1248 [NAICS 334113]

Dataram Corp., pp. Vol. II-1243, 1282 [NAICS 334112, 334412]

Datascope Corp., pp. Vol. II-1322, 1671, 1676 [NAICS 334510, 339112, 339113]

Datasis Corp., p. II-1381 [NAICS 334613]

DATAVOX Inc., p. III-1839 [NAICS 423690]

Daube's Bakery Inc., p. III-2089 [NAICS 445291]

Dauber Company Inc., p. I-767 [NAICS 327992]

Dauphin Precision Tool, pp. Vol. II-892, 1124, 1140 [NAICS 33221P, 333512, 333515]

Davalor Mold Corp., p. II-1119 [NAICS 333511]

Dave Bang Associates Inc., p. III-1883 [NAICS 423910]

Dave Steel Company Inc., pp. Vol. II-945, 964 [NAICS 332710, 33281M]

David Briggs Enterprises Inc., p. III-2097 [NAICS 445310]

David Gooding Inc., p. III-1847 [NAICS 423720]

David Hirschberg Company Inc., p. I-807 [NAICS 331314]

David Martin Inc., p. III-2186 [NAICS 453210]

David McDavid Auto Group, p. III-2011 [NAICS 441110]

David R Webb Company Inc., p. I-324 [NAICS 32121N]

David R Webb Inc., p. I-324 [NAICS 32121N]

David's Cookies, p. I-124 [NAICS 31182M]

David Sherman Corp., p. I-181 [NAICS 312140]

David Taylor Cadillac Co., p. III-2015 [NAICS 441120]

Davidson Pipe Supply Inc., p. III-1847 [NAICS 423720]

Daviess County Metal Sales Inc., p. I-863 [NAICS 332114]

Davis-Frost Inc., p. I-26 [NAICS 311225]

Davis-Lynch Inc., p. II-1039 [NAICS 33313M]

Davis Rubber Company Inc., p. I-660 [NAICS 32621M]

Davis-Standard Corp., pp. Vol. II-1129, 1134, 1152, 1337 [NAICS 333513, 333514, 333518, 334513]

Davis Vision Inc., p. II-1687 [NAICS 339115]

Davis Wire Corp., pp. Vol. I-793, Vol. II-939 [NAICS 33122M, 33261N]

Davisco International Inc., pp. Vol. I-76, 81, 152 [NAICS 311513, 311514, 31194M]

Davison Chemicals, p. I-595 [NAICS 32599N]

Dawahare's Inc., p. III-2132 [NAICS 448140]

Dawlen Corp., p. II-952 [NAICS 332721]

Dawn Food Products Inc., pp. Vol. I-68, 116, Vol. II-1061 [NAICS 31142M, 31181M, 33329N]

Dawson Manufacturing Co., p. I-670 [NAICS 32629M]

Day and Zimmermann Group Inc., p. II-997 [NAICS 332993]

Day-Glo Color Corp., pp. Vol. I-475, 554, 580 [NAICS 32513M, 325510, 325910]

Day Music Co., p. III-2159 [NAICS 451140]

Day Starter North America, pp. Vol. II-1442, 1447 [NAICS 335911, 335912]

Daybreak Coffee Roasters Inc., p. III-2094 [NAICS 445299]

Daybrook Fisheries Inc., p. I-110 [NAICS 31171M]

Daycon Products Company Inc., p. I-566 [NAICS 32561M]

Daystar Products International Inc., p. II-1519 [NAICS 336330]

Dayton Bag and Burlap Co., p. I-239 [NAICS 31491M]

Dayton Meat Products Inc., p. III-1946 [NAICS 424470]

Dayton Parts L.L.C., p. II-1486 [NAICS 336211]

Dayton-Phoenix Group Inc., p. II-1584 [NAICS 336510]

Dayton Steel Service Inc., pp. Vol. II-945, Vol. III-1824 [NAICS 332710, 423510]

Dayton Superior Corp., p. II-1033 [NAICS 333120]

Dayton Technologies L.L.C., p. I-621 [NAICS 326121]

Dayton Tire, p. I-660 [NAICS 32621M]

Dazor Manufacturing Corp., p. II-1386 [NAICS 335110]

DBB Marketing Co., p. III-1929 [NAICS 424420]

DBI SALA/PROTECTA, pp. Vol. I-251, 272 [NAICS 314999, 31522M]

DBK Concepts Inc., p. III-1831 [NAICS 423610]

DBM Technologies L.L.C., p. III-1762 [NAICS 423120]

DBT America Inc., p. II-1039 [NAICS 33313M]

DCA Manufacturing Corp., p. II-1292 [NAICS 334414]

DCI Biologicals Inc., p. I-549 [NAICS 325414]

DCI Furniture, p. II-1627 [NAICS 337127]

DCI Inc., p. II-923 [NAICS 332420]

DCI International, p. II-1682 [NAICS 339114]

DCI Marketing Inc., pp. Vol. I-420, Vol. II-1644, 1720 [NAICS 32311M, 337215, 339950]

DCS, p. II-1362 [NAICS 334518]

DDI Corp., pp. Vol. II-1257, 1262, 1282, Vol. III-1839 [NAICS 334210, 334220, 334412, 423690]

De Beukelaer Corp., p. I-124 [NAICS 31182M]

De Menno-Kerdoon, pp. Vol. I-443, 458 [NAICS 324110, 324191]

De Nora North America Inc., p. II-1463 [NAICS 335991]

De-Sta-Co Industries, pp. Vol. II-892, 933, 1112, 1140 [NAICS 33221P, 332510, 33341N, 333515]

De Wafelbakkers Inc., pp. Vol. I-62, 158 [NAICS 31141M, 31199M]

Deacon Industrial Supply Inc., p. III-1847 [NAICS 423720]

Dead River Co., p. III-1979 [NAICS 424720]

Dealer Tire L.L.C., p. III-1766 [NAICS 423130]

Dealers Supply and Lumber Inc., p. III-1782 [NAICS 423310]

Dealers Supply Co., p. III-1778 [NAICS 423220]

Dealers Truck Equipment Inc., pp. Vol. III-1859, 1879 [NAICS 423810, 423860]

Dean Co., p. I-324 [NAICS 32121N]

Dean Dairy Products Co., pp. Vol. I-86, 165 [NAICS 31151N, 31211M]

Dean Foods Co., pp. Vol. I-62, 68, 86, 92, 626 [NAICS 31141M, 31142M, 31151N, 311520, 326122]

Dean Machinery Co., p. III-1859 [NAICS 423810]

Dean Markley Electronics Inc., p. II-1731 [NAICS 339992]

Dean's RV Superstore Inc., p. III-2018 [NAICS 441210]

Dearborn Electronics Inc., p. II-1292 [NAICS 334414]

Deb Shops Inc., pp. Vol. III-2123, 2126 [NAICS 448110, 448120]

Debbie Supply Inc., p. III-2047 [NAICS 442299]

Numbers following p. or pp. are page references. Roman numerals indicate volume numbers. Bracketed items indicate industries. Page references are to the starting pages of company tables.

DeBruce Grain Inc., pp. Vol. III-1958, 1965 [NAICS 424510, 424590]

Decatur Plastic Products Inc., p. II-1536 [NAICS 336360]

Deccofelt Corp., p. I-224 [NAICS 313320]

Deck House Inc., pp. Vol. I-348, 353 [NAICS 321991, 321992]

Deckers Outdoor Corp., p. I-300 [NAICS 31621M]

Decko Products Inc., p. I-57 [NAICS 311340]

Deco Plate, p. II-933 [NAICS 332510]

Deco Tools Inc., p. II-1740 [NAICS 339994]

DecoArt Inc., pp. Vol. I-681, Vol. II-1714 [NAICS 327112, 33994M]

DecoGard Products Inc., p. I-415 [NAICS 322299]

Decor Inc., p. I-722 [NAICS 327215]

Decorative Decor Inc., p. III-2183 [NAICS 453110]

Decorator Industries Inc., p. I-234 [NAICS 31412M]

Decrane Aircraft Seating Inc., pp. Vol. II-945, 1536 [NAICS 332710, 336360]

Deen Meats and Cooked Foods, p. III-1946 [NAICS 424470]

Deep Creek Custom Packing Inc., p. I-110 [NAICS 31171M]

Deep South Products Inc., pp. Vol. I-124, 165 [NAICS 31182M, 31211M]

Deere and Co., pp. Vol. II-1023, 1028, 1033, 1194 [NAICS 333111, 333112, 333120, 33392M]

Deere Power Systems Group, p. II-1173 [NAICS 333618]

Deerfield Specialty Papers Inc., p. I-368 [NAICS 32212M]

Defiance Metal Products Co., pp. Vol. I-879, Vol. II-1014, 1134 [NAICS 33211P, 33299N, 333514]

Degen-Berglund Inc., p. III-2100 [NAICS 446110]

Degussa Corp., p. I-595 [NAICS 32599N]

Degussa Flavors & Fruit Systems, pp. Vol. I-152, 158 [NAICS 31194M, 31199M]

DeGussa Food Ingredients, pp. Vol. I-147, 152, 493 [NAICS 311930, 31194M, 32519M]

Degussa Stockhausen Inc., p. I-566 [NAICS 32561M]

Dehler Manufacturing Inc., pp. Vol. II-928, 1627 [NAICS 33243M, 337127]

Deitsch Plastic Company Inc., p. I-208 [NAICS 313230]

DeKalb Molded Plastics, p. I-636 [NAICS 326140]

DeKalb Office Environments, p. III-2037 [NAICS 442110]

Dekko Technologies Inc., p. I-767 [NAICS 327992]

Del Buono Bakery Inc., p. III-2089 [NAICS 445291]

Del City Wire Company Inc., p. II-1307 [NAICS 334417]

Del Laboratories Inc., pp. Vol. I-539, 575 [NAICS 325412, 325620]

Del Mar Food Products Corp., p. I-62 [NAICS 31141M]

Del Medical Imaging Corp., p. II-1357 [NAICS 334517]

Del Medical Systems Group, p. II-1357 [NAICS 334517]

Del Monte Foods Co., p. I-68 [NAICS 31142M]

Del Monte Fresh Produce, p. III-1950 [NAICS 424480]

Del Rey Tortilleria Inc., p. I-133 [NAICS 311830]

Del West Engineering Inc., p. II-1505 [NAICS 33631M]

Delafield Corp., pp. Vol. I-665, Vol. II-974 [NAICS 326220, 332913]

Delano Growers Grape Products, p. I-147 [NAICS 311930]

Delaplaine Creative, p. II-1381 [NAICS 334613]

Delaware Importers Inc., pp. Vol. III-1983, 1987 [NAICS 424810, 424820]

Delaware Public Auto Auction, p. III-2015 [NAICS 441120]

Delaware Technologies Inc., p. II-1297 [NAICS 334415]

Delaware Valley Sign Corp., p. I-239 [NAICS 31491M]

Delbar Products Inc., pp. Vol. I-722, Vol. II-1486 [NAICS 327215, 336211]

Delgasco Inc., p. III-1979 [NAICS 424720]

Delia's Corp., p. I-290 [NAICS 31599M]

Delicato Vineyards, p. I-177 [NAICS 312130]

Dell Inc., pp. Vol. II-1238, 1252, Vol. III-2211 [NAICS 334111, 334119, 454113]

Delmarva Millwork Corp., p. III-1782 [NAICS 423310]

Delnetics Inc., p. II-1302 [NAICS 334416]

DeLong Company Inc., pp. Vol. III-1958, 1991 [NAICS 424510, 424910]

DeLong Sportswear Inc., pp. Vol. I-279, 290 [NAICS 31523M, 31599M]

DeLonghi America Inc., p. III-1835 [NAICS 423620]

Delphi Corp., p. II-1551 [NAICS 336399]

Delroyd Worm Gear Products, p. II-1162 [NAICS 333612]

Delta Apparel Inc., pp. Vol. I-262, Vol. III-1913 [NAICS 31519M, 424310]

Delta Brands Inc., p. II-1152 [NAICS 333518]

Delta Colours Inc., p. III-1971 [NAICS 424690]

Delta Controls Inc., p. II-1342 [NAICS 334514]

Delta Design Inc., p. II-1347 [NAICS 334515]

Delta Engineering Corp., p. II-1589 [NAICS 336611]

Delta Faucet Co., p. II-974 [NAICS 332913]

Delta Foremost Chemical Corp., p. I-566 [NAICS 32561M]

Delta Galil USA, p. III-1919 [NAICS 424330]

Delta Gypsum Inc., p. III-1786 [NAICS 423320]

Delta Industries, p. II-1562 [NAICS 336412]

Delta Marine Industries Inc., p. II-1594 [NAICS 336612]

Delta Mold Inc., p. II-1119 [NAICS 333511]

Delta Oil Mill, p. I-31 [NAICS 31122N]

Delta Pacific Activewear Inc., pp. Vol. I-262, 267 [NAICS 31519M, 31521M]

Delta Petroleum Company Inc., pp. Vol. I-458, 463 [NAICS 324191, 324199]

Delta Plastics Inc., p. II-928 [NAICS 33243M]

Delta Pride Catfish Inc., p. I-110 [NAICS 31171M]

Delta Rubber Company Inc., p. I-665 [NAICS 326220]

Delta Scientific Corp., pp. Vol. II-939, 1342 [NAICS 33261M, 334514]

Delta Star Inc., p. II-1421 [NAICS 335311]

Delta Systems Inc., p. II-1432 [NAICS 335313]

Delta Tau Data Systems, p. II-1312 [NAICS 334418]

Delta Technical Coatings Inc., p. II-1714 [NAICS 33994M]

Delta Truss Inc., p. I-329 [NAICS 32121P]

Delta-V Ceramic Technologies, p. I-686 [NAICS 327113]

Delta Woodside Industries Inc., pp. Vol. I-198, 218, 272, 285, 290 [NAICS 313210, 31331M, 31522M, 31529M, 31599M]

Deltrol Controls, p. II-1362 [NAICS 334518]

Deluxe Corp., pp. Vol. I-420, Vol. II-1714 [NAICS 32311M, 33994M]

Deluxe Homes of P.A., p. I-353 [NAICS 321992]

Deluxe Office System Inc., p. III-1801 [NAICS 423420]

Demag Cranes & Components, p. II-1194 [NAICS 33392M]

Demco Products Inc., p. I-830 [NAICS 33142M]

Demeter Inc., p. III-1958 [NAICS 424510]

Demmer Corp., p. II-1541 [NAICS 336370]

DeMoulas Super Markets Inc., p. III-2076 [NAICS 445110]

DeMoulin Brothers and Co., p. I-285 [NAICS 31529M]

Den Hartog Industries Inc., pp. Vol. II-923, 1023 [NAICS 332420, 333111]

Den-Mat Corp., pp. Vol. I-566, 575, Vol. II-1682 [NAICS 32561M, 325620, 339114]

Denco Division Belcam, p. III-1843 [NAICS 423710]

Denison Hydraulics Inc., p. II-1157 [NAICS 333611]

Dennen Steel Corp., p. I-793 [NAICS 33122M]

Dennis Paper and Food Service, p. III-1875 [NAICS 423850]

Densitron Corp., p. II-1427 [NAICS 335312]

DENSO Mfg Tennessee Inc., pp. Vol. II-1347, 1437, 1512, 1551 [NAICS 334515, 335314, 33632M, 336399]

Dent Supply Neyteck, pp. Vol. II-1666, 1682 [NAICS 339111, 339114]

Dental Art Laboratories Inc., p. II-1692 [NAICS 339116]

Dental Arts Laboratory Inc., p. II-1682 [NAICS 339114]

Dentalez Inc., p. II-1682 [NAICS 339114]

DENTSPLY International Inc., pp. Vol. II-1671, 1676, 1682 [NAICS 339112, 339113, 339114]

DENTSPLY Rinn, pp. Vol. II-1357, 1682 [NAICS 334517, 339114]

Denver Fabrication Inc., p. III-1790 [NAICS 423330]

Denver Instrument Company Inc., p. II-1666 [NAICS 339111]

Denver Merchandise Mart, p. III-1894 [NAICS 423940]

Department 56 Inc., pp. Vol. I-681, 713 [NAICS 327112, 327212]

Depco Pump Company Inc., p. II-1179 [NAICS 333911]

Dependable Bagging Company, pp. Vol. I-703, 752 [NAICS 32712N, 327420]

Dependable Furniture Mfg Co., p. II-1616 [NAICS 337121]

Derby Cellular Products Inc., p. II-1725 [NAICS 339991]

Derby Computer Superstore, pp. Vol. III-2054, 2058 [NAICS 443112, 443120]

Derby Industries L.L.C., p. II-1749 [NAICS 339999]

Derecktor Shipyard Inc., p. II-1589 [NAICS 336611]

Deringer-Ney Inc., p. II-958 [NAICS 332722]

Numbers following p. or pp. are page references. Roman numerals indicate volume numbers. Bracketed items indicate industries. Page references are to the starting pages of company tables.

2329

DeRoyal Textile Inc., p. I-198 [NAICS 313210]

Derr Flooring Co., p. III-1778 [NAICS 423220]

Derrick Corp., p. II-1039 [NAICS 33313M]

Derse Inc., p. II-1720 [NAICS 339950]

Dervey Distributing Company Inc., p. III-1855 [NAICS 423740]

Des Champs Technologies, pp. Vol. II-1101, 1397 [NAICS 333414, 33521M]

DESA Heating L.L.C., pp. Vol. II-1101, 1427 [NAICS 333414, 335312]

DESA International L.L.C., pp. Vol. II-1207, 1427 [NAICS 333991, 335312]

Deschner Corp., p. II-1519 [NAICS 336330]

Deschutes Brewery Inc., p. I-172 [NAICS 312120]

DeSears Appliances Inc., pp. Vol. III-2050, 2054 [NAICS 443111, 443112]

Deseret Laboratories International, p. I-534 [NAICS 325411]

Desert Equipment Company Inc., p. III-1786 [NAICS 423320]

Desert Plastics L.L.C., p. I-589 [NAICS 325991]

Deshler Farmers Elevator Co., p. III-1958 [NAICS 424510]

Design/Focus By Glitterwrap, pp. Vol. I-203, 306, 368, 415 [NAICS 31322M, 31699M, 32212M, 322299]

Design Institute America Inc., p. II-1632 [NAICS 33712N]

Design Veronique, p. I-285 [NAICS 31529M]

Design Video Communications, p. II-1381 [NAICS 334613]

Designatronics Inc., p. II-1168 [NAICS 333613]

DesignCraft Fabric Corp., p. III-1913 [NAICS 424310]

Designed Mobile Systems, pp. Vol. I-348, 353 [NAICS 321991, 321992]

Designer Blinds of Omaha Inc., p. II-1662 [NAICS 337920]

Designer's Choice Unlimited Inc., p. III-2041 [NAICS 442210]

Designetics Inc., p. II-1740 [NAICS 339994]

Designs For Vision Inc., p. II-1687 [NAICS 339115]

Designtech International Inc., p. II-1512 [NAICS 33632M]

DesignTex Inc., p. I-198 [NAICS 313210]

DesignWorks Jewelry, p. II-1696 [NAICS 33991M]

Desks Inc., pp. Vol. III-1774, 2037 [NAICS 423210, 442110]

Dessert Inspirations, pp. Vol. I-92, 116 [NAICS 311520, 31181M]

Destination Harley-Davidson, p. III-2021 [NAICS 441221]

DET Distributing Co., p. III-1983 [NAICS 424810]

Detco Industries Inc., p. II-1397 [NAICS 33521M]

Deters Dairy, p. III-2094 [NAICS 445299]

Dethmers Manufacturing Co., pp. Vol. II-1184, 1524 [NAICS 333912, 336340]

Detrex Corp., pp. Vol. I-480, 488, 566, Vol. II-964 [NAICS 325181, 325188, 32561M, 33281M]

Detroit Broach Company Inc., pp. Vol. II-1124, 1140 [NAICS 333512, 333515]

Detroit Heading L.L.C., p. II-958 [NAICS 332722]

Detroit Quality Brush Mfg Inc., p. II-1740 [NAICS 339994]

Deublin Co., pp. Vol. II-1014, 1168, 1530 [NAICS 33299N, 333613, 336350]

Deutsch Advanced Interconnect, pp. Vol. II-1307, 1457 [NAICS 334417, 33593M]

Deutsch Inc, pp. Vol. II-1307, 1457 [NAICS 334417, 33593M]

Deutsch IPD Co., pp. Vol. II-1307, 1457 [NAICS 334417, 33593M]

Deutsche Nickel America Inc., p. I-830 [NAICS 33142M]

Devco Corp., p. III-1867 [NAICS 423830]

Devcon International Corp., pp. Vol. I-732, 737 [NAICS 327320, 32733M]

Devil Dog Manufacturing Inc., pp. Vol. I-267, 285 [NAICS 31521M, 31529M]

Devil's Tower Forest Products, p. I-312 [NAICS 32111M]

Devon Energy Corp., pp. Vol. I-443, 463 [NAICS 324110, 324199]

Devon Precision Industries Inc., p. II-952 [NAICS 332721]

Devro Inc., pp. Vol. I-510, 609, Vol. II-1061 [NAICS 32522M, 326112, 33329N]

DeWAL Industries Inc., p. I-224 [NAICS 313320]

Dewar of Virginia, p. I-703 [NAICS 32712N]

Dewied International Inc., p. I-621 [NAICS 326121]

Dewig Brothers Packing Inc., p. III-2083 [NAICS 445210]

DeWitt Company Inc., p. I-244 [NAICS 314991]

Dewitt Products Co., pp. Vol. I-453, 727 [NAICS 324122, 327310]

Dexta Corp., p. I-505 [NAICS 325212]

Dexter Co., p. II-1413 [NAICS 335224]

Dexter Fastener Technologies Inc., p. II-958 [NAICS 332722]

Dexter-Russell Inc., p. II-886 [NAICS 33221N]

Dey Inc., p. I-539 [NAICS 325412]

DF Electronics Inc., p. II-1342 [NAICS 334514]

DF Shoffner Mechanical, p. II-1009 [NAICS 332996]

D.F. Stauffer Biscuit Company Inc., p. I-124 [NAICS 31182M]

DFG Inc., pp. Vol. II-1687, 1702 [NAICS 339115, 339920]

DFI Technologies L.L.C., pp. Vol. II-1238, 1312 [NAICS 334111, 334418]

DFS Group Ltd., p. III-2190 [NAICS 453220]

DG Nicholas Co., p. III-1770 [NAICS 423140]

DG Yuengling and Son Inc., p. I-172 [NAICS 312120]

DGSE Companies Inc., pp. Vol. III-1894, 2144 [NAICS 423940, 448310]

DH Compounding Co., p. I-589 [NAICS 325991]

Di-An Enterprises Inc., p. II-1248 [NAICS 334113]

Di Giorgio Corp., p. III-1925 [NAICS 424410]

DI-MO Manufacturing Inc., p. II-1051 [NAICS 333220]

DI-NA-CAL Label Group, p. II-1212 [NAICS 333993]

Diablo Industries, p. II-1297 [NAICS 334415]

Diagnostic Hybrids Inc., p. I-544 [NAICS 325413]

Diagnostic Medical Systems, p. III-1813 [NAICS 423450]

Diagnostic Products Corp., pp. Vol. I-475, 544 [NAICS 32513M, 325413]

Diagnostic Ultrasound Corp., p. II-1357 [NAICS 334517]

Diagraph Corp., pp. Vol. I-580, Vol. II-1714 [NAICS 325910, 33994M]

Dial Corp., pp. Vol. I-102, 566, 575, Vol. III-1954 [NAICS 31161N, 32561M, 325620, 424490]

Diamet Corp., p. I-867 [NAICS 332117]

Diamond Animal Health Inc., p. I-549 [NAICS 325414]

Diamond Chain Co., pp. Vol. I-872, Vol. II-939, 1168, 1194 [NAICS 33211N, 33261M, 333613, 33392M]

Diamond Crystal Brands Inc., pp. Vol. I-40, 44 [NAICS 311313, 31131N]

Diamond Electric Mfg Corp., pp. Vol. II-1302, 1332 [NAICS 334416, 334512]

Diamond Foods Inc., p. I-137 [NAICS 31191M]

Diamond Fruit Growers, p. III-1950 [NAICS 424480]

Diamond Packaging Company Inc., p. I-609 [NAICS 326112]

Diamond Perforated Metals Inc., p. I-825 [NAICS 331419]

Diamond Pet Foods, p. I-4 [NAICS 311111]

Diana Dee's Stationery, pp. Vol. III-2186, 2190 [NAICS 453210, 453220]

Diana's Mexican Food Products, p. I-133 [NAICS 311830]

Dicar Inc., p. I-641 [NAICS 326150]

Dichtomatik North America, p. III-1867 [NAICS 423830]

Dick Gidron Ford Inc., p. III-2030 [NAICS 441310]

Dick's Sporting Goods Inc., p. III-2150 [NAICS 451110]

Dickey-Grabler Co., p. II-1541 [NAICS 336370]

Dickirson Corp., p. I-348 [NAICS 321991]

DiCon Fiberoptics Inc., p. II-1082 [NAICS 333314]

Dictaphone Healthcare Solutions, pp. Vol. II-1077, 1347, 1381 [NAICS 333313, 334515, 334613]

Didier Aaron Inc., p. III-2194 [NAICS 453310]

Diebold Inc., pp. Vol. II-1077, 1092, 1267, 1468 [NAICS 333313, 33331N, 334290, 335999]

Diedrich Coffee Inc., pp. Vol. I-143, Vol. III-2094 [NAICS 311920, 445299]

Diehl Inc., p. I-81 [NAICS 311514]

Diehl Machines Inc., p. II-1046 [NAICS 333210]

Diehl Woodworking Machinery, p. II-1046 [NAICS 333210]

Diesel Exchange Inc., p. II-1173 [NAICS 333618]

Dieterich Standard Inc., p. II-1342 [NAICS 334514]

Dietrich's Milk Products L.L.C., p. I-81 [NAICS 311514]

Dietz and Watson Inc., p. I-102 [NAICS 31161N]

Digene Corp., pp. Vol. I-544, Vol. II-1327, 1666 [NAICS 325413, 334511, 339111]

Diggs Packing Co., p. III-1946 [NAICS 424470]

Digi-Key Corp., p. III-2211 [NAICS 454113]

Digiorgio Costantini Partnership, p. III-1809 [NAICS 423440]

Digit Professional, p. II-1272 [NAICS 334310]

Digital Angel Corp., p. III-1909 [NAICS 424210]

Digital Excellence Inc., p. II-1381 [NAICS 334613]

Digital Recorders Inc., p. II-1272 [NAICS 334310]

Digital Storage Inc., p. III-1805 [NAICS 423430]

Digital Systems Corp., p. II-1238 [NAICS 334111]

Digital Video Services, p. II-1381 [NAICS 334613]

Numbers following p. or pp. are page references. Roman numerals indicate volume numbers. Bracketed items indicate industries. Page references are to the starting pages of company tables.

Digital Video Systems Inc., pp. Vol. II-1262, 1272 [NAICS 334220, 334310]

Digitec, p. II-1342 [NAICS 334514]

Digitek Computer Products Inc., p. III-1901 [NAICS 424120]

Digitron Electronics, p. II-1248 [NAICS 334113]

Dillard's Inc., p. III-2171 [NAICS 452111]

Dillman and Upton Inc., p. III-1794 [NAICS 423390]

Dillon Cross Tire Inc., p. III-1766 [NAICS 423130]

Dillon Yarn Corp., pp. Vol. I-192, 251 [NAICS 31311M, 314999]

Dilusso Baking, p. III-2089 [NAICS 445291]

DiMare Brothers Inc., p. III-1950 [NAICS 424480]

DiMare Florida, p. III-1950 [NAICS 424480]

Dimas North America Target Div., pp. Vol. I-448, 699, Vol. II-892, 1124, 1207 [NAICS 324121, 327123, 33221P, 333512, 333991]

DIMON Inc., p. III-2001 [NAICS 424940]

Dinastia International Corp., p. III-2058 [NAICS 443120]

Dingley Press, p. I-436 [NAICS 32312M]

Dinstuhl's Candies, p. III-2092 [NAICS 445292]

Diodes Inc., p. III-1839 [NAICS 423690]

Dionex Corp., pp. Vol. II-1337, 1352 [NAICS 334513, 334516]

Dioptics Medical Products Inc., p. II-1687 [NAICS 339115]

Diosynth Inc., p. I-480 [NAICS 325181]

Dippin' Dots Inc., p. I-92 [NAICS 311520]

Direct Mail Express Inc., p. I-436 [NAICS 32312M]

Directed Electronics Inc., p. III-1835 [NAICS 423620]

DISC Inc., p. II-1243 [NAICS 334112]

Disco Azteca Distributors Inc., p. III-2168 [NAICS 451220]

Discount City Home Center, p. III-2037 [NAICS 442110]

Discount Drug Mart Inc., p. III-2100 [NAICS 446110]

Discount Labels Inc., p. II-1714 [NAICS 33994M]

Discount Tire Co., pp. Vol. III-2030, 2211 [NAICS 441310, 454113]

Discovery Auto Parts Inc., p. III-1770 [NAICS 423140]

Discovery Communications Inc., p. III-2190 [NAICS 453220]

Disguise Inc., pp. Vol. I-285, 290 [NAICS 31529M, 31599M]

Dispatch Consumer Services Inc., p. I-420 [NAICS 32311M]

Dispersion Specialties Inc., p. I-580 [NAICS 325910]

Display Pack Inc., pp. Vol. I-403, 609 [NAICS 32223M, 326112]

Display Systems Inc., p. II-1720 [NAICS 339950]

Disston Co., pp. Vol. II-892, 1140 [NAICS 33221P, 333515]

Disston Precision Inc., p. I-830 [NAICS 33142M]

Distinctive Industries, pp. Vol. I-198, Vol. II-1536 [NAICS 313210, 336360]

Distinctive Marble Inc., p. I-762 [NAICS 327991]

Distribution International, pp. Vol. III-1790, 1871 [NAICS 423330, 423840]

Distribution Plus Inc., p. III-1954 [NAICS 424490]

Distribution Systems of America, p. III-1995 [NAICS 424920]

Distributors Warehouse Inc., p. III-2030 [NAICS 441310]

District Petroleum Products Inc., pp. Vol. III-1975, 2030, 2116 [NAICS 424710, 441310, 447110]

Dive Shop Inc., p. III-2150 [NAICS 451110]

Diversapack L.L.C., p. I-615 [NAICS 326113]

Diversi-Plast Products, pp. Vol. I-615, 631 [NAICS 326113, 326130]

Diversified Business Solutions Inc., p. III-1801 [NAICS 423420]

Diversified Chemical Technologies, p. I-458 [NAICS 324191]

Diversified CPC International, p. I-471 [NAICS 325120]

Diversified Diagnostic Products, p. II-1357 [NAICS 334517]

Diversified Flock Products Inc., pp. Vol. I-218, 224 [NAICS 31331M, 313320]

Diversified Foods & Seasonings, p. I-152 [NAICS 31194M]

Diversified Group Inc., pp. Vol. II-1092, 1589 [NAICS 33331N, 336611]

Diversified Heat Transfer Inc., p. II-918 [NAICS 332410]

Diversified Manufacturing Corp., pp. Vol. I-566, 575 [NAICS 32561M, 325620]

Diversified Systems Inc., p. II-1282 [NAICS 334412]

Diversified Traffic Products Inc., p. II-1451 [NAICS 33592M]

Divine Brothers Co., p. I-756 [NAICS 327910]

Dix Metals Inc., p. I-713 [NAICS 327212]

Dixie Brewing Company Inc., p. I-172 [NAICS 312120]

Dixie Building Supplies Inc., p. III-1790 [NAICS 423330]

Dixie Chili Inc., p. III-2094 [NAICS 445299]

Dixie Chopper, p. II-1028 [NAICS 333112]

Dixie Color Lab L.L.C., p. III-2062 [NAICS 443130]

Dixie Cut Stone and Marble Inc., pp. Vol. I-737, 762 [NAICS 32733M, 327991]

Dixie Dew Products Company Inc., p. I-81 [NAICS 311514]

Dixie Group Inc., pp. Vol. I-192, 229 [NAICS 31311M, 314110]

Dixie Sales Company Inc., p. III-1863 [NAICS 423820]

Dixie Seal and Stamp Inc., p. II-1714 [NAICS 33994M]

Dixien L.L.C., p. II-1134 [NAICS 333514]

Dixon Midland Lighting Co., p. III-1831 [NAICS 423610]

Dixon Ticonderoga Co., pp. Vol. I-458, 767, Vol. II-1714 [NAICS 324191, 327992, 33994M]

Dixon Valve and Coupling Co., pp. Vol. II-933, 980, 1009 [NAICS 332510, 33291N, 332996]

dj Orthopedics Inc., p. II-1676 [NAICS 339113]

DL French Company Inc., p. II-1051 [NAICS 333220]

DL Geary Brewing Company Inc., p. I-172 [NAICS 312120]

DLH Industries Inc., pp. Vol. I-510, 621 [NAICS 32522M, 326121]

D.M. Industries Ltd., p. II-1702 [NAICS 339920]

DM Merchandising Inc., p. III-1894 [NAICS 423940]

DME Corp., pp. Vol. II-1327, 1390, 1567 [NAICS 334511, 33512M, 336413]

DMG Equipment, p. I-448 [NAICS 324121]

DMI Furniture Inc., pp. Vol. II-1621, 1650 [NAICS 337122, 33721N]

DMV Stainless USA Inc., p. I-788 [NAICS 331210]

DNE World Fruit Sales Inc., p. III-1950 [NAICS 424480]

DNP America Inc., p. II-1381 [NAICS 334613]

Do It Best Corp., p. III-2065 [NAICS 444100]

Doable Products Inc., p. II-1644 [NAICS 337215]

DoAll Co., pp. Vol. III-1867, 1871 [NAICS 423830, 423840]

DoAll Industrial Supply, p. III-1843 [NAICS 423710]

Doane Pet Care Co., pp. Vol. I-4, 9 [NAICS 311111, 311119]

Doane Pet Care Inc., p. I-4 [NAICS 311111]

Dobbs, Arvin John, p. III-2050 [NAICS 443111]

Dober Chemical Corp., p. I-493 [NAICS 32519M]

Doble Engineering Company Inc., p. II-1352 [NAICS 334516]

Document Imaging Systems Corp., p. III-2186 [NAICS 453210]

DocuSource Inc., p. III-1801 [NAICS 423420]

Dodd Camera and Video, p. III-2062 [NAICS 443130]

Dodge-Regupol Inc., pp. Vol. I-229, 358, Vol. II-1725 [NAICS 314110, 321999, 339991]

Dodge Rockwell Automation, pp. Vol. I-872, Vol. II-1162, 1168 [NAICS 33211N, 333612, 333613]

Dodgen Industries Inc., pp. Vol. I-348, Vol. II-1500 [NAICS 321991, 336214]

Doe Run Resources Corp., p. I-807 [NAICS 331314]

Doeco Inc., p. III-1770 [NAICS 423140]

Dolby Laboratories Inc., pp. Vol. II-1267, 1317 [NAICS 334290, 334419]

Dolco Packaging, pp. Vol. I-609, 636 [NAICS 326112, 326140]

Dole and Bailey Inc., pp. Vol. III-1943, 1946, 1954 [NAICS 424460, 424470, 424490]

Dole Food Company Inc., pp. Vol. I-68, 137 [NAICS 31142M, 31191M]

Dole Packaged Frozen Food Inc., p. I-62 [NAICS 31141M]

Dole Refrigerating Co., p. II-1546 [NAICS 336391]

Dollar General Corp., pp. Vol. III-2047, 2132, 2180 [NAICS 442299, 448140, 452990]

Dollar Tree Stores Inc., p. III-2180 [NAICS 452990]

Dolle's Candyland Inc., pp. Vol. I-52, 57 [NAICS 311330, 311340]

Dolly Inc., p. I-239 [NAICS 31491M]

Dolly Madison Ice Cream Co., p. I-92 [NAICS 311520]

Dolphin Inc., p. I-852 [NAICS 33152N]

Dom-Ex Inc., p. III-1859 [NAICS 423810]

Domain Inc., p. I-4 [NAICS 311111]

Domaine Carneros Winery, p. I-177 [NAICS 312130]

Domaine Chandon, p. I-177 [NAICS 312130]

Dometic Sanitation Systems, pp. Vol. I-677, Vol. II-974 [NAICS 327111, 332913]

Dominance Industries Inc., p. I-319 [NAICS 321219]

Dominion Apparel, p. I-267 [NAICS 31521M]

Dominion Chemical Company Inc., p. I-480 [NAICS 325181]

Domino Amjet Inc., pp. Vol. I-580, Vol. II-1212 [NAICS 325910, 333993]

Domino Sugar, p. I-44 [NAICS 31131N]

Don Massey Cadillac Inc., p. III-2011 [NAICS 441110]

Don Pancho, p. I-133 [NAICS 311830]

Donahue Corp., p. II-1491 [NAICS 336212]

Donald E McNabb Carpet Co., p. III-1778 [NAICS 423220]

Donaldson Company Inc., pp. Vol. II-1112, 1229, 1332, 1551 [NAICS 33341N, 33399P, 334512, 336399]

Donatelle Plastics Inc., p. II-1119 [NAICS 333511]

Doncasters Inc, p. II-1562 [NAICS 336412]

Doncasters Inc. Storms Forge Div., p. I-872 [NAICS 33211N]

Donnelly Custom Manufacturing, p. II-1119 [NAICS 333511]

Donnkenny Apparel Inc., pp. Vol. I-279, 290 [NAICS 31523M, 31599M]

Donnkenny Inc., pp. Vol. I-272, 279, 290 [NAICS 31522M, 31523M, 31599M]

Donsco Inc., p. I-845 [NAICS 33151M]

Dooney and Bourke Inc., p. I-300 [NAICS 31621M]

Door County Coffee Inc., p. I-143 [NAICS 311920]

Door County Cooperative Inc., pp. Vol. III-1778, 2116 [NAICS 423220, 447110]

Door-Man Manufacturing Inc., p. II-1584 [NAICS 336510]

Doorway Manufacturing Co., p. I-334 [NAICS 32191M]

Dopaco California Inc., pp. Vol. I-379, 651 [NAICS 32221M, 32619M]

Dopaco Inc., pp. Vol. I-374, 379 [NAICS 322130, 32221M]

Dorma Architectural Hardware, p. II-933 [NAICS 332510]

Dormont Manufacturing Co., p. II-1009 [NAICS 332996]

Dorn Color Inc., p. I-395 [NAICS 32222P]

Dorsett Brothers Concrete Supply, p. I-732 [NAICS 327320]

Dorsett Industries L.P., p. I-229 [NAICS 314110]

Dorsey Trailer Co., pp. Vol. II-1486, 1491 [NAICS 336211, 336212]

Doskocil Manufacturing Inc., pp. Vol. I-306, Vol. II-1702 [NAICS 31699M, 339920]

Doster Warehouse Inc., p. III-1939 [NAICS 424450]

Dot Foods Inc., p. III-1925 [NAICS 424410]

Dot Hill Systems Corp., p. II-1243 [NAICS 334112]

Dot Line Corp., pp. Vol. III-1774, 1798 [NAICS 423210, 423410]

Dotronix Inc., p. II-1277 [NAICS 334411]

Doty Scientific Inc., p. II-1357 [NAICS 334517]

Double Envelope Co., p. I-403 [NAICS 32223M]

Doughnut Peddler, p. III-2089 [NAICS 445291]

Douglas Asphalt Co., p. I-453 [NAICS 324122]

Douglas Autotech Corp., p. II-1519 [NAICS 336330]

Douglas Machine, p. II-1212 [NAICS 333993]

Douglas Quikut, p. II-1397 [NAICS 33521M]

Douglass Fertilizer & Chemical, p. I-524 [NAICS 325314]

Douglass Frederick Designs, p. II-1731 [NAICS 339992]

Douron Inc., pp. Vol. III-1774, 1809 [NAICS 423210, 423440]

Dover Chemical Corp., pp. Vol. I-488, 493 [NAICS 325188, 32519M]

Dover Corp., pp. Vol. II-899, 1033, 1061, 1106, 1152, 1212 [NAICS 33231M, 333120, 33329N, 333415, 333518, 333993]

Dow Chemical Co., pp. Vol. I-475, 488, 500, 566, 626, 631, 641 [NAICS 32513M, 325188, 325211, 32561M, 326122, 326130, 326150]

Dow Chevrolet Oldsmobile Inc., p. III-2030 [NAICS 441310]

Down East Machine & Engin., p. II-1519 [NAICS 336330]

Down-Lite Products Inc., p. I-234 [NAICS 31412M]

Downey Creations L.L.C., p. III-1894 [NAICS 423940]

Dowty Aerospace, p. II-1222 [NAICS 33399N]

Doyle Equipment Co., p. III-1859 [NAICS 423810]

D.P. Associates Inc., p. II-1557 [NAICS 336411]

DPT Laboratories Ltd., p. I-575 [NAICS 325620]

Dpveen Company Inc., p. II-1056 [NAICS 333295]

Dr Bizer's Visionworld, p. III-2107 [NAICS 446130]

Dr Pepper & Seven Up Bottling, pp. Vol. I-165, Vol. III-1954 [NAICS 31211M, 424490]

Dr Smoothie Enterprises, p. I-147 [NAICS 311930]

Draeger Safety Inc., p. II-1367 [NAICS 334519]

Drafto Corp., p. II-1147 [NAICS 333516]

Drago Supply Company Inc., pp. Vol. II-1607, Vol. III-1867, 1871 [NAICS 336999, 423830, 423840]

Dragon Chemical Corp., p. I-529 [NAICS 325320]

Dragon Products Company Inc., pp. Vol. I-727, 732 [NAICS 327310, 327320]

Draka USA Corp., pp. Vol. I-793, 837 [NAICS 33122M, 33149M]

Drake Container Corp., p. I-374 [NAICS 322130]

Drake Corp., p. II-1046 [NAICS 333210]

Drake Petroleum Company Inc., p. III-1979 [NAICS 424720]

Drangle Foods Inc., p. I-76 [NAICS 311513]

Draper Valley Farms Inc., p. I-97 [NAICS 311615]

Dreamline Manufacturing Inc., p. II-1657 [NAICS 337910]

Dreco Inc., p. II-1397 [NAICS 33521M]

Dreisilker Electric Motors Inc., p. II-1162 [NAICS 333612]

Dreison International Inc., pp. Vol. II-1222, 1546 [NAICS 33399N, 336391]

Dress Barn Inc., p. III-2126 [NAICS 448120]

Dresser Flow Solutions, p. II-980 [NAICS 33291N]

Dresser Inc., pp. Vol. II-933, 980, 1009 [NAICS 332510, 33291N, 332996]

Dresser Instruments, pp. Vol. II-1140, 1332, 1337, 1457 [NAICS 333515, 334512, 334513, 33593M]

Dresser-Rand Co., pp. Vol. II-1157, 1184 [NAICS 333611, 333912]

Dresser Roots, p. II-1184 [NAICS 333912]

Dresser Wayne Dresser Inc., p. II-1189 [NAICS 333913]

Drew Foam Companies Inc., p. I-636 [NAICS 326140]

Drew Industries Inc., p. II-908 [NAICS 33232M]

Drexel Chemical Co., p. I-529 [NAICS 325320]

Drexel Heritage Furnishings Inc., p. II-1621 [NAICS 337122]

Drexel Technologies Inc., p. III-1901 [NAICS 424120]

Dreyer's Grand Ice Cream, p. I-92 [NAICS 311520]

Dri-Eaz Products Inc., pp. Vol. II-1217, 1397 [NAICS 333994, 33521M]

Driessen Aircraft Interior Systems, p. II-1567 [NAICS 336413]

Driggs Farms of Indiana Inc., p. I-92 [NAICS 311520]

Dril-Quip Inc., p. II-1039 [NAICS 33313M]

Driltech Mission L.L.C., pp. Vol. II-1039, 1194, 1207 [NAICS 33313M, 33392M, 333991]

DRIMARK Products Inc., p. II-1714 [NAICS 33994M]

Drinkmore Delivery Inc., p. I-181 [NAICS 312140]

Drivekore Inc., p. III-1794 [NAICS 423390]

Drives Inc., pp. Vol. I-872, Vol. II-892, 939, 1168 [NAICS 33211N, 33221P, 33261M, 333613]

DRS Optronics Inc., pp. Vol. II-1082, 1332, 1367, 1687 [NAICS 333314, 334512, 334519, 339115]

DRS Technologies Inc., pp. Vol. II-1243, 1317, 1327 [NAICS 334112, 334419, 334511]

DRT Manufacturing Co., p. II-1140 [NAICS 333515]

DrugMax Inc., p. III-1909 [NAICS 424210]

drugstore.com inc., p. III-2100 [NAICS 446110]

Drulane Palmer Smith Inc., p. I-224 [NAICS 313320]

Drummond Company Inc., p. I-463 [NAICS 324199]

Dry Creek Vineyard Inc., p. I-177 [NAICS 312130]

Dryvit Systems Inc., p. I-554 [NAICS 325510]

DS Manufacturing Inc., p. II-1599 [NAICS 336991]

DSI Toys Inc., p. II-1708 [NAICS 33993M]

DSL, p. II-1666 [NAICS 339111]

DSM Chemicals North America, pp. Vol. I-488, 595 [NAICS 325188, 32599N]

DSM Copolymer Inc., pp. Vol. I-458, 505, 595, Vol. II-1551 [NAICS 324191, 325212, 32599N, 336399]

DSM Pharma Chemical Inc., p. I-493 [NAICS 32519M]

DSP Group Inc., p. II-1262 [NAICS 334220]

DSW Inc., p. III-2141 [NAICS 448210]

DT Industries Inc., pp. Vol. II-1061, 1212 [NAICS 33329N, 333993]

Du-Co Ceramics Co., pp. Vol. I-686, 776 [NAICS 327113, 327999]

Duane Reade Inc., p. III-2100 [NAICS 446110]

Dublin Construction Company Inc., p. I-732 [NAICS 327320]

Ducane Products Co., p. II-1404 [NAICS 335221]

Ducarra Aviation Inc., p. II-1562 [NAICS 336412]

Duckwall-Alco Stores Inc., p. III-2180 [NAICS 452990]

Dudick Inc., p. I-699 [NAICS 327123]

Dudley Perkins Co., p. III-2021 [NAICS 441221]

Dudley Products Inc., p. I-575 [NAICS 325620]

Duferco Farrell Corp., pp. Vol. I-780, 793 [NAICS 33111M, 33122M]

Duferco Steel Inc., p. III-1824 [NAICS 423510]

Duffins-Langley Optical Inc., p. III-1817 [NAICS 423460]

Duffy Tool and Stamping L.L.C., pp. Vol. I-879, Vol. II-964 [NAICS 33211P, 33281M]

Duke Athletic Products, pp. Vol. I-256, 267 [NAICS 31511M, 31521M]

Dumac Business Systems Inc., p. III-1801 [NAICS 423420]

Dunaway Timber Co., p. I-343 [NAICS 321920]

Duncan Equipment Co., p. III-1871 [NAICS 423840]

Duncan Parking Technologies Inc., p. II-1342 [NAICS 334514]

Duni Corp., p. I-651 [NAICS 32619M]

Dunkin' Donuts, p. III-2089 [NAICS 445291]

Dunkin-Lewis Inc., p. III-1883 [NAICS 423910]

Dunlap Industries Inc., p. II-1735 [NAICS 339993]

Dunlo Motors Inc., p. III-2015 [NAICS 441120]

Dunlop Tire, pp. Vol. I-660, Vol. II-1599 [NAICS 32621M, 336991]

Dunn Edwards Corp., pp. Vol. I-554, Vol. III-2065 [NAICS 325510, 444100]

DuPage Machine Products Inc., p. II-952 [NAICS 332721]

DuPont iTechnologies, p. II-1282 [NAICS 334412]

DuPont Photomasks Inc., pp. Vol. I-713, Vol. II-1061, 1287 [NAICS 327212, 33329N, 334413]

DuPont Protein Technologies Intl, pp. Vol. I-26, 510, 539 [NAICS 311225, 32522M, 325412]

Dupont Teijin Films US L.L.P., p. I-615 [NAICS 326113]

Dura Automotive Systems Inc., p. II-1551 [NAICS 336399]

Dura Sales Inc., p. III-1786 [NAICS 423320]

Dura Supreme Inc., p. II-1611 [NAICS 337110]

Dura Wax Co., p. I-756 [NAICS 327910]

Durabag Company Inc., p. I-603 [NAICS 326111]

Durable Corp., p. I-229 [NAICS 314110]

Duracite, pp. Vol. I-762, Vol. II-1611 [NAICS 327991, 337110]

Durand Glass Manufacturing Inc., p. I-713 [NAICS 327212]

Durasys Corp., p. II-1248 [NAICS 334113]

DuraTech Industries, p. II-1720 [NAICS 339950]

DURECT Corp., p. I-549 [NAICS 325414]

Durham Co., p. II-1432 [NAICS 335313]

Durham Manufacturing Co., pp. Vol. II-1632, 1644, 1650 [NAICS 33712N, 337215, 33721N]

Duro Bag Manufacturing Inc., pp. Vol. I-395, 603 [NAICS 32222P, 326111]

Duro Dyne Corp., p. II-1101 [NAICS 333414]

Duro-Last Inc., pp. Vol. I-229, 453, 621 [NAICS 314110, 324122, 326121]

Duro-Med Industries Inc., pp. Vol. II-1671, 1676 [NAICS 339112, 339113]

Duro Textile L.L.C., p. I-198 [NAICS 313210]

Duroc USA, p. III-2007 [NAICS 424990]

Durol Western Manufacturing Inc., p. I-660 [NAICS 32621M]

Durr Industries Inc., p. II-1184 [NAICS 333912]

Dusek's Bakery Inc., p. III-2089 [NAICS 445291]

Dutch Gold Honey Inc., p. I-147 [NAICS 311930]

Dutch Made Inc., p. II-1632 [NAICS 33712N]

Dutch Prime Foods Inc., p. III-1946 [NAICS 424470]

Dutt and Wagner of Virginia Inc., p. III-1936 [NAICS 424440]

Dutton-Lainson Co., p. II-1500 [NAICS 336214]

Duty Free Americas Inc., p. III-2208 [NAICS 453998]

Duval Auto Auction Inc., p. III-1758 [NAICS 423110]

DVD Marketing Group, p. II-1381 [NAICS 334613]

Dvs Shoe Company Inc., pp. Vol. III-1875, 1922 [NAICS 423850, 424340]

DW Dickey and Son Inc., p. I-743 [NAICS 327390]

Dwan and Company Inc., p. III-1987 [NAICS 424820]

Dwight and Wilson Co., p. II-1584 [NAICS 336510]

Dwyer Instruments Inc., pp. Vol. II-1140, 1432, 1437, 1457 [NAICS 333515, 335313, 335314, 33593M]

Dwyer Kitchens, p. I-681 [NAICS 327112]

DX Chemical Service Co., pp. Vol. I-493, 595 [NAICS 32519M, 32599N]

DXP Enterprises Inc., p. III-1867 [NAICS 423830]

Dyecraftsmen Inc., p. I-218 [NAICS 31331M]

Dyer Fabrics Inc., p. I-218 [NAICS 31331M]

Dyer Quarry Inc., p. I-762 [NAICS 327991]

Dyke Industries Inc., p. III-1782 [NAICS 423310]

Dykes Feed, pp. Vol. I-4, 524 [NAICS 311111, 325314]

Dylon Industries Inc., pp. Vol. I-703, 767 [NAICS 32712N, 327992]

Dymax Corp., p. II-1189 [NAICS 333913]

Dyna-Empire Inc., p. II-1562 [NAICS 336412]

Dynabrade Inc., p. II-1207 [NAICS 333991]

Dynacast Inc., pp. Vol. I-852, 857, Vol. II-1134 [NAICS 33152N, 33152P, 333514]

DynaFlex of Missouri L.P., p. II-1682 [NAICS 339114]

Dynaloy Inc., p. I-560 [NAICS 325520]

Dynamax Corp., p. II-1500 [NAICS 336214]

Dynametal Technologies Inc., p. I-867 [NAICS 332117]

Dynamic Details Inc., p. II-1282 [NAICS 334412]

Dynamic Isolation Systems Inc., p. II-988 [NAICS 332991]

Dynamic Mfg Torque Converters, p. II-1530 [NAICS 336350]

Dynamix Group Inc., p. III-1805 [NAICS 423430]

Dynapower Corp., p. II-1302 [NAICS 334416]

Dynasty Apparel Industries Inc., p. I-267 [NAICS 31521M]

Dynasty Boats Inc., p. II-1594 [NAICS 336612]

DynaVox Systems L.L.C., p. II-1267 [NAICS 334290]

Dyne Systems Company L.L.C., p. II-1562 [NAICS 336412]

Dynegy Inc., p. I-443 [NAICS 324110]

Dynetic Systems Co., pp. Vol. II-1427, 1437 [NAICS 335312, 335314]

Dynisco L.L.C., pp. Vol. II-1140, 1337, 1347, 1367 [NAICS 333515, 334513, 334515, 334519]

Dyno Nobel Inc. (North America), p. I-585 [NAICS 325920]

Dyro Productions, p. III-1835 [NAICS 423620]

DyStar L.P., p. I-475 [NAICS 32513M]

E and B Paving Inc., pp. Vol. I-448, 743, Vol. II-908 [NAICS 324121, 327390, 33232M]

E and E Manufacturing Inc., p. II-1725 [NAICS 339991]

E and G Classics Inc., p. II-1536 [NAICS 336360]

E. and J. Gallo Winery, p. I-177 [NAICS 312130]

E Auto Parts Inc., p. III-2030 [NAICS 441310]

E Chabot Ltd., p. II-1696 [NAICS 33991M]

E Com Ventures Inc., pp. Vol. III-1909, 2208 [NAICS 424210, 453998]

E-Comms Inc., pp. Vol. II-1252, 1257, 1267 [NAICS 334119, 334210, 334290]

E Excel International Inc., p. I-534 [NAICS 325411]

E-Z-EM Inc., p. I-544 [NAICS 325413]

EA Pedersen Co., p. II-1432 [NAICS 335313]

EA Sween Deli Express, p. I-158 [NAICS 31199M]

EAB Industries, p. II-1740 [NAICS 339994]

EAC Corp., pp. Vol. II-1627, 1650 [NAICS 337127, 33721N]

EADS Barfield Inc., pp. Vol. II-1327, 1567 [NAICS 334511, 336413]

Eagle Bend Manufacturing Inc., p. II-1541 [NAICS 336370]

Eagle Box Co., p. I-626 [NAICS 326122]

Eagle Bridge Machine & Tool Inc., p. II-1584 [NAICS 336510]

Eagle Comtronics Inc., pp. Vol. II-1262, 1267, 1427 [NAICS 334220, 334290, 335312]

Eagle Creek Inc., p. I-510 [NAICS 32522M]

Eagle Glass Specialties Inc., p. I-709 [NAICS 327211]

Eagle Group Inc., p. II-1014 [NAICS 33299N]

Eagle Group Ltd., p. II-1051 [NAICS 333220]

Eagle Industries L.L.C., pp. Vol. II-1621, 1632, 1644 [NAICS 337122, 33712N, 337215]

Eagle Industries Unlimited Inc., pp. Vol. I-239, 306, 510, Vol. II-1702 [NAICS 31491M, 31699M, 32522M, 339920]

Eagle Maintenance & Janitorial, p. III-1875 [NAICS 423850]

Eagle Materials Inc., pp. Vol. I-727, 732, 743, 752 [NAICS 327310, 327320, 327390, 327420]

Eagle Ottawa L.L.C., pp. Vol. I-296, 306, Vol. II-1536 [NAICS 316110, 31699M, 336360]

Eagle Pet Products Inc., p. I-4 [NAICS 311111]

Eagle-Picher Automotive, p. II-1551 [NAICS 336399]

Eagle Wholesale L.P., pp. Vol. III-1939, 2001 [NAICS 424450, 424940]

Eagle Wings Industries Inc., pp. Vol. I-554, 879, Vol. II-1541 [NAICS 325510, 33211P, 336370]

Eaglehead Manufacturing Co., p. II-1207 [NAICS 333991]

EaglePicher Filtration & Minerals, p. I-767 [NAICS 327992]

EaglePitcher Automotive Hillsdale, pp. Vol. II-945, 1367 [NAICS 332710, 334519]

EAK Advertising, pp. Vol. II-1621, 1657 [NAICS 337122, 337910]

Earle Industries Inc., p. I-239 [NAICS 31491M]

Earle M. Jorgensen Co., pp. Vol. I-780, 811 [NAICS 33111M, 331316]

Earp Distribution, p. III-1946 [NAICS 424470]

Earth Brothers Ltd., pp. Vol. III-1950, 2087 [NAICS 424480, 445230]

Earth Color Inc. Kashan Litho Div., p. I-436 [NAICS 32312M]

Earth Tool Corp., p. II-1147 [NAICS 333516]

Earthgrains Co. (El Paso, TX), p. I-124 [NAICS 31182M]

East Bay Generator Co., p. II-1512 [NAICS 33632M]

East Central Iowa Cooperative, pp. Vol. III-1958, 1991 [NAICS 424510, 424910]

East Coast Automotive Industries, p. II-988 [NAICS 332991]

East Coast Lumber and Supply Co., p. I-329 [NAICS 32121P]

Numbers following p. or pp. are page references. Roman numerals indicate volume numbers. Bracketed items indicate industries. Page references are to the starting pages of company tables.

2333

East Coast Mill Sales Co., p. III-1794 [NAICS 423390]

East Coast Millwork Distributors, p. III-1782 [NAICS 423310]

East Coast Olive Oil Corp., p. I-26 [NAICS 311225]

East Coast Seafood Intern. Inc., p. III-1943 [NAICS 424460]

East Jordan Cooperative Co., p. III-1975 [NAICS 424710]

East Manufacturing Corp., pp. Vol. I-811, Vol. II-1194, 1486 [NAICS 331316, 33392M, 336211]

East Palestine China Co., p. I-681 [NAICS 327112]

East Pattern and Model Corp., p. I-752 [NAICS 327420]

East West Industrial Engineering, p. III-1871 [NAICS 423840]

East-West Label Company Inc., p. I-203 [NAICS 31322M]

Eastern Co., pp. Vol. I-334, Vol. II-933, 958, 1014 [NAICS 32191M, 332510, 332722, 33299N]

Eastern Computer Exchange Inc., p. III-2058 [NAICS 443120]

Eastern Decor Inc., p. III-1778 [NAICS 423220]

Eastern Fisheries Inc., p. I-110 [NAICS 31171M]

Eastern Iowa Supply Inc., p. III-1871 [NAICS 423840]

Eastern Pulp and Paper Corp., pp. Vol. I-363, 368 [NAICS 322110, 32212M]

Eastern Region of Supervalu, p. III-1925 [NAICS 424410]

Eastern Shipbuilding Group Inc., p. II-1589 [NAICS 336611]

Eastern Shore Poultry Inc., p. I-97 [NAICS 311615]

Eastern Shore Seafood Products, p. I-110 [NAICS 31171M]

Eastern Tools and Equipment Inc., p. III-1820 [NAICS 423490]

Eastland Shoe Corp., p. III-1922 [NAICS 424340]

Eastman Chemical Co., pp. Vol. I-475, 488, 500 [NAICS 32513M, 325188, 325211]

Eastman Gelatin Corp., p. II-1087 [NAICS 333315]

Eastman House, p. II-1657 [NAICS 337910]

Eastman Kodak Co., pp. Vol. I-615, 713, Vol. II-1087, 1252, 1322, 1337, 1347 [NAICS 326113, 327212, 333315, 334119, 334510, 334513, 334515]

Easton Sports Inc., pp. Vol. I-811, Vol. II-1702 [NAICS 331316, 339920]

Easton Technical Products Inc., p. II-1702 [NAICS 339920]

Easton Wholesale Company Inc., p. III-2004 [NAICS 424950]

Eastside Wholesale Supply Co., p. III-1778 [NAICS 423220]

Easy Gardener Products Ltd., pp. Vol. I-524, Vol. II-892 [NAICS 325314, 33221P]

Easy Way Products, p. I-229 [NAICS 314110]

Eaton Corp., pp. Vol. II-1437, 1551 [NAICS 335314, 336399]

Eaton Corp. Airflex Div., p. II-1168 [NAICS 333613]

Eaton Corp. Golf Grip Div., pp. Vol. II-1168, 1702 [NAICS 333613, 339920]

Eaton Metal Products Inc., p. II-923 [NAICS 332420]

Eatonform Inc., p. III-1901 [NAICS 424120]

E.B. Bradley Co., p. III-1843 [NAICS 423710]

EBAA Iron Inc., p. I-845 [NAICS 33151M]

Ebara International Corp., pp. Vol. II-1061, 1179 [NAICS 33329N, 333911]

Ebbtide Corp., p. II-1594 [NAICS 336612]

Eberbach Corp., p. I-718 [NAICS 327213]

EBG Inc., p. II-1297 [NAICS 334415]

EBI L.P., p. II-1322 [NAICS 334510]

EBM Industries, p. II-1112 [NAICS 33341N]

Ebner Furnaces Inc., pp. Vol. II-1101, 1217 [NAICS 333414, 333994]

EBSCO Industries Inc., pp. Vol. I-272, 290, 420, Vol. II-899, 908, 1001, 1644, 1650, 1702 [NAICS 31522M, 31599M, 32311M, 33231M, 33232M, 332994, 337215, 33721N, 339920]

Eby-Brown Co., pp. Vol. III-1909, 1925, 1939, 2001 [NAICS 424210, 424410, 424450, 424940]

E.C. Barton and Co., p. III-2065 [NAICS 444100]

EC Kitzel and Sons Inc., p. I-756 [NAICS 327910]

EC Styberg Engineering Co., p. II-1562 [NAICS 336412]

Ecco USA Inc., p. I-300 [NAICS 31621M]

Echelon Corp., p. II-1257 [NAICS 334210]

Echo Design Group Inc., pp. Vol. I-234, 251, 262, 290 [NAICS 31412M, 314999, 31519M, 31599M]

EchoStar Communications Corp., pp. Vol. III-1809, 1839 [NAICS 423440, 423690]

Eck Industries Inc., pp. Vol. I-852, 857, Vol. II-1134 [NAICS 33152N, 33152P, 333514]

Eck Supply Co., p. III-1831 [NAICS 423610]

Eckert TV and Appliances, p. III-2050 [NAICS 443111]

Eclipse Aviation Corp., p. II-1567 [NAICS 336413]

Eclipse Inc., pp. Vol. II-1033, 1101, 1112 [NAICS 333120, 333414, 33341N]

ECM Plastics Inc., p. I-589 [NAICS 325991]

ECM Publishers Inc., p. I-436 [NAICS 32312M]

Eco-Cycle Inc., p. I-363 [NAICS 322110]

Ecodyne MRM Inc., pp. Vol. I-879, Vol. II-918, 1009, 1106, 1217 [NAICS 33211P, 332410, 332996, 333415, 333994]

Ecolab Inc., p. I-566 [NAICS 32561M]

Ecolab Inc. Food & Beverage Div., p. III-1971 [NAICS 424690]

Ecological Fibers Inc., p. I-415 [NAICS 322299]

Econ-O-Copy Inc., p. III-1801 [NAICS 423420]

Economy Lumber Yard Inc., pp. Vol. III-1782, 1847 [NAICS 423310, 423720]

Economy Paper of Rochester, pp. Vol. III-1898, 1905, 1971 [NAICS 424110, 424130, 424690]

ECR International Inc., pp. Vol. II-918, 1106, 1217 [NAICS 332410, 333415, 333994]

Ectaco Inc., p. II-1238 [NAICS 334111]

E.D. Etnyre and Co., p. II-1491 [NAICS 336212]

Ed Kellum and Son Appliance Co., p. III-2054 [NAICS 443112]

Ed Phillips and Sons Co., p. III-1987 [NAICS 424820]

Edac Technologies Corp., p. II-1562 [NAICS 336412]

Edaron Inc., pp. Vol. I-374, 609 [NAICS 322130, 326112]

Eddington Thread Mfg Inc., p. I-192 [NAICS 31311M]

Edelsteins Better Furniture Inc., pp. Vol. III-2050, 2054 [NAICS 443111, 443112]

Edelweiss Manufacturing Inc., p. I-256 [NAICS 31511M]

Eden Foods Inc., pp. Vol. I-15, 124 [NAICS 31121M, 31182M]

Eden Oil Company Inc., p. III-1979 [NAICS 424720]

Eden Stone Company Inc., p. I-762 [NAICS 327991]

Edenton Dyeing & Finishing, p. I-218 [NAICS 31331M]

Edgar's Old Style Bakery, p. III-2089 [NAICS 445291]

Edge Industries Inc., p. II-1189 [NAICS 333913]

Edge Manufacturing Inc., p. II-886 [NAICS 33221N]

EdgeCraft Corp., p. II-1397 [NAICS 33521M]

Edimax Computer Co., p. II-1238 [NAICS 334111]

Edison Liquor Corp., p. III-1987 [NAICS 424820]

Edlund Company Inc., p. II-1397 [NAICS 33521M]

EDM Supplies Inc., p. II-1463 [NAICS 335991]

Edmar Manufacturing Inc., p. II-1129 [NAICS 333513]

Edmiston Brothers Inc., pp. Vol. III-1939, 2001 [NAICS 424450, 424940]

Edmunds Manufacturing Co., p. II-1129 [NAICS 333513]

EDO Corp., pp. Vol. II-1327, 1352 [NAICS 334511, 334516]

EDO Marine and Aircraft Systems, pp. Vol. II-1005, 1567 [NAICS 332995, 336413]

EDR/Beachwood Studios, p. II-1381 [NAICS 334613]

Edro Engineering Inc., p. II-1119 [NAICS 333511]

Edsal Manufacturing Company, pp. Vol. II-1644, 1650 [NAICS 337215, 33721N]

Educational Development Corp., pp. Vol. II-1376, Vol. III-2007 [NAICS 334612, 424990]

Educational Insights Inc., pp. Vol. II-1376, 1708 [NAICS 334612, 33993M]

EDW C Levy Co., p. I-767 [NAICS 327992]

Edward D. Sultan Company Ltd., pp. Vol. II-1696, Vol. III-2144 [NAICS 33991M, 448310]

Edward Don and Co., p. III-1875 [NAICS 423850]

Edward Fields Inc., p. III-1778 [NAICS 423220]

Edward George Co., p. III-1794 [NAICS 423390]

Edward Hines Lumber Co., pp. Vol. I-312, 329, 334, Vol. II-939, Vol. III-2065 [NAICS 32111M, 32121P, 32191M, 33261M, 444100]

Edwards and Associates Inc., p. II-1567 [NAICS 336413]

Edwards Brothers Inc., p. I-436 [NAICS 32312M]

Edwards Fruit Co., p. III-1950 [NAICS 424480]

Edwards Lifesciences Corp., p. II-1671 [NAICS 339112]

Edwards Technical Sales Inc., p. III-1879 [NAICS 423860]

Edwards Wood Products Inc., p. I-343 [NAICS 321920]

Edwin F Kalmus Company Inc., p. III-2159 [NAICS 451140]

E.E. Forbes and Sons Piano Inc., p. III-2159 [NAICS 451140]

E.E. Schenck Co., p. III-1913 [NAICS 424310]

Eemax Inc., p. II-1417 [NAICS 335228]

EFCO Corp., pp. Vol. I-743, Vol. II-1014 [NAICS 327390, 33299N]

Efficiency Production Inc., p. II-1033 [NAICS 333120]

Numbers following p. or pp. are page references. Roman numerals indicate volume numbers. Bracketed items indicate industries. Page references are to the starting pages of company tables.

Effingham Equity, pp. Vol. I-9, 15, 524, 529, Vol. III-1958, 1979 [NAICS 311119, 31121M, 325314, 325320, 424510, 424720]

EFI Electronics Corp., pp. Vol. II-1421, 1442 [NAICS 335311, 335911]

EFP Corp., pp. Vol. I-500, 609, 636, 641, 651 [NAICS 325211, 326112, 326140, 326150, 32619M]

EFTEC North America L.L.C., p. I-771 [NAICS 327993]

Efurd Machine of Mississippi, p. II-1046 [NAICS 333210]

EG and G Inc., p. II-1352 [NAICS 334516]

EGC Enterprises Inc., p. II-1463 [NAICS 335991]

EGE System Sun Control Inc., p. I-239 [NAICS 31491M]

Egenera Inc., p. II-1238 [NAICS 334111]

Egg Harbor Yacht L.L.C., p. II-1594 [NAICS 336612]

Eggers Industries Inc., pp. Vol. I-324, Vol. II-1621 [NAICS 32121N, 337122]

EH Burrell Company Inc., p. III-1770 [NAICS 423140]

EH Wachs Co., pp. Vol. II-1147, 1207 [NAICS 333516, 333991]

EH Walker Supply Company Inc., p. III-1898 [NAICS 424110]

Ehrlich, Gress and Co., p. III-1913 [NAICS 424310]

E.I. du Pont de Nemours & Co., pp. Vol. I-198, 443, 475, 488, 500, 510, 595 [NAICS 313210, 324110, 32513M, 325188, 325211, 32522M, 32599N]

Eide Industries Inc., p. I-239 [NAICS 31491M]

Eight In One Pet Products Inc., pp. Vol. I-4, 9 [NAICS 311111, 311119]

Einstein Bagels Inc., p. III-2089 [NAICS 445291]

Eisenmann Corp., pp. Vol. II-918, 1217 [NAICS 332410, 333994]

Eisner Associates Inc., p. III-2194 [NAICS 453310]

EJ Bartells, p. I-771 [NAICS 327993]

EJ Davis Company Inc., p. I-771 [NAICS 327993]

EJ Enterprises Inc., p. I-816 [NAICS 33131N]

EJ Footwear L.L.C., p. I-300 [NAICS 31621M]

EJ Murphy Co., p. II-1482 [NAICS 336120]

EJ Snyder and Company Inc., p. I-218 [NAICS 31331M]

EKCO Metals, p. III-1890 [NAICS 423930]

Eklund Appliance and TV, p. III-2050 [NAICS 443111]

El Burrito Mexican Food Products, p. I-22 [NAICS 311221]

El Dorado Furniture Co., p. III-2037 [NAICS 442110]

El Dorado Paper Bag Mfg Inc., p. I-395 [NAICS 32222P]

EL Harvey and Son Inc., p. I-363 [NAICS 322110]

El Metate Tortilla Factory, p. I-133 [NAICS 311830]

El Milagro Inc., p. I-133 [NAICS 311830]

El Paso Corp., p. I-443 [NAICS 324110]

El Popocatapetl Industries, p. I-133 [NAICS 311830]

El Toro Land and Cattle Co., p. III-1962 [NAICS 424520]

Elan Technology Inc., pp. Vol. I-681, 686 [NAICS 327112, 327113]

Elano Corp., pp. Vol. I-788, Vol. II-1009 [NAICS 331210, 332996]

Elastic Fabrics of America, p. I-213 [NAICS 31324M]

Elberta Crate and Box Co., pp. Vol. I-343, Vol. II-939 [NAICS 321920, 33261M]

Elcan Optical Technologies, pp. Vol. I-713, Vol. II-1687 [NAICS 327212, 339115]

Elcom Industries Inc., p. II-1248 [NAICS 334113]

ELDEC Corp., p. II-1457 [NAICS 33593M]

Elden Collection Inc., p. II-1657 [NAICS 337910]

Elden Enterprises, p. III-1798 [NAICS 423410]

Elder-Beerman Stores Corp., pp. Vol. III-2037, 2141, 2171 [NAICS 442110, 448210, 452111]

Elder Equipment Leasing of WY, p. III-1879 [NAICS 423860]

Elder Hosiery Mills Inc., p. I-256 [NAICS 31511M]

Elder Manufacturing Company Inc., pp. Vol. I-262, 285 [NAICS 31519M, 31529M]

Elderlee Inc., p. II-1720 [NAICS 339950]

Eldredge Lumber & Hardware Inc., p. III-1843 [NAICS 423710]

Elec-Tron Inc., p. II-1248 [NAICS 334113]

Election Systems and Software Inc., p. II-1077 [NAICS 333313]

Electric Cable Compounds Inc., p. I-505 [NAICS 325212]

Electric Fixture and Supply Co., p. III-1851 [NAICS 423730]

Electric Materials Co., pp. Vol. I-822, 830, 872 [NAICS 331411, 33142M, 33211N]

Electric Time Company Inc., p. II-1362 [NAICS 334518]

Electritek-AVT Inc., p. II-1442 [NAICS 335911]

Electro-Flex Heat Inc., p. II-1297 [NAICS 334415]

Electro-Graph Inc., p. II-1056 [NAICS 333295]

Electro Industries Inc., p. II-1101 [NAICS 333414]

Electro-Mechanical Corp., pp. Vol. I-811, Vol. II-1332, 1367, 1421, 1432 [NAICS 331316, 334512, 334519, 335311, 335313]

Electro-Methods Inc., pp. Vol. II-1327, 1562 [NAICS 334511, 336412]

Electro-Miniatures Corp., p. II-1463 [NAICS 335991]

Electro-Optical Instruments Inc., p. II-1056 [NAICS 333295]

Electro-Optical Products Corp., p. II-1252 [NAICS 334119]

Electro Rent Corporation Data, p. II-1347 [NAICS 334515]

Electro Scientific Industries Inc., pp. Vol. II-1061, 1194, 1322, 1337, 1347, 1468 [NAICS 33329N, 33392M, 334510, 334513, 334515, 335999]

Electro-Tec Corp., p. II-1463 [NAICS 335991]

Electrochemicals Inc., p. I-480 [NAICS 325181]

Electrocube Inc., p. II-1292 [NAICS 334414]

Electrodynamics Inc., p. II-1362 [NAICS 334518]

Electroglas Inc., p. II-1347 [NAICS 334515]

Electroimpact Inc., pp. Vol. II-1129, 1207, 1580 [NAICS 333513, 333991, 336419]

Electrolux Construction Products, pp. Vol. II-892, 1140 [NAICS 33221P, 333515]

Electrolux Home Products, pp. Vol. II-1028, 1413 [NAICS 333112, 335224]

Electrolux International, p. III-1835 [NAICS 423620]

Electron Coil Inc., p. II-1292 [NAICS 334414]

Electronic Assembly Corp., p. II-1317 [NAICS 334419]

Electronic Concepts Inc., p. II-1292 [NAICS 334414]

Electronic Office Systems, pp. Vol. III-1801, 2037 [NAICS 423420, 442110]

Electronic Systems Inc., p. II-1317 [NAICS 334419]

Electronic Theatre Controls Inc., p. II-1390 [NAICS 33512M]

Electronic Vision, p. II-1381 [NAICS 334613]

Electronics Boutique Inc., p. III-2058 [NAICS 443120]

Electronics For Imaging Inc., p. II-1252 [NAICS 334119]

ElectroOptical Industries Inc., p. II-1367 [NAICS 334519]

Elementis Pigments Inc., p. I-475 [NAICS 32513M]

Elenbaas Company Inc., p. I-4 [NAICS 311111]

ELG Metals Inc., p. I-807 [NAICS 331314]

Elgar Electronic Corp., pp. Vol. II-1302, 1421 [NAICS 334416, 335311]

Elgiloy Specialty Metals, p. I-825 [NAICS 331419]

Elgin Butler Brick Company Inc., pp. Vol. I-691, 699 [NAICS 327121, 327123]

Elgin Dairy Foods Inc., pp. Vol. I-81, Vol. III-1933 [NAICS 311514, 424430]

Elgin Sweeper Co., pp. Vol. II-1092, 1473 [NAICS 33331N, 336111]

Eli Lilly and Co., pp. Vol. I-9, 475, 534, 539, Vol. II-1357, 1671, Vol. III-1909 [NAICS 311119, 32513M, 325411, 325412, 334517, 339112, 424210]

Elite Lawn Irrigation, p. III-1863 [NAICS 423820]

Elite Spice Inc., p. I-152 [NAICS 31194M]

Elitegroup Computer Systems, p. II-1238 [NAICS 334111]

Elizabeth Arden Inc., pp. Vol. I-575, Vol. III-1909 [NAICS 325620, 424210]

Elizabeth Carbide Die Inc., pp. Vol. II-1119, 1134 [NAICS 333511, 333514]

Elizabeth Locke Jewels, p. III-2144 [NAICS 448310]

Elizabethton Herb and Metal, p. I-807 [NAICS 331314]

Elk Automotive L.L.C., p. II-1496 [NAICS 336213]

Elkay Manufacturing Co., pp. Vol. I-677, 780, Vol. II-974, 1014, 1106, 1611 [NAICS 327111, 33111M, 332913, 33299N, 333415, 337110]

Elkay Plastics Company Inc., p. I-603 [NAICS 326111]

ElkCorp., pp. Vol. I-453, Vol. II-1173, 1229 [NAICS 324122, 333618, 33399P]

Elkem Carbon-Keokuk, p. II-1463 [NAICS 335991]

Elkem Metals Company L.P., pp. Vol. I-803, 837 [NAICS 331312, 33149M]

Ellanef Manufacturing Corp., p. II-1580 [NAICS 336419]

Ellcon National Inc., pp. Vol. II-1524, 1584 [NAICS 336340, 336510]

Ellensburg Lamb Company Inc., p. I-102 [NAICS 31161N]

Elliff Motors Inc., p. III-2015 [NAICS 441120]

Ellingsworth Industries Ltd., p. I-374 [NAICS 322130]

Elliott Aviation Inc., p. III-1879 [NAICS 423860]

Elliott Bay Book Co., p. III-2162 [NAICS 451211]

Elliott Tool Technologies Ltd., p. II-1051 [NAICS 333220]

Elliott Turbomachinery Inc., pp. Vol. II-1157, 1184, 1337, 1562 [NAICS 333611, 333912, 334513, 336412]

Elliott-Williams Company Inc., p. II-1409 [NAICS 335222]

Ellis and Watts Inc., pp. Vol. I-348, Vol. II-918, 1496 [NAICS 321991, 332410, 336213]

Ellis Coffee Co., p. I-143 [NAICS 311920]

Ellis Hosiery Mills Inc., p. I-256 [NAICS 31511M]

Ellsworth Builders Supply Inc., pp. Vol. III-1794, 1843 [NAICS 423390, 423710]

Ellsworth Corp., p. III-1971 [NAICS 424690]

Ellsworth Ice Cream Inc., p. I-92 [NAICS 311520]

Ellwood Texas Forge L.P., p. I-872 [NAICS 33211N]

Elma Electronic Inc., p. I-879 [NAICS 33211P]

Elmar Window Fashions, p. II-1662 [NAICS 337920]

Elmco Supply, p. III-1847 [NAICS 423720]

Elmer's Candy Corp., p. I-52 [NAICS 311330]

Elmer's Crane and Dozer Inc., p. I-743 [NAICS 327390]

Elmet Technologies Inc., p. II-1386 [NAICS 335110]

Elmhurst Dairy Inc., p. I-86 [NAICS 31151N]

Elmo Greer and Sons Inc., p. I-448 [NAICS 324121]

Elna USA, pp. Vol. III-1835, 1913 [NAICS 423620, 424310]

Elopak Inc., pp. Vol. I-379, 415, Vol. II-1189, 1749 [NAICS 32221M, 322299, 333913, 339999]

Elpac Electronics Inc., p. II-1292 [NAICS 334414]

Elrene Home Fashions, p. I-234 [NAICS 31412M]

Eltec Instruments Inc., p. II-1297 [NAICS 334415]

Eltech Electronics Inc., pp. Vol. II-1282, 1312 [NAICS 334412, 334418]

Eltrex Industries Inc., p. II-1397 [NAICS 33521M]

Elwyn Inc., pp. Vol. II-1312, 1468, 1749 [NAICS 334418, 335999, 339999]

Elyria Manufacturing Corp., p. II-952 [NAICS 332721]

EMA Multimedia Inc., p. II-1381 [NAICS 334613]

Embassy Food Beverage, p. III-1801 [NAICS 423420]

Embedded Planet L.L.C., p. II-1248 [NAICS 334113]

Embrex Inc., p. I-549 [NAICS 325414]

EMC Corp., p. II-1243 [NAICS 334112]

EMCO Chemical Distributors Inc., p. III-1971 [NAICS 424690]

EMCO Enterprises Inc., pp. Vol. I-651, Vol. II-908 [NAICS 32619M, 33232M]

Emcore Corp., p. III-1831 [NAICS 423610]

EMD Chemicals, p. I-595 [NAICS 32599N]

Emerald Bio Agriculture Corp., p. I-529 [NAICS 325320]

Emerald Forest Products Inc., p. I-324 [NAICS 32121N]

Emerald International Corp., p. III-1828 [NAICS 423520]

Emerald Knits Inc., p. I-262 [NAICS 31519M]

Emeralds to Coconuts Inc., p. III-2126 [NAICS 448120]

Emergency One Inc., p. II-1486 [NAICS 336211]

Emerging Vision Inc., p. III-2107 [NAICS 446130]

Emerson & Cuming Composite, p. I-636 [NAICS 326140]

Emerson Appliance Controls, p. II-1332 [NAICS 334512]

Emerson Electric Co., pp. Vol. II-1427, 1437, 1468 [NAICS 335312, 335314, 335999]

Emerson Process Management, p. II-1222 [NAICS 33399N]

Emerson Radio Corp., p. II-1272 [NAICS 334310]

Emery Waterhouse Co., pp. Vol. III-1843, 2004 [NAICS 423710, 424950]

EMFCO, pp. Vol. II-964, 1009, 1562 [NAICS 33281M, 332996, 336412]

EMI Corp., p. II-1119 [NAICS 333511]

EMI Technologies Inc., p. II-1491 [NAICS 336212]

Emiliani Enterprises, p. III-1875 [NAICS 423850]

Eminence Speaker Corp., p. II-1272 [NAICS 334310]

Emmco Development Corp., p. II-988 [NAICS 332991]

Emmpak Foods Inc., p. I-102 [NAICS 31161N]

Empi Inc., pp. Vol. II-1671, 1676 [NAICS 339112, 339113]

Empire Art Products Co., p. II-1362 [NAICS 334518]

Empire Castings Inc., p. II-1051 [NAICS 333220]

Empire Comfort Systems Inc., pp. Vol. II-1101, 1702 [NAICS 333414, 339920]

Empire Container Corp., p. I-646 [NAICS 326160]

Empire Die Casting Company Inc., pp. Vol. I-852, 857 [NAICS 33152N, 33152P]

Empire Level Manufacturing Corp., pp. Vol. I-239, Vol. II-892, 1140 [NAICS 31491M, 33221P, 333515]

Empire New York, p. II-1447 [NAICS 335912]

Empire Optical of California Inc., p. II-1687 [NAICS 339115]

Empire Resources Inc., p. III-1824 [NAICS 423510]

Empire Screen Printing Inc., p. II-1720 [NAICS 339950]

Empire Southwest L.L.C., pp. Vol. III-1859, 1863 [NAICS 423810, 423820]

Empress International Ltd., p. III-1943 [NAICS 424460]

Empro Manufacturing Inc., p. II-1297 [NAICS 334415]

Ems Computing Inc., p. III-2058 [NAICS 443120]

EMS Technologies Inc., pp. Vol. II-1257, 1262, 1337, 1457 [NAICS 334210, 334220, 334513, 33593M]

Emsco Inc., pp. Vol. II-1397, 1740 [NAICS 33521M, 339994]

Emtech Laboratories Inc., p. I-771 [NAICS 327993]

Emulex Corp., pp. Vol. II-1243, 1252, 1257, Vol. III-1805 [NAICS 334112, 334119, 334210, 423430]

En-Fab Inc., pp. Vol. II-1157, 1342 [NAICS 333611, 334514]

En Pointe Technologies Inc., p. III-1805 [NAICS 423430]

Enabling Technologies Co., p. II-1248 [NAICS 334113]

Encon Safety Products, p. II-1676 [NAICS 339113]

Encore Development Inc., p. III-2058 [NAICS 443120]

Encore Manufacturing Inc., p. II-1028 [NAICS 333112]

Encore Medical Corp., p. II-1676 [NAICS 339113]

Encore Wire Corp., pp. Vol. I-830, 837 [NAICS 33142M, 33149M]

Encysive Pharmaceuticals Inc., p. I-549 [NAICS 325414]

Endicott Clay Products Co., pp. Vol. I-691, 699, 703 [NAICS 327121, 327123, 32712N]

Endress and Hauser Inc., pp. Vol. II-1337, 1342, 1352, 1367, 1437 [NAICS 334513, 334514, 334516, 334519, 335314]

Enerco Technical Products Inc, p. II-1397 [NAICS 33521M]

Enercon Industries Corp., pp. Vol. II-1212, 1292 [NAICS 333993, 334414]

Enercon Systems Inc., p. II-918 [NAICS 332410]

Enerfab Inc., p. II-923 [NAICS 332420]

Energizer Holdings Inc., pp. Vol. II-1390, 1749 [NAICS 33512M, 339999]

Energy Answers Corp., p. III-1890 [NAICS 423930]

Energy Conversion Devices Inc., pp. Vol. II-964, 1087, 1442 [NAICS 33281M, 333315, 335911]

Energy Conversion Systems, p. II-1512 [NAICS 33632M]

Energy Mate Homes, p. I-353 [NAICS 321992]

Energy Products Inc., p. II-1447 [NAICS 335912]

Energy Suspension, p. II-1519 [NAICS 336330]

Energy Transfer Partners L.P., pp. Vol. III-2208, 2222 [NAICS 453998, 454312]

Enersys, p. II-1442 [NAICS 335911]

EnerSys Energy Products Inc., p. II-1442 [NAICS 335911]

Enesco Group Inc., pp. Vol. III-2100, 2190 [NAICS 446110, 453220]

ENG Textiles Co., pp. Vol. I-218, 285 [NAICS 31331M, 31529M]

Engel Machinery Inc., p. II-1051 [NAICS 333220]

Engelhard-CLAL L.P., p. I-837 [NAICS 33149M]

Engelhard Corp., pp. Vol. I-475, 560, 780, 822, 837, Vol. II-964 [NAICS 32513M, 325520, 33111M, 331411, 33149M, 33281M]

Engine Power Components Inc., p. II-1505 [NAICS 33631M]

Engine Power Source Inc., pp. Vol. II-1173, 1505 [NAICS 333618, 33631M]

Engineered Carbons Inc., p. II-1463 [NAICS 335991]

Engineered Controls Intern. Inc., p. II-980 [NAICS 33291N]

Engineered Data Products Inc., p. II-1650 [NAICS 33721N]

Engineered Fabrics Corp., p. I-224 [NAICS 313320]

Engineered Machined Products, pp. Vol. II-1173, 1179 [NAICS 333618, 333911]

Engineered Storage Products Co., p. II-923 [NAICS 332420]

Engines Inc., p. II-1584 [NAICS 336510]

Engis Corp., pp. Vol. I-756, Vol. II-1124, 1140 [NAICS 327910, 333512, 333515]

Englefield Oil Co., pp. Vol. III-1975, 2116 [NAICS 424710, 447110]

English American Tailoring Co., p. I-279 [NAICS 31523M]

ENGlobal Corp., p. II-1238 [NAICS 334111]

Enhanced Laser Products, p. II-1087 [NAICS 333315]

ENI Products Group, pp. Vol. II-1262, 1302, 1307, 1427 [NAICS 334220, 334416, 334417, 335312]

Enkei America Inc., pp. Vol. I-811, 852 [NAICS 331316, 33152N]

Numbers following p. or pp. are page references. Roman numerals indicate volume numbers. Bracketed items indicate industries. Page references are to the starting pages of company tables.

2336

ENM Co., p. II-1342 [NAICS 334514]

Ennis Inc., pp. Vol. I-368, 388, 415, 420, Vol. II-1720 [NAICS 32212M, 32222N, 322299, 32311M, 339950]

Ennis Paint Inc., pp. Vol. I-554, Vol. II-1714 [NAICS 325510, 33994M]

Ennis Tag and Label Co., pp. Vol. I-368, Vol. III-1901 [NAICS 32212M, 424120]

Enodis Corp., pp. Vol. II-1061, 1092, 1106 [NAICS 33329N, 33331N, 333415]

Enogex Inc., p. I-443 [NAICS 324110]

Enova Systems Inc., p. II-1473 [NAICS 336111]

Enpath Medical Inc., p. II-1687 [NAICS 339115]

EnPro Industries Inc., p. II-1725 [NAICS 339991]

Enprotech Corp., p. III-1809 [NAICS 423440]

Ensign-Bickford Co. Trojan Div., p. I-585 [NAICS 325920]

Ensim Corp., p. III-1805 [NAICS 423430]

Enstrom Helicopter Corp., p. II-1557 [NAICS 336411]

Entegris Inc., pp. Vol. I-626, Vol. II-899, 1194, 1252 [NAICS 326122, 33231M, 33392M, 334119]

ENTEK International L.L.C., p. I-626 [NAICS 326122]

Enterasys Networks Inc., p. II-1267 [NAICS 334290]

Enterprise Automotive Systems, p. I-857 [NAICS 33152P]

Enterprise Co., p. II-886 [NAICS 33221N]

Enterprise Products Inc., pp. Vol. I-358, Vol. II-939, 1720 [NAICS 321999, 33261M, 339950]

Entrepreneurial Ventures Inc., p. III-2054 [NAICS 443112]

Environmental Elements Corp., p. II-1332 [NAICS 334512]

Environmental Inks and Coating, p. I-580 [NAICS 325910]

Environmental Lighting Concept, p. II-1386 [NAICS 335110]

Environmental Materials L.L.C., p. I-762 [NAICS 327991]

Environmental Stone L.L.C., p. I-762 [NAICS 327991]

Environmental Technologies Inc., p. II-1217 [NAICS 333994]

Envirotech International Inc., pp. Vol. III-1883, 2208 [NAICS 423910, 453998]

Envirotech Systems Worldwide, p. II-1417 [NAICS 335228]

Envision Product Design L.L.C., p. II-1357 [NAICS 334517]

Enzo Biochem Inc., p. I-534 [NAICS 325411]

Enzon Pharmaceuticals Inc., p. I-549 [NAICS 325414]

E.O. Habhegger Company Inc., p. III-1975 [NAICS 424710]

EO Schweitzer Manufacturing Inc., p. II-1342 [NAICS 334514]

E.P. Henry Corp., pp. Vol. I-737, 762 [NAICS 32733M, 327991]

EPCO, pp. Vol. II-1051, 1129 [NAICS 333220, 333513]

Epic Metals Corp., p. I-771 [NAICS 327993]

EPIX Pharmaceuticals Inc., p. I-544 [NAICS 325413]

Epoch BioSciences Inc., p. I-549 [NAICS 325414]

Epoch Corp., p. I-353 [NAICS 321992]

Eppendorf-5 Prime Inc., p. I-549 [NAICS 325414]

EPSCO International Inc., p. II-1009 [NAICS 332996]

Epson Electronics America Inc., p. II-1287 [NAICS 334413]

Equipment Concentration Site, p. III-1875 [NAICS 423850]

Equipment Sales Corp., pp. Vol. III-1847, 1851 [NAICS 423720, 423730]

E.R. Wagner Manufacturing Co., p. II-958 [NAICS 332722]

Erachem Comilog Inc., p. I-780 [NAICS 33111M]

ERB Industries Inc., p. I-267 [NAICS 31521M]

ERDCO Engineering Corp., p. II-1342 [NAICS 334514]

Erdmann Corp., p. III-1968 [NAICS 424610]

Ergon Inc., pp. Vol. I-443, 560, Vol. II-1317 [NAICS 324110, 325520, 334419]

Ergon Refining Inc., pp. Vol. I-443, 458 [NAICS 324110, 324191]

Eric Scott Leathers Ltd., p. I-306 [NAICS 31699M]

Erico International Corp., pp. Vol. II-933, 939, 958, 1457 [NAICS 332510, 33261M, 332722, 33593M]

Ericson Manufacturing Co., pp. Vol. II-1386, 1451 [NAICS 335110, 33592M]

Ericsson Amplifier Technologies, pp. Vol. II-1327, 1567 [NAICS 334511, 336413]

Erie Forge and Steel Inc., p. I-872 [NAICS 33211N]

Erie Industries Inc., p. II-1562 [NAICS 336412]

Ernest Paper Products Inc., p. III-1905 [NAICS 424130]

Ernie Ball Inc., p. II-1731 [NAICS 339992]

Ernie Green Industries Inc., pp. Vol. I-670, Vol. II-1505 [NAICS 32629M, 33631M]

Ervin Industries Inc., pp. Vol. I-756, 845 [NAICS 327910, 33151M]

Erving Paper Mills Inc., p. I-368 [NAICS 32212M]

Erway, Norman D Glass Blowing, p. I-709 [NAICS 327211]

Erwin Distributing Co., p. III-1987 [NAICS 424820]

Esam Inc., p. II-1451 [NAICS 33592M]

Escalade Inc., p. II-1702 [NAICS 339920]

ESCO Corp., pp. Vol. I-845, Vol. II-1033, 1039 [NAICS 33151M, 333120, 33313M]

ESCO Technologies Inc., pp. Vol. II-1005, 1317, 1327, 1572 [NAICS 332995, 334419, 334511, 336414]

ESE Inc., p. II-1362 [NAICS 334518]

Esleeck Manufacturing Inc., p. I-368 [NAICS 32212M]

Esperanza's Tortilleria, p. I-133 [NAICS 311830]

ESS Technology Inc., p. II-1282 [NAICS 334412]

Essendi, p. I-262 [NAICS 31519M]

Essex Brass Corp., p. II-974 [NAICS 332913]

Essex Grain Products Inc., p. III-1954 [NAICS 424490]

Essex Industries Inc., pp. Vol. II-923, 928, 1421, 1432 [NAICS 332420, 33243M, 335311, 335313]

Essick Air Products, p. II-1106 [NAICS 333415]

Essilor of America Inc., pp. Vol. I-651, Vol. II-1687 [NAICS 32619M, 339115]

Esslinger and Company Inc., p. III-1894 [NAICS 423940]

ESSROC Cement Corp., p. I-727 [NAICS 327310]

EST Co., p. I-852 [NAICS 33152N]

Estee Lauder Companies Inc., p. I-575 [NAICS 325620]

Esterline Technologies Corp., pp. Vol. II-933, 1061, 1124, 1229, 1337, 1347, 1567 [NAICS 332510, 33329N, 333512, 33399P, 334513, 334515, 336413]

Estes Inc., pp. Vol. II-1023, 1749, Vol. III-1991 [NAICS 333111, 339999, 424910]

Estes Park Brewery Inc., pp. Vol. I-172, Vol. III-2097, 2190 [NAICS 312120, 445310, 453220]

Estwing Manufacturing Inc., p. II-892 [NAICS 33221P]

ET Browne Drug Co., p. I-575 [NAICS 325620]

ETEC Durawear Inc., p. I-686 [NAICS 327113]

Ethan Allen Interiors Inc., pp. Vol. II-1616, 1621, Vol. III-2037 [NAICS 337121, 337122, 442110]

Ethel M Chocolates Master Foods, p. I-52 [NAICS 311330]

Ethyl Corp., p. I-475 [NAICS 32513M]

ETI Explosives Technologies Intl., p. I-585 [NAICS 325920]

ETI Systems, p. II-1297 [NAICS 334415]

Etienne Aigner Inc., pp. Vol. I-296, 300 [NAICS 316110, 31621M]

Etna Oil Company Inc., p. III-1975 [NAICS 424710]

Eton Corp., p. III-1835 [NAICS 423620]

Eugene Welding Co., p. I-788 [NAICS 331210]

Euphoria Chocolate Company Inc., p. I-48 [NAICS 311320]

Eureka Co., p. II-1397 [NAICS 33521M]

Euro American Trading-Merchants, p. III-1939 [NAICS 424450]

Eurojet US Ltd., p. III-1879 [NAICS 423860]

Eurokera North America Inc., p. I-681 [NAICS 327112]

Europackaging L.L.C., p. I-603 [NAICS 326111]

European Roasterie Inc., p. I-143 [NAICS 311920]

Eurostar Inc., p. III-2141 [NAICS 448210]

EV Group Inc., p. II-1056 [NAICS 333295]

Eva-Tone Inc., p. I-420 [NAICS 32311M]

Evanger Dog and Cat Food Inc., p. I-4 [NAICS 311111]

Evanite Fiber Corp., pp. Vol. I-626, 713 [NAICS 326122, 327212]

Evans Adhesive Corporation Ltd., p. I-560 [NAICS 325520]

Evans & Associates Construction, p. I-448 [NAICS 324121]

Evans & Sutherland Computer, pp. Vol. II-1238, 1248, 1468 [NAICS 334111, 334113, 335999]

Evans Cabinet Corp., pp. Vol. II-1611, 1632 [NAICS 337110, 33712N]

Evans Food Group Ltd., p. I-137 [NAICS 31191M]

Evans Industries Inc., p. II-928 [NAICS 33243M]

Evans Limestone Company Inc., p. I-762 [NAICS 327991]

Evans Lumber Co., pp. Vol. I-312, 334 [NAICS 32111M, 32191M]

Evans Machinery Inc., p. II-1046 [NAICS 333210]

EvapCo Inc., pp. Vol. II-918, 1229 [NAICS 332410, 33399P]

Evenflo Juvenile Furniture Co., pp. Vol. I-229, Vol. II-1536, 1621, 1657, 1708 [NAICS 314110, 336360, 337122, 337910, 33993M]

Numbers following p. or pp. are page references. Roman numerals indicate volume numbers. Bracketed items indicate industries. Page references are to the starting pages of company tables.

Evening Post Publishing Co., p. I-436 [NAICS 32312M]

Eventrentals, p. III-2190 [NAICS 453220]

Ever-Ready Oil Co., p. III-1979 [NAICS 424720]

Everbrite Inc., pp. Vol. II-1277, 1720 [NAICS 334411, 339950]

Everett J. Prescott Inc., p. III-1824 [NAICS 423510]

Everglades Lumber, pp. Vol. I-334, Vol. III-1794 [NAICS 32191M, 423390]

Evergreen Mills Inc., p. I-4 [NAICS 311111]

Evergreen Packaging Equipment, p. II-1212 [NAICS 333993]

Evergreen Slate Company Inc., p. I-453 [NAICS 324122]

Everhard Products Inc., p. II-886 [NAICS 33221N]

Everlast Worldwide Inc., pp. Vol. I-290, Vol. II-1702, Vol. III-1916, 1919 [NAICS 31599M, 339920, 424320, 424330]

Evolve One Inc., p. III-2001 [NAICS 424940]

Evvtex Company Inc., p. III-1894 [NAICS 423940]

Ewald Automotive Group Inc., p. III-2030 [NAICS 441310]

Ewald's Hartford Ford Lincoln, p. III-2030 [NAICS 441310]

Ewald's Mayfair Chrysler, p. III-2027 [NAICS 441229]

Ex-Cell Home Fashions Inc., p. I-677 [NAICS 327111]

Ex-L-Tube Inc., p. I-788 [NAICS 331210]

Exabyte Corp., p. II-1243 [NAICS 334112]

Exact Manufacturing, p. II-1134 [NAICS 333514]

EXAL Corp., pp. Vol. I-811, Vol. II-928 [NAICS 331316, 33243M]

Excalibur Electronics Inc., pp. Vol. III-1835, 2050 [NAICS 423620, 443111]

Excel Corp., p. I-102 [NAICS 31161N]

Excel Homes Inc., p. I-353 [NAICS 321992]

Excel Technology Inc., pp. Vol. II-1082, 1468 [NAICS 333314, 335999]

Excell Hallmark Sweet Co., p. II-1696 [NAICS 33991M]

Excellent Coffee Company Inc., p. I-143 [NAICS 311920]

Excello Specialty Co., p. I-388 [NAICS 32222N]

Excelpro Inc., p. I-81 [NAICS 311514]

Excelsior Mfg Supply Corp., pp. Vol. II-1101, 1106, 1112 [NAICS 333414, 333415, 33341N]

Excelsior Packaging Group, p. I-603 [NAICS 326111]

Excelso Coffee Co., p. I-143 [NAICS 311920]

Excimer Laser Systems Inc., p. II-1056 [NAICS 333295]

Executive Aviation Services Inc., p. III-1879 [NAICS 423860]

Executive Coach Builders Inc., pp. Vol. II-1496, 1607 [NAICS 336213, 336999]

Exercare Corp., p. III-1883 [NAICS 423910]

EXFO Burleigh Products Group, pp. Vol. II-1082, 1352, 1666 [NAICS 333314, 334516, 339111]

Exhibit Works Inc., p. II-1720 [NAICS 339950]

Exide Technologies, pp. Vol. II-1442, 1447 [NAICS 335911, 335912]

Exmark Manufacturing Inc., p. II-1028 [NAICS 333112]

Exopack, p. I-603 [NAICS 326111]

Exotic Automation and Supply, p. I-665 [NAICS 326220]

Experimental Applied Sciences, p. III-1909 [NAICS 424210]

Explorer Vans Co., p. II-1496 [NAICS 336213]

Express L.L.C., p. III-2126 [NAICS 448120]

Express-Med Inc., p. III-1813 [NAICS 423450]

Express Media Corp., p. II-1372 [NAICS 334611]

Express Scripts Inc., p. III-2100 [NAICS 446110]

Express-Times, p. III-1995 [NAICS 424920]

Exquisita Tortillas Inc., p. I-133 [NAICS 311830]

Extended Care Support Inc., p. III-2113 [NAICS 446199]

Exterior Wood Inc., p. I-312 [NAICS 32111M]

Extol of Ohio Inc., p. I-636 [NAICS 326140]

Extreme Networks Inc., pp. Vol. II-1252, 1317 [NAICS 334119, 334419]

Extrude Hone Corp., pp. Vol. II-945, 1124, 1140, 1152 [NAICS 332710, 333512, 333515, 333518]

Extruded Fiber Inc., pp. Vol. I-192, 510 [NAICS 31311M, 32522M]

Exx Inc., p. II-1708 [NAICS 33993M]

Exxon Mobil Corp., pp. Vol. I-443, Vol. III-2116 [NAICS 324110, 447110]

Eye Communication Systems Inc., p. III-1798 [NAICS 423410]

EYE DRx, p. III-2107 [NAICS 446130]

Eye Lighting Intern, pp. Vol. I-713, Vol. II-1386 [NAICS 327212, 335110]

Eye Med, pp. Vol. III-1817, 2107 [NAICS 423460, 446130]

Eyelematic Manufacturing Inc., pp. Vol. I-879, Vol. II-1735 [NAICS 33211P, 339993]

Eyelet Design Inc., p. II-1735 [NAICS 339993]

EZ Dumper Products L.L.C., p. II-1500 [NAICS 336214]

Ez-Flo International Inc., p. III-1847 [NAICS 423720]

E.Z. Gregory Inc., pp. Vol. III-1887, 1901 [NAICS 423920, 424120]

EZ-International Inc., pp. Vol. II-1599, 1607 [NAICS 336991, 336999]

EZ Loader Boat Trailers Inc, p. II-1500 [NAICS 336214]

EZ Pivot Transfer Machine, p. II-1657 [NAICS 337910]

EZCORP Inc., p. III-2194 [NAICS 453310]

Ezenia! Inc., p. II-1248 [NAICS 334113]

Ezon Inc., p. I-458 [NAICS 324191]

EzQuest Inc., p. II-1243 [NAICS 334112]

F and A Dairy of California Inc., p. I-76 [NAICS 311513]

F and B Manufacturing Co., p. II-1512 [NAICS 33632M]

F and M Mafco Inc., p. III-1859 [NAICS 423810]

F and P America Mfg Inc., pp. Vol. II-1519, 1524 [NAICS 336330, 336340]

F-D-C Corp., p. III-1820 [NAICS 423490]

F-D-S Manufacturing Inc., pp. Vol. I-374, 403 [NAICS 322130, 32223M]

F. Dohmen Co., p. III-1909 [NAICS 424210]

F Gavina and Sons Inc., p. I-143 [NAICS 311920]

F. Hoffmann-La Roche Ltd., pp. Vol. I-534, 539, 575 [NAICS 325411, 325412, 325620]

F.A. G Bearings Corp., pp. Vol. II-988, 1168 [NAICS 332991, 333613]

Fab Art Inc., p. II-1147 [NAICS 333516]

FAB Industries Inc., pp. Vol. I-198, 208, 213 [NAICS 313210, 313230, 31324M]

FABCO Equipment Inc., p. III-1859 [NAICS 423810]

FabCon, p. II-1473 [NAICS 336111]

Fabcon Inc., p. I-743 [NAICS 327390]

Faber Brothers Inc., p. III-1883 [NAICS 423910]

Fabreeka International Inc., pp. Vol. I-665, Vol. II-1519 [NAICS 326220, 336330]

Fabric Place, pp. Vol. III-2044, 2153, 2156 [NAICS 442291, 451120, 451130]

Fabrica International Inc., p. I-229 [NAICS 314110]

Fabricated Metals Co., pp. Vol. II-952, 1173, 1505 [NAICS 332721, 333618, 33631M]

Fabricated Metals Corp., p. I-816 [NAICS 33131N]

Fabricut Inc., pp. Vol. I-234, Vol. III-1913 [NAICS 31412M, 424310]

Fabrite Laminating Corp., p. I-224 [NAICS 313320]

Fabtex Inc., p. II-1662 [NAICS 337920]

Fabulous Furs, p. III-2135 [NAICS 448150]

Facemate Corp., p. I-239 [NAICS 31491M]

Factory 2-U Stores Inc., p. III-2132 [NAICS 448140]

Factory Direct Appliance Inc., p. III-1835 [NAICS 423620]

Factory Motor Parts Co., p. III-1762 [NAICS 423120]

Factory Motor Parts Inc., p. III-2030 [NAICS 441310]

Fadal Machining Centers L.L.C., p. II-1124 [NAICS 333512]

Fagen's Inc., pp. Vol. I-324, 329 [NAICS 32121N, 32121P]

Fagerdala-PacLite Inc., pp. Vol. I-603, 636 [NAICS 326111, 326140]

Fagerdala USA, pp. Vol. I-609, 636, 651 [NAICS 326112, 326140, 32619M]

FAI Inc., p. II-1512 [NAICS 33632M]

Fair-Rite Products Corp., pp. Vol. I-681, Vol. II-1468 [NAICS 327112, 335999]

Fairchild Corp., p. II-958 [NAICS 332722]

Fairchild Industrial Products Co., pp. Vol. II-1162, 1332 [NAICS 333612, 334512]

Fairchild Semiconductor Intern, p. II-1287 [NAICS 334413]

Fairey Finishing Plant Inc., pp. Vol. I-218, 256 [NAICS 31331M, 31511M]

Fairfax Kitchen and Bath Inc., pp. Vol. III-2047, 2050 [NAICS 442299, 443111]

Fairfield Chair Co., pp. Vol. II-1616, 1621 [NAICS 337121, 337122]

Fairfield Industries Inc., p. II-1367 [NAICS 334519]

Fairfield Manufacturing Inc., pp. Vol. II-1140, 1162, 1168, 1530 [NAICS 333515, 333612, 333613, 336350]

Fairfield Processing Corp., p. I-510 [NAICS 32522M]

Fairfield Textiles Corp., pp. Vol. I-213, 218, 251 [NAICS 31324M, 31331M, 314999]

Fairhaven Shipyard, p. II-1589 [NAICS 336611]

Fairport Yachts Ltd., p. II-1589 [NAICS 336611]

Fairway Building Products L.P., p. III-1786 [NAICS 423320]

Numbers following p. or pp. are page references. Roman numerals indicate volume numbers. Bracketed items indicate industries. Page references are to the starting pages of company tables.

Faith Enterprises, p. II-1056 [NAICS 333295]

Faiveley Rail Inc., p. II-1584 [NAICS 336510]

Falcon Fine Wire & Wire Products, p. III-1835 [NAICS 423620]

Falcon Industries Inc., p. III-2007 [NAICS 424990]

Falcon Lock, p. II-933 [NAICS 332510]

Falcon Plastics Inc., p. II-1119 [NAICS 333511]

Falcon Products Inc., pp. Vol. II-908, 939, 1627, 1644, 1650 [NAICS 33232M, 33261M, 337127, 337215, 33721N]

Falcon Shoe Co., p. I-300 [NAICS 31621M]

Fall River Group Inc., p. I-852 [NAICS 33152N]

Falley's Inc., p. III-2076 [NAICS 445110]

Falls Auto Parts and Supplies Inc., p. III-2030 [NAICS 441310]

Falstrom Co., p. II-1632 [NAICS 33712N]

Family Automotive Group Inc., pp. Vol. III-2011, 2021, 2027 [NAICS 441110, 441221, 441229]

Family Dollar Stores Inc., p. III-2180 [NAICS 452990]

Family Ford Sales Inc., p. III-2027 [NAICS 441229]

Famous Manufacturing Co., p. III-1851 [NAICS 423730]

Fantasy Activewear Inc., p. I-267 [NAICS 31521M]

Fantasy Entertainment Inc., p. II-1087 [NAICS 333315]

Fantasy Inc., p. II-1376 [NAICS 334612]

FANUC Robotics America Inc., pp. Vol. II-1061, 1337 [NAICS 33329N, 334513]

Fapp Brothers Petroleum Inc., p. III-1975 [NAICS 424710]

Far Niente Winery, p. I-177 [NAICS 312130]

Farbest Foods Inc., p. I-97 [NAICS 311615]

Fargo Assembly Co., p. II-1312 [NAICS 334418]

Fargo Assembly of Pennsylvania, pp. Vol. II-1312, 1457 [NAICS 334418, 33593M]

Fargo Electronics Inc., p. II-1238 [NAICS 334111]

Fargo Glass and Paint Co., pp. Vol. III-1778, 1794, 2004 [NAICS 423220, 423390, 424950]

Fargo Tank and Steel Co., p. II-923 [NAICS 332420]

Faribault Foods Inc., p. I-124 [NAICS 31182M]

Farm Boy Meats Inc., pp. Vol. I-102, Vol. III-1925 [NAICS 31161N, 424410]

Farm Country Co-Op, p. I-524 [NAICS 325314]

Farm-Oyl Company Inc., p. III-1863 [NAICS 423820]

Farmer Boy Ag Systems Inc., p. I-353 [NAICS 321992]

Farmer Brothers Co., pp. Vol. I-143, 147, Vol. II-1061 [NAICS 311920, 311930, 33329N]

Farmer John Brand Co., p. I-102 [NAICS 31161N]

Farmer's Mill and Elevator Inc., p. I-520 [NAICS 325312]

Farmers' Rice Coop., p. I-15 [NAICS 31121M]

Farmers Britt Co-Op, pp. Vol. III-1958, 1991, 2120 [NAICS 424510, 424910, 447190]

Farmers Cooperative, p. I-529 [NAICS 325320]

Farmers Cooperative Association, pp. Vol. III-1958, 1991 [NAICS 424510, 424910]

Farmers Cooperative Co., pp. Vol. III-1958, 1991 [NAICS 424510, 424910]

Farmers Cooperative Creamery, p. I-81 [NAICS 311514]

Farmers Cooperative Dairy Inc., p. III-1933 [NAICS 424430]

Farmers Cooperative Society Inc., p. I-9 [NAICS 311119]

Farmers Elevator and Supply Co., p. III-2222 [NAICS 454312]

Farmers Elevator Co., pp. Vol. I-15, 524, 529, Vol. III-1958, 2218 [NAICS 31121M, 325314, 325320, 424510, 454311]

Farmers Elevator Co-Op, p. I-524 [NAICS 325314]

Farmers Fertilizer, p. I-516 [NAICS 325311]

Farmers Furniture Company Inc., pp. Vol. III-1774, 2037 [NAICS 423210, 442110]

Farmers Pride Inc., p. I-97 [NAICS 311615]

Farmers Rice Milling Inc., p. I-15 [NAICS 31121M]

Farmers Supply Association Inc., p. III-2208 [NAICS 453998]

Farmers Supply Coop., p. III-1863 [NAICS 423820]

Farmers Union Cooperative, p. III-2218 [NAICS 454311]

Farmers Union Cooperative Oil Co., p. III-1975 [NAICS 424710]

Farmers Union Oil Co., pp. Vol. III-2116, 2222 [NAICS 447110, 454312]

Farmers Union Oil of Kenmare, p. III-1975 [NAICS 424710]

Farmers Union Oil of Valley City, pp. Vol. III-2072, 2222 [NAICS 444220, 454312]

Farmland Foods Inc., p. I-102 [NAICS 31161N]

Farnam Companies Inc., pp. Vol. I-529, 575, Vol. II-1023 [NAICS 325320, 325620, 333111]

Farner-Bocken Co., pp. Vol. III-1939, 2001 [NAICS 424450, 424940]

Faro Technologies Inc., pp. Vol. II-1327, 1367 [NAICS 334511, 334519]

Faroh Candies Inc., p. III-2092 [NAICS 445292]

Farouk Systems Inc., p. I-575 [NAICS 325620]

Farwest Steel Corp., p. III-1824 [NAICS 423510]

Fasco Mills Company Inc., pp. Vol. I-15, Vol. III-1958, 1991 [NAICS 31121M, 424510, 424910]

Fashion Inc., p. I-453 [NAICS 324122]

Fashion Trends Inc., pp. Vol. III-1894, 2007 [NAICS 423940, 424990]

Fashion World Inc., p. III-2123 [NAICS 448110]

Fastec Industrial, p. III-1843 [NAICS 423710]

Fastenal Co., p. II-958 [NAICS 332722]

Father's Produce Inc., p. III-1950 [NAICS 424480]

Father Sam's Bakery, p. I-133 [NAICS 311830]

Faultless Starch Bon AMI Co., pp. Vol. I-566, Vol. II-892, 933 [NAICS 32561M, 33221P, 332510]

Faurecia Automotive Seating In, p. II-1536 [NAICS 336360]

Favorite Plastic Corp., p. I-621 [NAICS 326121]

Fawn Industries Inc., p. II-1312 [NAICS 334418]

Fayblock Materials Inc., p. I-737 [NAICS 32733M]

FB Johnston Group, p. II-1720 [NAICS 339950]

F.B. McFadden Wholesale Inc., pp. Vol. III-1939, 2001 [NAICS 424450, 424940]

FB Productions Inc., p. I-374 [NAICS 322130]

F.B. Wright Co., p. III-1871 [NAICS 423840]

FBF Inc., p. III-1883 [NAICS 423910]

FC Phillips Inc., p. II-952 [NAICS 332721]

FCx Performance Inc., p. III-1867 [NAICS 423830]

F.D. Lawrence Electric Co., p. III-1831 [NAICS 423610]

FDP of Virginia, p. II-1524 [NAICS 336340]

FE Schumacher Co., p. I-811 [NAICS 331316]

F.E. Wheaton Lumber Co., p. III-2065 [NAICS 444100]

Feather Crest Farms Inc., p. III-1936 [NAICS 424440]

Featherlite Inc., p. II-1491 [NAICS 336212]

Fedcap Rehabilitation Services Inc., p. II-1468 [NAICS 335999]

Fedco Electronics Inc., p. II-1442 [NAICS 335911]

Fedders Corp., p. II-1106 [NAICS 333415]

Federal APD Inc., p. II-1189 [NAICS 333913]

Federal Cartridge Co., p. II-993 [NAICS 332992]

Federal Chicago Corp., pp. Vol. I-852, Vol. II-1119 [NAICS 33152N, 333511]

Federal Flavors Inc., p. I-152 [NAICS 31194M]

Federal Forge Inc., p. I-872 [NAICS 33211N]

Federal Fruit and Produce Co., p. III-1950 [NAICS 424480]

Federal International Inc., p. III-1890 [NAICS 423930]

Federal-Mogul Corp., pp. Vol. I-857, Vol. II-988, 1168, 1386, 1432, 1512, 1551, 1725 [NAICS 33152P, 332991, 333613, 335110, 335313, 33632M, 336399, 339991]

Federal Pacific Transformer, p. II-1302 [NAICS 334416]

Federal Plastics Corp., p. III-1968 [NAICS 424610]

Federal Process Corp., pp. Vol. III-1971, 1979 [NAICS 424690, 424720]

Federal Screw Works, pp. Vol. I-845, Vol. II-958, 1124, 1168 [NAICS 33151M, 332722, 333512, 333613]

Federal Sign Inc., p. II-1720 [NAICS 339950]

Federal Signal Corp., pp. Vol. II-1140, 1267, 1473, 1720 [NAICS 333515, 334290, 336111, 339950]

Federal Wine and Liquor Co., p. III-1987 [NAICS 424820]

Federated Co-Ops Inc., pp. Vol. I-15, 524 [NAICS 31121M, 325314]

Federated Department Stores Inc., pp. Vol. III-2171, 2211 [NAICS 452111, 454113]

Federated Group Inc., p. III-1925 [NAICS 424410]

Feeny Manufacturing Co., pp. Vol. II-908, 939 [NAICS 33232M, 33261M]

Fehr Foods Inc., p. I-124 [NAICS 31182M]

FEI Co., pp. Vol. II-1061, 1352 [NAICS 33329N, 334516]

Feintool Cincinnati Inc., pp. Vol. I-879, Vol. II-1134 [NAICS 33211P, 333514]

Feiss Industries, p. II-1390 [NAICS 33512M]

Feizy Import and Export Co., p. I-229 [NAICS 314110]

Felbro Food Products Inc., p. I-147 [NAICS 311930]

Feldmeier Equipment Inc., pp. Vol. II-918, 923 [NAICS 332410, 332420]

Feldspar Corp. E P K Clay Div., p. I-756 [NAICS 327910]

Felix Schoeller Technical Papers, pp. Vol. I-368, 415, Vol. II-1087 [NAICS 32212M, 322299, 333315]

Felker Brothers Corp., p. II-1009 [NAICS 332996]

Felknor International Inc., p. III-1939 [NAICS 424450]

Fellowes Inc., pp. Vol. II-1077, 1272 [NAICS 333313, 334310]

Felters Group, pp. Vol. I-251, Vol. II-1725 [NAICS 314999, 339991]

Felton Brush Inc., p. II-1740 [NAICS 339994]

Fenco Supply Company Inc., p. III-1855 [NAICS 423740]

Fender Musical Instruments Corp., pp. Vol. II-1272, 1731 [NAICS 334310, 339992]

Fenner Drives, pp. Vol. I-665, 857, Vol. II-1168, 1432 [NAICS 326220, 33152P, 333613, 335313]

Fenner Dunlop, pp. Vol. I-244, 665 [NAICS 314991, 326220]

Fenton and Lee Confections, p. I-48 [NAICS 311320]

Fenton Art Glass Co., pp. Vol. I-713, 722 [NAICS 327212, 327215]

Fenwal Safety Systems Inc., p. II-1676 [NAICS 339113]

Feralloy Corp., pp. Vol. I-780, Vol. II-908, 945, 964, Vol. III-1824 [NAICS 33111M, 33232M, 332710, 33281M, 423510]

Ferguson Enterprises Inc., p. III-1847 [NAICS 423720]

Ferguson Metals Inc., p. II-945 [NAICS 332710]

Ferguson Supply and Box Mfg Inc., p. III-1905 [NAICS 424130]

Fernco Inc., p. II-974 [NAICS 332913]

Ferno-Washington Inc., p. II-1014 [NAICS 33299N]

Feroleto Steel Company Inc., pp. Vol. I-793, Vol. III-1824 [NAICS 33122M, 423510]

Ferrara Fire Apparatus Inc., p. II-1482 [NAICS 336120]

Ferrara Foods and Confections Inc., p. I-57 [NAICS 311340]

Ferrara Pan Candy Company Inc., pp. Vol. I-52, 57 [NAICS 311330, 311340]

Ferrari-Carano Vineyards, p. I-177 [NAICS 312130]

Ferraz Shawmut Inc., p. II-1432 [NAICS 335313]

Ferrellgas Partners L.P., pp. Vol. I-443, Vol. III-1979, 2222 [NAICS 324110, 424720, 454312]

Ferrero USA Inc., pp. Vol. I-52, 57 [NAICS 311330, 311340]

Ferriot Inc., pp. Vol. II-1119, 1134 [NAICS 333511, 333514]

Ferris Industries Inc., p. II-1028 [NAICS 333112]

Ferrite International Co., pp. Vol. I-686, 776, Vol. II-1421 [NAICS 327113, 327999, 335311]

Ferro Corp., pp. Vol. I-500, 554 [NAICS 325211, 325510]

Ferro Electronics Materials, p. I-681 [NAICS 327112]

Ferronics Inc., pp. Vol. I-686, 776 [NAICS 327113, 327999]

Ferrotherm Company Inc., p. II-1562 [NAICS 336412]

Ferrous Metal Processing, pp. Vol. II-964, Vol. III-1824 [NAICS 33281M, 423510]

Ferrous Processing and Trading, pp. Vol. I-780, 807, 837 [NAICS 33111M, 331314, 33149M]

Ferry Cap and Set Screw Co., p. II-958 [NAICS 332722]

FES Systems Inc., p. II-1106 [NAICS 333415]

Fess Parker Winery and Vineyard, p. I-177 [NAICS 312130]

Fessenden Cooperative Association, pp. Vol. III-1958, 1991 [NAICS 424510, 424910]

Festive Designs, p. I-374 [NAICS 322130]

Festo Corp., pp. Vol. II-980, 1162, 1222 [NAICS 33291N, 333612, 33399N]

Fetzer Company-Restaurateurs, p. III-1855 [NAICS 423740]

FFP Operating Partners L.P., p. III-2116 [NAICS 447110]

FFR Inc., pp. Vol. III-1968, 2007 [NAICS 424610, 424990]

FHP Manufacturing Co., p. II-1217 [NAICS 333994]

Fiber Bond Corp., pp. Vol. I-510, 641, 756 [NAICS 32522M, 326150, 327910]

Fiber Innovation Technology Inc., p. I-510 [NAICS 32522M]

Fiber Innovations Inc., p. I-510 [NAICS 32522M]

Fiber Materials Inc., p. II-1463 [NAICS 335991]

Fiber Optic Center Inc., p. III-1820 [NAICS 423490]

Fiber Resources Unlimited Inc., p. III-1890 [NAICS 423930]

Fiber Systems Inc., p. III-1968 [NAICS 424610]

Fiber-Tech Industries Inc., pp. Vol. I-510, 631 [NAICS 32522M, 326130]

Fibercel, pp. Vol. I-22, 388 [NAICS 311221, 32222N]

FiberCore Inc., p. I-713 [NAICS 327212]

Fiberesin Industries Inc., pp. Vol. I-319, 415, Vol. II-1621, 1627 [NAICS 321219, 322299, 337122, 337127]

Fiberlite Centerfuge Inc., p. II-1666 [NAICS 339111]

FiberMark Inc., p. I-374 [NAICS 322130]

Fiberoptics Technology Inc., p. II-1451 [NAICS 33592M]

Fibre Converters Inc., pp. Vol. I-374, 395 [NAICS 322130, 32222P]

Fibre-Metal Products Co., p. II-1687 [NAICS 339115]

FIC America Corp., pp. Vol. I-879, Vol. II-1541 [NAICS 33211P, 336370]

FIC Corp., p. II-997 [NAICS 332993]

Field Container Company L.P., p. I-379 [NAICS 32221M]

Fieldale Farms Corp., pp. Vol. I-97, 102 [NAICS 311615, 31161N]

Fieldbrook Foods Inc., p. I-92 [NAICS 311520]

Fields Company L.L.C., pp. Vol. I-368, 453, 493 [NAICS 32212M, 324122, 32519M]

Fieldtex Products Inc., p. I-510 [NAICS 32522M]

Fiesta Gas Grills L.L.C., p. II-1404 [NAICS 335221]

Fiesta Mart Inc., p. III-2076 [NAICS 445110]

Fiesta Mexican Foods Inc., p. I-133 [NAICS 311830]

Fiesta Tortilla Factory, p. I-133 [NAICS 311830]

Fifkars Garden Tools, p. I-665 [NAICS 326220]

Figi Acquisition Company L.L.C., p. III-1778 [NAICS 423220]

Fikes Dairy Inc., p. I-92 [NAICS 311520]

Fil-Coil Company Inc., p. II-1248 [NAICS 334113]

Filene's Basement Corp., p. III-2171 [NAICS 452111]

Filler King Company Inc., p. I-329 [NAICS 32121P]

Filmdex Inc., p. III-1798 [NAICS 423410]

Filtech Inc., p. II-1277 [NAICS 334411]

Filter Fabrics Inc., p. I-192 [NAICS 31311M]

Filter Research Corp., p. II-1302 [NAICS 334416]

Filter Specialists Inc., pp. Vol. I-239, 395 [NAICS 31491M, 32222P]

Filtronetics Inc., p. II-1302 [NAICS 334416]

Filtronic ComTek Inc., pp. Vol. II-1302, 1312, 1317 [NAICS 334416, 334418, 334419]

Financial Equipment Company Inc., p. III-1801 [NAICS 423420]

Financial Profiles Inc., p. III-2058 [NAICS 443120]

Finch Services Inc., pp. Vol. III-1863, 2069 [NAICS 423820, 444210]

Finck Cigar Co., p. I-188 [NAICS 31222M]

Findings Inc., p. II-1696 [NAICS 33991M]

Findlay Industries Inc., pp. Vol. I-198, Vol. II-1536 [NAICS 313210, 336360]

Fine Art Lamps, p. II-1390 [NAICS 33512M]

Fine Arts Engraving Co., p. II-1696 [NAICS 33991M]

Fine Impressions, p. I-403 [NAICS 32223M]

Fine's, p. III-2123 [NAICS 448110]

Fine Toners Corp., p. I-580 [NAICS 325910]

Fine Wine Brokers Inc., p. III-1987 [NAICS 424820]

Finger Office Furniture, p. III-1774 [NAICS 423210]

Fingerhut Companies Inc., pp. Vol. I-68, 615, Vol. III-2211 [NAICS 31142M, 326113, 454113]

Finisar Corp., p. II-1267 [NAICS 334290]

Finish Line Inc., pp. Vol. III-2135, 2208 [NAICS 448150, 453998]

FinishMaster Automotive, p. III-2004 [NAICS 424950]

FinishMaster Inc., pp. Vol. I-554, Vol. III-2004 [NAICS 325510, 424950]

Finlay Enterprises Inc., p. III-2144 [NAICS 448310]

Finnaren and Haley Inc., p. I-453 [NAICS 324122]

Firearms Training Systems Inc., p. II-1468 [NAICS 335991]

FireKing International Inc., p. II-1650 [NAICS 33721N]

Fireline Inc., pp. Vol. I-510, 681, 686, 771 [NAICS 32522M, 327112, 327113, 327993]

Firestone Agricultural Tire Co., p. I-660 [NAICS 32621M]

Firestone Building Products Co., p. I-670 [NAICS 32629M]

Firestone Fibers and Textiles Co., p. I-248 [NAICS 314992]

Firestone Optics Inc., p. III-1817 [NAICS 423460]

Firestone Park Dental Lab Inc., p. II-1692 [NAICS 339116]

Firestone Vineyard L.L.C., p. I-177 [NAICS 312130]

Fireworks By Grucci Inc., p. I-585 [NAICS 325920]

Firmin's Office City, p. III-2186 [NAICS 453210]

First American Printing, pp. Vol. I-420, 436 [NAICS 32311M, 32312M]

First Aviation Services Inc., p. II-1562 [NAICS 336412]

First Cash Financial Services Inc., p. III-2194 [NAICS 453310]

First Coast Supply Inc., p. III-1835 [NAICS 423620]

First Colony Coffee and Tea Inc., p. I-143 [NAICS 311920]

First Cooperative Association, p. I-524 [NAICS 325314]

First District Association, p. I-81 [NAICS 311514]

First Press, p. II-1381 [NAICS 334613]

First Priority Inc., p. I-4 [NAICS 311111]

First Republic Corporation, pp. Vol. I-110, 192 [NAICS 31171M, 31311M]

First Solar L.L.C., p. II-1101 [NAICS 333414]

First Virtual Communications Inc., p. II-1248 [NAICS 334113]

Numbers following p. or pp. are page references. Roman numerals indicate volume numbers. Bracketed items indicate industries. Page references are to the starting pages of company tables.

2340

First Wave Inc., p. III-1879 [NAICS 423860]

First Wave Newpark Shipbuilding, pp. Vol. II-1589, 1594 [NAICS 336611, 336612]

First Years Inc., pp. Vol. II-1708, 1740 [NAICS 33993M, 339994]

Firstline Corp., pp. Vol. I-395, 554, 609, 615 [NAICS 32222P, 325510, 326112, 326113]

Fischer Engine Development Inc., p. II-1473 [NAICS 336111]

Fischer Imaging Corp., p. II-1357 [NAICS 334517]

Fischer Industries Inc., p. II-1357 [NAICS 334517]

Fish House Foods Inc., p. I-110 [NAICS 31171M]

Fisher and Company Inc., pp. Vol. II-933, 1536 [NAICS 332510, 336360]

Fisher Communications Inc., p. I-15 [NAICS 31121M]

Fisher Container Corp., pp. Vol. I-395, 603 [NAICS 32222P, 326111]

Fisher Manufacturing Co., p. II-974 [NAICS 332913]

Fisher-Price Inc., pp. Vol. II-1621, 1708 [NAICS 337122, 33993M]

Fisher Scientific, pp. Vol. II-1352, 1666 [NAICS 334516, 339111]

Fisher Scientific International Inc., pp. Vol. III-1813, 1820 [NAICS 423450, 423490]

Fisher Tank Co., p. II-923 [NAICS 332420]

Fisheries Supply Co., p. III-1879 [NAICS 423860]

Fishery Products International Inc., p. I-110 [NAICS 31171M]

Fishking Processors Inc., p. I-110 [NAICS 31171M]

Fishman Supply Co., pp. Vol. III-1901, 1905 [NAICS 424120, 424130]

Fishtech Solutions Inc., p. III-2058 [NAICS 443120]

Fisk Alloy Wire Inc., pp. Vol. I-825, 830 [NAICS 331419, 33142M]

Fiskars Brand Inc., pp. Vol. I-213, 239 [NAICS 31324M, 31491M]

Fiskars Brands Inc., pp. Vol. II-886, 892 [NAICS 33221N, 33221P]

Fiske Brothers Refining Inc., p. I-458 [NAICS 324191]

Fitch Dustdown Company Inc., p. III-1875 [NAICS 423850]

Fitec International Inc., p. I-244 [NAICS 314991]

Fittings Inc., p. II-1189 [NAICS 333913]

Fitz Chem Corp., p. III-1971 [NAICS 424690]

Five Star Coorperative, pp. Vol. I-9, 15, 516, 524, 529 [NAICS 311119, 31121M, 325311, 325314, 325320]

Five Star Custom Foods, p. I-158 [NAICS 31199M]

Five Star Food Services, p. III-2215 [NAICS 454210]

FKI Industries Inc., pp. Vol. II-899, 1194 [NAICS 33231M, 33392M]

FKI Logistex Automation, p. II-923 [NAICS 332420]

FL Smidth Inc., p. II-1184 [NAICS 333912]

Flambeau Inc., pp. Vol. I-651, Vol. II-928, 1119, 1708 [NAICS 32619M, 33243M, 333511, 33993M]

Flamemaster Corp., p. III-2004 [NAICS 424950]

Flanagan Industries, p. II-1557 [NAICS 336411]

Flanders Corp., p. II-1112 [NAICS 33341N]

Flanders Industries Inc., pp. Vol. I-811, Vol. II-1632 [NAICS 331316, 33712N]

Flanders Provision Company Inc., p. III-1929 [NAICS 424420]

Flanigan's Enterprises Inc., p. III-2097 [NAICS 445310]

Flash Electronics Inc., p. II-1282 [NAICS 334412]

Flat Rock Metal Inc., p. I-793 [NAICS 33122M]

Flavorchem Corp., p. I-147 [NAICS 311930]

Fleetwood Enterprises Inc., pp. Vol. I-348, Vol. II-1496, 1500 [NAICS 321991, 336213, 336214]

Fleetwood Folding Trailers Inc., p. II-1500 [NAICS 336214]

Fleetwood Motor Homes/Indiana, p. II-1496 [NAICS 336213]

Fleetwood Travel Trailers/CA, p. II-1500 [NAICS 336214]

Fleming Companies Inc., pp. Vol. III-1925, 2076 [NAICS 424410, 445110]

Flender Corp., p. II-1162 [NAICS 333612]

Flents Products Company Inc., pp. Vol. I-575, Vol. II-1082 [NAICS 325620, 333314]

Flesh Co., p. I-403 [NAICS 32223M]

Fletcher Granite Company L.L.C., p. I-762 [NAICS 327991]

Fletcher Jones Management Group, p. III-2011 [NAICS 441110]

Fletcher Machine Company Inc., p. II-1046 [NAICS 333210]

Fletcher's Medical Supplies Inc., p. III-2113 [NAICS 446199]

Flex-N-Gate L.L.C., p. II-1541 [NAICS 336370]

Flex-O-Glass Inc., pp. Vol. I-239, 603, 615 [NAICS 31491M, 326111, 326113]

Flex Products Inc., p. I-615 [NAICS 326113]

Flex-Tech Hose and Tubing Inc., p. I-665 [NAICS 326220]

Flex-Weld Inc., p. II-1307 [NAICS 334417]

Flexcon Industries Inc., p. II-923 [NAICS 332420]

Flexfab Horizons Intern, p. I-670 [NAICS 32629M]

Flexfab L.L.C., p. I-665 [NAICS 326220]

Flexi-Mat Corp., p. I-234 [NAICS 31412M]

Flexible Flyer, pp. Vol. II-1702, 1708 [NAICS 339920, 33993M]

Flexible Materials Inc., pp. Vol. I-324, 560, 631 [NAICS 32121N, 325520, 326130]

Flexon Industries Corp., pp. Vol. I-665, Vol. II-892 [NAICS 326220, 33221P]

Flexsteel Industries Inc., pp. Vol. II-1616, 1627, 1632 [NAICS 337121, 337127, 33712N]

Flextron Industries Inc., p. II-1519 [NAICS 336330]

Flextronics International Ltd., p. II-1312 [NAICS 334418]

Flight Systems Inc., p. II-1238 [NAICS 334111]

Flightline Systems, pp. Vol. II-1238, 1262, 1327, 1337, 1437 [NAICS 334111, 334220, 334511, 334513, 335314]

FlightSafety International, pp. Vol. II-1327, 1468 [NAICS 334511, 335999]

FlightSafety International Inc., p. II-1468 [NAICS 335999]

Flint Hills Resources L.P., p. I-443 [NAICS 324110]

Flint Ink Corp., pp. Vol. I-475, 580, 595 [NAICS 32513M, 325910, 32599N]

Flint River Mills Inc., pp. Vol. I-4, 9 [NAICS 311111, 311119]

FLIR Systems Inc., p. II-1327 [NAICS 334511]

Flo Dor Manufacturing Co., p. I-699 [NAICS 327123]

Flo-Tech L.L.C., p. III-2186 [NAICS 453210]

Flock Tex Inc., pp. Vol. I-218, 636 [NAICS 31331M, 326140]

Flood Co., pp. Vol. I-493, 560 [NAICS 32519M, 325520]

Flooring America, p. III-2047 [NAICS 442299]

Flora Inc., p. I-143 [NAICS 311920]

Floral Supply Syndicate, p. III-2208 [NAICS 453998]

Floribbean Wholesale Inc., p. III-1943 [NAICS 424460]

Florida Auto Auction, p. III-1758 [NAICS 423110]

Florida Extruders International Inc., p. I-811 [NAICS 331316]

Florida Favorite Fertilizer, pp. Vol. I-516, 520, 524 [NAICS 325311, 325312, 325314]

Florida Infusion Services Inc., p. III-1909 [NAICS 424210]

Florida Plywoods Inc., pp. Vol. I-319, Vol. II-1611 [NAICS 321219, 337110]

Florida Pneumatic Mfg Corp., p. II-1207 [NAICS 333991]

Florida Quality Truss Inc., p. I-329 [NAICS 32121P]

Florida RF Labs EMC Technology, p. II-1297 [NAICS 334415]

Florida Rock and Sand Co., pp. Vol. I-737, 743 [NAICS 32733M, 327390]

Florida Rock Industries Inc., pp. Vol. I-732, 737 [NAICS 327320, 32733M]

Florida's Natural Growers, p. I-68 [NAICS 31142M]

Florig Equipment Company Inc., p. II-1530 [NAICS 336350]

Florim USA, p. I-695 [NAICS 327122]

Flory Industries Inc., p. III-1863 [NAICS 423820]

Flotek Industries Inc., pp. Vol. II-1207, 1589 [NAICS 333991, 336611]

Floturn Inc., p. II-1009 [NAICS 332996]

Flour Shop Bakery and Pizza, p. III-2089 [NAICS 445291]

Flow International Corp., pp. Vol. II-1061, 1092, 1124, 1229 [NAICS 33329N, 33331N, 333512, 33399P]

Flow Polymers Inc., p. I-505 [NAICS 325212]

Flowers Auto Parts Co., pp. Vol. III-1762, 1871 [NAICS 423120, 423840]

Flowers Foods Inc., pp. Vol. I-116, 124 [NAICS 31181M, 31182M]

Flowers Industries Inc, p. I-116 [NAICS 31181M]

Flowserve Corp., pp. Vol. I-626, Vol. II-980, 1014, 1179, 1222, 1229 [NAICS 326122, 33291N, 33299N, 333911, 33399N, 33399P]

Flowtronex PSI Inc., pp. Vol. II-980, 1023, 1179, 1702 [NAICS 33291N, 333111, 333911, 339920]

Flue-Cured Tobacco Cooperative, p. I-185 [NAICS 312210]

Fluid Components International, p. II-1342 [NAICS 334514]

Fluid Energy Processing, p. I-767 [NAICS 327992]

Fluid Ink Technology Inc., p. I-580 [NAICS 325910]

Fluid Management Inc., p. II-1189 [NAICS 333913]

Fluidic Techniques, p. II-1342 [NAICS 334514]

Fluoresco Lighting-Sign, pp. Vol. II-1390, 1720 [NAICS 33512M, 339950]

Flush-Metal Partition Corp., p. I-681 [NAICS 327112]

Numbers following p. or pp. are page references. Roman numerals indicate volume numbers. Bracketed items indicate industries. Page references are to the starting pages of company tables.

2341

Company Index

Flying J Inc., pp. Vol. I-443, Vol. III-1979, 2116, 2180 [NAICS 324110, 424720, 447110, 452990]

FM Brush Company Inc., p. II-1740 [NAICS 339994]

FM Industries Inc., pp. Vol. II-945, 1134 [NAICS 332710, 333514]

FMC Corp., pp. Vol. I-147, 488, 529, 539, Vol. II-1567 [NAICS 311930, 325188, 325320, 325412, 336413]

FMC Technologies Inc., p. II-1039 [NAICS 33313M]

FMC Technologies Measurement, pp. Vol. II-1337, 1342, 1347, 1367, 1437 [NAICS 334513, 334514, 334515, 334519, 335314]

FMC Wyoming Corp., p. I-480 [NAICS 325181]

FMF Racing, p. II-1599 [NAICS 336991]

FN Manufacturing Inc., p. II-1001 [NAICS 332994]

FN Sheppard and Company Inc., p. I-665 [NAICS 326220]

FO Day Company Inc., p. I-448 [NAICS 324121]

Foam-Craft Inc., p. I-641 [NAICS 326150]

Foam Design Inc., p. I-641 [NAICS 326150]

Foam Fabricators Inc., p. I-636 [NAICS 326140]

Foam Factory and Upholstery Inc., pp. Vol. III-2007, 2208 [NAICS 424990, 453998]

Foam Products of San Antonio Inc., p. III-2007 [NAICS 424990]

Foam Rubber Products Inc., pp. Vol. I-234, 636, 641, Vol. II-1657 [NAICS 31412M, 326140, 326150, 337910]

Foam Seal Inc., p. I-229 [NAICS 314110]

Foam Supplies Inc., p. I-641 [NAICS 326150]

Foamade Industries Inc., p. I-641 [NAICS 326150]

Foamcraft Inc., p. I-641 [NAICS 326150]

Foamex International Inc., pp. Vol. I-500, 641 [NAICS 325211, 326150]

Focal Point Architectural Products, p. II-1119 [NAICS 333511]

Focal Point L.L.C., p. II-1386 [NAICS 335110]

FOCUS Enhancements Inc., p. II-1243 [NAICS 334112]

Focus Products Group L.L.C., p. III-1809 [NAICS 423440]

Foerster Instruments Inc., pp. Vol. II-1347, 1367 [NAICS 334515, 334519]

FOF Inc., pp. Vol. III-1975, 2116 [NAICS 424710, 447110]

FOF Products Inc., p. I-239 [NAICS 31491M]

Foilmark Holographics, p. I-395 [NAICS 32222P]

Foley's, p. III-2171 [NAICS 452111]

Follett Corp., pp. Vol. II-1189, Vol. III-1995, 2211 [NAICS 333913, 424920, 454113]

Follmer Development Inc., p. I-26 [NAICS 311225]

Fomo Products Inc., p. I-771 [NAICS 327993]

Fonda Group Inc., pp. Vol. I-368, 411 [NAICS 32212M, 322291]

Fontaine International Inc., pp. Vol. II-1491, Vol. III-1794 [NAICS 336212, 423390]

Fontaine Specialized, p. II-1491 [NAICS 336212]

Fontanini Meats, p. III-1946 [NAICS 424470]

Food 4 Less Holdings Inc., p. III-2076 [NAICS 445110]

Food Equipment Technologies Co., p. II-1397 [NAICS 33521M]

Food Lion L.L.C., p. III-2076 [NAICS 445110]

Food Market Merchandising Inc., p. III-1887 [NAICS 423920]

Food Services Inc., p. III-2215 [NAICS 454210]

Food Source Inc., pp. Vol. III-1905, 1929 [NAICS 424130, 424420]

Foodarama Supermarkets Inc., pp. Vol. I-68, 102, 116, 124, Vol. III-2072, 2076, 2097 [NAICS 31142M, 31161N, 31181M, 31182M, 444220, 445110, 445310]

Foodcraft Inc., p. I-143 [NAICS 311920]

Foods of New Mexico Inc., p. I-133 [NAICS 311830]

FoodSalesWest Inc., p. III-1929 [NAICS 424420]

Foot Locker Inc., pp. Vol. III-2132, 2141, 2211 [NAICS 448140, 448210, 454113]

Foote-Jones/Illinois Gear Div., p. II-1162 [NAICS 333612]

Footstar Inc., p. III-2141 [NAICS 448210]

For Bare Feet Inc., pp. Vol. I-256, 300 [NAICS 31511M, 31621M]

Forbes Custom Products L.L.C., p. I-239 [NAICS 31491M]

Forbes Industries Inc., p. II-1627 [NAICS 337127]

Forbo Industries Inc., p. III-1778 [NAICS 423220]

Force America Inc., p. II-1222 [NAICS 33399N]

Force Control Industries Inc., p. II-1524 [NAICS 336340]

Force Electronics Inc., p. III-1839 [NAICS 423690]

Ford Motor Co., pp. Vol. I-709, Vol. II-1194, 1473, 1486, 1551, Vol. III-1758, 1762 [NAICS 327211, 33392M, 336111, 336211, 336399, 423110, 423120]

Foreign Trade Corp., p. III-2054 [NAICS 443112]

Foremost Athletic Apparel, pp. Vol. III-1916, 1919, 1922 [NAICS 424320, 424330, 424340]

Foremost Farms USA Cooperative, pp. Vol. I-76, 81, 86 [NAICS 311513, 311514, 31151N]

Foremost Industries Inc., p. I-353 [NAICS 321992]

Foresight Technologies, p. II-1056 [NAICS 333295]

Forest City Enterprises Inc., p. III-1782 [NAICS 423310]

Forest City Technologies Inc., pp. Vol. I-554, 560, 636, Vol. II-964, 1725 [NAICS 325510, 325520, 326140, 33281M, 339991]

Forest Irving Products Inc., p. I-312 [NAICS 32111M]

Forest Laboratories Inc., p. I-539 [NAICS 325412]

Forest Pharmaceuticals Inc., p. I-539 [NAICS 325412]

Forest Products Inc., pp. Vol. I-312, 343, 358 [NAICS 32111M, 321920, 321999]

Forest Products Supply Inc., pp. Vol. I-324, 329 [NAICS 32121N, 32121P]

Foretravel Inc., p. II-1496 [NAICS 336213]

Forever Living Products Intern., p. III-2228 [NAICS 454390]

Forge Recording, p. II-1381 [NAICS 334613]

Forge Recording L.L.C., p. II-1376 [NAICS 334612]

Forged Metals Inc., p. I-872 [NAICS 33211N]

Fori Automation Inc., p. II-1152 [NAICS 333518]

Forks Prairie Mart Inc., p. III-2065 [NAICS 444100]

Form Services Inc., p. III-1786 [NAICS 423320]

Forman Inc., p. III-1905 [NAICS 424130]

Formed Fiber Technologies Inc., p. I-510 [NAICS 32522M]

Formetco Inc., p. II-1720 [NAICS 339950]

Formflex Inc., p. I-615 [NAICS 326113]

Formica Samples, p. I-631 [NAICS 326130]

Formosa Plastics Corporation USA, pp. Vol. I-500, 651 [NAICS 325211, 32619M]

Formosa U.S.A. Inc., p. III-1805 [NAICS 423430]

Forms Surfaces Company L.L.C., p. II-1632 [NAICS 33712N]

Formtech Enterprises Inc., p. I-621 [NAICS 326121]

Forney Industries Inc., pp. Vol. II-1427, 1468, 1512, 1740 [NAICS 335312, 335999, 33632M, 339994]

Forrer Supply Company Inc., p. III-1968 [NAICS 424610]

Forrest Machining Inc., p. II-1580 [NAICS 336419]

Fort Bragg Rent All Inc., p. III-2190 [NAICS 453220]

Fort Fudge Shop Inc., p. III-2092 [NAICS 445292]

Fort Miller Company Inc., p. I-743 [NAICS 327390]

Fort Wayne Foundry Corp., pp. Vol. I-852, 857 [NAICS 33152N, 33152P]

Fort Worth Lumber Co., p. III-1794 [NAICS 423390]

FORTA Corp., p. I-510 [NAICS 32522M]

Forth Technologies Inc., p. I-580 [NAICS 325910]

Fortrend Engineering Corp., p. II-1056 [NAICS 333295]

Fortune Brands Inc., pp. Vol. I-181, Vol. II-933, 939, 974, 1611, 1644, 1702 [NAICS 312140, 332510, 33261M, 332913, 337110, 337215, 339920]

Fortune Fashion Industries, p. I-251 [NAICS 314999]

Fortunoff Fine Jewelry, pp. Vol. III-2047, 2144 [NAICS 442299, 448310]

Forum Lighting Inc., p. II-1386 [NAICS 335110]

Forward Corp., p. III-2218 [NAICS 454311]

Forward Industries Inc., p. I-306 [NAICS 31699M]

Foseco Metallurgical Inc., pp. Vol. II-1119, 1147 [NAICS 333511, 333516]

Foss Co., pp. Vol. III-2097, 2100, 2132, 2150 [NAICS 445310, 446110, 448140, 451110]

Foss Manufacturing Company Inc., p. I-208 [NAICS 313230]

Foss North America Inc., pp. Vol. III-1820, 1875 [NAICS 423490, 423850]

Fossil Inc., pp. Vol. I-290, 306, Vol. II-1362 [NAICS 31599M, 31699M, 334518]

Fosta-Tek Optics Inc., p. II-1312 [NAICS 334418]

Foster Corp., p. I-589 [NAICS 325991]

Foster Manufacturing Inc., p. I-665 [NAICS 326220]

Foster Poultry Farms Inc., pp. Vol. I-9, 97 [NAICS 311119, 311615]

Foster Wheeler Energy Corp., p. II-899 [NAICS 33231M]

Foster Wheeler Ltd., pp. Vol. II-899, 1061, 1157, 1217 [NAICS 33231M, 33329N, 333611, 333994]

Fostoria Factory Outlet Co., p. III-2047 [NAICS 442299]

Fotoball USA Inc., p. III-2150 [NAICS 451110]

Foundry Networks Inc., pp. Vol. II-1077, 1252, 1257 [NAICS 333313, 334119, 334210]

Foundry Systems International, pp. Vol. I-852, 857, Vol. II-1505 [NAICS 33152N, 33152P, 33631M]

Fountain Powerboat Industries Inc., pp. Vol. II-1589, 1594 [NAICS 336611, 336612]

Fountainhead Group Inc., pp. Vol. II-892, 1184 [NAICS 33221P, 333912]

Four B Corp., p. III-2076 [NAICS 445110]

Four Leaf Textiles Inc., p. I-192 [NAICS 31311M]

Four M Corp., p. I-379 [NAICS 32221M]

Numbers following p. or pp. are page references. Roman numerals indicate volume numbers. Bracketed items indicate industries. Page references are to the starting pages of company tables.

2342

Four Seasons Cooperative, pp. Vol. III-2177, 2218, 2222 [NAICS 452910, 454311, 454312]

Four Winds International Inc., pp. Vol. II-1496, 1500 [NAICS 336213, 336214]

Four Winns Boats L.L.C., p. II-1594 [NAICS 336612]

Foursome Inc., pp. Vol. III-2132, 2141 [NAICS 448140, 448210]

Fowler Bottle Gas Service Inc., p. III-2222 [NAICS 454312]

Fownes Brothers and Company Inc., pp. Vol. I-262, 290 [NAICS 31519M, 31599M]

Fox Integrated Technologies Inc., p. III-1890 [NAICS 423930]

Fox Products Corp., p. II-1731 [NAICS 339992]

Fox River Mills Inc., p. I-256 [NAICS 31511M]

Fox River Paper Company L.L.C., pp. Vol. I-363, 415 [NAICS 322110, 322299]

Fox Run Craftsmen, p. II-886 [NAICS 33221N]

Fox Valley Fire and Safety Co., p. III-1831 [NAICS 423610]

Foxworth-Galbraith Lumber Co., p. III-2065 [NAICS 444100]

FP International, p. I-636 [NAICS 326140]

FPM Heat Treating, p. II-964 [NAICS 33281M]

Fraen Corp., p. II-952 [NAICS 332721]

Fraenkel Wholesale Furniture Inc., pp. Vol. II-1616, 1657, Vol. III-1774 [NAICS 337121, 337910, 423210]

Fralingers Inc., p. I-52 [NAICS 311330]

Framatome ANP Inc., pp. Vol. II-980, 1367, 1432 [NAICS 33291N, 334519, 335313]

Framed Pictures Enterprise Inc., pp. Vol. I-358, 722 [NAICS 321999, 327215]

Francis-Mustoe and Co., p. III-1929 [NAICS 424420]

Franco Manufacturing Inc., pp. Vol. I-234, 251 [NAICS 31412M, 314999]

Frank B. Fuhrer Wholesale Co., p. III-1983 [NAICS 424810]

Frank Edwards Co., p. III-1762 [NAICS 423120]

Frank L Wells Co., p. II-1152 [NAICS 333518]

Frank Lill and Son Inc., p. III-1847 [NAICS 423720]

Frank-Lin Distillers Products, p. I-181 [NAICS 312140]

Frank Mastoloni and Sons Inc., p. III-1894 [NAICS 423940]

Frank Miller Lumber Company, p. I-358 [NAICS 321999]

Frank Moran and Sons Inc., p. III-1887 [NAICS 423920]

Frank Parsons Paper Co., pp. Vol. III-1898, 1901 [NAICS 424110, 424120]

Frank's Nursery and Crafts Inc., p. III-2072 [NAICS 444220]

Frank's Quality Services Inc., p. III-1855 [NAICS 423740]

Frankford Candy & Chocolate Co., p. I-52 [NAICS 311330]

Frankfort Tower Industries Inc., pp. Vol. II-939, 1421 [NAICS 33261M, 335311]

Franklin Aluminum Company Inc., p. I-811 [NAICS 331316]

Franklin Baking Company Inc., p. I-116 [NAICS 31181M]

Franklin Cigar and Tobacco Inc., pp. Vol. III-1905, 1939, 2001 [NAICS 424130, 424450, 424940]

Franklin Corp., p. II-1616 [NAICS 337121]

Franklin Covey Co., pp. Vol. I-420, 436 [NAICS 32311M, 32312M]

Franklin Electric Company Inc., pp. Vol. II-1179, 1189, 1427, 1437 [NAICS 333911, 333913, 335312, 335314]

Franklin Electronic Publishers Inc., pp. Vol. II-1077, 1238 [NAICS 333313, 334111]

Franklin Equipment Inc, pp. Vol. II-1023, 1033 [NAICS 333111, 333120]

Franklin Homes USA Inc., p. I-348 [NAICS 321991]

Franklin Industries Co., p. I-788 [NAICS 331210]

Franklin Mint, pp. Vol. I-681, Vol. II-1696 [NAICS 327112, 33991M]

Frantz Mfg Co, p. II-1463 [NAICS 335991]

Franz Manufacturing Company Inc., p. II-1362 [NAICS 334518]

Franzia-Sanger Winery, p. I-177 [NAICS 312130]

Fraser Business Systems, p. III-1801 [NAICS 423420]

Fraser Shipyards Inc., p. II-1589 [NAICS 336611]

Frazee Industries Inc., p. I-554 [NAICS 325510]

Frazier and Frazier Industries Inc., p. I-845 [NAICS 33151M]

Fred Jones Enterprises L.L.C., p. III-1762 [NAICS 423120]

Fred's Inc., pp. Vol. III-2100, 2177, 2180 [NAICS 446110, 452910, 452990]

Freda's Fancy Florist Antiques Inc., p. III-2183 [NAICS 453110]

Frederick's of Hollywood Inc., p. III-2135 [NAICS 448150]

Fredericks Co., p. I-713 [NAICS 327212]

Fredericksburg Farmers Coop., p. I-524 [NAICS 325314]

Freeda Vitamins Inc., p. I-767 [NAICS 327992]

Freedman Seating Co., pp. Vol. II-1536, 1627, 1632 [NAICS 336360, 337127, 33712N]

Freedom Plastics Inc., pp. Vol. I-560, Vol. II-974 [NAICS 325520, 332913]

Freedom Wireless Inc., p. III-2054 [NAICS 443112]

Freeland Products Inc., p. II-1277 [NAICS 334411]

Freelin-Wade, p. I-621 [NAICS 326121]

Freeman Corp., p. I-324 [NAICS 32121N]

Freeman Cos., p. II-1720 [NAICS 339950]

Freeman Metal Products Inc., p. II-1745 [NAICS 339995]

Freeman Mfg and Supply Co., p. I-589 [NAICS 325991]

Freeport-McMoRan Copper, pp. Vol. I-443, 475, 822 [NAICS 324110, 32513M, 331411]

Freeport Refractories Inc., p. I-703 [NAICS 32712N]

FreightCar America Inc., p. II-1584 [NAICS 336510]

Freightliner L.L.C., pp. Vol. II-1194, 1473 [NAICS 33392M, 336111]

Freightliner of Charlotte, p. III-1758 [NAICS 423110]

Freightliner of Hartford Inc., pp. Vol. III-1758, 2015 [NAICS 423110, 441120]

Freightliner of San Antonio, p. III-1758 [NAICS 423110]

Freightliner Specialty Vehicle, p. II-1473 [NAICS 336111]

Freihofer Baking Co., p. I-116 [NAICS 31181M]

Freixenet USA, p. I-177 [NAICS 312130]

Fremont Beverage Inc., p. I-165 [NAICS 31211M]

Fremont Plastic Products Inc., p. II-1023 [NAICS 333111]

French Meadow Bakery Inc., p. I-133 [NAICS 311830]

French Toast, p. III-1919 [NAICS 424330]

Frenchman Valley Farmer's, p. III-1991 [NAICS 424910]

Frequency Electronics Inc., p. II-1347 [NAICS 334515]

Freres Lumber Company Inc., pp. Vol. I-312, 324 [NAICS 32111M, 32121N]

Fres-co System USA Inc., pp. Vol. I-560, Vol. II-1212 [NAICS 325520, 333993]

Fresca Mexican Foods Inc., p. I-133 [NAICS 311830]

Fresh Beginnings Inc., pp. Vol. I-57, 124 [NAICS 311340, 31182M]

Fresh Brands Distributing Inc., pp. Vol. I-165, Vol. III-1925, 1954 [NAICS 31211M, 424410, 424490]

Fresh Mark Inc., p. I-102 [NAICS 31161N]

Fresh Start Bakeries Inc., p. I-116 [NAICS 31181M]

Fresh Start Vitamins, p. I-534 [NAICS 325411]

FreshPoint Inc., p. III-1950 [NAICS 424480]

FreshPoint Southern California, pp. Vol. III-1929, 1950 [NAICS 424420, 424480]

Freshwater Farms Inc., p. I-110 [NAICS 31171M]

Fresno Distributing Co., p. III-1847 [NAICS 423720]

Fresno Truck Center A California, p. III-1758 [NAICS 423110]

Fresno Valves and Castings Inc., p. II-980 [NAICS 33291N]

Freudenberg Household Products, pp. Vol. II-1397, 1740 [NAICS 33521M, 339994]

Freudenberg Nonwovens Tough, p. I-208 [NAICS 313230]

Freund Baking Co., p. I-116 [NAICS 31181M]

Frieda's Inc., p. III-1950 [NAICS 424480]

Friedman Industries Inc., pp. Vol. I-793, Vol. II-1009, Vol. III-1824 [NAICS 33122M, 332996, 423510]

Friedman's Inc., p. III-2144 [NAICS 448310]

Friend Tire Co., p. III-1766 [NAICS 423130]

Friendly Ice Cream Corp., pp. Vol. I-68, 92 [NAICS 31142M, 311520]

Friends Enterprises, pp. Vol. III-2116, 2177 [NAICS 447110, 452910]

Friendship Dairies Inc., pp. Vol. I-76, 81, 86 [NAICS 311513, 311514, 31151N]

Frierson Bailey Lumber Supply, p. I-329 [NAICS 32121P]

Frigid Fluid Co., p. II-1745 [NAICS 339995]

Frit Industries Inc., pp. Vol. I-516, 520, 524 [NAICS 325311, 325312, 325314]

Fritsch USA Inc., p. II-1297 [NAICS 334415]

Fritz Company Inc., pp. Vol. III-1939, 2001 [NAICS 424450, 424940]

Fritz Industries Inc., p. I-695 [NAICS 327122]

Fromm Family Foods L.L.C., p. I-4 [NAICS 311111]

Fromm International, p. II-886 [NAICS 33221N]

Frontier Cooperative Co., pp. Vol. III 1958, 1991 [NAICS 424510, 424910]

Frontier Equity Exchange, p. III-2094 [NAICS 445299]

Numbers following p. or pp. are page references. Roman numerals indicate volume numbers. Bracketed items indicate industries. Page references are to the starting pages of company tables.

2343

Frontier FS Coop., pp. Vol. III-1958, 1975, 1991 [NAICS 424510, 424710, 424910]

Frontier F.S. Cooperative, pp. Vol. III-2218, 2222 [NAICS 454311, 454312]

Frontier Homes Inc., p. III-2203 [NAICS 453930]

Frontier Oil Corp., pp. Vol. I-443, Vol. III-1979 [NAICS 324110, 424720]

Frontier Refining & Marketing Inc., p. I-443 [NAICS 324110]

Frontier Spinning Mills L.L.C., p. I-192 [NAICS 31311M]

Frontier Trading Inc., pp. Vol. III-1958, 1991 [NAICS 424510, 424910]

Frost Inc., p. II-988 [NAICS 332991]

Frozen Specialties Inc., p. I-62 [NAICS 31141M]

Fruhauf Uniform Inc., p. I-285 [NAICS 31529M]

Fruit Growers Supply Co., p. III-1991 [NAICS 424910]

Fruit of the Loom Ltd., p. I-272 [NAICS 31522M]

Fruita Consumers Cooperative, p. I-516 [NAICS 325311]

Fry's Electronics Inc., pp. Vol. III-2054, 2211 [NAICS 443112, 454113]

Ft Pitt Acquisition Corp., p. II-886 [NAICS 33221N]

FT Precision Inc., p. II-1505 [NAICS 33631M]

FTD Group Inc., p. III-2183 [NAICS 453110]

Fuchs Lubricants Co., p. I-458 [NAICS 324191]

Fuchs Lubricants Inc. Century Div., p. I-458 [NAICS 324191]

FuelCell Energy Inc., pp. Vol. II-1442, 1447, 1512 [NAICS 335911, 335912, 33632M]

Fueltec United Inc., p. III-2222 [NAICS 454312]

Fuji American Advanced Sports, p. III-1883 [NAICS 423910]

Fuji Photo Film U.S.A. Inc., pp. Vol. II-1087, 1381 [NAICS 333315, 334613]

Fuji Vegetable Oil Inc., p. I-26 [NAICS 311225]

FUJIFILM Medical Systems USA, p. III-2007 [NAICS 424990]

Fujifilm Microdisks USA Inc., p. II-1381 [NAICS 334613]

Fujimi Corp., p. I-756 [NAICS 327910]

Fujipoly America Corp., p. I-505 [NAICS 325212]

Fujisawa Healthcare Inc., p. I-539 [NAICS 325412]

Fujitec America Inc., p. II-1194 [NAICS 33392M]

Fujitsu Microelectronics America, p. III-1839 [NAICS 423690]

Fujitsu Network Communications, pp. Vol. II-1257, 1262, 1317, 1451 [NAICS 334210, 334220, 334419, 33592M]

Fujitsu Transaction Solutions Inc., pp. Vol. II-1077, 1238 [NAICS 333313, 334111]

Fukuvi USA Inc., p. I-621 [NAICS 326121]

Fulcrum Incorporated, p. I-646 [NAICS 326160]

Fulflex Inc., p. I-192 [NAICS 31311M]

Fulghum Industries Inc., p. II-1046 [NAICS 333210]

Full Compass Systems Ltd., pp. Vol. III-1831, 1835 [NAICS 423610, 423620]

Full House Co., p. II-1046 [NAICS 333210]

Full Sail Brewing Co., pp. Vol. I-172, 181 [NAICS 312120, 312140]

Fuller Box Company Inc., p. II-928 [NAICS 33243M]

Fullerton Tool Company Inc., p. II-1207 [NAICS 333991]

Fulmer Company Inc., pp. Vol. II-945, Vol. III-1824 [NAICS 332710, 423510]

Fulton Bellows & Components, p. II-1332 [NAICS 334512]

Fulton Boiler Works Inc., p. II-918 [NAICS 332410]

Fulton Paper Company Inc., p. III-1905 [NAICS 424130]

Fulton Supply, p. I-312 [NAICS 32111M]

Fun Adventures Inc., p. III-1887 [NAICS 423920]

Fun Equipment Sales Inc., p. III-1887 [NAICS 423920]

Fun Kingdom Amusements L.L.C., p. III-2190 [NAICS 453220]

Funai Corp., pp. Vol. III-1801, 1805, 1835, 1839 [NAICS 423420, 423430, 423620, 423690]

Function Junction Inc., p. III-2047 [NAICS 442299]

Funder America Inc., pp. Vol. I-319, 631 [NAICS 321219, 326130]

Fuqua Homes Inc., p. I-348 [NAICS 321991]

Furman Foods Inc., p. I-158 [NAICS 31199M]

Furnace Parts L.L.C., p. I-681 [NAICS 327112]

Furniture Brands International Inc., pp. Vol. II-1616, 1621, 1627 [NAICS 337121, 337122, 337127]

Furniture By Thurston Inc., p. II-1632 [NAICS 33712N]

Furniture Works, p. III-1875 [NAICS 423850]

Furst-McNess Co., pp. Vol. I-9, 152, 158, 566, Vol. II-1397 [NAICS 311119, 31194M, 31199M, 32561M, 33521M]

Fusion U V Systems Inc., p. II-1189 [NAICS 333913]

Futon Shop, p. II-1657 [NAICS 337910]

Futter Lumber Corp., p. III-1782 [NAICS 423310]

Future Home Technology Inc., p. I-353 [NAICS 321992]

Future Media Productions Inc., p. II-1376 [NAICS 334612]

Future Metals Inc., p. III-1824 [NAICS 423510]

FW Ritter Sons Co., p. III-1998 [NAICS 424930]

FW Webb Co., pp. Vol. III-1847, 1851 [NAICS 423720, 423730]

Fyda Freightliner Columbus Inc., p. III-1758 [NAICS 423110]

Fyda Freightliner Youngstown Inc., p. III-1758 [NAICS 423110]

Fypon Ltd., p. I-334 [NAICS 32191M]

G and A Trading Co., p. III-1919 [NAICS 424330]

G and B Oil Company Inc., pp. Vol. III-1828, 1975 [NAICS 423520, 424710]

G and B Specialties Inc., p. I-872 [NAICS 33211N]

G and F Industries Inc., pp. Vol. I-879, Vol. II-1092, 1134 [NAICS 33211P, 33331N, 333514]

G and F Roof Supply Inc., p. III-1790 [NAICS 423330]

G and H Service Corp., p. III-1875 [NAICS 423850]

G and H Wire Co., p. II-1682 [NAICS 339114]

G and J Pepsi-Cola Bottlers Inc., p. I-165 [NAICS 31211M]

G and J Steel and Tubing, pp. Vol. I-788, Vol. II-1009 [NAICS 331210, 332996]

G and K Services Inc., pp. Vol. I-272, 290 [NAICS 31522M, 31599M]

G and L Musical Products, p. II-1731 [NAICS 339992]

G and M Oil Company Inc., p. III-1975 [NAICS 424710]

G and N Aircraft Inc., p. II-1562 [NAICS 336412]

G and O Manufacturing, pp. Vol. II-1101, 1106 [NAICS 333414, 333415]

G and S Sewing, p. I-267 [NAICS 31521M]

G and T Industries Inc., pp. Vol. I-641, Vol. III-2004 [NAICS 326150, 424950]

G and W Electric Co., p. II-1432 [NAICS 335313]

G and W Industries Corp., p. II-1376 [NAICS 334612]

G-III Apparel Group Ltd., pp. Vol. III-1916, 1919 [NAICS 424320, 424330]

G. Joannou Cycle Company Inc., p. III-1883 [NAICS 423910]

GA Fleet Associates Inc., p. II-1417 [NAICS 335228]

GA Heaton Co., p. III-1894 [NAICS 423940]

G.A. Sadowsky and Son Inc., pp. Vol. III-1766, 1975 [NAICS 423130, 424710]

GA Telesis Turbine Technology, p. III-1879 [NAICS 423860]

Gables Engineering Inc., p. II-1432 [NAICS 335313]

Gabriel Container Co., pp. Vol. I-374, 415 [NAICS 322130, 322299]

GACO Western Inc., p. I-641 [NAICS 326150]

Gage Brother's Concrete Products, pp. Vol. I-737, 743 [NAICS 32733M, 327390]

Gage, H L Sales Inc., p. III-1758 [NAICS 423110]

Gage Industries Inc., p. I-609 [NAICS 326112]

Gail Pittman Studios Inc., p. I-681 [NAICS 327112]

Gainey Vineyard, p. III-2097 [NAICS 445310]

Gaiser Tool Co., p. II-1140 [NAICS 333515]

Galamet Inc., p. I-807 [NAICS 331314]

Galaxy Industries Inc., pp. Vol. II-1119, 1207 [NAICS 333511, 333991]

Galaxy Nutritional Foods Inc., p. I-76 [NAICS 311513]

Galey and Lord Inc., p. I-198 [NAICS 313210]

Galgon Industries Inc., p. II-952 [NAICS 332721]

Galland Henning Nopak Inc., p. II-1152 [NAICS 333518]

Gallard-Schlesinger Industries Inc., p. III-1971 [NAICS 424690]

Galliker Quality Check Dairy, pp. Vol. I-86, 92, 143 [NAICS 31151N, 311520, 311920]

Galloway Company Corp., pp. Vol. I-81, 158 [NAICS 311514, 31199M]

Galpin Motors Inc., p. III-2011 [NAICS 441110]

Galvotec Alloys Inc., p. I-852 [NAICS 33152N]

Galyan's Trading Company Inc., p. III-2150 [NAICS 451110]

Gambrinus Company Inc., p. I-172 [NAICS 312120]

Gambro Renal Products Inc., p. II-1322 [NAICS 334510]

Gamco Products Co., p. I-857 [NAICS 33152P]

GameTime, p. II-1702 [NAICS 339920]

Gaming Partners Intern. Corp., pp. Vol. II-1627, 1708 [NAICS 337127, 33993M]

Gander Mountain Co., p. III-1883 [NAICS 423910]

Gans Ink and Supply Company Inc., p. I-580 [NAICS 325910]

Gap Inc., p. III-2132 [NAICS 448140]

GAP Supply Corp., p. III-1851 [NAICS 423730]

Garcia & Sons Auto & Used Part, p. III-1770 [NAICS 423140]

Numbers following p. or pp. are page references. Roman numerals indicate volume numbers. Bracketed items indicate industries. Page references are to the starting pages of company tables.

Garden Ridge Corp., pp. Vol. III-1778, 2047, 2177 [NAICS 423220, 442299, 452910]

Gardenburger Inc., p. I-81 [NAICS 311514]

Gardener's Supply Co., pp. Vol. I-358, 722, Vol. II-892 [NAICS 321999, 327215, 33221P]

Gardner Abrasives, p. I-756 [NAICS 327910]

Gardner and Benoit Inc., p. III-1855 [NAICS 423740]

Gardner Asphalt Corp., pp. Vol. I-448, 453 [NAICS 324121, 324122]

Gardner Denver Inc., pp. Vol. II-1112, 1179, 1184 [NAICS 33341N, 333911, 333912]

Gardner Glass Products Inc., pp. Vol. I-718, 722 [NAICS 327213, 327215]

Gare Bisquefire Inc., p. II-1119 [NAICS 333511]

Garelick Manufacturing Inc., p. II-1536 [NAICS 336360]

Garland C. Norris Co., p. III-1905 [NAICS 424130]

Garland Company Inc., p. I-453 [NAICS 324122]

Garland, Harwood, p. III-2058 [NAICS 443120]

Garment Corporation of America, p. I-279 [NAICS 31523M]

Garrity Industries Inc., p. II-1390 [NAICS 33512M]

Gary Farn Ltd., p. III-1909 [NAICS 424210]

Gary Merlino Construction Inc., pp. Vol. I-732, 743, 762, Vol. III-1786 [NAICS 327320, 327390, 327991, 423320]

Gary Metal Manufacturing L.L.C., pp. Vol. II-886, 1129, 1152 [NAICS 33221M, 333513, 333518]

Gary Plastic Packaging Corp., p. I-609 [NAICS 326112]

Gary-Williams Energy Corp., p. I-443 [NAICS 324110]

Gas America Services Inc., p. III-2116 [NAICS 447110]

Gas Atmospheres, p. II-1157 [NAICS 333611]

Gas Inc., pp. Vol. III-2050, 2222 [NAICS 443111, 454312]

Gasbarre Products Inc., pp. Vol. II-1129, 1217 [NAICS 333513, 333994]

Gasboy International L.L.C., p. II-1189 [NAICS 333913]

Gaska Tape Inc., p. I-203 [NAICS 31322M]

Gasket Engineering Company Inc., p. II-1541 [NAICS 336370]

GASL Inc., p. II-1572 [NAICS 336414]

Gaspro, pp. Vol. I-471, Vol. III-1813, 1867, 1979 [NAICS 325120, 423450, 423830, 424720]

Gasser Chair Company Inc., pp. Vol. II-1616, 1627 [NAICS 337121, 337127]

Gate City Beverage Distributors, pp. Vol. III-1954, 1983 [NAICS 424490, 424810]

Gate City Steel Inc., p. II-939 [NAICS 33261M]

Gate Concrete Products Co., p. I-743 [NAICS 327390]

Gate Pharmaceuticals, p. I-539 [NAICS 325412]

Gates Corp., pp. Vol. I-626, 665 [NAICS 326122, 326220]

Gates InterAmerica, p. I-665 [NAICS 326220]

Gateway CDI, pp. Vol. III-1916, 2007 [NAICS 424320, 424990]

Gateway Co-Op, p. III-1958 [NAICS 424510]

Gateway Inc., pp. Vol. II-1238, Vol. III-2211 [NAICS 334111, 454113]

Gateway Mastering Studios Inc., p. II-1381 [NAICS 334613]

Gateway Packaging of MO, p. I-395 [NAICS 32222P]

Gateway Supply Company Inc., pp. Vol. III-1847, 1851 [NAICS 423720, 423730]

Gatorade Co., p. I-165 [NAICS 31211M]

Gay and Robinson Inc., p. I-44 [NAICS 31131N]

Gay Johnson's Inc., pp. Vol. III-1766, 2116 [NAICS 423130, 447110]

Gayla Industries Inc., p. II-1708 [NAICS 33993M]

GBC Film Products, pp. Vol. I-560, 615 [NAICS 325520, 326113]

GBF Inc., p. I-544 [NAICS 325413]

GBS Corp., pp. Vol. I-388, 403, Vol. III-1901 [NAICS 32222N, 32223M, 424120]

GBS Filing Solutions Inc., p. I-403 [NAICS 32223M]

G.C. Broach Co., p. II-1217 [NAICS 333994]

G.C. Office Supply, p. III-2186 [NAICS 453210]

GC Quality Lubricants Inc., p. I-26 [NAICS 311225]

GCC Dacotah Inc., p. I-727 [NAICS 327310]

GCE Industries Inc., p. II-1207 [NAICS 333991]

GCM North American Aerospace, p. II-1557 [NAICS 336411]

GE Aircraft Engines, pp. Vol. II-1173, 1562 [NAICS 333618, 336412]

GE Control Products, p. II-1437 [NAICS 335314]

GE OEC Medical Systems Inc., pp. Vol. II-1322, 1357 [NAICS 334510, 334517]

GE Plastics, pp. Vol. I-388, 500, 615, 626, 631 [NAICS 32222N, 325211, 326113, 326122, 326130]

GE Power Systems, pp. Vol. I-681, 686 [NAICS 327112, 327113]

GE Richards Graphic Supplies Inc., p. III-2007 [NAICS 424990]

GE Sanuc Inc., pp. Vol. II-1282, 1312 [NAICS 334412, 334418]

GE Security Inc., p. II-1267 [NAICS 334290]

GE Supply, pp. Vol. III-1778, 1831 [NAICS 423220, 423610]

GE Supply Logistics, p. III-1843 [NAICS 423710]

GE Tri-Remanufacturing Inc., p. II-1562 [NAICS 336412]

GE Vallectios Nuclear Center, p. II-1357 [NAICS 334517]

Gear and Broach Inc., p. II-1162 [NAICS 333612]

Gear Products Inc., p. II-1162 [NAICS 333612]

Gear Works Inc., p. II-1162 [NAICS 333612]

Gebert Floor Covering Inc., p. III-1786 [NAICS 423320]

GECOM Corp., p. II-933 [NAICS 332510]

Geer Gas Corp., p. I-471 [NAICS 325120]

Geerlings and Wade Inc., p. III-2228 [NAICS 454312]

GEFCO, pp. Vol. II-1039, 1207 [NAICS 33313M, 333991]

Geffen Records, pp. Vol. II-1376, 1381 [NAICS 334612, 334613]

Gehl Co., pp. Vol. II-1023, 1033, 1194 [NAICS 333111, 333120, 33392M]

Gehl's Guernsey Farms Inc., pp. Vol. I-76, 81, 143 [NAICS 311513, 311514, 311920]

Gehr Industries Inc., p. II-1307 [NAICS 334417]

Gehring Textiles Inc., p. I-213 [NAICS 31324M]

Gel Spice Company Inc., p. I-152 [NAICS 31194M]

Gem-Dandy Inc., p. III-1916 [NAICS 424320]

Gem Gravure Company Inc., p. I-580 [NAICS 325910]

Gem Products Inc., pp. Vol. II-1106, 1332, 1397, 1413, 1417, 1427, Vol. III-1851 [NAICS 333415, 334512, 33521M, 335224, 335228, 335312, 423730]

Gem Seal Corp., p. I-453 [NAICS 324122]

Gemeinhardt Company L.L.C., p. II-1731 [NAICS 339992]

Gemini Industries Inc., p. II-1262 [NAICS 334220]

Gemline, pp. Vol. I-239, 306 [NAICS 31491M, 31699M]

Gen-Probe Inc., p. I-534 [NAICS 325411]

Genca Corp., p. II-1129 [NAICS 333513]

GenCorp Inc., pp. Vol. I-500, 626, Vol. II-1005, 1347, 1551, 1576, 1580 [NAICS 325211, 326122, 332995, 334515, 336399, 336415, 336419]

Genentech Inc., pp. Vol. I-539, 549 [NAICS 325412, 325414]

Generac Power Systems Corp., pp. Vol. II-1157, 1427, 1457 [NAICS 333611, 335312, 33593M]

General Air Corp., p. II-1056 [NAICS 333295]

General Aluminum Corp., pp. Vol. I-651, Vol. II-908 [NAICS 32619M, 33232M]

General Asphalt Company Inc., p. I-448 [NAICS 324121]

General Atomics, pp. Vol. II-1238, 1317, 1352 [NAICS 334111, 334419, 334516]

General Atomics Aeronautical, p. II-1567 [NAICS 336413]

General Automation Inc., p. II-952 [NAICS 332721]

General Automotive Mfg L.L.C., pp. Vol. II-952, 1173, 1512 [NAICS 332721, 333618, 33632M]

General Bag Corp., p. I-239 [NAICS 31491M]

General Bearing Corp., p. II-988 [NAICS 332991]

General Beverage Sales Co., pp. Vol. III-1983, 1987 [NAICS 424810, 424820]

General Binding Corp., pp. Vol. II-1061, Vol. III-1901 [NAICS 33329N, 424120]

General Building Systems Inc., p. I-329 [NAICS 32121P]

General Cable Corp., pp. Vol. I-837, Vol. II-1033, 1039 [NAICS 33149M, 333120, 33313M]

General Carbide Corp., pp. Vol. I-488, Vol. II-1134, 1140, 1168 [NAICS 325188, 333514, 333515, 333613]

General Chemical Corp., pp. Vol. I-475, 488, 595 [NAICS 32513M, 325188, 32599N]

General Chemical Industrial, pp. Vol. I-475, 480, 879, Vol. II-1229 [NAICS 32513M, 325181, 33211P, 33399P]

General Cigar Holdings Inc., p. I-188 [NAICS 31222M]

General Clay Products Corp., p. I-691 [NAICS 327121]

General Converters & Assemblers, p. I-343 [NAICS 321920]

General Devices Company Inc., pp. Vol. I-722, 879, Vol. II-928 [NAICS 327215, 33211P, 33243M]

General Die Casters Inc., p. I-852 [NAICS 33152N]

General Distributing Co., p. III-1983 [NAICS 424810]

General Distributing Company Inc., p. I-471 [NAICS 325120]

General Dynamics Corp., pp. Vol. II-1092, 1317, 1327, 1589, 1594, 1603 [NAICS 33331N, 334419, 334511, 336611, 336612, 336992]

General Dynamics Network, p. II-1267 [NAICS 334290]

General Econopak Inc., p. I-411 [NAICS 322291]

General Electric Co., pp. Vol. II-1357, 1390, 1417, 1427, 1468, 1562 [NAICS 334517, 33512M, 335228, 335312, 335999, 336412]

General Electric Transportation, p. II-1562 [NAICS 336412]

General Fibers and Fabrics Inc., p. I-510 [NAICS 32522M]

General Films Inc., p. I-621 [NAICS 326121]

General Foam Plastics Corp., pp. Vol. II-1702, 1749 [NAICS 339920, 339999]

General Machine Products Inc., pp. Vol. II-1207, 1451 [NAICS 333991, 33592M]

General Manufactured Housing, p. I-348 [NAICS 321991]

General Material Co., pp. Vol. I-703, 727 [NAICS 32712N, 327310]

General Mills Bakery & Food, p. I-15 [NAICS 31121M]

General Mills Inc., pp. Vol. I-36, 68, 92, 124 [NAICS 311230, 31142M, 311520, 31182M]

General Motors Corp., pp. Vol. II-1473, 1551, 1584 [NAICS 336111, 336399, 336510]

General Parts Inc., p. III-1762 [NAICS 423120]

General Plastics Manufacturing Co., p. II-1580 [NAICS 336419]

General Pool & S.p.A. Supply Inc., p. III-1883 [NAICS 423910]

General Porcelain Mfg Co., p. I-681 [NAICS 327112]

General Press Colors Ltd., p. I-580 [NAICS 325910]

General Produce Company Ltd., p. III-1950 [NAICS 424480]

General Products Corp., pp. Vol. I-857, 872 [NAICS 33152P, 33211N]

General Rubber & Plastics Of, p. III-1968 [NAICS 424610]

General Shale Brick Inc., pp. Vol. I-703, 737 [NAICS 32712N, 32733M]

General Thermodynamics, p. II-1101 [NAICS 333414]

General Tire Service, pp. Vol. III-1766, 2034 [NAICS 423130, 441320]

General Tool and Supply Co., pp. Vol. III-1843, 1871 [NAICS 423710, 423840]

General Wholesale Co., pp. Vol. III-1983, 1987 [NAICS 424810, 424820]

Generation II Locomotives Inc., p. II-1584 [NAICS 336510]

Genesco Inc., p. III-2141 [NAICS 448210]

Genesee Reserve Supply Inc., p. III-1794 [NAICS 423390]

Genesis Development Inc., p. II-1056 [NAICS 333295]

Genie Co., pp. Vol. II-1437, 1468 [NAICS 335314, 335999]

Genlyte Group Inc., pp. Vol. II-1386, 1390 [NAICS 335110, 33512M]

Genlyte Group Inc. Supply Div., p. II-1390 [NAICS 33512M]

Genmar Holdings Inc., p. II-1594 [NAICS 336612]

Genomic Solutions Inc., p. II-1666 [NAICS 339111]

Genova Products Inc., pp. Vol. I-453, Vol. II-939 [NAICS 324122, 33261M]

Genpak L.L.C., p. I-603 [NAICS 326111]

Genpak L.L.C. Continental, pp. Vol. I-379, 651 [NAICS 32221M, 32619M]

Gent-L-Kleen Products Inc., p. II-1189 [NAICS 333913]

GenTek Inc., pp. Vol. I-879, Vol. II-1229, 1551, Vol. III-1762 [NAICS 33211P, 33399P, 336399, 423120]

Gentex Corp., pp. Vol. I-290, 722, Vol. II-1082, 1267, 1317, 1687 [NAICS 31599M, 327215, 333314, 334290, 334419, 339115]

Genuine Parts Co., pp. Vol. III-1762, 1774, 1871, 1901 [NAICS 423120, 423210, 423840, 424120]

Genzyme Biosurgery, p. II-1671 [NAICS 339112]

Genzyme Corp., pp. Vol. I-539, 549, Vol. II-1671 [NAICS 325412, 325414, 339112]

GEO Heat Exchangers L.L.C., p. II-918 [NAICS 332410]

Geocel Corp., pp. Vol. I-636, 641 [NAICS 326140, 326150]

Geochron Enterprises Inc., p. II-1362 [NAICS 334518]

GeoPharma Inc., p. I-534 [NAICS 325411]

George A Mitchell Co., p. II-1147 [NAICS 333516]

George Fischer Sloane Inc., p. II-1009 [NAICS 332996]

George Koch Sons L.L.C., pp. Vol. I-771, Vol. II-1217 [NAICS 327993, 333994]

George P Johnson Co., p. II-1720 [NAICS 339950]

George Pfau's Sons Company Inc., p. I-458 [NAICS 324191]

George R. Pierce Inc., p. III-2203 [NAICS 453930]

George's Inc., p. I-97 [NAICS 311615]

George's Inc. Chicken Div., p. I-97 [NAICS 311615]

George's Music Room, p. III-2168 [NAICS 451220]

George W. Park Seed Inc., p. III-2072 [NAICS 444220]

George Weston Bakeries, p. III-2089 [NAICS 445291]

Georgia Boot L.L.C., p. I-300 [NAICS 31621M]

Georgia Carpet Finishers Inc., p. I-229 [NAICS 314110]

Georgia Crate and Basket Inc., p. I-343 [NAICS 321920]

Georgia Foam Inc., p. I-641 [NAICS 326150]

Georgia Gulf Corp., pp. Vol. I-475, 480, 488, 493, 500, 566 [NAICS 32513M, 325181, 325188, 32519M, 325211, 32561M]

Georgia Lighting, pp. Vol. III-1831, 2037 [NAICS 423610, 442110]

Georgia Narrow Fabrics Corp., p. I-203 [NAICS 31322M]

Georgia-Pacific Corp., pp. Vol. I-312, 324, 334, 363, 374, 379, 388, 411 [NAICS 32111M, 32121N, 32191M, 322110, 322130, 32221M, 32222N, 322291]

Georgia Tufters L.L.C., pp. Vol. I-229, 234 [NAICS 314110, 31412M]

Georgiou Studio, pp. Vol. I-279, Vol. III-2126, 2135 [NAICS 31523M, 448120, 448150]

GEPCO International Inc., p. II-1451 [NAICS 33592M]

Gerber AAA Plumbing Pottery, p. I-677 [NAICS 327111]

Gerber Childrenswear Inc., p. I-285 [NAICS 31529M]

Gerber Coburn Optical Inc., p. II-1252 [NAICS 334119]

Gerber Globe Union, pp. Vol. II-974, 980 [NAICS 332913, 33291N]

Gerber Plumbing Fixtures L.L.C., p. I-677 [NAICS 327111]

Gerber Radio Supply Co., p. III-1839 [NAICS 423690]

Gerber Scientific Inc., pp. Vol. II-1061, 1087, 1252, 1317, 1322 [NAICS 33329N, 333315, 334119, 334419, 334510]

Gerdau Ameristeel, pp. Vol. II-939, 1302 [NAICS 33261M, 334416]

Gerdau AmeriSteel Corp., p. I-780 [NAICS 33111M]

Gerdau-Ameristeel Sayreville Inc., p. II-939 [NAICS 33261M]

Gerhold Concrete Company Inc., p. I-737 [NAICS 32733M]

Germanow-Simon Co's, p. II-1082 [NAICS 333314]

Gerson and Gerson Inc., p. I-279 [NAICS 31523M]

Gerson Company Inc., pp. Vol. III-1894, 1998 [NAICS 423940, 424930]

Gesswein, p. III-1820 [NAICS 423490]

Getchell Brothers Inc., p. III-1933 [NAICS 424430]

Getinge USA Inc., p. II-1676 [NAICS 339113]

GF Goodman and Son Inc., p. II-1051 [NAICS 333220]

GF Office Furniture Ltd., pp. Vol. II-1616, 1650 [NAICS 337121, 33721N]

GFI America Inc., p. I-102 [NAICS 31161N]

GFS Chemicals Inc., p. II-1666 [NAICS 339111]

GH Stenner and Company Inc., p. II-1189 [NAICS 333913]

Ghent Manufacturing Inc., pp. Vol. II-1611, 1714 [NAICS 337110, 33994M]

Ghirardelli Chocolate Co., pp. Vol. I-48, 52 [NAICS 311320, 311330]

GHS Corp., p. II-1731 [NAICS 339992]

GHSP Inc., p. II-1457 [NAICS 33593M]

G.I. Joe's Inc., p. III-2177 [NAICS 452910]

Giant Cement Co., p. I-727 [NAICS 327310]

Giant Cement Holding Inc., p. I-727 [NAICS 327310]

Giant Eagle Inc., p. III-2076 [NAICS 445110]

Giant Food Inc., pp. Vol. I-86, 92, 116, 165, Vol. III-2076, 2100 [NAICS 31151N, 311520, 31181M, 31211N, 445110, 446110]

Giant Industries Inc., pp. Vol. I-411, 443, Vol. III-1979, 2076, 2116 [NAICS 322291, 324110, 424720, 445110, 447110]

Gibbs Die Casting Corp., pp. Vol. I-852, 857 [NAICS 33152N, 33152P]

Gibbs Oil Co., p. III-2116 [NAICS 447110]

Gibraltar Industries Inc., pp. Vol. I-780, Vol. II-899, Vol. III-1824 [NAICS 33111M, 33231M, 423510]

Gibson Farmers Coop., pp. Vol. III-1991, 2072 [NAICS 424910, 444220]

Gibson Laboratories Inc., p. I-549 [NAICS 325414]

Gibson Musical Intruments, p. II-1731 [NAICS 339992]

Gibson Wine Co., p. I-177 [NAICS 312130]

Giddings and Lewis L.L.C., pp. Vol. II-1061, 1124, 1140, 1152, 1437 [NAICS 33329N, 333512, 333515, 333518, 335314]

Gift Box Corporation of America, pp. Vol. I-203, 395 [NAICS 31322M, 32222P]

Giglio Distributing Co., pp. Vol. III-1983, 1987 [NAICS 424810, 424820]

Gilcrest/Jewett Lumber Co., p. III-2065 [NAICS 444100]

Gilead Sciences Inc., p. I-549 [NAICS 325414]

Giles Enterprises Inc., p. II-1397 [NAICS 33521M]

Giliberti Inc., p. II-1607 [NAICS 336999]

Gill Industries Inc., p. I-879 [NAICS 33211P]

Gillespie and Powers Inc., p. I-703 [NAICS 32712N]

Gillette Co., pp. Vol. I-575, Vol. II-886, 1442, 1740 [NAICS 325620, 33221N, 335911, 339994]

Gillig Corp., p. II-1486 [NAICS 336211]

Gilman Building Products L.L.C., p. I-312 [NAICS 32111M]

Gilman Engineering & Mfg L.L.C., pp. Vol. II-1092, 1229 [NAICS 33331N, 33399P]

Gilmore Brothers Inc., p. III-2171 [NAICS 452111]

Gilmour Manufacturing, pp. Vol. I-646, 665 [NAICS 326160, 326220]

Gilmour Manufacturing Co., pp. Vol. II-980, 1028 [NAICS 33291N, 333112]

Gilreath Manufacturing Inc., pp. Vol. I-615, 631 [NAICS 326113, 326130]

Gilster-Mary Lee Corp., p. I-158 [NAICS 31199M]

Gina Group L.L.C., p. I-256 [NAICS 31511M]

Giovanni Jewelry, p. II-1696 [NAICS 33991M]

Girard Extrusion, p. I-803 [NAICS 331312]

Girard Machine Company Inc., p. II-1147 [NAICS 333516]

Girard Plastics Company L.L.C., pp. Vol. II-974, 1708 [NAICS 332913, 33993M]

Girard Wood Products Inc., p. I-343 [NAICS 321920]

Gits Manufacturing Co., p. II-952 [NAICS 332721]

Gitto/Global Corp., p. I-589 [NAICS 325991]

Givaudan Flavors Inc., pp. Vol. I-81, 147, 152 [NAICS 311514, 311930, 31194M]

GIW Industries Inc., pp. Vol. I-857, Vol. II-1179 [NAICS 33152P, 333911]

G.J. Chemical Company Inc., p. III-1971 [NAICS 424690]

GKN Aerospace Chem-Tronics, pp. Vol. II-908, 1567, 1580 [NAICS 33232M, 336413, 336419]

GKN Aerospace Inc., pp. Vol. II-933, 1567 [NAICS 332510, 336413]

GKN Aerospace Transparency, pp. Vol. I-615, Vol. II-1567, 1580 [NAICS 326113, 336413, 336419]

GKN Armstrong Wheels Inc., p. II-1551 [NAICS 336399]

GKN Center Metals, p. I-867 [NAICS 332117]

GKN Sinter Metals-Germantown, pp. Vol. I-867, Vol. II-899 [NAICS 332117, 33231M]

GKN Sinter Metals-Saint Mary's, p. I-867 [NAICS 332117]

G.L. Turner Co., p. II-1028 [NAICS 333112]

Glacier Northwest Inc., pp. Vol. I-727, 732 [NAICS 327310, 327320]

Glacier Water Services Inc., pp. Vol. III-1809, 2215 [NAICS 423440, 454210]

Gladding Braided Products L.L.C., p. I-244 [NAICS 314991]

Glade and Grove Supply Inc., p. III-1863 [NAICS 423820]

Glade's Taffy Town Inc., p. I-52 [NAICS 311330]

Glade Sugar House, p. I-44 [NAICS 31131N]

Glaize Components, pp. Vol. I-324, 329 [NAICS 32121N, 32121P]

Glas-Col L.L.C., pp. Vol. II-918, 1666 [NAICS 332410, 339111]

Glaser Gas Inc., p. III-2222 [NAICS 454312]

Glasforms Inc., p. I-621 [NAICS 326121]

Glasgow Quarries Inc., p. I-748 [NAICS 327410]

Glass Etc., p. III-2190 [NAICS 453220]

Glass Surface Systems Inc., p. II-1386 [NAICS 335110]

Glassline Corp., p. II-1124 [NAICS 333512]

Glassmaster Co., p. I-631 [NAICS 326130]

Glassmasters Corp., p. I-681 [NAICS 327112]

Glasstone Inc., p. I-762 [NAICS 327991]

Glassworks WV L.L.C., pp. Vol. I-713, 722 [NAICS 327212, 327215]

Glastender Inc., p. II-1189 [NAICS 333913]

GlaxoSmithKline - USA, p. I-539 [NAICS 325412]

Glazed Products Inc., p. III-1794 [NAICS 423390]

Glazer's Wholesale Drug Inc., pp. Vol. III-1983, 1987 [NAICS 424810, 424820]

Glazier Foods Co., p. III-1929 [NAICS 424420]

Gleason Corp., pp. Vol. I-660, 670, Vol. II-908, 1033 [NAICS 32621M, 32629M, 33232M, 333120]

Gledhill Road Machinery Co., p. II-1028 [NAICS 333112]

Glen-Gery Corp., p. I-737 [NAICS 32733M]

Glen Oak Lumber and Milling Inc., pp. Vol. I-312, 324, 334, 358 [NAICS 32111M, 32121N, 32191M, 321999]

Glen Raven Inc., pp. Vol. I-198, 224 [NAICS 313210, 313320]

Glen Raven Technical Fabrics, p. I-218 [NAICS 31331N]

Glenbrook Technologies Inc., p. II-1357 [NAICS 334517]

Glencoe Equipment Inc., p. III-2069 [NAICS 444210]

Glencourt Inc., pp. Vol. I-76, 86, 116 [NAICS 311513, 31151N, 31181M]

Glendale Assn For Retarded, p. III-2190 [NAICS 453220]

Glendale Automotive Group, p. III-2018 [NAICS 441210]

Glenmac Inc., p. II-1028 [NAICS 333112]

Glenmark Industries Inc., p. I-395 [NAICS 32222P]

Glenoit L.L.C., p. I-229 [NAICS 314110]

Glenora Wine Cellars Inc., p. I-177 [NAICS 312130]

Glenroe Technologies Inc., p. II-1682 [NAICS 339114]

Glens Falls Lehigh Cement Inc., p. I-727 [NAICS 327310]

Glick Textiles Inc., p. III-1913 [NAICS 424310]

Glideaway Bed Carriage Mfg Co., p. II-1621 [NAICS 337122]

Glik Stores, p. III-2132 [NAICS 448140]

Global Accents Inc., p. III-1778 [NAICS 423220]

Global American Sales Inc., p. II-1248 [NAICS 334113]

Global Automotive Alliance, pp. Vol. I-665, 670 [NAICS 326220, 32629M]

Global Brand Marketing Inc., p. I-300 [NAICS 31621M]

Global Companies L.L.C., pp. Vol. III-1979, 2218 [NAICS 424720, 454311]

Global Finishing Solutions, p. II-1184 [NAICS 333912]

Global Gauge Corp., p. II-1357 [NAICS 334517]

Global Imaging Systems Inc., p. III-1801 [NAICS 423420]

Global Mart, p. III-2054 [NAICS 443112]

Global Packaging Inc., pp. Vol. I-395, 603, 636 [NAICS 32222P, 326111, 326140]

Global Payment Technologies Inc., p. II-1077 [NAICS 333313]

Global Power Equipment Group, pp. Vol. II-899, Vol. III-1867 [NAICS 33231M, 423830]

Global Stone James River Inc., p. I-762 [NAICS 327991]

Global Technology Group Ltd., pp. Vol. III-1916, 1919 [NAICS 424320, 424330]

Global Textile Services L.L.C., p. I-229 [NAICS 314110]

Global Tooling Systems Inc., p. II-952 [NAICS 332721]

Global Wire Group, p. I-830 [NAICS 33142M]

Globe Machine Manufacturing Co., p. II-1046 [NAICS 333210]

Globe Rubber Works Inc., p. I-505 [NAICS 325212]

Globe Ticket and Label Co., p. I-203 [NAICS 31322M]

Globe Turbochargers Specialties, pp. Vol. II-1562, 1584 [NAICS 336412, 336510]

Globecomm Systems Inc., p. II-1262 [NAICS 334220]

Glock Inc., p. II-1001 [NAICS 332994]

Glory Inc., p. III-1801 [NAICS 423420]

GloryBee Natural Sweetners Inc., p. I-44 [NAICS 31131N]

Glover Oil Company Inc., p. III-1975 [NAICS 424710]

Glover Truck Parts, p. III-1758 [NAICS 423110]

Glover Wholesale Inc., p. III-1875 [NAICS 423850]

Glowcore Acquisition Inc., p. II-1417 [NAICS 335228]

Glynn-Johnson Corp., p. II-933 [NAICS 332510]

GM Auto Recycling Inc., p. III-2030 [NAICS 441210]

GMF Industries Inc., p. II-1463 [NAICS 335991]

GMP Companies Inc., pp. Vol. I-539, Vol. III-1813 [NAICS 325412, 423450]

GMP Metal Products, pp. Vol. I-879, Vol. II-964, 1134, 1749 [NAICS 33211P, 33281M, 333514, 339999]

GNC Corp., pp. Vol. I-539, Vol. III-2094 [NAICS 325412, 445299]

Go-Crete, p. I-732 [NAICS 327320]

Godiva Chocolatier Inc., pp. Vol. I-48, 52 [NAICS 311320, 311330]

Godwin Pumps of America Inc., p. II-1179 [NAICS 333911]

Goetz & Sons Western Meat, pp. Vol. III 1936, 1943 [NAICS 424440, 424460]

Goetze's Candy Company Inc., p. I-57 [NAICS 311340]

Goffa International Corp., p. III-1887 [NAICS 423920]

Goglanian Bakeries Inc., p. I-116 [NAICS 31181M]

Gohmann Asphalt & Construction, p. I-448 [NAICS 324121]

GoIndustry Michael Fox Intern., p. III-1867 [NAICS 423830]

GOJO Industries Inc., p. I-575 [NAICS 325620]

Gold Bond Mattress, p. II-1657 [NAICS 337910]

Gold Circuit Inc., pp. Vol. III-1801, 2058, 2186 [NAICS 423420, 443120, 453210]

Gold Coast Beverage Distributors, pp. Vol. III-1954, 1983 [NAICS 424490, 424810]

Gold Eagle Co., pp. Vol. I-458, 566 [NAICS 324191, 32561M]

Gold Kist Holdings Inc., pp. Vol. I-4, 97, 102 [NAICS 311111, 311615, 31161N]

Gold Lumber Company Inc., p. III-1778 [NAICS 423220]

Gold'N Plump Poultry Inc., p. I-97 [NAICS 311615]

Gold Peak Industries, pp. Vol. II-1442, 1447 [NAICS 335911, 335912]

Gold Standard Enterprises Inc., pp. Vol. III-2094, 2097 [NAICS 445299, 445310]

Gold Type Business Machines Inc., p. III-1801 [NAICS 423420]

Golden Age of Foods Mfg, p. I-31 [NAICS 31122N]

Golden Alaska Seafoods Inc., p. I-110 [NAICS 31171M]

Golden Brand Bottling Inc., pp. Vol. III-1954, 1983 [NAICS 424490, 424810]

Golden Business Machines Inc., p. III-2186 [NAICS 453210]

Golden Chair Inc., p. II-1616 [NAICS 337121]

Golden Companies Inc., p. III-1839 [NAICS 423690]

Golden County Foods Inc., p. I-62 [NAICS 31141M]

Golden Enterprises Inc., pp. Vol. I-124, 137 [NAICS 31182M, 31191M]

Golden Foods & Golden Brands, p. I-26 [NAICS 311225]

Golden Furrow Fertilizer Inc., p. I-529 [NAICS 325320]

Golden Gate Foods Inc., p. I-26 [NAICS 311225]

Golden Gate Marketing, p. III-2190 [NAICS 453220]

Golden Grove Trading Inc., pp. Vol. III-1894, 2047 [NAICS 423940, 442299]

Golden Neo-Life Diamite Intern., p. I-534 [NAICS 325411]

Golden Peanut Company L.L.C., p. I-137 [NAICS 31191M]

Golden Shield Trading Inc., p. III-1883 [NAICS 423910]

Golden State Containers Inc., p. III-1905 [NAICS 424130]

Golden State Engineering Inc., p. II-952 [NAICS 332721]

Golden State Foods Corp., pp. Vol. I-68, 102, 116, 147, Vol. III-2007 [NAICS 31142M, 31161N, 31181M, 311930, 424990]

Golden State Porcelain Inc., p. I-681 [NAICS 327112]

Golden State Vintners Inc., pp. Vol. I-172, 177 [NAICS 312120, 312130]

Golden Stream Quality Foods Inc., pp. Vol. I-52, 137 [NAICS 311330, 31191M]

Golden Sun Feeds Inc., pp. Vol. I-4, 9 [NAICS 311111, 311119]

Golden West Equipment Inc., pp. Vol. III-1809, 1851, 1859 [NAICS 423440, 423730, 423810]

Golden West Nuts Inc., p. I-137 [NAICS 31191M]

Goldenberg Candy Co., p. I-57 [NAICS 311340]

GoldenRom Inc., p. II-1381 [NAICS 334613]

Goldfarb Electric Supply Inc., p. III-2208 [NAICS 453998]

Golding Farms Foods Inc., pp. Vol. I-31, 44 [NAICS 31122N, 31131N]

Golf Car Supply, p. III-1879 [NAICS 423860]

Golf Galaxy, p. III-2150 [NAICS 451110]

Golfsmith Intern. Holdings Inc., pp. Vol. III-1883, 2150 [NAICS 423910, 451110]

Golfsmith International Inc., pp. Vol. I-272, 290, Vol. II-1702 [NAICS 31522M, 31599M, 339920]

Golub Corp., p. III-2076 [NAICS 445110]

GOMACO Corp., p. II-1033 [NAICS 333120]

Good Cos., p. II-1657 [NAICS 337910]

Good Earth Organic Corp., pp. Vol. I-516, 524 [NAICS 325311, 325314]

Good Earth Tools Inc., p. II-1584 [NAICS 336510]

Good Food Co., pp. Vol. I-26, 44 [NAICS 311225, 31131N]

Good Guys Inc., p. III-2054 [NAICS 443112]

Good Humor-Breyers Ice Cream, p. I-92 [NAICS 311520]

Goodall Rubber Co., p. III-2007 [NAICS 424990]

Goodhart Sons Inc., pp. Vol. II-918, 928 [NAICS 332410, 33243M]

Goodin Co., pp. Vol. III-1847, 1851 [NAICS 423720, 423730]

Goodman Manufacturing L.P., p. II-1106 [NAICS 333415]

Goodman Packaging Equipment, pp. Vol. II-1152, 1212 [NAICS 333518, 333993]

Goodman's Inc., p. III-2037 [NAICS 442110]

Goodman Veneer and Lumber Co., pp. Vol. I-312, 324 [NAICS 32111M, 32121N]

Goodrich Actuation Systems, pp. Vol. II-1168, 1222 [NAICS 333613, 33399N]

Goodrich Corp., pp. Vol. I-500, 560, Vol. II-1168, 1184, 1562 [NAICS 325211, 325520, 333613, 333912, 336412]

Goodwill Industries, pp. Vol. I-234, Vol. III-2194 [NAICS 31412M, 453310]

Goodwill Industries Grand Rapids, p. III-2194 [NAICS 453310]

Goodwill Industries of Akron, p. I-285 [NAICS 31529M]

Goody-Goody Liquor Store Inc., pp. Vol. III-1983, 1987, 2097 [NAICS 424810, 424820, 445310]

Goody's Family Clothing Inc., p. III-2132 [NAICS 448140]

Goodyear Tire and Rubber Co., pp. Vol. I-500, 505, 660, 665, 670 [NAICS 325211, 325212, 32621M, 326220, 32629M]

Gopher Resource Corp., p. I-825 [NAICS 331419]

Gorant Candies Inc., p. I-52 [NAICS 311330]

Gordmans, p. III-2171 [NAICS 452111]

Gordon Aluminum Industries Inc., p. I-811 [NAICS 331316]

Gordon Brothers Corp., p. III-1894 [NAICS 423940]

Gordon Food Company Inc., pp. Vol. III-1933, 1946 [NAICS 424430, 424470]

Gordon Food Service Inc., pp. Vol. III-1925, 2076 [NAICS 424410, 445110]

Gordon Paper Company Inc., p. I-415 [NAICS 322299]

Gordon's Div., p. III-2144 [NAICS 448310]

Goria Enterprises, p. I-737 [NAICS 32733M]

Goria Enterprises Oldcastle APG, p. I-691 [NAICS 327121]

Gorilla Systems Inc., p. II-1248 [NAICS 334113]

Gorman-Rupp Co., pp. Vol. II-1092, 1179, 1189 [NAICS 33331N, 333911, 333913]

Gorman's Gallery Inc., p. III-2037 [NAICS 442110]

Gorton's, p. I-110 [NAICS 31171M]

Goshen Coach, pp. Vol. II-1486, 1607 [NAICS 336211, 336999]

Gospel Light Publications, p. II-1376 [NAICS 334612]

Gosport Manufacturing Inc., p. I-239 [NAICS 31491M]

Gossen Corp., p. I-353 [NAICS 321992]

Gossner Foods Inc., pp. Vol. I-76, 81, 86 [NAICS 311513, 311514, 31151N]

Gottschalks Inc., p. III-2171 [NAICS 452111]

Gould and Goodrich Leather Inc., p. I-510 [NAICS 32522M]

Gould Paper Corp., p. III-1898 [NAICS 424110]

Goulds Pumps Inc, p. II-1179 [NAICS 333911]

Goulston Technologies Inc., p. I-458 [NAICS 324191]

Gouverneur Talc Company Inc., p. I-767 [NAICS 327992]

Government Micro Resources Inc., p. II-1238 [NAICS 334111]

Government Supply Intern. Ltd., p. III-1813 [NAICS 423450]

Gowan Milling Company L.L.C., p. I-529 [NAICS 325320]

Goya Foods Inc., pp. Vol. I-26, 62, 68 [NAICS 311225, 31141M, 31142M]

GP Plastics Corp., p. I-603 [NAICS 326111]

GP Systems Inc., p. III-1835 [NAICS 423620]

GPC Capital Corp. II, p. I-626 [NAICS 326122]

GPD Global, pp. Vol. II-1129, 1189 [NAICS 333513, 333913]

GPrime Ltd., p. III-1839 [NAICS 423690]

Grabill Cabinet Company Inc., pp. Vol. II-1611, 1632 [NAICS 337110, 33712N]

Grace Pacific Corp., p. I-448 [NAICS 324121]

Graco Children's Products Inc, pp. Vol. II-1627, 1632, 1708 [NAICS 337127, 33712N, 33993M]

Graco Fertilizer Co., pp. Vol. I-516, 529 [NAICS 325311, 325320]

Graco Inc., pp. Vol. II-1092, 1179, 1184, 1189, 1229, 1432 [NAICS 33331N, 333911, 333912, 333913, 33399P, 335313]

Graeter's Inc., pp. Vol. I-52, 57, 92 [NAICS 311330, 311340, 311520]

Graftech International Ltd., p. II-1463 [NAICS 335991]

Grafton Village Cheese Co., p. III-2094 [NAICS 445299]

Graham Corp., p. II-1184 [NAICS 333912]

Numbers following p. or pp. are page references. Roman numerals indicate volume numbers. Bracketed items indicate industries. Page references are to the starting pages of company tables.

2348

Graham Manufacturing Inc., p. II-1184 [NAICS 333912]

Graham-White Manufacturing Inc., p. II-1217 [NAICS 333994]

Grain Millers Inc., p. I-36 [NAICS 311230]

Grain Processing Corp., pp. Vol. I-22, 172, 493, 500 [NAICS 311221, 312120, 32519M, 325211]

Gramercy Jewelry Mfg Corp., p. II-1696 [NAICS 33991M]

Grammer Dempsey & Hudson Inc., pp. Vol. II-945, 964, Vol. III-1824 [NAICS 332710, 33281M, 423510]

Granco Clark Inc., pp. Vol. II-1129, 1152 [NAICS 333513, 333518]

Grand Furniture Discount Stores, p. III-2037 [NAICS 442110]

Grand Home Furnishings, pp. Vol. III-2037, 2050, 2177 [NAICS 442110, 443111, 452910]

Grande Foods Corp., pp. Vol. I-133, 137 [NAICS 311830, 31191M]

Grandoe Corp., pp. Vol. I-296, Vol. II-1702, Vol. III-1916, 1919 [NAICS 316110, 339920, 424320, 424330]

Grandview Products Co., p. II-1611 [NAICS 337110]

Granger Farmers Cooperative, p. III-1933 [NAICS 424430]

Granite and Stone Solutions, p. I-762 [NAICS 327991]

Granite Bronze, p. I-762 [NAICS 327991]

Granite City Electric Supply Co., p. III-1831 [NAICS 423610]

Granite City Ready Mix Inc., p. III-1786 [NAICS 423320]

Granite Furniture Company Inc., pp. Vol. III-2037, 2041, 2044, 2054 [NAICS 442110, 442210, 442291, 443112]

Granite Rock Co., p. III-1786 [NAICS 423320]

Granitize Products Inc., p. III-1971 [NAICS 424690]

Grant Piston Rings, p. II-1505 [NAICS 33631M]

Grant Prideco Inc., pp. Vol. I-670, 788, Vol. II-1039 [NAICS 32629M, 331210, 33313M]

Graphaids Inc., p. III-1820 [NAICS 423490]

Graphel Corp., p. II-1463 [NAICS 335991]

Graphic Converting Inc., p. I-415 [NAICS 322299]

Graphic Engineering and Sales, p. II-1463 [NAICS 335991]

Graphic Image Inc., p. I-306 [NAICS 31699M]

Graphic Packaging International, pp. Vol. I-374, 379, 395 [NAICS 322130, 32221M, 32222P]

Graphic Sciences Inc., p. I-580 [NAICS 325910]

Graphic Systems Inc., p. III-1901 [NAICS 424120]

Graphic Technology Inc., p. I-388 [NAICS 32222N]

Graphite Die Mold Inc., p. II-1463 [NAICS 335991]

Graphite Electrodes Ltd., p. II-1603 [NAICS 336992]

Graphite Sales Inc., p. II-1463 [NAICS 335991]

GraphOn Corp., p. II-1248 [NAICS 334113]

Grasshopper Co., p. II-1028 [NAICS 333112]

Grassland Dairy Products Inc., pp. Vol. I-86, Vol. III-1933 [NAICS 31151N, 424430]

Graver Technologies Inc., pp. Vol. I-566, Vol. II-1229 [NAICS 32561M, 33399P]

Gray-Syracuse Inc., pp. Vol. I-837, 845, 857 [NAICS 33149M, 33151M, 33152P]

Graybar Electric Company Inc., p. III-1839 [NAICS 423690]

Grayhawk L.L.C., pp. Vol. I-752, 816 [NAICS 327420, 33131N]

Grayhill Inc., pp. Vol. II-1337, 1437, 1457 [NAICS 334513, 335314, 33593M]

Graymont of P.A., pp. Vol. I-748, Vol. II-1124 [NAICS 327410, 333512]

Grayson O Company Inc., p. II-886 [NAICS 33221N]

Great American Cookie Inc., p. I-124 [NAICS 31182M]

Great American Foods Corp., p. I-152 [NAICS 31194M]

Great American Wirebound Box, p. I-343 [NAICS 321920]

Great Atlantic and Pacific Tea Inc., pp. Vol. I-143, Vol. III-2076 [NAICS 311920, 445110]

Great Bend Cooperative, pp. Vol. III-1958, 2116 [NAICS 424510, 447110]

Great Dane Pub and Brewery, pp. Vol. I-172, Vol. III-1983 [NAICS 312120, 424810]

Great Foods of America Inc., p. I-26 [NAICS 311225]

Great Lakes Boat Top Inc., p. I-239 [NAICS 31491M]

Great Lakes Carbon Corp., p. I-463 [NAICS 324199]

Great Lakes Cheese Company Inc., p. I-76 [NAICS 311513]

Great Lakes Chemical Corp., pp. Vol. I-488, 560 [NAICS 325188, 325520]

Great Lakes Corrugated Corp., p. I-374 [NAICS 322130]

Great Lakes Die Cast Corp., p. I-852 [NAICS 33152N]

Great Lakes Fine Chemicals Inc., pp. Vol. I-471, 488 [NAICS 325120, 325188]

Great Lakes Industry Inc., p. II-1530 [NAICS 336350]

Great Lakes Intern. Recycling, pp. Vol. I-363, 807 [NAICS 322110, 331314]

Great Lakes L.L.C., p. II-1212 [NAICS 333993]

Great Lakes Pulp and Fiber Co., p. I-363 [NAICS 322110]

Great Lakes Rubber Company Inc., p. I-505 [NAICS 325212]

Great Lakes Tissue Company Inc., pp. Vol. I-368, 411 [NAICS 32212M, 322291]

Great Lakes Veneer Inc., p. I-324 [NAICS 32121N]

Great Lakes Waste Services Inc., p. III-1890 [NAICS 423930]

Great Neck Saw Manufacturers, pp. Vol. II-892, 1207, 1367 [NAICS 33221P, 333991, 334519]

Great Northern Corp., pp. Vol. I-379, 636, Vol. II-1720 [NAICS 32221M, 326140, 339950]

Great Plains-Coca Cola Btlng, p. I-165 [NAICS 31211M]

Great Plains Companies Inc., p. III-2065 [NAICS 444100]

Great Plains Industries Inc., pp. Vol. II-1222, 1342 [NAICS 33399N, 334514]

Great Planes Model Distributors, p. III-1887 [NAICS 423920]

Great River Food, p. III-1946 [NAICS 424470]

Great Southern Industries Inc., p. I-609 [NAICS 326112]

Great West Egg Industries, pp. Vol. III-1933, 1950 [NAICS 424430, 424480]

Great Western Malting Co., p. I-15 [NAICS 31121M]

Great Western Meats Inc., p. III-1946 [NAICS 424470]

Great Western Recycling Ind., p. I-807 [NAICS 331314]

Great Western Tortilla Co., p. I-133 [NAICS 311830]

Greater Kalamazoo Auto Auction, p. III-1758 [NAICS 423110]

Greater Rockford Auto Auction, pp. Vol. III-1758, 2027 [NAICS 423110, 441229]

Greco and Sons Inc., pp. Vol. III-1809, 2208 [NAICS 423440, 453998]

Grecon Dimter Inc., p. II-1046 [NAICS 333210]

Grede Foundries Inc., p. I-845 [NAICS 33151M]

Grede Foundry Inc., pp. Vol. I-845, 857 [NAICS 33151M, 33152P]

Green Bay Dressed Beef American, p. I-102 [NAICS 31161N]

Green Bay Packaging Inc., pp. Vol. I-368, 374, 379, 388, 415 [NAICS 32212M, 322130, 32221M, 32222N, 322299]

Green Dental Laboratories Inc., pp. Vol. II-1682, 1692 [NAICS 339114, 339116]

Green Mountain Coffee Roasters, p. I-143 [NAICS 311920]

Green Mountain Gringo, p. I-133 [NAICS 311830]

Green Orange Designs Inc., p. I-213 [NAICS 31324M]

Green Team of San Jose, p. III-1890 [NAICS 423930]

Green-Tek Inc., p. III-1998 [NAICS 424930]

Green Tokai Company Ltd., pp. Vol. I-621, 651, Vol. II-908, 1077, 1551 [NAICS 326121, 32619M, 33232M, 333313, 336399]

Green Tree Chemical Technologies, p. I-471 [NAICS 325120]

Green Tree Packing Co., p. I-110 [NAICS 31171M]

Green Valley Acquisition Co., pp. Vol. III-1979, 2116, 2177 [NAICS 424720, 447110, 452910]

Green Valley Chemical Corp., pp. Vol. I-471, 516 [NAICS 325120, 325311]

Greenbrier Companies Inc., p. II-1584 [NAICS 336510]

Greene Beverage Company Inc., p. III-1983 [NAICS 424810]

Greene Rubber Company Inc., p. III-2007 [NAICS 424990]

Greene, Tweed & Co., pp. Vol. II-980, 988, 1168, 1725 [NAICS 33291N, 332991, 333613, 339991]

Greenleaf Corp., pp. Vol. II-1124, 1134, 1140 [NAICS 333512, 333514, 333515]

Greenleaf Industries Inc., p. II-1051 [NAICS 333220]

Greenleaf Wholesale Florists, p. III-1998 [NAICS 424930]

Greenpages Inc., p. III-1805 [NAICS 423430]

Greensboro Auto Parts Inc., p. III-1770 [NAICS 423140]

Greenville Gravel Co., p. I-767 [NAICS 327992]

Greenwald Industries, p. II-1077 [NAICS 333313]

Greenway Co-Operative Service, p. III-1991 [NAICS 424910]

Greenwood Fire Apparatus Inc., p. II-1482 [NAICS 336120]

Greenwood Mills Inc., p. I-198 [NAICS 313210]

Greenwood Packing Plant, p. I-102 [NAICS 31161N]

Greer Citizen Inc., p. III-2186 [NAICS 453210]

Greer Lime Co., p. I-748 [NAICS 327410]

Greer Limestone, pp. Vol. I-448, 743, 748 [NAICS 324121, 327390, 327410]

Greetings and Readings Inc., p. III-2180 [NAICS 452990]

Gregory Industries Inc., p. I-863 [NAICS 332114]

Gregory Manufacturing Co., p. II-886 [NAICS 33221N]

Gregory Mountain Products, p. I-306 [NAICS 31699M]

Gregory Supply Company Inc., p. III-1794 [NAICS 423390]

Greif Inc., pp. Vol. I-334, 343, 379, 626, Vol. II-928 [NAICS 32191M, 321920, 32221M, 326122, 33243M]

Grenzebach AKI Corp., p. II-1046 [NAICS 333210]

Gresham Driving Aids Inc., p. II-1496 [NAICS 336213]

Gresham Petroleum Co., pp. Vol. III-1979, 2222 [NAICS 424720, 454312]

Grey Eagle Distributors Inc., p. III-1983 [NAICS 424810]

Greystar Corp., p. III-1867 [NAICS 423830]

Grieve Corp., p. II-1666 [NAICS 339111]

Griffin 88 Store Inc., p. III-2126 [NAICS 448120]

Griffin Food Co., pp. Vol. I-147, 152 [NAICS 311930, 31194M]

Griffin Industries Inc., p. I-102 [NAICS 31161N]

Griffin Land and Nurseries Inc., p. III-2072 [NAICS 444220]

Griffin Medical Products Inc., p. I-411 [NAICS 322291]

Griffin Wheel Co., p. II-1584 [NAICS 336510]

Griffin Wood Company Inc., p. III-1782 [NAICS 423310]

Griffith Laboratories Intern. Inc., pp. Vol. I-152, 158 [NAICS 31194M, 31199M]

Griffith Rubber Mills Inc., pp. Vol. II-1486, 1725 [NAICS 336211, 339991]

Griffiths Corp., p. I-879 [NAICS 33211P]

Griffon Corp., pp. Vol. I-334, 388, Vol. II-908, 1257 [NAICS 32191M, 32222N, 33232M, 334210]

Grindmaster Crathco Systems, pp. Vol. II-1189, 1397 [NAICS 333913, 33521M]

Griner Engineering Inc., p. II-952 [NAICS 332721]

Gro-Power Inc., pp. Vol. I-516, 529 [NAICS 325311, 325320]

Grob Inc., p. II-1046 [NAICS 333210]

Grobet File of America Inc., p. II-1682 [NAICS 339114]

Grocers Supply Co. Inc., pp. Vol. III-1909, 1925, 1939 [NAICS 424210, 424410, 424450]

Grocery Supply Co., pp. Vol. III-1925, 1939, 2001 [NAICS 424410, 424450, 424940]

Grooms Engines-Parts-Machining, p. II-1173 [NAICS 333618]

Gros-Ite Industries Div., p. II-1562 [NAICS 336412]

Gross Electric Inc., pp. Vol. III-1831, 2047 [NAICS 423610, 442299]

Grossel Tool Co., p. II-923 [NAICS 332420]

Grossenburg Implement Inc., p. III-1863 [NAICS 423820]

Grote Industries Inc., pp. Vol. I-722, Vol. II-1267, 1386, 1390, 1676 [NAICS 327215, 334290, 335110, 33512M, 339113]

Ground Control, p. I-218 [NAICS 31331M]

Group 1 Automotive Inc., pp. Vol. III-2011, 2027 [NAICS 441110, 441229]

Grow More Inc., pp. Vol. I-493, 520 [NAICS 32519M, 325312]

Growmark FS, p. I-520 [NAICS 325312]

GROWMARK Inc., pp. Vol. I-353, 524, Vol. II-899, Vol. III-2116 [NAICS 321992, 325314, 33231M, 447110]

Gruber Systems, pp. Vol. II-1014, 1061, 1134, 1179, 1194 [NAICS 33299N, 33329N, 333514, 333911, 33392M]

Gruett's Inc., p. I-348 [NAICS 321991]

Gruma Corp., p. I-137 [NAICS 31191M]

Grunau Company Inc., p. II-1009 [NAICS 332996]

Grupo Antolin Kentucky Inc., p. II-933 [NAICS 332510]

Grupo Deco California Corp., p. III-1875 [NAICS 423850]

GS Metals Corp., p. II-1584 [NAICS 336510]

GS Precision Inc., pp. Vol. II-1580, 1682 [NAICS 336419, 339114]

GSC Enterprises Inc., pp. Vol. III-1925, 2001 [NAICS 424410, 424940]

GT Equipment Technologies Inc., p. II-1056 [NAICS 333295]

GT Sales and Manufacturing Inc., p. I-670 [NAICS 32629M]

GTECH Holdings Corp., p. II-1077 [NAICS 333313]

GTI, p. I-544 [NAICS 325413]

GTSI Corp., p. III-1805 [NAICS 423430]

Guaranteed Foods Inc., p. III-2050 [NAICS 443111]

Guaranty Chevrolet-Pontiac, pp. Vol. II-1496, Vol. III-2011, 2018 [NAICS 336213, 441110, 441210]

Guard Line Inc., p. I-239 [NAICS 31491M]

Guardian Automotive, p. II-1541 [NAICS 336370]

Guardian Industries Corp., pp. Vol. I-709, Vol. II-1551 [NAICS 327211, 336399]

Gudebrod Inc., pp. Vol. I-192, 244 [NAICS 31311M, 314991]

Guerlain Inc., p. I-575 [NAICS 325620]

Guernsey Bel Inc., pp. Vol. I-57, 137 [NAICS 311340, 31191M]

Guernsey Dairy Stores Inc., p. I-92 [NAICS 311520]

Guess Inc., pp. Vol. I-272, 290, Vol. III-2123, 2126 [NAICS 31522M, 31599M, 448110, 448120]

Guggisberg Cheese Inc., p. I-76 [NAICS 311513]

Guhring Inc., pp. Vol. II-892, 1124, 1207 [NAICS 33221P, 333512, 333991]

Guidant Corp., p. II-1322 [NAICS 334510]

Guild Craft Furniture, pp. Vol. II-1616, 1621 [NAICS 337121, 337122]

Guilford Mills Inc., p. I-213 [NAICS 31324M]

Guinness UDV North America, p. I-181 [NAICS 312140]

Guitar Center Inc., p. III-2159 [NAICS 451140]

Guittard Chocolate Co., pp. Vol. I-52, 57, 124 [NAICS 311330, 311340, 31182M]

Gulbrandsen Manufacturing Inc., p. I-475 [NAICS 32513M]

Gulf Coast American Blind Corp., p. III-1778 [NAICS 423220]

Gulf Coast Pre-Stress Inc., p. I-743 [NAICS 327390]

Gulf Coast Regional Blood Center, pp. Vol. I-549, Vol. II-1676 [NAICS 325414, 339113]

Gulf Electroquip Inc., pp. Vol. II-1173, 1184, 1421 [NAICS 333618, 333912, 335311]

Gulf Island Fabrication Inc., p. II-1039 [NAICS 33313M]

Gulf Marine Repair Corp., p. II-1589 [NAICS 336611]

Gulf Oil L.P., p. III-1979 [NAICS 424720]

Gulf Pacific Rice Company Inc., p. III-1958 [NAICS 424510]

Gulf Performance Polymers Inc., p. I-589 [NAICS 325991]

Gulf States Asphalt Company Inc., pp. Vol. I-453, 560 [NAICS 324122, 325520]

Gulf States Paper Corp., pp. Vol. I-363, 374 [NAICS 322110, 322130]

Gulf States Toyota Inc., pp. Vol. III-1758, 1762 [NAICS 423110, 423120]

Gulf Stream Coach Inc., pp. Vol. II-1500, 1607 [NAICS 336214, 336999]

Gulf Stream Products Inc., p. I-677 [NAICS 327111]

Gulfside Supply Inc., p. III-1790 [NAICS 423330]

Gulfstream Aerospace Corp., pp. Vol. II-1557, 1580 [NAICS 336411, 336419]

Gull Industries Inc., pp. Vol. III-1979, 2116 [NAICS 424720, 447110]

Gund Inc., p. II-1708 [NAICS 33993M]

Gunderson Rail Services, pp. Vol. II-933, 1584, 1589 [NAICS 332510, 336510, 336611]

Gundlach-Bundschu Winery, p. I-177 [NAICS 312130]

Gundle/SLT Environmental Inc., p. I-615 [NAICS 326113]

Gunn Chevrolet Inc., p. III-2011 [NAICS 441110]

Gunnebo Johnson Corp., p. I-872 [NAICS 33211N]

Gunther International Ltd., p. II-1077 [NAICS 333313]

Gunton Corp., p. I-334 [NAICS 32191M]

Gunze USA Corp., p. II-1386 [NAICS 335110]

Gurley Precision Instruments, p. II-1342 [NAICS 334514]

Gusmer Machinery Group, p. II-1189 [NAICS 333913]

Gustafson's Dairy Inc., p. I-86 [NAICS 31151N]

Gutchess Lumber Company Inc., p. I-358 [NAICS 321999]

Guttermaker Inc., pp. Vol. I-863, Vol. II-1147 [NAICS 332114, 333516]

Guy Bennett Lumber Co., p. I-312 [NAICS 32111M]

GVM Inc., pp. Vol. II-1184, 1714 [NAICS 333912, 33994M]

Gwatney Chevrolet-Geo, p. III-2030 [NAICS 441310]

Gwatney Cos., p. III-2011 [NAICS 441110]

Gymboree Corp., p. III-2129 [NAICS 448130]

H. and E. Brothers Inc., p. III-1843 [NAICS 423710]

H and E Equipment Services, pp. Vol. III-1786, 1859 [NAICS 423320, 423810]

H and F Manufacturing Corp., p. I-453 [NAICS 324122]

H and H Furniture Co., p. I-1657 [NAICS 337910]

H and H Meat Products Inc., pp. Vol. I-102, Vol. III-1954 [NAICS 31161N, 424490]

Numbers following p. or pp. are page references. Roman numerals indicate volume numbers. Bracketed items indicate industries. Page references are to the starting pages of company tables.

2350

H and H Products Co., p. I-147 [NAICS 311930]

H and H Service Stores Inc., pp. Vol. III-2037, 2050, 2054 [NAICS 442110, 443111, 443112]

H and H Tube and Mfg Co., pp. Vol. I-830, 837, Vol. II-1009 [NAICS 33142M, 33149M, 332996]

H and K Dallas Inc., p. II-1627 [NAICS 337127]

H and L Poultry Processing L.L.C., p. I-97 [NAICS 311615]

H and L Tooth Co., p. II-1033 [NAICS 333120]

H and O Tool and Die Inc., p. II-1541 [NAICS 336370]

H and S Bakery Inc., p. I-116 [NAICS 31181M]

H and S Hardware, p. III-2065 [NAICS 444100]

H. Dennert Distributing Corp., p. III-1983 [NAICS 424810]

H-E-B Bakery Plant, pp. Vol. I-62, 116, 124 [NAICS 31141M, 31181M, 31182M]

H Heller and Company Inc., p. I-621 [NAICS 326121]

H Krevit and Company Inc., p. I-493 [NAICS 32519M]

H. Muehlstein and Company Inc., pp. Vol. III-1871, 1968 [NAICS 423840, 424610]

H. Smith Packing Corp., p. III-1950 [NAICS 424480]

H-Square Corp., p. II-1056 [NAICS 333295]

HA and Friend Company Inc., pp. Vol. III-1898, 1901, 1905 [NAICS 424110, 424120, 424130]

Haas Automation Inc., pp. Vol. II-1124, 1129 [NAICS 333512, 333513]

Haas Cabinet Company Inc., p. II-1611 [NAICS 337110]

HAB Industries Inc., p. I-218 [NAICS 31331M]

Habasit ABT Inc., p. I-665 [NAICS 326220]

Habbersett Sausage Inc., p. III-1946 [NAICS 424470]

Habersham Plantation Corp., p. II-1632 [NAICS 33712N]

HACCO Inc., p. I-529 [NAICS 325320]

HACH Ultra Analytics, pp. Vol. II-1082, 1342, 1352 [NAICS 333314, 334514, 334516]

Hacienda Mexican Foods L.L.C., p. I-133 [NAICS 311830]

Hadco Aluminum and Metals Corp., p. II-945 [NAICS 332710]

Hadco Inc., p. III-1835 [NAICS 423620]

Haden, Inc., pp. Vol. II-1217, 1740 [NAICS 333994, 339994]

Hader-Seitz Inc., p. II-923 [NAICS 332420]

Haeger Industries Inc., p. I-681 [NAICS 327112]

Haemonetics Corp., p. II-1671 [NAICS 339112]

Hagen Pet Foods Inc., p. I-4 [NAICS 311111]

Hager Co's, p. II-933 [NAICS 332510]

Haggar Clothing Co., p. I-272 [NAICS 31522M]

Haggar Corp., p. I-272 [NAICS 31522M]

Haggen Inc., p. III-2100 [NAICS 446110]

Hagopian and Sons Inc., p. III-2041 [NAICS 442210]

Hahn and Clay, p. II-923 [NAICS 332420]

Hahn Automotive Warehouse Inc., p. III-1762 [NAICS 423120]

Hail and Cotton Inc., p. III-1965 [NAICS 424590]

Hain Celestial Group Inc., p. I-68 [NAICS 31142M]

Haines and Kibblehouse Inc., p. I-448 [NAICS 324121]

Haines Equipment Inc., p. I-665 [NAICS 326220]

Hair U Wear, p. III-2007 [NAICS 424990]

Hajoca Corp., pp. Vol. III-1847, 1851 [NAICS 423720, 423730]

Haldeman-Homme Inc., p. III-1809 [NAICS 423440]

Haldex Brake Products Corp., p. II-1524 [NAICS 336340]

Haldor Topsoe Inc., pp. Vol. I-488, 516 [NAICS 325188, 325311]

Hale's Ales Ltd., p. I-172 [NAICS 312120]

Hale Trailer Brake and Wheel, pp. Vol. III-1758, 1762 [NAICS 423110, 423120]

Halifax Paving Inc., p. I-448 [NAICS 324121]

Hall, Bruce Corp., pp. Vol. III-2208, 2218 [NAICS 453998, 454311]

Hall Manufacturing Corp., p. I-621 [NAICS 326121]

Hall's Diving Center & Career, p. III-2150 [NAICS 451110]

Halliburton Co., p. II-1039 [NAICS 33313M]

Hallmark Building Supplies Inc., p. III-1794 [NAICS 423390]

Hallmark Cards Inc., pp. Vol. I-415, 780, Vol. II-1714, 1720, Vol. III-1898, 2186 [NAICS 322299, 33111M, 33994M, 339950, 424110, 453210]

Hallmark Sweet, p. II-1696 [NAICS 33991M]

Halls Merchandising Inc., p. III-2171 [NAICS 452111]

Hallsmith-Sysco Food Services, p. III-1925 [NAICS 424410]

Hallwood Group Inc., p. I-198 [NAICS 313210]

Halpin's Pharmacy Inc., p. III-2100 [NAICS 446110]

Halquist Stone Company Inc., p. I-762 [NAICS 327991]

Halron Oil Company Inc., pp. Vol. III-1979, 2116 [NAICS 424720, 447110]

Halton Co., pp. Vol. III-1859, 1879 [NAICS 423810, 423860]

Hamamatsu Corp., pp. Vol. II-1277, 1287, 1386 [NAICS 334411, 334413, 335110]

Hamel Forest Products Inc., p. I-358 [NAICS 321999]

Hamfab Products, p. I-771 [NAICS 327993]

Hamilton Fixture Co., p. II-1644 [NAICS 337215]

Hamilton Materials Inc., p. I-752 [NAICS 327420]

Hamilton Plastics Inc., p. I-609 [NAICS 326112]

Hamilton Products Inc., pp. Vol. I-306, 510 [NAICS 31699M, 32522M]

Hamilton Safe Products Inc., p. III-1820 [NAICS 423490]

Hamilton Sundstrand Corp., pp. Vol. II-1327, 1437, 1562, 1567, 1580 [NAICS 334511, 335314, 336412, 336413, 336419]

Hamlin Tool and Machine Inc., p. II-1541 [NAICS 336370]

Hammer and Wikan Inc., p. III-2177 [NAICS 452910]

Hammerhead Aviation L.L.C., p. III-1879 [NAICS 423860]

Hammill Manufacturing Inc., p. II-1134 [NAICS 333514]

Hammond Group Inc., pp. Vol. I-475, 825 [NAICS 32513M, 331419]

Hammond Lumber Co., p. I-312 [NAICS 32111M]

Hammond Machinery Inc., p. I-756 [NAICS 327910]

Hammons Products Company Inc., pp. Vol. I-137, Vol. III-1939 [NAICS 31191M, 424450]

Hamon Research-Cottrell Inc., p. I-699 [NAICS 327123]

Hampden Papers Inc., pp. Vol. I-368, 374 [NAICS 32212M, 322130]

Hampshire Chemical Corp., p. I-560 [NAICS 325520]

Hampshire Designers Inc., p. I-262 [NAICS 31519M]

Hampshire Group Ltd., pp. Vol. I-256, 262, 290 [NAICS 31511M, 31519M, 31599M]

Hampshire Manufacturing, p. I-267 [NAICS 31521M]

Hampton Affiliates, p. III-1782 [NAICS 423310]

Hampton Distribution Co's, p. III-1782 [NAICS 423310]

Hampton Transfer Prints Inc., p. II-1536 [NAICS 336360]

Hamrick Mills Inc., p. I-198 [NAICS 313210]

Hamrick's Inc., pp. Vol. I-290, Vol. III-2132 [NAICS 31599M, 448140]

Hamrock Inc., p. II-1644 [NAICS 337215]

Hamshaw Lumber Inc., p. III-1782 [NAICS 423310]

Hancock Fabrics Inc., pp. Vol. III-1913, 2156 [NAICS 424310, 451130]

Hancock Lumber Company Inc., p. I-312 [NAICS 32111M]

Hancor Inc., p. I-621 [NAICS 326121]

Handgards Inc., p. I-603 [NAICS 326111]

Handler Manufacturing Inc., p. II-1682 [NAICS 339114]

Handschy Industries Inc., pp. Vol. I-580, 595 [NAICS 325910, 32599N]

Handy and Harman, p. I-837 [NAICS 33149M]

Handy & Harman Electronic, p. II-1541 [NAICS 336370]

Handy Home Products, p. I-353 [NAICS 321992]

Hang-Em-All Products Corp., p. I-718 [NAICS 327121]

Hanger Orthopedic Group Inc., p. II-1676 [NAICS 339113]

Hangsterfers Laboratories Inc., p. I-458 [NAICS 324191]

Hanley Industries Inc., p. I-585 [NAICS 325920]

Hanna Instruments Inc., p. I-471 [NAICS 325120]

Hanna's Candle Co., p. III-2007 [NAICS 424990]

Hanna Steel Corp., pp. Vol. I-780, Vol. II-964 [NAICS 33111M, 33281M]

Hannaford Brothers Co., pp. Vol. III-2076, 2100 [NAICS 445110, 446110]

Hannan Supply Co., p. III-1831 [NAICS 423610]

Hannibal Industries Inc., pp. Vol. I-780, 788, 879 [NAICS 33111M, 331210, 33211P]

Hanover Direct Inc., p. III-2211 [NAICS 454113]

Hanover Foods Corp., pp. Vol. I-62, 68 [NAICS 31141M, 31142M]

Hanovia Inc., pp. Vol. II-1302, 1386 [NAICS 334416, 335110]

Hans Johnsen Co., p. III-1883 [NAICS 423910]

Hans Kissle Company Inc., p. I-92 [NAICS 311520]

Hansen Beverage Co., p. I-165 [NAICS 31211M]

Hansen Natural Corp., p. I-165 [NAICS 31211M]

Hansen's Surfboards Inc., p. III-1883 [NAICS 423910]

Hansol Multitech Inc., p. II-1248 [NAICS 334113]

Hanson Aggregates East Inc., p. I-748 [NAICS 327410]

Hanson Building Materials, pp. Vol. I-737, 743 [NAICS 32733M, 327390]

Hanson Permanente Cement, p. I-727 [NAICS 327310]

Hanson Pipe and Products Inc., p. I-737 [NAICS 32733M]

Hanson Tank, p. II-923 [NAICS 332420]

Hanson Tire Service Inc., p. III-1766 [NAICS 423130]

Hanson Truss Inc., p. I-329 [NAICS 32121P]

Happ Controls Inc., pp. Vol. II-1092, 1437, Vol. III-1875 [NAICS 33331N, 335314, 423850]

Happy Floors, p. III-1786 [NAICS 423320]

Happy Harry's Inc., p. III-2100 [NAICS 446110]

Harbison-Fischer Inc., pp. Vol. II-1039, 1179 [NAICS 33313M, 333911]

Harbison-Walker Refractories Co., pp. Vol. I-703, 727 [NAICS 32712N, 327310]

Harbor Auto Liquidators, p. III-2015 [NAICS 441120]

Harbor Industries Inc., p. II-1720 [NAICS 339950]

Harbor Linen, p. III-1778 [NAICS 423220]

Harbor Packaging Inc., p. III-1901 [NAICS 424120]

Harbor Sweets Inc., p. III-2092 [NAICS 445292]

Harbor Truck Sales & Service Inc., p. III-1758 [NAICS 423110]

Harbortown, p. II-1657 [NAICS 337910]

Harbour Industries Inc., p. II-1451 [NAICS 33592M]

Harco Brake Systems Inc., p. II-1524 [NAICS 336340]

Harco Industries Inc., p. II-1524 [NAICS 336340]

Harco Laboratories Inc., p. II-1332 [NAICS 334512]

Harcourt Outlines Inc., p. II-1714 [NAICS 33994M]

Harcourt Pencil Company Inc., p. II-1714 [NAICS 33994M]

Harcros Chemicals Inc., p. I-595 [NAICS 32599N]

Hard Manufacturing Company Inc., p. II-1657 [NAICS 337910]

Hardee's Food Systems Inc., pp. Vol. I-68, 102 [NAICS 31142M, 31161N]

Hardel Mutual Plywood Corp., p. I-324 [NAICS 32121N]

Harden Furniture Company Inc., pp. Vol. II-1621, 1650 [NAICS 337122, 33721N]

Harder Mechanical Contractors Inc., p. I-358 [NAICS 321999]

Hardie-Tynes Company Inc., p. II-1152 [NAICS 333518]

Hardigg Industries Inc., pp. Vol. I-670, Vol. II-928 [NAICS 32629M, 33243M]

Hardin Tubular Sales Inc., p. III-1968 [NAICS 424610]

Harding Energy Inc., pp. Vol. II-1442, 1447 [NAICS 335911, 335912]

Harding Metals Inc., p. III-1890 [NAICS 423930]

Hardinge Inc., pp. Vol. II-1061, 1124, 1140, 1152 [NAICS 33329N, 333512, 333515, 333518]

Hardrives Inc., p. I-453 [NAICS 324122]

Hardwick Clothes Inc., p. I-279 [NAICS 31523M]

Hardwick Knitted Fabrics Inc., p. I-213 [NAICS 31324M]

Hardwood Products Company L.P., p. I-358 [NAICS 321999]

Hardwoods of Michigan Inc., p. I-358 [NAICS 321999]

Harford Systems Inc., p. II-1023 [NAICS 333111]

Hargrove Inc., p. II-1720 [NAICS 339950]

Harker's Distribution Inc., pp. Vol. III-1929, 1936 [NAICS 424420, 424440]

Harlan Bakeries Inc., p. I-124 [NAICS 31182M]

Harley-Davidson Inc., p. II-1599 [NAICS 336991]

Harley Gray Stone Company Inc., p. I-762 [NAICS 327991]

Harman Consumer Products, p. II-1272 [NAICS 334310]

Harman Intern. Industries Inc., p. II-1272 [NAICS 334310]

Harmon Associates Corp., p. III-1890 [NAICS 423930]

Harmon Contract Inc., p. I-709 [NAICS 327211]

Harmonic Inc., pp. Vol. I-713, Vol. II-1257, 1262 [NAICS 327212, 334210, 334220]

Harmony Computers & Electronics, p. III-2058 [NAICS 443120]

Harmony Foods Corp., pp. Vol. I-57, 137 [NAICS 311340, 31191M]

Harmsco Inc., p. I-395 [NAICS 32222P]

Harodite Industries Inc., pp. Vol. I-218, 251 [NAICS 31331M, 314999]

Harold Beck and Sons Inc., p. II-1162 [NAICS 333612]

Harold Import Company Inc., p. III-1778 [NAICS 423220]

Harold Johnson Optical, p. I-709 [NAICS 327211]

Harold L. Keay and Son, p. III-2177 [NAICS 452910]

Harold's Stores Inc., pp. Vol. III-2123, 2126, 2211 [NAICS 448110, 448120, 454113]

Harold's Tire and Auto, p. III-1766 [NAICS 423130]

Harold Tymer Company Inc., p. III-2062 [NAICS 443130]

Harper Brush Works, pp. Vol. II-1397, 1740 [NAICS 33521M, 339994]

Harper Leather Goods Mfg Inc., p. I-306 [NAICS 31699M]

Harpoon Brewery, p. I-172 [NAICS 312120]

Harrell's Inc., pp. Vol. I-520, 524 [NAICS 325312, 325314]

Harrell-Swatty Cos., p. III-2011 [NAICS 441110]

Harrington and Co., pp. Vol. III-1786, 1843 [NAICS 423320, 423710]

Harris Corp., pp. Vol. II-1077, 1257, 1262, 1267, 1287, 1317 [NAICS 333313, 334210, 334220, 334290, 334413, 334419]

Harris Electric Inc., p. III-1831 [NAICS 423610]

Harris Environmental Systems Inc., p. II-1666 [NAICS 339111]

Harris Lighting, pp. Vol. II-1386, 1390 [NAICS 335110, 33512M]

Harris Ranch Beef Co., p. I-102 [NAICS 31161N]

Harris Steel Co., p. I-793 [NAICS 33122M]

Harris Teeter Inc., p. III-2076 [NAICS 445110]

Harris-Thomas Industries Inc., pp. Vol. I-872, Vol. II-1173, 1519 [NAICS 33211N, 333618, 336330]

Harrisburg Dairies Inc., p. I-81 [NAICS 311514]

Harrison Jet Guns II L.P., p. I-585 [NAICS 325920]

Harrison Poultry Inc., p. I-97 [NAICS 311615]

Harrison Steel Castings Co., p. I-845 [NAICS 33151M]

Harriss & Covington Hosiery Mills, p. I-256 [NAICS 31511M]

Harry J Rashti and Company Inc., p. I-285 [NAICS 31529M]

Harry London Candies Inc., pp. Vol. I-52, 57 [NAICS 311330, 311340]

Harry Winston Inc., pp. Vol. II-1696, Vol. III-2144 [NAICS 33991M, 448310]

Harsco Corp., pp. Vol. I-837, Vol. II-899, 908, 1009, 1092 [NAICS 33149M, 33231M, 33232M, 332996, 33331N]

Hart Furniture, pp. Vol. II-1632, 1657 [NAICS 33712N, 337910]

Hart Heat Transfer Products Inc., p. II-918 [NAICS 332410]

Hartford Concrete Products Inc., p. I-743 [NAICS 327390]

Hartford Distributors Inc., p. III-1983 [NAICS 424810]

Hartford Springfield Auction, p. III-1758 [NAICS 423110]

Hartmarx Corp., pp. Vol. I-272, 279, Vol. III-2123 [NAICS 31522M, 31523M, 448110]

Hartness International Inc., p. II-1212 [NAICS 333993]

Hartstrings, p. I-279 [NAICS 31523M]

Hartung Agalite Glass Co., p. I-709 [NAICS 327211]

Hartz Mountain Corp., pp. Vol. I-9, 137, Vol. II-1749 [NAICS 311119, 31191M, 339999]

Hartzell Propeller Inc., p. II-1567 [NAICS 336413]

Harvard Custom Mfg Inc., p. II-1312 [NAICS 334418]

Harvest Farms Inc., p. III-1929 [NAICS 424420]

Harvest Land Co-Op Inc., pp. Vol. I-9, 524, 529 [NAICS 311119, 325314, 325320]

Harvest Land Coop., p. I-524 [NAICS 325314]

Harvest Select Catfish, p. I-110 [NAICS 31171M]

Harvey Electronics Inc., p. III-2054 [NAICS 443112]

Harvey Fertilizer and Gas Inc., pp. Vol. I-516, 524 [NAICS 325311, 325314]

Harvey Gerstman & Associates, p. III-1843 [NAICS 423710]

Harvey Industries Inc., pp. Vol. II-908, Vol. III-1790 [NAICS 33232M, 423330]

Hasbro Inc., p. II-1708 [NAICS 33993M]

Haskel International Inc., p. II-1157 [NAICS 333611]

Haskell Livestock Auction Inc., p. III-1962 [NAICS 424520]

Haskell Office L.L.C., p. III-1774 [NAICS 423210]

Hastings Entertainment Inc., p. III-2168 [NAICS 451220]

Hastings Manufacturing Co., pp. Vol. I-458, Vol. II-892, 1505 [NAICS 324191, 33221P, 33631M]

Hastings Tile and Bath Inc., p. III-1786 [NAICS 423320]

Hat World Corp., p. I-290 [NAICS 31599M]

Hatch and Kirk Inc., p. II-1505 [NAICS 33631M]

Hatch Stamping Co., p. II-1134 [NAICS 333514]

HATCO, pp. Vol. I-272, 290, Vol. II-1696 [NAICS 31522M, 31599M, 33991M]

Hatco Corp., pp. Vol. II-1092, 1404, 1417, 1720 [NAICS 33331N, 335221, 335228, 339950]

Hatfield Quality Meats, p. I-102 [NAICS 31161N]

Hatley's Electronics, p. II-1277 [NAICS 334411]

Haulmark Industries Inc., pp. Vol. II-1491, 1500 [NAICS 336212, 336214]

Haumiller Engineering Co., p. II-1152 [NAICS 333518]

Havco Wood Products L.L.C., p. II-1491 [NAICS 336212]

Haven Homes Inc., p. I-353 [NAICS 321992]

Haverhill Paperboard, p. I-374 [NAICS 322130]

Haverty Furniture Companies Inc., p. III-2037 [NAICS 442110]

Hawaii Metal Recycling Co., p. I-807 [NAICS 331314]

Hawaiian Tropic, p. I-575 [NAICS 325620]

Hawk Corp., pp. Vol. II-933, 1567 [NAICS 332510, 336413]

Hawk Electronics, p. III-1839 [NAICS 423690]

Hawk-Eye Picture Tube Mfg Inc., p. II-1277 [NAICS 334411]

Hawker Pacific Aerospace, pp. Vol. II-1567, Vol. III-1879 [NAICS 336413, 423860]

Hawkeye Group Inc., p. II-1147 [NAICS 333516]

Hawkins Inc., pp. Vol. I-475, 566, Vol. III-1867 [NAICS 32513M, 32561M, 423830]

Haworth Inc., pp. Vol. II-1627, 1644, 1650 [NAICS 337127, 337215, 33721N]

Hawthorne Machinery Inc., pp. Vol. III-1831, 1867 [NAICS 423610, 423830]

Hayden's Sports Center Inc., p. III-1883 [NAICS 423910]

Haydock Caster Co., p. I-670 [NAICS 32629M]

Haydon Corp., p. I-863 [NAICS 332114]

Haydon Switch and Instrument, p. II-1332 [NAICS 334512]

Hayes Company Inc., pp. Vol. II-892, 1028 [NAICS 33221P, 333112]

Hayes Industries Inc., pp. Vol. I-621, Vol. II-1451 [NAICS 326121, 33592M]

Hayes Lemmerz International Inc., p. II-1551 [NAICS 336399]

Hayes Products L.L.C., p. II-1028 [NAICS 333112]

Haynes Corp., p. II-1173 [NAICS 333618]

Haynes International Inc., pp. Vol. I-554, 793, 837 [NAICS 325510, 33122M, 33149M]

Haysite Reinforced Plastics, pp. Vol. I-631, 771 [NAICS 326130, 327993]

Hayssen Packaging Technologies, p. II-1212 [NAICS 333993]

Hayward Industrial Products, pp. Vol. I-651, Vol. II-1112, 1702 [NAICS 32619M, 33341N, 339920]

Hazelett Strip-Casting Corp., p. II-1129 [NAICS 333513]

Hazen Paper Co., p. I-368 [NAICS 32212M]

Hazentec L.L.C., p. I-867 [NAICS 332117]

H.B. Fuller Co., pp. Vol. I-554, 560, Vol. II-964 [NAICS 325510, 325520, 33281M]

HB Mellott Estate Inc., pp. Vol. I-732, 748, 767 [NAICS 327320, 327410, 327992]

HBA Cast Products Company Inc., pp. Vol. I-852, 857 [NAICS 33152N, 33152P]

HBD Industries Inc., pp. Vol. I-665, 670, Vol. II-933 [NAICS 326220, 32629M, 332510]

HC Brill Company Inc., pp. Vol. I-147, 158, 566 [NAICS 311930, 31199M, 32561M]

H.C. Davis Company Inc., p. III-1933 [NAICS 424430]

H.C. Gabler Inc., p. III-1766 [NAICS 423130]

H.C. Lewis Oil Co., pp. Vol. III-1766, 1770, 1975 [NAICS 423130, 423140, 424710]

HC Merchandisers Inc., p. III-1879 [NAICS 423860]

HC Miller Co., p. I-403 [NAICS 32223M]

HC Power Inc., p. II-1421 [NAICS 335311]

HCC Inc., pp. Vol. II-892, 939, 1023 [NAICS 33221P, 33261M, 333111]

HCC Industries Inc., p. II-1317 [NAICS 334419]

HCI Direct Inc., p. I-256 [NAICS 31511M]

HCP Packaging, p. II-928 [NAICS 33243M]

H.D. Sheldon and Company Inc., p. III-1809 [NAICS 423440]

HDJ Company Inc., p. II-952 [NAICS 332721]

HDMG, p. II-1381 [NAICS 334613]

HE and M Inc., p. II-1046 [NAICS 333210]

H.E. Butt Grocery Co., p. III-2076 [NAICS 445110]

HE W Waste Recycling Inc., p. I-363 [NAICS 322110]

HE Williams Inc., pp. Vol. II-1386, 1390 [NAICS 335110, 33512M]

Head/Penn Racquet Sports, pp. Vol. II-1702, Vol. III-1883 [NAICS 339920, 423910]

Header Products Inc., p. II-952 [NAICS 332721]

Headwaters Inc., pp. Vol. I-463, Vol. II-1014 [NAICS 324199, 33299N]

Headway Research Inc., p. II-1056 [NAICS 333295]

Heafner Tires and Products 113, p. III-1766 [NAICS 423130]

Healy News Store Inc., p. III-2165 [NAICS 451212]

Heart Truss and Engineering Corp., p. I-329 [NAICS 32121P]

Heartland Co-op, pp. Vol. I-9, 524, 595, Vol. III-1958, 1991 [NAICS 311119, 325314, 32599N, 424510, 424910]

Heartland Corn Products, p. I-493 [NAICS 32519M]

Heartland Eps Inc., pp. Vol. I-636, 641 [NAICS 326140, 326150]

Heartland Paper Co., p. III-1898 [NAICS 424110]

Heartland USA Inc., p. I-244 [NAICS 314991]

HearUSA Inc., p. III-2208 [NAICS 453998]

Heat Seal L.L.C., p. II-1212 [NAICS 333993]

Heat Transfer Products, p. II-1417 [NAICS 335228]

Heatbath Corp., pp. Vol. II-1152, 1217 [NAICS 333518, 333994]

Heater Specialists L.L.C., pp. Vol. I-703; Vol. II-923 [NAICS 32712N, 332420]

Heath Consultants Inc., p. II-1327 [NAICS 334511]

Heatron Inc., p. II-1101 [NAICS 333414]

Hebco Products Inc., p. II-1524 [NAICS 336340]

Hebert Candies, pp. Vol. I-52, 57 [NAICS 311330, 311340]

Hedahls Parts Plus, p. III-2030 [NAICS 441310]

Hedb Corp., pp. Vol. II-1442, 1447 [NAICS 335911, 335912]

Hedman/TD Performance, p. III-1762 [NAICS 423120]

Hegar 4 Products Inc., p. II-1607 [NAICS 336999]

Heick Die Casting Corp., p. I-852 [NAICS 33152N]

HEICO Aerospace Holdings Corp., pp. Vol. II-1562, 1567 [NAICS 336412, 336413]

HEICO Corp., pp. Vol. II-1562, 1567 [NAICS 336412, 336413]

Heidelberg/Baumfolder Corp., p. II-1077 [NAICS 333313]

Heidelberg Web Systems, pp. Vol. II-1061, 1077 [NAICS 33329N, 333313]

Heidenhain Corp., p. III-1820 [NAICS 423490]

Heidtman Steel Products Inc., pp. Vol. II-908, 964, Vol. III-1824 [NAICS 33232M, 33281M, 423510]

Heil Trailer International, p. II-1194 [NAICS 33392M]

Heilig-Meyers Co., pp. Vol. III-2037, 2041, 2050, 2054 [NAICS 442110, 442210, 443111, 443112]

Heilind Electronics Inc., p. III-1839 [NAICS 423690]

Heim Bearings, pp. Vol. II-988, 1519 [NAICS 332991, 336330]

Heines Insulators Incorporated, p. III-1790 [NAICS 423330]

Heinkel's Packing Company Inc., p. III-1946 [NAICS 424470]

Heinz Frozen Food Co., p. I-62 [NAICS 31141M]

Heinz North America, pp. Vol. I-68, 152, 158 [NAICS 31142M, 31194M, 31199M]

Hekman Furniture Co., pp. Vol. II-1621, 1650 [NAICS 337122, 33721N]

Hekman Furniture Inc, pp. Vol. II-1611, 1621, 1650 [NAICS 337110, 337122, 33721N]

Helby Import Co., p. III-1894 [NAICS 423940]

Helen Grace Chocolates Inc., p. III-1939 [NAICS 424450]

Helen of Troy Ltd., pp. Vol. II-1397, Vol. III-1835, 1909, 1913 [NAICS 33521M, 423620, 424210, 424310]

Helen of Troy Texas Corp., pp. Vol. III-1835, 1909, 1913 [NAICS 423620, 424210, 424310]

Helena Chemical Co., pp. Vol. I-488, 493, 529 [NAICS 325188, 32519M, 325320]

Helena Industries Inc., pp. Vol. I-306, 343 [NAICS 31699M, 321920]

Helena Laboratories Corp., pp. Vol. I-544, Vol. II-1352, 1666 [NAICS 325413, 334516, 339111]

Helical Products Company Inc., p. II-1530 [NAICS 336350]

Helicomb International Inc., p. II-1557 [NAICS 336411]

Helio Precision Products Inc., p. II-1505 [NAICS 33631M]

Helix Technology Corp., pp. Vol. II-1179, 1184, 1327 [NAICS 333911, 333912, 334511]

Hella Electronics Corp., pp. Vol. II-1347, 1437, 1457 [NAICS 334515, 335314, 33593M]

Hella Lighting Corp., p. II-1386 [NAICS 335110]

Hella North America Inc., pp. Vol. II-933, 1106, 1332, 1437, 1512 [NAICS 332510, 333415, 334512, 335314, 33632M]

Heller Performance Polymers Inc., p. I-589 [NAICS 325991]

Heller's Carbonic West, p. I-471 [NAICS 325120]

Hellermanntyton Corp., pp. Vol. I-554, Vol. II-933, 939 [NAICS 325510, 332510, 33261M]

Helmer Labs Inc., p. II-1666 [NAICS 339111]

Helmerich and Payne Inc., p. I-475 [NAICS 32513M]

Heluva Good Cheese Inc., p. I-76 [NAICS 311513]

Helwig Carbon Products Inc., pp. Vol. II-939, 1463, 1740 [NAICS 33261M, 335991, 339994]

Helzberg's Diamond Shops Inc., p. III-2144 [NAICS 448310]

Hemagen Diagnostics Inc., p. I-544 [NAICS 325413]

Hemocue Inc., p. III-2113 [NAICS 446199]

Numbers following p. or pp. are page references. Roman numerals indicate volume numbers. Bracketed items indicate industries. Page references are to the starting pages of company tables.

2353

Hemophilia Health Services Inc., p. III-2100 [NAICS 446110]

Hempt Brothers Inc., pp. Vol. I-448, 732 [NAICS 324121, 327320]

Hendee Enterprises Inc., p. I-239 [NAICS 31491M]

Henderson Auctions Inc., p. III-1809 [NAICS 423440]

Henderson Coffee Corp., p. I-143 [NAICS 311920]

Henderson Engineering Inc., p. II-1217 [NAICS 333994]

Hendrick Automotive Group, p. III-2011 [NAICS 441110]

Hendrickson Truck Suspension, p. II-1486 [NAICS 336211]

Hendrix Manufacturing Inc., p. II-1039 [NAICS 33313M]

Hendrix Wire and Cable Inc., p. II-1451 [NAICS 33592M]

Hendry Corp., p. II-1589 [NAICS 336611]

Henkel Corp., pp. Vol. I-554, 560, 566, 575 [NAICS 325510, 325520, 32561M, 325620]

Henkel Loctite Corp., p. I-458 [NAICS 324191]

Henkel Technologies, p. I-560 [NAICS 325520]

Henkle Consumer Adhesives, pp. Vol. I-203, 388, 651, Vol. II-1077 [NAICS 31322M, 32222N, 32619M, 333313]

HENN, pp. Vol. I-343, Vol. II-1708 [NAICS 321920, 33993M]

Henningsen Foods Inc., pp. Vol. I-102, 158 [NAICS 31161N, 31199M]

Henri Bendel Inc., p. III-2126 [NAICS 448120]

Henri Studio Inc., p. I-681 [NAICS 327112]

Henry A. Fox Sales Co., p. III-1987 [NAICS 424820]

Henry and Henry Inc., p. I-147 [NAICS 311930]

Henry Brick Company Inc., p. I-691 [NAICS 327121]

Henry Company Inc., pp. Vol. I-453, 727 [NAICS 324122, 327310]

Henry Schein Inc., p. III-1813 [NAICS 423450]

Henry Technologies Inc., pp. Vol. II-1112, 1217, 1332 [NAICS 33341N, 333994, 334512]

Henry Wurst Inc., p. I-436 [NAICS 32312M]

Hensley Industries Inc., pp. Vol. I-845, Vol. II-1033 [NAICS 33151M, 333120]

Heraeus Electro-Nite Co., pp. Vol. II-1327, 1337 [NAICS 334511, 334513]

Heraeus Kulzer Inc., pp. Vol. I-752, Vol. II-1682 [NAICS 327420, 339114]

Heraeus Metal Processing Inc., p. II-1292 [NAICS 334414]

Heraeus Tenevo Inc., pp. Vol. I-713, Vol. II-1451 [NAICS 327212, 33592M]

Herb Chambers Cos., p. III-2011 [NAICS 441110]

Herbalife International Inc., pp. Vol. III-1909, 2094, 2228 [NAICS 424210, 445299, 454390]

Herbert Malarkey Roofing Co., p. I-453 [NAICS 324122]

Hercules Cement Co., p. I-727 [NAICS 327310]

Hercules Inc., pp. Vol. I-147, 493, 500, 510, 560, 566, 575, 595 [NAICS 311930, 32519M, 325211, 32522M, 325520, 32561M, 325620, 32599N]

Hercules Tire and Rubber Co., p. III-1766 [NAICS 423130]

Herff Jones Inc., pp. Vol. II-1696, 1749 [NAICS 33991M, 339999]

Heritage Communications Inc., p. III-2054 [NAICS 443112]

Heritage Dairy Stores Inc., p. III-2094 [NAICS 445299]

Heritage Ford Lincoln Mercury, p. III-2030 [NAICS 441310]

Heritage FS Inc., pp. Vol. III-1979, 1991, 2072, 2116 [NAICS 424720, 424910, 444220, 447110]

Heritage Homes of Nebraska Inc., p. I-353 [NAICS 321992]

Heritage Lace Inc., pp. Vol. III-1778, 1913 [NAICS 423220, 424310]

Heritage Operating L.P., p. III-2222 [NAICS 454312]

Heritage Paper Company Inc., pp. Vol. III-1898, 1905 [NAICS 424110, 424130]

Heritage Pontiac Buick GMC, p. III-1758 [NAICS 423110]

Heritage Products Inc., p. II-1519 [NAICS 336330]

Heritage Sportswear L.L.C., p. I-262 [NAICS 31519M]

Herley Industries Inc., p. II-1327 [NAICS 334511]

Herman Miller Greenhouse, p. II-1650 [NAICS 33721N]

Herman Miller Inc., pp. Vol. I-324, Vol. II-1627, 1644, 1650 [NAICS 32121N, 337127, 337215, 33721N]

Herman's Bakery and Coffee Shop, p. III-2089 [NAICS 445291]

Hermann Oak Leather Co., p. I-296 [NAICS 316110]

Hermes Abrasives L.P., p. I-756 [NAICS 327910]

Hermetic Switch Inc., p. II-1432 [NAICS 335313]

Herr Foods Inc., pp. Vol. I-137, 158 [NAICS 31191M, 31199M]

Herrick and White Ltd., p. II-1639 [NAICS 337212]

Herschel-Adams Inc., pp. Vol. II-892, 1023 [NAICS 33221P, 333111]

Hersey Meters, p. II-1342 [NAICS 334514]

Hershey Creamery Co., p. I-92 [NAICS 311520]

Hershey Foods Corp., pp. Vol. I-48, 52, 68, 147 [NAICS 311320, 311330, 31142M, 311930]

Hesco Parts Corp., p. II-1505 [NAICS 33631M]

Heska Corp., p. I-549 [NAICS 325414]

Hess Collection Winery Inc., p. I-177 [NAICS 312130]

Hesselberg Drug Co., p. III-2100 [NAICS 446110]

HETRA Secure Solutions Corp., p. II-1238 [NAICS 334111]

Heumann & Associates Dental, p. II-1692 [NAICS 339116]

Hewlett-Packard Co., pp. Vol. II-1238, 1252 [NAICS 334111, 334119]

Hexagram Inc., p. II-1332 [NAICS 334512]

Hexcel Corp., pp. Vol. I-198, 224, 500, 776, 879 [NAICS 313210, 313320, 325211, 327999, 33211P]

Heyco Metals Inc., p. I-879 [NAICS 33211P]

Heyman Corp., pp. Vol. III-1916, 1919 [NAICS 424320, 424330]

H.F. Coors China Co., p. I-681 [NAICS 327112]

H.H. Gregg Appliances, pp. Vol. III-2050, 2054 [NAICS 443111, 443112]

Hi-Lex Controls Inc., p. II-1432 [NAICS 335313]

Hi-Lex Corp., pp. Vol. I-837, Vol. II-1437 [NAICS 33149M, 335314]

HI PRO International Inc., p. I-453 [NAICS 324122]

Hi Rel Connectors Inc., p. II-1307 [NAICS 334417]

Hi-Shear Technology Corp., p. II-1005 [NAICS 332995]

Hi-Tec Sports USA Inc., p. III-1922 [NAICS 424340]

HI-Tech Housing Inc., pp. Vol. I-348, 353 [NAICS 321991, 321992]

Hi-Tech Mold and Engineering, p. II-1119 [NAICS 333511]

Hi-Tech Pharmacal Co. Inc., p. I-534 [NAICS 325411]

Hi-Tek Manufacturing Inc., pp. Vol. II-1505, 1562 [NAICS 33631M, 336412]

Hi-Temperature Insulation Inc., p. I-771 [NAICS 327993]

HI Way Auto Inc., p. III-1770 [NAICS 423140]

Hibbett Sporting Goods Inc., p. III-2150 [NAICS 451110]

Hickenbottom and Sons Inc., p. III-1950 [NAICS 424480]

Hickman, Williams and Co., p. III-1828 [NAICS 423520]

Hickory Brands Inc., pp. Vol. I-203, 244, Vol. III-1922 [NAICS 31322M, 314991, 424340]

Hickory Hill Furniture Inc., p. II-1616 [NAICS 337121]

Hickory Industries Inc., p. II-1404 [NAICS 335221]

Hickory Springs Mfg of California, p. I-641 [NAICS 326150]

Hickory Tech Corp., p. III-2208 [NAICS 453998]

Hickory Yarns, pp. Vol. I-192, 218 [NAICS 31311M, 31331M]

Hico Helium and Balloons, p. III-1887 [NAICS 423920]

Hidy Motors Inc., p. III-1758 [NAICS 423110]

Higbee Inc., p. I-771 [NAICS 327993]

Higdon Furniture Co., p. II-1657 [NAICS 337910]

Higgins Brick Co., p. I-737 [NAICS 32733M]

High Concrete Structures Inc., p. I-743 [NAICS 327390]

High Grade Beverage, pp. Vol. III-1954, 1983 [NAICS 424490, 424810]

High Life Sales Co., p. III-1983 [NAICS 424810]

High Performance Tube Inc., p. I-788 [NAICS 331210]

High Plains Corp., p. I-488 [NAICS 325188]

High Point Furniture Industries Inc., p. II-1616 [NAICS 337121]

High Quality Plastics Inc., p. II-1725 [NAICS 339991]

High Sierra Sport Co., p. I-262 [NAICS 31519M]

High Tech Elastomers Inc., p. I-505 [NAICS 325212]

High Technology Video Inc., pp. Vol. II-1376, 1381 [NAICS 334612, 334613]

Highland Containers Inc., p. II-928 [NAICS 33243M]

Highland Graphics Inc., p. I-762 [NAICS 327991]

Highland Manufacturing Co., p. I-348 [NAICS 321991]

Highland Mills Inc., p. I-256 [NAICS 31511M]

Highland Park Market Inc., p. III-2076 [NAICS 445110]

Highland Propane Co., p. III-2222 [NAICS 454312]

Highland Tank and Manufacturing, p. II-923 [NAICS 332420]

Highlight Industries Inc., p. II-1212 [NAICS 333993]

Highway Asphalt Co., p. I-448 [NAICS 324121]

Numbers following p. or pp. are page references. Roman numerals indicate volume numbers. Bracketed items indicate industries. Page references are to the starting pages of company tables.

2354

Hiland Dairy Foods L.L.C., pp. Vol. I-62, 86, 92, 646 [NAICS 31141M, 31151N, 311520, 326160]

Hilco, pp. Vol. II-892, 1082 [NAICS 33221P, 333314]

Hilite International, pp. Vol. II-1168, 1546 [NAICS 333613, 336391]

Hill Aircraft and Leasing Corp., p. III-1879 [NAICS 423860]

Hill Brothers Chemical Co., p. III-1971 [NAICS 424690]

Hill-Donnelly Corp., p. II-1243 [NAICS 334112]

Hill Meat Co., p. III-1946 [NAICS 424470]

Hill Phoenix Inc., p. II-1106 [NAICS 333415]

Hillary Peat Inc., p. I-524 [NAICS 325314]

Hillcrest Hi-Fidelity, p. III-2054 [NAICS 443112]

Hillenbrand Industries Inc., pp. Vol. I-306, Vol. II-933, 1627, 1650, 1657, 1745 [NAICS 31699M, 332510, 337127, 33721N, 337910, 339995]

Hills Materials Company Inc., pp. Vol. I-448, 732 [NAICS 324121, 327320]

Hillsboro Industries Inc., pp. Vol. II-1491, 1500 [NAICS 336212, 336214]

Hillside Plastics Inc., p. I-646 [NAICS 326160]

Hilltop Basic Resources Inc., p. I-732 [NAICS 327320]

Hillyard Industries, p. I-566 [NAICS 32561M]

Hilmar Cheese Company Inc., p. I-76 [NAICS 311513]

Hilord Chemical Corp., p. I-580 [NAICS 325910]

Hilti Inc., p. II-1207 [NAICS 333991]

Hinsdale Nurseries Inc., p. III-2072 [NAICS 444220]

Hinson Galleries Inc., p. III-2037 [NAICS 442110]

Hinton Lumber Products Inc., p. I-343 [NAICS 321920]

Hipp Wholesale Foods Inc., p. III-1929 [NAICS 424420]

Hired Hand Manufacturing Inc., pp. Vol. II-1101, 1112, 1152 [NAICS 333414, 33341N, 333518]

Hirsch Optical Corp., p. II-1687 [NAICS 339115]

Hirschvogel Inc., p. I-872 [NAICS 33211N]

Hirsh Industries Inc., pp. Vol. II-928, 1014, 1650 [NAICS 33243M, 33299N, 33721N]

Hirshfield's Inc., pp. Vol. I-554, Vol. III-2065 [NAICS 325510, 444100]

Hitachi America Ltd, p. II-1243 [NAICS 334112]

Hitachi Cable Indiana Inc., pp. Vol. II-933, 1519, 1524 [NAICS 332510, 336330, 336340]

Hitachi Computer Products, p. II-1243 [NAICS 334112]

Hitachi High Technologies, pp. Vol. II-1367, Vol. III-1820 [NAICS 334519, 423490]

Hitachi Medical Systems America, p. III-1813 [NAICS 423450]

Hitachi Metals America Ltd., pp. Vol. II-1014, 1061, 1140 [NAICS 33299N, 33329N, 333515]

Hitachi Metals North Carolina Ltd., p. I-686 [NAICS 327113]

Hitchcock Automotive Resources, p. III-2027 [NAICS 441229]

Hitchcock Industries Inc., pp. Vol. I-852, 857, Vol II-1134 [NAICS 33152N, 33152P, 333514]

Hite Co., pp. Vol. III-1831, 1835 [NAICS 423610, 423620]

Hix Corp., p. II-918 [NAICS 332410]

HJ Baker and Bro Inc., pp. Vol. I-9, 516, 520, 524 [NAICS 311119, 325311, 325312, 325314]

H.J. Heinz Co., pp. Vol. I-62, 68, 110 [NAICS 31141M, 31142M, 31171M]

HL Technologies Inc., p. III-1820 [NAICS 423490]

HM Electronics Inc., p. II-1362 [NAICS 334518]

HM Richards Inc., p. II-1616 [NAICS 337121]

HM Royal Inc., p. III-1828 [NAICS 423520]

HM White L.L.C., pp. Vol. II-1112, 1217, 1740 [NAICS 33341N, 333994, 339994]

HMC Corp., p. II-1046 [NAICS 333210]

HMC Shipping, p. III-1855 [NAICS 423740]

HMI Industries Inc., pp. Vol. I-788, Vol. II-1134, 1397 [NAICS 331210, 333514, 33521M]

HMP Industries Inc., p. II-952 [NAICS 332721]

HN Hinckley and Sons Inc., p. III-1847 [NAICS 423720]

HNI Corp., pp. Vol. I-743, Vol. II-933, 1014, 1101, 1627, 1650 [NAICS 327390, 332510, 33299N, 333414, 337127, 33721N]

H.O. Penn Machinery Inc., pp. Vol. III-1859, 1867, 1879 [NAICS 423810, 423830, 423860]

H.O. Trerice Co., pp. Vol. II-1332, 1352 [NAICS 334512, 334516]

Hoag Enterprises Inc., pp. Vol. III-1798, 2062 [NAICS 423410, 443130]

Hoban Foods Inc., pp. Vol. III-1929, 1933 [NAICS 424420, 424430]

Hobby Lobby Stores Inc., p. III-2153 [NAICS 451120]

Hobby Products International Inc., p. III-1887 [NAICS 423920]

Hoboken Wood Flooring Corp., pp. Vol. III-1778, 1782 [NAICS 423220, 423310]

Hockenberg Equipment Co., p. III-1855 [NAICS 423740]

Hockmeyer Equipment Corp., p. II-1740 [NAICS 339994]

Hodges Badge Company Inc., p. I-203 [NAICS 31322M]

Hoeganaes Corp., p. I-793 [NAICS 33122M]

Hoffer Flow Controls Inc., p. II-1342 [NAICS 334514]

Hoffman California Fabrics, p. III-1913 [NAICS 424310]

Hoffman Diamond Products Inc., p. I-756 [NAICS 327910]

Hoffman's Chocolate Shoppe, p. III-2092 [NAICS 445292]

Hoffman Tool and Die Inc., p. I-863 [NAICS 332114]

Hofley Manufacturing Co., p. II-1541 [NAICS 336370]

Hog Inc., pp. Vol. III-1863, 1965 [NAICS 423820, 424590]

Hog Slat Inc., pp. Vol. I-743, Vol. II-1023 [NAICS 327390, 333111]

Hoge Lumber Co., p. I-343 [NAICS 321920]

Hoge Warren Zimmerman Co., pp. Vol. I-776, Vol. II-1033 [NAICS 327999, 333120]

Hoida UBC, p. I-329 [NAICS 32121P]

Hol-Mac Corp., pp. Vol. II-1152, 1222 [NAICS 333518, 33399N]

Holcim Inc., p. I-727 [NAICS 327310]

Holcim (Texas) L.P., p. I-727 [NAICS 327310]

Holcim US Inc., p. I-743 [NAICS 327390]

Holcomb Freightliner Inc., p. III-1758 [NAICS 423110]

Holcomb Fuel Company Inc., p. III-2218 [NAICS 454311]

Holden Graphic Services, p. I-403 [NAICS 32223M]

Holiday Candy Corp., p. I-52 [NAICS 311330]

Holiday Companies Inc., pp. Vol. III-2076, 2116, 2150 [NAICS 445110, 447110, 451110]

Holiday Marketplace, p. I-510 [NAICS 32522M]

Holiday RV Superstores Inc., pp. Vol. III-2018, 2024 [NAICS 441210, 441222]

Holland American Wafer Inc., pp. Vol. I-15, 124 [NAICS 31121M, 31182M]

Holland Group Inc., pp. Vol. I-872, Vol. II-899, 1014, 1486, 1567 [NAICS 33211N, 33231M, 33299N, 336211, 336413]

Holland Manufacturing Corp., p. I-686 [NAICS 327113]

Holland USA, pp. Vol. II-1486, 1491 [NAICS 336211, 336212]

Hollar and Greene Produce Co., p. III-1950 [NAICS 424480]

Hollingsworth and Vose Co., pp. Vol. I-368, 415 [NAICS 32212M, 322299]

Hollins Organic Products Inc., p. I-516 [NAICS 325311]

Hollister Inc., pp. Vol. I-651, Vol. II-1322, 1671 [NAICS 32619M, 334510, 339112]

Holloway-Houston Inc., p. III-1879 [NAICS 423860]

Holloway Medical Sales Inc., p. III-1813 [NAICS 423450]

Holly Corp., p. I-443 [NAICS 324110]

Holly Park, p. I-348 [NAICS 321991]

Hollywood Film Co., p. II-1087 [NAICS 333315]

Hollywood Media Corp., p. III-2208 [NAICS 453998]

Holm Industries Inc., pp. Vol. I-621, Vol. II-1725 [NAICS 326121, 339991]

Holman Enterprises, p. III-2011 [NAICS 441110]

Holmberg Farms Inc., p. II-1023 [NAICS 333111]

Holmes Drywall Supply Inc., p. III-1794 [NAICS 423390]

Holmes Foods Inc., p. I-97 [NAICS 311615]

Holmes Lumber & Building Ctr, pp. Vol. I-329, 334, Vol. II-908, 1611 [NAICS 32121P, 32191M, 33232M, 337110]

Holmquist Lumber Inc., p. III-1790 [NAICS 423330]

Hologic Inc., pp. Vol. II-1087, 1357 [NAICS 333315, 334517]

Holox Ltd., p. I-471 [NAICS 325120]

Holston Gases Inc., p. III-1971 [NAICS 424690]

Holsum of Fort Wayne Inc., p. I-116 [NAICS 31181M]

Holt Cat, pp. Vol. II-1173, Vol. III-1859 [NAICS 333618, 423810]

Holt Paper and Chemical Inc., pp. Vol. III-1875, 1898 [NAICS 423850, 424110]

Holts Bakery Inc., p. III-2089 [NAICS 445291]

Homac Manufacturing Inc., p. II-1457 [NAICS 33593M]

Homaco Inc., pp. Vol. II-1432, 1451 [NAICS 335313, 33592M]

Homark Company Inc., p. I-348 [NAICS 321991]

Homasote Co., pp. Vol. I-319, 510, 771 [NAICS 321219, 32522M, 327993]

Home Care Equipment Inc., p. III-2113 [NAICS 446199]

Home Care Industries Inc., pp. Vol. I-395, Vol. II-1397 [NAICS 32222P, 33521M]

Home Care Service Inc., p. III-2113 [NAICS 446199]

Home Decor Outlet, pp. Vol. III-2044, 2047 [NAICS 442291, 442299]

Home Depot Inc., pp. Vol. III-2065, 2072 [NAICS 444100, 444220]

Home Fabric Mills Inc., p. III-2156 [NAICS 451130]

Home Oil Co., pp. Vol. III-1975, 2222 [NAICS 424710, 454312]

Home Products International Inc., p. II-939 [NAICS 33261M]

Home Style Industries, pp. Vol. I-234, Vol. II-1616, 1657, 1662 [NAICS 31412M, 337121, 337910, 337920]

Homecrest Industries Inc., p. II-1632 [NAICS 33712N]

Homedeq Inc., p. III-2113 [NAICS 446199]

HoMedics-USA Inc., p. III-1813 [NAICS 423450]

Homegrown Natural Foods Inc., p. I-31 [NAICS 31122N]

Homeland Security Network Inc., p. III-2015 [NAICS 441120]

HomeRight Corp., p. II-1740 [NAICS 339994]

Homeseekerscom Inc., p. III-2058 [NAICS 443120]

Homestead Dairies Inc., p. III-2094 [NAICS 445299]

Homestead Lawn and Tractor Co., p. III-2069 [NAICS 444210]

Hometown Auto Retailers Inc., p. III-2011 [NAICS 441110]

HON Co., pp. Vol. II-1627, 1650 [NAICS 337127, 33721N]

Honda of America Mfg Inc., pp. Vol. II-1473, 1599 [NAICS 336111, 336991]

Honeywell Aerospace, p. II-1347 [NAICS 334515]

Honeywell Hardware Product, p. III-1879 [NAICS 423860]

Honeywell International Inc., pp. Vol. I-475, 480, 500, 510, Vol. II-1317, 1327, 1352, 1551 [NAICS 32513M, 325181, 325211, 32522M, 334419, 334511, 334516, 336399]

Honickman Affiliates, pp. Vol. I-165, Vol. III-1954 [NAICS 31211M, 424490]

Honor Snack L.L.C., p. III-1939 [NAICS 424450]

Hood and Company Inc., p. I-825 [NAICS 331419]

Hood Packaging Corp., p. I-395 [NAICS 32222P]

Hood River Distillers Inc., p. I-181 [NAICS 312140]

Hook Industrial Sales Inc., p. II-1530 [NAICS 336350]

Hooker Furniture Corp., pp. Vol. II-1621, 1627, 1650 [NAICS 337122, 337127, 33721N]

Hooper Corporation., pp. Vol. II-1168, 1432 [NAICS 333613, 335313]

Hooper's Trailer Sales Inc., p. II-1491 [NAICS 336212]

Hoosier Racing Tire Corp., p. I-660 [NAICS 32621M]

Hoover and Strong Inc., p. I-825 [NAICS 331419]

Hoover Materials Handling Group, p. II-928 [NAICS 33243M]

Hoover's Jewelers Inc., p. III-2144 [NAICS 448310]

Hop Industries Corp., p. II-1077 [NAICS 333313]

Hope Global Co., pp. Vol. I-198, 203, 213 [NAICS 313210, 31322M, 31324M]

Hope Lumber and Supply Co., pp. Vol. I-312, 329, 334 [NAICS 32111M, 32121P, 32191M]

Hopf Equipment Inc., p. III-2021 [NAICS 441221]

Hopkins Distribution Company Inc., p. III-2007 [NAICS 424990]

Hopkins Furniture & Floor, p. III-2041 [NAICS 442210]

Hopkins Manufacturing Corp., pp. Vol. II-1512, 1740 [NAICS 33632M, 339994]

Hoquiam Plywood Company Inc., p. I-324 [NAICS 32121N]

Horiba Instruments Inc., p. II-1352 [NAICS 334516]

Horiba Jobin Yvon Inc., p. II-1352 [NAICS 334516]

Horiba Stec Inc., p. II-1337 [NAICS 334513]

Horizon, pp. Vol. III-1875, 1991, 2072 [NAICS 423850, 424910, 444220]

Horizon Milling L.L.C., p. I-15 [NAICS 31121M]

Horizon Music Inc., p. I-837 [NAICS 33149M]

Horizon Organic Holding Corp., p. I-86 [NAICS 31151N]

Horizon Sports Technologies Inc., p. II-1463 [NAICS 335991]

Horizons Inc., p. II-1087 [NAICS 333315]

Hormel Foods Corp., pp. Vol. I-68, 102 [NAICS 31142M, 31161N]

Hornady Manufacturing Co., p. II-993 [NAICS 332992]

HornerXpress, pp. Vol. II-1101, 1179 [NAICS 333414, 333911]

Hornwood Inc., pp. Vol. I-198, 251 [NAICS 313210, 314999]

Horsehead Industries Inc., pp. Vol. I-825, 837, Vol. II-1463 [NAICS 331419, 33149M, 335991]

Horton Automatics, pp. Vol. II-1229, 1437, 1468 [NAICS 33399P, 335314, 335999]

Horton Emergency Vehicles, p. II-1486 [NAICS 336211]

Horton Homes Inc., pp. Vol. I-348, 353 [NAICS 321991, 321992]

Horween Leather Co., p. I-296 [NAICS 316110]

Hosea O Weaver and Sons Inc., p. I-448 [NAICS 324121]

Hospi-Tel Manufacturing Co., p. II-1662 [NAICS 337920]

Hospital Forms and Systems Corp., p. I-403 [NAICS 32223M]

Hospital Specialty Co., pp. Vol. I-411, Vol. II-1189 [NAICS 322291, 333913]

Hospital Systems Inc., p. II-1322 [NAICS 334510]

Hospitality Mints L.L.C., p. I-57 [NAICS 311340]

Hostess Cake Div., p. I-116 [NAICS 31181M]

Hostmann-Steinberg Inc., p. I-580 [NAICS 325910]

Hot Topic Inc., pp. Vol. III-2123, 2135 [NAICS 448110, 448150]

Hotel Superstore, pp. Vol. III-1774, 1809, 1813 [NAICS 423210, 423440, 423450]

Hotwatt Inc., p. II-1217 [NAICS 333994]

Houchens Industries Inc., pp. Vol. III-1890, 2076, 2206 [NAICS 423930, 445110, 453991]

Houghton International Inc., pp. Vol. I-458, 554, 566, 595, Vol. II-964 [NAICS 324191, 325510, 32561M, 32599N, 33281M]

Houles USA Inc., p. III-1913 [NAICS 424310]

Houma Marine Fabricators, p. II-1589 [NAICS 336611]

Housatonic Curtain Company Inc., p. I-234 [NAICS 31412M]

Housby Mack Inc., p. III-1758 [NAICS 423110]

House-Autry Mills Inc., p. I-15 [NAICS 31121M]

House Foods America Corp., p. I-31 [NAICS 31122N]

House-Hasson Hardware Inc., p. III-1843 [NAICS 423710]

House of Blinds and Drapery, p. II-1662 [NAICS 337920]

House of Schwan Inc., p. III-1983 [NAICS 424810]

Housechem Inc., p. III-2007 [NAICS 424990]

Houston Foam Plastics Inc., p. I-636 [NAICS 326140]

Houston Hosiery Mills Inc., pp. Vol. I-213, 218 [NAICS 31324M, 31331M]

Houston's Inc., p. III-1809 [NAICS 423440]

How-Mac Manufacturing Inc., p. III-1968 [NAICS 424610]

Howard A. Davidson Lumber Co., pp. Vol. I-334, 343, 358, Vol. III-1782 [NAICS 32191M, 321920, 321999, 423310]

Howard Berger Company Inc., p. III-1843 [NAICS 423710]

Howard Fertilizer & Chemical Inc., p. I-524 [NAICS 325314]

Howard Leight Industries, p. II-1676 [NAICS 339113]

Howard Miller Clock Inc., pp. Vol. II-1362, 1367, 1611, 1644 [NAICS 334518, 334519, 337110, 337215]

Howe Coffee Co., p. III-2228 [NAICS 454390]

Howell Asphalt Co., p. I-448 [NAICS 324121]

Howmet Aluminum Casting Inc., p. I-852 [NAICS 33152N]

Howmet TMP Corp., p. II-1124 [NAICS 333512]

Howren Music Co., p. III-2159 [NAICS 451140]

Howse Implement Company Inc., p. II-1500 [NAICS 336214]

Hoya Corporation USA, pp. Vol. I-709, Vol. II-1082 [NAICS 327211, 333314]

Hoya Optical Inc., pp. Vol. II-1687, Vol. III-1817 [NAICS 339115, 423460]

HP Hood Inc., pp. Vol. I-76, 86, 92 [NAICS 311513, 31151N, 311520]

HP Pelzer Automotive Systems, p. I-771 [NAICS 327993]

HP Products Corp., p. III-1875 [NAICS 423850]

HP White Laboratory Inc., pp. Vol. II-993, 997, 1001, 1005 [NAICS 332992, 332993, 332994, 332995]

HPC Foodservice, p. III-1946 [NAICS 424470]

HPI Products Inc., p. I-529 [NAICS 325320]

HPM Building Supply, pp. Vol. I-453, Vol. III-1847, 2004 [NAICS 324122, 423720, 424950]

HR Textron Inc., pp. Vol. II-1327, 1567 [NAICS 334511, 336413]

HS White Corp., p. I-665 [NAICS 326220]

HSN L.P., p. III-2211 [NAICS 454113]

HSS Group, p. II-1725 [NAICS 339991]

H.T. Hackney Co., pp. Vol. III-1925, 1929, 2116 [NAICS 424410, 424420, 447110]

Hta Enterprises Inc., p. II-1056 [NAICS 333295]

Hub Construction Specialties Inc., p. III-1859 [NAICS 423810]

Hub Folding Box Company Inc., p. I-609 [NAICS 326112]

Hub Plastics Inc., p. I-646 [NAICS 326160]

Hub Servall Record Mfg Corp., p. II-1376 [NAICS 334612]

Hubbard Industrial Supply Co., p. III-1871 [NAICS 423840]

Hubbell Inc., pp. Vol. II-1257, 1267, 1307, 1317, 1367, 1390, 1437, 1457 [NAICS 334210, 334290, 334417, 334419, 334519, 33512M, 335314, 33593M]

Huber Orchard and Winery Inc., p. III-2089 [NAICS 445291]

Hubert Co., p. III-1809 [NAICS 423440]

Hubert Distributors Inc., p. III-1983 [NAICS 424810]

Huck Fasteners, p. II-958 [NAICS 332722]

Huck International Inc., p. II-958 [NAICS 332722]

Huck Spaulding Enterprises, p. II-1714 [NAICS 33994M]

Huckleberry People Inc., pp. Vol. I-57, Vol. III-2007 [NAICS 311340, 424990]

Huckleberry Press L.L.C., pp. Vol. II-1376, Vol. III-2153 [NAICS 334612, 451120]

Hudalla Assoc Inc., p. III-1883 [NAICS 423910]

Hudson Products Corp., p. II-1112 [NAICS 33341N]

Hudson-Sharp Machine Co., p. II-1051 [NAICS 333220]

Hudson Technologies Inc., p. III-1855 [NAICS 423740]

Hudson Valley Paper Co., pp. Vol. III-1898, 1901, 1905 [NAICS 424110, 424120, 424130]

Huey P Long Bridge Fleet Inc., p. II-1589 [NAICS 336611]

Huff United Paper Co., p. III-1905 [NAICS 424130]

Huffman Finishing Co., p. I-218 [NAICS 31331M]

Huffy Corp., pp. Vol. II-1599, 1702 [NAICS 336991, 339920]

Hughes-Anderson Heat Exchangers, p. II-918 [NAICS 332410]

Hughes Furniture Industries Inc., pp. Vol. II-1616, 1644 [NAICS 337121, 337215]

Hughes Hardwood International, p. II-1611 [NAICS 337110]

Hughes Network Systems Inc., pp. Vol. II-1257, 1267 [NAICS 334210, 334290]

Hughes Rental and Sales Inc., p. III-2144 [NAICS 448310]

Hughes Supply Inc., pp. Vol. III-1831, 1847, 1851 [NAICS 423610, 423720, 423730]

Hugo Boss USA Inc., p. I-272 [NAICS 31522M]

Hugo Neu-Proler Corp., p. III-1890 [NAICS 423930]

Hugo-Neu Schnitzer East, p. I-807 [NAICS 331314]

Huhtamaki Consumer Packaging, p. I-379 [NAICS 32221M]

Huish Detergents Inc., p. I-566 [NAICS 32561M]

Hukill Chemical Corp., pp. Vol. I-480, 516 [NAICS 325181, 325311]

Human-i-Tees Inc., p. III-2138 [NAICS 448190]

Humanicare International Inc., p. I-411 [NAICS 322291]

Humboldt Creamery Association, pp. Vol. I-81, 92 [NAICS 311514, 311520]

Humboldt Manufacturing Inc., p. II-1666 [NAICS 339111]

Humboldt Petroleum Inc., p. III-2116 [NAICS 447110]

Humco Holding Group Inc., pp. Vol. III-1909, 1971 [NAICS 424210, 424690]

Humphrey Products Company Inc., p. II-1222 [NAICS 33399N]

Humpty Dumpty Snack Foods Inc., p. I-137 [NAICS 31191M]

Hunkar Technologies, p. II-1212 [NAICS 333993]

Hunt Country Furniture Inc., p. II-1657 [NAICS 337910]

Hunt Forest Products Inc., pp. Vol. I-312, 324, 358 [NAICS 32111M, 32121N, 321999]

Hunt Petroleum Corp., p. I-443 [NAICS 324110]

Hunt Valve Company Inc., pp. Vol. II-1124, 1157 [NAICS 333512, 333611]

Hunter Automated Machinery, p. II-1051 [NAICS 333220]

Hunter Douglas Fabrication Co, p. I-234 [NAICS 31412M]

Hunter Douglas Intermountain, p. II-1662 [NAICS 337920]

Hunter Douglas Northwest, p. II-1662 [NAICS 337920]

Hunter Marine Corp., p. II-1594 [NAICS 336612]

Hunter's Specialties Inc., pp. Vol. I-244, 471, Vol. II-886 [NAICS 314991, 325120, 33221N]

Huntington Electric Inc., p. II-1297 [NAICS 334415]

Huntington Foam Corp., pp. Vol. I-636, 641 [NAICS 326140, 326150]

Huntington Tile Group L.P., p. III-1786 [NAICS 423320]

Hunts Point Auto Wreckers Inc., p. III-1770 [NAICS 423140]

Huntsman International L.L.C., pp. Vol. I-488, 493, 500, 534, 615 [NAICS 325188, 32519M, 325211, 325411, 326113]

Huntsville Rehabilitation, p. I-285 [NAICS 31529M]

Hurco Companies Inc., p. II-1337 [NAICS 334513]

Hurd Corp., p. II-1505 [NAICS 33631M]

Hurd Millwork Company Inc., pp. Vol. I-334, 651, Vol. II-908 [NAICS 32191M, 32619M, 33232M]

Huron Casting Inc., p. I-845 [NAICS 33151M]

Huron Valley Steel Corp., p. I-807 [NAICS 331314]

Hurricane Compressors, pp. Vol. II-1184, 1189 [NAICS 333912, 333913]

Hurst Boiler and Welding Inc., p. II-918 [NAICS 332410]

Hurst Tuff Stuff, p. II-1524 [NAICS 336340]

Hurwitz-Mintz Furniture Co., p. III-2037 [NAICS 442110]

Husco International Inc., p. II-980 [NAICS 33291N]

Huser-Paul Company Inc., pp. Vol. III-1939, 2001 [NAICS 424450, 424940]

Husky Trusses & Building Supply, p. I-329 [NAICS 32121P]

Hussey Copper Ltd., pp. Vol. I-822, 830, 857 [NAICS 331411, 33142M, 33152P]

Hussey Seating Company Inc., p. II-1627 [NAICS 337127]

Hutamaki Packaging, p. I-609 [NAICS 326112]

Hutchens Industries Inc., pp. Vol. II-1486, 1519 [NAICS 336211, 336330]

Hutchinson Fluid Transfer Systems, p. II-1546 [NAICS 336391]

Hutchinson FTS Inc., pp. Vol. II-923, 980, 1106, 1217, 1546 [NAICS 332420, 33291N, 333415, 333994, 336391]

Hutchinson Technology Inc., pp. Vol. II-1252, 1317 [NAICS 334119, 334419]

Huttig Building Products Inc., p. III-1782 [NAICS 423310]

Hvac Distributors Inc., p. III-1851 [NAICS 423730]

H.W. Jenkins Lumber Co., pp. Vol. III-1794, 2065 [NAICS 423390, 444100]

HW Rivett Flooring, p. III-2041 [NAICS 442210]

HWH Corp., p. II-1222 [NAICS 33399N]

Hy-Level Industries Inc., pp. Vol. II-952, 1124 [NAICS 332721, 333512]

Hy-Meg Corp., p. II-1297 [NAICS 334415]

Hy-Production Inc., p. II-952 [NAICS 332721]

Hy-Vee Inc., p. III-2076 [NAICS 445110]

Hybricon Corp., p. II-1212 [NAICS 333993]

Hycor Biomedical Inc., p. I-544 [NAICS 325413]

Hyde Manufacturing Company Inc., pp. Vol. II-892, 1140, 1207 [NAICS 33221P, 333515, 333991]

Hydra Rig, p. II-1505 [NAICS 33631M]

Hydradyne Hydraulics L.L.C., pp. Vol. II-945, 1222 [NAICS 332710, 33399N]

Hydraforce Inc., p. II-1222 [NAICS 33399N]

Hydralift AmClyde Inc., p. II-1033 [NAICS 333120]

Hydraulic Controls Inc., p. III-1867 [NAICS 423830]

Hydril Co., p. II-1039 [NAICS 33313M]

Hydro Aluminum Adrian, pp. Vol. I-811, 872 [NAICS 331316, 33211N]

Hydro Aluminum North America, pp. Vol. I-793, 811 [NAICS 33122M, 331316]

Hydro Aluminum Rockledge Inc., p. I-811 [NAICS 331316]

Hydro Automotive Structures Inc., p. I-811 [NAICS 331316]

Hydro Dynamics Inc., p. II-1157 [NAICS 333611]

Hydro-Quip, p. II-974 [NAICS 332913]

Hydro Systems Inc., p. II-1397 [NAICS 33521M]

Hydro-Temperature Corp., pp. Vol. II-1397, 1417 [NAICS 33521M, 335228]

Hydrosol Inc., p. I-471 [NAICS 325120]

Hydrox Laboratories, p. I-493 [NAICS 32519M]

Hyland Co., p. I-4 [NAICS 311111]

Hynite Corp., p. I-516 [NAICS 325311]

Hynix Semiconductor Mfg Am., p. II-1287 [NAICS 334413]

Hypercom Corp., pp. Vol. II-1077, 1257 [NAICS 333313, 334210]

Hypertherm Inc., pp. Vol. II-1124, 1140 [NAICS 333512, 333515]

Hyspan Precision Products Inc., p. II-1530 [NAICS 336350]

Hytrol Conveyor Company Inc., p. II-1194 [NAICS 33392M]

Hyundai Motor America, p. III-1758 [NAICS 423110]

I and D Auto Parts Warehouse, p. II-1530 [NAICS 336350]

I and I Sports Supply Co., p. III-2150 [NAICS 451110]

I Erlichman Company Inc., p. I-363 [NAICS 322110]

Numbers following p. or pp. are page references. Roman numerals indicate volume numbers. Bracketed items indicate industries. Page references are to the starting pages of company tables.

2357

I Lehrhoff and Company Inc., p. III-1835 [NAICS 423620]

I/N Kote, p. I-793 [NAICS 33122M]

I/OMagic Corp., p. II-1238 [NAICS 334111]

I-Sector Corp., pp. Vol. III-1805, 1839 [NAICS 423430, 423690]

I Tannenbaum Sons Inc., p. I-306 [NAICS 31699M]

IA Construction Corp., p. I-448 [NAICS 324121]

IAC/InterActiveCorp., p. III-2211 [NAICS 454113]

Iams Co., p. I-4 [NAICS 311111]

Iberia Sugar Cooperative Inc., pp. Vol. I-40, 44 [NAICS 311313, 31131N]

IBM Printing Systems Div., p. II-1252 [NAICS 334119]

IBM Rational Software Corp., p. III-1805 [NAICS 423430]

IBT Inc., p. III-1871 [NAICS 423840]

I.C. Isaacs and Company Inc., pp. Vol. I-262, 272, 290 [NAICS 31519M, 31522M, 31599M]

Ice Cap Inc., p. II-1101 [NAICS 333414]

Ice Cold Products, p. III-1855 [NAICS 423740]

Ice Cream Specialties Inc., p. I-92 [NAICS 311520]

Ice-O-Matic, p. III-1809 [NAICS 423440]

Icelandic USA Inc., p. I-110 [NAICS 31171M]

ICG Castings, p. I-852 [NAICS 33152N]

Ichikoh Manufacturing Inc., p. I-722 [NAICS 327215]

ICI Americas Inc., pp. Vol. I-500, 595, 615 [NAICS 325211, 32599N, 326113]

Icicle Seafoods Inc., p. I-110 [NAICS 31171M]

ICO Inc., p. II-964 [NAICS 33281M]

Icon Fitness Corp., p. II-1702 [NAICS 339920]

ICON Health and Fitness Inc., p. I-621 [NAICS 326121]

Icon Identity Solutions Inc., p. II-1720 [NAICS 339950]

ID Technology Corp., pp. Vol. II-1077, 1152, 1714 [NAICS 333313, 333518, 33994M]

Idacta, p. III-1809 [NAICS 423440]

Idaho Candy Co., pp. Vol. III-1909, 1939, 2001 [NAICS 424210, 424450, 424940]

Idaho Truck Specialties L.L.C., p. III-2030 [NAICS 441310]

IDC Corp., p. II-1248 [NAICS 334113]

IDC New York, p. II-1381 [NAICS 334613]

Ideal Automotive & Truck, p. III-2030 [NAICS 441310]

Ideal Box and Graphics Co., p. II-1720 [NAICS 339950]

Ideal Chemical and Supply Co., p. III-1971 [NAICS 424690]

Ideal Electric Co., p. II-1432 [NAICS 335313]

Ideal Fastener Corp., p. II-1735 [NAICS 339993]

Ideal Industries Inc., pp. Vol. II-1307, 1347, 1457 [NAICS 334417, 334515, 33593M]

Identix Inc., p. II-1468 [NAICS 335999]

IDEX Corp., pp. Vol. II-1124, 1179, 1184, 1229 [NAICS 333512, 333911, 333912, 33399P]

IDEXX Laboratories Inc., pp. Vol. I-539, 544, Vol. II-1671 [NAICS 325412, 325413, 339112]

IDI, p. I-631 [NAICS 326130]

IFM Efector Inc., p. III-1839 [NAICS 423690]

II Stanley Company Inc., pp. Vol. II-1077, 1512 [NAICS 333313, 33632M]

II-VI Inc., p. II-1082 [NAICS 333314]

IIMAK, p. II-1714 [NAICS 33994M]

IKA-Works Inc., p. III-1820 [NAICS 423490]

Ikelite Manufacturing Co., p. II-1386 [NAICS 335110]

IKON Office Solutions Inc., pp. Vol. I-420, Vol. III-1805 [NAICS 32311M, 423430]

IL Richer Company Inc., p. I-4 [NAICS 311111]

Ilapak Inc., p. III-1871 [NAICS 423840]

Ilford Imaging USA Inc., p. II-1087 [NAICS 333315]

Illbruck Inc., pp. Vol. I-636, 771 [NAICS 326140, 327993]

Illini F.S. Inc., pp. Vol. III-1975, 1991 [NAICS 424710, 424910]

Illinois Auto Electric Co., p. III-1867 [NAICS 423830]

Illinois Auto Truck Co., p. II-1530 [NAICS 336350]

Illinois Bottle Manufacturing, p. I-646 [NAICS 326160]

Illinois Capacitor Inc., p. II-1292 [NAICS 334414]

Illinois Tool Works Inc., pp. Vol. I-560, Vol. II-958, 1207, 1212, 1229 [NAICS 325520, 332722, 333991, 333993, 33399P]

Illinois Wholesale Cash Register, p. III-1801 [NAICS 423420]

ILLMO Rx Service Inc., p. III-1817 [NAICS 423460]

Illumina Inc., p. II-1352 [NAICS 334516]

Ilmor Engineering Inc., p. II-1505 [NAICS 33631M]

Ilpea Inc., p. II-1725 [NAICS 339991]

ILTACO-Chicago Avenue Pizza, p. I-133 [NAICS 311830]

Iluka Resources Inc., pp. Vol. I-767, 825 [NAICS 327992, 331419]

Image Asphalt Maintenance Inc., p. III-1786 [NAICS 423320]

Image Devices Inc., p. II-1277 [NAICS 334411]

Image IV Systems Inc., p. III-1801 [NAICS 423420]

Image Systems Corp., p. II-1248 [NAICS 334113]

Image Watches Inc., p. II-1362 [NAICS 334518]

ImagePoint, p. II-1720 [NAICS 339950]

Imagination Confections, p. I-57 [NAICS 311340]

Imaging Alliance Group L.L.C., p. III-1801 [NAICS 423420]

Imaging & Sensing Technology, pp. Vol. II-1087, 1277 [NAICS 333315, 334411]

Imaging Concepts of New Mexico, p. III-1801 [NAICS 423420]

Imaging Sciences International, p. II-1357 [NAICS 334517]

Imaging Supplies & Equipment, p. III-1798 [NAICS 423410]

Imaging Supplies Depot Inc., pp. Vol. III-1801, 2186 [NAICS 423420, 453210]

Imaging Technologies Services, p. I-436 [NAICS 32312M]

Imagistics International Inc., pp. Vol. II-1077, Vol. III-1801 [NAICS 333313, 423420]

Imation Corp., pp. Vol. II-1243, 1252, 1381 [NAICS 334112, 334119, 334613]

ImClone Systems Inc., p. I-539 [NAICS 325412]

Imeco Inc., p. II-1106 [NAICS 333415]

Imerys Pigments Inc., pp. Vol. I-488, 767 [NAICS 325188, 327992]

Imetal. CE Minerals, p. I-475 [NAICS 32513M]

IMI Cornelius Inc., pp. Vol. II-1061, 1189 [NAICS 33329N, 333913]

IMI Fabi L.L.C., p. I-767 [NAICS 327992]

IMI Norgren Inc., p. II-1222 [NAICS 33399N]

IMI-Stony Creek Stone Inc., p. I-748 [NAICS 327410]

Immco Diagnostics Inc., p. I-544 [NAICS 325413]

Immersive Media Co., p. II-1272 [NAICS 334310]

Immix Technologies L.L.C., p. I-505 [NAICS 325212]

Immucor Inc., p. I-544 [NAICS 325413]

Immuno Concepts Inc., p. I-544 [NAICS 325413]

Impact Forge Inc., p. I-872 [NAICS 33211N]

Impact Lighting Inc., p. III-1820 [NAICS 423490]

Impact Merchandising Corp., p. III-1835 [NAICS 423620]

Impact Products L.L.C., p. III-1875 [NAICS 423850]

Impaxx Inc., pp. Vol. I-374, 379 [NAICS 322130, 32221M]

IMPCO Machine Tools, p. II-1147 [NAICS 333516]

IMPCO Technologies Inc., p. II-1505 [NAICS 33631M]

Imperial Auto Auction, pp. Vol. III-1758, 2208 [NAICS 423110, 453998]

Imperial Commodities Corp., pp. Vol. III-1954, 2007 [NAICS 424490, 424990]

Imperial Company Inc., p. III-2116 [NAICS 447110]

Imperial Distributors Inc., p. III-1909 [NAICS 424210]

Imperial Electric Co., p. II-1427 [NAICS 335312]

Imperial Electronic Assembly Inc., p. II-1292 [NAICS 334414]

Imperial Graphics Inc., p. I-403 [NAICS 32223M]

Imperial Headwear Inc., pp. Vol. I-251, 290 [NAICS 314999, 31599M]

Imperial Marble Corp., p. I-762 [NAICS 327991]

Imperial Mfg Ice Cold Coolers Inc., p. I-353 [NAICS 321992]

Imperial Pools Inc., p. II-1702 [NAICS 339920]

Imperial Schrade Corp., p. II-886 [NAICS 33221N]

Imperial Sugar Co., pp. Vol. I-40, 44 [NAICS 311313, 31131N]

Imperial Toy Corp., p. II-1708 [NAICS 33993M]

Imperial Trading Co., pp. Vol. III-1909, 1925, 2001 [NAICS 424210, 424410, 424940]

Imperial Woodworking Co., pp. Vol. II-1611, 1639, 1644 [NAICS 337110, 337212, 337215]

Implement Sales L.L.C., p. III-1863 [NAICS 423820]

Impo International Inc., p. III-1922 [NAICS 424340]

Import Auto Clinic, p. III-1770 [NAICS 423140]

Importers Service Corp., pp. Vol. I-57, 147 [NAICS 311340, 311930]

Imports by Four Hands L.P., p. III-1774 [NAICS 423210]

Impreso Inc., pp. Vol. I-368, Vol. II-1087 [NAICS 32212M, 333315]

Impulse NC Inc., pp. Vol. II-1421, 1432 [NAICS 335311, 335313]

IMS Electrol Company Inc., pp. Vol. II-1307, 1312 [NAICS 334417, 334418]

In-Cide Technologies Inc., pp. Vol. I-748, 752 [NAICS 327410, 327420]

INA USA Corp., p. II-1168 [NAICS 333613]

INAMED Corp., pp. Vol. II-1671, 1676 [NAICS 339112, 339113]

Ince Distributing Inc., pp. Vol. III-1835, 1851 [NAICS 423620, 423730]

Numbers following p. or pp. are page references. Roman numerals indicate volume numbers. Bracketed items indicate industries. Page references are to the starting pages of company tables.

Incom Inc., p. II-1451 [NAICS 33592M]

Incredible Technologies Inc., p. II-1708 [NAICS 33993M]

Indalex Inc., p. I-811 [NAICS 331316]

INDEECO, p. II-918 [NAICS 332410]

Independence Corn By-Products, pp. Vol. I-756, Vol. II-1152 [NAICS 327910, 333518]

Independent Can Company Inc., p. II-928 [NAICS 332243M]

Independent Distribution Services, p. III-1778 [NAICS 423220]

Independent Salon Resource Inc., p. III-1875 [NAICS 423850]

Independent Stave Company Inc., p. I-343 [NAICS 321920]

Index Notion Company Inc., p. III-2190 [NAICS 453220]

Index Packaging Inc., pp. Vol. I-343, 636 [NAICS 321920, 326140]

Indian Head Industries Inc., pp. Vol. II-1222, 1524 [NAICS 33399N, 336340]

Indiana Botanic Gardens Inc., pp. Vol. I-143, 152, 534 [NAICS 311920, 31194M, 325411]

Indiana Industrial Services L.L.C., p. I-830 [NAICS 331142M]

Indiana Limestone Company Inc., p. I-762 [NAICS 327991]

Indiana Oxygen Company Inc., p. I-471 [NAICS 325120]

Indiana Packers Corp., p. I-102 [NAICS 311612]

Indiana Paging Network Inc., p. III-2054 [NAICS 443112]

Indiana Ribbon Inc., pp. Vol. I-203, 374 [NAICS 31322M, 322130]

Indiana Supply Corp., pp. Vol. III-1794, 1871 [NAICS 423390, 423840]

Indianapolis Dry Stripping, p. I-800 [NAICS 331311]

Indicon Corp., p. II-1432 [NAICS 335313]

Indies House, pp. Vol. I-348, Vol. II-1500 [NAICS 321991, 336214]

Indmar Products Company Inc., p. II-1173 [NAICS 333618]

Indpec Chemical Corp., p. I-475 [NAICS 32513M]

Industrial Acoustics Company Inc., pp. Vol. I-324, 771, Vol. II-1272, 1367 [NAICS 32121N, 327993, 334310, 334519]

Industrial Battery Engineering Inc., p. II-1442 [NAICS 335911]

Industrial Brush Corp., p. II-1740 [NAICS 339994]

Industrial Combustion Inc., pp. Vol. II-918, 1101 [NAICS 332410, 333414]

Industrial Data Entry Automation, p. II-1248 [NAICS 334113]

Industrial Distribution Group Inc., p. III-1871 [NAICS 423840]

Industrial Fiberglass Specialties, p. I-788 [NAICS 331210]

Industrial Furnace Interiors Inc., p. II-1277 [NAICS 334411]

Industrial Insulation Group, p. I-641 [NAICS 326150]

Industrial Laminates Norplex Inc., p. I-615 [NAICS 326113]

Industrial Metals and Surplus Inc., p. II-945 [NAICS 332710]

Industrial Noise Control Inc., p. I-771 [NAICS 327993]

Industrial Pallet Corp., p. I-343 [NAICS 321920]

Industrial Parts Depot L.L.C., p. II-1505 [NAICS 33631M]

Industrial Piping Inc., p. II-918 [NAICS 332410]

Industrial Polymers Corp., p. I-641 [NAICS 326150]

Industrial Powder Coatings Inc., pp. Vol. I-554, Vol. II-964 [NAICS 325510, 332810]

Industrial Rubber and Supply Inc., p. III-1913 [NAICS 424310]

Industrial Soap Co., pp. Vol. III-1875, 1971 [NAICS 321920, 423850, 424690]

Industrial Specialty Fabrics, pp. Vol. I-192, 251 [NAICS 31311M, 314999]

Industrial Television Services Inc., p. III-1798 [NAICS 423410]

Industrial Timer Co., p. II-1362 [NAICS 334518]

Industrial Truck Sales & Service, p. III-2208 [NAICS 453998]

Industrial Tube Corp., p. I-665 [NAICS 326220]

Industrial US L.L.C., p. III-1843 [NAICS 423710]

Industrial Video Corp., p. III-1798 [NAICS 423410]

Industrial Products Co., pp. Vol. II-1134, 1725 [NAICS 333514, 339991]

Industry-Railway Suppliers Inc., p. III-1879 [NAICS 423860]

INELCO, p. II-1302 [NAICS 334416]

Inergy Automotive Systems L.L.C., pp. Vol. I-651, Vol. II-1551 [NAICS 32619M, 336399]

Inergy L.P., pp. Vol. III-2218, 2222, 2228 [NAICS 454311, 454312, 454390]

Inex Vision Systems, p. II-1212 [NAICS 333993]

INFICON Holding AG, pp. Vol. II-1229, 1337 [NAICS 33399P, 334513]

Infimed Inc., p. II-1357 [NAICS 334517]

Infiniti Inc., p. I-285 [NAICS 31529M]

Infinity Products Inc., p. I-267 [NAICS 31521M]

Infinity Watch Corp., p. II-1362 [NAICS 334518]

InFocus Corp., pp. Vol. II-1087, 1317 [NAICS 33315, 334419]

INFOMotion, p. II-1381 [NAICS 334613]

Information Networks Inc., p. III-2058 [NAICS 443120]

Ingear Corp., pp. Vol. I-306, Vol. II-1702 [NAICS 31699M, 339920]

Ingersoll Cutting Tool Co., pp. Vol. II-1124, 1140, 1207 [NAICS 333512, 333515, 333991]

Ingersoll Machine Tools Inc., pp. Vol. II-1124, 1129 [NAICS 333512, 333513]

Ingersoll-Rand Co., pp. Vol. II-1179, 1207, 1222, 1229, 1337, 1740 [NAICS 333911, 333991, 33399N, 33399P, 334513, 339994]

Ingersoll-Rand Co. Rock Drill Div., pp. Vol. II-1033, 1039 [NAICS 333120, 33313M]

Ingles Markets Inc., pp. Vol. I-86, Vol. III-2076 [NAICS 31151N, 445110]

Ingram Auto Parts, p. III-1770 [NAICS 423140]

Ingram Industries Inc., p. III-1995 [NAICS 424920]

Ingram Micro Inc., p. III-1805 [NAICS 423430]

Initiative Foods, p. I-143 [NAICS 311920]

Injectronics Inc., p. I-436 [NAICS 32312M]

Ink Systems Inc., p. I-580 [NAICS 325910]

Ink Technology Corp., p. I-580 [NAICS 325910]

Inkley's Inc., pp. Vol. III-2054, 2062 [NAICS 443112, 443130]

Inkware Inc., p. I-580 [NAICS 325910]

Inland Asphalt Co., p. I-448 [NAICS 324121]

Inland Empire Paper Co., p. I-368 [NAICS 32212M]

Inland Enterprise Inc., p. I-703 [NAICS 32712N]

Inland Fruit Co., p. III-1950 [NAICS 424480]

Inland Industrial Tire North Inc., p. III-1766 [NAICS 423130]

Inland Northwest Dairies L.L.C., p. III-1933 [NAICS 424430]

Inland Products Inc., pp. Vol. I-26, 458 [NAICS 311225, 324191]

Inland Seafood Corp., p. III-1943 [NAICS 424460]

Inland Waters Pollution Control, p. III-1890 [NAICS 423930]

Inman Mills, p. I-192 [NAICS 31311M]

Innergy Power Corp., p. II-1442 [NAICS 335911]

Innertech-Nashville Inc., pp. Vol. II-933, 1551 [NAICS 332510, 336399]

Innodata Isogen Inc., p. I-436 [NAICS 334518]

Innova Electronics Inc., pp. Vol. II-1238, 1282, 1312 [NAICS 334111, 334412, 334418]

Innovation Associates Inc., p. II-1189 [NAICS 333913]

Innovation Specialties, p. I-362 [NAICS 334518]

Innovative Plastics Corp., p. I-306 [NAICS 31699M]

Innovative Robotics Solutions Inc., p. II-1056 [NAICS 333295]

Innovent Air Handling Equipment, p. II-918 [NAICS 332410]

Innoventions Inc., p. II-1292 [NAICS 334414]

Innovex Inc., p. II-1087 [NAICS 33315]

Innovo Group Inc., pp. Vol. I-239, 306 [NAICS 31491M, 31699M]

Innovis Inc., p. III-1801 [NAICS 423420]

INOAC Packaging Group Inc., p. I-646 [NAICS 326160]

Inolex Chemical Co., pp. Vol. I-488, 493 [NAICS 325188, 32519M]

Inoveris, p. II-1381 [NAICS 334613]

Inovision Holdings L.P., pp. Vol. II-1277, 1297 [NAICS 334411, 334415]

Inovys Corp., p. I-1056 [NAICS 333295]

Inpeake Packaging Inc., p. I-379 [NAICS 32221M]

Input/Output Inc., p. II-1367 [NAICS 334519]

Inservco Inc., p. II-1312 [NAICS 334418]

Insight Enterprises Inc., p. III-2211 [NAICS 454113]

Insight Technology Inc., p. II-1082 [NAICS 333314]

Instituform Technologies Inc., p. I-510 [NAICS 32522M]

Insl-X Bruning Paint Company Inc., p. I-554 [NAICS 325510]

Insl-X Products Corp., p. I-554 [NAICS 325510]

Inst For Develop Human Being, p. III-2200 [NAICS 453920]

Installed Products USA L.L.C., p. III-1790 [NAICS 423330]

Instant Photo Inc., p. III-1798 [NAICS 423410]

Numbers following p. or pp. are page references. Roman numerals indicate volume numbers. Bracketed items indicate industries. Page references are to the starting pages of company tables.

Insteel Industries Inc., pp. Vol. I-793, Vol. II-908, 939, 1014 [NAICS 33122M, 33232M, 33261M, 33299N]

Institutional Sales Associates; pp. Vol. III-1925, 1929 [NAICS 424410, 424420]

Institutional Wholesale Co., p. III-1875 [NAICS 423850]

Instrumentation Laboratory Co., p. I-544 [NAICS 325413]

Insulation Specialties of America, pp. Vol. I-686, 703, 771 [NAICS 327113, 32712N, 327993]

Insulation Supply Company Inc., p. III-1790 [NAICS 423330]

Insurance Auto Auctions Inc., pp. Vol. III-1758, 1762 [NAICS 423110, 423120]

Intat Precision Inc., p. I-845 [NAICS 33151M]

Intcomex, p. III-1805 [NAICS 423430]

Integrated Circuit Systems Inc., pp. Vol. II-1252, Vol. III-1839 [NAICS 334119, 423690]

Integrated Components Source, p. III-2058 [NAICS 443120]

Integrated Defense Technologies, pp. Vol. II-1267, 1327 [NAICS 334290, 334511]

Integrated Device Technology Inc., p. II-1287 [NAICS 334413]

Integrated Dynamics Engineering. p. II-1056 [NAICS 333295]

Integrated Logistics Solutions Inc., p. II-958 [NAICS 332722]

Integrated Microwave Corp., p. I-686 [NAICS 327113]

Integrated Packaging Corporation, pp. Vol. I-379, Vol. II-928 [NAICS 3221M, 33243M]

Integrated Resources Inc., p. I-343 [NAICS 321920]

Integrated Supply Network Inc., p. III-1762 [NAICS 423120]

Integrative Therapeutics Inc., p. III-1909 [NAICS 424210]

Integrity Media Inc., p. II-1376 [NAICS 334612]

Intel Corp., pp. Vol. II-1238, 1252, 1287, Vol. III-1805 [NAICS 334111, 334119, 334413, 423430]

Intelicoat Products, p. I-631 [NAICS 326130]

Intellectual Technology Inc., p. II-1248 [NAICS 334113]

Inter-American Transport, p. II-1023 [NAICS 333111]

Inter-Pacific Corp., pp. Vol. III-1919, 1922 [NAICS 424330, 424340]

Inter Parfums Inc., p. I-575 [NAICS 325620]

Inter-State Enterprises Co., p. III-1879 [NAICS 423860]

Inter-State Hardwoods Inc., p. I-358 [NAICS 321999]

Inter-Tel Inc., p. II-1257 [NAICS 334210]

Interbake Foods Inc., p. I-124 [NAICS 31182M]

Interbake Foods L.L.C., pp. Vol. I-116, 124 [NAICS 31181M, 31182M]

Intercard Corp., p. II-1248 [NAICS 334113]

Interceramic Inc., pp. Vol. III-1786, 2065 [NAICS 423320, 444100]

Interconnect Devices Inc., p. II-1347 [NAICS 334515]

Intercontinental Energy Group Inc., p. I-363 [NAICS 322110]

Interdynamics Inc., pp. Vol. I-471, Vol. II-1184 [NAICS 325120, 333912]

Interface Inc., pp. Vol. I-198, 229, 234, 475, 595, 626 [NAICS 313210, 314110, 31412M, 32513M, 32599N, 326122]

Integrated Industrial Systems Inc., pp. Vol. II-1147, 1162 [NAICS 333516, 333612]

Interior Investments L.L.C., p. III-1774 [NAICS 423210]

Interlake Material Handling Inc., pp. Vol. II-1194, 1644 [NAICS 33392M, 337215]

Interlectric Corp., p. II-1386 [NAICS 335110]

Interlink Electronics Inc., p. II-1297 [NAICS 334415]

Interlott Technologies Inc., p. II-1077 [NAICS 333313]

Intermagnetics General Corp., pp. Vol. I-686, 837, Vol. II-1014, 1106 [NAICS 327113, 33149M, 33299N, 333415]

Intermark Fabric Corp., pp. Vol. I-218, 224 [NAICS 31331M, 313320]

Intermatic Inc., pp. Vol. II-1287, 1317, 1332, 1437, 1457 [NAICS 334413, 334419, 334512, 335314, 33593M]

Intermet Corp., p. I-852 [NAICS 33152N]

Intermetra Corp., p. III-1839 [NAICS 423690]

Intermountain Scientific Corp., p. III-1820 [NAICS 423490]

Intern. Advanced Materials Inc., p. II-1292 [NAICS 334414]

Intern. Airline Support Group Inc., p. III-1879 [NAICS 423860]

Intern. Business Machines Corp., pp. Vol. II-1238, 1243, 1248, 1252, 1287 [NAICS 334111, 334112, 334113, 334119, 334413]

Intern. Construction Equipment, p. II-1207 [NAICS 333991]

Intern. Contract Furnishings Inc., p. III-1774 [NAICS 423210]

Intern. Engineering & Mfg Inc., p. II-1607 [NAICS 336999]

Intern. Flavors & Fragrances Inc., pp. Vol. I-147, 488, 575 [NAICS 311930, 325188, 325620]

Intern. Game Technology Inc., p. II-1749 [NAICS 339999]

Intern. Lottery & Totalizator Sys., p. II-1248 [NAICS 334113]

Intern. Molasses Corporation Ltd., p. I-44 [NAICS 311311]

Intern. Petroleum Corp of DE, p. I-443 [NAICS 324110]

Intern. Thermal Systems L.L.C., pp. Vol. II-1184, 1217 [NAICS 333912, 333994]

Intern. Trade American Consultant, p. III-1801 [NAICS 423420]

Intern. Truck Sales of Richmond, p. III-1758 [NAICS 423110]

International Abrasive Mfg Co., p. I-756 [NAICS 327910]

International AG Commodities Inc., p. III-1965 [NAICS 424590]

International Aluminum Corp., p. II-908 [NAICS 33232M]

International Carbonic Inc., p. II-1189 [NAICS 333913]

International Chimney Corp., p. I-699 [NAICS 327123]

International Coatings Inc., pp. Vol. I-560, 580 [NAICS 325520, 325910]

International Cold Storage Co., p. II-1106 [NAICS 333415]

International Components Corp., p. II-1292 [NAICS 334414]

International Control Services Inc., p. II-1282 [NAICS 334412]

International Crankshaft Inc., pp. Vol. I-872, Vol. II-1505 [NAICS 33211N, 33631M]

International Cryogenics Inc., p. I-471 [NAICS 325120]

International Cube, pp. Vol. I-403, 415 [NAICS 32223M, 322299]

International Decoratives Inc., p. III-1998 [NAICS 424930]

International Extrusion Corp., p. I-811 [NAICS 331316]

International Forest Products Corp., p. III-1905 [NAICS 424130]

International Furniture, pp. Vol. III-2027, 2037, 2050 [NAICS 441229, 442110, 443111]

International Garment Processors, p. I-218 [NAICS 31331M]

International Immunology Corp., p. I-549 [NAICS 325414]

International Knife and Saw Inc., p. II-1046 [NAICS 333210]

International Laser Group Inc., p. I-580 [NAICS 325910]

International Lease Finance Corp., p. III-1879 [NAICS 423860]

International Marketing Inc., p. I-660 [NAICS 32621M]

International Mfg Services Inc., p. II-1297 [NAICS 334415]

International Micro Systems Inc., p. III-2058 [NAICS 443120]

International Mill Service Inc., p. I-837 [NAICS 33149M]

International MultiFoods Corp., pp. Vol. I-15, 92, 124, Vol. III-1925 [NAICS 31121M, 311520, 31182M, 424410]

International Paper Co., pp. Vol. I-312, 363, 368, 374, 388, 403 [NAICS 32111M, 322110, 32212M, 322130, 32222N, 32223M]

International Patterns Inc., p. II-1627 [NAICS 337127]

International Piping Systems, pp. Vol. II-923, 928, 1009 [NAICS 332420, 33243M, 332996]

International Playthings Inc., p. III-1887 [NAICS 423920]

International Rectifier Corp., p. II-1287 [NAICS 334413]

International Resistive Co., p. II-1297 [NAICS 334415]

International Seal Company Inc., p. III-1867 [NAICS 423830]

International Speedway Corp., p. III-2190 [NAICS 453220]

International Staple & Machine, pp. Vol. II-1077, 1207 [NAICS 333313, 333991]

International Star Corp., p. I-771 [NAICS 327993]

International Thermoproducts, p. I-686 [NAICS 327113]

International Truck & Engine, pp. Vol. II-1173, 1473 [NAICS 333618, 336111]

International Turbine Service, p. III-1879 [NAICS 423860]

International Veneer Company Inc., p. I-324 [NAICS 32121N]

International Waters, pp. Vol. III-1916, 1919 [NAICS 424320, 424330]

International Wire Group Inc., p. I-837 [NAICS 33149M]

International Wood Industries Inc., pp. Vol. I-324, 358 [NAICS 32121N, 321999]

Interpane Glass Co., pp. Vol. I-709, 722 [NAICS 327211, 327215]

Interpharm Inc., p. I-534 [NAICS 325411]

Interplastic Corp., pp. I-500, 554 [NAICS 325211, 325510]

Interplex NAS Inc., p. I-879 [NAICS 33211P]

Interpoint Corp., p. II-1468 [NAICS 335999]

Interpower Corp., p. II-1302 [NAICS 334416]

Interserv Corp., p. II-1056 [NAICS 333295]

Intersil Corp., p. II-1287 [NAICS 334413]

Interstate Bakeries Corp., p. I-116 [NAICS 31181M]

Interstate Battery System of Dallas, p. III-1762 [NAICS 423120]

Interstate Brands Corp., p. I-116 [NAICS 31181M]

Interstate Brands Corp. Marketing, p. I-116 [NAICS 31181M]

Interstate Chemical Company Inc., pp. Vol. I-488, 493 [NAICS 325188, 32519M]

Interstate Co's Inc., pp. Vol. III-1831, 1867 [NAICS 423610, 423830]

Interstate Commodities Inc., p. III-1958 [NAICS 424510]

Interstate Concrete and Asphalt, pp. Vol. I-448, 732, 743 [NAICS 324121, 327320, 327390]

Interstate Diesel Service Inc., p. II-1505 [NAICS 33631M]

Interstate Meat Distributors Inc., p. III-1946 [NAICS 424470]

Interstate Paper Supply Inc., p. I-636 [NAICS 326140]

Interstate Resources Inc., p. I-379 [NAICS 32221M]

Interstate Supply Co., p. III-1778 [NAICS 423220]

Intersystems USA Inc., p. II-1248 [NAICS 334113]

Intervoice Inc., p. II-1257 [NAICS 334210]

inTEST Corp., p. II-1347 [NAICS 334515]

Intevac Inc., pp. Vol. II-1082, 1687 [NAICS 333314, 339115]

Intier Automotive Interiors, p. I-198 [NAICS 313210]

Intimate Brands Inc., pp. Vol. III-2126, 2135, 2211 [NAICS 448120, 448150, 454113]

Intoximeters Inc., p. II-1342 [NAICS 334514]

Intra-Coastal Packing Inc., p. III-1936 [NAICS 424440]

IntraAction Corp., p. I-771 [NAICS 327993]

Intracoastal City Dry Dock, p. II-1589 [NAICS 336611]

Intralox Inc., pp. Vol. II-939, 1168, 1194 [NAICS 33261M, 333613, 33392M]

Intrasonics Inc., p. II-1277 [NAICS 334411]

Intrepid Stone Inc., p. I-762 [NAICS 327991]

Intricon, p. II-1217 [NAICS 333994]

Intuitive Surgical Inc., pp. Vol. II-1671, 1676 [NAICS 339112, 339113]

Invacare Corp., p. II-1676 [NAICS 339113]

Invacare Technologies Corp., p. II-1676 [NAICS 339113]

Invensys Building Systems Inc., pp. Vol. II-1332, 1337, 1437 [NAICS 334512, 334513, 335314]

Invensys Inc., pp. Vol. II-918, 1033, 1061, 1179, 1217 [NAICS 332410, 333120, 33329N, 333911, 333994]

Invensys Systems Inc., p. II-1337 [NAICS 334513]

Inverness Medical Innovations Inc., p. I-544 [NAICS 325413]

Investacard, p. III-1887 [NAICS 423920]

Invisible Fence Inc., p. II-1421 [NAICS 335311]

Invisible Technologies Inc., pp. Vol. I-251, 306, Vol. II-1421 [NAICS 314999, 31699M, 335311]

Invitrogen Corp., pp. Vol. I-544, 549 [NAICS 325413, 325414]

Invivo Corp., p. II-1322 [NAICS 334510]

Inwood Office Furniture Inc., pp. Vol. II-1621, 1627, 1644, 1650 [NAICS 337122, 337127, 337215, 33721N]

INX International Ink Co., p. I-580 [NAICS 325910]

Iomega Corp., p. II-1243 [NAICS 334112]

Ionatron Inc., pp. Vol. I-208, Vol. III-2072 [NAICS 313230, 444220]

Ionics Inc., pp. Vol. I-165, Vol. II-1061, 1092 [NAICS 31211M, 33329N, 33331N]

Ionics Inc. Instrument Div., p. II-1352 [NAICS 334516]

Iowa Oil Co., pp. Vol. III-1979, 2218 [NAICS 424720, 454311]

Iowa Prestressed Concrete Inc., p. I-743 [NAICS 327390]

Iowa Turkey Products Inc., p. I-97 [NAICS 311615]

IPAC 2000, p. II-918 [NAICS 332410]

IPC Acquisition Corp., p. II-1257 [NAICS 334210]

IPC Communication Services Inc., p. II-1381 [NAICS 334613]

IPC Communications Inc., p. II-1267 [NAICS 334290]

IPC Information Systems Inc., pp. Vol. II-1257, 1267 [NAICS 334210, 334290]

IPC Power Resistors Intern. Inc., p. II-1297 [NAICS 334415]

IPG Photonics Corp., p. II-1468 [NAICS 335999]

Ipitek Photonic Technology, pp. Vol. II-1082, 1451 [NAICS 333314, 33592M]

IPS Corp., p. I-560 [NAICS 325520]

IPSCO Inc. (US), pp. Vol. II-1039, 1173 [NAICS 33313M, 333618]

Ipsen International Inc., p. II-1217 [NAICS 333994]

Ipswich Shellfish Company Inc., pp. Vol. I-110, Vol. III-1943 [NAICS 31171M, 424460]

IQ Products Company Inc., p. I-560 [NAICS 325520]

Ira Green Inc., p. I-251 [NAICS 314999]

Ira Higdon Grocery Company Inc., p. III-1954 [NAICS 424490]

Irby Steel, p. II-923 [NAICS 332420]

Ircon Inc., pp. Vol. II-1332, 1337, 1367, 1437 [NAICS 334512, 334513, 334519, 335314]

IRIS International Inc., p. II-1352 [NAICS 334516]

Iron Age Corp., p. I-300 [NAICS 31621M]

Iron and Metals Inc., p. I-807 [NAICS 331314]

Iron City Distributing Inc., p. III-1987 [NAICS 424820]

Ironwood Plastics Inc., p. II-1119 [NAICS 333511]

Irvin Aerospace Inc., p. I-251 [NAICS 314999]

Irvine Scientific Sales Inc., pp. Vol. I-544, 549 [NAICS 325413, 325414]

Irving Materials Inc., p. I-732 [NAICS 327320]

Irving Oil Corp., p. III-2218 [NAICS 454311]

Irving Tanning Co., p. I-296 [NAICS 316110]

Irwin International Inc., p. III-1817 [NAICS 423460]

Irwin Manufacturing Corp., p. I-285 [NAICS 31529M]

Irwin Seating Company Inc., pp. Vol. II-1616, 1627 [NAICS 337121, 337127]

ISCO Corp., p. III-2004 [NAICS 424950]

Isco Inc., pp. Vol. II-1352, Vol. III-1968 [NAICS 334516, 424610]

Island Recycling Inc., pp. Vol. I-363, 722, 807 [NAICS 322110, 327215, 331314]

Island Water Sports Inc., pp. Vol. III-2135, 2150 [NAICS 448150, 451110]

Isochem Colors Inc., p. I-580 [NAICS 325910]

Isolatek International, pp. Vol. I-415, 771 [NAICS 322299, 327993]

Isotope Products Co., p. I-544 [NAICS 325413]

ISP Elastomers, p. I-500 [NAICS 325211]

Ispat Inland Inc., pp. Vol. I-780, 793 [NAICS 33111M, 33122M]

Italian Peoples Bakery Inc., p. I-124 [NAICS 31182M]

ITD California Inc., p. III-1766 [NAICS 423130]

ITE Distributing, p. III-1801 [NAICS 423420]

Iten Chevrolet Co., p. III-2018 [NAICS 441210]

Iten Industries Inc., pp. Vol. I-631, 771, Vol. II-1725 [NAICS 326130, 327993, 339991]

Iteris Inc., pp. Vol. II-1243, 1666 [NAICS 334112, 339111]

ITG-MEDEV Inc., p. III-1909 [NAICS 424210]

ITOX Inc., pp. Vol. II-1248, 1312 [NAICS 334113, 334418]

Itron Corp., p. II-1307 [NAICS 334417]

Itron Inc., pp. Vol. II-1267, 1367, Vol. III-1805 [NAICS 334290, 334519, 423430]

Itronix Corp., p. II-1238 [NAICS 334111]

ITT Gilfillan Inc., p. II-1327 [NAICS 334511]

ITT Industries Inc., pp. Vol. II-1005, 1179, 1222, 1307, 1317, 1347, 1505, 1551, 1580 [NAICS 332995, 333911, 33399N, 334417, 334419, 334515, 33631M, 336399, 336419]

ITW Angleboard, p. I-374 [NAICS 322130]

ITW Bee Leitzke, p. II-958 [NAICS 332722]

ITW Fastex, p. II-958 [NAICS 332722]

ITW Hobart Brothers Co., pp. Vol. II-939, 1229, 1337 [NAICS 33261M, 33399P, 334513]

ITW Philadelphia Resins, p. I-560 [NAICS 325520]

ITW Ramset/Red Head, pp. Vol. I-560, 872 [NAICS 325520, 33211N]

Ivan Allen Workspace L.L.C., p. III-1774 [NAICS 423210]

IVAX Corp., p. I-539 [NAICS 325412]

IVAX Diagnostics Inc., p. I-544 [NAICS 325413]

IVC Industries Inc., p. I-534 [NAICS 325411]

IVCi L.L.C., p. III-1801 [NAICS 423420]

Ivek Corp., p. II-1189 [NAICS 333913]

Ivex Corp. Mill Div., p. I-374 [NAICS 322130]

Numbers following p. or pp. are page references. Roman numerals indicate volume numbers. Bracketed items indicate industries. Page references are to the starting pages of company tables.

2361

Ivoclar Vivadent Inc., p. II-1682 [NAICS 339114]

ivpcare Inc., pp. Vol. III-1813, 1909, 2100 [NAICS 423450, 424210, 446110]

Ivy Steel and Wire, pp. Vol. II-899, 939 [NAICS 33231M, 33261M]

IW Industries Inc., p. II-974 [NAICS 332913]

IWI Holding Ltd., p. II-1696 [NAICS 33991M]

Ixia, pp. Vol. II-1267, Vol. III-1839 [NAICS 334290, 423690]

Ixtlan Technology L.L.C., p. I-641 [NAICS 326150]

IXYS Corp., p. II-1337 [NAICS 334513]

Izzy Designs, p. II-1632 [NAICS 33712N]

J. Allan Steel Co., p. I-793 [NAICS 33122M]

J. Altis Ltd., p. III-2123 [NAICS 448110]

J and A Industries Inc., p. II-1584 [NAICS 336510]

J and B Meats Corp., p. III-1946 [NAICS 424470]

J and G Food Products Inc., p. III-1946 [NAICS 424470]

J and H Aluminum, p. III-1790 [NAICS 423330]

J and H Carpets Inc., p. I-229 [NAICS 314110]

J and H Oil Co., pp. Vol. III-1979, 2116 [NAICS 424720, 447110]

J and I Automotive Distributors, p. III-1770 [NAICS 423140]

J and J Amusements Inc., p. II-1607 [NAICS 336999]

J & J Snack Foods Corp., pp. Vol. I-62, 68, 124, 165, Vol. II-1061 [NAICS 31141M, 31142M, 31182M, 31211M, 33329N]

J and K Manufacturing Inc., p. II-1584 [NAICS 336510]

J and L Tank Inc., p. II-1491 [NAICS 336212]

J and M Industries Inc., p. I-239 [NAICS 31491M]

J and M Service Inc., pp. Vol. III-1782, 1859 [NAICS 423310, 423810]

J and S Plastics Inc., p. II-1056 [NAICS 333295]

J B'S Factory Carpet, p. III-2041 [NAICS 442210]

J D'Addario and Company Inc., p. II-1731 [NAICS 339992]

J. Hellman Produce Inc., p. III-1950 [NAICS 424480]

J Horst Manufacturing Inc., p. II-1147 [NAICS 333516]

J. Jill Group Inc., p. III-2211 [NAICS 454113]

J. Kings Food Service Profession., pp. Vol. III-1929, 1933, 1936, 1946 [NAICS 424420, 424430, 424440, 424470]

J Meyer and Sons Inc., pp. Vol. I-296, 589 [NAICS 316110, 325991]

J R Glidewell Dental Ceramics, p. II-1682 [NAICS 339114]

J. Richards Industries, p. II-1194 [NAICS 33392M]

J. Sosnick and Son Inc., pp. Vol. III-1939, 1987 [NAICS 424450, 424820]

J-Star Bodco Inc., p. III-1863 [NAICS 423820]

J-W Operating Co., p. II-1184 [NAICS 333912]

J. Weil and Co., p. III-1929 [NAICS 424420]

Jabil Circuit Inc., pp. Vol. II-1282, 1287 [NAICS 334412, 334413]

Jac Vandenberg Inc., p. III-1950 [NAICS 424480]

Jaciva's Inc., pp. Vol. III-2089, 2092 [NAICS 445291, 445292]

Jack Engle and Co., p. III-1890 [NAICS 423930]

Jack L Slagle Fire Equipment, p. II-1482 [NAICS 336120]

Jack Rubin and Sons Inc., p. III-1820 [NAICS 423490]

Jack Schwartz Shoes Inc., pp. Vol. I-300, Vol. III-1922 [NAICS 31621M, 424340]

Jack Williams Tire Company Inc., pp. Vol. III-1766, 2030 [NAICS 423130, 441310]

Jack Young Company Inc., p. III-1770 [NAICS 423140]

Jackson Flexible Products Inc., p. I-505 [NAICS 325212]

Jackson-Jennings Farm Bureau, p. III-1958 [NAICS 424510]

Jackson Manufacturing Co., p. II-1616 [NAICS 337121]

Jackson MSC Inc., p. II-1092 [NAICS 33331N]

Jackson Paper Company Inc., pp. Vol. III-1898, 1905 [NAICS 424110, 424130]

Jackson Paper Manufacturing Co., p. I-363 [NAICS 322110]

Jackson Produce Co., p. III-1950 [NAICS 424480]

Jackson Products Inc., pp. Vol. I-651, 722, Vol. II-1676, 1687 [NAICS 32619M, 327215, 339113, 339115]

Jackson's Lemmon Avenue Pottery, pp. Vol. III-2047, 2072 [NAICS 442299, 444220]

Jackson Tube Service Inc., pp. Vol. I-788, Vol. II-1009 [NAICS 331210, 332996]

Jackson Wheeler Metals Service, p. I-825 [NAICS 331419]

JacksonLea, p. I-756 [NAICS 327910]

Jaclyn Inc., pp. Vol. I-279, 306 [NAICS 31523M, 31699M]

Jaco Electronics Inc., pp. Vol. II-1282, 1332, 1347, 1457, Vol. III-1805, 1839 [NAICS 334412, 334512, 334515, 33593M, 423430, 423690]

Jaco Oil Co., p. III-2116 [NAICS 447110]

JACO Racing Products Inc., p. I-660 [NAICS 32621M]

Jacob Stern and Sons Inc., p. I-26 [NAICS 311225]

Jacobi Sales Inc., pp. Vol. III-1863, 2072 [NAICS 423820, 444220]

Jacobs Vehicle Systems, p. II-1173 [NAICS 333618]

Jacobsen Manufacturing Inc., p. I-348 [NAICS 321991]

Jacobson Capital Services Inc., p. III-1913 [NAICS 424310]

Jacobus Energy Inc., pp. Vol. III-1975, 2218 [NAICS 424710, 454311]

Jacquelynn's China Matching, p. III-2047 [NAICS 442299]

Jacuzzi Brands Inc., pp. Vol. I-879, Vol. II-933, 974, 1390, 1397 [NAICS 33211P, 332510, 332913, 33512M, 33521M]

Jade Apparel, p. I-279 [NAICS 31523M]

Jade Corp., p. II-1189 [NAICS 333913]

Jade Systems Corp., p. III-2058 [NAICS 443120]

Jado Sewing Machine Inc., p. II-1417 [NAICS 335228]

Jadtec Computer Group, p. III-2058 [NAICS 443120]

JAE Electronics Inc., p. I-1307 [NAICS 334417]

JaGee Corp., p. III-1958 [NAICS 424510]

JAKKS Pacific Inc., p. II-1708 [NAICS 33993M]

Jaks Famous Crawfish Seafoood, p. I-110 [NAICS 31171M]

Jameco Electronics Inc., p. II-1347 [NAICS 334515]

James A Kiley Company Inc., p. II-1482 [NAICS 336120]

James Austin Co., pp. Vol. I-516, 566 [NAICS 325311, 32561M]

James Burn International, p. I-374 [NAICS 322130]

James Calvetti Meats Inc., pp. Vol. III-1929, 1946 [NAICS 424420, 424470]

James Candy Company Inc., p. I-57 [NAICS 311340]

James Hardie Industries USA, p. I-727 [NAICS 327310]

James LTaylor Manufacturing Inc., pp. Vol. II-1046, 1189 [NAICS 333210, 333913]

James Thompson Inc., p. I-218 [NAICS 31331M]

Jamestown Implement Inc., p. III-1863 [NAICS 423820]

Jamieson Manufacturing Co., pp. Vol. III-1794, 1843 [NAICS 423390, 423710]

Jamison Bedding Inc., p. II-1657 [NAICS 337910]

Jamo Custom Building Products, pp. Vol. I-560, 727, 752 [NAICS 325520, 327310, 327420]

Jana's Classics Inc., p. I-124 [NAICS 31182M]

Janco Distributors Inc., p. III-1909 [NAICS 424210]

Jancy Engineering Inc., p. II-1207 [NAICS 333991]

Janel Glass Company Inc., p. I-713 [NAICS 327212]

Janes Inc., p. I-267 [NAICS 31521M]

Janesville-Sackner Group, p. I-641 [NAICS 326150]

Janovic Plaza Inc., p. III-2047 [NAICS 442299]

Janson Industries, p. II-1662 [NAICS 337920]

Jantz's Yard 4 Automotive Inc., p. III-1770 [NAICS 423140]

Japan America Beverage Co., p. I-181 [NAICS 312140]

Japs-Olson Company Inc., p. I-436 [NAICS 32312M]

Jarden Corp., pp. Vol. I-626, 670, 718, 879 [NAICS 326122, 32629M, 327213, 33211P]

Jardine Petroleum Co., p. III-1975 [NAICS 424710]

Jarritos Distributors, p. III-1954 [NAICS 424490]

Jarvis Steel and Lumber Inc., p. I-329 [NAICS 32121P]

Jason Industries Inc., p. II-1500 [NAICS 336214]

Jasper Seating Company Inc., pp. Vol. II-1621, 1627, 1650 [NAICS 337122, 337127, 33721N]

Jatco Inc., p. III-1968 [NAICS 424610]

Jawd Associates Inc., p. III-1936 [NAICS 424440]

Jax Asphalt Co., p. I-453 [NAICS 324122]

Jax USA, pp. Vol. I-458, Vol. III-1979 [NAICS 324191, 424720]

Jay C Food Stores, p. III-2076 [NAICS 445110]

Jay Franco and Sons Inc., p. I-234 [NAICS 31412M]

Jay Packaging Group Inc., p. I-609 [NAICS 326112]

Jay R. Smith Mfg. Co., p. II-974 [NAICS 332913]

Jayark Corp., p. I-262 [NAICS 31519M]

Jayco Inc., pp. Vol. II-1500, 1607 [NAICS 336214, 336999]

JBL Consumer Products, p. II-1272 [NAICS 334310]

JBR Inc., p. I-143 [NAICS 311920]

JC Newman Cigar Co., pp. Vol. I-188, Vol. III-2001 [NAICS 31222M, 424940]

J.C. Penney Company Inc., pp. Vol. III-2171, 2211 [NAICS 452111, 454113]

JC Produce Inc., p. III-1950 [NAICS 424480]

JC Snavely and Sons Inc., pp. Vol. I-324, 329 [NAICS 32121N, 32121P]

JcAIR Inc., p. II-1580 [NAICS 336419]

JCB Inc., pp. Vol. II-1033, 1194 [NAICS 333120, 33392M]

Numbers following p. or pp. are page references. Roman numerals indicate volume numbers. Bracketed items indicate industries. Page references are to the starting pages of company tables.

2362

JCM Industries Inc., pp. Vol. II-1194, 1644 [NAICS 33392M, 337215]

JCPenney Custom Decorating, p. I-234 [NAICS 31412M]

JD Calato Manufacturing Co., p. II-1731 [NAICS 339992]

JD Heiskell and Company Inc., p. I-9 [NAICS 311119]

JD Streett and Company Inc., pp. Vol. I-458, 595 [NAICS 324191, 32599N]

JDR Enterprises Inc., pp. Vol. I-244, Vol. II-974 [NAICS 314991, 332913]

JDS Uniphase Corp., pp. Vol. I-837, Vol. II-1257, 1287, 1322, 1468 [NAICS 33149M, 334210, 334413, 334510, 335999]

JDS Uniphase Corp. Epitaxx Div., p. II-1468 [NAICS 335999]

JE Berkowitz L.P., pp. Vol. I-709, 722 [NAICS 327211, 327215]

J.E. Higgins Lumber Co., p. III-1782 [NAICS 423310]

Jean Mart Inc., p. I-285 [NAICS 31529M]

Jean's Used Auto Parts, p. III-1770 [NAICS 423140]

Jeanerette Sugar Company Inc., pp. Vol. I-40, 44 [NAICS 311313, 31131N]

Jeff Wyler Dealer Group, p. III-2011 [NAICS 441110]

Jeffers Handbell Supply Inc., p. III-2159 [NAICS 451140]

Jefferson City Oil Company Inc., p. III-1975 [NAICS 424710]

Jefferson Homebuilders Inc., p. I-312 [NAICS 32111M]

Jefferson Industries Corp., p. II-1541 [NAICS 336370]

Jefferson Industries Inc., p. I-229 [NAICS 314110]

Jefferson Mills Inc., p. I-192 [NAICS 31311M]

Jefferson Supply Co., p. III-1875 [NAICS 423850]

Jel Sert Co., pp. Vol. I-92, 158 [NAICS 311520, 31199M]

Jelight Company Inc., p. II-1386 [NAICS 335110]

Jelly Belly Candy Co., p. I-57 [NAICS 311340]

Jem Engineering and Mfg Inc., p. I-788 [NAICS 331210]

Jenkins Brick Co., p. I-691 [NAICS 327121]

Jenkins Gas and Oil Company Inc., p. III-2222 [NAICS 454312]

Jennifer Convertibles Inc., p. II-1657 [NAICS 337910]

Jennmar Corp., pp. Vol. I-334, Vol. II-1039 [NAICS 32191M, 33313M]

Jensen Industries Inc., p. II-1682 [NAICS 339114]

Jensen Precast, p. I-743 [NAICS 327390]

Jensen's Inc., p. I-825 [NAICS 331419]

Jensen Scientific Products Inc., p. I-718 [NAICS 327213]

Jenss Department Stores Inc., p. III-2171 [NAICS 452111]

JEOL USA Inc., pp. Vol. II-1352, 1357 [NAICS 334516, 334517]

Jer-Co Industries Inc., p. II-1162 [NAICS 333612]

Jerald Manufacturing Company, p. II-1607 [NAICS 336999]

Jergens Inc., pp. Vol. I-857, Vol. II-988, 1140, 1222 [NAICS 33152P, 332991, 333515, 33399N]

Jernberg Industries Inc., pp. Vol. I-872, Vol. II-1486 [NAICS 33211N, 336211]

Jerome Cheese Co., p. I-76 [NAICS 311513]

Jerome Industries Corp., p. II-1302 [NAICS 334416]

Jerr-Dan Corp., p. II-1486 [NAICS 336211]

Jersey Shore Peterbilt Inc., pp. Vol. III-2027, 2030 [NAICS 441229, 441310]

Jersey Shore Steel Co., p. II-1147 [NAICS 333516]

Jervis B Webb Co., pp. Vol. II-1168, 1194, 1229, 1644 [NAICS 333613, 33392M, 33399P, 337215]

Jesse Engineering Co., pp. Vol. II-1129, 1147 [NAICS 333513, 333516]

Jessup Engineering Inc., p. II-1152 [NAICS 333518]

Jessup Manufacturing Co., p. I-505 [NAICS 325212]

Jesus People U S A Full Gospel, p. III-1790 [NAICS 423330]

Jet Fuel Oil Co., p. III-2218 [NAICS 454311]

Jet Plastica Industries Inc., p. I-636 [NAICS 326140]

Jeter Systems Corp., pp. Vol. I-403, Vol. II-1644, 1650 [NAICS 32223M, 337215, 33721N]

Jett Racing and Sales Inc., pp. Vol. III-1835, 2030, 2047, 2104, 2190 [NAICS 423620, 441310, 442299, 446120, 453220]

Jetta Corp., p. II-1611 [NAICS 337110]

Jeunique International Inc., pp. Vol. I-279, 575, Vol. II-1696 [NAICS 31523M, 325620, 33991M]

Jewel Case Corp., pp. Vol. I-306, Vol. II-928 [NAICS 31699M, 33243M]

Jewel Craft Of Utah, p. III-1894 [NAICS 423940]

Jewelry Corner Inc., pp. Vol. III-1894, 2144 [NAICS 423940, 448310]

Jewelry Manufacturers Outlet Inc., p. III-1894 [NAICS 423940]

Jewels Connection, p. III-1894 [NAICS 423940]

Jewett-Cameron Trading Ltd., p. III-2065 [NAICS 444100]

JF Allen Co., pp. Vol. I-732, 737, 762 [NAICS 327320, 32733M, 327991]

JFC International Inc., p. III-1954 [NAICS 424490]

JH Fletcher and Co., pp. Vol. II-1039, 1584 [NAICS 33313M, 336510]

J.H. Larson Co., pp. Vol. III-1831, 1847, 1851 [NAICS 423610, 423720, 423730]

JH Lynch and Sons Inc., p. I-448 [NAICS 324121]

JHM Engineering, p. II-1682 [NAICS 339114]

Jideco of Bardstown Inc., p. II-1427 [NAICS 335312]

Jilco Industries Inc., p. III-1879 [NAICS 423860]

Jim Barna Log Systems, p. I-353 [NAICS 321992]

Jim Beam Brands Co., p. I-181 [NAICS 312140]

Jim Click Ford Inc., p. III-2011 [NAICS 441110]

Jim Koons Management Co., p. III-2011 [NAICS 441110]

Jim L. Shetakis Distributing Co., p. III-1954 [NAICS 424490]

Jim Myers Drug Inc., p. III-2100 [NAICS 446110]

Jim's Formal Wear Co., p. III-1916 [NAICS 424320]

Jim's Supply Company Inc., pp. Vol. I-788, Vol. III-1863 [NAICS 331210, 423820]

Jim Smith Contracting, p. I-453 [NAICS 324122]

Jim Thompson Silk Co., p. III-1913 [NAICS 424310]

Jimlar Corp., p. III-1922 [NAICS 424340]

Jimmy Sanders Inc., pp. Vol. I-524, 529 [NAICS 325314, 325320]

Jinny Beauty Supply Company Inc., p. III-1875 [NAICS 423850]

Jirdon Agri Chemicals Inc., pp. Vol. III-1965, 2072 [NAICS 424590, 444220]

JJ Ferguson Sand and Gravel Inc., p. I-732 [NAICS 327320]

JJ Ryan Corp., p. I-872 [NAICS 33211N]

JJI Lighting Group Inc., p. II-1390 [NAICS 33512M]

J.J.R. Enterprises Inc., p. III-2054 [NAICS 443112]

JKL Components Corp., p. II-1082 [NAICS 333314]

JL Audio Inc., p. II-1272 [NAICS 334310]

JL Fisher Inc., p. II-1087 [NAICS 333315]

JL French Corp., pp. Vol. I-852, Vol. II-1749 [NAICS 33152N, 339999]

JL Shepherd and Associates, p. II-1357 [NAICS 334517]

JLG Industries Inc., p. II-1033 [NAICS 333120]

JLM Industries Inc., pp. Vol. I-475, 488, Vol. III-1971 [NAICS 32513M, 325188, 424690]

JM Family Enterprises Inc., p. III-2011 [NAICS 441110]

JM Fry Co., p. I-580 [NAICS 325910]

J.M. Huber Corp., pp. Vol. I-319, 358, 475, 500 [NAICS 321219, 321999, 32513M, 325211]

JM Martinac Shipbuilding Corp., p. II-1589 [NAICS 336611]

JM McConkey and Company Inc., p. III-2072 [NAICS 444220]

JM Murray Center Inc., pp. Vol. I-603, Vol. II-1682 [NAICS 326111, 339114]

J.M. Sealts Co., p. III-1929 [NAICS 424420]

JM Smith Corp., p. III-1909 [NAICS 424210]

J.M. Smucker Co., pp. Vol. I-68, 147 [NAICS 31142M, 311930]

J.M. Tull Metals Company Inc., p. III-1824 [NAICS 423510]

JMAC Inc., p. II-1551 [NAICS 336399]

JMK International Inc., pp. Vol. I-505, 670, Vol. II-1725 [NAICS 325212, 32629M, 339991]

JML Optical Industries Inc., pp. Vol. I-713, Vol. II-1082, 1087, 1687 [NAICS 327212, 333314, 333315, 339115]

Jo-Ann Stores Inc., p. II-2156 [NAICS 451130]

Jo-Bar Manufacturing Corp., p. II-1530 [NAICS 336350]

Joan and Gary's Original Bagel, p. III-2089 [NAICS 445291]

Jobe Concrete Products Inc., pp. Vol. I-448, 732 [NAICS 324121, 327320]

Jockey International Inc., pp. Vol. I-256, 262, 272, 279 [NAICS 31511M, 31519M, 31522M, 31523M]

Jodon Engineering Associates Inc., p. II-1277 [NAICS 334411]

Joe Myers Ford Inc., p. III-2011 [NAICS 441110]

Joe Patti Seafood Co., p. III-1943 [NAICS 424460]

Jofran Sales Inc., p. III-1774 [NAICS 423210]

Johann A Krause Inc., p. II-1124 [NAICS 333512]

Johanna Foods Inc., p. I-86 [NAICS 31151N]

Johanson Dielectrics Inc., p. II-1292 [NAICS 334414]

Johanson Manufacturing Corp., p. II-1292 [NAICS 334414]

John A. Van Den Bosch Co., p. I-4 [NAICS 311111]

John A Vassilaros and Sons Inc., p. I-143 [NAICS 311920]

John B. Sanfilippo and Son Inc., pp. Vol. I-52, 68, 137 [NAICS 311330, 31142M, 31191M]

John Boyle and Company Inc., pp. Vol. I-198, 224, 251 [NAICS 313210, 313320, 314999]

John C Nordt Company Inc., p. II-1696 [NAICS 33991M]

John Conti Coffee Co., p. I-143 [NAICS 311920]

John Day Co., p. III-1863 [NAICS 423820]

John Deer Sitting Group, p. II-1023 [NAICS 333111]

John Deere/Des Moines Works, pp. Vol. II-1023, 1061 [NAICS 333111, 33329N]

John Deere Landscapes, p. III-1998 [NAICS 424930]

John Deere Southeast Engineering, p. II-1028 [NAICS 333112]

John E. Koerner and Company Inc., p. III-1929 [NAICS 424420]

John F. Trompeter Co., pp. Vol. III-1939, 2001 [NAICS 424450, 424940]

John Fabick Tractor Co., pp. Vol. III-1859, 1863 [NAICS 423810, 423820]

John G Shelley Company Inc., p. I-505 [NAICS 325212]

John H. Burrows Inc., p. III-1950 [NAICS 424480]

John H. Harland Co., pp. Vol. I-420, Vol. II-1252 [NAICS 32311M, 334119]

John H. Myers and Son Inc., p. III-1782 [NAICS 423310]

John Hayes and Sons, p. III-1939 [NAICS 424450]

John J Steuby Co., p. II-952 [NAICS 332721]

John Johnson Company Inc., p. I-239 [NAICS 31491M]

John Kaldor Fabricmaker USA, p. III-1913 [NAICS 424310]

John Langenbacher Company Inc., p. II-1639 [NAICS 337212]

John Livacich Produce Inc., p. III-1950 [NAICS 424480]

John O. Butler Co., p. I-575 [NAICS 325620]

John Pryor Company Inc., pp. Vol. I-516, 520 [NAICS 325311, 325312]

John R Lyman Company Inc., p. I-411 [NAICS 322291]

John R. White Company Inc., p. III-1933 [NAICS 424430]

John Rogin Buick Inc., p. III-2030 [NAICS 441310]

John Romanowski & Associates, p. I-224 [NAICS 313320]

John's Kart Shop, p. II-1473 [NAICS 336111]

John Sullivan Dealerships, p. III-2011 [NAICS 441110]

John Taylor Fertilizers Co., pp. Vol. III-1863, 1991 [NAICS 423820, 424910]

John Wagner Associates Inc., p. II-958 [NAICS 332722]

JohnCo Hosiery Inc., p. I-256 [NAICS 31511M]

Johns Manville Corp., pp. Vol. I-368, 374, 771, Vol. II-1112 [NAICS 32212M, 322130, 327993, 33341N]

Johnson Acoustical and Supply, pp. Vol. I-752, 771 [NAICS 327420, 327993]

Johnson and Johnson, pp. Vol. I-534, 539, 566, 575, Vol. II-1676 [NAICS 325411, 325412, 32561M, 325620, 339113]

Johnson & Johnston Associates, p. I-631 [NAICS 326130]

Johnson Brass & Machine Foundry, p. II-1162 [NAICS 333612]

Johnson Brothers Co., p. III-1987 [NAICS 424820]

Johnson Controls Inc., pp. Vol. I-646, Vol. II-1332, 1437, 1442, 1447, 1627 [NAICS 326160, 334512, 335314, 335911, 335912, 337127]

Johnson Controls Interiors, p. II-933 [NAICS 332510]

Johnson Cooperative Grain Co., pp. Vol. III-1766, 1958, 1979, 1991 [NAICS 423130, 424510, 424720, 424910]

Johnson Corp., p. II-1168 [NAICS 333613]

Johnson Family Diamond Cellar, pp. Vol. II-1696, Vol. III-2144 [NAICS 33991M, 448310]

Johnson Gas Appliance Co., p. II-1217 [NAICS 333994]

Johnson Industries, p. III-1762 [NAICS 423120]

Johnson Level and Tool Mfg Co., pp. Vol. II-1134, 1714 [NAICS 333514, 33994M]

Johnson Matthey Inc, p. I-825 [NAICS 331419]

Johnson Oil Company of Gaylord, pp. Vol. III-1975, 2218 [NAICS 424710, 454311]

Johnson Outdoors Inc., pp. Vol. I-239, 244, 272, 290, 358, Vol. II-1342, 1367, 1427, 1594, 1702 [NAICS 31491M, 314991, 31522M, 31599M, 321999, 334514, 334519, 335312, 336612, 339920]

Johnson Power Ltd., p. II-1530 [NAICS 336350]

Johnson Rubber Co., pp. Vol. I-198, 670, Vol. II-1168, 1179, 1725 [NAICS 313210, 32629M, 333613, 333911, 339991]

Johnson Welded Products Inc., p. II-923 [NAICS 332420]

Johnson Wholesale Floors Inc., p. III-1778 [NAICS 423220]

JohnsonDiversey Inc., pp. Vol. I-595, Vol. II-1092 [NAICS 32599N, 33331N]

Johnsonville Sausage L.L.C., p. I-102 [NAICS 31161N]

Johnston Pump Company Inc., p. II-1179 [NAICS 333911]

Johnston Sweeper Co., pp. Vol. II-1092, 1478 [NAICS 33331N, 336112]

Johnstown Corp., p. I-852 [NAICS 33152N]

Joint Venture Piping Inc., pp. Vol. II-923, 1009 [NAICS 332420, 332996]

Jointa Galusha L.L.C., p. III-1786 [NAICS 423320]

Jolly Gardener Products Inc., p. I-524 [NAICS 325314]

Jomac Products Inc., p. I-267 [NAICS 31521M]

Jomar Corp., p. II-1051 [NAICS 333220]

Jon-Lin Foods Inc., p. I-62 [NAICS 31141M]

Jonathan Engineered Solutions, p. II-988 [NAICS 332991]

Jones and Sons Inc., p. I-737 [NAICS 32733M]

Jones Apparel Group Inc., pp. Vol. I-279, 290 [NAICS 31523M, 31599M]

Jones Boat Yard Inc., p. II-1589 [NAICS 336611]

Jones Co's Ltd., p. I-192 [NAICS 31311M]

Jonesboro Sun, p. I-732 [NAICS 327320]

Jonner Steel Industries Inc., p. II-886 [NAICS 33221N]

Jordache Enterprises Inc., pp. Vol. I-272, 279 [NAICS 31522M, 31523M]

Jordan Auto Parts Inc., p. III-1770 [NAICS 423140]

Jordan Automotive Group, p. III-2011 [NAICS 441110]

Jordan Group, p. III-2228 [NAICS 454390]

Jordan Lumber and Supply Inc., p. I-312 [NAICS 32111M]

Jordan Vineyard and Winery, p. I-177 [NAICS 312130]

Jordanos Inc., pp. Vol. III-1954, 1983 [NAICS 424490, 424810]

Jos. A. Bank Clothiers Inc., pp. Vol. III-2123, 2211 [NAICS 448110, 454113]

Josam Co., p. II-974 [NAICS 332913]

Joseph Davis Inc., p. I-343 [NAICS 321920]

Joseph F. Boente Sons Inc., pp. Vol. III-1979, 2116 [NAICS 424720, 447110]

Joseph Freedman Company Inc., p. I-807 [NAICS 331314]

Joseph Huber Brewing Inc., p. I-172 [NAICS 312120]

Joseph Industries Inc., p. II-1530 [NAICS 336350]

Joseph Lipic Pen Co., p. II-1714 [NAICS 33994M]

Joseph's Pasta Company Inc., p. I-124 [NAICS 31182M]

Joseph Schmidt Confections Inc., pp. Vol. I-52, 57 [NAICS 311330, 311340]

Joseph Trenk and Sons, p. III-1936 [NAICS 424440]

Joslyn Hi-Voltage Corp., p. II-1421 [NAICS 335311]

Jost International Corp., pp. Vol. II-1486, 1491 [NAICS 336211, 336212]

Jostens Inc., pp. Vol. I-306, Vol. II-1536, 1696 [NAICS 31699M, 336360, 33991M]

Journal Communications Inc., p. I-420 [NAICS 32311M]

Jowett Garments Factory Inc., p. I-279 [NAICS 31523M]

Joy Cone Co., p. I-158 [NAICS 31199M]

Joy Global Inc., pp. Vol. II-1033, 1039 [NAICS 333120, 33313M]

Joy-Mark Fiber Ceramics Inc., p. I-703 [NAICS 32712N]

Joyva Corp., p. I-57 [NAICS 311340]

JPM of Mississippi Inc., p. II-988 [NAICS 332991]

JR Johnson Supply Inc., pp. Vol. I-681, Vol. III-1998 [NAICS 327112, 424930]

J.R. Simplot Co., pp. Vol. I-62, 76, 516, 520, 529, 539 [NAICS 31141M, 311513, 325311, 325312, 325320, 325412]

JR Simplot Inc. Food Group Div., p. I-493 [NAICS 32519M]

J.R. Simplot Minerals & Chemicals, pp. Vol. I-516, 520 [NAICS 325311, 325312]

JR Wheel, p. I-811 [NAICS 331316]

JRB Company Inc., pp. Vol. II-928, 1033, 1584 [NAICS 33243M, 333120, 336510]

JRD Trading Inc., p. III-1794 [NAICS 423390]

JRH Biosciences Inc., p. I-549 [NAICS 325414]

JRM Industries Inc., p. I-203 [NAICS 31322M]

JS Apparel, p. I-267 [NAICS 31521M]

JS International Inc., p. III-1835 [NAICS 423620]

JSJ Corp., pp. Vol. I-857, 879, Vol. II-1140, 1194 [NAICS 33152P, 33211P, 333515, 33392M]

J.T. Davenport and Sons Inc., pp. Vol. III-1939, 2001 [NAICS 424450, 424940]

J.T. Eaton and Co., p. I-529 [NAICS 325320]

JT Thorpe Co., pp. Vol. I-703, 771 [NAICS 32712N, 327993]

JTB Furniture, p. II-1616 [NAICS 337121]

Numbers following p. or pp. are page references. Roman numerals indicate volume numbers. Bracketed items indicate industries. Page references are to the starting pages of company tables.

Juanita's Foods Corp., pp. Vol. I-152, 158 [NAICS 31194M, 31199M]

Juanitas Fine Foods, p. I-133 [NAICS 311830]

Judd Wire Inc., pp. Vol. I-793, Vol. II-1451, 1457 [NAICS 33122M, 33592M, 33593M]

Judith Leiber, pp. Vol. I-300, 306, Vol. II-1687 [NAICS 31621M, 31699M, 339115]

Judson-Atkinson Candies Inc., p. I-52 [NAICS 311330]

Judson Studios, p. I-695 [NAICS 327122]

Julian W. Perkins Inc., p. III-1975 [NAICS 424710]

Julie Hat Company Inc., p. I-267 [NAICS 31521M]

Julius Kraft Company Inc., pp. Vol. III-1916, 2007 [NAICS 424320, 424990]

Jump River Electric Coop., p. II-1417 [NAICS 335228]

Juniata Fabrics Inc., p. I-203 [NAICS 31322M]

Juniper Elbow Company Inc., p. II-1101 [NAICS 333414]

Juniper Networks Inc., p. II-1267 [NAICS 334290]

Juno Inc., p. I-651 [NAICS 32619M]

Juno Lighting Inc., p. II-1390 [NAICS 33512M]

Jupiter Aluminum Corp., p. I-816 [NAICS 33131N]

Just Born Inc., p. I-57 [NAICS 311340]

Just Diamonds, pp. Vol. III-1894, 2144 [NAICS 423940, 448310]

Just for Feet, p. III-2141 [NAICS 448210]

Just For Wraps, p. I-279 [NAICS 31523M]

Just In Time Distributors Inc., p. III-1835 [NAICS 423620]

Justin Industries Inc., pp. Vol. I-300, 691, 737, 743, Vol. III-2065 [NAICS 31621M, 327121, 32733M, 327390, 444100]

J.V. Products Co., p. II-1546 [NAICS 336391]

JVC Disc America, p. II-1381 [NAICS 334613]

JVC Professional Products Co., p. III-1839 [NAICS 423690]

J.W. Costello Beverage & S.W., p. III-1987 [NAICS 424820]

J.W. Jung Seed Company Inc., pp. Vol. III-2072, 2211 [NAICS 444220, 454113]

J.W. Pepper and Son Inc., p. III-2159 [NAICS 451140]

JW Performance Transmission Inc., p. II-1530 [NAICS 336350]

JW Peters Inc., p. I-743 [NAICS 327390]

J.W. Pierson Co., pp. Vol. III-1847, 2218 [NAICS 423720, 454311]

K and A Lumber Company Inc., pp. Vol. III-1782, 1794, 2065 [NAICS 423310, 423390, 444100]

K and F Industries Inc., pp. Vol. I-807, Vol. II-1567 [NAICS 331314, 336413]

K and F International Inc., pp. Vol. II-1129, 1714 [NAICS 333513, 33994M]

K and M Electronics Inc., p. II-1297 [NAICS 334415]

K and N Engineering Inc., pp. Vol. II-1112, 1229, 1599 [NAICS 33341N, 33399P, 336991]

K-Bin Inc., p. I-589 [NAICS 325991]

K-Mac Enterprises Inc., p. III-2058 [NAICS 443120]

K-Ply Inc., p. I-324 [NAICS 32121N]

K-Rain Manufacturing Corp., p. II-1362 [NAICS 334518]

K's Merchandise Mart Inc., pp. Vol. III-1894, 2177 [NAICS 423940, 452910]

K-Swiss Inc., p. I-300 [NAICS 31621M]

K-Tel International Inc., p. II-1376 [NAICS 334612]

K-Tron International Inc., pp. Vol. II-1023, 1194, 1337, 1347 [NAICS 333111, 33392M, 334513, 334515]

K-Tronics Inc., p. II-1297 [NAICS 334415]

K-Va-T Food Stores Inc., p. III-2076 [NAICS 445110]

K-Way Products Syca Systems Inc., p. II-1189 [NAICS 333913]

K. Yamada Distributors Ltd., p. III-1905 [NAICS 424130]

K-Z Inc., p. II-1500 [NAICS 336214]

K2 Inc., pp. Vol. I-239, 272, 290, Vol. II-1702 [NAICS 31491M, 31522M, 31599M, 339920]

KA Components, p. I-329 [NAICS 32121P]

KA Steel Chemicals Inc., p. I-480 [NAICS 325181]

Kaba Enterprises Inc., p. II-1372 [NAICS 334611]

Kaba Ilco Corp., pp. Vol. II-933, 1124 [NAICS 332510, 333512]

Kabana Inc., p. II-1696 [NAICS 33991M]

Kabat Textile Corp., p. III-1913 [NAICS 424310]

Kadant Inc., p. II-1061 [NAICS 33329N]

Kaelbel Wholesale Inc., pp. Vol. III-1929, 1943 [NAICS 424420, 424460]

Kaiser Aluminum Corp., pp. Vol. I-803, 811, 816 [NAICS 331312, 331316, 33131N]

Kaiser Compositek Inc., p. II-1580 [NAICS 336419]

Kaiser Wholesale Inc., pp. Vol. III-1875, 1939, 2001 [NAICS 423850, 424450, 424940]

Kalas Manufacturing Inc., pp. Vol. II-1451, 1512 [NAICS 33592M, 33632M]

Kalencom Corp., p. I-239 [NAICS 31491M]

Kalil Bottling Company Inc., p. III-1954 [NAICS 424490]

Kalmbach Feeds Inc., p. I-9 [NAICS 311119]

Kaltenberg Castle Brewery Inc., p. I-172 [NAICS 312120]

Kaman Corp., pp. Vol. II-1557, 1731, Vol. III-1871 [NAICS 336411, 339992, 423840]

Kaman Dayron Inc., pp. Vol. I-585, Vol. II-1432 [NAICS 325920, 335313]

Kamax, pp. Vol. I-793, Vol. II-958 [NAICS 33122M, 332722]

Kamp Implement Co., p. III-2027 [NAICS 441229]

Kamps Inc., p. I-343 [NAICS 321920]

Kanaflex Corp., p. I-665 [NAICS 326220]

Kanai Tofu Factory, p. I-31 [NAICS 31122N]

Kanawha Manufacturing Co., p. II-923 [NAICS 332420]

Kane Industries Corp., p. III-2177 [NAICS 452910]

Kane Magnetics International Inc., pp. Vol. I-686, Vol. II-1014 [NAICS 327113, 33299N]

Kane Miller Corp., p. I-26 [NAICS 311225]

Kaneb Pipe Line Partners L.P., p. III-1975 [NAICS 424710]

Kaneb Services L.L.C., p. III-1979 [NAICS 424720]

Kanematsu U.S.A. Inc., pp. Vol. III-1828, 1971 [NAICS 423520, 424690]

Kangaroo Technologies Corp., p. II-1248 [NAICS 334113]

Kansas City Aviation Center Inc, p. III-1879 [NAICS 423860]

Kaplan Co., p. III-2186 [NAICS 453210]

Kar Nut Products Co., p. I-137 [NAICS 31191M]

Kar Products, p. III-1843 [NAICS 423710]

Karavan Trailers Inc., pp. Vol. II-1500, 1607 [NAICS 336214, 336999]

Karen Kane Inc., p. I-279 [NAICS 31523M]

Karibe Inc., p. II-1536 [NAICS 336360]

Karl Ehmer Inc., p. I-143 [NAICS 311920]

Karl Kani Infinity Inc., pp. Vol. I-272, 279, 290 [NAICS 31522M, 31523M, 31599M]

Karl Schmidt Unisia Inc., pp. Vol. II-1505, 1551 [NAICS 33631M, 336399]

Karnak Corp., p. I-453 [NAICS 324122]

Karsten Manufacturing Corp., p. II-1702 [NAICS 339920]

Karsten of New Mexico L.L.C., p. I-353 [NAICS 321992]

Karsten Precision Inc., p. II-1702 [NAICS 339920]

Kasbar National Industries Inc., p. I-208 [NAICS 313230]

Kasco Manufacturing Inc., p. II-1046 [NAICS 333210]

Kasgro Rail Corp., p. II-1584 [NAICS 336510]

Kash N'Karry Food Stores Inc., p. III-2076 [NAICS 445110]

Kasha Industries Inc., p. I-589 [NAICS 325991]

Kashan Litho Inc., p. I-436 [NAICS 32312M]

Kason Industries Inc., p. II-1106 [NAICS 333415]

Kaspar and Esh Inc., p. II-1696 [NAICS 33991M]

Kasper A.S.L. Ltd., p. I-279 [NAICS 31523M]

Kasper's Meat Market Inc., p. III-2083 [NAICS 445210]

Kasson and Keller Inc., pp. Vol. I-651, Vol. II-908 [NAICS 32619M, 33232M]

Katahdin Paper Co., pp. Vol. I-363, 415 [NAICS 322110, 322299]

Kataman Metals Inc., p. III-1824 [NAICS 423510]

Katolight Corp., p. II-1157 [NAICS 333611]

Katy Industries Inc., pp. Vol. II-1046, 1061 [NAICS 333210, 33329N]

Kauffman Engineering Inc., p. II-1312 [NAICS 334418]

Kautex Textron North America, p. II-933 [NAICS 332510]

KaVo America Corp., p. III-1813 [NAICS 423450]

Kawai America Manufacturing, p. II-1731 [NAICS 339992]

Kay Home Products, p. II-1404 [NAICS 335221]

Kay Home Products Inc., p. II-1632 [NAICS 33712N]

Kay Inc., p. II-1056 [NAICS 333295]

Kay Toledo Tag Inc., p. I-415 [NAICS 322299]

Kaydon Corp., pp. Vol. II-988, 1229 [NAICS 332991, 33399P]

Kaye's Printing Inc., pp. Vol. I-403, 436 [NAICS 32223M, 32312M]

Kaye-Smith, p. I-403 [NAICS 32223M]

Kayem Foods Inc., p. I-102 [NAICS 31161N]

Kayser-Roth Corp., pp. Vol. I-256, Vol. II-1676 [NAICS 31511M, 339113]

KB Electronics Inc., p. II-1162 [NAICS 333612]

KB Holdings L.L.C., pp. Vol. III-1805, 2153, 2211 [NAICS 423430, 451120, 454113]

KBH Corp., p. II-1023 [NAICS 333111]

KC Company Inc., p. III-1782 [NAICS 423310]

KCI Konecranes Inc., p. II-1194 [NAICS 33392M]

KCS International Inc., p. II-1594 [NAICS 336612]

Numbers following p. or pp. are page references. Roman numerals indicate volume numbers. Bracketed items indicate industries. Page references are to the starting pages of company tables.

2365

KDC Systems/Dynalectric, p. II-1332 [NAICS 334512]

KDIndustries Inc., p. II-1189 [NAICS 333913]

KDS USA, p. II-1248 [NAICS 334113]

Kearfott Guidance & Navigation, pp. Vol. II-1262, 1327 [NAICS 334220, 334511]

Keasling's Drug Store, p. III-2100 [NAICS 446110]

Keeler Brass Company Inc., pp. Vol. I-857, Vol. II-958 [NAICS 33152P, 332722]

Keeney Manufacturing Co., pp. Vol. I-830, Vol. II-964, 1009 [NAICS 33142M, 33281M, 332996]

Keeper Corp., p. I-203 [NAICS 31322M]

Keepers International, p. I-256 [NAICS 31511M]

Kehe Food Distributors Inc., pp. Vol. III-1925, 1954 [NAICS 424410, 424490]

Keilson-Dayton Co., pp. Vol. III-1939, 2001 [NAICS 424450, 424940]

Keiser Industries Inc., p. I-353 [NAICS 321992]

Keithley Instruments Inc., pp. Vol. II-1337, 1347, 1352, 1367 [NAICS 334513, 334515, 334516, 334519]

Keithley Intern. Investment Corp., pp. Vol. II-1337, 1347, 1352, 1367 [NAICS 334513, 334515, 334516, 334519]

Kelch Corp., p. II-1152 [NAICS 333518]

Kelch Corp. Fuel Containment, p. II-1028 [NAICS 333112]

Kelco Industries Inc., p. I-670 [NAICS 32629M]

Kelderman Manufacturing Inc., p. II-1496 [NAICS 336213]

Kell Container Corp., p. II-1720 [NAICS 339950]

Keller-Crescent Company Inc., p. I-379 [NAICS 32221M]

Keller Group Inc., p. I-872 [NAICS 33211N]

Keller Laboratories Inc., p. II-1682 [NAICS 339114]

Keller Products Inc., p. II-1731 [NAICS 339992]

Keller Supply Co., p. III-1847 [NAICS 423720]

Kellerhaus Inc., p. III-2190 [NAICS 453220]

Kelley Automotive Group Inc., p. III-2011 [NAICS 441110]

Kelley Manufacturing Co., p. I-137 [NAICS 31191M]

Kellogg Brown and Root Inc., pp. Vol. I-343, 788, Vol. II-1039 [NAICS 321920, 331210, 33313M]

Kellogg Co., pp. Vol. I-62, 68, 116 [NAICS 31141M, 31142M, 31181M]

Kellogg Crankshaft Company Inc., p. II-1505 [NAICS 33631M]

Kellogg Garden Products, pp. Vol. I-516, 524 [NAICS 325311, 325314]

Kellwood Co., pp. Vol. I-234, 239, 272, 279, 290, Vol. II-1702 [NAICS 31412M, 31491M, 31522M, 31523M, 31599M, 339920]

Kelly Company Inc., p. II-1740 [NAICS 339994]

Kelly Flour Co., p. I-81 [NAICS 311514]

Kelly-Moore Paint Company Inc., pp. Vol. I-554, Vol. III-2065 [NAICS 325510, 444100]

Kelly Pipe Company L.L.C., pp. Vol. II-980, 1009 [NAICS 33291N, 332996]

Kelly Products Inc., p. III-1805 [NAICS 423430]

Kelly's Pipe and Supply Co., p. III-1847 [NAICS 423720]

Kelly's Sports Ltd., pp. Vol. III-1883, 2150 [NAICS 423910, 451110]

Kelly Tractor Co., p. III-1867 [NAICS 423830]

KEM Manufacturing Company Inc., p. II-1512 [NAICS 33632M]

Kemco Systems Inc., pp. Vol. II-923, 1332, 1417 [NAICS 332420, 334512, 335228]

KEMET Corp., p. II-1292 [NAICS 334414]

Kemira Chemicals Inc., pp. Vol. I-488, 493 [NAICS 325188, 32519M]

Kemps, pp. Vol. I-86, 92 [NAICS 31151N, 311520]

Kemps Foods L.L.C., p. I-92 [NAICS 311520]

Kencraft Inc., p. I-57 [NAICS 311340]

Kendale Industries Inc., p. II-988 [NAICS 332991]

Kendall LTP, p. III-1813 [NAICS 423450]

Kennametal Inc., pp. Vol. II-952, 1039, 1124, 1140, 1207 [NAICS 332721, 33313M, 333512, 333515, 333991]

Kennebunk Home, p. I-229 [NAICS 314110]

Kennedy Die Castings Inc., p. I-852 [NAICS 33152N]

Kennedy Diversified Inc., p. III-1770 [NAICS 423140]

Kennedy Ink Company Inc., p. I-580 [NAICS 325910]

Kennedy Manufacturing Inc., p. II-1627 [NAICS 337127]

Kennedy Oil Company Inc., p. III-2218 [NAICS 454311]

Kennedy's Bakery Inc., p. III-2089 [NAICS 445291]

Kennedy Tank and Mfg Inc., p. II-918 [NAICS 332410]

Kenneth Cole Productions Inc., pp. Vol. I-300, Vol. III-2135, 2141 [NAICS 31621M, 448150, 448210]

Kenneth Fox Supply Co., p. I-239 [NAICS 31491M]

Kenney Communications Inc., p. III-1995 [NAICS 424920]

Kenney Manufacturing Co., p. II-1662 [NAICS 337920]

Kenny's Candy Company Inc., p. I-57 [NAICS 311340]

Kenra L.L.C., p. II-886 [NAICS 33221N]

Kent Gypsum Supply Inc., p. III-1786 [NAICS 423320]

Kent Manufacturing Co., p. I-192 [NAICS 31311M]

Kent Moore Cabinets Limited Inc., p. II-1611 [NAICS 337110]

Kent's Tire Service Inc., p. III-1766 [NAICS 423130]

Kent Sporting Goods Company, p. II-1702 [NAICS 339920]

Kentec Inc., p. III-1843 [NAICS 423710]

Kentucky Bourbon Distillers Ltd., p. I-181 [NAICS 312140]

Kentucky-Indiana Lumber, pp. Vol. I-324, 329 [NAICS 32121N, 32121P]

Kentucky Textiles Inc., pp. Vol. I-262, 272, 279 [NAICS 31519M, 31522M, 31523M]

Kentucky Trailer, p. II-1491 [NAICS 336212]

Kenwal Steel Corp., p. III-1824 [NAICS 423510]

Kenway Distributors Inc., p. III-1875 [NAICS 423850]

Kenwood Vineyards, p. I-177 [NAICS 312130]

Kenworth of Dayton, p. III-2030 [NAICS 441310]

Kenworth of Tennessee Inc., pp. Vol. III-1758, 1867 [NAICS 423110, 423830]

Kenworth Sales Company Inc., pp. Vol. III-1758, 1762 [NAICS 423110, 423120]

Kenyon International Inc., p. II-1404 [NAICS 335221]

KepcoInc, p. I-762 [NAICS 327991]

Kerite Co., p. II-1451 [NAICS 33592M]

Kerley Ink, p. I-580 [NAICS 325910]

Kermit K. Kistler Inc., p. III-2027 [NAICS 441229]

Kern-Liebers USA Inc., p. II-939 [NAICS 33261M]

Kernersville News, p. III-2186 [NAICS 453210]

Kerns Manufacturing Corp., pp. Vol. II-1505, 1562 [NAICS 33631M, 336412]

Kerr Concentrates Inc., p. I-152 [NAICS 31194M]

Kerr Corp., p. II-1682 [NAICS 339114]

Kerr Group Inc., p. I-646 [NAICS 326160]

Kerr-McGee Corp., p. I-475 [NAICS 32513M]

Kerr-McGee Pigments Inc., pp. Vol. I-475, 752 [NAICS 32513M, 327420]

Kerr Pacific Corp., p. I-15 [NAICS 31121M]

Kerry Sweet Ingredients, p. I-36 [NAICS 311230]

Kershaw Knives, p. II-886 [NAICS 33221N]

Kerwin Paper Co., p. I-368 [NAICS 32212M]

Kesseli Morse Company Inc., p. III-1786 [NAICS 423320]

Kessler Containers Ltd., p. I-646 [NAICS 326160]

Kessler Industries Inc., pp. Vol. I-811, Vol. II-1632 [NAICS 331316, 33712N]

Kettle Foods Inc., p. I-137 [NAICS 31191M]

Kettle-Lakes Coop., pp. Vol. III-1991, 2072 [NAICS 424910, 444220]

Keurig Inc., p. II-1397 [NAICS 33521M]

Kevin Inc., p. III-2150 [NAICS 451110]

Kewaskum Frozen Foods Inc., pp. Vol. III-1929, 2083 [NAICS 424420, 445210]

Kewaunee Scientific Corp., pp. Vol. II-1627, 1666 [NAICS 337127, 339111]

Key Components L.L.C., p. II-1092 [NAICS 33331N]

Key Instruments, p. II-1342 [NAICS 334514]

Key Mechanical of Washington, p. III-1855 [NAICS 423740]

Key Plastics L.L.C., p. I-651 [NAICS 32619M]

Key Print Shop Inc., p. III-2186 [NAICS 453210]

Key Safety Systems Inc., p. II-1551 [NAICS 336399]

Key West Boats Inc., p. II-1594 [NAICS 336612]

Keymark Corp., pp. Vol. I-811, Vol. II-964 [NAICS 331316, 33281M]

Keys Fitness Products Inc., p. III-1883 [NAICS 423910]

Keyston Bros., p. I-198 [NAICS 313210]

Keystone Adjustable Cap Inc., p. I-411 [NAICS 322291]

Keystone Aggregate Products Co., p. III-1786 [NAICS 423320]

Keystone Automotive Industries, p. III-1762 [NAICS 423120]

Keystone Battery, p. II-1442 [NAICS 335911]

Keystone Cement Co., pp. Vol. I-703, 727, 762 [NAICS 32712N, 327310, 327991]

Keystone Consolidated Industries, pp. Vol. I-780, 793, Vol. II-939, 1014, 1463 [NAICS 33111M, 33122M, 33261M, 33299N, 335991]

Keystone Filler and Mfg Co., p. II-1463 [NAICS 335991]

Keystone Food Products Inc., pp. Vol. I-133, 137 [NAICS 311830, 31191M]

Numbers following p. or pp. are page references. Roman numerals indicate volume numbers. Bracketed items indicate industries. Page references are to the starting pages of company tables.

Keystone Foods L.L.C., pp. Vol. I-68, 97, 102 [NAICS 31142M, 311615, 31161N]

Keystone Industries, p. II-1682 [NAICS 339114]

Keystone Lime Co., p. I-748 [NAICS 327410]

Keystone North Inc., p. II-988 [NAICS 332991]

Keystone Plastics Inc., p. II-1740 [NAICS 339994]

Keystone Powdered Metal Co., pp. Vol. I-793, 867, Vol. II-1168 [NAICS 33122M, 332117, 333613]

Keystone Printing Ink Co., p. I-580 [NAICS 325910]

Keystops Inc., pp. Vol. III-1979, 2116 [NAICS 424720, 447110]

KEYTEC Inc., p. II-1248 [NAICS 334113]

KFP Corp., p. I-677 [NAICS 327111]

KHS-Inc, pp. Vol. II-1061, 1092, 1212 [NAICS 33329N, 33331N, 333993]

KI Inc., pp. Vol. II-1621, 1627, 1650 [NAICS 337122, 337127, 33721N]

KI Industries, p. II-974 [NAICS 332913]

KI (USA) Corp., pp. Vol. I-879, Vol. II-945 [NAICS 33211P, 332710]

Kia Motors America Inc., p. III-1758 [NAICS 423110]

KIB Enterprises Corp., p. II-1362 [NAICS 334518]

Kidde-Fenwal Inc., pp. Vol. II-1229, 1267, 1437, 1457 [NAICS 33399P, 334290, 335314, 33593M]

Kidde PLC, p. II-1749 [NAICS 339999]

Kidron, pp. Vol. II-1486, 1491 [NAICS 336211, 336212]

Kids II Inc., p. II-1708 [NAICS 33993M]

Kiefer Built Inc., pp. Vol. I-348, Vol. II-1491, 1500 [NAICS 321991, 336212, 336214]

Kiel Brothers Oil Co., p. III-1979 [NAICS 424720]

Kiewit Materials Co., pp. Vol. I-448, 732, Vol. III-1786 [NAICS 324121, 327320, 423320]

Kight's Medical Corp., p. III-1813 [NAICS 423450]

Kigre Inc., p. I-709 [NAICS 327211]

KIK Corp., p. I-646 [NAICS 326160]

KIK Technology Inc., p. II-1599 [NAICS 336991]

Kikiktagruk Inupiat Corp., p. III-2177 [NAICS 452910]

Kikkoman Foods Inc., pp. Vol. I-152, 158 [NAICS 31194M, 31199M]

Kilgore's Clear Lake Lumber Co., pp. Vol. III-2037, 2208 [NAICS 442110, 453998]

Killer Beads & Everything Else, p. III-1894 [NAICS 423940]

Kimal Lumber Co., p. I-329 [NAICS 32121P]

Kimball International, pp. Vol. II-1650, 1749 [NAICS 33721N, 339999]

Kimber Petroleum Corp., p. III-1979 [NAICS 424720]

Kimberly-Clark Corp., pp. Vol. I-368, 411, Vol. II-1676 [NAICS 32212M, 322291, 339113]

Kimble Glass Inc., pp. Vol. I-713, 718 [NAICS 327212, 327213]

Kimray Inc., pp. Vol. II-1039, 1179, 1332, 1421 [NAICS 33313M, 333911, 334512, 335311]

Kimwood Corp., p. II-1046 [NAICS 333210]

Kincaid Furniture Company Inc., p. II-1621 [NAICS 337122]

Kinder Morgan Snyder Gas Plant, p. I-471 [NAICS 325120]

Kindy Wood Manufacturing Inc., p. III-1774 [NAICS 423210]

Kinedyne Corp., pp. Vol. II-1194, 1337 [NAICS 33392M, 334513]

Kinergy Corp., p. II-1584 [NAICS 336510]

Kinetic Concepts Inc., pp. Vol. II-1627, 1657 [NAICS 337127, 337910]

Kinetics Thermal Systems, p. II-1666 [NAICS 339111]

Kinetronics Corp., p. III-1798 [NAICS 423410]

King Hickory Furniture Co., p. II-1616 [NAICS 337121]

King Instrument Company Inc., p. II-1342 [NAICS 334514]

King Koil, p. II-1657 [NAICS 337910]

King Koil Mid-Atlantic, p. II-1657 [NAICS 337910]

King Koil Northeast, p. II-1657 [NAICS 337910]

King Louie Intl, pp. Vol. I-279, 290 [NAICS 31523M, 31599M]

King Pharmaceuticals Inc., p. I-539 [NAICS 325412]

King's Custom Builders Inc., p. I-348 [NAICS 321991]

King's Peachtree Battle Drugs, p. III-2100 [NAICS 446110]

King Soopers Inc., pp. Vol. I-102, 116, 124, Vol. III-2076 [NAICS 31161N, 31181M, 31182M, 445110]

King Soopers Inc. Bakery Div., pp. Vol. I-116, 124 [NAICS 31181M, 31182M]

King Systems Corp., pp. Vol. I-621, Vol. II-1119 [NAICS 326121, 333511]

King Tire Service Inc., p. III-1766 [NAICS 423130]

Kings Delight Inc., p. I-97 [NAICS 311615]

Kings Liquor Inc., p. III-2097 [NAICS 445310]

Kingsbury Corp., p. II-1124 [NAICS 333512]

Kingsbury Inc., p. II-1168 [NAICS 333613]

Kingsdown Inc., p. II-1657 [NAICS 337910]

Kingsley Coach Inc., p. II-1496 [NAICS 336213]

Kingston Oil Supply Corp., p. III-2218 [NAICS 454311]

Kingston Technology Inc., pp. Vol. II-1243, 1252, 1287 [NAICS 334112, 334119, 334413]

Kinray Inc., p. III-1909 [NAICS 424210]

Kinsey Outdoors Inc., p. III-1883 [NAICS 423910]

Kinyo Company Inc., p. II-1087 [NAICS 333315]

Kipp Brothers Inc., p. III-1887 [NAICS 423920]

Kirchner Block and Brick Inc., p. I-737 [NAICS 32733M]

Kirk Expedx, p. III-1898 [NAICS 424110]

Kirk-Rudy Inc., pp. Vol. II-1077, 1212 [NAICS 333313, 333993]

Kirkegaard and Perry Labs Inc., pp. Vol. I-534, 549 [NAICS 325411, 325414]

Kirkland's Inc., p. III-1778 [NAICS 423220]

Kirlins Inc., pp. Vol. III-2092, 2190 [NAICS 445292, 453220]

Kistler Aerospace Corp., p. II-1576 [NAICS 336415]

Kitch Engineering Inc., p. II-1599 [NAICS 336991]

Kitchen Etc. Inc., p. III-2047 [NAICS 442299]

Kitchen Kompact Inc., p. II-1611 [NAICS 337110]

Kitchens Brothers Mfg Co., pp. Vol. I-312, 343, 358 [NAICS 32111M, 321920, 321999]

Kittle's Home Furnishings, p. III-2037 [NAICS 442110]

Kiva Designs Inc., p. III-1883 [NAICS 423910]

KLA-Tencor Corp., pp. Vol. II-1082, 1337 [NAICS 333314, 334513]

Klarity Multimedia Inc., p. II-1376 [NAICS 334612]

Klauber Brothers Inc., p. I-213 [NAICS 31324M]

Klauer Manufacturing Co., p. I-453 [NAICS 324122]

Klaussner Furniture of California, p. II-1616 [NAICS 337121]

Klear-Knit Inc., p. I-213 [NAICS 31324M]

Klear-Vu Corp., pp. Vol. I-234, Vol. II-1616 [NAICS 31412M, 337121]

Kleen Polymers Inc., p. I-505 [NAICS 325212]

Kleer-Fax Inc., p. I-403 [NAICS 32223M]

Klein Bicycle Corp., p. II-1599 [NAICS 336991]

Klein Camera and Hi-Fi Inc., p. III-2062 [NAICS 443130]

Klein Foods Inc., p. I-177 [NAICS 312130]

Klein Tools Inc., pp. Vol. I-251, 306, Vol. II-892, 939, 1676 [NAICS 314999, 31699M, 33221P, 33261M, 339113]

Kliklok-Woodman USA, p. II-1212 [NAICS 333993]

Klingensmith's Healthcare, p. III-1813 [NAICS 423450]

Klinginsmith TV and Appliance, p. III-2050 [NAICS 443111]

Klingspor Abrasives Inc., p. I-756 [NAICS 327910]

Klipsch Audio Technologies, p. II-1272 [NAICS 334310]

Klipsch L.L.C., p. II-1272 [NAICS 334310]

Klitzner Industries Inc., p. II-1696 [NAICS 33991M]

Klockner-Pentaplast of America, p. I-615 [NAICS 326113]

Klosterman Baking Company Inc., p. I-116 [NAICS 31181M]

Kluge Estate Winery and Vineyard, p. I-177 [NAICS 312130]

Kmart Corp., pp. Vol. III-2065, 2072, 2076, 2100, 2132, 2180 [NAICS 444100, 444220, 445110, 446110, 448140, 452990]

KMG Chemicals Inc., p. III-1971 [NAICS 424690]

Knape and Vogt Manufacturing, pp. Vol. II-933, 1644 [NAICS 332510, 337215]

Knapheide Manufacturing Co., pp. Vol. I-879, Vol. II-1486 [NAICS 33211P, 336211]

Knapp Vineyard Winery, pp. Vol. I-177, Vol. III-1987 [NAICS 312130, 424820]

Knauf Insulation GMBH, p. I-771 [NAICS 327993]

Knauf Polystyrene Inc., pp. Vol. I-636, 641 [NAICS 326140, 326150]

Knight & Carver YachtCenter Inc., pp. Vol. II-1589, 1594 [NAICS 336611, 336612]

Knight Rifles, p. II-1001 [NAICS 332994]

Knitcraft Corp., p. I-262 [NAICS 31519M]

Knoll Inc., pp. Vol. I-218, Vol. II-1627, 1644, 1650 [NAICS 31331M, 337127, 337215, 33721N]

Knouse Foods Cooperative Inc., pp. Vol. I-137, 152, 158 [NAICS 31191M, 31194M, 31199M]

Knowledge Unlimited Inc., p. II-1376 [NAICS 334612]

Knowles Electronics Holdings Inc., pp. Vol. II-1272, 1337, 1367 [NAICS 334310, 334513, 334519]

Knowlton Specialty Papers Inc., pp. Vol. I-368, 415 [NAICS 32212M, 322299]

Knox Fertilizer Company Inc., p. II-1028 [NAICS 333112]

Knud Nielsen Company Inc., p. III-1998 [NAICS 424930]

Knudson Manufacturing Inc., p. II-1147 [NAICS 333516]

Knurr Inc., pp. Vol. II-1644, 1650 [NAICS 337215, 33721N]

KO-REC-TYPE, pp. Vol. I-415, Vol. II-1714 [NAICS 322299, 33994M]

Koala Corp., p. II-1627 [NAICS 337127]

Kobe Precision Inc., pp. Vol. I-703, 811 [NAICS 32712N, 331316]

Kobe Wieland Copper Products, p. I-830 [NAICS 33142M]

Kobelco Compressors America, p. II-1562 [NAICS 336412]

Kobelco Stewart Bolling Inc., pp. Vol. II-1051, 1129 [NAICS 333220, 333513]

Kobrick's Coffee Company Inc., p. I-143 [NAICS 311920]

Kobrin Builders Supply Inc., p. III-1794 [NAICS 423390]

Kobrin Builders Supply of Sarasota, p. III-1786 [NAICS 423320]

Koch Entertainment Distribution, pp. Vol. II-1376, 1381 [NAICS 334612, 334613]

Koch Filter Corp., p. III-1851 [NAICS 423730]

Koch Foods, p. I-97 [NAICS 311615]

Koch Foods of Cumming, p. I-97 [NAICS 311615]

Koch Glitsch Inc., pp. Vol. I-879, Vol. II-933, 1033, 1725 [NAICS 33211P, 332510, 333120, 399991]

Koch Industries Inc., pp. Vol. I-595, 767 [NAICS 32599N, 327992]

Koch Membrane Systems Inc., p. II-1229 [NAICS 33399P]

Kocolene Marketing L.L.C., p. III-2116 [NAICS 447110]

Kocour Company Inc., p. I-756 [NAICS 327910]

Kodak Colorado Div., pp. Vol. I-368, Vol. II-1087 [NAICS 32212M, 333315]

Kodak Versamark Inc., p. I-580 [NAICS 325910]

Kodiak Northwest Inc., p. II-1028 [NAICS 333112]

Koellmann Gear Corp., p. II-1162 [NAICS 333612]

Koerner Distributors Inc., p. III-1987 [NAICS 424820]

Koetter Woodworking Inc., p. II-1611 [NAICS 337110]

Koeze Company Inc., pp. Vol. I-48, Vol. III-2092 [NAICS 311320, 445292]

Koh-I-Noor Inc., pp. Vol. II-1077, 1714 [NAICS 333313, 33994M]

Kohl's Corp., p. III-2171 [NAICS 452111]

Kohl's Department Stores Inc., p. III-2171 [NAICS 452111]

Kohler Co., pp. Vol. I-651, 677, Vol. II-974, 1014, 1173 [NAICS 32619M, 327111, 332913, 33299N, 333618]

Kohler Oil and Propane Co., p. III-1975 [NAICS 424710]

Kohlhepp Stone Center, pp. Vol. I-737, 762 [NAICS 32733M, 327991]

Koken Manufacturing Inc., pp. Vol. II-886, 1397, 1671, 1682 [NAICS 33221N, 33521M, 339112, 339114]

Kokoku Rubber Inc., p. II-1725 [NAICS 339991]

Kolb-Lena Cheese Co., p. I-76 [NAICS 311513]

Kolbe and Kolbe Millwork Inc., p. I-334 [NAICS 32191M]

Kolbe Cycle Sales, p. III-2021 [NAICS 441221]

Kolcraft Enterprises Inc., pp. Vol. II-1657, 1708 [NAICS 337910, 33993M]

Koldwave, p. II-918 [NAICS 332410]

Kollmorgen Corp., p. II-1352 [NAICS 334516]

Kollsman Inc., p. II-1327 [NAICS 334511]

Kolmar Laboratories Inc., p. I-575 [NAICS 325620]

Kolon America Inc., p. III-1916 [NAICS 424320]

Kolorcure Corp., p. I-580 [NAICS 325910]

Komag Inc., pp. Vol. II-1243, 1381 [NAICS 334112, 334613]

Komatsu Equipment Co., pp. Vol. I-879, Vol. III-1859 [NAICS 33211P, 423810]

Komatsu Forest L.L.C., p. II-1222 [NAICS 33399N]

Komatsu Forklift Intern. Corp., pp. Vol. II-1194, 1749 [NAICS 33392M, 399999]

Komfort Corp., p. II-1500 [NAICS 336214]

Komtek Inc., p. I-872 [NAICS 33211N]

Konarka Technologies Inc., p. II-1442 [NAICS 335911]

Kondex Corp., p. II-1028 [NAICS 333112]

KONE Inc., p. II-1194 [NAICS 33392M]

Konica Minolta Graphic Imaging, p. II-1087 [NAICS 333315]

Konica Minolta Photo Imaging, pp. Vol. I-388, Vol. II-1087 [NAICS 32222N, 333315]

Konop Companies Inc., p. III-2215 [NAICS 454210]

Konrad Marine Inc., p. II-1147 [NAICS 333516]

KOOLTRONIC Inc., p. II-918 [NAICS 332410]

Koontz-Wagner Electric Inc., pp. Vol. II-1427, 1432 [NAICS 335312, 335313]

Kopper's Chocolate Specialty Inc., pp. Vol. I-48, 52 [NAICS 311320, 311330]

Koppers Inc., pp. Vol. I-312, 388, 475, 484, 493, 743, Vol. II-1463 [NAICS 32111M, 32222N, 32513M, 325182, 32519M, 327390, 335991]

Korbel Champagne Cellars, pp. Vol. I-172, 177 [NAICS 312120, 312130]

Kordsa USA Inc., p. I-248 [NAICS 314992]

Koret of California Inc., p. I-290 [NAICS 31599M]

KoSa, pp. Vol. I-192, 510 [NAICS 31311M, 32522M]

Kosh Ophthalmic Inc., p. II-1687 [NAICS 339115]

Koss Corp., p. II-1272 [NAICS 334310]

Koval Marketing Inc., pp. Vol. III-1778, 1901, 2007 [NAICS 423220, 424120, 424990]

Kovatch Corp., p. II-1486 [NAICS 336211]

Koyo Corp, p. III-1867 [NAICS 423830]

Krackeler Scientific Inc., p. III-1820 [NAICS 423490]

Kraemer Textiles Inc., p. I-192 [NAICS 31311M]

Kraft Chemical Co., p. III-1971 [NAICS 424690]

Kraft Foods Inc., pp. Vol. I-68, 76, 102, 116, 124, 143 [NAICS 31142M, 311513, 31161N, 31181M, 31182M, 311920]

Kraft Hardware Inc., p. II-974 [NAICS 332913]

Kraft Tool Company Inc., p. II-1207 [NAICS 333991]

Kraftmaid Cabinetry Inc., pp. Vol. II-1611, 1621, 1632 [NAICS 337110, 337122, 33712N]

Kramer Beverage Company Inc., pp. Vol. III-1983, 1987 [NAICS 424810, 424820]

Kramer Ink Company Inc., p. I-580 [NAICS 325910]

Kranz Inc., p. III-1875 [NAICS 423850]

Krasdale Foods Inc., p. III-1925 [NAICS 424410]

Kreamer Feed Store Inc., p. I-4 [NAICS 311111]

Kreative Kamaaina Enterprises, p. III-1778 [NAICS 423220]

Kreider Corp., p. II-1541 [NAICS 336370]

Kreisler Manufacturing Corp., p. II-1562 [NAICS 336412]

Krell Development, p. III-2138 [NAICS 448190]

Krementz and Co., p. II-1696 [NAICS 33991M]

Kretchmar Bakery Inc., p. III-2089 [NAICS 445291]

Kretz Lumber Company Inc., p. I-358 [NAICS 321999]

Krispy Kreme Doughnuts Inc., p. I-116 [NAICS 31181M]

Kristel Corp., p. II-1248 [NAICS 334113]

KRL/Bantry Components Inc., p. II-1297 [NAICS 334415]

Kroehler Furniture Mfg Inc., p. II-1616 [NAICS 337121]

Kroger Co., pp. Vol. I-86, 92, 116, Vol. III-2076, 2144 [NAICS 31151N, 311520, 31181M, 445110, 448310]

Krohn Dairy Store, p. III-2094 [NAICS 445299]

Kronos Products Inc., p. I-116 [NAICS 31181M]

Kroot Corp., p. I-807 [NAICS 331314]

Krueger International Inc., p. II-1650 [NAICS 33721N]

KSM Electronics Inc., pp. Vol. II-939, 1307 [NAICS 33261M, 334417]

KT Industries L.L.C., p. I-203 [NAICS 31322M]

KTH Parts Industries Inc., p. II-1541 [NAICS 336370]

Kubic Marketing Inc., pp. Vol. III-1883, 1916, 1922 [NAICS 423910, 424320, 424340]

Kuert Concrete Inc., p. I-767 [NAICS 327992]

Kugler Oil Co., pp. Vol. I-524, Vol. III-2177, 2218 [NAICS 325314, 452910, 454311]

Kuhlman Electric Corp., pp. Vol. II-1302, 1421 [NAICS 334416, 335311]

Kuhn Knight Inc., pp. Vol. II-1023, 1033 [NAICS 333111, 333120]

Kulicke and Soffa Industries Inc., p. II-1061 [NAICS 33329N]

Kumho Tires U.S.A. Inc., p. III-1766 [NAICS 423130]

Kurdex Corp., p. II-1056 [NAICS 333295]

Kuriyama of America Inc., p. I-665 [NAICS 326220]

Kurt J Lesker Co., p. II-1140 [NAICS 333515]

Kurt Manufacturing Company Inc., pp. Vol. I-852, Vol. II-945, 1014, 1162 [NAICS 33152N, 332710, 33299N, 333612]

Kurt S. Adler Inc., p. III-2007 [NAICS 424990]

Kurt Versen Co., p. II-1390 [NAICS 33512M]

Kurtz Brothers, p. III-1820 [NAICS 423490]

Kurtz Gravel Company Inc., p. I-737 [NAICS 32733M]

Kurz-Hastings Inc., p. II-1129 [NAICS 333513]

KUS Inc. Zollner Div., pp. Vol. I-852, 857, Vol. II-1505 [NAICS 33152N, 33152P, 33631M]

Kustom Fit Hi-Tech Seating, pp. Vol. II-1486, 1536, 1650 [NAICS 336211, 336360, 33721N]

Kutol Products Co., p. II-1189 [NAICS 333913]

Kvaerner Pulping Inc., pp. Vol. I-788, Vol. II-908, 918, 1101, 1157 [NAICS 331210, 33232M, 332410, 333414, 333611]

KVAL Machinery, p. II-1046 [NAICS 333210]

KVH Industries Inc., p. II-1327 [NAICS 334511]

Numbers following p. or pp. are page references. Roman numerals indicate volume numbers. Bracketed items indicate industries. Page references are to the starting pages of company tables.

2368

KW Electric Inc., p. II-1584 [NAICS 336510]

Kwik Lok Corp., p. II-1212 [NAICS 333993]

Kyocera Industrial Ceramics Corp., p. I-776 [NAICS 327999]

Kyocera Solar Inc., p. II-1101 [NAICS 333414]

Kyphon Inc., p. II-1676 [NAICS 339113]

Kysor//Warren, p. II-1106 [NAICS 333415]

Kysor Panel Systems Inc., p. II-1106 [NAICS 333415]

L-3 Communications Holdings, pp. Vol. II-1262, 1327, 1332, 1337, 1347, 1580 [NAICS 334220, 334511, 334512, 334513, 334515, 336419]

L and E Bottling Company Inc., pp. Vol. I-165, Vol. III-1954 [NAICS 31211M, 424490]

L and J G Stickley Furniture Co., pp. Vol. II-1616, 1621, 1650 [NAICS 337121, 337122, 33721N]

L and J Technologies Inc., p. II-974 [NAICS 332913]

L and L Insulation and Supply Co., p. I-771 [NAICS 327993]

L and L Machinery Inc., p. II-1046 [NAICS 333210]

L and L Nursery Supply Inc., p. III-1998 [NAICS 424930]

L and L Products Inc., pp. Vol. I-560, Vol. II-1725 [NAICS 325520, 339991]

L & W Service Center Inc., pp. Vol. III-1766, 2034, 2050, 2054 [NAICS 423130, 441320, 443111, 443112]

L and W Stone Corp., p. III-1786 [NAICS 423320]

L'Garde Inc., p. II-1572 [NAICS 336414]

L'Oreal USA Inc., p. I-575 [NAICS 325620]

L-R Systems, p. II-1051 [NAICS 333220]

La Barca Tortilleria Inc., p. I-133 [NAICS 311830]

LA Burdick Chocolates, p. I-48 [NAICS 311320]

La Campana Tortilla Factory, p. I-133 [NAICS 311830]

La Canasta Mexican Food Products, p. I-133 [NAICS 311830]

La Chiquita Totrilla Mfg Co., p. I-133 [NAICS 311830]

La Colonial Tortilla Products Inc., p. I-133 [NAICS 311830]

La Corona Dye and Laundry, p. I-218 [NAICS 31331M]

LA Darling Co., p. II-1644 [NAICS 337215]

L.A. Dreyfus Co., p. I-57 [NAICS 311340]

LA East Studios, p. II-1376 [NAICS 334612]

La Espiga De Oro Tortilla Factory, p. I-133 [NAICS 311830]

La Fortaleza Inc., p. I-133 [NAICS 311830]

La Gloria Foods Corp., p. I-133 [NAICS 311830]

La Gloria Oil and Gas Co., p. I-443 [NAICS 324110]

La Mesa RV Center Inc., p. III-2018 [NAICS 441210]

La Mexicana Inc., p. I-133 [NAICS 311830]

La Mexicana Tortilleria Inc., p. I-133 [NAICS 311830]

La Pine Truck Sales Inc., p. III-2027 [NAICS 441229]

La Poblana Tortilla Factory Inc., p. I-133 [NAICS 311830]

La Rancherita Tortilla, p. I-133 [NAICS 311830]

La Rinascente Macaroni Inc., pp. Vol. I-15, 124 [NAICS 31121M, 31182M]

La Tapatia Tortilleria Inc., p. I-133 [NAICS 311830]

La Tolteca Foods Inc., p. I-133 [NAICS 311830]

La Vie Parisienne Inc., p. III-1894 [NAICS 423940]

La-Z-Boy Inc., pp. Vol. II-1616, 1650 [NAICS 337121, 33721N]

LA-Z Recliner Shop Inc., p. III-2037 [NAICS 442110]

LAB-InterLink Inc., p. II-1666 [NAICS 339111]

LaBarge Inc., pp. Vol. II-1312, 1327 [NAICS 334418, 334511]

Labatt USA Inc., p. III-1983 [NAICS 424810]

Labcon North America, p. II-1666 [NAICS 339111]

Label Maker Inc., p. I-203 [NAICS 31322M]

Label Specialties Inc., p. I-203 [NAICS 31322M]

Labella Strings, p. II-1731 [NAICS 339992]

Laboratory Supply Company Inc., p. III-1813 [NAICS 423450]

Lace Lastic Co., p. I-213 [NAICS 31324M]

Lacey Mills Inc., p. I-229 [NAICS 314110]

Lacie Ltd., p. II-1243 [NAICS 334112]

Lack Valley Stores Ltd., p. III-2037 [NAICS 442110]

Lacks Enterprises Inc., pp. Vol. I-631, 651, Vol. II-964 [NAICS 326130, 32619M, 33281M]

LaCrosse Footwear Inc., pp. Vol. I-300, 306 [NAICS 31621M, 31699M]

Lactoprot USA Inc., p. I-76 [NAICS 311513]

Lacy Diversified Industries, pp. Vol. I-334, Vol. III-1762 [NAICS 32191M, 423120]

Ladesco Inc., p. II-1302 [NAICS 334416]

Ladish Company Inc., p. I-872 [NAICS 33211N]

Lady Grace Stores Inc., p. III-2126 [NAICS 448120]

Laerdal Medical Corp., p. II-1671 [NAICS 339112]

Lafarge North America Inc., pp. Vol. I-448, 727, 732, 737, 743, 752, Vol. III-1786 [NAICS 324121, 327310, 327320, 32733M, 327390, 327420, 423320]

LaFavorita, p. I-133 [NAICS 311830]

Lafayette Dental Laboratory Inc., p. II-1692 [NAICS 339116]

Lafayette Venetian Blind Inc., pp. Vol. I-234, 334, Vol. II-1662 [NAICS 31412M, 32191M, 337920]

Lafayette Wire Products Inc., p. I-816 [NAICS 33131N]

LaForgia Fuel Oil Co., p. III-2218 [NAICS 454311]

Lafourche Sugars L.L.C., p. I-44 [NAICS 31131N]

Lagoon Corp., p. II-1376 [NAICS 334612]

Lagrange Molded Products Inc., p. I-229 [NAICS 314110]

Laguna Clay Co., pp. Vol. I-681, 767, Vol. III-2007 [NAICS 327112, 327992, 424990]

Laguna Corp., p. III-1835 [NAICS 423620]

Lagunitas Brewing Co., p. I-172 [NAICS 312120]

Lahaina Divers Inc., p. III-2150 [NAICS 451110]

Laid Back Enterprises Inc., p. I-267 [NAICS 31521M]

Laidlaw Corp., pp. Vol. I-609, Vol. II-939 [NAICS 326112, 33261M]

Lainiere De Picardie Inc., p. III-1968 [NAICS 424610]

Laird Plastics Inc., p. III-1968 [NAICS 424610]

Laird Technologies Inc., pp. Vol. I-879, Vol. II-1725 [NAICS 33211P, 339991]

Lake Beverage Corp., p. III-1983 [NAICS 424810]

Lake Business Products Inc., p. III-1801 [NAICS 423420]

Lake Country Foods, p. I-143 [NAICS 311920]

Lake Erie Recycling, p. I-807 [NAICS 331314]

Lake Erie Screw Corp., p. II-958 [NAICS 332722]

Lake Region Manufacturing Inc., pp. Vol. I-793, Vol. II-945, 1322 [NAICS 33122M, 332710, 334510]

Lake States Lumber Inc., p. III-1782 [NAICS 423310]

Lakeland Industries Inc., p. I-272 [NAICS 31522M]

Lakeland Tool and Engineering, pp. Vol. II-1119, 1134 [NAICS 333511, 333514]

Lakeridge Winery and Vineyards, p. III-2190 [NAICS 453220]

Lakeside Industries, p. I-448 [NAICS 324121]

Lakeside Oil Company Inc., p. III-1975 [NAICS 424710]

Lakeside Systems Inc., p. III-1863 [NAICS 423820]

Lakeview Farms Inc., p. I-76 [NAICS 311513]

Lakeway Manufacturing Inc., p. II-1147 [NAICS 333516]

Lakewood Engineering, pp. Vol. I-879, Vol. II-1101, 1112 [NAICS 33211P, 333414, 33341N]

LallyPak Inc., pp. Vol. I-609, 636 [NAICS 326112, 326140]

Lam Research Corp., p. II-1061 [NAICS 33329N]

LaMar Lighting Company Inc., p. II-1386 [NAICS 335110]

Lambda Research Optics Inc., p. I-713 [NAICS 327212]

Lambent Technologies Corp., p. I-566 [NAICS 32561M]

Lambert Coal Company Inc., p. III-1828 [NAICS 423520]

Laminart Plastics Corp., p. I-631 [NAICS 326130]

Laminated Industries Inc., p. I-363 [NAICS 322110]

Laminated Products Inc., p. I-762 [NAICS 327991]

Lamination Specialties Corp., pp. Vol. I-388, 793, Vol. II-1014, Vol. III-1824 [NAICS 32222N, 33122M, 33299N, 423510]

Laminations Inc., p. I-374 [NAICS 322130]

Lamons Gasket Co., p. II-1725 [NAICS 339991]

LaMotte Company Inc., p. II-1352 [NAICS 334516]

Lampert Yards Inc., p. III-2065 [NAICS 444100]

Lampire Biological Laboratories, p. I-544 [NAICS 325413]

Lamplight Farms Inc., pp. Vol. I-713, Vol. II-1390 [NAICS 327212, 33512M]

Lamps Plus Inc., p. III-2047 [NAICS 442299]

Lampson Tractor & Equipment, p. III-1863 [NAICS 423820]

Lamptronix Company Ltd., p. II-1386 [NAICS 335110]

Lamson and Goodnow Mfg Inc., p. II-886 [NAICS 33221N]

Lamson and Sessions Co., pp. Vol. I-626, Vol. II-908, 933, 980, 1257, 1457 [NAICS 326122, 33232M, 332510, 33291N, 334210, 33593M]

Lancaster Colony Corp., pp. Vol. I-62, 68, 713, Vol. II-1551, 1749 [NAICS 31141M, 31142M, 327212, 336399, 339999]

Lance Camper Mfg Corp., p. II-1500 [NAICS 336214]

Lance Inc., pp. Vol. I-52, 124, 137 [NAICS 311330, 31182M, 31191M]

Lance Ordnance Company Inc., pp. Vol. I-585, Vol. II-997 [NAICS 325920, 332993]

Lancer Corp., pp. Vol. II-1092, 1106, 1179, 1189 [NAICS 33331N, 333415, 333911, 333913]

Company Index

Lancer Dispersions Inc., p. I-589 [NAICS 325991]

Lanco Corp., pp. Vol. I-52, 57, Vol. III-2092 [NAICS 311330, 311340, 445292]

Land and Sea Inc., p. II-1607 [NAICS 336999]

Land and Sky Inc., p. II-1657 [NAICS 337910]

Land N Sea Inc., pp. Vol. I-279, 285, 290 [NAICS 31523M, 31529M, 31599M]

Land O' Frost Inc., p. I-102 [NAICS 31161N]

Land O' Lakes Western Region, pp. Vol. I-76, 86 [NAICS 311513, 31151N]

Land O'Lakes Inc., pp. Vol. I-9, 76, 86 [NAICS 311119, 311513, 31151N]

Land Reclamation Inc., pp. Vol. I-363, 807 [NAICS 322110, 331314]

Landaal Packaging Systems, pp. Vol. I-343, 395, 403 [NAICS 321920, 32222P, 32223M]

Landau Uniforms Inc., pp. Vol. I-272, 279, 285 [NAICS 31522M, 31523M, 31529M]

Landec Corp., p. I-500 [NAICS 325211]

Landis Grinding Systems, p. II-1124 [NAICS 333512]

Landis Gyr Inc., p. II-1347 [NAICS 334515]

Landmark International Trucks Inc., p. III-1758 [NAICS 423110]

Landmark Manufacturing Corp., pp. Vol. II-1134, 1541 [NAICS 333514, 336370]

Landmark Stone Supply Inc., p. III-1786 [NAICS 423320]

Landoll Corp., p. II-1023 [NAICS 333111]

Lands' End Inc., pp. Vol. III-2132, 2135, 2211 [NAICS 448140, 448150, 454113]

Landscape Structures Inc., p. II-1702 [NAICS 339920]

Lane Construction Corp., p. I-448 [NAICS 324121]

Lane Industries Inc., p. I-448 [NAICS 324121]

Lane Mountain Co., p. I-767 [NAICS 327992]

Lane's Bakery and Gifts Inc., p. III-2190 [NAICS 453220]

Laneko Roll Form Inc., p. I-863 [NAICS 332114]

Lang Exterior Co., p. I-713 [NAICS 327212]

Lang Manufacturing Co., p. II-1404 [NAICS 335221]

Langboard Inc., p. I-319 [NAICS 321219]

Langston Co., p. III-2171 [NAICS 452111]

Langston Companies Inc., pp. Vol. I-239, 395, 603 [NAICS 31491M, 32222P, 326111]

Lanier Worldwide Inc., pp. Vol. III-1798, 1801, 1805 [NAICS 423410, 423420, 423430]

Lankford-Sysco Food Services Inc., p. III-1925 [NAICS 424410]

Lanoga Corp., p. III-2065 [NAICS 444100]

Lansa USA Inc., p. III-1805 [NAICS 423430]

Lansco Colors, p. III-2004 [NAICS 424950]

Lantech.com L.L.C., p. II-1212 [NAICS 333993]

Lantis Eyewear Corp., p. II-1687 [NAICS 339115]

Lapeer Metal Stamping, p. II-1541 [NAICS 336370]

Lapeer Metal Stamping Companies, pp. Vol. I-879, Vol. II-1749 [NAICS 33211P, 339999]

Lapham-Hickey Steel Corp., pp. Vol. I-793, Vol. II-939, 964, 1014, Vol. III-1824 [NAICS 33122M, 33261M, 33281M, 33299N, 423510]

Lapp Insulator Company L.L.C., p. I-686 [NAICS 327113]

Lappin Electric Co., p. III-1831 [NAICS 423610]

Lares Research Inc., p. II-1682 [NAICS 339114]

LaRoche Industries Inc., p. III-1971 [NAICS 424690]

Larry H. Miller Group, p. III-2011 [NAICS 441110]

Larry Methvin Installation, p. I-722 [NAICS 327215]

Larry O Crother Inc., p. III-1790 [NAICS 423330]

Larry Pokras, p. III-1916 [NAICS 424320]

Larsen Cooperative Company Inc., p. III-2218 [NAICS 454311]

Larson Boats Inc., p. II-1594 [NAICS 336612]

Larson Distributing Company Inc., pp. Vol. III-1778, 2041 [NAICS 423220, 442210]

Larson Manufacturing Co., p. I-334 [NAICS 32191M]

Larter and Sons, p. II-1696 [NAICS 33991M]

Las Savell Jewelry Inc., p. III-2144 [NAICS 448310]

Las Vegas Golf and Tennis Inc., p. III-2150 [NAICS 451110]

LaSalle Bristol L.P., pp. Vol. II-1632, Vol. III-1774, 1778 [NAICS 33712N, 423210, 423220]

Lasco Bathware Inc., p. I-651 [NAICS 32619M]

Laser Technologies Inc., p. III-1801 [NAICS 423420]

LaserCard Corp., p. II-1243 [NAICS 334112]

Laserscope Inc., p. II-1322 [NAICS 334510]

Lasko Metal Products Inc., pp. Vol. II-1106, 1112, 1397 [NAICS 333415, 33341N, 33521M]

Lastec Inc., p. II-1028 [NAICS 333112]

Latco Inc., p. I-329 [NAICS 32121P]

Latex Foam International, pp. Vol. I-234, 641, Vol. II-1657 [NAICS 31412M, 326150, 337910]

Latham International, p. I-636 [NAICS 326140]

Lathem Time Corp., p. II-1362 [NAICS 334518]

Latin Percussion Inc., p. II-1731 [NAICS 339992]

Latitudes Inc., p. I-670 [NAICS 32629M]

Lau Industries Inc., p. II-1112 [NAICS 33341N]

Laufen-United States Ceramic Tile, p. I-695 [NAICS 327122]

Laurel Grocery Company Inc., p. III-1925 [NAICS 424410]

Laurel Valley Farms Inc., p. I-516 [NAICS 325311]

Lauremer Limited Inc., p. III-1894 [NAICS 423940]

Lausell Aluminum Jalousies Inc., p. I-722 [NAICS 327215]

Laux Sporting Goods Inc., p. III-2150 [NAICS 451110]

LaValley Building Supply Inc., p. I-353 [NAICS 321992]

Lavelle Industries Inc., p. I-589 [NAICS 325991]

Lavi Industries, pp. Vol. I-788, 830, Vol. II-1720 [NAICS 331210, 33142M, 339950]

Lavin Candy Company Inc., pp. Vol. III-1939, 2001 [NAICS 424450, 424940]

Law Enforcement Equipment Co., p. III-1820 [NAICS 423490]

Lawes Coal Company Inc., p. III-2218 [NAICS 454311]

Lawhon Farm Services Inc., p. I-524 [NAICS 325314]

Lawrence County Exchange, p. III-1958 [NAICS 424510]

Lawrence Marshall Chevrolet, p. III-2011 [NAICS 441110]

Lawrence Metal Products Inc., p. I-244 [NAICS 314991]

Lawson Products Inc., pp. Vol. III-1843, 1871, 1971 [NAICS 423710, 423840, 424690]

Laymon Candy Company Inc., p. III-1939 [NAICS 424450]

Lazare Kaplan International Inc., p. II-1696 [NAICS 33991M]

LB Electric Supply Company Inc., p. III-2047 [NAICS 442299]

L.B. Foster Co., pp. Vol. I-780, 845, Vol. II-899, 1009, 1584 [NAICS 33111M, 33151M, 33231M, 332996, 336510]

LB White Company Inc., pp. Vol. II-1101, 1397, 1627 [NAICS 333414, 33521M, 337127]

L.C. Manufacturing L.L.C., p. I-872 [NAICS 33211N]

LCI Ltd., p. III-1971 [NAICS 424690]

L.D. Amory and Company Inc., pp. Vol. III-1943, 2083 [NAICS 424460, 445210]

LD Brinkman and Co., p. III-1778 [NAICS 423220]

LD Willcox and Son Inc., pp. Vol. III-1766, 1770 [NAICS 423130, 423140]

LDG Electronics Inc., p. II-1248 [NAICS 334113]

LDM Technologies Inc., p. I-626 [NAICS 326122]

LDR Industries Inc., pp. Vol. I-665, Vol. II-958, 974 [NAICS 326220, 332722, 332913]

Le Creuset of America Inc., p. III-1809 [NAICS 423440]

Le-Jo Enterprises Inc., p. II-886 [NAICS 33221N]

LE Phillips Career Development, p. I-285 [NAICS 31529M]

LE Smith Co., p. II-1611 [NAICS 337110]

Le Sueur Cheese Co., pp. Vol. I-76, 81 [NAICS 311513, 311514]

Le Sueur Inc., pp. Vol. I-852, 857, Vol. II-1119 [NAICS 33152N, 33152P, 333511]

Lea-Wayne Knitting Mills Inc., p. I-256 [NAICS 31511M]

Leach & Garner General Findings, p. II-1696 [NAICS 33991M]

Leaders Manufacturing Inc., p. I-756 [NAICS 327910]

Leadertech Systems of Chicago, p. III-2058 [NAICS 443120]

Leahy/IFP, p. I-147 [NAICS 311930]

Leaman Building Materials L.P., p. III-2065 [NAICS 444100]

LeapFrog Enterprises Inc., p. II-1708 [NAICS 33993M]

Lear Corp., pp. Vol. I-290, 626, Vol. II-1536, 1541, 1551, 1627 [NAICS 31599M, 326122, 336360, 336370, 336399, 337127]

Learning Center, p. III-2058 [NAICS 443120]

Learning Labs Inc., pp. Vol. III-1820, 1901 [NAICS 423490, 424120]

Leath Furniture Inc., p. III-2037 [NAICS 442110]

Leather Factory Inc., pp. Vol. I-306, Vol. III-2007 [NAICS 31699M, 424990]

Leatherite Nylorite Mfg Outlet, pp. Vol. I-306, 510 [NAICS 31699M, 32522M]

Leavitt Tube Company L.L.C., pp. Vol. I-788, Vol. II-1009 [NAICS 331210, 332996]

Lebanon Seaboard Corp., p. I-524 [NAICS 325314]

LeCroy Corp., pp. Vol. II-1347, 1367 [NAICS 334515, 334519]

Lectro Engineering Co., p. II-1051 [NAICS 333220]

Lederle Machine Co., pp. Vol. II-1134, 1152 [NAICS 333514, 333518]

Ledtronics Inc., p. II-1386 [NAICS 335110]

Numbers following p. or pp. are page references. Roman numerals indicate volume numbers. Bracketed items indicate industries. Page references are to the starting pages of company tables.

Ledwell and Son Enterprises Inc., pp. Vol. II-923, 1486, 1491 [NAICS 332420, 336211, 336212]

Lee Brick and Tile Company Inc., p. I-691 [NAICS 327121]

Lee Co., pp. Vol. II-980, 1327 [NAICS 33291N, 334511]

Lee Industries Inc., p. II-1397 [NAICS 33521M]

Lee Iron and Metal Company Inc., p. I-807 [NAICS 331314]

Lee Pharmaceuticals Inc., p. II-1682 [NAICS 339114]

Lee Ray-Tarantino Company Inc., p. III-1950 [NAICS 424480]

Lee Supply Corp., pp. Vol. II-974, Vol. III-1847 [NAICS 332913, 423720]

Lee Williams Meats Inc., p. III-2083 [NAICS 445210]

Lee Yang Computers, p. III-2058 [NAICS 443120]

LeeBoy, p. II-1033 [NAICS 333120]

Leech Carbide, p. I-756 [NAICS 327910]

Leed's, pp. Vol. I-239, 306 [NAICS 31491M, 31699M]

Leedo Manufacturing Co., p. II-1611 [NAICS 337110]

Leelanau Fruit Co., p. III-1929 [NAICS 424420]

Leer Midwest, pp. Vol. I-651, Vol. II-1486 [NAICS 32619M, 336211]

Leevac Industries L.L.C., p. II-1589 [NAICS 336611]

LeFiell Manufacturing Co., p. I-788 [NAICS 331210]

Legacy Automotive Inc., p. III-2030 [NAICS 441310]

Legacy Cabinets L.L.C., p. II-1611 [NAICS 337110]

Legend Valve and Fitting Inc., p. III-1847 [NAICS 423720]

Legends Furniture Inc., p. III-1774 [NAICS 423210]

Leggett and Platt Inc., pp. Vol. I-780, 793, 852, Vol. II-1152, 1616, 1632, 1644, 1657 [NAICS 33111M, 33122M, 33152N, 333518, 337121, 33712N, 337215, 337910]

Lehigh Cement Co., pp. Vol. I-727, 743 [NAICS 327310, 327390]

Lehigh Group, pp. Vol. I-244, 872, Vol. II-958, 1735 [NAICS 314991, 33211N, 332722, 339993]

Lehigh Oil Co., p. III-2218 [NAICS 454311]

Lehigh Valley Plastics Inc., p. I-621 [NAICS 326121]

Lehman Pipe & Plumbing Supply, p. III-1863 [NAICS 423820]

Lehman-Roberts Co., p. I-448 [NAICS 324121]

Leigh Fibers Inc., p. I-251 [NAICS 314999]

Leiner Health Products L.L.C., pp. Vol. I-534, 539, 575 [NAICS 325411, 325412, 325620]

Leiss Tool and Die, p. II-1119 [NAICS 333511]

Leitch Inc., p. II-1432 [NAICS 335313]

Lektro Inc., p. II-1607 [NAICS 336999]

LeMans Corp., pp. Vol. III-1762, 1766 [NAICS 423120, 423130]

Lemco Mills Inc., p. I-256 [NAICS 31511M]

LeMica Corp., p. I-631 [NAICS 326130]

Lemon X Corp., p. I-143 [NAICS 311920]

Len Industries Inc., p. II-952 [NAICS 332721]

Lenape Forge Inc., p. I-872 [NAICS 33211N]

Lenaro Paper Company Inc., p. I-368 [NAICS 32212M]

Lenawee Stamping Corp., p. II-1541 [NAICS 336370]

Lenco PMC/CR Manufacturing, p. II-1134 [NAICS 333514]

Lending Trimming Company Inc., p. I-203 [NAICS 31322M]

Lennox International Inc., pp. Vol. II-1101, 1106 [NAICS 333414, 333415]

Lenoir Mirror Co., p. I-722 [NAICS 327215]

Lenox American Saw and Mfg Co., pp. Vol. II-892, 1046, 1207 [NAICS 33224P, 333210, 333991]

Lenox-Martell Inc., p. I-147 [NAICS 311930]

LensCrafters Inc., p. II-1687 [NAICS 339115]

Lenzing Fibers Corp., p. I-510 [NAICS 32522M]

Leo's Foods Inc., p. I-133 [NAICS 311830]

Leo Wolleman Inc., p. III-1894 [NAICS 423940]

Leon-Ferenbach Co., pp. Vol. I-192, 218 [NAICS 31311M, 31331M]

Leon Korol Co., p. III-1905 [NAICS 424130]

Leon Max Inc., pp. Vol. I-279, 290 [NAICS 31523M, 31599M]

Leon Plastics Inc., p. I-641 [NAICS 326150]

Leonard Peterson Inc., p. II-1666 [NAICS 339111]

Leonard's Bakery Ltd., p. III-2089 [NAICS 445291]

Leonard's Hardware Inc., p. III-1847 [NAICS 423720]

Leone Industries Inc., p. I-718 [NAICS 327213]

Lepage Bakeries Inc., p. I-116 [NAICS 31181M]

Lephart Imaging Systems Inc., p. III-2186 [NAICS 453210]

Leprino Foods Co., pp. Vol. I-76, 81, Vol. III-1958 [NAICS 311513, 311514, 424510]

Leroy Hill Coffee Company Inc., p. I-143 [NAICS 311920]

LesCare Kitchens, p. II-1611 [NAICS 337110]

LESCO Inc., pp. Vol. I-520, Vol. II-1023, 1028, 1033, 1390 [NAICS 325312, 333111, 333112, 333120, 33512M]

Lesley Roy Designs L.L.C., p. III-2190 [NAICS 453220]

Lester Building Systems, pp. Vol. I-324, 334, 353 [NAICS 32121N, 32191M, 321992]

Letica Corp., p. I-651 [NAICS 32619M]

Leupold and Stevens Inc., pp. Vol. II-1082, 1702 [NAICS 333314, 339920]

Levcor International Inc., pp. Vol. I-198, Vol. III-1913 [NAICS 313210, 424310]

Level Valley Creamery Inc., pp. Vol. I-76, 81, 86 [NAICS 311513, 311514, 31151N]

Levert-St John Inc., p. I-44 [NAICS 31131N]

Levi Strauss and Co., pp. Vol. I-272, 279, 290 [NAICS 31522M, 31523M, 31599M]

Leviton Lighting Controls, p. II-1390 [NAICS 33512M]

Leviton Manufacturing Inc., pp. Vol. II-1307, 1451, 1457, 1512 [NAICS 334417, 33592M, 33593M, 33632M]

Levitz Furniture Inc., p. III-2037 [NAICS 442110]

Levy Co., p. I-767 [NAICS 327992]

Levy Home Entertainment L.L.C., p. III-1995 [NAICS 424920]

Lew Horton Distributing Inc., p. III-2150 [NAICS 451110]

Lewan and Associates Inc., pp. Vol. III-1801, 1805 [NAICS 423420, 423430]

Lewco Inc., p. II-1217 [NAICS 333994]

Lewcott Corp., p. I-224 [NAICS 313320]

Lewis and Saunders Inc., p. II-1009 [NAICS 332996]

Lewis Brothers Bakeries, p. I-116 [NAICS 31181M]

Lewis Drug Inc., p. III-2100 [NAICS 446110]

Lewis-Goetz and Company Inc., p. III-2007 [NAICS 424990]

Lewis Marine Supply Inc., p. III-1879 [NAICS 423860]

Lewisburg Seating Systems Inc., p. II-1627 [NAICS 337127]

Lewright Meats Inc., p. III-2083 [NAICS 445210]

Lexar Media Inc., p. II-1087 [NAICS 333315]

Lexicon Genetics Inc., p. I-544 [NAICS 325413]

Lexidyne of P.A., p. I-411 [NAICS 322291]

Lexington Corp., p. II-1536 [NAICS 336360]

Lexington Home Brands, pp. Vol. II-1621, 1632, 1644 [NAICS 337122, 33712N, 337215]

Lexington Precision Corp., pp. Vol. I-670, 852, 857, Vol. II-1014 [NAICS 32629M, 33152N, 33152P, 33299N]

Lexmark Carpet Mills Inc., p. I-229 [NAICS 314110]

Lexmark International Inc., pp. Vol. II-1077, 1252, 1337 [NAICS 333313, 334119, 334513]

Lexus, p. III-1758 [NAICS 423110]

Leybold Vacuum USA Inc., pp. Vol. II-980, 1179, 1184 [NAICS 33291N, 333911, 333912]

Lezzer Lumber Inc., p. III-2065 [NAICS 444100]

LFD Inc., pp. Vol. III-2037, 2050 [NAICS 442110, 443111]

LGS Technologies, p. II-1725 [NAICS 339991]

LI-COR Biosciences, p. II-1352 [NAICS 334516]

Li'l Guy Foods Inc., p. I-133 [NAICS 311830]

Libbey Glass, p. I-713 [NAICS 327212]

Libbey Inc., pp. Vol. I-681, 713 [NAICS 327112, 327212]

Liberty Auto Salvage, p. III-1770 [NAICS 423140]

Liberty Business Forms, p. III-1901 [NAICS 424120]

Liberty Carton Co., p. I-374 [NAICS 322130]

Liberty Diversified Industries Inc., pp. Vol. I-379, Vol. II-908 [NAICS 32221M, 33232M]

Liberty Embroidery Inc., p. I-251 [NAICS 314999]

Liberty Envelope Corp., p. I-403 [NAICS 32223M]

Liberty Gold Fruit Co., pp. Vol. I-1936, 1943 [NAICS 424440, 424460]

Liberty Homes Inc., p. I-353 [NAICS 321992]

Liberty Inc., p. II-1500 [NAICS 336214]

Liberty Orchards Company Inc., p. I-57 [NAICS 311340]

Liberty-Pittsburgh Systems Inc., p. I-203 [NAICS 31322M]

Liberty Screenprinting Inc., p. I-251 [NAICS 314999]

Liberty Steel Products Inc., pp. Vol. I-879, Vol. II-945 [NAICS 33211P, 332710]

Liberty Tire and Rubber Inc., p. I-660 [NAICS 32621M]

Liberty Vegetable Oil Co., p. I-26 [NAICS 311225]

Libla Industries Inc., p. I-343 [NAICS 321920]

Libman Co., pp. Vol. II-1397, 1740 [NAICS 33521M, 339994]

Libra Industries Inc., p. II-1352 [NAICS 334516]

LiDestri Foods Inc., p. I-152 [NAICS 31194M]

Liechty Farm Equipment Inc., p. III-1863 [NAICS 423820]

Life-Like Products L.L.C., pp. Vol. I-636, 641, Vol. II-1708 [NAICS 326140, 326150, 33993M]

Numbers following p. or pp. are page references. Roman numerals indicate volume numbers. Bracketed items indicate industries. Page references are to the starting pages of company tables.

Life-Style Furniture Company Inc., p. II-1616 [NAICS 337121]

LifeCore Biomedical Inc., p. I-549 [NAICS 325414]

Lifeline Lifetech, p. III-2113 [NAICS 446199]

Lifeline Systems Inc., pp. Vol. II-1257, 1267 [NAICS 334210, 334290]

LifeScan Inc., pp. Vol. I-544, Vol. II-1322 [NAICS 325413, 334510]

Lifestyle Company Inc., p. III-1817 [NAICS 423460]

Lifetime Hoan Corp., p. II-886 [NAICS 33221N]

Lifetime Products Inc., pp. Vol. II-1621, 1627, 1702 [NAICS 337122, 337127, 339920]

Lift Parts Manufacturing Co., p. III-1867 [NAICS 423830]

Liftex Corp., pp. Vol. I-203, 251, 285 [NAICS 31322M, 314999, 31529M]

Light Process Co., p. II-1386 [NAICS 335110]

Light Sources Inc., pp. Vol. II-1386, 1702 [NAICS 335110, 339920]

Lighthouse For The Blind Inc., p. II-1714 [NAICS 33994M]

Lighting Components & Design, p. II-1421 [NAICS 335311]

Lights of America Inc., pp. Vol. II-1386, 1390 [NAICS 335110, 33512M]

Ligna Machinery Inc., p. II-1046 [NAICS 333210]

Lilli Group Inc., p. I-267 [NAICS 31521M]

Lillian Vernon Corp., p. III-1778 [NAICS 423220]

Lillie Rubin Affiliates Inc., p. III-2126 [NAICS 448120]

Limited Brands Inc., pp. Vol. III-2123, 2126, 2132, 2211 [NAICS 448110, 448120, 448140, 454113]

Limited Editions, p. III-1817 [NAICS 423460]

Limitorque Corp., pp. Vol. II-958, 1222 [NAICS 332722, 33399N]

Linatex Inc., p. I-665 [NAICS 326220]

Lincoln Brick and Supply Inc., p. III-1786 [NAICS 423320]

Lincoln, L H and Son Inc., p. I-296 [NAICS 316110]

Lincoln Laser Co., p. I-722 [NAICS 327215]

Lincoln Logs Ltd., p. I-353 [NAICS 321992]

Lincoln Pharmacy, p. III-2100 [NAICS 446110]

Lincoln Poultry and Egg Co., pp. Vol. III-1933, 1936 [NAICS 424430, 424440]

Lincoln Provision Inc., pp. Vol. III-1929, 1946 [NAICS 424420, 424470]

Lincoln Textile Products Inc., p. I-234 [NAICS 31412M]

Lincolnton Manufacturing Inc., p. I-262 [NAICS 31519M]

Lindal Cedar Homes Inc., p. I-353 [NAICS 321992]

Linde BOC Process Plants L.L.C., p. I-353 [NAICS 321992]

Linde Gas L.L.C., pp. Vol. I-471, Vol. II-1229 [NAICS 325120, 33399P]

Linden Industries Inc., p. II-1051 [NAICS 333220]

Linden Lumber Company Ltd., p. I-334 [NAICS 32191M]

Lindenmeyr Munroe, pp. Vol. III-1901, 1905 [NAICS 424120, 424130]

Linder Industrial Machinery Co., p. III-1859 [NAICS 423810]

Linderme Tube Co., pp. Vol. I-811, 830 [NAICS 331316, 33142M]

Lindquist Machine Corp., p. II-1152 [NAICS 333518]

Lindsay Manufacturing Co., p. II-1023 [NAICS 333111]

Lindt and Sprungli (USA) Inc., p. I-52 [NAICS 311330]

Line 6 Inc., p. II-1731 [NAICS 339992]

Linear Lighting, p. II-1390 [NAICS 33512M]

Linear Technology Corp., pp. Vol. II-1287, 1421, 1468 [NAICS 334413, 335311, 335999]

Linens 'n Things Inc., p. III-2047 [NAICS 442299]

Lingle Brothers Coffee Service, p. I-143 [NAICS 311920]

Link Belt Bearing, pp. Vol. II-988, 1168 [NAICS 332991, 333613]

Link-Belt Construction Equipment, pp. Vol. II-1033, 1194 [NAICS 333120, 33392M]

Linn Gear Co., p. II-1162 [NAICS 333612]

LINPAC Inc., pp. Vol. I-363, 379, 651 [NAICS 322110, 32221M, 32619M]

Linq Industrial Fabrics Inc., pp. Vol. I-198, 251 [NAICS 313210, 314999]

Linwood Mining & Minerals Corp., p. I-748 [NAICS 327410]

Liochem Inc., p. I-580 [NAICS 325910]

Lion Apparel Inc., pp. Vol. I-272, 279 [NAICS 31522M, 31523M]

Lion Brewery Inc., pp. Vol. I-165, 172 [NAICS 31211M, 312120]

Lion Oil El Dorado Refinery, pp. Vol. I-443, 453, 554, 727 [NAICS 324110, 324122, 325510, 327310]

Lion Recording Services Inc., p. II-1376 [NAICS 334612]

Lionel Lavallee Company Inc., p. III-1946 [NAICS 424470]

Lionetti Associates, p. III-1890 [NAICS 423930]

Lippert Corp., p. III-1786 [NAICS 423320]

Liqui-Box Corp., pp. Vol. I-379, Vol. II-1212 [NAICS 32221M, 333993]

Liquid Container\Plaxicon, pp. Vol. I-646, 651 [NAICS 326160, 32619M]

Liquid Control Corp., p. II-1189 [NAICS 333913]

Liquid Molding Systems Inc., pp. Vol. I-505, 631 [NAICS 325212, 326130]

Liquidmetal Technologies Inc., p. I-825 [NAICS 331419]

Lisbon Sausage Company Inc., p. III-1946 [NAICS 424470]

Lisle Corp., p. II-1124 [NAICS 333512]

List Industries Inc., p. II-1644 [NAICS 337215]

Litetronics International Inc., p. II-1386 [NAICS 335110]

Litex Industries Inc., p. III-1831 [NAICS 423610]

Lithia Motors Inc., p. III-2011 [NAICS 441110]

Lithia Of Sioux Falls, p. III-2030 [NAICS 441310]

Littelfuse Inc., p. II-1432 [NAICS 335313]

Littell International Inc., pp. Vol. II-1129, 1147, 1152 [NAICS 333513, 333516, 333518]

Litter Industries Inc., p. III-2222 [NAICS 454312]

Little Crow Foods, p. I-36 [NAICS 311230]

Little Hills Winery Gift Shop, pp. Vol. III-2097, 2190 [NAICS 445310, 453220]

Little Hocking Service Center, p. I-589 [NAICS 325991]

Little Lady Foods Inc., pp. Vol. I-62, 158 [NAICS 31141M, 31199M]

Little Professor Book Center, p. III-2162 [NAICS 451211]

Little Tikes, pp. Vol. I-626, Vol. II-1708 [NAICS 326122, 33993M]

Littlebrook Management Inc., p. II-974 [NAICS 332913]

Littleton Coin Company Inc., p. III-2208 [NAICS 453998]

Littman Dental Laboratory Inc., p. II-1692 [NAICS 339116]

Livers Bronze Co., p. II-1714 [NAICS 33994M]

Livingston and Haven L.L.C., p. II-1222 [NAICS 33399N]

Liz Claiborne Accessories, pp. Vol. I-290, 306 [NAICS 31599M, 31699M]

Liz Claiborne Inc., pp. Vol. I-272, 279, 290, 575 [NAICS 31522M, 31523M, 31599M, 325620]

Ljl Truck Center Inc., p. III-1758 [NAICS 423110]

L.L. Bean Inc., pp. Vol. I-272, 279, 285, 290, 306, Vol. III-2211 [NAICS 31522M, 31523M, 31529M, 31599M, 31699M, 454113]

LL Building Products Inc., pp. Vol. III-1824, 1867 [NAICS 423510, 423830]

Llamas Plastics Inc., p. I-631 [NAICS 326130]

Lloyd/Flanders Industries Inc., pp. Vol. II-1621, 1632 [NAICS 337122, 33712N]

Lloyd Manufacturing Corp., p. I-224 [NAICS 313320]

Lloyd's Florist, p. III-2183 [NAICS 453110]

LM Scofield Co., p. I-475 [NAICS 32513M]

LMI Aerospace Inc., p. II-1567 [NAICS 336413]

L.N. White and Company Inc., p. III-1943 [NAICS 424460]

Load King Manufacturing Co., pp. Vol. II-1627, 1720 [NAICS 337127, 339950]

Load Rite Trailers Inc., pp. Vol. II-1500, 1607 [NAICS 336214, 336999]

Local Oil Company of Anoka Inc., pp. Vol. III-1975, 2218 [NAICS 424710, 454311]

Lock Inspection Systems Inc., p. II-1357 [NAICS 334517]

Locke Insulators Inc., p. I-686 [NAICS 327113]

Lockhart Chemical Co., p. I-493 [NAICS 32519M]

Lockheed Martin Corp., pp. Vol. II-1262, 1267, 1327, 1557, 1567, 1572 [NAICS 334220, 334290, 334511, 336411, 336413, 336414]

Lockheed Martin Missiles/Fire Ctrl, p. II-1005 [NAICS 332995]

Lodan Electronics Inc., pp. Vol. II-1307, 1312 [NAICS 334417, 334418]

Loehmann's Holdings Inc., p. III-2126 [NAICS 448120]

Loews Corp., pp. Vol. I-188, Vol. III-1894 [NAICS 31222M, 423940]

Loftness U S Attachments, p. II-1028 [NAICS 333112]

Lofton Label Inc., p. I-203 [NAICS 31322M]

Logan Business Machines Inc., p. III-2186 [NAICS 453210]

Logan Clay Products Co., p. I-699 [NAICS 327123]

Logan Corp., p. III-1859 [NAICS 423810]

Logan Graphic Products Inc., pp. Vol. I-374, Vol. II-1124 [NAICS 322130, 333512]

Numbers following p. or pp. are page references. Roman numerals indicate volume numbers. Bracketed items indicate industries. Page references are to the starting pages of company tables.

Logan International II L.L.C., p. III-1929 [NAICS 424420]

Logan Oil Tools L.L.C., pp. Vol. II-1039, 1134 [NAICS 33313M, 333514]

Logantex Inc., p. III-1913 [NAICS 424310]

Logitech Inc., p. II-1252 [NAICS 334119]

Logo of The Americas, p. III-1817 [NAICS 423460]

LoJack Corp., pp. Vol. II-1262, 1267 [NAICS 334220, 334290]

Lombart Instruments U.S., p. III-2107 [NAICS 446130]

Lone Elm Sales Inc., pp. Vol. III-1929, 1933 [NAICS 424420, 424430]

Lone Star Bakery Inc., p. I-116 [NAICS 31181M]

Lone Star Industries Inc., pp. Vol. I-727, 732 [NAICS 327310, 327320]

Lone Star Racing Inc., pp. Vol. II-1162, 1473, 1519 [NAICS 333612, 336111, 336330]

Lone Star Technologies Inc., pp. Vol. I-788, 793, Vol. II-908, 1009, 1551 [NAICS 331210, 33122M, 33232M, 332996, 336399]

Long Agribusiness L.L.C., pp. Vol. II-1023, 1033 [NAICS 333111, 333120]

Long Beach Shavings, p. I-529 [NAICS 325320]

Long Rap Inc., pp. Vol. III-2123, 2126, 2135 [NAICS 448110, 448120, 448150]

Long Trail Brewing Co., p. I-172 [NAICS 312120]

Longaberger Co., pp. Vol. I-358, 681, Vol. II-1749, Vol. III-2211 [NAICS 321999, 327112, 339999, 454113]

Longo Electrical-Mechanical Inc., p. II-1162 [NAICS 333612]

Longs Drug Stores California Inc., p. III-2100 [NAICS 446110]

Longs Drug Stores Corp., p. III-2100 [NAICS 446110]

Longstreth Sporting Goods, p. III-1883 [NAICS 423910]

Longview Fibre Co., pp. Vol. I-363, 368, 379, 395, 510, Vol. II-928, 1720 [NAICS 322110, 32212M, 32221M, 32222P, 32522M, 33243M, 339950]

Longwood Engineered Products, p. I-670 [NAICS 32629M]

Lonza Inc., p. I-816 [NAICS 33131N]

Loomis Industries Inc., p. II-1056 [NAICS 333295]

Loos and Company Inc., pp. Vol. I-793, Vol. II-939, 1307 [NAICS 33122M, 33261M, 334417]

Lopez Foods Inc., p. I-102 [NAICS 31161N]

Lor-AL Products Inc., p. II-1023 [NAICS 333111]

Loral Space & Communications, p. II-1262 [NAICS 334220]

Loram Maintenance of Way Inc., p. II-1584 [NAICS 336510]

Lorann Oils Inc., p. I-26 [NAICS 311225]

Lorber Industries of California, pp. Vol. I-213, 251 [NAICS 31324M, 314999]

Loren Cook Co., p. II-1112 [NAICS 33341N]

Los Altos Food Products Inc., p. I-76 [NAICS 311513]

Los Altos Trophy Inc., pp. Vol. III-1894, 2208 [NAICS 423940, 453998]

Los Amigos Tortilla Mfg., p. I-133 [NAICS 311830]

Los Angeles Chemical Inc., p. III-1971 [NAICS 424690]

Los Angeles Lighting Mfg Co., p. II-1386 [NAICS 335110]

Los Angeles Nut House, p. III-1939 [NAICS 424450]

Los Bagels Inc., p. III-2089 [NAICS 445291]

Lost Coast Brewery and Cafe, p. I-172 [NAICS 312120]

Lotepro Corp., p. III-1971 [NAICS 424690]

Loth Mbi Inc., pp. Vol. III-1774, 2037 [NAICS 423210, 442110]

Lotte USA Inc., pp. Vol. I-52, 57, 124 [NAICS 311330, 311340, 31182M]

Lou Davis Wholesale, pp. Vol. III-1887, 2007 [NAICS 423920, 424990]

Lou Fusz Automotive Network, p. III-2011 [NAICS 441110]

LOUD Technologies Inc., pp. Vol. II-1262, 1272 [NAICS 334220, 334310]

Louis A Grant Inc., p. II-1101 [NAICS 333414]

Louis Foehrkolb Inc., pp. Vol. III-1929, 1943 [NAICS 424420, 424460]

Louis M Martini Winery, p. I-177 [NAICS 312130]

Louisa Food Products Inc., pp. Vol. I-124, 152 [NAICS 31182M, 31194M]

Louisiana Chemical Equipment, p. III-1971 [NAICS 424690]

Louisiana Compressor Maint., pp. Vol. II-980, 1157, 1184, 1505 [NAICS 33291N, 333611, 333912, 33631M]

Louisiana Office Products, p. III-1901 [NAICS 424120]

Louisiana-Pacific Corp., pp. Vol. I-312, 319, 324, 334 [NAICS 32111M, 321219, 32121N, 32191M]

Louisiana Plastic Converting Corp., p. I-589 [NAICS 325991]

Louisiana Sewn Products Inc., p. I-285 [NAICS 31529M]

Louisiana Sugar Cane Co-Op Inc., p. I-44 [NAICS 31131N]

Louisville Bedding Company Inc., pp. Vol. I-234, Vol. II-1702 [NAICS 31412M, 339920]

Louisville Pecan Company Inc., pp. Vol. III-1939, 1965, 2092 [NAICS 424450, 424590, 445292]

Louisville Tin and Stove Co., p. II-1101 [NAICS 333414]

Love and Quiches Desserts, p. I-116 [NAICS 31181M]

Love Box Company Inc., p. I-379 [NAICS 32221M]

Love's Travel Stops & Country, pp. Vol. III-2116, 2180 [NAICS 447110, 452990]

Low Cost Healthcare of Indiana, p. III-2100 [NAICS 446110]

Lowe's Companies Inc., pp. Vol. I-334, Vol. II-908, Vol. III-1782, 1794, 1843, 2050, 2065, 2072 [NAICS 32191M, 33232M, 423310, 423390, 423710, 443111, 444100, 444220]

Lowel-Light Manufacturing Inc., p. II-1386 [NAICS 335110]

Lowell Manufacturing Co., p. I-771 [NAICS 327993]

Lowen Corp., p. II-1720 [NAICS 339950]

Lowrance Electronics Inc., p. II-1327 [NAICS 334511]

Lowrey Organ Co., p. II-1731 [NAICS 339992]

Loxcreen Company Inc., pp. Vol. I-334, 621, 811 [NAICS 32191M, 326121, 331316]

Lozier Corp., pp. Vol. II-1611, 1644 [NAICS 337110, 337215]

LPS Industries Inc., p. I-403 [NAICS 32223M]

LPS Laboratories Inc., p. I-458 [NAICS 324191]

L.S. Starrett Co., pp. Vol. II-892, 1140, 1337, 1367 [NAICS 33221P, 333515, 334513, 334519]

LSB Industries Inc., pp. Vol. I-524, 585, Vol. II-988, 1106, 1124, 1168, 1184, 1725 [NAICS 325314, 325920, 332991, 333415, 333512, 333613, 333912, 339991]

LSI Corporation of America Inc., p. II-1611 [NAICS 337110]

LSI Industries Inc., pp. Vol. I-420, Vol. II-1390 [NAICS 32311M, 33512M]

LSI Lightron Inc., p. II-1390 [NAICS 33512M]

LSI Logic Corp., pp. Vol. II-1252, 1287 [NAICS 334119, 334413]

LSP Products Group, p. II-974 [NAICS 332913]

LTP Products and Services Inc., p. III-1875 [NAICS 423850]

LTV Copperweld, pp. Vol. I-788, Vol. II-939 [NAICS 331210, 33261M]

LTX Corp., pp. Vol. II-1337, 1347 [NAICS 334513, 334515]

Lubricating Specialties Co., p. I-458 [NAICS 324191]

Lubrication Engineers Inc., p. I-458 [NAICS 324191]

Lubrication Technology Inc., p. I-458 [NAICS 324191]

Lubrizol Corp., pp. Vol. I-458, 488, 595, 626 [NAICS 324191, 325188, 32599N, 326122]

Lucasbilt, p. III-1801 [NAICS 423420]

Lucchese Boot Company Inc., p. I-300 [NAICS 31621M]

Lucchese Inc., p. I-300 [NAICS 31621M]

Luce Schwab and Kase Inc., p. III-1855 [NAICS 423740]

Lucent Technologies Inc., p. II-1257 [NAICS 334210]

Luck Stone Corp., p. I-762 [NAICS 327991]

Luckett Tobaccos Inc., p. I-185 [NAICS 312210]

Lucks' Food Decorating Co., p. I-57 [NAICS 311340]

Lucky Coin, pp. Vol. III-1774, 1809, 1883 [NAICS 423210, 423440, 423910]

Lucky Farmers Inc., pp. Vol. I-9, Vol. III-1958, 1991 [NAICS 311119, 424510, 424910]

Ludlow Coated Products, pp. Vol. I-388, Vol. II-964 [NAICS 32222N, 33281M]

Ludlow Company L.P., p. I-368 [NAICS 32212M]

Ludlow Cooperative Elevator Inc., p. III-1958 [NAICS 424510]

Ludlow Corp., p. I-388 [NAICS 32222N]

Ludlow Textiles Company Inc., pp. Vol. I-192, 244 [NAICS 31311M, 314991]

Ludlum Measurements Inc., pp. Vol. II-1342, 1352, 1367 [NAICS 334514, 334516, 334519]

Ludowici Roof Tile, p. I-699 [NAICS 327123]

Lufkin Industries Inc., pp. Vol. I-845, Vol. II-1168, 1179, 1491 [NAICS 33151M, 333613, 333911, 336212]

Luhr Jensen and Sons Inc., p. II-1404 [NAICS 335221]

LuK Inc., pp. Vol. II-1530, 1551 [NAICS 336350, 336399]

Numbers following p. or pp. are page references. Roman numerals indicate volume numbers. Bracketed items indicate industries. Page references are to the starting pages of company tables.

2373

Lula Westfield L.L.C., p. I-44 [NAICS 31131N]

Lumber Inc., pp. Vol. I-324, 329 [NAICS 32121N, 32121P]

Lumber Specialties Ltd., p. I-329 [NAICS 32121P]

Lumberman's Inc., p. III-1782 [NAICS 423310]

Lumbermen's Inc., p. I-329 [NAICS 32121P]

Lumberyard Suppliers Inc., p. III-1794 [NAICS 423390]

Lumitex Inc., pp. Vol. II-1390, 1451 [NAICS 33512M, 33592M]

Lummus Corp., p. II-1129 [NAICS 333513]

Lummus Supply Co., p. III-2065 [NAICS 444100]

Luna Bianca USA Inc., p. III-1894 [NAICS 423940]

Luna Defense Systems Inc., p. II-1557 [NAICS 336411]

Lunaire Ltd., p. II-1468 [NAICS 335999]

Lund International, pp. Vol. I-879, Vol. II-1486 [NAICS 33211P, 336211]

Lunday-Thagard Co., p. I-453 [NAICS 324122]

Lundberg Family Farms, p. I-15 [NAICS 31121M]

Lundell Manufacturing Corp., p. I-636 [NAICS 326140]

Lunt Silversmiths Inc., pp. Vol. II-886, 1696 [NAICS 33221N, 33991M]

Lupient Automotive Group, p. III-2011 [NAICS 441110]

Lustre-Cal Nameplate Corp., p. I-816 [NAICS 33131N]

Luther P. Miller Inc., p. III-1975 [NAICS 424710]

Lutron Electronics Company Inc., pp. Vol. II-1437, 1457 [NAICS 335314, 33593M]

Luv n' care Ltd., pp. Vol. I-285, 646 [NAICS 31529M, 326160]

Luvel Dairy Products Inc., pp. Vol. I-81, 92 [NAICS 311514, 311520]

Luverne Truck Equipment Inc., pp. Vol. I-722, Vol. II-1486 [NAICS 327215, 336211]

Luwa Inc., pp. Vol. II-1106, 1112, 1217 [NAICS 333415, 33341N, 333994]

Lux Products Corp., p. II-1362 [NAICS 334518]

Luxfer Cylinders Inc., pp. Vol. II-899, 923 [NAICS 33231M, 332420]

Luxor, p. II-1632 [NAICS 33712N]

Luzenac America Inc., p. I-767 [NAICS 327992]

Luzerne Optical Laboratories, pp. Vol. II-1082, 1687 [NAICS 333314, 339115]

LVMH-Moet Hennessy Louis, p. I-177 [NAICS 312130]

LVS Sales Inc., p. II-1607 [NAICS 336999]

L.W. Barrett Company Inc., p. III-2007 [NAICS 424990]

Lycian Stage Lighting, p. II-1386 [NAICS 335110]

Lydall Inc., pp. Vol. I-374, 388, 510, 771 [NAICS 322130, 32222N, 32522M, 327993]

Lyle Industries Inc., p. II-1129 [NAICS 333513]

Lynn Ladder and Scaffolding Inc., p. I-358 [NAICS 321999]

Lynn Protein Inc., pp. Vol. I-76, 493 [NAICS 311513, 32519M]

Lyon and Healy Harps Inc., pp. Vol. II-1376, 1731 [NAICS 334612, 339992]

Lyon Conklin and Company Inc., pp. Vol. III-1824, 1847, 1851 [NAICS 423510, 423720, 423730]

Lyon County Cooperative Oil Co., pp. Vol. III-1975, 2218 [NAICS 424710, 454311]

Lyon Shipyard Inc., p. II-1589 [NAICS 336611]

Lyon Workspace Products L.L.C., pp. Vol. II-928, 1194, 1627, 1644, 1650 [NAICS 33243M, 33392M, 337127, 337215, 33721N]

Lyondell Chemical Co., pp. Vol. I-443, 493, 500 [NAICS 324110, 32519M, 325211]

LyTech Corp., p. II-1505 [NAICS 33631M]

M/A-Com Inc., p. II-1262 [NAICS 334220]

M/A/R/C Research, p. II-933 [NAICS 332510]

M and A Technology Inc., p. II-1238 [NAICS 334111]

M and F Worldwide Corp., p. I-147 [NAICS 311930]

M and G Electronics Corp., pp. Vol. II-1307, 1451, 1457, 1468 [NAICS 334417, 33592M, 33593M, 335999]

M and H Industries Inc., p. II-1541 [NAICS 336370]

M and I Electric Industries Inc., p. II-1421 [NAICS 335311]

M and J Industries L.L.C., p. II-1491 [NAICS 336212]

M and L Industries Inc., pp. Vol. III-1863, 2027 [NAICS 423820, 441229]

M and L Jewelry Mfg Inc., p. II-1696 [NAICS 33991M]

M and M Knopf Auto Parts Inc., pp. Vol. III-1762, 1770 [NAICS 423120, 423140]

M and P Industries Inc., p. I-727 [NAICS 327310]

M and R Industries Inc., p. I-788 [NAICS 331210]

M and R International Inc., p. III-1905 [NAICS 424130]

M and R Marking Systems Inc., p. II-1714 [NAICS 33994M]

M and S Manufacturing Inc., pp. Vol. II-952, 1162 [NAICS 332721, 333612]

M and S Systems L.P., p. II-1184 [NAICS 333912]

M and W Gear Co., pp. Vol. II-1028, 1157 [NAICS 333112, 333611]

M and W Sales Inc., p. III-2190 [NAICS 453220]

m-Audio, p. II-1282 [NAICS 334412]

M. Conley Co., pp. Vol. III-1875, 1905, 2007 [NAICS 423850, 424130, 424990]

M Cubed Technologies Inc., p. I-681 [NAICS 327112]

M D Both Industries Inc., p. I-580 [NAICS 325910]

M-D Building Material Inc., p. III-1843 [NAICS 423710]

M-D Building Products Inc., pp. Vol. I-621, 811, Vol. II-892, 933 [NAICS 326121, 331316, 33221P, 332510]

M D M Marketing Inc., p. II-1442 [NAICS 335911]

M D Moody and Sons Inc., p. III-1859 [NAICS 423810]

M-E-C Co., p. II-1023 [NAICS 333111]

M. Fabrikant and Sons Inc., p. III-1894 [NAICS 423940]

M-Flex, pp. Vol. II-1282, 1312 [NAICS 334412, 334418]

M. Foster Associates Inc., p. III-1919 [NAICS 424330]

M Geller Ltd., p. III-1894 [NAICS 423940]

M Hiller and Son Inc., p. III-1890 [NAICS 423930]

M-I L.L.C., p. I-458 [NAICS 324191]

M-Pulse Microwave Inc., p. II-1292 [NAICS 334414]

M-Ron Corp., p. II-1056 [NAICS 333295]

M7 Aerospace L.P., p. III-1879 [NAICS 423860]

M.A. Bruder and Sons Inc., p. I-554 [NAICS 325510]

MA Laboratories Inc., p. III-1805 [NAICS 423430]

M.A. Patout and Son Ltd., p. I-44 [NAICS 31131N]

Maac Machinery Inc., p. II-1051 [NAICS 333220]

MAAX-KSD Inc., p. II-1632 [NAICS 33712N]

MAAX Midwest, p. I-677 [NAICS 327111]

Mabis Healthcare Inc., p. III-1813 [NAICS 423450]

MAC Products Inc., p. II-1152 [NAICS 333518]

Mac Tools Inc., p. II-892 [NAICS 33221P]

Mac Trailer Manufacturing Inc., p. II-1491 [NAICS 336212]

MAC Valves Inc., p. II-980 [NAICS 33291N]

MacAlaster Bicknell Company Inc., p. III-1820 [NAICS 423490]

MacAndrews & Forbes Holdings, pp. Vol. I-147, 188 [NAICS 311930, 31222M]

MacBeath Hardwood Company, p. I-324 [NAICS 32121N]

MacCenter, p. III-2058 [NAICS 443120]

MacDermid Inc., pp. Vol. I-595, Vol. II-1252, 1282, 1287 [NAICS 32599N, 334119, 334412, 334413]

Mace Security International Inc., p. I-471 [NAICS 325120]

Macey's Inc., p. III-2100 [NAICS 446110]

Machine and Welding Supply Co., pp. Vol. III-1871, 1971 [NAICS 423840, 424690]

Machine Head, p. II-1376 [NAICS 334612]

Machine Service Inc., p. II-1530 [NAICS 336350]

Macho Products Inc., p. I-300 [NAICS 31621M]

Mack Boring and Parts Co., p. III-1809 [NAICS 423440]

Mack Technologies Inc., p. II-1238 [NAICS 334111]

Mack Trucks Inc., pp. Vol. II-1194, 1486 [NAICS 33392M, 336211]

Mackay Envelope Corp., p. I-403 [NAICS 32223M]

MacKenzie-Childs Ltd., p. I-681 [NAICS 327112]

MacKissic Inc., p. II-1028 [NAICS 333112]

Maclean Power Systems, p. I-771 [NAICS 327993]

Maclean Quality Composites, p. II-1463 [NAICS 335991]

Maco Furniture Inc., p. III-1774 [NAICS 423210]

Maco Group, p. I-603 [NAICS 326111]

Macomb Pipe and Supply Inc., p. III-1871 [NAICS 423840]

Macro Metallics, p. II-1277 [NAICS 334411]

Macrotech Polyseal Inc., p. II-1725 [NAICS 339991]

Madaris Hosiery Mills Inc., p. I-256 [NAICS 31511M]

Madden Communications Inc., p. I-436 [NAICS 32312M]

Madelaine Chocolate Novelties Inc., p. I-52 [NAICS 311330]

Madison Electric Co., p. III-1835 [NAICS 423620]

Madison Farmers Elevator Co., pp. Vol. III-1958, 1991 [NAICS 424510, 424910]

Madison Filter Inc., p. I-224 [NAICS 313320]

Madison Industries Inc., pp. Vol. I-229, 234 [NAICS 314110, 31412M]

Madison-Kipp Corp., pp. Vol. I-852, 857 [NAICS 33152N, 33152P]

Madison Paper Co., p. I-363 [NAICS 322110]

Madison Paper Industries Inc., pp. Vol. I-368, 415 [NAICS 32212M, 322299]

Madison Precision Products Inc., p. I-852 [NAICS 33152N]

Numbers following p. or pp. are page references. Roman numerals indicate volume numbers. Bracketed items indicate industries. Page references are to the starting pages of company tables.

2374

Madison Service Co., pp. Vol. I-516, 520, 529 [NAICS 325311, 325312, 325320]

Madras Packaging L.L.C., p. I-646 [NAICS 326160]

MAF Industries Inc., p. II-1212 [NAICS 333993]

Mag Instrument Inc., p. II-1390 [NAICS 33512M]

Mag-Nif Inc., p. II-1708 [NAICS 33993M]

Magee Plastics Company Inc., p. II-1584 [NAICS 336510]

Magee Rieter Automotive Systems, p. II-1749 [NAICS 339999]

Magenta Corp., pp. Vol. II-1189, 1666 [NAICS 333913, 339111]

Maggiore Wholesale, p. III-1987 [NAICS 424820]

Magi Inc., p. III-1950 [NAICS 424480]

Magic Aire, p. II-1101 [NAICS 333414]

Magic Hat Brewing & Performing, p. I-172 [NAICS 312120]

Magic Plastics Inc., p. II-1119 [NAICS 333511]

Magic Tilt Trailers Inc., p. II-1500 [NAICS 336214]

Magid Glove & Safety Mfg L.L.C., p. I-411 [NAICS 322291]

Magna Donnelly, pp. Vol. II-964, 1749 [NAICS 33281M, 339999]

Magna Donnelly Corp., pp. Vol. I-651, 722, Vol. II-1082 [NAICS 32619M, 327215, 333314]

Magneco Metrel Inc., pp. Vol. I-681, 703 [NAICS 327112, 32712N]

Magnesium Elektron Inc., pp. Vol. I-595, 825 [NAICS 32599N, 331419]

Magnesium Products of America, pp. Vol. II-1519, 1536 [NAICS 336330, 336360]

MAGNET L.L.C., p. II-1014 [NAICS 33299N]

Magnetek Inc., pp. Vol. II-1302, 1421 [NAICS 334416, 335311]

Magneti Marelli Powertrain USA, p. II-1505 [NAICS 33631M]

Magnetic Instrumentation Inc., p. II-1342 [NAICS 334514]

Magnetic Metals Corp., p. II-1129 [NAICS 333513]

Magnetics Spang & Magnetics, p. I-686 [NAICS 327113]

Magnetix Corp., pp. Vol. II-1376, 1381 [NAICS 334612, 334613]

Magnetrol International Inc., p. II-1457 [NAICS 33593M]

Magnevolt Inc., p. II-1447 [NAICS 335912]

Magnode Corp., pp. Vol. I-811, Vol. II-1720 [NAICS 331316, 339950]

Magnolia Homes, pp. Vol. I-348, 353 [NAICS 321991, 321992]

Magnolia Manufacturing Inc., p. I-192 [NAICS 31311M]

Magnolia Steel Company Inc., pp. Vol. III-1824, 2065 [NAICS 423510, 444100]

Magnolia Trailers Inc., p. II-1491 [NAICS 336212]

Magnum Tire Corp., p. III-1766 [NAICS 423130]

Magnum Venus Products, pp. Vol. II-1033, 1184, 1207, 1342 [NAICS 333120, 333912, 333991, 334514]

Magone Marine Service Inc., p. II-1589 [NAICS 336611]

Magotteaux Inc., pp. Vol. I-762, 857 [NAICS 327991, 33152P]

MagReTech Inc., p. I-807 [NAICS 331314]

Magtrol Inc., p. II-1524 [NAICS 336340]

Mahle Inc., p. II-1505 [NAICS 33631M]

Mahoney Environmental, p. I-26 [NAICS 311225]

Mahoney's Rocky Ledge Farm, pp. Vol. III-1998, 2072 [NAICS 424930, 444220]

Maida Development Co., p. I-1292 [NAICS 334414]

Maidenform Inc., p. I-279 [NAICS 31523M]

Main Iron Works Inc., p. II-1589 [NAICS 336611]

Maine Industrial Tires, p. I-660 [NAICS 32621M]

Maine Machine Products Inc., p. II-1005 [NAICS 332995]

Maine OXY-Acetylene Supply Co., pp. Vol. III-1971, 2222 [NAICS 424690, 454312]

Maine Potato Growers Inc., pp. Vol. I-395, 415 [NAICS 32222P, 322299]

Maines Paper and Food Service, pp. Vol. III-1898, 1905, 1925 [NAICS 424110, 424130, 424410]

Mainpro Inc., p. III-1820 [NAICS 423490]

Mainship Corp., p. II-1594 [NAICS 336612]

Maintenance Warehouse/America, p. III-1843 [NAICS 423710]

Majesti Watch Company Inc., p. II-1362 [NAICS 334518]

Majestic Athletic Wear Ltd., pp. Vol. I-267, 272, 279, 285 [NAICS 31521M, 31522M, 31523M, 31529M]

Majestic Distilling Company, Inc., p. I-181 [NAICS 312140]

Majestic Steel USA, p. I-780 [NAICS 33111M]

Majestic Van Corp., p. II-1496 [NAICS 336213]

Majilite Corp., p. I-224 [NAICS 313320]

Major Automotive Companies Inc., p. III-2011 [NAICS 441110]

Major Brands-Columbia, p. III-1987 [NAICS 424820]

Major Brands Inc., p. III-1987 [NAICS 424820]

Major Custom Cable Inc., p. II-1451 [NAICS 33592M]

Major-Prime Plastics Inc., p. III-1968 [NAICS 424610]

Major Tool and Machine Inc., p. II-1580 [NAICS 336419]

Major World Wide Ltd., pp. Vol. III-1894, 2007 [NAICS 423940, 424990]

Maker's Mark Distillery Inc., p. I-181 [NAICS 312140]

Makino Inc., pp. Vol. III-1843, 1867 [NAICS 423710, 423830]

Makita U.S.A. Inc., p. III-1843 [NAICS 423710]

Makray Manufacturing Inc., p. II-1119 [NAICS 333511]

Malco Products Inc., p. II-892 [NAICS 33221P]

Malden Mills Industries Inc., pp. Vol. I-208, 213 [NAICS 313230, 31324M]

Malibu Boats West Inc., p. II-1594 [NAICS 336612]

Malish Corp., p. II-1740 [NAICS 339994]

Malley's Chocolates, pp. Vol. I-48, Vol. III-2092 [NAICS 311320, 445292]

Mallinckrodt Inc., pp. Vol. I-475, 539, Vol. II-1322, 1671 [NAICS 32513M, 325412, 334510, 339112]

Mallory and Church Corp., p. I-256 [NAICS 31511M]

Malolo Beverages & Supplies Ltd., p. I-147 [NAICS 311930]

Malt-O-Meal Company Inc., p. I-36 [NAICS 311230]

Malt Products Corp., pp. Vol. I-15, 152 [NAICS 31121M, 31194M]

Malt River Brewing Co., p. I-172 [NAICS 312120]

Maly's Inc., p. III-1875 [NAICS 423850]

Mamco Corp., pp. Vol. II-1112, 1162, 1427 [NAICS 33341N, 333612, 335312]

MAN Roland Inc., p. II-1061 [NAICS 33329N]

Management Systems Inc., p. II-1342 [NAICS 334514]

Manatee Fruit Co., p. III-1998 [NAICS 424930]

Manchester Packaging Co., p. I-603 [NAICS 326111]

Manchester Paper Recycling, p. I-363 [NAICS 322110]

Manchester Tank & Equipment, pp. Vol. II-923, 1184 [NAICS 332420, 333912]

Manchester Technologies Inc., p. III-1805 [NAICS 423430]

Manchester Tool and Die Inc., pp. Vol. II-1129, 1147 [NAICS 333513, 333516]

Manco Power Sports, p. II-1607 [NAICS 336999]

Manda Fine Meats, p. I-97 [NAICS 311615]

Mane USA, pp. Vol. I-152, 575 [NAICS 31194M, 325620]

Maner Builders Supply Co., p. III-1782 [NAICS 423310]

Mangar Industries Inc., p. I-609 [NAICS 326112]

Mangia Italiano, p. III-2094 [NAICS 445299]

Manhattan Information Systems, p. III-2058 [NAICS 443120]

Manhattan Products Inc., p. I-566 [NAICS 32561M]

Manhiem Keystone Public Auto, p. III-2015 [NAICS 441120]

Manhill Food Service, p. III-2215 [NAICS 454210]

Manischewitz Foods, p. I-110 [NAICS 31171M]

Manistique Papers Inc., p. I-368 [NAICS 32212M]

Manitou North America, pp. Vol. II-1028, 1222 [NAICS 333112, 33399N]

Manitowoc Company Inc., pp. Vol. II-1033, 1106, 1194, 1589 [NAICS 333120, 333415, 33392M, 336611]

Manke Lumber Company Inc., p. I-312 [NAICS 32111M]

Manley Meats Inc., p. III-2083 [NAICS 445210]

Manley Performance Products Inc., p. II-1505 [NAICS 33631M]

Manley Toy Direct L.L.C., p. III-1887 [NAICS 423920]

Mann Corp., p. II-1292 [NAICS 334414]

Mannatech Inc., p. I-534 [NAICS 325411]

Manning Equipment Inc., pp. Vol. III-1758, 1762 [NAICS 423110, 423120]

Mannings USA Inc., p. II-1217 [NAICS 333994]

Mannington Commercial, p. I-229 [NAICS 314110]

Mannington Mills Inc., pp. Vol. I-229, 334, 626, 651, 695 [NAICS 314110, 32191M, 326122, 32619M, 327122]

Mannix Architectural Window, p. II-1639 [NAICS 337212]

Manny's Music, p. III-2159 [NAICS 451140]

Manor Industries Inc., p. II-1524 [NAICS 336340]

Manset Marine Supply Co., p. III-2024 [NAICS 441222]

Mansfield Paper Company Inc., p. III-1905 [NAICS 424130]

Mansfield Plumbing Products, pp. Vol. I-677, Vol. II-974 [NAICS 327111, 332913]

Mansour's Inc., p. III-2171 [NAICS 452111]

Numbers following p. or pp. are page references. Roman numerals indicate volume numbers. Bracketed items indicate industries. Page references are to the starting pages of company tables.

2375

Manta-Ray Inc., p. I-453 [NAICS 324122]

Mantex Corp., p. I-631 [NAICS 326130]

Manth-Brownell Inc., p. II-952 [NAICS 332721]

Manual Woodworkers & Weavers, pp. Vol. I-234, Vol. II-1616, 1621 [NAICS 31412M, 337121, 337122]

Manuels Mexican-Am Fine Foods, p. I-133 [NAICS 311830]

Manufactured Housing Enterprises, p. I-348 [NAICS 321991]

Manufacturers' Services Ltd., pp. Vol. II-1317, 1468 [NAICS 334419, 335999]

Manufacturers Industrial Group, p. II-1536 [NAICS 336360]

Manufacturers Products Inc., p. II-1541 [NAICS 336370]

Manufacturers Resources Inc., pp. Vol. I-192, 296 [NAICS 31311M, 316110]

Manufacturers Services Central US, p. II-1282 [NAICS 334412]

Manufacturing Sciences Corp., pp. Vol. I-811, 816, 837, 852, 857 [NAICS 331316, 33131N, 33149M, 33152N, 33152P]

Manufacturing Technology Inc., p. II-1152 [NAICS 333518]

Maola Milk and Ice Cream Co., pp. Vol. I-86, 92 [NAICS 31151N, 311520]

Mapes Piano String Co., p. II-1731 [NAICS 339992]

Maple City Ice Co., p. III-1983 [NAICS 424810]

Maple Donuts Inc., p. III-2089 [NAICS 445291]

Maple Grove Farms of Vermont, p. I-57 [NAICS 311340]

Maple Island Inc., p. I-81 [NAICS 311514]

Maple Leaf Bakery Inc., p. I-116 [NAICS 31181M]

Maple Leaf Farms Inc., p. I-97 [NAICS 311615]

Maple Press Co., p. I-436 [NAICS 32312M]

Maple Systems Inc., p. II-1248 [NAICS 334113]

Maple-Vail Book Mfg Group, p. I-436 [NAICS 32312M]

Maplehurst Bakeries Inc., p. I-116 [NAICS 31181M]

Maples Industries Inc., p. I-229 [NAICS 314110]

Mar-Jac Poultry Inc., p. I-97 [NAICS 311615]

Mar-Lees L.L.C., p. III-1943 [NAICS 424460]

Mar-Mac Protective Apparel Inc., pp. Vol. I-285, 411 [NAICS 31529M, 322291]

Mar-Ner Numismatics Ltd., pp. Vol. III-1894, 2208 [NAICS 423940, 453998]

Marathon Ashland Petroleum, p. I-443 [NAICS 324110]

Marathon Coach Inc., p. II-1500 [NAICS 336214]

Marathon Company Inc., p. II-1696 [NAICS 33991M]

Marathon Mfg and Supplys, p. I-218 [NAICS 31331M]

Marathon Norco Aerospace Inc., pp. Vol. II-1442, 1447, 1512 [NAICS 335911, 335912, 33632M]

Marathon Oil Corp., pp. Vol. I-443, 448, 595 [NAICS 324110, 324121, 32599N]

Marble-Era Products Inc., p. I-677 [NAICS 327111]

Marble Granite Tiles Inc., p. III-1786 [NAICS 423320]

Marble Knits Inc., p. I-262 [NAICS 31519M]

Marc Woodworking Inc., p. II-1639 [NAICS 337212]

Marcal Paper Mills Inc., pp. Vol. I-363, 368 [NAICS 322110, 32212M]

March Furniture Mfg Inc., p. II-1616 [NAICS 337121]

March Manufacturing Inc., p. II-1189 [NAICS 333913]

Marchon Eyewear Inc., p. II-1687 [NAICS 339115]

Marco Display Specialists Inc., p. II-1720 [NAICS 339950]

Marco Industries Inc., p. I-771 [NAICS 327993]

Marco Manufacturing Inc., p. II-1248 [NAICS 334113]

Marco Sales Inc., p. III-1851 [NAICS 423730]

Marconi Networks, pp. Vol. II-1014, 1252, 1257, 1317 [NAICS 33299N, 334119, 334210, 334419]

Marden Discount Store Inc., p. III-2177 [NAICS 452910]

Marelco Power Systems Inc., p. II-1302 [NAICS 334416]

Marfo Co., p. II-1696 [NAICS 33991M]

Marglen Industries, p. I-229 [NAICS 314110]

Marian Inc., pp. Vol. I-713, Vol. II-1725 [NAICS 327212, 339991]

Mariani Nut Company Inc., p. I-137 [NAICS 31191M]

Marietta Drapery & Window, p. II-1662 [NAICS 337920]

Marimon Business Systems Inc., pp. Vol. III-1801, 1901 [NAICS 423420, 424120]

Marine Construction & Design Co., p. II-1589 [NAICS 336611]

Marine Electrical Products Inc., pp. Vol. II-1312, 1512 [NAICS 334418, 33632M]

Marine Hydraulics Intern. Inc., p. II-1589 [NAICS 336611]

Marine Industries Northwest Inc., p. II-1589 [NAICS 336611]

Marine Products Corp., p. II-1594 [NAICS 336612]

Marine Specialty Company Inc., p. III-1968 [NAICS 424610]

Marine Travelift Inc., p. II-1594 [NAICS 336612]

MarineMax Inc., pp. Vol. III-2024, 2030 [NAICS 441222, 441310]

Mariner Health Care, Inc., p. III-2100 [NAICS 446110]

Marion Plywood Corp., pp. Vol. I-324, 343, 358 [NAICS 32121N, 321920, 321999]

Marisa Christina Inc., p. I-262 [NAICS 31519M]

Marisco Ltd., p. II-1589 [NAICS 336611]

Mark IV IDS Luminator Mass, p. II-1386 [NAICS 335110]

Mark IV Industries Inc., pp. Vol. I-626, Vol. II-1222, 1551 [NAICS 326122, 33399N, 336399]

Mark Line Industries, pp. Vol. I-348, 353 [NAICS 321991, 321992]

Mark Window Products, p. II-1662 [NAICS 337920]

Market Antiques, pp. Vol. III-2047, 2194 [NAICS 442299, 453310]

Market Street Recycling L.L.C., p. I-807 [NAICS 331314]

Marketfare Foods Inc., p. I-158 [NAICS 31199M]

Markey's Audio-Visual Inc., p. III-2054 [NAICS 443112]

Markin Tubing L.P., p. I-788 [NAICS 331210]

Markland Industries Inc., p. II-1599 [NAICS 336991]

Marks and Associates Inc., p. II-1056 [NAICS 333295]

Markstein Beverage Co., pp. Vol. III-1983, 1987 [NAICS 424810, 424820]

Marley Engineered Products, pp. Vol. II-1217, 1397 [NAICS 333994, 33521M]

Marlin Firearms Company Inc., pp. Vol. II-1001, 1005 [NAICS 332994, 332995]

Marlin Industries, p. III-1875 [NAICS 423850]

Marlin Manufacturing Corp., p. II-1342 [NAICS 334514]

Marlite, pp. Vol. I-324, Vol. II-1644, 1720 [NAICS 32121N, 337215, 339950]

Marlo Furniture Company Inc., p. III-2037 [NAICS 442110]

Marquardt and Company Inc., p. III-1898 [NAICS 424110]

Marquardt Switches Inc., p. II-1432 [NAICS 335313]

Marquette Tool and Die Co., p. II-1541 [NAICS 336370]

MarquipWardUnited, pp. Vol. II-1140, 1152, 1194, 1229 [NAICS 333515, 333518, 33392M, 33399P]

Marquis Spas, p. II-1702 [NAICS 339920]

Mars Controls Co., p. II-1362 [NAICS 334518]

Mars Electronics Intl Inc., pp. Vol. II-1077, 1212 [NAICS 333313, 333993]

Mars Inc., pp. Vol. I-4, 15, 52, 92 [NAICS 311111, 31121M, 311330, 311520]

Marsco Manufacturing L.L.C., pp. Vol. I-713, 722 [NAICS 327212, 327215]

Marsh Aviation Co., pp. Vol. II-1140, 1557 [NAICS 333515, 336411]

Marsh Bellofram Corp., pp. Vol. I-670, Vol. II-1140, 1222 [NAICS 32629M, 333515, 33399N]

Marsh-McBirney Inc., p. II-1342 [NAICS 334514]

Marsh Pottery L.L.C., pp. Vol. III-2037, 2047 [NAICS 442110, 442299]

Marsh Supermarkets Inc., pp. Vol. I-68, 102, Vol. III-2076, 2183 [NAICS 31142M, 31161N, 445110, 453110]

Marshall Brass Co., pp. Vol. II-974, 1421 [NAICS 332913, 335311]

Marshall Egg Products Inc., p. I-158 [NAICS 31199M]

Marshall Lab Inc., p. II-1056 [NAICS 333295]

Marshall Manufacturing Inc., pp. Vol. I-244, Vol. II-974 [NAICS 314991, 332913]

Marshall Pottery Inc., p. I-681 [NAICS 327112]

Marshall Steel Inc., p. II-1491 [NAICS 336212]

Marshalltown Co., p. II-892 [NAICS 33221P]

Marshfield Doorsystems Inc., pp. Vol. I-319, 334, Vol. II-1639 [NAICS 321219, 32191M, 337212]

Martco Inc., p. III-1831 [NAICS 423610]

Martco L.P., pp. Vol. I-312, 324, Vol. II-939 [NAICS 32111M, 32121N, 33261M]

Martech Medical Products Inc., p. I-621 [NAICS 326121]

Martek, p. I-529 [NAICS 325320]

Martek Biosciences Corp., p. I-549 [NAICS 325414]

Martha Pullen Company Inc., pp. Vol. III-1913, 2156 [NAICS 424310, 451130]

Martha Stewart Living Omnimedia, pp. Vol. II-1714, Vol. III-1778 [NAICS 33994M, 423220]

Martin Archery Inc., p. I-306 [NAICS 31699M]

Martin Automotive Group Inc., p. III-2011 [NAICS 441110]

Martin Cadillac Company Inc., p. III-2030 [NAICS 441310]

Martin Engineering, pp. Vol. II-1077, 1367 [NAICS 333313, 334519]

Martin Gilbert Woodworking Inc., pp. Vol. II-1632, 1650 [NAICS 33712N, 33721N]

Martin Greenfield Clothiers Ltd., p. I-267 [NAICS 31521M]

Martin Midstream Partners L.P., p. III-2222 [NAICS 454312]

Martin Preferred Foods L.P., p. I-97 [NAICS 311615]

Martin's Abattoir & Wholesale, p. I-15 [NAICS 31121M]

Martin's Potato Chips Inc., p. I-137 [NAICS 31191M]

Martin Tractor Company Inc., pp. Vol. III-1859, 1863, 2065 [NAICS 423810, 423820, 444100]

Martin Wheel Company Inc., p. I-660 [NAICS 32621M]

Martin Wine's Ltd., p. III-2097 [NAICS 445310]

Martinrea Industries Inc., p. II-1524 [NAICS 336340]

Marubeni America Corp., pp. Vol. III-1824, 1905, 1913, 2007 [NAICS 423510, 424130, 424310, 424990]

Maruchan Inc., p. I-158 [NAICS 31199M]

Marus Dental International, p. II-1682 [NAICS 339114]

Marval Industries Inc., p. I-589 [NAICS 325991]

Marvel Group, p. II-1720 [NAICS 339950]

Marvel Industries, p. II-1409 [NAICS 335222]

Marvin Hayes Fish Co., p. III-1943 [NAICS 424460]

Marvin L Walker & Associates Inc., p. III-1786 [NAICS 423320]

Marvin Windows & Doors, pp. Vol. I-312, 334 [NAICS 32111M, 32191M]

Mary Kay Inc., pp. Vol. I-575, Vol. III-1909, 2211 [NAICS 325620, 424210, 454113]

Mary Maxim Inc., pp. Vol. II-1714, Vol. III-2153 [NAICS 33994M, 451120]

Maryland/Alloy Wire Belt, pp. Vol. I-816, 867 [NAICS 33131N, 332117]

Maryland & Virginia Milk, p. I-86 [NAICS 31151N]

Maryland Ceramics & Steatite Inc., p. I-776 [NAICS 327999]

Maryland Seafood Inc., p. I-110 [NAICS 31171M]

Maryland Truck Parts Inc., p. III-2030 [NAICS 441310]

Masco Corp., pp. Vol. II-974, 1014, 1644 [NAICS 332913, 33299N, 337215]

Mascon Inc., p. II-1317 [NAICS 334419]

Mascot Pecan Shelling Inc., p. I-137 [NAICS 31191M]

Masland Carpets, p. I-229 [NAICS 314110]

Mason Dental Midwest Inc., p. II-1682 [NAICS 339114]

Mason Distributors, p. III-1909 [NAICS 424210]

Mason Industries Inc., pp. Vol. I-665, Vol. II-1307 [NAICS 326220, 334417]

Mason Shoe Manufacturing Co., p. I-300 [NAICS 31621M]

Masonite International Corp., pp. Vol. I-334, 651, Vol. II-908 [NAICS 32191M, 32619M, 33232M]

Masonry Center Inc., p. III-1786 [NAICS 423320]

Masotta Variety and Deli, pp. Vol. III-2094, 2180 [NAICS 445299, 452990]

Mass Movement, p. III-1883 [NAICS 423910]

MassEnvelopePlus Co., p. III-1901 [NAICS 424120]

Masson Cheese Corp., p. I-76 [NAICS 311513]

Master Automatic Machine Inc., p. II-952 [NAICS 332721]

Master Builders Inc., pp. Vol. I-566, 752 [NAICS 32561M, 327420]

Master Chemical Corp., p. I-458 [NAICS 324191]

Master Design Co., pp. Vol. I-395, Vol. II-1397 [NAICS 32222P, 33521M]

Master Fibers Inc., p. I-363 [NAICS 322110]

Master Marine, p. II-1589 [NAICS 336611]

Master Meter Inc., p. II-1342 [NAICS 334514]

Master Process Systems Inc., p. II-1056 [NAICS 333295]

Master Tow Inc., p. II-1607 [NAICS 336999]

Masterbuilt Manufacturing Inc., p. II-1404 [NAICS 335221]

Mastercraft Boat Company Inc., pp. Vol. II-1594, 1702 [NAICS 336612, 339920]

Mastercraft Fabrics L.L.C., p. I-198 [NAICS 313210]

Mastercraft Inc., p. II-1536 [NAICS 336360]

Mastercraft Industries Inc., p. II-1611 [NAICS 337110]

Masterfood USA, p. I-52 [NAICS 311330]

Masters of Design Inc., p. II-1696 [NAICS 33991M]

Masterson Company Inc., pp. Vol. I-137, 147, 152, 158 [NAICS 31191M, 311930, 31194M, 31199M]

Mastertaste, pp. Vol. I-62, 68, 152, 158 [NAICS 31141M, 31142M, 31194M, 31199M]

Mastex Industries, p. II-1708 [NAICS 33993M]

Masune First Aid and Safety Co., p. III-1813 [NAICS 423450]

Mat NuWood L.L.C., p. I-319 [NAICS 321219]

Matagorda Ventures Inc., pp. Vol. III-1894, 2144 [NAICS 423940, 448310]

Matchless Metal Polish Inc., p. I-756 [NAICS 327910]

Matchmaster Dyeing & Finishing, p. I-218 [NAICS 31331M]

Mate Precision Tooling, pp. Vol. II-1134, 1140 [NAICS 333514, 333515]

Material Sciences Corp., pp. Vol. I-615, Vol. II-964 [NAICS 326113, 33281M]

Matheny Motor Truck Co., p. III-1758 [NAICS 423110]

Mathey Dearman Inc., p. II-1147 [NAICS 333516]

Matritech Inc., p. I-544 [NAICS 325413]

Matrix Systems Inc., pp. Vol. II-1267, 1362 [NAICS 334290, 334518]

Matrixx Initiatives Inc., pp. Vol. I-57, 534 [NAICS 311340, 325411]

Matrx, pp. Vol. II-1184, 1682 [NAICS 333912, 339114]

Matson Lumber Co., p. I-343 [NAICS 321920]

Matt Parrott and Sons Co., p. III-1901 [NAICS 424120]

Matt Stone Inc., p. I-737 [NAICS 32733M]

Matt Umanov Guitars, p. III-2159 [NAICS 451140]

Mattel Inc., pp. Vol. I-670, Vol. II-1708 [NAICS 32629M, 33993M]

Matter of Fax, p. III-2054 [NAICS 443112]

Matthews Intern. Corp. Bronze, pp. Vol. I-852, 857 [NAICS 33152N, 33152P]

Matthews International Corp., pp. Vol. I-436, 857, Vol. II-1714, 1749 [NAICS 32312M, 33152P, 33994M, 339999]

Mattoon Precision Mfg Inc., p. II-1524 [NAICS 336340]

Mattos Inc., pp. Vol. III-1762, 2004 [NAICS 423120, 424950]

Mattress Discounters Corp., p. II-1657 [NAICS 337910]

Mattson Spray Equipment, p. II-1184 [NAICS 333912]

Mattson Technology Inc., p. II-1061 [NAICS 33329N]

Maule Air Inc., p. II-1557 [NAICS 336411]

Maurer Manufacturing, p. II-1500 [NAICS 336214]

Maurey Instrument Corp., p. II-1297 [NAICS 334415]

Maurice Electrical Supply Inc., p. III-1831 [NAICS 423610]

Maurice Lacroix U S A Inc., p. III-1894 [NAICS 423940]

Maurice Sporting Goods, p. III-1883 [NAICS 423910]

Maurices Inc., pp. Vol. III-2123, 2126 [NAICS 448110, 448120]

Maus & Elam Dental Laboratories, p. II-1692 [NAICS 339116]

Mautino Distributing Company, pp. Vol. III-1905, 1987 [NAICS 424130, 424820]

Maverick Boat Company Inc., p. II-1594 [NAICS 336612]

Maverick Machinery Company Inc., p. III-2194 [NAICS 453310]

Maverick Tube Corp., pp. Vol. I-780, 788 [NAICS 33111M, 331210]

Maverik Country Stores Inc., p. III-2116 [NAICS 447110]

Max Machinery Inc., pp. Vol. II-1189, 1342 [NAICS 333913, 334514]

Maxant Inc., p. II-1357 [NAICS 334517]

Maxco Inc., pp. Vol. I-743, Vol. II-1124, 1129 [NAICS 327390, 333512, 333513]

MAXCO Supply Inc., p. I-379 [NAICS 32221M]

Maxell Corp., p. II-1381 [NAICS 334613]

Maxfield Candy Co., p. I-57 [NAICS 311340]

Maxi-Aids Inc., p. III-2113 [NAICS 446199]

Maxim Integrated Products Inc., pp. Vol. II-1272, 1287, 1317 [NAICS 334310, 334413, 334419]

Maxim Lighting International, p. III-2007 [NAICS 424990]

Maxim Manufacturing Corp., p. II-1028 [NAICS 333112]

Maxima Technologies Inc., pp. Vol. II-1327, 1432 [NAICS 334511, 335313]

Maxine Swim Group Inc., p. I-279 [NAICS 31523M]

Maxitrol Co., pp. Vol. II-1332, 1421 [NAICS 334512, 335311]

Maxon Furniture Inc., p. II-1650 [NAICS 33721N]

Maxoptix Corp., p. II-1243 [NAICS 334112]

Maxtek Components Corp., pp. Vol. I-631, Vol. II-1282 [NAICS 326130, 334412]

Maxtor Corp., p. II-1243 [NAICS 334112]

Maxwell Technologies Inc., pp. Vol. II-1292, 1297 [NAICS 334414, 334415]

MAXXAM Inc., pp. Vol. I-803, 811, 816 [NAICS 331312, 331316, 33131N]

MAXXAM Property Inc., p. I-312 [NAICS 32111M]

Maxxis Corp., p. I-660 [NAICS 32621M]

MaxYield Coop., p. III-1958 [NAICS 424510]

May and Scofield Inc., p. II-1512 [NAICS 33632M]

May Department Stores Co., pp. Vol. III-1919, 2141, 2171 [NAICS 424330, 448210, 452111]

May's Drug Stores Inc., p. III-2100 [NAICS 446110]

Mayar Silk Inc., p. III-1913 [NAICS 424310]

Mayer Pollock Steel Corp., p. I-807 [NAICS 331314]

Mayes Printing Co., p. III-2186 [NAICS 453210]

Mayfair Plastics, p. I-646 [NAICS 326160]

Maynard Steel Casting Inc., p. I-845 [NAICS 33151M]

Mayo Global Tranportation, p. III-1758 [NAICS 423110]

Mayo Knitting Mills Inc., p. I-256 [NAICS 31511M]

Mays Chemical Company Inc., p. III-1971 [NAICS 424690]

Maytag Corp., pp. Vol. II-1092, 1397, 1404, 1413 [NAICS 33331N, 33521M, 335221, 335224]

Mayville Engineering Inc., pp. Vol. II-945, 952, 964 [NAICS 332710, 332721, 33281M]

Mazak Corp., pp. Vol. II-945, 1140, 1749 [NAICS 332710, 333515, 339999]

Mazer's Discount Home Centers, pp. Vol. III-2037, 2177 [NAICS 442110, 452910]

Mazzetta Co., p. III-1943 [NAICS 424460]

MBM Corp., p. III-1867 [NAICS 423830]

M.B.M. Corp., p. III-1954 [NAICS 424490]

MBR Industries Inc., p. III-1913 [NAICS 424310]

MBS Textbook Exchange Inc., p. III-1995 [NAICS 424920]

MBTM Limited Inc., p. I-239 [NAICS 31491M]

MC Assembly and Test Inc., p. II-1312 [NAICS 334418]

Mc Court Industries, p. III-1766 [NAICS 423130]

Mc Creary Modern Inc., p. II-1616 [NAICS 337121]

Mc Ginnis Inc., pp. Vol. II-945, 1589, 1607 [NAICS 332710, 336611, 336999]

Mc Kinney Drilling Company Inc., p. II-1033 [NAICS 333120]

MC Machinery Systems Inc., pp. Vol. II-1124, 1129 [NAICS 333512, 333513]

MC Steel Inc., p. II-1009 [NAICS 332996]

McAbee Construction Inc., pp. Vol. I-343, Vol. II-923 [NAICS 321920, 332420]

McAllister Equipment Co., p. III-1859 [NAICS 423810]

McBee Supply Corp., p. II-1505 [NAICS 33631M]

MCC Inc., p. I-732 [NAICS 327320]

McCabe's Quality Foods Inc., p. III-1925 [NAICS 424410]

McCadam Cheese Company Inc., p. I-76 [NAICS 311513]

McCain Snack Foods, pp. Vol. I-62, 137 [NAICS 31141M, 31191M]

McCall Oil and Chemical Co., pp. Vol. III-1971, 1975, 1979 [NAICS 424690, 424710, 424720]

McCann Industries Inc., p. III-1859 [NAICS 423810]

McCann Plastics Inc., p. I-589 [NAICS 325991]

McCann's Engineering & Mfg Inc., p. II-1189 [NAICS 333913]

McClancy Seasoning Co., p. I-124 [NAICS 31182M]

McClatchy Co., p. I-420 [NAICS 32311M]

McClesky Mills Inc., p. III-1965 [NAICS 424590]

McConnell Cabinets Inc., p. II-1611 [NAICS 337110]

McConway Foundry Inc., p. I-845 [NAICS 33151M]

McCorkle Machine Shop, p. II-1147 [NAICS 333516]

McCormick and Company Inc., pp. Vol. I-68, 147, 626, 646 [NAICS 31142M, 311930, 326122, 326160]

McCormick Distilling Inc., p. I-181 [NAICS 312140]

McCoy Miller, p. II-1486 [NAICS 336211]

McCracken Oil and Propane Co., p. III-1975 [NAICS 424710]

McCullagh Coffee, p. I-143 [NAICS 311920]

McCullough Industries Inc., p. II-1491 [NAICS 336212]

McDaniels Sales Co., p. III-2050 [NAICS 443111]

McDATA Corp., pp. Vol. II-1252, 1347, 1457, Vol. III-1805 [NAICS 334119, 334515, 33593M, 423430]

McDermott International Inc., pp. Vol. II-899, 908, 1092, 1427 [NAICS 33231M, 33232M, 33331N, 335312]

McDonald Metal/Roofing Supply, p. III-1790 [NAICS 423330]

McDonald's Meats Inc., p. III-2083 [NAICS 445210]

McDonald Technologies Intern, p. II-1307 [NAICS 334417]

McDonough Corp., pp. Vol. I-312, 358 [NAICS 32111M, 321999]

McElroy Manufacturing Inc., p. II-1077 [NAICS 333313]

McFarland Cascade, p. I-312 [NAICS 32111M]

McFarling Foods Inc., p. I-97 [NAICS 311615]

McGard Inc., p. II-958 [NAICS 332722]

McGrath Steel Co., p. II-939 [NAICS 33261M]

McGregor Co., p. I-520 [NAICS 325312]

McGregor-Surmount Corp., pp. Vol. II-1282, 1312 [NAICS 334412, 334418]

MCI Service Parts Inc., p. III-1762 [NAICS 423120]

McIntyre Group Ltd., p. I-566 [NAICS 32561M]

McJunkin Corp., pp. Vol. III-1831, 1847, 1859, 1867, 1871 [NAICS 423610, 423720, 423810, 423830, 423840]

McKamish Inc., p. II-1009 [NAICS 332996]

McKechnie Vehicle Components, pp. Vol. II-933, 964, 1009 [NAICS 332510, 33281M, 332996]

McKee Foods Corp., pp. Vol. I-36, 116, 124 [NAICS 311230, 31181M, 31182M]

McKenzie Forest Products L.L.C., p. I-324 [NAICS 32121N]

McKenzie Sports Products Inc., p. I-641 [NAICS 326150]

McKenzie Tank Lines Inc., pp. Vol. II-923, 1491 [NAICS 332420, 336212]

McKesson HBOC Inc., pp. Vol. I-165, 539, Vol. II-1749, Vol. III-1909 [NAICS 31211M, 325412, 339999, 424210]

McLane Company Inc., p. III-1925 [NAICS 424410]

McLaughlin and Moran Inc., p. III-1983 [NAICS 424810]

McLaughlin Body Co., pp. Vol. I-879, Vol. II-1023, 1033, 1486 [NAICS 33211P, 333111, 333120, 336211]

McLaughlin Gormley King Co., p. I-493 [NAICS 32519M]

McLaughlin Research Corp., p. II-1005 [NAICS 332995]

McLendon Hardware Inc., pp. Vol. III-1843, 2065 [NAICS 423710, 444100]

McLeod Belting Company Inc., pp. Vol. I-239, 867 [NAICS 31491M, 332117]

McMaster-Carr Supply Co., p. III-2211 [NAICS 454113]

McMenamin's Pubs and Breweries, p. I-172 [NAICS 312120]

McMichael Mills, p. I-192 [NAICS 31311M]

McMichael Mills Inc., pp. Vol. I-192, 203 [NAICS 31311M, 31322M]

McMillan Electric Co., p. II-1427 [NAICS 335312]

McMinn Loudan Farmers Coop., p. III-2072 [NAICS 444220]

McNaughton Inc., p. II-886 [NAICS 33221N]

McNaughton-McKay Electric Inc., p. III-1831 [NAICS 423610]

McNeil and NRM Inc., pp. Vol. II-1051, 1129 [NAICS 333220, 333513]

McNeil Consumer Health Care, p. I-539 [NAICS 325412]

McNeil Nutritionals, p. I-147 [NAICS 311930]

McNichols Co., pp. Vol. I-641, Vol. II-945, 1009 [NAICS 326150, 332710, 332996]

MCP Industries Inc., p. I-699 [NAICS 327123]

MCPc Inc., p. III-1901 [NAICS 424120]

McQueary Brothers Drug Co., p. III-1909 [NAICS 424210]

McQueeny-Lock Co., pp. Vol. III-2050, 2065 [NAICS 443111, 444100]

McRae Industries Inc., pp. Vol. I-300, Vol. III-1801 [NAICS 31621M, 423420]

McShane Enterprises Inc., p. III-1875 [NAICS 423850]

McWane Cast Iron Pipe Co., pp. Vol. I-845, Vol. II-1009 [NAICS 33151M, 332996]

McWane Corp., pp. Vol. I-845, Vol. II-899, 980, 1009 [NAICS 33151M, 33231M, 33291N, 332996]

Mdserve Inc., p. III-2058 [NAICS 443120]

MDU Resources Group Inc., p. I-471 [NAICS 325120]

M.E. Franks Inc., p. III-1933 [NAICS 424430]

Mead Technologies Inc., p. II-1297 [NAICS 334415]

Meade Instruments Corp., p. II-1082 [NAICS 333314]

Meaden Screw Products Co., p. II-952 [NAICS 332721]

Meadowbrook Orchards Inc., p. III-2089 [NAICS 445291]

Meadows Mills Inc., p. II-1046 [NAICS 333210]

Meadville Forging Co., p. I-872 [NAICS 33211N]

MeadWestvaco Corp., pp. Vol. I-368, 374, 379, 388, 415 [NAICS 32212M, 322130, 32221M, 32222N, 322299]

Mearthane Products Corp., pp. Vol. I-621, Vol. II-1599 [NAICS 326121, 336991]

Measurement Inc., p. I-436 [NAICS 32312M]

Measurement Specialties Inc., pp. Vol. II-1229, 1337, 1367, 1437 [NAICS 33399P, 334513, 334519, 335314]

Mechanical Industries Inc., p. I-665 [NAICS 326220]

Numbers following p. or pp. are page references. Roman numerals indicate volume numbers. Bracketed items indicate industries. Page references are to the starting pages of company tables.

Mechanical Rubber Products Co., p. I-505 [NAICS 325212]

Meco-Samsonite Corp., pp. Vol. II-1404, 1632 [NAICS 335221, 33712N]

Mectrol Corp., p. I-665 [NAICS 326220]

Med-Craft Inc., p. III-1879 [NAICS 423860]

Medal Distributing Co., pp. Vol. III-1843, 1847, 1871 [NAICS 423710, 423720, 423840]

Medallion Cabinetry Inc., p. II-1611 [NAICS 337110]

Medallion Watch L.L.C., p. III-2144 [NAICS 448310]

Medart Inc. (Fenton, Missouri), pp. Vol. III-1762, 1879 [NAICS 423120, 423860]

Medax International Inc., p. III-1820 [NAICS 423490]

Medco Health Solutions Inc., pp. Vol. I-500, Vol. III-2211 [NAICS 325211, 454113]

Medco Respiratory Instruments, p. III-1813 [NAICS 423450]

Media 100 Inc., pp. Vol. II-1087, 1376, 1381 [NAICS 333315, 334612, 334613]

Media Recovery Inc., p. II-1337 [NAICS 334513]

Media Sciences International Inc., p. I-580 [NAICS 325910]

Media That Delivers, p. III-1995 [NAICS 424920]

Medical Action Industries Inc., p. II-1676 [NAICS 339113]

Medical Analysis Systems Inc., p. I-544 [NAICS 325413]

Medical Coaches Inc., p. I-348 [NAICS 321991]

Medical Data Information Services, p. III-2062 [NAICS 443130]

Medical Elastomer Development, p. I-505 [NAICS 325212]

Medicia Corp., p. I-575 [NAICS 325620]

Medicine Shop, p. III-2100 [NAICS 446110]

MEDICMASTER, p. III-1813 [NAICS 423450]

Medico Industries Inc., pp. Vol. II-997, 1005 [NAICS 332993, 332995]

Medifast Inc., p. III-2094 [NAICS 445299]

MedImmune Inc., p. I-549 [NAICS 325414]

Medina Farmers Exchange Co., p. I-4 [NAICS 311111]

Medina Paper Recycling Inc., p. I-363 [NAICS 322110]

Medline Industries Inc., pp. Vol. II-1671, 1676 [NAICS 339112, 339113]

Medrad Inc., pp. Vol. II-1322, 1671, 1676 [NAICS 334510, 339112, 339113]

Medsep Corp., p. II-1671 [NAICS 339112]

Medtronic AVE Inc., pp. Vol. II-1287, 1322, 1671, 1676 [NAICS 334413, 334510, 339112, 339113]

Medtronic Inc., pp. Vol. II-1671, 1676 [NAICS 339112, 339113]

Medtronic Physio-Control Corp., p. II-1322 [NAICS 334510]

Medtronic Sofamor Danek Inc., p. II-1676 [NAICS 339113]

Medway Plastics Corp., p. II-1119 [NAICS 333511]

Mega Manufacturing Inc., pp. Vol. II-886, 1129 [NAICS 33221N, 333513]

Megadata Corp., p. II-1248 [NAICS 334113]

Meggitt USA, pp. Vol. II-980, 1262, 1327, 1451, 1580 [NAICS 33291N, 334220, 334511, 33592M, 336419]

MEGTEC Systems Inc., p. II-1217 [NAICS 333994]

Meguiar's, p. I-566 [NAICS 32561M]

Mehdi Dilmaghani Inc., p. III-2041 [NAICS 442210]

Meherrin Agricultural & Chemical, p. III-1971 [NAICS 424690]

Mehra Tube Inc., p. II-1009 [NAICS 332996]

Meier and Frank, p. III-2171 [NAICS 452111]

Meier Supply Company Inc., p. III-1855 [NAICS 423740]

Meijer Great Lakes L.P., pp. Vol. III-2076, 2177 [NAICS 445110, 452910]

Mel Cottons Sporting Goods, p. III-2150 [NAICS 451110]

Melco Embroidery Systems, p. II-1061 [NAICS 33329N]

Mele Cos., p. I-306 [NAICS 31699M]

Melles Griot Inc., pp. Vol. II-1082, 1322 [NAICS 333314, 334510]

Melling Tool Co., pp. Vol. II-952, 1179, 1437, 1505 [NAICS 332721, 333911, 335314, 33631M]

Melody Farms Inc., pp. Vol. III-1933, 1954 [NAICS 424430, 424490]

Melster Candies Inc., pp. Vol. I-52, 57 [NAICS 311330, 311340]

Melton Motors Inc., p. III-2030 [NAICS 441310]

MEMC Electronic Materials Inc., p. II-1287 [NAICS 334413]

Memec Inc., p. II-1287 [NAICS 334413]

Memox Corp., p. III-1894 [NAICS 423940]

Memphis Communications Corp., p. III-2186 [NAICS 453210]

Memphis New Holland Inc., p. III-2072 [NAICS 444220]

Memry Corp., pp. Vol. II-952, 1735 [NAICS 332721, 339993]

Men's Wearhouse Inc., p. III-2123 [NAICS 448110]

Menard Inc., pp. Vol. III-1843, 2004, 2065 [NAICS 423710, 424950, 444100]

Menasha Corp, pp. Vol. I-374, 415 [NAICS 322130, 322299]

Mendocino Brewing Company Inc., p. I-172 [NAICS 312120]

Mendocino Sea Vegetable Co., pp. Vol. III-1943, 1995 [NAICS 424460, 424920]

Menominee Saw and Supply Inc., p. II-1046 [NAICS 333210]

Menominee Tribal Enterprises, p. I-358 [NAICS 321999]

Menomonie Farmers Union Coop., pp. Vol. III-1979, 1991, 2072 [NAICS 424720, 424910, 444220]

Mentholatum Company Inc., p. I-575 [NAICS 325620]

Mentor Corp., p. II-1676 [NAICS 339113]

Mentor Lumber and Supply Inc., p. III-1794 [NAICS 423390]

Menzner Lumber and Supply Co., p. I-358 [NAICS 321999]

Meow Mix Co., p. I-4 [NAICS 311111]

Mepaco, p. II-923 [NAICS 332420]

Mer-Made Filter Inc., p. II-923 [NAICS 332420]

Meramec Industries Inc., pp. Vol. I-300, 306 [NAICS 31621M, 31699M]

Mercer Forge Corp., p. I-872 [NAICS 33211N]

Mercer International Inc., pp. Vol. I-363, 368 [NAICS 322110, 32212M]

Mercer Landmark Inc., pp. Vol. I-9, 15, 524 [NAICS 311119, 31121M, 325314]

Merchandising Incentives Corp., p. III-1820 [NAICS 423490]

Merchants Grocery Co., p. III-1925 [NAICS 424410]

Merck and Company Inc., pp. Vol. I-539, 549, 595 [NAICS 325412, 325414, 32599N]

Mercury Air Group Inc., p. III-1979 [NAICS 424720]

Mercury BE L.L.C., pp. Vol. III-1835, 2050, 2054 [NAICS 423620, 443111, 443112]

Mercury Instruments Inc., p. II-1077 [NAICS 333313]

Mercury Lighting Products Inc., p. II-1390 [NAICS 33512M]

Mercury Manufacturing Inc., p. II-1546 [NAICS 336391]

Mercury Marine Group, p. II-1173 [NAICS 333618]

Mercury Medical, pp. Vol. III-1813, 2113 [NAICS 423450, 446199]

Mercury Plastics Inc., pp. Vol. I-621, Vol. II-1725 [NAICS 326121, 339991]

Mercury Print Productions Inc., p. II-1376 [NAICS 334612]

Mercury Refining Company Inc., p. I-825 [NAICS 331419]

Mereen-Johnson Machine Co., pp. Vol. II-1046, 1051 [NAICS 333210, 333220]

Merial Ltd., pp. Vol. I-539, 544 [NAICS 325412, 325413]

Meridian Automotive Systems, p. II-1486 [NAICS 336211]

Meridian Automotive Systems Inc., p. II-1551 [NAICS 336399]

Meridian Bioscience Inc., pp. Vol. I-544, 549 [NAICS 325413, 325414]

Meridian Jet Prop Inc., p. III-2027 [NAICS 441229]

Meridian Medical Technologies, p. II-1322 [NAICS 334510]

Meridian Products, p. II-1611 [NAICS 337110]

Merillat Industries Inc., p. II-1611 [NAICS 337110]

Merisel Inc., p. III-1805 [NAICS 423430]

Merit Building Supply Inc., p. III-1790 [NAICS 423330]

Merit Industries Inc., p. II-1708 [NAICS 33993M]

Merit Medical Systems Inc., p. II-1671 [NAICS 339112]

Merix Corp., p. II-1282 [NAICS 334412]

Merkle-Korff Industries Inc., p. II-1162 [NAICS 333612]

Merle Norman Cosmetics Inc., pp. Vol. I-575, Vol. III-1909 [NAICS 325620, 424210]

Merlin Engineering Works Inc., p. III-1798 [NAICS 423410]

Merriam-Graves Corp., pp. Vol. III-1813, 1867, 1971 [NAICS 423450, 423830, 424690]

Merrill Corp., pp. Vol. I-420, 436 [NAICS 32311M, 32312M]

Merrill Stevens Dry Dock Co., p. II-1589 [NAICS 336611]

Merrill Y Landis Ltd., p. I-239 [NAICS 31491M]

Merrimac Paper Company Inc., p. I-415 [NAICS 322299]

Merritt Equipment Co., pp. Vol. II-928, 1486, 1500 [NAICS 33243M, 336211, 336214]

Merryvale Vineyards, p. I-177 [NAICS 312130]

Mervis Industries Inc, pp. Vol. I-363, 807 [NAICS 322110, 331314]

Mervis Industries Inc., p. I-837 [NAICS 33149M]

Mervyn's, p. III-2171 [NAICS 452111]

Mesa Fully Formed Inc., p. II-1611 [NAICS 337110]

Meshberger Brothers Stone Corp., p. I-748 [NAICS 327410]

Messer Griesheim Industries Inc., pp. Vol. I-471, Vol. II-1229 [NAICS 325120, 33399P]

Messier Services America Inc., pp. Vol. II-1562, 1567 [NAICS 336412, 336413]

Messina Hof Wine Cellars Inc., p. I-177 [NAICS 312130]

Messinger Bearings Corp., p. II-988 [NAICS 332991]

Mestek Inc., pp. Vol. II-899, 908, 1101, 1106, 1112, 1194 [NAICS 33231M, 33232M, 333414, 333415, 33341N, 33392M]

Met-Al Inc., p. I-807 [NAICS 331314]

Met-Pro Corp., pp. Vol. II-1112, 1222 [NAICS 33341N, 33399N]

Metabo Corp., p. I-756 [NAICS 327910]

Metagenics Inc., p. I-534 [NAICS 325411]

Metal Equipment Co., pp. Vol. I-816, Vol. II-1417 [NAICS 33131N, 335228]

Metal-Fab Inc., p. I-699 [NAICS 327123]

Metal Finishing Supply Inc., p. I-800 [NAICS 331311]

Metal Foils L.L.C., pp. Vol. I-803, 816, 822 [NAICS 331312, 33131N, 331411]

Metal Forming and Coining Corp., pp. Vol. II-1519, 1524, 1530 [NAICS 336330, 336340, 336350]

Metal Fusion Inc., pp. Vol. II-1397, 1404 [NAICS 33521M, 335221]

Metal Impact Corp., pp. Vol. I-793, 811 [NAICS 33122M, 331316]

Metal Management Inc., pp. Vol. II-1252, Vol. III-1890 [NAICS 334119, 423930]

Metal Powder Products Inc., p. I-867 [NAICS 332117]

Metal Seal and Product Inc., p. II-952 [NAICS 332721]

Metal Spinners Inc., p. I-863 [NAICS 332114]

Metal Ware Corp., pp. Vol. II-886, 1397 [NAICS 33221N, 33521M]

Metalcraft of Mayville, pp. Vol. II-945, 964, 1749 [NAICS 332710, 33281M, 339999]

Metaldyne Corp., pp. Vol. I-837, 872, 879, Vol. II-1129 [NAICS 33149M, 33211N, 33211P, 333513]

Metalex Corp., p. I-825 [NAICS 331419]

Metalforms Inc., p. II-918 [NAICS 332410]

Metallized Carbon Corp., p. II-1463 [NAICS 335991]

Metallurg Inc., p. I-780 [NAICS 33111M]

Metalor Technologies USA, p. I-867 [NAICS 332117]

Metalor USA Refining Corp., p. I-825 [NAICS 331419]

Metals USA Inc., pp. Vol. I-780, Vol. II-908, Vol. III-1824 [NAICS 33111M, 33232M, 423510]

Metals USA, Plates & Shapes, p. III-1824 [NAICS 423510]

Metals USA, Specialty Flat Rolled, p. I-830 [NAICS 33142M]

MetalsAmerica Inc., p. I-830 [NAICS 33142M]

Metalsco Inc,, p. III-1890 [NAICS 423930]

MetalTek International Inc., pp. Vol. I-845, 857 [NAICS 33151M, 33152P]

Metalworking Lubricants Co., p. I-458 [NAICS 324191]

Metalworking Products, pp. Vol. II-1124, 1129, 1140 [NAICS 333512, 333513, 333515]

Metamora Grain, pp. Vol. I-15, 524, Vol. III-1958, 1991 [NAICS 31121M, 325314, 424510, 424910]

Metech International L.L.C., p. I-807 [NAICS 331314]

Metecno-Aluma Shield Industries, pp. Vol. I-811, 816 [NAICS 331316, 33131N]

Metem Corp., p. II-1157 [NAICS 333611]

Meteor Glass Corp., p. I-718 [NAICS 327213]

Metform L.L.C., pp. Vol. I-872, Vol. II-958 [NAICS 33211N, 332722]

Methode Electronics Inc., pp. Vol. II-1297, 1307, 1317 [NAICS 334415, 334417, 334419]

Metl-Span I Ltd., p. I-631 [NAICS 326130]

Metokote Corp., p. II-964 [NAICS 33281M]

Metra Electronics Corp., pp. Vol. II-1134, 1312, 1512 [NAICS 333514, 334418, 33632M]

Metric & Multistandard, pp. Vol. III-1843, 1871 [NAICS 423710, 423840]

Metro Alloys Inc., p. I-807 [NAICS 331314]

Metro Electric Company Inc., p. II-1696 [NAICS 33991M]

Metro Kawasaki, p. III-2021 [NAICS 441221]

Metro Machine Corp., p. II-1589 [NAICS 336611]

Metro Mark Inc., pp. Vol. II-1386, 1463 [NAICS 335110, 335991]

Metro Metals Northwest, p. III-1890 [NAICS 423930]

Metro Office Products Inc., p. III-1901 [NAICS 424120]

Metro-Optix Inc., p. II-1243 [NAICS 334112]

Metro Ready Mix Concrete Inc., p. I-732 [NAICS 327320]

Metro Recycling Company Inc., p. III-1890 [NAICS 423930]

Metro Salvage, pp. Vol. III-1758, 2015 [NAICS 423110, 441120]

Metro Systems, p. III-1774 [NAICS 423210]

Metrolina Greenhouses Inc., p. III-1998 [NAICS 424930]

Metrologic Instruments Inc., p. II-1468 [NAICS 335999]

Metromont Materials, p. I-737 [NAICS 32733M]

Metromont Prestress Co., p. I-737 [NAICS 32733M]

Metropolitan Alloys Inc., p. I-825 [NAICS 331419]

Metropolitan Mining Company, p. I-807 [NAICS 331314]

Metropolitan Poultry & Seafood, pp. Vol. III-1936, 1943 [NAICS 424440, 424460]

Metropolitan Vacuum Cleaner Inc., p. II-1397 [NAICS 33521M]

Metsch Refractories Inc., pp. Vol. I-681, 703 [NAICS 327112, 32712N]

Metso Minerals Industries Inc., p. II-1039 [NAICS 33313M]

Metters Industries Inc., pp. Vol. II-1087, 1381 [NAICS 333315, 334613]

Mettler-Toledo Inc., p. II-1229 [NAICS 33399P]

Metuchen Capacitors Inc., p. II-1292 [NAICS 334414]

Metzeler Automotive Profile, p. II-1725 [NAICS 339991]

Mexican Accent Inc., p. I-133 [NAICS 311830]

Meyer International Trucks, p. II-1173 [NAICS 333618]

Meyer's Bakeries Inc., p. I-116 [NAICS 31181M]

Meyer Sound Laboratories Inc., p. II-1272 [NAICS 334310]

Meyer Tomatoes, p. III-1950 [NAICS 424480]

Meyer Tool Inc., pp. Vol. II-945, 1567 [NAICS 332710, 336413]

MFA Inc., p. III-1991 [NAICS 424910]

MFIC Corp., p. II-1666 [NAICS 339111]

MFM Industries Inc., p. I-767 [NAICS 327992]

MFRI Inc., pp. Vol. II-1009, 1112 [NAICS 332996, 33341N]

MG Concept, p. III-1809 [NAICS 423440]

MG Novelty Company Inc., p. III-2007 [NAICS 424990]

Mg's Original Products Co., pp. Vol. III-1809, 1913 [NAICS 423440, 424310]

MG Systems and Welding Inc., p. II-1124 [NAICS 333512]

MGB Engineering Co., p. II-1051 [NAICS 333220]

MGM Apparel Inc., p. I-285 [NAICS 31529M]

MGM Jewelry Manufacturers Inc., p. II-1696 [NAICS 33991M]

MGM Transformer Co., p. II-1421 [NAICS 335311]

MGP Ingredients Inc., pp. Vol. I-15, 22, 147, 172, 181 [NAICS 31121M, 311221, 311930, 312120, 312140]

MGS Group Inc., p. II-1152 [NAICS 333518]

MGS Inc., pp. Vol. II-1491, 1500 [NAICS 336212, 336214]

MH Detrick Co., p. I-703 [NAICS 32712N]

MH Eby Inc., pp. Vol. II-1486, 1491 [NAICS 336211, 336212]

Mi-Jack Products Inc., pp. Vol. II-1033, Vol. III-1859 [NAICS 333120, 423810]

Mi Mama's Tortillas L.L.C., p. I-133 [NAICS 311830]

Mi Rancho Tortilla Factory, pp. Vol. I-15, 133 [NAICS 31121M, 311830]

Mi Rancho Tortilla Inc., p. I-133 [NAICS 311830]

Mi-T-M Corp., p. II-1184 [NAICS 333912]

Miami-Luken Inc., p. III-1909 [NAICS 424210]

Miami Systems Corp., p. I-403 [NAICS 32223M]

Miami Tape Inc., p. II-1381 [NAICS 334613]

Miami Waste Paper Company Inc., p. I-363 [NAICS 322110]

MIC Group, p. II-945 [NAICS 332710]

MIC Industries Inc., pp. Vol. II-1061, 1152 [NAICS 33329N, 333518]

Micacraft Products Inc., p. II-1277 [NAICS 334411]

Miceli Dairy Products Co., p. I-76 [NAICS 311513]

Michael Anthony Jewelers Inc., p. II-1696 [NAICS 33991M]

Michael Day Enterprises Inc., p. I-589 [NAICS 325991]

Michael Foods Inc., pp. Vol. I-68, 86, 97 [NAICS 31142M, 31151N, 311615]

Michael L Merrill and Associates, p. III-2054 [NAICS 443112]

Michael's Naturopathic Programs, p. I-534 [NAICS 325411]

Michael Simon Inc., p. I-262 [NAICS 31519M]

Michael Stuart Inc., p. I-285 [NAICS 31529M]

Michael Weinig Inc., p. II-1046 [NAICS 333210]

Michaels of Oregon Co., p. II-1001 [NAICS 332994]

Michaels Stores Inc., p. III-2153 [NAICS 451120]

Michal Golan Inc., p. III-1894 [NAICS 423940]

Michalina's, p. I-62 [NAICS 31141M]

Michele Audio Corporation, pp. Vol. II-1376, 1381 [NAICS 334612, 334613]

Michelin Americas Research, p. I-660 [NAICS 32621M]

Michelin North America Inc., p. I-660 [NAICS 32621M]

Michelman Inc., p. I-488 [NAICS 325188]

Michels and Co., pp. Vol. II-1621, 1657 [NAICS 337122, 337910]

Michiana Box and Crate Inc., p. I-343 [NAICS 321920]

Michigan Agricultural, p. III-1958 [NAICS 424510]

Michigan Automotive Compressor, pp. Vol. II-1184, 1530 [NAICS 333912, 336350]

Michigan CAT, p. III-1859 [NAICS 423810]

Michigan City Baking, pp. Vol. I-116, 124 [NAICS 31181M, 31182M]

Michigan Paperboard L.P., p. I-395 [NAICS 32222P]

Michigan Production Machining, p. II-1129 [NAICS 333513]

Michigan Roll Form Inc., p. II-1147 [NAICS 333516]

Michigan Seat Co., pp. Vol. II-1028, 1194, 1536 [NAICS 333112, 33392M, 336360]

Michigan Tube Swagers, pp. Vol. II-1621, 1632, 1650 [NAICS 337122, 33712N, 33721N]

Michigan Turkey Producers, p. I-97 [NAICS 311615]

Michigan Wheel Corp., p. I-852 [NAICS 33152N]

Mickey Truck Bodies Inc., pp. Vol. II-1486, 1491 [NAICS 336211, 336212]

Mico West, p. II-1524 [NAICS 336340]

Micro-Aire Surgical Instruments, p. II-1207 [NAICS 333991]

Micro Bio-Medics Inc., p. III-1813 [NAICS 423450]

Micro Control Co., p. II-1352 [NAICS 334516]

Micro Craft Inc., pp. Vol. II-1432, 1457, 1468 [NAICS 335313, 33593M, 335999]

Micro Dynamics Corp., p. II-1292 [NAICS 334414]

Micro-Mech Inc., p. II-1463 [NAICS 335991]

Micro Memory L.L.C., p. II-1243 [NAICS 334112]

Micro Metals Inc., p. I-867 [NAICS 332117]

Micro Motors Inc., p. II-1682 [NAICS 339114]

Micro-Ohm Corp., p. II-1297 [NAICS 334415]

Micro Power Electronics Inc., p. II-1442 [NAICS 335911]

Micro Strategies Inc., p. III-2058 [NAICS 443120]

Micro-Tronics Inc., p. II-1463 [NAICS 335991]

Micro Warehouse Inc., p. III-2211 [NAICS 454113]

Microban Products Co., p. I-549 [NAICS 325414]

Microchip Technology Inc., p. II-1287 [NAICS 334413]

Microdyne Products Co., pp. Vol. I-471, Vol. II-1157 [NAICS 325120, 333611]

Microfibres Inc., pp. Vol. I-198, 208, 224 [NAICS 313210, 313230, 313320]

Microflex Inc., p. II-1307 [NAICS 334417]

Microframe Corp., p. II-1362 [NAICS 334518]

MicroGroup Inc., p. I-788 [NAICS 331210]

Micromall USA Inc., pp. Vol. III-1922, 2058 [NAICS 424340, 443120]

Micrometl Corp., p. I-453 [NAICS 324122]

Micromold Products Inc., p. I-788 [NAICS 331210]

Micron P.C. L.L.C., pp. Vol. II-1238, 1252 [NAICS 334111, 334119]

Micron Technology Inc., pp. Vol. II-1238, 1252, 1282, 1287 [NAICS 334111, 334119, 334412, 334413]

Micronetics Inc., p. II-1292 [NAICS 334414]

Microsoft Corp., p. II-1252 [NAICS 334119]

Microtek Medical Holdings Inc., pp. Vol. I-290, 566, Vol. II-1676 [NAICS 31599M, 32561M, 339113]

Microtool and Instrument Inc., p. I-756 [NAICS 327910]

Microwave Engineering Corp., p. II-1302 [NAICS 334416]

Mictron Inc., p. II-1277 [NAICS 334411]

Mid-AM Building Supply Inc., pp. Vol. III-1782, 1794 [NAICS 423310, 423390]

Mid-America Auto Auction Inc., p. III-1758 [NAICS 423110]

Mid-America Hardwoods Inc., pp. Vol. I-324, Vol. II-1621 [NAICS 32121N, 337122]

Mid America Lining Co., p. III-1968 [NAICS 424610]

Mid America Motors Inc., p. III-2030 [NAICS 441310]

Mid American Growers, p. III-1998 [NAICS 424930]

Mid-Carolina Steel Recycling Inc., pp. Vol. I-807, Vol. III-1794 [NAICS 331314, 423390]

Mid-City Iron and Metal Corp., p. III-1890 [NAICS 423930]

Mid-Continent Aircraft Corp., p. II-1557 [NAICS 336411]

Mid-Iowa Coop., p. I-9 [NAICS 311119]

Mid-Oklahoma Cooperative Inc., p. I-524 [NAICS 325314]

Mid-South Building Supply, pp. Vol. III-1790, 1794 [NAICS 423330, 423390]

Mid-South Electronics Inc., pp. Vol. II-1077, 1312, 1397 [NAICS 333313, 334418, 33521M]

Mid-South Industries Inc., p. II-1749 [NAICS 339999]

Mid-South Manufacturing Inc., p. II-1179 [NAICS 333911]

Mid-South Wire Company Inc., p. II-1512 [NAICS 33632M]

Mid-State Chemical & Supply, p. I-756 [NAICS 327910]

Mid-States Aluminum Corp., p. I-811 [NAICS 331316]

Mid-States Supply Company Inc., p. III-1871 [NAICS 423840]

Mid-Tenn Ford Truck Sales Inc., p. III-2030 [NAICS 441310]

Mid-Way Supply Inc., pp. Vol. III-1851, 1855 [NAICS 423730, 423740]

Mid-West Fabricating Co., p. II-1519 [NAICS 336330]

Mid-West Forge Corp., pp. Vol. I-872, Vol. II-1168, 1530 [NAICS 33211N, 333613, 336350]

Mid West Products, p. II-1028 [NAICS 333112]

Mid-Wood Inc., pp. Vol. III-2072, 2177 [NAICS 444220, 452910]

Midamar Corp., p. III-1946 [NAICS 424470]

Midcoast Aviation Inc., p. II-1173 [NAICS 333618]

Midcom Inc., p. II-1302 [NAICS 334416]

Middle America Management Inc., p. III-1887 [NAICS 423920]

Middle Tennessee Natural Gas, pp. Vol. III-1835, 1847 [NAICS 423620, 423720]

Middleby Corp., pp. Vol. II-1061, 1404 [NAICS 33329N, 335221]

Middlefield Cheese, pp. Vol. I-81, Vol. III-1933, 2094 [NAICS 311514, 424430, 445299]

Middleman Iron and Metal Co., p. III-1890 [NAICS 423930]

Middleton Doll Co., p. II-1708 [NAICS 33993M]

Middletown Tube Works Inc., p. II-1463 [NAICS 335991]

Midland 66 Oil Company Inc., pp. Vol. III-1975, 2222 [NAICS 424710, 454312]

Midland Asphalt & Materials Corp., p. I-448 [NAICS 324121]

Midland Bioproducts Corp., p. I-544 [NAICS 325413]

Midland Forge, p. I-872 [NAICS 33211N]

Midland-Impact L.L.P., pp. Vol. II-1061, Vol. III-2034, 2208 [NAICS 33329N, 441320, 453998]

Midland Manufacturing Inc., p. I-646 [NAICS 326160]

Midland Medical Supply Co., p. III-1813 [NAICS 423450]

Midland Optical, p. II-1687 [NAICS 339115]

Midland Steel Products Holding, p. II-1482 [NAICS 336120]

Midlands Millroom Supply Inc., p. II-1051 [NAICS 333220]

Midmac Systems Inc., p. II-1152 [NAICS 333518]

Midmark Corp., pp. Vol. II-1184, 1671, 1682 [NAICS 333912, 339112, 339114]

Midnight Auto Recycling L.L.C., p. III-1890 [NAICS 423930]

Midor Ltd., p. I-81 [NAICS 311514]

Midstate Mills Inc., pp. Vol. I-9, 15 [NAICS 311119, 31121M]

Midvale Industries Inc., p. III-1871 [NAICS 423840]

Midway Auto Parts Inc., p. III-1770 [NAICS 423140]

Midway Ford Truck Center Inc., p. III-2011 [NAICS 441110]

Midway Games Inc., p. II-1749 [NAICS 339999]

Midway Games West Inc., p. II-1749 [NAICS 339999]

Midway Products Group Inc., pp. Vol. I-879, Vol. II-1541 [NAICS 33211P, 336370]

Midwest Acoust-A-Fiber Inc., p. I-771 [NAICS 327993]

Midwest Asphalt Corporation Plant, p. I-448 [NAICS 324121]

Midwest Auto Parts, pp. Vol. III-1762, 2030 [NAICS 423120, 441310]

Midwest Brake Bond Company, p. II-1524 [NAICS 336340]

Midwest Bus Corp., p. II-1173 [NAICS 333618]

Midwest Canvas Corp., p. I-239 [NAICS 31491M]

Midwest Chemical and Supply Inc., p. III-1875 [NAICS 423850]

Numbers following p. or pp. are page references. Roman numerals indicate volume numbers. Bracketed items indicate industries. Page references are to the starting pages of company tables.

2381

Midwest Copier Exchange Inc., p. III-2194 [NAICS 453310]

Midwest Elastomers Inc., p. I-505 [NAICS 325212]

Midwest Equipment Company Inc., p. III-1809 [NAICS 423440]

Midwest Farmers Coop., pp. Vol. I-9, 15, 524 [NAICS 311119, 31121M, 325314]

Midwest Floor Coverings, pp. Vol. III-1778, 2041 [NAICS 423220, 442210]

Midwest Fluid Power L.L.C., p. II-974 [NAICS 332913]

Midwest Index & Marketing, p. I-403 [NAICS 32223M]

Midwest Industrial Rubber Inc., pp. Vol. I-665, Vol. II-1725 [NAICS 326220, 339991]

Midwest Industrial Supply Inc., p. I-493 [NAICS 32519M]

Midwest Industries Inc., p. II-1500 [NAICS 336214]

Midwest Ink Co., p. I-580 [NAICS 325910]

Midwest Iron and Metal Inc., p. III-1890 [NAICS 423930]

Midwest Manufacturing, p. I-334 [NAICS 32191M]

Midwest Manufacturing Co., p. II-1505 [NAICS 33631M]

Midwest Products & Engineering, p. II-1129 [NAICS 333513]

Midwest Roll Forming & Mfg Inc., p. I-863 [NAICS 332114]

Midwest Scientific Inc., p. III-1820 [NAICS 423490]

Midwest Stamping Inc., pp. Vol. I-879, Vol. II-933, 964, 1486, 1749 [NAICS 33211P, 332510, 33281M, 336211, 339999]

Midwest Technologies Illinois, pp. Vol. II-1023, 1179 [NAICS 333111, 333911]

Midwest Technology Inc., p. II-1557 [NAICS 336411]

Midwest Towers Inc., p. II-918 [NAICS 332410]

Midwest Trophy Mfg Inc., pp. Vol. II-1014, 1696 [NAICS 33299N, 33991M]

Midwest Veterinary Supply Inc., pp. Vol. III-1813, 1909 [NAICS 423450, 424210]

Midwest Wrecking Co., p. III-1770 [NAICS 423140]

Mielach Co., p. II-1639 [NAICS 337212]

Mies Equipment Inc., p. III-2018 [NAICS 441210]

MIFCO, pp. Vol. III-1979, 2218 [NAICS 424720, 454311]

Mighty Distributing System, p. III-1762 [NAICS 423120]

MII Inc., pp. Vol. II-1644, 1650 [NAICS 337215, 33721N]

Mikara Corp., pp. Vol. III-1875, 1909 [NAICS 423850, 424210]

Mike Balter Mallets, p. II-1731 [NAICS 339992]

Mike Crivello's Camera Centers, pp. Vol. III-1798, 2062 [NAICS 423410, 443130]

Mike Daugherty Chevrolet Inc., p. III-2030 [NAICS 441310]

Mike Hudson Distributing Inc., pp. Vol. III-1933, 1946 [NAICS 424430, 424470]

Mike-Sells Potato Chip Co., p. I-137 [NAICS 31191M]

Mike Sorrell Trucking & Materials, p. I-727 [NAICS 327310]

Miken Companies Inc., p. I-403 [NAICS 32223M]

Mikron Infrared Inc., p. II-1332 [NAICS 334512]

Milacron Inc., pp. Vol. I-458, 756, Vol. II-1061, 1092, 1140, 1152, 1337 [NAICS 324191, 327910, 33329N, 33331N, 333515, 333518, 334513]

Milacron Resin Abrasives Inc., p. I-756 [NAICS 327910]

Milbank Manufacturing Co., p. II-1457 [NAICS 33593M]

Milco Industries Inc., pp. Vol. I-213, 279 [NAICS 31324M, 31523M]

Milcom Systems Corp., p. II-1014 [NAICS 33299N]

Miles Farm Supply L.L.C., p. I-524 [NAICS 325314]

Miles Kimball Co., p. III-2211 [NAICS 454113]

Miles Treaster and Associates, p. III-1774 [NAICS 423210]

Milestone Contractors L.P., p. I-448 [NAICS 324121]

Military Sales and Service Co., p. III-1805 [NAICS 423430]

Milk Specialties Co., pp. Vol. I-4, 9 [NAICS 311111, 311119]

Milkco Inc., pp. Vol. I-62, 86, 646 [NAICS 31141M, 31151N, 326160]

Mill Creek Lumber and Supply Co., p. III-1782 [NAICS 423310]

Mill Masters Inc., p. II-1147 [NAICS 333516]

Mill-Rose Co., pp. Vol. I-756, Vol. II-1463, 1740 [NAICS 327910, 335991, 339994]

Mill Steel Co., pp. Vol. II-945, Vol. III-1824 [NAICS 332710, 423510]

Mill Supply Corp., p. III-1871 [NAICS 423840]

Millard Lumber Inc., p. III-2065 [NAICS 444100]

Millburn Bagel Inc., p. III-2089 [NAICS 445291]

Millcraft Paper Co. Cincinnati Div., p. III-1898 [NAICS 424110]

Mille Lacs Gourmet Foods, pp. Vol. I-52, 76 [NAICS 311330, 311513]

Millennium Chemicals Inc., pp. Vol. I-147, 471, 475, 488, 500, 626 [NAICS 311930, 325120, 32513M, 325188, 325211, 326122]

Millennium Industrial Tires, p. I-660 [NAICS 32621M]

Millennium Industries Corp., p. II-1505 [NAICS 33631M]

Millennium Pharmaceuticals Inc., p. I-539 [NAICS 325412]

Millennium Rail Inc., p. II-1584 [NAICS 336510]

Miller and Company Inc., pp. Vol. I-312, 334, Vol. III-1782 [NAICS 32111M, 32191M, 423310]

Miller and Holmes Inc., pp. Vol. III-2094, 2116 [NAICS 445299, 447110]

Miller Bearing Company Inc., p. II-988 [NAICS 332991]

Miller Bearings Inc., pp. Vol. III-1831, 1871 [NAICS 423610, 423840]

Miller Container Corp., p. I-379 [NAICS 32221M]

Miller-Cooper Co., p. I-580 [NAICS 325910]

Miller Corp., p. I-81 [NAICS 311514]

Miller Curtain Company Inc., p. I-234 [NAICS 31412M]

Miller Dial Corp., p. II-1720 [NAICS 339950]

Miller Distributing Inc., pp. Vol. III-1939, 2001 [NAICS 424450, 424940]

Miller Edge Inc., p. I-229 [NAICS 314110]

Miller Electric Co., p. I-713 [NAICS 327212]

Miller Engine and Machine Co., p. II-1157 [NAICS 333611]

Miller Industrial Products Inc., p. II-1524 [NAICS 336340]

Miller Industries Inc., p. II-1486 [NAICS 336211]

Miller Metals Service Corp., p. II-945 [NAICS 332710]

Miller Oil Co., p. III-1979 [NAICS 424720]

Miller's Carpet One, p. III-2041 [NAICS 442210]

Miller's Interiors Inc., p. III-2041 [NAICS 442210]

Miller Veneers Inc., p. I-324 [NAICS 32121N]

Millersburg Tire Service Inc., p. III-1766 [NAICS 423130]

Milliken and Co., pp. Vol. I-192, 198, 229, 234, 566 [NAICS 31311M, 313210, 314110, 31412M, 32561M]

Millionair Club Charity Inc., p. III-2194 [NAICS 453310]

Millipore Corp., pp. Vol. II-1337, 1352 [NAICS 334513, 334516]

Millman Lumber Co., p. I-334 [NAICS 32191M]

Mills Manufacturing Corp., p. I-251 [NAICS 314999]

Mills Resistor Co., p. II-1297 [NAICS 334415]

Millstar Electronic Publishing, p. II-1381 [NAICS 334613]

Millstone Coffee Inc., p. I-143 [NAICS 311920]

Millwork Distributors Inc., p. III-1782 [NAICS 423310]

Milmar Food Group L.L.C., p. I-62 [NAICS 31141M]

Milnot Co., p. I-81 [NAICS 311514]

Milport Enterprises Inc., p. I-480 [NAICS 325181]

Miltons Inc., p. III-2123 [NAICS 448110]

Miltope Group Inc., p. II-1243 [NAICS 334112]

Milwaukee Gear Co., p. II-1162 [NAICS 333612]

Milwaukee Resistor Corp., p. II-1297 [NAICS 334415]

Milwaukee Stove & Furnace, p. III-1794 [NAICS 423390]

Milwhite Inc., p. I-767 [NAICS 327992]

Min-Max Machine Ltd., p. II-1557 [NAICS 336411]

Minarik Corp., p. II-1437 [NAICS 335314]

MINCO, pp. Vol. I-686, 703 [NAICS 327113, 32712N]

Minco Inc., pp. Vol. I-488, 767 [NAICS 325188, 327992]

Minco Manufacturing Inc., pp. Vol. II-945, 1087 [NAICS 332710, 333315]

Mindrum Precision Products Inc., p. I-686 [NAICS 327113]

Mine and Mill Supply Inc., p. III-1859 [NAICS 423810]

Mine Safety Appliances Co., p. II-1676 [NAICS 339113]

Miner Enterprises Inc., pp. Vol. II-1584, Vol. III-1879 [NAICS 336510, 423860]

Mineral Resources International, p. I-534 [NAICS 325411]

Minerals Technologies Inc., pp. Vol. I-475, 595, 703 [NAICS 32513M, 32599N, 32712N]

Minerva Cheese Factory Inc., pp. Vol. I-76, 81, 86 [NAICS 311513, 311514, 31151N]

Ming Fung Jewelry Corp., p. III-1894 [NAICS 423940]

Minges Bottling Group, p. III-1954 [NAICS 424490]

Mingledorffs Inc., p. III-1851 [NAICS 423730]

Mini Cassia Factory, p. I-40 [NAICS 311313]

Numbers following p. or pp. are page references. Roman numerals indicate volume numbers. Bracketed items indicate industries. Page references are to the starting pages of company tables.

2382

Mini-Systems Inc., p. II-1297 [NAICS 334415]

Miniature Precision Components, p. II-1119 [NAICS 333511]

MiniFIBERS Inc., pp. Vol. I-192, 510 [NAICS 31311M, 32522M]

Minimax Corp., p. III-2058 [NAICS 443120]

Mining Resistors Inc., p. II-1297 [NAICS 334415]

Minka Group, p. II-1397 [NAICS 33521M]

Minkin Chandler Corp., p. III-1890 [NAICS 423930]

Minn-Dak Farmers Coop., pp. Vol. I-40, 44 [NAICS 311313, 31131N]

Minn-Dak Inc., p. III-1762 [NAICS 423120]

Minn-Kota Ag Products Inc., p. III-1991 [NAICS 424910]

Minncor Industries, p. II-945 [NAICS 332710]

Minnesota Air Inc., p. III-1851 [NAICS 423730]

Minnesota Automation, p. II-1212 [NAICS 333993]

Minnesota Diversified Industries, p. II-1312 [NAICS 334418]

Minnesota Electrical Supply Co., p. III-1851 [NAICS 423730]

Minnesota Tile, p. I-762 [NAICS 327991]

Minnesota Wire and Cable Co., p. II-1451 [NAICS 33592M]

Minolta Corp, p. II-1087 [NAICS 333315]

Minor Rubber Company Inc., p. I-665 [NAICS 326220]

Minson Corp., p. II-1632 [NAICS 33712N]

Minster Farmers Co-op Exchange, p. I-15 [NAICS 31121M]

Minster Farmers Cooperative, p. III-1933 [NAICS 424430]

Minster Machine Co., pp. Vol. II-1129, 1134 [NAICS 333513, 333514]

Minton Door Co., p. II-1639 [NAICS 337212]

Minuteman International Inc., p. I-566 [NAICS 32561M]

Minuteman Trucks Inc., p. III-1758 [NAICS 423110]

Minyard Food Stores Inc., p. III-2076 [NAICS 445110]

Miracle Ear Mfg and Services Inc., p. II-1322 [NAICS 334510]

Miracle Recreation Equipment Co., p. II-1702 [NAICS 339920]

Mirage Enterprises Inc., p. II-1491 [NAICS 336212]

Miroglio Textiles U.S.A. Inc., p. III-1913 [NAICS 424310]

Miskelly Furniture, p. III-2037 [NAICS 442110]

Misonix Inc., pp. Vol. II-1342, 1352, 1666 [NAICS 334514, 334516, 339111]

Mission Clay Products Corp., pp. Vol. I-699, Vol. II-1009 [NAICS 327123, 332996]

Mission Produce Inc., p. III-1950 [NAICS 424480]

Mississippi Chemical Corp., pp. Vol. I-471, 475, 516, 520, 595 [NAICS 325120, 32513M, 325311, 325312, 32599N]

Mississippi Phosphates Corp., p. I-475 [NAICS 32513M]

Mississippi Potash Inc., p. I-516 [NAICS 325311]

Mississippi Safety Services Inc., p. III-1995 [NAICS 424920]

Mississippi Sportwear Mfg Inc., p. I-285 [NAICS 31529M]

Mississippi Tank and Mfg Co., p. II-1500 [NAICS 336214]

Missouri Baking Co., p. III-2089 [NAICS 445291]

Missouri Forge Inc., p. I-872 [NAICS 33211N]

Missouri Petroleum Products, p. III-1979 [NAICS 424720]

Missouri Pressed Metals Inc., p. I-867 [NAICS 332117]

Mitann Inc., p. I-471 [NAICS 325120]

Mitchel and Scott Machine Inc., p. II-952 [NAICS 332721]

Mitchell Hughes Co., p. II-1056 [NAICS 333295]

Mitchell Lewis and Staver, pp. Vol. II-1184, 1207 [NAICS 333912, 333991]

Mitchell Rubber Products Inc., p. III-1871 [NAICS 423840]

Mitchell's Management Corp., p. III-2135 [NAICS 448150]

Mitchellace Inc., pp. Vol. I-203, 306 [NAICS 31322M, 31699M]

MITEK Oaktron Corp., p. II-1272 [NAICS 334310]

Mitsubishi Caterpillar Forklift, p. II-1194 [NAICS 33392M]

Mitsubishi Chemical America Inc, pp. Vol. I-580, 811 [NAICS 325910, 331316]

Mitsubishi Electric Power Products, p. II-1432 [NAICS 335313]

Mitsubishi Heavy Industries, pp. Vol. II-1184, 1332 [NAICS 333912, 334512]

Mitsubishi Motors North America, p. II-1473 [NAICS 336111]

Mitsubishi Polycrystaline Silicon, p. I-767 [NAICS 327992]

Mitsui and Company USA Inc., pp. Vol. I-251, Vol. II-899, 908 [NAICS 314999, 33231M, 33232M]

Mittler Supply Inc., p. I-471 [NAICS 325120]

Mitutoyo America Corp., pp. Vol. III-1820, 1867 [NAICS 423490, 423830]

Mity Enterprises Inc., pp. Vol. II-1627, 1650 [NAICS 337127, 33721N]

Mixon Fruit Farms Inc., p. III-2087 [NAICS 445230]

Mizell Corp., p. I-453 [NAICS 324122]

Mizuno USA Inc., p. II-1702 [NAICS 339920]

MJ Metal Inc., p. I-807 [NAICS 331314]

MJ Optical Inc., pp. Vol. I-713, Vol. II-1687 [NAICS 327212, 339115]

MJJ/Brilliant Jewelers Inc., p. II-1696 [NAICS 33991N]

MK Chambers Co., p. II-952 [NAICS 332721]

MK Diamond Products Inc., p. II-1140 [NAICS 333515]

MKM Machine Tool Company, p. II-952 [NAICS 332721]

MKS Instruments Inc., pp. Vol. II-1337, 1367, 1666 [NAICS 334513, 334519, 339111]

M.L. McDonald Sales Inc., p. III-2065 [NAICS 444100]

MLO Products Inc., pp. Vol. III-1939, 1954 [NAICS 424450, 424490]

MM Reif Ltd., pp. Vol. I-203, 239 [NAICS 31322M, 31491M]

MM Systems Corp., p. I-752 [NAICS 327420]

MMC Materials Inc., pp. Vol. I-732, 743 [NAICS 327320, 327390]

MMF Industries, pp. Vol. II-1077, 1650, 1714 [NAICS 333313, 33721N, 33994M]

MML Diagnostics Packaging Inc., p. I-544 [NAICS 325413]

MMM Carpets Unlimited Inc., p. III-2041 [NAICS 442210]

MMO Music Group Inc., p. II-1376 [NAICS 334612]

MMS, A Medical Supply Co., p. III-1813 [NAICS 423450]

MNP Corp., pp. Vol. II-958, 1725 [NAICS 332722, 339991]

Mobel Inc., p. II-1657 [NAICS 337910]

Mobile Home Stuff Store Inc., p. III-2203 [NAICS 453930]

Mobile Line Communications, p. III-2054 [NAICS 443112]

Mobile Register, p. I-420 [NAICS 32311M]

Mobile Rosin Oil Company Inc., p. I-505 [NAICS 325212]

Moby Enterprises Inc., p. II-1243 [NAICS 334112]

Mocaro Industries Inc., pp. Vol. I-213, 218 [NAICS 31324M, 31331M]

Mod-Ad Agency Inc., p. III-1887 [NAICS 423920]

Modar Inc., p. I-631 [NAICS 326130]

Model Imperial Fine Fragrances, p. III-1909 [NAICS 424210]

Modern Abrasive Corp., p. I-756 [NAICS 327910]

Modern Builders Supply Inc,, pp. Vol. III-2041, 2050 [NAICS 442210, 443111]

Modern Continental Companies, p. III-2094 [NAICS 445299]

Modern Development Co., pp. Vol. I-177, Vol. III-2208 [NAICS 312130, 453998]

Modern Dispersions Inc., p. I-589 [NAICS 325991]

Modern Drop Forge Co., p. I-872 [NAICS 33211N]

Modern Equipment Company Inc., pp. Vol. II-923, 928 [NAICS 332420, 33243M]

Modern Equipment Inc, pp. Vol. I-803, Vol. II-1112, 1152, 1217 [NAICS 331312, 33341N, 333518, 333994]

Modern Home Products Corp., p. II-1404 [NAICS 335221]

Modern Inc., pp. Vol. II-892, 1140 [NAICS 33221P, 333515]

Modern Line Products Co., p. III-1867 [NAICS 423830]

Modern Plastics Inc., p. III-1968 [NAICS 424610]

Modernfold Inc., pp. Vol. I-334, Vol. II-908 [NAICS 32191M, 33232M]

Modine Manufacturing Co., pp. Vol. II-899, 1106, 1551 [NAICS 33231M, 333415, 336399]

Modineer Company Inc., pp. Vol. I-863, Vol. II-1134 [NAICS 332114, 333514]

Modtech Holdings Inc., p. I-353 [NAICS 321992]

Modular Components National Inc., p. II-1357 [NAICS 334517]

Modular Gabions, pp. Vol. I-458, 615 [NAICS 324191, 326113]

Modular Structures of PA, p. I-353 [NAICS 321992]

Modutek Corp., p. II-1056 [NAICS 333295]

Moeller Aerospace Technology, p. II-1562 [NAICS 336412]

Moeller Manufacturing Inc., pp. Vol. II-1505, 1735 [NAICS 33631M, 339993]

Moeller Products Company Inc., p. II-1505 [NAICS 33631M]

Mohawk Industries Inc., p. I-229 [NAICS 314110]

Numbers following p. or pp. are page references. Roman numerals indicate volume numbers. Bracketed items indicate industries. Page references are to the starting pages of company tables.

2383

Mohawk Northern Plastics Inc., pp. Vol. I-603, 615 [NAICS 326111, 326113]

Mohawk Paper Mills Inc., pp. Vol. I-368, 388 [NAICS 32212M, 32222N]

Mokry-Tesmer Inc., p. II-1147 [NAICS 333516]

Mold Rite Plastics Inc., p. I-436 [NAICS 32312M]

Molded Rubber and Plastic Corp., p. I-505 [NAICS 325212]

Molecular BioProducts Inc., p. II-1666 [NAICS 339111]

Molecular Devices Corp., p. II-1352 [NAICS 334516]

Molex Inc., pp. Vol. II-1307, 1457 [NAICS 334417, 33593M]

Molex Inc. Industrial Div., p. II-1307 [NAICS 334417]

Momar Inc., pp. Vol. I-458, 529 [NAICS 324191, 325320]

Mona Slide Fasteners Inc., p. II-1735 [NAICS 339993]

Monaco Coach Corp., pp. Vol. II-1473, 1496 [NAICS 336111, 336213]

Monadnock Paper Mills Inc., p. I-368 [NAICS 32212M]

Monarch Art Plastics L.L.C., pp. Vol. I-544, 631 [NAICS 325413, 326130]

Monarch Cement Co., pp. Vol. I-727, 732 [NAICS 327310, 327320]

Monarch Ceramic Tile Mfg Inc., pp. Vol. I-681, 695 [NAICS 327112, 327122]

Monarch Color Corp., p. I-580 [NAICS 325910]

Monarch Hosiery Mills Inc, p. I-256 [NAICS 31511M]

Monarch Hydraulics Inc., p. II-1222 [NAICS 33399N]

Monarch Tool and Gauge L.L.C., p. I-867 [NAICS 332117]

Monin Gourmet Flavoring, p. I-147 [NAICS 311930]

Monode Marking Products Inc., p. I-580 [NAICS 325910]

Monona Wire Corp., p. II-1312 [NAICS 334418]

MonoSol L.L.C., p. I-615 [NAICS 326113]

Monroe Tractor and Implement, pp. Vol. III-1859, 1863 [NAICS 423810, 423820]

Monroe Truck Equipment Inc., pp. Vol. II-899, 1033, 1222, 1486, Vol. III-1762 [NAICS 33231M, 333120, 33399N, 336211, 423120]

Monsanto Co., pp. Vol. I-68, 147, 488, 500, 529, 539 [NAICS 31142M, 311930, 325188, 325211, 325320, 325412]

Monson Co's Inc., p. III-1971 [NAICS 424690]

Monster Cable Products Inc., pp. Vol. II-1272, 1451 [NAICS 334310, 33592M]

Montague Co., p. II-1404 [NAICS 335221]

Montana Coffee Traders Inc., p. I-143 [NAICS 311920]

Montana Quality Foods, p. III-1946 [NAICS 424470]

Montano Cigarettes, Candy, pp. Vol. III-1939, 2001 [NAICS 424450, 424940]

Monte Vista Cooperative Inc., pp. Vol. III-2116, 2222 [NAICS 447110, 454312]

Montebello Brands Inc., p. I-181 [NAICS 312140]

Montebello Container Corp., p. I-379 [NAICS 32221M]

Montena Taranto Foods Inc., p. I-76 [NAICS 311513]

Monterey Boats/Seabring Marine, p. II-1594 [NAICS 336612]

Monterey Carpets Inc., p. I-229 [NAICS 314110]

Monterey Gourmet Foods Inc.,.p. I-124 [NAICS 31182M]

Monterey Inc., pp. Vol. I-198, 213 [NAICS 313210, 31324M]

Montgomery Manufacturing Inc., p. II-1362 [NAICS 334518]

Montgomery Truss and Panel Inc., p. I-329 [NAICS 32121P]

MONTI Inc., p. I-771 [NAICS 327993]

Montola Growers Inc., p. I-26 [NAICS 311225]

Montour Industrial Supply Inc., p. III-1847 [NAICS 423720]

Moo Time Creamery Intl, p. I-92 [NAICS 311520]

Moody Creek Produce Inc., p. III-1950 [NAICS 424480]

Moog Inc., pp. Vol. II-1222, 1317, 1327, 1437, 1468, 1562, 1567 [NAICS 33399N, 334419, 334511, 335314, 335999, 336412, 336413]

Moon Distributors Inc., pp. Vol. III-1983, 1987 [NAICS 424810, 424820]

Moon Products Inc., p. II-1714 [NAICS 33994M]

Mooney Aerospace Group Ltd., p. II-1557 [NAICS 336411]

Mooney General Paper Co., pp. Vol. III-1905, 1968 [NAICS 424130, 424610]

Moonstruck Chocolate Co., pp. Vol. I-48, 52 [NAICS 311320, 311330]

Moore Brothers Inc., p. III-2007 [NAICS 424990]

Moore Food Distributors Inc., pp. Vol. III-1929, 1946, 1950 [NAICS 424420, 424470, 424480]

Moore-Handley Inc., p. III-1843 [NAICS 423710]

Moore Iron Works Inc., p. II-1584 [NAICS 336510]

Moore Knits Inc., pp. Vol. I-213, 267 [NAICS 31324M, 31521M]

Moore Medical Corp., p. III-1813 [NAICS 423450]

Moore Response Marketing, p. II-1720 [NAICS 339950]

Moore, Tony Automotive Parts, p. III-1770 [NAICS 423140]

Moorfeed Corp., p. II-1152 [NAICS 333518]

Moosehead Manufacturing Co., p. II-1657 [NAICS 337910]

Mootsies Tootsies, pp. Vol. I-300, Vol. III-1922 [NAICS 31621M, 424340]

Mor-Ryde Service Center, p. II-1519 [NAICS 336330]

Morbark Inc., pp. Vol. II-1023, 1046, 1152 [NAICS 333111, 333210, 333518]

Morehouse Continuum, p. III-1995 [NAICS 424920]

Morgan Adhesives Co., p. I-388 [NAICS 32222N]

Morgan Advanced Materials Inc, pp. Vol. I-681, 686, Vol. II-1168, 1463, 1725 [NAICS 327112, 327113, 333613, 335991, 339991]

Morgan AMT Carbon Technology, p. II-1463 [NAICS 335991]

Morgan Construction Company, pp. Vol. II-1092, 1147, 1162, 1168, 1217 [NAICS 33331N, 333516, 333612, 333613, 333994]

Morgan Crucible Company PLC, pp. Vol. I-703, Vol. III-1839, 2047 [NAICS 32712N, 423690, 442299]

Morgan Electro Ceramics, p. I-686 [NAICS 327113]

Morgan Saw Company Inc., p. II-1046 [NAICS 333210]

Morgan Street Brewery & Tavern, p. I-172 [NAICS 312120]

Morganite Inc., pp. Vol. II-1427, 1463 [NAICS 335312, 335991]

Morgro Inc., p. I-516 [NAICS 325311]

Moria Inc., p. III-1817 [NAICS 423460]

Morin Brick Company Inc., p. I-691 [NAICS 327121]

Morley Candy Makers Inc., pp. Vol. I-52, 57 [NAICS 311330, 311340]

Morley Sales Company Inc., p. III-1943 [NAICS 424460]

Morning Sun Inc., p. I-251 [NAICS 314999]

Moroni Feed Co., p. I-9 [NAICS 311119]

Moroso Performance Products Inc., pp. Vol. II-1473, 1512 [NAICS 336111, 33632M]

Morrell Inc., pp. Vol. II-1051, 1222, 1451 [NAICS 333220, 33399N, 33592M]

Morris Bean and Co., p. II-1530 [NAICS 336350]

Morris Brothers Metals Inc., p. I-807 [NAICS 331314]

Morris Export Services, p. I-343 [NAICS 321920]

Morris Industrial Corp., p. II-1046 [NAICS 333210]

Morris Manufacturing and Sales, p. II-952 [NAICS 332721]

Morris Printing Group Inc., p. I-436 [NAICS 32312M]

Morrisette Paper Company Inc., pp. Vol. I-403, 411, 415, 609, Vol. II-1212 [NAICS 32223M, 322291, 322299, 326112, 333993]

Morrison Industries Inc., p. III-1867 [NAICS 423830]

Morrison Milling Co., p. I-15 [NAICS 31121M]

Morrow County Grain Growers, pp. Vol. III-1863, 1958 [NAICS 423820, 424510]

Morse Automotive Corp., p. II-1524 [NAICS 336340]

Morse Brothers Inc., p. I-732 [NAICS 327320]

Morton Equipment Co., p. III-2069 [NAICS 444210]

Morton Grove Pharmaceuticals Inc., p. I-575 [NAICS 325620]

Morton Industrial Group Inc., p. II-1014 [NAICS 33299N]

Morton Mfg and Trade Inc., pp. Vol. III-1774, 2047 [NAICS 423210, 442299]

Morton Pharmaceuticals Inc., pp. Vol. I-471, 534 [NAICS 325120, 325411]

Morton Salt, p. I-595 [NAICS 32599N]

Mosaic Media Inc., p. II-1376 [NAICS 334612]

Mosebach Manufacturing Inc., p. II-1297 [NAICS 334415]

Moseley Associates Inc., p. II-1262 [NAICS 334220]

Moses Lake Industries Inc., p. I-566 [NAICS 32561M]

Mosler Auto Care Center, p. II-1473 [NAICS 336111]

Mossimo Inc., pp. Vol. II-1687, Vol. III-2123 [NAICS 339115, 448110]

Mosstype Corp., p. I-580 [NAICS 325910]

Mothers Work Inc., p. III-2126 [NAICS 448120]

Motion Control Engineering Inc., p. II-1432 [NAICS 335313]

Numbers following p. or pp. are page references. Roman numerals indicate volume numbers. Bracketed items indicate industries. Page references are to the starting pages of company tables.

2384

Motion Industries Inc., pp. Vol. I-458, Vol. II-1092, 1168, 1179, Vol. III-1871 [NAICS 324191, 33331N, 333613, 333911, 423840]

Motor Castings Co., pp. Vol. I-845, Vol. II-1463 [NAICS 33151M, 335991]

Motor Power Equipment Co., pp. Vol. III-1758, 2027 [NAICS 423110, 441229]

Motor Warehouse, p. III-1770 [NAICS 423140]

Motor Works Inc., pp. Vol. II-1173, 1505, 1512 [NAICS 333618, 33631M, 33632M]

Motorcar Parts America Inc., p. II-1512 [NAICS 33632M]

Motorcycle Stuff Inc., p. III-1762 [NAICS 423120]

Motorola Broadband, pp. Vol. II-1257, 1262 [NAICS 334210, 334220]

Motorola Inc., pp. Vol. II-1238, 1252, 1257, 1262, 1267, 1287, 1317, 1347 [NAICS 334111, 334119, 334210, 334220, 334290, 334413, 334419, 334515]

Mound City Industries Inc., pp. Vol. III-1939, 2001 [NAICS 424450, 424940]

Mount Horeb Implement Inc., p. III-2069 [NAICS 444210]

Mount Pleasant Seafood Co., pp. Vol. III-1943, 2083 [NAICS 424460, 445210]

Mount Vernon Mills Inc, pp. Vol. I-198, 234 [NAICS 313210, 31412M]

Mountain High Hosiery Ltd., p. I-256 [NAICS 31511M]

Mountain States Pipe & Supply, p. III-1847 [NAICS 423720]

Mountain Tarp and Awning Inc., pp. Vol. I-239, 510 [NAICS 31491M, 32522M]

Mountain View Coop., pp. Vol. III-1958, 1991 [NAICS 424510, 424910]

Mountain View Equipment Inc., p. III-1863 [NAICS 423820]

Mountain West Printing, p. III-1995 [NAICS 424920]

Mountainland Business Systems, p. III-1901 [NAICS 424120]

Mountainland Supply Co., pp. Vol. III-1847, 1863 [NAICS 423720, 423820]

Mountaire Corp., p. I-97 [NAICS 311615]

Mountaire Farms Inc., p. I-97 [NAICS 311615]

Mounthood Beverage Co., pp. Vol. III-1954, 1983, 1987 [NAICS 424490, 424810, 424820]

Mountville Mills Inc., p. I-229 [NAICS 314110]

Movado Group Inc., p. II-1362 [NAICS 334518]

Movie Star Inc., pp. Vol. I-279, Vol. III-1919 [NAICS 31523M, 424330]

Moya Terra Aqua Inc., p. II-1157 [NAICS 333611]

Moyco Technologies Inc., p. I-756 [NAICS 327910]

Moyer and Son Inc., p. III-1991 [NAICS 424910]

Moyer Packing Company Inc., pp. Vol. I-26, 102 [NAICS 311225, 31161N]

Mozzicato Pastry & Bake Shop, p. III-2089 [NAICS 445291]

MP Biomedicals Inc., p. I-549 [NAICS 325414]

MPC Products Corp., pp. Vol. II-1222, 1272, 1297, 1427, 1437 [NAICS 33399N, 334310, 334415, 335312, 335314]

MPD Inc., pp. Vol. II-1277, 1292, 1725 [NAICS 334411, 334414, 399991]

Mpower Software Services Inc., p. III-1805 [NAICS 423430]

MQ Whiteman, p. II-1033 [NAICS 333120]

Mr. Christmas Inc., p. II-1386 [NAICS 335110]

Mr Longarm Inc., pp. Vol. I-816, Vol. II-1740 [NAICS 33131N, 339994]

MRCI Worksource, p. I-609 [NAICS 326112]

MRL Industries Inc., p. II-1056 [NAICS 333295]

Mrs Clarks Foods L.C., p. I-152 [NAICS 31194M]

Mrs Fields Famous Brands, pp. Vol. I-92, 116, 124, 137 [NAICS 311520, 31181M, 31182M, 31191M]

MS Aerospace Inc., p. II-958 [NAICS 332722]

MS Walker Inc., p. I-181 [NAICS 312140]

MSC Industrial Direct Inc., p. II-1124 [NAICS 333512]

MSE Media Solutions, p. II-1381 [NAICS 334613]

MSI Electronics Inc., p. II-1056 [NAICS 333295]

Mt Carmel Sand and Gravel Inc., p. I-732 [NAICS 327320]

Mt Rushmore Black Hills Gold, p. II-1696 [NAICS 33991M]

MTD Products Inc., pp. Vol. I-879, Vol. II-1023, 1028, 1134 [NAICS 33211P, 333111, 333112, 333514]

MTD Southwest Inc., pp. Vol. II-892, 1028, 1207 [NAICS 33221P, 333112, 333991]

MTD Technologies Inc., p. II-1541 [NAICS 336370]

MTE Hydraulics Inc., p. II-1222 [NAICS 33399N]

MTI Electronics, pp. Vol. II-1347, 1468 [NAICS 334515, 335999]

MTI Technology Corp., p. II-1243 [NAICS 334112]

MTM Technologies Inc., p. III-2058 [NAICS 443120]

MTS Inc., pp. Vol. III-2162, 2168, 2208 [NAICS 451211, 451220, 453998]

MTS Systems Corp., pp. Vol. II-1337, 1347, 1367, 1437 [NAICS 334513, 334515, 334519, 335314]

MTX Audio, pp. Vol. II-1272, 1580 [NAICS 334310, 336419]

MU Inc., p. II-1277 [NAICS 334411]

Mueller Co., p. II-980 [NAICS 33291N]

Mueller Copper Tube Products Inc., p. I-830 [NAICS 33142M]

Mueller Industries Inc., pp. Vol. I-837, Vol. II-899, 980 [NAICS 33149M, 33231M, 33291N]

Muffin Town, p. III-1929 [NAICS 424420]

Muir-Roberts Company Inc., p. III-1950 [NAICS 424480]

Mulberry Metal Products Inc., p. II-928 [NAICS 33243M]

Muller Inc., p. III-1983 [NAICS 424810]

Mullinix Packages Inc., p. I-621 [NAICS 326121]

Mullins Food Products Inc., p. I-152 [NAICS 31194M]

Multi-Color Corp., p. I-388 [NAICS 32222N]

Multi-Flow Dispensers Inc., p. II-1189 [NAICS 333913]

Multi-Media Publishing, p. II-1381 [NAICS 334613]

Multi-Plex Inc., pp. Vol. I-879, Vol. II-1541 [NAICS 33211P, 336370]

Multi Precision Detail Inc., p. I-863 [NAICS 332114]

Multi-Seal Corp., p. I-660 [NAICS 32621M]

Multibase Inc., pp. Vol. I-475, 554, 589 [NAICS 32513M, 325510, 325991]

MultiLing Corp., p. III-1805 [NAICS 423430]

Multiplex Inc., p. II-1451 [NAICS 33592M]

Multiplex Technology Inc., p. II-1421 [NAICS 335311]

Multiplier Industries Corp., p. II-1442 [NAICS 335911]

Multiquip Inc., pp. Vol. II-1033, 1092, 1179, 1229, 1427 [NAICS 333120, 33331N, 333911, 33399P, 335312]

Multiseal Inc., p. II-1077 [NAICS 333313]

Multisorb Technologies Inc., p. I-767 [NAICS 327992]

Multiview Corp., p. III-2058 [NAICS 443120]

Mulzer Crushed Stone Inc., pp. Vol. I-732, 748 [NAICS 327320, 327410]

Munchkin Bottling Inc., p. I-718 [NAICS 327213]

Muncie Aviation Co., p. III-2027 [NAICS 441229]

Muncy Corp., p. II-1541 [NAICS 336370]

Muncy Homes Inc., p. I-353 [NAICS 321992]

Munich Welding Company Inc., p. I-816 [NAICS 33131N]

Munro and Company Inc., p. I-300 [NAICS 31621M]

Munroe Inc., p. II-1147 [NAICS 333516]

MUNROKids - Perfection Div., p. I-300 [NAICS 31621M]

Murata Electronics North America, p. II-1297 [NAICS 334415]

Murata Machinery USA Machine, pp. Vol. II-886, 1129 [NAICS 33221N, 333513]

Murco Wall Products Inc., pp. Vol. I-752, Vol. II-892, 1184, Vol. III-2004 [NAICS 327420, 33221P, 333912, 424950]

Murdock Webbing Company Inc., p. I-203 [NAICS 31322M]

Murphy-Brown L.L.C., p. I-9 [NAICS 311119]

Murphy Co., p. III-1798 [NAICS 423410]

Murphy Oil Corp., pp. Vol. I-443, Vol. III-2116 [NAICS 324110, 447110]

Murphy Plywood Co., p. I-324 [NAICS 32121N]

Murray Inc., pp. Vol. II-1028, 1599 [NAICS 333112, 336991]

Murray's Bargain Center, pp. Vol. III-2030, 2144 [NAICS 441310, 448310]

Musashi Auto Parts Michigan Inc., pp. Vol. II-1162, 1168, 1505 [NAICS 333612, 333613, 33631M]

Musashi South Carolina Inc., p. II-1162 [NAICS 333612]

Muscle Shoals Minerals Inc., pp. Vol. I-767, 825 [NAICS 327992, 331419]

Musco Sports Lighting, pp. Vol. II-892, 1140, 1386, 1390, 1720 [NAICS 33221P, 333515, 335110, 33512M, 339950]

Musgrave Pencil Co., p. II-1714 [NAICS 33994M]

Music Millenium Inc., p. III-2168 [NAICS 451220]

Muster Associates Inc., p. III-1875 [NAICS 423850]

Mutual Industries Inc., p. I-251 [NAICS 314999]

Mutual Liquid Gas & Equipment, p. III-2222 [NAICS 454312]

Mutual Materials, pp. Vol. I-691, 699, 737 [NAICS 327121, 327123, 32733M]

Mutual Trading Company Inc., p. III-1875 [NAICS 423850]

Muzak L.L.C., p. II-1376 [NAICS 334612]

MWI Corp., p. II-1222 [NAICS 33399N]

MWI Southern Graphite Inc., p. II-1463 [NAICS 335991]

Myers Industries Inc., pp. Vol. I-626, 780, Vol. III-1762 [NAICS 326122, 33111M, 423120]

Numbers following p. or pp. are page references. Roman numerals indicate volume numbers. Bracketed items indicate industries. Page references are to the starting pages of company tables.

2385

Company Index

Myers Tire Supply, pp. Vol. I-500, Vol. II-1092 [NAICS 325211, 33331N]

Mykrolis Corp., p. II-1229 [NAICS 33399P]

Mylan Laboratories Inc., p. I-539 [NAICS 325412]

Mylan Technologies Inc., p. I-534 [NAICS 325411]

Myogen Inc., p. I-549 [NAICS 325414]

Myriad, p. II-1056 [NAICS 333295]

Myriad Genetics Inc., p. I-544 [NAICS 325413]

Myron Manufacturing Corp., p. II-1714 [NAICS 33994M]

Myron's Dental Laboratories Inc., p. II-1692 [NAICS 339116]

Mytex Polymers GP, p. I-589 [NAICS 325991]

N. American Oil Seeds Products, p. I-31 [NAICS 31122N]

N and K Enterprises Inc., p. I-566 [NAICS 32561M]

N and S Tractor Co., p. III-1863 [NAICS 423820]

N. Siperstein Inc., p. III-2065 [NAICS 444100]

N Wasserstrom and Sons Inc., p. II-1014 [NAICS 33299N]

Nabi Biopharmaceuticals, pp. Vol. I-544, 549 [NAICS 325413, 325414]

NAC Carbon Products Inc., p. II-1463 [NAICS 335991]

NACCO Industries Inc., pp. Vol. II-1194, 1397, 1404 [NAICS 33392M, 33521M, 335221]

Nachi Machining Technology Co., pp. Vol. II-1162, 1217 [NAICS 333612, 333994]

Nackard, Fred Wholesale Liquor, pp. Vol. III-1987, 2215 [NAICS 424820, 454210]

NACOM Corp., p. II-1512 [NAICS 33632M]

Nagakura Engineering Works Inc., p. I-872 [NAICS 33211N]

Nagel Beverage Co., p. I-165 [NAICS 31211M]

Nagel Precision Inc., p. II-1152 [NAICS 333518]

Nagele Manufacturing Inc., p. II-1639 [NAICS 337212]

Nagl Manufacturing Co., p. II-1740 [NAICS 339994]

Nagle Paving Co., p. I-743 [NAICS 327390]

Nailer Industries, pp. Vol. II-1332, 1427 [NAICS 334512, 335312]

Nailor Industries of Texas Inc., p. II-1112 [NAICS 33341N]

Nalco Holding Co., pp. Vol. I-475, 595 [NAICS 32513M, 32599N]

Nalpac Enterprises Limited Inc., p. III-1871 [NAICS 423840]

Nambe Mills Inc., pp. Vol. I-713, Vol. II-886 [NAICS 327212, 33221N]

Nancy's Specialty Foods, pp. Vol. I-62, 92 [NAICS 31141M, 311520]

Nanometrics Inc., pp. Vol. II-1082, 1347, 1367 [NAICS 333314, 334515, 334519]

Nanophase Technologies Corp., p. I-691 [NAICS 327121]

Nantucket Bake Shop Inc., p. III-2089 [NAICS 445291]

NAPA Wine Co., p. I-177 [NAICS 312130]

NAPCO Inc., p. I-631 [NAICS 326130]

NAPCO Marketing Corp., pp. Vol. III-1998, 2007 [NAICS 424930, 424990]

Naples Lumber and Supply Inc., p. I-329 [NAICS 32121P]

Narragansett Imaging, p. II-1277 [NAICS 334411]

Narrow Fabric Industries Corp., pp. Vol. I-203, 213 [NAICS 31322M, 31324M]

Nash Finch Co., pp. Vol. III-1925, 1950, 2076, 2087 [NAICS 424410, 424480, 445110, 445230]

nash_elmo Industries L.L.C., pp. Vol. II-1179, 1184 [NAICS 333911, 333912]

Nashua Corp., pp. Vol. I-368, 388, 595, Vol. II-1087, 1243, Vol. III-1901 [NAICS 32212M, 32222N, 32599N, 333315, 334112, 424120]

Nashua Homes of Idaho Inc., pp. Vol. I-348, 353 [NAICS 321991, 321992]

Nassau Lens Company Inc., p. II-1082 [NAICS 333314]

Nassau Pools Construction Inc., p. III-1883 [NAICS 423910]

NASTRA Automotive Industries, pp. Vol. II-1512, 1524 [NAICS 33632M, 336340]

NATCO Group Inc., p. II-899 [NAICS 33231M]

Natco Products Corp., p. I-229 [NAICS 314110]

Naterra International Inc., p. II-886 [NAICS 33221N]

National Acme Co., p. II-1124 [NAICS 333512]

National Auto Credit Inc., p. III-2015 [NAICS 441120]

National Bedding Co., p. II-1657 [NAICS 337910]

National Beverage Corp., pp. Vol. I-68, 165, Vol. III-1954 [NAICS 31142M, 31211M, 424490]

National Bias Fabric Co., p. I-374 [NAICS 322130]

National Biological Corp., p. II-1386 [NAICS 335110]

National Bronze Manufacturing, pp. Vol. I-830, 867 [NAICS 33142M, 332117]

National Business Furniture Inc., p. III-1774 [NAICS 423210]

National By-Products Inc., p. I-9 [NAICS 311119]

National Center For Employment, pp. Vol. I-306, 510 [NAICS 31699M, 32522M]

National Cigar Corp., p. I-188 [NAICS 31222M]

National Cinema Supply Corp., pp. Vol. III-1798, 1939 [NAICS 423410, 424450]

National Communication Services, p. III-1839 [NAICS 423690]

National Computer Inc., p. II-1248 [NAICS 334113]

National Copper and Smelting Inc., p. I-830 [NAICS 33142M]

National Crane Shaft Co., pp. Vol. I-793, 872, Vol. II-945, 1014 [NAICS 33122M, 33211N, 332710, 33299N]

National Cycle Inc., p. II-1599 [NAICS 336991]

National Data Conversion Institute, p. II-1381 [NAICS 334613]

National-Detroit Inc., p. II-1046 [NAICS 333210]

National Diagnostics Inc., p. I-544 [NAICS 325413]

National Display Systems, p. II-1248 [NAICS 334113]

National Distributing Company, pp. Vol. III-1954, 1983, 1987 [NAICS 424490, 424810, 424820]

National Diversified Sales Inc., pp. Vol. I-743, Vol. II-980, 1023, 1028 [NAICS 327390, 33291N, 333111, 333112]

National Drying Machinery Co., p. II-1666 [NAICS 339111]

National Electric Coil Inc., pp. Vol. I-771, Vol. II-1173, 1512 [NAICS 327993, 333618, 33632M]

National Electrical Carbon Inc., p. II-1463 [NAICS 335991]

National Electrical Carbon Prods, p. II-1463 [NAICS 335991]

National Envelope Corp., p. I-403 [NAICS 32223M]

National Enzyme Co., p. I-147 [NAICS 311930]

National Filter Media Corp., pp. Vol. II-1112, 1229 [NAICS 33341N, 33399P]

National Flame and Forge Inc., pp. Vol. I-872, Vol. II-1505 [NAICS 33211N, 33631M]

National Frozen Foods Corp., p. I-62 [NAICS 31141M]

National Grape Cooperative, pp. Vol. I-68, 147, 152 [NAICS 31142M, 311930, 31194M]

National Guard Products Inc., p. II-1725 [NAICS 339991]

National Home Centers Inc., p. III-2065 [NAICS 444100]

National Instruments Corp., pp. Vol. II-1252, 1352 [NAICS 334119, 334516]

National Lumber Co., p. III-2065 [NAICS 444100]

National Machinery L.L.C., pp. Vol. II-892, 1129, 1152 [NAICS 33221P, 333513, 333518]

National Magnetics Group Inc., p. I-686 [NAICS 327113]

National Manufacturing Co., p. II-933 [NAICS 332510]

National Manufacturing Corp., pp. Vol. I-879, Vol. II-928 [NAICS 33211P, 33243M]

National Mills Inc., p. I-267 [NAICS 31521M]

National Nonwovens, p. I-208 [NAICS 313230]

National O Rings, p. II-1725 [NAICS 339991]

National Oilwell Inc., p. II-1039 [NAICS 33313M]

National Packaging Co., p. II-1720 [NAICS 339950]

National Pen Corp., p. III-1901 [NAICS 424120]

National Plastics Color Inc., p. I-589 [NAICS 325991]

National Posters Inc., p. I-251 [NAICS 314999]

National Presort Inc., pp. Vol. II-1077, 1212 [NAICS 333313, 333993]

National Presto Industries Inc., p. II-1397 [NAICS 33521M]

National Print Group Inc., p. II-1720 [NAICS 339950]

National Product Co., p. I-26 [NAICS 311225]

National Recovery Systems Inc., pp. Vol. I-767, 837 [NAICS 327992, 33149M]

National RV Holdings Inc., pp. Vol. II-1496, 1500 [NAICS 336213, 336214]

National RV Inc., pp. Vol. II-1496, 1500 [NAICS 336213, 336214]

National Seating Co., p. II-1536 [NAICS 336360]

National Semiconductor Corp., p. II-1287 [NAICS 334413]

National Service Industries Inc., pp. Vol. I-403, 566, Vol. II-1390 [NAICS 32223M, 32561M, 33512M]

National Spinning Company Inc., p. I-192 [NAICS 31311M]

National Spirit Group Corp., p. I-285 [NAICS 31529M]

National-Standard Co., pp. Vol. I-793, Vol. II-939 [NAICS 33122M, 33261M]

National Starch & Chemical Co, p. I-560 [NAICS 325520]

National Steel and Shipbuilding, p. II-1589 [NAICS 336611]

Numbers following p. or pp. are page references. Roman numerals indicate volume numbers. Bracketed items indicate industries. Page references are to the starting pages of company tables.

2386

National Steel Corp., pp. Vol. I-780, 793 [NAICS 33111M, 33122M]

National Store Fixtures, p. II-1644 [NAICS 337215]

National Tanning Supply, p. III-1875 [NAICS 423850]

National Time Recording, p. II-1362 [NAICS 334518]

National Tobacco Company L.P., pp. Vol. I-188, 415 [NAICS 31222M, 322299]

National Tool and Mfg Co., p. II-1119 [NAICS 333511]

National Tube Supply Co., pp. Vol. I-788, Vol. II-1009 [NAICS 331210, 332996]

National Vision Inc., p. III-2107 [NAICS 446130]

National Vitamin Company Inc., pp. Vol. I-534, 767 [NAICS 325411, 327992]

National Welders Supply Inc., pp. Vol. I-471, Vol. II-1229 [NAICS 325120, 33399P]

National Wood Products Inc., p. III-1782 [NAICS 423310]

Nationwide Homes Inc., p. I-353 [NAICS 321992]

Nationwide Vision Center, p. II-1687 [NAICS 339115]

Natl Oilwell Houston Scientific, pp. Vol. II-1317, 1347 [NAICS 334419, 334515]

Natrol Inc., p. III-1909 [NAICS 424210]

Natura Pet Products Inc., p. I-4 [NAICS 311111]

Natural Alternatives Intern. Inc., p. I-534 [NAICS 325411]

Natural Balance Inc., p. I-534 [NAICS 325411]

Natural Choice, pp. Vol. III-1875, 2215 [NAICS 423850, 454210]

Natural Energy Unlimited Inc., p. III-1950 [NAICS 424480]

Natural Fertilizer of America Inc., p. I-516 [NAICS 325311]

Natural Meat Specialties, p. III-1946 [NAICS 424470]

Naturally Fresh Company Inc., p. I-152 [NAICS 31194M]

Nature's Sunshine Products Inc., pp. Vol. I-534, 575 [NAICS 325411, 325620]

Nautica Enterprises Inc., pp. Vol. III-1916, 2123 [NAICS 424320, 448110]

Nautica International Inc., p. III-1916 [NAICS 424320]

Nautilus Group Inc., p. II-1702 [NAICS 339920]

Navarre Corp., p. III-1805 [NAICS 423430]

Navarro Discount Pharmacies, p. III-2100 [NAICS 446110]

Navarro Vineyards, pp. Vol. I-177, Vol. III-2097 [NAICS 312130, 445310]

Navatek Ltd., pp. Vol. II-1589, Vol. III-2024 [NAICS 336611, 441222]

Navistar International Corp., pp. Vol. II-1173, 1486 [NAICS 333618, 336211]

Naylor Pipe Co., p. I-788 [NAICS 331210]

NAZDAR Chicago Mfg Div., p. I-580 [NAICS 325910]

NAZDAR Co., p. I-580 [NAICS 325910]

NB Handy Company Inc., p. III-1790 [NAICS 423330]

NBI Inc., pp. Vol. I-713, 718 [NAICS 327212, 327213]

NBTY Inc., pp. Vol. I-534, 539 [NAICS 325411, 325412]

NC Filtration Corp., p. III-1851 [NAICS 423730]

NC Industries Inc., p. II-1140 [NAICS 333515]

NCH Corp., pp. Vol. I-566, Vol. II-974, 1229, 1687 [NAICS 32561M, 332913, 33399P, 339115]

NCI Building Systems Inc., p. II-899 [NAICS 33231M]

NCP Coatings Inc., p. I-554 [NAICS 325510]

NCP Solutions, p. I-436 [NAICS 32312M]

NCR Corp., pp. Vol. II-1077, 1238, 1243 [NAICS 333313, 334111, 334112]

NCS HealthCare Inc., p. III-2100 [NAICS 446110]

NCS Technologies Inc., p. II-1238 [NAICS 334111]

ND Industries Inc., pp. Vol. I-554, 560, Vol. II-958 [NAICS 325510, 325520, 332722]

ND Labs Inc., p. I-31 [NAICS 31122N]

NE Penna Salvage Company Inc., p. III-2015 [NAICS 441120]

Neapco Inc., pp. Vol. II-1530, 1551 [NAICS 336350, 336399]

Neatsfoot Oil Refineries Corp., p. I-26 [NAICS 311225]

Nebraska Beef Ltd., p. I-102 [NAICS 31161N]

Nebraska Boiler Co., p. II-918 [NAICS 332410]

Nebraska Book Company Inc., pp. Vol. III-1901, 1995, 2186, 2194 [NAICS 424120, 424920, 453210, 453310]

Nebraska Furniture Mart Inc., pp. Vol. III-2037, 2047, 2050, 2054, 2058 [NAICS 442110, 442299, 443111, 443112, 443120]

Nebraska Machinery Co., p. III-1859 [NAICS 423810]

NEC Business Communication, p. III-1839 [NAICS 423690]

NEC Electronics Inc., p. II-1287 [NAICS 334413]

NECCO Stark, pp. Vol. I-52, 57 [NAICS 311330, 311340]

Neeltran Inc., p. II-1302 [NAICS 334416]

Neenah Foundry Co., pp. Vol. I-845, Vol. II-964, 1014 [NAICS 33151M, 33281M, 33299N]

Neese Industries Inc., p. I-267 [NAICS 31521M]

Neff Motivation Inc., p. I-285 [NAICS 31529M]

Nehring Electrical Works Co., pp. Vol. I-816, 830, Vol. II-1451 [NAICS 33131N, 33142M, 33592M]

Neighborhood Manufacturing Co., pp. Vol. II-974, 1147 [NAICS 332913, 333516]

Neill Aircraft Co., p. II-1557 [NAICS 336411]

Neiman Marcus Group Inc., pp. Vol. III-2123, 2126, 2171 [NAICS 448110, 448120, 452111]

Nektar Therapeutics, p. II-1671 [NAICS 339112]

Nello L Teer Co., p. I-448 [NAICS 324121]

Nelson Irrigation Corp., p. II-1023 [NAICS 333111]

Nelson-Jameson Inc., pp. Vol. III-1863, 2007 [NAICS 423820, 424990]

Nelson Machine and Grinder Inc., p. II-1046 [NAICS 333210]

Nelson Paint of Michigan, p. II-1714 [NAICS 33994M]

Nelson Stud Welding Inc., p. II-958 [NAICS 332722]

Nemco Electronics Corp., p. II-1292 [NAICS 334414]

Nemschoff Chairs Inc., pp. Vol. II-1627, 1650 [NAICS 337127, 33721N]

NENSCO, p. II-1714 [NAICS 33994M]

Neogen Corp., p. I-544 [NAICS 325413]

Neon Graphics, p. II-1277 [NAICS 334411]

NeoResins Inc., p. I-500 [NAICS 325211]

NeoRx Corp., pp. Vol. I-544, 549 [NAICS 325413, 325414]

Neose Technologies Inc., p. I-44 [NAICS 31131N]

Neosource Manufacturing Inc., p. II-1639 [NAICS 337212]

Neoware Systems Inc., p. II-1248 [NAICS 334113]

NEPTCO Inc., pp. Vol. I-621, Vol. II-1082 [NAICS 326121, 333314]

Neptune Foods Inc., p. I-110 [NAICS 31171M]

Neptune Liquid Measurement Div., p. II-1342 [NAICS 334514]

Nerl Diagnostics Corp., p. I-534 [NAICS 325411]

Nesco Manufacturing Inc., pp. Vol. I-636, 762 [NAICS 326140, 327991]

Nestle USA - Beverages Division, pp. Vol. I-48, 52, 68, 143, 147 [NAICS 311320, 311330, 31142M, 311920, 311930]

Nestle USA Inc, p. I-62 [NAICS 31141M]

Net Products Solutions, p. III-1894 [NAICS 423940]

Netafim Irrigation Inc., p. II-1023 [NAICS 333111]

Netcom Inc., p. II-1302 [NAICS 334416]

Netopia Inc., p. II-1257 [NAICS 334210]

NetScreen Technologies Inc., p. II-1252 [NAICS 334119]

Network Appliance Inc., p. II-1243 [NAICS 334112]

Network Music L.L.C., p. II-1179 [NAICS 333911]

Networks Electronic Corp., pp. Vol. II-988, 1005, 1124, 1168, 1222 [NAICS 332991, 332995, 333512, 333613, 33399N]

Networks Plus Technology Group, p. III-1805 [NAICS 423430]

Neurocrine Biosciences Inc., p. I-549 [NAICS 325414]

Neuse Install, p. III-1790 [NAICS 423330]

Neuville Industries, p. I-256 [NAICS 31511M]

Neuville Industries Inc., p. I-256 [NAICS 31511M]

Nevada Beverage Co., p. III-1983 [NAICS 424810]

Nevamar Co. L.L.C., p. I-631 [NAICS 326130]

New Age Industrial Corp., p. I-803 [NAICS 331312]

New Balance Athletic Shoe Inc., pp. Vol. I-272, 290, 300 [NAICS 31522M, 31599M, 31621M]

New Belgium Brewing Inc., p. I-172 [NAICS 312120]

New Brunswick Scientific Inc., pp. Vol. II-1322, 1352, 1666 [NAICS 334510, 334516, 339111]

New Buffalo Shirt Factory Inc., pp. Vol. I-218, 251 [NAICS 31331M, 314999]

New Can Company Inc., pp. Vol. I-879, Vol. II-1009 [NAICS 33211P, 332996]

New Castle Refractories Inc., p. I-703 [NAICS 32712N]

New Centennial Inc., p. II-1491 [NAICS 336212]

NEW Cooperative Inc., pp. Vol. I-9, 15 [NAICS 311119, 31121M]

New Dimensions Precision, p. II-1222 [NAICS 33399N]

New Directions Slatwall, p. II-1644 [NAICS 337215]

New Energy Corp., pp. Vol. I-471, 493 [NAICS 325120, 32519M]

New England Business Service Inc., p. I-420 [NAICS 32311M]

Numbers following p. or pp. are page references. Roman numerals indicate volume numbers. Bracketed items indicate industries. Page references are to the starting pages of company tables.

2387

New England Confectionery Co., pp. Vol. I-48, 52 [NAICS 311320, 311330]

New England Controls Inc., p. III-1871 [NAICS 423840]

New England Homes Inc., p. I-353 [NAICS 321992]

New England Pottery Co., pp. Vol. III-1998, 2007 [NAICS 424930, 424990]

New England Recycling Inc., p. III-1890 [NAICS 423930]

New England Ropes Inc., p. I-244 [NAICS 314991]

New England Tea and Coffee Inc., p. I-143 [NAICS 311920]

New England Wire Technologies, pp. Vol. I-830, Vol. II-939, 1451, 1457 [NAICS 33142M, 33261M, 33592M, 33593M]

New England Wooden Ware Corp., p. II-1720 [NAICS 339950]

New Enterprise Stone & Lime Inc., p. I-732 [NAICS 327320]

New Era Building Systems Inc., p. I-353 [NAICS 321992]

New Era Cap Company Inc., pp. Vol. I-290, Vol. II-1702 [NAICS 31599M, 339920]

New Era Optical Company Inc., p. III-1817 [NAICS 423460]

New Focus Inc., p. II-1082 [NAICS 333314]

New Generations Furniture Inc., p. II-1616 [NAICS 337121]

New Hampshire Ball Bearings Inc, pp. Vol. I-857, Vol. II-945 [NAICS 33152P, 332710]

New Hampshire Ball Bearings Inc., p. II-988 [NAICS 332991]

New Hankey Company Inc., p. III-1883 [NAICS 423910]

New Hermes Inc., pp. Vol. III-1883, 1901 [NAICS 423910, 424120]

New Holland Concrete, p. I-737 [NAICS 32733M]

New Horizon FS Inc., p. III-1991 [NAICS 424910]

New Horizons Supply Cooperative, p. III-2218 [NAICS 454311]

New Jersey Porcelain Lenape, p. I-677 [NAICS 327111]

New Market Poultry Products Inc., p. I-97 [NAICS 311615]

New Mather Metals Inc., pp. Vol. I-872, Vol. II-939, 1519 [NAICS 33211N, 33261M, 336330]

New Mexico Metal Systems L.L.C., p. I-699 [NAICS 327123]

New NGC Inc., pp. Vol. I-319, 368, 388, 752 [NAICS 321219, 32212M, 32222N, 327420]

New Process Steel L.P., pp. Vol. I-436, Vol. II-945, Vol. III-1824 [NAICS 32312M, 332710, 423510]

New Products International Inc., p. II-1362 [NAICS 334518]

New River Industries Inc., pp. Vol. I-198, 251 [NAICS 313210, 314999]

New Riverside Ochre Inc., p. I-767 [NAICS 327992]

New South Companies Inc., pp. Vol. I-312, 334, 358 [NAICS 32111M, 32191M, 321999]

New South Lumber Incorporated, p. I-358 [NAICS 321999]

New Southern of Rocky Mount Inc., pp. I-26, 31 [NAICS 311225, 31122N]

New Tech Machinery Corp., p. II-1147 [NAICS 333516]

New Vision Coop., pp. Vol. III-1958, 1991 [NAICS 424510, 424910]

New WPI L.L.C., p. III-1774 [NAICS 423210]

New York Air Brake Corp., pp. Vol. II-1524, 1584 [NAICS 336340, 336510]

New York Blower Co., pp. Vol. II-1112, 1217 [NAICS 33341N, 333994]

New York Carpets, p. III-2041 [NAICS 442210]

New York Wire Company Inc., pp. Vol. I-816, 830, Vol. II-939 [NAICS 33131N, 33142M, 33261M]

NewAge Industries Inc., p. I-631 [NAICS 326130]

Newark Farmers Grain Co., p. III-1975 [NAICS 424710]

Newark Pacific Paperboard Corp., p. I-374 [NAICS 322130]

Neways Inc., p. I-534 [NAICS 325411]

Newburgh Dye and Printing Inc., p. I-218 [NAICS 31331M]

Newco Fibre Co., p. I-510 [NAICS 32522M]

Newco Inc., p. I-631 [NAICS 326130]

Newell Paper Co., pp. Vol. III-1898, 1905 [NAICS 424110, 424130]

Newell Porcelain Company Inc., p. I-686 [NAICS 327113]

Newell Recycling of San Antonio, p. I-807 [NAICS 331314]

Newell Rubbermaid Inc., pp. Vol. I-234, 713, Vol. II-933, 1229, 1662 [NAICS 31412M, 327212, 332510, 33399P, 337920]

Newhall Labs, p. I-534 [NAICS 325411]

Newly Weds Foods Inc., pp. Vol. I-92, 116, 152, 158 [NAICS 311520, 31181M, 31194M, 31199M]

Newman and Company Inc., pp. Vol. I-374, 395, 403, 415 [NAICS 322130, 32222P, 32223M, 322299]

Newman Auto Recyclers Inc., pp. Vol. III-1770, 1890 [NAICS 423140, 423930]

Newman Machine Company Inc., p. II-1046 [NAICS 333210]

Newman's Inc., p. III-1871 [NAICS 423840]

Newman Technology Inc., p. II-933 [NAICS 332510]

Newmar Corp., pp. Vol. II-1496, 1500 [NAICS 336213, 336214]

Newmark Rug Co., p. I-229 [NAICS 314110]

Newport Adhesives & Composites, p. I-560 [NAICS 325520]

Newport Corp., pp. Vol. II-1082, 1322, 1367, 1666 [NAICS 333314, 334510, 334519, 339111]

Newport Layton Home Fashions, p. I-234 [NAICS 31412M]

Newport News Shipbuilding Inc., p. II-1589 [NAICS 336611]

News and Record Inc., pp. Vol. I-420, 436 [NAICS 32311M, 32312M]

News Printing Co., p. I-436 [NAICS 32312M]

Newsom Oil Company Inc., p. III-2116 [NAICS 447110]

NEX, p. I-615 [NAICS 326113]

Nexergy Inc., pp. Vol. II-1307, 1312 [NAICS 334417, 334418]

Nexfor Fraser Papers, pp. Vol. I-363, 368 [NAICS 322110, 32212M]

Nexray Inc., p. II-1357 [NAICS 334517]

Next Day Blinds Corp., p. II-1662 [NAICS 337920]

Next Day Gormet & Superior, pp. Vol. III-1809, 1855 [NAICS 423440, 423740]

Next Specialty Resins Inc., p. I-589 [NAICS 325991]

Nextime Inc., p. III-1801 [NAICS 423420]

Nexus Plastics Inc., pp. Vol. I-603, 609, 621 [NAICS 326111, 326112, 326121]

NGK Ceramics USA Inc., p. I-686 [NAICS 327113]

NGK-Locke Inc., pp. Vol. II-1061, 1092, 1457 [NAICS 33329N, 33331N, 33593M]

NGK Metals Corp., pp. Vol. I-822, 825, 830 [NAICS 331411, 331419, 33142M]

NGK Spark Plugs (U.S.A.) Inc., pp. Vol. II-1140, 1512 [NAICS 333515, 33632M]

Niagara Blower Co., pp. Vol. II-918, 1397 [NAICS 332410, 33521M]

Niagara Corp., p. I-788 [NAICS 331210]

NIBCO Inc., pp. Vol. I-626, Vol. II-974, 980, 1009 [NAICS 326122, 332913, 33291N, 332996]

Nice Ball Bearings Inc., p. II-988 [NAICS 332991]

Nice Pak Products Inc., p. I-411 [NAICS 322291]

Nichirin Coupler TEC USA, p. III-1762 [NAICS 423120]

Nicholas Plastics Inc., p. I-621 [NAICS 326121]

Nichols and Stone Company Inc., pp. Vol. II-1632, 1657 [NAICS 33712N, 337910]

Nichols Tillage Tools Inc., p. I-872 [NAICS 33211N]

Nicholson Manufacturing Inc., pp. Vol. II-1023, 1046 [NAICS 333111, 333210]

Nick Sciabica and Sons, p. I-26 [NAICS 311225]

Nickerson Lumber Co., p. III-2065 [NAICS 444100]

Nidec America Corp, pp. Vol. II-1112, 1427, 1468 [NAICS 33341N, 335312, 335999]

NietoCom, p. III-2058 [NAICS 443120]

Nifco L.L.C., p. I-626 [NAICS 326122]

Nifty Products Inc., p. I-229 [NAICS 314110]

Night Hawk Frozen Foods Inc., p. I-62 [NAICS 31141M]

Nightscaping, p. II-1421 [NAICS 335311]

Nike Inc., pp. Vol. I-272, 290, 300, Vol. III-2141 [NAICS 31522M, 31599M, 31621M, 448210]

Nikko America Inc., p. III-1887 [NAICS 423920]

Niles Audio Corp., p. II-1272 [NAICS 334310]

Nilpeter, p. II-1212 [NAICS 333993]

Nimco Corp., p. I-374 [NAICS 322130]

Nina Plastics Inc., p. I-603 [NAICS 326111]

Ninja Jump Inc., p. III-2190 [NAICS 453220]

Nintendo of America Inc., p. II-1708 [NAICS 33993M]

Ninth Street Flowers Ltd., p. III-2072 [NAICS 444220]

Nirve Sports Ltd., p. III-2138 [NAICS 448190]

Nissan Forklift Corp, p. II-1194 [NAICS 33392M]

Nissho Iwai American Corp., pp. Vol. III-1762, 1871, 1971 [NAICS 423120, 423840, 424690]

Nissin Brake Ohio Inc., pp. Vol. I-852, Vol. II-945, 1524 [NAICS 33152N, 332710, 336340]

Nitches Inc., p. III-1919 [NAICS 424330]

Nitrogen Inc., p. I-529 [NAICS 325320]

NitroSteel Div., p. I-788 [NAICS 331210]

Nitterhouse Concrete Products Inc., p. I-737 [NAICS 32733M]

Niven Marketing Group, p. II-1720 [NAICS 339950]

N.K.S. Distributors Inc., pp. Vol. III-1983, 1987 [NAICS 424810, 424820]

NL Industries Inc., p. I-475 [NAICS 32513M]

NLX Corp., p. II-1468 [NAICS 335999]

NMC Group Inc., pp. Vol. I-510, Vol. III-1968 [NAICS 32522M, 424610]

NMS Communications Corp., p. II-1257 [NAICS 334210]

NN Inc., pp. Vol. I-780, Vol. II-988 [NAICS 33111M, 332991]

Noah Technologies Corp., p. I-493 [NAICS 32519M]

Noamco Inc., pp. Vol. I-621, 636 [NAICS 326121, 326140]

Nobel/Sysco Food Services Co., pp. Vol. III-1809, 1925 [NAICS 423440, 424410]

Nobility Homes Inc., p. I-348 [NAICS 321991]

Noble Americas Corp., pp. Vol. III-1828, 1954, 1991 [NAICS 423520, 424490, 424910]

Noble Gift Packaging, pp. Vol. III-1809, 1905 [NAICS 423440, 424130]

Noble-Met Ltd., p. II-1277 [NAICS 334411]

Noble Metals Precious Metals Div., p. I-825 [NAICS 331419]

Noble USA Inc., p. II-1297 [NAICS 334415]

Nobles County Cooperative Oil Co., p. III-2225 [NAICS 454319]

NOCO Energy Corp., pp. Vol. III-1975, 1979, 2116, 2218 [NAICS 424710, 424720, 447110, 454311]

Noel Woodcraft Inc., p. II-1362 [NAICS 334518]

Noffsinger Manufacturing Inc., p. I-665 [NAICS 326220]

Nokia Inc., pp. Vol. II-1252, 1257 [NAICS 334119, 334210]

Noland Co., pp. Vol. III-1847, 1851, 1855, 1867 [NAICS 423720, 423730, 423740, 423830]

Nomura and Company Inc., p. III-1958 [NAICS 424510]

Nonpareil Corp., p. I-158 [NAICS 31199M]

Noodles By Leonardo Inc., p. I-124 [NAICS 31182M]

Nor-Cal Produce Inc., p. III-1950 [NAICS 424480]

Nor-Cal Products Inc., p. II-1184 [NAICS 333912]

Nor-Cote International Inc., p. I-580 [NAICS 325910]

Nor-Lake Inc., p. II-1106 [NAICS 333415]

Nor Service Inc., p. I-863 [NAICS 332114]

Norac Company Inc., p. I-493 [NAICS 32519M]

Norampac Industries Inc., p. I-379 [NAICS 32221M]

Norampac New York City Inc., pp. Vol. I-403, Vol. II-1720 [NAICS 32223M, 339950]

Noranda Aluminum Inc., p. I-803 [NAICS 331312]

Norbert E. Mitchell Company Inc., p. III-2218 [NAICS 454311]

Norbest Inc., p. III-1936 [NAICS 424440]

Norbord Minnesota, p. I-319 [NAICS 321219]

Norca Corp., p. II-1491 [NAICS 336212]

Norcia Bakery, p. III-2089 [NAICS 445291]

Norcimbus Inc., p. II-1056 [NAICS 333295]

Norco Inc., pp. Vol. I-471, Vol. II-1229 [NAICS 325120, 33399P]

Norcold Inc., pp. Vol. II-1409, 1551 [NAICS 335222, 336399]

Norcostco Inc., p. I-285 [NAICS 31529M]

Nord Gear Corp., p. II-1162 [NAICS 333612]

NORDAM Group Inc., p. II-1567 [NAICS 336413]

Nordco Inc., p. II-1584 [NAICS 336510]

Nordenia USA Inc., pp. Vol. I-609, 615 [NAICS 326112, 326113]

Nordic Group of Companies Ltd., pp. Vol. I-626, Vol. II-1607 [NAICS 326122, 336999]

Nordic Ware, pp. Vol. I-713, Vol. II-886 [NAICS 327212, 33221N]

Nordson Corp., pp. Vol. II-1061, 1077, 1229, 1740 [NAICS 33329N, 333313, 33399P, 339994]

Nordstrom Auto Recycling, p. III-1770 [NAICS 423140]

Nordstrom Inc., pp. Vol. III-2123, 2132, 2171 [NAICS 448110, 448140, 452111]

Nordyne Inc., pp. Vol. II-1101, 1106, 1217 [NAICS 333414, 333415, 333994]

Norelco Consumer Products Co., p. II-1397 [NAICS 33521M]

Norfolk Iron and Metal, p. II-945 [NAICS 332710]

Norfolk Iron and Metal Co., pp. Vol. I-837, 879, Vol. II-945, 1009, Vol. III-1824 [NAICS 33149M, 33211P, 332710, 332996, 423510]

Norfolk Naval Shipyard, p. II-1589 [NAICS 336611]

Norfolk Shipbuilding & Drydock, p. II-1589 [NAICS 336611]

Noritsu America Corp., p. III-1798 [NAICS 423410]

Norka Futon, p. II-1657 [NAICS 337910]

Norkol Converting Corp., p. I-415 [NAICS 322299]

Norlake Manufacturing Co., p. II-1302 [NAICS 334416]

Norpac Food Sales, pp. Vol. III-1929, 1954 [NAICS 424420, 424490]

NORPAC Foods Inc., p. I-62 [NAICS 31141M]

Norplex Inc., pp. Vol. I-213, 395, Vol. III-1968 [NAICS 31324M, 32222P, 424610]

Norris Cylinder Co., p. II-923 [NAICS 332420]

Norse Dairy Systems, pp. Vol. I-609, Vol. II-1212 [NAICS 326112, 333993]

Nortec Industries Inc., p. II-1397 [NAICS 33521M]

Nortech Engineering Inc., p. II-1248 [NAICS 334113]

Nortech Systems Inc., pp. Vol. II-1248, 1322, 1512 [NAICS 334113, 334510, 33632M]

Nortek Holdings Inc., pp. Vol. I-709, Vol. II-1112, 1417, 1468 [NAICS 327211, 33341N, 335228, 335999]

Nortek Inc., pp. Vol. II-908, 1106, 1112, 1217 [NAICS 33232M, 333415, 33341N, 333994]

North Amercian Forest Products, p. III-1782 [NAICS 423310]

North America Ceramtec, p. I-686 [NAICS 327113]

North America Packaging Corp., p. I-651 [NAICS 32619M]

North American Bus Industries Inc., p. II-1486 [NAICS 336211]

North American Container Corp., pp. Vol. I-343, 379 [NAICS 321920, 32221M]

North American Enclosures Inc., p. I-358 [NAICS 321999]

North American Hoganas Inc., pp. Vol. I-803, 837, 867, Vol. II-1463 [NAICS 331312, 33149M, 332117, 335991]

North American Housing Corp., p. I-353 [NAICS 321992]

North American Lighting Inc., p. II-1512 [NAICS 33632M]

North American Manufacturing, pp. Vol. II-1101, 1512 [NAICS 333414, 33632M]

North American Nutrition Co's Inc., p. I-9 [NAICS 311119]

North American Shipbuilding, p. II-1589 [NAICS 336611]

North American Stainless, p. I-793 [NAICS 33122M]

North American Telecom Services, p. III-2054 [NAICS 443112]

North American Video & Sound, p. III-1798 [NAICS 423410]

North Carolina Granite Corp., p. I-762 [NAICS 327991]

North Carolina Mutual Wholesale, p. III-1909 [NAICS 424210]

North Central Cooperative Inc., pp. Vol. I-9, 443, 524, Vol. III-2222 [NAICS 311119, 324110, 325314, 454312]

North Coast Brewing Company, pp. Vol. I-172, Vol. III-2097 [NAICS 312120, 445310]

North Coast Medical Inc., p. III-1820 [NAICS 423490]

North Coast Nissan Inc., p. III-2027 [NAICS 441229]

North Coast Processing Inc., p. I-152 [NAICS 31194M]

North Country Harley-Davidson, p. III-2021 [NAICS 441221]

North Country Metals Inc., p. II-1607 [NAICS 336999]

North East Knitting Inc., pp. Vol. I-203, 213 [NAICS 31322M, 31324M]

North Florida Lumber Inc., p. I-324 [NAICS 32121N]

North Industries Inc., p. II-1417 [NAICS 335228]

North Landing Corp., p. III-1943 [NAICS 424460]

North Pacific Group Inc., pp. Vol. I-312, Vol. III-1782, 1794, 1824, 1991 [NAICS 32111M, 423310, 423390, 423510, 424910]

North Platte Telegraph, p. I-420 [NAICS 32311M]

North Safety Products L.L.C., p. I-290 [NAICS 31599M]

North Shore Bottling Company, p. III-1954 [NAICS 424490]

North Shore Laboratories Corp., p. I-660 [NAICS 32621M]

North Shore Sportswear Inc., p. III-1919 [NAICS 424330]

North Shore Strapping Inc., p. II-886 [NAICS 33221N]

North Star, p. III-1894 [NAICS 423940]

North Star Steel Texas Inc., pp. Vol. I-780, 793, Vol. II-899 [NAICS 33111M, 33122M, 33231M]

North State Cartons L.L.C., p. I-374 [NAICS 322130]

North State Recycling, p. III-1890 [NAICS 423930]

Northampton Farm Bureau, pp. Vol. III-2072, 2218 [NAICS 444220, 454311]

Northcoast Business Systems Inc., p. III-1801 [NAICS 423420]

Northeast Building Products Corp., p. I-713 [NAICS 327212]

Northeast Coop., p. III-2218 [NAICS 454311]

Northeast Distributors Inc., p. III-1855 [NAICS 423740]

Northeast Mississippi Coca-Cola, pp. Vol. I-165, Vol. III-2007 [NAICS 31211M, 424990]

Northern Concrete Pipe Inc., p. I-737 [NAICS 32733M]

Northern Contours Inc., p. II-1611 [NAICS 337110]

Northern Coop Services, p. III-1975 [NAICS 424710]

Northern Distributing Co., p. III-1983 [NAICS 424810]

Northern Hardwoods, p. I-324 [NAICS 32121N]

Northern Lakes Co-op Inc., pp. Vol. III-1975, 2171 [NAICS 424710, 452111]

Northern Marine Inc., p. II-1589 [NAICS 336611]

Northern Power Systems Inc., pp. Vol. II-1101, 1157 [NAICS 333414, 333611]

Northern Stamping Co., pp. Vol. I-879, Vol. II-1541, 1749 [NAICS 33211P, 336370, 339999]

Northern Stationers Inc., pp. Vol. III-1901, 2186 [NAICS 424120, 453210]

Northern Utah Manufacturing, p. I-81 [NAICS 311514]

Northern Video Systems Inc., pp. Vol. III-1835, 2054 [NAICS 423620, 443112]

Northern Wholesale Supply Inc., p. III-1758 [NAICS 423110]

Northfield Block Co., p. I-737 [NAICS 32733M]

Northland Plastics Inc., p. II-1051 [NAICS 333220]

Northrop Grumman Corp., pp. Vol. II-899, 1005, 1082, 1267, 1287, 1317, 1327, 1557, 1567, 1572, 1589 [NAICS 33231M, 332995, 333314, 334290, 334413, 334419, 334511, 336411, 336413, 336414, 336611]

Northrop Grumman Space, pp. Vol. II-1572, 1576, 1580 [NAICS 336414, 336415, 336419]

Northstar Aerospace, p. II-1536 [NAICS 336360]

Northstar Aerospace Inc., pp. Vol. II-1162, 1580 [NAICS 333612, 336419]

NorthStar Orthodontics Inc., p. II-1682 [NAICS 339114]

Northville Cider Mill Inc., p. I-177 [NAICS 312130]

Northville Industries Corp., p. III-1979 [NAICS 424720]

Northway Industries Inc., p. I-631 [NAICS 326130]

Northwest Aluminum Co., pp. Vol. I-803, 811 [NAICS 331312, 331316]

Northwest Automatic Products, p. II-952 [NAICS 332721]

Northwest Cheese Distributors Inc., pp. Vol. III-1905, 1933, 2094 [NAICS 424130, 424430, 445299]

Northwest Composites Inc., p. II-1327 [NAICS 334511]

Northwest Hills Pharmacy/Florist, pp. Vol. III-2100, 2183 [NAICS 446110, 453110]

Northwest Pet Products Inc., p. I-4 [NAICS 311111]

Northwest Pipe Co., pp. Vol. I-780, 788 [NAICS 33111M, 331210]

Northwest Tire Factory L.L.C., p. III-1766 [NAICS 423130]

Northwest Tool and Mfg Inc., p. I-803 [NAICS 331312]

Northwest Wholesale Inc., p. III-1991 [NAICS 424910]

Northwestern Industries Inc., pp. Vol. I-713, 722 [NAICS 327212, 327215]

Norton Ditto Inc., p. III-2123 [NAICS 448110]

Norton Metal Inc., p. III-2208 [NAICS 453998]

Norton Proppants, p. I-681 [NAICS 327112]

Norwalk Furniture Corp., p. II-1616 [NAICS 337121]

Norwood Promotional Products, p. III-1871 [NAICS 423840]

Nosler Inc., p. II-993 [NAICS 332992]

Noteworthy Industries Inc., pp. Vol. I-395, 603 [NAICS 32222P, 326111]

Nova Biomedical Corp., p. II-1352 [NAICS 334516]

Nova Drilling Services Inc., p. I-631 [NAICS 326130]

Nova Electronics Inc., p. II-1277 [NAICS 334411]

Novagen, p. I-549 [NAICS 325414]

Novamex, p. III-1954 [NAICS 424490]

Novar Controls Corp., pp. Vol. II-1267, 1437 [NAICS 334290, 335314]

Novartis Pharmaceuticals Corp., p. I-539 [NAICS 325412]

Novavax Inc., p. I-549 [NAICS 325414]

Novellus Systems Inc., p. II-1061 [NAICS 33329N]

Noveon Hilton Davis, pp. Vol. I-475, 554, 580 [NAICS 32513M, 325510, 325910]

Noveon International Inc., pp. Vol. I-147, 500, 554, 560, 595 [NAICS 311930, 325211, 325510, 325520, 32599N]

Noville Inc., p. I-152 [NAICS 31194M]

NOVITA, p. II-1696 [NAICS 33991M]

Novotechnik US Inc., p. II-1297 [NAICS 334415]

Novurania of America Inc., p. II-1594 [NAICS 336612]

Novus Inc., p. I-709 [NAICS 327211]

Now and Zen Inc., p. II-1362 [NAICS 334518]

NPK Construction Equipment Inc., p. II-886 [NAICS 33221N]

NRP-Jones, p. I-665 [NAICS 326220]

NRV Inc., p. I-81 [NAICS 311514]

NS Group Inc., pp. Vol. I-560, 780, 788 [NAICS 325520, 33111M, 331210]

NSC Diversified, p. III-2186 [NAICS 453210]

NSK Corp., pp. Vol. II-988, 1014, 1168, 1222 [NAICS 332991, 33299N, 333613, 33399N]

NSK Steering Systems America, p. II-1519 [NAICS 336330]

NSS Enterprises Inc., p. II-1217 [NAICS 333994]

nStor Corporation Inc., p. II-1243 [NAICS 334112]

NSW L.L.C., pp. Vol. I-609, 621, 665 [NAICS 326112, 326121, 326220]

NT International Inc., p. II-1342 [NAICS 334514]

NTE Electronics Inc., p. III-1839 [NAICS 423690]

NTELOS, p. III-2054 [NAICS 443112]

NTN-BCA Corp., p. II-988 [NAICS 332991]

NTN-Bower Corp., pp. Vol. II-988, 1168 [NAICS 332991, 333613]

NTN Driveshaft Incorporated CVJ, p. II-1530 [NAICS 336350]

Nu-Foam Products Inc., pp. Vol. I-229, 641 [NAICS 314110, 326150]

Nu Horizons Electronics Corp., p. III-1839 [NAICS 423690]

Nu-Kote International Inc., p. I-580 [NAICS 325910]

Nu-Look Fashions Inc., p. I-300 [NAICS 31621M]

Nu Skin Enterprises Inc., p. III-1909 [NAICS 424210]

Nu Skin International Inc., p. III-1909 [NAICS 424210]

Nu-Vu Food Service Systems, p. II-1404 [NAICS 335221]

Nu-Wa Industries Inc., p. II-1500 [NAICS 336214]

Nu-Way Concrete Forms Inc., pp. Vol. III-1786, 1794 [NAICS 423320, 423390]

Nuclear Fuel Services, p. I-488 [NAICS 325188]

Nuclear Measurements Corp., p. II-1277 [NAICS 334411]

NuCo2 Inc., p. III-1971 [NAICS 424690]

Nucor Corp., pp. Vol. I-780, Vol. II-899, 933, 958, 988 [NAICS 33111M, 33231M, 332510, 332722, 332991]

Nulco Lighting Corp., p. II-1390 [NAICS 33512M]

Null's Machine and Mfg Inc., p. II-1524 [NAICS 336340]

Numax Inc., p. III-1820 [NAICS 423490]

Numrich Gun Parts Corp., p. III-2150 [NAICS 451110]

Nunn Electric Supply Corp., pp. Vol. III-1831, 1835 [NAICS 423610, 423620]

Nunnery-Freeman Inc., p. II-1404 [NAICS 335221]

Nutra-Flo Co., p. I-524 [NAICS 325314]

Nutraceutical International Corp., p. I-534 [NAICS 325411]

Nutrilite, p. I-534 [NAICS 325411]

Nutrition 21 Inc., p. I-549 [NAICS 325414]

Nutrition Inc., pp. Vol. I-158, Vol. III-2215 [NAICS 31199M, 454210]

Nutrition Now Inc., p. III-1909 [NAICS 424210]

Nutritional Laboratories Intern., p. I-534 [NAICS 325411]

Nutro Corp., p. II-1740 [NAICS 339994]

Nuvex Ingredients Inc., pp. Vol. I-36, 137 [NAICS 311230, 31191M]

NVIDIA Corp., pp. Vol. II-1252, 1287 [NAICS 334119, 334413]

NWL Transformers Inc., pp. Vol. II-1282, 1302, 1332, 1421 [NAICS 334412, 334416, 334512, 335311]

NWP Manufacturing Inc., p. I-343 [NAICS 321920]

Ny-Glass Plastics Inc., p. II-1134 [NAICS 333514]

Nyer Medical Group Inc., p. III-2100 [NAICS 446110]

Nypro Atlanta, p. II-1119 [NAICS 333511]

Nypro Inc., pp. Vol. I-626, Vol. II-1468 [NAICS 326122, 335999]

NYX Inc., pp. Vol. I-609, 651, 670, Vol. II-1749 [NAICS 326112, 32619M, 32629M, 339999]

O and G Industries Inc., pp. Vol. I-448, 732, 743 [NAICS 324121, 327320, 327390]

O and S Research Inc., p. I-709 [NAICS 327211]

O-AT-KA Milk Products, pp. Vol. I-81, 86 [NAICS 311514, 31151N]

O. Berk Co., p. III-1871 [NAICS 423840]

O'Brien Corp., p. I-306 [NAICS 31699M]

O'Bryan Brothers Inc., p. I-262 [NAICS 31519M]

O-Cedar Brands Inc., p. II-1740 [NAICS 339994]

O'Connor Truck Sales Inc., p. III-1770 [NAICS 423140]

O'Day Equipment Inc., p. II-1189 [NAICS 333913]

O'Krent Floor Covering Co., pp. Vol. III-2041, 2044 [NAICS 442210, 442291]

O'Neal Steel Inc., p. III-1824 [NAICS 423510]

O'Reilly Automotive Inc., pp. Vol. II-1092, Vol. III-1762, 2030 [NAICS 33331N, 423120, 441310]

O'Sullivan Industries Holdings, pp. Vol. II-1621, 1632 [NAICS 337122, 33712N]

Oak Hall Industries L.P., p. I-285 [NAICS 31529M]

Oak State Products Inc., p. I-124 [NAICS 31182M]

Oakdale Cotton Mills, pp. Vol. I-192, 244 [NAICS 31311M, 314991]

Oakley Inc., pp. Vol. II-1362, 1687, 1702 [NAICS 334518, 339115, 339920]

Oakwood Group, p. II-1541 [NAICS 336370]

Oasis Corp., pp. Vol. II-1106, 1397 [NAICS 333415, 33521M]

Oasis Foods Co., pp. Vol. I-26, 152 [NAICS 311225, 31194M]

OBC Northwest Inc., p. I-239 [NAICS 31491M]

Oberg Industries Inc., pp. Vol. I-879, Vol. II-1119, 1134 [NAICS 33211P, 333511, 333514]

Ocala Recycling Co., pp. Vol. I-363, 807 [NAICS 322110, 331314]

Occidental Petroleum Corp., pp. Vol. I-443, 480, 595 [NAICS 324110, 325181, 32599N]

OCCK Inc., p. II-1386 [NAICS 335110]

Oce-USA Inc., pp. Vol. II-1061, 1077, 1087, 1252 [NAICS 33329N, 333313, 333315, 334119]

Ocean Beauty Seafoods Inc., p. I-110 [NAICS 31171M]

Ocean Crest Seafoods Inc., p. III-1943 [NAICS 424460]

Ocean Design Inc., p. II-1307 [NAICS 334417]

Ocean Gold Seafoods Inc., pp. Vol. I-110, Vol. III-1943 [NAICS 31171M, 424460]

Ocean Optics Inc., pp. Vol. II-1082, 1352 [NAICS 333314, 334516]

Ocean Organics Corp., p. I-516 [NAICS 325311]

Ocean Pacific Apparel Corp., pp. Vol. III-1916, 1919 [NAICS 424320, 424330]

Ocean Spray Cranberries Inc., p. I-68 [NAICS 31142M]

Ocean To Ocean, p. I-110 [NAICS 31171M]

Ocean Yachts Inc., p. II-1589 [NAICS 336611]

Oceaneering International Inc., pp. Vol. I-665, Vol. II-933, 980 [NAICS 326220, 332510, 33291N]

Oceaneering Space Systems Inc., pp. Vol. II-1005, 1580 [NAICS 332995, 336419]

OCI Chemical Corp., p. I-480 [NAICS 325181]

Oconomowoc Manufacturing Corp., p. II-988 [NAICS 332991]

OCTA Inc., p. I-863 [NAICS 332114]

Ocular Sciences Inc., p. II-1687 [NAICS 339115]

Odama Systems Inc., p. III-2058 [NAICS 443120]

ODB Company Inc., pp. Vol. II-1184, 1740 [NAICS 333912, 339994]

Odd Job Stores Inc., p. III-2177 [NAICS 452910]

ODL Inc., pp. Vol. I-713, 811 [NAICS 327212, 331316]

Odom Corp., pp. Vol. III-1954, 1983, 1987 [NAICS 424490, 424810, 424820]

OEM/Miller, p. I-621 [NAICS 326121]

O.F. Mossberg and Sons Inc., p. II-1001 [NAICS 332994]

Office Connection Inc., p. III-2186 [NAICS 453210]

Office Depot Inc., pp. Vol. I-420, 436, Vol. III-2037, 2054, 2058, 2186 [NAICS 32311M, 32312M, 442110, 443112, 443120, 453210]

Office Depot Inc. Bus Serv, pp. Vol. III-1774, 1901 [NAICS 423210, 424120]

Office Paper Systems Inc., p. I-363 [NAICS 322110]

Office Pavilion, p. III-1774 [NAICS 423210]

Office Pavilion Inc., p. III-2037 [NAICS 442110]

Office Service Co., p. III-1901 [NAICS 424120]

Office World Inc., pp. Vol. III-1801, 1901 [NAICS 423420, 424120]

OfficeMax Inc., pp. Vol. I-319, 324, 368 [NAICS 321219, 32121N, 32212M]

Offset Paperback Manufacturers, p. I-420 [NAICS 32311M]

Offshore Energy Services Inc., p. II-1009 [NAICS 332996]

Offshore Specialty Fabricators Inc., p. II-1589 [NAICS 336611]

Offtech Inc., pp. Vol. III-1801, 1901 [NAICS 423420, 424120]

OFS, p. II-1451 [NAICS 33592M]

OFS Plant 1, pp. Vol. II-1627, 1650 [NAICS 337127, 33721N]

Ogden Newspapers Inc., pp. Vol. I-420, 436 [NAICS 32311M, 32312M]

Ogihara America Corp., pp. Vol. I-879, Vol. II-1541 [NAICS 33211P, 336370]

Ogura Corp., p. II-1546 [NAICS 336391]

Ohi Automotive of America Corp., pp. Vol. I-879, Vol. II-1541, 1551 [NAICS 33211P, 336370, 336399]

Ohio Art Co., p. II-1708 [NAICS 33993M]

Ohio Calculating Inc., p. III-1801 [NAICS 423420]

Ohio Carbon Blank, p. II-1463 [NAICS 335991]

Ohio Decorative Products Inc., pp. Vol. I-852, 857, Vol. II-964 [NAICS 33152N, 33152P, 33281M]

Ohio Fresh Eggs L.L.C., p. I-158 [NAICS 31199M]

Ohio Metal Working Products Inc., p. I-756 [NAICS 327910]

Ohio Pet Foods Inc., p. I-4 [NAICS 311111]

Ohio Pulp Mills Inc., p. I-363 [NAICS 322110]

Ohio Road Paving Co., p. I-453 [NAICS 324122]

Ohio Valley Goodwill Industries, p. II-1087 [NAICS 333315]

Ohio Valley Plastics Inc., p. I-589 [NAICS 325991]

Ohio Valley Supply Co., p. III-1968 [NAICS 424610]

Ohmcraft Inc., p. II-1297 [NAICS 334415]

Ohmstede-United Industrial, p. II-918 [NAICS 332410]

Oil Air Products Inc., p. I-665 [NAICS 326220]

Oil Center Research Inc., pp. Vol. I-458, 560 [NAICS 324191, 325520]

Oil-Dri Corporation of America, p. I-767 [NAICS 327992]

Oil Equipment Company Inc., p. II-1189 [NAICS 333913]

Oil States International Inc., pp. Vol. II-1039, 1432 [NAICS 33313M, 335313]

Oilgear Co., pp. Vol. II-1179, 1342 [NAICS 333911, 334514]

OK Industries Inc., p. I-97 [NAICS 311615]

Oki Telecom Inc., p. II-1282 [NAICS 334412]

Oklahoma Goodwill Industries Inc., p. III-2180 [NAICS 452990]

Oklahoma Respiratory Care Inc., p. III-2113 [NAICS 446199]

Okonite Co., pp. Vol. II-1451, 1457 [NAICS 33592M, 33593M]

Okuhara Foods Inc., p. III-1943 [NAICS 424460]

Olcott Plastics Inc., p. I-646 [NAICS 326160]

Old Castle Glass, pp. Vol. I-420, 709, 713, 722 [NAICS 32311M, 327211, 327212, 327215]

Old Colony Envelope Co., p. I-403 [NAICS 32223M]

Old Dominion Floor Company Inc., p. III-2041 [NAICS 442210]

Old Dominion Peanut Corp., p. I-57 [NAICS 311340]

Old Europe Cheese Inc., p. I-76 [NAICS 311513]

Old Fashioned Foods Inc., pp. Vol. I-76, 152 [NAICS 311513, 31194M]

Old Home Foods Inc., p. I-76 [NAICS 311513]

Old Market Pub and Brewery, p. III-2097 [NAICS 445310]

Old Mill Winery, p. I-177 [NAICS 312130]

Old Navy, pp. Vol. III-2123, 2126 [NAICS 448110, 448120]

Old Nutfield Brewing Limited Inc., p. I-172 [NAICS 312120]

Old Virginia Brick Company Inc., p. I-691 [NAICS 327121]

Oldcastle APG National Inc., p. III-1786 [NAICS 423320]

Oldcastle Glass, p. I-709 [NAICS 327211]

Oldcastle Glass-New York, pp. Vol. I-709, 713, 722 [NAICS 327211, 327212, 327215]

Oldcastle Glass of Los Angeles, pp. Vol. I-709, 713, 722 [NAICS 327211, 327212, 327215]

Oldcastle Precast Inc., p. I-737 [NAICS 32733M]

Oldcastle Stone Products, p. I-762 [NAICS 327991]

Oldenburg Stamler Corp., pp. Vol. II-1039, 1222, 1432 [NAICS 33313M, 33399N, 335313]

Ole' Mexican Foods Inc., pp. Vol. I-116, 133, 137 [NAICS 31181M, 311830, 31191M]

Ole Hickory Pits, p. II-1404 [NAICS 335221]

Olin Corp., pp. Vol. I-480, 595, 830, 837, Vol. II-993, 997, 1317 [NAICS 325181, 32599N, 33142M, 33149M, 332992, 332993, 334419]

Olinger Distributing Co., p. III-1987 [NAICS 424820]

Oliver Equipment Company Inc., p. II-1157 [NAICS 333611]

Oliver Products Company Inc., p. II-1212 [NAICS 333993]

Oliver Rubber Co., pp. Vol. I-660, 670 [NAICS 32621M, 32629M]

Oliver's Candies L.L.C., p. I-48 [NAICS 311320]

Oliver Wine Company Inc., p. I-177 [NAICS 312130]

Olla Beauty Supply Inc., p. III-1875 [NAICS 423850]

Olsen Distributing Co., p. III-1998 [NAICS 424930]

Olson Floor Covering Inc., p. III-2041 [NAICS 442210]

Olson Trailer and Body L.L.C., pp. Vol. II-1482, 1496 [NAICS 336120, 336213]

Olsun Electrics Corp., pp. Vol. II-1302, 1421 [NAICS 334416, 335311]

Olum's of Binghamton Inc., pp. Vol. III-2037, 2050 [NAICS 442110, 443111]

Olympia Group Inc., pp. Vol. I-756, Vol. II-1207 [NAICS 327910, 333991]

Olympian Co., pp. Vol. III-1975, 2116 [NAICS 424710, 447110]

Olympic Oil Ltd., p. I-458 [NAICS 324191]

Olympic Steel Inc., p. III-1824 [NAICS 423510]

OM Group Inc., p. I-475 [NAICS 32513M]

Omaha Bedding Co., p. II-1657 [NAICS 337910]

Omaha Beef Company Inc., pp. Vol. III-1933, 1946 [NAICS 424430, 424470]

Numbers following p. or pp. are page references. Roman numerals indicate volume numbers. Bracketed items indicate industries. Page references are to the starting pages of company tables.

2391

Company Index

Omaha Compound Co., p. III-1875 [NAICS 423850]

Omaha Standard Inc., pp. Vol. I-879, Vol. II-1486 [NAICS 33211P, 336211]

Omaha World Herald Inc., p. I-420 [NAICS 32311M]

Omega Extruding Corporation, p. I-603 [NAICS 326111]

Omega Optical Inc., p. II-1082 [NAICS 333314]

Omega Products, p. I-665 [NAICS 326220]

Omega Protein Corp., p. I-26 [NAICS 311225]

OMEGA Pultrusions Inc., p. I-631 [NAICS 326130]

Omni Connection International Inc., p. II-1512 [NAICS 33632M]

Omni Plastics Inc., p. II-1119 [NAICS 333511]

Omni-X Inc., p. II-1147 [NAICS 333516]

Omnicare Inc., p. III-1909 [NAICS 424210]

Omnicell Inc., p. III-1813 [NAICS 423450]

Omnii Oral Pharmaceuticals Inc., p. II-1682 [NAICS 339114]

OmniSource Corp., p. III-1890 [NAICS 423930]

Omnitech Robotics Inc., pp. Vol. II-1282, 1337 [NAICS 334412, 334513]

Omnium, p. I-529 [NAICS 325320]

OmniVision Technologies Inc., p. II-1287 [NAICS 334413]

Omnova Solutions Inc., pp. Vol. I-224, 453, 626 [NAICS 313320, 324122, 326122]

Omron Electronics L.L.C., pp. Vol. II-1287, 1437 [NAICS 334413, 335314]

Omron Healthcare Inc., p. III-1813 [NAICS 423450]

ON Semiconductor Corp., p. II-1287 [NAICS 334413]

On Time Promotions Inc., p. II-1362 [NAICS 334518]

One Lambda Inc., p. I-544 [NAICS 325413]

One Price Clothing Stores Inc., pp. Vol. III-2126, 2129, 2135 [NAICS 448120, 448130, 448150]

One Voice Productions Inc., p. II-1376 [NAICS 334612]

ONEOK Inc., p. I-443 [NAICS 324110]

Oneonta Trading Corp., p. III-1950 [NAICS 424480]

Onicon Inc., p. II-1342 [NAICS 334514]

Ono Industries Inc., p. I-510 [NAICS 32522M]

Onquest Technologies Inc., p. III-2058 [NAICS 443120]

Onsrud Cutter L.P., p. II-1129 [NAICS 333513]

Ontario Die Company of America, p. II-1129 [NAICS 333513]

Onyx Collection Inc., p. I-762 [NAICS 327991]

OPEX Corp., p. II-1077 [NAICS 333313]

OPI Products Inc., p. I-575 [NAICS 325620]

Oplink Communications Inc., p. II-1082 [NAICS 333314]

OPTIA, p. II-1252 [NAICS 334119]

Optical Cable Corp., p. I-713 [NAICS 327212]

Optical Coating Laboratory Inc., pp. Vol. II-1082, 1087, 1252, 1287 [NAICS 333314, 333315, 334119, 334413]

Optical Disc Corp., pp. Vol. II-1376, 1381 [NAICS 334612, 334613]

Optical Gaging Products Inc., pp. Vol. II-1082, 1087 [NAICS 333314, 333315]

Optical Supply Inc., pp. Vol. I-713, Vol. II-1687 [NAICS 327212, 339115]

Optics Inc., p. III-1817 [NAICS 423460]

Optidisc Solutions L.L.C., pp. Vol. II-1376, 1381 [NAICS 334612, 334613]

Optima Chemical Group L.L.C., p. I-493 [NAICS 32519M]

Optimum Technologies Inc., p. I-505 [NAICS 325212]

Optogenics of Syracuse, pp. Vol. I-713, Vol. II-1687 [NAICS 327212, 339115]

Optomart, p. II-1687 [NAICS 339115]

Oral Arts Dental Laboratories Inc., pp. Vol. II-1682, 1692 [NAICS 339114, 339116]

Oral Health Products Inc., p. II-1740 [NAICS 339994]

Orange County Container Corp., pp. Vol. I-379, 388 [NAICS 32221M, 32222N]

Orange Glo International Inc., pp. Vol. I-566, Vol. II-1740 [NAICS 32561M, 339994]

OraSure Technologies Inc., p. I-544 [NAICS 325413]

Orbit Irrigation Products Inc., p. II-1023 [NAICS 333111]

Orbital Sciences Corp., pp. Vol. II-1005, 1262, 1327, 1367, 1580 [NAICS 332995, 334220, 334511, 334519, 336419]

Orbseal L.L.C., p. I-560 [NAICS 325520]

Orca Bay Seafoods Inc., p. I-110 [NAICS 31171M]

Orchard Supply Hardware Stores, pp. Vol. III-2065, 2072 [NAICS 444100, 444220]

Orco Block Company Inc., p. I-737 [NAICS 32733M]

Orcon Corp., pp. Vol. I-224, 615, 771 [NAICS 313320, 326113, 327993]

Orcon Industries Corp., p. I-636 [NAICS 326140]

Order-Matic Corp., pp. Vol. II-1077, 1252, 1317 [NAICS 333313, 334119, 334419]

Ore-Cal Corp., p. III-1943 [NAICS 424460]

Oreck Corp., pp. Vol. II-1092, 1397 [NAICS 33331N, 33521M]

Oregon Aero Inc., p. II-1536 [NAICS 336360]

Oregon Glass Co., p. I-713 [NAICS 327212]

Oregon Pacific Building Products, p. III-1794 [NAICS 423390]

Oregon Select Inc., p. II-1046 [NAICS 333210]

Oregon Steel Mills Inc., p. I-780 [NAICS 33111M]

Oren Elliott Products Inc., p. II-1292 [NAICS 334414]

OrePac Building Products, p. III-1794 [NAICS 423390]

Orgain Building Supply Co., p. I-329 [NAICS 32121P]

Organic Valley, pp. Vol. I-76, 102, 158 [NAICS 311513, 31161N, 31199M]

Orgil-Frederick Trading Co., pp. Vol. III-1843, 1847 [NAICS 423710, 423720]

Orian Rugs Inc., p. I-229 [NAICS 314110]

Orica USA Inc., p. I-585 [NAICS 325920]

Oriental Weavers Rug Mfg Inc., p. I-229 [NAICS 314110]

Original Bradford Soap Works Inc., pp. Vol. I-566, 595 [NAICS 32561M, 32599N]

Original Herkimer County Cheese, p. I-76 [NAICS 311513]

Orion America Inc., pp. Vol. II-1272, 1312 [NAICS 334310, 334418]

Orion Corp., p. II-1168 [NAICS 333613]

Orion Industries, pp. Vol. II-1541, 1557 [NAICS 336370, 336411]

Orion Pacific Inc., p. I-589 [NAICS 325991]

Orion South Inc., p. II-1039 [NAICS 33313M]

Orlando Auto Auction Inc., p. III-1758 [NAICS 423110]

Orleans Furniture Inc., p. II-1621 [NAICS 337122]

Orlotronics Corp., p. II-1005 [NAICS 332995]

Ormco Corp., p. II-1682 [NAICS 339114]

Ormet Aluminum Mill Products, pp. Vol. I-816, Vol. II-1302 [NAICS 33131N, 334416]

Ormet Corp., pp. Vol. I-803, 816, 825 [NAICS 331312, 33131N, 331419]

Ornamental Products Inc., p. II-1639 [NAICS 337212]

Orrefors Kosta Boda, p. III-1778 [NAICS 423220]

Ortec Inc., pp. Vol. I-500, 595 [NAICS 325211, 32599N]

Orthodontic Technologies Inc., p. II-1692 [NAICS 339116]

Orthofix Inc., p. II-1676 [NAICS 339113]

Osborn International, pp. Vol. I-756, Vol. II-1740 [NAICS 327910, 339994]

Osborne Distributing Company, p. III-1991 [NAICS 424910]

Oscar Mayer Foods Corp., pp. Vol. I-68, 102 [NAICS 31142M, 31161N]

Oscarware Inc., p. II-1404 [NAICS 335221]

Osco Inc., p. II-1051 [NAICS 333220]

OSCO Industries Inc., p. I-845 [NAICS 33151M]

OSG Tap and Die Inc., pp. Vol. II-892, 1124, 1134, 1140, 1207 [NAICS 33221P, 333512, 333514, 333515, 333991]

Osgood Industries Inc., p. II-1212 [NAICS 333993]

OshKosh B'Gosh Inc., pp. Vol. I-272, 285, 300, Vol. III-2129 [NAICS 31522M, 31529M, 31621M, 448130]

Oshkosh Truck Corp., pp. Vol. II-1194, 1473 [NAICS 33392M, 336111]

OSI Pharmaceuticals Inc., p. I-544 [NAICS 325413]

OSI Sealants Inc., p. I-560 [NAICS 325520]

Osmic Inc., p. II-1357 [NAICS 334517]

Osmose Inc., pp. Vol. I-493, 595 [NAICS 32519M, 32599N]

OSO Lumber and Hardware Co., p. I-329 [NAICS 32121P]

Osram Sylvania Inc., p. II-1390 [NAICS 33512M]

Osteotech Inc., p. I-549 [NAICS 325414]

Ostrow Co., pp. Vol. III-1778, 2047 [NAICS 423220, 442299]

Oswego Wire Inc., p. I-830 [NAICS 33142M]

Oticon Inc., p. II-1322 [NAICS 334510]

Otis Spunkmeyer Inc., p. I-116 [NAICS 31181M]

Ottawa Cooperative Association, p. III-1958 [NAICS 424510]

Ottawa Dental Labs Inc., p. II-1682 [NAICS 339114]

Ottawa Truck Inc., pp. Vol. II-1194, 1457, 1486 [NAICS 33392M, 33593M, 336211]

Otter Creek Brewing Inc., p. I-172 [NAICS 312120]

Ouachita Coca-Cola Bottling Co., pp. Vol. I-147, 165 [NAICS 311930, 31211M]

Ouachita Coca-Cola Enterprises, p. I-165 [NAICS 31211M]

Ourisman Automotive Enterprises, p. III-2011 [NAICS 441110]

Numbers following p. or pp. are page references. Roman numerals indicate volume numbers. Bracketed items indicate industries. Page references are to the starting pages of company tables.

Outdoor Recreation Group Inc., p. I-239 [NAICS 31491M]

Outdoor Technolgies Inc., p. I-621 [NAICS 326121]

Outdoor Venture Corp., p. I-239 [NAICS 31491M]

Outlook Group Corp., p. I-415 [NAICS 322299]

Outokumpu American Brass Inc., pp. Vol. I-822, 830, 837 [NAICS 331411, 33142M, 33149M]

Outokumpu Copper Franklin Inc., p. I-830 [NAICS 33142M]

Outside The Box Interactive L.L.C., p. II-1381 [NAICS 334613]

Outwater Plastics Industries Inc., p. III-1968 [NAICS 424610]

Ovation Instruments, p. II-1731 [NAICS 339992]

Overbilt Trailer Co., p. II-1491 [NAICS 336212]

Overhead Door Corp., pp. Vol. I-334, Vol. II-908, 1491 [NAICS 32191M, 33232M, 336212]

Overhill Farms Inc., p. I-62 [NAICS 31141M]

Overland Storage Inc., p. II-1243 [NAICS 334112]

Overly Manufacturing Co., p. I-453 [NAICS 324122]

Overstock.com Inc., p. III-2208 [NAICS 453998]

O.W. and B.S. Look Company Inc., p. III-1943 [NAICS 424460]

Owen Oil Tools Inc., p. II-1039 [NAICS 33313M]

Owens and Minor Inc., pp. Vol. III-1813, 1909 [NAICS 423450, 424210]

Owens Corning, pp. Vol. I-198, 453, 500, 713, 771, Vol. II-908 [NAICS 313210, 324122, 325211, 327212, 327993, 33232M]

Owens-Illinois Inc., pp. Vol. I-626, 718 [NAICS 326122, 327213]

Owens Research Inc., p. II-1147 [NAICS 333516]

Owensboro Brick and Tile Co., p. I-703 [NAICS 32712N]

Owensboro Grain Company Inc., p. I-31 [NAICS 31122N]

Owl Intern. Global Associates, p. II-1589 [NAICS 336611]

Owl Wire and Cable Inc., pp. Vol. I-830, Vol. II-1451 [NAICS 33142M, 33592M]

OWT Industries, pp. Vol. II-1028, 1207 [NAICS 333112, 333991]

Oxarc Inc., p. I-471 [NAICS 325120]

Oxberry L.L.C., p. II-1386 [NAICS 335110]

Oxbo International Corp., p. II-1023 [NAICS 333111]

Oxbow Corp., p. III-1975 [NAICS 424710]

Oxford Automotive Inc., pp. Vol. II-1541, 1551 [NAICS 336370, 336399]

Oxford Homes Inc., p. I-353 [NAICS 321992]

Oxford Industries Inc., pp. Vol. I-262, 272, 279, 290 [NAICS 31519M, 31522M, 31523M, 31599M]

Oxy U. S. A Inc., p. I-443 [NAICS 324110]

Ozark Aircraft Systems L.L.C., p. II-1557 [NAICS 336411]

Ozarka Spring Water Co., p. I-165 [NAICS 31211M]

Ozuna Food Products Corp., p. I-133 [NAICS 311830]

P and F Industries Inc., pp. Vol. II-1101, 1124, 1207, 1417 [NAICS 333414, 333512, 333991, 335228]

P and H Mining Equipment Inc., pp. Vol. II-1033, 1039 [NAICS 333120, 33313M]

P and R Specialty Inc., p. I-374 [NAICS 322130]

P Stone Inc., p. I-748 [NAICS 327410]

PA Landers Inc., p. I-732 [NAICS 327320]

PABCO Gypsum, p. I-752 [NAICS 327420]

Pabco Roofing Products, p. I-453 [NAICS 324122]

Pabst Brewing Co., p. I-172 [NAICS 312120]

PAC Foundries, pp. Vol. I-845, 852 [NAICS 33151M, 33152N]

Pacamor Bearings Inc., p. II-988 [NAICS 332991]

PacAstro, p. II-1572 [NAICS 336414]

PACCAR Inc., pp. Vol. II-1473, 1486 [NAICS 336111, 336211]

PACCAR Inc. Parts Div., p. III-1762 [NAICS 423120]

Pace American Inc., p. II-1491 [NAICS 336212]

Pace International L.L.C., p. I-524 [NAICS 325314]

Pace Supply Corp., p. III-1790 [NAICS 423330]

Pacer Technology, p. I-646 [NAICS 326160]

Pacesetter Steel Service Inc., pp. Vol. I-436, Vol. II-964, Vol. III-1824 [NAICS 32312M, 33281M, 423510]

Pacific Aerospace & Electronics, pp. Vol. I-852, Vol. II-964 [NAICS 33152N, 33281M]

Pacific Allied Products Ltd., p. I-646 [NAICS 326160]

Pacific Beverage Company Inc., p. III-1983 [NAICS 424810]

Pacific Clay Products Inc., p. I-699 [NAICS 327123]

Pacific Clutch and Brake, pp. Vol. II-1524, 1530 [NAICS 336340, 336350]

Pacific Coast Feather Co., pp. Vol. I-234, 251 [NAICS 31412M, 314999]

Pacific Coast Producers, p. I-68 [NAICS 31142M]

Pacific Coast Supply L.L.C., pp. Vol. III-1786, 1790 [NAICS 423320, 423330]

Pacific Consolidated Industries, p. I-471 [NAICS 325120]

Pacific Cornetta Inc., p. III-1879 [NAICS 423860]

Pacific Cycle L.L.C., p. II-1599 [NAICS 336991]

Pacific Cycle L.L.C. Roadmaster, p. III-1883 [NAICS 423910]

Pacific Digital Corp., pp. Vol. II-1272, Vol. III-1809 [NAICS 334310, 423440]

Pacific Echo Inc., p. I-665 [NAICS 326220]

Pacific Golf Accessories Inc., p. III-1883 [NAICS 423910]

Pacific Insulation Co., p. III-1790 [NAICS 423330]

Pacific Koast Graphics Inc., p. III-1905 [NAICS 424130]

Pacific Magtron International Inc., p. III-1805 [NAICS 423430]

Pacific Medical Inc., p. III-1813 [NAICS 423450]

Pacific Mutual Door Co., p. III-1782 [NAICS 423310]

Pacific Packaging Products Inc., p. III-1905 [NAICS 424130]

Pacific Pipe Company Inc., p. III-1871 [NAICS 423840]

Pacific Piston Ring Company Inc., p. II-1505 [NAICS 33631M]

Pacific Precision Metals Inc, p. II-1632 [NAICS 33712N]

Pacific Press Technologies, p. II-886 [NAICS 33221N]

Pacific Rim Import Corp., p. III-1774 [NAICS 423210]

Pacific Seacraft Corp., p. II-1589 [NAICS 336611]

Pacific Seafood Group, p. I-110 [NAICS 31171M]

Pacific Ship Repair & Fabrication, p. II-1589 [NAICS 336611]

Pacific Ship Yards International, p. II-1589 [NAICS 336611]

Pacific Shipyards Intl, p. II-1173 [NAICS 333618]

Pacific Shrimp, p. I-110 [NAICS 31171M]

Pacific Sintered Metals, p. I-867 [NAICS 332117]

Pacific Southwest Container, p. I-379 [NAICS 32221M]

Pacific Star Seafoods Inc., p. I-110 [NAICS 31171M]

Pacific Steel Casting Co., pp. Vol. I-845, 857 [NAICS 33151M, 33152P]

Pacific Sunwear of California Inc., pp. Vol. III-2123, 2126 [NAICS 448110, 448120]

Pacific Supply, pp. Vol. III-1782, 1786, 1790 [NAICS 423310, 423320, 423330]

Pacific Topsoils Inc., p. II-1028 [NAICS 333112]

Pacific Trail Inc., pp. Vol. III-1916, 1919 [NAICS 424320, 424330]

Pacific Transformer Corp., p. II-1421 [NAICS 335311]

Pacific Trinetics Corp., p. II-1056 [NAICS 333295]

Pacific Western Systems Inc., p. II-1056 [NAICS 333295]

Pacific Wood Laminates Inc., p. I-324 [NAICS 32121N]

Pacifico Group, p. III-2011 [NAICS 441110]

Packaging Concepts Inc., pp. Vol. I-395, 415 [NAICS 32222P, 322299]

Packaging Corporation of America, p. I-379 [NAICS 32221M]

Packaging Personified Inc., pp. Vol. I-603, 609, 621 [NAICS 326111, 326112, 326121]

Packaging Resources, pp. Vol. I-343, 636 [NAICS 321920, 326140]

Packaging Services Inc., pp. Vol. I-379, Vol. II-928, 1720 [NAICS 32221M, 33243M, 339950]

Packaging Services Industries, pp. Vol. I-609, 636 [NAICS 326112, 326140]

Packaging Technologies Inc., p. II-1212 [NAICS 333993]

Packless Metal Hose Inc., p. II-918 [NAICS 332410]

Pacon Corp., pp. Vol. I-403, 415, Vol. III-1898 [NAICS 32223M, 322299, 424110]

Pacon Manufacturing Corp., pp. Vol. I-411, 415, Vol. II-886 [NAICS 322291, 322299, 33221N]

Pacor Inc., p. I-771 [NAICS 327993]

Pactiv Corp., pp. Vol. I-374, 379, 395, 403, 816 [NAICS 322130, 32221M, 32222P, 32223M, 33131N]

Padre Island Brewing Inc., p. I-172 [NAICS 312120]

Page International Inc., p. I-665 [NAICS 326220]

Paget Equipment Co., p. II-918 [NAICS 332410]

PAI Industries Inc., p. II-1505 [NAICS 33631M]

Paige Electric Company L.P., p. II-945 [NAICS 332710]

Pain Enterprises, p. I-471 [NAICS 325120]

Paint Supply Co., p. III-2004 [NAICS 424950]

Painters Supply Company Inc., p. III-2004 [NAICS 424950]

Painting Machinery, p. III-1863 [NAICS 423820]

PAKO Inc., pp. Vol. II-1505, 1562 [NAICS 33631M, 336412]

Pala International Inc., p. III-2144 [NAICS 448310]

Numbers following p. or pp. are page references. Roman numerals indicate volume numbers. Bracketed items indicate industries. Page references are to the starting pages of company tables.

2393

Palco Telecom Service Inc., pp. Vol. II-1257, 1262 [NAICS 334210, 334220]

Palermo Supply Company Inc., p. III-1847 [NAICS 423720]

Pall Corp., pp. Vol. II-1112, 1229, 1551 [NAICS 33341N, 33399P, 336399]

Pallet Factory Inc., p. I-343 [NAICS 321920]

Pallet Management Systems Inc., p. I-343 [NAICS 321920]

PalletOne, p. I-343 [NAICS 321920]

Palm Harbor Homes Inc., pp. Vol. I-348, 353 [NAICS 321991, 321992]

Palm Peterbilt-GMC Trucks Inc., p. II-1491 [NAICS 336212]

Palmer Auto Salvage, p. III-1770 [NAICS 423140]

Palmer Manufacturing Co., p. II-1580 [NAICS 336419]

Palmetto Ford Inc., p. III-2030 [NAICS 441310]

PalmOne Inc., p. II-1248 [NAICS 334113]

Palmor Products Inc., p. II-1028 [NAICS 333112]

Palomar Medical Technologies, pp. Vol. II-1282, 1322 [NAICS 334412, 334510]

Palson's Inc., p. III-2186 [NAICS 453210]

Pam Oil Inc., p. III-1762 [NAICS 423120]

Pamarco Technologies Inc., p. II-1714 [NAICS 33994M]

Pamplin Entertainment Corp., p. II-1376 [NAICS 334612]

Pan De Vida Inc., p. III-1887 [NAICS 423920]

Pan-O-Gold Baking Company Inc., p. I-116 [NAICS 31181M]

Pan Osprey Inc., p. III-1883 [NAICS 423910]

Pan Pacific Enterprises Inc., p. II-1005 [NAICS 332995]

Panasonic Consumer Electronics, p. III-1839 [NAICS 423690]

Panasonic Speech Technology, p. II-1257 [NAICS 334210]

Panavision Inc., p. II-1087 [NAICS 333315]

Panavision International L.P., pp. Vol. II-1087, 1390 [NAICS 333315, 33512M]

Pancho's Management Inc., pp. Vol. III-1946, 1950 [NAICS 424470, 424480]

Pandjiris Inc., p. II-1147 [NAICS 333516]

Panef Corp., p. I-26 [NAICS 311225]

Panolam Industries Inc., p. I-631 [NAICS 326130]

Pantronix Corp., pp. Vol. II-1312, 1451 [NAICS 334418, 33592M]

Pantry Inc., p. III-2076 [NAICS 445110]

Papa 51 Limited Co., p. II-1557 [NAICS 336411]

Papa John's International Inc., p. I-68 [NAICS 31142M]

Pape Pecan House, pp. Vol. III-1939, 2092, 2094 [NAICS 424450, 445292, 445299]

Paper Corporation of the U.S., p. III-1898 [NAICS 424110]

Paper Machinery Corp., p. II-1051 [NAICS 333220]

Paper Mart, pp. Vol. III-1875, 1901, 1905 [NAICS 423850, 424120, 424130]

Paper Place, p. III-2186 [NAICS 453210]

Paper Products Company Inc., pp. Vol. III-1905, 1968 [NAICS 424130, 424610]

Paper Systems Inc., p. I-415 [NAICS 322299]

Paper Warehouse Inc., p. III-2153 [NAICS 451120]

PaperPak Products Inc., p. I-411 [NAICS 322291]

Paperwork Co., p. III-2186 [NAICS 453210]

Papsco Inc., p. I-609 [NAICS 326112]

Par-Foam Products Inc., p. I-641 [NAICS 326150]

Par Ltd., p. I-267 [NAICS 31521M]

Par Pharmaceutical Companies Inc., p. I-539 [NAICS 325412]

PaR Systems Inc., p. II-1061 [NAICS 33329N]

PAR Technology Corp., p. II-1077 [NAICS 333313]

Paraclipse Inc., p. I-529 [NAICS 325320]

Paraco Gas Corp., p. III-1979 [NAICS 424720]

Paradies Shops Inc., pp. Vol. III-2153, 2190 [NAICS 451120, 453220]

Paradise Inc., pp. Vol. I-52, 641 [NAICS 311330, 326150]

Paradyne Networks Inc., p. II-1257 [NAICS 334210]

Paragon Development Systems Inc., p. II-1238 [NAICS 334111]

Paragon Die and Engineering Inc., p. II-1119 [NAICS 333511]

Paragon Films Inc., p. I-615 [NAICS 326113]

Paragon Glass Works Inc., p. II-1386 [NAICS 335110]

Paragon Media Inc., p. II-1381 [NAICS 334613]

Paragon Medical Inc., p. I-306 [NAICS 31699M]

Paragon Music Center Inc., p. III-2159 [NAICS 451140]

Paragon Packaging Inc., p. I-646 [NAICS 326160]

Paramit Corp., p. II-1312 [NAICS 334418]

Paramount Apparel Intern. Inc., p. I-251 [NAICS 314999]

Paramount Can Company Inc., p. III-1968 [NAICS 424610]

Paramount Export Co., pp. Vol. III-1950, 1954 [NAICS 424480, 424490]

Paramount Farms, p. I-137 [NAICS 31191M]

Paramount Petroleum Corp., p. I-443 [NAICS 324110]

Paramount Restaurant Supply, p. III-1875 [NAICS 423850]

Paramount Stone Company Inc., p. III-1786 [NAICS 423320]

Parco Foods L.L.C., p. I-124 [NAICS 31182M]

Parco Inc., p. II-1725 [NAICS 339991]

Paris Foods Corp., p. III-1929 [NAICS 424420]

Parisi Royal, p. II-1639 [NAICS 337212]

Park 100 Foods Inc., p. I-152 [NAICS 31194M]

Park Air Corp., p. II-1051 [NAICS 333220]

Park Electrochemical Corp., pp. Vol. I-388, Vol. II-964, 1262 [NAICS 32222N, 33281M, 334220]

Park Industries Inc., pp. Vol. II-1124, 1207 [NAICS 333512, 333991]

Park-Ohio Holdings Corp., pp. Vol. I-505, 626, 756, 872, Vol. II-928, 1217 [NAICS 325212, 326122, 327910, 33211N, 33243M, 333994]

Park Pharmacy Corp., p. III-2100 [NAICS 446110]

Parkdale Mills Inc., pp. Vol. I-192, 290 [NAICS 31311M, 31599M]

Parker Drilling Co., pp. Vol. II-1039, 1092 [NAICS 33313M, 33331N]

Parker-Hannifin, p. II-1725 [NAICS 339991]

Parker Hannifin Corp., pp. Vol. II-980, 1222, 1551, 1567 [NAICS 33291N, 33399N, 336399, 336413]

Parker Hannifin Corp. Abex NWL, pp. Vol. II-1332, 1567, 1580 [NAICS 334512, 336413, 336419]

Parker Hannifin Corp. Airborne, pp. Vol. II-1421, 1562 [NAICS 335311, 336412]

Parker Hannifin Corp. JBL Div., p. II-1725 [NAICS 339991]

Parker Hannifin Corp. Racor Div., pp. Vol. II-1112, 1567 [NAICS 33341N, 336413]

Parker Hosiery Company Inc., p. I-256 [NAICS 31511M]

Parker Paint Manufacturing Inc., p. I-554 [NAICS 325510]

Parkson Corp., p. II-1092 [NAICS 33331N]

Parkview Metal Products Inc., p. II-1134 [NAICS 333514]

Parkway Drugs Inc., p. III-2100 [NAICS 446110]

Parkway Plastics Inc., p. I-646 [NAICS 326160]

Parlec Inc., p. II-1207 [NAICS 333991]

Parlex Corp., pp. Vol. I-837, Vol. II-1282, 1457 [NAICS 33149M, 334412, 33593M]

Parlux Fragrances Inc., p. I-575 [NAICS 325620]

Parma International Inc., p. II-1708 [NAICS 33993M]

Parmalat New Atlanta Dairies, pp. Vol. I-86, 92 [NAICS 31151N, 311520]

Parmalat Sunnydale Farms Inc., pp. Vol. I-62, 86 [NAICS 31141M, 31151N]

Parnell-Martin Co., p. III-1847 [NAICS 423720]

Parr Instrument Co., pp. Vol. II-923, 1342, 1666 [NAICS 332420, 334514, 339111]

Parron-Hall Corp., p. III-1774 [NAICS 423210]

Parrot-Ice Drink Products, p. II-1189 [NAICS 333913]

Pars International Computer Inc., p. III-1809 [NAICS 423440]

Parsons Sales Company Inc., p. III-1790 [NAICS 423330]

Partec Inc., p. II-1708 [NAICS 33993M]

ParTech Inc., p. II-1077 [NAICS 333313]

Particle Measuring Systems Inc., p. II-1352 [NAICS 334516]

Partitions and Accessories Co., pp. Vol. III-1809, 2047, 2208 [NAICS 423440, 442299, 453998]

Partitions Specialties Inc., p. III-1809 [NAICS 423440]

Parts Now! L.L.C., pp. Vol. III-1805, 1867 [NAICS 423430, 423830]

Parts Unlimited Inc., p. II-1536 [NAICS 336360]

Parts Warehouse Inc., p. III-1762 [NAICS 423120]

Party Bazaar, p. III-2190 [NAICS 453220]

Party City Corp., pp. Vol. I-420, Vol. III-2208, 2228 [NAICS 32311M, 453998, 454390]

Party People Limited Inc., p. III-2190 [NAICS 453220]

Pasadena Paper Company L.P., p. I-403 [NAICS 32223M]

Pasadena Tank Corp., p. II-923 [NAICS 332420]

Paslin Company Inc., pp. Vol. II-1134, 1140 [NAICS 333514, 333515]

Pass and Seymour/Legrand, pp. Vol. II-1307, 1317, 1437, 1451, 1457 [NAICS 334417, 334419, 335314, 33592M, 33593M]

Pass Pets Ltd., p. III-2208 [NAICS 453998]

Passaic Rubber Co., p. I-224 [NAICS 313320]

Pastaworks, p. III-2094 [NAICS 445299]

Pastian's Bakery, p. III-2089 [NAICS 445291]

Numbers following p. or pp. are page references. Roman numerals indicate volume numbers. Bracketed items indicate industries. Page references are to the starting pages of company tables.

Pastorelli Food Products Inc., p. I-26 [NAICS 311225]

Patagonia Inc., p. III-2211 [NAICS 454113]

Patent Construction Systems, p. II-1033 [NAICS 333120]

Patented Systems Inc., p. II-1157 [NAICS 333611]

Pathmark Stores Inc., p. III-2076 [NAICS 445110]

Patio Enclosures Inc., p. I-722 [NAICS 327215]

Patrick Industries Inc., pp. Vol. II-1611, Vol. III-1782, 1790, 1794 [NAICS 337110, 423310, 423330, 423390]

Patten Industries Inc., p. III-1859 [NAICS 423810]

Patten Power Systems Inc., pp. Vol. II-1173, 1427, Vol. III-1867 [NAICS 333618, 335312, 423830]

Patterson Companies Inc., p. III-1813 [NAICS 423450]

Patterson Frozen Foods Inc., p. I-62 [NAICS 31141M]

Patterson-Kelley, pp. Vol. II-918, 1417 [NAICS 332410, 335228]

Patterson Oil Co., pp. Vol. III-1979, 2218, 2222 [NAICS 424720, 454311, 454312]

Patterson Pump Co., p. II-1179 [NAICS 333911]

Patton Music Company Inc., pp. Vol. III-2206, 2215 [NAICS 453991, 454210]

Patuxent Materials Inc., p. III-1786 [NAICS 423320]

Paul deLima Company Inc., p. I-143 [NAICS 311920]

Paul Mueller Co., pp. Vol. II-1106, 1666 [NAICS 333415, 339111]

Paul Reed Smith Guitars Ltd., p. II-1731 [NAICS 339992]

Paul's TV - King Of Big Screen, p. III-2054 [NAICS 443112]

Paul Stuart Inc., pp. Vol. III-2123, 2126 [NAICS 448110, 448120]

Paulo Products Co., p. II-1217 [NAICS 333994]

Paulsen Inc., p. I-732 [NAICS 327320]

Paulstra CRC Corp., p. I-670 [NAICS 32629M]

Pauluhn Electric Manufacturing, pp. Vol. II-1386, 1432, 1512 [NAICS 335110, 335313, 33632M]

Pauwels Transformers Inc., p. II-1421 [NAICS 335311]

PAV Republic Inc., pp. Vol. I-780, 793, Vol. II-964, 1014 [NAICS 33111M, 33122M, 33281M, 33299N]

Pavco Inc., pp. Vol. I-475, 488, Vol. II-1457 [NAICS 32513M, 325188, 33593M]

Pavermodule of Florida Inc., pp. Vol. I-691, 737 [NAICS 327121, 32733M]

Pavilion Furniture Inc., p. II-1632 [NAICS 33712N]

Pawling Corp., pp. Vol. I-488, 505, 621 [NAICS 325188, 325212, 326121]

PAXAR Corp., pp. Vol. I-203, 388, 420, Vol. II-1212 [NAICS 31322M, 32222N, 32311M, 333993]

Paxar Corp., Woven Label Group, p. I-203 [NAICS 31322M]

Paxton Company Inc., p. III-1879 [NAICS 423860]

Payless Office Supply Inc., p. III-2186 [NAICS 453210]

Payless ShoeSource Inc., p. III-2141 [NAICS 448210]

PB Fasteners, pp. Vol. II-958, 1580 [NAICS 332722, 336419]

P.B.D. Inc., p. III-1995 [NAICS 424920]

PBI Market Equipment Inc., pp. Vol. III-1809, 1875 [NAICS 423440, 423850]

PBM Graphics Inc., p. I-436 [NAICS 32312M]

PBR Columbia L.L.C., p. II-1524 [NAICS 336340]

PC Connection Inc., p. III-2211 [NAICS 454113]

PC Mall Inc., p. III-2211 [NAICS 454113]

PC Professional Inc., p. III-2058 [NAICS 443120]

P.C. T Systems Inc., p. II-1056 [NAICS 333295]

PCC Airfoils Inc., p. II-1567 [NAICS 336413]

PCC Ceramics Group, pp. Vol. I-681, 776 [NAICS 327112, 327999]

PCC Flow Technologies Inc., p. II-1179 [NAICS 333911]

PCC Structurals Inc., pp. Vol. I-845, 857 [NAICS 33151M, 33152P]

PCDC Inc., p. I-4 [NAICS 311111]

PCG Trading L.L.C., pp. Vol. III-1805, 1831 [NAICS 423430, 423610]

PCI Energy Services Inc., p. II-945 [NAICS 332710]

PCM Image-Tek, p. II-1212 [NAICS 333993]

PDC Glass and Metal Services Inc., p. III-1782 [NAICS 423310]

PDM Steel Service Centers Inc., p. III-1824 [NAICS 423510]

PDQ Sewing Contractors, p. I-285 [NAICS 31529M]

PDVSA Services Inc., p. I-443 [NAICS 324110]

Peace Textile America Inc., p. I-218 [NAICS 31331M]

Peach State Truck Center, pp. Vol. III-1758, 1762 [NAICS 423110, 423120]

Peachtree Doors and Windows Inc., p. I-334 [NAICS 32191M]

Peachtree Fabrics Inc., p. III-1913 [NAICS 424310]

Peachtree Industries Inc., p. III-2138 [NAICS 448190]

Peak Minerals-Azomite Inc., p. I-516 [NAICS 325311]

Peaker Services Inc., p. II-1584 [NAICS 336510]

Peanut Processors Inc., p. I-137 [NAICS 31191M]

Pearce Industries Inc., p. III-1859 [NAICS 423810]

Pearson NCS Inc., p. II-1082 [NAICS 333314]

Pearson's Candy Co., pp. Vol. I-52, 57 [NAICS 311330, 311340]

Pease and Curren Inc., p. I-825 [NAICS 331419]

Peavey Electronics Corp., pp. Vol. II-1272, 1451, 1731 [NAICS 334310, 33592M, 339992]

Pech Optical Corp., p. II-1687 [NAICS 339115]

Pechin Shopping Village, pp. Vol. III-2065, 2180 [NAICS 444100, 452990]

Peck Road Ford Truck Sales Inc., p. III-1758 [NAICS 423110]

Peckham Industries Inc., pp. Vol. I-448, 743 [NAICS 324121, 327390]

PEDCO, pp. Vol. II-1173, 1530 [NAICS 333618, 336350]

Peddinghaus Corp., p. II-1152 [NAICS 333518]

Peddinghaus Modern Technology, p. I-872 [NAICS 33211N]

Pedro Companies Inc., p. I-306 [NAICS 31699M]

Peebles Inc., p. III-2171 [NAICS 452111]

Peer Bearing Co., pp. Vol. II-988, 1168 [NAICS 332991, 333613]

Peerless Chain Co., p. II-939 [NAICS 33261M]

Peerless Coffee Co., p. I-143 [NAICS 311920]

Peerless Confection Co., p. I-57 [NAICS 311340]

Peerless Lighting, p. II-1390 [NAICS 33512M]

Peerless Manufacturing, pp. Vol. I-788, Vol. II-918, 1217 [NAICS 331210, 332410, 333994]

Peerless Manufacturing Co., pp. Vol. II-1039, 1332 [NAICS 33313M, 334512]

Peerless Pottery Inc., p. I-677 [NAICS 327111]

Peerless-Premier Appliance Co., p. II-1404 [NAICS 335221]

Peerless Pump Company Inc., pp. Vol. II-1162, 1179 [NAICS 333612, 333911]

Peerless Tyre Co., pp. Vol. III-2030, 2116 [NAICS 441310, 447110]

Peerless Water Treatment, p. III-2050 [NAICS 443111]

Peerless-Winsmith Inc., pp. Vol. II-1014, 1112, 1427 [NAICS 33299N, 33341N, 335312]

Peet's Coffee and Tea Inc., pp. Vol. I-143, Vol. III-1954 [NAICS 311920, 424490]

Peg-Perego USA Inc., p. II-1708 [NAICS 33993M]

Pegasus Laboratories Inc., pp. Vol. I-4, 9 [NAICS 311111, 311119]

Pegler-Sysco Food Services Co., pp. Vol. III-1809, 1813 [NAICS 423440, 423450]

Pelican Optical Labs Inc., p. III-1817 [NAICS 423460]

Pelican Products Inc., pp. Vol. I-306, Vol. II-1390 [NAICS 31699M, 33512M]

Pella Corp., pp. Vol. I-334, 358, Vol. II-908 [NAICS 32191M, 321999, 33232M]

Pellerin Laundry Machinery Sales, p. III-1875 [NAICS 423850]

Pellet America Corp., p. I-589 [NAICS 325991]

Pelmor Laboratories Inc., p. I-505 [NAICS 325212]

Peltier Glass Company Inc., p. I-709 [NAICS 327211]

Pelton and Crane Co., p. II-1682 [NAICS 339114]

Pemco Aviation Group Inc., pp. Vol. II-1557, 1567, 1572 [NAICS 336411, 336413, 336414]

Pemco World Air Services, p. II-1562 [NAICS 336412]

PEMSTAR Inc., pp. Vol. II-1282, 1457 [NAICS 334412, 33593M]

Penco Corp., pp. Vol. III-1847, 1851 [NAICS 423720, 423730]

PENCO Products Inc., pp. Vol. II-928, 1627, 1644 [NAICS 33243M, 337127, 337215]

Pencoa, p. II-1714 [NAICS 33994M]

Penda Corp., pp. Vol. I-229, Vol. II-1486, 1500 [NAICS 314110, 336211, 336214]

Penda Inc., p. II-1500 [NAICS 336214]

Pendleton Flour Mills L.L.C., p. I-15 [NAICS 31121M]

Pendleton Woolen Mills Inc., p. I-198 [NAICS 313210]

Pendu Manufacturing Inc., p. II-1046 [NAICS 333210]

Penford Corp., pp. Vol. I-22, 534, 595 [NAICS 311221, 325411, 32599N]

Pengrove Building Systems Inc., p. I-353 [NAICS 321992]

Peninsula Floor Inc., p. I-229 [NAICS 314110]

Peninsular Paper Company Inc., pp. Vol. III-1905, 1971 [NAICS 424130, 424690]

Penn Aluminum International Inc., pp. Vol. I-803, 811 [NAICS 331312, 331316]

Penn Co's, pp. Vol. I-251, Vol. II-1212 [NAICS 314999, 333993]

Penn Detroit Diesel Allison Inc., pp. Vol. II-1168, 1173, 1505 [NAICS 333613, 333618, 33631M]

Penn Fishing Tackle Mfg Co., p. II-1702 [NAICS 339920]

Penn Machine Co., pp. Vol. II-945, 1039, 1147, 1162, 1551 [NAICS 332710, 33313M, 333516, 333612, 336399]

Penn Maid-Crowley Foods, pp. Vol. I-76, 86 [NAICS 311513, 31151N]

Penn Octane Corp., p. III-1979 [NAICS 424720]

Penn Refrigeration Service Corp., p. I-631 [NAICS 326130]

Penn Summit Manufacturing, p. I-788 [NAICS 331210]

Penn Telecom Inc., p. III-1839 [NAICS 423690]

Penn-Union Corp., p. II-1457 [NAICS 33593M]

Penn United Technology Inc., pp. Vol. I-488, Vol. II-1124, 1134 [NAICS 325188, 333512, 333514]

Pennfield Corp., p. I-9 [NAICS 311119]

Pennsylvania Brewing Inc., p. I-172 [NAICS 312120]

Pennsylvania House Furniture, pp. Vol. II-1616, 1621 [NAICS 337121, 337122]

Pennsylvania Transformer, pp. Vol. II-1302, 1421 [NAICS 334416, 335311]

PennTecQ Inc., p. I-863 [NAICS 332114]

Penny Plate Inc., p. II-928 [NAICS 33243M]

Penske Jasper Engines, p. II-1505 [NAICS 33631M]

Pentafab Inc., p. I-218 [NAICS 31331M]

Pentair Inc., pp. Vol. I-334, 368, Vol. II-908, 980, 993, 1046, 1179, 1207 [NAICS 32191M, 32212M, 33232M, 33291N, 332992, 333210, 333911, 333991]

Pentair Water, pp. Vol. II-1179, 1222 [NAICS 333911, 33399N]

Pentel of America Ltd., p. II-1714 [NAICS 33994M]

Penthouse Manufacturing Co., p. I-575 [NAICS 325620]

Pentron Corp., p. II-1682 [NAICS 339114]

People's Pharmacy Inc., p. III-2100 [NAICS 446110]

Peopleclick Inc., p. III-2058 [NAICS 443120]

Peopleloungers Inc., pp. Vol. II-1616, 1627 [NAICS 337121, 337127]

Peoples Gas and Oil Company Inc., p. III-2222 [NAICS 454312]

Pep Boys-Manny, Moe and Jack, p. III-2030 [NAICS 441310]

Pep Threads, p. I-285 [NAICS 31529M]

Pepin-Ireco Inc., p. I-585 [NAICS 325920]

Pepperl Fuchs Inc., p. II-1332 [NAICS 334512]

Pepsi Bottling Group Inc., p. I-165 [NAICS 31211M]

Pepsi Bottling Ventures L.L.C., p. I-165 [NAICS 31211M]

Pepsi-Cola Batavia Bottling Corp., p. III-1954 [NAICS 424490]

Pepsi-Cola Bottling Co., pp. Vol. I-165, Vol. III-1954 [NAICS 31211M, 424490]

Pepsi Cola Bottling of Central VA, p. I-165 [NAICS 31211M]

Pepsi-Cola Bottling of Conway, p. I-165 [NAICS 31211M]

Pepsi-Cola Bottling of Florence, pp. Vol. I-147, 165 [NAICS 311930, 31211M]

Pepsi-Cola Buffalo Bottling Co., p. I-165 [NAICS 31211M]

Pepsi-Cola General Bottlers, pp. Vol. I-165, Vol. III-1954 [NAICS 31211M, 424490]

Pepsi-Cola Metro Bottling Co., p. I-165 [NAICS 31211M]

Pepsi MidAmerica, pp. Vol. I-147, 165 [NAICS 311930, 31211M]

PepsiAmericas Inc., pp. Vol. I-165, Vol. II-1106 [NAICS 31211M, 333415]

PepsiCo Inc., pp. Vol. I-68, 137, 165 [NAICS 31142M, 31191M, 31211M]

Pequea Machine Inc., p. II-1162 [NAICS 333612]

Perceptron Inc., p. II-1082 [NAICS 333314]

Perdue Company Inc., p. III-2186 [NAICS 453210]

Perdue Farms Inc., pp. Vol. I-9, 26, 97 [NAICS 311119, 311225, 311615]

Perez Trading Company Inc., pp. Vol. III-1898, 1905 [NAICS 424110, 424130]

Perfect Plastic Printing Corp., pp. Vol. I-631, Vol. II-892, 1720 [NAICS 326130, 33221P, 339950]

Perfection Bakeries Inc., p. I-116 [NAICS 31181M]

Perfection Clutch, p. II-1530 [NAICS 336350]

Perfection Spring & Stamping, p. II-1541 [NAICS 336370]

Perfecto Manufacturing Inc., pp. Vol. I-358, 713, 722 [NAICS 321999, 327212, 327215]

Perfetti Van Melle USA Inc., p. I-57 [NAICS 311340]

Performance Contracting Group, p. II-1014 [NAICS 33299N]

Performance Contractors Inc., p. II-1009 [NAICS 332996]

Performance Films Distributing, p. III-1798 [NAICS 423410]

Performance Food Group Co., pp. Vol. III-1809, 1925, 1929, 1950 [NAICS 423440, 424410, 424420, 424480]

Performance Inc., p. III-2150 [NAICS 451110]

Performance Machine Inc., pp. Vol. II-1524, 1599 [NAICS 336340, 336991]

Performance Materials Corp., p. I-510 [NAICS 32522M]

Performance Technologies Inc., p. II-1282 [NAICS 334412]

PerkinElmer Belfab, p. II-1725 [NAICS 339991]

PerkinElmer Fluid Sciences Inc., pp. Vol. II-1567, 1580, 1725 [NAICS 336413, 336419, 339991]

PerkinElmer Inc., pp. Vol. II-1082, 1267, 1317, 1337 [NAICS 333314, 334290, 334419, 334513]

Perkins Engines Inc., p. II-1173 [NAICS 333618]

Perma Glas-Mesh Inc., pp. Vol. I-224, 713 [NAICS 313320, 327212]

Perma R Products Inc., p. I-636 [NAICS 326140]

Permacor Inc., pp. Vol. I-686, 867 [NAICS 327113, 332117]

Permco, pp. Vol. II-1162, 1168, 1179, 1222, 1567 [NAICS 333612, 333613, 333911, 33399N, 336413]

Permian Tank Inc., p. II-923 [NAICS 332420]

Pernod Ricard USA, pp. Vol. I-177, 181 [NAICS 312130, 312140]

Perrigo Co., pp. Vol. I-539, 575 [NAICS 325412, 325620]

Perry Bancshares Inc., p. I-732 [NAICS 327320]

Perry Chemical and Mfg Inc., pp. Vol. I-641, 756 [NAICS 326150, 327910]

Perry Dell Farms, p. III-2080 [NAICS 445120]

Perry Ellis International Inc., p. I-272 [NAICS 31522M]

Perry Judd's Inc., p. I-420 [NAICS 32311M]

Perry Manufacturing Company Inc., p. I-279 [NAICS 31523M]

Perry's Ice Cream Company Inc., p. I-92 [NAICS 311520]

Perryton Equity Exchange, pp. Vol. III-1958, 1979, 1991 [NAICS 424510, 424720, 424910]

Persinger Supply Co., pp. Vol. III-1835, 1871 [NAICS 423620, 423840]

Persona Inc., p. II-1720 [NAICS 339950]

Persons-Majestic Mfg Co., p. II-1599 [NAICS 336991]

Perstorp Polyols Inc., pp. Vol. I-488, 493 [NAICS 325188, 32519M]

Pet Food Services Inc., p. I-4 [NAICS 311111]

Pet Magic Inc., p. I-4 [NAICS 311111]

Petco Animal Supplies Inc., p. III-2208 [NAICS 453998]

Pete Moore Appliance Inc., pp. Vol. III-2037, 2050 [NAICS 442110, 443111]

Peter Pan Seafoods Inc., p. I-110 [NAICS 31171M]

Peterbilt of Utah Inc., p. III-1758 [NAICS 423110]

Petersen Aluminum Corp., pp. Vol. I-453, 811, 816, Vol. II-964 [NAICS 324122, 331316, 33131N, 33281M]

Peterson and Company Inc., p. I-830 [NAICS 33142M]

Peterson Farms Inc., pp. Vol. I-9, 97 [NAICS 311119, 311615]

Peterson Industries Inc., p. II-1500 [NAICS 336214]

Peterson Medical, p. III-1813 [NAICS 423450]

Peterson Spring Inc., p. II-939 [NAICS 33261M]

Peterson Tractor Co., p. III-1859 [NAICS 423810]

Petit Jean Poultry Inc., p. I-97 [NAICS 311615]

Petitto Mine Equipment Inc., p. II-1584 [NAICS 336510]

Petri Baking Products Inc., p. I-124 [NAICS 31182M]

Petricca Industries Inc., pp. Vol. I-732, 743 [NAICS 327320, 327390]

Petrik Laboratories Inc., p. I-516 [NAICS 325311]

Petro Holdings Inc., pp. Vol. III-2208, 2218, 2225 [NAICS 453998, 454311, 454319]

Petro Stopping Centers L.P., pp. Vol. III-2116, 2180 [NAICS 447110, 452990]

Petroferm Inc., p. I-566 [NAICS 32561M]

Petroleum Marketers Inc., pp. Vol. III-1975, 2218 [NAICS 424710, 454311]

Petroleum Service Co., pp. Vol. III-1867, 1979 [NAICS 423830, 424720]

PETsMART Inc., p. III-2208 [NAICS 453998]

Pettibone Traverse Lift L.L.C., p. II-1194 [NAICS 33392M]

Petting Zoo Inc., p. III-1887 [NAICS 423920]

Pettit's Pastry Inc., p. III-2089 [NAICS 445291]

Petty Enterprises II L.L.C., pp. Vol. II-1473, 1486, 1505 [NAICS 336111, 336211, 33631M]

Petzl America Inc., p. III-1883 [NAICS 423910]

Pferd Milwaukee Brush Inc., p. II-1740 [NAICS 339994]

PFFJ Inc., p. I-9 [NAICS 311119]

P.F.G. Lester Company Inc., pp. Vol. III-1809, 1971 [NAICS 423440, 424690]

Pfizer, pp. Vol. I-529, 539, 595 [NAICS 325320, 325412, 32599N]

Pfizer Inc., pp. Vol. I-529, 534, 539, Vol. II-1676, Vol. III-1909 [NAICS 325320, 325411, 325412, 339113, 424210]

PGT Industries Inc., pp. Vol. I-651, 722, Vol. II-908 [NAICS 32619M, 327215, 33232M]

P.H. Glatfelter Co., pp. Vol. I-363, 368 [NAICS 322110, 32212M]

Phamatech Inc., p. III-1813 [NAICS 423450]

Pharmaceutical Innovations Inc., p. II-1357 [NAICS 334517]

Pharmasol Corp., p. I-471 [NAICS 325120]

Pharmavite Corp., pp. Vol. I-534, 575 [NAICS 325411, 325620]

PharMerica Inc., p. III-1909 [NAICS 424210]

PharMingen, p. I-549 [NAICS 325414]

Pharr Brand Name Apparel L.L.C., p. I-285 [NAICS 31529M]

Pharr Yarns Inc., p. I-192 [NAICS 31311M]

Phase Technology Corp., p. II-1272 [NAICS 334310]

PHB Inc. Phb Tool and Die Div., pp. Vol. I-852, 857 [NAICS 33152N, 33152P]

PHC Industries Inc., p. I-306 [NAICS 31699M]

PHD Inc., p. II-1222 [NAICS 33399N]

Phelps Dodge Corp., pp. Vol. I-484, 822, 857, Vol. II-1551 [NAICS 325182, 331411, 33152P, 336399]

Phelps Dodge Magnet Wire Co., pp. Vol. I-803, 816, 830, 837, Vol. II-939 [NAICS 331312, 33131N, 33142M, 33149M, 33261M]

Phelps Time Recording Lock Corp., p. II-1362 [NAICS 334518]

Phelps Tire Co., pp. Vol. I-660, Vol. III-2034 [NAICS 32621M, 441320]

Phenomenex Inc., pp. Vol. II-1352, 1666 [NAICS 334516, 339111]

Phibro Animal Health Corp., pp. Vol. I-4, 488 [NAICS 311111, 325188]

Phifer Wire Products Inc., pp. Vol. I-811, Vol. II-939 [NAICS 331316, 33261M]

Philadelphia Bourse Inc., pp. Vol. II-1567, Vol. III-2208 [NAICS 336413, 453998]

Philadelphia Candies Inc., p. III-2092 [NAICS 445292]

Philadelphia Coca-Cola Bottling, p. I-165 [NAICS 31211M]

Philadelphia Gear Corp., pp. Vol. II-980, 1162, 1427 [NAICS 33291N, 333612, 335312]

Philadelphia Tramrail Co., p. II-1584 [NAICS 336510]

Philadelphia Turf Co., p. III-1863 [NAICS 423820]

Philip Services Corp., pp. Vol. I-488, 595, Vol. III-1890 [NAICS 325188, 32599N, 423930]

Philip Specialty Co., pp. Vol. II-997, 1005 [NAICS 332993, 332995]

Philips Consumer Electronics, pp. Vol. II-1267, 1272, Vol. III-1809 [NAICS 334290, 334310, 423440]

Philips Products Inc., pp. Vol. I-651, Vol. II-908 [NAICS 32619M, 33232M]

Philips Semiconductors, p. II-1287 [NAICS 334413]

Philips Semiconductors Inc., p. II-1287 [NAICS 334413]

Phillip Metals Inc., p. III-1890 [NAICS 423930]

Phillips and Temro Industries Inc., pp. Vol. II-1222, 1546 [NAICS 33399N, 336391]

Phillips Beverage Co., p. I-181 [NAICS 312140]

Phillips Components, pp. Vol. I-686, Vol. II-1297 [NAICS 327113, 334415]

Phillips Service Industries Inc., pp. Vol. II-928, 1207 [NAICS 33243M, 333991]

Phillips Sew and Assembly Inc., p. I-267 [NAICS 31521M]

Phillips-Van Heusen Corp., pp. Vol. I-272, 279, 290, 300, Vol. III-1916, 1919, 1922, 2123, 2126, 2141 [NAICS 31522M, 31523M, 31599M, 31621M, 424320, 424330, 424340, 448110, 448120, 448210]

Philly's Famous Water Ice Inc., p. III-1933 [NAICS 424430]

Phoenix Aerospace Inc., p. III-1879 [NAICS 423860]

Phoenix Cement Co., p. I-727 [NAICS 327310]

Phoenix Coca-Cola Bottling Co., pp. Vol. I-165, Vol. II-928, Vol. III-1954 [NAICS 31211M, 33243M, 424490]

Phoenix Company of Chicago Inc., p. II-1307 [NAICS 334417]

Phoenix Electric Corp., p. II-1297 [NAICS 334415]

Phoenix Electric Manufacturing, p. II-1463 [NAICS 335991]

Phoenix Equipment Inc., p. III-1820 [NAICS 423490]

Phoenix Footwear Group Inc., p. I-300 [NAICS 31621M]

Phoenix L.L.C., p. III-2186 [NAICS 453210]

Phoenix Metals Co., pp. Vol. II-1092, Vol. III-1824 [NAICS 33331N, 423510]

Phoenix Process Equipment Inc., p. II-1129 [NAICS 333513]

Phoenix Products Co., p. III-1971 [NAICS 424690]

Phoenix Sewing Co., p. I-285 [NAICS 31529M]

Phoenix Textile Corp., p. III-1778 [NAICS 423220]

PHONEXTRA INC., p. III-2208 [NAICS 453998]

Photo Sciences Inc., pp. Vol. I-703, Vol. II-1056, 1082, 1451 [NAICS 32712N, 333295, 333314, 33592M]

Photo Stencil L.L.C., p. II-1714 [NAICS 33994M]

Photo Systems Inc., p. III-1798 [NAICS 423410]

Photo Video Network, p. II-1376 [NAICS 334612]

Photocircuits Corp., p. II-1282 [NAICS 334412]

Photon Dynamics Inc., p. II-1347 [NAICS 334515]

Photronics Inc., pp. Vol. I-713, Vol. II-1061, 1287 [NAICS 327212, 33329N, 334413]

Phylrich International Inc., p. II-974 [NAICS 332913]

Physician Sales and Service Inc., p. III-1813 [NAICS 423450]

Piano and Organ Distributors Inc., p. III-2159 [NAICS 451140]

PIC Design L.L.C., p. I-665 [NAICS 326220]

Picanol of America Inc., p. III-1867 [NAICS 423830]

Pickelner Fuel Company Inc., pp. Vol. III-2218, 2222 [NAICS 454311, 454312]

Picker International Inc., p. III-1813 [NAICS 423450]

Pickett Hosiery Mills Inc., p. I-256 [NAICS 31511M]

Pickett Measurement Systems, p. II-1342 [NAICS 334514]

Picolight Inc., pp. Vol. II-1267, Vol. III-1839 [NAICS 334290, 423690]

Pictsweet Co., p. I-62 [NAICS 31141M]

Picture Galleries Inc., p. III-2200 [NAICS 453920]

Pictures and More Inc., p. III-1778 [NAICS 423220]

Piedmont Home Textile Inc., pp. Vol. I-234, 251 [NAICS 31412M, 314999]

Piedmont Laboratories Inc., p. I-471 [NAICS 325120]

Pieper Electric Inc., pp. Vol. II-1327, 1337, 1432, 1437 [NAICS 334511, 334513, 335313, 335314]

Pier 1 Imports Inc., pp. Vol. III-2037, 2047, 2132 [NAICS 442110, 442299, 448140]

Pier 1 Imports (U.S.) Inc., pp. Vol. III-2037, 2047, 2132, 2144 [NAICS 442110, 442299, 448140, 448310]

Pier 19 Inc., p. III-2047 [NAICS 442299]

Pier-Mac Plastics Inc., p. I-863 [NAICS 332114]

Pieratt's Inc., pp. Vol. II-1352, Vol. III-2050, 2054 [NAICS 334516, 443111, 443112]

Pierce Industries, p. II-923 [NAICS 332420]

Pierce-Spafford Metals Inc., p. III-1770 [NAICS 423140]

Piercing Pagoda Inc., p. III-2144 [NAICS 448310]

Pierre Part Store Inc., pp. Vol. III-2177, 2190 [NAICS 452910, 453220]

Pierre's French Ice Cream Co., p. I-92 [NAICS 311520]

Piggly Wiggly Carolina Inc., p. III-1925 [NAICS 424410]

Pik Rite Inc., p. II-1589 [NAICS 336611]

Pike Distributors Inc., p. III-1987 [NAICS 424820]

Pilgrim's Pride, p. I-97 [NAICS 311615]

Pilgrim's Pride Corp., pp. Vol. I-62, 97 [NAICS 31141M, 311615]

Pilkington North America Inc., pp. Vol. I-709, 722 [NAICS 327211, 327215]

Pillar Data Systems Inc., p. II-1243 [NAICS 334112]

Pillar Induction Company L.L.C., p. II-1217 [NAICS 333994]

Pilot Chemical Co., p. I-566 [NAICS 32561M]

Pilot Corporation of America, p. II-1714 [NAICS 33994M]

Pina Cellars, p. I-177 [NAICS 312130]

Pine Bluff Arsenal, pp. Vol. II-993, 1005 [NAICS 332992, 332995]

Pine Grove Manufactured Homes, pp. Vol. I-348, 353 [NAICS 321991, 321992]

Pine Island Sportswear Ltd., p. I-262 [NAICS 31519M]

Pine Lesser and Sons Inc., pp. Vol. III-1939, 2001 [NAICS 424450, 424940]

Pine Ridge Winery L.L.C., p. I-177 [NAICS 312130]

Pine Tree Lumber L.P., p. III-1843 [NAICS 423710]

Pines Manufacturing Inc., pp. Vol. II-1129, 1147, 1152 [NAICS 333513, 333516, 333518]

Pinkerton Building Supplies Inc., p. III-1794 [NAICS 423390]

Pinnacle Frames and Accents Inc., p. I-358 [NAICS 321999]

Pinnacle Systems Inc., p. II-1087 [NAICS 333315]

Pint Size Corp., p. III-1933 [NAICS 424430]

Pioneer Aerospace Corp., pp. Vol. I-251, 343, Vol. II-908, 1676 [NAICS 314999, 321920, 33232M, 339113]

Numbers following p. or pp. are page references. Roman numerals indicate volume numbers. Bracketed items indicate industries. Page references are to the starting pages of company tables.

Pioneer Automotive Technologies, p. II-1272 [NAICS 334310]

Pioneer Companies Inc., pp. Vol. I-475, 480 [NAICS 32513M, 325181]

Pioneer Flour Mills, pp. Vol. I-15, 158 [NAICS 31121M, 31199M]

Pioneer Hi-Bred International Inc., p. I-529 [NAICS 325320]

Pioneer Industries L.L.C., p. III-1794 [NAICS 423390]

Pioneer Metal Finishing Corp., p. II-964 [NAICS 33281M]

Pioneer National Latex Co., pp. Vol. I-589, 670, Vol. II-1708 [NAICS 325991, 32629M, 33993M]

Pioneer Natural Resources USA, p. I-443 [NAICS 324110]

Pioneer New Media Technologies, pp. Vol. II-1243, 1272 [NAICS 334112, 334310]

Pioneer Paper Corp., p. I-379 [NAICS 32221M]

Pioneer Photo Albums Inc., p. III-1798 [NAICS 423410]

Pioneer Plastics Corp., pp. Vol. I-388, 631 [NAICS 32222N, 326130]

Pioneer Power Systems Inc., pp. Vol. II-1292, 1302, 1421 [NAICS 334414, 334416, 335311]

Pioneer Snacks Inc., pp. Vol. I-102, 137 [NAICS 31161N, 31191M]

Piper Products Inc., p. II-1404 [NAICS 335221]

Piping Technology and Products, p. II-923 [NAICS 332420]

Piqua Materials Inc., p. I-771 [NAICS 327993]

Pirelli Communications Cables, p. II-1451 [NAICS 33592M]

Pisani Enterprises Inc., pp. Vol. III-1894, 2190, 2208 [NAICS 423940, 453220, 453998]

Pisgah Yarn and Dyeing Inc., p. I-218 [NAICS 31331M]

Pistorius Machine Company Inc., p. II-1046 [NAICS 333210]

Pitney Bowes Inc., p. II-1077 [NAICS 333313]

Pitt Penn Oil Co., p. I-458 [NAICS 324191]

Pitt Plastics Inc., p. I-615 [NAICS 326113]

Pittsburg Tank and Tower Inc., p. II-923 [NAICS 332420]

Pittsburgh Brewing Company Inc., p. I-172 [NAICS 312120]

Pittsburgh Snax and Nut Inc., p. III-2094 [NAICS 445299]

Pittsburgh Vision Services, p. II-1740 [NAICS 339994]

Pittsfield Weaving Company Inc., pp. Vol. I-192, 203 [NAICS 31311M, 31322M]

Pivot Interiors, p. III-1774 [NAICS 423210]

Pixelink Corp., p. II-1248 [NAICS 334113]

PK USA Inc., pp. Vol. I-641, Vol. II-933, 1473 [NAICS 326150, 332510, 336111]

PL Rohrer and Bro Inc., pp. Vol. III-2069, 2072 [NAICS 444210, 444220]

Plaid Enterprises Inc., pp. Vol. I-554, Vol. II-1714 [NAICS 325510, 33994M]

Plain & Fancy Custom Cabinetry, p. II-1611 [NAICS 337110]

Plains Equity Exchange, pp. Vol. III-1975, 2072 [NAICS 424710, 444220]

Plainview Batteries Inc., p. II-1447 [NAICS 335912]

Plant Health Care Inc., p. I-516 [NAICS 325311]

Plant Maintenance Service Corp., pp. Vol. II-918, 923, 1217 [NAICS 332410, 332420, 333994]

Plant Sitters Inc., p. III-2183 [NAICS 453110]

Plantation Pecan and Gift Inc., p. I-57 [NAICS 311340]

Planters Cotton Oil Mill, pp. Vol. I-31, 137 [NAICS 31122N, 31191M]

Plantronics Inc., pp. Vol. II-1257, 1317 [NAICS 334210, 334419]

Plasco, pp. Vol. II-1119, 1307 [NAICS 333511, 334417]

Plasco Inc., p. II-1119 [NAICS 333511]

Plaskolite Inc., pp. Vol. I-615, 621 [NAICS 326113, 326121]

Plasmon Inc., p. II-1243 [NAICS 334112]

Plaspack USA Inc., p. I-603 [NAICS 326111]

Plaspros Inc., p. I-609 [NAICS 326112]

Plasser American Corp., p. II-1584 [NAICS 336510]

Plastag Corp., p. I-631 [NAICS 326130]

Plastech, p. II-1119 [NAICS 333511]

Plasti-Form Inc., p. I-651 [NAICS 32619M]

Plastic Engineering & Tech Svs, p. II-1051 [NAICS 333220]

Plastic Fabricating Company Inc., p. II-1632 [NAICS 33712N]

Plastic Industries Inc., p. I-646 [NAICS 326160]

Plastic Packaging Inc., pp. Vol. I-603, 631 [NAICS 326111, 326130]

Plastic Packaging Technology, p. I-603 [NAICS 326111]

Plastic Processors Inc., p. I-208 [NAICS 313230]

Plastic Suppliers Inc., p. I-615 [NAICS 326113]

Plastic Trim L.L.C., pp. Vol. I-621, Vol. II-933 [NAICS 326121, 332510]

Plasticolor Molded Products Inc., p. I-229 [NAICS 314110]

Plastics Engineering Company Inc., pp. Vol. I-500, 595 [NAICS 325211, 32599N]

PlastiFab Inc., p. II-1968 [NAICS 424610]

Plastiflex Company Inc., p. I-665 [NAICS 326220]

Plastikon Industries, p. II-1119 [NAICS 333511]

Plastipak Packaging Inc., p. I-626 [NAICS 326122]

Plastirun Corp., p. I-411 [NAICS 322291]

Plastival Inc., p. III-1794 [NAICS 423390]

Plastomer Corp., pp. Vol. I-636, 641, Vol. II-1725 [NAICS 326140, 326150, 339991]

Plastrglas Inc., p. I-703 [NAICS 32712N]

Plastronics Interconnections Inc., p. II-1056 [NAICS 333295]

PlastxWorld Inc., p. I-589 [NAICS 325991]

Platt Brothers and Company Inc., p. II-1735 [NAICS 339993]

Platt Electric Supply Inc., p. III-1831 [NAICS 423610]

Platypus Inc., p. III-2047 [NAICS 442299]

Play-Mor Trailers Inc., p. II-1491 [NAICS 336212]

Player Wire Wheels Ltd., p. III-1766 [NAICS 423130]

Players Lounge, p. III-2097 [NAICS 445310]

Playmobil USA Inc., p. III-1887 [NAICS 423920]

Playtex Products Inc., pp. Vol. I-272, 279, 290, 411, 626, 670 [NAICS 31522M, 31523M, 31599M, 322291, 326122, 32629M]

Playworld Systems Inc., p. II-1702 [NAICS 339920]

Plaza Bakery Haagen Dazs, p. III-2094 [NAICS 445299]

Plaza Materials Corp., p. I-748 [NAICS 327410]

PLCS Inc., p. II-1147 [NAICS 333516]

Pleasants Hardware Co., p. III-1843 [NAICS 423710]

Pleasure Craft Marine Engine Co., p. II-1505 [NAICS 33631M]

Plee-Zing Inc., p. III-1929 [NAICS 424420]

Plexus Corp., pp. Vol. II-1282, 1317 [NAICS 334412, 334419]

Pliana Inc., p. I-192 [NAICS 31311M]

Pliant Corp., p. I-388 [NAICS 32222N]

Plote Co's Inc., p. I-453 [NAICS 324122]

Plum Creek Timber Company Inc., p. I-312 [NAICS 32111M]

Plumrose USA Inc., p. I-102 [NAICS 31161N]

Plunkett Furniture Co., pp. Vol. III-2037, 2041 [NAICS 442110, 442210]

PLUS Vision Corp. of America, pp. Vol. II-1087, Vol. III-1901 [NAICS 333315, 424120]

Pluto Corp., p. I-646 [NAICS 326160]

Plymouth Foam Inc., p. I-771 [NAICS 327993]

Plymouth Rubber Company Inc., pp. Vol. I-224, 670, Vol. II-1243, 1468 [NAICS 313320, 32629M, 334112, 335999]

Plymouth Tube Co., pp. Vol. I-780, 793 [NAICS 33111M, 33122M]

PMC Global Inc., pp. Vol. I-493, 626, 641 [NAICS 32519M, 326122, 326150]

PMG International Inc., p. III-1995 [NAICS 424920]

PMI, p. I-646 [NAICS 326160]

PMX Industries Inc., pp. Vol. I-822, 830, 857 [NAICS 331411, 33142M, 33152P]

Pneumatic Scale Corp., p. II-1212 [NAICS 333993]

PNY Technologies Inc., p. II-1287 [NAICS 334413]

Pobco Inc., p. II-988 [NAICS 332991]

Pocahontas Foods USA Inc., p. III-1929 [NAICS 424420]

Pohlman Inc., p. II-952 [NAICS 332721]

Point Adams Packing Co., p. I-110 [NAICS 31171M]

Pokka USA, p. I-143 [NAICS 311920]

Polar Corp., pp. Vol. I-165, Vol. III-1954 [NAICS 31211M, 424490]

Polar Tank Trailers Inc., p. II-1491 [NAICS 336212]

Polaris Industries Inc., pp. Vol. II-1594, 1607 [NAICS 336612, 336999]

Polaroid Corp., pp. Vol. II-1082, 1087 [NAICS 333314, 333315]

Polk County Farmers Co-Op, pp. Vol. III-1863, 2120 [NAICS 423820, 447190]

Pollock Paper and Packaging Co., pp. Vol. I-374, 379, 388, Vol. III-1905 [NAICS 322130, 32221M, 32222N, 424130]

Polo Ralph Lauren Corp., pp. Vol. III-1916, 1919, 2132 [NAICS 424320, 424330, 448140]

Polson Rubber Company Inc., p. I-660 [NAICS 32621M]

Poly-America L.P., pp. Vol. I-603, 615 [NAICS 326111, 326113]

Poly Design International Inc., p. II-1056 [NAICS 333295]

Poly Foam Inc., pp. Vol. I-609, 636 [NAICS 326112, 326140]

Poly Hi Solidur Inc., pp. Vol. I-500, 615, 621 [NAICS 325211, 326113, 326121]

Numbers following p. or pp. are page references. Roman numerals indicate volume numbers. Bracketed items indicate industries. Page references are to the starting pages of company tables.

2398

Poly-Optical Products Inc., pp. Vol. II-1386, 1451 [NAICS 335110, 33592M]

Poly Pak America Inc., pp. Vol. I-395, 403, 615 [NAICS 32222P, 32223M, 326113]

Poly Portables Inc., p. II-1119 [NAICS 333511]

Poly Processing Co., p. II-923 [NAICS 332420]

Poly-Tainer Inc., p. I-646 [NAICS 326160]

Poly Vinyl Company Inc., p. I-621 [NAICS 326121]

Polycast Industries Inc., p. II-1056 [NAICS 333295]

Polychem Alloy Inc., p. I-589 [NAICS 325991]

Polychem Corp., pp. Vol. I-198, 872 [NAICS 313210, 33211N]

Polychem Dispersions Inc., p. I-505 [NAICS 325212]

Polycom Inc., pp. Vol. II-1252, 1272 [NAICS 334119, 334310]

Polyfil Corp., p. I-589 [NAICS 325991]

Polyflex, p. I-589 [NAICS 325991]

Polyfoam Corp., p. I-636 [NAICS 326140]

Polygenex International Inc., p. I-203 [NAICS 31322M]

PolyMedica Corp., pp. Vol. I-539, Vol. II-1671, Vol. III-2211 [NAICS 325412, 339112, 454113]

Polymer Enterprises Inc., pp. Vol. I-660, 670 [NAICS 32621M, 32629M]

Polymer Group Inc., pp. Vol. I-198, 208, 244 [NAICS 313210, 313230, 314991]

Polymeric Imaging Inc., p. I-580 [NAICS 325910]

Polymeric Resources Corp., p. I-510 [NAICS 32522M]

Polymerics Inc., p. I-505 [NAICS 325212]

PolyOne Corp., pp. Vol. I-500, 554, 560, 589 [NAICS 325211, 325510, 325520, 325991]

Polypack Inc., p. II-1212 [NAICS 333993]

Polypros Inc., p. II-1056 [NAICS 333295]

Polysciences Inc., p. I-493 [NAICS 32519M]

Polytek Development Corp., pp. Vol. I-505, 589 [NAICS 325212, 325991]

Polytex Environmental Inks Ltd., p. I-580 [NAICS 325910]

Polytex Fibers Corp., p. I-603 [NAICS 326111]

Polytone Musical Instruments Inc., p. II-1731 [NAICS 339992]

Polyvinyl Films Inc., p. I-609 [NAICS 326112]

Pomeroy IT Solutions Inc., p. III-1805 [NAICS 423430]

Ponder's Inc., p. III-2186 [NAICS 453210]

Ponderay Newsprint Co., p. I-368 [NAICS 32212M]

Poof-Slinky Inc., p. II-1708 [NAICS 33993M]

Pool Water Products Inc., p. III-1883 [NAICS 423910]

Poole Ventura Inc., p. II-1056 [NAICS 333295]

Poolmaster Inc., p. II-1708 [NAICS 33993M]

PoolPak International, p. II-1397 [NAICS 33521M]

Poore Brothers Inc., p. III-1939 [NAICS 424450]

Pope and Talbot Inc., pp. Vol. I-312, 363, 368 [NAICS 32111M, 322110, 32212M]

Popp Cement Tile Products, p. I-699 [NAICS 327123]

Popper and Sons Inc., p. II-1352 [NAICS 334516]

Popular Dry Goods Co., p. III-2171 [NAICS 452111]

Popular Mattress Factory Inc., p. II-1657 [NAICS 337910]

Porcelain Products Co., pp. Vol. I-686, Vol. II-1421 [NAICS 327113, 335311]

Porous Media Corp., p. II-1229 [NAICS 33399P]

Port Plastics Inc., p. III-1968 [NAICS 424610]

Porta-Kamp Construction Inc., p. I-353 [NAICS 321992]

Porta Systems Corp., p. II-1421 [NAICS 335311]

Portage Electric Products Inc., p. II-1332 [NAICS 334512]

PORTEC Pathfinder, p. II-1519 [NAICS 336330]

Portec Rail Products Inc., p. II-1584 [NAICS 336510]

Porter Engineered Systems Ohio, p. II-1541 [NAICS 336370]

Porter Henderson Implement Co., p. III-2069 [NAICS 444210]

Porter Instrument Company Inc., pp. Vol. II-1342, 1421 [NAICS 334514, 335311]

Porter Of Racine, p. III-2037 [NAICS 442110]

Porter Oil Company Inc., p. III-1975 [NAICS 424710]

Porter Pipe and Supply Co., p. III-1851 [NAICS 423730]

PorterCorp, pp. Vol. I-324, 641 [NAICS 32121N, 326150]

Portola Packaging Inc., p. I-646 [NAICS 326160]

Posey County Farm Bureau Coop., p. I-524 [NAICS 325314]

Positran Manufacturing Inc., p. II-1473 [NAICS 336111]

Post Oak Pharmacy Inc., p. III-2100 [NAICS 446110]

Poston Packing of Florence Inc., p. III-1946 [NAICS 424470]

Potential Industries Inc., p. III-1890 [NAICS 423930]

Potlatch Corp., pp. Vol. I-334, 358, 368, 374, 403 [NAICS 32191M, 321999, 32212M, 322130, 32223M]

Potlatch Corp. Pulp & Paperboard, pp. Vol. I-363, 374 [NAICS 322110, 322130]

Potlatch Corp. Wood Products, p. I-312 [NAICS 32111M]

Potomac Supply Corp., pp. Vol. I-312, 343 [NAICS 32111M, 321920]

Potters Industries Inc., p. I-722 [NAICS 327215]

Poulsbo RV Inc., p. III-2018 [NAICS 441210]

Poultry Products North East Inc., p. I-97 [NAICS 311615]

Powell Distributing Company Inc., pp. Vol. III-1975, 1979 [NAICS 424710, 424720]

Powell Electronics Inc., p. II-1312 [NAICS 334418]

Powell Industries Inc., pp. Vol. II-1157, 1421, 1432 [NAICS 333611, 335311, 335313]

Powell's Books Inc., p. III-2162 [NAICS 451211]

Powell Structural Systems, p. I-329 [NAICS 32121P]

Power and Telephone Supply Inc., p. III-1839 [NAICS 423690]

Power Battery Company Inc., pp. Vol. II-1442, 1447 [NAICS 335911, 335912]

Power Curbers Inc., p. II-1033 [NAICS 333120]

Power Film Systems Inc., p. II-1297 [NAICS 334415]

Power Flame Inc., p. II-1101 [NAICS 333414]

Power-Lite Electric Supplies, p. III-1831 [NAICS 423610]

Power Motive Corp., p. III-1859 [NAICS 423810]

Power-One Inc., p. II-1317 [NAICS 334419]

Power-Packer U.S., p. II-1222 [NAICS 33399N]

Power Technology Southeast Inc., p. II-1157 [NAICS 333611]

Power Train Service Company Inc., pp. Vol. II-1162, 1530 [NAICS 333612, 336350]

PowerBar, p. I-158 [NAICS 31199M]

Powercon Corp., p. II-1432 [NAICS 335313]

PowerLight Corp., p. II-1101 [NAICS 333414]

Powerohm Resistors Inc., p. II-1297 [NAICS 334415]

Powers Distributing Company Inc., p. III-1983 [NAICS 424810]

Powers Fasteners Inc., p. II-958 [NAICS 332722]

Powervar Inc., p. II-1447 [NAICS 335912]

Powerware Corp., p. II-1468 [NAICS 335999]

Powerwave Technologies Inc., p. II-1262 [NAICS 334220]

Pozzi Window Co., p. III-1782 [NAICS 423310]

PPC Industries Inc., p. I-603 [NAICS 326111]

PPG Industries Inc., pp. Vol. I-480, 488, 554, 709 [NAICS 325181, 325188, 325510, 327211]

PPM, p. I-713 [NAICS 327212]

PQ Acquisition Company Inc., p. III-2007 [NAICS 424990]

PQ Corp., p. I-722 [NAICS 327215]

Prairie AG Coop., pp. Vol. I-516, 520 [NAICS 325311, 325312]

Prairie Farms Dairy Inc., pp. Vol. I-81, 86, 92 [NAICS 311514, 31151N, 311520]

Prairie Farms Dairy Inc. Ice Cream, p. III-1933 [NAICS 424430]

Prairie Livestock L.L.C., p. III-1962 [NAICS 424520]

Prairie Material Sales Inc., pp. Vol. I-732, 737, 743 [NAICS 327320, 32733M, 327390]

Prairie Packaging Inc., p. I-636 [NAICS 326140]

Prajin 1 Stop Distributors Inc., p. III-2168 [NAICS 451220]

Pratt and Whitney PSD, p. II-1562 [NAICS 336412]

Pratt & Whitney Space Propulsion, p. II-1580 [NAICS 336419]

Pratt Feed and Supply Co., p. III-2197 [NAICS 453910]

Pratt Industries Inc, p. I-379 [NAICS 32221M]

Pratte Building Systems L.L.C., p. I-329 [NAICS 32121P]

Praxair Inc., pp. Vol. I-471, 691, 780 [NAICS 325120, 327121, 33111M]

PRD Company Inc., p. II-1147 [NAICS 333516]

Pre-Mix Industries Inc, p. I-732 [NAICS 327320]

Precious Gems and Jewels, p. III-1894 [NAICS 423940]

Precise Optics/P M E Inc., p. II-1357 [NAICS 334517]

Precision and Elamex USA Co., pp. Vol. I-879, Vol. II-945, 958, 1009, 1134 [NAICS 33211P, 332710, 332722, 332996, 333514]

Precision Castparts Corp., pp. Vol. I-845, Vol. II-1562 [NAICS 33151M, 336412]

Precision Countertops Inc., p. I-631 [NAICS 326130]

Precision Dynamics Corp., pp. Vol. I-234, 411, Vol. II-1714 [NAICS 31412M, 322291, 33994M]

Precision Electronic Glass Inc., p. I-713 [NAICS 327212]

Precision Finishing Inc., pp. Vol. I-756, Vol. II-1152 [NAICS 327910, 333518]

Precision Foods Inc., pp. Vol. I-68, 152, 158 [NAICS 31142M, 31194M, 31199M]

Numbers following p. or pp. are page references. Roman numerals indicate volume numbers. Bracketed items indicate industries. Page references are to the starting pages of company tables.

2399

Precision Husky Corp., p. II-1046 [NAICS 333210]

Precision Industrial Automation, p. II-1129 [NAICS 333513]

Precision Interconnect, p. I-837 [NAICS 33149M]

Precision Machined Engines Inc., p. II-1562 [NAICS 336412]

Precision Medical Inc., p. II-1342 [NAICS 334514]

Precision Metal Products Inc., p. I-872 [NAICS 33211N]

Precision Metalsmiths Inc., p. I-852 [NAICS 33152N]

Precision Parts & Remanufacturing, p. II-1512 [NAICS 33632M]

Precision Power House Inc., pp. Vol. II-1376, 1381 [NAICS 334612, 334613]

Precision Products Inc., pp. Vol. II-892, 1028 [NAICS 33221P, 333112]

Precision Rebuilders Inc., p. II-1524 [NAICS 336340]

Precision Resistive Products Inc., p. II-1297 [NAICS 334415]

Precision Resistor Company Inc., p. II-1297 [NAICS 334415]

Precision Resource Inc., p. I-879 [NAICS 33211P]

Precision Rolled Products Inc., pp. Vol. I-825, 837 [NAICS 331419, 33149M]

Precision Silicones Inc., p. I-505 [NAICS 325212]

Precision Strip Inc., p. II-945 [NAICS 332710]

Precision Timer Company Inc., p. II-1362 [NAICS 334518]

Precision Tube Inc., p. II-952 [NAICS 332721]

Precision Walls Inc., pp. Vol. I-722, 752, Vol. II-1644 [NAICS 327215, 327420, 337215]

Precisionform Inc., p. II-952 [NAICS 332721]

Precix Inc., pp. Vol. I-290, 300, Vol. II-1702 [NAICS 31599M, 31621M, 339920]

Precoat Metals, p. II-964 [NAICS 33281M]

Precor Inc., p. II-1702 [NAICS 339920]

Preferred Machine & Tool Prods, p. II-1157 [NAICS 333611]

Preferred Meal Systems Inc., pp. Vol. I-62, 158 [NAICS 31141M, 31199M]

Prejean Winery Inc., p. I-177 [NAICS 312130]

Premarc Corp., pp. Vol. I-695, 699, 737 [NAICS 327122, 327123, 32733M]

Premcor Inc., p. I-443 [NAICS 324110]

Premcor Refining Group Inc., p. I-443 [NAICS 324110]

Premier Boxboard Limited L.L.C., p. I-368 [NAICS 32212M]

Premier Circuit Assembly Inc., p. II-1512 [NAICS 33632M]

Premier Gear & Machine Works, p. II-1046 [NAICS 333210]

Premier Industries Inc., pp. Vol. I-641, 646 [NAICS 326150, 326160]

Premier Ink Systems Inc., p. I-580 [NAICS 325910]

Premier Manufacturing Corp., pp. Vol. I-670, Vol. II-939 [NAICS 32629M, 33261M]

Premier Marine Inc., p. II-1594 [NAICS 336612]

Premier Pan Co., p. II-886 [NAICS 33221N]

Premier Technology Inc., p. III-1809 [NAICS 423440]

Premier Tool and Die Cast Corp., p. I-852 [NAICS 33152N]

Premier Yarn Dyers Inc., p. I-218 [NAICS 31331M]

Premiere Candy Co., p. I-52 [NAICS 311330]

Premio Computer Inc., pp. Vol. II-1077, 1238 [NAICS 333313, 334111]

Premium Oil Co., p. III-2116 [NAICS 447110]

Premium Protein Products, p. I-97 [NAICS 311615]

Premium Standard Farms Inc., p. I-102 [NAICS 31161N]

PremiumWear Inc., p. I-290 [NAICS 31599M]

Premtec Inc., p. I-665 [NAICS 326220]

Pres-On Tape and Gasket Corp., p. I-636 [NAICS 326140]

Presco Products, pp. Vol. I-615, Vol. II-1714 [NAICS 326113, 33994M]

Prescolite Inc., p. II-1390 [NAICS 33512M]

Prescotech Industries Inc., pp. Vol. I-374, 641 [NAICS 322130, 326150]

President Container Inc., p. I-379 [NAICS 32221M]

President Global Corp., p. I-124 [NAICS 31182M]

Presidio Components Inc., p. II-1292 [NAICS 334414]

Presrite Corp., p. I-872 [NAICS 33211N]

Pressco Technology Inc., p. II-1082 [NAICS 333314]

Presstek Inc., pp. Vol. I-436, Vol. II-1087 [NAICS 32312M, 333315]

Pressure BioSciences Inc., p. I-544 [NAICS 325413]

Pressure Products Company Inc., p. I-709 [NAICS 327211]

Pressure Systems Inc., pp. Vol. I-837, Vol. II-923, 1580 [NAICS 33149M, 332420, 336419]

Prestige Automotive Group, p. III-2011 [NAICS 441110]

Prestige Fabricators Inc., pp. Vol. I-641, Vol. II-1657 [NAICS 326150, 337910]

Prestige Inc., p. II-1611 [NAICS 337110]

Prestige Lumber and Supplies Inc., pp. Vol. III-1782, 1794 [NAICS 423310, 423390]

Prestige Packaging Inc., p. III-1968 [NAICS 424610]

Prestige Stamping Inc., p. II-1541 [NAICS 336370]

Prestige Window Fashions, pp. Vol. I-234, Vol. II-1662 [NAICS 31412M, 337920]

Prestolite Electric Inc., pp. Vol. II-1194, 1457, 1512 [NAICS 33392M, 33593M, 33632M]

Prestolite Wire Corp., p. II-1451 [NAICS 33592M]

Prestress Services Industries, p. I-743 [NAICS 327390]

Pretium Packaging L.L.C., p. I-646 [NAICS 326160]

Pretty Products Inc., pp. Vol. I-229, 670 [NAICS 314110, 32629M]

Pretzels Inc., p. I-137 [NAICS 31191M]

Prewett Associated Mills, p. I-256 [NAICS 31511M]

PRI-Pak Inc., pp. Vol. I-177, 181 [NAICS 312130, 312140]

Price and Pierce International Inc., p. III-1898 [NAICS 424110]

Price Brothers Co., pp. Vol. I-737, 743 [NAICS 32733M, 327390]

PriceSmart Inc., p. I-411 [NAICS 322291]

Pride Container Corp., p. II-1720 [NAICS 339950]

PRIDE Industries Inc., p. II-1312 [NAICS 334418]

Pride of The Pond, p. I-110 [NAICS 31171M]

Pride of The South Catfish Inc., p. I-110 [NAICS 31171M]

Pridgeon and Clay Inc., pp. Vol. II-980, 1541, 1749 [NAICS 33291N, 336370, 339999]

Priefert Manufacturing Inc., p. II-1023 [NAICS 333111]

Priester Pecan Company Inc., p. I-137 [NAICS 31191M]

Primary Steel Inc., p. III-1824 [NAICS 423510]

Prime Alliance Inc., p. III-1968 [NAICS 424610]

Prime Art and Jewel, p. III-1894 [NAICS 423940]

Prime Industries L.L.P., p. I-646 [NAICS 326160]

Prime Quality Feeds, p. I-4 [NAICS 311111]

Prime Tanning Corp., p. I-296 [NAICS 316110]

Prime Time Manufacturing Inc., p. II-1696 [NAICS 33991M]

Prime Time Thermographics Inc., pp. Vol. III-1867, 1898 [NAICS 423830, 424110]

Prime Wire and Cable Inc., p. II-1307 [NAICS 334417]

Primepak Co., p. III-1905 [NAICS 424130]

Primetv L.L.C., p. III-2054 [NAICS 443112]

Primewood Inc., pp. Vol. I-324, Vol. II-1611 [NAICS 32121N, 337110]

Primex Plastics Corp., p. I-621 [NAICS 326121]

Primrose Candy Company Inc., p. I-57 [NAICS 311340]

Primrose Oil Co., p. I-458 [NAICS 324191]

Prince Castle Inc., pp. Vol. II-1092, 1627 [NAICS 33331N, 337127]

Prince Corp., pp. Vol. I-4, 9 [NAICS 311111, 311119]

Prince Industries Inc., p. II-952 [NAICS 332721]

Prince Manufacturing Co., pp. Vol. I-475, 529, 767, 780 [NAICS 32513M, 325320, 327992, 33111M]

Prince of Peace Enterprises Inc., p. III-1939 [NAICS 424450]

Prince Rubber and Plastics Inc., p. III-1968 [NAICS 424610]

Princess Fabrics, p. III-1913 [NAICS 424310]

Princess House Inc., p. III-1778 [NAICS 423220]

Princeton Gamma-Tech Inc., p. II-1357 [NAICS 334517]

Principle Business Enterprises Inc., pp. Vol. I-300, 411, 631, 641 [NAICS 31621M, 322291, 326130, 326150]

Print Inc., p. III-2058 [NAICS 443120]

Printex Packaging Corp., p. I-636 [NAICS 326140]

Printpack Inc., pp. Vol. I-388, 395, 626, 641 [NAICS 32222N, 32222P, 326122, 326150]

Printpal Inc., pp. Vol. III-1901, 2058 [NAICS 424120, 443120]

Prinz Ltd., p. III-1798 [NAICS 423410]

Priority Healthcare Corp., p. III-1909 [NAICS 424210]

Pritchard Amps, p. II-1731 [NAICS 339992]

Private Label Cosmetics Inc., p. I-575 [NAICS 325620]

PRN Pharmaceutical Services Inc., p. III-1909 [NAICS 424210]

Pro Company Sound Inc., pp. Vol. II-1307, 1451 [NAICS 334417, 33592M]

Pro-Cut International L.L.C., p. III-2228 [NAICS 454390]

Pro-Dentec, p. II-1682 [NAICS 339114]

Pro-Dex Inc., p. II-1682 [NAICS 339114]

Pro-Foods International L.L.C., p. I-97 [NAICS 311615]

Pro Golf Discount Inc., p. III-2150 [NAICS 451110]

Numbers following p. or pp. are page references. Roman numerals indicate volume numbers. Bracketed items indicate industries. Page references are to the starting pages of company tables.

2400

Pro-Line Corp., p. I-575 [NAICS 325620]

Pro Pac Labs Inc., p. I-534 [NAICS 325411]

Pro-Pet L.L.C., p. I-4 [NAICS 311111]

Pro Power Products Inc., p. II-1442 [NAICS 335911]

Pro-Serve Inc., p. I-529 [NAICS 325320]

Pro Vac Inc., p. II-1056 [NAICS 333295]

Proactive Net Inc., p. III-2058 [NAICS 443120]

Probe 2000 Inc., p. II-1056 [NAICS 333295]

Probest Paint, p. II-1740 [NAICS 339994]

Process Combustion Corp., p. II-1101 [NAICS 333414]

Process Displays Co., p. II-1720 [NAICS 339950]

Process Equipment and Service Inc., p. II-1039 [NAICS 33313M]

Process Industries Consortium Inc., p. II-1162 [NAICS 333612]

Process Technology Inc., pp. Vol. II-1101, 1217, 1302, 1332 [NAICS 333414, 333994, 334416, 334512]

Processed Plastic Co., p. II-1708 [NAICS 33993M]

Processing Technologies Inc., pp. Vol. II-1051, 1129 [NAICS 333220, 333513]

Procter and Gamble Co., pp. Vol. I-137, 143, 165, 368, 411, 539, 566, 575 [NAICS 31191M, 311920, 31211M, 32212M, 322291, 325412, 32561M, 325620]

Prodelin Corp., pp. Vol. II-899, 908, 1262 [NAICS 33231M, 33232M, 334220]

Prodenco Group Inc., p. II-1682 [NAICS 339114]

Prodesco Inc., p. I-213 [NAICS 31324M]

Produce Supply Express, p. III-1950 [NAICS 424480]

Producers Rice Mill Inc., pp. Vol. I-15, 68 [NAICS 31121M, 31142M]

Production Castings Inc., p. I-852 [NAICS 33152N]

Production Department Inc., p. I-279 [NAICS 31523M]

Production Management Industries, pp. Vol. I-343, Vol. II-1039, 1194 [NAICS 321920, 33313M, 33392M]

Production Tech Industries Inc., p. II-1530 [NAICS 336350]

Production Technology Inc., p. II-1357 [NAICS 334517]

Production Tool Supply, pp. Vol. III-1867, 1871 [NAICS 423830, 423840]

Productive and Moore Co., pp. Vol. II-1124, 1134 [NAICS 333512, 333514]

Productive Plastics Inc., p. I-615 [NAICS 326113]

Productivity Technologies Corp., p. II-1129 [NAICS 333513]

Producto, p. II-1134 [NAICS 333514]

Producto Dieco Corp., p. II-1124 [NAICS 333512]

Products Carousel Inc., p. I-4 [NAICS 311111]

Professional Audio Design Inc., p. III-2054 [NAICS 443112]

Professional Housewares, p. III-1835 [NAICS 423620]

Professional Office Services Inc., p. I-403 [NAICS 32223M]

Profile Rubber Corp., p. I-505 [NAICS 325212]

Programmer's Paradise Inc., pp. Vol. III 1805, 1820 [NAICS 423430, 423490]

Progress Casting Group Inc., pp. Vol. I-852, 857 [NAICS 33152N, 33152P]

Progress Industries Inc., p. II-1046 [NAICS 333210]

Progress Printing Company Inc., p. I-436 [NAICS 32312M]

Progress Rail Services Corp., p. II-1584 [NAICS 336510]

Progressive Balloons Inc., p. III-1887 [NAICS 423920]

Progressive Business Equipment, p. III-1901 [NAICS 424120]

Progressive Companies Inc., pp. Vol. I-110, Vol. III-1943 [NAICS 31171M, 424460]

Progressive Concepts Inc., p. III-1839 [NAICS 423690]

Progressive Farmers Coop., pp. Vol. III-1975, 1991 [NAICS 424710, 424910]

Progressive Furniture Inc., pp. Vol. II-1621, 1632 [NAICS 337122, 33712N]

Progressive Gaming Intern. Corp., pp. Vol. II-1720, 1749 [NAICS 339950, 339999]

Progressive Lighting Inc., p. III-2047 [NAICS 442299]

Progressive Plastics Inc., p. I-646 [NAICS 326160]

Progressive Produce Co., p. III-1950 [NAICS 424480]

Progressive Tool & Industries Co, pp. Vol. II-1061, 1134, 1229 [NAICS 33329N, 333514, 33399P]

Prolerized New England Co., pp. Vol. I-807, 837 [NAICS 331314, 33149M]

Proliant Inc., p. I-147 [NAICS 311930]

Proligo L.L.C., p. I-549 [NAICS 325414]

Promega Biosciences Inc., p. I-544 [NAICS 325413]

Promex Industries Inc., p. II-1312 [NAICS 334418]

Proper Mold and Engineering Inc., pp. Vol. II-1119, 1134 [NAICS 333511, 333514]

Propet USA Inc., p. I-300 [NAICS 31621M]

Proseed Inc., p. III-1813 [NAICS 423450]

PROSOCO Inc., pp. Vol. I-554, 560, 566 [NAICS 325510, 325520, 32561M]

Protect-All Inc., p. I-609 [NAICS 326112]

Protection Services Inc., pp. Vol. I-651, Vol. II-1014, 1390, 1720 [NAICS 32619M, 33299N, 33512M, 339950]

Protein Design Labs Inc., p. I-549 [NAICS 325414]

Protein Sciences Corp., p. I-549 [NAICS 325414]

Protein Technologies Intl, p. I-9 [NAICS 311119]

Protel Inc., p. III-2215 [NAICS 454210]

Proteus Industries Inc., p. II-1342 [NAICS 334514]

Protient, p. I-81 [NAICS 311514]

Provena Foods Inc., p. I-124 [NAICS 31182M]

Provence Breads, p. III-2089 [NAICS 445291]

Provia Software Inc., p. II-1243 [NAICS 334112]

Providence Home Services, p. III-2208 [NAICS 453998]

Proxim Corp., p. II-1267 [NAICS 334290]

Prudential Lighting Corp., p. II-1386 [NAICS 335110]

PSB Co., pp. Vol. II-908, 1014, 1627 [NAICS 33232M, 33299N, 337127]

PSC Metals Inc., p. III-1890 [NAICS 423930]

PSI, p. I-631 [NAICS 326130]

PSI Aerospace Bearings, pp. Vol. II-988, 1580 [NAICS 332991, 336419]

PSI Sales Inc., p. III-1859 [NAICS 423810]

PSS World Medical Inc., p. III-1813 [NAICS 423450]

PT O'Malley Lumber Inc., p. I-343 [NAICS 321920]

PT Tech Inc., p. II-1524 [NAICS 336340]

PTC Alliance, p. I-788 [NAICS 331210]

PTS Electronics Corp., pp. Vol. II-1262, 1267, 1272, 1307 [NAICS 334220, 334290, 334310, 334417]

Publishers Group West Inc., p. III-1995 [NAICS 424920]

Publishers Printing L.L.C., p. I-436 [NAICS 32312M]

Publix Super Markets Inc., pp. Vol. I-86, 102, 116, Vol. III-2076 [NAICS 31151N, 31161N, 31181M, 445110]

Puckett Machinery Co., p. III-1859 [NAICS 423810]

Pulaski Furniture Corp., pp. Vol. II-1621, 1627 [NAICS 337122, 337127]

Pulltarps Manufacturing, p. I-239 [NAICS 31491M]

Pulpdent Corp., p. II-1682 [NAICS 339114]

Pump Engineering Inc., p. II-1157 [NAICS 333611]

Punch Tech Inc., p. II-1735 [NAICS 339993]

Puratos Corp., pp. Vol. I-124, 158 [NAICS 31182M, 31199M]

Purcell Murray Company Inc., p. III-1835 [NAICS 423620]

Purchased Parts Group Inc., p. II-958 [NAICS 332722]

Purdue Pharma L.P., p. I-539 [NAICS 325412]

Pure World Inc., p. I-534 [NAICS 325411]

Purina Mills Inc., p. I-4 [NAICS 311111]

Purina Mills L.L.C., pp. Vol. I-4, 9, 22 [NAICS 311111, 311119, 311221]

Purity Products Inc., p. I-26 [NAICS 311225]

Purity Wholesale Grocers Inc., pp. Vol. III-1909, 1925, 1929, 1933 [NAICS 424210, 424410, 424420, 424430]

Pursell Technologies Inc., p. I-524 [NAICS 325314]

Pursley Turf Farms, pp. Vol. III-1998, 2072 [NAICS 424930, 444220]

Putney Paper Company Inc., pp. Vol. I-368, 411, 415 [NAICS 32212M, 322291, 322299]

Putzmeister Inc., p. II-1179 [NAICS 333911]

PVC Compounders Inc., p. I-589 [NAICS 325991]

PVC Container Corp., pp. Vol. I-448, 646 [NAICS 324121, 326160]

PVS Chemicals Inc., p. I-488 [NAICS 325188]

PW Eagle Inc., p. I-626 [NAICS 326122]

PWI Inc., p. II-1386 [NAICS 335110]

Pye's Auto Sales Inc., p. III-2015 [NAICS 441120]

Pyramid Breweries Inc., pp. Vol. I-172, Vol. III-1983 [NAICS 312120, 424810]

Pyramid Technologies L.L.C., p. II-1362 [NAICS 334518]

Pyro Industrial Services Inc., pp. Vol. I-686, 703 [NAICS 327113, 32712N]

Pyromatics Corp., p. I-703 [NAICS 32712N]

Pyromation Inc., p. II-1332 [NAICS 334512]

Pyrosequencing Inc., p. III-1820 [NAICS 423490]

Pyrotechnic Specialties Inc., p. I-585 [NAICS 325920]

Q3 Industries Inc., p. II-1541 [NAICS 336370]

Q3 JMC Inc., pp. Vol. II-923, 1486 [NAICS 332420, 336211]

QCA Inc., p. II-1376 [NAICS 334612]

QDS-Henshen Inc., p. II-1530 [NAICS 336350]

QED Environmental Systems Inc., pp. Vol. II-1112, 1229, 1352 [NAICS 33341N, 33399P, 334516]

Numbers following p. or pp. are page references. Roman numerals indicate volume numbers. Bracketed items indicate industries. Page references are to the starting pages of company tables.

2401

Q.E.P. Company Inc., pp. Vol. II-892, Vol. III-1843 [NAICS 33221P, 423710]

QK Healthcare Inc., p. III-1909 [NAICS 424210]

QLogic Corp., p. II-1287 [NAICS 334413]

QP Semiconductor, p. II-1056 [NAICS 333295]

QRS Music Technologies Inc., p. II-1731 [NAICS 339992]

Qsc Systems Inc., p. II-1277 [NAICS 334411]

QSE Inc., p. II-1302 [NAICS 334416]

QSN Manufacturing Inc., p. II-1735 [NAICS 339993]

QST Inc., p. I-505 [NAICS 325212]

Quabaug Corp., p. I-306 [NAICS 31699M]

Quabbin Wire and Cable Inc., p. II-1451 [NAICS 33592M]

Quad/Graphics Inc., p. I-420 [NAICS 32311M]

Quadrant Engineering Plastic, pp. Vol. I-500, 615, 651, Vol. II-933, 1168 [NAICS 325211, 326113, 32619M, 332510, 333613]

Quaker Chemical Corp., pp. Vol. I-458, 595 [NAICS 324191, 32599N]

Quaker City Castings Inc., pp. Vol. I-845, 857 [NAICS 33151M, 33152P]

Quaker Fabric Corp., p. I-198 [NAICS 313210]

Quaker Manufacturing Corp., p. II-1541 [NAICS 336370]

Quaker Plastic Corp., p. I-621 [NAICS 326121]

Quaker Window Products Co., p. I-334 [NAICS 32191M]

Quala-Die Inc., p. I-867 [NAICS 332117]

QUALCOMM Inc., p. II-1262 [NAICS 334220]

Quali-Tech Manufacturing Co., p. II-1740 [NAICS 339994]

Qualico Steel Company Inc., p. II-945 [NAICS 332710]

Qualitel Corp., pp. Vol. II-1282, 1312 [NAICS 334412, 334418]

Quality Accents Inc., pp. Vol. III-1887, 2153 [NAICS 423920, 451120]

Quality Bearing Service of Nevada, p. II-988 [NAICS 332991]

Quality Beverage Inc., p. III-1983 [NAICS 424810]

Quality Cabinet and Fixture Co., p. II-1639 [NAICS 337212]

Quality Candy Shoppes/Buddy, pp. Vol. III-1939, 2092 [NAICS 424450, 445292]

Quality Candy Shoppes Inc., pp. Vol. I-48, 52 [NAICS 311320, 311330]

Quality Carpet Cushions, p. I-229 [NAICS 314110]

Quality Castings Co., p. I-845 [NAICS 33151M]

Quality Chef, pp. Vol. I-62, 152 [NAICS 31141M, 31194M]

Quality Co's Inc., p. III-2215 [NAICS 454210]

Quality Components Inc., p. II-1292 [NAICS 334414]

Quality Container, p. I-646 [NAICS 326160]

Quality Control Corp., pp. Vol. II-952, 1725 [NAICS 332721, 339991]

Quality Custom Cabinetry Inc., p. II-1611 [NAICS 337110]

Quality Foam Packaging Inc., p. I-636 [NAICS 326140]

Quality Food Centers Inc., p. III-2076 [NAICS 445110]

Quality Imaging Products, p. III-2058 [NAICS 443120]

Quality Inks Inc., p. I-580 [NAICS 325910]

Quality King Distributors Inc., p. III-1909 [NAICS 424210]

Quality Maintenance Enterprises, p. III-2050 [NAICS 443111]

Quality Oil Company L.L.C., pp. Vol. III-1979, 2218 [NAICS 424720, 454311]

Quality Pipe Products Inc., p. II-974 [NAICS 332913]

Quality Plastic of Prescott Inc., p. I-646 [NAICS 326160]

Quality Pool Supply Co., p. III-1883 [NAICS 423910]

Quality Pork International Inc., p. I-102 [NAICS 31161N]

Quality Printing & Office Supply, p. III-2186 [NAICS 453210]

Quality Quick Bindery Services, pp. Vol. III-1898, 1905 [NAICS 424110, 424130]

Quality Roofing Supplies Inc., p. III-1790 [NAICS 423330]

Quality Rubber Co., p. II-1519 [NAICS 336330]

Quality S Manufacturing Inc., p. II-1607 [NAICS 336999]

Quality Synthetic Rubber Inc., pp. Vol. I-500, 670 [NAICS 325211, 32629M]

Quality Systems Integrated Corp., p. II-1312 [NAICS 334418]

Quality Trailer Products Corp., pp. Vol. II-899, 1500 [NAICS 33231M, 336214]

Quality Transmission Components, pp. Vol. II-1162, 1168 [NAICS 333612, 333613]

Quality Transparent Bag Co., pp. Vol. I-603, 621 [NAICS 326111, 326121]

Quality Truck Tires Inc., p. III-1766 [NAICS 423130]

Quality Wood Products Inc., p. II-1611 [NAICS 337110]

QualServ Corp., pp. Vol. II-1627, 1644 [NAICS 337127, 337215]

Qualserv/Food Service Supplies, pp. Vol. II-1014, 1611, 1627 [NAICS 33299N, 337110, 337127]

Qualstar Corp., p. II-1243 [NAICS 334112]

Quanex Corp., pp. Vol. I-780, 788, 793, 816, Vol. II-908 [NAICS 33111M, 331210, 33122M, 33131N, 33232M]

Quantegy Inc., pp. Vol. II-1272, 1381 [NAICS 334310, 334613]

Quantum Corp., pp. Vol. II-1238, 1243 [NAICS 334111, 334112]

Quantum-Dynamics Company Inc., p. I-471 [NAICS 325120]

Quantum Engineering Inc., p. II-1584 [NAICS 336510]

Quantum Instruments Inc., pp. Vol. II-1087, 1442 [NAICS 333315, 335911]

Quantum3D Inc., p. II-1381 [NAICS 334613]

Quartz Scientific Inc., pp. Vol. I-703, 767 [NAICS 32712N, 327992]

Quebecor World George Rice, p. I-436 [NAICS 32312M]

Queen City TV & Appliance, p. III-2054 [NAICS 443112]

Queen City Wholesale Inc., pp. Vol. III-1939, 2001 [NAICS 424450, 424940]

Queen Helene, p. II-886 [NAICS 33221N]

Queens City LaCrosse Co., pp. Vol. III-1916, 1919, 2135 [NAICS 424320, 424330, 448150]

Queens Commercial Service, p. III-1790 [NAICS 423330]

Queenstake Jerritt Canyone Mine, p. I-825 [NAICS 331419]

Quentzel Henry Plumbing Supply, p. III-1847 [NAICS 423720]

Quest Corp., p. II-1147 [NAICS 333516]

Questar Corp., p. I-463 [NAICS 324199]

Questcor Pharmaceuticals Inc., p. I-534 [NAICS 325411]

Questech Services Corp., p. II-1297 [NAICS 334415]

Quickbeam Systems Inc., p. III-2208 [NAICS 453998]

Quickie Manufacturing Corp., pp. Vol. II-1397, 1740 [NAICS 33521M, 339994]

Quicksilver Truck Liners, p. I-703 [NAICS 32712N]

Quidel Corp., p. I-544 [NAICS 325413]

Quigley Corp., p. I-52 [NAICS 311330]

Quik Stop Markets Inc., p. III-2116 [NAICS 447110]

Quikey Manufacturing Inc., p. I-203 [NAICS 31322M]

Quikrete Co's, pp. Vol. I-691, 727 [NAICS 327121, 327310]

Quiksilver Inc., pp. Vol. I-272, 279, 290, Vol. II-1702 [NAICS 31522M, 31523M, 31599M, 339920]

QuikTrip Corp., pp. Vol. III-2076, 2116 [NAICS 445110, 447110]

Quill Computer Div., p. III-2058 [NAICS 443120]

Quilt In A Day, p. III-2156 [NAICS 451130]

Quinault Pride Seafoods, pp. Vol. III-1943, 2085 [NAICS 424460, 445220]

Quincy Compressor Div., p. II-1184 [NAICS 333912]

Quinn Group Inc., pp. Vol. III-1859, 1863 [NAICS 423810, 423820]

Quintel Corp., p. II-1056 [NAICS 333295]

Quinton Cardiology Systems Inc., p. II-1322 [NAICS 334510]

Quixote Corp., p. II-1607 [NAICS 336999]

QVC Inc., p. III-2211 [NAICS 454113]

R and B Plastics Machinery L.L.C., p. II-1051 [NAICS 333220]

R & B Wholesale Distributors Inc., p. III-1835 [NAICS 423620]

R and D Batteries Inc., p. II-1442 [NAICS 335911]

R and D Dynamics Corp., p. II-1157 [NAICS 333611]

R and D Tool and Engineering Inc., p. II-1119 [NAICS 333511]

R and K Building Supplies Inc., p. III-1782 [NAICS 423310]

R and M Energy Systems, p. II-1039 [NAICS 33313M]

R and N Knitted Headwear Inc., p. I-262 [NAICS 31519M]

R and R Manufacturing Inc., p. II-952 [NAICS 332721]

R and R Marketing L.L.C., p. III-1987 [NAICS 424820]

R and R Products Inc., p. II-1028 [NAICS 333112]

R and R Professsional Moving Inc., p. III-1875 [NAICS 423850]

R & S Mexican Food Products Inc., p. I-133 [NAICS 311830]

R-Group International Inc., p. II-1357 [NAICS 334517]

R Twining and Company Ltd., p. I-143 [NAICS 311920]

R-Y Timber Inc., pp. Vol. I-312, Vol. III-1782 [NAICS 32111M, 423310]

RA Jones and Company Inc., p. II-1212 [NAICS 333993]

R.A. Pearson Company Inc., pp. Vol. II-1129, 1212 [NAICS 333513, 333993]

Rabideaux's Sausage Kitchen Inc., pp. Vol. III-2047, 2083 [NAICS 442299, 445210]

Racemark International L.P., p. I-229 [NAICS 314110]

RaceTrac Petroleum Inc., pp. Vol. III-1975, 1979, 2116, 2180 [NAICS 424710, 424720, 447110, 452990]

Rada Manufacturing Company, p. II-886 [NAICS 33221N]

Radcal Corp., p. II-1357 [NAICS 334517]

Rademann Stone & Landscape Inc., p. I-762 [NAICS 327991]

Radford Co., p. III-1782 [NAICS 423310]

Radiac Abrasives Inc., p. I-756 [NAICS 327910]

Radiall America, p. III-1831 [NAICS 423610]

Radian Corp., p. II-1282 [NAICS 334412]

Radiator Specialty Co., p. I-566 [NAICS 32561M]

Radici Spandex, p. I-192 [NAICS 31311M]

Radio Flyer Inc., p. II-1708 [NAICS 33993M]

Radio Satellite Integrators Corp., p. II-1262 [NAICS 334220]

Radio Sound Inc., p. II-1599 [NAICS 336991]

Radiology Support Devices, p. II-1357 [NAICS 334517]

RadioShack Corp., pp. Vol. II-1238, Vol. III-2054 [NAICS 334111, 443112]

Radix Corp., p. II-1238 [NAICS 334111]

Radix Wire Co., p. II-1451 [NAICS 33592M]

Radnor Alloys Inc., p. III-1820 [NAICS 423490]

Radware, p. III-1805 [NAICS 423430]

RAE Corp., p. II-1106 [NAICS 333415]

RAE Products and Chemical Inc., p. III-2004 [NAICS 424950]

Rae Storage Battery Co., p. II-1442 [NAICS 335911]

Rafferty-Brown Steel Inc., p. III-1824 [NAICS 423510]

Rafi Systems Inc., p. II-1687 [NAICS 339115]

Rafter Equipment Corp., p. II-1147 [NAICS 333516]

Rag Shops Inc., pp. Vol. III-2153, 2156 [NAICS 451120, 451130]

Ragle Dental Laboratory Inc., p. II-1692 [NAICS 339116]

Rahco International Inc., p. II-1023 [NAICS 333111]

Rainbo Records Inc., p. II-1376 [NAICS 334612]

Rainbo Records Mfg Corp., p. II-1376 [NAICS 334612]

Rainbow Inc., p. III-1929 [NAICS 424420]

Rainbow Play Systems Inc., p. II-1702 [NAICS 339920]

Rainbow Sales Distributing, pp. Vol. III-1798, 1817 [NAICS 423410, 423460]

Rainier Industries Ltd., p. I-239 [NAICS 31491M]

Rainin Instrument L.L.C., pp. Vol. II-1337, 1367 [NAICS 334513, 334519]

Rainsweet, p. III-1929 [NAICS 424420]

RAK Industries, p. III-1871 [NAICS 423840]

Ralcorp Holdings Inc., pp. Vol. I-36, 68, 124 [NAICS 311230, 31142M, 31182M]

Raleigh America, p. III-1883 [NAICS 423910]

Raleigh Metal Processors Inc., p. I-807 [NAICS 331314]

Raleigh Mine & Industrial Supply, p. III-2208 [NAICS 453998]

Raley's Inc., pp. Vol. III-2076, 2100 [NAICS 445110, 446110]

Ralph's Foods, p. III-2171 [NAICS 452111]

Ralph's Power Sewing Machine, p. III-2050 [NAICS 443111]

Ralphs Grocery Co., p. III-2076 [NAICS 445110]

Ralston Foods Inc., p. I-124 [NAICS 31182M]

Raltron Electronics Corp., p. II-1297 [NAICS 334415]

Ram Freezers and Coolers Mfg Inc., p. II-1409 [NAICS 335222]

RAM Industries Inc., pp. Vol. II-1162, 1427, 1432, 1457 [NAICS 333612, 335312, 335313, 33593M]

Ram Tool and Supply Co., p. III-1843 [NAICS 423710]

Ramar Industries Incorporated, p. II-1362 [NAICS 334518]

Ramcar Batteries Inc., p. II-1442 [NAICS 335911]

Ramona's Mexican Food Products, p. I-133 [NAICS 311830]

Ramsey Winch Co., p. II-1162 [NAICS 333612]

Ramtex Inc., pp. Vol. I-192, 251 [NAICS 31311M, 314999]

Rance Industries Inc., p. II-1147 [NAICS 333516]

Rand Intern. Leisure Products Ltd., p. III-1883 [NAICS 423910]

Rand-Whitney Container L.L.C., p. I-379 [NAICS 32221M]

Randall Bearings Inc., p. II-988 [NAICS 332991]

Randall Brothers Inc., p. II-1639 [NAICS 337212]

Randall Foods Inc., p. I-97 [NAICS 311615]

Randolph Jewelers, p. III-2144 [NAICS 448310]

Ranew's Truck & Equipment, p. II-1491 [NAICS 336212]

Range Cooperatives Inc., p. III-2222 [NAICS 454312]

Range Resources Corp., pp. Vol. I-443, Vol. II-1039 [NAICS 324110, 33313M]

Ranger All-Season Corp., p. II-1607 [NAICS 336999]

Ranger Boat Co., pp. Vol. I-358, Vol. II-1500, 1594 [NAICS 321999, 336214, 336612]

Ranger Construction Industries Inc., p. I-448 [NAICS 324121]

Ranger Joe's International, pp. Vol. III-2150, 2180 [NAICS 451110, 452990]

Ranger Manufacturing Co., pp. Vol. II-1332, 1386 [NAICS 334512, 335110]

Ranir Corp., p. II-1682 [NAICS 339114]

Rank Technology Corp., p. II-1243 [NAICS 334112]

Rankin County Unit System, p. III-1859 [NAICS 423810]

Ranpak Corp., p. II-1212 [NAICS 333993]

RaPac Inc., p. I-609 [NAICS 326112]

Rapair Inc., p. II-1173 [NAICS 333618]

Rapak Inc., p. I-603 [NAICS 326111]

Rapco International Inc., pp. Vol. II-1307, 1512 [NAICS 334417, 33632M]

Rapid Engineering Inc., p. II-1152 [NAICS 333518]

Rapid Granulator Inc., p. II-1051 [NAICS 333220]

Rapid Industrial Plastics Inc., p. III-1968 [NAICS 424610]

Rapid Processing L.L.C., p. III-1890 [NAICS 423930]

Rashti and Rashti, p. I-285 [NAICS 31529M]

Rave Computer Association Inc., p. III-1809 [NAICS 423440]

Raven Industries Inc., pp. Vol. I-615, Vol. II-1282, 1327, 1337, 1347 [NAICS 326113, 334412, 334511, 334513, 334515]

Rawlings Sporting Goods Inc., p. II-1702 [NAICS 339920]

Ray-O-Lite, p. I-718 [NAICS 327213]

Raymarine Inc., p. II-933 [NAICS 332510]

Raymond Corp., p. II-1194 [NAICS 33392M]

Raymond Oil Co., p. III-2222 [NAICS 454312]

Raymour & Flanigan Furniture Co., p. III-2037 [NAICS 442110]

Rayonier Inc., pp. Vol. I-312, 324, 334, 363, 510 [NAICS 32111M, 32121N, 32191M, 322110, 32522M]

Rayovac Corp., pp. Vol. II-1390, 1442, 1447, 1468 [NAICS 33512M, 335911, 335912, 335999]

Raytech Corp., p. I-776 [NAICS 327999]

Raytheon Co., pp. Vol. II-1287, 1317, 1327, 1397, 1557, 1567, 1572 [NAICS 334413, 334419, 334511, 33521M, 336411, 336413, 336414]

Raytheon Engineers/Constructors, pp. Vol. II-1287, 1317, 1327, 1567, 1572 [NAICS 334413, 334419, 334511, 336413, 336414]

Rayvex, p. II-1028 [NAICS 333112]

RB Industries Inc., p. II-1046 [NAICS 333210]

R.B. Matheson Trucking Inc., p. III-1762 [NAICS 423120]

RB Rubber Products Inc., p. I-670 [NAICS 32629M]

RBC Bremen Bearings Inc., p. II-988 [NAICS 332991]

Rbs Business Solutions L.L.C., p. III-1801 [NAICS 423420]

RBT Services Inc., p. II-1584 [NAICS 336510]

RC Aluminum Industries Inc., p. I-811 [NAICS 331316]

RC Bigelow Inc., p. I-143 [NAICS 311920]

RC Owen Co's, p. I-188 [NAICS 31222M]

RC2 Corp., p. III-1887 [NAICS 423920]

RC2 Racing Champions Ertl Inc., p. III-1887 [NAICS 423920]

R.C.A. Rubber Co., p. I-670 [NAICS 32629M]

RCC Koozie Norwood, pp. Vol. I-290, 395, 651, 722 [NAICS 31599M, 32222P, 32619M, 327215]

RCD Components Inc., pp. Vol. II-1297, 1302, 1427 [NAICS 334415, 334416, 335312]

Rch Associates Inc., p. II-1056 [NAICS 333295]

RCP Block and Brick Inc., pp. Vol. I-737, 743 [NAICS 32733M, 327390]

RD Fixtures, p. III-1809 [NAICS 423440]

R.D. Offutt Co., p. III-1950 [NAICS 424480]

RDO Equipment Co., pp. Vol. III-1859, 1863 [NAICS 423810, 423820]

Numbers following p. or pp. are page references. Roman numerals indicate volume numbers. Bracketed items indicate industries. Page references are to the starting pages of company tables.

2403

RDS Manufacturing Inc., pp. Vol. II-923, 1562 [NAICS 332420, 336412]

RE Darling Co., p. I-665 [NAICS 326220]

R.E. Michel Company Inc., pp. Vol. III-1847, 1851, 1855 [NAICS 423720, 423730, 423740]

RE Phelon Company Inc., pp. Vol. I-811, Vol. II-1028, 1437 [NAICS 331316, 333112, 335314]

RE Service Company Inc., p. I-816 [NAICS 33131N]

RE Snader and Associates Inc., p. III-1798 [NAICS 423410]

Re:Source New Jersey, p. III-1778 [NAICS 423220]

Rea Magnet Wire Company Inc., pp. Vol. I-803, 830 [NAICS 331312, 33142M]

Reaction Technology Inc., p. II-1056 [NAICS 333295]

Reade Advanced Materials, p. I-776 [NAICS 327999]

Reade Manufacturing Co., p. I-825 [NAICS 331419]

Reader's Digest Association Inc., p. III-2211 [NAICS 454113]

Reader's Wholesale Distributors, p. III-1778 [NAICS 423220]

Reading Eagle Co., p. I-436 [NAICS 32312M]

Ready Ice, p. I-165 [NAICS 31211M]

Ready Metal Manufacturing Co., p. II-1644 [NAICS 337215]

Ready Mix USA, p. I-732 [NAICS 327320]

Real Mex Foods Inc., p. I-133 [NAICS 311830]

Realistic Furniture Industries, p. II-1616 [NAICS 337121]

Reaves and Company Inc., p. I-239 [NAICS 31491M]

Rebco Inc., p. I-867 [NAICS 332117]

Rebel Party Rents, p. III-2190 [NAICS 453220]

Recarbco, p. II-1505 [NAICS 33631M]

Reckart Equipment Co., p. II-1046 [NAICS 333210]

Reckitt Benckiser Inc., pp. Vol. I-137, 152, 158 [NAICS 31191M, 31194M, 31199M]

Recognition Systems Inc., p. III-1798 [NAICS 423410]

Recon Optical Inc., pp. Vol. II-1082, 1194, 1287, 1327, 1437 [NAICS 333314, 33392M, 334413, 334511, 335314]

Record Exchange of Roanoke Inc., p. III-2168 [NAICS 451220]

Record Technology Inc., p. II-1376 [NAICS 334612]

Recording For The Blind, pp. Vol. II-1376, Vol. III-1995 [NAICS 334612, 424920]

Recreational Equipment Inc., pp. Vol. III-2132, 2150, 2211 [NAICS 448140, 451110, 454113]

Rectorseal Corp., pp. Vol. I-458, 727 [NAICS 324191, 327310]

Recycled Fibers Eastern Region, p. I-363 [NAICS 322110]

Recycled Wood Products, pp. Vol. III-2007, 2072 [NAICS 424990, 444220]

Recycling Center Inc., p. I-363 [NAICS 322110]

Recycling Works Inc., p. I-363 [NAICS 322110]

Red Ball Oxygen Company Inc., pp. Vol. I-471, 480 [NAICS 325120, 325181]

Red Bud Industries Inc., p. II-1152 [NAICS 333518]

Red Gold Inc., pp. Vol. I-68, 152 [NAICS 31142M, 31194M]

Red Hill Studios, p. II-1381 [NAICS 334613]

Red Line Research Laboratories, p. II-1442 [NAICS 335911]

Red Mile Inc., p. III-1965 [NAICS 424590]

Red Newt Cellars Inc., p. III-2097 [NAICS 445310]

Red Rhino Manufacturing, p. II-1491 [NAICS 336212]

Red River Motor Co., p. III-2030 [NAICS 441310]

Red's Market Inc., p. III-1950 [NAICS 424480]

Red Seal Electric Co., p. I-771 [NAICS 327993]

Red Spot Paint and Varnish Inc., p. I-554 [NAICS 325510]

Red Star Oil Co., p. I-443 [NAICS 324110]

Red Wing Shoe Co., p. I-300 [NAICS 31621M]

RedBack Networks Inc., pp. Vol. II-1267, Vol. III-1839 [NAICS 334290, 423690]

Redburn Tire, p. III-1766 [NAICS 423130]

Reddaway Manufacturing Inc., p. II-1524 [NAICS 336340]

Reddy Ice Holdings Inc., pp. Vol. I-165, Vol. II-1106 [NAICS 31211M, 333415]

Redhook Ale Brewery Inc., p. I-172 [NAICS 312120]

Redington Counters Inc., pp. Vol. II-1342, 1362 [NAICS 334514, 334518]

Redland Brick Incorporated, p. I-691 [NAICS 327121]

Redman Homes Inc., p. I-348 [NAICS 321991]

Redwood Empire Inc., p. III-1782 [NAICS 423310]

Reebok International Ltd., pp. Vol. I-272, 300, Vol. II-1702, Vol. III-1916, 1919, 1922 [NAICS 31522M, 31621M, 339920, 424320, 424330, 424340]

Reece Oil Co., p. III-1975 [NAICS 424710]

Reed and Barton Corp., p. II-1696 [NAICS 33991M]

Reed-Rico, pp. Vol. II-1124, 1134 [NAICS 333512, 333514]

Reeder Distributors Inc., p. III-1975 [NAICS 424710]

Reeds Jewelers Inc., p. III-2144 [NAICS 448310]

Reell Precision Mfg Corp., pp. Vol. II-1168, 1524 [NAICS 333613, 336340]

Reese Enterprises Inc., p. I-229 [NAICS 314110]

Reeves Brothers Inc., pp. Vol. I-198, 203, 224, 251 [NAICS 313210, 31322M, 313320, 314999]

Refractory Specialties Inc., pp. Vol. I-703, 771 [NAICS 32712N, 327993]

Refrigeration & Electric Supply, p. III-1855 [NAICS 423740]

Refrigeration Sales Corp., pp. Vol. III-1851, 1855 [NAICS 423730, 423740]

Refrigeration Supplies Distributor, p. III-1855 [NAICS 423740]

Refron Inc., p. III-2225 [NAICS 454319]

Regal-Beloit Corp., pp. Vol. II-1124, 1140, 1512, 1551 [NAICS 333512, 333515, 33632M, 336399]

Regal-Beloit Corp. Durst Div., p. II-1162 [NAICS 333612]

Regal Chemical Co., p. I-529 [NAICS 325320]

Regal Kitchens Inc., p. II-1611 [NAICS 337110]

Regal Manufacturing Company, p. I-192 [NAICS 31311M]

Regal Marine Industries Inc., p. II-1594 [NAICS 336612]

Regal Originals Inc., p. I-285 [NAICS 31529M]

Regal Plastic Supply Co., p. III-1968 [NAICS 424610]

Reganis Auto Center Inc., p. III-1758 [NAICS 423110]

Regen Technologies L.L.C., pp. Vol. II-1173, 1222 [NAICS 333618, 33399N]

Regency Cap and Gown Co., p. I-285 [NAICS 31529M]

Regency Thermographers, p. I-436 [NAICS 32312M]

Regent Aerospace Corp., pp. Vol. II-1536, 1567 [NAICS 336360, 336413]

Regent Sports Corp., p. III-1883 [NAICS 423910]

Regina Press, p. III-1995 [NAICS 424920]

Regional International Corp., p. III-1758 [NAICS 423110]

Regional Medical Rental and Sales, p. III-1813 [NAICS 423450]

Rehau Inc., p. I-651 [NAICS 32619M]

Rehrig International Inc., pp. Vol. I-631, Vol. II-1194, 1720 [NAICS 326130, 33392M, 339950]

Reichert Ophthalmic Instruments, p. II-1687 [NAICS 339115]

Reichert Stamping Co., p. II-1541 [NAICS 336370]

Reichhold Inc., pp. Vol. I-500, 560, 595 [NAICS 325211, 325520, 32599N]

Reid Tool Supply Co., p. III-1871 [NAICS 423840]

Reilly Dairy and Food Co., p. III-1933 [NAICS 424430]

Reilly Foam Corp., p. I-641 [NAICS 326150]

Reilly Industries Inc., pp. Vol. I-453, 467, 554, 595, Vol. II-1033 [NAICS 324122, 325110, 325510, 32599N, 333120]

Reily Foods Co., pp. Vol. I-26, 143, 152, 158 [NAICS 311225, 311920, 31194M, 31199M]

Reines R.V. Center Inc., p. III-2018 [NAICS 441210]

Reinke Manufacturing Inc., p. II-1023 [NAICS 333111]

Reiss Corp., p. I-636 [NAICS 326140]

Reisterstown Lumber Inc., p. I-329 [NAICS 32121P]

Reliable Automatic Sprinkler Co., p. II-1229 [NAICS 33399P]

Reliable Biopharmaceutical Corp., p. I-534 [NAICS 325411]

Reliable Capacitors Inc., p. II-1292 [NAICS 334414]

Reliable of Milwaukee, pp. Vol. I-213, 262 [NAICS 31324M, 31519M]

Reliable Parts, p. III-1835 [NAICS 423620]

Reliable Rubber & Plastic, p. II-1051 [NAICS 333220]

Reliable Tire Distributors Inc., p. III-1766 [NAICS 423130]

Reliable Tool and Machine Inc., pp. Vol. II-1524, 1530 [NAICS 336340, 336350]

Reliable Tractor Inc., pp. Vol. III-1863, 2027 [NAICS 423820, 441229]

Reliable Truss and Lumber Inc., p. I-329 [NAICS 32121P]

Reliance Machine Products Inc., p. II-1056 [NAICS 333295]

Reliance Steel and Aluminum Co., p. III-1824 [NAICS 423510]

Reliance Trailer Company L.L.C., p. II-1491 [NAICS 336212]

Reliance Trailer Manufacturing, p. II-1491 [NAICS 336212]

Reliant Industries Inc., p. II-958 [NAICS 332722]

Relio's Jewelry Co., p. II-1696 [NAICS 33991M]

Reliv' International Inc., pp. Vol. III-1909, 1954 [NAICS 424210, 424490]

Numbers following p. or pp. are page references. Roman numerals indicate volume numbers. Bracketed items indicate industries. Page references are to the starting pages of company tables.

Reliv' World Corp., p. III-1909 [NAICS 424210]

Remco Industries International Inc., p. II-1404 [NAICS 335221]

REMEC Inc., pp. Vol. II-1262, 1267, 1287, 1317 [NAICS 334220, 334290, 334413, 334419]

REMEC Veritek Inc., p. II-1312 [NAICS 334418]

Remee Casting Co., p. I-762 [NAICS 327991]

Remington Arms Company Inc., pp. Vol. I-244, Vol. II-993, 1001, 1702 [NAICS 314991, 332992, 332994, 339920]

Remington Industries Inc., p. I-229 [NAICS 314110]

REMPAC Foam Corp., p. I-636 [NAICS 326140]

Remtec Inc., p. II-1297 [NAICS 334415]

Remtec International, p. I-471 [NAICS 325120]

Remy International Inc., pp. Vol. II-1427, 1437, 1442, 1512, 1551 [NAICS 335312, 335314, 335911, 33632M, 336399]

Rena-Ware Distributors Inc., p. III-2228 [NAICS 454390]

Renaissance Publishing Inc., p. I-420 [NAICS 32311M]

Renault Winery Inc., p. I-177 [NAICS 312130]

Renfro Corp., p. I-256 [NAICS 31511M]

Reno Agriculture & Electronics, p. II-1584 [NAICS 336510]

Reno Rendering Co., p. I-26 [NAICS 311225]

Renold Ajax Inc., p. II-1162 [NAICS 333612]

Renold Jeffrey, pp. Vol. II-939, 1168 [NAICS 33261M, 333613]

Renovators Supply Inc., p. II-974 [NAICS 332913]

Rentech Boiler Services Inc., p. II-918 [NAICS 332410]

Reorganized Sale OKWD Inc., pp. Vol. I-348, Vol. III-2203 [NAICS 321991, 453930]

Replogle Enterprises, p. I-324 [NAICS 32121N]

Reprographic Technologies, pp. Vol. I-388, 436 [NAICS 32222N, 32312M]

Reptron Electronics Inc., pp. Vol. II-1282, Vol. III-1839 [NAICS 334412, 423690]

Republic Engineered Products, p. I-780 [NAICS 33111M]

Republic Foil-Garmco USA, p. I-816 [NAICS 33131N]

Republic Packaging Corp., p. I-626 [NAICS 326122]

Republic Services Inc., p. III-1824 [NAICS 423510]

Republic Storage Systems Inc., p. II-1644 [NAICS 337215]

Republic Tobacco L.P., pp. Vol. III-1905, 2001 [NAICS 424130, 424940]

Requa Inc., p. I-756 [NAICS 327910]

Request Foods Inc., pp. Vol. I-62, 158 [NAICS 31141M, 31199M]

Res-Net Microwave Inc., pp. Vol. II-1297, 1312, 1451 [NAICS 334415, 334418, 33592M]

Research & Advanced Methods, p. II-1119 [NAICS 333511]

Research Corporation Tech, p. I-488 [NAICS 325188]

Research Electro-Optics Inc., p. II-1082 [NAICS 333314]

Research Manufacturing Corp., p. I-670 [NAICS 32629M]

Research Products Intern. Corp., p. III-1820 [NAICS 423490]

Reser's Fine Foods Inc., pp. Vol. I-102, 158 [NAICS 31161N, 31199M]

Resnick Supermarket Equipment, pp. Vol. III-1809, 1855 [NAICS 423440, 423740]

Resource One Computer Systems, p. III-2058 [NAICS 443120]

Respironics Inc., pp. Vol. II-1322, 1671, 1676 [NAICS 334510, 339112, 339113]

Restek Corp., p. II-1666 [NAICS 339111]

Restonic Mattress Corp., p. II-1657 [NAICS 337910]

Restoragen Inc., p. I-549 [NAICS 325414]

Restoration Hardware Inc., pp. Vol. II-1627, Vol. III-2208 [NAICS 337127, 453998]

Retail Distributors Inc., pp. Vol. III-1883, 1887 [NAICS 423910, 423920]

Retail Ventures Inc., p. III-2180 [NAICS 452990]

Reuland Electric Company Inc., p. II-1162 [NAICS 333612]

Reunion Industries Inc., p. I-589 [NAICS 325991]

Revak Turbomachinery Services, pp. Vol. II-1157, 1179, 1427 [NAICS 333611, 333911, 335312]

Revell-Monogram L.L.C., pp. Vol. I-651, Vol. II-1708 [NAICS 32619M, 33993M]

Revels Tractor Company Inc., p. III-2072 [NAICS 444220]

Revere Industries L.L.C., p. I-816 [NAICS 33131N]

Reviva, p. II-1173 [NAICS 333618]

Revlon Inc., p. I-575 [NAICS 325620]

Rex Cut Products Inc., p. I-756 [NAICS 327910]

Rex Oil Company Inc., p. III-1979 [NAICS 424720]

Rex Pipe and Supply Co., p. III-1968 [NAICS 424610]

REX Stores Corp., pp. Vol. III-2050, 2054 [NAICS 443111, 443112]

Rexall Sundown Inc., pp. Vol. I-539, Vol. III-1909, 2211 [NAICS 325412, 424210, 454113]

Rexam Inc., pp. Vol. I-420, 615, 626 [NAICS 32311M, 326113, 326122]

Rexarc International Inc., p. II-1157 [NAICS 333611]

Rexel Inc., p. III-1839 [NAICS 423690]

Rexhall Industries Inc., p. II-1496 [NAICS 336213]

Rexnord Corp., pp. Vol. II-1530, 1551 [NAICS 336350, 336399]

Reyes Industries Inc., pp. Vol. I-239, Vol. II-1657 [NAICS 31491M, 337910]

Reynolds and Company Inc., pp. Vol. I-756, Vol. II-1046 [NAICS 327910, 333210]

Reynolds International L.P., pp. Vol. II-1023, 1033, 1039 [NAICS 333111, 333120, 33313M]

RF Micro Devices Inc., pp. Vol. II-1257, 1287 [NAICS 334210, 334413]

RF Techniques Inc., p. II-1297 [NAICS 334415]

R.G. Barry Corp., pp. Vol. I-224, 300 [NAICS 313320, 31621M]

RG Group Manufacturing, p. II-1524 [NAICS 336340]

RGA, p. III-1831 [NAICS 423610]

RGM Products Company Inc., pp. Vol. I-448, 453 [NAICS 324121, 324122]

R H Barringer Distributing Inc., pp. Vol. III-1939, 1983 [NAICS 424450, 424810]

R.H. Kuhn Co., p. III-2037 [NAICS 442110]

RH Phillips-Hogue, pp. Vol. I-177, Vol. III-1987 [NAICS 312130, 424820]

Rheem Manufacturing Co., pp. Vol. II-1101, 1106 [NAICS 333414, 333415]

Rhino Linings Of Wausau, p. III-1766 [NAICS 423130]

Rhinotek, p. III-1805 [NAICS 423430]

Rhode Island Mack Sales and Serv, p. III-2030 [NAICS 441310]

Rhodes Supply Company Inc., pp. Vol. III-1790, 1794 [NAICS 423330, 423390]

Rhodia ChiRex Inc., p. I-534 [NAICS 325411]

Rhopac Fabricators Inc., p. I-403 [NAICS 32223M]

R.I. Lampus Co., p. I-737 [NAICS 32733M]

Ribbon Webbing Corp., pp. Vol. I-203, 244, 510 [NAICS 31322M, 314991, 32522M]

Ribco Manufacturing Inc., p. II-1735 [NAICS 339993]

Rica Foods Inc., p. I-97 [NAICS 311615]

Ricart Automotive, p. III-2011 [NAICS 441110]

Ricart Chrysler Plymouth, p. III-2011 [NAICS 441110]

Riccar America Co., p. III-1835 [NAICS 423620]

Rice Lake Weighing Systems Inc., pp. Vol. II-1168, 1347 [NAICS 333613, 334515]

Rice Oil Company Inc., p. I-165 [NAICS 31211M]

Rice Packaging Inc., p. I-374 [NAICS 322130]

Riceland Cabinet Inc., p. I-762 [NAICS 327991]

Riceland Foods, p. I-15 [NAICS 31121M]

Riceland Foods Inc., pp. Vol. I-15, 26, 31 [NAICS 31121M, 311225, 31122N]

Riceland Foods Inc. Lecithin Div., p. I-26 [NAICS 311225]

Rich Ice Cream Co., p. I-92 [NAICS 311520]

Rich Products Corp., pp. Vol. I-62, 68, 81, 110 [NAICS 31141M, 31142M, 311514, 31171M]

Rich's/Lazarus/Goldsmith's, p. III-2171 [NAICS 452111]

Rich-United Corp., p. III-2228 [NAICS 454390]

Richard A Johnson Cedar Products, p. III-1794 [NAICS 423390]

Richard J Cassidy Inc., p. III-1770 [NAICS 423140]

Richard O'Brien Co's Inc., p. III-1859 [NAICS 423810]

Richard, P.C. and Son Long Island, p. III-2050 [NAICS 443111]

Richard S Hatfield Inc., p. III-1855 [NAICS 423740]

Richards & Ellis Graphics Group, p. III-1798 [NAICS 423410]

Richards Battery Company Inc., p. II-1442 [NAICS 335911]

Richards Brick Co., p. I-691 [NAICS 327121]

Richards Brothers Supermarket Inc., p. III-2177 [NAICS 452910]

Richards Corp., p. II-1087 [NAICS 333315]

Richards Industries Inc., p. II-1421 [NAICS 335311]

Richards Products Inc., p. III-1909 [NAICS 424210]

Richards-Wilcox Inc., pp. Vol. II-1168, 1644 [NAICS 333613, 337215]

Richardson and Partners, p. III-2011 [NAICS 441110]

Richardson Electronics Ltd., p. III-1839 [NAICS 423690]

Richardson Industries Inc., pp. Vol. I-312, 329, Vol. II-1611, 1621 [NAICS 32111M, 32121P, 337110, 337122]

Numbers following p. or pp. are page references. Roman numerals indicate volume numbers. Bracketed items indicate industries. Page references are to the starting pages of company tables.

Company Index

2405

Richardson Sales and Consulting, p. II-1124 [NAICS 333512]

Richelieu Partners Group, p. I-158 [NAICS 31199M]

Richloom Fabrics Corp., p. III-2180 [NAICS 452990]

Richmond Apothecaries Inc., p. III-2100 [NAICS 446110]

Richmond Ford L.L.C., p. III-1758 [NAICS 423110]

Richmond Optical Company Inc., p. III-1817 [NAICS 423460]

Richmond Yarns Inc., p. I-192 [NAICS 31311M]

Ricoh Electronics Inc., p. II-1077 [NAICS 333313]

Ridewell Corp., p. II-1519 [NAICS 336330]

Ridgeview Industries, p. I-879 [NAICS 33211P]

Ridgway's Ltd., pp. Vol. I-420, 436 [NAICS 32311M, 32312M]

Riedon Inc., p. II-1297 [NAICS 334415]

Riefler Concrete Products L.L.C., pp. Vol. I-737, 743 [NAICS 32733M, 327390]

Riegel By-Products Company Inc., p. I-26 [NAICS 311225]

Riegsecker's Inc., p. II-1607 [NAICS 336999]

Rieke Packaging Systems Inc., pp. Vol. I-879, Vol. II-1189, 1457, 1725 [NAICS 33211P, 333913, 33593M, 339991]

Riekes Equipment Co., p. III-1867 [NAICS 423830]

Rieman & Arszman Custom, p. III-1835 [NAICS 423620]

Rigaku MSC Inc., pp. Vol. II-1357, Vol. III-1813 [NAICS 334517, 423450]

Rigel Computer Systems Inc., p. III-2058 [NAICS 443120]

Riggins Inc., p. III-2218 [NAICS 454311]

Riggs Supply Corp., p. III-1794 [NAICS 423390]

Right Cooperative Association Inc., pp. Vol. I-15, 31, 524 [NAICS 31121M, 31122N, 325314]

Right Honda, p. III-1758 [NAICS 423110]

Rightway Fasteners Inc., p. II-958 [NAICS 332722]

Riley Creek Lumber Co., p. I-312 [NAICS 32111M]

Rima Manufacturing Company, p. II-952 [NAICS 332721]

Rimage Corp., p. II-1087 [NAICS 333315]

Rimtec Corp., p. I-589 [NAICS 325991]

Rinderer's Drug Stores Inc., p. III-2100 [NAICS 446110]

Ring Container Technologies Inc., p. I-646 [NAICS 326160]

Ringwood Co., p. II-1189 [NAICS 333913]

Rinker Boat Co., p. II-1594 [NAICS 336612]

Rino Manufacturing Inc., p. II-1248 [NAICS 334113]

Rio Brands Inc., p. II-1632 [NAICS 33712N]

Rio Grande Valley Sugar Growers, p. I-44 [NAICS 31131N]

Rippey Corp., p. II-1056 [NAICS 333295]

RISO Inc., p. II-1252 [NAICS 334119]

Rita's Italian Ice, p. III-2094 [NAICS 445299]

Ritchey Produce Company Inc., p. III-1950 [NAICS 424480]

Ritchey's Dairy Inc., p. I-143 [NAICS 311920]

Rite Aid Corp., pp. Vol. III-2030, 2100, 2162 [NAICS 441310, 446110, 451211]

Rite-Hite Corp., pp. Vol. I-251, 670, Vol. II-899, 908, 1676 [NAICS 314999, 32629M, 33231M, 33232M, 339113]

Rite-Style Optical Co., p. II-1687 [NAICS 339115]

Rite Temperature Associates Inc., p. III-1855 [NAICS 423740]

Rite Way Oil and Gas Inc., p. III-2116 [NAICS 447110]

Riteway Magic Supply Inc., p. II-1740 [NAICS 339994]

Ritron Inc., pp. Vol. II-1262, 1267, 1272 [NAICS 334220, 334290, 334310]

Rittal Corp., pp. Vol. I-879, Vol. II-1457 [NAICS 33211P, 33593M]

Ritter Manufacturing Company Inc., p. II-1046 [NAICS 333210]

Ritz Camera Centers Inc., pp. Vol. III-2024, 2062 [NAICS 441222, 443130]

Ritz-Craft Corporation, pp. Vol. I-348, 353 [NAICS 321991, 321992]

Ritz Messwandler, p. II-1421 [NAICS 335311]

Riva Jewelry Manufacturing Inc., p. I-825 [NAICS 331419]

Riva World, pp. Vol. III-1758, 2021 [NAICS 423110, 441221]

River Birch Homes Inc., p. I-348 [NAICS 321991]

River City Brewery Inc., p. I-172 [NAICS 312120]

River City Truck Parts Inc., p. III-1770 [NAICS 423140]

River Country Coop., p. III-1975 [NAICS 424710]

River Run Computers Inc., p. II-1238 [NAICS 334111]

River Valley Co-Op, pp. Vol. I-9, 15 [NAICS 311119, 31121M]

Riverhead Building Supply Corp., p. III-2065 [NAICS 444100]

Riverside Brick and Supply, pp. Vol. I-691, 695 [NAICS 327121, 327122]

Riverside Electronics Ltd., p. II-1282 [NAICS 334412]

Riverside Engineering, p. I-872 [NAICS 33211N]

Riverside Furniture Corp., pp. Vol. II-1616, 1621 [NAICS 337121, 337122]

Riverside Refractories Inc., p. I-703 [NAICS 32712N]

Riverside Scrap, p. III-1890 [NAICS 423930]

Riverside Scrap Iron & Metal, p. III-1890 [NAICS 423930]

Riviana Foods Inc., pp. Vol. I-15, Vol. III-1950, 1954 [NAICS 31121M, 424480, 424490]

Riviera Tool Co., pp. Vol. II-1152, 1541 [NAICS 333518, 336370]

RJ Lee Group Inc., p. II-1352 [NAICS 334516]

R.J. Reynolds Tobacco Holdings, p. I-188 [NAICS 31222M]

R.J. Rous Inc., p. III-1933 [NAICS 424430]

RJ Singer International Inc., p. II-1212 [NAICS 333993]

RJR Packaging, pp. Vol. I-379, 388, 395, 420 [NAICS 32221M, 32222N, 32222P, 32311M]

RK Black Inc., p. III-1801 [NAICS 423420]

RK Miles Inc., p. III-1782 [NAICS 423310]

RKA Petroleum Companies Inc., pp. Vol. III-1975, 1979 [NAICS 424710, 424720]

RKI Inc., pp. Vol. I-879, Vol. II-1486 [NAICS 33211P, 336211]

RL Industries Inc., p. II-1051 [NAICS 333220]

RL Ryerson Company Inc., p. III-2018 [NAICS 441210]

RL Schreiber Inc., p. I-152 [NAICS 31194M]

RM Hendrick Graduate Supply, p. I-285 [NAICS 31529M]

RMC Carolina Materials Inc., p. I-737 [NAICS 32733M]

RMC Ewell, Inc., pp. Vol. I-732, 737, 743 [NAICS 327320, 32733M, 327390]

RMC Florida Group, pp. Vol. I-732, 737 [NAICS 327320, 32733M]

RMC Inc, p. III-2197 [NAICS 453910]

RMC Metromont, p. I-737 [NAICS 32733M]

RMC Pacific Materials Inc., pp. Vol. I-732, 756 [NAICS 327320, 327910]

RMD Inc., p. II-1357 [NAICS 334517]

RMF Steel Products Co., p. II-1212 [NAICS 333993]

RMO Inc., p. II-1682 [NAICS 339114]

RMS Co., pp. Vol. II-945, 1580, 1671 [NAICS 332710, 336419, 339112]

RMS Communications Group Inc., p. III-1839 [NAICS 423690]

Ro-An Industries Corp., p. II-1051 [NAICS 333220]

Ro Do Company Inc., p. III-2089 [NAICS 445291]

Ro-Mac Lumber and Supply Inc., p. III-2065 [NAICS 444100]

Ro-Vic Inc., p. III-1875 [NAICS 423850]

Road Machinery Co., p. III-1859 [NAICS 423810]

Road Rescue Inc., p. II-1473 [NAICS 336111]

Road Systems Inc., p. II-1491 [NAICS 336212]

Roadside Lumber & Hardware Inc., p. III-1843 [NAICS 423710]

Roanoke Cement Co., p. I-727 [NAICS 327310]

Roanoke Electric Steel Corp., p. I-780 [NAICS 33111M]

Roanoke Gas Co., p. III-2222 [NAICS 454312]

Roaring Spring Paper Products, pp. Vol. I-379, 415 [NAICS 32221M, 322299]

Robbins and Myers Inc., pp. Vol. II-1179, 1427 [NAICS 333911, 335312]

Robbins Co., p. II-1124 [NAICS 333512]

Robbins Inc., p. I-358 [NAICS 321999]

Robbins L.L.C., pp. Vol. I-505, 660 [NAICS 325212, 32621M]

Robbins Lumber Inc., p. I-363 [NAICS 322110]

Robbins Manufacturing Inc., p. I-312 [NAICS 32111M]

ROBC Inc., p. I-165 [NAICS 31211M]

Robert Abbey Inc., p. II-1390 [NAICS 33512M]

Robert and William Inc., p. I-4 [NAICS 311111]

Robert Bosch Corp., p. II-1551 [NAICS 336399]

Robert Bosch Tool Corp., pp. Vol. II-892, 1028, 1207 [NAICS 33221P, 333112, 333991]

Robert BoshTool Corp., pp. Vol. II-1092, 1207 [NAICS 33331N, 333991]

Robert Crist and Company RV, p. III-2018 [NAICS 441210]

Robert F Henry Tile Company Inc., p. III-1786 [NAICS 423320]

Robert H Ham Associates Ltd., p. III-1809 [NAICS 423440]

Robert J Matthews Company Inc., pp. Vol. III-1820, 2007 [NAICS 423490, 424990]

Robert M Hadley Company Inc., p. II-1292 [NAICS 334414]

Robert Manufacturing Inc., p. II-974 [NAICS 332913]

Robert Mucha Jr A, p. III-1883 [NAICS 423910]

Robert Orr-Sysco Food Services, p. III-1925 [NAICS 424410]

Robert's Oxygen Inc, p. I-471 [NAICS 325120]

Robert Weed Plywood Corp., pp. Vol. I-324, Vol. II-1611, 1644 [NAICS 32121N, 337110, 337215]

Robertet Fragrances Inc., p. I-575 [NAICS 325620]

Roberts Aircraft Company Nevada, p. III-1879 [NAICS 423860]

Roberts Company Inc., pp. Vol. I-699, Vol. II-899, 1594 [NAICS 327123, 33231M, 336612]

Roberts Foods Inc., pp. Vol. III-1929, 1936, 1950 [NAICS 424420, 424440, 424480]

Roberts Oxygen Company Inc., p. III-1867 [NAICS 423830]

Robertshaw Uni-Line, p. III-1851 [NAICS 423730]

Robertson Optical Labratories Inc., p. III-1817 [NAICS 423460]

Robertson Worldwide Co., p. II-1421 [NAICS 335311]

Robin International USA Inc., pp. Vol. III-1916, 1919 [NAICS 424320, 424330]

Robin-Lynn Mills Inc., p. I-256 [NAICS 31511M]

Robinson Brick Co., pp. Vol. I-691, Vol. III-1786 [NAICS 327121, 423320]

Robinson Hosiery Mill, p. I-256 [NAICS 31511M]

Robinson Knife Manufacturing Inc., p. III-1778 [NAICS 423220]

Robinson Latva L.L.P., pp. Vol. I-845, 852 [NAICS 33151M, 33152N]

Robinson Manufacturing Inc., pp. Vol. I-272, 279 [NAICS 31522M, 31523M]

Robinson Ransbottom Pottery Co., p. I-681 [NAICS 327112]

Robinson Steel Company Inc., pp. Vol. I-793, Vol. II-945 [NAICS 33122M, 332710]

Robinsons-May, p. III-2171 [NAICS 452111]

Robison-Anton Textile Co., p. I-192 [NAICS 31311M]

Robison Oil Corp., p. III-2218 [NAICS 454311]

Robison Tire Company Inc., p. III-1766 [NAICS 423130]

Robotics Inc., p. II-1189 [NAICS 333913]

Robroy Industries Inc., p. I-631 [NAICS 326130]

ROC Carbon Co., p. II-1157 [NAICS 333611]

Roche Pharmaceuticals, p. I-539 [NAICS 325412]

Rochelle Foods Inc., p. I-102 [NAICS 31161N]

Rochester 100 Inc., p. I-603 [NAICS 326111]

Rochester Big & Tall Clothing, p. III-2123 [NAICS 448110]

Rochester Liquor Corp., p. III-1987 [NAICS 424820]

Rochester-Syracuse Auto Auction, p. III-1758 [NAICS 423110]

Rock Island Corp., p. III-1843 [NAICS 423710]

Rock of Ages Corp., pp. Vol. I-762, Vol. II-1749 [NAICS 327991, 339999]

Rock-Tenn Co., pp. Vol. I-374, 379 [NAICS 322130, 32221M]

Rockbestos-Surprenant Cable, p. II-1451 [NAICS 33592M]

Rockbridge Farmers Coop., pp. Vol. III-1975, 2072, 2218 [NAICS 424710, 444220, 454311]

Rockford Acromatic Products, pp. Vol. II-952, 1168, 1530 [NAICS 332721, 333613, 336350]

Rockford Blacktop Construction, p. I-448 [NAICS 324121]

Rockford Corp., p. II-1272 [NAICS 334310]

Rockford International Inc., p. III-1843 [NAICS 423710]

Rockford Powertrain Inc., pp. Vol. II-1162, 1168, 1530 [NAICS 333612, 333613, 336350]

Rockford Rigging Inc., p. I-825 [NAICS 331419]

Rockies Brewing Company Inc., p. I-172 [NAICS 312120]

Rockland Corp., p. I-767 [NAICS 327992]

Rockland Immunochemicals Inc., p. I-544 [NAICS 325413]

Rockland Industries Inc., p. I-251 [NAICS 314999]

Rockview Farms Inc., p. I-86 [NAICS 31151N]

Rockwell Automation Inc., pp. Vol. II-1168, 1229, 1427, 1437 [NAICS 333613, 33399P, 335312, 335314]

Rockwell Collins Inc., pp. Vol. II-1262, 1267, 1327, 1437, 1580 [NAICS 334220, 334290, 334511, 335314, 336419]

Rockwood Automatic Machine, p. II-952 [NAICS 332721]

Rockwood Pigments Davis Colors, p. I-475 [NAICS 32513M]

Rocky Mount Cord Co., p. I-244 [NAICS 314991]

Rocky Mountain Chocolate Factory, pp. Vol. I-48, 52 [NAICS 311320, 311330]

Rocky Mountain Fabrication Inc., p. II-923 [NAICS 332420]

Rocky Mountain Recycling, p. I-807 [NAICS 331314]

Rocky Mountain Steel, pp. Vol. I-780, Vol. II-899, 908, 939, 1147 [NAICS 33111M, 33231M, 33232M, 33261M, 333516]

Rocky Mountain Welding, p. II-1129 [NAICS 333513]

Rocky Mtn Chocolate Factory, p. III-2092 [NAICS 445292]

Rocky Shoes and Boots Inc., p. I-300 [NAICS 31621M]

Rockydale Quarries Corp., p. I-748 [NAICS 327410]

Rodda Paint Co., p. I-554 [NAICS 325510]

Rodgers Instruments L.L.C., p. II-1731 [NAICS 339992]

Rodman Industries, p. I-319 [NAICS 321219]

Rodney Hunt Co., p. I-845 [NAICS 33151M]

Rodney Strong Vineyards, p. I-177 [NAICS 312130]

roemner Co., p. II-1666 [NAICS 339111]

Roesch Inc., p. I-681 [NAICS 327112]

Rofin-Sinar Inc., p. II-1468 [NAICS 335999]

Roger Shawn Houck, p. III-1863 [NAICS 423820]

Rogers Brothers Wholesale Inc., pp. Vol. III-1929, 1946, 1950 [NAICS 424420, 424470, 424480]

Rogers Corp., pp. Vol. I-500, 626, Vol. II-1282, 1287, 1307, 1317, 1457, 1725 [NAICS 325211, 326122, 334412, 334413, 334417, 334419, 33593M, 339991]

Rogers Corp. Adv Circuit Material, p. II-1282 [NAICS 334412]

Rogers Foam Corp., p. I-641 [NAICS 326150]

Rogers Group Inc., p. I-448 [NAICS 324121]

Rogers Industrial Products Inc., pp. Vol. II-1051, 1129 [NAICS 333220, 333513]

Rogers Iron and Metal Corp., p. I-807 [NAICS 331314]

Rogers Machinery Company Inc., pp. Vol. III-1809, 1867 [NAICS 423440, 423830]

Rogers Manufacturing Inc., p. II-1491 [NAICS 336212]

Rogue Ales Public House, p. I-172 [NAICS 312120]

Rohm and Haas Co., pp. Vol. I-488, 500, 529, 626 [NAICS 325188, 325211, 325320, 326122]

Rohm and Haas Morton Salt, p. I-152 [NAICS 31194M]

Rohmax USA Inc., pp. Vol. I-458, 595 [NAICS 324191, 32599N]

Roho Group, p. I-234 [NAICS 31412M]

Rohrbach Brewing Co., p. I-172 [NAICS 312120]

Rohrer Corp., pp. Vol. I-374, 395, 403, 415, 609 [NAICS 322130, 32222P, 32223M, 322299, 326112]

ROL Mfg of America Inc., p. II-1077 [NAICS 333313]

Roland Machinery Co., p. III-1859 [NAICS 423810]

Rolf's Patisserie Inc., p. III-1954 [NAICS 424490]

Roll Former Corp., pp. Vol. I-863, Vol. II-1147 [NAICS 332114, 333516]

Roll-Kraft, pp. Vol. II-1129, 1147 [NAICS 333513, 333516]

Roll-Tech Inc., p. I-660 [NAICS 32621M]

Rollac Shutter of Texas Inc., p. I-239 [NAICS 31491M]

Rolled Alloys Inc., pp. Vol. I-788, 857 [NAICS 331210, 33152P]

Roller Derby Skate Corp., p. III-1883 [NAICS 423910]

Roller Fabrics, p. I-213 [NAICS 31324M]

Rollex Corp., p. I-811 [NAICS 331316]

Rollform of Jamestown Inc., p. I-863 [NAICS 332114]

Rolligon Corp., p. I-660 [NAICS 32621M]

Rolling Hills Fs Inc., p. III-1958 [NAICS 424510]

Rolling Pin Pastry Company Inc., p. III-2089 [NAICS 445292]

Rolls Battery of New England, p. II-1442 [NAICS 335911]

Rollx Vans, p. II-1496 [NAICS 336213]

ROM Corp., p. I-239 [NAICS 31491M]

Roman Inc., p. III-2007 [NAICS 424990]

Roman Meal Milling Company Inc., p. I-36 [NAICS 311230]

Roman Research Inc., p. II-886 [NAICS 33221N]

Romanelli and Son Inc., p. III-1979 [NAICS 424720]

Romans Interiors Inc., p. III-2041 [NAICS 442210]

Rome Plow Co., pp. Vol. II-1023, 1033 [NAICS 333111, 333120]

Rome Tool and Die Company Inc., p. II-1524 [NAICS 336340]

Romero's Food Products Inc., p. I-133 [NAICS 311830]

Ron Jon Surf Shop, pp. Vol. III-2132, 2150 [NAICS 448140, 451110]

Rondele Specialty Foods, p. I-76 [NAICS 311513]

Rondy and Company Inc., p. I-505 [NAICS 325212]

Roney Oatman Inc., p. III-1933 [NAICS 424430]

Ronile Inc., p. I-218 [NAICS 31331M]

Ronk Electrical Industries Inc., p. II-1292 [NAICS 334414]

Numbers following p. or pp. are page references. Roman numerals indicate volume numbers. Bracketed items indicate industries. Page references are to the starting pages of company tables.

2407

Ronken Industries Inc., p. II-1292 [NAICS 334414]

Ronpak Inc., p. I-395 [NAICS 32222P]

Ronsley Inc., p. III-2183 [NAICS 453110]

Ronson Corp., p. I-458 [NAICS 324191]

Roofing Supply Ltd., p. III-1790 [NAICS 423330]

Roofing Supply of Atlanta Inc., p. III-1790 [NAICS 423330]

Roofline Inc., p. III-1790 [NAICS 423330]

Rooms To Go Inc., p. III-2037 [NAICS 442110]

Root Group Inc., p. II-1238 [NAICS 334111]

Root-Lowell Manufacturing Co., p. II-1184 [NAICS 333912]

Root Spring Scraper Co., p. II-1028 [NAICS 333112]

Ropak Corp., p. I-651 [NAICS 32619M]

Ropak Northwest Inc., p. III-1871 [NAICS 423840]

Roper Industries Inc., pp. Vol. II-980, 1179, 1337, 1352, 1367, 1437 [NAICS 33291N, 333911, 334513, 334516, 334519, 335314]

Roper Whitney of Rockford Inc., pp. Vol. II-886, 1129 [NAICS 33221N, 333513]

Roplast Industries Inc., p. I-603 [NAICS 326111]

Rorke Data Inc., pp. Vol. II-1243, 1248 [NAICS 334112, 334113]

Rosauer's Supermarkets Inc., pp. Vol. III-2076, 2100 [NAICS 445110, 446110]

Rosboro Lumber Co., p. I-324 [NAICS 32121N]

Rose Acquisition Group L.L.C., p. I-807 [NAICS 331314]

Rose Acre Farms Inc., pp. Vol. I-31, 158 [NAICS 31122N, 31199M]

Rose and Walker Supply Inc., pp. Vol. III-1786, 1790 [NAICS 423320, 423330]

Rose Brick and Materials Inc., p. III-2218 [NAICS 454311]

Rose City Chevrolet Inc., p. III-2030 [NAICS 441310]

Rose Industries Inc., p. III-1883 [NAICS 423910]

Rose, Morris Auto Parts Inc., p. III-1770 [NAICS 423140]

Rose Tree, p. I-234 [NAICS 31412M]

Roseburg Forest Products Co., pp. Vol. I-319, 324 [NAICS 321219, 32121N]

Rosemark Bakery Inc., p. III-2089 [NAICS 445291]

Rosemont Industries Inc., p. I-756 [NAICS 327910]

Rosenberger's Dairies Inc., p. I-86 [NAICS 31151N]

Rosenfeld Concrete Corp., p. I-732 [NAICS 327320]

Rosenlew Inc., p. I-603 [NAICS 326111]

Rosenthal Automotive Cos., p. III-2011 [NAICS 441110]

Rosenthal Jewelers Supply Corp., p. III-1894 [NAICS 423940]

Roses Southwest Papers Inc., pp. Vol. I-368, 395, 411 [NAICS 32212M, 32222P, 322291]

Roskam Baking Company Inc., p. I-36 [NAICS 311230]

Roskamp Champion, pp. Vol. I-793, Vol. II-1124, 1147 [NAICS 33122M, 333512, 333516]

Ross Aluminum Foundry L.L.C., pp. Vol. I-852, 857 [NAICS 33152N, 33152P]

Ross & Wallace Paper Products, p. I-395 [NAICS 32222P]

Ross Bicycles USA Ltd., pp. Vol. II-1599, Vol. III-1883 [NAICS 336991, 423910]

Ross Lighting Corp., p. II-1390 [NAICS 33512M]

Ross Mould Inc., p. II-1119 [NAICS 333511]

Ross Stores Inc., p. III-2132 [NAICS 448140]

Rossborough-Remacor L.L.C., p. II-1147 [NAICS 333516]

Rostra Precision Controls Inc., p. II-1162 [NAICS 333612]

Rosy Brothers Inc., p. III-2069 [NAICS 444210]

Rotary Corp., pp. Vol. II-892, 1028, 1112 [NAICS 33221P, 333112, 33341N]

Rotary Pen Corp., p. II-1714 [NAICS 33994M]

Rotation Products Corp., p. II-988 [NAICS 332991]

Rotek Inc., pp. Vol. I-845, Vol. II-988 [NAICS 33151M, 332991]

Rotella's Italian Bakery Inc., p. I-116 [NAICS 31181M]

Roth Kase USA Ltd., p. I-76 [NAICS 311513]

Rotometals Inc., p. I-825 [NAICS 331419]

Rotor Clip Company Inc., pp. Vol. I-793, Vol. II-939, 1505 [NAICS 33122M, 33261M, 33631M]

Rott-Keller Supply Co., pp. Vol. III-1766, 1998 [NAICS 423130, 424930]

Round Hill Cellars, p. I-177 [NAICS 312130]

Roundy's Inc., p. III-1925 [NAICS 424410]

Roush Industries Inc., p. II-1119 [NAICS 333511]

Rovanco Piping Systems Inc., p. I-788 [NAICS 331210]

Rowan Companies Inc., pp. Vol. II-899, 1033, 1039 [NAICS 33231M, 333120, 33313M]

Rowe Companies, pp. Vol. II-1616, 1621, Vol. III-2037 [NAICS 337121, 337122, 442110]

Rowe Furniture Inc., pp. Vol. II-1616, 1621 [NAICS 337121, 337122]

Rowe Machinery and Mfg Co., p. II-1152 [NAICS 333518]

Rowenta Inc., p. III-1835 [NAICS 423620]

Rowland Coffee Roasters Inc., p. I-143 [NAICS 311920]

Rowley Spring and Stamping Corp., p. II-1302 [NAICS 334416]

Roy Houff and Co., p. III-1998 [NAICS 424930]

Roy Robinson Chevrolet Subaru, p. III-2018 [NAICS 441210]

Royal American Company L.L.C., p. I-244 [NAICS 314991]

Royal Appliance Mfg Co., pp. Vol. II-1092, 1397 [NAICS 33331N, 33521M]

Royal Baths Manufacturing Inc., pp. Vol. I-762, Vol. II-974, 1702 [NAICS 327991, 332913, 339920]

Royal Brass and Hose Inc., p. III-1863 [NAICS 423920]

Royal Cabinets, p. II-1611 [NAICS 337110]

Royal Canin USA Inc., p. I-4 [NAICS 311111]

Royal Chemical Company Ltd., pp. Vol. I-566, 595 [NAICS 32561M, 32599N]

Royal China & Porcelain, p. I-681 [NAICS 327112]

Royal Concrete Pipe Inc., p. I-737 [NAICS 32733M]

Royal Consumer Information, p. III-1801 [NAICS 423420]

Royal Crest Dairy Inc., p. I-86 [NAICS 31151N]

Royal Crown Bottling Co., p. I-165 [NAICS 31211M]

Royal Crown Bottling Corp., p. I-165 [NAICS 31211M]

Royal Cup Inc., p. I-143 [NAICS 311920]

Royal Dental Manufacturing Inc., p. II-1682 [NAICS 339114]

Royal Group Inc., p. I-379 [NAICS 32221M]

Royal Home Fashions Inc., p. I-234 [NAICS 31412M]

Royal Metal Products Inc., p. II-1101 [NAICS 333414]

Royal Oak Industries Inc., p. II-1140 [NAICS 333515]

Royal Palm Corp., p. I-256 [NAICS 31511M]

Royal Paper Stock Company Inc., p. I-363 [NAICS 322110]

Royal Park Uniforms Inc., p. I-267 [NAICS 31521M]

Royal Seating Ltd., pp. Vol. II-1627, 1632, 1650 [NAICS 337127, 33712N, 33721N]

Royal Window Coverings USA, p. II-1662 [NAICS 337920]

Royalty Carpet Mills Inc., p. I-229 [NAICS 314110]

Royce Hosiery L.L.C., pp. Vol. III-1916, 1919 [NAICS 424320, 424330]

Royce Photo Graphics Inc., p. III-1798 [NAICS 423410]

Royce Rolls Ringer Company Inc., p. II-1740 [NAICS 339994]

Royersford Foundry & Machine, p. II-988 [NAICS 332991]

Royle Systems Group, p. II-1129 [NAICS 333513]

Royster-Clark Inc., pp. Vol. I-516, Vol. III-1991 [NAICS 325311, 424910]

Royster-Clark Nitrogen Inc., pp. Vol. I-471, 516 [NAICS 325120, 325311]

Rozier Mercantile Co., p. III-2171 [NAICS 452111]

RP Johnson and Son Inc., pp. Vol. III-1794, 1843 [NAICS 423390, 423710]

R.P. Lumber Company Inc., p. III-2065 [NAICS 444100]

RPC Inc., p. II-1594 [NAICS 336612]

Rpg Diffusor Systems Inc., p. I-771 [NAICS 327993]

RPM International Inc., pp. Vol. I-272, 554, 560 [NAICS 31522M, 325510, 325520]

RPS Engineering Inc., p. I-453 [NAICS 324122]

RPS Imaging Inc., p. II-1357 [NAICS 334517]

R.R. Donnelley and Sons Co., p. I-420 [NAICS 32311M]

RRR Development Co., p. II-1051 [NAICS 333220]

RS Co., p. III-1894 [NAICS 423940]

RS Electronics Inc., p. III-1831 [NAICS 423610]

RS Roofing and Sheet Metal Inc., p. III-1790 [NAICS 423330]

RS Technical Services Inc., p. II-1087 [NAICS 333315]

RSA Security Inc., p. II-1252 [NAICS 334119]

RSDC Of Michigan L.L.C., p. III-1824 [NAICS 423510]

RSG Forest Products, p. I-312 [NAICS 32111M]

RSG Forest Products Inc., p. I-312 [NAICS 32111M]

RSI Home Products, p. I-762 [NAICS 327991]

RSL Woodworking Products Inc., p. II-1639 [NAICS 337212]

RSM Sensitron Semiconductor, p. II-1312 [NAICS 334418]

RSR Wholesale Guns Inc., p. III-1883 [NAICS 423910]

RTI International Metals Inc., pp. Vol. I-837, 872, Vol. II-908, 1014, 1567 [NAICS 33149M, 33211N, 33232M, 33299N, 336413]

RTKL International Ltd., p. III-2208 [NAICS 453998]

RTP Co., pp. Vol. I-500, 589 [NAICS 325211, 325991]

RTS Packaging L.L.C., p. I-374 [NAICS 322130]

Rubber and Gasket of America Inc., p. I-665 [NAICS 326220]

Rubber Applications Inc., p. I-699 [NAICS 327123]

Rubber Enterprises Inc., pp. Vol. I-665, 670 [NAICS 326220, 32629M]

Rubber Specialties Inc., p. I-505 [NAICS 325212]

Rubberlite Inc., pp. Vol. I-560, Vol. II-1725 [NAICS 325520, 339991]

Rubbermaid Home Products Div., pp. Vol. I-626, 670 [NAICS 326122, 32629M]

Rubens and Marble Inc., p. I-262 [NAICS 31519M]

Rubenstein Brothers Inc., pp. Vol. III-2123, 2141 [NAICS 448110, 448210]

Rubigo Cosmetics, p. II-1740 [NAICS 339994]

Ruddick Corp., pp. Vol. I-192, Vol. III-2076 [NAICS 31311M, 445110]

Rudolph Foods Company Inc., p. I-137 [NAICS 31191M]

Rudolph Technologies Inc., p. II-1367 [NAICS 334519]

RUE Educational Publishers Inc., p. II-1376 [NAICS 334612]

Rueff Lighting Co., p. II-1386 [NAICS 335110]

Ruffin and Payne Inc., p. III-1790 [NAICS 423330]

Ruger Investment Castings Div., p. I-845 [NAICS 33151M]

Ruggedtronics Inc., pp. Vol. II-1238, 1252 [NAICS 334111, 334119]

Ruggiero Seafood Inc., p. I-110 [NAICS 31171M]

Ruiz Food Products Inc., pp. Vol. I-62, 133, 158 [NAICS 31141M, 311830, 31199M]

Ruiz Mexican Foods Inc., p. I-133 [NAICS 311830]

RunTex Inc., p. III-2141 [NAICS 448210]

Ruppe Hosiery Inc., p. I-256 [NAICS 31511M]

Rush Communications of NY Inc., p. III-2135 [NAICS 448150]

Rush Enterprises Inc., pp. Vol. III-1762, 1863, 2027 [NAICS 423120, 423820, 441229]

Rush Metals Inc., p. I-867 [NAICS 332117]

Russ Berrie and Company Inc., pp. Vol. I-358, 681, Vol. II-1708, 1749 [NAICS 321999, 327112, 33993M, 339999]

Russelectric Inc., pp. Vol. II-1432, 1457 [NAICS 335313, 33593M]

Russell and Miller Inc., p. II-1720 [NAICS 339950]

Russell Corp., pp. Vol. I-262, 272, 290 [NAICS 31519M, 31522M, 31599M]

Russell Standard Corp., pp. Vol. I-453, 554 [NAICS 324122, 325510]

Russell-William Ltd., p. II-1720 [NAICS 339950]

Russell Yarn L.L.C., p. I-198 [NAICS 313210]

Russound Fmp Inc., p. II-1421 [NAICS 335311]

Rust Wholesale Company Inc., p. III-2007 [NAICS 424990]

Rutgers Organics Corp., p. I-493 [NAICS 32519M]

Rutland Plywood Corp., p. I-324 [NAICS 32121N]

RVL Packaging Inc., pp. Vol. I-203, Vol. II-1536 [NAICS 31322M, 336360]

RVSI Acuity CiMatrix Div., p. II-1337 [NAICS 334513]

RW Bowman Corp., p. III-2050 [NAICS 443111]

RW Garcia Company Inc., p. I-133 [NAICS 311830]

R.W. Sauder Inc., p. I-97 [NAICS 311615]

RWC Inc., p. II-1152 [NAICS 333518]

RWE Schott Solar Inc., p. II-1101 [NAICS 333414]

Ryan Trading L.L.C., p. II-1312 [NAICS 334418]

Ryerson Tull Inc., pp. Vol. I-780, Vol. III-1824 [NAICS 33111M, 423510]

Ryko Manufacturing Company Inc., p. II-1092 [NAICS 33331N]

Ryobi Die Castings USA Inc., pp. Vol. I-852, Vol. II-1505 [NAICS 33152N, 33631M]

Ryobi Technologies Inc., p. II-1207 [NAICS 333991]

S and C Ford, p. III-2011 [NAICS 441110]

S and D Coffee Inc., pp. Vol. I-68, 143, Vol. III-1925, 1954 [NAICS 31142M, 311920, 424410, 424490]

S and G Mfg Group L.L.C., p. II-1627 [NAICS 337127]

S and H Trailer Manufacturing Inc., p. II-1500 [NAICS 336214]

S and J Industrial Supply Co., p. I-756 [NAICS 327910]

S and K Famous Brands Inc., p. III-2123 [NAICS 448110]

S and S Blue Ridge Copiers Inc., p. III-2186 [NAICS 453210]

S and S Fire Apparatus Inc., p. II-1482 [NAICS 336120]

S and S Steel Services Inc., pp. Vol. II-945, 1749 [NAICS 332710, 339999]

S and S Technology, p. II-1357 [NAICS 334517]

S and S Time Corp., p. II-1362 [NAICS 334518]

S and W Manufacturing Inc., p. I-403 [NAICS 32223M]

S and Z Tool and Die Inc., p. II-1134 [NAICS 333514]

S. Joseph and Sons Inc., p. III-2144 [NAICS 448310]

S. Schwab Company Inc., pp. Vol. I-279, 285 [NAICS 31523M, 31529M]

S. Shamash and Sons, p. III-1965 [NAICS 424590]

S-TEC Corp., p. II-1327 [NAICS 334511]

S. Woods Enterprises Inc., p. III-2011 [NAICS 441110]

S Zitner Co., p. I-57 [NAICS 311340]

Saab Aircraft of America Inc., p. III-1879 [NAICS 423860]

Saab Cars USA Inc., p. III-2011 [NAICS 441110]

Saba Textiles Inc., p. I-218 [NAICS 31331M]

Sabina Farmers Exchange, pp. Vol. I-15, 524 [NAICS 31121M, 325314]

Sabreliner Corp., pp. Vol. II-1173, 1557, 1567 [NAICS 333618, 336411, 336413]

Sabritec, pp. Vol. II-1307, 1580 [NAICS 334417, 336419]

Sabroso Foods, p. I-133 [NAICS 311830]

Sacramento Brewing Co's Oasis, p. I-172 [NAICS 312120]

Sacramento Rendering Co., p. I-26 [NAICS 311225]

Sadler's Barbecue Sales Inc., p. I-152 [NAICS 31194M]

S.A.E. Circuits Colorado Inc., p. II-1282 [NAICS 334412]

SAE Power, p. II-1302 [NAICS 334416]

Safariland Ltd. Inc., p. I-306 [NAICS 31699M]

Safco Industries Inc., p. II-1248 [NAICS 334113]

Safeguard Chemical Corp., p. I-529 [NAICS 325320]

Safelite Glass Corp., pp. Vol. I-709, 722 [NAICS 327211, 327215]

SafeNet Inc., p. II-1262 [NAICS 334220]

Safer Textiles and Kuttner Prints, pp. Vol. I-218, 251 [NAICS 31331M, 314999]

Safety Components Intern. Inc., pp. Vol. I-198, Vol. II-1005, Vol. III-1762 [NAICS 313210, 332995, 423120]

Safety Steel Service Inc., p. II-1009 [NAICS 332996]

Safeway Inc., p. III-2076 [NAICS 445110]

Safier's Inc., pp. Vol. III-1939, 2001 [NAICS 424450, 424940]

Saftronics Inc., p. II-1162 [NAICS 333612]

Sag Harbor, p. I-279 [NAICS 31523M]

Sage Laboratories Inc., p. II-1307 [NAICS 334417]

Sagem Morpho Inc., p. II-1749 [NAICS 339999]

Sager Computer, p. II-1238 [NAICS 334111]

Sager Electronics Inc., p. III-1831 [NAICS 423610]

Saginaw Asphalt Paving Co., p. III-1786 [NAICS 423320]

Saginaw Control & Engineering, p. II-1432 [NAICS 335313]

Sagoma Plastics Inc., p. II-1708 [NAICS 33993M]

Saint Elizabeth Home Medical, pp. Vol. III-1813, 2054 [NAICS 423450, 443112]

Saint-Gobain Abrasives Inc., p. I-756 [NAICS 327910]

Saint-Gobain Advanced Ceramics, pp. Vol. I-681, 686, 703 [NAICS 327112, 327113, 32712N]

Saint-Gobain Calmar Inc., pp. Vol. I-651, Vol. II-1189 [NAICS 32619M, 333913]

Saint-Gobain Container Inc., p. I-718 [NAICS 327213]

Saint-Gobain Crystals & Detectors, p. II-1277 [NAICS 334411]

Saint-Gobain Technical Fabrics, pp. Vol. I-224, 554, 722 [NAICS 313320, 325510, 327215]

Saint-Gobain Universal Abrasives, p. I-756 [NAICS 327910]

St. James Gourmet Inc., p. III-1946 [NAICS 424470]

St. Joe Co., p. I-312 [NAICS 32111M]

St. John Knits International Inc., pp. Vol. I-279, 290, 300, 306, 575, Vol. II-1696 [NAICS 31523M, 31599M, 31621M, 31699M, 325620, 33991M]

St. Jude Medical Cardiac Rhythm, p. II-1322 [NAICS 334510]

St. Jude Medical Inc., pp. Vol. II-1322, 1676 [NAICS 334510, 339113]

St. Martin Oil and Gas Inc., p. III-1975 [NAICS 424710]

Sakrete Inc., p. I-752 [NAICS 327420]

Saks Inc., p. III-2132 [NAICS 448140]

Salem Equipment Inc., p. II-1046 [NAICS 333210]

Salem Packing Co., p. III-1946 [NAICS 424470]

Salem-Republic Rubber Co., pp. Vol. I-224, 505, 665 [NAICS 313320, 325212, 326220]

Salem Suede Inc., p. I-296 [NAICS 316110]

Salem Tube Inc., p. I-788 [NAICS 331210]

Salinas Tallow Company Inc., p. I-26 [NAICS 311225]

Salinas Valley Ford Sales Inc., p. III-2011 [NAICS 441110]

Numbers following p. or pp. are page references. Roman numerals indicate volume numbers. Bracketed items indicate industries. Page references are to the starting pages of company tables.

2409

Salt River Pima Maricopa Indian, p. I-727 [NAICS 327310]

Salta's Tire Company Inc., pp. Vol. III-1766, 2034 [NAICS 423130, 441320]

Salton Inc., pp. Vol. II-1397, 1404, 1417 [NAICS 33521M, 335221, 335228]

Salvajor Company Inc., p. II-1417 [NAICS 335228]

Salvati Foods Inc., p. III-1933 [NAICS 424430]

Sam Ash Music Corp., pp. Vol. III-2058, 2159 [NAICS 443120, 451140]

Sam Kane Beef Processors Inc., p. I-102 [NAICS 31161N]

Sam Levitz Furniture Co., p. III-2037 [NAICS 442110]

SAM'S Club, pp. Vol. III-2030, 2100, 2162 [NAICS 441310, 446110, 451211]

Samaritan Wholesale Tire Inc., p. III-1766 [NAICS 423130]

Sampson Coatings Inc., p. I-554 [NAICS 325510]

Samson Investment Co., p. I-443 [NAICS 324110]

Samson Rope Technologies, p. I-244 [NAICS 314991]

Samsonite Corp., p. I-306 [NAICS 31699M]

Samsung Electronics America Inc., p. III-1835 [NAICS 423620]

Samsung Opto-Electronics Am., pp. Vol. III-1798, 1867, 1894 [NAICS 423410, 423830, 423940]

Samuel Aaron International Inc., p. II-1696 [NAICS 33991M]

Samuel Feldman Lumber Inc., p. III-1782 [NAICS 423310]

Samuel Frank Metal Company Inc., p. III-1890 [NAICS 423930]

Samuel Son and Co., p. I-793 [NAICS 33122M]

Samuel Strapping Systems Inc., pp. Vol. II-892, 1212 [NAICS 33221P, 333993]

Samuels Glass Co., p. I-709 [NAICS 327211]

Samuels Jewelers Inc., p. III-2144 [NAICS 448310]

Samuels Recycling Co., p. I-807 [NAICS 331314]

Samy's Camera Inc., p. III-2062 [NAICS 443130]

San Antonio Aerospace Inc., pp. Vol. II-1567, 1580 [NAICS 336413, 336419]

San Antonio Winery Inc., p. I-177 [NAICS 312130]

San Francisco Drydock Inc., p. II-1589 [NAICS 336611]

SAN Holdings Inc., p. II-1243 [NAICS 334112]

San Joaquin Refining Inc., p. I-443 [NAICS 324110]

San Joaquin Supply Company Inc., p. III-1875 [NAICS 423850]

San Luis Obisbo Eye Assoc A ME, p. III-2107 [NAICS 446130]

Sancap Abrasives, p. I-756 [NAICS 327910]

Sancoa International Company, p. I-388 [NAICS 32222N]

Sand Seed Service Inc., pp. Vol. I-15, 31 [NAICS 31121M, 31122N]

Sanden International Inc., pp. Vol. II-1106, 1184 [NAICS 333415, 333912]

Sanders Gallery, p. III-2047 [NAICS 442299]

Sanderson Farms Inc., pp. Vol. I-62, 68, 97, 102 [NAICS 31141M, 31142M, 311615, 31161N]

Sanderson Ford Inc., p. III-2011 [NAICS 441110]

Sanderson Ford Trucks, pp. Vol. III-1758, 1867, 2011 [NAICS 423110, 423830, 441110]

Sanderson-MacLeod Inc., pp. Vol. I-510, 830, Vol. II-1740 [NAICS 32522M, 33142M, 339994]

Sanderson Plumbing Products Inc., p. I-358 [NAICS 321999]

SanDisk Corp., p. II-1243 [NAICS 334112]

Sandpiper Knitting Inc., p. I-262 [NAICS 31519M]

Sandridge Food Corp., p. I-92 [NAICS 311520]

Sandusky Athol International, p. I-224 [NAICS 313320]

Sandvik Sorting Systems Inc., p. II-1077 [NAICS 333313]

Sandvik Special Metals Corp., pp. Vol. I-788, 825 [NAICS 331210, 331419]

Sanese Svs & Catering By Design, pp. Vol. I-137, 158 [NAICS 31191M, 31199M]

SangStat Medical Corp., pp. Vol. I-549, Vol. II-1671 [NAICS 325414, 339112]

Sanmina S.C.I., pp. Vol. II-1238, 1312 [NAICS 334111, 334418]

Sanmina-SCI Corp., p. II-1282 [NAICS 334412]

Sans Pareil Inc., p. III-1817 [NAICS 423460]

Sansegal Sportswear Inc., p. I-251 [NAICS 314999]

Sanson Co., p. III-1950 [NAICS 424480]

Santa Cruz Biotechnology Inc., p. I-549 [NAICS 325414]

Santa Cruz Guitar Co., p. II-1731 [NAICS 339992]

Santa Fe Jewelers, p. III-1894 [NAICS 423940]

Santa Fe Textiles Inc., p. I-203 [NAICS 31322M]

Santa Fe Tortilla Company Inc., p. I-133 [NAICS 311830]

Santana and Laminations Inc., pp. Vol. I-615, 631 [NAICS 326113, 326130]

Santee Dairies Inc., p. I-86 [NAICS 31151N]

Santee Industries, p. II-1599 [NAICS 336991]

Santee Print Works Co., p. I-218 [NAICS 31331M]

Santens of America Inc., p. I-234 [NAICS 31412M]

SANYO Fisher Co., pp. Vol. II-1238, 1272, 1397 [NAICS 334111, 334310, 33521M]

Sanyo Foods Corporation, p. I-158 [NAICS 31199M]

Sanyo Laser Products Inc., pp. Vol. II-1243, 1376 [NAICS 334112, 334612]

Sapa Inc., pp. Vol. I-811, Vol. II-964 [NAICS 331316, 33281M]

Saputo Cheese USA Inc., p. I-76 [NAICS 311513]

Sara Lee Branded Apparel, p. I-256 [NAICS 31511M]

Sara Lee Coffee and Tea, p. I-143 [NAICS 311920]

Sara Lee Corp., pp. Vol. I-68, 102, 116, 143, 165, 256, 262, 529 [NAICS 31142M, 31161N, 31181M, 311920, 31211M, 31511M, 31519M, 325320]

Sara Lee Refrigerated Foods, p. I-97 [NAICS 311615]

Sara Mana Business Products Inc., p. III-2186 [NAICS 453210]

Sardelli International, p. II-1696 [NAICS 33991M]

Sardello Inc., pp. Vol. II-1173, 1584 [NAICS 333618, 336510]

Sargent Fletcher Inc., p. II-1567 [NAICS 336413]

Sargent Manufacturing Inc., p. II-933 [NAICS 332510]

Sargent-Welch Scientific Co., p. III-1820 [NAICS 423490]

Sarnoff Corp., pp. Vol. II-1267, 1272 [NAICS 334290, 334310]

Sarris Candies Inc., pp. Vol. I-52, 57 [NAICS 311330, 311340]

Sarstedt Inc., p. II-1666 [NAICS 339111]

Sartori Foods, p. I-76 [NAICS 311513]

Sartorius BBI Systems Inc., p. II-1666 [NAICS 339111]

S.A.S. Conway Co., p. I-300 [NAICS 31621M]

Sasol North America Inc., pp. Vol. I-566, 595 [NAICS 32561M, 32599N]

Satco Inc., p. I-703 [NAICS 32712N]

Satis Vacuum of America, p. III-1817 [NAICS 423460]

Saturday Knight Ltd., pp. Vol. I-234, 251, Vol. III-2047 [NAICS 31412M, 314999, 442299]

Saturn Electronics & Engineering, pp. Vol. II-1282, 1317 [NAICS 334412, 334419]

Sauber Manufacturing Co., p. II-1500 [NAICS 336214]

Saucony Inc., pp. Vol. I-300, Vol. III-2150 [NAICS 31621M, 451110]

Sauder Manufacturing Co., pp. Vol. I-251, Vol. II-899, 964 [NAICS 314999, 33231M, 33281M]

Sauder Woodworking Co., pp. Vol. I-319, Vol. II-1621, 1627, 1644, 1650 [NAICS 321219, 337122, 337127, 337215, 33721N]

Saudi Electric Supply Inc., p. III-1831 [NAICS 423610]

Sauer-Danfoss Inc., pp. Vol. II-1168, 1189, 1505 [NAICS 333613, 333913, 33631M]

Sauereisen Inc., pp. Vol. I-703, 752 [NAICS 32712N, 327420]

Sault Printing Company Inc., p. III-2186 [NAICS 453210]

Saunders Brothers Inc., pp. Vol. I-358, Vol. II-1644 [NAICS 321999, 337215]

Saunders Corp., p. I-756 [NAICS 327910]

Saunders Engine Co., p. II-1173 [NAICS 333618]

Sav-On Discount Office Supplies, p. III-2186 [NAICS 453210]

Sava Industries Inc., pp. Vol. II-1307, 1312 [NAICS 334417, 334418]

Savage Arms Inc., p. II-1001 [NAICS 332994]

Savannah Distributing Inc., p. III-1987 [NAICS 424820]

Savannah Foods and Industries Inc., pp. Vol. I-40, 44, 62, 68 [NAICS 311313, 31131N, 31141M, 31142M]

Savannah Luggage Works, pp. Vol. I-239, 510 [NAICS 31491M, 32522M]

Save Mart Supermarkets, p. III-2076 [NAICS 445110]

Savient Pharmaceuticals Inc., p. I-534 [NAICS 325411]

Savin Corp., p. III-1801 [NAICS 423420]

Saxonburg Ceramics Inc., pp. Vol. I-681, 686, 703, 776 [NAICS 327112, 327113, 32712N, 327999]

Saxony Ice Co., p. I-471 [NAICS 325120]

Sayers Group L.L.C., p. III-1805 [NAICS 423430]

SBC Communications Inc., p. II-1257 [NAICS 334210]

SBC Group Inc., p. III-1798 [NAICS 423410]

SBP Image Solutions, p. III-2186 [NAICS 453210]

SBS Technologies Inc., p. II-1238 [NAICS 334111]

S.C. Industrial Resource Group Inc., p. II-1046 [NAICS 333210]

Numbers following p. or pp. are page references. Roman numerals indicate volume numbers. Bracketed items indicate industries. Page references are to the starting pages of company tables.

S.C. Johnson & Son Inc., pp. Vol. I-395, 500, 529, 566, 575 [NAICS 32222P, 325211, 325320, 32561M, 325620]

S.C. Johnson & Son Inc. Waxdale, pp. Vol. I-493, 500, 529, 566 [NAICS 32519M, 325211, 325320, 32561M]

S.C.A. Personal Care, p. I-411 [NAICS 322291]

Scaccianoce Inc., p. I-137 [NAICS 31191M]

Scalamandre Silks Inc., p. I-203 [NAICS 31322M]

Scale Models, p. II-1708 [NAICS 33993M]

Scales Air Compressor Corp., p. II-1184 [NAICS 333912]

ScanSource Inc., p. III-1805 [NAICS 423430]

Scantibodies Laboratory Inc., pp. Vol. I-544, Vol. II-1322 [NAICS 325413, 334510]

Scantron Corp., p. II-1248 [NAICS 334113]

Scapa North America Inc., I-670 [NAICS 32629M]

Scariano Brothers L.L.C., pp. Vol. III-1929, 1946 [NAICS 424420, 424470]

Scenic Fruit Company Inc., p. I-62 [NAICS 31141M]

Schaeff Lift Truck Inc., p. II-1491 [NAICS 336212]

Schaeperkoetter Store Inc., p. III-2177 [NAICS 452910]

Schaffner Manufacturing Inc., pp. Vol. I-756, Vol. II-1152 [NAICS 327910, 333518]

Scharffen Berger Chocolate Maker, p. I-48 [NAICS 311320]

Schatz Bearing Corp., p. II-988 [NAICS 332991]

Schawk Inc., pp. Vol. I-395, 420, 436 [NAICS 32222P, 32311M, 32312M]

Scheels All Sports Inc., pp. Vol. III-2065, 2150 [NAICS 444100, 451110]

Schefenacker Inc., p. I-722 [NAICS 327215]

Schefer Gear Works Inc., p. II-1162 [NAICS 333612]

Scheid Vineyards Inc., p. I-177 [NAICS 312130]

Schenck Accurate Inc., pp. Vol. II-1189, 1342 [NAICS 333913, 334514]

Schenck RoTec Corp., p. II-1152 [NAICS 333518]

Schenone Specialty Foods Inc., pp. Vol. I-48, Vol. III-2092 [NAICS 311320, 445292]

Scherer Brothers Lumber Co., p. III-2065 [NAICS 444100]

Schering-Plough Corp., pp. Vol. I-539, Vol. II-1676, Vol. III-1909 [NAICS 325412, 339113, 424210]

Schermerhorn Brothers Co., p. III-1871 [NAICS 423840]

Scheu Steel Supply Co., p. III-1770 [NAICS 423140]

Schewel Furniture Company Inc., p. III-2037 [NAICS 442110]

Schick Technologies Inc., p. II-1357 [NAICS 334517]

Schick Wilkinson Sword, p. II-886 [NAICS 33221N]

Schiebout Tire Co., p. III-1766 [NAICS 423130]

Schiff's Restaurant Service Inc., p. III-1954 [NAICS 424490]

Schiffer Dental Care Products, p. II-1740 [NAICS 339994]

Schildberg Construction Inc., p. I-762 [NAICS 327991]

Schilling Forge Inc., pp. Vol. II-886, 1682 [NAICS 33221N, 339114]

Schils America Inc., p. I-9 [NAICS 311119]

Schindler Elevator Corp., p. II-1194 [NAICS 33392M]

Schirm USA Inc., p. I-529 [NAICS 325320]

Schlegel Systems Inc., pp. Vol. I-251, 641, Vol. II-1725 [NAICS 314999, 326150, 339991]

Schleicher & Schuell BioScience, pp. Vol. I-544, Vol. II-1666 [NAICS 325413, 339111]

Schleicher/Schuell MicroScience, pp. Vol. I-549, Vol. II-1666 [NAICS 325414, 339111]

Schlessman Seed Co., p. I-31 [NAICS 31122N]

Schlumberger, p. II-1451 [NAICS 33592M]

Schlumger Co., p. II-1451 [NAICS 33592M]

Schmelzer Industries Inc., p. I-203 [NAICS 31322M]

Schmidt Baking Company Inc., p. I-116 [NAICS 31181M]

Schmidt Group Inc., pp. Vol. I-631, Vol. II-939, Vol. III-1867, 1871 [NAICS 326130, 33261M, 423830, 423840]

Schmidt Printing Inc., p. I-420 [NAICS 32311M]

Schmidt's Wholesale Inc., pp. Vol. III-1847, 1871 [NAICS 423720, 423840]

Schmuckal Oil Co., pp. Vol. III-2116, 2218 [NAICS 447110, 454311]

Schnadig Corp., pp. Vol. II-1616, 1621 [NAICS 337121, 337122]

Schneider Cheese Inc., p. I-76 [NAICS 311513]

Schneider Electric Co., pp. Vol. II-1162, 1432, 1437, 1457 [NAICS 333612, 335313, 335314, 33593M]

Schneider's Bakery Inc., p. III-2089 [NAICS 445291]

Schneider's Dairy, pp. Vol. I-86, 92 [NAICS 31151N, 311520]

Schneller Inc., p. I-224 [NAICS 313320]

Schnitzer Steel Industries Inc., p. I-780 [NAICS 33111M]

Schnuck Markets Inc., p. III-2076 [NAICS 445110]

Scholars Inn Bakehouse, p. III-2089 [NAICS 445291]

Scholle Corp., pp. Vol. I-554, 609 [NAICS 325510, 326112]

Scholle Custom Packaging Inc., p. I-603 [NAICS 326111]

School Specialty Inc., pp. Vol. III-1774, 1801, 1901 [NAICS 423210, 423420, 424120]

Schott Fiber Optics, pp. Vol. II-1082, 1367, 1451 [NAICS 333314, 334519, 33592M]

Schott Glass Technologies Inc., pp. Vol. I-709, 713, Vol. II-1082, 1687 [NAICS 327211, 327212, 333314, 339115]

Schott International Inc., p. III-1913 [NAICS 424310]

Schott North Am Technical Glass, p. I-879 [NAICS 33211P]

SCHOTT North America Inc, p. II-1082 [NAICS 333314]

Schott North America Technical, pp. Vol. I-722, Vol. II-1287, 1457 [NAICS 327215, 334413, 33593M]

Schottenstein Stores Corp., pp. Vol. III-2030, 2047, 2171 [NAICS 441310, 442299, 452111]

Schram Auto and Truck Parts Inc., p. III-1770 [NAICS 423140]

Schramsberg Vineyards, p. I-177 [NAICS 312130]

Schreiber Foods Inc., pp. Vol. I-62, 76, Vol. II-1061 [NAICS 31141M, 311513, 33329N]

Schuessler Knitting Mills Inc., pp. Vol. I-213, 262 [NAICS 31324M, 31519M]

Schuette Mfg and Steel Sales Inc., p. II-1023 [NAICS 333111]

Schuetz Container Systems Inc., pp. Vol. I-646, 651 [NAICS 326160, 32619M]

Schulmerich Carillons Inc., pp. Vol. II-1362, 1731 [NAICS 334518, 339992]

Schulte Storage, pp. Vol. II-928, 1644 [NAICS 33243M, 337215]

Schumacher Electric Corp., pp. Vol. II-1302, 1421, 1468 [NAICS 334416, 335311, 335999]

Schunk Graphite Technology, pp. Vol. I-458, Vol. II-1463 [NAICS 324191, 335991]

Schupan and Sons Inc., pp. Vol. I-807, 837 [NAICS 331314, 33149M]

Schuster Concerte L.L.C., p. I-732 [NAICS 327320]

Schutte and Koerting L.L.C., p. II-1342 [NAICS 334514]

Schuylkill Haven Casket Inc., p. II-1745 [NAICS 339995]

Schwan Food Co., pp. Vol. I-62, 92, Vol. III-2228 [NAICS 31141M, 311520, 454390]

Schwan's Food Service Inc., p. II-1189 [NAICS 333913]

Schwans Bakery of Stilwell, p. I-116 [NAICS 31181M]

Schwans Sales, p. III-1929 [NAICS 424420]

Schwartz Industries Inc., p. II-1473 [NAICS 336111]

Schwartz Manufacturing Co., p. I-208 [NAICS 313230]

Schwartzman Co., p. I-807 [NAICS 331314]

Schwarz, p. I-420 [NAICS 32311M]

Schwarzschild Jewelers Inc., p. III-2144 [NAICS 448310]

Schwebel Baking Co., p. I-116 [NAICS 31181M]

Schweigert Foods, p. I-97 [NAICS 311615]

Schweitzer-Mauduit Intern. Inc., pp. Vol. I-368, Vol. II-1714 [NAICS 32212M, 33994M]

Schweizer Aircraft Corp., pp. Vol. II-1557, 1580 [NAICS 336411, 336419]

Schwing America Inc., p. II-1179 [NAICS 333911]

Scientemp Corp., p. II-1409 [NAICS 335222]

Scientific-Atlanta Inc., p. II-1262 [NAICS 334220]

Scientific Microscopes Inc., p. III-1820 [NAICS 423490]

Scientific Plastics Ltd., p. II-1662 [NAICS 337920]

Scientific Services Company Inc., p. II-1277 [NAICS 334411]

Scientific Supplies & Technology, p. III-1820 [NAICS 423490]

Scientific Technologies Inc., pp. Vol. II-1248, 1347, 1421 [NAICS 334113, 334515, 335311]

Scientifics, pp. Vol. III-2208, 2211 [NAICS 453998, 454111]

SCM Group USA Inc., p. II-1046 [NAICS 333210]

Scolari's Food and Drug Co., p. III-2076 [NAICS 445110]

SCOOTER Store Inc., p. III-2228 [NAICS 454390]

Scope Imports Inc., p. III-1916 [NAICS 424320]

Scope Industries Inc., p. I-4 [NAICS 311111]

Score Acquisitions Corp., pp. Vol. I-52, Vol. III-1939 [NAICS 311330, 424450]

Scot Inc., pp. Vol. II-1005, 1302 [NAICS 332995, 334416]

Scotchman Industries Inc., pp. Vol. II-1152, 1207 [NAICS 333518, 333991]

Scotsman Industries Inc., p. II-1106 [NAICS 333415]

Scott Brass Inc., pp. Vol. I-793, 857 [NAICS 33122M, 33152P]

Numbers following p. or pp. are page references. Roman numerals indicate volume numbers. Bracketed items indicate industries. Page references are to the starting pages of company tables.

2411

Scott Company of California Inc., p. II-908 [NAICS 33232M]

Scott Construction Equipment, p. III-1859 [NAICS 423810]

Scott Fetzer Co., pp. Vol. II-1092, 1101, 1179, 1184 [NAICS 33331N, 333414, 333911, 333912]

Scott Industrial Systems Inc., p. III-1867 [NAICS 423830]

Scott Industries Inc., p. I-771 [NAICS 327993]

Scott Industries of KY L.L.C., p. III-1968 [NAICS 424610]

Scott Lumber Inc., p. I-343 [NAICS 321920]

Scott-McRae Automotive Group, p. III-2011 [NAICS 441110]

Scott Paint Co., p. I-554 [NAICS 325510]

Scott Pet Products Inc., p. I-4 [NAICS 311111]

Scott Process Systems Inc., p. II-923 [NAICS 332420]

Scott Resources Inc., pp. Vol. II-1376, 1708 [NAICS 334612, 33993M]

Scott Rice of Kansas City Inc., p. III-2037 [NAICS 442110]

Scott's Liquid Gold Inc., p. I-493 [NAICS 32519M]

Scott's of Wisconsin, pp. Vol. I-52, 57 [NAICS 311330, 311340]

Scott Semiconductor Gases Inc., p. I-471 [NAICS 325120]

Scott Truck and Tractor Inc., pp. Vol. III-1859, 1863 [NAICS 423810, 423820]

Scotts Miracle-Gro Co., pp. Vol. I-516, 520, 524, 529 [NAICS 325311, 325312, 325314, 325320]

Scottsboro Aluminum L.L.C., pp. Vol. I-811, 816, Vol. II-1009 [NAICS 331316, 33131N, 332996]

Scotty's Fashions Cutting Inc., pp. Vol. I-272, 279 [NAICS 31522M, 31523M]

Scotty's Inc., p. III-2065 [NAICS 444100]

Scoular Co., pp. Vol. III-1958, 1991 [NAICS 424510, 424910]

Scovill Fasteners Inc., p. II-1735 [NAICS 339993]

SCP Pool Corp., p. III-1883 [NAICS 423910]

Scrap All Inc., p. I-807 [NAICS 331314]

Screen Works Ltd., pp. Vol. II-1087, 1714 [NAICS 333315, 33994M]

SD Ireland Concrete Construction, p. I-732 [NAICS 327320]

SD Myers Inc., pp. Vol. II-1112, 1302, 1421 [NAICS 33341N, 334416, 335311]

SDI Technologies Inc., p. II-1272 [NAICS 334310]

SDS Lumber Co., pp. Vol. I-312, 324 [NAICS 32111M, 32121N]

S.E. Johnson Companies Inc., p. I-448 [NAICS 324121]

Sea Coast Supply, p. III-1790 [NAICS 423330]

Sea Lion Technology Inc., p. I-493 [NAICS 32519M]

Sea-Pro Boats Inc., p. II-1594 [NAICS 336612]

Sea Ray Boats Inc., p. II-1594 [NAICS 336612]

Sea Safari Ltd., p. I-110 [NAICS 31171M]

Sea Vision USA, p. II-1687 [NAICS 339115]

Seaboard Asphalt Products Co., p. I-453 [NAICS 324122]

Seaboard Atlantic Garment Inc., p. I-218 [NAICS 31331M]

Seaboard Corp., pp. Vol. I-97, 102, Vol. III-1958 [NAICS 311615, 31161N, 424510]

Seaboard Folding Box Corp., p. I-379 [NAICS 32221M]

Seabrook Seafood Inc., p. I-110 [NAICS 31171M]

Seabrook Wallcoverings Inc., p. III-2004 [NAICS 424950]

SeaChange International Inc., p. II-1262 [NAICS 334220]

Seafood Producers Coop., p. I-110 [NAICS 31171M]

Seagate Technology, p. II-1243 [NAICS 334112]

Seagrave Fire Apparatus L.L.C., pp. Vol. II-1014, 1179, 1194, 1486 [NAICS 33299N, 333911, 33392M, 336211]

Seal-it Inc., p. I-609 [NAICS 326112]

Seal Master Corp., pp. Vol. I-505, 665, Vol. II-1725 [NAICS 325212, 326220, 339991]

Seal Rite Door, p. III-1782 [NAICS 423310]

Seal Tek Inc., p. I-224 [NAICS 313320]

Seal-Tite Plastic Packaging Co., p. I-603 [NAICS 326111]

Sealant Equipment & Engineering, p. II-1189 [NAICS 333913]

Sealco Commercial Vehicle, p. II-1524 [NAICS 336340]

Sealed Air Corp., p. I-615 [NAICS 326113]

Sealed Air Cryovac Div., pp. Vol. I-395, 615 [NAICS 32222P, 326113]

Sealfons Inc., pp. Vol. III-2126, 2129 [NAICS 448120, 448130]

Sealy Corp., p. II-1657 [NAICS 337910]

Sealy Mattress Company of NJ, p. II-1657 [NAICS 337910]

Seaman Corp., pp. Vol. I-224, 554 [NAICS 313320, 325510]

Seaman Paper of Massachusetts, p. I-368 [NAICS 32212M]

Seaman Timber Company Inc., p. I-343 [NAICS 321920]

Seamens Medical Solutions, p. III-1813 [NAICS 423450]

Seamless Siding Management, p. III-1790 [NAICS 423330]

Seaquist Closures L.L.C., p. II-1179 [NAICS 333911]

Sears Home Services Group, p. III-2058 [NAICS 443120]

Sears, Roebuck and Co., pp. Vol. III-1843, 2030, 2107, 2171, 2211 [NAICS 423710, 441310, 446130, 452111, 454113]

Seasons 4 Inc., p. II-1217 [NAICS 333994]

Seaswirl Boats Inc., p. II-1594 [NAICS 336612]

Seattle Aero L.L.C., p. III-1879 [NAICS 423860]

Seattle Gourmet Foods Inc., p. I-48 [NAICS 311320]

Seattle Lighting Fixture, p. III-1831 [NAICS 423610]

Seattle Office Furniture L.L.C., p. III-2037 [NAICS 442110]

Seaward Trellborg Engineered, pp. Vol. I-651, Vol. II-933 [NAICS 32619M, 332510]

Seawatch International Ltd., p. I-110 [NAICS 31171M]

Sebastian International Inc., p. I-575 [NAICS 325620]

Sebastiani Vineyards, pp. Vol. I-177, Vol. III-1987 [NAICS 312130, 424820]

SECO Industries, p. II-1212 [NAICS 333993]

Second Source Inc., p. II-1056 [NAICS 333295]

Securcam Inc., p. III-1835 [NAICS 423620]

Security Gold Exchange Inc., p. III-1894 [NAICS 423940]

Security Supply Corp., p. III-1847 [NAICS 423720]

SED International Holdings Inc., pp. Vol. III-1805, 1839 [NAICS 423430, 423690]

SED International Inc., pp. Vol. III-1805, 1839 [NAICS 423430, 423690]

Sedia Inc., p. I-224 [NAICS 313320]

Seegott Inc., p. III-1971 [NAICS 424690]

Seelye Plastics Inc, p. I-788 [NAICS 331210]

Segye Times Inc., p. III-2200 [NAICS 453920]

SEI Capacitors Inc., p. II-1292 [NAICS 334414]

SEI Electronics Inc., p. II-1297 [NAICS 334415]

Seibert Powder Coatings Inc., p. I-554 [NAICS 325510]

Seiko Corporation of America, p. II-1362 [NAICS 334518]

Seitz Corp., p. II-1189 [NAICS 333913]

Sekisui America Corp. Voltek Div., p. I-636 [NAICS 326140]

Selco Custom Time Corp., p. II-1362 [NAICS 334518]

Select Comfort Corp., p. II-1657 [NAICS 337910]

Select Copy Systems, p. III-1801 [NAICS 423420]

Select Optical, p. II-1687 [NAICS 339115]

Selecto-Flash Inc., p. I-218 [NAICS 31331M]

Selee Corp., pp. Vol. I-686, Vol. II-1217, 1229 [NAICS 327113, 333994, 33399P]

Self Industries Inc., pp. Vol. I-793, Vol. II-928 [NAICS 33122M, 33243M]

Sellars Absorbent Materials Inc., p. I-251 [NAICS 314999]

Sellars Nonwoven, p. I-208 [NAICS 313230]

Sellstrom Manufacturing Co., p. II-1687 [NAICS 339115]

Selmet Inc., p. I-857 [NAICS 33152P]

Semblex Corp., pp. Vol. I-793, Vol. II-958 [NAICS 33122M, 332722]

Semco Enterprises Inc., p. I-825 [NAICS 331419]

Semco Inc., pp. Vol. I-771, Vol. II-1112, 1397 [NAICS 327993, 33341N, 33521M]

Semco Plastic Co., p. II-1134 [NAICS 333514]

Semiconductor Equipment Corp., p. II-1056 [NAICS 333295]

Semling-Menke Company Inc., p. I-334 [NAICS 32191M]

Sempac Systems Inc., p. I-388 [NAICS 32222N]

Semtech Corp., p. II-1287 [NAICS 334413]

Seneca Foods Corp., p. I-68 [NAICS 31142M]

Seneca Sawmill Co., p. I-312 [NAICS 32111M]

Senez Roofing and Builder, Ernest, p. III-1790 [NAICS 423330]

Senior Aerospace Metal Bellows, p. II-1184 [NAICS 333912]

Senior Operations Inc., pp. Vol. I-699, Vol. II-1229 [NAICS 327123, 33399P]

Senoret Chemical Company Inc., p. I-529 [NAICS 325320]

Sensient Technologies Corp., pp. Vol. I-68, 147, 539, 575 [NAICS 31142M, 311930, 325412, 325620]

SensorMedics Corp., p. II-1322 [NAICS 334510]

Sensus Metering Systems, pp. Vol. II-1317, 1342 [NAICS 334419, 334514]

Numbers following p. or pp. are page references. Roman numerals indicate volume numbers. Bracketed items indicate industries. Page references are to the starting pages of company tables.

2412

Sensus Precision Die Casting Inc., p. II-1342 [NAICS 334514]

SenTech Medical Systems Inc., p. II-1657 [NAICS 337910]

Sentinel Consumer Products Inc., p. I-306 [NAICS 31699M]

Sentinel Lubricants Inc., p. I-458 [NAICS 324191]

Sentry Equipment Corp., p. II-918 [NAICS 332410]

Sentry Group, pp. Vol. II-928, 1650 [NAICS 33243M, 33721N]

Sentry Products Inc., p. II-1267 [NAICS 334290]

Sepracor Inc., pp. Vol. I-539, 544 [NAICS 325412, 325413]

Sequa Corp., pp. Vol. I-595, Vol. II-964, 1157, 1327, 1551, 1576, 1580 [NAICS 32599N, 33281M, 333611, 334511, 336399, 336415, 336419]

Sequel Corp., pp. Vol. II-1173, 1505 [NAICS 333618, 33631M]

Sequoia Industries Inc., p. II-1530 [NAICS 336350]

Sequoit Harbor Marina, p. I-239 [NAICS 31491M]

Sermatech-Ethylene, pp. Vol. I-631, 771 [NAICS 326130, 327993]

Sermatech-Lehr, p. II-1562 [NAICS 336412]

Serologicals Corp., p. I-549 [NAICS 325414]

Serra Corp., pp. Vol. I-879, Vol. II-1312 [NAICS 33211P, 334418]

Serta Inc., p. II-1657 [NAICS 337910]

Serta Mattress Company Inc., p. II-1657 [NAICS 337910]

Serta Restokraft Mattress I, p. II-1657 [NAICS 337910]

Serv-All Recycling, p. I-363 [NAICS 322110]

Servants Inc., pp. Vol. I-343, Vol. III-1905 [NAICS 321920, 424130]

Servco Pacific Inc., pp. Vol. III-1801, 1901, 2011 [NAICS 423420, 424120, 441110]

Service Construction Supply Inc., p. III-1786 [NAICS 423320]

Service Industries Inc., p. II-1157 [NAICS 333611]

Service Manufacturing Corp., p. I-239 [NAICS 31491M]

Service Oil Inc., pp. Vol. III-1975, 2116 [NAICS 424710, 447110]

Services Group of America Inc., pp. Vol. III-1925, 1950 [NAICS 424410, 424480]

Servo Instrument Corp., p. II-1297 [NAICS 334415]

Servotronics Inc., p. II-886 [NAICS 33221N]

Sessions Company Inc., pp. Vol. I-26, 137 [NAICS 311225, 31191M]

Setex Inc., p. II-1536 [NAICS 336360]

Seton Company Inc., pp. Vol. I-306, Vol. II-1551 [NAICS 31699M, 336399]

Setton Pistachio of Terra Bella Inc., p. I-137 [NAICS 31191M]

Setton's International Foods, pp. Vol. I-52, 57, 92, 137 [NAICS 311330, 311340, 311520, 31191M]

Setzers and Company Inc., pp. Vol. III-1778, 1835 [NAICS 423220, 423620]

Seven D Wholesale, pp. Vol. III-1782, 1790 [NAICS 423310, 423330]

Severance Tool Industries Inc., p. I-867 [NAICS 332117]

Severn Peanut Company Inc., p. I-137 [NAICS 31191M]

Severn Trent Water Purification, p. II-1092 [NAICS 33331N]

Seville Flexpack Corp., pp. Vol. I-609, 636, 641 [NAICS 326112, 326140, 326150]

SFA Inc., pp. Vol. II-945, 1312 [NAICS 332710, 334418]

SFI-Delaware L.L.C., pp. Vol. I-420, 436 [NAICS 32311M, 32312M]

SG Supply Co., p. III-1847 [NAICS 423720]

SGL Carbon L.L.C., p. II-1463 [NAICS 335991]

Shadowhawk Inc., p. III-1890 [NAICS 423930]

Shafer Electronics Co., pp. Vol. II-1307, 1312 [NAICS 334417, 334418]

Shakespeare, p. I-510 [NAICS 32522M]

Shakespeare and Co., pp. Vol. III-2162, 2194 [NAICS 451211, 453310]

Shakespeare Fishing Tackle, p. II-1702 [NAICS 339920]

Shakespeare Machine Stamping, p. I-756 [NAICS 327910]

Shaklee Corp., pp. Vol. I-539, 566, 575 [NAICS 325412, 32561M, 325620]

Shako Inc., pp. Vol. I-621, 665 [NAICS 326121, 326220]

Shamrock Foods Co., pp. Vol. I-76, 86, 92, Vol. III-1925, 1929, 1933, 1943, 1946, 1950, 1954 [NAICS 311513, 31151N, 311520, 424410, 424420, 424430, 424460, 424470, 424480, 424490]

Shamrock Ford Lincoln Mercury, p. III-2030 [NAICS 441310]

Shanklin Corp., p. II-1212 [NAICS 333993]

Shar Systems, p. II-1463 [NAICS 335991]

Sharp Energy Inc., p. III-2222 [NAICS 454312]

Sharp Microelectronics Group, p. II-1243 [NAICS 334112]

Sharpe Dry Goods Co., pp. Vol. II-1692, Vol. III-2123, 2126, 2141 [NAICS 339116, 448110, 448120, 448210]

Sharper Image Corp., p. III-2211 [NAICS 454113]

Shasta Industries Inc., p. III-2208 [NAICS 453998]

Shaver Specialty Company Inc., p. II-1473 [NAICS 336111]

Shaw Group Inc., p. II-1009 [NAICS 332996]

Shaw's Supermarkets Inc., p. III-2076 [NAICS 445110]

Shawmut Corp., p. I-631 [NAICS 326130]

Sheaffer Pen, p. II-1714 [NAICS 33994M]

Shealy Sales and Vending Inc., p. III-2215 [NAICS 454210]

Sheetz Inc., pp. Vol. III-2116, 2180 [NAICS 447110, 452990]

Sheffield Bronze Paint Corp., p. I-830 [NAICS 33142M]

Sheffield Laboratory, p. I-534 [NAICS 325411]

Sheffield Steel Corp., pp. Vol. I-780, 793 [NAICS 33111M, 33122M]

Shelburne Plastics, p. I-646 [NAICS 326160]

Shelby Contracting Company Inc., p. I-448 [NAICS 324121]

Shelby Enterprises Inc., p. II-1009 [NAICS 332996]

Shelby-Skipwith Inc., p. III-1855 [NAICS 423740]

Shell Factory Museum Inc., p. III-2190 [NAICS 453220]

Shelley's Septic Tank, p. III-1786 [NAICS 423320]

Shelly and Sands Inc., p. I-732 [NAICS 327320]

Shelly Enterprises Inc., pp. Vol. I-324, 329, 334 [NAICS 32121N, 32121P, 32191M]

Shelter Systems Ltd., p. I-329 [NAICS 32121P]

Shepher Distributors & Sales Corp., p. III-1887 [NAICS 423920]

Shepherd Construction Inc., p. I-448 [NAICS 324121]

Shepherd Products Co., p. III-1913 [NAICS 424310]

Sheplers Inc., p. III-2135 [NAICS 448150]

Sheridan Books Inc., pp. Vol. I-420, 436 [NAICS 32311M, 32312M]

Sheridan Press Inc., p. I-436 [NAICS 32312M]

Sherline Products Inc., p. II-1046 [NAICS 333210]

Sherman and Reilly Inc., p. II-1152 [NAICS 333518]

Sherman, Clay and Co., p. III-2159 [NAICS 451140]

Sherman Industries Inc., pp. Vol. I-732, 737, 743 [NAICS 327320, 32733M, 327390]

Sherman International Corp., p. I-737 [NAICS 32733M]

Sherman Prestressed Concrete, p. I-743 [NAICS 327390]

Sherrill Furniture Company Inc., p. II-1616 [NAICS 337121]

Sherrod Vans Inc., p. II-1496 [NAICS 336213]

Sherry Designs Inc., p. II-1496 [NAICS 336213]

Sherry Resortwear, pp. Vol. I-218, 234 [NAICS 31331M, 31412M]

Sherwin-Williams Co., pp. Vol. I-475, 493, 500, 554, 560, Vol. III-2065 [NAICS 32513M, 32519M, 325211, 325510, 325520, 444100]

Sherwood Brands Inc., pp. Vol. I-48, 52, 124 [NAICS 311320, 311330, 31182M]

Sherwood Food Distributors, pp. Vol. III-1929, 1936, 1946 [NAICS 424420, 424440, 424470]

SHI, p. III-1805 [NAICS 423430]

Shield Pack Inc., p. I-603 [NAICS 326111]

Shiloh Industries Inc., pp. Vol. I-872, Vol. II-1541 [NAICS 33211N, 336370]

Shimadzu Scientific Instruments, pp. Vol. II-1352, Vol. III-1820 [NAICS 334516, 423490]

Shimano American Corp., pp. Vol. II-1599, 1702, Vol. III-1883 [NAICS 336991, 339920, 423910]

Shincor Silicones Inc., pp. Vol. I-505, 767 [NAICS 325212, 327992]

Shine Brothers Corp., p. I-807 [NAICS 331314]

Shintech Inc., pp. Vol. I-500, 589 [NAICS 325211, 325991]

Shipley Company L.L.C., p. I-595 [NAICS 32599N]

Shipman Elevator Co., p. III-1991 [NAICS 424910]

Shirley Oil and Supply Inc., p. III-2116 [NAICS 447110]

Shivvers Manufacturing Inc., p. II-1028 [NAICS 333112]

Shoals Technologies Group Inc., p. II-1541 [NAICS 336370]

Shock-Tech Inc., p. II-1519 [NAICS 336330]

Shockley Engineering and Mfg, p. I-646 [NAICS 326160]

Shoe Carnival Inc., p. III-2141 [NAICS 448210]

Shoe Pavilion Inc., p. III-2141 [NAICS 448210]

Shook and Fletcher Insulation Co., p. III-1790 [NAICS 423330]

Shoosmith Brothers Inc., p. I-448 [NAICS 324121]

ShopKo Stores Inc., pp. Vol. III-2171, 2180 [NAICS 452111, 452990]

Numbers following p. or pp. are page references. Roman numerals indicate volume numbers. Bracketed items indicate industries. Page references are to the starting pages of company tables.

2413

Company Index

Shopnet.com Inc., p. I-285 [NAICS 31529M]

Shopper's Food Warehouse Corp., p. III-2076 [NAICS 445110]

Shopsmith Inc., p. II-1046 [NAICS 333210]

Shor-Line, p. II-1023 [NAICS 333111]

Shore Chemical, p. I-549 [NAICS 325414]

Shoreline Glass Company Inc., p. III-1794 [NAICS 423390]

Shorr Packaging, pp. Vol. III-1898, 1905 [NAICS 424110, 424130]

Showa Aluminum Corporation, pp. Vol. II-918, 1546 [NAICS 332410, 336391]

Shredded Products Corp., p. III-1890 [NAICS 423930]

Shreves Engine Rebuilding, p. II-1173 [NAICS 333618]

Shuford Mills Inc., p. I-192 [NAICS 31311M]

Shultz Foods Co., pp. Vol. I-137, Vol. III-2208 [NAICS 31191M, 453998]

Shur-Co Inc., p. I-239 [NAICS 31491M]

Shurtape Technologies Inc., pp. Vol. I-388, 670 [NAICS 32222N, 32629M]

SI Corp., p. I-208 [NAICS 313230]

SI Jacobson Manufacturing, p. I-609 [NAICS 326112]

Siano Appliance Distributors Inc., p. III-1835 [NAICS 423620]

SICO America Inc., pp. Vol. II-1621, 1657 [NAICS 337122, 337910]

Sicor Inc., pp. Vol. I-539, Vol. III-1813 [NAICS 325412, 423450]

SICPA Securink Corp., p. I-580 [NAICS 325910]

Sidari's Italian Foods, p. III-1929 [NAICS 424420]

Sidel, p. II-1212 [NAICS 333993]

Sidler Inc. Sidler Laotto Mfg Div., pp. Vol. II-1386, 1390, 1437, 1457 [NAICS 335110, 33512M, 335314, 33593M]

Sidley Diamond Tool Co., p. I-756 [NAICS 327910]

Siegel Roberts of Tennessee, p. II-964 [NAICS 33281M]

Sieger Engineering Inc., p. II-1671 [NAICS 339112]

Siegwerk Inc., p. I-580 [NAICS 325910]

Siemans Logistics and Assembly, pp. Vol. II-1194, 1229, 1644 [NAICS 33392M, 33399P, 337215]

Siemens Applied Automation, p. II-1352 [NAICS 334516]

Siemens Building Technologies, pp. Vol. II-1332, 1337, 1437 [NAICS 334512, 334513, 335314]

Siemens Energy & Automation, pp. Vol. II-1162, 1432, 1437 [NAICS 333612, 335313, 335314]

Siemens Industrial Automation Inc., pp. Vol. II-1437, 1551 [NAICS 335314, 336399]

Siemens Machine Tool Business, pp. Vol. II-1162, 1312, 1332 [NAICS 333612, 334418, 334512]

Siemens Medical Solutions, pp. Vol. II-1322, 1357 [NAICS 334510, 334517]

Siemens Medical Solutions Inc., pp. Vol. II-1322, 1468 [NAICS 334510, 335999]

Siemens Motion Controlled, p. II-1332 [NAICS 334512]

Siemens Power Transmission, p. II-1432 [NAICS 335313]

Siemens Ultrasound Div., p. II-1322 [NAICS 334510]

Siemens VDO Automotive, pp. Vol. II-1222, 1505 [NAICS 33399N, 33631M]

Siemens Westinghouse Power, pp. Vol. II-1157, 1427 [NAICS 333611, 335312]

Siemer's Distributing Co., p. III-1946 [NAICS 424470]

Siemon Company Inc., pp. Vol. II-1257, 1307, 1457, 1468 [NAICS 334210, 334417, 33593M, 335999]

Sierra Alloys Co., pp. Vol. I-788, 803 [NAICS 331210, 331312]

Sierra Aluminum Co., pp. Vol. I-811, 852 [NAICS 331316, 33152N]

Sierra Bullets L.L.C., p. II-993 [NAICS 332992]

Sierra Chemical Co., pp. Vol. I-480, Vol. III-1971 [NAICS 325181, 424690]

Sierra Design Group, p. II-1749 [NAICS 339999]

Sierra Nevada Corp., p. II-1262 [NAICS 334220]

Sierra Office Supplies and Printing, p. III-1901 [NAICS 424120]

Sierra Pacific Industries, pp. Vol. I-312, 334, 358 [NAICS 32111M, 32191M, 321999]

Sierra Pine L.P., pp. Vol. I-319, 334 [NAICS 321219, 32191M]

Sierra Seafood Co., p. III-1943 [NAICS 424460]

Sierracin/Sylmar, p. I-722 [NAICS 327215]

SierraPine Ltd. Ampine Div., p. I-319 [NAICS 321219]

SierraPine Ltd. Medite Div., p. I-319 [NAICS 321219]

SIFCO Industries Inc., pp. Vol. I-811, 872, Vol. II-964, 1092 [NAICS 331316, 33211N, 33281M, 33331N]

Sifton Motorcycle Products Inc., p. II-1599 [NAICS 336991]

Sights Denim Systems Inc., pp. Vol. I-218, 251 [NAICS 31331M, 314999]

Sigma-Aldrich Corp., pp. Vol. I-595, Vol. III-1971 [NAICS 32599N, 424690]

Sigma Extruding Corp., p. I-609 [NAICS 326112]

Sigma-Genosys, p. I-549 [NAICS 325414]

Sigma Plastics Group, pp. Vol. I-395, 626 [NAICS 32222P, 326122]

Sigma Probe Inc., p. II-1292 [NAICS 334414]

SigmaTel Inc., p. II-1347 [NAICS 334515]

SigmaTron International Inc., pp. Vol. II-1092, 1262, 1282 [NAICS 33331N, 334220, 334412]

Sigmund Cohn Corp., p. I-825 [NAICS 331419]

Signatrol Inc., p. II-1362 [NAICS 334518]

Signature Brands Group, p. II-886 [NAICS 33221N]

Signature Eyewear Inc., p. II-1687 [NAICS 339115]

Signet Armorlite Inc., p. II-1687 [NAICS 339115]

Signode Packaging Systems, pp. Vol. I-388, 670, Vol. II-892, 1014 [NAICS 32222N, 32629M, 33221P, 33299N]

Signtronix, p. II-1720 [NAICS 339950]

Sika Corp., pp. Vol. I-560, 743 [NAICS 325520, 327390]

Sikora's Religious Art, p. III-1820 [NAICS 423490]

Sikorsky Aircraft Corp., p. II-1557 [NAICS 336411]

Silarx Pharmaceuticals Inc., p. I-534 [NAICS 325411]

Silberline Manufacturing Inc., pp. Vol. I-475, 488 [NAICS 32513M, 325188]

Silbond Corp., pp. Vol. I-488, 493 [NAICS 325188, 32519M]

Silbrico Corp., p. I-771 [NAICS 327993]

Silco Oil Co., pp. Vol. III-1979, 2116 [NAICS 424720, 447110]

Silgan Containers Corp., pp. Vol. II-899, 928 [NAICS 33231M, 33243M]

Silgan Holdings Inc., pp. Vol. I-626, Vol. II-928 [NAICS 326122, 33243M]

Silicon Graphics Inc., p. II-1238 [NAICS 334111]

Silicon Optix Inc., p. I-825 [NAICS 331419]

Silicon Storage Technology Inc., pp. Vol. II-1243, 1287 [NAICS 334112, 334413]

Siliconix Inc., pp. Vol. II-1287, Vol. III-1839 [NAICS 334413, 423690]

Silk and Morgan Inc., p. III-1998 [NAICS 424930]

Silmix Inc., p. I-505 [NAICS 325212]

Silvanus Products Inc., p. I-306 [NAICS 31699M]

Silvas Oil Company Inc., p. I-443 [NAICS 324110]

Silver City Brewing Company Inc., p. I-172 [NAICS 312120]

Silver Fox Inc., pp. Vol. III-2126, 2135 [NAICS 448120, 448150]

Silver King Refrigeration Inc., pp. Vol. II-1061, 1106, 1644 [NAICS 33329N, 333415, 337215]

Silver Spring Gardens, p. I-152 [NAICS 31194M]

Silver Star Trailers, p. II-1607 [NAICS 336999]

Silver State Liquor and Wine, p. III-1987 [NAICS 424820]

Silvercrest, p. I-348 [NAICS 321991]

Silverman Brothers Inc., p. III-2171 [NAICS 452111]

Silverton Marine Corp., p. II-1594 [NAICS 336612]

Simcala Inc., p. I-767 [NAICS 327992]

Simclar Inc., p. II-1282 [NAICS 334412]

Simeus Foods International Inc., p. I-62 [NAICS 31141M]

Simkar L.L.C., pp. Vol. II-1386, 1390 [NAICS 335110, 33512M]

Simkins Industries Inc., pp. Vol. I-374, 379 [NAICS 322130, 32221M]

Simmons Farm Raised Catfish Inc., p. I-110 [NAICS 31171M]

Simmons Foods Inc., pp. Vol. I-9, 97 [NAICS 311119, 311615]

Simmons Juvenile Products Co., pp. Vol. II-1621, 1657 [NAICS 337122, 337910]

Simon Pearce US Inc., pp. Vol. I-681, 713 [NAICS 327112, 327212]

Simon's Specialty Cheese Inc., p. III-2094 [NAICS 445299]

Simonds International Corp., pp. Vol. II-892, 1140 [NAICS 33221P, 333515]

Simple Designs Manufacturing Inc., p. II-1616 [NAICS 337121]

Simple Soyman, p. I-31 [NAICS 31122N]

Simple Wisdom Inc., p. III-2100 [NAICS 446110]

SimpleTech Inc., p. II-1252 [NAICS 334119]

Simplex Inc., p. II-923 [NAICS 332420]

Simplex Industries Inc., p. I-353 [NAICS 321992]

Simplicity Manufacturing Inc., pp. Vol. II-892, 1023, 1028 [NAICS 33221P, 333111, 333112]

Simplot Phosphates, pp. Vol. I-488, 520 [NAICS 325188, 325312]

Simpson Electric Co., pp. Vol. II-1332, 1342, 1367, 1432, 1437 [NAICS 334512, 334514, 334519, 335313, 335314]

Simpson Manufacturing Inc., pp. Vol. I-358, Vol. II-908, 933 [NAICS 321999, 33232M, 332510]

Simpson Norton Corp., p. III-1863 [NAICS 423820]

Simpson Paper Co., pp. Vol. I-368, 388 [NAICS 32212M, 32222N]

Simpson Strong-Tie Company Inc., p. II-933 [NAICS 332510]

Simula Inc., pp. Vol. II-1567, 1627 [NAICS 336413, 337127]

Sinar-Bron Inc., p. III-1798 [NAICS 423410]

Sinclair Casper Refining Co., p. I-443 [NAICS 324110]

Sinclair Oil Corp., pp. Vol. I-443, Vol. III-2116 [NAICS 324110, 447110]

Singer Equipment Company Inc., pp. Vol. III-1809, 1875 [NAICS 423440, 423850]

Singleton Seafood Co., p. I-110 [NAICS 31171M]

Sino-Swearingen Aircraft Corp., p. II-1557 [NAICS 336411]

Sintering Technologies Inc., p. I-867 [NAICS 332117]

Sioux City Foundry Co., p. III-1824 [NAICS 423510]

Sioux City Stationery Inc., pp. Vol. III-1898, 1901 [NAICS 424110, 424120]

Sioux Steam Cleaner Corp., p. II-1157 [NAICS 333611]

Sioux Vocational Services Inc., p. I-343 [NAICS 321920]

Siouxland Farmers Coop., pp. Vol. I-9, 15 [NAICS 311119, 31121M]

Sipi Metals Corp., pp. Vol. I-822, 825, 830 [NAICS 331411, 331419, 33142M]

Sippican Inc., p. II-1322 [NAICS 334510]

Sircle Spring Co., p. II-1051 [NAICS 333220]

Sirenza Microdevices Inc., p. II-1282 [NAICS 334412]

SiRF Technology Holdings Inc., p. II-1327 [NAICS 334511]

SIS-USA Inc., p. III-1801 [NAICS 423420]

Sitex Corp., p. III-1875 [NAICS 423850]

Sitka Sound Seafoods, p. I-110 [NAICS 31171M]

Sivalls Inc., p. II-1039 [NAICS 33313M]

Sivyer Steel Corp., p. I-845 [NAICS 33151M]

Siya Inc., pp. Vol. III-1875, 1887 [NAICS 423850, 423920]

SK Hand Tool Corp., p. II-892 [NAICS 33221P]

SK Textiles Inc., pp. Vol. I-198, 234 [NAICS 313210, 31412M]

Skandia Window Fashions, p. II-1662 [NAICS 337920]

Skaps Industries Inc., p. I-244 [NAICS 314991]

SKB Corp., p. I-306 [NAICS 31699M]

Skechers U.S.A. Inc., pp. Vol. I-300, Vol. III-1922 [NAICS 31621M, 424340]

Skeeter Products Inc., p. II-1589 [NAICS 336611]

SKF Aero Bearing Service Center, p. II-1562 [NAICS 336412]

SKF International Inc., p. III-1894 [NAICS 423940]

S.K.H. Management Co., pp. Vol. III-1950, 1991, 2072 [NAICS 424480, 424910, 444220]

Skidmore, p. II-918 [NAICS 332410]

Skier's Choice, p. II-1594 [NAICS 336612]

Skill Tool and Die Corp., pp. Vol. I-879, Vol. II-1134 [NAICS 33211P, 333514]

Skinner Inc., p. III-2194 [NAICS 453310]

Skip's Cutting Inc., p. I-267 [NAICS 31521M]

Skipperliner Industries Inc., p. II-1594 [NAICS 336612]

Sklar Corp., p. III-1813 [NAICS 423450]

Skokie Valley Beverage Co., p. III-1983 [NAICS 424810]

Sks Bottle and Packaging Inc., p. III-1905 [NAICS 424130]

Sky Trak International Inc., pp. Vol. I-343, Vol. II-1033 [NAICS 321920, 333120]

Skyline Corp., pp. Vol. I-348, Vol. II-899, 1500 [NAICS 321991, 33231M, 336214]

Skyline Corp. Nomad Div, p. II-1500 [NAICS 336214]

Skyway Technology Group Inc., p. III-2194 [NAICS 453310]

Skyworks Solutions Inc., p. II-1287 [NAICS 334413]

Skyy Spirits L.L.C., p. I-181 [NAICS 312140]

SL Industries Inc., pp. Vol. II-1427, 1457, 1562 [NAICS 335312, 33593M, 336412]

S.L. Outerbanks L.L.C., pp. Vol. I-251, 262, 272 [NAICS 314999, 31519M, 31522M]

Slade Gorton and Company Inc., p. III-1943 [NAICS 424460]

Slane Hosiery Mills Inc., p. I-256 [NAICS 31511M]

Slant Fin Corp., pp. Vol. II-918, 1101 [NAICS 332410, 333414]

Slater Dye Works Inc., p. I-218 [NAICS 31331M]

Sleepeck Printing Co., p. I-436 [NAICS 32312M]

Sleeping Beauty Turquoise, p. III-2144 [NAICS 448310]

Sleeptronics Sleep Products, p. II-1657 [NAICS 337910]

Sli Lighting Products, pp. Vol. II-1386, 1390 [NAICS 335110, 33512M]

Slidell Inc., p. II-1212 [NAICS 333993]

Sligh Furniture Co., p. II-1362 [NAICS 334518]

Sloan and Company Inc., p. II-1639 [NAICS 337212]

Sloan Transportation Products, pp. Vol. II-1505, 1524 [NAICS 33631M, 336340]

Sloan Valve Co., pp. Vol. II-974, 980 [NAICS 332913, 33291N]

Small Precision Tools Inc., p. II-1140 [NAICS 333515]

Smalley Steel Ring Co., p. I-830 [NAICS 33142M]

Smart and Final Inc., pp. Vol. III-1925, 2076 [NAICS 424410, 445110]

Smart and Final Stores Corp., pp. Vol. III-1925, 2076 [NAICS 424410, 445110]

SMART Modular Technologies, pp. Vol. II-1243, 1252, 1287 [NAICS 334112, 334119, 334413]

Smart Papers L.L.C., pp. Vol. I-368, 388, 395, 415, 436 [NAICS 32212M, 32222N, 32222P, 322299, 32312M]

Smarte Carte Inc., pp. Vol. II-1644, 1708 [NAICS 337215, 33993M]

SMC Corp., p. II-1496 [NAICS 336213]

SMC Corporation of America, pp. Vol. II-923, 1112, 1222, 1229, 1421 [NAICS 332420, 33341N, 33399N, 33399P, 335311]

SMC Inc., pp. Vol. II-1282, 1312 [NAICS 334412, 334418]

Smead Manufacturing Co., pp. Vol. I-368, 403, 420, 436, Vol. II-1650 [NAICS 32212M, 32223M, 32311M, 32312M, 33721N]

Smeal Fire Apparatus Co., pp. Vol. II-1014, 1482 [NAICS 33299N, 336120]

Smede-Son Steel and Supply Inc., pp. Vol. II-945, Vol. III-2065 [NAICS 332710, 444100]

Smelter Service Corp., p. III-1890 [NAICS 423930]

SMI, p. III-1817 [NAICS 423460]

SMI Manufacturing Inc., p. II-1039 [NAICS 33313M]

Smith & Associates Intern. Inc., p. III-1839 [NAICS 423690]

Smith & Nephew Inc., pp. Vol. I-575, Vol. II-1322, 1676 [NAICS 325620, 334510, 339113]

Smith and Wesson Corp., pp. Vol. II-1001, Vol. III-1883 [NAICS 332994, 423910]

Smith and Wesson Holding Corp., p. II-1001 [NAICS 332994]

Smith Dairy, p. I-92 [NAICS 311520]

Smith Detroit Diesel Allison Inc., p. II-1173 [NAICS 333618]

Smith Equipment, p. II-1421 [NAICS 335311]

Smith Equipment and Supply Co., p. II-1740 [NAICS 339994]

Smith Garden Products Inc., p. I-524 [NAICS 325314]

Smith International Inc., pp. Vol. II-1039, 1207 [NAICS 33313M, 333991]

Smith-Lee Company Inc., p. I-411 [NAICS 322291]

Smith-Victor Corp., p. II-1087 [NAICS 333315]

Smithco West Inc., p. II-1028 [NAICS 333112]

Smithfield Foods Inc., pp. Vol. I-97, 102 [NAICS 311615, 31161N]

Smithfield Packing Company Inc., p. I-102 [NAICS 31161N]

Smiths Aerospace Actuation, p. II-1222 [NAICS 33399N]

Smiths Aerospace Components, pp. Vol. II-1157, 1505, 1749 [NAICS 333611, 33631M, 339999]

Smiths Aerospace Electronic, p. II-1580 [NAICS 336419]

Smiths Detection, p. II-1666 [NAICS 339111]

Smiths Medical ASD Inc., pp. Vol. I-488, Vol. II-1671, 1676 [NAICS 325188, 339112, 339113]

Smokey Mountain Chew Inc., p. I-188 [NAICS 31222M]

Smulekoff Furniture Company Inc., p. III-2037 [NAICS 442110]

Smurfit-Stone Container Corp., pp. Vol. I-324, 363, 374, 379 [NAICS 32121N, 322110, 322130, 32221M]

SMV Industries Inc., p. III-1863 [NAICS 423820]

S.N.A.C.C. Distributing Co., p. III-1939 [NAICS 424450]

Snacks Alliance, p. I-137 [NAICS 31191M]

Snap-On Inc., pp. Vol. I-879, Vol. II-892, 928, 1207, 1347, 1367 [NAICS 33211P, 33221P, 33243M, 333991, 334515, 334519]

Snap-Tite Inc., pp. Vol. I-665, Vol. II-933, 1486 [NAICS 326220, 332510, 336211]

Snapco Manufacturing Corp., p. II-1735 [NAICS 339993]

Snapple Beverage Group Inc., p. I-165 [NAICS 31211M]

Snavely Forest Products Inc., pp. Vol. I-334, Vol. III-1782 [NAICS 32191M, 423310]

Numbers following p. or pp. are page references. Roman numerals indicate volume numbers. Bracketed items indicate industries. Page references are to the starting pages of company tables.

2415

S.N.C. Manufacturing Inc., pp. Vol. II-1302, 1421 [NAICS 334416, 335311]

SNE Enterprises Inc., pp. Vol. I-334, 651, Vol. II-908 [NAICS 32191M, 32619M, 33232M]

Snecma USA Inc., p. I-857 [NAICS 33152P]

Sno-Way International Inc., p. II-1028 [NAICS 333112]

Snoke Special Products Inc., pp. Vol. I-830, Vol. II-1106 [NAICS 33142M, 333415]

Snow Aviation International, pp. Vol. II-1557, 1562 [NAICS 336411, 336412]

Snow Ball Foods Inc., p. I-97 [NAICS 311615]

Snugtop, p. II-1500 [NAICS 336214]

Snyder Manufacturing Inc., p. I-631 [NAICS 326130]

Snyder's Drug Stores Inc., p. III-2100 [NAICS 446110]

Snyder's of Hanover Inc., p. I-137 [NAICS 31191M]

Sodak Gaming Inc., p. II-1708 [NAICS 33993M]

Soderberg Inc., pp. Vol. II-1687, Vol. III-1817 [NAICS 339115, 423460]

Sodetal USA Inc., p. I-248 [NAICS 314992]

Sofanou Inc., p. I-621 [NAICS 326121]

Software House International Inc., p. III-1805 [NAICS 423430]

Software Spectrum Inc., p. III-1805 [NAICS 423430]

Sohn Manufacturing Inc., pp. Vol. I-580, Vol. II-1212 [NAICS 325910, 333993]

Soil Mender Products, p. I-516 [NAICS 325311]

Sokkia Corp., p. III-1859 [NAICS 423810]

Sola Communications Inc., p. III-1831 [NAICS 423610]

Sola International Inc., pp. Vol. II-1687, Vol. III-1817 [NAICS 339115, 423460]

Solar Turbines Inc., pp. Vol. II-1157, 1184 [NAICS 333611, 333912]

Solarcom, p. III-1805 [NAICS 423430]

Solectron Corp., pp. Vol. II-1282, 1287, 1317 [NAICS 334412, 334413, 334419]

Solid State Equipment Corp., p. II-1056 [NAICS 333295]

Solideal Tire Inc., p. III-1766 [NAICS 423130]

Solo Cup Co., pp. Vol. I-379, 415, 636, 651 [NAICS 32221M, 322299, 326140, 32619M]

Solomon Corp., pp. Vol. II-1302, 1421 [NAICS 334416, 335311]

Solon Manufacturing Company, p. I-358 [NAICS 321999]

Soloy Corp., p. II-1557 [NAICS 336411]

Soltex International Inc., p. III-1913 [NAICS 424310]

Solutek Corp., p. II-1087 [NAICS 333315]

Solutia Inc., p. I-595 [NAICS 32599N]

Solvay Advanced Polymers, p. III-1968 [NAICS 424610]

Solvay Interox, Inc., p. I-475 [NAICS 32513M]

Solvay Paperboard L.L.C., p. I-374 [NAICS 322130]

Solvay Solexis, p. I-589 [NAICS 325991]

Somera Communications Inc., p. III-1839 [NAICS 423690]

Somerset Pharmaceuticals Inc., p. III-1909 [NAICS 424210]

Somerset Recycling Service Inc., p. I-363 [NAICS 322110]

Somerset Refinery Inc., p. I-443 [NAICS 324110]

Sommer Brothers Seed Co., p. I-15 [NAICS 31121M]

Sonant Corp., p. II-1267 [NAICS 334290]

Sonic Automotive Inc., p. III-2011 [NAICS 441110]

Sonic Studios, p. II-1442 [NAICS 335911]

SONICblue Inc., pp. Vol. II-1252, 1272 [NAICS 334119, 334310]

Sonobond Ultrasonics Inc., p. I-224 [NAICS 313320]

Sonoco Products Co., pp. Vol. I-374, 379, 395, 560 [NAICS 322130, 32221M, 32222P, 325520]

Sonoma Flower Co., p. III-2183 [NAICS 453110]

SonoSite Inc., p. II-1322 [NAICS 334510]

Sonstegard Foods Co., p. I-158 [NAICS 31199M]

Sonus Networks Inc., p. II-1257 [NAICS 334210]

Sopark Corp., pp. Vol. II-1307, 1312, 1512 [NAICS 334417, 334418, 33632M]

Sorbee International Ltd., pp. Vol. I-52, 57 [NAICS 311330, 311340]

Sorrento Lactalis Inc., p. I-76 [NAICS 311513]

Sorrento Networks Corp., p. II-1082 [NAICS 333314]

SOS Metals Inc., pp. Vol. I-780, 793, Vol. III-1824 [NAICS 33111M, 33122M, 423510]

SOS Products Company Inc., p. II-974 [NAICS 332913]

Sosmetal Products Inc., pp. Vol. III-1762, 1770 [NAICS 423120, 423140]

Soudan Metals Co., p. I-793 [NAICS 33122M]

Sound Around Electronics Inc., p. II-1512 [NAICS 33632M]

Sound Battery Company Inc., p. II-1442 [NAICS 335911]

Sound Enhancements Inc., p. II-1731 [NAICS 339992]

Sound Inc., p. III-1831 [NAICS 423610]

Sound of Market Street, pp. Vol. III-2054, 2168 [NAICS 443112, 451220]

Sound Recorders Inc., p. II-1376 [NAICS 334612]

Sound Refining Inc., p. I-443 [NAICS 324110]

Sound Seal, p. I-771 [NAICS 327993]

Soundcast Co., p. I-857 [NAICS 33152P]

Soundcoat Company Inc., p. I-771 [NAICS 327993]

Source 4, pp. Vol. I-251, Vol. III-1901 [NAICS 314999, 424120]

Source Code Corp., p. II-1238 [NAICS 334111]

Source Inc., p. III-2208 [NAICS 453998]

Source Management Inc., p. III-1901 [NAICS 424120]

South Atlantic Services Inc., pp. Vol. I-529, 646 [NAICS 325320, 326160]

South Bay Cable, pp. Vol. I-793, 837 [NAICS 33122M, 33149M]

South Carolina Prestress Corp., p. I-737 [NAICS 32733M]

South Central Printing Inc., p. I-203 [NAICS 31322M]

South Coast Lumber and Affiliates, p. I-324 [NAICS 32121N]

South Coast Terminals L.P., p. I-458 [NAICS 324191]

South Dakota Soybean Processors, p. I-31 [NAICS 31122N]

South Florida Ford New Holland, p. III-2072 [NAICS 444220]

South Peninsula Sales Inc., p. III-2215 [NAICS 454210]

South Tech Plastics Inc., p. I-631 [NAICS 326130]

South Texas Shrimp Processors, p. I-110 [NAICS 31171M]

Southbend Sporting Goods Inc., p. III-1883 [NAICS 423910]

Southcoast Cabinet Inc., p. II-1611 [NAICS 337110]

Southeast Air Control Inc., p. II-1546 [NAICS 336391]

Southeast-Atlantic Beverage, p. I-165 [NAICS 31211M]

Southeast Frozen Food Co., p. III-1929 [NAICS 424420]

Southeast Texas Industries Inc., p. II-923 [NAICS 332420]

Southeast Toyota Distributors Inc., pp. Vol. III-1758, 1762 [NAICS 423110, 423120]

Southeastern Container Inc., p. I-646 [NAICS 326160]

Southeastern Equipment Inc., p. III-1859 [NAICS 423810]

Southeastern Family Publishers, p. III-1995 [NAICS 424920]

Southeastern Materials Inc., p. I-329 [NAICS 32121P]

Southeastern Mills Inc., pp. Vol. I-15, 124 [NAICS 31121M, 31182M]

Southeastern Protein Inc., p. I-31 [NAICS 31122N]

Southern Agricultural Insecticides, pp. Vol. I-524, 529 [NAICS 325314, 325320]

Southern Beverage Company Inc., p. III-1954 [NAICS 424490]

Southern Clay Products Inc., pp. Vol. I-681, 703 [NAICS 327112, 32712N]

Southern Colorchrome Inc., p. III-1798 [NAICS 423410]

Southern Comfort Conversion Inc., pp. Vol. II-1496, 1607 [NAICS 336213, 336999]

Southern Energy Homes Inc., p. I-348 [NAICS 321991]

Southern Film Extruders Inc., p. I-621 [NAICS 326121]

Southern Finishing Co., pp. Vol. I-324, Vol. II-1611 [NAICS 32121N, 337110]

Southern Foods Group L.P., pp. Vol. I-86, 92 [NAICS 31151N, 311520]

Southern Furniture of Conover Inc., pp. Vol. II-1616, 1621 [NAICS 337121, 337122]

Southern Grout and Mortars Inc., pp. Vol. I-453, 727, 752 [NAICS 324122, 327310, 327420]

Southern Heat Exchanger Corp., p. II-918 [NAICS 332410]

Southern Hens Inc., p. I-97 [NAICS 311615]

Southern Holdings Inc., p. III-1890 [NAICS 423930]

Southern Hosiery Mill Inc., p. I-256 [NAICS 31511M]

Southern L.P. Gas Inc., pp. Vol. III-2050, 2222 [NAICS 443111, 454312]

Southern Mills Inc., pp. Vol. I-224, 239 [NAICS 313320, 31491M]

Southern Minnesota Beet Sugar, pp. Vol. I-40, 44 [NAICS 311313, 31131N]

Southern Missouri Containers Inc., p. I-609 [NAICS 326112]

Southern Motion Inc., p. II-1616 [NAICS 337121]

Southern Office Furniture, p. III-1774 [NAICS 423210]

Numbers following p. or pp. are page references. Roman numerals indicate volume numbers. Bracketed items indicate industries. Page references are to the starting pages of company tables.

Southern Pride, p. II-1404 [NAICS 335221]

Southern Pride Catfish Inc., p. I-110 [NAICS 31171M]

Southern Products and Silica Inc., p. I-767 [NAICS 327992]

Southern Provision Company Inc., p. III-1946 [NAICS 424470]

Southern Pump and Tank Co., p. III-1762 [NAICS 423120]

Southern Refrigeration Corp., pp. Vol. III-1851, 1855 [NAICS 423730, 423740]

Southern Scrap Material L.L.C., p. I-807 [NAICS 331314]

Southern States Cooperative Inc., p. III-1991 [NAICS 424910]

Southern Steel and Wire Inc., p. II-939 [NAICS 33261M]

Southern Tea Inc., p. I-143 [NAICS 311920]

Southern Weaving Co., p. I-203 [NAICS 31322M]

Southern Webbing Mills Inc., p. I-203 [NAICS 31322M]

Southern Wine & Spirits, pp. Vol. III-1983, 1987 [NAICS 424810, 424820]

Southern Wool and Skin, p. I-296 [NAICS 316110]

Southern Yarn Dyers Inc., pp. Vol. I-192, 218 [NAICS 31311M, 31331M]

SouthFresh Aquaculture L.L.C., p. I-110 [NAICS 31171M]

Southland Oil Co., p. I-443 [NAICS 324110]

Southland Pine Needles L.L.C., p. I-767 [NAICS 327992]

Southside Recycling Inc., p. III-1890 [NAICS 423930]

Southwall Technologies Inc., p. I-615 [NAICS 326113]

Southwest Ag Inc., p. III-1809 [NAICS 423440]

Southwest Canners Inc., p. I-165 [NAICS 31211M]

Southwest Cupid, p. I-279 [NAICS 31523M]

Southwest Energy Distributors Inc., p. III-2116 [NAICS 447110]

Southwest Lens Corp., p. III-1817 [NAICS 423460]

Southwest Plastic Binding Inc., p. I-374 [NAICS 322130]

Southwest Products Co., p. II-1519 [NAICS 336330]

Southwest Stone Supply Inc., p. III-1786 [NAICS 423320]

Southwest United Industries Inc., p. II-1173 [NAICS 333618]

Southwest Windpower Inc., p. II-1157 [NAICS 333611]

Southwestern Industries Inc., p. II-1124 [NAICS 333512]

Southwestern Petroleum Corp., pp. Vol. I-26, 453, 458 [NAICS 311225, 324122, 324191]

Southwestern Stationery & Bank, p. III-1901 [NAICS 424120]

Southwire Building Wire, p. II-1451 [NAICS 33592M]

Southwire Co., pp. Vol. I-803, 822, 837 [NAICS 331312, 331411, 33149M]

Southwire Co. NSA Div., pp. Vol. I-803, 852 [NAICS 331312, 33152N]

Southwood Furniture Corp., p. II-1616 [NAICS 337121]

Southworth Co., pp. Vol. I-363, 368, 415 [NAICS 322110, 32212M, 322299]

Southworth International Group, p. I-505 [NAICS 325212]

Sovereign Specialty Chemicals, pp. Vol. I-554, 560 [NAICS 325510, 325520]

SP Industries, p. II-1666 [NAICS 339111]

SP Industries Inc., pp. Vol. I-713, 722, Vol. II-1666 [NAICS 327212, 327215, 339111]

SP Newsprint Co., p. I-363 [NAICS 322110]

S.P. Richards Co., pp. Vol. III-1774, 1901 [NAICS 423210, 424120]

S.p.A. Manufacturing Inc., p. II-1051 [NAICS 333220]

Space Coast Truss Inc., p. I-329 [NAICS 32121P]

Space Maintainers Laboratory, p. II-1692 [NAICS 339116]

SpaceDev Inc., p. II-1572 [NAICS 336414]

Spacehab Inc., pp. Vol. II-1572, 1580 [NAICS 336414, 336419]

SpaceLabs Medical Inc., p. II-1322 [NAICS 334510]

Spahn and Rose Lumber Co., pp. Vol. I-329, Vol. III-2065 [NAICS 32121P, 444100]

Spalding Holdings Corp., pp. Vol. I-272, 300, Vol. III-1883, 1922, 2150 [NAICS 31522M, 31621M, 423910, 424340, 451110]

Span-America Medical Systems, p. I-641 [NAICS 326150]

Spang and Company Inc., p. II-1337 [NAICS 334513]

Spangler Candy Co., pp. Vol. I-52, 57 [NAICS 311330, 311340]

Spangler Racing, p. II-1473 [NAICS 336111]

Spangler Valve Co., p. II-1342 [NAICS 334514]

Spantek, p. I-825 [NAICS 331419]

Sparkle Flavors, pp. Vol. III-1939, 1950 [NAICS 424450, 424480]

Sparkletts D S Waters L.P., p. III-2228 [NAICS 454390]

Spartan Distributors Inc., p. III-1863 [NAICS 423820]

Spartan Light Metal Products, p. I-857 [NAICS 33152P]

Spartan Light Metal Products Inc., pp. Vol. I-852, 857, Vol. II-958, 964 [NAICS 33152N, 33152P, 332722, 33281M]

Spartan Motors Inc., p. II-1473 [NAICS 336111]

Spartan Stores Inc., p. III-1925 [NAICS 424410]

Spartan Supply Co., p. III-1790 [NAICS 423330]

Spartanburg Automotive Steel Inc., pp. Vol. II-1541, 1749 [NAICS 336370, 339999]

Spartanics Ltd., pp. Vol. II-886, 1342 [NAICS 33221N, 334514]

Spartech Corp., pp. Vol. I-500, 615, 626, 631 [NAICS 325211, 326113, 326122, 326130]

Spartech Polycom, p. I-589 [NAICS 325991]

Spartech Polycom Inc., pp. Vol. I-589, 631 [NAICS 325991, 326130]

Sparton Corp., pp. Vol. II-1262, 1327, 1367 [NAICS 334220, 334511, 334519]

Spates Fabricators Inc., p. I-329 [NAICS 32121P]

Spaulding Composites Inc., p. I-771 [NAICS 327993]

Speakman Company Inc., p. II-974 [NAICS 332913]

Spear and Jackson Inc., p. II-892 [NAICS 33221P]

Spec's Family Partner's, pp. Vol. I-116, Vol. III-2083, 2097 [NAICS 31181M, 445210, 445310]

Special Devices Inc., pp. Vol. II-997, 1367 [NAICS 332993, 334519]

Special Equipment Engineering, p. II-1056 [NAICS 333295]

Special Projects Inc., p. I-681 [NAICS 327112]

Specialized Bicycle Components, p. II-1599 [NAICS 336991]

Specialized Packaging Group Inc., p. I-379 [NAICS 32221M]

Specialized Plastic Sealings Inc., p. II-1657 [NAICS 337910]

Specialized Products Co., pp. Vol. I-306, Vol. II-1347, Vol. III-2007 [NAICS 31699M, 334515, 424990]

Specialty Bar Products Co., pp. Vol. II-945, 958, 964 [NAICS 332710, 332722, 33281M]

Specialty Coating Systems Inc., pp. Vol. I-554, Vol. II-964, 1092, 1386 [NAICS 325510, 33281M, 33331N, 335110]

Specialty Container Corp., p. I-603 [NAICS 326111]

Specialty Feeds Inc., p. I-4 [NAICS 311111]

Specialty Gases Inc., p. I-471 [NAICS 325120]

Specialty Industries Inc., p. II-928 [NAICS 33243M]

Specialty Ink Company Inc., p. I-580 [NAICS 325910]

Specialty Merchandise Corp., p. III-2007 [NAICS 424990]

Specialty Polymers Inc., p. I-560 [NAICS 325520]

Specialty Screw Corp., p. II-958 [NAICS 332722]

Specialty Shearing and Dyeing Inc., p. I-224 [NAICS 313320]

Specialty Silicone Fabricators Inc., pp. Vol. I-500, 670 [NAICS 325211, 32629M]

Specialty Store Services Inc., p. III-1809 [NAICS 423440]

Speck Sales Inc., pp. Vol. III-1766, 2034 [NAICS 423130, 441320]

Spectacular Products Inc., p. III-1820 [NAICS 423490]

Specto-Optical Co., p. III-1817 [NAICS 423460]

Spectra Gases, p. I-471 [NAICS 325120]

Spectra Logic Corp., p. II-1243 [NAICS 334112]

Spectra-Physics Lasers Inc., pp. Vol. II-1322, 1468 [NAICS 334510, 335999]

Spectracom Corp., p. II-1362 [NAICS 334518]

Spectral Response Inc., p. II-1312 [NAICS 334418]

Spectranetics Corp., p. III-1813 [NAICS 423450]

Spectro Coating Corp., p. I-218 [NAICS 31331M]

Spectronics Corp., p. II-1357 [NAICS 334517]

Spectrum Astro Inc., pp. Vol. II-1572, 1580 [NAICS 336414, 336419]

Spectrum Control Inc., pp. Vol. II-1307, 1468 [NAICS 334417, 335999]

Spectrum Dyed Yarns Inc., pp. Vol. I-192, 218 [NAICS 31311M, 31331M]

Speedline Athletic Wear Inc., p. I-285 [NAICS 31529M]

Speedline Technologies, p. II-1229 [NAICS 33399P]

Speedling Inc. EPS Div., p. I-500 [NAICS 325211]

Speedway Motorsports Inc., pp. Vol. II-1708, Vol. III-2190 [NAICS 33993M, 453220]

Speidel Inc., p. III-1894 [NAICS 423940]

Numbers following p. or pp. are page references. Roman numerals indicate volume numbers. Bracketed items indicate industries. Page references are to the starting pages of company tables.

2417

Company Index

Spellman High Voltage Electronics, p. II-1468 [NAICS 335999]

Spence Engineering Company Inc., pp. Vol. II-980, 1421 [NAICS 33291N, 335311]

Spencer Press Inc., p. I-436 [NAICS 32312M]

Spencer Products Co., p. II-1735 [NAICS 339993]

Spencers Inc., pp. Vol. I-279, 285, 388 [NAICS 31523M, 31529M, 32222N]

Spentech Plastic Containers Inc., p. I-646 [NAICS 326160]

Sperry and Rice Mfg L.L.C., pp. Vol. I-505, 621, 641, 670, Vol. II-1725 [NAICS 325212, 326121, 326150, 32629M, 339991]

SPI Polyols Inc., pp. Vol. I-147, 595 [NAICS 311930, 32599N]

Spiller Spring Co., p. II-939 [NAICS 33261M]

Spina Electric Co., p. III-1835 [NAICS 423620]

Spinco Metal Products Inc., p. I-793 [NAICS 33122M]

Spiral Inc., pp. Vol. I-388, 395 [NAICS 32222N, 32222P]

Spiralkote Inc., p. I-395 [NAICS 32222P]

Spirol International Corp., pp. Vol. I-857, Vol. II-958, 1124, 1140 [NAICS 33152P, 332722, 333512, 333515]

Spitzer Management Inc., p. III-2011 [NAICS 441110]

SPM Flow Control Inc., p. II-1039 [NAICS 33313M]

Spokane Seed Co., p. III-1958 [NAICS 424510]

Sponge-Cushion Inc., p. I-229 [NAICS 314110]

Spongex Corp., pp. Vol. I-636, 771 [NAICS 326140, 327993]

Spontex Inc., p. I-296 [NAICS 316110]

Sporlan Valve Co., p. II-1332 [NAICS 334512]

Sport Chalet Inc., p. III-2150 [NAICS 451110]

Sport Supply Group Inc., pp. Vol. I-872, Vol. II-1702 [NAICS 33211N, 339920]

Sport Truck USA-Coldwater Inc., p. III-2015 [NAICS 441120]

Sportco Manufacturing Inc., p. III-1883 [NAICS 423910]

Sportpharma USA Inc., p. III-1909 [NAICS 424210]

Sportrack L.L.C., pp. Vol. I-651, Vol. II-1119, 1749 [NAICS 32619M, 333511, 339999]

Sports Authority Inc., pp. Vol. III-2150, 2211 [NAICS 451110, 454113]

Sports Molding Inc., p. II-1119 [NAICS 333511]

Sportsman's Guide Inc., p. III-2150 [NAICS 451110]

Sportsstuff Inc., p. III-1883 [NAICS 423910]

Spray-N-Grow Inc., p. I-516 [NAICS 325311]

Spraying Systems Co., pp. Vol. II-980, 1184, 1207 [NAICS 33291N, 333912, 333991]

Spraylat Corp., p. I-554 [NAICS 325510]

Sprecher Brewing Company Inc., pp. Vol. I-172, Vol. III-2190 [NAICS 312120, 453220]

Spring Air Co., p. II-1657 [NAICS 337910]

Spring Air Mattress Corp., p. II-1657 [NAICS 337910]

Spring Air Partners California, p. II-1657 [NAICS 337910]

Spring Air Partners-TX Inc., p. II-1657 [NAICS 337910]

Spring Arbor Distribution Inc., pp. Vol. III-1839, 1995, 2007 [NAICS 423690, 424920, 424990]

Springdale Farm Market Inc., pp. Vol. III-2087, 2183, 2190 [NAICS 445230, 453110, 453220]

Springdale Specialty Plastics, p. I-646 [NAICS 326160]

Springfield Creamery Inc., p. I-26 [NAICS 311225]

Springfield Inc., p. II-1001 [NAICS 332994]

Springfield Wire Inc., pp. Vol. I-837, Vol. II-1217, 1312, 1457 [NAICS 33149M, 333994, 334418, 33593M]

Springs Basic Bedding, p. I-234 [NAICS 31412M]

Springs Industries Inc., pp. Vol. I-198, 234, 713, Vol. II-1662 [NAICS 313210, 31412M, 327212, 337920]

Springs Window Fashions L.P., pp. Vol. I-334, Vol. II-1662 [NAICS 32191M, 337920]

Springswood Fashions, p. II-1662 [NAICS 337920]

Spruce Pine Mica Co., p. I-776 [NAICS 327999]

SPS Spinco Inc., p. II-1287 [NAICS 334413]

SPS Technologies L.L.C., pp. Vol. I-837, Vol. II-958, 1014, 1580 [NAICS 33149M, 332722, 33299N, 336419]

SPX Corp., pp. Vol. II-980, 1262, 1421, 1427, 1437 [NAICS 33291N, 334220, 335311, 335312, 335314]

Squid Ink Manufacturing Inc., p. I-580 [NAICS 325910]

Squire Cogswell/Aeros Instruments, p. II-1184 [NAICS 333912]

SRI Sports Technology, p. I-229 [NAICS 314110]

SS Kemp and Co., p. III-1809 [NAICS 423440]

SSG Precision Optronics Inc., p. II-1082 [NAICS 333314]

SSS Lumber Company Inc., p. I-748 [NAICS 327410]

SST Corp., pp. Vol. III-1909, 1971 [NAICS 424210, 424690]

St Augustine Marine Canvas, p. I-239 [NAICS 31491M]

St Clair Plastics Co., pp. Vol. II-1119, 1162 [NAICS 333511, 333612]

St George Crystal Ltd., pp. Vol. I-713, 722, Vol. II-1390 [NAICS 327212, 327215, 33512M]

St Henry Tile Company Inc., p. I-737 [NAICS 32733M]

St Ives Inc., pp. Vol. I-420, 436 [NAICS 32311M, 32312M]

St Ives USA Inc., p. I-420 [NAICS 32311M]

St Jude Shop Inc., p. III-1820 [NAICS 423490]

St Laurent Brothers Inc., p. I-31 [NAICS 31122N]

St Lawrence Cement, p. I-727 [NAICS 327310]

St Lawrence Explosive Corp., p. I-585 [NAICS 325920]

St Louis Crafts Inc., pp. Vol. III-1887, 2153 [NAICS 423920, 451120]

St Louis Music Inc., p. II-1272 [NAICS 334310]

St Mary Sugar Cooperative Inc., p. I-44 [NAICS 31131N]

St Marys Carbon Company Inc., pp. Vol. I-857, Vol. II-1463, 1725 [NAICS 33152P, 335991, 339991]

St Mobile Aerospace Engineering, p. II-1557 [NAICS 336411]

St Supery Vineyards and Winery, p. I-177 [NAICS 312130]

STA Industries Inc., p. II-1212 [NAICS 333993]

STAAR Surgical Co., p. II-1687 [NAICS 339115]

Staber Industries Inc., p. II-1413 [NAICS 335224]

Staco Energy Products Co., p. II-1302 [NAICS 334416]

Stag/Parkway Inc., p. III-1762 [NAICS 423120]

Stag's Leap Wine Cellars, p. I-177 [NAICS 312130]

Stage Stores Inc., p. III-2132 [NAICS 448140]

Stahl's Bakery Inc., p. III-2089 [NAICS 445291]

Stahmann Farms Inc., pp. Vol. I-52, 57, 137, Vol. III-2092 [NAICS 311330, 311340, 31191M, 445292]

Staiman Recycling Corp., pp. Vol. I-363, 807 [NAICS 322110, 331314]

Stainless Fabrication Inc., p. II-923 [NAICS 332420]

Stainless Foundry & Engineering, p. I-845 [NAICS 33151M]

Staker and Parson Cos., pp. Vol. I-448, 732 [NAICS 324121, 327320]

Stalcop L.P., p. I-863 [NAICS 332114]

Stamco Industries Inc., pp. Vol. II-1129, 1541 [NAICS 333513, 336370]

Stanadyne Corp., p. II-1505 [NAICS 33631M]

Stanbury Uniforms Inc., p. I-285 [NAICS 31529M]

Standale Lumber and Supply Co., p. III-2047 [NAICS 442299]

Standard Air and Lite Corp., p. III-1851 [NAICS 423730]

Standard Beverage Corp., pp. Vol. III-1983, 1987 [NAICS 424810, 424820]

Standard Candy Company Inc., pp. Vol. I-52, 57 [NAICS 311330, 311340]

Standard Commercial Corp., pp. Vol. I-185, 192, Vol. III-1965 [NAICS 312210, 31311M, 424590]

Standard Companies Inc., pp. Vol. III-2050, 2065 [NAICS 443111, 444100]

Standard Construction Inc., p. I-448 [NAICS 324121]

Standard Diamond, p. I-756 [NAICS 327910]

Standard Die Supply Inc., p. II-1051 [NAICS 333220]

Standard Drug Co., p. III-2100 [NAICS 446110]

Standard Duplicating Machine, p. III-1801 [NAICS 423420]

Standard Furniture Mfg Inc., pp. Vol. II-1621, 1657 [NAICS 337122, 337910]

Standard Homeopathic Co., p. I-534 [NAICS 325411]

Standard Iron and Metal Inc., p. III-1890 [NAICS 423930]

Standard Machine and Mfg Co., p. II-1189 [NAICS 333913]

Standard Microsystems Corp., pp. Vol. II-1061, 1267, 1282 [NAICS 33329N, 334290, 334412]

Standard Motor Products Inc., p. II-1551 [NAICS 336399]

Standard Parts Corp., p. II-1530 [NAICS 336350]

Standard Process Inc., p. I-147 [NAICS 311930]

Standard Register Co., pp. Vol. I-388, 420, Vol. II-1077, 1252, 1342 [NAICS 32222N, 32311M, 333313, 334119, 334514]

Standard Roofings Inc., p. III-1790 [NAICS 423330]

Standard Rubber Products Co., p. I-589 [NAICS 325991]

Standard Rubber Products Inc., p. I-505 [NAICS 325212]

Standard Textile Company Inc., pp. Vol. I-234, 272, 279, Vol. II-1676 [NAICS 31412M, 31522M, 31523M, 339113]

Standard-Thomson Corp., p. II-1332 [NAICS 334512]

Standby Screw Machine Products, p. II-952 [NAICS 332721]

Standex International Corp., pp. Vol. II-899, 1061, 1106, Vol. III-2211 [NAICS 33231M, 33329N, 333415, 454113]

Standex International Corp. Fed Ind, p. II-1106 [NAICS 333415]

Standridge Color Corp., p. I-475 [NAICS 32513M]

Stanek Plating Rack Company Inc., p. II-1740 [NAICS 339994]

Stanford Home Centre, p. III-1782 [NAICS 423310]

Stanhope Products Co., p. II-1541 [NAICS 336370]

Stanion Wholesale Electric Inc., p. III-1831 [NAICS 423610]

Stanislaus Farm Supply Co., pp. Vol. III-1991, 2072 [NAICS 424910, 444220]

Stanley Furniture Company Inc., p. II-1621 [NAICS 337122]

Stanley Steemer International Inc., p. II-1092 [NAICS 33331N]

Stanley Works, pp. Vol. II-892, 933, 1207, 1468 [NAICS 33221P, 332510, 333991, 335999]

Stant Manufacturing Inc., pp. Vol. II-933, 1551 [NAICS 332510, 336399]

Staplcotn Cooperative Association, p. III-1965 [NAICS 424590]

Staples Inc., pp. Vol. III-2037, 2186, 2208 [NAICS 442110, 453210, 453998]

Star America Inc., p. I-256 [NAICS 31511M]

Star Automation Inc., p. II-1051 [NAICS 333220]

Star-Byte Inc., p. II-1381 [NAICS 334613]

Star Extruded Shapes Inc., p. I-811 [NAICS 331316]

Star Fine Foods Inc., p. I-26 [NAICS 311225]

Star Gas Partners L.P., p. III-2222 [NAICS 454312]

Star Guide Corp., p. III-1820 [NAICS 423490]

Star Headlight and Lantern Inc., pp. Vol. II-1386, 1390, 1584 [NAICS 335110, 33512M, 336510]

Star-Lite Manufacturing Inc., pp. Vol. I-615, 816 [NAICS 326113, 33131N]

Star Lucky Industries Inc., p. III-1835 [NAICS 423620]

Star Lumbers New Home, pp. Vol. III-1782, 2208 [NAICS 423310, 453998]

Star Mfg International Inc., p. II-1189 [NAICS 333913]

Star Milling Co., pp. Vol. I-9, 15 [NAICS 311119, 31121M]

Star of The West Milling Inc., pp. Vol. I-15, 124 [NAICS 31121M, 31182M]

Star Packaging Corp., p. I-609 [NAICS 326112]

Star Printing Company L.L.C., p. I-203 [NAICS 31322M]

Star Sales Company Inc., pp. Vol. III-1843, 1887, 1894 [NAICS 423710, 423920, 423940]

Star Scientific Inc., p. I-188 [NAICS 31222M]

Star Styled Dancing Supplies Inc., p. I-285 [NAICS 31529M]

Star Supply Co., p. III-1851 [NAICS 423730]

Star Trac by Unisen Inc., p. II-1702 [NAICS 339920]

Star X-Ray Company Inc., p. II-1357 [NAICS 334517]

Starboard Inc., p. III-1943 [NAICS 424460]

Starbucks Corp., pp. Vol. I-143, Vol. III-1954, 2094 [NAICS 311920, 424490, 445299]

Stargel Office Systems Inc., p. III-1801 [NAICS 423420]

Stark Carpet Corp., p. III-1778 [NAICS 423220]

Stark Ceramics Inc., pp. Vol. I-681, 691, 695 [NAICS 327112, 327121, 327122]

StarKist Foods Inc., p. I-4 [NAICS 311111]

Starline Manufacturing Inc., p. II-974 [NAICS 332913]

StarMark Cabinetry, p. II-1611 [NAICS 337110]

Starrow Enterprises Inc., p. I-762 [NAICS 327991]

Starting Line Products Inc., p. II-1607 [NAICS 336999]

Starvaggi Industries Inc., p. I-767 [NAICS 327992]

Starwest Botanicals Inc., p. I-534 [NAICS 325411]

Stash Tea Co., p. I-143 [NAICS 311920]

State Electric Supply Co., p. III-1831 [NAICS 423610]

State Electronics Parts Corp., p. II-1297 [NAICS 334415]

State Fair Foods Inc., p. I-62 [NAICS 31141M]

State Industrial Products, pp. Vol. I-453, 458, 566, Vol. II-892, 1092 [NAICS 324122, 324191, 32561M, 33221P, 33331N]

State Line Scrap Company Inc., p. III-1890 [NAICS 423930]

State of the Art Inc., p. II-1297 [NAICS 334415]

State Pipe & Supply Inc, p. III-1770 [NAICS 423140]

State Seal Co., p. III-1968 [NAICS 424610]

Stateline Coop., pp. Vol. I-9, 524 [NAICS 311119, 325314]

Stater Bros. Markets, p. III-2076 [NAICS 445110]

Statewide Wholesale Inc., p. III-1790 [NAICS 423330]

Statham Commercial Tire, pp. Vol. I-660, Vol. III-1766 [NAICS 32621M, 423130]

Static Control Components Inc., p. II-1468 [NAICS 335999]

Staubli Corp. Prevost Div., p. III-1867 [NAICS 423830]

Staveley NDT, pp. Vol. II-1357, 1367, 1468 [NAICS 334517, 334519, 335999]

Stayfast Inc., p. II-1735 [NAICS 339993]

Steam Turbine Alternative, p. II-1157 [NAICS 333611]

Stearns Products Development, p. II-918 [NAICS 332410]

Steel and Pipe Supply Inc., p. III-1824 [NAICS 423510]

Steel City Corp., pp. Vol. II-1627, 1644 [NAICS 337127, 337215]

Steel Dynamics Inc., pp. Vol. I-780, 793 [NAICS 33111M, 33122M]

Steel King Industries Inc., pp. Vol. II-928, 1644 [NAICS 33243M, 337215]

Steel of West Virginia Inc., pp. Vol. I-334, Vol. II-1014 [NAICS 32191M, 33299N]

Steel Related Technology L.L.C., p. II-945 [NAICS 332710]

Steel Technologies Inc., pp. Vol. I-780, 793, Vol. II-1014 [NAICS 33111M, 33122M, 33299N]

Steelcase Inc., pp. Vol. II-1627, 1650 [NAICS 337127, 33721N]

Steelcraft, p. II-1147 [NAICS 333516]

Steelcraft Manufacturing Co., p. II-1014 [NAICS 33299N]

Steelweld Equipment Co., pp. Vol. II-1486, 1644 [NAICS 336211, 337215]

Steen Armament Research Inc., p. III-1883 [NAICS 423910]

Stegner Food Products Co., p. I-603 [NAICS 326111]

Stein Garden and Gifts, pp. Vol. III-1998, 2072, 2183 [NAICS 424930, 444220, 453110]

Stein Mart Inc., p. III-2132 [NAICS 448140]

Stein Seal Co., pp. Vol. II-1463, 1725 [NAICS 335991, 339991]

Steiner Corp., pp. Vol. I-198, 272, 290, Vol. II-1332 [NAICS 313210, 31522M, 31599M, 334512]

Steiner Electric Co., pp. Vol. III-1831, 1839 [NAICS 423610, 423690]

Steinerfilm Inc., p. II-1292 [NAICS 334414]

Steinhafels Inc., pp. Vol. III-2037, 2041 [NAICS 442110, 442210]

Steinwall Inc., p. II-1119 [NAICS 333511]

Steinway Musical Instruments Inc., p. II-1731 [NAICS 339992]

Stella D' Oro Biscuit Company Inc., pp. Vol. I-116, 124 [NAICS 31181M, 31182M]

Stella Golden Inc., p. III-1894 [NAICS 423940]

Stelrema Corp., p. II-1119 [NAICS 333511]

Stelwagon Manufacturing Co., pp. Vol. III-1790, 1794 [NAICS 423330, 423390]

Stem Brothers Inc., p. III-2222 [NAICS 454312]

Stemco Inc., pp. Vol. II-1486, 1725 [NAICS 336211, 339991]

Stemmerich Inc., p. I-788 [NAICS 331210]

Stenograph L.L.C., pp. Vol. I-415, Vol. II-1077 [NAICS 322299, 333313]

Step2 Co., pp. Vol. II-892, 1708 [NAICS 33221P, 33993M]

Stepan Co., pp. Vol. I-488, 500, 566 [NAICS 325188, 325211, 32561M]

STERIS Corp., pp. Vol. II-1671, 1676 [NAICS 339112, 339113]

Steris Laboratories Inc., p. I-534 [NAICS 325411]

Sterling Chemicals Inc., pp. Vol. I-488, 493, 500, 626 [NAICS 325188, 32519M, 325211, 326122]

Sterling Construction Company, p. III-1762 [NAICS 423120]

Sterling Distributing Co., p. III-1987 [NAICS 424820]

Sterling Inc., p. II-1332 [NAICS 334512]

Sterling Plumbing, p. II-974 [NAICS 332913]

Sterling Sugars Inc., p. I-44 [NAICS 31131N]

Sterlingwear of Boston Inc., p. I-267 [NAICS 31521M]

Stern and Stern Industries Inc., p. I-218 [NAICS 31331M]

Stern Leach Co., p. I-825 [NAICS 331419]

Stetron International Inc., p. II-1297 [NAICS 334415]

Steuben Foods Inc., pp. Vol. I-81, Vol. II-945 [NAICS 311514, 332710]

Steve's Shoes Inc., p. III-2141 [NAICS 448210]

Steven Fabrics Co., p. II-1662 [NAICS 337920]

Steven Madden Ltd., pp. Vol. I-300, Vol. III-1922, 2141 [NAICS 31621M, 424340, 448210]

Steven-Windsor Inc., p. III-2123 [NAICS 448110]

Stevens Aviation Inc., p. III-2027 [NAICS 441229]

Numbers following p. or pp. are page references. Roman numerals indicate volume numbers. Bracketed items indicate industries. Page references are to the starting pages of company tables.

2419

Company Index

Stevens Industries Inc., pp. Vol. I-324, Vol. II-1611, 1627, 1644 [NAICS 32121N, 337110, 337127, 337215]

Stevens Office Interiors, p. III-2037 [NAICS 442110]

Stevenson Tractor Inc., p. III-2069 [NAICS 444210]

Steward Inc., pp. Vol. II-1277, 1302 [NAICS 334411, 334416]

Steward Machine Company Inc., p. II-1147 [NAICS 333516]

Stewart & Stevenson Services Inc., pp. Vol. II-1039, 1157, 1607, Vol. III-1867, 1879 [NAICS 33313M, 333611, 336999, 423830, 423860]

Stewart Audio, p. II-1272 [NAICS 334310]

Stewart Connector Systems Inc., p. II-1307 [NAICS 334417]

Stewart Distributors Inc., p. III-1778 [NAICS 423220]

Stewart Enterprises Inc., p. II-1745 [NAICS 339995]

Stewart Filmscreen Corp., p. II-1087 [NAICS 333315]

Stewart Industries Inc., p. II-1134 [NAICS 333514]

Stewart Sutherland Inc., p. I-395 [NAICS 32222P]

Stewarts Private Blend Foods, p. I-143 [NAICS 311920]

Sticker Corp., p. II-1147 [NAICS 333516]

Stiles Machinery Inc., p. III-1867 [NAICS 423830]

Stimple and Ward Co., p. I-830 [NAICS 33142M]

Stimpson Co., pp. Vol. II-958, 1735 [NAICS 332722, 339993]

Stingray Boats Co., p. II-1594 [NAICS 336612]

Stinson Seafood 2001 Inc., p. I-110 [NAICS 31171M]

STL Technology Partners, p. III-2058 [NAICS 443120]

Stock Building Supply Holdings, p. III-2065 [NAICS 444100]

Stock Components, p. I-329 [NAICS 32121P]

StockerYale Inc., pp. Vol. II-1082, 1243, 1362 [NAICS 333314, 334112, 334518]

Stockton Poultry Market, p. III-2083 [NAICS 445210]

Stoffel Seals Corp., pp. Vol. I-251, 388 [NAICS 314999, 32222N]

Stolle Machinery Company L.L.C., p. II-1129 [NAICS 333513]

Stone Construction Equipment Inc., pp. Vol. II-892, 1033, 1367 [NAICS 33221P, 333120, 334519]

Stone Hill Wine Company Inc., p. I-177 [NAICS 312130]

Stoneridge Inc., p. II-1551 [NAICS 336399]

Stoneridge Motorsports L.L.C., pp. Vol. III-2021, 2027 [NAICS 441221, 441229]

Stonewall Kitchens L.L.C., p. I-26 [NAICS 311225]

Stoneway Electric Supply Co., p. III-1831 [NAICS 423610]

Stora Enso, p. I-388 [NAICS 32222N]

Stora Enso Duluth Paper Mill, p. I-368 [NAICS 32212M]

Stora Enso North America, pp. Vol. I-368, 374, 379, 388, 395 [NAICS 32212M, 322130, 32221M, 32222N, 32222P]

Storage Battery Systems Inc., p. II-1442 [NAICS 335911]

Storage Technology Corp., pp. Vol. II-1243, 1252, Vol. III-1805 [NAICS 334112, 334119, 423430]

Store Kraft Manufacturing Co., p. II-1644 [NAICS 337215]

Store Supply Warehouse Inc., p. III-1809 [NAICS 423440]

Storis Inc., p. III-1843 [NAICS 423710]

Stork H and E Turbo Blading Inc., p. II-1157 [NAICS 333611]

Storopack, p. I-636 [NAICS 326140]

Story and Clark Piano, p. II-1731 [NAICS 339992]

Story-Wright Inc., p. III-2186 [NAICS 453210]

Stoudt Brewing Co., p. I-172 [NAICS 312120]

Stoughton Trailers L.L.C., pp. Vol. II-928, 1482, 1491 [NAICS 33243M, 336120, 336212]

Stout Marketing Inc., p. I-816 [NAICS 33131N]

Stowe-Pharr Mills Inc, p. I-192 [NAICS 31311M]

Stowers Machinery Corp., p. III-1859 [NAICS 423810]

Strainrite Co's, p. I-395 [NAICS 32222P]

Stratagene Cloning Systems Inc., p. II-1352 [NAICS 334512]

Strataglass L.L.C., p. II-1589 [NAICS 336611]

Strategic Diagnostics Inc., p. I-544 [NAICS 325413]

Strategic Minerals Corp., p. I-837 [NAICS 33149M]

Stratex Networks Inc., pp. Vol. II-1262, 1267 [NAICS 334220, 334290]

Stratford Homes L.P., p. I-353 [NAICS 321992]

Strathmore Pharmacy Inc., p. III-2100 [NAICS 446110]

Strattec Security Corp., p. II-933 [NAICS 332510]

Stratus Technologies Inc., pp. Vol. II-1252, 1267 [NAICS 334119, 334290]

Straub International Inc., p. III-1863 [NAICS 423820]

Streamfeeder L.L.C., pp. Vol. II-1077, 1229 [NAICS 333313, 33399P]

Streator Industrial Handling Inc., pp. Vol. I-343, Vol. II-1491, 1644 [NAICS 321920, 336212, 337215]

Streck Laboratories Inc., pp. Vol. II-1332, 1666 [NAICS 334512, 339111]

Streicher Mobile Fueling Inc., p. III-1979 [NAICS 424720]

Stremick's Heritage Foods L.L.C., pp. Vol. I-86, 92 [NAICS 31151N, 311520]

Stresau Laboratory Inc., p. I-585 [NAICS 325920]

Stresscon Corp., p. I-743 [NAICS 327390]

Stribling Equipment L.L.C., p. III-1859 [NAICS 423810]

Stride Rite Corp., pp. Vol. I-300, Vol. III-2141 [NAICS 31621M, 448210]

Stride Rite International Corp., p. I-300 [NAICS 31621M]

Stride Tool Inc., p. II-1207 [NAICS 333991]

Strine Printing Company Inc., pp. Vol. I-388, 436 [NAICS 32222N, 32312M]

Strippit LVD, p. II-1152 [NAICS 333518]

Stroh Die Casting Company Inc., p. I-852 [NAICS 33152N]

Stroheim and Romann Inc., pp. Vol. I-198, 229, 388 [NAICS 313210, 314110, 32222N]

Stromag Inc., p. II-1524 [NAICS 336340]

Stromberg's Architectural Prods, pp. Vol. I-752, 762 [NAICS 327420, 327991]

Strongwell Corp., p. II-958 [NAICS 332722]

Strossner's Bakery Inc., p. III-2183 [NAICS 453110]

Stroupe Mirror Company Inc., p. I-722 [NAICS 327215]

Structural Component Systems Inc., p. I-329 [NAICS 32121P]

Structural Systems Inc., pp. Vol. I-329, 353 [NAICS 32121P, 321992]

Struthers Industries Inc., pp. Vol. II-918, 923, 1217 [NAICS 332410, 332420, 333994]

Struve Distributing Company Inc., p. III-1809 [NAICS 423440]

Stryker Corp., pp. Vol. II-1357, 1671, 1676 [NAICS 334517, 339112, 339113]

Stuart C. Irby Co., p. III-1831 [NAICS 423610]

Stuart's of Eldorado Inc., p. III-2186 [NAICS 453210]

Stuarts' Petroleum Corp., p. III-1975 [NAICS 424710]

Stuebing Automatic Machine Co., p. I-374 [NAICS 322130]

Stuller Settings Inc., p. II-1696 [NAICS 33991M]

Stulz Air Technology Systems Inc., pp. Vol. II-1106, 1112 [NAICS 333415, 33341N]

Sturges Manufacturing Inc., p. I-203 [NAICS 31322M]

Sturgis Iron and Metal Inc., p. I-807 [NAICS 331314]

Sturm, Ruger and Company Inc., pp. Vol. I-845, 857, Vol. II-1001 [NAICS 33151M, 33152P, 332994]

Style Craft, p. II-1616 [NAICS 337121]

Style Crest Products, pp. Vol. I-872, Vol. II-958 [NAICS 33211N, 332722]

Style Solutions Inc., p. I-670 [NAICS 32629M]

Stylebuilt Accessories Inc., p. II-1189 [NAICS 333913]

Stylex Inc., p. II-1650 [NAICS 33721N]

Styline Industries Inc., pp. Vol. II-1621, 1650 [NAICS 337122, 33721N]

Stylors Inc., pp. Vol. I-510, Vol. II-886 [NAICS 32522M, 33221N]

Styrotech Inc., p. I-636 [NAICS 326140]

Subaru of America Inc., pp. Vol. III-1758, 1762 [NAICS 423110, 423120]

Subaru of America Inc. West, p. III-1758 [NAICS 423110]

Subaru of Indiana Automotive Inc., p. II-1473 [NAICS 336111]

Subcon Industries, p. I-343 [NAICS 321920]

Sublette Cooperative Inc., p. III-2116 [NAICS 447110]

Suburban Marble and Granite Inc., p. III-1786 [NAICS 423320]

Suburban Propane L.P., p. III-2222 [NAICS 454312]

Suburban Surgical Company Inc., pp. Vol. II-1023, 1650 [NAICS 333111, 33721N]

Successories Inc., p. III-2208 [NAICS 453998]

Sue-Lynn Textiles Inc., p. I-256 [NAICS 31511M]

Suever Stone Co., p. I-748 [NAICS 327410]

Sugar Creek Packing Co., p. I-102 [NAICS 31161N]

Sugar Plum Bakery, p. III-2089 [NAICS 445291]

Sugar Services Corp., p. I-40 [NAICS 311313]

Sugo Music Co., p. II-1376 [NAICS 334612]

Suhner Industrial Products Corp., pp. Vol. I-756, Vol. II-1124, 1162, 1207 [NAICS 327910, 333512, 333612, 333991]

Suit-Kote Corp., p. I-448 [NAICS 324121]

Numbers following p. or pp. are page references. Roman numerals indicate volume numbers. Bracketed items indicate industries. Page references are to the starting pages of company tables.

Sukup Manufacturing Co., p. II-1023 [NAICS 333111]

Sullivan Paper Company Inc., p. I-415 [NAICS 322299]

SullivanArc, p. I-609 [NAICS 326112]

Sullivans, p. III-2007 [NAICS 424990]

Sultan Chemists Inc., p. II-1682 [NAICS 339114]

Sulzer Inc., pp. Vol. II-1061, 1322, 1676 [NAICS 33329N, 334510, 339113]

Sulzer Medica USA Inc., p. II-1322 [NAICS 334510]

Sulzer Pumps Inc., p. II-1179 [NAICS 333911]

Sumerset Custom Houseboats Inc., p. II-1594 [NAICS 336612]

Sumitomo Electric Wintec Am., p. I-830 [NAICS 33142M]

Sumitomo Machinery Corporation, pp. Vol. II-1162, 1168 [NAICS 333612, 333613]

Sumitomo Plastics Machinery Mfg, p. II-1051 [NAICS 333220]

Summers Fuel Inc., p. III-1828 [NAICS 423520]

Summers Optical/EMS Contract, p. II-1687 [NAICS 339115]

Summit Air Industries Inc., p. III-1851 [NAICS 423730]

Summit Aviation Inc., p. III-1879 [NAICS 423860]

Summit Electric Supply Inc., p. III-1831 [NAICS 423610]

Summit Import Corp., pp. Vol. III-1929, 1954 [NAICS 424420, 424490]

Summit Radio Corp., p. III-1879 [NAICS 423860]

Summitville Tiles Inc., pp. Vol. I-691, 695, 727, 752 [NAICS 327121, 327122, 327310, 327420]

Sun Chemical Corp. Pigments Div., p. I-475 [NAICS 32513M]

Sun Coast Calamari Inc., p. I-110 [NAICS 31171M]

Sun Coatings Inc., p. I-453 [NAICS 324122]

Sun Devil Fire Equipment Inc., p. III-1871 [NAICS 423840]

Sun Frost, p. II-1409 [NAICS 335222]

Sun Gro Horticulture Distribution, p. III-1863 [NAICS 423820]

Sun Hydraulics Corp., pp. Vol. II-980, 1009 [NAICS 33291N, 332996]

Sun Land Beef Co., p. I-102 [NAICS 31161N]

Sun Marble At Fresno Inc., p. III-1786 [NAICS 423320]

Sun Metal Products Inc., p. I-660 [NAICS 32621M]

Sun MicroStamping Technologies, pp. Vol. II-1119, 1152 [NAICS 333511, 333518]

Sun Microsystems Inc., pp. Vol. II-1238, 1248 [NAICS 334111, 334113]

Sun Nuclear Corp., p. II-1357 [NAICS 334517]

Sun Optics, p. III-1817 [NAICS 423460]

Sun Pacific Industries, p. III-1968 [NAICS 424610]

Sun Publications of Florida Inc., p. I-436 [NAICS 32312M]

Sun Rams Products Inc., p. II-1687 [NAICS 339115]

Sun Records, p. II-1376 [NAICS 334612]

Sun Remanufacturing Corp., p. II-1714 [NAICS 33994M]

Sun River Service Corp., p. I-4 [NAICS 311111]

Sun-Rys Distributing Corp., pp. Vol. III-1851, 2004 [NAICS 423730, 424950]

Sun Seed Company Inc., p. I-4 [NAICS 311111]

Sun State Intern. Trucks L.L.C., p. III-2027 [NAICS 441229]

Sun Steel Company L.L.C., pp. Vol. I-793, Vol. II-945 [NAICS 33122M, 332710]

Sun Ten Laboratories Inc., p. I-534 [NAICS 325411]

Sun Valley Inc., p. II-1500 [NAICS 336214]

Sunbelt Marketing Inc., p. III-1847 [NAICS 423720]

Sunbury Textile Mills Inc., p. I-251 [NAICS 314999]

Suncast Corp., pp. Vol. II-1028, 1644 [NAICS 333112, 337215]

Suncoast Medical Clinic, pp. Vol. I-713, Vol. II-1082, 1687 [NAICS 327212, 333314, 339115]

SunCoast Merchandise Corp., pp. Vol. III-1801, 1835, 1839, 1894 [NAICS 423420, 423620, 423690, 423940]

Suncoast Post-Tension, p. II-939 [NAICS 33261M]

Suncoast Window Treatments Inc., p. II-1662 [NAICS 337920]

Sunday River Brewing Inc., pp. Vol. I-172, Vol. III-2097 [NAICS 312120, 445310]

Sundowner Interiors Inc., p. II-1500 [NAICS 336214]

Sundowner Trailers Inc., p. II-1500 [NAICS 336214]

Sundstrom Pressed Steel Co., p. II-1584 [NAICS 336510]

Sundyne Corp., pp. Vol. II-1112, 1179, 1184, Vol. III-1867 [NAICS 33341N, 333911, 333912, 423830]

Sunflower Restaurant Supply Inc., p. III-1809 [NAICS 423440]

Sunfresh Inc., pp. Vol. III-1929, 1950 [NAICS 424420, 424480]

Sunkist Growers Inc., pp. Vol. I-68, III-1929, 1950, 1954 [NAICS 31142M, 424420, 424480, 424490]

Sunland Optical Company Inc., p. III-2107 [NAICS 446130]

Sunlife Systems International Inc., p. I-453 [NAICS 324122]

Sunline Coach Company Inc., p. II-1500 [NAICS 336214]

Sunnen Products Co., pp. Vol. I-756, Vol. II-1124, 1140 [NAICS 327910, 333512, 333515]

Sunniland Corp., pp. Vol. I-524, Vol. III-1790 [NAICS 325314, 423330]

Sunnybrook RV Inc., p. II-1500 [NAICS 336214]

Sunnyside Farms, pp. Vol. I-92, 549 [NAICS 311520, 325414]

Sunoco Inc., pp. Vol. I-443, Vol. III-1979 [NAICS 324110, 424720]

Sunoco Logistics Partners L.P., p. III-1975 [NAICS 424710]

Sunoptic Technologies, pp. Vol. II-1082, 1451, 1666 [NAICS 333314, 33592M, 339111]

Sunpower Inc., p. II-1157 [NAICS 333611]

Sunray Coop., pp. Vol. III-1958, 1991 [NAICS 424510, 424910]

Sunrich Inc., pp. Vol. I-31, 124 [NAICS 31122N, 31182M]

Sunrise AG Cooperative, p. III-1933 [NAICS 424430]

Sunrise Cooperative Inc., pp. Vol. I-9, 524, Vol. III-1958 [NAICS 311119, 325314, 424510]

Sunrise Enterprises Of Roseburg, p. III-2194 [NAICS 453310]

Sunrise Imaging Inc., p. II-1087 [NAICS 333315]

Sunrise Medical Long Term Care, pp. Vol. II-1611, 1627, 1650 [NAICS 337110, 337127, 33721N]

Sunset Industries Inc., p. II-1157 [NAICS 333611]

Sunsetter Products L.P., p. I-239 [NAICS 31491M]

Sunshine Drapery & Interior, p. II-1662 [NAICS 337920]

Sunshine Kitchens Inc., p. II-1611 [NAICS 337110]

Sunshine Manufactured Structures, p. I-348 [NAICS 321991]

SunSource Inc., pp. Vol. II-980, 1222, Vol. III-1762 [NAICS 33291N, 33399N, 423120]

Sunstone Imports Inc., p. II-1696 [NAICS 33991M]

Sunteca Systems Inc., p. II-1662 [NAICS 337920]

Suntron Corp., pp. Vol. II-1282, 1317 [NAICS 334412, 334419]

Super Lopez Food Products, p. I-133 [NAICS 311830]

Super Products Corp., p. II-1184 [NAICS 333912]

Super Shoe Stores Inc., pp. Vol. III-1922, 2141 [NAICS 424340, 448210]

Super Steel, p. II-1457 [NAICS 33593M]

Super-Tek Products Inc., p. I-752 [NAICS 327420]

Super Vacuum Manufacturing Inc., p. II-1482 [NAICS 336120]

Superbag Corp., p. I-603 [NAICS 326111]

Supercircuits Inc., p. III-1798 [NAICS 423410]

Superior Aluminum Alloys L.L.C., p. I-803 [NAICS 331312]

Superior Battery Mfg Inc., pp. Vol. II-1442, 1447 [NAICS 335911, 335912]

Superior Clay Corp., pp. Vol. I-681, 691, 699 [NAICS 327112, 327121, 327123]

Superior Confections Inc., pp. Vol. I-48, 52 [NAICS 311320, 311330]

Superior Dairies Inc., p. III-1933 [NAICS 424430]

Superior Dental Laboratories Inc., p. II-1692 [NAICS 339116]

Superior-Deshler Inc., pp. Vol. III-2050, 2222 [NAICS 443111, 454312]

Superior Die Set Corp., p. II-1124 [NAICS 333512]

Superior Distributing Co., p. III-1983 [NAICS 424810]

Superior Essex Inc., pp. Vol. I-837, Vol. II-1257 [NAICS 33149M, 334210]

Superior Fabrics Co., pp. Vol. I-198, 208, Vol. II-1662 [NAICS 313210, 313230, 337920]

Superior Forge and Steel Corp., p. I-793 [NAICS 33122M]

Superior Glass Fibers Inc., p. I-229 [NAICS 314110]

Superior Graphite Co., pp. Vol. I-458, Vol. II-1463 [NAICS 324191, 335991]

Superior Homes L.L.C., p. I-348 [NAICS 321991]

Superior Industries Intern. Inc., p. II-1551 [NAICS 336399]

Superior Mills Inc., p. I-256 [NAICS 31511M]

Superior-MPM Technologies Inc., p. II-1051 [NAICS 333220]

Superior Printing Ink Company, p. I-580 [NAICS 325910]

Superior Quartz Products Inc., p. II-1386 [NAICS 335110]

Superior Ready Mix Concrete L.P., p. I-732 [NAICS 327320]

Superior Scaffold Services Inc., p. III-1794 [NAICS 423390]

Numbers following p. or pp. are page references. Roman numerals indicate volume numbers. Bracketed items indicate industries. Page references are to the starting pages of company tables.

2421

Superior Soft Water Inc., p. III-1847 [NAICS 423720]

Superior Technical Ceramics Corp., p. I-713 [NAICS 327212]

Superior Tire and Rubber Corp., p. I-660 [NAICS 32621M]

Superior Uniform Group Inc., pp. Vol. I-272, 290 [NAICS 31522M, 31599M]

Superior Wheels, p. III-1770 [NAICS 423140]

SUPERVALU Champaign, pp. Vol. III-1925, 2076, 2100 [NAICS 424410, 445110, 446110]

SUPERVALU Inc., pp. Vol. I-68, Vol. III-1909, 1925, 2076 [NAICS 31142M, 424210, 424410, 445110]

Supply House Inc., p. III-2047 [NAICS 442299]

Supply Room Companies Inc., p. III-1901 [NAICS 424120]

Supreme Bay Insulation, pp. Vol. I-631, 771 [NAICS 326130, 327993]

Supreme Industries Inc., p. II-1486 [NAICS 336211]

Supreme Machined Products Inc., p. II-952 [NAICS 332721]

Supreme Rice Mill Inc., p. I-15 [NAICS 31121M]

Sure Fit Inc., p. I-234 [NAICS 31412M]

Sure Heat Manufacturing Co., pp. Vol. II-1101, 1404 [NAICS 333414, 335221]

SureFed Ltd., p. I-9 [NAICS 311119]

Surefire L.L.C., p. II-1390 [NAICS 33512M]

Surface Combustion Inc., p. II-1217 [NAICS 333994]

Surface Protection Industries Inc., p. I-554 [NAICS 325510]

Surge Components Inc., p. II-1292 [NAICS 334414]

Surgical Appliance Industries Inc., p. I-279 [NAICS 31523M]

Surgient Inc., p. II-1243 [NAICS 334112]

SurModics Inc., p. I-560 [NAICS 325520]

Surner Heating Company Inc., p. III-1979 [NAICS 424720]

Surplus Sourcing Group Inc., p. III-2058 [NAICS 443120]

Suscon Inc., p. I-646 [NAICS 326160]

Suspa Inc., p. II-923 [NAICS 332420]

Susquehanna Pfaltzgraff Co., p. I-681 [NAICS 327112]

Sussman-Automatic Corp., pp. Vol. II-918, 1157 [NAICS 332410, 333611]

Sustainable Resources L.L.C., pp. Vol. I-493, 807, Vol. III-1890 [NAICS 32519M, 331314, 423930]

Sutherland Foodservice Inc., p. III-1936 [NAICS 424440]

Sutphen Corp., p. II-1482 [NAICS 336120]

Sutron Corp., p. II-1666 [NAICS 339111]

Sutton Cooperative Grain Co., p. III-2177 [NAICS 452910]

Sutton Group, pp. Vol. III-1916, 1919 [NAICS 424320, 424330]

Suzanne L Kilmer, p. III-1820 [NAICS 423490]

Swagelok Co., pp. Vol. II-980, 1009, 1092, 1222 [NAICS 33291N, 332996, 33331N, 33399N]

Swaim Inc., p. II-1616 [NAICS 337121]

Swales Thermal Systems, pp. Vol. II-1567, 1580 [NAICS 336413, 336419]

Swan Finishing Company Inc., p. I-218 [NAICS 31331M]

Swank Inc., pp. Vol. I-290, 306, 575, Vol. II-1696 [NAICS 31599M, 31699M, 325620, 33991M]

Swanson Group Inc., pp. Vol. I-312, 324 [NAICS 32111M, 32121N]

Swarovski North America Ltd., pp. Vol. I-722, Vol. II-1696 [NAICS 327215, 33991M]

SWD Corp., pp. Vol. III-1939, 2001 [NAICS 424450, 424940]

Sweda Company L.L.C., pp. Vol. I-306, Vol. II-1077, 1362, 1714 [NAICS 31699M, 333313, 334518, 33994M]

Swedish Hill Winery, p. I-177 [NAICS 312130]

Sweet Candy Co., p. I-52 [NAICS 311330]

Sweet Dreams Enterprises, p. III-2186 [NAICS 453210]

Sweet Shop USA, pp. Vol. I-52, 57 [NAICS 311330, 311340]

Sweet Street Desserts Inc., pp. Vol. I-116, 158 [NAICS 31181M, 31199M]

Sweetheart Bakery Inc., p. III-2089 [NAICS 445291]

Sweetman Construction Co., p. III-1794 [NAICS 423390]

Swenson Spreader Co., p. II-1028 [NAICS 333112]

SWH Supply Co., pp. Vol. III-1851, 1855 [NAICS 423730, 423740]

Swift and Co., p. I-102 [NAICS 31161N]

Swift Lumber Inc., p. I-358 [NAICS 321999]

Swift Shipbuilders L.L.C., pp. Vol. II-1589, 1594 [NAICS 336611, 336612]

Swift Spinning Mills Inc., pp. Vol. I-192, 198 [NAICS 31311M, 313210]

Swift Textile Metalizing L.L.C., pp. Vol. I-208, 213, 224 [NAICS 313230, 31324M, 313320]

Swiger Coil Systems Inc., p. II-1302 [NAICS 334416]

Swim 'N Sport, p. III-2135 [NAICS 448150]

SwimWays Corp., p. II-1708 [NAICS 33993M]

Swimwear Anywhere Inc., p. I-279 [NAICS 31523M]

Swing-A-Way Manufacturing Co., p. II-892 [NAICS 33221P]

Swisher International Group Inc., p. I-188 [NAICS 31222M]

Swisher Mower and Machine Inc., p. II-1028 [NAICS 333112]

Swiss Tech, p. III-1894 [NAICS 423940]

Swiss-Tech L.L.C., p. II-952 [NAICS 332721]

Swiss Valley Farms Co., pp. Vol. I-76, 86 [NAICS 311513, 31151N]

Swiss Watch International Inc., p. III-1894 [NAICS 423940]

SwissRay International Inc., p. II-1357 [NAICS 334517]

Swisstex Inc., p. I-208 [NAICS 313230]

Switching Power Inc., p. II-1421 [NAICS 335311]

Swoboda Inc., p. II-1512 [NAICS 33632M]

Syar Industries Inc., p. III-1794 [NAICS 423390]

Sylvania Yarn Systems Inc., p. I-192 [NAICS 31311M]

Sylvest Farms Inc., p. I-97 [NAICS 311615]

Sylvester Materials Co., p. III-1786 [NAICS 423320]

Symbol Mattress Co., p. II-1657 [NAICS 337910]

Symbol Technologies Inc., p. II-1252 [NAICS 334119]

Symetrics Industries Inc., p. II-1282 [NAICS 334412]

Symmco Inc., p. I-867 [NAICS 332117]

SymmetriCom Inc., pp. Vol. II-1257, 1347 [NAICS 334210, 334515]

SYMMETRY Medical, p. I-872 [NAICS 33211N]

Symmetry Ultrexx, p. II-1140 [NAICS 333515]

Symrise, pp. Vol. I-152, 575 [NAICS 31194M, 325620]

Symrise Inc., p. I-152 [NAICS 31194M]

Syms Corp., pp. Vol. III-1919, 2123, 2132, 2135 [NAICS 424330, 448110, 448140, 448150]

Syn-Tech Systems Inc., p. II-1189 [NAICS 333913]

Synalloy Corp., pp. Vol. I-475, 488, 493 [NAICS 32513M, 325188, 32519M]

Synbiotics Corp., pp. Vol. I-534, 544 [NAICS 325411, 325413]

Synchronicity Mastering Services, p. II-1376 [NAICS 334612]

Syncro Corp., p. II-1512 [NAICS 33632M]

Syndicate Sales Inc., p. I-636 [NAICS 326140]

Synergetix, p. II-1307 [NAICS 334417]

Synergis Technologies Group, pp. Vol. II-1134, 1140 [NAICS 333514, 333515]

Synergy Foods L.L.C., p. I-31 [NAICS 31122N]

Synergy Gold Group Inc., p. III-1894 [NAICS 423940]

Synergy Microwave Corp., p. II-1282 [NAICS 334412]

Syngenta Crop Protection Inc., p. I-529 [NAICS 325320]

SYNNEX Corp., pp. Vol. II-1243, 1248, 1252 [NAICS 334112, 334113, 334119]

Synrad Inc., pp. Vol. II-1082, 1468 [NAICS 333314, 335999]

Syntegra USA Inc., p. II-1238 [NAICS 334111]

Synthes, pp. Vol. II-1671, 1676 [NAICS 339112, 339113]

Synthetech Inc., p. I-549 [NAICS 325414]

Synthetic Thread Company Inc., p. I-192 [NAICS 31311M]

Syntron Bioresearch Inc., p. I-544 [NAICS 325413]

Sypris Solutions Inc., pp. Vol. II-1262, 1282, 1337 [NAICS 334220, 334412, 334513]

Syracuse China Co., p. I-681 [NAICS 327112]

Syratech Corp., pp. Vol. I-722, 852, Vol. II-886, 1632, 1696 [NAICS 327215, 33152N, 33221N, 33712N, 33991M]

SYSCO Corp., pp. Vol. III-1925, 1929, 1936, 1943, 1946, 1950, 1954 [NAICS 424410, 424420, 424440, 424460, 424470, 424480, 424490]

Sysco Food Serv San Francisco, p. III-1925 [NAICS 424410]

Sysco Food Service of Jamestown, p. III-1929 [NAICS 424420]

SYSCO Food Services, p. III-1925 [NAICS 424410]

Sysco Food Services-Jacksonville, p. III-1925 [NAICS 424410]

Sysco Food Services of Baraboo, p. III-1925 [NAICS 424410]

Sysco Food Services of Houston, p. III-1925 [NAICS 424410]

Sysco Food Services of Kansas, p. III-1925 [NAICS 424410]

Syscom Co., p. III-2058 [NAICS 443120]

Sysmex Corporation of America, p. III-1813 [NAICS 423450]

Numbers following p. or pp. are page references. Roman numerals indicate volume numbers. Bracketed items indicate industries. Page references are to the starting pages of company tables.

2422

System Components Inc., p. II-1530 [NAICS 336350]

Systemax Inc., p. III-2211 [NAICS 454113]

Systems and Electronics Inc., pp. Vol. II-1005, 1367, 1567 [NAICS 332995, 334519, 336413]

Systems Manufacturing Corp., p. II-1248 [NAICS 334113]

T-3 Energy Services Inc., pp. Vol. II-980, 1302 [NAICS 33291N, 334416]

T and L Automatics Inc., p. II-952 [NAICS 332721]

T-L Irrigation Co., pp. Vol. II-964, 974, 1023 [NAICS 33281M, 332913, 333111]

T-Systems International Inc., p. I-665 [NAICS 326220]

T-Thermal Co, p. II-1217 [NAICS 333994]

TA Systems Inc., p. II-1051 [NAICS 333220]

Tab of Northeast Florida Inc., p. III-1901 [NAICS 424120]

TAB Products Co., pp. Vol. I-403, Vol. II-1077, 1650, Vol. III-1774, 1901 [NAICS 32223M, 333313, 33721N, 423210, 424120]

TABC Inc., pp. Vol. I-879, Vol. II-1486 [NAICS 33211P, 336211]

TAC Americas Inc., pp. Vol. II-1112, 1337, 1437 [NAICS 33341N, 334513, 335314]

Taco Inc., pp. Vol. II-918, 1179, 1332 [NAICS 332410, 333911, 334512]

Taco Metals Inc., p. I-621 [NAICS 326121]

Tacoma Fixture Company Inc., p. II-1611 [NAICS 337110]

Taconic, p. II-1282 [NAICS 334412]

Tacony Corp., pp. Vol. II-1397, 1417 [NAICS 33521M, 335228]

Tactica International Inc., p. II-1749 [NAICS 339999]

Tadin Herb and Tea Co., p. I-143 [NAICS 311920]

Tadpole Computer Inc., p. II-1238 [NAICS 334111]

Tag-It Pacific Inc., p. III-1913 [NAICS 424310]

Tag Trade Associates Group Ltd., pp. Vol. I-234, 681 [NAICS 31412M, 327112]

TAH Industries Inc., p. II-1189 [NAICS 333913]

Tahari Ltd., p. III-1919 [NAICS 424330]

Taiho Corporation of America, pp. Vol. II-1168, 1546 [NAICS 333613, 336391]

Takane USA Inc., p. II-1362 [NAICS 334518]

Takata/Highland Industries, p. I-251 [NAICS 314999]

Take-A-Ticket Inc., p. II-1189 [NAICS 333913]

Taku Store, p. III-2085 [NAICS 445220]

Talaria L.L.C. Hinckley Co. Div., p. II-1594 [NAICS 336612]

Talbert Manufacturing Inc., p. II-1491 [NAICS 336212]

Talbots Inc., pp. Vol. III-2126, 2211 [NAICS 448120, 454113]

Talking Devices Co., p. II-1381 [NAICS 334613]

Talley Defense Systems Inc., pp. Vol. II-1001, 1229, 1576 [NAICS 332994, 33399P, 336415]

Tamaqua Cable Products Corp., p. II-1451 [NAICS 33592M]

Tamko Roofing Products Inc., pp. Vol. I-312, 448, 453 [NAICS 32111M, 324121, 324122]

Tamms Industries Inc., p. I-727 [NAICS 327310]

Tampa Armature Works Inc., p. II-1427 [NAICS 335312]

Tampa Bay Fisheries Inc., p. I-110 [NAICS 31171M]

Tampa Bay Hardwoods & Lumber, p. III-1782 [NAICS 423310]

Tampa Bay Shipbuilding & Repair, p. II-1589 [NAICS 336611]

Tampa Bay Steel Corp., p. II-945 [NAICS 332710]

Tampa Bay Systems Sales Inc., p. III-1851 [NAICS 423730]

TAMRAC Inc., pp. Vol. I-306, Vol. II-1087 [NAICS 31699M, 333315]

Tamron USA Inc., p. II-1087 [NAICS 333315]

Tandberg Educational Inc., p. II-1248 [NAICS 334113]

Tandy Brands Accessories Inc., pp. Vol. I-290, 306 [NAICS 31599M, 31699M]

Tantalum Pellet Company Inc., p. II-1292 [NAICS 334414]

TAP Pharmaceuticals Inc., p. I-539 [NAICS 325412]

Tape and Label Engineering Inc., p. II-1189 [NAICS 333913]

Tape-Craft Corp., p. I-203 [NAICS 31322M]

Tape Resources Inc., p. II-1381 [NAICS 334613]

Tape Specialty Inc., p. II-1376 [NAICS 334612]

TAPEMARK Company Inc., p. I-415 [NAICS 322299]

Tappan Wire and Cable Inc., p. II-1451 [NAICS 33592M]

Tappins Inc., p. III-2144 [NAICS 448310]

TARC Industries, p. I-681 [NAICS 327112]

Target Corp., pp. Vol. III-2076, 2132, 2171, 2177, 2180, 2211 [NAICS 445110, 448140, 452111, 452910, 452990, 454113]

Target Distributing Co., p. III-1835 [NAICS 423620]

Target Marketing Systems Inc., p. III-1770 [NAICS 423140]

Target Stores Inc., p. III-2171 [NAICS 452111]

Targeted Genetics Corp., p. I-549 [NAICS 325414]

Tarkett Inc., pp. Vol. III-1778, 1968 [NAICS 423220, 424610]

Tarkett Wood Inc., p. I-334 [NAICS 32191M]

Tarrant Apparel Group, pp. Vol. I-262, 290 [NAICS 31519M, 31599M]

Tarter Gate Wood Products Inc., p. I-343 [NAICS 321920]

Tasler Inc., pp. Vol. I-343, 609 [NAICS 321920, 326112]

Tastefully Simple Inc., p. III-2228 [NAICS 454390]

Tasty Baking Co., pp. Vol. I-116, 124 [NAICS 31181M, 31182M]

Taubensee Steel and Wire Co., pp. Vol. I-793, Vol. II-939 [NAICS 33122M, 33261M]

Tawas Tool Company Inc., p. II-1140 [NAICS 333515]

Taylor and Fenn Co., pp. Vol. I-845, 857 [NAICS 33151M, 33152P]

Taylor Brothers, p. I-188 [NAICS 31222M]

Taylor Corp., p. I-420 [NAICS 32311M]

Taylor Dynamometer Inc., p. II-1473 [NAICS 336111]

Taylor Excel, p. I-102 [NAICS 31161N]

Taylor-Listug Inc., p. II-1731 [NAICS 339992]

Taylor Machine Works Inc., pp. Vol. II-1033, 1194 [NAICS 333120, 33392M]

Taylor Products Company Inc., p. II-1212 [NAICS 333993]

Taylor Publishing Co., p. I-420 [NAICS 32311M]

Taylor's Industrial Services, p. II-1129 [NAICS 333513]

Taylor Utlimate Services Co., p. III-1809 [NAICS 423440]

Taylor-Winfield Corp., pp. Vol. II-1129, 1217 [NAICS 333513, 333994]

TaylorMade Adidas Golf Inc., p. II-1702 [NAICS 339920]

Taymark, pp. Vol. III-1905, 2007 [NAICS 424130, 424990]

Tazo Tea, p. I-143 [NAICS 311920]

TB Wood's Corp., p. II-1229 [NAICS 33399P]

TBC Corp., pp. Vol. III-1762, 1766 [NAICS 423120, 423130]

TBDN Tennessee Co., p. II-1112 [NAICS 33341N]

TCI America, p. I-493 [NAICS 32519M]

TCRS Inc., p. II-1530 [NAICS 336350]

TCT Stainless Steel Inc., pp. Vol. I-793, Vol. II-945, 964 [NAICS 33122M, 332710, 33281M]

T.D. Williamson Inc., p. II-1039 [NAICS 33313M]

TEAC America Inc, pp. Vol. II-1243, 1272, Vol. III-1835 [NAICS 334112, 334310, 423620]

Teak Isle Inc., pp. Vol. I-358, 641, Vol. II-1594 [NAICS 321999, 326150, 336612]

Team Inc., p. II-933 [NAICS 332510]

TEAM Industries Inc., p. II-923 [NAICS 332420]

Team Schierl Cos., pp. Vol. III-2030, 2094, 2218 [NAICS 441310, 445299, 454311]

Team Technologies Inc., pp. Vol. II-1682, 1714, 1740 [NAICS 339114, 33994M, 339994]

Teasley Drug, p. III-2100 [NAICS 446110]

TEC America Inc., pp. Vol. III-1801, 1809 [NAICS 423420, 423440]

TEC Specialty Products Inc., pp. Vol. I-560, 703, 743 [NAICS 325520, 32712N, 327390]

Tech Data Corp., p. III-1805 [NAICS 423430]

Tech Development Inc., pp. Vol. II-1157, 1505 [NAICS 333611, 33631M]

Tech-Etch Inc., p. II-1696 [NAICS 33991M]

Tech International, pp. Vol. I-560, 660 [NAICS 325520, 32621M]

Tech-Mark Inc., p. II-1404 [NAICS 335221]

Tech Mold Inc., p. II-1119 [NAICS 333511]

Tech/Ops Sevcon Inc., p. II-1332 [NAICS 334512]

Tech Supply Inc., p. III-1766 [NAICS 423130]

Techalloy Company Inc., pp. Vol. I-554, Vol. II-939, 1101 [NAICS 325510, 33261M, 333414]

TechFab L.L.C., pp. Vol. I-208, 510 [NAICS 313230, 32522M]

Techko Inc., pp. Vol. I-403, Vol. II-1134, 1267, 1676 [NAICS 32223M, 333514, 334290, 339113]

Techmer PM L.L.C., pp. Vol. I-500, 554, 651 [NAICS 325211, 325510, 32619M]

Technic Inc., pp. Vol. I-793, 825 [NAICS 33122M, 331419]

Technical Building Services Inc., p. III-1831 [NAICS 423610]

Technical Oil Products Inc., p. I-26 [NAICS 311225]

Technical Ordnance Inc., pp. Vol. I-585, Vol. II-997, 1005 [NAICS 325920, 332993, 332995]

Technical Products Engineering, p. II-1442 [NAICS 335911]

Technicar Inc., p. III-2030 [NAICS 441310]

Technicolor Thompson Group, p. II-1376 [NAICS 334612]

Technicon Industries Inc., p. I-771 [NAICS 327993]

Technitrol Inc., pp. Vol. I-879, Vol. II-1229, 1317, 1367, 1421, 1457 [NAICS 33211P, 33399P, 334419, 334519, 335311, 33593M]

Techno-Aide L.L.C., p. II-1357 [NAICS 334517]

Techno Inc., p. II-1124 [NAICS 333512]

Technoland Inc., p. III-2058 [NAICS 443120]

Technology Alternatives Corp., p. II-1248 [NAICS 334113]

Technology Assessment/Transfer, p. I-686 [NAICS 327113]

Technology Research Corp., p. II-1421 [NAICS 335311]

Technuity Inc., p. III-2208 [NAICS 453998]

TechWorks Inc., pp. Vol. II-1243, Vol. III-1798 [NAICS 334112, 423410]

Tecniflex Inc., p. III-1801 [NAICS 423420]

Tecnifoam Inc., p. I-771 [NAICS 327993]

Teco Diagnostics Inc., p. I-544 [NAICS 325413]

TECO-Westinghouse Motor Co., p. II-1427 [NAICS 335312]

TECT Utica Corp., p. II-1580 [NAICS 336419]

Tectum Inc., pp. Vol. I-319, 713, Vol. II-1390 [NAICS 321219, 327212, 33512M]

Tecumseh Products Co., pp. Vol. II-1106, 1173, 1179, 1184, 1427, 1551 [NAICS 333415, 333618, 333911, 333912, 335312, 336399]

Ted Britt Ford, p. III-2011 [NAICS 441110]

Ted Lansing Corp., p. III-1794 [NAICS 423390]

Tedia Company Inc., p. I-529 [NAICS 325320]

Tee Group Films Inc., p. I-615 [NAICS 326113]

Tee Jays Manufacturing Inc., pp. Vol. I-203, 213, 251 [NAICS 31322M, 31324M, 314999]

Teel Plastics Company Inc., p. I-621 [NAICS 326121]

Teepak L.L.C., p. I-510 [NAICS 32522M]

Tegam Inc., p. II-1342 [NAICS 334514]

TEI Electronics Inc., p. II-1731 [NAICS 339992]

Tekelec, pp. Vol. II-1262, 1267, 1347 [NAICS 334220, 334290, 334515]

Teknol Inc., p. III-2004 [NAICS 424950]

Teknor Apex Co., pp. Vol. I-475, 505, 589, 665, 670 [NAICS 32513M, 325212, 325991, 326220, 32629M]

Tekonsha Engineering Co., pp. Vol. I-488, Vol. II-1194 [NAICS 325188, 33392M]

Tekra Corp., p. III-1971 [NAICS 424690]

Teksid Aluminum Foundry Inc., pp. Vol. I-845, 852, Vol. II-1505 [NAICS 33151M, 33152N, 33631M]

Tektronix Inc., pp. Vol. II-1243, 1252, 1347, Vol. III-1805 [NAICS 334112, 334119, 334515, 423430]

Tele Vue Optics Inc., p. I-709 [NAICS 327211]

Telechron of North Carolina Inc., p. II-1362 [NAICS 334518]

Telecom Engineering Consultants, p. III-1839 [NAICS 423690]

Telect Inc., p. II-1257 [NAICS 334210]

Teledata Communications Inc., p. II-1077 [NAICS 333313]

Teledyne Continental Morots, p. II-1442 [NAICS 335911]

Teledyne Controls, p. II-1567 [NAICS 336413]

Teledyne Electronic Technology, p. II-1342 [NAICS 334514]

Teledyne Technologies Inc., pp. Vol. II-1267, 1562, 1580 [NAICS 334290, 336412, 336419]

Teleflex Fluid Systems Inc., p. I-665 [NAICS 326220]

Teleflex Inc., pp. Vol. II-1092, 1157, 1327, 1332, 1437, 1671 [NAICS 33331N, 333611, 334511, 334512, 335314, 339112]

Teleflex Marine Inc., p. II-1222 [NAICS 33399N]

Telemechanics Inc., p. II-1248 [NAICS 334113]

Telephonics Inc., p. II-1267 [NAICS 334290]

TeleVideo Inc., p. II-1248 [NAICS 334113]

Telex Communications Inc., pp. Vol. II-1257, 1262, 1267, 1317, 1580 [NAICS 334210, 334220, 334290, 334419, 336419]

Tell Steel Inc., p. III-1770 [NAICS 423140]

Tellabs Inc., pp. Vol. II-1257, 1262, 1267 [NAICS 334210, 334220, 334290]

Tellog Systems Inc., p. II-1362 [NAICS 334518]

Tellurian Technologies Inc., p. II-1362 [NAICS 334518]

Telquest International Corp., p. III-1839 [NAICS 423690]

Teltron Technologies Inc., pp. Vol. II-1277, 1357 [NAICS 334411, 334517]

Temo Inc., p. I-722 [NAICS 327215]

Tempco Electric Heater Corp., p. II-1217 [NAICS 333994]

Tempel Steel Co., pp. Vol. I-560, 631, 780, Vol. II-1014, Vol. III-1824 [NAICS 325520, 326130, 33111M, 33299N, 423510]

Temperature Equipment Corp., pp. Vol. III-1847, 1851, 1855 [NAICS 423720, 423730, 423740]

Temperature Systems Inc., p. III-1851 [NAICS 423730]

Temple-Inland Forest Products, pp. Vol. I-312, 319, 324, 752 [NAICS 32111M, 321219, 32121N, 327420]

Temple-Inland Inc., pp. Vol. I-374, 379 [NAICS 322130, 32221M]

Temple's Sporting Goods, p. III-2150 [NAICS 451110]

Templeton Coal Inc. Glas-Col Div., pp. Vol. I-358, Vol. II-1101, 1666, 1749 [NAICS 321999, 333414, 339111, 339999]

Temtex Industries Inc., pp. Vol. I-691, Vol. II-1101 [NAICS 327121, 333414]

Ten X Technology Inc., p. II-1082 [NAICS 333314]

Tenax Corp., p. I-244 [NAICS 314991]

TenBrook Sales Inc., p. III-2222 [NAICS 454312]

Tender Corp., p. I-529 [NAICS 325320]

Tenere Inc., p. II-1134 [NAICS 333514]

Tenex Corp., p. II-1714 [NAICS 33994M]

Tennant Co., p. II-1092 [NAICS 33331N]

Tenneco Automotive Inc., p. II-1551 [NAICS 336399]

Tennessee Apparel Corp., p. I-272 [NAICS 31522M]

Tennessee Electroplating Co., p. I-722 [NAICS 327215]

Tennessee Farmers Cooperative, pp. Vol. I-15, 524 [NAICS 31121M, 325314]

Tennessee Mat Company Inc., p. I-229 [NAICS 314110]

Tennessee Sewing Machine, p. II-1417 [NAICS 335228]

Tennessee Shell Co., p. III-1943 [NAICS 424460]

Tennessee SteelSummit, pp. Vol. I-780, 879 [NAICS 33111M, 33211P]

Tennessee Valley Recycling, p. I-807 [NAICS 331314]

Tennessee Wheel and Rubber Co., p. I-660 [NAICS 32621M]

Tennsco Corp., pp. Vol. II-1644, 1650 [NAICS 337215, 33721N]

Tension Envelope Corp., p. I-403 [NAICS 32223M]

Tentina Window Fashions Inc., p. II-1662 [NAICS 337920]

TEPPCO Partners L.P., p. III-1975 [NAICS 424710]

Tepro Florida Inc., p. II-1297 [NAICS 334415]

Tepro Inc., p. I-670 [NAICS 32629M]

Teradyne Inc., pp. Vol. II-1257, 1307, 1317, 1347 [NAICS 334210, 334417, 334419, 334515]

TeraStor Corp., p. II-1243 [NAICS 334112]

Terayon Communications Systems, p. II-1257 [NAICS 334210]

Terex Corp., pp. Vol. II-1033, 1194, 1491 [NAICS 333120, 33392M, 336212]

Terex Telelect Inc., p. II-1222 [NAICS 33399N]

Terminal Amusement Co., p. III-2215 [NAICS 454210]

Terra Industries Inc., p. I-529 [NAICS 325320]

Terra Marc Industries, p. II-1023 [NAICS 333111]

Terra Nitrogen Company L.P., pp. Vol. I-516, 529 [NAICS 325311, 325320]

Terrace Supply Co., p. III-2004 [NAICS 424950]

Terramarr Inc., p. III-1813 [NAICS 423450]

Terre Hill Concrete Products, p. I-737 [NAICS 32733M]

Terry Dees Enterprises Inc., p. III-1766 [NAICS 423130]

Terryberry Co., p. II-1696 [NAICS 33991M]

Terumo Cardiovascular Systems, pp. Vol. II-1322, 1671 [NAICS 334510, 339112]

Tesa Tape Inc., p. I-388 [NAICS 32222N]

Tesma Sterling Heights, pp. Vol. II-1473, 1541 [NAICS 336111, 336370]

Tesoro Hawaii Corp., p. I-443 [NAICS 324110]

Tesoro Alaska Co., p. I-443 [NAICS 324110]

Tesoro Petroleum Corp., pp. Vol. I-443, Vol. III-2218 [NAICS 324110, 454311]

Tessco Technologies Inc., pp. Vol. I-756, Vol. III-1839 [NAICS 327910, 423690]

Tessler and Weiss Premesco Inc., p. II-1696 [NAICS 33991M]

Test Technology Inc., pp. Vol. II-1282, 1312 [NAICS 334412, 334418]

Testa Interactive, p. III-1805 [NAICS 423430]

Testa Machine Company Inc., p. II-1147 [NAICS 333516]

Testrite Instrument Company Inc., pp. Vol. II-1082, 1087, 1687, 1714 [NAICS 333314, 333315, 339115, 33994M]

Tetley USA Inc., p. I-143 [NAICS 311920]

Teton Homes, p. II-1500 [NAICS 336214]

Tetra-Holdings Inc., pp. Vol. I-722, Vol. II-1417 [NAICS 327215, 335228]

Teva Pharmaceuticals USA Inc., p. I-539 [NAICS 325412]

Numbers following p. or pp. are page references. Roman numerals indicate volume numbers. Bracketed items indicate industries. Page references are to the starting pages of company tables.

Tex-Mastic International Inc., p. I-453 [NAICS 324122]

Tex-Tech Industries Inc., pp. Vol. I-203, 251, 395, Vol. II-1112 [NAICS 31322M, 314999, 32222P, 33341N]

Tex-Tenn Corp., p. I-213 [NAICS 31324M]

Tex-Tube Co., p. II-1009 [NAICS 332996]

Texas Aerospace Services Inc., p. II-1557 [NAICS 336411]

Texas Arai, p. II-1168 [NAICS 333613]

Texas Architectural Aggregates, p. I-762 [NAICS 327991]

Texas Boot Inc., p. I-300 [NAICS 31621M]

Texas Brine Company L.L.C., p. I-152 [NAICS 31194M]

Texas Cement Products Inc., p. I-752 [NAICS 327420]

Texas Citrus Exchange, p. I-147 [NAICS 311930]

Texas Coffee Company Inc., p. I-143 [NAICS 311920]

Texas Concrete Co., p. II-1584 [NAICS 336510]

Texas Farm Products Co., pp. Vol. I-4, 524, 529 [NAICS 311111, 325314, 325320]

Texas Industries Inc., pp. Vol. I-727, 737, 762, 780, Vol. II-899 [NAICS 327310, 32733M, 327991, 33111M, 33231M]

Texas Instruments Inc., pp. Vol. II-1287, 1437 [NAICS 334413, 335314]

Texas Lehigh Cement L.P., p. I-727 [NAICS 327310]

Texas Molecular L.P., p. III-1971 [NAICS 424690]

Texas Petrochemicals L.P., pp. Vol. I-443, 505, 595 [NAICS 324110, 325212, 32599N]

Texas Recreation Corp., p. I-267 [NAICS 31521M]

Texas Refinery Corp., p. I-453 [NAICS 324122]

Texas Stagecoach, p. II-1607 [NAICS 336999]

Texollini Inc., p. I-198 [NAICS 313210]

Textile Piece Dyeing Company, p. I-218 [NAICS 31331M]

Textile Rubber and Chemical Inc., pp. Vol. I-500, 589 [NAICS 325211, 325991]

Textileather Corp., pp. Vol. I-224, 615 [NAICS 313320, 326113]

Textron Inc., pp. Vol. II-958, 1551, 1557, 1562, 1567, 1580, 1702 [NAICS 332722, 336399, 336411, 336412, 336413, 336419, 339920]

Texturing Services Inc., p. I-192 [NAICS 31311M]

T.F. Hudgins Inc., pp. Vol. II-974, Vol. III-1871 [NAICS 332913, 423840]

TG Kentucky L.L.C., p. I-670 [NAICS 32629M]

TG Missouri Corp., pp. Vol. I-651, Vol. II-1519 [NAICS 32619M, 336330]

TH Foods Inc., pp. Vol. I-124, 137 [NAICS 31182M, 31191M]

T.H. Rogers Lumber Co., pp. Vol. III-1782, 1794, 2065 [NAICS 423310, 423390, 444100]

Thaler Machine Co., p. II-952 [NAICS 332721]

Thaler Oil Company Inc., p. III-1975 [NAICS 424710]

Thales Avionics Inflight Systems, p. II-1272 [NAICS 334310]

Thales Communications Inc., pp. Vol. II-1262, 1267, 1272 [NAICS 334220, 334290, 334310]

Thalheimer Brothers Inc., p. I-807 [NAICS 331314]

Tharpe Company Inc., p. II-1696 [NAICS 33991M]

The MAC Group, p. III-1798 [NAICS 423410]

Theis Enterprises Corp., p. II-1056 [NAICS 333295]

Thelen Sand and Gravel Inc., pp. Vol. I-524, 732 [NAICS 325314, 327320]

Ther-A-Pedic Sleep Products, p. II-1657 [NAICS 337910]

TheraSense Inc., p. II-1671 [NAICS 339112]

Therm-O-Disc Inc., p. II-1332 [NAICS 334512]

Therm-O-Link Inc., pp. Vol. II-939, 1451 [NAICS 33261M, 33592M]

Therm-O-Rock East Inc., p. I-767 [NAICS 327992]

Therma-Flow Inc., pp. Vol. II-918, 1417 [NAICS 332410, 335228]

Therma-Tron-X Inc., p. II-1152 [NAICS 333518]

Therma-Tru Corp., pp. Vol. I-651, Vol. II-908 [NAICS 32619M, 33232M]

Therma-Wave Inc., p. II-1056 [NAICS 333295]

Thermadyne Holdings Corp., pp. Vol. I-595, Vol. II-1152, 1229 [NAICS 32599N, 333518, 33399P]

Thermafiber Inc., p. I-771 [NAICS 327993]

Thermal Circuits Inc., pp. Vol. II-1101, 1217 [NAICS 333414, 333994]

Thermal Dynamics Inc., p. II-918 [NAICS 332410]

Thermal Engineering Corp., p. II-918 [NAICS 332410]

Thermal Foams Inc., p. I-636 [NAICS 326140]

Thermal Industries Inc., p. I-651 [NAICS 32619M]

Thermal Supply Inc., pp. Vol. III-1851, 1855 [NAICS 423730, 423740]

Thermal Ventures Inc., p. I-771 [NAICS 327993]

Thermo Electron Corp., pp. Vol. II-1061, 1322, 1367, 1666 [NAICS 33329N, 334510, 334519, 339111]

Thermo Industries Inc., p. III-1851 [NAICS 423730]

Thermo King of Houston L.L.P., p. III-1855 [NAICS 423740]

Thermo King of Philadelphia, p. II-1546 [NAICS 336391]

Thermo-Kool & Mid, p. II-1409 [NAICS 335222]

Thermo Products L.L.C., p. II-1106 [NAICS 333415]

Thermo-Twin Industries Inc., p. I-709 [NAICS 327211]

Thermocoax Inc., p. III-1831 [NAICS 423610]

Thermodyne Food Service Prods, p. II-1404 [NAICS 335221]

ThermoGenesis Corp., p. II-1666 [NAICS 339111]

Thermon Industries Inc., pp. Vol. II-918, 1451 [NAICS 332410, 33592M]

Thermoplastic Services Inc., p. III-1968 [NAICS 424610]

Thermopol Inc., p. I-665 [NAICS 326220]

Thermos L.L.C., pp. Vol. I-646, 718, Vol. II-928 [NAICS 326160, 327213, 33243M]

Thermoseal Glass Corp., p. I-709 [NAICS 327211]

Theros Equipment Inc., p. III-1859 [NAICS 423810]

Thetford Corp., pp. Vol. I-566, 651, Vol. II-1014 [NAICS 32561M, 32619M, 33299N]

Thibiant International Inc., p. I-575 [NAICS 325620]

Thin Film Technology Corp., p. II-1297 [NAICS 334415]

Things Remembered Inc., pp. Vol. I-251, Vol. II-964 [NAICS 314999, 33281M]

Third Street Sportswear Mfg Inc., p. I-285 [NAICS 31529M]

THL Bedding Holding Co., pp. Vol. I-234, Vol. II-1397, 1621, 1657 [NAICS 31412M, 33521M, 337122, 337910]

Thomas and Betts Corp., pp. Vol. II-1307, 1457 [NAICS 334417, 33593M]

Thomas and Skinner Inc., p. I-631 [NAICS 326130]

Thomas C Wilson Inc., p. II-1051 [NAICS 333220]

Thomas Electronics, p. II-1302 [NAICS 334416]

Thomas Electronics Inc., p. II-1277 [NAICS 334411]

Thomas Electronics of New York, p. II-1277 [NAICS 334411]

Thomas Engineering Inc., p. II-1134 [NAICS 333514]

Thomas G Faria Corp., pp. Vol. II-1140, 1432 [NAICS 333515, 335313]

Thomas Industries Inc., pp. Vol. II-1179, 1184, 1390 [NAICS 333911, 333912, 33512M]

Thomas Interior Systems Inc., p. III-1774 [NAICS 423210]

Thomas Mc Lean Inc., p. III-1790 [NAICS 423330]

Thomas Nelson Inc., pp. Vol. II-1376, Vol. III-1839, 1901 [NAICS 334612, 423690, 424120]

Thomas Plastics Inc., p. I-646 [NAICS 326160]

Thomas Roofing Supply Co., p. III-1790 [NAICS 423330]

Thomas Scientific, pp. Vol. III-1820, 1971 [NAICS 423490, 424690]

Thomas Steel Strip Corp., pp. Vol. I-793, 825, 830, Vol. II-964 [NAICS 33122M, 331419, 33142M, 33281M]

Thomas W. Ruff of Florida Inc., p. III-1774 [NAICS 423210]

Thombert Inc., p. I-660 [NAICS 32621M]

Thompson Building Materials Inc., p. I-737 [NAICS 32733M]

Thompson Candy Acquisition, pp. Vol. I-52, 57 [NAICS 311330, 311340]

Thompson Equipment Inc., p. II-1342 [NAICS 334514]

Thompson Lift Truck Co., p. III-2027 [NAICS 441229]

Thompson Pump and Mfg Inc., p. II-1222 [NAICS 33399N]

Thompson Steel Company Inc., p. I-793 [NAICS 33122M]

Thona N C Inc., p. I-505 [NAICS 325212]

Thor Industries Inc., pp. Vol. II-1473, 1496 [NAICS 336111, 336213]

THOR-LO Inc., p. I-256 [NAICS 31511M]

Thoratec Corp., pp. Vol. II-1322, 1671, 1676 [NAICS 334510, 339112, 339113]

Thorgren Tool and Molding Inc., p. I-510 [NAICS 32522M]

Thorlabs Inc., pp. Vol. II-1082, 1451 [NAICS 333314, 33592M]

Thorp Seed Co., p. I-31 [NAICS 31122N]

Thos. Somerville Co., pp. Vol. III-1847, 1851 [NAICS 423720, 423730]

THP United Enterprises Inc., p. III-1971 [NAICS 424690]

Three Dimensional Chemical Corp., p. I-580 [NAICS 325910]

Three Dog Bakery Inc., p. I-4 [NAICS 311111]

Three-G Enterprises Inc., p. I-756 [NAICS 327910]

Three Rivers Optical Co., p. I-709 [NAICS 327211]

Three States Supply Co., p. III-1851 [NAICS 423730]

Threshold Rehabilitation Services, p. I-267 [NAICS 31521M]

Thrifty Discount Liquor and Wines, p. III-2097 [NAICS 445310]

Thrifty Drug Stores, p. III-2100 [NAICS 446110]

Thrush Aircraft Inc., p. II-1557 [NAICS 336411]

Thrush Company Inc., p. II-974 [NAICS 332913]

Thruway Fasteners Inc., p. III-1843 [NAICS 423710]

Thruway Food Market & Shopping, p. III-2177 [NAICS 452910]

Thule Inc., p. II-1014 [NAICS 33299N]

ThyssenKrupp Budd Detroit, pp. Vol. I-879, Vol. II-1473, 1541 [NAICS 33211P, 336111, 336370]

ThyssenKrupp Gerlach Co., pp. Vol. I-872, Vol. II-1505 [NAICS 33211N, 33631M]

ThyssenKrupp Inc., p. I-845 [NAICS 33151M]

ThyssenKrupp Materials N.A. Inc., pp. Vol. I-651, 857, Vol. II-908, Vol. III-1824, 1968 [NAICS 32619M, 33152P, 33232M, 423510, 424610]

ThyssenKrupp Rubber Machinery, p. II-1051 [NAICS 333220]

ThyssenKrupp Stahl Co., pp. Vol. I-852, 857, Vol. II-1129, 1217 [NAICS 33152N, 33152P, 333513, 333994]

Tiara Yachts Inc., p. II-1594 [NAICS 336612]

Tidel Technologies Inc., p. II-1077 [NAICS 333313]

Tidewater Companies Inc., p. III-1863 [NAICS 423820]

Tidewater Inc., p. II-1589 [NAICS 336611]

Tidewater Skanska Inc., p. II-899 [NAICS 33231M]

Tidewater Wholesalers Inc., pp. Vol. III-1939, 2001 [NAICS 424450, 424940]

Tie Down Engineering Inc., pp. Vol. II-1500, 1524, 1530 [NAICS 336214, 336340, 336350]

Tied House Brewing, p. I-172 [NAICS 312120]

Tien-Hu Knitting Company Inc., p. I-262 [NAICS 31519M]

Tierney Brothers Inc., p. II-1714 [NAICS 33994M]

Tiffany and Co., p. III-2144 [NAICS 448310]

Tiffen Manufacturing Corp., pp. Vol. II-1087, 1112 [NAICS 333315, 33341N]

Tiffin Motor Homes Inc., p. II-1496 [NAICS 336213]

Tifton Ophthalmology Inc., p. III-1820 [NAICS 423490]

Tiger Accessory Group, p. II-1740 [NAICS 339994]

Tigerflex Corp., p. I-665 [NAICS 326220]

Tigerpoly Manufacturing Inc., pp. Vol. I-670, Vol. II-1427, 1505 [NAICS 32629M, 335312, 33631M]

TII Network Technologies Inc., pp. Vol. II-1302, 1421, 1432 [NAICS 334416, 335311, 335313]

Til-Mar Inc., p. III-2007 [NAICS 424990]

Tilcon Connecticut Inc., p. I-448 [NAICS 324121]

Tillamook Country Smoker Inc., p. I-137 [NAICS 31191M]

Tillamook County Creamery, pp. Vol. I-76, 86, 92 [NAICS 311513, 31151N, 311520]

Tillie's Flower Shop, p. III-2183 [NAICS 453110]

Tillotson Rubber Company Inc., pp. Vol. I-670, Vol. II-1676 [NAICS 32629M, 339113]

TIM Plastics Inc., p. I-646 [NAICS 326160]

TimBar Packaging & Display, pp. Vol. I-379, 388, Vol. II-928, 1720 [NAICS 32221M, 32222N, 33243M, 339950]

Timber Creek Resouce L.L.C., p. I-343 [NAICS 321920]

Timber Harvester Inc., p. II-1046 [NAICS 333210]

Timber Products Co., pp. Vol. I-324, Vol. III-1782 [NAICS 32121N, 423310]

Timber Truss Housing Systems, pp. Vol. I-329, 353 [NAICS 32121P, 321992]

Timberland Co., pp. Vol. I-272, 290, 300 [NAICS 31522M, 31599M, 31621M]

Timberland Machines, p. III-1863 [NAICS 423820]

TIMCO Aviation Services Inc., pp. Vol. II-1557, Vol. III-1879 [NAICS 336411, 423860]

TIMCO Standard Tandem Inc., pp. Vol. I-803, 807 [NAICS 331312, 331314]

Time Life Inc., p. II-1376 [NAICS 334612]

Time Oil Co., pp. Vol. III-2116, 2225 [NAICS 447110, 454319]

Time Service Inc., p. III-1894 [NAICS 423940]

Times-Citizen Communications, p. I-436 [NAICS 32312M]

Times Communications Systems, p. III-2054 [NAICS 443112]

Times Microwave Systems, pp. Vol. II-1307, 1312, 1451 [NAICS 334417, 334418, 33592M]

Times Printing Company Inc., p. I-436 [NAICS 32312M]

Timesavers Inc., p. II-1046 [NAICS 333210]

Timeworks Inc., p. II-1362 [NAICS 334518]

Timken Aerospace & Super Prec., pp. Vol. II-988, 1168 [NAICS 332991, 333613]

Timken Co., pp. Vol. I-780, 837, Vol. II-988, 1168 [NAICS 33111M, 33149M, 332991, 333613]

Tincher Dental Laboratory, p. II-1692 [NAICS 339116]

Tingley Rubber Corp., p. I-300 [NAICS 31621M]

Tip Top Poultry Inc., p. I-97 [NAICS 311615]

Tishken Products Co., p. II-1147 [NAICS 333516]

Tissurama Industries Inc., pp. Vol. I-213, 218, 251 [NAICS 31324M, 31331M, 314999]

Titan America Inc., pp. Vol. I-727, 732 [NAICS 327310, 327320]

Titan International Inc., p. I-780 [NAICS 33111M]

Titan Machinery L.L.C., p. III-2069 [NAICS 444210]

Titan Tire Corp., p. I-660 [NAICS 32621M]

Titan Trailer Manufacturing Inc., p. II-1491 [NAICS 336212]

Titanium Metals Corp., p. I-837 [NAICS 33149M]

TIW Corp., pp. Vol. II-933, 980, 1039, 1676 [NAICS 332510, 33291N, 33313M, 339113]

TJ Hale Company Inc., p. II-1639 [NAICS 337212]

T.J.T. Inc., pp. Vol. I-660, Vol. III-1790 [NAICS 32621M, 423330]

TJX Companies Inc., p. III-2132 [NAICS 448140]

Tk Coatings L.L.C., p. I-453 [NAICS 324122]

TL Administration Corp., p. I-147 [NAICS 311930]

TL Industries Inc., p. II-1332 [NAICS 334512]

TM Poly-Film Inc., pp. Vol. I-603, 621 [NAICS 326111, 326121]

TM Tire Company Inc., p. III-1766 [NAICS 423130]

TMD Friction Inc., p. II-1524 [NAICS 336340]

TMI Systems Design Corp., pp. Vol. II-1611, 1621 [NAICS 337110, 337122]

Tnemec Company Inc., p. I-554 [NAICS 325510]

TNR Technical Inc., pp. Vol. II-1442, 1447 [NAICS 335911, 335912]

TNT Custom Marine Co., pp. Vol. II-1173, 1589, 1594 [NAICS 333618, 336611, 336612]

TNT Fireworks, p. III-1887 [NAICS 423920]

TNT Plastic Molding Inc., p. II-1119 [NAICS 333511]

Tobacco Processors Inc., p. I-185 [NAICS 312210]

Tobacco Technology Inc., p. I-185 [NAICS 312210]

Tobin Productions Inc., p. II-1381 [NAICS 334613]

Toby Sexton Tire Company Inc., p. III-1766 [NAICS 423130]

Toce Brothers Inc., p. III-1766 [NAICS 423130]

Today's Office Inc., p. III-2186 [NAICS 453210]

Todd Holding Co., p. III-2076 [NAICS 445110]

Todd's Enterprises, pp. Vol. I-62, 152 [NAICS 31141M, 31194M]

Todd Shipyards Corp., p. II-1589 [NAICS 336611]

Todd Systems Inc., p. II-1302 [NAICS 334416]

Todhunter International Inc., pp. Vol. I-172, 177, 181 [NAICS 312120, 312130, 312140]

Tokico (USA) Inc., p. II-1551 [NAICS 336399]

Tokusen USA Inc., p. I-248 [NAICS 314992]

Tol-O-Matic Inc., p. II-1332 [NAICS 334512]

Tolas Health Care Packaging, pp. Vol. I-609, 631 [NAICS 326112, 326130]

Tolco Corp., p. II-1189 [NAICS 333913]

Toledo Molding and Die Inc., pp. Vol. II-1119, 1749 [NAICS 333511, 339999]

Tolerance Masters Inc., p. II-1562 [NAICS 336412]

Tolleson Lumber Company Inc., p. I-312 [NAICS 32111M]

Tom Arbron Associates, p. I-776 [NAICS 327999]

Tom Barrow Company Inc., p. III-1851 [NAICS 423730]

Tom's Foods Inc., pp. Vol. I-52, 57, 116, 137 [NAICS 311330, 311340, 31181M, 31191M]

Tom Smith Industries Inc., p. II-1119 [NAICS 333511]

Toma-Tek Inc., p. I-158 [NAICS 31199M]

Tomar Electronics Inc., p. II-1386 [NAICS 335110]

Tomasco Mulciber Inc., p. II-1541 [NAICS 336370]

Tomba Communications, p. III-1805 [NAICS 423430]

Tomco Auto Products Inc., p. II-1512 [NAICS 33632M]

Tomco2 Equipment Co., p. II-923 [NAICS 332420]

Tomen America Inc., pp. Vol. III-1867, 1913, 1968, 1971 [NAICS 423830, 424310, 424610, 424690]

Tomen-Ein Inc., p. I-224 [NAICS 313320]

Tomlinson Industries, pp. Vol. I-852, Vol. II-928, 1189, 1627 [NAICS 33152N, 33243M, 333913, 337127]

Tommy Hilfiger USA Inc., p. III-1916 [NAICS 424320]

Tommyknocker Brewery and Pub, p. I-172 [NAICS 312120]

Tompkins Industries, p. I-665 [NAICS 326220]

Tonini Church Supply Co., p. III-1820 [NAICS 423490]

Tonneau Master, p. I-239 [NAICS 31491M]

Tonner Doll Company Inc., p. II-1708 [NAICS 33993M]

Tony Downs Foods Co., pp. Vol. I-97, 158 [NAICS 311615, 31199M]

Tony Lama Boot Co., p. I-300 [NAICS 31621M]

Tony's Fine Foods, pp. Vol. III-1933, 1946, 1954 [NAICS 424430, 424470, 424490]

Numbers following p. or pp. are page references. Roman numerals indicate volume numbers. Bracketed items indicate industries. Page references are to the starting pages of company tables.

Tony's Seafood Ltd., pp. Vol. I-110, Vol. III-2085 [NAICS 31171M, 445220]

Too Inc., p. III-2129 [NAICS 448130]

Tool Automation Enterprises Corp., p. II-1584 [NAICS 336510]

Tools For Bending Inc., p. II-1129 [NAICS 333513]

Tootsie Roll Industries Inc., p. I-52 [NAICS 311330]

Top Flight Inc., pp. Vol. I-403, 415 [NAICS 32223M, 322299]

Top Flite Golf Co., p. II-1702 [NAICS 339920]

Top Line Distributing Inc., p. III-1887 [NAICS 423920]

Top Shape Steel Rule Die Corp., p. I-374 [NAICS 322130]

Top South Inc., p. I-762 [NAICS 327991]

TOP Tobacco L.P., p. I-188 [NAICS 31222M]

Top Water Feed, p. I-4 [NAICS 311111]

Topco Associates Inc., pp. Vol. III-1925, 1954 [NAICS 424410, 424490]

Topcon America Corp., pp. Vol. II-1082, 1327, 1352, 1367 [NAICS 333314, 334511, 334516, 334519]

Topmost Chemical and Paper, p. III-1971 [NAICS 424690]

Topp Construction Services Inc., p. II-1106 [NAICS 333415]

Topps Company Inc., pp. Vol. I-52, 57, 420, Vol. II-1708 [NAICS 311330, 311340, 32311M, 33993M]

Tops Markets Inc., p. III-2076 [NAICS 445110]

Topsville Inc., p. III-1919 [NAICS 424330]

Torani Specialty Beverages, pp. Vol. I-147, 152, 158 [NAICS 311930, 31194M, 31199M]

Toray Composites (America) Inc., pp. Vol. I-510, Vol. II-1463 [NAICS 32522M, 335991]

Toray Plastics America Inc., p. I-615 [NAICS 326113]

Toresco Enterprises Inc., p. III-2011 [NAICS 441110]

Tork Inc., p. II-1386 [NAICS 335110]

Torkan Inc., p. III-2041 [NAICS 442210]

Torn and Glasser Inc., pp. Vol. III-1939, 1954, 1958 [NAICS 424450, 424490, 424510]

Toro Co., pp. Vol. II-892, 1023, 1028 [NAICS 33221P, 333111, 333112]

Torrington Research Co., p. II-1342 [NAICS 334514]

Torrington Supply Company Inc., p. III-1847 [NAICS 423720]

Tortilla King Inc., p. I-133 [NAICS 311830]

Tortillas Inc., p. I-133 [NAICS 311830]

Tortillas Mexico Mexico Inc., p. I-133 [NAICS 311830]

Tortilleria El Maizal Inc., p. I-133 [NAICS 311830]

Toshiba America Electronic, p. III-1839 [NAICS 423690]

Toshiba America Inc., p. II-1272 [NAICS 334310]

Toshiba America Medical Systems, p. III-1813 [NAICS 423450]

Toshiba International Corp., pp. Vol. II-1157, 1322, 1427 [NAICS 333611, 334510, 335312]

Tosoh Set Inc., pp. Vol. I-681, Vol. II-1056 [NAICS 327112, 333295]

Tosoh SMD Inc., p. I-825 [NAICS 331419]

Total Beverage Corp., p. III-2097 [NAICS 445310]

Total Componet Solutions Corp., p. II-1530 [NAICS 336350]

Total Control Solutions Inc., p. II-1248 [NAICS 334113]

Total Door Supply Inc., p. III-1843 [NAICS 423710]

Total Electronics L.L.C., p. II-1332 [NAICS 334512]

Total Fire and Safety Inc., p. III-1809 [NAICS 423440]

Total Identity Corp., pp. Vol. III-2153, 2162, 2194 [NAICS 451120, 451211, 453310]

Total Lubricants USA, p. I-458 [NAICS 324191]

Total Safety Inc., pp. Vol. II-1676, 1749 [NAICS 339113, 339999]

Totaline of Florida Inc., p. III-1855 [NAICS 423740]

Toter Inc., pp. Vol. I-879, Vol. II-928 [NAICS 33211P, 33243M]

Totten Tubes Inc., p. III-1843 [NAICS 423710]

Touch of Lace, p. I-213 [NAICS 31324M]

Touchtunes Music Corp., p. II-1376 [NAICS 334612]

Tower Automotive Inc., p. II-1541 [NAICS 336370]

Tower Manufacturing Corp., p. II-1302 [NAICS 334416]

Town And Country Coop., pp. Vol. III-1958, 2116 [NAICS 424510, 447110]

Town and Country Living, p. I-234 [NAICS 31412M]

Town Food Service Equipment, p. II-1404 [NAICS 335221]

Town House Home Furnishings, p. III-1774 [NAICS 423210]

Townley Manufacturing Inc., pp. Vol. II-1009, 1033, 1039 [NAICS 332996, 333120, 33313M]

Toy Wonders Inc., p. III-1887 [NAICS 423920]

Toyo Seat USA Corp., pp. Vol. II-933, 1536 [NAICS 332510, 336360]

Toyota Industrial Equipment Mfg, p. II-1194 [NAICS 33392M]

Toyota Motor Mfg Kentucky, pp. Vol. II-1473, 1486 [NAICS 336111, 336211]

Toyota Motor Sales U.S.A. Inc., p. III-1758 [NAICS 423110]

Toyota On The Heights, p. III-1758 [NAICS 423110]

Toys 'R' Us Inc., pp. Vol. III-2129, 2153 [NAICS 448130, 451120]

Toys and Treasures International, p. III-2153 [NAICS 451120]

TPI Composites Inc., p. II-1594 [NAICS 336612]

TPI Corp., pp. Vol. II-1101, 1106, 1112 [NAICS 333414, 333415, 33341N]

Trace Die Cast Inc., p. I-852 [NAICS 33152N]

Tracer Corp., p. III-1879 [NAICS 423860]

Tracewell Systems Inc., p. II-1243 [NAICS 334112]

Tracker Marine L.L.C., p. II-1594 [NAICS 336612]

Trackmobile Inc., p. II-1584 [NAICS 336510]

TRACO, pp. Vol. I-722, Vol. II-908 [NAICS 327215, 33232M]

Traco Manufacturing Inc., pp. Vol. I-22, 603, 609, Vol. II-892, 1212 [NAICS 311221, 326111, 326112, 33221P, 333993]

Tractech, pp. Vol. II-1524, 1530 [NAICS 336340, 336350]

Tractor and Equipment Co., p. III-1867 [NAICS 423830]

Tractor Supply Co., p. III-2072 [NAICS 444220]

Tracy Industries Inc., pp. Vol. II-1173, 1512, Vol. III-1770 [NAICS 333618, 33632M, 423140]

Trade AM International Inc., p. I-229 [NAICS 314110]

Trade Winds Rehabilitation Center, p. I-285 [NAICS 31529M]

tradeair.com Inc., p. III-2228 [NAICS 454390]

Tradehome Shoe Stores Inc., p. III-2141 [NAICS 448210]

Trader Joe's Co., p. III-2097 [NAICS 445310]

Traeger Industries Inc., p. II-1404 [NAICS 335221]

Trailstar Manufacturing Corp., p. II-1491 [NAICS 336212]

Trainor Grain and Supply Co., p. III-1958 [NAICS 424510]

TRAM Inc., pp. Vol. II-1312, 1317, 1457 [NAICS 334418, 334419, 33593M]

Trans-Industries Inc., p. II-1720 [NAICS 339950]

Trans-Lux Corp., p. II-1720 [NAICS 339950]

Trans-Ocean Products Inc., p. I-110 [NAICS 31171M]

Trans-Pak Inc., p. I-343 [NAICS 321920]

Trans-Tec Services Inc., p. III-1979 [NAICS 424720]

Trans Western Polymers Inc., p. I-603 [NAICS 326111]

Trans World Entertainment Corp., pp. Vol. III-2168, 2211 [NAICS 451220, 454113]

Transammonia Inc., pp. Vol. III-1979, 1991 [NAICS 424720, 424910]

Transcat Inc., p. II-1347 [NAICS 334515]

Transco Inc., pp. Vol. I-771, Vol. II-1272 [NAICS 327993, 334310]

Transcontinental Printing USA Inc., p. I-403 [NAICS 32223M]

Transcraft Corp., p. II-1491 [NAICS 336212]

Transform Automotive L.L.C., pp. Vol. I-665, Vol. II-1530 [NAICS 326220, 336350]

Transformer Manufacturers Inc., p. II-1302 [NAICS 334416]

Transgenomic Inc., pp. Vol. II-1352, 1666 [NAICS 334516, 339111]

Transilwrap Company Inc., pp. Vol. I-615, 631 [NAICS 326113, 326130]

Transistor Devices Inc., pp. Vol. II-1367, 1468 [NAICS 334519, 335999]

Transition Products Inc., p. III-1901 [NAICS 424120]

Transmudo Company Inc., p. III-1946 [NAICS 424470]

TransNet Corp., p. III-2058 [NAICS 443120]

Transparent Container Inc., p. I-609 [NAICS 326112]

Transply Inc., p. III-1871 [NAICS 423840]

Transpo Electronics Inc., pp. Vol. II-1421, 1432, 1437, 1512 [NAICS 335311, 335313, 335314, 33632M]

Transport Diesel Service Inc., p. II-1173 [NAICS 333618]

Transport Refrigeration Sales, p. III-1855 [NAICS 423740]

Transpro Inc., p. II-1217 [NAICS 333994]

TransTechnology Corp., pp. Vol. II-958, 1033, 1580 [NAICS 332722, 333120, 336419]

Transtector System Inc., p. II-1421 [NAICS 335311]

Travel Supreme Inc., pp. Vol. II-1496, 1500 [NAICS 336213, 336214]

Travis Boats and Motors Inc., pp. Vol. III-2024, 2030 [NAICS 441222, 441310]

Numbers following p. or pp. are page references. Roman numerals indicate volume numbers. Bracketed items indicate industries. Page references are to the starting pages of company tables.

2427

Travis Pattern and Foundry Inc., pp. Vol. I-803, 852, Vol. II-1023, 1432 [NAICS 331312, 33152N, 333111, 335313]

TRC Manufacturing Inc., p. II-1740 [NAICS 339994]

Treadwell Corp., p. II-1357 [NAICS 334517]

TreatCo Inc., p. I-4 [NAICS 311111]

Treaty City Industries Inc., p. I-709 [NAICS 327211]

Trebor Instrument Corp., p. II-1056 [NAICS 333295]

Tredegar Corp., pp. Vol. I-615, 626, 811 [NAICS 326113, 326122, 331316]

Tredegar Film Products, p. I-615 [NAICS 326113]

Tree of Life Inc., p. III-1925 [NAICS 424410]

TreeCon Resources Inc., p. III-1863 [NAICS 423820]

Treeland Nursery Co., p. III-2072 [NAICS 444220]

Trefethen Vineyards Winery, p. I-177 [NAICS 312130]

Trefilarbed Arkansas Inc., p. II-939 [NAICS 33261M]

Trega Foods Inc., p. I-76 [NAICS 311513]

Trelleborg Palmer Chenard, p. II-1580 [NAICS 336419]

Tremco Inc., pp. Vol. I-448, 453, 493, 554, 560 [NAICS 324121, 324122, 32519M, 325510, 325520]

Trend Technologies L.L.C., pp. Vol. I-651, Vol. II-908 [NAICS 32619M, 33232M]

Trendway Corp., pp. Vol. II-1621, 1650 [NAICS 337122, 33721N]

Trent Tube Inc., p. I-788 [NAICS 331210]

Trenwyth Industries, pp. Vol. I-737, 743, 771 [NAICS 32733M, 327390, 327993]

Tressa Inc., p. II-886 [NAICS 33221N]

Tri Aerospace L.L.C., p. II-1562 [NAICS 336412]

Tri-Con Industries Ltd., p. II-1536 [NAICS 336360]

Tri County Beverage Co., p. III-1983 [NAICS 424810]

Tri-County Custom Sports Inc., p. III-1883 [NAICS 423910]

Tri-County Limestone Co., p. I-748 [NAICS 327410]

Tri-Delta Technology Inc., p. I-646 [NAICS 326160]

Tri Electronics Inc., p. III-2054 [NAICS 443112]

Tri Medica International Inc., p. I-534 [NAICS 325411]

Tri-Seal A Tekni-Plex Co., p. I-641 [NAICS 326150]

Tri-State Brick and Tile Inc., pp. Vol. I-691, 703 [NAICS 327121, 32712N]

Tri-State Cut Stone and Brick Co., p. I-762 [NAICS 327991]

Tri-State Foam Products Inc., p. I-636 [NAICS 326140]

Tri-State Iron and Metal Co., p. I-363 [NAICS 322110]

Tri-State Plant Food Inc., p. I-520 [NAICS 325312]

Tri-State Recycling Inc., p. I-363 [NAICS 322110]

Tri-State Surgical Supply, p. III-1813 [NAICS 423450]

Tri-Supreme Optical, p. I-713 [NAICS 327212]

Tri Tech Laboratories Inc., pp. Vol. I-575, Vol. II-1397 [NAICS 325620, 33521M]

Tri Tool Inc., p. II-1124 [NAICS 333512]

Triad Energy Resources Inc., p. I-516 [NAICS 325311]

Triad Machinery Inc., p. III-1859 [NAICS 423810]

Trialco Inc., p. I-803 [NAICS 331312]

Triangle Gas, p. I-471 [NAICS 325120]

Triangle Tool Corp., p. II-1119 [NAICS 333511]

Triangle Truss Inc., p. I-329 [NAICS 32121P]

Tribology Tech Lube Inc., p. I-458 [NAICS 324191]

Tribune Co., p. III-1890 [NAICS 423930]

Tricon Chemical Corp., p. I-480 [NAICS 325181]

Tricon Industries Inc., pp. Vol. II-1312, 1432 [NAICS 334418, 335313]

TriContinent Scientific Inc., p. II-1666 [NAICS 339111]

TricorBraun, p. III-1968 [NAICS 424610]

TriCounty Farm Service Inc., p. III-2222 [NAICS 454312]

Trident Co., pp. Vol. II-945, 964, 1749, Vol. III-1824 [NAICS 332710, 33281M, 339999, 423510]

Trident Seafoods Corp., p. I-110 [NAICS 31171M]

Trilithic Inc., p. II-1272 [NAICS 334310]

Trilogy Communications Inc., p. II-1451 [NAICS 33592M]

Trim Systems L.L.C., pp. Vol. II-933, 1486 [NAICS 332510, 336211]

Trimaco, pp. Vol. I-239, Vol. II-1740 [NAICS 31491M, 339994]

TriMark Corp., pp. Vol. I-358, Vol. III-1843 [NAICS 321999, 423710]

TriMas Corp., pp. Vol. II-899, 1140, 1168, 1222, 1229, 1427, 1607, 1725 [NAICS 33231M, 333515, 333613, 33399N, 33399P, 335312, 336999, 339991]

Trimble Navigation Ltd., pp. Vol. II-1327, 1367 [NAICS 334511, 334519]

Trimfoot Co., p. I-300 [NAICS 31621M]

Trimtex Company Inc., p. I-213 [NAICS 31324M]

Trinchero Family Estates, p. I-177 [NAICS 312130]

TRINDCO, p. I-762 [NAICS 327991]

Trine Products, p. II-1731 [NAICS 339992]

Trinidad Benham Corp., pp. Vol. III-1958, 2007 [NAICS 424510, 424990]

Trinity, pp. Vol. II-980, 1009 [NAICS 33291N, 332996]

Trinity Forge Inc., p. I-872 [NAICS 33211N]

Trinity Industries Inc., pp. Vol. II-899, 928, 1584, 1589 [NAICS 33231M, 33243M, 336510, 336611]

Trinity Packaging Corp., p. I-603 [NAICS 326111]

Trinity Rail Group, p. II-1584 [NAICS 336510]

Trinity Tool Company Inc., p. I-756 [NAICS 327910]

Trinity Trailer Manufacturing Inc., pp. Vol. II-1482, 1491 [NAICS 336120, 336212]

Trintex Corp., p. I-660 [NAICS 32621M]

Trio Packaging Corp., pp. Vol. II-1077, 1212 [NAICS 333313, 333993]

Trionix Research Laboratory Inc., p. II-1357 [NAICS 334517]

TriPath Imaging Inc., p. II-1352 [NAICS 334516]

Tripifoods Inc., p. III-1950 [NAICS 424480]

Triple D Equipment Inc., p. III-2072 [NAICS 444220]

Triple F Inc., p. I-31 [NAICS 31122N]

Triple H Food Processors Inc., pp. Vol. I-152, 158 [NAICS 31194M, 31199M]

Tripoli Bakery Inc., p. III-2089 [NAICS 445291]

TriQuint Semiconductor Inc., p. II-1287 [NAICS 334413]

Trireme Manufacturing Inc., p. II-1157 [NAICS 333611]

Tris USA Inc., p. II-1463 [NAICS 335991]

Triton Boat Company L.P., p. II-1594 [NAICS 336612]

Triton Electron Technology Div., p. II-1277 [NAICS 334411]

Triton Systems Inc., pp. Vol. II-1077, 1457 [NAICS 333313, 33593M]

Triumph Corp., p. II-1541 [NAICS 336370]

Triumph Group Inc., p. II-1567 [NAICS 336413]

Triumph Pet Industries Inc., p. I-4 [NAICS 311111]

Triumph Twist Drill Company Inc., pp. Vol. II-1039, 1140, 1207 [NAICS 33313M, 333515, 333991]

Triversity Corp., p. III-1801 [NAICS 423420]

TRM Corp., p. III-1801 [NAICS 423420]

TRM Manufacturing Inc., p. I-603 [NAICS 326111]

Trojan Battery Co., pp. Vol. II-1442, 1447 [NAICS 335911, 335912]

Tronair Inc., p. II-923 [NAICS 332420]

Tropar Manufacturing Inc., p. II-1362 [NAICS 334518]

Tropical Nut and Fruit Co., p. I-137 [NAICS 31191M]

Tropical Sportswear Intern. Corp., pp. Vol. I-272, 279 [NAICS 31522M, 31523M]

Tropicana Products Inc., pp. Vol. I-9, 62, 68, 718 [NAICS 311119, 31141M, 31142M, 327213]

Tropitone Furniture Company Inc., p. II-1632 [NAICS 33712N]

Troutman Brothers, p. III-1946 [NAICS 424470]

Troutman's Emporium, p. III-2171 [NAICS 452111]

Troy Manufacturing Texas Inc., p. I-699 [NAICS 327123]

Troyer Foods Inc., pp. Vol. III-1929, 1936, 1943, 1946 [NAICS 424420, 424440, 424460, 424470]

Troyer Potato Products Inc., p. I-137 [NAICS 31191M]

Tru-Kay Manufacturing Inc., p. II-1696 [NAICS 33991M]

Tru-Wood Cabinets Inc., p. II-1611 [NAICS 337110]

Truan's Candies Inc., p. III-2092 [NAICS 445292]

Truck Country of Rockford Inc., p. III-2011 [NAICS 441110]

Truck-Lite Company Inc., pp. Vol. II-1390, 1512 [NAICS 33512M, 33632M]

Truck Parts and Equipment Co., p. III-1758 [NAICS 423110]

Truck Trailer Transit Inc., p. II-1524 [NAICS 336340]

Trudy Corp., p. II-1376 [NAICS 334612]

True Fitness Technology Inc., p. II-1702 [NAICS 339920]

True House Inc., p. I-329 [NAICS 32121P]

True Temper Sports Inc., p. II-1702 [NAICS 339920]

True Value Co., pp. Vol. I-554, Vol. II-933, Vol. III-1778, 1843, 1863 [NAICS 325510, 332510, 423220, 423710, 423820]

True Value Manufacturing Co., p. I-554 [NAICS 325510]

Truesoups L.L.C., p. I-62 [NAICS 31141M]

TruHeat L.L.C., pp. Vol. II-1101, 1217 [NAICS 333414, 333994]

Truman Arnold Companies Inc., p. III-1975 [NAICS 424710]

Trumbull Industries Inc., pp. Vol. III-1847, 1871 [NAICS 423720, 423840]

Numbers following p. or pp. are page references. Roman numerals indicate volume numbers. Bracketed items indicate industries. Page references are to the starting pages of company tables.

Truss Manufacturing Company Inc., p. I-329 [NAICS 32121P]

Truss Specialists Inc., p. I-329 [NAICS 32121P]

Truss Tech Industries Inc., p. I-329 [NAICS 32121P]

Trussway Ltd., p. I-329 [NAICS 32121P]

Truth Hardware, pp. Vol. II-908, 933 [NAICS 33232M, 332510]

TSF Sportswear, p. I-285 [NAICS 31529M]

TST Impreso Inc., p. I-368 [NAICS 32212M]

TT Technology Inc., p. III-1859 [NAICS 423810]

TTC Trammell Company Inc., p. II-1735 [NAICS 339993]

TTM Technologies Inc., p. II-1282 [NAICS 334412]

TTP Diesel Power and Machine, p. III-1770 [NAICS 423140]

Tu-K Industries Inc., p. II-886 [NAICS 33221N]

Tubbs Cordage Co., p. I-244 [NAICS 314991]

Tube City L.L.C., pp. Vol. I-837, Vol. III-1770, 1890 [NAICS 33149M, 423140, 423930]

Tube Forming and Machine Inc., p. II-1147 [NAICS 333516]

Tube Methods Inc., p. I-788 [NAICS 331210]

Tube Monitor Co., p. II-1277 [NAICS 334411]

Tubular Products Co., p. II-1009 [NAICS 332996]

Tubular Services L.P., p. II-958 [NAICS 332722]

Tubular Steel Inc., pp. Vol. I-788, Vol. III-1824 [NAICS 331210, 423510]

Tucker Technology Inc., p. II-1541 [NAICS 336370]

Tuesday Morning Corp., p. III-2180 [NAICS 452990]

Tufco Technologies Inc., pp. Vol. I-368, 411, 415 [NAICS 32212M, 322291, 322299]

Tuff Torq Corp., pp. Vol. II-892, 1028, 1168 [NAICS 33221P, 333112, 333613]

Tulnoy Lumber Inc., p. III-1843 [NAICS 423710]

Tulsa Dynaspan Inc., p. I-743 [NAICS 327390]

Tulstar Products Inc., p. III-1971 [NAICS 424690]

Tunnessen's Automotive, p. III-1770 [NAICS 423140]

Tupperware Corp., p. I-626 [NAICS 326122]

Tupperware U.S. Inc., p. III-2228 [NAICS 454390]

Tur-Pak Foods Inc., p. I-97 [NAICS 311615]

Turblex Inc., p. II-1157 [NAICS 333611]

Turbo Air Inc., p. II-1562 [NAICS 336412]

Turbo Dynamics Corp., p. II-1157 [NAICS 333611]

Turbo Start Battery, p. II-1442 [NAICS 335911]

Turbocare Inc., pp. Vol. II-980, 1157, 1725 [NAICS 33291N, 333611, 339991]

Turbon International Inc., p. II-1714 [NAICS 33994M]

Turbotechnology Services Corp., p. II-1157 [NAICS 333611]

Turf Equipment and Supply Inc., p. III-1863 [NAICS 423820]

Turf Products Corp., p. III-1863 [NAICS 423820]

Turmatic Systems Inc., p. II-1152 [NAICS 333518]

Turner Bellows Inc., p. II-1087 [NAICS 333315]

Turner Dairy Farms Inc., p. III-2094 [NAICS 445299]

Turner Holdings L.L.C., pp. Vol. I-68, 86, 92 [NAICS 31142M, 31151N, 311520]

Turner New Zealand Inc., pp. Vol. III-1943, 2094 [NAICS 424460, 445299]

Tursso Company Inc., p. I-395 [NAICS 32222P]

Tuscarora Yarns Inc., p. I-192 [NAICS 31311M]

Tusco Grocers Inc., pp. Vol. III-1929, 1933, 1946 [NAICS 424420, 424430, 424470]

Tusonix Inc., pp. Vol. I-686, Vol. II-1292 [NAICS 327113, 334414]

TUTCO Inc., p. II-1101 [NAICS 333414]

Tuthill Corp., pp. Vol. II-958, 980, 1112, 1179, 1307 [NAICS 332722, 33291N, 33341N, 333911, 334417]

Tuthill Energy Systems, pp. Vol. II-1101, 1112, 1157 [NAICS 333414, 33341N, 333611]

Tuthill Linkage Group, pp. Vol. II-958, 1168, 1530 [NAICS 332722, 333613, 336350]

Tuthill Transport Technologies, p. II-939 [NAICS 33261M]

Tuthill Vacuum & Blower Systems, p. II-1184 [NAICS 333912]

Tuttle-Click Automotive Group, p. III-2011 [NAICS 441110]

T.W. Hager Lumber Company Inc., pp. Vol. I-319, 358 [NAICS 321219, 321999]

TW Inc., p. III-2168 [NAICS 451220]

TW Metals Inc., p. III-1824 [NAICS 423510]

Tweeter Home Entertainment, p. III-2054 [NAICS 443112]

Twenty-First Century Healthcare, p. I-534 [NAICS 325411]

Twigg Corp., p. II-1580 [NAICS 336419]

Twin Brothers Marine L.L.C., p. II-1589 [NAICS 336611]

Twin City Bagels Inc., p. III-2089 [NAICS 445291]

Twin City Bottle Inc., pp. Vol. III-1778, 1786 [NAICS 423220, 423320]

Twin City Die Castings Inc., pp. Vol. I-852, 857 [NAICS 33152N, 33152P]

Twin City Fan Companies Ltd., p. II-1112 [NAICS 33341N]

Twin City Foods Inc., p. I-62 [NAICS 31141M]

Twin City Hide Inc., p. I-296 [NAICS 316110]

Twin City Knitting Company Inc., p. I-256 [NAICS 31511M]

Twin City Optical Co., p. II-1687 [NAICS 339115]

Twin City Oxygen Inc., p. I-471 [NAICS 325120]

Twin Disc Inc., pp. Vol. II-1162, 1168 [NAICS 333612, 333613]

Twin Hills Collectables L.L.C., pp. Vol. III-1887, 2190 [NAICS 423920, 453220]

Twin Rivers Technologies L.P., p. I-493 [NAICS 32519M]

Twin State Inc., p. I-524 [NAICS 325314]

Twincraft Inc., pp. Vol. I-566, Vol. II-945 [NAICS 32561M, 332710]

Twitchell Corp., pp. Vol. I-198, 368 [NAICS 313210, 32212M]

Two Creeks Ski Shop Snowmass, p. III-2150 [NAICS 451110]

Two Rivers F S, pp. Vol. I-9, 15, 524 [NAICS 311119, 31121M, 325314]

Two Stroke International, p. II-1562 [NAICS 336412]

Two Technologies Inc., p. II-1248 [NAICS 334113]

Twomey Co., p. III-1991 [NAICS 424910]

TXE Inc., p. II-1376 [NAICS 334612]

TXF Products, pp. Vol. II-1397, 1740 [NAICS 33521M, 339994]

TXI Corp., p. I-737 [NAICS 32733M]

TXU Corp., p. I-443 [NAICS 324110]

Ty Inc., p. II-1708 [NAICS 33993M]

Tyan Computer Corp., p. II-1282 [NAICS 334412]

Tyco Adhesives Betham Div., pp. Vol. I-388, Vol. II-1676 [NAICS 32222N, 339113]

Tyco Electronics, pp. Vol. I-899, 964, 1257 [NAICS 33231M, 33281M, 334210]

Tyco Electronics-Printed Circuit, p. II-1282 [NAICS 334412]

TYCO Specialty Films, pp. Vol. I-609, 615 [NAICS 326112, 326113]

TYCO Telecommunications Inc., pp. Vol. II-1367, 1451 [NAICS 334519, 33592M]

Tyco Telecommunications Ltd., p. II-1267 [NAICS 334290]

Tyco Valves and Controls, pp. Vol. II-980, Vol. III-1871 [NAICS 33291N, 423840]

TYK AMERICA Inc., pp. Vol. I-703, Vol. II-1463 [NAICS 32712N, 335991]

Tyldin Corp., p. III-1766 [NAICS 423130]

Tyler Meat Co., p. III-1946 [NAICS 424470]

Tyler Mountain Water Inc., p. I-646 [NAICS 326160]

Tyler Pipe Co., p. II-1009 [NAICS 332996]

Tyr Sport Inc., pp. Vol. III-1883, 1916 [NAICS 423910, 424320]

Tyrolit Wickman Inc., p. I-756 [NAICS 327910]

Tyson Foods Inc., pp. Vol. I-62, 97 [NAICS 31141M, 311615]

Tyson Fresh Meats Inc., p. I-102 [NAICS 31161N]

U-Line Corp., pp. Vol. II-1409, 1417 [NAICS 335222, 335228]

U-Pull-It, p. III-1770 [NAICS 423140]

U2 Technology, p. II-1357 [NAICS 334517]

UAP Holding Corp., p. I-529 [NAICS 325320]

UB Machine Inc., p. II-1473 [NAICS 336111]

UBE Machinery Inc., p. II-1051 [NAICS 333220]

UCB Films Inc., pp. Vol. I-510, 615 [NAICS 32522M, 326113]

Uchiyama America Inc., p. II-1725 [NAICS 339991]

UFP Technologies Inc., p. I-641 [NAICS 326150]

Ugine Stainless and Alloys Inc., pp. Vol. I-793, 845 [NAICS 33122M, 33151M]

Uinta Business Systems Inc., p. III-1801 [NAICS 423420]

UIS Inc., pp. Vol. I-52, 334, Vol. II-1512, 1551 [NAICS 311330, 32191M, 33632M, 336399]

Ulbrich Stainless Steels, pp. Vol. I-780, 837 [NAICS 33111M, 33149M]

Ulrich Chemical Inc., p. III-1971 [NAICS 424690]

Ultimate Electronics Inc., p. III-2054 [NAICS 443112]

Ultra-Cast Inc., p. I-788 [NAICS 331210]

Ultra Flex Packaging Corp., p. I-609 [NAICS 326112]

Ultra Palm Optical, p. III-1820 [NAICS 423490]

Ultra Panel Marine Inc., p. II-1594 [NAICS 336612]

Ultra-Poly Corp., p. I-589 [NAICS 325991]

Ultralife Batteries Inc., pp. Vol. II-1442, 1447, Vol. III-2007 [NAICS 335911, 335912, 424990]

Ultron Systems Inc., p. II-1056 [NAICS 333295]

UM Holdings Inc., p. II-1702 [NAICS 339920]

Umberger's Of Fontana Inc., p. III-2069 [NAICS 444210]

UMBRA TCH, pp. Vol. II-1627, 1662 [NAICS 337127, 337920]

UMI Racing, p. II-1599 [NAICS 336991]

UMI Tech Inc., p. III-1798 [NAICS 423410]

Umpqua Dairy Products Co., p. I-92 [NAICS 311520]

Unaka Company Inc., pp. Vol. II-1404, 1632 [NAICS 335221, 33712N]

Unarco Industries, p. II-939 [NAICS 33261M]

Unarco Material Handling Inc., p. II-1644 [NAICS 337215]

Uncle Bum's Gourmet Sauces, p. I-152 [NAICS 31194M]

UndercoverWear Inc., p. III-2228 [NAICS 454390]

Underwood Equipment Inc., p. III-1863 [NAICS 423820]

Uneeda Enterprizes Inc., p. I-756 [NAICS 327910]

Uni-Bond Brake Inc., p. II-1524 [NAICS 336340]

Uni-Form Components Co., pp. Vol. II-1491, 1584 [NAICS 336212, 336510]

Uni-Glide Manufacturing Co., p. I-348 [NAICS 321991]

Uni-Hydro Inc., p. II-1152 [NAICS 333518]

Unibilt Industries Inc., p. I-353 [NAICS 321992]

Uniboring Company Inc., pp. Vol. II-945, 1749 [NAICS 332710, 339999]

Unical Aviation Inc., p. III-1879 [NAICS 423860]

Unicep Packaging Inc., p. II-1682 [NAICS 339114]

UNICHEM Corp., p. I-480 [NAICS 325181]

UNICOR, pp. Vol. I-234, Vol. II-1644, 1650 [NAICS 31412M, 337215, 33721N]

UNIFAB International Inc., pp. Vol. II-1039, 1589 [NAICS 33313M, 336611]

Unifi Inc., pp. Vol. I-192, 198 [NAICS 31311M, 313210]

Unified Western Grocers Inc., pp. Vol. III-1925, 1929 [NAICS 424410, 424420]

Unifirst Corp., p. I-272 [NAICS 31522M]

Uniflex Inc., p. I-395 [NAICS 32222P]

Unifoil Corp., p. I-395 [NAICS 32222P]

Unifrax Corp., p. I-686 [NAICS 327113]

Unilux Inc., p. II-1277 [NAICS 334411]

Unimac Graphics, p. I-436 [NAICS 32312M]

Uninterruptible Power Products, pp. Vol. II-1442, 1447 [NAICS 335911, 335912]

Union Asphalt, pp. Vol. I-727, 732 [NAICS 327310, 327320]

Union Carbide Corp., pp. Vol. I-471, 488, 500 [NAICS 325120, 325188, 325211]

Union City Filament Corp., p. II-1277 [NAICS 334411]

Union City Mirror and Table Co., p. II-1657 [NAICS 337910]

Union Foundry Co., pp. Vol. I-845, Vol. II-923 [NAICS 33151M, 332420]

Union Metal Corp., pp. Vol. I-743, 811, Vol. II-1390 [NAICS 327390, 331316, 33512M]

Union Process Inc., p. I-580 [NAICS 325910]

Union Switch and Signal Inc., p. II-1267 [NAICS 334290]

Union Tank Car Co., p. II-1584 [NAICS 336510]

Union Technology Corp., p. II-1292 [NAICS 334414]

Union Wadding Company Inc., pp. Vol. I-208, 368, 415 [NAICS 313230, 32212M, 322299]

Unipac Inc., p. I-306 [NAICS 31699M]

Unipres Southeast USA Inc., p. II-1473 [NAICS 336111]

Unipres USA Inc., pp. Vol. I-879, Vol. II-1541 [NAICS 33211P, 336370]

Unipress Corp., p. II-1413 [NAICS 335224]

Uniqema, pp. Vol. I-458, 488 [NAICS 324191, 325188]

Unique Binders Inc., pp. Vol. III-1898, 1905 [NAICS 424110, 424130]

Unique Electronics Inc., p. II-1451 [NAICS 33592M]

Unique Fabricating Inc., pp. Vol. I-609, 771, Vol. II-1725 [NAICS 326112, 327993, 339991]

Unique Functional Products, p. II-1530 [NAICS 336350]

Unique Machine and Tool Co., p. II-1046 [NAICS 333210]

Unique Plastic Packaging L.L.C., p. I-646 [NAICS 326160]

Unique Tool and Mfg Inc., p. II-1541 [NAICS 336370]

Uniroyal Engineered Products, p. I-224 [NAICS 313320]

Uniroyal Technology Corp., p. I-224 [NAICS 313320]

UniSea Inc., p. I-110 [NAICS 31171M]

Uniseal, p. I-641 [NAICS 326150]

Unisource Midwest Inc., pp. Vol. III-1875, 1898 [NAICS 423850, 424110]

Unisource Worldwide Inc., pp. Vol. I-415, Vol. II-1212, Vol. III-1867, 1871, 1875, 1898, 1905 [NAICS 322299, 333993, 423830, 423840, 423850, 424110, 424130]

Unisys Corp., pp. Vol. II-1238, 1248, 1252 [NAICS 334111, 334113, 334119]

Unit Drop Forge Company Inc., p. I-872 [NAICS 33211N]

Unit Parts Co., pp. Vol. II-1437, 1512 [NAICS 335314, 33632M]

Unitech USA, p. III-1820 [NAICS 423490]

United Abrasives Inc., pp. Vol. I-665, 756, Vol. II-1046 [NAICS 326220, 327910, 333210]

United Air Specialists Inc., pp. Vol. II-1112, 1184 [NAICS 33341N, 333912]

United Aluminum Corp., p. I-816 [NAICS 33131N]

United American Video Corp., p. II-1381 [NAICS 334613]

United Audio Video Group Inc., p. II-1381 [NAICS 334613]

United Brick and Tile Co., p. I-691 [NAICS 327121]

United Building Centers, p. III-2065 [NAICS 444100]

United Capital Corp., p. II-1421 [NAICS 335311]

United Central Supply, p. III-1871 [NAICS 423840]

United Chemi-Con Inc., p. II-1292 [NAICS 334414]

United Corporate Furnishings Inc., p. III-1774 [NAICS 423210]

United Dairy Farmers Inc., pp. Vol. I-86, 92 [NAICS 31151N, 311520]

United Dairy Inc., pp. Vol. I-86, 165 [NAICS 31151N, 31211M]

United Dairymen of Arizona Inc., p. I-81 [NAICS 311514]

United Defense Industries Inc., pp. Vol. II-1005, 1327, 1572, 1603 [NAICS 332995, 334511, 336414, 336992]

United Dental Laboratories Inc., p. II-1682 [NAICS 339114]

United Design Corp., p. I-681 [NAICS 327112]

United Drug Service Inc., p. III-1913 [NAICS 424310]

United Elastic Corp. Stuart Div., p. I-203 [NAICS 31322M]

United Elchem Industries, p. I-703 [NAICS 32712N]

United Engines L.L.C., p. II-1173 [NAICS 333618]

United Furniture Industries, p. II-1616 [NAICS 337121]

United Gilsonite Laboratories Inc., p. I-554 [NAICS 325510]

United Hardware Distributing Co., pp. Vol. III-1794, 1843, 1863, 1883 [NAICS 423390, 423710, 423820, 423910]

United Health Care Services Inc., p. III-1813 [NAICS 423450]

United Industrial Corp., pp. Vol. I-631, Vol. II-1005, 1327, 1347, 1468 [NAICS 326130, 332995, 334511, 334515, 335999]

United Knitting L.P., p. I-213 [NAICS 31324M]

United Knitting Machine Co., p. II-1584 [NAICS 336510]

United Learning Inc., p. III-1995 [NAICS 424920]

United Lens Company Inc., pp. Vol. II-1082, 1687 [NAICS 333314, 339115]

United McGill Corp., pp. Vol. I-560, Vol. II-923, 1112, 1217 [NAICS 325520, 332420, 33341N, 333994]

United Meat Company Inc., pp. Vol. III-1936, 1946 [NAICS 424440, 424470]

United Natural Foods Inc., p. I-68 [NAICS 31142M]

United Pacific Pet L.L.C., p. III-2007 [NAICS 424990]

United Pipe and Steel Corp., p. III-1847 [NAICS 423720]

United Plastic Fabricating Inc., pp. Vol. I-500, 651 [NAICS 325211, 32619M]

United Plastics Group Inc., pp. Vol. I-626, Vol. II-1134 [NAICS 326122, 333514]

United Plastics Machinery L.L.C., p. II-1051 [NAICS 333220]

United Producers Inc., p. III-1962 [NAICS 424520]

United Refining and Smelting Co., p. I-825 [NAICS 331419]

United Retail Group Inc., p. III-2126 [NAICS 448120]

United Sales, p. III-1831 [NAICS 423610]

United Salt Corp., p. I-152 [NAICS 31194M]

United Shellfish Company Inc., p. I-110 [NAICS 31171M]

United Sleep Products Inc., pp. Vol. II-1621, 1657 [NAICS 337122, 337910]

United Southern Industries Inc., p. II-1028 [NAICS 333112]

United State Fire-Arms Mfg Inc., p. II-1001 [NAICS 332994]

United States Alumoweld Inc., p. I-816 [NAICS 33131N]

United States Antimony Corp., p. I-825 [NAICS 331419]

United States Box Corp., p. III-1905 [NAICS 424130]

U.S. Concrete Inc., p. I-743 [NAICS 327390]

United States Container Corp., p. III-1905 [NAICS 424130]

United States Electric Co., p. III-1855 [NAICS 423740]

U.S. Factory Outlets Inc., p. III-2171 [NAICS 452111]

U.S. Fitness Products, p. III-2150 [NAICS 451110]

U.S. Home Systems Inc., p. III-2037 [NAICS 442110]

U.S. Lock Corp., p. III-1843 [NAICS 423710]

United States Marine Repair Inc., p. II-1589 [NAICS 336611]

U.S. Music Corp., p. II-1731 [NAICS 339992]

United States Pipe and Foundry, pp. Vol. I-845, Vol. II-899, 980, 1009 [NAICS 33151M, 33231M, 33291N, 332996]

U.S. Precast Corp., p. I-743 [NAICS 327390]

U.S. Printing Supply Co., p. III-1898 [NAICS 424110]

U.S. Repeating Arms Company, p. II-1001 [NAICS 332994]

United States Steel Corp., p. I-780 [NAICS 33111M]

United States Strong Tool Co., pp. Vol. III-1867, 1871 [NAICS 423830, 423840]

United States Sugar Corp., p. I-44 [NAICS 31131N]

United States Surgical Corp, pp. Vol. II-939, 1671, 1676 [NAICS 33261M, 339112, 339113]

U.S. Tile, pp. Vol. I-691, 699 [NAICS 327121, 327123]

United Stationers Inc., pp. Vol. III-1774, 1801, 1901 [NAICS 423210, 423420, 424120]

United Subcontractors Inc., p. III-1790 [NAICS 423330]

United Supply Co., pp. Vol. II-1662, Vol. III-1778 [NAICS 337920, 423220]

United Technologies Corp., pp. Vol. II-1106, 1194, 1473, 1562 [NAICS 333415, 33392M, 336111, 336412]

United Titanium Inc., p. I-825 [NAICS 331419]

UnitedAuto Group Inc., p. III-2011 [NAICS 441110]

Univar USA, p. I-493 [NAICS 32519M]

Univar USA Inc., p. III-1971 [NAICS 424690]

Univenture Inc., p. I-641 [NAICS 326150]

Universal Alloy, pp. Vol. I-811, Vol. II-1580 [NAICS 331316, 336419]

Universal American Flowers, p. III-1998 [NAICS 424930]

Universal Automotive Industries, p. III-1762 [NAICS 423120]

Universal Avionics Systems Corp., p. II-1327 [NAICS 334511]

Universal Bearings Inc., pp. Vol. I-358, 845, Vol. II-958, 988, 1168 [NAICS 321999, 33151M, 332722, 332991, 333613]

Universal Blanchers L.L.C., p. I-137 [NAICS 31191M]

Universal Clay Products, pp. Vol. I-686, 703, 776 [NAICS 327113, 32712N, 327999]

Universal Compression Inc., p. II-945 [NAICS 332710]

Universal Cooperative Inc., pp. Vol. III-1762, 1843, 1958, 1971 [NAICS 423120, 423710, 424510, 424690]

Universal Corp., pp. Vol. I-595, Vol. III-1782, 1939, 1954, 1965, 2007 [NAICS 32599N, 423310, 424450, 424490, 424590, 424990]

Universal Display Corp., p. II-1248 [NAICS 334113]

Universal Electronics Inc., p. II-1272 [NAICS 334310]

Universal Fiber Systems L.L.C., pp. Vol. I-192, 218 [NAICS 31311M, 31331M]

Universal Flow Monitors Inc., p. II-1342 [NAICS 334514]

Universal Forest Products Inc., p. I-312 [NAICS 32111M]

Universal Furniture House Inc., pp. Vol. III-2037, 2050 [NAICS 442110, 443111]

Universal Furniture Intern. Inc., pp. Vol. II-1616, 1621 [NAICS 337121, 337122]

Universal Lighting Technologies, p. II-1421 [NAICS 335311]

Universal Molding Co, pp. Vol. I-811, Vol. II-964 [NAICS 331316, 33281M]

Universal Photonics Inc., pp. Vol. I-756, Vol. II-1124 [NAICS 327910, 333512]

Universal Refractories Inc., p. I-703 [NAICS 32712N]

Universal Scrap Metal Inc., p. I-807 [NAICS 331314]

Universal Semiconductor Inc., p. II-1297 [NAICS 334415]

Universal Sewing Machine Inc., p. I-267 [NAICS 31521M]

Universal Stainless & Alloy, p. I-788 [NAICS 331210]

Universal Strap Inc., p. I-203 [NAICS 31322M]

Universal Superabrasives Inc., pp. Vol. I-756, Vol. II-892, 1140 [NAICS 327910, 33221P, 333515]

Universal Uniseal Inc., p. II-974 [NAICS 332913]

Universal Urethane Inc., p. II-1119 [NAICS 333511]

Universal Veneer Mill Corp., p. I-324 [NAICS 32121N]

University Automotive Group, p. III-1758 [NAICS 423110]

University Book Store Inc., pp. Vol. III-2162, 2177 [NAICS 451211, 452910]

University Cooperative Society Inc., pp. Vol. III-2162, 2177 [NAICS 451211, 452910]

Uniway Of Augusta Inc., p. III-2180 [NAICS 452990]

Uniweld Products Inc., p. II-1421 [NAICS 335311]

Unkefer Homer Farm Equipment, p. III-2021 [NAICS 441221]

Unocal Corp., pp. Vol. I-443, Vol. II-1463 [NAICS 324110, 335991]

UNOVA Inc., pp. Vol. II-1092, 1229 [NAICS 33331N, 33399P]

Unverferth Manufacturing Inc., p. II-1023 [NAICS 333111]

Upco Inc., p. II-1168 [NAICS 333613]

UPF Corp., p. I-771 [NAICS 327993]

UPS Supply Chain Soloutions, p. III-1879 [NAICS 423860]

Urban Outfitters Inc., pp. Vol. III-2123, 2126, 2132 [NAICS 448110, 448120, 448140]

Uretech International Inc., p. II-1524 [NAICS 336340]

Urethane Contractors Supply, p. III-1790 [NAICS 423330]

U.R.M. Stores Inc., p. III-1925 [NAICS 424410]

Urwiler Oil and Fertilizer Inc., p. III-2116 [NAICS 447110]

Urys Corp., p. I-133 [NAICS 311830]

US Agri-Chemicals Corp., p. I-520 [NAICS 325312]

US Airways Group Inc., p. III-1879 [NAICS 423860]

US Airweld, p. I-471 [NAICS 325120]

US Auto Parts Network Inc., p. III-2030 [NAICS 441310]

US Axle Inc., p. II-1530 [NAICS 336350]

US Business Interiors Inc., p. III-1774 [NAICS 423210]

US Button Corp., p. II-1735 [NAICS 339993]

US Diamond Wheel, pp. Vol. I-756, Vol. II-1124 [NAICS 327910, 333512]

US Distilled Products, p. I-181 [NAICS 312140]

US Dyeing and Finishing Inc., p. I-218 [NAICS 31331M]

US Elastomer, p. I-505 [NAICS 325212]

US Fence, p. I-312 [NAICS 32111M]

US Fence Inc., p. I-636 [NAICS 326140]

US Fiberglass Inc., p. III-1863 [NAICS 423820]

US Filter Corp., pp. Vol. III-1847, 1971 [NAICS 423720, 424690]

US. Filter/Johnson Screen, pp. Vol. II-1039, 1229 [NAICS 33313M, 33399P]

US. Filter Wheelabrator Corp., pp. Vol. II-1061, 1092 [NAICS 33329N, 33331N]

US FoodService Inc. Carolina Div., p. III-1925 [NAICS 424410]

US Games Systems Inc., p. II-1708 [NAICS 33993M]

US Ink, p. I-580 [NAICS 325910]

US Leisure, p. II-1632 [NAICS 33712N]

US Magnesium L.L.C., p. I-825 [NAICS 331419]

US Manufacturing Corp., pp. Vol. I-837, 872 [NAICS 33149M, 33211N]

US Mills Inc., p. I-36 [NAICS 311230]

US Molding Machinery Co., p. II-1051 [NAICS 333220]

US Natural Resources Hemco Div., p. II-1046 [NAICS 333210]

US Oil and Refining Co., pp. Vol. I-443, 448 [NAICS 324110, 324121]

US Oil Company Inc., pp. Vol. III-1762, 1851, 1979, 2116 [NAICS 423120, 423730, 424720, 447110]

US Optical Disc, p. II-1381 [NAICS 334613]

US Pole, p. II-1390 [NAICS 33512M]

US Poly Enterprises Inc., p. I-505 [NAICS 325212]

US Reclamation Bureau, p. III-1847 [NAICS 423720]

US Ring, p. I-374 [NAICS 322130]

US Safety, p. II-1687 [NAICS 339115]

US Samica Inc., p. I-776 [NAICS 327999]

US Tanker and Fire Apparatus Inc., p. II-1482 [NAICS 336120]

US Textile Corp., pp. Vol. I-388, 609 [NAICS 32222N, 326112]

US Tool Grinding Inc., p. II-1207 [NAICS 333991]

US Tsubaki Inc., pp. Vol. II-1168, 1530 [NAICS 333613, 336350]

US Underwater Services Inc., p. III-2150 [NAICS 451110]

US Union Tool, p. II-1207 [NAICS 333991]

USA Dubs, p. II-1381 [NAICS 334613]

Numbers following p. or pp. are page references. Roman numerals indicate volume numbers. Bracketed items indicate industries. Page references are to the starting pages of company tables.

2431

Company Index

USA Instruments Inc., p. II-1302 [NAICS 334416]

USA Knit Inc., p. I-256 [NAICS 31511M]

USANA Health Sciences Inc., pp. Vol. I-68, 534, 575 [NAICS 31142M, 325411, 325620]

USEC Inc., p. I-475 [NAICS 32513M]

USFilter Envirex Products, p. II-1092 [NAICS 33331N]

USG Corp., pp. Vol. I-626, 752, 771 [NAICS 326122, 327420, 327993]

Ushio America Inc., pp. Vol. II-939, 1033, 1386, 1390, 1468 [NAICS 33261M, 333120, 335110, 33512M, 335999]

USI Inc., pp. Vol. III-1798, 1801 [NAICS 423410, 423420]

USN Corp., p. III-2144 [NAICS 448310]

USPAR Enterprises Inc., p. II-1386 [NAICS 335110]

USR Industries Inc., p. II-1362 [NAICS 334518]

USR Optonix Inc., pp. Vol. I-475, 488, 595 [NAICS 32513M, 325188, 32599N]

USS-POSCO Industries, pp. Vol. I-780, 793, Vol. II-908 [NAICS 33111M, 33122M, 33232M]

UST Inc., pp. Vol. I-177, 185, 188 [NAICS 312130, 312210, 31222M]

Utah Metal Works Inc., p. I-807 [NAICS 331314]

Utah Paperbox Company Inc., p. I-395 [NAICS 32222P]

UTEX Industries Inc., pp. Vol. I-670, Vol. II-1725 [NAICS 32629M, 339991]

UTI Corp., p. I-837 [NAICS 33149M]

Utica Cutlery Co., p. II-886 [NAICS 33221N]

Utilimaster Corp., pp. Vol. II-1478, 1486 [NAICS 336112, 336211]

Utility Manufacturing, p. III-1867 [NAICS 423830]

Utility Trailers Of Indianapolis Inc., p. III-1758 [NAICS 423110]

Utobia Systems Inc., p. II-1248 [NAICS 334113]

UTStarcom Inc., pp. Vol. II-1252, 1267 [NAICS 334119, 334290]

Uttermost Company Inc., pp. Vol. I-722, Vol. II-1362 [NAICS 327215, 334518]

UV Process Supply Inc., p. III-1798 [NAICS 423410]

UVP Inc., pp. Vol. II-1386, 1666 [NAICS 335110, 339111]

V and E Kohnstamm Inc., p. I-147 [NAICS 311930]

V and F Transformers Corp., pp. Vol. II-1302, 1421 [NAICS 334416, 335311]

V-Line Corporation L.L.C., pp. Vol. III-1786, 1790 [NAICS 423320, 423330]

V. Santoni and Co., p. III-1987 [NAICS 424820]

V Sattui Winery, pp. Vol. I-177, Vol. III-2094, 2097 [NAICS 312130, 445299, 445310]

V-T Industries Inc., pp. Vol. II-1611, 1644 [NAICS 337110, 337215]

Vac-Con Inc., p. II-1152 [NAICS 333518]

Vac Magnetics Corp., pp. Vol. I-686, 767 [NAICS 327113, 327992]

Vac Pac Manufacturing Inc., p. I-244 [NAICS 314991]

Vacationland Vendors Inc., p. III-2215 [NAICS 454210]

Valassis Communications Inc., p. I-420 [NAICS 32311M]

Valco Cincinnati Inc., pp. Vol. II-1077, 1189, 1212, 1740 [NAICS 333313, 333913, 333993, 339994]

Valco/Valley Tool and Die Inc., p. II-1541 [NAICS 336370]

Valcom Inc., pp. Vol. II-1262, 1272 [NAICS 334220, 334310]

Valeant Pharmaceuticals Intl., p. I-539 [NAICS 325412]

Valence Technology Inc., p. II-1442 [NAICS 335911]

Valero Energy Corp., pp. Vol. I-443, Vol. III-2218 [NAICS 324110, 454311]

Valhi Inc., pp. Vol. I-475, Vol. II-1627 [NAICS 32513M, 337127]

Valiant Yachts, p. II-1589 [NAICS 336611]

Valk Industries Inc., p. I-609 [NAICS 326112]

Valk Manufacturing Co., pp. Vol. II-1028, 1140 [NAICS 333112, 333515]

Vallot Food Service Inc., p. III-1936 [NAICS 424440]

Valley Automotive L.L.C., pp. Vol. II-1014, 1500 [NAICS 33299N, 336214]

Valley Blox Inc, pp. Vol. I-329, 334, 737, 743 [NAICS 32121P, 32191M, 32733M, 327390]

Valley Cabinet Inc., p. II-1611 [NAICS 337110]

Valley Caliche Products Inc., p. III-1786 [NAICS 423320]

Valley Crest Tree Co., p. III-1998 [NAICS 424930]

Valley Dairy, p. III-2094 [NAICS 445299]

Valley Detroit Diesel Allison, pp. Vol. II-1157, 1179 [NAICS 333611, 333911]

Valley Fertilizer and Chemical Inc., pp. Vol. I-529, 748 [NAICS 325320, 327410]

Valley Forge Brewing L.P., p. I-172 [NAICS 312120]

Valley Fresh Inc., p. I-97 [NAICS 311615]

Valley Joist Inc., p. II-899 [NAICS 33231M]

Valley Knit Inc., p. I-256 [NAICS 31511M]

Valley Manufactured Housing Inc., p. I-348 [NAICS 321991]

Valley Mills Inc., p. I-256 [NAICS 31511M]

Valley National Gases Inc., pp. Vol. I-471, Vol. III-1971, 1979 [NAICS 325120, 424690, 424720]

Valley Oil Division, p. III-2218 [NAICS 454311]

Valley Processing, p. I-505 [NAICS 325212]

Valley Products Co., p. I-566 [NAICS 32561M]

Valley Proteins Inc., p. I-102 [NAICS 31161N]

Valley Queen Cheese Factory Inc., p. I-81 [NAICS 311514]

Valley Recyclers, p. I-807 [NAICS 331314]

Valley Rubber Mixing Inc., p. I-505 [NAICS 325212]

Valley Truck Parts Inc., pp. Vol. II-1173, 1427 [NAICS 333618, 335312]

Valley Vending Service Inc., p. III-2001 [NAICS 424940]

Valley Welders Supply Inc., p. III-1867 [NAICS 423830]

Valley Wholesale Supply Corp., p. III-1778 [NAICS 423220]

Valleycast Inc., p. I-830 [NAICS 33142M]

Vallorbs Jewel Co., p. II-952 [NAICS 332721]

Valmont Industries Inc., pp. Vol. I-780, Vol. II-899, 1014, 1023, 1421 [NAICS 33111M, 33231M, 33299N, 333111, 335311]

Valspar Corp., pp. Vol. I-500, 554 [NAICS 325211, 325510]

Valtex L.L.C., p. I-285 [NAICS 31529M]

Value City Furniture Div., pp. Vol. III-1774, 2037 [NAICS 423210, 442110]

Value Frozen Foods Inc., p. I-62 [NAICS 31141M]

Value Line Textiles Inc., p. I-256 [NAICS 31511M]

Valuecomm Corp., p. III-1809 [NAICS 423440]

ValueVision Media Inc., p. III-2211 [NAICS 454113]

Valvoline, p. I-458 [NAICS 324191]

VAM PTS Co., p. II-958 [NAICS 332722]

Vamistor Corp., p. II-1297 [NAICS 334415]

Van Bebber Brothers Inc., p. III-1770 [NAICS 423140]

Van Bortel Aircraft Inc., p. III-1879 [NAICS 423860]

Van Boxtel Ford Inc., pp. Vol. III-2018, 2027 [NAICS 441210, 441229]

Van Diest Supply Co., pp. Vol. I-524, 529 [NAICS 325314, 325320]

Van Hoecks Shoes, p. III-2141 [NAICS 448210]

Van Kleeck's Tire Inc., pp. Vol. III-1766, 2034 [NAICS 423130, 441320]

Van Roy Coffee Co., p. I-40 [NAICS 311313]

Van's Electrical Systems, p. III-1770 [NAICS 423140]

Van Solkema Produce Inc., p. III-1950 [NAICS 424480]

Van Son Holland Ink Corporation, p. I-580 [NAICS 325910]

VANCO USA L.L.C., p. II-1491 [NAICS 336212]

Vancouver Iron and Steel Inc., p. I-845 [NAICS 33151M]

Vandervoort Dairy Food Co., pp. Vol. I-92, 165 [NAICS 311520, 31211M]

Vanex Inc., p. I-453 [NAICS 324122]

Vanguard International Inc., p. III-1950 [NAICS 424480]

Vanguard Legato A California, pp. Vol. III-1774, 1778 [NAICS 423210, 423220]

Vanguard L.L.C., p. II-1500 [NAICS 336214]

Vanguard Piping Systems, p. II-974 [NAICS 332913]

Vanson Leathers Inc., p. I-285 [NAICS 31529M]

Vantage Mobility International, p. II-1486 [NAICS 336211]

Varbros Corp., p. II-1541 [NAICS 336370]

Varco International Inc., p. II-1039 [NAICS 33313M]

Varel International Inc., pp. Vol. II-1039, 1140 [NAICS 33313M, 333515]

Varga Enterprises Inc., p. III-1766 [NAICS 423130]

Vari-Tronics Company Inc., p. II-1451 [NAICS 33592M]

Vari-Wall Tube Specialists, p. II-1599 [NAICS 336991]

Varian Inc., pp. Vol. II-1061, 1352 [NAICS 33329N, 334516]

Varian Medical Systems Inc., pp. Vol. II-1322, 1357 [NAICS 334510, 334517]

Varian Oncology Systems, p. II-1671 [NAICS 339112]

Varian Semiconductor Equipment, p. II-1317 [NAICS 334419]

Varian Vacuum Technologies, p. II-1397 [NAICS 33521M]

Variety Foods Inc., p. I-137 [NAICS 31191M]

Variflex Inc., p. II-1702 [NAICS 339920]

Varsity Brands Inc., p. II-1702 [NAICS 339920]

Varsity Spirit Corp., p. I-290 [NAICS 31599M]

Numbers following p. or pp. are page references. Roman numerals indicate volume numbers. Bracketed items indicate industries. Page references are to the starting pages of company tables.

2432

Varsity Spirit Fashions & Supplies, p. I-290 [NAICS 31599M]

Vartan Pedian and Sons, p. III-2041 [NAICS 442210]

Vaughan and Sons Inc., pp. Vol. III-1782, 1786, 2065 [NAICS 423310, 423320, 444100]

Vaughan Furniture Company Inc., p. II-1621 [NAICS 337122]

Vaughn Manufacturing, p. II-1417 [NAICS 335228]

Vaupell Precision Machining, pp. Vol. II-945, 1134 [NAICS 332710, 333514]

VCI Capital Inc., p. II-1229 [NAICS 33399P]

Veada Industries Inc., pp. Vol. I-234, 239, Vol. II-1536, 1594 [NAICS 31412M, 31491M, 336360, 336612]

VEC Technology Inc., p. I-510 [NAICS 32522M]

Vector Marketing Corp., p. III-1778 [NAICS 423220]

Vector Technology Corp., p, III-1805 [NAICS 423430]

Vectorply Corp., p. I-218 [NAICS 31331M]

Veeco Instruments Inc., pp. Vol. II-1061, 1347 [NAICS 33329N, 334515]

Veeco Slider MTI Group, p. I-756 [NAICS 327910]

Vegas Fastener Manufacturing, p. III-1871 [NAICS 423840]

Vegas Golf Inc., p. III-2150 [NAICS 451110]

Vel Tye L.L.C., pp. Vol. I-203, Vol. II-1735 [NAICS 31322M, 339993]

Veldheer Tulip Garden Inc., p. III-2072 [NAICS 444220]

Vellano Brothers Inc., p. III-1871 [NAICS 423840]

Velocity Graphics, p. II-1077 [NAICS 333313]

Velsicol Chemical Corp., p. I-493 [NAICS 32519M]

Veltec Inc., p. I-505 [NAICS 325212]

Veltek Associates Inc., pp. Vol. I-493, 534 [NAICS 32519M, 325411]

Velux-America Inc., p. II-908 [NAICS 33232M]

VELVAC Inc., p. II-1524 [NAICS 336340]

Vend-A-Snack Of Clarksdale Inc., p. III-2215 [NAICS 454210]

Vend-Omack Sales Inc., p. III-2215 [NAICS 454210]

Vendome Copper & Brass Works, p. II-918 [NAICS 332410]

Vendura Industries Inc., p. I-762 [NAICS 327991]

Venetian Marble Inc., p. I-762 [NAICS 327991]

Ventamatic Ltd., p. II-1157 [NAICS 333611]

Ventana Distributing Company, p. III-1855 [NAICS 423740]

Ventana Medical Systems Inc., pp. Vol. II-1352, 1671 [NAICS 334516, 339112]

Ventura Coastal Corp., p. I-152 [NAICS 31194M]

Venture Tape Corp., pp. Vol. I-203, 224 [NAICS 31322M, 313320]

Venus Trimming and Binding Co., p. I-203 [NAICS 31322M]

Ver-Mac Industries Inc., p. I-863 [NAICS 332114]

Verdin Company Inc., pp. Vol. II-1362, 1731 [NAICS 334518, 339992]

VerHalen Inc., p. III-1782 [NAICS 423310]

VeriFone Inc., pp. Vol. II-1077, 1457 [NAICS 333313, 33593M]

Vermeer Manufacturing Inc., pp. Vol. II-1023, 1033 [NAICS 333111, 333120]

Vermont Composites Inc., p. I-510 [NAICS 32522M]

Vermont Country Store, pp. Vol. III-2037, 2047 [NAICS 442110, 442299]

Vermont Pure Holdings Ltd., p. III-1954 [NAICS 424490]

Vermont Teddy Bear Company, p. II-1708 [NAICS 33993M]

Vern Dale Products Inc., p. I-81 [NAICS 311514]

Veronica Foods Co., pp. Vol. III-1950, 1954 [NAICS 424480, 424490]

Versa Products Company Inc., p. II-1222 [NAICS 33399N]

Versatech Industries Inc., p. II-1277 [NAICS 334411]

Vertical Health Solutions Inc., p. III-2100 [NAICS 446110]

Very Special Chocolats Inc., p. I-52 [NAICS 311330]

Vesco Oil Corp., p. III-1979 [NAICS 424720]

Vestil Manufacturing Corp., p. II-928 [NAICS 33243M]

Vesuvius Hi-Tech Ceramics, p. I-686 [NAICS 327113]

Vesuvius McDanel Co., pp. Vol. I-686, Vol. II-1292 [NAICS 327113, 334414]

Vesuvius Monofrax Inc., p. I-703 [NAICS 32712N]

Vet Pharm Inc., p. III-1820 [NAICS 423490]

Vetline Inc., p. III-2100 [NAICS 446110]

Vetter Equipment Co., p. III-1863 [NAICS 423820]

V.F. Corp., pp. Vol. I-262, 272, 290 [NAICS 31519M, 31522M, 31599M]

VF Grace Inc., p. III-1883 [NAICS 423910]

V.H.. Associates Inc., pp. Vol. III-1958, 1991 [NAICS 424510, 424910]

Viam Manufacturing Inc., p. I-229 [NAICS 314110]

Viansa Winery and Tuscan Club, p. I-177 [NAICS 312130]

ViaSat Inc., pp. Vol. II-1262, 1267 [NAICS 334220, 334290]

VIASYS Healthcare Inc., pp. Vol. II-1671, Vol. III-1813 [NAICS 339112, 423450]

Viasystems Group Inc., p. II-1282 [NAICS 334412]

Viatech Publishing Solutions Inc., p. I-436 [NAICS 32312M]

Vibro/Dynamics Corp., p. II-1519 [NAICS 336330]

Vic Trenco Inc., p. III-1809 [NAICS 423440]

Vicam L.P., p. I-544 [NAICS 325413]

Vicente Foods Inc., p. III-2097 [NAICS 445310]

Vicor Corp., p. II-1468 [NAICS 335999]

Victaulic Co., pp. Vol. I-780, 857, Vol. II-980, 1009 [NAICS 33111M, 33152P, 33291N, 332996]

Victor Envelope Manufacturing, p. I-403 [NAICS 32223M]

Victor Insulators Inc., p. I-686 [NAICS 327113]

Victor's Settings, p. II-1696 [NAICS 33991M]

Victoria's Secret Stores Inc., p. III-2135 [NAICS 448150]

Victorian Homes, p. I-348 [NAICS 321991]

Victory Brewing Company Inc., p. I-172 [NAICS 312120]

Victory Plastics Intl, p. I-631 [NAICS 326130]

Victory White Metal Co., p. I-825 [NAICS 331419]

Victron Inc., p. II-1282 [NAICS 334412]

Vicuron Pharmaceuticals Inc., p. I-549 [NAICS 325414]

Vidalia Naval Stores Co., pp. Vol. III-1782, 2065 [NAICS 423310, 444100]

Video Display Corp., p. II-1277 [NAICS 334411]

Video-Matic USA Inc., pp. Vol. II-1376, 1381 [NAICS 334612, 334613]

Videotek Inc., pp. Vol. II-1272, 1432 [NAICS 334310, 335313]

Vie de France Yamazaki Inc., pp. Vol. I-62, 116 [NAICS 31141M, 31181M]

Vie-Del Corp., p. I-177 [NAICS 312130]

ViewSonic Corp., p. II-1252 [NAICS 334119]

Vigobyte International Corp., p. II-1381 [NAICS 334613]

Viking Acoustical Corp., pp. Vol. I-771, Vol. II-1243 [NAICS 327993, 334112]

Viking Aluminum Products Inc., p. II-1632 [NAICS 33712N]

Viking Automatic Sprinkler Co., p. II-1229 [NAICS 33399P]

Viking Cabinetry Group, pp. Vol. II-1611, 1632 [NAICS 337110, 33712N]

Viking Drill and Tool Inc., p. II-1207 [NAICS 333991]

Viking Electronics Inc., p. II-1307 [NAICS 334417]

Viking Engineering Company Inc., p. II-1157 [NAICS 333611]

Viking Explosives and Supply Inc., p. I-585 [NAICS 325920]

Viking Industrial Corp., p. III-1770 [NAICS 423140]

Viking Office Products Inc., p. III-1901 [NAICS 424120]

Viking Range Corp., pp. Vol. II-1404, 1417 [NAICS 335221, 335228]

Viking Sink Company L.L.C., p. I-677 [NAICS 327111]

Viking Technologies Ltd., p. II-1292 [NAICS 334414]

Viking Yacht Co., p. II-1594 [NAICS 336612]

Villa Furniture Manufacturing Inc., p. II-1536 [NAICS 336360]

Village Green Inc., pp. Vol. III-1998, 2183 [NAICS 424930, 453110]

Village Super Market Inc., p. III-2097 [NAICS 445310]

Villeroy and Boch USA Inc., p. III-2047 [NAICS 442299]

Vineland Syrup Inc., p. I-147 [NAICS 311930]

Vintage Air Inc., p. II-1546 [NAICS 336391]

Vintage Petroleum Inc., p. I-443 [NAICS 324110]

Vintage Sales Stables Inc., p. III-1962 [NAICS 424520]

Vintwood International Ltd., p. III-1987 [NAICS 424820]

Vinyl Building Products Inc., pp. Vol. I-334, 651 [NAICS 32191M, 32619M]

Vinylex Corp., p. I-621 [NAICS 326121]

VinylSource, p. I-621 [NAICS 326121]

Vinylume Products Inc., p. I-709 [NAICS 327211]

VIP Boats, pp. Vol. II-1500, 1594 [NAICS 336214, 336612]

VIP Foodservice, pp. Vol. III-1929, 1950 [NAICS 424420, 424480]

Virco Manufacturing Corp., pp. Vol. II-1627, 1650 [NAICS 337127, 33721N]

Virgin Records, p. II-1376 [NAICS 334612]

Virginia Dare Extract Inc., p. I-152 [NAICS 31194M]

Virginia Glass Products Corp., p. I-713 [NAICS 327212]

Virginia Homes Mfg Corp., p. I-353 [NAICS 321992]

Virginia Industries Inc., p. II-988 [NAICS 332991]

Virginia Marble Manufacturers Inc., p. I-762 [NAICS 327991]

Virginia Metalcrafters Inc., p. I-830 [NAICS 33142M]

Virginia Mirror Company Inc., p. I-722 [NAICS 327215]

Virginia Transformer Corp., pp. Vol. II-1302, 1421 [NAICS 334416, 335311]

Virginia Vermiculite Ltd., p. I-767 [NAICS 327992]

Visalia Sales Yard Inc., p. III-1962 [NAICS 424520]

VISCO Inc., p. I-788 [NAICS 331210]

Vishay Dale Electronics Inc., pp. Vol. II-1297, 1337, 1432 [NAICS 334415, 334513, 335313]

Vishay Intertechnology Inc., pp. Vol. II-1292, 1302, 1307, 1367 [NAICS 334414, 334416, 334417, 334519]

Vision's Edge Inc., p. II-1376 [NAICS 334612]

Vision Sciences Research Corp., p. III-1817 [NAICS 423460]

Vision, Solutions, Impact L.L.C., p. III-1894 [NAICS 423940]

Visionaire Corp., p. II-1557 [NAICS 336411]

Visionweb L.P., p. III-1817 [NAICS 423460]

Visitor Information Center, p. III-2190 [NAICS 453220]

Viskase Companies Inc., pp. Vol. I-379, 615, Vol. II-886 [NAICS 32221M, 326113, 33122N]

Visoy Food Inc., p. I-31 [NAICS 31122N]

Vista Fibers, p. III-1890 [NAICS 423930]

Vista Ford, p. III-2030 [NAICS 441310]

Vista Metals Inc., p. I-807 [NAICS 331314]

Vista Oil Co., p. III-1766 [NAICS 423130]

Vista Paint Corp., p. I-554 [NAICS 325510]

Visteon Corp., p. III-1762 [NAICS 423120]

Visual Sound Inc., pp. Vol. III-1835, 2168 [NAICS 423620, 451220]

VISX Inc., p. II-1322 [NAICS 334510]

Vita Craft Corp., p. II-886 [NAICS 33221N]

Vita Food Products Inc., p. I-110 [NAICS 31171M]

Vitacost Holdings Inc., p. III-2208 [NAICS 453998]

Vitafom Inc., p. I-198 [NAICS 313210]

Vital Signs Inc., pp. Vol. II-1671, 1676 [NAICS 339112, 339113]

Vitality Food Service Inc., p. II-1189 [NAICS 333913]

Vitasoy USA Inc., p. I-31 [NAICS 31122N]

Vitatech International Inc., p. I-534 [NAICS 325411]

Vitesse Semiconductor Corp., p. II-1342 [NAICS 334514]

Vitronic/Four Seasons, pp. Vol. I-285, 420 [NAICS 31529M, 32311M]

Vitta Corp., p. I-203 [NAICS 31322M]

Viva Foam Products, p. I-636 [NAICS 326140]

VIVA Life Science Inc., p. III-1909 [NAICS 424210]

Viziflex Seels Inc., p. II-1725 [NAICS 339991]

VJ Mattson Co., p. I-703 [NAICS 32712N]

VLP Holding Co., p. III-1859 [NAICS 423810]

VLSIP Technologies Inc., p. II-1312 [NAICS 334418]

VMI Americas Inc., p. II-1051 [NAICS 333220]

VMV Paducahbilt, p. II-1173 [NAICS 333618]

Vocollect Inc., p. II-1238 [NAICS 334111]

Voertman's, pp. Vol. III-2162, 2190 [NAICS 451211, 453220]

Vogelsang USA, p. II-1179 [NAICS 333911]

Vogler Motor Company Inc., p. III-2030 [NAICS 441310]

Voice of God Recordings Inc., p. II-1376 [NAICS 334612]

Voith Fabrics, p. I-208 [NAICS 313230]

Voith Fabrics Inc., p. I-208 [NAICS 313230]

Voith Paper Inc., p. II-1061 [NAICS 33329N]

Voith Siemens Hydro Power, pp. Vol. II-1092, 1157, 1222 [NAICS 33331N, 333611, 33399N]

Volckening Inc., p. II-1740 [NAICS 339994]

Volex Inc., pp. Vol. II-1307, 1317 [NAICS 334417, 334419]

Vollrath Company L.L.C., p. II-886 [NAICS 33221N]

Volt Information Sciences Inc., p. II-1061 [NAICS 33329N]

Voltek L.L.C., p. I-636 [NAICS 326140]

Voltronics Corp., p. II-1292 [NAICS 334414]

Voltronics Inc., p. II-1297 [NAICS 334415]

Voluntary Purchasing Group Inc., pp. Vol. I-524, 529 [NAICS 325314, 325320]

Von Hoffmann Corp., p. I-420 [NAICS 32311M]

Von Maur Inc., p. III-2171 [NAICS 452111]

VonHoffmann Corp., p. I-436 [NAICS 32312M]

Voorwood Co., p. II-1046 [NAICS 333210]

Voss Industries Inc., p. II-958 [NAICS 332722]

Voss Steel, pp. Vol. I-780, Vol. II-908, 945, 964, Vol. III-1824 [NAICS 33111M, 33232M, 332710, 33281M, 423510]

Vox Medica Inc., p. II-1536 [NAICS 336360]

Voyager Inc., p. II-1536 [NAICS 336360]

VPI L.L.C., p. II-1468 [NAICS 335999]

VPI Mirrex Corp., p. I-615 [NAICS 326113]

VSM Abrasives Corp., p. I-756 [NAICS 327910]

VT Inc., pp. Vol. III-2011, 2024 [NAICS 441110, 441222]

Vtech Innovation L.P., p. III-1835 [NAICS 423620]

VU Media Duplication Inc., pp. Vol. II-1376, 1381 [NAICS 334612, 334613]

Vulcan Electric Co., p. I-703 [NAICS 32712N]

Vulcan Engineering Co., p. II-1119 [NAICS 333511]

Vulcan Information Packaging Inc., p. I-403 [NAICS 32223M]

Vulcan Machinery Corp., p. II-1051 [NAICS 333220]

Vulcan Materials Co., pp. Vol. I-448, 480 [NAICS 324121, 325181]

Vutec Corp., p. II-1087 [NAICS 333315]

VWR Scientific Products Corp., pp. Vol. III-1798, 1820 [NAICS 423410, 423490]

VyTech Industries Inc., p. I-224 [NAICS 313320]

W-D Bryant and Son Inc., p. III-2050 [NAICS 443111]

W-Industries Inc., pp. Vol. II-1222, 1432 [NAICS 33399N, 335313]

W Kost Manufacturing Co., pp. Vol. I-329, 353 [NAICS 32121P, 321992]

W Silver Investments & Holding, p. I-807 [NAICS 331314]

W Terr of The Salvation Army, p. III-2194 [NAICS 453310]

W.A. Roosevelt Co., pp. Vol. III-1847, 1851, 1855 [NAICS 423720, 423730, 423740]

W.A. Wilson INC., p. III-1794 [NAICS 423390]

Wabash Alloys L.L.C., pp. Vol. I-807, 837, 857 [NAICS 331314, 33149M, 33152P]

Wabash Asphalt Company Inc., p. I-453 [NAICS 324122]

Wabash MPI, pp. Vol. II-1051, 1129, 1666 [NAICS 333220, 333513, 339111]

Wabash National Corp., pp. Vol. II-1491, 1551 [NAICS 336212, 336399]

Wabash National Trailer Centers, p. III-1875 [NAICS 423850]

Wabash Valley Services Co., p. III-2208 [NAICS 453998]

Wabash Wood Products, p. II-1491 [NAICS 336212]

Wacker Chemical Corp., p. III-1971 [NAICS 424120]

Wacker Corp., pp. Vol. II-1033, 1061, 1179, 1207, 1427 [NAICS 333120, 33329N, 333911, 333991, 335312]

Wacker Silicones Corp., pp. Vol. I-475, 500, 505, 554, 560 [NAICS 32513M, 325211, 325212, 325510, 325520]

Waco Meat Service Inc., p. III-1946 [NAICS 424470]

Wadena Timber Roots, p. I-329 [NAICS 32121P]

Wades Dairy Inc., p. III-1933 [NAICS 424430]

Wafer Process Systems Inc., p. II-1056 [NAICS 333295]

Wafertech L.L.C., p. II-1287 [NAICS 334413]

Wagner Knitting Inc., p. I-213 [NAICS 31324M]

Wagner Spray Tech, p. II-1184 [NAICS 333912]

Wagner Vineyards & Brewing Co., pp. Vol. I-172, 177 [NAICS 312120, 312130]

Wahl Clipper Corp., pp. Vol. II-886, 892, 1207, 1397, 1468 [NAICS 33221N, 33221P, 333991, 33521M, 335999]

Wahl Refractories Inc., p. I-703 [NAICS 32712N]

Wahltek Inc., p. III-1809 [NAICS 423440]

Wal-Mart Stores Inc., pp. Vol. III-2076, 2100, 2171, 2177, 2180 [NAICS 445110, 446110, 452111, 452910, 452990]

Wal-Mart.com USA L.L.C., p. III-2211 [NAICS 454113]

Walbash Alloys, p. I-807 [NAICS 331314]

Walbro Engine Management, p. II-1512 [NAICS 33632M]

Walden Structures Inc., p. I-353 [NAICS 321992]

Waldinger Corp., p. II-1009 [NAICS 332996]

Walgreen Co., p. III-2100 [NAICS 446110]

Walker and Associates Inc., p. III-1831 [NAICS 423610]

Walker Die Casting Inc., p. I-852 [NAICS 33152N]

Walker Forge Inc., p. I-872 [NAICS 33211N]

Walker Manufacturing Co., p. II-1028 [NAICS 333112]

Walker Power Systems Inc., p. II-1157 [NAICS 333611]

Walker Products Inc., pp. Vol. II-1332, 1505 [NAICS 334512, 33631M]

Walker Racing Inc., p. II-1473 [NAICS 336111]

Walkers Farm and Garden Inc., p. III-2069 [NAICS 444210]

Wall Colmonoy Corp., pp. Vol. II-964, 1567 [NAICS 33281M, 336413]

Wall Drug Store Inc., pp. Vol. III-2100, 2144, 2162, 2190 [NAICS 446110, 448310, 451211, 453220]

Wall Industries Inc., p. I-244 [NAICS 314991]

Wallace Packaging Corp., p. II-1708 [NAICS 33993M]

Wallace Refiners Inc., p. I-825 [NAICS 331419]

Wallis Oil Co., pp. Vol. III-1979, 2076 [NAICS 424720, 445110]

Wallner Tooling\Expac Inc., pp. Vol. I-825, Vol. II-1152 [NAICS 331419, 333518]

Wallover Oil Company Inc., p. I-458 [NAICS 324191]

Walman Optical Co., p. II-1687 [NAICS 339115]

Walpole Feed and Supply Co., p. III-2069 [NAICS 444210]

Walpole Woodworkers Inc., pp. Vol. I-358, Vol. II-1621, 1632 [NAICS 321999, 337122, 33712N]

Walt Disney Co., p. III-2190 [NAICS 453220]

Waltco Truck Equipment Inc., pp. Vol. II-1194, 1222, 1486, 1551 [NAICS 33392M, 33399N, 336211, 336399]

Walter Craig Inc., pp. Vol. III-1883, 2150 [NAICS 423910, 451110]

Walter Industries Inc., pp. Vol. I-353, 780 [NAICS 321992, 33111M]

Walter Meier Holdings Corp., p. III-1867 [NAICS 423830]

Walter Meier Inc., p. III-1943 [NAICS 424460]

Walter's Tire Service Inc., pp. Vol. I-660, Vol. III-1766, 2034 [NAICS 32621M, 423130, 441320]

Walton Feed Inc., p. I-516 [NAICS 325311]

Walton Tribune, p. I-436 [NAICS 32312M]

Walz Craft Inc., pp. Vol. I-343, Vol. II-1611 [NAICS 321920, 337110]

Wamco Inc., p. III-1879 [NAICS 423860]

War Eagle Mill Inc., p. III-2190 [NAICS 453220]

Ward/Kraft Inc., pp. Vol. I-388, 436 [NAICS 32222N, 32312M]

Ward Manufacturing Inc., pp. Vol. I-845, Vol. II-1009, 1229 [NAICS 33151M, 332996, 33399P]

Ward Process Inc., p. I-771 [NAICS 327993]

Warehouse One Inc., p. III-1774 [NAICS 423210]

Warlock Records Music Group, p. II-1376 [NAICS 334612]

Warnaco Group Inc., pp. Vol. I-272, 279 [NAICS 31522M, 31523M]

Warner Electric, pp. Vol. II-1427, 1437 [NAICS 335312, 335314]

Warner Electric Co., p. II-1302 [NAICS 334416]

Warner Manufacturing Co., p. II-1740 [NAICS 339994]

Warner Power Conversion L.L.C., p. II-1421 [NAICS 335311]

Warner Robins Supply Inc., p. I-329 [NAICS 32121P]

Warnock Automotive Group Inc., p. III-2011 [NAICS 441110]

Warnock Food Products Inc., p. I-133 [NAICS 311830]

Warp Brothers, p. I-609 [NAICS 326112]

Warren CAT, p. III-1859 [NAICS 423810]

Warren Fabricating Corp., pp. Vol. II-1039, 1147 [NAICS 33313M, 333516]

Warren Featherbone Co., p. I-285 [NAICS 31529M]

Warren Fire Equipment Inc., p. III-1875 [NAICS 423850]

Warren Industries Inc., p. II-1708 [NAICS 33993M]

Warren Manufacturing Inc., p. II-1491 [NAICS 336212]

Warren Power and Machinery L.P., p. III-1867 [NAICS 423830]

Warren Technology Inc., p. II-1101 [NAICS 333414]

Warsaw Chemical Company Inc., pp. Vol. I-480, 560 [NAICS 325181, 325520]

Warsaw Coil Company Inc., p. II-1302 [NAICS 334416]

Wasatch Brew Pub, pp. Vol. I-172, Vol. III-1983 [NAICS 312120, 424810]

Washing Equipment Of Texas Ltd., p. III-2050 [NAICS 443111]

Washington Beef L.L.C., p. I-102 [NAICS 31161N]

Washington Crab Producers Inc., p. I-110 [NAICS 31171M]

Washington Energy Services Co., p. III-1831 [NAICS 423610]

Washington Group Intern. Inc., p. II-1584 [NAICS 336510]

Washington Music Sales Center, p. III-2159 [NAICS 451140]

Washington Penn Plastic Inc., p. I-500 [NAICS 325211]

Washington Quality Food Products, p. I-15 [NAICS 31121M]

Wasserstrom Co., pp. Vol. III-1774, 1809 [NAICS 423210, 423440]

Waste Management of Iowa Inc., p. III-1890 [NAICS 423930]

Waste Minimization, p. I-471 [NAICS 325120]

Waste Paper Service, pp. Vol. I-363, 807 [NAICS 322110, 331314]

Watec America Corp., p. II-1087 [NAICS 333315]

Water Gremlin Co., p. II-1702 [NAICS 339920]

Water Heater Innovations Inc., p. II-1417 [NAICS 335228]

Water Pik Technologies Inc., pp. Vol. II-1457, 1682 [NAICS 33593M, 339114]

Water Saver Faucet Co., pp. Vol. II-974, 1666 [NAICS 332913, 339111]

Water Services of America Inc., p. II-1106 [NAICS 333415]

Water Street Seafood Inc., p. III-1943 [NAICS 424460]

Waterbury Companies Inc., p. I-529 [NAICS 325320]

Waterford-Wedgwood U.S.A., p. III-1778 [NAICS 423220]

Waterhouse nc., pp. Vol. III-2062, 2190 [NAICS 443130, 453220]

Waterloo Mills Co., p. I-4 [NAICS 311111]

Waterlox Coatings Corp., p. I-224 [NAICS 313320]

Watermark Books, p. III-2162 [NAICS 451211]

Watermark Paddle Sports Inc., p. II-1594 [NAICS 336612]

Waterous Co., pp. Vol. I-845, Vol. II-1179 [NAICS 33151M, 333911]

Waters Corp., pp. Vol. I-549, Vol. II-1352 [NAICS 325414, 334516]

Waters Instruments Inc., p. II-1421 [NAICS 335311]

Watkins Inc., p. I-152 [NAICS 31194M]

Watlow Co., pp. Vol. II-1432, 1451 [NAICS 335313, 33592M]

Watlow Industries, pp. Vol. II-1101, 1217 [NAICS 333414, 333994]

Watlow Winona Inc., pp. Vol. II-1332, 1432, 1666 [NAICS 334512, 335313, 339111]

Watonwan Farm Services, pp. Vol. III-1991, 2116 [NAICS 424910, 447110]

Watsco Inc., pp. Vol. II-1332, Vol. III-1851 [NAICS 334512, 423730]

Watson and Associates, p. III-1835 [NAICS 423620]

Watson Foods Company Inc., pp. Vol. I-147, 152 [NAICS 311930, 31194M]

Watson Laboratories Inc. - Ohio, p. I-539 [NAICS 325412]

Watson Pharmaceuticals Inc., p. I-539 [NAICS 325412]

Watson Truck and Supply Inc., p. III-2030 [NAICS 441310]

Watt Stopper Inc., pp. Vol. II-1390, 1457 [NAICS 33512M, 33593M]

Watts Water Technologies Inc., p. II-980 [NAICS 33291N]

Wauconda Tool & Engineering, p. II-958 [NAICS 332722]

Waukesha Engine Dresser Inc., pp. Vol. II-1173, 1427, 1437 [NAICS 333618, 335312, 335314]

Waupaca Foundry Inc., p. I-845 [NAICS 33151M]

Wausau Concrete Company Inc., p. I-737 [NAICS 32733M]

Wausau-Mosinee Paper Corp., p. I-368 [NAICS 32212M]

Wausau Papers of New Hampshire, p. I-368 [NAICS 32212M]

Wausau Steel Corp., pp. Vol. I-807, Vol. II-945, Vol. III-1824 [NAICS 331314, 332710, 423510]

Wausau Tile Inc., pp. Vol. I-743, Vol. II-1621, 1627, 1702 [NAICS 327390, 337122, 337127, 339920]

Wausaukee Composites Inc., pp. Vol. I-251, 636, 641 [NAICS 314999, 326140, 326150]

Wauseon Machine and Mfg, p. II-1147 [NAICS 333516]

Waverly Mills Inc., p. I-192 [NAICS 31311M]

Wawa Inc., pp. Vol. I-86, 92, Vol. III-2076, 2116 [NAICS 31151N, 311520, 445110, 447110]

Wawona Frozen Foods Inc., p. I-62 [NAICS 31141M]

Waxie Sanitary Supply, p. III-1971 [NAICS 424690]

Waxman Industries Inc., p. III-1847 [NAICS 423720]

Waycross Molded Products, p. I-229 [NAICS 314110]

Waymouth Farms Inc., pp. Vol. I-4, 52, 57, 137 [NAICS 311111, 311330, 311340, 31191M]

Wayne County Rubber Inc., p. I-505 [NAICS 325212]

Wayne-Dalton Corp., pp. Vol. I-334, Vol. II-908 [NAICS 32191M, 33232M]

Wayne Densch Inc., p. III-1983 [NAICS 424810]

Wayne Farms, p. I-9 [NAICS 311119]

Wayne Farms L.L.C., p. I-97 [NAICS 311615]

Wayne Machine and Die Inc., p. II-1051 [NAICS 333220]

Wayne Mills Company Inc., pp. Vol. I-203, 224 [NAICS 31322M, 313320]

Wayne Wire Cloth Products Inc., p. II-952 [NAICS 332721]

W.B. McGuire Company Inc., p. II-1212 [NAICS 333993]

Numbers following p. or pp. are page references. Roman numerals indicate volume numbers. Bracketed items indicate industries. Page references are to the starting pages of company tables.

2435

WB Place, pp. Vol. I-285, 296 [NAICS 31529M, 316110]

W.B. Wood Co., p. III-1774 [NAICS 423210]

WCCO Belting Inc., p. I-665 [NAICS 326220]

WD-40 Co., p. I-458 [NAICS 324191]

W.D. Larson Companies Limited, p. III-1758 [NAICS 423110]

W.D. Music Products Inc., p. II-1731 [NAICS 339992]

WE Neal Slate Co., p. I-752 [NAICS 327420]

Weasler Engineering Inc., pp. Vol. II-1168, 1530 [NAICS 333613, 336350]

Weastec Inc., pp. Vol. II-1432, 1457, 1512 [NAICS 335313, 33593M, 33632M]

Weather Shield Manufacturing Inc., pp. Vol. I-334, 651, Vol. II-908 [NAICS 32191M, 32619M, 33232M]

Weather Tec Corp., p. II-974 [NAICS 332913]

Weatherby Inc., p. II-1001 [NAICS 332994]

Weatherford Completion Systems, p. II-1039 [NAICS 33313M]

Weatherford CPS, p. II-1039 [NAICS 33313M]

Weatherford International Inc., p. II-1039 [NAICS 33313M]

Weatherford International Ltd., p. II-1179 [NAICS 333911]

Weatherford Pearland Mfg Inc., pp. Vol. I-788, Vol. II-1039, 1124 [NAICS 331210, 33313M, 333512]

Weaver Industries Inc., p. II-1463 [NAICS 335991]

Weaver Popcorn Company Inc., p. I-137 [NAICS 31191M]

Weavexx Corp., p. I-251 [NAICS 314999]

Web Graphics, p. I-403 [NAICS 32223M]

Web Printing Controls Inc., p. II-1332 [NAICS 334512]

Web Service Company Inc., pp. Vol. II-1092, 1413 [NAICS 33331N, 335224]

Webb Corp., p. II-1147 [NAICS 333516]

Webb Furniture Enterprises Inc, p. I-319 [NAICS 321219]

Webb Wheel Products Inc., p. II-1524 [NAICS 336340]

Webber Oil Co., p. III-1979 [NAICS 424720]

Webco Industries Inc., p. I-788 [NAICS 331210]

Weber Display and Packaging, p. II-1720 [NAICS 339950]

Weber Intern. Packaging L.L.C., p. I-646 [NAICS 326160]

Weber Knapp Co., pp. Vol. II-933, 1644 [NAICS 332510, 337215]

Weber Metals Inc., p. I-872 [NAICS 33211N]

Weber Processing Plant Inc., pp. Vol. III-1946, 2083 [NAICS 424470, 445210]

Weber-Stephen Products Co., p. II-1404 [NAICS 335221]

Webs Precision Metal Corp., p. II-1731 [NAICS 339992]

Websource, p. III-1898 [NAICS 424110]

Webster Industries Inc., p. I-395 [NAICS 32222P]

Wedemeyer Bakery Inc., p. III-2089 [NAICS 445291]

Wedron Silica Co., p. I-756 [NAICS 327910]

Weekend Warrior Trailers Inc., p. II-1500 [NAICS 336214]

Weekley Asphalt Paving Inc., p. I-448 [NAICS 324121]

Weems and Plath Inc., p. II-1362 [NAICS 334518]

Weetabix Company Inc., p. I-36 [NAICS 311230]

Wegmans Food Markets Inc., p. III-2076 [NAICS 445110]

Wehadkee Yarn Mills, p. I-192 [NAICS 31311M]

WEI Long Electric Industrial Co., p. II-1442 [NAICS 335911]

Weibel Inc., p. I-177 [NAICS 312130]

Weider Nutrition International Inc., pp. Vol. I-147, 165, 534, Vol. III-1954 [NAICS 311930, 31211M, 325411, 424490]

Weigh-Tronix Inc., p. II-1342 [NAICS 334514]

Weil-McLain, p. II-918 [NAICS 332410]

Weiler Corp., pp. Vol. I-756, Vol. II-1740 [NAICS 327910, 339994]

Weiler Engineering Inc., p. II-1212 [NAICS 333993]

Weiler Welding Company Inc., p. I-471 [NAICS 325120]

Weiman's Bakery Inc., p. III-2089 [NAICS 445291]

Weimer Bearing and Transmission, p. II-1168 [NAICS 333613]

Weinbrenner Shoe Company Inc., p. I-300 [NAICS 31621M]

Weir Floway Pumps Inc., p. II-1179 [NAICS 333911]

Weir's Furniture Village, p. III-2037 [NAICS 442110]

Weir Specialty Pumps, pp. Vol. I-670, Vol. II-1179 [NAICS 32629M, 333911]

Weir Valves and Controls USA, p. II-980 [NAICS 33291N]

Weis Markets Inc., p. III-2076 [NAICS 445110]

Weiss-Aug Company Inc., p. II-1051 [NAICS 333220]

Weissman's Theatrical Supplies, p. I-285 [NAICS 31529M]

Welch Allyn Inc., pp. Vol. I-544, Vol. II-1671 [NAICS 325413, 339112]

Welch Foods Inc., pp. Vol. I-62, 68 [NAICS 31141M, 31142M]

Welch Packaging Inc., p. II-1720 [NAICS 339950]

Welco Gases Corp., p. I-471 [NAICS 325120]

Welco Manufacturing Inc., p. I-752 [NAICS 327420]

Welcome Industrial Corporation, pp. Vol. III-1778, 1835, 1887 [NAICS 423220, 423620, 423920]

Weld Wheel Industries, p. I-660 [NAICS 32621M]

Welded Ring Products Co., pp. Vol. I-863, Vol. II-1580 [NAICS 332114, 336419]

Welded Tubes Inc., p. I-788 [NAICS 331210]

Welex Inc., p. II-1061 [NAICS 33329N]

Welker Engineering Company Inc., p. II-1129 [NAICS 333513]

Wellborn Cabinet Inc., pp. Vol. II-1611, 1621, 1632 [NAICS 337110, 337122, 33712N]

Wellco Enterprises Inc., p. I-300 [NAICS 31621M]

Wellington Cordage, p. I-244 [NAICS 314991]

Wellington Industries Inc., p. II-1541 [NAICS 336370]

Wellman Inc., pp. Vol. I-198, 510, Vol. III-1890 [NAICS 313210, 32522M, 423930]

Wellman Products Group, pp. Vol. II-1168, 1567, 1599 [NAICS 333613, 336413, 336991]

Wellman Thermal Systems Corp., pp. Vol. II-892, 1101, 1217 [NAICS 33221P, 333414, 333994]

Wellons Inc., pp. Vol. II-928, 1217 [NAICS 33243M, 333994]

Wells' Dairy Inc., pp. Vol. I-86, 92 [NAICS 31151N, 311520]

Wells Cargo Inc., p. II-1194 [NAICS 33392M]

Wells-Gardner Electronics Corp., p. II-1248 [NAICS 334113]

Wells Mfg Dura-Bar Div., pp. Vol. I-845, 857 [NAICS 33151M, 33152P]

Wellsaw Inc., p. II-1046 [NAICS 333210]

Wellston Aerosol Mfg Inc., p. I-471 [NAICS 325120]

WELSCO Inc., p. III-2222 [NAICS 454312]

Wen Technology Corp., p. II-1238 [NAICS 334111]

Wencor West Inc., p. III-1879 [NAICS 423860]

Wendell August Forge Inc., p. III-2190 [NAICS 453220]

Wendt Dunnington Co., p. I-756 [NAICS 327910]

Wenger Corp., pp. Vol. II-1632, 1731 [NAICS 33712N, 339992]

Wenger Manufacturing Inc., pp. Vol. II-1129, 1217 [NAICS 333513, 333994]

Wenner Bread Products Inc., p. I-116 [NAICS 31181M]

Wente Family Estates, pp. Vol. I-177, Vol. III-2097 [NAICS 312130, 445310]

Wenzel Farm Sausage, pp. Vol. III-1933, 1946 [NAICS 424430, 424470]

Werthan Packaging Inc., p. I-395 [NAICS 32222P]

Wescast Industries Cordele, p. I-845 [NAICS 33151M]

Weschler Instruments, pp. Vol. II-1302, 1342 [NAICS 334416, 334514]

Wesco Cedar Inc., p. III-1790 [NAICS 423330]

Wesco Electrical Co., p. II-1292 [NAICS 334414]

Wesco Fabrics Inc., p. III-1913 [NAICS 424310]

Wesco Financial Corp., p. III-1824 [NAICS 423510]

Wesco Industrial Products, pp. Vol. II-974, 1352 [NAICS 332913, 334516]

WESCO Industries, p. I-343 [NAICS 321920]

WESCO International Inc., pp. Vol. III-1831, 1867, 1871 [NAICS 423610, 423830, 423840]

Wesley Hall Inc., p. II-1616 [NAICS 337121]

West Agro Inc., pp. Vol. I-595, Vol. II-1671 [NAICS 32599N, 339112]

West Barcelona Inc., p. III-1883 [NAICS 423910]

West Bend Equipment Inc., p. II-1607 [NAICS 336999]

West Bond Inc., p. II-1056 [NAICS 333295]

West Central Coop., p. I-31 [NAICS 31122N]

West Central Turkeys Inc., p. I-97 [NAICS 311615]

West Coast Accudyne Inc., p. II-1129 [NAICS 333513]

West Coast Copper and Supply Inc., p. III-1851 [NAICS 423730]

West Coast Glass Products, p. I-709 [NAICS 327211]

West Coast Industrial Systems Inc., p. II-1046 [NAICS 333210]

West Coast Ingredients Inc., p. I-81 [NAICS 311514]

West Coast Paper Co., pp. Vol. III-1898, 1905 [NAICS 424110, 424130]

West Coast Plastics Inc., p. I-646 [NAICS 326160]

West Coast Tube and Pipe, p. I-788 [NAICS 331210]

West Coast Wire and Steel Inc., pp. Vol. II-1207, 1749 [NAICS 333991, 339999]

Numbers following p. or pp. are page references. Roman numerals indicate volume numbers. Bracketed items indicate industries. Page references are to the starting pages of company tables.

2436

West Coast Wire Rope & Rigging, p. III-1824 [NAICS 423510]

West Electronics Inc., p. II-1005 [NAICS 332995]

West Elizabeth Lumber Co., p. I-324 [NAICS 32121N]

West Irving Die Cast, pp. Vol. I-852, 857, Vol. II-1119, 1134 [NAICS 33152N, 33152P, 333511, 333514]

West L.A. Music, p. III-2159 [NAICS 451140]

West Liberty Foods, p. I-97 [NAICS 311615]

West Linn Paper Company Inc., p. I-388 [NAICS 32222N]

West Marine Inc., pp. Vol. III-2024, 2211 [NAICS 441222, 454113]

West Pharmaceutical Services Inc., p. III-1813 [NAICS 423450]

West Virginia Brewing L.L.C., p. I-172 [NAICS 312120]

Westan, p. I-296 [NAICS 316110]

Westar Contract Kitchen & Bath, p. III-1835 [NAICS 423620]

Westbury Ltd., p. I-262 [NAICS 31519M]

Westby Co-Operative Creamery, p. I-81 [NAICS 311514]

Westchester Lace Inc., p. I-213 [NAICS 31324M]

Westchester Modular Homes Inc., p. I-353 [NAICS 321992]

Westell Technologies Inc., p. II-1257 [NAICS 334210]

Westerbeke Corp., p. II-1173 [NAICS 333618]

Western Aircraft Inc., p. III-1879 [NAICS 423860]

Western American Inc., p. II-1189 [NAICS 333913]

Western Cooperative Co., pp. Vol. III-2072, 2225 [NAICS 444220, 454319]

Western-Cullen-Hayes Inc., p. II-1584 [NAICS 336510]

Western Digital Corp., pp. Vol. II-1243, 1252, 1287 [NAICS 334112, 334119, 334413]

Western Distributing Co., pp. Vol. III-1983, 1987 [NAICS 424810, 424820]

Western Extralite Co., p. III-1831 [NAICS 423610]

Western Family Foods Inc., p. III-1925 [NAICS 424410]

Western Gas Resources Inc., p. I-443 [NAICS 324110]

Western Industries Chilton, p. II-923 [NAICS 332420]

Western Industries Corp., p. I-641 [NAICS 326150]

Western Intern, p. I-471 [NAICS 325120]

Western Iowa Coop., pp. Vol. I-9, 524 [NAICS 311119, 325314]

Western Natural Gas Co., pp. Vol. III-2050, 2222 [NAICS 443111, 454312]

Western NonWovens Commerce, p. I-510 [NAICS 32522M]

Western Pacific Building Materials, p. III-1794 [NAICS 423390]

Western Pacific Pulp and Paper, p. III-1890 [NAICS 423930]

Western Plastics Inc., pp. Vol. I-609, 816 [NAICS 326112, 33131N]

Western Pneumatic Tube Co., p. I-788 [NAICS 331210]

Western Polymer Corp., p. I-22 [NAICS 311221]

Western Power & Equipment, p. III-1859 [NAICS 423810]

Western Printing Ink Corp., p. I-580 [NAICS 325910]

Western Products, p. II-1028 [NAICS 333112]

Western Products Inc., pp. Vol. III-1782, 1790, 2065 [NAICS 423310, 423330, 444100]

Western Quality Food Products, p. I-92 [NAICS 311520]

Western Recreational Vehicles Inc., pp. Vol. II-1496, 1500 [NAICS 336213, 336214]

Western Reserve Farm Co-Op, pp. Vol. I-524, 529, Vol. III-2208 [NAICS 325314, 325320, 453998]

Western Shower Door Inc., pp. Vol. I-722, Vol. II-1644 [NAICS 327215, 337215]

Western States Envelope Co., pp. Vol. I-388, 403 [NAICS 32222N, 32223M]

Western States Equipment, pp. Vol. III-1762, 1831 [NAICS 423120, 423610]

Western States Manufacturing Inc., p. I-660 [NAICS 32621M]

Western Stockmen's, pp. Vol. I-4, Vol. III-1820 [NAICS 311111, 423490]

Western Synthetic Fiber Inc., p. I-510 [NAICS 32522M]

Western Tire Centers Inc., p. III-1766 [NAICS 423130]

Western Trailers Co., p. II-1491 [NAICS 336212]

Western Truck Parts & Equipment, p. III-2011 [NAICS 441110]

Western Window and Door Corp., pp. Vol. I-709, 722 [NAICS 327211, 327215]

Western Zirconium, p. I-825 [NAICS 331419]

Westfalia Separator Inc., pp. Vol. II-899, 1023, 1092, 1229 [NAICS 33231M, 333111, 33331N, 33399P]

Westfalia Surge Inc., p. II-1023 [NAICS 333111]

Westheffer Company Inc., p. II-1189 [NAICS 333913]

Westin Automotive Products Inc., pp. Vol. II-1486, 1512 [NAICS 336211, 33632M]

Westin Fey Automotive Products, p. II-1486 [NAICS 336211]

Westin Foods, pp. Vol. I-62, 152 [NAICS 31141M, 31194M]

Westing House Lighting, pp. Vol. II-1386, 1390 [NAICS 335110, 33512M]

Westinghouse Air Brake, p. II-1584 [NAICS 336510]

Westinghouse Savannah River Co., p. II-1367 [NAICS 334519]

Westland Industries Inc., p. I-239 [NAICS 31491M]

Westling Manufacturing Inc., pp. Vol. II-1427, 1512 [NAICS 335312, 33632M]

Westmark Products Inc., p. II-1632 [NAICS 33712N]

Westmed Inc., p. I-621 [NAICS 326121]

WestPoint Stevens Inc., p. I-234 [NAICS 31412M]

Westport Axle Corp., p. II-1530 [NAICS 336350]

Westport Research Associates, p. II-1248 [NAICS 334113]

Westport Shipyard Inc., p. II-1589 [NAICS 336611]

Westrex Corporation Inc., p. II-1277 [NAICS 334411]

Westrex International, p. II-1248 [NAICS 334113]

Westshore Glass Corp., p. III-1794 [NAICS 423390]

Westward Seafoods Inc., p. I-110 [NAICS 31171M]

Westwood Group, pp. Vol. I-709, Vol. II-1056 [NAICS 327211, 333295]

Westye Group-Southeast Inc., p. III-1835 [NAICS 423620]

Wet Seal Inc., p. III-2126 [NAICS 448120]

Wetherill Associates Inc., p. II-1512 [NAICS 33632M]

Weyerhaeuser Co., pp. Vol. I-312, 334, 363, 368, 374, 415 [NAICS 32111M, 32191M, 322110, 32212M, 322130, 322299]

Weyerhaeuser Paper Co, pp. Vol. I-374, 379 [NAICS 322130, 32221M]

Weyerhauser Samill, p. I-324 [NAICS 32121N]

WF Miller Turf & Industrial, p. III-2069 [NAICS 444210]

WFI Industries Ltd., pp. Vol. II-1101, 1217 [NAICS 333414, 333994]

WGI Inc., p. II-1562 [NAICS 336412]

WH Industries Inc., p. II-1505 [NAICS 33631M]

Whaling Manufacturing Inc., p. I-267 [NAICS 31521M]

Whatcom Farmers Co-Op, pp. Vol. I-516, Vol. III-2007 [NAICS 325311, 424990]

Whatever It Takes Transmission, pp. Vol. II-1512, 1530 [NAICS 33632M, 336350]

Whayne Supply Co., pp. Vol. III-1859, 1863 [NAICS 423810, 423820]

Wheaton Science Products Inc., p. I-718 [NAICS 327213]

Wheatstone Corp., pp. Vol. II-1272, 1650 [NAICS 334310, 33721N]

Wheel City, p. III-1766 [NAICS 423130]

Wheeler Brothers Grain Inc., pp. Vol. III-1958, 1991 [NAICS 424510, 424910]

Wheeler's Las Vegas RV, p. III-2018 [NAICS 441210]

Wheeling Brake Block Mfg Co., p. II-1524 [NAICS 336340]

Wheeling-Pittsburgh Steel Corp., pp. Vol. I-780, 793 [NAICS 33111M, 33122M]

WheelWorks, pp. Vol. III-1766, 2030 [NAICS 423130, 441310]

Whelen Engineering Co., pp. Vol. II-1302, 1390, 1512 [NAICS 334416, 33512M, 33632M]

Whelen Engineering Inc., pp. Vol. II-1267, 1277, 1386, 1390, 1512 [NAICS 334290, 334411, 335110, 33512M, 33632M]

Whip Mix Corp., pp. Vol. I-752, 845, Vol. II-1666, 1682 [NAICS 327420, 33151M, 339111, 339114]

Whirlaway Corp., p. II-952 [NAICS 332721]

Whirley Industries Inc., p. I-646 [NAICS 326160]

Whirlpool Corp., pp. Vol. II-1404, 1409, 1413 [NAICS 335221, 335222, 335224]

Whirltronics Inc., p. II-1028 [NAICS 333112]

Whirlwind Music Distributors Inc., pp. Vol. II-1307, 1451 [NAICS 334417, 33592M]

Whit Corp., p. II-1740 [NAICS 339994]

Whitaker Brothers Business, p. III-1801 [NAICS 423420]

Whitaker House Publishing, p. III-1995 [NAICS 424920]

Whitaker Oil Co., p. III-1979 [NAICS 424720]

White Brothers Inc., p. III-2021 [NAICS 441221]

White Cap Industries Inc., p. III-1843 [NAICS 423710]

Company Index

Numbers following p. or pp. are page references. Roman numerals indicate volume numbers. Bracketed items indicate industries. Page references are to the starting pages of company tables.

2437

White Clover Dairy Inc., pp. Vol. I-4, 9, 76, 86 [NAICS 311111, 311119, 311513, 31151N]

White Coffee Corp., p. I-143 [NAICS 311920]

White Engineering Surfaces Corp., p. II-952 [NAICS 332721]

White Hydraulics Inc., p. II-1222 [NAICS 33399N]

White Lily Foods Co., pp. Vol. I-15, 124 [NAICS 31121M, 31182M]

White Oak Mills Inc., p. I-15 [NAICS 31121M]

White Outdoor Products Co., p. III-1843 [NAICS 423710]

White Pigeon Paper Company Inc., p. I-395 [NAICS 32222P]

White Rock Distilleries Inc., p. I-181 [NAICS 312140]

White's Boots Inc., p. I-300 [NAICS 31621M]

White's Old Mill Garden Center, p. III-2072 [NAICS 444220]

White's Tractor and Truck Inc., p. III-1863 [NAICS 423820]

White Wave Inc., pp. Vol. I-62, 68 [NAICS 31141M, 31142M]

Whitehall Industries Inc., p. I-837 [NAICS 33149M]

Whitehall Jewellers Inc., p. III-2144 [NAICS 448310]

Whitesell Corp., p. II-958 [NAICS 332722]

Whitestone Acquisition Corp., p. I-411 [NAICS 322291]

Whitewater Processing Co., p. I-97 [NAICS 311615]

Whitfield Foods Inc., p. I-147 [NAICS 311930]

Whiting Door Manufacturing Corp., pp. Vol. II-1486, 1491 [NAICS 336211, 336212]

Whiting Manufacturing Inc., p. I-234 [NAICS 31412M]

Whitlam Label Company Inc., p. I-415 [NAICS 322299]

Whitley Manufacturing Inc., p. I-348 [NAICS 321991]

Whitmire Container Corp., p. I-646 [NAICS 326160]

Whitney Blake Co., p. II-1302 [NAICS 334416]

Whitney Design Inc., p. III-2007 [NAICS 424990]

Whittaker Controls Inc., p. II-1222 [NAICS 33399N]

Whole Foods Market Inc., pp. Vol. III-2076, 2094 [NAICS 445110, 445299]

Whole Foods Market S Pacific, p. III-2094 [NAICS 445299]

Wholesale Glass Distributors Inc., pp. Vol. I-713, Vol. III-1794 [NAICS 327212, 423390]

Wholesale Roofing Supply Inc., p. III-1790 [NAICS 423330]

Wholesale Supply Group Inc., pp. Vol. III-1847, 2050, 2065 [NAICS 423720, 443111, 444100]

WHX Corp., pp. Vol. I-780, 793 [NAICS 33111M, 33122M]

Wichita Falls Nunn Electrical, p. III-1831 [NAICS 423610]

Wickes Furniture Company Inc., p. III-2037 [NAICS 442110]

Wickes Lumber, pp. Vol. I-334, Vol. III-2065 [NAICS 32191M, 444100]

Wickett and Craig of America Inc., p. I-296 [NAICS 316110]

WICO Metal Products Inc., pp. Vol. II-958, 1134, 1541 [NAICS 332722, 333514, 336370]

WICOR Inc., pp. Vol. II-980, 1179 [NAICS 33291N, 333911]

Widezone International Inc., p. I-26 [NAICS 311225]

Wieland Electric Inc., pp. Vol. II-1307, 1457, 1714 [NAICS 334417, 33593M, 33994M]

Wieland Metals Inc., p. I-830 [NAICS 33142M]

Wiemuth and Son Company Inc., pp. Vol. III-1939, 2001 [NAICS 424450, 424940]

Wiggins Airways Inc., pp. Vol. III-1879, 2027 [NAICS 423860, 441229]

Wiggins Lift Company Inc., p. II-1607 [NAICS 336999]

Wika Instrument Corp., p. II-1725 [NAICS 339991]

Wikoff Color Corp., p. I-580 [NAICS 325910]

Wilbert Funeral Services Inc., p. I-681 [NAICS 327112]

Wilbrecht Electronics Inc, p. II-1297 [NAICS 334415]

Wilbur Chocolate Company Inc., pp. Vol. I-52, 57 [NAICS 311330, 311340]

Wilbur-Ellis Co., p. III-1991 [NAICS 424910]

Wilco Farmers, pp. Vol. III-1958, 1979, 1991 [NAICS 424510, 424720, 424910]

Wilcox Bait and Tackle Inc., pp. Vol. III-2024, 2150 [NAICS 441222, 451110]

Wilcox Frozen Foods Inc., p. III-1929 [NAICS 424420]

Wild Birds Unlimited Inc., p. III-2208 [NAICS 453998]

Wild Oats Markets Inc., p. III-2094 [NAICS 445299]

Wild Turkey Distillery, p. I-181 [NAICS 312140]

Wilden Pump and Engineering Inc., p. II-1179 [NAICS 333911]

Wildish Land Co., p. III-1786 [NAICS 423320]

Wilen Professional Cleaning, pp. Vol. II-1397, 1740 [NAICS 33521M, 339994]

Wiley X, p. III-1817 [NAICS 423460]

Wilkens-Anderson Co., p. III-1820 [NAICS 423490]

Wilkens Industries Inc., p. II-1491 [NAICS 336212]

Wilkinson Manufacturing Co., p. II-928 [NAICS 33243M]

Will-Burt Co., pp. Vol. II-945, 1390 [NAICS 332710, 33512M]

Will Poultry Company Inc., pp. Vol. III-1929, 1936, 1943, 1946 [NAICS 424420, 424440, 424460, 424470]

Willamina Lumber Co., p. I-312 [NAICS 32111M]

Willard Milling Inc., p. I-4 [NAICS 311111]

Willard Packaging Company Inc., p. I-636 [NAICS 326140]

Willbanks Metals Inc., p. II-945 [NAICS 332710]

Wille Brothers Co., pp. Vol. III-1782, 1794 [NAICS 423310, 423390]

Wille Electric Supply Co., pp. Vol. III-1831, 2065 [NAICS 423610, 444100]

Willert Home Products Inc., pp. Vol. I-529, 566 [NAICS 325320, 32561M]

William Arthur Inc., pp. Vol. I-368, 403 [NAICS 32212M, 32223M]

William Barnet and Son L.L.C., pp. Vol. I-198, 510 [NAICS 313210, 32522M]

William George Company Inc., pp. Vol. III-1929, 1950 [NAICS 424420, 424480]

William H. Harvey Co., pp. Vol. I-458, Vol. II-958, 1725 [NAICS 324191, 332722, 339991]

William Kenyon and Sons Inc., p. I-244 [NAICS 314991]

William Thies and Sons Inc., p. III-1983 [NAICS 424810]

Williamette Valley Co., pp. Vol. I-493, 554, 670 [NAICS 32519M, 325510, 32629M]

Williams and Wells Co., p. III-1879 [NAICS 423860]

Williams Enterprise of Georgia, p. II-899 [NAICS 33231M]

Williams Foods Inc., p. I-152 [NAICS 31194M]

Williams Furniture & Design, pp. Vol. III-2041, 2044 [NAICS 442210, 442291]

Williams Industries Inc., p. I-743 [NAICS 327390]

Williams International L.L.C., p. II-1562 [NAICS 336412]

Williams Kitchen and Bath, pp. Vol. III-1782, 2065 [NAICS 423310, 444100]

Williams Panel Brick Inc., p. I-703 [NAICS 32712N]

Williams-Sonoma Inc., pp. Vol. III-2047, 2072, 2144, 2211 [NAICS 442299, 444220, 448310, 454113]

Williams Thin Film Products, p. I-691 [NAICS 327121]

Williams White and Co., p. II-1129 [NAICS 333513]

Williamsville Brewery Ltd., p. III-2097 [NAICS 445310]

Willick Engineering Company Inc., p. II-1357 [NAICS 334517]

Willimantic Waste Paper Inc., pp. Vol. I-363, 722, 807 [NAICS 322110, 327215, 331314]

Willis Lease Finance Corp., p. III-1879 [NAICS 423860]

Willmar Poultry Farms Inc., p. I-9 [NAICS 311119]

Willoughby Brewing Co., p. I-172 [NAICS 312120]

Willow Brook Foods Inc., p. I-102 [NAICS 31161N]

Willow Green Company Inc., p. I-681 [NAICS 327112]

Willy Wonka Candy Factory, p. I-57 [NAICS 311340]

Wilmes Window Mfg Co., p. I-709 [NAICS 327211]

Wilmington Machinery Inc., p. II-1051 [NAICS 333220]

Wilson Electronics Inc., p. II-1262 [NAICS 334220]

Wilson Foods Company L.L.C., p. III-1929 [NAICS 424420]

Wilson Greatbatch Technologies, p. II-1447 [NAICS 335912]

Wilson Group Ltd., p. III-1774 [NAICS 423210]

Wilson-Hurd Manufacturing Co., p. II-1720 [NAICS 339950]

Wilson Lumber Company Inc., p. III-2065 [NAICS 444100]

Wilson of Wallingford Inc., p. III-2218 [NAICS 454311]

Wilson Plywood and Door Inc., p. III-1782 [NAICS 423310]

Wilson Sporting Goods Co., p. II-1702 [NAICS 339920]

Wilson Supply & Tristate Propane, p. I-471 [NAICS 325120]

Wilson Trailer Co., pp. Vol. II-1194, 1500 [NAICS 33392M, 336214]

Wilson Wholesale Supply Co., p. III-1790 [NAICS 423330]

Wilsons The Leather Experts Inc., p. III-2147 [NAICS 448320]

Numbers following p. or pp. are page references. Roman numerals indicate volume numbers. Bracketed items indicate industries. Page references are to the starting pages of company tables.

2438

Wilwood Engineering Inc., p. II-1524 [NAICS 336340]

Winchell's Donut Houses, p. I-116 [NAICS 31181M]

Winchester Electronics, pp. Vol. I-837, Vol. II-1307, 1457 [NAICS 33149M, 334417, 33593M]

Winchester Optical Co., p. II-1687 [NAICS 339115]

Winchester Pacific Batteries USA, p. II-1442 [NAICS 335911]

Winco Distributors Inc., p. III-1782 [NAICS 423310]

WinCo Foods Inc., p. III-2076 [NAICS 445110]

Wincraft Inc., pp. Vol. I-234, 251, Vol. II-1735 [NAICS 31412M, 314999, 339993]

WinCup Inc., p. I-651 [NAICS 32619M]

Winder Dairy Inc., p. I-116 [NAICS 31181M]

Windham House Inc., p. III-2047 [NAICS 442299]

Window Technologies L.L.C., p. I-709 [NAICS 327211]

Windquest Companies Inc., pp. Vol. I-358, 631 [NAICS 321999, 326130]

Windsor Vineyards, pp. Vol. I-177, Vol. III-1987 [NAICS 312130, 424820]

Windway Capital Corp., pp. Vol. I-379, 681, Vol. II-1594 [NAICS 32221M, 327112, 336612]

Winegard Co., pp. Vol. II-1262, 1427 [NAICS 334220, 335312]

Winesellers Ltd., p. III-1987 [NAICS 424820]

Winfield Consumer Products Inc., p. III-2030 [NAICS 441310]

Winfrey's Olde English Fudge Inc., p. I-48 [NAICS 311320]

Winkie Manufacturing Inc., p. I-285 [NAICS 31529M]

Winmark Corp., pp. Vol. II-1731, Vol. III-1883, 2129 [NAICS 339992, 423910, 448130]

Winn-Dixie Stores Inc., p. III-2076 [NAICS 445110]

Winnebago Industries Inc., p. II-1496 [NAICS 336213]

Winnemucca Farms, p. I-15 [NAICS 31121M]

Winner Steel Inc., p. II-1302 [NAICS 334416]

Winners Circle Systems, p. III-2058 [NAICS 443120]

Winpak Films Inc., p. I-615 [NAICS 326113]

Winpak Lane Inc., p. II-1212 [NAICS 333993]

Winroc Corporation Midwest, p. III-1794 [NAICS 423390]

Winsert Inc., p. II-1173 [NAICS 333618]

Winslow Automatics Inc., p. II-1562 [NAICS 336412]

Winston Brothers, p. III-1890 [NAICS 423930]

Winston Weaver Company Inc., p. I-520 [NAICS 325312]

Winter-Wolff International Inc., p. I-816 [NAICS 33131N]

Winthrop-Atkins Company Inc., p. II-1708 [NAICS 33993M]

Winthrop Printing Company Inc., p. I-403 [NAICS 32223M]

Wip-X Systems Inc., p. I-218 [NAICS 31331M]

Wire Technologies Inc., p. I-837 [NAICS 33149M]

Wiremold Co., pp. Vol. I-793, Vol. II-939, 1457 [NAICS 33122M, 33261M, 33593M]

Wirerope Works Inc., p. II-939 [NAICS 33261M]

Wirtz Group of Co's, p. II-1119 [NAICS 333511]

Wis-Pak Inc., p. I-165 [NAICS 31211M]

Wisconsin Aluminum Foundry, pp. Vol. I-852, 857, Vol. II-886 [NAICS 33152N, 33152P, 33221N]

Wisconsin Distributors Inc., p. III-1983 [NAICS 424810]

Wisconsin Film and Bag Inc., p. I-603 [NAICS 326111]

Wisconsin Homes Inc., p. I-353 [NAICS 321992]

Wisconsin Lift Truck Corp., p. III-1867 [NAICS 423830]

Wisconsin Metal Products Co., p. II-1541 [NAICS 336370]

Wisconsin Packaging Group, p. I-420 [NAICS 32311M]

Wisconsin Paperboard Corp., pp. Vol. I-363, 415 [NAICS 322110, 322299]

Wisconsin Steel and Tube Corp., pp. Vol. I-811, Vol. II-1009 [NAICS 331316, 332996]

Wisconsin Truss Inc., p. I-329 [NAICS 32121P]

Wisconsin TV Tube Sales Inc., p. II-1277 [NAICS 334411]

Wisconsin Veneer & Plywood Inc., p. I-324 [NAICS 32121N]

Wise Alloys L.L.C., p. II-908 [NAICS 33232M]

Wise Company Inc., p. II-1627 [NAICS 337127]

Wise El Santo Company Inc., pp. Vol. III-1916, 2007 [NAICS 424320, 424990]

Witex USA Inc., p. III-1786 [NAICS 423320]

Witt Co., pp. Vol. III-1798, 1801 [NAICS 423410, 423420]

Witt Industries Inc., p. II-928 [NAICS 33243M]

Witt Lining Systems, p. I-699 [NAICS 327123]

Wittern Group, p. II-1092 [NAICS 33331N]

Wittichen Supply Co., p. III-1855 [NAICS 423740]

WJ Bullock Inc., p. I-803 [NAICS 331312]

WJ Ruscoe Co., p. I-703 [NAICS 32712N]

WJS Enterprises Inc., p. III-1801 [NAICS 423420]

WKI Holding Company Inc., pp. Vol. I-681, 713, 722, Vol. II-886 [NAICS 327112, 327212, 327215, 33221N]

WL Construction and Paving Inc., p. I-448 [NAICS 324121]

WL Gore and Associates, p. I-621 [NAICS 326121]

W.L. Gore and Associates Inc., pp. Vol. I-793, Vol. II-1282, 1307, 1327, 1451 [NAICS 33122M, 334412, 334417, 334511, 33592M]

W.L. Halsey Company Inc., pp. Vol. III-1871, 1905 [NAICS 423840, 424130]

WL Jenkins Co, p. II-1731 [NAICS 339992]

WM Barr and Company Inc., p. I-554 [NAICS 325510]

Wm. K. Walthers Inc., pp. Vol. II-1708, Vol. III-1887 [NAICS 33993M, 423920]

WM Management Inc., p. III-1820 [NAICS 423490]

Wm. Wrigley Jr. Co., p. I-57 [NAICS 311340]

WMI/TSH, p. II-1023 [NAICS 333111]

WMS Gaming Inc., p. II-1749 [NAICS 339999]

WMS Industries Inc., p. II-1749 [NAICS 339999]

WmT Burnett and Co., pp. Vol. I-636, 641 [NAICS 326140, 326150]

WNA American Plastic Industries, p. I-603 [NAICS 326111]

WNC Pallet & Forest Products Inc., p. I-343 [NAICS 321920]

Wohlt Cheese Corp., p. I-76 [NAICS 311513]

Wold Trona Company Inc., p. I-480 [NAICS 325181]

Wolf Machine Co., p. I-192 [NAICS 31311M]

Wolf Manufacturing Inc., p. III-1770 [NAICS 423140]

Wolf X-Ray Corp., p. II-1357 [NAICS 334517]

Wolff Brothers Supply Inc., pp. Vol. III-1831, 1847, 1851 [NAICS 423610, 423720, 423730]

Wolff Shoe Co., p. III-1922 [NAICS 424340]

Wolohan Lumber Co., p. III-2065 [NAICS 444100]

Wolverine Brass Inc., p. II-974 [NAICS 332913]

Wolverine Tractor & Equipment, p. III-1859 [NAICS 423810]

Wolverine Tube Inc., p. I-830 [NAICS 33142M]

Wolverine World Wide Inc., p. I-300 [NAICS 31621M]

Wonalancet Co., p. III-1965 [NAICS 424590]

Wood and Hyde Leather Inc., p. I-296 [NAICS 316110]

Wood Group Component Repair, p. II-1157 [NAICS 333611]

Wood Group ESP, p. II-1039 [NAICS 33313M]

Wood Group Pratt & Whitney, p. II-1173 [NAICS 333618]

Wood Group Pressure Control Inc., pp. Vol. II-980, 1039 [NAICS 33291N, 33313M]

Wood Group Turbo Power L.L.C., p. II-1173 [NAICS 333618]

Wood-Mizer Products Inc., pp. Vol. II-1028, 1046, 1217 [NAICS 333112, 333210, 333994]

Wood-Mode Inc., p. II-1611 [NAICS 337110]

Wood Stone Corp., p. II-1404 [NAICS 335221]

Wood Structures Inc., p. I-329 [NAICS 32121P]

Wood Ventures Inc., p. II-1404 [NAICS 335221]

Woodbine Alaska Fish Co., p. I-110 [NAICS 31171M]

Woodbridge Foam Fabricating, p. I-641 [NAICS 326150]

Woodbridge Group, p. I-641 [NAICS 326150]

Woodbury Business Forms Inc., p. I-403 [NAICS 32223M]

Woodcraft Inc., p. I-631 [NAICS 326130]

Woodcraft Industries Inc., p. I-334 [NAICS 32191M]

Wooden Pallets Ltd., p. I-343 [NAICS 321920]

Woodland Products Company Inc., p. III-1782 [NAICS 423310]

Woodmart Window Coverings, p. III-1778 [NAICS 423220]

Woodruff Energy Co., p. III-2218 [NAICS 454311]

Woodstock Percussion Inc., p. II-1731 [NAICS 339992]

Woodward FST Inc., pp. Vol. II-1342, 1567 [NAICS 334514, 336413]

Woodward Governor Company, pp. Vol. II-1157, 1173, 1427, 1437, 1468, 1562 [NAICS 333611, 333618, 335312, 335314, 335999, 336412]

Woolrich Inc., pp. Vol. I-198, 234 [NAICS 313210, 31412M]

Woonsocket Spinning Co., pp. Vol. I-192, 203 [NAICS 31311M, 31322M]

Wooten Oil Co., p. III-1975 [NAICS 424710]

Worcester Envelope Company Inc., p. I-403 [NAICS 32223M]

Worcester Sand and Gravel Inc., p. III-1786 [NAICS 423320]

Work Services Corp., p. I-358 [NAICS 321999]

Workflow Management Inc., p. I-420 [NAICS 32311M]

Numbers following p. or pp. are page references. Roman numerals indicate volume numbers. Bracketed items indicate industries. Page references are to the starting pages of company tables.

2439

Company Index

Workshare Technology Inc., p. III-2058 [NAICS 443120]

Workshops of Gerald E Henn, p. I-681 [NAICS 327112]

Workspace Development L.L.C., p. III-1774 [NAICS 423210]

World Cycling Productions Inc., p. III-2150 [NAICS 451110]

World Electronics Inc., p. II-1277 [NAICS 334411]

World Emblem International Inc., p. I-251 [NAICS 314999]

World Fuel Services Corp., p. III-1979 [NAICS 424720]

World Manufacturing Inc., pp. Vol. II-1112, 1720 [NAICS 33341N, 339950]

World Media Group Inc., p. II-1376 [NAICS 334612]

World Oil Co., pp. Vol. I-443, 453 [NAICS 324110, 324122]

World Plastic Extruders Inc., p. I-621 [NAICS 326121]

World Resource Recovery Systems, p. I-363 [NAICS 322110]

World's Finest Chocolate Inc., pp. Vol. I-52, 158 [NAICS 311330, 31199M]

World Wide Container Services, p. I-343 [NAICS 321920]

World Wide Technology Inc., p. III-1805 [NAICS 423430]

Worldtex Inc., pp. Vol. I-192, 203 [NAICS 31311M, 31322M]

Worldwide Aeros Corp., p. II-1557 [NAICS 336411]

Worldwide Refractories Inc., p. I-703 [NAICS 32712N]

Worldwide Retail Exchange L.L.C., p. III-2007 [NAICS 424990]

Worldwide Security Service Inc., p. II-1357 [NAICS 334517]

Wornick Co., pp. Vol. I-76, 158 [NAICS 311513, 31199M]

Worth Inc., p. II-1702 [NAICS 339920]

Worthington Bio Chemical Corp., p. I-549 [NAICS 325414]

Worthington Industries Inc., pp. Vol. I-626, 780, 793, 845, Vol. III-1824 [NAICS 326122, 33111M, 33122M, 33151M, 423510]

Worthington Precision Metals, p. II-952 [NAICS 332721]

Worzalla Publishing Co., p. I-436 [NAICS 32312M]

WOTCO Inc., p. II-1039 [NAICS 33313M]

Woven Electronics Corp., pp. Vol. II-1307, 1312 [NAICS 334417, 334418]

Wozniak Industries Inc., pp. Vol. I-872, 879 [NAICS 33211N, 33211P]

W.P. Ballard and Co., p. III-2007 [NAICS 424990]

WP Law Inc., p. III-1847 [NAICS 423720]

WPI Inc., p. II-1307 [NAICS 334417]

W.R. Grace and Co., pp. Vol. I-475, 615, 626, 641 [NAICS 32513M, 326113, 326122, 326150]

W.R. Grace Co. Cryovac-Texas, p. I-626 [NAICS 326122]

Wrangell Seafood Inc., p. I-110 [NAICS 31171M]

Wright and McGill Co., p. III-2208 [NAICS 453998]

Wright and Wilhelmy Inc., pp. Vol. III-1843, 1847, 1991 [NAICS 423710, 423720, 424910]

Wright Business Graphics Inc., p. I-403 [NAICS 32223M]

Wright Capacitors Inc., p. II-1292 [NAICS 334414]

Wright Chemical Corp., p. I-493 [NAICS 32519M]

Wright Images, p. III-2062 [NAICS 443130]

Wright Industries Inc., pp. Vol. II-1140, 1152 [NAICS 333515, 333518]

Wright Manufacturing Inc., p. II-1028 [NAICS 333112]

Wright Medical Group Inc., pp. Vol. II-1322, 1676 [NAICS 334510, 339113]

Wright Metal Products Inc., p. II-945 [NAICS 332710]

Wright Packaging Inc., p. I-395 [NAICS 32222P]

Wright Products, p. I-852 [NAICS 33152N]

Wrights Knitwear Corp., p. I-272 [NAICS 31522M]

Wrought Washer Mfg Inc., p. II-958 [NAICS 332722]

W.S. Badcock Corp., p. III-1778 [NAICS 423220]

W.S. Lee and Sons Inc., pp. Vol. III-1875, 1929, 1933 [NAICS 423850, 424420, 424430]

WS Packaging Group, p. I-388 [NAICS 32222N]

WTC Machinery Inc., p. II-1147 [NAICS 333516]

W.W. Grainger Inc., pp. Vol. III-1831, 1851, 1867 [NAICS 423610, 423730, 423830]

WW Trailer Manufacturers Inc., p. II-1500 [NAICS 336214]

WY Shugart and Sons Inc., p. I-256 [NAICS 31511M]

Wyandot Inc., pp. Vol. I-133, 137 [NAICS 311830, 31191M]

Wyeth, pp. Vol. I-534, 539, 575 [NAICS 325411, 325412, 325620]

Wyeth Nutritionals Inc., p. I-81 [NAICS 311514]

Wyeth Pharmaceuticals, p. I-539 [NAICS 325412]

Wyko Inc., p. II-1051 [NAICS 333220]

Wyle Electronics, pp. Vol. III-1805, 1839 [NAICS 423430, 423690]

Wynkoop Brewing Company Inc., p. I-172 [NAICS 312120]

Wynn Fire & Rescue Equipment, p. III-2208 [NAICS 453998]

Wyoming Refining Co., p. I-443 [NAICS 324110]

X-Cel Contacts Inc., p. II-1687 [NAICS 339115]

X-Cel Feeds Inc., p. I-4 [NAICS 311111]

X-Cel Optical Co., p. I-713 [NAICS 327212]

X-L Plastics Inc., pp. Vol. I-603, 615 [NAICS 326111, 326113]

X-L Specialized Trailers Inc., p. II-1491 [NAICS 336212]

X-Ray Cassette Repair Co., p. II-1357 [NAICS 334517]

X-Rite Inc., pp. Vol. I-837, Vol. II-1082, 1087, 1337, 1357, 1367, 1671 [NAICS 33149M, 333314, 333315, 334513, 334517, 334519, 339112]

Xaloy Inc., pp. Vol. II-928, 958 [NAICS 33243M, 332722]

Xerographic Solutions Inc., p. III-1820 [NAICS 423490]

Xerox Corp., pp. Vol. II-1077, 1087, 1252 [NAICS 333313, 333315, 334119]

Xerxes Computer Corp., p. III-2058 [NAICS 443120]

Xicon Passive Components, p. II-1297 [NAICS 334415]

Xilinx Inc., pp. Vol. II-1287, 1317 [NAICS 334413, 334419]

XiTec Holdings L.L.C., p. II-1357 [NAICS 334517]

XKD Corp., p. II-1248 [NAICS 334113]

XL Adhesives L.L.C., p. I-224 [NAICS 313320]

Xtek Inc., pp. Vol. II-1147, 1162 [NAICS 333516, 333612]

Xymox Technologies Inc., p. II-1302 [NAICS 334416]

Yacht Club Trailers, pp. Vol. II-1500, 1607 [NAICS 336214, 336999]

Yale Security Group, pp. Vol. I-879, Vol. II-933 [NAICS 33211P, 332510]

Yamada North America Inc., pp. Vol. II-1179, 1519, 1530 [NAICS 333911, 336330, 336350]

Yamaha Music Manufacturing Inc., p. II-1731 [NAICS 339992]

Yancey's Fancy Inc., p. I-76 [NAICS 311513]

Yank Waste Company Inc., p. I-363 [NAICS 322110]

Yanke Energy Inc., p. II-1157 [NAICS 333611]

Yankee Candle Company Inc., pp. Vol. II-1749, Vol. III-2208 [NAICS 339999, 453998]

Yankee Hill Brick & Tile Mfg Co., pp. Vol. I-691, 695 [NAICS 327121, 327122]

YANMAR America Corp., pp. Vol. II-1173, Vol. III-1859 [NAICS 333618, 423810]

Yarde Metals Inc., pp. Vol. II-945, Vol. III-1824 [NAICS 332710, 423510]

Yardney Technical Products Inc., pp. Vol. II-1442, 1447 [NAICS 335911, 335912]

Yardville Supply Co., pp. Vol. III-1786, 1863 [NAICS 423320, 423820]

Yarnell Ice Cream Company Inc., p. I-92 [NAICS 311520]

Yaskawa Electric America Inc., p. II-1427 [NAICS 335312]

Yasutomo and Company Inc., p. III-1901 [NAICS 424120]

Yates-American Machine Inc., p. II-1046 [NAICS 333210]

Yates Bleachery Co., p. I-218 [NAICS 31331M]

Yates Foil USA Inc., p. I-816 [NAICS 33131N]

Yazaki North America Inc., pp. Vol. II-1140, 1468, 1512 [NAICS 333515, 335999, 33632M]

Yeager Skanska Inc., p. I-448 [NAICS 324121]

Year One Inc., p. III-2030 [NAICS 441310]

Yessick's Design Center, p. III-2190 [NAICS 453220]

Yield Engineering Systems Inc., p. II-1056 [NAICS 333295]

Yingling Aircraft Inc., p. III-1879 [NAICS 423860]

YKK Snap Fasteners America, pp. Vol. II-958, 1061, 1077, 1735 [NAICS 332722, 33329N, 333313, 339993]

Yoder Industries Inc., p. I-852 [NAICS 33152N]

Yoder Lumber Company Inc., p. I-358 [NAICS 321999]

Yoder Manufacturing Co., p. II-1147 [NAICS 333516]

Yoder Oil Company Inc., pp. Vol. III-1975, 2116 [NAICS 424710, 447110]

Yokogawa Corporation of America, pp. Vol. II-1243, 1337, 1342, 1367 [NAICS 334112, 334513, 334514, 334519]

Yomega Corp., p. II-1708 [NAICS 33993M]

Numbers following p. or pp. are page references. Roman numerals indicate volume numbers. Bracketed items indicate industries. Page references are to the starting pages of company tables.

York Building Products Inc., p. I-737 [NAICS 32733M]

York Casket Co., p. II-1745 [NAICS 339995]

York Corrugating Co., p. I-863 [NAICS 332114]

York Electronics Corp., p. II-1292 [NAICS 334414]

York International Corp., p. II-1106 [NAICS 333415]

York Refrigerations-Frick, pp. Vol. II-980, 1106, 1409 [NAICS 33291N, 333415, 335222]

York Shipley Global, p. II-918 [NAICS 332410]

Yorktowne Inc., p. II-1611 [NAICS 337110]

Yorktowne Paperboard Corp., p. I-374 [NAICS 322130]

Yorozu Automotive Tennessee Inc., p. II-1541 [NAICS 336370]

Young and Bertke Air Systems Co., p. II-1740 [NAICS 339994]

Young and Franklin Inc., p. II-1222 [NAICS 33399N]

Young Forever Inc., p. III-1887 [NAICS 423920]

Young Innovations Inc., pp. Vol. II-1357, 1682 [NAICS 334517, 339114]

Young Pecan Co., p. I-137 [NAICS 31191M]

Young's Manufacturing Inc., p. I-285 [NAICS 31529M]

Young's Market Company L.L.C., pp. Vol. III-1983, 1987 [NAICS 424810, 424820]

Young Supply Co., p. III-1855 [NAICS 423740]

Younger Brothers Components Inc., p. I-329 [NAICS 32121P]

Youngstown Iron and Metal Inc., p. III-1890 [NAICS 423930]

Youngstown-Kenworth Inc., p. II-1486 [NAICS 336211]

Youngstown Plastic Tooling, p. II-1051 [NAICS 333220]

Your Name Professsional Brands, p. I-575 [NAICS 325620]

YS and CH Enterprises Inc., p. III-2083 [NAICS 445210]

YSD Industries Inc., p. II-1584 [NAICS 336510]

YSI Inc., pp. Vol. II-1352, 1367 [NAICS 334516, 334519]

YSK Corp., pp. Vol. II-1519, 1530 [NAICS 336330, 336350]

Yukon Equipment Inc., p. III-1859 [NAICS 423810]

Yurman Design Inc., p. II-1696 [NAICS 33991M]

Yves Delorme Inc., p. III-1778 [NAICS 423220]

YXLON International Inc., p. II-1357 [NAICS 334517]

Zabatt Engine Services Inc., p. II-1173 [NAICS 333618]

Zabin Industries Inc., p. II-1735 [NAICS 339993]

Zachary Confections Inc., pp. Vol. I-52, 57 [NAICS 311330, 311340]

Zaclon Inc., p. I-480 [NAICS 325181]

Zahars Inc., p. III-2092 [NAICS 445292]

Zak Designs Inc., p. I-681 [NAICS 327112]

Zale Corp., p. III-2144 [NAICS 448310]

Zamaroni Quarry Inc., p. III-2072 [NAICS 444220]

Zamzow Manufacturing Inc., pp. Vol. I-239, 285, 510 [NAICS 31491M, 31529M, 32522M]

Zander's Creamery Inc., p. I-26 [NAICS 311225]

Zanios Foods Inc., pp. Vol. III-1933, 1936, 1943, 1946 [NAICS 424430, 424440, 424460, 424470]

ZAP, p. II-1599 [NAICS 336991]

Zapata Corp., p. I-26 [NAICS 311225]

Zapf Creation Inc., p. III-1887 [NAICS 423920]

Zaro's Bake Shop, p. I-124 [NAICS 31182M]

Zebra Pen Corp., p. III-1901 [NAICS 424120]

Zebra Technologies Corp., pp. Vol. I-420, Vol. II-1252, 1714 [NAICS 32311M, 334119, 33994M]

Zed Industries Inc., p. II-1051 [NAICS 333220]

Zeeco Inc., pp. Vol. II-1101, 1217 [NAICS 333414, 333994]

Zeeland Lumber and Supply Inc., p. III-2065 [NAICS 444100]

Zeiger Enterprises Inc., pp. Vol. III-1916, 1919, 1922 [NAICS 424320, 424330, 424340]

Zelco Industries Inc., p. II-1362 [NAICS 334518]

Zenith Specialty Bag Company, pp. Vol. I-395, 415 [NAICS 32222P, 322299]

Zephyr Manufacturing Inc., p. II-1207 [NAICS 333991]

Zero Products Div., p. II-1152 [NAICS 333518]

Zesco Products Inc., p. III-1875 [NAICS 423850]

Zeus Scientific Inc., p. I-544 [NAICS 325413]

ZF Industries Inc., p. III-1879 [NAICS 423860]

Zf Lemforder Corp., pp. Vol. II-1519, 1530 [NAICS 336330, 336350]

Zhone Technologies Inc., pp. Vol. II-1257, 1432 [NAICS 334210, 335313]

Zidell Marine Corp., p. II-1589 [NAICS 336611]

Zieger and Sons Inc., p. III-1998 [NAICS 424930]

Ziegler Bolt and Parts Co., p. III-1843 [NAICS 423710]

Ziehm Imaging Inc., p. II-1357 [NAICS 334517]

Zila Inc., p. III-1813 [NAICS 423450]

Zim's Bagging Co., pp. Vol. I-395, 603, 636 [NAICS 32222P, 326111, 326140]

Zimmer Holdings Inc., p. II-1676 [NAICS 339113]

Zinpro Corp., p. I-767 [NAICS 327992]

Zippo Manufacturing Company, pp. Vol. I-306, Vol. II-939, 1714, 1749 [NAICS 31699M, 33261M, 33994M, 339999]

Zman Magnetics Inc., p. II-1302 [NAICS 334416]

Zocalo Imports Inc., pp. Vol. III-1774, 1778 [NAICS 423210, 423220]

Zoeller Co., pp. Vol. II-980, 1179 [NAICS 33291N, 333911]

ZOLL Medical Corp., pp. Vol. II-1322, 1671 [NAICS 334510, 339112]

Zomax Inc., p. II-1376 [NAICS 334612]

Zondervan Corp., pp. Vol. II-1087, 1272 [NAICS 333315, 334310]

Zones Inc., p. III-2211 [NAICS 454113]

Zook Enterprises L.L.C., p. II-1463 [NAICS 335991]

Zoran Corp., p. II-1287 [NAICS 334413]

Zrike Co., p. I-681 [NAICS 327112]

ZTR Control Systems Inc., p. II-1584 [NAICS 336510]

Zuckerman-Honickman Inc., p. III-1871 [NAICS 423840]

Zunicom Inc., p. III-1831 [NAICS 423610]

Zurn Wilkins, p. II-974 [NAICS 332913]

Z.V. Pate Inc., pp. Vol. III-2072, 2177 [NAICS 444220, 452910]

Zy-Tech Global Industries, p. III-1871 [NAICS 423840]

Zygo Corp., pp. Vol. II-1082, 1322, 1327, 1347, 1367 [NAICS 333314, 334510, 334511, 334515, 334519]

Zyloware Corp., p. II-1687 [NAICS 339115]

ZymoGenetics Inc., p. I-549 [NAICS 325414]

Appendices

ASM NAICS TO 2002 NAICS CONVERSION GUIDE

2002 NAICS TO ASM NAICS CONVERSION GUIDE

ASM NAICS to 2002 NAICS Conversion Guide

This index shows the *Annual Survey of Manufactures'* (ASM) NAICS codes and descriptions along with their corresponding 2002 Federal Government NAICS codes and descriptions. Nec stands for 'not elsewhere classified.' ASM NAICS are in bold.

311111 Dog and cat food manufacturing
311111 Dog and cat food manufacturing

311119 Animal food manufacturing, nec
311119 Other animal food manufacturing

31121M Flour milling and malt manufacturing
311211 Flour milling
311212 Rice milling
311313 Malt manufacturing

311221 Wet corn milling
311221 Wet corn milling

311225 Fats and oils refining and blending
311225 Fats and oils refining and blending

31122N Soybean and other oilseed processing
311222 Soybean processing
311223 Other oilseeed processing

311230 Breakfast cereal manufacturing
311230 Breakfast cereal manufacturing

31131N Sugar cane mills and refining
311311 Sugar cane mills
311312 Cane sugar refining

311313 Beet sugar manufacturing
311313 Beet sugar manufacturing

311320 Chocolate and confectionery manufacturing from cacao beans
311320 Chocolate and confectionery manufacturing from cacao beans

311330 Confectionery manufacturing from purchased chocolate
311330 Confectionery manufacturing from purchased chocolate

311340 Nonchocolate confectionery manufacturing
311340 Nonchocolate confectionery manufacturing

31141M Frozen food manufacturing
311411 Frozen fruit, juice, and vegetable manufacturing
311412 Frozen specialty food manufacturing

31142M Fruit and vegetable canning, pickling, and drying
311421 Fruit and vegetable canning
311422 Specialty canning
311423 Dried and dehydrated food manufacturing

31151N Fluid milk and butter manufacturing
311511 Fluid milk manufacturing
311512 Creamery butter manufacturing

311513 Cheese manufacturing
311513 Cheese manufacturing

311514 Dry, condensed, and evaporated dairy product manufacturing
311514 Dry, condensed, and evaporated dairy product manufacturing

311520 Ice cream and frozen dessert manufacturing
311520 Ice cream and frozen dessert manufacturing

31161N Animal (except poultry) slaughtering and processing
311611 Animal (except poultry) slaughtering
311612 Meat processed from carcasses
311613 Rendering and meat byproduct processing

311615 Poultry processing
311615 Poultry processing

31171M Seafood product preparation and packaging
311711 Seafood canning
311712 Fresh and frozen seafood processing

31181M Bread and bakery product manufacturing
311811 Retail bakeries
311812 Commercial bakeries
311813 Frozen cakes, pies, and other pastries manufacturing

31182M Cookie, cracker, and pasta manufacturing
311821 Cookie and cracker manufacturing
311822 Flour mixes and dough manufacturing from purchased flour
311823 Dry pasta manufacturing

311830 Tortilla manufacturing
311830 Tortilla manufacturing

31191M Snack food manufacturing
311911 Roasted nuts and peanut butter manufacturing
311919 Other snack food manufacturing

311920 Coffee and tea manufacturing
311920 Coffee and tea manufacturing

311930 Flavoring syrup and concentrate manufacturing
311930 Flavoring syrup and concentrate manufacturing

31194M Seasoning and dressing manufacturing
311941 Mayonnaise, dressing, and other prepared sauce manufacturing
311942 Spice and extract manufacturing

31199M Food manufacturing, nec
311991 Perishable prepared food manufacturing
311999 All other miscellaneous food manufacturing

31211M Soft drink and ice manufacturing
312111 Soft drink manufacturing
312112 Bottled water manufacturing
312113 Ice manufacturing

312120 Breweries
312120 Breweries

312130 Wineries
312130 Wineries

312140 Distilleries
312140 Distilleries

312210 Tobacco stemming and redrying
312210 Tobacco stemming and redrying

31222M Tobacco product manufacturing
312221 Cigarette manufacturing
312229 Other tobacco product manufacturing

31311M Fiber, yarn, and thread mills
313111 Yarn spinning mills
313112 Yarn texturing, throwing, and twisting mills
313113 Thread mills

313210 Broadwoven fabric mills
313210 Broadwoven fabric mills

31322M Narrow fabric mills and schiffli machine embroidery
313221 Narrow fabric mills
313222 Schiffli machine embroidery

313230 Nonwoven fabric mills
313230 Nonwoven fabric mills

31324M Knit fabric mills
313241 Weft knit fabric mills
313249 Other knit fabric and lace mills

31331M Textile and fabric finishing mills
311311 Broadwoven fabric finishing mills
311312 Textile and fabric finishing (except broadwoven fabric) mills

313320 Fabric coating mills
311320 Fabric coating mills

314110 Carpet and rug mills
314110 Carpet and rug mills

31412M Curtain and linen mills
314121 Curtain and drapery mills
314129 Other household textile product mills

31491M Textile bag and canvas mills
314911 Textile bag mills
314912 Canvas and related product mills

314991 Rope, cordage, and twine mills
314991 Rope, cordage, and twine mills

314992 Tire cord and tire fabric mills
314992 Tire cord and tire fabric mills

314999 Textile product mills, nec
314999 All other miscellaneous textile product mills

31511M Hosiery and sock mills
315111 Sheer hosiery mills
315119 Other hosiery and sock mills

31519M Apparel knitting mills, nec
315191 Outerwear knitting mills
315192 Underwear and nightwear knitting mills

31521M Cut and sew apparel contractors
315211 Men's and boys' cut and sew apparel contractors
315212 Women's, girl's, and infants' cut and sew apparel contractors

31522M Men's and boys' cut and sew apparel manufacturing
315221 Men's and boys' cut and sew underwear and nightwear manufacturing
315222 Men's and boys' cut and sew suit, coat, and overcoat manufacturing
315223 Men's and boys' cut and sew shirt (except work shirt) manufacturing
315224 Men's and boys' cut and sew trouser, slack, and jean manufacturing

315225 Men's and boys' cut and sew work clothing manufacturing
315228 Men's and boys' cut and sew other outerwear manufacturing

31523M Women's and girls' cut and sew apparel manufacturing
315231 Women's and girls' cut and sew lingerie, loungewear, and nightwear manufacturing
315232 Women's and girls' cut and sew blouse and shirt manufacturing
315233 Women's and girls' cut and sew dress manufacturing
315234 Women's and girls' cut and sew suit, coat, tailored jacket, and skirt manufacturing
315239 Women's and girls' cut and sew other outerwear manufacturing

31529M Cut and sew apparel manufacturing, nec
315291 Infants' cut and sew apparel manufacturing
315292 Fur and leather apparel manufacturing
315299 All other cut and sew apparel manufacturing

31599M Apparel accessories and other apparel manufacturing
315991 Hat, cap, and millinery manufacturing
315992 Glove and mitten manufacturing
315993 Men's and boys' neckwear manufacturing
315999 Other apparel accessories and other apparel manu-facturing

316110 Leather and hide tanning and finishing
316110 Leather and hide tanning and finishing

31621M Footwear manufacturing
316211 Rubber and plastics footwear manufacturing
316212 House slipper manufacturing
316213 Men's footwear (except athletic) manufacturing
316214 Women's footwear (except athletic) manufacturing
316219 Other footwear manufacturing

31699M Leather and allied product manufacturing, nec
316991 Luggage manufacturing
316992 Women's handbag and purse manufacturing
316993 Personal leather good (except women's handbag and purse) manu-facturing
316999 All other leather good manufacturing

32111M Sawmills and wood preservation
321113 Sawmills
321114 Wood preservation

321219 Reconstituted wood product manufacturing
321219 Reconstituted wood product manufacturing

32121N Veneer and plywood manufacturing
321211 Hardwood veneer and plywood manufacturing
321212 Softwood veneer and plywood manufacturing

32121P Engineered wood product manufacturing
321213 Engineered wood member (except truss) manufacturing
321214 Truss manufacturing

32191M Millwork
321911 Wood window and door manufacturing
321912 Cut stock, resawing lumber, and planing
321918 Other millwork (including flooring)

321920 Wood container and pallet manufacturing
321920 Wood container and pallet manufacturing

321991 Manufactured home (mobile home) manufacturing
321991 Manufactured home (mobile home) manufacturing

321992 Prefabricated wood building manufacturing
321992 Prefabricated wood building manufacturing

321999 Wood product manufacturing, nec
321999 All other miscellaneous wood product manufacturing

322110 Pulp mills
322110 Pulp mills

32212M Paper and newsprint mills
322121 Paper (except newsprint) mills
322122 Newsprint mills

322130 Paperboard mills
322130 Paperboard mills

32221M Paperboard container mills
322211 Corrugated and solid fiber box manufacturing
322212 Folding paperboard box manufacturing
322213 Setup paperboard box manufacturing
322214 Fiber can, tube, drum, and similar products manufacturing
322215 Nonfolding sanitary food container manufacturing

32222N Coated and laminated paper and packaging manufacturing
322221 Coated and laminated packaging paper and plastics film manufacturing
322222 Coated and laminated paper manufacturing

32222P Coated, uncoated and multiwall bag and packaging manufacturing
322223 Plastics, foil, and coated paper bag manufacturing
322224 Uncoated paper and multiwall bag manufacturing
322225 Laminated aluminum foil manufacturing for flexible packaging uses
322226 Surface-coated paperboard manufacturing

32223M Stationery product manufacturing
322231 Die-cut paper and paperboard office supplies manufacturing
322232 Envelope manufacturing
322233 Stationery, tablet, and related product manufacturing

322291 Sanitary paper product manufacturing
322291 Sanitary paper product manufacturing

322299 Converted paper product manufacturing, nec
322299 All other converted paper product manufacturing

32311M Printing
323110 Commercial lithographic printing
323111 Commercial gravure printing
323112 Commercial flexographic printing
323113 Commercial screen printing
323114 Quick printing
323115 Digital printing
323116 Manifold business form printing
323117 Books printing
323118 Blankbook, loose-leaf binders, and devices manufacturing
323119 Other commercial printing

32312M Support activities for printing
323121 Trade binding and related work
323122 Prepress services

324110 Petroleum refineries
324110 Petroleum refineries

324121 Asphalt paving mixture and block manufacturing
324121 Asphalt paving mixture and block manufacturing

324122 Asphalt shingle and coating materials manufacturing
324122 Asphalt shingle and coating materials manufacturing

324191 Petroleum lubricating oil and grease manufacturing
324191 Petroleum lubricating oil and grease manufacturing

324199 Petroleum and coal products manufacturing, nec
324199 All other petroleum and coal products manufacturing

325110 Petrochemical manufacturing
325110 Petrochemical manufacturing

325120 Industrial gas manufacturing
325120 Industrial gas manufacturing

32513M Synthetic dye and pigment manufacturing
325131 Inorganic dye and pigment manufacturing
325132 Synthetic organic dye and pigment manufacturing

325181 Alkalies and chlorine manufacturing
325181 Alkalies and chlorine manufacturing

325182 Carbon black manufacturing
325182 Carbon black manufacturing

325188 Basic inorganic chemical manufacturing, nec
325188 All other basic inorganic chemical manufacturing

32519M Basic organic chemical manufacturing, nec
325191 Gum and wood chemical manufacturing
325192 Cyclic crude and intermediate manufacturing
325193 Ethyl alcohol manufacturing
325199 All other basic organic chemical manufacturing

325211 Plastics material and resin manufacturing
325211 Plastics material and resin manufacturing

325212 Synthetic rubber manufacturing
325212 Synthetic rubber manufacturing

32522M Artificial and synthetic fibers and filaments manufacturing
325221 Cellulosic organic fiber manufacturing
325222 Noncellulosic organic fiber manufacturing

325311 Nitrogenous fertilizer manufacturing
325311 Nitrogenous fertilizer manufacturing

325312 Phosphatic fertilizer manufacturing
325312 Phosphatic fertilizer manufacturing

325314 Fertilizer (mixing only) manufacturing
325314 Fertilizer (mixing only) manufacturing

325320 Pesticide and other agricultural chemical manufacturing
325320 Pesticide and other agricultural chemical manufacturing

325411 Medicinal and botanical manufacturing
325411 Medicinal and botanical manufacturing

325412 Pharmaceutical preparation manufacturing
325412 Pharmaceutical preparation manufacturing

325413 In-vitro diagnostic substance manufacturing
325413 In-vitro diagnostic substance manufacturing

325414 Biological product (except diagnostic) manufacturing
325414 Biological product (except diagnostic) manufacturing

325510 Paint and coating manufacturing
325510 Paint and coating manufacturing

325520 Adhesive manufacturing
325520 Adhesive manufacturing

32561M Soap and cleaning compound manufacturing
325611 Soap and other detergent manufacturing
325612 Polish and other sanitation goods manufacturing
325613 Surface active agent manufacturing

325620 Toilet preparation manufacturing
325620 Toilet preparation manufacturing

325910 Printing ink manufacturing
325910 Printing ink manufacturing

325920 Explosives manufacturing
325920 Explosives manufacturing

325991 Custom compounding of purchased resins
325991 Custom compounding of purchased resins

ASM NAICS/2002 NAICS Conversion Guide

32599N Chemical product and preparation manufacturing, nec
325992 Photographic film, paper, plate, and chemical manufacturing
325998 All other miscellaneous chemical product and preparation manufacturing

326111 Plastics bag manufacturing
326111 Plastics bag manufacturing

326112 Plastics packaging film and sheet manufacturing
326112 Plastics packaging film and sheet manufacturing

326113 Unlaminated plastics film and sheet (except packaging) manufacturing
326113 Unlaminated plastics film and sheet (except packaging) manufacturing

326121 Unsupported plastics profile shape manufacturing
326121 Unlaminated plastics profile shape manufacturing

326122 Plastics pipe and pipe fitting manufacturing
326122 Plastics pipe and pipe fitting manufacturing

326130 Laminated plastics plate, sheet, and shape manufacturing
326130 Laminated plastics plate, sheet (except packaging), and shape manufacturing

326140 Polystyrene foam product manufacturing
326140 Polystyrene foam product manufacturing

326150 Urethane and other foam product (except polystyrene) manufacturing
326150 Urethane and other foam product (except polystyrene) manufacturing

326160 Plastics bottle manufacturing
326160 Plastics bottle manufacturing

32619M Plastics product manufacturing, nec
326191 Plastics plumbing fixture manufacturing
326192 Resilient floor covering manufacturing
326199 All other plastics product manufacturing

32621M Tire manufacturing
326211 Tire manufacturing (except retreading)
326212 Tire retreading

326220 Rubber and plastics hoses and belting manufacturing
326220 Rubber and plastics hoses and belting manufacturing

32629M Rubber product manufacturing, nec
326291 Rubber product manufacturing for mechanical use
326299 All other rubber product manufacturing

327111 Vitreous china plumbing fixture and china and earthenware bathroom accessories manufacturing
327111 Vitreous china plumbing fixture and china and earthenware bathroom accessories manufacturing

327112 Vitreous china, fine earthenware, and other pottery product manufacturing
327112 Vitreous china, fine earthenware, and other pottery product manufacturing

327113 Porcelain electrical supply manufacturing
327113 Porcelain electrical supply manufacturing

327121 Brick and structural clay tile manufacturing
327121 Brick and structural clay tile manufacturing

327122 Ceramic wall and floor tile manufacturing
327122 Ceramic wall and floor tile manufacturing

327123 Structural clay product manufacturing, nec
327123 Other structural clay product manufacturing

32712N Refractory manufacturing
327124 Clay refractory manufacturing
327125 Nonclay refractory manufacturing

327211 Flat glass manufacturing
327211 Flat glass manufacturing

327212 Pressed and blown glass and glassware manufacturing, nec
327212 Other pressed and blown glass and glassware manufacturing

327213 Glass container manufacturing
327213 Glass container manufacturing

327215 Glass product manufacturing made of purchased glass
327215 Glass product manufacturing made of purchased glass

327310 Cement manufacturing
327310 Cement manufacturing

327320 Ready-mix concrete manufacturing
327320 Ready-mix concrete manufacturing

32733M Concrete pipe, brick, and block manufacturing
327331 Concrete block and brick manufacturing
327332 Concrete pipe manufacturing

327390 Concrete product manufacturing, nec
327390 Other concrete product manufacturing

327410 Lime manufacturing
327410 Lime manufacturing

327420 Gypsum product manufacturing
327420 Gypsum product manufacturing

327910 Abrasive product manufacturing
327910 Abrasive product manufacturing

327991 Cut stone and stone product manufacturing
327991 Cut stone and stone product manufacturing

327992 Ground or treated mineral and earth manufacturing
327992 Ground or treated mineral and earth manufacturing

327993 Mineral wool manufacturing
327993 Mineral wool manufacturing

327999 Nonmetallic mineral product manufacturing, nec
327999 All other miscellaneous nonmetallic mineral product manufacturing

33111M Iron and steel mills and ferroalloy manufacturing
331111 Iron and steel mills
331112 Electrometallurgical ferroalloy product manufacturing

331210 Iron and steel pipe and tube manufacturing from purchased steel
331210 Iron and steel pipe and tube manufacturing from purchased steel

33122M Rolling and drawing of purchased steel
331221 Rolled steel shape manufacturing
331222 Steel wire drawing

331311 Alumina refining
331311 Alumina refining

331312 Primary aluminum production
331312 Primary aluminum production

331314 Secondary smelting and alloying of aluminum
331314 Secondary smelting and alloying of aluminum

331316 Aluminum extruded product manufacturing
331316 Aluminum extruded product manufacturing

33131N Aluminum rolling and drawing
331315 Aluminum sheet, plate, and foil manufacturing
331319 Other aluminum rolling and drawing

331411 Primary smelting and refining of copper
331411 Primary smelting and refining of copper

331419 Primary smelting and refining of nonferrous metal (except copper and aluminum)
331419 Primary smelting and refining of nonferrous metal (except copper and aluminum)

33142M Copper rolling, drawing, extruding, and alloying
331421 Copper rolling, drawing, and extruding
331422 Copper wire (except mechanical) drawing
331423 Secondary smelting, refining, and alloying of copper

33149M Nonferrous metal (except copper and aluminum) rolling, drawing, extruding, and alloying
331491 Nonferrous metal (except copper and aluminum) rolling, drawing, and extruding
331492 Secondary smelting, refining, and alloying of nonferrous metal (except copper and aluminum)

33151M Ferrous metal foundries
331511 Iron foundries
331512 Steel investment foundries
331513 Steel foundries (except investment)

33152N Aluminum foundries
331521 Aluminum die-casting foundries
331524 Aluminum foundries (except die-casting)

33152P Nonaluminum Foundries
331522 Nonferrous (except aluminum) die-casting foundries
331525 Copper foundries (except die-casting)
331528 Other nonferrous foundries (except die-casting)

332114 Custom roll forming
332114 Custom roll forming

332117 Powder metallurgy parts manufacturing
332117 Powder metallurgy parts manufacturing

33211N Forging
332111 Iron and steel forging
332112 Nonferrous forging

33211P Crown, closure and metal stamping manufacturing
332115 Crown and closure manufacturing
332116 Metal stamping

33221N Cutlery, kitchen utensil, pot and pan manufacturing
332211 Cutlery and flatware (except precious) manufacturing
332214 Kitchen utensil, pot, and pan manufacturing

33221P Hand tool and saw blade manufacturing
332212 Hand and edge tool manufacturing
332213 Saw blade and handsaw manufacturing

33231M Plate work and fabricated structural product manufacturing
332311 Prefabricated metal building and component manufacturing
332312 Fabricated structural metal manufacturing
332313 Plate work manufacturing

33232M Ornamental, sheet and architectural metal work manufacturing
332321 Metal window and door manufacturing
332322 Sheet metal work manufacturing
332323 Ornamental and architectural metal work manufacturing

332410 Power boiler and heat exchanger manufacturing
332410 Power boiler and heat exchanger manufacturing

332420 Metal tank (heavy gauge) manufacturing
332420 Metal tank (heavy gauge) manufacturing

33243M Metal can, box, and other metal container (light gauge) manufacturing
332431 Metal can manufacturing
332439 Other metal container manufacturing

332510 Hardware manufacturing
332510 Hardware manufacturing

33261M Spring and wire product manufacturing
332611 Spring (heavy gauge) manufacturing
332612 Spring (light gauge) manufacturing
332618 Other fabricated wire product manufacturing

332710 Machine shops
332710 Machine shops

332721 Precision turned product manufacturing
332721 Precision turned product manufacturing

332722 Bolt, nut, screw, rivet, and washer manufacturing
332722 Bolt, nut, screw, rivet, and washer manufacturing

33281M Coating, engraving, heat treating, and allied activities
332811 Metal heat treating
332812 Metal coating, engraving (except jewelry and silverware), and allied services to manufacturers
332813 Electroplating, plating, polishing, anodizing, and coloring

332913 Plumbing fixture fitting and trim manufacturing
332913 Plumbing fixture fitting and trim manufacturing

33291N Valves and fittings manufacturing, nonplumbing
332911 Industrial valve manufacturing
332912 Fluid power valve and hose fitting manufacturing
332919 Other metal valve and pipe fitting manufacturing

332991 Ball and roller bearing manufacturing
332991 Ball and roller bearing manufacturing

332992 Small arms ammunition manufacturing
332992 Small arms ammunition manufacturing

332993 Ammunition (except small arms) manufacturing
332993 Ammunition (except small arms) manufacturing

332994 Small arms manufacturing
332994 Small arms manufacturing

332995 Ordnance and accessories manufacturing, nec
332995 Other ordnance and accessories manufacturing

332996 Fabricated pipe and pipe fitting manufacturing
332996 Fabricated pipe and pipe fitting manufacturing

33299N Fabricated metal products manufacturing, nec
332997 Industrial pattern manufacturing
332998 Enameled iron and metal sanitary ware manufacturing
332999 All other miscellaneous fabricated metal product manufacturing

333111 Farm machinery and equipment manufacturing
333111 Farm machinery and equipment manufacturing

333112 Lawn and garden tractor and home lawn and garden equipment manufacturing
333112 Lawn and garden tractor and home lawn and garden equipment manufacturing

333120 Construction machinery manufacturing
333120 Construction machinery manufacturing

33313M Mining and oil and gas field machinery manufacturing
333131 Mining machinery and equipment manufacturing
333132 Oil and gas field machinery and equipment manufacturing

333210 Sawmill and woodworking machinery manufacturing
333210 Sawmill and woodworking machinery manufacturing

333220 Plastics and rubber industry machinery manufacturing
333220 Plastics and rubber industry machinery manufacturing

333295 Semiconductor machinery manufacturing
333295 Semiconductor machinery manufacturing

33329N Machinery manufacturing, nec
  333291 Paper industry machinery manufacturing
  333292 Textile machinery manufacturing
  333293 Printing machinery and equipment manufacturing
  333294 Food product machinery manufacturing
  333298 All other industrial machinery manufacturing

333313 Office machinery manufacturing
  333313 Office machinery manufacturing

333314 Optical instrument and lens manufacturing
  333314 Optical instrument and lens manufacturing

333315 Photographic and photocopying equipment manufacturing
  333315 Photographic and photocopying equipment manufacturing

33331N Other commercial and service industry machinery manufacturng, nec
  333311 Automatic vending machine manufacturing
  333312 Commercial laundry, dry cleaning, and pressing machine manufacturing
  333319 Other commercial and service industry machinery manufacturing

333414 Heating equipment (except warm air furnaces) manufacturing
  333414 Heating equipment (except warm air furnaces) manufacturing

333415 Air-conditioning and warm air heating equipment and commercial and industrial refrigeration equipment manufacturing
  333415 Air-conditioning and warm air heating equipment and commercial and industrial refrigeration equipment manufacturing

33341N Ventilation equipment manufacturing
  333411 Air purification equipment manufacturing
  333412 Industrial and commercial fan and blower manufacturing

333511 Industrial mold manufacturing
  333511 Industrial mold manufacturing

333512 Machine tool (metal cutting types) manufacturing
  333512 Machine tool (metal cutting types) manufacturing

333513 Machine tool (metal forming types) manufacturing
  333513 Machine tool (metal forming types) manufacturing

333514 Special die and tool, die set, jig, and fixture manufacturing
  333514 Special die and tool, die set, jig, and fixture manufacturing

333515 Cutting tool and machine tool accessory manufacturing
  333515 Cutting tool and machine tool accessory manufacturing

333516 Rolling mill machinery and equipment manufacturing
  333516 Rolling mill machinery and equipment manufacturing

333518 Metalworking machinery manufacturing, nec
  333518 Other metalworking machinery manufacturing

333611 Turbine and turbine generator set unit manufacturing
  333611 Turbine and turbine generator set units manufacturing

333612 Speed changer, industrial high-speed drive, and gear manufacturing
  333612 Speed changer, industrial high-speed drive, and gear manufacturing

333613 Mechanical power transmission equipment manufacturing
  333613 Mechanical power transmission equipment manufacturing

333618 Engine equipment manufacturing, nec
  333618 Other engine equipment manufacturing

333911 Pump and pumping equipment manufacturing
  333911 Pump and pumping equipment manufacturing

333912 Air and gas compressor manufacturing
  333912 Air and gas compressor manufacturing

333913 Measuring and dispensing pump manufacturing
  333913 Measuring and dispensing pump manufacturing

33392M Material handling equipment manufacturing
  333921 Elevator and moving stairway manufacturing
  333922 Conveyor and conveying equipment manufacturing
  333923 Overhead traveling crane, hoist, and monorail system manufacturing
  333924 Industrial truck, tractor, trailer, and stacker machinery manufacturing

333991 Power-driven hand tool manufacturing
  333991 Power-driven hand tool manufacturing

333993 Packaging machinery manufacturing
  333993 Packaging machinery manufacturing

333994 Industrial process furnace and oven manufacturing
  333994 Industrial process furnace and oven manufacturing

33399N Fluid power equipment manufacturing
  333995 Fluid power cylinder and actuator manufacturing
  333996 Fluid power pump and motor manufacturing

33399P General purpose machinery manufacturing, nec
  333992 Welding and soldering equipment manufacturing
  333997 Scale and balance (except laboratory) manufacturing
  333999 All other miscellaneous general-purpose machinery manufacturing

334111 Electronic computer manufacturing
  334111 Electronic computer manufacturing

334112 Computer storage device manufacturing
  334112 Computer storage device manufacturing

334113 Computer terminal manufacturing
  334113 Computer terminal manufacturing

334119 Computer peripheral equipment manufacturing, nec
  334119 Other computer peripheral equipment manufacturing

334210 Telephone apparatus manufacturing
  334210 Telephone apparatus manufacturing

334220 Radio and television broadcasting and wireless communications equipment manufacturing
  334220 Radio and television broadcasting and wireless commuinications equipment manufacturing

334290 Communications equipment manufacturing, nec
  334290 Other communications equipment manufacturing

334310 Audio and video equipment manufacturing
  334310 Audio and video equipment manufacturing

334411 Electron tube manufacturing
  334411 Electron tube manufacturing

334412 Bare printed circuit board manufacturing
  334412 Bare printed circuit board manufacturing

334413 Semiconductor and related device manufacturing
  334413 Semiconductor and related device manufacturing

334414 Electronic capacitor manufacturing
  334414 Electronic capacitor manufacturing

334415 Electronic resistor manufacturing
  334415 Electronic resistor manufacturing

334416 Electronic coil, transformer, and other inductor manufacturing
  334416 Electronic coil, transformer, and other inductor manufacturing

334417 Electronic connector manufacturing
  334417 Electronic connector manufacturing

334418 Printed circuit assembly (electronic assembly) manufacturing
  334418 Printed circuit assembly (electronic assembly) manufacturing

334419 Other electronic component manufacturing
  334419 Other electronic component manufacturing

334510 Electromedical and electrotherapeutic apparatus manufacturing
    334510 Electromedical and electrotherapeutic apparatus manufacturing

334511 Search, detection, navigation, guidance, aeronautical, and nautical system and instrument manufacturing
    334511 Search, detection, navigation, guidance, aeronautical, and nautical system and instrument manufacturing

334512 Automatic environmental control manufacturing for residential, commercial, and appliance use
    334512 Automatic environmental control manufacturing for residential, commercial, and appliance use

334513 Instruments and related products manufacturing for measuring, displaying, and controlling industrial process variables
    334513 Instruments and related products manufacturing for measuring, displaying, and controlling industrial process variables

334514 Totalizing fluid meter and counting device manufacturing
    334514 Totalizing fluid meter and counting device manufacturing

334515 Instrument manufacturing for measuring and testing electricity and electrical signals
    334515 Instrument manufacturing for measuring and testing electricity and electrical signals

334516 Analytical laboratory instrument manufacturing
    334516 Analytical laboratory instrument manufacturing

334517 Irradiation apparatus manufacturing
    334517 Irradiation apparatus manufacturing

334518 Watch, clock, and parts manufacturing
    334518 Watch, clock, and part manufacturing

334519 Measuring and controlling device manufacturing, nec
    334519 Other measuring and controlling device manufacturing

334611 Software reproducing
    334611 Software reproducing

334612 Prerecorded compact disc (except software), tape, and record reproducing
    334612 Prerecorded compact disc (except software), tape, and record reproducing

334613 Magnetic and optical recording media manufacturing
    334613 Magnetic and optical recording media manufacturing

335110 Electric lamp bulb and parts manufacturing
    335110 Electric lamp bulb and part manufacturing

33512M Lighting fixture manufacturing
    335121 Residential electric lighting fixture manufacturing
    335122 Commercial, industrial, and institutional electric lighting fixture manufacturing
    335129 Other lighting equipment manufacturing

33521M Small electrical appliance manufacturing
    335211 Electric house wares and household fan manufacturing
    335212 Household vacuum cleaner manufacturing

335221 Household cooking appliance manufacturing
    335221 Household cooking appliance manufacturing

335222 Household refrigerator and home freezer manufacturing
    335222 Household refrigerator and home freezer manufacturing

335224 Household laundry equipment manufacturing
    335224 Household laundry equipment manufacturing

335228 Major household appliance manufacturing, nec
    335224 Other major household appliance manufacturing

335311 Power, distribution, and specialty transformer manufacturing
    335311 Power, distribution, and specialty transformer manufacturing

335312 Motor and generator manufacturing
    335312 Motor and generator manufacturing

335313 Switchgear and switchboard apparatus manufacturing
    335313 Switchgear and switchboard apparatus manufacturing

335314 Relay and industrial control manufacturing
    335314 Relay and industrial control manufacturing

335911 Storage battery manufacturing
    335911 Storage battery manufacturing

335912 Primary battery manufacturing
    335912 Primary battery manufacturing

33592M Communication and energy wire and cable manufacturing
    335921 Fiber optic cable manufacturing
    335929 Other communication and energy wire manufacturing

33593M Wiring device manufacturing
    335931 Current-carrying wiring device manufacturing
    335932 Noncurrent-carrying wiring device manufacturing

335991 Carbon and graphite product manufacturing
    335991 Carbon and graphite product manufacturing

335999 Electrical equipment and component manufacturing, nec
    335999 All other miscellaneous electrical equipment and component manufacturing

336111 Automobile manufacturing
    336111 Automobile manufacturing

336112 Light truck and utility vehicle manufacturing
    336112 Light truck and utility vehicle manufacturing

336120 Heavy duty truck manufacturing
    336120 Heavy duty truck manufacturing

336211 Motor vehicle body manufacturing
    336211 Motor vehicle body manufacturing

336212 Truck trailer manufacturing
    336212 Truck trailer manufacturing

336213 Motor home manufacturing
    336213 Motor home manufacturing

336214 Travel trailer and camper manufacturing
    336214 Travel trailer and camper manufacturing

33631M Motor vehicle gasoline engine and engine parts manufacturing
    336311 Carburetor, piston, piston ring, and valve manufacturing
    336312 Gasoline engine and engine parts manufacturing

33632M Motor vehicle electrical and electronic equipment manufacturing
    336321 Vehicular lighting equipment manufacturing
    336322 Other motor vehicle electrical and electronic equipment manufacturing

336330 Motor vehicle steering and suspension component (except spring) manufacturing
    336330 Motor vehicle steering and suspension component (except spring) manufacturing

336340 Motor vehicle brake system manufacturing
    336340 Motor vehicle brake system manufacturing

336350 Motor vehicle transmission and power train parts manufacturing
    336350 Motor vehicle transmission and power train parts manufacturing

336360 Motor vehicle seating and interior trim manufacturing
    336360 Motor vehicle seating and interior trim manufacturing

336370 Motor vehicle metal stamping
336370 Motor vehicle metal stamping

336391 Motor vehicle air-conditioning manufacturing
336391 Motor vehicle air-conditioning manufacturing

336399 Motor vehicle parts manufacturing, nec
336399 All other motor vehicle parts manufacturing

336411 Aircraft manufacturing
336411 Aircraft manufacturing

336412 Aircraft engine and engine parts manufacturing
336412 Aircraft engine and engine parts manufacturing

336413 Other aircraft parts and auxiliary equipment manufacturing
336413 Other aircraft parts and auxiliary equipment manufacturing

336414 Guided missile and space vehicle manufacturing
336414 Guided missile and space vehicle manufacturing

336415 Guided missile and space vehicle propulsion unit and propulsion unit parts manufacturing
336415 Guided missile and space vehicle propulsion unit and propulsion unit parts manufacturing

336419 Guided missile and space vehicle parts and auxiliary equipment manufacturing, nec
336419 Other guided missile and space vehicle parts and auxiliary equipment manufacturing

336510 Railroad rolling stock manufacturing
336510 Railroad rolling stock manufacturing

336611 Ship building and repairing
336611 Ship building and repairing

336612 Boat building
336612 Boat building

336991 Motorcycle, bicycle, and parts manufacturing
336991 Motorcycle, bicycle, and parts manufacturing

336992 Military armored vehicle, tank, and tank component manufacturing
336992 Military armored vehicle, tank, and tank component manufacturing

336999 All other transportation equipment manufacturing
336999 All other transportation equipment manufacturing

337110 Wood kitchen cabinet and counter top manufacturing
337110 Wood kitchen cabinet and counter top manufacturing

337121 Upholstered household furniture manufacturing
337121 Upholstered household furniture manufacturing

337122 Nonupholstered wood household furniture manufacturing
337122 Nonupholstered wood household furniture manufacturing

337127 Institutional furniture
337127 Institutional furniture

33712N Household nonupholstered furniture, nec
337124 Metal household furniture manufacturing
337125 Household furniture (except wood and metal) manufacturing
337129 Wood television, radio, and sewing machine cabinet manufacturing

337212 Custom architectural woodwork and millwork manufacturing
337212 Custom architectural woodwork and millwork manufacturing

337215 Showcase, partition, shelving, and locker manufacturing
337215 Showcase, partition, shelving, and locker manufacturing

33721N Office furniture manufacturing
337211 Wood office furniture manufacturing
337214 Office furniture (except wood) manufacturing

337910 Mattress manufacturing
337910 Mattress manufacturing

337920 Blind and shade manufacturing
337920 Blind and shade manufacturing

339111 Laboratory apparatus and furniture manufacturing
339111 Laboratory apparatus and furniture manufacturing **339112 Surgical and medical instrument manufacturing**
339112 Surgical and medical instrument manufacturing

339113 Surgical appliance and supplies manufacturing
339113 Surgical appliance and supplies manufacturing

339114 Dental equipment and supplies manufacturing
339114 Dental equipment and supplies manufacturing

339115 Ophthalmic goods manufacturing
339115 Ophthalmic goods manufacturing

339116 Dental laboratories
339116 Dental laboratories

33991M Jewelry and silverware manufacturing
339911 Jewelry (except costume) manufacturing
339912 Silverware and hollowware manufacturing
339913 Jewelers' material and lapidary work manufacturing
339914 Costume jewelry and novelty manufacturing

339920 Sporting and athletic goods manufacturing
339920 Sporting and athletic goods manufacturing

33993M Doll, toy, and game manufacturing
339931 Doll and stuffed toy manufacturing
339932 Game, toy, and children's vehicle manufacturing

33994M Office supplies (except paper) manufacturing
339941 Pen and mechanical pencil manufacturing
339942 Lead pencil and art good manufacturing
339943 Marking device manufacturing
339944 Carbon paper and inked ribbon manufacturing

339950 Sign manufacturing
339950 Sign manufacturing

339991 Gasket, packing, and sealing device manufacturing
339991 Gasket, packing, and sealing device manufacturing

339992 Musical instrument manufacturing
339992 Musical instrument manufacturing

339993 Fastener, button, needle, and pin manufacturing
339993 Fastener, button, needle, and pin manufacturing

339994 Broom, brush, and mop manufacturing
339994 Broom, brush, and mop manufacturing

339995 Burial casket manufacturing
339995 Burial casket manufacturing

339999 Miscellaneous manufacturing, nec
339999 Miscellaneous manufacturing, nec

2002 NAICS to ASM NAICS Conversion Guide

This index shows the 2002 Federal Government NAICS codes and descriptions along with their corresponding *Annual Survey of Manufactures'* (ASM) NAICS codes and descriptions. Nec stands for 'not elsewhere classified.' 2002 Federal Government NAICS are in bold.

311111 Dog and cat food manufacturing
311111 Dog and cat food manufacturing

311119 Other animal food manufacturing
311119 Animal food manufacturing, nec

311211 Flour milling
31121M Flour milling and malt manufacturing (part)

311212 Rice milling
31121M Flour milling and malt manufacturing (part)

311313 Malt manufacturing
31121M Flour milling and malt manufacturing (part)

311221 Wet corn milling
311221 Wet corn milling

311222 Soybean processing
31122N Soybean and other oilseed processing (part)

311223 Other oilseeed processing
31122N Soybean and other oilseed processing (part)

311225 Fats and oils refining and blending
311225 Fats and oils refining and blending

311230 Breakfast cereal manufacturing
311230 Breakfast cereal manufacturing

311311 Sugar cane mills
31131N Sugar cane mills and refining (part)

311312 Cane sugar refining
31131N Sugar cane mills and refining (part)

311313 Beet sugar manufacturing
311313 Beet sugar manufacturing

311320 Chocolate and confectionery manufacturing from cacao beans
311320 Chocolate and confectionery manufacturing from cacao beans

311330 Confectionery manufacturing from purchased chocolate
311330 Confectionery manufacturing from purchased chocolate

311340 Nonchocolate confectionery manufacturing
311340 Nonchocolate confectionery manufacturing

311411 Frozen fruit, juice, and vegetable manufacturing
31141M Frozen food manufacturing (part)

311412 Frozen specialty food manufacturing
31141M Frozen food manufacturing (part)

311421 Fruit and vegetable canning
31142M Fruit and vegetable canning, pickling, and drying (part)

311422 Specialty canning
31142M Fruit and vegetable canning, pickling, and drying (part)

311423 Dried and dehydrated food manufacturing
31142M Fruit and vegetable canning, pickling, and drying (part)

311511 Fluid milk manufacturing
31151N Fluid milk and butter manufacturing (part)

311512 Creamery butter manufacturing
31151N Fluid milk and butter manufacturing (part)

311513 Cheese manufacturing
311513 Cheese manufacturing

311514 Dry, condensed, and evaporated dairy product manufacturing
311514 Dry, condensed, and evaporated dairy product manufacturing

311520 Ice cream and frozen dessert manufacturing
311520 Ice cream and frozen dessert manufacturing

311611 Animal (except poultry) slaughtering
31161N Animal (except poultry) slaughtering and processing (part)

311612 Meat processed from carcasses
31161N Animal (except poultry) slaughtering and processing (part)

311613 Rendering and meat byproduct processing
31161N Animal (except poultry) slaughtering and processing (part)

311615 Poultry processing
311615 Poultry processing

311711 Seafood canning
31171M Seafood product preparation and packaging (part)

311712 Fresh and frozen seafood processing
31171M Seafood product preparation and packaging (part)

311811 Retail bakeries
31181M Bread and bakery product manufacturing (part)

311812 Commercial bakeries
31181M Bread and bakery product manufacturing (part)

311813 Frozen cakes, pies, and other pastries manufacturing
31181M Bread and bakery product manufacturing (part)

311821 Cookie and cracker manufacturing
31182M Cookie, cracker, and pasta manufacturing (part)

311822 Flour mixes and dough manufacturing from purchased flour
31182M Cookie, cracker, and pasta manufacturing (part)

311823 Dry pasta manufacturing
31182M Cookie, cracker, and pasta manufacturing (part)

311830 Tortilla manufacturing
311830 Tortilla manufacturing

311911 Roasted nuts and peanut butter manufacturing
31191M Snack food manufacturing (part)

311919 Other snack food manufacturing
31191M Snack food manufacturing (part)

311920 Coffee and tea manufacturing
311920 Coffee and tea manufacturing

311930 Flavoring syrup and concentrate manufacturing
311930 Flavoring syrup and concentrate manufacturing

311941 Mayonnaise, dressing, and other prepared sauce manufacturing
31194M Seasoning and dressing manufacturing (part)

311942 Spice and extract manufacturing
31194M Seasoning and dressing manufacturing (part)

311991 Perishable prepared food manufacturing
31199M Food manufacturing, nec (part)

311999 All other miscellaneous food manufacturing
31199M Food manufacturing, nec (part)

312111 Soft drink manufacturing
31211M Soft drink and ice manufacturing (part)

312112 Bottled water manufacturing
31211M Soft drink and ice manufacturing (part)

312113 Ice manufacturing
31211M Soft drink and ice manufacturing (part)

312120 Breweries
312120 Breweries

312130 Wineries
312130 Wineries

312140 Distilleries
312140 Distilleries

312210 Tobacco stemming and redrying
312210 Tobacco stemming and redrying

312221 Cigarette manufacturing
31222M Tobacco product manufacturing (part)

312229 Other tobacco product manufacturing
31222M Tobacco product manufacturing (part)

313111 Yarn spinning mills
31311M Fiber, yarn, and thread mills (part)

313112 Yarn texturing, throwing, and twisting mills
31311M Fiber, yarn, and thread mills (part)

313113 Thread mills
31311M Fiber, yarn, and thread mills (part)

313210 Broadwoven fabric mills
313210 Broadwoven fabric mills

313221 Narrow fabric mills
31322M Narrow fabric mills and schiffli machine embroidery (part)

313222 Schiffli machine embroidery
31322M Narrow fabric mills and schiffli machine embroidery (part)

313230 Nonwoven fabric mills
313230 Nonwoven fabric mills

313241 Weft knit fabric mills
31324M Knit fabric mills (part)

313249 Other knit fabric and lace mills
31324M Knit fabric mills (part)

311311 Broadwoven fabric finishing mills
31331M Textile and fabric finishing mills (part)

311312 Textile and fabric finishing (except broadwoven fabric) mills
31331M Textile and fabric finishing mills (part)

313320 Fabric coating mills
311320 Fabric coating mills

314110 Carpet and rug mills
314110 Carpet and rug mills

314121 Curtain and drapery mills
31412M Curtain and linen mills (part)

314129 Other household textile product mills
31412M Curtain and linen mills (part)

314911 Textile bag mills
31491M Textile bag and canvas mills (part)

314912 Canvas and related product mills
31491M Textile bag and canvas mills (part)

314991 Rope, cordage, and twine mills
314991 Rope, cordage, and twine mills

314992 Tire cord and tire fabric mills
314992 Tire cord and tire fabric mills

314999 All other miscellaneous textile product mills
314999 Textile product mills, nec

315111 Sheer hosiery mills
31511M Hosiery and sock mills (part)

315119 Other hosiery and sock mills
31511M Hosiery and sock mills (part)

315191 Outerwear knitting mills
31519M Apparel knitting mills, nec (part)

315192 Underwear and nightwear knitting mills
31519M Apparel knitting mills, nec (part)

315211 Men's and boys' cut and sew apparel contractors
31521M Cut and sew apparel contractors (part)

315212 Women's, girl's, and infants' cut and sew apparel contractors
31521M Cut and sew apparel contractors (part)

315221 Men's and boys' cut and sew underwear and nightwear manufacturing
31522M Men's and boys' cut and sew apparel manufacturing (part)

315222 Men's and boys' cut and sew suit, coat, and overcoat manufacturing
31522M Men's and boys' cut and sew apparel manufacturing (part)

315223 Men's and boys' cut and sew shirt (except work shirt) manufacturing
31522M Men's and boys' cut and sew apparel manufacturing (part)

315224 Men's and boys' cut and sew trouser, slack, and jean manufacturing
31522M Men's and boys' cut and sew apparel manufacturing (part)

315225 Men's and boys' cut and sew work clothing manufacturing
31522M Men's and boys' cut and sew apparel manufacturing (part)

315228 Men's and boys' cut and sew other outerwear manufacturing
31522M Men's and boys' cut and sew apparel manufacturing (part)

315231 Women's and girls' cut and sew lingerie, loungewear, and nightwear manufacturing
31523M Women's and girls' cut and sew apparel manufacturing (part)

315232 Women's and girls' cut and sew blouse and shirt manufacturing
31523M Women's and girls' cut and sew apparel manufacturing (part)

315233 Women's and girls' cut and sew dress manufacturing
31523M Women's and girls' cut and sew apparel manufacturing (part)

315234 Women's and girls' cut and sew suit, coat, tailored jacket, and skirt manufacturing
31523M Women's and girls' cut and sew apparel manufacturing (part)

315239 Women's and girls' cut and sew other outerwear manufacturing
31523M Women's and girls' cut and sew apparel manufacturing (part)

315291 Infants' cut and sew apparel manufacturing
31529M Cut and sew apparel manufacturing, nec (part)

315292 Fur and leather apparel manufacturing
31529M Cut and sew apparel manufacturing, nec (part)

315299 All other cut and sew apparel manufacturing
31529M Cut and sew apparel manufacturing, nec (part)

315991 Hat, cap, and millinery manufacturing
31599M Apparel accessories and other apparel manufacturing (part)

315992 Glove and mitten manufacturing
31599M Apparel accessories and other apparel manufacturing (part)

315993 Men's and boys' neckwear manufacturing
31599M Apparel accessories and other apparel manufacturing (part)

315999 Other apparel accessories and other apparel manufacturing
31599M Apparel accessories and other apparel manufacturing (part)

316110 Leather and hide tanning and finishing
316110 Leather and hide tanning and finishing

316211 Rubber and plastics footwear manufacturing
31621M Footwear manufacturing (part)

316212 House slipper manufacturing
31621M Footwear manufacturing (part)

316213 Men's footwear (except athletic) manufacturing
31621M Footwear manufacturing (part)

316214 Women's footwear (except athletic) manufacturing
31621M Footwear manufacturing (part)

316219 Other footwear manufacturing
31621M Footwear manufacturing (part)

316991 Luggage manufacturing
31699M Leather and allied product manufacturing, nec (part)

316992 Women's handbag and purse manufacturing
31699M Leather and allied product manufacturing, nec (part)

316993 Personal leather good (except women's handbag and purse) manufacturing
31699M Leather and allied product manufacturing, nec (part)

316999 All other leather good manufacturing
31699M Leather and allied product manufacturing, nec (part)

321113 Sawmills
32111M Sawmills and wood preservation (part)

321114 Wood preservation
32111M Sawmills and wood preservation (part)

321211 Hardwood veneer and plywood manufacturing
32121N Veneer and plywood manufacturing (part)

321212 Softwood veneer and plywood manufacturing
32121N Veneer and plywood manufacturing (part)

321213 Engineered wood member (except truss) manufacturing
32121P Engineered wood product manufacturing (part)

321214 Truss manufacturing
32121P Engineered wood product manufacturing (part)

321219 Reconstituted wood product manufacturing
321219 Reconstituted wood product manufacturing

321911 Wood window and door manufacturing
32191M Millwork (part)

321912 Cut stock, resawing lumber, and planing
32191M Millwork (part)

321918 Other millwork (including flooring)
32191M Millwork (part)

321920 Wood container and pallet manufacturing
321920 Wood container and pallet manufacturing

321991 Manufactured home (mobile home) manufacturing
321991 Manufactured home (mobile home) manufacturing

321992 Prefabricated wood building manufacturing
321992 Prefabricated wood building manufacturing

321999 All other miscellaneous wood product manufacturing
321999 Wood product manufacturing, nec

322110 Pulp mills
322110 Pulp mills

322121 Paper (except newsprint) mills
32212M Paper and newsprint mills (part)

322122 Newsprint mills
32212M Paper and newsprint mills (part)

322130 Paperboard mills
322130 Paperboard mills

322211 Corrugated and solid fiber box manufacturing
32221M Paperboard container mills (part)

322212 Folding paperboard box manufacturing
32221M Paperboard container mills (part)

322213 Setup paperboard box manufacturing
32221M Paperboard container mills (part)

322214 Fiber can, tube, drum, and similar products manufacturing
32221M Paperboard container mills (part)

322215 Nonfolding sanitary food container manufacturing
32221M Paperboard container mills (part)

322221 Coated and laminated packaging paper and plastics film manufacturing
32222N Coated and laminated paper and packaging manufacturing (part)

322222 Coated and laminated paper manufacturing
32222N Coated and laminated paper and packaging manufacturing (part)

322223 Plastics, foil, and coated paper bag manufacturing
32222P Coated, uncoated and multiwall bag and packaging manufacturing (part)

322224 Uncoated paper and multiwall bag manufacturing
32222P Coated, uncoated and multiwall bag and packaging manufacturing (part)

322225 Laminated aluminum foil manufacturing for flexible packaging uses
32222P Coated, uncoated and multiwall bag and packaging manufacturing (part)

322226 Surface-coated paperboard manufacturing
32222P Coated, uncoated and multiwall bag and packaging manufacturing (part)

322231 Die-cut paper and paperboard office supplies manufacturing
32223M Stationery product manufacturing (part)

322232 Envelope manufacturing
32223M Stationery product manufacturing (part)

322233 Stationery, tablet, and related product manufacturing
32223M Stationery product manufacturing (part)

322291 Sanitary paper product manufacturing
322291 Sanitary paper product manufacturing

322299 All other converted paper product manufacturing
322299 Converted paper product manufacturing, nec

323110 Commercial lithographic printing
32311M Printing (part)

323111 Commercial gravure printing
32311M Printing (part)

323112 Commercial flexographic printing
32311M Printing (part)

323113 Commercial screen printing
32311M Printing (part)

323114 Quick printing
32311M Printing (part)

323115 Digital printing
32311M Printing (part)

323116 Manifold business form printing
32311M Printing (part)

323117 Books printing
32311M Printing (part)

323118 Blankbook, loose-leaf binders, and devices manufacturing
32311M Printing (part)

323119 Other commercial printing
32311M Printing (part)

323121 Trade binding and related work
32312M Support activities for printing (part)

323122 Prepress services
32312M Support activities for printing (part)

324110 Petroleum refineries
324110 Petroleum refineries

324121 Asphalt paving mixture and block manufacturing
324121 Asphalt paving mixture and block manufacturing

324122 Asphalt shingle and coating materials manufacturing
324122 Asphalt shingle and coating materials manufacturing

324191 Petroleum lubricating oil and grease manufacturing
324191 Petroleum lubricating oil and grease manufacturing

324199 All other petroleum and coal products manufacturing
324199 Petroleum and coal products manufacturing, nec

325110 Petrochemical manufacturing
325110 Petrochemical manufacturing

5120 Industrial gas manufacturing
35120 Industrial gas manufacturing

norganic dye and pigment manufacturing
Synthetic dye and pigment manufacturing (part)

ic organic dye and pigment manufacturing
ic dye and pigment manufacturing (part)

325181 Alkalies and chlorine manufacturing
325181 Alkalies and chlorine manufacturing

325182 Carbon black manufacturing
325182 Carbon black manufacturing

325188 All other basic inorganic chemical manufacturing
325188 Basic inorganic chemical manufacturing, nec

325191 Gum and wood chemical manufacturing
32519M Other basic organic chemical manufacturing (part)

325192 Cyclic crude and intermediate manufacturing
32519M Other basic organic chemical manufacturing (part)

325193 Ethyl alcohol manufacturing
32519M Other basic organic chemical manufacturing (part)

325199 All other basic organic chemical manufacturing
32519M Other basic organic chemical manufacturing (part)

325211 Plastics material and resin manufacturing
325211 Plastics material and resin manufacturing

325212 Synthetic rubber manufacturing
325212 Synthetic rubber manufacturing

325221 Cellulosic organic fiber manufacturing
32522M Artificial and synthetic fibers and filaments manufacturing (part)

325222 Noncellulosic organic fiber manufacturing
32522M Artificial and synthetic fibers and filaments manufacturing (part)

325311 Nitrogenous fertilizer manufacturing
325311 Nitrogenous fertilizer manufacturing

325312 Phosphatic fertilizer manufacturing
325312 Phosphatic fertilizer manufacturing

325314 Fertilizer (mixing only) manufacturing
325314 Fertilizer (mixing only) manufacturing

325320 Pesticide and other agricultural chemical manufacturing
325320 Pesticide and other agricultural chemical manufacturing

325411 Medicinal and botanical manufacturing
325411 Medicinal and botanical manufacturing

325412 Pharmaceutical preparation manufacturing
325412 Pharmaceutical preparation manufacturing

325413 In-vitro diagnostic substance manufacturing
325413 In-vitro diagnostic substance manufacturing

325414 Biological product (except diagnostic) manufacturing
325414 Biological product (except diagnostic) manufacturing

325510 Paint and coating manufacturing
325510 Paint and coating manufacturing

325520 Adhesive manufacturing
325520 Adhesive manufacturing

325611 Soap and other detergent manufacturing
32561M Soap and cleaning compound manufacturing (part)

325612 Polish and other sanitation goods manufacturing
32561M Soap and cleaning compound manufacturing (part)

325613 Surface active agent manufacturing
32561M Soap and cleaning compound manufacturing (part)

325620 Toilet preparation manufacturing
325620 Toilet preparation manufacturing

325910 Printing ink manufacturing
325910 Printing ink manufacturing

325920 Explosives manufacturing
325920 Explosives manufacturing

325991 Custom compounding of purchased resins
325991 Custom compounding of purchased resins

325992 Photographic film, paper, plate, and chemical manufacturing
32599N Chemical product and preparation manufacturing, nec (part)

325998 All other miscellaneous chemical product and preparation manufacturing
32599N Chemical product and preparation manufacturing, nec (part)

326111 Plastics bag manufacturing
326111 Unsupported plastics bag manufacturing

326112 Plastics packaging film and sheet (including laminated) manufacturing
326112 Unsupported plastics packaging film and sheet manufacturing

326113 Unlaminated plastics film and sheet (except packaging) manufacturing
326113 Unsupported plastics film and sheet (except packaging) manufacturing

326121 Unlaminated plastics profile shape manufacturing
326121 Unsupported plastics profile shape manufacturing

326122 Plastics pipe and pipe fitting manufacturing
326122 Plastics pipe and pipe fitting manufacturing

326130 Laminated plastics plate, sheet (except packaging), and shape manufacturing
326130 Laminated plastics plate, sheet, and shape manufacturing

326140 Polystyrene foam product manufacturing
326140 Polystyrene foam product manufacturing

326150 Urethane and other foam product (except polystyrene) manufacturing
326150 Urethane and other foam product (except polystyrene) manufacturing

326160 Plastics bottle manufacturing
326160 Plastics bottle manufacturing

326191 Plastics plumbing fixture manufacturing
32619M Plastics product manufacturing, nec (part)

326192 Resilient floor covering manufacturing
32619M Plastics product manufacturing, nec (part)

326199 All other plastics product manufacturing
32619M Plastics product manufacturing, nec (part)

326211 Tire manufacturing (except retreading)
32621M Tire manufacturing (part)

326212 Tire retreading
32621M Tire manufacturing (part)

326220 Rubber and plastics hoses and belting manufacturing
326220 Rubber and plastics hoses and belting manufacturing

326291 Rubber product manufacturing for mechanical use
32629M Rubber product manufacturing, nec (part)

326299 All other rubber product manufacturing
32629M Rubber product manufacturing, nec (part)

327111 Vitreous china plumbing fixture and china and earthenware bathroom accessories manufacturing
327111 Vitreous china plumbing fixture and china and earthenware bathroom accessories manufacturing

327112 Vitreous china, fine earthenware, and other pottery product manufacturing
327112 Vitreous china, fine earthenware, and other pottery product manufacturing

327113 Porcelain electrical supply manufacturing
327113 Porcelain electrical supply manufacturing

327121 Brick and structural clay tile manufacturing
327121 Brick and structural clay tile manufacturing

327122 Ceramic wall and floor tile manufacturing
327122 Ceramic wall and floor tile manufacturing

327123 Other structural clay product manufacturing
327123 Structural clay product manufacturing, nec

327124 Clay refractory manufacturing
32712N Refractory manufacturing (part)

327125 Nonclay refractory manufacturing
32712N Refractory manufacturing (part)

327211 Flat glass manufacturing
327211 Flat glass manufacturing

327212 Other pressed and blown glass and glassware manufacturing
327212 Pressed and blown glass and glassware manufacturing, nec

327213 Glass container manufacturing
327213 Glass container manufacturing

327215 Glass product manufacturing made of purchased glass
327215 Glass product manufacturing made of purchased glass

327310 Cement manufacturing
327310 Cement manufacturing

327320 Ready-mix concrete manufacturing
327320 Ready-mix concrete manufacturing

327331 Concrete block and brick manufacturing
32733M Concrete pipe, brick, and block manufacturing (part)

327332 Concrete pipe manufacturing
32733M Concrete pipe, brick, and block manufacturing (part)

327390 Other concrete product manufacturing
327390 Concrete product manufacturing, nec

327410 Lime manufacturing
327410 Lime manufacturing

327420 Gypsum product manufacturing
327420 Gypsum product manufacturing

327910 Abrasive product manufacturing
327910 Abrasive product manufacturing

327991 Cut stone and stone product manufacturing
327991 Cut stone and stone product manufacturing

327992 Ground or treated mineral and earth manufacturing
327992 Ground or treated mineral and earth manufacturing

327993 Mineral wool manufacturing
327993 Mineral wool manufacturing

327999 All other miscellaneous nonmetallic mineral product manufacturing
327999 Nonmetallic mineral product manufacturing, nec

331111 Iron and steel mills
33111M Iron and steel mills and ferroalloy manufacturing (part)

331112 Electrometallurgical ferroalloy product manufacturing
33111M Iron and steel mills and ferroalloy manufacturing (part)

331210 Iron and steel pipe and tube manufacturing from purchased steel
331210 Iron and steel pipe and tube manufacturing from purchased steel

331221 Rolled steel shape manufacturing
33122M Rolling and drawing of purchased steel (part)

331222 Steel wire drawing
33122M Rolling and drawing of purchased steel (part)

331311 Alumina refining
331311 Alumina refining

331312 Primary aluminum production
331312 Primary aluminum production

331314 Secondary smelting and alloying of aluminum
331314 Secondary smelting and alloying of aluminum

331315 Aluminum sheet, plate, and foil manufacturing
33131N Aluminum rolling and drawing (part)

331316 Aluminum extruded product manufacturing
331316 Aluminum extruded product manufacturing

331319 Other aluminum rolling and drawing
33131N Aluminum rolling and drawing (part)

331411 Primary smelting and refining of copper
331411 Primary smelting and refining of copper

331419 Primary smelting and refining of nonferrous metal (except copper and aluminum)
331419 Primary smelting and refining of nonferrous metal (except copper and aluminum)

331421 Copper rolling, drawing, and extruding
33142M Copper rolling, drawing, extruding, and alloying (part)

331422 Copper wire (except mechanical) drawing
33142M Copper rolling, drawing, extruding, and alloying (part)

331423 Secondary smelting, refining, and alloying of copper
33142M Copper rolling, drawing, extruding, and alloying (part)

331491 Nonferrous metal (except copper and aluminum) rolling, drawing, and extruding
33149M Nonferrous metal (except copper and aluminum) rolling, drawing, extruding, and alloying (part)

331492 Secondary smelting, refining, and alloying of nonferrous metal (except copper and aluminum)
33149M Nonferrous metal (except copper and aluminum) rolling, drawing, extruding, and alloying (part)

331511 Iron foundries
33151M Ferrous metal foundries (part)

331512 Steel investment foundries
33151M Ferrous metal foundries (part)

331513 Steel foundries (except investment)
33151M Ferrous metal foundries (part)

331521 Aluminum die-casting foundries
33152N Aluminum foundries (part)

331524 Aluminum foundries (except die-casting)
33152N Aluminum foundries (part)

331522 Nonferrous (except aluminum) die-casting foundries
33152P Nonaluminum foundries (part)

331525 Copper foundries (except die-casting)
33152P Nonaluminum foundries (part)

331528 Other nonferrous foundries (except die-casting)
33152P Nonaluminum foundries (part)

332111 Iron and steel forging
33211N Forging (part)

332112 Nonferrous forging
33211N Forging (part)

332114 Custom roll forming
332114 Custom roll forming

332115 Crown and closure manufacturing
33211P Crown, closure and metal stamping manufacturing (part)

332116 Metal stamping
33211P Crown, closure and metal stamping manufacturing (part)

332117 Powder metallurgy parts manufacturing
332117 Powder metallurgy parts manufacturing

332211 Cutlery and flatware (except precious) manufacturing
33221N Cutlery, kitchen utensil, pot and pan manufacturing (part)

332212 Hand and edge tool manufacturing
33221P Hand tool and saw blade manufacturing (part)

332213 Saw blade and handsaw manufacturing
33221P Hand tool and saw blade manufacturing (part)

332214 Kitchen utensil, pot, and pan manufacturing
33221N Cutlery, kitchen utensil, pot and pan manufacturing (part)

332311 Prefabricated metal building and component manufacturing
33231M Plate work and fabricated structural product manufacturing (part)

332312 Fabricated structural metal manufacturing
33231M Plate work and fabricated structural product manufacturing (part)

332313 Plate work manufacturing
33231M Plate work and fabricated structural product manufacturing (part)

332321 Metal window and door manufacturing
33232M Ornamental, sheet and architectural metal work manufacturing (part)

332322 Sheet metal work manufacturing
33232M Ornamental, sheet and architectural metal work manufacturing (part)

332323 Ornamental and architectural metal work manufacturing
33232M Ornamental, sheet and architectural metal work manufacturing (part)

332410 Power boiler and heat exchanger manufacturing
332410 Power boiler and heat exchanger manufacturing

332420 Metal tank (heavy gauge) manufacturing
332420 Metal tank (heavy gauge) manufacturing

332431 Metal can manufacturing
33243M Metal can, box, and other metal container (light gauge) manufacturing (part)

332439 Other metal container manufacturing
33243M Metal can, box, and other metal container (light gauge) manufacturing (part)

332510 Hardware manufacturing
332510 Hardware manufacturing

332611 Spring (heavy gauge) manufacturing
33261M Spring and wire product manufacturing (part)

332612 Spring (light gauge) manufacturing
33261M Spring and wire product manufacturing (part)

332618 Other fabricated wire product manufacturing
33261M Spring and wire product manufacturing (part)

332710 Machine shops
332710 Machine shops

332721 Precision turned product manufacturing
332721 Precision turned product manufacturing

332722 Bolt, nut, screw, rivet, and washer manufacturing
332722 Bolt, nut, screw, rivet, and washer manufacturing

332811 Metal heat treating
33281M Coating, engraving, heat treating, and allied activities (part)

332812 Metal coating, engraving (except jewelry and silverware), and allied services to manufacturers
33281M Coating, engraving, heat treating, and allied activities (part)

332813 Electroplating, plating, polishing, anodizing, and coloring
33281M Coating, engraving, heat treating, and allied activities (part)

332911 Industrial valve manufacturing
33291N Valves and fittings manufacturing, nonplumbing (part)

332912 Fluid power valve and hose fitting manufacturing
33291N Valves and fittings manufacturing, nonplumbing (part)

332913 Plumbing fixture fitting and trim manufacturing
332913 Plumbing fixture fitting and trim manufacturing

332919 Other metal valve and pipe fitting manufacturing
33291N Valves and fittings manufacturing, nonplumbing (part)

332991 Ball and roller bearing manufacturing
332991 Ball and roller bearing manufacturing

332992 Small arms ammunition manufacturing
332992 Small arms ammunition manufacturing

332993 Ammunition (except small arms) manufacturing
332993 Ammunition (except small arms) manufacturing

332994 Small arms manufacturing
332994 Small arms manufacturing

332995 Other ordnance and accessories manufacturing
332995 Ordnance and accessories manufacturing, nec

332996 Fabricated pipe and pipe fitting manufacturing
332996 Fabricated pipe and pipe fitting manufacturing

332997 Industrial pattern manufacturing
33299N Fabricated metal products manufacturing, nec (part)

332998 Enameled iron and metal sanitary ware manufacturing
33299N Fabricated metal products manufacturing, nec (part)

332999 All other miscellaneous fabricated metal product manufacturing
33299N Fabricated metal products manufacturing, nec (part)

333111 Farm machinery and equipment manufacturing
333111 Farm machinery and equipment manufacturing

333112 Lawn and garden tractor and home lawn and garden equipment manufacturing
333112 Lawn and garden tractor and home lawn and garden equipment manufacturing

333120 Construction machinery manufacturing
333120 Construction machinery manufacturing

333131 Mining machinery and equipment manufacturing
33313M Mining and oil and gas field machinery manufacturing (part)

333132 Oil and gas field machinery and equipment manufacturing
33313M Mining and oil and gas field machinery manufacturing (part)

333210 Sawmill and woodworking machinery manufacturing
333210 Sawmill and woodworking machinery manufacturing

333220 Plastics and rubber industry machinery manufacturing
333220 Plastics and rubber industry machinery manufacturing

333295 Semiconductor machinery manufacturing
333295 Semiconductor machinery manufacturing

333291 Paper industry machinery manufacturing
33329N Machinery manufacturing, nec (part)

333292 Textile machinery manufacturing
33329N Machinery manufacturing, nec (part)

333293 Printing machinery and equipment manufacturing
33329N Machinery manufacturing, nec (part)

333294 Food product machinery manufacturing
33329N Machinery manufacturing, nec (part)

333295 Semiconductor machinery manufacturing
333295 Semiconductor machinery manufacturing

333298 All other industrial machinery manufacturing
33329N Machinery manufacturing, nec (part)

333311 Automatic vending machine manufacturing
33331N Other commercial and service industry machinery manufacturng, nec

333312 Commercial laundry, dry cleaning, and pressing machine manufacturing
33331N Other commercial and service industry machinery manufacturng, nec (part)

333313 Office machinery manufacturing
333313 Office machinery manufacturing

333314 Optical instrument and lens manufacturing
333314 Optical instrument and lens manufacturing

333315 Photographic and photocopying equipment manufacturing
333315 Photographic and photocopying equipment manufacturing

333319 Other commercial and service industry machinery manufacturing
33331N Other commercial and service industry machinery manufacturng, nec (part)

333411 Air purification equipment manufacturing
33341N Ventilation equipment manufacturing (part)

333412 Industrial and commercial fan and blower manufacturing
33341N Ventilation equipment manufacturing (part)

333414 Heating equipment (except warm air furnaces) manufacturing
333414 Heating equipment (except warm air furnaces) manufacturing

333415 Air-conditioning and warm air heating equipment and commercial and industrial refrigeration equipment manufacturing
333415 Air-conditioning and warm air heating equipment and commercial and industrial refrigeration equipment manufacturing

333511 Industrial mold manufacturing
333511 Industrial mold manufacturing

333512 Machine tool (metal cutting types) manufacturing
333512 Machine tool (metal cutting types) manufacturing

333513 Machine tool (metal forming types) manufacturing
333513 Machine tool (metal forming types) manufacturing

333514 Special die and tool, die set, jig, and fixture manufacturing
333514 Special die and tool, die set, jig, and fixture manufacturing

333515 Cutting tool and machine tool accessory manufacturing
333515 Cutting tool and machine tool accessory manufacturing

333516 Rolling mill machinery and equipment manufacturing
333516 Rolling mill machinery and equipment manufacturing

333518 Other metalworking machinery manufacturing
333518 Metalworking machinery manufacturing, nec

333611 Turbine and turbine generator set units manufacturing
333611 Turbine and turbine generator set units manufacturing

333612 Speed changer, industrial high-speed drive, and gear manufacturing
333612 Speed changer, industrial high-speed drive, and gear manufacturing

333613 Mechanical power transmission equipment manufacturing
333613 Mechanical power transmission equipment manufacturing

333618 Other engine equipment manufacturing
333618 Engine equipment manufacturing, nec

333911 Pump and pumping equipment manufacturing
333911 Pump and pumping equipment manufacturing

333912 Air and gas compressor manufacturing
333912 Air and gas compressor manufacturing

333913 Measuring and dispensing pump manufacturing
333913 Measuring and dispensing pump manufacturing

333921 Elevator and moving stairway manufacturing
33392M Material handling equipment manufacturing (part)

333922 Conveyor and conveying equipment manufacturing
33392M Material handling equipment manufacturing (part)

333923 Overhead traveling crane, hoist, and monorail system manufacturing
33392M Material handling equipment manufacturing (part)

333924 Industrial truck, tractor, trailer, and stacker machinery manufacturing
33392M Material handling equipment manufacturing (part)

333991 Power-driven hand tool manufacturing
333991 Power-driven hand tool manufacturing

333992 Welding and soldering equipment manufacturing
33399P General purpose machinery manufacturing, nec (part)

333993 Packaging machinery manufacturing
333993 Packaging machinery manufacturing

333994 Industrial process furnace and oven manufacturing
333994 Industrial process furnace and oven manufacturing

333995 Fluid power cylinder and actuator manufacturing
33399N Fluid power equipment manufacturing (part)

333996 Fluid power pump and motor manufacturing
33399N Fluid power equipment manufacturing (part)

333997 Scale and balance (except laboratory) manufacturing
33399P General purpose machinery manufacturing, nec (part)

333999 All other miscellaneous general-purpose machinery manufacturing
33399P General-purpose machinery manufacturing, nec (part)

334111 Electronic computer manufacturing
334111 Electronic computer manufacturing

334112 Computer storage device manufacturing
334112 Computer storage device manufacturing

334113 Computer terminal manufacturing
334113 Computer terminal manufacturing

334119 Other computer peripheral equipment manufacturing
334119 Computer peripheral equipment manufacturing, nec

334210 Telephone apparatus manufacturing
334210 Telephone apparatus manufacturing

334220 Radio and television broadcasting and wireless communications equipment manufacturing
334220 Radio and television broadcasting and wireless commuinications equipment manufacturing

334290 Other communications equipment manufacturing
334290 Communications equipment manufacturing, nec

334310 Audio and video equipment manufacturing
334310 Audio and video equipment manufacturing

334411 Electron tube manufacturing
334411 Electron tube manufacturing

334412 Bare printed circuit board manufacturing
334412 Bare printed circuit board manufacturing

334413 Semiconductor and related device manufacturing
334413 Semiconductor and related device manufacturing

334414 Electronic capacitor manufacturing
334414 Electronic capacitor manufacturing

334415 Electronic resistor manufacturing
334415 Electronic resistor manufacturing

334416 Electronic coil, transformer, and other inductor manufacturing
334416 Electronic coil, transformer, and other inductor manufacturing

334417 Electronic connector manufacturing
334417 Electronic connector manufacturing

334418 Printed circuit assembly (electronic assembly) manufacturing
334418 Printed circuit assembly (electronic assembly) manufacturing

334419 Other electronic component manufacturing
334419 Other electronic component manufacturing

334510 Electromedical and electrotherapeutic apparatus manufacturing
334510 Electromedical and electrotherapeutic apparatus manufacturing

334511 Search, detection, navigation, guidance, aeronautical, and nautical system and instrument manufacturing
334511 Search, detection, navigation, guidance, aeronautical, and nautical system and instrument manufacturing

334512 Automatic environmental control manufacturing for residential, commercial, and appliance use
334512 Automatic environmental control manufacturing for residential, commercial, and appliance use

334513 Instruments and related products manufacturing for measuring, displaying, and controlling industrial process variables
334513 Instruments and related products manufacturing for measuring, displaying, and controlling industrial process variables

334514 Totalizing fluid meter and counting device manufacturing
334514 Totalizing fluid meter and counting device manufacturing

334515 Instrument manufacturing for measuring and testing electricity and electrical signals
334515 Instrument manufacturing for measuring and testing electricity and electrical signals

334516 Analytical laboratory instrument manufacturing
334516 Analytical laboratory instrument manufacturing

334517 Irradiation apparatus manufacturing
334517 Irradiation apparatus manufacturing

334518 Watch, clock, and part manufacturing
334518 Watch, clock, and parts manufacturing

334519 Other measuring and controlling device manufacturing
334519 Measuring and controlling device manufacturing, nec

334611 Software reproducing
334611 Software reproducing

334612 Prerecorded compact disc (except software), tape, and record reproducing
334612 Prerecorded compact disc (except software), tape, and record reproducing

334613 Magnetic and optical recording media manufacturing
334613 Magnetic and optical recording media manufacturing

335110 Electric lamp bulb and part manufacturing
335110 Electric lamp bulb and parts manufacturing

335121 Residential electric lighting fixture manufacturing
33512M Lighting fixture manufacturing (part)

335122 Commercial, industrial, and institutional electric lighting fixture manufacturing
33512M Lighting fixture manufacturing (part)

335129 Other lighting equipment manufacturing
33512M Lighting fixture manufacturing (part)

335211 Electric house wares and household fan manufacturing
33521M Small electrical appliance manufacturing (part)

335212 Household vacuum cleaner manufacturing
33521M Small electrical appliance manufacturing (part)

335221 Household cooking appliance manufacturing
335221 Household cooking appliance manufacturing

335222 Household refrigerator and home freezer manufacturing
335222 Household refrigerator and home freezer manufacturing

335224 Household laundry equipment manufacturing
335224 Household laundry equipment manufacturing

335228 Other major household appliance manufacturing
335224 Major household appliance manufacturing, nec

335311 Power, distribution, and specialty transformer manufacturing
335311 Power, distribution, and specialty transformer manufacturing

335312 Motor and generator manufacturing
335312 Motor and generator manufacturing

335313 Switchgear and switchboard apparatus manufacturing
335313 Switchgear and switchboard apparatus manufacturing

335314 Relay and industrial control manufacturing
335314 Relay and industrial control manufacturing

335911 Storage battery manufacturing
335911 Storage battery manufacturing

335912 Primary battery manufacturing
335912 Primary battery manufacturing

335921 Fiber optic cable manufacturing
33592M Communication and energy wire and cable manufacturing (part)

335929 Other communication and energy wire manufacturing
33592M Communication and energy wire and cable manufacturing (part)

335931 Current-carrying wiring device manufacturing
33593M Wiring device manufacturing (part)

335932 Noncurrent-carrying wiring device manufacturing
33593M Wiring device manufacturing (part)

335991 Carbon and graphite product manufacturing
335991 Carbon and graphite product manufacturing

335999 All other miscellaneous electrical equipment and component manufacturing
335999 Electrical equipment and component manufacturing, nec

336111 Automobile manufacturing
336111 Automobile manufacturing

336112 Light truck and utility vehicle manufacturing
336112 Light truck and utility vehicle manufacturing

336120 Heavy duty truck manufacturing
336120 Heavy duty truck manufacturing

336211 Motor vehicle body manufacturing
336211 Motor vehicle body manufacturing

336212 Truck trailer manufacturing
336212 Truck trailer manufacturing

336213 Motor home manufacturing
336213 Motor home manufacturing

336214 Travel trailer and camper manufacturing
336214 Travel trailer and camper manufacturing

336311 Carburetor, piston, piston ring, and valve manufacturing
33631M Motor vehicle gasoline engine and engine parts manufacturing (part)

336312 Gasoline engine and engine parts manufacturing
33631M Motor vehicle gasoline engine and engine parts manufacturing (part)

336321 Vehicular lighting equipment manufacturing
33632M Motor vehicle electrical and electronic equipment manufacturing (part)

336322 Other motor vehicle electrical and electronic equipment manufacturing
33632M Motor vehicle electrical and electronic equipment manufacturing (part)

336330 Motor vehicle steering and suspension component (except spring) manufacturing
336330 Motor vehicle steering and suspension component (except spring) manufacturing

336340 Motor vehicle brake system manufacturing
336340 Motor vehicle brake system manufacturing

336350 Motor vehicle transmission and power train parts manufacturing
336350 Motor vehicle transmission and power train parts manufacturing

336360 Motor vehicle seating and interior trim manufacturing
336360 Motor vehicle seating and interior trim manufacturing

336370 Motor vehicle metal stamping
336370 Motor vehicle metal stamping

336391 Motor vehicle air-conditioning manufacturing
336391 Motor vehicle air-conditioning manufacturing

336399 All other motor vehicle parts manufacturing
336399 Motor vehicle parts manufacturing, nec

336411 Aircraft manufacturing
336411 Aircraft manufacturing

336412 Aircraft engine and engine parts manufacturing
336412 Aircraft engine and engine parts manufacturing

336413 Other aircraft parts and auxiliary equipment manufacturing
336413 Other aircraft parts and auxiliary equipment manufacturing

336414 Guided missile and space vehicle manufacturing
336414 Guided missile and space vehicle manufacturing

336415 Guided missile and space vehicle propulsion unit and propulsion unit parts manufacturing
336415 Guided missile and space vehicle propulsion unit and propulsion unit parts manufacturing

336419 Other guided missile and space vehicle parts and auxiliary equipment manufacturing
336419   Guided missile and space vehicle parts and auxiliary equipment manufacturing, nec

336510 Railroad rolling stock manufacturing
336510   Railroad rolling stock manufacturing

336611 Ship building and repairing
336611   Ship building and repairing

336612 Boat building
336612   Boat building

336991 Motorcycle, bicycle, and parts manufacturing
336991   Motorcycle, bicycle, and parts manufacturing

336992 Military armored vehicle, tank, and tank component manufacturing
336992   Military armored vehicle, tank, and tank component manufacturing

336999 All other transportation equipment manufacturing
336999   Transportation equipment manufacturing, nec

337110 Wood kitchen cabinet and counter top manufacturing
337110   Wood kitchen cabinet and counter top manufacturing

337121 Upholstered household furniture manufacturing
337121   Upholstered household furniture manufacturing

337122 Nonupholstered wood household furniture manufacturing
337122   Nonupholstered wood household furniture manufacturing

337124 Metal household furniture manufacturing
33712N   Other household nonupholstered furniture (part)

337125 Household furniture (except wood and metal) manufacturing
33712N   Other household nonupholstered furniture (part)

337127 Institutional furniture
337127   Institutional furniture

337129 Wood television, radio, and sewing machine cabinet manufacturing
33712N   Other household nonupholstered furniture (part)

337211 Wood office furniture manufacturing
33721N   Office furniture manufacturing (part)

337212 Custom architectural woodwork and millwork manufacturing
337212   Custom architectural woodwork and millwork manufacturing

337214 Office furniture (except wood) manufacturing
33721N   Office furniture manufacturing (part)

337215 Showcase, partition, shelving, and locker manufacturing
337215   Showcase, partition, shelving, and locker manufacturing

337910 Mattress manufacturing
337910   Mattress manufacturing

337920 Blind and shade manufacturing
337920   Blind and shade manufacturing

339111 Laboratory apparatus and furniture manufacturing
339111   Laboratory apparatus and furniture manufacturing

339112 Surgical and medical instrument manufacturing
339112   Surgical and medical instrument manufacturing

339113 Surgical appliance and supplies manufacturing
339113   Surgical appliance and supplies manufacturing

339114 Dental equipment and supplies manufacturing
339114   Dental equipment and supplies manufacturing

339115 Ophthalmic goods manufacturing
339115   Ophthalmic goods manufacturing

339116 Dental laboratories
339116   Dental laboratories

339911 Jewelry (except costume) manufacturing
33991M   Jewelry and silverware manufacturing (part)

339912 Silverware and hollowware manufacturing
33991M   Jewelry and silverware manufacturing (part)

339913 Jewelers' material and lapidary work manufacturing
33991M   Jewelry and silverware manufacturing (part)

339914 Costume jewelry and novelty manufacturing
33991M   Jewelry and silverware manufacturing (part)

339920 Sporting and athletic goods manufacturing
339920   Sporting and athletic goods manufacturing

339931 Doll and stuffed toy manufacturing
33993M   Doll, toy, and game manufacturing (part)

339932 Game, toy, and children's vehicle manufacturing
33993M   Doll, toy, and game manufacturing (part)

339941 Pen and mechanical pencil manufacturing
33994M   Office supplies (except paper) manufacturing (part)

339942 Lead pencil and art good manufacturing
33994M   Office supplies (except paper) manufacturing (part)

339943 Marking device manufacturing
33994M   Office supplies (except paper) manufacturing (part)

339944 Carbon paper and inked ribbon manufacturing
33994M   Office supplies (except paper) manufacturing (part)

339950 Sign manufacturing
339950   Sign manufacturing

339991 Gasket, packing, and sealing device manufacturing
339991   Gasket, packing, and sealing device manufacturing

339992 Musical instrument manufacturing
339992   Musical instrument manufacturing

339993 Fastener, button, needle, and pin manufacturing
339993   Fastener, button, needle, and pin manufacturing

339994 Broom, brush, and mop manufacturing
339994   Broom, brush, and mop manufacturing

339995 Burial casket manufacturing
339995   Burial casket manufacturing

339999 All other miscellaneous manufacturing
339999   Miscellaneous manufacturing, nec